I have revised this translation line by line, and word by word.... It is the only one which I have corrected.

J. H. Merle d'Aubigné

[See page iv.]

HISTORY

OF

THE REFORMATION

OF THE

SIXTEENTH CENTURY.

By J. H. MERLE D'AUBIGNÉ, D. D.,

PRESIDENT OF THE THEOLOGICAL SCHOOL OF GENEVA, AND VICE-PRESIDENT OF

THE SOCIÉTÉ EVANGÉLIQUE:

VOLUMES I. TO V.

VOLUMES I., II., AND III., TRANSLATED BY H. WHITE, B.A. TRINITY COLLEGE, CAMBRIDGE, M.A.
AND PH. DR. HEIDELBERG, AND CAREFULLY REVISED BY THE AUTHOR, WHO HAS MADE
NUMEROUS IMPORTANT ADDITIONS NOT TO BE FOUND IN ANY OTHER TRANSLATION;

VOL. IV. THE ENGLISH ORIGINAL BY DR. MERLE D'AUBIGNÉ, ASSISTED BY DR. WHITE; AND VOL. V.
TRANSLATED BY DR. WHITE, AND CAREFULLY REVISED BY THE AUTHOR.

HARTLAND INSTITUTE
P.O. Box 1, Rapidan, VA 22733

J'appelle accessoire, l'estat des affaires de ceste vie caduque et transitoire. J'appelle principat, le gouvernement spirituel auquel reluit souverainement la providence de Dieu.—*Théodore de Bèze.*

By accessory, I mean the state of affairs in this frail and transitory life; by principal, the spiritual government in which God's providence rules supreme.—*Theodore Beza.*

ISBN: 0-923309-14-4

Reprinted from the edition
issued in London in 1846

Printed in the United States of America

PREFACE

OLIVER & BOYD'S EDITION REVISED BY THE AUTHOR.

I HAVE been often requested to publish an English Edition of the first three volumes of my History of the Reformation, carefully revised and corrected by myself, and which might thus become a *Standard Edition* in Great Britain.

I have acknowledged the necessity of this task. In fact, without overlooking the merit of the different English translations of this work ; even the best, I am compelled to say, have failed in conveying my thoughts in several passages ; and in some cases this inaccuracy has been of serious consequence. I will mention one instance.

At the end of the year 1844, I received several letters from the United States, informing me that, besides 75,000 copies of my History put in circulation by different American booksellers, *The American Tract Society* had printed an edition of 24,000 copies, which they sold through the instrumentality of more than a hundred hawkers (*colporteurs*), principally in the *New Settlements*, which no bookseller can reach, but whither the pope ceases not from sending active emissaries ; they added, that the committee of this society, composed of different denominations, and among others of Episcopalians and Baptists, were rendered uneasy by certain passages in my history, and had thought proper, with the best intentions, either to modify or retrench them ; they informed me, lastly, that two Presbyterian synods, astonished at these changes, had publicly accused the Society of mutilating the work, and that there had arisen (wrote one of the most respectable men in the United States, himself a Presbyterian, and not a member of the Society) so violent a discussion, that " the Committee will inevitably be ruined unless *you* interfere to rescue it."

I thought it my duty to do so without sacrificing, however, any of the facts or any of the opinions I had put forth. And the following is one of the means to which I had recourse :—

On closely examining the inculpated passages, I found that in some cases those which had offended either the Episcopalians or the Baptists, were incorrectly rendered in the English translation which the New York Committee had before it.

Thus in vol. iii. book ix. chap. 4, the Committee had been stopped by this expression : " It is the *Episcopal authority* itself that Luther calls to the bar of judgment in the person of the German primate."

The Committee consequently altered this phrase, and wrote : " It is *the authority of Rome itself* that Luther calls to the bar of judgment in the person of the German primate."

This is no doubt an important alteration, but the first translator had himself changed my idea. The French reads thus : " *C'est l'épiscopat tout entier que Luther traduit à sa barre dans la personne du primat germanique.*" (Vol. iii. p. 34, l. 8.)

There is no question of episcopal authority, but *of the whole body of the Roman-catholic bishops.* I pronounce neither for nor against the episcopal authority : I am content to point out an inaccuracy in the translation.

Here is another instance :—

In vol. iii. book ix. chap. 11, the New York Committee were stopped by this expression, which they found in the English translation : " The ancient structure of the *Church* was thus tottering ;" and they substituted, " The ancient structure of *Popery* was thus tottering."

In the French there occurs neither *Church* nor *Popery*, but simply : " *l'ancien édifice s'écroulait.*" (Vol. iii. p. 150, last line.) Nevertheless the Committee's rendering is preferable. It is not the Church of Christ that was tottering, since the gates of hell cannot prevail against it : it is the Papal Church, as is evident from the context.

Most of the other passages changed by the American Society were no doubt originally translated with tolerable fidelity; but it was sufficient that some were not so, to make the author feel the necessity of a new edition carefully revised by himself.

This I have done in the present Edition. I have revised this translation line by line, and word by word; and I have restored the sense wherever I did not find it clearly rendered. It is the only one which I have corrected. I declare in consequence, that I acknowledge this translation as the only faithful expression of my thoughts in the English language, and I recommend it as such to all my readers.

Farther, I have in this Edition made numerous corrections and additions, frequently of importance. Some facts have been related that have not been introduced elsewhere, so that it will thus have an indisputable authority over all others.

It is almost unnecessary for me to add, that if the other translations appear to me somewhat defective, I accuse neither the publishers nor the translators: this is an inevitable disadvantage when the work is not revised by the author. There are some publishers in particular with whom I have had pleasing intercourse, and whom (I feel compelled to say) I am delighted in reckoning among the number of my friends.

I seize the present opportunity of adding, that neither the evangelical Episcopalians nor the Baptists can find any thing in this work contrary to their principles. Certainly I am a Presbyterian; certainly this work is opposed to a dogmatic and sectarian Episcopacy, which maintains that, in order to be united to Christ, you must be united to a bishop; but it is by no means opposed to the evangelical and constitutional Episcopacy,—to the Episcopacy of Leighton, Scott, J. Newton, Simeon, and Cecil,—which, faithful to the Word of God, desires to lay no other foundation than Jesus Christ.

There is an error with regard to the Baptists that has misled many individuals. They have imagined that the Anabaptists in the time of the Reformation and the Baptists of our days are the same sect. But they are two sects that, both in doctrine and history, are as distinct as possible. When the English Baptists separated from the Episcopal establishment in the sixteenth century, they did so without being in any way influenced by the Anabaptists of the Continent. The example of the latter would rather have prevented their separation.

I should here render justice to the evangelical Episcopalians and Baptists of Great Britain. They have acknowledged (at least I have heard nothing to the contrary) that the work of God narrated in these volumes had a claim to their entire sympathy. Christianity is neither an abstract doctrine nor an external organization. It is a life from God communicated to mankind, or rather to the Church. This new life is contained essentially in the person of Jesus Christ, and it is given to all those who are united to him, whether Episcopalians, Presbyterians, Baptists, or others. For this union is effected neither by the baptism of adults, nor by the episcopacy, nor by general assemblies; but solely by faith in certain Divine facts that Christ has accomplished, his humble incarnation, his atoning death, and his glorious resurrection. From this intimate union of Christians with Christ there necessarily results an intimate union of Christians with all those who receive the life of Christ; for the life that is in one is the life that is in all; and all together, Episcopalians, Presbyterians, Congregationalists, Baptists, &c., form not a simple plurality, but also, and chief of all, a living and organic unity.

The history of the Reformation is the history of one of the greatest outpourings of the life that cometh from God. May this work contribute to unite always more and more all those who are partakers of that Divine life.

J. H. Merle d'Aubigné

EAUX VIVES, NEAR GENEVA, *February* 1846.

CONTENTS TO VOLUME FIRST.

BOOK I.

STATE OF EUROPE BEFORE THE REFORMATION.

CHAPTER I.

Christianity—Two distinctive Principles—Rise of the Papacy —Early Encroachments—Influence of Rome—Co-opera-tion of the Bishops and of the Sects—Visible Unity of the Church—Invisible Unity of the Church—Primacy of St. Peter—Patriarchates—Co-operation of Princes—Influence of the Barbarians—Rome invokes the aid of the Franks— Secular Power—Pepin and Charlemagne—The Decretals —Disorders of Rome—The Emperor, the Pope's Suze-rain—Hildebrand — His Character — Celibacy — Struggle with the Empire — Emancipation of the Pope — Hil-debrand's Successors—The Crusades—The Empire—The Church, ... Page 7

CHAPTER II.

Grace—Dead Faith—Works—Unity and Duality—Pelagian-ism—Salvation at the hands of the Priests—Penance— Flagellations—Indulgences—Works of Supererogation — Purgatory—The Tariff—Jubilee—The Papacy and Chris-tianity—State of Christendom, . . . 14

CHAPTER III.

Religion—Relics—Easter Revels—Morals—Corruption—Dis-orders of the Priests, Bishops, and Popes—A Papal Family —Alexander VI.—Cæsar Borgia—Education—Ignorance— Ciceronians, ... 17

CHAPTER IV.

Imperishable Nature of Christianity—Two Laws of God— Apparent Strength of Rome—Secret Opposition—Decline —Threefold Opposition—Kings and People—Transforma-tion of the Church—The Pope judged in Italy—Discoveries of Kings and their Subjects—Frederick the Wise—Mode-ration and Expectation, ... 20

CHAPTER V.

Popular Feeling—The Empire—Providential Preparations —Impulse of the Reformation—Peace—The Commonalty —National Character—Papal Yoke—State of the Empire —Opposition at Rome—Middle Classes—Switzerland— Courage—Liberty—Smaller Cantons—Italy—Obstacles to the Reform — Spain — Obstacles—Portugal—France—Pre-

parations—Disappointment—The Low Countries—Eng-land—Scotland—The North—Russia—Poland—Bohemia —Hungary, ... Page 23

CHAPTER VI.

Roman Theology—Remains of Life—Justification by Faith —Witnesses to the Truth—Claudius—The Mystics—The Waldenses—Valdo—Wickliffe — Huss — Prediction — Pro-testantism before the Reformation—Anselm—Arnoldi— Utenheim—Martin—New Witnesses in the Church—Tho-mas Conecte—The Cardinal of Crayn—Institoris—Savo-narola—Justification by Faith—John Vitrarius—John Lailier—John of Wesalia—John of Goch—John Wessel— Protestantism before the Reformation—The Bohemian Brethren—Prophecy of Proles—Prophecy of the Eisenach Franciscan, ... 28

CHAPTER VII.

Third Preparation—Letters—Revival—Recollections of An-tiquity in Italy—Influence of the Humanists—Christia-nity of Dante—Valla—Infidelity in Italy—Platonic Philo-sophy—Commencement of Learning in Germany—Young Students—Printing—Characteristics of German Litera-ture—The Learned and the Schoolmen—A New World —Reuchlin—Reuchlin in Italy—His Labours—His Influ-ence in Germany—Mysticism—Contest with the Domini-cans, ... 34

CHAPTER VIII.

Erasmus—Erasmus a Canon—At Paris—His Genius—His Reputation—His Influence—Popular Attack—Praise of Folly—Gibes—Churchmen—Saints—Folly and the Popes —Attack on Science—Principles—Greek New Testament —His Profession of Faith—His Labours and Influence— His Failings—Two Parties—Reform without Violence— Was such possible?—Unreformed Church—His Timidity —His Indecision—Erasmus loses his Influence with all Parties, ... 40

CHAPTER IX.

The Nobility—Different Motives—Hütten—Literary League —Literæ Obscurorum Virorum—Their Effect—Luther's Opinion—Hütten at Brussels—His Letters—Sickingen— War—His Death—Cronberg—Hans Sachs—General Fer-ment 45

BOOK II.

THE YOUTH, CONVERSION, AND EARLY LABOURS OF LUTHER—1483-1517.

CHAPTER I.

Luther's Descent—His Parents—His Birth—His Poverty—Paternal Home—Severity—First Knowledge—School of Magdeburg — Hardships — Eisenach — The Shunamite — House of Cotta—Arts—Recollections of these Times—His Studies—Trebonius—The University, . . Page 49

CHAPTER II.

The University—Scholastic Divinity and the Classics—Luther's Piety—Discovery of the Bible—Illness—Luther admitted M.A.—Conscience—Death of Alexis—The Thunder-Storm—Providence—Farewell—Luther enters a Convent, ... 53

CHAPTER III.

His Father's Anger—Pardon—Humiliations—The Sack and the Cell—Endurance—Luther's Studies—St. Augustine—Peter d'Ailly—Occam—Gerson—The chained Bible—Lyra—Hebrew and Greek—Daily Prayers—Asceticism—Mental Struggles—Luther during Mass—Useless Observances—Luther in a Fainting-fit, ... 56

CHAPTER IV.

Pious Monks—Staupitz—His Piety—Visitation—Conversations—The Grace of Christ—Repentance—Power of Sin—Sweetness of Repentance — Election — Providence — The Bible—The aged Monk—Forgiveness of Sins—Ordination—The Dinner—Festival of Corpus Christi—Luther made Professor at Wittemberg, ... 60

CHAPTER V.

The University of Wittemberg—First Instructions—Biblical Lectures—Sensation—Luther preaches at Wittemberg—The Old Chapel—Impression produced by his Sermons, 65

CHAPTER VI.

Journey to Rome—Convent on the Po—Sickness at Bologna—Recollections of Rome—Julius II.—Superstitious Devotion — Profanity of the Clergy — Conversations — Roman

Scandals—Biblical Studies—Pilate's Staircase—Effects on Luther's Faith and on the Reformation—Gate of Paradise—Luther's Confession, ... Page 67

CHAPTER VII.

Luther Returns to Wittemberg—Made Doctor of Divinity—Carlstadt—Luther's Oath—Principle of the Reformation—Luther's Courage—Early Views of Reformation—The Schoolmen — Spalatin — Reuchlin's Quarrel with the Monks, ... 71

CHAPTER VIII.

Faith—Popular Declamations—Academic Teaching—Luther's Purity of Life—German Theology or Mysticism—The Monk Spenlein—Justification by Faith—Luther on Erasmus — Faith and Works — Erasmus — Necessity of Works—Luther's Charity, ... 74

CHAPTER IX.

Luther's first Theses—The Old Adam and Grace—Visitation of the Convents—Luther at Dresden and Erfurth—Tornator—Peace and the Cross—Results of Luther's Journey—His Labours—The Plague, ... 78

CHAPTER X.

The Relics—Relations of Luther with the Elector—Advice to the Chaplain—Duke George—His Character—Luther's Sermon before the Court—Dinner at Court—Evening with Emser, ... 80

CHAPTER XI.

Return to Wittemberg—Theses—Free-Will—Nature of Man—Rationalism—Proposal to the University of Erfurth—Eck—Urban Regius—Luther's Modesty—Effect of the Theses, ... 82

BOOK III.

THE INDULGENCES AND THE THESES. 1517—MAY 1518.

CHAPTER I.

Procession—Tetzel — Tetzel's Sermon — Confession — Four Graces—Sale—Public Penance—Letter of Indulgence—Exceptions—Amusements and Dissipation, . Page 85

CHAPTER II.

The Franciscan Confessor—The Soul in the Burial-ground—The Shoemaker of Hagenau—The Students—Myconius—Conversation with Tetzel—Trick of a Nobleman—Remarks of the Wise and of the People—A Miner of Schneeberg, ... 89

CHAPTER III.

Leo X.—The Pope's Necessities—Albert—His Character—Farming the Indulgences—Franciscans and Dominicans, ... 92

CHAPTER IV.

Tetzel approaches—Luther in the Confessional—Tetzel's Anger—Luther has no Plan—Jealousy of Orders—Luther's Sermon—The Elector's Dream, . . Page 93

CHAPTER V.

Festival of All-Saints—Theses—Their Strength—Moderation—Providence—Letter to Albert—Indifference of the Bishops—Dissemination of the Theses, . . 96

CHAPTER VI.

Reuchlin—Erasmus—Flek—Bibra—The Emperor—The Pope—Myconius—The Monks—Apprehensions—Adelman—An aged Priest—The Bishop—The Elector—The Townspeople of Erfurth—Luther's Answer—Disorder—Luther's Mainspring, ... 101

CONTENTS.

CHAPTER VII.

Tetzel's Attack—Luther's Reply—Good Works—Luther and Spalatin—Study of Scripture—Scheurl and Luther—Doubts on the Theses—Luther pleads for the People—A New Coat, ... Page 105

CHAPTER VIII.

Frankfort Discussion — Tetzel's Theses — Menaces — Knipstrow's Opposition—Luther's Theses burnt—The Monks—Luther's Peace—Tetzel's Theses burnt—Grief of Luther, ... 108

CHAPTER IX.

Prierio—System of Rome—Dialogue—System of Reform—Answer to Prierio—The Word—The Pope and the Church

—Hochstraten—The Monks—Luther Replies—Eck—The School—The Obelisks—Luther's Sentiments—The Asterisks—Rupture, ... Page 111

CHAPTER X.

Popular Writings—The Lord's Prayer—Our Father—Who art in Heaven—Hallowed be thy Name—Thy Kingdom come—Thy Will be done—Our Daily Bread—Sermon on Repentance—Remission of Sins cometh from Christ, 116

CHAPTER XI.

Apprehensions of his Friends—Journey to Heidelberg—Bibra—Palatine Palace—Rupture—The Paradoxes—Disputation—The Audience—Bucer—Brentz—Snepf—Conversations with Luther—Labours of these young Doctors—Effects on Luther—The aged Professor—The True Light—Arrival, ... 118

BOOK IV.

LUTHER BEFORE THE LEGATE.—MAY TO DECEMBER 1518.

CHAPTER I.

The Resolutions—Repentance—Papacy—Leo X.—Luther to his Bishop—Luther to the Pope—Luther to the Vicar-General—Rovera to the Elector—Sermon on Excommunication—Influence and Strength of Luther, . Page 122

CHAPTER II.

Diet at Augsburg—The Emperor to the Pope—The Elector to Rovera—Luther summoned to Rome—Luther's Peace—Intercession of the University—Papal Brief—Luther's Indignation—The Pope to the Elector, . . 126

CHAPTER III.

The Armourer Schwartzerd—His Wife—Philip—His Genius and Studies—The Bible—Call to Wittemberg—Melancthon's Departure and Journey—Leipsic—Mistake—Luther's Joy—Parallel—Revolution in Education—Study of Greek, ... 129

CHAPTER IV.

Sentiments of Luther and Staupitz—Summons to appear—Alarm and Courage—The Elector with the Legate—Departure for Augsburg—Sojourn at Weimar—Nuremberg—Arrival at Augsburg, ... 132

CHAPTER V.

De Vio—His Character—Serra Longa—Preliminary Conversation—Visit of the Councillors—Return of Serra Longa — The Prior — Luther's Discretion — Luther and Serra Longa—The Safe-conduct—Luther to Melancthon, 135

CHAPTER VI.

First Appearance—First Words—Conditions of Rome—Propositions to be retracted—Luther's Answer—He withdraws—Impression on both Parties—Arrival of Staupitz, Page 138

CHAPTER VII.

Second Interview—Luther's Declaration—The Legate's Answer—His Volubility—Luther's Request, . . 141

CHAPTER VIII.

Third Interview—Treasure of Indulgences—Faith—Humble Petition—Legate's Reply—Luther's Answer—The Legate's Anger—Luther withdraws—First Defection, . 143

CHAPTER IX.

De Vio and Staupitz—Staupitz and Luther—Luther to Spalatin—Luther to Carlstadt—The Communion—Link and De Vio—Departure of Link and Staupitz—Luther to Cajetan—Cardinal's Silence—Luther's Farewell—Departure—Appeal to Rome, ... 145

CHAPTER X.

Luther's Flight—Admiration—Luther's Desire—The Legate to the Elector—The Elector to the Legate—Prosperity of the University, ... 149

CHAPTER XI.

Thoughts on Departure—Farewell to the Church—Critical Moment—Deliverance—Luther's Courage—Dissatisfaction at Rome—Bull—Appeal to a Council, 152

CONTENTS TO VOLUME SECOND.

BOOK V.

THE LEIPSIC DISPUTATION.—1519.

CHAPTER I.

Luther's Danger—God preserves Luther—The Pope sends a Chamberlain — The Legate's Journey — Roman Briefs — Circumstances favourable to the Reform—Miltitz with Spalatin—Tetzel's Alarm—Miltitz's Flattery—Demands a Retractation—Luther refuses, but offers to keep Silence —Agreement between Luther and the Nuncio—The Legate's Kiss—Tetzel reproached by the Legate—Luther to the Pope—Nature of the Reformation—Luther opposes Separation—De Vio and Miltitz at Treves—Luther's Cause extends over various Countries—Luther's Writings begin the Reformation, ... Page 155

CHAPTER II.

Pause in Germany—Eck revives the Contest—Disputation between Eck and Carlstadt—Question of the Pope—Luther replies—Fears of Luther's Friends—Luther's Courage —The Truth triumphs unaided—Refusal of Duke George —Gaiety of Mosellanus—Fears of Erasmus, . 161

CHAPTER III.

Arrival of Eck and of the Wittembergers—Amsdorff—The Students—Carlstadt's Accident—Placard—Eck and Luther—The Pleissenburg—Judges proposed—Luther objects —He consents at last, ... 164

CHAPTER IV.

Opening of the Disputation—Speech of Mosellanus—*Veni, Sancte Spiritus*—Portraits of Luther and Carlstadt—Doctor Eck—Carlstadt's Books—Merit of Congruity—Natural Powers—Scholastic Distinction—Point at which Rome and the Reformation diverge—Liberty given to Man by Grace—Carlstadt's Notes—Clamour of the Spectators—

Melancthon during the Disputation—His Opinion—Eck's Manœuvres—Luther Preaches—Citizens of Leipsic—Quarrels between the Students and Doctors, . Page 166

CHAPTER V.

The Hierarchy and Rationalism—The Two Peasants' Sons —Eck and Luther begin—The Head of the Church—Primacy of Rome—Equality of Bishops—Peter the Foundation-stone—Christ the Corner-stone—Eck insinuates that Luther is a Hussite—Luther on the doctrine of Huss—Agitation among the Hearers—The Word alone—The Court-fool—Luther at Mass—Saying of the Duke—Purgatory—Close of the Discussion, ... 170

CHAPTER VI.

Interest felt by the Laity—Luther's Opinion—Confession and Boasts of Doctor Eck—Effects of the Disputation—Poliander—Cellarius—The Young Prince of Anhalt—The Students of Leipsic—Cruciger—Melancthon's Call—Luther's Emancipation, ... 175

CHAPTER VII.

Eck attacks Melancthon—Melancthon's Defence—Interpretation of Holy Scripture—Luther's Firmness—The Bohemian Brothers—Emser—Staupitz, . . . 177

CHAPTER VIII.

The Epistle to the Galatians—Christ for us—Blindness of Luther's Opponents—Earliest Ideas on the Lord's Supper —Is the Sacrament without Faith sufficient?—Luther a Bohemian—Eck attacked—Eck goes to Rome, . 179

BOOK VI.

THE PAPAL BULL.—1520.

CHAPTER I.

Character of Maximilian—Candidates for the Empire—Charles—Francis I.—Disposition of the Germans—The Crown offered to Frederick — Charles elected Emperor, ... Page 181

CHAPTER II.

Luther's Letter to the Emperor—His Danger—Frederick's Instructions to his Envoy at Rome—Luther's Sentiments —Melancthon's Fears—The German Nobles favour the Reformation—Schaumburg—Sickingen—Ulric of Hütten —Luther's Confidence—Erasmus defends Luther—Abstemius — Hedio — Luther becomes more free—Faith the Source of Works—What gives Faith?—Luther judging his own Writings, ... 183

CHAPTER III.

The Papacy Attacked—Appeal to the Nobility—The three Walls—All Christians are Priests—The Magistrate should chastise the Clergy—Roman Corruptions—Ruin of Italy—Dangers of Germany—The Pope — The Legates — The Monks—Marriage of Priests—Celibacy— Festivals—The Bohemians—Charity—The Universities — The Empire—The Emperor should retake Rome—Unpublished Book—Luther's Moderation—Success of the Address, . 187

CHAPTER IV.

Preparations at Rome—Motives for Papal Resistance—Eck at Rome—The King of Crowns—Eck prevails—The Pope is the World—God brings about the Separation—A Swiss Priest pleads for Luther—The Roman Consistory—Exordium of the Bull—Luther condemned, . . . 191

CHAPTER V.

Wittemberg—Melancthon—His Marriage—Catherine—Domestic Life—Benevolence—Good Humour—Christ and Antiquity—Labour—Love of Letters—His Mother—Revolt of the Students, ... Page 195

CHAPTER VI.

The Gospel in Italy—Sermon on the Mass—Babylonish Captivity of the Church—Baptism—Abolition of other Vows—Progress of Reform, . . . 197

CHAPTER VII.

Fresh Negotiations—The Augustines at Eisleben—Miltitz—Deputation to Luther—Miltitz and the Elector—Conference at Lichtemberg—Luther's Letter to the Pope—Book presented to the Pope—Union of Christ with the Believer—Liberty and Bondage, . . . 198

CHAPTER VIII.

The Bull in Germany—Eck's Reception—The Bull at Wittemberg—Zwingle's Intervention, . . . 202

CHAPTER IX.

Luther's Appeal to God—His Opinion of the Bull—A Neutral Family—Luther on the Bull—Against the Bull of Antichrist—The Pope forbids Faith—Effects of the Bull—The Burning Pile of Louvain, . . . Page 204

CHAPTER X.

Decisive Step of the Reformer—Luther's Appeal to a General Council—Close Combat—The Bull burnt by Luther—Meaning of this daring Act—Luther in the Academy—Luther against the Pope—New Work by Melancthon—How Luther encourages his Friends—Progress of the Struggle—Melancthon's Opinions on the Weak-hearted—Luther's Treatise on the Bible—Doctrine of Grace—Luther's Recantation, ... 207

CHAPTER XI.

Coronation of Charles the Fifth—The Nuncio Aleander—Shall Luther's Books be Burnt?—Aleander and the Emperor—The Nuncios and the Elector—Duke John's Son in Behalf of Luther—Luther's Calmness—The Elector protects Luther—Reply of the Nuncios—Frasmus at Cologne—Erasmus at the Elector's—Declaration of Erasmus—Advice of Erasmus—System of Charles V. . . 210

CHAPTER XII.

Luther on Confession—Real Absolution—Antichrist—Luther's Popularity—Satires—Ulrich of Hütten—Lucas Cranach—The Carnival at Wittemberg—Staupitz intimidated—Luther's Labours—His Humility—Progress of the Reformation, ... 214

BOOK VII.

THE DIET OF WORMS.—1521, JANUARY TO MAY.

CHAPTER I.

Victories of the Word of God—The Diet of Worms—Policy of Rome—Difficulties—Charles demands Luther—The Elector to Charles V.—State of Feeling—Alarm of Aleander—The Elector departs without Luther—Aleander arouses Rome—Excommunication of Pope and Communion with Christ—Fulminations of the Bull—Luther's Motives in the Reformation, . . Page 218

CHAPTER II.

A Foreign Prince—Council of Politicians—Conference between the Confessor and the Chancellor—Inutility of these Manœuvres—Aleander's Activity—Luther's Words—Charles yields to the Pope, . . . 222

CHAPTER III.

Aleander introduced to the Diet—Aleander's Speech—Luther is accused—Rome is justified—Appeal to Charles against Luther—Effect of the Nuncio's Speech, . 225

CHAPTER IV.

Sentiments of the Princes—Speech of Duke George—Character of the Reformation—One Hundred and One Grievances—Charles gives Way—Aleander's Stratagems—The Grandees of Spain—Peace of Luther—Death and no Retractation, ... 227

CHAPTER V.

Shall Luther have a Safe-conduct—The Safe-conduct—Will Luther come—Holy Thursday at Rome—The Pope and Luther, ... 229

CHAPTER VI.

Luther's Courage—Bugenhagen at Wittemberg—Persecutions in Pomerania—Melancthon desires to accompany Luther—Amsdorff, Schurff and Suaven—Hütten to Charles V. . . . . . . Page 232

CHAPTER VII.

Departure for the Diet of Worms—Luther's Farewell—His Condemnation is posted up—Cavalcade near Erfurth—Meeting between Jonas and Luther—Luther in his former Convent—Luther preaches at Erfurth—Incident—Faith and Works—Concourse of People and Luther's Courage—Luther's Letter to Spalatin—Stay at Frankfort—Fears at Worms—Plan of the Imperialists—Luther's Firmness, ... 234

CHAPTER VIII.

Entry into Worms—Death-Song—Charles's Council—Capito and the Temporizers—Luther's numerous Visiters—Citation—Hütten to Luther—Luther proceeds to the Diet—Saying of Freundsberg—Imposing Assembly—The Chancellor's Speech—Luther's Reply—His Discretion—Saying of Charles V.—Alarm—Triumph—Luther's Firmness—Violence of the Spaniards—Advice—Luther's Struggles and Prayer—Strength of the Reformation—His Vow to the Scriptures—The Court of the Diet—Luther's Speech—Three Classes of Writings—He requires Proof of his Errors—Serious Warnings—He repeats his Speech in Latin—Here I stand: I can say no more—The Weakness of God stronger than Man—A new Attempt—Victory, . 238

CHAPTER IX.

Tumult and Calmness—The Flagon of Duke Eric—The Elector and Spalatin—The Emperor's Message—Proposal to violate the Safe-conduct—Violent Opposition—Enthusiasm in favour of Luther—Language of Conciliation—Fears of the Elector—Luther's numerous Visiters—Philip of Hesse, ... 246

CHAPTER X.

Conference with the Archbishop of Treves—Wehe's Exhortation to Luther—Luther's Replies—Private Conversation—Visit of Cochlœus—Supper at the Archbishop's—Conference at the Hotel of the Knights of Rhodes—A Council proposed—Luther's last Interview with the Archbishop—Visit to a sick Friend—Luther receives Orders to leave Worms—Luther's Departure, . Page 249

CHAPTER XI.

The Conflict at Worms—Luther's Letter to Cranach—Luther's Letter to Charles V.—Luther with the Abbot of Hirschfeldt—The Parish Priest of Eisenach—Several Princes leave the Diet—Charles signs Luther's Condemnation—The Edict of Worms—Luther with his Parents—Luther attacked and carried away—The Ways of God—The Wartburg—Luther a Prisoner, . . Page 252

BOOK VIII.

THE SWISS. 1484—1522.

CHAPTER I.

Movement in Switzerland—Source of the Reformation—Its democratic Character—Foreign Service—Morality—The Tockenburg—A Chalet on the Alps—A Family of Shepherds—Young Ulrich, ... Page 257

CHAPTER II.

Ulrich at Wesen and Basle—Ulrich at Berne—The Dominican Convent—Jetzer—The Apparitions—Passion of the Lay-brother—Imposture—Discovery and Punishment—Zwingle at Vienna and Basle—Music at Basle—Wittembach proclaims the Gospel—Leo Juda—The Priest of Glaris, ... 259

CHAPTER III.

Fondness for War—Schinner—Pension from the Pope—The Labyrinth—Zwingle in Italy—Principle of Reform—Zwingle and Luther—Zwingle and Erasmus—Zwingle and the ancient Classics—Paris and Glaris, . . 262

CHAPTER IV.

Zwingle to Erasmus—Oswald Myconius—The Robbers—Œcolampadius—Zwingle at Marignan—Zwingle and Italy—Zwingle's Method—Commencement of the Reform—Discovery—Passage from one World to the other, . 265

CHAPTER V.

Our Lady of Einsidlen—Zwingle's Call—The Abbot—Geroldsek—A learned Society—The Bible copied—Zwingle and Superstition—First Opposition to Error—Sensation—Hedio—Zwingle and the Legates—The Honours of Rome—The Bishop of Constance—Samson and the Indulgences—Stapfer—Zwingle's Charity—His Friends, . 268

CHAPTER VI.

The Canons' College—Election to the Cathedral—Fable—Accusations—Zwingle's Confession—Development of God's Purposes—Farewell to Einsidlen—Arrival at Zurich—Zwingle's bold Declaration—First Sermons—Their Effect—Opposition—Zwingle's Character—Taste for Music—Arrangement of the Day—The Book-hawker, . 272

CHAPTER VII.

The Indulgences—Samson at Berne and at Baden—The Dean of Bremgarten—Young Henry Bullinger—Samson and the Dean—Zwingle's internal Struggles—Zwingle opposes the Indulgences—Samson is sent back, . . 276

CHAPTER VIII.

Zwingle's Toils and Fatigue—The Baths of Pfeffers—The Moment of God—The Great Death—Zwingle attacked by the Plague—His Adversaries—His Friends—Convalescence—General Joy—Effects of the Pestilence—Myconius at Lucerne—Oswald encourages Zwingle—Zwingle at Basle—Capito invited to Mentz—Hedio at Basle—The Unnatural Son—Preparations for the Struggle, Page 279

CHAPTER IX.

The Two Reformers—The Fall of Man—Expiation of the Man-God—No Merit in Works—Objections refuted—Power of Love for Christ—Election—Christ the sole Master—Effects of this Preaching—Dejection and Courage—First Act of the Magistrate—Church and State—Attacks—Gaister, ... 283

CHAPTER X.

A new Combatant—The Reformer of Berne—Zwingle encourages Haller—The Gospel at Lucerne—Oswald persecuted—Zwingle's Preaching—Henry Hullinger and Gerold of Knonau—Rubli at Basle—The Chaplain of the Hospital—War in Italy—Zwingle protests against the Capitulations, ... 286

CHAPTER XI.

Zwingle opposes Human Traditions—Commotion during Lent—Truth triumphs amidst Opposition—The Bishop's Deputies—Accusation before the Clergy and the Council—Appeal to the Great Council—The Coadjutor and Zwingle—Zwingle's Reply—Decree of the Great Council—Posture of Affairs—Hoffman's Attack, . . . 290

CHAPTER XII.

Mourning and Joy in Germany—Plots against Zwingle—The Bishop's Mandate—Archeteles—The Bishop's Appeal to the Diet—Injunction against attacking the Monks—Zwingle's Declaration—The Nuns of Œtenbach—Zwingle's Address to Schwytz, ... 293

CHAPTER XIII.

A French Monk—He teaches in Switzerland—Dispute between Zwingle and the Monk—Discourse of the Commander of the Johannites—The Carnival at Berne—The Eaters of the Dead—The Skull of St. Anne—Appenzel—The Grisons—Murder and Adultery—Zwingle's Marriage, ... 295

CHAPTER XIV.

How the Truth triumphs—Meeting at Einsidlen—Petition to the Bishop and Confederates—The Men of Einsidlen separate—Scene in a Convent—Dinner with Myconius—The Strength of the Reformers—Effect of the Petitions to Lucerne—The Council of the Diet—Haller at the Townhall—Friburg—Oswald's Destitution—Zwingle consoles him—Oswald quits Lucerne—The Diet's first Act of Severity—Consternation of Zwingle's Brothers—Zwingle's Resolution—The Future—Zwingle's Prayer, . 298

CONTENTS TO VOLUME THIRD.

BOOK IX.

FIRST REFORMS.—1521 AND 1522.

CHAPTER I.

Progress of the Reformation—New Period—Usefulness of Luther's Captivity in the Wartburg—Agitation in Germany—Melancthon and Luther—Enthusiasm,   Page 309

CHAPTER II.

Luther in the Wartburg—Object of his Captivity—Anxiety—Sickness—Luther's Labours—On Confession—Reply to Latomus—His daily Walks, ... 312

CHAPTER III.

Commencement of the Reform—Marriage of Feldkirchen—The Marriage of Monks—Theses—Tract against Monachism—Luther no longer a Monk, . . 315

CHAPTER IV.

Archbishop Albert—The Idol of Halle—Luther's Indignation—Alarm of the Court—Luther's Letter to the Archbishop—Albert's Reply—Joachim of Brandenburg, 316

CHAPTER V.

Translation of the Bible—Wants of the Church—Principles of the Reformation—Temptations of the Devil—Luther's Works condemned by the Sorbonne—Melancthon's Reply—Luther Visits Wittemberg, . . 319

CHAPTER VI.

Fresh Reforms—Gabriel Zwilling on the Mass—The University—Melancthon's Propositions—The Elector—Monastic Institutions attacked—Emancipation of the Monks—Disturbances—Chapter of the Augustine Monks—Carlstadt and the Mass—First Celebration of the Lord's Supper—Importance of the Mass in the Romish System, 322

CHAPTER VII.

False Reform—The New Prophets—The Prophets at Wittemberg—Melancthon—The Elector—Luther—Carlstadt and the Images—Disturbances—Luther is called for—He does not hesitate—Dangers, . . Page 326

CHAPTER VIII.

Departure from the Wartburg—New Position—Luther and Primitive Catholicism—Meeting at the Black Bear—Luther's Letter to the Elector—Return to Wittemberg—Sermon at Wittemberg—Charity—The Word—How the Reformation was brought about—Faith in Christ—Its Effects—Didymus—Carlstadt—The Prophets—Interview with Luther—End of the Struggle, . . 330

CHAPTER IX.

Translation of the New Testament—Faith and Scripture—Opposition—Importance of this Publication—Necessity for a systematic Arrangement—Melancthon's Loci Communes—Original Sin—Salvation—Free Will—Effects of the Loci Communes, . . . 337

CHAPTER X.

Opposition—Henry VIII.—Wolsey—The Queen—Fisher—Sir Thomas More—Luther's Books burnt—Henry's attack on Luther—Presented to the Pope—Its Effect on Luther—Energy and Violence—Luther's Reply—Answer by the Bishop of Rochester—Reply of Sir Thomas More—Henry's Proceedings, ... 340

CHAPTER XI.

General Movement—The Monks—How the Reformation was carried on—Unlearned Believer—The Old and the New Doctors—Printing and Literature—Bookselling and Colportage, ... 345

CHAPTER XII.

Luther at Zwickau—The Castle of Freyberg—Worms—Frankfort—Universal Movement—Wittemberg the Centre of the Reformation—Luther's Sentiments, . 348

BOOK X.

AGITATION, REVERSES, AND PROGRESS. 1522—1526.

CHAPTER I.

Political Element—Want of Enthusiasm at Rome—Siege of Pampeluna—Courage of Ignatius—Transition—Luther and Loyola—Visions—Two Principles, . Page 351

CHAPTER II.

Victory of the Pope—Death of Leo X.—The Oratory of Divine Love—Adrian VI.—Plan of Reform—Opposition, 355

CHAPTER III.

Diet of Nuremberg—Soliman's Invasion—The Nuncio calls for Luther's Death—The Nuremberg Preachers—Promise of Reform—The Nuncio's Alarm—Grievances of the Nation—Decree of the Diet—Fulminating Letter of the Pope—Luther's Advice, . . . 356

CHAPTER IV.

Persecution—Exertions of Duke George—The Convent at Antwerp—Miltenberg—The Three Monks of Antwerp—The Scaffold—The Martyrs of Brussels, . Page 360

CHAPTER V.

The New Pope, Clement VII.—The Legate Campeggio—Diet of Nuremberg—Demand of the Legate—Reply of the Diet—A Secular Council projected—Alarm and Exertions of the Pope—Bavaria—League of Ratisbon—Campeggio's Dishonesty—Severity and Reforms—Political Schism—Opposition—Intrigues of Rome—Decree of Burgos—Rupture, ... 363

CHAPTER VI.

Persecution—Gaspard Tauber—A Bookseller—Cruelties in Wurtemberg, Salzburg, and Bavaria—Pomerania—Henry of Zuphten, ... 366

CHAPTER VII.

Divisions — The Lord's Supper—Two Extremes — Hoen's Discovery—Wessel on the Lord's Supper—Carlstadt—Luther—Mysticism of the Anabaptists—Carlstadt at Orlamund—Luther's Mission—Interview at Table—The Conference of Orlamund—Carlstadt Banished, . Page 368

CHAPTER VIII.

Progress—Resistance against the Ratisbon Leaguers—Meeting between Philip of Hesse and Melancthon—The Landgrave converted to the Gospel—The Palatinate—Luneburg —Holstein—The Grand-Master at Wittemberg, . 372

CHAPTER IX.

Reforms—All-Saints Church—Fall of the Mass—Learning—Christian Schools—Learning extended to the Laity—The Arts — Moral Religion — Esthetical Religion — Music — Poetry—Painting, ... 374

CHAPTER X.

Political Ferment — Luther against Rebellion — Thomas Munzer—Agitation—The Black Forest—The Twelve Articles—Luther's Opinion — Helfenstein — March of the Peasants—March of the Imperial Army—Defeat of the Peasants—Cruelty of the Princes, . . Page 377

CHAPTER XI.

Munzer at Mulhausen—Appeal to the People—March of the Princes—End of the Revolt—Influence of the Reformers—Sufferings—Changes—Two Results, . . 382

CHAPTER XII.

Death of the Elector Frederick—The Prince and the Reformer—Roman-catholic Alliance—Plans of Charles the Fifth—Dangers, ... 386

CHAPTER XIII.

The Nuns of Nimptsch—Luther's Sentiments—The Convent dissolved—Luther's Marriage—Domestic Happiness, 387

CHAPTER XIV.

The Landgrave—The Elector—Prussia—Reformation—Secularization—The Archbishop of Mentz—Conference at Friedwalt—Diet—Alliance of Torgau—Resistance of the Reformers—Alliance of Magdeburg—The Catholics redouble their Exertions—The Emperor's Marriage—Threatening Letters—The Two Parties, . . . 389

BOOK XI.

DIVISIONS.

SWITZERLAND—GERMANY. 1523—1527.

CHAPTER I.

Unity in Diversity—Primitive Fidelity and Liberty—Formation of Romish Unity—Leo Juda and the Monk—Zwingle's Theses—The Disputation of January, Page 393

CHAPTER II.

Papal Temptations—Progress of the Reformation—The Idol at Stadelhofen — Sacrilege — The Ornaments of the Saints, ... 395

CHAPTER III.

The Disputation of October—Zwingle on the Church—The Church—Commencement of Presbyterianism—Discussion on the Mass—Enthusiasts—The Language of Discretion —Victory—A Characteristic of the Swiss Reformation—Moderation—Oswald Myconius at Zurich—Revival of Literature—Thomas Plater of the Valais, . . 397

CHAPTER IV.

Diet of Lucerne—Hottinger arrested—His Death—Deputation from the Diet to Zurich—Abolition of Religious Processions—Abolition of Images—The Two Reformations—Appeal to the People, . . 400

CHAPTER V.

New Opposition—Abduction of Œxlin—The Family of the Wirths—The Populace at the Convent of Ittingen—The Diet of Zug—The Wirths apprehended and given up to the Diet—Their Condemnation, . . 403

CHAPTER VI.

Abolition of the Mass—Zwingle's Dream—Celebration of the Lord's Supper—Fraternal Charity—Original Sin—The Oligarchs opposed to the Reform—Various Attacks, 406

CHAPTER VII.

Berne—The Provost Watteville—First Successes of the Reformed Doctrines—Haller at the Convent—Accusation and Deliverance—The Monastery of Königsfeldt—Margaret Watteville to Zwingle—The Convent opened—Two Champions—Clara May and the Provost Watteville, 408

CHAPTER VIII.

Basle—Œcolampadius—He visits Augsburg—Enters a Convent—Retires to Sickingen's Castle—Returns to Basle—Ulrich Hütten—His Plans—Last Effort of Chivalry—Hütten dies at Ufnau, ... Page 411

CHAPTER IX.

Erasmus and Luther—Vacillations of Erasmus—Luther to Erasmus — Erasmus's Treatise against Luther on Free Will—Three Opinions—Effect upon Luther—Luther on Free Will—The Jansenists and the Reformers—Homage to Erasmus—His Anger—The Three Days, 413

CHAPTER X.

The Three Adversaries—Source of Truth—Anabaptism—Anabaptism and Zwingle—Constitution of the Church—Prison—The Prophet Blaurock — Anabaptism at Saint Gall—An Anabaptist Family—Discussion at Zurich—The Limits of the Reformation—Punishment of the Anabaptists, ... 415

CHAPTER XI.

Progression and Immobility—Zwingle and Luther—The Netherlanders at Zurich—Result of Zwingle's inquiries—Luther's Return to Scholasticism—Respect for Tradition —Occam—Contrary Tendency in Zwingle—Beginning of the Controversy—Œcolampadius and the Swabian Syngramma—Strasburg mediates, . . 421

CHAPTER XII.

The Tockenburg—An Assembly of the People—Reformation —The Grisons—Disputation at Ilantz—Results—Reformation at Zurich, ... 425

CHAPTER XIII.

The Oligarchs—Deputation to Berne—Bernese Mandate of 1526 in favour of the Papacy—Discussion at Baden—Regulations of the Discussion—Riches and Poverty—Eck and Œcolampadius—Discussion—Zwingle's Share in the Discussion—Vaunts of the Romanists—Abusive Language of a Monk—Close of the Disputation, . . 427

CHAPTER XIV.

Consequences at Basle, Berne, Saint Gall, and other Places —Diet at Zurich—The small Cantons—Threats against Berne—Foreign Support, . . . 429

BOOK XII.

THE FRENCH. 1500—1526.

CHAPTER I.

Universality of Christianity—Enemies of the Reform in France—Heresy and Persecution in Dauphiny—A country Mansion—The Farel Family—Pilgrimage to the Holy Cross—Immorality and Superstition—William desires to become a Student, ... Page 432

CHAPTER II.

Louis XII. and the Assembly of Tours—Francis and Margaret—Learned Men—Lefevre—His Courses at the University—Meeting between Lefevre and Farel—Farel's Hesitation and Researches—First Awakening—Lefevre's Prophecy—Teaches Justification by Faith—Objections—Disorder of the Colleges—Effects on Farel—Election—Sanctification of Life, ... 435

CHAPTER III.

Farel and the Saints—The University—Farel's Conversion—Farel and Luther—Other Disciples—Date of the Reform in France—Spontaneous Rise of the different Reforms—Which was the first?—Lefevre's Place, . 440

CHAPTER IV.

Character of Francis I.—Commencement of Modern Times—Liberty and Obedience—Margaret of Valois—The Court—Briçonnet, Count of Montbrun—Lefevre commends him to the Bible—Francis I. and "his Children"—The Gospel brought to Margaret—Conversion—Adoration—Margaret's Character, ... 442

CHAPTER V.

Enemies of the Reformation—Louisa—Duprat—Concordat of Bologna—Opposition of the Parliament and the University—The Sorbonne—Beda—His Character—His Tyranny—Berquin, the most learned of the Nobility—The Intriguers of the Sorbonne—Heresy of the three Magdalens—Luther condemned at Paris—Address of the Sorbonne to the King—Lefevre quits Paris for Meaux, 445

CHAPTER VI.

Briçonnet visits his Diocese—Reform—The Doctors persecuted in Paris—Philiberta of Savoy—Correspondence between Margaret and Briçonnet, . . . 449

CHAPTER VII.

Beginning of the Church at Meaux—The Scriptures in French—The Artisans and the Bishop—Evangelical Harvest—The Epistles of St. Paul sent to the King—Lefevre and Roma—The Monks before the Bishop—The Monks before the Parliament—Briçonnet's first fall—Lefevre and Farel—Persecution—Francis Lambert—His Noviciate and Apostolic Labours—His Early Struggles—He quits Avignon, ... 452

CHAPTER VIII.

Lefevre and Farel persecuted—Difference between the Lutheran and Reformed Churches—Leclerc posts up his Placards—Leclerc branded—Berquin's Zeal—Berquin before the Parliament—Rescued by Francis I.—Mazurier's Apostacy—Fall and Remorse of Pavanne—Metz—Agrippa and Chatelain—Lambert at Wittemberg—Evangelical Press at Hamburg—Lambert marries—He longs to return to France—The Lots—Peter Toussaint becomes attentive—Leclerc breaks the Images—Leclerc's Condemnation and Torture—Martyrdom of Chatelain—Flight, Page 457

CHAPTER IX.

Farel and his Brothers—Farel expelled from Gap—He preaches in the Fields—The Knight Anemond of Coct—The Minorite—Anemond quits France—Luther to the Duke of Savoy—Farel quits France, . . 464

CHAPTER X.

Catholicity of the Reformation—Friendship between Farel and Œcolampadius—Farel and Erasmus—Altercation—Farel demands a Disputation—Theses—Scripture and Faith—Discussion, ... 467

CHAPTER XI.

New Campaign—Farel's Call to the Ministry—An Outpost—Lyons—Sebville at Grenoble—Conventicles—Preaching at Lyons—Maigret in Prison—Margaret intimidated, 470

CHAPTER XII.

The French at Basle—Encouragement of the Swiss—Fears of Discord—Translating and Printing at Basle—Bibles and Tracts disseminated in France, . . 473

CHAPTER XIII.

Progress at Montbeliard—Resistance and Commotion—Toussaint leaves Œcolampadius—The Image of Saint Anthony—Death of Anemond—Strasburg—Lambert's Letter to Francis I.—Successive Defeats, . 475

CHAPTER XIV.

Francis made Prisoner at Pavia—Margaret's anxiety for her Brother—Allegorical Letter—Reaction against the Reformation—Louisa consults the Sorbonne—Commission against the Heretics—Charges against Briçonnet—The Faculty of Paris—The Bishop's Alarm—Appeals to the Parliament—Temptation—His second fall—Consequences—Recantation—Briçonnet and Fénelon—Lefevre accused—Condemnation and Flight—Lefevre at Strasburg—Louis Berquin imprisoned—Erasmus attacked—He appeals to the King and the Emperor—Esch imprisoned—Schuch at Nancy—His Martyrdom—Beda's Struggle with Caroli—Sorrow of Pavanne—His Martyrdom—A Christian Hermit—Concourse at Notre Dame, ... 479

CHAPTER XV.

A Student of Noyon—Character of young Calvin—Early Education—Consecrated to Theology—The Bishop gives him the Tonsure—He leaves Noyon on Account of the Plague—The Two Calvins—Slanders—The Reformation creates new Languages—Persecution and Terror—Margaret's Letter to her Brother—Toussaint put in Prison—The Persecution more furious—Death of Du Blet, Moulin, and Papillon—God saves the Church—Margaret's Project—Her Departure for Spain, ... 489

CONTENTS TO VOLUME FOURTH.

BOOK XIII.

THE PROTEST AND THE CONFERENCE. 1526—1529.

CHAPTER I.

Twofold Movement of Reform—Reform the Work of God—First Diet of Spires—Palladium of Reform—Firmness of the Reformers—Proceedings of the Diet—Report of the Commissioners—The Papacy painted and described by Luther—The Destruction of Jerusalem—Instructions of Seville—Change of Policy—Holy League—Religious Liberty proposed—Crisis of the Reformation, . Page 499

CHAPTER II.

Italian War—The Emperor's Manifesto—March on Rome—Revolt of the Troops—The Sack of Rome—German Humours—Violence of the Spaniards—Clement VII. capitulates, ... 503

CHAPTER III.

Profitable Calm—Constitution of the Church—Philip of Hesse—The Monk of Marburg—Lambert's Paradoxes—Friar Boniface—Disputation at Hamburg—Triumph of the Gospel in Hesse- -Constitution of the Church—Bishops—Synods—Two Elements of the Church—Luther on the Ministry—Organization of the Church—Luther's Contradictions on State Interference—Luther to the Elector—German Mass—Melancthon's Instructions—Disaffection—Visitation of the Reformed Churches—Results—The Reformation advances—Elizabeth of Brandenburg, 506

CHAPTER IV.

Edict of Ofen—Persecutions—Winchler, Carpenter, and Keyser—Alarm in Germany—Pack's Forgery—League of the Reformed Princes—Advice of the Reformers—Luther's Pacific Council—Surprise of the Papist Princes—Pack's Scheme not improbable—Vigour of the Reformation, 513

CHAPTER V.

Alliance between Charles and Clement VII.—Omens—Hostility of the Papists—Arbitrary Proposition of Charles-Resolutions of the Diet—The Reformation in Danger—Decision of the Princes—Violence of Ferdinand—The Schism completed, ... Page 517

CHAPTER VI.

The Protest—Principles of the Protest—Supremacy of the Gospel—Christian Union—Ferdinand rejects the Protest—Attempt at Conciliation—Exultation of the Papists—Evangelical Appeal—Christian Unity a Reality—Dangers of the Protestants—The Protestants leave Spires—The Princes the True Reformers—Germany and Reform, 520

CHAPTER VII.

Union necessary to Reform—Luther's Doctrine on the Lord's Supper—A Lutheran Warning—Proposed Conference at Marburg—Melancthon and Zwingle—Zwingle leaves Zurich—Rumours in Zurich—The Reformers at Marburg—Carlstadt's Petition—Preliminary Discussions—Holy Ghost—Original Sin—Baptism—Luther, Melancthon. and Zwingle—Opening of the Conference—The Prayer of the Church—Hoc est Corpus Meum—Syllogism of Œcolampadius—The Flesh profiteth nothing—Lambert convinced—Luther's Old Song—Agitation in the Conference—Arrival of new Deputies—Christ's Humanity finite—Mathematics and Popery—Testimony of the Fathers—Testimony of Augustine—Argument of the Velvet Cover—End of the Conference—The Landgrave mediates—Necessity of Union—Luther rejects Zwingle's Hand—Sectarian Spirit of the Germans—Bucer's Dilemma—Christian Charity prevails—Luther's Report—Unity of Doctrine—Unity in Diversity—Signatures—Two Extremes—Three Views—Germ of Popery—Departure—Luther's Dejection—Turks before Vienna—Luther's Battle-Sermon and Agony—Luther's Firmness—Victory—Exasperation of the Papists—Threatening Prospects, . . 524

BOOK XIV.

THE AUGSBURG CONFESSION.—1530.

CHAPTER I.

Two striking Lessons—Charles V. in Italy—The German Envoys—Their Boldness—The Landgrave's Present—The Envoys under Arrest—Their Release and Departure—Meeting of Charles and Clement—Gattinara's Proposition—Clement's Arms—War imminent—Luther's Objections—The Saviour is coming—Charles's Conciliatory Language—The Emperor's Motives, ... Page 537

CHAPTER II.

The Coronation—The Emperor made a Deacon—The Romish Church and the State—Alarm of the Protestants—Luther advocates Passive Resistance—Brück's noble Advice—Articles of Faith prepared—Luther's Strong Tower—Luther at Coburg—Charles at Innspruck—Two Parties at Court—Gattinara—The King of Denmark won over by Charles—Piety of the Elector—Wiles of the Romanists, ... 541

CHAPTER III.

Augsburg—The Gospel Preached—The Emperor's Message—The Sermons prohibited—Firmness of the Elector—The Elector's Reply—Preparation of the Confession—Luther's Sinai—His Son and his Father—Luther's Merriment—Luther's Diet at Coburg—Saxony, a Paradise below—To the Bishops—Travail of the Church—Charles—The Pope's Letter—Melancthon on Fasting—The Church, the Judge—The Landgrave's catholic Spirit, . . Page 545

CHAPTER IV.

Agitation in Augsburg—Violence of the Imperialists—Charles at Munich—Charles's Arrival—The Nuncio's Blessing—The Imperial Procession—Charles's Appearance—Enters Augsburg—Te Deum—The Benediction—Charles desires the Sermons to be discontinued—Brandenburg offers his Head—The Emperor's Request for Corpus Christi—Refusal of the Princes—Agitation of Charles—The Princes oppose Tradition—Procession of Corpus Christi—Exasperation of Charles, . 550

CHAPTER V.

The Sermons prohibited—Compromise proposed and accepted—The Herald—Curiosity of the Citizens—The new Preachers—The Medley of Popery—Luther encourages the Princes—Veni Spiritus—Mass of the Holy Ghost—The Sermon—Opening of the Diet—The Elector's Prayer—Insidious Plan of the Romanists—Valdez and Melancthon—No Public Discussion—Evangelical firmness prevails, ... 554

CHAPTER VI.

The Elector's Zeal—The Signing of the Confession—Courage of the Princes—Melancthon's Weakness—The Legate's Speech—Delays—The C nfession in Danger—The Protestants are firm — Melancthon's Despondency — Luther's Prayer and Anxiety—Luther's Texts—His Letter to Melancthon—Faith, ... Page 559

CHAPTER VII.

The 25th June 1530—The Palatine Chapel—Recollections and Contrast—The Confession—Prologue—Justification—The Church—Free Will and Works—Faith—Interest of the Hearers—The Princes become Preachers—The Confession—Abuses—Church and State—The two Governments — Epilogue — Argumentation — Prudence — Church and State—The Sword—Moderate Tone of the Confession—Its Defects—A new Baptism, ... 563

CHAPTER VIII.

Effect on the Romanists—Luther demands Religious Liberty—His dominant Idea—Song of Triumph—Ingenuous Confessions—Hopes of the Protestants—Failure of the Popish Intrigues—The Emperor's Council—Violent Discussions—A Refutation proposed—Its Authors—Rome and the Civil Power—Perils of the Confessors—Melancthon's Minimum—The Emperor's Sister—Melancthon's Fall—Luther opposes Concession—The Legate repels Melancthon—The Pope's Decision—Question—Melancthon's School-matters—Answer, ... 568

CHAPTER IX.

The Refutation—Charles's Dissatisfaction—Interview with the Princes—The Swiss at Augsburg—Tetrapolitan Confession—Zwingle's Confession—Afflicting Divisions—The Elector's Faith—His Peace—The Lion's Skin—The Refutation—One Concession—Scripture and the Hierarchy—Imperial Commands—Interview between Melancthon and Campeggio—Policy of Charles—Stormy Meeting—Resolutions of the Consistory—The Prayers of the Church—Two Miracles—The Emperor's Menace—The Prince's Courage—The Mask—Negotiations—The Spectres at Spires—Tumult in Augsburg, ... Page 574

CHAPTER X.

Philip of Hesse—Temptation—Union resisted—The Landgrave's Dissimulation—The Emperor's Order to the Protestants—Brandenburg's threatening Speeches—Resolution of Philip of Hesse—Flight from Augsburg—Discovery—Charles's Emotion—Revolution in the Diet—Metamorphosis—Unusual Moderation—Peace! Peace! . . 580

CHAPTER XI.

The Mixed Commission—The Three Points—Romish Dissimulation—Abuses—Concessions—The Main Question—Bishops and Pope conceded—Danger of Concession—Opposition to the pretended Concord—Luther's opposing Letters—The Word above the Church—Melancthon's Blindness—Papist Infatuation—A new Commission—Be Men and not Women—The Two Phantoms—Concessions—The Three Points—The great Antithesis—Failure of Conciliation—The Gordian Knot—A Council granted—Charles's Summons—Menaces—Altercations—Peace or War—Romanism concedes—Protestantism resists—Luther recalls his Friends, ... 584

CHAPTER XII.

The Elector's Preparatives and Indignation—Recess of Augsburg—Irritating Language—Apology of the Confession—Intimidation—Final Interview—Messages of Peace—Exasperation of the Papists—Restoration of Popery—Tumult in the Church—Union of the Churches—The Pope and the Emperor—Close of the Diet—Armaments—Attack on Geneva—Joy of the Evangelicals—Establishment of Protestantism, ... 591

BOOK XV.

SWITZERLAND——CONQUESTS. 1526—1530.

CHAPTER I.

Originality of the Swiss Reform—Change—Three Periods of Reform—Switzerland Romande—The two Movements in the Church—Aggressive Spirit—The Schoolmaster—Farel's new Baptism—Mysticism and Scholasticism—A Door is opened—Opposition—Lausanne—Manners of the Clergy—Farel to Galeotto—Farel and the Monk—The Tribunal—The Monk cries for Pardon—Opposition of the Ormonds—A false Convert—Christian Unity, . Page 596

CHAPTER II.

State—Religion in Berne—Irresolution of Berne—Almanack of Heretics—Evangelical Majority—Haller—Zwingle's Signal—Anabaptists in Berne—Victory of the Gospel—Papist Provocations—The City Companies—Proposed Disputation—Objections of the Forest Cantons—The Church, the Judge of Controversies—Unequal Contest—Zwingle—A Christian Band—The Cordeliers' Church—Opening of the Conference—The sole Head—Unity of Error—A Priest converted at the Altar—St. Vincent's Day—The Butchers—A strange Argument—Papist Bitterness—Necessity of Reform—Zwingle's Sermon—Visit of the King of kings—Edict of Reform—Was the Reformation Political? 602

CHAPTER III.

The Reform accepted by the People—Faith, Purity, and Charity—First Evangelical Communion—Bernese Proposition to the Diet—Cavern, and Head of Beatus—Threatening Storm from the Mountains—Revolt—Confusion in Berne—Unterwalden crosses the Brunig—Energy of Berne—Victory—Political Advantages, . . . 608

CHAPTER IV.

Reformation of St. Gall—Nuns of St. Catherine—Reformation of Glaris, Berne, Appenzell, the Grisons, Schaffhausen, and the Rhine District—A Popish Miracle—Obstacles in Basle—Zeal of the Citizens—Œcolampadius marries—Witticism of Erasmus—First Action—Half Measures—Petition of the Reformed, ... 612

CHAPTER V.

Crisis in Basle—Half-measures rejected—Reformed Propositions—A Night of Terror—Idols broken in the Cathedral—The Hour of Madness—Idols broken in all the Churches—Reform legalized—Erasmus in Basle—A great Transformation—Revolution and Reformation, . Page 814

CHAPTER VI.

Farel's Commission—Farel at Lausanne and Morat—Neufchatel—Farel preaches at Serrière—Enters Neufchatel—Sermon—The Monks—Farel's Preaching—Popery in Neufchatel—Canons and Monks unite—Farel at Morat and in the Vully—Reformation of the Bishopric of Basle—Farel again in Neufchatel—Placards—The Hospital Chapel—Civil Power invoked by the Romanists, 815

CHAPTER VII.

Valangin—Guillemette de Vergy—Farel goes to the Val de Ruz—The Mass interrupted—Farel dragged to the River—Farel in Prison—Apostles and Reformers compared—Farel preaching at Neufchatel—Installed in the Cathedral—A Whirlwind sweeps over the People—The Idols destroyed—Interposition of the Governor—Triumph of the Reformed, ... 822

CHAPTER VIII.

The Romanists demand a Ballot—The Bernese in Favour of the Reform—Both Parties come to the Poll—The Prud-hommes of Neufchatel—Proposed Delay—The Romanists grasp the Sword—The Voting—Majority for Reform—Protestantism perpetual—The Image of Saint John—A Miracle—Retreat of the Canons—Popery and the Gospel, ... 625

CHAPTER IX.

Reaction preparing—Failure of the Plot—Farel in Valangin and near the Lake—De Bély at Fontaine—Farel's Sufferings—Marcourt at Valangin—Disgraceful Expedient—Vengeance—The Reform established—French Switzerland characterized—Gathering Tempest, 628

BOOK XVI.

SWITZERLAND—CATASTROPHE. 1528—1531.

CHAPTER I.

Two great Lessons—Christian Warfare—Zwingle, Pastor, Statesman, and General—His noble Character—Persecutions—Swiss Catholics seek an Alliance with Austria—Great Dissatisfaction—Deputation to the Forest Canto—Zwingle's Proposal—Moderation of Berne—Keyse. Martyrdom—Zwingle and War—Zwingle's Error, Page 631

CHAPTER II.

Free Preaching of the Gospel in Switzerland—Zwingle supports the common Bailiwicks—War—Zwingle joins the Army—The Zurich Army threatens Zug—The Landamman Aebli—Bernese Interposition—Zwingle's Opposition—Swiss Cordiality—Order in the Zurich Camp—A Conference—Peace restored—Austrian Treaty torn—Zwingle's Hymn—Nuns of Saint Catherine, .   .   .   634

CHAPTER III.

Conquests of Reform in Schaffhausen and Zurzack—Reform in Glaris—To-day the Cowl, To-morrow the Reverse—Italian Bailiwicks—The Monk of Como—Egidio's Hope for Italy—Call of the Monk of Locarno—Hopes of reforming Italy—The Monks of Wettingen—Abbey of Saint Gall—Kilian Kouffi—Saint Gall recovers its Liberty—The Reform in Soleure—Miracle of Saint Ours—Popery triumphs—The Grisons invaded by the Spaniards—Address of the Ministers to the Romish Cantons—God's Word the Means of Unity — Œcolampadius for Spiritual Influence—Autonomy of the Church, .   .   .   638

CHAPTER IV.

Zwingle and the Christian State—Zwingle's double Part—Zwingle and Luther in Relation to Politics—Philip of Hesse and the Free Cities—Projected Union between Zwingle and Luther—Zwingle's political Action—Project of Alliance against the Emperor—Zwingle advocates active Resistance—He destines the Imperial Crown for Philip—Faults of the Reformation—Embassy to Venice—Giddiness of the Reformation—Projected Alliance with France—Zwingle's Plan of Alliance—Approaching Ruin—Slanders in the Five Cantons—Violence—Mysterious Paper—Berne and Basle vote for Peace—General Diet at Baden—Evangelical Diet at Zurich—Political Reformation of Switzerland—Activity of Zurich, .   .   644

CHAPTER V.

Diet of Arau—Helvetic Unity—Berne proposes to close the Markets—Opposition of Zurich—Proposition agreed to and published—Zwingle's War Sermon—Blockade of the

CHAPTER VI.

Waldstettes—No Bread, no Wine, no Salt—Indignation of the Forest Cantons—The Roads blockaded—Processions—Cry of Despair—France tries to conciliate—Diet at Bremgarten — Hope — The Cantons inflexible — The Strength of Zurich broken—Discontent—Zwingle's false Position—Zwingle demands his Dismission—The Council remonstrate—He remains—Zwingle at Bremgarten—Zwingle's Farewell to Bullinger—Zwingle's Agony—The Forest Cantons reject all Conciliation—Frightful Omens—The Comet—Zwingle's Tranquillity, .   Page 651

CHAPTER VI.

The Five Cantons decide for War—Deceitful Calm—Fatal Inactivity—Zurich forewarned—Banner of Lucerne planted—Manifesto—The Bailiwicks pillaged—The Monastery of Cappel—Letter—Infatuation of Zurich—New Warnings—The War begins—The Tocsin—A fearful Night—The War—Banner and Army of Zurich—Zwingle's Departure—Zwingle's Horse—Anna Zwingle, .   .   .   657

CHAPTER VII.

The Scene of War—The Enemy at Zug—Declaration of War—Council—Army of the Forest Cantons appears—The first Gun fired—Zwingle's Gravity and Sorrow—Zurich Army ascending the Albis—Halt and Council at the Beech Tree—They quicken their March—Jauch's Reconnaissance—His Appeal—Ambuscade, ...   662

CHAPTER VIII.

Unforeseen Change—The whole Army advances—Universal Disorder—The Banneret's Death—The Banner in Danger—The Banner saved—Terrible Slaughter—Slaughter of the Pastors—Zwingle's last Words—Barbarity of the Victors—The Furnace of Trial—Zwingle's dying Moments—Day after the Battle—Homage and Outrage, .   665

CHAPTER IX.

Consternation in Zurich—Violence of the Populace—Grief and Distress—Zwingle is dead!—Funeral Oration—Army of Zurich—Another Reverse on the Goubel—Inactivity of the Bernese—Hopes and Plan of Charles V.—End of the War—Treaty of Peace, ...   669

CHAPTER X.

Restoration of Popery at Bremgarten and Rapperschwyl—Priests and Monks every where—Sorrow of Œcolampadius—A tranquil Scene—Peaceful Death of Œcolampadius—Henry Bullinger at Zurich—Contrition and Exultation—The great Lesson—Conclusion. .   .   673

CONTENTS TO VOLUME FIFTH.

BOOK XVII.

ENGLAND BEFORE THE REFORMATION.

CHAPTER I.

Introduction—Work of the Sixteenth Century—Unity and Diversity—Necessity of considering the entire Religious History of England—Establishment of Christianity in Great Britain—Formation of Ecclesiastical Catholicism in the Roman Empire—Spiritual Christianity received by Britain—Slavery and Conversion of Succat—His Mission to Ireland—Anglo-Saxons re-establish Paganism in England—Columba at Iona—Evangelical Teaching—Presbytery and Episcopacy in Great Britain—Continental Missions of the Britons—An Omission, . Page 677

CHAPTER II.

Pope Gregory the Great—Desires to reduce Britain—Policy of Gregory and Augustine—Arrival of the Mission—Appreciation—Britain superior to Rome—Dionoth at Bangor—First and Second Romish Aggressions—Anguish of the Britons—Pride of Rome—Rome has recourse to the Sword—Massacre—Saint Peter scourges an Archbishop—Oswald—His Victory—Corman—Mission of Oswald and Aidan—Death of Oswald, ... 682

CHAPTER III.

Character of Oswy—Death of Aidan—Wilfrid at Rome—At Oswald's Court—Finan and Colman—Independence of the Church attacked—Oswy's Conquests and Troubles—*Synodus Pharensis*—Cedda—Degeneration—The Disputation—Peter, the Gatekeeper—Triumph of Rome—Grief of the Britons—Popedom organized in England—Papal Exultation—Archbishop Theodore — Cedda re-ordained—Discord in the Church—Disgrace and Treachery of Wilfrid—His end—Scotland attacked—Adamnan—Iona resists—A King converted by Architects — The Monk Egbert at Iona—His History—Monkish Visions — Fall of Iona, ... 687

CHAPTER IV.

Clement—Struggle between a Scotchman and an Englishman—Word of God only—Clement's Success—His Condemnation—Virgil and the Antipodes—John Scotus and Philosophical Religion—Alfred and the Bible—Darkness and Popery—William the Conqueror—Wulston at Edward's Tomb—Struggle between William and Hildebrand—The Pope yields—Cæsaropapia, ... 694

CHAPTER V.

Anselm's Firmness—Becket's Austerity—The King scourged—John becomes the Pope's Vassal—Collision between Popery and Liberty—The Vassal King ravages his Kingdom—Religion of the Senses and Superstition, . 697

CHAPTER VI.

Reaction—Grostète—Principles of Reform—Contest with the Pope—Sewal—Progress of the Nation—Opposition to the Papacy—Conversion of Bradwardine—Grace is Supreme—Edward III.—Statutes of *Provisors* and *Præmunire*, ... 700

CHAPTER VII.

The Mendicant Friars—Their Disorders and Popular Indignation—Wickliffe—His Success—Speeches of the Peers against the Papal Tribute—Agreement of Bruges—Courtenay and Lancaster—Wickliffe before the Convocation—Altercation between Lancaster and Courtenay—Riot—Three Briefs against Wickliffe—Wickliffe at Lambeth—Mission of the *Poor Priests*—Their Preachings and Persecutions—Wickliffe and the Four Regents, . Page 702

CHAPTER VIII.

The Bible—Wickliffe's Translation—Effects of its Publication—Opposition of the Clergy—Wickliffe's Fourth Phasis — Transubstantiation — Excommunication — Wickliffe's Firmness—Wat Tyler—The Synod—The Condemned Propositions—Wickliffe's Petition—Wickliffe before the Primate at Oxford—Wickliffe summoned to Rome—His Answer—The Trialogue—His Death—And Character—His Teaching—His Ecclesiastical Views—A Prophecy, . 706

CHAPTER IX.

The Wickliffites—Call for Reform—Richard II.—The first Martyr—Lord Cobham—Appears before Henry V.—Before the Archbishop—His Confession and Death—The Lollards, ... 711

CHAPTER X.

Learning at Florence—The Tudors—Erasmus visits England—Sir Thomas More—Dean Colet—Erasmus and young Henry—Prince Arthur and Catherine—Marriage and Death—Catherine betrothed to Henry—Accession of Henry VIII.—Enthusiasm of the Learned—Erasmus recalled to England—Cromwell before the Pope—Catherine proposed to Henry—Their Marriage and Court—Tournaments—Henry's Danger, ... 714

CHAPTER XI.

The Pope excites to War—Colet's Sermon at St Paul's—The Flemish Campaign—Marriage of Louis XII. and Princess Mary—Letter from Anne Boleyn—Marriage of Brandon and Mary—Oxford—Sir Thomas More at Court—Attack upon the Monasteries—Colet's Household—He preaches Reform—The Greeks and Trojans, ... 719

CHAPTER XII.

Wolsey—His first Commission—His Complaisance and Dioceses—Cardinal, Chancellor, and Legate—Ostentation and Necromancy—His Spies and Enmity—Pretensions of the Clergy, ... 722

CHAPTER XIII.

The Wolves—Richard Hun—A Murder—Verdict of the Jury—Hun condemned, and his Character vindicated—The Gravesend Passage-boat—A Festival disturbed—Brown tortured—Visit from his Wife—A Martyr—Character of Erasmus—1516 and 1517—Erasmus goes to Basle, . 724

BOOK XVIII.

THE REVIVAL OF THE CHURCH.

CHAPTER I.

Four reforming Powers—Which reformed England?—Papal Reform—Episcopal Reform?—Royal Reform?—What is required in a legitimate Reform—The Share of the Kingly Power—Share of the Episcopal Authority—High and Low Church—Political Events—The Greek and Latin New Testament—Thoughts of Erasmus — Enthusiasm and Anger—Desire of Erasmus—Clamours of the Priests—Their Attack at Court—Astonishment of Erasmus—His Labours for this Work—Edward Lee; his Character—Lee's *Tragedy*—Conspiracy. . . . . . Page 728

CHAPTER II.

Effects of the New Testament in the Universities—Conversations—A Cambridge Fellow—Bilney buys the New Testament—The first Passage—His Conversion—Protestantism. the Fruit of the Gospel—The Vale of the Severn—William Tyndale — Evangelization at Oxford — Bilney teaches at Cambridge—Fryth—Is Conversion Possible?—True Consecration—The Reformation has begun, 732

CHAPTER III.

Alarm of the Clergy—The Two Days—Thomas Man's Preaching—True real Presence—Persecutions at Coventry—Standish Preaches at St Paul's—His Petition to the King and Queen—His Arguments and Defeat—Wolsey's Ambition—First Overtures—Henry and Francis Candidates for the Empire—Conference between Francis I. and Sir T. Boleyn—The Tiara promised to Wolsey—The Cardinal's Intrigues with Charles and Francis, . . . 735

CHAPTER IV.

Tyndale—Sodbury Hall—Sir John and Lady Walsh—Table-Talk—The Holy Scriptures—The Images—The Anchor of Faith—A Roman Camp—Preaching of Faith and Works—Tyndale accused by the Priests—They tear up what he has planted—Tyndale resolves to translate the Bible—His first Triumph—The Priests in the Taverns—Tyndale summoned before the Chancellor of Worcester—Consoled by an aged Doctor—Attacked by a Schoolman—His Secret becomes known—He leaves Sodbury Hall, . . 738

CHAPTER V.

Luther's Works in England—Consultation of the Bishops—The Bull of Leo X. published in England—Luther's Books burnt—Letter of Henry VIII.—He undertakes to write against Luther—Cry of Alarm—Tradition and Sacramentalism—Prudence of Sir T. More—The Book presented to the Pope—*Defender of the Faith*—Exultation of the King, ... 742

CHAPTER VI.

Wolsey's Machinations to obtain the Tiara — He gains Charles V.—Alliance between Henry and Charles—Wolsey offers to command the Troops—Treaty of Bruges—Henry believes himself King of France—Victories of Francis I.—Death of Leo X. 745

CHAPTER VII.

The Just Men of Lincolnshire—Their Assemblies and Teaching—Agnes and Morden—Itinerant Libraries—Polemical Conversations—Sarcasm—Royal Decree and Terror—Depositions and Condemnations—Four Martyrs—A Conclave—Charles consoles Wolsey. . . . Page 747

CHAPTER VIII.

Character of Tyndale—He arrives in London—He preaches—The Cloth and the Ell—The Bishop of London gives Audience to Tyndale—He is dismissed—A Christian Merchant of London—Spirit of Love in the Reformation—Tyndale in Monmouth's House—Fryth helps him to translate the New Testament—Importunities of the Bishop of Lincoln—Persecution in London—Tyndale's resolution—He departs—His Indignation against the Prelates—His Hopes, ... 749

CHAPTER IX.

Bilney at Cambridge—Conversions—The University Cross-Bearer—A Leicestershire Farmer—A Party of Students—Superstitious Practices—An obstinate Papist—The Sophists—Latimer attacks Stafford—Bilney's Resolution—Latimer hears Bilney's Confession—Confessor converted—New Life in Latimer—Bilney preaches Grace—Nature of the Ministry—Latimer's Character and Teaching—Works of Charity—Three Classes of Adversaries—Clark and Dalaber, ... 753

CHAPTER X.

Wolsey seeks the Tiara—Clement VII. is elected—Wolsey's Dissimulation—Charles offers France to Henry—Pace's Mission on this Subject—Wolsey reforms the Convents—His secret Alliances—Treaty between France and England—Taxation and Insurrection—False Charges against the Reformers—Latimer's Defence—Tenterden Steeple, 758

CHAPTER XI.

Tyndale at Hamburg—First two Gospels—Embarrassment—Tyndale at Wittemberg—At Cologne—The New Testament at Press—Sudden Interruption—Cochlœus at Cologne—Rupert's Manuscripts—Discovery of Cochlœus—His inquiries—His Alarm—Rincke and the Senate's Prohibition—Consternation and Decision of Tyndale—Cochlœus writes to England—Tyndale ascends the Rhine—Prints two Editions at Worms—Tyndale's Prayer, 761

CHAPTER XII.

Worms and Cambridge—St Paul resuscitated—Latimer's Preaching—Never Man spake like this Man—Joy and Vexation at Cambridge—Sermon by Prior Buckingham—Irony—Latimer's Reply to Buckingham—The Students threatened—Latimer preaches before the Bishop—He is forbidden to preach—The most zealous of Bishops—Barnes the Restorer of Letters—Bilney undertakes to convert him—Barnes offers his Pulpit to Latimer—Fryth's Thirst for God—Christmas Eve, 1525—Storm against Barnes—Ferment in the Colleges—Germany at Cambridge—Meetings at Oxford—General Expectation, . 764

BOOK XIX.

THE ENGLISH NEW TESTAMENT AND THE COURT OF ROME.

CHAPTER I.

Church and State essentially distinct—Their fundamental Principles—What restores Life to the Church—Separation from Rome necessary—Reform and Liberty—The New Testament crosses the Sea—Is hidden in London—Garret's Preaching and Zeal—Dissemination of Scripture—What the People find in it—The Effects it produces—Tyndale's Explanations—Roper, More's Son-in-law—Garret carries Tyndale's Testament to Oxford—Henry and his Valet—The Supplication of the Beggars—Two Sorts of Beggars—Evils caused by Priests—More's Supplications of the Souls in Purgatory, ... Page 770

CHAPTER II.

The two Authorities—Commencement of the Search—Garret at Oxford—His Flight—His Return and Imprisonment—Escapes and takes refuge with Dalaber—Garret and Dalaber at Prayer—The *Magnificat*—Surprise among the Doctors—Clark's Advice—Fraternal Love at Oxford—Alarm of Dalaber—His Arrest and Examination—He is tortured—Garret and twenty Fellows imprisoned—The Cellar—Condemnation and Humiliation, . . 774

CHAPTER III.

Persecution at Cambridge—Barnes arrested—A grand Search—Barnes at Wolsey's Palace—Interrogated by the Cardinal—Conversation between Wolsey and Barnes—Barnes threatened with the Stake—His Fall and public Penance—Richard Bayfield—His Faith and Imprisonment—Visits Cambridge—Joins Tyndale—The Confessors in the Cellar at Oxford—Four of them die—The rest liberated, . 778

CHAPTER IV.

Luther's Letter to the King—Henry's Anger—His Reply—Luther's Resolution—Persecutions—Barnes escapes—Proclamations against the New Testament—W. Roy to Caiaphas—Third Edition of the New Testament—The Triumph of Law and Liberty—Hackett attacks the Printer—Hackett's Complaints—A Seizure—The Year 1526 in England, ... 782

CHAPTER V.

Wolsey desires to be revenged—The Divorce suggested—Henry's Sentiments towards the Queen—Wolsey's first Steps—Longland's Proceedings—Refusal of Margaret of Valois—Objection of the Bishop of Tarbes—Henry's Uneasiness—Catherine's Alarm—Mission to Spain, . 785

CHAPTER VI.

Anne Boleyn appointed Maid of Honour to Catherine—Lord Percy becomes attached to her—Wolsey separates them—Anne enters Margaret's Household—Siege of Rome ; Cromwell—Wolsey's Intercession for the Popedom—He demands the Hand of Renée of France for Henry—Failure—Anne reappears at Court—Repels the King's Advances—Henry's Letter—He resolves to accelerate the Divorce—Two Motives which induce Anne to refuse the Crown—Wolsey's Opposition, ... Page 787

CHAPTER VII.

Bilney's Preaching—His Arrest—Arthur's Preaching and Imprisonment—Bilney's Examination—Contest between the Judge and the Prisoner—Bilney's Weakness and Fall—His Terrors—Two Wants—Arrival of the Fourth Edition of the New Testament—Joy among the Believers, 791

CHAPTER VIII.

The Papacy intercepts the Gospel—The King consults Sir Thomas More—Ecclesiastical Conferences about the Divorce—The Universities—Clark—The Nun of Kent—Wolsey decides to do the King's Will—Mission to the Pope—Four Documents—Embarrassment of Charles V.—Francis Philip at Madrid—Distress and Resolution of Charles—He turns away from the Reformation—Conference at the Castle of St Angelo—Knight arrives in Italy—His Flight—Treaty between the Pope and the Emperor—Escape of the Pope—Confusion of Henry VIII.—Wolsey's Orders—His Entreaties, ... 794

CHAPTER IX.

The English Envoys at Orvieto—Their Oration to the Pope—Clement gains time—The Envoys and Cardinal Sanctorum Quatuor—Stratagem of the Pope—Knight discovers it and returns—The Transformations of Antichrist—The English obtain a new Document—Fresh Stratagem—Demand of a second Cardinal-legate—The Pope's new Expedient—End of the Campaign, ... 797

CHAPTER X.

Disappointment in England—War declared against Charles V.—Wolsey desires to get him deposed by the Pope—A new Scheme—Embassy of Fox and Gardiner—Their Arrival at Orvieto—Their first Interview with Clement—The Pope reads a Treatise by Henry—Gardiner's Threats and Clement's Promise—The Modern Fabius—Fresh Interview and Menaces—The Pope has not *the Key*—Gardiner's Proposition—Difficulties and Delays of the Cardinals—Gardiner's last Blows—Reverses of Charles V. in Italy—The Pope's Terror and Concession—The *Commission* granted—Wolsey demands the *Engagement*—A Loophole—The Pope's Distress, ... 801

CHAPTER XI.

Fox's Report to Henry and Anne—Wolsey's Impression—He demands the Decretal—One of the Cardinal's petty Manœuvres—He sets his Conscience at Rest—Gardiner fails at Rome—Wolsey's new Perfidy—The King's Anger against the Pope—Sir T. More predicts Religious Liberty—Immorality of Ultramontane Socialism—Erasmus invited—Wolsey's last Flight—Energetic Efforts at Rome—Clement grants all—Wolsey triumphs—Union of Rome and England, ... 805

BOOK XX.

THE TWO DIVORCES.

CHAPTER I.

Progress of the Reformation—The two Divorces—Entreaties to Anne Boleyn—The Letters in the Vatican—Henry to Anne—Henry's Second Letter—Third—Fourth—Wolsey's Alarm—His fruitless Proceedings—He turns—The Sweating Sickness—Henry's Fears—New Letters to Anne—Anne falls sick; her Peace—Henry writes to her—Wolsey's Terror—Campeggio does not arrive—All dissemble at Court, ... Page 8.9

CHAPTER II.

Coverdale and Inspiration—He undertakes to translate the Scriptures—His Joy and Spiritual Songs—Tyball and the Laymen—Coverdale preaches at Brumstead—Revival at Colchester—Incomplete Societies and the New Testament —Persecution—Monmouth arrested and released, . 814

CHAPTER III.

Political Changes—Fresh Instructions from the Pope to Campeggio—His Delays—He unbosoms himself to Francis —A Prediction—Arrival of Campeggio—Wolsey's Uneasiness—Henry's Satisfaction—The Cardinal's Project—Campeggio's Reception—First Interview with the Queen and with the King—Useless Efforts to make Campeggio part with the Decretal—The Nuncio's Conscience—Public Opinion—Measures taken by the King—His Speech to the Lords and Aldermen—Festivities—Wolsey seeks French Support—Contrariety, ... 817

CHAPTER IV.

True Catholicity—Wolsey—Harman's Matter—West sent to Cologne—Labours of Tyndale and Fryth—Rincke at Frankfort—He makes a Discovery—Tyndale at Marburg—West returns to England—His Tortures in the Monastery, ... 823

CHAPTER V.

Necessity of the Reformation—Wolsey's Earnestness with Da Casale—An Audience with Clement VII.—Cruel Position of the Pope—A Judas' Kiss—A new Brief—Bryan and Vannes sent to Rome—Henry and Du Bellay—Wolsey's Reasons against the Brief—Excitement in London—Metamorphosis—Wolsey's Decline—His Anguish, . 826

CHAPTER VI.

The Pope's Illness—Wolsey's Desire—Conference about the Members of the Conclave—Wolsey's Instructions—The Pope recovers—Speech of the English Envoys to the Pope —Clement willing to abandon England—The English demand the Pope's Denial of the Brief—Wolsey's Alarm—Intrigues—Bryan's Clearsightedness—Henry's Threats—Wolsey's new Efforts—He calls for an Appeal to Rome, and retracts—Wolsey and Du Bellay at Richmond—The Ship of the State, ... 828

CHAPTER VII.

Discussion between the Evangelicals and the Catholics—Union of Learning and Life—The Laity; Tewkesbury—His Appearance before the Bishop's Court—He is tortured —Two Classes of Opponents—A Theological Duel—Scripture and the Church—Emancipation of the Mind—Mission to the Low Countries—Tyndale's Embarrassment—Tonstall wishes to buy the Books—Packington's Stratagem—Tyndale departs for Antwerp—His Shipwreck—Arrival at Hamburg—Meets Coverdale, ... Page 832

CHAPTER VIII.

The Royal Session—Sitting of the 18th June; the Queen's Protest—Sitting of the 21st June—Summons to the King and Queen—Catherine's Speech—She retires—Impression on the Audience—The King's Declaration—Wolsey's Protest—Quarrel between the Bishops—New Sitting—Apparition to the Maid of Kent—Wolsey chafed by Henry—The Earl of Wiltshire at Wolsey's—Private Conference between Catherine and the two Legates, . . . 836

CHAPTER IX.

The Trial resumed—Catherine summoned—Twelve Articles—The Witnesses' Evidence—Arthur and Catherine really married—Campeggio opposes the argument of Divine Right—Other Arguments—The Legates required to deliver Judgment—Their Tergiversations—Change in Men's Minds—Final Session—General Expectation—Adjournment during Harvest—Campeggio excuses this Impertinence—The King's Indignation—Suffolk's Violence—Wolsey's Reply—He is ruined—General Accusations—The Cardinal turns to an Episcopal Life, . . . 839

CHAPTER X.

Anne Boleyn at Hever—She Reads the Obedience of a Christian Man—Is recalled to Court—Miss Gainsford and George Zouch—Tyndale's Book converts Zouch—Zouch in the Chapel-Royal—The Book seized—Anne applies to Henry —The King reads the Book—Pretended Influence of the Book on Henry—The Court at Woodstock—The Park and its Goblins—Henry's Esteem for Anne, . . . 842

CHAPTER XI.

Embarrassment of the Pope—The Triumphs of Charles decide him—He traverses the Cause to Rome—Wolsey's Dejection—Henry's Wrath—His Fears—Wolsey obtains Comfort—Arrival of the two Legates at Grafton—Wolsey's Reception by Henry—Wolsey and Norfolk at Dinner—Henry with Anne—Conference between the King and the Cardinal—Wolsey's Joy and Grief—The Supper at Euston—Campeggio's Farewell Audience—Wolsey's Disgrace—Campeggio at Dover—He is accused by the Courtiers—Leaves England—Wolsey foresees his own Fall and that of the Papacy, ... 845

CHAPTER XII.

A Meeting at Waltham—Youth of Thomas Cranmer—His early Education—Studies Scripture for three Years—His Functions as Examiner—The Supper at Waltham—New View of the Divorce—Fox communicates it to Henry—Cranmer's Vexation—Conference with the King—Cranmer at the Boleyns, ... 850

CHAPTER XIII.

Wolsey in the Court of Chancery—Accused by the Dukes—Refuses to give up the Great Seal—His Despair—He gives up the Seal—Order to depart—His Inventory—Alarm—The Scene of Departure—Favourable Message from the King—Wolsey's Joy—His Fool—Arrival at Esher, . Page 852

CHAPTER XIV.

Thomas More elected Chancellor—A Lay Government one of the great facts of the Reformation—Wolsey accused of subordinating England to the Pope—He implores the King's Clemency—His Condemnation—Cromwell at Esher —His Character—He sets out for London—Sir Christopher Hales recommends him to the King—Cromwell's Interview with Henry in the Park—A new Theory—Cromwell elected Member of Parliament—Opened by Sir Thomas More—Attack on Ecclesiastical Abuses—Reforms pronounced by the Convocation—Three Bills—Rochester attacks them—Resistance of the House of Commons—Struggles—Henry Sanctions the Three Bills—Alarm of the Clergy and Disturbances, ... 855

CHAPTER XV.

The Last Hour—More's Fanaticism—Debates in Convocation—Royal Proclamation—The Bishop of Norwich—Sentences condemned—Latimer's Opposition—The New Testament Burnt—The Persecution begins—Hitton—Bayfield --Tonstall and Packington—Bayfield arrested—The Rector Patmore—Lollards' Tower—Tyndale and Patmore—A Musician—Freese the Painter—Placards and Martyrdom of Bennet—Thomas More and John Petit—Bilney, ... Page 858

CHAPTER XVI.

Wolsey's Terror—Impeachment by the Peers—Cromwell saves him—The Cardinal's illness—Ambition returns to him—His practices in Yorkshire—He is arrested by Northumberland—His departure—Arrival of the Constable of the Tower—Wolsey at Leicester Abbey—Persecuting language—He dies—Three Movements: Supremacy, Scripture, and Faith, ... 864

PREFACE.

THE history of one of the greatest revolutions that has ever been accomplished in human affairs—of a mighty impulse communicated to the world three centuries ago, and whose influence is still visible on every side—and not the history of a mere party, is the object of my present undertaking. The history of the Reformation is distinct from that of Protestantism. In the former every thing bears the mark of a regeneration of the human race—of a religious and social change emanating from God himself. In the latter we too often witness a glaring degeneracy from first principles, the struggles of parties, a sectarian spirit, and the traces of petty individualities. The history of Protestantism may have an interest for Protestants only; the history of the Reformation addresses itself to all Christians, or rather to all mankind.

An historian may choose his subject in the wide field presented to his labours: he may describe the great events which have changed the aspect of a people or of the world; or on the other hand he may record that tranquil onward course of a nation, of the Church, or of mankind, which usually succeeds every great social change. Both these departments of history are of vast importance; yet public interest has ever been more strongly attracted to those epochs which, under the name of revolutions, have given fresh life to a nation, or created a new era for society in general.

It is a transformation of the latter kind that, with very humble powers, I have undertaken to describe, not without a hope that the beauty of the subject may compensate for my own deficiencies. The term " revolution," which I here apply to it, has of late fallen into discredit with many individuals, who almost confound it with revolt. But they are wrong: for a revolution is merely a change in the affairs of men,—something new unfolded (*revolutus*) from the bosom of humanity; and this very word, previous to the end of the last century, was more frequently used in a good than in a bad sense: a happy, a wonderful revolution, were the terms employed. The Reformation was quite the opposite of a revolt: it was the re-esta-

blishment of the principles of primitive Christianity. It was a *regenerative* movement with respect to all that was destined to revive; a *conservative* movement as regards all that will exist for ever. While Christianity and the Reformation established the great principle of the equality of souls in the eyes of God, and overthrew the usurpations of a haughty priesthood that assumed to place itself between the Creator and his creature, they both laid down this fundamental rule of social order, that all power is derived from God, and called upon all men to " love the brotherhood, fear God, and honour the king."

The Reformation is eminently distinguished from all the revolutions of antiquity, and from most of those of modern times. Political changes—the consolidation or the overthrow of the power of the one or of the many—were the object of the latter. The love of truth, of holiness, of immortality, was the simple yet mighty spring which set in motion that which I have to describe. It indicates a forward movement in human nature. In truth, man advances—he improves, whenever he aims at higher objects, and seeks for immaterial and imperishable blessings, instead of pursuing material, temporal, and earthly advantages. The Reformation is one of the brightest days of this glorious progress. It is a guarantee that the new struggle, which is receiving its accomplishment under our own eyes, will terminate on the side of truth, in a purer, more spiritual, and still nobler triumph.

Primitive Christianity and the Reformation are the two greatest revolutions in history. They were not limited to one nation only, as were the various political movements that history records; but their influence extended over many, and their effects are destined to be felt to the utmost limits of the world.

Primitive Christianity and the Reformation are one and the same revolution, brought about at different epochs and under different circumstances. Although not alike in their secondary features, they are identical in their primary and chief characteristics. One is a repetition of the other. The former put an end to the old world; the latter be-

1

gan the new : between them lie the Middle Ages. One is the parent of the other ; and although the daughter may in some instances bear marks of inferiority, she has characters that are peculiarly her own.

One of them is the rapidity of its action. The great revolutions that have led to the fall of a monarchy, or wrought an entire change in a political system, or which have launched the human mind on a new career of development, have been slowly and gradually prepared. The old-established power has long been undermined : one by one its chief supports have given way. This was the case at the introduction of Christianity. But the Reformation, at the first glance, seems to present a different aspect. The church of Rome under Leo X. appears in the height of its power and glory. A monk speaks—and in one half of Europe this mighty glory and power crumble into dust. In this revolution we are reminded of the words by which the Son of God foretells his second advent : " As the lightning cometh out of the east, and shineth even to the west, so shall the coming of the Son of Man be."

Such rapidity of action is inexplicable to those who see in this event nothing more than a reform ; who look upon it simply as an act of critical sagacity, which consisted in making a choice among various doctrines —rejecting some, preserving others, and arranging those which were retained so as to combine them into a new system.

But how could a whole people, how could many nations have so promptly executed this laborious task ? How could this critical examination have kindled the fire and enthusiasm so necessary for great and above all for sudden revolutions ? The Reformation, as its history will show, was altogether different. It was a new outpouring of that life which Christianity brought into the world. It was the triumph of the greatest of its doctrines,—of that which animates all who embrace it with the purest and most intense enthusiasm,—the doctrine of Faith, the doctrine of Grace. Had the Reformation been what many Romanists and Protestants of our days imagine it,—had it been that negative system of negative reason which, like a fretful child, rejects whatever is displeasing to it, and disowns the grand truths and leading ideas of universal Christianity, it would never have crossed the threshold of the schools, or been known beyond the narrow limits of the cloister or perhaps of the friar's cell. But with Protestantism, as many understand the word, it had no connexion. Far from being an emaciated, an enervated body, it rose up like a man, full of strength and energy.

Two considerations will account for the suddenness and extent of this revolution. One must be sought in God ; the other among men. The impulse was given by an invisible and mighty hand : the change accomplished was the work of Omnipotence. An impartial and attentive observer, who looks beyond the surface, must necessarily be led to this conclusion. But as God works by second causes, another task remains for the historian. Many circumstances which have often passed unnoticed, gradually prepared the world for the great transformation of the sixteenth century, so that the human mind was ripe when the hour of its emancipation arrived.

It is the historian's duty to combine these two great elements in the picture he presents to his readers. This has been my endeavour in the following pages. I shall be easily understood so long as I am occupied in investigating the secondary causes that concurred in producing the revolution I have undertaken to describe. Many perhaps will understand me less clearly, and will even be tempted to charge me with superstition, when I ascribe the completion of the work to God. It is a conviction, however, that I fondly cherish. These volumes, as well as the motto I have prefixed to them, lay down in the chief and foremost place this simple and pregnant principle : GOD IN HISTORY. But as it is a principle that has been generally neglected and sometimes disputed, it may be right for me to explain my views on this subject, and by this means justify the method I have adopted.

History can no longer remain in our days that dead letter of events, to the detail of which the majority of earlier writers restricted themselves. It is now understood that in history, as in man, there are two elements—matter and spirit. Unwilling to resign themselves to the task of producing a simple recital of facts, which would have been but a barren chronicle, our great modern historians have sought for a vital principle to animate the materials of past ages.

Some have borrowed this principle from the rules of art : they have aimed at being ingenuous, exact, and picturesque in description, and have endeavoured to give life to their narrative by the characteristic details of the events themselves.

Others have sought in philosophy the principle that should fertilize their labours. With the relation of events they have interwoven extended views, instructive lessons, political and philosophical truths ; and have given animation to their narrative by the idea they have drawn from it, and by the theory they have been able to associate with it.

Both these methods, undoubtedly, are good, and should be employed within certain limits. But there is another source to which, above all, we must look for the intelligence, spirit, and life of past ages ; and this source is Religion. History should live by that life which belongs to it, and that life is God. In history, God should be acknowledged and proclaimed. The history of the world should be set forth as the annals of the government of the Sovereign King.

I have gone down into the lists whither the recitals of our historians have invited me. There I have witnessed the actions of men and of nations, developing themselves with energy, and contending in violent collision. I have heard a strange din of arms, but I have been nowhere shown the majestic countenance of the presiding Judge.

And yet there is a living principle, emanating from God, in every national movement. God is ever present on that vast theatre where successive generations of men meet and struggle. It is true he is unseen; but if the heedless multitude pass by without caring for him because he is "a God that dwelleth in the thick darkness," thoughtful men, who yearn for the very principle of their existence, seek for him the more ardently, and are not satisfied until they lie prostrate at his feet. And their inquiries meet with a rich reward. For from the height to which they have been compelled to soar to meet their God, the history of the world, instead of presenting to their eyes a confused chaos, as it does to the ignorant crowd, appears as a majestic temple, on which the invisible hand of God himself is at work, and which rises to his glory above the rock of humanity.

Shall we not recognise the hand of God in those grand manifestations, those great men, those mighty nations, which arise, and start as it were from the dust of the earth, and communicate a fresh impulse, a new form and destiny to the human race? Shall we not acknowledge him in those heroes who spring from society at appointed epochs—who display a strength and activity beyond the ordinary limits of humanity—and around whom, as around a superior and mysterious power, nations and individuals unhesitatingly gather? Who has launched into the expanse of time, those huge comets with their fiery trains, which appear but at distant intervals, scattering among the superstitious crowd abundance and joy, calamity and terror? Who, if not God? Alexander sought his origin in the abodes of the Divinity. And in the most irreligious age there has been no eminent glory that has not endeavoured in some way or other to connect itself with heaven.

And do not those revolutions which hurl kings from their thrones, and precipitate whole nations to the dust,—do not those wide-spread ruins which the traveller meets with among the sands of the desert,—do not those majestic relic which the field of humanity presents to our view—do they not all declare aloud—a God in history? Gibbon, seated among the ruins of the Capitol, and contemplating its august remains, owned the intervention of a superior destiny. He saw it—he felt it: in vain would he avert his eyes. That shadow of a mysterious power started

from behind every broken pillar; and he conceived the design of describing its influence in the history of the disorganisation, decline, and corruption of that Roman dominion which had enslaved the world. Shall not we discern amidst the great ruins of humanity that almighty hand which a man of noble genius —one who had never bent the knee to Christ —perceived amid the scattered fragments of the monuments of Romulus, the sculptured marbles of Aurelius, the busts of Cicero and Virgil, the statues of Cæsar and Augustus, Pompey's horses, and the trophies of Trajan, —and shall we not confess it to be the hand of God?

What a startling fact, that men brought up amid the elevated ideas of Christianity, regard as mere superstition that Divine intervention in human affairs which the very heathens had admitted!

The name given by ancient Greece to the Sovereign Ruler shows it to have received primeval revelations of the great truth of a God, who is the principle of history and the life of nations. He was styled *Zeus*,[1] or the *life-giver* to all that lives,—to nations as well as to individuals. On his altars kings and people swore their solemn oaths; and from his mysterious inspirations Minos and other legislators pretended to have received their laws. This is not all: this great truth is figured forth by one of the most beautiful fables of heathen antiquity. Even mythology might teach a lesson to the philosophers of our days; and I may be allowed to establish the fact, as perhaps there are readers who will feel less prejudice against the instructions of paganism than of Christianity itself. This Zeus, this supreme Ruler, this Eternal Spirit, this life-giving Principle, is the father of Clio, the muse of history, whose mother is Mnemosyne or Memory. Thus, according to the notions of antiquity, history combines a heavenly with an earthly nature. She is the daughter of God and man; but, alas! the purblind philosophy of our proud age is far from having attained the lofty views of that heathen wisdom. Her divine paternity has been denied; and the illegitimate child now wanders up and down the world, like a shameless adventurer, hardly knowing whence she comes or whither she is going.

But this God of pagan antiquity is only a faint reflection, a dim shadow of Jehovah— of the Eternal One. The true God whom the Hebrews worship, willing to impress on the minds of all nations that he reigns continually upon earth, gave with this intent, if I may venture the expression, a bodily form to this sovereignty in the midst of Israel. A visible theocracy was appointed to exist once upon the earth, that it might unceasingly remind us of that invisible theocracy which shall for ever govern the world.

[1] Zeus, from ζάω, I live.

3

And see what lustre this great truth (God in history) receives under the Christian dispensation. What is Jesus Christ, if he be not God in history? It was this discovery of Jesus Christ which enabled John Müller, the greatest of modern historians, fully to comprehend his subject. " The Gospel," said he, " is the fulfilment of every hope, the perfection of all philosophy, the interpreter of every revolution, the key to all the seeming contradictions in the physical and moral world : it is life and immortality. Since I have known the Saviour, every thing is clear to my eyes : with him, there is no difficulty I cannot solve." [1]

Thus wrote this eminent historian; and is not this great truth, that God has appeared in human nature, in reality the keystone of the arch,—the mysterious link which binds all earthly things together, and connects them with heaven? History records a birth of God, and yet God has no part in history! Jesus Christ is the true God of man's history; it is shown by the very meanness of his advent. When man would raise a shelter against the weather—a shade from the heat of the sun—what preparation of materials, what scaffolding and crowds of workmen, what trenches and heaps of rubbish !—but when God would do the same, he takes the smallest seed that a new-born child might clasp in its feeble hand, deposits it in the bosom of the earth, and from that grain, scarcely distinguishable in its commencement, he produces the stately tree, under whose spreading branches the families of men may find a refuge. To effect great results by imperceptible means—such is the law of God.

In Jesus Christ is found the most glorious fulfilment of this law. Christianity has now taken possession of the gates of every people. It reigns or hovers over all the tribes of the earth, from the rising to the setting sun ; and even a sceptical philosophy is compelled to acknowledge it as the social and spiritual law of the world. And yet what was the commencement of this religion, the noblest of all things under the vault of heaven—nay, in the "infinite immense" of creation ? A child born in the smallest town of the most despised nation in the world—a child whose mother had not what even the most indigent and wretched woman of our towns possesses, a room to shelter her in the hour of travail— a child born in a stable and cradled in a manger ! In this, O God, I acknowledge and adore thee !

The Reformation recognised this divine law, and was conscious of fulfilling it. The idea that " God is in history " was often put forth by the reformers. We find it particularly expressed by Luther in one of those homely and quaint, yet not undignified similitudes, which he was fond of using that he might be understood by the people. " The world," said he one day at table with his friends, " is a vast and magnificent game of cards, made up of emperors, kings, princes, &c. The pope for many centuries beat the emperors, kings, and princes. They yielded and fell before him. Then came our Lord God. He dealt the cards : he took the lowest (Luther) for himself, and with it he beat the pope, that vanquisher of the kings of the earth......This is the ace of God. As Mary said : ' He hath put down the mighty from their seats, and exalted them of low degree.' " [1]

The epoch whose history I am desirous of retracing is important for the present generation. When a man becomes sensible of his own weakness, he is generally inclined to look for support in the institutions he sees flourishing around him, or else in the bold devices of his imagination. The history of the Reformation shows that nothing new can be made out of things old; and that if, according to our Saviour's expression, we require new bottles for new wine, we must also have new wine for new bottles. It directs man to God as the universal agent in history,—to that Divine word, ever old by the eternal nature of the truths it contains, ever new by the regenerative influence that it exerts; which purified society three centuries ago, which restored faith in God to souls enfeebled by superstition, and which, at every epoch in the history of man, is the fountain whence floweth salvation.

It is singular to witness a great number of men, agitated by a vague desire of believing in something fixed, addressing themselves in our days to the erroneous Catholicism of Rome. In one sense this movement is natural ; religion is so little known among them, that they think it can only be found where they see it inscribed in large letters on a banner that time has rendered venerable. I do not say that all Catholicism is incapable of bestowing on man what he stands in need of. I think we should carefully distinguish between Catholicism and Popery. The latter, in my opinion, is an erroneous and destructive system ; but I am far from confounding it with Catholicism. How many worthy men, how many true Christians, has not the catholic church contained within its bosom ! What important services were rendered by Catholicism to the existing states of Europe, at the moment of their formation—at a period when it was still deeply impregnated with the Gospel, and when Popery was as yet only hovering over it like a faint shadow ! But we live no longer in those days. Strenuous endeavours are now making to reunite Catholicism with Popery ; and if catholic and christian truths are put forward, they are merely to

---

[1] Letter to Charles Bonnet.

[1] Colloquia, or Table-talk.

serve as baits to draw us into the nets of the hierarchy. We have nothing, then, to hope for on that side. Has Popery renounced one of its observances, of its doctrines, or of its assumptions? Will that religion which was insupportable in former times, be less so in ours? What regeneration has ever been known to emanate from Rome? Is it from a pontifical hierarchy, overflowing with earthly passions, that can proceed the spirit of faith, hope, and charity, which alone can save us? Is it an exhausted system, that has no vitality for itself, which is everywhere in the struggles of death, and which exists only by external aid, that can impart life to others, or animate christian society with the heavenly inspiration that it requires?

Will this yearning of the heart and mind that begins to be felt by many of our contemporaries, lead others to apply to the new Protestantism which in many places has succeeded the powerful teaching of the apostles and reformers? A great vagueness of doctrine prevails in many of those reformed churches whose first members sealed with their blood the clear and living faith that inspired them. Men distinguished for their information, and sensible to all the beauties which this world presents, are carried away into strange aberrations. A general faith in the divinity of the Gospel is the only standard they are willing to uphold. But what is this Gospel? that is the vital question; and yet on this, either they are silent, or else every one answers it according to his own opinions. What avails it to know that God has placed in the midst of all nations a vessel containing a remedy for our souls, if we care not to know its contents, or if we do not strive to appropriate them to ourselves? This system cannot fill up the void of the present times. Whilst the faith of the apostles and reformers appears every where active and effectual for the conversion of the world, this vague system does nothing—enlightens nothing—vivifies nothing.

But let us not be without hope. Does not Roman-catholicism confess the great doctrines of Christianity,—God the Father, Son, and Holy Ghost—Creator, Saviour, and Sanctifier, who is the Truth? And does not this vague Protestantism hold in its hand the Book of Life, which is sufficient for doctrine, correction, and instruction in righteousness? And how many upright souls, honoured in the eyes of men, lovely in the sight of God, are there not to be found among those subjected to these two systems? How can we forbear loving them? How not ardently desire their complete emancipation from human elements? Charity is infinite: it embraces the most distant opinions, to draw them to the feet of Christ.

Already there are indications that these two extreme opinions are moving nearer to Christ, who is the centre of truth. Are there not some Roman-catholic churches in which the reading of the Bible is recommended and practised? And what steps has not Protestant rationalism already made! It did not spring from the Reformation: for the history of that great revolution will prove it to have been an epoch of faith. But may we not hope it is drawing nearer to it? Will not the might of truth go forth to it from the word of God, and will not this rationalism be transformed by it? Already we often witness in it a religious feeling, inadequate doubtless, but still it is a movement towards sound doctrine, and which may lead us to hope for some definite progress.

But the new Protestantism and the old Catholicism are of themselves irrelevant and ineffectual. We require something else to restore the saving power to the men of our days. We need something which is not of man—something that comes from God. " Give me," said Archimedes, ' a point without the world, and I will lift it from its poles." True Christianity is this point, which raises the heart of man from its double pivot of selfishness and sensuality, and which will one day turn the whole world from its evil ways, and make it revolve on a new axis of righteousness and peace.

Whenever religion has been under discussion, there have been three points to which our attention has been directed; God, Man, and the Priest. There can only be three kinds of religion upon earth, according as God, Man, or the Priest, is its author and its head. I denominate that the religion of the priest, which is invented by the priest, for the glory of the priest, and in which a sacerdotal caste is dominant. By the religion of man, I mean those various systems and opinions which human reason has framed, and which, being the offspring of human infirmity, are consequently devoid of all healing power. The term divine religion I apply to the truth such as God gave it,—the end and aim of which are the glory of God and the salvation of man.

Hierarchism, or the religion of the priest —Christianity, or the religion of God—Rationalism, or the religion of man, are the three doctrines that divide Christendom in our days. There is no salvation, either for man or for society, in the first or in the last. Christianity alone can give life to the world; and, unhappily, of the three prevailing systems, it is not that which has the greatest number of followers.

Some, however, it has. Christianity is operating its work of regeneration among many Catholics in Germany, and no doubt in other countries also. It is accomplishing its task with greater purity and vigour, in my opinion, among the evangelical Christians of Switzerland, France, Great Britain, and the United States. God be praised that these individual or social regenerations, produced by the Gospel, are no longer such rarities as must be sought in ancient annals.

It is the history of the Reformation in general that I desire to write. I purpose tracing it among different nations, to show that the same truths have every where produced the same results, and also to point out the diversities arising from the dissimilar characters of the people. It is especially in Germany that we find the primitive type of this reform; there it presents the most organic developments,—there chiefly it bears the character of a revolution not limited to a particular nation, but which concerns the whole world. The Reformation in Germany is the fundamental history of the reform—it is the primary planet; the other reformations are secondary planets, revolving with it, deriving light from the same source, forming part of the same system, but each having a separate existence, shedding each a different radiance, and always possessing a peculiar beauty. We may apply the language of St Paul to these reforms of the sixteenth century : " There is one glory of the sun, and another glory of the moon, and another glory of the stars ; for one star differeth from another star in glory." (1 Cor. xv. 41.) The Swiss Reformation occurred at the same time as the German, but was independent of it. It presented, at a later period especially, some of the great features observable in that of Germany. The Reformation in Great Britain recommends itself in a very especial manner to our attention, from the powerful influence which the churches of that country are exerting at the present day over all the world. But recollections of ancestry and of refuge—the remembrance of struggles, suffering, and exile endured in the cause of the Reformation in France, lend a particular attraction, in my eyes, to the French reform. Considered by itself, and with respect to the date of its origin, it presents beauties that are peculiarly its own.

I believe the Reformation to be the work of God : his hand is every where visible in it. Still I hope to be impartial in retracing its history. I think I have spoken of the principal Roman-catholic actors in this great drama—of Leo X., Albert of Magdeburg, Charles V., and Doctor Eck, for instance, more favourably than the majority of historians have done. On the other hand, I have had no desire to conceal the faults and errors of the reformers.

As early as the winter of 1831–32, I delivered a course of public lectures on the epoch of the Reformation. I then published my opening discourse.[1] These lectures were a preparatory labour for the history I now lay before the public.

This history is compiled from the original sources with which a long residence in Germany, the Netherlands, and Switzerland, has rendered me familiar ; as well as from the study, in their original languages, of the documents relating to the religious history of Great Britain and other countries. As these sources will be pointed out in the course of the work, it will be unnecessary to enumerate them here.

I should have wished to authenticate the various portions of my work by many original notes ; but I feared that if they were long and frequent, they would prove a disagreeable interruption to my readers. I have therefore confined myself to such passages as seemed calculated to give them a clearer view of the history I have undertaken to write.

I address this history to those who love to see past events exactly as they occurred, and not by the aid of that magic glass of genius which colours and magnifies, but which sometimes also diminishes and changes them. Neither the philosophy of the eighteenth nor the romanticism of the nineteenth century will guide my judgments or supply my colours. The history of the Reformation is written in the spirit of the work itself. Principles, it is said, have no modesty. It is their nature to rule, and they steadily assert their privilege. Do they encounter other principles in their paths that would dispute their empire, they give battle immediately. A principle never rests until it has gained the victory ; and it cannot be otherwise—with it to reign is to live. If it does not reign supreme, it dies. Thus, at the same time that I declare my inability and unwillingness to enter into rivalry with other historians of the Reformation, I make an exception in favour of the principles on which this history is founded, and I firmly maintain their superiority.

Up to this hour we do not possess, as far as I am aware, any complete history of the memorable epoch that is about to employ my pen. Nothing indicated that this deficiency would be supplied when I began this work. This is the only circumstance that could have induced me to undertake it, and I here put it forward as my justification. This deficiency still exists ; and I pray to Him from whom cometh every good and perfect gift, to grant that this humble work may not be profitless to my readers.

EAUX-VIVES, near GENEVA, }
August 1835. }

---

[1] Discours sur l'Etude de l'Histoire du Christianisme, et son Utilité pour l'Epoque actuelle. Paris, 1832, chez J. J. Risler.

HISTORY OF THE REFORMATION.

VOLUME FIRST.

~~~~~~~~~~~~~~~~~~~~~~~~~~

BOOK I.

STATE OF EUROPE BEFORE THE REFORMATION.

CHAPTER I.

Christianity—Two distinctive Principles—Rise of the Papacy—Early Encroachments—Influence of Rome—Co-operation of the Bishops and of the Sects—Visible Unity of the Church—Invisible Unity of the Church—Primacy of St. Peter—Patriarchates—Co-operation of Princes—Influence of the Barbarians—Rome invokes the aid of the Franks—Secular Power—Pepin and Charlemagne—The Decretals—Disorders of Rome—The Emperor, the Pope's Suzerain—Hildebrand—His Character—Celibacy—Struggle with the Empire—Emancipation of the Pope—Hildebrand's Successors—The Crusades—The Empire—The Church.

THE enfeebled world was tottering on its foundations when Christianity appeared. The national religions which had satisfied the parents, no longer proved sufficient for their children. The new generations could not repose contented within the ancient forms. The gods of every nation, when transported to Rome, there lost their oracles, as the nations themselves had there lost their liberty. Brought face to face in the Capitol, they had destroyed each other, and their divinity had vanished. A great void was occasioned in the religion of the world.

A kind of deism, destitute alike of spirit and of life, floated for a time above the abyss in which the vigorous superstitions of antiquity had been engulfed. But like all negative creeds, it had no power to reconstruct. National prepossessions disappeared with the fall of the national gods. The various kingdoms melted one into the other. In Europe, Asia, and Africa, there was but one vast empire, and the human race began to feel its universality and unity.

Then the Word was made flesh.

God appeared among men, and as man, to save that which was lost. In Jesus of Nazareth dwelt all the fulness of the Godhead bodily.

This is the greatest event in the annals of the world. Former ages had prepared the way for it: the latter ages flow from it. It is their centre and their bond of unity.

Henceforward the popular superstitions had no meaning, and the slight fragments preserved from the general wreck of incredulity vanished before the majestic orb of eternal truth.

The Son of Man lived thirty-three years on earth, healing the sick, converting sinners, not having where to lay his head, and displaying in the midst of this humiliation such greatness and holiness, such power and divinity, as the world had never witnessed before. He suffered and died—he rose again and ascended into heaven. His disciples, beginning at Jerusalem, travelled over the Roman empire and the world, every where proclaiming their Master as the author of everlasting life. From the midst of a people who despised all nations, came forth a mercy that invited and embraced all men. A great number of Asiatics, of Greeks, and of Romans, hitherto dragged by their priests to the feet of dumb idols, believed the Word. It suddenly enlightened the whole earth, like a beam of the sun. [1] A breath of life began to move over this wide field of death. A new people, a holy nation, was formed upon the earth; and the astonished world beheld in the disciples of the Galilean a purity and self-denial, a charity and heroism, of which it had retained no idea.

Two principles especially distinguished the new religion from all the human systems that fled before it. One had reference to the ministers of its worship, the other to its doctrines.

The ministers of paganism were almost the gods of these human religions. The

[1] Οἵα τις ἡλίου βολή. Eusebius, Hist. Eccles. ll. 3.

7

priests of Egypt, Gaul, Dacia, Germany, Britain, and India, led the people, so long at least as their eyes were not opened. Jesus Christ, indeed, established a ministry, but he did not found a separate priesthood: he dethroned these living idols of the world, destroyed an overbearing hierarchy, took away from man what he had taken from God, and re-established the soul in immediate connexion with the divine fountain of truth, by proclaiming himself sole Master and sole Mediator. "One is your master, even Christ; and all ye are brethren."[1]

As regards doctrine, human systems had taught that salvation is of man: the religions of the earth had devised an earthly salvation. They had told men that heaven would be given to them as a reward: they had fixed its price; and what a price! The religion of God taught that salvation comes from him alone; that it is a gift from heaven; that it emanates from an amnesty—from the grace of the Sovereign Ruler: "God hath given to us eternal life."[2]

Undoubtedly Christianity cannot be summed up in these two points; but they seem to govern the subject, as far as history is concerned. And as it is impossible for me to trace the opposition between truth and error in all its features, I have been compelled to select the most prominent.

Such were the two constituent principles of the religion that then took possession of the Roman empire and of the world. With these we are within the true limits of Christianity, and beyond them Christianity disappears. On their preservation or their loss depended its greatness or its fall. They are closely connected: for we cannot exalt the priests of the Church or the works of the faithful without lowering Christ in his twofold quality of Mediator and Redeemer. One of these principles was to predominate in the history of the religion; the other in its doctrine. They both reigned at the beginning. Let us inquire how they were lost; and let us commence by tracing the destiny of the former.

The Church was in the beginning a community of brethren, guided by a few of the brethren. All were taught of God, and each had the privilege of drawing for himself from the divine fountain of light.[3] The Epistles which then settled the great questions of doctrine did not bear the pompous title of a single man—of a ruler. We learn from the Holy Scriptures, that they began simply with these words: "The apostles and elders and brethren send greeting unto the brethren."[4]

But these very writings of the apostles already foretell that from the midst of this brotherhood there shall arise a power that will destroy this simple and primitive order.[5]

Let us contemplate the formation and trace the development of this power so alien to the Church.

Paul of Tarsus, one of the greatest apostles of the new religion, had arrived at Rome, the capital of the empire and of the world, preaching in bondage the salvation which cometh from God. A Church was formed beside the throne of the Cæsars. Composed at first of a few converted Jews, Greeks, and Roman citizens, it was rendered famous by the teaching and the death of the Apostle of the Gentiles. For a time it shone out brightly, as a beacon upon a hill. Its faith was everywhere celebrated; but erelong it declined from its primitive condition. It was by small beginnings that both imperial and Christian Rome advanced to the usurped dominion of the world.

The first pastors or bishops of Rome early employed themselves in converting the neighbouring cities and towns. The necessity which the bishops and pastors of the Campagna felt of applying in cases of difficulty to an enlightened guide, and the gratitude they owed to the church of the metropolis, led them to maintain a close union with it. As it has always happened in analogous circumstances, this reasonable union soon degenerated into dependence. The bishops of Rome considered as a *right* that superiority which the surrounding Churches had freely yielded. The encroachments of power form a great part of history; as the resistance of those whose liberties are invaded forms the other portion. The ecclesiastical power could not escape the intoxication which impels all who are lifted up to seek to mount still higher. It obeyed this general law of human nature.

Nevertheless the supremacy of the Roman bishops was at that period limited to the superintendence of the Churches within the civil jurisdiction of the prefect of Rome.[1] But the rank which this imperial city held in the world offered a prospect of still greater destinies to the ambition of its first pastor. The respect enjoyed by the various Christian bishops in the second century was proportionate to the rank of the city in which they resided. Now Rome was the largest, richest, and most powerful city in the world. It was the seat of empire, the mother of nations. "All the inhabitants of the earth belong to her," said Julian;[2] and Claudian declared her to be "the fountain of laws."[3]

If Rome is the queen of cities, why should not her pastor be the king of bishops? Why should not the Roman church be the mother of Christendom? Why should not all nations be her children, and her authority their sovereign law? It was easy for the ambitious heart of man to reason thus. Ambitious Rome did so.

---

[1] Matthew xxiii. 8. [2] 1 John v. 11. [3] John vi. 45.
[4] Acts xv. 23. [5] 2 Thess. ii.

[1] Suburbicaria loca.—See the sixth canon of the Nicene Council, thus quoted by Rufinus (Hist. Eccles. x. 6); Et ut apud Alexandriam et in urbe Roma, vetusta consuetudo servetur, ut vel ille Ægypti, vel hic suburbicariarum ecclesiarum solicitudinem gerat, &c.
[2] Julian. Orat. I.
[3] Claudian in Paneg. Stilichonis, lib. 3.

Thus, when pagan Rome fell, she bequeathed to the humble minister of the God of peace, sitting in the midst of her ruins, the proud titles which her invincible sword had won from the nations of the earth.

The bishops of the different parts of the empire, fascinated by that charm which Rome had exercised for ages over all nations, followed the example of the Campagna, and aided this work of usurpation. They felt a pleasure in yielding to the bishop of Rome some portion of that honour which was due to the queen of the world. There was originally no dependence implied in the honour thus paid. They treated the Roman pastor as if they were on a level with him.[1] But usurped power increases like an avalanche. Admonitions, at first simply fraternal, soon became absolute commands in the mouth of the pontiff. A foremost place among equals appeared to him a throne.

The Western bishops favoured this encroachment of the Roman pastors, either from jealousy of the Eastern bishops, or because they preferred submitting to the supremacy of a pope, rather than to the dominion of a temporal power.

On the other hand, the theological sects that distracted the East, strove, each for itself, to interest Rome in its favour; they looked for victory in the support of the principal church of the West.

Rome carefully enregistered these applications and intercessions, and smiled to see all nations voluntarily throwing themselves into her arms. She neglected no opportunity of increasing and extending her power. The praises and flattery, the exaggerated compliments and consultations of other Churches, became in her eyes and in her hands the titles and documents of her authority. Such is man exalted to a throne: the incense of courts intoxicates him, his brain grows dizzy. What he possesses becomes a motive for attaining still more.

The doctrine of the Church and the necessity of its visible unity, which had begun to gain ground in the third century, favoured the pretensions of Rome. The Church is, above all things, the assembly of "them that are sanctified in Christ Jesus" (1 Cor. i. 2)— "the assembly of the first-born which are written in heaven" (Heb. xii. 23). Yet the Church of our Lord is not simply inward and invisible; it is necessary that it should be manifested, and it is with a view to this manifestation that the sacraments of Baptism and the Lord's Supper were instituted. The visible Church has features different from those which distinguish it as an invisible Church. The invisible Church, which is the body of Christ, is necessarily and eternally one. The visible Church no doubt partakes of the unity of the former; but, considered by itself, plurality is a characteristic

already ascribed to it in the New Testament. While speaking of one Church of God,[1] it no sooner refers to its manifestation to the world, than it enumerates "the Churches of Galatia, of Macedonia, of Judea, all Churches of the saints."[2] These Churches may undoubtedly, to a certain extent, look for visible unity; but if this union be wanting, they lose none of the essential qualities of the Church of Christ. The strong bond which originally united the members of the Church, was that living faith of the heart which connected them all with Christ as their common head. Different causes soon concurred to originate and develop the idea of a necessity for external union. Men accustomed to the political forms and associations of an earthly country, carried their views and habits into the spiritual and eternal kingdom of Christ. Persecution, powerless to destroy or even to shake this new community, made it only the more sensible of its own strength, and pressed it into a more compact body. To the errors that sprung up in the theosophic schools and in the various sects, was opposed the one and universal truth received from the apostles, and preserved in the Church. This was well, so long as the invisible and spiritual Church was identical with the visible and external Church. But a great separation took place erelong: the form and the life became disunited. The semblance of an identical and exterior organization was gradually substituted for that interior and spiritual communion, which is the essence of the religion of God. Men forsook the precious perfume of faith, and bowed down before the empty vessel that had contained it. They sought other bonds of union, for faith in the heart no longer connected the members of the Church; and they were united by means of bishops, archbishops, popes, mitres, canons, and ceremonies. The living Church retiring gradually within the lonely sanctuary of a few solitary hearts, an external Church was substituted in its place, and all its forms were declared to be of divine appointment. Salvation no longer flowing from the Word, which was henceforward put out of sight, the priests affirmed that it was conveyed by means of the forms they had themselves invented, and that no one could attain it except by these channels. No one, said they, can by his own faith attain to everlasting life. Christ communicated to the apostles, and these to the bishops, the unction of the Holy Spirit; and this spirit is to be procured only in that order of succession! Originally, whoever possessed the spirit of Jesus Christ was a member of the Church; now the terms were inverted, and it was maintained that he only who was a member of the Church could receive the Spirit.[3]

---

[1] Eusebius, Hist. Eccles. l. 5. c. 24; Socrat. Hist. Eccles. c. 21; Cyprian, ep. 59, 72, 75.

[1] 1 Cor. xv. 9. 1 Tim. iii. 15.
[2] 1 Cor. xvi. 1. 2 Cor. viii. 1. Gal. i. 22. 1 Cor. xiv. 33.
[3] Ubi ecclesia, ibi et spiritus Dei. Ubi spiritus Dei, illic ecclesia. Irenæus.

C

As these ideas became established, the distinction between the people and the clergy was more strongly marked. The salvation of souls no longer depended entirely on faith in Christ, but also, and in a more especial manner, on union with the Church. The representatives and heads of the Church were made partakers of the trust that should be placed in Christ alone, and became the real mediators of their flocks. The idea of a universal Christian priesthood was gradually lost sight of; the servants of the Church of Christ were compared to the priests of the old covenant; and those who separated from the bishop were placed in the same rank with Korah, Dathan, and Abiram! From a peculiar priesthood, such as was then formed in the Church, to a sovereign priesthood, such as Rome claims, the transition was easy.

In fact, no sooner was the erroneous notion of the necessity for a visible unity of the Church established, than another appeared— the necessity for an outward representation of that union. Although we find no traces in the Gospel of Peter's superiority over the other apostles; although the very idea of a primacy is opposed to the fraternal relations which united the brethren, and even to the spirit of the Gospel dispensation, which on the contrary requires all the children of the Father to " minister one to another," acknowledging only one teacher and one master; although Christ had strongly rebuked his disciples, whenever ambitious desires of pre-eminence were conceived in their carnal hearts : the primacy of St. Peter was invented and supported by texts wrongly interpreted, and men next acknowledged in this apostle and in his self-styled successors at Rome, the visible representatives of visible unity—the heads of the universal Church.

The constitution of the Patriarchate contributed in like manner to the exaltation of the Papacy. As early as the three first centuries the metropolitan Churches had enjoyed peculiar honour. The council of Nice, in its sixth canon, mentions three cities, whose Churches, according to it, exercised a long-established authority over those of the surrounding provinces : these were Alexandria, Rome, and Antioch. The political origin of this distinction is indicated by the name which was at first given to the bishops of these cities : they were called *Exarchs*, from the title of the civil governors.[1] Somewhat later they received the more ecclesiastical appellation of *Patriarchs*. We find this title first employed at the council of Constantinople, but in a different sense from that which it afterwards received. It was not until shortly before the council of Chalcedon that it was given exclusively to the great metropolitans. The second general council created a new patriarchate, that of Constan-

tinople itself, the new Rome, the second capital of the empire. The church of Byzantium, so long obscure, enjoyed the same privileges, and was placed by the council of Chalcedon in the same rank as the Church of Rome. Rome at that time shared the patriarchal supremacy with these three churches. But when the Mahometan invasion had destroyed the sees of Alexandria and of Antioch,—when the see of Constantinople fell away, and in later times even separated from the West, Rome remained alone, and the circumstances of the times gathered all the Western Churches around her see, which from that time has been without a rival.

New and more powerful friends than all the rest soon came to her assistance. Ignorance and superstition took possession of the Church, and delivered it, fettered and blindfold, into the hands of Rome.

Yet this bondage was not effected without a struggle. Frequently did the Churches proclaim their independence; and their courageous voices were especially heard from Proconsular Africa and from the East.[1]

But Rome found new allies to stifle the cries of the Churches. Princes, whom those stormy times often shook upon their thrones, offered their protection if Rome would in its turn support them. They conceded to her the spiritual authority, provided she would make a return in secular power. They were lavish of the souls of men, in the hope that she would aid them against their enemies. The power of the hierarchy which was ascending, and the imperial power which was declining, leant thus one upon the other, and by this alliance accelerated their twofold destiny.

Rome could not lose by it. An edict of Theodosius II. and of Valentinian III. proclaimed the Roman bishop " rector of the whole Church."[2] Justinian published a similar decree. These edicts did not contain all that the popes pretended to see in them; but in those times of ignorance it was easy for them to secure that interpretation which was most favourable to themselves. The dominion of the emperors in Italy becoming daily more precarious, the bishops of Rome took advantage of this circumstance to free themselves from their dependence.

But already had issued from the forests of the North the most effectual promoters of the

[1] Cyprian, bishop of Carthage, writes thus of Stephen, bishop of Rome :—Magis ac magis ejus *errorem* denotabis, qui hæreticorum causam contra Christianos et contra *Ecclesiam Dei* asserere conatur....qui unitatem et veritatem de divina lege venientem non tenens....Consuetudo sine veritate, vetustas erroris est. Epist. 74.
Firmilian, bishop of Cæsarea in Cappadocia, said also in the latter half of the third century : Eos autem qui Romæ sunt, non ea in omnibus observare quæ sunt ab origine tradita, et frustra auctoritatem apostolorum prætendere....Ceterum nos (i. e. the bishops of the Asiatic churches, which were more ancient than that of Rome) veritati et consuetudinem jungimus, et consuetudini Romanorum, consuetudinem sed *veritatis* opponimus ; ab initio hoc tenentes quod a Christo et ab apostolo traditum est. Cypr. Ep. 75. These are testimonies of great importance.
[2] Rector totius ecclesiæ.

papal power. The barbarians who had invaded and settled in the West, after being satiated with blood and plunder, lowered their reeking swords before the intellectual power that met them face to face. Recently converted to Christianity, ignorant of the spiritual character of the Church, and feeling the want of a certain external pomp in religion, they prostrated themselves, half savage and half heathen as they were, at the feet of the high-priest of Rome. With their aid the West was in his power. At first the Vandals, then the Ostrogoths, somewhat later the Burgundians and Alans, next the Visigoths, and lastly the Lombards and Anglo-Saxons, came and bent the knee to the Roman pontiff. It was the sturdy shoulders of these children of the idolatrous north that succeeded in placing on the supreme throne of Christendom a pastor of the banks of the Tiber.

At the beginning of the seventh century these events were accomplishing in the West, precisely at the period when the power of Mahomet arose in the East, prepared to invade another quarter of the world.

From this time the evil continued to increase. In the eighth century we see the Roman bishops resisting on the one hand the Greek emperors, their lawful sovereigns, and endeavouring to expel them from Italy, while with the other they court the mayors of the palace in France, begging from this new power, just beginning to rise in the West, a share in the wreck of the empire. Rome founded her usurped authority between the East, which she repelled, and the West, which she summoned to her aid. She raised her throne between two revolts. Startled by the shouts of the Arabs, now become masters of Spain, and who boasted that they would speedily arrive in Italy by the gates of the Pyrenees and Alps, and proclaim the name of Mahomet on the Seven Hills; alarmed at the insolence of Astolphus, who at the head of his Lombards, roaring like a lion, and brandishing his sword before the gates of the eternal city, threatened to put every Roman to death:[1] Rome, in the prospect of ruin, turned her frightened eyes around her, and threw herself into the arms of the Franks. The usurper Pepin demanded her pretended sanction of his new authority; it was granted, and the Papacy obtained in return his promise to be the defender of the "Republic of God." Pepin wrested from the Lombards the cities they had taken from the Greek emperor; yet, instead of restoring them to that prince, he laid their keys on St. Peter's altar, and swore with uplifted hands that he had not taken up arms for man, but to obtain from God the remission of his sins, and to do homage for his conquests to St. Peter. Thus did France establish the temporal power of the popes.

Charlemagne appeared; the first time he ascends the stairs to the basilic of St. Peter, devoutly kissing each step. A second time he presents himself, lord of all the nations that formed the empire of the West, and of Rome itself. Leo III. thought fit to bestow the imperial title on him who already possessed the power; and on Christmas day, in the year 800, he placed the diadem of the Roman emperors on the brow of the son of Pepin.[1] From this time the pope belongs to the empire of the Franks: his connexion with the East is ended. He broke off from a decayed and fallen tree to graft himself upon a wild and vigorous sapling. A future elevation, to which he would have never dared aspire, awaits him among these German tribes with whom he now unites himself.

Charlemagne bequeathed to his feeble successors only the wrecks of his power. In the ninth century disunion every where weakened the civil authority. Rome saw that this was the moment to exalt herself. When could the Church hope for a more favourable opportunity of becoming independent of the state, than when the crown which Charles had worn was broken, and its fragments lay scattered over his former empire?

Then appeared the False Decretals of Isidore. In this collection of the pretended decrees of the popes, the most ancient bishops, who were contemporary with Tacitus and Quintilian, were made to speak the barbarous Latin of the ninth century. The customs and constitutions of the Franks were seriously attributed to the Romans in the time of the emperors. Popes quoted the Bible in the Latin translation of Jerome, who had lived one, two, or three centuries after them; and Victor, bishop of Rome, in the year 192, wrote to Theophilus, who was archbishop of Alexandria in 385. The impostor who had fabricated this collection endeavoured to prove that all bishops derived their authority from the bishop of Rome, who held his own immediately from Christ. He not only recorded all the successive conquests of the pontiffs, but even carried them back to the earliest times. The popes were not ashamed to avail themselves of this contemptible imposture. As early as 865, Nicholas I. drew from its stores the weapons by which to combat princes and bishops.[2] This impudent invention was for ages the arsenal of Rome.

Nevertheless, the vices and crimes of the pontiffs suspended for a time the effects of the decretals. The Papacy celebrated its admission to the table of kings by shameful orgies. She became intoxicated: her senses were lost in the midst of drunken revellings. It is about this period that tradition places

---

[1] Fremens ut leo....asserens omnes uno gladio jugulari. Anastasius, Bibl. Vit. Pontif. p. 83.

[1] Visum est et ipsi Apostolico Leoni....ut ipsum Carolum, imperatorem nominare debuisset, qui ipsam Romam tenebat, ubi semper Cæsares sedere soliti erant, et reliquas sedes.... Annalista Lambecianus, ad an. 801.
[2] See Ep. ad Univers. Episc. Gall. Mansi xv.

upon the papal throne a woman named Joan, who had taken refuge in Rome with her lover, and whose sex was betrayed by the pangs of childbirth during a solemn procession. But let us not needlessly augment the shame of the pontifical court. Abandoned women at this time governed Rome; and that throne which pretended to rise above the majesty of kings was sunk deep in the dregs of vice. Theodora and Marozia installed and deposed at their pleasure the self-styled masters of the Church of Christ, and placed their lovers, sons, and grandsons, in St. Peter's chair. These scandals, which are but too well authenticated, may perhaps have given rise to the tradition of Pope Joan.

Rome became one wide theatre of disorders, the possession of which was disputed by the most powerful families of Italy. The counts of Tuscany were generally victorious. In 1033, this house dared to place on the pontifical throne, under the name of Benedict IX., a youth brought up in debauchery. This boy of twelve years old continued, when pope, the same horrible and degrading vices.[1] Another party chose Sylvester III. in his stead; and Benedict, whose conscience was loaded with adulteries, and whose hands were stained with murder,[2] at last sold the Papacy to a Roman ecclesiastic.

The emperors of Germany, filled with indignation at such enormities, purged Rome with the sword. The empire, asserting its paramount rights, drew the triple crown from the mire into which it had fallen, and saved the degraded papacy by giving it respectable men as its chiefs. Henry III. deposed three popes in 1046, and his finger, decorated with the ring of the Roman patricians, pointed out the bishop to whom the keys of St. Peter should be confided. Four popes, all Germans, and nominated by the emperor, succeeded. When the Roman pontiff died, the deputies of that church repaired to the imperial court, like the envoys of other dioceses, to solicit a new bishop. With joy the emperor beheld the popes reforming abuses, strengthening the Church, holding councils, installing and deposing prelates, in defiance of foreign monarchs: the Papacy by these pretensions did but exalt the power of the emperor, its lord paramount. But to allow of such practices was to expose his own authority to great danger. The power which the popes thus gradually recovered might be turned suddenly against the emperor himself. When the reptile had gained strength, it might wound the bosom that had cherished it: and this result followed.

And now begins a new era for the papacy. It rises from its humiliation, and soon trample the princes of the earth under foot.

To exalt the Papacy is to exalt the Church, to advance religion, to ensure to the spirit the victory over the flesh, and to God the conquest of the world. Such are its maxims: in these ambition finds its advantage, and fanaticism its excuse.

The whole of this new policy is personified in one man: Hildebrand.

This pope, who has been by turns indiscreetly exalted or unjustly traduced, is the personification of the Roman pontificate in all its strength and glory. He is one of those normal characters in history, which include within themselves a new order of things, similar to those presented in other spheres by Charlemagne, Luther, and Napoleon.

This monk, the son of a carpenter of Savoy, was brought up in a Roman convent, and had quitted Rome at the period when Henry III. had there deposed three popes, and taken refuge in France in the austere convent of Cluny. In 1048, Bruno, bishop of Toul, having been nominated pope by the emperor at Worms, who was holding the German Diet in tha. city, assumed the pontifical habits, and took the name of Leo IX.; but Hildebrand, who had hastened thither, refused to recognise him, since it was (said he) from the secular power that he held the tiara.[1] Leo, yielding to the irresistible power of a strong mind and of a deep conviction, immediately humbled himself, laid aside his sacerdotal ornaments, and clad in the garb of a pilgrim, set out barefoot for Rome along with Hildebrand (says an historian), in order to be there legitimately elected by the clergy and the Roman people. From this time Hildebrand was the soul of the Papacy, until he became pope himself. He had governed the Church under the name of several pontiffs, before he reigned in person as Gregory VII. One grand idea had taken possession of this great genius. He desired to establish a visible theocracy, of which the pope, as vicar of Jesus Christ, should be the head. The recollection of the universal dominion of heathen Rome haunted his imigination and animated his zeal. He wished to restore to papal Rome all that imperial Rome had lost. "What Marius and Cæsar," said his flatterers, "could not effect by torrents of blood, thou hast accomplished by a word."

Gregory VII. was not directed by the spirit of the Lord. That spirit of truth, humility, and long-suffering, was unknown to him. He sacrificed the truth whenever he judged it necessary to his policy. This he did particularly in the case of Berenger, archdeacon of Angers. But a spirit far superior to that of the generality of pontiffs—a deep conviction of the justice of his cause—undoubtedly animated him. He was bold, ambitious, per-

---

[1] Cujus quidem post adeptum sacerdotium vita quam turpis, quam fœda, quamque execranda exstiterit, horresco referre. Desiderius (abbot of Cassino, afterwards Pope Victor III.), De Miraculis a S. Benedicto, &c., lib. iii. init.
[2] Theophylactus....cum post multa adulteria et homicidia manibus suis perpetrata, &c. Bonizo (bishop of Sutri, afterwards of Placenza), Liber ad Amicum.

[1] Quia non secundum canonicam institutionem, sed per sæcularem et regiam potestatem, Romanam ecclesiam arripere velis. Bruno de Segni, Vita Leonis. Otho of Freysingen, an historian who lived a century later, places at Cluny this meeting of Leo and Hildebrand. This is probably an error.

severing in his designs, and at the same time skilful and politic in the use of the means that would ensure success.

His first task was to organize the militia of the Church. It was necessary to gain strength before attacking the empire. A council held at Rome removed the pastors from their families, and compelled them to become the devoted adherents of the hierarchy. The law of celibacy, planned and carried out by popes, who were themselves monks, changed the clergy into a sort of monastic order. Gregory VII. claimed the same power over all the bishops and priests of Christendom, that an abbot of Cluny exercises in the order over which he presides. The legates of Hildebrand, who compared themselves to the proconsuls of ancient Rome, travelled through the provinces, depriving the pastors of their legitimate wives; and, if necessary, the pope himself raised the populace against the married clergy.[1]

But chief of all, Gregory designed emancipating Rome from its subjection to the empire. Never would he have dared conceive so bold a scheme, if the troubles that afflicted the minority of Henry IV., and the revolt of the German princes against that young emperor, had not favoured its execution. The pope was at this time one of the magnates of the empire. Making common cause with the other great vassals, he strengthened himself by the aristocratic interest, and then forbade all ecclesiastics, under pain of excommunication, to receive investiture from the emperor. He broke the ancient ties that connected the Churches and their pastors with the royal authority, but it was to bind them all to the pontifical throne. To this throne he undertook to chain priests, kings, and people, and to make the pope a universal monarch. It was Rome alone that every priest should fear: it was in Rome alone that he should hope. The kingdoms and principalities of the earth are her domain. All kings were to tremble at the thunderbolts hurled by the Jupiter of modern Rome. Woe to him who resists. Subjects are released from their oaths of allegiance; the whole country is placed under an interdict; public worship ceases; the churches are closed; the bells are mute; the sacraments are no longer administered; and the malediction extends even to the dead, to whom the earth, at the command of a haughty pontiff, denies the repose of the tomb.

The pope, subordinate from the very beginning of his existence successively to the Roman, Frank, and German emperors, was now free, and he trod for the first time as their equal, if not their master. Yet Gregory VII. was humbled in his turn: Rome was taken, and Hildebrand compelled to flee.

He died at Salerno, exclaiming, " I have loved righteousness and hated iniquity, therefore do I die in exile."[1] Who shall dare charge with hypocrisy these words uttered on the very brink of the grave?

The successors of Gregory, like soldiers arriving after a victory, threw themselves as conquerors on the enslaved Churches. Spain rescued from Islamism, Prussia reclaimed from idolatry, fell into the arms of the crowned priest. The Crusades, which were undertaken at his instigation, extended and confirmed his authority. The pious pilgrims, who in imagination had seen saints and angels leading their armed bands,—who, entering humble and barefoot within the walls of Jerusalem, burnt the Jews in their synagogue, and watered with the blood of thousands of Saracens the places where they came to trace the sacred footsteps of the Prince of Peace,—carried into the East the name of the pope, who had been forgotten there since he had exchanged the supremacy of the Greeks for that of the Franks.

In another quarter the power of the Church effected what the arms of the republic and of the empire had been unable to accomplish. The Germans laid at the feet of a bishop those tributes which their ancestors had refused to the most powerful generals. Their princes, on succeeding to the imperial dignity, imagined they received a crown from the popes, but it was a yoke that was placed upon their necks. The kingdoms of Christendom, already subject to the spiritual authority of Rome, now became her serfs and tributaries.

Thus every thing was changed in the Church.

It was at first a community of brethren, and now an absolute monarchy was established in its bosom. All Christians were priests of the living God,[2] with humble pastors as their guides. But a haughty head is upraised in the midst of these pastors; a mysterious voice utters words full of pride; an iron hand compels all men, great and small, rich and poor, bond and free, to wear the badge of its power. The holy and primitive equality of souls before God is lost sight of. At the voice of one man Christendom is divided into two unequal parties: on the one side is a separate caste of priests, daring to usurp the name of the Church', and claiming to be invested with peculiar privileges in the eyes of the Lord; and, on the other, servile flocks reduced to a blind and passive submission—a people gagged and fettered, and given over to a haughty caste. Every tribe, language, and nation of Christendom, submits to the dominion of this spiritual king, who has received power to conquer.

---

[1] Hi quocumque prodeunt, clamores insultantium. digitos ostendentium, colaphos pulsantium, perferunt. Alii membris mutilati; alii per longos cruciatus superbe necati, &c. Martene and Durand. Thesaurus Nov. Anecd. i. 231.

[1] Dilexi justitiam et odivi iniquitatem, propterea mortuʃ in exilio.
[2] 1 Peter ii. 9.

CHAPTER II.

Grace—Dead Faith—Works—Unity and Duality—Pelagianism—Salvation at the hands of the Priests—Penance—Flagellations—Indulgences—Works of Supererogation—Purgatory—The Tariff—Jubilee—The Papacy and Christianity—State of Christendom.

But side by side with the principle that should pervade the history of Christianity, was found another that should preside over its doctrine. This was the great idea of Christianity—the idea of grace, of pardon, of amnesty, of the gift of eternal life. This idea supposed in man an alienation from God, and an inability of returning by any power of his own into communion with that infinitely holy being. The opposition between the true and the false doctrine undoubtedly cannot be entirely summed up in the question of salvation by faith or by works. Nevertheless it is its most striking characteristic. But further, salvation considered as coming from man, is the creative principle of every error and abuse. The excesses produced by this fundamental error led to the Reformation, and by the profession of the contrary principle it was carried out. This feature should therefore be very prominent in an introduction to the history of that reform.

Salvation by grace was the second characteristic which essentially distinguished the religion of God from all human systems. What had now become of it? Had the Church preserved, as a precious deposit, this great and primordial thought? Let us trace its history.

The inhabitants of Jerusalem, of Asia, of Greece, and of Rome, in the time of the first emperors, heard these glad tidings: "By grace are ye saved through faith; and that not of yourselves; it is the gift of God."[1] At this proclamation of peace, at this joyful news, at this word of power, many guilty souls believed, and were drawn to Him who is the source of peace; and numerous Christian Churches were formed in the midst of the degenerate nations of that age.

But a great mistake was soon made as to the nature of this saving faith. Faith, according to St. Paul, is the means by which the whole being of the believer—his understanding, heart, and will—enter into possession of the salvation purchased for him by the incarnation and death of the Son of God. Jesus Christ is apprehended by faith, and from that hour becomes all things to man and in man. He communicates a divine life to our human nature; and man thus renewed, and freed from the chains of sin and self, feels new affections and performs new works. Faith, says the theologian in order to express his ideas, is the subjective appropriation of the objective work of Christ. If faith be not an appropriation of salvation, it is nothing; all the Christian economy is thrown into confusion, the fountains of the new life are sealed, and Christianity is overturned from its foundations.

And this is what did happen. This practical view of faith was gradually forgotten. Soon it became, what it still is to many persons, a simple act of the understanding, a mere submission to a superior authority.

From this first error there necessarily proceeded a second. Faith being thus stripped of its practical character, it was impossible to say that it alone had power to save: as works no longer were its fruits, they were of necessity placed side by side with it, and the doctrine that man is justified by faith and by works prevailed in the Church. In place of that Christian unity which comprises in a single principle justification and works, grace and the law, doctrine and duty, succeeded that melancholy duality which regards religion and morality as two entirely distinct things—that fatal error, which, by separating things that cannot live unless united, and by putting the soul on one side and the body on the other, is the cause of spiritual death. The words of the apostle, re-echoing across the interval of ages are —"Having begun in the spirit, are ye now made perfect by the flesh?"

Another great error contributed still further to unsettle the doctrine of grace: this was Pelagianism. Pelagius asserted that human nature is not fallen—that there is no hereditary corruption, and that man, having received the power to do good, has only to will in order to perform.[1] If good works consist only in external acts, Pelagius is right. But if we look to the motives whence these outward acts proceed, we find every where in man's nature selfishness, forgetfulness of God, pollution, and impotency. The Pelagian doctrine, expelled by Augustine from the Church when it had presented itself boldly, insinuated itself as demi-Pelagianism, and under the mask of the Augustine forms of expression. This error spread with astonishing rapidity throughout Christendom. The danger of the doctrine was particularly manifested in this,—that by placing goodness without, and not within, the heart, it set a great value on external actions, legal observances, and penitential works. The more these practices were observed, the more righteous man became: by them heaven was gained; and soon the extravagant idea prevailed that there are men who have advanced in holiness beyond what was required of them.

Whilst Pelagianism corrupted the Christian doctrine, it strengthened the hierarchy. The hand that lowered grace, exalted the Church: for grace is God, the Church is man.

[1] Ephes. ii. 8.

[1] Velle et esse ad hominem referenda sunt, quia de arbitrii fonte descendunt. Pelagius in Aug. De Gratia Dei cap. 4.

The more we feel the truth that all men are guilty before God, the more also shall we cling to Christ as the only source of grace. How could we then place the Church in the same rank with Christ, since it is but an assembly of all those who are found in the same wretched state by nature? But so soon as we attribute to man a peculiar holiness, a personal merit, every thing is changed. The clergy and the monks are looked upon as the most natural channels through which to receive the grace of God. This was what happened often after the times of Pelagius. Salvation, taken from the hands of God, fell into those of the priests, who set themselves in the place of our Lord. Souls thirsting for pardon were no more to look to heaven, but to the Church, and above all to its pretended head. To these blinded souls the Roman pontiff was God. Hence the greatness of the popes—hence unutterable abuses. The evil spread still further. When Pelagianism laid down the doctrine that man could attain a state of perfect sanctification, it affirmed also that the merits of saints and martyrs might be applied to the Church. A peculiar power was attributed to their intercession. Prayers were made to them; their aid was invoked in all the sorrows of life; and a real idolatry thus supplanted the adoration of the living and true God.

At the same time, Pelagianism multiplied rites and ceremonies. Man, imagining that he could and that he ought by good works to render himself deserving of grace, saw no fitter means of meriting it than acts of external worship. The ceremonial law became infinitely complicated, and was soon put on a level, to say the least, with the moral law. Thus were the consciences of Christians burdened anew with a yoke that had been declared insupportable in the times of the apostles.[1]

But it was especially by the system of penance, which flowed immediately from Pelagianism, that Christianity was perverted. At first, penance had consisted in certain public expressions of repentance, required by the Church from those who had been excluded on account of scandals, and who desired to be received again into its bosom.

By degrees penance was extended to every sin, even to the most secret, and was considered as a sort of punishment to which it was necessary to submit, in order to obtain the forgiveness of God through the priest's absolution.

Ecclesiastical penance was thus confounded with Christian repentance, without which there can be neither justification nor sanctification.

Instead of looking to Christ for pardon through faith alone, it was sought for principally in the Church through penitential works.

Great importance was soon attached to external marks of repentance—to tears, fasting, and mortification of the flesh; and the inward regeneration of the heart, which alone constitutes a real conversion, was forgotten.

As confession and penance are easier than the extirpation of sin and the abandonment of vice, many ceased contending against the lusts of the flesh, and preferred gratifying them at the expense of a few mortifications.

The penitential works, thus substituted for the salvation of God, were multiplied in the Church from Tertullian down to the thirteenth century. Men were required to fast, to go barefoot, to wear no linen, &c.; to quit their homes and their native land for distant countries; or to renounce the world and embrace a monastic life.

In the eleventh century voluntary flagellations were superadded to these practices: somewhat later they became quite a mania in Italy, which was then in a very disturbed state. Nobles and peasants, old and young, even children of five years of age, whose only covering was a cloth tied round the middle, went in pairs, by hundreds, thousands, and tens of thousands, through the towns and villages, visiting the churches in the depth of winter. Armed with scourges, they flogged each other without pity, and the streets resounded with cries and groans that drew tears from all who heard them.

Still, long before the disease had reached such a height, the priest-ridden world had sighed for deliverance. The priests themselves had found out, that if they did not apply a remedy their usurped power would slip from their hands. They accordingly invented that system of barter celebrated under the title of Indulgences. They said to their penitents: " You cannot accomplish the tasks imposed on you. Well! we, the priests of God and your pastors, will take this heavy burden upon ourselves. For a seven weeks' fast," said Regino, abbot of Prum, " you shall pay twenty pence, if you are rich; ten, if less wealthy; and three pence if you are poor; and so on for other matters."[1] Courageous men raised their voices against this traffic, but in vain!

The pope soon discovered what advantages could be derived from these indulgences. Alexander Hales, the irrefragable doctor, invented in the thirteenth century a doctrine well calculated to secure these vast revenues to the Papacy. A bull of Clement VII. declared it an article of faith. Jesus Christ, it was said, had done much more than was necessary to reconcile God to man. One single drop of his blood would have been sufficient. But he shed it copiously, in order to form a treasure for his Church that eternity can never exhaust. The supererogatory merits of the saints, the reward of the good works they had done beyond their obligation, have

---

[1] Acts xv. 10.

[1] Libri duo de Ecclesiasticis Disciplinis.

still further augmented this treasure. Its keeping and management were confided to Christ's vicar upon earth. He applies to each sinner, for the sins committed after baptism, these merits of Jesus Christ and of the saints, according to the measure and the quantity his sins require. Who would venture to attack a custom of such holy origin?

This inconceivable traffic was soon extended and complicated. The philosophers of Alexandria had spoken of a fire in which men were to be purified. Many ancient doctors had adopted this notion; and Rome declared this philosophical opinion a tenet of the Church. The pope by a bull annexed Purgatory to his domain. In that place, he declared, men would have to expiate the sins that could not be expiated here on earth; but that indulgences would liberate their souls from that intermediate state in which their sins would detain them. Thomas Aquinas set forth this doctrine in his famous *Summa Theologiæ.* No means were spared to fill the mind with terror. The priests depicted in horrible colours the torments inflicted by this purifying fire on all who became its prey. In many Roman-catholic countries we may still see paintings exhibited in the churches and public places, wherein poor souls, from the midst of glowing flames, invoke with anguish some alleviation of their pain. Who could refuse the ransom which, falling into the treasury of Rome, would redeem the soul from such torments?

Somewhat later, in order to reduce this traffic to a system, they invented (probably under John XXII.) the celebrated and scandalous Tariff of Indulgences, which has gone through more than forty editions. The least delicate ears would be offended by an enumeration of all the horrors it contains. Incest, if not detected, was to cost five groats; and six, if it was known. There was a stated price for murder, infanticide, adultery, perjury, burglary, &c. "O disgrace of Rome!" exclaims Claude d'Espence, a Roman divine: and we may add, O disgrace of human nature! for we can utter no reproach against Rome that does not recoil on man himself. Rome is human nature exalted in some of its worst propensities. We say this that we may speak the truth; we say it also, that we may be just.

Boniface VIII., the most daring and ambitious pontiff after Gregory VII., was enabled to effect still more than his predecessors.

In the year 1300, he published a bull, in which he declared to the Church that every hundred years all who made a pilgrimage to Rome should receive a plenary indulgence. From all parts, from Italy, Sicily, Sardinia, Corsica, France, Spain, Germany, and Hungary, people flocked in crowds. Old men of sixty and seventy undertook the journey, and in one month two hundred thousand pilgrims visited Rome. All these strangers brought rich offerings; and the pope and the Romans saw their coffers replenished.

Roman avarice soon fixed each Jubilee at fifty, then at thirty-three, and lastly at twenty-five years' interval. Then, for the greater convenience of purchasers, and the greater profit of the sellers, both the jubilee and its indulgences were transported from Rome to every market-place in Christendom. It was no longer necessary to leave one's home. What others had gone in search of beyond the Alps, each man could now buy at his own door.

The evil could not become greater.

Then the Reformer appeared.

We have seen what had become of the principle that was destined to govern the history of Christianity; we have seen also what became of that which should have pervaded its doctrines: both were lost.

To set up a mediatorial caste between God and man—to obtain by works, by penance, and by money, the salvation which is the free gift of God—such is Popery.

To open to all, through Jesus Christ, without any human mediator, without that power which calls itself the Church, free access to the great boon of eternal life which God offers to man—such is Christianity and the Reformation.

Popery is a lofty barrier erected by the labour of ages between God and man. If any one desires to scale it, he must pay or he must suffer; and even then he will not surmount it.

The Reformation is the power that has overthrown this barrier, that has restored Christ to man, and has thus opened a level path by which he may reach his Creator.

Popery interposes the Church between God and man.

Primitive Christianity and the Reformation bring God and man face to face.

Popery separates them—the Gospel unites them.

After having thus traced the history of the decline and fall of the two great principles that were to distinguish the religion of God from all human systems, let us see what were some of the consequences of this immense transformation.

But first let us pay due honour to the Church of the Middle Ages, which succeeded that of the apostles and of the fathers, and which preceded that of the reformers. The Church was still the Church, although fallen, and daily more and more enslaved: that is to say, she was always the greatest friend of man. Her hands, though bound, could still be raised to bless. Eminent servants of Jesus Christ, who were true Protestants as regards the essential doctrines of Christianity, diffused a cheering light during the dark ages; and in the humblest convent, in the remotest parish, might be found poor monks and poor priests to alleviate great sufferings. The Catholic church was not the Papacy. The latter was the oppressor, the former the oppressed. The Reformation, which declared war against the one, came to deliver the other. And it must be confessed that the Papacy itself became at times in the hands of God, who brings good out of evil, a necessary counterpoise to the power and ambition of princes.

CHAPTER III.

Religion—Relics—Easter Revels—Morals—Corruption—Disorders of the Priests, Bishops, and Popes—A Papal Family—Alexander VI.—Cæsar Borgia—Education—Ignorance—Ciceronians.

LET us now see what was the state of the Church previous to the Reformation.

The nations of Christendom no longer looked to a holy and living God for the free gift of eternal life. To obtain it, they were obliged to have recourse to all the means that a superstitious, fearful, and alarmed imagination could devise. Heaven was filled with saints and mediators, whose duty it was to solicit this mercy. Earth was filled with pious works, sacrifices, observances, and ceremonies, by which it was to be obtained. Here is a picture of the religion of this period transmitted to us by one who was long a monk, and afterwards a fellow-labourer of Luther's—by Myconius :—

"The sufferings and merits of Christ were looked upon as an idle tale, or as the fictions of Homer. There was no thought of the faith by which we become partakers of the Saviour's righteousness and of the heritage of eternal life. Christ was looked upon as a severe judge, prepared to condemn all who should not have recourse to the intercession of the saints, or to the papal indulgences. Other intercessors appeared in his place :—first the Virgin Mary, like the Diana of paganism, and then the saints, whose numbers were continually augmented by the popes. These mediators granted their intercession only to such applicants as had deserved well of the orders founded by them. For this it was necessary to do, not what God had commanded in his Word, but to perform a number of works invented by monks and priests, and which brought money to the treasury. These works were Ave-Marias, the prayers of Saint Ursula and of Saint Bridget: they must chant and cry night and day. There were as many resorts for pilgrims as there were mountains, forests, and valleys. But these penances might be compounded for with money. The people, therefore, brought to the convents and to the priests money and every thing that had any value—fowls, ducks, geese, eggs, wax, straw, butter, and

cheese. Then the hymns resounded, the bells rang, incense filled the sanctuary, sacrifices were offered up, the larders overflowed, the glasses went round, and masses terminated and concealed these pious orgies. The bishops no longer preached, but they consecrated priests, bells, monks, churches, chapels, images, books, and cemeteries ; and all this brought in a large revenue. Bones, arms, and feet were preserved in gold and silver boxes ; they were given out during mass for the faithful to kiss, and this too was a source of great profit.

"All these people maintained that the pope, 'sitting as God in the temple of God,'[1] could not err, and they would not suffer any contradiction."[2]

In the church of All Saints at Wittemberg was shown a fragment of Noah's ark, some soot from the furnace of the Three Children, a piece of wood from the cradle of Jesus Christ, some hair from the beard of St. Christopher, and nineteen thousand other relics of greater or less value. At Schaffhausen was exhibited the breath of St. Joseph that Nicodemus had received in his glove. In Wurtemberg you might meet a seller of indulgences, vending his merchandise, his head adorned with a large feather plucked from the wing of St. Michael.[3] But it was not necessary to travel far in search of these precious treasures. Men who farmed the relics traversed the whole country, hawking them about the rural districts (as has since been the case with the Holy Scriptures), and carrying them to the houses of the faithful, to spare them the trouble and expense of a pilgrimage. They were exhibited with pomp in the churches. These wandering hawkers paid a stipulated sum to the owners of the relics,—a per-centage on their profits. The kingdom of heaven had disappeared, and in its place a market of abominations had been opened upon earth.

Thus a spirit of profanity had invaded religion ; and the holiest recollections of the Church, the seasons which more particularly summoned the faithful to holy meditation and love, were disgraced by buffoonery and heathenish profanation. The " Revels of Easter " held a distinguished place in the records of the Church. As the festival of the resurrection of Christ ought to be celebrated with joy, the preachers studied in their sermons every thing that might raise a laugh among their hearers. One imitated the note of the cuckoo ; another hissed like a goose. One dragged to the altar a layman robed in a monk's frock ; a second related the most indecent stories ; and a third recounted the tricks of St. Peter, and among others, how in a tavern he had cheated his host by not paying his reckoning.[4] The

[1] 2 Thessalonians, ii. 4.
[2] Myconius, History of the Reformation ; and Seckendorf. History of Lutheranism.
[3] Müller's Reliquien, vol. iii. p. 22.
[4] Œcolampad., De Risu Paschali.

lower clergy took advantage of this opportunity to ridicule their superiors. The churches were converted into a mere stage for mountebanks, and the priests into buffoons.

If such was the state of religion, what must have been the state of morals?

Undoubtedly the corruption was not at that time universal. Justice requires that this should not be forgotten. The Reformation elicited numerous examples of piety, righteousness, and strength of mind. The spontaneous action of God's power was the cause; but how can we deny that he had beforehand deposited the seeds of this new life in the bosom of the Church? If in our days we should bring together all the immoralities, all the turpitudes committed in a single country, the mass of corruption would doubtless shock us still. Nevertheless, the evil at this period wore a character and universality that it has not borne subsequently. And, above all, the mystery of iniquity desolated the holy places, as it has not been permitted to do since the days of the Reformation.

Morality had declined with the decline of faith. The tidings of the gift of eternal life is the power of God to regenerate man. Take away the salvation which God has given, and you take away sanctification and good works. And this result followed.

The doctrine and the sale of indulgences were powerful incentives to evil among an ignorant people. True, according to the Church, indulgences could benefit those only who promised to amend their lives, and who kept their word. But what could be expected from a tenet invented solely with a view to the profit that might be derived from it? The venders of indulgences were naturally tempted, for the better sale of their merchandise, to present their wares to the people in the most attractive and seducing aspect. The learned themselves did not fully understand the doctrine. All that the multitude saw in them was, that they permitted men to sin; and the merchants were not over eager to dissipate an error so favourable to their sale.

What disorders and crimes were committed in these dark ages, when impunity was to be purchased by money! What had man to fear, when a small contribution towards building a church secured him from the fear of punishment in the world to come? What hope could there be of revival when all communication between God and man was cut off, and man, an alien from God, who is the spirit and the life, moved only in a round of paltry ceremonies and sensual observances, in an atmosphere of death!

The priests were the first who yielded to this corrupting influence. By desiring to exalt themselves they became abased. They had aimed at robbing God of a ray of his glory, and placing it in their own bosoms; but their attempt had proved vain, and they had only hidden there a leaven of corruption stolen from the power of evil. The history of the age swarms with scandals. In many places, the people were delighted at seeing a priest keep a mistress, that the married women might be safe from his seductions.[1] What humiliating scenes did the house of a pastor in those days present! The wretched man supported the woman and the children she had borne him with the tithes and offerings.[2] His conscience was troubled: he blushed in the presence of the people, before his domestics, and before God. The mother, fearing to come to want if the priest should die, made provision against it beforehand, and robbed her own house. Her honour was lost. Her children were ever a living accusation against her. Despised by all, they plunged into quarrels and debauchery. Such was the family of the priest!......These were frightful scenes, by which the people knew how to profit.[3]

The rural districts were the scene of numerous disorders. The abodes of the clergy were often dens of corruption. Corneille Adrian at Bruges,[4] the abbot Trinkler at Cappel,[5] imitated the manners of the East, and had their harems. Priests, consorting with dissolute characters, frequented the taverns, played at dice, and crowned their orgies with quarrels and blasphemy.[6]

The council of Schaffhausen forbade the priests to dance in public, except at marriages, and to carry more than one kind of arms: they decreed also that all who were found in houses of ill fame should be unfrocked.[7] In the archbishopric of Mentz, they scaled the walls by night, and created all kinds of disorder and confusion in the inns and taverns, and broke the doors and locks.[8] In many places the priest paid the bishop a regular tax for the woman with whom he lived, and for each child he had by her. A German bishop said publicly one day, at a great entertainment, that in one year eleven thousand priests had presented themselves before him for that purpose. It is Erasmus who relates this.[9]

If we go higher in the hierarchical order, we find the corruption not less great. The dignitaries of the Church preferred the tumult of camps to the hymns of the altar. To be able, lance in hand, to reduce his neighbours to obedience, was one of the chief qualifications of a bishop. Baldwin, archbishop of Treves, was continually at war with his neighbours and his vassals: he demolished their castles, built strongholds, and thought of nothing but the extension of his territory

[1] Nicol. De Clemangis, de Præsullb. Simoniacis.
[2] The words of Seb. Stor., pastor of Lichstall in 1524.
[3] Füsslin Beytræge, ii. 224.
[4] Metern. Nederl. Hist. viii.
[5] Hottinger, Hist. Eccles. ix. 305.
[6] Mandate of Hugo, bishop of Constance, 3d March 1517.
[7] Müller's Reliq., iii. 251.
[8] Steubing, Gesch. der Nass. Oran. Lande.
[9] Uno anno ad se delata undecim millia sacerdotum palam concubinariorum. Erasmi Opp. ix. 401.

18

A certain bishop of Eichstadt, when administering justice, wore a coat of mail under his robes, and held a large sword in his hand. He used to say he was not afraid of five barbarians, provided they did but attack him in fair fight. [1] Everywhere the bishops were continually at war with their towns. The citizens demanded liberty, the bishops required implicit obedience. If the latter gained the victory, they punished the revolters by sacrificing numerous victims to their vengeance; but the flame of insurrection burst out again, at the very moment when it was thought to be extinguished.

And what a spectacle was presented by the pontifical throne in the times immediately preceding the Reformation! Rome, it must be acknowledged, had seldom witnessed so much infamy.

Rodrigo Borgia, after having lived with a Roman lady, had continued the same illicit connexion with one of her daughters, named Rosa Vanozza, by whom he had five children. He was a cardinal and archbishop, living at Rome with Vanozza and other women, visiting the churches and the hospitals, when the death of Innocent VIII. created a vacancy in the pontifical chair. He succeeded in obtaining it by bribing each cardinal at a stipulated price. Four mules laden with silver publicly entered the palace of Sforza, one of the most influential of the cardinals. Borgia became pope under the name of Alexander VI., and rejoiced in thus attaining the summit of earthly felicity.

On the day of his coronation, his son Cæsar, a youth of ferocious and dissolute manners, was created archbishop of Valencia and bishop of Pampeluna. He next celebrated in the Vatican the marriage of his daughter Lucretia, by festivities at which his mistress, Julia Bella, was present, and which were enlivened by licentious plays and songs. "All the clergy," says an historian,[2] "kept mistresses, and all the convents of the capital were houses of ill fame." Cæsar Borgia espoused the cause of the Guelfs; and when by their assistance he had destroyed the Ghibellines, he turned upon the Guelfs and crushed them in their turn. But he desired to share alone in all these spoils. In 1497, Alexander gave the duchy of Benevento to his eldest son. The duke suddenly disappeared. A faggot-dealer, on the banks of the Tiber, one George Schiavoni, had seen a dead body thrown into the stream during the night; but he said nothing of it, as being a common occurrence. The body of the duke was found. His brother Cæsar had been the instigator of his death.[3] This was not enough. His brother-in-law stood in his way: one day Cæsar caused him to be stabbed on the very stairs of the pontifical

palace. He was carried bleeding to his own apartments. His wife and sister did not leave him; and fearful that Cæsar would employ poison, they prepared his meals with their own hands. Alexander set a guard on the doors; but Cæsar ridiculed these precautions, and remarked, as the pope was about to pay a visit to his son-in-law, "What is not done at dinner, will be done at supper." Accordingly, one day he gained admittance to the chamber of the convalescent, turned out the wife and sister, and calling in his executioner Michilotto, the only man in whom he placed any confidence, ordered his brother-in-law to be strangled before his eyes.[1] Alexander had a favourite, Perotto, whose influence also offended the young duke. He rushed upon him: Perotto took refuge under the pontifical mantle, and clasped the pope in his arms. Cæsar stabbed him, and the blood of his victim spirted in the face of the pontiff.[2] "The pope," adds a contemporary and eye-witness of these scenes, "loves the duke his son, and lives in great fear of him."

Cæsar was the handsomest and strongest man of his age. Six wild bulls fell easily beneath his blows in single combat. Every morning some new victim was found, who had been assassinated during the night in the Roman streets. Poison carried off those whom the dagger could not reach. No one dared move or breathe in Rome, for fear that his turn should come next. Cæsar Borgia was the hero of crime. That spot of earth in which iniquity had attained such a height was the throne of the pontiffs. When man gives himself up to the powers of evil, the higher he claims to be exalted before God, the lower he sinks into the abyss of hell. The dissolute entertainments given by the pope, his son Cæsar, and his daughter Lucretia, in the pontifical palace, cannot be described or even thought of without shuddering. The impure groves of antiquity saw nothing like them. Historians have accused Alexander and Lucretia of incest; but this charge does not appear sufficiently established. The pope had prepared poison in a box of sweetmeats that was to be served up after a sumptuous repast: the cardinal for whom it was intended being forewarned, gained over the attendant, and the poisoned box was set before Alexander.[3] He ate of it and died. "The whole city ran together, and could not satiate their eyes with gazing on this dead viper."[4]

Such was the man who filled the papal chair at the beginning of the century in which the Reformation burst forth.

Thus had the clergy brought not only themselves but religion into disrepute. Well might a powerful voice exclaim: "The

[1] Schmidt, Gesch. der Deutschen, vol. v.
[2] Infessura.
[3] Amazzò il fratello ducha di Gandia e lo fa butar nel Tevere. MS. of Capello, ambassador at Rome in 1500, extracted by Ranke.

[1] Intro in camera......fe ussir la moglie e sorella......estrangolò dito zovene. MS. of Capello, Ranke.
[2] Adeo il sangue il saltò in la faza del papa. Ibid.
[3] E messe la scutola venenata avante il papa. Sanato.
[4] Gordon, Tomasi, Infessura, Guicciardini, &c.

ecclesiastical order is opposed to God and to his glory. The people know it well; and this is but too plainly shown by the many songs, proverbs, and jokes against the priests, that are current among the commonalty, and all those caricatures of monks and priests on every wall, and even on the playing-cards. Every one feels a loathing on seeing or hearing a priest in the distance." It is Luther who speaks thus. [1]

The evil had spread through all ranks: " a strong delusion" had been sent among men; [2] the corruption of manners corresponded with the corruption of faith. A mystery of iniquity oppressed the enslaved Church of Christ.

Another consequence necessarily flowed from the neglect into which the fundamental doctrine of the Gospel had fallen. Ignorance of the understanding accompanied the corruption of the heart. The priests having taken into their hands the distribution of a salvation that belongs only to God, had secured a sufficient title to the respect of the people. What need had they to study sacred learning? It was no longer a question of explaining the Scriptures, but of granting letters of indulgence; and for this ministry it was not necessary to have acquired much learning.

In country places, they chose for preachers, says Wimpheling, "miserable wretches whom they had previously raised from beggary, and who had been cooks, musicians, huntsmen, stable-boys, and even worse." [3]

The superior clergy themselves were often sunk in great ignorance. A bishop of Dunfeld congratulated himself on having never learnt either Greek or Hebrew. The monks asserted that all heresies arose from those two languages, and particularly from the Greek. " The New Testament," said one of them, " is a book full of serpents and thorns. Greek," continued he, "is a new and recently invented language, and we must be upon our guard against it. As for Hebrew, my dear brethren, it is certain that all who learn it, immediately become Jews." Heresbach, a friend of Erasmus, and a respectable author, reports these expressions. Thomas Linacer, a learned and celebrated ecclesiastic, had never read the New Testament. In his latter days (in 1524), he called for a copy, but quickly threw it away from him with an oath, because on opening it his eyes had glanced upon these words: " But I say unto you, Swear not at all." Now he was a great swearer. " Either this is not the Gospel," said he, " or else we are not Christians." [4] Even the faculty of theology at Paris scrupled not to declare to the parliament: " Re-

ligion is ruined, if you permit the study of Greek and Hebrew."

If any learning was found here and there among the clergy, it was not in sacred literature. The Ciceronians of Italy affected a great contempt for the Bible on account of its style. Pretended priests of the Church of Christ translated the writings of holy men, inspired by the Spirit of God, in the style of Virgil and of Horace, to accommodate their language to the ears of good society. Cardinal Bembo, instead of the *Holy Ghost*, used to write *the breath of the heavenly zephyr*; for the expression *to forgive sins—to bend the manes and the sovereign gods*; and for *Christ, the Son of God—Minerva sprung from the head of Jupiter*. Finding one day the worthy Sadolet engaged in translating the Epistle to the Romans, he said to him: " Leave these childish matters: such fooleries do not become a sensible man." [1]

These were some of the consequences of the system that then oppressed Christendom. This picture undoubtedly demonstrates the corruption of the Church, and the necessity for a reformation. Such was our design in writing this sketch. The vital doctrines of Christianity had almost entirely disappeared, and with them the life and light that constitute the essence of the religion of God. The material strength of the Church was gone. It lay an exhausted, enfeebled, and almost lifeless body, extended over that part of the world which the Roman empire had occupied.

CHAPTER IV.

Imperishable Nature of Christianity—Two Laws of God—Apparent Strength of Rome—Secret Opposition—Decline—Threefold Opposition—Kings and People—Transformation of the Church—The Pope judged in Italy—Discoveries of Kings and their Subjects—Frederick the Wise—Moderation and Expectation.

THE evils which thus afflicted Christendom; superstition, unbelief, ignorance, vain speculations, and corruption of morals—the natural fruits of the heart of man—were not new upon the earth. Often had they appeared in the history of nations. They had invaded, especially in the East, the different religious systems that had seen their day of glory. Those enervated systems had sunk under these evils, had fallen under their attack, and not one of them had ever risen again.

Was Christianity now to undergo the same fate? Would it be lost like these old national religions? Would the blow that had caused their death be sufficient to deprive it of life? Could nothing save it? Will these hostile powers that overwhelm it, and which have already overthrown so many

---

[1] Da man an alle Wände, auf allerley Zeddel, zuletzt auch auf den Kartenspielen, Pfaffen, und Münche malete. Luth. Epp. ii. 674.
[2] 2 Thess. ii. 11.
[3] Apologia pro Rep. Christ.
[4] Müller's Reliq. iii. 253.

[1] Felleri. Mon. ined. p. 400.

various systems of worship, be able to seat themselves without resistance on the ruins of the Church of Jesus Christ?

No! There is in Christianity what none of these national systems possessed. It does not, like them, present certain general ideas mingled with tradition and fable, destined to fall sooner or later under the assault of reason: it contains a pure and undefiled truth, founded on facts capable of bearing the examination of every upright and enlightened mind. Christianity does not propose merely to excite in man certain vague religious feelings, whose charm once lost can never be recovered: its object is to satisfy, and it does really satisfy, all the religious wants of human nature, whatever may be the degree of development which it has attained. It is not the work of man, whose labours pass away and are forgotten; it is the work of God, who upholds what he has created; and it has the promise of its Divine Head as the pledge of its duration.

It is impossible for human nature ever to rise superior to Christianity. And if for a time man thought he could do without it, it soon appeared to him with fresh youth and a new life, as the only remedy for souls. The degenerate nations then returned with new ardour towards those ancient, simple, and powerful truths, which in the hour of their infatuation they had despised.

In fact, Christianity manifested in the sixteenth century the same regenerative power that it had exercised at first. After fifteen centuries the same truths produced the same effects. In the day of the Reformation, as in the time of Peter and Paul, the Gospel overthrew mighty obstacles with irresistible force. Its sovereign power displayed its efficacy from north to south among nations the most dissimilar in manners, character, and intellectual development. Then, as in the times of Stephen and James, it kindled the fire of enthusiasm and devotedness in the lifeless nations, and elevated them to the height of martyrdom.

How was this revival of the Church accomplished?

We observe here two laws by which God governs the Church in all times.

First he prepares slowly and from afar that which he designs to accomplish. He has ages in which to work.

Then, when the time is come, he effects the greatest results by the smallest means. It is thus he acts in nature and in history. When he wishes to produce a majestic tree, he deposits a small seed in the bosom of the earth; when he wishes to renovate his Church, he employs the meanest instruments to accomplish what emperors and learned and distinguished men in the Church could not effect. We shall soon go in search of, and we shall discover, that small seed which a Divine hand placed in the earth in the days of the Reformation. But we must here distinguish and recognise the different means by which God prepared the way for this great revolution.

At the period when the Reformation was about to burst forth, Rome appeared in peace and security. One might have said that nothing could ever disturb her in her triumph: great victories had been achieved by her. The general councils—those upper and lower chambers of Catholicism—had been subdued. The Waldenses and the Hussites had been crushed. No university, except perhaps that of Paris, which sometimes raised its voice at the signal of its kings, doubted the infallibility of the oracles of Rome. Every one seemed to have taken his own share of its power. The higher orders of the clergy preferred giving to a distant chief the tithe of their revenues, and tranquilly to consume the remainder, to risking all for an independence that would cost them dear and would bring them little profit. The inferior clergy, attracted by the prospect of brilliant stations, which their ambition painted and discovered in the distance, willingly purchased by a little slavery the flattering hopes they cherished. Besides, they were every where so oppressed by the chiefs of the hierarchy, that they could scarcely stir under their powerful hands, and much less raise themselves and make head against them. The people bent the knee before the Roman altar; and even kings themselves, who began in secret to despise the bishop of Rome, would not have dared lay hands upon his power for fear of the imputation of sacrilege.

But if external opposition appeared to have subsided, or even to have entirely ceased, when the Reformation broke out, its internal strength had increased. If we take a nearer view of the edifice, we discover more than one symptom that foreboded its destruction. The cessation of the general councils had scattered their principles throughout the Church, and carried disunion into the camp of their opponents. The defenders of the hierarchy were divided into two parties; those who maintained the system of absolute papal dominion, according to the maxims of Hildebrand; and those who desired a constitutional papal government, offering securities and liberty to the several Churches.

And more than this, in both parties faith in the infallibility of the Roman bishop had been rudely shaken. If no voice was raised to attack it, it was because every one felt anxious rather to preserve the little faith he still possessed. They dreaded the slightest shock, lest it should overthrow the whole edifice. Christendom held its breath; but it was to prevent a calamity in which it feared to perish. From the moment that man trembles to abandon a long-worshipped persuasion, he possesses it no more. And he will not much longer keep up the appearance that he wishes to maintain.

The Reformation had been gradually prepared by God's providence in three different spheres—the political, the ecclesiastical, and the literary. Princes and their subjects, Christians and divines, the learned and the wise, contributed to bring about this revolution of the sixteenth century. Let us pass in review this triple classification, finishing with that of literature, which was perhaps the most powerful in the times immediately preceding the reform.

And, firstly, Rome had lost much of her ancient credit in the eyes of nations and of kings. Of this the Church itself was the primary cause. The errors and superstitions which she had introduced into Christianity were not, properly speaking, what had inflicted the mortal wound. The Christian world must have been raised above the clergy in intellectual and religious development, to have been able to judge of it in this point of view. But there was an order of things within the comprehension of the laity, and by this the Church was judged. It had become altogether earthly. That sacerdotal dominion which lorded over the nations, and which could not exist except by the delusion of its subjects, and by the halo that encircled it, had forgotten its nature, left heaven and its spheres of light and glory to mingle in the vulgar interests of citizens and princes. The priests, born to be the representatives of the Spirit, had bartered it away for the flesh. They had abandoned the treasures of science and the spiritual power of the Word, for the brute force and false glory of the age.

This happened naturally enough. It was in truth the spiritual order which the Church had at first undertaken to defend. But to protect it against the resistance and attacks of the people, she had recourse to earthly means, to vulgar arms, which a false policy had induced her to take up. When once the Church had begun to handle such weapons, her spirituality was at an end. Her arm could not become temporal and her heart not become temporal also. Erelong was seen apparently the reverse of what had been at first. After resolving to employ earth to defend heaven, she made use of heaven to defend the earth. Theocratic forms became in her hands the means of accomplishing worldly enterprises. The offerings which the people laid at the feet of the sovereign pontiff of Christendom were employed in maintaining the splendour of his court and in paying his armies. His spiritual power served as steps by which to place the kings and nations of the earth under his feet. The charm ceased, and the power of the Church was lost, so soon as the men of those days could say, She is become as one of us.

The great were the first to scrutinize the titles of this imaginary power.[1] This very examination might perhaps have been suffi-

cient for the overthrow of Rome. But fortunately for her the education of the princes was every where in the hands of her adepts. who inspired their august pupils with sentiments of veneration towards the Roman pontiff. The rulers of the people grew up in the sanctuary of the Church. Princes of ordinary capacity never entirely got beyond it: many longed only to return to it at the hour of death. They preferred dying in a friar's cowl to dying beneath a crown.

Italy—that European apple of discord—contributed perhaps more than anything else to open the eyes of kings. They had to contract alliances with the pope, which had reference to the temporal prince of the States of the Church, and not to the bishop of bishops. Kings were astonished at seeing the popes ready to sacrifice the rights belonging to the pontiff, in order that they might preserve some advantage to the prince. They perceived that these pretended organs of the truth had recourse to all the paltry wiles of policy,—to deceit, dissimulation, and perjury.[1] Then fell off the bandage which education had bound over the eyes of princes. Then the artful Ferdinand of Aragon played stratagem against stratagem. Then the impetuous Louis XII. had a medal struck, with the inscription, *Perdam Babylonis Nomen.*[2] And the good Maximilian of Austria, grieved at hearing of the treachery of Leo X., said openly: " This pope also, in my opinion, is a scoundrel. Now may I say, that never in my life has any pope kept his faith or his word with me....I hope, God willing, this will be the last of them."[3]

Kings and people then began to feel impatient under the heavy burden the popes had laid upon them. They demanded that Rome should relieve them from tithes, tributes, and annates, which exhausted their resources. Already had France opposed Rome with the Pragmatic Sanction, and the chiefs of the empire claimed the like immunity. The emperor was present in person at the council of Pisa in 1511, and even for a time entertained the idea of securing the Papacy to himself. But of all these leaders, none was so useful to the Reformation as he in whose states it was destined to commence.

Frederick of Saxony, surnamed the Wise, was at that time the most powerful of all the Electors. Coming to the government of the hereditary states of his family in 1487, he had received the electoral dignity from the emperor; and in 1493, having gone on a pilgrimage to Jerusalem, he was there made a knight of the Holy Sepulchre. The influence he exercised, his wealth and liberality, raised him above his equals. God chose him to serve as a tree under whose shelter the seeds of truth might put forth their first

---

[1] Adrien Baillet, Hist. des Démêlés de Boniface VIII. avec Philippe le Bel. Paris, 1708.

[1] Guicciardini, Storia d'Italia.
[2] I will destroy the name of Babylon.
[3] Scultet. Annal. ad ann. 1520.

shoots, without being uprooted by the tempests around them.[1]

No one was better adapted for this noble ministry. Frederick possessed the esteem of all, and enjoyed the full confidence of the emperor. He even supplied his place when Maximilian was absent from Germany. His wisdom did not consist in the skilful exercise of a crafty policy, but in an enlightened, far-seeing prudence; the first principle of which was never from interested motives to infringe the laws of honour and of religion.

At the same time, he felt the power of God's word in his heart. One day, when the vicar-general Staupitz was with him, the conversation turned on those who were in the habit of delivering empty declamations from the pulpit. "All discourses," said the elector, "that are filled only with subtleties and human traditions, are wonderfully cold and unimpressive; since no subtlety can be advanced, that another subtlety cannot overthrow. The Holy Scriptures alone are clothed with such power and majesty, that, destroying all our learned reasoning-machines, they press us close, and compel us to say, Never man spake like this man." Staupitz having expressed himself entirely of that opinion, the elector shook him cordially by the hand and said: "Promise me that you will always think the same."[2]

Frederick was precisely the prince required at the beginning of the Reformation. Too much weakness on the part of the friends of this work would have allowed of its being crushed. Too much precipitation would have made the storm burst forth sooner, which from its very commencement began to gather in secret against it. Frederick was moderate but firm. He possessed that virtue which God requires at all times in those who love his ways: he waited for God. He put in practice the wise counsel of Gamaliel: "If this work be of men, it will come to nought; but if it be of God, ye cannot overthrow it."[3] "Things are come to such a pass," said this prince to Spengler of Nuremberg, one of the most enlightened men of his day, "that man can do no more; God alone must act. For this reason we place in his powerful hands these mighty works that are too difficult for us." Providence claims our admiration in the choice it made of such a ruler to protect its rising work.

[1] Qui præ multis pollebat principibus aliis, auctoritate, opibus, potentia, liberalitate et magnificentia. Cochlœus, Acta L., p. 2.
[2] Luth. Epp.   [3] Acts v. 38, 39.

CHAPTER V.

Popular Feeling—The Empire—Providential Preparations—Impulse of the Reformation—Peace—The Commonalty—National Character—Papal Yoke—State of the Empire—Opposition at Rome—Middle Classes—Switzerland—Courage—Liberty—Smaller Cantons—Italy—Obstacles to the Reform—Spain—Obstacles—Portugal—France—Preparations—Disappointment—The Low Countries—England—Scotland—The North—Russia—Poland—Bohemia—Hungary.

WE have seen God's preparations among the princes for the work he was about to accomplish: let us now consider what they were among their subjects. It would have been of less importance for the chiefs to have been ready, if the nations themselves had not been so. The discoveries made by the kings had acted gradually upon the people. The wisest of them began to grow accustomed to the idea that the bishop of Rome was a mere man, and sometimes even a very bad man. The people in general began to suspect that he was not much holier than their own bishops, whose reputation was very equivocal. The licentiousness of the popes excited the indignation of Christendom, and a hatred of the Roman name was deeply seated in the hearts of nations.[1]

Numerous causes at the same time facilitated the emancipation of the various countries of the West. Let us cast a glance over their condition at this period.

The Empire was a confederation of different states, having an emperor at their head, and each possessing sovereignty within its own territories. The Imperial Diet, composed of all the princes or sovereign states, exercised the legislative power for all the Germanic body. It was the emperor's duty to ratify the laws, decrees, and *recesses* of this assembly, and he had the charge of applying them and putting them into execution. The seven most powerful princes, under the title of Electors, had the privilege of conferring the imperial crown.

The north of Germany, inhabited principally by the ancient Saxon race, had acquired the greatest portion of liberty. The emperor, whose hereditary possessions were continually harassed by the Turks, was compelled to keep on good terms with these princes and their courageous subjects, who were at that time necessary to him. Several free cities in the north, west, and south of the empire, had by their commerce, manufactures, and industry, attained a high degree of prosperity, and consequently of independence. The powerful house of Austria, which wore the imperial crown, held most of the states of southern Germany in its power, and narrowly watched every movement. It was preparing to extend its dominion over the whole of the empire, and even beyond it, when the Reformation raised a powerful

[1] Odium Romani nominis, penitus infixum esse multarum gentium animis opinor, ob ea, quæ vulgo de moribus ejus urbis jactantur. Erasm. Epp. lib. xii. p. 634.

barrier against its encroachments, and saved the independence of Europe.

As Judæa, when Christianity first appeared, was in the centre of the old world, so Germany was the centre of Christendom. It touched, at the same time, on the Low Countries, England, France, Switzerland, Italy, Hungary, Bohemia, Poland, Denmark, and all the North. It was in the very heart of Europe that this principle of life was destined to be developed, and its pulsations were to circulate through the arteries of this great body the generous blood that was appointed to vivify all its members.

The particular form of constitution which the empire had received, conformably with the dispensations of Providence, favoured the propagation of new ideas. If Germany had been a monarchy strictly so called, like France or England, the arbitrary will of the sovereign might have sufficed to check for a while the progress of the Gospel. But it was a confederation. The truth, opposed in one state, might be received with favour in another.

The internal peace that Maximilian had secured to the empire was no less favourable to the Reformation. For a long time, the numerous members of the Germanic body seemed to have taken a pleasure in tearing each other to pieces. Nothing had been seen but confusion, discord, and wars incessantly renewed. Neighbours were against neighbours, town against town, nobles against nobles. Maximilian had laid a firm foundation of public order in the Imperial Chamber, an institution appointed to decide all differences between the various states. The German nations, after so many disorders and anxieties, saw the beginning of a new era of security and repose. Nevertheless Germany, when Luther appeared, still presented to the eye of the observer that motion which agitates the sea after a storm of long continuance. The calm was yet uncertain. The first breeze might make the tempest burst forth anew. Of this we shall see more than one example. The Reformation, by communicating a new impulse to the German race, for ever destroyed the old causes of agitation. It put an end to the barbarous system that had hitherto prevailed, and gave a new one to Europe.

Meanwhile the religion of Jesus Christ had exerted on Germany its peculiar influence. The third estate (the commonalty) had rapidly advanced. In the different parts of the empire, particularly in the free cities, numerous institutions arose, calculated to develop this imposing mass of the people. There the arts flourished: the burghers devoted themselves in security to the tranquil labours and sweet relations of social life. They became more and more accessible to information. Thus they daily acquired greater respect and influence. It was not magistrates, who are often compelled to adapt their conduct to the political exigencies of the times; or nobles passionately fond of military glory above all things; or an ambitious and greedy priesthood, trading with religion as its peculiar property, that were to found the Reformation in Germany. It was to be the work of the middle classes—of the people—of the whole nation.

The peculiar character of the Germans seemed especially favourable to a religious reformation. They had not been enervated by a false civilisation. The precious seeds that the fear of God deposits among a people had not been scattered to the winds. Ancient manners still survived. In Germany was found that uprightness, fidelity, and industry—that perseverance and religious disposition, which still flourishes there, and which promises greater success to the Gospel than the fickle, scornful, and sensual character of other European nations.

The Germans had received from Rome that great element of modern civilisation—the faith. Instruction, knowledge, legislation—all except their courage and their arms—had come to them from the sacerdotal city. Strong ties had from that time connected Germany with the Papacy. The former was a spiritual conquest of the latter, and we know to what use Rome has always applied her conquests. Other nations, who had possessed the faith and civilisation before the Roman Pontiff existed, had maintained a greater independence with respect to it. But this subjection of the Germans was destined only to make the reaction more powerful at the moment of awakening. When the eyes of Germany should be opened, she would tear away the trammels in which she had so long been held captive. The slavery she had endured would give her a greater longing for deliverance and liberty, and the hardy champions of truth would go forth from that prison of restraint and discipline in which for ages her people had been confined.

There was at that time in Germany something very nearly resembling what in the political language of our days is termed " a see-saw system." When the head of the empire was of an energetic character, his power increased; when on the contrary he possessed little ability, the influence and authority of the princes and electors were augmented. Never had the latter felt more independent of their chief than under Maximilian at the period of the Reformation. And their leader having taken part against it, it is easy to understand how that very circumstance was favourable to the propagation of the Gospel.

In addition to this, Germany was weary of what Rome contemptuously denominated " the patience of the Germans." The latter had in truth shown much patience since the time of Louis of Bavaria. From that period the emperors had laid down their arms, and the tiara had been placed without resistance above the crown of the Cæsars. But the strife had only changed its scene of action. It had descended to lower ground. These same struggles, of which popes and emperors had set the world an example, were soon renewed on a smaller scale in every city of Germany between the bishops and the magistrates. The burghers had taken up the sword which the chiefs of the empire had let fall. As early as 1329, the citizens of Frankfort-on-the-Oder had resisted with intrepidity all their ecclesiastical superiors. Having been excommunicated for their fidelity to the Margrave Louis, they had remained for twenty-eight years without masses, baptism, marriage ceremonies, or funeral rites. The return of the priests and monks was greeted with laughter, like a comedy or farce. A deplorable error, no doubt, but the priests themselves were the cause of it. At the period of the Reformation these oppositions between the magistrates and the ecclesiastics had increased. Every hour the privileges and temporal assumptions of the clergy brought these two bodies into collision.

But it was not only among the burgomasters, councillors, and secretaries of the cities that Rome and her clergy found opponents. About the same time the indignation was at work among the populace. It broke out in 1493, and later in 1502, in the Rhenish provinces : the peasants, exasperated at the heavy yoke imposed upon them by their ecclesiastical sovereigns, formed among themselves what has been called the " League of the Shoes." They began to assemble by night in Alsace, repairing by unfrequented paths to isolated hills, where they swore to pay in future no taxes but such as they had freely consented to, to abolish all tolls and *jalage*,[1] to limit the power of the priests, and to plunder the Jews. Then placing a peasant's shoe on the end of a pole by way of standard, they marched against the town of Schlettstadt, proposing to call to their assistance the free confederation of the Swiss : but they were soon dispersed. This was only one of the symptoms of the general fermentation that agitated the castles, towns, and rural districts of the empire.

Thus, every where, from high to low, was heard a hollow murmur, forerunner of the thunderbolt that was soon to fall. Germany appeared ripe for the appointed task of the sixteenth century. Providence in its slow progress had prepared every thing ; and even the passions which God condemns, were directed by his almighty hand to the accomplishment of his designs.

Let us take a·glance at the other nations of Europe.

Thirteen small republics, placed with their allies in the centre of Europe, among mountains which seemed to form its citadel, composed a simple and brave nation. Who

would have looked in those sequestered valleys for the men whom God would choose to be the liberators of the Church conjointly with the children of the Germans? Who would have thought that small unknown cities—scarcely raised above barbarism, hidden behind inaccessible mountains, on the shores of lakes that had found no name in history—would surpass, as regards Christianity, even Jerusalem, Antioch, Ephesus, Corinth, and Rome? Nevertheless, such was the will of Him who " causeth it to rain upon one piece of land, and the piece of land whereupon it raineth not, withereth."[1]

Other circumstances besides seemed destined to oppose numerous obstacles to the progress of the Reformation in the bosom of the Helvetic population. If the obstructions of power were to be dreaded in a monarchy, the precipitancy of the people was to be feared in a democracy.

But in Switzerland, also, the way had been prepared for the truth. It was a wild but generous stock, that had been sheltered in her deep valleys, to be grafted one day with a fruit of great value. Providence had scattered among these new people principles of courage, independence, and liberty, that were to be developed in all their majesty, so soon as the day of battle against Rome should arrive. The pope had conferred upon the Swiss the title of Protectors of the Liberty of the Church. But they seem to have understood this honourable appellation in a sense somewhat different from the pontiff. If their soldiers guarded the pope beneath the shadow of the ancient Capitol, their citizens carefully protected in the bosom of the Alps their own religious liberties against the assaults of the pope and of the clergy. The ecclesiastics were forbidden to have recourse to any foreign jurisdiction. The " Letter of the Priests " (Pfaffenbrief, 1370) was a strong protest of Swiss independence against the abuses and power of the clergy. Zurich was distinguished among all the states by its courageous resistance to the claims of Rome. Geneva, at the other extremity of Switzerland, was contending with its bishop. These two cities distinguished themselves above all the others in the great struggle that we have undertaken to describe.

But if the Helvetian towns, accessible to every amelioration, were to be drawn into the reform movement, it was not to be the case with the inhabitants of the mountains. Knowledge had not yet reached them. These cantons, the founders of Swiss liberty, proud of the part they had taken in the great struggle for independence, were not easily disposed to imitate their younger brothers of the plain. Why should they change that faith under which they had expelled the Austrian, and which had consecrated by

---

[1] The *jalage* was a seignorial duty levied upon wine sold by retail.

[1] Amos iv. 7.

altars all the scenes of their triumphs? Their priests were the only enlightened guides to whom they could have recourse: their worship and their festivals relieved the monotony of their tranquil hours, and agreeably disturbed the silence of their peaceful homes. They remained steadfast against all religious innovations.

Passing the Alps, we find ourselves in that Italy which was in the eyes of the majority the holy land of Christendom. Whence could Europe have looked for the good of the Church if not from Italy—if not from Rome? Might not that power which raised successively so many different characters to the pontifical chair, some day place in it a pontiff who would become an instrument of blessing to the heritage of the Lord? If even there was no hope in the pontiffs, were there not bishops and councils that might reform the Church? Nothing good can come out of Nazareth: but from Jerusalem,—from Rome! ... Such might have been the ideas of men; but "God's thoughts are not as their thoughts." He said, "He that is filthy let him be filthy still;"[1] and abandoned Italy to her unrighteousness. That land of ancient renown was by turns the victim of intestine war and of foreign invasion. The stratagems of policy, the violence of factions, the strife of arms, seemed alone destined to prevail there, and to banish for a long season the peace of the Gospel.

Italy, broken to pieces, dismembered, and without unity, appeared but little suited to receive one general impulse. Each frontier was a new barrier where the truth would be stopped.

And if the truth was destined to come from the North, how could the Italians, with so refined a taste, and with social habits so delicate in their own eyes, condescend to receive any thing from the barbarous Germans? Were the men who bestowed more admiration on the regular cadence of a sonnet than on the majesty and simplicity of the Scriptures, a proper soil for the seed of the word of God? A false civilisation is, of all the various conditions of a nation, that which is most repugnant to the Gospel.

Finally, whatever might be the state of affairs, Rome was always Rome to Italy. The temporal power of the popes not only led the different Italian states to court their alliance and their favour at any cost, but the universal dominion of Rome offered more than one inducement to the avarice and vanity of the ultra-montane states. As soon as it became a question of emancipating the rest of the world from Rome, Italy would become Italy again; domestic quarrels would not prevail to the advantage of a foreign system; and attacks aimed against the chief of the peninsular family would be sufficient to awaken common interests and affections from their long slumber.

[1] Revelation xxii. 11.

The Reformation had thus little prospect of success on that side of the Alps. Nevertheless, there were found beyond these mountains souls prepared to receive the light of the Gospel, and Italy was not at that hour entirely disinherited.

Spain possessed what Italy did not—a serious, noble-minded, and religiously disposed population. In every age this people has reckoned pious and learned men among the members of its clergy, and it was sufficiently remote from Rome to be able to throw off its yoke without difficulty. There are few nations in which we might have more reasonably hoped for a revival of that primitive Christianity which Spain had received perhaps from the hands of St. Paul himself. And yet Spain did not rise up among the nations. She was to fulfil this prophecy of Divine wisdom: *The first shall be last.* Various circumstances led to this mournful result.

Spain, considering its isolated position and distance from Germany, would be affected only in a slight degree by the shocks of that great earthquake which so violently agitated the empire. It was occupied, besides, with very different treasures from those which the word of God was then offering to the nations. The new world eclipsed the eternal world. A virgin soil, which seemed to consist of gold and silver, inflamed the imaginations of all. An eager thirst for wealth left no room in the Spanish heart for nobler thoughts. A powerful clergy, having scaffolds and treasures at its disposal, ruled in the peninsula. Spain willingly rendered a servile obedience to her priests, which, by releasing her from every spiritual anxiety, left her free to give way to her passions,—to go in pursuit of riches, discoveries, and new continents. Victorious over the Moors, she had, at the cost of her noblest blood, torn the crescent from the walls of Granada and many other cities, and planted the cross of Christ in its place. This great zeal for Christianity, which appeared destined to afford the liveliest expectations, turned against the truth. How could Catholic Spain, which had crushed infidelity, fail to oppose heresy? How could those who had driven Mahomet from their beautiful country allow Luther to penetrate into it? Their kings did even more: they equipped fleets against the Reformation, and went to Holland and England in search of it, that they might subdue it. But these attacks elevated the nations assailed; and erelong Spain was crushed by their united power. Thus, in consequence of the Reformation, did this Catholic country lose that temporal prosperity which had made it at first reject the spiritual liberty of the Gospel. Nevertheless, the dwellers beyond the Pyrenees were a brave and generous race. Many of its noble children, with the same ardour, but with more knowledge than those whose blood had stained the Moorish swords, came and laid down their lives as a sacrifice on the burning piles of the Inquisition.

The case was nearly the same in Portugal as in Spain. Emanuel the Fortunate gave it a " golden age," which unfitted it for the self-denial required by the Gospel. The Portuguese thronged the newly discovered roads to the East Indies and Brazil, and turned their backs on Europe and the Reformation.

Few countries seemed better disposed for the reception of the evangelical doctrines than France. In that country almost all the intellectual and spiritual life of the Middle Ages had been concentrated. One might have been led to say, that paths had been opened in every direction for a great manifestation of the truth. Men of the most opposite characters, and whose influence had been most extensive over the French nation, were found to have some affinity with the Reformation. St. Bernard had given an example of that faith of the heart, of that inward piety, which is the noblest feature of the Reformation. Abelard had carried into the study of theology that rational principle, which, incapable of building up what is true, is powerful to destroy what is false. Numerous pretended heretics had rekindled the flames of the word of God in the provinces. The university of Paris had stood up against the Church, and had not feared to oppose it. At the commencement of the fifteenth century the Clemangis and the Gersons had spoken out with boldness. The Pragmatic Sanction had been a great act of independence, and seemed destined to be the palladium of the Gallican liberties. The French nobles, so numerous and so jealous of their pre-eminence, and who at this period had seen their privileges gradually taken away to augment the kingly power, must have been favourably disposed to a religious revolution that might have restored some portion of the independence they had lost. The people, quick, intelligent, and susceptible of generous emotions, were as accessible to the truth as any other, if not more so. The Reformation in this country seemed likely to crown the long travail of many centuries. But the chariot of France, which appeared for so many generations to be hastening onwards in the same direction, suddenly turned aside at the epoch of the Reformation, and took quite a contrary course. Such is the will of Him who is the guide of nations and of their rulers. The prince who was then seated in the chariot and held the reins, and who, as a patron of literature, seemed of all the chiefs of Roman-catholicism likely to be the foremost in promoting the Reformation, threw his subjects into another path. The symptoms of many centuries proved fallacious, and the impulse given to France was unavailing against the ambition and fanaticism of her kings. The house of

Valois deprived her of that which should have belonged to her. Perhaps had she received the Gospel, she would have become too powerful. It was God's will to select weaker nations—nations just rising into existence, to be the depositories of his truth. France, after having been almost entirely reformed, found herself Roman-catholic in the end. The sword of her princes thrown into the balance made it incline towards Rome. Alas! another sword—that of the Reformers themselves—completed the destruction of the Reformation. Hands that had been used to wield the sword, ceased to be raised to heaven in prayer. It is by the blood of its confessors, and not of its adversaries, that the Gospel triumphs.

At the era of the Reformation the Netherlands was one of the most flourishing countries of Europe. Its people were industrious, enlightened in consequence of the numerous relations they maintained with the different parts of the world, full of courage, and enthusiastic in the cause of their independence, privileges, and liberties. Situated at the very gates of Germany, it would be one of the first to hear the report of the Reformation. Two very distinct parties composed its population. The more southern portion, that overflowed with wealth, gave way. How could all these manufactures carried to the highest degree of perfection—this immense commerce by land and sea—Bruges, that great mart of the northern trade—Antwerp, the queen of merchant cities—how could all these resign themselves to a long and bloody struggle about questions of faith? On the contrary, the northern provinces, defended by their sand-hills, the sea, and their canals, and still more by the simplicity of their manners, and their determination to lose every thing rather than the Gospel, not only preserved their freedom, their privileges, and their faith, but even achieved their independence and a glorious nationality.

England gave but little promise of what she afterwards became. Driven out of the Continent, where she had long and obstinately attempted the conquest of France, she began to turn her eyes towards the sea, as to a kingdom destined to be the real object of her conquests, and whose inheritance was reserved for her. Twice converted to Christianity—once under the ancient Britons, and again under the Anglo-Saxons—she paid with great devotion the annual tribute of St. Peter's pence. Yet high destinies were in reserve for her. Mistress of the ocean, and touching at once upon all quarters of the globe, she was to become one day, with the nation to which she should give birth, the hand of God to scatter the seeds of life in the most distant islands and over the widest continents. Already there were a few circumstances foreboding her mighty destiny: great learning had shone in the British islands, and some glimmerings of it still remained. A crowd of foreigners—artists, merchants, and artisans—coming from the Low Countries, Germany, and other places, filled their cities and their havens. The new religious ideas would thus easily be carried thither. Finally, England had then for king an eccentric prince, who, endowed with some information and great courage, changed his projects and his ideas every hour, and turned from one side to the other according to the direction in which his violent passions drove him. It was possible that one of the Eighth Henry's caprices might some day be favourable to the Reformation.

Scotland was at this time distracted by factions. A king of five years old, a queen-regent, ambitious nobles, and an influential clergy, harassed this courageous people in every direction. They were destined, however, erelong to shine in the first rank among those who should receive the Reformation.

The three kingdoms of the North—Denmark, Sweden, and Norway—were united under a common sceptre. These rude and warlike people seemed to have little connexion with the doctrine of love and peace. Yet by their very energy they were perhaps better disposed than the nations of the South to receive the power of the Gospel. But these sons of warriors and of pirates brought, methinks, too warlike a character into that protestant cause, which their swords in later times so heroically defended.

Russia, driven into the extremity of Europe, had but few relations with the other states. Besides, she belonged to the Greek communion; and the Reformation effected in the Western, exerted little or no influence on the Eastern church.

Poland seemed well prepared for a reform. The neighbourhood of the Bohemian and Moravian Christians had disposed it to receive the evangelical impulse, which by its vicinity to Germany was likely to be promptly communicated. As early as 1500 the nobility of Great Poland had demanded that the cup should be given to the laity, by appealing to the customs of the primitive Church. The liberty enjoyed in its cities, the independence of its nobles, made it a secure asylum for all Christians who had been persecuted in their own country. The truth they carried with them was joyfully received by a great number of the inhabitants. Yet it is one of the countries which, in our days, possesses the fewest confessors.

The flame of the Reformation, which had long burnt brightly in Bohemia, had been nearly extinguished in blood. Nevertheless, some precious remnants, escaped from the slaughter, were still alive to see the day which Huss had foretold.

Hungary had been torn in pieces by intestine wars under the government of princes without ability or experience, and who had eventually bound the fate of their subjects to Austria, by enrolling this powerful family among the heirs to their crown.

Such was the state of Europe at the beginning of the sixteenth century, which was destined to produce so great a transformation in christian society.

CHAPTER VI.

Roman Theology—Remains of Life—Justification by Faith—Witnesses to the Truth—Claudius—The Mystics—The Waldenses—Valdo—Wickliffe—Huss—Prediction—Protestantism before the Reformation—Anselm—Arnoldi—Utenheim—Martin—New Witnesses in the Church—Thomas Conecte—The Cardinal of Crayn—Institoris—Savonarola—Justification by Faith—John Vitrarius—John Lallier—John of Wesalia—John of Goch—John Wessel—Protestantism before the Reformation—The Bohemian Brethren—Prophecy of Proles—Prophecy of the Eisenach Franciscan.

HAVING described the condition of the nations and princes of Europe, we now proceed to the preparations for the great Reform which existed in theology and in the Church.

The singular system of theology that was established in the Church, was destined to contribute powerfully to open the eyes of the new generation. Formed for an age of darkness, as if that age would last for ever, that system was to be left behind, and to be rent in every direction, so soon as the age grew in understanding. This was the result. The popes had added now this and now that to the Christian doctrines. They had neither changed nor removed anything except it would not square with their hierarchical system; what was not contrary to their plans might remain until further orders. It contained certain true doctrines, such as Redemption and the power of the Holy Ghost, of which a skilful divine, if there was one to be found at that time, might have availed himself to combat and overthrow all the others. The pure gold mingled with the base alloy in the treasures of the Vatican, might have easily led to the discovery of the fraud. It is true, that if any courageous adversary turned his attention towards it, the winnowing-fan of Rome immediately swept away this pure grain. But these very condemnations only served to augment the confusion.

This confusion was immense, and the pretended unity was but one wide disorder. At Rome there were the doctrines of the court and the doctrines of the church. The faith of the metropolis differed from that of the provinces. In the latter, too, this diversity was infinite. There was the faith of the princes, of the people, and of the religious orders. There was a distinction between the opinions of this convent and of that district, of this doctor and of that monk.

In order that the truth might exist peaceably in the ages when Rome would have crushed her with its iron sceptre, she had followed the example of the insect that weaves a chrysalis of its threads in which to shelter itself during the inclement season. And, strange to say, the instruments employed by divine truth to this end were the so-much decried schoolmen. These industrious artisans of thought had unravelled every theological idea, and of all their threads had woven a web, under which it would have been difficult for more skilful persons than their contemporaries to recognise the truth in its pristine purity. We may regret that the insect, so full of life, and glowing with the brightest colours, should enclose itself, to all appearance dead, in its dark cell ; but in this covering is its safety. The case was the same with truth. If the interested and suspicious policy of Rome, in the day of its power, had seen her unveiled, it would have crushed her, or at least endeavoured so to do. Disguised as she was by the theologians of the time, under endless subtleties and distinctions, the popes did not recognise her, or saw that in this condition she could not injure them. They took the work and the workmen under their protection. But the season might come in which this hidden truth would raise her head, and throw off the toils that had covered her. Having gained new strength in her apparent tomb, she would be seen in the day of her resurrection gaining the victory over Rome and its errors. This spring-time arrived. At the very period when these absurd coverings of the schoolmen were falling one after another under the skilful attacks and the sneers of the new generation, the truth issued from them, blooming in youth and beauty.

It was not alone from the writings of the schoolmen that powerful testimony was given to the truth. Christianity had every where mingled something of its own life with the life of the people. The Church of Christ was a dilapidated building ; but in digging around it, a portion of the living rock on which it had been originally built was discovered among its foundations. Numerous institutions dating from the pure ages of the Church still existed, and could not fail to awaken in many souls evangelical sentiments opposed to the prevailing superstition. Inspired men, the old doctors of the Church, whose writings were deposited in various libraries, raised here and there a solitary voice. We may hope that it was listened to in silence by many an attentive ear. Let us not doubt that the Christians—and how pleasing is the thought!—had many brethren and sisters in those monasteries, where we too easily discover little else than hypocrisy and licentiousness.

The Church had fallen, because the great doctrine of justification by faith in the Saviour had been taken away from her. It was necessary, therefore, before she could rise again, that this doctrine should be restored to her. As soon as this fundamental truth should be re-established in Christendom, all the errors and observances that had taken its place—all that multitude of saints, of works, penances, masses, indulgences, &c., would disappear. As soon as the one only Mediator and his only sacrifice were acknowledged, all other mediators and sacrifices would vanish. "This article of justification," says a man whom we may consider enlightened on the matter,[1] " is what creates the Church, nourishes it, edifies it, preserves and defends it : no one can teach worthily in the Church, or oppose an adversary with success, if he does not adhere to this truth. This," adds the writer whom we quote, in allusion to the earliest prophecy, "is the heel that shall bruise the head of the serpent."

God, who was preparing his work, raised up during the course of ages a long line of witnesses to the truth. But of this truth to which these generous men bore witness, they had not a sufficiently clear knowledge, or at least were not able to set it forth with adequate distinctness. Unable to accomplish this task, they were all that they should have been to prepare the way for it. Let us add, however, that if they were not ready for the work, the work was not ready for them. The measure was not yet full : the ages had not yet accomplished their prescribed course; the need of the true remedy was not as yet generally felt.

Scarcely had Rome usurped her power, before a strong opposition was formed against her, which was continued during the Middle Ages.

Archbishop Claudius of Turin, in the ninth century ; Pierre de Bruys, his disciple Henry, and Arnold of Brescia, in the twelfth century, in France and in Italy, laboured to re-establish the worship of God in spirit and in truth ; but for the most part they looked for this worship too much in the absence of images and of outward observances.

The Mystics, who have existed in almost every age, seeking in silence for holiness of heart, righteousness of life, and tranquil communion with God, beheld with sorrow and affright the abominations of the Church. They carefully abstained from the quarrels of the schools and from the useless discussions under which real piety had been buried. They endeavoured to withdraw men from the vain formality of external worship, from the noise and pomp of ceremonies, to lead them to that inward repose of a soul which looks to God for all its happiness. They could not do this without coming into collision on every side with the received opinions, and without laying bare the wounds of the Church. But at the same time they had not a clear notion of the doctrine of justification by faith.

The Waldenses, far superior to the Mystics

[1] Luther to Brentius.

in purity of doctrine, compose a long line of witnesses to the truth. Men more unfettered than the rest of the Church seem from the most distant times to have inhabited the summits of the Piedmontese Alps; their number was augmented and their doctrine purified by the disciples of Valdo. From their mountain-heights the Waldenses protested during a long series of ages against the superstitions of Rome.[1] "They contend for the lively hope which they have in God through Christ—for the regeneration and interior revival by faith, hope, and charity—for the merits of Jesus Christ, and the all-sufficiency of his grace and righteousness."[2]

Yet this primal truth of the justification of sinners,—this main doctrine, that should have risen from the midst of all the rest like Mont Blanc from the bosom of the Alps, was not sufficiently prominent in their system. Its summit was not yet raised high enough.

Pierre Vaud or Valdo, a rich merchant of Lyons (1170), sold all his goods and gave them to the poor. He and his friends appear to have aimed at re-establishing the perfection of primitive Christianity in the common affairs of life. He therefore began also with the branches and not with the roots. Nevertheless his preaching was powerful because he appealed to Scripture, and it shook the Roman hierarchy to its very foundations.

Wickliffe arose in England in 1360, and appealed from the pope to the word of God: but the real internal wound in the body of the Church was in his eyes only one of the numerous symptoms of the disease.

John Huss preached in Bohemia a century before Luther preached in Saxony. He seems to have penetrated deeper than his predecessors into the essence of christian truth. He prayed to Christ for grace to glory only in his cross and in the inestimable humiliation of his sufferings. But his attacks were directed less against the errors of the Romish church than the scandalous lives of the clergy. Yet he was, if we may be allowed the expression, the John-Baptist of the Reformation. The flames of his pile kindled a fire in the Church that cast a brilliant light into the surrounding darkness, and whose glimmerings were not to be so readily extinguished.

John Huss did more: prophetic words issued from the depths of his dungeon. He foresaw that a real reformation of the Church was at hand. When driven out of Prague and compelled to wander through the fields of Bohemia, where an immense crowd followed his steps and hung upon his words, he had cried out: "The wicked have begun by preparing a treacherous snare for the goose.[3] But if even the goose, which is only a

domestic bird, a peaceful animal, and whose flight is not very high in the air, has nevertheless broken through their toils, other birds, soaring more boldly towards the sky, will break through them with still greater force. Instead of a feeble goose, the truth will send forth eagles and keen-eyed vultures."[1] This prediction was fulfilled by the reformers.

When the venerable priest had been summoned by Sigismund's order before the council of Constance, and had been thrown into prison, the chapel of Bethlehem in which he had proclaimed the Gospel, and the future triumphs of Christ, occupied his mind much more than his own defence. One night, the holy martyr saw in imagination, from the depths of his dungeon, the pictures of Christ that he had had painted on the walls of his oratory, effaced by the pope and his bishops. This vision distressed him: but on the next day he saw many painters occupied in restoring these figures in greater number and in brighter colours. As soon as their task was ended, the painters, who were surrounded by an immense crowd, exclaimed: "Now let the popes and bishops come! they shall never efface them more!" And many people rejoiced in Bethlehem, and I with them, adds John Huss.—"Busy yourself with your defence rather than with your dreams," said his faithful friend, the knight of Chlum, to whom he had communicated this vision. "I am no dreamer," replied Huss, "but I maintain this for certain, that the image of Christ will never be effaced. They have wished to destroy it, but it shall be painted afresh in all hearts by much better preachers than myself. The nation that loves Christ will rejoice at this. And I, awaking from among the dead, and rising, so to speak, from my grave, shall leap with great joy."[2]

A century passed away; and the torch of the Gospel, lighted up anew by the reformers, illuminated indeed many nations, that rejoiced in its brightness.

But it was not only among those whom the church of Rome looks upon as her adversaries that the word of life was heard during these ages. Catholicism itself—let us say it for our consolation—counts numerous witnesses to the truth within its pale. The primitive building had been consumed; but a generous fire smouldered beneath its ashes, and from time to time sent forth many brilliant sparks.

It is an error to believe that Christianity did not exist before the Reformation, save under the Roman-catholic form, and that it was not till then that a section of the Church assumed the form of Protestantism.

Among the doctors who flourished prior to the sixteenth century, a great number no doubt had a leaning towards the system

---

[1] Nobla Leyson.
[2] Treatise on Antichrist, a work contemporary with the Nobla Leyson.
[3] Huss in the Bohemian language signifies *goose*.

[1] Epist. J. Hüss. tempore anathematis scripta.
[2] Hüss, Epp. sub. temp. concilii scriptæ.

which the Council of Trent put forth in 1562; but many also inclined towards the doctrines professed at Augsburg by the Protestants in 1530; and the majority perhaps oscillated between these two poles.

Anselm of Canterbury laid down, as the very essence of Christianity, the doctrines of the incarnation and atonement;[1] and in a work, in which he teaches us how to die, he says to the departing soul: "Look only to the merits of Jesus Christ." St. Bernard proclaimed with a powerful voice the mysteries of Redemption. "If my sin cometh from another," says he, "why should not my righteousness be granted me in the same manner? Assuredly it is better for me that it should be given me, than that it should be innate."[2] Many schoolmen, and in later times the Chancellor Gerson, vigorously attacked the errors and abuses of the Church.

But let us reflect above all on the thousands of souls, obscure and unknown to the world, who have nevertheless been partakers of the real life of Christ.

A monk named Arnoldi every day offered up this fervent prayer in his quiet cell: "O Lord Jesus Christ! I believe that thou alone art my redemption and my righteousness."[3]

Christopher of Utenheim, a pious bishop of Basle, had his name inscribed on a picture painted on glass, which is still in that city, and surrounded it with this motto, which he desired to have continually before his eyes: "My hope is in the cross of Christ; I seek grace and not works."[4]

A poor Carthusian friar, named Martin, wrote a touching confession, in which he says: "O most merciful God! I know that I cannot be saved and satisfy thy righteousness otherwise than by the merits, by the most innocent passion, and by the death of thy dearly beloved Son......Holy Jesus! all my salvation is in thy hands. Thou canst not turn away from me the hands of thy love, for they have created me, formed me, and redeemed me. Thou hast written my name with an iron pen, in great mercy and in an indelible manner, on thy side, on thy hands, and on thy feet," &c. &c. Then the good Carthusian placed his confession in a wooden box, and enclosed it in a hole he made in the wall of his cell.[5]

The piety of brother Martin would never have been known, if the box had not been discovered on the 21st December 1776, as some workmen were pulling down an old building that had formed part of the Carthusian convent at Basle. How many convents may not have concealed such treasures!

But these holy men possessed this touching faith for themselves alone, and knew not how to communicate it to others. Living in retirement, they could say more or less what brother Martin confided to his box: "And if I cannot confess these things with my mouth, I confess them at least with my pen and with my heart."[1] The word of truth was in the sanctuary of a few pious souls; but, to use the language of the Gospel, it had not "free course" in the world.

However, if they did not always confess aloud the doctrine of salvation, they were not afraid at least to protest openly, even in the bosom of the Church of Rome, against the abuses that disgraced it.

Scarcely had the Councils of Constance and Basle, in which Huss and his disciples had been condemned, terminated their sittings, when this noble line of witnesses against Rome, which we have pointed out, recommenced with greater brilliancy. Men of generous dispositions, shocked at the abominations of the papacy, arose like the Old-Testament prophets, whose fate they also shared, and uttered like them their denunciations in a voice of thunder. Their blood stained the scaffolds, and their ashes were scattered to the winds.

Thomas Conecte, a Carmelite friar, appeared in Flanders. He declared that "the grossest abominations were practised at Rome, that the Church required a reform, and that so long as we served God, we should not fear the pope's excommunications."[2] All the country listened with enthusiasm; Rome condemned him to the stake in 1432, and his contemporaries declared that he had been translated to heaven.[3]

Cardinal Andrew, archbishop of Crayn, being sent to Rome as the emperor's ambassador, was struck with dismay at discovering that the papal sanctity, in which he had devoutly believed, was a mere fiction; and in his simplicity he addressed Sixtus IV. in the language of evangelical remonstrance. Mockery and persecution were his only answer. Upon this he endeavoured in 1482 to assemble a new council at Basle. "The whole Church," said he, "is shaken by divisions, heresies, sins, vices, unrighteousness, errors, and countless evils, so as to be nigh swallowed up by the devouring abyss of damnation.[4] For this reason we proclaim a general council for the reformation of the Catholic faith and the purification of morals." The archbishop was thrown into prison at Basle, where he died. The inquisitor, Henry Institoris, who was the first to oppose him, uttered these remarkable words: "All the world cries out and demands a council; but

1 Cur Deus homo?
2 Et sane mihi tutior donata quam innata. De Erroribus Abælardi, cap. 6.
3 Credo quod tu mi Domine Jesu Christe, solus es mea justitia et redemptio. Leibnitz. script. Brunsw. iii. 396.
4 Spes mea crux Christi; gratiam, non opera quæro.
5 Sciens posse me aliter non salvari, et tibi satisfacere nisi per meritum, &c. For these and similar quotations, see Flacius, Catal. Test. Veritatis; Wolfii Lect. Memorabiles; Müller's Reliquien, &c.

1 Et si hæc prædicta confiteri non possum lingua, confiteor tamen corde et scripto.
2 Bertrand d'Argentré, Histoire de Bretaigne, p. 788. Paris, 1618.
3 Ille summo vivit Olympo. Baptista Mantuanus, De Beata vitâ, in fine.
4 A sorbente gurgite damnationis subtrahi. J. H. Hottingeri Hist. Eccl. Sæcul., xv. 347.

there is no human power that can reform the Church by a council. The Most High will find other means, which are at present unknown to us, although they may be at our very doors, to bring back the Church to its pristine condition.[1] This remarkable prophecy, delivered by an inquisitor, at the very period of Luther's birth, is the best apology for the Reformation.

Jerome Savonarola shortly after entering the Dominican order at Bologna in 1475, devoted himself to continual prayers, fasting, and mortification, and cried, " Thou, O God, art good, and in thy goodness teach me thy righteousness."[2] He preached with energy in Florence, to which city he had removed in 1489. His voice carried conviction; his countenance was lit up with enthusiasm; and his action possessed enchanting grace. " We must regenerate the Church," said he; and he professed the great principle that alone could effect this regeneration. " God," he exclaimed, " remits the sins of men, and justifies them by his mercy. There are as many compassions in heaven as there are justified men upon earth; for none are saved by their own works. No man can boast of himself; and if, in the presence of God, we could ask all these justified sinners—Have you been saved by your own strength?—all would reply as with one voice, ' Not unto us, O Lord! not unto us; but to thy name be the glory!'—Therefore, O God, do I seek thy mercy, and I bring not unto thee my own righteousness; but when by thy grace thou justifiest me, then thy righteousness belongs unto me; for grace is the righteousness of God.—So long, O man, so long as thou believest not, thou art, because of thy sin, destitute of grace.—O God, save me by thy righteousness, that is to say, in thy Son, who alone among men was found without sin!"[3] Thus did the grand and holy doctrine of justification by faith gladden Savonarola's heart. In vain did the presidents of the Churches oppose him;[4] he knew that the oracles of God were far above the visible Church, and that he must proclaim these oracles with the aid of the Church, without it, or even in spite of it. " Fly," cried he, " fly far from Babylon!" and it was Rome that he thus designated, and Rome erelong replied in her usual manner. In 1497, the infamous Alexander VI. issued a brief against him; and in 1498, torture and the stake terminated this reformer's life.

John Vitrarius, a Franciscan monk of Tournay, whose monastic spirit does not appear to have been of a very lofty range, vigorously attacked the corruptions of the Church. " It is better to cut a child's throat (he said) than to place him in a religious order that is not reformed.[1]—If thy curate, or any other priest, detains a woman in his house, you should go and drag the woman by force, or otherwise, out of the house.—There are some who repeat certain prayers to the Virgin Mary, that they may see her at the hour of death. But thou shalt see the devil, and not the virgin." A recantation was required, and the monk gave way in 1498.

John Lallier, doctor of the Sorbonne, stood forth in 1484 against the tyrannical dominion of the hierarchy. " All the clergy," said he, " have received equal power from Christ.—The Roman Church is not the head of other Churches.—You should keep the commandments of God and of the apostles: and as for the commandments of bishops and all the other lords of the Church......they are but straw! They have ruined the Church by their crafty devices.[2] The priests of the Eastern Church sin not by marrying, and I believe that in the Western Church we should not sin were we also to marry.—Since the time of Sylvester, the Romish Church is no longer the Church of Christ, but a state-church—a money-getting church.—We are not bound to believe in the legends of the saints, any more than in the Chronicles of France."

John of Wesalia, doctor of divinity at Erfurth, a man distinguished for his energy and talents, attacked the errors on which the hierarchy was founded, and proclaimed the Holy Scriptures as the only source of faith. " It is not religion (by which he meant a monastic life) that saves us," said he to the monks; " it is the grace of God.—God from all eternity has established a book in which he has written the names of all his elect. Whoever is not inscribed therein, will never be so; and whoever is therein inscribed, will never see his name blotted out.—It is by the grace of God alone that the elect are saved. He whom God is willing to save by the gift of his grace, will be saved, though all the priests in the world should wish to condemn and excommunicate him. And he whom God will condemn, though all should wish to save him, will nevertheless be condemned.[3]—By what audacity do the successors of the apostles enjoin, not what Christ has prescribed in his holy books, but what they themselves have devised, carried away, as they are, by thirst for gold and by the desire of ruling?—I despise the Pope, the Church and the Councils, and I give Christ the glory." Wesalia, having arrived gradually at these convictions, pro-

---

[1] Alium modum Altissimus procurabit, nobis quidem pro nunc incognitum, licet heu! præ foribus existat, ut ad pristinum statum ecclesia redeat. T. H. Hotting. Hist. Eccl. Sæc. xv. p. 413.
[2] Bonus es tu, et in bonitate tua, doce me justificationes tuas. Batesius, Vitæ Selectorum Virorum, p. 112, Lond. 1681.
[3] Meditationes in Psalmos; Prediche sopra il Salmo; Quam bonus Israël, &c.; Sermones supra Archam Noe, &c.
[4] Inter omnes vero persecutores, potissimum Ecclesiæ præsides. Batesius, p. 118.

[1] D'Argentré, Collectio Judiciorum de Novis Erroribus, ii. 340.
[2] Ibidem.
[3] Et quem Deus vult damnare, si omnes vellent hunc salvare, adhuc iste damnaretur. Paradoxa Damnata, &c., 1749. Moguntiæ.

fessed them boldly from the pulpit, and entered into communication with the delegates from the Hussites. Feeble, and bending under the weight of years, a prey to sickness, and leaning upon his staff, this courageous old man appeared with tottering steps before the Inquisition, and perished in its dungeons in 1482.

John of Goch, prior of Malines, about the same period, extolled christian liberty as the essence of every virtue. He charged the prevailing doctrines with Pelagianism, and denominated Thomas Aquinas " the prince of error." " The canonical scriptures alone," said he, " are entitled to a sure confidence, and have an undeniable authority. The writings of the ancient Fathers have no authority, but so far as they are conformable with canonical truth.[1] The common proverb says truly : *Satan would be ashamed to think of what a monk dares undertake.*"

But the most remarkable of these forerunners of the Reformation was undoubtedly John Wessel, surnamed " the Light of the World," a man full of courage and of love for the truth, who was doctor in divinity successively at Cologne, Louvain, Paris, Heidelberg, and Groningen, and of whom Luther says : " Had I read his works sooner, my enemies might have thought I had derived every thing from Wessel, so much are we of one mind."[2]—" St. Paul and St. James," says Wessel, " preach different but not contrary doctrines. Both maintain that ' the just shall live by faith ;' but by a faith working by charity. He who, at the sound of the Gospel, believes, desires, hopes, trusts in the glad tidings, and loves Him who justifies and blesses him, forthwith yields himself up entirely to Him whom he loves, and attributes no merit to himself, since he knows that of himself he has nothing.[3]—The sheep must discern the things on which he feeds, and avoid a corrupted nutriment, even when presented by the shepherd himself. The people should follow the shepherd into the pastures; but when he ceases to lead them into the pastures, he is no longer a shepherd, and then, since he does not fulfil his duty, the flock is not bound to follow him. Nothing is more effectual to the destruction of the Church than a corrupted clergy. All Christians, even the humblest and most simple, are bound to resist those who are destroying the Church.[4] We must obey the precepts of doctors and of prelates only according to the measure laid down by St. Paul (1 Thess. v.

21) ; that is to say, so far as, ' sitting in Moses' seat,' they teach according to Moses. We are God's servants, and not the pope's, as it is said : *Thou shalt worship the Lord thy God and him only shalt thou serve.* The Holy Spirit has reserved to himself the duty of renewing, vivifying, preserving, and increasing the unity of the Church, and has not abandoned it to the Roman pontiff, who frequently cares nothing about it.—Even her sex does not prevent a woman if she is faithful and prudent, and if she has charity shed abroad in her heart, from being able to feel, judge, approve, and decide by a judgment that God will ratify."

Thus, in proportion as the Reformation drew nigh, were the voices multiplied that proclaimed the truth. We might be led to say that the Church intended showing by these means that the Reformation existed before Luther. Protestantism arose in the Church on the very day in which the germs of Popery showed themselves ; as in the political world conservative principles have existed from the very moment when the despotism of nobles or the disorders of factions have raised their heads. Protestantism was sometimes even stronger than the Papacy in the centuries immediately preceding the Reformation. What could Rome oppose to all the witnesses we have just heard, at the time when their voices re-echoed through the earth ?—A few monks without either learning or piety.

To this we may add, that the Reformation had taken root, not only among the doctors of the Church, but also among the people. The opinions of Wickliffe, issuing from Oxford, had spread over all Christendom, and had found adherents in Bavaria, Swabia, Franconia, and Prussia. In Bohemia, from the very bosom of discord and of war, had come forth at last a peaceful and christian community, reminding the world of the primitive Church, and giving powerful testimony to the grand principle of Gospel opposition, that " Christ, and not Peter, and his successors, is the rock on which the Church is founded." Belonging equally to the German and Sclavonic races, these simple Christians had sent forth missionaries into the midst of the various nations who spoke their language, noiselessly to gain over followers to their opinions. Nicholas Kuss, who was twice visited by them at Rostock, began in 1511 to preach openly against the pope.[1]

It is important to notice this state of affairs. When the Wisdom from on high shall utter his lessons in a still louder voice, there will be minds and hearts everywhere to listen to them. When the Husbandman, who has been continually traversing his Church, shall go forth to a new and to a greater sowing, the soil will be prepared to receive the grain. When the trumpet of the

---

[1] Antiquorum patrum scripta tantum habent auctoritatis, quantum canonicæ veritati sunt conformia. Epist. Apologet. Antwerp, 1521.
[2] Adeo spiritus utriusque concordat. Farrago Wesseli, in præf.
[3] Extentus totus et propensus in eum quem amat, a quo credit, cupit, sperat, confidit, justificatur, nihil sibi ipsi tribuit, qui scit nihil habere ex se. De Magnit. Passionis, cap. xlvi. Opera, p. 553.
[4] Nemo magis Ecclesiam destruit, quam corruptus clerus. Destruentibus Ecclesiam omnes Christiani tenentur resistere. De Potestate Eccles. Opp., p. 769.

[1] Wolfii Lect. Memorab., ii. p. 17.

Angel of the covenant, that has never ceased to be heard in the world, shall send forth a louder peal, numbers will gird themselves to the battle.

The Church already had a presentiment that the hour of combat was approaching. If more than one philosopher announced in some measure, during the last century, the revolution in which it closed, shall we be astonished that many doctors at the end of the fifteenth century had foreseen the approaching change that would regenerate the Church?

Andrew Proles, provincial of the Augustines, who for nearly half a century presided over that congregation, and who, with unshaken firmness, maintained in his order the doctrines of St. Augustine, being assembled with his brethren in the convent of Himmelspforte, near Wernigerode, used often to stop them while reading the word of God, and say: " My brethren! ye hear the testimony of the Holy Scriptures! They declare that by grace we are what we are, and that by it alone we hold all that we possess. Whence then proceed so much darkness and such horrible superstitions?......Oh, my brethren! Christianity needs a bold and a great reform, and methinks I see it already approaching." Then would the monks cry out, " Why do you not begin this reform yourself, and oppose such a cloud of errors?" —" You see, my brethren," replied the aged provincial, " that I am bent with the weight of years, and weak in body, and that I have not the learning, ability, and eloquence, that so great an undertaking requires. But God will raise up a hero, who by his age, strength, talents, learning, genius, and eloquence, shall hold the foremost place. He will begin the Reformation; he will oppose error, and God will give him boldness to resist the mighty ones of the earth."[1] An old monk of Himmelspforte, who had often heard these words, communicated them to Flacius. It was in the very order of which Proles was provincial that the Christian hero was foretold to appear.

A monk named John Hilten was an inmate of the Franciscan convent at Eisenach in Thuringia. The prophecies of Daniel and the Revelation of St. John were his especial study. He even wrote a commentary on these works, and censured the most flagrant abuses of the monastic life. The exasperated monks threw him into prison. His advanced age and the filthiness of his dungeon brought on a dangerous illness: he asked for the superior, and the latter had scarcely arrived before he burst into a violent passion, and without listening to the prisoner's complaints, bitterly abused his doctrine, that was opposed, adds the chronicle, to the monk's kitchen. The Franciscan, forgetting his malady, and groaning heavily, replied: " I

bear your insults calmly for the love of Christ; for I have said nothing that can endanger the monastic state: I have only censured its most crying abuses. But," continued he (according to what Melancthon records in his Apology for the Augsburg Confession of Faith), " *another man will arise in the year of our Lord* 1516: *he will destroy you, and you shall not be able to resist him.*"[1] John Hilten, who had prophesied that the end of the world would come in 1651, was less mistaken in pointing out the year when the future Reformer would appear. Not long after, he was born in a small village at a little distance from the monk's dungeon: in this very town of Eisenach he commenced his studies, and only one year later than the imprisoned friar had stated, he publicly entered upon the Reformation.

CHAPTER VII.

Third Preparation—Letters—Revival—Recollections of Antiquity in Italy—Influence of the Humanists—Christianity of Dante—Valla—Infidelity in Italy—Platonic Philosophy—Commencement of Learning in Germany—Young Students—Printing—Characteristics of German Literature—The Learned and the Schoolmen—A New World—Reuchlin—Reuchlin in Italy—His Labours—His Influence in Germany—Mysticism—Contest with the Dominicans.

THUS princes and people, living members of the Church and theologians, were labouring each in their sphere to prepare the work which the sixteenth century was to accomplish. But the Reformation was destined to find another auxiliary in learning. The human mind was gaining strength. This circumstance alone would have wrought its emancipation. Let but a small seed fall near a time-eaten wall, and as the tree grows up, the wall will be overthrown.

The Roman pontiff had constituted himself the guardian of the people, and his superior intelligence rendered this an easy task. For a long time he had kept them in a state of pupilage, but now they were breaking bounds on every side. This venerable guardianship, which derived its origin from the principles of eternal life and civilisation that Rome had communicated to the barbarous nations, could no longer be exercised without opposition. A formidable antagonist had taken up his position against it, in order to control it. The natural tendency of the human mind to expand, to examine, to learn, had given birth to this new power. Men's eyes were opened: they demanded a reason for each step taken by this long-venerated guide, under whose direction they had walked in silence, so long as their eyes were closed. The nations of modern Europe had passed the age of infancy;

---

[1] Excitabit Dominus heroem, ætate, viribus. Flacii Catal. Testium Veritatis, p. 843.

[1] Alius quidem veniet... Apologia Conf. Aug. xiii. De Votis Monasticis.

their manhood was beginning. Their artless and credulous simplicity had given way to an inquiring spirit,—to a reason impatient to fathom things to the very bottom. They asked what had been God's object in making a revelation to the world, and whether men had a right to set themselves up as mediators between God and their brethren.

One thing only could have saved the Church: this was to elevate itself still higher than the people. To be on a level with them was not sufficient. But men soon found, on the contrary, that she was much below them. She began to take a downward course, at the very time that they were ascending. When men began to soar towards the regions of intelligence, the priesthood was found engrossed in earthly pursuits and human interests. It is a phenomenon that has often been renewed in history. The eaglet's wings had grown; and there was no man whose hand could reach it and stay its flight.

It was in Italy that the human mind first began to soar above the earth.

The doctrines of the schoolmen and romantic poetry had never reigned undisturbed in that peninsula. Some faint recollections of antiquity had always remained in Italy, —recollections that were revived in great strength towards the end of the Middle Ages, and which ere long communicated a fresh impulse to the human mind.

Already in the fourteenth century had Dante and Petrarch revived the credit of the ancient Roman poets; at the same time the former placed the mightiest popes in his "Inferno," and the second called with boldness for the primitive constitution of the Church. At the beginning of the fifteenth century John of Ravenna taught the Latin literature with great renown at Padua and Florence; and Chrysoloras interpreted the masterpieces of Greece at Florence and at Pavia.

While learning was thus issuing from the prisons in which it had been held captive in Europe, the East imparted fresh light to the West. The standard of Mahomet, planted on the walls of Constantinople in 1453, had driven its learned men into exile. They had carried the learning of Greece with them into Italy. The torch of the ancients rekindled the minds that had been for ages quenched in darkness. George of Trebizond, Argyropolos, Bessarion, Lascaris, Chalcondylas, and many others, inspired the West with their own love for Greece and its noble works of genius. The patriotism of the Italians was awakened; and there arose in Italy a great number of learned men, among whom shone Gasparino, Aurispa, Aretino, Poggio, and Valla, who endeavoured in like manner to restore the writers of ancient Rome to the honour they merited. There was at that period a great burst of light, and Rome was doomed to suffer by it.

This passion for antiquity which took possession of the *humanists*, shook in the most elevated minds their attachment to the Church, for "no man can serve two masters." At the same time the studies to which they devoted themselves, placed at the disposition of these learned men a method entirely new and unknown to the schoolmen, of examining and judging the teaching of the Church. Finding in the Bible, much more than in the works of theologians, the beauties that charmed them in the classic authors, the *humanists* were fully inclined to place the Bible above the doctors. They reformed the taste, and thus prepared the way for the Reformation of the faith.

These scholars, it is true, loudly protested that their studies did not strike at the faith of the Church; yet they attacked the schoolmen long before the Reformers did, and turned into ridicule those barbarians, those "Teutons," who had existed but not lived.[1] Some even proclaimed the doctrines of the Gospel, and laid hands on what Rome held most dear. Dante, although adhering to many Romish doctrines, had already proclaimed the power of faith, as did the reformers. "It is true faith that renders us citizens of heaven," said he.[2] "Faith according to the Gospel is the principle of life; it is the spark that, spreading daily more and more, becomes a living flame, and shines on us, like a star in heaven. Without faith there is no good work, nor upright life, that can avail us. However great be the sin, the arms of Divine grace are wider still, and embrace all who turn to God.[3] The soul is not lost through the anathemas of the pontiff; and eternal love can still reach it, so long as hope retains her verdant blossom.[4] From God, from God alone, cometh our righteousness by faith." And speaking of the Church, Dante exclaims: "O my bark, how deeply art thou laden! O Constantine, what mischief has been engendered, I will not say by thy conversion, but by that offering which the wealthy father then received from thee!"

Somewhat later, Laurentius Valla applied the study of antiquity to the opinions of the Church: he denied the authenticity of the correspondence between Christ and King Abgar; he rejected the tradition of the drawing up of the Apostles' Creed; and sapped the foundation on which reposed the pretended donation of Constantine.[5]

Still this great light which the study of antiquity threw out in the fifteenth century was calculated only to destroy: it could not build up. Neither Homer nor Virgil could

---

[1] Qui ne viventes quidem vivebant. Politiani Epp. ix. 3.
[2] Parad. xxiv. 44.
[3] Orribil furon li peccati miei :
Ma la bontà infinita ha sì gran braccia,
Che prende ciò che si rivolve a lei. Purgator. iii. 121-124.
[4] Per lor maladizion sì non si perde,
Che non possa tornar l'eterno amore,
Mentre che la speranza ha fior del verde. Ibid. 134-136.
[5] De ementita Constantini donatione declamatio ad Papam. Opp. Basil. 1543.

build up. Neither Homer nor Virgil could save the Church. The revival of learning, sciences, and arts, was not the principle of the Reformation. The paganism of the poets, as it reappeared in Italy, rather confirmed the paganism of the heart. The scepticism of the followers of Aristotle, and the contempt for every thing that did not appertain to philology, took possession of many literary men, and engendered an incredulity which, even while affecting submission to the Church, attacked the most important truths of religion. Peter Pompomatius, the most distinguished representative of this impious tendency, publicly taught at Bologna and Padua that the immortality of the soul and the doctrine of providence were mere philosophical problems.[1] John Francis Pico, nephew of Pico of Mirandola, speaks of one pope who did not believe in God;[2] and of another who, having acknowledged to a friend his disbelief in the immortality of the soul, appeared to him one night after death, and said: " Alas! the eternal fire that is now consuming me makes me feel but too sensibly the immortality of that soul which I had thought would die with the body!" This may remind us of those remarkable words spoken, it is asserted, by Leo. X. to his secretary Bembo : " Every age knows how useful this fable of Christ has been to us and ours"[3]......Contemptible superstitions were attacked, but incredulity with its disdainful and mocking sneer was set up in their place. To laugh at every thing, even at what was most holy, was the fashion and the badge of a freethinker. Religion was considered only as a means of governing the world. " I fear," said Erasmus in 1516, " that with the study of ancient literature, the olden paganism will reappear."

It is true that then, as after the ridicule of the Augustan age, and as even in our days after the sneers of the last century, a new Platonism arose and attacked this rash scepticism, and sought, like the philosophy of the present times, to inspire a certain degree of respect for Christianity, and to rekindle a religious feeling in the heart. The Medici at Florence encouraged these efforts of the Platonists. But no merely philosophical religion can ever regenerate the Church or the world. It may lose its strength in a kind of mystical enthusiasm ; but as it is supercilious, and despises the preaching of the cross of Christ, pretending to see in the Gospel doctrines little else but figures and symbols, incomprehensible to the majority of mankind, it will ever be powerless to reform and save.

What then would have been the result, had real Christianity not reappeared in the world, and if faith had not once more filled all hearts with its own strength and holiness ? The Reformation preserved both religion and society. If the Church of Rome had had God's glory and the welfare of the people at heart, she would have welcomed the Reformation with joy. But what was this to a Leo the Tenth ?

And yet a torch could not be lighted in Italy without its rays shining beyond the Alps. The affairs of the church kept up a continual intercourse between this peninsula and the other parts of Christendom. The *barbarians* felt erelong the superiority and superciliousness of the Italians, and began to be ashamed of their defects of language and of style. A few young noblemen, such as Dalberg, Langen, and Spiegelberg, burning with the desire of knowledge, visited Italy, and brought back to Germany and imparted to their friends the learning, the grammar, and the classic authors they so much desired.[1] Soon there appeared a man of distinguished talents, Rodolph Agricola, whose learning and genius won for him as great veneration as if he had lived in the age of Augustus or of Pericles. The ardour of his mind and the fatigues of the school wore him out in a few years ; but in the intercourse of private life he had trained up noble disciples, who carried their master's zeal over all Germany. Often when assembled around him had they deplored the darkness of the Church, and asked why St. Paul so frequently repeats that men are justified by faith and not by works.[2]......At the feet of these new teachers was soon gathered a youthful but rude band of scholars, living upon alms, studying without books ; and who, divided into societies of priests of Bacchus, arquebusiers, and others, passed in disorderly troops from town to town, and from school to school. No matter ; these strange companies were the beginning of a literary public. Gradually the masterpieces of antiquity issued from the German presses and supplanted the schoolmen ; and the art of printing, discovered at Mentz in 1440, multiplied the voices that boldly remonstrated against the corruptions of the Church, and those not less powerful, which invited the human mind into new paths of inquiry.

The study of ancient literature produced very different effects in Germany from those which followed it in Italy and in France: it was there combined with faith. The Germans immediately looked for the advantage that might accrue to religion from these new literary pursuits. What had produced in Italian minds little more than a minute and barren refinement of the understanding, pervaded the whole being of the Germans, warmed their hearts, and prepared them for

---

[1] De Immortalitate Animæ, De Prædestinatione et Providentia, &c.

[2] Qui nullum Deum credens. J. F. Pici de Fide, Opp. ii. 820.

[3] Ra de Christo fabula. Mornæi Hist. Papatus, p. 820.

[1] Hamelmann, Relatio Hist. This first impulse has been erroneously ascribed to Thomas à Kempis. Delprat over G. Groote, p. 280.

[2] Fide justos esse. Melancth. Decl. i. 602.

a brighter light. The first restorers of learning in Italy and in France were remarkable for their levity, and frequently also for their immorality. Their successors in Germany, animated by a serious feeling, zealously went in search of truth. Italy, offering up her incense to literature and profane learning, beheld the rise of a sceptical opposition. Germany, occupied with deep theological questions, and thrown back upon herself, saw the rise of an opposition based on faith. In the one country the foundations of the Church were undermined; in the other they were re-established on their true basis. A remarkable society was formed in the empire, composed of liberal, generous-minded, and learned men, who counted princes among their number, and who endeavoured to make learning profitable to religion. Some brought to their studies the humble faith of children; others, an enlightened and penetrating intellect, inclined perhaps to overstep the bounds of legitimate freedom and criticism: yet both contributed to clear the entrance of the temple from the superstitions that had encumbered it.

The monkish theologians perceived their danger, and began to clamour against these very studies which they had tolerated in Italy and France, because they had there gone hand in hand with frivolity and profligacy. A conspiracy was formed amongst them against literature and science, for behind them faith was seen advancing. A monk, cautioning a person against the heresies of Erasmus, was asked in what they consisted. He acknowledged that he had not read the work of which he was speaking, and could only say that "it was written in too pure Latinity."

The disciples of learning and the scholastic divines soon came to open war. The latter beheld with alarm the movement that was taking place in the realms of intellect, and thought that immobility and darkness would be the surest guardians of the Church. It was to save Rome that they opposed the revival of letters; but in this they contributed to its fall. Rome herself had a great share in producing this result. Momentarily led astray under the pontificate of Leo X., she deserted her old friends, and clasped her young adversaries in her arms. Popery and learning formed an alliance that seemed likely to dissolve the union between the monastic orders and the hierarchy. The popes did not at the first glance perceive that what they had taken for a plaything was in reality a sword that might cause their death. In like manner, during the last century, princes were seen welcoming to their courts political and philosophical principles which, had they yielded to all their influences, would have overturned their thrones. Such an alliance was not of long duration. Learning went forward, without a care as to what might endanger the power of its patron. The monks

and schoolmen were well aware that to desert the pope would be to abandon themselves: and the pope, notwithstanding the brief patronage he accorded to the fine arts, was not less active, when he saw the danger, in taking measures the most contrary to the spirit of the times.

The universities defended themselves, as best they could, against the intrusion of this new light. Rhagius was expelled from Cologne, Celtes from Leipsic, and Hermann von dem Busch from Rostock. Still the new doctors, and the ancient classics with them, gradually established themselves, and frequently with the aid of the ruling princes, in these superior academies. In despite of the schoolmen, societies of grammarians and of poets were soon formed in them. Every thing was to be converted into Greek and Latin, even to their very names. How could the admirers of Sophocles and of Virgil be known by such barbarous appellations as Krachenberger or Schwarzerd? At the same time a spirit of independence spread through the universities. The students were no longer seen in seminarist fashion, with their books under their arms, walking demurely, respectfully, and with downcast eyes, behind their masters. The petulance of Martial and of Ovid had passed into these new disciples of the Muses. They hailed with transport the ridicule heaped on the dialectic theologians; and the heads of the literary movement were sometimes accused of favouring, and even of exciting the disorderly proceedings of the scholars.

Thus a new world, sprung out of antiquity, had arisen in the midst of the world of the Middle Ages. The two parties could not avoid coming to blows: a struggle was at hand. It was the mildest champion of literature, an old man drawing near the close of his peaceful career, who was to begin the conflict.

In order that the truth might prove triumphant, it was necessary first that the weapons by which she was to conquer should be brought forth from the arsenals where they had lain buried for ages. These weapons were the Holy Scriptures of the Old and New Testament. It was necessary to revive in Christendom the love and the study of sacred Greek and Hebrew learning. The man whom the providence of God selected for this task was named John Reuchlin.

The sweet voice of a child had been remarked in the choir of the church at Pforzheim, and had attracted the notice of the Margrave of Baden. It was that of John Reuchlin, a boy of agreeable manners and lively disposition, the son of a worthy burgess of that town. The margrave soon showed him especial favour, and made choice of him in 1473 to accompany his son Frederick to the university of Paris.

The son of the usher of Pforzheim, in transports of joy, arrived with the prince at this school, then the most celebrated of the West. Here he found the Spartan Hermonymos and John Wessel, *the light of the world;* and had now an opportunity of studying Greek and Hebrew under able masters, of which languages there was at that time no professor in Germany, and of which he was one day to be the restorer in the home of the Reformation. The young and indigent German transcribed for richer students the rhapsodies of Homer and the orations of Isocrates, gaining thus the means of prosecuting his own studies and of purchasing books.

But he heard other things from the mouth of Wessel, that made a deep impression on his mind. "The popes may err. All human satisfactions are blasphemy against Christ, who has reconciled and completely justified the human race. To God alone belongs the power of giving plenary absolution. It is not necessary to confess our sins to the priest. There is no purgatory unless it be God himself, who is a devouring fire, and who cleanseth from all impurity."

Reuchlin had barely attained the age of twenty years, when he taught philosophy and Greek and Latin at Basle; and—what then passed for a miracle—a German was heard speaking Greek.

The partisans of Rome began to feel uneasy, when they saw these generous spirits searching into the ancient treasures. "The Romans make wry faces," said Reuchlin, "and cry out, pretending that all these literary pursuits are contrary to the Romish piety, because the Greeks are schismatics. Oh! what toil and suffering must be undergone to restore wisdom and learning to Germany!"

Not long after, Eberhard of Wurtemberg invited Reuchlin to Tubingen to adorn that rising university. In 1483, he took him with him into Italy. Chalcondylas, Aurispa, and John Pico of Mirandola, were his friends and companions at Florence. At Rome, when Eberhard had a solemn audience of the pope, surrounded by his cardinals, Reuchlin delivered an address in such pure and elegant Latinity, that the assembly, who expected nothing of the kind from a barbarous German, was filled with astonishment, and the pontiff exclaimed: "This man certainly deserves to rank with the best orators of France and Italy."

Ten years later Reuchlin was compelled to take refuge at Heidelberg, at the court of the Elector Philip, to escape the vengeance of Eberhard's successor. Philip, in conjunction with John of Dalberg, bishop of Worms, his friend and chancellor, endeavoured to diffuse the light that was beginning to dawn in every part of Germany. Dalberg had founded a library, which was open to all the learned. On this new stage Reuchlin made great efforts to destroy the barbarism of his countrymen.

Having been sent by the elector in 1498 on an important mission to Rome, he employed all the time and money he could spare, either in improving himself in the Hebrew language under the learned Israelite, Abdias Sphorna, or in purchasing all the Greek and Hebrew manuscripts he could find, with a view of employing them as so many torches to increase in his own country the light which was already beginning to appear.

Argyropolos, an illustrious Greek, was then at Rome explaining to a numerous auditory the ancient marvels of his national literature. The learned ambassador proceeded with his attendants to the hall where this doctor was lecturing, and on his entrance saluted the master, and deplored the misfortunes of Greece, then expiring under the blows of the Ottomans. The astonished scholar asked his visiter, "Where do you come from, and do you understand Greek?" Reuchlin answered, "I am a German, and I am not entirely ignorant of your language." At the request of Argyropolos, he read and explained a passage from Thucydides, which the professor happened to have before him. Upon this Argyropolos, struck with astonishment and grief, exclaimed, "Alas! alas! the fugitive and exiled Greece has gone to hide herself beyond the Alps!"

It was thus that the sons of barbarous Germany and of ancient and learned Greece met in the palaces of Rome; thus the East and the West embraced in this resort of the world, and the one poured into the lap of the other those intellectual treasures which it had snatched from the barbarism of the Ottomans. God, whenever his plans require it, brings together in an instant, by some great catastrophe, the things which seemed destined to remain for ever separated.

Reuchlin, on his return to Germany, was able to take up his residence again at Wurtemberg. It was at this time he accomplished those labours that were so useful to Luther and to the Reformation. This man, who, as Count Palatine, occupied a distinguished place in the empire, and who, as philosopher, contributed to lower Aristotle and exalt Plato, drew up a Latin dictionary which superseded those of the schoolmen; wrote a Greek grammar which greatly facilitated the study of that language; translated and explained the Penitential Psalms; corrected the Vulgate; and—which is his chief merit and glory—was the first to publish in Germany a Hebrew grammar and dictionary. Reuchlin by this labour reopened the long-sealed books of the old covenant, and thus raised, as he says himself, "a monument more durable than brass."

But Reuchlin endeavoured to promote the cause of truth as much by his life as by his writings. By his lofty stature, his commanding person, and his engaging address, he immediately gained the confidence of all with whom he had to deal. His thirst for knowledge was only equalled by his zeal in communicating what he had learnt. He spared neither money nor labour to introduce into Germany the editions of the classic writers as they issued from the Italian presses ; and thus the usher's son did more to enlighten his fellow-countrymen than rich corporations or mighty princes. His influence over youth was very extensive ; and who can estimate all that the Reformation owes to him in that respect ? We will mention only one instance. His cousin, a young man, the son of a skilful and celebrated armourer named *Schwarzerd*, came to reside with his sister Elisabeth, in order to study under his direction. Reuchlin, delighted at beholding the genius and industry of his youthful scholar, adopted him as his son. Good advice, presents of books, example,—nothing was spared to make his relative useful to the Church and to his country. He was charmed at seeing the work prosper under his eyes ; and finding the German name of *Schwarzerd* too harsh, he translated it into Greek, according to the fashion of the times, and named the young student *Melancthon*. This was the illustrious friend of Luther.

But grammatical studies could not satisfy Reuchlin. Imitating his Jewish teachers, he began to study the mystic meaning of the Word. "God is a spirit," said he, "the Word is a breath, man breathes, God is the Word. The names which He has given to himself are an echo of eternity."[1] He thought with the Cabalists that man can ascend from symbol to symbol, and from form to form to the last and purest of all forms,— to that which regulates the kingdom of the spirit.[2]

While Reuchlin was bewildering himself in these peaceful and abstract researches, the hostility of the schoolmen, suddenly and very much against his will, forced him into a violent contest that was one of the preludes to the Reformation.

There dwelt at Cologne one Pfefferkorn, a baptized rabbi, and intimately connected with the inquisitor Hochstraten. This man and the Dominicans solicited and obtained from the Emperor Maximilian—perhaps with very good intentions—an order by virtue of which the Jews were to bring all their Hebrew books (the Bible only excepted) to the town-hall of the place in which they resided. Here these writings were to be burnt. The motive put forward was, that they were full of blasphemies against Jesus Christ. It must be acknowledged they were at least full of absurdities, and that the Jews themselves would have been no great losers by the proposed measure.

The emperor invited Reuchlin to give his opinion upon these works. The learned doctor particularly singled out the books written against Christianity, leaving them

to their destined fate ; but he endeavoured to save the rest. "The best way to convert the Israelites," added he, "would be to establish two professors of the Hebrew language in each university, who should teach the theologians to read the Bible in Hebrew, and thus to refute the Jewish doctors." In consequence of this advice the Jews had their books restored to them.

The proselyte and the inquisitor, like hungry ravens who see their prey escaping them, raised a furious clamour. They picked out different passages from Reuchlin's work, perverted their meaning, declared the author a heretic, accused him of a secret inclination to Judaism, and threatened him with the dungeons of the Inquisition. Reuchlin at first gave way to alarm ; but as these men became daily more insolent, and prescribed disgraceful conditions, he published in 1513 a "Defence against his Cologne Slanderers," in which he described the whole party in the liveliest colours.

The Dominicans swore to be avenged, and hoped, by a stroke of authority, to uphold their tottering power. Hochstraten had a tribunal formed at Mentz against Reuchlin, and the writings of this learned man were committed to the flames. Then the innovators, the masters and disciples of the new school, feeling themselves all attacked in the person of Reuchlin, rose up like one man. The times were changed : Germany and literature were not Spain and the Inquisition. This great literary movement had called a public opinion into existence. Even the superior clergy were almost entirely gained over to it. Reuchlin appealed to Leo X. This pope, who was no friend to the ignorant and fanatical monks, referred the whole matter to the Bishop of Spires, who declared Reuchlin innocent, and condemned the monks to pay the expenses of the investigation. The Dominicans, those stanch supporters of the Papacy, had recourse in their exasperation to the infallible decrees of Rome ; and Leo X., not knowing how to act between these two hostile powers, issued a mandate *de supersedendo*.

This union of learning with faith is one of the features of the Reformation, and distinguishes it both from the establishment of Christianity and from the religious revivals of the present day. The Christians contemporary with the Apostles had against them all the refinement of their age ; and, with very few exceptions, it is the same with those of our times. The majority of learned men were with the reformers. Even public opinion was favourable to them. The work thus gained in extent ; but perhaps it lost in depth.

Luther, acknowledging all that Reuchlin had done, wrote to him shortly after his victory over the Dominicans : "The Lord has been at work in you, that the light of Holy Scripture might begin to shine in that

---

[1] De Verbo Mirifico. [2] De Arte Cabalistica.

Germany where for so many ages, alas ! it was not only stifled but entirely extinct."[1]

CHAPTER VIII.

Erasmus—Erasmus a Canon—At Paris—His Genius—His Reputation—His Influence—Popular Attack—Praise of Folly—Gibes—Churchmen—Saints—Folly and the Popes—Attack on Science—Principles—Greek New Testament—His Profession of Faith—His Labours and Influence—His Failings—Two Parties—Reform without Violence—Was such possible ?—Unreformed Church—His Timidity—His Indecision—Erasmus loses his Influence with all Parties.

ONE man—the great writer of the opposition at the beginning of the sixteenth century—had already appeared, who considered it as the grand affair of his life to attack the doctrines of the schools and of the convents.

Reuchlin, was not twelve years old when this great genius of the age was born. A man of no small vivacity and wit, named Gerard, a native of Gouda in the Low Countries, loved a physician's daughter. The principles of Christianity did not govern his life, or at least his passions silenced them. His parents and his nine brothers urged him to embrace a monastic life. He fled from his home, leaving the object of his affections on the point of becoming a mother, and repaired to Rome. The frail Margaret gave birth to a son. Gerard was not informed of it ; and some time after he received from his parents the intelligence that she whom he had loved was no more. Overwhelmed with grief, he entered the priesthood, and devoted himself entirely to the service of God. He returned to Holland : Margaret was still living ! She would not marry another, and Gerard remained faithful to his sacerdotal vows. Their affection was concentrated on their son. His mother had taken the tenderest care of him : the father, after his return, sent him to school, although he was only four years old. He was not yet thirteen, when his teacher, Sinthemius of Deventer, one day embraced him with rapture, exclaiming, " This child will attain the highest pinnacle of learning ! " It was Erasmus of Rotterdam.

About this time his mother died, and not long after his broken-hearted father followed her to the grave.

The youthful Erasmus[2] was now alone. He entertained the greatest dislike for a monastic life, which his guardians urged him to embrace, but to which, from his very birth, we might say, he had been opposed. At last, he was persuaded to enter a convent of canons regular, and scarcely had he done so when he felt himself oppressed by the weight of his vows. He recovered a little liberty, and we soon find him at the court of the Archbishop of Cambray, and somewhat later at the university of Paris. He there pursued his studies in extreme poverty, but with the most indefatigable industry. As soon as he could procure any money, he employed it in purchasing—first, Greek works, and then clothes. Frequently did the indigent Hollander solicit in vain the generosity of his protectors ; and hence, in after-life, it was his greatest delight to furnish the means of support to youthful but poor students. Engaged without intermission in the pursuit of truth and of knowledge, he reluctantly assisted in the scholastic disputes, and shrank from the study of theology, lest he should discover any errors in it, and be in consequence denounced as a heretic.

It was at this period that Erasmus became conscious of his powers. In the study of the ancients he acquired a correctness and elegance of style, that placed him far above the most eminent scholars of Paris. He began to teach ; and thus gained powerful friends. He published some writings, and was rewarded by admiration and applause. He knew the public taste, and shaking off the last ties of the schools and of the cloister, he devoted himself entirely to literature, displaying in all his writings those shrewd observations, that clear, lively, and enlightened wit which at once amuse and instruct.

The habit of application, which he contracted at this period, clung to him all his life : even in his journeys, which were usually on horseback, he was not idle. He used to compose on the road, while riding across the country, and as soon as he reached the inn, committed his thoughts to writing. It was thus he composed his celebrated Praise of Folly, in a journey from Italy to England.[1]

Erasmus early acquired a great reputation among the learned : but the exasperated monks vowed deadly vengeance against him. Courted by princes, he was inexhaustible in finding excuses to escape from their invitations. He preferred gaining his living with the printer Frobenius by correcting books, to living surrounded with luxury and favour in the splendid courts of Charles V., Henry VIII., or Francis I., or to encircling his head with the cardinal's hat that was offered him.[2]

Henry the Eighth having ascended the throne in 1509, Lord Mountjoy invited Erasmus, who had already been in England, to come and cultivate literature under the sceptre of their Octavius. In 1510 he lectured at Cambridge, maintaining with Archbishop Warham, John Colet, and Sir Thomas More, those friendly relations which continued until their death. In 1516 he visited Basle, where he took up his abode in 1521.

---

[1] Mal Vita J. Reuchlin. Francf. 1687.—Mayerhoff, J. Reuchlin und seine Zeit. Berlin, 1830.
[2] His name was properly *Gerard*, like his father's. This Dutch name he translated into Latin (*Desiderius*, Well-beloved), and into Greek (*Erasmus*).

[1] 'Εγκώμιον μωρίας. Seven editions of this work were sold in a few months.
[2] A principibus facile mihi contingeret fortuna, nisi mihi nimium dulcis esset libertas. Epist. ad Pirck.

What was his influence on the Reformation?

It has been overrated by one party, and depreciated by another. Erasmus never was, and never could have been, a reformer; but he prepared the way for others. Not only did he diffuse over his age a love of learning, and a spirit of inquiry and examination that led others much farther than he went himself;—but still more, under the protection of great prelates and powerful princes, he was able to unveil and combat the vices of the Church by the most cutting satires.

Erasmus, in fact, attacked the monks and the prevailing abuses in two ways. He first adopted a popular method. This fair little man, whose half-closed blue eyes keenly observed all that was passing,—on whose lips was ever a slight sarcastic smile,—whose manner was timid and embarrassed,—and whom, it seemed, that a puff of wind would blow down,—scattered in every direction his elegant and biting sarcasms against the theology and devotion of his age. His natural character and the events of his life had rendered this disposition habitual. Even in those writings where we should have least expected it, his sarcastic humour suddenly breaks out, and he immolated, as with needle-points, those schoolmen and those ignorant monks against whom he had declared war. There are many points of resemblance between Voltaire and Erasmus. Preceding authors had already popularized the idea of that element of folly which has crept into all the opinions and actions of human life. Erasmus seized upon it, and introduced Folly in her own person, *Moria*, daughter of Plutus, born in the Fortunate Isles, fed on drunkenness and impertinence, and queen of a powerful empire. She gives a description of it. She depicts successively all the states in the world that belong to her, but she dwells particularly on the churchmen, who will not acknowledge her benefits, though she loads them with her favours. She overwhelms with her gibes and sarcasms that labyrinth of dialectics in which the theologians had bewildered themselves, and those extravagant syllogisms, by which they pretended to support the Church. She unveils the disorders, ignorance, filthy habits, and absurdities of the monks.

"They all belong to me," says she, "those folks whose greatest pleasure is in relating miracles, or listening to marvellous lies, and who make use of them in an especial manner to beguile the dulness of others, and to fill their own purses (I speak particularly of priests and preachers)! In the same category are those who enjoy the foolish but sweet persuasion that if they chance to see a piece of wood or a picture representing Polyphemus or Christopher, they will not die that day......"

"Alas! what follies," continues Moria;

"I am almost ashamed of them myself! Do we not see every country claiming its peculiar *saint*? Each trouble has its saint, and every saint his candle. This cures the toothach; that assists women in childbed; a third restores what a thief has stolen; a fourth preserves you in shipwreck; and a fifth protects your flocks. There are some who have many virtues at once, and especially the Virgin-mother of God, in whom the people place more confidence than in her Son.[1]......If in the midst of all these mummeries some wise man should rise and give utterance to these harsh truths: 'You shall not perish miserably if you live like Christians;[2]—you shall redeem your sins, if to your alms you add repentance, tears, watchings, prayer, fasting, and a complete change in your way of life;—this saint will protect you, if you imitate his conduct;'—If, I say, some wise man should charitably utter these things in their ears, oh! of what happiness would he not rob their souls, and into what trouble, what distress would he not plunge them!......The mind of man is so constituted that imposture has more hold upon it than truth.[3] If there is one saint more apocryphal than another—a St. George, St. Christopher, or St. Barbara—you will see him worshipped with greater fervency than St. Peter, St. Paul, or even than Christ himself."[4]

But Moria does not stop here: she attacks the bishops "who run more after gold than after souls, and who think they have done enough for Jesus Christ, when they take their seats complacently and with theatrical pomp, like Holy Fathers to whom adoration belongs, and utter blessings or anathemas." The daughter of the Fortunate Isles even ventures to attack the Court of Rome and the pope himself, who, passing his time in amusements, leaves the duties of his ministry to St. Peter and St. Paul. "Can there be any greater enemies to the Church than these unholy pontiffs, who by their silence allow Jesus Christ to be forgotten; who bind him by their mercenary regulations; who falsify his doctrine by forced interpretations; and crucify him a second time by their scandalous lives?"[5]

Holbein added the most grotesque illustrations to the Praise of Folly, in which the pope figured with his triple crown. Perhaps no work has ever been so thoroughly adapted to the wants of the age. It is impossible to describe the impression this little book produced throughout Christendom. Twenty-seven editions appeared in the life-time of

1 Præcipue Deipara Virgo, cui vulgus hominum plus prope tribuit quam Filio. Encomium Moriæ, Opp. iv. 444.
2 Non male peribis, si bene vixeris. Ibid.
3 Sic sculptus est hominis animus, ut longe magis fucis quam veris capiatur. Ibid. 450.
4 Aut ipsum Christum. Ibid.
5 Quasi sint illi hostes ecclesiæ perniciores quam impii pontifices, qui et silentio Christum sinunt abolescere, et quæstuariis legibus alligant, et coactis interpretationibus adulterant, et pestilente vita jugulant. Enc. Moriæ, Ibid.

Erasmus: it was translated into every European language, and contributed more than any other to confirm the anti-sacerdotal tendency of the age.

But to the popular attack of sarcasm Erasmus united science and learning. The study of Greek and Latin literature had opened a new prospect to the modern genius that was beginning to awaken from its slumber in Europe. Erasmus eagerly embraced the idea of the Italians that the sciences ought to be studied in the schools of the ancients, and that, laying aside the inadequate and absurd works that had hitherto been in use, men should study geography in Strabo, medicine in Hippocrates, philosophy in Plato, mythology in Ovid, and natural history in Pliny. But he went a step further, and it was the step of a giant, and must necessarily have led to the discovery of a new world of greater importance to the interests of humanity than that which Columbus had recently added to the old. Erasmus, following out his principle, required that men should no longer study theology in Scotus and Aquinas, but go and learn it in the writings of the Fathers of the Church, and above all in the New Testament. He showed that they must not even rest contented with the Vulgate, which swarmed with errors.; and he rendered an incalculable service to truth by publishing his critical edition of the Greek text of the New Testament—a text as little known in the West as if it had never existed. This work appeared at Basle in 1516, one year before the Reformation. Erasmus thus did for the New Testament what Reuchlin had done for the Old. Henceforward divines were able to read the Word of God in the original languages, and at a later period to recognise the purity of the Reformed doctrines.

"It is my desire," said Erasmus, on publishing his New Testament, "to lead back that cold disputer of words, styled theology, to its real fountain. Would to God that this work may bear as much fruit to Christianity as it has cost me toil and application!" This wish was realized. In vain did the monks cry out, "He presumes to correct the Holy Ghost!" The New Testament of Erasmus gave out a bright flash of light. His paraphrases on the Epistles, and on the Gospels of St. Matthew and St. John; his editions of Cyprian and Jerome; his translations of Origen, Athanasius, and Chrysostom; his *Principles of True Theology*,[1] his *Preacher*,[2] and his Commentaries on various Psalms, contributed powerfully to diffuse a taste for the Word of God and for pure theology. The result of his labours even went beyond his intentions. Reuchlin and Erasmus gave the Bible to the learned; Luther, to the people.

Erasmus did still more: by his restoration of the New Testament, he restored what that revelation taught. "The most exalted aim in the revival of philosophical studies," said he, "will be to obtain a knowledge of the pure and simple Christianity of the Bible." A noble sentiment! and would to God that the organs of our modern philosophy under stood their mission as well as he did! "'I am firmly resolved," said he again, "to die in the study of the Scriptures; in them are all my joy and all my peace."[1] "The sum of all christian philosophy," said he on another occasion, "amounts to this:—to place all our hopes in God alone, who by his free grace, without any merit of our own, gives us every thing through Christ Jesus; to know that we are redeemed by the death of his Son; to be dead to worldly lusts; and to walk in conformity with his doctrine and example, not only injuring no man, but doing good to all; to support our trials patiently in the hope of a future reward; and finally, to claim no merit to ourselves on account of our virtues, but to give thanks to God for all our strength and for all our works. This is what should be instilled into man, until it becomes a second nature."[2]

Then raising his voice against that mass of church-regulations about dress, fasting, feast-days, vows, marriage, and confession, which oppressed the people d enriched the priests, Erasmus exclaims: "In the churches they scarcely ever think of explaining the Gospel.[3] The greater part of their sermons must be drawn up to please the commissaries of indulgences. The most holy doctrine of Christ must be suppressed or perverted to their profit. There is no longer any hope of cure, unless Christ himself should turn the hearts of rulers and of pontiffs, and excite them to seek for real piety."

The writings of Erasmus followed one another in rapid succession. He laboured unceasingly, and his works were read just as they came from his pen. This animation, this native energy, this intellect so rich and so delicate, so witty and so bold, that was poured without any reserve in such copious streams upon his contemporaries, led away and enchanted the immense public who devoured the works of the philosopher of Rotterdam. He soon became the most influential man in Christendom, and crowns and pensions were showered upon him from every side.

If we cast our eyes on the great revolution that somewhat later renewed the Church, we cannot help acknowledging that Erasmus served as a bridge to many minds. Numbers who would have been alarmed by the evangelical truths presented in all their strength and purity, allowed themselves to be drawn

---

[1] Ratio Veræ Theologiæ.
[2] Ecclesiasticus, seu de Ratione Concionandi.

[1] Ad Servatium.
[2] Ad Joh. Slechtam, 1519. Hæc sunt animis hominum inculcanda, sic, ut velut in naturam transeant. Er. Epp. L 680.
[3] In templis vix vacat Evangelium interpretari. Annot ad Matth. xi. 30. *Jugum meum suave.*

along by him, and ultimately became the most zealous partisans of the Reformation.

But the very circumstances that fitted him for the work of preparation, disqualified him for its accomplishment. "Erasmus is very capable of exposing error," said Luther, "but he knows not how to teach the truth." The Gospel of Christ was not the fire at which he kindled and sustained his energy,—the centre whence his activity radiated. He was in an eminent degree a man of learning, and only in consequence of that was he a Christian. He was too much the slave of vanity to acquire a decided influence over his age. He anxiously calculated the result that each step he took might have upon his reputation. There was nothing he liked better than to talk about himself and his fame. "The pope," wrote he with childish vanity to an intimate friend, at the period when he declared himself the opponent of Luther, "the pope has sent me a diploma full of kindness and honourable testimonials. His secretary declares that this is an unprecedented honour, and that the pope dictated every word himself."

Erasmus and Luther, viewed in connexion with the Reformation, are the representatives of two great ideas,—of two great parties in their age, and indeed in every age. The one is composed of men of timid prudence ; the other, of men of resolution and courage. These two parties were in existence at that epoch, and they are personified in their illustrious chiefs. The men of prudence thought that the study of theological science would gradually bring about a reformation of the Church, and that, too, without violence. The men of action thought that the diffusion of more correct ideas among the learned would not put an end to the superstitions of the people, and that the correction of this or of that abuse, so long as the whole life of the Church was not renewed, would be of little effect.

"A disadvantageous peace," Erasmus used to say, "is better than the most righteous war."[1] He thought—and how many Erasmuses have lived since, and are living even in our own days ! he thought that a reformation which might shake the Church would endanger its overthrow ; he witnessed with alarm men's passions aroused into activity ; evil every where mixed up with the little good that might be effected ; existing institutions destroyed without the possibility of others being set up in their place ; and the vessel of the Church, leaking on every side, at last swallowed up by the tempest. "Those who bring the sea into new beds," said he, "often attempt a work that deceives their expectations ; for the terrible element, once let in, does not go where they would wish it, but rushes whithersoever it

pleases, and causes great devastation."[1] "Be that as it may," added he, "let troubles be every where avoided ! It is better to put up with ungodly princes, than to increase the evil by any change."[2]

But the courageous portion of his contemporaries were prepared with an answer. History had sufficiently proved that a free exposition of the truth and a decided struggle against falsehood could alone ensure the victory. If they had temporized, the artifices of policy and the wiles of the papal court would have extinguished the truth in its first glimmerings. Had not conciliatory measures been employed for ages ? Had not council after council been convoked to reform the Church ? All had been unavailing. Why now pretend to repeat an experiment that had so often failed ?

Undoubtedly a thorough reform could not be accomplished without violence. But when has anything good or great ever appeared among men without causing some agitation ? Would not this fear of seeing evil mingled with good, even had it been reasonable, have checked the noblest and the holiest undertakings ? We must not fear the evil that may arise out of a great agitation, but we must take courage to resist and to overcome it.

Is there not besides an essential difference between the commotion originating in human passions, and that which emanates from the Spirit of God ? One shakes society, the other strengthens it. What an error to imagine with Erasmus that in the then existing state of Christendom,—with that mixture of contrary elements, of truth and falsehood, life and death—a violent collision could be prevented ! As well strive to close the crater of Vesuvius when the angry elements are already warring in its bosom ! The Middle Ages had seen more than one violent commotion, when the sky was less threatening with storms than at the time of the Reformation. Men had not then to think of checking and of repressing, but of directing and guiding.

Who can tell what frightful ruin might not have occurred if the Reformation had not burst forth ? Society, the prey of a thousand elements of destruction, destitute of any regenerating or conservative qualities, would have been terribly convulsed. Certainly this would have really been a reform in Erasmus's fashion, and such as many moderate but timid men of our days still dream of, which would have overturned christian society. The people, wanting that knowledge and that piety which the Reformation brought down even to the lowest ranks, abandoned to their violent passions, and to a restless spirit of revolt, would have been let loose, like a

---

[1] Malo hunc, qualisqualis est, rerum humanarum statum quam novos excitari tumultus, said he on another occasion. Epp. i. 953.

[1] Semel admissum non ea fertur, qua destinarat admissor. .... Er. Epp. i. 953.
[2] Præstat ferre principes impios, quam novatis rebus gravius malum accersere.... Ad Matth. xi. 30.

furious and exasperated wild beast, whose rage no chains can any longer control.

The Reformation was no other than an interposition of the Spirit of God among men, —a regulating principle that God sent upon earth. It is true that it might stir up the fermenting elements hidden in the heart of man ; but God overruled them. The evangelical doctrines, the truth of God, penetrating the masses of the people, destroyed what was destined to perish, but every where strengthened what ought to be maintained. The effect of the Reformation on society was to reconstruct ; prejudice alone could say that it was an instrument of destruction. It has been said with reason, with reference to the work of reform, that " the ploughshare might as well think that it injures the earth it breaks up, while it is only fertilizing it."

The leading principle of Erasmus was : " Give light, and the darkness will disappear of itself." This principle is good, and Luther acted upon it. But when the enemies of the light endeavour to extinguish it, or to wrest the torch from the hand of him who bears it, must we (for the sake of peace) allow him to do so ? must we not resist the wicked ?

Erasmus was deficient in courage. Now, that quality is as indispensable to effect a reformation as to take a town. There was much timidity in his character. From his early youth·he trembled at the name of death. He took the most extraordinary care of his health. He spared no sacrifice to remove from a place in which a contagious malady was reigning. The desire of enjoying the comforts of life exceeded even his vanity, and this was his motive for rejecting more than one brilliant offer.

He had,therefore, no claims to the character of a reformer. " If the corrupted morals of the court of Rome call for a prompt and vigorous remedy, that is no business of mine," said he, " nor of those who are like me." [1] He had not that strength of faith which animated Luther. While the latter was ever prepared to lay down his life for the truth, Erasmus candidly observed, " Let others aspire to martyrdom : as for me, I do not think myself worthy of such an honour. [2] I fear that if any disturbance were to arise, I should imitate Peter in his fall."

By his conversation and by his writings Erasmus had prepared the way for the Reformation more than any other man ; and yet he trembled when he saw the approach of that very tempest which he himself had raised. He would have given anything to restore the calm of former times, even with all its dense vapours. But it was too late : the dike was broken. It was no longer in man's power to arrest the flood that was at once to cleanse and fertilize the world. Erasmus

was powerful as God's instrument ; when he ceased to be that, he was nothing.

Ultimately Erasmus knew not what party to adopt. None pleased him, and he feared all. " It is dangerous to speak," said he, " and it is dangerous to be silent." In every great religious movement there will be found these wavering characters,—respectable on many accounts, but injurious to the truth, and who, from their unwillingness to displease any, offend all.

What would have become of the Truth, had not God raised up more courageous champions than Erasmus ? Listen to the advice he gives Viglius Zuichem, who was afterwards president of the supreme court at Brussels, as to the manner in which he should behave towards the sectarians—for thus he had already begun to denominate the Reformers : " My friendship for you leads me to desire that you will keep aloof from the contagion of the sects, and that you will give them no opportunity of saying, Zuichem is become one of us. If you approve of their teaching, you should at least dissemble, and, above all, avoid discussions with them. A lawyer should finesse with these people, as the dying man did with the devil, who asked him, What do you believe ? The poor man, fearful of being caught in some heresy, if he should make a confession of his faith, replied, What the Church believes. The devil demanded, And what does the Church believe ? —What I believe.—Once more he was questioned, What do you believe ?—and the expiring man answered once more, What the Church believes !" [1] Thus Duke George of Saxony, Luther's mortal enemy, having received an equivocal answer to a question he had put to Erasmus, said to him, " My dear Erasmus, wash me the fur without wetting it !" Secundus Curio, in one of his works, describes two heavens—the papal and the christian. He found Erasmus in neither, but discovered him revolving between both in never-ending orbits.

Such was Erasmus. He needed that inward emancipation which alone gives perfect liberty. How different would he have been had he abandoned *self*, and sacrificed all for truth ! But after having endeavoured to effect certain reforms with the approbation of the heads of the Church ; after having deserted the Reformation for Rome, when he saw that these two things could not go hand in hand ;—he lost ground with all parties. On the one side, his recantations could not repress the anger of the fanatical partisans of the papacy : they felt all the evil he had done them, and would not pardon him. Furious monks loaded him with abuse from the pulpits : they called him a second Lucian —a fox that had laid waste the Lord's vineyard. A doctor of Constance had hung the portrait of Erasmus in his study, that he

---

[1] Ingens aliquod et præsens remedium, certe meum non est. Er. Epp. l. 653.
[2] Ego me non arbitror hoc honore dignum. Ibid.

[1] Erasm. Epp. 274. Append. Edit. Lugd. Bat.

might be able at any moment to spit in his face.—But, on the other hand, Erasmus, deserting the standard of the Gospel, lost the affection and esteem of the noblest men of the age in which he lived, and was forced to renounce, there can be little doubt, those heavenly consolations which God sheds in the heart of those who act as good soldiers of Christ. This at least seems to be indicated by those bitter tears, those painful vigils, that broken sleep, that tasteless food, that loathing of the study of the Muses, (formerly his only consolation), those saddened features, that pale face, those sorrowful and downcast eyes, that hatred of existence which he calls " a cruel life," and those longings after death, which he describes to his friends.[1] Unhappy Erasmus !

The enemies of Erasmus went, in my opinion, a little beyond the truth, when they exclaimed on Luther's appearance: " Erasmus laid the egg, and Luther hatched it."[2]

CHAPTER IX.

The Nobility—Different Motives—Hütten—Literary League Literæ Obscurorum Virorum—Their Effect—Luther's Opinion—Hütten at Brussels—His Letters—Sickingen—War—His Death—Cronberg—Hans Sachs—General Ferment.

THE same symptoms of regeneration that we have seen among princes, bishops, and learned men, were also found among men of the world,—among nobles, knights, and warriors. The German nobility played an important part in the Reformation. Several of the most illustrious sons of Germany formed a close alliance with the men of letters, and inflamed by an ardent, frequently by an excessive zeal, they strove to deliver their country from the Roman yoke.

Various causes contributed to raise up friends to the Reformation among the ranks of the nobles. Some having frequented the universities, had there received into their bosoms the fire with which the learned were animated. Others, brought up in generous sentiments, had hearts predisposed to receive the glorious lessons of the Gospel. Many discovered in the Reformation a certain chivalrous character that fascinated them and carried them along with it. And others, we must freely acknowledge, were offended with the clergy, who, in the reign of Maximilian,

had powerfully contributed to deprive them of their ancient independence, and bring them under subjection to their princes. They were full of enthusiasm, and looked upon the Reformation as the prelude to a great political renovation ; they saw in imagination the empire emerging with new splendour from this crisis, and hailed a better state, brilliant with the purest glory, that was on the eve of being established in the world, not less by the swords of the knights than by the Word of God.[1]

Ulrich of Hütten, who has been called the German Demosthenes, on account of his philippics against the Papacy, forms, as it were, the link that unites the knights with the men of letters. He distinguished himself by his writings not less than by his sword. Descended from an ancient Franconian family, he was sent at the age of eleven years to the convent of Foulda, in which he was to become a monk. But Ulrich, who felt no inclination for this profession, ran away from the convent at sixteen, and repaired to the university of Cologne, where he devoted himself to the study of languages and poetry. Somewhat later he led a wandering life, and was present, as a common soldier, at the siege of Padua in 1513, beheld Rome and all her scandalous abuses, and there sharpened those arrows which he afterwards discharged against her.

On his return to Germany, Hütten composed a treatise against Rome, entitled " The Roman Trinity." In this work he unveils the disorders of the papal court, and points out the necessity of putting an end to her tyranny by force. " There are three things," says a traveller named Vadiscus, who figures in the treatise,—" there are three things that are usually brought away from Rome : a bad conscience, a disordered stomach, and an empty purse. There are three things in which Rome does not believe : the immortality of the soul, the resurrection of the dead, and hell. There are three things in which Rome traffics : the grace of Christ, ecclesiastical dignities, and women." The publication of this work compelled Hütten to leave the court of the Archbishop of Mentz, where he had composed it.

Reuchlin's affair with the Dominicans was the signal that brought together all the men of letters, magistrates, and nobles, who were opposed to the monks. The defeat of the inquisitors, who, it was said, had escaped a definite and absolute condemnation only by means of bribery and intrigue, had emboldened their adversaries. Councillors of the empire : patricians of the most considerable cities,—Pickheimer of Nuremberg, Peutinger of Augsburg, and Stuss of Cologne ; distinguished preachers, such as Capito and Œcolampadius ;

---

[1] Vigiliæ molestæ, somnus irrequietus, cibus insipidus omnis, ipsum quoque musarum studium......ipsa frontis meæ mœstitia, vultus pallor, oculorum subtristis dejectio. Erasm. Epp. i. 1380.

[2] The works of Erasmus were published by John Le Clerc, at Liege, 1703, in ten vols. folio. For his life, consult Burigny, Vie d'Erasme, Paris, 1757 ; A. Müller, Leben des Erasmus, Hamb. 1828 ; and the Biography inserted by Le Clerc in his Bibliothèque Choisie. See also the beautiful and impartial essay of M. Nisard (Revue des Deux Mondes), who seems to me, however, to be mistaken in his estimate of Erasmus and Luther.

[1] Animus ingens et ferox, viribus pollens.—Nam si consilia et conatus Hütteni non defecissent, quasi nervi copiarum atque potentiæ, jam mutatio omnium rerum exstitisset, et quasi orbis status publici fuisset conversus. Camer. Vita Melancthonis.

doctors of medicine and historians ; all the literary men, orators, and poets, at whose head shone Ulrich of Hütten, composed that *army of Reuchlinists*, of which a list was even published.[1] The most remarkable production of this learned league was the famous popular satire entitled—*The Letters of Obscure Men.* The principal authors of this work were Hütten, and Crotus Robianus, one of his college friends ; but it is hard to say which of them first conceived the idea, even if it did not originate with the learned printer Angst, and if Hütten took any share in the first part of the work. Several *humanists*, assembled in the fortress of Ebernburg, appear to have contributed to the second. It is a bold sketch, a caricature often too rudely coloured, but full of truth and strength, of striking resemblance, and in characters of fire. Its effect was prodigious. The monks, the adversaries of Reuchlin, the supposed writers of these letters, discuss the affairs of the day and theological matters after their own fashion and in barbarous latinity. They addressed the silliest and most useless questions to their correspondent Ortuin Gratius, professor at Cologne, and a friend of Pfefferkorn. With the most artless simplicity they betray their gross ignorance, incredulity, and superstition ; their low and vulgar spirit ; the coarse gluttony by which they make a god of their bellies ; and at the same time their pride, and fanatical, persecuting zeal. They relate many of their droll adventures, of their excesses and profligacy, with various scandalous incidents in the lives of Hochstraten, Pfefferkorn, and other chiefs of their party. The tone of these letters—at one time hypocritical, at another quite childish—gives them a very comic effect : and yet the whole is so natural, that the English Dominicans and Franciscans received the work with the greatest approbation, and thought it really composed on the principles and in the defence of their orders. A certain prior of Brabant, in his credulous simplicity, even purchased a great number of copies, and sent them as presents to the most distinguished of the Dominicans. The monks, more and more exasperated, applied to the pope for a severe bull against all who should dare to read these letters ; but Leo X. would not grant their request. They were forced to bear with the general ridicule, and to smother their anger. No work ever inflicted a more terrible blow on these supporters of the Papacy. But it was not by satire and by jests that the Gospel was to triumph. Had men continued walking in this path ; had the Reformation had recourse to the jeering spirit of the world, instead of attacking error with the arms of God, its cause would have been lost. Luther boldly condemned these satires. One of his friends having sent him *The Tenour of Pasquin's Supplication,*

he replied, " The nonsense you have forwarded me seems to have been composed by an ill-regulated mind. I have communicated it to a circle of friends, and all have come to the same conclusion."[1] And speaking of the same work, he writes to another correspondent : " This *Supplication* appears to me to have been written by the author of the *Letters of Obscure Men.* I approve of his design, but not of his work, since he cannot refrain from insults and abuse."[2] This judgment is severe, but it shows Luther's disposition, and how superior he was to his contemporaries. We must add, however, that he did not always follow such wise maxims.

Ulrich having been compelled to resign the protection of the Archbishop of Mentz, sought that of Charles V., who was then at variance with the pope. He accordingly repaired to Brussels, where the emperor was holding his court. But far from obtaining anything, he learnt that the pope had called upon Charles to send him bound hand and foot to Rome. The inquisitor Hochstraten, Reuchlin's persecutor, was one of those whom Leo X. had charged to bring him to trial. Ulrich quitted Brabant in indignation at such a request having been made to the emperor. He had scarcely left Brussels, when he met Hochstraten on the highroad. The terrified inquisitor fell on his knees, and commended his soul to God and the saints. " No !" said the knight, " I will not soil my weapon with thy blood !" He gave him a few strokes with the flat of his sword, and allowed him to proceed in peace.

Hütten took refuge in the castle of Ebernburg, where Francis of Sickingen offered an asylum to all who were persecuted by the ultra-montanists. It was here that his burning zeal for the emancipation of his country dictated those remarkable letters which he addressed to Charles V., to the Elector Frederick of Saxony, to Albert, archbishop of Mentz, and to the princes and nobles,—letters that place him in the foremost ranks of authorship. Here, too, he composed all those works intended to be read and understood by the people, and which inspired all the German states with horror of Rome, and with the love of liberty. Ardently devoted to the cause of the Reformation, his design was to lead the nobles to take up arms in favour of the Gospel, and to fall with the sword upon that Rome which Luther aimed at destroying solely by the Word of God, and by the invincible power of the truth.

Yet amidst all this warlike enthusiasm, we are charmed at finding in Hütten mild and delicate sentiments. On the death of his parents, he made over to his brothers all the family property, although he was the eldest son, and even begged them not to write to him or send him any money, lest, notwithstanding their innocence, they should be

[1] *Exercitus Reuchlinistarum*, at the head of the collection of letters addressed to Reuchlin on this subject.

[1] Luth. Epp. i. 37.　　[2] Ibid. 38.

exposed to suffer by the malice of his enemies, and fall with him into the pit.

If Truth cannot acknowledge Hütten as one of her children, for her walk is ever with holiness of life and charity of heart, she will at least accord him honourable mention as one of the most formidable antagonists of error.[1]

The same may be said of Francis of Sickingen, his illustrious friend and protector. This noble knight, whom many of his contemporaries judged worthy of the imperial crown, shines in the first rank among those warriors who were the adversaries of Rome. Although delighting in the uproar of battle, he was filled with an ardent love of learning and with veneration for its professors. When at the head of an army that menaced Wurtemberg, he gave orders that, in case Stuttgard should be taken by assault, the house and property of that great scholar, John Reuchlin, should be spared. Sickingen afterwards invited him to his camp, and embracing him, offered to support him in his quarrel with the monks of Cologne. For a long time chivalry had prided itself on despising literature. The epoch whose history we are retracing presents to us a new spectacle. Under the weighty cuirasses of the Hüttens and Sickingens we perceive that intellectual movement which was beginning to make itself felt in every quarter. The first fruits that the Reformation gave to the world were warriors that were the friends of the peaceful arts.

Hütten, who on his return from Brussels had taken refuge in the castle of Sickingen, invited the worthy knight to study the evangelical doctrines, and explained to him the foundations on which they rest. "And is there any man," asked he in astonishment, "who dares attempt to overthrow such an edifice?...Who could do it?..."

Many individuals, who were afterwards celebrated as reformers, found an asylum in his castle; among others, Martin Bucer, Aquila, Schwebel, and Œcolampadius, so that Hütten with justice used to call Ebernburg "the resting-place of the righteous." It was the duty of Œcolampadius to preach daily in the castle. The warriors who were there assembled at last grew weary of hearing so much said about the meek virtues of Christianity: the sermons appeared to them too long, however brief Œcolampadius endeavoured to be. They repaired, it is true, almost every day to the church, but it was for little else than to hear the benediction and to repeat a short prayer, so that Œcolampadius used to exclaim: "Alas! the Word of God is sown here upon stony ground!"

Erelong Sickingen, wishing to serve the cause of truth after his own fashion, declared war against the Archbishop of Treves, "in order," as he said, "to open a door for the Gospel." In vain did Luther, who had already appeared, strive to dissuade him from it: he attacked Treves with 5000 horse and 1000 foot. The courageous archbishop, with the aid of the Elector Palatine and the Landgrave of Hesse, compelled him to retire. In the following spring the allied princes attacked him in his castle of Landstein. After a bloody assault, Sickingen was obliged to surrender: he had been mortally wounded. The three princes entered the fortress, and after searching through it, discovered the stout-hearted knight in a vault, lying on his bed of death. He stretched out his hand to the Elector Palatine, without seeming to notice the princes who accompanied him; but these overwhelmed him with questions and reproaches: "Leave me in repose," said he, "for I must now prepare to answer a more powerful lord than you!......" When Luther heard of his death, he exclaimed: "The Lord is righteous and greatly to be praised! It is not by the sword that he will have his Gospel propagated."

Such was the melancholy end of a warrior, who, as elector or emperor, might perhaps have raised Germany to a high degree of glory; but who, confined within a narrow circle, wasted the great powers with which he had been endowed. But it was not in the tumultuous bosoms of these warriors that the divine truth, coming down from heaven, was to take up her abode. It was not by their arms that she was to prevail; and God, by bringing to nought Sickingen's mad projects, confirmed anew the testimony of St. Paul: *The weapons of our warfare are not carnal, but mighty through God* (2 Cor. x. 4).

Another knight, Harmut of Cronberg, a friend of Hütten and Sickingen, appears to have had more wisdom and a deeper knowledge of the truth. He wrote with great modesty to Leo X., exhorting him to restore his temporal power to its rightful owner, namely, the emperor. Addressing his subjects as a father, he endeavoured to explain to them the doctrines of the Gospel, and exhorted them to faith, obedience, and trust in Jesus Christ, "who is the Lord of all," added he. He resigned into the Emperor's hand a pension of 200 ducats, "because he would no longer serve one who lent his ear to the enemies of the truth." We find an expression of his recorded that seems to place him far above Hütten and Sickingen: "Our heavenly doctor, the Holy Ghost, can, whenever he pleases, teach in one hour more of the faith that is in Christ Jesus, than could be learnt at the university of Paris in ten years."

Those who look for the friends of the Reformation only on the steps of thrones,[1] or in cathedrals and in colleges, and who maintain that it had no friends among the

---

[1] Hütten's Works were published at Berlin by Munchen, 1822-1825. in 5 vols. 8vo.

[1] See Châteaubriand's Etudes Historiques.

people, are greatly mistaken. God, who was preparing the hearts of the wise and the powerful, was also preparing in the homes of the people many simple and humble-minded men, who were one day to become the ministers of his Word. The history of the period shows the ferment then agitating the lower orders. The tendency of popular literature before the Reformation was in direct opposition to the prevailing spirit of the Church. In the *Eulenspiegel*, a celebrated popular poem of the times, there is a perpetual current of ridicule against brutal and gluttonous priests, who were fond of pretty housekeepers, fine horses, and a well-filled larder. In the *Reynard Reineke*, the priests' houses with their families of little children are a prominent feature; another popular writer thunders with all his might against those ministers of Christ who ride spirited horses, but who will not fight against the infidels; and John Rosenblut, in one of his carnival plays, introduces the Grand Turk in person to deliver a seasonable address to the states of Christendom.

It was in reality in the bosoms of the people that the revolution so soon to break forth was violently fermenting. Not only do we see youths issuing from their ranks and seizing upon the highest stations in the Church; but there are those who remained all their lives engaged in the humblest occupations, and yet powerfully contributing to the great revival of Christendom. We proceed to recall a few features in the life of one of these individuals.

Hans Sachs, son of a tailor of Nuremberg, was born on the 5th November 1494. He was named Hans (John) after his father, and had made some little progress in learning, when a severe malady compelled him to renounce his studies and take up the business of a shoemaker. Young Hans profited by the liberty which this humble trade allowed to his mind, to penetrate into that higher world in which his soul delighted. The songs that had ceased to be heard in the castles of the nobles, sought and found an asylum among the inhabitants of the merry towns of Germany. A singing school was held in the church of Nuremberg. These exercises, in which Hans used to join, opened his heart to religious impressions, and helped to awaken in him a taste for poetry and music. But the young man's genius could not long remain confined within the walls of his workshop. He wished to see with his own eyes that world of which he had read so much in books,—of which his comrades related so many stories,—and which his imagination peopled with wonders. In 1511, with a small bundle of necessaries, he sets out and directs his steps towards the south. Erelong the youthful traveller, who had met with jovial companions, students roaming from town to town, and with many dangerous temptations, feels a terrible struggle beginning within him.

The lusts of life and his holy resolutions are contending for the mastery. Trembling for the result, he takes flight and hides himself in the small town of Wels in Austria (1513), where he lived in retirement, devoting himself to the cultivation of the fine arts. The Emperor Maximilian chanced to pass through this town with a brilliant retinue, and the young poet allowed himself to be carried away by the splendour of the court. The prince placed him in his hunting-train; and in the noisy halls of the palace of Inspruck, Hans again forgot all his resolutions. But his conscience once more cried aloud. Immediately the young huntsman lays aside his brilliant livery, quits the court, and repairs to Schwatz, and afterwards to Munich. It was in the latter town that, at the age of twenty years (1514), he composed his first hymn " in honour of God " to a remarkable air. He was covered with applause. During his travels he had had many opportunities of observing the numerous and melancholy proofs of the abuses under which religion was buried.

On his return to Nuremberg, Hans settled, married, and became a father. When the Reformation broke out, he lent an attentive ear. He clung to the Holy Scriptures, which were already dear to him as a poet, but in which he no longer sought merely for images and songs, but for the light of truth. To this truth erelong he consecrated his lyre, and from an humble workshop, near the gates of the imperial city of Nuremberg, issued tones that re-echoed throughout Germany, preparing men's minds for a new era, and every where endearing to the people the mighty revolution that was going forward. The spiritual songs of Hans Sachs and his Bible in verse were a powerful help to this great work. It would, perhaps, be hard to decide who did the most for it—the Prince-elector of Saxony, administrator of the empire, or the Nuremberg shoemaker!

Thus, then, was there in every class something that announced the Reformation. Warnings appeared on every side, and events were hastening on which threatened to destroy the work of ages of darkness, and to " make all things new." The hierarchical form, which the efforts of many centuries had stamped upon the world, was shaken, and its fall was nigh. The light that had been just discovered spread a multitude of new ideas through every country with inconceivable rapidity. In every grade of society a new life was in motion. " What an age !" exclaimed Hütten; " studies flourish—minds are awakening: it is a joy merely to be alive !" Minds that had lain dormant for so many generations, seemed desirous of redeeming by their activity the time they had lost. To leave them unemployed, and without food, or to present them only with such as had long supported their languishing existence, would have betrayed ignorance of man's nature. Already did the human mind clearly perceive what was and what should be, and surveyed with a daring glance the immense gulf which separated these two worlds. Great princes filled the thrones; the time-worn colossus of Rome was tottering under its own weight; the ancient spirit of chivalry was dead, and its place supplied by a new spirit which breathed at once from the sanctuaries of learning and from the homes of the lowly. The printed Word had taken wings that carried it, as the wind wafts the light seed, even to the most distant places. The discovery of the two Indies extended the boundaries of the world. Everything announced a great revolution.

But whence is to proceed the blow that shall throw down the ancient building, and raise a new one from its ruins? No one knew. Who possessed greater wisdom than Frederick, greater learning than Reuchlin, greater talents than Erasmus, more wit and energy than Hütten, more valour than Sickingen, or was more virtuous than Cronberg? And yet it was not from Frederick, or Reuchlin, or Erasmus, or Hütten, or Sickingen, or Cronberg!............ Learned men, princes, warriors, nay the Church itself—all had undermined some of the foundations; but there they had stopped. In no direction could be seen the powerful hand that was to be the instrument of God.

And yet all men had a presentiment that it would soon appear. Some pretended to have discovered in the stars unerring indications of its approach. Some, as they looked upon the miserable state of religion, foretold the near coming of Antichrist. Others, on the contrary predicted a reformation to be close at hand. The world waited in expectation. Luther appeared.

BOOK II.

THE YOUTH, CONVERSION, AND EARLY LABOURS OF LUTHER.—1483–1517.

CHAPTER I.

Luther's Descent—His Parents—His Birth—His Poverty—Paternal Home—Severity—First Knowledge—School of Magdeburg—Hardships—Eisenach—The Shunamite—House of Cotta—Arts—Recollections of these Times—His Studies—Trebonius—The University.

ALL was ready. God who prepares his work through ages, accomplishes it by the weakest instruments, when His time is come. To effect great results by the smallest means—such is the law of God. This law, which prevails every where in nature, is found also in history. God selected the reformers of the Church from the same class whence he had taken the apostles. He chose them from among that lower rank, which, although not the meanest, does not reach the level of the middle classes. Everything was thus intended to manifest to the world that the work was not of man but of God. The reformer Zwingle emerged from an Alpine shepherd's hut; Melancthon, the theologian of the Reformation, from an armourer's shop; and Luther from the cottage of a poor miner.

The first period in man's life—that in which he is formed and moulded under the hand of God—is always important. It is eminently so in the career of Luther. The whole of the Reformation is included in it. The different phases of this work succeeded one another in the soul of him who was to be the instrument for effecting it, before they were accomplished in the world. The knowledge of the change that took place in Luther's heart can alone furnish the key to the reformation of the Church. It is only by studying the particulars that we can understand the general work. Those who neglect the former will be ignorant of the latter except in its outward appearance. They may acquire a knowledge of certain events and certain results, but they will never comprehend the intrinsic nature of that revival, because the principle of life, that was its very soul, remains unknown to them. Let us therefore study the Reformation in Luther himself, before we proceed to the events that changed the face of Christendom.

In the village of Mora, near the Thuringian forests, and not far from the spot where Boniface, the apostle of Germany, began to proclaim the Gospel, had dwelt, doubtless for many centuries, an ancient and numerous family of the name of Luther.[1] As was customary with the Thuringian peasants, the eldest son always inherited the dwelling and the paternal fields, while the other children departed elsewhere in quest of a livelihood. One of these, by name John Luther, married Margaret Lindemann, the daughter of an inhabitant of Neustadt, in the see of Wurzburg. The married pair quitted the plains

[1] Vetus familia est et late propagata mediocrium hominum. Melancth. Vita Luth.

49

of Eisenach, and went to settle in the little town of Eisleben in Saxony, to earn their bread by the sweat of their brows.

Seckendorf relates, on the testimony of Rebhan, superintendent at Eisenach in 1601, that Luther's mother, thinking her time still distant, had gone to the fair of Eisleben, and that contrary to her expectation she there gave birth to a son. Notwithstanding the credit that is due to Seckendorf, this account does not appear to be correct: in fact, none of the oldest of Luther's historians mention it; and besides, it is about twenty-four leagues from Mora to Eisleben, and in the condition of Luther's mother at that time, people do not readily make up their minds to travel such a distance *to see a fair;* and, lastly, the evidence of Luther himself appears in direct opposition to this assertion.[1]

John Luther was an upright man, diligent in business, frank, and carrying the firmness of his character even to obstinacy. With a more cultivated mind than that of most men of his class, he used to read much. Books were then rare; but John omitted no opportunity of procuring them. They formed his relaxation in the intervals of repose, snatched from his severe and constant labours. Margaret possessed all the virtues that can adorn a good and pious woman. Her modesty, her fear of God, and her prayerful spirit, were particularly remarked. She was looked upon by the matrons of the neighbourhood as a model whom they should strive to imitate.[2]

It is not precisely known how long the married pair had been living at Eisleben, when, on the 10th November, one hour before midnight, Margaret gave birth to a son. Melancthon once questioned his friend's mother as to the period of his birth. "I well remember the day and the hour," replied she, "but I am not certain about the year." But Luther's brother James, an honest and upright man, has recorded, that in the opinion of the whole family the future reformer was born on St. Martin's eve, 10th November 1483,[3] And Luther himself wrote on a Hebrew Psalter which is still in existence: "I was born in the year 1483."[4] The first thought of his pious parents was to dedicate to God by the holy rite of baptism the child that he had given them. On the morrow, which happened to be Tuesday, the father with gratitude and joy carried his son to St. Peter's church, and there he received the seal of his consecration to the Lord. They called him Martin in commemoration of the day.

The child was not six months old, when his parents quitted Eisleben to repair to Mansfeldt, which is only five leagues distant.

The mines of that neighbourhood were then very celebrated. John Luther, who was a hard-working man, feeling that perhaps he would be called upon to bring up a numerous family, hoped to gain a better livelihood for himself and his children in that town. It was here that the understanding and strength of young Luther received their first development; here his activity began to display itself, and here his character was declared in his words and in his actions. The plains of Mansfeldt, the banks of the Wipper, were the theatre of his first sports with the children of the neighbourhood.

The first period of their abode at Mansfeldt was full of difficulty to the worthy John and his wife. At first they lived in great poverty. "My parents," said the Reformer, "were very poor. My father was a poor wood-cutter, and my mother has often carried wood upon her back, that she might procure the means of bringing up her children. They endured the severest labour for our sakes." The example of the parents whom he revered, the habits they inspired in him, early accustomed Luther to labour and frugality. How many times, doubtless, he accompanied his mother to the wood, there to gather up his little faggot!

There are promises of blessing on the labour of the righteous, and John Luther experienced their realization. Having attained somewhat easier circumstances, he established two smelting furnaces at Mansfeldt. Beside these furnaces little Martin grew in strength, and with the produce of this labour his father afterwards provided for his studies. "It was from a miner's family," says the good Mathesius, "that the spiritual *founder* of Christendom was to go forth: an image of what God would do in purifying the sons of Levi through him, and refining them like gold in his furnaces." Respected by all for his integrity, for his spotless life, and good sense, John Luther was made councillor of Mansfeldt, capital of the earldom of that name. Excessive misery might have crushed the child's spirit: the competence of his paternal home expanded his heart and elevated his character.

John took advantage of his new position to court the society which he preferred. He had a great esteem for learned men, and often invited to his table the clergy and schoolmasters of the place. His house offered a picture of those social meetings of his fellow-citizens, which did honour to Germany at the commencement of the sixteenth century. It was a mirror in which were reflected the numerous images that followed one another on the agitated scene of the times. The child profited by them. No doubt the sight of these men, to whom so much respect was shown in his father's house, excited more than once in little Martin's heart the

---

[1] Ego natus sum in Eisleben, baptisatusque apud Sanctum-Petrum ibidem. Parentes mei de prope Isenaco illuc migrarunt. Luth. Epp. i. 390.
[2] Intuebanturque in eam cæteræ honestæ mulieres, ut in exemplar virtutum. Melancth. Vita Lutheri.
[3] Ibid.
[4] Anno 1483, natus ego. Psalter in the Dantzic Library.

[1] Drumb musste dieser geistliche Schmelzer. Mathesius, Historien, 1565, p. 3.

ambitious desire of becoming himself one day a schoolmaster or a learned man.

As soon as he was old enough to receive instruction, his parents endeavoured to impart to him the knowledge of God, to train him up in His fear, and to mould him to christian virtues. They exerted all their care in this earliest domestic education.[1] The father would often kneel at the child's bedside, and fervently pray aloud, begging the Lord that his son might remember His name and one day contribute to the propagation of the truth.[2] The parent's prayer was most graciously listened to. And yet his tender solicitude was not confined to this.

His father, anxious to see him acquire the elements of that learning for which he himself had so much esteem, invoked God's blessing upon him, and sent him to school. Martin was still very young. His father, or Nicholas Emler, a young man of Mansfeldt, often carried him in their arms to the house of George Emilius, and afterwards returned to fetch him home. Emler in afteryears married one of Luther's sisters.

His parents' piety, their activity and austere virtue, gave the boy a happy impulse, and formed in him an attentive and serious disposition. The system of education which then prevailed made use of chastisement and fear as the principal incentives to study. Margaret, although sometimes approving the too great severity of her husband, frequently opened her maternal arms to console her son to console him in his tears. Yet even she herself overstept the limits of that wise precept: *He that loveth his son, chasteneth him betimes.* Martin's impetuous character gave frequent occasion for punishment and reprimand. " My parents," said Luther in afterlife, " treated me harshly, so that I became very timid. My mother one day chastised me so severely about a nut, that the blood came. They seriously thought that they were doing right ; but they could not distinguish character, which however is very necessary in order to know when, or where, or how chastisement should be inflicted. It is necessary to punish ; but the apple should be placed beside the rod." [3]

At school the poor child met with treatment no less severe. His master flogged him fifteen times successively in one morning. " We must," said Luther, when relating this circumstance—" we must whip children, but we must at the same time love them." With such an education Luther learnt early to despise the charms of a merely sensual life. " What is to become great, should begin small," justly observes one of his oldest biographers; " and if children are brought up too delicately and with too much

kindness from their youth, they are injured for life." [1]

Martin learnt something at school. He was taught the heads of his Catechism, the Ten Commandments, the Apostles' Creed, the Lord's Prayer, some hymns, some forms of prayer, and a Latin grammar written in the fourth century by Donatus, who was St. Jerome's master, and which, improved in the eleventh century by one Remigius, a French monk, was long held in great repute in every school. He further studied the calendar of Cisio Janus, a very singular work, composed in the tenth or eleventh century : in fine, he learnt all that could be taught in the Latin school of Mansfeldt.

But the child's thoughts do not appear to have been there directed to God. The only religious sentiment that could then be discovered in him was fear. Every time he heard Jesus Christ spoken of, he turned pale with affright ; for the Saviour had only been represented to him as an offended judge. This servile fear—so alien to true religion— may perhaps have prepared him for the glad tidings of the Gospel, and for that joy which he afterwards felt, when he learnt to know Him who is meek and lowly in heart.

John Luther wished to make his son a scholar. The day that was every where beginning to dawn, had penetrated even into the house of the Mansfeldt miner, and there awakened ambitious thoughts. The remarkable disposition, the persevering application of his son, made John conceive the liveliest expectations. Accordingly, in 1497, when Martin had attained the age of fourteen years, his father resolved to part with him, and send him to the Franciscan school at Magdeburg. His mother was forced to consent, and Martin prepared to quit the paternal roof.

Magdeburg was like a new world to Martin. In the midst of numerous privations, for he scarcely had enough to live upon, he inquired—he listened. Andrew Proles, provincial of the Augustine order, was at that time warmly advocating the necessity of reforming religion and the Church. It was not he, however, who deposited in the young man's heart the first germ of the ideas that were afterwards developed there.

This was a rude apprenticeship for Luther. Thrown upon the world at the age of fourteen, without friends or protectors, he trembled in the presence of his masters, and in the hours of recreation he painfully begged his bread in company with children poorer than himself. " I used to beg with my companions for a little food," said he, " that we might have the means of providing for our wants. One day, at the time the Church celebrates the festival of Christ's nativity, we were wandering together through the neighbouring villages, going from house to

1 Ad agnitionem et timorem Dei....domestica institutione diligenter assuefecerunt. Melancth. Vita Luth.
2 Conrad Schlusselburg, Orat. de Vita et Morte Lutheri.
3 Sed non poterant discernere ingenia, secundum quæ essent temperandæ correctiones. L. Opp. W. xxii. p. 1785.
1 Was gross sol werden, muss klein angehen. Mathesius, Hist. p. 3.

house, and singing in four parts the usual carols on the infant Jesus, born at Bethlehem. We stopped before a peasant's house that stood by itself at the extremity of the village. The farmer, hearing us sing our Christmas hymns, came out with some victuals which he intended to give us, and called out in a high voice and with a harsh tone, Boys, where are you? Frightened at these words, we ran off as fast as our legs would carry us. We had no reason to be alarmed, for the farmer offered us assistance with great kindness; but our hearts, no doubt, were rendered timorous by the menaces and tyranny with which the teachers were then accustomed to rule over their pupils, so that a sudden panic had seized us. At last, however, as the farmer continued calling after us, we stopped, forgot our fears, ran back to him, and received from his hands the food intended for us. It is thus," adds Luther, " that we are accustomed to tremble and flee, when our conscience is guilty and alarmed. In such a case we are afraid even of the assistance that is offered us, and of those who are our friends, and who would willingly do us every good."[1]

A year had scarcely passed away, when John and Margaret, hearing what difficulty their son found in supporting himself at Magdeburg, sent him to Eisenach, where there was a celebrated school, and in which town they had many relatives.[2] They had other children; and although their means had increased, they could not maintain their son in a place where he was unknown. The furnaces and the industry of John Luther did little more than provide for the support of his family. He hoped that when Martin arrived at Eisenach, he would more easily find the means of subsistence; but he was not more fortunate in this town. His relations who dwelt there took no care about him, or perhaps, being very poor themselves, they could not give him any assistance.

When the young scholar was pinched by hunger, he was compelled, as at Magdeburg, to join with his schoolfellows in singing from door to door to obtain a morsel of bread. This custom of Luther's days is still preserved in many German cities: sometimes the voices of the youths form an harmonious concert. Often, instead of food, the poor and modest Martin received nothing but harsh words. Then, overwhelmed with sorrow, he shed many tears in secret, and thought with anxiety of the future.

One day, in particular, he had already been repulsed from three houses, and was preparing to return fasting to his lodgings, when, having reached the square of St. George, he stopped motionless, plunged in melancholy reflections, before the house of a worthy citizen. Must he for want of bread renounce

his studies, and return to labour with his father in the mines of Mansfeldt?......Suddenly a door opens—a woman appears on the threshold: it is Ursula, the wife of Conrad Cotta, and daughter of the burgomaster of Ilefeld.[1] The Eisenach chronicles style her "the pious *Shunamite*," in remembrance of her who so earnestly constrained the prophet Elisha to stay and eat bread with her. The christian Shunamite had already more than once remarked the youthful Martin in the assemblies of the faithful; she had been affected by the sweetness of his voice and by his devotion.[2] She had heard the harsh words that had been addressed to the poor scholar, and seeing him stand thus sadly before her door, she came to his aid, beckoned him to enter, and gave him food to appease his hunger.

Conrad approved of his wife's benevolence: he even found so much pleasure in the boy's society, that a few days after he took him to live entirely with him. Henceforward his studies were secured. He is not obliged to return to the mines of Mansfeldt, and bury the talents that God has intrusted to him. At a time when he knew not what would become of him, God opened the heart and the house of a christian family. This event disposed his soul to that confidence in God which the severest trials could not after wards shake.

Luther passed in Cotta's house a very different kind of life from that which he had hitherto known. His existence glided away calmly, exempt from want and care: his mind became more serene, his character more cheerful, and his heart more open. All his faculties awoke at the mild rays of charity, and he began to exult with life, joy, and happiness. His prayers were more fervent, his thirst for knowledge greater, and his progress in study more rapid.

To literature and science he added the charms of the fine arts; for they also were advancing in Germany. The men whom God destines to act upon their contemporaries, are themselves at first influenced and carried away by all the tendencies of the age in which they live. Luther learned to play on the flute and on the lute. With this latter instrument he used often to accompany his fine alto voice, and thus cheered his heart in the hours of sadness. He took delight in testifying by his melody his lively gratitude towards his adoptive mother, who was passionately fond of music. He himself loved the art even to old age, and composed the words and airs of some of the finest hymns that Germany possesses. Many have even passed into our language.

These were happy times for young Luther: he could never think of them without emotion. One of Conrad's sons coming many

---

[1] Lutheri Opera (Walch.) ii. 2347.
[2] Isenacum enim pene totam parentelam meam habet. Epp. i. 39c.

[1] Lingk's Reisegesch. Luth.
[2] Dieweil sie umb seines Singen und herzlichen Gebets willen. Mathesius, p. 3.

years after to study at Wittemberg, when the poor scholar of Eisenach had become the first doctor of the age, was received with joy at his table and under his roof. He wished to make some return to the son for the kindness he had received from the parents. It was in remembrance of this christian woman who had fed him when all the world repulsed him, that he gave utterance to this beautiful thought : " There is nothing sweeter on earth than the heart of a woman in which piety dwells."

Luther was never ashamed of these days in which, oppressed by hunger, he used in sadness to beg the bread necessary for his studies and his livelihood. Far from that, he used to reflect with gratitude on the extreme poverty of his youth. He looked upon it as one of the means that God had employed to make him what he afterwards became, and he accordingly thanked him for it. The poor children who were obliged to follow the same kind of life, touched his heart. " Do not despise," said he, " the boys who go singing through the streets, begging a little bread for the love of God (*panem propter Deum*): I also have done the same. It is true that somewhat later my father supported me with much love and kindness at the university of Erfurth, maintaining me by the sweat of his brow ; yet I have been a poor beggar. And now, by means of my pen, I have risen so high, that I would not change lots with the Grand Turk himself. Nay more, should all the riches of the earth be heaped one upon another, I would not take them in exchange for what I possess. And yet I should not be where I am, if I had not gone to school— if I had not learnt to write."—Thus did this great man see in these his first humble beginnings the origin of all his glory. He feared not to recall to mind that the voice whose accents thrilled the empire and the world, once used to beg for a morsel of bread in the streets of a small town. The Christian finds a pleasure in such recollections, because they remind him that it is in God alone he should glory.

The strength of his understanding, the liveliness of his imagination, the excellence of his memory, soon carried him beyond all his schoolfellows.[1] He made rapid progress especially in Latin, in eloquence, and in poetry. He wrote speeches and composed verses. As he was cheerful, obliging, and had what is called " a good heart," he was beloved by his masters and by his schoolfellows.

Among the professors he attached himself particularly to John Trebonius, a learned man, of an agreeable address, and who had all that regard for youth which is so well calculated to encourage them.

Martin had noticed that whenever Trebonius entered the schoolroom, he raised his cap to salute the pupils. A great condescension in those pedantic times ! This had delighted the young man. He saw that he was something. The respect of the master had elevated the scholar in his own estimation. The colleagues of Trebonius, who did not adopt the same custom, having one day expressed their astonishment at his extreme condescension, he replied (and his answer did not the less strike the youthful Luther) : " There are among these boys men of whom God will one day make burgomasters, chancellors, doctors, and magistrates. Although you do not yet see them with the badges of their dignity, it is right that you should treat them with respect." Doubtless the young scholar listened with pleasure to these words, and perhaps imagined himself already with the doctor's cap upon his head !

CHAPTER II.

The University—Scholastic Divinity and the Classics—Luther's Piety—Discovery of the Bible—Illness—Luther admitted M.A.—Conscience—Death of Alexis—The Thunder-Storm—Providence—Farewell—Luther enters a Convent.

LUTHER had now reached his eighteenth year. He had tasted the sweets of literature ; he burnt with a desire of knowledge ; he sighed for a university education, and wished to repair to one of those fountains of learning where he could slake his thirst for letters. His father required him to study the law. Full of hope in the talents of his son, he wished that he should cultivate them and make them generally known. He already pictured him discharging the most honourable functions among his fellow-citizens, gaining the favour of princes, and shining on the theatre of the world. It was determined that the young man should go to Erfurth.

Luther arrived at this university in 1501. Jodocus, surnamed the Doctor of Eisenach, was teaching there the scholastic philosophy with great success. Melancthon regrets that at that time nothing was taught at Erfurth but a system of dialectics bristling with difficulties. He thinks that if Luther had met with other professors, if they had taught him the milder and calmer discipline of true philosophy, the violence of his nature might have been moderated and softened.[2] The new disciple applied himself to study the philosophy of the Middle Ages in the works of Occam, Scotus, Bonaventure, and Thomas

---

[1] Cumque et vis ingenii acerrima esset, et imprimis ad eloquentiam idonea, celeriter æqualibus suis præcurrit. Melancth. Vita Luth.

[1] Degustata igitur literarum dulcedine, natura flagrans cupiditate discendi appetit academiam. Mel. Vit. Luth.
[2] Et fortassis ad leniendam vehementiam naturæ mitiora studia veræ philosophiæ. Mel. Vit. Luth.

Aquinas. In later times all this scholastic divinity was his aversion. He trembled with indignation whenever Aristotle's name was pronounced in his presence, and he went so far as to say that if Aristotle had not been a man, he should not have hesitated to take him for the devil. But a mind so eager for learning as his required other aliments; he began to study the masterpieces of antiquity, the writings of Cicero, Virgil, and other classic authors. He was not content, like the majority of students, with learning their productions by heart: he endeavoured to fathom their thoughts, to imbibe the spirit which animated them, to appropriate their wisdom to himself, to comprehend the object of their writings, and to enrich his mind with their pregnant sentences and brilliant images. He often addressed questions to his professors, and soon outstripped all his fellow-students.[1] Blessed with a retentive memory and a strong imagination, all that he read or heard remained constantly present to his mind; it was as if he had seen it himself. "Thus shone Luther in his early years. The whole university," says Melancthon, "admired his genius." [2]

But even at this period the young man of eighteen did not study merely to cultivate his intellect: he had those serious thoughts, that heart directed heavenwards, which God gives to those of whom he resolves to make his most zealous ministers. Luther was sensible of his entire dependence upon God, —simple and powerful conviction, which is at once the cause of deep humility and of great actions ! He fervently invoked the divine blessing upon his labours. Every morning he began the day with prayer; he then went to church, and afterwards applied to his studies, losing not a moment in the whole course of the day. "To pray well," he was in the habit of saying, "is the better half of study." [3]

The young student passed in the university library all the time he could snatch from his academical pursuits. Books were as yet rare, and it was a great privilege for him to profit by the treasures brought together in this vast collection. One day—he had then been two years at Erfurth, and was twenty years old—he opens many books in the library one after another, to learn their writers' names. One volume that he comes to attracts his attention. He has never until this hour seen its like. He reads the title —it is a Bible! a rare book, unknown in those times.[4] His interest is greatly excited: he is filled with astonishment at finding other matters than those fragments of the gospels and epistles that the Church has selected to be read to the people during public worship every Sunday throughout the year. Until this day he had imagined that they composed the whole Word of God. And now he sees so many pages, so many chapters, so many books of which he had had no idea ! His heart beats as he holds the divinely inspired volume in his hand. With eagerness and with indescribable emotion he turns over these leaves from God. The first page on which he fixes his attention narrates the story of Hannah and of the young Samuel. He reads—and his soul can hardly contain the joy it feels. This child, whom his parents lend to the Lord as long as he liveth; the song of Hannah, in which she declares that Jehovah "raiseth up the poor out of the dust, and lifteth the beggar from the dunghill, to set them among princes ;" this child, who grew up in the temple in the presence of the Lord; those sacrificers, the sons of Heli, who are wicked men, who live in debauchery, and "make the Lord's people to transgress ;" —all this history, all this revelation that he has just discovered, excites feelings till then unknown. He returns home with a full heart. " Oh ! that God would give me such a book for myself," thought he.[1] Luther was as yet ignorant both of Greek and Hebrew. It is scarcely probable that he had studied these languages during the first two or three years of his residence at the university. The Bible that had filled him with such transports was in Latin. He soon returned to the library to pore over his treasure. He read it again and again, and then, in his astonishment and joy, he returned to read it once more. The first glimmerings of a new truth were then beginning to dawn upon his mind.

Thus had God led him to the discovery of his Word—of that book of which he was one day to give his fellow-countrymen that admirable translation in which Germany has for three centuries perused the oracles of God. Perhaps for the first time this precious volume has now been taken down from the place it occupied in the library of Erfurth. This book, deposited upon the unknown shelves of a gloomy hall, is about to become the book of life to a whole nation. In that Bible the Reformation lay hid.

It was in the same year that Luther took his first academical degree—that of bachelor. The excessive labour to which he had devoted himself in order to pass his examination, occasioned a dangerous illness. Death seemed approaching him : serious reflections occupied his mind. He thought that his earthly existence was drawing to an end. The young man excited general interest. "It is a pity," they thought, " to see so many expectations so early blighted." Many friends came to visit him on his bed of sickness. Among their number was a venerable and

---

[1] Et quidem inter primos, ut ingenio studioque multos œæqualium antecellebat. Cochlœus, Acta Lutheri. p. 1.
[2] Sic igitur in juventute eminebat, ut toti academiæ Lutheri ingenium admirationi esset. Vita Luth.
[3] Fleissig Gebet, ist uber die Helfft studirt. Mathes. 3.
[4] Auff ein Zeyt, wie er die Bücher fein nacheinander besieht....kombt er über die lateinische Biblia. Mathes. 3.

[1] Avide percurrit, cœpitque optare ut olim talem librum et ipse nancisci posset. M. Adami Vit. Luth. p. 103.

aged priest, who had watched with interest the student of Mansfeldt in his labours and in his academic career. Luther could not conceal the thoughts that occupied his mind. "Soon," said he, "I shall be called away from this world." But the old man kindly replied, "My dear bachelor, take courage; you will not die of this illness. Our God will yet make of you a man who, in turn, shall console many.[1] For God layeth his cross upon those whom he loveth, and they who bear it patiently acquire much wisdom." These words struck the young invalid. It was when he was so near death that he heard the voice of a priest remind him that God, as Samuel's mother said, raiseth up the miserable. The old man had poured sweet consolation into his heart, had revived his spirits; never will he forget it. "This was the first prediction that the worthy doctor heard," says Mathesius, Luther's friend, who records the fact, "and he often used to call it to mind." We may easily comprehend in what sense Mathesius calls these words a prediction.

When Luther recovered, there was a great change in him. The Bible, his illness, the words of the aged priest, seem to have made a new appeal to him: but as yet there was nothing decided in his mind. Another circumstance awakened serious thoughts within him. It was the festival of Easter, probably in the year 1503. Luther was going to pass a short time with his family, and wore a sword according to the custom of the age. He struck against it with his foot, the blade fell out, and cut one of the principal arteries. Luther, whose only companion had run off in haste to seek for assistance, finding himself alone, and seeing the blood flowing copiously without being able to check it, lay down on his back, and put his finger on the wound; but the blood escaped in despite of his exertions, and Luther, feeling the approach of death, cried out, "O Mary, help me!" At last a surgeon arrived from Erfurth, who bound up the cut. The wound opened in the night, and Luther fainted, again calling loudly upon the Virgin. "At that time," said he in after-years, "I should have died relying upon Mary." Erelong he abandoned that superstition, and invoked a more powerful Saviour. He continued his studies. In 1505 he was admitted M.A. and doctor of philosophy. The university of Erfurth was then the most celebrated in all Germany. The others were but inferior schools in comparison with it. The ceremony was conducted, as usual, with great pomp. A procession by torchlight came to pay honour to Luther.[2] The festival was magnificent. It was a general rejoicing. Luther, encouraged perhaps by these honours,

felt disposed to apply himself entirely to the law, in conformity with his father's wishes.

But the will of God was different. While Luther was occupied with various studies, and beginning to teach the physics and ethics of Aristotle, with other branches of philosophy, his heart ceased not from crying to him that religion was the one thing needful, and that above all things he should secure his salvation. He knew the displeasure that God manifests against sin; he called to mind the penalties that his Word denounces against the sinner; and he asked himself, with apprehension, whether he was sure of possessing the divine favour. His conscience answered, No! His character was prompt and decided: he resolved to do all that might ensure him a firm hope of immortality. Two events occurred, one after the other, to disturb his soul, and to hasten his resolution.

Among his university friends was one named Alexis, with whom he lived in the closest intimacy. One morning a report was spread in Erfurth that Alexis had been assassinated. Luther hastens to ascertain the truth of this rumour. This sudden loss of his friend agitated him, and the question he asked himself, What would become of me, if I were thus called away without warning? fills his mind with the keenest terrors.[1]

It was in the summer of the year 1505 that Luther, whom the ordinary university vacations left at liberty, resolved to go to Mansfeldt, to revisit the dear scenes of his childhood and to embrace his parents. Perhaps also he wished to open his heart to his father, to sound him on the plan that he was forming in his mind, and obtain his permission to engage in another profession. He foresaw all the difficulties that awaited him. The idle life of the majority of priests was displeasing to the active miner of Mansfeldt. Besides, the ecclesiastics were but little esteemed in the world; for the most part their revenues were scanty; and the father, who had made great sacrifices to maintain his son at the university, and who now saw him teaching publicly in a celebrated school, although only in his twentieth year, was not likely to renounce the proud hopes he had cherished.

We are ignorant of what passed during Luther's stay at Mansfeldt. Perhaps the decided wish of his father made him fear to open his heart to him. He again quitted his father's house to take his seat on the benches of the academy. He was already within a short distance of Erfurth, when he was overtaken by a violent storm, such as often occurs in these mountains. The lightning flashed—the bolt fell at his feet. Luther threw himself upon his knees. His hour, perhaps, is come. Death, the judgment, and eternity summon him with all their terrors.

[1] Deus te virum faciet qui alios multos iterum consolabitur. M. Adami Vit. Luth. p. 103.
[2] Luth. Opp. W. xxii. p. 2229.

[1] Interitu sodalis sui contristatus. Cochlœus, l.

and he hears a voice that he can no longer resist. "Encompassed with the anguish and terror of death," as he says himself,[1] he makes a vow, if the Lord delivers him from this danger, to abandon the world, and devote himself entirely to God. After rising from the ground, having still present to him that death which must one day overtake him, he examines himself seriously, and asks what he ought to do.[2] The thoughts that once agitated him now return with greater force. He has endeavoured, it is true, to fulfil all his duties, but what is the state of his soul? Can he appear before the tribunal of a terrible God with an impure heart? He must become holy. He has now as great a thirst for holiness, as he had formerly for knowledge. But where can he find it, or how can he attain it? The university provided him with the means of satisfying his first desires. Who shall calm that anguish —who shall quench the fire that now consumes him? To what school of holiness shall he direct his steps? He will enter a cloister: the monastic life will save him. Oftentimes has he heard speak of its power to transform the heart, to sanctify the sinner, to make man perfect! He will enter a monastic order. He will there become holy: thus will he secure eternal life.[3]

Such was the event that changed the calling, the whole destiny of Luther. In this we perceive the finger of God. It was his powerful hand that on the highway cast down the young master of arts, the candidate for the bar, the future lawyer, to give an entirely new direction to his life. Rubianus, one of Luther's friends at the university of Erfurth, wrote thus to him in after-life: "Divine Providence looked at what you were one day to become, when on your return from your parents, the fire from heaven threw you to the ground, like another Paul, near the city of Erfurth, and withdrawing you from our society, drove you into the Augustine order." Analagous circumstances have marked the conversion of the two greatest instruments that Divine Providence has made use of in the two greatest revolutions that have been effected upon the earth: Saint Paul and Luther.[4]

Luther re-enters Erfurth. His resolution is unalterable. Still it is not without a pang that he prepares to break the ties so dear to him. He communicates his intention to no one. But one evening he invites his university friends to a cheerful but frugal supper. Music once more enlivens their social meeting. It is Luther's farewell to the world. Henceforth, instead of these amiable companions of his pleasures and his studies, he will have monks; instead of this gay and witty conversation—the silence of the cloister; and for these merry songs—the solemn strains of the quiet chapel. God calls him, and he must sacrifice everything. Still, for the last time, let him share in the joys of his youth! The repast excites his friends: Luther himself is the soul of the party. But at the very moment that they are giving way without restraint to their gaiety, the young man can no longer control the serious thoughts that fill his mind. He speaks—he makes known his intention to his astonished friends. They endeavour to shake it, but in vain. And that very night Luther, fearful perhaps of their importunate solicitations, quits his lodgings. He leaves behind him all his clothes and books, taking with him only Virgil and Plautus; he had no Bible as yet. Virgil and Plautus! an epic poem and comedies! striking picture of Luther's mind! There had in effect taken place in him a whole epic—a beautiful, grand, and sublime poem; but as he had a disposition inclined to gaiety, wit, and humour, he combined more than one familiar feature with the serious and stately groundwork of his life.

Provided with these two books, he repairs alone, in the darkness of night, to the convent of the hermits of St. Augustine. He asks admittance. The gate opens and closes again. Behold him separated for ever from his parents, from the companions of his studies, and from the world! It was the 17th August 1505: Luther was then twenty-one years and nine months old.

CHAPTER III.

His Father's Anger—Pardon—Humiliations—The Sack and the Cell—Endurance—Luther's Studies—St. Augustine—Peter d'Ailly—Occam—Gerson—The chained Bible—Lyra—Hebrew and Greek—Daily Prayers—Asceticism—Mental Struggles—Luther during Mass—Useless Observances—Luther in a Fainting-fit.

LUTHER was with God at last. His soul was in safety. He was now about to find that holiness which he so much desired. The monks were astonished at the sight of the youthful doctor, and extolled his courage and his contempt of the world.[1] He did not, however, forget his friends. He wrote to them, bidding farewell to them and to the world; and on the next day he sent these letters, with the clothes he had worn till then, and returned to the university his ring of master of arts, that nothing might remind him of the world he had renounced.

---

[1] Mit Erschrecken und Angst des Todes umgeben. L. Epp. ii. 101.
[2] Cum esset in campo, fulminis ictu territus. Cochlœus, 1.
[3] Occasio autem fuit ingrediendi illud vitæ genus, quod pietati et studiis doctrinæ de Deo, existimavit esse convenientius. Mel. Vit. Luth.
[4] Some historians record that Alexis was killed by the thunderbolt that alarmed Luther; but two of his contemporaries, Mathesius (p. 4), and Selneccer (in Orat. de Luth.), distinguish between these two events; we may even add the testimony of Melancthon to theirs: he says—"Sodalem nescio quo casu interfectum." Vit. Luth.

[1] Hujus mundi contemptu, ingressus est repente, multis admirantibus, monasterium. Cochlœus, 1.

56

His friends at Erfurth were struck with astonishment. Must so eminent a genius go and hide himself in that monastic state, which is a partial death?[1] Filled with the liveliest sorrow, they hastily repair to the convent, in the hope of inducing Luther to retrace so afflicting a step: but all was useless. For two whole days they surrounded the convent and almost besieged it, in the hope of seeing Luther come forth. But the gates remained closely shut and barred. A month elapsed without any one being able to see or speak to the new monk.

Luther had also hastened to communicate to his parents the great change that had taken place in his life. His father was amazed. He trembled for his son, as Luther himself tells us in the dedication of his work on monastic vows addressed to his father. His weakness, his youth, the violence of his passions, all led John Luther to fear that when the first moment of enthusiasm was over, the idle habits of the cloister would make the young man fall either into despair or into some great sin. He knew that this kind of life had already been the destruction of many. Besides, the councillor-miner of Mansfeldt had formed very different plans for his son. He had hoped that he would contract a rich and honourable marriage. And now all his ambitious projects are overthrown in one night by this imprudent step.

John wrote a very angry letter to his son, in which he spoke to him in a contemptuous tone, as Luther informs us, while he had addressed him always in a friendly manner after he had taken his master-of-arts degree. He withdrew all his favour, and declared him disinherited from his paternal affection. In vain did his father's friends, and doubtless his wife, endeavour to soften him; in vain did they say: " If you would offer a sacrifice to God, let it be what you hold best and dearest,—even your son, your Isaac." The inexorable councillor of Mansfeldt would listen to nothing.

Not long after, however (as Luther tells us in a sermon preached at Wittemberg, 20th January 1544), the plague appeared, and deprived John Luther of two of his sons. About this time some one came and told the bereaved father, the monk of Erfurth is dead also !......His friends seized the opportunity of reconciling the father to the young novice. " If it should be a false alarm," said they to him, " at least sanctify your affliction by cordially consenting to your son's becoming a monk !"—" Well ! so be it !" replied John Luther, with a heart bruised, yet still half rebellious, " and God grant he may prosper !" Some time after this, when Luther, who had been reconciled to his father, related to him the event that had induced him to enter a monastic order : " God grant," replied the worthy miner, " that you may not have

taken for a sign from heaven what was merely a delusion of the devil."[1]

There was not then in Luther that which was afterwards to make him the reformer of the Church. Of this his entrance into the convent is a strong proof. It was a proceeding in conformity with the tendencies of the age from which he was soon to contribute his endeavours to liberate the Church. He who was destined to become the great teacher of the world, was as yet its slavish imitator. A new stone had been added to the edifice of superstition by the very man who was erelong to destroy it. Luther looked to himself for salvation, to human works and observances. He knew not that salvation cometh wholly from God. He sought after his own glory and righteousness, unmindful of the righteousness and glory of the Lord. But what he was ignorant of as yet, he learnt soon after. It was in the cloister of Erfurth that this immense transformation was brought about, which substituted in his heart God and his wisdom for the world and its traditions, and that prepared the mighty revolution of which he was to be the most illustrious instrument.

When Martin Luther entered the convent, he changed his name, and assumed that of Augustine.

The monks had received him with joy. It was no slight gratification to their vanity to see one of the most esteemed doctors of the age abandon the university for a house be longing to their order. Nevertheless they treated him harshly, and imposed on him the meanest occupations. They wished to humble the doctor of philosophy, and to teach him that his learning did not raise him above his brethren. They imagined, besides, by this means to prevent him from devoting himself so much to his studies, from which the convent could reap no advantage. The former master of arts had to perform the offices of porter, to open and shut the gates, to wind up the clock, to sweep the church, and to clean out the cells.[2] Then, when the poor monk, who was at once doorkeeper, sexton, and menial servant of the cloister, had finished his work : *Cum sacco per civitatem !* Away with your wallet through the town ! cried the friars ; and laden with his bread-bag, he wandered through all the streets of Erfurth, begging from house to house, obliged perhaps to present himself at the doors of those who had once been his friends or his inferiors. On his return, he had either to shut himself up in a low and narrow cell, whence he could see nothing but a small garden a few feet square, or recommence his humble tasks. But he put up with all. Naturally disposed to devote himself entirely to whatever he undertook, he

[1] Gott geb dass es nicht ein Betrug und teuflisch Gespenst sey ! L. Epp. ii. 101.
[2] Loca immunda purgare coactus est. M. Adami Vita Luth. p. 103.

57

had become a monk with all his soul. Besides, how could he have a thought of sparing his body, or have had any regard for what might please the flesh? It was not thus that he could acquire the humility, the sanctity which he had come to seek within the walls of the cloister.

The poor monk, oppressed with toil, hastened to employ in study all the moments that he could steal from these mean occupations. He voluntarily withdrew from the society of the brethren to give himself up to his beloved pursuits; but they soon found it out, and surrounding him with murmurs, tore him from his books, exclaiming, "Come, come! It is not by studying, but by begging bread, corn, eggs, fish, meat, and money that a monk renders himself useful to the cloister."[1] Luther submitted: he laid aside his books, and took up his bag again. Far from repenting at having taken upon himself such a yoke, he is willing to go through with his task. It was then that the inflexible perseverance with which he always carried out the resolutions he had once formed, began to be developed in his mind. The resistance he made to these rude assaults gave a stronger temper to his will. God tried him in small things, that he might learn to remain unshaken in great ones. Besides, to be able to deliver his age from the miserable superstitions under which it groaned, it was necessary for him first to feel their weight. To drain the cup, he must drink it to the very dregs.

This severe apprenticeship did not, however, last so long as Luther might have feared. The prior of the convent, at the intercession of the university to which Luther belonged, freed him from the humiliating duties that had been laid upon him. The youthful monk then returned to his studies with new zeal. The works of the Fathers of the Church, especially of St. Augustine, attracted his attention. The exposition of the Psalms by this illustrious doctor, and his book *On the Letter and the Spirit*, were his favourite study. Nothing struck him more than the sentiments of this Father on the corruption of man's will and on Divine Grace. He felt by his own experience the reality of that corruption and the necessity for that grace. The words of St. Augustine corresponded with the sentiments of his heart. If he could have belonged to any other school than that of Jesus Christ, it would undoubtedly have been to that of the doctor of Hippo. He almost knew by rote the works of Peter d'Ailly and of Gabriel Biel. He was much taken with a saying of the former, that, if the Church had not decided to the contrary, it would have been preferable to concede that the bread and wine were really taken in the Lord's supper, and not mere accidents.

He also carefully studied the theologians Occam and Gerson, who both express themselves so freely on the authority of the popes. To this course of reading he added other exercises. He was heard in the public discussions unravelling the most complicated trains of reasoning, and extricating himself from a labyrinth whence none but he could have found an outlet. All his auditors were filled with astonishment.[1]

But he had not entered the cloister to acquire the reputation of a great genius: it was to seek food for his piety.[2] He therefore regarded these labours as mere digressions.

He loved above all things to draw wisdom from the pure source of the Word of God. He found in the convent a Bible fastened by a chain, and to this chained Bible he was continually returning. He had but little understanding of the Word, yet was it his most pleasing study. It sometimes happened that he passed a whole day meditating upon a single passage. At other times he learned fragments of the Prophets by heart. He especially desired to acquire from the writings of the Prophets and of the Apostles a perfect knowledge of God's will; to grow up in greater fear of His name; and to nourish his faith by the sure testimony of the Word.[3]

It would appear that about this time he began to study the Scriptures in their original languages, and to lay the foundation of the most perfect and most useful of his labours—the translation of the Bible. He made use of Reuchlin's Hebrew Lexicon, that had just appeared. John Lange, one of the friars of the convent, a man skilled in Greek and Hebrew, and with whom he always remained closely connected, probably was his first instructor.[4] He also made much use of the learned commentaries of Nicholas Lyra, who died in 1340. It was from this circumstance that Pflug, afterwards bishop of Naumburg, said: *Si Lyra non lyrasset, Lutherus non saltasset.*[5]

The young monk studied with such industry and zeal that it often happened that he did not repeat the daily prayers for three or four weeks together. But he soon grew alarmed at the thought that he had transgressed the rules of his order. He then shut himself up to repair his negligence, and began to repeat conscientiously all the prayers he had omitted, without a thought of either eating or drinking. Once even, for seven weeks together, he scarcely closed his eyes in sleep.

Burning with desire to attain that holiness

[1] In disputationibus publicis labyrinthos aliis inextricabiles, disserte multis admirantibus explicabat. Melancth. Vita Luth.
[2] In eo vitæ genere non famam ingenii, sed alimenta pietatis quærebat. Ibid.
[3] Et firmis testimoniis aleret timorem et fidem. Ibid.
[4] Gesch. d. deutsch. Bibelübersetzung.
[5] If Lyra had not touched his lyre, Luther had never danced.

[1] Selncceri Orat. de Luth.—Mathesius, p. 5.

in quest of which he had entered the cloister, Luther gave way to all the rigour of an ascetic life. He endeavoured to crucify the flesh by fastings, mortifications, and watchings.[1] Shut up in his cell, as in a prison, he struggled unceasingly against the deceitful thoughts and the evil inclinations of his heart. A little bread and a small herring were often his only food. Besides, he was naturally of very abstemious habits. Thus he was frequently seen by his friends, long after he had ceased to think of purchasing heaven by his abstinence, content himself with the poorest viands, and remain even four days in succession without eating or drinking.[2] This we have on the testimony of Melancthon, a witness in every respect worthy of credit. We may judge from this circumstance of the little value we ought to attach to the fables that ignorance and prejudice have circulated as to Luther's intemperance. At the period of which we are speaking, nothing was too great a sacrifice that might enable him to become a saint —to acquire heaven. Never did the Romish church possess a more pious monk. Never did cloister witness more severe or indefatigable exertions to purchase eternal happiness.[3] When Luther had become a reformer, and had declared that heaven was not to be obtained by such means as these, he knew very well what he was saying. "I was indeed a pious monk," wrote he to Duke George of Saxony, "and followed the rules of my order more strictly than I can express. If ever monk could obtain heaven by his monkish works, I should certainly have been entitled to it. Of this all the friars who have known me can testify. If it had continued much longer, I should have carried my mortifications even to death, by means of my watchings, prayers, reading, and other labours."[4]

We are approaching the epoch which made Luther a new man, and which, by revealing to him the infinity of God's love, put him in a condition to declare it to the world.

Luther did not find in the tranquillity of the cloister and in monkish perfection that peace of mind which he had looked for there. He wished to have the assurance of his salvation : this was the great want of his soul. Without it, there was no repose for him. But the fears that had agitated him in the world pursue him to his cell. Nay, they were increased. The faintest cry of his heart re-echoed loud beneath the silent arches of the cloister. God had led him thither, that he might learn to know himself, and to despair of his own strength and virtue. His conscience, enlightened by the Divine Word,

told him what it was to be holy ; but he was filled with terror at finding, neither in his heart nor in his life, that image of holiness which he had contemplated with admiration in the Word of God. A sad discovery, and one that is made by every sincere man ! No righteousness within, no righteousness without ! all was omission, sin, impurity !...... The more ardent the character of Luther, the stronger was that secret and constant resistance which man's nature opposes to good ; and it plunged him into despair.

The monks and divines of the day encouraged him to satisfy the divine righteousness by meritorious works. But what works, thought he, can come from a heart like mine ? How can I stand before the holiness of my judge with works polluted in their very source ? "I saw that I was a great sinner in the eyes of God," said he, "and I did not think it possible for me to propitiate him by my own merits."

He was agitated and yet dejected, avoiding the trifling and stupid conversation of the monks. The latter, unable to comprehend the storms that tossed his soul, looked upon him with surprise,[1] and reproached him for his silence and his gloomy air. One day, Cochlœus tells us, as they were saying mass in the chapel, Luther had carried thither all his anxiety, and was in the choir in the midst of the brethren, sad and heart-stricken. Already the priest had prostrated himself, the incense had been burnt before the altar, the *Gloria* sung, and they were reading the Gospel, when the poor monk, unable any longer to repress his anguish, cried out in a mournful tone, as he fell on his knees, "It is not I—it is not I."[2] All were thunderstruck : and the ceremony was interrupted for a moment. Perhaps Luther thought he heard some reproach of which he knew himself innocent ; perhaps he declared his unworthiness of being one of those to whom Christ's death had brought the gift of eternal life. Cochlœus says, they were then reading the story of the dumb man from whom Christ expelled a devil. It is possible that this cry of Luther, if the account be true, had reference to this circumstance, and that, although speechless like the dumb man, he protested by such an exclamation, that his silence came from other causes than demoniacal possession. Indeed, Cochlœus tells us that the monks sometimes attributed the sufferings of their brother to a secret intercourse with the devil, and this writer himself entertained that opinion.[3]

A tender conscience inclined Luther to regard the slightest fault as a great sin. He had hardly discovered it, before he endeavoured to expiate it by the severest mortifications, which only served to point out to

---

[1] Summa disciplinæ severitate se ipse regit. et omnibus exercitiis lectionum, disputationum, jejuniorum, precum, omnes longe superat. Melancth. Vit. Luth.
[2] Erat enim natura, valde modici cibi et potus ; vidi continuis quatuor diebus, cum quidem recte valeret, prorsus nihil edentem aut bibentem. Ibid.
[3] Strenue in studiis et exercitiis spiritualibus, militavit ibi Deo annis quatuor. Cochlœus
[4] L. Opp. (W.) xix. 2299.

[1] Visus est fratribus non nihil singularitatis habere. Cochlœus, l.
[2] Cum......repente ceciderit vociferans, "Non sum ! non sum !" Ibid.
[3] Ex occulto aliquo cum dæmone commercio. Ibid.

him the inutility of all human remedies. "I tortured myself almost to death," said he, "in order to procure peace with God for my troubled heart and agitated conscience; but surrounded with thick darkness, I found peace nowhere."

The practices of monastic holiness, which had lulled so many consciences to sleep, and to which Luther himself had had recourse in his distress, soon appeared to him the unavailing remedies of an empirical and deceptive religion. "While I was yet a monk, I no sooner felt assailed by any temptation than I cried out—I am lost! Immediately I had recourse to a thousand methods to stifle the cries of my conscience. I went every day to confession, but that was of no use to me. Then bowed down by sorrow, I tortured myself by the multitude of my thoughts.—Look, exclaimed I, thou art still envious, impatient, passionate!...It profiteth thee nothing, O wretched man, to have entered this sacred order."

And yet Luther, imbued with the prejudices of his time, had from early youth considered the observances, whose worthlessness he had now discovered, as a certain remedy for diseased souls. What can he think of the strange discovery he has just made in the solitude of the cloister? It is possible, then, to dwell within the sanctuary, and yet bear in one's bosom a man of sin!......He has received another garment, but not another heart. His expectations are disappointed. Where can he stop? Can all these rules and observances be mere human inventions? Such a supposition appears to him, at one time, a temptation of the devil, and at another, an irresistible truth. By turns contending with the holy voice that spake to his heart, and with the venerable institutions that time had sanctioned, Luther passed his life in a continual struggle. The young monk crept like a shadow through the long galleries of the cloister, that re-echoed with his sorrowful moanings. His body wasted away; his strength began to fail him; it sometimes happened that he remained like one dead.[1]

On one occasion, overwhelmed with sorrow, he shut himself up in his cell, and for several days and nights allowed no one to approach him. One of his friends, Lucas Edemberger, feeling anxious about the unhappy monk, and having a presentiment of the condition in which he was, took with him some boys who were in the habit of singing in the choirs, and knocked at the door of the cell. No one opens—no one answers. The good Edemberger, still more alarmed, breaks open the door. Luther lies insensible upon the floor, and giving no signs of life. His friend strives in vain to recall him to his senses: he is still motionless.

Then the choristers begin to sing a sweet hymn. Their clear voices act like a charm on the poor monk, to whom music was ever one of his greatest pleasures: gradually he recovers his strength, his consciousness, and life.[1] But if music could restore his serenity for a few moments, he requires another and a stronger remedy to heal him thoroughly: he needs that mild and subtle sound[2] of the Gospel, which is the voice of God himself. He knew it well. And therefore his troubles and his terrors led him to study with fresh zeal the writings of the prophets and of the apostles.[3]

CHAPTER IV.

Pious Monks—Staupitz—His Piety—Visitation—Conversations—The Grace of Christ—Repentance—Power of Sin—Sweetness of Repentance— Election — Providence — The Bible—The aged Monk—Forgiveness of Sins—Ordination—The Dinner— Festival of Corpus Christi—Luther made Professor at Wittemberg.

LUTHER was not the first monk who had undergone such trials. The gloomy walls of the cloisters often concealed the most abominable vices, that would have made every upright mind shudder, had they been revealed; but often, also, they hid christian virtues that expanded there in silence, and which, had they been exposed to the eyes of the world, would have excited universal admiration. The possessors of these virtues, living only with themselves and with God, attracted no attention, and were often unknown to the modest convent in which they were enclosed: their lives were known only to God. Sometimes these humble solitaries fell into that mystic theology,—sad disease of the noblest minds! which in earlier ages had been the delight of the first monks on the banks of the Nile, and which unprofitably consumes the souls of those who become its victims.

Yet if one of these men was called to some high station, he there displayed virtues whose salutary influence was long and widely felt. The candle was set on a candlestick, and it illumined the whole house. Many were awakened by this light. Thus from generation to generation were these pious souls propagated; they were seen shining like isolated torches at the very times when the cloisters were often little other than impure receptacles of the deepest darkness.

A young man had been thus distinguished in one of the German convents. His name was John Staupitz, and he was descended from a noble Misnian family. From his

---

[1] Sæpe eum cogitantem attentius de ira Dei, aut de mirandis pœnarum exemplis, subito tanti terrores concutiebant, ut pene exanimaretur. Melancth. Vita Luth.

[1] Seckend. p. 53.   [2] 1 Kings xix. 12.
[3] Hoc studium ut magis expeteret, illis suis doloribus et pavoribus movebatur. Melancth. Vita Luth.

tenderest youth he had had a taste for knowledge and a love of virtue.[1] He felt the need of retirement to devote himself to letters. He soon discovered that philosophy and the study of nature could not do much towards eternal salvation. He therefore began to learn divinity; but especially endeavoured to unite practice with knowledge. "For," says one of his biographers, "it is in vain that we assume the name of divine, if we do not confirm that noble title by our lives."[2] The study of the Bible and of the Augustine theology, the knowledge of himself, the battles that he, like Luther, had had to fight against the deceits and lusts of his heart, led him to the Redeemer. He found peace to his soul in faith in Christ. The doctrine of election by grace had taken strong hold of his mind. The integrity of his life, the extent of his knowledge, the eloquence of his speech, not less than a striking exterior and dignified manners,[3] recommended him to his contemporaries. Frederick the Wise, elector of Saxony, made him his friend, employed him in various embassies, and founded the university of Wittemberg under his direction. This disciple of St. Paul and St. Augustine was the first dean of the theological faculty of that school whence the light was one day to issue to illumine the schools and churches of so many nations. He was present at the Lateran council, as proxy of the Archbishop of Saltzburg, became provincial of his order in Thuringia and Saxony, and afterwards vicar-general of the Augustines for all Germany.

Staupitz was grieved at the corruption of morals and the errors of doctrine that were devastating the Church. His writings on the love of God, on christian faith, and on conformity with the death of Christ, and the testimony of Luther, confirm this. But he considered the former evil of more importance than the latter. Besides the mildness and indecision of his character, his desire not to go beyond the sphere of action he thought assigned to him, made him fitter to be the restorer of a convent than the reformer of the Church. He would have wished to raise none but distinguished men to important offices; but not finding them, he submitted to employ others. "We must plough," said he, " with such horses as we can find; and with oxen, if there are no horses."[4]

We have witnessed the anguish and the internal struggles to which Luther was a prey in the convent of Erfurth. At this period a visitation of the vicar-general was announced. In fact Staupitz came to make his usual inspection. This friend of Frederick, the founder of the university of Wittemberg, and chief of the Augustines, exhibited much kindness to those monks who were under his authority. One of these brothers soon attracted his attention. He was a young man of middle height, whom study, fasting, and prolonged vigils had so wasted away that all his bones might be counted.[1] His eyes, that in after-years were compared to a falcon's, were sunken; his manner was dejected; his countenance betrayed an agitated mind, the prey of a thousand struggles, but yet strong and resolute. His whole appearance was grave, melancholy, and solemn: Staupitz, whose discernment had been exercised by long experience, easily discovered what was passing in his mind, and distinguished the youthful monk above all who surrounded him. He felt drawn towards him, had a presentiment of his great destiny, and entertained quite a paternal interest for his inferior. He had had to struggle, like Luther, and therefore he could understand him. Above all, he could point out to him the road to peace, which he himself had found. What he learnt of the circumstances that had brought the young Augustine into the convent, still more increased his sympathy. He requested the prior to treat him with greater mildness, and took advantage of the opportunities afforded by his station to win the confidence of the youthful brother. Approaching him with affection, he endeavoured by every means to dispel his timidity, which was increased by the respect and fear that a man of such exalted rank as Staupitz must necessarily inspire.

Luther's heart, which harsh treatment had closed till then, opened at last and expanded under the mild beams of charity. "As in water face answereth to face, so the heart of man to man."[2] Luther's heart found an echo in that of Staupitz. The vicar-general understood him, and the monk felt a confidence towards him, that he had as yet experienced for none. He unbosomed to him the cause of his dejection, described the horrible thoughts that perplexed him, and then began in the cloister of Erfurth those conversations so full of wisdom and of instruction. Up to this time no one had understood Luther. One day, when at table in the refectory, the young monk, dejected and silent, scarcely touched his food. Staupitz, who looked earnestly at him, said at last, "Why are you so sad, brother Martin?"— "Ah!" replied he, with a deep sigh, "I do not know what will become of me!"— "These temptations," resumed Staupitz, "are more necessary to you than eating and drinking." These two men did not stop there; and erelong in the silence of the cloister took place that intimate intercourse, which powerfully contributed to lead forth the future reformer from his state of darkness.

[1] A. teneris unguiculis, generoso animi impetu, ad virtutem et eruditam doctrinam contendit. Melch. Adam. Vita Staupizii.
[2] Ibid.
[3] Corporis forma atque statura conspicuus. Cochlœus, 3.
[4] L. Opp. (W.) v. 2819.

[1] P. Mosellani Epist.   [2] Proverbs xxvii. 19.

"It is in vain," said Luther despondingly to Staupitz, "that I make promises to God: sin is ever the strongest."

"O my friend!" replied the vicar-general, looking back on his own experience; "more than a thousand times have I sworn to our holy God to live piously, and I have never kept my vows. Now I swear no longer, for I know I cannot keep my solemn promises. If God will not be merciful towards me for the love of Christ, and grant me a happy departure, when I must quit this world, I shall never, with the aid of all my vows and all my good works, stand before him. I must perish."[1]

The young monk is terrified at the thought of divine justice. He lays open all his fears to the vicar-general. He is alarmed at the unspeakable holiness of God and his sovereign majesty. "Who may abide the day of his coming? and who shall stand when he appeareth?" (Mal. iii. 2.)

Staupitz resumes: he knows where he had found peace, and he will point it out to the young man. "Why," said he, "do you torment yourself with all these speculations and these high thoughts?......Look at the wounds of Jesus Christ, to the blood that he has shed for you: it is there that the grace of God will appear to you. Instead of torturing yourself on account of your sins, throw yourself into the Redeemer's arms. Trust in him—in the righteousness of his life—in the atonement of his death. Do not shrink back; God is not angry with you, it is you who are angry with God. Listen to the Son of God. He became man to give you the assurance of divine favour. He says to you, You are my sheep; you hear my voice; no man shall pluck you out of my hand."[2]

But Luther does not find in himself the repentance which he thinks necessary for salvation: and replies he, it is the usual answer of distressed and timid minds: "How can I dare believe in the favour of God, so long as there is no real conversion in me? I must be changed, before he will accept me."

His venerable guide shows him that there can be no real conversion, so long as man fears God as a severe judge. "What will you say then," asks Luther, "to so many consciences to which a thousand insupportable tasks are prescribed in order that they may gain heaven?"

Then he hears this reply of the vicar-general, or rather he does not believe that it comes from man: it seems to him like a voice from heaven.[3] "There is no real repentance except that which begins with the love of God and of righteousness.[4] What others imagine to be the end and accomplishment of repentance, is on the contrary only

its beginning. In order that you may be filled with the love of what is good, you must first be filled with love for God. If you desire to be converted, do not be curious about all these mortifications and all these tortures. Love him who first loved you!"

Luther listens—he listens again. These consolations fill him with joy till then unknown, and impart new light. "It is Jesus Christ," thinks he in his heart: "yes, it is Jesus Christ himself who so wonderfully consoles me by these sweet and healing words."[1]

These words, indeed, penetrated to the bottom of the young monk's heart, like the sharp arrow of a strong man.[2] In order to repent, we must love God. Guided by this new light, he begins to compare the Scriptures. He looks out all the passages that treat of repentance and conversion. These words, till then so dreaded, to use his own expression, "are become to him an agreeable pastime and the sweetest of recreations. All the passages of Scripture that used to alarm him, seem now to run to him from every part,—to smile and sport around him."[3]

"Hitherto," exclaims he, "although I carefully dissembled the state of my soul before God, and endeavoured to express towards him a love which was a mere constraint and a fiction, there was no expression in Scripture so bitter to me as that of repentance. But now there is none so sweet or more acceptable.[4] Oh! how delightful are all God's precepts when we read them not only in books, but also in our Saviour's precious wounds!"[5]

Although Luther had been consoled by Staupitz' words, he nevertheless fell sometimes into despondency. Sin was again felt in his timid conscience, and then all his previous despair banished the joy of salvation. "O my sin! my sin! my sin!" cried the young monk one day in the presence of the vicar-general, with a tone of profound anguish. "Well! would you only be a sinner in appearance," replied the latter, "and have also a Saviour only in appearance? Then," added Staupitz with authority, "know that Jesus Christ is the Saviour even of those who are great, real sinners, and deserving of utter condemnation."

It was not alone the sin he discovered in his heart that agitated Luther; the troubles of his conscience were augmented by those of reason. If the holy precepts of the Bible alarmed him, some of the doctrines of that divine book still more increased his tortures.

[1] L. Opp. (W.) viii. 2725.   [2] Ibid. ii. 264.
[3] Te velut e cœlo sonantem accepimus. L. Epp. i. 115. ad Staupitzium, 30 May, 1518.
[4] Pœnitentia vero non est, nisi quæ ab amore justitiæ et Dei incipit, &c. Ibid.

[1] Memini inter jucundissimas et salutares fabulas tuas, quibus me solet Dominus Jesus mirifice consolari. L. Epp. i. 115. ad Staupitzium, 30 May, 1518.
[2] Hæsit hoc verbum tuum in me, sicut sagitta potentis acuta. Ibid.
[3] Ecce jucundissimum ludum, verba undique mihi colludebant, planeque huic sententiæ arridebant et assultabant. L. Epp. i. 115.
[4] Nunc nihil dulcius aut gratius mihi sonet quam pœnitentia, &c. Ibid.
[5] Ita enim dulcescunt præcepta Dei, quando non in libris tantum, sed in vulneribus dulcissimi Salvatoris legenda intelligimus. Ibid.

The Truth, which is the great medium by which God confers peace on man, must necessarily begin by taking away from him the false security that destroys him. The doctrine of Election particularly disturbed the young man, and launched him into a boundless field of inquiry. Must he believe that it was man who first chose God for his portion, or that God first elected man? The Bible, history, daily experience, the works of Augustine,—all had shown him that we must always and in every case ascend to that first cause, to that sovereign will by which every thing exists, and on which every thing depends. But his ardent spirit would have desired to go still further; he would have wished to penetrate into the secret councils of God, unveiled his mysteries, seen the invisible, and comprehended the incomprehensible. Staupitz checked him. He told him not to presume to fathom the hidden God, but to confine himself to what he has manifested to us in Jesus Christ. " Look at Christ's wounds," said he, " and then will you see God's counsel towards man shine brightly forth. We cannot understand God out of Jesus Christ. In him, the Lord has said, you will find what I am, and what I require. Nowhere else, neither in heaven nor in earth, will you discover it."[1]

The vicar-general did still more. He showed Luther the paternal designs of Providence in permitting these temptations and these various struggles that his soul was to undergo. He made him view them in a light well calculated to revive his courage. By such trials God prepares for himself the souls that he destines for some important work. We must prove the vessel before we launch it into the wide sea. If there is an education necessary for every man, there is a particular one for those who are destined to act upon their generation. This is what Staupitz represented to the monk of Erfurth. " It is not in vain," said he to him, " that God exercises you in so many conflicts: you will see that he will employ you, as his servant, for great purposes."

These words, to which Luther listened with astonishment and humility, inspired him with courage, and led him to discover strength in himself which he had not even suspected. The wisdom and prudence of an enlightened friend gradually revealed the strong man to himself. Staupitz went further: he gave him many valuable directions for his studies, exhorting him, henceforward, to derive all his theology from the Bible, and to put away the systems of the schools. " Let the study of the Scriptures," said he, " be your favourite occupation." Never was good advice better followed out. What particularly delighted Luther, was the present Staupitz made him of a Bible: but it was not that Latin one, bound in red leather, the pro-

perty of the convent, and which it was all his desire to possess, and to be able to carry about with him, because he was so familiar with its pages, and knew where to find each passage.[1] Nevertheless, at length he is master of the treasure of God. Henceforward he studies the Scriptures, and especially the epistles of St. Paul, with ever-increasing zeal. To these he adds the works of St. Augustine alone. All that he reads is imprinted deeply in his mind. His struggles have prepared his heart to understand the Word. The soil has been ploughed deep: the incorruptible seed sinks into it with power. When Staupitz quitted Erfurth, a new dawn had risen upon Luther.

But the work was not yet finished. The vicar-general had prepared the way: God reserved its accomplishment for an humbler instrument. The conscience of the young Augustine had not yet found repose. His body gave way at last under the conflict and the tension of his soul. He was attacked by an illness that brought him to the brink of the grave. This was in the second year of his abode in the convent. All his distresses and all his fears were aroused at the approach of death. His own impurity and the holiness of God again disturbed his mind. One day, as he lay overwhelmed with despair, an aged monk entered his cell, and addressed a few words of comfort to him. Luther opened his heart to him, and made known the fears by which he was tormented. The venerable old man was incapable of following up that soul in all its doubts, as Staupitz had done; but he knew his *Credo*, and had found in it much consolation to his heart. He will therefore apply the same remedy to his young brother. Leading him back to that Apostles' creed which Luther had learnt in early childhood at the school of Mansfeldt, the aged monk repeated this article with kind good-nature: *I believe in the forgiveness of sins.* These simple words, which the pious brother pronounced with sincerity in this decisive moment, diffused great consolation in Luther's heart. " I believe," he repeated to himself erelong on his bed of sickness, " I believe in the forgiveness of sins!"—"Ah!" said the monk, " you must believe not only in the forgiveness of David's and of Peter's sins, for this even the devils believe. It is God's command that we believe our own sins are forgiven us."[2] How delightful did this commandment seem to poor Luther! " Hear what St. Bernard says in his discourse on the Annunciation," added the aged brother: " The testimony of the Holy Ghost in thy heart is this: Thy sins are forgiven thee."

From this moment light sprung up in the heart of the young monk of Erfurth. The word of grace had been pronounced: he had

[1] L. Opp. (W.) xxii. 489.

[1] Seckend. p. 52.
[2] Davidi aut Petro....Sed mandatum Dei esse, ut singuli homines nobis remitti peccata credamus. Melancth. Vita Luth.

believed in it. He disclaims all merit of salvation, and resigns himself confidingly to the grace of God in Jesus Christ. He does not at first perceive the consequences of the principle he has admitted; he is still sincere in his attachment to the Church, and yet he has no further need of her; for he has received salvation immediately from God himself, and henceforth Roman-catholicism is virtually destroyed in him. He advances,—he seeks in the writings of the apostles and prophets for all that can strengthen the hope which fills his heart. Each day he invokes support from on high, and each day also the light increases in his soul.

Luther's mental health restored that of his body, and he soon rose from his bed of sickness. He had received a new life in a twofold sense. The festival of Christmas, that soon came, gave him an opportunity of abundantly tasting all the consolations of faith. He took part in these holy solemnities with sweet emotion; and when in the ceremonial of the day he had to chant these words: *O beata culpa quœ talem meruisti Redemptorem!*[1] his whole being responded *Amen*, and thrilled with joy.

Luther had been two years in the cloister, and was to be ordained priest. He had received much, and saw with delight the prospect afforded by the sacerdotal office of freely distributing what he had freely received. He wished to take advantage of the ceremony that was about to take place to become thoroughly reconciled with his father. He invited him to be present, and even requested him to fix the day. John Luther, who was not yet entirely pacified with regard to his son, nevertheless accepted the invitation, and named Sunday, 2d May, 1507.

Among the number of Luther's friends was the vicar of Eisenach, John Braun, who had been a faithful counsellor to him during his residence in that city. Luther wrote to him on the 22d April. This is the oldest letter of the reformer, and it bears the following address: "To John Braun, holy and venerable priest of Christ and of Mary." It is only in Luther's two earliest letters that the name of Mary is found.

"God, who is glorious and holy in all his works," says the candidate for the priesthood, "having most graciously condescended to raise me up—me, a wretched and in all respects unworthy sinner, and to call me by his sole and most free mercy to his sublime ministry; I ought, in order to testify my gratitude for such divine and magnificent goodness (as far at least as mere dust and ashes can do it) to fulfil with my whole heart the duties of the office intrusted to me."

At last the day arrived. The miner of Mansfeldt did not fail to be present at his son's ordination. He gave him indeed no unequivocal mark of his affection and of his generosity by presenting him on this occasion with twenty florins.

The ceremony took place. Hieronymus, bishop of Brandenburg, officiated. At the moment of conferring on Luther the power of celebrating mass, he placed the chalice in his hands, and uttered these solemn words, *Accipe potestatem sacrificandi pro vivis et mortuis:* "Receive the power of sacrificing for the quick and the dead." Luther at that time listened calmly to these words, which conferred on him the power of doing the work of the Son of God; but he shuddered at them in after-years. "If the earth did not then open and swallow us both up," said he, "it was owing to the great patience and long-suffering of the Lord."[1]

The father afterwards dined at the convent with his son, the young priest's friends, and the monks. The conversation fell on Martin's entrance into the monastery. The brothers loudly extolled it as a most meritorious work; upon which the inflexible John, turning to his son, asked him: "Have you not read in Scripture, that you should obey your father and mother?"[2] These words struck Luther; they presented in quite a new aspect the action that had brought him into the bosom of the convent, and they long re-echoed in his heart.

Shortly after his ordination, Luther, by the advice of Staupitz, made little excursions on foot into the neighbouring parishes and convents, either to divert his mind and give his body the necessary exercise, or to accustom him to preaching.

The festival of Corpus Christi was to be celebrated with great pomp at Eisleben. The vicar-general would be present, and Luther repaired there also. He had still need of Staupitz, and sought every opportunity of meeting this enlightened guide who directed his soul into the path of life. The procession was numerous and brilliant. Staupitz himself bore the consecrated host, Luther following in his sacerdotal robes. The thought that it was Jesus Christ himself whom the vicar-general carried, the idea that the Saviour was there in person before him, suddenly struck Luther's imagination, and filled him with such terror that he could scarcely proceed. The perspiration fell drop by drop from his face; he staggered, and thought he should die of anguish and affright. At length the procession was over; the host, that had awakened all the fears of the monk, was solemnly deposited in the sanctuary; and Luther, finding himself alone with Staupitz, fell into his arms and confessed his dread. Then the good vicar-general, who had long known that gentle Saviour, who does not break the bruised reed, said to him mildly: "It was not Jesus Christ, my brother; he

[1] Oh blessed fault, that has merited such a Redeemer! Mathesius, p. 5.

[1] Opp. xvi. (W.) 1144.   [2] Ei, hast du nicht auch gehört dass man Eltern soll gehorsam seyn. L. Epp. ii. 101.

64

does not alarm; he gives consolation only." [1]

Luther was not destined to remain hidden in an obscure convent. The time was come for his removal to a wider stage. Staupitz, with whom he always remained in close communication, saw clearly that the young monk's disposition was too active to be confined within so narrow a circle. He spoke of him to the Elector Frederick of Saxony: and this enlightened prince invited Luther in 1508, probably about the end of the year, to become professor at the university of Wittemberg. This was the field on which he was to fight many hard battles. Luther felt that his true vocation was there. He was requested to repair to his new post with all speed: he replied to the call without delay, and in the hurry of his removal he had not time to write to him whom he styled his master and well-beloved father,—John Braun, curate of Eisenach. He did so however a few months later. "My departure was so hasty," said he, "that those with whom I was living were almost ignorant of it. I am farther away, I confess: but the better part of me remains with you." [2] Luther had been three years in the cloister at Erfurth.

CHAPTER V.

The University of Wittemberg—First Instructions—Biblical Lectures—Sensation—Luther preaches at Wittemberg—The Old Chapel—Impression produced by his Sermons.

In the year 1502, Frederick the Elector founded a new university at Wittemberg. He declared in the charter confirming the privileges of this high school, that he and his people would look to it as to an oracle. At that time he had little thought in how remarkable a manner this language would be verified. Two men belonging to the opposition that had been formed against the scholastic system,—Pollich of Mellerstadt, doctor of medicine, law, and philosophy, and Staupitz—had had great influence in the establishment of this academy. The university declared that it selected St. Augustine for its patron,—a choice that was very significant. This new institution, which possessed great liberty, and which was considered as a court of final appeal in all cases of difficulty, was admirably fitted to become the cradle of the Reformation, and it powerfully contributed to the development of Luther and of Luther's work.

On his arrival at Wittemberg, he repaired to the Augustine convent, where a cell was allotted to him; for though a professor, he did not cease to be a monk. He had been

called to teach physics and dialectics. In assigning him this duty, regard had probably been paid to the philosophical studies he had pursued at Erfurth, and to the degree of Master of Arts which he had taken. Thus Luther, who hungered and thirsted after the Word of God, was compelled to devote himself almost exclusively to the study of the Aristotelian scholastic philosophy. He had need of that bread of life which God gives to the world, and yet he must occupy himself with human subtleties. What a restraint! and what sighs it called forth! "By God's grace, I am well," wrote he to Braun, "except that I have to study philosophy with all my might. From the first moment of my arrival at Wittemberg, I was earnestly desirous of exchanging it for that of theology; but," added he, lest it should be supposed he meant the theology of the day, "it is of a theology which seeks the kernel in the nut, the wheat in the husk, the marrow in the bones, that I am speaking. [1] Be that as it may, God is God," continues he with that confidence which was the soul of his life; "man is almost always mistaken in his judgments; but this is our God. He will lead us with goodness for ever and ever." The studies that Luther was then obliged to pursue were of great service to him, in enabling him in after-years to combat the errors of the schoolmen.

But he could not stop there. The desire of his heart was about to be accomplished. That same power, which some years before had driven Luther from the bar into a monastic life, was now impelling him from philosophy towards the Bible. He zealously applied himself to the acquisition of the ancient languages, and particularly of Greek and Hebrew, in order to draw knowledge and learning from the very springs whence they gushed forth. He was all his life indefatigable in labour. [2] A few months after his arrival at the university, he solicited the degree of bachelor of divinity. He obtained it at the end of March 1509, with the particular summons to devote himself to biblical theology,—ad Biblia.

Every day, at one in the afternoon, Luther was called to lecture on the Bible: a precious hour both for the professor and his pupils, and which led them deeper and deeper into the divine meaning of those revelations so long lost to the people and to the schools!

He began his course by explaining the Psalms, and thence passed to the Epistle to the Romans. It was more particularly while meditating on this portion of Scripture, that the light of truth penetrated his heart. In the retirement of his quiet cell, he used to consecrate whole hours to the study of the

---

[1] Theologia quæ nucleum nucis, et medullam tritici, et medullam ossium scrutatur. L. Epp. i. 6.
[2] In studiis literarum, corpore ac mente indefessus. Pallavicini, Hist. Conc. Trident. i. 16

[.] Es ist nicht Christus, denn Christus schreckt nicht, sondern tröstet nur. L. Opp. (W.) xxii. pp. 513, 724.
[2] L. Epp. i. p. 5. March 17, 1509.

Divine Word, this epistle of St. Paul lying open before him. On one occasion, having reached the seventeenth verse of the first chapter, he read this passage from the prophet Habakkuk : *The just shall live by faith.* This precept struck him. There is then for the just a life different from that of other men : and this life is the gift of faith. This promise, which he received into his heart, as if God himself had placed it there, unveils to him the mystery of the christian life, and increases this life in him. Years after, in the midst of his numerous occupations, he imagined he still heard these words : The just shall live by faith.[1]

Luther's lectures thus prepared had little similarity with what had been heard till then. It was not an eloquent rhetorician or a pedantic schoolman that spoke ; but a Christian who had felt the power of revealed truths,—who drew them forth from the Bible,—poured them out from the treasures of his heart,—and presented them all full of life to his astonished hearers. It was not the teaching of a man, but of God.

This entirely new method of expounding the truth made a great noise ; the news of it spread far and wide, and attracted to the newly established university a crowd of youthful foreign students. Even many professors attended Luther's lectures, and among others Mellerstadt, frequently styled *the light of the world,* first rector of the university, who already at Leipsic, where he had been previously, had earnestly combated the ridiculous instructions of scholasticism, had denied that "the light created on the first day was Theology," and had maintained that the study of literature should be the foundation of that science. "This monk," said he, "will put all the doctors to shame ; he will bring in a new doctrine, and reform the whole church ; for he builds upon the Word of Christ, and no one in the world can either resist or overthrow that Word, even should he attack it with all the arms of philosophy, of the sophists, Scotists, Albertists, Thomists, and with all the Tartaretus."[2]

Staupitz, who was the instrument of God to develop all the gifts and treasures hidden in Luther, requested him to preach in the church of the Augustines. The young professor shrunk from this proposal. He desired to confine himself to his academical duties, he trembled at the thought of increasing them by those of the ministry. In vain did Staupitz solicit him : "No ! no !" replied he, "it is no slight thing to speak before men in the place of God."[3] What affecting humility in this great reformer of the Church ! Staupitz persisted ; but the ingenious Luther, says one of his biographers, found fifteen

arguments, pretexts, and evasions to defend himself against this invitation. At length, the chief of the Augustines persevering in his attack, Luther said : "Ah, doctor, by doing this you deprive me of life. I shall not be able to hold out three months."—"Well ! so be it in God's name," replied the vicar-general, "for our Lord God has also need on high of devoted and skilful men." Luther was forced to yield.

In the middle of the square at Wittemberg stood an ancient wooden chapel, thirty feet long and twenty wide, whose walls propped up on all sides were falling into ruin. An old pulpit made of planks, and three feet high, received the preacher. It was in this wretched place that the preaching of the Reformation began. It was God's will that that which was to restore his glory should have the humblest beginnings. The foundations of the new Augustine Church had just been laid, and in the meanwhile this miserable place of worship was made use of. "This building," adds Myconius, one of Luther's contemporaries, who records these circumstances, "may well be compared to the stable in which Christ was born. It was in this wretched enclosure, that God willed, so to speak, that his well-beloved Son should be born a second time. Among those thousands of cathedrals and parish churches with which the world is filled, there was not one at that time which God chose for the glorious preaching of eternal life."

Luther preaches : every thing is striking in the new minister. His expressive countenance, his noble air, his clear and sonorous voice, captivate all his hearers. Before his time, the majority of preachers had sought rather what might amuse their congregation, than what would convert them. The great seriousness that pervaded all Luther's sermons, and the joy with which the knowledge of the Gospel had filled his heart, imparted to his eloquence an authority, a warmth, and an unction that his predecessors had not possessed. "Endowed with a ready and lively genius," says one of his opponents,[1] "with a good memory, and employing his mother tongue with wonderful facility, Luther was inferior to none of his contemporaries in eloquence. Speaking from the pulpit, as if he were agitated by some violent emotion, suiting the action to his words, he affected his hearers' minds in a surprising manner, and carried them like a torrent wherever he pleased. So much strength, grace, and eloquence are rarely found in these children of the North."—"He had," says Bossuet, "a lively and impetuous eloquence that charmed and led away the people."[2]

Soon the little chapel could not hold the hearers who crowded to it. The council of Wittemberg then nominated Luther their

[1] Seckend., p. 55.
[2] Melch. Adam. Vita Lutheri. 104.—The *Tartaretus, Sermones Discipuli,* and *Dormi securè,* were favourite works with the scholastic divines in the Middle Ages.
[3] Fabricius centifol. Luth. 33.—Math. 6.

[1] Florimond Raymond, Hist. Hæres., cap. 5.
[2] Hist. des Variations, l.

chaplain, and invited him to preach in the city church. The impression he there produced was greater still. The energy of his genius, the eloquence of his style, and the excellency of the doctrines that he proclaimed, equally astonished his hearers. His reputation extended far and wide, and Frederick the Wise himself came once to Wittemberg to hear him.

This was the beginning of a new life for Luther. The slothfulness of the cloister had been succeeded by great activity. Freedom, labour, the earnest and constant action to which he could now devote himself at Wittemberg, succeeded in re-establishing harmony and peace within him. Now he was in his place, and the work of God was soon to display its majestic progress.

CHAPTER VI.

Journey to Rome—Convent on the Po—Sickness at Bologna—Recollections of Rome—Julius II.—Superstitious Devotion—Profanity of the Clergy—Conversations—Roman Scandals—Biblical Studies—Pilate's Staircase—Effects on Luther's Faith and on the Reformation—Gate of Paradise—Luther's Confession.

LUTHER was teaching both in the academical hall and in the church, when he was interrupted in his labours. In 1510, or according to others in 1511 or 1512, he was sent to Rome. Seven convents of his order were at variance on certain points with the vicar-general.[1] The acuteness of Luther's mind, his powerful language, and his talents for discussion, were the cause of his selection as agent for these seven monasteries before the pope.[2] This divine dispensation was necessary for Luther. It was requisite that he should know Rome. Full of the prejudices and delusions of the cloister, he had always imagined it to be the abode of sanctity.

He set out and crossed the Alps. But he had scarcely descended into the plains of the rich and voluptuous Italy, before he found at every step subjects of astonishment and scandal. The poor German monk was entertained in a wealthy convent of the Benedictines on the banks of the Po, in Lombardy. The revenues of this monastery amounted to 36,000 ducats; 12,000 were devoted to the table, 12,000 were set apart for the buildings, and the remainder for the wants of the monks.[3] The splendour of the apartments, the richness of their dress, and the delicacy of their food, confounded Luther. Marble, silk, luxury in all its forms—what a novel sight for the humble brother of the poor convent of Wittemberg! He was astonished and was silent; but when Friday came, what was his surprise at seeing the Benedictine table groaning under a load of meat. Upon this he resolved to speak. "The Church and the pope," said he, "forbid such things." The Benedictines were irritated at this reprimand of the unpolished German. But Luther having persisted, and perhaps threatened to make their irregularities known, some thought the simplest course would be to get rid of their importunate guest. The porter of the convent forewarned him of the danger he incurred by a longer stay. He accordingly quitted this epicurean monastery, and reached Bologna, where he fell dangerously ill. Some have attributed this to the effects of poison; but it is more reasonable to suppose that the change of diet affected the frugal monk of Wittemberg, whose usual food was bread and herrings. This sickness was not to be unto death, but to the glory of God. He again relapsed into the sorrow and dejection so natural to him. To die thus, far from Germany, under this burning sky, and in a foreign land—what a sad fate! The distress of mind that he had felt at Erfurth returned with fresh force. The sense of his sinfulness troubled him; the prospect of God's judgment filled him with dread. But at the very moment that these terrors had reached their highest pitch, the words of St. Paul, that had already struck him at Wittemberg, *The just shall live by faith,* recurred forcibly to his memory, and enlightened his soul like a ray from heaven. Thus restored and comforted, he soon regained his health, and resumed his journey towards Rome, expecting to find there a very different manner of life from that of the Lombard convents, and impatient to efface, by the sight of Roman holiness, the melancholy impressions left on his mind by his sojourn on the banks of the Po.

At length, after a toilsome journey under a burning Italian sun, at the beginning of summer, he drew near the seven-hilled city. His heart was moved within him: his eyes sought after the queen of the world and of the Church. As soon as he discovered the eternal city in the distance,—the city of St. Peter and St. Paul,—the metropolis of Catholicism,—he fell on his knees, exclaiming, "Holy Rome, I salute thee!"[1]

Luther is in Rome: the Wittemberg professor stands in the midst of the eloquent ruins of consular and imperial Rome—of the Rome of so many martyrs and confessors of Jesus Christ. Here had lived that Plautus and that Virgil whose works he had carried with him into the cloister, and all those great men at whose history his heart had so often beat with emotion. He beholds their statues,—the ruins of the monuments that bear witness to their glory. But all that glory—all that power has fled; his feet

[1] Quod septem conventus a vicario in quibusdam dissentirent. Cochlœus, 2.
[2] Quod esset acer ingenio et ad contradicendum audax et vehemens. Ibid.
[3] L. Opp. (W.) xxii. 1468.

[1] Matth. Dresser. Hist. Lutheri.

trample on their dust. At each step he calls to mind the sad presentiments of Scipio shedding tears as he looked upon the ruins—the burning palaces and tottering walls of Carthage, and exclaimed, "Thus will it one day be with Rome!" "And in truth," said Luther, "the Rome of the Scipios and Cæsars has become a corpse. There are such heaps of rubbish that the foundations of the houses are now where once stood the roofs. It is there," added he, as he threw a melancholy glance over these ruins, "it is there that once the riches and the treasures of the world were gathered together."[1] All these fragments, against which his feet stumble at every step, proclaim to Luther within the very walls of Rome, that what is strongest in the eyes of man may be easily destroyed by the breath of the Lord.

But with these profane ashes are mingled other and holier ones: he recals them to mind. The burial-place of the martyrs is not far from that of the generals of Rome and of her conquerors. Christian Rome with its sufferings has more power over the heart of the Saxon monk than pagan Rome with all its glory. Here that letter arrived in which Paul wrote, *The just shall live by faith.* He is not far from Appii Forum and the Three Taverns. Here is the house of Narcissus—there the palace of Cæsar, where the Lord delivered the Apostle from the jaws of the lion. Oh, how these recollections strengthen the heart of the monk of Wittemberg!

But Rome at this time presented a very different aspect. The warlike Julius II. filled the papal chair, and not Leo X., as some distinguished German historians have said, doubtless through inattention. Luther has often related a trait in the character of this pope. When the news reached him that his army had been defeated by the French before Ravenna, he was repeating his daily prayers: he flung away the book, exclaiming with a terrible oath: "And thou too art become a Frenchman...... Is it thus thou dost protect thy Church?......" Then turning in the direction of the country to whose arms he thought to have recourse, he added: "Saint Switzer, pray for us!"[2] Ignorance, levity, and dissolute manners, a profane spirit, a contempt for all that is sacred, a scandalous traffic in divine things—such was the spectacle afforded by this unhappy city. Yet the pious monk remained for some time longer in his delusions.

Having arrived about the period of the feast of St. John, he heard the Romans repeating around him a proverb current among them: "Happy the mother whose son performs mass on St. John's eve!"—"Oh, how should I rejoice to render my mother happy!" said Luther to himself. Margaret's pious son endeavoured to repeat a mass on that day; but he could not, the throng was too great.[1]

Fervent and meek, he visited all the churches and chapels; he believed in all the falsehoods that were told him; he devoutly performed all the holy practices that were required there, happy in being able to execute so many good works from which his fellow-countrymen were debarred. "Oh! how I regret," said the pious German to himself, "that my father and mother are still alive! What pleasure I should have in delivering them from the fire of purgatory by my masses, my prayers, and by so many other admirable works!"[2] He had found the light; but the darkness was far from being entirely expelled from his understanding. His heart was converted; his mind was not yet enlightened: he had faith and love, but he wanted knowledge. It was no trifling matter to emerge from that thick night which had covered the earth for so many centuries.

Luther several times repeated mass at Rome. He officiated with all the unction and dignity that such an action appeared to him to require. But what affliction seized the heart of the Saxon monk at witnessing the sad and profane mechanism of the Roman priests, as they celebrated the sacrament of the altar! These on their part laughed at his simplicity. One day when he was officiating he found that the priests at an adjoining altar had already repeated seven masses before he had finished one. "Quick, quick!" cried one of them, "send our Lady back her Son;" making an impious allusion to the transubstantiation of the bread into the body and blood of Jesus Christ. At another time Luther had only just reached the Gospel, when the priest at his side had already terminated the mass. "Passa, passa!" cried the latter to him, "make haste! have done with it at once."[3]

His astonishment was still greater, when he found in the dignitaries of the papacy what he had already observed in the inferior clergy. He had hoped better things of them.

It was the fashion at the papal court to attack Christianity, and you could not pass for a well-bred man, unless you entertained some erroneous or heretical opinion on the doctrines of the Church.[4] They had endeavoured to convince Erasmus, by means of certain extracts from Pliny, that there was no difference between the souls of men and of beasts;[5] and some of the pope's youthful courtiers maintained that the orthodox faith was the result of the crafty devices of a few saints.[6]

[1] L. Opp. (W.) xxii. 2374, 2377.
[2] Sancte Swizere! ora pro nobis. Ibid. 1314, 1332.

[1] L. Opp. (W.) Dedication of Ps. 117. vol. vi. L. g.
[2] Ibid.
[3] L. Opp. (W.) xix. von der Winkelmesse. Mathesius, p. 6.
[4] In quel tempo non pareva fosse galantuomo e buon cortegiano colui che di dogmi della chiesa non aveva qualche opinione erronea ed heretica. Caracciola, Vit. MS. Paul IV., quoted by Ranke.
[5] Burigny, Vie d'Erasme, i. 139.
[6] E medio Romanæ curiæ, sectam juvenum....qui assero-

Luther's quality of envoy from the German Augustines procured him invitations to numerous meetings of distinguished ecclesiastics. One day, in particular, he was at table with several prelates, who displayed openly before him their buffoonery and impious conversation, and did not scruple to utter in his presence a thousand mockeries, thinking, no doubt, that he was of the same mind as themselves. Among other things, they related before the monk, laughing and priding themselves upon it, how, when they were repeating mass at the altar, instead of the sacramental words that were to transform the bread and wine into the flesh and blood of our Saviour, they pronounced over the elements this derisive expression : *Panis es, et panis manebis ; vinum es, et vinum manebis.*[1] Then, continued they, we elevate the host, and all the people bow down and worship it. Luther could hardly believe his ears. His disposition, although full of animation and even gaiety in the society of friends, was remarkably serious whenever sacred matters were concerned. The mockeries of Rome were a stumbling-block to him. "I was," said he, "a thoughtful and pious young monk. Such language grieved me bitterly. If 'tis thus they speak at Rome, freely and publicly at the dinner-table, thought I to myself, what would it be if their actions corresponded to their words, and if all—pope, cardinals, and courtiers—thus repeat the mass! And how they must have deceived me, who have heard them read devoutly so great a number !"[2]

Luther often mixed with the monks and citizens of Rome. If some few extolled the pope and his party, the majority gave a free course to their complaints and to their sarcasms. What stories had they not to tell about the reigning pope, or Alexander VI., or about so many others! One day his Roman friends related how Cæsar Borgia, having fled from Rome, was taken in Spain. As they were going to try him, he called for mercy, and asked for a confessor to visit him in his prison. A monk was sent to him, whom he slew, put on his hood, and escaped. "I heard that at Rome; and it is a positive fact," says Luther.[3] Another day, passing down a wide street leading to St. Peter's, he halted in astonishment before a stone statue, representing a pope under the figure of a woman, holding a sceptre, clothed in the papal mantle, and carrying a child in her arms. It is a young woman of Mentz, he was told, whom the cardinals elected pope, and who was delivered of a child opposite this place. No pope, therefore, passes along that street. "I am surprised," says Luther,

"that the popes allow such a statue to remain."[1]

Luther had thought to find the edifice of the Church encompassed with splendour and strength, but its doors were broken down, and the walls damaged by fire. He witnessed the desolation of the sanctuary, and drew back with horror. All his dreams had been of holiness,—he had discovered nought but profanation.

The disorders without the churches were not less shocking to him. "The police of Rome is very strict and severe," said he. "The judge or captain patrols the city every night on horseback with three hundred followers ; he arrests every one that is found in the streets : if they meet an armed man, he is hung, or thrown into the Tiber. And yet the city is filled with disorder and murder ; whilst in those places where the Word of God is preached uprightly and in purity, peace and order prevail, without calling for the severity of the law."[2]—"No one can imagine what sins and infamous actions are committed in Rome," said he at another time ; "they must be seen and heard to be believed. Thus, they are in the habit of saying, If there is a hell, Rome is built over it : it is an abyss whence issues every kind of sin."[3]

This spectacle made a deep impression even then upon Luther's mind ; it was increased erelong. "The nearer we approach Rome, the greater number of bad Christians we meet with," said he, many years after. "There is a vulgar proverb, that he who goes to Rome the first time, looks out for a knave ; the second time, he finds him ; and the third, he brings him away with him. But people are now become so clever, that they make these three journeys in one."[4] Machiavelli, one of the most profound geniuses of Italy, but also one of unenviable notoriety, who was living at Florence when Luther passed through that city on his way to Rome, has made the same remark : "The strongest symptom," said he, "of the approaching ruin of Christianity (by which he means Roman-catholicism) is, that the nearer people approach the capital of Christendom, the less Christian spirit is found in them. The scandalous examples and the crimes of the court of Rome are the cause why Italy has lost every principle of piety and all religious feeling. We Italians," continues this great historian, "are indebted principally to the Church and the priests for having become impious and immoral."[5] Luther, somewhat later, was sensible of the very great importance of this journey. "If they would give me one hundred thousand florins," said

bant, nostram fidem orthodoxam potius quibusdam sanctorum astutiis subsistere. Paul Canensius, Vita Pauli II.
1 Bread thou art, and bread thou shalt remain ; wine thou art, and wine thou shalt remain.
2 Luth. Opp. (W.) xix. von der Winkelmesse.
3 Das habe Ich zu Rom für gewiss gehört. Luth. Opp. (W.) xxii. 1322.

1 Es nimmt mich wunder, das die Päbste solches Bild leiden können. Luth. Opp. (W.) xxii. 1320.
2 L. Opp. (W.) xxii. 2376.
3 Ist irgend eine Hoelle, so muss Rom darauf gebaut seyn. Luth. Opp. (W.) xxii. 2377.
4 Address to the Christian Nobles of Germany.
5 Dissert. on the 1st Dec. of Livy.

he, " I would not have missed seeing Rome!"[1]

This visit was also very advantageous to him in regard to learning. Like Reuchlin, Luther took advantage of his residence in Italy to penetrate deeper into the meaning of the Holy Scriptures. He took lessons in Hebrew from a celebrated rabbi, named Elias Levita. It was at Rome that he partly acquired that knowledge of the Divine Word, under the attacks of which Rome was destined to fall.

But this journey was most important to Luther in another respect. Not only was the veil withdrawn, and the sardonic sneer, the mocking incredulity which lay concealed behind the Romish superstitions revealed to the future reformer, but the living faith that God had implanted in him was there powerfully strengthened.

We have seen how he at first gave himself up to all the vain observances which the Church enjoined for the expiation of sin. One day, among others, wishing to obtain an indulgence promised by the pope to all who should ascend on their knees what is called Pilate's Staircase, the poor Saxon monk was humbly creeping up those steps, which he was told had been miraculously transported from Jerusalem to Rome. But while he was performing this meritorious act, he thought he heard a voice of thunder crying from the bottom of his heart, as at Wittemberg and Bologna, *The just shall live by faith.* These words, that twice before had struck him like the voice of an angel from God, resounded unceasingly and powerfully within him. He rises in amazement from the steps up which he was dragging his body : he shudders at himself ; he is ashamed of seeing to what a depth superstition had plunged him. He flies far from the scene of his folly.[2]

This powerful text has a mysterious influence on the life of Luther. It was a *creative* sentence both for the reformer and for the Reformation. It was in these words God then said, Let there be light ! and there was light.

It is frequently necessary for a truth to be presented many times to our minds in order that it may produce the due effect. Luther had profoundly studied the Epistle to the Romans, and yet the doctrine of justification by faith there taught had never appeared so clear to him. Now he comprehends that righteousness which alone can stand before God ; now he receives for himself from the hand of Christ that obedience which God of his free gift imputes to the sinner, as soon as he raises his eyes with humility to the crucified Son of Man. This was the decisive epoch of Luther's inner life. That faith which had saved him from the terrors of death, became the very soul of his theology,

his stronghold in every danger ; the principle which gave energy to his preaching and strength to his charity ; the foundation of his peace, the encouragement to his labours, his comfort in life and in death.

But this great doctrine of a salvation proceeding from God and not from man, was not only the power of God to save Luther's soul ; it became in a still greater degree the power of God to reform the Church :—an effectual weapon wielded by the apostles,—a weapon too long neglected, but taken at last, in all its primitive brightness, from the arsenal of the omnipotent God. At the very moment when Luther uprose from his knees on Pilate's Staircase, in agitation and amazement at those words which Paul had addressed fifteen centuries before to the inhabitants of that metropolis,—Truth, till then a melancholy captive, and fettered in the Church, uprose also to fall no more.

We should here listen to what Luther himself says on the matter. "Although I was a holy and blameless monk, my conscience was nevertheless full of trouble and anguish. I could not endure those words— the righteousness of God. I had no love for that holy and just God who punishes sinners. I was filled with secret anger against him : I hated him, because, not content with frightening by the law and the miseries of life us wretched sinners, already ruined by original sin, he still further increased our tortures by the Gospel......But when, by the Spirit of God, I understood these words,—when I learnt how the justification of the sinner proceeds from the free mercy of our Lord through faith,[1]......then I felt born again like a new man ; I entered through the open doors into the very paradise of God.[2] Henceforward, also, I saw the beloved and Holy Scriptures with other eyes. I perused the Bible,—I brought together a great number of passages that taught me the nature of God's work. And as previously I had detested with all my heart these words,—The righteousness of God, I began from that hour to value them and to love them, as the sweetest and most consoling words in the Bible. In very truth, this language of St. Paul was to me the true gate of Paradise."

Thus when he was called on solemn occasions to confess this doctrine, Luther always recovered his enthusiasm and rough energy. " I see," observed he at an important moment,[3] " that the devil is continually attacking this fundamental article by means of his doctors, and that in this respect he can never cease or take any repose. Well then, I, Doctor Martin Luther, unworthy herald of the Gospel of our Lord Jesus Christ, confess this article, that *faith alone without*

---

[1] 100,000 Gulden.—L. Opp. (W.) xxii. 2374.
[2] Seckendorf, p. 56.

[1] Quâ vos Deus misericors justificat per fidem....L. Opp. Lat. in præf.
[2] Hic me prorsus renatum esse sensi, et apertis portis in ipsum paradisum intrasse. Ibid.
[3] Comment on the Imperial Edict, 1531. L. Opp. (L.) vol. xx.

works justifies before God; and I declare that it shall stand and remain for ever in despite of the emperor of the Romans, the emperor of the Turks, the emperor of the Tartars, the emperor of the Persians,—in spite of the pope and all the cardinals, with the bishops, priests, monks, and nuns,—in spite of kings, princes, and nobles,—and in spite of all the world and of the devils themselves; and that if they endeavour to fight against this truth, they will draw the fires of hell upon their heads. This is the true and holy Gospel, and the declaration of me, Doctor Luther, according to the teaching of the Holy Ghost ....There is no one," continues he, " who has died for our sins, if not Jesus Christ the Son of God. I say it once again, should all the world and all the devils tear each other to pieces and burst with rage, that it is not the less true. And if it is He alone that taketh away our sins, it cannot be ourselves and our own works. But good works follow redemption, as the fruit grows on the tree. That is our doctrine—that is what is taught by the Holy Ghost and by all the communion of saints. We hold fast to it in the name of God. Amen !"

It was thus Luther found what had been overlooked, at least to a certain degree, by all doctors and reformers, even by the most illustrious of them. It was in Rome that God gave him this clear view of the fundamental doctrine of Christianity. He had gone to the city of the pontiffs for the solution of certain difficulties concerning a monastic order : he brought away from it in his heart the salvation of the church.

CHAPTER VII.

Luther Returns to Wittemberg—Made Doctor of Divinity—Carlstadt—Luther's Oath—Principle of the Reformation—Luther's Courage—Early Views of Reformation—The Schoolmen — Spalatin — Reuchlin's Quarrel with the Monks.

LUTHER quitted Rome, and returned to Wittemberg : his heart was full of sorrow and indignation. Turning his eyes with disgust from the pontifical city, he directed them with hope to the Holy Scriptures—to that new life which the Word of God seemed then to promise to the world. This word increased in his heart by all that the Church lost. He separated from the one to cling to the other. The whole of the Reformation was in that one movement. It set God in the place of the priest.

Staupitz and the elector did not lose sight of the monk whom they had called to the university of Wittemberg. It appears as if the vicar-general had a presentiment of the work that was to be done in the world, and

that, finding it too difficult for himself, he wished to urge Luther towards it. There is nothing more remarkable —nothing, perhaps, more mysterious than this person, who is seen every where urging forward Luther in the path where God calls him, and then going to end his days sadly in a cloister. The preaching of the young professor had made a deep impression on the prince ; he had admired the strength of his understanding, the forcibleness of his eloquence, and the excellency of the matters that he expounded. [1] The elector and his friend, desirous of advancing a man of such great promise, resolved that he should take the high degree of doctor of divinity. Staupitz repaired to the convent, and took Luther into the garden, where, alone with him under a tree that Luther in after-years delighted to point out to his disciples, [2] the venerable father said to him: "My friend, you must now become Doctor of the Holy Scriptures." Luther shrunk at the very thought : this eminent honour startled him. " Seek a more worthy person," replied he. " As for me, I cannot consent to it." The vicar-general persisted : " Our Lord God has much to do in the Church : he has need at this time of young and vigorous doctors." These words, adds Melancthon, were perhaps said playfully, yet the event corresponded with them ; for generally many omens precede all great revolutions. [3] It is not necessary to suppose that Melancthon here speaks of miraculous prophecies. The most incredulous age—that which preceded the present one—saw an exemplification of this remark. How many presages, without there being any thing miraculous in them, announced the revolution in which it closed !

" But I am weak and sickly," replied Luther. " I have not long to live. Look out for some strong man."—" The Lord has work in heaven as well as on earth," replied the vicar-general: " dead or alive, He has need of you in his council." [4]

" It is the Holy Ghost alone that can make a doctor of divinity," [5] then urged the monk still more alarmed. " Do what your convent requires," said Staupitz, " and what I, your vicar-general, command ; for you have promised to obey us."—" But my poverty," resumed the brother: " I have no means of defraying the expenses incidental to such a promotion."—" Do not be uneasy about that," replied his friend : " the prince has done you the favour to take all the charges upon himself." Pressed on every side, Luther thought it his duty to give way.

It was about the end of the summer of 1512

[1] Vim ingenii, nervos orationis, ac rerum bonitatem expositarum in concionibus admiratus fuerat. Melancth. Vita Luth.
[2] Unter einem Baum, den er mir und andern gezeigt. Math. p. 6.
[3] Multa præcedunt mutationes præsagia. Vita Luth.
[4] Ihr lebet nun oder sterbet, so darff euch Gott in seinem Rathe. Mathes. p. 6.
[5] Neminem nisi Spiritum Sanctum creare posse doctorem theologiæ. Weismanni Hist. Eccl. i. 1404.

that Luther set out for Leipsic to receive from the elector's treasurers the money necessary for his promotion. But according to court custom, the money did not arrive. The brother growing impatient wished to depart, but monastic obedience detained him. At length, on the 4th October, he received fifty florins from Pfeffinger and John Doltzig. In the receipt which he gave them, he employs no other title than that of monk. "I, Martin," wrote he, "brother of the order of Hermits."[1] Luther hastened to return to Wittemberg.

Andrew Bodenstein of the city of Carlstadt was at that time dean of the theological faculty, and it is by the name of Carlstadt that this doctor is generally known. He was also called A. B. C. Melancthon first gave him this designation on account of the three initials of his name. Bodenstein acquired in his native country the first elements of learning. He was of a serious and gloomy character, perhaps inclined to jealousy, and of a restless temper, but full of desire for knowledge, and of great capacity. He frequented several universities to augment his stores of learning, and studied theology at Rome. On his return from Italy, he settled at Wittemberg, and became doctor of divinity. "At this time," he said afterwards, "I had not yet read the Holy Scriptures."[2] This remark gives us a very correct idea of what theology then was. Carlstadt, besides his functions of professor, was canon and archdeacon. Such was the man who in after-years was destined to create a schism in the Reformation. At this time he saw in Luther only an inferior; but the Augustine erelong became an object of jealousy to him. "I will not be less great than Luther," said he one day.[3] Very far from anticipating at that period the great destinies of the young professor, Carlstadt conferred on his future rival the highest dignity of the university.

On the 18th October 1512, Luther was received licentiate in divinity, and took the following oath: "I swear to defend the evangelical truth with all my might."[4] On the day following, Bodenstein solemnly conferred on him, in the presence of a numerous assembly, the insignia of doctor of divinity. He was made a biblical doctor, and not a doctor of sentences; and was thus called to devote himself to the study of the Bible, and not to that of human traditions.[5] He then pledged himself by an oath, as he himself relates,[6] to his well-beloved and Holy Scriptures. He promised to preach them faithfully, to teach them with purity, to study them all his life, and to defend them, both in disputation and in writing, against all false teachers, so far as God should give him ability.

1 L. Epp. l. 11.
2 Weismann, Hist. Eccl. p. 1416.
3 Ibid.
4 Juro me veritatem evangelicam viriliter defensurum.
5 Doctor biblicus *and not* sententiarius.—Melancth.
6 L. Opp. (W.) xvi. 2061.—Mathesius, p. 7.

This solemn oath was Luther's call to the Reformation. By imposing on his conscience the holy obligation of searching freely and boldly proclaiming the Christian truth, this oath raised the new doctor above the narrow limits to which his monastic vow would perhaps have confined him. Called by the university, by his sovereign, in the name of imperial majesty and of the see of Rome itself, and bound before God by the most solemn oath, he became from that hour the most intrepid herald of the Word of Life. On that memorable day Luther was armed champion of the Bible.

We may accordingly look upon this oath, sworn to the Holy Scriptures, as one of the causes of the revival of the Church. The sole and infallible authority of the Word of God was the primary and fundamental principle of the Reformation. Every reform in detail that was afterwards carried out in the doctrine, morals, or government of the Church, and in its worship, was but a consequence of this first principle. In these days we can scarcely imagine the sensation produced by this elementary and simple but long-neglected truth. A few men of more enlarged views than the common, alone foresaw its immense consequences. Erelong the courageous voices of all the Reformers proclaimed this mighty principle, at the sound of which Rome shall crumble into dust: "The Christians receive no other doctrines than those founded on the express words of Jesus Christ, of the Apostles, and of the Prophets. No man, no assembly of doctors, has a right to prescribe new ones."

Luther's position was changed. The summons that he had received became to the reformer as one of those extraordinary calls which the Lord addressed to the Prophets under the Old Covenant, and to the apostles under the New. The solemn engagement that he made produced so deep an impression upon his soul that the recollection of this oath was sufficient, in after-years, to console him in the midst of the greatest dangers and of the fiercest conflicts. And when he saw all Europe agitated and shaken by the Word that he had proclaimed; when the accusations of Rome, the reproaches of many pious men, the doubts and fears of his own too sensible heart, seemed likely to make him hesitate, fear, and fall into despair,—he called to mind the oath that he had taken, and remained steadfast, calm, and full of joy. "I have gone forward in the Lord's name," said he in a critical moment, "and I have placed myself in his hands. His will be done! Who prayed him to make me a doctor?...If it was He who created me such, let him support me; or else if he repent of what he has done, let him deprive me of my office. ......This tribulation, therefore, alarms me not. I seek one thing only, which is to preserve the favour of God in all that he has called me to do with him." At another time he said: "He who undertakes any thing without a Divine call, seeks his own glory. But I, Doctor Martin Luther, was forced to become a doctor. Popery desired to stop me in the performance of my duty: but you see what has happened to it, and worse still will befall it. They cannot defend themselves against me. I am determined, in God's name, to tread upon the lions, to trample dragons and serpents under foot. This will begin during my life, and will be accomplished after my death."[1]

From the period of his oath, Luther no longer sought the truth for himself alone: he sought it also for the Church. Still full of the recollections of Rome, he saw confusedly before him a path in which he had promised to walk with all the energy of his soul. The spiritual life that had hitherto been manifested only within him, now extended itself without. This was the third epoch of his development. His entrance into the cloister had turned his thoughts towards God; the knowledge of the remission of sins and of the righteousness of faith had emancipated his soul; his doctor's oath gave him that baptism of fire by which he became a reformer of the Church.

His ideas were soon directed in a general manner towards the Reformation. In an address that he had written, as it would seem, to be delivered by the provost of Lietzkau at the Lateran council, he declared that the corruption of the world originated in the priests' teaching so many fables and traditions, instead of preaching the pure Word of God. The Word of Life, in his view, alone had the power of effecting the spiritual regeneration of man. Thus then already he made the salvation of the world depend upon the re-establishment of sound doctrine, and not upon a mere reformation of manners. Yet Luther was not entirely consistent with himself; he still entertained contradictory opinions: but a spirit of power beamed from all his writings; he courageously broke the bonds with which the systems of the schools had fettered the thoughts of men; he every where passed beyond the limits within which previous ages had so closely confined him, and opened up new paths. God was with him.

The first adversaries that he attacked were those famous schoolmen, whom he had himself so much studied, and who then reigned supreme in all the academies. He accused them of Pelagianism, and forcibly inveighing against Aristotle, the father of the schools, and against Thomas Aquinas, he undertook to hurl them both from the throne whence they governed, the one philosophy, and the other theology.[2]

"Aristotle, Porphyry, the sententiary divines (the schoolmen)," he wrote to Lange,

"are useless studies in our days. I desire nothing more earnestly than to unveil to the world that comedian who has deceived the Church by assuming a Greek mask, and to show his deformity to all."[1] In every public discussion he was heard repeating: "The writings of the apostles and prophets are surer and more sublime than all the sophisms and all the divinity of the schools." Such language was new, but men gradually became used to it. About a year after he was able to write with exultation: "God is at work. Our theology and St. Augustine advance admirably and prevail in our university. Aristotle is declining: he is tottering towards his eternal ruin that is near at hand. The lectures on the Sentences produce nothing but weariness. No one can hope for hearers, unless he professes the Biblical theology."[2] Happy the university of which such testimony can be given!

At the same time that Luther was attacking Aristotle, he took the side of Erasmus and Reuchlin against their enemies. He entered into communication with these great men and with other scholars, such as Pirckheimer, Mutianus, and Hütten, who belonged more or less to the same party. He also about this period, formed another friendship that was of great importance through the whole course of his life.

There was at that time at the elector's court a person remarkable for his wisdom and his candour: this was George Spalatin. He was born at Spalatus or Spalt in the bishopric of Eichstadt, and had been originally curate of the village of Hohenkirch, near the Thuringian forests. He was afterwards chosen by Frederick the Wise to be his secretary, chaplain, and tutor to his nephew, John Frederick, who was one day to wear the electoral crown. Spalatin was a simple-hearted man in the midst of the court: he appeared timid in the presence of great events; circumspect and prudent, like his master,[3] before the ardent Luther, with whom he corresponded daily. Like Staupitz, he was better suited for peaceful times. Such men are necessary: they are like those delicate substances in which jewels and crystal are wrapped to secure them from the injuries of transport. They seem useless; and yet without them all these precious objects would be broken and lost. Spalatin was not a man to effect great undertakings; but he faithfully and noiselessly performed the task imposed upon him.[4] He was at first one of the principal aids of his master in collecting those relics of saints, of which Frederick was so long a great admirer. But he, as well as the prince, turned by degrees towards the truth. The faith, which then reappeared in

[1] L. Opp. (W.) xxi. 2061.
[2] Aristotelem in philosophicis, Sanctum Thomam in theologicis, evertendos suceperat. Pallavicini, i. 16.

[1] Perdita studia nostri sæculi. Epp. i. 16. (8tl. February 1516.)
[2] Ep. i. 57. (18th May 1517.)
[3] Secundum genium heri sui. Weismann, Hist. Eccles. i. 1434.
[4] Fideliter et sine strepitu fungens. Ibid.

73

the Church, did not lay such violent hold upon him as upon Luther: it guided him by slower methods. He became Luther's friend at court; the minister through whom passed all matters between the reformer and the princes; the mediator between the Church and the State. The elector honoured Spalatin with great intimacy: they always travelled together in the same carriage.[1] Nevertheless the atmosphere of the court oppressed the good chaplain: he was affected by profound melancholy; he could have desired to quit all these honours, and become once more a simple pastor in the forests of Thuringia. But Luther consoled him, and exhorted him to remain firm at his post. Spalatin acquired general esteem: princes and learned men showed him the most sincere regard. Erasmus used to say, " I inscribe Spalatin's name not only among those of my principal friends, but still further among those of my most honoured protectors; and that, not upon paper, but on my heart."[2]

Reuchlin's quarrel with the monks was then making a great noise in Germany. The most pious men were often undecided what part they should take; for the monks were eager to destroy the Hebrew books in which blasphemies against Christ were to be found. The elector commissioned his chaplain to consult the doctor of Wittemberg on this matter, as his reputation was already great. Here is Luther's answer: it is the first letter he addressed to the court-preacher:—

" What shall I say? These monks pretend to cast out Beelzebub, but it is not by the finger of God. I cease not from groaning and lamenting over it. We Christians are beginning to be wise outwardly, and mad inwardly.[3] There are in every part of our Jerusalem blasphemies a hundred times worse than those of the Jews, and all there are filled with spiritual idols. It is our duty with holy zeal to carry out and destroy these internal enemies. But we neglect that which is most urgent; and the devil himself persuades us to abandon what belongs to us, at the same time that he prevents us from correcting what belongs to others."

CHAPTER VIII.

Faith—Popular Declamations—Academic Teaching—Luther's Purity of Life—German Theology or Mysticism—The Monk Spenlein—Justification by Faith—Luther on Erasmus—Faith and Works.—Erasmus—Necessity of Works—Luther's Charity.

LUTHER did not lose himself in this quarrel. A living faith in Christ filled his heart and

his life. " Within my heart," said he, " reigns alone (and it ought thus to reign alone) faith in my Lord Jesus Christ, who is the beginning, middle, and end of all the thoughts that occupy my mind by day and night."[1]

All his hearers listened with admiration as he spoke, whether from the professor's chair or from the pulpit, of that faith in Jesus Christ. His teaching diffused great light. Men were astonished that they had not earlier acknowledged truths that appeared so evident in his mouth. " The desire of self-justification," said he, " is the cause of all the distresses of the heart. But he who receives Jesus Christ as a Saviour, enjoys peace ; and not only peace, but purity of heart. All sanctification of the heart is a fruit of faith. For faith is a divine work in us, which changes us and gives us a new birth, emanating from God himself. It kills the old Adam in us ; and, by the Holy Ghost which is communicated to us, it gives us a new heart and makes us new men. It is not by empty speculations," he again exclaimed, " but by this practical method that we can obtain a saving knowledge of Jesus Christ."[2]

It was at this time that Luther preached those discourses on the Ten Commandments that have come down to us under the title of *Popular Declamations*. They contain errors no doubt; Luther became enlightened only by degrees. " *The path of the just is as the shining light, that shineth more and more unto the perfect day.*"[3] But what truth, simplicity, and eloquence are found in these discourses ! How well can we understand the effect that the new preacher must have produced upon his audience and upon his age ! We will quote but one passage taken from the beginning.

Luther ascends the pulpit of Wittemberg, and reads these words : " *Thou shalt have no other gods before me*" (Exod. xx. 3). Then turning to the people who crowded the sanctuary, he says, " All the sons of Adam are idolaters, and have sinned against this first commandment."[4]

Doubtless this strange assertion startled his hearers. He proceeds to justify it, and the speaker continues : " There are two kinds of idolatry—one external, the other internal.

" The external, in which man bows down to wood and stone, to beasts and to the heavenly host.

" The internal, in which man, fearful of punishment, or seeking his own pleasure, does not worship the creature, but loves him in his heart, and trusts in him......

[1] Qui cum principe in rheda sive lectico solitus est ferri. Corpus Reformatorum, i. 33.
[2] Melch. Ad. Vita Spalat. p. 100.
[3] Foris sapere, et domi desipere. L. Epp. i. 8.

[1] Præf. ad Galat.
[2] Non per speculationem, sed per hanc viam practicam.
[3] Prov. iv. 18.
[4] Omnes filii Adæ sunt idololatræ. Decem Præcepta Wittembergensi populo prædicata per R. P. D. Martinum Lutherum, Aug. anno 1516. These discourses were preached in German ; the quotations are from the Latin edition, i. 1.

" What kind of religion is this? You do not bend the knee before riches and honours, but you offer them your heart, the noblest portion of yourselves.........Alas! you worship God in body, but the creature in spirit.

" This idolatry prevails in every man until he is healed by the free gift of the faith that is in Christ Jesus.

" And how shall this cure be accomplished?

" Listen. Faith in Christ takes away from you all trust in your own wisdom, righteousness, and strength; it teaches you that if Christ had not died for you, and had not thus saved you, neither you nor any other creature would have been able to do it.[1] Then you learn to despise all those things that are unavailing to you.

" Nothing now remains to you but Jesus Christ—Christ alone,—Christ all-sufficient for your soul. Hoping for nothing from any creature, you have only Christ, from whom you hope for every thing, and whom you love above every thing.

" Now Christ is the one, sole, and true God. When you have him for your God, you have no other gods."[2]

It is in this manner Luther shows how the soul is brought back to God, his sovereign good, by the Gospel, according to the words of Jesus Christ: *I am the way; no man cometh unto the Father but by me.* The man who speaks thus to his age aims at something more than the correction of a few abuses; he is earnest above all things to establish true religion. His work is not merely negative; it is primarily positive.

Luther afterwards turns his discourse against the superstitions which then filled Christendom;—the signs and mysterious characters, the observance of certain days and months, familiar spirits, phantoms, the influence of the stars, witchcraft, metamorphoses, incubi and succubi, the patronage of saints, &c. &c. &c.; one after another he attacks these idols, and with vigorous arm overthrows all these false gods.

But it was particularly in his lecture-room, before an enlightened and youthful audience, hungering for the truth, that he displayed all the treasures of God's Word. " He explained Scripture in such a manner," says his illustrious friend Melancthon, " that, in the judgment of all pious and well-informed men, it was as if a new morn had risen upon the doctrine after a long night of darkness. He showed the difference that existed between the Law and the Gospel. He refuted the then prevalent error of the churches and of the schools, that men by their works merit the remission of sins, and become righteous before God by an outward discipline. He thus led men's hearts back to the Son of God.[1] Like John the Baptist, he pointed to the Lamb of God that has taken away the sins of the world; he explained how sin is freely pardoned on account of the Son of God, and that man receives this blessing through faith. He made no change in the ceremonies. On the contrary, the established discipline had not in his order a more faithful observer and defender. But he endeavoured more and more to make all understand these grand and essential doctrines of conversion, of the remission of sins, of faith, and of the true consolation that is to be found in the cross. Pious minds were struck and penetrated by the sweetness of this doctrine; the learned received it with joy.[2] One might have said that Christ, the apostles, and the prophets, were now issuing from the obscurity of some impure dungeon."[3]

The firmness with which Luther relied on the Holy Scriptures imparted great authority to his teaching. But other circumstances added still more to his strength. In him every action of his life corresponded with his words. It was known that these discourses did not proceed merely from his lips:[4] they had their source in his heart, and were practised in all his works. And when, somewhat later, the Reformation burst forth, many influential men, who saw with regret these divisions in the Church, won over beforehand by the holiness of the reformer's life and by the beauty of his genius, not only did not oppose him, but, further still, embraced that doctrine to which he gave testimony by his works.[5] The more men loved christian virtues, the more they inclined to the reformer. All honest divines were in his favour.[6] This is what was said by those who knew him, and particularly by the wisest man of his age, Melancthon, and by Erasmus, the illustrious opponent of Luther. Envy and prejudice have dared to speak of his disorderly life. Wittemberg was changed by this preaching of faith, and that city became the focus of a light that was soon to illumine all Germany, and to shine on all the Church.

It was in 1516 that Luther published the work of an anonymous mystic theologian (probably Ebland, priest at Frankfort), entitled *German Theology,* in which the author shows how man may attain perfection by the three methods of purification, illumination, and communion. Luther never gave himself up to the mystic theology, but he received from it a salutary impression. It confirmed him in his disgust for the dry teaching of the schoolmen, in his contempt for the works and observances so much

<hr/>

[1] Nisi ipse pro te mortuus esset, teque servaret, nec tu, nec omnis creatura tibi posset prodesse. Decem Præc. l. l.
[2] At Jesus est verus, unus, solus Deus, quem cum habes, non habes alienum deum. Ibid.

[1] Revocavit igitur Lutherus hominum mentes ad Filium Dei. Melancth. Vita Luth.
[2] Hujus doctrinæ dulcedine pii omnes valde capiebantur, et eruditis gratum erat. Melancth. Vita Luth.
[3] Quasi ex tenebris, carcere, squalore, educi Christum, prophetas, apostolos. Ibid.
[4] Oratio non in labris nasci, sed in pectore. Ibid.
[5] Eique propter auctoritatem, quam sanctitate morum antea pepererat, adsenserunt. Ibid.
[6] Puto et hodie theologos omnes probos favere Luthero Erasm. Epp. i. 652.

trumpeted by the Church, and in the conviction that he felt of man's spiritual helplessness and of the necessity of grace, and in his attachment to the Bible. "I prefer," wrote he to Staupitz, "the mystics and the Bible to all the schoolmen;"[1] thus placing the former teachers in the next rank to the sacred writers. Perhaps, also, the *German Theology* aided him in forming a sounder idea on the sacraments, and above all on the mass; for the author maintains that the eucharist gives Christ to man, and does not offer up Christ to God. Luther accompanied this publication by a preface, in which he declared that, next to the Bible and St. Augustine, he had never met with a book in which he had learnt more of God, Christ, man, and of all things. Already many doctors began to speak ill of the Wittemberg professors, and accused them of innovation. "One would say," continues Luther, "that there had never lived men before us who taught as we teach. Yes, in truth, there have been many. But the anger of God, which our sins have deserved, has prevented us from seeing and hearing them. For a long time the universities have banished the Word of God into a corner. Let them read this book, and then let them say whether our theology is new, for this is not a new book."[2]

But if Luther derived from the mystic divinity whatever good it contained, he did not take the bad also. The great error of mysticism is to overlook the free gift of salvation. We are about to notice a remarkable example of the purity of his faith.

Luther had an affectionate and tender heart, and desired to see those whom he loved in possession of that light which had guided him into the paths of peace. He took advantage of every opportunity that occurred, as professor, preacher, or monk, as well as of his extensive correspondence, to communicate his treasure to others. One of his former brethren in the convent of Erfurth, the monk George Spenlein, was then residing in the convent of Memmingen, perhaps after having spent a short time at Wittemberg. Spenlein had commissioned the doctor to sell various articles that he had left with him—a tunic of Brussels cloth, a work by an Eisenach doctor, and a hood. Luther carefully discharged this commission. He received, says he in a letter to Spenlein, dated the 7th April 1516, one florin for the tunic, half a florin for the book, and a florin for the hood, and had remitted the amount to the father-vicar, to whom Spenlein owed three florins. But Luther quickly passes from this account of a monk's wardrobe to a more important subject.

"I should be very glad to know," wrote he to friar George, "what is the state of your soul. Is it not tired of its own righteousness? does it not breathe freely at last, and does it not confide in the righteousness of Christ? In our days, pride seduces many, and especially those who labour with all their might to become righteous. Not understanding the righteousness of God that is given to us freely in Christ Jesus, they wish to stand before Him on their own merits. But that cannot be. When you were living with me, you were in that error, and so was I. I am yet struggling unceasingly against it, and I have not yet entirely triumphed over it.

"Oh, my dear brother, learn to know Christ, and him crucified. Learn to sing unto him a new song, to despair of yourself, and to say to him : Thou, Lord Jesus Christ, art my righteousness, and I am thy sin. Thou hast taken what was mine, and hast given me what was thine.[1] What thou wast not, thou didst become, in order that I might become what I was not!—Beware, my dear George, of pretending to such purity as no longer to confess yourself a sinner : for Christ dwells only with sinners. He came down from heaven, where he was living among the righteous, in order to live also among sinners. Meditate carefully upon this love of Christ, and you will taste all its unspeakable consolation. If our labours and afflictions could give peace to the conscience, why should Christ have died? You will not find peace, save in him, by despairing of yourself and of your works, and in learning with what love he opens his arms to you, taking all your sins upon himself, and giving thee all his righteousness."

Thus the powerful doctrine that had already saved the world in the apostolic age, and which was destined to save it a second time in the days of the Reformation, was clearly and forcibly explained by Luther. Passing over the many ages of ignorance and superstition that had intervened, in this he gave his hand to Saint Paul.

Spenlein was not the only man whom he sought to instruct in this fundamental doctrine. The little truth that he found in this respect in the writings of Erasmus, made him uneasy. It was of great importance to enlighten a man whose authority was so great, and whose genius was so admirable. But how was he to do it? His court-friend, the Elector's chaplain, was much respected by Erasmus : it is to him that Luther applies. "What displeases me in Erasmus, who is a man of such extensive learning, is, my dear Spalatin," wrote Luther, " that by the righteousness of works and of the law, of which the apostle speaks, he understands the fulfilling of the ceremonial law. The righteousness of the law consists not only in ceremonies, but in all the works of the Decalogue. Even if these works should be accomplished without faith in Christ, they

[1] Illis præfero mysticos et Biblia. L. Epp. i. 107.
[2] Die Deutsche Theologie. Strasburg, 1519. Preface.

[1] Tu, Domine Jesu, es justitia mea ; ego autem sum peccatum tuum : tu assumpsisti meum, et dedisti mihi tuum. L. Epp. i. 17.

may, it is true, produce a Fabricius, a Regulus, and other men perfectly upright in the eyes of the world; but they then deserve as little to be styled *righteousness*, as the fruit of the medlar to be called a fig. For we do not become righteous, as Aristotle maintains, by performing righteous works; but when we are become righteous, then we perform such works.[1] The man must first be changed, and afterwards the works. Abel was first accepted by God, and then his sacrifice." Luther continues: "Fulfil, I beseech you, the duty of a friend and of a Christian by communicating these matters to Erasmus." This letter is thus dated: "In haste, from the corner of our convent, 19th October 1516." It places in its true light the relation between Luther and Erasmus. It shows the sincere interest he felt in what he thought would be really beneficial to this illustrious writer. Undoubtedly, the opposition shown by Erasmus to the truth compelled Luther somewhat later to combat him openly; but he did not do so until he had sought to enlighten his antagonist.

At last then were heard explained ideas at once clear and deep on the nature of goodness. Then was declared the principle, that what constitutes the real goodness of an action is not its outward appearance, but the spirit in which it is performed. This was aiming a deadly blow at all those superstitious observances which for ages had oppressed the Church, and prevented christian virtues from growing up and flourishing within it.

"I am reading Erasmus," says Luther on another occasion, "but he daily loses his credit with me. I like to see him rebuke with so much firmness and learning the grovelling ignorance of the priests and monks; but I fear that he does not render great service to the doctrine of Jesus Christ. What is of man is dearer to him than what is of God.[2] We are living in dangerous times. A man is not a good and judicious Christian because he understands Greek and Hebrew. Jerome who knew five languages, is inferior to Augustine who understood but one; although Erasmus thinks the contrary. I very carefully conceal my opinions concerning Erasmus, through fear of giving advantage to his adversaries. Perhaps the Lord will give him understanding in His time."[3]

The helplessness of man—the omnipotence of God, were the two truths that Luther desired to re-establish. That is but a sad religion and a wretched philosophy by which man is directed to his own natural strength. Ages have tried in vain this so much boasted strength; and while man has, by his own natural powers, arrived at great excellence in all that concerns his earthly existence, he

has never been able to scatter the darkness that conceals from his soul the knowledge of the true God, or to change a single inclination of his heart. The highest degree of wisdom attained by ambitious minds, or by souls thirsting with the desire of perfection, has been to despair of themselves.[1] It is therefore a generous, a comforting, and supremely true doctrine which unveils our own impotency in order to proclaim a power from God by which we can do all things. That truly is a great reformation which vindicates on earth the glory of heaven, and which pleads before man the rights of the Almighty God.

No one knew better than Luther the intimate and indissoluble bond that unites the gratuitous salvation of God with the free works of man. No one showed more plainly than he, that it is only by receiving all from Christ, that man can impart much to his brethren. He always represented these two actions—that of God and that of man—in the same picture. And thus it is, that after explaining to the friar Spenlein what is meant by saving righteousness, he adds, "If thou firmly believest those things, as is thy duty (for cursed is he who does not believe them), receive thy brethren who are still ignorant and in error, as Jesus Christ has received thee. Bear with them patiently. Make their sins thine own; and if thou hast any good thing, impart it to them. 'Receive ye one another,' says the apostle, 'as Christ also received us, to the glory of God.' (Rom. xv. 7.) It is a deplorable righteousness that cannot bear with others because it finds them wicked, and which thinks only of seeking the solitude of the desert, instead of doing them good by long-suffering, prayer, and example. If thou art the lily and the rose of Christ, know that thy dwelling-place is among thorns. Only take care lest by thy impatience, by thy rash judgments, and thy secret pride, thou dost not thyself become a thorn. Christ reigns in the midst of his enemies. If he had desired to live only among the good, and to die for those only who loved him, for whom, I pray, would he have died, and among whom would he have lived?"

It is affecting to see how Luther practised these charitable precepts. An Augustine monk of Erfurth, George Leiffer, was exposed to many trials. Luther became informed of this, and within a week after writing the preceding letter to Spenlein, he came to him with words of comfort. "I learn that you are agitated by many tempests, and that your soul is tossed to and fro by the waves. ......The cross of Christ is divided among all the world, and each man has his share. You should not, therefore, reject that which has

---

[1] Non enim justa agendo justi efficimur; sed justi fiendo et essendo, operamur justa. L. Epp. l. 22.
[2] Humana prævalent in eo plusquam divina.
[3] Dabit ei Dominus intellectum suo forte tempore. Ibid.

[1] Τί οὖν; δυνατὸν ἀναμάρτητον εἶναι ἤδη; What! is it possible to be without sin? asked Epictetus (iv. 12. 19.) Ἀμήχανον. Impossible! replied he.

fallen to you. Receive it rather as a holy relic, not in a vessel of silver or of gold, but in what is far better—in a heart of gold,—in a heart full of meekness. If the wood of the cross has been so sanctified by the body and blood of Christ, that we consider it as the most venerable relic, how much more should the wrongs, persecutions, sufferings, and hatred of men, be holy relics unto us, since they have not only been touched by Christ's flesh, but have been embraced, kissed, and blessed by his infinite charity."[1]

CHAPTER IX.

Luther's first Theses—The Old Adam and Grace—Visitation of the Convents—Luther at Dresden and Erfurth—Tornator—Peace and the Cross—Results of Luther's Journey—His Labours—The Plague.

LUTHER'S teaching produced its natural fruits. Many of his disciples already felt themselves impelled to profess publicly the truths which their master's lessons had revealed to them. Among his hearers was a young scholar, Bernard of Feldkirchen, professor of Aristotle's physics in the university, and who five years later was the first of the evangelical ecclesiastics who entered into the bonds of matrimony.

It was Luther's wish that Feldkirchen should maintain, under his presidence, certain theses or propositions in which his principles were laid down. The doctrines professed by Luther thus gained additional publicity. The disputation took place in 1516.

This was Luther's first attack upon the dominion of the sophists and upon the papacy, as he himself characterizes it. Weak as it was, it caused him some uneasiness. "I allow these propositions to be printed," said he many years after, when publishing them in his works, "principally that the greatness of my cause, and the success with which God has crowned it, may not make me vain. For they fully manifest my humiliation, that is to say, the infirmity and ignorance, the fear and trembling with which I began this conflict. I was alone: I had thrown myself imprudently into this business. Unable to retract, I conceded many important points to the pope, and I even adored him."[2]

Some of the propositions were as follows :[3]

" The old Adam is the vanity of vanities ; he is the universal vanity ; and he renders all other creatures vain, however good they may be.

" The old Adam is called *the flesh*, not only because he is led by the lusts of the flesh,

but further, because should he be chaste, prudent, and righteous, he is not born again of God by the Holy Ghost.

" A man who has no part in the grace of God, cannot keep the commandments of God, or prepare himself, either wholly or in part, to receive grace, but he rests of necessity under the power of sin.

" The will of man without grace is not free, but is enslaved, and that too with its own consent.

" Jesus Christ, our strength and our righteousness, he who trieth the heart and reins, is the only discerner and judge of our merits.

" Since all is possible, by Christ, to the believer, it is superstitious to seek for other help, either in man's will or in the saints."[1]

This disputation made a great noise, and it has been considered as the beginning of the Reformation.

The hour drew nigh in which the Reformation was to burst forth. God hastened to prepare the instrument that he had determined to employ. The elector, having built a new church at Wittemberg, to which he gave the name of All Saints, sent Staupitz into the Low Countries to collect relics for the ornament of the new edifice. The vicar-general commissioned Luther to replace him during his absence, and in particular to make a visitation of the forty monasteries of Misnia and Thuringia.

Luther repaired first to Grimma, and thence to Dresden. Every where he endeavoured to establish the truths that he had discovered, and to enlighten the members of his order. —" Do not bind yourselves to Aristotle, or to any other teacher of a deceitful philosophy," said he to the monks, " but read the Word of God with diligence. Do not look for salvation in your own strength or in your good works, but in the merits of Christ and in God's grace."[2]

An Augustine monk of Dresden had fled from his convent, and was at Mentz, where the prior of the Augustines had received him. Luther wrote to the latter,[3] begging him to send back the stray sheep, and added these words so full of charity and truth : " I know that offences must needs come. It is no marvel that man falls ; but it is so that he rises again and stands upright. Peter fell that he might know he was but a man. Even in our days the cedars of Lebanon are seen to fall. The very angels—a thing that exceeds all imagination!—have fallen in heaven, and Adam in paradise. Why then should we be surprised if a reed is shaken by the whirlwind, or if a smoking taper is extinguished?"

From Dresden Luther proceeded to Erfurth, and reappeared to discharge the functions of vicar-general in that very convent

---

1 Sanctissimæ reliquiæ......deificæ voluntatis suæ charitate amplexæ osculatæ. L. Epp. i. 18.
2 Sed etiam ultro adorabam. L. Opp. Lat. i. 50.
4 L. Opp. (L.) xvii. 142, and in the Latin editioa, vol. i. 51.

1 Cum credenti omnia sint, auctore Christo possibilia, superstitoisum est, humano arbitrio, aliis sanctis, alia deputari auxilia. L. Opp. (L.) xvii. 142.
2 Hilscher's Luther's Anwesenheit in Alt-Dresden, 1728.
3 Epp. i. 20, dated May 1, 1516.

where, eleven years before, he had wound up the clock, opened the gates, and swept out the church. He nominated to the priorship of the convent his friend the bachelor John Lange, a learned and pious but severe man: he exhorted him to affability and patience. " Put on," wrote he to him shortly after, " put on a spirit of meekness towards the prior of Nuremberg: this is but proper, seeing that he has assumed a spirit of bitterness and harshness. Bitterness is not expelled by bitterness, that is to say, the devil by the devil; but sweetness dispels bitterness, that is to say, the finger of God casts out the evil spirit."[1] We must, perhaps, regret that Luther did not on various occasions remember this excellent advice.

At Neustadt on the Orla there was nothing but disunion. Dissensions and quarrels reigned in the convent, and all the monks were at war with their prior. They assailed Luther with their complaints. The prior Michael Dressel, or Tornator, as Luther calls him, translating his name into Latin, on his side laid all his troubles before the doctor. "Peace, peace!" said he. "You seek peace," replied Luther; " but it is the peace of the world, and not the peace of Christ that you seek. Do you not know that our God has set his peace in the midst of war? He whom no one disturbs has not peace. But he who, troubled by all men and by the things of this life, bears all with tranquillity and joy—he possesses the true peace. You say with Israel: Peace, peace! and there is no peace. Say rather with Christ: The cross, the cross! and there will be no cross. For the cross ceases to be a cross, as soon as we can say with love: O blessed cross, there is no wood like thine!"[2] On his return to Wittemberg, Luther, desiring to put an end to these dissensions, permitted the monks to elect another prior.

Luther returned to Wittemberg after an absence of six weeks. He was afflicted at all that he had seen; but the journey gave him a better knowledge of the Church and of the world, increased his confidence in his intercourse with society, and afforded him many opportunities of founding schools, of pressing this fundamental truth that "Holy Scripture alone shows us the way to heaven," and of exhorting the brethren to live together in holiness, chastity, and peace.[3] There is no doubt that much good seed was sown in the different Augustine convents during this journey of the reformer. The monastic orders, which had long been the support of Rome, did perhaps more for the Reformation than against it. This is true in particular of the Augustines. Almost all the pious men

of liberal and elevated mind, who were living in the cloisters, turned towards the Gospel. A new and generous blood erelong circulated through these orders, which were, so to speak; the arteries of the German Church. As yet nothing was known in the world of the new ideas of the Wittemberg Augustine, while they were already the chief topic of conversation in the chapters and monasteries. Many a cloister thus became a nursery of reformers. As soon as the great struggle took place, pious and able men issued from their obscurity, and abandoned the seclusion of a monastic life for the active career of ministers of God's Word. At the period of this inspection of 1516 Luther awakened many drowsy souls by his words. Hence this year has been named " the morning star of the gospel-day."

Luther resumed his usual occupation. He was at this period overwhelmed with labour: it was not enough that he was professor, preacher, and confessor; he was burdened still further by many temporal occupations having reference to his order and his convent. " I have need almost continually," writes he, " of two secretaries; for I do nothing else all the day long but write letters. I am preacher to the convent, I read the prayers at table, I am pastor and parish minister, director of studies, the prior's vicar (that is to say, prior eleven times over!) inspector of the fish-ponds at Litzkau, counsel to the inns of Herzberg at Torgau, lecturer on Saint Paul, and commentator on the Psalms...... I have rarely time to repeat the daily prayers and to sing a hymn; without speaking of my struggles with flesh and blood, with the devil and the world......Learn from this what an idle man I am!"[1]

About this time the plague broke out in Wittemberg. A great number of the students and teachers quitted the city. Luther remained. " I am not certain," wrote he to his friend at Erfurth, " if the plague will let me finish the Epistle to the Galatians. Its attacks are sudden and violent: it is making great ravages among the young in particular. You advise me to fly. Whither shall I fly? I hope that the world will not come to an end, if brother Martin dies.[2] If the pestilence spreads, I shall disperse the brothers in every direction; but as for me, my place is here; duty does not permit me to desert my post, until He who has called me shall summon me away. Not that I have no fear of death (for I am not Paul, I am only his commentator); but I hope that the Lord will deliver me from fear." Such was the resolution of the Wittemberg doctor. Shall he whom the pestilence could not force to retire a single step, shrink before Rome? Shall he yield through fear of the scaffold?

---

[1] Non enim asper asperum, id est non diabolus diabolum; sed suavis asperum, id est digitus Dei ejicit dæmonia. L. Epp. i. 36.
[2] Tam cito enim crux cessat esse crux, quam cito lætus dixeris: Crux benedicta! inter ligna nullum tale. Epp. i. 27.
[3] Heiliglich, friedlich und züchtig. Math. p. 10.

[1] Letter to Lange, 26th October 1516. Epp. i. 41.
[2] Quo fugiam! spero quod non corruet orbis, ruente fratre Martino. Ibid. 42.

CHAPTER X.

The Relics—Relations of Luther with the Elector—Advice to the Chaplain—Duke George—His Character—Luther's Sermon before the Court—Dinner at Court—Evening with Emser.

LUTHER displayed the same courage before the mighty of this world, that he had shown amidst the most formidable evils. The elector was much pleased with the vicar-general, who had made a rich harvest of relics in the Low Countries. Luther gives an account of them to Spalatin; and this affair of the relics, occurring at the very moment when the Reformation is about to begin, is a singular circumstance. Most certainly, the reformers had little idea to what point they were tending. A bishopric appeared to the elector the only recompense worthy the services of the vicar-general. Luther, to whom Spalatin wrote on the subject, strongly disapproved of such an idea. "There are many things which please your prince," replied he, "and which, nevertheless, are displeasing to God.[1] I do not deny that he is skilful in the matters of this world; but in what concerns God and the salvation of souls, I account him, as well as his councillor Pfeffinger, sevenfold blind. I do not say this behind their backs, like a slanderer; do not conceal it from them, for I am ready myself, and on all occasions, to tell it them both to their faces. Why would you," continues he, "surround this man (Staupitz) with all the whirlwinds and tempests of episcopal cares?"

The elector was not offended with Luther's frankness. "The prince," wrote Spalatin, "often speaks of you, and in honourable terms." Frederick sent the monk some very fine cloth for a gown. "It would be too fine," said Luther, "if it were not a prince's gift. I am not worthy that any man should think of me, much less a prince, and so great a prince as he. Those are my best friends who think the worst of me.[2] Thank our prince for his kindness to me; but I cannot allow myself to be praised either by you or by any man; for all praise of man is vain, and only that which comes from God is true."

The excellent chaplain was unwilling to confine himself to his court functions. He wished to make himself useful to the people; but like many individuals in every age, he desired to do it without offence and without irritation, by conciliating the general favour. "Point out," wrote he to Luther, "some work that I may translate into our mother tongue; one that shall give general satisfaction, and at the same time be useful." "Agreeable and useful!" replied Luther; "such a question is beyond my ability. The better things are the less they please.[1] What is more salutary than Jesus Christ? and yet he is to the majority a savour of death. You will tell me that you wish to be useful only to those who love what is good. In that case make them hear the voice of Jesus Christ: you will be useful and agreeable, depend upon it, to a very small number only; for the sheep are rare in this region of wolves."

Luther, however, recommended to his friend the sermons of the Dominican Tauler. "I have never read," said he, "either in Latin or in our own language, a theology sounder, or more in conformity with the Gospel. Taste, then, and see how sweet the Lord is, but not till after you have first tasted and felt how bitter is every thing that we are ourselves."[2]

It was in the course of the year 1517 that Luther entered into communication with Duke George of Saxony. The house of Saxony had at that time two chiefs. Two princes, Ernest and Albert, carried off in their youth from the castle of Altenburg by Kunz of Kaufungen, had, by the treaty of Leipsic, become the founders of the two houses which still bear their names. The Elector Frederick, son of Ernest, was at the period we are describing, the head of the Ernestine branch; and his cousin Duke George, of the Albertine. Dresden and Leipsic were both situated in the states of this duke, whose residence was in the former of these cities. His mother, Sidonia, was daughter of George Podiebrad, king of Bohemia. The long struggle that Bohemia had maintained with Rome, since the time of John Huss, had not been without influence on the prince of Saxony. He had often manifested a desire for a Reformation. "He has imbibed it with his mother's milk," said the priests; "he is by birth an enemy of the clergy."[3] He annoyed the bishops, abbots, canons, and monks in many ways; and his cousin, the Elector Frederick, was compelled more than once to interfere in their behalf. It seemed that Duke George would be one of the warmest partisans of a Reformation. The devout Frederick, on the other hand, who had in former years worn the spurs of Godfrey in the Holy Sepulchre, and girding himself with the long and heavy sword of the conqueror of Jerusalem, had made oath to fight for the Church, like that ancient and valiant knight, appeared destined to be the most ardent champion of Rome. But in all that concerns the Gospel, the anticipations of human wisdom are frequently disappointed. The reverse of what we might have supposed took place. The duke would have been delighted to humiliate the Church and the clergy, to humble the bishops, whose princely retinue far surpassed his own; but it was another thing to receive into his heart

[1] Multa placent principi tuo, quæ Deo displicent. L. Epp. i. 26.
[2] Il mihi maxime prosunt, qui mei pessime meminerint. Ibid. 45.

[3] Quo sunt aliqua salubriora, eo minus placent. L. Epp. i. 46.
[2] Quam amarum est, quicquid nos sumus. Ibid.
[3] L. Opp. (W.) xxii. 1849.

the evangelical doctrine that would humble it, to acknowledge himself a guilty sinner, incapable of being saved, except by grace alone. He would willingly have reformed others, but he cared not to reform himself. He would perhaps have set his hand to the task of compelling the Bishop of Mentz to be contented with a single bishopric, and to keep no more than fourteen horses in his stables, as he said more than once;[1] but when he saw another than himself step forward as a reformer, —when he beheld a simple monk undertake this work, and the Reformation gaining numerous partisans among the people, the haughty grandson of the Hussite king became the most violent adversary of the reform to which he had before shown himself favourable.

In the month of July 1517, Duke George requested Staupitz to send him an eloquent and learned preacher. Luther was recommended to him as a man of extensive learning and irreproachable conduct. The prince invited him to preach at Dresden in the castle-chapel, on the feast of St. James the Elder.

The day arrived. The duke and his court repaired to the chapel to hear the Wittemberg preacher. Luther joyfully seized this opportunity of testifying to the truth before such an assemblage. He selected his text from the Gospel of the day: *Then came to him the mother of Zebedee's children with her sons,"* &c. (Matt. xx. 20–23). He preached on the unreasonable desires and prayers of men; and then spoke emphatically on the assurance of salvation. He established it on this foundation, that those who receive the Word of God with faith are the true disciples of Jesus Christ, elected to eternal life. He next treated of gratuitous election, and showed that this doctrine, if presented in union with the work of Christ, has great power to dispel the terrors of conscience; so that men, instead of flying far from the righteous God, at the sight of their own unworthiness, are gently led to seek their refuge in Him. In conclusion, he related an allegory of three virgins, from which he deduced edifying instructions.

The word of truth made a deep impression on his hearers. Two of them in particular seemed to pay very great attention to the sermon of the Wittemberg monk. The first was a lady of respectable appearance, who was seated on the court benches, and on whose features a profound emotion might be traced. It was Madame de la Sale, first lady to the duchess. The other was a licentiate in canon law, Jerome Emser, councillor and secretary to the duke. Emser possessed great talents and extensive information. A courtier and skilful politician, he would have desired to be on good terms with the two contending parties—to pass at Rome for a

defender of the papacy, and at the same time shine in Germany among the learned men of the age. But under this pliant mind was concealed a violent character. It was in the palace-chapel at Dresden that Luther and Emser first met; they were afterwards to break more than one lance together.

The dinner hour arrived for the inhabitants of the palace, and in a short time the ducal family and the persons attached to the court were assembled at table. The conversation naturally fell on the preacher of the morning. "How were you pleased with the sermon?" said the duke to Madame de la Sale.—"If I could hear but one more like it," replied she, "I should die in peace."— "And I," replied George angrily, "would rather give a large sum not to have heard it; for such discourses are only calculated to make people sin with assurance."

The master having thus made known his opinion, the courtiers gave way uncontrolled to their dissatisfaction. Each one had his censure ready. Some maintained that in his allegory of the three virgins, Luther had in view three ladies of the court; on which there arose interminable babbling. They rallied the three ladies whom the monk of Wittemberg had thus, they said, publicly pointed out.[1] He is an ignorant fellow, said some; he is a proud monk said others. Each one made his comment on the sermon, and put what he pleased into the preacher's mouth. The truth had fallen into the midst of a court that was little prepared to receive it. Every one mangled it after his own fashion. But while the Word of God was thus an occasion of stumbling to many, it was for the first lady a stone of uprising. Falling sick a month after, she confidently embraced the grace of the Saviour, and died with joy.[2]

As for the duke, it was not perhaps in vain that he heard this testimony to the truth. Whatever may have been his opposition to the Reformation during his life, we know that at his death he declared that he had no hope save in the merits of Jesus Christ.

It was natural that Emser should do the honours to Luther in his master's name. He invited him to supper. Luther refused; but Emser persisted, and prevailed on him to come. Luther thought he should only meet a few friends; but he soon perceived that a trap had been laid for him.[3] A master of arts from Leipsic and several Dominicans were with the prince's secretary. The master of arts, having no mean opinion of himself, and full of hatred towards Luther, addressed him in a friendly and honied manner; but he soon got into a passion, and began to shout with all his might.[4] The combat began. The dispute turned, says

[1] L. Opp. (W.) xxii. 1849.

[1] Has tres postes in aula principis a me notatas garrierunt. L. Epp. i. 85.
[2] Keith, Leb. Luth. p. 32.
[3] Inter medias me insidias conjectum. L. Epp. i. 85.
[4] In me acriter et clamose invectus est. Ibid.

Luther, on the trumpery of Aristotle and St. Thomas. [1] At last Luther defied the master of arts to define with all the learning of the Thomists what is the fulfilling of God's commandments. The embarrassed disputant put a good face on the matter. "Pay me my fee," said he holding out his hand, "*da pastum.*" One would have said that he wished to give a regular lesson, taking his fellow-guests for his pupils. "At this foolish reply," adds the reformer, "we all burst into laughter, and then we parted."

During this conversation a Dominican was listening at the door. He longed to enter and spit in Luther's face: [2] but he checked himself, and boasted of it afterwards. Emser, charmed at seeing his guests disputing, and appearing himself to preserve a due moderation, was earnest in excuses to Luther for the manner in which the evening had passed. [3] The latter returned to Wittemberg.

CHAPTER XI.

Return to Wittemberg—Theses—Free-Will—Nature of Man —Rationalism—Proposal to the University of Erfurth— Eck—Urban Regius—Luther's Modesty—Effect of the Theses.

LUTHER returned zealously to work. He was preparing six or seven young theologians who were shortly to undergo an examination for a license to teach. What rejoiced him most of all was, that their promotion would tend to the discredit of Aristotle. "I could desire to multiply the number of his enemies as soon as possible," said he. [4] With this intent he published certain theses about that time which merit our attention.

Free-will was the great subject treated of. He had already touched upon it in the Feldkirchen theses; he now went deeper into the question. There had been, from the very commencement of Christianity, a struggle more or less keen between the two doctrines of man's liberty and his enslavement. Some schoolmen had taught, like Pelagius and other doctors, that man possessed of himself the liberty or the power of loving God and of performing good works. Luther denied this liberty; not to deprive man of it, but in order that he might obtain it. The struggle in this great question is not therefore, as is generally said, between liberty and slavery: it is between a liberty proceeding from man, and one that comes from God. Those who style themselves the partisans of liberty say to man: "Thou hast the power of performing good works; thou hast no need of greater

liberty." The others, who are called the partisans of servitude, say on the contrary: "True liberty is what thou needest, and God offers it thee in his Gospel." On the one side, they speak of liberty to perpetuate slavery; on the other, they speak of slavery to give liberty. Such was the contest in the times of St. Paul, of St. Augustine, and of Luther. Those who say, "Change nothing," are the champions of slavery: the others who say, "Let your fetters fall off," are the champions of liberty.

But we should deceive ourselves were we to sum up all the Reformation in that particular question. It is one of the numerous doctrines maintained by the Wittemberg doctor, and that is all. It would be indulging in a strange delusion to pretend that the Reformation was a fatalism,—an opposition to liberty. It was a noble emancipation of the human mind. Snapping the numerous bonds with which the hierarchy had bound men's minds,—restoring the ideas of liberty, of right, of free examination, it set free its own age, ourselves, and the remotest posterity. But let it not be said that the Reformation delivered man from every human despotism, but made him a slave by proclaiming the sovereignty of Grace. It desired, no doubt, to lead back the human will, to confound it with and render it entirely subject to the Divine will; but what kind of philosophy is that which does not know that an entire conformity with the will of God is the sole, supreme, and perfect liberty; and that man will be really free, only when sovereign righteousness and eternal truth alone have dominion over him?

The following are some of the ninety-nine propositions that Luther put forth in the Church against the Pelagian rationalism of the scholastic theology :—

"It is true that man who has become a corrupt tree, can will or do naught but evil.

"It is false that the will, left to itself, can do good as well as evil; for it is not free, but in bondage.

"It is not in the power of Man's will to choose or reject whatever is offered to it.

"Man cannot of his own nature will God to be God. He would prefer to be God himself, and that God were not God.

"The excellent, infallible, and sole preparation for grace, is the eternal election and predestination of God. [1]

"It is false to say that if man does all that he can, he removes the obstacles to grace.

"In a word, nature possesses neither a pure reason nor a good will. [2]

"On the side of man there is nothing that goes before grace, unless it be impotency and even rebellion.

---

1 Super Aristotelis et Thomæ nugis. L. Epp. i. 85.
2 Ne prodiret et in faciem meam spueret. Ibid.
3 Enixe sese excusavit. Ibid.
4 Cujus vellem hostes cito quamplurimos fieri. Ibid. 59.

1 Optima et infallibilis ad gratiam præparatio et unica dispositio, est eterna Dei electio et prædestinatio. L. Opp. Lat. i. 56.
2 Breviter, nec rectum dictamen habet natura, nec bonam voluntatem. Ibid.

" There is no moral virtue without pride or without sorrow, that is to say, without sin.

" From beginning to end, we are not masters of our actions, but their slaves.

" We do not become righteous by doing what is righteous; but having become righteous, we do what is righteous.

" He who says that a divine, who is not a logician, is a heretic and an empiric, maintains an empirical and heretical proposition.

" There is no form of reasoning (of syllogism) that holds with the things of God.[1]

" If the form of the syllogism could be applied to Divine things, we should have *knowledge* and not *belief* of the article of the Holy Trinity.

" In a word, Aristotle is to divinity, as darkness to light.

" Man is a greater enemy to the grace of God than he is to the law itself.

" He who is without God's grace sins continually, even should he neither rob, murder, nor commit adultery.

" He sins, in that he does not fulfil the law spiritually.

" Not to kill, not to commit adultery, externally only and with regard to the actions, is the righteousness of hypocrites.

" The law of God and the will of man are two adversaries, that without the grace of God can never be reconciled.[2]

" What the law commands, the will never wishes, unless through fear or love it puts on the appearance of willing.

" The law is the task-master of the will, who is not overcome but by the Child that is born unto us. (Isaiah ix. 6.)[3]

" The law makes sin abound, for it exasperates and repels the will.

" But the grace of God makes righteousness abound through Jesus Christ, who causes us to love the law.

" Every work of the law appears good outwardly, but inwardly it is sin.

" The will, when it turns towards the law without the grace of God, does so in its own interest alone.

" Cursed are all those who perform the works of the law.

" Blessed are all those who perform the works of God's grace.

" The law which is good, and in which we have life, is the love of God shed abroad in our hearts by the Holy Ghost. (Rom. v. 5.)

" Grace is not given in order that the work may be done more frequently and more easily, but because without grace there can be no work of love.

" To love God is to hate oneself and to know nothing out of God."[4]

Thus Luther ascribes to God all the good that man can do. There is no question of repairing, of patching up, if we may use the expression, man's will : an entirely new one must be given him. God only has been able to say this, because God alone can accomplish it. This is one of the greatest and most important truths that the human mind can conceive.

But while Luther proclaimed the powerlessness of man, he did not fall into the other extreme. He says in the eighth thesis : " It does not hence follow that the will is naturally depraved ; that is to say, that its nature is that of evil itself, as the Manichees have taught."[1] Originally man's nature was essentially good : it has turned away from the good, which is God, and inclined towards evil. Yet its holy and glorious origin still remains ; and it is capable, by the power of God, of recovering this origin. It is the business of Christianity to restore it to him. It is true that the Gospel displays man in a state of humiliation and impotency, but between two glories and two grandeurs : a past glory from which he has been precipitated, and a future glory to which he is called. There lies the truth : man is aware of it, and if he reflects ever so little, he easily discovers that all which is told him of his present purity, power, and glory is but a fiction with which to lull and sooth his pride.

Luther in his theses protested not only against the pretended goodness of man's will, but still more against the pretended light of his understanding in respect to Divine things. In truth, scholasticism as well as his will. This theology, as some of its doctors have represented it, was at bottom nothing but a kind of rationalism. This is indicated by the propositions we have cited. One might fancy them directed against the rationalism of our days. In the theses that were the signal of the Reformation, Luther censured the Church and the popular superstitions which had added indulgences, purgatory, and so many other abuses to the Gospel. In those we have just quoted, he assailed the schools and rationalism, which had taken away from that very Gospel the doctrine of the sovereignty of God, of his revelation, and of his grace. The Reformation attacked rationalism before it turned against superstition. It proclaimed the rights of God, before it cut off the excrescences of man. It was positive before it became negative. This has not been sufficiently observed ; and yet if we do not notice it, we cannot justly appreciate that religious revolution and its true nature.

However this may be, the truths that Luther had just enunciated with so much energy were very novel. It would have been an easy matter to support these propo-

---

[1] Nulla forma syllogistica tenet in terminis divinis. L. Opp. Lat. i. 56.
[2] Lex et voluntas sunt adversarii duo, sine gratia Dei implacabiles. Ibid. 57.
[3] Lex est exactor voluntatis, qui non superatur nisi per Parvulum qui natus est nobis. Ibid.
[4] L. Opp. Lips. xvii. 143, and Opp. Lat. i.

[1] Nec ideo sequitur quod sit naturaliter mala, id est natura mali, secundum Manichæos. L. Opp. Lips. xvii. 141. and Opp. Lat. i.

sitions at Wittemberg; for there his influence predominated. But it might have been said that he had chosen a field where he knew that no combatant would dare appear. By offering battle in another university, he would give them greater publicity; and it was by publicity that the Reformation was effected. He turned his eyes to Erfurth, whose theologians had shown themselves so irritated against him.

He therefore transmitted these propositions to John Lange, prior of Erfurth, and wrote to him: "My suspense as to your decision upon these paradoxes is great, extreme, too great perhaps, and full of anxiety. I strongly suspect that your theologians will consider as paradoxical, and even as *kakodoxical*,[1] what is in my opinion very orthodox. Pray inform me, as soon as possible, of your sentiments upon them. Have the goodness to declare to the faculty of theology, and to all, that I am prepared to visit you, and to maintain these propositions publicly, either in the university or in the monastery." It does not appear that Luther's challenge was accepted. The monks of Erfurth were contented to let him know that these propositions had greatly displeased them.

But he desired to send them also into another quarter of Germany. For this purpose he turned his eyes on an individual who plays a great part in the history of the Reformation, and whom we must learn to know.

A distinguished professor, by name John Meyer, was then teaching at the university of Ingolstadt in Bavaria. He was born at Eck, a village in Swabia, and was commonly styled Doctor Eck. He was a friend of Luther, who esteemed his talents and his information. He was full of intelligence, had read much, and possessed an excellent memory. He united learning with eloquence. His gestures and his voice expressed the vivacity of his genius. Eck, as regards talent, was in the south of Germany what Luther was in the north. They were the two most remarkable theologians of that epoch, although having very different tendencies. Ingolstadt was almost the rival of Wittemberg. The reputation of these two doctors attracted from every quarter, to the universities where they taught, a crowd of students eager to listen to their teaching. Their personal qualities, not less than their learning, endeared them to their disciples. The character of Dr Eck has been attacked; but one trait of his life will show that, at this period at least, his heart was not closed against generous impulses.

Among the students whom his reputation had attracted to Ingolstadt, was a young man named Urban Regius, born on the shores of an Alpine lake. He had studied first at the university of Friburg in Brisgau. On his arrival at Ingolstadt, Urban followed the philosophical courses, and gained the professor's favour. Compelled to provide for his own wants, he was obliged to undertake the charge of some young noblemen. He had not only to watch over their conduct and their studies, but even to provide with his own money the books and clothing that they stood in need of. These youths dressed with elegance, and were fond of good living. Regius, in his embarrassed condition, entreated the parents to withdraw their sons. —" Take courage," was their reply. His debts increased; his creditors became pressing: he knew not what to do. The emperor was at that time collecting an army against the Turks. Recruiting parties arrived at Ingolstadt, and in his despair Urban enlisted. Dressed in his military uniform, he appeared in the ranks at their final review previous to leaving the town. At that moment Dr Eck came into the square with several of his colleagues. To his great surprise he recognised his pupil among the recruits. "Urban Regius!" said he, fixing on him a piercing glance. "Here!" replied the young soldier. "Pray, what is the cause of this change?" The young man told his story. "I will take the matter upon myself," replied Eck, who then took away his halbert, and bought him off. The parents, threatened by the doctor with their prince's displeasure, sent the money necessary to pay their children's expenses. Urban Regius was saved, and became somewhat later one of the bulwarks of the Reformation.

It was through Dr Eck that Luther thought of making his propositions on Pelagianism and scholastic rationalism known in the south of the empire. He did not, however, send them direct to the Ingolstadt professor, but forwarded them to a common friend, the excellent Christopher Scheurl, secretary to the city of Nuremberg, begging him to transmit them to Eck at Ingolstadt, which was not far from Nuremberg. "I forward you," said he, "my propositions, which are altogether paradoxical, and even kakistodoxical (κακιστόδοξας), as it would appear to many. Communicate them to our dear Eck, that most learned and ingenious man, in order that I may see and hear what he thinks of them."[1] It was thus Luther spoke at that time of Dr Eck: such was the friendship that united them. It was not Luther that broke it off.

But it was not on this field that the battle was to be fought. These propositions turned on doctrines of perhaps greater importance than those which two months later set the Church in flames; and yet, in despite of Luther's challenges, they passed unnoticed. At most, they were read within the walls of the schools, and created no sensation beyond

[1] Imo cacodoxa (unsound doctrine) videri suspicor. L. Epp. i. 60.

[1] Eccio nostro, eruditissimo et ingeniosissimo viro exhibete, ut audiam et videam quid vocet illas. L. Epp. i. 63.

them. It was because they were only university propositions, or theological doctrines; while the theses which followed had reference to an evil that had grown up among the people, and which was then breaking bounds on every side throughout Germany. So long as Luther was content to revive forgotten doctrines, men were silent; but when he pointed out abuses that injured all the world, everybody listened.

And yet in neither case did Luther propose more than to excite one of those theological discussions so frequent in the universities. This was the circle to which his thoughts

were restricted. He had no idea of becoming a reformer. He was humble, and his humility bordered on distrust and anxiety. "Considering my ignorance," said he, "I deserve only to be hidden in some corner, without being known to any one under the sun."[1] But a mighty hand drew him from this corner in which he would have desired to remain unknown to the world. A circumstance, independent of Luther's will, threw him into the field of battle, and the war began. It is this providential circumstance which the course of events now calls upon us to relate.

[1] L. Opp. (W.) xviii. 1944.

<hr>

BOOK III.

THE INDULGENCES AND THE THESES. 1517—MAY 1518.

CHAPTER I.

Procession—Tetzel—Tetzel's Sermon—Confession—Four Graces—Sale—Public Penance—Letter of Indulgence—Exceptions—Amusements and Dissipation.

A GREAT agitation prevailed at that time among the German people. The Church had opened a vast market upon earth. From the crowds of purchasers, and the shouts and jokes of the sellers, it might have been called a fair, but a fair conducted by monks. The merchandise that they were extolling, and which they offered at a reduced price, was, said they, the salvation of souls!

These dealers traversed the country in a handsome carriage, accompanied by three horsemen, living in great state, and spending freely. One might have thought it some archbishop on a progress through his diocese, with his retinue and officers, and not a common chapman or a begging monk. When the procession approached a town, a deputy waited on the magistrate, and said, "The Grace of God and of the Holy Father is at your gates." Instantly everything was in motion in the place. The clergy, the priests and nuns, the council, the schoolmasters and their pupils, the trades with their banners, men and women, young and old, went out to meet these merchants, bearing lighted tapers in their hands, and advancing to the sound of music and of all the bells, "so that they could not have received God himself with greater honour," says an historian. The salutations being exchanged, the procession moved towards the church. The pontiff's bull of grace was carried in front on a velvet cushion, or on cloth of gold. The chief of the indulgence-merchants came next, holding

a large red wooden cross in his hand. All the procession thus moved along amidst singing, prayers, and the smoke of incense. The sound of the organ, and loud music, welcomed the merchant-monk and his attendants into the temple. The cross that he had carried was placed in front of the altar: on it were suspended the arms of the pope, and so long as it remained there, the clergy of the place, the penitentiaries, and the under-commissaries with white wands, came daily after vespers, or before the salutation, to render it homage.[1] This great affair excited a lively sensation in the quiet cities of Germany.

One person in particular attracted the attention of the spectators at these sales. It was he who carried the red cross, and who played the chief part. He was robed in the Dominican dress, and moved with an air of arrogance. His voice was sonorous, and seemed in its full strength, although he had already attained his sixty-third year.[2] This man, the son of a Leipsic goldsmith named Diez, was known as John Diezel, or Tetzel. He had studied in his native city, had taken the degree of bachelor in 1487, and two years after had entered the Dominican order. Numerous honours had been heaped upon his head. Bachelor of divinity, prior of the Dominicans, apostolic commissary, inquisitor (hæreticæ pravitatis inquisitor), he had from the year 1502 uninterruptedly filled the office of dealer in indulgences. The skill that he had acquired as subordinate had soon procured him the nomination as chief commis-

[1] Mit weissen Stæblein. Instructions of the Archbishop of Mentz to the Under-commissaries of Indulgences, &c. Art. 8.
[2] Ingenio ferox et corpore robustus. Cochl. 5.

sary. He received eighty florins a-month; all his expenses were paid; a carriage and three horses were at his disposal; but his subsidiary profits, as may be easily imagined, far exceeded his stipend. In 1507 he gained at Friburg two thousand florins in two days. If he had the office of a mountebank, he possessed the manners also. Convicted at Inspruck of adultery and infamous conduct, his vices had nearly caused his death. The Emperor Maximilian had ordered him to be put into a sack and thrown into the river. The Elector Frederick of Saxony interfered and obtained his pardon.[1] But the lesson that he had received had not taught him modesty. He led two of his children about with him. Miltitz, the pope's legate, mentions this fact in one of his letters.[2] It would have been difficult to find in all the convents of Germany a man better qualified than Tetzel for the business with which he was charged. To the theology of a monk, to the zeal and spirit of an inquisitor, he united the greatest effrontery; and the circumstance that most especially facilitated his task, was his skill in inventing those extravagant stories by which the people's minds are captivated. To him all means were good that filled his chest. Raising his voice, and displaying the eloquence of a mountebank, he offered his indulgences to all comers, and knew better than any tradesman how to extol his wares.[3]

When the cross had been erected, and the arms of the pope suspended from it, Tetzel went into the pulpit, and with a tone of assurance began to extol the value of indulgences, in the presence of a crowd whom the ceremony had attracted to the holy place. The people listened and stared as they heard of the admirable virtues that he announced. A Jesuit historian, speaking of the Dominican monks whom Tetzel had taken with him, says: "Some of these preachers failed not, as usual, to go beyond the matter they were treating of, and so far to exaggerate the worth of indulgences, that they gave the people cause to believe that they were assured of their salvation, and of the deliverance of souls from purgatory, so soon as they had given their money."[4] If such were the disciples, we may easily imagine what the master must have been. Let us listen to one of the harangues he delivered after the elevation of the cross.

"Indulgences (said he) are the most precious and the most noble of God's gifts.

"This cross (pointing to the red cross) has as much efficacy as the very cross of Jesus Christ.[5]

"Come and I will give you letters, all properly sealed, by which even the sins that you intend to commit may be pardoned.

"I would not change my privileges for those of St. Peter in heaven; for I have saved more souls by my indulgences than the apostle by his sermons.

"There is no sin so great, that an indulgence cannot remit; and even if any one (which is doubtless impossible) had offered violence to the blessed Virgin Mary, mother of God, let him pay—only let him pay well, and all will be forgiven him.[1]

"Reflect then, that for every mortal sin you must, after confession and contrition, do penance for seven years, either in this life or in purgatory: now, how many mortal sins are there not committed in a day, how many in a week, how many in a month, how many in a year, how many in a whole life![2] ......
Alas! these sins are almost infinite, and they entail an infinite penalty in the fires of purgatory. And now, by means of these letters of indulgence, you can once in your life, in every case except four, which are reserved for the apostolic see, and afterwards in the article of death, obtain a plenary remission of all your penalties and all your sins!"

Tetzel even entered into financial calculations. "Do you not know," said he, "that if any one desires to visit Rome, or any country where travellers incur danger, he sends his money to the bank, and for every hundred florins that he wishes to have, he gives five or six or ten more, that by means of the letters of this bank he may be safely repaid his money at Rome or elsewhere......
And you, for a quarter of a florin, will not receive these letters of indulgence, by means of which you may introduce into paradise, not a vile metal, but a divine and immortal soul, without its running any risk.[3]

Tetzel then passed to another subject.

"But more than this," said he: "indulgences avail not only for the living, but for the dead.

"For that, repentance is not even necessary.

"Priest! noble! merchant! wife! youth! maiden! do you not hear your parents and your other friends who are dead, and who cry from the bottom of the abyss: We are suffering horrible torments! a trifling alms would deliver us; you can give it, and you will not!"

All shuddered at these words uttered by the thundering voice of the impostor-monk.

"At the very instant," continued Tetzel,

[1] Welchen Churfurst Friederich vom Sack zu Inspruck erbeten hatte. Mathes. 10.
[2] L. Opp. (W.) xv. 862.
[3] Circumferuntur venales indulgentiæ in his regionibus a Tecelio Dominicano impudentissimo sycophanta. Melancth. Vita Luth.
[4] Hist. du Lutheranisme par le P. Maimbourg, de la compagnie de Jésus, 1681, p. 21.
[5] L. Opp. (W.) xxii. 1393.

[1] Tetzel defends and maintains this assertion in his *Anti-theses*, published the same year. Th. 99, 100, and 101. "Sub-commissariis insuper ac prædicatoribus veniarum imponere, ut si quis per impossibile Dei genetricem semper virginem violasset, quod eundem indulgentiarum vigore absolvere possent, luce clarius est."—Positiones fratris J. Tezelii quibus defendit indulgentias contra Lutherum.
[2] Quot peccata mortalia committuntur in die....Löscher's Reformations Act. i. 418.
[3] Si contingat aliquem ire Romam, vel ad alias periculosas partes, mittat pecunias suas in banco, et ille proquolibet centum dat quinque, aut sex, aut decem, &c. Ibid.

" that the money rattles at the bottom of the chest, the soul escapes from purgatory, and flies liberated to heaven. [1]

" O stupid and brutish people, who do not understand the grace so richly offered ! Now heaven is every where opened !......Do you refuse to enter now ? When, then, will you enter ?......Now you can ransom so many souls !......Stiffnecked and thoughtless man ! with twelve groats you can deliver your father from purgatory, and you are ungrateful enough not to save him ! I shall be justified in the day of judgment ; but you,—you will be punished so much the more severely for having neglected so great salvation. I declare to you, though you should have but a single coat, you ought to strip it off and sell it, in order to obtain this grace......The Lord our God no longer reigns. He has resigned all power to the pope."

Then seeking to make use of other arms besides, he added : " Do you know why our most Holy Lord distributes so rich a grace ? It is to restore the ruined Church of St. Peter and St. Paul, so that it may not have its equal in the world. This Church contains the bodies of the holy apostles Peter and Paul, and those of a multitude of martyrs. These saintly bodies, through the present state of the building, are now, alas !...... beaten upon, inundated, polluted, dishonoured, reduced to rottenness, by the rain and the hail......Alas ! shall these sacred ashes remain longer in the mire and in degradation ? " [2]

This description failed not to produce an impression on many, who burned with a desire to come to the aid of poor Leo X., who had not the means of sheltering the bodies of St. Peter and St. Paul from the weather.

The orator next turned against the cavillers and traitors who opposed his work : " I declare them excommunicated ! " exclaimed he.

Then addressing the docile souls, and making an impious application of scripture, he exclaimed : " Blessed are the eyes which see the things that ye see : for I tell you, that many prophets and kings have desired to see those things which ye see, and have not seen them ; and to hear those things which ye hear, and have not heard them ! " And in conclusion, pointing to the strong box in which the money was received, he generally finished his pathetic discourse by three appeals to his auditory : " Bring— bring—bring ! "—" He used to shout these words with such a horrible bellowing," wrote Luther, " that one would have said it was a mad bull rushing on the people and goring them with his horns." [3] When his speech was ended, he left the pulpit, ran towards the money-box, and in sight of all the people

flung into it a piece of money, taking care that it should rattle loudly. [1]

Such were the discourses that Germany listened to with astonishment in the days when God was preparing Luther.

The speech being concluded, the indulgence was considered as " having established its throne in the place with due solemnity." Confessionals decorated with the pope's arms were ranged about : the under-commissaries and the confessors whom they selected were considered the representatives of the apostolic penitentiaries of Rome at the time of a great jubilee ; and on each of their confessionals were posted in large characters, their names, surnames, and titles. [2]

Then thronged the crowd around the confessors. Each came with a piece of money in his hand. Men, women, and children, the poor, and even those who lived on alms—all found money. The penitentiaries, after having explained anew to each individual privately the greatness of the indulgence, addressed this question to the penitents : " How much money can you conscientiously spare to obtain so complete a remission ? " The demand, said the Instructions of the Archbishop of Mentz to the Commissaries, should be made at this moment, in order that the penitents might be better disposed to contribute.

Four precious graces were promised to those who should aid in building the basilic of St. Peter. " The first grace that we announce to you," said the commissaries, in accordance with the letter of their instructions, " is the full pardon of every sin." [3] Next followed three other graces : *first,* the right of choosing a confessor, who, whenever the hour of death appeared at hand, should give absolution from all sin, and even from the greatest crimes reserved for the apostolic see : [4] *secondly,* a participation in all the blessings, works, and merits of the Catholic Church, prayers, fasts, alms, and pilgrimages ; [5] *thirdly,* redemption of the souls that are in purgatory.

To obtain the first of these graces, it was requisite to have contrition of heart and confession of mouth, or at least an intention of confessing. But as for the three others, they might be obtained without contrition, without confession, simply by paying. Christopher Columbus, extolling the value of gold, had said ere this with great seriousness : " Whoever possesses it can introduce souls into paradise." Such was the doctrine taught by the Archbishop of Mentz and by the papal commissaries.

" As for those," said they, " who wish to deliver souls from purgatory and procure the pardon of all their offences, let them put money into the chest ; contrition of heart or

---

[1] Thesis 56. Positiones fratris J. Tezelii quibus defendit Indulgentias contra Lutherum.
[2] Instructions of the Archbishop of Mentz, &c.
[3] Resol. on thesis 32.

[1] Tentzel, Reformationsgesch.—Myconius, Ref. Hist.— Instr. of Archbishop of Mentz to the Under-commissaries. —Luther's Theses.
[2] Instruct., &c. 5, 69.
[3] Ibid. 19.
[4] Ibid. 30.
[5] Ibid. 35.

confession of mouth is not necessary.[1] Let them only hasten to bring their money; for thus will they perform a work most useful to the souls of the dead, and to the building of the Church of St. Peter." Greater blessings could not be offered at a lower rate.

The confession over, and that was soon done, the faithful hastened to the vendor. One alone was charged with the sale. His stall was near the cross. He cast inquiring looks on those who approached him. He examined their manner, their gait, their dress, and he required a sum proportionate to the appearance of the individual who presented himself. Kings, queens, princes, archbishops, bishops, were, according to the scale, to pay twenty-five ducats for an ordinary indulgence. Abbots, counts, and barons, ten. The other nobles, the rectors, and all those who possessed an income of five hundred florins, paid six. Those who had two hundred florins a-year paid one; and others, only a half. Moreover, if this tariff could not be carried out to the letter, full powers were given the apostolical commissionary; and all was to be arranged according to the data of " sound reason," and the generosity of the donor.[2] For particular sins, Tetzel had a particular tax. For polygamy it was six ducats; for sacrilege and perjury, nine ducats; for murder, eight ducats; for witchcraft, two ducats. Samson, who exercised the same trade in Switzerland as Tetzel in Germany, had a somewhat different scale. For infanticide he required four *livres tournois;* and for parricide or fratricide, one ducat.[3]

The apostolical commissaries sometimes met with difficulties in their trade. It frequently happened, both in towns and villages, that the men were opposed to this traffic, and forbade their wives to give anything to these merchants. What could their pious spouses do? " Have you not your dowry, or other property, at your own disposal?" asked the vendors. " In that case you can dispose of it for so holy a work, against the will of your husbands."[4]

The hand that had given the indulgence could not receive the money; this was forbidden under the severest penalties: there were good reasons to fear lest that hand should prove unfaithful. The penitent was himself to drop the price of his pardon into the chest.[5] They showed an angry countenance against all who daringly kept their purses closed.[6]

If among the crowd of those who thronged the confessionals there should be found a man whose crime had been public, though it was one that the civil laws could not reach, he was to begin by doing public penance. They first led him into a chapel or the vestry; there they stripped off his garments, took off his shoes, and left him nothing but his shirt. They crossed his arms over his bosom: placed a taper in one hand, and a rod in the other. The penitent then walked at the head of a procession to the red cross. Here he remained kneeling until the chants and the offertory were over. After this the commissary struck up the psalm, *Miserere Mei!* The confessors immediately drew near the penitent, and conducted him through the station towards the commissary, who, taking the rod and striking him thrice gently on the back,[1] said to him: " God have pity on thee, and pardon thy sin !" He then began to sing the *Kyrie eleison:*[2] the penitent was led to the front of the cross, where the confessor gave him the apostolical absolution, and declared him reinstated in the communion of the faithful. Sad mummery, concluded by the words of Holy Scripture, that, in such a moment, were mere profanity!

We give one of these letters of absolution. It is worth while learning the contents of these diplomas which led to the Reformation of the Church.

" May our Lord Jesus Christ have pity on thee, N. N., and absolve thee by the merits of his most holy passion! And I, in virtue of the apostolical power that has been confided to me, absolve thee from all ecclesiastical censures, judgments, and penalties which thou mayst have incurred; moreover, from all excesses, sins, and crimes that thou mayst have committed, however great and enormous they may be, and from whatsoever cause, were they even reserved for our most holy father the pope and for the apostolic see. I blot out all the stains of inability and all marks of infamy that thou mayst have drawn upon thyself on this occasion. I remit the penalties that thou shouldst have endured in purgatory. I restore thee anew to participation in the sacraments of the Church. I incorporate thee afresh in the communion of saints, and re-establish thee in the purity and innocence which thou hadst at thy baptism. So that in the hour of death, the gate by which sinners enter the place of torments and punishment shall be closed against thee, and, on the contrary, the gate leading to the paradise of joy shall be open. And if thou shouldst not die for long years, this grace will remain unalterable until thy last hour shall arrive.

" In the name of the Father, Son, and Holy Ghost. Amen.

" Friar JOHN TETZEL, commissary, has signed this with his own hand."

With what skill are presumptuous and lying words here foisted in between holy and christian expressions!

All the believers were required to confess in the place where the red cross was set up. None were excepted but the sick and aged, and pregnant women. If, however, there chanced to be in the neighbourhood some noble in his castle, some great personage in his palace, there was also an exemption for him,[1] as he would not like to be mixed up with this crowd, and his money was well worth the pains of fetching from his mansion.

Was there any convent whose chiefs, opposed to Tetzel's commerce, forbade their monks to visit the places where the Indulgence had set up its throne, they found means of remedying the evil by sending them confessors, who were empowered to absolve them contrary to the rules of their order and the will of their superiors.[2] There was no vein in the gold mine that they did not find the means of working.

Then came what was the end and aim of the whole business: the reckoning of the money. For greater security, the chest had three keys: one was in Tetzel's keeping; the second in that of a treasurer delegated by the house of Fugger of Augsburg, to whom this vast enterprise had been consigned; the third was confided to the civil authority. When the time was come, the money-boxes were opened before a public notary, and the contents were duly counted and registered. Must not Christ arise and drive out these profane money-changers from the sanctuary?

When the mission was over, the dealers relaxed from their toils. The instructions of the commissary-general forbade them, it is true, to frequent taverns and places of bad repute;[3] but they cared little for this prohibition. Sin could have but few terrors for those who made so easy a traffic in it. "The collectors led a disorderly life," says a Romanist historian; "they squandered in taverns, gambling-houses, and places of ill-fame, all that the people had saved from their necessities."[4] It has even been asserted, that when they were in the taverns they would often stake the salvation of souls on a throw of the dice.[5]

CHAPTER II.

The Franciscan Confessor—The Soul in the Burial-ground—The Shoemaker of Hagenau—The Students—Myconius—Conversation with Tetzel—Trick of a Nobleman—Remarks of the Wise and of the People—A Miner of Schneeberg.

BUT now let us turn to the scenes which this sale of the pardon of sins at that time gave rise to in Germany. There are characteristics which, of themselves alone, depict the times. We prefer using the language of the men whose history we are narrating.

At Magdeburg, Tetzel refused to absolve a rich lady, unless (as he declared to her) she would pay one hundred florins in advance. She requested the advice of her usual confessor, who was a Franciscan: "God grants the remission of sins gratuitously," replied the monk, "he does not sell it." He begged her, however, not to communicate to Tetzel the counsel she had received from him. But this merchant having notwithstanding heard a report of this opinion so contrary to his interests, exclaimed: "Such a counsellor deserves to be banished or to be burnt."[1]

Tetzel rarely found men enlightened enough, and still more rarely men who were bold enough, to resist him. In general he easily managed the superstitious crowd. He had set up the red cross of the indulgences at Zwickau, and the worthy parishioners had hastened to drop into his strong-box the money that would deliver them. He was about to leave with a well-stored purse, when, on the eve of his departure, the chaplains and their acolytes asked him for a farewell supper. The request was just. But how contrive it? the money was already counted and sealed up. On the morrow he caused the great bell to be tolled. The crowd rushed into the church; each one imagined something extraordinary had happened, seeing that the business was over. "I had resolved," said he, "to depart this morning; but last night I was awakened by groans. I listened attentively......they came from the cemetery......Alas! it was some poor soul calling upon me and earnestly entreating me to deliver it from the torments by which it is consumed! I shall stay, therefore, one day longer, in order to move the compassion of all christian hearts in favour of this unhappy soul. I myself will be the first to give, and he that does not follow my example will merit condemnation." What heart would not have replied to this appeal? Who knows, besides, what soul it is thus crying from the cemetery? The offerings were abundant, and Tetzel entertained the chaplains and their acolytes with a joyous repast, the expense of which was defrayed by the offerings given in behalf of the soul of Zwickau.[2]

The indulgence-merchants had visited Hagenau in 1517. The wife of a shoemaker, taking advantage of the authorization given in the commissary-general's instructions, had procured a letter of indulgence, contrary to her husband's will, and had paid a gold florin. She died shortly after. As the husband had not caused a mass to be said for the repose of her soul, the priest charged him with contempt of religion, and the magistrate of

1 Instruction 9.   2 Ibid. 69.   3 Ibid. 4.
4 Sarpi, Council of Trent, 5.
5 Schrock, K. G. v. d. R. i. 116.

1 Scultet. Annal. Evangel. 4.
2 Löscher's Ref. Act. i. 404.   L. Opp. xv. 443, &c.

Hagenau summoned him to appear in court. The shoemaker put his wife's indulgence in his pocket, and went to answer the accusation.—" Is your wife dead?" asked the magistrate.—" Yes," replied he.—" What have you done for her?"—" I have buried her body, and commended her soul to God."—" But have you had a mass said for the repose of her soul?"—" I have not: it was of no use: she entered heaven at the moment of her death."—" How do you know that?"—" Here is the proof." As he said these words, he drew the indulgence from his pocket, and the magistrate, in presence of the priest, read in so many words, that, at the moment of her death, the woman who had received it would not go into purgatory, but would at once enter into heaven. " If the reverend gentleman maintains that a mass is still necessary," added the widower, " my wife has been deceived by our most holy father the pope ; if she has not been, it is the priest who deceives me." There was no reply to this, and the shoemaker was acquitted. Thus did the plain sense of the people condemn these pious frauds. [1]

One day as Tetzel was preaching at Leipsic, and mingling with his sermon some of these stories of which we have given a specimen, two students quitted the church in indignation, exclaiming: " It is impossible for us to listen any longer to this monk's jokes and puerilities." [2] One of them, we are informed, was the youthful Camerarius, who afterwards became Melancthon's intimate friend and biographer.

But of all the young men of the age, the one on whom Tetzel made the deepest impression was doubtless Myconius, afterwards celebrated as a reformer and historian of the Reformation. He had received a christian education. " My son," his father, a pious Franconian, would often say to him, " pray frequently ; for all things are given to us gratuitously from God alone. The blood of Christ," added he, " is the only ransom for the sins of the whole world. O my son, though three men only should be saved by Christ's blood, believe, and believe with assurance, that thou art one of those three men. [3] It is an insult to the Saviour's blood to doubt that he can save." And then, cautioning his son against the traffic that was now beginning to be established in Germany : " Roman indulgences," said he again, " are nets to catch silver, and which serve to deceive the simple-minded. Remission of sins and eternal life are not to be purchased with money."

At the age of thirteen Frederick was sent to the school at Annaberg to finish his studies. Tetzel arrived in this city shortly after, and

remained there two years. The people flocked in crowds to hear his sermons. " There is no other means of obtaining eternal life," cried Tetzel in a voice of thunder, " than the satisfaction of works. But this satisfaction is impossible for man. He can therefore only purchase it from the Roman pontiff." [1]

When Tetzel was about to quit Annaberg, his sermons became more earnest. " Soon," cried he in threatening accents, " I shall take down the cross, shut the gates of heaven, [2] and extinguish the brightness of the sun of grace that beams before your eyes." And then assuming a tender tone of exhortation : " Now is the accepted time; behold, now is the day of salvation." Again raising his voice, the priestly Stentor, [3] who was addressing the inhabitants of a country whose wealth consisted in its mines, shouted out : " Bring your money, citizens of Annaberg ! contribute bounteously in favour of indulgences, and your mines and your mountains shall be filled with pure silver !" Finally, at Whitsuntide, he declared that he would distribute his letters to the poor gratuitously, and for the love of God.

The youthful Myconius was one of Tetzel's hearers. He felt an ardent desire to take advantage of this offer. " I am a poor sinner," said he to the commissaries in Latin, " and I have need of a gratuitous pardon."—" Those alone," replied the merchants, " can have part in Christ's merits who lend a helping hand to the Church, that is to say, who give money."—" What is the meaning, then," asked Myconius, " of those promises of a free gift posted on the gates and walls of the churches ?"—" Give at least a groat," said Tetzel's people, after having vainly interceded with their master in favour of the young man. " I cannot."—" Only six deniers."—" I am not worth so much." The Dominicans begin to fear that he came on purpose to entrap them. " Listen," said they, " we will make you a present of the six deniers." The young man replied indignantly : " I will have no bought indulgences. If I desired to buy them, I should only have to sell one of my schoolbooks. I desire a gratuitous pardon, and for the love of God alone. You will render an account to God for having allowed a soul to be lost for six deniers."—" Who sent you to entrap us ?" exclaimed the vendors.—" Nothing but the desire of receiving God's pardon could have made me appear before such great gentlemen," replied the young man, as he withdrew.

" I was very sad at being thus sent away unpitied. But I felt, however, a comforter within me, who said that there was a God in heaven who pardons repentant souls without

1 Musculi Loci Communes, 362.
2 Hoffman's Reformationsgesch. v. Leipzick, 32.
3 Si tantum tres homines essent salvandi per sanguinem Christi, certo statueret unum se esse ex tribus illis. Melch. Adam. Vita Myconii.

1 Si nummis redimatur a pontifice Romano. Melch Adam.
2 Clausurum januam cœli. Ibid.
3 Stentor pontificius. Ibid.

money and without price, for the love of his Son Jesus Christ. As I took leave of these folks, the Holy Spirit touched my heart. I burst into tears, and prayed to the Lord with anguish: O God! cried I, since these men have refused to remit my sins, because I wanted money to pay them, do thou, Lord, have pity on me, and pardon them of thy pure grace. I repaired to my chamber; I prayed to my crucifix which was lying on my desk; I put it on a chair, and fell down before it. I cannot describe to you what I experienced. I begged God to be a father to me, and to do with me whatever he pleased. I felt my nature changed, converted, transformed. What had delighted me before, now became an object of disgust. To live with God and to please him was my earnest, my sole desire."[1]

Thus did Tetzel himself prepare the Reformation. By flagrant abuses, he cleared the way for a purer doctrine; and the indignation he aroused in a generous youth was one day to burst forth with power. We may form some idea of this by the following anecdote.

A Saxon nobleman, who had heard Tetzel at Leipsic, was much displeased by his falsehoods. Approaching the monk, he asked him if he had the power of pardoning sins that men have an intention of committing. "Most assuredly," replied Tetzel, "I have received full powers from his holiness for that purpose."—"Well, then," answered the knight, "I am desirous of taking a slight revenge on one of my enemies, without endangering his life. I will give you ten crowns if you will give me a letter of indulgence that shall fully justify me." Tetzel made some objections; they came, however, to an arrangement by the aid of thirty crowns. The monk quitted Leipsic shortly after. The nobleman and his attendants lay in wait for him in a wood between Jüterbock and Treblin; they fell upon him, gave him a slight beating, and took away the well-stored indulgence-chest the inquisitor was carrying with him. Tetzel made a violent outcry, and carried his complaint before the courts. But the nobleman showed the letter which Tetzel had signed himself, and which exempted him beforehand from every penalty. Duke George, whom this action had at first exceedingly exasperated, no sooner read the document than he ordered the accused to be acquitted.[2]

This traffic every where occupied men's thoughts, and was every where talked of. It was the topic of conversation in castles, in academies, and in the burghers' houses, as well as in taverns, inns, and all places of public resort.[3] Opinions were divided; some

believed, others felt indignant. As for the sensible part of the nation, they rejected with disgust the system of indulgences. This doctrine was so opposed to the Holy Scriptures and to morality, that every man who had any knowledge of the Bible, or any natural light, internally condemned it, and only waited for a signal to oppose it. On the other hand, the scoffers found ample food for raillery. The people, whom the dissolute lives of the priests had irritated for many years, and whom the fear of punishment still kept within certain bounds, gave vent to all their hatred. Complaints and sarcasms might every where be heard on the love of money that devoured the clergy.

They did not stop there. They attacked the power of the keys and the authority of the sovereign pontiff. "Why," said they, does not the pope deliver at once all the souls from purgatory by a holy charity and on account of their great wretchedness, since he delivers so many for love of perishable money and of the cathedral of St. Peter? Why are they always celebrating festivals and anniversaries for the dead? Why does not the pope restore or permit the resumption of the benefices and prebends founded in favour of the dead, since it is now useless and even reprehensible to pray for those whom the indulgences have delivered for ever? What means this new holiness of God and of the pope, that for love of money they grant to an impious man, and an enemy of God, to deliver from purgatory a pious soul, the beloved of the Lord, rather than deliver it themselves gratuitously through love, and because of its great misery?"[1]

Stories were told of the gross and immoral conduct of the traffickers in indulgences. To pay their bills to the carriers who transported them and their merchandise, the innkeepers with whom they lodged, or whoever had done them any service, they gave a letter of indulgence for four souls, for five, or for any number according to circumstances. Thus these certificates of salvation circulated in the inns and markets like bank notes or other paper money. "Pay! pay!" said the people, "that is the head, belly, tail, and all the contents of their sermons."[2]

A miner of Schneeberg met a seller of indulgences. "Must we credit," asked he, "what you have so often told us of the power of indulgences and of the papal authority, and believe that we can, by throwing a penny into the chest, ransom a soul from purgatory?" The merchant affirmed it was so. "Ah!" resumed the miner, "what a merciless man, then, the pope must be, since for want of a wretched penny he leaves a poor soul crying in the flames so long! If he has no ready money, let him store up some hundred thousand crowns, and deliver all these

[1] Myconius's Letter to Eberus in Hechtii Vita Tezelii, Wittemb. 114.
[2] Albinus, Meissn. Chronik. L. W. (W.) xv. 446, &c., Hechtius in Vit. Tezelii.
[3] L. Opp. (Leipz.) xvii. 111, 116.

[1] Luther, Theses on Indulgences. 82, 83, 84.
[2] L. Opp. (Leips.) xvii. 79.

souls at once. We poor people would very readily repay him both interest and capital."

The Germans were wearied with this scandalous traffic that was carried on in the midst of them. They could not longer endure the impositions of these master-cheats of Rome, as Luther called them.[1] No bishop, no theologian, however, dared oppose their quackery and their frauds. All minds were in suspense. Men asked one another if God would not raise up some mighty man for the work that was to be done: but nowhere did he appear.

CHAPTER III.

Leo X.—The Pope's Necessities—Albert—His Character—Farming the Indulgences—Franciscans and Dominicans.

THE pope who then sat in St. Peter's chair was not a Borgia, but Leo X. of the illustrious family of the Medici. He was clever, sincere, full of gentleness and meekness. His manners were affable, his liberality unbounded, his morals superior to those of his court; Cardinal Pallavicini however acknowledges that they were not beyond reproach. To this amiable character he united many of the qualities of a great prince. He was a friend to the arts and sciences. In his presence were represented the first Italian comedies ; and there were few of his time that he had not seen performed. He was passionately fond of music ; every day his palace re-echoed with the sound of instruments, and he was frequently heard humming the airs that had been executed before him. He loved magnificence, he spared no expense in festivals, sports, theatres, presents, or rewards. No court surpassed in splendour and in luxury that of the sovereign pontiff. Hence, when it was known that Julian Medici thought of taking up his abode at Rome with his young wife : "Thank God!" exclaimed Cardinal Bibliena, the most influential of Leo's councillors ; for nothing was wanting but a court of ladies."[2] A court of ladies was the necessary complement of the court of the pope. But to religious feelings Leo was quite a stranger. " He possessed such charming manners," said Sarpi,[3] " that he would have been a perfect man, if he had had some knowledge of religion and greater inclination to piety, about which he never troubled himself much."

[1] Fessi erant Germani omnes, ferendis explicationibus, nundinationibus, et infinitis imposturis Romanensium nebulonum. L. Opp. Lat. in Præf.
[2] Ranke, Rœmische Pæbste, i. 71.
[3] Council of Trent, 4. Pallavicini, while endeavouring to confute Sarpi, confirms and even heightens his testimony: Suo plane officio defuit, (Leo)....venationes, facetias, pompas adeo frequentes....Conc. Trid. Hist. i. s, 9.

Leo required large sums of money. He had to provide for his great expenses, find means for his extensive liberality, fill the purse of gold which he flung daily among the people, keep up the licentious shows of the Vatican, satisfy the numerous calls of his relatives and of his courtiers, who were addicted to pleasures, endow his sister who had married Prince Cibo, natural son of Pope Innocent VIII., and defray the cost of his taste for literature, the arts, and luxury. His cousin, Cardinal Pucci, who was as skilful in the science of amassing as Leo in that of squandering money, advised him to have recourse to indulgences. The pope, therefore, published a bull, announcing a general indulgence, the produce of which should be applied (said he) to the building of St. Peter's, that monument of sacerdotal magnificence. In a letter given at Rome, under the seal of the Fisherman, in November 1517, Leo requires of his commissary of indulgences 147 gold ducats, to purchase a manuscript of the thirty-third book of Livy. Of all the uses to which he applied the money of the Germans, this was undoubtedly the best. Yet it was a strange thing to deliver souls from purgatory to procure the means of purchasing a manuscript of the history of the Roman wars.

There was at that time in Germany a youthful prince who in many respects was the very image of Leo X.: this was Albert, younger brother of the Elector Joachim of Brandenburg. This young man at the age of twenty-four years had been created archbishop and elector of Mentz and of Magdeburg ; two years later he was made cardinal. Albert had neither the virtues nor the vices that are often met with in the superior dignitaries of the church. Young, frivolous, and worldly, but not without generous sentiments, he saw clearly many of the abuses of Romanism, and cared little for the fanatical monks who surrounded him. His equity inclined him to acknowledge, in part at least, the justice of the demands of the friends of the Gospel. At the bottom of his heart he was not violently opposed to Luther. Capito, one of the most distinguished reformers, was long his chaplain, his counsellor, and his intimate confidant. Albert regularly attended at his sermons. " He did not despise the Gospel," said Capito ; " on the contrary he highly esteemed it, and for a long time prevented the monks from attacking Luther." But he would have desired the latter not to compromise him, and that, while pointing out doctrinal errors and the vices of the inferior clergy, he should beware of exposing the failings of bishops and of princes. Above all, he feared to see his name mixed up in the matter. " Consider," said the confiding Capito to Luther, deceiving himself as many have done in similar circumstances, " consider the example of Jesus Christ and of the Apostles : they blamed the Pharisees and the incestuous Corinthians ; but they never named the offenders. You do not know what is passing in the hearts of the bishops. There is much more good in them than perhaps you imagine." But Albert's profane and frivolous disposition, much more than the susceptibilities and fears of his self-love, was destined to alienate him from the Reformation. Affable, witty, handsome, sumptuous, extravagant, delighting in the luxuries of the table, in costly equipages, in magnificent buildings, in licentious pleasures, and in the society of literary men, this young archbishop-elector was in Germany what Leo X. was in Rome. His court was one of the most magnificent in the empire. He was ready to sacrifice to pleasure and to greatness all the presentiments of truth that might have stolen into his heart. Nevertheless, even to the last, he evinced a certain resistance and better convictions; more than once he gave proofs of his moderation and of his equity.

Albert, like Leo, had need of money. Some rich merchants of Augsburg, named Fugger, had made him advances. He was called upon to pay his debts. Besides, although he had monopolized two archbishoprics and one bishopric, he had not the means of paying for his *pallium*. This ornament, made of white wool, besprinkled with black crosses, and blessed by the pope, who sent it to the archbishops as an emblem of their dignity, cost them 26,000, or, according to some accounts, 30,000 florins. Albert very naturally formed the project of resorting to the same means as the pontiff to obtain money. He solicited the general farming of indulgences, or, " of the sins of the Germans," as they said at Rome.

Sometimes the popes themselves worked them; at other times they farmed them, as some governments still farm gambling-houses. Albert proposed sharing the profits of this business with Leo. The pope, in accepting the terms, exacted immediate payment of the price of the pallium. Albert, who was reckoning on the indulgences to meet this demand, again applied to the Fuggers, who thinking it a safe speculation made the required advance on certain conditions, and were named treasurers of this undertaking. They were the royal bankers of this epoch: they were afterwards created counts for the services they had rendered.

The pope and the archbishop having thus divided before hand the spoils of the good souls of Germany, it was next a question who should be commissioned to realize the investment. It was at first offered to the Franciscans, and their superior was associated with Albert. But these monks wished to have no share in it, for it was already in bad odour among all good people. The Augustines, who were more enlightened than the other religious orders, cared still less about it. The Franciscans, however, feared to displease the pope, who had jus' sent a Cardinal's hat to their general Forli, —a hat that had cost this poor mendicant order 30,000 florins. The superior judged it more prudent not to refuse openly; but he made all kinds of objections to Albert. They could never come to an understanding; and accordingly the elector joyfully accepted the proposition to take the whole matter to him self. The Dominicans, on their part, coveted a share in the general enterprise about to be set on foot. Tetzel, who had already acquired great reputation in this trade, hastened to Mentz, and offered his services to the elector. They called to mind the ability he had shown in publishing the indulgences for the knights of the Teutonic order of Prussia and Livonia; his proposals were accepted, and thus the whole traffic passed into the hands of his order. [1]

CHAPTER IV.

Tetzel approaches—Luther in the Confessional—Tetzel's Anger—Luther has no Plan—Jealousy of Orders—Luther's Sermon—The Elector's Dream.

LUTHER, as far as we are acquainted, heard of Tetzel for the first time at Grimma in 1516, just as he was commencing his visitation of the churches. It was reported to Staupitz, who was still with Luther, that there was a seller of indulgences at Würzen named Tetzel, who was making a great noise. Some of his extravagant expressions were quoted, and Luther exclaimed with indignation: " If God permit, I will make a hole in his drum." [2]

Tetzel was returning from Berlin, where he had met with the most friendly reception from the Elector Joachim, the farmer-general's brother, when he took his station at Juterbock. Staupitz, taking advantage of the confidence the Elector Frederick placed in him, had often called his attention to the abuses of the indulgences and the scandalous lives of the vendors. [3] The princes of Saxony, indignant at this disgraceful traffic, had forbidden the merchant to enter their provinces. He was therefore compelled to remain in the territories of his patron the Archbishop of Magdeburg; but he approached Saxony as near as he could. Juterbock was only four miles from Wittemberg. " This great purse-thresher," said Luther, " began to thresh[4] bravely throughout the country, so that the money began to leap and fall tinkling into the box." The people flocked in crowds from Wittemberg to the indulgence-market of Juterbock.

1 Seckendorf, 42.
2 Lingke, Reisegesch. Luthers. 27.
3 Instillans ejus pectori frequentes indulgentiarum abusus. Cochlœus, 4.
4 Dreschen. Luth. Opp. xvii.

At this period Luther was still full of respect for the Church and the pope. "I was at that time," said he, "a monk, and a most furious papist, so intoxicated, nay, so drowned in the Roman doctrines, that I would have willingly aided, if I could, in killing any one who should have had the audacity to refuse the slightest obedience to the pope.[1] I was a very Saul, as there are many still." But at the same time his heart was ready to catch fire for everything that he recognised as truth, and against everything he believed to be error. "I was a young doctor fresh from the forge, ardent and rejoicing in the Word of the Lord."[2]

Luther was one day seated in the confessional at Wittemberg. Many of the townspeople came successively, and confessed themselves guilty of great excesses. Adultery, licentiousness, usury, ill-gotten gains,—such are the crimes acknowledged to the minister of the Word by those souls of which he will one day have to give an account. He reprimands, corrects, instructs. But what is his astonishment when these individuals reply that they will not abandon their sins?......
Greatly shocked, the pious monk declares that since they will not promise to change their lives, he cannot absolve them. The unhappy creatures then appeal to their letters of indulgence; they show them, and maintain their virtue. But Luther replies that he has nothing to do with these papers, and adds: *Except ye repent, ye shall all likewise perish.* They cry out and protest; but the doctor is immovable. They must cease to do evil, and learn to do well, or else there is no absolution. "Have a care," added he, "how you listen to the clamours of these indulgence-merchants: you have better things to do than buy these licenses which they sell at so vile a price."[3]

The inhabitants of Wittemberg, in great alarm, hastily returned to Tetzel: they told him that an Augustine monk had treated his letters with contempt. The Dominican at this intelligence bellowed with anger. He stormed from the pulpit, employing insults and curses;[4] and to strike the people with greater terror, he had a fire lighted several times in the market-place, declaring that he had received an order from the pope to burn all heretics who presumed to oppose his most holy indulgences.

Such is the fact that was, not the cause, but the first occasion of the Reformation. A pastor, seeing the sheep of his fold in a course in which they must perish, seeks to withdraw them from it. As yet he has no thought of reforming the church and the

world. He has seen Rome and her corruptions; but still he does not rise up against her. He has a presentiment of some of the abuses under which Christendom groans; but he does not think of correcting them. He does not desire to become a reformer.[1] He has no more plan for the reformation of the Church than he had had for the reformation of himself. God wills a reform, and elects Luther to be its instrument. The same remedy which had been so efficacious in healing his own wounds, the hand of God will apply by him to the sores of Christendom. He remains tranquil in the sphere that is assigned to him. He walks simply wherever his Master calls him. He fulfils at Wittemberg the duties of professor, preacher, and pastor. He is seated in the temple where the members of his church come and open their hearts to him. It is there—on that field—that the evil attacks him, and error seeks him out. They would prevent him from executing his office. His conscience, bound to the Word of God, revolts. Is it not God who calls him? To resist is a duty: it is therefore a right. He must speak. Thus, says Mathesius, were the events ordained by that God who desired to restore Christendom by means of the forgemaster's son, and to pass through his furnaces the impure doctrine of the Church in order to purify it.[2]

It is not requisite, after this statement, to refute a lying imputation, invented by some of Luther's enemies, but not till after his death. It has been said, that the jealousy peculiar to religious orders,—that vexation at seeing a disgraceful and reprobated traffic confided to the Dominicans rather than to the Augustines, who had hitherto possessed it,—led the Wittemberg professor to attack Tetzel and his doctrines. The well-established fact, that this speculation had been first offered to the Franciscans, who would have nothing to do with it, is sufficient to refute this fable repeated by writers who have copied one another. Cardinal Pallavicini himself affirms that the Augustines had never held this commission.[3] Besides, we have witnessed the travail of Luther's soul. His conduct needs no other interpretation. It was necessary for him to confess aloud the doctrine to which he owed his happiness. In Christianity, when a man has found a treasure for himself, he desires to impart it to others. In our days we should give up these puerile and unworthy explanations of the great revolution of the 16th century. It requires a more powerful lever to raise the world. The Reformation was not in Luther only; his age must have given it birth. Luther, who was impelled equally by

[1] In Præf. Opp. Witt. i. Monachum, et papistam insanissimum ita ebrium, imo submersum in dogmatibus papæ, &c.
[2] L. Opp. (W.) xxii.
[3] Cœpi dissuadere populis et eos dehortari ne indulgentiariorum clamoribus aurem præberent. L. Opp. Lat. in Præf.
[4] Wütet, schilt und maledeit gräulich auf dem Predigtstuhl. Myconius, Reformationsgesch.

[1] Hæc initia fuerunt hujus controversiæ, in qua Lutherus, nihil adhuc suspicans aut somnians de futura mutatione rituum. Mel. Vit. Luth.
[2] Die verseurte Lehr durch den Ofen gehen. 10.
[3] Falsum est consuevisse hoc munus injungi Eremitanis S. Augustini, 14.

obedience to the Word of God and charity towards men, ascended the pulpit. He fore-armed his hearers, but with gentleness, as he says himself.[1] His prince had obtained from the pope special indulgences for the castle-chapel at Wittemberg. Some of the blows that he was aiming at the inquisitor's indulgences might fall on those of the elector. It matters not! he will hazard disgrace. If he sought to please men, he would not be Christ's servant.

" No one can prove by Scripture, that the righteousness of God requires a penalty or satisfaction from the sinner," said the faithful minister of the Word to the people of Wittemberg. " The only duty it imposes is a true repentance, a sincere conversion, a resolution to bear the cross of Christ, and to perform good works. It is a great error to pretend of oneself to make satisfaction for our sins to God's righteousness ; God pardons them gratuitously by his inestimable grace. " The Christian Church, it is true, requires something of the sinner, and which consequently can be remitted. But that is all. ......Yet farther, these indulgences of the Church are tolerated only because of the idle and imperfect Christians who will not zealously perform good works; for they move no one to sanctification, but leave each man in his imperfection."

Next attacking the pretences under which indulgences are published, he continued : " They would do much better to contribute for love of God to the building of St. Peter's, than to buy indulgences with this intention. ......But, say you, shall we then never purchase any ?......I have already told you, and I repeat it, my advice is that no one should buy them. Leave them for drowsy Christians : but you should walk apart and for yourselves ! We must turn the faithful aside from indulgences, and exhort them to the works which they neglect."

Finally, glancing at his adversaries, Luther concluded in these words : " And should any cry out that I am a heretic (for the truth I preach is very prejudicial to their strong box), I care but little for their clamours. They are gloomy and sick brains, men who have never tasted the Bible, never read the christian doctrine, never comprehended their own doctors, and who lie rotting in the rags and tatters of their own vain opinions......[2] May God grant both them and us a sound understanding! Amen." After these words the doctor quitted the pulpit, leaving his hearers in great emotion at such daring language.

This sermon was printed, and made a profound impression on all who read it. Tetzel replied to it, and Luther answered again ; but these discussions did not take place till the year 1518.

The festival of All-Saints was approaching. The chronicles of the time relate a circumstance, which, although of little importance to the history of this period, may still serve to characterize it. It is a dream of the elector's, the essence of which is no doubt true, although some circumstances may have been added by those who related it. A respectable writer observes, that the fear of giving his adversaries an opportunity of saying that Luther's doctrine was founded on dreams, has no doubt hindered many historians from mentioning it.[1]

The Elector Frederick of Saxony, say the chronicles of the time, was at his palace of Schweinitz, six leagues from Wittemberg, when, on the 31st October, early in the morning, being with his brother Duke John, who was then co-regent, and who reigned alone after his death, and with his chancellor, the elector said—" I must tell you of a dream, brother, which I had last night, and of which I should like to know the meaning. It is so firmly graven in my memory that I should never forget it, even were I to live a thousand years; for it came three times, and always with new circumstances."

DUKE JOHN.—" Was it a good or a bad dream ?"

THE ELECTOR. — " I cannot tell: God knows."

DUKE JOHN.—" Do not be uneasy about it: let me hear it."

THE ELECTOR.—" Having gone to bed last night, tired and dispirited, I soon fell asleep after saying my prayers, and slept calmly for about two hours and a half. I then awoke, and all kinds of thoughts occupied me till midnight. I reflected how I should keep the festival of All-Saints; I prayed for the wretched souls in purgatory, and begged that God would direct me, my councils, and my people, according to the truth. I then fell asleep again, and dreamt that the Almighty sent me a monk. who was a true son of Paul the Apostle. He was accompanied by all the saints, in obedience to God's command, to bear him testimony, and to assure me that he did not come with any fraudulent design, but that all he should do was conformable to the will of God. They asked my gracious permission to let him write something on the doors of the palace-chapel at Wittemberg, which I conceded through my chancellor. Upon this, the monk repaired thither and began to write; so large were the characters, that I could read from Schweinitz what he was writing. The pen he used was so long that its extremity reached as far as Rome, where it pierced the ears of a lion[2] which lay there, and shook

---

[1] Säuberlich.
[2] Sondern in ihren Löcherichen und zerrissenen Opinien, viel nahe verwesen. L. Opp. (L.) xvii. 119.

[1] Seckendorf. It will be found in Löscher, 1. 46, &c.; Tenzel's Anf. und Fortg. der Ref.; Jünker's Ehrenged. 148; Lehmann's Beshr. de Meissn. Erzgeb. &c.; and in a MS. among the Weimar State Papers, taken down from Spalatin's mouth. Our account of the dream is from this MS. published at the last jubilee of the Reformation, 1817.
[2] Leo X.

the triple crown on the pope's head. All the cardinals and princes ran up hastily and endeavoured to support it. You and I both tendered our assistance : I stretched out my arm......that moment I awoke with my arm extended, in great alarm and very angry with this monk, who could not guide his pen better. I recovered myself a little......it was only a dream.

" I was still half asleep, and once more closed my eyes. The dream came again. The lion, still disturbed by the pen, began to roar with all his might, until the whole city of Rome, and all the states of the Holy Empire, ran up to know what was the matter. The pope called upon us to oppose this monk, and addressed himself particularly to me, because the friar was living in my dominions. I again awoke, repeated the Lord's prayer, entreated God to preserve his holiness, and fell asleep......

" I then dreamt that all the princes of the empire, and we along with them, hastened to Rome, and endeavoured one after another to break this pen; but the greater our exertions, the stronger it became : it crackled as if it had been made of iron : we gave it up as hopeless. I then asked the monk (for I was now at Rome, now at Wittemberg) where he had got that pen, and how it came to be so strong. ' This pen,' replied he, ' belonged to a Bohemian goose a hundred years old.[1] I had it from one of my old schoolmasters. It is so strong, because no one can take the pith out of it, and I am myself quite astonished at it.' On a sudden I heard a loud cry : from the monk's long pen had issued a host of other pens......I awoke a third time : it was daylight."

DUKE JOHN.—" What is your opinion, Mr Chancellor ? Would that we had here a Joseph, or a Daniel, taught of God !"

THE CHANCELLOR. — " Your highnesses know the vulgar proverb, that the dreams of young women, wise men, and great lords, have generally some hidden meaning. But we shall not learn the signification of this for some time, until the events have come to pass to which it relates. For this reason, confide its accomplishment to God, and commit all things into his hands."

DUKE JOHN.—" My opinion is the same as yours, Mr Chancellor ; it is not proper for us to rack our brains to discover the interpretation of this dream : God will direct everything to his own glory."

THE ELECTOR.—" May our faithful God do even so ! Still I shall never forget this dream. I have thought of one interpretation......but I shall keep it to myself. Time will show, perhaps, whether I have conjectured rightly."

Thus, according to the Weimar manuscript, passed the morning of the 31st Octo-

ber at Schweinitz ; let us see how the evening was spent at Wittemberg. We are now returning entirely to the domain of history.

CHAPTER V.

Festival of All-Saints—Theses—Their Strength—Moderation—Providence—Letter to Albert—Indifference of the Bishops—Dissemination of the Theses.

LUTHER'S words had produced little effect. Tetzel continued his traffic and his impious discourses without disturbing himself.[1] Will Luther resign himself to these crying abuses, and will he keep silence ? As pastor, he has earnestly exhorted those who had recourse to his services ; as preacher, he has uttered a warning voice from the pulpit. It still remains for him to speak as a theologian ; he has yet to address not merely a few souls in the confessional, not merely the assembly of the faithful at Wittemberg, but all those who are, like himself, teachers of the Word of God. His resolution is taken.

It is not the Church he thinks of attacking ; it is not the pope he is bringing to the bar ; on the contrary, it is his respect for the pope that will not allow him to be silent longer on the monstrous claims by which the pontiff is discredited. He must take the pope's part against those impudent men who dare mingle up his venerable name with their scandalous traffic. Far from thinking of a revolution which should overthrow the primacy of Rome, Luther believes he has the pope and catholicism for his allies against these barefaced monks.[2]

The festival of All-Saints was a very important day for Wittemberg, and, above all, for the church the elector had built there, and which he had filled with relics. On that day the priests used to bring out these relics, ornamented with gold, silver, and precious stones, and exhibit them before the people, who were astonished and dazzled at such magnificence.[3] Whoever visited the church on that festival and made confession, obtained a rich indulgence. Accordingly, on this great anniversary, pilgrims came to Wittemberg in crowds.

On the 31st October 1517, at noon on the day preceding the festival,[4] Luther, who had already made up his mind, walks boldly towards the church, to which a superstitious crowd of pilgrims was repairing, and posts upon the door ninety-five theses or proposi-

---

[1] John Huss. This circumstance may have been added later, in allusion to the words of Huss we have quoted above, p. 30.

[1] Cujus impiis et nefariis concionibus incitatus Lutherus, studio pietatis ardens edidit propositiones de indulgentiis. Melancth. Vita Luth.
[2] Et in iis certus mihi videbar, me habiturum patronum papam, cujus fiducia tunc fortiter nitebar. L. Opp. Lat. in Præf.
[3] Quas magnifico apparatu publice populis ostendi cura vit. Cochlœus, 4.
[4] Cursus, Schles. Chronikon. i. 241.

tions against the doctrine of indulgences. Neither the Elector, nor Staupitz, nor Spalatin, nor any even of his most intimate friends, had been made acquainted with his intentions. [1]

Luther therein declares, in a kind of preface, that he has written these theses with the express desire of setting the truth in the full light of day. He declares himself ready to defend them on the morrow, in the university, against all opponents. Great was the attention they excited : they were read, and passed from mouth to mouth. Erelong the pilgrims, the university, and the whole city, were in commotion.

We give some of these propositions, written with the pen of the monk, and posted on the door of the church of Wittemberg :—

I. " When our Lord and Master Jesus Christ says *repent*, he means that the whole life of believers upon earth should be a constant and perpetual repentance.

2. " This word cannot be understood of the sacrament of penance (*i. e.* confession and satisfaction), as administered by the priest.

3. " Still the Lord does not mean to speak in this place solely of internal repentance ; internal repentance is null, if it produce not externally every kind of mortification of the flesh.

4. " Repentance and sorrow—*i. e.* true penance—endure as long as a man is displeased with himself—that is, until he passes from this life into eternity.

5. " The pope is unable and desires not to remit any other penalty than that which he has imposed of his own good pleasure, or conformably to the canons—*i. e.* the papal ordinances.

6. " The pope cannot remit any condemnation, but only declare and confirm the remission of God, except in the cases that appertain to himself. If he does otherwise, the condemnation remains entirely the same.

8. " The laws of ecclesiastical penance ought to be imposed solely on the living, and have no regard to the dead.

21. " The commissaries of indulgences are in error when they say, that by the papal indulgence a man is delivered from every punishment and is saved.

25. " The same power that the pope has over purgatory throughout the Church, each bishop possesses individually in his own diocese, and each priest in his own parish.

27. " They preach mere human follies who maintain, that as soon as the money rattles in the strong box, the soul flies out of purgatory.

28. " This is certain, that as soon as the money tinkles, avarice and love of gain arrive, increase, and multiply. But the support and prayers of the Church depend solely on God's will and good pleasure.

[1] Cum hujus disputationis nullus etiam intimorum amicorum fuerit conscius. L. Epp. i. 186.

32. " Those who fancy themselves sure of salvation by indulgences will go to perdition along with those who teach them so.

35. " They are teachers of antichristian doctrines who pretend that to deliver a soul from purgatory, or to buy an indulgence, there is no need of either sorrow or repentance.

36. " Every Christian who truly repents of his sins, enjoys an entire remission both of the penalty and of the guilt, without any need of indulgences.

37. " Every true Christian, whether dead or alive, participates in all the blessings of Christ or of the Church, by God's gift, and without a letter of indulgence.

38. " Still we should not contemn the papal dispensation and pardon ; for this pardon is a declaration of the pardon of God.

40. " True repentance and sorrow seek and love the punishment ; but the mildness of indulgence absolves from the punishment, and begets hatred against it.

42. " We should teach Christians that the pope has no thought or desire of comparing in any respect the act of buying indulgences with any work of mercy.

43. " We should teach Christians that he who gives to the poor, or lends to the needy, does better than he who purchases an indulgence.

44. " For the work of charity increaseth charity, and renders a man more pious ; whereas the indulgence does not make him better, but only renders him more self-confident, and more secure from punishment.

45. " We should teach Christians that whoever sees his neighbour in want, and yet buys an indulgence, does not buy the pope's indulgence, but incurs God's anger.

46. " We should teach Christians that if they have no superfluity, they are bound to keep for their own households the means of procuring necessaries, and ought not to squander their money in indulgences.

47. " We should teach Christians that the purchase of an indulgence is a matter of free choice and not of commandment.

48. " We should teach Christians that the pope, having more need of prayers offered up in faith than of money, desires prayer more than money when he dispenses indulgences.

49. " We should teach Christians that the pope's indulgence is good, if we put no confidence in it ; but that nothing is more hurtful, if it diminishes our piety.

50. " We should teach Christians that if the pope knew of the extortions of the preachers of indulgences, he would rather the mother-church of St. Peter were burnt and reduced to ashes, than see it built up with the skin, the flesh, and the bones of his flock.

51. " We should teach Christians that the pope (as it is his duty) would distribute his own money to the poor whom the indulgence-sellers are now stripping of their last farthing,

even were he compelled to sell the mother-church of St. Peter.

52. " To hope to be saved by indulgences, is a lying and an empty hope ; although even the commissary of indulgences, nay farther, the pope himself, should pledge their souls to guarantee it.

53. " They are the enemies of the pope and of Jesus Christ, who, by reason of the preaching of indulgences, forbid the preaching of the Word of God.

55. " The pope can have no other thought than this : If the indulgence, which is a lesser matter, be celebrated with ringing of a bell, with pomp and ceremony, much more should we honour and celebrate the Gospel, which is a greater thing, with a hundred bells, and with a hundred pomps and ceremonies.

62. " The true and precious treasure of the Church is the Holy Gospel of the glory and grace of God.

65. " The treasures of the Gospel are nets in which in former times the rich and those in easy circumstances were caught.

66. " But the treasures of the indulgence are nets with which they now catch the riches of the people.

67. " It is the duty of bishops and pastors to receive the commissaries of the apostolical indulgences with every mark of respect.

68. " But it is still more their duty to ascertain with their eyes and ears that the said commissaries do not preach the dreams of their own imagination, instead of the orders of the pope.

71. " Cursed be he who speaks against the indulgence of the pope.

72. " But blessed be he who speaks against the foolish and impudent language of the preachers of indulgences.

76. " The indulgence of the pope cannot take away the smallest daily sin, as far as regards the guilt or the offence.

79. " It is blasphemy to say that the cross adorned with the arms of the pope is as effectual as the cross of Christ.

80. " The bishops, pastors, and theologians who permit such things to be told the people, will have to render an account of them.

81. " This shameless preaching, these impudent commendations of indulgences, make it difficult for the learned to defend the dignity and honour of the pope against the calumnies of the preachers, and the subtle and crafty questions of the common people.

86. " Why, say they, does not the pope, who is richer than the richest Crœsus, build the mother-church of St. Peter with his own money, rather than with that of poor Christians ?

92. " Would that we were quit of all these preachers who say to the Church : Peace ! peace ! and there is no peace.

94. " We should exhort Christians to diligence in following Christ, their head, through crosses, death, and hell.

95. " For it is far better to enter into the kingdom of heaven through much tribulation, than to acquire a carnal security by the consolations of a false peace."

Such was the commencement of the work. The germs of the Reformation were contained in these propositions of Luther's. The abuses of indulgences were attacked therein, and this is their most striking feature ; but beneath these attacks there was a principle which, although attracting the attention of the multitude in a less degree, was one day to overthrow the edifice of popery. The evangelical doctrine of a free and gratuitous remission of sins was there for the first time publicly professed. The work must now increase in strength. It was evident, indeed, that whoever had this faith in the remission of sins, announced by the Wittemberg doctor ; that whoever had this repentance, this conversion, and this sanctification, the necessity of which he so earnestly inculcated, would no longer care for human ordinances would escape from the toils and swaddling-bands of Rome, and would acquire the liberty of the children of God. All errors would fall down before this truth. By it, light had begun to enter Luther's mind ; by it, also, the light would be diffused over the Church. A clear knowledge of this truth is what preceding reformers had wanted ; and hence the unfruitfulness of their exertions. Luther himself acknowledged afterwards, that in proclaiming justification by faith, he had laid the axe to the root of the tree. " It is doctrine we attack in the adherents of the papacy," said he. " Huss and Wickliffe only attacked their lives ; but in attacking their doctrine we take the goose by the neck.[1] Every thing depends on the Word, which the pope has taken from us and falsified. I have vanquished the pope, because my doctrine is of God, and his is of the devil."

In our own days, too, we have forgotten this main doctrine of justification by faith. although in a sense opposed to that of our fathers. " In the time of Luther," observes one of our contemporaries,[2] " the remission of sins cost money at least ; but in our days, each man supplies himself gratis." There is a great similarity between these two errors. There is perhaps more forgetfulness of God in ours, than in that of the 16th century. The principle of justification by the grace of God, which brought the Church out of so much darkness at the period of the Reformation, can alone renew our generation, put an end to its doubts and waverings, destroy the selfishness that preys upon it, establish righteousness and morality among the nations, and, in short, reunite the world to God from whom it has been dissevered.

But if Luther's theses were strong by the

[1] Wenn man die Lehre angreifft, so wird die Gans am Krage gegriffen. L. Opp. (W.) xxii. 1369
[2] Harms of Kiel.

strength of the truth they proclaimed, they were not the less so by the faith of their champion. He had boldly drawn the sword of the Word: he had done so in reliance on the power of truth. He had felt that by leaning on God's promises, he could afford to risk something, to use the language of the world. "Let him who desires to begin a good work," said he when speaking of this daring attack, "undertake it with confidence in the goodness of his cause, and not, which God forbid! expecting the support and consolation of the world. Moreover, let him have no fear of man, or of the whole world; for these words will never lie: *It is good to trust in the Lord, and assuredly he that trusteth in the Lord shall not be confounded.* But let him that will not or who cannot risk something with confidence in God, take heed how he undertakes any thing."[1] Luther, after having posted his theses on the gate of All-Saints' Church, retired, no doubt, to his tranquil cell, full of the peace and joy that spring from an action done in the Lord's name, and for the sake of eternal truth.

Whatever be the boldness that prevails in these propositions, they still bespeak the monk who refuses to admit a single doubt on the authority of the see of Rome. But, while attacking the doctrine of indulgences, Luther had unwittingly touched on certain errors, whose discovery could not be agreeable to the pope, seeing that sooner or later they would call his supremacy in question. Luther was not so far-sighted; but he was sensible of the extreme boldness of the step he had just taken, and consequently thought it his duty to soften down their audacity, as far as he could in conformity with the truth. He therefore set forth these theses as doubtful propositions on which he solicited the information of the learned; and appended to them, conformably with the established usage, a solemn declaration that he did not mean to affirm or say any thing contrary to the Holy Scriptures, the Fathers of the Church, and the rights and decretals of the Roman See.

Frequently, in after-years, as he contemplated the immense and unexpected consequences of this courageous attack, Luther was astonished at himself, and could not understand how he had ventured to make it. An invisible and mightier hand than his held the clue, and led the herald of truth along a path that was still hidden from him, and from the difficulties of which he would perhaps have shrunk, if he had foreseen them, and if he had advanced alone and of his own accord. "I entered into this controversy," said he, "without any definite plan, without knowledge or inclination; I was taken quite unawares, and I call God, the searcher of hearts, to witness."[2]

Luther had become acquainted with the source of these abuses. Some one brought him a little book, adorned with the arms of the Archbishop of Mentz and Magdeburg, which contained the regulations to be followed in the sale of indulgences. It was this young prelate, then, this graceful prince, who had prescribed, or at least sanctioned, all this quackery. In him Luther saw only a superior whom he should fear and respect.[1] Not wishing to beat the air at hazard, but rather to address those who are charged with the government of the Church, Luther sent him a letter, abounding at once in frankness and humility. It was on the very day he posted up the theses that the doctor wrote to Albert:—

"Pardon me, most reverend father in Christ and most illustrious prince," said he, "if I, who am but the dregs of men,[2] have the presumption to write to your Sublime Highness. The Lord Jesus Christ is my witness that, feeling how small and despicable I am, I have long put off doing it...... May your Highness condescend to cast a single glance on a grain of dust, and of your episcopal mildness graciously receive my petition.

"Certain individuals are hawking the papal indulgences up and down the country, in your Grace's name. I am unwilling so much to blame the clamours of these preachers (for I have not heard them), as the false ideas of the simple and ignorant people, who, in purchasing indulgences, fancy themselves assured of salvation......

"The souls intrusted to your care, most excellent Father, are taught, not unto life, but unto death. The severe and just account that will be required of you increases from day to day......I could no longer be silent. No! Man is not saved by the work or the office of his bishop......Even the righteous are saved with difficulty, and narrow is the way which leadeth unto life. Wherefore, then, do these preachers of indulgences by their empty fables inspire the people with a carnal security?

"Indulgences alone, to hear them, ought to be proclaimed and extolled......What! is it not the principal, the sole duty of the bishops to instruct the people in the Gospel, and in the charity of Christ Jesus?[3] Christ himself has nowhere ordained the preaching of indulgences; but he has forcibly commanded the preaching of the Gospel.[4] How dreadful, then, and how dangerous, for a bishop to allow the Gospel to be silent, and that the noise of indulgences alone should re-echo incessantly in the ears of his flock!...

"Most worthy Father in God, in the in-

---

[1] L. Opp. (Leips.) vi. 518.
[2] Casu enim, non voluntate nec studio, in has turbas incidi, Deum ipsum testor. L. Opp. Lat. in Præf.

[1] Domino suo et pastori in Christo venerabiliter metuendo. (The address on the letter.) To his reverently to be feared Lord and Pastor in Christ. Epp. i. 68.
[2] Fæx hominum. Ibid.
[3] Ut populus Evangelium discat atque charitatem Christi. Ibid.
[4] Vehementer præcipit. Ibid.

structions to the commissaries, which have been published in your Grace's name (no doubt without your knowledge), it is said, that the indulgences are the most precious treasure—that by them man is reconciled to God, and that repentance is not necessary to those who purchase them.

"What can I, what ought I to do, most worthy Bishop, most serene Prince? I beg your Highness, in the name of our Lord Jesus Christ, to cast a look of paternal vigilance on this affair, to suppress the book entirely, and to order the preachers to deliver other sermons before the people. If you do not so, fear lest you should one day hear some voice uplifted in refutation of these preachers, to the great dishonour of your most serene Highness."

Luther, at the same time, forwarded his theses to the archbishop, and added a postscript inviting him to read them, in order to convince himself on how slight a foundation the doctrine of indulgences was based.

Thus, Luther's whole desire was for the sentinels of the Church to awaken and resolve to put an end to the evils that were laying it waste. Nothing could be more noble and more respectful than this letter from a monk to one of the greatest princes of the Church and of the Empire. Never did man act more in accordance with this precept of Christ; " Render to Cæsar the things that are Cæsar's, and to God the things that are God's." This is not the course of those fiery revolutionists who "despise dominion and speak evil of dignities." It is the cry of a christian conscience—of a priest who gives honour to all, but who fears God above every thing. All his prayers, all his entreaties, were unavailing. The youthful Albert, engrossed by pleasures and ambitious designs, made no reply to so solemn an appeal. The Bishop of Brandenburg, Luther's ordinary, a learned and pious man, to whom he sent his theses, replied that he was attacking the power of the Church; that he would bring upon himself much trouble and vexation; that the thing was above his strength; and he earnestly advised him to keep quiet.[1] The princes of the Church stopped their ears against the voice of God, which was manifested with such energy and tenderness through the mouth of Luther. They would not understand the signs of the times; they were struck with that blindness which has caused the ruin of so many powers and dignities. "They both thought," said Luther afterwards, "that the pope would be too strong for a poor mendicant friar like me."

But Luther could judge better than the bishops of the disastrous effects of indulgences on the manners and lives of the people, for he was in direct communication with them. He saw continually and near at hand what the bishops knew only through unfaithful reports. Although the bishops failed him, God did not. The Head of the Church, who sitteth in the heavens, and to whom all power is given upon earth, had himself prepared the soil and deposited the seed in the hands of his minister; he gave wings to the seeds of truth, and he scattered it in an instant throughout the length and breadth of his Church.

No one appeared next day at the university to attack Luther's propositions. The Tetzel traffic was too much decried, and too shameful, for any one but himself or his followers to dare take up the glove. But these theses were destined to be heard elsewhere than under the arched roof of an academic hall. Scarcely had they been nailed to the church door of Wittemberg, than the feeble sounds of the hammer were followed throughout all Germany by a mighty blow that reached even the foundations of haughty Rome, threatening with sudden ruin the walls, the gates, and pillars of popery, stunning and terrifying her champions, and at the same time awakening thousands from the sleep of error.[1]

These theses spread with the rapidity of lightning. A month had not elapsed before they were at Rome. " In a fortnight," says a contemporary historian, "they were in every part of Germany, and in four weeks they had traversed nearly the whole of Christendom, as if the very angels had been their messengers, and had placed them before the eyes of all men. No one can believe the noise they made."[2] Somewhat later they were translated into Dutch and Spanish, and a traveller sold them in Jerusalem. " Every one," said Luther, " complained of the indulgences: and as all the bishops and doctors had kept silence, and nobody was willing to bell the cat, poor Luther became a famous doctor, because (as they said) there came one at last who ventured to do it. But I did not like this glory, and the tune was nearly too high for my voice."[3]

Many of the pilgrims, who had thronged to Wittemberg from every quarter for the feast of All-Saints, carried back with them, instead of indulgences, the famous theses of the Augustine monk. By this means they contributed to their circulation. Every one read them, meditated and commented on them. Men conversed about them in all the convents and in all the universities.[4] The pious monks, who had entered the cloisters to save their souls,—all upright and honourable men, were delighted at this simple and striking confession of the truth, and heartily desired that Luther would continue the work he had begun. At length one man had found courage to undertake the perilous struggle. This was a reparation accorded

---

[1] Er sollte still halten; es wäre eine grosse Sache. Math. R.

[1] Walther, Nachr. v. Luther, p. 45.
[2] Myconius, Hist. Ref. p. 23.
[3] Das Lied wollte meiner Stimme zu hoch werden. (L. Opp.)
[4] In alle hohe Schulen und Klöster. Math. 13.

to Christendom: the public conscience was satisfied. Piety saw in these theses a blow aimed at every superstition; the new theology hailed in it the defeat of the scholastic dogmas; princes and magistrates considered them as a barrier raised against the invasions of the ecclesiastical power; and the nation rejoiced at seeing so positive a *veto* opposed by this monk to the cupidity of the Roman chancery. "When Luther attacked this fable," remarked to Duke George of Saxony, a man very worthy of belief, and one of the principal rivals of the reformer, namely Erasmus, "the whole world applauded, and there was a general assent." "I observe," said he at another time to Cardinal Campeggio, "that the greater their evangelical piety and the purer their morals, the less are men opposed to Luther. His life is praised even by those who cannot endure his faith. The world was weary of a doctrine so full of puerile fables and human ordinances, and thirsted for that living, pure, and hidden water which springs from the veins of the evangelists and apostles. Luther's genius was fitted to accomplish these things, and his zeal would naturally catch fire at so glorious an enterprise."[1]

CHAPTER VI.

Reuchlin—Erasmus—Flek—Bibra—The Emperor—The Pope—Myconius—The Monks—Apprehensions—Adelman—An aged Priest—The Bishop—The Elector—The Townspeople of Erfurth—Luther's Answer—Disorder—Luther's Mainspring.

WE must follow these propositions into whatever place they penetrated,—into the studies of the learned, the cells of the monks, and the halls of princes, to form an idea of the various but prodigious effects they produced in Germany.

Reuchlin received them. He was wearied of the rude combat he had to fight against the monks. The strength displayed by the new combatant in his theses reanimated the dispirited champion of literature, and restored joy to his desponding heart. "Thanks be to God!" exclaimed he after reading them, "at last they have found a man who will give them so much to do, that they will be compelled to let my old age end in peace."

The cautious Erasmus was in the Low Countries when these propositions reached him. He internally rejoiced at witnessing his secret wishes for the rectifying of abuses expressed with so much courage: he approved of the author, exhorting him only to greater moderation and prudence. Never-

theless, when some one reproached Luther's violence in his presence: "God," said he, "has given men a physician who cuts deep into the flesh, because the malady would otherwise be incurable." And when a little later the Elector of Saxony asked his opinion on Luther's business, he replied with a smile: "I am not at all surprised that it has made so much noise; for he has committed two unpardonable crimes; he has attacked the pope's tiara and the monks' bellies."[1]

Doctor Flek, prior of the monastery of Steinlausitz, had long discontinued reading the Mass, but without telling any one the real cause. One day he found Luther's theses posted up in the refectory: he went up to them, began to read, and had only perused a few, when, unable to contain his joy, he exclaimed: "Ah! ah! he whom we have so long expected is come at last, and he will show you monks a trick or two!" Then looking into the future, says Mathesius, and playing on the meaning of the name Wittemberg: "All the world," said he, "will go and seek wisdom on that mountain and will find it."[2] He wrote to the doctor to continue the glorious struggle with boldness. Luther styles him a man full of joy and consolation.

The ancient and renowned episcopal see of Wurzburg was filled at that time by Lorenzo de Bibra, a pious, wise, and worthy man, according to the testimony of his contemporaries. When a gentleman came and informed him that he intended placing his daughter in a convent: "Rather give her a husband," said he. And then he added: "If you require money for her dowry, I will lend it you." The emperor and all the princes held him in the highest esteem. He mourned over the disorders of the Church, and above all, over those of the convents. The theses reached his palace also: he read them with great joy, and publicly declared that he approved of Luther. Somewhat later, he wrote to the Elector Frederick: "Do not let the pious Doctor Martin go, for they do him wrong." The elector was delighted at this testimony, and communicated it to the reformer with his own hand.

The Emperor Maximilian, predecessor of Charles the Fifth, read and admired the theses of the monk of Wittemberg; he perceived his ability, and foresaw that this obscure Augustine might one day become a powerful ally for Germany in her struggle against Rome. He accordingly said to the Elector of Saxony through his envoy: "Take great care of the monk Luther, for the time may come when we shall have need of him."[3] And shortly after, being in diet with Pfeffinger, the elector's privy counsellor, he said

---

[1] Ad hoc præstandum mihi videbatur ille, et natura compositus et accensus studio. Erasm. Epp. Campegio Cardinali, i. 650.

[1] Müller's Denkw. iv. 256.
[2] Alle Welt von diessem Weissenberg, Weissheit holen und bekommen, p. 13. *Wittemberg* (or Weissenberg) signifies *the mountain of wisdom.*
[3] Dass er uns den Munch Luther fleisig beware. Math 15.

to him: "Well! what is your Augustine doing? In truth his propositions are not contemptible. He will play the monks a pretty game."[1]

At Rome, even in the Vatican, these theses were not so badly received as might have been imagined. Leo X. judged rather as a patron of letters than as pope. The amusement they gave him made him forget the severe truths they contained; and as Sylvester Prierio, the master of the sacred palace, who had the charge of examining the books, requested him to treat Luther as a heretic, he replied: "Brother Martin Luther is a very fine genius, and all that is said against him is mere monkish jealousy."[2]

There were few men on whom Luther's theses produced a deeper impression than the scholar of Annaberg, whom Tetzel had so mercilessly repulsed. Myconius had entered a convent. On the very night of his arrival he dreamt he saw immense fields of wheat all glistening with ripe ears. "Cut," said the voice of his guide; and when he alleged his want of skill, his conductor showed him a reaper working with inconceivable activity. "Follow him, and do as he does," said the guide.[3] Myconius, as eager after holiness as Luther had been, devoted himself while in the monastery to all the vigils, fasts, mortifications, and practices invented by men. But at last he despaired of ever attaining his object by his own exertions. He neglected his studies, and employed himself in manual labours only. At one time he would bind books; at another, work at the turner's lathe, or any laborious occupation. This outward activity was unable to quiet his troubled conscience. God had spoken to him, and he could no longer fall back into his previous lethargy. This state of anguish endured several years. It has been sometimes imagined that the paths of the reformers were smooth, and that when they had renounced the observances of the Church, nothing but pleasure and comfort awaited them. It is not considered that they arrived at the truth through internal struggles a thousand times more painful than the observances to which slavish minds easily submitted.

At length the year 1517 arrived; Luther's theses were published; they were circulated through Christendom, and penetrated also into the monastery where the scholar of Annaberg was concealed. He hid himself in a corner of the cloister with another monk, John Voigt, that he might read them at his ease.[4] Here were the selfsame truths he had heard from his father; his eyes were opened; he felt a voice within him responding to that which was then re-echoing through Germany,

and great consolation filled his heart. "I see plainly," said he, "that Martin Luther is the reaper I saw in my dream, and who taught me to gather the ears." He began immediately to profess the doctrine that Luther had proclaimed. The monks grew alarmed, as they heard him; they argued with him, and declared against Luther and against his convent. "This convent," replied Myconius, "is like our Lord's sepulchre: they wish to prevent Christ's resurrection, but they will fail." At last his superiors, finding they could not convince him, interdicted him for a year and a half from all intercourse with the world, permitting him neither to write nor receive letters, and threatening him with imprisonment for life. But the hour of his deliverance was at hand. Being afterwards nominated pastor of Zwickau, he was the first who declared against the papacy in the churches of Thuringia. "Then," said he, "was I enabled to labour with my venerable father Luther in the Gospel-harvest." Jonas describes him as a man capable of doing everything he undertook.[1]

No doubt there were others besides to whose souls Luther's propositions were a signal of life. They kindled a new flame in many cells, cottages, and palaces. While those who had entered the convents in quest of good cheer, an idle life, or respect and honours, says Mathesius, began to load the name of Luther with reproaches, the monks who lived in prayer, fasting, and mortification, returned thanks to God, as soon as they heard the cry of that eagle whom Huss had announced a century before.[2] Even the common-people, who did not clearly understand the theological question, but who only knew that this man assailed the empire of the lazy and mendicant monks, welcomed him with bursts of acclamation. An immense sensation was produced in Germany by these daring propositions. Some of the reformer's contemporaries, however, foresaw the serious consequences to which they might lead, and the numerous obstacles they would encounter. They expressed their fears aloud, and rejoiced with trembling.

"I am much afraid," wrote the excellent canon of Augsburg, Bernard Adelmann, to his friend Pirckheimer, "that the worthy man must give way at last before the avarice and power of the partisans of indulgences. His representations have produced so little effect, that the Bishop of Augsburg, our primate and metropolitan,[3] has just ordered, in the pope's name, fresh indulgences for St. Peter's at Rome. Let him haste to secure the aid of princes; let him beware of tempting God; for he must be void of common sense if he overlooks the imminent peril he

---

[1] Schmidt, Brand. Reformationsgesch, p. 124.
[2] Che frate Martino Luthero haveva un bellissimo ingegno, e che coteste erano invidie fratesche. Brandelli, Leo's contemporary and a Dominican, Hist. trag. pars 3.
[3] Melch. Adami Vita Myconii.
[4] Legit tunc cum Joanne Voito in angulum abditus, libellos Lutheri. Melch. Adam.

[1] Qui potuit quod voluit.
[2] Darvon Magister Johann Huss geweissaget. Math. 13.
[3] Totque uxorum vir (and the husband of so many wives) added he. Heumani Documenta litt. 167.

incurs." Adelmann was delighted on hearing it rumoured that Henry VIII. had invited Luther to England. "In that country," thought the canon, "he will be able to teach the truth in peace." Many thus imagined that the doctrine of the Gospel required the support of the civil power. They knew not that it advances without this power, and is often trammelled and enfeebled by it.

Albert Kranz, the famous historian, was at Hamburg on his deathbed, when Luther's theses were brought to him: "Thou art right, Brother Martin," said he, "but thou wilt not succeed......Poor monk! Go to thy cell and cry: Lord! have mercy upon me!"[1]

An aged priest of Hexter in Westphalia, having received and read the theses in his parsonage, shook his head and said in Low German: "Dear Brother Martin! if you succeed in overthrowing this purgatory and all these paper-dealers, you will be a fine fellow indeed!" Erbenius, who lived a century later, wrote the following doggerel under these words:—

> "What would the worthy parson say,
> If he were living at this day?"[2]

Not only did a great number of Luther's friends entertain fears as to this proceeding, but many even expressed their disapprobation. The Bishop of Brandenburg, grieved at seeing so violent a quarrel break out in his diocese, would have desired to stifle it. He resolved to effect this by mildness. "In your theses on indulgences," said he to Luther, through the Abbot of Lenin, "I see nothing opposed to the Catholic truth; I myself condemn these indiscreet proclamations; but for the love of peace and for regard to your bishop, discontinue writing upon this subject." Luther was confounded at being addressed with such humility by so great a dignitary. Led away by the first impulse of his heart, he replied with emotion: "I consent: I would rather obey than perform miracles if that were possible."[3]

The elector beheld with regret the commencement of a combat that was justifiable no doubt, but the results of which could not be foreseen. No prince was more desirous of maintaining the public peace than Frederick. Yet, what an immense conflagration might not be kindled by this spark! What violent discord, what rending of nations, might not this monkish quarrel produce! The elector gave Luther frequent intimations of the uneasiness he felt.[4]

Even in his own order and in his own convent at Wittemberg, Luther met with disapprobation. The prior and sub-prior were terrified at the outcry made by Tetzel and his companions. They repaired trembling and alarmed to Brother Martin's cell, and said: "Pray do not bring disgrace upon our order! The other orders, and especially the Dominicans, are already overjoyed to think that they will not be alone in their shame." Luther was moved at these words; but he soon recovered, and replied: "Dear fathers! if this work be not of God, it will come to naught; but if it be, let it go forwards." The prior and sub-prior made no answer. "The work is still going forwards," added Luther, after recounting this anecdote, "and, God willing, it will go on better and better unto the end. Amen."[1]

Luther had many other attacks to endure. At Erfurth, he was blamed for the violent and haughty manner in which he condemned the opinions of others: this is the reproach usually made against those men who possess that strength of conviction which proceeds from the Word of God. He was also accused of precipitation and levity.

"They require moderation in me," answered Luther, "and they trample it under foot in the judgment they pass on me!...... We can always see the mote in our brother's eye, and we overlook the beam in our own ......Truth will not gain more by my moderation, than it will lose by my rashness. I desire to know (continues he, addressing Lange) what errors you and your theologians have found in my theses? Who does not know that a man rarely puts forth any new idea without having some appearance of pride, and without being accused of exciting quarrels? If humility herself should undertake something new, her opponents would accuse her of pride![2] Why were Christ and all the martyrs put to death? Because they seemed to be proud contemners of the wisdom of the time, and because they advanced novelties, without having first humbly taken counsel of the oracles of the ancient opinions.

"Do not let the wise of our days expect from me humility, or rather hypocrisy, enough to ask their advice, before publishing what duty compels me to say. Whatever I do will be done, not by the prudence of men, but by the counsel of God. If the work be of God, who shall stop it? if it be not, who can forward it? Not my will, nor theirs, nor ours; but thy will, O Holy Father, which art in heaven."—What courage, what noble enthusiasm, what confidence in God, and above all, what truth in these words, and what truth for all ages!

The reproaches and accusations which were showered upon Luther from every quarter, could not fail, however, to produce some impression on his mind. He had been deceived in his hopes. He had expected to see the heads of the Church and the most dis-

---

[1] Frater, abi in cellam, et dic: Miserere mei. Lindner in Luther's Leben, 93.
[2] Quid vero nunc si vivere
Bonus iste clericus diceret.
[3] Bene sum contentus: malo obedire quam miracula facere, etiam si possem. Epp. i. 71.
[4] Suumque dolorem sæpe significavit, metuens discordias majores. Melancth. Vita Luth.

[1] L. Opp. (L.) vi. 518.
[2] Finge enim ipsam humilitatem nova conari, statim superbiæ subjicietur ab iis qui aliter sapiunt. L. Epp. i. 73.

tinguished scholars in the nation publicly unite with him; but the case was far otherwise. A word of approbation which escaped in the first moment of astonishment was all the best disposed accorded him; on the contrary, many whom he had hitherto respected the most, were loudest in their censure. He felt himself alone in the Church, alone against Rome, alone at the foot of that ancient and formidable building whose foundations penetrated to the centre of the earth, whose walls soared to the clouds, and against which he had aimed so daring a blow.[1] He was troubled and dispirited. Doubts, which he fancied he had overcome, returned to his mind with fresh force. He trembled at the thought that he had the whole authority of the Church against him: to withdraw from that authority, to be deaf to that voice which people had obeyed for centuries, to set himself in opposition to that Church which he had been accustomed from his infancy to venerate as the mother of the faithful,.........he, an insignificant monk.........was an effort too great for human power![2] No step cost him dearer than this. And it was this, accordingly, which decided the Reformation.

No one can paint better than himself the combat in his own soul:—" I began this business," said he, " with great fear and trembling. Who was I then, I, a poor, wretched, contemptible friar, more like a corpse than a man;[3] who was I to oppose the majesty of the pope, before whom not only the kings of the earth and the whole world trembled, but even, if I may so speak, heaven and hell were constrained to obey the signal of his eyes?.........No one can know what my heart suffered during these first two years, and into what despondency, I may say into what despair, I was sunk. Those haughty spirits who have since attacked the pope with such great hardihood can form no idea of it, although with all their skill they would have been unable to do him the least harm, if Jesus Christ had not already inflicted through me, his weak and unworthy instrument, a wound that shall never be healed.........But while they were content to look on and leave me alone in the danger, I was not so cheerful, so tranquil, nor so confident; for at that time I was ignorant of many things which now, thank God, I know. There were, it is true, many pious Christians who were pleased with my propositions, and valued them highly; but I could not acknowledge them and consider them as the instruments of the Holy Ghost; I looked only to the pope, to

the cardinals, bishops, theologians, lawyers, monks, and priests.........It was from them I expected to witness the influence of the Spirit. However, after gaining the victory over all their arguments by Scripture, I at last surmounted through Christ's grace, but with great anguish, toil, and pain, the only argument that still checked me, namely, that I should " listen to the Church;"[1] for, from the bottom of my heart, I reverenced the pope's Church as the true Church; and I did so with far more sincerity and veneration than all those scandalous and infamous corrupters who, to oppose me, now extol it so mightily. If I had despised the pope, as those men really despise him in their hearts who praise him so much with their lips, I should have trembled lest the earth should have instantly opened and swallowed me up alive like Korah and his company."

How honourable are these combats to Luther! What sincerity, what uprightness of mind they display! and by these painful assaults which he had to sustain from within and from without, he is rendered more worthy of our esteem than he would have been by an intrepidity unaccompanied by any such struggles. This travail of his soul clearly demonstrates the truth and Divinity of his work. We see that the cause and the principle were both in heaven. Who will dare assert, after all the features we have pointed out, that the Reformation was a political affair? No; it was not the effect of man's policy, but of God's power. If Luther had been urged forward solely by human passions, he would have sunk under his fears; his errors, his scruples, would have smothered the fire kindled in his soul; and he would have shed upon the Church a mere passing ray, as many zealous and pious men have done whose names have been handed down to us. But now God's time was come; the work could not be stopped; the emancipation of the Church must be accomplished. Luther was appointed at least to prepare the way for that complete enfranchisement and those extensive developments which are promised to the reign of Jesus Christ. He experienced, accordingly, the truth of that glorious promise: *Even the youths shall faint and be weary and the young men shall utterly fall: but they that wait upon the Lord shall renew their strength; they shall mount up with wings as eagles.* That Divine power which filled the heart of the Wittemberg doctor, and which had impelled him to the combat, soon restored to him all his early resolution.

[1] Solus primo eram. L. Opp. Lat. in Præf.
[2] Consilium immanis audaciæ plenum. Pallavicini, i. 17.
[3] Miserrimus tunc fraterculus, cadaveri similior quam homini. L. Opp. Lat. i. 49.

[1] Et cum omnia argumenta superassem per scripturas, hoc unum cum summa difficultate et angustia, tandem Christo favente, vix superavi, Ecclesiam scilicet esse audiendam. L. Opp. Lat. i. 49.

CHAPTER VII.

Tetzel's Attack—Luther's Reply—Good Works—Luther and Spalatin—Study of Scripture—Scheurl and Luther—Doubts on the Theses—Luther pleads for the People—A New Coat.

THE reproaches, the timidity, and the silence of his friends had discouraged Luther ; the attacks of his enemies produced a contrary effect : this is a case of frequent occurrence. The adversaries of the truth, who hope by their violence to do their own work, are doing that of God himself. [1] Tetzel took up the gauntlet, but with a feeble hand. Luther's sermon, which had been for the people what the theses had been for the learned, was the object of his first reply. He refuted this discourse point by point, after his own fashion ; he then announced that he was preparing to meet his adversary more fully in certain theses which he would maintain at the university of Frankfort-on-the-Oder. " Then," said he, replying to the conclusion of Luther's sermon, " each man will be able to judge who is the heresiarch, heretic, schismatic ; who is mistaken, rash, and slanderous. Then it will be clear to the eyes of all who it is that has a dull brain, that has never felt the Bible, never read the christian doctrines, never understood his own doctors......In support of the propositions I advance, I am ready to suffer all things— prisons, scourging, drowning, and the stake."

One thing strikes us, as we read Tetzel's reply—the difference between the German employed by him and Luther. One might say they were several ages apart. A foreigner, in particular, sometimes finds it difficult to understand Tetzel, while Luther's language is almost entirely that of our own days. A comparison of their writings is sufficient to show that Luther is the creator of the German language. This is, no doubt, one of his least merits, but still it is one.

Luther replied without naming Tetzel ; Tetzel had not named him. But there was no one in Germany who could not write at the head of their publications the names they thought proper to conceal. Tetzel, in order to set a higher value upon his indulgences, endeavoured to confound the repentance required by God with the penance imposed by the Church. Luther sought to clear up this point.

" To save words," said he, in his picturesque language, " I throw to the winds (which, besides, have more leisure than I) his other remarks, which are mere artificial flowers and dry leaves, and will content myself with examining the foundations of his edifice of burs.

" The penance imposed by the holy father cannot be that required by Christ ; for what the holy father imposes he can dispense with ; and if these two penances were one and the same thing, it would follow that the pope takes away what Christ imposes, and destroys the commandment of God......Well ! if he likes it, let him abuse me (continues Luther, after quoting other erroneous interpretations by Tetzel), let him call me heretic, schismatic, slanderer, and whatever he pleases : I shall not be his enemy for that, and I shall pray for him as for a friend...... But I cannot suffer him to treat the Holy Scriptures, our consolation (Rom. xv. 4), as a sow treats a sack of oats."[1]

We must accustom ourselves to find Luther sometimes making use of coarse expressions, and such as are too familiar for our age : it was the fashion of the times ; and there will generally be found under these words, which would now shock the conventional usages of language, a strength and propriety which redeem their vulgarity. He thus continues :—

" He who purchases indulgences, repeat our adversaries, does better than he who gives alms to a poor man who is not reduced to the last extremity.—Now, should we hear the news that the Turks are profaning our churches and our crosses, we could hear it without shuddering ; for we have in the midst of us the worst of Turks, who profane and annihilate the only real sanctuary, the Word of God, that sanctifieth all things.— Let him who desires to follow this precept, beware of feeding the hungry, or of clothing the naked, before they die, and consequently have no more need of assistance."

It is important to compare Luther's zeal for good works with what he says on justification by faith. The man that has any experience and any knowledge of Christianity, does nor require this new proof of a truth, the evidence of which he has himself felt : namely, the more we are attached to justification by faith, the more we see the necessity of works, and the more we become attached to their practice ; whilst any laxity with regard to the doctrine of faith necessarily brings with it laxity of morals. Luther, and Saint Paul before him and Howard after him, are proofs of the first assertion ; every man without faith, and there are many such in the world, is a proof of the second.

When Luther comes to Tetzel's invectives, he answers them in this manner. " When I hear these invectives, I fancy it is an ass braying at me. I am delighted with them, and I should be very sorry were such people to call me a good Christian." We must represent Luther as he was, with all his weaknesses. A turn for jesting, and even for coarse jesting, was one of them. The Reformer was a great man, a man of God, no

---

[1] Hi furores Tezelli et ejus satellitum imponunt necessitatem Luthero, de rebus iisdem copiosius disserendi et tuendæ veritatis. Melancth. Vita Luth.

[1] Dass er die Schrift, unsern Trost, nicht anders behandelt wie die Sau einen Habersack.

doubt; but he was still a man and not an angel, and he was not even a perfect man. Who has the right to require perfection in him?

" Finally," added he, challenging his adversary to battle, " although it is not usual to burn heretics for such matters, here am I at Wittemberg, I, Doctor Martin Luther! Is there any inquisitor who is determined to chew iron and to blow up rocks? I beg to inform him that he has a safe-conduct to come hither, open gates, bed and board secured to him, and all by the gracious cares of our worthy prince, Duke Frederick, elector of Saxony, who will never protect heresy." [1]

We see that Luther was not wanting in courage. He relied upon the Word of God; and it is a rock that never fails us in the storm. But God in his faithfulness afforded him other assistance. The burst of joy by which the multitude welcomed Luther's theses, had been soon followed by a gloomy silence. The learned had timidly retreated before the calumnies and abuse of Tetzel and the Dominicans. The bishops, who had previously exclaimed against the abuse of indulgences, seeing them attacked at last, had not failed, by a contradiction that is by no means rare, to discover that the attack was unseasonable. The greater portion of the reformer's friends were alarmed. Many had fled away. But when the first terror was over, a contrary movement took place in their minds. The monk of Wittemberg, who for some time had been almost alone in the midst of the Church, soon gathered around him again a numerous body of friends and admirers.

There was one who, although timid, yet remained faithful during this crisis, and whose friendship was his consolation and support. This was Spalatin. Their correspondence was not interrupted. " I thank you," said Luther, speaking of a particular mark of friendship that he had received, " but what am I not indebted to you? [2] It was on the 11th November 1517, eleven days after the publication of the theses, and consequently at the very time when the fermentation of men's minds was greatest, that Luther delighted thus to pour out his gratitude into his friend's heart. It is interesting to witness in this very letter to Spalatin, this strong man, who had just performed the bravest action, declaring whence all his strength was derived. " We can do nothing of ourselves: we can do everything by God's grace. All ignorance is invincible for us: no ignorance is invincible for the grace of God. The more we endeavour, of ourselves, to attain wisdom, the nearer we approach to folly. [3] It is untrue that this invincible ignorance excuses the sinner; otherwise there would be no sin in the world."

Luther had not sent his propositions either to the prince or to any of his court. It would appear that the chaplain expressed some astonishment to his friend in consequence. " I was unwilling," replied Luther, " that my theses should reach our most illustrious prince, or any of his court, before they had been received by those who think themselves especially designated in them, for fear they should believe I had published them by the prince's order, or to conciliate his favour, and from opposition to the Bishop of Mentz. I understand there are many persons who dream such things. But now I can safely swear, that my theses were published without the knowledge of Duke Frederick." [1]

If Spalatin consoled his friend and supported him by his influence, Luther, on his part, endeavoured to answer the questions put to him by the unassuming chaplain. Among others, the latter asked one that has been often proposed in our days: " What is the best method of studying Scripture?"

" As yet, most excellent Spalatin," Luther replied, " you have only asked me things that were in my power. But to direct you in the study of the Holy Scriptures is beyond my ability. If, however, you absolutely wish to know my method, I will not conceal it from you.

" It is very certain, that we cannot attain to the understanding of Scripture either by study or by the intellect. Your first duty is to begin by prayer. [2] Entreat the Lord to grant you, of his great mercy, the true understanding of his Word. There is no other interpreter of the Word of God than the Author of this Word, as he himself has said: *They shall be all taught of God.* Hope for nothing from your own labours, from your own understanding: trust solely in God, and in the influence of his Spirit. Believe this on the word of a man who has had experience." [3] We here see how Luther arrived at the possession of the truth which he preached. It was not, as some pretend, by trusting to a presumptuous reason; is was not, as others maintain, by giving way to malignant passions. The purest, the sublimest, the holiest source—God himself, consulted in humility, confidence, and prayer,—was that at which he drank. But in our days he has found few imitators, and hence it is there are not many who understand him. To every serious mind these words of Luther's are of themselves a justification of the Reformation.

Luther found further consolation in the friendship of respectable laymen. Christopher Scheurl, the excellent secretary of the imperial city of Nuremberg, gave him the

[1] Luth. Opp. (L.) xvii. 132.
[2] Tibi gratias ago: imo quid tibi non debeo? L. Epp. i. 74.
[3] Quanto magis conamur ex nobis ad sapientiam, tanto amplius appropinquamus insipientiæ. Ibid.

[1] Sed salvum est nunc etiam jurare, quod sine scitu Ducis Frederici exierint. L. Epp. i. 76.
[2] Primum id certissimum est, sacras literas non posse vel studio, vel ingenio penetrari. Ideo primum officium est, ut ab oratione incipias.
[3] Igitur de tuo studio desperes oportet omnino, simul et ingenio. Deo autem soli confidas et influxui Spiritus. Experto crede ista. L. Epp. i. 88, dated 18th January.

most affecting marks of his regard.[1] We know how dear are the expressions of sympathy to a man's heart when he sees himself attacked on every side. The secretary of Nuremberg did still more: he desired to increase the number of Luther's friends, and with this intent requested him to dedicate one of his works to Jerome Ebner, a celebrated Nuremberg lawyer. "You entertain a high opinion of my studies," modestly answered the reformer; "but I have a very mean one of them. Nevertheless, I have desired to conform with your wishes. I have sought...... but among all my stores, that I have never found so paltry before, nothing presented itself that did not appear utterly unworthy of being dedicated to so great a man by so mean a person as myself." Affecting humility! It is Luther who speaks, and it is to Doctor Ebner, whose name is unknown to us, that he compares himself. Posterity has not ratified this decision.

Luther, who had done nothing to circulate his theses, had not sent them to Scheurl any more than to the Elector and his court. The secretary of Nuremberg expressed his astonishment at this. "My design," answered Luther, "was not to give my theses such publicity. I only desired to confer on their contents with some of those who remain with us or near us.[2] If they had been condemned, I would have destroyed them. If they had been approved of, I purposed publishing them. But they have now been printed over and over again, and circulated so far beyond all my hopes, that I repent of my offspring;[3] not because I fear the truth should be made known to the people, 'twas this alone I sought; but that is not the way to instruct them. They contain questions that are still doubtful to me, and if I had thought my theses would have created such a sensation, there are some things I should have omitted, and others I should have asserted with greater confidence." In after-years Luther thought differently. Far from fearing he had said too much, he declared that he ought to have said much more. But the apprehensions he manifested to Scheurl do honour to his sincerity. They show that he had no premeditated plan, no party spirit, no self-conceit, and that he sought for truth alone. When he had discovered it fully, he changed his tone. "You will find in my earlier writings," said he many years after, "that I very humbly conceded many things to the pope, and even important things, that now I regard and detest as abominable and blasphemous."[4]

Scheurl was not the only respectable layman who, at this time, gave testimony of his friendship for Luther. The celebrated painter, Albert Durer, sent him a present, perhaps one of his pictures, and the doctor warmly expressed his gratitude for the kindness.[1]

Thus Luther practically experienced the truth of these words of Divine wisdom: *A friend loveth at all times; and a brother is born for adversity.* But he remembered them also for others, and pleaded the cause of the whole nation. The elector had just imposed one tax, and there was a talk of another, probably by the advice of his counsellor Pfeffinger, against whom Luther often vented his biting sarcasms. The doctor boldly placed himself in the breach: "Let not your highness despise the prayer of a poor beggar," said he. "I beseech you, in God's name, not to impose a new tax. My heart was bruised as well as the hearts of many of those who are most devoted to you, when they saw how far the last had injured your good fame, and the popularity your highness enjoyed. It is true that the Lord has given you an exalted understanding, so that you see into these matters farther than I or your subjects can. But perhaps it is God's will that a mean understanding should instruct a greater, in order that no one should trust to himself, but solely in the Lord our God, whom I pray to preserve your health of body for our good, and your soul for eternal blessedness. Amen.' Thus it is that the Gospel, which calls upon us to honour kings, makes us also plead the cause of the people. To a nation it proclaims its duties; and reminds the prince of his subjects' rights. The voice of a Christian like Luther, resounding in the cabinet of a sovereign, might often supply the place of a whole assembly of legislators.

In this same letter, in which Luther addresses a severe lesson to the elector, he does not fear to make a request, or rather to remind him of a promise to give him a new coat. This freedom of Luther, at a time when he might fear he had displeased Frederick, does equal honour to the prince and to the reformer. "But if it is Pfeffinger who has charge of it," added he, "let him give it me in reality, not in protestations of friendship. He knows how to spin fine speeches, but they never produce good cloth." Luther imagined that by the faithful counsel he had given his prince, he had well earned his court-dress.[2] But, however that may be, he had not received it two years after, and he asked for it again.[3] This seems to indicate that Frederick was not so much influenced by Luther as has been supposed.

[1] Literæ tuæ animum tuum erga meam parvitatem candidum et longe ultra merita benevolentissimum probaverunt. L. Epp. i. 79. "Your letters," wrote Luther on 11th Dec. 1517, " have shown the candour of your mind, and your unmerited benevolence towards my low estate."
[2] Non fuit consilium neque votum eas evulgari, sed cum paucis apud et circum nos habitantibus primum super ipsis conferri. L. Epp. i. 95.
[3] Ut me pœniteat hujus fœturæ. Ibid.
[4] Quæ istis temporibus pro summa blasphemia et abominatione habeo et execror. L. Opp. Lat. (W.) in Præf.

[1] Accepi simul et donum insignis viri Alberti Durer. L. Epp. i. 95.
[2] Mein Hofkleid verdienen. Epp. L. i. 77, 78.
[3] Ibid. 283.

CHAPTER VIII.

Frankfort Discussion — Tetzel's Theses — Menaces — Knipstrow's Opposition—Luther's Theses burnt—The Monks —Luther's Peace—Tetzel's Theses burnt—Grief of Luther.

MEN's minds had thus recovered a little from their first alarm. Luther himself felt inclined to declare that his theses had not the scope attributed to them. New events might turn aside the general attention, and this blow aimed at the Romish doctrine be lost in air like so many others. But the partisans of Rome prevented the affair from ending thus. They fanned the flame instead of quenching it.

Tetzel and the Dominicans replied with insolence to the attack that had been made on them. Burning with the desire of crushing the impudent monk who had dared to trouble their commerce, and of conciliating the favour of the Roman pontiff, they uttered a cry of rage; they maintained that to attack the indulgence ordained by the pope, was to attack the pope himself, and they summoned to their aid all the monks and divines of their school.[1] Tetzel indeed felt that an adversary like Luther was too much for him alone. Greatly disconcerted at the doctor's attack, and exasperated to the highest degree, he quitted the vicinity of Wittemberg, and repaired to Frankfort-on-the-Oder, where he arrived in the month of November 1517. The university of this city, was of recent date; but it had been founded by the opposite party. Conrad Wimpina, an eloquent man, the ancient rival of Pollich of Mellerstadt, and one of the most distinguished theologians of the age, was a professor there. Wimpina cast an envious glance on the doctor and university of Wittemberg. Their reputation galled him. Tetzel requested him to answer Luther's theses, and Wimpina wrote two lists of antitheses, the object of the first being to defend the doctrine of indulgences, and the second, the authority of the pope.

On the 20th January 1518 took place that disputation prepared so long beforehand, announced with so much pomp, and on which Tetzel founded such great hopes. On every side he had beaten up for recruits. Monks had been sent from all the cloisters in the neighbourhood, and they met to the number of about three hundred. Tetzel read his theses. They even contained this declaration, "that whoever says that the soul does not escape out of purgatory so soon as the money tinkles in the chest, is in error."[2]

But above all, he put forward propositions according to which the pope seemed actually *seated as God in the temple of God,* according

to the apostle's expression. It was convenient for this shameless trafficker to take shelter, with all his disorders and scandals, under the mantle of the pope.

He declared himself ready to maintain the following propositions before the numerous assembly by which he was surrounded:—

3. "We should teach Christians that the pope, by the greatness of his power, is above the whole universal Church, and superior to the councils, and that we should implicitly obey his decrees.

4. "We should teach Christians that the pope alone has the right of deciding in all matters of christian faith; that he alone and no one besides him has power to interpret the meaning of Scripture according to his own views, and to approve or condemn all the words or writings of other men.

5. "We should teach Christians that the judgment of the pope cannot err, in matters concerning the christian faith, or which are necessary to the salvation of the human race.

6. "We should teach Christians that, in matters of faith, we should rely and repose more on the pope's sentiments, as made known by his decisions, than on the opinions of all the learned, which are derived merely from Scripture.

8. "We should teach Christians that those who injure the honour or dignity of the pope, are guilty of high-treason, and deserve to be accursed.

17. "We should teach Christians that there are many things which the Church regards as indisputable articles of universal truth, although they are not to be found in the canon of the Bible or in the writings of the ancient doctors.

44. "We should teach Christians to regard as obstinate heretics all who declare by their words, acts, or writings, that they will not retract their heretical propositions, even should excommunication fall upon them like hail or rain.

48. "We should teach Christians that those who protect the errors of heretics, and who, by their authority, prevent them from being brought before the judge who has a right to hear them, are excommunicated; that if in the space of a year they do not change their conduct, they will be declared infamous, and cruelly punished with divers chastisements, according to the law, and for a warning to other men.[1]

50. "We should teach Christians that those who scribble so many books and waste so much paper, who dispute and preach publicly and wickedly about oral confession, the satisfaction of works, the rich and great indulgences of the Bishop of Rome, and his power; that the persons who take part with those who preach or write such things, who

---

[1] Suum senatum convocat; monachos aliquot et theologos sua sophistica utcunque tinctos. Mel. Vita Luth.
[2] Quisquis ergo dicit, non citius posse animam volare, quam in fundo cistæ denarius possit tinnire, errat. Positiones Fratris Joh. Tezelii, pos. 56. L. Opp. i. 94.

[1] Pro infamibus sunt tenendi, qui etiam per juris capitula terribiliter multis plectentur pœnis in omnium hominum terrorem. Positiones fratris Joh. Tezelii, pos. 56. L. Opp. i. 98.

are pleased with their writings, and circulate them among the people and over the world; that those who speak in private of these things, in a contemptuous and shameless manner—should expect to incur the penalties before mentioned, and to precipitate themselves, and others with them, into eternal condemnation at the judgment day, and into merited disgrace even in this world. For ' if so much as a beast touch the mountain, it shall be stoned.' "

We see that Tetzel did not attack Luther only. He probably had the Elector of Saxony in view in his 48th thesis. These propositions, besides, savour strongly of the Dominican. To threaten every contradictor with cruel punishments, was the argument of an inquisitor, to which there were no means of replying. The three hundred monks whom Tetzel had collected stared and listened with admiration to what he had said. The theologians of the university were too fearful of being ranked with the abettors of heresy, or else were too strongly attached to Wimpina's principles, openly to attack the astonishing theses that had just been read.

All this affair, about which there had been so much noise, seemed then destined to be a mere sham fight; but among the crowd of students present at the disputation was a youth about twenty years of age, named John Knipstrow. He had read Luther's theses, and had found them conformable to the doctrines of Scripture. Indignant at beholding the truth publicly trodden under foot, without any one appearing in its defence, this young man raised his voice, to the great astonishment of all the assembly, and attacked the presumptuous Tetzel. The poor Dominican, who had not reckoned on any opposition, was quite confused. After a few exertions, he deserted the field of battle, and gave way to Wimpina. The latter resisted more vigorously; but Knipstrow pressed him so closely, that to finish a struggle so unbecoming in his eyes, the president (Wimpina himself) declared the disputation over, and immediately proceeded to confer the degree of doctor upon Tetzel in recompense of this glorious combat. In order to get rid of the young orator, Wimpina had him sent to the convent of Pyritz in Pomerania, with an order that he should be strictly watched. But this dawning light was removed from the banks of the Oder, only to diffuse not long after a greater brilliancy throughout Pomerania.[1] When God thinks fit, he employs even learners to confound the teachers.

Tetzel, wishing to retrieve the check he had experienced, had recourse to the *ultima ratio* of Rome and of the inquisitors,—to fire. He caused a pulpit and a scaffold to be erected in one of the public walks in the environs of Frankfort. Thither he repaired in solemn procession, with his insignia of in-

quisitor of the faith. He gave vent to all his violence from the pulpit. He hurled thunderbolts, and exclaimed with his stentorian voice, that the heretic Luther deserved to suffer death at the stake. Next, placing the doctor's propositions and sermon on the scaffold, he burnt them.[1] He knew better how to do this than to maintain his theses. At this time he met with no gainsayers: his victory was complete. The impudent Dominican re-entered Frankfort in triumph. When powerful parties are vanquished, they have recourse to certain demonstrations, which we may well accord to them as some consolation for their disgrace.

These second theses of Tetzel's form an important epoch in the Reformation. They changed the ground of dispute: they transported it from the indulgence-markets to the halls of the Vatican, and diverted it from Tetzel to the pope. In the place of that despicable broker whom Luther had so firmly grasped, they substituted the sacred person of the head of the Church. Luther was filled with astonishment. It is probable that he would erelong have taken this step himself; but his enemies spared him the trouble. It was henceforward no question of a discredited traffic, but of Rome itself; and the blow by which a daring hand had tried to demolish Tetzel's shop, shook the very foundations of the pontifical throne.

Tetzel's theses served as a rallying cry to the troops of Rome. An uproar against Luther broke out among the monks, infuriate at the appearance of a more formidable adversary than either Reuchlin or Erasmus. Luther's name resounded every where from the pulpits of the Dominicans, who addressed themselves to the passions of the people. They called the bold doctor a madman, a seducer, and a demoniac. His doctrine was cried down as the most horrible heresy. " Only wait a fortnight, or a month at most," said they, " and this notorious heretic will be burnt." If it had depended solely on the Dominicans, the fate of Jerome and of Huss would soon have been that of the Saxon doctor also; but God was watching over him. His life was destined to accomplish what the ashes of the Bohemian reformer had begun; for each does the work of God, one by his death, the other by his life. Many began already to exclaim that the whole university of Wittemberg was deeply tainted with heresy, and pronounced it infamous.[2] " Let us drive out that villain and all his partisans," continued they. In many places these cries succeeded in exciting the passions of the multitude. The public attention was directed against those who shared Luther's

1 Fulmina in Lutherum torquet : vociferatur ubique hunc hereticum igni perdendum esse : propositiones etiam Lutheri et concionem de indulgentiis publice conjicit in flammas. Melancth. Vita Luth.
2 Eo furunt usque, ut Universitatem Wittembergensem propter me infamem conantur facere et hæreticam. L. Epp. I. 92.

opinions; and wherever the monks were the strongest, the friends of the Gospel experienced the effects of their hatred. It was thus, with regard to the Reformation, that our Saviour's prophecy began to be accomplished : *Men will revile you, and persecute you, and say all manner of evil against you falsely, for my sake.* In every age this is the recompense bestowed by the world on the decided friends of the Gospel.

When Luther was informed of Tetzel's theses, and of the general attack of which they were the signal, his courage immediately took fire. He felt the necessity of opposing such adversaries face to face ; and his intrepid soul had no difficulty in coming to such a decision. But at the same time their weakness revealed to him his own strength, and inspired him with the consciousness of what he really was.

He did not, however, give way to those sentiments of pride so natural to man's heart. "I have more difficulty to refrain from despising my adversaries," wrote he about this time to Spalatin, "and from sinning in this way against Jesus Christ, than I should have in conquering them. They are so ignorant of human and divine things, that it is disgraceful to have to fight against them. And yet it is this very ignorance which gives them their inconceivable arrogance and their brazen face."[1] But the strongest encouragement to his heart, in the midst of this general hostility, was the intimate conviction that his cause was that of truth. "Do not be surprised," wrote he to Spalatin at the beginning of 1518, "that I am so grossly insulted. I listen to their abuse with joy. If they did not curse me, we could not be so firmly assured that the cause I have undertaken is that of God himself.[2] Christ has been set up for a sign to be spoken against."—"I know," said he on another occasion, "that from the very beginning of the world, the Word of God has been of such a nature, that whoever desired to publish it to the world has been compelled, like the Apostles, to abandon all things, and to expect death. If it were not so it would not be the Word of Jesus Christ."[3] This peace in the midst of agitation is a thing unknown to the heroes of the world. We see men who are at the head of a government, or of a political party, sink under their toils and vexations. The Christian generally acquires new vigour in his struggle. It is because he possesses a mysterious source of repose and of courage unknown to him whose eyes are closed against the Gospel.

One thing, however, sometimes agitated Luther : the thought of the dissensions his courageous opposition might produce. He knew that a single word might set the world on fire. At times his imagination beheld prince arrayed against prince, and perhaps people against people. His patriotic heart was saddened; his christian charity alarmed. He would have desired peace; and yet he must speak, for such was the Lord's will. "I tremble," said he, "I shudder at the idea that I may be an occasion of discord between such mighty princes."[1]

He still kept silence with regard to Tetzel's propositions concerning the pope. Had he been carried away by passion, he would, no doubt, have instantly fallen upon that astonishing doctrine, under the shelter of which his adversary sought to protect himself. But he did not; and in his delay, his reserve and silence, there is something grave and solemn, which sufficiently reveals the spirit that animated him. He waited, but not from weakness : for the blow was all the stronger.

Tetzel, after his *auto-da-fé* at Frankfort, had hastened to send his theses into Saxony. They will serve as an antidote (thought he) against Luther's. A man from Halle, commissioned by the inquisitor to circulate his theses, arrived at Wittemberg. The students of the university, still indignant that Tetzel should have burnt their master's propositions, had scarcely heard of his arrival, before they sought him out, surrounded him, mobbed and frightened him. "How can you dare bring such things here?" said they. Some of them bought part of the copies he had with him, others seized the remainder. They thus became masters of his whole stock, amounting to eight hundred copies ; and then, unknown to the elector, the senate, the rector, Luther, and all the professors,[2] they posted the following words on the university boards : "Whoever desires to be present at the burning and funeral of Tetzel's theses, must come to the market-place at two o'clock."

Crowds assembled at the appointed hour, and the Dominican's propositions were consigned to the flames in the midst of noisy acclamations. One copy escaped the conflagration, which Luther sent afterwards to his friend Lange of Erfurth. These generous but imprudent youths followed the precept of the ancients—*Eye for eye, and tooth for tooth*, and not that of Jesus Christ. But when doctors and professors set the example at Frankfort, can we be astonished that it was followed by young students at Wittemberg? The news of this academical execution soon spread through all Germany, and made a great noise.[3] Luther was deeply pained at it.

"I am surprised," wrote he to his old

[1] Epp. Luth. i. 92.
[2] Nisi maledicerer, non crederem ex Deo esse quæ tracto. L. Epp. i. 85.
[3] "The Word of God was purchased by death," continues he in his energetic language, "proclaimed by death, preserved by death, and by death must it be preserved and published." Morte emptum est (verbum Dei), mortibus vulgatum, mortibus servatum, mortibus quoque servandum aut referendum est.

[1] Inter tantos principes dissidii origo esse, valde horreo et timeo. L. Epp. i. 93.
[2] Hæc inscio principe, senatu, rectore, denique omnibus nobis. Ibid. 99.
[3] Fit ex ea re ingens undique fabula. Ibid.

master, Jodocus, at Erfurth, " you should have believed I allowed Tetzel's theses to be burnt! Do you think I have so taken leave of my senses? But what could I do? When I am concerned, everybody believes whatever is told of me.[1] Can I stop the mouths of the whole world? Well! let them say, hear, and believe whatever they like concerning me. I shall work so long as God gives me strength, and with His help I shall fear nothing."— " What will come of it," said he to Lange, " I know not, except that the peril in which I am involved becomes greater on this very account."[2] This act shows how the hearts of the young already glowed for the cause which Luther defended. This was a sign of great importance ; for a movement which has taken place among the youth is soon of necessity propagated throughout the whole nation.

The theses of Tetzel and of Wimpina, although little esteemed, produced a certain effect. They aggravated the dispute; they widened the rent in the mantle of the Church ; they brought questions of the highest interest into the controversy. The chiefs of the Church began, accordingly, to take a nearer view of the matter, and to declare strongly against the Reformer. " Truly, I do not know on whom Luther relies," said the Bishop of Brandenburg, " since he thus ventures to attack the power of the bishops." Perceiving that this new conjuncture called for new measures, the bishop came himself to Wittemberg. But he found Luther animated with that interior joy which springs from a good conscience, and determined to give battle. The bishop saw that the Augustine monk obeyed a power superior to his own, and returned in anger to Brandenburg. One day during the winter of 1518, as he was seated before the fire, he said, turning to those who surrounded him : " I will not lay my head down in peace, until I have thrown Martin into the fire, like this brand ;" and he flung the billet into the flames. The revolution of the sixteenth century was not destined to be accomplished by the heads of the Church, any more than that of the first century had been by the sanhedrim and by the synagogue. The chiefs of the clergy in the sixteenth century were opposed to Luther, to the Reformation, and to its ministers ; as they had been to Jesus Christ, to the Gospel, to his Apostles, and, as too frequently happens in every age, to the truth.—" The Bishops," said Luther, speaking of the visit the prelate of Brandenburg had paid him, " begin to perceive that they ought to have done what I am doing, and they are ashamed of it. They call me proud and arrogant—I will not deny that I am so ; but they are not the people to know either what God is, or what we are."[3]

[1] Omnes omnibus omnia credunt de me. L. Epp. i. 109.
[2] Ibid. 9b.
[3] Quid vel Deus vel ipsi sumus. L. Epp. i. 224.

CHAPTER IX.

Prierio—System of Rome—Dialogue—System of Reform— Answer to Prierio—The Word—The Pope and the Church —Hochstraten—The Monks—Luther Replies—Eck—The School—The Obelisks—Luther's Sentiments—The Asterisks—Rupture.

A more formidable resistance than that made by Tetzel was already opposed to Luther Rome had answered. A reply had gone forth from the walls of the sacred palace. It was not Leo X. who had condescended to speak of theology : " 'Tis a mere monkish squabble," he said one day ; " the best way is not to meddle with it." And at another time he observed, " It is a drunken German that has written these theses : when the fumes have passed off, he will talk very differently."[1] A Roman Dominican, Sylvester Mazzolini of Prierio or Prierias, master of the sacred palace, filled the office of censor and it was in this capacity that he first became acquainted with the theses of the Saxon monk.

A Romish censor and Luther's theses, what a contrast! Freedom of speech, freedom of inquiry, freedom of belief, come into collision in the city of Rome with that power which claims to hold in its hands the monopoly of intelligence, and to open and shut at pleasure the mouth of Christendom. The struggle of christian liberty which engenders children of God, with pontifical despotism which produces slaves of Rome, is typified, as it were, in the first days of the Reformation, in the encounter of Luther and Prierio.

The Roman censor, prior-general of the Dominicans, empowered to decide on what Christendom should profess or conceal, and on what it ought to know or be ignorant of, hastened to reply. He published a writing, which he dedicated to Leo X. In it he spoke contemptuously of the German monk, and declared with Romish assurance " that he should like to know whether this Martin had an iron nose or a brazen head, which cannot be broken ! "[2] And then, under the form of a dialogue, he attacked Luther's theses, employing by turns ridicule, insult, and menaces.

This combat between the Augustine of Wittemberg and the Dominican of Rome was waged on the very question that is the principle of the Reformation, namely : " What is the sole infallible authority for Christians ? " Here is the system of the Church, as set forth by its most independent organs :—[3]

The letter of the written Word is dead without the spirit of interpretation, which alone reveals its hidden meaning. Now,

[1] Ein voller trunkener Deutscher. L. Opp. (W.) xxii. 1337.
[2] An ferreum nasum aut caput æneum gerat iste Lutherus, ut effringi non possit. Sylv. Prieratis Dialogus.
[3] See John Gerson's Propositiones de Sensu Litterali S Scripturæ. Opp. tom. i.

this spirit is not given to every Christian, but to the Church—that is, to the priests. It is great presumption to say, that He who promised the Church to be with her always, even to the end of the world, could have abandoned her to the power of error. It will be said, perhaps, that the doctrine and constitution of the Church are no longer such as we find them in the sacred oracles. Undoubtedly: but this change is only in appearance; it extends only to the form and not to the substance. We may go further: this change is progressive. The vivifying power of the Divine Spirit has given a reality to what in Scripture was merely an idea; it has filled up the outline of the Word; it has put a finishing touch to its rude sketches; it has completed the work of which the Bible only gave the first rough draft. We must therefore understand the sense of the Holy Scriptures as settled by the Church, under the guidance of the Holy Spirit. From this point the catholic doctors diverge. General councils, said some (and Gerson was one of them), are the representatives of the Church. The pope, said others, is the depositary of the spirit of interpretation, and no one has a right to understand the Scriptures otherwise than as decreed by the Roman pontiff. This was the opinion of Prierio.

Such was the doctrine opposed by the master of the sacred palace to the infant Reformation. He put forward propositions, on the power of the Church and of the pope, at which the most shameless flatterers of the Church of Rome would have blushed. Here is one of the principles he advanced at the head of his writing: "Whoever relies not on the teaching of the Roman Church, and of the Roman pontiff, as the infallible rule of faith, from which the Holy Scriptures themselves derive their strength and their authority, is a heretic."[1]

Then, in a dialogue in which Luther and Sylvester are the speakers, the latter seeks to refute the doctor's propositions. The opinions of the Saxon monk were altogether strange to a Roman censor; and, accordingly, Prierio shows that he understood neither the emotions of his heart, nor the springs of his conduct. He measured the doctor of the truth by the petty standard of the servants of Rome. "My dear Luther," said he, "if you were to receive from our lord the pope a good bishopric and a plenary indulgence for repairing your Church, you would sing in a softer strain, and you would extol the indulgences you are now disparaging!" The Italian, so proud of his elegant manners, occasionally assumes the most scurrilous tone: "If it is the nature of dogs to bite," said he to Luther, "I fear you had a dog for your father."[2] The Dominican at last won-

ders at his own condescension in speaking to the rebellious monk; and ends by showing his adversary the cruel teeth of an inquisitor. "The Roman Church," says he, "the apex of whose spiritual and temporal power is in the pope, may constrain by the secular arm those who, having once received the faith, afterwards go astray. It is not bound to employ reason to combat and vanquish rebels."[1]

These words, traced by the pen of a dignitary of the Roman court, were very significant. Still, they did not frighten Luther. He believed, or feigned to believe, that this dialogue was not written by Prierio, but by Ulric Hütten, or by another of the contributors to the *Letters of some Obscure Men*; who, said he, in his satirical humour, and in order to excite Luther against Prierio, had compiled this mass of absurdities.[2] He had no desire to behold the see of Rome excited against him. However, after having kept silence for some time, his doubts (if he had any) were dispelled: he set to work, and his answer was ready in two days.[3]

The Bible had moulded the reformer and begun the Reformation. Luther needed not the testimony of the Church in order to believe. His faith had come from the Bible itself; from within and not from without. He was so intimately convinced that the evangelical doctrine was immovably founded on the Word of God, that in his eyes all external authority was useless. This experiment made by Luther opened a new futurity to the Church. The living source that had welled forth for the monk of Wittemberg was to become a river to slake the thirst of nations.

In order that we may comprehend the Word, the Spirit of God must give understanding, said the Church; and it was right so far. But its error had been in considering the Holy Spirit as a monopoly accorded to a certain class, and supposing that it could be confined exclusively within assemblies or colleges, in a city or in a conclave. *The wind bloweth where it listeth*, had said the Son of God, speaking of God's Spirit; in another place, *they shall* ALL *be taught of God*. The corruption of the Church, the ambition of the pontiffs, the passions of the councils, the quarrels of the clergy, the pomp of the prelates, had banished far from the sacerdotal abodes that Holy Ghost, that spirit of humility and peace. It had deserted the assemblies of the proud, the palaces of the mighty ones of the Church, and had taken up its dwelling with simple Christians and humble priests. It had fled from a domineering hierarchy, that had often trampled under foot and shed the blood of the poor; from a proud

---

[1] A qua etiam Sacra Scriptura robur trahit et auctoritatem, hæreticus est. Fundamentum tertium.
[2] Si mordere canum est proprium, vereor ne tibi pater canis fuerit. Sylv. Prier. Dial.

[1] Seculari brachio potest eos compescere, nec tenetur rationibus certare ad vincendos protervientes. Sylv. Prier. Dial.
[2] Convenit inter nos, esse personatum aliquem Sylvestrum ex obscuris viris, qui tantas ineptias in hominem luserit ad provocandum me adversus eum. Epp. i. p. 87, 14th January.
[3] T. i. (W.) Lat., p. 170.

and ignorant clergy, whose chiefs were better skilled in using the sword than the Bible; and dwelt at one time with despised sects, and at another with men of intelligence and learning. The holy cloud, that had departed from the sumptuous basilics and proud cathedrals, had descended into the obscure abodes of the humble, or into the quiet studies, those tranquil witnesses of a conscientious inquiry. The Church, degraded by its love of power and of riches, dishonoured in the eyes of the people by the venal use it made of the doctrine of life; the Church, which sold salvation to replenish the treasuries drained by its haughtiness and debauchery,—had forfeited all respect, and sensible men no longer attached any value to her testimony. Despising so debased an authority, they joyfully turned towards the Divine Word, and to its infallible authority, as toward the only refuge remaining to them in such a general disorder.

The age, therefore, was prepared. The bold movement by which Luther changed the resting-place of the sublimest hopes of the human heart, and with a hand of power transported them from the walls of the Vatican to the rock of the Word of God, was saluted with enthusiasm. This is the work that the reformer had in view in his reply to Prierio.

He passes over the principles which the Dominican had set forth in the beginning of his work : " But," said he, " following your example, I will also lay down certain fundamental principles.

"The first is this expression of St. Paul : *Though we, or an angel from heaven, preach any other Gospel unto you than that which we have preached unto you, let him be accursed.*

" The second is this passage from St. Augustine to St. Jerome : ' I have learnt to render to the canonical books alone the honour of believing most firmly that none of them has erred ; as for the others, I do not believe in what they teach, simply because it is they who teach them.' "

Here we see Luther laying down with a firm hand the essential principles of the Reformation : the Word of God, the whole Word of God, nothing but the Word of God. " If you clearly understand these points," continues he, " you will also understand that your Dialogue is wholly overturned by them ; for you have only brought forward the expressions and the opinions of St. Thomas." Then, attacking his adversary's axioms, he frankly declares that he believes popes and councils can err. He complains of the flatteries of the Roman courtiers, who ascribe both temporal and spiritual power to the pope. He declares that the Church exists virtually in Christ alone, and representatively in the councils. [1] And then coming

to Prierio's insinuation : " No doubt you judge of me after yourself," said he, " but if I aspired to an episcopal station, of a surety I should not use the language that is so grating to your ears. Do you imagine I am ignorant how bishoprics and the priesthood are obtained at Rome ? Do not the very children sing in the streets those well-known words :—[1]

Of all foul spots the world around,
The foulest spot in Rome is found."

Such songs as these had been current at Rome before the election of one of the latter popes. Nevertheless, Luther speaks of Leo with respect : " I know," said he, " that we may compare him to Daniel in Babylon ; his innocence has often endangered his life." He concludes by a few words in reply to Prierio's threats : " Finally, you say that the pope is at once pontiff and emperor, and that he is mighty to compel obedience by the secular arm. Do you thirst for blood ?...... I protest that you will not frighten me either by your rhodomontades or by the threatening noise of your words. If I am put to death, Christ lives, Christ my Lord, and the Lord of all, blessed for evermore. Amen." [2]

Thus, with a firm hand, Luther erects against the infidel altar of the papacy the altar of the only infallible and Holy Word of God, before which he would have every knee to bow, and on which he declares himself ready to offer up his life.

Prierio published an answer, and then a third book " On the Irrefragable Truth of the Church and of the Roman Pontiff," in which, relying upon the ecclesiastical law, he asserted, that although the pope should make the whole world go with him to hell, he could neither be condemned nor deposed.[3] The pope was at last obliged to impose silence on Prierio.

A new adversary erelong entered the lists ; he also was a Dominican. James Hochstraten, inquisitor at Cologne, whom we have already seen opposing Reuchlin and the friends of letters, shuddered at Luther's boldness. It was necessary for monkish darkness and fanaticism to come in contact with him who was destined to give them a mortal blow. Monachism had sprung up as the primitive truth began to disappear. Since then, monks and errors had grown up side by side. The man had now appeared who was to accelerate their ruin ; but these robust champions could not abandon the field of battle without a struggle. It lasted all the reformer's life ; but in Hochstraten this combat is singularly personified : Hochstraten and Luther ; the free and courageous

---

[1] Ego ecclesiam virtualiter non scio nisi in Christo, representative non nisi in concilio. L. Opp. Lat. p. 174.

[1] Quando hanc pueri in omnibus plateis urbis cantant: Denique nunc facta est......fœdissima Roma. L. Opp. Lat. p. 183.
[2] Si occidor, vivit Christus, Dominus meus et omnium. Ibid. p. 186.
[3] De Juridica et Irrefragabili Veritate Romanæ Ecclesiæ, lib. tertius, cap. 12.

Christian with the impetuous slave of monkish superstitions! Hochstraten lost his temper, grew furious, and called loudly for the heretic's death......It is by the stake he wished to secure the triumph of Rome. " It is high-treason against the Church," exclaimed he, " to allow so horrible a heretic to live one hour longer. Let the scaffold be instantly erected for him !" This murderous advice was, alas ! but too effectually carried out in many countries; the voices of numerous martyrs, as in the primitive times of the Church, gave testimony to the truth, even in the midst of flames. But in vain were the sword and the stake invoked against Luther. The Angel of the Lord kept watch continually around him, and preserved him.

Luther answered Hochstraten in few words, but with great energy : " Go," said he in conclusion, " go, thou raving murderer, who criest for the blood of thy brethren ; it is my earnest desire that thou forbearest to call me Christian and faithful, and that thou continuest, on the contrary, to decry me as a heretic. Understandest thou these things, blood-thirsty man ! enemy of the truth ! and if thy mad rage should hurry thee to undertake anything against me, take care to act with circumspection, and to choose thy time well. God knows what is my purpose, if he grant me life...,...My hope and my expectation, God willing, will not deceive me."[1] Hochstraten was silent.

A more painful attack awaited the reformer. Doctor Eck, the celebrated professor of Ingolstadt, the deliverer of Urban Regius, and Luther's friend, had received the famous theses. Eck was not a man to defend the abuse of indulgences ; but he was a doctor of the schools and not of the Bible ; well versed in the scholastic writings, but not in the Word of God. If Prierio had represented Rome, if Hochstraten had represented the monks, Eck represented the schoolmen. The schools, which for five centuries past had domineered over Christendom, far from giving way at the first blow of the reformer, rose up haughtily to crush the man who dared pour out upon them the floods of his contempt. Eck and Luther, the School and the Word, had more than one struggle ; but it was now that the combat began.

Eck could not but find errors in many of Luther's positions. Nothing leads us to doubt the sincerity of his convictions. He as enthusiastically maintained the scholastic opinions, as Luther did the declarations of the Word of God. We may even suppose that he felt no little pain when he found himself obliged to oppose his old friend ; it would seem, however, from the manner of his attack, that passion and jealousy had some share in his motives.

He gave the name of *Obelisks* to his remarks against Luther's theses. Desirous at first of saving appearances, he did not publish his work, but was satisfied with communicating it confidentially to his ordinary, the Bishop of Eichstadt. But the *Obelisks* were soon extensively circulated, either through the indiscretion of the bishop or by the doctor himself. A copy fell into the hands of Link, a friend of Luther and preacher at Nuremberg. The latter hastened to send it to the reformer. Eck was a far more formidable adversary than Tetzel, Prierio, or Hochstraten : the more his work surpassed theirs in learning and in subtlety, the more dangerous it was. He assumed a tone of compassion towards his " feeble adversary," being well aware that pity inflicts more harm than anger. He insinuated that Luther's propositions circulated the Bohemian poison, that they savoured of Bohemia, and by these malicious allusions, he drew upon Luther the unpopularity and hatred attached in Germany to the name of Huss and to the schismatics of his country.

The malice that pervaded this treatise exasperated Luther ; but the thought that this blow came from an old friend grieved him still more. Is it then at the cost of his friend's affections that he must uphold the truth ? Luther poured out the deep sorrow of his heart in a letter to Egranus, pastor at Zwickau. " In the *Obelisks* I am styled a venomous man, a Bohemian, a heretic, a seditious, insolent, rash person......I pass by the milder insults, such as drowsy-headed, stupid, ignorant, contemner of the sovereign pontiff, &c. This book is brimful of the blackest outrages. Yet he who penned them is a distinguished man, with a spirit full of learning, and a learning full of spirit; and, what causes me the deepest vexation, he is a man who was united to me by a great and recently contracted friendship :[1] it is John Eck, doctor of divinity, chancellor of Ingolstadt, a man celebrated and illustrious by his writings. If I did not know Satan's thoughts, I should be astonished at the fury which has led this man to break off so sweet and so new a friendship,[2] and that, too, without warning me, without writing to me, without saying a single word."

But if Luther's heart was wounded, his courage was not cast down. On the contrary, he rose up invigorated for the contest. " Rejoice, my brother," said he to Egranus, whom a violent enemy had likewise attacked,. " rejoice, and do not let these flying leaves affright thee. The more my adversaries give way to their fury, the farther I advance. I leave the things that are behind me, in order that they may bay at them, and I pursue what lies before me, that they may bay at them in their turn."

---

[1] L. Opp. (Leips.) xvii. 140.

[1] Et quod magis urit, antea mihi magna recenterque contracta amicitia conjunctus. L. Epp. i. 100.
[2] Quo furore ille amicitias recentissimas et jucundissimas solveret. Ibid.

Eck was sensible how disgraceful his conduct had been, and endeavoured to vindicate himself in a letter to Carlstadt. In it he styled Luther "their common friend," and cast all the blame on the Bishop of Eichstadt, at whose solicitation he pretended to have written his work. He said that it had not been his intention to publish the *Obelisks;* that he would have felt more regard for the bonds of friendship that united him to Luther; and demanded in conclusion, that Luther, instead of disputing publicly with him, should turn his weapons against the Frankfort divines. The professor of Ingolstadt, who had not feared to strike the first blow, began to be alarmed when he reflected on the strength of that adversary whom he had so imprudently attacked. Willingly would he have eluded the struggle; but it was too late.

All these fine phrases did not persuade Luther, who was yet inclined to remain silent. " I will swallow patiently," said he, "this sop, worthy of Cerberus."[1] But his friends differed from him: they solicited, they even constrained him to answer. He therefore replied to the *Obelisks* by his *Asterisks,* opposing (as he said, playing on the words) to the rust and livid hue of the Ingoldstadt doctor's *Obelisks,* the light and dazzling brightness of the stars of heaven. In this work he treated his adversary with less severity than he had shown his previous antagonists; but his indignation pierced through his words.

He showed that in these chaotic *Obelisks* there was nothing from the Holy Scriptures, nothing from the Fathers of the Church, nothing from the ecclesiastical canons; that they were filled with scholastic glosses, opinions, mere opinions and empty dreams;[2] in a word, the very things that Luther had attacked. The *Asterisks* are full of life and animation. The author is indignant at the errors of his friend's book; but he pities the man.[3] He professes anew the fundamental principle which he laid down in his answer to Prierio: "The supreme pontiff is a man, and may be led into error; but God is truth, and cannot err."[4] Farther on, employing the *argumentum ad hominem* against the scholastic doctor, he says to him, " It would be great impudence assuredly for any one to teach in the philosophy of Aristotle, what he cannot prove by the authority of that ancient author.—You grant it.—It is, *a fortiori,* the

most impudent of all impudence to affirm in the Church and among Christians what Christ himself has not taught.[1] Now, where is it found in the Bible that the treasure of Christ's merits is in the hands of the pope?"

He adds farther: " As for the malicious reproach of Bohemian heresy, I bear this calumny with patience through love of Christ. I live in a celebrated university, in a well-famed city, in a respectable bishopric, in a powerful duchy, where all are orthodox, and where, undoubtedly, so wicked a heretic would not be tolerated."

Luther did not publish the *Asterisks;* he communicated them solely to his friends. They were not given to the public till long after.[2]

This rupture between the two doctors of Ingoldstadt and Wittemberg made a great sensation in Germany. They had many friends in common. Scheurl especially, who appears to have been the man by whom the two doctors had been connected, was alarmed. He was one of those who desired to see a thorough reform in the German Church by means of its most distinguished organs. But if, at the very outset, the most eminent theologians of the day should fall to blows; if, while Luther came forward with novelties, Eck became the representative of antiquity, what disruption might not be feared! Would not numerous partisans rally round each of these two chiefs, and would not two hostile camps be formed in the bosom of the empire?

Scheurl endeavoured therefore to reconcile Eck and Luther. The latter declared his willingness to forget everything; that he loved the genius, that he admired the learning of Doctor Eck,[3] and that what his old friend had done had caused him more pain than anger. " I am ready," said he to Scheurl, " for peace and for war: but I prefer peace. Apply yourself to the task grieve with us that the devil has thrown among us this beginning of discord, and afterwards rejoice that Christ in his mercy has crushed it." About the same time he wrote Eck a letter full of affection:[4] but Eck made no reply; he did not even send him any message.[5] It was no longer a season for reconciliation. The contest daily grew warmer. Eck's pride and implacable spirit soon broke entirely the last ties of that friendship which every day grew weaker.

---

[1] Volui tamen hanc offam Cerbero dignam absorbere patientia. L. Epp. i. 100.
[2] Omnia scholasticissima, opiniosissima, meraque somnia. Asterici, Opp. L. Lat. i. 145.
[3] Indignor rei et misereor hominis. Ibid. p. 150.
[4] Homo est summus pontifex, falli potest. Sed veritas est Deus, qui falli non potest. Ibid. p. 155.

[1] Longe ergo impudentissima omnium temeritas est, aliquid in ecclesia asserere, et inter Christianos, quod non docuit Christus. Asterici, Opp. L. Lat. i. 156.
[2] Cum privatim dederim Asteriscos meos non fit ei respondendi necessitas. L. Epp. p. 126.
[3] Diligimus hominis ingenium et admiramur eruditionem. L. Epp. ad Scheurlum, 15th June 1518, vol. i. 125.
[4] Quod ad me attinet, scripsi ad eum ipsum has, ut vides, amicissimas et plenas litteras humanitate erga eum. Ibid.
[5] Nihil neque litterarum neque verborum me participem fecit. Ibid.

CHAPTER X.

Popular Writings—The Lord's Prayer—Our Father—Who art in Heaven—Hallowed be thy Name—Thy Kingdom come—Thy Will be done—Our Daily Bread—Sermon on Repentance—Remission of Sins cometh from Christ.

Such were the struggles that the champion of the Word of God had to sustain at the very entrance of his career. But these contests with the leaders of society, these academical disputes, are of little account to the Christian. Human teachers imagine they have gained the noblest triumph, when they succeed in filling a few journals or a few drawing-rooms with the noise of their systems. Since it is with them a mere question of self-love or of party rather than of the welfare of humanity, they are satisfied with this worldly success. Their labours are accordingly like smoke, which, after blinding the eyes, passes away, leaving no trace behind. They have neglected depositing the fire among the masses; they have but skimmed the surface of human society.

It is not so with the Christian; he thinks not of a party, or of academical success, but of the salvation of souls. He therefore willingly neglects the brilliant contest in which he might engage at his ease with the champions of the world, and prefers the obscure labours which carry light and life to the cottages and homes of the people. This was what Luther did, or rather, following the precept of his Divine Master, *he did this, and left not other things undone.* At the time he was combating with inquisitors, university chancellors, and masters of the sacred palace, he endeavoured to diffuse sound knowledge on religious subjects among the multitude. This is the aim of many of the popular works he published about this time, such as his *Sermons on the Ten Commandments,* delivered two years before in the church of Wittemberg, and of which we have already spoken, and his *Explanation of the Lord's Prayer for simple and ignorant Laymen.* [1] Who would not be pleased to know how the reformer addressed the people at this period? We will therefore quote some of the expressions that he put forth " to run through the land," as he says in the preface to the latter work.

Prayer, that interior act of the heart, will undoubtedly ever be one of the points by which a true and vital reformation will begin; Luther accordingly occupied himself on this subject without delay. It is impossible to translate his energetic style, and the strength of that language which grew, so to speak, under his pen, as he wrote; we will however make the attempt.

" When thou prayest," said he, " let thy words be few, but thy thoughts and affections many, and above all let them be profound.

[1] Opp. (Leips.) vii. 1086.

The less thou speakest the better thou prayest. Few words and many thoughts, is christian: many words and few thoughts, is heathenish......

" External and bodily prayer is that buzzing of the lips, that outward babble which is gone through without any attention, and which strikes the eyes and the ears of men; but prayer in spirit and in truth is the inward desire, the motions, the sighs, which issue from the depths of the heart. The former is the prayer of hypocrites, and of all those who trust in themselves: the latter is the prayer of the children of God, who walk in his fear."

Then passing on to the first words of the Lord's Prayer, *Our Father,* he expresses himself thus:—

" There is no name among all names which more inclines us towards God, than the name of Father. We should not feel so much happiness and consolation in calling him our Lord, or God, or Judge.........By this word Father the bowels of the Lord are moved; for there is no voice more lovely or more endearing to a father than that of his child.

" *Who art in heaven.*—He who confesses that he has a Father in heaven, acknowledges himself a stranger upon earth. Hence there arises an ardent longing in his heart, like that of a child who dwells far from his father's country, among strangers, in wretchedness and in mourning. It is as if he said: Alas! my Father! thou art in heaven, and I, thy unhappy child, am on the earth, far from thee, in the midst of danger, necessity, and tribulation.

" *Hallowed be thy name.*—He who is passionate, envious, an evil-speaker, a calumniator, dishonours that name of God in which he was baptized. Putting to an impious use the vessel that God hath consecrated to himself, he is like a priest who would take the holy cup and with it give drink to a sow, or gather dung......

" *Thy kingdom come.*—Those who amass wealth, who build sumptuous houses, who seek all that the world can give, and pronounce this prayer with their lips, resemble large organ-pipes which peal loudly and incessantly in the churches, without either speech, feeling, or reason......"

Further on Luther attacks the then very popular error of pilgrimages: " One goes to Rome, another to St. James'; this man builds a chapel, that one endows a religious foundation, in order to attain the kingdom of God; but all neglect the essential point, which is to become His kingdom themselves. Why goest thou beyond the seas in search of God's kingdom?......It is in thine own heart that it should be found.

" It is a terrible thing," continues he, " to hear this prayer offered up: *Thy will be done!* Where in the Church do we see this will of God performed?......One bishop rises up against another bishop, one church against another church. Priests, monks, and nuns, quarrel, fight, and battle. In every place there is nought but discord. And yet each party exclaim that their meaning is good, their intention upright; and thus to the honour and glory of God they all together perform a work of the devil......

"Wherefore do we say *Our bread?*" continues he in explanation of the words, *Give us this day our daily bread.* "Because we pray not to have the ordinary bread that pagans eat, and which God gives to all men, but for *our* bread, ours who are children of the heavenly father.

"And what, then, is this bread of God? —It is Jesus Christ our Lord : *I am the living bread which cometh down from heaven, and giveth life unto the world.* For this reason (and let us not deceive ourselves), all sermons and all instructions that do not set Jesus Christ before us and teach us to know him, cannot be the daily bread and the nourishment of our souls......

"To what use will such bread have been prepared for us, if it is not offered to us, and so we cannot taste it ?......It is as if a magnificent banquet had been prepared, and there was no one to serve the bread, to hand round the dishes, to pour out the wine, so that the guests must feed themselves on the sight and the smell of the viands......For this cause we must preach Jesus Christ alone.

"But what is it, then, to know Jesus Christ, sayest thou, and what advantage is derived from it?......I reply : To learn and to know Jesus Christ is to understand what the apostle says : *Christ is made unto us of God, wisdom, and righteousness, and sanctification, and redemption.* Now this you understand, if you acknowledge all your wisdom to be a condemnable folly, your own righteousness a condemnable iniquity, your own holiness a condemnable impurity, your own redemption a miserable condemnation ; if you feel that you are really before God and before all creatures a fool, a sinner, an impure, a condemned man, and if you show, not only by your words, but from the bottom of your heart, and by your works, that you have no consolation and no salvation remaining except in Jesus Christ. To believe is none other than to eat this bread from heaven."

Thus did Luther remain faithful to his resolution of opening the eyes of a blind people whom the priests were leading at their pleasure. His writings, circulating rapidly through all Germany, called up a new light, and scattered abundantly the seeds of truth in a soil well prepared for it. But while thinking of those who were afar off, he did not forget those who were near at hand.

From every pulpit the Dominicans condemned the infamous heretic. Luther, the man of the people, and who, had he been willing, might with a few words have aroused the popular waves, always disdained such triumphs, and thought only of instructing his hearers.

His reputation, which extended more and more, and the courage with which he raised the banner of Christ in the midst of the enslaved Church, caused his sermons to be listened to with ever increasing interest. Never had the crowd of hearers been so great. Luther went straight to the mark. One day, having gone into the pulpit at Wittemberg, he undertook to establish the doctrine of repentance, and on this occasion, he delivered a sermon which afterwards became very celebrated, and in which he laid many of the foundations of the evangelical doctrine.

He first contrasts the pardon of men with the pardon of Heaven. "There are two kinds of remission," said he, "remission of the penalty, and remission of the sin. The first reconciles man externally with the Christian Church. The second, which is the heavenly indulgence, reconciles man to God. If a man does not experience within himself that peace of conscience, that joy of heart which proceeds from the remission of God, there are no indulgences that can aid him, even should he purchase all that have ever been offered upon earth."

He continues thus : "They desire to do good works before their sins are forgiven whilst it is necessary for sin to be forgiven before men can perform good works. It is not the works that expel sin ; but the sin once expelled, good works will follow ![1] For good works must be performed with a joyful heart, with a good conscience towards God, that is, with remission of sins."

He then comes to the principal object of his sermon, and it was also the great aim of the entire Reformation. The Church had been set in the place of God and of his Word ; he challenges this claim, and makes every thing depend on faith in the Word of God.

"The remission of the sin is in the power neither of the pope, nor of the bishop, nor of the priest, nor of any other man, but reposes solely on the Word of Christ, and on your own faith. For Christ designed not to build our consolation, our salvation, on the word or on the work of man, but solely on himself, on His work and on His Word......Thy repentance and thy works may deceive thee, but Christ, thy God, will not deceive thee, he will not falter, and the devil shall not overthrow his words.[2]

"A pope or a bishop has no more power than the lowliest priest, as regards remission of sins. And even were there no priest, each Christian, even a woman or a child,[3] can do

---

[1] Nicht die Werke treiben die Sünde aus; sondern die Austreibung der Sünde thut gute Werke. L. Opp. (L.) xvii. 162.
[2] Christus dein Gott wird dir nicht lügen, noch wanken. Ibid.
[3] Ob es schon ein Weib oder ein Kind wäre. Ibid.

the same thing. For if a simple Christian says to you, ' God pardons sin in the name of Jesus Christ,' and you receive this word with a firm faith, and as if God himself were addressing you, you are absolved......

" If you do not believe your sins are forgiven, you make God a liar, and you put more confidence in your own vain thoughts, than in God and his Word......

" Under the Old Testament, neither prophet, priest, nor king had the power of proclaiming remission of sins. But under the New, each believer has this power. The Church is overflowing with remission of sins![1] If a pious Christian consoles thy conscience with the word of the cross, let it be man or woman, young or old, receive this consolation with such faith as rather to die many deaths than to doubt that it will be so before God......Repent, do all the works in thy power; but let the faith thou hast in pardon through Jesus Christ be in the foremost rank, and command alone on the field of battle."[2]

Thus spoke Luther to his astonished and enraptured hearers. All the scaffolding that impudent priests had raised to their profit between God and the soul of man, was thrown down, and man was brought face to face with his God. The word of forgiveness descended pure from on high, without passing through a thousand corrupting channels. In order that the testimony of God should be efficacious, it was no longer necessary for men to set their delusive seal to it. The monopoly of the sacerdotal caste was abolished; the Church was emancipated.

CHAPTER XI.

Apprehensions of his Friends—Journey to Heidelberg—Bibra—Palatine Palace—Rupture—The Paradoxes—Disputation—The Audience—Bucer—Brentz—Snepf—Conversations with Luther—Labours of these young Doctors—Effects on Luther—The aged Professor—The True Light—Arrival.

MEANWHILE it had become necessary for the fire that had been lighted at Wittemberg to be kindled in other places. Luther, not content with announcing the Gospel truth in the place of his residence, both to the students of the academy and to the people, was desirous of scattering elsewhere the seed of sound doctrine. In the spring of 1518, a general chapter of the Augustine order was to be held at Heidelberg. Luther was summoned to it as one of the most distinguished men of the order. His friends did all they could to dissuade him from undertaking this journey. In truth, the monks had endeavoured to

render Luther's name odious in all the places through which he would have to pass. To insults they added menaces. It would require but little to excite a popular tumult on his journey of which he might be the victim. " Or else," said his friends, " they will effect by fraud and stratagem, what they dare not do by violence."[1] But Luther never suffered himself to be hindered in the accomplishment of a duty by the fear of danger, however imminent. He therefore closed his ears to the timid observations of his friends: he pointed to Him in whom he trusted, and under whose guardianship he was ready to undertake so formidable a journey. Immediately after the festival of Easter, he set out calmly on foot,[2] the 13th April 1518.

He took with him a guide named Urban, who carried his little baggage, and who was to accompany him as far as Wurtzburg. What thoughts must have crowded into the heart of this servant of the Lord during his journey ! At Weissenfels, the pastor, whom he did not know, immediately recognised him as the Wittemberg doctor, and gave him a hearty welcome.[3] At Erfurth, two other brothers of the Augustine order joined him. At Judenbach, they fell in with the elector's privy councillor, Degenhard Pfeffinger, who entertained them at the inn where they had found him. " I had the pleasure," wrote Luther to Spalatin, " of making this rich lord a few groats poorer ; you know how I like on every opportunity to levy contributions on the rich for the benefit of the poor, especially if the rich are my friends."[4] He reached Coburg, overwhelmed with fatigue. " All goes well, by God's grace," wrote he, " except that I acknowledge having sinned in undertaking this journey on foot. But for that sin I have no need, I think, of the remission of indulgences ; for my contrition is perfect, and the satisfaction plenary. I am overcome with fatigue, and all the conveyances are full. Is not this enough, and more than enough, of penance, contrition, and satisfaction ?"[5]

The reformer of Germany, unable to find room in the public conveyances, and no one being willing to give up his place, was compelled, notwithstanding his weariness, to leave Coburg the next morning humbly on foot. He reached Wurtzburg the second Sunday after Easter, towards evening. Here he sent back his guide.

In this city resided the Bishop of Bibra, who had received his theses with so much approbation. Luther was the bearer of a letter to him from the Elector of Saxony. The bishop, delighted at the opportunity of becoming personally acquainted with this bold champion of the truth, immediately invited him to the episcopal palace. He went and met him at the door, conversed affection-

---

[1] Also siehst du dass die ganze Kirche voll von Vergebung der Sünden ist. L. Opp. (L.) xvii. 162.
[2] Und Hauptmann im Felde bleibe. Ibid.

[1] L. Epp. i. 98.
[2] Pedester veniam. Ibid.
[3] Ibid. 105.   [4] Ibid. 104.   [5] Ibid. 106.

ately with him, and offered to provide him with a guide to Heidelberg. But at Wurtzburg Luther had met his two friends, the vicar-general Staupitz, and Lange, the prior of Erfurth, who had offered him a place in their carriage. He therefore thanked Bibra for his kindness; and on the morrow the three friends quitted Wurtzburg. They thus travelled together for three days, conversing with one another. On the 21st April they arrived at Heidelberg. Luther went and lodged at the Augustine convent.

The Elector of Saxony had given him a letter for the Count Palatine Wolfgang, duke of Bavaria. Luther repaired to his magnificent castle, the situation of which excites, even to this day, the admiration of strangers. The monk from the plains of Saxony had a heart to admire the situation of Heidelberg, where the two beautiful valleys of the Rhine and the Neckar unite. He delivered his letter to James Simler, steward of the household. The latter on reading it observed: "In truth you have here a valuable letter of credit."[1] The count-palatine received Luther with much kindness, and frequently invited him to his table, together with Lange and Staupitz. So friendly a reception was a source of great comfort to Luther. "We were very happy, and amused one another with agreeable and pleasant conversation," said he; "eating and drinking, examining all the beauties of the palatine palace, admiring the ornaments, arms, cuirasses; in fine, everything remarkable contained in this celebrated and truly regal castle."[2]

But Luther had another task to perform. He must work while it is yet day. Having arrived at a university which exercised great influence over the west and south of Germany, he was there to strike a blow that should shake the churches of these countries. He began, therefore, to write some theses which he purposed maintaining in a public disputation. Such discussions were not unusual; but Luther felt that this one, to be useful, should lay forcible hold upon men's minds. His disposition, besides, naturally led him to present truth under a paradoxical form. The professors of the university would not permit the discussion to take place in their large theatre; and Luther was obliged to take a hall in the Augustine convent. The 26th April was the day appointed for the disputation.

Heidelberg, at a later period, received the evangelical doctrine: those who were present at the conference in the convent might have foreseen that it would one day bear fruit.

Luther's reputation had attracted a large audience; professors, students, courtiers, citizens, came in crowds. The following are some of the doctor's *Paradoxes;* for so he designated his theses. Perhaps even in our days they would still bear this name; it would, however, be easy to translate them into obvious propositions:—

1. "The law of God is a salutary doctrine of life. Nevertheless, it cannot aid man in attaining to righteousness; on the contrary, it impedes him.

3. "Man's works, however fair and good they may be, are, however, to all appearance, nothing but deadly sins.

4. "God's works, however unsightly and bad they may appear, have however an everlasting merit.

7. "The works of the righteous themselves would be mortal sins, unless, being filled with a holy reverence for the Lord, they feared that their works might in truth be mortal sins.[1]

9. "To say that works done out of Christ are truly dead, but not deadly, is a dangerous forgetfulness of the fear of God.

13. "Since the fall of man, free-will is but an idle word; and if man does all he can, he still sins mortally.

16. "A man who imagines to arrive at grace by doing all that he is able to do, adds sin to sin, and is doubly guilty.

18. "It is certain that man must altogether despair of himself, in order to be made capable of receiving Christ's grace.

21. "A theologian of the world calls evil good, and good evil; but a theologian of the cross teaches aright on the matter.

22. "The wisdom which endeavours to learn the invisible perfections of God in his works, puffs up, hardens, and blinds a man.

23. "The law calls forth God's anger, kills, curses, accuses, judges, and condemns whatsoever is not in Christ.[2]

24. "Yet this wisdom (§ 22) is not evil; and the law (§ 23) is not to be rejected; but the man who studies not the knowledge of God under the cross, turns to evil whatever is good.

25. "That man is not justified who performs many works; but he who, without works, has much faith in Christ.

26. "The law says, Do this! and what it commands is never done. Grace says, Believe in Him! and immediately all things are done.[3]

28. "The love of God finds nothing in man, but creates in him what he loves. The love of man proceeds from its well-beloved."[4]

Five doctors of divinity attacked these theses. They had read them with all the astonishment that novelty excites. Such theology appeared very extravagant; and yet they discussed these points, according to Luther's own testimony, with a courtesy that inspired him with much esteem for

---

[1] Ihr habt bei Gott einen köstlichen Credenz. L. Epp. i. 111. [2] Ibid.

[1] Justorum opera essent mortalia, nisi pio Dei timore, ab ipsismet justis, ut mortalia timerentur. L. Opp. Lat. i. 55.
[2] Lex iram Dei operatur, occidit, maledicit, reum facit, judicat, damnat, quicquid non est in Christo. Ibid.
[3] Lex dicit: Fac hoc! et nunquam fit. Gratia dicit: Crede in hunc! et jam facta sunt omnia. Ibid.
[4] Amor Dei non invenit, sed creat suum diligibile; amor hominis fit a suo diligibili. Ibid.

them, but at the same time with earnestness and discernment. Luther, on his side, displayed wonderful mildness in his replies, unrivalled patience in listening to the objections of his adversaries, and all the quickness of St. Paul in solving the difficulties opposed to him. His replies were short, but full of the Word of God, and excited the admiration of his hearers. " He is in all respects like Erasmus," said many ; " but surpasses him in one thing : he openly professes what Erasmus is content merely to insinuate." [1]

The disputation was drawing to an end. Luther's adversaries had retired with honour from the field ; the youngest of them, Doctor George Niger, alone continued the struggle with the powerful champion. Alarmed at the daring propositions of the monk, and not knowing what further arguments to have recourse to, he exclaimed, with an accent of fear : " If our peasants heard such things, they would stone you to death ! " [2] At these words the whole auditory burst into a loud laugh.

Never had an assembly listened with so much attention to a theological discussion. The first words of the reformer had aroused their minds. Questions which shortly before would have been treated with indifference, were now full of interest. On the countenances of many of the hearers a looker-on might have seen reflected the new ideas which the bold assertions of the Saxon doctor had awakened in their minds.

Three young men in particular were deeply moved. One of them, Martin Bucer by name, was a Dominican, twenty-seven years of age, who, notwithstanding the prejudices of his order, appeared unwilling to lose one of the doctor's words. He was born in a small town of Alsace, and had entered a convent at sixteen. He soon displayed such capacity that the most enlightened monks entertained the highest expectations of him : [3] " He will one day be the ornament of our order," said they. His superiors had sent him to Heidelberg to study philosophy, theology, Greek, and Hebrew. At that period Erasmus published several of his works, which Bucer read with avidity.

Soon appeared the earliest writings of Luther. The Alsacian student hastened to compare the reformer's doctrines with the Holy Scriptures. Some misgivings as to the truth of the Popish religion arose in his mind. [4] It was thus that the light was diffused in those days. The elector-palatine took particular notice of the young man. His strong and sonorous voice, his graceful manners and eloquent language, the freedom with which he attacked the vices of the day, made him a

distinguished preacher. He was appointed chaplain to the court, and was fulfilling his functions when Luther's journey to Heidelberg was announced. What joy for Bucer ! No one repaired with greater eagerness to the hall of the Augustine convent. He took with him paper, pens, and ink, intending to take down what the doctor said. But while his hand was swiftly tracing Luther's words, the finger of God, in more indelible characters, wrote on his heart the great truths he heard. The first gleams of the doctrine of grace were diffused through his soul during this memorable hour. [1] The Dominican was gained over to Christ.

Not far from Bucer stood John Brentz or Brentius, then nineteen years of age. He was the son of a magistrate in a city of Swabia, and at thirteen had been entered as student at Heidelberg. None manifested greater application. He rose at midnight and began to study. This habit became so confirmed, that during his whole life he could not sleep after that hour. In later years he consecrated these tranquil moments to meditation on the Scriptures. Brentz was one of the first to perceive the new light then dawning on Germany. He welcomed it with a heart abounding in love. [2] He eagerly perused Luther's works But what was his delight when he could hear the writer himself at Heidelberg ! One of the doctor's propositions more especially startled the youthful scholar ; it was this : " That man is not justified before God who performs many works ; but he who, without works, has much faith in Jesus Christ."

A pious woman of Heilbronn on the Neckar, wife of a senator of that town, named Snepf, had imitated Hannah's example, and consecrated her first-born son to the Lord, with a fervent desire to see him devote himself to the study of theology. This young man, who was born in 1495, made rapid progress in learning ; but either from taste, or from ambition, or in compliance with his father's wishes, he applied to the study of jurisprudence. The pious mother was grieved to behold her child, her Ehrhard, pursuing another career than that to which she had consecrated him. She admonished him, entreated him, prayed him continually to remember the vow she had made on the day of his birth. [3] Overcome at last by his mother's perseverance, Ehrhard Snepf gave way. Erelong he felt such a taste for his new studies, that nothing in the world could have diverted him from them.

He was very intimate with Bucer and Brentz, and they were friends until death ; " for," says one of their biographers, " friendships based on the love of letters and of

1 Bucer, in Scultet's Annal. Evang. Renovat. p. 22.
2 Si rustici hæc audirent, certe lapidibus vos obruerent et interficerent. L. Epp. i. 111.
3 Prudentioribus monachis spem de se præclaram excitavit. Melch. Adam. Vit. Buceri, p. 211.
4 Cum doctrinam in eis traditam cum sacris litteris contullisset, quædam in pontificia religione suspecta habere cœpit. Ibid.

1 Primam lucem purioris sententiæ de justificatione in suo pectore sensit. Melch. Adam. Vit. Buceri, p. 211.
2 Ingens Dei beneficium lætus Brentius agnovit, et grate mente amplexus est. Ibid.
3 Crebris interpellationibus eum voti quod de nato ipso fecerat, admoneret ; et a studio juris ad theologiam quasi conviciis avocaret. Melch. Adam. Snepfii Vita.

virtue never fail." He was present with his two friends at the Heidelberg discussion. The Paradoxes and courage of the Wittemberg doctor gave him a new impulse. Rejecting the vain opinion of human merits, he embraced the doctrine of the free justification of the sinner.

The next day Bucer went to Luther. " I had a familiar and private conversation with him," said Bucer; " a most exquisite repast, not of dainties, but of truths that were set before me. To whatever objection I made, the doctor had a reply, and explained everything with the greatest clearness. Oh! would to God that I had time to write more!"[1] Luther himself was touched with Bucer's sentiments. " He is the only brother of his order," wrote he to Spalatin, " who is sincere; he is a young man of great promise. He received me with simplicity, and conversed with me very earnestly. He is worthy of our confidence and love."[2]

Brentz, Snepf, and many others, excited by the new truths that began to dawn upon their minds, also visited Luther; they talked and conferred with him; they begged for explanations on what they did not understand. The reformer replied, strengthening his arguments by the Word of God. Each sentence imparted fresh light to their minds. A new world was opening before them.

After Luther's departure, these noble-minded men began to teach at Heidelberg. They felt it their duty to continue what the man of God had begun, and not allow the flame to expire which he had lighted up. The scholars will speak, when the teachers are silent. Brentz, although still so young, explained the Gospel of St. Matthew, at first in his own room, and afterwards, when the chamber became too small, in the theatre of philosophy. The theologians, envious at the crowd of hearers this young man drew around him, became irritated. Brentz then took orders, and transferred his lectures to the college of the Canons of the Holy Ghost. Thus the fire already kindled up in Saxony now glowed in Heidelberg. The centres of light increased in number. This period has been denominated the seedtime of the Palatinate.

But it was not the Palatinate alone that reaped the fruits of the Heidelberg disputation. These courageous friends of the truth soon became shining lights in the Church. They all attained to exalted stations, and took part in many of the debates which the Reformation occasioned. Strasburg, and England a little later, were indebted to Bucer for a purer knowledge of the truth. Snepf first declared it at Marburg, then at Stuttgart, Tubingen, and Jena. Brentz, after having taught at Heidelberg, continued his labours for a long period at Tubingen, and at Halle in Swabia. We shall meet with these three men again in the course of our history.

[1] Gerdesius, Monument. Antiq., &c.   [2] L. Epp. i. 412.

This disputation carried forward Luther himself. He increased daily in the knowledge of the truth. " I belong to those," said he, " who improve by writing and by teaching others, and not to those who from nothing become on a sudden great and learned doctors."

He was overjoyed at seeing with what avidity the students of the schools received the dawning truth, and this consoled him when he found the old doctors so deep-rooted in their opinions. " I have the glorious hope," said he, " that as Christ, when rejected by the Jews, turned to the Gentiles, we shall now also behold the new theology, that has been rejected by these graybeards with their empty and fantastical notions, welcomed by the rising generation."[1]

The chapter being ended, Luther thought of returning to Wittemberg. The count-palatine gave him a letter for the elector, dated 1st of May, in which he said " that Luther had shown so much skill in the disputation, as greatly to contribute to the renown of the university of Wittemberg." He was not allowed to return on foot.[2] The Nuremberg Augustines conducted him as far as Wurtzburg, from whence he proceeded to Erfurth with the friars from that city. As soon as he arrived he repaired to the house of his old teacher, Jodocus. The aged professor, much grieved and scandalized at the path his disciple had taken, was in the habit of placing before all Luther's propositions a *theta*, the letter employed by the Greeks to denote condemnation.[3] He had written to the young doctor in terms of reproach, and the latter desired to reply in person to these letters. Not having been admitted, he wrote to Jodocus: " All the university, with the exception of one licentiate, think as I do. More than this; the prince, the bishop, many other prelates, and all our most enlightened citizens, declare with one voice, that up to the present time they had neither known nor understood Jesus Christ and his Gospel. I am ready to receive your corrections; and although they should be severe, they will appear to me very gentle. Open your heart, therefore, without fear; unburden your anger. I will not and I cannot be vexed with you. God and my conscience are my witnesses!"[4]

The old doctor was moved by these expressions of his former pupil. He was willing to try if there were no means of removing the damnatory theta. They conversed on the matter, but the result was unfavourable. " I made him understand at least," said Luther, " that all their *sentences* were like that beast which is said to devour itself. But talking to a deaf man is labour in vain. These doc-

[1] L. Epp. i. 112.
[2] Veni autem curru, qui ieram pedester. Ibid. 110.
[3] Omnibus placitis meis nigrum theta præfigit. Ibid. 111. The Greeks used to place the initial letter of the word Ϧανατος, death, opposite the names of criminals condemned to die.
[4] Ibid.

tors obstinately cling to their petty distinctions, although they confess there is nothing to confirm them but the light of natural reason, as they call it—a dark chaos truly to us who preach no other light than Jesus Christ, the true and only light."[1]

Luther quitted Erfurth in the carriage belonging to the convent, which took him to Eisleben. From thence the Augustines of the place, proud of a doctor who had shed such glory on their order and on their city, his native place, conveyed him to Wittem-

[1] Nisi dictamine rationis naturalis, quod apud nos idem est, quod chaos tenebratum, qui non prædicamus aliam lucem, quam Christum Jesum lucem veram et solam. L. Epp. i. 111.

berg with their own horses and at their own expense. Every one desired to bestow some mark of affection and esteem on this extraordinary man, whose fame was constantly increasing.

He arrived on the Saturday after Ascension day. The journey had done him good, and his friends thought him improved in appearance and stronger than before his departure.[1] They were delighted at all he had to tell them. Luther rested some time after the fatigues of his journey and his dispute at Heidelberg; but this rest was only a preparation for severer toils.

[1] Ita ut nonnullis videar factus habitior et corpulentior. L. Epp. i. 111.

BOOK IV.

LUTHER BEFORE THE LEGATE.—MAY TO DECEMBER 1518.

CHAPTER I.

The Resolutions—Repentance—Papacy—Leo X.—Luther to his Bishop—Luther to the Pope—Luther to the Vicar-General—Rovera to the Elector—Sermon on Excommunication—Influence and Strength of Luther.

TRUTH at last had raised her head in the midst of Christendom. Victorious over the inferior ministers of the papacy, she was now to enter upon a struggle with its chief in person. We are about to contemplate Luther contending with Rome.

It was after his return from Heidelberg that he took this bold step. His early theses on the indulgences had been misunderstood. He determined to explain their meaning with greater clearness. From the clamours that a blind hatred extorted from his enemies, he had learnt how important it was to win over the most enlightened part of the nation to the truth: he therefore resolved to appeal to its judgment, by setting forth the bases on which his new convictions were founded. It was requisite at once to challenge the decision of Rome: he did not hesitate to send his explanations thither. While he presented them with one hand to the enlightened and impartial readers of his nation, with the other he laid them before the throne of the sovereign pontiff.

These explanations of his theses, which he styled *Resolutions*,[1] were written in a very moderate tone. Luther endeavoured to soften down the passages that had occasioned the greatest irritation, and thus gave proof of

[1] Luth. Opp. (Leips.) xvii. 29-113.

genuine humility. But at the same time he showed himself to be unshaken in his convictions, and courageously defended all the propositions which truth obliged him to maintain. He repeated once more, that every truly penitent Christian possesses remission of sins without papal indulgences; that the pope, like the meanest priest, can do no more than simply declare what God has already pardoned; that the treasury of the merits of the saints, administered by the pope, was a pure chimera, and that the Holy Scriptures were the sole rule of faith. But let us hear his own statement on some of these points.

He begins by establishing the nature of real repentance, and contrasts that act of God which regenerates man with the mummeries of the Church of Rome. "The Greek word μετανοϊτε," said he, "signifies, put on a new spirit, a new mind, take a new nature, so that ceasing to be earthly, you may become heavenly......Christ is a teacher of the spirit and not of the letter, and his words are spirit and life. He teaches therefore a repentance in spirit and in truth, and not those outward penances that can be performed by the proudest sinners without humiliation; he wills a repentance that can be effected in every situation of life,—under the kingly purple, under the priest's cassock, under the prince's hat,—in the midst of those pomps of Babylon where a Daniel lived, as well as under the monk's frock and the beggar's rags."[1]

Further on we meet with this bold lan-

[1] On the first Thesis.

guage: "I care not for what pleases or displeases the pope. He is a man like other men. There have been many popes who loved not only errors and vices, but still more extraordinary things. I listen to the pope as pope, that is to say, when he speaks in the canons, according to the canons, or when he decrees some article in conjunction with a council, but not when he speaks after his own ideas. Were I to do otherwise, ought I not to say with those who know not Christ, that the horrible massacres of Christians by which Julius II. was stained, were the good deeds of a gentle shepherd towards Christ's flock?[1]

"I cannot help wondering," continues Luther, "at the simplicity of those who have asserted that the two swords of the Gospel represent, one the spiritual, the other the secular power. Yes! the pope wields a sword of iron; it is thus he exhibits himself to Christendom, not as a tender father, but as a formidable tyrant. Alas! an angry God has given us the sword we longed for, and taken away that which we despised. In no part of the world have there been more terrible wars than among Christians......Why did not that acute mind which discovered this fine commentary, interpret in the same subtle manner the history of the two keys intrusted to St. Peter, and lay it down as a doctrine of the Church, that one key serves to open the treasures of heaven, the other the treasures of the earth?"[2]

"It is impossible," says Luther in another place, "for a man to be a Christian without having Christ; and if he has Christ, he possesses at the same time all that belongs to Christ. What gives peace to our consciences is this—by faith our sins are no longer ours, but Christ's, on whom God has laid them all; and, on the other hand, all Christ's righteousness belongs to us, to whom God has given it. Christ lays his hand on us, and we are healed. He casts his mantle over us, and we are sheltered; for he is the glorious Saviour, blessed for evermore."[3]

With such views of the riches of salvation by Jesus Christ, there was no longer any need of indulgences.

While Luther attacks the papacy, he speaks honourably of Leo X. "The times in which we live are so evil," said he, "that even the most exalted individuals have no power to help the Church. We have at present a very good pope in Leo X. His sincerity, his learning, inspire us with joy. But what can be done by this one man, amiable and gracious as he is? He was worthy of being pope in better days. In our age we deserve none but such men as Julius II. and Alexander VI."

He then comes to the point: "I will say what I mean, boldly and briefly: the Church needs a reformation. And this cannot be the

work either of a single man, as the pope, or of many men, as the cardinals and councils; but it must be that of the whole world, or rather it is a work that belongs to God alone. As for the time in which such a reformation should begin, he alone knows who has created all time......The dike is broken, and it is no longer in our power to restrain the impetuous and overwhelming billows."

This is a sample of the declarations and ideas which Luther addressed to his enlightened fellow-countrymen. The festival of Whitsuntide was approaching; and at the same period in which the apostles gave to the risen Saviour the first testimony of their faith, Luther, the new apostle, published this spirit-stirring book, in which he ardently called for a resurrection of the Church. On Saturday, 22d May 1518, the eve of Pentecost, he sent the work to his ordinary the bishop of Brandenburg with the following letter:—

"Most worthy Father in God! It is now some time since a new and unheard-of doctrine touching the apostolic indulgences began to make a noise in this country; the learned and the ignorant were troubled by it; and many persons, some known, some personally unknown to me, begged me to declare by sermon or by writing what I thought of the novelty, I will not say the impudence, of this doctrine. At first I was silent and kept in the background. But at last things came to such a pass, that the pope's holiness was compromised.

"What could I do? I thought it my duty neither to approve nor condemn these doctrines, but to originate a discussion on this important subject, until the Holy Church should decide.

"As no one accepted the challenge I had given to the whole world, and since my theses have been considered, not as matters for discussion, but as positive assertions,[1] I find myself compelled to publish an explanation of them. Condescend therefore to receive these trifles,[2] which I present to you, most merciful bishop. And that all the world may see that I do not act presumptuously, I entreat your reverence to take pen and ink, and blot out, or even throw into the fire and burn, anything that may offend you. I know that Jesus Christ needs neither my labours nor my services, and that he will know how to proclaim his glad tidings to the Church without my aid. Not that the bulls and the threats of my enemies alarm me; quite the contrary. If they were not so impudent, so shameless, no one should hear of me; I would hide myself in a corner, and there study alone for my own good. If this affair is not God's, it certainly shall no longer be mine or any other man's, but a thing of nought. Let the honour and the glory be his to whom alone they belong!"

---

[1] Thesis 26.   [2] Thesis 60.   [3] Thesis 37.

[1] Non ut disputabilia sed asserta acciperentur. L. Epp. i. 114.   [2] Ineptias.

Luther was still filled with respect for the head of the Church. He supposed Leo to be a just man and a sincere lover of the truth. He resolved, therefore, to write to him. A week after, on Trinity Sunday, 30th May 1518, he penned a letter, of which we give a few specimens.

"To the most blessed Father Leo X. sovereign bishop, Martin Luther, an Augustine friar, wishes eternal salvation.

"I am informed, most holy Father, that wicked reports are in circulation about me, and that my name is in bad odour with your holiness. I am called a heretic, apostate, traitor, and a thousand other insulting names. What I see fills me with surprise, what I learn fills me with alarm. But the only foundation of my tranquillity remains,—a pure and peaceful conscience. Deign to listen to me, most holy Father,—to me who am but a child and unlearned."

After relating the origin of the whole matter, Luther thus continues :—

"In all the taverns nothing was heard but complaints against the avarice of the priests, and attacks against the power of the keys and of the sovereign bishop. Of this the whole of Germany is a witness. When I was informed of these things, my zeal was aroused for the glory of Christ, as it appeared to me ; or, if another explanation be sought, my young and warm blood was inflamed.

"I forewarned several princes of the Church ; but some laughed at me, and others turned a deaf ear. The terror of your name seemed to restrain every one. I then published my disputation.

"And behold, most holy Father, the conflagration that is reported to have set the whole world on fire.

"Now what shall I do ? I cannot retract, and I see that this publication draws down upon me an inconceivable hatred from every side. I have no wish to appear before the world ; for I have no learning, no genius, and am far too little for such great matters ; above all, in this illustrious age, in which Cicero himself, were he living, would be compelled to hide himself in some dark corner.[1]

"But in order to quiet my adversaries, and to reply to the solicitations of many friends, I here publish my thoughts. I publish them, holy Father, that I may be in greater safety under the shadow of your wings. All those who desire it will thus understand with what simplicity of heart I have called upon the ecclesiastical authority to instruct me, and what respect I have shown to the power of the keys.[2] If I had not behaved with propriety, it would have been impossible for the most serene lord

Frederick, duke and elector of Saxony, who shines among the friends of the apostolic and christian truth, to have ever endured in his university of Wittemberg a man so dangerous as I am asserted to be.

"For this reason, most holy Father, I fall at the feet of your holiness, and submit myself to you, with all that I have and with all that I am. Destroy my cause, or espouse it : declare me right or wrong ; take away my life or restore it, as you please. I shall acknowledge your voice as the voice of Jesus Christ, who presides and speaks through you. If I have merited death, I shall not refuse to die ;[1] the earth is the Lord's, and all that is therein. May he be praised through all eternity ! Amen. May he uphold you for ever ! Amen.

"Written the day of the Holy Trinity, in the year 1518.

"MARTIN LUTHER, Augustine Friar."

What humility and truth in Luther's fear, or rather in the avowal he makes that his warm young blood was perhaps too hastily inflamed ! In this we behold the sincerity of a man who, presuming not on himself, dreads the influence of his passions in the very acts most in conformity with the Word of God. This language is widely different from that of a proud fanatic. We behold in Luther an earnest desire to gain over Leo to the cause of truth, to prevent all schism, and to cause the Reformation, the necessity of which he proclaims, to proceed from the head of the church. Assuredly it is not he who should be accused of destroying that unity in the Western Church which so many persons of all parties have since regretted. He sacrificed everything to maintain it ;—everything except the truth. It was not he, it was his adversaries, who, by refusing to acknowledge the fulness and sufficiency of the salvation wrought by Jesus Christ, rent our Saviour's vesture, even at the foot of the cross.

After writing this letter, and on the very same day, Luther wrote to his friend Staupitz, vicar-general of his order. It was by his instrumentality that he desired the Solutions and letter should reach Leo.

"I beg of you," says he, " to accept with kindness these trifles[2] that I send you, and to forward them to the excellent Pope Leo X. Not that I desire by this to draw you into the peril in which I am involved ; I am determined to encounter the danger alone. Jesus Christ will see if what I have said proceeds from Him or from me—Jesus Christ, without whose will the pope's tongue cannot move, and the hearts of kings cannot decide.

"As to those who threaten me, I reply in the words of Reuchlin : ' He who is poor has

---

[1] Luther adds: but necessity compels me to cackle like a goose among swans. Sed cogit necessitas me anserem strepere inter olores. L. Epp. i. 121.
[2] Quam pure simpliciterque ecclesiasticam potestatem et reverentiam clavium quæsierim et coluerim. Ibid.

[1] Quare, beatissime Pater, prostratum me pedibus tuæ beatitudinis offero, cum omnibus quæ sum et habeo : vivifica, occide ; voca, revoca ; approba, reproba, ut placuerit. Vocem tuam, vocem Christi in te præsidentis et loquentis agnoscam. Si mortem merui, mori non recusabo. L. Epp. i. 121.
[2] His Solutions.

nothing to fear, since he has nothing to lose."[1] I have neither property nor money, and I do not desire any. If formerly I possessed any honour, any reputation, let Him who has begun to deprive me of them complete his task. All that is left to me is a wretched body, weakened by many trials. Should they kill me by stratagem or by force, to God be the glory! They will thus, perhaps, shorten my life by an hour or two. It is enough for me that I have a precious Redeemer, a powerful High Priest, Jesus Christ my Lord. As long as I live will I praise him. If another will not unite with me in these praises, what is that to me?"

In these words we read Luther's inmost heart.

While he was thus looking with confidence towards Rome, Rome already entertained thoughts of vengeance against him. As early as the 3d of April, Cardinal Raphael of Rovera had written to the Elector Frederick, in the pope's name, intimating that his orthodoxy was suspected, and cautioning him against protecting Luther. "Cardinal Raphael," said the latter, "would have had great pleasure in seeing me burnt by Frederick."[2] Thus was Rome beginning to sharpen her weapons against Luther. It was through his protector's mind that she resolved to aim the first blow. If she succeeded in destroying that shelter under which the monk of Wittemberg was reposing, he would become an easy prey to her.

The German princes were very tenacious of their reputation for orthodoxy. The slightest suspicion of heresy filled them with alarm. The court of Rome had skilfully taken advantage of this disposition. Frederick, moreover, had always been attached to the religion of his forefathers, and hence Raphael's letter made a deep impression on his mind. But it was a rule with the elector never to act precipitately. He knew that truth was not always on the side of the strongest. The disputes between the empire and Rome had taught him to mistrust the interested views of that court. He had found out that to be a christian prince, it was not necessary to be the pope's slave.

"He was not one of those profane persons," said Melancthon, "who order all changes to be arrested at their very commencement.[3] Frederick submitted himself to God. He carefully perused the writings that appeared, and did not allow that to be destroyed which he believed to be true."[4] It was not from want of power; for, besides being sovereign in his own states, he enjoyed in the empire a respect very little inferior to that which was paid to the emperor himself.

It is probable that Luther gained some information of this letter of Cardinal Raphael's, transmitted to the elector on the 7th July. Perhaps, it was the prospect of excommunication which this Roman missive seemed to forbode, that induced him to enter the pulpit of Wittemberg on the 15th of the same month, and to deliver a sermon on that subject, which made a deep impression. He drew a distinction between external and internal excommunication; the former excluding only from the services of the Church, the latter from communion with God. "No one," said he, "can reconcile the fallen sinner with God, except the Eternal One. No one can separate man from God, except man himself by his own sins. Blessed is he who dies under an unjust excommunication! While he suffers a grievous punishment at the hands of men for righteousness' sake, he receives from the hand of God the crown of everlasting happiness."

Some of the hearers loudly commended this bold language; others were still more exasperated by it.

But Luther no longer stood alone; and although his faith required no other support than that of God, a phalanx which defended him against his enemies had grown up around him. The German people had heard the voice of the reformer. From his sermons and writings issued those flashes of light which aroused and illumined his contemporaries. The energy of his faith poured forth in torrents of fire on their frozen hearts. The life that God had placed in this extraordinary mind communicated itself to the dead body of the Church. Christendom, motionless for so many centuries, became animated with religious enthusiasm. The people's attachment to the Romish superstitions diminished day by day; there were always fewer hands that offered money to purchase forgiveness;[1] and at the same time Luther's reputation continued to increase. The people turned towards him, and saluted him with love and respect, as the intrepid defender of truth and liberty.[2] Undoubtedly, all men did not see the depth of the doctrines he proclaimed. For the greater number it was sufficient to know that he stood up against the pope, and that the dominion of the priests and monks was shaken by the might of his word. In their eyes, Luther's attack was like those beacon fires kindled on the mountains, which announce to a whole nation that the time to burst their chains has arrived. The reformer was not aware of what he had done, until the noble-minded portion of the nation had already hailed him as their leader. But for a great number also, Luther's coming was something more than this. The Word of God, which he so skilfully wielded, pierced

1 Qui pauper est nihil timet, nihil potest perdere. L. Epp. l. 118. 2 L. Opp. (W.) xv. 339.
3 Noc profana judicia sequens quæ tenera initia omnium mutationum celerrime opprimi jubent. Mel. Vit. Luth.
4 Deo cessit, et ea quæ vera esse judicavit, deleri non voluit. Ibid.

1 Rarescebant manus largentium. Cochlœus, 7.
2 Luthero autem contra augebatur auctoritas, favor, fides, existimatio, fama: quod tam liber acerque videretur veritatis assertor. Ibid.

their hearts like a two-edged sword. In many bosoms was kindled an earnest desire of obtaining the assurance of pardon and eternal life. Since the primitive ages, the Church had never witnessed such hungering and thirsting after righteousness. If the eloquence of Peter the Hermit and of St. Bernard had inspired the people of the Middle Ages to assume a perishable cross, the eloquence of Luther prevailed on those of his day to take up the real cross,—the truth which saves. The scaffolding which then encumbered the Church had stifled everything; the form had destroyed the life. The powerful language given to this man diffused a quickening breath over the soil of Christendom. At the first outburst, Luther's writings had carried away believers and unbelievers alike: the unbelievers, because the positive doctrines that were afterwards to be settled had not been as yet fully developed; the believers, because their germs were found in that living faith which his writings proclaimed with so much power. Accordingly, the influence of these writings was immense; they filled in an instant Germany and the world. Every where prevailed a secret conviction that men were about to witness, not the establishment of a sect, but a new birth of the Church and of society. Those who were born of the breath of the Holy Ghost rallied around him who was its organ. Christendom was divided into two parties: the one contended with the spirit against the form, and the other with the form against the spirit. On the side of the form were, it is true, all the appearances of strength and grandeur; on the side of the spirit were helplessness and insignificance. But form, void of spirit, is but a feeble body, which the first breath of wind may throw down. Its apparent power serves but to excite hostility and to precipitate its destruction. Thus, the simple Word of truth had raised a powerful army for Luther.

CHAPTER II.

Diet at Augsburg—The Emperor to the Pope—The Elector to Rovera—Luther summoned to Rome—Luther's Peace—Intercession of the University—Papal Brief—Luther's Indignation—The Pope to the Elector.

THIS army was very necessary, for the nobles began to be alarmed, and the empire and the Church were already uniting their power to get rid of this troublesome monk. If a strong and courageous prince had then filled the imperial throne, he might have taken advantage of this religious agitation, and in reliance upon the Word of God and upon the nation, have given a fresh impulse to the ancient opposition against the papacy. But Maximilian was too old, and he had determined besides on making every sacrifice in order to attain the great object of his life, the aggrandizement of his house, and consequently the elevation of his grandson. The emperor was at that time holding an imperial diet at Augsburg. Six electors had gone thither in person at his summons. All the Germanic states were there represented. The kings of France, Hungary, and Poland had sent their ambassadors. These princes and envoys displayed great magnificence. The Turkish war was one of the causes for which the diet had been assembled. The legate of Leo X. earnestly urged the meeting on this point. The states, learning wisdom from the bad use that had formerly been made of their contributions, and wisely counselled by the Elector Frederick, were satisfied with declaring they would reflect on the matter, and at the same time produced fresh complaints against Rome. A Latin discourse, published during the diet, boldly pointed out the real danger to the German princes. "You desire to put the Turk to flight," said the author. "This is well; but I am very much afraid that you are mistaken in the person. You should look for him in Italy, and not in Asia."[1]

Another affair of no less importance was to occupy the diet. Maximilian desired to have his grandson Charles, already king of Spain and Naples, proclaimed king of the Romans, and his successor in the imperial dignity. The pope knew his own interests too well to desire to see the imperial throne filled by a prince whose power in Italy might be dangerous to himself. The emperor imagined he had already won over most of the electors and of the states; but he met with a vigorous resistance from Frederick. All solicitations proved unavailing; in vain did the ministers and the best friends of the elector unite their entreaties to those of the emperor; he was immovable, and showed on this occasion (as it has been remarked) that he had firmness of mind not to swerve from a resolution which he had once acknowledged to be just. The emperor's design failed.

Henceforward this prince sought to gain the good-will of the pope, in order to render him favourable to his plans; and, to give a more striking proof of his attachment, he wrote to him as follows, on the 5th August: "Most holy Father, we have learnt these few days since that a friar of the Augustine order, named Martin Luther, has presumed to maintain certain propositions on the traffic of indulgences; a matter that displeases us the more because this friar has found many protectors, among whom are persons of exalted station.[2] If your holiness and the very reverend fathers of the Church (i. e. the cardinals) do not soon exert your authority to put an end to these scandals, these pernicious

[1] Schröck, K. Gesch. n. d. R. l. 156.
[2] Defensores et patronos etiam potentes quos dictus frater consecutus est. Raynald ad an. 1518.

teachers will not only seduce the simple people, but they will involve great princes in their destruction. We will take care that whatever your holiness may decree in this matter for the glory of God Almighty shall be enforced throughout the whole empire."

This letter must have been written immediately after some warm discussion between Maximilian and Frederick. On the same day, the elector wrote to Raphael of Rovera. He had learnt, no doubt, that the emperor was writing to the Roman pontiff, and to parry the blow, he put himself in communication with Rome.

"I shall never have any other desire," says he, "than to show my submission to the universal Church.

"Accordingly, I have never defended either the writings or the sermons of Doctor Martin Luther. I learn, besides, that he has always offered to appear, under a safe-conduct, before impartial, learned, and christian judges, in order to defend his doctrine, and to submit, in case he should be convicted of error by the Scriptures themselves."[1]

Leo X., who up to this time had let the business follow its natural course, aroused by the clamours of the theologians and monks, nominated an ecclesiastical commission at Rome empowered to try Luther, and in which Sylvester Prierio, the reformer's great enemy, was at once accuser and judge. The case was soon prepared, and the court summoned Luther to appear before it in person within sixty days.

Luther was tranquilly awaiting at Wittemberg the good effects that he imagined his submissive letter to the pope would produce, when on the 7th August, two days only after the letters of Maximilian and of Frederick were sent off, he received the summons of the Roman tribunal. "At the very moment I was expecting a blessing," said he, "I saw the thunderbolt fall upon me. I was the lamb that troubled the water the wolf was drinking. Tetzel escaped, and I was to permit myself to be devoured."

This summons caused general alarm in Wittemberg ; for whatever course Luther might take he could not escape danger. If he went to Rome, he would there become the victim of his enemies. If he refused to appear, he would be condemned for contumacy, as was usual, without the power of escaping; for it was known that the legate had received orders to do every thing he could to exasperate the emperor and the German princes against the doctor. His friends were filled with consternation. Shall the preacher of truth risk his life in that great city *drunk with the blood of the saints and of the martyrs of Jesus?* Shall a head be raised in the midst of enslaved Christendom, only to fall? Shall this man also be struck down—this man whom God appears to have

formed to withstand a power that hitherto nothing had been able to resist? Luther himself saw that no one could save him but the elector; yet he would rather die than compromise his prince. At last his friends agreed on an expedient that would not endanger Frederick. Let him refuse Luther a safe-conduct, and then the reformer would have a legitimate excuse for not appearing at Rome.

On the 8th August, Luther wrote to Spalatin begging him to employ his influence with the elector to have his cause heard in Germany. "See what snares they are laying for me," wrote he also to Staupitz, "and how I am surrounded with thorns. But Christ lives and reigns, the same yesterday, to-day, and for ever. My conscience assures me that I have been teaching the truth, although it appears still more odious because I teach it. The Church is the womb of Rebecca. The children must struggle together, even to the risk of the mother's life.[1] As for the rest, pray the Lord that I feel not too much joy in this trial. May God not lay this sin to their charge."

Luther's friends did not confine themselves to consultations and complaints. Spalatin wrote, on the part of the elector, to Renner the emperor's secretary : "Doctor Martin Luther willingly consents to be judged by all the universities of Germany, except Leipsic, Erfurth, and Frankfort-on-the-Oder, which have shown themselves partial. It is impossible for him to appear at Rome in person."[2]

The university of Wittemberg wrote a letter of intercession to the pope : "The weakness of his frame," they said, speaking of Luther, "and the dangers of the journey, render it difficult and even impossible for him to obey the order of your holiness. His distress and his prayers incline us to sympathize with him. We therefore entreat you, most holy Father, as obedient children, to look upon him as a man who has never been tainted with doctrines opposed to the tenets of the Roman Church."

The university, in its solicitude, wrote the same day to Charles of Miltitz, a Saxon gentleman and the pope's chamberlain, in high estimation with Leo X. In this letter they gave Luther a more decided testimony than they had ventured to insert in the first. "The reverend father Martin Luther, an Augustine," it ran, "is the noblest and most distinguished member of our university. For many years we have seen and known his talents, his learning, his profound acquaintance with the arts and literature, his irreproachable morals, and his truly christian behaviour."[3]

This active charity shown by all who surrounded Luther is his noblest panegyric.

---

[1] Uterus Rebeccæ est : parvulos in eo collidi necesse est etiam usque ad periculum matris. L. Epp. i. 138.
[2] L. Opp. (L.) xvii. 173.
[3] L. Opp. Lat. i. 183, 184. L. Opp. (L.) xvii. 171, 172.

While men were anxiously looking for the result of this affair, it was terminated more easily than might have been expected. The legate De Vio, mortified at his ill success in the commission he had received to excite a general war against the Turks, wished to exalt and give lustre to his embassy in Germany by some other brilliant act. He thought that if he could extinguish heresy he should return to Rome with honour. He therefore entreated the pope to intrust this business to him. Leo for his part was highly pleased with Frederick for his strong opposition to the election of the youthful Charles. He felt that he might yet stand in need of his support. Without farther reference to the summons, he commissioned the legate, by a brief dated 23d August, to investigate the affair in Germany. The pope lost nothing by this course of proceeding; and even if Luther could not be prevailed on to retract, the noise and scandal that his presence at Rome must have occasioned would be avoided.

"We charge you," said Leo, "to summon personally before you, to prosecute and constrain without any delay, and as soon as you shall have received this paper from us, the said Luther, who has already been declared a heretic by our dear brother Jerome, bishop of Ascoli."[1]

The pope then proceeded to utter the severest threats against Luther:

"Invoke for this purpose the arm and the aid of our very dear son in Christ, Maximilian, and of the other princes of Germany, and of all the communities, universities, and potentates, ecclesiastic or secular. And, if you get possession of his person, keep him in safe custody, that he may be brought before us."[2]

We see that this indulgent concession from the pope was only a surer way of inveigling Luther to Rome. Next followed milder measures:

"If he return to his duty, and beg forgiveness for so great a misdeed, of his own accord and without solicitation, we give you power to receive him into the unity of our holy mother the Church."

The pope soon returned to his maledictions:

"If he persist in his obstinacy, and you cannot secure his person, we authorize you to proscribe him in every part of Germany; to banish, curse, and excommunicate all those who are attached to him; and to order all Christians to flee from their presence."

Still this was not enough:

"And in order that this contagious disease may be the more effectually eradicated," continued the pope, "you will excommunicate all prelates, religious orders, universi-

ties, communities, counts, dukes, and potentates (the Emperor Maximilian always excepted), who shall not aid in seizing the aforesaid Martin Luther and his adherents, and send them to you under good and safe guard.—And if, which God forbid, the said princes, communities, universities, and potentates, or any belonging to them, shall in any manner offer an asylum to the said Martin and his adherents, give him privately or publicly, by themselves or by others, succour and counsel, we lay under interdict all these princes, communities, universities, and potentates, with their cities, towns, countries and villages, as well as the cities, towns, countries, and villages in which the said Martin may take refuge, so long as he shall remain there, and three days after he shall have quitted them."

This audacious see, which claims to be the earthly representative of him who said: *God sent not his Son into the world to condemn the world, but that the world through him might be saved,* continues its anathemas; and after pronouncing the penalties against ecclesiastics, goes on to say:

"As for the laymen, if they do not immediately obey your orders without delay or opposition, we declare them infamous (the most worthy emperor always excepted), incapable of performing any lawful act, deprived of christian burial, and stripped of all the fiefs they may hold either from the apostolic see, or from any lord whatsoever."[1]

Such was the fate destined for Luther. The monarch of Rome has invoked every thing for his destruction. Nothing was spared, not even the quiet of the grave. His ruin appears certain. How can he escape from this vast conspiracy? But Rome was deceived; the movement, begun by the Spirit of God, cannot be checked by the decrees of her chancery.

The pope had not even preserved the appearances of a just and impartial examination. Luther had been declared a heretic, not only before he had been heard, but even before the expiration of the time allowed for his appearance. The passions, and never do they show themselves more violently than in religious discussions, overleap all forms of justice. It is not only in the Roman church, but in the Protestant churches that have turned aside from the Gospel, and wherever the truth is not found, that we meet with such strange proceedings in this respect. Every thing is lawful against the Gospel. We frequently see men who in every other case would scruple to commit the least injustice, not fearing to trample under foot all rule and law, whenever Christianity, or the testimony that is paid to it, is concerned.

When Luther became acquainted with this brief, he thus expressed his indignation:

[1] Dictum Lutherum hæreticum per prædictum auditorem iam declaratum. Breve Leonis X. ad Thomam.
[2] Brachio cogas atque compellas, et eo in potestate tua redacto eum sub fideli custodia retineas, ut coram nobis sistatur. Ibid.

[1] Infamiæ et inhabilitatis ad omnes actus legitimos, ecclesiasticæ sepulturæ, privationis quoque feudorum. Breve Leonis X. ad Thomam.

" This is the most remarkable part of the affair : the brief was issued on the 23d August—I was summoned on the 7th—so that between the brief and the summons sixteen days elapsed. Now, make the calculation, and you will find that my Lord Jerome, bishop of Ascoli, proceeded against me, pronounced judgment, condemned me, and declared me a heretic, before the summons reached me, or at the most within sixteen days after it had been forwarded to me. Now, where are the sixty days accorded me in the summons ? They began on the 7th August, they should end on the 7th October.........Is this the style and fashion of the Roman court, which on the same day summons, exhorts, accuses, judges, condemns, and declares a man guilty who is so far from Rome, and who knows nothing of all these things ? What reply can they make to this ? No doubt they forgot to clear their brains with hellebore before having recourse to such trickery."[1]

But while Rome secretly deposited her thunders in the hands of her legate, she sought by sweet and flattering words to detach from Luther's cause the prince whose power she dreaded most. On the same day (23d August 1518), the pope wrote to the Elector of Saxony. He had recourse to the wiles of that ancient policy which we have already noticed, and endeavoured to flatter the prince's vanity.

" Dear son," wrote the pontiff, " when we think of your noble and worthy family ; of you who are its ornament and head ; when we call to mind how you and your ancestors have always desired to uphold the christian faith, and the honour and dignity of the holy see, we cannot believe that a man who abandons the faith can rely upon your highness's favour, and daringly give the rein to his wickedness. Yet it is reported to us from every quarter that a certain friar, Martin Luther, hermit of the order of St. Augustine, has forgotten, like a child of the evil one and despiser of God, his habit and his order, which consist in humility and obedience, and that he boasts of fearing neither the authority nor the punishment of any man, being assured of your favour and protection.

" But as we know that he is deceived, we have thought fit to write to your highness, and to exhort you in the Lord to watch over the honour of your name, as a christian prince ; the ornament, glory, and sweet savour of your noble family ; to defend yourself from these calumnies ; and to guard yourself not only from so serious a crime as that imputed to you, but still further even from the suspicion that the rash presumption of this friar tends to bring upon you."

Leo X. at the same time informed the elector that he had commissioned the cardinal of St. Sixtus to investigate the matter, and requested him to deliver Luther into the legate's hands, " for fear," added he, still returning to his first argument, " the pious people of our own or of future times should one day lament and say : The most pernicious heresy with which the Church of God has been afflicted sprung up under the favour and support of that high and worthy family."[1]

Thus had Rome taken her measures. With one hand she scattered the intoxicating incense of flattery ; in the other she held concealed her terrors and revenge.

All the powers of the earth, emperor, pope, princes, and legates, began to rise up against this humble friar of Erfurth, whose internal struggles we have already witnessed. *The kings of the earth set themselves, and the rulers take counsel against the Lord, and against his anointed.*

CHAPTER III.

The Armourer Schwartzerd—His Wife—Philip—His Genius and Studies—The Bible—Call to Wittemberg—Melancthon's Departure and Journey—Leipsic—Mistake—Luther's Joy—Parallel—Revolution in Education—Study of Greek.

BEFORE this letter and the brief had reached Germany, and while Luther was still afraid of being compelled to appear at Rome, a fortunate event brought consolation to his heart. He needed a friend into whose bosom he could pour out his sorrows, and whose faithful affection would comfort him in his hours of dejection. God gave him such a friend in Melancthon.

George Schwartzerd was a skilful master-armourer of Bretten, a small town in the palatinate. On the 14th of February 1497, his wife bore him a son, who was named Philip, and who became famous in after-years under the name of Melancthon. George, who was highly esteemed by the palatine princes, and by those of Bavaria and Saxony, was a man of perfect integrity. Frequently he would refuse from purchasers the price they offered him ; and if he found they were poor, would compel them to take back their money. It was his habit to leave his bed at midnight, and offer a fervent prayer upon his knees. If the morning came without his having performed this pious duty, he was dissatisfied with himself all the rest of the day. His wife Barbara was the daughter of a respectable magistrate named John Reutér. She possessed a tender disposition, rather inclined to superstition, but in other respects discreet and prudent. To her we are indebted for these well-known German rhymes :—

[1] Luth. Opp. (L.) xvii. 176.   [1] Luth. Opp. (L.) xvii. 173.

129

Alms-giving impoverisheth not.
Church-going hindereth not.
To grease the car delayeth not.
Ill-gotten wealth profiteth not.
God's book deceiveth not.

And the following rhymes also :—

Those who love to squander
More than their fields render,
Will surely come to ruin,
Or a rope be their undoing.[1]

Philip was not eleven years old when his father died. Two days before he expired, George called his son to his bedside, and exhorted him to have the fear of God constantly before his eyes. " I foresee," said the dying armourer, " that terrible tempests are about to shake the world. I have witnessed great things, but greater still are preparing. May God direct and guide thee !" After Philip had received his father's blessing, he was sent to Spire that he might not be present at his parent's death. He departed weeping bitterly.

The lad's grandfather, the worthy bailiff Reuter, who himself had a son, performed a father's duty to Philip, and took him and his brother George into his own house. Shortly after this he engaged John Hungarus to teach the three boys. The tutor was an excellent man, and in after-years proclaimed the Gospel with great energy, even to an advanced age. He overlooked nothing in the young man. He punished him for every fault, but with discretion : " It is thus," said Melancthon in 1554, " that he made a scholar of me. He loved me as a son, I loved him as a father ; and we shall meet, I hope, in heaven."[2]

Philip was remarkable for the excellence of his understanding, and his facility in learning and explaining what he had learnt. He could not remain idle, and was always looking for some one to discuss with him the things he had heard.[3] It frequently happened that well-educated foreigners passed through Bretten and visited Reuter. Immediately the bailiff's grandson would go up to them, enter into conversation, and press them so hard in the discussion that the hearers were filled with admiration. With strength of genius he united great gentleness, and thus won the favour of all. He stammered ; but like the illustrious Grecian orator, he so diligently set about correcting this defect, that in after-life no traces of it could be perceived.

On the death of his grandfather, the youthful Philip with his brother and his young uncle John, was sent to the school at Pforzheim. These lads resided with one of their relations, sister to the famous Reuchlin. Eager in the pursuit of knowledge, Philip, under the tuition of George Simmler, made

rapid progress in learning, and particularly in Greek, of which he was passionately fond. Reuchlin frequently came to Pforzheim. At his sister's house he became acquainted with her young boarders, and was soon struck with Philip's replies. He presented him with a Greek Grammar and a Bible. These two books were to be the study of his whole life.

When Reuchlin returned from his second journey to Italy, his young relative, then twelve years old, celebrated the day of his arrival by representing before him, with the aid of some friends, a Latin comedy which he had himself composed. Reuchlin, charmed with the young man's talents, tenderly embraced him, called him his dear son, and placed sportively upon his head the red hat he had received when he had been made doctor. It was at this time that Reuchlin changed the name of Schwartzerd into that of Melancthon ; both words, the one in German and the other in Greek, signifying *black earth*. Most of the learned men of that age thus translated their names into Greek or Latin.

Melancthon, at twelve years of age, went to the University of Heidelberg, and here he began to slake his ardent thirst for knowledge. He took his bachelor's degree at fourteen. In 1512, Reuchlin invited him to Tubingen, where many learned men were assembled. He attended by turns the lectures of the theologians, doctors, and lawyers. There was no branch of knowledge that he deemed unworthy his study. Praise was not his object, but the possession and the fruits of learning.

The Holy Scriptures especially engaged his attention. Those who frequented the church of Tubingen had remarked that he frequently held a book in his hands, which he was occupied in reading between the services. This unknown volume appeared larger than the prayer books, and a report was circulated that Philip used to read profane authors during those intervals. But the suspected book proved to be a copy of the Holy Scriptures, printed shortly before at Basle by John Frobenius. All his life he continued this study with the most unceasing application. He always carried this precious volume with him, even to the public assemblies to which he was invited.[1] Rejecting the empty systems of the schoolmen, he adhered to the plain word of the Gospel. " I entertain the most distinguished and splendid expectations of Melancthon," wrote Erasmus to OEcolampadius about this time ; " God grant that this young man may long survive us. He will entirely eclipse Erasmus."[2] Nevertheless, Melancthon shared in the errors of his age. " I shudder," he observed at an advanced period of his life,

---

[1] Almosen geben armt nicht, etc. Wer mehr will verzhren, etc. Müller's Reliquien.
[2] Dilexit me ut filium, et ego eum ut patrem ; et conveniemus, spero, in vita æterna. Melancth. Explicat. Evang.
[3] Quiescere non poterat, sed quærebat ubique aliquem cum quo de auditis disputaret. Camer. Vit. Mel. p. 7.

[1] Camer. Vita Phil. Mel. p. 16.
[2] Is prorsus obscurabit Erasmum. Err. Epp. i. 405.

" when I think of the honour I paid to images, while I was yet a papist." [1]

In 1514, he was made doctor of philosophy, and then began to teach. He was seventeen years old. The grace and charm that he imparted to his lessons, formed the most striking contrast to the tasteless method which the doctors, and above all the monks, had pursued till then. He took an active part in the struggle in which Reuchlin was engaged with the learning-haters of the day. Agreeable in conversation, mild and elegant in his manners, beloved by all who knew him, he soon acquired great authority and solid reputation in the learned world.

It was at this time that the elector formed the design of inviting some distinguished scholar to the university of Wittemberg, as professor of the ancient languages. He applied to Reuchlin, who recommended Melancthon. Frederick foresaw the celebrity that this young man would confer on an institution so dear to him, and Reuchlin, charmed at beholding so noble a career opening before his young friend, wrote to him these words of the Almighty to Abraham : " *Get thee out of thy country, and from thy kindred, and from thy father's house, and I will make thy name great, and thou shalt be a blessing.* Yea," continued the old man, " I hope that it will be so with thee, my dear Philip, my handiwork and my consolation." [2] In this invitation Melancthon acknowledged a call from God. At his departure the university was filled with sorrow ; yet it contained individuals who were jealous and envious of him. He left his native place, exclaiming : " The Lord's will be done !" He was then twenty-one years of age.

Melancthon travelled on horseback, in company with several Saxon merchants, as a traveller joins a caravan in the deserts ; for, says Reuchlin, he was unacquainted both with the roads and the country. [3] He presented his respects to the elector, whom he found at Augsburg. At Nuremberg he saw the excellent Pirckheimer, whom he had known before ; at Leipsic he formed an acquaintance with the learned hellenist Mosellanus. The university of this last city gave a banquet in his honour. The repast was academical. The dishes succeeded one another in great variety, and at each new dish one of the professors rose and addressed Melancthon in a Latin speech he had prepared before hand. The latter immediately replied extemporaneously. At last, wearied with so much eloquence, he said : " Most illustrious men, permit me to reply to your harangues once for all ; for, being unprepared, I cannot put such varieties into my answers as you have done in your addresses."

After this, the dishes were brought in without the accompaniment of a speech. [1]

Reuchlin's youthful relative arrived in Wittemberg on the 25th August 1518, two days after Leo X. had signed the brief addressed to Cajetan, and the letter to the elector.

The Wittemberg professors did not receive Melancthon so favourably as those of Leipsic had done. The first impression he made on them did not correspond with their expectations. They saw a young man, who appeared younger than he really was, of small stature, and with a feeble and timid air. Was this the illustrious doctor whom Erasmus and Reuchlin, the greatest men of the day, extolled so highly ? Neither Luther, with whom he first became acquainted, nor his colleagues, entertained any great hopes of him when they saw his youth, his shyness, and his diffident manners.

On the 29th August, four days after his arrival, he delivered his inaugural discourse. All the university was assembled. This lad, as Luther calls him, [2] spoke in such elegant latinity, and showed so much learning, an understanding so cultivated, and a judgment so sound, that all his hearers were struck with admiration.

When the speech was finished, all crowded round him with congratulations ; but no one felt more joy than Luther. He hastened to impart to his friends the sentiments that filled his heart. " Melancthon," wrote he to Spalatin on the 31st August, " delivered four days after his arrival so learned and so beautiful a discourse, that every one listened with astonishment and admiration. We soon recovered from the prejudices excited by his stature and appearance ; we now praise and admire his eloquence ; we return our thanks to you and to the prince for the service you have done us. I ask for no other Greek master. But I fear that his delicate frame will be unable to support our mode of living, and that we shall be unable to keep him long on account of the smallness of his salary. I hear that the Leipsic people are already boasting of their power to take him from us. O my dear Spalatin, beware of despising his age and his personal appearance. He is a man worthy of every honour." [3]

Melancthon began immediately to lecture on Homer and the Epistle of St. Paul to Titus. He was full of ardour. " I will make every effort," wrote he to Spalatin, " to conciliate the favour of all those in Wittemberg who love learning and virtue." [4] Four days after his inauguration, Luther wrote again to Spalatin: " I most particularly recommend to you the very learned and very amiable Grecian, Philip. His lecture-room is always full. All

---

[1] Cohorresco quando cogito quomodo ipse accesserim ad statuas in papatu. Explic. Evangel.
[2] Meum opus et meum solatium. Corp. Ref. i. 33.
[3] Des Wegs und der Orte unbekannt. Ibid. 30.

[1] Camer. Vita Mel. 26.
[2] Puer et adolescentulus, si ætatem consideres. L. Epp. i. 141.
[3] Ibid. 135.
[4] Ut Wittembergam literatis ac bonis omnibus concilliem. Corp. Ref. i. 51.

the theologians in particular go to hear him. He is making every class, upper, lower, and middle, begin to read Greek."[1]

Melancthon was able to respond to Luther's affection. He soon found in him a kindness of disposition, a strength of mind, a courage, a discretion, that he had never found till then in any man. He venerated, he loved him. "If there is any one," said he, "whom I dearly love, and whom I embrace with my whole heart, it is Martin Luther."[2]

Thus did Luther and Melancthon meet; they were friends until death. We cannot too much admire the goodness and wisdom of God, in bringing together two men so different, and yet so necessary to one another. Luther possessed warmth, vigour, and strength; Melancthon clearness, discretion, and mildness. Luther gave energy to Melancthon, Melancthon moderated Luther. They were like substances in a state of positive and negative electricity, which mutually act upon each other. If Luther had been without Melancthon, perhaps the torrent would have overflowed its banks; Melancthon, when Luther was taken from him by death, hesitated and gave way, even where he should not have yielded.[3] Luther did much by power; Melancthon perhaps did no less by following a gentler and more tranquil method. Both were upright, open-hearted, generous; both ardently loved the Word of eternal life, and obeyed it with a fidelity and devotion that governed their whole lives.

Melancthon's arrival at Wittemberg effected a revolution not only in that university, but in the whole of Germany and in all the learned world. The attention he had bestowed on the Greek and Latin classics and on philosophy had given a regularity, clearness, and precision to his ideas, which shed a new light and an indescribable beauty on every subject that he took in hand. The mild spirit of the Gospel fertilized and animated his meditations, and in his lectures the driest pursuits were clothed with a surpassing grace that captivated all hearers. The barrenness that scholasticism had cast over education was at an end. A new manner of teaching and of studying began with Melancthon. "Thanks to him," says an illustrious German historian,[4] "Wittemberg became the school of the nation."

It was indeed highly important that a man who knew Greek thoroughly should teach in that university, where the new developments of theology called upon masters and pupils to study in their original language the earliest documents of the christian faith. From

this time Luther zealously applied to the task. The meaning of a Greek word, of which he had been ignorant until then, suddenly cleared up his theological ideas. What consolation and what joy did he not feel, when he saw, for instance, that the Greek word μείάνοια, which, according to the Latin Church, signifies a *penance*, a satisfaction required by the Church, a human expiation, really meant in Greek a transformation or conversion of the heart! A thick mist was suddenly rolled away from before his eyes. The two significations given to this word suffice of themselves to characterize the two Churches.

The impulse Melancthon gave to Luther in the translation of the Bible is one of the most remarkable circumstances of the friendship between these two great men. As early as 1517, Luther had made some attempts at translation. He had procured as many Greek and Latin books as were within his reach. And now, with the aid of his dear Philip, he applied to his task with fresh energy. Luther compelled Melancthon to share in his researches; consulted him on the difficult passages: and the work, which was destined to be one of the great labours of the reformer, advanced more safely and more speedily.

Melancthon, on his side, became acquainted with the new theology. The beautiful and profound doctrine of justification by faith filled him with astonishment and joy; but he received with independence the system taught by Luther, and moulded it to the peculiar form of his mind; for, although he was only twenty-one years old, he was one of those precocious geniuses who attain early to a full possession of all their powers, and who think for themselves from the very first.

The zeal of the teachers was soon communicated to the disciples. It was decided to reform the method of instruction. With the elector's consent, certain courses that possessed a merely scholastic importance were suppressed; at the same time the study of the classics received a fresh impulse. The school of Wittemberg was transformed, and the contrast with other universities became daily more striking. All this, however, took place within the limits of the Church, and none suspected they were on the eve of a great contest with the pope.

---

[1] Summos cum mediis et infimis, studiosos facit Græcitatis. L. Epp. i. 140.
[2] Martinum, si omnino in rebus humanis quidquam, vehementissime diligo, et animo integerrimo complector. Mel. Epp. i. 411.
[3] Calvin writes to Sleidan: Dominus eum fortiore spiritu instruat, ne gravem ex ejus timiditate jacturam sentiat posteritas. May the Lord give him a more determined spirit, lest through his timidity our posterity suffer a serious injury.
[4] Plank.

CHAPTER IV.

Sentiments of Luther and Staupitz—Summons to appear—Alarm and Courage—The Elector with the Legate—Departure for Augsburg—Sojourn at Weimar—Nuremberg—Arrival at Augsburg.

No doubt Melancthon's arrival at a moment so critical brought a pleasing change to the current of Luther's thoughts; no doubt, in the sweet outpourings of a dawning friendship, and in the midst of the biblical labours to which he devoted himself with fresh zeal, he sometimes forgot Rome, Prierio, Leo, and the ecclesiastical court before which he was to appear. Yet these were but fugitive moments, and his thoughts always returned to that formidable tribunal before which his implacable enemies had summoned him. With what terror would not such thoughts have filled a soul whose object had been any thing else than the truth! But Luther did not tremble; confident in the faithfulness and power of God, he remained firm, and was ready to expose himself alone to the anger of enemies more terrible than those who had kindled John Huss's pile.

A few days after Melancthon's arrival, and before the resolution of the pope transferring Luther's citation from Rome to Augsburg could be known, the latter wrote thus to Spalatin: " I do not require that our sovereign should do the least thing in defence of my theses; I am willing to be given up and thrown into the hands of my adversaries. Let him permit all the storm to burst upon me. What I have undertaken to defend, I hope to be able to maintain, with the help of Christ. As for violence, we must needs yield to that, but without abandoning the truth."[1]

Luther's courage was infectious: the mildest and most timid men, as they beheld the danger that threatened this witness to the truth, found language full of energy and indignation. The prudent, the pacific Staupitz wrote to Spalatin on the 7th September: " Do not cease to exhort the prince, your master and mine, not to allow himself to be frightened by the roaring of the lions. Let him defend the truth, without anxiety either about Luther, Staupitz, or the order. Let there be one place at least where men may speak freely and without fear. I know that the plague of Babylon, I was nearly saying of Rome, is let loose against whoever attacks the abuses of those who sell Jesus Christ. I have myself seen a preacher thrown from the pulpit for teaching the truth; I saw him, although it was a festival, bound and dragged to prison. Others have witnessed still more cruel sights. For this reason, dearest Spalatin, prevail upon his highness to continue in his present sentiments."[2]

At last the order to appear before the cardinal-legate at Augsburg arrived. It was now with one of the princes of the Roman Church that Luther had to deal. All his friends entreated him not to set out.[3] They feared that even during the journey snares might be laid for his life. Some busied themselves in finding an asylum for him. Staupitz himself, the timid Staupitz, was moved at the thought of the dangers to which brother Martin would be exposed— that brother whom he had dragged from the seclusion of the cloister, and whom he had launched on that agitated sea in which his life was now endangered. Alas! would it not have been better for the poor brother to have remained for ever unknown! It was too late. At least he would do everything in his power to save him. Accordingly he wrote from his convent at Salzburg, on the 15th September, soliciting Luther to flee and seek an asylum with him. " It appears to me," said he, " that the whole world is enraged and combined against the truth. The crucified Jesus was hated in like manner. I do not see that you have anything else to expect but persecution. Erelong no one will be able without the pope's permission to search the Scriptures, and therein look for Jesus Christ, which Jesus Christ however commands. You have but few friends: I would to God that fear of your adversaries did not prevent those few from declaring themselves in your favour! The wisest course is for you to abandon Wittemberg for a season and come to me. Then we shall live and die together. This is also the prince's opinion," adds Staupitz.[1]

From different quarters Luther received the most alarming intelligence. Count Albert of Mansfeldt bid him beware of undertaking the journey, for several powerful lords had sworn to seize his person, and strangle or drown him.[2] But nothing could frighten him. He had no intention of profiting by the vicar-general's offer. He will not go and conceal himself in the obscurity of a convent at Salzburg; he will remain faithfully on that stormy scene where the hand of God has placed him. It is by persevering in despite of his adversaries, by proclaiming the truth aloud in the midst of the world, that the reign of this truth advances. Why then should he flee? He is not one of those who draw back to perish, but of those who keep the faith to the saving of their souls. This expression of the Master whom he desires to serve, and whom he loves more than life, re-echoes incessantly in his heart: *Whosoever shall confess me before men, him will I also confess before my Father who is in heaven.* At all times do we find in Luther and in the Reformation this intrepid courage, this exalted morality, this infinite charity, which the first advent of Christianity had already made known to the world. " I am like Jeremiah," says Luther at the time of which we are speaking, " a man of strife and contention; but the more their threats increase, the more my joy is multiplied. My wife and my children are well provided for; my fields, my

[1] L. Epp. 1. 139.   [2] Jen. Aug. 1. 384.
[3] Contra omnium amicorum consilium comparui.

[1] Epp. 1. 61.
[2] Ut vel stranguler, vel baptizer ad mortem. L. Epp. 1 129.

houses, and my goods are in order.[1] They have already destroyed my honour and my reputation. One single thing remains; it is my wretched body: let them take it; they will thus shorten my life by a few hours. But as for my soul, they cannot take that. He who desires to proclaim the Word of Christ to the world, must expect death at every moment; for our husband is a bloody husband to us.[2]

The elector was then at Augsburg. Shortly before quitting the diet in that city, he had paid the legate a visit. The cardinal, highly flattered with this condescension from so illustrious a prince, promised Frederick, that if the monk appeared before him, he would listen to him in a paternal manner, and dismiss him kindly. Spalatin, by the prince's order, wrote to his friend, that the pope had appointed a commission to hear him in Germany; that the elector would not permit him to be dragged to Rome; and that he must prepare for his journey to Augsburg. Luther resolved to obey. The notice he had received from the count of Mansfeldt induced him to ask a safe-conduct from Frederick. The latter replied that it was unnecessary, and sent him only letters of recommendation to some of the most distinguished councillors of Augsburg. He also provided him with money for the journey; and the poor defenceless reformer set out on foot to place himself in the hands of his enemies.[3]

What must have been his feelings as he quitted Wittemberg and took the road to Augsburg, where the pope's legate awaited him! The object of this journey was not like that to Heidelberg, a friendly meeting; he was about to appear before the Roman delegate without a safe-conduct; perhaps he was going to death. But his faith was not one of mere outward show; with him it was a reality. Hence it gave him peace, and he could advance without fear, in the name of the Lord of hosts, to bear his testimony to the Gospel.

He arrived at Weimar on the 28th September, and lodged in the Cordeliers' monastery. One of the monks could not take his eyes off him; it was Myconius. He then saw Luther for the first time; he wished to approach him, to say that he was indebted to him for peace of mind, and that his whole desire was to labour with him. But Myconius was too strictly watched by his superiors: he was not allowed to speak to Luther.[4]

The Elector of Saxony was then holding his court at Weimar, and it is on this account probably that the Cordeliers gave the doctor a welcome. The day following his arrival

was the festival of St. Michael. Luther said mass, and was invited to preach in the palace-chapel. This was a mark of favour his prince loved to confer on him. He preached extempore, in presence of the court, selecting his text (Matthew, chap. xviii. verses 1 to 11) from the gospel of the day. He spoke forcibly against hypocrites, and those who boast of their own righteousness. But he said not a word about angels, although such was the custom on St. Michael's day.

The courage of the Wittemberg doctor, who was going quietly and on foot to answer a summons which had terminated in death to so many of his predecessors, astonished all who saw him. Interest, admiration, and sympathy prevailed by turns in their hearts. John Kestner, purveyor to the Cordeliers, struck with apprehension at the thought of the dangers which awaited his guest, said to him: "Brother, in Augsburg you will meet with Italians, who are learned men and subtle antagonists, and who will give you enough to do. I fear you will not be able to defend your cause against them. They will cast you into the fire, and their flames will consume you."[1] Luther solemnly replied: "Dear friend, pray to our Lord God who is in heaven, and put up a *paternoster* for me and for his dear Son Jesus, whose cause is mine, that he may be favourable to him. If He maintain his cause, mine is maintained; but if he will not maintain it, of a truth it is not I who can maintain it, and it is he who will bear the dishonour."

Luther continued his journey on foot, and arrived at Nuremberg. As he was about to present himself before a prince of the Church, he wished to appear in a becoming dress. His own was old, and all the worse for the journey. He therefore borrowed a frock from his faithful friend Wenceslas Link, preacher at Nuremberg.

Luther doubtless did not confine his visits to Link; he saw in like manner his other Nuremberg friends, Scheurl the town-clerk, the illustrious painter Albert Durer (to whose memory that city has recently erected a statue), and others besides. He derived strength from the conversation of these excellent ones of the earth, while many monks and laymen felt alarmed at his journey, and endeavoured to shake his resolution, beseeching him to retrace his steps. The letters he wrote from this city show the spirit which then animated him: "I have met," said he, "with pusillanimous men who wish to persuade me not to go to Augsburg; but I am resolved to proceed. The Lord's will be done! Even at Augsburg, even in the midst of his enemies, Christ reigns. Let Christ live; let Luther die,[2] and every sinner, ac-

---

1 Uxor mea et liberi mei provisi sunt. L. Epp. i. 129. He had neither wife nor children at this time.
2 Sic enim sponsus noster, sponsus sanguinum nobis est. Ibid. See Exodus iv. 25.
3 Veni igitur pedester et pauper Augustam. L. Opp. Lat. in Præf.
4 Ibi Myconius primum videt Lutherum : sed ab accessu et colloquio ejus tunc est prohibitus. M. Adami Vita Myconii, p. 176.

1 Profecto in ignem te conjicient et flammis exurent. Melch. Adam. Vit. Myc. p. 176. Myconis Ref. Hist. p. 39.
2 Vivat Christus, moriatur Martinus. Weismanni, Hist. Sacr. Nov. Test. p. 1465. Weismann had read this letter in manuscript. It is not to be found in the collection of M. de Wette.

cording as it is written! May the God of my salvation be exalted! Farewell! persevere, stand fast; for it is necessary to be rejected either by God or by man: but God is true, and man is a liar."

Link and an Augustine monk named Leonard could not make up their minds to permit Luther to go alone to face the dangers that threatened him. They knew his disposition, and were aware that, abounding as he did in determination and courage, he would probably be wanting in prudence. They therefore accompanied him. When they were about five leagues from Augsburg, Luther, whom the fatigues of the journey and the various agitations of his mind had probably exhausted, was seized with violent pains in the stomach. He thought he should die. His two friends in great alarm hired a waggon in which they placed the doctor. On the evening of the 7th October they reached Augsburg, and alighted at the Augustine convent. Luther was very tired; but he soon recovered. No doubt his faith and the vivacity of his mind speedily recruited his weakened body.

CHAPTER V.

De Vio—His Character—Serra Longa—Preliminary Conversation—Visit of the Councillors—Return of Serra Longa — The Prior — Luther's Discretion — Luther and Serra Longa—The Safe-conduct—Luther to Melancthon.

IMMEDIATELY on his arrival, and before seeing any one, Luther, desirous of showing the legate all due respect, begged Link to go and announce his presence. Link did so, and respectfully informed the cardinal, on the part of the Wittemberg doctor, that the latter was ready to appear before him whenever he should give the order. The legate was delighted at this news. At last he had this impetuous heretic within his reach, and promised himself that the reformer should not quit the walls of Augsburg as he had entered them. At the same time that Link waited upon the legate, the monk Leonard went to inform Staupitz of Luther's arrival. The vicar-general had written to the doctor that he would certainly come and see him as soon as he knew that he had reached Augsburg. Luther was unwilling to lose a minute in informing him of his presence. [1]

The diet was over. The emperor and the electors had already separated. The emperor, it is true, had not yet quitted the place, but was hunting in the neighbourhood. The ambassador of Rome remained alone in Augsburg. If Luther had gone thither during the diet, he would have met with powerful supporters; but everything now seemed destined to bend beneath the weight of the papal authority.

The name of the judge before whom Luther was to appear was not calculated to encourage him. Thomas de Vio, surnamed Cajetan, from the town of Gaeta in the kingdom of Naples, where he was born in 1469, had given great promise from his youth. At sixteen, he had entered the Dominican order, contrary to the express will of his parents. He had afterwards become general of his order, and cardinal of the Roman Church. But what was worse for Luther, this learned doctor was one of the most zealous defenders of that scholastic theology which the reformer had always treated so unmercifully. His mother, we are informed, had dreamt during her pregnancy that St. Thomas in person would instruct the child to which she was about to give birth, and would introduce him into heaven. Accordingly De Vio, when he became a Dominican, had changed his name from James to Thomas. He had zealously defended the prerogatives of the papacy, and the doctrines of Thomas Aquinas, whom he looked upon as the pearl of theologians. [1] Fond of pageantry and show, he construed almost seriously the Roman maxim, that legates are above kings, and surrounded himself with a brilliant train. On the 1st August, he had performed a solemn mass in the cathedral of Augsburg, and, in presence of all the princes of the empire, had placed the cardinal's hat on the head of the Archbishop of Mentz, who knelt before him, and had delivered to the emperor himself the hat and sword which the pope had consecrated. Such was the man before whom the Wittemberg monk was about to appear, dressed in a frock that did not belong to him. Further, the legate's learning, the austerity of his disposition, and the purity of his morals, ensured him an influence and authority in Germany that other Roman courtiers would not easily have obtained. It was no doubt to this reputation for sanctity that he owed this mission. Rome perceived that it would admirably forward her designs. Thus even the good qualities of Cajetan rendered him still more formidable. Besides, the affair intrusted to him was by no means complicated. Luther was already declared a heretic. If he would not retract, the legate must send him to prison; and if he escaped, whoever should give him an asylum was to be excommunicated. This was what the dignitary of the Church before whom Luther was summoned, had to perform on behalf of Rome. [2]

Luther had recovered his strength during the night. On Saturday morning (8th October), being already reinvigorated after his journey, he began to consider his strange

[1] Divi Thomæ Summa cum Commentariis Thomæ de Vio Lugduni, 1587.
[2] The pope's bull. L. Opp. (L.) xvii. 174.

L. Epp. i. 144.

position. He was resigned, and awaited the manifestation of God's will by the course of events. He had not long to wait. A person, unknown to him, sent to say (as if entirely devoted to him) that he was about to pay him a visit, and that Luther should avoid appearing before the legate until after this interview. The message proceeded from an Italian courtier named Urban of Serra Longa, who had often visited Germany as envoy from the Margrave of Montferrat. He had known the Elector of Saxony, to whom he had been accredited, and after the margrave's death, he had attached himself to the Cardinal de Vio.

The art and address of this individual presented the most striking contrast with the noble frankness and generous integrity of Luther. The Italian soon arrived at the Augustine monastery. The cardinal had sent him to sound the reformer, and prepare him for the recantation expected from him. Serra Longa imagined that his sojourn in Germany had given him a great advantage over the other courtiers in the legate's train; he hoped to make short work with this German monk. He arrived attended by two domestics, and professed to have come of his own accord, from friendship towards a favourite of the Elector of Saxony, and from attachment to the holy Church. After having most cordially saluted Luther, the diplomatist added in an affectionate manner:

"I am come to offer you good advice. Be wise, and become reconciled with the Church. Submit to the cardinal without reserve. Retract your offensive language. Remember the Abbot Joachim of Florence: he had published, as you know, many heretical things, and yet he was declared no heretic, because he retracted his errors."

Upon this Luther spoke of justifying what he had done.

Serra Longa.—" Beware of that !...... Would you enter the lists against the legate of his holiness ?"

Luther.—" If they convince me of having taught anything contrary to the Roman Church, I shall be my own judge, and immediately retract. The essential point will be to know whether the legate relies on the authority of St. Thomas more than the faith will sanction. If he does so, I will not yield."

Serra Longa.—" Oh, oh ! You intend to break a lance then !"

The Italian then began to use language which Luther styles horrible. He argued that one might maintain false propositions, provided they brought in money and filled the treasury; that all discussion in the universities against the pope's authority must be avoided; that, on the contrary, it should be asserted that the pope could, by a single nod, change or suppress articles of faith; [1]

and so he ran on, in a similar strain. But the wily Italian soon perceived that he was forgetting himself; and returning to his mild language, he endeavoured to persuade Luther to submit to the legate in all things, and to retract his doctrine, his oaths, and his theses.

The doctor, who was at first disposed to credit the fair professions of the orator Urban (as he calls him in his narrative), was now convinced that they were of little worth, and that he was much more on the legate's side than on his. He consequently became less communicative, and was content to say, that he was disposed to show all humility, to give proofs of his obedience, and render satisfaction in those things in which he might have erred. At these words Serra Longa exclaimed joyfully: " I shall hasten to the legate; you will follow me presently. Everything will go well, and all will soon be settled." [1]

He went away. The Saxon monk, who had more discernment than the Roman courtier, thought to himself: " This crafty Sinon has been badly taught and trained by his Greeks." [2] Luther was in suspense between hope and fear; yet hope prevailed. The visit and the strange professions of Serra Longa, whom he afterwards called a bungling mediator, [3] revived his courage.

The councillors and other inhabitants of Augsburg, to whom the elector had recommended Luther, were all eager to see the monk whose name already resounded throughout Germany. Peutinger, the imperial councillor, one of the most eminent patricians of the city, who frequently invited Luther to his table; the councillor Langemantel; Doctor Auerbach of Leipsic; the two brothers Adelmann, both canons, and many more, repaired to the Augustine convent. They cordially saluted this extraordinary man who had undertaken so long a journey to place himself in the hands of the Roman agents. " Have you a safe conduct?" asked they.—" No," replied the intrepid monk. " What boldness!" they all exclaimed.—" It was a polite expression," says Luther, " to designate my rashness and folly." All unanimously entreated him not to visit the legate before obtaining a safe-conduct from the emperor himself. It is probable the public had already heard something of the pope's brief, of which the legate was the bearer.

" But," replied Luther, " I set out for Augsburg without a safe-conduct, and have arrived safely."

" The elector has recommended you to us; you ought therefore to obey us, and do all that we tell you," answered Langemantel affectionately but firmly.

Doctor Auerbach coincided with these views, and added: " We know that at the

[1] Et nutu solo omnia abrogare, etiam ea quæ fidei essent. L. Epp. i. 144.

[1] L. Opp. (L.) xvii. 179.
[2] Hunc Sinonem parum consulte instructum arte pelasga. L. Epp. i. 144. See Virgil's Æneid, book ii.
[3] Mediator ineptus. Ibid.

bottom of his heart the cardinal is exceedingly irritated against you.[1] One cannot trust these Italians."[2]

The canon Adelmann urged the same thing: "You have been sent without protection, and they have forgotten to provide you with that which you needed most."[3]

His friends undertook to obtain the requisite safe-conduct from the emperor. They then told Luther how many persons, even in elevated rank, had a leaning in his favour. "The minister of France himself, who left Augsburg a few days ago, has spoken of you in the most honourable manner."[4] This remark struck Luther, and he remembered it afterwards. Thus several of the most respectable citizens in one of the first cities of the Empire were already gained over to the Reformation.

The conversation had reached this point when Serra Longa returned. "Come," said he to Luther, "the cardinal is waiting for you. I will myself conduct you to him. But you must first learn how to appear in his presence: when you enter the room in which he is, you will prostrate yourself with your face to the ground; when he tells you to rise, you will kneel before him; and you will wait his further orders before you stand up.[5] Remember you are about to appear before a prince of the Church. As for the rest, fear nothing: all will speedily be settled without difficulty."

Luther, who had promised to follow this Italian as soon as he was invited, found himself in a dilemma. However, he did not hesitate to inform him of the advice of his Augsburg friends, and spoke of a safe-conduct.

"Beware of asking for anything of the kind," immediately replied Serra Longa; "you do not require one. The legate is kindly disposed towards you, and ready to end this business in a friendly manner. If you ask for a safe-conduct, you will ruin everything."[6]

"My gracious lord, the Elector of Saxony," replied Luther, "recommended me to several honourable men in this city. They advise me to undertake nothing without a safe-conduct: I ought to follow their advice. For if I did not, and anything should happen, they will write to the elector, my master, that I would not listen to them."

Luther persisted in his determination, and Serra Longa was compelled to return to his chief, and announce the shoal on which his mission had struck, at the very moment he flattered himself with success.

Thus terminated the conferences of that day with the orator of Montferrat.

Another invitation was sent to Luther, but with a very different view. John Frosch,

prior of the Carmelites, was an old friend. Two years before, as licentiate in theology, he had defended some theses, under the presidence of Luther. He came to see him, and begged him earnestly to come and stay with him. He claimed the honour of entertaining the doctor of Germany as his guest. Already men did not fear to pay him homage even in the face of Rome; already the weak had become the stronger. Luther accepted the invitation, and left the convent of the Augustines for that of the Carmelites.

The day did not close without serious reflections. Serra Longa's eagerness and the fears of the councillors alike pointed out the difficulties of Luther's position. Nevertheless, he had God in heaven for his protector; guarded by Him he could sleep without fear.

The next day was Sunday,[1] on which he obtained a little more repose. Yet he had to endure fatigues of another kind. All the talk of the city was about Doctor Luther, and everybody desired to see, as he wrote to Melancthon, "this new Erostratus, who had caused so vast a conflagration."[2] They crowded round him in his walks, and the good doctor smiled, no doubt, at this singular excitement.

But he had to undergo importunities of another kind. If the people were desirous of seeing him, they had a still greater wish to hear him. He was requested on all sides to preach. Luther had no greater joy than to proclaim the Gospel. It would have delighted him to preach Jesus Christ in this large city, and in the solemn circumstances in which he was placed. But he evinced on this occasion, as on many others, a just sentiment of propriety, and great respect for his superiors. He refused to preach, for fear the legate should think he did it to annoy and to brave him. This moderation and this discretion were assuredly as good as a sermon.

The cardinal's people, however, did not permit him to remain quiet. They renewed their persuasions. "The cardinal," said they, "gives you assurances of his grace and favour: what are you afraid of?" They employed a thousand reasons to persuade him to wait upon De Vio. "He is a very merciful father," said one of these envoys. But another approached and whispered in his ear: "Do not believe what they tell you. He never keeps his word."[3] Luther persisted in his resolution.

On Monday morning (10th October), Serra Longa again returned to the charge. The courtier had made it a point of honour to succeed in his negotiation. He had scarcely arrived when he said in Latin: "Why do you not wait upon the cardinal? He is ex-

[1] Sciunt enim eum in me exacerbatissimum intus, quicquid simulet foris. L. Epp. i. 143.
[2] L. Opp. (L.) xvii. 201.   [3] Ibid. 203.
[4] Seckend. p. 144.   [5] Ibid. 130.
[6] L. Opp. (L.) 179.

[1] 9th October.
[2] Omnes cupiunt videre hominem, tanti incendii Heros tratum. L. Epp. i. 146.
[3] L. Opp. (L.) xvii. 205.

pecting you most indulgently: the whole matter lies in six letters: REVOCA, retract. Come! you have nothing to fear."

Luther thought to himself that these six letters were very important ones; but without entering into any discussion on the merits of the things to be retracted, he replied: "I will appear as soon as I have a safe-conduct."

Serra Longa lost his temper on hearing these words. He insisted—he made fresh representations; but Luther was immovable. Becoming still more angry, he exclaimed: "You imagine, no doubt, that the elector will take up arms in your defence, and for your sake run the risk of losing the territories he received from his forefathers?"

LUTHER.—"God forbid!"

SERRA LONGA.—"When all forsake you, where will you take refuge?"

LUTHER, *looking to heaven with an eye of faith*, "Under heaven."[1]

Serra Longa was silent for a moment, struck with the sublimity of this unexpected answer. He then resumed the conversation: "What would you do if you held the legate, pope, and cardinals in your hands, as they have you now in theirs?"

LUTHER.—"I would show them all possible honour and respect. But with me the Word of God is before everything."

SERRA LONGA, *smiling, and snapping his fingers in the manner of the Italians:* "Eh, eh! all honour!......I do not believe a word of it."

He then went out, sprung into his saddle, and disappeared.

Serra Longa did not return to Luther; but he long remembered the resistance he had met with from the reformer, and that which his master was soon after to experience in person. We shall find him at a later period loudly calling for Luther's blood.

Serra Longa had not long quitted the doctor when the safe-conduct arrived. Luther's friends had obtained it from the imperial councillors. It is probable that the latter had consulted the emperor on the subject, as he was not far from Augsburg. It would even appear from what the cardinal said afterwards, that from unwillingness to displease him, his consent also had been asked. Perhaps this was the reason why Serra Longa was set to work upon Luther; for open opposition to the security of a safe-conduct would have disclosed intentions that it was desirable to keep secret. It was a safer plan to induce Luther himself to desist from the demand. But they soon found out that the Saxon monk was not a man to give way.

Luther was now to appear. In demanding a safe-conduct, he did not lean upon an arm of flesh; for he was fully aware that an imperial safe-conduct had not preserved John Huss from the stake. He only wished to do his duty by submitting to the advice of his master's friends. The Lord will decide his fate. If God should require his life, he is ready joyfully to resign it. At this solemn moment, he felt the need of communing once again with his friends, above all with Melancthon, who was so dear to his heart, and he took advantage of a few moments of leisure to write to him.

"Show yourself a man," said he, "as you do at all times. Teach our beloved youths what is upright and acceptable to God. As for me, I am going to be sacrificed for you and for them, if such is the Lord's will.[1] I would rather die, and even (which would be my greatest misfortune) be for ever deprived of your sweet society, than retract what I felt it my duty to teach, and thus ruin perhaps by my own fault the excellent studies to which we are now devoting ourselves.

"Italy, like Egypt in times of old, is plunged in darkness so thick that it may be felt. No one in that country knows anything of Christ, or of what belongs to him; and yet they are our lords and our masters in faith and in morals. Thus the wrath of God is fulfilled among us, as the prophet saith: *I will give children to be their princes, and babes shall rule over them.* Do your duty to God, my dear Philip, and avert his anger by pure and fervent prayer."

The legate, being informed that Luther would appear before him on the morrow assembled the Italians and Germans in whom he had the greatest confidence, in order to concert with them the method he should pursue with the Saxon monk. Their opinions were divided. We must compel him to retract, said one; we must seize him and put him in prison, said another; it would be better to put him out of the way, thought a third; they should try to win him over by gentleness and mildness, was the opinion of a fourth. The cardinal seems to have resolved on beginning with the last method.[2]

CHAPTER VI.

First Appearance—First Words—Conditions of Rome—Propositions to be retracted—Luther's Answer—He withdraws—Impression on both Parties—Arrival of Staupitz.

THE day fixed for the interview arrived at last.[3] The legate knowing that Luther had declared himself willing to retract everything that could be proved contrary to the truth, was full of hope; he doubted not that it would be easy for a man of his rank and learning to reclaim this monk to obedience to the Church.

Luther repaired to the legate's residence, accompanied by the prior of the Carmelites,

---

[1] Et ubi manebis?....Respondi: Sub cœlo. L. Opp. in Praef.

[1] Ego pro illis et vobis vado immolari. L. Epp. i. 146.
[2] L. Opp. (L.) xvii. 183.
[3] Tuesday, 11th October.

his host and his friend; by two friars of the same convent; by Doctor Link and an Augustine, probably the one that had come from Nuremberg with him. He had scarcely entered the legate's palace, when all the Italians who formed the train of this prince of the Church crowded round him; every one desired to see the famous doctor, and they thronged him so much that he could with difficulty proceed. Luther found the apostolic nuncio and Serra Longa in the hall where the cardinal was waiting for him. His reception was cold, but civil, and conformable with Roman etiquette. Luther, in accordance with the advice he had received from Serra Longa, prostrated himself before the cardinal; when the latter told him to rise, he remained on his knees; and at a fresh order from the legate, he stood up. Many of the most distinguished Italians in the legate's court found their way into the hall in order to be present during the interview; they particularly desired to see the German monk humble himself before the pope's representative.

The legate remained silent. He hated Luther as an adversary of the theological supremacy of St. Thomas, and as the chief of a new, active, and hostile party in a rising university, whose first steps had disquieted the Thomists. He was pleased at seeing Luther fall down before him, and thought, as a contemporary observes, that he was about to recant. The doctor on his part humbly waited for the prince to address him; but as he did not speak, Luther understood this silence as an invitation to begin, and he did so in these words:

"Most worthy Father, in obedience to the summons of his papal holiness, and in compliance with the orders of my gracious lord the Elector of Saxony, I appear before you as a submissive and dutiful son of the holy Christian Church, and acknowledge that I have published the propositions and theses ascribed to me. I am ready to listen most obediently to my accusation, and if I have erred, to submit to instruction in the truth."

The cardinal, who had determined to assume the appearance of a tender and compassionate father towards an erring child, then adopted the most friendly tone; he praised and expressed his delight at Luther's humility, and said to him: "My dear son, you have disturbed all Germany by your dispute on indulgences. I understand that you are a very learned doctor in the Holy Scriptures, and that you have many followers. For this reason, if you desire to be a member of the Church, and to find a gracious father in the pope, listen to me."

After this prelude, the legate did not hesitate to declare at once what he expected of him, so confident was he of Luther's submission. "Here are three articles," said he, "which by the command of our holy Father, Pope Leo X., I have to set before you. *First,*

You must bethink yourself, own your faults, and retract your errors, propositions, and sermons; *secondly,* You must promise to abstain in future from propagating your opinions; and, *thirdly,* bind yourself to behave with greater moderation, and avoid everything that may grieve or disturb the Church."

LUTHER.—"Most holy Father, I beg you will show me the pope's brief, by virtue of which you have received full powers to treat of this matter."

Serra Longa and the other Italians opened their eyes with astonishment at this demand, and although the German monk had already appeared to them a very strange kind of man, they could not conceal their amazement at such a daring request. Christians, accustomed to ideas of justice, desire that justice should be observed towards others and towards themselves; but those who act habitually in an arbitrary manner, are surprised when they are called upon to proceed according to the usual rules, formalities, and laws.

DE VIO.—"This request, my dear son, cannot be granted. You must confess your errors, keep a strict watch upon your words for the future, and not return like a dog to his vomit, so that we may sleep without anxiety or disturbance; then, in accordance with the order and authorization of our most holy Father the Pope, I will arrange the whole business."

LUTHER.—"Condescend, then, to inform me in what I have erred."

At this new request, the Italian courtiers, who had expected to see the poor German fall down on his knees and beg pardon, were still more astonished than before. None of them would have deigned to reply to so impertinent a question. But De Vio, who thought it ungenerous to crush this petty monk with the weight of his authority, and who, besides, trusted to gain an easy victory by his learning, consented to tell Luther of what he was accused, and even to enter into discussion with him. We must do justice to the general of the Dominicans. We must acknowledge that he showed more equity, a greater sense of propriety, and less passion, than have been often shown in similar matters since. He replied in a condescending tone:

"Most dear son! here are two propositions that you have advanced, and which you must retract before all: 1*st,* The treasure of indulgences does not consist of the sufferings and merits of our Lord Jesus Christ; 2*d.* The man who receives the holy sacrament must have faith in the grace that is presented to him."

Each of these propositions, in truth, struck a mortal blow at the Romish commerce. If the pope had not the power of dispensing at his pleasure the merits of the Saviour; if, in receiving the drafts which the brokers of the Church negotiated, men did not receive a portion of this infinite righteousness, this paper-money would lose its value, and would be as worthless as a heap of rags. It was the same with the sacraments. Indulgences were more or less an extraordinary branch of Roman commerce; the sacraments were a staple commodity. The revenue they produced was of no small amount. To assert that faith was necessary before they could confer a real benefit on the soul of a Christian, took away all their charms in the eyes of the people; for it is not the pope who gives faith: it is beyond his province; it proceeds from God alone. To declare its necessity was therefore depriving Rome both of the speculation and the profit. By attacking these two doctrines, Luther had imitated Jesus Christ, who at the very beginning of his ministry had overthrown the tables of the money-changers, and driven the dealers out of the temple. *Make not my Father's house a house of merchandise,* he had said.

"In confuting your errors," said Cajetan, "I will not appeal to the authority of St. Thomas and other doctors of the schools; I will rely entirely on Holy Scripture, and talk with you in all friendliness."

But De Vio had scarcely begun to bring forward his proofs before he departed from the rule he had declared that he would follow. [1] He combated Luther's first proposition by an *Extravagance* [2] of Pope Clement, and the second by all sorts of opinions from the schoolmen. The discussion turned first on this papal constitution in favour of indulgences. Luther, indignant at hearing what authority the legate ascribed to a decree of Rome, exclaimed :—

"I cannot receive such constitutions as sufficient proofs on matters so important. For they pervert the Holy Scriptures, and never quote them to the purpose."

De Vio.—"The pope has power and authority over all things."

Luther, *quickly.*—"Except Scripture !" [3]

De Vio, *sneering.*—"Except Scripture ! ......Do you not know that the pope is above councils; he has recently condemned and punished the Council of Basle."

Luther.—"The university of Paris has appealed from this sentence."

De Vio.—"These Paris gentlemen will receive their deserts."

The dispute between the cardinal and Luther then turned upon the second point, namely, the faith that Luther declared necessary for the efficacy of the sacraments. Luther, according to his custom, quoted various passages of Scripture in favour of the opinion he maintained; but the legate treated them with ridicule. "It is of faith in general that you are speaking," said he.— "No," replied Luther.—One of the Italians,

the legate's master of the ceremonies, irritated at Luther's resistance and replies, was burning with the desire to speak. He continually endeavoured to put in a word, but the legate imposed silence on him. At last he was compelled to reprimand him so sharply, that the master of the ceremonies quitted the hall in confusion. [1]

"As for indulgences," said Luther to the legate, "if it can be shown that I am mistaken, I am very ready to receive instruction. We may pass over that and yet be good Christians. But as to the article of faith, if I made the slightest concession, I should renounce Jesus Christ. I cannot—I will not yield on this point, and with God's grace I will never yield."

De Vio, *growing angry.*—"Whether you will, or whether you will not, you must retract that article this very day, or, upon that article alone, I shall reject and condemn your whole doctrine."

Luther.—"I have no will but the Lord's. Let him do with me as seemeth good to him. But if I had four hundred heads, I would rather lose them all than retract the testimony which I have borne to the holy Christian faith."

De Vio.—"I did not come here to dispute with you. Retract, or prepare to suffer the penalty you have deserved." [2]

Luther saw clearly that it was impossible to put an end to the subject by a conference. His opponent sat before him as if he were himself pope, and pretended that he would receive humbly and submissively all that was said to him; and yet he listened to Luther's replies, even when they were founded on Holy Scripture, with shrugging of shoulders, and every mark of irony and contempt. He thought the wiser plan would be to answer the cardinal in writing. This means, thought he, gives at least one consolation to the oppressed. Others will be able to judge of the matter, and the unjust adversary, who by his clamours remains master of the field of battle, may be frightened at the consequences. [3]

Luther having shown a disposition to retire, the legate said, "Do you wish me to give you a safe-conduct to go to Rome?"

Nothing would have pleased Cajetan better than the acceptance of this offer. He would thus have been freed from a task of which he now began to perceive the difficulties; and Luther, with his heresy, would have fallen into hands that would soon have arranged everything. But the reformer, who saw the dangers that surrounded him, even in Augsburg, took care not to accept an offer that would have delivered him up, bound hand and foot, to the vengeance of his enemies. He therefore rejected it, as often as De Vio proposed it; and he did so very frequently. The legate dissembled his vexation at Luther's

---

[1] L. Opp. (L.) xvii. 190.
[2] A name applied to certain papal constitutions collected and subjoined to the body of the canon law.
[3] Salva Scriptura.

[1] L. Opp. (L.) xvii. 180.   [2] Ibid. 190, 183, 206, &c.
[3] Ibid. 209.

refusal he took refuge in his dignity, and dismissed the monk with a compassionate smile, under which he endeavoured to conceal his disappointment, and at the same time with the politeness of a man who hopes for better success another time.

Luther had scarcely reached the court of the palace before that babbling Italian, the master of the ceremonies, whom his lord's reprimands had compelled to quit the hall of conference, overjoyed at being able to speak without being observed by Cajetan, and burning with desire to confound the abominable heretic with his luminous reasonings, ran after him, and began, as he walked along, to deal out his sophisms. But Luther, disgusted with this foolish individual, replied to him by one of those sarcasms which he had so much at command, and the poor master slunk away abashed, and returned in confusion to the cardinal's palace.

Luther did not carry away a very exalted opinion of his adversary. He had heard from him, as he wrote afterwards to Spalatin, propositions quite opposed to sound theology, and which in the mouth of another would have been considered arch-heresies. And yet De Vio was reckoned the most learned of the Dominicans. Next after him was Prierio. "We may conclude from this," says Luther, "what they must be who are in the tenth or the hundredth rank."[1]

On the other hand, the noble and decided bearing of the Wittemberg doctor had greatly surprised the cardinal and his courtiers. Instead of a poor monk asking pardon as a favour, they had found a man of independence, a firm Christian, an enlightened doctor, who required that unjust accusations should be supported by proofs, and who victoriously defended his own doctrine. Every one in Cajetan's palace cried out against the pride, obstinacy, and effrontery of the heretic. Luther and De Vio had learned to know each other, and both prepared for their second interview.

A very agreeable surprise awaited Luther on his return to the Carmelite convent. The vicar-general of the Augustine order, his friend and father, Staupitz, had arrived at Augsburg. Unable to prevent Luther's journey to that city, Staupitz gave his friend a new and touching proof of his attachment by going thither himself in the hope of being useful to him. This excellent man foresaw that the conference with the legate might have the most serious consequences. He was equally agitated by his fears and by his friendship for Luther. After so painful an interview, it was a great comfort to the doctor to embrace so dear a friend. He told him how impossible it had been to obtain an answer of any value, and how the cardinal had insisted solely upon a recantation, without having essayed to convince him. "You

must positively," said Staupitz, "reply to the legate in writing."

After what he had learnt of the first interview, Staupitz entertained but little hopes from another. He therefore resolved upon an act which he now thought necessary; he determined to release Luther from the obligations of his order. By this means Staupitz thought to attain two objects: if, as everything seemed to forebode, Luther should fail in this undertaking, he would thus prevent the disgrace of his condemnation from being reflected on the whole order: and if the cardinal should order him to force Luther to be silent or to retract, he would have an excuse for not doing so.[1] The ceremony was performed with the usual formalities. Luther saw clearly what he must now expect. His soul was deeply moved at the breaking of those bonds which he had taken upon him in the enthusiasm of youth. The order he had chosen rejects him; his natural protectors forsake him. He is already become a stranger among his brethren. But although his heart was filled with sadness at the thought, all his joy returned when he directed his eyes to the promises of a faithful God, who has said: *I will never leave thee nor forsake thee.*

The emperor's councillors having informed the legate, through the Bishop of Trent, that Luther was provided with an imperial safe-conduct, and having at the same time enjoined him to take no proceedings against the doctor, De Vio lost his temper, and abruptly answered in this truly Romish language: "It is well; but I will execute the pope's orders."[2] We know what they were.

CHAPTER VII.

Second Interview—Luther's Declaration—The Legate's Answer—His Volubility—Luther's Request.

THE next day[3] both parties prepared for a second interview, which it seemed would be decisive. Luther's friends, who were resolved to accompany him to the legate's palace, went to the Carmelite convent. Peutinger and the Dean of Trent, both imperial councillors, and Staupitz, arrived successively. Shortly after, the doctor had the pleasure of seeing them joined by the knight Philip of Feilitzsch and Doctor Ruhel, councillors of the elector, who had received their master's order to be present at the conferences, and to protect Luther's liberty. They had reached Augsburg the previous evening. They were to keep close to him, says Ma-

---

[1] Luth. Epp. i. 173.

[1] Darinn ihn Dr Staupitz von dem Kloster-Gehorsam absolvirt. Math. 15.
[2] L. Opp. (L.) xvii. 201.
[3] Wednesday, 12th October.

thesius, as the knight of Chlum stood by John Huss at Constance. The doctor moreover took a notary, and, accompanied by all his friends, he repaired to the legate's palace.

At this moment Staupitz approached him: he fully comprehended Luther's position ; he knew that unless his eyes were fixed on the Lord, who is the deliverer of his people, he must fall. " My dear brother," said he, seriously, " bear constantly in mind that you have begun these things in the name of the Lord Jesus Christ."[1] Thus did God environ his humble servant with consolation and encouragement.

When Luther arrived at the cardinal's, he found a new adversary : this was the prior of the Dominicans of Augsburg, who sat beside his chief. Luther, conformably with the resolution he had taken, had written his answer. The customary salutations being finished, he read the following declaration with a loud voice :—

" I declare that I honour the holy Roman Church, and that I shall continue to honour her. I have sought after truth in my public disputations, and everything that I have said I still consider as right, true, and christian. Yet I am but a· man, and may be deceived. I am therefore willing to receive instruction and correction in those things wherein I may have erred. I declare myself ready to reply orally or in writing to all the objections and charges that the lord legate may bring against me. I declare myself ready to submit my theses to the four universities of Basle, Friburg in Brisgau, Louvain, and Paris, and to retract, whatever they shall declare erroneous. In a word, I am ready to do all that can be required of a Christian. But I solemnly protest against the method that has been pursued in this affair, and against the strange pretension of compelling me to retract without having refuted me."[2]

Undoubtedly nothing could be more reasonable than these propositions of Luther's, and they must have greatly embarrassed a judge who had been tutored beforehand as to the judgment he should pronounce. The legate, who had not expected this protest, endeavoured to hide his confusion by affecting to smile at it, and by assuming an appearance of mildness. " This protest," said he to Luther, with a smile, " is unnecessary ; I have no desire to dispute with you either privately or publicly ; but I propose arranging this matter with the kindness of a parent." The sum of the cardinal's policy consisted in laying aside the stricter forms of justice, which protect the accused, and treating the whole affair as one of mere administration between a superior and an inferior : a convenient method, that opens a wider field for arbitrary proceedings.

Continuing with the most affectionate air,

De Vio said : " My dear friend, abandon, I beseech you, so useless an undertaking : bethink yourself, acknowledge the truth, and I am prepared to reconcile you with the Church and the sovereign bishop.........Retract, my friend, retract ; such is the pope's wish. Whether you will or whether you will not, is of little consequence. It would be a hard matter for you to kick against the pricks."

Luther, who saw himself treated as if he were already a rebellious child and an outcast from the Church, exclaimed : " I cannot retract ! but I offer to reply, and that too in writing. We had debating enough yesterday."[1]

De Vio was irritated at this expression, which reminded him that he had not acted with sufficient prudence ; but he recovered himself, and said with a smile : " Debated ! my dear son, I have not debated with you : besides, I have no wish to debate ; but, to please the most serene Elector Frederick, I am ready to listen to you, and to exhort you in a friendly and paternal manner."

Luther could not understand why the legate was so much scandalized at the term he had employed ; for (thought he), if I had not wished to speak with politeness, I ought to have said, not *debated*, but *disputed* and *wrangled*, for that is what we really did yesterday.

De Vio, who felt that in the presence of the respectable witnesses who attended this conference, he must at least appear anxious to convince Luther, reverted to the two propositions, which he had pointed out as fundamental errors, being firmly resolved to permit the reformer to speak as little as possible. Availing himself of his Italian volubility, he overwhelmed the doctor with objections, without waiting for any reply. At one time he jeered, at another scolded ; he declaimed with passionate warmth ; mingled together the most heterogeneous matters ; quoted St. Thomas and Aristotle ; clamoured, stormed against all who thought differently from himself ; and apostrophized Luther. More than ten times did the latter try to speak ; but the legate immediately interrupted him and overwhelmed him with threats. Retract ! retract ! this was all that was required of him. He raved, he domineered, he alone was permitted to speak.[2] Staupitz took upon himself to check the legate. " Pray, allow brother Martin time to reply to you," said he. But De Vio began again ; he quoted the Extravagances and the opinions of St. Thomas ; he had resolved to have all the talk to himself during this interview. If he could not convince, and if he dared not strike, he would do his best to stun by his violence.

Luther and Staupitz saw very clearly that they must renounce all hope, not only of en-

<hr/>

[1] Seckend. p. 137.
[2] Löscher, ii. 463 ; L. Opp. (L.) xvii. 181, 209.

[1] Digladiatum, *battled.* L. Epp. i. 181.
[2] Decies fere cœpi ut loquerer, toties rursus tonabat et solus regnabat. L. Opp. (L.) xvii. 181, 209.

lightening De Vio by discussion, but still more of making any useful confession of faith. Luther therefore reverted to the request he had made at the beginning of the sitting, and which the cardinal had then eluded. Since he was not permitted to speak, he begged that he might at least be permitted to transmit a written reply to the legate. Staupitz seconded this petition; several of the spectators joined their entreaties to his, and Cajetan, notwithstanding his repugnance to every thing that was written, for he remembered that such writings are lasting (*scripta manent*) at length consented. The meeting broke up. The hopes that had been entertained of seeing the matter arranged at this interview were deferred; they must wait and see the issue of the next conference.

The permission which the general of the Dominicans had given Luther to take time for his reply, and to write his answer, to the two distinct accusations touching indulgences and faith, was no more than strict justice required, and yet we must give De Vio credit for this mark of moderation and impartiality.

Luther quitted the cardinal, delighted that his request had been granted. On his way to Cajetan, and on his return, he was the object of public attention. All enlightened men were as much interested in his affair as if they were to be tried themselves. It was felt that the cause of the Gospel, of justice, and of liberty, was then pleading at Augsburg. The lower classes alone held with Cajetan, and they no doubt gave the Reformer some significant proofs of their sentiments, for he took notice of them.[1]

It became more evident every day that the legate would hear no other words from Luther than these: "I retract," and Luther was resolved not to pronounce them. What will be the issue of so unequal a struggle? How can it be imagined that all the power of Rome matched against a single man should fail to crush him? Luther sees this; he feels the weight of that terrible hand under which he has voluntarily placed himself; he loses all hope of returning to Wittemberg, of seeing his dear Philip again, of mingling once more with those generous youths in whose hearts he so delighted to scatter the seeds of life. He beholds the sentence of excommunication suspended over his head, and doubts not that it will soon fall upon him.[2] These prospects afflict his soul, but he is not cast down. His trust in God is not shaken. God can break the instrument he has been pleased to make use of until this hour; but he will uphold the truth. Happen what may, Luther must defend it to the last. He therefore begins to prepare the protest that he intends presenting to the legate. It would appear that he devoted part of the 13th October to this task.

CHAPTER VIII.

Third Interview—Treasure of Indulgences—Faith—Humble Petition—Legate's Reply—Luther's Answer—The Legate's Anger—Luther withdraws—First Defection.

On Friday (14th October) Luther returned to the cardinal, accompanied by the elector's councillors. The Italians crowded around him as usual, and were present at the conference in great numbers. Luther advanced and presented his protest to the cardinal. His courtiers regarded this paper with astonishment—a paper so presumptuous in their eyes. This is what the Wittemberg doctor declared to their master:— [1]

"You attack me on two points. First, you oppose to me the constitution of Pope Clement VI., in which it is said that the treasure of indulgences is the merit of the Lord Jesus Christ and of the saints—which I deny in my theses.

"Panormitanus [2] declares in his first book that in whatever concerns the holy faith, not only a general council, but still further, each believer, is above the pope, if he can bring forward the declarations of Scripture and allege better reasons than the pope.[3] The voice of our Lord Jesus Christ is far above the voice of all men, whatever be the names they bear.

"My greatest cause of grief and of serious reflection is, that this constitution contains doctrines entirely at variance with the truth. It declares that the merits of the saints are a treasure, while the whole of Scripture bears witness that God rewards us far more richly than we deserve. The prophet exclaims: *Enter not into judgment with thy servant, O Lord, for in thy sight shall no man living be justified!*[4] 'Woe be to men, however honourable and however praiseworthy their lives may have been,' says Augustine, 'if a judgment from which mercy was excluded should be pronounced upon them!'[5]

"Thus the saints are not saved by their merits, but solely by God's mercy, as I have declared. I maintain this, and in it I stand fast. The words of Holy Scripture, which declare that the saints have not merit enough, must be set above the words of men, which affirm that they have an excess. For the pope is not above the Word of God, but below it."

Luther does not stop here: he shows that if indulgences cannot be the merits of the saints, they cannot any the more be the merits of Christ. He proves that indulgences

[1] L. Opp. (L.) xvii. 187.
[2] By Panormitanus Luther indicates Ives, author of the famous collection of ecclesiastical law entitled *Panormia*, and bishop of Chartres towards the close of the eleventh century.
[3] Ostendit in materia fidei. non modo generale concilium esse super papam, sed etiam quemlibet fidelium, si melioribus nitatur auctoritate et ratione quam papa. L. Opp. Lat. i. 209.
[4] Psalm cxliii.   [5] Confess. ix.

are barren and fruitless, since their only effect is to exempt men from performing good works, such as prayer and alms-giving. "No," exclaims he, " the merits of Jesus Christ are not a treasure of indulgence exempting man from good works, but a treasure of grace which quickeneth. The merits of Christ are applied to the believer without indulgences, without the keys, by the Holy Ghost alone, and not by the pope. If any one has an opinion better founded than mine," adds he, terminating what referred to this first point, " let him make it known to me, and then will I retract."

" I affirm," said he, coming to the second article, " that no man can be justified before God if he has not faith; so that it is necessary for a man to believe with a perfect assurance that he has obtained grace. To doubt of this grace is to reject it. The faith of the righteous is his righteousness and his life." [1]

Luther proves his proposition by a multitude of declarations from Scripture.

" Condescend, therefore, to intercede for me with our most holy father the pope," adds he " in order that he may not treat me with such harshness. My soul is seeking for the light of truth. I am not so proud or so vainglorious as to be ashamed of retracting if I have taught false doctrines. My greatest joy will be to witness the triumph of what is according to God's Word. Only let not men force me to do anything that is against the voice of my conscience."

The legate took the declaration from Luther's hands. After glancing over it, he said coldly : " You have indulged in useless verbiage : you have penned many idle words; you have replied in a foolish manner to the two articles, and have blackened your paper with a great number of passages from Scripture that have no connexion with the subject." Then, with an air of contempt, De Vio flung Luther's protest aside, as if it were of no value, and recommencing in the tone which had been so successful in the previous interview, he began to exclaim with all his might that Luther ought to retract. The latter was immovable. " Brother ! brother ! " then cried De Vio in Italian, " on the last occasion you were very tractable, but now you are very obstinate." The cardinal then began a long speech, extracted from the writings of St. Thomas; he again extolled the constitution of Clement VI. ; and persisted in maintaining that by virtue of this constitution it is the very merits of Jesus Christ that are dispensed to the believer by means of indulgences. He thought he had reduced Luther to silence: the latter sometimes interrupted him ; but De Vio raved and stormed without intermission, and claimed, as on the previous day, the sole right of speaking.

This method had partially succeeded the first time ; but Luther was not a man to submit to it on a second occasion. His indignation burst out at last; it is his turn to astonish the spectators, who believe him already conquered by the prelate's volubility. He raises his sonorous voice, seizes upon the cardinal's favourite objection, and makes him pay dearly for his rashness in venturing to enter into discussion with him. " Retract, retract!" repeated De Vio, pointing to the papal constitution. " Well, if it can be proved by this constitution," said Luther, " that the treasure of indulgences is the very merits of Jesus Christ, I consent to retract, according to your Eminence's good-will and pleasure."

The Italians, who had expected nothing of the kind, opened their eyes in astonishment at these words, and could not contain their joy at seeing their adversary caught in the net. As for the cardinal, he was beside himself ; he laughed aloud, but with a laugh in which anger and indignation were mingled ; he sprang forward, seized the book which contained this famous constitution; looked for it, found it, and, exulting in the victory he thought certain, read the passage aloud with panting eagerness.[1] The Italians were elated ; the elector's councillors were uneasy and embarrassed ; Luther was waiting for his adversary. At last, when the cardinal came to these words : " The Lord Jesus Christ has acquired this treasure by his sufferings," Luther stopped him : " Most worthy father," said he, " pray, meditate and weigh these words carefully : *He has acquired.* [2] Christ has acquired a treasure by his merits; the merits, therefore, are not the treasure ; for, to speak philosophically, the cause and effect are very different matters. The merits of Jesus Christ have acquired for the pope the power of giving certain indulgences to the people ; but it is not the very merits of our Lord that the hand of the pontiff distributes. Thus, then, my conclusion is the true one, and this constitution, which you invoke with so much noise, testifies with me to the truth I proclaim."

De Vio still held the book in his hands, his eyes resting on the fatal passage; he could make no reply. He was caught in the very snare he had laid, and Luther held him there with a strong hand, to the inexpressible astonishment of the Italian courtiers around him. The legate would have eluded the difficulty, but had not the means : he had long abandoned the testimony of Scripture and of the Fathers ; he had taken refuge in this Extravagance of Clement VI., and lo ! he was caught. Yet he was too cunning to betray his confusion. Desirous of concealing his disgrace, the prince of the Church suddenly quitted this subject, and violently attacked other articles. Luther, who perceived

<hr>

[1] Justitia justi et vita ejus, est fides ejus. L. Opp. Lat. i. 211.

[1] Legit fervens et anhelans. L. Epp. i. 145.
[2] Acquisivit. Ibid.

this skilful manœuvre, did not permit him to escape; he tightened and closed on every side the net in which he had taken the cardinal, and rendered all escape impossible. "Most reverend Father," said he, with an ironical, yet very respectful tone, "your eminence cannot, however, imagine that we Germans are ignorant of grammar: to be a treasure, and to acquire a treasure, are two very different things."

"Retract!" said De Vio; "retract! or if you do not. I shall send you to Rome to appear before judges commissioned to take cognizance of your affair. I shall excommunicate you with all your partisans, with all who are or who may be favourable to you, and reject them from the Church. All power has been given me in this respect by the holy apostolic see.[1] Think you that your protectors will stop me? Do you imagine that the pope cares anything for Germany? The pope's little finger is stronger than all the German princes put together."[2]

"Deign," replies Luther, "to forward to Pope Leo X., with my humble prayers, the answer which I have transmitted you in writing."

At these words, the legate, highly pleased at finding a moment's release, again assumed an air of dignity, and said to Luther with pride and anger:

"Retract, or return no more."[3]

These words struck Luther. This time he will reply in another way than by speeches: he bowed and left the hall, followed by the elector's councillors. The cardinal and the Italians, remaining alone, looked at one another in confusion at such a result.

Thus the Dominican system, covered with the brilliancy of the Roman purple, had haughtily dismissed its humble adversary. But Luther was conscious that there was a power—the Christian doctrine, the truth—that no secular or spiritual authority could ever subdue. Of the two combatants, he who withdrew remained master of the field of battle.

This is the first step by which the Church separated from the papacy.

Luther and De Vio did not meet again; but the reformer had made a deep impression on the legate, which was never effaced. What Luther had said about faith, what De Vio read in the subsequent writings of the Wittemberg doctor, greatly modified the cardinal's opinions. The theologians of Rome beheld with surprise and discontent the sentiments he advanced on justification in his commentary on the Epistle to the Romans. The Reformation did not recede, did not retract; but its judge, he who had not ceased from crying, Retract! retract! changed his views, and indirectly retracted his errors. Thus was crowned the unshaken fidelity of the Reformer.

Luther returned to the monastery where he had been entertained. He had stood fast; he had given testimony to the truth; he had done his duty. God will perform the rest! His heart overflowed with peace and joy.

CHAPTER IX.

De Vio and Staupitz—Staupitz and Luther—Luther to Spalatin—Luther to Carlstadt—The Communion—Link and De Vio—Departure of Link and Staupitz—Luther to Cajetan—Cardinal's Silence—Luther's Farewell—Departure—Appeal to Rome.

YET the rumours that reached him were not very encouraging: it was reported in the city, that if he did not retract, he was to be seized and thrown into a dungeon. The vicar-general of his order, Staupitz himself, it was affirmed, had given his consent.[1] Luther cannot believe what is said of his friend. No! Staupitz will not deceive him! As for the cardinal's designs, to judge from his words, there could be no doubt about them. Yet he will not flee from the danger; his life, like the truth itself, is in powerful hands, and, despite the threatening peril, he is resolved not to quit Augsburg.

The legate soon repented of his violence; he felt that he had gone beyond his part, and endeavoured to retrace his steps. Staupitz had scarcely finished his dinner (on the morning of the interview, and the dinner-hour was noon), before he received a message from the cardinal, inviting him to his palace. Staupitz went thither attended by Wenceslas Link.[2] The vicar-general found the legate alone with Serra Longa. De Vio immediately approached Staupitz, and addressed him in the mildest language. "Endeavour," said he, "to prevail upon your monk, and induce him to retract. Really, in other respects, I am well pleased with him, and he has no better friend than myself."[3]

STAUPITZ.—"I have already done so, and I will again advise him to submit to the Church in all humility."

DE VIO.—"You will have to reply to the arguments he derives from the Holy Scriptures."

STAUPITZ.—"I must confess, my lord, that is a task beyond my abilities: for Doctor Martin Luther is superior to me both in genius and knowledge of the Holy Scriptures."

The cardinal smiled, no doubt, at the vicar-general's frankness. Besides, he knew himself how difficult it would be to convince Luther. He continued, addressing both Staupitz and Link:—

---

[1] L. Opp. (L.) xvii. 197. [2] Ibid. (W.) xxii. 1331.
[3] Revoca, aut non revertere. Ibid. (L.) xvii. 202.

[1] L. Opp. (L.) xvii. 210. [2] Ibid. 204. [3] Ibid. 185

" Are you aware, that, as partisans of an heretical doctrine, you are yourselves liable to the penalties of the Church?"

STAUPITZ.—" Condescend to resume the conference with Luther, and order a public discussion on the controverted points."

DE VIO, *alarmed at the very thought.*—" I will no longer dispute with that beast, for it has deep eyes and wonderful speculations in its head."[1]

Staupitz at length prevailed on the cardinal to transmit to Luther in writing what he was required to retract.

The vicar-general returned to Luther. Staggered by the representations of the cardinal, he endeavoured to persuade him to come to an arrangement. " Refute, then," said Luther, " the declarations of Scripture that I have advanced."—" It is beyond my ability," said Staupitz.—" Well then!" replied Luther, " it is against my conscience to retract, so long as these passages of Scripture are not explained differently. What!" continued he, " the cardinal professes, as you inform me, that he is desirous of arranging this affair without any disgrace or detriment to me! Ah! these are Roman expressions, which signify in good German that it will be my eternal shame and ruin. What else can he expect who, through fear of men and against the voice of his conscience, denies the truth?"[2]

Staupitz did not persist; he only informed Luther that the cardinal had consented to transmit to him in writing the points which he would be required to retract. He then no doubt informed him also of his intention of quitting Augsburg, where he had no longer anything to do. Luther communicated to him a plan he had formed for comforting and strengthening their souls. Staupitz promised to return, and they separated for a short time.

Alone in his cell, Luther turned his thoughts towards the friends dearest to his heart. His ideas wandered to Weimar and to Wittemberg. He desired to inform the elector of what was passing; and, fearful of being indiscreet by addressing the prince himself, he wrote to Spalatin, and begged the chaplain to inform his master of the state of affairs. He detailed the whole transaction, even to the promise given by the legate to send him the controverted points in writing, and finished by saying: " This is the posture of affairs; but I have neither hope nor confidence in the legate. I will not retract a syllable. I will publish the reply I gave him, in order that, if he should proceed to violence, he may be covered with shame in all Christendom."[3]

The doctor then profited by the few moments that still remained to write to his Wittemberg friends.

" Peace and happiness," wrote he to Doctor Carlstadt. " Accept these few words as if they were a long letter, for time and events are pressing. At a better opportunity I will write to you and others more fully. Three days my business has been in hand, and matters are now at such a point that I have no longer any hope of returning to you, and I have nothing to look for but excommunication. The legate positively will not allow me to dispute either publicly or privately. He desires not to be a judge," says he, " but a father to me; and yet he will hear no other words from me than these: 'I retract, and acknowledge my error.' And these I will not utter.

" The dangers of my cause are so much the greater that its judges are not only implacable enemies, but, still further, men incapable of understanding it. Yet the Lord God lives and reigns: to his protection I commit myself, and I doubt not that, in answer to the prayers of a few pious souls, he will send me deliverance; I imagine I feel them praying for me.

" Either I shall return to you without having suffered any harm; or else, struck with excommunication, I shall have to seek a refuge elsewhere.

" However that may be, conduct yourself valiantly, stand fast, and glorify Christ boldly and joyfully......

" The cardinal always styles me his dear son. I know how much I must believe of that. I am nevertheless persuaded that I should be the most acceptable and dearest man to him in the world, if I would pronounce the single word *Revoco*, I retract. But I will not become a heretic by renouncing the faith by which I became a Christian. I would rather be exiled, accursed, and burnt to death.

" Farewell, my dear doctor; show this letter to our theologians, to Amsdorff, to Philip, to Otten, and the rest, in order that you may pray for me and also for yourselves; for it is your cause that I am pleading here. It is that of faith in the Lord Jesus Christ, and in the grace of God."[1]

Sweet thought, which ever fills with consolation and with peace all those who have borne witness to Jesus Christ, to his divinity, to his grace, when the world pours upon them from every side its judgments, its exclusions, and its disgrace: " Our cause is that of faith in the Lord!" And what sweetness also in the conviction expressed by the Reformer: " I feel that they are praying for me!" The Reformation was the work of piety and prayer. The struggle between Luther and De Vio was that of a religious element which reappeared full of life with the expiring relics of the wordy dialectics of the middle ages.

Thus did Luther converse with his absent friends. Staupitz soon returned; Doctor

---

[1] Ego nolo amplius cum hac bestia disputare. Habet enim profundos oculos et mirabiles speculationes in capite suo. Myconius. 35.
[2] I. Opp. (L.) xvii. 210. [3] L. Epp. i. 149.

[1] L. Epp. i. 159.

Ruhel and the Knight of Feilitzsch, both envoys from the elector, also called upon Luther after taking leave of the cardinal. Some other friends of the Gospel joined them. Luther, seeing thus assembled these generous men, who were on the point of separating, and from whom he was perhaps to part for ever, proposed that they should celebrate the Lord's Supper together. They agreed, and this little band of faithful men communicated in the body and blood of Jesus Christ. What feelings swelled the hearts of the reformer's friends at the moment when, celebrating the Eucharist with him, they thought it was perhaps the last time they would be permitted to do so! What joy, what love animated Luther's heart, as he beheld himself so graciously accepted by his Master at the very moment that men rejected him! How solemn must have been that communion! How holy that evening![1]

The next day,[2] Luther waited for the articles the legate was to send him; but not receiving any message, he begged his friend Wenceslas Link to go to the cardinal. De Vio received Link in the most affable manner, and assured him that he had no desire but to act like a friend. He said, "I no longer regard Luther as a heretic. I will not excommunicate him this time, unless I receive further orders from Rome. I have sent his reply to the pope by an express." And then, to show his friendly intentions, he added: "If Doctor Luther would only retract what concerns indulgences, the matter would soon be finished; for, as to what concerns faith in the sacraments, it is an article that each one may understand and interpret in his own fashion." Spalatin, who records these words, adds this shrewd but just remark: "It follows clearly that Rome looks to money rather than to the holy faith and the salvation of souls."[3]

Link returned to Luther: he found Staupitz with him, and gave them an account of his visit. When he came to the unexpected concession of the legate: "It would have been well," said Staupitz, "if Doctor Wenceslas had had a notary and witnesses with him to take down these words in writing; for, if such a proposal were made known, it would be very prejudicial to the Romans."

However, in proportion to the mildness of the prelate's language, the less confidence did these worthy Germans place in him. Many of the good men to whom Luther had been recommended held counsel together: "The legate," said they, "is preparing some mischief by this courier of whom he speaks, and it is very much to be feared that you will all be seized and thrown into prison."

Staupitz and Wenceslas therefore resolved to quit the city; they embraced Luther, who persisted in remaining at Augsburg, and departed hastily for Nuremberg, by two different roads, not without much anxiety respecting the fate of the courageous witness they were leaving behind them.

Sunday passed off quietly enough. But Luther in vain waited for the legate's message: the latter sent none. At last he determined to write. Staupitz and Link, before setting out, had begged him to treat the cardinal with all possible respect. Luther had not yet made trial of Rome and of her envoys: this is his first experiment. If deference did not succeed, he would take a warning from it. Now at least he must make the attempt. For his own part, not a day passed in which he did not condemn himself, and groan over his facility in giving utterance to expressions stronger than the occasion required: why should he not confess to the cardinal what he confessed daily to God? Besides, Luther's heart was easily moved, and he suspected no evil. He took up his pen, and with a sentiment of the most respectful goodwill, wrote to the cardinal as follows:[1]—

"Most worthy Father in God, once more I approach you, not in person, but by letter, entreating your paternal goodness to listen to me graciously. The reverend Dr Staupitz, my very dear father in Christ, has called upon me to humble myself, to renounce my own sentiments, and to submit my opinions to the judgment of pious and impartial men. He has also praised your fatherly kindness, and has thoroughly convinced me of your favourable disposition towards me. This news has filled me with joy.

"Now, therefore, most worthy Father, I confess, as I have already done before, that I have not shown (as has been reported) sufficient modesty, meekness, or respect for the name of the sovereign pontiff; and, although I have been greatly provoked, I see that it would have been better for me to have conducted my cause with greater humility, mildness, and reverence, and not *to have answered a fool according to his folly, lest I should be like unto him.*

"This grieves me very much, and I ask forgiveness. I will publicly confess it to the people from the pulpit, as indeed I have often done before. I will endeavour, by God's grace, to speak differently. Nay more: I am ready to promise, freely and of my own accord, not to utter another word on the subject of indulgences, if this business is arranged. But also, let those who made me begin, be compelled on their part to be more moderate henceforth in their sermons, or to be silent.

"As for the truth of my doctrine, the authority of St. Thomas and other doctors cannot satisfy me. I must hear (if I am worthy to do so) the voice of the bride, which is the Church. For it is certain that she hears the voice of the Bridegroom, which is Christ.

"In all humility and submission, I there-

[1] L. Opp. (L.) xvii. 178.   [2] Saturday, 15th October.
[3] L. Opp. (L.) xvii. 182   [1] This letter is dated 17th October.

147

fore entreat your paternal love to refer all this business, so unsettled up to this day, to our most holy lord Leo X., in order that the Church may decide, pronounce, and ordain, and that I may retract with a good conscience, or believe with sincerity."[1]

As we read this letter, another reflection occurs to us. We see that Luther was not acting on a preconceived plan, but solely by virtue of convictions impressed successively on his mind and on his heart. Far from having any settled system, any well arranged opposition, he frequently and unsuspectingly contradicted himself. Old convictions still reigned in his mind, although opposite convictions had already entered it. And yet, it is in these marks of sincerity and truth that men have sought for arguments against the Reformation; it is because it followed the necessary laws of progression which are imposed upon all things in the human mind, that some have written the history of its variations; it is in these very features, that show its sincerity and which consequently make it honourable, that one of the most eminent christian geniuses has found his strongest objections![2] Inconceivable perversity of the human mind!

Luther received no answer to his letter. Cajetan and his courtiers, after being so violently agitated, had suddenly become motionless. What could be the reason? Might it not be the calm that precedes the storm? Some persons were of Pallavicini's opinion: "The cardinal was waiting," he observes, "until this proud monk, like an inflated bellows, should gradually lose the wind that filled him, and become thoroughly humble."[3] Others, imagining they understood the ways of Rome better, felt sure that the legate intended to arrest Luther, but that, not daring to proceed to such extremities on his own account, because of the imperial safe-conduct, he was waiting a reply from Rome to his message. Others could not believe that the cardinal would delay so long. The Emperor Maximilian, said they (and this may really be the truth), will have no more scruple to deliver Luther over to the judgment of the Church, notwithstanding the safe-conduct, than Sigismond had to surrender Huss to the Council of Constance. The legate is perhaps even now negotiating with the emperor. Maximilian's authorization may arrive every minute. The more he was opposed to the pope before, the more will he seem to flatter him now, until the imperial crown encircles his grandchild's head. There is not a moment to be lost. "Draw up an appeal to the pope," said the noble-minded men who surrounded Luther, "and quit Augsburg without delay."

Luther, whose presence in this city had been useless during the last four days, and who had sufficiently proved, by his remaining after the departure of the Saxon councillors sent by the elector to watch over his safety, that he feared nothing, and that he was ready to answer any charge, yielded at length to his friends' solicitations. But first he resolved to inform De Vio of his intention: he wrote to him on Tuesday, the eve of his departure. This second letter is in a firmer tone than the other. It would appear that Luther, seeing all his advances were unavailing, began to lift up his head in the consciousness of his integrity and of the injustice of his enemies.

"Most worthy Father in God," wrote he to De Vio, "your paternal kindness has witnessed,—I repeat it, witnessed and sufficiently acknowledged my obedience. I have undertaken a long journey, through great dangers, in great weakness of body, and despite of my extreme poverty; at the command of our most holy lord, Leo X., I have appeared in person before your eminence; lastly, I have thrown myself at the feet of his holiness, and I now wait his good pleasure, ready to submit to his judgment, whether he should condemn or acquit me. I therefore feel that I have omitted nothing which it becomes an obedient child of the Church to do.

"I think, consequently, that I ought not uselessly to prolong my sojourn in this town; besides, it would be impossible; my resources are failing me; and your paternal goodness has loudly forbidden me to appear before you again, unless I will retract.

"I therefore depart in the name of the Lord, desiring, if possible, to find some spot where I may dwell in peace. Many persons, of greater importance than myself, have requested me to appeal from your paternal kindness, and even from our most holy lord, Leo X., ill informed, to the pope when better informed.[1] Although I know that such an appeal will be far more acceptable to our most serene highness the elector than a retractation, nevertheless, if I had consulted my own feelings only, I should not have done so......I have committed no fault; I ought therefore to fear nothing."

Luther having written this letter, which was not given to the legate until after his departure, prepared to quit Augsburg. God had preserved him till this hour, and he praised the Lord for it with all his heart; but he must not tempt God. He embraced his friends Peutinger, Langemantel, and the Adelmanns, Auerbach, and the prior of the Carmelites, who had shown him such christian hospitality. On Wednesday, before daybreak, he was up and ready to set out. His friends had recommended him to take every precaution for fear that he should be prevented, if his intentions were known. He followed their advice as far as possible. A

[1] L. Opp. (L.) p. 198.
[2] Bossuet's Histoire des Variations. Liv. 1. 25. &c.
[3] Ut follis ille ventosa elatione distentus, p. 40.

[1] Ut a R. P. tua, immo a Sanctissimo Domino nostro Leone X. male informato ad melius informandum appellem. L. Epp. i. 161.

pony, that Staupitz had left for him, was brought to the door of the convent. Once more he bids his brethren adieu; he then mounts and sets off, without a bridle for his horse, without boots or spurs, and unarmed. The magistrate of the city had sent him as a guide one of the horse-police who was well acquainted with the roads. This servant conducts him in the dark through the silent streets of Augsburg. They direct their course to a small gate in the wall of the city. One of the councillors, Langemantel, had given orders that it should be opened. He is still in the power of the legate. The hand of Rome may grasp him yet. No doubt, if the Italians knew their prey was escaping them, they would utter a cry of rage. Who can say that the intrepid adversary of Rome will not yet be seized and thrown into a dungeon?......At length Luther and his guide arrive at the little gate; they pass through. They are out of Augsburg; and soon they put their horses to a gallop, and ride speedily away.

Luther, on his departure, had left his appeal to the pope in the hands of the prior of Pomesaw. His friends had recommended that it should not be transmitted to the legate. The prior was commissioned to have it posted upon the cathedral gates two or three days after the doctor's departure, in the presence of a notary and witnesses. This was done.

In this paper, Luther declares that he appeals from the most holy Father the Pope, ill informed, to the most holy lord and Father in Christ, Leo X. of that name, by the grace of God, better informed.[1] This appeal had been drawn up in the customary form and style, by aid of the imperial notary, Gall of Herbrachtingen, in presence of two Augustine monks, Bartholomew Utzmair, and Wenzel Steinbies. It was dated the 16th October.

When the cardinal was informed of Luther's departure, he was thunderstruck, and even frightened and alarmed, as he assured the elector in his letter. Indeed there was good cause to be annoyed. This departure, which so abruptly terminated the negotiations, disconcerted the hopes with which he had so long flattered his pride. He had been ambitious of the honour of healing the wounds of the Church, of restoring the tottering influence of the pope in Germany; and the heretic had escaped not only unpunished, but even without being humbled. The conference had served only to exhibit in a stronger light, on the one hand, Luther's simplicity, integrity, and firmness; and, on the other, the imperious and unreasonable proceedings of the pope and his ambassador. Since Rome had gained nothing, she had lost; her authority, not having been strengthened, had received a fresh check. What will

they say in the Vatican? What messages will be received from Rome? The difficulties of his position will be forgotten; the unlucky issue of this affair will be attributed to his want of skill. Serra Longa and the Italians were furious at seeing themselves with all their dexterity, outwitted by a German monk. De Vio could hardly conceal his irritation. Such an insult called for vengeance, and we shall soon witness him breathing out his wrath in a letter to the elector.

CHAPTER X.

Luther's Flight—Admiration—Luther's Desire—The Legate to the Elector—The Elector to the Legate—Prosperity of the University.

LUTHER and his guide continued their flight far from the walls of Augsburg. He spurred his horse, and galloped as fast as the poor animal's strength would permit. He called to mind the real or supposed flight of John Huss, the manner in which he was caught, and the assertion of his adversaries, who pretended that Huss having by his flight annulled the emperor's safe-conduct, they had the right of condemning him to the flames.[1] These anxious thoughts, however, did not long occupy Luther's mind. Having escaped from a city in which he had passed ten days under the terrible hand of Rome, which had already crushed so many thousand witnesses to the truth, and sprinkled all around it with blood,—now that he is free, now that he inhales the fresh breezes of the country, traverses the villages and rural districts, and beholds himself wonderfully delivered by the arm of the Lord, his whole being returns thanks to the Almighty. It is truly he who can now say : *Our soul is escaped as a bird out of the snare of the fowlers ; the snare is broken, and we are escaped. Our help is in the name of the Lord, who made heaven and earth.*[2] Thus was Luther's heart overflowing with joy. But his thoughts were turned on De Vio also: "The cardinal would have liked to have me in his hands to send me to Rome. He is vexed, no doubt, at my escape. He imagined I was in his power at Augsburg; he thought he had me; but he was holding an eel by the tail. Is it not disgraceful that these people set so high a value upon me? They would give a heap of crowns to have me in their clutches, while our Lord Jesus Christ was sold for thirty pieces of silver."[3]

The first day he travelled fourteen leagues. When he reached the inn where he was to pass the night, he was so fatigued (his horse was a very hard trotter, an historian tells

---

[1] Melius informandum. L. Opp. Lat. i. 219.

[1] Weissmann, Hist. Eccles. i. 1237.
[2] Psalm cxxiv. 7.   [3] L. Opp. (L.) xvii. 202.

us) that, when he dismounted, he could not stand upright, and lay down upon a bundle of straw. He nevertheless obtained some repose. On the morrow he continued his journey. At Nuremberg he met with Staupitz, who was visiting the convents of his order. It was in this city that he first saw the brief sent by the pope to Cajetan about him. He was indignant at it, and it is very probable that if he had seen this brief before leaving Wittemberg, he would never have gone to the cardinal. "It is impossible to believe," said he, "that any thing so monstrous could have proceeded from any sovereign pontiff."[1]

All along the road Luther was an object of general interest. He had not yet yielded in any one point. Such a victory, gained by a mendicant monk over the representative of Rome, filled every heart with admiration. Germany seemed avenged of the contempt of Italy. The eternal Word had received more honour than the word of the pope. This vast power, which for so many centuries tyrannized over the world, had received a formidable check. Luther's journey was like a triumph. Men rejoiced at the obstinacy of Rome, in the hope that it would lead to her destruction. If she had not insisted on preserving her shameful gains; if she had been wise enough not to despise the Germans; if she had reformed crying abuses: perhaps, according to human views, all would have returned to that death-like state from which Luther had awakened. But the papacy will not yield; and the doctor will see himself compelled to bring to light many other errors, and to go forward in the knowledge and manifestation of the truth.

On the 26th of October Luther reached Græfenthal, on the verge of the Thuringian forests. Here he met with Count Albert of Mansfeldt, the same person who had so strongly dissuaded him from going to Augsburg. The count, laughing heartily at his singular equipage, compelled him to stop and be his guest. Luther soon resumed his journey.

He hastened forward, desiring to be at Wittemberg on the 31st October, under the impression that the elector would be there for the festival of All-Saints, and that he should see him. The brief which he had read at Nuremberg had disclosed to him all the perils of his situation. In fact, being already condemned at Rome, he could not hope either to stay at Wittemberg, to obtain an asylum in a convent, or to find peace and security in any other place. The elector's protection might perhaps be able to defend him; but he was far from being sure of it. He could no longer expect anything from the two friends whom he had possessed hitherto at the court of this prince. Staupitz had lost the favour he had so long enjoyed, and was

quitting Saxony. Spalatin was beloved by Frederick, but had not much influence over him. The elector himself was not sufficiently acquainted with the doctrine of the Gospel to encounter manifest danger for its sake. Luther thought, however, that he could not do better than return to Wittemberg, and there await what the eternal and merciful God would do with him. If, as many expected, he were left unmolested, he resolved to devote himself entirely to study and to the education of youth.[1]

Luther re-entered Wittemberg on the 30th of October. All his expedition had been to no purpose. Neither the elector nor Spalatin had come to the feast. His friends were overjoyed at seeing him again amongst them. He hastened to inform Spalatin of his arrival. "I returned to Wittemberg to-day safe and sound, by the grace of God," said he, "but how long I shall stay here I do not know... ...I am filled with joy and peace, and can hardly conceive that the trial which I endure can appear so great to so many distinguished personages."

De Vio had not waited long after Luther's departure to pour forth all his indignation to the elector. His letter breathes vengeance. He gives Frederick an account of the conference with an air of assurance. "Since brother Martin," says he in conclusion, "cannot be induced by paternal measures to acknowledge his error, and remain faithful to the catholic Church, I beg your highness will send him to Rome, or expel him from your states. Be assured that this difficult, mischievous, and envenomed business cannot be protracted much longer; for so soon as I have informed our most holy lord of all this artifice and wickedness, it will be brought to an end." In a postscript, written with his own hand, the cardinal entreats the elector not to tarnish his honour and that of his illustrious ancestors for the sake of a miserable little friar.[2]

Never perhaps did Luther's soul feel a nobler indignation than when he read the copy of this letter forwarded to him by the elector. The thought of the sufferings he is destined to undergo, the value of the truth for which he is contending, contempt inspired by the conduct of the Roman legate,—all agitated his heart together. His reply, written in the midst of this agitation, is full of that courage, sublimity, and faith which he always displayed in the most trying circumstances of his life. He gives, in his turn, an account of the Augsburg conference; and after describing the cardinal's behaviour, he continues thus:—

"I should like to answer the legate in the place of the elector:

"Prove that you speak of what you understand," I would say to him; "let the whole matter be committed to writing: then I will

[1] Tale quid monstri a summo Pontifice egredi. L. Epp. 166.

[1] L. Opp. (L.) xvii. 183.   [2] Ibid. 203.

150

send brother Martin to Rome, or else I will myself seize him and put him to death. I will take care of my conscience and of my honour, and will permit no stain to tarnish my glory. But so long as your positive knowledge shuns the light, and is made known by its clamours only, I can put no faith in darkness.

"It is thus I would reply, most excellent prince.

"Let the reverend legate, or the pope himself, specify my errors in writing; let them give their reasons; let them instruct me, for I am a man who desires instruction, who begs and longs for it, so that even a Turk would not refuse to grant it. If I do not retract and condemn myself when they have proved that the passages which I have cited ought to be understood in a different sense from mine, then, most excellent elector, let your highness be the first to prosecute and expel me; let the university reject me, and overwhelm me with its anger......Nay more, and I call heaven and earth to witness, may the Lord Jesus Christ cast me out and condemn me!......The words that I utter are not dictated by vain presumption, but by an unshaken conviction. I am willing that the Lord God withdraw his grace from me, and that every one of God's creatures refuse me his countenance, if, when a better doctrine has been shown me, I do not embrace it.

"If they despise me on account of my low estate, me a poor little mendicant friar, and if they refuse to instruct me in the way of truth, then let your highness entreat the legate to inform you in writing wherein I have erred; and if they refuse even your highness this favour, let them write their views either to his imperial majesty, or to some archbishop of Germany. What can I or what ought I to say more?

"Let your highness listen to the voice of your conscience and of your honour, and not send me to Rome. No man can require you to do so, for it is impossible I can be safe in Rome. The pope himself is not safe there. It would be commanding you to betray christian blood. They have paper, pens, and ink: they have also notaries without number. It is easy for them to write wherein and wherefore I have erred. It will cost them less to instruct me when absent by writing, than to put me to death by stratagem when among them.

"I resign myself to banishment. My adversaries are laying their snares on every side, so that I can nowhere live in security. In order that no evil may happen to you on my account, I leave your territories in God's name. I will go wherever the eternal and merciful God will have me. Let him do with me according to his pleasure!

"Thus then, most serene Elector, I reverently bid you farewell. I commend you to the everlasting God, and give you eternal thanks for all your kindness towards me.

Whatever be the people among whom I shall dwell in future, I shall ever remember you, and pray continually and gratefully for the happiness of yourself and of your family.[1] ......I am still, thanks be to God, full of joy: and praise him because Christ, the Son of God, thinks me worthy to suffer in such a cause. May he ever protect your illustrious highness! Amen."

This letter, so abounding in truth, made a deep impression on the elector. "He was shaken by a very eloquent letter," says Maimbourg. Never could he have thought of surrendering an innocent man to the hands of Rome; perhaps he would have desired Luther to conceal himself for a time, but he resolved not to appear to yield in any manner to the legate's menaces. He wrote to his councillor Pfeffinger, who was at the emperor's court, telling him to inform this prince of the real state of affairs, and to beg him to write to Rome, so that the business might be concluded, or at least that it might be settled in Germany by impartial judges.[2]

A few days after, the elector replied to the legate: "Since Doctor Martin has appeared before you at Augsburg, you should be satisfied. We did not expect that you would endeavour to make him retract, without having convinced him of his errors. None of the learned men in our principality have informed me that Martin's doctrine is impious, antichristian, or heretical." The prince refused, moreover, to send Luther to Rome, or to expel him from his states.

This letter, which was communicated to Luther, filled him with joy. "Gracious God!" wrote he to Spalatin, "with what de light I have read it again and again! I know what confidence may be put in these words, at once so forcible and moderate. I fear that the Romans will not understand their full bearing; but they will at least understand that what they think already finished is as yet hardly begun. Pray, return my thanks to the prince. It is strange that he (De Vio) who, a short time ago, was a mendicant monk like myself, does not fear to address the mightiest princes disrespectfully, to call them to account, to threaten, to command them, and to treat them with such inconceivable haughtiness. Let him learn that the temporal power is of God, and that its glory may not be trampled under foot."[3]

What had doubtless encouraged the elector to reply to the legate in a tone the latter had not expected, was a letter addressed to him by the university of Wittemberg. It had good reason to declare in the doctor's favour, for it flourished daily more and more, and was eclipsing all the other schools. A crowd of students flocked thither from all parts of Germany to hear this extraordinary man,

[1] Ego enim ubicumque ero gentium, illustrissimæ Dominationis tuæ nunquam non ero memor. L. Epp. i. 187.
[2] L. Opp. (L.) xvii. 244.
[3] Et suos non licere honores conculcari. L. Epp. i. 198.

whose teaching appeared to open a new era to religion and learning. These youths who came from every province, halted as soon as they discovered the steeples of Wittemberg in the distance; they raised their hands to heaven, and praised God for having caused the light of truth to shine forth from this city, as from Sion in times of old, and whence it spread even to the most distant countries.[1] A life and activity till then unknown animated the university. "Our students here are as busy as ants," wrote Luther.[2]

CHAPTER XI.

Thoughts on Departure—Farewell to the Church—Critical Moment—Deliverance—Luther's Courage—Dissatisfaction at Rome—Bull—Appeal to a Council.

LUTHER, imagining he might soon be expelled from Germany, was engaged in publishing a report of the Augsburg conference. He desired that it should remain as a testimony of the struggle between him and Rome. He saw the storm ready to burst, but did not fear it. He waited from day to day for the anathemas that were to be sent from Italy; and he put everything in order, that he might be prepared when they arrived. "Having tucked up my robe and girt my loins," said he, "I am ready to depart, like Abraham, without knowing whither I go; or rather well knowing, since God is every where."[3] He intended leaving a farewell letter behind him. "Be bold enough," wrote he to Spalatin, "to read the letter of an accursed and excommunicated man."

His friends felt great anxiety and fear on his account. They entreated him to deliver up himself as a prisoner into the elector's hands, in order that this prince might keep him somewhere in security.[4]

His enemies could not understand whence he derived this confidence. One day as the conversation turned upon him at the court of the Bishop of Brandenburg, and it was asked on what support he could rely: "On Erasmus," said some; "on Capito, and other learned men who are in his confidence."—"No, no," replied the bishop, "the pope would care very little about those folks. It is in the university of Wittemberg and the Duke of Saxony that he trusts." Thus both parties were ignorant of the stronghold in which the reformer had taken refuge.

Thoughts of departure passed through Luther's mind. They did not originate in fear of danger, but in foresight of the continually increasing obstacles that a free confession of the truth would meet with in Germany. "If I remain here," said he, "the liberty of speaking and writing many things will be torn from me. If I depart, I shall freely pour forth the thoughts of my heart, and devote my life to Christ."[1]

France was the country where Luther hoped to have the power of announcing the truth without opposition. The liberty enjoyed by the doctors and university of Paris, appeared to him worthy of envy. Besides, he agreed with them on many points. What would have happened had he been removed from Wittemberg to France? Would the Reformation have been established there, as in Germany? Would the power of Rome have been dethroned there; and would France, which was destined to see the hierarchical principles of Rome and the destructive principles of an irreligious philosophy long contend within her bosom, have become a great centre of evangelical light? It is useless to indulge in vain conjectures on this subject; but perhaps Luther at Paris might have changed in some degree the destinies of Europe and of France.

Luther's soul was deeply moved. He used to preach frequently in the city church, in the room of Simon Heyens Pontanus, pastor of Wittemberg, who was almost always sick. He thought it his duty, at all events, to take leave of that congregation to whom he had so frequently announced salvation. He said in the pulpit one day: "I am a very unstable and uncertain preacher. How often already have I not left you without bidding you farewell?.........If this case should happen again, and that I cannot return, accept my farewell now." Then, after adding a few words, he concluded by saying with moderation and gentleness: "Finally, I warn you not to be alarmed, should the papal censures be discharged upon me. Do not blame the pope, or bear any ill-will, either to him or to any other man; but trust all to God."[2]

The moment seemed to have come at last. The prince informed Luther that he desired him to leave Wittemberg. The wishes of the elector were too sacred for him not to hasten to comply with them. He therefore made preparations for his departure, without well knowing whither he should direct his steps. He desired however to see his friends once more around him, and with this intent prepared a farewell repast. Seated at the same table with them, he still enjoys their sweet conversation, their tender and anxious friendship. A letter is brought to him...... It comes from the court. He opens it and reads; his heart sinks; it contains a fresh order for his departure. The prince inquires, "why he delays so long." His soul was overwhelmed with sadness. Yet he resumed his courage, and raising his head, said firmly

---

[1] Scultet. Annal. i. 17.
[2] Studium nostrum more formicarum fervet. L. Epp. i. 93.
[3] Quia Deus ubique. Ibid. 188.
[4] Ut principi me in captivitatem darem. Ibid. 189.

[1] Si iero totum effundam et vitam offeram Christo. L. Epp. i. 190.
[2] Deo rem committerent. Ibid. 191.

and joyfully, as he turned his eyes on those about him: "Father and mother abandon me, but the Lord takes me up."[1] Leave he must. His friends were deeply moved.— What would become of him? If Luther's protector rejects him, who will receive him? And the Gospel, the truth, and this admirable work......all will doubtless perish with its illustrious witness. The Reformation seems to hang upon a thread, and at the moment Luther quits the walls of Wittemberg, will not this thread break? Luther and his friends said little. Struck with the blow that had fallen upon their brother, tears roll down their cheeks. But shortly after, a new messenger arrives. Luther opens the letter, not doubting that it contains a fresh order. But, O powerful hand of the Lord! for a time he is saved. Everything is changed. "Since the pope's new envoy hopes that all may be arranged by a conference, remain for the present."[2] How important was this hour! and what would have happened if Luther, ever anxious to obey his sovereign's will, had left Wittemberg immediately on receiving the first letter? Never were Luther and the cause of the Reformation lower than at this moment. It appeared that their fate was decided: an instant sufficed to change it. Having reached the lowest degree of his career, the Wittemberg doctor rose rapidly, and his influence from this time continued increasing. The Almighty commands (in the language of the prophet), and his servants go down to the depths, and mount up again to heaven.

By Frederick's order, Spalatin summoned Luther to Lichtemberg, to have an interview with him. They conversed a long time on the situation of affairs. "If the censures arrive from Rome," said Luther, "certainly I shall not stay at Wittemberg."—"Beware," said Spalatin, "of being too precipitate in going to France!"[3] He left him, telling him to wait for further orders. "Only commend my soul to Christ," said Luther to his friends. "I see that my adversaries are still more determined in their designs to ruin me; but meanwhile Christ strengthens me in my resolution to concede nothing."[4]

Luther now published his *Report of the Conference at Augsburg*. Spalatin had written to him, on the part of the elector, not to do so; but the letter came too late. As soon as the publication had taken place, the prince gave his sanction: "Great God!" said Luther in his preface, "what a new, what an amazing crime to seek for light and truth! ......and above all in the Church, that is to say, in the kingdom of truth."—"I send you my *Report*," wrote he to Link: "it is keener no doubt than the legate expects; but my pen is ready to produce much greater things.

I do not know myself whence these thoughts arise. In my opinion, the work is not yet begun,[1] so far are the great ones at Rome mistaken in looking for the end. I will send you what I have written, in order that you may judge whether I have guessed rightly that the Antichrist of whom St. Paul speaks now reigns in the court of Rome. I think I shall be able to show that he is worse now-a-days than the Turks themselves.

Sinister reports reached Luther from every side. One of his friends wrote to him that the new envoy from Rome had received an order to lay hold of him and deliver him up to the pope. Another related, that while travelling he had met with a courtier, and that the conversation turning on the matters that were now occupying all Germany, the latter declared that he had undertaken to deliver Luther into the hands of the sovereign pontiff. "But the more their fury and their violence increase," wrote the reformer, "the less I tremble."[2]

At Rome they were much displeased with Cajetan. The vexation felt at the ill-success of this business was at first vented on him. The Roman courtiers thought they had reason to reproach him for having been deficient in that prudence and address which, if we must believe them, were the chief qualities in a legate, and for not having relaxed, on so important an occasion, the strictness of his scholastic theology. It is all his fault, said they. His clumsy pedantry spoiled all. Why did he exasperate Luther by insults and threats, instead of alluring him by the promise of a rich bishopric, or even of a cardinal's hat?[3] These mercenaries judged of the reformer by themselves. Still the failure must be retrieved. On the one hand, Rome must declare herself; on the other, she must conciliate the elector, who might be very serviceable to her in the choice they would soon have to make of an emperor. As it was impossible for Roman ecclesiastics to suspect whence Luther derived his courage and his strength, they imagined that the elector was implicated more deeply in the affair than he really was. The pope therefore resolved to pursue another course. He caused a bull to be published in Germany by his legate, in which he confirmed the doctrine of indulgences, precisely in the points attacked, but in which he made no mention either of Luther or of the elector. As the reformer had always declared that he would submit to the decision of the Roman church, the pope imagined that he would now either keep his word, or exhibit himself openly as a disturber of the peace of the Church, and a contemner of the holy apostolic see. In either case, the pope could not but gain; no advantage however is derived by obstinately opposing the

---

[1] Vater und Mutter verlassen mich, aber der Herr nimmt mich auf.
[2] L. Opp. xv. 824.
[3] Ne tam cito in Galliam irem. L. Epp. 1. 195.
[4] Firmat Christus propositum non cedendi in me. Ibid.

[1] Res ista necdum habet initium suum meo judicio. L. Epp. i. 193.
[2] Quo illi magis furunt, et vi affectant viam eo minus ego terreor. Ibid. 191.
[3] Sarpi, Council of Trent, p. 8.

truth. In vain had the pope threatened with excommunication whoever should teach otherwise than he ordained ; the light is not stopped by such orders. It would have been wiser to moderate by certain restrictions the pretensions of the sellers of indulgences. This decree from Rome was therefore a new fault. By legalizing crying abuses, it irritated all wise men, and rendered Luther's reconciliation impossible. " It was thought," says a Roman-catholic historian, a great enemy to the Reformation,[1] " that this bull had been issued solely for the benefit of the pope and the begging friars, who began to find that no one would purchase their indulgences."

Cardinal De Vio published the decree at Lintz, in Austria, on the 13th December 1518 ; but Luther had already placed himself beyond its reach. On the 28th November, he had appealed, in the chapel of *Corpus Christi*, at Wittemberg, from the pope to a general council of the Church. He foresaw the storm that was about to burst upon him ; he knew that God alone could disperse it ; but he did what it was his duty to do. He must, no doubt, quit Wittemberg, if only on the elector's account, as soon as the Roman anathemas arrive : he would not, however, leave Saxony and Germany without a striking protest. He therefore drew one up, and that it might be ready for circulation as soon

as the Roman thunders reached him, as he expresses it, he had it printed under the express condition that the bookseller should deposit all the copies with him. But this man, covetous of gain, sold almost every one, while Luther was calmly waiting to receive them. The doctor was vexed, but the thing was done. This bold protest was soon circulated every where. In it Luther declared anew that he had no intention of saying any thing against the holy Church or the authority of the apostolic see, and of the pope when well-advised. " But," continues he, " seeing that the pope, who is God's vicar upon earth, may, like any other man, err, sin, and lie, and that an appeal to a general council is the only means of safety against that injustice which it is impossible to resist, I am obliged to have recourse to this step."[1]

Here we see the Reformation launched on a new career. It is no longer made dependent on the pope and on his resolutions, but on a general council. Luther addresses the whole Church, and the voice that proceeds from the chapel of *Corpus Christi* must be heard throughout all the Lord's fold. The reformer is not wanting in courage ; of this he has just given a new proof. Will God be wanting to him ? This we shall learn from the different periods of the Reformation that still remain to be displayed before our eyes.

[1] Maimbourg, p. 38.

[1] Löscher. Ref. Act.

HISTORY OF THE REFORMATION.

VOLUME SECOND.

BOOK V.

THE LEIPSIC DISPUTATION.—1519.

CHAPTER I.

Luther's Danger—God preserves Luther—The Pope sends a Chamberlain — The Legate's Journey — Roman Briefs — Circumstances favourable to the Reform—Miltitz with Spalatin—Tetzel's Alarm—Miltitz's Flattery—Demands a Retractation—Luther refuses, but offers to keep Silence —Agreement between Luther and the Nuncio—The Legate's Kiss—Tetzel reproached by the Legate—Luther to the Pope—Nature of the Reformation—Luther opposes Separation—De Vio and Miltitz at Treves—Luther's Cause extends over various Countries—Luther's Writings begin the Reformation.

DANGERS had gathered round Luther and the Reformation. The appeal of the Wittemberg doctor to a general council was a new assault upon the papal power. A bull of Pius II. had pronounced the greater excommunication even against the emperors who should dare be guilty of such an act of revolt. Frederick of Saxony, as yet weak in the evangelical doctrine, was ready to banish Luther from his states.[1] A new message from Leo X. would therefore have driven the reformer among strangers, who might have feared to compromise themselves by receiving a monk lying under the anathema of Rome. And if any of the nobles had drawn the sword in his defence, these simple knights, despised by the mighty princes of Germany, would soon have been crushed in their perilous enterprise.

But at the very moment that the courtiers of Leo X. were urging him to measures of severity, and when another blow would have placed his adversary in his hands, this pope suddenly changed his policy, and entered upon a course of conciliation and apparent

mildness.[1] We may reasonably presume that he was deceived as to the elector's sentiments, and thought them more favourable to Luther than they really were; we may admit that the public voice and the spirit of the age—powers then quite new—appeared to surround Luther with an impregnable rampart; we may suppose, as one of his historians has done,[2] that he followed the impulses of his judgment and of his heart, which inclined to mildness and moderation; but this new mode of action, adopted by Rome at such a moment, is so strange, that it is impossible not to recognise in it a higher and a mightier hand.

A Saxon noble, the pope's chamberlain, and canon of Mentz, Treves, and Meissen, was then at the Roman court. He had contrived to make himself of importance. He boasted of being distantly related to the Saxon princes, so that the Roman courtiers sometimes gave him the title of Duke of Saxony. In Italy, he made a foolish display of his German nobility; in Germany, he was an awkward imitator of the elegance and manners of the Italians. He was fond of wine,[3] and his residence at the court of Rome had increased this vice. The Roman courtiers, however, entertained great expectations of him. His German origin, his insinuating manners, his skill in business,— all led them to hope that Charles of Miltitz (for such was his name) would by his pru-

[1] Letter from the Elector to his envoy at Rome. L. Opp. (L.) xvii. 298.

[1] Rationem agendi prorsus oppositam inire statuit. Cardinal Pallavicini, Hist. Concil. Trident. i. 51.
[2] Roscoe, Life of Leo X., chap. xix.
[3] Nec ab usu immoderato vini abstinuit. Pallavicini, Hist. Concil. Trid. i. 69.

dence succeed in arresting the mighty revolution that threatened to shake the world.

It was of importance to conceal the real object of the mission of the Roman chamberlain. This was effected without difficulty. Four years previously, the pious elector had petitioned the pope for the Golden Rose. This rose, the most beautiful of flowers, represented the body of Jesus Christ; it was consecrated yearly by the sovereign pontiff, and sent to one of the chief princes in Europe. It was resolved to give it this year to the elector. Miltitz departed with a commission to examine the state of affairs, and to gain over Spalatin and Pfeffinger, the elector's councillors. He carried private letters for them. In this manner, by seeking to conciliate those who surrounded the prince, Rome hoped erelong to have her formidable adversary in her power.

The new legate, who arrived in Germany in December 1518, was engaged during his journey in sounding the public opinion. To his great surprise he found, that wherever he went, the majority of the inhabitants were partisans of the Reformation.[1] They spoke of Luther with enthusiasm. For one person favourable to the pope, there were three favourable to the reformer.[2] Luther has transmitted to us one of the incidents of his mission. "What do you think of the papal chair?" the legate would frequently ask the landladies and maidservants at the inns. On one occasion one of these poor women artlessly replied: "What can we know of the papal chair, whether it is of wood or of stone?"[3]

The mere rumour of the new legate's arrival filled the elector's court, the university and town of Wittemberg, and the whole of Saxony, with suspicion and distrust. "Thanks be to God, Luther is still alive," wrote Melancthon in affright.[4] It was affirmed that the Roman legate had received orders to get Luther into his power either by violence or stratagem. Every one recommended the doctor to be on his guard against the treachery of Miltitz. "He is coming," said they, "to seize you and give you up to the pope. Trustworthy persons have seen the briefs he is bringing with him."—"I await God's will," replied Luther.[5]

Miltitz indeed came bearing letters for the elector, for his councillors, and for the bishops and the burgomaster of Wittemberg. He brought with him seventy apostolical briefs. If the flattery and the favours of Rome attained their end,—if Frederick delivered Luther into his hands, these seventy briefs were, in some measure, to serve as passports.

He would produce and post up one in each of the cities through which he would have to pass, and by this means he hoped to succeed in dragging his prisoner to Rome without opposition.[1]

The pope appeared to have taken every precaution. Already in the electoral court they did not know what course to adopt. They would have resisted violence; but how could they oppose the head of Christendom, who spoke with so much mildness, and with so great an appearance of reason? Would it not be desirable, they said, for Luther to conceal himself, until the storm had passed over? An unexpected event extricated Luther, the elector, and the Reformation, from this difficult position. The aspect of the world suddenly changed.

On the 12th of January 1519, Maximilian. emperor of Germany, expired. Frederick of Saxony, in conformity with the Germanic constitution, became administrator of the empire. Henceforth the elector no longer feared the projects of nuncios. New interests began to agitate the court of Rome, which forced it to be cautious in its negotiations with Frederick, and arrested the blow that Miltitz and De Vio undoubtedly were meditating.

The pope earnestly desired to prevent Charles of Austria, already king of Naples, from filling the imperial throne. He thought that a neighbouring king was more to be feared than a German monk. Desirous of securing the elector. who might be of great use to him in this affair, he resolved to let the monk rest, that he might the better oppose the king; but both advanced in despite of him. Thus changed Leo X.

Another circumstance also contributed to turn aside the storm that threatened the Reformation. Political troubles broke out immediately after Maximilian's death. In the south of the empire, the Swabian confederation desired to punish Ulric of Wurtemberg, who had been unfaithful to it; in the north, the Bishop of Hildesheim threw himself with an armed force upon the bishopric of Minden and on the territories of the Duke of Brunswick. In the midst of all this agitation, how could the great ones of the age attach any importance to a dispute about the remission of sins? But God especially advanced the cause of the Reformation by the wisdom of the elector, now become vicar of the empire, and by the protection he granted to the new teachers. "The tempest suspended its rage," says Luther, "the papal excommunication began to fall into contempt. Under the shadow of the elector's viceroyalty, the Gospel circulated far and wide, and popery suffered great damage in consequence."[2]

Besides, during an interregnum the severest prohibitions naturally lost their force.

---

[1] Seiscitatus per viam Miltitzius quanam esset in æstimatione Lutherus....sensit de eo cum admiratione homines loqui. Pallavicini, Hist. Concil. Trid. i. 51.
[2] Ecce ubi unum pro papa stare inveni, tres pro te contra papam stabant. L. Opp. Lat. in Præf.
[3] Quid nos scire possumus quales vos Romæ habeatis sellas, ligneasne an lapideas? Ibid.
[4] Martinus noster, Deo gratias, adhuc spirat. Corpus Reformatorum edidit Bretschneider, i. 61.
[5] Expecto consilium Dei. L. Epp. i. 191.

[1] Per singula oppida affigeret unum, et ita tutus me per duceret Romam. L. Opp. Lat. in Præf.
[2] Tunc desiit paululum sævire tempestas, &c. Ibid.

All became easier and more free. The ray of liberty that shone upon these beginnings of the Reformation powerfully developed the yet tender plant ; and already it might have been seen how favourable political liberty would be to the progress of evangelical Christianity.

Miltitz, who had reached Saxony before the death of Maximilian, had hastened to visit his old friend Spalatin ; but he had no sooner begun his complaints against Luther, than Spalatin broke out against Tetzel. He made the nuncio acquainted with the falsehoods and blasphemies of the indulgence-merchant, and declared that all Germany ascribed to the Dominican the divisions by which the Church was rent.

Miltitz was astonished. Instead of being the accuser, he found himself the accused. All his anger was immediately directed against Tetzel. He summoned him to appear at Altenburg and justify his conduct.

The Dominican, as cowardly as he was boastful, fearing the people whom his impositions had exasperated, had discontinued passing from town to town, and had hidden himself in the college of St. Paul at Leipsic. He turned pale on receiving Miltitz's letter. Even Rome abandons him ; she threatens and condemns him ; she wishes to draw him from the only asylum in which he thinks himself secure, and to expose him to the anger of his enemies. Tetzel refused to obey the nuncio's summons. " Certainly," wrote he to Miltitz on the 31st of December 1518, " I should not care about the fatigue of the journey, if I could leave Leipsic without danger to my life ; but the Augustine Martin Luther has so excited and aroused the men of power against me, that I am nowhere safe. A great number of Luther's partisans have sworn my death ; I cannot, therefore, come to you." [1] What a striking contrast is here between these two men, the one residing in the college of St. Paul at Leipsic, the other in the Augustine cloister at Wittemberg ! The servant of God displayed an intrepid courage in the presence of danger ; the servant of men, a contemptible cowardice.

Miltitz had been ordered to employ persuasive measures in the first instance ; and it was only when these failed that he was to produce his seventy briefs, and at the same time make use of all the favours of Rome to induce the elector to restrain Luther. He therefore intimated his desire to have an interview with the reformer. Their common friend, Spalatin, offered his house for that purpose, and Luther quitted Wittemberg on the 2d or 3d of January to visit Altenburg.

In this interview Miltitz exhausted all the cunning of a diplomatist and of a Roman courtier. Luther had scarcely arrived when the nuncio approached him with great demonstrations of friendship. " Oh !" thought Luther, " how his violence is changed into gentleness ! This new Saul came to Germany, armed with more than seventy apostolical briefs, to drag me alive and in chains to that murderous Rome ; but the Lord has thrown him to the ground by the way." [1]

" My dear Martin," said the pope's chamberlain, in a fawning tone, " I thought you were an old theologian who, seated quietly at his fireside, was labouring under some theological crotchet ; but I see you are still a young man and in the prime of life. [2] Do you know," continued he, assuming a graver tone, " that you have drawn away everybody from the pope and attached them to yourself ?" [3] Miltitz was not ignorant that the best way of seducing mankind is to flatter their pride ; but he did not know the man he had to deal with. " If I had an army of 25,000 men," added he, " I do not think I should be able to carry you to Rome." [4] Rome with all her power was sensible of her weakness compared with this poor monk ; and the monk felt strong compared with Rome. " God stays the waves of the sea upon the shore," said Luther, " and he stays them—with sand !" [5]

The nuncio, believing he had now prepared his adversary's mind, continued in these terms : " Bind up the wound that you yourself have inflicted on the Church, and that you alone can heal. Beware," said he, dropping a few tears, " beware of raising a tempest that would cause the destruction of Christendom." [6] He then gradually proceeded to hint that a retractation alone could repair the mischief ; but he immediately softened down whatever was objectionable in this word, by giving Luther to understand that he felt the highest esteem for him, and by storming against Tetzel. The snare was laid by a skilful hand : how could it fail to catch the prey ? " If, at the outset, the Archbishop of Mentz had spoken to me in this manner," said the reformer afterwards, " this business would not have created so much disturbance." [7]

Luther then replied, and set forth with calmness, but with dignity and force, the just complaints of the Church ; he did not conceal his great indignation against the Archbishop of Mentz, and complained in a noble manner of the unworthy treatment he had received from Rome, notwithstanding the purity of his intentions. Miltitz, who had not expected to hear such decided language, was able however to suppress his anger.

[1] Sed per viam a Domino prostratus......mutavit violentiam in benevolentiam fallacissime simulatam. L. Epp. i. 206.
[2] O Martine, ego credebam te esse senem aliquem theologum, qui post fornacem sedens (sitting behind the stove), &c. L. Opp. Lat. in Præf.
[3] Quod orbem totum mihi conjunxerim et papæ abstraxerim. L. Epp. i. 231.
[4] Si haberem xxv. millia armatorum, non confiderem te posse a me Romam perduci. L. Opp. Lat. in Præf.
[5] L. Opp. (W.) xxii.
[6] Profusis lacrymis ipsum oravit, ne tam perniciosam Christiano generi tempestatem cieret. Pallavicini, i. 52.
[7] Non evasisset res in tantum tumultum. L. Opp. Lat. in Præf.

[1] Löscher, ii. 567.

" I offer," resumed Luther, " to be silent for the future on this matter, and to let it die away of itself,[1] provided my opponents are silent on their part; but if they continue attacking me, a serious struggle will soon arise out of a trifling quarrel. My weapons are quite prepared."—" I will do still more," he added a moment after; " I will write to his holiness, acknowledging I have been a little too violent, and I will declare to him that it is as a faithful son of the Church that I opposed discourses which drew upon them the mockeries and insults of the people. I even consent to publish a writing desiring all those who read my works not to see in them any attacks upon the Roman Church, and to continue under its authority. Yes! I am willing to do and to bear everything; but as for a retractation. never expect one from me."

Miltitz saw by Luther's firm tone that the wisest course would be to appear satisfied with what the reformer so readily promised. He merely proposed they should choose an archbishop to arbitrate on some points that were still to be discussed. " Be it so," said Luther; " but I am very much afraid that the pope will not accept any judge; in that case I will not abide by the pope's decision, and then the struggle will begin again. The pope will give the text, and I shall make my own comments upon it."

Thus ended the first interview between Luther and Miltitz. They had a second meeting, in which the truce or rather the peace was signed. Luther immediately informed the elector of what had taken place. " Most serene prince and most gracious lord," wrote he, I hasten most humbly to acquaint your electoral highness that Charles of Miltitz and myself are at last agreed, and have terminated this matter by deciding upon the following articles :—

1. Both parties are forbidden to preach, write, or do anything further in the discussion that has been raised.

2. Miltitz will immediately inform the holy Father of the state of affairs. His holiness will empower an enlightened bishop to investigate the matter, and to point out the erroneous articles I should retract. If they prove me to be in error I shall willingly recant, and will do nothing derogatory to the honour or authority of the holy Roman Church."[2]

When the agreement had been thus effected, Miltitz appeared overjoyed. " These hundred years past," exclaimed he, " no question has occasioned more anxiety to the cardinals and Roman courtiers than this. They would rather have given ten thousand ducats than consent to its being prolonged."[3] The pope's chamberlain spared no marks

of attention to the monk of Wittemberg. At one time he manifested his joy, at another he shed tears. This show of sensibility moved the reformer but little; still he avoided showing what he thought of it. " I pretended not to understand the meaning of these crocodile's tears," said he.[1]

Miltitz gave Luther an invitation to supper, which the latter accepted. His host laid aside all the severity connected with his mission, and Luther indulged in all the cheerfulness of his disposition. The repast was joyous,[2] and when the moment of departure was come, the legate opened his arms to the heretical doctor, and kissed him.[3] " A Judas kiss," thought Luther; " I pretended not to understand these Italian artifices," wrote he to Staupitz.[4]

Was that kiss destined to reconcile Rome and the dawning Reformation? Miltitz hoped so, and was delighted at the thought; for he had a nearer view than the Roman courtiers of the terrible consequences the papacy might suffer from the Reformation. If Luther and his adversaries are silenced, thought he, the dispute will be ended; and Rome, by calling up favourable circumstances, will regain all her former influence. It appeared, then, that the termination of the contest was at hand. Rome had opened her arms, and the reformer seemed to have cast himself into them. But this work was not of man, but of God. The error of Rome lay in regarding as a mere monkish quarrel what was in reality an awakening of the Church. The kisses of a papal chamberlain could not check the renewal of Christendom.

Miltitz being of opinion that he would by this means reclaim the erring Lutherans, behaved most graciously to all of them, accepted their invitations, and sat down to table with the heretics; but soon becoming inebriated (it is a pope who relates this),[5] the pontifical nuncio was no longer master of his tongue. The Saxons led him to speak of the pope and the court of Rome, and Miltitz, confirming the old proverb, *in vino veritas*,[6] gave an account in the openness of his heart of all the practices and disorders of the papacy.[7] His companions smiled, urging and pressing him to continue; everything was exposed; they took notes of what he said; and these scandals were afterwards made matter of public reproach against the Romans. at the Diet of Worms, in the presence of all Germany. Pope Paul III. com-

1 Und die Sache sich zu Tode bluten. L. Epp. i. 207.
2 Ibid. 209.
3 Ab integro jam sæculo nullum negotium Ecclesiæ contigisse quod majorem illi solicitudinem incussisset. Pallavicini, i. 52.

1 Ego dissimulabam has crocodili lacrymas a me intelligi. L. Epp. i. 216. The crocodile is said to weep when he cannot seize his prey.
2 Atque vesperi, me accepto, convivio lætati sumus. Ibid. 231.
3 Sic amice discessimus etiam cum osculo (Judæ scilicet). Ibid. 216.
4 Has italitates. Ibid. 231.
5 Sæpe perturbatos vino. Instructio data episcopo Mutinæ Pauli III. nuntio, 24th October 1536. The MS. was discovered by Ranke in a library at Rome.
6 When the wine is in, the wit comes out. Old Eng. Prov.
7 Ea effutire de pontifice et Romana curia a Saxonibus inducebatur. Instructio, &c.

plained, alleging they had put things in his envoy's mouth that were utterly destitute of foundation, and in consequence ordered his nuncios, whenever they were invited out, to make a pretence of accepting the invitations, to behave graciously, and to be guarded in their conversation.[1]

Miltitz, faithful to the arrangement he had just concluded, went from Altenburg to Leipsic, where Tetzel was residing. There was no necessity to silence him, for sooner than speak he would have concealed himself if possible in the centre of the earth. But the nuncio resolved to vent all his anger on him. As soon as he reached Leipsic, he summoned the wretched Tetzel before him, overwhelmed him with reproaches, accused him of being the author of all his trouble, and threatened him with the pope's displeasure.[2] This was not enough. An agent from the house of Fugger, who was then in the city, was confronted with him. Miltitz laid before the Dominican the accounts of this establishment, the papers he had himself signed, and proved that he had squandered or stolen considerable sums of money. The unhappy man, whom in the day of his triumph nothing could alarm, bent under the weight of these just accusations: he fell into despair, his health suffered, he knew not where to hide his shame. Luther was informed of the wretched condition of his old adversary, and he alone was affected by it. "I am sorry for Tetzel," wrote he to Spalatin.[3] He did not confine himself to words: it was not the man but his actions that he hated. At the very moment that Rome was venting her wrath on the Dominican, Luther sent him a letter full of consolation. But all was unavailing. Tetzel, a prey to remorse, terrified by the reproaches of his best friends, and dreading the pope's anger, died very miserably not long after. It was believed that grief accelerated his death.[4]

Luther, in accordance with the promise he had given Miltitz, wrote the following letter to the pope on the 3d March:—

"Blessed Father! May your holiness condescend to incline your paternal ear, which is that of Christ himself, towards your poor sheep, and listen kindly to his bleating. What shall I do, most holy Father? I cannot bear the lightnings of your anger, and I know not how to escape them. I am called upon to retract. I would most readily do so, could that lead to the desired result. But the persecutions of my adversaries have circulated my writings far and wide, and they are too deeply graven on the hearts of men, to be by any possibility erazed. A recantation would only still more dishonour the Church of Rome, and draw from the lips of all a cry of accusation against her. Most holy Father! I declare in the presence of God and of all His creatures, that I have never desired, and that I shall never desire, to weaken, either by force or stratagem, the power of the Roman Church or of your holiness. I confess that nothing in heaven or in earth should be preferred above that Church, except Jesus Christ alone—the Lord of all."[1]

These words might appear strange and even reprehensible in Luther's mouth, did we not remember that he reached the light not suddenly, but by a slow and progressive course. They are a very important evidence, that the Reformation was not simply an opposition to the papacy, it was not a war waged against certain forms; nor was it the result of a merely negative tendency. Opposition to the pope was in the second line of the battle: a new life, a positive doctrine was the generating principle. "Jesus Christ, the Lord of all, and who must be preferred above all," even above Rome itself, as Luther writes at the end of his letter, was the essential cause of the Revolution of the sixteenth century.

It is probable that shortly before this time the pope would not have passed over unnoticed a letter in which the monk of Wittemberg plainly refused to retract. But Maximilian was dead: men's minds were occupied with the choice of his successor, and in the midst of the intrigues which then agitated the pontifical city, Luther's letter was disregarded.

The reformer made a better use of his time than his powerful adversary. Whilst Leo X. was occupied with his interests as a temporal prince, and was making every exertion to exclude a formidable neighbour from the throne, Luther grew each day in knowledge and in faith. He studied the papal decrees, and the discoveries he made therein greatly modified his ideas. "I am reading the decrees of the pontiffs," wrote he to Spalatin, "and (I whisper this in your ear) I do not know whether the pope is Antichrist himself or his apostle,[2] so greatly is Christ misrepresented and crucified in them."

Yet he still felt esteem for the ancient Church of Rome, and had no thought of separating from it. "That the Roman Church," said he in the explanation which he had promised Miltitz to publish, "is honoured by God above all others is what we cannot doubt. Saint Peter, Saint Paul, forty-six popes, many hundreds of thousands of martyrs, have shed their blood in its bosom, and have overcome hell and the world, so that God's eye regards it with especial favour. Although every thing is now in a very

[1] Hilari quidem vultu accipere si *fingant* invitationes. Instructio, &c.
[2] Verbis minisque pontificiis ita fregit hominem hactenus, terribilem cunctis et imperterritum stentorem. L. Opp. in Præf.
[3] Doleo Tetzelium. L. Epp. i. 223.
[4] Sed conscientia indignitate Papæ forte occubuit. L. Opp. in Præf.

[1] Præter unum Jesum Christum Dominum omnium. L Epp. i. 234.
[2] Nescio an Papa sit Antichristus ipse vel apostolus ejus. Ibid. 239.

wretched state there, this is not a sufficient reason for separating from it. On the contrary, the worse things are going on within it, the more should we cling to it; for it is not by separation that we shall make it better. We must not desert God on account of the devil; or abandon the children of God who are still in the Roman communion, because of the multitude of the ungodly. There is no sin, there is no evil that should destroy charity or break the bond of union. For charity can do all things, and to unity nothing is difficult."[1]

It was not Luther who separated from Rome: it was Rome that separated from Luther, and thus rejected the ancient faith of the Catholic Church, of which he was then the representative. It was not Luther who deprived Rome of her power, and made her bishop descend from a throne which he had usurped: the doctrines he proclaimed, the word of the apostles which God manifested anew in the Universal Church with great power and admirable purity, could alone prevail against that dominion which had for centuries enslaved the Church.

These declarations, which were published by Luther at the end of February, did not entirely satisfy Miltitz and De Vio. These two vultures, who had both seen their prey escape from their talons, had retired within the ancient walls of Treves. There, assisted by the prince-archbishop, they hoped to accomplish together the object in which each of them had failed separately. The two nuncios felt clearly that nothing more was to be expected from Frederick, now invested with supreme power in the empire. They saw that Luther persisted in his refusal to retract. The only means of success were to deprive the heretical monk of the elector's protection, and entice him into their hands. Once at Treves, in the states of an ecclesiastical prince, the reformer will be very skilful if he escapes without having fully satisfied the demands of the sovereign pontiff. They immediately applied themselves to the task. "Luther," said Miltitz to the Elector-archbishop of Treves, "has accepted your Grace as arbitrator. Summon him before you." The Elector of Treves accordingly wrote on the 3d May to the Elector of Saxony, requesting him to send Luther to him. De Vio, and afterwards Miltitz himself, wrote also to Frederick, informing him that the Golden Rose had arrived at Augsburg. This (thought they) is the moment for striking a decisive blow.

But circumstances had changed: neither Frederick nor Luther permitted himself to be shaken. The elector comprehended his new position. He no longer feared the pope, much less his agents. The reformer, seeing Miltitz and De Vio united, foresaw the fate that awaited him if he complied with their invitation. "Everywhere," said he, "and in every manner they seek after my life."[1] Besides, he had appealed to the pope, and the pope, busied in intrigues with crowned heads, had not replied. Luther wrote to Miltitz: "How can I set out without an order from Rome, in the midst of the troubles by which the Empire is agitated? How can I encounter so many dangers, and incur such heavy expense, seeing that I am the poorest of men?"

The Elector of Treves, a prudent and moderate man, and a friend of Frederick's, was desirous of keeping on good terms with the latter. Besides, he had no desire to interfere in this matter, unless he was positively called upon. He therefore arranged with the Elector of Saxony to put off the inquiry until the next diet, which did not take place until two years after, when it assembled at Worms.

Whilst a providential hand thus warded off, one by one, the dangers by which Luther was threatened, he himself was boldly advancing towards a goal which he did not suspect. His reputation increased; the cause of truth grew in strength; the number of students at Wittemberg was augmented. and among them were the most distinguished young men of Germany. "Our town." wrote Luther. "can hardly receive all those who are flocking to it;"—and on another occasion: "The number of students increases considerably, like an overflowing river."[2]

But it was no longer in Germany alone that the reformer's voice was heard. It had passed the frontiers of the empire, and begun to shake, among the different nations of Europe, the foundations of the Romish power. Frobenius, a celebrated printer at Basle, had published a collection of Luther's works. It was rapidly circulated. At Basle. the bishop himself commended Luther. The cardinal of Sion, after reading his works, exclaimed with a slight tone of irony, playing upon his name: "O Luther! thou art a real Luther!"[3]

Erasmus was at Louvain when Luther's writings reached the Low Countries. The prior of the Augustines of Antwerp, who had studied at Wittemberg, and who, according to the testimony of Erasmus, was a follower of true primitive Christianity, read them with eagerness, as did other Belgians. But those who consulted their own interests only, remarks the sage of Rotterdam, and who fed the people with old wives' tales, broke out into gloomy fanaticism. "I cannot describe to you," wrote Erasmus to Luther, "the emotion, the truly tragic sensation which your writings have occasioned."[4]

Frobenius sent six hundred copies of these

[1] L Opp. L. xvii. 224.

[1] Video ubique, undique, quocumque modo, animam meam quæri. L. Epp. i. 274. May 16.
[2] Sicut aqua inundans. Ibid. 278, 279.
[3] Lauterer, purifier, refiner.
[4] Nullo sermone consequi queam, quas tragœdias hic excitarint tui libelli. Erasm. Epp. vi. 4.

works into France and Spain. They were sold publicly in Paris. The doctors of the Sorbonne, as it would appear, read them with approbation. "It is high time," said some of them, "that those who devote themselves to biblical studies should speak out freely." In England these books were received with still greater eagerness. Some Spanish merchants translated them into their mother-tongue, and forwarded them from Antwerp to their own country. "Certainly these merchants must have been of Moorish descent," says Pallavicini. [1]

Calvi, a learned bookseller of Pavia, carried a great number of copies to Italy, and circulated them in all the transalpine cities. It was not the love of gain that inspired this man of letters, but a desire of contributing to the revival of piety. The energy with which Luther maintained the cause of Christ filled him with joy. "All the learned men of Italy," wrote he, "will unite with me, and we will send you verses composed by our most distinguished writers."

Frobenius, in transmitting a copy of his publication to Luther, related all these joyful tidings, and added : "I have sold every copy, except ten; and I have never made so good a speculation." Other letters informed Luther of the joy caused by his works. "I am delighted," said he, "that the truth is so pleasing, although she speaks with so little learning and in so barbarous a tone." [2]

Such was the commencement of the awakening in the various countries of Europe. If we except Switzerland, and even France, where the Gospel had already been preached, the arrival of the Wittemberg doctor's writings every where forms the first page in the history of the Reformation. A printer of Basle scattered the first germs of truth. At the very moment when the Roman pontiff thought to stifle the work in Germany, it began in France, the Low Countries, Italy, Spain, England, and Switzerland. What matters it, even should Rome cut down the parent stem ?......the seeds are already scattered over every land.

CHAPTER II.

Pause in Germany—Eck revives the Contest—Disputation between Eck and Carlstadt—Question of the Pope—Luther replies—Fears of Luther's Friends—Luther's Courage—The Truth triumphs unaided—Refusal of Duke George—Gaiety of Mosellanus—Fears of Erasmus.

WHILE the combat was beginning beyond the confines of the empire, it appeared dying away within. The most impetuous of the

Roman champions, the Franciscans of Juterböck, who had imprudently attacked Luther, had hastily become silent after the reformer's vigorous reply. The papal partisans were mute : Tetzel was no longer in a condition to fight. Luther was entreated by his friends not to continue the discussion, and he had promised compliance. The theses were passing into oblivion. This treacherous peace rendered the eloquence of the reformer powerless. The Reformation appeared checked. "But," said Luther somewhat later, when speaking of this epoch, "men imagine vain things; for the Lord awoke to judge the people. [1]—God does not guide me," he said in another place; "he pushes me forward, he carries me away. I am not master of myself. I desire to live in repose; but I am thrown into the midst of tumults and revolutions." [2]

Eck the scholastic, Luther's old friend, and author of the *Obelisks*, was the man who recommended the combat. He was sincerely attached to the papacy, but seems to have had no true religious sentiments, and to have been one of that class of men, so numerous in every age, who look upon science, and even theology and religion, as the means of acquiring worldly reputation. Vain glory lies hid under the priest's cassock no less than under the warrior's coat of mail. Eck had studied the art of disputation according to the rules of the schoolmen, and had become a master in this sort of controversy. While the knights of the middle ages and the warriors in the time of the Reformation sought for glory in the tournament, the schoolmen struggled for it in syllogistic disputations,—a spectacle of frequent occurrence in the universities. Eck, who entertained no mean idea of himself, and who was proud of his talents, of the popularity of his cause, and of the victories he had gained in eight universities of Hungary, Lombardy, and Germany, ardently desired to have an opportunity of trying his strength and skill against the reformer. He had spared no exertion to acquire the reputation of being one of the most learned men of the age. He was constantly endeavouring to excite some new discussion, to make a sensation, and aimed at procuring, by means of his exploits, all the enjoyments of life. A journey that he had made to Italy had been, according to his own account, one long series of triumphs. The most learned scholars had been forced to subscribe to his theses. This experienced gladiator fixed his eyes on a new field of battle, in which he thought the victory already secure. The *little monk* who had suddenly grown into a giant,—that Luther, whom hitherto no one had been able to vanquish, galled his pride

---

[1] Maurorum stirpe prognatis. Pallav. i. 91.
[2] In his id gaudeo, quod veritas tam barbare et indocte oquens, adeo placet. L. Epp. i. 255.

[1] Dominus evigilavit et stat ad judicandos populos. L. Opp. Lat. in Præf.
[2] Deus rapuit, pellit, nedum ducit me : non sum compos mei ; volo esse quietus et rapior in medios tumultus. L. Epp. i. 231.

and excited his jealousy.[1] Perhaps in seeking his own glory, Eck might ruin Rome. But his scholastic vanity was not to be checked by such a consideration. Theologians, as well as princes, have more than once sacrificed the general interest to their personal glory. We shall see what circumstances afforded the Ingoldstadt doctor the means of entering the lists with his importunate rival.

The zealous but too ardent Carlstadt was still on friendly terms with Luther. These two theologians were closely united by their attachment to the doctrine of grace, and by their admiration for Saint Augustine. Carlstadt was inclined to enthusiasm, and possessed little discretion: he was not a man to be restrained by the skill and policy of a Miltitz. He had published some theses in reply to Dr. Eck's *Obelisks*, in which he defended Luther and their common faith. Eck had answered him; but Carlstadt did not let him have the last word.[2] The discussion grew warm. Eck, desirous of profiting by so favourable an opportunity, had thrown down the gauntlet, and the impetuous Carlstadt had taken it up. God made use of the passions of these two men to accomplish His purposes. Luther had not interfered in their disputes, and yet he was destined to be the hero of the fight. There are men who by the force of circumstances are always brought upon the stage. It was agreed that the discussion should take place at Leipsic. Such was the origin of that Leipsic disputation which became so famous.

Eck cared little for disputing with and even conquering Carlstadt: Luther was his great aim. He therefore made every exertion to allure him to the field of battle, and with this view published thirteen theses,[3] which he pointed expressly against the chief doctrines already set forth by the reformer. The thirteenth was thus drawn up: " We deny that the Roman Church was not raised above the other churches before the time of Pope Sylvester; and we acknowledge in every age, as the successor of St. Peter and the vicar of Jesus Christ, him who has filled the chair and held the faith of St. Peter." Sylvester lived in the time of Constantine the Great; by this thesis, Eck denied, therefore, that the primacy enjoyed by Rome had been conferred on it by that emperor.

Luther, who had reluctantly consented to remain silent, was deeply moved as he read these propositions. He saw that they were aimed at him, and felt that he could not honourably avoid the contest. " This man," said he, " calls Carlstadt his antagonist, and at the same time attacks me. But God reigns. He knows what He will bring out of this tra-

gedy.[1] It is neither Doctor Eck nor myself that will be at stake: God's purpose will be accomplished. Thanks to Eck, this affair, which hitherto has been mere play, will become serious, and inflict a deadly blow on the tyranny of Rome and of the Roman pontiff."

Rome herself had broken the truce. She did more; in renewing the signal of battle, she began the contest on a point that Luther had not yet attacked. It was the papal supremacy to which Doctor Eck drew the attention of his adversaries. In this he followed the dangerous example that Tetzel had already set.[2] Rome invited the blows of the gladiator; and, if she left some of her members quivering on the arena, it was because she had drawn upon herself his formidable arm.

The pontifical supremacy once overthrown, the whole edifice would crumble into ruin. The greatest danger was impending over the papacy, and yet neither Miltitz nor Cajetan took any steps to prevent this new struggle. Did they imagine that the Reformation would be vanquished, or were they struck with that blindness which often hurries along the mighty to their destruction ?

Luther, who had set a rare example of moderation by remaining silent so long, fearlessly replied to the challenge of his antagonist. He immediately published some new theses in opposition to those of Doctor Eck. The last was conceived in these words: " It is by contemptible decretals of Roman pontiffs, composed within the last four centuries, that they would prove the primacy of the Church of Rome; but this primacy is opposed by all the credible history of eleven centuries,—by the declarations of Holy Scripture,—and by the resolutions of the Council of Nice, the holiest of all councils."[3]

" God knows," wrote he at the same time to the elector, " that I was firmly resolved to keep silence, and that I was glad to see this struggle terminated at last. I have so strictly adhered to the treaty concluded with the papal commissary, that I have not replied to Sylvester Prierio, notwithstanding the insults of my adversaries, and the advice of my friends. But now Doctor Eck attacks me, and not only me, but the university of Wittemberg also. I cannot suffer the truth to be thus covered with opprobrium."[4]

At the same time Luther wrote to Carlstadt: " Most excellent Andrew, I would not have you enter upon this dispute, since they are aiming at me. I shall joyfully lay aside my serious occupations to take my part in the sports of these flatterers of the Roman pontiff."[5]—Then addressing his adversary,

---

[1] Nihil cupiebat ardentius, quam sui specimen præbere in solemni disputatione cum æmulo. Pallavicini, tom. i. 63.
[2] Defensio adversus Eckii monomachiam.
[3] L. Opp. (L.) xvii. 242.

[1] Sed Deus in medio deorum ; ipse novit quid ex ea tragœdia deducere voluerit. L. Epp. i. 230, 232.
[2] See vol. i. pp. 108-109.
[3] L. Opp. L. xvii. 245.
[4] L. Epp. i. 237.
[5] Gaudens et ridens posthabeo istorum mea seria ludo. Ibid. 251.

he cries disdainfully from Wittemberg to Ingolstadt: " Now, my dear Eck, be brave, and gird thy sword upon thy thigh, thou mighty man!¹ If I could not please thee as mediator, perhaps I shall please thee better as antagonist. Not that I imagine I can vanquish thee ; but because, after all the triumphs thou hast gained in Hungary, Lombardy, and Bavaria (if at least we are to believe thee), I shall give thee opportunity of gaining the title of conqueror of Saxony and Misnia, so that thou shalt for ever be hailed with the glorious title of August."²

All Luther's friends did not share in his courage ; for no one had hitherto been able to resist the sophisms of Doctor Eck. But their greatest cause of alarm was the subject of the discussion : the pope's primacy. How can the poor monk of Wittemberg dare oppose that giant who for ages has crushed all his enemies? The courtiers of the elector were alarmed. Spalatin, the prince's confidant and Luther's intimate friend, was filled with anxiety. Frederick was uneasy : even the sword of the knight of the holy sepulchre, with which he had been invested at Jerusalem,³ would be of little avail in this war. The reformer alone did not blench. *The Lord* (thought he) *will deliver him into my hands.* The faith by which he was animated gave him the means of encouraging his friends : " I entreat you, my dear Spalatin," said he, " do not give way to fear. You well know that if Christ had not been on my side, all that I have hitherto done must have been my ruin. Quite recently has not the Duke of Pomerania's chancellor received news from Italy, that I had turned Rome topsy-turvy, and that they knew not how to quiet the agitation ? so that it was resolved to attack me, not according to the rules of justice, but by Roman artifices (such was the expression used), meaning, I suppose, poison, ambush, or assassination.

" I restrain myself, and from love to the elector and the university suppress many things that I would publish against Babylon, if I were elsewhere. O my poor Spalatin, it is impossible to speak with truth of the Scriptures and of the Church without arousing the beast. Never expect to see me free from danger, unless I abandon the teaching of sound divinity. If this matter be of God, it will not come to an end before all my friends have forsaken me, as Christ was forsaken by his disciples. Truth will stand alone, and will triumph by its own right hand, not by mine, nor yours, nor any other man's.⁴ If I perish, the world will not perish with me. But, wretch that I am, I fear I am unworthy to die in such a cause."—

" Rome," he wrote again about the same time, " Rome is eagerly longing to kill me, and I am wasting my time in braving her. I have been assured that an effigy of Martin Luther was publicly burnt in the Campo di Fiore at Rome, after being loaded with execrations. I await their furious rage.¹ The whole world," he continued, " is moved, and totters in body and mind ; what will happen, God only knows. For my part, I foresee wars and disasters. The Lord have mercy on us!"²

Luther wrote letter upon letter to duke George,³ begging this prince, in whose states Leipsic was situated, to give him permission to go and take part in the disputation ; but he received no answer. The grandson of the Bohemian king, alarmed by Luther's proposition on the papal anthority, and fearing the recurrence of those wars in Saxony of which Bohemia had so long been the theatre, would not consent to the doctor's request. The latter therefore resolved to publish an explanation of the 13th thesis. But this writing, far from persuading the duke, made him only the more resolved ; he positively refused the sanction required by the reformer to take a share in the disputation, allowing him only to be present as a spectator.⁴ This annoyed Luther very much : yet he had but one desire,—to obey God. He resolved to go—to look on—and to wait his opportunity.

At the same time the prince forwarded to his utmost ability the disputation between Eck and Carlstadt. George was attached to the old doctrine ; but he was upright, sincere, a friend to free inquiry, and did not think that every opinion should be judged heretical, simply because it was offensive to the court of Rome. More than this, the elector used his influence with his cousin ; and George, gaining confidence from Frederick's language, ordered that the disputation should take place.⁵

Adolphus, bishop of Merseburg, in whose diocese Leipsic was situated, saw more clearly than Miltitz and Cajetan the danger of leaving such important questions to the chances of single combat. Rome dared not expose to such hazard the hard-earned fruits of many centuries. All the Leipsic theologians felt no less alarm, and entreated their bishop to prevent the discussion. Upon this, Adolphus made the most energetic representations to Duke George, who very sensibly replied : " I am surprised that a bishop should have so great a dread of the ancient and praiseworthy custom of our fathers,—the investigation of doubtful questions in matters of faith. If your theologians refuse to defend their doctrines, it would be better to employ

---

¹ Esto vir fortis et accingere gladio tuo super femur tuum, potentissime! L. Epp. i. 251.
² Ac si voles semper Augustus saluteris in æternum. Ibid.
³ See vol. l. pp. 22-81.
⁴ Ea sola sit veritas, quæ salvet se dextera sua, non mea, non tua, non ullius hominis. L. Epp. i. 261.

¹ Expecto furorem illorum. L. Epp. i. 280. May 30, 1519.
² Totus orbis nutat et movetur, tam corpore quam anima. Ibid.
³ Ternis literis, a duce Georgio non potui certum obtinere responsum. Ibid. 282.
⁴ Ita ut non disputator, sed spectator futurus Lipsiam ingrederer. L. Opp. in Præf.
⁵ Principis nostri verbo firmatus. L. Epp. i. 255.

the money spent on them in maintaining old women and children, who at least could spin while they were singing."[1]

This letter had but little effect on the bishop and his theologians. There is a secret consciousness in error that makes it shrink from examination, even when talking most of free inquiry. After having imprudently advanced, it retreated with cowardice. Truth gave no challenge, but it stood firm: error challenged to the combat, and ran away. Besides, the prosperity of Wittemberg was an object of jealousy to the university of Leipsic. The monks and priests of the latter city begged and entreated their flocks from the pulpit to flee from the new heretics. They vilified Luther; they depicted him and his friends in the blackest colours, in order to excite the ignorant classes against the doctors of the Reformation.[2] Tetzel, who was still living, awoke to cry out from the depth of his retreat: "It is the devil who urges them to this contest."[3]

All the Leipsic professors did not, however, entertain the same opinions: some belonged to the class of indifferents, always ready to laugh at the faults of both parties. Among this body was the Greek professor, Peter Mosellanus. He cared very little about either John Eck, Carlstadt, or Martin Luther; but he flattered himself that he would derive much amusement from their disputation. "John Eck, the most illustrious of goose-quill gladiators and of braggadocios," wrote he to his friend Erasmus, "John Eck, who like the Aristophanic Socrates despises even the gods themselves, will have a bout with Andrew Carlstadt. The match will end in loud cries. Ten such men as Democritus would find matter for laughter in it."[4]

The timid Erasmus, on the contrary, was alarmed at the very idea of a combat, and his prudence would have prevented the discussion. "If you would take Erasmus's word," wrote he to Melancthon, "you would labour rather in cultivating literature than in disputing with its enemies.[5] I think that we should make greater progress by this means. Above all, let us never forget that we ought to conquer not only by our eloquence, but also by mildness and moderation." Neither the alarm of the priests nor the discretion of the pacificators could any longer prevent the combat. Each man got his arms ready.

1 Scheinder, Lips. Chr. iv. 168.
2 Theologi interim me proscindunt....populum Lipsiæ inclamant. L. Epp. i. 255.
3 Das walt der Teufel. Ibid.
4 Seckend. p. 201.
5 Malim te plus operæ sumere in asserendis bonis literis, quam in sectandis harum hostibus. Corpus Reformatorum, edit. Bretschneider, i. 78, April 22, 1519.

CHAPTER III.

Arrival of Eck and of the Wittembergers—Amsdorff—The Students—Carlstadt's Accident—Placard—Eck and Luther—The Pleissenburg—Judges proposed—Luther objects —He consents at last.

WHILE the electors were meeting at Frankfort to choose an Emperor (June 1519), the theologians assembled at Leipsic for an act, unnoticed by the world at large, but whose importance was destined to be quite as great for posterity.

Eck came first to the rendezvous. On the 21st of June he entered Leipsic with Poliander, a young man whom he had brought from Ingolstadt to write an account of the disputation. Every mark of respect was paid to the scholastic doctor. Robed in his sacerdotal garments, and at the head of a numerous procession, he paraded the streets of the city on the festival of Corpus Christi. All were eager to see him: the inhabitants were on his side, he tells us himself, "yet," adds he, "a report was current in the town that I should be beaten in this combat."

On the day succeeding the festival (Friday, 24th June), which was the feast of Saint John, the Wittembergers arrived. Carlstadt, who was to contend with Dr Eck, sat alone in his carriage, and preceded all the rest. Duke Barnim of Pomerania, who was then studying at Wittemberg, and who had been named honorary rector of the university, came next in an open carriage: at each side were seated the two great divines—the fathers of the Reformation—Luther and Melancthon. The latter would not quit his friend. "Martin, the soldier of the Lord," he had said to Spalatin, "has stirred up this fetid pool.[1] My spirit is vexed when I think of the disgraceful conduct of the papal theologians. Be firm, and abide with us!" Luther himself had wished that his Achates, as he called him, should accompany him.

John Lange, vicar of the Augustines, many doctors of law, several masters of arts, two licentiates in theology, and other ecclesiastics, among whom was Nicholas Amsdorff, closed the procession. Amsdorff, sprung from a noble family, valuing little the brilliant career to which his illustrious birth might have called him, had dedicated himself to theology. The theses on indulgences had brought him to a knowledge of the truth. He had immediately made a bold confession of faith.[2] Possessing a strong mind and an ardent character, Amsdorff frequently excited Luther, who was naturally vehement enough, to acts that were perhaps imprudent. Born in exalted rank, he had no fear of the great, and he sometimes spoke to them with

1 Martinus, Domini miles, hanc camarinam movit. Corp Ref. i. 82.
2 Nec cum carne et sanguine diu contulit, sed statim palam ad alios, fidei confessionem constanter edidit. M. Adami Vita Amsdorff.

a freedom bordering on rudeness. "The Gospel of Jesus Christ," said he one day before an assembly of nobles, "belongs to the poor and afflicted—not to you, princes, lords, and courtiers, who live continually in luxury and pleasures."[1]

But these persons alone did not form the procession from Wittemberg. A great number of students followed their teachers: Eck affirms that they amounted to two hundred. Armed with pikes and halberds, they surrounded the carriages of the doctors, ready to defend them, and proud of their cause.

Such was the order in which the *cortège* of the reformers arrived in Leipsic. They had already entered by the Grimma gate, and advanced as far as St. Paul's cemetery, when one of the wheels of Carlstadt's carriage gave way. The archdeacon, whose vanity was delighted at so solemn an entry, rolled into the mud. He was not hurt, but was compelled to proceed to his lodgings on foot. Luther's carriage, which followed next, rapidly outstripped him, and bore the reformer in safety to his quarters. The inhabitants of Leipsic, who had assembled to witness the entry of the Wittemberg champions, looked upon this accident as an evil omen to Carlstadt: and erelong the whole city was of opinion that he would be vanquished in the combat, but that Luther would come off victorious.[2]

Adolphus of Merseburg was not idle. As soon as he heard of the approach of Luther and Carlstadt, and even before they had alighted from their carriages, he ordered placards to be posted upon the doors of all the churches, forbidding the opening of the disputation under pain of excommunication. Duke George, astonished at this audacity, commanded the town-council to tear down the placards, and committed to prison the bold agent who had ventured to execute the bishop's order.[3] George had repaired to Leipsic, attended by all his court, among whom was that Jerome Emser, at whose house in Dresden Luther had passed a remarkable evening.[4] George made the customary presents to the respective combatants. "The duke," observed Eck with vanity, "gave me a fine deer; but he only gave a fawn to Carlstadt."[5]

Immediately on hearing of Luther's arrival, Eck went to visit the Wittemberg doctor. "What is this!" asked he; "I am told that you refuse to dispute with me!"

LUTHER.—"How can I, since the duke has forbidden me?"

ECK.—"If I cannot dispute with you, I care little about meeting Carlstadt. It was on your account I came here."[6] Then after

a moment's silence he added: "If I can procure you the duke's permission, will you enter the lists with me?"

LUTHER, *joyfully.*—"Procure it for me, and we will fight."

Eck immediately waited on the duke, and endeavoured to remove his fears. He represented to him that he was certain of victory, and that the papal authority, far from suffering in the dispute, would come forth covered with glory. The ringleader must be attacked: if Luther remains standing, all stands with him; if he falls, everything will fall with him. George granted the required permission.

The duke had caused a large hall to be prepared in his palace of the Pleissenburg. Two pulpits had been erected opposite each other; tables were placed for the notaries commissioned to take down the discussion, and benches had been arranged for the spectators. The pulpits and benches were covered with handsome hangings. Over the pulpit of the Wittemberg doctor was suspended the portrait of Saint Martin, whose name he bore; over that of Doctor Eck, a representation of Saint George the champion. "We shall see," said the presumptuous Eck, as he looked at this emblem, "whether I shall not ride over my enemies." Every thing announced the importance that was attached to this contest.

On the 25th June, both parties met at the palace to hear the regulations that were to be observed during the disputation. Eck, who had more confidence in his declamations and gestures than in his arguments, exclaimed, "We will dispute freely and extemporaneously; and the notaries shall not take down our words in writing."

CARLSTADT.—"It has been agreed that the disputation should be reported, published, and submitted to the judgment of all men."

ECK.—"To take down every thing that is said is dispiriting to the combatants, and prolongs the battle. There is an end to that animation which such a discussion requires. Do not check the flow of eloquence."[1]

The friends of Doctor Eck supported his proposition, but Carlstadt persisted in his objections. The champion of Rome was obliged to give way.

ECK.—"Be it so; it shall be taken down. But do not let the notes be published before they have been submitted to the examination of chosen judges."

LUTHER.—"Does then the truth of Doctor Eck and his followers dread the light?"

ECK.—"We must have judges."

LUTHER.—"What judges?"

ECK.—"When the disputation is finished, we will arrange about selecting them."

The object of the partisans of Rome was evident. If the Wittemberg divines accepted judges, they were lost: for their adversaries

[1] Weismann, Hist. Eccl. l. 1444.
[2] Seb. Fröschel vom Priesterthum. Wittemb. 1585. In the Preface.
[3] L. Opp. (L.) xvii, 245.
[4] See vol. i. p. 81.
[5] Seckend. p. 190.
[6] Si tecum non licet disputare, neque cum Carlstatio volo; propter te enim huc veni. (L. Opp. in Præf.)

[1] Melancth. Opp. i. 139. Koethe's edition.

were sure beforehand of those who would be applied to. If they refused these judges, they would be covered with shame, for their opponents would circulate the report that they were afraid to submit their opinions to impartial arbitrators.

The judges whom the reformers demanded were, not any particular individual, whose opinion had been previously formed, but all Christendom. They appealed to this universal suffrage. Besides, it is a slight matter to them if they are condemned, if, while pleading their cause before the whole world, they have brought a few souls to the knowledge of the truth. " Luther," says a Romanist historian, " required all men for his judges ; that is, such a tribunal that no urn could have been vast enough to contain the votes."[1]

They separated. " See what artifices they employ," said Luther and his friends one to another. " They desire no doubt to have the pope or the universities for judges."

In fact, on the next morning the Romanist divines sent one of their number to Luther, who was commissioned to propose that their judge should be—the pope !......" The pope !" said Luther ; " how can I possibly agree to this ?"

" Beware," exclaimed all his friends, " of acceding to conditions so unjust." Eck and his party held another council. They gave up the pope, and proposed certain universities. " Do not deprive us of the liberty which you had previously granted," answered Luther. — " We cannot give way on this point," replied they. — " Well then !" exclaimed Luther, " I will take no part in the discussion !"[2]

Again the parties separated, and this matter was a general topic of conversation throughout the city. " Luther," everywhere exclaimed the Romanists, " Luther will not dispute !......He will not acknowledge any judge !" His words were commented on and misrepresented, and his adversaries endeavoured to place them in the most unfavourable light. " What ! does he really decline the discussion ?" said the reformer's best friends. They went to him and expressed their alarm. " You refuse to take any part in the discussion !" cried they. " Your refusal will bring everlasting disgrace on your university and on your cause." This was attacking Luther on his weakest side.— " Well, then !" replied he, his heart overflowing with indignation, " I accept the conditions imposed upon me ; but I reserve the right of appeal, and except against the court of Rome."[3]

[1] Alebat, ad universos mortales pertinere judicium, hoc est ad tribunal cujus colligendis calculis nulla urna satis capax. Pallavicini, i. 55.
[2] L. Opp. (L.) xvii. 245.   [3] Ibid.

CHAPTER IV.

Opening of the Disputation—Speech of Mosellanus—*Veni, Sancte Spiritus*—Portraits of Luther and Carlstadt—Doctor Eck—Carlstadt's Books—Merit of Congruity—Natural Powers—Scholastic Distinction—Point at which Rome and the Reformation diverge—Liberty given to Man by Grace—Carlstadt's Notes—Clamour of the Spectators—Melancthon during the Disputation—His Opinion—Eck's Manœuvres—Luther Preaches—Citizens of Leipsic—Quarrels between the Students and Doctors.

THE 27th of June was the day appointed for the opening of the discussion. Early in the morning the two parties assembled in the college of the university, and thence went in procession to the Church of Saint Thomas, where a solemn mass was performed by order and at the expense of the duke. After the service they proceeded to the ducal palace. At their head were Duke George and the Duke of Pomerania ; after them came counts, abbots, knights, and other persons of distinction, and last of all the doctors of the two parties. A guard composed of seventy-six citizens, armed with halberds, accompanied the train, with banners flying, and to the sound of martial music. It halted at the castle-gates.

The procession having reached the palace, each took his station in the hall appointed for the discussion. Duke George, the hereditary Prince John, Prince George of Anhalt, then twelve years old, and the Duke of Pomerania, occupied the seats assigned them.

Mosellanus ascended the pulpit to remind the theologians, by the duke's order, in what manner they were to dispute. " If you fall to quarrelling," said the speaker, " what difference will there be between a theologian in discussion and a shameless duellist ? What is your object in gaining the victory, if it be not to recover a brother from the error of his ways ?......It appears to me that each of you should desire less to conquer than to be conquered !"[1]

When this address was terminated, sacred music resounded through the halls of the Pleissenburg ; all the assembly knelt down, and the ancient hymn of invocation to the Holy Ghost, *Veni Sancte Spiritus*[2] was sung. This was a solemn moment in the annals of the Reformation. Thrice the invocation was repeated, and while this solemn strain was heard, the defenders of the old doctrine and the champions of the new : the churchmen of the Middle Ages and those who sought to restore the church of the Apostles, here assembled and confounded with one another, humbly bent their heads to the earth. The ancient tie of one and the same communion still bound together all those different minds ; the same prayer still proceeded from all those lips, as if pronounced by one heart.

These were the last moments of outward —of dead unity : a new unity of spirit and

[1] Seckend. p. 209.   [2] Come, Holy Spirit.

of life was about to begin. The Holy Ghost was invoked upon the Church, and was preparing to answer and to renovate Christendom.

The singing and the prayers being ended, they all rose up. The discussion was about to open; but as it was past the hour of noon, it was deferred until two o'clock.

The duke invited to his table the principal persons who were to be present at the discussion. After the repast, they returned to the castle. The great hall was filled with spectators. Disputations of this kind were the public meetings of that age. It was here that the representatives of their day agitated the questions that occupied all minds. The speakers were soon at their posts. That the reader may form a better idea of their appearance, we will give their portraits as drawn by one of the most impartial witnesses of the contest.

"Martin Luther is of middle stature, and so thin, in consequence of his studies, that his bones may almost be counted. He is in the prime of life, and has a clear and sonorous voice. His knowledge and understanding of the Holy Scriptures is unparalleled; he has the Word of God at his fingers' ends.[1] Besides this, he possesses great store of arguments and ideas. One might perhaps desire a little more judgment in arranging his subjects. In conversation he is pleasing and affable; there is nothing harsh or austere about him; he can accommodate himself to every one; his manner of speaking is agreeable and unembarrassed. He displays firmness, and has always a cheerful air, whatever may be his adversaries' threats; so that it is difficult to believe that he could undertake such great things without the Divine protection. He is blamed, however, for being more caustic, when reproving others, than becomes a theologian, particularly when putting forward novelties in religion.

"Carlstadt is of shorter stature; his complexion is dark and sun-burnt, his voice unpleasing, his memory less trust-worthy than Luther's, and he is more inclined to anger. He possesses, however, though in a smaller degree, the qualities that distinguish his friend.

"Eck is tall, broad-shouldered, and has a strong and thorough German voice. He has good lungs, so that he would be heard well in a theatre, and would even make an excellent town-crier. His accent is rather vulgar than elegant. He has not that gracefulness so much extolled by Fabius and Cicero. His mouth, his eyes, and his whole countenance give you the idea of a soldier or a butcher rather than of a divine.[2] He has an excellent memory, and if he had only as

much understanding, he would be really a perfect man. But he is slow of comprehension, and is wanting in judgment, without which all other qualities are useless. Hence, in disputing, he heaps together, without selection or discernment, a mass of passages from the Bible, quotations from the Fathers, and proofs of all kinds. He has, besides, an impudence almost beyond conception. If he is embarrassed, he breaks off from the subject he is treating of, and plunges into another; he sometimes even takes up his adversary's opinion, clothing it in other words, and with extraordinary skill attributes to his opponent the absurdity he had been himself defending."

Such, according to Mosellanus, were the men at that time attracting the attention of the crowd which thronged the great hall of the Pleissenburg.

The dispute began between Eck and Carlstadt.

Eck's eyes were fixed for a moment on certain objects that lay on the desk of his adversary's pulpit, and which seemed to disturb him; they were the Bible and the holy Fathers. "I decline the discussion," exclaimed he suddenly, "if you are permitted to bring your books with you." Surprising that a divine should have recourse to books in order to dispute! Eck's astonishment was still more marvellous. "It is the fig-leaf which this Adam makes use of to hide his shame,"[1] said Luther. "Did not Augustine consult his books when arguing with the Manicheans?" What did that matter? Eck's partisans raised a great clamour. The other side did the same. "The man has no memory," said Eck. At last it was arranged, according to the wish of the Chancellor of Ingolstadt, that each should rely upon his memory and his tongue only. "Thus, then," said many, "the object of this disputation will not be to discover the truth, but what praise is to be conferred on the tongue and the memory of the disputants."

As we are unable to give the details of this discussion, which lasted seventeen days, we shall, as an historian expresses it, imitate the painters, who, when they have to represent a battle, set the most memorable actions in the foreground, and leave the others in the distance.[2]

The subject of discussion between Eck and Carlstadt was important. "Man's will, before his conversion," said Carlstadt, "can perform no good work: every good work comes entirely and exclusively from God, who gives man first the will to do, and then the power of accomplishing." This truth had been proclaimed by Scripture, which says: *It is God which worketh in you both to will and to do of his good pleasure;*[3] and by Saint Augustine, who, in his dispute with

---

[1] Seine Gelehrsamkeit aber und Verstand in heiliger Schrift ist unvergleichlich, so dass er fast alles im Griff hat. Mosellanus in Seckend. p. 206.
[2] Das Maul, Augen und ganze Gesicht, presentirt ehe einen Fleischer oder Soldaten, als einen Theologum. Ibid.

[1] Prætexit tamen et hic Adam ille folium fici pulcherrimum. L. Epp. i. 294.
[2] Pallavicini, i. 65.   [3] Philippians ii. 13.

the Pelagians, had enunciated it in nearly the same terms. Every work in which the love of God and obedience towards Him do not exist is deprived in the eyes of the Almighty of all that can render it good, even should it originate in the best of human motives. Now there is in man a natural opposition to God—an opposition that the unaided strength of man cannot surmount. He has neither the will nor the power to overcome it. This must therefore be effected by the Divine will.

This is the whole question of free will—so simple, and yet so decried by the world. Such had been the doctrine of the Church. But the schoolmen had so explained it that it was not recognisable. Undoubtedly (said they) the natural will of man can do nothing really pleasing to God; but it can do much towards rendering men meet to receive the grace of God, and more worthy to obtain it. They called these preparations a merit of congruity:[1] "because it is *congruous*," said Thomas Aquinas, "that God should treat with particular favour him who makes a good use of his own will." And, as regards the conversion to be effected in man, undoubtedly it must be accomplished by the grace of God, which (according to the schoolmen) should bring it about, but not to the exclusion of his natural powers. These powers (said they) were not destroyed by sin: sin only opposes an obstacle to their development; but so soon as this obstacle is removed (and it was this, in their opinion, that the grace of God had to effect) the action of these powers begins again. The bird, to use one of their favourite comparisons, that has been tied for some time, has in this state neither lost its ability nor forgotten the art of flying; but some hand must loose the bonds, in order that he may again make use of his wings. This is the case with man, said they.[2]

Such was the question agitated between Eck and Carlstadt. At first Eck had appeared to oppose all Carlstadt's propositions on this subject; but finding his position untenable, he said: "I grant that the will has not the power of doing a good work, and that it receives this power from God."— "Do you acknowledge then," asked Carlstadt, overjoyed at obtaining so important a concession, "that every good work comes entirely from God?"—"The *whole* good work really proceeds from God, but not *wholly*," cunningly replied the scholastic doctor.—"Truly, this is a discovery not unworthy of the science of divinity," exclaimed Melancthon.—"An entire apple," continued Eck, "is produced by the sun, but not entirely and without the co-operation of the plant."[3] Most certainly it has never yet

been maintained that an apple is produced solely by the sun.

Well then, said the opponents, plunging deeper into this important and delicate question of philosophy and religion, let us inquire how God acts upon man, and how man conducts himself under this action. "I acknowledge," said Eck, "that the first impulse in man's conversion proceeds from God, and that the will of man in this instance is entirely passive."[1] Thus far the two parties were agreed. "I acknowledge," said Carlstadt, "that after this first impulse which proceeds from God, something must come on the part of man,—something that St. Paul denominates *will*, and which the fathers entitle *consent*." Here again they were both agreed: but from this point they diverged. "This consent of man," said Eck, "comes partly from our natural will, and partly from God's grace."[2]—"No," said Carlstadt; "God must entirely create this will in man."[3]— Upon this Eck manifested anger and astonishment at hearing words so fitted to make man sensible of his nothingness. "Your doctrine," exclaimed he, "converts a man into a stone, a log, incapable of any reaction!"— "What!" replied the reformers, "the faculty of receiving this strength which God produces in him, this faculty which (according to us) man possesses, does not sufficiently distinguish him from a log or a stone?"— "But," said their antagonist, "by denying that man has any natural ability, you contradict all experience."—"We do not deny," replied they, "that man possesses a certain ability, and that he has the power of reflection, meditation, and choice. We consider this power and ability as mere instruments that can produce no good work, until the hand of God has set them in motion. They are like a saw in the hands of a sawyer."[4]

The great doctrine of free will was here discussed; and it was easy to demonstrate that the doctrine of the reformers did not deprive man of his liberty as a moral agent, and make him a mere passive machine. The liberty of a moral agent consists in his power of acting conformably to his choice. Every action performed without external constraint, and in consequence of the determination of the soul itself, is a free action. The soul is determined by motives; but we continually observe the same motives acting differently on different minds. Many men do not act in conformity with the motives of which, however, they acknowledge the full force. This inefficacy of motives proceeds from the obstacles opposed to them by the corruption of the understanding and of the heart. But God, by giving man a new heart and a new spirit, removes these obstacles; and by re-

---

[1] Meritum congruum.
[2] Planck, i. 176.
[3] Quanquam totum opus Dei sit, non tamen *totaliter* a Deo esse quemadmodum totum pomum efficitur a sole, sed non a sole *totaliter* et sine plantæ efficentia. Pallavicini, L 56

[1] Motionem seu inspirationem prevenientem esse a solo Deo; et ibi liberum arbitrium habet se passive.
[2] Partim a Deo, partim a libero arbitrio.
[3] Consentit homo, sed consensus est donum Dei. Consentire non est agere.
[4] Ut serra in manu hominis trahentis.

moving them, far from depriving him of his liberty, He takes away, on the contrary, everything that would prevent him from acting freely, from listening to the voice of his conscience, and, in the words of the Gospel, makes him *free indeed* (John viii. 36.)

A trivial circumstance interrupted the discussion. We learn from Eck,[1] that Carlstadt had prepared a number of arguments; and, like many public speakers of our own day, he was reading what he had written. Eck saw in this the tactics of a mere learner, and objected to it. Carlstadt, embarrassed, and fearing that he should break down if he were deprived of his papers, persisted. "Ah!" exclaimed the schoolman, proud of the advantage he thought he had obtained, "his memory is not so good as mine." The point was referred to the arbitrators, who permitted the reading of extracts from the Fathers, but decided that in other respects the disputants should speak extempore.

This first part of the disputation was often interrupted by the noise of the spectators. They were in commotion, and frequently raised their voices. Any proposition that offended the ears of the majority immediately excited their clamours, and then, as in our own days, the galleries were often called to order. The disputants themselves were sometimes carried away by the heat of discussion.

Near Luther sat Melancthon, who attracted almost as much attention as his neighbour. He was of small stature, and appeared little more than eighteen years old. Luther, who was a head taller, seemed connected with him in the closest friendship; they came in, went out, and took their walks together. "To look at Melancthon," wrote a Swiss theologian who studied at Wittemberg,[2] "you would say he was a mere boy; but in understanding, learning, and talent, he is a giant, and I cannot comprehend how such heights of wisdom and genius can be found in so small a body." Between the sittings, Melancthon conversed with Carlstadt and Luther. He aided them in preparing for the combat, and suggested the arguments with which his extensive learning furnished him; but during the discussion he remained quietly seated among the spectators, and carefully listened to the words of the theologians.[3] From time to time, however, he came to the assistance of Carlstadt; and when the latter was near giving way under the powerful declamation of the Chancellor of Ingolstadt, the young professor whispered a word, or slipped him a piece of paper, on which the answer was written. Eck having perceived this on one occasion, and feeling indignant that this grammarian, as he called him,

should dare interfere in the discussion, turned towards him and said haughtily: "Hold your tongue, Philip; mind your studies, and do not disturb me."[1] Perhaps Eck at that time foresaw how formidable an opponent he would afterwards find in this young man. Luther was offended at the gross insult directed against his friend. "Philip's judgment," said he, "has greater weight with me than that of a thousand Doctor Ecks."

The calm Melancthon easily detected the weak points of the discussion. "We cannot help feeling surprised," said he, with that wisdom and beauty which we find in all his words, "when we think of the violence with which these subjects were treated. How could any one expect to derive any profit from it? The Spirit of God loves retirement and silence: it is then that he penetrates deep into our hearts. The bride of Christ does not dwell in the streets and market-places, but leads her Spouse into the house of her mother."[2]

Each party claimed the victory. Eck strained every nerve to appear the conqueror. As the points of divergence almost touched each other, he frequently exclaimed that he had convinced his opponent; or else, like another Proteus (said Luther), he suddenly turned round, put forth Carlstadt's opinions in other words, and asked him, with a tone of triumph, if he did not find himself compelled to yield. And the unskilful auditors, who could not detect the manœuvre of the sophist, applauded and exulted with him. In many respects they were not equally matched. Carlstadt was slow, and on some occasions did not reply to his adversary's objections until the next day. Eck, on the contrary, was a master in his science, and found whatever he required at the very instant. He entered the hall with a disdainful air; ascended the rostrum with a firm step; and there he tossed himself about, paced to and fro, spoke at the full pitch of his sonorous voice, had a reply ready for every argument, and bewildered his hearers by his memory and skill. And yet, without perceiving it, Eck conceded during the discussion much more than he had intended. His partisans laughed aloud at each of his devices; "but (said Luther) I seriously believe that their laughter was mere pretence, and that in their hearts they were annoyed at seeing their chief, who had commenced the battle with so many bravados, abandon his standard, desert his army, and become a shameless runaway."[3]

Three or four days after the opening of the conference, the disputation was interrupted by the festival of Peter and Paul the apostles.

On this occasion the Duke of Pomerania

---

[1] Seckendorf, p. 192.
[2] John Kessler, afterwards the reformer of Saint Gall.
[3] Lipsicæ pugnæ otiosus spectator in reliquo vulgo sedi. Corp. Ref. i. 111.

[1] Tace tu, Philippe, ac tua studia cura, nec me perturba Corp. Ref. i. 149.
[2] Melancth. Opp. p. 134.
[3] Relictis signis desertorem exercitus et transfugam factum. L. Opp. i. 295.

requested Luther to preach before him in his chapel. Luther cheerfully consented. But the place was soon crowded, and as the number of hearers kept increasing, the assembly was transferred to the great hall of the castle, in which the discussion was held. Luther chose his text from the gospel of the day, and preached on the grace of God and the power of Saint Peter. What Luther ordinarily maintained before an audience composed of men of learning, he then set before the people. Christianity causes the light of truth to shine upon the humblest as well as the most elevated minds; it is this which distinguishes it from every other religion and from every system of philosophy. The theologians of Leipsic, who had heard Luther preach, hastened to report to Eck the scandalous words with which their ears had been shocked. "You must reply," exclaimed they; "you must publicly refute these subtle errors." Eck desired nothing better. All the churches were open to him, and four times in succession he went into the pulpit to cry down Luther and his sermon. Luther's friends were indignant at this. They demanded that the Wittemberg divine should be heard in his turn. But it was all in vain. The pulpits were open to the adversaries of the evangelical doctrine; they were closed against those who proclaimed it. "I was silent," said Luther, "and was forced to suffer myself to be attacked, insulted, and calumniated, without even the power of excusing or defending myself."[1]

It was not only the ecclesiastics who manifested their opposition to the evangelical doctors: the citizens of Leipsic were, in this respect, of the same opinion as the clergy. A blind fanaticism had rendered them the dupes of the falsehood and hatred that the priests were attempting to propagate. The principal inhabitants did not visit either Luther or Carlstadt. If they met them in the street, they did not salute them, and endeavoured to prejudice the duke against them. But on the contrary they paid frequent visits to the Doctor of Ingolstadt, and ate and drank with him. The latter feasted with them, entertaining them with a description of the costly banquets to which he had been invited in Germany and Italy, sneering at Luther who had imprudently rushed upon his invincible sword, slowly quaffing the beer of Saxony the better to compare it with that of Bavaria, and casting amorous glances (he boasts of it himself) on the frail fair ones of Leipsic. His manners, which were rather free, did not give a favourable idea of his morals.[2] They were satisfied with offering Luther the wine usually presented to the disputants. Those who were favourably

disposed towards him, concealed their feelings from the public; many, like Nicodemus of old, visited him stealthily and by night. Two men alone honourably distinguished themselves by publicly declaring their friendship for him. They were Doctor Auerbach, whom we have already seen at Augsburg, and Doctor Pistor the younger.

The greatest agitation prevailed in the city. The two parties were like two hostile camps, and they sometimes came to blows. Frequent quarrels took place in the taverns between the students of Leipsic and those of Wittemberg. It was generally reported, even in the meetings of the clergy, that Luther carried a devil about with him shut up in a little box. "I don't know whether the devil is in the box or merely under his frock," said Eck insidiously; "but he is certainly in one or the other."

Several doctors of the two parties had lodgings during the disputation in the house of the printer Herbipolis. They became so outrageous, that their host was compelled to station a police-officer, armed with a halberd, at the head of the table, with orders to prevent the guests from coming to blows. One day Baumgartner, an indulgence-merchant, quarrelled with a gentleman, a friend of Luther's, and gave way to such a violent fit of anger that he expired. "I was one of those who carried him to his grave," said Froschel, who relates the circumstance.[1] In this manner did the general ferment in men's minds display itself. Then, as in our own times, the speeches in the pulpits found an echo in the drawing-room and in the streets.

Duke George, although strongly biassed in Eck's favour, did not display so much passion as his subjects. He invited Eck, Luther, and Carlstadt to meet each other at his table. He even begged Luther to come and see him in private; but it was not long before he displayed all the prejudices with which he had been inspired against the reformer. "By your work on the Lord's Prayer," said the duke with displeasure, "you have misled the consciences of many. There are some people who complain that they have not been able to repeat a single *pater-noster* for four days together."

CHAPTER V.

The Hierarchy and Rationalism—The Two Peasants' Sons —Eck and Luther begin—The Head of the Church—Primacy of Rome—Equality of Bishops—Peter the Foundation-stone—Christ the Corner-stone—Eck insinuates that Luther is a Hussite—Luther on the doctrine of Huss— Agitation among the Hearers—The Word alone—The Court-fool—Luther at Mass—Saying of the Duke—Purgatory—Close of the Discussion.

ON the 4th of July the discussion between Eck and Luther commenced. Everything

---

[1] Mich verklagen, schelten und schmæhen. L. Opp. (L.) xvii. 247.
[2] Eck to Haven and Bourkard, 1st July 1519 Walch. xv. 1456.

[1] Löscher, iii. 278.

seemed to promise that it would be more violent, more decisive, and more interesting than that which had just concluded, and which had gradually thinned the hall. The two combatants entered the arena resolved not to lay down their arms until victory declared in favour of one or the other. The general expectation was aroused, for the papal primacy was to be the subject of discussion. Christianity has two great adversaries : hierarchism and rationalism. Rationalism, in its application to the doctrine of man's ability, had been attacked by the reformers in the previous part of the Leipsic disputation. Hierarchism, considered in what is at once its summit and its base,—the doctrine of papal authority,—was to be contested in the second. On the one side appeared Eck, the champion of the established religion, vaunting of the discussions he had maintained, as a general boasts of his campaigns.[1] On the other side advanced Luther, who seemed destined to reap persecution and ignominy from this struggle, but who still presented himself with a good conscience, a firm resolution to sacrifice everything in the cause of truth, and an assurance grounded in faith in God, and in the deliverance He grants to all who trust in Him. New convictions had sunk deep into his soul; they were not as yet arranged into a system ; but in the heat of the combat they flashed forth like lightning. Serious and daring, he showed a resolution that made light of every obstacle. On his features might be seen the traces of the storms his soul had encountered, and the courage with which he was prepared to meet fresh tempests. These combatants, both sons of peasants, and the representatives of the two tendencies that still divide Christendom, were about to enter upon a contest on which depended, in great measure, the future prospects of the State and of the Church. At seven in the morning the two disputants were in their pulpits, surrounded by a numerous and attentive assembly.

Luther stood up, and with a necessary precaution, he said modestly :—

" In the name of the Lord, Amen ! I declare that the respect I bear to the sovereign pontiff would have prevented my entering upon this discussion, if the excellent Dr. Eck had not dragged me into it."

Eck.—" In thy name, gentle Jesus ! before descending into the lists, I protest before you, most noble lords, that all that I may say is in submission to the judgment of the first of all sees, and of him who is its possessor."

After a brief silence, Eck continued :

" There is in the Church of God a primacy that cometh from Christ himself. The Church militant was formed in the image of the Church triumphant. Now, the latter is a monarchy in which the hierarchy ascends step by step up to God, its sole chief. For this reason Christ has established a similar order upon earth. What a monster the Church would be if it were without a head ! "[1]

Luther, *turning towards the assembly.*— " When Dr. Eck declares that the universal Church must have a head, he says well. If there is any one among us who maintains the contrary, let him stand up ! As for me, it is no concern of mine."

Eck.—" If the Church militant has never been without a head, I should like to know who it can be, if not the Roman pontiff ? "

Luther.—" The head of the Church militant is Christ himself, and not a man. I believe this on the testimony of God's Word. *He must reign*, says Scripture, *till he hath put all enemies under his feet.*[2] Let us not listen to those who banish Christ to the Church triumphant in heaven. His kingdom is a kingdom of faith. We cannot see our Head, and yet we have one."[3]

Eck, who did not consider himself beaten, had recourse to other arguments, and resumed :

" It is from Rome, according to Saint Cyprian, that sacerdotal unity has proceeded. "[4]

Luther.—" For the Western Church, I grant it. But is not this same Roman Church the offspring of that of Jerusalem ? It is the latter, properly speaking, that is the nursing-mother of all the churches."[5]

Eck.—" Saint Jerome declares that if an extraordinary power, superior to all others, were not given to the pope,[6] there would be in the churches as many sects as there were pontiffs."

Luther.—" *Given :* that is to say, if all the rest of believers consent to it, this power might be conceded to the chief pontiff *by human right.*[7] And I will not deny, that if all the believers in the world agree in recognising as first and supreme pontiff either the Bishop of Rome, or of Paris, or of Magdeburg, we should acknowledge him as such from the respect due to this general agreement of the Church ; but that has never been seen yet, and never will be seen. Even in our own days, does not the Greek Church refuse its assent to Rome ? "

Luther was at that time prepared to acknowledge the pope as chief magistrate of the Church, freely elected by it ; but he denied that he was pope of Divine right. It

---

[1] Nam quod monstrum esset, Ecclesiam esse acephalam! L. Opp. Lat. i. 243.
[2] 1 Corinthians xv. 25.
[3] Prorsus audiendi non sunt qui Christum extra Ecclesiam militantem tendunt in triumphantem, cum sit regnum fidei. Caput nostrum non videmus; tamen habemus. L. Opp. Lat. i. p. 243.
[4] Unde sacerdotalis unitas exorta est. Ibid.
[5] Hæc est matrix proprie omnium ecclesiarum. Ibid. 244.
[6] Cui si non exsors quædam et ab omnibus eminens detur potestas. Ibid. 243.
[7] *Detur*, inquit hoc est jure humano, posset fieri, consentientibus cæteris omnibus fidelibus. Ibid. 244.

---

[1] Faciebat hoc Eccius quia certam sibi gloriam propositam cernebat, propter propositionem meam, in qua negabam Papam esse jure divino caput Ecclesiæ : hic patuit ei campus magnus. L. Opp. in Præf.

was not till much later that he denied that submission was in any way due to him : and this step he was led to take by the Leipsic disputation. But Eck had ventured on ground better known to Luther than to himself. The latter could not, indeed, maintain his thesis that the papacy had existed during the preceding four centuries only. Eck quoted authorities of an earlier date, to which Luther could not reply. Criticism had not yet attacked the False Decretals. But the nearer the discussion approached the primitive ages of the Church, the greater was Luther's strength. Eck appealed to the Fathers ; Luther replied to him from the Fathers, and all the bystanders were struck with his superiority over his rival.

" That the opinions I set forth are those of Saint Jerome," said he, " I prove by the epistle of St. Jerome himself to Evagrius : ' Every bishop,' says he, ' whether at Rome, Eugubium, Constantinople, Rhegium, Tanis, or Alexandria, is partaker of the same merit and of the same priesthood.[1] The power of riches, the humiliation of poverty, are the only things that make a difference in the rank of the bishops.'"

From the writings of the Fathers, Luther passed to the decisions of the councils, which consider the Bishop of Rome as only the first among his peers.[2]

" We read," said he, " in the decree of the Council of Africa, ' The bishop of the first see shall neither be called prince of the pontiffs, nor sovereign pontiff, nor by any other name of that kind ; but only bishop of the first see.' If the monarchy of the Bishop of Rome was of Divine right," continued Luther, " would not this be an heretical injunction ? "

Eck replied by one of those subtle distinctions that were so familiar to him :—

" The bishop of Rome, if you will have it so, is not universal bishop, but bishop of the universal Church."[3]

Luther.—" I shall make no reply to this : let our hearers form their own opinion of it."

—" Certainly," added he directly, " this is an explanation very worthy of a theologian, and calculated to satisfy a disputant who thirsts for glory. It is not for nothing, it seems, that I have remained at great expense at Leipsic, since I have learnt that the pope is not, in truth, the universal bishop, but the bishop of the universal Church ! "[4]

Eck.—" Well then, I will come to the point. The worthy doctor calls upon me to prove that the primacy of the Church of Rome is of Divine right. I will prove it by this expression of Christ : *Thou art Peter, and on this rock will I build my Church.* Saint Augustine, in one of his epistles, has thus

explained the meaning of this passage : " Thou art Peter, and on this *rock* (that is to say, *on Peter*) I will build my Church.' It is true that in another place the same father has explained that by this *rock* we should understand Christ himself, but he has not retracted his former exposition."

Luther.—" If the reverend doctor desires to attack me, let him first reconcile these contradictions in Saint Augustine. For it is most certain that Augustine has said *many times* that the rock was Christ, and perhaps not more than *once* that it was Peter himself. But even should Saint Augustine and all the Fathers say that the Apostle is the rock of which Christ speaks, I would resist them, single-handed, in reliance upon the Holy Scriptures, that is, on Divine right ;[1] for it is written : *Other foundation can no man lay than that is laid, which is Jesus Christ.*[2] Peter himself terms Christ *the chief cornerstone, and a living stone on which we are built up a spiritual house.*"[3]

Eck.—" I am surprised at the humility and modesty with which the reverend doctor undertakes to oppose, alone, so many illustrious Fathers, and pretends to know more than the sovereign pontiffs, the councils, the doctors, and the universities !......It would be surprising, no doubt, if God had hidden the truth from so many saints and martyrs —until the advent of the reverend father ! "

Luther.—" The Fathers are not against me. Saint Augustine and Saint Ambrose, both most excellent doctors, teach as I teach. *Super isto articulo fidei, fundata est Ecclesia,*[4] says Saint Ambrose, when explaining what is meant by the rock on which the Church is built. Let my opponent then set a curb upon his tongue. To express himself as he does, will only serve to excite contention, and not be to discuss like a true doctor."

Eck had no idea that his opponent's learning was so extensive, and that he would be able to extricate himself from the toils that were drawn around him. " The reverend doctor," said he, " has come well armed into the lists. I beg your lordships to excuse me, if I do not exhibit such accuracy of research. I came here to discuss, and not to make a book."—Eck was surprised but not beaten. As he had no more arguments to adduce, he had recourse to a wretched and spiteful trick, which, if it did not vanquish his antagonist, must at least embarrass him greatly. If the accusation of being Bohemian, a heretic, a Hussite, can be fixed upon Luther, he is vanquished ; for the Bohemians were objects of abhorrence in the Church. The scene of combat was not far from the frontiers of Bohemia ; Saxony, after the sentence pronounced on John Huss by the Council of

---

[1] Ejusdem meriti et ejusdem sacerdotii est. L. Opp. Lat. i. 244.
[2] Primus inter pares.
[3] Non episcopus universalis, sed universalis Ecclesiæ episcopus. Ibid. 246.
[4] Ego glorior me tot expensis non frustra. L. Epp. i. 299.

[1] Resistam eis ego unus, auctoritate apostoli, id est, divino jure. L. Opp. Lat. i. 137.
[2] 1 Corinthians iii. 11.
[3] 1 Peter ii. 4, 5, 6.
[4] The Church is founded on that article of faith. L. Op. Lat. i. 254.

Constance, had been exposed to all the horrors of a long and ruinous war; it was its boast to have resisted the Hussites at that time; the university of Leipsic had been founded in opposition to the tendencies of John Huss; and this discussion was going on in the presence of princes, nobles, and citizens, whose fathers had fallen in that celebrated contest. To insinuate that Luther and Huss are of one mind, will be to inflict a most terrible blow on the former. It is to this stratagem that the Ingolstadt doctor now has recourse: "From the earliest times, all good Christians have acknowledged that the Church of Rome derives its primacy direct from Christ himself, and not from human right. I must confess, however, that the Bohemians, while they obstinately defended their errors, attacked this doctrine. I beg the worthy father's pardon, if I am an enemy of the Bohemians, because they are enemies of the Church, and if the present discussion has called these heretics to my recollection; for, in my humble opinion, the doctor's conclusions are in every way favourable to these errors. It is even asserted that the Hussites are loudly boasting of it."[1]

Eck had calculated well: his partisans received this perfidious insinuation with the greatest favour. There was a movement of joy among the audience. "These insults," said the reformer afterwards, "tickled them much more agreeably than the discussion itself."

LUTHER.—"I do not like and I never shall like a schism. Since on their own authority the Bohemians have separated from our unity, they have done wrong, even if the Divine right had pronounced in favour of their doctrines; for the supreme Divine right is charity and oneness of mind."[2]

It was during the morning sitting of the 5th of July that Luther had made use of this language. The meeting broke up shortly after, as it was the hour of dinner. Luther felt ill at ease. Had he not gone too far in thus condemning the Christians of Bohemia? Did they not hold the doctrines that Luther was now maintaining? He saw all the difficulties of his position. Shall he rise up against a council that condemned John Huss, or shall he deny that sublime idea of a universal Christian Church which had taken full possession of his mind? The unshaken Luther did not hesitate. He would do his duty, whatever might be the consequences. Accordingly when the assembly met again at two in the afternoon, he was the first to speak. He said with firmness:

"Among the articles of faith held by John Huss and the Bohemians, there are some that are most christian. This is a positive certainty. Here, for instance, is one: 'That

there is but one universal Church;' and here is another: 'It is not necessary for salvation to believe the Roman Church superior to all others.' It is of little consequence to me whether these things were said by Wickliffe or by Huss......they are truth."

Luther's declaration produced a great sensation among his hearers. Huss—Wickliffe—those odious names, pronounced with approbation by a monk in the midst of a catholic assembly! An almost general murmur ran round the hall. Duke George himself felt alarmed. He fancied he saw that banner of civil war upraised in Saxony which had for so many years desolated the states of his maternal ancestors. Unable to suppress his emotion, he placed his hands on his hips, shook his head, and exclaimed aloud, so that all the assembly heard him, "He is carried away by rage!"[1] The whole meeting was agitated: they rose up, each man speaking to his neighbour. Those who had given way to drowsiness awoke. Luther's friends were in great perplexity; while his enemies exulted. Many who had thus far listened to him with pleasure began to entertain doubts of his orthodoxy. The impression produced on Duke George's mind by these words was never effaced; from this moment he looked upon the reformer with an evil eye, and became his enemy.[2]

Luther did not suffer himself to be intimidated by these murmurs. One of his principal arguments was, that the Greeks had never recognised the pope, and yet they had never been declared heretics; that the Greek Church had existed, still existed, and would exist, without the pope, and that it as much belonged to Christ as the Church of Rome did. Eck, on the contrary, impudently maintained that the Christian and the Roman Church were one and the same; that the Greeks and Orientals, in abandoning the pope, had also abandoned the christian faith, and were indisputably heretics. "What!" exclaimed Luther, "are not Gregory of Nazianzum, Basil the Great, Epiphanius, Chrysostom, and an immense number besides of Greek bishops—are they not saved? and yet they did not believe that the Church of Rome was above the other Churches!......It is not in the power of the Roman pontiffs to make new articles of faith. The christian believer acknowledges no other authority than Holy Scripture. This alone is the *right Divine*.[3] I beg the worthy doctor to concede that the Roman pontiffs were men, and that he will not make them gods."

Eck then resorted to one of those jests which give a specious air of triumph to him who employs them.

"The reverend father is a very poor cook," said he; "he has made a terrible hodge-podge

[1] Et, ut fama est, de hoc plurimum gratulantur. L. Opp. Lat. i. 250.
[2] Nunquam mihi placuit, nec in æternum placebit quodcunque schisma....Cum supremum jus divinum sit charitas et unitas spiritus. Ibid.

[1] Das Walt die Sucht!
[2] Nam adhuc erat Dux Georgius mihi non inimicus, quod sciebam certo. L. Opp. in Præf.
[3] Nec potest fidelis Christianus cogi ultra sacram Scripturam, quæ est proprie jus divinum. L. Opp. Lat. i. 252.

of Greek saints and heretics; so that the odour of sanctity in the one prevents us from smelling the poison of the others."[1]

LUTHER, *interrupting Eck with warmth.*— "The worthy doctor is becoming abusive. In my opinion, there can be no communion between Christ and Belial."

Luther had made a great stride in advance. In 1516 and 1517, he had only attacked the sermons of the indulgence-hawkers and the scholastic doctrines, but had respected the papal decrees. Somewhat later he had rejected these decrees, and had appealed to a council. Now he had thrown off even this latter authority, declaring that no council could lay down a new article of faith, and claim to be infallible. Thus had all human authorities fallen successively before him; the sands that the rain and the torrents carry with them had disappeared; and for rebuilding the ruined house of the Lord nothing remained but the everlasting rock of the Word of God. "Reverend father," said Eck, "if you believe that a council, regularly assembled, can err, you are in my eyes nothing better than a heathen and a publican!"

Such were the discussions that occupied the two doctors. The assembly listened with earnestness; but their attention sometimes flagged, and the bystanders were delighted when any incident occurred to amuse and excite them. It often happens that the most serious matters are mixed up with others the most ridiculous. This was the case at Leipsic.

Duke George, according to the custom of the times, had a court-fool. Some wags said to him: "Luther maintains that a court-fool may marry, while Eck says that he cannot." Upon this, the fool took a great dislike to Eck, and every time he entered the hall in the duke's train, he looked at the theologian with a threatening air. The Chancellor of Ingolstadt, who was not above indulging in buffoonery, closed one eye (the fool was blind of an eye) and with the other began to squint at the little gentleman, who, losing his temper, overwhelmed the doctor with abuse. The whole assembly (says Peifer) burst into laughter, and this interlude somewhat diminished the extreme tension of their minds.[2]

At the same time scenes were enacting in the city and in the churches, that showed the horror inspired in the Romish partisans by Luther's bold assertions. It was from the convents attached to the pope's interest that the loudest clamours proceeded. One Sunday, the Wittemberg doctor entered the Dominican church before high mass. There were present only a few monks repeating low mass at the smaller altars. As soon as it was known in the cloister that the heretic

Luther was in the church, the monks ran in hastily, snatched up the remonstrance, and carrying it to the tabernacle,[1] there shut it up carefully, watching over it lest the host should be profaned by the heretical eyes of the Wittemberg Augustine. At the same time those who were reading mass hurriedly caught up the various ornaments employed in the service, deserted the altar, fled across the church, and took refuge in the vestry, as if, says an historian, Satan had been at their heels.

The subject of the discussion furnished matter for conversation in every place. In the inns, the university, and the court, each man expressed his opinion. However great might have been Duke George's exasperation, he did not obstinately refuse to be convinced. One day, as Eck and Luther were dining with him, he interrupted their conversation by saying: "Whether the pope be pope by human or by Divine right, nevertheless, he is pope."[2] Luther was much pleased at these words. "The prince," said he, "would never have made use of them, had he not been struck by my arguments."

The discussion on the papal primacy had lasted five days. On the 8th of July, they proceeded to the doctrine of Purgatory. This occupied rather more than two days. Luther still admitted this doctrine; but denied that it was taught in Scripture or in the Fathers in the manner that his opponent and the schoolmen pretended. "Our Doctor Eck," said he, alluding to the superficial character of his adversary's mind, "has this day skimmed over Scripture almost without touching it—as a spider runs upon water."

On the 11th of July they came to Indulgences. "It was a mere joke," said Luther; "the dispute was ridiculous. The indulgences fell outright, and Eck was nearly of my opinion."[3] Eck himself said: "If I had not disputed with Doctor Martin on the papal supremacy, I should almost have agreed with him."[4]

The discussion next turned on Repentance, Absolution of the Priest, and Satisfactions. Eck, according to his usual practice, quoted the scholastic doctors, the Dominicans, and the pope's canons. Luther closed the disputation with these words: "The reverend doctor flees from the Scriptures, as the devil from before the cross. As for me, with all due respect to the Fathers, I prefer the

---

[1] At Rev. Pater, *artis coquinariæ* minus instructus, commiscet sanctos Græcos cum schismaticis et hæreticis, ut fuco sanctitatis Patrum hæreticorum tueatur perfidiam. L. Opp. Lat. i. 252.
[2] L. Opp. (W.) xv. 1440.—2 Löscher, iii. 281.

[1] The *tabernacle* is an octagonal shaped case, standing in the centre of the altar, and made of polished brass, marble, silver, gold, or at least gilded wood. Its size varies from eighteen inches to four feet in height, and from one foot to three in diameter. In it are deposited the *pix*, containing the large consecrated wafer intended to be exhibited for the adoration of worshippers, and the *ciborium* in which are the small ones prepared for the communicants. The *remonstrance* is a highly ornamented stand with a circular opening to receive the larger wafer used in the elevation of the host.
[2] Ita ut ipse dux Georgius inter prandendum, ad Eccium et me dicat: "Sive sit jure humano, sive sit jure divino, papa; ipse est papa." L. Opp. in Præf.
[3] L. Opp. (L.) xvii. 246.
[4] So wollt'er fast einig mit mir gewest seyn. Ibid.

authority of Holy Writ, and this test I would recommend to our judges."[1]

Here ended the dispute between Eck and Luther. Carlstadt and the Ingolstadt doctor kept up the discussion two days longer on human merits in good works. On the 16th of July the business was concluded, after having lasted twenty days, by a speech from the rector of the university. As soon as he had finished, loud music was heard, and the solemnity was concluded by singing the *Te Deum*.

But during the chanting of this solemn thanksgiving, men's minds were no longer as they had been during the *Veni Spiritus* at the opening of the discussion. Already the presentiments of many had been realized. The blows that the champions of the two doctrines had aimed at each other, had inflicted a deep wound upon the papacy.

CHAPTER VI.

Interest felt by the Laity—Luther's Opinion—Confession and Boasts of Doctor Eck—Effects of the Disputation—Poliander—Cellarius—The Young Prince of Anhalt—The Students of Leipsic—Cruciger—Melancthon's Call—Luther's Emancipation.

THESE theological disputes, to which the men of the world would now be unwilling to consecrate a few brief moments, had been followed and listened to for twenty successive days with great attention; laymen, knights, and princes had manifested a constant interest. Duke Barnim of Pomerania and Duke George were remarkably regular in their attendance. But, on the contrary, some of the Leipsic theologians, friends of Doctor Eck, slept soundly, as an eyewitness informs us. It was necessary to wake them up at the close of the disputation, for fear they should lose their dinners.

Luther quitted Leipsic first; Carlstadt followed him; but Eck remained several days after their departure.

No decision had been come to on the discussion.[2] Every one commented on it according to his own feelings. "At Leipsic," said Luther, "there was great loss of time, but no seeking after truth. We have been examining the doctrines of our adversaries these two years past, so that we have counted all their bones. Eck, on the contrary, has hardly grazed the surface;[3] but he made more noise

in one hour than we have in two long years."

In his private letters to his friends, Eck confessed his defeat on certain points; but he had abundant reasons to account for it. "The Wittembergers," wrote he to Hoch straten on the 24th July, "conquered me on several points;[1] first, because they brought their books with them; secondly, because some of their friends took notes of the discussion, which they examined at their leisure; thirdly, because they were many; two doctors (Carlstadt and Luther), Lange, vicar of the Augustines; two licentiates, Amsdorff, and a very presumptuous nephew of Reuchlin (Melancthon); three doctors of law, and several masters of arts, all of whom aided in the discussion, either in public or in private. But as for me, I appeared alone, the justice of my cause being my sole companion." Eck forgot Emser, and the bishop and doctors of Leipsic.

If such avowals escaped from Eck in his familiar correspondence, his behaviour in public was very different. The doctor of Ingolstadt and the Leipsic divines loudly vaunted of what they called *their victory*. They circulated false reports in every direction. All the mouthpieces of their party repeated their self-congratulations. "Eck is triumphing every where," wrote Luther.[2] But in the camp of Rome each man disputed his share of the laurels. "If we had not come to Eck's support," said the men of Leipsic, "the illustrious doctor would have been overthrown."—"The Leipsic divines are very good sort of people," said the Ingolstadt doctor, "but I expected too much of them. I did every thing single-handed."—"You see," said Luther to Spalatin, "that they are singing a new Iliad and a new Æneid.[3] They are so kind as to make a Hector or a Turnus of me, while Eck, in their eyes, is Achilles or Æneas. They have but one doubt remaining, whether the victory was gained by the arms of Eck or by those of Leipsic. All that I can say to clear up the subject is this, Doctor Eck never ceased bawling, and the Leipsic divines did nothing but hold their tongues."

"Eck is conqueror in the eyes of those who do not understand the matter, and who have grown gray under the old schoolmen," said the elegant, witty, and wise Mosellanus; "but Luther and Carlstadt are victorious in the opinion of those who possess any learning, understanding, and modesty."[4]

The Leipsic disputation was not destined, however, to pass away in smoke. Every work performed with devotion bears fruit. Luther's words had sunk with irresistible power into the minds of his hearers. Many

---

[1] Videtur fugere a facie Scripturarum, sicut diabolus crucem. Quare, salvis reverentiis Patrum, præfero ego auctoritatem Scripturæ, quod commendo judicibus futuris. L. Opp. Lat. i. 291.
[2] Ad exitum certaminis, uti solet, nulla prodiit decisio. Pallavicini, i. 65.
[3] Totam istam conclusionum cohortem multo acrius et validius nostri Wittembergenses....oppugnaverunt et ita examinaverunt ut ossa eorum numerare licuerit, quas Eccius vix in facie cutis leviter perstrinxit. L. Epp. i. 291.

[1] Verum in multis me obruerunt. Corp. Ref. i. 83.
[2] Eccius triumphat ubique. L. Epp. i. 290.
[3] Novam quandam Iliada et Æneida illos cantare. Ibid. 305.
[4] Lutheri Sieg sey um so veil weniger berühmt, weil der Gelehrten, Verstandigen, und derer die sich selbst nicht hoch rühmen, wenig seyen. Seckendorf, p. 207.

of those who daily thronged the hall of the castle were subdued by the truth. It was especially in the midst of its most determined adversaries that its victories were gained. Doctor Eck's secretary, familiar friend, and disciple, Poliander, was won to the Reformation ; and in the year 1522, he publicly preached the Gospel at Leipsic. John Cellarius, professor of Hebrew, a man violently opposed to the reformed doctrines, was touched by the words of the eloquent doctor, and began to search the Scriptures more deeply. Erelong he gave up his station, and went to Wittemberg to study humbly at Luther's feet. Some time after he was pastor at Frankfort and at Dresden.

Among those who had taken their seats on the benches reserved for the court, and who surrounded Duke George, was George of Anhalt, a young prince, twelve years old, descended from a family celebrated for their combats against the Saracens. He was then studying at Leipsic under a private tutor. An eager desire for learning and an ardent thirst for truth already distinguished this illustrious youth. He was frequently heard repeating these words of Solomon : *Lying lips become not a prince.* The discussion at Leipsic awakened serious reflections in this boy, and excited a decided partiality for Luther. [1] Some time after, he was offered a bishopric. His brothers and all his relations entreated him to accept it, wishing to push him to the highest dignities in the Church. But he was determined in his refusal. On the death of his pious mother, who was secretly well disposed towards Luther, he became possessed of all the reformer's writings. He offered up constant and fervent prayers to God, beseeching him to turn his heart to the truth, and often, in the solitude of his closet, he exclaimed with tears : *Deal with thy servant according to thy mercy, and teach me thy statutes.* [2] His prayers were heard. Convinced and carried away, he fearlessly ranged himself on the side of the Gospel. In vain did his guardians, and particularly Duke George, besiege him with entreaties and remonstrances. He was inflexible, and George exclaimed, half convinced by the reasoning of his ward: "I cannot answer him ; but I will still remain in my own Church, for it is a hard matter to break in an old dog." We shall meet again with this amiable prince, one of the noblest characters of the Reformation, who preached in person to his subjects the words of everlasting life, and to whom has been applied the saying of Dion on the Emperor Marcus Antoninus : " He was consistent during the whole of his life ; he was a good man, one in whom there was no guile." [3]

But it was the students in particular who received Luther's words with enthusiasm. They felt the difference between the spirit and energy of the Wittemberg doctor, and the sophistical distinctions, the empty speculations of the Chancellor of Ingolstadt. They saw that Luther relied upon the Word of God, and that Eck's opinions were grounded on human tradition. The effect was instantaneous. The lecture-rooms of the university of Leipsic were speedily deserted after the disputation. One circumstance, indeed, contributed to this result : the plague seemed on the point of breaking out in that city. But there were other universities (Erfurth, Ingolstadt, &c.) to which the students might have gone. The power of truth drew them to Wittemberg, where the number of students was soon doubled. [1]

Among those who removed from the one university to the other, was observed a youth of sixteen years, of melancholy disposition, speaking seldom, and who, in the midst of the conversations and sports of his fellow-students, often appeared absorbed in his own reflections. [2] His parents had at first thought him of weak intellect ; but soon found him so quick in learning, and so constantly occupied with his studies, that they formed the greatest expectations of him. His uprightness and candour, his modesty and piety, won him the affection of all, and Mosellanus pointed him out as a model to the whole university. His name was Gaspard Cruciger, a native of Leipsic. The new student of Wittemberg was afterwards the friend of Melancthon, and Luther's assistant in the translation of the Bible.

The Leipsic disputation bore still greater fruits. Here it was that the theologian of the Reformation received his call. Melancthon sat modest and silent listening to the discussion, in which he took very little part. Till that time literature had been his sole occupation. The conference gave him a new impulse, and launched the eloquent professor into the career of theology. From that hour his extensive learning bowed before the Word of God. He received the evangelical truths with the simplicity of a child ; explained the doctrine of salvation with a grace and perspicuity that charmed all his hearers ; and trod boldly in that path so new to him, for, said he, " Christ will never abandon his followers." [3] Henceforward the two friends walked together, contending for liberty and truth,—the one with the energy of St. Paul, the other with the meekness of St. John. Luther has admirably expressed the difference of their callings. " I was born," said he, " to contend on the field of battle with factions and with wicked spirits. This is why my works abound with war and tempests-

[1] L. Opp. (W.) xv. 1440.
[2] A Deo petivit, flecti pectus suum ad veritatem, ac lacrymans sæpe hæc verba repetivit....M. Adami, Vita Georgii Anhalt, p. 248.
[3] "Ομοιος διὰ πάντων ἐγίνετο, ἀγαθὸς δὲ ἦν, καὶ ὑδὶν προσποίηλον εἶχεν. Melch. Adam. p. 255.

[1] Peifer, Histor. Lipsiensis, p. 366.
[2] Et cogitabundus et sæpe in medios sodalitios quasi peregrinante animo. Melch. Adami, Vita Crucigeri, p. 193.
[3] Christus suis non deerit. Corp. Ref. i. 104.

It is my task to uproot the stock and the stem, to clear away the briars and underwood. to fill up the pools and the marshes. I am the rough woodman who has to prepare the way and smooth the road. But Philip advances quietly and softly; he tills and plants the ground; sows and waters it joyfully, according to the gifts that God has given him with so liberal a hand."[1]

If Melancthon, the tranquil sower, was called to the work by the disputation of Leipsic, Luther, the hardy woodman, felt his arm strengthened by it, and his courage reinvigorated. The greatest effect of this discussion was that wrought in Luther himself. " The scales of scholastic theology," said he, " fell then entirely from before my eyes, under the triumphant presidence of Doctor Eck." The veil which the School and the Church had conjointly drawn before the sanctuary was rent for the reformer from top to bottom. Driven to new inquiries, he arrived at unexpected discoveries. With as much indignation as astonishment, he saw the evil in all its magnitude. Searching into the annals of the Church, he discovered that the supremacy of Rome had no other origin than ambition on the one hand, and ignorant credulity on the other. The narrow point of view under which he had hitherto looked upon the Church was succeeded by a deeper and more extended range. He recognised in the Christians of Greece and of the East true members of the Catholic Church; and instead of a visible chief, seated on the banks of the Tiber, he adored, as sole chief of the people of God, an invisible and eternal Redeemer, who, according to his promise, is daily in the midst of every nation upon earth, with all who believe in His name. The Latin Church was no longer in Luther's estimation the universal Church; he saw the narrow barriers of Rome fall down, and exulted in discovering beyond them the glorious dominions of Christ. From that time he comprehended how a man might be a member of Christ's Church, without belonging to the pope's. But, above all, the writings of John Huss produced a deep impression upon him. He there found, to his great surprise, the doctrine of St. Paul and of St. Augustine,—that doctrine at which he himself had arrived after so many struggles. " I believed and I taught all the doctrines of John Huss without being aware of it:[2] and so did Staupitz. In short, although unconscious of it, we are all Hussites. Paul and Augustine were so themselves. I am confounded, and know not what to think.—Oh! how terribly have men deserved the judgments of God, seeing that the Gospel truth, which has been unveiled and published this century past, has been condemned, burnt, and stifled......Wo, wo to the world!"

Luther separated from the papacy, and then felt towards it a decided aversion and holy indignation; and all the witnesses that in every age had risen up against Rome came in turns before him and testified against her, each revealing some abuse or error. " Oh! what thick darkness!" exclaimed he.

He was not allowed to be silent on this sad discovery. The insolence of his adversaries, their pretended triumph, and the efforts they made to extinguish the light, decided his soul. He advanced along the path in which God conducted him, without anxiety as to the goal to which it would lead him. Luther has pointed to this moment as that of his emancipation from the papal yoke. " Learn from me," said he, " how difficult a thing it is to throw off errors confirmed by the example of all the world,[1] and which, through long habit, have become a second nature to us. I had then been seven years reading and publicly explaining the Holy Scriptures with great zeal, so that I knew them almost by heart.[2] I had also all the first-fruits of knowledge and faith in our Lord Jesus Christ; that is to say, I knew that we are justified and saved not by our works, but by faith in Christ; and I even maintained openly that the pope is not the head of the Christian Church by Divine right. And yet I could not see the consequences that flowed from this; namely, that the pope is necessarily and certainly of the devil. For what is not of God must needs be of the devil."[3] Luther adds further on: " I no longer permit myself to be indignant against those who are still attached to the pope, since I, who had for so many years studied the Holy Scriptures so attentively, still clung with so much obstinacy to popery."[4]

Such were the real results of the Leipsic disputation,—results of more importance than the disputation itself. It was like those first successes which discipline an army and excite its courage.

CHAPTER VII.

Eck attacks Melancthon—Melancthon's Defence—Interpretation of Holy Scripture—Luther's Firmness—The Bohemian Brothers—Emser—Staupitz.

Eck gave way to all the intoxication of what he wished to represent as a victory. He inveighed against Luther; heaped charge upon charge against him;[5] wrote to Frede-

[1] L. Opp. (W.) xiv. 200.
[2] Ego imprudens hucusque omnia Johannis Huss et docui et tenui. L. Epp. ii. 452.

[1] Quam difficile sit eluctari et emergere ex erroribus, totius orbis exemplo firmatis....L. Opp. Lat. in Præf.
[2] Per septem annos, ita ut memoriter pene omnia tenerem. Ibid.
[3] Quod enim ex Deo non est, necesse est ex diabolo esse. Ibid.
[4] Cum ego tot annis sacra legens diligentissime, tamen ita hæsi tenaciter. Ibid.
[5] Proscidit, post abitum nostrum, Martinum inhumanissime. Melancth. Corp. Ref. i. 106.

rick ; and desired, like a skilful general, to take advantage of the confusion that always follows a battle, to obtain important concessions from that prince. While waiting for the measures that were to be taken against his adversary's person, he called down fire upon his writings, even on those he had not read. He begged the elector to summon a provincial council : " Let us exterminate these vermin," said the coarse doctor, " before they multiply beyond all bounds."[1]

It was not against Luther alone that he vented his anger. His imprudence called Melancthon into the lists. The latter, connected by tender ties of friendship with the excellent Œcolampadius, wrote him an account of the disputation, speaking of Dr. Eck in terms of commendation.[2] Nevertheless, the pride of the Chancellor of Ingolstadt was wounded. He immediately took up the pen against " that grammarian of Wittemberg, who was not ignorant, indeed, of Latin and Greek, but who had dared publish a letter in which he had insulted him.........Dr. Eck."[3]

Melancthon replied, and this was his first theological writing. It is characterized by all that exquisite urbanity which distinguished this excellent man. Laying down the fundamental principles of hermeneutics,[4] he showed that we ought not to interpret Scripture by the Fathers, but the Fathers by Scripture. " How often has not Jerome been mistaken!" said he ; " how frequently Augustine ! how frequently Ambrose ! how often their opinions are different ! and how often they retract their errors ! There is but one Scripture, inspired by the Holy Ghost, and pure and true in all things.[5]

" Luther does not follow certain ambiguous explanations of the ancients, say they ; and why should he ? When he explains the passage of Saint Matthew : *Thou art Peter, and upon this rock I will build my Church*, he says the same thing as Origen, who alone is a host ; as Augustine in his homily ; and as Ambrose in his sixth book upon Saint Luke ; I will mention no others.—What then, will you say the Fathers contradict one another ? —And is there any thing astonishing in that ?[6] I believe in the Fathers, because I believe in Scripture. The meaning of Scripture is one and simple, like heavenly truth itself. It is obtained by comparing scripture with scripture : it is deduced from the thread and connexion of the discourse.[7] There is a philosophy that is enjoined us as regards Holy Scripture : and that is, to bring all human opinions and maxims to it, as to a touchstone by which to try them."[1]

For a very long period such powerful truths had not been set forth with so much elegance. The Word of God was restored to its place, and the Fathers to theirs. The simple method by which we may arrive at the real meaning of Scripture was firmly laid down. The Word floated above all the difficulties and all the explanations of the School. Melancthon furnished the means of replying to all those who, like Dr. Eck, should perplex this subject, even to the most distant ages. The feeble *grammarian* had risen up ; and the broad and sturdy shoulders of the scholastic gladiator had bent under the first movement of his arm.

The weaker Eck was, the louder he clamoured. By his boastings and his accusations, he hoped to secure the victory that he had lost in his discussions. The monks and all the partisans of Rome re-echoed his clamours. From every part of Germany, reproaches were poured upon Luther ; but he remained unaffected by them. " The more I find my name covered with opprobrium, the more do I glory in it," said he at the conclusion of the explanations he published on the Leipsic propositions. " The truth, that is to say Christ, must needs increase, and I must decrease. The voice of the Bride and the Bridegroom causes me a joy that far surpasses the terrors inspired by their clamours. Men are not the authors of my sufferings, and I entertain no hatred towards them. It is Satan, the prince of wickedness, who desires to terrify me. But He who is within us is mightier than he that is in the world. The judgment of our contemporaries is bad, that of posterity will be better."[2]

If the Leipsic disputation augmented Luther's enemies in Germany, it also increased the number of his friends in foreign countries. " What Huss was in Bohemia in other days, you now are in Saxony, dear Martin," wrote the Bohemian brethren to him ; " for this reason, pray and be strong in the Lord ! "

About this time the war broke out between Luther and Emser, then professor at Leipsic. The latter wrote to Dr. Zack, a zealous Roman-catholic of Prague, a letter in which his design appeared to be to deprive the Hussites of their notion that Luther belonged to their party. Luther could not doubt that by seeming to justify him, the learned Leipsicker was endeavouring to fix upon him the suspicion of adhering to the Bohemian heresy, and he accordingly resolved to tear aside the veil under which his former host of Dresden desired to conceal his hostility. With this intent he published a letter, addressed " To Emser the Goat " (his adversary's crest was a goat), and concluded by these words, so

[1] Ehe das Ungeziffer uberhand nehme. L. Opp. (L.) xvii. 271.
[2] Eccius ob varias et insignes ingenii dotes. L. Opp. Lat. i. 337.
[3] Ausus est grammaticus Wittembergensis, Græce et Latine sane non indoctus, epistolam edere. Ibid. 338.
[4] The art of interpreting the Holy Scriptures.
[5] Una est Scriptura, cœlestis spiritus, pura, et per omnia verax. Contra Eckium Defensio, Corp. Ref. i. 115.
[6] Quid igitur ? Ipsi secum pugnant ! quid mirum ? Ibid.
[7] Quem coliatis Scripturis e filo ductuque orationis licet assequi. Ibid. p. 114.

[1] Ut hominum sententias, decretaque, ad ipsas, ceu ad Lydium lapidem, exigamus. Corp. Ref. i. 115.
[2] Præsens male judicat ætas ; judicium melius posteritatis erit. L. Opp. Lat. i. 310.

clearly depicting his character : " My maxim is,—to love all men, but to fear none."[1]

While new friends and enemies thus sprung up around Luther, his old friends seemed to be deserting him. Staupitz, who had brought the reformer from the obscurity of his cloister at Erfurth, began to evince some coolness towards him. Luther had soared too high for Staupitz, who could not follow him. " You abandon me," wrote Luther to him. " All day long I have been very sad on your account, as a weaned child cries after its mother.[2] I dreamt of you last night (continues the reformer) : you were leaving me, while I groaned and shed bitter tears. But you stretched out your hand, bade me be calm, and promised to return to me again."

The pacificator Miltitz was desirous of making a fresh attempt to calm the agitation of men's minds. But what hold could he have over men still agitated by the emotions the struggle had excited ? His endeavours proved unavailing. He was the bearer of the famous Golden Rose presented to the elector, but the latter did not condescend to receive it in person.[3] Frederick knew the artifices of Rome, and all hope of deceiving him was relinquished.[4]

CHAPTER VIII.

The Epistle to the Galatians—Christ for us—Blindness of Luther's Opponents—Earliest Ideas on the Lord's Supper —Is the Sacrament without Faith sufficient ?—Luther a Bohemian—Eck attacked—Eck goes to Rome.

LUTHER, far from retreating, advanced daily. It was at this time that he aimed one of his most violent blows against error in his Commentary on the Epistle to the Galatians.[5] The second Commentary is undoubtedly superior to the first ; but in the first he expounded with great power the doctrine of justification by faith. Each expression of the new apostle was full of life, and God made use of him to introduce a knowledge of Himself into the hearts of the people. " Christ gave himself for our sins," said Luther to his contemporaries.[6] " It was not silver or gold that He gave for us ; it was not a man ; it was not all the angels ; it was himself that He gave, out of whom there is nothing great. And He gave this inestimable treasure—for our sins. Where now are those who vaunt of the power of our

will ?—where are all the lessons of moral philosophy ?—where are the power and the strength of the law ? Since our sins were so great that nothing could take them away except a ransom so immeasurable, shall we still claim to obtain righteousness by the strength of our own will, by the power of the law, or by the teaching of men ? What shall we do with all these artifices, with all these delusions ? Alas ! we shall cover our iniquities with a false righteousness, and we shall make hypocrites of ourselves, whom nothing in the world can save."

But while Luther was thus laying down the doctrine that there is no salvation for men out of Christ, he also showed that this salvation transforms man, and makes him abound in good works. " He who has truly heard the Word of Christ (said the Reformer), and who keeps it, is immediately clothed with the spirit of charity. If you love the man who has made you a present of twenty florins, or done you any important service, or in any other manner testified his affection, how much more ought you to love Him who has given you not gold or silver, but himself, who has even received so many wounds for your sake, who for you has sweated drops of blood, and who died for you ; in a word, who, by paying for all your sins, has swallowed up death, and obtained for you in heaven a Father full of love!......If you love Him not, you have not heard with your heart the things that He has done ; you have not believed them, for faith worketh by love."— " This Epistle is my epistle," said Luther, speaking of the Epistle to the Galatians : " I am wedded to it."

His adversaries compelled him to advance more quickly than he would have done without them. At this period Eck incited the Franciscans of Juterbock to attack him again. Luther, in his reply,[1] not content with repeating what he had already taught, attacked errors that he had newly discovered. " I should like to know," said he, " in what part of Scripture the power of canonizing the saints has been given to the popes ; and also what necessity, what utility there is in canonizing them......For that matter," added he sarcastically, " let them canonize as much as they like ! "[2]

Luther's new attacks remained unanswered. The blindness of his enemies was as favourable to him as his own courage. They passionately defended secondary matters, and when Luther laid his hand on the foundations of the Roman doctrine, they saw them shaken without uttering a word. They busied themselves in defending the outworks, while their intrepid adversary was advancing into the body of the place, and there boldly planting the standard of truth. Accordingly, they were afterwards astonished when they

---

[1] L. Opp. Lat. i. 252.
[2] Ego super te, sicut ablactatus super matre sua, tristissimus hac die fui. Epp. i. 342.
[3] Rosam quam vocant auream nullo honore dignatus est ; imo pro ridicula habuit. L. Opp. Lat. in Præf.
[4] Intellexit princeps artes Romanæ curiæ et eos (legatos) digne tractare novit. Ibid.
[5] September 1519.
[6] L. Opp. (L.) x. 461.

[1] Defensio contra malignum Eccii judicium. L. Opp. Lat i. 356.
[2] Canoniset quisque quantum volet. Ibid. 367.

beheld the fortress they were defending undermined and on fire, and crumbling into ruins in the midst of the flames, while they were flattering themselves that it was impregnable, and were still braving those who led the assault. Thus are all great catastrophes effected.

The Sacrament of the Lord's Supper was now beginning to occupy Luther's thoughts. He looked in vain for this holy supper in the Mass. One day, shortly after his return from Leipsic, he went into the pulpit. Let us listen to his words, for they are the first he uttered on a subject that has since rent the Church of the Reformation into two parties. He said: "In the holy sacrament of the altar there are three things we must observe: the sign, which should be outward, visible, and in a bodily shape; the thing signified, which is inward, spiritual, and in the mind of man; and faith, which makes use of both."[1] If definitions had been carried no farther, unity would not have been destroyed.

Luther continued: "It would be a good thing if the Church, by a general council, should order both kinds to be given to the believer; not however that one kind is not sufficient, for faith alone would suffice." This bold language pleased his hearers. A few of them were however alarmed and irritated. "It is false and scandalous," said they.[2]

The preacher continued: "There is no closer, deeper, or more indivisible union than that which takes place between the food and the body which the food nourishes. Christ is so united to us in the sacrament, that he acts as if he were ourselves. Our sins assail him; his righteousness defends us."

But Luther was not satisfied with setting forth the truth; he attacked one of the most fundamental errors of Rome.[3] That Church maintains that the Sacrament operates of itself, independently of the disposition of the communicant. Nothing can be more convenient than such an opinion. Hence the ardour with which the sacrament is sought, —hence the profits of the Romish clergy. Luther attacked this doctrine,[4] and opposed it by the contrary doctrine,[5] by virtue of which faith and the concurrence of the heart are necessary.

This energetic protest was of a nature to overthrow the ancient superstitions; and yet it is most astonishing that no one paid any attention to it. Rome passed by that which should have called up a shriek of distress, and fell impetuously on the unimportant remark Luther had made at the beginning of his discourse, touching the communion in both kinds. This sermon having been published in December, a cry of heresy was raised in every quarter. "It is nothing more nor less than the doctrine of Prague,' was the observation at the court of Dresden, where the sermon arrived during the festival of Christmas; "the work, besides, is in German, in order that the common people may understand it."[1] The prince's devotion was disturbed, and on the third day of the festival he wrote to his cousin Frederick: "Since the publication of this sermon, the number of those who receive the Eucharist in both kinds has increased in Bohemia by six thousand. Your Luther, from being a professor at Wittemberg, is about to become bishop of Prague and arch-heretic!"—"He was born in Bohemia!" said some, "of Bohemian parents; he was brought up in Prague, and taught from Wickliffe's books!"

Luther thought it his duty to contradict these rumours in a writing wherein he seriously gives an account of his family. "I was born at Eisleben,"[2] said he, "and christened in St. Peter's Church. Dresden is the nearest place to Bohemia that I have ever visited."

Duke George's letter did not estrange the elector from Luther. A few days after, this prince invited the doctor to a splendid banquet which he gave the Spanish ambassador, and there Luther valiantly contended against Charles's minister.[3] The elector had begged him, through his chaplain, to defend his cause with moderation. "Too much folly is displeasing to men," replied Luther to Spalatin; "but too much discretion is displeasing to God. The Gospel cannot be defended without tumult and without scandal. The Word of God is a sword,—a war,—a ruin, —a stumbling-block,—a destruction,—a poison;[4] and, as Amos says, it meets us like a bear in the road or a lioness in the forest. I seek nothing, I ask nothing. There is One greater than I, who seeketh and asketh. If He should fall, I lose nothing; if He stand, I am profited nothing."[5]

Every thing announced that Luther would need faith and courage now more than ever. Eck was forming plans of revenge. Instead of the laurels that he had reckoned on gaining, the Leipsic gladiator had become the laughing-stock of all the sensible men of his nation. Several biting satires were published against him One was the *Epistle of Ignorant Canons*, written by Œcolampadius, and which cut Eck to the quick. Another was a *Complaint against Eck*, probably from the pen of the excellent Pirckheimer of Nuremberg, overflowing with a sarcasm and dignity of which Pascal's *Provincial Letters* can alone give us any idea.

---

1 L. Opp. (L.) xvii. 272.
2 Ibid. 281.
3 Si quis dixerit per ipsa novæ legis sacramenta *ex opere operato* non conferri gratiam, sed solam fidem divinæ promissionis, ad gratiam consequendam sufficere, anathema sit. Concil. Trident. Session 7, canon 8.
4 Known as the *opus operatum*.
5 That of the *opus operantis*.

1 L. Opp. (L.) xvii. 281.
2 Cæterum ego natus sum in Eisleben. Luth. Epp. l. 383.
3 Cum quo heri ego et Philippus certavimus, splendide invitati. Ibid. 388.
4 Verbum Dei gladius est, bellum est, ruina est, scandalum est, perditio est, venenum est. L. Epp. i. 417.
5 Ego nihil quæro: est, qui quærat. Stet ergo, sive cadat: ego nihil lucror, aut amitto. Itid. 418.

Luther manifested his displeasure at several of these writings. "It is better to attack openly," said he, "than to bite from behind a hedge."[1]

What a disappointment for the Chancellor of Ingolstadt! His fellow-countrymen abandoned him. He prepared to cross the Alps to seek foreign support. Wherever he went, he vented his threats against Luther, Melancthon, Carlstadt, and the elector himself. "From his lofty language," said the Wittemberg doctor, "one might take him to be God Almighty."[2] Inflamed with anger and the desire of revenge, Eck published, in February 1520, a work on the primacy of St. Peter. In this treatise, which was utterly destitute of all sound criticism, he maintained that this apostle was the first of the popes, and had dwelt twenty-five years in Rome. After this he set out for Italy, to receive the reward of his pretended triumphs, and to forge in Rome, under the shadow of

[1] Melior est aperta criminatio, quam iste sub sepe morsus. L. Epp. i. 426.
[2] Deum crederes Omnipotentem loqui. Ibid. 380.

the papal capitol, more powerful thunderbolts than the frail weapons of the schoolmen that had shivered in his hands.

Luther foresaw all the perils that his opponent's journey might draw upon him; but he feared not. Spalatin, in alarm, begged him to propose peace. "No," replied Luther, "so long as he continues his clamours, I cannot withdraw my hands from the contest. I trust every thing to God. I consign my bark to the winds and to the waves. The battle is the Lord's.[1] Why should you imagine that Christ will advance his cause by peace? Did he not fight with his own blood, and all the martyrs after him?"

Such, at the opening of the year 1520, was the position of the combatants of Leipsic. The one was rousing all the papacy to crush his rival: the other waited for war with the same calmness that men look for peace. The new year was destined to see the storm burst forth.

[1] Cogor rem Deo committere, data flatibus et fluctibus nave. Bellum Domini est. L. Epp. i. 425.

BOOK VI.

THE PAPAL BULL—1520.

CHAPTER I.

Character of Maximilian—Candidates for the Empire—Charles—Francis I.—Disposition of the Germans—The Crown offered to Frederick—Charles elected Emperor.

A NEW actor was about to appear on the stage. God designed to bring the Wittemberg monk face to face with the most powerful monarch that had appeared in Christendom since the days of Charlemagne. He selected a prince in the vigour of youth, and to whom every thing seemed to announce a long reign—a prince whose sceptre extended over a considerable part of the old world, and even over the new, so that (according to a celebrated saying) the sun never went down on his vast dominions; and to him He opposed that lowly Reformation, begun in the secluded cell of a convent at Erfurth by the anguish and the sighs of a poor monk. The history of this monarch and of his reign was destined, it would seem, to teach the world an important lesson. It was to show the nothingness of all the strength of man when it presumes to measure itself with the weakness of God. If a prince, a friend to Luther, had been called to the imperial throne, the success of the Reformation might

have been ascribed to his protection. If even an emperor opposed to the new doctrines, but yet a weak ruler, had worn the diadem, the triumph of this work might have been accounted for by the weakness of the monarch. But it was the haughty conqueror at Pavia who was destined to vail his pride before the power of God's Word; and the whole world beheld the man, who found it an easy task to drag Francis I. a prisoner to Madrid, obliged to lower his sword before the son of a poor miner.

The emperor Maximilian was dead, and the electors had met at Frankfort to choose a successor. This was an important event for all Europe under the existing circumstances. All Christendom was occupied with this election. Maximilian had not been a great prince; but his memory was dear to the people. They were delighted to call to recollection his presence of mind and his good nature. Luther used often to converse with his friends about him, and one day related the following anecdote of this monarch ·

A mendicant was once following him and begging alms, calling him *brother*; "for (said he) we are both descended from the same father, Adam. I am poor (continued he), but you are rich, and you ought therefore to help me." The emperor turned round at these words, and said to him : " There is a penny for you; go to all your other brothers, and, if each one gives you as much, you will be richer than I am."[1]

It was not a good-natured Maximilian that was destined to wear the imperial crown. The times were changing ; men of overweening ambition were about to dispute the throne of the emperors of the West; a strong hand was to grasp the reins of the empire, and long and bloody wars were on the point of succeeding a profound peace.

Three kings claimed the crown of the Cæsars from the assembly at Frankfort. A youthful prince, grandson of the last emperor, born in the first year of the century, and consequently nineteen years old, appeared first. His name was Charles, and he was born at Ghent. His paternal grandmother, Mary, daughter of Charles the Bold, had bequeathed to him Flanders and the rich domains of Burgundy. His mother, Joanna, daughter of Ferdinand of Aragon and Isabella of Castile, and wife of Philip the Emperor Maximilian's son, had transmitted to him the united crowns of the two Spains, Naples, and Sicily, to which Christopher Columbus had recently added a new world. His grandfather's death now put him in possession of the hereditary states of Austria. This young prince, endowed with great intelligence, and amiable whenever it pleased him to be so, joined to a taste for military exercises, in which the famous dukes of Burgundy had long distinguished themselves,—to the subtlety and penetration of the Italians,—to the respect for existing institutions which still characterizes the house of Austria, and which promised a firm defender to the papacy, —an extensive knowledge of public affairs which he had acquired under the direction of Chièvres ; for, from the age of fifteen years, he had attended all the deliberations of his councils.[2] Qualities so various were covered and concealed, as it were, by his Spanish taciturnity and reserve ; there was an air of melancholy in his long visage. " He was pious and silent," said Luther ; " I will wager that he does not talk so much in a year as I do in a day."[3] If Charles had grown up under free and christian influences, he would perhaps have been one of the most meritorious princes recorded in history ; but politics absorbed his whole life, and blighted his naturally amiable character.

The youthful Charles, not content with the sceptres he already grasped in his hand, aspired to the imperial dignity. " It is a beam of sunshine that casts a splendour upon the house on which it falls," said many ; " but stretch forth the hand to seize it, and you find nothing." Charles, on the contrary,

looked upon it as the summit of all earthly grandeur, and a means of obtaining a magical influence over the minds of nations.

Francis I., king of France, was the second candidate. The young paladins of the court of this chivalrous sovereign were ever repeating that he ought, like Charlemagne, to be emperor of all the West, and, reviving the exploits of the knights of old, to attack the Crescent that threatened the empire, crush the infidels, and recover the Holy Sepulchre. " You should convince the dukes of Austria that the imperial crown is not hereditary," said the ambassadors of Francis to the electors. " Besides, in the present state of affairs, Germany requires, not a youth of nineteen, but a prince who with a tried judgment combines talents already proved. Francis will unite the arms of France and Lombardy with those of Germany to make war on the Mussulmans. As sovereign of the duchy of Milan, he is already a member of the empire." The French ambassadors strengthened their arguments by four hundred thousand crowns which they expended in buying votes, and in banquets which the guest generally quitted in a state of inebriation.

Lastly, Henry VIII. of England, jealous of the influence the choice of the electors would give Francis or Charles, also entered the lists ; but he soon left these two powerful rivals to dispute the crown between them.

The electors were not very favourably disposed towards either. " Our people," thought they, " will consider the King of France as a foreign master, and this master may wrest even from us that independence of which the great lords of his own kingdom have recently been deprived." As for Charles, it was an old maxim with the electors never to select a prince who already played an important part in the empire. The pope participated in these fears. He was opposed to the King of Naples, his neighbour, and to the King of France, whose enterprising spirit alarmed him. " Choose rather one of yourselves," was the advice he sent to the electors. The Elector of Treves proposed to nominate Frederick of Saxony ; and the imperial crown was laid at the feet of this friend to Luther.

Such a choice would have gained the approbation of the whole of Germany. Frederick's wisdom and love for the people were well known. During the revolt of Erfurth, he had been advised to take the city by storm. He refused, that he might avoid bloodshed. " But it will not cost five men," was the reply.—" A single man would be too many," answered the prince.[1] It appeared that the election of the protector of the Reformation would secure the triumph of that work. Ought not Frederick to have seen a call from God in this wish of the electors? Who could

[1] L. Opp. (W.) xxii. 1869.
[2] Mémoires de Du Bellay. i. 45.
[3] L. Opp. (W.) xxii. 1874.

[1] L. Opp. (W.) xxii. 1858.

have been better suited to preside over the destinies of the empire than this wise prince? Who could have been stronger against the Turks than a truly Christian emperor? The refusal of the Elector of Saxony, so extolled by historians, may have been a fault on the part of this prince. Perhaps to him must be partly ascribed the contests that devastated Germany in after days. But it is a difficult matter to decide whether Frederick deserves to be blamed for want of faith, or honoured for his humility. He thought that the very safety of the empire required him to refuse the crown.[1] "We need an emperor more powerful than myself to preserve Germany," said this modest and disinterested prince. "The Turk is at our gates. The King of Spain, whose hereditary possessions of Austria border on the threatened frontier, is its natural defender."

The Roman legate, seeing that Charles would be elected, declared that the pope withdrew his objections; and on the 28th of June the grandson of Maximilian was nominated emperor. "God," said Frederick not long after, "hath given him to us in His favour and in His anger."[2] The Spanish envoys offered 30,000 gold florins to the Elector of Saxony, as a testimonial of their master's gratitude; but this prince refused them, and forbade his ministers to accept of any present. At the same time, he secured the liberties of Germany by a capitulation to which Charles's envoys swore in his name. The circumstances under which the latter assumed the imperial crown seemed, moreover, to give a stronger pledge than these oaths in favour of German liberty and of the work of the Reformation. This youthful prince was jealous of the laurels that his rival Francis I. had gathered at Marignan. The struggle would still be continued in Italy, and the interval thus employed would doubtless suffice for the Reformation to gain strength. Charles quitted Spain in May 1520, and was crowned at Aix-la-Chapelle on the 22d of October.

CHAPTER II.

Luther's Letter to the Emperor—His Danger—Frederick's Instructions to his Envoy at Rome—Luther's Sentiments —Melancthon's Fears—The German Nobles favour the Reformation—Schaumburg—Sickingen—Ulric of Hütten —Luther's Confidence—Erasmus defends Luther—Abstemius — Hedio — Luther becomes more free — Faith the Source of Works—What gives Faith?—Luther judging his own Writings.

LUTHER had foreseen that the cause of the Reformation would soon be carried before the new emperor. He wrote to Charles, while this prince was yet at Madrid: "If

[1] Is vero heroica plane moderatione animi magnifice repudiavit. Pallavicini, i. 79.
[2] L. Opp. (W.) xxii. 1896.

the cause that I defend," said he, "is worthy of appearing before the throne of the Majesty of heaven, it ought not to be unworthy of engaging the attention of a prince of this world. O Charles! first of the kings of the earth! I throw myself a suppliant at the feet of your most serene majesty. Deign to receive under the shadow of your wings, not me, but the cause of that eternal truth, for the defence of which God has intrusted you with the sword."[1] The young monarch laid aside this singular letter from a German monk, and made no reply to it.

While Luther was vainly turning towards Madrid, the storm seemed to increase around him. Fanaticism was kindling in Germany. Hochstraten, indefatigable in his attempts at persecution, had extracted certain theses from Luther's writings. At his demand, the universities of Cologne and Louvain had condemned these works. That of Erfurth, still exasperated at Luther's preference for Wittemberg, was about to follow their example. But having been informed of it, the doctor wrote to Lange so spirited a letter, that the Erfurth divines were dismayed and kept silent. The condemnation pronounced at Cologne and Louvain sufficed, however, to inflame men's minds. Nay, more: the priests of Meissen, who had espoused Emser's quarrel, said publicly (Melancthon is our authority) that he who should kill Luther would be without sin.[2] "Now is the time," said Luther, "when men will think they do Christ a service by putting us to death." These homicidal words were destined to produce their fruit in due season.

One day, says a biographer, as Luther was in front of the Augustine cloister, a stranger, who held a pistol concealed under his cloak, accosted him in these words: "Why do you go thus alone?"—"I am in God's hands," replied Luther. "He is my strength and my shield. What can man do unto me?"[3] Upon this the stranger turned pale (adds the historian), and fled away trembling. Serra Longa, the ambassador at the Augsburg conference, wrote to the elector about this time: "Let not Luther find an asylum in the states of your highness; let him be rejected of all, and stoned in the face of heaven; that will be more pleasing to me than if I received ten thousand crowns from you."[4]

But it was particularly in the direction of Rome that the storm was gathering. Valentine Teutleben, a Thuringian nobleman, vicar to the Archbishop of Mentz, and a zealous partisan of the papacy, was the Elector of Saxony's representative at the papal court. Teutleben, ashamed of the protection accorded by his master to an heretical monk, was im-

[1] Causam ipsam veritatis. L. Epp. i. 392. 15th January 1520.
[2] Ut sine peccato esse eum censebant qui me interfecerit. L. Epp. i. 383.
[3] Was kann mir ein Mensch thun? Keith, L. Umstände, p. 89.
[4] Tenzel, Hist. Bericht vom Anfang und Torbg. den Reform. Lutheri, ii. 16s.

patient at seeing his mission paralyzed by this imprudent conduct. He imagined that, by alarming the elector, he would induce him to abandon the rebellious divine. " They will not listen to me here," wrote he to his master, " because of the protection you show to Luther." But the Romans were deceived if they thought to frighten the prudent Frederick. This prince was aware that the will of God and the movements of nations were more irresistible than the decrees of the papal chancery. He ordered his envoy to intimate to the pope that, far from defending Luther, he had always left him to defend himself; besides, he had already called upon him to quit Saxony and the university; that the doctor had declared his willingness to obey, and that he would not then be in the electoral states, if the legate himself, Charles of Miltitz, had not entreated the prince to keep him near at hand, for fear that, by going to other countries, Luther would act with greater liberty than even in Saxony.[1] Frederick went farther than this: he desired to enlighten Rome. " Germany," continues he in his letter, " now possesses a great number of learned men, well taught in every language and science; the laity themselves begin to have understanding, and to love the Holy Scriptures; if, therefore, the reasonable conditions of Dr. Luther are rejected, there is great cause to fear that peace will never be re-established. Luther's doctrine has struck deep root into many hearts. If, instead of refuting it by the testimony of the Bible, you strive to destroy him by the thunderbolts of the ecclesiastical authority, great scandals will arise, and ruinous and terrible revolts will be excited."[2]

The elector, having the greatest confidence in Luther, communicated Teutleben's letter to him, with another that he had received from Cardinal Saint George. The reformer was agitated as he read them. He immediately perceived the dangers by which he was surrounded. His soul was for a time quite overwhelmed. But it was in such moments that the whole strength of his faith shone forth. Often weak, and ready to fall into dejection, he rose again, and appeared greater in the midst of the tempest. He longed to be delivered from such trials; but he saw at what price peace was offered to him, and he indignantly rejected it. " Hold my peace!" exclaimed he, " I am disposed to do so, if they will permit me: that is, if they will make others keep silence. If any one desires my places, let him take them; if any one desires to destroy my writings, let him burn them, I am ready to keep quiet, provided they do not require that the truth of the Gospel should be silent also.[3] I do not

ask for a cardinal's hat; I ask not for gold, or for anything that Rome values. There is nothing in the world they cannot obtain from me, provided they will not shut up the way of salvation against Christians.[1] Their threats do not alarm me, their promises cannot seduce me."

Animated with such sentiments, Luther soon recovered his militant disposition, and preferred the christian warfare to the calm of solitude. One night was sufficient to bring back his desire of overthrowing Rome. " I have taken my part," wrote he on the morrow; " I despise the fury of Rome, and contemn her favours. No more reconciliation, no more communication with her for ever.[2] Let her condemn me, let her burn my writings! In my turn, I will condemn and publicly burn the pontifical law,—that nest of every heresy. The moderation I have hitherto shown has been unavailing; I now renounce it!"

His friends were far from being thus tranquil. Great was the consternation at Wittemberg. " We are in a state of extraordinary expectation," said Melancthon; " I would rather die than be separated from Luther. [3] If God does not help us, we shall all perish."—" Our dear Luther is still alive," wrote he a month later, in his anxiety; " may it please God to grant him a long life![4] for the Roman sycophants are making every exertion to put him to death. Let us pray that this sole avenger of sacred theology may long survive."

These prayers were heard. The warning the elector had given Rome through his envoy was not without foundation. Luther's words had found an echo every where—in cottages and convents, in the homes of the citizens and in the castles of the nobles, in the universities and in the palaces of kings. " If my life," he had said to Duke John of Saxony, " has been instrumental to the conversion of a single man, I shall willingly consent to see all my books perish."[5] It was not one man, it was a great multitude, that had found the light in the writings of the humble doctor. Every where, accordingly, were men to be found ready to protect him. The sword intended to slay him was forging in the Vatican; but heroes were springing up in Germany to shield him with their bodies. At the moment when the bishops were chafing with rage, when princes kept silence, when the people were in expectation, and when the first murmurs of the thunder were beginning to be heard from the Seven Hills, God aroused the German nobles to make a rampart for his servant.

[1] Da er viel freyer und sicherer schreiben und handeln möchte was er wollte. L. Opp. (L.) xvii. 208.
[2] Schreckliche, grausame, schädliche und verderbliche Empörungen erregen. Ibid.
[3] Semper quiescere paratus, modo veritatem evangelicam non jubeant quiescere. L. Epp. i. 462.

[1] Si salutis viam Christianis permittant esse liberam, hoc unum peto ab illis, ac præterea nihil. L. Epp. i. 462.
[2] Nolo eis reconciliari nec communicare in perpetuum. Ibid. 466. 10th July 1520.
[3] Emori mallem, quam ab hoc viro avelli. Corp. Ref. i. 160, 163.
[4] Martinus noster spirat, atque utinam diu. Ibid. 190, 208. [5] L. Opp. (L.) xvii. 392.

Sylvester of Schaumburg, one of the most powerful knights of Franconia, sent his son to Wittemberg at this time with a letter for the reformer. " Your life is in danger," wrote he. " If the support of the electors, princes, or magistrates fail you, I entreat you to beware of going to Bohemia, where in former times learned men have had much to undergo; rather come to me. God willing, I shall soon have collected more than a hundred gentlemen, and with their help I shall be able to protect you from every danger." [1]

Francis of Sickingen, the hero of his age,[2] of whose intrepid courage we have already been witnesses,[3] loved the reformer, because he found him worthy of being loved, and also because he was hated by the monks.[4] " My services, my goods, and my body, all that I possess," wrote he to Luther, " are at your disposal. You desire to maintain the christian truth : I am ready to aid you in the work." [5] Harmurth of Cronberg held the same language. Lastly, Ulric of Hütten, the poet and valiant knight of the sixteenth century, never ceased speaking in Luther's favour. But what a contrast between these two men! Hütten wrote to the reformer : " It is with swords and with bows, with javelins and bombs, that we must crush the fury of the devil." Luther on receiving these letters exclaimed : " I will not have recourse to arms and bloodshed in defence of the Gospel. By the Word the earth has been subdued ; by the Word the Church has been saved ; and by the Word also it shall be re-established."—" I do not despise his offer," said he at another time on receiving Schaumburg's letter, which we have mentioned above, " but I will rely upon none but Jesus Christ." [6] It was not thus the Roman pontiffs spoke when they waded in the blood of the Waldenses and Albigenses. Hütten felt the difference between his cause and Luther's, and he accordingly wrote to him with noble-mindedness : " As for me, I am busied with the affairs of men ; but you soar far higher, and are occupied solely with those of God." [7] He then set out to win, if possible, Charles and Ferdinand to the side of truth. [8]

Luther at this time met with a still more illustrious protector. Erasmus, whom the Romanists so often quote against the Reformation, raised his voice and undertook the reformer's defence, after his own fashion, however, that is to say, without any show of defending him. On the 1st of November 1519, this patriarch of learning wrote to Albert, elector of Mentz and primate of all Germany, a letter in which, after describing in vivid colours the corruption of the Church, he says : " This is what stirred up Luther, and made him oppose the intolerable imprudence of certain doctors. For what other motive can we ascribe to a man who seeks not honours and who cares not for money ? [1] Luther has dared doubt the virtue of indulgences ; but others before him had most unblushingly affirmed it. He feared not to speak, certainly with little moderation, against the power of the Roman pontiff ; but others before him had extolled it without reserve. He has dared contemn the decrees of St. Thomas, but the Dominicans had set them almost above the Gospel. He has dared give utterance to his scruples about confession, but the monks continually made use of this ordinance as a net in which to catch and enslave the consciences of men. Pious souls were grieved at hearing that in the universities there was little mention of the evangelical doctrine ; that in the assemblies of Christians very little was heard of Christ ; [2] that nothing was there talked of, except the power of the pontiff, and the opinions of the Romish doctors ; and that the whole sermon was a mere matter of lucre, flattery, ambition, and imposture.[3] It is to such a state of affairs that we should ascribe Luther's violent language." Such was Erasmus's opinion on the state of the Church and on the reformer. This letter, which was published by Ulric Hütten, then residing at the court of Mentz, made a profound impression.

At the same time, men more obscure than Erasmus and than all the knights, but who were destined to be more powerful auxiliaries, rallied round Luther in every direction. Doctor Botzhemus Abstemius, canon of Constance, wrote to him thus : " Now that you have become the friend of the universe, or at least of the better part of the world, that is to say, of good and true Christians, you must also become mine, whether you will or not! [4] I am so delighted with your writings, that nothing gives me greater pleasure than to be living at a time when not only profane but also sacred literature is resuming its pristine splendour." [5] And at nearly the same period Gaspard Hedio, preacher at Basle, wrote to the reformer : " Most dear sir, I see that your doctrine is of God, and that it cannot be destroyed ; that it becomes daily more efficacious ; and that every hour it is winning souls to Christ by turning them

[1] Denn Ich, und hundert von Adel, die Ich (ob Gott will) aufbringen will, euch redlich anhalten. L. Opp. (L.) xvii. 381.
[2] Equitum Germaniæ rarum decus (a peerless ornament of German knighthood), says Melancthon on this occasion. Corp. Ref. i. 201.
[3] See vol i. p. 47.
[4] Et ob id invisus illis. Corp. Ref. i. 139.
[5] Ibid.
[6] Nolo nisi Christo protectore niti. L. Epp. i. 148.
[7] Mea humana sunt: tu perfectior, jam totus ex divinis pendes. L. Opp. Lat. ii. 175.
[8] Viam facturus libertati (cod. Bavar. veritati) per maximos principes. Corp. Ref. i. 201.

[1] Quid enim aliud suspicer de eo qui nec honores ambit, nec pecuniam cupit? Erasm. Opp. iii. 315.
[2] Imo in sacris concionibus minimum audiri de Christo. Ibid.
[3] Totam orationem jam palam quæstum, adulationem, ambitionem, ac fucum præ se ferre. Ibid.
[4] Postquam orbi, aut saltem potiori orbis parti, hoc est, bonis et vere christianis amicus factus es, meus quoque amicus eris, velis, nolis. Botzheim and his Friends, by Walchner, p. 107.
[5] Et divinæ pristinum nitorem recuperant. Ibid.

away from sin and attracting them to real piety.[1] Do not halt therefore, O liberator, but exert all your power to restore the yoke of Christ, so light and easy to bear. Be yourself the general, and we will follow after you, like soldiers whom nothing can tear from you."[2]

Thus at one time Luther's enemies oppress him, at another his friends spring up to defend him. "My bark," said he, "floats to and fro, the sport of the winds; hope and fear prevail by turns; but what matters it!"[3] And yet these testimonies of sympathy were not without influence upon his mind. "The Lord reigns," said he, "I see him there, as if I could touch him."[4] Luther felt that he was not alone; his words had borne fruit, and this thought filled him with fresh courage. The fear of compromising the elector no longer checked him, when he found other defenders ready to brave the anger of Rome. He became more free, and if possible more determined. This is an important epoch in the development of Luther's character. "Rome ought to understand," wrote he at this period to the elector's chaplain, "that, even should she succeed by her threats in expelling me from Wittemberg, she would only injure her cause. It is not in Bohemia, but in the very heart of Germany that those are to be found who are ready to defend me against the thunders of the papacy. If I have not done my enemies all the harm I am preparing for them, they must ascribe it neither to my moderation nor to their tyranny, but to the elector's name and to the interests of the university of Wittemberg, which I feared to compromise: now that I have such fears no longer, they will see me fall with fresh vigour upon Rome and upon her courtiers."[5]

And yet it was not on the great that Luther fixed his hopes. He had been often solicited to dedicate a book to Duke John, the elector's brother. He had not done so. "I am afraid," said he, "that the suggestion comes from himself. Holy Scripture should subserve the glory of God's name alone."[6] Luther now recovered from his fears, and dedicated his sermon on Good Works to Duke John. This is one of the writings in which the reformer lays down with the greatest force the doctrine of justification by faith, —that powerful truth, whose strength he sets far above the sword of Hütten, the army of Sickengen, and the protection of dukes and electors.

"The first, the noblest, the sublimest of all works," says he, "is faith in Jesus Christ.[7] It is from this work that all other

works must proceed: they are but the vassals of faith, and receive their efficacy from it alone.

"If a man feels in his heart the assurance that what he has done is acceptable to God. the work is good, if it were merely the lifting up of a straw; but if he have not this assurance, his work is not good, even should he raise the dead. A heathen, a Jew, a Turk, a sinner, can perform all the other works; but to trust firmly in God, and to feel an assurance that we are accepted by him, is what a Christian, strong in grace, alone is capable of doing.

"A Christian who possesses faith in God does everything with liberty and joy; while the man who is not at one with God is full of care and kept in bondage; he asks himself with anguish how many works he should perform; he runs to and fro; he questions this man and that; he nowhere finds peace, and does everything with sorrow and fear.

"Consequently, I have always extolled faith. But in the world it is otherwise. There, the essential thing is to have many works—works high and great, and of every dimension, without caring whether they are quickened by faith. Thus, men build their peace, not on God's good pleasure, but on their own merits, that is to say, on sand. (Matthew vii. 27.)

"To preach faith (it has been said) is to prevent good works; but if a man should possess the strength of all men united, or even of all creatures,[1] this sole obligation of living in faith would be a task too great for him ever to accomplish. If I say to a sick man: 'Be well, and thou shalt have the use of thy limbs,' will any one say that I forbid him to use his limbs? Must not health precede labour? It is the same when we preach faith: it should go before works, in order that the works themselves should exist.

"Where then, you will say, can we find this faith, and how can we receive it? This is in truth what it is most important to know. Faith comes solely from Jesus, who was promised and given freely.

"O man! figure Jesus Christ to yourself, and contemplate how God in him has shown thee his mercy, without any merit on thy part going before.[2] Draw from this image of his grace the faith and assurance that all thy sins are forgiven thee. Works cannot produce it. It flows from the blood, and wounds, and death of Christ; thence it wells forth into our hearts. Christ is the rock whence flow milk and honey. (Deut. xxxii.)

As we cannot notice all Luther's writings, we have quoted a few short passages from this discourse on Good Works, in consequence of the opinion the reformer himself entertained of it. "In my own judgment,"

[1] Lucri facit Christo, abducit a vitiis, asserit veræ pietati. Kappens Nachlese, ii. 433.
[2] Tu dux esto, nos indivulsi milites erimus. Ibid.
[3] Ita fluctuat navis mea: nunc spes, nunc timor regnat. L. Epp. i. 443.
[4] Dominus regnat, ut palpare possimus. Ibid. 451.
[5] Sævius in Romanenses grassaturus. Ibid. 465.
[6] Scripturam sacram nolim alicujus nomini nisi Dei servire. Ibid. 431.
[7] Das erste und höchste, alleredelste....gute Werck ist der Glaube in Christum. L. Opp. (L.) xvii. 394.

[1] Wenn ein Mensch tausend, oder alle Menschen, oder alle Creaturen wäre. L. Opp. (L.) xvii. 398.
[2] Siehe, also must du Christum in dich bilden, und sehen wie in Ihm Gott seine Barmherzigkeit dir fürhält und anbeut. Ibid. 401.

said he, " it is the best I ever published."
And he added immediately this deep reflec-
tion : " But I know that when I please my-
self with what I write, the infection of that
bad leaven hinders it from pleasing others."[1]
Melancthon, in forwarding this discourse to
a friend, accompanied it with these words :
" There is no one among all the Greek and
Latin writers who has come nearer than
Luther to the spirit of St. Paul."[2]

CHAPTER III.

The Papacy attacked—Appeal to the Nobility—The three
Walls—All Christians are Priests—The Magistrate should
chastise the Clergy—Roman Corruptions—Ruin of Italy—
Dangers of Germany—The Pope—The Legates—The
Monks—Marriage of Priests—Celibacy—Festivals—The
Bohemians—Charity—The Universities—The Empire—
The Emperor should retake Rome—Unpublished Book—
Luther's Moderation—Success of the Address.

BUT there was another evil in the Church
besides the substitution of a system of meritorious works for the grand idea of grace and
amnesty.[3] A haughty power had arisen in
the midst of the shepherds of Christ's flock.
Luther prepared to attack this usurped authority. Already a vague and distant rumour
announced the success of Dr. Eck's intrigues
at Rome. This rumour aroused the militant
spirit of the reformer, who, in the midst of
all his troubles, had studied in his retirement
the rise, progress, and usurpations of the
papacy. His discoveries had filled him with
surprise. He no longer hesitated to make
them known, and to strike the blow which,
like Moses' rod in ancient times, was to
awaken a people who had long slumbered in
captivity. Even before Rome had time to
publish her formidable bull, it was he who
hurled his declaration of war against her.
" The time to be silent is past," exclaimed
he ; " the time to speak is come ! At last,
we must unveil the mysteries of Antichrist."
On the 23d of June 1520, he published his
famous *Appeal to his Imperial Majesty and
to the Christian Nobility of the German Nation, on the Reformation of Christianity.*[4] This
work was the signal of the attack that was
to decide both the rupture and the victory.
" It is not through presumption," said he
at the opening of this address, " that I, a
man of the people, venture to speak to your
lordships. The misery and oppression that
at this hour weigh down all the states of
Christendom, and particularly Germany, extort from me a cry of distress. I must call
for help ; I must see if God will not give his

[1] Erit, meo judicio. omnium quæ ediderim optimum :
quanquam scio quæ mihi mea placent, hoc ipso fermento
infecta, non solere aliis placere. L. Epp. i. 431.
[2] Quo ad Pauli spiritum nemo propius accessit. Corp.
Ref. i. 202.
[3] See vol. i. p. 7, seqq.
[4] L. Opp. (L.) xvii. 457-502.

Spirit to some man in our own country, and
thus stretch forth his hand to save our
wretched nation. God has placed over us a
young and generous prince,[1] and has thus
filled our hearts with great expectations.
But on our parts we must do every thing
that lies in our power.
" Now the first requisite is, not to trust in
our own strength, or in our lofty wisdom.
If we begin a good work with confidence in
ourselves, God overthrows and destroys it.
Frederick I., Frederick II., and many other
emperors besides, before whom the world
trembled, have been trodden under foot by
the popes, because they trusted more in their
own strength than in God. Therefore they
could not but fall. It is against the powers
of hell that we have to contend in this
struggle. Hoping nothing from the strength
of arms, humbly trusting in the Lord, looking more to the distress of Christendom than
to the crimes of the wicked—*this* is how we
must set to work. Otherwise the work will
have a prosperous look at the beginning ; but
suddenly, in the midst of the contest, confusion will enter in, evil minds will cause incalculable disasters, and the whole world will
be deluged with blood. The greater our
power, the greater also is our danger, if we
do not walk in the fear of the Lord."
After this prelude, Luther continues thus
" The Romans have raised around themselves three walls to protect them against
every kind of reformation. Have they been
attacked by the temporal power ?—they have
asserted that it had no authority over them,
and that the spiritual power was superior to
it. Have they been rebuked by Holy Scripture ?—they have replied that no one is able
to interpret it except the pope. Have they
been threatened with a council ?—no one
(said they) but the sovereign pontiff has
authority to convoke one.
" They have thus despoiled us of the three
rods destined to correct them, and have given
themselves up to every wickedness. But
now may God be our helper, and give us one
of those trumpets that overthrew the walls
of Jericho. With our breath let us throw
down those barriers of paper and straw which
the Romans have built around them, and upraise the rods which punish the wicked, by
exposing the wiles of the devil."
Luther now begins the attack. He shakes
to its foundation that papal monarchy which
for ages had combined the people of the West
in one body under the sceptre of the Roman
bishop. That there is no sacerdotal caste in
Christianity, is the truth which he powerfully sets forth at the beginning,—a truth
hidden from the eyes of the Church from the
earliest ages.
" It has been said," writes Luther, " that
the pope, the bishops, the priests, and all
those who people the convents, form the spi-

[1] The emperor Charles V.—Gott hat uns ein junges edles
Blut zum Haupt gegeben. L. Opp. (L.) xvii. 457.

ritual or ecclesiastical state; and that the princes, the nobility, the citizens, and peasants, form the secular or lay estate. This is a fine story. Let no person, however, be startled at it. All Christians belong to the spiritual state, and there is no other difference between them than that arising from the functions which they discharge. We have all one baptism, one faith; and this it is which constitutes the spiritual man. The unction, the tonsure, ordination, consecration by the bishop or the pope, may make a hypocrite, but never a spiritual man. We are all consecrated priests by baptism, as Saint Peter says: *Ye are priests and kings*, although it does not belong to all to exercise such offices, for no one can take what is common to all without the consent of the community. But if we possess not this Divine consecration, the pope's anointing can never make a priest. If ten brothers, sons of a king, having equal claims to the inheritance, select one of them to administer it for them, they would all be kings, and yet only one of them would be the administrator of their common power. So it is with the Church. If a few pious laymen were banished to a desert place, and if, not having among them a priest consecrated by a bishop, they should agree to choose one of their own number, married or not, this man would be as truly a priest as if all the bishops in the world had consecrated him. Thus Augustine, Ambrose, and Cyprian, were elected.

" Hence it follows that laymen and priests, princes and bishops, or, as they say, the clergy and laity, have nothing but their functions to distinguish them. They have all the same estate, but have not all the same work to perform.

" If this be true, why should not the magistrate chastise the clergy? The secular power was established by God to punish the wicked and to protect the good. And it must be allowed to act throughout all Christendom, whomsoever it may touch, be he pope, bishop, priest, monk, or nun. St. Paul says to all Christians: *Let every one*[1] (and consequently the pope also) *be subject unto the higher powers, for they bear not the sword in vain.*"

Luther, having in like manner overthrown the two other walls, passes in review all the corruptions of Rome. He sets forth, in an eminently popular style of eloquence, the evils that had been pointed out for centuries past. Never had a nobler protest been heard. The assembly before which Luther spoke was the Church; the power whose corruptions he attacked was that papacy which for ages had oppressed all nations with its weight; and the reformation he so loudly called for was destined to exercise its powerful influence over all Christendom,—in all the world, so long as the human race shall endure.

He begins with the pope. "It is a horrible thing," says he, "to behold the man who styles himself Christ's vicegerent displaying a magnificence that no emperor can equal. Is this being like the poor Jesus, or the humble Peter? He is (say they) the lord of the world! But Christ, whose vicar he boasts of being, has said, *My kingdom is not of this world*. Can the dominions of a vicar extend beyond those of his superior?"

Luther now proceeds to describe the effects of the papal rule. "Do you know what is the use of cardinals? I will tell you. Italy and Germany have many convents, religious foundations, and richly endowed benefices. How can this wealth be drawn to Rome? Cardinals have been created; these cloisters and prelacies have been given to them; and now......Italy is almost deserted, the convents are in ruins, the bishoprics devoured, the cities decayed, the inhabitants corrupted, religious worship is expiring, and preaching abolished!......And why is this? Because all the wealth of the churches must go to Rome. The Turk himself would never have so ruined Italy!"

Luther next turns to his fellow-country men:

" And now that they have thus sucked all the blood of their own nation, they come into Germany; they begin tenderly; but let us be on our guard, or Germany will erelong be like Italy! We have already a few cardinals. Before the dull Germans comprehend our design (think they) they will no longer have either bishopric, convent, or benefice, penny or farthing left. Antichrist must possess the treasures of the earth. Thirty or forty cardinals will be created in one day. Bamberg will be given to one, the bishopric of Wurtzburg to another; rich cures will be attached to them, until the cities and churches are desolate. And then the pope will say: I am Christ's vicar, and the shepherd of his flocks. Let the Germans be submissive!"

Luther's indignation is kindled:

"What! shall we Germans endure such robberies and such extortions from the pope? If the kingdom of France has been able to defend itself, why should we permit ourselves to be thus ridiculed and laughed at? Oh! if they only despoiled us of our goods! But they lay waste the churches, fleece the sheep of Christ, abolish religious worship, and annihilate the Word of God."

Luther here exposes "the practices of Rome" to obtain the money and the revenues of Germany. Annats, palliums, commendams, administrations, reversions, incorporations, reserves, &c.—he passes them all in review; and then he says: "Let us endeavour to check such desolation and wretchedness. If we desire to march against the Turks, let us march against those who are the worst Turks of all. If we hang thieves, and decapitate highway robbers, let us not

---

[1] Πᾶσα ψυχή, every soul. Rom. xiii. 1, 4.

permit Romish avarice to escape, which is the greatest of thieves and robbers, and that too in the name of St. Peter and of Jesus Christ! Who can suffer this? Who can be silent? All that the pope possesses, has he not gained by plunder? For he has neither bought it, nor inherited it from St. Peter, nor gained it by the sweat of his brow? Whence then has he all this?"

Luther proposes remedies for these evils, and calls energetically upon the nobility of Germany to put an end to these Romish depredations. He then comes to the reformation of the pope himself: "Is it not ridiculous," says he, "that the pope pretends to be the lawful heir to the empire? Who gave it him? Was it Jesus Christ, when he said: *The kings of the Gentiles exercise lordship over them, but it shall not be so among you?*[1] (Luke xxii. 25, 26.) How is it possible to govern an empire, and at the same time preach, pray, study, and take care of the poor? Jesus Christ forbade his ministers to carry with them either gold or two coats, because they would be unable to discharge the duties of their ministry if they were not free from all other care; and yet the pope would govern the empire and still remain pope."

Luther continues stripping the sovereign pontiff: "Let the pope renounce every claim on the kingdom of Naples and Sicily. He has no more right to it than I have. It is unjustly and in opposition to all the commandments of Christ that he possesses Bologna, Imola, Ravenna, the Romagna, the March of Ancona, &c. *No man that warreth,* says Saint Paul, *entangleth himself with the affairs of this life.* (2 Tim. ii. 4.) Yet the pope, who pretends to be the leader of the Church militant, entangles himself with the affairs of this life more than any emperor or king. We must relieve him from all this toil. Let the emperor put the bible and a prayer-book into the pope's hands, in order that he may leave the cares of government to kings, and confine himself to preaching and praying."[2]

Luther will no more suffer the pope's spiritual power in Germany than his temporal power in Italy. "First of all," says he, "we must expel from every German state those papal legates, with their pretended benefits which they sell us at their weight in gold, and which are downright impositions. They take our money, and for what? to legalize their ill-gotten gains, to absolve from all oaths, to teach us to be wanting in fidelity, to instruct us how to sin, and to lead us direct to hell. Hearest thou this, O pope! not most holy, but most sinful pope!—May God from his throne in heaven soon hurl thee from thy throne into the bottomless pit!"

The christian tribune pursues his course. After having called the pope to his bar, he summons before him all the corruptions that form the papal train, and purposes sweeping from the floor of the Church the rubbish by which it was encumbered. He begins with the monks:—

"And now then I come to that sluggish troop which promises much but does little. Do not be angry, my dear sirs, my intentions are good: what I have to say is a truth at once sweet and bitter: namely, no more cloisters must be built for mendicant friars. We have, indeed, too many already, and would to God that they were all pulled down. Strolling through a country like beggars never has done and never can do good."

The marriage of the clergy now has its turn, and this is the first time Luther speaks of it:—

"To what a sad state have the clergy fallen, and how many priests do we not find burdened with women, and children, and remorse, and yet no one comes to their aid! It is all very well for the pope and the bishops to let things go on as before, and for that to continue lost which is lost; but I am determined to save my conscience, and to open my mouth freely: after that, let the pope, the bishops, and any one who pleases, take offence at it!.........I assert, then, that according to the appointment of Christ and his apostles, each city should have a pastor or bishop, and that this pastor may have a wife, as Saint Paul writes to Timothy: *A bishop must be the husband of one wife* (1 Tim. iii. 2), and as is still practised in the Greek Church. But the devil has persuaded the pope, as the same apostle says to Timothy (1 Tim. iv. 1 to 3), to forbid the clergy to marry. And hence have proceeded miseries so numerous that we cannot mention all. What is to be done? How can we save so many pastors, in whom we have no fault to find, except that they live with a woman, to whom they would with all their heart be legitimately married? Ah! let them quiet their consciences! let them take this woman as their lawful wife, and let them live virtuously with her, not troubling themselves whether the pope is pleased or not. The salvation of your soul is of greater consequence to you than tyrannical and arbitrary laws, that do not emanate from the Lord."

It is in this way that the Reformation aimed at restoring purity of morals in the Church. The reformer continues:—

"Let all festivals be abolished, and let none but Sunday be observed; or if people desire to keep the great Christian festivals, let them be celebrated only in the morning, and let the rest of the day be like any other working-day. For as on those days men do nothing but drink, gamble, indulge in every sin, or remain idle, they offend God on the festivals more than at other times."

---

[1] 'Τμεῖς δὲ οὐχ οὕτως (sub. ἔσῃ). See Matthew xx. 26.

[2] Ihm die Biblien und Betbücher dafür anzeigen....und er predige und bete. L. Opp. xvii. 472.

He next attacks the commemorations,[1] which he styles mere taverns; and after them the fasts and religious fraternities.— He not only desires to put an end to abuses, he wishes also to put away schism. "It is high time," says he, "that we busied ourselves seriously with the cause of the Bohemians,—that we put a stop to envy and hatred,—and that we united with them." After proposing some excellent means of reconciliation, he adds: "We must convince heretics by Scripture, as did the ancient Fathers, and not subdue them by fire. In this latter system, the executioners would be the most learned doctors in the world...... Oh! would to God that on both sides we stretched forth our hands in brotherly humility, instead of being inflexible in the sentiment of our strength and of our right! Charity is more necessary than the papacy of Rome. I have now done all that is in my power. If the pope and his adherents oppose this, the responsibility will fall on them. The pope should be ready to renounce his papacy, all his possessions, and all his honours, if he could by that means save a single soul. But he would rather see all the world perish than bate even a hair's-breadth of the power he has usurped![2]......I am clear of these things."

Luther next proceeds to the universities and schools:—

"I am much afraid that the universities will prove to be the great gates of hell, unless they diligently labour in explaining the Holy Scriptures, and engraving them in the hearts of youth. I advise no one to place his child where the Scriptures do not reign paramount. Every institution in which men are not unceasingly occupied with the Word of God must become corrupt."[3] Weighty words, upon which governments, learned men, and parents in every age should seriously meditate!

Towards the end of this appeal he returns to the empire and to the emperor:—

"The pope, unable to manage at his will the ancient masters of the Roman empire, conceived a plan of taking away their title and their empire, and bestowing them on us Germans. Thus it happened that we became the vassals of the pope. For the pope took possession of Rome, and compelled the emperor by an oath never to reside there; whence it is that the emperor is emperor of Rome, without Rome. We possess the name: the pope has the country and the cities. We have the title and arms of the empire; the pope has its treasures, power, privileges, and liberties. The pope eats the fruit, and we play with the husk. It is thus that the

pride and tyranny of the Romans have always abused our simplicity.

"But now may God, who has given us such an empire, be our helper! Let us act in conformity with our name, title, and arms; let us preserve our liberty; and let the Romans learn to appreciate what God has given us by their hands! They boast of having given us an empire. Well, then, let us take what belongs to us! Let the pope resign to us Rome and every portion of the empire that he still holds! Let him put an end to his taxes and extortions! Let him restore our liberty, our power, our property, our honour, our souls, and our bodies! Let the empire be all that an empire ought to be, and let the sword of princes no longer be constrained to bow before the hypocritical pretensions of a pope!"

In these words there are not only energy and enthusiasm, but also a lofty strain of reasoning. Did any orator ever speak thus to the nobility of the empire, and to the emperor himself? Far from being surprised that so many German states separated from Rome, ought we not rather to feel astonished that all Germany did not march to the banks of the Tiber to resume that imperial power whose attributes the popes had so imprudently placed on the brow of its sovereign?

Luther concludes this courageous appeal in these words:—

"I can very well imagine that I have pitched my song too high, proposed many things that will seem impossible, and attacked many errors rather too violently. But what can I do? Let the world be offended with me, rather than God!......They can but take away my life. I have often proposed peace to my adversaries. But God, by their instrumentality, has compelled me continually to cry louder and louder against them. I have still another song in reserve against Rome. If their ears itch, I will sing it them, and loudly too. Dost thou clearly understand, O Rome, what I mean?"......

This is probably an allusion to a work on the papacy that Luther had some intention of publishing, but which was withheld. About this time the Rector Burkhardt wrote to Spengler: "There is also a little treatise *De execranda Venere Romanorum;* but it is kept in reserve." The title promised something very offensive; and we should rejoice that Luther had the moderation not to publish this writing.

"If my cause is just," continues he, "it will be condemned by all the world, and justified only by Christ in heaven. Let them come on, then, pope, bishops, priests, monks, and doctors! let them put forth all their zeal! let them give the rein to all their fury! These are, in truth, the men who ought to persecute the truth, as every age has witnessed."

Whence did this monk acquire so clear an understanding of public affairs, which even

---

[1] Yearly festivals in commemoration of the dedication or opening of a church: the Belgian *kermess*.
[2] Nun liess er ehe die Welt untergehen, ehe er ein Haarbrett seiner vermessenen Gewalt liesse abbrechen. L. Opp. (L.) xvii. 483.
[3] Es muss verderben, alles was nicht Gottes Wort ohn Unterlass treibt. Ibid. 486.

the states of the empire often found so difficult to elucidate? Whence did this German derive the courage which made him raise his head in the midst of a nation so long enslaved, and aim such violent blows at the papacy? What was the mysterious power that animated him? Might we not be led to say that he had heard these words addressed by God to a man of the olden time: *Behold, I have made thy face strong against their faces. As an adamant harder than flint have I made thy forehead: fear them not, neither be dismayed at their looks.*

This exhortation, which was addressed to the German nobility, soon reached all those for whom it had been written. It circulated through Germany with inconceivable rapidity. Luther's friends trembled; Staupitz and those who desired to employ mild measures found the blow too severe. "In our days," replied Luther, "every thing that is handled gently falls into oblivion, and no one cares about it."[1] At the same time he gave striking evidence of single-mindedness and humility. He did not yet know himself. "I cannot tell what to say of myself," wrote he. "Perhaps I am Philip's (Melancthon's) forerunner. I am preparing the way for him, like Elias, in spirit and in power. It is he who will one day trouble Israel and the house of Ahab."[2]

But there was no need to wait for another than him who had already appeared. The house of Ahab was already shaken. The *Appeal to the German Nobility* was published on the 26th June 1520; in a short time four thousand copies were sold, a number unprecedented in those days. The astonishment was universal. This writing produced a powerful sensation among the people. The vigour, life, perspicuity, and generous boldness that breathed throughout, made it a truly popular work. The people felt at last that he who spoke to them loved them also. The confused views of a great number of wise men were cleared up. The Romish usurpations became evident to every mind. No one at Wittemberg any longer doubted that the pope was Antichrist. Even the elector's court, so circumspect and timid, did not disapprove of the reformer: it waited patiently. But the nobility and the people did not wait. The nation was reanimated. Luther's voice had shaken it; it was won over, and rallied round the standard that he had uplifted. Nothing could have been more advantageous to the reformer than this publication. In the palaces and castles, in the homes of the citizens and the cottages of the peasants, all were now prepared, and defended as it were with a breastplate, against the sentence of condemnation that was about to fall upon this prophet of the people. All Germany was on fire. Let the bull arrive! not by such means will the conflagration be extinguished.

CHAPTER IV.

Preparations at Rome—Motives for Papal Resistance—Eck at Rome—The King of Crowns—Eck prevails—The Pope is the World—God brings about the Separation—A Swiss Priest pleads for Luther—The Roman Consistory—Exordium of the Bull—Luther condemned.

EVERY preparation was made at Rome for condemning the defender of the liberty of the Church. That Church had long been living in a state of haughty security. For several years the monks had been accusing Leo X. of caring only for luxury and pleasure, of occupying himself solely with the chase, the theatre, and music,[1] while the Church was tottering to its fall. At length, aroused by the clamours of Dr Eck, who had come from Leipsic to invoke the power of the Vatican, pope, cardinals, monks, and all Rome, awoke, and thought of saving the papacy.

Rome indeed was compelled to have recourse to the severest measures. The gauntlet had been thrown down; the combat must be to the death. Luther did not attack the abuses of the Roman pontificate, but the pontificate itself. At his command he would have had the pope descend humbly from his throne, and become a simple pastor or bishop on the banks of the Tiber. All the dignitaries of the Roman hierarchy were to renounce their wealth and their worldly glory, and become elders and deacons of the churches of Italy. All that splendour and power, which for ages had dazzled the West, was to vanish and give place to the humble simplicity of the primitive christian worship. God might have brought this about; He will do so in his own time; but it could not be expected from man. And even should any pope have been so disinterested or bold as to be willing to overthrow the ancient and costly edifice of the Roman Church, thousands of priests and bishops would have stretched out their hands to prevent its fall. The pope had received his power on the express condition of maintaining what was confided to him. Rome thought herself divinely appointed to the government of the Church. We cannot therefore be astonished that she prepared to strike the most terrible blows. And yet she hesitated at first. Many cardinals and the pope himself were opposed to violent measures. The skilful Leo saw clearly that a decision, the execution of which depended on the very doubtful compliance of the civil power, might seriously compromise the authority of the Church. He was aware, besides, that violent measures hitherto employed had only served to aggravate the mischief. Is it not possible to gain over this Saxon monk? asked the Roman politicians of one another. Will all the power of the Church, will all the craft of Italy fail?—They must negotiate still.

Eck accordingly met with powerful ob-

---

[1] Quæ nostro sæculo quiete tractantur, mox cadere in oblivionem. L. Epp. i. 479. [2] Ibid. 478.

[1] E sopra tutto musico eccellentissimo, e quando el canta con qualche uno. li fa donar cento e più ducati. Zorsi MS

stacles. He neglected nothing that might prevent such impious concessions. In every quarter of Rome he vented his rage, and called for revenge. The fanatical portion of the monks soon leagued with him. Strengthened by their alliance, he assailed the pope and cardinals with fresh courage. In his opinion, every attempt at conciliation would be useless. These (said he) are idle dreams with which you soothe yourselves at a distance from the danger. He knew the peril, for he had contended with the audacious monk. He saw that there should be no delay in cutting off this gangrened limb, for fear the disease should infect the whole body. The impetuous disputant of Leipsic parried objection after objection, and with difficulty persuaded the pope.[1] He desired to save Rome in spite of herself. He made every exertion, passing many hours together in deliberation in the pontiff's cabinet.[2] He excited the court and the cloisters, the people and the Church. "Eck is stirring up the bottomless pit against me," said Luther; "he is setting fire to the forests of Lebanon."[3]

But the victory, at the very moment Dr. Eck made most sure of it, appeared suddenly to escape from his hands. There existed even in Rome a respectable party to a certain extent favourable to Luther. On this point we have the testimony of a Roman citizen, one of whose letters, written in January 1521, has fortunately been preserved. "You should know," says he, "that in Rome there is scarcely an individual, at least among men of sound judgment, who is not aware that in many respects Luther speaks the truth."[4] These respectable persons resisted the demands of Dr. Eck. "We should take more time for reflection," said they; "Luther should be opposed by moderation and by reason, and not by anathemas." Leo X. was again staggered. But immediately all that was bad in Rome burst out into violent fury.[5] Eck mustered his recruits, and from all quarters, but especially from among the Dominicans, auxiliaries rallied round him, overflowing with anger and apprehension lest their victim should escape. "It is unbecoming the dignity of the Roman pontiff," said they, "to give a reason to every little wretch that presumes to raise his head;[6] on the contrary, these obstinate people should be crushed by force, lest others, after them, should imitate their audacity. It was in this way that the punishment of John Huss, and of his disciple Jerome, terrified many; and if the same thing had been done to

Reuchlin, Luther would never have dared what he has done."

At the same time the theologians of Cologne, Louvain, and other universities, and even princes of Germany, either by letter or through their envoys, daily urged the pope in private by the most pressing entreaties. But the most earnest solicitations proceeded from a banker who, by his wealth, possessed great influence at Rome, and who was familiarly styled "the king of crowns."[1] The papacy has always been more or less in the hands of those who have lent it money. This banker was Fugger, the treasurer of the indulgences. Inflamed with anger against Luther, and very uneasy about his profits and his wares,[2] the Augsburg merchant strained every nerve to exasperate the pope: "Employ force against Luther," said he, "and I will promise you the alliance and support of several princes." It would even appear that it was he who had sent Eck to Rome.[3]

This gave the decisive blow. The "king of crowns" was victor in the pontifical city. It was not the sword of the Gaul, but well-stored purses that were on this occasion thrown into the balance. Eck prevailed at last. The politicians were defeated by the fanatics in the papal councils. Leo gave way, and Luther's condemnation was resolved upon. Eck breathed again. His pride was flattered by the thought that it was he who had decided the destruction of his heretical rival, and thus saved the Church. "It was fortunate," said he, "that I came to Rome at this time,[4] for they were but little acquainted with Luther's errors. It will one day be known how much I have done in this cause."

Few were more active in supporting Doctor Eck than Sylvester Mazzolini de Prierio, master of the sacred palace. He had just published a work in which he maintained that not only did the infallible decision of all controverted points belong to the pope alone, but that the papal dominion was the fifth monarchy prophesied by Daniel, and the only true monarchy; that the pope was the first of all ecclesiastical princes, the father of all secular rulers, the chief of the world, and, essentially, the world itself.[5] In another writing, he affirmed that the pope is as much superior to the emperor, as gold is more precious than lead;[6] that the pope may elect and depose both emperors and electors; establish and annul positive rights, and that the emperor, though backed by all the laws and nations of Christendom, cannot

[1] Sarpi, Council of Trent.
[2] Stetimus nuper, papa, duo cardinales....et ego per quinque horas in deliberatione. Eckii Epistola (3d May), in Luth. Opp. Lat. ii. 48.
[3] Impetraturus abyssos abyssorum....succensurus saltum Libani. L. Epp. i. 421-429.
[4] Scias, neminem Romæ esse, si saltem sapiat, qui non certo certius sciat et cognoscat Martinum in plurimis veritatem dicere. Riederer's Nachrichten zur Kirchen Gelehrten und Buchergeschichte, i. 179.
[5] Mali vero, quia veritatem audire coguntur insaniunt. Ibid.
[6] Non decere Rom. Pont. unicuique vilissimo homunculo rationem reddere debere. Ibid.

[1] Super omnia vero mercator ille Fuckerus, qui plurimum ob pecunias Romæ potest, utpote quem summorum regem vocare solent. Riederer's Nachrichten, i. 179.
[2] De quæstu suo ac beneficiorum mercatura sollicitus. Ibid.
[3] Ejusce rei causa Eckium illum suum Romam misit. Ibid.
[4] Bonum fuit me venisse hoc tempore Romam. Ep. Eckii. Ibid.
[5] Caput orbis et consequenter orbis totus in virtute. De juridica et irrefragabili veritate Romanæ Ecclesiæ. Bibl. Max. xix. cap. iv.
[6] Papa est imperatore major dignitate plus quam aurum plombo. De Papa et ejus potestate, p. 371.

decide the least thing against the pope's will. Such was the voice that issued from the palace of the sovereign pontiff; such was the monstrous fiction which, combined with the scholastic doctrines, pretended to extinguish the dawning truth. If this fable had not been unmasked as it has been, and even by learned men in the Romish communion, there would have been neither true religion nor true history. The papacy is not only a lie in the face of the Bible; it is so even in the face of the annals of all nations. Thus the Reformation, by breaking its charm, emancipated not only the Church, but also kings and people. It has been said that the Reformation was a political work; in this sense it is true; but this is only a secondary sense.

Thus did God send forth a spirit of infatuation on the Roman doctors. The separation between truth and error had now become necessary; and error was the instrument of its accomplishment. If they had come to an agreement, it could only have been at the expense of truth; but to take away the smallest part of itself, is to prepare the way for its complete annihilation. It is like the insect which is said to die if one of its antennæ be removed. Truth requires to be entire in all its members, in order to display that energy by which it is enabled to gain wide and salutary victories, and to propagate itself through future ages. To mingle a little error with truth is like throwing a grain of poison into a well-filled dish; this one grain is sufficient to change the nature of the food, and will cause death, slowly perhaps, but surely. Those who defend Christ's doctrine against the attacks of its adversaries, as jealously keep watch upon its remotest outworks as upon the body of the place; for no sooner has the enemy gained a footing in the least of these positions, than his victory is not far distant. The Roman pontiff resolved, at the period we have now reached, to rend the Church, and the fragment that remains in his grasp, however splendid it may be, ineffectually conceals under its gorgeous ornaments the malignant principle by which it is attacked. Wherever the Word of God is, there is life. Luther, however great his courage, would probably have kept silence, if Rome had been silent herself, and had affected to make a few apparent concessions. But God had not abandoned the Reformation to the weak heart of man. Luther was in the hands of One more far-sighted than himself. Divine Providence made use of the pope to break every link between the past and the future, and to turn the reformer into a new path, unknown and undistinguishable to his eyes, the approaches of which he never could have found unaided. The pontifical bull was the letter of divorcement that Rome gave to the pure Church of Jesus Christ in the person of him who was then its humble but faithful representative; and the Church accepted it,

from that hour to depend solely on her Head who is in heaven.

While, at Rome, Luther's condemnation was urged forward with so much violence that an humble priest, living in one of the simple towns of Helvetia, and who had never held any communication with the reformer, was deeply affected at the thought of the blow impending over him; and, while the friends of the Wittemberg doctor trembled and remained silent, this child of the Swiss mountains resolved to employ every means in his power to arrest the formidable bull. His name was Ulrich Zwingle. William des Faucons, secretary to the pope's legate in Switzerland, and who, in the legate's absence, was intrusted with the affairs of Rome, was his friend. "So long as I live," had said the nuncio *ad interim* to him a few days before, "you may count on my doing all that can be expected from a true friend." The Helvetian priest, trusting to this assurance, went to the nuncio's office (such at least is the conclusion we draw from one of his letters.) He had no fear on his own part of the dangers to which the evangelical faith exposed him; he knew that a disciple of Christ should always be ready to lay down his life. "All that I ask of Christ for myself," said he to a friend to whose bosom he confided his anxiety about Luther, "is, that I may endure with the heart of a man the evils that await me. I am a vessel of clay in His hands; let Him dash me in pieces or strengthen me, as seemeth good to Him."[1] But the Swiss evangelist feared for the Christian Church, if so formidable a blow should strike the reformer. He endeavoured to persuade the representative of Rome to enlighten the pope, and to employ all the means in his power to prevent Luther's excommunication.[2] "The dignity of the holy see itself is interested in this," said Zwingle, "for if matters should come to such a point, Germany, overflowing with enthusiasm for the Gospel and for the doctor who preaches it, will despise the pope and his anathemas."[3] This intervention proved of no effect: it would appear also that, even at the time it was made, the blow had been already struck. Such was the first occasion in which the paths of the Saxon doctor and of the Swiss priest met. We shall again find the latter in the course of this history, and see him growing up and increasing to a lofty stature in the Church of the Lord.

Luther's condemnation being once resolved upon, new difficulties were raised in the consistory. The theologians were of opinion that the fulmination should be issued immediately; the lawyers, on the contrary, that

[1] Hoc unum Christum obtestans, ut masculo omnra pectore ferre donet, et me figulinum suum rumpat aut firmet, ut illi placitum sit. Zwinglii Epistolæ, curantibus Schulero et Schulthessio, p. 144.
[2] Ut pontificem admoneat, ne excommunicationem ferat. Ibid.
[3] Nam si feratur, auguror Germanos cum excommunicatione pontificem quoque contempturos. Ibid.

it should be preceded by a summons. "Was not Adam first summoned?" said they to their theological colleagues; "so too was Cain: *Where is thy brother Abel?* demanded the Almighty." To these singular arguments drawn from the Holy Scriptures the canonists added motives derived from the natural law: "The evidence of a crime," said they, "cannot deprive a criminal of his right of defence."[1] It is pleasing to find these principles of justice in a Roman assembly. But these scruples were not to the taste of the divines in the assembly, who, instigated by passion, thought only of going immediately to work. One man in particular then came forward whose opinions must of necessity have had great influence: this was De Vio, cardinal Cajetan, still labouring under extreme vexation at his defeat in Augsburg, and the little honour or profit he had derived from his German mission. De Vio, who had returned to Rome in ill health, was carried to the assembly on his couch. He would not miss this paltry triumph, which afforded him some little consolation. Although defeated at Augsburg, he desired to take part at Rome in condemning this indomitable monk, before whom he had witnessed the failure of all his learning, skill, and authority. Luther was not there to reply: De Vio thought himself invincible. "I have seen enough to know," said he, "that if the Germans are not kept under by fire and sword, they will entirely throw off the yoke of the Roman Church."[2] Such a declaration from Cajetan could not fail to have great weight. The cardinal was avenged of his defeat and of the contempt of Germany. A final conference, which Eck attended, was held in the pope's presence at his villa of Malliano. On the 15th of June the Sacred College decided on the condemnation, and sanctioned the famous bull.

"Arise, O Lord," said the Roman pontiff, speaking at this solemn moment as God's vicegerent and head of the Church, "arise, judge thy cause, and call to mind the opprobrium which madmen continually heap on thee! Arise, O Peter; remember thy Holy Roman Church, mother of all churches, and queen of the faith! Arise, O Paul, for behold a new Porphyry attacks thy doctrines and the holy popes, our predecessors. Lastly, arise, ye assembly of saints, the holy Church of God, and intercede with the Almighty!"[3]
The pope then proceeds to quote from Luther's works forty-one pernicious, scandalous, and poisonous propositions, in which

the latter set forth the holy doctrines of the Gospel. The following propositions are included in the list:—

"To deny that sin remains in the child after baptism, is to trample under foot both Saint Paul and our Lord Jesus Christ."
"A new life is the best and sublimest penance."
"To burn heretics is contrary to the will of the Holy Ghost," &c. &c.
"So soon as this bull shall be published," continues the pope, "the bishops shall make diligent search after the writings of Martin Luther that contain these errors, and burn them publicly and solemnly in the presence of the clergy and laity. As for Martin himself, what have we not done? Imitating the long-suffering of God Almighty, we are still ready to receive him again into the bosom of the Church, and we grant him sixty days in which to forward us his recantation in a paper, sealed by two prelates; or else, which would be far more agreeable to us, for him to come to Rome in person, in order that no one may entertain any doubts of his obedience. Meanwhile, and from this very moment, he must give up preaching, teaching, and writing, and commit his works to the flames. And if he does not retract in the space of sixty days, we by these presents condemn both him and his adherents as open and obstinate heretics." The pope then pronounces a number of excommunications, maledictions, and interdicts, against Luther and his partisans, with orders to seize their persons and send them to Rome.[1] We may easily conceive what would have become of these noble-minded confessors of the Gospel in the papal dungeons.

Thus was the tempest gathering over Luther's head. It might have been imagined, after the affair of Reuchlin, that the court of Rome would no longer make common cause with the Dominicans and the Inquisition. But now the latter had the ascendancy, and the ancient alliance was solemnly renewed. The bull was published; and for centuries Rome had not pronounced a sentence of condemnation that her arm had not followed up with death. This murderous message was about to leave the Seven Hills, and reach the Saxon monk in his cell. The moment was aptly chosen. It might be supposed that the new emperor, who had so many reasons for courting the pope's friendship, would be eager to deserve it by sacrificing to him an obscure monk. Already Leo X., the cardinals, nay all Rome, exulted in their victory, and fancied they saw their enemy at their feet.

---

[1] Sarpi, Council of Trent, i. 12.
[2] Compertum igitur se habere dicebat nisi igne et gladio Germani compescerentur, omnino jugum Romanæ Ecclesiæ excussuros. Riederer's Nachrichten, i. 179.
[3] L. Opp. (L.) xvii. 305, and Opp. Lat. i. 32.

[1] Sub prædictis pœnis, præfatum Lutherum, complices, adherentes, receptatores et fautatores, personaliter capiant et ad nos mittant. Bulla Leonis, loc. cit.

CHAPTER V.

Wittemberg—Melancthon—His Marriage—Catherine—Domestic Life—Benevolence—Good Humour—Christ and Antiquity—Labour—Love of Letters—His Mother—Revolt of the Students.

WHILE the inhabitants of the eternal city were thus agitated, more tranquil scenes were passing at Wittemberg. Melancthon was there diffusing a mild but brilliant light. From fifteen hundred to two thousand auditors, assembling from Germany, England, the Low Countries, France, Italy, Hungary, and Greece, were often gathered round him. He was twenty-four years of age, and had not entered the ecclesiastical state. There were none in Wittemberg who were not delighted to receive the visits of this young professor, at once so learned and so amiable. Foreign universities, Ingolstadt in particular, desired to attract him within their walls. His Wittemberg friends were eager to retain him among them by the ties of marriage. Although Luther wished that his dear friend Philip might find a consort, he openly declared that he would not be his adviser in this matter. Others took this task upon themselves. The young doctor frequented, in particular, the house of the burgomaster Krapp, who belonged to an ancient family. Krapp had a daughter named Catherine, a woman of mild character and great sensibility. Melancthon's friends urged him to demand her in marriage; but the young scholar was absorbed in his books, and would hear no mention of anything besides. His Greek authors and his Testament were his delight. The arguments of his friends he met with other arguments. At length they extorted his consent. All the preliminary steps were arranged, and Catherine was given him to wife. He received her very coldly,[1] and said with a sigh: "It is God's will! I must renounce my studies and my pleasures to comply with the wishes of my friends."[2] He appreciated, however, Catherine's good qualities. "The young woman," said he, "has just such a character and education as I should have asked of God: διξιᾷ ὁ Θεὸς τικμαίροιῇο.[3] Certainly she deserves a better husband." Matters were settled in the month of August; the betrothal took place on the 25th of September, and at the end of November the wedding was celebrated. Old John Luther with his wife and daughters visited Wittemberg on this occasion.[4] Many learned men and people of note were present at the nuptials.

The young bride felt as much affection as the young professor gave evidence of coldness. Always anxious about her husband Catherine grew alarmed at the least prospect of any danger that threatened her dear partner. Whenever Melancthon proposed taking any step of such a nature as to compromise himself, she overwhelmed him with entreaties to renounce it. "I was compelled," wrote Melancthon on one such occasion, "to give way to her weakness......such is our lot." How many infidelities in the Church may have had a similar origin! Perhaps we should ascribe to Catherine's influence the timidity and fears with which her husband has so often been reproached. Catherine was an affectionate mother as well as loving wife. She was liberal in her alms to the poor. "O God! do not abandon me in my old age, when my hair begins to turn gray!" such was the daily prayer of this pious and timid woman. Melancthon was soon conquered by his wife's affection. When he had once tasted the joys of domestic life, he felt all their sweetness: he was formed for such pleasures. Nowhere did he feel himself happier than with Catherine and his children. A French traveller one day finding " the master of Germany" rocking his child's cradle with one hand, and holding a book in the other, started back with surprise. But Melancthon, without being disconcerted, explained to him with so much warmth the value of children in the eyes of God, that the stranger quitted the house wiser (to use his own words) than he had entered it.

Melancthon's marriage gave a domestic circle to the Reformation. There was from this time one house in Wittemberg always open to those who were inspired by the new life. The concourse of strangers was immense.[1] They came to Melancthon on a thousand different matters; and the established regulations of his household enjoined him to refuse nothing to any one.[2] The young professor was extremely disinterested whenever good was to be done. When all his money was spent, he would secretly carry his plate to some merchant, caring little about depriving himself of it, since it gave him wherewithal to comfort the distressed. "Accordingly it would have been impossible for him to provide for the wants of himself and family," says his friend Camerarius, "if a Divine and secret blessing had not from time to time furnished him the means." His good nature was extreme. He possessed several ancient gold and silver medals, remarkable for their inscriptions and figures. He showed them one day to a stranger who called upon him. "Take any one you like," said Melancthon.—"I should like them all," replied the stranger. I confess (says Philip) that this unreasonable request displeased me

---

[1] Uxor enim datur mihi non dico quam frigenti. Corp. Ref. i. 211.
[2] Ego meis studiis, mea me voluptate fraudo. Ibid. 265.
[3] May God, by his right hand, prosper this matter! Ibid. 212.
[4] Parentes mei cum sororibus nuptias honorarunt Philippi. L. Epp. i. 528.

[1] Videres in ædibus illis perpetuo accedentes et introeuntes et discedentes atque exeuntes aliquos. Camerar. Vita Melancth. p. 40.
[2] Ea domus disciplina erat, ut nihil cuiquam negaretur. Ibid.

a little at first; I nevertheless gave them to him.[1]

There was in Melancthon's writings a perfume of antiquity, which did not however prevent the sweet savour of Christ from exhaling from every part, and which communicated to them an inexpressible charm. There is not one of his letters addressed to his friends in which we are not reminded in the most natural manner of the wisdom of Homer, Plato, Cicero, and Pliny, Christ ever remaining his Master and his God. Spalatin had asked him the meaning of this expression of Jesus Christ, *Without me ye can do nothing* (John xv. 5). Melancthon referred him to Luther. " *Cur agam gestum, spectante Roscio?* to use Cicero's words,"[2] said he. He then continues : " This passage signifies that we must be absorbed in Christ, so that we ourselves no longer act, but Christ lives in us. As the Divine nature was incorporated with the human in the person of Christ, so man must be incorporated with Jesus Christ by faith."

The illustrious scholar generally retired to rest shortly after supper. At two or three o'clock in the morning he was again at his studies.[3] It was during these early hours that his best works were written. His manuscripts usually lay on the table exposed to the view of every visiter, so that he was robbed of several. When he had invited any of his friends to his house, he used to beg one of them to read before sitting down to table some small composition in prose or verse. He always took some young men with him during his journeys, and conversing with them in a manner at once amusing and instructive. If the conversation languished, each of them had to recite in turn passages extracted from the ancient poets. He made frequent use of irony, tempering it, however, with great mildness. " He scratches and bites," said he of himself, " and yet he does no harm."

Learning was his passion. The great object of his life was to diffuse literature and knowledge. Let us not forget that in his estimation the Holy Scriptures ranked far above the writings of pagan authors. " I apply myself solely to one thing," said he, " the defence of letters. By our example we must excite youth to the admiration of learning, and induce them to love it for its own sake, and not for the advantage that may be derived from it. The destruction of learning brings with it the ruin of everything that is good : religion, morals, Divine and human

things.[1] The better a man is, the greater his ardour in the preservation of learning ; for he knows that of all plagues ignorance is the most pernicious."

Some time after his marriage, Melancthon, in company with Camerarius and other friends, made a journey to Bretten in the Palatinate, to visit his beloved mother. As soon as he caught sight of his birthplace, he got off his horse, fell on his knees, and returned thanks to God for having permitted him to see it once more. Margaret almost fainted with joy as she embraced her son. She wished him to stay at Bretten, and begged him earnestly to adhere to the faith of his fathers. Melancthon excused himself in this respect, but with great delicacy, lest he should wound his mother's feelings. He had much difficulty in leaving her again ; and whenever a traveller brought him news from his natal city, he was as delighted as if he had once more returned (to use his own words) to the joys of his childhood. Such was the private life of one of the greatest instruments of the religious Revolution of the sixteenth century.

A disturbance, however, occurred to trouble these domestic scenes and the studious activity of Wittemberg. The students came to blows with the citizens. The rector displayed great weakness. We may imagine what was Melancthon's sorrow at beholding the excesses committed by these disciples of learning. Luther was indignant : he was far from desiring to gain popularity by an unbecoming conciliation. The opprobrium these disorders reflected on the university pierced him to the heart.[2] He went into the pulpit, and preached forcibly against these seditions, calling upon both parties to submit to the magistrates.[3] His sermon occasioned great irritation : " Satan," said he in one of his letters, " being unable to attack us from without, desires to injure us from within. I am not afraid of him ; but I fear lest God's anger should light upon us, because we have not becomingly received His Word. These last three years I have been thrice exposed to great danger ; at Augsburg in 1518, at Leipsic in 1519, and now in 1520 at Wittemberg. It is neither by wisdom nor by arms that the renovation of the Church will be accomplished, but by humble prayers, by a faith full of courage, that puts Christ on our side.[4] My dear friend, unite thy prayers with mine, for fear the wicked spirit should make use of this small spark to kindle a great conflagration."

---

[1] Sed dedisse nihilominus illos. Camerar. Vita Melancth. p. 43.
[2] How can I declaim in the presence of Roscius? Corp. Ref. Epp. 13th April 1520.
[3] Surgebat mox aut non longo intervallo post mediam noctem. Camerar. p. 56.

[1] Religionem, mores, humana divinaque omnia labefactat literarum inscitia. Corp. Ref. i. 207. 22d July 1520.
[2] Urit me ista confusio academiæ nostræ. L. Epp. i. 467.
[3] Commendans potestatem magistratuum. Ibid.
[4] .... Nec prudentia nec armis, sed humili oratione et forti fide, quibus obtineamus Christum pro nobis. Ibid. 469.

CHAPTER VI.

The Gospel in Italy—Sermon on the Mass—Babylonish Captivity of the Church—Baptism—Abolition of other Vows—Progress of Reform.

But more terrible combats than these awaited Luther. Rome was brandishing the sword with which she was about to strike the Gospel. The rumour of the condemnation that was destined to fall upon him, far from dispiriting the reformer, augmented his courage. He manifested no anxiety to parry the blows of this haughty power. It is by inflicting more terrible blows himself that he will neutralize those of his adversaries. While the transalpine assemblies are thundering out anathemas against him, he will bear the sword of the Word into the midst of the Italian people. Letters from Venice spoke of the favour with which Luther's sentiments were received there. He burnt with desire to send the Gospel across the Alps. Evangelists were wanted to carry it thither. " I wish," said he, " that we had living books, that is, preachers,[1] and that we could multiply and protect them every where, in order that they might convey to the people a knowledge of holy things. The prince could not undertake a more glorious task. If the people of Italy should receive the truth, our cause would then be impregnable." It does not appear that Luther's project was realized. In later years, it is true, evangelical men, even Calvin himself, sojourned for a short period in Italy; but for the present Luther's designs were not carried out. He had addressed one of the mighty princes of the world: if he had appealed to men of humble rank, but full of zeal for the kingdom of God, the result might have been different. At that period, the idea generally prevailed, that every thing should be done by governments; and the association of simple individuals,— that power which is now effecting such great things in Christendom,—was almost unknown.

If Luther did not succeed in his projects for propagating the truth in distant countries, he was only the more zealous in announcing it himself. It was at this time that he preached, at Wittemberg, his sermon on the Mass.[2] In this discourse he inveighs against the numerous sects of the Romish Church, and reproaches it, with reason, for its want of unity. " The multiplicity of spiritual laws," says he, " has filled the world with sects and divisions. Priests, monks, and laymen have come to hate each other more than the Christians hate the Turks. What do I say? Priests against priests, and monks against monks, are deadly enemies. Each one is attached to his own sect, and despises all others. The unity and charity of Christ are at an end."—He next attacks the doctrine that the mass is a sacrifice, and has some virtue in itself. " What is most precious in every sacrament, and consequently in the eucharist," says he, " is the promises and the Word of God. Without faith in this Word and these promises, the sacrament is dead: it is a body without a soul, a vessel without wine, a purse without money, a type without fulfilment, a letter without spirit, a casket without jewels, a scabbard without a sword."

Luther's voice was not, however, confined to Wittemberg; and if he did not find missionaries to bear his instructions to distant lands, God had provided a missionary of a new kind. The printing-press was the successor of the Evangelists. This was the breaching-battery employed against the Roman fortress. Luther had prepared a mine the explosion of which shook the edifice of Rome to its lowest foundations. This was the publication of his famous book on the *Babylonish Captivity of the Church*, which appeared on the 6th of October 1520.[1] Never did man, in so critical a position, display greater courage.

In this work he first sets forth with haughty irony all the advantages for which he is indebted to his enemies :—

" Whether I will it or not," said he, " I become wiser every day, urged on as I am by so many illustrious masters. Two years ago, I attacked indulgences, but with so much indecision and fear, that I am now ashamed of it. There is no cause for astonishment in this, for I was alone when I set this stone rolling." He thanks Prierio, Eck, Emser, and his other adversaries: " I denied," continued he, " that the papacy was of Divine origin, but I granted that it was of human right. Now, after reading all the subtleties on which these gentry have set up their idol, I know that the papacy is none other than the kingdom of Babylon, and the violence of Nimrod the mighty hunter. I therefore beseech all my friends and all the booksellers to burn the books that I have written on this subject, and to substitute this one proposition in their place: *The papacy is a vigorous chase led by the Roman bishop, to catch and destroy souls.*"[2]

Luther next proceeds to attack the prevailing errors on the sacraments, monastic vows, &c. He reduces the seven sacraments of the Church to three; namely, Baptism, Penance, and the Lord's Supper. After explaining the true nature of this Supper, he passes on to baptism; and it is here in particular that he lays down the excellence of faith, and vigorously attacks Rome. " God," says he, " has preserved this sacrament alone free from human traditions. God has said: *He that believeth and is baptized shall be*

---

[1] Si vivos libros, hoc est, concionatores possemus multiplicare. L. Epp. i. 491.
[2] L. Opp. (L.) xvii. 490.

[1] L. Opp. Lat. ii. 63; and Leips. xvii. 511.
[2] Papatus est robusta venatio Romani episcopi. L. Opp. Lat. ii. 64.

saved. This promise of God should be preferred before all the glory of works, all vows, all satisfactions, all indulgences, and all inventions of man. Now, upon this promise, if we receive it with faith, depends our whole salvation. If we believe, our hearts are strengthened by the Divine promise; and though the believer should be forsaken of all, this promise in which he believes will never forsake him. With it, he will resist the adversary who lies in wait for his soul, and be prepared to meet remorseless death, and stand before the judgment-seat of God. It will be his consolation in all his trials to say : God's promises never deceive ; of their truth I received a pledge at my baptism ; if God is for me, who shall be against me? Oh, how rich is the Christian that has been baptized ! Nothing can destroy him except he refuse to believe.

" Perhaps to what I have said on the necessity of faith, they will object to me the baptism of little children. But as the Word of God is mighty to change even the heart of a wicked man, who is however neither less deaf nor ignorant than a little child ; in like manner also the prayers of the Church, to which all things are possible, change the little child, by the faith that it pleases God to pour into his heart, and thus purifies and renews it." [1]

After having thus explained the doctrine of baptism, Luther wields it as a weapon of offence against the papacy. In fact, if the Christian finds all his salvation in the renewal of his baptism by faith, what need has he of the Romish ordinances ?

" For this reason, I declare," says Luther, " that neither the pope, nor the bishop, nor any man whatsoever, has authority to impose the least thing on a Christian, unless it be with his own consent. All that is done without it is an act of tyranny. [2] We are free as regards all men. The vow that we made at our baptism is sufficient of itself, and is more than we can ever fulfil. [3] All other vows may therefore be abolished. Let every man who enters the priesthood or any religious order clearly understand, that the works of a monk or a priest differ in no respect before God from those of a peasant who tills his fields, or of a woman who manages her house. [4] God estimates all things by the standard of faith. And it often happens that the simple labour of a serving man or maiden is more acceptable to

God than the fasts and works of a monk, because the latter are void of faith......Christians are God's true people, led captive to Babylon, where every thing has been taken from them which baptism hath given."

Such were the weapons by which that religious revolution whose history we are retracing was effected. First, the necessity of faith was re-established, and then the reformers employed it as a weapon to dash to atoms every superstition. It is with this power of God, which removes mountains, that they attacked so many errors. These words of Luther, and many others like them, circulating through cities, convents, and rural districts, were the leaven that leavened the whole mass.

Luther terminates this famous writing on the *Captivity of Babylon* with these words :—
" I hear that new papal excommunications are about to be fabricated against me. If it be true, this present book must be considered as part of my future recantation. The remainder will soon follow, to prove my obedience ; and the complete work will form, with Christ's aid, such a whole as Rome has never heard or seen the like."

CHAPTER VII.

Fresh Negotiations—The Augustines at Eisleben—Miltitz—Deputation to Luther—Miltitz and the Elector—Conference at Lichtemberg—Luther's Letter to the Pope—Book presented to the Pope—Union of Christ with the Believer—Liberty and Bondage.

AFTER such a publication, all hope of reconciliation between Luther and the pope must of necessity have vanished. The incompatibility of the reformer's faith with the doctrines of the Church must have struck the least discerning ; but precisely at that very time fresh negotiations had been opened. Five weeks before the publication of the *Captivity of Babylon*, at the end of August 1520, the general chapter of the Augustine monks was held at Eisleben. The venerable Staupitz there resigned the general vicarship of the order, and it was conferred on Wenceslas Link, the same who had accompanied Luther to Augsburg.[1] The indefatigable Miltitz suddenly arrived in the midst of the proceedings.[2] He was ardently desirous of reconciling Luther with the pope. His vanity, his avarice, and above all, his jealousy and hatred, were deeply interested in this result. Eck and his boastings annoyed him ; he knew that the Ingolstadt doctor had been decrying him at Rome, and he

---

[1] Sicut enim Verbum Dei potens est dum sonat, etiam impii cor immutare, quod non minus est surdum et incapax quam ullus parvulus ; ita per orationem Ecclesiæ offerentis et credentis, parvulus, fide infusa, mutatur, mundatur et renovatur. L. Opp. Lat. ii. 77.
[2] Dico itaque, neque papa, neque episcopus, neque ullus hominum habet jus unius syllabæ constituendæ super Christianum honinem, nisi id fiat ejusdem consensu ; quidquid aliter fit, tyrannico spiritu fit. Ibid.
[3] Generali edicto tollere vota....abunde enim vovimus in baptismo, et plus quam possimus implere. Ibid. 78.
[4] Opera quantum libet sacra et ardua religiosorum et sacerdotum, in oculis Dei prorsus nihil distare ab operibus rustici in agro laborantis, aut mulieris in domo sua curantis. Ibid.

[1] See vol. i. p. 134.
[2] Nondum tot pressus difficultatibus animum desponderat Miltitius....dignus profecto non mediocri laude. Pallavicini, i. 68.

would have made every sacrifice to baffle, by a peace that should be promptly concluded, the schemes of this importunate rival. The interests of religion were mere secondary matters in his eyes. One day, as he relates, he was dining with the Bishop of Leissen. The guests had already made pretty copious libations, when a new work of Luther's was laid before them. It was opened and read; the bishop grew angry; the official swore; but Miltitz burst into a hearty laugh.[1] He dealt with the Reformation as a man of the world; Eck as a theologian.

Aroused by the arrival of Dr. Eck, Miltitz addressed the chapter of the Augustines in a speech, delivered with a strong Italian accent,[2] thinking thus to impose on his simple fellow-countrymen. "The whole Augustine order," said he, "is compromised in this affair. 'Show me the means of restraining Luther."[3]—"We have nothing to do with the doctor," replied the fathers, "and cannot give you advice." They relied no doubt on the release from the obligations to his order which Staupitz had given Luther at Augsburg. Miltitz persisted: "Let a deputation from this venerable chapter wait upon Luther, and entreat him to write to the pope, assuring him that he has never plotted against his person.[4] That will be sufficient to put an end to the matter." The chapter complied with the nuncio's demand, and commissioned, no doubt at his own request, the former vicar-general and his successor (Staupitz and Link) to speak to Luther. This deputation immediately set out for Wittemberg, bearing a letter from Miltitz to the doctor, filled with expressions of the greatest respect. "There is no time to lose," said he; "the thunder-storm, already gathering over the reformer's head, will soon burst forth; and then all will be over."

Neither Luther nor the deputies who shared in his sentiments[5] expected any success from a letter to the pope. But that was an additional reason for not refusing to write one. Such a letter could only be a mere matter of form, which would set the justice of Luther's cause in a still stronger light. "This Italianized Saxon (Miltitz)," thought Luther, "is no doubt looking to his own private interest in making the request. Well, then, let it be so! I will write, in conformity with the truth, that I have never entertained any designs against the pope's person. I must be on my guard against attacking the see of Rome itself too violently. Yet I will sprinkle it with its own salt."[6]

But not long after, the doctor was informed of the arrival of the bull in Germany; on the 3d of October, he told Spalatin that he would not write to the pope, and on the 6th of the same month, he published his book on the *Captivity of Babylon*. Miltitz was not even yet discouraged. The desire of humbling Eck made him believe in impossibilities. On the second of October, he had written to the elector full of hope: "All will go on well; but, for the love of God, do not delay any longer to pay me the pension that you and your brother have given me these several years past. I require money to gain new friends at Rome. Write to the pope, pay homage to the young cardinals, the relations of his holiness, in gold and silver pieces from the electoral mint, and add to them a few for me also, for I have been robbed of those that you gave me."[1]

Even after Luther had been informed of the bull, the intriguing Miltitz was not discouraged. He requested to have a conference with Luther at Lichtemberg. The elector ordered the latter to go there;[2] but his friends, and above all, the affectionate Melancthon, opposed it.[3] "What!" thought they; "accept a conference with the nuncio in so distant a place, at the very moment when the bull is to appear which commands Luther to be seized and carried to Rome! Is it not clear that, as Dr. Eck is unable to approach the reformer on account of the open manner in which he has shown his hatred, the crafty chamberlain has taken upon himself to catch Luther in his toils?"

These fears had no power to stop the Wittemberg doctor. The prince has commanded, and he will obey. "I am setting out for Lichtemberg," he wrote to the chaplain on the 11th of October; "pray for me." His friends would not abandon him. Towards evening of the same day, he entered Lichtemberg on horseback, accompanied by thirty cavaliers, among whom was Melancthon. The papal nuncio arrived about the same time with a train of four persons.[4] Was not this moderate escort a mere trick to inspire confidence in Luther and his friends?

Miltitz was very pressing in his solicitations, assuring Luther that the blame would be thrown on Eck and his foolish vaunting,[5] and that all would be concluded to the satisfaction of both parties. "Well then!" replied Luther, "I offer to keep silence henceforward, provided my adversaries are silent likewise. For the sake of peace, I will do every thing in my power."[6]

Miltitz was filled with joy. He accompanied Luther as far as Wittemberg. The reformer and the nuncio entered side by side into that city which Doctor Eck was already

---

[1] Der Bischof entrüstet, der Official geflucht er aber gelachet habe. Seckend. p. 266.
[2] Orationem habuit Italica pronunciatione vestitam. L. Epp. i. 483.
[3] Petens consilium super me compescendo. Ibid.
[4] Nihil me in personam suam fuisse molitam. Ibid. 484.
[5] Quibus omnibus causa mea non displicet. Ibid. 486.
[6] Aspergetur tamen sale suo. Ibid.

[1] Den Pabsts Nepoten, zwei oder drei Churfürstliche Gold und Silberstücke, zu verehren. Seckend. p. 267.
[2] Sicut princeps ordinavit. L. Epp. i. 455.
[3] Invito præceptore (*Melancthon*) nescio quanta metuente. Ibid.
[4] Jener von mehr als dreissig, diser aber kaum mit vier Pferden begleitet. Seckend. p. 268.
[5] Totum pondus in Eccium versurus. L. Epp. i. 496.
[6] Ut nihil videar omittere quod in me ad pacem quoquo modo facere possit. Ibid.

199

approaching, presenting with a threatening hand the formidable bull that was intended to crush the Reformation. "We shall bring this business to a happy conclusion," wrote Miltitz to the elector immediately; "thank the pope for the rose, and at the same time send forty or fifty florins to the Cardinal *Quatuor Sanctorum.*"[1]

Luther had now to fulfil his promise of writing to the pope. Before bidding Rome farewell for ever, he was desirous of proclaiming to her once more some important and salutary truths. Many readers, from ignorance of the sentiments that animated the writer, will consider his letter as a caustic writing, a bitter and insolent satire.

All the evils that afflicted Christendom he sincerely ascribed to Rome; on this ground, his language cannot be regarded as insolent, but as containing the most solemn warnings. The greater his affection for Leo, and the greater his love for the Church of Christ, the more he desires to lay bare the extent of its wound. The energy of his expressions is a scale by which to measure the energy of his affections. The moment is come for striking a decisive blow. We may almost imagine we see a prophet going round the city for the last time, reproaching it with its abominations, revealing the judgments of the Almighty, and calling out "Yet a few days more!"

The following is Luther's letter:—

"To the most holy Father in God, Leo X., Pope at Rome. be all health in Christ Jesus our Lord. Amen.

"From the midst of the violent battle which for three years I have been fighting against dissolute men, I cannot hinder myself from sometimes looking towards you, O Leo, most holy Father in God! And although the madness of your impious flatterers has constrained me to appeal from your judgment to a future council, my heart has never been alienated from your holiness, and I have never ceased praying constantly and with deep groaning for your prosperity and for that of your pontificate.[2]

"It is true that I have attacked certain antichristian doctrines, and have inflicted a deep wound upon my adversaries, because of their impiety. I do not repent of this, for I have the example of Christ before me. What is the use of salt, if it hath lost its pungency; or of the edge of the sword, if it cuts not?[3] Cursed be the man who does the Lord's work coldly! Most excellent Leo, far from ever having entertained an evil thought with reference to you, I wish you the most precious blessings for eternity. I have done but one thing—upheld the Word of truth. I am ready to submit to you in every thing; but as for this Word, I will not—I cannot aban-

don it.[1] He who thinks differently from me thinks erroneously.

"It is true that I have attacked the court of Rome; but neither you nor any man on earth can deny that it is more corrupt than Sodom and Gomorrah; and that the impiety prevailing there is past all hope of cure. Yes! I have been filled with horror at seeing that under your name the poor people of Christ have been made a sport of. This I opposed, and I will oppose it again; not that I imagine I shall be able, despite the opposition of flatterers, to prosper in anything connected with this Babylon, which is confusion itself; but I owe it to my brethren, in order that some may escape, if possible, from these terrible scourges.

"You are aware that Rome for many years past has inundated the world with all that could destroy both body and soul. The Church of Rome, once the foremost in sanctity, is become the most licentious den of robbers, the most shameless of all brothels, the kingdom of sin, of death, and of hell,[2] which Antichrist himself, if he were to appear, could not increase in wickedness. All this is clearer than the sun at noonday.

"And yet, O Leo! you sit like a lamb in the midst of wolves, like Daniel in the lions' den! What can you do alone against such monsters? Perhaps there are three or four cardinals who combine learning with virtue. But what are they against so great a number! You would all die of poison, before being able to make trial of any remedy. The fate of the court of Rome is decreed; God's wrath is upon it, and will consume it.[3] It hates good advice, dreads reform, will not mitigate the fury of its impiety, and thus deserves that men should speak of this city as of its mother: *We would have healed Babylon, but she is not healed: forsake her.*[4] It was for you and your cardinals to have applied the remedy; but the sick man mocks the physician, and the horse will not obey the rein.

"Full of affection for you, most excellent Leo, I have always regretted that you, who are worthy of better times, should have been raised to the pontificate in such days as these. Rome merits you not, nor those who resemble you; she deserves to have Satan himself for her king. So true it is that he reigns more than you in that Babylon. Would to God that, laying aside that glory which your enemies so loudly extol, you would exchange it for some small living, or would support yourself on your paternal inheritance; for none but Iscariots deserve such honour......O my dear Leo, of what use are you in this Roman court, except that the basest men employ your name and

[1] Seckend. p. 268.
[2] Ut non totis viribus sedulis atque quantum in me fuit gemebundis precibus apud Deum quæsterim. L. Epp. i. 498.
[3] Quid prodierit sal, si non mordeat? Quid os gladii, si non cædat? Ibid. 499.

[1] Verbum deserere et negare nec possum, nec volo. L. Epp. i. 499.
[2] Facta est.... spelunca latronum licentiosissima, lupanar omnium impudentissimi, regnum peccati, mortis, et inferni. Ibid. 500.
[3] Actum est de Romana curia; pervenit in eam ira Dei usque in finem. Ibid.
[4] Jeremiah li. 9.

power to ruin fortunes, destroy souls, multiply crimes, oppress the faith, the truth, and the whole Church of God? O Leo! Leo! you are the most unhappy of men, and you sit on the most dangerous of thrones! I tell you the truth because I mean you well.

"Is it not true that under the spreading firmament of heaven there is nothing more corrupt or more detestable than the Romish court? It infinitely exceeds the Turks in vices and corruption. Once it was the gate of heaven, now it is the mouth of hell; a mouth which the wrath of God keeps open so wide,[1] that on witnessing the unhappy people rushing into it, I cannot but utter a warning cry, as in a tempest, that some at least may be saved from the terrible gulf.

"Behold, O Leo, my Father! why I have inveighed against this death-dealing see. Far from rising up against your person, I thought I was labouring for your safety, by valiantly attacking that prison, or rather that hell, in which you are shut up. To inflict all possible mischief on the court of Rome, is performing *your* duty. To cover it with shame, is to do Christ honour; in a word, to *be a Christian, is not to be a Roman.*

"Yet finding that by succouring the see of Rome I lose both my labour and my pains, I transmitted to it this writing of divorcement, and said: Farewell, Rome! *He that is unjust, let him be unjust still; and he which is filthy, let him be filthy still!*[2] and I devoted myself to the tranquil and solitary study of the Holy Scripture. Then Satan opened his eyes, and awoke his servant John Eck, a great adversary of Jesus Christ, in order to challenge me again to the lists. He was desirous of establishing, not the primacy of Saint Peter, but his own, and for that purpose to lead the conquered Luther in his triumphal train. His be the blame of all the disgrace with which the see of Rome is covered."

Luther relates his communications with De Vio, Miltitz, and Eck; and then continues:—

"Now then, I come to you, most holy Father, and, prostrate at your feet, I beseech you to curb, if that be possible, these enemies of peace. But I cannot retract my doctrine. I cannot permit any rules of interpretation to be imposed on the Scriptures. The Word of God, which is the fountain whence all true liberty flows, must not be bound.[3]

"O Leo! my Father! listen not to those flattering sirens who would persuade you that you are not a mere man, but a demi-god, and can command and require whatever you please. You are the servant of servants, and the place where you are seated is the most dangerous and miserable of all. Believe those who depreciate you, and not those who extol you. I am perhaps too bold in presuming to teach so exalted a majesty, which ought to instruct all men. But I see the dangers that surround you at Rome; I see you driven to and fro, like the waves of the sea in a storm. Charity urges me, and it is my duty to utter a cry of warning and of safety.

"That I may not appear empty-handed before your holiness, I present you a small book which I have dedicated to you, and which will inform you of the subjects on which I should be engaged, if your parasites permitted me. It is a little matter, if its size be considered; but a great one, if we regard its contents; for the sum of the christian life is therein contained. I am poor, and have nothing else to offer you; besides, have you need of any other than spiritual gifts? I commend myself to your holiness, whom may the Lord Jesus preserve for ever! Amen!"

The little book which Luther presented to the pope was his discourse on *Christian Liberty*, in which the reformer demonstrates incontrovertibly, how, without infringing the liberty given by faith, a Christian may submit to all external ordinances in a spirit of liberty and charity. Two truths serve as a foundation to the whole argument: "The Christian is free and master in all things. The Christian is in bondage and a servant in all and to all. He is free and a master by faith; he is a servant and a slave by love."

He first explains the power of faith to make a Christian free: "Faith unites the soul to Christ, as a wife to her husband," says Luther to the pope. "All that Christ has, becomes the property of the believing soul; all that the soul has, becomes the property of Christ. Christ possesses every blessing and eternal salvation: they are henceforward the property of the soul. The soul possesses every vice and sin: they become henceforth the property of Christ. It is then the blessed exchange commences: Christ, who is God and man, Christ who has never sinned, and whose holiness is immaculate, Christ the Almighty and Everlasting, appropriating by his nuptial ring, that is, by faith, all the sins of the believer's soul, these sins are swallowed up and lost in Him; for there is no sin that can stand before his infinite righteousness. Thus, by means of faith, the soul is delivered from every sin, and clothed with the eternal righteousness of her husband, Jesus Christ. Blessed union! the rich, noble, and holy spouse, Jesus Christ, unites in marriage with that poor, guilty, and despised wife,[1] delivers her from every ill, and adorns her with the most costly blessings...
...Christ, a priest and king, shares this honour and glory with every Christian. The

---

[1] Olim janua cœli, nunc patens quoddam os inferni, et tale os, quod urgente ira Dei, obstrui non potest. L. Epp. i. 501.
[2] Revelation xxii. 11.
[3] Leges interpretandi verbi Dei non patior, cum oporteat verbum Dei esse non alligatum, quod libertatem docet. L. Epp. i. 504.

[1] Ist nun das nicht eine fröhliche Wirthschafft, da der reiche, edle, fromme Bräutigam Christus, das arme, verachtete, böse Huhrlein zur Ehe nimmt. L. Opp. (L.) xvii. 3so.

Christian is a king, and consequently possesses all things; he is a priest, and consequently possesses God. And it is faith, and not works, that brings him to such honour. The Christian is free of all things, above all things, faith giving him abundantly of every thing."

In the second part of his discourse, Luther gives another view of the truth. "Although the Christian is thus made free, he voluntarily becomes a slave, to act towards his brethren as God has acted towards him through Jesus Christ. I desire (says he) to serve freely, joyfully, and gratuitously, a Father who has thus lavished upon me all the abundance of his blessings: I wish to become all things for my neighbour, as Christ has become all things for me."—"From faith," continues Luther, "proceeds the love of God; from love proceeds a life full of liberty, charity, and joy. Oh! how noble and elevated is the christian life! But, alas! no one knows it, no one preaches it. By faith the Christian ascends to God: by love, he descends even to man, and yet he abides ever with God. This is true liberty—a liberty which surpasses all others as much as the heavens are above the earth."

Such is the work with which Luther accompanied his letter to Leo.

CHAPTER VIII.

The Bull in Germany—Eck's Reception—The Bull at Wittemberg—Zwingle's Intervention.

WHILE the reformer was thus addressing the Roman pontiff for the last time, the bull which anathematized him was already in the hands of the chiefs of the German Church, and at the threshold of Luther's dwelling-place. It would appear that no doubts were entertained at Rome of the success of the step just taken against the Reformation. The pope had commissioned two high functionaries of his court, Caraccioli and Aleander, to bear it to the Archbishop of Mentz, desiring him to see it put in execution. But Eck himself appeared in Saxony as the herald and agent of the great pontifical work.

The choice had long been doubtful. "Eck," wrote an inhabitant of Rome about this time, "was peculiarly adapted for this mission by his impudence, his dissimulation, his lies, his flattery, and other vices, that are held in high esteem at Rome: but his fondness for drinking (a failing towards which the Italians entertain a great aversion), was rather against his election."[1] The influence, however, of his patron Fugger, "the king of crowns," prevailed in the end. This bad habit was even metamorphosed into a virtue in the case of Dr. Eck. "He is just the man we want," said many of the Romans; "for these drunken Germans, what can be better than a drunken legate?[1] Their temerity can only be checked by an equal degree of temerity." Further, it was whispered about that no man of sincerity and good sense would undertake such a mission; and that even could such a man be found, the magnitude of the danger would soon make him abandon the place. The idea of nominating Aleander as Dr. Eck's colleague seemed most excellent. "A worthy pair of ambassadors," said some; "both are admirably suited for this work, and perfectly matched in effrontery, impudence, and debauchery."[2]

The doctor of Ingolstadt had felt more than any other man the force of Luther's attack; he had seen the danger, and stretched forth his hand to steady the tottering edifice of Rome. He was, in his own opinion, the Atlas destined to bear on his sturdy shoulders the ancient Roman world now threatening to fall to ruins. Proud of the success of his journey to Rome,—proud of the commission he had received from the sovereign pontiff,—proud of appearing in Germany with the new title of protonotary and pontifical nuncio,—proud of the bull he held in his hands, and which contained the condemnation of his indomitable rival, his present mission was a more magnificent triumph than all the victories he had gained in Hungary, Bavaria, Lombardy, and Saxony, and from which he had previously derived so much renown. But this pride was soon to be brought low. The pope, by confiding the publication of the bull to Eck, had committed a fault destined to destroy its effect. So great a distinction, accorded to a man not filling an elevated station in the Church, offended all sensible men. The bishops, accustomed to receive the bulls direct from the Roman pontiff, were displeased that this should be published in their dioceses by a nuncio created for the occasion. The nation, that had laughed at the pretended conqueror at Leipsic at the moment of his flight to Italy, was astonished and indignant at seeing him recross the Alps, bearing the insignia of a papal nuncio, and furnished with power to crush her chosen men. Luther considered this judgment brought by his implacable opponent, as an act of personal revenge; this condemnation was in his idea (says Pallavicini) the treacherous dagger of a mortal enemy, and not the lawful axe of a Roman lictor.[3] This paper was no

[1] Temeritate, audacia, mendaciis simulatione, adulatione, et cæteris vitiis curiæ aptis egregie pollet. Verum sola obstabat ebrietas, Italis (ut nosti) perquam odiosa. Riederer, Nachrichten zum kirchen-geschichten, i. 179.

[1] Nihil magis Germanos temulentos quam temulentum decere legatum. Riederer, Nachrichten zum kirchen-geschichten, i. 179.
[2] Egregium profecto oratorum par, et causæ perquam conveniens, impudentiaque, temeritate, et vitæ flagitiis simile. Ibid.
[3] Non tanquam a securi legitimi lictoris, sed e telo infensissimi hostis. Pallavicini, i. 74.

longer regarded as the bull of the supreme pontiff, but as the bull of Doctor Eck. Thus the edge was blunted and weakened beforehand by the very man who had prepared it.

The Chancellor of Ingolstadt had made all haste to Saxony. 'Twas there he had fought; 'twas there he wished to publish his victory. He succeeded in posting up the bull at Meissen, Merseburg, and Brandenburg, towards the end of September. But in the first of these cities it was stuck up in a place where no one could read it, and the bishops of the three sees did not press its publication. Even his great protector, Duke George, forbade the council of Leipsic to make it generally known before receiving an order from the Bishop of Merseburg; and this order did not come till the following year. "These difficulties are merely for form's sake," thought John Eck at first; for every thing in other respects seemed to smile upon him. Duke George himself sent him a gilt cup filled with ducats. Even Miltitz, who had hastened to Leipsic at the news of his rival's presence, invited him to dinner. The two legates were boon companions, and Miltitz thought he could more effectually sound his rival over the bottle. "When he had drunk pretty freely, he began," says the pope's chamberlain, "to boast at a fine rate; he displayed his bull, and related how he intended bringing that scoundrel Martin to reason."[1] But erelong the Ingolstadt doctor observed that the wind was changing. A great alteration had taken place in Leipsic during the past year.[2] On St. Michael's day, some students posted up placards in ten different places, in which the new nuncio was sharply attacked. In alarm he fled to the cloister of St. Paul, in which Tetzel had already taken refuge, refused to see any one, and prevailed upon the rector to bring these youthful adversaries to account. But poor Eck gained little by this. The students wrote a ballad upon him, which they sung in the streets: Eck heard it from his retreat. Upon this he lost all his courage; the formidable champion trembled in every limb. Each day he received threatening letters. One hundred and fifty students arrived from Wittemberg, boldly exclaiming against the papal envoy. The wretched apostolical nuncio could hold out no longer. "I have no wish to see him killed," said Luther, "but I am desirous that his schemes should fail."[3] Eck quitted his asylum by night, escaped secretly from Leipsic, and went and hid himself at Coburg. Miltitz, who relates this, boasted of it more than the reformer. This triumph was not of long duration; all the conciliatory plans of the chamberlain failed,

and he came to a melancholy end. Miltitz, being intoxicated, fell into the Rhine at Mentz, and was drowned.

Gradually, however, Eck's courage revived. He repaired to Erfurth, whose theologians had given the Wittemberg doctor several proofs of their jealousy. He insisted that the bull should be published in this city; but the students seized the copies, tore them in pieces, and flung the fragments into the river, saying: "Since it is a bull (a bubble), let it float!"[1] "Now," said Luther, when he was informed of this, "the pope's paper is a real bull (bubble)."

Eck did not dare appear at Wittemberg; he sent the bull to the rector, threatening to destroy the university if he did not conform to it. At the same time he wrote to Duke John, Frederick's brother and co-regent: "Do not misconstrue my proceedings," said he; "for I am fighting on behalf of the faith, which costs me much care, toil, and money."[2]

The Bishop of Brandenburg could not, even had he so wished, act in Wittemberg in his quality of ordinary; for the university was protected by its privileges. Luther and Carlstadt, both condemned by the bull, were invited to be present at the deliberations that took place on its contents. The rector declared that, as the bull was not accompanied by a letter from the pope, he would not publish it. The university already enjoyed in the surrounding countries a greater authority than the pontiff himself. Its declaration served as a model for the elector's government. Thus the spirit that was in Luther triumphed over the bull of Rome.

While this affair was thus violently agitating the public mind in Germany, a solemn voice was heard in another country of Europe. One man, foreseeing the immense schism that the papal bull would cause in the Church, stood forward to utter a serious warning and to defend the reformer. It was the same Swiss priest whom we have mentioned before, Ulrich Zwingle, who, without any relations of friendship with Luther, published a writing full of wisdom and dignity,—the first of his numerous works.[3] A brotherly affection seemed to attract him towards the reformer of Wittemberg. "The piety of the pontiff," said he, "calls upon him to sacrifice gladly all that he holds dearest, for the glory of Christ his king and the public peace of the Church. Nothing is more injurious to his dignity than his defending it by bribery or by terror. Before even Luther's writings had been read, he was cried down among the people as a heretic, a schismatic, and as

---

[1] Nachdem (writes Miltitz) er nun tapfer getrunken hatte, fieng er gleich an trefflich von seiner Ordre zu prahlen, &c. Seckend. p. 238.
[2] Longe aliam faciem et mentem Lipsiæ eum invenire quam sperasset. *Ib.* Epp. i. 492.
[3] Nollem eum occidi, quanquam optem ejus consilia irrita fieri. Ibid.

[1] L. Epp. i. 520. A studiosis discerpta et in aquam projecta, dicentibus; Bulla est, in aquam natet! playing on the word *bulla*, which means a *bubble*, the seal appended to the bull, and hence the *bull* itself.
[2] Mit viel Mühe, Arbeit und Kosten. L. Opp. (L.) xvii. 317.
[3] Consilium cujusdam ex animo cupientis esse consultum et pontificis dignitati, et Christianæ religionis tranquillitati.—Zw. Opp. cur. Schulero et Schulthessio, iii. 1-5.

Antichrist himself. No one had given him warning, no one had refuted him ; he begged for a discussion, and they were content to condemn him. The bull that is now published against him displeases even those who honour the pope's grandeur ; for throughout it betrays signs of the impotent hatred of a few monks, and not those becoming the mildness of a pontiff, the vicar of a Saviour full of compassion. All men acknowledge that the true doctrine of the Gospel of Jesus Christ has greatly degenerated, and that we need a striking public revival of laws and morality.[1] Look to all men of learning and virtue ; the greater their sincerity, the stronger is their attachment to the evangelical truth, and the less are they scandalized at Luther's writings. There is no one but confesses that these books have made him a better man,[2] although perhaps they may contain passages that he does not approve of.—Let men of pure doctrine and acknowledged probity be chosen ; let those princes above all suspicion, the Emperor Charles, the King of England, and the King of Hungary, themselves appoint the arbitrators ; let these men read Luther's writings, hear him personally, and let their decision be ratified ! Νικησάτω ἡ τοῦ Χριστοῦ παιδεία καὶ ἀλήθεια ! "[3]

This proposition emanating from the country of the Swiss led to no results. The great divorce must be accomplished ; Christendom must be rent in twain ; and even in its wounds will the remedy for all its ills be found.

CHAPTER IX.

Luther's Appeal to God—His Opinion of the Bull—A Neutral Family—Luther on the Bull—Against the Bull of Antichrist—The Pope forbids Faith—Effects of the Bull—The Burning Pile of Louvain.

In truth, what signified all this resistance of students, rectors, and priests ? If the mighty hand of Charles unites with the pope's, will they not crush these scholars and grammarians ? Who shall withstand the power of the pontiff of Christendom, and of the Emperor of the West ? The bolt is discharged ; Luther is cut off from the Church ; the Gospel seems lost. At this solemn moment, the reformer does not conceal from himself the perils that surround him. He casts his looks to heaven. He prepares to receive, as from the hand of the Lord, the blow that seems destined to destroy him. His soul reposes at the foot of the throne of God. " What will happen ? " said he. " I know not, and I care not to know, feeling sure that He who sitteth in heaven hath foreseen from all eternity the beginning, continuation, and end of all this affair. Wherever the blow may reach me, I fear not. The leaf of a tree does not fall to the ground without the will of our Father. How much less we ourselves...... It is a little matter to die for the Word, since this WORD, which was made flesh for us, died itself at first. We shall arise with it, if we die with it, and passing where it has gone before, we shall arrive where it has arrived, and abide with it through all eternity."[1]

Sometimes, however, Luther cannot restrain the contempt inspired by the manœuvres of his enemies ; we then find in him that mixture of sublimity and irony which characterizes him. " I know nothing of Eck," said he, except that he has arrived with a long beard, a long bull, and a long purse ; but I laugh at his bull."[2]

On the 3d of October he was informed of the papal brief. " It is come at last, this Roman bull," said he. " I despise and attack it as impious, false, and in every respect worthy of Eck. It is Christ himself who is condemned therein. No reasons are given in it : I am cited to Rome, not to be heard, but that I may eat my words. I shall treat it as a forgery, although I believe it true. Oh, that Charles V. would act like a man ! and that for the love of Christ he would attack these wicked spirits ![3] I rejoice in having to bear such ills for the best of causes. Already I feel greater liberty in my heart ; for at last I know that the pope is Antichrist, and that his throne is that of Satan himself."

It was not in Saxony alone that the thunders of Rome had caused alarm. A tranquil family of Swabia, one that had remained neutral, found its peace suddenly disturbed. Bilibald Pirckheimer of Nuremberg, one of the most distinguished men of his day, early bereft of his beloved wife Crescentia, was attached by the closest ties of affection to his two young sisters, Charity, abbess of Saint Claire, and Clara, a nun in the same convent. These two pious young women served God in this seclusion, and divided their time between study, the care of the poor, and meditation on eternal life. Bilibald, a statesman, found some relaxation from his public cares in the correspondence he kept up with them. They were learned, read Latin, and studied the Fathers ; but there was nothing they loved so much as the Holy Scriptures. They had never had any other instructor than their brother. Charity's

---

[1] Multum degenerasse ab illa sincera Christi evangelica doctrina, adeo ut nemo non fateatur opus esse publica aliqua et insigni legum ac morum instauratione. Zw. Opp. iii. 3.
[2] Nemo non fatetur se ex illius libris factum esse meliorem. Ibid. 4.
[3] May the teaching and the truth of Christ prevail !

[1] Parum est nos pro Verbo mori, cum ipsum incarnatum pro nobis prius mortuum sit. L. Epp. i. 490.
[2] Venisse eum barbatum, bullatum, nummatum. Ridebo et ego bullam sive ampullam. Ibid. 488.
[3] Utinam Carolus vir esset, et pro Christo hos Satanas aggrederetur. Ibid. 494.

letters bear the impress of a delicate and loving mind. Full of the tenderest affection for Bilibald, she feared the least danger on his account. Pirckheimer, to encourage this timid creature, composed a dialogue between Charitas and Veritas (Charity and Truth), in which Veritas strives to give confidence to Charitas.[1] Nothing could have been more touching, or better adapted to console a tender and anxious heart.

What must have been Charity's alarm when she heard it rumoured that Bilibald's name was posted up under the pope's bull on the gates of the cathedral beside that of Luther! In fact, Eck, impelled by blind fury, had associated with Luther six of the most distinguished men in Germany, Carlstadt, Feldkirchen, Egranus, who cared little about it, Adelmann, Pirckheimer, and his friend Spengler, whom the public functions with which they were invested rendered particularly sensible to this indignity. Great was the agitation in the convent of St. Claire. How could they endure Bilibald's shame? Nothing is so painful to relatives as trials of this nature. The danger was truly urgent. In vain did the city of Nuremberg, the Bishop of Bamberg, and even the Dukes of Bavaria, intercede in favour of Spengler and Pirckheimer: these noble-minded men were compelled to humble themselves before Dr. Eck, who made them feel all the importance of a Roman protonotary, and compelled them to write a letter to the pope, in which they declared that they did not adhere to the doctrines of Luther, except so far as they were conformable with the christian faith. At the same time Adelmann, with whom Eck had once disputed, as he rose from table, after a discussion on the great question then filling every mind, was forced to appear before the bishop of Augsburg, and clear himself upon oath from all participation in the Lutheran heresy. Yet vengeance and anger proved bad counsellors to Eck. The names of Bilibald and of his friends brought discredit on the bull. The character of these eminent men, and their numerous connexions, served to increase the general irritation.

Luther at first pretended to doubt the authenticity of the bull. "I hear," says he in the first of his writings on the subject, "that Eck has brought a new bull from Rome, which resembles him so much that it might be called *Doctor Eck*,—so full is it of falsehood and error. He would have us believe that it is the pope's doing, while it is only a forgery." After having set forth the reasons for his doubts, Luther concludes by saying: "I must see with my own eyes the lead, the seal, the strings, the clause, the signature of the bull, in fact the whole of it, before I value all these clamours even at a straw!"[2]

But no one doubted, not even Luther himself, that it really emanated from the pope.

Germany waited to see what the reformer would do. Would he stand firm? All eyes were fixed on Wittemberg. Luther did not keep his contemporaries long in suspense. He replied with a terrible discharge of artillery, publishing on the 4th of November 1520 his treatise *Against the bull of Antichrist*.

"What errors, what deceptions," says he, "have crept among the poor people under the mantle of the Church and of the pretended infallibility of the pope! How many souls have thus been lost! how much blood spilt! how many murders committed! how many kingdoms devastated!......

"I can pretty clearly distinguish," says he ironically, a little further on, "between skill and malice, and I set no high value on a malice so unskilful. To burn books is so easy a matter that even children can do it; much more, then, the holy Father and his doctors.[1] It would be well for them to show greater ability than that which is required to burn books......Besides, let them destroy my works! I desire nothing better; for all my wish has been to lead souls to the Bible, so that they might afterwards neglect my writings.[2] Great God! if we had a knowledge of Scripture, what need would there be of any books of mine?......I am free, by the grace of God, and bulls neither console nor alarm me. My strength and my consolation are in a place where neither men nor devils can reach them."

Luther's tenth proposition, condemned by the pope, was thus drawn up: "no man's sins are forgiven, unless he believes they are forgiven when the priest absolves him." By condemning this, the pope denied that faith was necessary in the sacrament. "They pretend," exclaims Luther, "that we must not believe our sins are forgiven when we receive absolution from the priest. And what then ought we to do?......Listen, Christians, to this news from Rome. Condemnation is pronounced against that article of faith which we profess when we say: 'I believe in the Holy Ghost, the Holy Catholic Church, the forgiveness of sins.' If I were certain that the pope had really issued this bull at Rome (and he had no doubt about it), and that it was not invented by Eck, that prince of liars, I should like to proclaim to all Christians that they ought to consider the pope as the real Antichrist spoken of in Scripture. And if he would not discontinue publicly to proscribe the faith of the Church, then...... let even the temporal sword resist *him*, rather than the Turk!......For the Turk permits us to believe, but the pope forbids it."

While Luther was speaking thus forcibly, his dangers were increasing. His enemies' plan was to expel him from Wittemberg. If Luther and Wittemberg can be separated,

---

[1] Pirckheimeri Opp. Franckfort.
[2] Oder nicht ein Haarbreit geben. L. Opp. (L.) xvii. 323.

[1] So ist Bücher verbrennen so leicht, dass es auch Kinder können, schweig denn der heilige Vater Pabst. L. Opp. (L.) xvii. 324.
[2] In Biblien zu führen, dass man derselben Verstand erlangte, und denn meine Büchlein verschwinden liess. Ibid.

Luther and Wittemberg will be ruined. One blow would thus free Rome both from the heretical doctor and the heretical university. Duke George, the Bishop of Merseburg, and the Leipsic theologians secretly applied themselves to the task.[1] When Luther heard of it, he said: "I place the whole matter in God's hands."[2] These intrigues were not entirely ineffectual: Adrian, Hebrew professor at Wittemberg, suddenly turned against the doctor. Great strength of faith was required to bear up against the blow inflicted by the court of Rome. There are some characters that will go along with the truth only to a certain point. Such was Adrian. Alarmed by this condemnation, he quitted Wittemberg, and repaired to Dr. Eck at Leipsic.

The bull was beginning to be carried into execution. The voice of the pontiff of Christendom was not powerless. For ages, fire and sword had taught submission to his decrees. The burning piles were erected at his voice. Every thing seemed to announce that a terrible catastrophe would shortly put an end to the daring revolt of this Augustine monk. In October 1520 Luther's books were taken away from all the booksellers' shops in Ingolstadt, and put under seal. The Elector-archbishop of Mentz, moderate as he was, felt obliged to banish Ulrich of Hütten from his court, and to imprison his printer. The papal nuncios had besieged the youthful emperor: Charles declared that he would protect the old religion;[3] and in some of his hereditary possessions scaffolds were erected, on which the writings of the heretic were to be reduced to ashes. Princes of the Church and councillors of state were present at these autos-da-fé.

Eck behaved with insolence, in every quarter threatening the great and the learned, and "filling every thing with his smoke," as Erasmus says.[4] "The pope," said Eck, "who has overthrown so many counts and dukes, will know how to bring these wretched grammarians to their senses.[5] We must tell the Emperor Charles himself: *You are but a cobbler.*"[6] And his colleague Aleander, frowning like a schoolmaster who threatens his pupils with the rod,[7] said to Erasmus: "We shall know how to get at this Duke Frederick, and teach him reason." Aleander was quite elated with his success. To hear the haughty nuncio talk, one would have thought that the fire which consumed Luther's books at Mentz was "the beginning of the

end." These flames (said they one to another at Rome) will spread terror far and wide. It was so with many timid and superstitious minds; but even in the hereditary states of Charles, the only places in which they dared carry out the bull, the people, and sometimes the nobles, often replied to these pontifical demonstrations by ridicule or by expressions of indignation. "Luther," said the doctors of Louvain, when they appeared before Margaret, governor of the Netherlands, "Luther is overturning the christian faith."—"Who is Luther?" asked the princess.—"An ignorant monk."—"Well, then," replied she, "do you who are so wise and so numerous write against him. The world will rather believe many wise men than an isolated and unlearned man." The Louvain doctors preferred an easier method. They erected a vast pile at their own expense. A great multitude thronged the place of execution. Students and citizens might be seen hastily traversing the crowd, bearing large volumes under their arms, which they threw into the flames. Their zeal edified both monks and doctors; but the trick was afterwards discovered—it was the *Sermones Discipuli, Tartaretus*, and other scholastic and papistical works, they had been throwing into the fire, instead of Luther's writings![1]

The Count of Nassau, viceroy of Holland, replied to the Dominicans who solicited permission to burn the doctor's books: "Go and preach the Gospel with as much purity as Luther does, and you will have to complain of nobody." As the conversation turned upon the reformer at a banquet when the leading princes of the empire were present, the Lord of Ravenstein said aloud: "In the space of four centuries, a single Christian has ventured to raise his head, and him the pope wishes to put to death!"[2]

Luther, sensible of the strength of his cause, remained traquil in the midst of the tumult the bull had created.[3] "If you did not press me so earnestly," said he to Spalatin, "I should keep silence, well knowing that the work must be accomplished by the counsel and power of God."[4] The timid man was for speaking out, the strong desired to remain silent. Luther discerned a power that escaped the eyes of his friend. "Be of good cheer," continues the reformer. "It is Christ who has begun these things, and it is He that will accomplish them, whether I be banished or put to death. Jesus Christ is here present, and He who is within us is greater than he who is in the world."[5]

1 Ut Wittemberga pellerer. L. Epp. i. 519.
2 Id quod in manum Dei refero. Ibid. 520.
3 A ministris pontificiis mature præoccupatus, declaravit se vello veterem fidem tutari. Pallavicini, i. 80.
4 Omnia suis fumis complens. Hardt. Hist. Lit. Ref. i. 169.
5 Tres pediculosos grammatistas. Ibid.
6 Pontifex potest dicere Cæsari Carolo: Tu es cerdo. Ibid.
7 Eo vultu quo solent tetrici literatores pueris minari virgas. Ibid.

1 Seckend. p. 289.
2 Es ist in vierhundert Jahren ein christlicher Mann aufgestanden, den will der Pabst todt haben. Ibid. p. 288.
3 In bullosis illis tumultibus. L. Epp. i. 519.
4 Rem totam Deo committerem. Ibid. 521.
5 Christus ista cœpit, ipse perficiet, etiam me sive extincto, sive fugato. Ibid. 526.

CHAPTER X.

Decisive Step of the Reformer—Luther's Appeal to a General Council—Close Combat—The Bull burnt by Luther—Meaning of this daring Act—Luther in the Academy—Luther against the Pope—New Work by Melancthon—How Luther encourages his Friends—Progress of the Struggle—Melancthon's Opinions on the Weak-hearted—Luther's Treatise on the Bible—Doctrine of Grace—Luther's Recantation.

Duty obliged Luther to speak, that the truth might be manifested to the world. Rome has struck the blow: he will show how he has received it. The pope has put him under the ban of the Church; he will put the pope under the ban of Christendom. Hitherto the pontiff's commands have been all-powerful; he will oppose sentence to sentence, and the world shall know which has the greater strength. " I desire," said he, " to set my conscience at rest, by disclosing to all men the danger that threatens them;"[1] and at the same time he prepared to make a fresh appeal to a general council. An appeal from the pope to a council was a crime. It is therefore by a new attack on the pontifical power that Luther presumes to justify those by which it had been preceded.

On the 17th of November, a notary and five witnesses, among whom was Cruciger, met at ten o'clock in the morning in one of the halls of the Augustine convent where Luther resided. There, the public officer (Sarctor of Eisleben) immediately proceeding to draw up the minute of his protest, the reformer in presence of these witnesses said with a solemn tone of voice :—

" Considering that a general council of the Christian Church is above the pope, especially in matters of faith ;

" Considering that the power of the pope is not above but inferior to Scripture ; and that he has no right to slaughter the sheep of Christ's flock, and throw them into the jaws of the wolf ;

" I, Martin Luther, an Augustine friar, doctor of the Holy Scriptures at Wittemberg, appeal by these presents, in behalf of myself and of those who are or who shall be with me, from the most holy pope Leo to a future general and christian council.

" I appeal from the said pope, *first*, as an unjust, rash, and tyrannical judge, who condemns me without a hearing, and without giving any reasons for his judgment; *secondly*, as a heretic and an apostate, misled, hardened, and condemned by the Holy Scriptures, who commands me to deny that christian faith is necessary in the use of the sacraments ;[2] *thirdly*, as an enemy, an antichrist, an adversary, an oppressor of Holy Scripture,[3] who dares set his own words in opposition to the Word of God ; *fourthly*, as a despiser, a calumniator, a blasphemer of the holy Christian Church and of a free council, who maintains that a council is nothing of itself.

" For this reason, with all humility, I entreat the most serene, most illustrious, excellent, generous, noble, powerful, wise, and prudent lords, namely, Charles emperor of Rome, the electors, princes, counts, barons, knights, gentlemen, councillors, cities and communities of the whole German nation, to adhere to my protest, and to resist with me the antichristian conduct of the pope, for the glory of God, the defence of the Church and of the christian doctrine, and for the maintenance of the free councils of Christendom ; and Christ, our Lord, will reward them bountifully by his everlasting grace. But if there be any who scorn my prayer, and continue to obey that impious man the pope, rather than God,[4] I reject by these presents all responsibility, having faithfully warned their consciences, and I abandon them, as well as the pope and his adherents, to the supreme judgment of God."

Such is Luther's bill of divorce; such is his reply to the pontiff's bull. A great seriousness pervades the whole of this declaration. The charges he brings against the pope are of the gravest description, and it is not heedlessly that he makes them. This protest was circulated through Germany, and sent to most of the courts of Christendom.

Luther had, however, a still more daring step in reserve, although this which he had just taken appeared the extreme of audacity. He would in no respect be behindhand with Rome. The monk of Wittemberg will do all that the sovereign pontiff dares do. He gives judgment for judgment ; he raises pile for pile. The son of the Medici and the son of the miner of Mansfeldt have gone down into the lists ; and in this desperate struggle, which shakes the world, one does not strike a blow which the other does not return. On the 10th of December, a placard was posted on the walls of the university of Wittemberg, inviting the professors and students to be present at nine o'clock in the morning, at the Eastern gate, near the Holy Cross. A great number of doctors and students assembled, and Luther, walking at their head, conducted the procession to the appointed place. How many burning piles has Rome erected during the course of ages ! Luther resolves to make a better application of the great Roman principle. It is only a few old papers that are about to be destroyed ; and fire, thinks he, is intended for that purpose. A scaffold had been prepared. One of the oldest masters of arts set fire to it. As the flames rose high into the air, the formidable Augustine, wearing his frock, approached the pile, carrying the Canon Law, the Decretals, the Clemen-

---

[1] Ut meam conscientiam redimam. L. Epp. i. 522.
[2] Ab erroneo, indurato, per Scripturas sanctas damnato, hæretico et apostata. L. Opp. Lat. ii. 50. See also L. Opp. (L.) xvii. 332. There are some paragraphs in the German that are not in the Latin text.
[3] Oppressore totius Sacræ Scripturæ. Ibid.

[1] Et papæ, impio homini, plus quam Deo obediant. L. Opp. Lat. ii. 50. L. Opp. (L.) xvii. 332.

tines, the papal Extravagants, some writings by Eck and Emser, and the pope's bull. The Decretals having been first consumed, Luther held up the bull, and said : " Since thou hast vexed the Holy One of the Lord, may everlasting fire vex and consume thee ! " He then flung it into the flames. Never had war been declared with greater energy and resolution. After this Luther calmly returned to the city, and the crowd of doctors, professors, and students, testifying their approval by loud cheers, re-entered Wittemberg with him. " The Decretals," said Luther, " resemble a body whose face is meek as a young maiden's, whose limbs are full of violence like those of a lion, and whose tail is filled with wiles like a serpent. Among all the laws of the popes, there is not one word that teaches us who is Jesus Christ." [1] " My enemies," said he on another occasion, " have been able, by burning my books, to injure the cause of truth in the minds of the common people, and destroy their souls ; for this reason, I consumed their books in return. A serious struggle has just begun. Hitherto I have been only playing with the pope. I began this work in God's name ; it will be ended without me and by His might. If they dare burn my books, in which more of the Gospel is to be found (I speak without boasting) than in all the books of the pope, I can with much greater reason burn theirs, in which no good can be discovered."

If Luther had commenced the Reformation in this manner, such a step would undoubtedly have entailed the most deplorable results. Fanaticism might have been aroused by it, and the Church thrown into a course of violence and disorder. But the reformer had prefaced his work by seriously explaining the lessons of Scripture. The foundations had been wisely laid. Now, a powerful blow, such as he had just given, might not only be without inconvenience, but even accelerate the moment in which Christendom would throw off its bonds.

Luther thus solemnly declared that he separated from the pope and his church. This might appear necessary to him after his letter to Leo X. He accepted the excommunication that Rome had pronounced. He showed the christian world that there was now war unto death between him and the pope. He burnt his ships upon the beach, thus imposing on himself the necessity of advancing and of combating.

Luther had re-entered Wittemberg. On the morrow, the lecture-room was more crowded than usual. All minds were in a state of excitement ; a solemn feeling pervaded the assembly ; they waited expecting an address from the doctor. He lectured on the Psalms,—a course that he had commenced in the month of March in the preceding year. Having finished his explanations, he

remained silent a few minutes, and then continued energetically : " Be on your guard against the laws and statutes of the pope. I have burnt his Decretals, but this is merely child's play. It is time, and more than time, that the pope were burnt ; that is (explaining himself immediately), the see of Rome, with all its doctrines and abominations." Then assuming a more solemn tone, he added : " If you do not contend with your whole heart against the impious government of the pope, you cannot be saved. Whoever takes delight in the religion and worship of popery, will be eternally lost in the world to come." [1]

" If you reject it," continued he, " you must expect to incur every kind of danger, and even to lose your lives. But it is far better to be exposed to such perils in this world than to keep silence ! So long as I live, I will denounce to my brethren the sore and the plague of Babylon, for fear that many who are with us should fall back like the rest into the bottomless pit."

We can scarcely imagine the effect produced on the assembly by this discourse, the energy of which surprises us. " Not one among us," adds the candid student who has handed it down, " unless he be a senseless log of wood (as all the papists are, he says parenthetically), doubts that this is truth pure and undefiled. It is evident to all believers that Dr. Luther is an angel of the living God, called to feed Christ's wandering sheep with the Word of God." [2]

This discourse and the act by which it was crowned mark an important epoch in the Reformation. The dispute at Leipsic had inwardly detached Luther from the pope. But the moment in which he burnt the bull was that in which he declared in the most formal manner his entire separation from the Bishop of Rome and his church, and his attachment to the universal Church, such as it had been founded by the apostles of Jesus Christ. At the eastern gate of the city he lit up a fire that has been burning for three centuries.

" The pope," said he, " has three crowns ; and for this reason : the first is against God, for he condemns religion ; the second against the emperor, for he condemns the secular power ; the third is against society, for he condemns marriage." [3] When he was reproached with inveighing too severely against popery : " Alas ! " replied he, " would that I could speak against it with a voice of thunder, and that each of my words was a thunderbolt ! " [4]

The firmness spread to Luther's friends and fellow-countrymen. A whole nation rallied around him. The university of Wittem-

[1] Muss ewig in jenem Leben verlohren seyn. L. Opp. (L.) xvii. 333.
[2] Lutherum esse Dei viventis angelum qui palabundas Christi oves pascat. L. Opp. Lat. ii. 123.
[3] L. Opp. (W.) xxii. 1313.
[4] Und ein jeglich Wort eine Donneraxt ärwe. Ibid. 1350.

[1] L. Opp. (W.) xxii. 1493-1496.

berg in particular grew daily more attached to this hero, to whom it was indebted for its importance and glory. Carlstadt then raised his voice against that "furious lion of Florence," which tore all human and divine laws, and trampled under foot the principles of eternal truth. Melancthon, also, about this time addressed the states of the empire in a writing characterized by the elegance and wisdom peculiar to this amiable man. It was in reply to a work attributed to Emser, but published under the name of Rhadinus, a Roman divine. Never had Luther himself spoken with greater energy; and yet there was a grace in Melancthon's language that won its way to every heart.

After showing by various passages of Scripture that the pope is not superior to the other bishops: "What is it," says he to the states of the empire, "that prevents our depriving the pope of the rights that we have given him? It matters little to Luther whether our riches, that is to say, the treasures of Europe, are sent to Rome; but the great cause of his grief and ours is, that the laws of the pontiffs and the reign of the pope not only endanger the souls of men but entirely ruin them. Each one may judge for himself whether it is becoming or not to contribute his money for the maintenance of Roman luxury; but to judge of religion and its sacred mysteries is not within the scope of the commonalty. It is on this ground, then, that Luther appeals to your faith and zeal, and that all pious men unite with him, —some aloud, others with sighs and groans. Call to remembrance that you are Christians, ye princes of a christian people, and wrest these sad relics of Christendom from the tyranny of Antichrist. They are deceivers who pretend that you have no authority over priests. That same spirit which animated Jehu against the priests of Baal, urges you, by this precedent, to abolish the Roman superstition, which is much more horrible than the idolatry of Baal."[2] Thus spoke the gentle Melancthon to the princes of Germany.

A few cries of alarm were heard among the friends of the Reformation. Timid minds inclined to extreme measures of conciliation, and Staupitz, in particular, expressed the deepest anxiety. "All this matter has been hitherto mere play," wrote Luther to him. "You have said yourself, that if God does not do these things, it is impossible they can be done. The tumult becomes more and more tumultuous, and I do not think it will ever be appeased, except at the last day."[3] Thus did Luther encourage these affrighted minds. Three centuries have passed away, and the tumult has not yet subsided!

"The papacy," continued he, "is no longer what it was yesterday and the day before. Let it excommunicate and burn my writings! ......let it slay me!......it shall not check that which is advancing. Some great portent is at our doors.[1] I burnt the bull, at first with great trembling, but now I experience more joy from it than from any action I have ever done in my life."[2]

We involuntarily stop, and are delighted at reading in Luther's great soul the mighty future that was preparing. "O my father," said he to Staupitz in conclusion, "pray for the Word of God and for me. I am carried away and tossed about by these waves."[3]

Thus war was declared on both sides. The combatants threw away their scabbards. The Word of God reasserted its rights, and deposed him who had taken the place of God himself. Society was shaken. In every age selfish men are not wanting who would let human society sleep on in error and corruption; but wise men, although they may be timid, think differently. "We are well aware," said the gentle and moderate Melancthon, "that statesmen have a dread of innovation; and it must be acknowledged that, in this sad confusion which is denominated human life, controversies, and even those which proceed from the justest causes, are always tainted with some evil. It is requisite, however, that in the Church, the Word and commandments of God should be preferred to every mortal thing.[4] God threatens with his eternal anger those who endeavour to suppress the truth. For this reason it was a duty, a christian duty, incumbent on Luther, and from which he could not draw back, especially as he was a doctor of the Church of God, to reprove the pernicious errors which unprincipled men were disseminating with inconceivable effrontery. If controversy engenders many evils, as I see to my great sorrow," adds the wise Philip, "it is the fault of those who at first propagated error, and of those who, filled with diabolical hatred, are now seeking to uphold it."

But all men did not think thus. Luther was overwhelmed with reproaches: the storm burst upon him from every quarter of heaven. "He is quite alone," said some; "he is a teacher of novelties," said others.

"Who knows," replied Luther, sensible of the call that was addressed to him from on high, "if God has not chosen and called me,[5] and if they ought not to fear that, by despising me, they despise God himself? Moses was alone at the departure from Egypt; Elijah was alone in the reign of King Ahab;

---

[1] Quid obstat quominus papæ quod dedimus jus adimamus? Corp. Ref. i. 337.
[2] Ut extinguaris illam, multo tetriorem Baalis idololatria, Romanam superstitionem. Ibid.
[3] Tumultus egregie tumultuatur, ut nisi extremo die sedari mihi posse non videatur. L. Epp. i. 541.

[1] Omnino aliquid portenti præ foribus est. L. Epp. i. 512. What a presentiment of the future!
[2] Primum trepidus et orans, sed nunc lætior quam ullo totius vitæ meæ facto. Ibid.
[3] Ego fluctibus his rapior et volvor. Ibid.
[4] Sed tamen in Ecclesia necesse est anteferri mandatum Dei omnibus rebus humanis. Melancth. Vita Lutheri.
[5] Wer weiss ob mich Gott dazu berufen und erwählt hat. Foundation of the articles condemned by the bull of Rome. L. Opp. (L.) xvii. 338.

Isaiah alone in Jerusalem; Ezekiel alone in Babylon......God never selected as a prophet either the high-priest or any other great personage; but ordinarily he chose low and despised men, once even the shepherd Amos. In every age, the saints have had to reprove the great, kings, princes, priests, and wise men, at the peril of their lives......And was it not the same under the New Testament? Ambrose was alone in his time; after him, Jerome was alone; later still, Augustine was alone......I do not say that I am a prophet;[1] but I say that they ought to fear, precisely because I am alone and they are many. I am sure of this, that the Word of God is with me, and that it is not with them.

"It is said also," continues he, "that I put forward novelties, and that it is impossible to believe that all the other doctors were so long in error.

"No! I do not preach novelties. But I say that all christian doctrines have been lost sight of by those who should have preserved them; namely, the learned and the bishops. Still I doubt not that the truth remained in a few hearts, even were it with infants in the cradle.[2] Poor peasants and simple children now understand Jesus Christ better than the pope, the bishops, and the doctors.

"I am accused of rejecting the holy doctors of the Church. I do not reject them; but, since all these doctors endeavour to prove their writings by Holy Scripture, Scripture must be clearer and surer than they are. Who would think of proving an obscure passage by one that was obscurer still? Thus, then, necessity obliges me to have recourse to the Bible, as all the doctors have done, and to call upon it to pronounce upon their writings; for the Bible alone is lord and master.

"But (say they) men of power persecute him. Is it not clear, according to Scripture, that the persecutors are generally wrong, and the persecuted right; that the majority has ever been on the side of falsehood, and the minority on that of truth? Truth has in every age caused an outcry."[3]

Luther next examines the propositions condemned in the bull as heretical, and demonstrates their truth by proofs drawn from the Holy Scriptures. With what vigour especially does he not maintain the doctrine of Grace!

"What! before and without grace, nature can hate sin, avoid it, and repent of it; while even after grace is come, this nature loves sin, seeks it, longs for it, and never ceases contending against grace, and being angry with it; a state which all the saints mourn over continually!......It is as if men said

that a strong tree, which I cannot bend by the exertion of all my strength, would bend of itself, as soon as I left it, or that a torrent which no dikes or barriers can check, would cease running as soon as it was left alone. ......No! it is not by reflecting on sin and its consequences that we arrive at repentance; but it is by contemplating Jesus Christ, his wounds, and his infinite love.[1] The knowledge of sin must proceed from repentance, and not repentance from the knowledge of sin. Knowledge is the fruit, repentance is the tree. In my country, the fruit grows on the tree; but it would appear that in the states of the holy Father the tree grows on the fruit."

The courageous doctor, although he protests, still retracts some of his propositions. Our astonishment will cease when we see the manner in which he does it. After quoting the four propositions on indulgences, condemned by the bull,[2] he simply adds:—

"In submission to the holy and learned bull, I retract all that I have ever taught concerning indulgences. If my books have been justly burnt, it is certainly because I made concessions to the pope on the doctrine of indulgences; for this reason I condemn them to the flames."

He retracts also with respect to John Huss: "I now say that not a *few* articles, but *all* the articles of John Huss are wholly christian. By condemning John Huss, the pope has condemned the Gospel. I have done five times more than he, and yet I much fear I have not done enough. Huss only said that a wicked pope is not a member of Christendom; but if Peter himself were now sitting at Rome, I should deny that he was pope by Divine appointment."

CHAPTER XI.

Coronation of Charles the Fifth—The Nuncio Aleander—Shall Luther's Books be Burnt?—Aleander and the Emperor—The Nuncios and the Elector—Duke John's Son in Behalf of Luther—Luther's Calmness—The Elector protects Luther—Reply of the Nuncios—Erasmus at Cologne—Erasmus at the Elector's—Declaration of Erasmus—Advice of Erasmus—System of Charles V.

THE mighty words of the reformer sunk deep into men's hearts, and contributed to their emancipation. The sparks that flew from every one of them were communicated to the whole nation. But still a greater question remained to be solved. Would the prince in whose states Luther was residing, favour or oppose the execution of the bull? The reply appeared doubtful. The elector, as well as all the princes of the empire, was at Aix-

[1] Ich sage nicht dass Ich ein Prophet sey. L. Opp. (L.) xvii. 338.
[2] Und sollten's eitel Kinder in der Wiege seyn. Ibid. 539.
[3] Warheit hat allezeit rumort. Ibid. 340.

[1] Man soll zuvor Christum in seine Wunden sehen, und aus denselben seine Liebe gegen uns. L. Opp. (L.) xvii. 351.
[2] Props. 19 to 22. Ibid. 363.

la-Chapelle. Here the crown of Charlemagne was placed on the head of the youngest but most powerful monarch of Christendom. An unusual pomp and magnificence were displayed in this ceremony. Charles V., Frederick, princes, ministers, and ambassadors, repaired immediately to Cologne. Aix-la-Chapelle, where the plague was raging, seemed to pour its whole population into this ancient city on the banks of the Rhine.

Among the crowd of strangers who thronged this city were the two papal nuncios, Marino Caraccioli and Jerome Aleander. Caraccioli, who had already been ambassador at the court of Maximilian, was commissioned to congratulate the new emperor, and to treat with him on political matters. But Rome had discovered that, to succeed in extinguishing the Reformation, it was necessary to send into Germany a nuncio specially accredited for this work, and of a character, skill, and activity fitted for its accomplishment. Aleander had been selected.[1] This man, afterwards invested with the purple of the cardinals, would appear to have been descended from a family of respectable antiquity, and not from Jewish parents, as it has been said. The guilty Borgia invited him to Rome to be the secretary of his son—of that Cæsar before whose murderous sword all Rome trembled.[2] "Like master, like man," says an historian, who thus compares Aleander to Alexander VI. This judgment is in our opinion too severe. After Borgia's death, Aleander applied to his studies with fresh ardour. His knowledge of Greek, Hebrew, Chaldee, and Arabic, gained him the reputation of being the most learned man of his age. He devoted himself with his whole heart to every thing he undertook. The zeal with which he studied languages was by no means inferior to that which he exerted afterwards in persecuting the Reformation. Leo X. attached him to his own service. Some historians speak of his epicurean manners; Romanists, of the integrity of his life.[3] It would appear that he was fond of luxury, parade, and amusement. "Aleander is living at Venice like a grovelling epicurean, and in high dignity," wrote his old friend Erasmus concerning him. All are agreed in confessing that he was violent, prompt in his actions, full of ardour, indefatigable, imperious, and devoted to the pope. Eck was the fiery and intrepid champion of the schools: Aleander, the haughty ambassador of the proud court of the pontiffs. He seemed born to be a nuncio.

Rome had made every preparation to destroy the monk of Wittemberg. The duty of attending the coronation of the emperor, as the pope's representative, was a mere secondary mission in Aleander's eyes, yet calculated to facilitate his task by the respect it secured for him. But he was specially charged to prevail upon Charles to crush the rising Reformation.[1]

As soon as Aleander arrived at Cologne, he and Caraccioli set every wheel in motion to have Luther's heretical works burnt throughout the empire, but particularly under the eyes of the German princes assembled in that city. Charles V. had already given his consent with regard to his hereditary states. The agitation of men's minds was excessive. "Such measures," said they to Charles's ministers and the nuncios themselves, "far from healing the wound, will only increase it. Do you imagine that Luther's doctrines are found only in those books that you are throwing into the fire? They are written, where you cannot reach them, in the hearts of the nation.[2]......If you desire to employ force, it must be that of countless swords unsheathed to massacre a whole nation.[3] A few logs of wood piled up to burn a few sheets of paper will effect nothing; and such arms are unbecoming the dignity of an emperor and of a pontiff." The nuncio defended his burning piles: "These flames," said he, "are a sentence of condemnation written in colossal characters, equally intelligible to those who are near and those who are afar off,—to the learned and ignorant,—and even to those who cannot read."

But it was not in reality papers and books that the nuncio wanted: it was Luther himself. "These flames," resumed he, "are not sufficient to purify the infected air of Germany.[4] If they terrify the simple, they do not punish the wicked. We require an imperial edict against Luther's person."[5]

Aleander did not find the emperor so compliant when the reformer's life was in question, as when his books only were concerned. "As I have but recently ascended the throne," said he to Aleander, "I cannot without the advice of my councillors and the consent of the princes strike such a blow as this against a numerous faction surrounded by so many powerful defenders. Let us first learn what our father, the Elector of Saxony, thinks of this matter;[6] we shall afterwards see what reply we can make to the pope." The nuncios, therefore, proceeded to make trial of their artifices and eloquence on the elector.

The first Sunday in November, Frederick having attended mass in the Greyfriars' con-

[1] Studium flagrantissimum religionis, ardor indolis.... incredibile quanta solertia....Pallavicini, i. 84.
[2] See vol. i. p. 19. Capello, Venetian Ambassador at Rome in 1500, says of Cæsar: Tutta Roma trema di esso ducha non li faza amazzar....Extracted by Ranke from a MS. *Relations* in the archives of Vienna.
[3] Er wird übel als ein gebohrner Jude und schændlicher Epicurer beschrieben. Seckend. 288. Integritas vitæ qua prænoscebatur. Pallavicini, i. 84.

[1] Cui tota sollicitudo inniteretur nascentis hæresis evellendæ. Pallavicini, i. 83.
[2] Altiusque insculptam in mentibus universæ fere Germaniæ. Ibid. i. 88.
[3] In vi innumerabilium gladiorum qui infinitum populum trucidarent. Ibid.
[4] Non satis ad expurgandum aerem Germaniæ jam tabificum. Ibid. p. 89.
[5] Cæsaris edictum in caput....Lutheri. Ibid
[6] Audiamus antea hac in re patrem nostrum Fredericum. L. Opp. Lat. ii. 117.

vent, Caraccioli and Aleander begged an audience. He received them in the presence of the Bishop of Trent and several of his councillors. Caraccioli first presented the papal brief. Of a milder disposition than Aleander, he thought it his duty to win over the prince by his flatteries, and began by eulogizing him and his ancestors. "It is to you," said he, "that we look for the salvation of the Roman Church and of the Roman Empire."

But the impetuous Aleander, wishing to come to the point, hastily stepped forward and interrupted his colleague, who modestly gave way :[1] "It is to me and Eck," said he, "that this business of Martin's has been intrusted. Look at the imminent dangers into which this man is plunging the christian republic. If we do not make haste to apply some remedy, the empire is ruined. Why were the Greeks destroyed, but because they abandoned the pope? You cannot remain united to Luther without separating from Jesus Christ.[2] I require two things of you, in the name of his holiness : *first*, that you will burn Luther's writings ; *secondly*, that you will inflict on him the punishment he deserves, or at least that you will deliver him up to the pope.[3] The emperor and all the princes of the empire have declared their willingness to accede to our request ; you alone hesitate still."

Frederick replied, through the medium of the Bishop of Trent : "This matter is too serious to be settled now. We will let you know our determination."

The situation in which Frederick was placed was a difficult one. What part ought he to take? On the one side were the emperor, the princes of the empire, and the supreme pontiff of Christendom, whose authority the elector had as yet no idea of throwing off ; on the other, a monk, a feeble monk ; for it was he only that they demanded. Charles's reign had just commenced. Ought Frederick, the oldest and wisest of all the princes of Germany, to sow disunion in the empire? Besides, how could he renounce that ancient piety which led him even to the sepulchre of Christ?

Other voices were then heard. A young prince, who afterwards wore the electoral crown, and whose reign was signalized by the greatest misfortunes, John Frederick, son of Duke John, the elector's nephew, and Spalatin's pupil, a youth seventeen years of age, had received in his heart a sincere love for the truth, and was firmly attached to Luther.[4] When he saw the reformer struck by the Roman anathemas, he embraced his cause with the warmth of a young Christian and of a youthful prince. He wrote to the doctor and to his uncle, nobly entreating the latter to protect Luther against his enemies. On the other hand, Spalatin, frequently it is true very dejected, Pontanus, and the other councillors who were with the elector at Cologne, represented to the prince that he ought not to abandon the reformer.[1]

In the midst of this general agitation, one man alone remained tranquil : it was Luther. While it was sought to preserve him by the influence of the great, the monk in his cloister at Wittemberg thought that it was rather for him to save the great ones of this world. "If the Gospel," wrote he to Spalatin, "was of a nature to be propagated or maintained by the powers of this world, God would not have intrusted it to fishermen.[2] It belongs not to the princes and pontiffs of this age to defend the Word of God. They have enough to do to shelter themselves from the judgments of the Lord and of his Anointed. If I speak, it is in order that they may attain a knowledge of the Divine Word, and that by it they may be saved."

Luther's expectation was not to be deceived. That faith, which a convent at Wittemberg concealed, exerted its power in the palaces of Cologne. Frederick's heart, shaken perhaps for a moment, grew stronger by degrees. He was indignant that the pope, in defiance of his earnest entreaties to examine into the matter in Germany, had decided upon it at Rome at the request of a personal enemy of the reformer, and that in his absence this opponent should have dared publish in Saxony a bull that threatened the existence of the university and the peace of his subjects. Besides, the elector was convinced that Luther was wronged. He shuddered at the thought of delivering an innocent man into the hands of his cruel enemies. Justice was the principle on which he acted, and not the wishes of the pope. He came to the determination of not giving way to Rome. On the 4th of November, Frederick's councillors (in the presence of the bishop of Trent), replied that he had seen with much pain the advantage that Dr. Eck had taken of his absence to involve in the condemnation several persons who were not named in the bull ; that since his departure from Saxony, it was possible that an immense number of learned and ignorant men, of the clergy and laity, might have united and adhered to the cause and appeal of Luther ;[3] that neither his imperial majesty nor any other person had shown that Luther's writings had been refuted, and that they only deserved to be thrown into the fire ; and finally he requested

[1] Cui ita loquenti de improviso sese addit Aleander. L. Opp. Lat. ii. 117.
[2] Non posse oum Luthero conjungi, quin sejungeretur a Christo. Pallav. i. 86.
[3] Ut de eo supplicium sumeret, vel captum pontifici transmitteret. L. Opp. Lat. ii. 117.
[4] Sonderliche Gunst und Gnade zu mir unwirdiglich und den grossen Willen und Lust zu der heiligen göttlichen Wahrheit. L. Epp. i. 548. Letter to John Frederick, 30th October 1520.

[1] Assiduo flabello ministrorum, illi jugiter suadentium ne Lutherum desereret. Pallav. i. 86.
[2] Evangelium si tale esset, quod potentatibus mundi aut propagaretur aut servaretur, non illud piscatoribus Deus demandasset. L. Epp. i. 621.
[3] Ut ingens vis populi, doctorum et rudium, sacrorum et profanorum, sese conjunxerint. L. Opp. Lat. ii. 116.

that Doctor Luther should be furnished with a safe-conduct, so that he might appear before a tribunal of learned, pious, and impartial judges.

After this declaration, Aleander, Caraccioli, and their followers, retired to deliberate.[1] This was the first time that the elector had publicly made known his intentions with regard to the reformer. The nuncios had expected quite a different course from him. Now (they had thought) that the elector, by maintaining his character for impartiality, would draw dangers upon himself the whole extent of which he could not foresee, he will not hesitate to sacrifice the monk. Thus Rome had reasoned. But her machinations were doomed to fail before a force that did not enter into her calculations, —the love of justice and of truth.

Being re-admitted into the presence of the elector's councillors, the imperious Aleander said : " I should like to know what the elector would think, if one of his subjects should choose the king of France, or any other foreign prince, for judge." Seeing that nothing could shake the Saxon councillors, he said : " We will execute the bull ; we will hunt out and burn Luther's writings. As for his person," added he, affecting a contemptuous indifference, " the pope is not desirous of staining his hands with the blood of the wretched man."

The news of the reply the elector had made to the nuncios having reached Wittemberg, Luther's friends were filled with joy. Melancthon and Amsdorff, especially, indulged in the most flattering anticipations. " The German nobility," said Melancthon, " will direct their course by the example of this prince, whom they follow in all things, as their Nestor. If Homer styled his hero *the bulwark of the Greeks*, why should we not call Frederick *the bulwark of the Germans?*"[2]

The oracle of courts, the torch of the schools, the light of the world, Erasmus, was then at Cologne. Many princes had invited him, to be guided by his advice. At the epoch of the Reformation, Erasmus was the leader of the moderates ; he imagined himself to be so, but without just cause ; for when truth and error meet face to face, justice lies not between them. He was the chief of that philosophical and academical party which, for ages, had attempted to correct Rome, but had never succeeded ; he was the representative of human wisdom, but that wisdom was too weak to batter down the high places of Popery. It needed that wisdom from God, which men often call foolishness, but at whose voice mountains crumble into dust. Erasmus would neither throw himself into the arms of Luther, nor sit at the pope's feet. He hesitated, and

often wavered between these two powers, attracted at one time towards Luther, then suddenly repelled in the direction of the pope. " The last spark of christian piety seems nearly extinguished," said he in his letter to Albert ; " and 'tis this which has moved Luther's heart. He cares neither for money nor honours."[1] But this letter, which the imprudent Ulrich of Hütten had published, caused Erasmus so much annoyance, that he determined to be more cautious in future. Besides, he was accused of being Luther's accomplice, and the latter offended him by his imprudent language. " Almost all good men are for Luther,"[2] said he ; " but I see that we are tending towards a revolt......I would not have my name joined with his. That would injure me without serving him."[3] " So be it," replied Luther ; " since that annoys you, I promise never to make mention either of you or of your friends." Such was the man to whom both the partisans and enemies of the Reformation applied.

The elector, knowing that the opinion of a man so much respected as Erasmus would have great influence, invited the illustrious Dutchman to visit him. Erasmus obeyed the order. This was on the 5th December. Luther's friends could not see this step without secret uneasiness. The elector was standing before the fire, with Spalatin at his side, when Erasmus was introduced. " What is your opinion of Luther?" immediately demanded Frederick. The prudent Erasmus, surprised at so direct a question, sought at first to elude replying. He screwed up his mouth, bit his lips, and said not a word. Upon this the elector, raising his eyebrows, as was his custom when he spoke to people from whom he desired to have a precise answer (says Spalatin), fixed his piercing glance on Erasmus.[4] The latter, not knowing how to escape from his confusion, said at last, in a half jocular tone : " Luther has committed two great faults : he has attacked the crown of the pope and the bellies of the monks."[5] The elector smiled, but gave his visiter to understand that he was in earnest. Erasmus then laying aside his reserve, said : " The cause of all this dispute is the hatred of the monks towards learning, and the fear they have of seeing their tyranny destroyed. What weapons are they using against Luther ?—clamour, cabals, hatred, and libels. The more virtuous a man is, and the greater his attachment to the Gospel, the less is he opposed to Luther.[6] The severity of the

---

[1] Quo audito, Marinus et Aleander seorsim cum suis locuti sunt. L. Opp. Lat. ii. 117.
[2] Homerica appellatione murum Germaniæ. Corp. Ref. i. 272.

[1] Et futurum erat....ut tandem prorsus extingueretur illa scintilla Christianæ pietatis ; hæc moverunt animum Lutheri....qui nec honores ambit, nec pecuniam cupit. Erasm. Epp. Lond. 1642, p. 586.
[2] Favent vero ferme boni omnes. Corp. Ref. i. 205.
[3] Er will von mir ungennent seyn. L. Epp. i. 525. Nam ea res me gravat, et Lutherum-non sublevat. Corp. Ref. i 206.
[4] Da sperret auch wahrlich mein gnädister Herr seine Augen nur wohl auf....Spalatin, Hist. MS. in Seckend. p . 291.
[5] Lutherus peccavit in duobus, nempe quod tetigit coronam pontificis et ventres monachorum.
[6] Cum optimus quisque et evangelicæ doctrinæ proximus

bull has aroused the indignation of all good men, and no one can recognise in it the gentleness of a vicar of Christ.[1] Two only, out of all the universities, have condemned Luther; and they have only *condemned* him, not *proved* him in the wrong. Do not be deceived; the danger is greater than some men imagine. Arduous and difficult things are pressing on.[2] To begin Charles's reign by so odious an act as Luther's imprisonment, would be a mournful omen. The world is thirsting for evangelical truth;[3] let us beware of setting up a blamable opposition. Let this affair be inquired into by serious men,—men of sound judgment; this will be the course most consistent with the dignity of the pope himself!"

Thus spoke Erasmus to the elector. Such frankness may perhaps astonish the reader; but Erasmus knew whom he was addressing. Spalatin was delighted. He went out with Erasmus, and accompanied him as far as the house of the Count of Nuenar, provost of Cologne, where Erasmus was residing. The latter, in an impulse of frankness, on retiring to his study, took a pen, sat down, wrote a summary of what he had said to the elector, and forwarded the paper to Spalatin; but erelong the fear of Aleander came over the timid Erasmus; the courage that the presence of the elector and his chaplain had communicated to him had evaporated; and he begged Spalatin to return the too daring paper, for fear it should fall into the hands of the terrible nuncio. But it was too late.

The elector, feeling re-assured by the opinion of Erasmus, spoke to the emperor in a more decided tone. Erasmus himself endeavoured, in nocturnal conferences,[4] like those of Nicodemus of old, to persuade Charles's councillors that the whole business should be referred to impartial judges. Perhaps he hoped to be named arbitrator in a cause which threatened to divide the christian world. His vanity would have been flattered by such an office. But at the same time, and not to lose his credit at Rome, he wrote the most submissive letters to Leo, who replied with a kindness that seriously mortified Aleander.[5] From love to the pope, the nuncio would willingly have reprimanded the pope; for Erasmus communicated these letters from the pontiff, and they added still more to his credit. The nuncio complained of it to Rome. "Pretend not to notice this man's wickedness," was the reply; "prudence enjoins this: we must leave a door open to repentance."[6]

Charles at the same time adopted a "see-

saw" system, which consisted in flattering the pope and the elector, and appearing to incline by turns towards each, according to the necessities of the moment. One of his ministers, whom he had sent to Rome on Spanish business, arrived at the very moment that Doctor Eck was clamorously urging on Luther's condemnation. The wily ambassador immediately saw what advantage his master might derive from the Saxon monk. "Your Majesty," he wrote on the 12th May 1520 to the emperor, who was still in Spain, "ought to go into Germany, and show some favour to a certain Martin Luther, who is at the Saxon court, and who by the sermons he preaches gives much anxiety to the court of Rome."[1] Such from the commencement was the view Charles took of the Reformation. It was of no importance for him to know on which side truth or error might be found, or to discern what the great interests of the German nation required. His only question was, what policy demanded, and what should be done to induce the pope to support the emperor. And this was well known at Rome. Charles's ministers intimated to Aleander the course their master intended following. "The emperor," said they, "will behave towards the pope as he behaves towards the emperor;[2] for he has no desire to increase the power of his rivals, and particularly of the King of France." At these words the imperious nuncio gave way to his indignation. "What!" replied he, "supposing the pope should abandon the emperor, must the latter renounce his religion? If Charles wishes to avenge himself thus......let him tremble! this baseness will turn against himself." But the nuncio's threats did not shake the imperial diplomatists.

CHAPTER XII.

Luther on Confession—Real Absolution—Antichrist—Luther's Popularity—Satires—Ulrich of Hütten—Lucas Cranach—The Carnival at Wittemberg—Staupitz intimidated—Luther's Labours—His Humility—Progress of the Reformation.

IF the legates of Rome failed with the mighty ones of this world, the inferior agents of the papacy succeeded in spreading trouble among the lower ranks. The army of Rome had heard the commands of its chief. Fanatical priests made use of the bull to alarm timid consciences, and well-meaning but unenlightened ecclesiastics considered it a sacred duty to act in conformity with the instructions of the pope. It was in the confessional that Luther had commenced his

---

dicatur, minime offensus Luthero. **Axiomata Erasmi in**
L. Opp. Lat. ii. 115.
[1] Bullæ sævitia probos omnes offendit, ut indigna mitissimo Christi vicario. Ibid.
[2] Urgent ardua negotia. Ibid.
[3] Mundus sitit veritatem evangelicam. Ibid.
[4] Sollicitatis per nocturnos congressus.... Pallav. i. 87.
[5] Quæ male torquebant Aleandrum. Ibid.
[6] Prudentis erat consilii, hominis pravitatem dissimulare. Ibid. 88.

[1] Despatches of Manuel Llorente. 1. 398.
[2] Cæsarem ita se gesturum erga Pontificem, uti æ Pontifex erga Cæsarem gereret. Pallav. i. 91.

struggle against Rome;[1] it was in the confessional that Rome contended against the reformer's adherents. Scouted in the face of the world, the bull became powerful in these solitary tribunals. "Have you read Luther's works?" asked the confessors; "do you possess any of them? do you regard them as true or heretical?" And if the penitent hesitated to pronounce the anathema, the priest refused absolution. Many consciences were troubled. Great agitation prevailed among the people. This skilful manœuvre bade fair to restore to the papal yoke the people already won over to the Gospel. Rome congratulated herself on having in the thirteenth century erected this tribunal, so skilfully adapted to render the free consciences of Christians the slaves of the priests.[2] So long as this remains standing, her reign is not over.

Luther was informed of these proceedings. What can he do, unaided, to baffle this manœuvre? The Word, the Word proclaimed loudly and courageously, shall be his weapon. The Word will find access to those alarmed consciences, those terrified souls, and give them strength. A powerful impulse was necessary, and Luther's voice made itself heard. He addressed the penitents with fearless dignity, with a noble disdain of all secondary considerations. "When you are asked whether you approve of my books or not," said he, "reply: 'You are a confessor, and not an inquisitor or a gaoler. My duty is to confess what my conscience leads me to say: yours is not to sound and extort the secrets of my heart. Give me absolution, and then dispute with Luther, with the pope, with whomsoever you please; but do not convert the sacrament of penance into a quarrel and a combat.'—And if the confessor will not give way, then (continues Luther) I would rather go without absolution. Do not be uneasy: if man does not absolve you, God will. Rejoice that you are absolved by God himself, and appear at the altar without fear. At the last judgment the priest will have to give an account of the absolution he has refused you. They may deprive us of the sacrament, but they cannot deprive us of the strength and grace that God has connected with it. It is not in their will or in their power, but in our own faith, that God has placed salvation. Dispense with the sacrament, altar, priest, and church; the Word of God, condemned by the bull, is more than all these things. The soul can do without the sacrament, but it cannot live without the Word. Christ, the true bishop, will undertake to give you spiritual food."[3]

Thus did Luther's voice sink into every alarmed conscience, and make its way into every troubled family, imparting courage and faith. But he was not content simply with defending himself; he felt that he ought to become the assailant, and return blow for blow. A Romish theologian, Ambrose Catharinus, had written against him. "I will stir up the bile of this Italian beast," said Luther.[1] He kept his word. In his reply, he proved, by the revelations of Daniel and St. John, by the epistles of St. Paul, St. Peter, and St. Jude, that the reign of Antichrist, predicted and described in the Bible, was the Papacy. "I know for certain," said he in conclusion, "that our Lord Jesus Christ lives and reigns. Strong in this assurance, I should not fear many thousands of popes. May God visit us at last according to his infinite power, and show forth the day of the glorious advent of his Son, in which he will destroy the wicked one.[2] And let all the people say, Amen!"

And all the people did say, Amen! A holy terror seized upon their souls. It was Antichrist whom they beheld seated on the pontifical throne. This new idea, which derived greater strength from the prophetic descriptions launched forth by Luther into the midst of his contemporaries, inflicted the most terrible blow on Rome. Faith in the Word of God took the place of that faith which the Church alone had hitherto enjoyed; and the power of the pope, long the object of adoration among nations, had now become a source of terror and detestation.

Germany replied to the papal bull by overwhelming Luther with its acclamations. Although the plague was raging at Wittemberg, new students arrived every day, and from four to six hundred disciples habitually sat at the feet of Luther and Melancthon in the halls of the academy. The two churches belonging to the convent and the city were not large enough for the crowd that hung listening to the reformer's words. The prior of the Augustines was fearful that these temples would fall under the weight of the hearers.[3] But this spiritual movement was not confined within the walls of Wittemberg; it spread through Germany. Princes, nobles, and learned men from every quarter, addressed Luther in letters breathing consolation and faith. The doctor showed the chaplain more than thirty years.[4]

The Margrave of Brandenburg came one day to Wittemberg, with several other princes, to visit Luther. "They desired to see the man," said the latter.[5] In truth, all were desirous of *seeing the man* whose words had moved the people, and made the pontiff of the West totter upon his throne.

The enthusiasm of Luther's friends in-

---

[1] See vol. i. p. 94.
[2] In 1215 by the Fourth Lateran Council, under Innocent III.
[3] Und wird dich der rechte Bischoff Christus selber speisen.... L. Opp. (L.) xvii. 565.

[1] Italicæ bestiæ bilem movebo. L. Epp. i. 570.
[2] Ostendat illum diem adventus gloriæ Filii sui, quo destruatur iniquus iste. L. Opp. Lat. ii. 162.
[3] Es möchte noch gar die Kirche und Capelle um der Menge willen einfallen. Spalatin in Seckend. p. 295.
[4] Mehr als dreyssig Briefe von Fürsten.... Ibid.
[5] Videre enim hominem voluerunt. L. Epp. i. 544, dated 16th January 1521.

creased every day. "What unheard-of foolishness in Emser," exclaimed Melancthon, "who has ventured to measure himself with our Hercules, not perceiving the finger of God in every one of Luther's actions,[1] as Pharaoh would not see it in those of Moses." The gentle Melancthon found words of power to arouse those who seemed to be retrograding or even remaining stationary. "Luther has stood up for the truth," wrote he to John Hess, "and yet you keep silence!......He is alive and prospering still, although the lion (Leo) is chafing and roaring. Bear in mind that it is impossible for Roman impiety to approve of the Gospel.[2] How can this age be wanting in men like Judas, Caiaphas, Pilate, or Herod? Arm yourself, therefore, with the weapons of God's Word against such adversaries."

All Luther's writings, his Lord's Prayer, and particularly his new edition of the German Theology,[3] were perused with avidity. Reading clubs were formed for the circulation of his works among their members. His friends reprinted them, and got them distributed by hawkers. They were recommended from the pulpit. There was a general wish for a German Church; and the people demanded that no one should henceforth be invested with any ecclesiastical dignity, unless he could preach to the people in the vulgar tongue, and that in every quarter the bishops of Germany should resist the papal power.

Nor was this all: biting satires against the principal ultramontanists were circulated throughout the provinces of the empire. The opposition rallied all its forces around this new doctrine, which gave it precisely what it stood in need of......a justification in the eyes of religion. Most of the lawyers, wearied by the encroachments of the ecclesiastical tribunals, attached themselves to the reform, but the humanists, in particular, eagerly embraced this party. Ulrich Hütten was indefatigable. He addressed letters to Luther, to the legates, and to the most considerable men in Germany. "I tell you, and repeat it, Marino," said he to the legate Caraccioli, in one of his works, "the darkness with which you had covered our eyes is dispersed; the Gospel is preached; the truth is proclaimed; the absurdities of Rome are overwhelmed with contempt; your decrees languish and die; liberty is beginning to dawn upon us!"[4]

Not content with employing prose, Hütten had recourse to verse also. He published his *Outcry on the Lutheran Conflagration*,[5] in

which, appealing to Jesus Christ, he beseeches him to consume with the brightness of his countenance all who dared deny his authority. Above all, he set about writing in German. "Hitherto," said he, "I have written in Latin, a tongue not intelligible to every one; but now I address all my fellow-countrymen!" His German *rhymes* unveiled to the people the long and disgraceful catalogue of the sins of the Roman court. But Hütten did not wish to confine himself to mere words; he was eager to interfere in the struggle with the sword; and he thought that the vengeance of God should be accomplished by the swords and halberds of those valiant warriors of whom Germany was so proud. Luther opposed this mad project: "I desire not," said he, "to fight for the Gospel with violence and bloodshed. I have written to Hütten to this effect."[1]

The celebrated painter Lucas Cranach published, under the title of the *Passion of Christ and Antichrist*, a set of engravings which represented on one side the glory and magnificence of the pope, and on the other the humiliation and sufferings of the Redeemer. The inscriptions were written by Luther. These engravings, designed with considerable skill, produced an effect beyond all previous example. The people withdrew from a church that appeared in every respect so opposed to the spirit of its Founder. "This is a very good work for the laity," said Luther.[2]

Many persons wielded weapons against the papacy, that had but little connexion with the holiness of a christian life. Emser had replied to Luther's book (*To the Goat of Leipsic*) by another whose title was *To the Bull of Wittemberg*. The name was not ill-chosen. But at Magdeburg Emser's work was suspended to the common gibbet, with this inscription: "The book is worthy of the place," and a scourge was hung at its side, to indicate the punishment the author merited.[3] At Dœblin some persons wrote under the papal bull, in ridicule of its ineffectual thunders, "The nest is here, but the birds have flown."[4]

The students at Wittemberg, taking advantage of the license of the carnival, dressed up one of their number in a costume similar to the pope's, and paraded him with great pomp through the streets of the city, but in a manner somewhat too ludicrous, as Luther observes.[5] When they reached the great square, they approached the river, and some,

---

[1] Dei digitum esse quæ a Martino fiant. Corp. Ref. 1. 282.
[2] Non posse Evangelium Romanæ impietati probari. Ibid. 280.
[3] See vol. 1. p. 75.
[4] Ablata illa est a vobis inducta olim nostris oculis caligo, prædicatur Evangelium.... spes est libertatis. Ulrich ab Hütten Eques, Mar. Carrac. L. Opp. Lat. ii. 176.
[5] ....Quo tu oculos, pie Christe, tuos, frontisque severæ
Tende supercilium, teque esse ostende neganti.
Qui te contemnunt igitur, mediumque tonanti
Ostendunt digitum, tandem iis te ostende potentem.
Te

Te videat ferus ille Leo, te tota malorum
Sentiat illuvies, scelerataque Roma tremiscat,
Ultorem scelerum discant te vivere saltem,
Qui regnare negant.
In Incendium Lutheranum Exclamatio Ulrichi Hütteni Equitis, Mar. Carac. L. Opp. Lat. ii. 176.
[1] Nollem vi et cæde pro Evangelio certari; ita ut scripsi ad hominem. L. Epp. i. 543.
[2] Bonus est pro laicis liber. L. Epp. i. 571. This book, which deserves reprinting, I found in the library of Zurich.
[3] In publico infamiæ loco affixus. Ibid. 560.
[4] Das Nest iste hie, die Vögel sind ausgeflogen. Ibid. 570.
[5] Nimis ludicre Papam personatum circumvenerunt sublimem et pompaticum. Ibid. 561.

pretending a sudden attack, appeared desirous of throwing the pope into the water. But the pontiff, having little inclination for such a bath, took to his heels; his cardinals, bishops, and familiars imitated his example, dispersing into every quarter of the city. The students pursued them through the streets; and there was hardly a corner in Wittemberg where some Roman dignitary had not taken refuge from the shouts and laughter of the excited populace.[1] " The enemy of Christ," says Luther, " who makes a mockery of kings, and even of Christ, richly deserves to be thus mocked himself." In our opinion he is wrong; truth is too beautiful to be thus profaned. She should combat without the aid of ballads, caricatures, and the masquerades of a carnival. Perhaps, without these popular demonstrations, her success would be less apparent; but it would be purer, and consequently more lasting. However that may be, the imprudent and prejudiced conduct of the Roman court had excited universal antipathy; and this very bull, by which the papacy thought to crush the whole reformation, was precisely that which made the revolt burst out in every quarter.

Yet the reformer did not find intoxication and triumph in every thing. Behind that chariot in which he was dragged by a people excited and transported with admiration, there was not wanting the slave to remind him of his miserable state. Some of his friends seemed inclined to retrace their steps. Staupitz, whom he designated his father, appeared shaken. The pope had accused him, and Staupitz had declared his willingness to submit to the decision of his holiness. " I fear," wrote Luther to him, " that by accepting the pope for judge, you seem to reject me and the doctrines I have maintained. If Christ loves you, he will constrain you to recall your letter. Christ is condemned, stripped, and blasphemed; this is a time not to fear, but to raise the voice.[2] For this reason, while you exhort me to be humble, I exhort you to be proud; for you have too much humility, as I have too much pride. The world may call me proud, covetous, an adulterer, a murderer, antipope, one who is guilty of every crime......What matters it! provided I am not reproached with having wickedly kept silence at the moment our Lord said with sorrow: *I looked on my right hand, and beheld, but there was no man that would know me.* (Ps. cxlii.) The Word of Jesus Christ is a Word not of peace but of the sword. If you will not follow Jesus Christ, I will walk alone, will advance alone, and alone will I carry the fortress."[3]

Thus Luther, like a general at the head of an army, surveyed the whole field of battle;

and while his voice inspirited new soldiers to the conflict, he discovered those of his troops who appeared weak, and recalled them to the line of duty. His exhortations were heard every where. His letters rapidly followed each other. Three presses were constantly occupied in multiplying his writings.[1] His words ran through the people, strengthening the alarmed consciences in the confessionals, upholding in the convents timid souls that were ready to faint, and maintaining the rights of truth in the palaces of princes.

" In the midst of the storms that assail me," wrote Luther to the elector, " I hoped to find peace at last. But now I see that this was the vain thought of a man. From day to day the waters rise, and already I am entirely surrounded by the waves. The tempest is bursting upon me with frightful tumult.[2] In one hand I grasp the sword, with the other I build up the walls of Zion."[3] His ancient ties are broken: the hand that had hurled against him the thunders of excommunication had snapped them asunder. " Excommunicated by the bull," said he, " I am absolved from the authority of the pope and of the monastic laws. Joyfully do I welcome this deliverance. But I shall neither quit the habit of my order nor the convent."[4] And yet, amid this agitation, he does not lose sight of the dangers to which his soul is exposed in the struggle. He perceives the necessity of keeping a strict watch over himself. " You do well to pray for me," wrote he to Pellican, who resided at Basle. " I cannot devote sufficient time to holy exercises; life is a cross to me. You do well to exhort me to modesty: I feel its necessity; but I am not master of myself; I am carried away by mysterious impulses. I wish no one ill;[5] but my enemies press on me with such fury, that I do not sufficiently guard against the temptations of Satan. Pray, then, for me!"

Thus the reformer and the Reformation were hastening towards the goal whither God called them. The agitation was gaining ground. The men who seemed likely to be most faithful to the hierarchy began to be moved. "Those very persons,' says Eck ingenuously enough, " who hold the best livings and the richest prebends from the pope, remain as mute as fishes. Many of them even extol Luther as a man filled with the Divine spirit, and style the defenders of the pope mere sophists and flatterers."[6] The Church, apparently full of vigour, supported by treasures, governments, and armies, but in reality exhausted and feeble, having no love for God, no christian life, no enthusiasm for the truth, found itself

---

1 .... Fugitivum cum cardinalibus, episcopis, familiisque suis, in diversas partes oppidi disperserunt et insecuti sunt. L. Epp. i. 17th Feb. 1521.
2 Non enim hoc tempus timendi sed clamandi. Ibid. 557.
3 Quod si tu non vis sequi, sine me ire et rapi. Ibid. 558.

1 Cum tria prela solus ego occupare cogar. L. Epp. i. 558
2 Videns rem tumultuosissimo tumultu tumultuantem Ibid. 546.
3 Una manu gladium apprehendens et altera murum ædificaturus. Ibid. 565.
4 Ab ordinis et Papæ legibus solutus....quod gaudeo et amplector. Ibid. 558.
5 Compos mei non sum, rapior nescio quo spiritu, cum nemini me male velle conscius sim. Ibid. 556.
6 Reynald Epist. J. Eckii ad Cardinalem Contarenum.

face to face with men who were simple but courageous, and who, knowing that God is with those who contend in behalf of his Word, had no doubt of victory. In every age it has been seen how great is the strength of an idea to penetrate the masses, to stir up nations, and to hurry them, if required, by thousands to the battle-field and to death. But if so great be the strength of a human idea, what power must not a heaven-descended idea possess, when God opens to it the gates of the heart! The world has not often seen so much power at work; it was seen, however, in the early days of Chris-tianity, and in the time of the Reformation; and it will be seen in future ages. Men who despised the riches and grandeur of the world, who were contented with a life of sorrow and poverty, began to be moved in favour of all that was holiest upon earth,—the doctrine of faith and of grace. All the religious elements were fermenting beneath the agitated surface of society; and the fire of enthusiasm urged souls to spring forward with courage into this new life, this epoch of renovation, which had just opened before them with so much grandeur, and toward which Providence was hurrying the nations.

BOOK VII.

THE DIET OF WORMS.—1521, JANUARY TO MAY.

CHAPTER I.

Victories of the Word of God—The Diet of Worms—Policy of Rome—Difficulties—Charles demands Luther—The Elector to Charles V.—State of Feeling—Alarm of Aleander—The Elector departs without Luther—Aleander arouses Rome—Excommunication of Pope and Communion with Christ—Fulminations of the Bull—Luther's Motives in the Reformation.

THE Reformation, commenced by the struggles of an humble spirit in the cell of a cloister at Erfurth, had continually increased. An obscure individual, bearing in his hand the Word of Life, had stood firm before the mighty ones of the world, and they had shaken before him. He had wielded this arm of the Word of God, first against Tetzel and his numerous army; and those greedy merchants, after a brief struggle, had fled away: he next employed it against the Roman legate at Augsburg; and the legate in amazement had allowed the prey to escape him: somewhat later with its aid he contended against the champions of learning in the halls of Leipsic; and the astonished theologians had beheld their syllogistic weapons shivered in their hands: and, lastly, with this single arm, he had opposed the pope, when the latter, disturbed in his slumbers, had risen on his throne to blast the unfortunate monk with his thunders; and this same Word had paralyzed all the power of this head of Christendom. A final struggle remained to be undergone. The Word was destined to triumph over the emperor of the West, over the kings and princes of the earth; and then, victorious over all the powers of the world, to uprise in the Church, and reign as the very Word of God.

The entire nation was agitated. Princes and nobles, knights and citizens, clergy and laity, town and country,—all participated in the struggle. A mighty religious revolution, of which God himself was the prime mover, but which was also deeply rooted in the lives of the people, threatened to overthrow the long-venerated chief of the Roman hierarchy. A new generation of a serious, deep, active, and energetic spirit, filled the universities, cities, courts, castles, rural districts, and frequently even the cloisters. A presentiment that a great transformation of society was at hand, inspired all minds with holy enthusiasm. What would be the position of the emperor with regard to this movement of the age? and what would be the end of this formidable impulse by which all men were carried along?......

A solemn diet was about to be opened: this was the first assembly of the empire over which Charles was to preside. As Nuremberg, where it should have been held, in accordance with the Golden Bull, was suffering from the plague, it was convoked to meet at Worms on the 6th January 1521.[1] Never before had so many princes met together in diet; each one was desirous of participating in this first act of the young emperor's government, and was pleased at the opportunity of displaying his power. The youthful landgrave Philip of Hesse, among others, who was afterwards to play so important a part in the Reformation, arrived at Worms, about the middle of January, with six hundred horsemen, among whom were warriors celebrated for their valour.

[1] Sleidan, vol. I. 80.

218

But a much stronger motive inclined the electors, dukes, archbishops, landgraves, margraves, counts, bishops, barons, and lords of the empire, as well as the deputies of the towns, and the ambassadors of the kings of Christendom, to throng with their brilliant trains the roads that led to Worms. It had been announced that, among other important matters to be laid before the diet, would be the nomination of a council of regency to govern the empire during Charles's absence, and the jurisdiction of the imperial chamber; but public attention was more particularly directed to another question, which the emperor had also mentioned in his letters of convocation: that of the Reformation. The great interests of worldly policy grew pale before the cause of the monk of Wittemberg. It was this which formed the principal topic of conversation between the noble personages who arrived at Worms.

Every thing announced that the diet would be stormy, and difficult to manage. Charles, who was hardldy twenty years of age, was pale, of weak health, and yet a graceful horseman, able to break a lance like others of his time; his character was as yet undeveloped; his air was grave and melancholy, although of a kindly expression, and he had not hitherto shown any remarkable talent, and did not appear to have adopted any decided line of conduct. The skilful and active William de Croi, lord of Chièvres, his high chamberlain, tutor, and prime minister, who enjoyed an absolute authority at court, died at Worms: numerous ambitions here met; many passions came into collision; the Spaniards and the Belgians vied with each other in their exertions to insinuate themselves into the councils of the young prince; the nuncios multiplied their intrigues; the German princes spoke out boldly. It might easily be foreseen that the underhanded practices of parties would have a principal share in the struggle.[1]

But over all these scenes of agitation hovered a terrible will—the Roman papacy, which, inflexible as the destiny of the ancients, had unceasingly crushed for ages past every doctor, king, or people that had opposed its tyrannous progress. A letter written at Rome in the month of January 1521, and by a Roman citizen, reveals its intentions. "If I am not mistaken, the only business in your diet will be this affair of Luther, which gives us much more trouble than the Turk himself. We shall endeavour to gain over the young emperor by threats, by prayers, and feigned caresses. We shall strive to win the Germans by extolling the piety of their ancestors, and by making them rich presents, and by lavish promises. If these methods do not succeed, we shall depose the emperor; absolve the people from their obedience; elect another (and he will be one that suits us) in

his place; stir up civil war among the Germans, as we have just done in Spain;[1] and summon to our aid the armies of the kings of France, England, and all the nations of the earth.[2] Probity, honour, religion, Christ —we shall make light of all, provided our tyranny be saved."[3] A very slight familiarity with the history of the papacy is sufficient to show that these words are a faithful description of its policy. It is identically what Rome has always done when she has had the power: only the times were now a little changed. We shall soon behold her busy at her task.

Charles opened the diet on the 28th January 1521, the festival of Charlemagne. His mind was filled with the high importance of the imperial dignity. He said, in his opening discourse, that no monarchy could be compared with the Roman empire, to which nearly the whole world had submitted in former times; that unfortunately this empire was a mere shadow of what it once had been; but that, by means of his kingdoms and powerful alliances, he hoped to restore it to its ancient glory.

But numerous difficulties immediately presented themselves to the young emperor. What must he do, placed between the papal nuncio and the elector to whom he was indebted for his crown? How can he avoid displeasing either Aleander or Frederick? The first entreated the emperor to execute the pope's bull, and the second besought him to take no steps against the monk until he had been heard. Desirous of pleasing both parties, the young prince, during his stay at Oppenheim, had written to the elector to bring Luther with him to the diet, assuring him that no injustice should be shown to the reformer, that no violence should be used towards him, and that learned men should confer with him.

This letter, accompanied by others from Chièvres and the count of Nassau, threw the elector into great perplexity. At every moment the alliance of the pope might become necessary to the young and ambitious emperor, and then Luther s fate was sealed. If Frederick should take the reformer to Worms, he might be leading him to the scaffold. And yet Charles's orders were precise. The elector commanded Spalatin to communicate to Luther the letters he had received. "The adversaries," said the chaplain to him, "are making every exertion to hasten on this affair."[4]

Luther's friends were alarmed, but he himself did not tremble. His health was at that

---

[1] Es gieng aber auf diesem Reichstag gar schlüpferig zu. ...Seckend. p. 326.

[1] Robertson's History of Charles V., book iii.
[2] Cæsarem deponemus, populos subjectione debita liberabimus, seditionem inter Germanos, quemadmodum nunc inter Hispanos, concitabimus, Gallum, Anglum, et omnes terræ reges ad arma convocabimus. Riederer, Nachrichten, i. 179.
[3] Tantum ut voti compotes evadere valeamus, nihil pensi apud nos erit, non Christus, neque fides, pietas, honestas, probitas, dummodo tyrannis nostra sit salva. Ibid.
[4] Adversarios omnia moliri ad maturandum id negotii. L. Epp. i. 534.

time very weak; but that was a trifling matter for him. "If I cannot go to Worms in good health," replied he to the elector, "I will be carried there, sick as I am. For if the emperor calls me, I cannot doubt that it is the call of God himself. If they desire to use violence against me, and that is very probable (for it is not for their instruction that they order me to appear), I place the matter in the Lord's hands. He still lives and reigns who preserved the three young men in the burning fiery furnace. If He will not save me, my life is of little consequence. Let us only prevent the Gospel from being exposed to the scorn of the wicked, and let us shed our blood for it, for fear they should triumph. It is not for me to decide whether my life or my death will contribute most to the salvation of all. Let us pray God that our young emperor may not begin his reign by imbruing his hands in my blood. I would rather perish by the sword of the Romans. You know what chastisement was inflicted on the Emperor Sigismund after the murder of John Huss. You may expect every thing from me...... except flight and recantation.[1] Fly I cannot, and still less retract!

Before receiving Luther's reply, the elector had formed his resolution. This prince, who was advancing in the knowledge of the Gospel, now became more decided in his conduct. He felt that the conference at Worms would not have a favourable result. "It appears a difficult matter," he wrote in reply to Charles, "to bring Luther with me to Worms; I beseech you to relieve me from this anxiety. Furthermore, I have never been willing to defend his doctrine, but only to prevent his being condemned without a hearing. The legates, without waiting for your orders, have permitted themselves to take a step at once dishonouring Luther and myself; and I much fear that they thus provoked him to commit a very imprudent act which might expose him to great danger, if he were to appear before the diet." The elector alluded to the burning of the papal bull.

But the rumour of Luther's coming was already current through the city. Men eager for novelty were delighted; the emperor's courtiers were alarmed; but none showed greater indignation than the papal legate. On his journey, Aleander had been able to discover how far the Gospel announced by Luther had found an echo in all classes of society. Men of letters, lawyers, nobles, the inferior clergy, the regular orders, and the people, were gained over to the Reformation.[2] These friends of the new doctrine walked boldly with heads erect; their language was fearless and daring; an invincible

terror froze the hearts of the partisans of Rome. The papacy was still standing, but its buttresses were tottering; for their ears already distinguished a presage of destruction, like that indistinct murmur heard ere the mountain falls and crumbles into dust.[1] Aleander on the road to Worms was frequently unable to contain himself. If he desired to dine or sleep in any place, neither the learned, the nobles, nor the priests, even among the supposed partisans of Rome, dared receive him; and the haughty nuncio was obliged to seek a lodging at inns of the lowest class.[2] Aleander was frightened, and began to think his life in danger. Thus he arrived at Worms, and to his Roman fanaticism was then superadded the feeling of the personal indignities he had suffered. He immediately used every exertion to prevent the appearance of the bold and formidable Luther. "Would it not be scandalous," said he, "to behold laymen examining anew a cause already condemned by the pope?" Nothing is so alarming to a Roman courtier as inquiry; and yet, should this take place in Germany, and not at Rome, how great would be the humiliation, even were Luther's condemnation to be agreed upon unanimously; but such a result appeared by no means certain. Will not Luther's powerful eloquence, which has already committed such ravages, drag many princes and lords into inevitable destruction? Aleander pressed Charles closely: he entreated, threatened, and spoke as the nuncio of the head of the Church.[3] Charles submitted, and wrote to the elector that the time accorded to Luther having already elapsed, this monk lay under the papal excommunication, so that, if he would not retract what he had written, Frederick must leave him behind at Wittemberg. But this prince had already quitted Saxony without Luther. "I pray the Lord to be favourable to our elector," said Melancthon, as he saw him depart. "It is on him all our hopes for the restoration of Christendom repose. His enemies will dare anything, and they will not leave a stone unturned;[4] but God will confound the councils of Ahithophel. As for us, let us maintain our share of the combat by our teaching and by our prayers." Luther was deeply grieved at being forbidden to come to Worms.[5]

It was not sufficient for Aleander that Luther did not appear at Worms; he desired his condemnation. He was continually soliciting the princes, prelates, and different members of the diet; he accused the Augustine monk not only of disobedience and

<hr/>

[1] Omnia de me præsumas præter fugam et palinodiam. L. Epp. i. 536.
[2] Multitudo....turba pauperum, nobilium....grammatici ....causidici....inferiores ecclesiastici....factio multorum regularium....Pallav. i. 93.

[1] Hæ omnes conditiones petulanter grassantium....motum cuilibet incutiebant. Pallav. i. 93.
[2] Neminem nactus qui auderet ipsum excipere, ad vilia sordidaque hospitia ægre divertit. Ibid.
[3] Legati Romani nolunt ut audiatur homo hæreticus. Minantur multa. Zw. Epp. p. 157.
[4] Καὶ πάντα λίθον κινησομίνους. Corp. Ref. i. 279. 24th January.
[5] Cum dolore legi novissimas Caroli .teras. L. Epp. i. 512.

heresy, but even of sedition, rebellion, impiety, and blasphemy. But the very tone of his voice betrayed the passions by which he was animated. " He is moved by hatred and vengeance, much more than by zeal and piety," was the general remark;[1] and frequent and violent as were his speeches, he made no converts to his sentiments.[2] Some persons observed to him that the papal bull had only condemned Luther conditionally; others could not altogether conceal the joy they felt at this humiliation of the haughtiness of Rome. The emperor's ministers on the one hand, the ecclesiastical electors on the other, showed a marked coldness; the former, that the pope might feel the necessity of leaguing with their master; the latter, that the pontiff might purchase their support at a dearer price. A feeling of Luther's innocence predominated in the assembly; and Aleander could not contain his indignation.

But the coldness of the diet made the legate less impatient than the coldness of Rome. Rome, which had had so much difficulty in taking a serious view of this quarrel of a " drunken German," did not imagine that the bull of the sovereign pontiff would be ineffectual to humiliate and reduce him. She had resumed all her carelessness,[3] and sent neither additional bulls nor money. But how could they bring this matter to an issue without money?[4] Rome must be awakened. Aleander uttered a cry of alarm. " Germany is separating from Rome," wrote he to the Cardinal de Medicis; " the princes are separating from the pope. Yet a little more delay, yet a little more negotiation, and hope will be gone. Money! money! or Germany is lost."[5]

Rome awoke at this cry; the vassals of the papacy, casting off their torpor, hastily forged their redoubtable thunderbolts in the Vatican. The pope issued a new bull;[6] and the excommunication, with which the heretical doctor had as yet been only threatened, was decidedly pronounced against him and all his adherents. Rome, by breaking the last tie which still bound him to the Church, augmented Luther's liberty, and with increased liberty came an increase of strength. Cursed by the pope, he took refuge with fresh love at the feet of Christ. Ejected from the outward courts of the temple, he felt more strongly that he was himself a temple in which dwelt the living God.

" It is a great glory," said he, " that we sinners, by believing in Christ, and by eating his flesh, possess within us, in all their

vigour, his power, wisdom, and righteousness, as it is written, *Whoso believeth in me, in him do I dwell.* Wonderful abiding-place! marvellous tabernacle! far superior to that of Moses, and magnificently adorned within, with beautiful hangings, curtains of purple, and ornaments of gold; while without, as on the tabernacle that God commanded to be built in the desert of Sinai, we perceive nought but a rude covering of goats' hair and rams' skins.[1] Often do Christians stumble, and, to look at them outwardly, they seem all weakness and reproach. But this matters not, for beneath this weakness and this foolishness dwells in secret a power that the world cannot know, and which yet overcometh the world; for Christ dwelleth in us. I have sometimes beheld Christians walking lamely and with great feebleness; but when came the hour of conflict or of appearing before the bar of the world, Christ suddenly stirred within them, and they became so strong and so resolute, that Satan fled away frightened from before their face."[2]

Such an hour would soon strike for Luther; and Christ, in whose communion he dwelt, could not fail him. Meantime Rome rejected him with violence. The reformer and all his partisans were accursed, whatever their rank and power, and dispossessed, with their inheritors, of all their honours and goods. Every faithful Christian, who valued the salvation of his soul, was to flee at the sight of this accursed band. Wherever the heresy had been introduced, the priests were enjoined, on Sundays and festivals, at the hour when the churches were thronged with worshippers, to publish the excommunication with due solemnity. The altars were to be stripped of their ornaments and sacred vessels; the cross to be laid on the ground; twelve priests holding tapers in their hands were first to light them, and immediately dashing them violently to the earth, to extinguish them under their feet; the bishop was then to proclaim the condemnation of these unbelievers; all the bells were to be rung; the bishops and priests were to utter their anathemas and maledictions, and preach boldly against Luther and his adherents.

The excommunication had been published in Rome twenty-two days, but probably had not yet reached Germany, when Luther, being informed that there was some talk of summoning him to Worms, wrote a letter to the elector, drawn up in such a manner that Frederick might show it to the diet. Luther was desirous of correcting the erroneous ideas of the princes, and of frankly laying before this august tribunal the true nature of a cause so misunderstood. " I rejoice with all my heart, most serene Lord," says he, " that his imperial majesty desires to summon me before him touching this affair. I call Jesus

1 Magis invidia et vindictæ libidine quam zelo pietatis. Historia Johannis Cochlœi, de actis et scriptis Martini Lutheri, Paris, 1565, p. 27, verso. Cochlœus was all his life one of the most inveterate of Luther's enemies. He will soon appear upon the stage.
2 Vehementibus suis orationibus parum promovit. Cochlœus.
3 Negligens quædam securitas Romam pervaserat. Pallav. i. 94.
4 Nec pecunia ad varios pro eadem sumptus. Ibid.
5 Periculum denique amittendæ Germaniæ ex parcimonia monetæ cujusdam. Ibid.
6 Decet Romanum Pontificem, &c. Bullarium Romanum.

1 Exodus xxvi. 7, 14.
2 So regete sich der Christus, dass sie so fest wurden, dass der Teufel fliehen musste. L. Opp. ix. 613, on John vi. 56.

Christ to witness, that it is the cause of the whole German nation, of the universal Church, of the christian world, nay, of God himself......and not of an individual, especially such a one as myself.[1] I am ready to go to Worms, provided I have a safe-conduct, and learned, pious, and impartial judges. I am ready to answer......for it is not from a presumptuous spirit, or with any view to personal advantage, that I have taught the doctrine with which I am reproached: it is in obedience to my conscience and to my oath as doctor of the Holy Scriptures: it is for the glory of God, for the salvation of the Christian Church, for the good of the German nation, and for the extirpation of so much superstition, abuse, evil, scandal, tyranny, blasphemy, and impiety."

This declaration, drawn up at a moment so solemn for Luther, merits particular attention. Such were the motives of his actions, and the inward springs that led to the revival of christian society. This is very different from the jealousy of a monk or the desire of marriage!

CHAPTER II.

A Foreign Prince—Council of Politicians—Conference between the Confessor and the Chancellor—Inutility of these Manœuvres—Aleander's Activity—Luther's Words —Charles yields to the Pope.

But all this was of little consequence to politicians. However noble might have been the idea Charles had formed of the imperial dignity, Germany was not the centre of his interests and of his policy. He understood neither the spirit nor the language of Germany. He was always a Duke of Burgundy, who to many other sceptres had united the first crown of Christendom. It was a remarkable circumstance that, at the moment of its most intimate transformation, Germany should elect a foreign prince, to whom the necessities and tendencies of the nation were but of secondary importance. Undoubtedly the emperor was not indifferent to the religious movement, but it had no meaning in his eyes, except so far as it threatened the pope. War between Charles and Francis I. was inevitable; the principal scene of that war would be Italy. The alliance of the pope became therefore daily more necessary to Charles's projects. He would have preferred detaching Frederick from Luther, or satisfying the pope without offending Frederick. Many of his courtiers manifested in the affair of the Augustine monk that disdainful coldness which politicians generally

affect when there is any question of religion. " Let us avoid all extreme measures," said they. " Let us entangle Luther by negotiations, and reduce him to silence by some trifling concessions. The proper course is to stifle and not to fan the flame. If the monk falls into the net, we are victorious! By accepting a compromise, he will silence himself and ruin his cause. For form's sake we will decree certain exterior reforms; the elector will be satisfied: the pope will be gained; and matters will resume their ordinary course."

Such was the project formed by the emperor's confidants. The Wittemberg doctors seem to have divined this new policy. " They are trying to win men over secretly," said Melancthon, " and are working in the dark."[1] Charles's confessor, John Glapio, a man of great weight, a skilful courtier, and a wily monk, took upon himself the execution of the scheme. Glapio possessed the full confidence of Charles; and this prince, imitating the Spanish customs in this particular, intrusted him almost entirely with the care of matters pertaining to religion. As soon as Charles had been named emperor, Leo hastened to win over Glapio by favours which the confessor very gratefully acknowledged.[2] He could make no better return to the pontiff's generosity than by crushing this heresy, and he applied himself to the task.[3]

Among the elector's councillors was Gregory Bruck, or Pontanus, the chancellor, a man of intelligence, decision, and courage, who was a better theological scholar than many doctors, and whose wisdom was capable of resisting the wiles of the monks in Charles's court. Glapio, knowing the chancellor's influence, requested an interview with him, and introducing himself as if he had been a friend of the reformer, said with an air of kindness: " I was filled with joy, in reading Luther's first writings; I thought him a vigorous tree, which had put forth goodly branches, and gave promise to the Church of the most precious fruit. Many people, it is true, have entertained the same views before his time; yet no one but himself has had the noble courage to publish the truth without fear. But when I read his book on the *Captivity of Babylon*, I felt like one overwhelmed with blows from head to foot. I do not think," added the monk, " that brother Martin will acknowledge himself to be the author of it; I do not find in it either his usual style or learning." After some discussion, the confessor continued: " Introduce me to the elector, and in your presence I will show him Luther's errors."

The chancellor replied that the business of

[1] Causam, quæ, Christo teste, Dei, christiani orbis, ecclesiæ catholicæ, et totius Germanicæ nationis, et non unius si privati est hominis. L. Epp. i. 551.

[1] Clanculum tentent et experiantur. Corp. Ref. i. 2ol. 3d Feb.

[2] Benignis officiis recens a Pontifice delinitus. Pallav. i. 90.

[3] Et sane in eo toto negotio singulare probitatis ardorisque specimen dedit. Ibid

the diet left his highness no leisure, and besides he did not mix himself up with this matter. The monk was vexed at seeing his demand rejected. "Nevertheless," continued the chancellor, "since you say there is no evil without a remedy, explain yourself."

Assuming a confidential air, the confessor replied: "The emperor earnestly desires to see a man like Luther reconciled with the Church; for his books (previous to the publication of the treatise on the *Captivity of Babylon*) were rather agreeable to his majesty......[1] The irritation caused by the bull no doubt excited Luther to write the latter work. Let him then declare that he had no intention of troubling the repose of the Church, and the learned of every nation will side with him. Procure me an audience with his highness."

The chancellor went to Frederick. The elector well knew that any retractation whatsoever was impossible: "Tell the confessor," answered he, "that I cannot comply with his request; but continue your conference."

Glapio received this message with every demonstration of respect; and changing his line of attack, he said: "Let the elector name some confidential persons to deliberate on this affair."

THE CHANCELLOR.—"The elector does not profess to defend Luther's cause."

THE CONFESSOR.—"Well, then, you at least can discuss it with me......Jesus Christ is my witness that I make this proposition from love to the Church and Luther, who has opened so many hearts to the truth."[2]

The chancellor, having refused to undertake a task which belonged to the reformer, prepared to withdraw.

"Stay," said the monk.

THE CHANCELLOR.—"What remains to be done?"

THE CONFESSOR.—"Let Luther deny that he wrote the *Captivity of Babylon*."

THE CHANCELLOR.—"But the pope's bull condemns all his other writings."

THE CONFESSOR.—"That is because of his obstinacy. If he disclaims this book, the pope in his omnipotence can easily pardon him. What hopes may we not entertain now that we have so excellent an emperor!"......

Perceiving that these words had produced some effect on the chancellor, the monk hastily added: "Luther always desires to argue from the Bible. The Bible......it is like wax, you may stretch it and bend it as you please. I would undertake to find in the Bible opinions more extravagant even than Luther's. He is mistaken when he changes every word of Christ into a commandment." And then, wishing to act upon the fears of his hearer, he added: "What would be the result if to-day or to-morrow the emperor should have recourse to arms? Reflec upon this." He then permitted Pontanus to retire.

The confessor laid fresh snares. "A man might live ten years with him, and not know him at last," said Erasmus.

"What an excellent book is that of Luther's on Christian Liberty," said he to the chancellor, whom he saw again a few days after; "what wisdom! what talent! what wit! it is thus that a real scholar ought to write......Let both sides choose men of irreproachable character, and let the pope and Luther refer the whole matter to their decision. There is no doubt that Luther would come off victorious on many points.[1] I will speak about it to the emperor. Believe me, I do not mention these things solely on my own authority. I have told the emperor that God would chastise him and all the princes, if the Church, which is the spouse of Christ, be not cleansed from all the stains that defile her. I added, that God himself had sent Luther, and commissioned him to reprove men for their offences, employing him as a scourge to punish the sins of the world."[2]

The chancellor, on hearing these words (which reflected the feelings of the age, and showed the opinion entertained of Luther even by his adversaries), could not forbear expressing his astonishment that his master was not treated with more respect. "There are daily consultations with the emperor on this affair," said he, "and yet the elector is not invited to them. He thinks it strange that the emperor, who is not a little indebted to him, should exclude him from his councils."

THE CONFESSOR.—"I have been present only once at these deliberations, and then heard the emperor resist the solicitations of the nuncios. Five years hence it will be seen what Charles has done for the reformation of the Church."

"The elector," answered Pontanus, "is unacquainted with Luther's intentions. Let him be summoned and have a hearing."

The confessor replied with a deep sigh:[3] "I call God to witness how ardently I desire to see the reformation of Christendom accomplished."

To protract the affair and to keep the reformer silent was all that Glapio proposed. In any case, Luther must not come to Worms. A dead man returning from the other world and appearing in the midst of the diet would have been less alarming to the nuncios, the monks, and all the papal host, than the presence of the Wittemberg doctor.

"How many days does it take to travel

---

[1] Es haben dessen Bücher Ihre Majestät....um etwas gefallen. Weimar State Papers. Seckend. p. 315.
[2] Der andern das Hertz zu vielem Guten eröffnet....Ibid.

[1] Es sey nicht zu zweifeln dass Luthers in vielen Artickeln werde den Sieg davon tragen....Seckend. p. 319.
[2] Dass Gott diesen Mann gesandt....dass er eine Geissel seye um der Sünden willen. Weimar State Papers, ibid. 320.
[3] Glapio that hierauf einen tiefen Seufzer, un rufte Gott zum Zeugen.....Ibid. 321.

from Wittemberg to Worms?" asked the confessor with an assumed air of indifference; and then, begging Pontanus to present his most humble salutations to the elector, he retired.

Such were the manœuvres resorted to by the courtiers. They were disconcerted by the firmness of Pontanus. That just man was immovable as a rock during all these negotiations. The Roman monks themselves fell into the snares they had laid for their enemies. "The Christian," said Luther in his figurative language, " is like a bird tied near a trap. The wolves and foxes prowl round it, and spring on it to devour it; but they fall into the pit and perish, while the timid bird remains unhurt. It is thus the holy angels keep watch around us, and those devouring wolves, the hypocrites and persecutors, cannot harm us."[1] Not only were the artifices of the confessor ineffectual, but his admissions still more confirmed Frederick in his opinion that Luther was right, and that it was his duty to protect him.

Men's hearts daily inclined more and more towards the Gospel. A Dominican prior suggested that the emperor, the kings of France, Spain, England, Portugal, Hungary, and Poland, with the pope and the electors, should name representatives to whom the arrangement of this affair should be confided. " Never," said he, " has implicit reliance been placed on the pope alone."[2] The public feeling became such that it seemed impossible to condemn Luther without having heard and confuted him.[3]

Aleander grew uneasy, and displayed unusual energy. It was no longer against the elector and Luther alone that he had to contend. He beheld with horror the secret negotiations of the confessor, the proposition of the prior, the consent of Charles's ministers, the extreme coldness of Roman piety, even among the most devoted friends of the pontiff, " so that one might have thought," says Pallavicini, " that a torrent of iced water had gushed over them."[4] He had at length received from Rome the money he had demanded; he held in his hand the energetic briefs addressed to the most powerful men in the empire.[5] Fearing to see his prey escape, he felt that now was the time to strike a decisive blow. He forwarded the briefs, scattered the money profusely, and made the most alluring promises; " and, armed with this threefold weapon," says the historian, Cardinal Pallavicini, " he made a fresh attempt to bias the wavering assembly of electors in the pope's favour."[5] But around the emperor in particular he laid his snares. He took advantage

of the dissensions existing between the Belgian and Spanish ministers. He besieged his monarch unceasingly. All the partisans of Rome, awakened by his voice, solicited Charles. " Daily deliberations," wrote the elector to his brother John, " are held against Luther; they demand that he shall be placed under the ban of the pope and of the emperor; they endeavour to injure him in every way. Those who parade in their red hats, the Romans, with all their followers, display indefatigable zeal in this task."[1]

Aleander did in reality urge the condemnation of the reformer with a violence that Luther characterizes as marvellous fury.[2] The apostate nuncio,[3] as Luther styles him, transported by anger beyond the bounds of prudence, one day exclaimed: " If you Germans pretend to shake off the yoke of obedience to Rome, we will act in such a manner that, exterminated by mutual slaughter, you shall perish in your own blood."[4]— " This is how the pope feeds Christ's sheep," adds the reformer.

But such was not his own language. He asked nothing for himself. " Luther is ready," said Melancthon, " to purchase at the cost of his own life the glory and advancement of the Gospel."[5] But he trembled when he thought of the calamities that might be the consequence of his death. He pictured to himself a misled people revenging perhaps his martyrdom in the blood of his adversaries, and especially of the priests. He shrank from so dreadful a responsibility. " God," said he, " checks the fury of his enemies; but if it breaks forth......then shall we see a storm burst upon the priests like that which has devastated Bohemia......My hands are clear of this, for I have earnestly entreated the German nobility to oppose the Romans by wisdom, and not by the sword.[6] To make war upon the priests,—a class without courage or strength,—would be to fight against women and children."

Charles V. could not resist the solicitations of the nuncio. His Belgian and Spanish devotion had been developed by his preceptor Adrian, who afterwards occupied the pontifical throne. The pope had addressed him in a brief, entreating him to give the power of law to the bull by an imperial edict. " To no purpose will God have invested you with the sword of the supreme power," said he, " if you do not employ it, not only against the infidels, but against the heretics also, who are far worse than they." Accordingly, one day in the beginning of February, at the moment when every one in Worms was

[1] L. Opp. (W.) xxii. 1655.
[2] Und niemals dem Papst allein geglaubt. Seck. p. 323.
[3] Spalatinus scribit tantum favoris Evangelio esse istic ut me inaudito et inconvicto damnari non speret. L. Epp. i. 556, Feb. 9.
[4] Hinc aqua manabat, quæ succensæ pietatis æstum restinguebat. Pallav. i. 96.
[5] Mandata, pecuniis ac diplomata. Ibid. 95.
[6] Triplici hac industria nunc Aleander....Ibid.

[1] Das thun die in rothen Hüten prangen. Seck. p. 364.
[2] Miro furore Papistæ moliuntur mihi mala. L. Epp. i. 556.
[3] Nuntius apostaticus (a play upon the words " apostolicus and apostaticus," apostolic and apostate) agit summis viribus. Ibid. 569.
[4] Ut mutuis cædibus absumpti, vestro cruore pereatis. L. Epp. i. 556.
[5] Libenter etiam morte sua Evangelii gloriam et profectum emerit. Corp. Ref. i. 285.
[6] Non ferro, sed consiliis et edictis. L. Epp. i. 563.

making preparations for a splendid tournament, and when the emperor's tent was already erected, the princes who were arming themselves to take part in the brilliant show were summoned to the imperial palace. After listening to the reading of the papal bull, a stringent edict was laid before them, enjoining its immediate execution. " If you can recommend any better course," added the emperor, following the usual custom, " I am ready to hear you."

An animated debate immediately took place in the assembly. " This monk," wrote a deputy from one of the free cities of Germany, "gives us plenty of occupation. Some would like to crucify him, and I think that he will not escape; only it is to be feared that he will rise again the third day." The emperor had imagined that he would be able to publish his edict without opposition from the states; but such was not the case. Their minds were not prepared. It was necessary to gain over the diet. " Convince this assembly," said the youthful monarch to the nuncio. This was all that Aleander desired; and he was promised a hearing before the diet on the 13th of February.

CHAPTER III.

Aleander introduced to the Diet—Aleander's Speech—Luther is accused—Rome is justified—Appeal to Charles against Luther—Effect of the Nuncio's Speech.

THE nuncio prepared for this solemn audience. This was an important duty, but Aleander was not unworthy of it. He was not only ambassador from the sovereign pontiff, and surrounded with all the splendour of his high office, but also one of the most eloquent men of his age. The friends of the Reformation looked forward to this sitting with apprehension. The elector, pretending indisposition, was not present; but he gave some of his councillors orders to attend, and take notes of the nuncio's speech.

When the day arrived, Aleander proceeded towards the assembly of the princes. The feelings of all were excited; many were reminded of Annas and Caiaphas going to Pilate's judgment-seat and calling for the death of *this fellow who perverted the nation.*[1] " Just as the nuncio was about to cross the threshold, the usher of the diet," says Pallavicini, " approaching him rudely, thrust him back by a blow on the breast."[2] " He was a Lutheran at heart," adds the Romanist historian. If this story be true, it shows no doubt an excess of passion; but at the same time it furnishes us with a standard by which to measure the influence that Luther's words

[1] Luke xxiii. 2.
[2] Pugnis ejus pectori admotis repulerit. Pallav. i. 112.

had excited even in those who guarded the doors of the imperial council. The proud Aleander, recovering himself with dignity, walked forward and entered the hall. Never had Rome been called to make its defence before so august an assembly. The nuncio placed before him the documents that he had judged necessary, namely, Luther's works and the papal bulls; and, as soon as the diet was silent, he began :—

" Most august emperor, most mighty princes, most excellent deputies ! I appear before you in defence of a cause for which my heart glows with the most ardent affection. It is to retain on my master's head that triple crown which you all adore : to maintain that papal throne for which I should be willing to deliver my body to the flames, if the monster, that has engendered this growing heresy that I am now to combat, could be consumed at the same stake and mingle his ashes with mine.[1]

" No! the whole difference between Luther and the pope does not turn on the papal interests. I have Luther's books before me, and a man only needs have eyes in his head to see that he attacks the holy doctrines of the Church. He teaches that those alone communicate worthily whose consciences are overwhelmed with sorrow and confusion because of their sins, and that no one is justified by baptism, if he has not faith in the promise of which baptism is the pledge.[2] He denies the necessity of works to obtain heavenly glory. He denies that we have the liberty and power of obeying the natural and Divine law. He asserts that we sin of necessity in every one of our actions. Has the arsenal of hell ever sent forth weapons better calculated to break the bonds of decency ?......He preaches in favour of the abolition of monastic vows. Can we imagine any greater sacrilegious impiety ?......What desolation should we not witness in the world, were those who are the salt of the earth to throw aside their sacred garments, desert the temples that re-echo with their holy songs, and plunge into adultery, incest, and every vice !......

" Shall I enumerate all the crimes of this Augustine monk ? He sins against the dead, for he denies purgatory; he sins against heaven, for he says that he would not believe even an angel from heaven; he sins against the Church, for he maintains that all Christians are priests; he sins against the saints, for he despises their venerable writings; he

[1] Dummodo mecum una monstrum nascentis hæresis arderet. Pallav. i. 97. Seckendorff and many Protestant historians after him, have asserted that Pallavicini himself composed the speech he puts into Aleander's mouth. It is true that the cardinal states he had arranged it in the form in which he presents it to his readers; but he points out the sources whence he had taken it, and in particular, Aleander's letters deposited in the Archives of the Vatican (Acta Wormatiæ, fol. 66 and 99); in my opinion, therefore, I should betray partiality by rejecting it wholly. I quote some of the features of this speech from Protestant and Romanist sources.
[2] Baptismum neminem justificare, sed fidem in verbum promissionis, cui additur Baptismus. Cochlœus, Act. Luth. i. 2s.

sins against councils, for he designates that of Constance an assembly of devils; he sins against the world, for he forbids the punishment of death to be inflicted on any who have not committed a deadly sin.[1] Some of you may say that he is a pious man......I have no desire to attack his private life, but only to remind this assembly that the devil often deceives people in the garb of truth."

Aleander, having spoken of the doctrine of purgatory condemned by the Council of Florence, laid it at the emperor's feet the papal bull on this council. The Archbishop of Mentz took it up, and gave it to the Archbishops of Treves and Cologne, who received it reverently, and passed it to the other princes. The nuncio, after having thus accused Luther, proceeded to the second point, which was to justify Rome:—

"At Rome, says Luther, the mouth promises one thing, the hand does another. If this were true, must we not come to the very opposite conclusion? If the ministers of a religion live conformably to its precepts, it is a sign that the religion is false. Such was the religion of the ancient Romans...... Such is that of Mahomet and of Luther himself; but such is not the religion which the Roman pontiffs teach us. Yes, the doctrine they profess condemns them all, as having committed faults; many, as guilty; and some (I will speak frankly) as criminal.[2] ......This doctrine exposes their actions to the censure of men during their lives, to the brand of history after their death.[3] Now, I would ask what pleasure or profit could the popes have found in inventing such a religion?

"The Church, it may be said, was not governed by the Roman pontiffs in the primitive ages.—What conclusion shall we draw from this? With such arguments we might persuade men to feed on acorns, and princesses to wash their own linen."[4]

But his adversary—the reformer—was the special object of the nuncio's hatred. Boiling with indignation against those who said that he ought to be heard, he exclaimed: "Luther will not allow himself to be instructed by any one. The pope had already summoned him to Rome, and he did not comply. Next, the pope cited him before the legate at Augsburg, and he did not appear until he had procured a safe-conduct, that is to say, after the legate's hands were tied, and his tongue alone was left unfettered......[5] Ah!" said Aleander, turning towards Charles V.,

"I entreat your imperial Majesty to do nothing that may lead to your reproach. Do not interfere in a matter which does not concern the laity. Perform your own duties! Let Luther's doctrines be interdicted by you throughout the length and breadth of the empire: let his writings be burnt every where. Fear not! In Luther's errors there is enough to burn a hundred thousand heretics......[1] And what have we to fear? The multitude?......Its insolence makes it appear terrible before the conflict, but in the battle its cowardice renders it contemptible. Foreign princes?......But the King of France has forbidden the introduction of Luther's doctrines into his kingdom; and the King of England is preparing an assault with his own royal hand. You know what are the sentiments of Hungary, Italy, and Spain, and there is not one of your neighbours, however much he may hate you, who wishes you so much evil as this heresy would cause you. For if our adversary's house adjoins our own, we may desire it to be visited with fever, but not with the plague......What are all these Lutherans? A crew of insolent pedagogues, corrupt priests, dissolute monks, ignorant lawyers, and degraded nobles, with the common people, whom they have misled and perverted. How far superior to them is the catholic party in number, ability, and power! A unanimous decree from this illustrious assembly will enlighten the simple, warn the imprudent, decide the wavering, and give strength to the weak......But if the axe is not laid to the roots of this poisonous tree, if the death-blow is not struck, then......I see it overshadowing the heritage of Jesus Christ with its branches, changing our Lord's vineyard into a gloomy forest, transforming the kingdom of God into a den of wild beasts, and reducing Germany to that frightful state of barbarism and desolation which has been brought upon Asia by the superstition of Mahomet."

The nuncio was silent. He had spoken for three hours. The enthusiasm of his language had produced a deep impression on the assembly. The princes looked at each other, excited and alarmed, says Cochlœus, and murmurs soon arose from every side against Luther and his partisans.[2] If the eloquent Luther had been present; if he had been able to reply to this speech; if, profiting by the avowals extorted from the Roman nuncio by the recollection of his former master, the infamous Borgia, he had shown that these very arguments, intended to defend Rome, were of themselves its condemnation; if he had shown that the doctrine which proved its iniquity was not invented by him, as the orator said, but was that religion which Christ had given to the world, and

---

[1] Weil er verbiete jemand mit Todes Strafe zu belegen, der nicht eine Todtsünde begangen. Seckend. p. 333.
[2] Multos ut quadantenus reos, nonnullos (dicam ingenue) ut scelestos. Pallav. i. 101.
[3] Linguarum vituperationi dum vivunt, historiarum infamiæ post mortem. Ibid.
[4] In the Odyssey, Homer represents the princess Nausicaa going with her maidens to the river side to wash her garments. The classical reader will be familiar with the allusion to acorns, which the heathen writers supposed to be the earliest food of the human race, "when first in woods the naked savage ran."
[5] Quod idem erat, ac revinctis legati brachiis, et lingua solum soluta. Ibid. 109.

[1] Dass 100,000 Ketzer ihrethalben verbrannt werden Seck. p. 332.
[2] Vehementer exterriti atque commoti, alter alterum intuebantur, atque in Lutherum ejusque fautores murmurare cœperunt. Cochlœus, p. 26.

which the Reformation was re-establishing in its primitive splendour; if he had presented a faithful and animated picture of the errors and abuses of the papacy, and had shown how the religion of Christ had been made an instrument of self-interest and rapacity; the effect of the nuncio's harangue would have been instantly nullified. But no one rose to speak. The assembly remained under the impression produced by this speech; and, agitated and transported, showed itself ready to extirpate Luther's heresy by force from the soil of the empire.[1]

Nevertheless, it was a victory only in appearance. It was among the purposes of God that Rome should have an opportunity of displaying her reasons and her power. The greatest of her orators had spoken in the assembly of the princes; he had given utterance to all that Rome had to say. But it was precisely this last effort of the papacy that became a signal of defeat in the eyes of many who had listened to it. If a bold confession is necessary for the triumph of truth, the surest means of destroying error is to make it known without reserve. Neither the one nor the other, to run its course, should be concealed. The light tests all things.

CHAPTER IV.

Sentiments of the Princes—Speech of Duke George—Character of the Reformation—One Hundred and One Grievances—Charles gives Way—Aleander's Stratagems—The Grandees of Spain—Peace of Luther—Death and no Retractation.

A few days were sufficient to dissipate the first impression, as is ever the case when an orator conceals the emptiness of his arguments by high-sounding words.

The majority of the princes were ready to sacrifice Luther; but no one desired to immolate the rights of the empire and the grievances of the Germanic nation. They were very ready to give up the insolent monk who had dared speak so boldly; but they were the more resolved to make the pope feel the justice of a reform demanded by the chiefs of the nation. It was accordingly Luther's most determined personal enemy, Duke George of Saxony, who spoke with the greatest energy against the encroachments of Rome. The grandson of Podiebrad, king of Bohemia, although offended by the doctrine of Grace preached by the reformer, had not yet lost the hope of a moral and ecclesiastical reform. The principal cause of his irritation against the monk of Wittemberg was, that by his despised doctrines he was spoiling the whole affair. But now, seeing

the nuncio affecting to involve Luther and the reform of the Church in one and the same condemnation, George suddenly rose in the assembly of the princes, to the great astonishment of those who knew his hatred of the reformer. "The diet," said he, "must not forget its grievances against the court of Rome. How many abuses have crept into our states! The annats, which the emperor granted voluntarily for the good of Christianity, now exacted as a due; the Roman courtiers daily inventing new regulations to monopolize, sell, and lease the ecclesiastical benefices; a multitude of transgressions connived at; rich transgressors undeservedly tolerated, while those who have no money to purchase impunity are punished without mercy; the popes continually bestowing on their courtiers reversions and reserves, to the detriment of those to whom the benefices belong; the *commendams* of the abbeys and convents of Rome conferred on cardinals, bishops, and prelates, who appropriate their revenues, so that not a single monk is to be found in a convent where there should be twenty or thirty; stations multiplied to infinity, and stalls for the sale of indulgences set up in every street and public place of our cities—stalls of Saint Anthony, of the Holy Ghost, of Saint Hubert, of Saint Cornelius, of Saint Vincent, and so forth; companies purchasing at Rome the right to hold such markets, then buying permission of their bishop to display their wares, and squeezing and draining the pockets of the poor to obtain money; the indulgence, that ought only to be granted for the salvation of souls, and that should be earned by prayer, fasting, and works of charity, sold according to a tariff; the bishops' officials oppressing the lowly with penances for blasphemy, adultery, debauchery, and the violation of any festival, but not even reprimanding the clergy who commit similar crimes; penalties imposed on those who repent, and devised in such a manner that they soon fall again into the same error and give more money:[1] ......these are some of the abuses that cry out against Rome. All shame has been put aside, and their only object is......money! money! money!......so that the preachers who should teach the truth utter nothing but falsehoods, and are not only tolerated, but rewarded, because the greater their lies the greater their gain. It is from this foul spring that such tainted waters flow. Debauchery stretches out the hand to avarice. The officials invite women to their dwellings under various pretexts, and endeavour to seduce them, at one time by threats, at another by presents, or if they cannot succeed, they ruin their good fame.[2] Alas! it is the

---

[1] Lutheranam hæresim esse funditus evellendam. Pallav. i. 101; Roscoe's Leo X. chap. xix.

[1] Sondern dass er es bald wieder begehe und mehr Geld erlegen müsse. Weimar State Papers, Seckend. p. 328.
[2] Dass sie Weibesbilder unter mancherley Schein beschicken, selbige sodann mit Drohungen und Geschenken zu fällen suchen, oder in einen bösen Verdacht bringen. Ibid. p. 330.

scandal caused by the clergy that hurls so many poor souls into eternal condemnation ! A general reform must be effected. An œcumenical council must be called to bring about this reform. For these reasons, most excellent princes and lords, I humbly entreat you to take this matter into your immediate consideration." Duke George then handed in a list of the grievances he had enumerated. This was some days after Aleander's speech. The important catalogue has been preserved in the archives of Weimar.

Even Luther had not spoken with greater force against the abuses of Rome; but he had done something more. The duke pointed out the evil; Luther had pointed out both the cause and the remedy. He had demonstrated that the sinner receives the true indulgence, that which cometh from God, solely by faith in the grace and merits of Jesus Christ; and this simple but powerful doctrine had overthrown all the markets established by the priests. "How can a man become pious?" asked he one day. "A gray friar will reply, By putting on a gray hood and girding yourself with a cord. A Roman will answer, By hearing mass and by fasting. But a Christian will say, Faith in Christ alone justifies and saves. Before works, we must have eternal life. But when we are born again, and made children of God by the Word of grace, then we perform good works."[1]

The duke's speech was that of a secular prince; Luther's that of a reformer. The great evil in the church had been its excessive devotion to outward forms, its having made of all its works and graces mere external and material things. The indulgences were the extreme point of this course; and that which was most spiritual in Christianity, namely, pardon, might be purchased in shops like any other commodity. Luther's great work consisted in employing this extreme degeneration of religion to lead men and the Church back to the primitive sources of life, and to restore the kingdom of the Holy Ghost in the sanctuary of the heart. Here, as often happens in other cases, the remedy was found in the disease itself, and the two extremes met. From that time forward, the Church, that for so many centuries had been developed externally in human ceremonies, observances, and practices, began to be developed internally in faith, hope, and charity.

The duke's speech produced a proportionally greater impression, as his hostility to Luther was notorious. Other members of the diet brought forward their respective grievances, which received the support of the ecclesiastical princes themselves.[2] "We have a pontiff who loves only the chase and his pleasures," said they; "the benefices of the German nation are given away at Rome

to gunners, falconers, footmen, ass-drivers, grooms, guardsmen, and other people of this class, ignorant, inexperienced, and strangers to Germany."[1]

The diet appointed a committee to draw up all these grievances; they were found to amount to a hundred and one. A deputation, composed of secular and ecclesiastical princes, presented the report to the emperor, conjuring him to see them rectified, as he had engaged to do in his capitulation. "What a loss of Christian souls!" said they to Charles V.; "what depredations! what extortions, on account of the scandals by which the spiritual head of Christendom is surrounded! It is our duty to prevent the ruin and dishonour of our people. For this reason we most humbly but most urgently entreat you to order a general reformation, and to undertake its accomplishment."[2] There was at that time in christian society an unknown power operating on princes and people alike, a wisdom from on high, influencing even the adversaries of the Reformation, and preparing for that emancipation whose hour was come at last.

Charles could not be insensible to the remonstrances of the empire. Neither he nor the nuncio had expected them. Even his confessor had threatened him with the vengeance of Heaven, unless he reformed the Church. The emperor immediately recalled the edict commanding Luther's writings to be burnt throughout the empire, and substituted a provisional order to deliver these books into the keeping of the magistrates.

This did not satisfy the assembly, which desired the appearance of the reformer. It is unjust, said his friends, to condemn Luther without a hearing, and without learning from his own mouth whether he is the author of the books that are ordered to be burnt. His doctrines, said his adversaries, have so taken hold of men's minds, that it is impossible to check their progress, unless we hear them from himself. There shall be no discussion with him; and if he avows his writings, and refuses to retract them, then we will all with one accord, electors, princes, estates of the holy empire, true to the faith of our ancestors. assist your majesty to the utmost of our power in the execution of your decrees.[3]

Aleander in alarm, and fearing every thing from Luther's intrepidity and the ignorance of the princes, instantly strained every nerve to prevent the reformer's appearance. He went from Charles's ministers to the princes most favourably inclined to the pope, and from them to the emperor himself.[4] "It is not lawful," said he, "to question what the sovereign pontiff has decreed. There shall

---

[1] L. Opp. (W.) xxii. 748, 752.
[2] Seckend. Vorrede von Frick.

[1] Büchsenmeistern, Falknern, Pfistern, Eseltreibern, Stallknechten, Trabanten....Kapp's Nachlese nützl. Ref. Urkunden. iii. 262.
[2] Dass eine Besserung und gemeine Reformation geschehe. Ibid. 262.
[3] L. Opp. (L.) xxii. 567.
[4] Quam ob rem sedulo contestatus est apud Cæsaris administros. Pallav. i. 113.

be no discussion with Luther, you say; but," continued he, "will not the energy of this audacious man, the fire of his eyes, the eloquence of his language, and the mysterious spirit by which he is animated, be sufficient to excite a tumult?[1] Already many adore him as a saint, and in every place you may see his portrait surrounded with a glory like that which encircles the heads of the blessed ......If you are resolved to summon him before you, at least do not put him under the protection of the public faith!"[2] These latter words were meant either to intimidate Luther, or to prepare the way for his destruction.

The nuncio found an easy access to the grandees of Spain. In Spain, as in Germany, the opposition to the Dominican inquisitors was national. The yoke of the inquisition, that had been thrown off for a time, had just been replaced on their necks by Charles. A numerous party in that peninsula sympathized with Luther; but it was not thus with the grandees, who had discovered on the banks of the Rhine what they had hated beyond the Pyrenees. Inflamed with the most ardent fanaticism, they were impatient to destroy the new heresy. Frederick, duke of Alva, in particular, was transported with rage whenever he heard the Reformation mentioned.[3] He would gladly have waded in the blood of all these sectarians. Luther was not yet summoned to appear, but already had his mere name powerfully stirred the lords of Christendom assembled at Worms.

The man who thus moved all the powers of the earth seemed alone undisturbed. The news from Worms was alarming. Luther's friends were terrified. "There remains nothing for us but your good wishes and prayers," wrote Melancthon to Spalatin. "Oh! that God would deign to purchase at the price of our blood the salvation of the christian world!"[4] But Luther was a stranger to fear; shutting himself up in his quiet cell, he there meditated on and applied to himself those words in which Mary, the mother of Jesus, exclaims: *My soul doth magnify the Lord, and my spirit hath rejoiced in God my Saviour. For he that is mighty hath done to me great things; and holy is his name. He hath showed strength with his arm; he hath put down the mighty from their seats, and exalted them of low degree.*[5] These are some of the reflections that filled Luther's heart: "HE THAT IS MIGHTY......says Mary. What great boldness on the part of a young girl! With a single word she brands all the strong with weakness, all the mighty with feebleness, all the wise with folly, all those whose name is glorious upon earth with disgrace, and casts all strength, all might, all wisdom, and all glory at the feet of God.[1] *His arm*, continues she, meaning by this the power by which he acts of himself, without the aid of any of his creatures: mysterious power!......which is exerted in secrecy and in silence until His designs are accomplished. Destruction is at hand, when no one has seen it coming: relief is there, and no one had suspected it. He leaves His children in oppression and weakness, so that every man says: They are lost! ......But it is then He is strongest; for where the strength of men ends, there begins that of God. Only let faith wait upon him...... And, on the other hand, God permits his adversaries to increase in grandeur and power. He withdraws his support, and suffers them to be puffed up with their own.[2] He empties them of His eternal wisdom, and lets them be filled with their own, which is but for a day. And while they are rising in the brightness of their power, the arm of the Lord is taken away, and their work vanishes as a bubble bursting in the air."

It was on the 10th of March, at the very moment when the imperial city of Worms was filled with dread at his name, that Luther concluded this explanation of the *Magnificat*.

He was not left quiet in his retreat. Spalatin, in conformity with the elector's orders, sent him a note of the articles, which he would be required to retract. A retractation, after his refusal at Augsburg!......"Fear not," wrote he to Spalatin, "that I shall retract a single syllable, since their only argument is, that my works are opposed to the rites of what they call the Church. If the Emperor Charles summons me only that I may retract, I shall reply that I will remain here, and it will be the same as if I had gone to Worms and returned. But, on the contrary, if the emperor summons me that I may be put to death as an enemy of the empire, I am ready to comply with his call;[3] for, with the help of Christ, I will never desert the Word on the battle-field. I am well aware that these bloodthirsty men will never rest until they have taken away my life. Would that it were the papists alone that would be guilty of my blood!"

CHAPTER V.

Shall Luther have a Safe-conduct—The Safe-conduct—Will Luther come—Holy Thursday at Rome—The Pope and Luther.

AT last the emperor made up his mind. Luther's appearance before the diet seemed the

[1] Lingua promptus, ardore vultus, et oris spiritu ad concitandam seditionem. Pallav. i. 113.
[2] Haud certe fidem publicam illi præbendam..Ibid.
[3] Albæ dux videbatur aliquando furentibus modis agitari. ..Ibid. 362.
[4] Utinam Deus redimat nostro sanguine salutem Christiani populi. Corp. Ref. i. 362.
[5] Luke i. 46-55.

[1] *Magnificat.* L. Opp. Wittemb. Deutsch. Ausg. iii. 11, &c.
[2] Er zieht seine Krafft heraus und lässt sie von eigener Krafft sich aufblasen. Ibid. &c.
[3] Si ad me occidendum deinceps vocare velit....offeram me venturum. L. Epp. i. 574.

only means calculated to terminate an affair which engaged the attention of all the empire. Charles V. resolved to summon him, but without granting him a safe-conduct. Here Frederick was again compelled to assume the character of a protector. The dangers by which the reformer was threatened were apparent to all. Luther's friends, says Cochlœus, feared that he would be delivered into the pope's hands, or that the emperor himself would put him to death, as undeserving, on account of his heresy, that any faith should be kept with him.[1] On this question there was a long and violent debate[2] between the princes. Struck at last by the extensive agitation then stirring up the people in every part of Germany, and fearing that during Luther's journey some unexpected tumult or dangerous commotion might burst forth in favour of the reformer,[3] the princes thought the wisest course would be to tranquillize the public feelings on this subject; and not only the emperor, but also the Elector of Saxony, Duke George, and the Landgrave of Hesse, through whose territories he would have to pass, gave him each a safe-conduct.

On the 6th of March, 1521, Charles V. signed the following summons addressed to Luther:—

"Charles, by the grace of God Emperor elect of the Romans, always August, &c. &c.

"Honourable, well-beloved, and pious! We and the States of the Holy Empire here assembled, having resolved to institute an inquiry touching the doctrine and the books that thou hast lately published, have issued, for thy coming hither and thy return to a place of security, our safe-conduct and that of the empire, which we send thee herewith. Our sincere desire is, that thou shouldst prepare immediately for this journey, in order that within the space of the twenty-one days fixed by our safe-conduct, thou mayst without fail be present before us. Fear neither injustice nor violence. We will firmly abide by our aforesaid safe-conduct, and expect that thou wilt comply with our summons. In so doing, thou wilt obey our earnest wishes.

"Given in our imperial city of Worms, this sixth day of March, in the year of our Lord 1521, and the second of our reign.

"CHARLES.

"By order of my Lord the Emperor, witness my hand, ALBERT, Cardinal of Mentz, High-chancellor.

"NICHOLAS ZWIL."

The safe-conduct contained in the letter was directed: "To the honourable, our well-beloved and pious Doctor Martin Luther, of the order of Augustines."

It began thus:

"We, Charles, the fifth of that name, by the grace of God Emperor elect of the Romans, always August, King of Spain, of the Two Sicilies, of Jerusalem, of Hungary, of Dalmatia, of Croatia, &c., Archduke of Austria, Duke of Burgundy, Count of Hapsburg, of Flanders, of the Tyrol," &c. &c.

Then the king of so many states, intimating that he had cited before him an Augustine monk named Luther, enjoined all princes, lords, magistrates, and others, to respect the safe-conduct which had been given him, under pain of the displeasure of the emperor and the empire.[1]

Thus did the emperor confer the titles of "well-beloved, honourable, and pious," on a man whom the head of the Church had excommunicated. This document had been thus drawn up, purposely to remove all distrust from the mind of Luther and his friends. Gaspard Sturm was commissioned to bear this message to the reformer, and accompany him to Worms. The elector, apprehending some outburst of public indignation, wrote on the 12th of March to the magistrates of Wittemberg to provide for the security of the emperor's officer, and to give him a guard, if it was judged necessary. The herald departed.

Thus were God's designs fulfilled. It was His will that this light, which he had kindled in the world, should be set upon a hill; and emperor, kings, and princes, immediately began to carry out His purpose without knowing it. It costs Him little to elevate what is lowliest. A single act of His power suffices to raise the humble native of Mansfeldt from an obscure cottage to the palaces in which kings were assembled. In His sight there is neither small nor great, and, in His good time, Charles and Luther meet.

But will Luther comply with this citation? His best friends were doubtful about it. "Doctor Martin has been summoned here," wrote the elector to his brother on the 25th March; "but I do know whether he will come. I cannot augur any good from it." Three weeks later (on the 16th of April), this excellent prince, seeing the danger increase, wrote again to Duke John: "Orders against Luther are placarded on the walls. The cardinals and bishops are attacking him very harshly:[2] God grant that all may turn out well! Would to God that I could procure him a favourable hearing!"

While these events were taking place at Worms and Wittemberg, the Papacy redoubled its attacks. On the 28th of March (which was the Thursday before Easter), Rome re-echoed with a solemn excommunication. It was the custom to publish at that season the terrible bull In Cœna Domini, which is a long series of maledictions. On that day the approaches to the temple in

---

[1] Tanquam perfido hæretico nulla sit servanda fides. Cochlœus, p. 28.
[2] Longa consultatio difficilisque disceptatio. Ibid.
[3] Cum autem grandis ubique per Germaniam fere totam excitata est....animorum commotio. Ibid.

[1] Lucas Cranach's Stammbuch, &c. herausgegeben v. Chr v. Mecheln. p. 12.
[2] Die Cardinäle und Bischöfe sind ihm hart zuwieder... Seckend. p. 365.

which the sovereign pontiff was to officiate were early occupied with the papal guards, and by a crowd of people that had flocked together from all parts of Italy to receive the benediction of the holy father. Branches of laurel and myrtle decorated the open space in front of the cathedral; tapers were lighted on the balcony of the temple, and there the remonstrance was elevated. On a sudden the air re-echoes with the loud pealing of bells; the pope, wearing his pontifical robes, and borne in an arm-chair, appears on the balcony; the people kneel down, all heads are uncovered, the colours are lowered, the soldiers ground their arms, and a solemn silence prevails. A few moments after, the pope slowly stretches out his hands, raises them towards heaven, and then as slowly bends them towards the earth, making the sign of the cross. Thrice he repeats this movement. Again the noise of bells reverberates through the air, proclaiming far and wide the benediction of the pontiff; some priests now hastily step forward, each holding a lighted taper in his hand : these they reverse, and after tossing them violently, dash them away, as if they were the flames of hell; the people are moved and agitated; and the words of malediction are hurled down from the roof of the temple. [1]

As soon as Luther was informed of this excommunication, he published its tenor, with a few remarks written in that cutting style of which he was so great a master. Although this publication did not appear till sometime afterwards, we will insert in this place a few of its most striking features. We shall hear the high-priest of Christendom on the balcony of the cathedral, and the Wittemberg monk answering him from the farthest part of Germany.[2]

There is something characteristic in the contrast of these two voices.

THE POPE.—" Leo, bishop"......

LUTHER.—" Bishop!......yes, as the wolf is a shepherd : for the bishop should exhort according to the doctrine of salvation, and not vomit forth imprecations and maledictions."......

THE POPE.—" Servant of all the servants of God"......

LUTHER.—" At night, when we are drunk; but in the morning, our name is Leo, lord of all lords."

THE POPE.—" The Roman bishops, our predecessors, have been accustomed on this festival to employ the arms of righteousness......

LUTHER.—" Which, according to your account, are excommunication and anathema; but, according to Saint Paul, long-suffering, kindness, and love." (2 Cor. vi. 6, 7.)

[1] This ceremony is described in various works; among others in the " *Tagebuch einer Reise durch Deutschland und Italien.* Berlin, 1817, iv. 94. The principal features are of earlier date than the 16th century.
[2] For the bull and Luther's commentary, see *Die Bulla vom Abendfressen.* L. Opp. (L.) xviii. 1.

THE POPE.—" According to the duties of the apostolic office, and to maintain the purity of the christian faith"......

LUTHER.—" That is to say, the temporal possessions of the pope."

THE POPE.—" And its unity, which consists in the union of the members with Christ, their head,.....and with his vicar"....

LUTHER.—" For Christ is not sufficient: we must have another besides."

THE POPE.—" To preserve the holy communion of believers, we follow the ancient custom, and excommunicate and curse, in the name of Almighty God, the Father".....

LUTHER.—" Of whom it is said: *God sent not his Son into the world to condemn the world."* (John iii. 17.)

THE POPE.—" The Son, and the Holy Ghost, and according to the power of the apostles Peter and Paul......and our own" ...

LUTHER.—" *Our own!* says the ravenous wolf, as if the power of God was too weak without him."

THE POPE.—" We curse all heretics,— Garasi,[1] Patarins, Poor Men of Lyons, Arnoldists, Speronists, Passageni, Wickliffites, Hussites, Fratricelli"......

LUTHER.—" For they desired to possess the Holy Scriptures, and required the pope to be sober and preach the Word of God."

THE POPE.—" And Martin Luther, recently condemned by us for a similar heresy, as well as all his adherents, and all those whosoever they may be, who show him any countenance."......

LUTHER.—" I thank thee, most gracious pontiff, for condemning me along with all these Christians! It is very honourable for me to have my name proclaimed at Rome on a day of festival, in so glorious a manner, that it may run through the world in conjunction with the names of these humble confessors of Jesus Christ."

THE POPE.—" In like manner, we excommunicate and curse all pirates and corsairs"......

LUTHER.—" Who can be a greater corsair and pirate than he that robs souls, imprisons them, and puts them to death ? "

THE POPE.—" Particularly those who navigate our seas"......

LUTHER.—" Our seas!......Saint Peter, *our* predecessor, said : *Silver and gold have I none* (Acts iii. 6); and Jesus Christ said: *The kings of the Gentiles exercise lordship over them; but ye shall not be so* (Luke xxii. 25). But if a waggon filled with hay must give place on the road to a drunken man, how much more must Saint Peter and Christ himself give way to the pope!"

THE POPE.—" In like manner we excommunicate and curse all those who falsify our bulls and our apostolical letters"......

LUTHER.—" But God's letters, the Holy Scriptures, all the world may condemn and burn."

[1] This name has been altered; read *Gasari* or *Cathari.*

THE POPE.—" In like manner we excommunicate and curse all those who intercept the provisions that are coming to the court of Rome"......

LUTHER.—" He snarls and snaps, like a dog that fears his bone will be taken from him."[1]

THE POPE.—" In like manner we condemn and curse all those who withhold any judiciary dues, fruits, tithes, or revenues, belonging to the clergy"......

LUTHER.—" For Christ has said : *If any man will sue thee at the law, and take away thy coat, let him have thy cloak also* (Matt. v. 40), and this is our commentary."

THE POPE.—" Whatever be their station, dignity, order, power, or rank ; were they even bishops or kings"......

LUTHER.—" *For there shall be false teachers among you, who despise dominion and speak evil of dignities*, says Scripture." (Jude 8.)

THE POPE.—" In like manner we condemn and curse all those who, in any manner whatsoever, do prejudice to the city of Rome, the kingdom of Sicily, the islands Sardinia and Corsica, the patrimony of St. Peter in Tuscany, the duchy of Spoleto, the marquisate of Ancona, the Campagna, the cities of Ferrara and Benevento, and all other cities or countries belonging to the Church of Rome."

LUTHER.—" O Peter ! thou poor fisherman ! whence didst thou get Rome and all these kingdoms ? all hail, Peter ! king of Sicily !......and fisherman at Bethsaida ! "

THE POPE.—" We excommunicate and curse all chancellors, councillors, parliaments, procurators, governors, officials, bishops, and others, who oppose our letters of exhortation, invitation, prohibition, mediation, execution."......

LUTHER.—" For the holy see desires only to live in idleness, in magnificence, and debauchery ; to command, to intimidate, to deceive, to lie, to dishonour, to seduce, and commit every kind of wickedness in peace and security......

" Oh Lord, arise ! it is not as the papists pretend ; thou hast not forsaken us ; thou hast not turned away thine eyes from us ! "

Thus spoke Leo at Rome and Luther at Wittemberg.

The pontiff having ended these maledictions, the parchment on which they were written was torn in pieces, and the fragments scattered among the people. Immediately the crowd began to be violently agitated, each one rushing forward and endeavouring to seize a scrap of this terrible bull. These were the holy relics that the Papacy offered to its faithful adherents on the eve of the great day of grace and expiation. The multitude soon dispersed, and the neighbourhood of the cathedral became deserted and

silent as before. Let us now return to Wittemberg.

CHAPTER VI.

Luther's Courage—Bugenhagen at Wittemberg—Persecutions in Pomerania—Melancthon desires to accompany Luther—Amsdorff, Schurff and Suaven—Hütten to Charles V.

IT was now the 24th of March. At last the imperial herald had passed the gate of the city in which Luther resided. Gaspard Sturm waited upon the doctor, and delivered the citation from Charles V. What a serious and solemn moment for the reformer ! All his friends were in consternation. No prince, without excepting Frederick the Wise, had declared for him. The knights, it is true, had given utterance to their threats ; but them the powerful Charles despised. Luther, however, was not discomposed. " The papists," said he,· on seeing the anguish of his friends, " do not desire my coming to Worms, but my condemnation and my death.[1] It matters not ! Pray, not for me, but for the Word of God. Before my blood has grown cold, thousands of men in the whole world will have become responsible for having shed it ! The most holy adversary of Christ, the father, the master, the generalissimo of murderers, insists on its being shed. So be it ! Let God's will be done ! Christ will give me his Spirit to overcome these ministers of error. I despise them during my life ; I shall triumph over them by my death.[2] They are busy at Worms about compelling me to retract ; and this shall be my retraction : I said formerly that the pope was Christ's vicar ; now I assert that he is our Lord's adversary, and the devil's apostle.' And when he was apprized that all the pulpits of the Franciscans and Dominicans resounded with imprecations and maledictions against him : " Oh ! what deep joy do I feel ! " exclaimed he.[3] He knew that he had done God's will, and that God was with him ; why then should he not set out with courage ? Such purity of intention, such liberty of conscience, is a hidden but incalculable support, that never fails the servant of God, and renders him more invulnerable than if protected by coats of mail and armed hosts.

At this time there arrived at Wittemberg a man who, like Melancthon, was destined to be Luther's friend all his life, and to comfort him at the moment of his departure.[4] This was a priest named Bugenhagen, thirty-

---

[1] Gleich wie ein Hund ums Beines willen. L. Opp. (L.) xviii. 12.

[1] Damnatum et perditum. L. Epp. i. 556.
[2] Ut hos Satanæ ministros et contemnam vivens et vincam moriens. Ibid. 579.
[3] Quod mire quam gaudeam. Ibid. 567.
[4] Venit Wittembergam paulo ante iter Lutheri ad comitia Wormatiæ indicta. Melch. Adami Vita Bugenhagii, p. 314

six years of age, who had fled from the severities which the Bishop of Camin and Prince Bogislas of Pomerania exercised on the friends of the Gospel, whether ecclesiastics, citizens, or men of letters.[1] Sprung from a senatorial family, and born at Wollin in Pomerania (whence he is commonly called Pomeranus), Bugenhagen had been teaching at Treptow from the age of twenty years. The young eagerly crowded around him; the nobles and the learned emulated each other in courting his society. He diligently studied the Holy Scriptures, praying God to enlighten him.[2] One day towards the end of December 1520, Luther's book on the *Captivity of Babylon* was put into his hands as he sat at supper with several of his friends. "Since the death of Christ," said he, after running his eye over the pages, "many heretics have infested the Church; but never yet has there existed such a pest as the author of this work." Having taken the book home and perused it two or three times, all his opinions were changed; truths quite new to him presented themselves to his mind; and on returning some days after to his colleagues, he said, "The whole world is lying in the thickest darkness. This man alone sees the light."[3] Several priests, a deacon, and the abbot himself, received the pure doctrine of salvation, and in a short time, by the power of their preaching, they led their hearers (says an historian) back from human superstitions to the sole and effectual merits of Jesus Christ.[4] Upon this a persecution broke out. Already the prisons re-echoed with the groans of many individuals. Bugenhagen fled from his enemies and arrived at Wittemberg. "He is suffering for love to the Gospel," wrote Melancthon to the elector's chaplain. "Whither could he fly, but to our ἄσυλον (asylum), and to the protection of our prince?"[5]

But no one welcomed Bugenhagen with greater joy than Luther. It was agreed between them, that immediately after the departure of the reformer, Bugenhagen should begin to lecture on the Psalms. It was thus Divine Providence led this able man to supply in some measure the place of him whom Wittemberg was about to lose. A year later, Bugenhagen was placed at the head of the Church in this city, over which he presided thirty-six years. Luther styled him in an especial manner *The Pastor*.

Luther was about to depart. His friends, in alarm, thought that if God did not interpose in a miraculous manner, he was going to certain death. Melancthon, far removed from his native town, was attached to Luther

with all the affection of a susceptible heart. "Luther," said he, "supplies the place of all my friends; he is greater and more admirable for me than I can dare express. You know how Alcibiades admired Socrates;[1] but I admire Luther after another and in a christian fashion." He then added these beautiful and sublime words: "Every time I contemplate Luther, I find him constantly greater than himself."[2] Melancthon desired to accompany Luther in his dangers; but their common friends, and no doubt the doctor himself, opposed his wishes. Ought not Philip to fill his friend's place? and if the latter never returned, who then would there be to direct the work of the Reformation? "Would to God," said Melancthon, resigned, yet disappointed, "that he had allowed me to go with him."[3]

The impetuous Amsdorff immediately declared that he would accompany the doctor. His strong mind found pleasure in confronting danger. His boldness permitted him to appear fearlessly before an assembly of kings. The elector had invited to Wittemberg, as professor of jurisprudence, Jerome Schurff, the son of a physician at St. Gall, a celebrated man, of gentle manners, and very intimate with Luther. "He has not yet been able to make up his mind," said Luther, to pronounce sentence of death on a single malefactor."[4] This timid man, however, desired to assist the doctor by his advice in this perilous journey. A young Danish student, Peter Suaven, who resided with Melancthon, and who afterwards became celebrated by his evangelical labours in Pomerania and Denmark, likewise declared that he would accompany his master. The youth of the schools were also to have their representative at the side of the champion of truth.

Germany was moved at the sight of the perils that menaced the representative of her people. She found a suitable voice to give utterance to her fears. Ulrich of Hütten shuddered at the thought of the blow about to be inflicted on his country. On the 1st of April, he wrote to Charles V. himself: "Most excellent emperor," said he, "you are on the point of destroying us, and yourself with us. What is proposed to be done in this affair of Luther's, except to ruin our liberty, and to crush your power? In the whole extent of the empire there is not a single upright man that does not feel the deepest interest in this matter.[5] The priests alone set themselves against Luther, because he has opposed their enormous power, their scandalous luxury, and their depraved lives;

[1] Sacerdotes, cives et scholasticos in vincula conjecit. Mel. Adami Vita Bugenhagii, p. 313.
[2] Precesque adjunxit, quibus divinitus se regi ac doceri petivit. Ibid. p. 312.
[3] In Cimmeriis tenebris versatur: hic vir unus et solus verum videt. Ibid. p. 313.
[4] A superstitionibus ad unicum Christi meritum traducere. Ibid.
[5] Corp. Ref. i. 361.

[1] Alcibiades was convinced that the society of Socrates was a support the gods had given him for his instruction and security. Plutarch—Alcibiades.
[2] Quem quoties contemplor, se ipso subinde majorem judico. Corp. Ref. i. 264.
[3] Utinam licuisset mihi una proficisci. Ibid. 365.
[4] L. Opp. (W.) xxii. 2067. 1819.
[5] Neque enim quam lata est Germania, ulli boni sunt, &c. L. Opp. Lat. ii. 182, verso.

and because he has pleaded, in behalf of Christ's doctrine, for the liberty of our country, and for purity of morals.

"O emperor! discard from your presence these Roman ambassadors, bishops, and cardinals, who desire to prevent all reformation. Did you not observe the sorrow of the people as they saw you arrive on the banks of the Rhine, surrounded by these red-hatted gentry......and by a band of priests, instead of a troop of valiant warriors ?......

"Do not surrender your sovereign majesty to those who desire to trample it under foot! Have pity on us! Do not drag yourself and the whole nation into one common destruction. Lead us into the midst of the greatest dangers, under the weapons of your soldiers, to the canon's mouth;[1] let all nations conspire against us; let every army assail us, so that we can show our valour in the light of day, rather than that we should be thus vanquished and enslaved obscurely and stealthily, like women, without arms and unresisting......Alas! we had hoped that you would deliver us from the Roman yoke, and overthrow the tyranny of the pontiff. God grant that the future may be better than these beginnings!

"All Germany falls prostrate at your feet;[2] with tears we entreat and implore your help, your compassion, your faithfulness; and by the holy memory of those Germans who, when all the world was subject to Rome, did not bow their heads before that haughty city, we conjure you to save us, to restore us to ourselves, to deliver us from bondage, and take revenge upon our tyrants!"

Thus, by the mouth of this knight, spoke the German nation to Charles V. The emperor paid no attention to this epistle, and probably cast it disdainfully to one of his secretaries. He was a Fleming, and not a German. His personal aggrandizement, and not the liberty and glory of the empire, was the object of all his desires.

CHAPTER VII.

Departure for the Diet of Worms—Luther's Farewell—His Condemnation is posted up—Cavalcade near Erfurth—Meeting between Jonas and Luther—Luther in his former Convent—Luther preaches at Erfurth—Incident—Faith and Works—Concourse of People and Luther's Courage—Luther's Letter to Spalatin—Stay at Frankfort—Fears at Worms—Plan of the Imperialists—Luther's Firmness.

It was now the 2d of April, and Luther had to take leave of his friends. After apprizing Lange, by a note, that he would spend the Thursday or Friday following at Erfurth,[3] he

bade farewell to his colleagues. Turning to Melancthon, he said with an agitated voice, "My dear brother, if I do not return, and should my enemies put me to death, continue to teach, and stand fast in the truth. Labour in my stead, since I shall no longer be able to labour for myself. If you survive, my death will be of little consequence." Then, committing his soul to the hands of Him who is faithful, Luther got into the car and quitted Wittemberg. The town-council had provided him with a modest conveyance, covered with an awning, which the travellers could set up or remove at pleasure. The imperial herald, wearing his robe of office, and carrying the imperial eagle, rode on horseback in front, attended by his servant. Next came Luther, Schurff, Amsdorff, and Suaven, in the car. The friends of the Gospel and the citizens of Wittemberg were deeply agitated,—and, invoking God's aid, burst into tears. Thus Luther began his journey.

He soon discovered that gloomy presentiments filled the hearts of all he met. At Leipsic no respect was shown him, and the magistrates merely presented him with the customary cup of wine. At Naumburg he met a priest, probably J. Langer, a man of stern zeal, who carefully preserved in his study a portrait of the famous Jerome Savonarola (who was burnt at Florence in 1498 by order of Pope Alexander VI.), as a martyr to freedom and morality, as well as a confessor of the evangelical truth. Having taken down the portrait of the Italian martyr, the priest approached Luther, and held it out to him in silence. The latter understood what this mute representation was intended to announce, but his intrepid soul remained firm. "It is Satan," said he, "that would prevent, by these terrors, the confession of the truth in the assembly of princes, for he foresees the blow it would inflict upon his kingdom."[1] "Stand firm in the truth thou hast proclaimed," said the priest solemnly, "and God will as firmly stand by thee!"[2]

After passing the night at Naumburg, where he had been hospitably entertained by the burgomaster, Luther arrived the next evening at Weimar. He had hardly been a minute in the town, when he heard loud cries in every direction: it was the publication of his condemnation. "Look there!" said the herald. He turned his eyes, and with astonishment saw the imperial messengers going from street to street, every where posting up the emperor's edict commanding his writings to be deposited with the magistrates. Luther doubted not that this unseasonable display of severity was intended to frighten him from undertaking the journey, so that he might be condemned as having refused to appear. "Well, doctor! will you

---

[1] Duc nos in manifestum potius periculum, duc in ferrum, duc in ignes. L. Opp. Lat. ii. 183.
[2] Omnem nunc Germaniam quasi ad genua provolutam :ibi. Ibid. 184.
[3] L. Epp. i. 580.

[1] Terrorem hunc a Sathana sibi dixit afferri....M. Adami, p. 117.
[2] E: wolle bey der erkandten Wahrheyt mit breytem Fuss a:shalten....Mathesius Historien, p. 23. We quote the first edition of 1566.

proceed?" asked the imperial herald in alarm. "Yes!" replied Luther; "although interdicted in every city, I shall go on! I rely upon the emperor's safe-conduct."

At Weimar, Luther had an audience with Duke John, brother to the Elector of Saxony, who resided there. The prince invited him to preach, and the reformer consented. Words of life flowed from the doctor's agitated heart. A Franciscan monk, who heard him, by name John Voït, the friend of Frederick Myconius, was then converted to the evangelical doctrine. He left his convent two years after, and somewhat later became professor of theology at Wittemberg. The duke furnished Luther with the money necessary for his journey.

From Weimar the reformer proceeded to Erfurth. This was the city of his youth. Here he hoped to meet his friend Lange, if, as he had written to him, he might enter the city without danger.[1] When about three or four leagues from the city, near the village of Nora, he perceived a troop of horsemen approaching in the distance. Were they friends or enemies? In a short time Crotus, rector of the university, Eobanus Hesse, the friend of Melancthon, and whom Luther styled the prince of poets, Euricius Cordus, John Draco, and others, to the number of forty, senators, members of the university, and burghers, greeted him with acclamations. A multitude of the inhabitants of Erfurth thronged the road, and gave utterance to their joy. All were eager to see the man who had dared to declare war against the pope.

A man about twenty-eight years old, by name Justus Jonas, had outstripped the cavalcade.[2] Jonas, after studying the law at Erfurth, had been appointed rector of that university in 1519. Receiving the light of the Gospel, which was shining forth in every direction, he had entertained the desire of becoming a theologian. "I think," wrote Erasmus to him, "that God has elected you as an instrument to make known the glory of his son Jesus."[3] All his thoughts were turned towards Wittemberg and Luther. Some years before, when he was as yet a law-student, Jonas, who was a man of active and enterprising spirit, had set out on foot in company with a few friends, and had crossed forests infested with robbers, and cities devastated by the plague, in order to visit Erasmus, who was then at Brussels. Shall he now hesitate to confront other dangers by accompanying the reformer to Worms? He earnestly begged the favour to be granted him, and Luther consented. Thus met these two doctors, who were to labour together all their lives in the task of renovating the

Church. Divine Providence gathered round Luther men who were destined to be the light of Germany: Melancthon, Amsdorff, Bugenhagen, and Jonas. On his return from Worms, Jonas was elected provost of the Church of Wittemberg, and doctor of divinity. "Jonas," said Luther, "is a man whose life is worth purchasing at a large price, in order to retain him on earth."[1] No preacher ever surpassed him in his power of captivating his hearers.—"Pomeranus is a critic," said Melancthon; "I am a dialectician, Jonas is an orator. Words flow from his lips with admirable beauty, and his eloquence is full of energy. But Luther surpasses us all."[2] It appears that about this time a friend of Luther's childhood, and also one of his brothers, increased the number of his escort.

The deputation from Erfurth had turned their horses' heads. Luther's carriage entered within the walls of the city, surrounded by horsemen and pedestrians. At the gate, in the public places, in the streets where the poor monk had so often begged his bread, the crowd of spectators was immense. Luther alighted at the convent of the Augustines, where the Gospel had first given consolation to his heart. Lange joyfully received him; Usingen, and some of the elder fathers, showed him much coldness. There was a great desire to hear him preach; the pulpit had been forbidden him, but the herald, sharing the enthusiasm of those about him, gave his consent.

On the Sunday after Easter the church of the Augustines of Erfurth was filled to overflowing. This friar, who had been accustomed in former times to unclose the doors and sweep out the church, went up into the pulpit, and opening the Bible, read these words:—*Peace be unto you. And when he had so said, he showed unto them his hands and his side* (John xx. 19, 20.) "Philosophers, doctors, and writers," said he, "have endeavoured to teach men the way to obtain everlasting life, and they have not succeeded. I will now tell it to you."

This has been the great question in every age; accordingly Luther's hearers redoubled their attention.

"There are two kinds of works," continued the reformer: "works not of ourselves, and these are good; our own works, and they are of little worth. One man builds a church: another goes on a pilgrimage to St. Jago of Compostella or St. Peter's; a third fasts, prays, takes the cowl, and goes barefoot; another does something else. All these works are nothingness, and will come to nought; for our own works have no virtue in them. But I am now going to tell you what is the true work. God has raised one

[1] Nisi periculum sit Erfordiam ingredi. L. Epp. i. 580.
[2] Hos inter, qui nos prævenerat, ibat Jonas,
Ille decus nostri, primaque fama Chori.
Eob. Hessi Elegia Secunda.
[3] Velut organum quoddam electum ad illustrandam filii tui Jesu gloriam. Erasm. Epp. v. 27.

[1] Vir est quem oportuit multo pretio emptum et servatum in terra. Weismann, i. 1436.
[2] Pomeranus est grammaticus, ego sum dialecticus, Jonas est orator......Lutherus vero nobis omnibus antecellit. Knapp Narrat. de J. Jona, p. 581.

man from the dead, the Lord Jesus Christ, that He might destroy death, extirpate sin, and shut the gates of hell. This is the work of salvation. The devil thought he had the Lord in his power, when he saw Him hanging between two thieves, suffering the most disgraceful martyrdom, accursed of God and of men......But the Godhead displayed its power, and destroyed death, sin, and hell......
" Christ has vanquished! this is the joyful news! and we are saved by his work, and not by our own. The pope says differently: but I affirm that the holy mother of God herself was saved, neither by her virginity, nor by her maternity, nor by her purity, nor by her works, but solely by the instrumentality of faith and the works of God."

While Luther was speaking, a sudden noise was heard; one of the galleries cracked, and it was feared that it would break down under the pressure of the crowd. This incident occasioned a great disturbance in the congregation. Some ran out from their places; others stood motionless through fright. The preacher stopped a moment, and then stretching out his hand, exclaimed with a loud voice : " Fear nothing! there is no danger : it is thus the devil seeks to hinder me from proclaiming the Gospel, but he will not succeed." [1] At these words, those who were flying halted in astonishment and surprise; the assembly again became calm, and Luther, undisturbed by these efforts of the devil, continued thus: " You say a great deal about faith (you may perhaps reply to me): show us how we may obtain it. Well, I will teach you. Our Lord Jesus Christ said : *Peace be unto you! behold my hands,* that is to say, Behold, O man! it is I, I alone, who have taken away thy sin, and ransomed thee; and now thou hast peace, saith the Lord.

" I have not eaten of the fruit of the forbidden tree," resumed Luther, " nor have you; but we have all partaken of the sin that Adam has transmitted to us, and have gone astray. In like manner, I have not suffered on the cross, neither have you; but Christ has suffered for us; we are justified by God's work, and not by our own......I am (saith the Lord) thy righteousness and thy redemption.

" Let us believe in the Gospel and in the epistles of St. Paul, and not in the letters and decretals of the popes."

After proclaiming faith as the cause of the sinner's justification, Luther proclaims works as the consequence and manifestation of salvation.

" Since God has saved us," continues he, " let us so order our works that they may be acceptable to him. Art thou rich? let thy goods administer to the necessities of the poor! Art thou poor? let thy services be acceptable to the rich! If thy labour is

useful to thyself alone, the service that thou pretendest to render unto God is a lie." [1]

In the whole of this sermon there is not a word about himself; not a single allusion to the circumstances in which he is placed : nothing about Worms, or Charles, or the nuncios; he preaches Christ, and Christ only. At this moment, when the eyes of all the world are upon him, he has no thought of himself : this stamps him as a true servant of God.

Luther departed from Erfurth, and passed through Gotha, where he preached another sermon. Myconius adds, that as the people were leaving the church, the devil threw down from the pediment some stones that had not moved for two hundred years. The doctor slept at the convent of the Benedictines at Reinhardsbrunn, and from thence proceeded to Eisenach, where he felt indisposed. Amsdorff, Jonas, Schurff, and all his friends were alarmed. He was bled; they tended him with the most affectionate anxiety, and John Oswald, the *schultheiss* of the town, brought him a cordial. Luther having drunk a portion fell asleep, and, reinvigorated by this repose he was enabled to continue his journey on the following morning.

His progress resembled that of a victorious general. The people gazed with emotion on this daring man, who was going to lay his head at the feet of the emperor and the empire.[2] An immense crowd flocked eagerly around him.[3] " Ah!" said some, " there are so many bishops and cardinals at Worms !......They will burn you, and reduce your body to ashes, as they did with John Huss." But nothing frightened the monk. " Though they should kindle a fire," said he, " all the way from Worms to Wittemberg, the flames of which reached to heaven, I would walk through it in the name of the Lord,—I would appear before them,—I would enter the jaws of this Behemoth, and break his teeth, confessing the Lord Jesus Christ." [4]

One day, just as he had entered an inn, and the crowd was pressing around him as usual, an officer advanced and said: " Are you the man that has undertaken to reform the papacy? How can you hope to succeed?" —" Yes," replied Luther, " I am the man. I trust in God Almighty, whose Word and commandment I have before me." The officer was touched, and looking at him with a milder air, said: " My dear friend, what you say is a great matter. I am the servant of Charles, but your Master is greater than mine. He will aid and preserve you." [5] Such was the impression produced by Luther.

[1] Agnosco insidias, hostis acerbe, tuas. Hessi Eleg. iii.

[1] L. Opp. (L.) xii. 485.
[2] Quocunque iter faciebant, frequens erat concursus hominum, videndi Lutheri studio. Cochlœus, p. 29.
[3] Iter facienti occurrebant populi. Pallav. Hist. C. Tr. i. 114.
[4] Ein Feuer das bis an den Himmel reichte....Keil, i. 98.
[5] Nun habt Ihr einen grössern Herrn, denn ich. Ibid. 99.

Even his enemies were struck at the sight of the multitudes that thronged around him; but they depicted his journey in far different colours.[1] The doctor arrived at Frankfort on Sunday the 14th of April.

Already the news of Luther's journey had reached Worms. The friends of the pope had thought that he would not obey the emperor's summons. Albert, cardinal-archbishop of Mentz would have given any thing to stop him on the road. New intrigues were put in motion to attain this result.

As soon as Luther arrived in Frankfort, he took some repose, and afterwards gave intelligence of his approach to Spalatin, who was then at Worms with the elector. This was the only letter he wrote during his journey. "I am coming," said he, "although Satan endeavoured to stop me on the road by sickness. Since I left Eisenach I have been in a feeble state, and am still as I never was before. I learn that Charles has published an edict to frighten me. But Christ lives, and I shall enter Worms in despite of all the gates of hell, and of the powers of the air.[2] Have the goodness, therefore, to prepare a lodging for me."

The next day Luther went to visit the school of the learned William Nesse, a celebrated geographer of that period. "Apply to the study of the Bible, and to the investigation of truth," said he to the pupils. And then putting his right hand on one of the children, and his left upon another, he pronounced a benediction on the whole school.

If Luther blessed the young, he was also the hope of the aged. Catherine of Holzhausen, a widow far advanced in years, and who served God, approached him and said: "My parents told me that God would raise up a man who should oppose the papal vanities and preserve His Word. I hope thou art that man, and I pray for the grace and Holy Spirit of God upon thy work."[3]

These were far from being the general sentiments in Frankfort. John Cochlœus, dean of the church of Our Lady, was one of the most devoted partizans of the papacy. He could not repress his apprehensions when he saw Luther pass through Frankfort on his road to Worms. He thought that the Church had need of devoted champions. It is true no one had summoned him; but that mattered not. Luther had scarcely quitted the city, when Cochlœus followed him, ready (said he) to sacrifice his life in defence of the honour of the Church.[4]

The alarm was universal in the camp of the pope's friends. The heresiarch was arriving; every day and every hour brought him nearer to Worms. If he entered, all might perhaps be lost. Archbishop Albert, the confessor Glapio, and the politicians who surrounded the emperor, were confounded. How could they hinder this monk from coming? To carry him off by force was impossible, for he had Charles's safe-conduct. Stratagem alone could stop him. These artful men immediately conceived the following plan. The emperor's confessor and his head chamberlain, Paul of Amsdorff, hastily quitted Worms.[1] They directed their course towards the castle of Ebernburg, about ten leagues from the city, the residence of Francis of Sickingen,—that knight who had offered an asylum to Luther. Bucer, a youthful Dominican, chaplain to the elector-palatine, and who had been converted to the evangelical doctrine by the disputation at Heidelberg,[2] had taken refuge in this "resting-place of the righteous." The knight, who did not understand much about religious matters, was easily deceived, and the character of the palatine chaplain facilitated the confessor's designs. In fact, Bucer was a man of pacific character. Making a distinction between fundamental and secondary points, he thought that the latter might be given up for the sake of unity and peace.[3]

The chamberlain and Charles's confessor began their attack. They gave Sickingen and Bucer to understand, that Luther was lost if he entered Worms. They declared that the emperor was ready to send a few learned men to Ebernburg to confer with the doctor. "Both parties," said they to the knight, "will place themselves under your protection." "We agree with Luther on all essential points," said they to Bucer; "it is now a question of merely secondary matters. and you shall mediate between us." The knight and the doctor were staggered. The confessor and the chamberlain continued: "Luther's invitation must proceed from you." said they to Sickingen, "and Bucer shall carry it to him."[4] Everything was arranged according to their wishes. Only let the too credulous Luther go to Ebernburg, his safe-conduct will soon have expired, and then who shall defend him?

Luther had arrived at Oppenheim. His safe-conduct was available for only three days more. He saw a troop of horsemen approaching him, and at their head soon recognised Bucer, with whom he had held such intimate conversations at Heidelberg.[5]

---

[1] In diversoriis multa propinatio, læta compotatio, musices quoque gaudia: adeo ut Lutherus ipse alicubi sonora testudine ludens omnium in se oculos converteret, velut Orpheus quidam, sed rasus adhuc et cucullatus, eoque mirabilior. Cochlœus, p. 29. In the taverns there was good cheer, joyous potations, and even the charms of music: so that Luther, playing upon the harp, drew all eyes upon himself, like a very Orpheus, and the more wonderful as he was shorn and wore a cowl.
[2] Intrabimus Wormatiam, invitis omnibus portis inferni et potentatibus aeris. L. Opp. i. 987.
[3] Ich hoffe dass du der Verheissene....Cypr. Hilar. Ev. p. 608.
[4] Lutherum illac transeuntem subsequutus, ut pro honore

Ecclesiæ vitam suam....exponeret. Cochlœus, p. 36. This is the writer whom we quote so frequently.
[1] Dass der Keyser seinen Beichtvater und Ihrer Majest. Ober-Kammerling, zu Sickingen schickt. L. Opp. xvii. 587.
[2] See vol. i. p. 120.
[3] Condocefaciebat τὰ ἀναγκαῖα a probabilibus distinguere, ut scirent quæ retinenda....M. Adami Vita Buceri. p. 223.
[4] Dass er sollte den Luther zu sich fodern. L. Opp. xvii. 587,
[5] Da kam Bucer zu, mit etlichen Reutern. Ibid.

" These cavaliers belong to Francis of Sickingen," said Bucer, after the first interchange of friendship; " he has sent me to conduct you to his castle.[1] The emperor's confessor desires to have an interview with you. His influence over Charles is unlimited; everything may yet be arranged. But beware of Aleander!" Jonas, Schurff, and Amsdorff knew not what to think. Bucer was pressing; but Luther felt no hesitation. " I shall continue my journey," replied he to Bucer; " and if the emperor's confessor has anything to say to me, he will find me at Worms. I go whither I am summoned."

In the mean while, Spalatin himself began to be anxious and to fear. Surrounded at Worms by the enemies of the Reformation, he heard it said that the safe-conduct of a heretic ought not to be respected. He became alarmed for his friend. At the moment when the latter was approaching the city, a messenger appeared before him, with this advice from the chaplain: " Do not enter Worms!" And this from his best friend—the elector's confidant—from Spalatin himself!......But Luther, undismayed, turned his eyes on the messenger, and replied: " Go and tell your master, that even should there be as many devils in Worms as tiles on the house-tops, still I would enter it!"[2] Never, perhaps, has Luther been so sublime! The messenger returned to Worms with this astounding answer. " I was then undaunted," said Luther, a few days before his death; " I feared nothing. God can indeed render a man intrepid at any time; but I know not whether I should now have so much liberty and joy."—" When our cause is good," adds his disciple Mathesius, " the heart expands, and gives courage and energy to evangelists as well as to soldiers." [3]

CHAPTER VIII.

Entry into Worms—Death-Song—Charles's Council—Capito and the Temporizers—Luther's numerous Visiters—Citation—Hütten to Luther—Luther proceeds to the Diet—Saving of Freundsberg—Imposing Assembly—The Chancellor's Speech—Luther's Reply—His Discretion—Saying of Charles V.—Alarm—Triumph—Luther's Firmness—Violence of the Spaniards—Advice—Luther's Struggles and Prayer—Strength of the Reformation—His Vow to the Scriptures—The Court of the Diet—Luther's Speech—Three Classes of Writings—He requires Proof of his Errors—Serious Warnings—He repeats his Speech in Latin—Here I stand: I can say no more—The Weakness of God stronger than Man—A new Attempt—Victory.

At length, on the morning of the 16th of April, Luther discovered the walls of the ancient city. All were expecting him. One absorbing thought prevailed in Worms.

Some young nobles, Bernard of Hirschfeldt, Albert of Lindenau, with six knights and other gentlemen in the train of the princes, to the number of a hundred (if we may believe Pallavicini), unable to restrain their impatience, rode out on horseback to meet him, and surrounded him, to form an escort at the moment of his entrance. He drew near. Before him pranced the imperial herald, in full costume. Luther came next in his modest car. Jonas followed him on horseback, and the cavaliers were on both sides of him. A great crowd was waiting for him at the gates. It was near mid-day when he passed those walls, from which so many persons had predicted he would never come forth alive. Every one was at table; but as soon as the watchman on the tower of the cathedral sounded his trumpet, all ran into the streets to see the monk. Luther was now in Worms.

Two thousand persons accompanied him through the streets of the city. The citizens eagerly pressed forward to see him: every moment the crowd was increasing. It was much greater than at the public entry of the emperor. On a sudden, says an historian, a man dressed in a singular costume, and bearing a large cross, such as is employed in funeral processions, made way through the crowd, advanced towards Luther, and then with a loud voice, and in that plaintive, measured tone in which mass is said for the repose of the soul, he sang these words, as if he were uttering them from the abode of the dead :—

> Advenisti, O desiderabilis!
> Quem expectabamus in tenebris![1]

Thus a *requiem* was Luther's welcome to Worms. It was the court-fool of one of the dukes of Bavaria, who, if the story be true, gave Luther one of those warnings, replete at once with sagacity and irony, of which the history of these individuals furnishes so many examples. But the shouts of the multitude soon drowned the *De Profundis* of the cross-bearer. The procession made its way with difficulty through the crowd. At last, the herald of the empire stopped before the hotel of the knights of Rhodes. There resided the two councillors of the elector, Frederick of Thun and Philip of Feilitsch, as well as the marshal of the empire, Ulrich of Pappenheim. Luther alighted from his car, and said as he touched the ground: " God will be my defence."[2]—" I entered Worms in a covered waggon, and in my monk's gown," said he at a later period. " All the people came out into the streets to get a sight of Friar Martin."[3]

The news of his arrival filled both the Elector of Saxony and Aleander with alarm.

---

[1] Und wollte mir überreden zu Sickingen gen Ebernburg zu kommen. L. Opp. xvii. 587.
[2] Wenn so viel Teufel zu Worms wären, als Ziegel auf den Dächern noch wollt ich hinein. Ibid.
[3] So wächst das Herz im Leibe....Math. p. 24.

[1] At last thou'rt come, long looked-for one, whom we have waited for in the darkness of the grave. M. Adami Vita Lutheri, p. 118.
[2] Deus stabit pro me. Pallav. i. 114.
[3] L. Opp. xvii. 587.

The young and graceful Archbishop Albert, who kept a middle position between the two parties, was confounded at such boldness. " If I had possessed no more courage than he," said Luther, " it is true they would never have seen me at Worms."

Charles V. immediately summoned his council. The emperor's privy-councillors hastily repaired to the palace, for the alarm had reached them also. " Luther is come," said Charles; " what must we do?"

Modo, bishop of Palermo, and chancellor of Flanders, replied, if we may credit the testimony of Luther himself: " We have long consulted on this matter. Let your imperial majesty get rid of this man at once. Did not Sigismund cause John Huss to be burnt? We are not bound either to give or to observe the safe-conduct of a heretic."[1]— " No!" said Charles, " we must keep our promise." They submitted, therefore, to the reformer's appearance before the diet.

While the councils of the great were thus agitated on account of Luther, there were many persons in Worms who were delighted at the opportunity of at length beholding this illustrious servant of God. Capito, chaplain and councillor to the Archbishop of Mentz, was the foremost among them. This remarkable man, who, shortly before, had preached the Gospel in Switzerland with great freedom,[2] thought it becoming the station he then filled to act in a manner which led to his being accused of cowardice by the Evangelicals, and of dissimulation by the Romanists.[3] Yet at Mentz he had proclaimed the doctrine of grace with much clearness. At the moment of his departure, he had succeeded in supplying his place by a young and zealous preacher named Hedio. The Word of God was not bound in that city, the ancient seat of the primacy of the German Church. The Gospel was listened to with eagerness; in vain did the monks endeavour to preach from the Holy Scriptures after their manner, and employ all the means in their power to check the impulse given to men's minds: they could not succeed.[4] But while proclaiming the new doctrine, Capito attempted to remain friendly with those who persecuted it. He flattered himself, as others did who shared in his opinions, that he might in this way be of great service to the Church. To judge by their talk, if Luther was not burnt, if all the Lutherans were not excommunicated, it was owing to Capito's influence with the Archbishop Albert.[5] Cochlœus, dean of Frankfort, who reached Worms about the same time as Luther, im-

mediately waited on Capito. The latter, who was, outwardly at least, on very friendly terms with Aleander, presented Cochlœus to him, thus serving as a link between the two greatest enemies of the reformer.[1] Capito no doubt thought he was advancing Christ's cause by all these temporizing expedients, but we cannot find that they led to any good result. The event almost always baffles these calculations of human wisdom, and proves that a decided course, while it is the most frank, is also the wisest.

Meantime, the crowd still continued round the hotel of Rhodes, where Luther had alighted. To some he was a prodigy of wisdom, to others a monster of iniquity. All the city longed to see him.[2] They allowed him, however, a few hours after his arrival to recruit his strength, and to converse with his most intimate friends. But as soon as the evening came, counts, barons, knights, gentlemen, ecclesiastics, and citizens, flocked about him. All, even his greatest enemies, were struck with the boldness of his manner, the joy that seemed to animate him, the power of his language, and that imposing elevation and enthusiasm which gave this simple monk an irresistible authority. But while some ascribed this grandeur to something divine, the friends of the pope loudly exclaimed that he was possessed by a devil.[3] Visiters rapidly succeeded each other, and this crowd of curious individuals kept Luther from his bed until a late hour of the night.

On the next morning, Wednesday the 17th of April, the hereditary marshal of the empire, Ulrich of Pappenheim, cited him to appear at four in the afternoon before his imperial majesty and the states of the empire. Luther received this message with profound respect.

Thus everything was arranged; he was about to stand for Jesus Christ before the most august assembly in the world. Encouragements were not wanting to him. The impetuous knight, Ulrich Hütten, was then in the castle of Ebernburg. Unable to visit Worms (for Leo X. had called upon Charles V. to send him bound hand and foot to Rome), he resolved at least to stretch out the hand of friendship to Luther; and on this very day (17th April) he wrote to him, adopting the language of a king of Israel:[4] " *The Lord hear thee in the day of trouble; the name of the God of Jacob defend thee. Send thee help from the sanctuary, and strengthen thee out of Zion. Grant thee according to thine own heart, and fulfil all thy counsel.* Dearly beloved Luther! my venerable father!......fear not, and stand firm. The counsel of the wicked has beset you, and they have opened

---

[1] Dass Ihre Majestät den Luther aufs erste beyseit thäte und umbringen liess.... L. Opp. xvii. 587.
[2] See below, Book viii.
[3] Astutia plusquam vulpina vehementer callidum....Lutherismum versutissime dissimulabat. Cochlœus, p. 36.
[4] Evangelium audiunt avidissime, Verbum Dei alligatum non est.... Caspar Hedio, Zw. Epp. p. 157.
[5] Lutherus in hoc districtu dudum esset combustus, Lutherani ἀσσυνάγωγαι, nisi Capito aliter persuasisset principi. Ibid. p. 148.

[1] Hic (Capito) illum (Cochlœum) insinuavit Hieronyme Aleandro, nuncio Leonis X. Cochlœus, p. 36.
[2] Eadem die tota civitas solicite confluxit. Pallav. i. 114.
[3] Nescio quid divinum suspicabantur; ex adverso alii, malo dæmone obsessam existimabant. Ibid.
[4] David in the 20th Psalm.

their mouths against you like roaring lions. But the Lord will arise against the unrighteous, and put them to confusion. Fight, therefore, valiantly in Christ's cause. As for me, I too will combat boldly. Would to God that I were permitted to see how they frown. But the Lord will purge his vineyard, which the wild boar of the forest has laid waste......May Christ preserve you !"[1] Bucer did what Hütten was unable to do ; he came from Ebernburg to Worms, and did not leave his friend during the time of his sojourn in that city.[2]

Four o'clock arrived. The marshal of the empire appeared ; Luther prepared to set out with him. He was agitated at the thought of the solemn congress before which he was about to appear. The herald walked first ; after him the marshal of the empire ; and the reformer came last. The crowd that filled the streets was still greater than on the preceding day. It was impossible to advance ; in vain were orders given to make way ; the crowd still kept increasing. At length the herald, seeing the difficulty of reaching the town-hall, ordered some private houses to be opened, and led Luther through the gardens and private passages to the place where the diet was sitting.[3] The people who witnessed this, rushed into the houses after the monk of Wittemberg, ran to the windows that overlooked the gardens, and a great number climbed on the roofs. The tops of the houses and the pavements of the streets, above and below, all were covered with spectators.[4]

Having reached the town-hall at last, Luther and those who accompanied him were again prevented by the crowd from crossing the threshold. They cried, " Make way ! make way !" but no one moved. Upon this the imperial soldiers by main force cleared a road, through which Luther passed. As the people rushed forward to enter with him, the soldiers kept them back with their halberds. Luther entered the interior of the hall ; but even there every corner was crowded. In the antechambers and deep recesses of the windows there were more than five thousand spectators,—Germans, Italians, Spaniards, and others. Luther advanced with difficulty. At last, as he drew near the door which was about to admit him into the presence of his judges, he met a valiant knight, the celebrated George of Freundsberg, who, four years later, at the head of his German lansquenets, bent the knee with his soldiers on the field of Pavia, and then charging the left of the French army, drove it into the Ticino, and in a great measure decided the captivity of the King of France. The old general, seeing Luther pass, tapped him on the shoulder, and shaking his head,

blanched in many battles, said kindly : " Poor monk ! poor monk ! thou art now going to make a nobler stand than I or any other captains have ever made in the bloodiest of our battles ! But if thy cause is just, and thou art sure of it, go forward in God's name, and fear nothing ! God will not forsake thee ! "[1] A noble tribute of respect paid by the courage of the sword to the courage of the mind ! *He that ruleth his spirit is greater than he that taketh a city*, were the words of a king.[2]

At length the doors of the hall were opened. Luther went in, and with him entered many persons who formed no portion of the diet. Never had man appeared before so imposing an assembly. The Emperor Charles V., whose sovereignty extended over great part of the old and new world ; his brother the Archduke Ferdinand ; six electors of the empire, most of whose descendants now wear the kingly crown ; twenty-four dukes, the majority of whom were independent sovereigns over countries more or less extensive, and among whom were some whose names afterwards became formidable to the Reformation,—the Duke of Alva and his two sons ; eight margraves ; thirty archbishops, bishops, and abbots ; seven ambassadors, including those from the kings of France and England ; the deputies of ten free cities ; a great number of princes, counts, and sovereign barons ; the papal nuncios ;— in all two hundred and four persons : such was the imposing court before which appeared Martin Luther.

This appearance was of itself a signal victory over the papacy. The pope had condemned the man, and yet there he stood before a tribunal which, by this very act, set itself above the pope. The pope had laid him under an interdict, and cut him off from all human society ; and yet he was summoned in respectful language, and received before the most august assembly in the world. The pope had condemned him to perpetual silence, and yet he was now about to speak before thousands of attentive hearers drawn together from the farthest parts of Christendom. An immense revolution had thus been effected by Luther's instrumentality. Rome was already descending from her throne, and it was the voice of a monk that caused this humiliation.

Some of the princes, when they saw the emotion of this son of the lowly miner of Mansfeldt in the presence of this assembly of kings, approached him kindly, and one of them said to him : " *Fear not them which kill the body, but are not able to kill the soul.*" And another added : *When ye shall be brought before governors and kings for my sake, the spirit*

---

[1] Servet te Christus. L. Opp. ii. 175.
[2] Bucerus eodem venit. M. Adami Vita Buceri, p. 212.
[3] Und ward also durch heimliche Gänge geführt. L. Opp. (L.) xvii. 574.
[4] Doch lief das Volk häufig zu, und stieg sogar auf Dächer. Seck. p. 348.

[1] Münchlein ! münchlein ! du gehest jetzt einen Gang, einen solchen Stand zu thun, dergleichen ich und mancher Obrister, auch in unser allerernestesten Schlacht-Ordnung nicht gethan haben.... Seck. p. 348.
[2] Proverbs xvi. 32.

of your Father shall speak in you." [1] Thus was the reformer comforted with his Master's words by the princes of this world.

Meanwhile the guards made way for Luther. He advanced and stood before the throne of Charles V. The sight of so august an assembly appeared for an instant to dazzle and intimidate him. All eyes were fixed on him. The confusion gradually subsided, and a deep silence followed. "Say nothing," said the marshal of the empire to him, "before you are questioned." Luther was left alone.

After a moment of solemn silence, the chancellor of the Archbishop of Treves, John ab Eck, the friend of Aleander, and who must not be confounded with the theologian of the same name, rose and said with a loud and clear voice, first in Latin and then in German: "Martin Luther! his sacred and invincible imperial majesty has cited you before his throne, in accordance with the advice and counsel of the states of the holy Roman empire, to require you to answer two questions: First, Do you acknowledge these books to have been written by you?"—At the same time the imperial speaker pointed with his finger to about twenty volumes placed on a table in the middle of the hall, directly in front of Luther. "I do not know how they could have procured them," said Luther, relating this circumstance. It was Aleander who had taken this trouble. "Secondly," continued the chancellor, "Are you prepared to retract these books, and their contents, or do you persist in the opinions you have advanced in them?"

Luther, having no mistrust, was about to answer the first of these questions in the affirmative, when his counsel, Jerome Schurff, hastily interrupting him, exclaimed aloud: "Let the titles of the books be read!" [2]

The Chancellor approached the table and read the titles. There were among their number many devotional works, quite foreign to the controversy.

Their enumeration being finished, Luther said first in Latin, and then in German:

"Most gracious emperor! Gracious princes and lords!

"His imperial majesty has asked me two questions.

"As to the first, I acknowledge as mine the books that have just been named: I cannot deny them.

"As to the second, seeing that it is a question which concerns faith and the salvation of souls, and in which the Word of God, the greatest and most precious treasure either in heaven or earth,[3] is interested, I should act imprudently were I to reply without reflection. I might affirm less than the circum-

stance demands, or more than truth requires, and so sin against this saying of Christ:— *Whosoever shall deny me before men, him will I also deny before my Father which is heaven.* For this reason I entreat your imperial majesty, with all humility, to allow me time, that I may answer without offending against the Word of God."

This reply, far from giving grounds to suppose that Luther felt any hesitation, was worthy of the reformer and of the assembly. It was right that he should appear calm and circumspect in so important a matter, and lay aside every thing in this solemn moment that might cause a suspicion of passion or rashness. Besides, by taking reasonable time, he would give a stronger proof of the unalterable firmness of his resolution. In history we read of many men who by a hasty expression have brought great misfortunes upon themselves and upon the world. Luther restrained his own naturally impetuous disposition; he controlled his tongue, ever too ready to speak; he checked himself at a time when all the feelings by which he was animated were eager for utterance. This restraint, this calmness, so surprising in such a man, multiplied his strength a hundredfold, and put him in a position to reply, at a later period, with such wisdom, power, and dignity, as to deceive the expectations of his adversaries, and confound their malice and their pride.

And yet, because he had spoken in a respectful manner, and in a low tone of voice, many thought that he hesitated, and even that he was dismayed. A ray of hope beamed on the minds of the partisans of Rome. Charles, impatient to know the man whose words had stirred the empire, had not taken his eyes off him. He turned to one of his courtiers, and said disdainfully, "Certainly this man will never make a heretic of me." [1] Then rising from his seat, the youthful emperor withdrew with his ministers into a council-room; the electors with the princes retired into another; and the deputies of the free cities, into a third. When the diet assembled again, it was agreed to comply with Luther's request. This was a great miscalculation in men actuated by passion.

"Martin Luther," said the Chancellor of Treves, "his imperial majesty, of his natural goodness, is very willing to grant you another day, but under condition that you make your reply *vivâ voce*, and not in writing."

The imperial herald now stepped forward and conducted Luther back to his hotel. Menaces and shouts of joy were heard by turns on his passage. The most sinister rumours circulated among Luther's friends. "The diet is dissatisfied," said they; "the papal envoys have triumphed; the reformer

---

[1] Einige aus denen Reichs-Gliedern sprachen Ihm einen Muth, mit Christi Worten, ein......Matthew x. 28, 18, 20. Seckendorf, p. 348.
[2] Legantur tituli librorum. L. Opp. (L.) xvii. 568.
[3] Weil dies eine Frage vom Glauben und der Seelen Seligkeit ist, und Gottes Wort belanget....Ibid. 573.

[1] Hic certe nunquam efficeret ut hæreticus evaderem. Pallav. i. 115.

will be sacrificed." Men's passions were inflamed. Many gentlemen hastened to Luther's lodgings: "Doctor," said they, with emotion, "what is this? It is said they are determined to burn you!"[1]..."If they do so," continued these knights, "it will cost them their lives!"—"And that certainly would have happened," said Luther, as, twenty years after, he quoted these words at Eisleben.

On the other hand, Luther's enemies exulted. "He has asked for time," said they; "he will retract. At a distance, his speech was arrogant; now his courage fails him......He is conquered."

Perhaps Luther was the only man that felt tranquil at Worms. Shortly after his return from the diet, he wrote to Cuspianus, the imperial Councillor: "I write to you from the midst of the tumult (alluding probably to the noise made by the crowd in front of the hotel). I have just made my appearance before the emperor and his brother.[2]......I confessed myself the author of my books, and declared that I would reply to-morrow touching my retractation. With Christ's help, I shall never retract one tittle of my works."[3]

The emotion of the people and of the foreign soldiers increased every hour. While the opposing parties were proceeding calmly in the diet, they were breaking out into acts of violence in the streets. The insolence of the haughty and merciless Spanish soldiers offended the citizens. One of these myrmidons of Charles, finding in a bookseller's shop the pope's bull with a commentary written by Hütten, took the book and tore it in pieces, and then throwing the fragments on the ground, trampled them under foot. Others having discovered several copies of Luther's writing on the *Captivity of Babylon*, took them away and destroyed them. The indignant people fell upon the soldiers and compelled them to take to flight. At another time, a Spaniard on horseback pursued, sword in hand, through one of the principal streets of Worms, a German who fled before him, and the affrighted people dared not stop the furious man.[4]

Some politicians thought they had found means of saving Luther. "Retract your doctrinal errors," said they; "but persist in all that you have said against the pope and his court, and you are safe." Aleander shuddered with alarm at this counsel. But Luther, immovable in his resolution, declared that he had no great opinion of a political reform that was not based upon faith.

Glapio, the Chancellor ab Eck, and Aleander, by Charles's order, met early on the morning of the 18th to concert the measures to be taken with regard to Luther.

For a moment Luther had felt dismay, when he was about to appear the preceding day before so august an assembly. His heart had been troubled in the presence of so many great princes, before whom nations humbly bent the knee. The reflection that he was about to refuse to submit to these men, whom God had invested with sovereign power, disturbed his soul; and he felt the necessity of looking for strength from on high. "The man who, when he is attacked by the enemy, protects himself with the shield of faith," said he one day, "is like Perseus with the Gorgon's head. Whoever looked at it fell dead. In like manner should we present the Son of God to the snares of the devil."[1] On the morning of the 18th of April, he was not without his moments of trial, in which the face of God seemed hidden from him. His faith grew weak; his enemies multiplied before him; his imagination was overwhelmed at the sight......His soul was as a ship tossed by a violent tempest, which reels and sinks to the bottom of the abyss, and then mounts up again to heaven. In this hour of bitter sorrow, in which he drinks the cup of Christ, and which was to him a little garden of Gethsemane, he falls to the earth, and utters these broken cries, which we cannot understand unless we can figure to ourselves the depth of the anguish whence they ascend to God:—[2]

"O Almighty and Everlasting God! How terrible is this world! Behold, it openeth its mouth to swallow me up, and I have so little trust in Thee!......How weak is the flesh, and how powerful is Satan! If it is in the strength of this world only that I must put my trust, all is over!......My last hour is come,[3] my condemnation has been pronounced!......O God! O God!......O God! do thou help me against all the wisdom of the world! Do this; thou shouldest do this ......thou alone......for this is not my work, but Thine. I have nothing to do here, nothing to contend for with these great ones of the world! I should desire to see my days flow on peaceful and happy. But the cause is Thine......and it is a righteous and eternal cause. O Lord! help me! Faithful and unchangeable God! In no man do I place my trust. It would be vain! All that is of man is uncertain; all that cometh of man fails......O God! my God, hearest Thou me not?......My God, art Thou dead? .....No! Thou canst not die! Thou hidest thyself only! Thou hast chosen me for this work. I know it well!......Act, then, O God...... stand at my side, for the sake of thy well-beloved Jesus Christ, who is my defence, my shield, and my strong tower."

[1] Wie geht's? man sagt sie wollen euch verbrennen.... L. Opp. (L.) xvii. 588.
[2] Hac hora coram Cæsare et fratre Romano constiti. L. Epp. i. 587.
[3] Verum ego ne apicem quidem revocabo. Ibid.
[4] Kappen's Ref. Urkunden., ii. 448.

[1] Also sollen wir den Sohn Gottes als Gorgonis Haupt.... L. Opp. (W.) xxii. 1659.
[2] See L. Opp. (L.) xvii. 589.
[3] Die Glocke ist schon gegossen: lit. the bell is already founded. Ibid.

After a moment of silent struggle, he thus continues:

"Lord! where stayest Thou?......O my God! where art Thou?......Come! come! I am ready!......I am ready to lay down my life for Thy truth......patient as a lamb. For it is the cause of justice—it is thine!......I will never separate myself from Thee, neither now nor through eternity!......And though the world should be filled with devils,—though my body, which is still the work of Thy hands, should be slain, be stretched upon the pavement, be cut in pieces......reduced to ashes......my soul is Thine![1]...... Yes! I have the assurance of Thy Word. My soul belongs to Thee! It shall abide for ever with Thee......Amen!......O God! help me!......Amen!"

This prayer explains Luther and the Reformation. History here raises the veil of the sanctuary, and discloses to our view the secret place whence strength and courage were imparted to this humble and despised man, who was the instrument of God to emancipate the soul and the thoughts of men, and to open a new era. Luther and the Reformation are here brought before us. We discover their most secret springs. We see whence their power was derived. This out-pouring of a soul that offers itself up in the cause of truth is to be found in a collection of documents relative to Luther's appearance at Worms, under Number XVI., in the midst of safe-conducts and other papers of a similar nature. One of his friends had no doubt overheard it, and has transmitted it to posterity. In our opinion, it is one of the most precious documents in all history.

After he had thus prayed, Luther found that peace of mind without which man can effect nothing great. He then read the Word of God, looked over his writings, and sought to draw up his reply in a suitable form. The thought that he was about to bear testimony to Jesus Christ and his Word, in the presence of the emperor and of the empire, filled his heart with joy. As the hour for his appearance was not far off, he drew near the Holy Scriptures that lay open on the table, and with emotion placed his left hand on the sacred volume, and raising his right towards heaven, swore to remain faithful to the Gospel, and freely to confess his faith, even should he seal his testimony with his blood. After this he felt still more at peace.

At four o'clock the herald appeared and conducted him to the place where the diet was sitting. The curiosity of the people had increased, for the answer was to be decisive. As the diet was occupied, Luther was compelled to wait in the court in the midst of an immense crowd, which heaved to and fro like the sea in a storm, and pressed the reformer with its waves. Two long

hours elapsed, while the doctor stood in this multitude so eager to catch a glimpse of him. "I was not accustomed," said he, "to those manners and to all this noise."[1] It would have been a sad preparation, indeed, for an ordinary man. But God was with Luther. His countenance was serene; his features tranquil; the Everlasting One had raised him on a rock. The night began to fall. Torches were lighted in the hall of the assembly. Their glimmering rays shone through the ancient windows into the court. Every thing assumed a solemn aspect. At last the doctor was introduced. Many persons entered with him, for every one desired to hear his answer. Men's minds were on the stretch; all impatiently awaited the decisive moment that was approaching. This time Luther was calm, free, and confident, without the least perceptible mark of embarrassment. His prayer had borne fruit. The princes having taken their seats, though not without some difficulty, for many of their places had been occupied, and the monk of Wittemberg finding himself again standing before Charles V., the chancellor of the Elector of Treves began by saying:

"Martin Luther! yesterday you begged for a delay that has now expired. Assuredly it ought not to have been conceded, as every man, and especially you, who are so great and learned a doctor in the Holy Scriptures, should always be ready to answer any questions touching his faith.......Now, therefore, reply to the question put by his majesty, who has behaved to you with so much mildness. Will you defend your books as a whole, or are you ready to disavow some of them?"

After having said these words in Latin, the chancellor repeated them in German.

"Upon this, Dr. Martin Luther," say the Acts of Worms, "replied in the most submissive and humble manner. He did not bawl, or speak with violence; but with decency, mildness, suitability, and moderation, and yet with much joy and christian firmness."[2]

"Most serene emperor! illustrious princes! gracious lords!" said Luther, turning his eyes on Charles and on the assembly, "I appear before you this day, in conformity with the order given me yesterday, and by God's mercies I conjure your majesty and your august highnesses to listen graciously to the defence of a cause which I am assured is just and true. If, through ignorance, I should transgress the usages and proprieties of courts, I entreat you to pardon me; for I was not brought up in the palaces of kings, but in the seclusion of a convent.

"Yesterday, two questions were put to me on behalf of his imperial majesty: the first,

---

[1] Die Seele ist dein. L. Opp. (L.) xvii. 589

[1] Des Getümmels und Wesens war Ich gar nicht gewohnt. L. Opp. xvii. 535, 588.
[2] Schreyt nicht sehr noch heftig, sondern redet fein, sittlich, züchtig und bescheiden. L. Opp. (L.) xvii. 576.

if I was the author of the books whose titles were enumerated; the second, if I would retract or defend the doctrine I had taught in them. To the first question I then made answer, and I persevere in that reply.

" As for the second, I have written works on many different subjects. There are some in which I have treated of faith and good works, in a manner at once so pure, so simple, and so scriptural, that even my adversaries, far from finding anything to censure in them, allow that these works are useful, and worthy of being read by all pious men. The papal bull, however violent it may be, acknowledges this. If, therefore, I were to retract these, what should I do?...... Wretched man! Among all men, I alone should abandon truths that friends and enemies approve, and I should oppose what the whole world glories in confessing......

" Secondly, I have written books against the papacy, in which I have attacked those who, by their false doctrine, their evil lives, or their scandalous example, afflict the christian world, and destroy both body and soul. The complaints of all who fear God are confirmatory of this. Is it not evident that the laws and human doctrines of the popes entangle, torment, and vex the consciences of believers, while the crying and perpetual extortions of Rome swallow up the wealth and the riches of Christendom, and especially of this illustrious nation?......

" Were I to retract what I have said on this subject, what should I do but lend additional strength to this tyranny, and open the floodgates to a torrent of impiety?[1] Overflowing with still greater fury than before, we should see these insolent men increase in number, behave more tyrannically, and domineer more and more. And not only would the yoke that now weighs upon the christian people be rendered heavier by my retractation, but it would become, so to speak, more legitimate, for by this very retractation it would receive the confirmation of your most serene majesty and of all the states of the holy empire. Gracious God! I should thus become a vile cloak to cover and conceal every kind of malice and tyranny!......

" Lastly, I have written books against individuals who desired to defend the Romish tyranny and to destroy the faith. I frankly confess that I may have attacked them with more acrimony than is becoming my ecclesiastical profession. I do not consider myself a saint; but I cannot disavow these writings, for by so doing I should sanction the impiety of my adversaries, and they would seize the opportunity of oppressing the people of God with still greater cruelty.

" Yet I am but a mere man, and not God; I shall therefore defend myself as Christ did. *If I have spoken evil, bear witness of the evil* (John xviii. 23), said he. How much more

should I, who am but dust and ashes, and who may so easily go astray, desire every man to state his objections to my doctrine!

" For this reason, most serene emperor, and you, most illustrious princes, and all men of every degree, I conjure you, by the mercy of God, to prove from the writings of the prophets and apostles that I have erred. As soon as I am convinced of this, I will retract every error, and be the first to lay hold of my books and throw them into the fire.

" What I have just said plainly shows, I hope, that I have carefully weighed and considered the dangers to which I expose myself; but, far from being dismayed, I rejoice to see that the Gospel is now, as in former times, a cause of trouble and dissension. This is the character—this is the destiny of the Word of God. *I came not to send peace on earth, but a sword,* said Jesus Christ (Math. x. 34). God is wonderful and terrible in his counsels; beware lest, by presuming to quench dissensions, you should persecute the holy Word of God, and draw down upon yourselves a frightful deluge of insurmountable dangers, of present disasters, and eternal desolation......You should fear lest the reign of this young and noble prince, on whom (under God) we build such lofty expectations, not only should begin, but continue and close under the most gloomy auspices. I might quote many examples from the oracles of God," continued Luther, speaking with a noble courage in the presence of the greatest monarch of the world:

" I might speak of the Pharaohs, the kings of Babylon, and those of Israel, whose labours never more effectually contributed to their own destruction than when they sought by counsels, to all appearance most wise, to strengthen their dominion. *God removeth mountains, and they know it not; which overturneth them in his anger* (Job ix. 5).

" If I say these things, it is not because I think that such great princes need my poor advice, but because I desire to render unto Germany what she has a right to expect from her children. Thus, commending myself to your august majesty and to your most serene highnesses, I humbly entreat you not to suffer the hatred of my enemies to pour out upon me an indignation that I have not merited."[1]

Luther had pronounced these words in German with modesty, but with great warmth and firmness;[2] he was ordered to repeat them in Latin. The emperor did not like the German tongue. The imposing assembly that surrounded the reformer, the noise, and his own emotion, had fatigued him. " I was in a great perspiration," said he, " heated by the tumult, standing in the midst of the princes." Frederick of Thun,

---

[1] Nicht allein die Fenster, sondern auch Thür und Thor aufthäte. L. Opp. (L.) xvii. 573.

[1] This speech, as well as all the other expressions we quote, is taken literally from authentic documents. See L. Opp. (L.) xvii. 776-780.
[2] Non clamose at modeste, non tamen sine christiana animositate et constantia. L. Opp. Lat. ii. 165.

privy councillor to the Elector of Saxony, who was stationed by his master's orders at the side of the reformer, to watch over him that no violence might be employed against him, seeing the condition of the poor monk, said: " If you cannot repeat what you have said, that will do, doctor." But Luther, after a brief pause to take breath, began again, and repeated his speech in Latin with the same energy as at first.[1]

" This gave great pleasure to the Elector Frederick," says the reformer.

When he had ceased speaking, the Chancellor of Treves, the orator of the diet, said indignantly : " You have not answered the question put to you. You were not summoned hither to call in question the decisions of councils. You are required to give a clear and precise answer. Will you, or will you not, retract?" Upon this Luther replied without hesitation : " Since your most serene majesty and your high mightinesses require from me a clear, simple, and precise answer, I will give you one,[2] and it is this : I cannot submit my faith either to the pope or to the councils, because it is clear as the day that they have frequently erred and contradicted each other. Unless therefore I am convinced by the testimony of Scripture, or by the clearest reasoning,—unless I am persuaded by means of the passages I have quoted,—and unless they thus render my conscience bound by the Word of God, *I cannot and I will not retract*, for it is unsafe for a Christian to speak against his conscience." And then, looking round on this assembly before which he stood, and which held his life in its hands, he said: " HERE I STAND, I CAN DO NO OTHER ; MAY GOD HELP ME ! AMEN !"[3]

Luther, constrained to obey his faith, led by his conscience to death, impelled by the noblest necessity, the slave of his belief, and under this slavery still supremely free, like the ship tossed by a violent tempest, and which, to save that which is more precious than itself, runs and is dashed upon the rocks, thus uttered these sublime words which still thrill our hearts at an interval of three centuries: thus spoke a monk before the emperor and the mighty ones of the nation ; and this feeble and despised man, alone, but relying on the grace of the Most High, appeared greater and mightier than them all. His words contain a power against which all these mighty rulers can do nothing. This is the weakness of God, which is stronger than man. The empire and the Church on the one hand, and this obscure man on the other, had met. God had brought together these kings and these prelates publicly to confound their wisdom. The battle is lost, and the consequences of this defeat of the great ones of the earth will be felt among every nation and in every age to the end of time.

The assembly was thunderstruck. Many of the princes found it difficult to conceal their admiration. The emperor, recovering from his first impression, exclaimed : " This monk speaks with an intrepid heart and unshaken courage."[1] The Spaniards and Italians alone felt confounded, and soon began to ridicule a greatness of soul which they could not comprehend.

" If you do not retract," said the chancellor, as soon as the diet had recovered from the impression produced by Luther's speech, " the emperor and the states of the empire will consult what course to adopt against an incorrigible heretic." At these words Luther's friends began to tremble ; but the monk repeated : " May God be my helper ; for I can retract nothing."[2]

After this Luther withdrew, and the princes deliberated. Each one felt that this was a critical moment for Christendom. The *yes* or the *no* of this monk would decide, perhaps for ages, the repose of the Church and of the world. His adversaries had endeavoured to alarm him, and they had only exalted him before the nation ; they had thought to give greater publicity to his defeat, and they had but increased the glory of his victory. The partisans of Rome could not make up their mind to submit to this humiliation. Luther was again called in, and the orator of the diet said to him : " Martin, you have not spoken with the modesty becoming your position. The distinction you have made between your books was futile ; for if you retracted those that contained your errors, the emperor would not allow the others to be burnt. It is extravagant in you to demand to be refuted by Scripture, when you are reviving heresies condemned by the general council of Constance. The emperor, therefore, calls upon you to declare simply, yes or no, whether you presume to maintain what you have advanced, or whether you will retract a portion ?"—" I have no other reply to make than that which I have already made," answered Luther calmly. His meaning was understood. Firm as a rock, all the waves of human power dashed ineffectually against him. The strength of his words, his bold bearing, his piercing eyes, the unshaken firmness legible on the rough outlines of his truly German features, had produced the deepest impression on this illustrious assembly. There was no longer any hope. The Spaniards, the Belgians, and even the Romans, were dumb. The monk had vanquished these great ones of the earth. He had said *no* to the Church and to the empire. Charles V. arose, and all the assembly with him : " The diet will meet again to-morrow to hear

[1] L. Opp. Lat. ii. 165-167.
[2] Dabo illud neque dentatum, neque cornutum. Ibid. p. 166. I will give you one that shall have neither horns nor teeth.
[3] Hier stehe ich : Ich kann nicht anders ; Gott nelfe mir. Amen. L. Opp. (L.) xvii. 580.

[1] Der Mönch redet unerschrocken, mit getrostem Muth Seck. 350.
[2] L. Opp. (W.) xv. 2236.

the emperor's opinion," said the chancellor with a loud voice.

CHAPTER IX.

Tumult and Calmness—The Flagon of Duke Eric—The Elector and Spalatin—The Emperor's Message—Proposal to violate the Safe-conduct—Violent Opposition—Enthusiasm in favour of Luther—Language of Conciliation—Fears of the Elector—Luther's numerous Visiters—Philip of Hesse.

NIGHT had closed in. Each man retired to his home in darkness. Two imperial officers formed Luther's escort. Some persons imagined that his fate was decided, that they were leading him to prison, whence he would never come forth but to mount the scaffold: an immense tumult broke out. Several gentlemen exclaimed: " Are they taking him to prison?"—" No," replied Luther, " they are accompanying me to my hotel." At these words the agitation subsided. Some Spanish soldiers of the emperor's household followed this bold man through the streets by which he had to pass, with shouts and mockery, while others howled and roared like wild beasts robbed of their prey.[1] But Luther remained calm and firm.

Such was the scene at Worms. The intrepid monk, who had hitherto boldly braved all his enemies, spoke on this occasion, when he found himself in the presence of those who thirsted for his blood, with calmness, dignity, and humility. There was no exaggeration, no mere human enthusiasm, no anger; overflowing with the liveliest emotion, he was still at peace; modest, though withstanding the powers of the earth; great in presence of all the grandeur of the world. This is an indisputable mark that Luther obeyed God, and not the suggestions of his own pride. In the hall of the diet there was one greater than Charles and than Luther. *When ye shall be brought before governors and kings for my sake, take no thought how or what ye shall speak,* saith Jesus Christ, *for it is not ye that speak.*[2] Never perhaps had this promise been more clearly fulfilled.

A profound impression had been produced on the chiefs of the empire. This Luther had noticed, and it had increased his courage. The pope's ministers were provoked because John ab Eck had not sooner interrupted the guilty monk. Many lords and princes were won over to a cause supported with such conviction. With some, it is true, the impression was transient; but others, on the contrary, who concealed their sentiments at that time, at an after-period declared themselves with great courage.

Luther had returned to his hotel, seeking to recruit his body fatigued by so severe a trial. Spalatin and other friends surrounded him, and all together gave thanks to God. As they were conversing, a servant entered, bearing a silver flagon filled with Eimbeck beer. " My master," said he, as he offered it to Luther, " invites you to refresh yourself with this draught."—" Who is the prince," said the Wittemberg doctor, " who so graciously remembers me?" It was the aged Duke Eric of Brunswick. The reformer was affected by this present from so powerful a lord, belonging to the pope's party. " His highness," continued the servant, " has condescended to taste it before sending it to you." Upon this Luther, who was thirsty, poured out some of the duke's beer, and after drinking it, he said: " As this day Duke Eric has remembered me, so may our Lord Jesus Christ remember him in the hour of his last struggle."[1] It was a present of trifling value; but Luther, desirous of showing his gratitude to a prince who remembered him at such a moment, gave him such as he had—a prayer. The servant returned with this message to his master. At the moment of his death the aged duke called these words to mind, and addressing a young page, Francis of Kramm, who was standing at his bedside: " Take the Bible," said he, " and read it to me." The child read these words of Christ, and the soul of the dying man was comforted: *Whosoever shall give you a cup of water to drink in my name, because ye belong to Christ, verily I say unto you, he shall not lose his reward.*

Hardly had the Duke of Brunswick's servant gone away, when a messenger from the Elector of Saxony came with orders for Spalatin to come to him immediately. Frederick had gone to the diet filled with great uneasiness. He had imagined that in the presence of the emperor, Luther's courage would fail him; and hence he had been deeply moved by the resolute bearing of the reformer. He was proud of being the protector of such a man. When the chaplain arrived, the table was spread; the elector was just sitting down to supper with his court, and already the servants had brought in the water for their hands. As he saw Spalatin enter, he motioned him to follow, and as soon as he was alone with the chaplain in his bedchamber, he said: " Oh! how Father Luther spoke before the emperor, and before all the states of the empire! I only trembled lest he should be too bold."[2] Frederick then formed the resolution of protecting the doctor more courageously in future.

Aleander saw the impression Luther had produced; there was no time to lose; he must induce the emperor to act with vigour. The opportunity was favourable; war with

[1] Subsannatione hominem Dei et longo rugitu prosecuti sunt. L. Opp. Lat. ii. 166.
[2] Matt. x. 18, 20.

[1] Also gedenckě seiner unser Herr Christus in seinem letzten Kampff. Seck. p. 354.
[2] O wie schön hat Pater Martinus geredet. Ibid. 356.

France was imminent. Leo X., desirous of enlarging his states, and caring little for the peace of Christendom, was secretly negotiating two treaties at the same time,—one with Charles against Francis, the other with Francis against Charles.[1] In the former, he claimed of the emperor, for himself, the territories of Parma, Placentia, and Ferrara; in the second, he stipulated with the king for a portion of the kingdom of Naples, which would thus be taken from Charles. The latter felt the importance of gaining Leo to his side, in order to have his alliance in the war against his rival of France. It was a mere trifle to purchase the mighty pontiff's friendship at the cost of Luther's life.

On the day following Luther's appearance (Friday, 19th April), the emperor ordered a message to be read to the diet, which he had written in French with his own hand.[2] "Descended from the christian emperors of Germany," said he, "from the catholic kings of Spain, from the archdukes of Austria, and from the dukes of Burgundy, who have all been renowned as defenders of the Roman faith, I am firmly resolved to imitate the example of my ancestors. A single monk, misled by his own folly, has risen against the faith of Christendom. To stay such impiety I will sacrifice my kingdoms, my treasures, my friends, my body, my blood, my soul, and my life.[3] I am about to dismiss the Augustine Luther, forbidding him to cause the least disorder among the people; I shall then proceed against him and his adherents, as contumacious heretics, by excommunication, by interdict, and by every means calculated to destroy them.[4] I call on the members of the states to behave like faithful Christians."

This address did not please every one. Charles, young and hasty, had not complied with the usual forms; he should first have consulted with the diet. Two extreme opinions immediately declared themselves. The creatures of the pope, the Elector of Brandenburg, and several ecclesiastical princes, demanded that the safe-conduct given to Luther should not be respected.[5] "The Rhine," said they, "should receive his ashes, as it had received those of John Huss a century ago." Charles, if we may credit an historian, bitterly repented in after-years that he did not adopt this infamous suggestion. "I confess," said he, towards the close of his life, "that I committed a great fault by permitting Luther to live. I was not obliged to keep my promise with him; that

heretic had offended a Master greater than I,—God himself. I might and I ought to have broken my word, and to have avenged the insult he had committed against God: it is because I did not put him to death that heresy has not ceased to advance. His death would have stifled it in the cradle."[1]

So horrible a proposition filled the elector and all Luther's friends with dismay. "The punishment of John Huss," said the elector-palatine, "has brought too many misfortunes on the German nation for us ever to raise such a scaffold a second time."—"The princes of Germany," exclaimed even George of Saxony, Luther's inveterate enemy, "will not permit a safe-conduct to be violated. This diet, the first held by our new emperor, will not be guilty of so base an action. Such perfidy does not accord with the ancient German integrity." The princes of Bavaria, though attached to the Church of Rome, supported this protest. The prospect of death that Luther's friends had already before their eyes appeared to recede.

The rumour of these discussions, which lasted two days, circulated through the city. Party-spirit ran high. Some gentlemen, partisans of the reform, began to speak firmly against the treachery solicited by Aleander. "The emperor," said they, "is a young man whom the papists and bishops by their flatteries manage at their will."[2] Pallavicini speaks of four hundred nobles ready to enforce Luther's safe-conduct with the sword. On Saturday morning placards were seen posted on the gates of houses and in the public places,—some against Luther, and others in his favour. On one of them might be read merely these expressive words of the Preacher: *Woe to thee, O land, when thy king is a child.*[3] Sickingen, it was reported, had assembled at a few leagues from Worms, behind the impregnable ramparts of his stronghold, many knights and soldiers, and was only waiting to know the result of the affair before proceeding to action. The enthusiasm of the people, not only in Worms, but also in the most distant cities of the empire;[4] the intrepidity of the knights; the attachment felt by many princes to the cause of the reformer, were all of a nature to show Charles and the diet that the course suggested by the Romanists might compromise the supreme authority, excite revolts, and even shake the empire.[5] It was only the burning of a simple monk that was in ques-

[1] Guicciardini, lib. xiv. 175; Dumont, Corp. Dipl. vol. iv. 96. Dicesi del papa Leone, che quando l'aveva fatto lega con alcuno, prima soleva dir che pero non si dovea restar de tratar con lo altro principe opposto. Suriano, Venetian Ambassador at Rome, MS. in the archives of Venice.
[2] Autographum in lingua Burgundica, ab ipsomet enarratum. Cochlœus, p. 32.
[3] Regna, thesauros, amicos, corpus, sanguinem, vitam, spiritumque profundere. Pallav. i. 118.
[4] Und andern Wegen sie zu vertilgen. L. Opp. (L.) xvii 581.
[5] Dass Luthero das sichere Geleit nicht möchte gehalten werden. Seckend. p. 357.

[1] Sandoval, Hist. de Carlos V. quoted in Llorente's History of the Inquisition, ii. 57. According to Llorente, the supposition that, towards the end of his life, Charles inclined to evangelical opinions, is a mere invention of the Protestants and of the enemies of Philip II. This question is an historical problem which Llorente's numerous quotations seem unhappily to solve entirely in accordance with his statements.
[2] Eum esse puerum, qui nutu et blanditiis Papistarum et Episcoporum trahatur quocunque velint. Cochlœus, p. 33.
[3] Eccles. x. 16.
[4] Verum etiam in longinquis Germaniæ civitatibus, motus et murmura plebium. Cochlœus, p. 33.
[5] Es wäre ein Aufruhr daraus worden, says Luther. Thereupon an insurrection would have broken out.

tion; but the princes and the partisans of Rome had not, all together, sufficient strength or courage to do this. There can be no doubt, also, that Charles V., who was then young, feared to commit perjury. This would seem to be indicated by a saying, if it is true, which, according to some historians, he uttered on this occasion : " Though honour and faith should be banished from all the world, they ought to find a refuge in the hearts of princes." It is mournful to reflect that he may have forgotten these words when on the brink of the grave. But other motives besides may have influenced the emperor. The Florentine Vettori, the friend of Leo X. and of Machiavelli, asserts that Charles spared Luther only that he might thus keep the pope in check. [1]

In the sitting of Saturday, the violent propositions of Aleander were rejected. Luther was beloved ; there was a general desire to preserve this simple-minded man, whose confidence in God was so affecting ; but there was also a desire to save the Church. Men shuddered at the thought of the consequences that might ensue, as well from the triumph as from the punishment of the reformer. Plans of conciliation were put forward ; it was proposed to make a new effort with the doctor of Wittemberg. The Archbishop-elector of Mentz himself, the young and extravagant Albert, more devout than bold, says Pallavicini, [2] had become alarmed at the interest shown by the people and nobility towards the Saxon monk. Capito, his chaplain, who during his sojourn at Basle had formed an intimacy with the evangelical priest of Zurich, named Zwingle, a bold man in the defence of truth, and of whom we have already had occasion to speak, had also, there can be no doubt, represented to Albert the justice of the reformer's cause. The worldly archbishop had one of those returns to christian sentiments which we sometimes notice in his life, and consented to wait on the emperor, to ask permission to make a last attempt. But Charles refused every thing. On Monday, the 22d of April, the princes went in a body to repeat Albert's request. " I will not depart from what I have determined," replied the emperor. " I will authorize no one to communicate officially with Luther. But," added he, to Aleander's great vexation, " I will grant that man three days for reflection ; during which time, you may exhort him privately." [3] This was all that they required. The reformer, thought they, elevated by the solemnity of his appearance before the diet, will give way in a more friendly conference, and perhaps will be saved from the abyss into which he is about to fall

The Elector of Saxony knew the contrary, and hence was filled with apprehension. " If it were in my power," wrote he the next day to his brother Duke John, " I should be ready to defend Luther. You cannot imagine how far the partisans of Rome carry their attacks against me. Were I to tell you all, you would hear some most astonishing matters.[1] They are resolved upon his destruction ; and whoever manifests any interest for his safety, is immediately set down as a heretic. May God, who never abandons the cause of justice, bring all things to a happy end !" Frederick, without showing his kindly feelings towards the reformer, confined himself to observing every one of his movements.

It was not the same with men of every rank in society who were then at Worms. They fearlessly displayed their sympathy. On Friday a number of princes, counts, barons, knights, gentlemen, ecclesiastics, laymen, and of the common people, collected before the hotel where the reformer was staying ; they went in and out one after another, and could hardly satisfy themselves with gazing on him.[2] He had become the man of Germany. Even those who thought him in error were affected by the nobleness of soul that led him to sacrifice his life to the voice of his conscience. With many persons then present at Worms, the chosen men of the nation, Luther held conversations abounding in that salt with which all his words were seasoned. None quitted him without feeling animated by a generous enthusiasm for the truth. " How many things I shall have to tell you !" wrote George Vogler, private secretary to Casimir, margrave of Brandenburg, to one of his friends. " What conversations, how full of piety and kindness, has Luther had with me and others ! What a charming person he is !"[3]

One day a young prince, seventeen years of age, came prancing into the court of the hotel ; it was Philip, who for two years had ruled in Hesse. This youthful sovereign was of prompt and enterprising character, wise beyond his years, warlike, impetuous, and unwilling to be guided by any ideas but his own. Struck by Luther's speeches, he wished to have a nearer view of him. " He, however, was not yet on my side," said Luther, as he related this circumstance.[4] He leapt from his horse, unceremoniously ascended to the reformer's chamber, and addressing him, said : " Well ! dear doctor, how goes it ?" " Gracious lord," answered Luther, " I hope all will go well." " From what I hear of you, doctor," resumed the landgrave smiling, " you teach that a woman may leave her husband and take another,

[1] Carlo si excusò di non poter procedere piu oltre, rispetto al salvocondotto, ma la verità fu che conoscendo che il Papa temeva molto di questa doctrina di Luthero, lo volle tenere con questo freno. Vettori, Istoria d'Italia, MS. in the Corsini Library at Rome, extracted by Ranke.
[2] Qui pio magis animo erat quam forti. Pallavicini, p. 118.
[3] Quibus privatim exhortari hominem possent. Ibid. 119.

[1] Wunder hören werden. Seckend. p. 365.
[2] Und konnten nicht satt werden ihn zu sehen. L. Opp. xvii. 581.
[3] Wie eine holdselige Person er ist. Meuzel, Magaz. i. 207.
[4] War noch nicht auf meiner Seite. L. Opp. xvii. 589.

when the former is become too old!" It was some members of the imperial court who had told this story to the landgrave. The enemies of truth never fail to invent and propagate fables on the pretended doctrines of christian teachers. " No, my lord," replied Luther seriously ; " I entreat your highness not to talk thus!" Upon this the young prince hastily held out his hand to the doctor, shook it heartily, and said: " Dear doctor, if you are in the right, may God help you!" He then left the room, sprung on his horse, and rode off. This was the first interview between these two men, who were afterwards destined to be at the head of the Reformation, and to defend it,—the one with the sword of the Word, the other with the sword of princes.

CHAPTER X.

Conference with the Archbishop of Treves—Wehe's Exhortation to Luther—Luther's Replies—Private Conversation—Visit of Cochlœus—Supper at the Archbishop's—Conference at the Hotel of the Knights of Rhodes—A Council proposed—Luther's last Interview with the Archbishop—Visit to a sick Friend—Luther receives Orders to leave Worms—Luther's Departure.

RICHARD of Greiffenklau, archbishop of Treves, had with the permission of Charles V. undertaken the office of mediator. Richard, who was on very intimate terms with the Elector of Saxony, and a good Roman-catholic, desired by settling this affair to render a service to his friend as well as to his Church. On Monday evening (22d April), just as Luther was sitting down to table, a messenger came from the archbishop, informing him that this prelate desired to see him on the next morning but one (Wednesday) at six o'clock.

The chaplain and Sturm the imperial herald waited on Luther before six o'clock on that day. But as early as four in the morning, Aleander had sent for Cochlœus. The nuncio had soon discovered in the man whom Capito had introduced to him, a devoted instrument of the court of Rome, on whom he might count as upon himself. As he could not be present at this interview, Aleander desired to find a substitute. " Go to the residence of the Archbishop of Treves," said he to the Dean of Frankfort ; " do not enter into discussion with Luther, but listen attentively to all that is said, so as to give me a faithful report."[1] The reformer with some of his friends arrived at the archbishop's, where he found the prelate surrounded by Joachim, margrave of Brandenburg, Duke George of Saxony, the bishops of Brandenburg and Augsburg, with several nobles, deputies of the free cities, lawyers, and theologians, among whom were Cochlœus and Jerome Wehe, chancellor of Baden. This skilful lawyer was anxious for a reformation in morals and discipline ; he even went further : " the Word of God," said he, " that has been so long hidden under a bushel, must reappear in all its brightness."[1] It was this conciliatory person who was charged with the conference. Turning kindly to Luther, he said : " We have not sent for you to dispute with you, but to exhort you in a fraternal tone. You know how carefully the Scriptures call upon us to beware of *the arrow that flieth by day, and the destruction that wasteth at noonday.* That enemy of mankind has excited you to publish many things contrary to true religion. Reflect on your own safety and that of the empire. Beware lest those whom Christ by his blood has redeemed from eternal death should be misled by you, and perish everlastingly......Do not oppose the holy councils. If we did not uphold the decrees of our fathers, there would be nothing but confusion in the Church. The eminent princes who hear me feel a special interest in your welfare ; but if you persist, then the emperor will expel you from the empire,[2] and no place in the world will offer you an asylum......Reflect on the fate that awaits you !"

" Most serene princes," replied Luther, " I thank you for your solicitude on my account ; for I am but a poor man, and too mean to be exhorted by such great lords."[3] He then continued : " I have not blamed all the councils, but only that of Constance, because by condemning this doctrine of John Huss, *That the Christian Church is the assembly of all those who are predestined to salvation,*[4] it has condemned this article of our faith, *I believe in the Holy Catholic Church,* and the Word of God itself. It is said my teaching is a cause of offence," added he ; " I reply that the Gospel of Christ cannot be preached without offence. Why then should the fear or apprehension of danger separate me from the Lord and from that Divine Word which alone is truth ? No ! I would rather give up my body, my blood, and my life !"

The princes and doctors having deliberated, Luther was again called in, and Wehe mildly resumed : " We must honour the powers that be, even when they are in error, and make great sacrifices for the sake of charity." And then with greater earnestness of manner, he said : " Leave it to the emperor's decision, and fear not."

LUTHER.—" I consent with all my heart that the emperor, the princes, and even the

---

[1] Aleander, mane hora quarta vocaverit ad se Cochlœum, lubens ut....audiret solum....Cochlœus. p. 36.

[1] Dass das Wort Gottes, welches so lange unter dem Scheffel verborgen gesteckt, heller scheine .... Seckend. p. 364.
[2] Und aus dem Reich verstossen. L. Opp. (L.) xvii. 589; Sleidan, i. 97.
[3] Agnosco enim me homuncionem, longe viliorem esse, quam ut a tantis principibus....L. Opp. Lat. p. 167.
[4] Ecclesia Christi est universitas prædestinatorum. Ibid.

meanest Christian, should examine and judge my works ; but on one condition, that they take the Word of God for their standard. Men have nothing to do but to obey it. Do not offer violence to my conscience, which is bound and chained up with the Holy Scriptures."[1]

THE ELECTOR OF BRANDENBURG.—"If I rightly understand you, doctor, you will acknowledge no other judge than the Holy Scriptures ? "

LUTHER—"Precisely so, my lord, and on them I take my stand."[2]

Upon this the princes and doctors withdrew; but the excellent Archbishop of Treves could not make up his mind to abandon his undertaking. "Follow me," said he to Luther, as he passed into his private room ; and at the same time ordered John ab Eck and Cochlœus on the one side, and Schurff and Amsdorff on the other, to come after. "Why do you always appeal to Scripture," asked Eck with warmth ; "it is the source of all heresies." But Luther, says his friend Mathesius, remained firm as a rock, which is based on the *true rock*,—the Word of the Lord. "The pope," replied he, "is no judge in the things belonging to the Word of God. Every Christian should see and decide for himself how he ought to live and die."[3] They separated. The partisans of the Papacy felt Luther's superiority, and attributed it to there being no one present capable of answering him. "If the emperor had acted wisely," says Cochlœus, "when summoning Luther to Worms, he would also have invited theologians to refute his errors."

The Archbishop of Treves repaired to the diet, and announced the failure of his mediation. The astonishment of the young emperor was equal to his indignation. " It is time to put an end to this business," said he. The archbishop pressed for two days more ; all the diet joined in the petition ; Charles V. gave way. Aleander, no longer able to restrain himself, burst out into violent reproaches.[4]

While these scenes were passing in the diet, Cochlœus burned to gain a victory in which kings and prelates had been unsuccessful. Although he had from time to time dropped a few words at the archbishop's, he was restrained by Aleander's injunction to keep silence. He resolved to find compensation, and as soon as he had rendered a faithful account of his mission to the papal nuncio, he called on Luther. He went up to him in the most friendly manner, and expressed the vexation he felt at the emperor's resolution. After dinner, the conversation became animated.[5] Cochlœus urged Luther

to retract. The latter shook his head. Several nobles who were at table with him could hardly contain themselves. They were indignant that the partisans of Rome should insist, not upon convincing Luther by Scripture, but on constraining him by force. "Well, then," said Cochlœus to Luther, impatient under these reproaches, "I offer to dispute publicly with you, if you will renounce your safe-conduct."[1] All that Luther demanded was a public disputation. What ought he to do? To renounce the safe-conduct would be to endanger his life ; to refuse this challenge would appear to throw doubts on the justice of his cause. His guests perceived in this proposal a plot framed with Aleander, whom the Dean of Frankfort had just quitted. One of them, Vollrat of Watzdorf by name, extricated Luther from the embarrassment occasioned by so difficult a choice. This fiery lord, indignant at a snare, the sole object of which was to deliver Luther into the hands of the executioner,[2] rose hastily, seized the frightened priest, and pushed him out of the room ; and blood no doubt would have been spilt, if the other guests had not left the table at the same moment, and mediated between the furious knight and Cochlœus, who trembled with alarm.[3] The latter retired in confusion from the hotel of the Knights of Rhodes. Most probably it was in the heat of discussion that these words had fallen from the dean, and there had been no preconcerted plan formed between him and Aleander to entice Luther into so treacherous a snare. This Cochlœus denies, and we are inclined to credit his testimony. And yet just before going to Luther's lodging he had been in conference with Aleander.

In the evening, the Archbishop of Treves assembled at supper the persons who had attended that morning's conference : he thought that this would be a means of unbending their minds, and bringing them closer together. Luther, so firm and intrepid before arbitrators and judges, in private life was so good-humoured and jovial, that they might reasonably hope any thing from him. The archbishop's chancellor, who had been so formal in his official capacity, lent himself to this new essay, and towards the end of the repast proposed Luther's health. The latter prepared to return the compliment ; the wine was poured out, and, according to his usual custom, he had made the sign of the cross on his glass, when suddenly it burst in his hands, and the wine was spilt upon the table. The guests were astonished. " It must have contained poison ! "[4] exclaimed

[1] Sie wollten sein Gewissen, das mit Gottes Wort und heiliger Schrift gebunden und gefangen wäre, nicht dringen. Matt. p. 27.
[2] Ja darauf stehe Ich. L. Opp. (L.) xvii. 588.
[3] Ein Christenmensch muss zusehen und richten....L. Epp. i. 604.
[4] De iis Aleander acerrime conquestus est. Pallav. i. 120.
[5] Peracto prandio. Cochlœus, p. 36.

[1] Und wollte mit mir disputiren, ich sollte allein das Geleit aufsagen. L. Opp. (L.) xvii. 589.
[2] Atque ita traderet eum carnificinæ. Cochlœus, p. 36.
[3] Das Ihm das Blut über den Kopf gelaufen wäre, wo man nicht gewehret hätte. L. Opp. (L.) xvii. 589.
[4] Es müsse Gift darinnen gewesen seyn.—Luther does not speak of this circumstance ; but Razeberg, a friend of Luther's, and physician to the Elector John Frederick, mentions it in a manuscript in the library at Gotha, and says that he had it from an eye-witness.

some of Luther's friends aloud. But the doctor, without betraying any agitation, replied with a smile: "My dear Sirs, either this wine was not intended for me, or else it would have disagreed with me." And then he added calmly: "There is no doubt the glass broke because after washing it it was dipped too soon into cold water." These words, although so simple, under such circumstances are not devoid of grandeur, and show an unalterable peace of mind. We cannot imagine that the Roman-catholics would have desired to poison Luther, especially under the roof of the Archbishop of Treves. This repast neither estranged nor approximated the two parties. Neither the favour nor the hatred of men had any influence over the reformer's resolution: it proceeded from a higher source.

On the morning of Thursday, the 25th of April, the Chancellor Wehe, and Doctor Peutinger of Augsburg, the emperor's councillor, who had shown great affection for Luther at the period of his interview with De Vio, repaired to the hotel of the Knights of Rhodes. The Elector of Saxony sent Frederick of Thun and another of his councillors to be present at the conference. "Place yourself in our hands," said with emotion both Wehe and Peutinger, who would willingly have made every sacrifice to prevent the division that was about to rend the Church. "We pledge you our word, that this affair shall be concluded in a christian-like manner."—"Here is my answer in two words," replied Luther. "I consent to renounce my safe-conduct.[1] I place my person and my life in the emperor's hands, but the Word of God......never!" Frederick of Thun rose in emotion, and said to the envoys: "Is not this enough? Is not the sacrifice large enough?" And after declaring he would not hear a single word more, he left the room. Upon this, Wehe and Peutinger, hoping to succeed more easily with the doctor, came and sat down by his side. "Place yourself in the hands of the diet," said they. "No," replied he, "for *cursed be the man that trusteth in man!*" (Jeremiah xvii. 5.) Wehe and Peutinger became more earnest in their exhortations and attacks; they urged the reformer more pressingly. Luther, wearied out, rose and dismissed them, saying: "I will never permit any man to set himself above the Word of God."[2]—"Reflect upon our proposal," said they, as they withdrew; "we will return in the evening."

They came; but feeling convinced that Luther would not give way, they brought a new proposition. Luther had refused to acknowledge, first the pope, then the emperor, and lastly the diet; there still remained one judge whom he himself had once demanded: a general council. Doubtless such a proposal would have offended Rome: but it was their last hope of safety. The delegates offered a council to Luther. The latter might have accepted it without specifying anything. Years would have passed away before the difficulties could have been set aside which the convocation of a council would have met with on the part of the pope. To gain time was for the reformer and the Reformation to gain every thing. God and the lapse of years would have brought about great changes. But Luther set plain dealing above all things; he would not save himself at the expense of truth, even were silence alone necessary to dissemble it.—"I consent," replied he, "but" (and to make such a request was to refuse a council) "on condition that the council shall decide only according to Scripture."[1]

Peutinger and Wehe, not imagining that a council could decide otherwise, ran quite overjoyed to the archbishop: "Doctor Martin," said they, "submits his books to a council." The archbishop was on the point of carrying these glad tidings to the emperor, when he felt some doubt, and ordered Luther to be brought to him.

Richard of Greiffenklau was alone when the doctor arrived. "Dear doctor," said the archbishop, with great kindness and feeling,[2] "my doctors inform me that you consent to submit, unreservedly, your cause to a council."—"My lord," replied Luther, "I can endure every thing, but I cannot abandon the Holy Scriptures." The bishop perceived that Wehe and Peutinger had stated the matter incorrectly. Rome could never consent to a council that decided only according to Scripture. "It was like telling a shortsighted man," says Pallavicini, "to read very small print, and at the same time refusing him a pair of spectacles."[3] The worthy archbishop sighed: "It was a fortunate thing that I sent for you," said he. "What would have become of me, if I had immediately carried this news to the emperor?"

Luther's immovable firmness and inflexibility are doubtless surprising; but they will be understood and respected by all those who know the law of God. Seldom has a nobler homage been paid to the unchangeable Word from heaven; and that, too, at the peril of the liberty and life of the man who bore this testimony.

"Well, then," said the venerable prelate to Luther, "point out a remedy yourself."

LUTHER, *after a moment's silence.*—"My lord, I know no better than this of Gamaliel: *If this work be of men, it will come to nought: but if it be of God, ye cannot overthrow it; lest*

---

[1] Er wollte ehe das Geleit aufsagen....L. Opp. (L.) xvii. 589.
[2] Er wollte kurtzrum Menschen über Gottes Wort nicht erkennen. L. Opp. (L.) xvii. 583.

[1] Das darüber aus der heiligen Schrifft gesprochen. L. Opp. (L.) xvii. 584.
[2] Ganz gut und mehr denn gnädig. L. Epp. i. 604.
[3] Simulque conspiciliorum omnium usum negare. Ibid. 110.

haply ye be found even to fight against God.
Let the emperor, the electors, the princes,
and states of the empire, write this answer
to the pope."

THE ARCHBISHOP.—" Retract at least some
articles."

LUTHER.—" Provided they are none of
those which the Council of Constance has
already condemned."

THE ARCHBISHOP.—" I am afraid it is precisely those that you would be called upon
to retract."

LUTHER.—" In that case I would rather
lose my life,—rather have my arms and legs
cut off, than forsake the clear and true Word
of God."[1]

The archbishop understood Luther at last.
" You may retire," said he, still with the
same kind manner. " My lord," resumed
Luther, " may I beg you to have the goodness to see that his majesty provides me
with the safe-conduct necessary for my return."—" I will see to it," replied the good
archbishop, and so they parted.

Thus ended these negotiations. The whole
empire had turned towards this man[2] with
the most ardent prayers and with the most
terrible threats, and he had not faltered.
His refusal to bend beneath the iron yoke of
the pope emancipated the Church and began
the new times. The interposition of Providence was manifest. This is one of those
grand scenes in history over which hovers
and rises the majestic presence of the Divinity. Luther withdrew in company with
Spalatin, who had arrived at the Archbishop's
during the interview. John Minkwitz, councillor to the Elector of Saxony, had fallen ill
at Worms. The two friends went to visit
him. Luther gave the sick man the most
affectionate consolations. " Farewell!" said
he, as he retired, " to-morrow I shall leave
Worms."

Luther was not deceived. Hardly had he
returned three hours to the hotel of the
Knights of Rhodes, when the Chancellor ab
Eck, accompanied by the imperial chancellor
and a notary, appeared before him.

The chancellor said to him : " Martin Luther, his imperial majesty, the electors,
princes, and states of the empire, having at
sundry times and in various forms exhorted
you to submission, but always in vain, the
emperor, in his capacity of advocate and defender of the Catholic faith, finds himself
compelled to resort to other measures. He
therefore commands you to return home in
the space of twenty-one days, and forbids you
to disturb the public peace on your road,
either by preaching or by writing."

Luther felt clearly that this message was
the beginning of his condemnation : " As the
Lord pleases," answered he meekly, " blessed

be the name of the Lord !" He then added :
" Before all things, humbly and from the bottom of my heart do I thank his majesty, the
electors, princes, and other states of the empire, for having listened to me so kindly. I
desire, and have ever desired, but one thing
—a reformation of the Church according to
Holy Scripture. I am ready to do and to
suffer everything in humble obedience to the
emperor's will. Life or death, evil or good
report—it is all the same to me, with one
reservation—the preaching of the Gospel ;
for, says St. Paul, the Word of God must not
be bound." The deputies retired.

On the morning of Friday the 26th of
April, the friends of the reformer with several
lords met at Luther's hotel.[1] They were
delighted at seeing the christian firmness
with which he had opposed Charles and the
empire ; and recognised in him the features
of that celebrated portrait of antiquity :

Justum ac tenacem propositi virum,
Non civium ardor prava jubentium,
Non vultus instantis tyranni
Mente quatit solida....[2]

They desired once more, perhaps for the
last time, to say farewell to this intrepid
monk. Luther partook of a humble repast.
But now he had to take leave of his friends,
and fly far from them, beneath a sky lowering with tempests. This solemn moment
he desired to pass in the presence of God.
He lifted up his soul in prayer, blessing
those who stood around him.[3] As it struck
ten, Luther issued from the hotel with the
friends who had accompanied him to Worms.
Twenty gentlemen on horseback surrounded
his car. A great crowd of people accompanied him beyond the walls of the city. Some
time after he was overtaken by Sturm, the
imperial herald, at Oppenheim, and on the
next day they arrived at Frankfort.

CHAPTER XI.

The Conflict at Worms—Luther's Letter to Cranach—Lu-
ther's Letter to Charles V.—Luther with the Abbot of
Hirschfeldt—.The Parish Priest of Eisenach—Several
Princes leave the Diet—Charles signs Luther's Condem-
nation—The Edict of Worms—Luther with his Parents—
Luther attacked and carried away—The Ways of God—
The Wartburg—Luther a Prisoner.

THUS had Luther escaped from these walls of
Worms, that seemed destined to be his sepulchre. With all his heart he gave God
the glory. " The devil himself," said he,
" guarded the pope's citadel ; but Christ has

[1] Ehe Stumpf und Stiel fahren lassen....L. Opp. (I.) xvii.
184.
[2] Totum imperium ad se conversum spectabat. Pallav.
t. 120.

[1] Salutatis patronis et amicis qui eum frequentissimi con-
venerunt. L. Opp. Lat. ii. 168.
[2] The man that's resolute and just,
Firm to his principles and trust,
Nor hopes nor fears can bend ;
Nor parties, for revenge engaged,
Nor threatenings of a court enraged,
Can shake his steady mind.—Horat. Od. iii. 3.
[3] Seine Freunde gesegnet. Mathesius, p. 27.

made a wide breach in it, and Satan was constrained to confess that the Lord is mightier than he."[1]

"The day of the Diet of Worms," says the pious Mathesius, Luther's disciple and friend, "is one of the greatest and most glorious days given to the earth before the end of the world."[2] The battle that had been fought at Worms resounded far and wide, and at its noise which spread through all Christendom, from the regions of the North to the mountains of Switzerland, and the towns of England, France, and Italy, many eagerly grasped the powerful weapons of the Word of God.

Luther, who reached Frankfort on the evening of Saturday the 27th of April, took advantage the next day of a leisure moment, the first that he had enjoyed for a long time, to write a familiar and expressive note to his friend at Wittemberg, the celebrated painter Lucas Cranach. "Your servant, dear gossip Lucas," said he. "I thought his majesty would have assembled some fifty doctors at Worms to convict the monk outright. But not at all.—Are these your books?—Yes! —Will you retract them?—No!—Well, then, be gone!—There's the whole history. O blind Germans !......how childishly we act, to allow ourselves to be the dupes and sport of Rome !......The Jews must sing their Yo! Yo! Yo! But a day of redemption is coming for us also, and then will we sing hallelujah !³......For a season we must suffer in silence. *A little while, and ye shall not see me: and again a little while, and ye shall see me*, said Jesus Christ (John xvi. 16). I hope that it will be the same with me. Farewell. I commend you all to the Lord. May he preserve in Christ your understanding and your faith against the attacks of the wolves and the dragons of Rome. Amen !"

After having written this somewhat enigmatical letter, Luther, as the time pressed, immediately set out for Friedberg, which is six leagues distant from Frankfort. On the next day Luther again collected his thoughts. He desired to write once more to Charles, as he had no wish to be confounded with guilty rebels. In his letter to the emperor he set forth clearly what is the obedience due to kings, and that which is due to God, and what is the limit at which the former should cease and give place to the latter. As we read this epistle, we are involuntarily reminded of the words of the greatest autocrat of modern times : "My dominion ends where that of conscience begins."[4]

"God, who is the searcher of hearts, is my witness," says Luther, "that I am ready most earnestly to obey your majesty, in honour or in dishonour, in life or in death, and with no exception save the Word of God, by which man lives. In all the affairs of this present life, my fidelity shall be unshaken, for here to lose or to gain is of no consequence to salvation. But when eternal interests are concerned, God wills not that man should submit unto man. For such submission in spiritual matters is a real worship, and ought to be rendered solely to the Creator."[1]

Luther wrote also, but in German, a letter addressed to the states of the empire. Its contents were nearly similar to that which he had just written to the emperor. In it he related all that had passed at Worms. This letter was copied several times and circulated throughout Germany ; "every where," says Cochlœus, "it excited the indignation of the people against the emperor and the superior clergy."[2]

Early the next day Luther wrote a note to Spalatin, enclosing the two letters he had written the evening before ; he sent back to Worms the herald Sturm, won over to the cause of the Gospel ; and after embracing him, departed hastily for Grunberg.

On Tuesday, at about two leagues from Hirschfeldt, he met the chancellor of the prince-abbot of that town, who came to welcome him. Soon after there appeared a troop of horsemen with the abbot at their head. The latter dismounted, and Luther got out of his waggon. The prince and the reformer embraced, and afterwards entered Hirschfeldt together. The senate received them at the gates of the city.[3] The princes of the Church came out to meet a monk anathematized by the pope, and the chief men of the people bent their heads before a man under the ban of the emperor.

"At five in the morning we shall be at church," said the prince at night as he rose from the table to which he had invited the reformer. The abbot insisted on his sleeping in his own bed. The next day Luther preached, and this dignitary of the church, with all his train, escorted him on his way.

In the evening Luther reached Eisenach, the scene of his childhood. All his friends in this city surrounded him, entreating him to preach, and the next day accompanied him to the church. Upon this the priest of the parish appeared, attended by a notary and witnesses ; he came forward trembling, divided between the fear of losing his place, and of opposing the powerful man that stood before him. "I protest against the liberty that you are taking," said the priest at last,

---

1 Aber Christus macht ein Loch derein. L. Opp. (L.) xvii. 589.
2 Diss ist der herrlichen grossen Tag einer vorm Ende der Welt. Mathes. p. 28.
3 Es müssen die Juden einmal singen: Io, Io, Io! ...L. Epp. i. 589. The shouts of joy uttered by the Jews at the time of the crucifixion represent the triumphal songs of the papal partisans at the catastrophe that awaited Luther; but the reformer hears in the distance the hallelujahs of deliverance.
4 Napoleon to the Protestant deputation after his accession to the empire.

1 Nam ea fides et submissio proprie est vera illa latria et adoratio Dei....L. Epp. i. 592.
2 Per chalcographos multiplicata et in populos dispersa est ea epistola....Cæsari autem et clericis odium populare, &c. Cochlœus, p. 38.
3 Senatus intra portas nos excepit. L. Epp. ii. 6.

in an embarrassed tone. Luther went up into the pulpit, and that voice which, twenty-three years before, had sung in the streets of this town to procure a morsel of bread, sounded beneath the arched roof of the ancient church those notes that were beginning to agitate the world. After the sermon, the priest with confusion went up to Luther. The notary had drawn up the protest, the witnesses had signed it, all was properly arranged to secure the incumbent's place. "Pardon me," said he to the doctor humbly; "I am acting thus to protect me from the resentment of the tyrants who oppress the Church."[1]

And there were in truth strong grounds for apprehension. The aspect of affairs at Worms was changed: Aleander alone seemed to rule there. "Banishment is Luther's only prospect," wrote Frederick to his brother, Duke John; "nothing can save him. If God permits me to return to you, I shall have matters to relate that are almost beyond belief. It is not only Annas and Caiaphas, but Pilate and Herod also, that have combined against him." Frederick had little desire to remain longer at Worms; he departed, and the elector-palatine did the same. The elector-archbishop of Cologne also quitted the diet. Their example was followed by many princes of inferior rank. As they deemed it impossible to avert the blow, they preferred (and in this perhaps they were wrong) abandoning the place. The Spaniards, the Italians, and the most *ultra-montane* German princes alone remained.

The field was now free—Aleander triumphed. He laid before Charles the outline of an edict intended by him as a model of that which the diet ought to issue against the monk. The nuncio's project pleased the exasperated emperor. He assembled the remaining members of the diet in his chamber, and there had Aleander's edict read over to them; it was accepted (Pallavicini informs us) by all who were present.

The next day, which was a great festival, the emperor went to the cathedral, attended by all the lords of his court. When the religious ceremonies were over, and a crowd of people still thronged the sanctuary, Aleander, robed in all the insignia of his dignity, approached Charles V.[2] He held in his hand two copies of the edict against Luther, one in Latin, the other in German, and kneeling before his imperial majesty, entreated him to affix to them his signature and the seal of the empire. It was at the moment when the sacrifice had been offered, when the incense still filled the temple, while the sacred chants were still re-echoing through its long-drawn aisles, and as it were in the presence of the Deity, that the destruction of the

enemy of Rome was to be sealed. The emperor, assuming a very gracious air,[1] took the pen and wrote his name. Aleander withdrew in triumph, immediately sent the decree to the printers, and forwarded it to every part of Christendom.[2] This crowning act of the toils of Rome had cost the papacy no little trouble. Pallavicini himself informs us, that this edict, although bearing date the 8th of May, was not signed till later; but it was antedated to make it appear that the signature was affixed at a period when all the members of the diet were assembled.

"We, CHARLES THE FIFTH," said the emperor (and then came his titles), "to all electors, princes, prelates, and others whom it may concern.

"The Almighty having confided to us, for the defence of the holy faith, more kingdoms and greater authority than He has ever given to any of our predecessors, we purpose employing every means in our power to prevent our holy empire from being polluted by any heresy.

"The Augustine monk, Martin Luther, notwithstanding our exhortation, has rushed like a madman on our holy Church, and attempted to destroy it by books overflowing with blasphemy. He has shamefully polluted the indestructible law of holy matrimony; he has endeavoured to excite the laity to dye their hands in the blood of the clergy;[3] and, setting at nought all authority, has incessantly urged the people to revolt, schism, war, murder, robbery, incendiarism, and to the utter ruin of the christian faith......In a word, not to mention his many other evil practices, this man, who is in truth not a man, but Satan himself under the form of a man and dressed in a monk's frock,[4] has collected into one stinking slough all the vilest heresies of past times, and has added to them new ones of his own......

"We have therefore dismissed from our presence this Luther, whom all pious and sensible men deem a madman, or one possessed by the devil; and we enjoin that, on the expiration of his safe-conduct, immediate recourse be had to effectual measures to check his furious rage.

"For this reason, under pain of incurring the penalties due to the crime of high-treason, we forbid you to harbour the said Luther after the appointed term shall be expired, to conceal him, to give him food or drink, or to furnish him, by word or by deed, publicly or secretly, with any kind of succour whatsoever. We enjoin you, moreover, to seize him, or cause him to be seized, wherever you may find him, to bring him before us without any delay, or to keep him in safe custody,

---

[1] Humiliter tamen excusante....ob metum tyrannorum suorum. L. Epp. ii. 6.
[2] Cum Cæsar in templo adesset....processit illi obviam Aleander. Pallav. i. 122.

[1] Festivissimo vultu. Pallav. i. 122.
[2] Et undique pervulgata. Ibid.
[3] Ihre Hände in der Priester Blut zu waschen. L. Opp. (L.) xvii. 598.
[4] Nicht ein Mensch, sondern als der böse Feind in Gestalt eines Menschen mit angenommenen Mönchskütten.... Ibid.

until you have learned from us in what manner you are to act towards him, and have received the reward due to your labours in so holy a work.

"As for his adherents, you will apprehend them, confine them, and confiscate their property.

"As for his writings, if the best nutriment becomes the detestation of all men as soon as one drop of poison is mingled with it, how much more ought such books, which contain a deadly poison for the soul, be not only rejected, but destroyed! You will therefore burn them, or utterly destroy them in any other manner.

"As for the authors, poets, printers, painters, buyers or sellers of placards, papers, or pictures, against the pope or the Church, you will seize them, body and goods, and will deal with them according to your good pleasure.

"And if any person, whatever be his dignity, should dare act in contradiction to the decree of our imperial majesty, we order him to be placed under the ban of the empire.

"Let every man behave according to this decree."

Such was the edict signed in the cathedral of Worms. It was more than a bull of Rome, which, although published in Italy, could not be executed in Germany. The emperor himself had spoken, and the diet had ratified his decree. All the partisans of Rome burst into a shout of triumph. "It is the end of the tragedy!" exclaimed they.— "In my opinion," said Alphonso Valdez, a Spaniard at Charles's court, "it is not the end, but only the beginning."[1] Valdez perceived that the movement was in the Church, in the people, and in the age, and that, even should Luther perish, his cause would not perish with him. But no one was blind to the imminent and inevitable danger in which the reformer himself was placed; and the great majority of superstitious persons were filled with horror at the thought of that incarnate devil, covered with a monk's hood, whom the emperor pointed out to the nation.

The man against whom the mighty ones of the earth were thus forging their thunderbolts had quitted the church of Eisenach, and was preparing to bid farewell to some of his dearest friends. He did not take the road to Gotha and Erfurth, but proceeded to the village of Mora, his father's native place, once more to see his aged grandmother, who died four months after, and to visit his uncle, Henry Luther, and some other relations. Schurff, Jonas, and Suaven set out for Wittemberg; Luther got into the waggon with Amsdorff, who still remained with him, and entered the forests of Thuringia.[2]

The same evening he arrived at the village of his sires. The poor old peasant clasped in her arms that grandson who had withstood Charles the emperor and Leo the pope. Luther spent the next day with his relations; happy, after the tumult at Worms, in this sweet tranquillity. On the next morning he resumed his journey, accompanied by Amsdorff and his brother James. In this lonely spot the reformer's fate was to be decided. They skirted the woods of Thuringia, following the road to Waltershausen. As the waggon was moving through a hollow way, near the deserted church of Glisbach, at a short distance from the castle of Altenstein, a sudden noise was heard, and immediately five horsemen, masked and armed from head to foot, sprung upon the travellers. His brother James, as soon as he caught sight of the assailants, leaped from the waggon and ran away as fast as his legs would carry him, without uttering a single word. The driver would have resisted. "Stop!" cried one of the strangers with a terrible voice, falling upon him and throwing him to the ground.[1] A second mask laid hold of Amsdorff and kept him at a distance. Meanwhile the three remaining horsemen seized upon Luther, maintaining a profound silence. They pulled him violently from the waggon, threw a military cloak over his shoulders, and placed him on a led horse. The two other masks now quitted Amsdorff and the waggoner; all five leaped to their saddles— one dropped his hat, but they did not even stop to pick it up—and in the twinkling of an eye vanished with their prisoner into the gloomy forest. At first they took the road to Broderode, but soon retraced their steps by another path; and without quitting the wood, made so many windings in every direction as utterly to baffle any attempt to track them. Luther, little accustomed to be on horseback, was soon overcome with fatigue.[2] They permitted him to alight for a few minutes: he lay down near a beech-tree, where he drank some water from a spring which is still called after his name. His brother James, continuing his flight, arrived at Waltershausen in the evening. The affrighted waggoner jumped into the car, which Amsdorff had again mounted, and whipping his horses, drove rapidly away from the spot, and conducted Luther's friend to Wittemberg. At Waltershausen, at Wittemberg, in the country, villages, and towns along their road, they spread the news of the violent abduction of the doctor. This intelligence, which delighted some, struck the greater number with astonishment and indignation. A cry of grief soon resounded through all Germany: "Luther has fallen into the hands of his enemies!"

After the violent combat that Luther had just sustained, God had been pleased to conduct him to a place of repose and peace. After having exhibited him on the brilliant

---

[1] Non finem, sed initium. P. Martyris Epp. p. 412.
[2] Ad carnem meam trans sylvam profectus. L. Epp. ii. 7.

[1] Dejectoque in solum auriga et verberato. Pallav. l. 122.
[2] Longo itinere, novus eques, fessus. L. Epp. ii. 3.

theatre of Worms, where all the powers of the reformer's soul had been strung to so high a pitch, He gave him the secluded and humiliating retreat of a prison. God draws from the deepest seclusion the weak instruments by which He purposes to accomplish great things; and then, when He has permitted them to glitter for a season with dazzling brilliancy on an illustrious stage, He dismisses them again to the deepest obscurity. The Reformation was to be accomplished by other means than violent struggles or pompous appearances before diets. It is not thus that the leaven penetrates the mass of the people : the Spirit of God seeks more tranquil paths. The man, whom the Roman champions were persecuting without mercy, was to disappear for a time from the world. It was requisite that this great individuality should fade away, in order that the revolution then accomplishing might not bear the stamp of an individual. It was necessary for the man to retire, that God might remain alone to move by His Spirit upon the deep waters in which the darkness of the Middle Ages was already engulfed, and to say : *Let there be light,* so that there might be light.

As soon as it grew dark, and no one could track their footsteps, Luther's guards took a new road. About one hour before midnight they reached the foot of a mountain.[1] The horses ascended slowly. On the summit was an old castle, surrounded on all sides, save that by which it was approached, by the black forests that cover the mountains of Thuringia.

It was to this lofty and isolated fortress, named the Wartburg, where in former times the ancient landgraves had sheltered themselves, that Luther was conducted. The bolts were drawn back, the iron bars fell, the gates opened ; the reformer crossed the threshold ; the doors were closed behind him. He dismounted in the court. One of the horsemen, Burkhardt of Hund, lord of Altenstein, withdrew ; another, John of Berlepsch, provost of the Wartburg, led the doctor into the chamber that was to be his prison, and where he found a knight's uniform and a sword. The three other cavaliers, the pro-

vost's attendants, took away his ecclesiastical robes, and dressed him in the military garments that had been prepared for him, enjoining him to let his beard and hair grow,[1] in order that no one in the castle might discover who he was. The people in the Wartburg were to know the prisoner only by the name of Knight George. Luther scarcely recognised himself in his new dress.[2] At last he was left alone, and his mind could reflect by turns on the astonishing events that had just taken place at Worms, on the uncertain future that awaited him, and on his new and strange residence. From the narrow loopholes of his turret, his eye roamed over the gloomy, solitary, and extensive forests that surrounded him. "It was there," says Mathesius, his friend and biographer, "that the doctor abode, like St. Paul in his prison at Rome."

Frederick of Thun, Philip Feilitsch, and Spalatin, in a private conversation they had had with Luther at Worms by the elector's orders, had not concealed from him that his liberty must be sacrificed to the anger of Charles and of the pope.[3] And yet this abduction had been so mysteriously contrived, that even Frederick was for a long time ignorant of the place where Luther was shut up. The grief of the friends of the Reformation was prolonged. The spring passed away ; summer, autumn, and winter succeeded ; the sun had accomplished its annual course, and still the walls of the Wartburg enclosed their prisoner. Truth had been interdicted by the diet; its defender, confined within the ramparts of a castle, had disappeared from the stage of the world, and no one knew what had become of him : Aleander triumphed ; the reformation appeared lost.........But God reigns, and the blow that seemed as if it would destroy the cause of the Gospel, did but contribute to save its courageous minister, and to extend the light of faith to distant countries.

Let us quit Luther, a captive in Germany, on the rocky heights of the Wartburg, to see what God was doing in other countries of Christendom.

---

[1] Hora ferme undecima ad mansionem noctis perveni in tenebris. L. Epp. ii. 3.

[1] Exutus vestibus meis et equestribus indutus, comam et barbam nutriens ..... L. Epp. ii. 7.
[2] Cum ipse me jamdudum non noverim. Ibid.
[3] Seckend. p. 365.

BOOK VIII.

THE SWISS. 1484—1522.

CHAPTER I.

Movement in Switzerland—Source of the Reformation—Its democratic Character—Foreign Service—Morality—The Tockenburg—A Chalet on the Alps—A Family of Shepherds—Young Ulrich.

AT the moment when the decree of the Diet of Worms appeared, a continually increasing movement began to disturb the quiet valleys of Switzerland. The voices that resounded over the plains of Upper and Lower Saxony were re-echoed from the bosom of the Helvetic mountains by the energetic voices of its priests, of its shepherds, and of the inhabitants of its warlike cities. The partisans of Rome were filled with apprehension, and exclaimed that a wide and terrible conspiracy was forming every where in the Church against the Church. The exulting friends of the Gospel said that, as in spring the breath of life is felt from the shores of the sea to the mountain top, so the Spirit of God was now melting throughout Christendom the ices of a lengthened winter, and covering it with fresh flowers and verdure, from its lowest plains to its most barren and its steepest rocks.

It was not Germany that communicated the light of truth to Switzerland, Switzerland to France, and France to England: all these countries received it from God; just as one part of the world does not communicate the light of day to the other, but the same brilliant orb imparts it direct to all the earth. Infinitely exalted above men, Christ, *the day-spring from on high,* was at the epoch of the Reformation, as he had been at the establishment of Christianity, the Divine fire whence emanated the life of the world. One and the same doctrine was suddenly established, in the sixteenth century, at the hearths and altars of the most distant and dissimilar nations; it was every where the same spirit, every where producing the same faith.

The Reformation of Germany and that of Switzerland demonstrate this truth. Zwingle had no communication with Luther. There was no doubt a connecting link between these two men; but we must not look for it upon earth: it was above. He who from heaven gave the truth to Luther, gave it to Zwingle also. Their bond of union was God. "I began to preach the Gospel," says Zwingle, "in the year of grace 1516, that is to say, at a time when Luther's name had never been heard in this country. It is not from Luther that I learnt the doctrine of Christ, but from the Word of God. If Luther preaches Christ, he does what I am doing; and that is all." [1]

But if the different reformations derived a striking unity from the same Spirit whence they all proceeded, they also received certain particular marks from the different nations among whom they were effected.

We have already given an outline of the condition of Switzerland at the epoch of the Reformation. [2] We shall add but little to what has been already said. In Germany the monarchical principle predominated, in Switzerland the democratic. In Germany the Reformation had to struggle with the will of princes; in Switzerland, against the wishes of the people. An assembly of men, more easily carried away than a single individual, is also more rapid in its decisions. The victory over the papacy, which cost years of struggle beyond the Rhine, required on this side but a few months, and sometimes only a few days.

In Germany, the person of Luther towers imposingly above the Saxon people; he seems to be alone in his attacks upon the Roman colossus; and wherever the conflict is raging, we discern from afar his lofty stature rising high above the battle. Luther is the monarch, so to speak, of the revolution that is accomplishing. In Switzerland, the struggle begins in different cantons at the same time; there is a confederation of reformers; their number surprises us; doubtless one head overtops the others, but no one commands; it is a republican senate, in which all appear with their original features and distinct influences. They were a host: Wittembach, Zwingle, Capito, Haller, Œcolampadius, Oswald Myconius, Leo Juda, Farel, Calvin; their stage was Glaris, Basle, Zurich, Berne, Neufchatel, Geneva, Lucerne, Schafhausen, Appenzel, Saint Gall, and the Grisons. In the German reformation there is but one stage, flat and uniform as the country itself; in Switzerland, the Reformation is divided, like the region itself, by its thousand mountains. Each valley, so to speak, has its own awakening, and each peak of the Alps, its own light from heaven.

A lamentable epoch for the Swiss had begun after their exploits against the dukes of

[1] 1516 eo scilicet tempore, quum Lutheri nomen in nostris regionibus inauditum adhuc erat . . . doctrinam Christi non a Luthero, sed ex verbo Dei didici. Zwinglii Opera cur. Schulero et Schulthessio, Turici, 1829, vol. i. 273, 276.
[2] Vol. i. p. 25.

Burgundy. Europe, which had discovered the strength of their arms, had enticed them from their mountains, and had robbed them of their independence, by rendering them the arbitrators of the fate of nations on the battle-field. The hand of a Swiss pointed the sword at the breast of his fellow-countryman on the plains of Italy and of France, and the intrigues of foreigners had filled with jealousy and dissension those lofty valleys of the Alps so long the abode of simplicity and peace. Attracted by the charms of gold, sons, labourers, and serving-men, stealthily quitted their Alpine pastures for the banks of the Rhone or the Po. Helvetian unity was broken under the slow steps of mules laden with gold. . The Reformation (for in Switzerland also it had its political bearings), proposed to restore the unity and the ancient virtues of the cantons. Its first cry was for the Swiss to rend the perfidious toils of the stranger, and to embrace one another in close union at the foot of the cross. But its generous accents were unheeded. Rome, accustomed to purchase in these valleys the blood she shed to increase her power, rose up in anger. She excited Swiss against Swiss; and passions hitherto unknown sprang up and rent the body of the nation.

Switzerland needed a reform. There was, it is true, among the Helvetians, a simplicity and good nature that seemed ridiculous to the refined Italians; but at the same time they had the reputation of being the people that most habitually transgressed the laws of chastity. This astrologers attributed to the constellations;[1] philosophers, to the strength of temperament among those indomitable people; moralists, to the Swiss principles, which looked upon deceit, dishonesty, and calumny, as sins of a much deeper die than impurity.[2] Marriage was forbidden the priests; but it would have been difficult to find one who lived in a state of real celibacy. They were required to behave, not chastely, but prudently. This was one of the earliest disorders against which the Reformation was directed.

It is now time to trace the dawnings of the new day in these valleys of the Alps.

About the middle of the eleventh century two hermits made their way from Saint Gall towards the mountains that lie to the south of this ancient monastery, and arrived at a desert valley about ten leagues long.[3] On the north, the lofty mountains of the Sentis, Sommerigkopf, and the Old Man, separate this valley from the canton of Appenzel; on the south, the Kuhfirsten with its seven peaks rises between it and the Wallensee, Sargans, and the Grisons; on the east, the valley slopes away to the rays of the rising sun, and displays the magnificent prospect of the Tyrolese Alps. These two hermits, having reached the springs of the little river Thur, erected their two cells. By degrees the valley was peopled; on its most elevated portion, 2010 feet above the level of Lake Zurich, there arose around a church a village named *Wildhaus*, or the *Wild-house*, upon which now depend two hamlets, Lisighaus, or Elizabeth's house, and Schönenboden. The fruits of the earth grow not upon these heights. A green turf of alpine freshness covers the whole valley, ascending the sides of the mountains, above which enormous masses of rock rise in savage grandeur to the skies.

About a quarter of a league from the church, near Lisighaus, by the side of a path that leads to the pasture-grounds beyond the river, may still be seen a peasant's cottage. Tradition narrates that the wood necessary for its construction was felled on the very spot.[1] Everything seems to indicate that it was built in the most remote times. The walls are thin, the windows are composed of small round panes of glass; the roof is formed of shingles, loaded with stones to prevent their being carried away by the wind. Before the house gushes forth a limpid stream.

About the end of the fifteenth century, this house was inhabited by a man named Zwingle, amman or bailiff of the parish. The family of the Zwingles or Zwingli was ancient, and in great esteem among the inhabitants of these mountains.[2] Bartholomew, the bailiff's brother, at first incumbent of the parish, and from the year 1487 dean of Wesen, enjoyed a certain celebrity in the country.[3] The wife of the amman of Wildhaus, Margaret Meili (whose brother John was somewhat later abbot of the convent of Fischingen in Thurgovia), had already borne him two sons, Henry and Klaus, when on New Year's day 1484, seven weeks after the birth of Luther, a third son, who was christened Ulrich, was born in this lonely chalet.[4] Five other sons, John, Wolfgang, Bartholomew, James, Andrew, and an only daughter, Anna, increased the number of this Alpine family. No one in the whole district was more respected than the amman Zwingle.[5] His character, his office, and his numerous children, made him the patriarch of the mountains. He was a shepherd, as were his sons. No sooner had the first days of May clothed the mountains with verdure,

1 Wirz, Helvetische Kirchen Geschichte, iii. 201.
2 Sodomitis melius erit in die judicii, quam rerum vel honoris ablatoribus. Hemmerlin, de anno jubilæo.
3 The Tockenburg.

1 Schuler's Zwingli's Bildungs Gesch., p. 290.
2 Diss Geschlächt der Zwinglinen, wass in guter Achtung diesser Landen, als ein gut alt ehrlich Geschlächt. H. Bullinger's Hist. Beschreibung der Eidg. Geschichten. I am indebted to the kindness of Mr J. G. Hess for the communication of this valuable work, which in 1837 existed only in manuscript. It has since been published by some friends of history at Zurich. In my quotations I have preserved the orthography of the original.
3 Ein verrumbter Mann. Ibid.
4 Quadragesimum octavum agimus (I am in my forty-eighth year), wrote Zwingle to Vadianus, on the 17th of September 1531.
5 Clarus fuit pater ob spectatam vitæ sanctimoniam. Oswald Myconius, Vita Zwinglii.

than the father and his children would set off for the pasture-grounds with their flocks, rising gradually from station to station, and reaching in this way, by the end of July, the highest summits of the Alps. They then began to return gradually towards the valleys, and in autumn the whole population of the Wildhaus re-entered their humble cottages. Sometimes, during the summer, the young people who should have stayed at home, longing to enjoy the fresh breezes of the mountains, set out in companies for the chalets, accompanying their voices with the melodious notes of their rustic instruments; for all were musicians. When they reached the Alps, the shepherds welcomed them from afar with their horns and songs, and spread before them a repast of milk; and then the joyous troop, after many devious windings, returned to their valleys to the sound of the bagpipe. In his early youth, Ulrich doubtless sometimes shared in these amusements. He grew up at the foot of these rocks that seemed everlasting, and whose summits pointed to the skies. "I have often thought," said one of his friends, "that being brought near to heaven on these sublime heights, he there contracted something heavenly and divine."[1]

Long were the winter evenings in the cottages of the Wildhaus. At such a season the youthful Ulrich listened, at the paternal hearth, to the conversations between the bailiff and the elders of the parish. He heard them relate how the inhabitants of the valley had in former times groaned beneath a heavy yoke. He thrilled with joy at the thought of the independence the Tockenburg had won for itself, and which its alliance with the Swiss had secured. The love of country kindled in his heart; Switzerland became dear to him; and if any one chanced to drop a word unfavourable to the confederates, the child would immediately rise up and warmly defend their cause.[2] Often, too, might he be seen, during these long evenings, quietly seated at the feet of his pious grandmother, listening, with his eyes fixed on her, to her scripture stories and her pious legends, and eagerly receiving them into his heart.

[1] Divinitatis nonnihil cœlo propiorem contraxisse. Oswald Myconius, Vita Zw.
[2] Schuler's Zw. Bildung. p. 291.

CHAPTER II.

Ulrich at Wesen and Basle—Ulrich at Berne—The Dominican Convent—Jetzer—The Apparitions—Passion of the Lay-brother—Imposture—Discovery and Punishment—Zwingle at Vienna and Basle—Music at Basle—Wittembach proclaims the Gospel—Leo Juda—The Priest of Glaris.

THE good amman was charmed at the promising disposition of his son. He perceived that Ulrich might one day do something better than tend herds on Mount Sentis, to the sound of the shepherd's song (ranz des vaches). One day he took him by the hand and led him to Wesen. He crossed the grassy flanks of the Ammon, and descended the bold and savage rocks that border the Lake of Wallenstadt; on reaching the town, he entered the house of his brother the dean, and intrusted the young mountaineer to his care, that he might examine his capacity.[1] Ulrich was particularly distinguished by a natural horror of falsehood, and a great love for truth. He tells us himself, that one day, when he began to reflect, the thought occurred to him that "lying ought to be punished more severely than theft;" for, adds he, "truth is the mother of all virtues." The dean soon loved his nephew like a son; and, charmed with his vivacity, he confided his education to a schoolmaster, who in a short time taught him all he knew himself. At ten years of age, the marks of a superior mind were already noticed in the young Ulrich.[2] His father and his uncle resolved to send him to Basle.

When the child of the Tockenburg arrived in this celebrated city, with that singlemindedness and simplicity of heart which he seems to have inhaled with the pure air of his native mountains, but which really came from a higher source, a new world opened before him. The celebrity of the famous Council of Basle, the university which Pius II. had founded in this city in 1460, the printing-presses which then resuscitated the masterpieces of antiquity, and circulated through the world the first fruits of the revival of letters; the distinguished men who resided in it, Wessel, Wittembach, and especially of that prince of scholars, that sun of the schools, Erasmus, all rendered Basle, at the epoch of the Reformation, one of the great centres of light in the West.

Ulrich was placed at St. Theodore's school. Gregory Binzli was then at its head,—a man of feeling heart, and gentleness rarely found at that period among teachers. Young Zwingle made rapid progress. The learned disputations, then in fashion among the doctors, had descended even to the children in the schools. Ulrich took part in them; he

[1] Tenerrimum adhuc ad fratrem sacrificum adduxit, ut ingenii ejus periculum faceret. Melch. Adami Vita Zw. p. 25.
[2] Und in Ihm erschinen merkliche Zeichen eines edlen Gemüths. Bullinger Chronick.

disciplined his growing powers against the pupils of other establishments, and was always conqueror in these struggles, which were a prelude to those by which he was to overthrow the papacy in Switzerland.[1] This success filled his elder rivals with jealousy. He soon outgrew the school of Basle, as he had that of Wesen.

Lupulus, a distinguished scholar, had just opened at Berne the first learned institution in Switzerland. The bailiff of Wildhaus and the priest of Wesen resolved to send the boy to it; Zwingle, in 1497, left the smiling plains of Basle, and again approached those Upper Alps where his infancy had been spent, and whose snowy tops, gilded by the sun, might be seen from Berne. Lupulus, himself a distinguished poet, introduced his pupil into the sanctuary of classic learning,—a treasure then unknown, and whose threshold had been passed only by a few.[2] The young neophyte ardently inhaled these perfumes of antiquity. His mind expanded, his style was formed, he became a poet.

Among the convents of Berne, that of the Dominicans was the most celebrated. These monks were engaged in a serious quarrel with the Franciscans. The latter maintained the immaculate conception of the Virgin, which the former denied. Wherever they went, before the dazzling altars that adorned their church, and between the twelve columns that supported its fretted roof, the Dominicans had but one thought—how they might humble their rivals. They had remarked Zwingle's beautiful voice; they had heard of his precocious understanding, and thinking that he might give lustre to their order, endeavoured to attract him among them,[3] and invited him to remain in their convent until he was old enough to pass his noviciate. All Zwingle's future career was at stake. The amman of Wildhaus being informed of the lures to which the Dominicans had resorted, trembled for the inexperience of his son, and ordered him to quit Berne immediately. Zwingle thus escaped from these monastic walls within which Luther had entered of his own free-will. What transpired somewhat later may serve to show the imminent danger Zwingle then incurred.

In 1507, a great agitation reigned in the city of Berne. A young man of Zurzach, named John Jetzer, having one day presented himself at this same Dominican convent, had been repulsed. The poor dejected youth made another attempt, and said, holding out fifty-three florins and some pieces of silk, "It is all I possess; take it, and receive me into your order." He was admitted on the

6th of January among the lay brethren But on the first night, a strange noise in his cell filled him with terror. He fled to the convent of the Carthusians, whence he was sent back to the Dominicans.

On the following night, the eve of the festival of Saint Matthias, he was awoke by deep groans; he opened his eyes, and saw a tall white spectral form standing beside his bed. " I am," said a sepulchral voice, " a soul escaped from the fires of purgatory." The lay brother tremblingly replied: "God help thee! I can do nothing." The phantom then advanced towards the poor brother, and seizing him by the throat, indignantly reproached him for his refusal. Jetzer, full of alarm, exclaimed : " What can I do to save thee ?" " Scourge thyself eight days in succession until the blood comes, and lie prostrate on the earth in the Chapel of Saint John." The spectre answered thus and vanished. The lay brother confided the particulars of this apparition to his confessor, the convent-preacher, and, by his advice, submitted to the discipline required. It was soon reported through the whole city that a soul had applied to the Dominicans in order to be delivered from purgatory. The Franciscans were deserted, and the people ran in crowds to the church, where the holy man was to be seen prostrate on the pavement. The soul from purgatory had announced its re-appearance in eight days. On the appointed night, it came again, attended by two spirits that tormented it, extorting from it the most frightful groans. " Scotus," said the disturbed spirit, " Scotus, the inventor of the Franciscan doctrine of the immaculate conception of the Virgin, is among those who suffer like horrible torments with me." At this news, which soon spread through Berne, the partisans of the Franciscans were still more dismayed. But the soul, at the moment of disappearing, had announced a visit from the Virgin herself. In effect, on the day fixed, the astonished brother saw Mary appear in his cell. He could not believe his eyes. She approached him kindly, gave him three of our Saviour's tears, and as many drops of his blood, with a crucifix and a letter addressed to Pope Julius II., " who, said she, " is the man selected by God to abolish the festival of His pretended immaculate conception." And then, drawing still nearer the bed on which the brother lay, she informed him in a solemn voice that he was about to experience a signal favour, and at the same time pierced his hand with a nail. The brother uttered a horrible shriek; but Mary wrapt his hand in a cloth that her Son (as she said) had worn at the time of the flight into Egypt. This one wound was not enough; in order that the glory of the Dominicans might at least equal that of the Franciscans, Jetzer must have the five wounds of Christ and of St. Francis on his hands, his feet, and his side. The four

---

[1] In disputationibus, quæ pro more tum erant inter pueros usitatæ, victoriam semper reportavit. Osw. Myc. Vita Zw.

[2] Ab eo in adyta classicorum scriptorum introductus. Ibid.

[3] Und alss er wol singen kœndt, lœkten ihn die prediger mœnchen in dass Kloster. Bullinger Chronik.

others were inflicted, and then, after giving him some drink, he was placed in a hall hung with pictures representing our Lord's passion ; here he spent many long days without food, and his imagination soon became greatly excited. The monks from time to time opened the doors of this chamber to the people, who came in crowds to contemplate with devout astonishment the brother with his five wounds, stretching out his arms, bending his head, and imitating by his postures and movements the crucifixion of our Lord. At times, he was quite out of his senses ; he foamed at the mouth, and appeared ready to give up the ghost. " He is suffering the cross of Christ," murmured the spectators. The multitude, eager in pursuit of miracles, thronged the convent incessantly. Men who deserve our highest esteem, even Lupulus himself, Zwingle's teacher, were overcome with fear ; and the Dominicans, from their pulpits, boasted of the glory God had conferred upon their order.

For many years this order had felt the necessity of humbling the Franciscans and of increasing by means of miracles the respect and liberality of the people. The theatre selected for these operations was Berne, " a simple, rude, and ignorant city," as it had been styled by the sub-prior of Berne in a chapter held at Wimpfen on the Neckar. To the prior, sub-prior, chaplain, and purveyor of the convent were assigned the principal parts, but they were not able to play them out. A new apparition of Mary having taken place, Jetzer fancied he recognised his confessor's voice ; and on saying so aloud, Mary disappeared. She came again to censure the incredulous brother. " This time it is the prior," exclaimed Jetzer, rushing on him with a knife in his hand. The saint flung a pewter platter at the head of the poor brother, and vanished.

Alarmed at the discovery Jetzer had made, the Dominicans endeavoured to get rid of him by poison. He detected their treachery, and having escaped from the convent, revealed their imposture. They put a good face on the matter, and sent deputies to Rome. The pope empowered his legate in Switzerland, and the bishops of Lausanne and Sion, to inquire into the affair. The four Dominicans were convicted and condemned to be burnt alive, and on the 1st of May 1509, they perished at the stake in the presence of more than thirty thousand spectators. The rumour of this imposture circulated through Europe, and by laying bare one of the greatest sores of the Church, prepared the way for the Reformation.[1]

Such were the men from whose hands the youthful Ulrich Zwingle escaped. He had studied polite letters at Berne ; he had now

to study philosophy, and for this purpose went to Vienna in Austria. The companions of Ulrich's studies and amusements in the capital of Austria were a young man of Saint Gall, Joachim Vadian, whose genius promised to adorn Switzerland with a learned scholar and a distinguished statesman ; Henry Loréti, of the canton of Glaris, better known as Glarean, and who appeared destined to shine as a poet ; and a young Swabian, John Heigerlin, the son of a blacksmith, and hence called Faber, a man of pliant character, proud of honours and renown, and who gave promise of all the qualities requisite to form a courtier.

Zwingle returned to Wildhaus in 1502 ; but on revisiting his native mountains, he felt that he had quaffed of the cup of learning, and that he could not live amidst the songs of his brothers and the lowing of their herds. Being now eighteen years of age, he again repaired to Basle[1] to continue his literary pursuits ; and there, at once master and scholar, he taught in Saint Martin's school, and studied at the university ; from that time he was able to do without the assistance of his parents. Not long after he took the degree of Master of Arts. An Alsatian, Capito by name, who was his senior by nine years, was one of his greatest friends.

Zwingle now applied to the study of scholastic divinity ; for as he would one day be called to expose its sophistry, it was necessary that he should first explore its gloomy labyrinths. But the joyous student of the Sentis mountains might be seen suddenly shaking off the dust of the schools, and changing his philosophic toils for innocent amusements ; he would take up one of his numerous musical instruments (the lute, harp, violin, flute, dulcimer, or hunting horn), draw from them some cheerful air, as in the pasture-grounds of Lisighaus ; make his own chamber or that of his friends re-echo with the tunes of his native place, and accompany them with his songs. In his love for music he was a real child of the Tockenburg,—a master among many.[2] He played on other instruments besides those we have already named. Enthusiastic in the art, he spread a taste for it through the university ; not that he was fond of dissipation, but because he liked by this means to relax his mind, fatigued by serious study, and to put himself in a condition to return with greater zeal to such arduous pursuits.[3] None possessed a livelier disposition, or more amiable character, or more attractive conversational powers.[4] He was like a vigorous Alpine tree, expanding in all its strength and beauty, and which,

1 Ne diutius ab exercitio literarum cessaret. Osw. Myc. Vita Zw.
2 Ich habe auch nie von Keinem gehœrt, der in der Kunst Musica .....so erfahren gewesen. B. Weysen, Füsslin Beyträge zur Ref. Gesch. iv. 35.
3 Ut ingenium seriis defatigatum recrearetur et paratius ad solita studia rediretur.....Melch. Adami Vita Zw.
4 Ingenio amœnus, et ore jucundus, supra quam dici pos sit, erat. Osw. Myc. Vita Zw.

1 Wirz, Helvetische Kirchen, Gesch. iii. 387; Anshelm's Chronik, iii. and iv. No transaction of that day ever gave rise to so many publications. See Haller's Biblioth. der Schw. Gesch. iii.

as yet unpruned, throws out its healthy branches in every direction. The time will come for these branches to shoot with fresh vigour towards heaven.

After having plunged into the scholastic divinity, he quitted its barren wastes with weariness and disgust, having found therein nothing but a medley of confused ideas, empty babbling, vain-glory, and barbarism, without one atom of sound doctrine. "It is a mere loss of time," said he ; and he waited his hour.

In November 1505, Thomas Wittembach, son of a burgomaster of Bienne, arrived at Basle. Hitherto he had been teaching at Tubingen, at the side of Reuchlin. He was in the flower of life, sincere, pious, skilled in the liberal arts, the mathematics, and in the knowledge of Scripture. Zwingle and all the youths of the academy immediately flocked around him. An energy till then unknown animated his lectures, and prophetic words fell from his lips. "The hour is not far distant," said he, "in which the scholastic theology will be set aside, and the old doctrines of the Church revived."[1]—"Christ's death," added he, "is the only ransom for our souls."[2] Zwingle's heart eagerly received these seeds of life.[3] This was at the period when classical studies were beginning every where to supersede the scholasticism of the Middle Ages. Zwingle, like his master and his friends, rushed into this new path.

Among the students who were most attentive to the lessons of the new doctor, was a young man twenty-three years old, of small stature, of weak and sickly frame, but whose looks announced both gentleness and intrepidity. This was Leo Juda, the son of an Alsatian parish-priest, and whose uncle had died at Rhodes fighting under the banners of the Teutonic knights in the defence of Christendom. Leo and Ulrich became intimate friends. Leo played on the dulcimer, and had a very fine voice. Often did his chamber re-echo with the cheerful songs of these young friends of the arts. Leo Juda afterwards became Zwingle's colleague, and even death could not destroy so holy a friendship.

The office of pastor of Glaris became vacant at this time. One of the pope's youthful courtiers, Henri Goldli, his Holiness's equerry, and who was already the possessor of several benefices, hastened to Glaris with the pontiff's letter of nomination. But the shepherds of Glaris, proud of the antiquity of their race and of their struggles in the cause of liberty, did not feel inclined to bend their heads before a slip of parchment from Rome. Wildhaus is not far from Glaris, and Wesen,

of which Zwingle's uncle was the incumbent, is the place where these people hold their markets. The reputation of the young master of arts of Basle had extended even to these mountains, and him the people of Glaris desired to have for their priest. They invited him in 1506. Zwingle was ordained at Constance by the bishop, preached his first sermon at Rapperswyl, read his first mass at Wildhaus on St. Michael's day, in the presence of all his relations and the friends of his family, and about the end of the year arrived at Glaris.

CHAPTER III.

Fondness for War—Schinner—Pension from the Pope—The Labyrinth—Zwingle in Italy—Principle of Reform—Zwingle and Luther—Zwingle and Erasmus—Zwingle and the ancient Classics—Paris and Glaris.

Zwingle immediately applied himself with zeal to the duties of his large parish. Yet he was but twenty-two years old, and often permitted himself to be led away by dissipation, and by the relaxed ideas of the age. As a Romish priest, he did not differ from all the surrounding clergy. But even at this time, when the evangelical doctrine had not changed his heart, he was never guilty of those scandals which often afflicted the Church,[1] and always felt the necessity of subjecting his passions to the holy standard of the Gospel.

A fondness for war at that time inflamed the tranquil valleys of Glaris. There dwelt the families of heroes—the Tchudis, the Walas, the Œblis, whose blood had flowed on the field of battle. The aged warriors would relate to the youths, delighted at these recitals, their exploits in the wars of Burgundy and Swabia, and the combats of St. Jacques and of Ragaz. But, alas! it was no longer against the enemies of their independence that these warlike shepherds took up arms. They might be seen, at the voice of the king of France, of the emperor, of the duke of Milan, or even of the holy father himself, descending like an avalanche from the Alps, and dashing with a noise of thunder against the troops drawn up in the plains.

As a poor boy named Matthew Schinner, who attended the school of Sion, in the Valais (about the middle of the second half of the fifteenth century), was singing one day in the streets, as the young Martin Luther did a little later, he heard his name called by an old man. The latter struck by the freedom with which the child answered his questions, said to him with that prophetic tone which a man is thought sometimes to possess on the

[1] Et doctrinam Ecclesiæ veterem....instaurari oporteat. Gualterus, Misc. Tig. iii. 102.
[2] Der Tod Christy sey die einige Bezahlung für unsere Sünde....Füsslin Beytr. ii. 268.
[3] Quum a tanto viro semina quædam....Zwingliano pectori injecta essent. Leo Jud. in Præf. ad. Ann. Zw. in N. T.

[1] Sic reverentia pudoris, imprimis autem officii divini, perpetuo cavit. Osw. Myc. Vit. Zw.

262

brink of the grave: "Thou shalt be a bishop and a prince."[1] These words made a deep impression on the youthful mendicant, and from that moment a boundless ambition took possession of his soul. At Zurich and at Como he made such progress as to surprise his masters. He became priest of a small parish in the Valais, rose rapidly, and being sent to Rome somewhat later to demand of the pope the confirmation of a bishop of Sion, who had just been elected, he obtained this bishopric for himself, and encircled his brows with the episcopal mitre. This ambitious and crafty though often noble-minded and generous man, never considered any dignity but as a step to mount still higher. Having offered his services to Louis XII., and at the same time naming his price: "It is too much for one man," said the king. "I will show him," replied the exasperated Bishop of Sion, "that I, alone, am worth many men." In effect, he turned towards Pope Julius II., who gladly welcomed him; and, in 1510, Schinner succeeded in attaching the whole Swiss confederation to the policy of this warlike pontiff. The bishop was rewarded with a cardinal's hat, and he smiled as he now saw but one step between him and the papal throne.

Schinner's eyes wandered continually over the cantons of Switzerland, and as soon as he discovered an influential man in any place, he hastened to attach him to himself. The pastor of Glaris fixed his attention, and Zwingle learnt erelong that the pope had granted him a yearly pension of fifty florins, to encourage him in his literary pursuits. His poverty did not permit him to buy books; this money, during the short time Ulrich received it, was entirely devoted to the purchase of classical or theological works, which he procured from Basle.[2] Zwingle from that time attached himself to the cardinal, and thus entered the Roman party. Schinner and Julius II. at last betrayed the object of their intrigues; eight thousand Swiss, whom the eloquence of the cardinal-bishop had enlisted, crossed the Alps; but want of provisions, with the arms and money of the French, made them return ingloriously to their mountains. They carried back with them the usual concomitants of these foreign wars—distrust, licentiousness, party-spirit, violence, and disorders of every kind. Citizens refused to obey their magistrates; children their parents; agriculture and the cares of their flocks and herds were neglected; luxury and beggary increased side by side; the holiest ties were broken, and the Confederation seemed on the brink of dissolution.

Then were the eyes of the young priest of Glaris opened, and his indignation burst forth. His powerful voice was raised to warn the people of the gulf into which they were about to fall. It was in the year 1510 that he published his poem entitled *The Labyrinth.* Within the mazes of this mysterious garden, Minos has concealed the Minotaur, that monster, half-man, half-bull, whom he feeds with the bodies of the young Athenians. "This Minotaur," says Zwingle, "represents the sins, the vices, the irreligion, the foreign service of the Swiss, which devour the sons of the nation."

A bold man, Theseus, determines to rescue his country; but numerous obstacles arrest him:—first, a one-eyed lion; this is Spain and Aragon:—then a crowned eagle, whose beak opens to swallow him up; this is the Empire:—then a cock, raising its crest, and seeming to challenge to the fight; this is France. The hero surmounts all these obstacles, reaches the monster, slays him, and saves his country.

"In like manner," exclaims the poet, "are men now wandering in a labyrinth, but, as they have no clue, they cannot regain the light. Nowhere do we find an imitation of Jesus Christ. A little glory leads us to risk our lives, torment our neighbour, and rush into disputes, war, and battle.......One might imagine that the furies had broken loose from the abyss of hell."[1]

A Theseus, a reformer was needed; this Zwingle perceived clearly, and henceforth he felt a presentiment of his mission. Shortly after, he composed an allegory, the meaning of which was less enigmatical.[2]

In April 1512, the confederates again arose at the voice of the cardinal for the defence of the Church. Glaris was in the foremost rank. The whole parish took the field under their banner, with the landamman and their pastor. Zwingle was compelled to march with them. The army passed the Alps, and the cardinal appeared in the midst of the confederates decorated with the pontiff's presents;—a ducal cap ornamented with pearls and gold, and surmounted by the Holy Ghost represented under the form of a dove. The Swiss scaled the ramparts of fortresses and the walls of cities; and in the presence of their enemies swam naked across rivers, halberd in hand. The French were defeated at every point; bells and trumpets pealed their notes of triumph; the people crowded around them from all quarters; the nobles furnished the army with wine and fruits in abundance; monks and priests mounted the pulpits, and proclaimed that the confederates were the people of God, who avenged the Bride of the Lord on her enemies; and the pope a prophet like Caiaphas of old, conferred on them the title of "Defenders of the Liberty of the Church."[3]

---

[1] Helvet. Kirch. Gesch. von Wirz, iii. 314.
[2] Welches er an die Bücher verwändet. Bullinger Chronik.

[1] Das wir die hœllschen wüterinn'n
Mœgend denken abbrochen syn.
Zw. Opp. (Edit. Schüler et Schulthess), ii. second part, 250.
[2] Fabelgedicht vom Ochsen und etlichen Thieren, lez loufender dinge begriffenlich. Ibid. 257.
[3] De Gestis inter Gallos et Helvetios, relatio H. Zwinglii.

This sojourn in Italy was not without its influence on Zwingle as regards his call to the Reformation. On his return from this campaign, he began to study Greek, "in order (as he said) to be able to draw from the fountain-head of truth the doctrines of Jesus Christ.[1] I am determined to apply myself to Greek," wrote he to Vadian on the 23d of February 1513, "that no one shall be able to turn me aside from it, except God: I do it, not for glory, but for the love of sacred learning." Somewhat later, a worthy priest, who had been his schoolfellow, coming to see him: "Master Ulrich," said he, "I am informed that you are falling into this new error; that you are a Lutheran."—"I am not a Lutheran," said Zwingle, "for I learned Greek before I had ever heard the name of Luther."[2] To know Greek, to study the Gospel in the original language, was, in Zwingle's opinion, the basis of the Reformation.

Zwingle went farther than merely acknowledging at this early period the grand principle of evangelical Christianity,—the infallible authority of Holy Scripture. He perceived, moreover, how we should determine the sense of the Divine Word : "They have a very mean idea of the Gospel," said he, "who consider as frivolous, vain, and unjust, all that they imagine does not accord with their own reason.[3] Men are not permitted to wrest the Gospel at pleasure that it may square with their own sentiments and interpretation."[4]—"Zwingle turned his eyes to heaven," says his best friend, "for he would have no other interpreter than the Holy Ghost himself."[5]

Such, at the commencement of his career, was the man whom certain persons have not hesitated to represent as having desired to subject the Bible to human reason. "Philosophy and divinity," said he, "were always raising objections. At last I said to myself: I must neglect all these matters, and look for God's will in his Word alone. I began (continues he) earnestly to entreat the Lord to grant me his light, and although I read the Scriptures only, they became clearer to me than if I had read all the commentators." He compared Scripture with itself, explaining obscure passages by those that are clear.[6] He soon knew the Bible thoroughly, and particularly the New Testament.[7] When Zwingle thus turned towards Holy Scripture, Switzerland took its first step towards the

Reformation. Accordingly, when he explained the Scriptures, every one felt that his teaching came from God, and not from man.[1] "All-divine work!" exclaimed Oswald Myconius; "it is thus we recovered the knowledge of the truth from heaven !"

Zwingle did not, however, contemn the explanations of the most celebrated doctors : in after-years he studied Origen, Ambrose, Jerome, Augustine, and Chrysostom, but not as authorities. "I study the doctors," said he, "with the same end as when we ask a friend: How do you understand this passage?" Holy Scripture, in his opinion, was the touchstone by which to test the holiest doctors themselves.[2]

Zwingle's course was slow, but progressive. He did not arrive at the truth, like Luther, by those storms which impel the soul to run hastily to its harbour of refuge ; he reached it by the peaceful influence of Scripture, whose power expands gradually in the heart. Luther attained the wished-for shore through the storms of the wide ocean ; Zwingle by gliding softly down the stream. These are the two principal ways by which the Almighty leads men. Zwingle was not fully converted to God and to his Gospel until the earlier years of his residence at Zurich ; yet the moment when in 1514 or 1515, this strong man bent the knee before God, in prayer for the understanding of his Word, was that in which appeared the first glimmering rays of the bright day that afterwards beamed upon him.

About this period one of Erasmus's poems, in which Jesus Christ is introduced addressing mankind perishing through their own fault, made a deep impression on Zwingle. Alone in his closet, he repeated to himself that passage in which Jesus complains that men do not seek every grace from him, although he is the source of all that is good. "ALL," said Zwingle, "ALL." And this word was ever present to his mind. "Are there, then, any creatures, any saints of whom we should beg assistance ? No: Christ is our only treasure."[3]

Zwingle did not restrict himself to the study of christian letters. One of the characteristic features of the reformers of the sixteenth century is their profound study of the Greek and Roman writers. The poems of Hesiod, Homer, and Pindar, possessed great charms for Zwingle, and he has left some commentaries or characteristics of the two last poets. It seemed to him that Pindar spoke of the gods in so sublime a strain that he must have felt a presentiment of the true God. He studied Demosthenes and Cicero thoroughly, and in their writings learnt the art of oratory and the duties of a citizen. He

---

[1] Ante decem annos, operam dedi græcis literis, ut ex fontibus doctrinam Christi haurire possem. Zw. Opp. i. 274, in his Explan. Artic. which bears the date of 1523.
[2] Ich hab græcæ können, ehe ich ni nüt von Luther gehöt hab. Salat. Chronik. MS.
[3] Nihil sublimius de evangelio sentiunt, quam quod, quidquid eorum rationi non est consentaneum, hoc iniquum, vanum et frivolum existimant. Zw. Opp. i. 202.
[4] Nec posse evangelium ad sensum et interpretationem hominum redigi. Ibid. 215.
[5] In cœlum suspexit, doctorem quærens Spiritum. Osw. Myc. Vita Zw.
[6] Scripta contulit et obscura claris elucidavit. Ibid.
[7] In summa, er macht im, die H. Schrifft, Insonders dass N. T. gantz gemein. Bullinger MS.

[1] Ut nemo non videret Spiritum doctorem, non hominem. Osw. Myc. Vita Zw.
[2] Scriptura canonica, seu Lydio lapide probandos. Ibid.
[3] Dass Christus unser armen seelen ein einziger Schatz sey. Zw. Opp. i. 298. Zwingle said in 1523 that he had read this poem of Erasmus's some eight or nine years before.

called Seneca a holy man. The child of the Swiss mountains delighted also to investigate the mysteries of nature in the works of Pliny. Thucydides, Sallust, Livy, Cæsar, Suetonius, Plutarch, and Tacitus, taught him the knowledge of mankind. He has been reproached with his enthusiasm for the great men of antiquity, and it is true that some of his expressions on this subject admit of no justification. But if he honoured them so highly, it was because he fancied he discerned in them, not mere human virtues, but the influence of the Holy Ghost. In his opinion, God's influence, far from being limited in ancient times by the boundaries of Palestine, extended over the whole world.[1] " Plato," said he, " has also drunk at this heavenly spring. And if the two Catos, Scipio, and Camillus, had not been truly religious, could they have been so high-minded ?"[2]

Zwingle communicated a taste for letters to all around him. Many intelligent young men were educated at his school. " You have offered me not only books, but yourself also," wrote Valentine Tschudi, son of one of the heroes in the Burgundian wars ; and this young man, who had already studied at Vienna and Basle, under the most celebrated doctors, added : " I have found no one who could explain the classic authors with such acumen and profundity as yourself."[3] Tschudi went to Paris, and thus was able to compare the spirit that prevailed in this university with that which he had found in a narrow valley of the Alps, above which towered the gigantic summits and eternal snows of the Dodi, the Glarnisch, the Viggis and the Freyberg. " In what frivolities do they educate the French youth !" said he. No poison can equal the sophistical art that they are taught. It dulls the senses, weakens the judgment, and brutalizes the man, who then becomes, as it were, a mere echo, an empty sound. Ten women could not make head against one of these rhetoricians.[4] Even in their prayers, I am certain they bring their sophisms before God, and by their syllogisms presume to constrain the Holy Spirit to answer them." Such were at that time Paris, the intellectual metropolis of Christendom, and Glaris, a village of herdmen among the Alps. One ray of light from God's Word enlightens more than all the wisdom of man.

1 Spiritus ille cœlestis non solam Palestinam vel creaverat vel fovebat, sed mundum universum. Œcol. and Zw. Epp. p. 9.
2 Nisi religiosi, nunquam fuissent magnanimi. Ibid.
3 Nam qui sit acrioris in enodandis auctoribus judicii, vidi neminem. Zw. Epp. p. 13.
4 Ut nec decem mulierculæ....uni sophistæ adæquari queant. Ibid. p. 45.

CHAPTER IV.

Zwingle to Erasmus—Oswald Myconius—The Robbers—Œcolampadius—Zwingle at Marignan—Zwingle and Italy—Zwingle's Method—Commencement of the Reform—Discovery—Passage from one World to the other.

A GREAT man of that age, Erasmus, exercised much influence over Zwingle. No sooner did one of his writings appear than Zwingle hastened to purchase it. In 1514, Erasmus arrived in Basle, where the bishop received him with every mark of esteem. All the friends of learning immediately assembled around him. But the prince of the schools had easily discovered him who was to be the glory of Switzerland. " I congratulate the Helvetians," wrote he to Zwingle, " that you are labouring to polish and civilize them by your studies and your morals, which are alike of the highest order."[1] Zwingle earnestly longed to see him. " Spaniards and Gauls went to Rome to see Livy," said he, and set out. On arriving at Basle, he found there a man about forty years of age, of small stature, weak frame, and delicate appearance, but exceedingly amiable and polite.[2] It was Erasmus. His agreeable manners soon banished Zwingle's timidity ; the power of his genius subdued him. " Poor as Æschines," said he, " when each of Socrates' disciples offered their master a present, I give you what Æschines gave......I give you myself !"

Among the men of learning who then formed the court of Erasmus,—such as Amerbach, Rhenanus, Frobenius, Nessenus, and Glarean,—Zwingle noticed one Oswald Geisshüssler, a young man of Lucerne, twenty-seven years old. Erasmus hellenized his name, and called him Myconius. We shall generally speak of him by his baptismal appellation, to distinguish the friend of Zwingle from Frederick Myconius, the disciple of Luther. Oswald, after studying at Rothwyl with a youth of his own age, named Berthold Haller, and next at Berne and at Basle, had become rector of Saint Theodore's school, and afterwards of St. Peter's in the latter city. The humble schoolmaster, though possessed of a scanty income, had married a young woman whose simplicity and purity of mind won all hearts. We have already seen that this was a time of trouble in Switzerland, in which foreign wars gave rise to violent disorders, and the soldiers, returning to their country, brought back with them their campaigning habits of licentiousness and brutality. One dark and cloudy day in winter, some of these ruffians attacked Oswald's quiet dwelling in his absence. They knocked at the door, threw stones, and called for his modest wife in the most indecent

1 Tu, tuique similes optimis etiam studiis ac moribus et expolietis et nobilitabitis. Zw. Epp. p. 10.
2 Et corpusculo hoc tuo minuto, verum minime inconcinno, urbanissime gestientem videre videar. Ibid.

language; at last they dashed in the windows, and entering the schoolroom, broke every thing they could find, and then retired. Oswald returned shortly after. His son, little Felix, ran to meet him with loud cries, and his wife, unable to speak, made signs of the utmost horror. He perceived what had happened to him. At the same moment, a noise was heard in the street. Unable to control his feelings, the schoolmaster seized a weapon, and pursued the rioters to the cemetery. They took refuge within it, prepared to defend themselves: three of their number fell upon Myconius, and wounded him; and while his wound was dressing, those wretches again broke into his house with furious cries. Oswald says no more.[1] Such were the scenes that took place in the cities of Switzerland at the beginning of the sixteenth century, and before the Reformation had softened and disciplined the manners.

The integrity of Oswald Myconius, and his thirst for knowledge and virtue, brought him into contact with Zwingle. The rector of the school of Basle recognised the superiority of the priest of Glaris. In his humility he shrunk from the praises lavished on him both by Zwingle and Erasmus. The latter would often say: "I look upon you schoolmasters as the peers of kings." But the modest Myconius was of a different opinion. "I do but crawl upon the earth; from my childhood, there has been something humble and mean about me."[2]

A preacher who had arrived in Basle at nearly the same time as Zwingle, was then attracting general attention. Of a mild and peaceful disposition, he loved a traquil life; slow and circumspect in action, his chief delight was to labour in his study and to promote concord among all Christians.[3] His name was John Hausschein, in Greek Œcolampadius, or "the light of the house;" he was born in Franconia, of rich parents, a year before Zwingle. His pious mother desired to consecrate to learning and to God the only child that Providence had left her. His father at first destined him to business, and then to jurisprudence. But after Œcolampadius had returned from Bologna, where he had been studying the law, the Lord, who was pleased to make him a light in the Church,[4] called him to the study of theology. He was preaching in his native town, when Capito, who had known him at Heidelberg, got him appointed preacher at Basle. He there proclaimed Christ with an eloquence which filled his hearers with admiration.[5] Erasmus admitted him into his intimacy.

Œcolampadius was charmed with the hours he passed in the society of this great genius. "There is but one thing," said the monarch of learning to him, "that we should look for in Holy Scripture, and that is Jesus Christ."[1] He gave the youthful preacher, as a memorial of his friendship, the commencement of the Gospel of St. John. Œcolampadius would often kiss this pledge of so valued an affection, and kept it suspended to his crucifix, "in order," said he, "that I may always remember Erasmus in my prayers."

Zwingle returned to his native mountains, his heart and mind full of all he had seen and heard at Basle. "I should be unable to sleep," wrote he to Erasmus shortly after his return, "if I had not held some conversation with you. There is nothing I am prouder of than of having seen Erasmus." Zwingle had received a new impulse. Such journeys often exercise a great influence over the career of a Christian. Zwingle's pupils —Valentine, Jost, with Louis Peter and Egidius Tschudi; his friends—the landamman Æbli, the priest Binzli of Wesen, Fridolin Brunner, and the celebrated professor Glarean, were delighted to see him increase in knowledge and in wisdom. The old respected him as a courageous patriot; the faithful pastors, as a zealous minister of the Lord. Nothing was done in the country without his being first consulted. All good people hoped that the ancient virtues of Switzerland would be one day revived by him.[2]

Francis I. having ascended the throne. and desiring to avenge in Italy the honour of the French name, the pope in consternation endeavoured to gain over the cantons. Thus, in 1515, Ulrich again visited the plains of Italy in the midst of the phalanxes of his countrymen. But the dissensions that the intrigues of the French sowed in the confederate army wrung his heart. Often might he be seen in the midst of the camp haranguing with energy, and at the same time with great wisdom, an audience armed from head to foot, and ready for the fight.[3] On the 8th of September, five days before the battle of Marignan, he preached in the square of Monza, where the Swiss soldiers who had remained faithful to their colours were assembled. "If we had then, and even later, followed Zwingle's advice," said Werner Steiner of Zug, "what evils would our country have been spared!" But all ears were shut against the voice of concord, prudence, and submission. The impetuous eloquence of Cardinal Schinner electrified the confederates, and impelled them to rush like a torrent to the fatal field of Marignan. The flower of the Helvetian youth perished there.

---

[1] Erasmi Laus Stultitiæ, cum annot. Myconii.
[2] Equidem humi repere didici hactenus, et est natura nescio quid humile vel a cunabulis in me. Osw. Myc. Vita Zw.
[3] Ingenio miti et tranquillo, pacis et concordiæ studiosissimus. Melch. Ad. Vit. Œcol. p. 58.
[4] Flectente et vocante Deo, qui eo in domo sua pro lampade usurus erat. Ibid. 46.
[5] Omnium vere spiritualium et eruditorum admiratione Christum prædicavit. Ibid.

[1] Nihil in sacris literis præter Christum quærendum. Erasm. Epp. p. 403.
[2] Justitiam avitam per hunc olim restitutam iri. Osw. Myc. Vita Zw.
[3] In dem Heerlager hat er Flyssig geprediget. Bullinger Chron.

Zwingle, who had been unable to prevent such disasters, threw himself, in the cause of Rome, into the midst of danger. His hand wielded the sword.[1] A melancholy error! A minister of Christ, he forgot more than once that he should fight only with the weapons of the Spirit, and he was destined to see fulfilled, in his own person, this prophecy of our Lord : *They that take the sword, shall perish with the sword.*

Zwingle and the Swiss had been unable to save Rome. The ambassador of Venice was the first in the pontifical city to hear of the defeat at Marignan. Quite elated, he repaired early in the morning to the Vatican. The pope left his chamber half dressed to give him an audience. When Leo X. heard the news, he did not conceal his terror. In this moment of alarm he saw only Francis I., and had no hope but in him : " My lord ambassador," said he tremblingly to Zorsi, " we must throw ourselves into the arms of the king, and cry for mercy!"[2] Luther and Zwingle, in their dangers, knew another arm, and invoked another mercy.

This second visit to Italy was not unprofitable to Zwingle. He remarked the difference between the Ambrosian ritual in use at Milan and that of Rome. He collected and compared with each other the most ancient canons of the mass. Thus a spirit of inquiry was developed in him, even amid the tumult of camps. At the same time the sight of the children of his fatherland, led beyond the Alps and delivered up to slaughter like their herds, filled him with indignation. It was a common saying, that " the flesh of the confederates was cheaper than that of their kine." The faithlessness and ambition of the pope,[3] the avarice and ignorance of the priests, the licentiousness and dissipation of the monks, the pride and luxury of the prelates, the corruption and venality that infected the Swiss on every side—all these evils forced themselves upon his attention, and made him feel more keenly than ever the necessity of a reform in the Church.

From this time Zwingle preached the Word of God more clearly. He explained the portions of the Gospels and Epistles selected for the public services, always comparing scripture with scripture.[4] He spoke with animation and with power,[5] and pursued with his hearers the same course that God had adopted with him. He did not, like Luther, expose the sores of the Church ; but in proportion as the study of the Bible discovered to him any useful lesson, he communicated it to his

flock. He endeavoured to instil the truth into their hearts, and then relied on it for the result that it was destined to produce.[1] " If the people understand what is true," thought he, " they will soon discern what is false." This maxim is good in the commencement of a reformation ; but there comes a time when error should be boldly pointed out. This Zwingle knew full well. " The spring is the season for sowing," said he ; and it was then seed-time with him.

Zwingle has indicated this period (1516) as the beginning of the Swiss Reformation. In effect, if four years before he had bent his head over the book of God, he now raised it, and turned towards his people to impart to them the light that he had found therein. This is a new and important epoch in the history of the development of the religious revolution in these countries; but it has been erroneously concluded from these dates that Zwingle's reform preceded that of Luther. Perhaps Zwingle preached the Gospel a year previous to the publication of Luther's theses, but Luther himself preached four years before those celebrated propositions.[2] If Luther and Zwingle had strictly confined themselves to preaching, the Reformation would not so rapidly have spread through the Church. Luther and Zwingle were neither the first monk nor the first priest that had taught a purer doctrine than the schoolmen. But Luther was the first to uplift publicly and with indomitable courage the standard of truth against the dominion of error ; to direct general attention to the fundamental doctrine of the Gospel,—salvation through grace ; to lead his generation into that new way of knowledge, faith, and life, from which a new world has issued ; in a word, to begin a salutary and real revolution. The great struggle, of which the theses of 1517 were the signal, really gave birth to the Reformation, and imparted to it both a soul and a body. Luther was the first reformer.

A spirit of inquiry was beginning to breathe on the mountains of Switzerland. One day the priest of Glaris, chancing to be in the delighful country of Mollis, at the house of Adam the priest of the place, together with Bunzli, priest of Wesen, and Varschon, priest of Kerensen, these friends discovered an old liturgy, in which they read these words : " After the child is baptized, let him partake of the sacrament of the Eucharist and likewise of the cup."[3]—" So then," said Zwingle, " the sacrament was at that time given in our churches under both kinds." This liturgy, which was about two hundred years old, was a great discovery for these Alpine priests.

The defeat at Marignan produced its natural results in the cantons. The victorious

---

In den Schachten sich redlich und dapfer gestellt mit Rathen, Worten und Thaten. Bullinger Chron.
[2] Domine orator, vederemo quel fara il re Christianissimo se metteremo in le so man dimandando misericordia. Zorsi Relatione MS.
[3] Bellissimo parlador (Leo X.) prometea assa ma non atendea. Relatione MS. di Gradenigo, venuto orator di Roma.
[4] Non hominum commentis, sed sola scripturarum biblicarum collatione. Zw. Opp. i. 273.
[5] Sondern auch mit predigen, dorrinen er heftig waas. Bullinger MS.

[1] Volebat veritatem cognitam in cordibus auditorum agere suum officium. Osw. Myc. Vit. Zw.
[2] Vol. i. 72, &c.
[3] Detur Eucharistiæ sacramentum, similiter poculum sanguinis. Zw. Opp. i. 266.

Francis I. was prodigal of gold and flatteries to win over the confederates, and the emperor conjured them by their honour, by the tears of widows and orphans, and by the blood of their brethren, not to sell themselves to their murderers. The French party had the upperhand in Glaris, and from that time this residence became burdensome to Ulrich.

Had Zwingle remained at Glaris, he might possibly have been a mere man of the age. Party intrigue, political prejudices, the empire, France, and the Duke of Milan, might have almost absorbed his life. God never leaves in the midst of the tumult of the world those whom He is training for his people. He leads them aside; He places them in some solitude, where they find themselves face to face with God and themselves, and whence they derive inexhaustible instruction. The Son of God himself, a type in this respect of the course He pursues with his servants, passed forty days in the wilderness. It was now time to withdraw Zwingle from this political movement which, by constant repetition in his soul, would have quenched the Spirit of God. The hour had come to prepare him for another stage than that on which courtiers, cabinets, and factions contended, and where he would have uselessly wasted a strength worthy of a higher occupation. His fellow-countrymen had need of something better. It was necessary that a new life should now descend from heaven, and that the instrument of its transmission should unlearn the things of earth, to learn those of heaven. These two spheres are entirely distinct: a wide gulf separates the two worlds; and before passing wholly from one to the other, Zwingle was to sojourn for a time on a neutral territory,—an intermediate and preparatory state, there to be taught of God. God at this time removed him from among the factions of Glaris, and conducted him, for his noviciate, to the solitude of a hermitage. He confined within the narrow walls of an abbey this generous seed of the Reformation, which, transplanted to a better soil, was soon to cover the mountains with its shadow.

CHAPTER V.

Our Lady of Einsidlen—Zwingle's Call—The Abbot—Geroldsek—A learned Society—The Bible copied—Zwingle and Superstition—First Opposition to Error—Sensation—Hedio—Zwingle and the Legates—The Honours of Rome—The Bishop of Constance—Samson and the Indulgences—Stapfer—Zwingle's Charity—His Friends.

ABOUT the middle of the ninth century, a German monk, Meinrad of Hohenzollern, had passed between the lakes of Zurich and Wallenstadt, and halted on a little hill in front of an amphitheatre of pines, where he built a cell. Ruffians imbrued their hands in the blood of the saint. The polluted cell long remained deserted. About the end of the tenth century, a convent and church in honour of the Virgin were built on this sacred spot. About midnight on the eve of the day of consecration, the Bishop of Constance and his priests were at prayers in the church: a heavenly strain, proceeding from invisible beings, suddenly resounded through the chapel. They listened prostrate and with admiration. On the morrow, as the bishop was about to consecrate the building, a voice repeated thrice: " Stop! stop! God himself has consecrated it!"[1] Christ in person (it was said) had blessed it during the night: the strains they had heard were those of the angels, apostles, and saints; and the Virgin standing above the altar shone with the brightness of lightning. A bull of Leo VIII. had forbidden the faithful to doubt the truth of this legend. From that time an immense crowd of pilgrims had annually visited our Lady of the Hermits for the festival of " the Consecration of the Angels." Delphi and Ephesus in ancient times, and Loretto in more recent days, have alone equalled the renown of Einsidlen. It was in this extraordinary place that, in 1516, Ulrich Zwingle was invited to be priest and preacher.

Zwingle did not hesitate. " It is neither ambition nor covetousness," said he, " that takes me there, but the intrigues of the French."[2] Reasons of a higher kind determined him. On the one hand, having more solitude, more tranquillity, and a less extensive parish, he would be able to devote more time to study and meditation; on the other, this resort of pilgrims offered him an easy means of spreading a knowledge of Jesus Christ into the most distant countries.[3]

The friends of evangelical preaching at Glaris loudly expressed their grief. " What more distressing can happen to Glaris," said Peter Tschudi, one of the most distinguished citizens of the canton, " than to be deprived of so great a man ?"[4] His parishioners, seeing that he was inflexible, resolved to leave him the title of pastor of Glaris, with a portion of the stipend, and the power of returning whenever he chose.[5]

Conrad of Rechberg, a gentleman descended from an ancient family, serious, frank, intrepid, and sometimes, perhaps, a little rough, was one of the most celebrated huntsmen of the country to which Zwingle was going. In one of his farms (the Silthal) he had established a stud where he raised a breed of horses that became famous in Italy

[1] Cessa, cessa, frater, divinitus capella consecrata est. Hartm. Annal. Einsidl. p. 51.
[2] Locum mutavimus non cupidinis aut cupiditatis moti stimulis, verum Gallorum technis. Zw. Epp. p. 24.
[3] Christum et veritatem ejus in regiones et varias et remotas divulgari tam felici oportunitate. Osw. Myc. Vita Zw.
[4] Quid enim Glareanæ nostræ tristius accidere poterat, tanto videlicet privari viro. Zw. Epp. p. 16.
[5] For two years after this Zwingle still signed his name: Pastor Glaronæ, Minister Eremi. Ibid. p. 30.

Such was the abbot of Our Lady of the Hermits. Rechberg held in equal detestation the pretensions of Rome and theological discussions. One day when, during a visitation of the order, some observations were made to him: " I am master here, and not you," said he, somewhat rudely ; " go your ways." At another time, as Leo Juda was discussing some intricate question at table with the administrator of the convent, the hunting abbot exclaimed: " Leave off your disputes ! I cry with David : *Have mercy upon me, O God, according to thy loving kindness, and enter not into judgment with thy servant.* I desire to know nothing more.[1]

The manager of the monastery was Baron Theobald of Geroldsek ; a man of mild character, sincere piety, and great love for letters. His favourite plan was to assemble in his convent a body of learned men ; and with this view he had invited Zwingle. Eager for instruction and reading, he begged his new friend to direct him. " Study the Holy Scriptures," replied Zwingle, " and that you may better understand them, read Saint Jerome. However (added he) a time will come (and that soon, with God's help) when Christians will not set great store either by Saint Jerome or any other doctor, but solely by the Word of God." [2] Geroldsek's conduct gave indication of his progress in faith. He permitted the nuns in a convent depending on Einsidlen to read the Bible in the vulgar tongue ; and some years later Geroldsek went and lived at Zurich beside Zwingle, and died with him on the field of Cappel. The same charm erelong tenderly attached to Zwingle not only Geroldsek, but also Zink the chaplain, the worthy Œxlin, Lucas, and other inmates of the abbey. These studious men, far removed from the tumult of parties, used to unite in reading the Scriptures, the fathers of the Church, the masterpieces of antiquity, and the writings of the restorers of learning. This interesting circle was often increased by friends from distant parts. Among others, Capito one day arrived at Einsidlen. The two old friends of Basle walked over the convent together, and strolled about its wild environs, absorbed in conversation, examining the Scriptures, and seeking to learn God's will. There was one point upon which they were agreed, and it was this : " The pope of Rome must fall!" Capito was at this time a bolder man than he was afterwards.

In this calm retreat Zwingle enjoyed rest, leisure, books, and friends, and grew in understanding and in faith. It was then (May 1517) that he commenced a work that proved very useful to him. As in ancient days the kings of Israel transcribed God's law with their own hands, so Zwingle with

his copied out the Epistles of St. Paul. At that time there existed none but voluminous editions of the New Testament, and Zwingle wished to be able to carry it with him always. [1] He learned these Epistles by heart, and somewhat later the other books of the New Testament and part of the Old. His soul thus grew daily more attached to the supreme authority of the Word of God. He was not content simply to acknowledge this authority; he resolved sincerely to subject his life to it. He entered gradually into a more christian path. The purpose for which he had been brought into this desert was accomplishing. Doubtless, it was not until his residence at Zurich that the power of a christian life penetrated all his being ; but already at Einsidlen he had made evident progress in sanctification. At Glaris, he had been seen to take part in worldly amusements ; at Einsidlen, he sought more and more after a life pure from every stain and from all worldliness; he began to have a better understanding of the great spiritual interests of the people, and learned by degrees what God designed to teach him.

Providence, in bringing him to Einsidlen, had also other aims. He was to have a nearer view of the superstitions and abuses which had invaded the Church. The image of the Virgin, carefully preserved in the monastery, had, it was said, the power of working miracles. Over the gate of the abbey might be read this presumptuous inscription: "Here a plenary remission of sins may be obtained." A crowd of pilgrims flocked to Einsidlen from every part of Christendom to merit this grace by their pilgrimage at the festival of the Virgin. The church, the abbey, and all the valley, were filled with her devout worshippers. But it was particularly at the great feast of " the Consecration of the Angels" that the crowd thronged the hermitage. Many thousand individuals of both sexes climbed in long files the slopes of the mountain leading to the oratory, singing hymns or counting their beads. These devout pilgrims crowded eagerly into the church, imagining themselves nearer to God there than elsewhere.

Zwingle's residence at Einsidlen, as regards a knowledge of the abuses of the papacy, produced an analogous effect to that resulting from Luther's visit to Rome. In this monastery he completed his education as a reformer. God alone is the source of salvation, and He is every where : this was what he learned at Einsidlen, and these two truths became the fundamental articles of Zwingle's theology. The seriousness he had acquired in his soul soon manifested itself in his actions. Struck by the knowledge of so many evils, he resolved to oppose them boldly. He did not hesitate between his conscience and his interests: he stood forth with courage,

[1] Wirz, K. Gesch. iii. 363 ; Zwinglis Bildung v. Schüler, p. 174; Miscell. Tigur. iii. 28.
[2] Fore, idque brevi, Deo sic juvante, ut neque Hieronymus neque cæteri, sed sola Scriptura divina apud Christianos in pretio sit futura. Zw. Opp. i. 273.

[1] This manuscript is still extant in the public library of Zurich.

and his energetic eloquence uncompromisingly attacked the superstitions of the crowd that surrounded him. "Do not imagine," said he from the pulpit, "that God is in this temple more than in any other part of creation. Whatever be the country in which you dwell, God is around you, and hears you, as well as at Our Lady's of Einsidlen. Can unprofitable works, long pilgrimages, offerings, images, the invocation of the Virgin, or of the saints, secure for you the grace of God?......What avails the multitude of words with which we embody our prayers? What efficacy has a glossy cowl, a smooth-shorn head, a long and flowing robe, or gold-embroidered slippers!......God looks at the heart, and our hearts are far from Him!"[1]

But Zwingle desired to do more than merely inveigh against superstition; he wished to satisfy the ardent yearnings for reconciliation with God, experienced by many pilgrims who flocked to the chapel of Our Lady of Einsidlen. "Christ," exclaimed he, like John the Baptist in this new desert of the mountains of Judea, "Christ, who was once offered upon the cross, is the sacrifice (*host*) and victim, that makes satisfaction for the sins of believers to all eternity."[2] Thus Zwingle advanced. On the day when such bold language was first heard in the most venerated sanctuary of Switzerland, the standard uplifted against Rome began to rise more distinctly above its mountains, and there was, so to speak, an earthquake of reformation that shook their very foundations.

In effect, universal astonishment filled the crowd as they listened to the words of the eloquent priest. Some withdrew in horror; others hesitated between the faith of their sires and this doctrine which was to ensure peace; many went to Jesus who was preached to them as meek and gentle, and carried back the tapers they had brought to present to the Virgin. A crowd of pilgrims returned to their homes, every where announcing what they had heard at Einsidlen: "Christ ALONE saves, and he saves EVERY WHERE." Often did whole bands, amazed at these reports, turn back without completing their pilgrimage. Mary's worshippers diminished in number daily. It was their offerings that made up in great measure the stipends of Zwingle and Geroldsek. But this bold witness to the truth felt happy in impoverishing himself, if he could spiritually enrich souls.

Among Zwingle's numerous hearers at the feast of Whitsuntide in 1518, was Gaspard Hedio, doctor of divinity at Basle, a learned man, of mild character and active charity. Zwingle was preaching on the narrative of the paralytic (Luke v.), in which occurs this declaration of our Lord: *The Son of Man*

hath power upon earth to forgive sins—words well adapted to strike the crowd assembled in the temple of the Virgin. The preacher's sermon stirred, charmed, and inspired his congregation, and particularly the Basle doctor.[1] For a long while after, Hedio was accustomed to speak of it with admiration. "How beautiful is this discourse," said he: "how profound, solemn, copious, penetrating, and evangelical! how it reminds us of the ἐνέργεια (the force) of the ancient doctors!"[2] From this moment Hedio admired and loved Zwingle.[3] He would have liked to have spoken with him, to have unbosomed himself to him; he wandered round the abbey, yet dared not advance, being held back (he says) by superstitious timidity. He remounted his horse, and retired slowly, often turning his head towards the walls that enclosed so great a treasure, and bearing away in his heart the keenest regret.[4]

Thus preached Zwingle; certainly with less force, but with more moderation and not less success than Luther: he precipitated nothing; he shocked men's minds far less than the Saxon reformer: he expected everything from the power of truth. He behaved with the same discretion in his intercourse with the heads of the Church. Far from showing himself immediately as their adversary, like Luther, he long remained their friend. The latter humoured him exceedingly, not only on account of his learning and talents (Luther had the same claims to the respect of the Bishops of Mentz and Brandenburg), but especially because of his attachment to the political party of the pope, and the influence such a man as Zwingle possessed in a republican state.

Several cantons, indeed, disgusted with the papal service, were on the point of breaking with it. But the legates flattered themselves they would retain many by gaining Zwingle, as they had already gained Erasmus, by pensions and honours. The legates Ennius and Pucci paid frequent visits to Einsidlen, whence, considering its vicinity to the democratic cantons, their negotiations with these states were easier. But Zwingle, far from sacrificing the truth to the demands and offers of Rome, let no opportunity escape of defending the Gospel. The famous Schinner, whose diocese was then in a disturbed state, spent some time at Einsidlen. "The popedom," said Zwingle one day, "reposes on a bad foundation:[5] apply yourselves to the work; reject all errors and abuses, or else you will see the whole edifice fall with a tremendous crash."[6]

---

[1] Is sermo ita me inflammavit.... Zw. Epp. p. 9C.
[2] Elegans ille, doctus, gravis, copiosus, penetrans et evangelicus.... Ibid. p. 89.
[3] Ut inciperem Zwinglium arctissime complecti, suscipere et admirari. Ibid.
[4] Sicque abequitavi, non sine molestia, quam tamen ipse mihi pepereram. Ibid. p. 90.
[5] Dass das ganz Papstum einen schlechten Grund habe. Zw. Opp. ii. part. i. p. 7.
[6] Oder aber sy werdind mit grosser unrüw selbs umfallen, Ibid.

[1] Vestis oblonga et plicis plena, mult auro ornati....Cor vero interim procul a Deo est. Zw. Opp. i. 236.
[2] Christus qui sese semel in cruce obtulit, hostia est et victima satisfaciens in æternum, pro peccatis omnium fidelium. Ibid. 263.

He spoke with the same freedom to Cardinal Pucci. Four times he returned to the charge. " With God's aid," said he, " I will continue to preach the Gospel, and this preaching will make Rome totter." He then explained to the prelate what ought to be done in order to save the Church. Pucci promised everything, but did nothing. Zwingle declared that he would resign the pope's pension. The legate entreated him to keep it, and Zwingle, who had no intention at that time of setting himself in open hostility against the head of the Church, consented to receive it for three years longer. " But do not imagine," added he " that for love of money I retract a single syllable of the truth."[1] Pucci in alarm procured for the reformer the nomination of acolyte to the pope. This was a step to further honours. Rome aimed at frightening Luther by her judgments, and at gaining Zwingle by her favours. Against the one she hurled her excommunications ; to the other she cast her gold and splendours. These were two different ways of attaining the same end, and of silencing the bold tongues that dared, in the pope's despite, proclaim the Word of God in Germany and in Switzerland. The latter was the more skilful policy : but neither was successful. The emancipated souls of the preachers of the truth were equally beyond the reach of vengeance or of favour.

Another Swiss prelate, Hugo of Landenberg, bishop of Constance, about this time excited hopes in Zwingle's breast. He ordered a general visitation of the churches. But Landenberg, a man of no decision of character, permitted himself to be guided at one time by Faber his vicar, and at another by a vicious woman whose influence he could not shake off. Sometimes he appeared to honour the Gospel, and yet he looked upon any man as a disturber of the people who ventured to preach it boldly. He was one of those men, too common in the Church, who, although they prefer truth to error, show more regard to error than to truth, and often end by turning against those by whose sides they should have fought. Zwingle applied to him, but in vain. He was destined to make the same experiment as Luther, and to acknowledge that it was useless to invoke the assistance of the heads of the Church, and that the only way of reviving Christianity was to act as a faithful teacher of the Word of God. The opportunity soon came.

Along the heights of Saint Gothard, over those elevated roads that have been cut with incredible toil through the steep rocks that separate Switzerland from Italy, journeyed a Franciscan monk, in the month of August 1518. Emerging from an Italian convent, he was the bearer of the papal indulgences which he had been empowered to sell to the good Christians of the Helvetic Confederation. The brilliant successes gained under the two preceding popes had conferred honour on this scandalous traffic. Accompanied by men appointed to puff off the wares he had for sale, he crossed these snows and icy glaciers as old as the world. This greedy train, whose appearance was wretched enough, and not unlike a band of adventurers in search of plunder, advanced silently to the noise of the impetuous torrents that form the Rhine, the Rhone, the Ticino, and other rivers, meditating the spoliation of the simple inhabitants of Switzerland. Samson, for such was the Franciscan's name, and his troop, arrived first in Uri, and there opened their trade. They had soon finished with these poor mountaineers, and then passed on to Schwytz. Zwingle resided in this canton— and here the combat was to take place between the two servants of two very different masters. " I can pardon all sins," said the Italian monk, the Tetzel of Switzerland, addressing the inhabitants of the capital. " Heaven and hell are subject to my power; and I sell the merits of Christ to any who will purchase them by buying an indulgence for ready money."

Zwingle's zeal took fire as he heard of these discourses. He preached with energy, saying ; " Jesus Christ, the Son of God, has said, *Come* UNTO ME *all ye that are weary and heavy laden, and I will give you rest.* Is it not then, most presumptuous folly and senseless temerity to declare, on the contrary : ' Buy letters of indulgence ! hasten to Rome ! give to the monks ! sacrifice to the priests ! and if thou doest these things, I absolve thee from thy sins ?'[1] Jesus Christ is the only oblation; the only sacrifice; the only way !"[2]

Throughout Schwytz, Samson erelong was called a cheat and seducer. He took the road to Zug, and for a time the two champions did not meet.

Scarcely had Samson left Schwytz, when Stapfer, a citizen of this canton, a man of distinguished character, and afterwards secretary of state, was suddenly reduced with his family to great distress. " Alas ! " said he, addressing Zwingle in his anguish, " I know not how to satisfy my hunger, and that of my poor children."[3] Zwingle could give when Rome could take, and he was as ready to practise good works, as he was to combat those who taught that salvation was to be gained by them. Every day he carried Stapfer abundant supplies.[4] " It is God," said he, desirous of taking no praise to himself, " it is God who begets charity in the faithful, and gives at once the thought, the resolve, and the work itself. Whatever good

---

[1] *Frustra sperari me vel verbulum de veritate diminutu-rum esse, pecuniæ gratia.* Zw. Opp. i. 365.

[1] *Romam curre ! redime literas indulgentiarum ! da tan-tumdem monachis ! offer sacerdotibus,* &c. Zw. Opp. i. 222.
[2] *Christus una est oblatio, unum sacrificium, una via.* Ibid. 201.
[3] *Ut meæ, meorumque liberorum inediæ corporali sub veniretis.* Zw. Epp. p. 234.
[4] *Largas mihi quotidie suppetias tulistis.* Ibid.

work the just man doeth, it is God who doeth it by his own power.[1] Stapfer remained attached to Zwingle all his life, and when four years later he had become secretary of state at Schwytz, and felt impelled by more elevated desires, he turned towards Zwingle, saying with nobleness and candour: " Since it was you who provided for my temporal wants, how much more may I now expect from you the food that shall satisfy my soul ! "

Zwingle's friends increased in number. It was not only at Glaris, Basle, and Schwytz that souls were found in harmony with his : in Uri, there was Schmidt, the secretary of state ; at Zug, Colin, Müller, and Werner Steiner, an old fellow-soldier at Marignan ; at Lucerne, Xyloctect and Kilchmeyer ; at Bienne, Wittembach; and many others in other places besides. But the priest of Einsidlen had no friend more devoted than Oswald Myconius. Oswald had quitted Basle in 1516, to superintend the cathedral school at Zurich. At that time this city possessed neither learned men nor learned schools. Oswald laboured, in conjunction with several other well-disposed men, among whom was Utinger, the pope's notary, to rescue the Zurich people from their ignorance, and to initiate them in the literature of the ancients. At the same time he upheld the immutable truth of the Holy Scriptures, and declared that if the pope and the emperor commanded any thing in opposition to the Gospel, man is bound to obey God alone, who is above the emperor and the pope.

CHAPTER VI.

The Canons' College—Election to the Cathedral—Fable—Accusations—Zwingle's Confession—Development of God's Purposes — Farewell to Einsidlen — Arrival at Zurich — Zwingle's bold Declaration—First Sermons—Their Effect — Opposition — Zwingle's Character — Taste for Music—Arrangement of the Day—The Book-hawker.

SEVEN centuries before, Charlemagne had attached a college of canons to the cathedral of Zurich, the school belonging to which was under the direction of Myconius. These canons having declined from their primitive institution, and desiring to enjoy their benefices in the sweets of an indolent life, used to elect a priest to whom they confided the preaching and the cure of souls. This post became vacant shortly after the arrival of Myconius, who immediately thought of his friend. What a gain it would be to Zurich ! Zwingle's exterior was in his favour. He was a handsome man,[2] of graceful manners,

and pleasing conversation ; he had already become celebrated for his eloquence, and excelled throughout the Confederation by the splendour of his genius. Myconius spoke of him to Felix Frey, the provost of the chapter, who was prepossessed by Zwingle's talents and appearance ;[1] to Utinger, an old man, highly respected, and to the canon Hoffmann, a person of upright and open character, who, from having long preached against the foreign service, was already well disposed in Ulrich's favour. Other Zurichers had, on different occasions, heard Zwingle at Einsidlen, and had returned full of admiration. The election of a preacher for the cathedral soon put everybody in Zurich in motion. The different parties began to bestir themselves. Many laboured day and night to procure the election of the eloquent preacher of Our Lady of the Hermits.[2] Myconius informed his friend of this...... " Wednesday next, I shall go and dine at Zurich," replied Zwingle, " and then we will talk this matter over." He came accordingly. While paying a visit to one of the canons, the latter said, " Can you not come and preach the Word of God among us ?"— " I can," replied he, " but I will not come, unless I am called." He then returned to his abbey.

This visit spread alarm in the camp of his enemies. They pressed several priests to become candidates for the vacant post. A Swabian, Lawrence Fable, even delivered a probationary sermon, and a report was circulated that he had been elected. " It is very true, then," said Zwingle, on being apprized of this, " that no man is a prophet in his own country, since a Swabian is preferred to a Swiss. I know what the applause of the people is worth."[3] Immediately after, Zwingle received a letter from Cardinal Schinner's secretary, informing him that the election had not yet taken place. But the false intelligence that had reached him first piqued the chaplain of Einsidlen. Knowing that a man so unworthy as this Fable aspired to the station, he became the more eager for it himself, and wrote about it to Myconius. Oswald replied on the following day : " Fable will always remain a fable ; our gentlemen have learnt that he is the father of six boys, and already holds I know not how many livings."[4]

Zwingle's enemies, however, did not consider themselves beaten. All agreed in extolling to the clouds the extent of his acquirements ;[5] but some said, " He is too fond of music ! " Others, " He loves company and

---

[1] Caritatem ingenerat Deus, consilium, propositum et opus. Quidquid boni præstat justus, hoc Deus sua virtute præstat. Zw. Opp. i. 226.
[2] Dan Zwingli vom lyb ein hubscher man wass. Bullinger Chron.

[1] Und als Imme seine Gestalt und geschiklichkeit wol gefiel, gab er Im syn stimm. Bullinger Chron.
[2] Qui dies et noctes laborarent ut vir ille subrogaretur. Osw. Myc. Vit. Zw.
[3] Scio vulgi acclamationes et illud blandum Euge! Euge! Zw. Epp. p. 53.
[4] Fabula manebit fabula; quem domini mei acceperunt sex pueris esse patrem....Ibid.
[5] Neminem tamen, qui tuam doctrinam non ad cœlum ferat....Ibid.

pleasure!" And others again, "He was once too intimate with persons of light conduct!" One man even accused him of seduction. Zwingle was not blameless, and although less erring than the ecclesiastics of his day, he had more than once, in the first years of his ministry, allowed himself to be led astray by the passions of youth. We cannot easily form an idea of the influence upon the soul of the corrupt atmosphere in which it lives. There existed in the papacy, and among the priests, disorders that were established, allowed, and authorized, as conformable to the laws of nature. A saying of Æneas Sylvius, afterwards pope under the title of Pius II., gives some notion of the degraded state of public manners at this epoch.[1] Disorder had come to be the generally admitted order of things.

Oswald exerted incredible activity in his friend's behalf; he employed all his powers to justify him, and luckily succeeded.[2] He visited the Burgomaster Roust, Hoffman, Frey, and Utinger; he lauded the probity, decorum, and purity of Zwingle's conduct, and confirmed the Zurichers in the favourable impression they entertained towards the priests of Einsidlen. Little credit was paid to the stories of his adversaries. The most influential men said that Zwingle would be preacher at Zurich. The canons said the same, but in an under-tone. "Hope on," wrote Oswald with a rising heart; "hope on, for I hope." He nevertheless informed him of the accusations of his enemies. Although Zwingle had not yet become altogether a new man, he was one of those whose conscience is awakened, who may fall into sin, but never without a struggle and without remorse. Often had he resolved to lead a holy life, alone among his kind, in the midst of the world. But when he found himself accused, he would not boast of being without sin. "Having no one to walk with me in the resolutions I had formed," wrote he to the canon Utinger, "many even of those about me being offended at them, alas! I fell, and like the dog of which St. Peter speaks (2 Pet. ii. 22), I turned again to my vomit.[3] The Lord knows with what shame and anguish I have dragged these faults from the bottom of my heart, and laid them before that great Being to whom, however, I confess my wretchedness far more willingly than to man."[4] But if Zwingle acknowledged himself a sinner, he vindicated himself from the odious accusations that had been made against him. He declared that he had always banished far from him the thought of adultery or of seducing the innocent,[1]—grievous excesses which were then too common. "I call to witness," says he, "all those with whom I have ever lived."[2]

The election took place on the 11th of December. Zwingle was appointed by a majority of seventeen votes out of twenty-four. It was time that the Reformation began in Switzerland. The chosen instrument that Providence had been preparing for three years in the hermitage of Einsidlen was ready; the hour was come for him to be stationed elsewhere. God, who had chosen the new university of Wittemberg, situated in the heart of Germany, under the protection of one of the wisest of princes, *there* to call Luther, selected in Helvetia the city of Zurich, regarded as the head of the confederation, *there* to station Zwingle. In that place he would be in communication not only with one of the most intelligent and simple-hearted, the strongest and the most energetic people in Switzerland, but still more with all the cantons that collected around this ancient and powerful state. The hand that had led a young herdsman from the Sentis to the school of Wesen, was now setting him, mighty in word and in deed, in the face of all, that he might regenerate his nation. Zurich was about to become the centre of light to the whole of Switzerland.

It was a day of mingled joy and sorrow at Einsidlen, when its inmates were informed of Zwingle's nomination. The society which had been formed there was about to be broken up by the removal of its most valuable member; and who could say that superstition might not again prevail in this ancient resort of pilgrims?......The state-council of Schwytz transmitted to Ulrich the expression of their sentiments, styling him "reverend, most learned, very gracious lord and good friend."[3] —"Give us at least a successor worthy of yourself," said the heart-broken Geroldsek to Zwingle.—"I have a little *lion* for you," replied he, "one who is simple-minded and prudent, and deep in the mysteries of Scripture."—"I will have him," said the administrator. It was Leo Juda, that mild and intrepid man, with whom Zwingle had been so intimate at Basle. Leo accepted this invitation which brought him nearer his dear Ulrich. The latter embraced his friends, quitted the solitude of Einsidlen, and arrived at that delightful spot where rises the cheerful and animated city of Zurich, with its amphitheatre of hills, covered with vineyards, or adorned with pastures and orchards, and crowned with forests, above which appear the highest summits of the Albis.

Zurich, the centre of the political interests of Switzerland, and in which were often collected the most influential men in the nation,

[1] Non esse qui vigesimum annum excessit, nec virginem tetigerit. Zw. Epp. p. 57.
[2] Reprimo hæc pro viribus, imo et repressi. Ibid. p. 54.
[3] Quippe neminem habens comitem hujus instituti, scandalisantes, vero non paucos, heu! cecidi et factus sum canis ad vomitum. Ibid. p. 55.
[4] En, cum verecundia (Deus novit!) magna hæc ex pectoris specubus depromsi, apud eum scilicet, cum quo etiam coram minus quam cum ullo ferme mortalium confiteri vererer. Ibid.

[1] Ea ratio nobis perpetuo fuit, nec alienum thorum conscendere, nec virginem vitiare. Zw. Epp. p. 55.
[2] Testes invoco cunctos, quibuscum vixi. Ibid.
[3] Reverende, perdocte, admodum gratiose domine ac bone amice. Ibid. p. 60.

was the spot best adapted for acting upon Helvetia, and scattering the seeds of truth through all the cantons. Accordingly, the friends of learning and of the Bible joyfully hailed Zwingle's nomination. At Paris, in particular, the Swiss students, who were very numerous, thrilled with joy at this intelligence.[1] But if at Zurich a great victory lay before Zwingle, he had also to expect a hard struggle. Glarean wrote to him from Paris: "I foresee that your learning will excite great hatred;[2] but be of good cheer, and like Hercules you will subdue the monsters."

On the 27th of December 1518, Zwingle arrived at Zurich, and alighted at the hotel of Einsidlen. He received a hearty and an honourable welcome.[3] The canons immediately assembled, and invited him to take his place among them. Felix Frey presided; the canons, friends or enemies to Zwingle, sat indiscriminately around their provost. Unusual excitement prevailed in the assembly; for every one felt, unconsciously perhaps, how serious was the beginning of this ministry. As they feared the innovating spirit of the young priest, it was agreed to explain to him the most important duties of his charge. "You will make every exertion," they said to him gravely, "to collect the revenues of the chapter, without overlooking the least. You will exhort the faithful, both from the pulpit and in the confessional, to pay all tithes and dues, and to show by their offerings their affection to the Church. You will be diligent in increasing the income arising from the sick, from masses, and in general from every ecclesiastical ordinance." The chapter added : "As for the administration of the sacraments, the preaching and the care of the flock, these are also the duties of the chaplain. But for these you may employ a substitute, and particularly in preaching. You should administer the sacraments to none but persons of note, and only when called upon ; you are forbidden to do so without distinction of persons."[4]

What a regulation for Zwingle! money! money, nothing but money!......Did Christ establish his ministry for this ? Prudence, however, moderated his zeal ; he knew that he could not at once deposit the seed in the earth, behold the tree grow up, and gather its fruits. Without any remark on the duties imposed upon him, Zwingle, after humbly expressing his gratitude for their flattering selection, announced what he intended doing: "The life of Christ," said he, "has been too long hidden from the people. I shall preach upon the whole of the Gospel of St. Matthew, chapter after chapter, according to the inspiration of the Holy Ghost, without human commentaries, drawing solely from the fountains of Scripture,[1] sounding its depths, comparing one passage with another, and seeking for understanding by constant and earnest prayer.[2] It is to God's glory, to the praise of his only Son, to the real salvation of souls, and to their edification in the true faith, that I shall consecrate my ministry."[3] Language so novel made a deep impression on the chapter. Some testified their joy ; but the majority evinced sorrow.[4] "This way of preaching is an innovation," exclaimed they; "one innovation will lead to another, and where shall we stop?" The canon Hoffman, especially, thought it his duty to prevent the melancholy consequences of an election for which he himself had been so earnest. "This explanation of Scripture," said he, "will be more injurious than useful to the people."—"It is not a new manner," replied Zwingle, "it is the old custom. Call to mind the homilies of Chrysostom on St. Matthew, and of Augustine on St. John. Besides, I will speak with moderation, and give no person just cause to complain of it."

Thus did Zwingle abandon the exclusive use of the fragments of the Gospels read since the time of Charlemagne : by restoring the Holy Scriptures to their ancient rights, he bound the Reformation from the very commencement of his ministry to the primitive times of Christianity, and laid a foundation by which future ages might study the Word of God. But we may go further : the firm and independent position he took up as regards the Gospel, announced a new work; the figure of the reformer stood in bold outline before the eyes of his people, and the reform advanced.

Hoffman, having failed in the chapter, addressed a written request to the provost, praying him to forbid Zwingle to disturb the faith of the people. The provost called the new preacher before him, and spoke to him very affectionately. But no human power could close Zwingle's lips. On the 31st December, he wrote to the council of Glaris, resigning entirely the cure they had reserved for him up to this time : he was all for Zurich, and for the work that God was preparing for him in this city.

On Saturday, the 1st day of the year 1519, and it was also his thirty-fifth birthday, Zwingle went into the cathedral pulpit. A great crowd, eager to see this celebrated man, and to hear this new Gospel, which was a general topic of conversation, crowded the temple. "It is to Christ," said Zwingle,

[1] Omnes adeo quotquot ex Helvetiis adsunt juvenes fremere et gaudere. Zw. Epp. p. 63.
[2] Quantum invidiæ tibi inter istos eruditio tua conflabit. Ibid. p. 64.
[3] Do er ehrlich und wol empfangen ward. Bullinger Chronik.
[4] Schuler's Zwingli's Bildung. p. 227.

[1] Absque humanis commentationibus, ex solis fontibus Scripturæ sacræ. Zw. Opp. i. 273.
[2] Sed mente Spiritus, quam diligenti Scripturarum collectione, precibusque ex corde fusis. se nacturum. Osw. Myc. Vita Zw.
[3] Alles Gott und seinen einigen Sohn zu Lob und Ehren und zu rechten Heil der Seelen, zur Underrichtung im rechten Glauben. Bull. MS.
[4] Quibus auditis, mœror simul et lætitia. Osw. Myc.

"that I desire to lead you; to Christ, the true source of salvation. His Divine Word is the only food that I wish to set before your hearts and souls." He then gave out that on the following day, the first Sunday in the year, he would begin to explain the Gospel according to St. Matthew. The next morning, the preacher and a still more numerous congregation were at their posts. Zwingle opened the Gospel—so long a sealed book—and read the first page. Discoursing on the history of the patriarchs and prophets (1st chapter of St. Matthew), he explained it in such a manner that his wondering and enraptured hearers exclaimed: "We never heard the like of this before!"[1]

He continued thus to explain St. Matthew according to the Greek text. He showed how all the Bible found at once its explanation and its application in the very nature of man. Setting forth the highest truths of the Gospel in simple language, his preaching reached all classes, the wise and learned, as well as the ignorant and foolish.[2] He extolled the infinite mercies of God the Father, and conjured all his hearers to place their sole trust in Jesus Christ, as their only Saviour.[3] At the same time, he called them most earnestly to repentance; he forcibly attacked the prevailing errors among his people; and inveighed courageously against luxury, intemperance, costly garments, the oppression of the poor, idleness, foreign service, and pensions from the princes. "In the pulpit," said one of his contemporaries, "he spared no one, neither pope, emperor, kings, dukes, princes, lords, nor even the confederates themselves. All his strength and all the delight of his heart was in God; and accordingly he exhorted all the city of Zurich to trust solely in Him."[4] "Never had they heard a man speak with such authority," said Oswald Myconius, who followed his friend's labours with great joy and hope.

It was impossible that the Gospel could be preached in Zurich to no purpose. An ever increasing multitude of all classes, and particularly of the lower orders, flocked to hear him.[5] Many Zurichers had ceased to frequent the public worship. "I derive no instruction from the sermons of these priests," said Füsslin, the poet, historian, and councillor of state; "they do not preach the things belonging to salvation, because they understand them not. I can see in these men nothing but avarice and licentiousness." Henry Räuschlin, treasurer of state, a constant reader of scripture, thought the same:

"The priests," said he, "met in thousands at the Council of Constance......to burn the best of them all." These distinguished men, attracted by curiosity, came to hear Zwingle's first sermon. On their features might be read the emotion with which they listened to the preacher. "Glory be to God!" said they, as they retired; "this man is a preacher of the truth. He will be our Moses to lead us forth from this Egyptian darkness."[1] From this moment they became the intimate friends of the reformer. "Ye mighty ones of the world," said Füsslin, "cease to proscribe the doctrine of Christ! When Christ, the Son of God, had been put to death, fishermen rose up to fill his place. And now, if you destroy the preachers of the truth, you will see glaziers, millers, potters, founders, shoemakers, and tailors, teaching in their stead."[2]

For a time there was but one cry of admiration in Zurich; but as soon as the first moments of enthusiasm were passed, the adversaries resumed their courage. Many well-meaning men, alarmed by the fear of a reformation, gradually became estranged from Zwingle. The violence of the monks, suppressed for a while, burst forth again, and the college of the canons resounded with complaints. Zwingle was immovable. His friends, as they contemplated his courage, imagined they saw a man of the apostolic age reappearing before them.[3] Among his enemies, some laughed and joked, others gave utterance to violent threats; but he endured all with christian patience.[4] "If we desire to gain over the wicked to Jesus Christ," he was accustomed to say, "we must shut our eyes against many things."[5] An admirable saying, which should not be lost!

His character and his deportment towards all men contributed, as much as his discourses, to win their hearts. He was at once a true Christian and a true republican. The equality of mankind was not with him a mere conventional term; it was written in his heart, and shown by his life. He had neither that pharasaical pride nor that monastic coarseness which offends equally the simple and the wise of this world; they felt attracted towards him, and were at ease in his society. Bold and energetic in the pulpit, he was affable to all whom he met in the streets or public places; he was often seen in the halls where the companies and trades used to meet, explaining to the citizens the chief features of the christian doctrine, or conversing familiarly with them. He ad-

---

[1] Dessgleichen wie jederman redt, nie gehört worden war. B. Weise (Zwingle's contemporary), Füsslin Beyträge, iv. 36.
[2] Nam ita simplices æqualiter cum prudentissimis et acutissimis quibusque, proficiebant. Osw. Myc. Vita Zw.
[3] In welchem er Gott den Vater presset und alle Menschen allein tuff Issum Christum, als den einigen Heiland verthrauwen lehrte. Bullinger Chron.
[4] All sein Trost stuhnd allein mit frölichem Gemüth zu Gott....B. Weise, Füsslin Beytr. iv. 36.
[5] Do ward bald ein gross Gelauff von allerley menschen, Innsonders von dem gemeinen Mann.. Bullinger Chron.

[1] Und unser Moses seyn der uns aus Egypten führt. Bullinger Chron.
[2] Werden die Gläser, Müller, Haffner, Giesser, Shuhmacher und Schneider lehren. Müller's Reliq. iii. 185.
[3] Nobis apostolici illius sæculi virum repræsentas. Zw. Epp. p. 74.
[4] Obganniunt quidam, rident, minantur, petulanter incessunt....at tu vere, christiana patientia, suffers omnia. Ibid. May 7, 1519.
[5] Connivendum ad multa ei, qui velit malos Christo lucri facere....Ibid.

dressed peasants and patricians with the same cordiality. " He invited the country-people to dine with him," said one of his most violent enemies, " walked with them, talked to them of God, put the devil in their hearts, and his books into their pockets. He succeeded so well that the notables of Zurich used to visit the peasants, drink with them, show them about the city, and pay them every mark of attention."[1]

He continued to cultivate music " with moderation," says Bullinger ; nevertheless the opponents of the Gospel took advantage of this, and called him " the evangelical lute-player and fifer."[2] Faber having one day censured him for this taste, he replied with noble frankness : " My dear Faber you do not know what music is. True, I have learnt to play on the lute, the violin, and other instruments, and they serve me to quiet little children ;[3] but you are too holy for music !......Do you not know that David was a sk[i]ll[f]ul player on the harp, and how by this me..s he drove the evil spirit out of Saul ?......Ah ! if you did but know the sounds of the heavenly lyre, the wicked spirit of ambition and love of riches which possesses you would soon depart from you likewise." Perhaps this may have been a weakness in Zwingle ; still it was with a spirit of cheerfulness and evangelical liberty that he cultivated this art, which religion has always associated with her sublimest devotion. He set to music some of his christian poems, and was not ashamed from time to time to amuse the little ones of his flock with his lute. He conducted himself in the same kindly manner towards the poor. " He would eat and drink with all who invited him," says one of his contemporaries ; " he despised no one ; he was compassionate to the poor, always steadfast and cheerful in good and evil fortune. No misfortune alarmed him ; his conversation was at all times full of consolation, and his heart firm."[4] Thus Zwingle's popularity was ever on the increase ; sitting by times at the tables of the poor and at the banquets of the rich, as his Master had done in former days, and every where doing the work to which God had called him.

He was indefatigable in study. From day-break until ten o'clock he used to read, write, and translate ; at that time Hebrew was the special object of his studies. After dinner he listened to those who had any news to give him or who required his advice ; he then would walk out with some of his friends and visit his flock. At two o'clock he resumed his studies. He took a short walk after supper, and then wrote his letters,

which often occupied him till midnight. He always worked standing, and never permitted himself to be disturbed except for some very important cause.[1]

But the exertions of more than one man were required. A man named Lucian called on him one day with the works of the German reformer. Rhenanus, a scholar then residing at Basle, and indefatigable in circulating Luther's writings in Switzerland, had sent him to Zwingle. Rhenanus had perceived that the hawking of books was a powerful means of spreading the evangelical doctrines. Lucian had travelled over almost the whole of Switzerland, and knew nearly everybody. " Ascertain," said Rhenanus to Zwingle, " whether this man possesses sufficient prudence and skill ; if so, let him carry from city to city, from town to town, from village to village, and even from house to house, among the Swiss, the works of Luther, and especially his exposition of the Lord's prayer written for the laity.[2] The more they are known, the more purchasers they will find. But you must take care not to let him hawk any other books ; for if he has only Luther's, he will sell them so much the faster." By this means a ray of light penetrated the humble dwelling of many a Swiss family. There was however one book that Zwingle should have caused to be distributed along with Luther's—the Gospel of Jesus Christ.

CHAPTER VII.

The Indulgences—Samson at Berne and at Baden—The Dean of Bremgarten—Young Henry Bullinger—Samson and the Dean—Zwingle's internal Struggles—Zwingle opposes the Indulgences—Samson is sent back.

AN opportunity of displaying Zwingle's zeal in a new vocation presented itself. Samson, the famous indulgence merchant, was slowly approaching Zurich. This wretched trafficker had left Schwytz and arrived at Zug on the 20th of September 1518, and had remained there three days. An immense crowd had gathered round him. The poorest were the most eager, and thus prevented the rich from getting near him. This did not suit the monk's views ; and accordingly one of his attendants began to cry out to the populace : " Good folks, do not crowd so much ! make way for those who have money ! We will afterwards endeavour to satisfy those who have none." From Zug, Samson and his band proceeded to Lucerne ; from Lucerne to Unterwalden ; and then,

---

[1] Dass der Rath gemeldete Bauern besucht .... Salat's Chronik, p. 155.
[2] Der Lauthenschlager und evangelischer Pfyffer. Bullinger Chron.
[3] Dass kombt mir Ja wol die Kind zu geschweizen. Ibid.
[4] War allwegen trostlichen Gemüths und tapferer Red. B. Weise, Füssl. Beytr. iv. 36.

[1] Certas studiis vindicans horas, quas etiam non omisit, nisi seriis coactus. Osw. Myc. Vita Zw.
[2] Oppidatim, municipatim, vicatim, imo domesticatim per Helvetios circumferat. Zw. Epp. 81.

after crossing fertile mountains and rich valleys, skirting the everlasting snows of the Oberland, and displaying their Romish merchandise in these most beautiful portions of Switzerland, they arrived in the neighbourhood of Berne. The monk was at first forbidden to enter the city; but eventually, by means of certain friends he had there, he succeeded in gaining admission, and set up his stall in St. Vincent's Church. Here he began to bawl out more lustily than before: "Here," said he to the rich, "are indulgences on parchment for a crown."—"There," said he to the poor, "are absolutions on common paper for two batz!"[1] One day a celebrated knight, Jacques de Stein, appeared before him, prancing on a dapple-gray horse,[2] which the monk admired very much. "Give me," said the knight, "an indulgence for myself, for my troop, five hundred strong, for all my vassals at Belp, and for all my ancestors, and you shall have my dapple-gray charger in exchange." This was asking a high price for a horse; but as it pleased the Franciscan, they soon came to terms; the charger was led to the monk's stable, and all those souls were declared for ever exempt from hell. Another day, a citizen purchased of him for thirteen florins an indulgence empowering his confessor to absolve him, among other matters, from every kind of perjury.[3] So much respect was felt for Samson, that the councillor De May, an aged and enlightened man, who had spoken irreverently of him, was compelled to beg pardon of the haughty monk on his knees.

On the last day of his stay the noisy sound of bells proclaimed the departure of the monk from Berne. Samson was in the church, standing on the steps of the high altar. The canon Henry Lupulus, formerly Zwingle's teacher, was his interpreter. "When the wolf and the fox prowl about together," said the canon Anselm, turning to the schultheiss De Watteville, "your safest plan, my gracious lord, is to shut up your sheep and your geese." But the monk cared little for such remarks, which, moreover, did not reach his ears: "Kneel down," said he to the superstitious crowd, "recite three *Paters*, three *Aves*, and your souls will immediately be as pure as at the moment of your baptism." Upon this all the people fell on their knees. Samson, desirous of surpassing himself, exclaimed: "I deliver from the torments of purgatory and of hell all the souls of the Bernese who are dead, whatever may have been the manner and the place of their death!" These mountebanks, like their brothers of the fairs, kept their best trick till the last.

Samson, laden with money, proceeded through Argovia and Baden towards Zurich.

At every step, this monk, whose appearance had been so wretched when first he crossed the Alps, displayed greater haughtiness and splendour. The Bishop of Constance, who was irritated because Samson would not have his bulls legalized by him, had forbidden all the priests of his diocese to open their churches to him. At Baden, however, the priest of the parish dared not make any opposition to his traffic. The effrontery of the monk was redoubled. Heading a procession round the cemetery, he seemed to fix his eyes upon some object in the air, while his acolytes were chanting the hymn for the dead; and pretending to see the souls escaping from the cemetery to heaven, he exclaimed: "*Ecce volant!* See how they fly!" One day a man went into the belfry and ascended to the top; erelong a cloud of white feathers, floating in the air, covered the astonished procession: "See how they fly!" exclaimed this wag, shaking a cushion on the summit of the tower. Many persons burst out laughing.[1] Samson flew into a passion, and was not to be appeased until he was told that the man's wits were sometimes disordered. He left Baden quite abashed.

He continued his journey, and about the end of February 1519, arrived at Bremgarten, which the schultheiss and junior priest of the town, who had seen him at Baden, had invited him to visit. In all that district no one enjoyed a better reputation than Dean Bullinger. This man, although ill informed in the Word of God and in the errors of the Church, was frank, zealous, eloquent, charitable to the poor, ready to do a kindness to the little ones of his flock, and was generally beloved. In his youth he had formed a conscientious union with the daughter of a councillor in the town. This was a practice not unusual among priests who were unwilling to lead a scandalous life. Anna had borne him five sons, and this numerous family had by no means diminished the respect felt towards him. In all Switzerland there was not a more hospitable house than his. He was fond of hunting, and might often be seen with a pack of ten or twelve hounds, and accompanied by the lords of Hallwyll, the abbot of Mury, and the patricians of Zurich, scouring the neighbouring fields and forests. His table was free to all comers, and none of his guests was gayer than himself. When the deputies to the diet were going to Baden by way of Bremgarten, they were always entertained by the dean. "Bullinger," said they, "holds a court like the most powerful lord."

Strangers had remarked in this house a child with intelligent features. Henry, one of the dean's sons, had incurred many dangers from his earliest infancy. At one time he was attacked by the plague, and he was about to be buried, when some feeble signs

---

[1] A batz is worth about three-halfpence.
[2] Um einen Kuttgrowen Hengst. Anshelm, v. 335; J. J. Hotting. Helv. K. Gesch. iii. 29.
[3] A quovis perjurio. Muller's Reliq. iv. 402.

[1] Dessen viel Luth gnug lachten. Bullinger Chronik.

of life restored joy to his parents' hearts. On another occasion, a vagabond, having attracted him by his caresses, was carrying him away, when some passers-by recognised and rescued him. At three years old, he knew the Lord's prayer and the Apostles' creed; and creeping into the church, he would go into his father's pulpit, gravely take his station, and repeat at the full strength of his voice: " I believe in God the Father," &c. At twelve years of age his parents sent him to the grammar school of Emmeric; their hearts were filled with apprehension, for the times were dangerous for an inexperienced boy. When the regulations of a university appeared to them too severe, the students might often be seen quitting the school in troops, taking little children with them, and encamping in the woods, whence they would send the youngest of their number to beg bread, or else, with arms in their hands, would fall upon travellers, whom they robbed, and then consumed the fruits of their plunder in debauchery. Fortunately Henry was preserved from evil in this distant place. Like Luther, he gained his bread by singing from door to door, for his father wished him to learn to live on his own resources. He was sixteen years old when he opened a New Testament. " I there found," said he, " all that is necessary for man's salvation, and from that time I adhered to this principle, that we must follow the sacred Scriptures alone, and reject all human additions. I believe neither the Fathers nor myself, but explain scripture by scripture, without adding or taking away anything."[1] Thus did God prepare this young man, who was one day to be Zwingle's successor. He is the author of the chronicle so often quoted by us.

About this time Samson arrived at Bremgarten with all his train. The bold dean, whom this little Italian army did not dismay, forbade the monk to sell his merchandise in his deanery. The schultheiss, the town-council, and the junior pastor,—all friends to Samson,—were met together in a chamber of the inn where the latter had alighted, and, greatly disconcerted, had gathered round the impatient monk when the dean arrived. " Here are the papal bulls," said the monk; " open your church !"

THE DEAN.—" I will not permit the purses of my parishioners to be drained by unauthenticated letters; for the bishop has not legalized them."

THE MONK, solemnly.—" The pope is above the bishop. I forbid you to deprive your flock of so signal a favour."

THE DEAN.—" Should it cost me my life, I will not open my church."

THE MONK, indignantly. — " Rebellious priest ! in the name of our most holy lord the pope, I pronounce against you the greater

excommunication, and will not absolve you until you have redeemed such unprecedented rashness by paying three hundred ducats.".......

THE DEAN, turning his back and quitting the room.—" I shall know how to reply to my lawful judges: as for you and your excommunication, I care not for either."

THE MONK, in a passion. — " Impudent brute ! I am going to Zurich, and I will there lay my complaint before the deputies of the confederation."[1]

THE DEAN.—" I can appear there as well as you, and will go thither immediately."

While these events were taking place at Bremgarten, Zwingle, who saw the enemy gradually approaching, preached energetically against the indulgences.[2] The vicar, Faber of Constance, encouraged him, promising him the bishop's support.[3] " I am aware," said Samson, as he was moving towards Zurich, " that Zwingle will speak against me, but I will stop his mouth." In effect, Zwingle felt too deeply all the sweetness of Christ's forgiveness, not to attack the paper indulgences of these foolish men. Like Luther, he often trembled because of his sinfulness, but he found in the Lord a deliverance from every fear. This modest but resolute man increased in the knowledge of God. " When Satan frightens me," said he, " by crying out : ' You have not done this or that, which God commands !' forthwith the gentle voice of the Gospel consoles me, by saying : ' What thou canst not do (and certainly thou canst do nothing), Christ has done and perfected.' Yes (continued the pious evangelist), when my heart is troubled because of my helplessness and the weakness of my flesh, my spirit is revived at the sound of these glad tidings : Christ is thy innocence ! Christ is thy righteousness ! Christ is thy salvation ! Thou art nothing, thou canst do nothing ! Christ is the Alpha and Omega ; Christ is the First and the Last; Christ is all things ; he can do all things.[4] All created things will forsake and deceive thee ; but Christ, the innocent and righteous one, will receive and justify thee......Yes ! it is he," exclaimed Zwingle, " who is our righteousness, and the righteousness of all those who shall ever appear justified before the throne of God !".......

In the presence of such truths, the indulgences fell of themselves : Zwingle accordingly feared not to attack them. " No man," said he, " can remit sins ; Christ, who is very God and very man, alone has this power.[5] Go ! buy indulgences......but be as-

[1] Bulling. Epp. Franz's Merkw. Zuge, p. 19.

[1] Du freche Bestie....&c. Bull. Chronik.
[2] Ich prengete streng wider des Pabsts Ablass....Zw. Opp. ii. part i. p. 7.
[3] Und hat mich darin gestärkt : er welle mir mit aller trüw byston. Ibid.
[4] Christus est innocentia tua ; Christus est justitia et puritas tua ; Christus est salus tua ; tu nihil es, tu nihil potes ; Christus est A et Ω ; Christus est prora et puppis (the prow and the stern) ; Christus est omnia....Ibid. i. 207.
[5] Nisi Christus Jesus, verus Deus et verus homo....Zw. Opp. i. 412.

sured, that you are not absolved. Those who sell remission of sins for money, are the companions of Simon the magician, the friends of Balaam, and the ambassadors of Satan."

Dean Bullinger, still heated by his conversation with the monk, arrived at Zurich before him. He came to lay his complaints before the diet against this shameless merchant and his traffic. He found some envoys from the bishop who were there with the same motives, and made common cause with them. All promised to support him. The spirit that animated Zwingle pervaded the city. The council of state resolved to oppose the monk's entry into Zurich.

Samson had reached the suburbs and alighted at an inn. He was preparing to mount his horse to make his solemn entry, and had already one foot in the stirrup, when deputies from the council appeared before him, offering him the honorary cup of wine as envoy from the pope, and informing him that he might dispense with entering Zurich. " I have something to communicate to the diet in the name of his holiness," replied the monk. This was a mere trick. It was agreed, however, to receive him ; but as he spoke of nothing but papal bulls, he was dismissed after being compelled to withdraw the excommunication pronounced against the dean of Bremgarten. He quitted the hall fuming with anger, and soon after the pope recalled him to Italy. A waggon, drawn by three horses, and laden with the money that his falsehoods had wrung from the poor, preceded him on those steep paths of the St. Gothard that he had crossed eight months before, without money or parade, and burdened with only a few papers.[1]

The Helvetic diet showed more resolution than the German. It was because neither bishops nor cardinals had a seat in it. And hence the pope, deprived of these supporters, acted more mildly towards Switzerland than towards Germany. But the affair of the indulgences, which played so important a part in the German, was merely an episode in the Swiss Reformation.

CHAPTER VIII.

Zwingle's Toils and Fatigue—The Baths of Pfeffers—The Moment of God—The Great Death—Zwingle attacked by the Plague—His Adversaries — His Friends—Convalescence.—General Joy—Effects of the Pestilence—Myconius at Lucerne—Oswald encourages Zwingle—Zwingle at Basle—Capito invited to Mentz—Hedio at Basle—The Unnatural Son—Preparations for the Struggle.

ZWINGLE did not spare himself. Such great and continued toil called for relaxation, and

he was ordered to repair to the baths of Pfeffers. " Oh ! had I a hundred tongues, a hundred mouths, and a voice of iron, as Virgil says ; or rather had I the eloquence of Cicero, how could I express all that I owe to you, and the pain this separation causes me ? "[1] Such were the parting words of Herus, one of the pupils resident in his house, and who thus gave utterance to the feelings of all who knew Zwingle. He departed, and reached Pfeffers through the frightful gorge formed by the impetuous torrent of the Jamina. He descended into that infernal gulf, as Daniel the hermit terms it, and arrived at those baths, perpetually shaken by the fall of the torrent, and moistened by the spray of its broken waters. Torches were required to be burned at noonday in the house where Zwingle lodged. It was even asserted by the inhabitants, that frightful spectres appeared sometimes amid the gloom.

And yet even here he found an opportunity of serving his Master. His affability won the hearts of many of the invalids. Among their number was the celebrated poet Philip Ingentinus, professor at Friburg, in Brisgau,[2] who from that time became a zealous supporter of the Reformation.

God was watching over his work, and designed to accelerate it. Strong in frame, in character, and in talents, Zwingle, whose defect consisted in this strength, was destined to see it prostrated, that he might become such an instrument as God loves. He needed the baptism of adversity and infirmity, of weakness and pain. Luther had received it in that hour of anguish when his cell and the long galleries of the convent at Erfurth re-echoed with his piercing cries. Zwingle was appointed to receive it by being brought into contact with sickness and death. There is a moment in the history of the heroes of this world, of such as Charles XII. or Napoleon, which decides their career and their renown ; it is that in which their strength is suddenly revealed to them. An analogous moment exists in the life of God's heroes, but it is in a contrary direction ; it is that in which they first recognise their helplessness and nothingness ; from that hour they receive the strength of God from on high. A work like that of which Zwingle was to be the instrument is never accomplished by the natural strength of man ; it would wither immediately, like a tree transplanted in all its maturity and vigour. A plant must be feeble or it will not take root, and a grain must die in the earth before it can become fruitful. God conducted Zwingle, and with him the work that depended on him, to the gates of the sepulchre. It is from among the dry bones, the darkness, and the

---

[1] Und führt mit Ihm ein threspendiger Schatz an Gelt, den er armen Lüthen abgelogen hat. Bullinger Chronik.

[1] Etiamsi mihi sint linguæ centum, sint oraque centum, ferrea vox, ut Virgilius ait, aut potius Ciceroniana eloquentia. Zw. Epp. p. 84.
[2] Illic tum comitatem tuam e sinu uberrimo profluentem, non injucunde sum expertus. Ibid. p. 119.

dust of death, that God is pleased to select the instruments by means of which he designs to scatter over the earth his light, regeneration, and life.

Zwingle was hidden among those colossal rocks that encircle the furious torrent of the Jamina, when he was suddenly informed that the plague, or the *great death*,[1] as it was called, had broken out at Zurich. It appeared in all its terror in the month of August, on St. Lawrence's day, and lasted till Candlemas, sweeping off two thousand five hundred inhabitants. The young men who resided in Zwingle's house had quitted it immediately, in accordance with the directions he had left behind him. His house was deserted; but it was his time to return to it. He hastily quitted Pfeffers, and reappeared in the midst of his flock, which the malady had decimated, and his younger brother Andrew, who had waited for him, he immediately sent back to Wildhaus, and from that hour devoted himself entirely to the victims of this frightful scourge. Every day he proclaimed Christ and his consolations to the sick.[2] His friends, delighted to see him unharmed amid so many deadly arrows,[3] experienced, however, a secret alarm. "Do your duty," said a letter from Basle, written by Conrad Brunner, who himself died of the plague a few months afterwards, "but at the same time remember to take care of your own life." This caution came too late; Zwingle was attacked by the plague. The great preacher of Switzerland lay stretched on a bed from which he seemed likely never to rise. His thoughts were turned inwards; his eyes were directed to heaven. He knew that God had given him a sure inheritance, and venting the feelings of his heart in a hymn, overflowing with unction and simplicity, of which, though we cannot transfer the antique and natural language, we will endeavour at least to exhibit its rhythm and *literal* meaning,—he exclaimed :—

Lo! at the door
    I hear death's knock![4]
Shield me, O Lord,
    My strength and rock.

The hand once nailed
    Upon the tree,
Jesus, uplift—
    And shelter me.

Willest thou, then,
    Death conquer me[5]
In my noonday!....
    So let it be!

---

[1] Der grosse Tod. Bullinger Chronik.
[2] Ut in majori periculo sis, quod in die te novo exponas, dum invisis ægrotos. Bullinger Chronik, p. 87. Chateaubriand had forgotten this and a thousand similar facts, when he wrote that "the protestant pastor abandons the necessitous on the bed of death, and never risks his life in the midst of the pestilence." Essai sur la littérature Anglaise.
[3] Plurimum gaudeo, te inter tot jactus telorum versantem, illæsum hactenus evasisse. Ibid.
[4] Ich mein der Tod,
Syg an der Thür, &c. Zw. Opp. ii. part ii. 270.
In rendering this and the other specimens of poetry contained in this history, the translator has aimed solely at giving a *faithful transcript* of the original.
[5] Willt du dann glych
Tod haben mich
In mitts der Tagen min
So soll's willig sin. Ibid.

Oh! may I die,
    Since I am thine;
Thy home is made
    For faith like mine.

Meantime his disease increased in virulence; his despairing friends beheld this man, the hope of Switzerland and of the Church, about to fall a prey to the tomb. His senses and his strength forsook him. His heart was dismayed, but he still found strength sufficient to turn towards God and to cry :—

My pains increase:
    Lord, stand thou near.
Body and soul
    Dissolve with fear.

Now death is near,
    My tongue is dumb;
Fight for me, Lord,
    Mine hour is come![1]

See Satan's net
    Is o'er me tost—
I feel his hand....
    Must I be lost?

His shafts, his voice
    Alarm no more,
For here I lie
    Thy cross before.

Canon Hoffman sincerely attached to his creed, could not bear the idea of seeing Zwingle die in the errors which he had preached. He called on the provost of the chapter, and said to him: "Think of the danger to which his soul is exposed. Has he not designated as innovators and fantastical all the doctors who have taught these three hundred and eighty years past and more—Alexander Hales, Bonaventure, Albertus Magnus, Thomas Aquinas, and all the canonists? Does not he maintain that their docrines are mere visions, which they dreamt in their cowls within the walls of their cloisters?......Alas! it would have been better for the city of Zurich had Zwingle ruined our vintage and our harvest for many years! Now he is at death's door.........I entreat you to save his poor soul!" It would appear that the provost, who was more enlightened than the canon, did not think it necessary to convert Zwingle to Bonaventure and Albertus Magnus. He was left in peace."

The city was filled with distress. The believers cried to God night and day, praying Him to restore their faithful pastor.[2] The alarm had spread from Zurich to the mountains of the Tockenburg. The pestilence had made its appearance even on those lofty hills. Seven or eight persons had died in the village, among whom was a servant of Zwingle's brother Nicholas.[3] No letter was received from the reformer. "Tell me," wrote young Andrew Zwingle, "in what state you are, my dear brother. The abbot and all our brothers salute thee." It would

---

[1] Nun ist es um
Min Zung ist stumm.
* * * * *
Darum ist Zyt
Das du min stryt. Ibid. 271.
[2] Alle Glaubige rufften Gott treuwillich an, dass er Ihren getreüwen Hirten wieder ufrichte. Bullinger Chronik.
[3] Nicolao vero germano nostro etiam obiit servus suus, attamen non in ædibus suis. Zw. Epp. p. 88.

appear that Zwingle's parents were dead, from there being no mention of them here.

The news of Zwingle's malady, and even the report of his death, were circulated through Switzerland and Germany. "Alas!" exclaimed Hedio in tears, "the preserver of our country, the trumpet of the Gospel, the magnanimous herald of truth, is cut down in the flower and spring-tide of his life!"[1] When the news of Zwingle's decease reached Basle, the whole city resounded with lamentations and mourning.[2]

Yet the spark of life that still remained began to burn more brightly. Although his frame was weak, his soul felt the unalterable conviction that God had called him to replace the candle of His Word on the empty candlestick of the Church. The plague had forsaken its victim, and Zwingle exclaims with emotion:—

> My God, my Sire,
> Heal'd by thy hand,
> Upon the earth
> Once more I stand.
>
> From guilt and sin
> May I be free!
> My mouth shall sing
> Alone of thee!
>
> The uncertain hour
> For me will come...
> O'erwhelm'd perchance
> With deeper gloom.[3]
>
> It matters not!
> With joy I'll bear
> My yoke, until
> I reach heaven's sphere.[4]

In the beginning of November, as soon as he could hold a pen, Zwingle wrote to his family. This gave unutterable joy to his friends,[5] particularly to his young brother Andrew, who himself died of the plague in the following year, and at whose death Ulrich wept and groaned (as he himself observes) with more than woman's sorrow.[6] At Basle, Conrad Brunner, Zwingle's friend, and Bruno Amerbach, the celebrated printer, both young men, had died after three days' illness. It was believed in that city that Zwingle also had fallen. The university felt the deepest dejection. "Whom the gods love die young," said they.[7] But who can describe their delight when Collins, a student from Lucerne, and after him a merchant from

Zurich, brought intelligence that Zwingle had escaped from the jaws of death![1] The vicar of the Bishop of Constance, John Faber, that old friend of Zwingle's, who was subsequently his most violent antagonist, wrote to him: "Oh! my beloved Ulrich, what joy I feel at learning that you have been saved from the grasp of cruel death! When you are in danger, the christian commonwealth is threatened. The Lord has pleased to urge you by these trials to seek more earnestly for eternal life."

This was indeed the aim of the trials by which God had proved Zwingle, and this end was obtained, but in a different manner from that imagined by Faber. This pestilence of 1519, which committed such frightful ravages in the north of Switzerland, was in the hands of God a powerful means for the conversion of many souls.[2] But on no one did it exercise so powerful an influence as on Zwingle. The Gospel, which had hitherto been too much regarded by him as a mere doctrine, now became a great reality. He arose from the darkness of the sepulchre with a new heart. His zeal became more active; his life more holy; his preaching more free, more christian, and more powerful. This was the epoch of Zwingle's complete emancipation; henceforward he consecrated himself entirely to God. But the Reformation of Switzerland received a new life at the same time as the reformer. The scourge of God, *the great death*, as it swept over these mountains and descended into its valleys, gave a holier character to the movement that was there taking place. The Reformation, as well as Zwingle, was baptized in the waters of affliction and of grace, and came forth purer and more vigorous. It was a memorable day in the counsels of God for the regeneration of this people.

Zwingle derived fresh strength, of which he stood so much in need, from communion with his friends. To Myconius especially he was united by the strongest affection. They walked in reliance on each other, like Luther and Melancthon. Oswald was happy at Zurich. True, his position there was embarrassed, but tempered by the virtues of his modest wife. It was of her that Glarean said: "If I could meet with a young woman like her, I should prefer her to a king's daughter." Yet a faithful monitor often broke in upon the sweet affection of Zwingle and Myconius. It was the canon Xyloctect inviting Oswald to return to Lucerne, his native place. "Zurich is not your country," said he, "it is Lucerne! You tell me that the Zurichers are your friends; I do not deny it. But do you know what will be the end of it? Serve your country: This I would advise and entreat you, and, if I may, I

---

[1] Quis enim non doleat, publicam patriæ salutem, tubam Evangelii, magnanimum veritatis buccinatorem languere, intercidere. Zw. Epp. p. 90.
[2] Heu quantum luctus, fatis Zwinglium concessiase, importunus ille rumor suo vehementi impetu divulgavit. Ibid. p. 91.
[3] These words were strikingly fulfilled, twelve years later, on the blood-stained field of Cappel.
[4] So will ich doch
Den Trutz und Poch
In diser Welt
Tragen frölich
Um widergelt.
Although these three fragments of poetry bear date " at the beginning, the middle, and the end of his malady," and express the sentiments Zwingle really felt at these three periods, it is most probable that they were not put into the shape in which they have come down to us until after his recovery. See Bullinger Chronik.
[5] Inspectis tuis literis, incredibilis quidam æstus lætitiæ pectus meum subiit. Zw. Epp. p. 88.
[6] Ejulatum et luctum plusquam femineum. Ibid. p. 155.
[7] Ὃν τι θεοὶ φιλίουσι, νεανίσκος τελευτᾷ. Ibid. p. 90.

[1] E diris te mortis faucibus feliciter ereptum negotiator quidam Tigurinus....Zw. Epp. p. 91.
[2] Als die Pestilentz in Jahre 1519, in diesser Gegend grassirte, viele neigten sich zu einem bessern Leben. George Vögelin, Ref. Hist. Füsslin Beytr. iv. 174.

would command you!"[1] Xyloctect, joining actions with words, procured his nomination as head-master of the collegiate school at Lucerne. Oswald hesitated no longer ; he saw the finger of God in this appointment, and however great the sacrifice, he resolved to make it. Who could tell that he might not be an instrument in the hand of the Lord to introduce the doctrine of peace into the warlike city of Lucerne ? But what a sad farewell was that of Zwingle and Myconius ! They parted in tears. "Your departure," wrote Ulrich to his friend shortly after, "has inflicted a blow on the cause I am defending, like that suffered by an army in battle-array when one of its wings is destroyed.[2] Alas ! now I feel all the value of my Myconius, and how often, without my knowing it, he has upheld the cause of Christ."

Zwingle felt the loss of his friend the more deeply, as the plague had left him in a state of extreme weakness. "It has enfeebled my memory," wrote he on the 30th of November 1519, "and depressed my spirits." He was hardly convalescent before he resumed all his duties. "But," said he, "when I am preaching, I often lose the thread of my discourse. All my limbs are oppressed with languor, and I am almost like a corpse." Besides this, Zwingle's opposition to indulgences had aroused the hostility of their partisans. Oswald encouraged his friend by the letters he wrote from Lucerne. Was not the Lord, at this very moment, giving a pledge of his support by the protection He afforded in Saxony to the powerful champion who had gained such signal victories over Rome ?......" What is your opinion," said Myconius to Zwingle, " of Luther's cause ? As for me, I have no fear either for the Gospel or for him. If God does not protect His truth, who shall protect it ? All that I ask of the Lord is, that He will not withdraw his hand from those who hold nothing dearer than his Gospel. Continue as you have begun, and an abundant reward shall be conferred upon you in heaven !"

The arrival of an old friend consoled Zwingle for the departure of Myconius. Bunzli, who had been Ulrich's instructor at Basle, and who had succeeded the Dean of Wesen, the reformer's uncle, visited Zurich in the first week of the year 1520, and Zwingle and he formed a project of going to Basle to see their common friends.[3] Zwingle's sojourn in that city was not fruitless. "Oh ! my dear Zwingle," wrote John Glother not long after, "never can I forget you. I am bound to you by that kindness with which, during your stay in Basle, you came to see me,—me, a poor schoolmaster, an obscure man, without learning, merit, and of low

estate ! You have won my affections by that gracefulness of manner, that inexpressible suavity with which you subdue all hearts,—nay, even the stones, if I may so speak.[1] But Zwingle's old friends profited still more by his visit. Capito, Hedio, and many others, were electrified by his powerful language ; and the former, commencing in Basle, a work similar to that which Zwingle was carrying on in Zurich, began to explain the Gospel according to St. Matthew, before an ever-increasing auditory. The doctrine of Christ penetrated and warmed their hearts. The people received it gladly, and hailed with acclamations the revival of Christianity.[2] This was the dawn of the Reformation ; and accordingly a conspiracy of priests and monks was soon formed against Capito. It was at this period that Albert, the youthful cardinal-archbishop of Mentz, desirous of attaching so great a scholar to his person, invited him to his court. [3] Capito, seeing the difficulties that were opposed to him, accepted the invitation. The people were excited ; their indignation was roused against the priests, and a violent commotion broke out in the city. [4] Hedio was thought of as his successor ; but some objected to his youth, and others said, " He is Capito's disciple !" "The truth stings," said Hedio ; " it is not safe to wound tender ears by preaching it. [5] But it matters not ! Nothing shall make me swerve from the straight road." The monks redoubled their efforts : " Do not believe those,' exclaimed they from the pulpit, " who tell you that the sum of christian doctrine is found in the Gospel and in St. Paul. Scotus has been more serviceable to Christianity than St. Paul himself. All the learned things that have been ever said or printed were stolen from Scotus. All that these hunters after glory have been able to do, is merely to add a few Greek or Hebrew words to obscure the whole matter."[6]

The disturbance increased, and there was cause to fear that, after Capito's departure, the opposition would become still more powerful. "I shall be almost alone," thought Hedio ;—" I, a weak and wretched man, to struggle unaided with these pestilent monsters." [7] In these circumstances he called to God for succour, and wrote to Zwingle : " Animate my courage by frequent letters. Learning and Christianity are now between the hammer and the anvil. Luther has just been condemned by the universities of Lou-

1 Patriam cole, suadeo et obsecro, et, si hoc possum, jubeo. Xyloctectus Myconio.
2 Nam res meæ, te abeunte, non sunt minus accisæ, quam si exercitui in procinctu stanti altera alarum abstergatur. Zw. Epp. p. 98.
3 Ibid. pp. 103, 111.

1 Morum tuorum elegantia, suavitasque incredibilis, qua omnes tibi devincis, etiam lapides, ut sic dixerim. Zw. Epp. p. 133.
2 Renascenti Christianismo mirum quam faveant. Ibid. p. 120.
3 Cardinalis illic invitavit amplissimis conditionibus. Ibid.
4 Tumultus exoritur et maxima indignatio vulgi erga ἱεςεῖς. Ibid.
5 Auriculas teneras mordaci radere vero, non usque adeo tutum est. Ibid.
6 Scotum plus profuisse rei Christianæ quam ipsum Paulum.... quicquid eruditum, furatum ex Scoto....Ibid
7 Cum pestilentissimis monstris. Ibid. p. 121.

vain and Cologne. If ever the Church was in imminent danger, it is now."[1]

Capito left Basle for Mentz on the 28th of April, and was succeeded by Hedio. Not content with the public assemblies in the church, where he continued the explanation of St. Matthew, Hedio proposed in the month of June (as he writes to Luther) to have private meetings in his house, for the more familiar communication of evangelical instruction to those who felt its necessity. This powerful means of edification in the truth, and of exciting the interest and zeal of believers for Divine things, could not fail, then as in all times, to arouse opposition among worldly minded people and domineering priests, both which classes, though from different motives, are unwilling that God should be worshipped anywhere except within the boundary of certain walls. But Hedio was immovable.

At the period when he was forming this good resolution at Basle, there arrived at Zurich one of those characters who, in all revolutions, are thrown up, like a foul scum, on the surface of society.

The senator Grebel, a man highly respected in Zurich, had a son named Conrad, a youth of remarkable talents, a violent enemy of ignorance and superstition, which he attacked with the most cutting satire; he was blustering and passionate, caustic and ill-natured in his speech; void of natural affection, dissipated, speaking loudly and frequently of his own innocence, and seeing nothing but evil in his neighbours. We mention him here, because he was afterwards destined to play a melancholy part. Just at this time, Vadian married one of Conrad's sisters. The latter, who was studying at Paris, where his misconduct had rendered him incapable of walking, feeling a desire to be present at the marriage, suddenly (about the middle of June) appeared in the midst of his family. The poor father received his prodigal son with a kind smile; his tender mother, with a flood of tears. The affection of his parents could not change his unnatural heart. His good but unhappy mother having some time afterwards been brought to the verge of the grave, Conrad wrote to his brother-in-law Vadian: "My mother has recovered; she is again ruler of the house; she sleeps, rises, scolds, breakfasts, quarrels, dines, disputes, sups, and is always a trouble to us. She trots about, roasts and bakes, heaps and hoards, toils and wearies herself to death, and will soon bring on a relapse."[2] Such was the man who somewhat later presumed to domineer over Zwingle, and became notorious as one of the chiefs of the fanatical Anabaptists. It may be that Divine Providence allowed such characters to appear at the epoch of the Reformation, to form a contrast by their very excesses with the wise, christian, and regulated spirit of the reformers.

Every thing seemed to indicate that the battle between the Gospel and popery was about to begin. "Let us stir up the temporizers," wrote Hedio to Zwingle; "the truce is broken. Let us put on our breastplates; for we shall have to fight against the most formidable enemies."[1] Myconius wrote to Ulrich in the same strain; but the latter replied to these warlike appeals with admirable mildness: "I would allure these obstinate men," said he, "by kindness and friendly proceedings, rather than overthrow them by violent controversy.[2] For if they call our doctrine (which is in truth not ours) a devilish doctrine, it is all very natural, and by this I know that we are really ambassadors from God. The devils cannot be silent in Christ's presence."

CHAPTER IX.

The Two Reformers—The Fall of Man—Expiation of the Man-God—No Merit in Works—Objections refuted—Power of Love for Christ—Election—Christ the sole Master—Effects of this Preaching—Dejection and Courage—First Act of the Magistrate—Church and State—Attacks—Galster.

ALTHOUGH Zwingle desired to follow a mild course, he did not remain inactive. After his illness, his preaching had become more profound and more vivifying. Upwards of two thousand persons in Zurich had received the Word of God in their hearts, confessed the evangelical doctrine, and were already qualified to announce it themselves.[3]

Zwingle held the same faith as Luther, but a faith depending on deeper reasoning. In Luther it was all impulse; in Zwingle, perspicuity of argument prevailed. We find in Luther's writings an internal and private conviction of the value of the cross of Jesus Christ to himself individually; and this conviction, so full of energy and life, animates all that he says. The same sentiment, undoubtedly, is found in Zwingle, but in a less degree. He was rather attracted by the harmony of the christian doctrine: he admired it for its exquisite beauty, for the light it sheds upon the soul of man, and for the everlasting life it brings into the world. The one is moved by the heart, the other by the understanding; and this is why those who have not felt by their own experience the

---

[1] Si unquam imminebat periculum, jam imminet. Zw. Epp. p. 121, 17th March 1520.
[2] Sie regiert das Haus, schläft, steht auf, zankt, frühstückt, keift .... Simml. Samml. iv.; Wirz, i. 76.

[1] Armemus pectora nostra! pugnandum erit contra te-terrimos hostes. Zw. Epp. p. 101.
[2] Benevolentia honestoque obsequio potius allici, quam animosa oppugnatione trahi. Ibid. p. 103.
[3] Non enim soli sumus: Tiguri plus duobus millibus per-multorum est rationalium, qui lac jam spirituale sugentes .... Ibid. 104.

faith that animated these two great disciples of the same Lord have fallen into the gross error of representing one as a mystic and the other as a rationalist. Possibly, the one is more pathetic in the exposition of his faith, the other, more philosophical; but both believe in the same truths. It may be true that they do not regard secondary questions in the same light; but that faith which is one,—that faith which renews and justifies its possessor,—that faith which no confession, no articles can express,—exists in both alike. Zwingle's doctrines have been so often misrepresented, that it will not be irrelevant to glance at what he was then preaching to the people who daily thronged the cathedral of Zurich.

In the fall of the first man Zwingle found a key to the history of the human race. "Before the fall," said he one day, "man had been created with a free will, so that, had he been willing, he might have kept the law; his nature was pure; the disease of sin had not yet reached him; his life was in his own hands. But having desired to be as God, he died......and not he alone, but all his posterity. Since then in Adam all men are dead, no one can recal them to life, until the Spirit, which is God himself, raises them from the dead."[1]

The inhabitants of Zurich, who listened eagerly to this powerful orator, were overwhelmed with sorrow as he unfolded before their eyes that state of sin in which mankind are involved; but soon they heard the words of consolation, and the remedy was pointed out to them, which alone can restore man to life. "Christ, very man and very God,"[2] said the eloquent voice of this son of the Tockenburg herdsman, "has purchased for us a never ending redemption. For since it was the eternal God who died for us, his passion is therefore an eternal sacrifice, and everlastingly effectual to heal;[3] it satisfies the Divine justice for ever in behalf of all those who rely upon it with firm and unshaken faith. Wherever sin is," exclaimed the reformer, "death of necessity follows. Christ was without sin, and guile was not found in his mouth; and yet he died!...... This death he suffered in our stead! He was willing to die that he might restore us to life; and as he had no sins of his own, the all-merciful Father laid ours upon him.[4]...... Seeing that the will of man," said the christian orator again, "had rebelled against the Most High, it was necessary for the re-establishment of eternal order and for the salva-

tion of man, that the human will should submit in Christ's person to the Divine will."[1] He would often remark that the expiatory death of Jesus Christ had taken place in behalf of believers, of the people of God.[2]

The souls that thirsted after salvation in the city of Zurich found repose at the sound of these glad tidings; but there still existed in their minds some long-established errors which it was necessary to eradicate. Starting from the great truth that salvation is the gift of God, Zwingle inveighed powerfully against the pretended merit of human works. "Since eternal salvation," said he "proceeds solely from the merits and death of Jesus Christ, it follows that the merit of our own works is mere vanity and folly, not to say impiety and senseless impudence.[3] If we could have been saved by our own works, it would not have been necessary for Christ to die. All who have ever come to God have come to him through the death of Jesus Christ."[4]

Zwingle foresaw the objections this doctrine would excite among some of his hearers. They waited on him and laid them before him. He replied to them from the pulpit: "Some people, perhaps more dainty than pious, object that this doctrine renders men careless and dissolute. But of what importance are the fears and objections that the daintiness of men may suggest? Whosoever believes in Jesus Christ is assured that all that cometh from God is necessarily good. If, therefore, the Gospel is of God, it is good.[5] And what other power besides could implant righteousness, truth, and love among men?.........O God, most gracious, most righteous Father of all mercies," exclaimed he in a transport of piety, "with what charity Thou hast embraced us, thine enemies![6]......With what lofty and unfailing hopes hast thou filled us, who deserved to feel nothing but despair! and to what glory hast thou called, in thy Son, our meanness and our nothingness!......Thou willest, by this unspeakable love, to constrain us to return thee love for love!"

Following out this idea, he proceeded to show that love to the Redeemer is a law more powerful than the commandments. "The Christian," said he, "delivered from the law, depends entirely on Jesus Christ. Christ is his reason, his counsel, his righteousness, and his whole salvation. Christ lives and acts in him.[7] Christ alone is

[1] Quum ergo omnes homines in Adamo mortui sunt.... donec per Spiritum et gratiam Dei ad vitam quæ Deus est excitentur. Zw. Opp. i. 203. This passage, and others we have quoted, or which we may have occasion to quote, are taken from a work Zwingle published in 1523, and in which he reduced to order the doctrines he had been preaching for several years past.—Hic recensere cœpi (he says) quæ ex verbo Dei prædicavi. Ibid. p. 228.
[2] Christus verus homo et verus Deus....Ibid. 206.
[3] Deus enim æternus, quum sit qui pro nobis moritur, passionem ejus æternam et perpetuo salutarem esse oportet. Ibid.
[4] Mori voluit ut nos vitæ restitueret....Ibid. 204.

[1] Necesse fuit ut voluntas humana in Christo se divinæ submitteret. Zw. Opp. i. 204.
[2] Hostia est et victima, satisfaciens in æternum pro peccatis omnium fidelium. Ibid. 253. Expurgata peccata multitudinis, hoc est, fidelis populi. Ibid. 264.
[3] Sequitur meritum nostrorum operum, nihil esse quam vanitatem et stultitiam, ne dicam impietatem et ignorantem impudentiam. Ibid. 290.
[4] Quotquot ad Deum venerunt unquam, per mortem Christi ad Deum venisse. Ibid.
[5] Certus ad quod quidquid ex Deo est, bonum sit. Si ergo Evangelium ex Deo, bonum est. Ibid. 208.
[6] Quanta caritate nos fures et perduelles....Ibid. 207.
[7] Tum enim totus a Christo pendet. Christus est ei ratio, consilium, justitia, innocentia et tota salus. Christus in eo vivit, in eo agit. Ibid. 233

his leader, and he needs no other guide." And then making use of a comparison within the range of his hearers' intelligence, he added: " If a government forbids its citizens under pain of death to receive any pension or largess from the hands of foreigners, how mild and easy is this law to those who, from love to their country and their liberty, voluntarily abstain from so culpable an action! But, on the contrary, how vexatious and oppressive it is to those who consult their own interest alone! Thus the righteous man lives free and joyful in the love of righteousness, and the unrighteous man walks murmuring under the heavy burden of the law that oppresses him!"[1]

In the cathedral of Zurich there were many old soldiers who felt the truth of these words. Is not love the most powerful of lawgivers? Are not its commands immediately fulfilled? Does not He whom we love dwell in our hearts, and there perform all that he has ordained? Accordingly Zwingle, growing bolder, proclaimed to the people of Zurich that love to the Redeemer was alone capable of impelling a man to perform works acceptable to God. "Works done out of Jesus Christ are worthless," said the christian orator. "Since every thing is done of him, in him, and by him, what can we lay claim to for ourselves? Wherever there is faith in God, there God is; and wherever God abideth, there a zeal exists urging and impelling men to good works.[2] Take care only that Christ is in thee, and that thou art in Christ, and doubt not that then he is at work in thee. The life of a Christian is one perpetual good work which God begins, continues, and completes."[3]

Deeply affected by the greatness of that love of God, which is from everlasting, the herald of grace raised his voice in louder accents of invitation to irresolute and timid souls. "Are you afraid," said he, "to approach this tender Father who has elected you? Why has he chosen us of his grace? Why has he called us? Why has he drawn us to him? Is it that we should fear to approach him?"[4]

Such was Zwingle's doctrine: the doctrine of Christ himself. " If Luther preaches Christ, he does what I am doing," said the preacher of Zurich; "those whom he has brought to Christ are more numerous than those whom I have led. But this matters not: I will bear no other name than that of Christ, whose soldier I am, and who alone is my chief. Never has one single word been written by me to Luther, nor by Luther to

me. And why?......that it might be shown how much the Spirit of God is in unison with itself, since both of us, without any collusion, teach the doctrine of Christ with such uniformity."[1]

Thus did Zwingle preach with courage and enthusiasm.[2] The vast cathedral could not contain the multitude of his hearers. All praised God for the new life that was beginning to reanimate the lifeless body of the Church. Many of the Swiss from every canton, who came to Zurich either to attend the diet or for other motives, impressed by this new preaching, carried its precious seeds, into all the valleys of their native country. A shout of rejoicing rose from every city and mountain. "Switzerland," wrote Nicholas Hageus from Lucerne to Zurich, " Switzerland has hitherto given birth to such as Brutus, Scipio, and Cæsar; but she has hardly produced a man who really knew Jesus Christ, and who nourished our souls, not with vain disputes, but with the Word of God. Now that Divine Providence has given Switzerland a Zwingle for preacher and an Oswald Myconius for teacher, virtue and sacred learning are reviving among us. O fortunate Helvetia! if at last thou wouldst rest from war, and, already illustrious by thy arms, become more illustrious still by righteousness and peace!"[3]—" There was a report," wrote Myconius to Zwingle, " that your voice could not be heard three paces off. But I see now that it was a falsehood, for all Switzerland hears you!"[4]—" Thou hast armed thyself with an intrepid courage," wrote Hedio from Basle; " I will follow thee as far as I am able."[5]—" I have heard thee," wrote Sebastain Hofmeister of Schaffhausen from Constance. " Would to God that Zurich, which is at the head of our happy confederation, were healed of its disease, so that the whole body might be at length restored to health!"[6]

But Zwingle met with adversaries as well as admirers. "Why," said some, " does he busy himself with the affairs of Switzerland?"......" Why," said others, " does he repeat the same things in every sermon?" In the midst of all this opposition, dejection often came over Zwingle's soul. Everything seemed in his eyes falling into confusion, and society to be on the eve of a general convulsion.[7] He thought it impossible for any new truth to appear, without its antagonistic error springing up immediately.[8] If any hope arose in his heart, fear grew up by

---

[1] Bonus vir in amore justitiæ liber et lætus vivit. Zw. Opp. i. 234.
[2] Ubi Deus, illic cura est et studium, ad opera bona urgens et impellens....Ibid. 213.
[3] Vita ergo pii hominis nihil aliud est, nisi perpetua quædam et indefessa boni operatio, quam Deus incipit, ducit, et absolvit....Ibid. 295.
[4] Quum ergo Deus pater nos elegit ex gratia sua, traxitque et vocavit, cur ad eum accedere non auderemus? Ibid. 287.

[1] Quam concors sit spiritus Dei, dum nos tam procul dissiti, nihil colludentes, tam concorditer Christi doctrinam docemus. Zw. Opp. i. 276.
[2] Quam fortis sis in Christo prædicando. Zw. Epp. p. 160.
[3] O Helvetiam longe feliciorem, si tandem liceat te a bellis conquiescere! Ibid. p. 128.
[4] At video mendacium esse, cum audiaris per totam Helvetiam. Ibid. p. 135.
[5] Sequar te quoad potero....Ibid. p. 134.
[6] Ut capite felicis patriæ nostræ a morbo erepto, sanitas tandem in reliqua membra reciperetur. Ibid. p. 147.
[7] Omnia sursum deorsumque moventur. Ibid. p. 142.
[8] Ut nihil proferre caput queat, cujus non contrariunæ regione emergat. Ibid.

its side. He soon, however, threw off his dejection. " The life of man here below is a continual war," said he ; " whoever desires to obtain glory must face the world, and, like David, force this haughty Goliath, so proud of his stature, to bite the dust. The Church," said he, as Luther had done, " was purchased by blood, and by blood must be restored.[1] The more numerous are its impurities, the more men like Hercules must we call up to cleanse these Augean stables.[2] I am under no apprehensions for Luther," added he, " even should he be struck by the thunderbolts of this (Romish) Jupiter."[3]

Zwingle had need of repose, and repaired to the waters of Baden. The priest of this town, formerly one of the pope's guards, a man of kindly disposition but of the greatest ignorance, had obtained his benefice by carrying the halberd. Faithful to his military habits, he used to pass the day and part of the night in jovial company, while his curate Stäheli was indefatigable in performing all the duties of his charge.[4] Zwingle sent for him and said : " I have need of Swiss helpers ;" and from that moment Stäheli was his fellow-labourer. Zwingle, Stäheli, and Luti subsequently pastor at Winterthour, lived under the same roof.

Zwingle's devotion was not unrewarded. The Word of Christ, preached with so much energy, was destined to bear fruit. Many magistrates were gained over ; they had found in God's Word their consolation and their strength. Afflicted at observing the priests, and above all the monks, uttering shamelessly from the pulpit whatever came into their heads, the council published a decree ordering them to preach nothing in their sermons " that they had not drawn from the sacred fountains of the Old and New Testaments."[5] It was in 1520 that the civil authority thus interfered for the first time in the work of the Reformation ; acting as a christian magistrate (in the opinion of some), since it is the primary duty of the magistrate to defend the Word of God and to protect the dearest interests of the citizens ;— depriving the Church of its liberty (in the opinion of others), subjecting it to the secular power, and giving the signal of that long train of evils which the union of Church and State has since engendered. We will not here decide on this great controversy, which in our own days is maintained with so much warmth in many countries. It is sufficient for us to mark its origin at the epoch of the Reformation. But there is still another thing to be pointed out ; the act of these magistrates was of itself an effect of the preaching of the Word of God. The Reformation in Switzerland then emerged from simple individualities, and became a national work. Born in the hearts of a few priests and learned men, it extended, rose up, and took its station on higher ground. Like the waters of the sea, it rose gradually, until it had covered a vast expanse.

The monks were confounded : they had been ordered to preach the Word of God only, and most of them had never read it. One opposition provokes another. This decree became the signal for the most violent attacks against the Reformation. Plots began to be formed against the priest of Zurich : his life was in danger. One day, as Zwingle and his curates were quietly conversing in their house, some citizens entered hastily, saying : " Have you strong bolts to your doors ? Be on your guard to-night."—" We often had such alarms as these," adds Stäheli ; " but we were well armed,[1] and a patrol was stationed in the street to protect us."

In other places recourse was had to still more violent measures. An aged man of Schaffhausen, named Galster, possessing a just spirit and a fervour rare at his age, and rejoicing in the light he had found in the Gospel, endeavoured to communicate it to his wife and children ; in his zeal, which may have been indiscreet, he openly attacked the relics, priests, and superstition with which his canton abounded. He soon became an object of hatred and terror even to his own family. The old man, anticipating mischief, left his house broken-hearted, and fled to the neighbouring forests. Here he remained some days sustaining life upon what he could find, when suddenly, on the last night of the year 1520, torches flashed through the forest in every direction, and the shouts of men and the cry of savage dogs re-echoed through its gloomy shades. The council had ordered a grand chase in the forest to discover the wretched man. The hounds caught their prey. The unhappy Galster was dragged before the magistrate, and summoned to abjure his faith ; as he continued steadfast, he was beheaded.[2]

CHAPTER X.

A new Combatant—The Reformer of Berne—Zwingle encourages Haller—The Gospel at Lucerne—Oswald persecuted—Zwingle's Preaching—Henry Bullinger and Gerold of Knonau—Rubli at Basle—The Chaplain of the Hospital—War in Italy—Zwingle protests against the Capitulations.

THE year thus inaugurated by this bloody execution had hardly begun, when Zwingle

---

[1] Ecclesiam puto, ut sanguine parta est, ita sanguine instaurari. Zw. Epp. p. 143.
[2] Eo plures armabis Hercules qui fimum tot hactenus boum efferant. Ibid. p. 144.
[3] Etiamsi fulmine Jovis istius fulminetur. Ibid.
[4] Misc. Tig. ii. 679-696 ; Wirz. i. 78, 79.
[5] Vetuit eos Senatus quicquam prædicare quod non ex sacrarum literarum utriusque Testamenti fontibus hausissent. Zw. Opp. iii. 28.

[1] Wir waren aber gut gerüstet. Misc. Tig. ii. 681 ; Wirz i. 334.
[2] Wirz. i. 510 ; Sebast. Wagner, von Kirchhofer, p. 18.

received a visit at Zurich from a young man about twenty-eight years of age, of tall stature, and whose exterior denoted candour, simplicity, and diffidence.[1] He introduced himself as Berthold Haller, and on hearing his name Zwingle embraced the celebrated preacher of Berne with that affability which imparted such a charm to his manners. Haller was born at Aldingen in Wurtemberg,[2] and had studied first at Rotwyl under Rubellus, and next at Pforzheim, where Simmler was his preceptor, and Melancthon his fellow-pupil. The Bernese had about that time resolved on attracting literary men to their republic, which had already become so famous by its feats of arms. Rubellus and Berthold, who was then only twenty-one years old, repaired thither. Subsequently Haller was named canon, and shortly after preacher, of the cathedral. The Gospel taught by Zwingle had reached Berne; Haller believed, and from that hour desired to see the mighty man whom he already respected as a father. He went to Zurich, where Myconius had announced him. Thus did Haller and Zwingle meet. Haller, a man of meek disposition, confided to Zwingle all his trials; and Zwingle, the strong man, inspired him with courage. "My soul," said Berthold to Zwingle one day, "is overwhelmed;......I cannot support such unjust treatment. I am determined to resign my pulpit and retire to Basle, and there in Wittembach's society, devote myself wholly to sacred learning." "Alas!" replied Zwingle, "and I too feel discouragement creep over me when I see myself unjustly assailed; but Christ awakens my conscience by the powerful stimulus of his terrors and promises. He alarms me by saying: *Whosoever shall be ashamed of me before men, of him shall I be ashamed before my Father*: and he restores me to tranquillity by adding: *Whosoever shall confess me before men, him also will I confess before my Father*. O my dear Berthold, take courage! Our names are written in imperishable characters in the annals of the citizens on high.[3] I am ready to die for Christ.[4]......Oh! that your fierce bear-cubs," added he, "would hear the doctrine of Jesus Christ, then would they grow tame.[5] But you must undertake this duty with great gentleness, lest they should turn round furiously, and rend you in pieces." Haller's courage revived. "My soul," wrote he to Zwingle, "has awakened from its slumber. I must preach the Gospel. Jesus Christ must be restored to this city, whence He has

been so long exiled."[1] Thus did the flame that glowed so brightly in Zwingle's bosom rekindle that of Berthold, and the timid Haller rushed into the midst of the savage bears, that grinding their teeth (says Zwingle) sought to devour him.

It was in another quarter, however, that the persecution was to break out in Switzerland. The warlike Lucerne stood forward as an adversary armed cap-a-pie and lance in rest. The military spirit prevailed in this canton, the advocate of foreign service; and the leading men of the capital knit their brows whenever they heard one word of peace calculated to restrain their warlike disposition. When Luther's works reached this city, some of the inhabitants began to read them, and were struck with horror. They appeared to have been penned by the hand of a demon; their imagination took fright, their eyes wandered, and they fancied their chambers were filled with devils, surrounding and gazing upon them with a sarcastic leer.[2]......They hastily closed the volume and flung it aside in terror. Oswald, who had heard of these singular visions, never spoke of Luther, except to his most intimate friends, and was content simply to announce the Gospel of Christ. Yet notwithstanding this moderation, loud cries were heard in the city: "We must burn Luther and the schoolmaster (Myconius)!"[3]......" I am assailed by my adversary, like a ship in a hurricane at sea," said Oswald to one of his friends.[4] One day in the beginning of the year 1520, he was suddenly called before the council. "You are enjoined," said they, "never to read Luther's works to your pupils, never to mention him before them, and never even to think of him."[5] The lords of Lucerne presumed, it will be seen, to extend their jurisdiction very widely. Shortly after this, a preacher declaimed from the pulpit against heresy. All the assembly was moved; every eye was turned on Oswald, for whom could the preacher have had in view but him? Oswald remained quietly in his place, as if the matter did not concern him. But on leaving the church, as he was walking with his friend the Canon Xyloctect, one of the councillors, who had not yet recovered from his agitation, passed near them. "Well! you disciples of Luther," said he angrily, "why do you not defend your master?" They made no reply. "I live," said Myconius, "in the midst of savage wolves; but I have this consolation, that most of them have lost their teeth. They would bite if they could; but as they cannot, they merely howl."

---

[1] Animi tui candorem simplicem et simplicitatem candidissimam, hac tua pusilla quidem epistola....Zw. Epp. p. 186.
[2] Ita ipse in literis MS. J. J. Hott. iii. 54.
[3] Scripta tamen habeatur in fastis supernorum civium. Zw. Epp. p. 196.
[4] Ut mori pro Christo non usque adeo detrectem apud me. Ibid. p. 187.
[5] Ut ursi tui ferociusculi, audita Christi doctrina, mansuescere incipiant. Ibid. The reader will remember that a bear figures in the shield of Berne.

[1] Donec Christum, cucullatis nugis longe a nobis exulem ....pro virili restituerim. Zw. Epp. p. 187.
[2] Dum Lutherum semel legerint, ut putarent stubellam suam plenam esse dæmonibus. Ibid. 137.
[3] Clamatur hic per totam civitatem: Lutherum comburendum et ludi magistrum. Ibid. 153.
[4] Non aliter me impellunt quam procellæ marinæ navem aliquam. Ibid. 159.
[5] Imo ne in mentem eum admitterem. Ibid.

The senate was called together, for the tumult among the people kept increasing. "He is a Lutheran!" said one of the councillors. "He is a teacher of novelties!" said another. "He is a seducer of youth," said a third..........." Let him appear! let him appear!" cried all. The poor schoolmaster came before them, and heard fresh menaces and prohibitions. His simple spirit was wounded and depressed. His gentle wife could only console him by her tears. "Every one is against me," exclaimed he in his anguish. "Assailed by so many tempests, whither shall I turn, or how shall I escape them?...If Christ were not with me, I should long ago have fallen beneath their blows." [1]......" What matters it whether Lucerne will keep you or not?" wrote Dr. Sebastian Hofmeister, in a letter dated from Constance. "The earth is the Lord's. Every country is the home of the brave. Even were we the vilest of men, our cause is just, for we teach the Gospel of Christ."

Whilst the truth thus met with so many obstacles at Lucerne, it was triumphant at Zurich. Zwingle laboured unceasingly. Desirous of meditating on the whole of Scripture in the original languages, he applied himself diligently to the study of Hebrew under the direction of John Boschenstein, Reuchlin's pupil. But his object in studying the Scriptures was to preach them. On Fridays, the peasants who came in crowds, bringing their produce to the market of the city, showed great eagerness for the Word of God. To satisfy their wants, Zwingle had begun, in the month of December 1520, to expound the Psalms every market-day, preparing his sermon by previous meditation on each particular text. The reformers always combined learned pursuits with their practical labours: these labours were their end, their studies were but the means. They were not less zealous in the closet than before the people. The union of learning and love is a characteristic feature of this epoch. With reference to his Sunday preachings, Zwingle, after having expounded the life of our Lord according to St. Matthew, proceeded to show, by explaining the Acts of the Apostles, how the doctrine of Christ had been propagated. He next set forth the rule of a christian life, as inculcated in the Epistles to Timothy; he made use of the Epistle to the Galatians to combat doctrinal errors, and combined with it the two Epistles of Peter, to demonstrate to the contemners of St. Paul how the same spirit animated both these apostles; he concluded with the Epistle to the Hebrews, that he might explain to their fullest extent all the blessings which flow from the gift of Jesus Christ, the great high-priest of the Christian.

But Zwingle did not confine himself to adult men alone; he endeavoured to kindle in the young also a sacred fire by which they should be animated. One day in the year 1521, as he was engaged in his closet studying the Fathers of the Church, extracting the most remarkable passages, and carefully classifying them in a thick volume, he saw a young man enter whose features strongly interested him. [1] It was Henry Bullinger, who, having returned from Germany, had come to see him, impatient to know that teacher of his native land whose name was already celebrated in Christendom. The handsome youth fixed his eyes successively on the reformer and his books, and felt a call to follow Zwingle's example. The latter welcomed him with that cordiality which won every heart. This first visit had a powerful influence over the whole life of the student, after he had returned to his father's hearth. Another young man had also gained Zwingle's affection; this was Gerold Meyer von Knonau. His mother, Anna Reinhardt, who subsequently occupied an important place in the life of the reformer, had been a great beauty, and was still distinguished by her virtues. A young man of noble family, John Meyer von Knonau, who had been brought up at the court of the Bishop of Constance, to whom he was related, had conceived an ardent affection for Anna; but she belonged to a plebeian family. The elder Meyer von Knonau had refused his consent to their union, and disinherited his son after the marriage. In 1513, Anna was left a widow with one son and two daughters, and she now lived solely for the education of the poor orphans. Their grandfather was inexorable. One day, however, the widow's servant took young Gerold out with her, a lively and graceful boy, then only three years old, and as she stopped with him in the fish-market, the elder Meyer, who chanced to be at the window, [2] noticed him, watched every movement, and asked to whom this beautiful child, so buoyant with life and freshness, belonged. "It is your son's," was the reply. The old man's heart was touched—the ice was melted—everything was forgotten, and he clasped in his arms the wife and the children of his son. Zwingle had become attached as if he were his own child to the young, noble, and courageous Gerold, who was destined to expire in the flower of his age at the reformer's side, his hand upon the sword, and surrounded, alas! by the dead bodies of his enemies. Thinking that Gerold could not find in Zurich sufficient resources for study, Zwingle in 1521 sent him to Basle.

[1] Si Christus non esset, jam olim defecissem. Zw. Epp. p. 160.

[1] Ich hab by Im ein gross Buch gesehen, *Locorum communium*; als ich by Ihm wass, anno 1521, dorinnen er *Sententias* und *Dogmata Patrum*, flyssig jedes an seinem ort verzeichnet. Bullinger Chronik.
[2] Lüget des Kindts Grossvater zum fänster uss, und ersach das Kind in der Fischer-bränten (Kufe), so fräch (frisch) und frölich sitzen....Archives des Meyer de Knonau, quoted in a notice of *Anna Reinhardt*, Erlangen, 1835, by M. Gerold Meyer von Knonau. I am indebted to the kindness of this friend for the elucidation of several obscure passages in the life of Zwingle.

The young Von Knonau did not find Hedio, Zwingle's friend, in that city. As Capito was obliged to accompany the Archbishop Albert to the coronation of Charles V., he had engaged Hedio to supply his place at Mentz. Basle thus successively lost her most faithful preachers; the Church seemed abandoned, but other men appeared. Four thousand hearers crowded the church of William Rubli, priest of St. Alban's. He attacked the doctrine of the mass, purgatory, and the invocation of saints. But this man, who was turbulent and greedy of public applause, inveighed against error rather than contended for the truth. On the festival of Corpus Christi he joined the great procession, but instead of the relics, which it was customary to parade through the streets, there was carried before him a copy of the Holy Scriptures, handsomely bound, and with this inscription in large letters: "The Bible; this is the true relic, all others are but dead men's bones." Courage adorns the servant of God: ostentation disfigures him. The work of an evangelist is to preach the Bible and not to make a pompous display of it. The enraged priests accused Rubli before the council. A crowd immediately filled the square of the Cordeliers. "Protect our preacher," said the citizens to the council. Fifty ladies of distinction interposed in his favour, but Rubli was compelled to leave Basle. Somewhat later he was implicated, like Grebel, in the disorders of the Anabaptists. As the Reformation was evolved, it every where rejected the chaff that was mixed up with the good grain.

At this time, from the lowliest of chapels was heard an humble voice distinctly proclaiming the Gospel doctrines. It was that of the youthful Wolfgang Wissemburger, the son of a councillor of state, and chaplain to the hospital. All the inhabitants of Basle, who felt new desires, experienced a deeper affection for the meek chaplain than they had for the haughty Rubli himself. Wolfgang began to read mass in German. The monks renewed their clamours; but this time they failed, and Wissemburger was enabled to continue preaching the Gospel; "for," says an old chronicler, "he was a citizen and his father a councillor."[1] This first success of the Reformation at Basle was an omen of still greater. At the same time, it was of much importance to the progress of the work throughout the confederation. Zurich was not alone. The learned Basle began to be charmed at the sound of the new doctrine. The foundations of the new temple were extending. The Reformation in Switzerland was attaining a higher stage of development.

Zurich was, however, the centre of the movement. But in the year 1521, important political events, that grieved Zwingle's heart, in some measure diverted men's minds from the preaching of the Gospel. Leo X., who had offered his alliance simultaneously to Charles V. and Francis I., had at length decided for the emperor. The war between these two rivals was about to burst forth in Italy. "The pope shall have nothing left but his ears," said the French general Lautrec.[1] This ill-timed jest increased the pontiff's anger. The King of France claimed the support of the Swiss cantons, which, with the exception of Zurich, were in alliance with him: his call was obeyed. The pope flattered himself with the hope of engaging Zurich in his cause, and the Cardinal of Sion, who was always intriguing, in full confidence in his dexterity and eloquence, hastened to this city to procure soldiers for his master. But he met with a resolute opposition from his old friend Zwingle. The latter was indignant at the thought of seeing the Swiss sell their blood to the foreigner; his imagination already conjured up the sight of the Zurichers under the standards of the pope and the emperor crossing their swords in the plains of Italy with the confederates assembled under the banner of France; and at this fratricidal picture his patriotic and christian soul thrilled with horror. He thundered from the pulpit: "Will you," exclaimed he "tear in pieces and destroy the confederation?[2]......We hunt down the wolves that ravage our flocks, but we make no resistance to those who prowl around us to devour men!......It is not without reason that the mantles and the hats they wear are red; shake these garments, and down will fall ducats and crowns; but if you wring them, you will see them dripping with the blood of your brothers, your fathers, your sons, and your dearest friends!"[3]......In vain did Zwingle raise his manly voice. The cardinal with his red hat succeeded, and two thousand seven hundred Zurichers departed under the command of George Berguer. Zwingle's heart was wrung. His influence was not, however, lost. For many years after the banners of Zurich were not unfolded and carried through the gates of the city in behalf of foreign princes.

[1] Disse che M. di Lutrech et M. de l'Escu havia ditto che ʼl voleva che le recchia del papa fusse la major parte retasse di la so persona. Gradenigo, the Venetian ambassador at Rome, MS. 1523.

[2] Sagt wie es ein fromme Eidtgnosschafft zertrennen und umbkehren würde. Bull. Chronik.

[3] Sie tragen billig rothe hüt und mäntel, dan schüte man sie, so fallen Cronen und Duggaten heraus, winde man sie. so rünt deines Bruders, Vaters, Sohns und guten Freunds Blut heraus. Ibid.

[1] Diewell er ein Burger war und sein Vater des Raths. Fridolin Ryff's Chronik.

CHAPTER XI.

Zwingle opposes Human Traditions—Commotion during Lent—Truth triumphs amidst Opposition—The Bishop's Deputies—Accusation before the Clergy and the Council—Appeal to the Great Council—The Coadjutor and Zwingle—Zwingle's Reply—Decree of the Great Council—Posture of Affairs—Hoffman's Attack.

WOUNDED in his feelings as a citizen, Zwingle devoted himself with fresh zeal to the preaching of the Gospel. His sermons increased in energy. "I will never cease labouring to restore the primitive unity of the Church of Christ," said he.[1] He began the year 1522 by showing the difference between the precepts of the Gospel and those of men. When the season of Lent came round, he preached with still greater vigour. After having laid the foundations of the new building, he was desirous of sweeping away the rubbish of the old. " For four years," said he to the crowd assembled in the cathedral, " you have eagerly received the holy doctrine of the Gospel. Glowing with the fire of charity, fed with the sweets of the heavenly manna, it is impossible you can now find any savour in the wretched nutriment of human traditions."[2] And then attacking the compulsory abstinence from meat at certain seasons, he exclaimed with his artless eloquence: "There are some who maintain that to eat meat is a fault, and even a great sin, although God has never forbidden it, and yet they think it not a crime to sell human flesh to the foreigner, and drag it to slaughter ! "[3] ......At this daring language the partisans of the military capitulations, who were present in the assembly, shuddered with indignation and anger, and vowed never to forget it.

While Zwingle was preaching thus energetically, he still continued to say mass ; he observed the established usages of the Church, and even abstained from meat on the appointed days. He was of opinion that the people should be enlightened previously. But there were some turbulent persons who did not act so prudently. Rubli, who had taken refuge at Zurich, permitted himself to be led astray by an extravagant zeal. The former curate of Saint Alban's, a Bernese captain, and Conrad Huber, a member of the great council, were accustomed to meet at the house of the latter to eat meat on Friday and Saturday. On this they greatly prided themselves. The question of fasting engrossed every mind. An inhabitant of Lucerne having come to Zurich, said to one of his friends in this city : " You worthy confederates of Zurich are wrong in eating meat during Lent."—The Zuricher replied : " You gentlemen of Lucerne, however, take the

liberty to eat meat on the prohibited days." —" We have purchased it from the pope."— " And we, from the butcher......If it be an affair of money, one is certainly as good as the other."[1] The council having received a complaint against the transgressors of the ecclesiastical ordinances, requested the opinion of the parish priest. Zwingle replied that the practice of eating meat every day was not blamable of itself ; but that the people ought to abstain from doing so until a competent authority should have come to some decision on the matter. The other members of the clergy concurred in his sentiments.

The enemies of the truth took advantage of this fortunate circumstance. Their influence was declining ; the victory would remain with Zwingle, unless they made haste to strike a vigorous blow. They importuned the Bishop of Constance. " Zwingle," exclaimed they, " is the destroyer and not the keeper of the Lord's fold."[2]

The ambitious Faber, Zwingle's old friend, had just returned from Rome full of fresh zeal for the papacy. From the inspirations of this haughty city were destined to proceed the first religious troubles in Switzerland. A decisive struggle between the evangelical truth and the representatives of the Roman pontiff was now to take place. Truth acquires its chief strength in the attacks that are made upon it. It was under the shade of opposition and persecution that Christianity at its rise acquired the power that eventually overthrew all its enemies. At the epoch of its revival, which forms the subject of our history, it was the will of God to conduct His truth in like manner through these rugged paths. The priests then stood up, as in the days of the apostles, against the new doctrine. Without these attacks, it would probably have remained hidden and obscure in a few faithful souls. But God was watching the hour to manifest it to the world. Opposition opened new roads for it, launched it on a new career, and fixed the eyes of the nation upon it. This opposition was like a gust of wind, scattering the seeds to a distance, which would otherwise have remained lifeless on the spot where they had fallen. The tree, that was destined to shelter the people of Switzerland, had been deeply planted in her valleys, but storms were necessary to strengthen its roots and extend its branches. The partisans of the papacy, seeing the fire already smouldering in Zurich, rushed forward to extinguish it, but they only made the conflagration fiercer and more extensive.

In the afternoon of the 7th of April 1522, three ecclesiastical deputies from the Bishop of Constance entered Zurich ; two of them

---

[1] Ego veterem Christi Ecclesiæ unitatem instaurare non desinam. Zw. Opp. iii. 47.
[2] Gustum non aliquis humanarum traditionum cibus vobis arridere potuerit. Ibid. i. 2.
[3] Aber menschenfleisch verkoufen und ze Tod schlahen.. ..Ibid. ii. part ii. p. 301.

[1] So haben wir's von dem Metzger erkaufft......Bull. Chronik.
[2] Ovilis dominici populator esse, non custos aut pastor. Zw. Opp. iii. 28.

had an austere and angry look; the third appeared of milder disposition; they were Melchior Battli, the bishop's coadjutor, Doctor Brendi, and John Vanner, preacher of the cathedral, an evangelical man, and who preserved silence during the whole of the business.[1] It was already dark when Luti ran to Zwingle and said : " The bishop's commissioners have arrived; some great blow is preparing; all the partisans of the old customs are stirring. A notary is summoning all the priests for an early meeting to-morrow in the hall of the chapter."

The assembly of the clergy accordingly took place on the following day, when the coadjutor rose and delivered a speech which his opponents described as haughty and violent;[2] he studiously refrained, however, from uttering Zwingle's name. A few priests, recently gained over to the Gospel, were thunderstruck; their pallid features, their silence, and their sighs betrayed their total loss of courage.[3] Zwingle now stood up and answered in a manner that effectually silenced his adversaries. At Zurich, as in the other cantons, the most violent enemies of the new doctrine were to be found in the Smaller Council. The deputation, worsted before the clergy, laid their complaints before the magistrates; Zwingle was absent, and accordingly they had no reply to fear. The result appeared decisive. They were about to condemn the Gospel without its defender being heard. Never had the Reformation of Switzerland been in greater danger. It was on the point of being stifled in its cradle. The councillors who were friendly to Zwingle then appealed to the jurisdiction of the Great Council; this was the only remaining chance of safety, and God made use of it to save the cause of the Gospel. The Two Hundred were convened. The partisans of the papacy made every exertion to prevent Zwingle's admission; he struggled hard to obtain a hearing, knocking at every door, and leaving not a stone unturned,[4] to use his own expression; but in vain !...... " It is impossible," said the burgomasters; " the council has decided to the contrary."— " Upon this," says Zwingle, " I remained tranquil, and with deep sighs laid the matter before Him who heareth the groans of the captive, beseeching him to defend his Gospel."[5] The patient and submissive expectation of the servants of God has never deceived them.

On the 9th of April, the Two Hundred met. " We desire to have our pastors here," immediately said the friends of the Reformation who belonged to it. The Smaller Council resisted; but the Great Council decided that the pastors should be present at the accusation, and even reply if they thought fit. The deputies of Constance were first introduced, and next the three priests of Zurich; Zwingle, Engelhard, and the aged Rœschli.

After these antagonists, thus brought face to face, had scrutinized each other's appearance, the coadjutor stood up. " If his heart and head had only been equal to his voice," says Zwingle, " he would have excelled Apollo and Orpheus in sweetness, and the Gracchi and Demosthenes in power."

" The civil constitution," said this champion of the papacy, " and the christian faith itself are endangered. Men have recently appeared who teach novel, revolting, and seditious doctrines." At the end of a long speech, he fixed his eyes on the assembled senators, and said, " Remain in the Church ! —remain in the Church !—Out of it no one can be saved. Its ceremonies alone are capable of bringing the simple to a knowledge of salvation;[1] and the shepherds of the flock have nothing more to do than explain their meaning to the people."

As soon as the coadjutor had finished his speech, he prepared to leave the council-room with his colleagues, when Zwingle said earnestly: " Most worthy coadjutor, and you, his companions, stay, I entreat you, until I have vindicated myself."

THE COADJUTOR.—" We have no commission to dispute with any one."

ZWINGLE —" I have no wish to dispute, but to state fearlessly what I have been teaching up to this hour."

THE BURGOMASTER ROUST, *addressing the deputation from Constance.*—" I beseech you to listen to the reply the pastor desires to make."

THE COADJUTOR.—" I know too well the man I have to deal with. Ulrich Zwingle is too violent for any discussion to be held with him."

ZWINGLE.—" How long since has it been customary to accuse an innocent man with such violence, and then refuse to hear his defence ? In the name of our common faith, of the baptism we have both received, of Christ the author of salvation and of life, listen to me.[2] If you cannot as deputies, at least do so as Christians."

After firing her guns in the air, Rome was hastily retreating from the field of battle. The reformer wanted only to be heard, and the agents of the papacy thought of nothing but running away. A cause thus pleaded was already gained by the one side and lost by the other. The Two Hundred could no

---

[1] Zw. Opp. iii. 8.—J. J. Hottinger, iii. 77.—Ruchat, i. 134, 2d edition, and others say, that Faber headed this deputation. Zwingle names the three deputies, but does not mention Faber. These writers have probably confounded two different offices of the Roman hierarchy, those of coadjutor and of vicar-general.
[2] Erat tota oratio vehemens et stomachi supercilique plena. Zw. Opp. iii. 8.
[3] Infirmos quosdam nuper Christo lucrifactos sacerdotes offensos ea sentirem, ex tacitis palloribus ac suspiriis. Ibid. 9.
[4] Frustra diu movi omnem lapidem. Ibid.
[5] Ibi ego quiescere ac suspiriis rem agere cœpi apud eum qui audit gemitum compeditorum. Ibid.

[1] Unicas esse per quas simplices christiani ad agnitionem salutis inducerentur. Zw. Opp. iii. 10.
[2] Ob communem fidem, ob communem baptismum, ob Christum vitæ salutisque auctorem. Ibid. li.

longer contain their indignation; a murmur was heard in the assembly;[1] again the burgomaster entreated the deputies to remain. Abashed and speechless, they returned to their places, when Zwingle said:—

"The reverend coadjutor speaks of doctrines that are seditious and subversive of the civil laws. Let him learn that Zurich is more tranquil and more obedient to the laws than any other city of the Helvetians,—a circumstance which all good citizens ascribe to the Gospel. Is not Christianity the strongest bulwark of justice among a nation?[2] What is the result of all ceremonies, but shamefully to disguise the features of Christ and of his disciples?[3] Yes!—there is another way, besides these vain observances, to bring the unlearned people to the knowledge of the truth. It is that which Christ and his apostles followed......the Gospel itself! Let us not fear that the people cannot understand it. He who believes, understands. The people can believe, they can therefore understand. This is a work of the Holy Ghost, and not of mere human reason.[4] As for that matter, let him who is not satisfied with forty days, fast all the year if he pleases: it is a matter of indifference to me. All that I require is, that no one should be compelled to fast, and that for so trivial an observance the Zurichers should not be accused of withdrawing from the communion of Christians."

"I did not say that," exclaimed the coadjutor.—"No," said his colleague Dr. Brendi, "he did not say so." But all the senate confirmed Zwingle's assertion.

"Excellent citizens," continued the latter, "let not this charge alarm you! The foundation of the Church is that rock, that Christ, who gave Peter his name because he confessed him faithfully. In every nation whoever sincerely believes in the Lord Jesus is saved. It is out of *this* Church that no one can have everlasting life.[5] To explain the Gospel and to follow it is our whole duty as ministers of Christ. Let those who live upon ceremonies undertake to explain them!" This was probing the wound to the quick.

The coadjutor blushed and remained silent. The council of the Two Hundred then broke up. On the same day they came to the resolution that the pope and the cardinals should be requested to explain the controverted point, and that in the meanwhile the people should abstain from eating meat during Lent. This was leaving the matter *in statu quo*, and replying to the bishop by seeking to gain time.

This discussion had forwarded the work of the Reformation. The champions of Rome and those of the new doctrine had met face to face, as it were, in the presence of the whole people; and the advantage had not remained on the side of the pope. This was the first skirmish in a campaign that promised to be long and severe, and alternated with many vicissitudes of mourning and joy. But the first success at the beginning of a contest gives courage to the whole army and intimidates the enemy. The Reformation had seized upon a ground from which it was never to be dislodged. If the council thought themselves still obliged to act with caution, the people loudly proclaimed the defeat of Rome. "Never," said they in the exultation of the moment, "will she be able to rally her scattered and defeated troops."[1] "With the energy of St. Paul," said they to Zwingle, "you have attacked these false apostles and their Ananiahs—those whited walls...... The satellites of Antichrist can never do more than gnash their teeth at you!" From the farthest parts of Germany came voices proclaiming him with joy—"the glory of reviving theology."[2]

But at the same time the enemies of the Gospel were rallying their forces. There was no time to lose if they desired to suppress it; for it would soon be beyond the reach of their blows. Hoffman laid before the chapter a voluminous accusation against the reformer. "Suppose," he said, "the priest could prove by witnesses what sins or what disorders had been committed by ecclesiastics in certain convents, streets, or taverns, he ought to name no one! Why would he have us understand (it is true I have scarcely ever heard him myself) that he alone derives his doctrine from the fountain-head, and that others seek it only in kennels and puddles?[5] Is it not impossible, considering the diversity of men's minds, that every preacher should preach alike?"

Zwingle answered this accusation in a full meeting of the chapter, scattering his adversaries' charges, "as a bull with his horns tosses straw in the air."[3] The matter which had appeared so serious, ended in loud bursts of laughter at the canon's expense. But Zwingle did not stop there; on the 16th of April he published a treatise *on the free use of meats.*[5]

[1] Cœpit murmur audiri civium indignantium. Zw. Opp. iii 11.
[2] Imo Christianismum ad communem justitiam servandam esse potentissimum. Ibid. 13.
[3] Ceremonias haud quicquam aliud agere, quam et Christo et ejus fidelibus os oblinere. Ibid.
[4] Quicquid hic agitur divino fit afflatu, non humano ratiocinio. Ibid.
[5] Extra illam neminem salvari. Ibid. 15.

- Ut vulgo jactatum sit, nunquam ultra copias sarturos. Zw. Epp. p. 203.
[2] Vale renascentis Theologiæ decus. Letter of Urban Regius. Ibid. 225.
[3] Die andern aber aus Rinnen und Pfützen. Simml. Samml. Wirz. i. 244.
[4] Ut cornu vehemens taurus aristas. Zw. Epp. p. 203.
[5] De delectu et libero ciborum usu. Zw. Opp. i. 1.

CHAPTER XII.

Mourning and Joy in Germany—Plots against Zwingle—The Bishop's Mandate—Archeteles—The Bishop's Appeal to the Diet—Injunction against attacking the Monks—Zwingle's Declaration—The Nuns of Œtenbach—Zwingle's Address to Schwytz.

ZWINGLE's indomitable firmness delighted the friends of truth, and particularly the evangelical Christians of Germany, so long deprived, by his captivity in the Wartburg, of the mighty apostle who had first arisen in the bosom of the Church. Already many pastors and believers, exiled in consequence of the merciless decree which the papacy had extorted from Charles V. at Worms, had found an Asylum at Zurich. Nesse, the professor of Frankfort, whom Luther had visited on his road to Worms, wrote to Zwingle: "Oh! the joy that I feel at hearing with what authority you proclaim Jesus Christ! Strengthen by your exhortations those whom the cruelty of wicked bishops has compelled to flee far from our desolate churches."[1]

But it was not in Germany alone that the adversaries were plotting against the friends of the Reformation. Not an hour passed in which the means of getting rid of Zwingle were not discussed.[2] One day he received an anonymous letter, which he communicated immediately to his two curates. "Snares surround you on every side," wrote his secret friend; "a deadly poison has been prepared to take away your life.[3] Never eat food but in your own house, and only what has been prepared by your own cook. The walls of Zurich contain men who are plotting your destruction. The oracle that has revealed this to me is more worthy of credit than that of Delphi. I am your friend; you shall know me hereafter."[4]

On the next day after that in which Zwingle had received this mysterious epistle, just as Stäheli was entering the Water-church, a chaplain stopped him and said: "Leave Zwingle's house forthwith; a catastrophe is at hand!" Certain fanatics, who despaired of seeing the Reformation checked by words, were arming themselves with poniards. Whenever mighty revolutions are taking place in society, assassins ordinarily spring from the foul dregs of the agitated people. God watched over Zwingle.

Whilst the murderers were beholding the failure of their plots, the legitimate organs of the papacy were again in commotion. The bishop and his councillors resolved to renew the war. Intelligence of this reached Zwingle from every quarter. The reformer, in full reliance on the Word of God, said with noble intrepidity: "I fear them......as a lofty rock fears the roaring waves......σὺν τῷ Θιῷ, with the aid of God!" added he.[1] On the 2d of May, the Bishop of Constance published a mandate, in which, without naming either Zwingle or Zurich, he complained that speculative persons were reviving doctrines already condemned, and that both learned and ignorant were in the habit of discussing in every place the deepest mysteries. John Vanner, preacher of the cathedral at Constance, was the first attacked: "I prefer," said he, "being a Christian with the hatred of many, to abandoning Christ for the friendship of the world."[2]

But it was at Zurich that the rising heresy required to be crushed. Faber and the bishop knew that Zwingle had many enemies among the canons. They resolved to take advantage of this enmity. Towards the end of May a letter from the bishop arrived at Zurich; it was addressed to the provost and chapter. "Sons of the Church," wrote the prelate, "let those perish who will perish! but let no one seduce you from the Church."[3] At the same time the bishop entreated the canons to prevent those culpable doctrines, which engendered pernicious sects, from being preached or discussed among them, either in private or in public. When this letter was read in the chapter, all eyes were fixed on Zwingle. The latter, understanding the meaning of this look, said to them: "I see that you think this letter refers to me; please to give it me, and, God willing, I will answer it."

Zwingle replied in his *Archeteles*, a word which signifies "the beginning and the end;"......"for," said he, "I hope this first answer will also be the last." In this work he spoke of the bishop in a very respectful manner, and ascribed all the attacks of his enemies to a few intriguing men. "What have I done?" said he; "I have called all men to a knowledge of their own infirmities; I have endeavoured to conduct them to the only true God and to Jesus Christ his Son. To this end, I have not made use of captious arguments, but of plain and sincere language, such as the children of Switzerland can understand." And then, passing from a defensive to an offensive attitude, he added with great beauty: "When Julius Cæsar felt the mortal wound, he folded his garments around him, that he might fall with dignity. The downfall of your ceremonies is at hand! I see at least that they fall decently, and that light be every where promptly substituted for darkness."[4]

---

[1] Et ut iis, qui ob malorum episcoporum sævitiam a nobis submoventur, prodesse velis. Zw. Epp. p. 208.
[2] Nulla præteriit hora, in qua non fierent....consultationes insidiosissimæ. Osw. Myc. Vita Zw.
[3] Ἕτοιμα φάρμακα λυγρά. Zw. Epp. p. 199.
[4] Σός εἰμι, agnosces me postea. Ibid.

[1] Quos ita metuo, ut littus altum fluctuum undas minacium. Zw. Epp. p. 203.
[2] Malo esse Christianus cum multorum invidia, quam relinquere Christum propter mundanorum amicitiam. Ibid. p. 200, dated 22d May.
[3] Nemo vos filios ecclesiæ de ecclesia tollat! Zw. Opp. iii. 35.
[4] In umbrarum locum, lux quam ocissime inducatur. Ibid. 69.

This was the sole result of the bishop's letter to the chapter of Zurich. Since every friendly remonstrance had proved vain, it was necessary to strike a more vigorous blow. Upon this, Faber and Landenberg cast their eyes around them, fixing them at last on the diet, the supreme council of the Helvetic nation.[1] Deputies from the bishop appeared before this body, stating that their master had issued a mandate forbidding the priests in his diocese to make any innovation in matters of doctrine; that his authority had been despised, and that he now invoked the support of the chiefs of the confederation to aid him in reducing the rebels to obedience, and in defending the true and ancient faith.[2] The enemies of the Reformation had the majority in this first assembly of the nation. Not long before, it had published a decree interdicting all those priests from preaching, whose sermons, in its opinion, were a cause of dissension among the people. This injunction of the diet, which then for the first time interfered with the Reformation, fell to the ground; but now, being resolved to act with severity, this assembly summoned before them Urban Weiss, pastor of Fislispach near Baden, whom the general report accused of preaching the new faith and rejecting the old. Weiss was set at liberty for a season at the intercession of several individuals, and under bail of a hundred florins offered by his parishioners.

But the diet had taken its position: of this we have just been witnesses; every where the monks and priests began to recover their courage. At Zurich they had shown themselves more imperious immediately after the first decree of this assembly. Several members of the council were in the habit of visiting the three convents night and morning, and even of taking their meals there. The monks tampered with these well-meaning guests, and solicited them to procure an injunction from the government in their favour. " If Zwingle will not hold his tongue," said they, " we will bawl louder than he." The diet had sided with the oppressors. The council of Zurich knew not what to do. On the 7th of June they voted an ordinance forbidding any one to preach against the monks; but this decree had scarcely passed " when a sudden noise was heard in the council-chamber," says Bullinger's chronicle, " which made them all look at one another."[3] Tranquillity was not restored; the battle that was fought from the pulpit every day grew hotter. The council nominated a deputation before which the pastors of Zurich and the readers and preachers of the convents were summoned to appear in the provost's house; after a lively debate, the burgomaster en-

joined both parties to preach nothing that might endanger the public peace. " I can not comply with this injunction," said Zwingle ; " I am resolved to preach the Gospel freely and unconditionally, in conformity with the previous ordinance. I am bishop and pastor of Zurich ; to me has been confided the cure of souls It is I who have taken oath, and not the monks. They ought to yield, and not I. If they preach lies, I will contradict them, even in the pulpits of their own convents. If I myself teach a doctrine contrary to the holy Gospel, then I desire to be rebuked, not only by the chapter, but by any citizen whatsoever ;[1] and moreover to be punished by the council."—" We demand permission," said the monks, " to preach the doctrines of St. Thomas." The committee of the council determined, after proper deliberation, "That Thomas (Aquinas), Scotus, and the other doctors should be laid aside, and that nothing should be preached but the Gospel." Thus did the truth once more prevail. But the anger of the papal partisans was augmented. The *ultramontane* canons could not conceal their rage. They stared insolently at Zwingle in the chapter, and seemed to be thirsting for his blood.[2]

These menaces did not check Zwingle. There was still one place in Zurich where, thanks to the Dominicans, the light had not yet penetrated : this was the nunnery of Œtenbach. Here the daughters of the first families of Zurich were accustomed to take the veil. It seemed unjust that these poor women, shut up within the walls of their convent, should be the only persons that did not hear the Word of God. The Great Council ordered Zwingle to visit them. The reformer went into that pulpit which had hitherto been confined to the Dominicans, and preached "on the clearness and certainty of the Word of God."[3] He subsequently published this remarkable discourse, which did not fall on barren ground, and which still further exasperated the monks.

A circumstance now occurred that extended this hostility, and communicated it to many other hearts. The Swiss, under the command of Stein and Winkelried, had just suffered a bloody defeat at the Bicocca. They had made a desperate charge upon the enemy, but Pescara's artillery and the lansquenets of that Freundsberg whom Luther had met at the door of the hall of assembly at Worms, had overthrown both commanders and standards, while whole companies had been mown down and suddenly exterminated. Winkelried and Stein, with members of the noble families of Mulinen, Diesbach, Bonstetten, Tschudi, and Pfyffer, had been left on the field of battle. Schwytz especially

---

1 Nam er ein anderen weg an die Hand; schike seine Boten, &c. Bullinger Chronik.
2 Und den wahren alten glauben erhalten. Ibid.
3 Liess die Rathstuben einen grossen Knall. Ibid.

1 Sondern von einem jedem Bürger wyssen. Bull. Chronik.
2 Oculos in me procacius torquent, ut cujus caput peti gauderent. Zw. Opp. iii. 29.
3 De claritate et certitudine verbi Dei. Ibid. i. 66.

had been decimated. The bloody relics of this frightful combat had returned to Switzerland, carrying mourning in their train. A cry of woe resounded from the Alps to the Jura, and from the Rhone to the Rhine.

But no one felt so keen a pain as Zwingle. He immediately wrote an address to Schwytz dissuading the citizens of this canton from foreign service. " Your ancestors," said he with all the warmth of a patriot's heart, " fought with their enemies in defence of liberty; but they never put Christians to death for mere gain. These foreign wars bring innumerable calamities on our country. The scourge of God chastises our confederate nations, and Helvetian liberty is on the verge of expiring between the interested caresses and the deadly hatred of foreign princes." [1] Zwingle gave the hand to Nicholas de Flue, [2] and followed up the exhortations of this man of peace. This address having been presented to the assembly of the people of Schwytz, produced such an effect, that they resolved to abstain provisionally from every foreign alliance for the next twenty-five years. But erelong the French party procured the repeal of this generous resolution, and Schwytz, from that hour, became the canton most opposed to Zwingle and his work. Even the disgrace that the partisans of these foreign treaties brought upon their native land only served to increase the hatred of these men against the intrepid minister who was endeavouring to avert from his country so many misfortunes and such deep shame. An opposition, growing more violent every day, was formed in the confederation against Zwingle and Zurich. The usages of the Church and the practices of the recruiting officers, as they were attacked conjointly, mutually supported each other in withstanding the impetuous blast of that reform which threatened to overthrow them both. At the same time enemies from without were multiplying. It was not only the pope, but other foreign princes also, who vowed a pitiless hostility to the Reformation. Did it not pretend to withdraw from their ranks those Helvetian halberds to which their ambition and pride had been indebted for so many triumphs? But on the side of the Gospel there remained ......God and the most excellent of the people: this was enough. Besides, from different countries, Divine Providence was bringing to its aid men who had been persecuted for their faith.

[1] Ein göttlich Vermanung an die cersamen, etc. Eidgnossen zu Schywz. Zw. Opp. part ii. 206.
[2] In 1481, the confederates were on the brink of civil war, when a hermit of Unterwalden (Nicholas de Flue) repaired to Stanz, where the diet were assembled, calmed their angry passions, and restored tranquillity and peace.

CHAPTER XIII.

A French Monk—He teaches in Switzerland—Dispute between Zwingle and the Monk—Discourse of the Commander of the Johannites—The Carnival at Berne—The Eaters of the Dead—The Skull of St. Anne—Appenzel—The Grisons—Murder and Adultery—Zwingle's Marriage.

On Saturday the 12th of July there appeared in the streets of Zurich a monk of tall, thin, and rigid frame, wearing the gray frock of the Cordeliers, of foreign air, and mounted on an ass, which hardly lifted his bare feet off the ground. [1] In this manner he had journeyed from Avignon, without knowing a word of German. By means of his Latin, however, he was able to make himself understood. Francis Lambert, for such was his name, asked for Zwingle, and handed him a letter from Berthold Haller. " This Franciscan father," said the Bernese parish priest, " who is no other than the apostolical preacher of the convent-general of Avignon, has been teaching the christian truth for these last five years; he has preached in Latin before our priests at Geneva, at Lausanne before the bishop, at Friburg, and lastly at Berne, touching the church, the priesthood, the sacrifice of the mass, the traditions of the Romish bishops, and the superstitions of the religious orders. It seems most astonishing to me to hear such things from a gray friar and a Frenchman......characters that presuppose, as you are aware, a whole sea of superstitions." [2] The Frenchman related to Zwingle how Luther's writings having been discovered in his cell, he had been compelled to quit Avignon without delay; how, at first, he had preached the Gospel in the city of Geneva, and afterwards at Lausanne, on the shores of the same lake. Zwingle, highly delighted, opened the church of Our Lady to the monk, and made him sit in the choir on a seat in front of the high altar. In this church Lambert delivered four sermons, in which he inveighed forcibly against the errors of Rome; but in the fourth, he defended the invocation of Mary and the saints.

" Brother! thou art mistaken," [3] immediately exclaimed an animated voice. It was Zwingle's. Canons and chaplains thrilled with joy at the prospect of a dispute between the Frenchman and the heretical priest. " He has attacked you," said they all to Lambert; " demand a public discussion with him." The monk of Avignon did so, and at ten o'clock on the 22d of July the two champions met in the conference hall of the canons. Zwingle opened the Old and New Testament in Greek and Latin; he continued discussing and explaining until two o'clock, when the French monk, clasping his hands and raising

[1] ....Kam ein langer, gerader, barfüsser Mönch....ritte auf einer Eselin. Füsslin Beyträge, iv. 39.
[2] A tali Franciscano, Gallo, quæ omnia mare superstitionum confluere faciunt, inaudita. Zw. Epp. p. 207.
[3] Bruder, da irrest du. Füsslin Beytr. iv. 40.

them to heaven,[1] exclaimed: "I thank thee, O God, that by means of such an illustrious instrument thou hast brought me to so clear a knowledge of the truth! Henceforth," added he, turning to the assembly, "in all my tribulations I will call on God alone, and will throw aside my beads. To-morrow I shall resume my journey; I am going to Basle to see Erasmus of Rotterdam, and from thence to Wittemberg to visit Martin Luther, the Augustine monk." And accordingly he departed on his ass. We shall meet with him again. He was the first man who, for the cause of the Gospel, went forth from France into Switzerland and Germany: the humble forerunner of many thousands of refugees and confessors.

Myconius had no such consolations: on the contrary, he was destined to see Sebastian Hofmeister, who had come from Constance to Lucerne, and there boldly preached the Gospel, forced to leave the city. Upon this Oswald's sorrow increased. The humid climate of Lucerne was against him; a fever preyed upon him; the physicians declared that unless he removed to some other place, he would die. "Nowhere have I a greater desire to be than near you," wrote he to Zwingle, "and nowhere less than at Lucerne. Men torment me, and the climate is wasting me away. My malady, they say, is the penalty of my iniquity: alas! whatever I say, whatever I do, turns to poison with them......There is ONE in heaven on whom all my hopes repose."[2]

This hope was not delusive. It was about the end of March, and the feast of the Annunciation was approaching. The day before the eve of this anniversary a great festival was observed in commemoration of a fire which in 1340 had reduced the greater part of the city to ashes. The streets of Lucerne were already crowded with a vast concourse of people from the surrounding districts, and several hundreds of priests were assembled. The sermon at this solemn feast was usually delivered by some celebrated preacher. The commander of the Johannites, Conrad Schmidt of Küssnacht, arrived to perform this duty. An immense congregation filled the church. Who shall describe the general astonishment, when the commander, laying aside the custom of preaching in Latin, spoke in German, so that all might understand him,[3] explaining with authority and holy fervour the love of God in sending his Son, and proving eloquently that mere external works have no power to save, and that the promises of God are truly the essence of the Gospel! "God forbid," exclaimed Conrad before the astonished people, "that we should acknowledge for our head a chief

so full of sin as the Bishop of Rome, and reject Christ![1] If the Bishop of Rome distributes the nourishment of the Gospel, let us acknowledge him as our pastor, but not as chief; and if he distribute it not, let us in nowise acknowledge him." Oswald could not contain himself for joy. "What a man!" cried he, "what a sermon! what majesty! what authority! how full of the spirit of Christ!" The effect was general. A solemn silence succeeded the agitation that filled the city; but this was merely transient. If the people stop their ears to the voice of God, his calls become less frequent every day, and even cease entirely. This was the case with Lucerne.

Whilst the truth was thus proclaimed from the pulpit at Berne, the papacy was attacked in the festive meetings of the people. Nicholas Manuel, a distinguished layman, celebrated for his poetical talents, and who had reached the highest offices of state, indignant at seeing his fellow-countrymen so unmercifully plundered by Samson, composed some carnival dramas, in which he assailed the covetousness, pomp, and haughtiness of the pope and clergy with the stinging weapons of satire. On the Shrove Tuesday " of the lords" (the lords were then the clergy, and began their Lent eight days before the people), nothing was talked of in Berne but a drama or mystery, entitled, *The Eaters of the Dead*, which some young persons were to act in the Rue de la Croix. The citizens crowded to the show. As a matter of art, these dramatic sketches at the commencement of the sixteenth century possess some interest; but it is with a very different view that we quote them in this place. We should prefer, doubtless, not to be obliged to quote, on the part of the Reformation, attacks of this nature; it is by other arms that truth prevails. But history does not create, she can only adduce what she finds.

At last the show begins, to the great delight of the impatient crowd assembled in the Rue de la Croix. First appears the pope, covered with glittering robes, and sitting on a throne. Around him stand his courtiers, his guards, and a motley crowd of priests of every degree; behind them are nobles, laymen, and mendicants. Soon a funeral procession appears; it is a wealthy farmer they are carrying to his last home. Two of his relatives walk slowly in front of the coffin, with handkerchiefs in their hands. When the procession came before the pope, the bier was placed at his feet, and the acting began:—

FIRST RELATION, *in a sorrowful tone.*

Noble army of the saints!
Hear, oh! hear our sad complaints:
Our cousin's dead....the yawning tomb
Has swallow'd him in life's first bloom.

---

[1] Dass er beyde Hände zusammen hob. Füsslin, Beytr. Iv. 40.
[2] Quicquid facio venenum est illis. Sed est in quem omnis spes mea reclinat. Zw. Epp. p. 192.
[3] Wolt er keine pracht tryben mit latein schwätzen, sondern gut teutsch reden. Bullinger Chronik.

[1] Absit a grege Christiano, ut caput tam lutulentum et peccatis plenum acceptans, Christum abjiciat. Zw. Epp. p. 195.

SECOND RELATION.

No cost to monk or priest we'll spare;
We've a hundred crowns for mass and prayer,
If thus from purgatorial fire
We can but save our 'parted sire.[1]

THE SEXTON, *coming out of the crowd around the pope, and running hastily to the parish priest.*
ROBERT MORE-AND-MORE.

A trifle to drink, sir priest, I crave!
A farmer stout now goes to his grave.

THE PRIEST.

But *one!*....I only thirst the more!
One dead!....would it were half a score!
The more the merrier then live we![2]
Death is the best of games for me.

THE SEXTON.

Would it were so! 'twould then be well!
I'd rather toll a dead man's knell
Than from morn to night a field be tilling:
He never complains, and to pay is willing.

THE PRIEST.

If the death-knell opes the gate of heaven
I know not.—But what's that to me!
With salmon and pike, with barbel and trout,
It fills my house right merrily.

THE PRIEST'S NIECE.[3]

'Tis well! But, look ye, I claim my share;
To-day this soul must for me prepare
A gown of white, black, green, or red,
And a pretty kerchief to deck my head.

CARDINAL HIGH-PRIDE, *wearing a red hat, and standing near the pope.*

Did we not love the heritage of death,
Could we sweep off, in life's young prime
On corpse-encumbered field such countless bands,
Lured by intrigue, or else by envy urged?[4]
On Christian blood Rome fattens. Hence my hat
And robe derive their sanguinary hue.
My honours and my wealth are gain'd from death.

BISHOP WOLF'S-BELLY.

In the pope's laws firm will I live and die.
My robes are silken and my purse is full;
The tournament and chase are my delight.
In former times, when yet the Church was young,
Clothed as simple villagers we went.[5]
We priests were shepherds—now, the peers of kings.
And yet at times a shepherd's life I love.

A VOICE.

A shepherd's life!

BISHOP WOLF'S-BELLY.

Ay! at shearing time.—Shepherds and wolves are we:
They, the poor sheep; and if they feed us not,
They fall, unpitied by our ruthless fangs.
Connubial sweets we are forbid to taste.
'Tis well!—beneath this heavy yoke
The purest falter;—this is better still.
Scandals!—I heed them not; they fill my purse,
And serve but to augment my princely train.
The smallest profit never comes amiss.
A priest with money only has to choose
Among the fair—pays florins four—I'm blind.
Has he a child?—again his purse must bleed.
'Tis thus a good round sum I net each year,—
Two thousand florins; but not e'en two pence[6]
Would fall to me, were they discreet and wise.
All honour to the pope! With bended knee
I bow before him. In his faith I'll live,
Defend his church, and own him as my god.

THE POPE.

Now doth the faithless world at last believe,
That an ambitious priest can ope or shut,
At will, the gates of heaven. Preach faithfully
The ordinances of the conclave's choice.

1 Kein kosten soll uns dauern dran,
  Wo wir Mönch und Priester mögen ha'n
  Und sollt'es kosten hundert kronen....
      Bern. Mausol. iv. Wirz. K. Gesch. i. 353.
2 Je mehr, je besser! Kämen doch noch zehn! Ibid.
3 The German word (*Pfaffenmetze*) is more expressive, but less decent.
4 Wenn mir nicht wär' mit Todten wohl,
  So läg nicht mancher Acker voll, etc. Ibid.
5 Wenn es stünd, wie im Anfang der Kilchen,
  Ich trüge vielleicht grobes Tuch und Zwilchen. Ibid.
6 The German is very expressive:—
  So bin Ich auf gut Deutsch ein Hurenwirth, &c. &c.
Ibid.

Now are we kings—the layman, a dull thrall.
Wave but the Gospel standard in the air,
And we are lost. To offer sacrifice
Or fee the priest, the Gospel teacheth not.
Did we obey its precepts, we should live—
Alas!—in poverty, and meanly die.
Ah! then farewell to richly harness'd steeds,
To sumptuous chariots—then a sullen ass
Would bear the portly majesty of Rome.[1]....
No!—firmly Saint Peter's rights I'll guard,
And rash intruders with my thunders blast.
Let us but will—the universe is ours,
And prostrate nations worship us as God.
I walk upon their bodies to my throne.
Avaunt, ye unclean laymen, from our treasure...
Three drops of holy water fill your measure.

We will not continue our translation of Manuel's drama. The anguish of the clergy on discovering the efforts of the reformers, and their anger against those who threatened to put a stop to their disorders, are painted in the liveliest colours. The dissolute manners, of which this mystery presents so vivid an image, were too common for each one not to be struck with the truth of the representation. The people were excited. Many were their jests as they departed from the show in the Rue de la Croix; but some individuals were more seriously affected; they spoke of christian liberty and of the papal despotism; they contrasted the simplicity of the Gospel with the pomp of Rome. The contempt of the people soon went beyond all bounds. On Ash Wednesday the indulgences were paraded through the streets, accompanied with satirical songs. A heavy blow had been struck in Berne and in all Switzerland at the ancient edifice of Popery.

Not long after this representation, another comedy was acted at Berne; but in this there was nothing invented. The clergy, council, and citizens were assembled in front of the Upper Gate, awaiting the skull or Saint Anne, which the famous knight Albert of Stein had gone to fetch from Lyons. At length Stein appeared, carrying the holy relic enveloped in a silken cloth, before which the Bishop of Lausanne had humbly bent the knee as it passed through his city. The precious skull was borne in procession to the Dominican church; the bells rang out; the train filed into the temple; and with great solemnity the skull of Mary's mother was placed on an altar specially consecrated to it, and behind a sumptuous trellis work. But in the midst of these rejoicings, a letter was received from the abbot of the convent of Lyons, in which reposed the relics of the saint, announcing that the monks had sold the knight a profane skull taken from the cemetery, from among the scattered fragments of the dead. This mystification deeply incensed the inhabitants or the illustrious city of Berne.

The Reformation was advancing in other parts of Switzerland. In 1521, a young man of Appenzel, Walter Klarer by name, returned from the university of Paris to his native canton. Luther's works fell into his

1 Wir möchten fast kaum ein Eselein ha'n. Bern Mausol. iv. Wirz. K. Gesch. i. 383.

hands, and in 1522 he preached the evangelical doctrine with all the energy of a youthful Christian. An innkeeper named Rausberg, member of the council of Appenzel, a rich and pious man, opened his house to all the friends of truth. A famous captain, Bartholomew Berweger, who had fought for Julius II. and Leo X., having returned from Rome about this time, persecuted the evangelical ministers. One day, however, remembering what wickedness he had seen at Rome, he began to read his Bible, and to attend the sermons of the new preachers: his eyes were opened, and he embraced the Gospel. On witnessing the crowds that could not find room in the churches, he said: " Let the ministers preach in the fields and public places ; " and despite a violent opposition, the meadows, hills, and mountains of Appenzel often afterwards re-echoed with the tidings of salvation.

This doctrine, proceeding upwards along the banks of the Rhine, spread even as far as the ancient Rhætia. One day a stranger coming from Zurich crossed the stream, and entered the house of a saddler in Flasch, the first village of the Grisons. The saddler, Christian Anhorn, listened with astonishment to the language of his guest. The whole village invited the stranger, whose name was Jacques Burkli, to preach to them. He took his station in front of the altar ; a troop of armed men, with Anhorn at their head, stood round to protect him from any sudden attack while he was proclaiming the Gospel. The rumour of this preaching spread far and wide, and on the following Sunday an immense crowd flocked to the church. In a brief space a large proportion of the inhabitants of these districts demanded the Eucharist according to our Lord's institution. But on a sudden the tocsin rang in Mayenfeldt ; the affrighted people ran together to know the cause ; the priests described the danger that threatened the Church ; and then at the head of this fanatic crowd, ran hastily to Flasch. Anhorn, who was working in the fields, surprised at hearing the sound of bells at so unusual a time, returned home immediately, and hid Burkli in a deep hole in his cellar. The house was surrounded, the doors burst in ; they sought for the heretical preacher, but in vain : at last, the persecutors left the place.[1]

The Word of God spread through the whole league of the ten jurisdictions. The priest of Mayenfeldt having returned from Rome, whither he had gone in his irritation at the progress of the Gospel, exclaimed : " Rome has made me evangelical ! " and he became a fervent reformer. Erelong the Reformation extended over the league of " the house of God ; " " Oh ! that you could see how the dwellers in the Rhætian mountains are

throwing off the yoke of the Babylonian captivity ! " wrote Salandronius to Vadian.

Disorders of a revolting character hastened the time when Zurich and the neighbouring cantons snapped asunder the Roman yoke. A married schoolmaster, desiring to enter holy orders, obtained his wife's consent with this view, and they separated. The new priest, finding it impossible to observe his vow of celibacy, and unwilling to wound his wife's feelings, quitted the place where she lived, and went into the see of Constance, where he formed a criminal connexion. His wife heard of this, and followed him. The poor priest had compassion on her, and dismissing the woman who had usurped her rights, took his lawful spouse into his house. The *procurator-fiscal* immediately drew up a complaint ; the vicar-general was in a ferment ; the councillors of the consistory deliberated......and ordered the curate to forsake either his wife or his benefice. The poor wife left her husband's house in tears, and her rival re-entered it in triumph. The Church declared itself satisfied, and from that time the adulterous priest was left undisturbed.[1]

Not long after, a parish priest of Lucerne seduced a married woman and lived with her. The husband, having returned to Lucerne, availed himself of the priest's absence to recover his wife. As he was taking her home, the seducer met them ; fell upon the injured husband, and inflicted a wound of which the latter died.[2] All pious men felt the necessity of re-establishing the law of God, which declares *marriage honourable in all*.[3] The evangelical ministers had discovered that the law of celibacy was of human origin, imposed by the pontiffs, and contrary to the Word of God, which, describing a faithful bishop, represents him as a husband and father (1 Timothy iii. 2, 4). At the same time they observed, that of all abuses that had crept into the Church, none had been a cause of more vice and scandal. They thought, therefore, that it was not only lawful, but, even more, a duty to God to reject it. Many of them now returned to this ancient usage of apostolical times. Xyloctect was married. Zwingle also took a wife about this period.

No woman had been more respected in Zurich than Anna Reinhardt, the widow of Meyer von Knonau, Gerold's mother. From Zwingle's arrival, she had been one of his most attentive hearers ; she lived near him, and he had noticed her piety, her modesty, and affection for her children. The young Gerold, who had become, as it were, his adopted son, drew him still closer to the mother. The sufferings undergone by this christian woman, who was one day to be more cruelly tried than any of her sex re-

[1] Anhorn Wiedergeburt der Ev. Kirchen in den 3 Bündten. Chur. 1680 ; Wirz. L. 557.

[1] Simml. Samml. vi. ; Wirz. K. Gesch. 1. 275.
[2] Hinc cum scorto redeuntem in itinere deprehendit, aggreditur, lethiferoque vulnere cædit et tandem moritur. Zw. Epp. p. 206.
[3] Hebrews xiii. 4.

corded in history, had communicated a seriousness that contributed to show forth her evangelical virtues more brightly.[1] At this time she was about thirty-five years old, and her fortune only amounted to four hundred florins. It was on her that Zwingle fixed his eyes as a companion for life. He comprehended all the sacredness and sympathy of the conjugal state. He entitled it "a most holy alliance."[2]—" In like manner," said he, " as Christ died for his followers, and gave himself entirely for them, so should married persons do all and suffer all for one another." But Zwingle, when he took Anna Reinhardt to wife, did not make his marriage known. This is undoubtedly a blamable weakness in a man at other times so resolute. The light that he and his friends had acquired on the question of celibacy was not general. Weak minds might have been scandalized. He feared that his usefulness in the Church would be paralyzed, if his marriage were made public.[3] He sacrificed a portion of his happiness to these fears, excusable perhaps, but which he ought to have shaken off.[4]

CHAPTER XIV.

How the Truth triumphs—Meeting at Einsidlen—Petition to the Bishop and Confederates—The Men of Einsidlen separate—Scene in a Convent—Dinner with Myconius——The Strength of the Reformers—Effect of the Petitions to Lucerne—The Council of the Diet—Haller at the Townhall—Friburg—Oswald's Destitution—Zwingle consoles him—Oswald quits Lucerne—The Diet's first Act of Severity—Consternation of Zwingle's Brothers—Zwingle's Resolution—The Future—Zwingle's Prayer.

BUT far higher interests than these occupied the minds of the friends of truth. The diet,

1 Anna Reinhard, von Gerold Meyer von Knonau, p. 25.
2 Ein hochheiliges Bündniss. Ibid.
3 Qui veritus sis, te marito non tam feliciter usurum Christum in negotio verbi sui. Zw. Epp. p. 335.
4 Biographers, respectable historians, and all the writers who have copied them, place Zwingle's marriage two years later, in April 1524. Without any intention of stating here all the reasons that have convinced me of their error, I shall put down simply the most decisive authorities. A letter from Myconius, Zwingle's intimate friend, dated 22d July 1522, has these words: *Vale cum uxore quam felicissime*. In another letter from the same, written about the end of the year, we read: *Vale cum uxore*. The very contents of these letters prove the accuracy of their respective dates. But what is stronger still is a letter written from Strasburg by Bucer, at the very time Zwingle's marriage was made public, the 14th April 1524 (the date of the year is wanting, but internal evidence proves it to have been written in 1524), containing several passages which show that Zwingle must have been married some time: here are several, besides that quoted in the preceding note :—" Professum *palam* te maritum legi. Unum hoc desiderabam in te.—Quæ multo facilius quam *connubii tui confessionem* Antichristus posset ferre. —Αγαμον, ab eo, quod cum fratribus....episcopo Constantiensi congressus es, nullus credidi.—Qua ratione id *tam diu celares*....non dubitarim, rationibus huc adductum, quæ apud virum evangelicum non queant omnino repudiari," &c. Zw. Epp. p. 335. Zwingle, therefore, did not marry in 1524; but he then made his marriage known, if having been contracted two years before. The learned editors of Zwingle's letters say : " Num forte jam Zwinglius Annam Reinhardam clandestino in matrimonio habebat ?" p. 210. This does not appear to be a doubtful point, but a fact which combines all the truth required in history.

as we have seen, pressed by the enemies of the Reformation, had enjoined the evangelical preachers to preach no doctrines likely to disturb the people. Zwingle felt that the moment for action had arrived; and with his characteristic energy convened a meeting at Einsidlen of the ministers of the Lord who were friendly to the Gospel. The Christian's strength consists neither in the power of arms, nor in the flames of the burning pile, nor in factious intrigues, nor in the support of the mighty ones of the earth; it is a simple, but bold and unanimous confession of those great truths to which the world must one day be subjected. God especially calls those who serve him to uphold these doctrines firmly before the people, without permitting themselves to be alarmed by the clamours of their adversaries. These truths have in themselves an assurance of their triumph; and idols fall before them, as in former times before the ark of God. The hour was come in which God willed the great truth of salvation to be thus confessed in Switzerland; it was requisite that the Gospel standard should be planted on some high place. Providence was about to draw from their secluded retreats many humble but intrepid men, and cause them to give a noble testimony in the presence of the nation.

Towards the end of June and the beginning of July 1522, pious ministers were seen journeying from every side on a new pilgrimage towards the celebrated chapel of Einsidlen.[1] From Art in the canton of Schwytz, came its priest Balthasar Trachsel; from Weiningen, near Baden, the priest Stäheli; from Zug, Werner Steiner; from Lucerne, the canon Kilchmeyer; from Uster, the incumbent Pfister; from Hongg, near Zurich, the priest Stumpff; and from Zurich itself, the canon Fabricius, the chaplain Schmidt, Grossman, the preacher of the hospital, and Zwingle. Leo Juda, the priest of Einsidlen, joyfully received all these ministers of Jesus Christ into the old abbey. Subsequently to Zwingle's residence, this place had become the stronghold of truth, and a dwelling-place for the righteous." [2] Thus, two hundred and fifteen years before, thirty-three brave patriots had met in the solitary plain of the Grutli, resolved to break the yoke of Austria. At Einsidlen they met to burst in sunder the yoke of human authority in Divine things. Zwingle proposed that his friends should address an urgent petition to the cantons and the bishop, with a view of obtaining the free preaching of the Gospel, and at the same time the abolition of compulsory celibacy, the source of such criminal disorders. All concurred in his opinion.[3] Ulrich had himself prepared the

1 Thaten sich zusammen etliche priester. Bull. Chronik.
2 Zu Einsidlen hatten sie alle Sicherheit dahin zu gehen und dort zu wohnen. J. J. Hottinger Helv. K. Gesh. iii. 86.
3 Und wurden eins an den Bischoff zu Constantz und gmein Eidtgnossen ein Supplication zu stellen. Bull. Chronik.

addresses. The petition to the bishop was first read, and on the 2d of July it was signed by all the evangelists named above. A cordial affection knit together the preachers of the Gospel in Switzerland. There were many others who sympathized with the men who had met at Einsidlen; such were Haller, Myconius, Hedio, Capito, Œcolampadius, Sebastian Meyer, Hoffmeister, and Vanner. This harmony is one of the most beautiful features of the Swiss Reformation. These excellent persons ever acted as one man, and remained friends until death.

The men of Einsidlen felt that it was only by the power of faith that the members of the Confederation, divided by the foreign capitulations, could become a single body. But their eyes were directed to heaven. "The heavenly teaching," said they to their ecclesiastical superior in the address of the 2d of July, "that truth which God the Creator has manifested by his Son to the human race immersed in sin, has been long veiled from our eyes by the ignorance, not to say the wickedness, of a few men. But this same Almighty God has resolved to re-establish it in its primitive estate. Unite, then, with those who desire that the whole body of Christians should return to their Head, which is Christ. [1]......On our part we are determined to proclaim his Gospel with indefatigable perseverance, and at the same time with such discretion that no one shall complain of it. [2] Favour this—astonishing it may be, but not rash undertaking. Be like Moses, in the way, at the head of the people when they went out of Egypt, and with your own hands overthrow every obstacle that opposes the triumphant progress of the truth."

After this spirited appeal, the evangelists assembled at Einsidlen came to the question of celibacy. Zwingle had nothing to ask in this respect; he had such a wife as, according to Saint Paul's description, the wife of a minister of Christ should be—*grave, sober, faithful in all things.* (1 Tim. iii. 11.) But he thought of his brethren, whose consciences were not as yet, like his own, emancipated from human ordinances. He longed, moreover, for the time when all the servants of God might live openly and fearlessly in the bosom of their families, *having their children in subjection with all gravity.* (1 Tim. iii. 4.) "You cannot be ignorant," said the men of Einsidlen, "how deplorably the laws of chastity have hitherto been violated by the priests. When in the consecration of the ministers of the Lord, they ask of him who speaks for all the rest: Are those whom you present to us righteous men?—he answers: They are righteous.—Are they learned?—They are learned. But when he is asked:

Are they chaste? He replies: As far as human weakness permits. [1] The New Testament every where condemns licentious intercourse: every where it sanctions marriage." Here follows a great number of quotations. "It is for this reason," continued they, "we entreat you, by the love of Christ, by the liberty he has purchased for us, by the wretchedness of so many feeble and wavering souls, by the wounds of so many ulcerated consciences, by all divine and human motives......to permit what has been rashly enacted to be wisely repealed; for fear the majestic edifice of the Church should fall with a frightful crash, and spread destruction far and wide. [2] Behold with what storms the world is threatened! If wisdom does not interfere, the ruin of the priestly order is certain."

The petition to the confederation was longer still. [3] "Excellent sirs," thus spoke the allies of Einsidlen to the confederates at the end of their appeal, "we are all Swiss, and you are our fathers. There are some among us who have been faithful in the field of battle, in the chambers of pestilence, and in the midst of other calamities. It is in the name of sincere chastity that we address you. Who is unaware that we should better satisfy the lust of the flesh by not submitting to the regulations of lawful wedlock? But we must put an end to the scandals that afflict the Church of Christ. If the tyranny of the Roman pontiff is resolved to oppress us, fear nothing, brave heroes! The authority of the Word of God, the rights of christian liberty, and the sovereign power of grace, will surround and protect us. [4] We have all the same country, the same faith; we are Swiss, and the virtue of our illustrious ancestors has always displayed its power by an invincible defence of those who are unjustly oppressed."

Thus in Einsidlen itself, in that ancient stronghold of superstition, which in our days is one of he most famous sanctuaries of Roman observances, did Zwingle and his friends boldly uplift the banner of truth and liberty. They appealed to the heads of the state and of the Church. They placarded their theses like Luther, but at the gates of the episcopal palace and of the national council. The band of friends at Einsidlen separated calm, rejoicing, and full of hope in that God in whose hands they had placed their cause; and retiring, some by the battle-field of Morgarten, others, over the chain of the Albis, and the rest, by different valleys and mountains, returned each man to his post.

---

[1] Ut universa Christianorum multitudo ad caput suum, quod Christus est, redeat. Supplicatio quorundum apud Helvetios Evangelistarum. Zw. Opp. iii. 18.
[2] Evangelium irremisso tenore promulgare statuimus.... Ibid.

[1] Suntne casti? reddidit: Quatenus humana imbecillitas permittit. Supplicatio, &c. Zw. Opp. iii. 18.
[2] Ne quando moles ista non ex patris cœlestis sententia constructa, cum fragore longe perniciosiore corruat. Ibid. 24.
[3] Amica et pia parænesis ad communem Helvetiorum civitatem scripta, ne evangelicæ doctrinæ cursum impediant, &c. Ibid. i. 39.
[4] Divini enim verbi auctoritatem, libertatis christianæ et divinæ gratiæ præsidium nobis adesse conspicietis. Ibid 63.

" It was something really sublime for those times,"[1] says Henry Bullinger, " that these men should have thus dared stand forth, and rallying round the Gospel, expose themselves to every danger. But God preserved them all, so that no harm befell them; for God always preserves his own." It was indeed sublime : it was a bold step in the progress of the Reformation, one of the brightest days of the religious regeneration of Switzerland. A holy confederation was formed at Einsidlen. Humble but intrepid men had grasped the sword of the Spirit, which is the Word of God, and the shield of faith. The gauntlet was thrown down—the challenge was given—not only by one man, but by men of different cantons, prepared to sacrifice their lives : they must await the struggle.

Every thing seemed to forebode that the contest would be severe. It was but five days after, on the 7th of July, that the magistrates of Zurich, desirous of offering some satisfaction to the Roman party, summoned before them Conrad Grebel and Claus Hottinger, two of those violent men who appeared desirous of overstepping the bounds of a prudent Reformation. " We forbid you," said the burgomaster Roust, " to speak against the monks and on the controverted questions." At these words a loud noise was heard in the chamber, says an old chronicle. God so manifested himself throughout all this work, that the people saw signs of his intervention in every thing. Each man looked around him in astonishment, without being able to discover the cause of this mysterious circumstance.[2]

But it was in the convents especially that the indignation was greatest. Every meeting that was held in them either for discussion or amusement, saw some new attack burst forth. One day there was a great banquet at the convent of Fraubrunn; and as the wine had got into the heads of the guests, they began to launch the most envenomed darts against the Gospel.[3] What most incensed the priests and monks was the evangelical doctrine that, in the Christian Church there ought not to be any sacerdotal caste raised above the believers. One single friend of the Reformation was present, Macrinus, a layman, and master of the school at Soleure. At first he avoided the discussion, passing from one table to the other. But at length, unable to endure the violent language of the guests, he rose boldly and said aloud : " Yes! all true Christians are priests and sacrificers, as St. Peter says : Ye are priests and kings." At these words one of the loudest bawlers, the Dean of Burgdorff, a tall strong man with a voice of thunder, burst out laughing : " So then you

Greeklings and pedagogues are the royal priesthood ?......a pretty priesthood, forsooth ! ......beggarly kings......priests without prebends or livings!"[1] And at the very instant priests and monks with one accord fell on the imprudent layman.

It was in Lucerne, however, that the bold step of the men of Einsidlen was destined to produce the greatest commotion. The diet had met in this city, and complaints arrived from every quarter against these daring preachers, who would prevent Helvetia from quietly selling the blood of her children to the stranger. On the 22d of July 1522, as Oswald Myconius was at dinner in his own house with the canon Kilchmeyer and others favourably disposed to the Gospel, a youth sent by Zwingle stood at his door.[2] He brought the two famous petitions of Einsidlen, and a letter from Zwingle, calling upon Oswald to circulate them in Lucerne. " It is my advice," added the reformer, " that this should be done quietly, gradually, rather than all at once ; for we must learn to give up every thing—even one's wife—for Christ's sake."

The critical moment was approaching in Lucerne ; the shell had fallen in the midst of the city, and was about to explode. Oswald's guests read the petitions. " May God prosper this beginning !"[3] exclaimed Oswald, looking up to heaven, and adding immediately : " From this very hour this prayer should be the constant occupation of our hearts. The petitions were circulated immediately, perhaps with more ardour than Zwingle had required. But the moment was extraordinary. Eleven men, the flower of the clergy, had placed themselves in the breach ; it was desirable to enlighten men's minds, to decide the wavering, and to win over the most influential members of the diet.

Oswald, in the midst of his exertions, did not forget his friends. The youthful messenger had told him of the attacks Zwingle had to put up with on the part of the monks of Zurich. " The truth of the Holy Ghost is invincible," wrote Myconius to him on the same day. " Shielded with the buckler of Scripture, you have conquered not only in one contest, nor in two, but in three, and the fourth is now beginning......Grasp those powerful arms which are harder than adamant ! Christ, to protect his followers, requires nothing but his Word. Your struggles impart unflinching courage to all who have devoted themselves to Jesus Christ."[4]

The two petitions did not produce the desired effect in Lucerne. Some pious men approved of them ; but their numbers were few. Many, fearing to compromise them-

[1] Es was zwahren gros zu denen Zyten....Bull. Chronik.
[2] Da liess die Stube einen grossen Knall. Füsslin Beytr. iv. 39.
[3] Cum invalescente Baccho, disputationes, imo verius jurgia....Zw. Epp. p. 230.

[1] Estote ergo Græculi ac Donatistæ regale sacerdotium ....Zw. Epp. p. 230.
[2] Venit puer, quem mississi, inter prandendum. Ibid. 209
[3] Deus cœpta fortunet! Ibid.
[4] Is permaneas, qui es, in Christo Jesu....Ibid. 210.

selves, would neither praise nor blame them.[1] " These folks," said others, " will never succeed in this business!" All the priests murmured, and whispered against them; and the people became violent against the Gospel. The passion for a military life had been revived in Lucerne after the bloody defeat of the Bicocca, and war alone filled every mind.[2] Oswald, who watched attentively these different impressions, felt his courage sinking. The evangelical future that he had dreamed of for Lucerne and Switzerland, seemed to vanish. " Our countrymen are blind as regards heavenly things," said he with a deep sigh: " We can hope nothing from the Swiss, which concerns the glory of Christ."[3]

In the council and the diet the irritation was greatest. The pope, France, England, the empire—all were in commotion around Switzerland after the defeat of the Bicocca and the evacuation of Lombardy by the French, under the orders of Lautrec. Were not political affairs complicated enough, that these eleven men should come with their petitions and superadd mere religious questions? The deputies of Zurich alone inclined in favour of the Gospel. The canon Xyloctect, fearing for the safety of himself and his wife (for he had married a daughter of one of the first families in the country), had shed tears of regret, as he refused to go to Einsidlen and sign the addresses. The canon Kilchmeyer was bolder, and he had every thing to fear. On the 13th of August he wrote to Zwingle : " Sentence threatens me, but I await it with courage"...... As his pen was tracing these words, the usher of the council entered his room, and summoned him to appear on the morrow.[4] " If they throw me into prison," said he, continuing his letter, " I shall claim your help ; but it will be easier to transport a rock from our Alps than to remove me a finger's breadth from the Word of Jesus Christ." The respect due to his family, and the determination of the council to make the storm burst on Oswald, saved the canon.

Berthold Haller had not signed the petitions, perhaps because he was not a Swiss. But with unyielding courage he explained the Gospel of St. Matthew, after Zwingle's example. A great crowd filled the cathedral of Berne. The Word of God operated more powerfully on the people than Manuel's dramas. Haller was summoned to the town-hall ; the people escorted this meek man thither, and remained assembled in the square in front. The council were divided in their sentiments. " It is a matter that concerns the bishop," said the most influential members. " We must give him up to Monseigneur of Lausanne." Haller's friends trembled at these words, and besought him to withdraw as soon as possible. The people surrounded him, and accompanied him home, and a great body of armed citizens remained before his house, determined to form a rampart for their humble pastor with their bodies. The bishop and council shrunk back at this spirited demonstration, and Haller was saved. He did not, however, combat alone in Berne. Sebastian Meyer refuted the pastoral letter of the Bishop of Constance, and especially the hackneyed charge, " that the disciples of the Gospel teach a new doctrine ; and that the old is the true one."—" To have been a thousand years wrong," said he, " will not make us right for one single hour ; or else the pagans should have kept to their creed. If the most ancient doctrines ought to be preferred, fifteen hundred years are more than five hundred, and the Gospel is older than the decrees of the pope."[1]

About this time, the magistrates of Friburg intercepted some letters addressed to Haller and Meyer by a canon of that town, named John Hollard, a native of Orbe. They imprisoned him, deprived him of his office, and finally banished him. John Vannius, a chorister of the cathedral, soon declared in favour of the evangelical doctrine ; for in this war no soldier fell whose place was not immediately filled by another. " How can the muddy water of the Tiber," said Vannius, " subsist beside the pure stream that Luther has drawn from the springs of St. Paul?" But the mouth of the chorister also was shut. " In all Switzerland you will hardly find men more unfavourably disposed towards sound doctrine than the Friburgers," wrote Myconius to Zwingle.[2]

An exception must however be made as regards Lucerne ; and this Myconius knew well. He had not signed the famous petitions ; but if he did not, his friends did, and a victim was wanted. The ancient literature of Greece and Rome was beginning, through his exertions, to shed its light upon Lucerne ; students resorted thither from various quarters to hear the learned professor ; and the friends of peace listened with delight to milder sounds than the clash of halberds, swords, and breastplates, with which alone this warlike city had hitherto re-echoed. Oswald had sacrificed everything for his country ;—he had quitted Zurich and Zwingle ; —he had lost his health ;—his wife was ailing ;[3]—his child was young ;—should Lucerne once cast him forth, he could nowhere look for an asylum. But this they heeded not : factions are pitiless, and what should excite their compassion does but inflame their anger. Hertenstein, burgomaster of Lucerne,

[1] Boni, qui pauci sunt, commendant libellos vestros ; alii nec laudant nec vituperant. Zw. Epp. p. 210.
[2] Belli furor occupat omnia. Ibid.
[3] Nihil ob id apud Helvetios agendum de iis rebus quæ Christi gloriam possunt augere. Ibid.
[4] Tu vero audi. Hæc dum scriberem, irruit præco, a Senatoribus missus.... Ibid. 213.

[1] Simml. Samml. vi.
[2] Hoc audio vix alios esse per Helvetiam, qui pejus velint sanæ doctrinæ. Zw. Epp. p. 226.
[3] Conjux infirma. Ibid. 192.

an old and valiant warrior, who had become celebrated in the Swabian and Burgundian wars, proposed the schoolmaster's dismissal, and wished to drive him from the canton with his Greek, his Latin, and his Gospel. He succeeded. As he left the meeting of the council in which Myconius had been deprived of his post, Hertenstein met Berguer the Zurich deputy : " We send you back your schoolmaster," said he ironically : " prepare a comfortable lodging for him."—" We will not let him sleep in the open air,"[1] immediately replied the courageous deputy. But Berguer promised more than he could perform.

The burgomaster's tidings were but too true, and they were soon made known to the unhappy Myconius. He is stripped of his appointment,.........banished ; and the only crime with which he is reproached is being Luther's disciple.[2] He turns his eyes around him, and nowhere finds a shelter. He beholds his wife, his son, and himself,—weak and sickly creatures,—driven from their country ......and around him Switzerland agitated by a violent tempest, breaking and shattering all that resists it. " Here," said he then to Zwingle, " here is your poor Myconius banished by the council of Lucerne.[3]......Whither shall I go ?......I know not......Assailed yourself by such furious storms, how can you shelter me ? In my tribulation I cry to that God who is my chief hope. Ever rich, ever kind, He does not permit any who call upon him to turn away unheard. May He provide for my wants !"

Thus wrote Oswald. He had not long to wait for the word of consolation. There was one man in Switzerland inured to the battles of faith. Zwingle drew nigh to his friend and raised him up. " So rude are the blows by which men strive to overthrow the house of God," said Zwingle, " and so frequent are their attacks, that it is not only the wind and rain that burst upon it, as our Lord predicts (Matth. vii. 27), but also the hail and the thunder.[4] If I did not see that the Lord kept watch over the ship, I should long since have abandoned the helm ; but I see him, through the storm, strengthening the tackling, handing the yards, spreading the sails ; nay more, commanding the very winds...... Should I not be a coward and unworthy the name of a man if I abandoned my post, and sought a disgraceful death in flight ? I confide entirely in his sovereign goodness. Let Him govern,—let Him carry us forward,— let Him hasten or delay,—let Him plunge us even to the bottom of the deep......we will fear nothing.[5] We are vessels that belong to Him. He can make use of us as he pleases, for honour or dishonour." After these words, so full of the sincerest faith, Zwingle continues : " As for yourself, this is my advice. Appear before the council, and deliver an address worthy of you and of Christ ; that is to say, calculated to melt and not irritate their feelings. Deny that you are Luther's disciple ; confess that you are Christ's. Let your pupils surround you and speak too ; and if this does not succeed, then come to your friend,—come to Zwingle,—and look upon our city as your home !"

Encouraged by this language, Oswald followed the noble advice of the reformer ; but all his efforts were unavailing. This witness to the truth was compelled to leave his country ; and the people of Lucerne decried him so much that in every quarter the magistrates prevented his finding an asylum. " Nothing remains for me but to beg my bread from door to door,"[1] exclaimed this confessor of Christ, whose heart was crushed at the sight of so much hostility. But erelong the friend of Zwingle and his most powerful auxiliary, the first man in Switzerland who had combined learning with a love to the Gospel, the reformer of Lucerne, and subsequently one of the heads of the Helvetian church, was with his sick wife and infant child compelled to leave that ungrateful city, where of all his family, one only of his sisters had received the Gospel. He crossed its ancient bridge : he bade farewell to those mountains which appear to rise from the bosom of the Walstatter lake into the clouds. The canons Xyloctect and Kilchmeyer, the only friends whom the Reformation yet counted among his fellow-countrymen, followed him not long after. And at the moment when this poor man, accompanied by two feeble creatures, whose existence depended upon him, with eyes turned towards the lake, and shedding tears over his blinded country, bade adieu to those sublime scenes of nature, the majesty of which had surrounded his cradle, the Gospel itself departed from Lucerne, and Rome reigns there even to this day.

Shortly after, the diet then sitting at Baden, excited by the severity shown to Myconius, incensed by the petitions from Einsidlen, which were now printed and every where producing a great sensation, and solicited by the Bishop of Constance, who called upon them to crush the reformer, had recourse to persecution, ordered the authorities of the common bailiwicks to denounce all the priests and laymen who should dare speak against the faith, caused the preacher who happened to be nearest to be immediately arrested, namely Urban Weiss, pastor of Fislispach, who had been previously liberated on bail, and had him taken to Constance, where he was delivered up to the bishop, who detained

---

[1] Veniat! efficiemus enim ne dormiendum sit ei sub dio. Zw. Epp. p. 216.
[2] Nil exprobarunt nisi quod sim Lutheranus. Ibid.
[3] Expe litur ecce miser Myconius a Senatu Lucernano. Ibid. 215.
[4] Nec ventos esse, nec imbres, sed grandines et fulmina. Ibid. p. 217.
[5] Regat, vehat, festinet, maneat, acceleret, moretur, mergat !....Ibid.

[1] Ostiatim quærere quod edam. Zw. Epp. p. 245.

him a long while in prison. "It was thus," says Bullinger's chronicle, "that the persecutions of the confederates against the Gospel began: and this took place at the instigation of the clergy, who in every age have dragged Jesus Christ before the judgment-seat of Herod and of Pilate."[1]

Nor did Zwingle himself escape trial. About this time he was wounded in the tenderest point. The rumour of his doctrines and of his struggles had passed the Sentis, penetrated the Tockenburg, and reached the heights of Wildhaus. The family of herdsmen from which the reformer had sprung, was deeply moved. Of Zwingle's five brothers, some had continued their peaceful mountain labours; others, to their brother's great regret, had taken up arms, quitted their herds, and served a foreign prince. Both were alike astonished at the reports that reached their chalets. Already they pictured to themselves their brother dragged to Constance before the bishop, and a pile erected for his destruction on the same spot where John Huss had perished in the flames. These proud herdsmen could not endure the idea of being called the brothers of a heretic. They wrote to Zwingle, describing their pain and their fears. Zwingle replied to them as follows: "So long as God shall permit me, I will execute the task which he has confided to me, without fearing the world and its haughty tyrants. I know every thing that can befall me. There is no danger, no misfortune that I have not carefully weighed long ago. My own strength is nothingness itself, and I know the power of my enemies; but I know also that I can do every thing in Christ, who strengthens me. Though I should be silent, another would be constrained to do what God is now doing through me, and I should be punished by the Almighty. Banish all anxiety, my dear brothers. If I have any fear, it is lest I have been milder and gentler than suits our times.[2] What reproach (say you) will be cast upon our family, if you are burnt, or put to death in any other way![3] Oh! my beloved brothers, the Gospel derives from the blood of Christ this remarkable property, that the most violent persecutions, far from checking its progress, serve but to accelerate it. Those alone are the true soldiers of Christ, who do not fear to bear in their body the wounds of their Master. All my labours have no other aim than to proclaim to men the treasures of happiness that Christ hath purchased for us, that all might take refuge in the Father, through the death of his Son.

If this doctrine scandalizes you, your anger cannot stop me. You are my brothers—yes!—my own brothers, sons of the same father, fruit of the same womb;......but if you were not my brothers in Christ and in the work of faith, then my grief would be so violent, that nothing could equal it. Farewell.—I shall never cease to be your affectionate brother, if only you will not cease yourselves to be the brethren of Jesus Christ."[1]

The confederates appeared to rise, like one man, against the Gospel. The addresses of Einsidlen had given the signal. Zwingle, agitated at the fate of Myconius, saw, in his misfortunes, the beginning of calamities. Enemies in Zurich, enemies without; a man's own relatives becoming his opponents; a furious opposition on the part of the monks and priests; violent measures in the diet and councils; coarse and perhaps bloody attacks from the partisans of foreign service; the highest valleys of Switzerland, that cradle of the confederation, pouring forth its invincible phalanxes, to save Rome, and annihilate at the cost of their lives the rising faith of the sons of the Reformation:—such was the picture the penetrating eye of the reformer discovered in the distance, and he shuddered at the prospect. What a future! Was the work, hardly begun, about to be destroyed? Zwingle, thoughtful and agitated, laid all his anguish before the throne of God: "O Jesus," said he, "thou seest how the wicked and the blasphemers stun thy people's ears with their clamours.[2] Thou knowest how from my childhood I have hated all dispute, and yet, in despite of myself, Thou has not ceased to impel me to the conflict.........Therefore do I call upon Thee with confidence to complete what Thou hast begun. If I have built up any thing wrongly, do Thou throw it down with thy mighty hand. If I have laid any other foundation than Thee, let thy powerful arm destroy it.[3] O vine abounding in sweetness, whose husbandman is the Father, and whose branches we are, do not abandon thy shoots![4] For Thou hast promised to be with us until the end of the world!"

It was on the 22d of August 1522 that Ulrich Zwingle, the reformer of Switzerland, seeing the storms descending from the mountains on the frail bark of the faith, thus poured forth before God the troubles and desires of his soul.

[1] Uss anstiften der geistlichen, Die zu allen Zyten, Christum Pilato und Herodi vürstellen. Chronik.
[2] Plus enim metuo ne forte lenior, mitiorque fuerim. De semper casta virgine Maria. Zw. Opp. i. 104.
[3] Si vel igni vel alio quodam supplicii genere tollaris e medio. Ibid.

[1] Frater vester germanus nunquam desinam, si modo vos fratres Christi esse perrexeritis. Zw. Opp. i. 107.
[2] Vides enim, piissime Jesu, aures eorum septas esse nequissimis susurronibus, sycophantis, lucrionibus.... Ibid. iii. 74.
[3] Si fundamentum aliud præter te jecero, demoliaris. Ibid.
[4] O suavissima vitis, cujus vinitor pater palmites vere nos sumus, sationem tuam ne deseras! Ibid.

PREFACE TO VOLUME THIRD.

A SPIRIT of examination and inquiry is in our days constantly urging the literary men of France, Switzerland, Germany, and England to search after the original documents which form the basis of Modern History. I desire to add my mite to the accomplishment of the important task which our age appears to have undertaken. Hitherto I have not been content merely with reading the works of contemporary historians: I have examined eye-witnesses, letters, and original narratives; and have made use of several manuscripts, particularly that of Bullinger, which has been printed since the appearance of the Second Volume of this Work in France. [1]

But the necessity of having recourse to unpublished documents became more urgent when I approached (as I do in the Twelfth Book) the history of the Reformation in France. On this subject we possess but few printed memoirs, in consequence of the perpetual trials in which the Reformed Church of that country has existed. In the spring of 1838 I examined, as far as was in my power, the manuscripts preserved in the public libraries of Paris, and it will be seen that a manuscript in the Royal Library, hitherto I believe unknown, throws much light on the early stages of the Reformation; and in the autumn of 1839 I consulted the manuscripts in the library belonging to the consistory of the pastors of Neufchatel, a collection exceedingly rich with regard to this period, as having inherited the manuscripts of Farel's library; and through the kindness of the Chatelain of Meuron I obtained the use of a manuscript life of Farel written by Choupard, into which most of these documents have been copied. These materials have enabled me to reconstruct an entire phasis of the Reformation in France. In addition to these aids, and to those supplied by the Library of Geneva, I made an appeal, in the columns of the *Archives du Christianisme*, to all friends of history and of the Reformation who might have any manuscripts at their disposal; and I here gratefully acknowledge the different communications that have been made to me, in particular by M. Ladevèze, pastor at Meaux. But although religious wars and persecutions have destroyed many precious documents, a number still exist, no doubt, in various parts of France, which would be of vast importance for the history of the Reformation; and I earnestly call upon all those who may possess or have any knowledge of them, kindly to communicate with me on the subject. It is felt now-a-days that these documents are public property; and on this account I hope my appeal will not be made in vain.

It may be thought that in writing a general History of the Reformation, I have entered into an unnecessary detail of its first dawnings in France. But these particulars are almost unknown, the events that form the subject of my Twelfth Book, occupying only four pages in the *Histoire Ecclesiastique des Églises réformées au Royaume de France*, by Theodore Beza; and other historians have confined themselves almost entirely to the political progress of the nation. Unquestionably the scenes that I have discovered, and which I am now about to relate, are not so imposing as the Diet of Worms. Nevertheless, independently of the christian interest that is attached to them, the humble but heaven-descended movement that I have endeavoured to describe, has probably exerted a greater influence over the destinies of France than the celebrated wars of Francis I. and Charles V. In a large machine, it is not that which makes the greatest show that is always the most essential part, but the most hidden springs.

Complaints have been made of the delay that has taken place in the publication of this third volume; and some persons would have had me keep back the first until the whole was completed. There are, possibly, certain superior intellects to which conditions may be prescribed; but there are others whose weakness must give them, and to this number the author belongs. To publish a volume at one time, and then a second whenever I was able, and after that a third, is the course that my important duties and my poor ability allow me to take. Other cir-

[1] Bullinger's Chronik, Frauenfeld, 1838-1840.

cumstances, moreover, have interposed ; severe afflictions have on two occasions interrupted the composition of this third volume, and gathered all my affections and all my thoughts over the graves of beloved children. The reflection that it was my duty to glorify that adorable Master who addressed me in such powerful appeals, and who vouchsafed me such Divine consolation, could alone have given me the courage required for the completion of my task.

I have thought these explanations due to the kindness with which this Work has been received both in France and England, and especially in the latter country. The approbation of the Protestant Christians of Great Britain, the representatives of evangelical principles and doctrines in the most distant parts of the world, is most highly valued by me ; and I feel a pleasure in telling them that it is an inestimable encouragement to my labours.

The cause of truth recompenses those who embrace and defend it ; and such has been the result with the nations who received the Reformation. In the eighteenth century, at the very moment when Rome thought to triumph by the Jesuits and the scaffold, the victory slipped from her grasp. Rome fell, like Naples, Portugal, and Spain, into inextricable difficulties ; and at the same time two Protestant nations arose and began to exercise an influence over Europe that had hitherto belonged to the Roman-catholic powers. England came forth victorious from those attacks of the French and Spaniards which the pope had so long been stirring up against her, and the Elector of Brandenburg, in spite of the wrath of Clement XI., encircled his head with a kingly crown. Since that time England has extended her dominion in every quarter of the globe, and Prussia has taken a new rank among the continental states, while a third power, Russia, also separated from Rome, has been growing up in her immense deserts. In this manner have evangelical principles exerted their influence over the countries that have embraced them, and *righteousness hath exalted the nations* (Prov. xiv. 34). Let the evangelical nations be well assured that to Protestantism they are indebted for their greatness. From the moment they abandon the position that God has given them, and incline again towards Rome, they will lose their glory and their power. Rome is now endeavouring to win them over, employing flattery and threats by turns ; she would, like Delilah, lull them to sleep upon her knees,......but it would be to cut off their locks, that their adversaries might put out their eyes and bind them with fetters of brass.

Here, too, is a great lesson for that country with which the author feels himself so intimately connected by the ties of ancestry. Should France, imitating her different go-

vernments, turn again towards the papacy, it will be, in our belief, the signal of great disasters. Whoever attaches himself to the papacy will be compromised in its destruction. France has no prospect of strength or of greatness but by turning towards the Gospel. May this great truth be rightly understood by the people and their leaders !

It is true that in our days popery is making a great stir. Although labouring under an incurable consumption, she would by a hectic flush and feverish activity persuade others and herself too that she is still in full vigour. This a theologian in Turin has endeavoured to do in a work occasioned by this History, and in which we are ready to acknowledge a certain talent in bringing forward testimonies, even the most feeble, with a tone of candour to which we are little accustomed, and in a becoming style, with the exception, however, of the culpable facility with which the author in his twelfth chapter revives accusations against the reformers, the falsehood of which has been so authentically demonstrated and so fully acknowledged.[1]

As a sequel to his Biography of Luther, M. Audin has recently published a Life of Calvin, written under the influence of lamentable prejudices, and in which we can hardly recognise the reformers and the Reformation. Nevertheless, we do not find in this author the shameful charges against Calvin to which we have just alluded ; he has passed them over in praiseworthy silence. No man that has any self-respect can now venture to bring forward these gross and foolish calumnies.

Perhaps on some other occasion we shall add a few words to what we have already said in our First Book on the origin of popery. Here they would be out of place.

I shall only remark, in a general way, that it is precisely the *human* and very rational causes that so clearly explain its origin, to which the papacy has recourse to prove its *divine* institution. Thus christian antiquity declares that the universal episcopacy was committed to all the bishops, so that the bishops of Jerusalem, Alexandria, Antioch, Ephesus, Rome, Carthage, Lyons, Arles, Milan, Hippo, Cæsarea, &c., were interested and interfered in all that took place in the christian world. Rome immediately claims for herself that duty which was incumbent on all, and reasoning as if no one but herself were concerned in it, employs it to demonstrate her primacy.

Let us take another example. The christian churches, established in the large cities of the empire, sent missionaries to the countries with which they were connected. This was done first of all by Jerusalem ; then by

[1] La Papauté considérée dans son origine et dans son développement au moyen âge, ou réponse aux allégations de M. Merle D'Aubigné dans son Histoire de la Réformation au seizième siècle, par l'abbé C. Magnin, docteur en théologie. Genève, chez Berthier-Guers, 1840.

Antioch, Alexandria, and Ephesus; and finally by Rome: and Rome forthwith concludes from what she had done after the others, and to a less extent than the others, that she was entitled to set herself above the others. These examples will suffice.

Let us only remark further, that Rome possessed alone in the West the honour that had been shared in the East by Corinth, Philippi, Thessalonica, Ephesus, Antioch, and, in a much higher degree, by Jerusalem;[1] namely, that of having had one apostle or many among its first teachers. Accordingly, the Latin Churches must naturally have felt a certain respect towards Rome. But the Eastern Christians, who honoured her as the Church of the political metropolis of the empire, would never acknowledge her ecclesiastical superiority. The famous General Council of Chalcedon ascribed to Constantinople, formerly the obscure Byzantium, the same privileges ($\tau\grave{\alpha}$ $\check{\iota}\sigma\alpha$ $\pi\rho\epsilon\sigma\mathcal{C}\tilde{\epsilon}\iota\alpha$) as to Rome, and declared that she ought to be elevated *like her*. And hence when the papacy was definitively formed in Rome, the East would not acknowledge a master of whom it had never heard mention; and, standing on the ancient footing of its catholicity, it abandoned the West to the power of the new sect which had sprung up in its bosom. The East even to this day calls itself emphatically catholic and orthodox; and whenever you ask one of the Eastern Christians, whom Rome has gained by her numerous concessions, if he is a catholic? "No," replies he directly, "I am papistian (a papist)."[2]

If this History has been criticized by the Romish party, it seems also to have met with others who have regarded it in a purely literary light. Men for whom I feel much esteem appear to attach greater importance to a literary or political history of the Refor-

mation, than to an exposition grounded on its spiritual principles and its interior springs of action. I can well understand this way of viewing my subject, but I cannot participate in it. In my opinion, the very essence of the Reformation is its doctrines and its inward life. Every work in which these two things do not hold the chief place may be showy, but it will not be faithfully and candidly historical. It would be like a philosopher who, in describing a man, should detail with great accuracy and picturesque beauty all that concerns the body, but should give only a subordinate place to that divine inhabitant the soul.

There are no doubt great defects in the feeble work of which I here present another fragment to the christian public; and I could desire that it were still more copiously imbued with the spirit of the Reformation. The better I have succeeded in pointing out whatever manifests the glory of Christ, the more faithful I shall have been to history. I willingly adopt as my law those words, which an historian of the sixteenth century, a man of the sword still more than of the pen, after writing a portion of the history of that Protestantism in France which I do not purpose narrating, addresses to those who might think of completing his task: "I would give them that law which I acknowledge myself: that, in seeking the glory of this precious instrument, their principal aim should be that of the arm which has prepared, employed, and wielded it at His good pleasure. For all praise given to princes is unseasonable and misplaced, if it have not for leaf and root that of the living God, to whom alone belong honour and dominion for ever and ever."[1]

---

[1] St. Epiphany says, that our Lord committed to James the Elder at Jerusalem his throne on earth ($\tau\grave{o}\nu$ $\vartheta\rho\acute{o}\nu o\nu$ $\alpha\upsilon\tau o\tilde{\upsilon}$ $\grave{\epsilon}\pi\grave{\iota}$ $\tau\tilde{\eta}\varsigma$ $\gamma\tilde{\eta}\varsigma$) : and speaking of the bishops assembled at Jerusalem, he declares that the whole world ($\pi\alpha\nu\tau\alpha$ $\varkappa o\sigma\mu o\nu$) ought to submit to their authority. Epiph. Hæres., 70, 10; 78, 7.

[2] Journal of the Rev. Joseph Wolff. London, 1839, p. 225.

[1] As the French original does not indicate the source whence this quotation is taken, it may not be improper to mention that it will be found in the *Histoire Universelle* of Theodore Agrippa D'Aubigné, 3 vols. folio, Amsterdam, 1626. D'Aubigné was then a refugee at Geneva, and in the preface to this work, which contains a history of the world and more especially of France and French Protestantism during his lifetime, he bequeaths to his children the task of completing the history he had partially traced out, and prescribes to them (in the passage quoted above) the spirit in which it should be performed. He little thought that two centuries and a half would pass away before his legacy would be accepted and the history of Protestantism completed. [*Note by the Translator.*]

HISTORY OF THE REFORMATION.

VOLUME THIRD.

<hr>

BOOK IX.

FIRST REFORMS.—1521 AND 1522.

CHAPTER I.

Progress of the Reformation—New Period—Usefulness of Luther's Captivity in the Wartburg—Agitation in Germany—Melancthon and Luther—Enthusiasm.

FOR four years an old doctrine had been again proclaimed in the Church. The great tidings of *salvation by grace*, published in earlier times in Asia, Greece, and Italy, by Paul and his brethren, and after many ages re-discovered in the Bible by a monk of Wittemberg, had resounded from the plains of Saxony as far as Rome, Paris, and London; and the lofty mountains of Switzerland had re-echoed its powerful accents. The springs of truth, of liberty, and of life, had been re-opened to the human race. Thither had the nations hastened in crowds, and drunk gladly; but those who had there so eagerly quenched their thirst, were unchanged in appearance. All *within* was new, and yet every thing *without* seemed to have remained the same.

The constitution of the Church, its ritual, its discipline, had undergone no change. In Saxony, and even at Wittemberg, wherever the new ideas had penetrated, the papal worship continued with its usual pomp; the priest before the altar, offering the host to God, appeared to effect an ineffable transubstantiation; monks and nuns entered the convents and took their eternal vows; the pastors of the flocks lived without families; religious brotherhoods met together; pilgrimages were undertaken; believers hung their votive offerings on the pillars of the chapels; and all the ceremonies, even to the most insignificant observances of the sanctuary, were celebrated as before. There was a new life in the world, but it had not yet created a new body. The language of the priest formed the most striking contrast with his actions. He might be heard thundering from the pulpit against the mass, as being an idolatrous worship; and then might be seen coming down to the altar, and scrupulously performing the pomps of this mystery. In every quarter the new Gospel sounded in the midst of the ancient rites. The priest himself did not perceive this strange contradiction; and the people, who had listened with admiration to the bold language of the new preachers, devoutly practised the old observances, as if they were never to lay them aside. Every thing remained the same, at the domestic hearth and in social life, as in the house of God. There was a new faith in the world, but not new works. The sun of spring had shone forth, but winter still seemed to bind all nature; there were no flowers, no foliage, nothing outwardly that gave token of the change of season. But these appearances were deceitful; a vigorous sap was circulating unperceived below the surface, and was about to change the aspect of the world.

It is perhaps to this prudent progress that the Reformation is indebted for its triumphs. Every revolution should be accomplished in the mind before it is carried out externally. The inconsistency we have noticed did not even strike Luther at first. It seemed to him quite natural that the people, who read his works with enthusiasm, should remain devoutly attached to the abuses which they assailed. One might almost fancy he had sketched his plan beforehand, and had resolved to change the mind before changing the forms. But this would be ascribing to him a wisdom the honour of which belongs to a higher Intelligence. He carried out a plan that he had not himself conceived. At a later period he could recognise and discern these things : but he did not imagine them, and did not arrange them so. God led the way : it was Luther's duty to follow.

If Luther had begun by an external reform ; if, as soon as he had spoken, he had attempted to abolish monastic vows, the mass, confession, and forms of worship, most assuredly he would have met with a vigorous resistance. Man requires time to accommodate himself to great revolutions. But Luther was by no means the violent, imprudent, daring innovator that some historians have described.[1] The people, seeing no change in their customary devotions, fearlessly abandoned themselves to their new teacher. They were even surprised at the attacks directed against a man who still left them their mass, their beads, their confessor; and attributed them to the low jealousy of obscure rivals, or to the cruel injustice of powerful adversaries. Yet Luther's opinions agitated their minds, renewed their hearts, and so undermined the ancient edifice that it soon fell of itself, without human agency. Ideas do not act instantaneously : they make their way in silence, like the waters that, filtering behind the rocks of the Alps, loosen them from the mountain on which they rest. Suddenly the work done in secret reveals itself, and a single day is sufficient to lay bare the agency of many years, perhaps of many centuries.

A new era is beginning for the Reformation. Already truth is restored in its doctrine ; now the doctrine is about to restore truth in all the forms of the Church and of society. The agitation is too great for men's minds to remain fixed and immovable at the point they have attained. Upon those dogmas, now so mightily shaken, were based customs that are already tottering to their fall, and which must disappear with them. There is too much courage and life in the new generation for it to continue silent before error. Sacraments, public worship, hierarchy, vows, constitution, domestic and public life,—all are about to be modified. The ship, slowly and laboriously constructed, is about to quit the docks and to be launched on the open sea. We shall have to follow its progress through many shoals.

The captivity of the Wartburg separates these two periods. Providence, which was making ready to give so great an impulse to the Reformation, had prepared its progress by leading into profound retirement the instrument destined to effect it. The work seemed for a time buried with the workman; but the seed must be laid in the earth, that it may bring forth fruit ; and from this pri-

son, which seemed to be the reformer's tomb, the Reformation was destined to go forth to new conquests, and to spread erelong over the whole world.

Hitherto the Reformation had been centred in the person of Luther. His appearance before the Diet of Worms was doubtless the sublimest day of his life. His character appeared at that time almost spotless ; and it is this which has given rise to the observation, that if God, who concealed the reformer for ten months within the walls of the Wartburg, had that instant removed him for ever from the eyes of the world, his end would have been as an apotheosis. But God designs no apotheosis for his servants ; and Luther was preserved to the Church, in order to teach, by his very faults, that the faith of Christians should be based solely on the Word of God. He was transported suddenly far from the stage on which the great revolution of the sixteenth century was taking place ; the truth, that for four years he had so powerfully proclaimed, continued in his absence to act upon Christendom : and the work, of which he was but the feeble instrument, henceforward bore the seal not of man, but of God himself.

Germany was moved at Luther's captivity. The most contradictory rumours were circulated in the provinces. The reformer's absence excited men's minds more than his presence could have done. In one place it was said that friends from France had placed him in safety on the other bank of the Rhine;[1] in another, that he had fallen by the dagger of the assassin. Even in the smallest villages inquiries were made about Luther ; travellers were stopped and questioned ; and groups collected in the public places. At times some unknown orator would recount in a spirit-stirring narrative how the doctor had been carried off; he would describe the cruel horsemen tying their prisoner's hands, spurring their horses, and dragging him after them on foot, until his strength was exhausted, stopping their ears to his cries, and forcing the blood from his limbs.[2] " Luther's body," added he, " has been seen pierced through and through."[3] As they heard this, the listeners uttered cries of sorrow. " Alas ! " said they, " we shall never see or hear that noble-minded man again, whose voice stirred our very hearts ! " Luther's friends trembled with indignation, and swore to avenge his death. Women, children, men of peace, and the aged, beheld with affright the prospect of new struggles. Nothing could equal the alarm of the partisans of Rome. The priests and monks, who at first had not been able to conceal their exultation, thinking themselves

---

[1] Hume and others.

[1] Hic....invalescit opinio, me esse ab amicis captum e Francia missis. L. Epp. ii. 5.
[2] Et inter festinantes cursu equites ipsum pedestrem raptim tractum fuisse ut sanguis e digitis erumperet. Cochlœus, p. 39.
[3] Fuit qui testatus sit, visum a se Lutheri cadaver transfossum....Pallavicini, Hist. Conc. Trid. i. 122.

secure of victory because one man was dead, and who had raised their heads with an insulting air of triumph, would now have fled far from the threatening anger of the people.[1] These men, who, while Luther was free, had given the reins to their fury, trembled now that he was a captive.[2] Aleander, especially, was astounded. "The only remaining way of saving ourselves," wrote a Roman-catholic to the Archbishop of Mentz, "is to light torches and hunt for Luther through the whole world, to restore him to the nation that is calling for him."[3] One might have said that the pale ghost of the reformer, dragging his chains, was spreading terror around, and calling for vengeance. "Luther's death," exclaimed some, "will cause torrents of blood to be shed."[4]

In no place was there such commotion as in Worms itself; resolute murmurs were heard among both people and princes. Ulrich Hütten and Hermann Busch filled the country with their plaintiff strains and songs of battle. Charles V. and the nuncios were publicly accused. The nation took up the cause of the poor monk, who, by the strength of his faith, had become their champion.

At Wittemberg, his colleagues and friends, and especially Melancthon, were at first sunk in the deepest affliction. Luther had imparted to this young scholar the treasures of that holy theology which had thenceforward wholly occupied his mind. Luther had given substance and life to that purely intellectual cultivation which Melancthon had brought to Wittemberg. The depth of the reformer's teaching had struck the youthful Hellenist, and the doctor's courage in maintaining the rights of the everlasting Gospel against all human authority had filled him with enthusiasm. He had become a partner in his labours; he had taken up the pen, and with that purity of style which he derived from the study of the ancients, had successively, and with a hand of power, humbled the authority of the fathers and councils before the sovereign word of God.

Melancthon showed the same decision in his learning that Luther displayed in his actions. Never were there two men of greater diversity, and at the same time of greater unity. "Scripture," said Melancthon, "imparts to the soul a holy and marvellous delight: it is the heavenly ambrosia."[5]— "The Word of God," exclaimed Luther, "is a sword, a war, a destruction; it falls upon the children of Ephraim like a lioness in the forest." Thus, one saw in the Scriptures a power to console, and the other a violent opposition against the corruptions of the world. But both esteemed it the greatest thing on earth; and hence they agreed in perfect harmony. "Melancthon," said Luther, "is a wonder; all men confess it now. He is the most formidable enemy of Satan and the schoolmen, for he knows their foolishness, and Christ the rock. The little Grecian surpasses even me in divinity; he will be as serviceable to you as many Luthers." And he added that he was ready to abandon any opinion of which Philip did not approve. On his part, too, Melancthon, filled with admiration at Luther's knowledge of Scripture, set him far above the fathers of the Church. He would make excuses for the jests with which Luther was reproached, and compared him to an earthen vessel that contains a precious treasure beneath its coarse exterior. "I should be very unwilling to reprove him inconsiderately in this matter," said Melancthon.[1]

But now, these two hearts, so closely united, were separated. These two valiant soldiers can no longer march side by side to the deliverance of the Church. Luther has disappeared; perhaps he is lost for ever. The consternation at Wittemberg was extreme: like that of an army, with gloomy and dejected looks, before the blood-stained body of their general who was leading them on to victory.

Suddenly more comforting news arrived. "Our beloved father lives,"[2] exclaimed Philip in the joy of his soul; "take courage and be firm." But it was not long before their dejection returned. Luther was alive, but in prison. The edict of Worms, with its terrible proscriptions,[3] was circulated by thousands throughout the empire, and even among the mountains of the Tyrol.[4] Would not the Reformation be crushed by the iron hand that was weighing upon it? Melancthon's gentle spirit was overwhelmed with sorrow.

But the influence of a mightier hand was felt above the hand of man; God himself deprived the formidable edict of all its strength. The German princes, who had always sought to diminish the power of Rome in the empire, trembled at the alliance between the emperor and the pope, and feared that it would terminate in the destruction of their liberty. Accordingly, while Charles in his journey through the Low Countries greeted with an ironical smile the burning piles which flatterers and fanatics kindled on the public places with Luther's works, these very writings were read in Germany with a continually increasing eagerness, and numerous pamphlets in favour of the reform were daily inflicting some new blow on the papacy.

---

[1] Molem vulgi imminentis ferre non possunt. L. Epp. ii. 13.
[2] Qui me libero insanierunt, nunc me captivo ita formidant ut incipiant mitigare. Ibid.
[3] Nos vitam vix redempturos, nisi accensis candelis undique eum requiramus. Ibid.
[4] Gerbelii Ep. in MS. Heckelianis. Lindner, Leb. Luth. p. 244.
[5] Mirabilis in iis voluptas, immo ambrosia quædam cælestia. Corp. Ref i. 128.

[1] Spiritum Martini nolim temere in hac causa interpellare. Corp. Ref. i. 211.
[2] Pater noster carissimus vivit. Ibid. 389.
[3] Dicitur parari proscriptio horrenda. Ibid.
[4] Dicuntur signatæ chartæ proscriptionis bis mille missa quoque ad Insbruck. Ibid.

The nuncios were distracted at seeing this edict, the fruit of so many intrigues, producing so little effect. " The ink with which Charles V. signed his arrest," said they bitterly, " is scarcely dry, and yet the imperial decree is every where torn in pieces." The people were becoming more and more attached to the admirable man who, heedless of the thunders of Charles and of the pope, had confessed his faith with the courage of a martyr. " He offered to retract," said they, " if he were refuted, and no one dared undertake the task. Does not this prove the truth of his doctrines ? " Thus the first movement of alarm was succeeded in Wittemberg and the whole empire by a movement of enthusiasm. Even the Archbishop of Mentz, witnessing this outburst of popular sympathy, dared not give the Cordeliers permission to preach against the reformer. The university, that seemed on the point of being crushed, raised its head. The new doctrines were too firmly established for them to be shaken by Luther's absence ; and the halls of the academy could hardly contain the crowd of hearers.[1]

CHAPTER II.

Luther in the Wartburg—Object of his Captivity—Anxiety—Sickness—Luther's Labours— On Confession—Reply to Latomus—His daily Walks.

MEANTIME the Knight George, for by that name Luther was called in the Wartburg, lived solitary and unknown. " If you were to see me," wrote he to Melancthon, " you would take me for a soldier, and even *you* would hardly recognise me."[2] Luther at first indulged in repose, enjoying a leisure which had not hitherto been allowed him. He wandered freely through the fortress, but could not go beyond the walls.[3] All his wishes were attended to, and he had never been better treated.[4] A crowd of thoughts filled his soul ; but none had power to trouble him. By turns he looked down upon the forests that surrounded him, and raised his eyes towards heaven. " A strange prisoner am I," exclaimed he, " a captive with and against my will !"[5]

"Pray for me," wrote he to Spalatin ; " your prayers are the only thing I need. I do not grieve for any thing that may be said of me in the world. At last I am at rest."[6]

This letter, as well as many others of the same period, is dated from the island of Patmos. Luther compared the Wartburg to that celebrated island to which the wrath of Domitian in former times had banished the Apostle John.

In the midst of the dark forests of Thuringia the reformer reposed from the violent struggles that had agitated his soul. There he studied christian truth, not for the purpose of contention, but as a means of regeneration and life. The beginning of the Reformation was of necessity polemical ; new times required new labours. After cutting down the thorns and the thickets, it was requisite to sow the Word of God peaceably in the heart. If Luther had been incessantly called upon to fight fresh battles, he would not have accomplished a durable work in the Church. Thus by his captivity he escaped a danger which might possibly have ruined the Reformation,—that of always attacking and destroying without ever defending or building up.

This humble retreat had a still more precious result. Uplifted by his countrymen, as on a shield, he was on the verge of the abyss; the least giddiness might have plunged him into it headlong. Some of the first promoters of the Reformation both in Germany and Switzerland, ran upon the shoal of spiritual pride and fanaticism. Luther was a man very subject to the infirmities of our nature, and he was unable to escape altogether from these dangers. The hand of God, however, delivered him for a time, by suddenly removing him from the sphere of intoxicating ovations, and throwing him into an unknown retreat. There his soul was wrapt in pious meditation at God's footstool ; it was again tempered in the waters of adversity ; its sufferings and humiliation compelled him to walk, for a time at least, with the humble ; and the principles of a christian life were thenceforward evolved in his soul with greater energy and freedom.

Luther's calmness was not of long duration. Seated in loneliness on the ramparts of the Wartburg, he remained whole days lost in deep meditation. At one time the Church appeared before him, displaying all her wretchedness ;[1] at another, directing his eyes hopefully towards heaven, he could exclaim : " Wherefore, O Lord, hast thou made all men in vain ?" (Psalm lxxxix. 48.) And then, giving way to despair, he cried with dejection : " Alas ! there is no one in this latter day of his anger, to stand like a wall before the Lord, and save Israel !"

Then recurring to his own destiny, he feared lest he should be accused of deserting the field of battle ;[2] and this supposition weighed down his soul. " I would rather,"

<hr>

[1] Scholastici quorum supra millia ibi tunc fuerunt. Spalatini Annales, 1521, October.
[2] Equitem videres ac ipse vix agnosceres. L. Epp. ii. 11.
[3] Nunc sum hic otiosus, sicut inter captivos liber. Ibid. 3, 12th May.
[4] Quanquam et hilariter et libenter omnia mihi ministret. Ibid. 13, 15th August.
[5] Ego mirabilis captivus qui et volens et nolens hic sedeo. Ibid, 4, 12th May.
[6] Tu fac ut pro me ores: hac una re opus mihi est. Quic-

quid de me fit in publico, nihil mœror; ego in quiete tandem sedeo. L. Epp. ii. 10th June 1521.
[1] Ego hic sedens tota die faciem Ecclesiæ ante me constituo. Ibid. 1.
[2] Verebar ego ne aciem deserere viderer. Ibid.

said he, " be stretched on coals of fire, than lie here half-dead." [1]

Transporting himself in imagination to Worms and Wittemberg, into the midst of his adversaries, he regretted having yielded to the advice of his friends, that he had quitted the world, and that he had not presented his bosom to the fury of men. [2] "Alas!" said he, " there is nothing I desire more than to appear before my cruelest enemies." [3]

Gentler thoughts, however, brought a truce to such anxiety. Every thing was not storm and tempest for Luther; from time to time his agitated mind found tranquillity and comfort. Next to the certainty of God's help, one thing consoled him in his sorrows; it was the recollection of Melancthon. " If I perish," wrote he, " the Gospel will lose nothing: [4] you will succeed me as Elisha did Elijah, with a double portion of my spirit." But calling to mind Philip's timidity, he exclaimed with energy: " Minister of the Word! keep the walls and towers of Jerusalem, until you are struck down by the enemy. As yet we stand alone upon the field of battle; after me, they will aim their blows at you." [5]

The thought of the final attack Rome was about to make on the infant Church, renewed his anxieties. The poor monk, solitary and a prisoner, had many a combat to fight alone. But a hope of deliverance speedily dawned upon him. It appeared to him that the assaults of the Papacy would raise the whole German nation, and that the victorious soldiers of the Gospel would surround the Wartburg, and restore the prisoner to liberty. " If the pope," said he, " lays his hand on all those who are on my side, there will be a disturbance in Germany; the greater his haste to crush us, the sooner will come the end of the pope and his followers. And I ......I shall be restored to you. [6] God is awakening the hearts of many, and stirring up the nations. Only let our enemies clasp our affair in their arms and try to stifle it; it will gather strength under their pressure, and come forth ten times more formidable."

But sickness brought him down from those high places on which his courage and his faith had placed him. He had already suffered much at Worms; his disease increased in solitude. [7] He could not endure the food at the Wartburg, which was less coarse than that of his convent; they were compelled to give him the meagre diet to which he had been accustomed. He passed whole nights without sleep. Anxieties of mind were superadded to the pains of the body. No great work is ever accomplished without suffering and martyrdom. Luther, alone upon his rock, endured in his strong frame a passion that the emancipation of the human race rendered necessary. " Seated by night in my chamber," says he, " I uttered groans, like a woman in her travail; torn, wounded, and bleeding"[1]......then breaking off his complaints, touched with the thought that his sufferings are a blessing from God, he exclaimed with love: " Thanks be to Thee, O Christ, that thou wilt not leave me without the precious marks of thy cross!" [2] But soon, growing angry with himself, he cried out: " Madman and hard-hearted that I am! Woe is me! I pray seldom, I seldom wrestle with the Lord, I groan not for the Church of God! [3] Instead of being fervent in spirit, my passions take fire; I live in idleness, in sleep, and indolence!" Then, not knowing to what he should attribute this state, and accustomed to expect every thing from the affection of his brethren, he exclaimed in the desolation of his heart: " O my friends! do you then forget to pray for me, that God is thus far from me?"

Those who were around him, as well as his friends at Wittemberg and at the elector's court, were uneasy and alarmed at this state of suffering. They feared lest they should see the life they had rescued from the flames of the pope and the sword of Charles V. decline sadly and expire. Was the Wartburg destined to be Luther's tomb? " I fear," said Melancthon, " that the grief he feels for the Church will cause his death. A fire has been kindled by him in Israel; if he dies, what hope will remain for us? Would to God, that at the cost of my own wretched life, I could retain in the world that soul which is its fairest ornament! [4]—Oh! wha. a man!" exclaimed he, as if already standing beside his grave; " we never appreciated him rightly!"

What Luther denominated the shameful indolence of his prison was a task that almost exceeded the strength of one man. " I am here all the day," wrote he on the 14th of May, " in idleness and pleasures (alluding doubtless to the better diet that was provided him at first). I am reading the Bible in Hebrew and Greek; I am going to write a treatise in German on Auricular Confession; I shall continue the translation of the Psalms, and compose a volume of sermons, so soon as I have received what I want from Wittemberg. I am writing without intermission." [5] And yet this was but a part of his labours.

His enemies thought that, if he were not

[1] Mallem inter carbones vivos ardere, quam solus semivivus, atque utinam non mortuus putere. L. Epp. ii. 10.
[2] Cervicem esse objectandam publico furori. Ibid. 89.
[3] Nihil magis opto, quam furoribus adversariorum occurrere, objecto jugulo. Ibid. 1.
[4] Etiam si peream, nihil peribit Evangelio. Ibid. 10.
[5] Nos soli adhuc stamus in acie: te quærent post me. Ibid. 2.
[6] Quo citius id tentaverit, hoc citius et ipse et sui peribunt, et ego revertar. Ibid. 10.
[7] Auctum est malum, quo Wormatiæ laborabam. Ibid. 17.

[1] Sedeo dolens, sicut puerpera, lacer et saucius et cruentus. L. Epp. ii. 50, 9th Sept.
[2] Gratias Christo, qui me sine reliquiis sanctæ crucis non derelinquit. Ibid.
[3] Nihil gemens pro ecclesia Dei. Ibid. 22, 13th July.
[4] Utinam hac vili anima mea ipsius vitam emere queam. Corp. Ref. i. 415, 6th July.
[5] Sine intermissione scribo. L. Epp. ii. 6, 16.

dead, at least they should hear no more of him; but their joy was not of long duration, and there could be no doubt that he was alive. A multitude of writings, composed in the Wartburg, succeeded each other rapidly, and the beloved voice of the reformer was every where hailed with enthusiasm. Luther published simultaneously works calculated to edify the Church, and polemical tracts which troubled the too eager exultation of his enemies. For nearly a whole year, he by turns instructed, exhorted, reproved, and thundered from his mountain-retreat; and his amazed adversaries asked one another if there was not something supernatural, some mystery, in this prodigious activity. "He could never have taken any rest," says Cochlœus.[1]

But there was no other mystery than the imprudence of the partisans of Rome. They hastened to take advantage of the edict of Worms, and to strike a decisive blow at the Reformation; while Luther, condemned, under the ban of the empire, and a prisoner in the Wartburg, undertook to defend the sound doctrine, as if he were still victorious and at liberty. It was especially at the tribunal of penance that the priests endeavoured to rivet the chains of their docile parishioners; and accordingly the confessional was the object of Luther's first attack. "They bring forward," said he, "these words of St. James: *Confess your faults to one another.* Singular confessor! his name is *One Another.* Whence it would follow that the confessors should also confess themselves to their penitents; that each Christian should be, in his turn, pope, bishop, priest; and that the pope himself should confess to all!"[2]

Luther had scarcely finished this tract when he began another. A theologian of Louvain, by name Latomus, already notorious by his opposition to Reuchlin and Erasmus, had attacked the reformer's opinions. In twelve days, Luther's refutation was ready, and it is a masterpiece. He clears himself of the reproach that he was wanting in moderation. "The moderation of the day," said he, "is to bend the knee before sacrilegious pontiffs and impious sophists, and to say to them: Gracious lord! Excellent master! Then, when you have so done, you may put any one you please to death; you may even convulse the world, and you will be none the less a man of moderation......Away with such moderation! I would rather be frank and deceive no one. The shell may be hard, but the kernel is soft and tender."[3]

As Luther's health continued feeble, he

thought of leaving the place of his confinement. But how could he manage it? To appear in public would be exposing his life. The back of the mountain on which the fortress stood was crossed by numerous footways, bordered by tufts of strawberries. The heavy gate of the castle opened, and the prisoner ventured, not without fear, to gather some of the fruit.[1] By degrees he grew bolder, and in his knight's garb began to wander through the surrounding country, attended by one of the guards of the castle, a worthy but somewhat churlish man. One day, having entered an inn, Luther threw aside his sword, which encumbered him, and hastily took up some books that lay there. His nature got the better of his prudence. His guardian trembled lest a movement, so extraordinary in a soldier, should excite suspicions that the doctor was not really a knight. At another time the two comrades alighted at the convent of Reinhardsbrunn, where Luther had slept a few months before on his road to Worms.[2] Suddenly one of the lay-brothers uttered a cry of surprise. Luther was recognised. His attendant perceived it, and dragged him hastily away; and already they were galloping far from the cloister before the astonished brother had recovered from his amazement.

The military life of the doctor had at intervals something about it truly theological. One day the nets were made ready—the gates of the fortress opened—the long-eared dogs rushed forth. Luther desired to taste the pleasures of the chase. The huntsmen soon grew animated; the dogs sprang forward, driving the game from the covers. In the midst of all this uproar, the Knight George stands motionless: his mind is occupied with serious thoughts; the objects around him fill his heart with sorrow.[3] "Is not this," says he, "the image of the devil setting on his dogs—that is, the bishops, those representatives of Antichrist, and urging them in pursuit of poor souls?"[4] A young hare was caught: delighted at the prospect of liberating it, he wrapped it carefully in his cloak, and set it down in the midst of a thicket; but hardly had he taken a few steps away from the spot before the dogs scented the animal and killed it. Luther, attracted by the noise, uttered a groan of sorrow, and exclaimed: "O pope! and thou, too, Satan! thus it is ye endeavour to destroy even those souls that have been saved from death!"[5]

---

[1] Cum quiescere non posset. Cochl. Act. Luth. p. 39.
[2] Und der Pabst müsse ihm beichten. L. Opp. xvii. 701.
[3] Cortex meus esse potest durior, sed nucleus meus mollis et dulcis est. Ibid. Lat. ii. 213.

[1] Zu zeiten gehet er inn die Erdbeer am Schlossberg. Mathes. p. 33.
[2] Vol. ii. p. 237.
[3] Theologisabar etiam ibi inter retia et canes....tantum misericordiæ et doloris miscuit mysterium. L. Epp. ii. 43.
[4] Quid enim ista imago, nisi Diabolum significat per insidias suas et impios magistros canes suos....Ibid.
[5] Sic sævit Papa et Satan ut servatas etiam animas perdant. Ibid. 44.

CHAPTER III.

Commencement of the Reform—Marriage of Feldkirchen—The Marriage of Monks—Theses—Tract against Monachism—Luther no longer a Monk.

WHILE the doctor of Wittemberg, thus dead to the world, was seeking relaxation in these sports in the neighbourhood of the Wartburg, the work was going on as if of itself: the Reform was beginning; it was no longer restricted to doctrine, it entered deeply into men's actions. Bernard Feldkirchen, pastor of Kemberg, the first under Luther's directions to attack the errors of Rome,[1] was also the first to throw off the yoke of its institutions. He married.

The Germans are fond of social life and domestic joys; and hence, of all the papal ordinances, compulsory celibacy was that which produced the saddest consequences. This law, which had been first imposed on the heads of the clergy, had prevented the ecclesiastical fiefs from becoming hereditary. But when extended by Gregory VII. to the inferior clergy, it was attended with the most deplorable results. Many priests had evaded the obligations imposed upon them by the most scandalous disorders, and had drawn contempt and hatred on the whole body; while those who had submitted to Hildebrand's law were inwardly exasperated against the Church, because, while conferring on its superior dignitaries so much power, wealth, and earthly enjoyment, it bound its humbler ministers, who were its most useful supporters, to a self-denial so contrary to the Gospel.

"Neither popes nor councils," said Feldkirchen and another pastor named Seidler, who had followed his example, "can impose any commandment on the Church that endangers body and soul. The obligation of keeping God's law compels me to violate the traditions of men."[2] The re-establishment of marriage in the sixteenth century was a homage paid to the moral law. The ecclesiastical authority became alarmed, and immediately fulminated its decrees against these two priests. Seidler, who was in the territories of Duke George, was given up to his superiors, and died in prison. But the Elector Frederick refused to surrender Feldkirchen to the Archbishop of Magdeburg. "His highness," said Spalatin, "declines to act the part of a constable." Feldkirchen therefore continued pastor of his flock, although a husband and a father.

The first emotion of the reformer when he heard of this was to give way to exultation: "I admire this new bridegroom of Kemberg," said he, "who fears nothing, and hastens forward in the midst of the uproar." Luther was of opinion that priests ought to marry. But this question led to another,—the marriage of monks; and here Luther had to support one of those internal struggles of which his whole life was composed; for every reform must first be won by a spiritual struggle. Melancthon and Carlstadt, the one a layman, the other a priest, thought that the liberty of contracting the bonds of wedlock should be as free for the monks as for the priests. The monk Luther did not think so at first. One day the governor of the Wartburg having brought him Carlstadt's theses on celibacy: "Gracious God!" exclaimed he, "our Wittembergers then will give wives even to the monks!"......This thought surprised and confounded him; his heart was troubled. He rejected for himself the liberty that he claimed for others. "Ah!" said he indignantly, "they will not force *me* at least to take a wife."[1] This expression is doubtless unknown to those who assert that Luther preached the Reformation that he might marry. Inquiring for truth, not with passion, but with uprightness of purpose, he maintained what seemed to him true, although contrary to the whole of his system. He walked in a mixture of error and truth, until error had fallen and truth remained alone.

There was, indeed, a great difference between the two questions. The marriage of priests was not the destruction of the priesthood; on the contrary, this of itself might restore to the secular clergy the respect of the people; but the marriage of monks was the downfal of monachism. It became a question, therefore, whether it was desirable to disband and break up that powerful army which the popes had under their orders. "Priests," wrote Luther to Melancthon, "are of divine appointment, and consequently are free as regards human commandments. But of their own free will the monks adopted celibacy; they are not therefore at liberty to withdraw from the yoke they voluntarily imposed on themselves."[2]

The reformer was destined to advance, and carry by a fresh struggle this new position of the enemy. Already had he trodden under foot a host of Roman abuses, and even Rome herself; but monachism still remained standing. Monachism, that had once carried life into so many deserts, and which, passing through so many centuries, was now filling the cloisters with sloth, and often with licentiousness, seemed to have embodied itself, and gone to defend its rights in that castle of Thuringia, where the question of its life and death was discussed in the conscience of one man. Luther struggled with it: at one moment he was on the point of gaining the victory, at another he was nearly overcome.

---

[1] Vol. i. p. 78.
[2] Coegit me ergo ut humanas traditiones violarem, necessitas servandi juris divini. Corp. Ref. i. 141.

[1] At mihi non obtrudent uxorem. L. Epp. ii. 40.
[2] Me enim vehementer movet, quod sacerdotum ordo a Deo institutus, est liber, non autem monachorum qui sua sponte statum eligerunt. Ibid. 34.

At length, unable longer to maintain the contest, he flung himself in prayer at the feet of Jesus Christ, exclaiming: "Teach us, deliver us, establish us, by Thy mercy, in the liberty that belongs to us; for of a surety we are thy people!"[1]

He had not long to wait for deliverance; an important revolution was effected in the reformer's mind; and again it was the doctrine of justification by faith that gave him victory. That arm which had overthrown the indulgences, the practices of Rome, and the pope himself, also wrought the downfal of the monks in Luther's mind and throughout Christendom. Luther saw that monachism was in violent opposition to the doctrine of salvation by grace, and that a monastic life was founded entirely on the pretended merits of man. Feeling convinced, from that hour, that Christ's glory was interested in this question, he heard a voice incessantly repeating in his conscience: "Monachism must fall!"—"So long as the doctrine of justification by faith remains pure and undefiled in the Church, no one can become a monk," said he.[2] This conviction daily grew stronger in his heart, and about the beginning of September he sent "to the bishops and deacons of the Church of Wittemberg," the following theses, which were his declaration of war against a monastic life:—

"Whatsoever is not of faith is sin (Rom. xiv. 23).

"Whosoever maketh a vow of virginity, of chastity, of service to God without faith, maketh an impious and idolatrous vow—a vow to the devil himself.

"To make such vows is worse than the priests of Cybele or the vestals of the pagans; for the monks make their vows in the thought of being justified and saved by these vows; and what ought to be ascribed solely to the mercy of God, is thus attributed to meritorious works.

"We must utterly overthrow such convents, as being the abodes of the devil.

"There is but one order that is holy and makes man holy, and that is Christianity or faith.[3]

"For convents to be useful they should be converted into schools, where children should be brought up to man's estate; instead of which they are houses where adult men become children, and remain so for ever."

We see that Luther would still have tolerated convents as places of education; but erelong his attacks against these establishments became more violent. The immorality and shameful practices that prevailed in the cloisters recurred forcibly to his thoughts. "I am resolved," wrote he to Spalatin on the 11th of November, "to deliver the young

from the hellish fires of celibacy."[1] He now wrote a book against monastic vows, which he dedicated to his father:—

"Do you desire," said he in his dedication to the old man at Mansfeldt, "do you still desire to rescue me from a monastic life? You have the right, for you are still my father, and I am still your son. But that is no longer necessary: God has been beforehand with you, and has Himself delivered me by his power. What matters it whether I wear or lay aside the tonsure and the cowl? Is it the cowl—is it the tonsure—that makes the monk? *All things are yours,* says St. Paul, *and you are Christ's.* I do not belong to the cowl, but the cowl to me. I am a monk, and yet not a monk; I am a new creature, not of the pope, but of Jesus Christ. Christ, alone and without any go-between, is my bishop, my abbot, my prior, my lord, my father, and my master; and I know no other. What matters it to me if the pope should condemn me and put me to death? He cannot call me from the grave and kill me a second time......The great day is drawing near in which the kingdom of abominations shall be overthrown. Would to God that it were worth while for the pope to put us all to death! Our blood would cry out to heaven against him, and thus his condemnation would be hastened, and his end be near."[2]

The transformation had already been effected in Luther himself; he was no longer a monk. It was not outward circumstances, or earthly passions, or carnal precipitation that had wrought this change. There had been a struggle: at first Luther had taken the side of monachism; but truth also had gone down into the lists, and monachism had fallen before it. The victories that passion gains are ephemeral; those of truth are lasting and decisive.

CHAPTER IV.

Archbishop Albert—The Idol of Halle—Luther's Indignation—Alarm of the Court—Luther's Letter to the Archbishop—Albert's Reply—Joachim of Brandenburg.

WHILE Luther was thus preparing the way for one of the greatest revolutions that were destined to be effected in the Church, and the Reformation was beginning to enter powerfully into the lives of Christians, the Romish partisans, blind as those generally are who have been long in the possession of power, imagined that, because Luther was in the Wartburg, the Reform was dead and

---

[1] Dominus Jesus erudiat et liberet nos, per misericordiam suam, in libertatem nostram. To Melancthon, on Celibacy, 6th August 1521. L. Epp. ii. 40.
[2] L. Opp. (W.) xxii. 1466.
[3] Es ist nicht mehr denn eine einige Geistlichkeit, die da heilig ist, und heilig macht....L. Opp. xvii. 718.

[1] Adolescentes liberare ex isto inferno cœlibatus. L. Opp ii. 95.
[2] Dass unser Blut möcht schreien, und dringen sein Gericht, dass sein Bald ein Ende würde. L. Epp. ii. 105.

for ever extinct; and fancied they should be able quietly to resume their ancient practices, that had been for a moment disturbed by the monk of Wittemberg. Albert, elector-archbishop of Mentz, was one of those weak men who, all things being equal, decide for the truth; but who, as soon as their interest is put in the balance, are ready to take part with error. His most important aim was to have a court as brilliant as that of any prince in Germany, his equipages as rich, and his table as well furnished: the traffic in indulgences served admirably to promote this object. Accordingly, the decree against Luther had scarcely issued from the imperial chancery, before Albert, who was then residing with his court at Halle, summoned the vendors of indulgences, who were still alarmed at the words of the reformer, and endeavoured to encourage them by such language as this: "Fear nothing, we have silenced him; let us begin to shear the flock in peace; the monk is a prisoner; he is confined by bolts and bars; this time he will be very clever if he comes again to disturb us in our affairs." The market was reopened, the merchandise was displayed for sale, and again the churches of Halle re-echoed with the speeches of the mountebanks.

But Luther was still alive, and his voice was powerful enough to pass beyond the walls and gratings behind which he had been hidden. Nothing could have roused his indignation to a higher pitch. What! the most violent battles have been fought: he has confronted every danger: the truth remains victorious, and yet they dare trample it under foot, as if it had been vanquished! ......That voice shall again be heard, which has once already put an end to this criminal traffic. "I shall enjoy no rest," wrote he to Spalatin, "until I have attacked the idol of Mentz with its brothel at Halle."[1]

Luther set to work immediately; he cared little about the mystery with which some sought to envelop his residence in the Wartburg. He was like Elijah in the desert forging fresh thunderbolts against the impious Ahab. On the first of November he finished his treatise *Against the New Idol of Halle.*

Intelligence of Luther's plans reached the archbishop. Alarmed and in emotion at the very idea, he sent about the middle of October two of his attendants (Capito and Auerbach) to Wittemberg to avert the storm. "Luther must moderate his impetuosity," said they to Melancthon, who received them cordially. But Melancthon, although mild himself, was not one of those who imagine that wisdom consists in perpetual concession, tergiversation, and silence. "It is God who moves him," replied he, "and our

age needs a bitter and pungent salt."[1] Upon this Capito turned to Jonas, and endeavoured through him to act upon the court. The news of Luther's intention was already known there, and produced great amazement. "What!" said the courtiers: "rekindle the fire that we have had so much trouble to extinguish! Luther can only be saved by being forgotten, and yet he is rising up against the first prince in the empire!"—"I will not suffer Luther to write against the Archbishop of Mentz, and thus disturb the public tranquillity," said the elector. [2]

Luther was annoyed when these words were repeated to him. Is it not enough to imprison his body, but they will enchain his mind also, and the truth with it?......Do they fancy that he hides himself through fear, and that his retirement is an avowal of defeat? He maintains that it is a victory. Who dared stand up against him at Worms and oppose the truth? Accordingly when the captive in the Wartburg had read the chaplain's letter, informing him of the prince's sentiments, he flung it aside, determined to make no reply. But he could not long contain himself; he took up the epistle and wrote to Spalatin: "The elector will not suffer!......and I too will not suffer the elector *not* to permit me to write......Rather would I destroy yourself, the elector, nay, every creature in the world![3] If I have resisted the pope, who is the creator of your cardinal, why should I give way before his creature? It is very fine, forsooth, to hear you say that we must not disturb the public tranquillity, while you allow the everlasting peace of God to be disturbed!......Spalatin, it shall not be so! Prince, it shall not be so![4] I send you a book I had already prepared against the cardinal when I received your letter. Forward it to Melancthon."

Spalatin trembled as he read this manuscript; again he represented to the reformer how imprudent it would be to publish a work that would force the imperial government to lay aside its apparent ignorance of Luther's fate, and punish a prisoner who dared attack the greatest prince in the empire and the Church. If Luther persevered in his designs, the tranquillity would again be disturbed, and the Reformation perhaps be lost. Luther consented to delay the publication of his treatise, and even permitted Melancthon to erase the most violent passages.[5] But, irritated at his friend's timidity, he wrote to the chaplain: "The Lord lives and reigns, that Lord in whom you court-folks do not believe, unless he so accommodate His works to your reason, that there is no longer any necessity

---

[1] Non continebor quin idolum Moguntinum invadam, cum suo lupanari Hallensi. L. Epp. ii. 59, 7th October.

[1] Huic seculo opus esse acerrimo sale. Corp. Ref. i. 463.
[2] Non passurum principem scribi in Moguntinum. L. Epp. ii. 94.
[3] Potius te et principem ipsum perdam et omnem creaturam. Ibid.
[4] Non sic, Spalatine; non sic, princeps. Ibid.
[5] Ut acerbiora radat. Ibid. 110.

to believe." He then resolved to write direct to the cardinal.

It is the whole episcopal body that Luther thus brings to the bar in the person of the German primate. His words are those of a bold man, ardent in zeal for the truth, and who feels that he is speaking in the name of God himself.

" Your electoral highness," wrote he from the depth of the retreat in which he was hidden, " has set up again in Halle the idol that swallows the money and the souls of poor Christians. You think, perhaps, that I am disabled, and that the emperor will easily stifle the cries of the poor monk......But know that I shall discharge the duties that christian charity has imposed upon me, without fearing the gates of hell, and much less the pope, his bishops, and cardinals.

" For this reason my humble prayer is, that your electoral highness would remember the beginning of this affair—how from one tiny spark proceeded so terrible a conflagration. All the world was at that time in a state of security. This poor begging friar (thought they), who unaided would attack the pope, is too weak for such an undertaking. But God interposed ; and he caused the pope more labour and anxiety than he had ever felt since he had taken his place in the temple of God to tyrannize over the Church. This same God still lives : let none doubt it.[1] He will know how to withstand a cardinal of Mentz, even were he supported by four emperors ; for He is pleased above all things to hew down the lofty cedars and to abase the haughty Pharaohs.

" For this reason I inform your highness by letter, that if the idol is not thrown down, I must, in obedience to God's teaching, publicly attack your highness, as I have attacked the pope himself. Let your highness conduct yourself in accordance with this advice ; I shall wait a fortnight for an early and favourable reply. Given in my wilderness, the Sunday after St. Catherine's day (15th November) 1521.

" From your electoral highness's devoted and obedient servant,

" MARTIN LUTHER."

This letter was sent to Wittemberg, and from Wittemberg to Halle, where the cardinal-elector was then residing ; for no one ventured to intercept it, foreseeing the storm that would be aroused by so daring an act. But Melancthon accompanied it by a letter addressed to the prudent Capito, in which he endeavoured to prepare the way for a favourable termination of this difficult business.

It is impossible to describe the feelings of the youthful and weak archbishop on receiving the reformer's letter. The work announced *against the idol of Halle* was like a

[1] Derselbig Gott lebet noch, da zweifel nur niemand an ..L. Epp. ii. 113.

sword suspended over his head. And, at the same time, what anger must have been kindled in his heart by the insolence of this peasant's son,—of this excommunicated monk, who dared make use of such language to a prince of the house of Brandenburg,—the primate of the German Church? Capito besought the archbishop to satisfy the monk. Alarm, pride, and the voice of conscience which he could not stifle, struggled fearfully in Albert's bosom. At length dread of the book, and perhaps remorse also, prevailed ; he humbled himself : he put together all he thought calculated to appease the man of the Wartburg, and a fortnight had barely elapsed when Luther received the following letter, still more astonishing than his own terrible epistle :—

" My dear Doctor,—I have received and read your letter, and have taken it in good part. But I think the motive that has led you to write me such an epistle has long ceased to exist. I desire, with God's help, to conduct myself as a pious bishop and a christian prince, and I confess my need of the grace of God. I do not deny that I am a sinner, liable to sin and error, sinning and erring daily. I am well assured that without God's grace I am worthless and offensive mire, even as other men, if not more so. In replying to your letter, I would not conceal this gracious disposition ; for I am more than desirous of showing you all kindness and favour, for love of Christ. I know how to receive a christian and fraternal rebuke.

" With my own hand. ALBERT."

Such was the language addressed to the excommunicated monk of the Wartburg by the Elector-archbishop of Mentz and Magdeburg, commissioned to represent and maintain in Germany the constitution of the Church. Did Albert, in writing it, obey the generous impulses of his conscience, or his slavish fears? In the first case, it is a noble letter ; in the second, it merits our contempt. We would rather suppose it originated in the better feelings of his heart. However that may be, it shows the immeasurable superiority of God's servants over all the great ones of the earth. While Luther alone, a prisoner and condemned, derived invincible courage from his faith, the archbishop, elector and cardinal, environed with all the power and favours of the world, trembled on his throne. This contrast appears continually, and is the key to the strange enigma offered by the history of the Reformation. The Christian is not called upon to count his forces, and to number his means of victory. The only thing he should be anxious about is to know whether the cause he upholds is really that of God, and whether he looks only to his Master's glory. Unquestionably he has an inquiry to make ; but this is wholly spiritual,—the Christian looks at the heart, and not the arm; he weighs the justice of his cause, and not its outward strength. And when this question is once settled, his path is clear. He must move forward boldly, were it even against the world and all its armed hosts, in the unshaken conviction that God himself will fight for him.

The enemies of the Reformation thus passed from extreme severity to extreme weakness; they had already done the same at Worms; and these sudden transitions are of continual occurrence in the battle that error wages against truth. Every cause destined to fall is attacked with an internal uneasiness which makes it tottering and uncertain, and drives it by turns from one pole to the other. Steadiness of purpose and energy are far better; they would thus perhaps precipitate its fall, but at least if it did fall, it would fall with glory.

One of Albert's brothers, Joachim I., elector of Brandenburg, gave an example of that strength of character which is so rare, particularly in our own times. Immovable in his principles, firm in action, knowing how to resist when necessary the encroachments of the pope, he opposed an iron hand to the progress of the Reformation. At Worms he had insisted that Luther should not be heard, and that he ought to be punished as a heretic, in despite of his safe-conduct. Scarcely had the edict of Worms been issued, when he ordered that it should be strictly enforced throughout his states. Luther could appreciate so energetic a character, and making a distinction between Joachim and his other adversaries, he said: "We may still pray for the Elector of Brandenburg."[1] The disposition of this prince seemed to have been communicated to his people. Berlin and Brandenburg long remained closed against the Reformation. But what is received slowly is held faithfully.[2] While other countries, which then hailed the Gospel with joy, —Belgium for instance, and Westphalia,— were soon to abandon it, Brandenburg, the last of the German states to enter on the narrow way of faith, was destined in after-years to stand in the foremost ranks of the Reformation.

Luther did not read Cardinal Albert's letter without a suspicion that it was dictated by hypocrisy, and in accordance with the advice of Capito. He kept silence, however, being content with declaring to the latter, that so long as the archbishop, who was hardly capable of managing a small parish, did not lay aside his cardinal's mask and episcopal pomp, and become a simple minister of the Word, it was impossible that he could be in the way of salvation.[3]

[1] Helwing, Gesh. der Brandeb. ii. 605.
[2] Hoc enim proprium est illorum hominum (ex March. Brandeburg), ut quam semel in religione sententiam approbaverint, non facile deserant. Leutingeri Opp. i. 41.
[3] Larvam cardinalatus et pompam episcopalem ablegare. L. Epp. ii. 132.

CHAPTER V.

Translation of the Bible—Wants of the Church—Principles of the Reformation—Temptations of the Devil—Luther's Works condemned by the Sorbonne—Melancthon's Reply —Luther Visits Wittemberg.

WHILE Luther was thus struggling against error, as if he were still in the midst of the battle, he was also labouring in his retirement of the Wartburg, as if he had no concern in what was going on in the world. The hour had come in which the Reformation, from being a mere theological question, was to become the life of the people; and yet the great engine by which this progress was to be effected was not yet in being. This powerful and mighty instrument, destined to hurl its thunderbolts from every side against the proud edifice of Rome, throw down its walls, cast off the enormous weight of the Papacy under which the Church lay stifled, and communicate an impulse to the whole human race which would still be felt until the end of time,—this instrument was to go forth from the old castle of the Wartburg, and enter the world on the same day that terminated the reformer's captivity.

The farther the Church was removed from the time when Jesus, the true Light of the world, was on the earth, the greater was her need of the torch of God's Word, ordained to transmit the brightness of Jesus Christ to the men of the latter days. But this Divine Word was at that time hidden from the people. Several unsuccessful attempts at translation from the Vulgate had been made in 1477, 1490, and in 1518; they were almost unintelligible, and from their high price beyond the reach of the people. It had even been prohibited to give the German Church the Bible in the vulgar tongue.[1] Besides which, the number of those who were able to read did not become considerable until there existed in the German language a book of lively and universal interest.

Luther was called to present his nation with the Scriptures of God. That same God who had conducted St. John to Patmos, there to write his revelation, had confined Luther in the Wartburg, there to translate His Word. This great task, which it would have been difficult for him to have undertaken in the midst of the cares and occupations of Wittemberg, was to establish the new building on the primitive rock, and, after the lapse of so many ages, lead Christians back from the subtleties of the schoolmen to the pure fountain-head of redemption and salvation.

The wants of the Church spoke loudly; they called for this great work; and Luther, by his own inward experience, was to be led to perform it. In truth, he discovered in faith

[1] Codex Diplom. Ecclesiæ Magunt. iv. 460.

that repose of the soul which his agitated conscience and his monastic ideas had long induced him to seek in his own merits and holiness. The doctrine of the Church, the scholastic theology, knew nothing of the consolations that proceed from faith; but the Scriptures proclaim them with great force, and there it was that he had found them. Faith in the Word of God had made him free. By it he felt emancipated from the dogmatical authority of the Church, from its hierarchy and traditions, from the opinions of the schoolmen, the power of prejudice, and from every human ordinance. Those strong and numerous bonds which for centuries had enchained and stifled Christendom, were snapped asunder, broken in pieces, and scattered round him; and he nobly raised his head freed from all authority except that of the Word. This independence of man, this submission to God, which he had learned in the Holy Scriptures, he desired to impart to the Church. But before he could communicate them, it was necessary to set before it the revelations of God. A powerful hand was wanted to unlock the massive gates of that arsenal of God's Word from which Luther had taken his arms, and to open to the people against the day of battle those vaults and antique halls which for many ages no foot had ever trod.

Luther had already translated several fragments of the Holy Scripture; the seven penitential Psalms had been his first task.[1] John the Baptist, Christ himself, and the Reformation, had begun alike by calling men to repentance. It is the principle of every regeneration in the individual man, and in the whole human race. These essays had been eagerly received; men longed to have more; and this voice of the people was considered by Luther as the voice of God himself. He resolved to reply to the call. He is a prisoner within those lofty walls; what of that! he will devote his leisure to translating the Word of God into the language of his countrymen. Erelong this Word will be seen descending from the Wartburg with him; circulating among the people of Germany, and putting them in possession of those spiritual treasures hitherto shut up within the hearts of a few pious men. "Would that this one book," exclaimed Luther, "were in every language, in every hand, before the eyes, and in the ears and hearts of all men!"[2] Admirable words, which, after a lapse of three centuries an illustrious body,[3] translating the Bible into the mother-tongue of every nation upon earth, has undertaken to realize. "Scripture without any comment," said he again, "is the sun whence all teachers receive their light."

Such are the principles of Christianity and of the Reformation. According to these venerable words, we should not consult the Fathers to throw light upon Scripture, but Scripture to explain the Fathers. The reformers and the apostles set up the Word of God as the only light, as they exalt the sacrifice of Christ as the only righteousness. By mingling any authority of man with this absolute authority of God, or any human righteousness with this perfect righteousness of Christ, we vitiate both the foundations of Christianity. These are the two fundamental heresies of Rome, and which, although doubtless in a smaller degree, some teachers were desirous of introducing into the bosom of the Reformation.

Luther opened the Greek originals of the evangelists and apostles, and undertook the difficult task of making these divine teachers speak his mother tongue. Important crisis in the history of the Reformation! from that time the Reformation was no longer in the hands of the reformer. The Bible came forward; Luther withdrew. God appeared, and man disappeared. The reformer placed THE BOOK in the hands of his contemporaries. Each one may now hear the voice of God for himself; as for Luther, henceforth he mingles with the crowd, and takes his station in the ranks of those who come to draw from the common fountain of light and life.

In translating the Holy Scriptures, Luther found that consolation and strength, of which he stood so much in need. Solitary, in ill health, and saddened by the exertions of his enemies and the extravagances of some of his followers,—seeing his life wearing away in the gloom of that old castle, he had occasionally to endure terrible struggles. In those times, men were inclined to carry into the visible world the conflicts that the soul sustains with its spiritual enemies; Luther's lively imagination easily embodied the emotions of his heart, and the superstitions of the Middle Ages had still some hold upon his mind, so that we might say of him, as it has been said of Calvin with regard to the punishment inflicted on heretics: there was yet a remnant of popery in him.[1] Satan was not in Luther's view simply an invisible though real being; he thought that this adversary of God appeared to men as he had appeared to Jesus Christ. Although the authenticity of many of the stories on this subject contained in the Table-talk and elsewhere is more than doubtful, history must still record this failing in the reformer. Never was he more assailed by these gloomy ideas than in the solitude of the Wartburg. In the days of his strength he had braved the devil in Worms; but now all the reformer's power seemed broken and his glory tarnished. He was thrown aside; Satan was victorious in his turn, and in the anguish

---

[1] Psalms 6, 32, 38, 51, 102, 130, 147.
[2] Et solus hic liber omnium lingua, manu, oculis, auribus, cordibus versaretur. L. Epp. ii. 116.
[3] The Bible Society.

[1] Michelet, in his *Mémoires de Luther*, devotes more than thirty pages to the various accounts of these Satanic visitations.

of his soul Luther imagined he saw his giant form standing before him, lifting his finger in threatening attitude, exulting with a bitter and hellish sneer, and gnashing his teeth in fearful rage. One day especially, it is said, as Luther was engaged on his translation of the New Testament, he fancied he beheld Satan, filled with horror at his work, tormenting him, and prowling round him like a lion about to spring upon his prey. Luther, alarmed and incensed, snatched up his inkstand and flung it at the head of his enemy. The figure disappeared, and the missile was dashed in pieces against the wall. [1]

Luther's sojourn in the Wartburg began to be insupportable to him. He felt indignant at the timidity of his protectors. Sometimes he would remain a whole day plunged in deep and silent meditation, and awakened from it only to exclaim, " Oh, that I were at Wittemberg!" At length he could hold out no longer; there had been caution enough; he must see his friends again, hear them, and converse with them. True, he ran the risk of falling into the hands of his enemies, but nothing could stop him. About the end of November, he secretly quitted the Wartburg, and set out for Wittemberg. [2]

A fresh storm had just burst upon him. At last the Sorbonne had spoken out. That celebrated school of Paris, the first authority in the Church after the pope, the ancient and venerable source whence theological learning had proceeded, had given its verdict against the Reformation.

The following are some of the propositions condemned by this learned body. Luther had said, " God ever pardons and remits sins gratuitously, and requires nothing of us in return, except that in future we should live according to righteousness." And he had added, " Of all deadly sins, this is the most deadly, namely, that any one should think he is not guilty of a damnable and deadly sin before God." He had said in another place, " Burning heretics is contrary to the will of the Holy Ghost."

To these three propositions, and to many others besides, which they quoted, the theological faculty of Paris replied, " Heresy!— let him be accursed!"[3]

But a young man, twenty-four years of age, of short stature, diffident, and plain in appearance, dared take up the gauntlet which the first college in the world had thrown down. They knew pretty well at Wittemberg what should be thought of these pompous censures: they knew that Rome had yielded to the suggestions of the Dominicans, and that the Sorbonne had been mis-

led by two or three fanatical doctors who were designated at Paris by satirical nicknames. [1] Accordingly, in his Apology, Melancthon did not confine himself to defending Luther; but, with the boldness which characterizes his writings, carried the war into the enemy's camp. " You say he is a Manichean!—he is a Montanist!—let fire and faggot repress his foolishness! And who is Montanist? Luther, who would have us believe in Holy Scripture alone, or you, who would have men believe in the opinions of their fellow-creatures rather than in the Word of God?"[2]

To ascribe more importance to the word of a man than to the Word of God was in very truth the heresy of Montanus, as it still is that of the pope and of all those who set the hierarchical authority of the Church or the interior inspirations of mysticism far above the positive declarations of the Sacred Writings. Accordingly the youthful master of arts, who had said, " I would rather lay down my life than my faith,"[3] did not stop there. He accused the Sorbonne of having obscured the Gospel, extinguished faith. and substituted an empty philosophy in the place of Christianity. [4] After this work of Melancthon's, the position of the dispute was changed; he proved unanswerably that the heresy was at Paris and Rome, and the catholic truth at Wittemberg.

Meanwhile Luther, caring little for the condemnations of the Sorbonne, was proceeding in his military equipment to the university. He was greatly distressed by various reports which reached him on the road of a spirit of impatience and independence that was showing itself among some of his adherents. [5] At length he arrived at Wittemberg without being recognised, and stopped at Amsdorff's house. Immediately all his friends were secretly called together; [6] and Melancthon among the first, who had so often said, " I would rather die than lose him."[7] They came!—What a meeting!— what joy!—The captive of the Wartburg tasted in their society all the sweetness of christian friendship. He learnt the spread of the Reformation, the hopes of his brethren; and, delighted at what he saw and heard, [8] offered up a prayer,—returned thanks to God,—and then with brief delay returned to the Wartburg.

---

[1] The keeper of the Wartburg still carefully directs the traveller's attention to the spots made by Luther's inkstand.
[2] Machete er sich heimlich aus seiner Patmo auf. L. Opp. xviii. 238.
[3] Determinatio theologorum Parisiensium super doctrina Lutherana. Corp. Ref. i. 366-388.

[1] Damnarunt triumviri Beda, *Quercus*, et *Christophorus*. Nomina sunt horum monstrorum etiam vulgo nunc nota *Belua, Stercus, Christotomus*. Zwinglii Epp. i. 176.
[2] Corp. Ref. i. 396.
[3] Scias me positurum animam citius quam fidem. Ibid.
[4] Evangelium obscuratum est, fides extincta....Ex Christianismo. contra omnem sensum spiritus, facta est quædam philosophiæ vivendi ratio. Ibid. 400.
[5] Per viam vexatus rumore vario de nostrorum quorundam importunitate. L. Epp. ii. 109.
[6] Liess in der Stille seine Freunde fodern. L. Opp. xviii. 238.
[7] Quo si mihi carendum est, mortem fortius tulero. Corp. Ref. i. 453, 455.
[8] Omnia vehementer placent quæ video et audio. L. Epp. ii. 109.

CHAPTER VI.

Fresh Reforms—Gabriel Zwilling on the Mass—The University—Melancthon's Propositions—The Elector—Monastic Institutions attacked—Emancipation of the Monks—Disturbances—Chapter of the Augustine Monks—Carlstadt and the Mass—First Celebration of the Lord's Supper—Importance of the Mass in the Romish System.

LUTHER'S joy was well-founded. The work of the Reformation was then making a great stride. Feldkirchen, always in the van, had led the assault; now the main body was in motion, and that power which carried the Reformation from the doctrine it had purified into the worship, life, and constitution of the Church, now manifested itself by a new explosion, more formidable to the papacy than even the first had been.

Rome, having got rid of the reformer, thought the heresy was at an end. But in a short time everything was changed. Death removed from the pontifical throne the man who had put Luther under the ban of the Church. Disturbances occurred in Spain, and compelled Charles to visit his kingdom beyond the Pyrenees. War broke out between this prince and Francis I., and as if that were not enough to occupy the emperor, Soliman made an incursion into Hungary. Charles, thus attacked on all sides, was forced to forget the monk of Worms and his religious innovations.

About the same time, the vessel of the Reformation, which, driven in every direction by contrary winds, was on the verge of foundering, righted itself, and floated proudly above the waters.

It was in the convent of the Augustines at Wittemberg that the Reformation broke out. We ought not to feel surprise at this: it is true the reformer was there no longer; but no human power could drive out the spirit that had animated him.

For some time the Church in which Luther had so often preached re-echoed with strange doctrines. Gabriel Zwilling, a zealous monk and chaplain to the convent, was there energetically proclaiming the Reformation. As if Luther, whose name was at that time every where celebrated, had become too strong and too illustrious, God selected feeble and obscure men to begin the Reformation which that renowned doctor had prepared. "Jesus Christ," said the preacher, "instituted the sacrament of the altar in remembrance of his death, and not to make it an object of adoration. To worship it is a real idolatry. The priest who communicates alone commits a sin. No prior has the right to compel a monk to say mass alone. Let one, two, or three officiate, and let the others receive the Lord's sacrament under both kinds."[1]

This is what Friar Gabriel required, and this daring language was listened to approvingly by the other brethren, and particularly by those who came from the Low Countries.[1] They were disciples of the Gospel, and why should they not conform in every thing to its commands? Had not Luther himself written to Melancthon in the month of August: "Henceforth and for ever I will say no more private masses?"[2] Thus the monks, the soldiers of the hierarchy, emancipated by the Word, boldly took part against Rome.

At Wittemberg they met with a violent resistance from the prior. Calling to mind that all things should be done in an orderly manner, they gave way, but with a declaration that to uphold the mass was to oppose the Gospel of God.

The prior had gained the day: one man had been stronger than them all. It might seem, therefore, that this movement of the Augustines was one of those caprices of insubordination so frequently occurring in monasteries. But it was in reality the Spirit of God itself which was then agitating all Christendom. A solitary cry, uttered in the bosom of a convent, found its echo in a thousand voices; and that which men would have desired to confine within the walls of a cloister, went forth and took a bodily form in the very midst of the city.

Rumours of the dissensions among the friars soon spread through the town. The citizens and students of the university took part, some with, some against the mass. The elector's court was troubled. Frederick in surprise sent his chancellor Pontanus to Wittemberg with orders to reduce the monks to obedience, by putting them, if necessary, on bread and water;[3] and on the 12th of October, at seven in the morning, a deputation from the professors, of which Melancthon formed a part, visited the convent, exhorting the brethren to attempt no innovations,[4] or at least to wait a little longer. Upon this all their zeal revived: as they were unanimous in their faith, except the prior who combated them, they appealed to Scripture, to the understanding of believers, and to the conscience of the theologians; and two days after handed in a written declaration.

The doctors now examined the question more closely, and found that the monks had truth on their side. They had gone to convince, and were convinced themselves. What ought they to do? their consciences cried aloud; their anxiety kept increasing: at last, after long hesitation, they formed a courageous resolution.

On the 20th of October, the university made their report to the elector. "Let your

---

[1] Einem 2 oder 3 befehlen Mess zu halten und die andern 12 von denen, das Sacrament *sub utraque specie*, mit empfahen. Corp. Ref. i. 460.

[1] Der meiste Theil jener Parthei Niederländer seyn. Corp. Ref. i. 476.
[2] Sed et ego amplius non faciam missam privatam in æternum. L. Epp. ii. 36.
[3] Wollen die Mönche nicht Mess halten, sie werden's bald in der Küchen und Keller empfinden. Corp. Ref. i. 461.
[4] Mit dem Mess halten keine Neuerung machen. Ibid.

electoral highness," said they, after setting forth the errors of the mass, " put an end to every abuse, lest Christ in the day of judgment should rebuke us as he did the people of Capernaum."

Thus it is no longer a few obscure monks who are speaking; it is that university which for several years has been hailed by all the wise as the school of the nation; and the very means employed to check the Reformation are those which will now contribute to its extension.

Melancthon, with that boldness which he carried into learning, published fifty-five propositions calculated to enlighten men's minds.

" Just as looking at a cross," said he, is not performing a good work, but simply contemplating a sign that reminds us of Christ's death ;

" Just as looking at the sun is not performing a good work, but simply contemplating a sign that reminds us of Christ and of his Gospel;

" So, partaking of the Lord's Supper is not performing a good work, but simply making use of a sign that reminds us of the grace that has been given us through Christ.

" But here is the difference, namely, that the symbols invented by men simply remind us of what they signify ; while the signs given us by God, not only remind us of the things themselves, but assure our hearts of the will of God.[1]

" As the sight of a cross does not justify, so the mass does not justify.

" As the sight of a cross is not a sacrifice either for our sins or for the sins of others, so the mass is not a sacrifice.

" There is but one sacrifice,—but one satisfaction,—Jesus Christ. Besides him, there is none.

" Let such bishops as do not oppose the impiety of the mass be accursed."

Thus spoke the pious and gentle Philip. The elector was amazed. He had desired to reduce some young friars,—and now the whole university, headed by Melancthon, rose in their defence. To wait seemed to him in all things the surest means of success. He did not like sudden reforms, and desired that every opinion should make its way without obstruction. " Time alone," thought he, " clears up all things and brings them to maturity." And yet in spite of him the Reformation was advancing with hasty steps, and threatened to carry every thing along with it. Frederick made every exertion to arrest its progress. His authority, the influence of his character, the reasons that appeared to him the most convincing, were all set in operation. " Do not be too hasty," said he to the theologians ; " your number is too small to carry such a reform. If it is

based upon the Gospel, others will discover it also, and you will put an end to abuses with the aid of the whole Church. Talk, debate, preach on these matters as much as you like, but keep up the ancient usages."

Such was the battle fought on the subject of the mass. The monks had bravely led the assault ; the theologians, undecided for a moment, had soon come to their support. The prince and his ministers alone defended the place. It has been asserted that the Reformation was accomplished by the power and authority of the elector ; but far from that, the assailants shrunk back at the sound of his voice, and the mass was saved for a few days.

The heat of the attack had already been directed against another point. Friar Gabriel still continued his heart-stirring sermons in the Church of the Augustines. Monachism was now the object of his reiterated blows ; if the mass was the stronghold of the Roman doctrines, the monastic orders were the support of the hierarchy. These, then, were the two first positions that must be carried.

" No one," said Gabriel, according to the prior's report, "no dweller in the convents keeps the commandments of God ; no one can be saved under a cowl ;[1] every man that enters a cloister enters it in the name of the devil. The vows of chastity, poverty, and obedience, are contrary to the Gospel."

This extraordinary language was reported to the prior, who avoided going to church for fear he should hear it.

" Gabriel," said they, " desires that every exertion should be made to empty the cloisters. He says if a monk is met in the streets, the people should pull him by the frock and laugh at him; and that if they cannot be driven out of the convents by ridicule, they should be expelled by force. Break open pull down, utterly destroy the monasteries (says he), so that not a single trace of them may remain; and that not one of those stones, that have contributed to shelter so much sloth and superstition, may be found in the spot they so long occupied."[2]

The friars were astonished ; their consciences told them that Gabriel's words were but too true, that a monkish life was not in conformity with the will of God, and that no one could dispose of their persons but themselves.

Thirteen Augustines quitted the convent together, and laying aside the costume of their order, assumed a lay dress. Those who possessed any learning attended the lectures of the university, in order one day to be serviceable to the Church ; and those whose minds were uncultivated, endeavoured to gain a livelihood by the work of their own

---

[1] Signa ab hominibus reperta admonent tantum ; signa a Deo tradita, præterquam quod admonent, certificant etiam cor de voluntate Dei. Corp. Ref. i. 478.

[1] Kein Mönch werde in der Kappe selig. Corp. Ref. i. 433.
[2] Dass man nicht oben Stück von einem Kloster da sey gestanden, merken möge. Ibid. 483.

hands, according to the injunctions of the apostle, and the example of the good citizens of Wittemberg.[1] One of them, who understood the business of a joiner, applied for the freedom of the city, and resolved to take a wife.

If Luther's entry into the Augustine convent at Erfurth had been the germ of the Reformation, the departure of these thirteen monks from the convent of the Augustines at Wittemberg was the signal of its entering into possession of Christendom. For thirty years past Erasmus had been unveiling the uselessness, the folly, and the vices of the monks; and all Europe laughed and grew angry with him: but sarcasm was required no longer. Thirteen high-minded and bold men returned into the midst of the world, to render themselves profitable to society and fulfil the commandments of God. Feldkirchen's marriage had been the first defeat of the hierarchy; the emancipation of these thirteen Augustines was the second. Monachism, which had arisen at the time when the Church entered upon its period of enslavement and error, was destined to fall at the dawning of liberty and truth.

This daring step excited universal ferment in Wittemberg. Admiration was felt towards those men who thus came to take their part in the general labours, and they were received as brethren. At the same time a few outcries were heard against those who persisted in remaining lazily sheltered behind the walls of their monastery. The monks who remained faithful to their prior trembled in their cells; and the latter, carried away by the general movement, stopped the celebration of the low masses.

The smallest concession in so critical a moment necessarily precipitated the course of events. The prior's order created a great sensation in the town and university, and produced a sudden explosion. Among the students and citizens of Wittemberg were found some of those turbulent men whom the least excitement arouses and hurries into criminal disorders. They were exasperated at the idea of the low masses, which even the superstitious prior had suspended, still being said in the parish church; and on Tuesday the 3d of December, as the mass was about to be read, they suddenly advanced to the altar, took away the books, and drove the priests out of the chapel. The council and university were annoyed, and met to punish the authors of these misdeeds. But the passions once aroused are not easily quelled. The Cordeliers had not taken part in this movement of the Augustines. On the following day, the students posted a threatening placard on the gates of their convent; after that forty students entered their church, and although they refrained

from violence, they ridiculed the monks, so that the latter dared not say mass except in the choir. Towards evening the fathers were told to be upon their guard: "The students (it was said) are resolved to attack the monastery!" The frightened religioners, not knowing how to shelter themselves from these real or supposed attacks, hastily besought the council to protect them; a guard of soldiers was sent, but the enemy did not appear. The university caused the students who had taken part in these disturbances to be arrested. It was discovered that some were from Erfurth, where they had become notorious for their insubordination.[1] The penalties of the university were inflicted upon them.

And yet the necessity was felt of inquiring carefully into the lawfulness of monastic vows. A chapter of Augustine monks from Misnia and Thuringia assembled at Wittemberg in the month of December. They came to the same opinion as Luther. On the one hand they declared that monastic vows were not criminal, but on the other that they were not obligatory. "In Christ," said they, "there is neither layman nor monk; each one is at liberty to quit the monastery or to stay in it. Let him who goes forth beware lest he abuse his liberty; let him who remains obey his superiors, but through love." They next abolished mendicancy and the saying of masses for money; they also decreed that the best instructed among them should devote themselves to the teaching of the Word of God, and that the rest should support their brethren by the work of their own hands.[2]

Thus the question of vows appeared settled; but that of the mass was undecided. The elector still resisted the torrent, and protected an institution which he saw standing in all Christendom. The orders of so indulgent a prince could not long restrain the public feeling. Carlstadt's head in particular was affected by the general fermentation. Zealous, upright, and bold, ready, like Luther, to sacrifice every thing for the truth, he was inferior to the reformer in wisdom and moderation; he was not entirely exempt from vain-glory, and with a disposition inclined to examine matters to the bottom, he was defective in judgment and in clearness of ideas. Luther had dragged him from the mire of scholasticism, and directed him to the study of Scripture; but Carlstadt had not acknowledged with his friend the all-sufficiency of the Word of God. Accordingly he was often seen adopting the most singular interpretations. So long as Luther was at his side, the superiority of the master kept the scholar within due bounds. But now Carlstadt was free. In the university, in the

[1] Etliche unter den Bürgern, etliche unter den Studenten, says the prior in his complaint to the Elector. Corp. Ref. I. 483

[1] In summa es sollen die Aufruhr etliche Studenten von Erffurth erwerckt haben. Corp. Ref. i. 490.
[2] Corp. Ref. i. 456. The editors assign this decree to the month of October before the friars had quitted the convent at Wittemberg.

324

church, every where in Wittemberg, this little dark-featured man, who had never excelled in eloquence, might be heard proclaiming with great fervour ideas that were sometimes profound, but often enthusiastic and exaggerated. " What madness," exclaimed he, " to think that one must leave the Reformation to God's working alone ! A new order of things is beginning. The hand of man should interfere. Woe be to him who lags behind, and does not mount the breach in the cause of the Almighty."

The archdeacon's language communicated to others the impatience he felt himself. " All that the popes have ordained is impious," said certain upright and sincere men who followed his example. " Let us not become partakers in those abominations by allowing them to subsist any longer. What is condemned by the Word of God ought to be put down in the whole of Christendom, whatever may be the ordinances of men. If the heads of the State and of the Church will not do their duty, let us do ours. Let us renounce all negotiations, conferences, theses, and disputations, and let us apply the effectual remedy to so many evils. We need a second Elijah to throw down the altars of Baal."

The re-establishment of the Lord's Supper, in this moment of ferment and enthusiasm, unquestionably could not present the solemnity and holiness of its first institution by the Son of God, on the eve of his death, and almost at the foot of the cross. But if God now made use of weak and perhaps passionate men, it was nevertheless his hand that revived in the Church the feast of his love.

In the previous October, Carlstadt had already celebrated the Lord's Supper in private with twelve of his friends, in accordance with Christ's institution. On the Sunday before Christmas he gave out from the pulpit that on the day of our Lord's circumcision (the first day of the year) he would distribute the eucharist in both kinds (bread and wine) to all who might present themselves at the altar ; that he would omit all useless forms,[1] and in celebrating this mass would wear neither cope nor chasuble.

The affrighted council entreated the councillor Beyer to prevent such a flagrant irregularity ; and upon this Carlstadt resolved not to wait until the appointed time. On Christmas-day, 1521, he preached in the parish church on the necessity of quitting the mass and receiving the sacrament in both kinds. After the sermon he went to the altar ; pronounced the words of consecration in German, and then turning towards the attentive people, said with a solemn voice : " Whosoever feels the burden of his sins, and hungers and thirsts for the grace of God, let him come and receive the body

and blood of our Lord."[1] And then, without elevating the host, he distributed the bread and wine to all, saying ; " This is the cup of my blood, the blood of the new and everlasting Covenant."

Antagonist sentiments prevailed in the assembly. Some, feeling that a new grace from God had been given to the Church, approached the altar in silence and emotion. Others, attracted chiefly by the novelty, drew nigh with a certain sense of agitation and impatience. Five communicants alone had presented themselves in the confessional : the rest simply took part in the public confession of sins. Carlstadt gave a public absolution to all, imposing on them no other penance than this : " Sin no more." They concluded with singing the Agnus Dei.[2]

No one opposed Carlstadt ; these reforms had already obtained general assent. The archdeacon administered the Lord's Supper again on New Year's day, and on the Sunday following, and from that time it was regularly celebrated. Einsidlen, one of the elector's councillors, having reproached Carlstadt with seeking his own glory rather than the salvation of his hearers : " Mighty lord," replied he, " there is no form of death that can make me withdraw from Scripture. The Word has come upon me with such promptitude......Woe be to me if I preach it not !"[3] Shortly after, Carlstadt married.

In the month of January 1522, the council and university of Wittemberg regulated the celebration of the Lord's Supper according to the new ritual. They were, at the same time, engaged on the means of reviving the moral influence of religion ; for the Reformation was destined to restore simultaneously faith, worship, and morality. It was decreed not to tolerate mendicants, whether they were begging friars or not ; and that in every street there should be some pious man commissioned to take care of the poor, and summon open sinners before the university and the council.[4]

Thus fell the mass—the principal bulwark of Rome ; thus the Reformation passed from simple teaching into public worship. For three centuries the mass and transubstantiation had been peremptorily established.[5] From that period every thing in the Church had taken a new direction ; all things tended to the glory of man and the worship of the priest. The Holy Sacrament had been adored ; festivals had been instituted in honour of the sublimest of miracles ; the adoration of Mary had acquired a high importance ; the priest who, on his consecration, received the wonderful power of " making

---

[1] Und die anderen *Schirymstege* alle aussen lassen. Corp. Ref. i. 512.

[1] Wer mit Sünden beschwert und nach der Gnade Gottes hungrig und durstig. Corp. Ref. i. 540.
[2] Wenn man communicirt hat, so singt man : *Agnus Dei* carmen. Ibid.
[3] Mir ist das Wort fast in grosser Geschwindigkeit eingefallen. Ibid. 545.
[4] Keinen offenbaren Sünder zu dulden....Ibid. 540.
[5] By the Council of Lateran, in 1215.

the body of Christ," had been separated from the laity, and had become, according to Thomas Aquinas, a mediator between God and man;[1] celibacy had been proclaimed as an inviolable law; auricular confession had been enforced upon the people, and the cup denied them; for how could humble laymen be placed in the same rank as priests invested with the most august ministry? The mass was an insult to the Son of God: it was opposed to the perfect grace of His cross, and the spotless glory of His everlasting kingdom. But if it lowered the Saviour, it exalted the priest, whom it invested with the unparalleled power of reproducing, in his hand and at his will, the Sovereign Creator. From that time the Church seemed to exist not to preach the Gospel, but simply to reproduce Christ bodily.[2] The Roman pontiff, whose humblest servants created at pleasure the body of God himself, sat as God in the temple of God, and claimed a spiritual treasure, from which he drew at will indulgences for the pardon of souls.

Such were the gross errors which, for three centuries, had been imposed on the Church in conjunction with the mass. When the Reformation abolished this institution of man, it abolished these abuses also. The step taken by the archdeacon of Wittemberg was therefore one of a very extended range. The splendid festivals that used to amuse the people, the worship of the Virgin, the pride of the priesthood, the authority of the pope—all tottered with the mass. The glory was withdrawn from the priests, to return to Jesus Christ, and the Reformation took an immense stride in advance.

CHAPTER VII.

False Reform—The New Prophets—The Prophets at Wittemberg—Melancthon—The Elector—Luther—Carlstadt and the Images—Disturbances—Luther is called for—He does not hesitate—Dangers.

PREJUDICED men might have seen nothing in the work that was going on but the effects of an empty enthusiasm. The very facts were to prove the contrary, and demonstrate that there is a wide gulf between a Reformation based on the Word of God and a fanatical excitement.

Whenever a great religious ferment takes place in the Church, some impure elements always appear with the manifestations of truth. We see the rise of one or more false reforms proceeding from man, and which serve as a testimony or countersign to the

real reform. Thus many false messiahs in the time of Christ testified that the real Messiah had appeared. The Reformation of the sixteenth century could not be accomplished without presenting a similar phenomenon. In the small town of Zwickau it was first manifested.

In that place there lived a few men who, agitated by the great events that were then stirring all Christendom, aspired at direct revelations from the Deity, instead of meekly desiring sanctification of heart, and who asserted that they were called to complete the Reformation so feebly sketched out by Luther. " What is the use," said they, " of clinging so closely to the Bible? The Bible! always the Bible! Can the Bible preach to us? Is it sufficient for our instruction? If God had designed to instruct us by a book, would he not have sent us a Bible from heaven? It is by the Spirit alone that we can be enlightened. God himself speaks to us. God himself reveals to us what we should do, and what we should preach." Thus did these fanatics, like the adherents of Rome, attack the fundamental principle on which the entire Reformation is founded —the all-sufficiency of the Word of God.

A simple clothier, Nicholas Storch by name, announced that the angel Gabriel had appeared to him during the night,[1] and that after communicating matters which he could not yet reveal, said to him : " Thou shalt sit on my throne." A former student of Wittemberg, one Mark Stubner, joined Storch, and immediately forsook his studies; for he had received direct from God (said he) the gift of interpreting the Holy Scriptures. Another weaver, Mark Thomas, was added to their number; and a new adept, Thomas Munzer, a man of fanatical character, gave a regular organization to this rising sect. Storch, desirous of following Christ's example, selected from among his followers twelve apostles and seventy-two disciples. All loudly declared, as a sect in our own days has done, that apostles and prophets were at length restored to the Church of God.[2]

The new prophets, pretending to walk in the footsteps of those of old, began to proclaim their mission : " Woe ! woe !" said they; " a Church governed by men so corrupt as the bishops cannot be the Church of Christ. The impious rulers of Christendom will be overthrown. In five, six, or seven years, a universal desolation will come upon the world. The Turk will seize upon Germany; all the priests will be put to death, even those who are married. No ungodly man, no sinner will remain alive; and after the earth has been purified by blood, God will then set up a kingdom; Storch will be put in possession of the supreme authority,

---

[1] Sacerdos constituitur medius inter Deum et populum. Th. Aquin. Summa, iii. 22.
[2] Perfectio hujus sacramenti non est in usu fidelium, sed in consecratione materiæ. Ibid. Quest. 80.

[1] Advolasse Gabrielem Angelum. Camerarii Vita. Mel. p. 48.
[2] Breviter, de sese prædicant viros esse propheticos et apostolicos. Corp. Ref. i. 514. The author alludes to the followers of Irving.—Tr.

and commit the government of the nations to the saints.[1] Then there will be one faith, one baptism. The day of the Lord is at hand, and the end of the world draweth nigh. Woe! woe! woe!" Then declaring that infant baptism was valueless, the new prophets called upon all men to come and receive from their hands the true baptism, as a sign of their introduction into the new Church of God.

This language made a deep impression on the people. Many pious souls were stirred by the thought that prophets were again restored to the Church, and all those who were fond of the marvellous threw themselves into the arms of the fanatics of Zwickau.

But scarcely had this old heresy, which had already appeared in the days of Montanism and in the Middle Ages, found followers, when it met with a powerful antagonist in the Reformation. Nicholas Hausmann, of whom Luther gave this powerful testimony, "What we preach, he practises,"[2] was pastor of Zwickau. This good man did not allow himself to be misled by the pretensions of the false prophets. He checked the innovations that Storch and his followers desired to introduce, and his two deacons acted in unison with him. The fanatics, rejected by the ministers of the Church, fell into another extravagance. They formed meetings in which revolutionary doctrines were professed. The people were agitated, and disturbances broke out. A priest, carrying the host, was pelted with stones;[3] the civil authority interfered, and cast the ringleaders into prison.[4] Exasperated by this proceeding, and eager to vindicate themselves and to obtain redress, Storch, Mark Thomas, and Stubner repaired to Wittemberg.[5]

They arrived there on the 27th of December 1521. Storch led the way with the gait and bearing of a trooper.[6] Mark Thomas and Stubner followed him. The disorder then prevailing in Wittemberg was favourable to their designs. The youths of the academy and the citizens, already profoundly agitated and in a state of excitement, were a soil well fitted to receive these new prophets.

Thinking themselves sure of support, they immediately called on the professors of the university, in order to obtain their sanction. "We are sent by God to instruct the people," said they. "We have held familiar conversations with the Lord; we know what will happen;[7] in a word, we are apostles and prophets, and appeal to Dr Luther." This strange language astonished the professors.

"Who has commissioned you to preach?" asked Melancthon of his old pupil Stubner, whom he received into his house. "The Lord our God."—"Have you written any books?"—"The Lord our God has forbidden me to do so." Melancthon was agitated: he grew alarmed and astonished.

"There are, indeed, extraordinary spirits in these men," said he; "but what spirits? ......Luther alone can decide. On the one hand, let us beware of quenching the Spirit of God, and, on the other, of being led astray by the spirit of Satan."

Storch, being of a restless disposition, soon quitted Wittemberg. Stubner remained. Animated by an eager spirit of proselytism, he went through the city, speaking now to one, then to another; and many acknowledged him as a prophet from God. He addressed himself more particularly to a Swabian named Cellarius, a friend of Melancthon's, who kept a school in which he used to instruct a great number of young people, and who soon fully acknowledged the mission of the new prophets.

Melancthon now became still more perplexed and uneasy. It was not so much the visions of the Zwickau prophets that disturbed him, as their new doctrine on baptism. It seemed to him conformable with reason, and he thought that it was deserving examination; "for" said he, "we must neither admit nor reject any thing lightly."[1]

Such is the spirit of the Reformation. Melancthon's hesitation and anxiety are a proof of the uprightness of his heart, more honourable to him, perhaps, than any systematic opposition would have been.

The elector himself, whom Melancthon styled "the lamp of Israel,"[2] hesitated. Prophets and apostles in the electorate of Saxony as in Jerusalem of old! "This is a great matter," said he; "and as a layman, I cannot understand it. But rather than fight against God, I would take a staff in my hand, and descend from my throne."

At length he informed the professors, by his councillors, that they had sufficient trouble in hand at Wittemberg; that in all probability these pretensions of the Zwickau prophets were only a temptation of the devil; and that the wisest course, in his opinion, would be to let the matter drop of itself; nevertheless that, under all circumstances, whenever his highness should clearly perceive God's will, he would take counsel of neither brother nor mother, and that he was ready to suffer every thing in the cause of truth.[3]

Luther in the Wartburg was apprized of

---

[1] Ut rerum potiatur et instauret sacra et respublicas tradat sanctis viris tenendas. Camerar. Vita Mel. p. 45.
[2] Quod nos docemus, ille facit.
[3] Einen Priester der das Venerabile getragen mit Steinen geworfen. Seck. p. 482.
[4] Sunt et illic in vincula conjecti. Mel. Corp. Ref. i. 513.
[5] Huc advolarunt tres viri, duo lanifices, literarum rudes, literatus tertius est. Ibid.
[6] Incedens more et habitu militum istorum quos Lansknecht dicimus. L. Epp. ii. 245.
[7] Esse sibi cum Deo familiaria colloquia, videre futura ... Mel. Electori, 27th Dec. 1521. Corp. Ref. i. 514.

[1] Censebat enim neque admittendum neque rejiciendum quicquam temere. Camer. Vita Mel. p. 49.
[2] Electori lucernæ Israel. Ibid. p. 513.
[3] Darüber auch leiden was S. C. G. leiden sollt. Ibid. p. 537.

the agitation prevailing in the court and at Wittemberg. Strange men had appeared, and the source whence their mission proceeded was unknown. He saw immediately that God had permitted these afflicting events to humble his servants, and to excite them by trials to strive more earnestly after sanctification.

"Your electoral grace," wrote he to Frederick, "has for many years been collecting relics from every country. God has satisfied your desire, and sent you, without cost or trouble, a whole *cross*, with nails, spears, and scourges......Health and prosperity to the new relic!......Only let your highness fearlessly stretch out your arm, and suffer the nails to enter your flesh!...... I always expected that Satan would send us this plague."

But at the same time nothing appeared to him more urgent than to secure for others the liberty that he claimed for himself. He had not two weights and two measures. "Beware of throwing them into prison," wrote he to Spalatin. "Let not the prince dip his hand in the blood of these new prophets."[1] Luther went far beyond his age, and even beyond many other reformers, on the subject of religious liberty.

Circumstances were becoming every day more serious in Wittemberg.[2]

Carlstadt rejected many of the doctrines of the new prophets, and particularly their anabaptism ; but there is a contagion in religious enthusiasm that a head like his could not easily resist. From the arrival of the men of Zwickau in Wittemberg, Carlstadt accelerated his movements in the direction of violent reforms. "We must fall upon every ungodly practice, and overthrow them all in a day," said he.[3] He brought together all the passages of Scripture against images, and inveighed with increasing energy against the idolatry of Rome. "They fall down— they crawl before these idols," exclaimed he; "they burn tapers before them, and make them offerings......Let us arise and tear them from the altars!"

These words were not uttered in vain before the people. They entered the churches, carried away the images, broke them in pieces, and burnt them.[4] It would have been better to wait until their abolition had been legally proclaimed; but some thought that the caution of the chiefs would compromise the Reformation itself.

To judge by the language of these enthusiasts, there were no true Christians in Wittemberg save those who went not to confession, who attacked the priests, and who ate meat on fast days. If any one was suspected of not rejecting all the rites of the Church as an invention of the devil, he was set down as a worshipper of Baal. "We must form a Church," cried they, "composed of saints only!"

The citizens of Wittemberg laid before the council certain articles which it was forced to accept. Many of these regulations were conformable to evangelical morals. They required more particularly that all houses of public amusement should be closed.

But Carlstadt soon went still farther : he began to despise learning ; and the old professor was heard from his chair advising his pupils to return home, to take up the spade, to guide the plough, and quietly cultivate the earth, because man was ordained to eat bread in the sweat of his brow. George Mohr, the master of the boys' school at Wittemberg, led away by the same fanaticism, called to the assembled citizens from the window of his schoolroom to come and take away their children. Why should they be made study, since Storch and Stubner had never been at the university, and yet they were prophets?......A mechanic, therefore, was as well qualified as all the doctors in the world, and perhaps better, to preach the Gospel.

Thus arose doctrines in direct opposition to the Reformation, which had been prepared by the revival of letters. It was with the weapons of theological learning that Luther had attacked Rome ; and the enthusiasts of Wittemberg, like the fanatical monks with whom Erasmus and Reuchlin had contended, presumed to trample all human learning under foot. If this vandalism succeeded in holding its ground, the hopes of the world were lost ; and another irruption of barbarians would extinguish the light that God had kindled in Christendom.

The results of these strange discourses soon showed themselves. Men's minds were absorbed, agitated, diverted from the Gospel; the university became disorganized ; the demoralized students broke the bonds of discipline and dispersed ; and the governments of Germany recalled their subjects.[1] Thus the men who desired to reform and vivify every thing, were on the point of ruining all.[2] One struggle more (exclaimed the friends of Rome, who on all sides were regaining their confidence), one last struggle, and all will be ours!

Promptly to check the excesses of these fanatics was the only means of saving the Reformation. But who could do it ? Melancthon ? He was too young, too weak, too much agitated himself by these strange phenomena. The elector ? He was the most pacific man of his age. To build castles at Altenburg, Weimar, Lochau, and Coburg ; to adorn churches with the beautiful pictures

---

[1] Ne princeps manus cruentet in prophetis. L. Epp. ii. 135.
[2] Ubi fiebant omnia in dies difficiliora. Camer. Vita Mel. p. 49.
[3] Irruendum et demoliendum statim. Ibid.
[4] Die Bilder zu stürmen und aus den Kirchen zu werfen. Math. p. 31.

[1] Etliche Fürsten ihre Bewandten abgefordert. Corp. Ref. i. 560.
[2] Perdita et funditus diruta. Camer. Vit. Mel. p. 52.

of Lucas Cranach ; to improve the singing in the chapels ; to advance the prosperity of his university ; to promote the happiness of his subjects ; to stop in the midst of the children whom he met playing in the streets, and give them little presents :—such were the gentle occupations of his life. And now in his advanced age, would he contend with fanatics—would he oppose violence to violence ? How could the good and pious Frederick make up his mind to this ?

The disease continued to spread, and no one stood forward to check it. Luther was far from Wittemberg. Confusion and ruin had taken hold of the city. The Reformation had seen an enemy spring from its own bosom more formidable than popes and emperors. It was on the very verge of the abyss.

Luther! Luther! was the general and unanimous cry at Wittemberg. The citizens called for him earnestly ; the professors desired his advice ; the prophets themselves appealed to him. All entreated him to return.[1]

We may imagine what was passing in the reformer's mind. All the terrors of Rome were nothing in comparison with what now wrung his heart. It is from the very midst of the Reformation that its enemies have gone forth. It is preying upon its own vitals ; and that doctrine, which alone had brought peace to his troubled heart, becomes the occasion of fatal disturbances to the Church.

"If I knew," he had once said, "that my doctrine injured one man, one single man, however lowly and obscure (which it cannot, for it is the Gospel itself), I would rather die ten times than not retract it."[2] And now a whole city, and that city Wittemberg, is falling into disorder ! True, his doctrine has no share in this ; but from every quarter of Germany voices are heard accusing him of it. Pains more keen than he had ever felt before assail him now, and new temptations agitate him. "Can such then be the end of this great work of the Reformation ?" said he to himself. Impossible !—he rejects these doubts. God has begun,......God will perfect the work. " I creep in deep humility to the grace of the Lord,"[3] exclaimed he, " and beseech him that his name may remain attached to this work ; and that if anything impure be mixed up with it, he will remember that I am a sinful man."

The news communicated to Luther of the inspiration of these new prophets, and of their sublime interviews with God, did not stagger him one moment. He knew the depth, the anguish, the humiliation of the spiritual life : at Erfurth and Wittemberg he had made trial of the power of God, which

did not so easily permit him to believe that God appeared to his creatures and conversed with them. " Ask these prophets," wrote he to Melancthon, " whether they have felt those spiritual torments, those creations of God, those deaths and hells which accompany a real regeneration......[1] And if they speak to you only of agreeable things, of tranquil impressions, of devotion and piety, as they say, do not believe them, although they should pretend to have been transported to the third heaven. Before Christ could attain his glory, he was compelled to suffer death ; and in like manner the believer must go through the bitterness of sin before he can obtain peace. Do you desire to know the time, place, and manner in which God talks with men ? Listen : *As a lion so hath he broken all my bones : I am cast out from before his face, and my soul is abased even to the gates of hell......*No ! The Divine Majesty (as they call Him) does not speak face to face with men, so that they may see Him ; for *no man* (says He) *can see my face and live.*"

But his firm conviction of the delusion under which these prophets were labouring, served but to augment Luther's grief. Has the great truth of salvation by grace so quickly lost its charms that men turn aside from it to follow fables? He begins to feel that the work is not so easy as he had thought at first. He stumbles at the first stone that the deceitfulness of the human heart had placed in his path ; he is bowed down by grief and anxiety. He resolves, at the hazard of his life, to remove it out of the way of his people, and decides on returning to Wittemberg.

At that time he was threatened by imminent dangers. The enemies of the Reformation fancied themselves on the very eve of destroying it. George of Saxony, equally indisposed towards Rome and Wittemberg, had written, as early as the 16th of October 1521, to Duke John, the elector's brother, to draw him over to the side of the enemies of the Reformation. " Some," said he, " deny that the soul is immortal. Others (and these are monks !) attach bells to swine and set them to drag the relics of St. Anthony through the streets, and then throw them into the mire.[2] All this is the fruit of Luther's teaching ! Entreat your brother the elector either to punish the ungodly authors of these innovations, or at least publicly to declare his opinion of them. Our changing beard and hair remind us that we have reached the latter portion of our course. and urge us to put an end to such great evils."

After this George departed to take his seat in the imperial government at Nuremberg.

---

[1] Lutherum revocavimus ex heremo suo magnis de causis. Corp. Ref. i. 566.
[2] Möchte ich ehe zehn Tode leyden. *Wieder Emser.* L. Opp. xviii. 613.
[3] Ich krieche zu seiner Gnaden. Ibid. 615.

[1] Quæras num experti sint spirituales illas angustias et nativitates divinas, mortes infernosque. L. Epp. ii. 215.
[2] Mit Schweinen und Schellen ...in Koth geworfen Weimar Ann. Seck. p. 482.

He had scarcely arrived when he made every exertion to urge it to adopt measures of severity. In effect, on the 21st of January, this body passed an edict, in which it complained bitterly that the priests said mass without being robed in their sacerdotal garments, consecrated the sacrament in German, administered it without having received the requisite confession from the communicants, placed it in the hands of laymen,[1] and were not even careful to ascertain that those who stood forward to receive it were fasting.

Accordingly the imperial government desired the bishops to seek out and punish severely all the innovators within their respective dioceses. The latter hastened to comply with these orders.

Such was the moment selected by Luther for his reappearance on the stage. He saw the danger; he foreboded incalculable disasters. " Erelong," said he, " there will be a disturbance in the empire, carrying princes, magistrates, and bishops before it. The people have eyes: they will not, they cannot be led by force. All Germany will run blood.[2] Let us stand up as a wall to preserve our nation in this dreadful day of God's anger."

CHAPTER VIII.

Departure from the Wartburg—New Position—Luther and Primitive Catholicism — Meeting at the Black Bear — Luther's Letter to the Elector—Return to Wittemberg— Sermon at Wittemberg — Charity—The Word—How the Reformation was brought about — Faith in Christ—Its Effects—Didymus—Carlstadt—The Prophets—Interview with Luther—End of the Struggle.

SUCH were Luther's thoughts; but he beheld a still more imminent danger. At Wittemberg, the conflagration, far from dying away, became fiercer every day. From the heights of the Wartburg, Luther could perceive in the horizon the frightful gleams, the signal of devastation, shooting at intervals through the air. Is not he the only one who can give aid in this extremity? Shall he not throw himself into the midst of the flames to quench their fury? In vain his enemies prepare to strike the decisive blow; in vain the elector entreats him not to leave the Wartburg, and to prepare his justification against the next diet. He has a more important task to perform — to justify the Gospel itself. " More serious intelligence reaches me every day," wrote he. " I shall set out: circumstances positively require me to do so."[3]

Accordingly, he rose on the 3d of March

with the determination of leaving the Wartburg for ever. He bade adieu to its time-worn towers and gloomy forests. He passed beyond those walls where the excommunications of Leo X. and the sword of Charles V. were unable to reach him. He descended the mountain. The world that lay at his feet and in the midst of which he was about to appear again, would soon perhaps call loudly for his death. But that mattered not! he went forward rejoicing: for in the name of the Lord he was returning among his fellowmen. [1]

Time had moved on. Luther was quitting the Wartburg for a cause very different from that for which he had entered it. He had gone thither as the assailant of the old tradition and of the ancient doctors; he left it as the defender of the doctrine of the apostles against new adversaries. He had entered it as an innovator, and as an impugner of the ancient hierarchy; he left it as a conservative and champion of the faith of Christians. Hitherto Luther had seen but one thing in his work,—the triumph of justification by faith; and with this weapon he had thrown down mighty superstitions. But if there was a time for destroying, there was also a time for building up. Beneath those ruins with which his strong arm had strewn the plain,—beneath those crumpled letters of indulgence, those broken tiaras and tattered cowls,—beneath so many Roman abuses and errors that lay in confusion upon the field of battle, he discerned and discovered the primitive Catholic Church, reappearing still the same, and coming forth as from a long period of trial, with its unchangeable doctrines and heavenly accents. He could distinguish it from Rome, welcoming and embracing it with joy. Luther effected nothing new in the world, as he has been falsely charged, he did not raise a building for the future that had no connexion with the past; he uncovered, he opened to the light of day the ancient foundations, on which thorns and thistles had sprung up, and continuing the construction of the temple, he built simply on the foundations laid by the apostles. Luther perceived that the ancient and primitive Church of the apostles must, on the one hand, be restored in opposition to the Papacy, by which it had been so long oppressed; and on the other, be defended against enthusiasts and unbelievers, who pretended to disown it, and who, regardless of all that God had done in times past, were desirous of beginning an entirely new work. Luther was no longer exclusively the man of one doctrine,—that of justification,—although he always assigned it the highest place; he became the man of the whole Christian theology; and while he still believed that the Church was essentially the congregation of saints, he was careful not to despise the visible Church, and ac-

[1] In ihre falsche Hände reiche. L. Opp. xviii. 285.
[2] Germaniam in sanguine natare. L. Epp. ii. 157
[3] Ita enim res postulat ipsa. Ibid. 135.

[1] So machte er sich mit unglaublicher Freudigkeit des Geistes, im Nähmen Gottes auf den Weg. Seck. p. 458.

knowledged the assembly of the elect as the kingdom of God. Thus was a great change effected, at this time, in Luther's heart, in his theology, and in the work of renovation that God was carrying on in the world. The Roman hierarchy might perhaps have driven the reformer to extremes; the sects which then so boldly raised their heads brought him back to the true path of moderation. The sojourn in the Wartburg divides the history of the Reformation into two periods.

Luther was riding slowly on the road to Wittemberg: it was already the second day of his journey, and Shrove Tuesday. Towards evening a terrible storm burst forth, and the roads were flooded. Two Swiss youths, who were travelling in the same direction as himself, were hastening onwards to find a shelter in the city of Jena. They had studied at Basle, and the celebrity of Wittemberg attracted them to that university. Travelling on foot, fatigued, and wet through, John Kessler of St. Gall and his companion quickened their steps. The city was all in commotion with the amusements of the carnival; balls, masquerades, and noisy feasting engrossed the people of Jena; and when the two travellers arrived, they could find no room at any of the inns. At last they were directed to the *Black Bear*, outside the city gates. Dejected and harassed, they repaired thither slowly. The landlord received them kindly.[1] They took their seats near the open door of the public room, ashamed of the state in which the storm had placed them, and not venturing to go in. At one of the tables sat a solitary man in a knight's dress, wearing a red cap on his head and breeches over which fell the skirts of his doublet; his right hand rested on the pommel of his sword, his left grasped the hilt; and before him lay an open book, which he appeared to be reading with great attention.[2] At the noise made by the entrance of these two young men, he raised his head, saluted them affably, and invited them to come and sit at his table; then presenting them with a glass of beer, and alluding to their accent, he said: "You are Swiss, I perceive; but from what canton?"—"From St. Gall."—"If you are going to Wittemberg, you will there meet with a fellow-countryman, Doctor Schurff."—Encouraged by this kind reception, they added: "Sir, could you inform us where Martin Luther is at present?"—"I know for certain," replied the knight, "that he is not at Wittemberg; but he will be there shortly. Philip Melancthon is there. Study Greek and Hebrew, that you may clearly understand the Holy Scriptures."—"If God spare our lives," observed one of the young men, "we will not return home without having seen and heard Doctor Luther; for it is on his account that we have undertaken this long journey. We know that he desires to abolish the priesthood and the mass; and as our parents destined us to the priesthood from our infancy, we should like to know clearly on what grounds he rests his proposition." The knight was silent for a moment, and then resumed: "Where have you been studying hitherto?"—"At Basle."—"Is Erasmus of Rotterdam still there? what is he doing?" They replied to his questions, and there was another pause. The two Swiss knew not what to think. "Is it not strange," thought they, "that this knight talks to us of Schurff, Melancthon, and Erasmus, and on the necessity of learning Greek and Hebrew."—"My dear friends," said the unknown suddenly, "what do they think of Luther in Switzerland?"—"Sir," replied Kessler, "opinions are very divided about him there as every where else. Some cannot extol him enough; and others condemn him as an abominable heretic."—"Ha! the priests, no doubt," said the stranger.

The knight's cordiality had put the students at their ease. They longed to know what book he was reading at the moment of their arrival. The knight had closed it, and placed it by his side. At last Kessler's companion ventured to take it up. To the great astonishment of the two young men, it was the Hebrew Psalter! The student laid it down immediately, and as if to divert attention from the liberty he had taken, said: "I would willingly give one of my fingers to know that language."—"You will attain your wish," said the stranger, "if you will only take the trouble to learn it."

A few minutes after, Kessler heard the landlord calling him; the poor Swiss youth feared something had gone wrong; but the host whispered to him: "I perceive that you have a great desire to see and hear Luther; well! it is he who is seated beside you." Kessler took this for a joke, and said: "Mr Landlord, you want to make a fool of me."—"It is he in very truth," replied the host; "but do not let him see that you know him." Kessler made no answer, but returned into the room and took his seat at the table, burning to repeat to his comrade what he had just heard. But how could he manage it? At last he thought of leaning forward, as if he were looking towards the door, and then whispered into his friend's ear: "The landlord assures me that this man is Luther."—"Perhaps he said Hütten," replied his comrade; "you did not hear him distinctly."—"It may be so," returned Kessler; "the host said: It is Hütten; the two names are pretty much alike, and I mistook one for the other."

At that moment the noise of horses was heard before the inn: two merchants, who

331

desired a lodging, entered the room; they took off their spurs, laid down their cloaks, and one of them placed beside him on the table an unbound book, which soon attracted the knight's notice. " What book is that ? " asked he.—" A commentary on some of the Gospels and Epistles by Doctor Luther," replied the merchant; " it is just published." —" I shall procure it shortly," said the knight.

At this moment the host came to announce that supper was ready. The two students, fearing the expense of such a meal in company with the knight Ulrich of Hütten and two wealthy merchants, took the landlord aside, and begged him to serve them with something apart. " Come along, my friends," replied the landlord of the Black Bear; " take your place at table beside this gentleman; I will charge you moderately." —" Come along," said the knight, " I will settle the score."

During this meal, the stranger knight uttered many simple and edifying remarks. The students and the merchants were all ears, and paid more attention to his words than to the dishes set before them. " Luther must either be an angel from heaven or a devil from hell," said one of the merchants in course of conversation ; " I would readily give ten florins if I could meet Luther and confess to him."

When supper was over, the merchants left the table; the two Swiss remained alone with the knight, who, taking a large glass of beer, rose and said solemnly, after the manner of the country: " Swiss, one glass more for thanks." As Kessler was about to take the glass, the unknown set it down again, and offered him one filled with wine, saying: " You are not accustomed to beer."

He then arose, flung a military cloak over his shoulders, and extending his hand to the students, said to them: " When you reach Wittemberg, salute Dr Schurff on my part." —" Most willingly," replied they; " but what name shall we give ?"—" Tell him simply," added Luther, " He that is to come salutes you." With these words he quitted the room, leaving them full of admiration at his kindness and good nature.

Luther, for it was really he, continued his journey. It will be remembered that he had been laid under the ban of the empire; whoever met and recognised him, might seize him. But at the time when he was engaged in an undertaking that exposed him to every risk, he was calm and serene, and conversed cheerfully with those whom he met on the road.

It was not that he deceived himself: he saw the future big with storms. " Satan," said he, " is enraged, and all around are plotting death and hell.[1] Nevertheless, I go forward, and throw myself in the way of the emperor and of the pope, having no protector save God in heaven. Power has been given to all men to kill me wherever they find me. But Christ is the Lord of all; if it be His will that I be put to death, so be it ! "

On that same day, Ash-Wednesday, Luther reached Borna, a small town near Leipsic. He felt it his duty to inform the prince of the bold step he was about to take; and accordingly alighted at the Guide Hotel and wrote the following letter :—

" Grace and peace from God our Father, and from our Lord Jesus Christ !

" Most serene Elector, gracious Lord ! The events that have taken place at Wittemberg, to the great reproach of the Gospel, have caused me such pain that if I were not confident of the truth of our cause, I should have given way to despair.

" Your highness knows this, or if not, be it known to you now, that I received the Gospel not from men but from heaven, through our Lord Jesus Christ. If I called for discussion, it was not because I had any doubts of the truth, but in humility, and in the hope to win over others. But since my humility is turned against the Gospel, my conscience compels me now to act otherwise. I have sufficiently given way to your highness by passing this year in retirement. The devil knows well that I did not do so through fear. I should have entered Worms had there been as many devils in the city as tiles on the house-tops. Now Duke George, with whom your highness frightens me, is yet much less to be feared than a single devil. If that which is passing at Wittemberg were taking place at Leipsic (the duke's residence), I would immediately mount my horse to go thither, although (may your highness pardon these words) for nine whole days together it were to rain nothing but Duke Georges, and each one nine times more furious than he is. What is he thinking of in attacking me ? Does he take Christ my Lord for a man of straw ?[1] O Lord, be pleased to avert the terrible judgment which is impending over him !

" Be it known to your highness that I am going to Wittemberg under a protection far higher than that of princes and electors. I think not of soliciting your highness's support, and, far from desiring your protection, I would rather protect you myself. If I knew that your highness could or would protect me, I would not go to Wittemberg at all. There is no sword that can further this cause. God alone must do every thing without the help or concurrence of man. He who has the greatest faith is he who is most able to protect. But I observe that your highness is still weak in faith.

" But since your highness desires to know what you have to do, I will answer with all deference : your highness has already done

---

[1] Furit Satanas; et fremunt vicini undique, nescio quot mortibus et infernis. L. Epp. ii. 153.

[1] Er hält meinen Herrn Christum für ein Mann aus Stroh geflochten. L. Epp. ii. 139.

too much, and ought to do nothing at all. God will not and cannot endure either your cares and labours or mine. Let your highness's conduct be guided by this.

" As for what concerns me, your highness must act as an elector; you must let the orders of his imperial majesty take their course in your towns and rural districts. You must offer no resistance if men desire to seize or kill me;[1] for no one should resist dominions except He who has established them.

" Let your highness leave the gates open, and respect safe-conducts, if my enemies in person or their envoys come in search of me into your highness's states. Every thing shall be done without trouble or danger to yourself.

" I have written this letter in haste, that you may not be made uneasy at hearing of my arrival. I have to do with a very different man from Duke George. He knows me well, and I know him pretty well.

" Given at Borna, at the inn of the Guide, this Ash-Wednesday 1522.

" Your electoral highness's
" Very humble servant,
" MARTIN LUTHER."

It was thus Luther drew nigh to Wittemberg. He wrote to his prince, but not to excuse himself. An imperturbable confidence filled his heart. He saw the hand of God in this cause, and that was sufficient for him. The heroism of faith can never be carried farther. One of the editions of Luther's works has the following remark in the margin of this letter: " This is a wonderful writing of the third and last Elias!"[2]

Luther re-entered Wittemberg on Friday the 7th March, having been five days on the way from Eisenach. Doctors, students, and citizens, all broke forth in rejoicings; for they had recovered the pilot who alone could extricate the vessel from the shoals among which it was entangled.

The elector, who was at Lockau with his court, felt great emotion as he read the reformer's letter. He was desirous of vindicating him before the diet: " Let him address me a letter," wrote the prince to Schurff, " explaining the motives of his return to Wittemberg, and let him say also that he returned without my permission." Luther consented.

" I am ready to incur the displeasure of your highness and the anger of the whole world," wrote he to the prince. " Are not the Wittembergers my sheep? Has not God intrusted them to me? And ought I not, if necessary, to expose myself to death for their sakes? Besides, I fear to see a terrible outbreak in Germany by which God will punish

our nation. Let your highness be well assured, and doubt not that the decrees of heaven are very different from those of Nuremberg."[1] This letter was written on the very day of Luther's arrival at Wittemberg.

On the following day, being the eve of the first Sunday in Lent, Luther visited Jerome Schurff. Melancthon, Jonas, Amsdorff, and Augustin Schurff, Jerome's brother, were there assembled. Luther eagerly questioned them, and they were informing him of all that had taken place, when two foreign students were announced, desiring to speak with Dr. Jerome. On entering this assembly of doctors, the two young men of St. Gall were at first abashed; but they soon recovered themselves on discovering the knight of the Black Bear among them. The latter immediately went up to them, greeted them as old acquaintances, and smiled as he pointed to one of the doctors: " This is Philip Melancthon, whom I mentioned to you." The two Swiss remained all day with the doctors of Wittemberg, in remembrance of the meeting at Jena.

One great thought absorbed the reformer's mind, and checked the joy he felt at meeting his friends once more. Unquestionably the character in which he was now to appear was obscure: he was about to raise his voice in a small town of Saxony, and yet his undertaking had all the importance of an event which was to influence the destinies of the world. Many nations and many ages were to feel its effects. It was a question whether that doctrine which he had derived from the Word of God, and which was ordained to exert so mighty an influence on the future development of the human race, would be stronger than the destructive principles that threatened its existence. It was a question whether it were possible to reform without destroying, and clear the way to new developments without annihilating the old. To silence fanatical men inspired by the energy of a first enthusiasm; to master an unbridled multitude, to calm it down, to lead it back to order, peace, and truth; to break the course of the impetuous torrent which threatened to overthrow the rising edifice of the Reformation, and to scatter its ruins far and wide:—such was the task for which Luther had returned to Wittemberg. But would his influence be sufficient for this? The event alone could show.

The reformer's heart shuddered at the thought of the struggle that awaited him. He raised his head as a lion provoked to fight shakes his long mane. " We must now trample Satan under foot, and contend against the angel of darkness," said he. " If our adversaries do not retire of their own accord, Christ will know how to compel them. We

[1] Und ja nicht wehren....so sie mich fahen oder tödten will. L. Epp. ii. 140.
[2] Der wahre, dritte und lezte Elias....L. Opp. (L.) xviii. 271.

[1] L. Epp. ii. 143. Luther was forced to alter this expression at the elector's request.

who trust in the Lord of life and of death are ourselves lords of life and of death."[1]

But at the same time the impetuous reformer, as if restrained by a superior power, refused to employ the anathemas and thunders of the Word, and became an humble pastor, a gentle shepherd of souls. "It is with the Word that we must fight," said he, "by the Word must we overthrow and destroy what has been set up by violence. I will not make use of force against the superstitious and unbelieving. Let him who believeth draw nigh! let him who believeth not keep afar off! no one must be constrained. Liberty is the very essence of faith."[2]

The next day was Sunday. On that day the doctor, whom for nearly a year the lofty ramparts of the Wartburg have concealed from every eye, will reappear before the people in the pulpit of the church. It was rumoured in Wittemberg that Luther was come back, and that he was going to preach. This news alone, passing from mouth to mouth, had already given a powerful diversion to the ideas by which the people were misled. They are going to see the hero of Worms. The people crowded together, and were affected by various emotions. On Sunday morning the church was filled with an attentive and excited crowd.

Luther divines all the sentiments of his congregation; he goes up into the pulpit; there he stands in the presence of the flock that he had once led as a docile sheep, but which has broken from him like an untamed bull. His language is simple, noble, yet full of strength and gentleness: one might have supposed him to be a tender father returning to his children, inquiring into their conduct, and kindly telling them what report he had heard about them. He candidly acknowledges the progress they have made in faith; and by this means prepares and captivates their minds. He then continues in these words:—

"But we need something more than faith; we need charity. If a man who bears a sword in his hand be alone, it is of little consequence whether it be sheathed or not; but if he is in the midst of a crowd, he should act so as to wound nobody.

"What does a mother do to her infant? At first she gives it milk, then some very light food. If she were to begin by giving it meat and wine, what would be the consequence?......

"So should we act towards our brethren. My friend, have you been long enough at the breast? It is well! but permit your brother to drink as long as yourself.

"Observe the sun! He dispenses two things, light and heat. There is no king powerful enough to bend aside his rays; they come straight to us; but heat is radiated and communicated in every direction. Thus faith, like light, should always be straight and inflexible; but charity, like heat, should radiate on every side, and bend to all the wants of our brethren."

Luther having thus prepared his hearers, began to press them more closely:

"The abolition of the mass, say you, is in conformity with Scripture: Agreed! But what order, what decency have you observed? It behoved you to offer up fervent prayers to the Lord, and apply to the public authority; then might every man have acknowledged that the thing was of God."

Thus spake Luther. This dauntless man, who at Worms had withstood the princes of the earth, produced a deep impression on the minds of his hearers by these words of wisdom and of peace. Carlstadt and the prophets of Zwickau, so great and powerful for a few weeks, and who had tyrannized over and agitated Wittemberg, had shrunk into pigmies beside the captive of the Wartburg.

"The mass," continued he, "is a bad thing; God is opposed to it; it ought to be abolished; and I would that throughout the whole world it were replaced by the Supper of the Gospel. But let no one be torn from it by force. We must leave the matter in God's hands. His Word must act, and not we. And why so, you will ask? Because I do not hold men's hearts in my hand, as the potter holds the clay. We have a right to speak; we have not the right to act. Let us preach: the rest belongs unto God. Were I to employ force, what should I gain? Grimace, formality, apings, human ordinances, and hypocrisy......But there would be no sincerity of heart, nor faith, nor charity. Where these three are wanting, all is wanting, and I would not give a pear-stalk for such a result.[1]

"Our first object must be to win men's hearts; and for that purpose we must preach the Gospel. To-day the Word will fall into one heart, to-morrow into another, and it will operate in such a manner that each one will withdraw from the mass and abandon it. God does more by his Word than you and I and all the world by our united strength. God lays hold upon the heart; and when the heart is taken, all is won.

"I do not say this for the restoration of the mass. Since it is down, in God's name there let it lie! But should you have gone to work as you did? Paul, arriving one day in the powerful city of Athens, found there altars raised to false gods. He went from one to the other, and observed them without touching one. But he walked peaceably into the middle of the market-place, and declared to the people that all their gods were idols. His language took possession of their

[1] Domini enim sumus vitæ et mortis. L. Epp. ii. 150.
[2] Non enim ad fidem et ad ea quæ fidei sunt. ullus cogendus est....Ibid. 151

[1] Ich wollte nicht einen Birnstiel drauf geben. L. Opp (L.) xviii. 225.

hearts, and the idols fell without Paul's having touched them.

" I will preach, discuss, and write; but I will constrain none, for faith is a voluntary act. See what I have done! I stood up against the pope, indulgences, and papists, but without violence or tumult. I put forward God's Word; I preached and wrote —this was all I did. And yet while I was asleep, or seated familiarly at table with Amsdorff and Melancthon, drinking and gossiping over our Wittemberg beer, the Word that I had preached overthrew popery, so that neither prince nor emperor has done it so much harm. And yet I did nothing: the Word alone did all. If I had wished to appeal to force, the whole of Germany would perhaps have been deluged with blood. But what would have been the result? Ruin and desolation both to body and soul. I therefore kept quiet, and left the Word to run through the world alone. Do you know what the devil thinks when he sees men resort to violence to propagate the Gospel through the world? Seated with folded arms behind the fire of hell, Satan says, with malignant looks and frightful grin: ' Ah! how wise these madmen are to play my game!' But when he sees the Word running and contending alone on the field of battle, then he is troubled, and his knees knock together; he shudders and faints with fear."

Luther went into the pulpit again on Tuesday; and his powerful voice resounded once more through the agitated crowd. He preached again on the five succeeding days. He took a review of the destruction of images, distinction of meats, the institution of the Lord's Supper, the restoration of the cup, the abolition of confession. He showed that these points were of far less importance than the mass, and that the originators of the disorders that had taken place in Wittemberg had grossly abused their liberty. He employed by turns the language of christian charity and bursts of holy indignation.

He inveighed more especially against those who partook thoughtlessly of Christ's Supper. " It is not the outward manducation that maketh a Christian," said he, " but the inward and spiritual eating that worketh by faith, and without which all forms are mere show and grimace. Now this faith consists in a firm belief that Jesus Christ is the Son of God; that having taken our sins and iniquities upon himself, and having borne them on the cross, he is himself our sole and almighty atonement; that he stands continually before God, that he reconcileth us with the Father, and that he hath given us the sacrament of his body to strengthen our faith in this unspeakable mercy. If I believe in these things, God is my defender; with him, I brave sin, death, hell, and devils; they can do me no harm, nor disturb a single hair of my head. This spiritual bread is the conso-

lation of the afflicted, health to the sick, life to the dying, food to the hungry, riches to the poor. He who does not groan under his sins must not approach that altar: what can he do there? Ah! let our conscience accuse us, let our hearts be rent in twain at the thought of our sins, and then we shall not so presumptuously approach the holy sacrament."

The crowd ceased not to fill the temple; people flocked from the neighbouring towns to hear the new Elijah. Among others, Capito spent two days at Wittemberg, and heard two of the doctor's sermons. Never had Luther and Cardinal Albert's chaplain been so well agreed. Melancthon, the magistrates, the professors, and all the inhabitants, were delighted.[1] Schurff, charmed at the result of so gloomy an affair, hastened to communicate it to the elector. On Friday the 15th March, the day on which Luther delivered his sixth sermon, he wrote: " Oh, what joy has Dr. Martin's return diffused among us! His words, through Divine mercy, every day are bringing back our poor misguided people into the way of truth. It is clear as the sun that the Spirit of God is in him, and that by His special providence he returned to Wittemberg."[2]

In truth, these sermons are models of popular eloquence, but not of that which in the times of Demosthenes, or even of Savonarola, fired men's hearts. The task of the Wittemberg orator was more difficult. It is easier to rouse the fury of a wild beast than to allay it. Luther had to soothe a fanaticized multitude, to tame its unbridled passions; and in this he succeeded. In his eight discourses, the reformer did not allow one offensive word to escape him against the originators of these disorders,—not one unpleasant allusion. But the greater his moderation, the greater also was his strength; the more caution he used towards these deluded men, the more powerful was his vindication of offended truth. How could the people of Wittemberg resist his powerful eloquence? Men usually ascribe to timidity, fear, and compromise, those speeches that advocate moderation. Here there was nothing of the sort. Luther appeared before the inhabitants of Wittemberg braving the excommunication of the pope and the proscription of the emperor. He had returned in despite of the prohibition of the elector, who had declared his inability to defend him. Even at Worms, Luther had not shown so much courage. He confronted the most imminent dangers; and accordingly his words were not disregarded: the man who braved the scaffold had a right to exhort to submission. That man may boldly speak of obedience to God, who, to do so, defies all the persecution of man. At Luther's voice all objections vanished, the tumult subsided, sedi-

[1] Grosse Freude und Frohlocken unter Gelahrten und Ungelahrten. L. Opp. xviii. 266.
[2] Aus sonderlicher Schickung des Allmachtigen....Ibid

tious cries were heard no longer, and the citizens of Wittemberg returned quietly to their dwellings.

Gabriel Didymus, who had shown himself the most enthusiastic of all the Augustine friars, did not lose one of the reformer's words. "Do you not think Luther a wonderful teacher?" asked a hearer in great emotion. "Ah!" replied he, "I seem to listen to the voice, not of a man, but of an angel."[1] Erelong Didymus openly acknowledged that he had been deceived. "He is quite another man," said Luther.[2]

It was not so at first with Carlstadt. Despising learning, pretending to frequent the workshops of the Wittemberg mechanics to receive understanding of the Holy Scriptures, he was mortified at seeing his work crumble away at Luther's appearance.[3] In his eyes this was checking the reform itself. Hence his air was always dejected, gloomy, and dissatisfied. Yet he sacrificed his self-love for the sake of peace; he restrained his desires of vengeance, and became reconciled, outwardly at least, with his colleague, and shortly after resumed his lectures in the university.[4]

The chief prophets were not at Wittemberg when Luther returned. Nicholas Storch was wandering through the country; Mark Stubner had quitted Melancthon's hospitable roof. Perhaps their prophetic spirit had disappeared, and they had had *neither voice nor answer*,[5] so soon as they learnt that the new Elijah was directing his steps towards this new Carmel. The old schoolmaster Cellarius alone had remained. Stubner, however, being informed that the sheep of his fold were scattered, hastily returned. Those who were still faithful to "the heavenly prophecy" gathered round their master, reported Luther's speeches to him, and asked him anxiously what they were to think and do.[6] Stubner exhorted them to remain firm in their faith. "Let him appear," cried Cellarius, "let him grant us a conference,—let him only permit us to set forth our doctrine, and then we shall see......"

Luther cared little to meet such men as these; he knew them to be of violent, impatient, and haughty dispositions, who could not endure even kind admonition, and who required that every one should submit at the first word, as to a supreme authority.[7] Such are enthusiasts in every age. And yet, as they desired an interview, the doctor could not refuse it. Besides, it might be of use to the weak ones of the flock were he to unmask the imposture of the prophets. The

conference took place. Stubner opened the proceedings by explaining in what manner he desired to regenerate the Church and transform the world. Luther listened to him with great calmness.[1] "Nothing that you have advanced," replied he at last gravely, "is based upon Holy Scripture.—It is all a mere fable." At these words Cellarius could contain himself no longer; he raised his voice, gesticulated like a madman, stamped, and struck the table with his fist,[2] and exclaimed, in a passion, that it was an insult to speak thus to a man of God. Upon this Luther observed: "St. Paul declares that the proofs of his apostleship were made known by miracles; prove yours in like manner."—"We will do so," answered the prophets.[3] "The God whom I worship," said Luther, "will know how to bridle your gods." Stubner, who had preserved his tranquillity, then fixed his eyes on the reformer, and said to him with an air of inspiration, "Martin Luther! I will declare what is now passing in thy soul......Thou art beginning to believe that my doctrine is true." Luther, after a brief pause, exclaimed: "God chastise thee, Satan!" At these words all the prophets were as if distracted. "The Spirit, the Spirit!" cried they. Luther, adopting that cool tone of contempt and that cutting and homely language so familiar to him, said, "I slap your *spirit* on the snout."[4] Their clamours now increased; Cellarius, in particular, distinguished himself by his violence. He foamed and trembled with anger.[5] They could not hear one another in the room where they met in conference. At length the three prophets abandoned the field and left Wittemberg the same day.

Thus had Luther accomplished the work for which he had left his retreat. He had made a stand against fanaticism, and expelled from the bosom of the renovated Church the enthusiasm and disorder by which it had been invaded. If with one hand the Reformation threw down the dusty decretals of Rome, with the other it rejected the assumptions of the mystics, and established, on the ground it had won, the living and unchangeable Word of God. The character of the Reformation was thus firmly settled. It was destined to walk for ever between these two extremes, equally remote from the convulsions of the fanatics and the death-like torpor of the papacy.

A whole population excited, deluded, and unrestrained, had at once become tranquil, calm, and submissive; and the most perfect quiet again reigned in that city which a few days before had been like the troubled ocean. Perfect liberty was immediately establish-

---

[1] Imo, inquit, angeli, non hominis vocem mihi audisse videor. Camer. p. 12.
[2] In alium virum mutatus est. L. Epp. ii. 156.
[3] Ego Carlstadium offendi, quod ordinationes suas cessavi. Ibid. 177.
[4] Philippi et Carlstadii lectiones, ut sunt optimæ. Ibid. 384.
[5] 1 Kings xviii. 29.
[6] Rursum ad ipsum confluere....Camer. p. 52.
[7] Vehementer superbus et impatiens....credi vult plena auctoritate, ad primam vocem....L. Epp. ij. 179.

[1] Audivit Lutherus placide. Camer. p. 52.
[2] Cum et solum pedibus et propositam mensulam manibus feriret. Ibid.
[3] Quid pollicentes de mirabilibus affectionibus. Ibid. p. 53.
[4] Ihren Geist haue er über die Schnauze. L. Opp. Altenburg. Ausg. iii. 137.
[5] Spumabat et fremebat et furebat. L. Epp. ii. 179.

ed at Wittemberg. Luther still continued to reside in the convent and wear his monastic dress; but every one was free to do otherwise. In communicating at the Lord's table, a general absolution was sufficient, or a particular one might be obtained. It was laid down as a principle to reject nothing but what was opposed to the clear and formal declaration of the Holy Scriptures.[1] This was not indifference; on the contrary, religion was thus restored to what constitutes its very essence; the sentiment of religion withdrew from the accessory forms in which it had well nigh perished, and transferred itself to its true basis. Thus the Reformation was saved, and its teaching enabled to continue its development in the bosom of the Church in charity and truth.

CHAPTER IX.

Translation of the New Testament—Faith and Scripture—Opposition—Importance of this Publication—Necessity for a systematic Arrangement—Melancthon's Loci Communes—Original Sin—Salvation—Free Will—Effects of the Loci Communes.

TRANQUILLITY was hardly established when the reformer turned to his dear Melancthon, and demanded his assistance in the final revision of the New Testament which he had brought with him from the Wartburg.[2] As early as the year 1519 Melancthon had laid down the grand principle, that the Fathers must be explained according to Scripture, and not Scripture according to the Fathers.[3] Meditating more profoundly every day on the books of the New Testament, he felt at once charmed by their simplicity and impressed by their depth. " There alone can we find the true food of the soul," boldly asserted this man so familiar with all the philosophy of the ancients. Accordingly he readily complied with Luther's invitation; and from that time the two friends passed many long hours together studying and translating the inspired Word. Often would they pause in their laborious researches to give way to their admiration. Luther said one day, " Reason thinks, Oh! if I could once hear God speak! I would run from one end of the world to the other to hear him...... Listen then, my brother man! God, the Creator of the heavens and the earth, speaks to thee."

The printing of the New Testament was carried on with unexampled zeal.[4] One would have said that the very workmen felt the importance of the task in which they were engaged. Three presses were employed in this labour, and ten thousand sheets, says Luther, were printed daily.[1]

At length, on the 21st of September 1522, appeared the complete edition of three thousand copies, in two folio volumes, with this simple title : THE NEW TESTAMENT—GERMAN—WITTEMBERG. It bore no name of man. Every German might henceforward procure the Word of God at a moderate price.[2]

The new translation, written in the very tone of the holy writings, in a language yet in its youthful vigour, and which for the first time displayed its great beauties, interested, charmed, and moved the lowest as well as the highest ranks. It was a national work; the book of the people; nay more—it was in very truth the Book of God. Even opponents could not refuse their approbation to this wonderful work, and some indiscreet friends of the reformer, impressed by the beauty of the translation, imagined they could recognise in it a second inspiration. This version served more than all Luther's writings to the spread of christian piety. The work of the sixteenth century was thus placed on a foundation where nothing could shake it. The Bible, given to the people, recalled the mind of man, which had been wandering for ages in the tortuous labyrinth of scholasticism, to the Divine fountain of salvation. Accordingly the success of this work was prodigious. In a short time every copy was sold. A second edition appeared in the month of December; and in 1533 seventeen editions had been printed at Wittemberg, thirteen at Augsburg, twelve at Basle, one at Erfurth, one at Grimma, one at Leipsic, and thirteen at Strasburg.[3] Such were the powerful levers that uplifted and transformed the Church and the world.

While the first edition of the New Testament was going through the press, Luther undertook a translation of the Old. This labour, begun in 1522, was continued without interruption. He published his translation in parts as they were finished, the more speedily to gratify public impatience, and to enable the poor to procure the book.

From Scripture and faith, two sources which in reality are but one, the life of the Gospel has flowed, and is still spreading over the world. These two principles combated two fundamental errors. Faith was opposed to the Pelagian tendency of Roman-catholicism; Scripture, to the theory of tradition and the authority of Rome. Scripture led man to faith, and faith led him back to Scripture. " Man can do no meritorious work; the free grace of God, which he receives by faith in Christ, alone saves him." Such was the doctrine proclaimed in Christendom.

---

[1] Ganz klare und gründliche Schrift.
[2] Verum omnia nunc elimare cœpimus, Philippus et ego. L. Epp. ii. 176.
[3] See vol. ii. p. 178.
[4] Ingenti labore et studio. L. Epp. ii. 236.

[1] Ante Michaelis non absolvetur, quanquam singulis diebus decies millia chartarum sub tribus prelis excudant ....L. Epp. ii. 236.
[2] A florin and a half, about half a crown.
[3] Gesch. d. deutsch. Bibel Uebersetz.

But this doctrine could not fail to impel Christendom to the study of Scripture. In truth, if faith in Christ is every thing in Christianity, if the practices and ordinances of the Church are nothing, it is not to the teaching of the Church that we should adhere, but to the teaching of Christ. The bond that unites to Christ will become everything to the believer. What matters to him the outward link that connects him with an outward church enslaved by the opinions of men?......Thus, as the doctrine of the Bible had impelled Luther's contemporaries towards Jesus Christ, so in turn the love they felt to Jesus Christ impelled them to the Bible. It was not, as has been supposed in our days, from a philosophical principle, or in consequence of doubt, or from the necessity of inquiry, that they returned to Scripture; it was because they there found the Word of Him they loved. "You have preached Christ to us," said they to the reformer, "let us now hear him himself." And they seized the pages that were spread before them, as a letter coming from heaven.

But if the Bible was thus gladly received by those who loved Christ, it was scornfully rejected by those who preferred the traditions and observances of men. A violent persecution was waged against this work of the reformer's. At the news of Luther's publication, Rome trembled. The pen which had transcribed the sacred oracles was really that which Frederick had seen in his dream, and which, reaching to the Seven Hills, had shaken the tiara of the papacy.[1] The monk in his cell, the prince on his throne, uttered a cry of anger. Ignorant priests shuddered at the thought that every citizen, nay every peasant, would now be able to dispute with them on the precepts of our Lord. The King of England denounced the work to the Elector Frederick and to Duke George of Saxony. But as early as the month of November the duke had ordered his subjects to deposit every copy of Luther's New Testament in the hands of the magistrates. Bavaria, Brandenburg, Austria, and all the states devoted to Rome, published similar decrees. In some places they made sacrilegious bonfires of these sacred books in the public places.[2] Thus did Rome in the sixteenth century renew the efforts by which paganism had attempted to destroy the religion of Jesus Christ, at the moment when the dominion was escaping from the priests and their idols. But who can check the triumphant progress of the Gospel? "Even after my prohibition," wrote Duke George, "many thousand copies were sold and read in my states."

God even made use of those hands to circulate his Word that were endeavouring to destroy it. When the Romanist theologians saw that they could not prohibit the reformer's work, they themselves published a translation of the New Testament. It was Luther's version, altered here and there by the publishers. There was no hindrance to its being read. Rome as yet knew not that wherever the Word of God is established, there her power is shaken. Joachim of Brandenburg permitted all his subjects to read any translation of the Bible, in Latin or in German, provided it did not come from Wittemberg. The people of Germany, and those of Brandenburg in particular, thus made great progress in the knowledge of the truth.

The publication of the New Testament in the vulgar tongue is an important epoch in the Reformation. If Feldkirchen's marriage was the first step in the progress of the Reformation from doctrine into social life; if the abolition of monastic vows was the second; if the re-establishment of the Lord's Supper was the third,—the publication of the New Testament was perhaps the most important of all. It worked an entire change in society: not only in the presbytery of the priest, in the monk's cell, and in the sanctuary of our Lord; but also in the mansions of the great, in the houses of the citizens, and in the cottages of the peasants. When the Bible began to be read in the families of Christendom, Christendom itself was changed. Then arose other habits, other manners, other conversations, and another life. With the publication of the New Testament, the Reformation left the School and the Church to take possession of the hearths of the people.

The effect produced was immense. The Christianity of the primitive Church, drawn by the publication of the Holy Scriptures from the oblivion of centuries in which it had lain, was thus presented before the eyes of the nation; and this view was sufficient to justify the attacks that had been made against Rome. The simplest men, provided they knew how to read, women, and mechanics (our informant is a contemporary and violent opponent of the Reformation) eagerly studied the New Testament.[1] They carried it about with them; soon they knew it by heart, and the pages of this book loudly proclaimed the perfect unison of Luther's Reformation with the Divine revelation.

And yet it was only by fragments that the doctrine of the Bible and of the Reformation had been set forth hitherto. A certain truth had been put forward in one writing; a certain error attacked in another. On one vast plain lay sattered and confused the ruins of the old edifice and the materials of the new: but the new edifice was wanting. The publication of the New Testament undoubtedly satisfied this want. The Reformation could say, as it gave this book: Here is my

[1] Vol. i. p. 95.
[2] Qui et alicubi in unum congesti rogum publice combusti sunt.

[1] Ut sutores, mulieres, et quilibet idiotæ....avidissime legerent. Cochlœus, p. 50.

system! But as every man is at liberty to assert that his system is that of the Bible, the Reformation was called to arrange what it had found in Scripture. And this Melancthon now did in its name.

He had walked with regular but confident steps in the development of his theology, and had from time to time published the results of his inquiries. Before this, in 1520, he had declared that in several of the seven sacraments he could see nothing but an imitation of the Jewish ceremonies; and in the infallibility of the pope, a haughty presumption equally opposed to the Holy Scriptures and to good sense. "To contend against these doctrines," he had said, "we require more than one Hercules."[1] Thus had Melancthon reached the same point as Luther, although by a calmer and more scientific process. The time had come in which he was to confess his faith in his turn.

In 1521, during Luther's captivity, Melancthon's celebrated work, "On the Common-places of Theology," had presented to christian Europe a body of doctrine of solid foundations and admirable proportions. A simple and majestic unity appeared before the astonished eyes of the new generation. The translation of the Testament justified the Reformation to the people; Melancthon's Common-places justified it in the opinion of the learned.

For fifteen centuries the Church had existed, and had never seen such a work. Forsaking the ordinary developments of scholastic theology, Luther's friend at last gave the world a theological system derived solely from Scripture. In it there reigned a breath of life, a vitality of understanding, a strength of conviction, and a simplicity of statement, that form a striking contrast with the subtle and pedantic systems of the schools. Men of the most philosophic minds, as well as the strictest theologians, were equally filled with admiration.

Erasmus entitled this work a wondrous army drawn up in battle array against the tyrannous battalions of the false doctors;[2] and while he avowed his dissent from the author on several points, he added, that although he had always loved him, he had never loved him so much as after reading this work. "So true it is," said Calvin when presenting it subsequently to France, "that the greatest simplicity is the greatest virtue in treating of the christian doctrine."[3]

But no one felt such joy as Luther. Throughout life this work was the object of his admiration. The disconnected sounds that his hand, in the deep emotion of his soul, had drawn from the harp of the prophets and apostles, were here blended together into one enchanting harmony. Those scattered stones, which he had laboriously hewn from the quarries of Scripture, were now combined into a majestic edifice. Hence he never ceased recommending the study of this work to the youths who came to Wittemberg in search of knowledge: "If you desire to become theologians," he would say, "read Melancthon."[1]

According to Melancthon, a deep conviction of the wretched state to which man is reduced by sin is the foundation on which the edifice of christian theology should be raised. This universal evil is the primary fact, the leading idea on which the science is based; it is the characteristic that distinguishes theology from those sciences whose only instrument is reason.

The christian divine, diving into the heart of man, explains its laws and mysterious attractions, as another philosopher in after-years explained the laws and attraction of bodies. "Original sin," said he, "is an inclination born with us,—a certain impulse which is agreeable to us,—a certain force leading us to sin, and which has been communicated by Adam to all his posterity. As in fire there is a native energy impelling it to mount upward, as there is in the loadstone a natural quality by which iron is attracted; so also there is in man a primitive force that inclines him to evil. I grant that in Socrates, Xenocrates, and Zeno, were found temperance, firmness, and chastity; these shadows of virtues were found in impure hearts and originated in self-love. This is why we should regard them not as real virtues, but as vices."[2] This language may seem harsh; but not so if we apprehend Melancthon's meaning aright. No one was more willing to acknowledge virtues in the pagans that entitled them to the esteem of man; but he laid down this great truth, that the sovereign law given by God to all his creatures, is to love Him above all things. Now, if man, in doing that which God commands, does it not from love to God, but from love of self, can God accept him for daring to substitute himself in the place of His infinite Majesty? and can there be no sinfulness in an action that is express rebellion against the supreme Deity?

The Wittemberg divine then proceeds to show how man is saved from this wretchedness. "The apostle," said he, "invites thee to contemplate the Son of God sitting at the right hand of the Father, mediating and interceding for us;[3] and calls upon thee to feel assured that thy sins are forgiven thee, that thou art reputed righteous, and accepted

[1] Adversus quas non uno nobis, ut ita dicam, Hercule opus est. Corp. Ref. i. 137.
[2] Video dogmatum aciem pulchre instructam adversus tyrannidem pharisaicam. Er. Epp. p. 949.
[3] La Somme de Theologie, par Philippe Melancthon, Genève, 1551. Jehan Calvin aux Lecteurs.

[1] Librum invictum (said he on another occasion) non solum immortalitate sed et canone ecclesiastico dignum De Servo Arbitrio.
[2] Loci Communes Theologici, Basle, 1521, p. 35. This edition is very rare. For the subsequent revisions consult that of Erlangen, 1828, founded on that of Basle, 1561.
[3] Vult te intueri Filium Dei sedentem ad dextram Patris, mediatorem interpellantem pro nobis. Ibid.

by the Father for the sake of that Son who suffered for us on the cross."

The first edition of the *Common-places* is especially remarkable for the manner in which the theologian of Germany speaks of free will. He saw more clearly perhaps than Luther, for he was a better theologian, that this doctrine could not be separated from that which constituted the very essence of the Reformation. Man's justification before God proceeds from faith alone : this is the first point. This faith enters man's heart by the grace of God alone : here is the second. Melancthon saw clearly that if he allowed that man had any natural ability to believe, he would be throwing down in the second point that great doctrine of grace which he had stated in the first. He had too much discernment and understanding of the Holy Scriptures to be mistaken in so important a matter. But he went too far. Instead of confining himself within the limits of the religious question, he entered upon metaphysics. He established a fatalism which might tend to represent God as the author of evil,—a doctrine which has no foundation in Scripture. " As all things which happen," said he, " happen necessarily, according to the Divine predestination, there is no such thing as liberty in our wills."[1]

But the object Melancthon had particularly in view was to present theology as a system of piety. The schoolmen had so dried up the doctrine as to leave no traces of vitality in it. The task of the Reformation was therefore to reanimate this lifeless doctrine. In the subsequent editions, Melancthon felt the necessity of expounding these doctrines with greater clearness.[2] But such was not precisely the case in 1521. " To know Christ," said he, " is to know his blessings.[3] Paul, in his epistle to the Romans, desiring to give a summary of the christian doctrines, does not philosophize on the mystery of the Trinity, on the mode of incarnation, on active or passive creation ; of what then does he speak ?—of the law,—of sin,—of grace. On this our knowledge of Christ depends."

The publication of this body of theology was of inestimable value to the cause of truth. Calumnies were refuted ; prejudices swept away. In the churches, palaces, and universities, Melancthon's genius found admirers, who esteemed the graces of his character. Even those who knew not the author were attracted to his creed by his book. The roughness and occasional violence of Luther's language had often repelled many. But here was a man who explained those mighty truths whose sudden explosion had shaken the world, with great elegance of style, exquisite taste, admirable perspicuity, and perfect order. The work was sought after and read with avidity, and studied with ardour. Such gentleness and moderation won all hearts. Such nobility and force commanded their respect ; and the superior classes of society, hitherto undecided, were gained over to a wisdom that made use of such beautiful language.

On the other hand, the adversaries of truth, whom Luther's terrible blows had not yet humbled, remained for a time silent and disconcerted at the appearance of Melancthon's treatise. They saw that there was another man as worthy of their hatred as Luther himself. " Alas ! " exclaimed they, " unhappy Germany ! to what extremity wilt thou be brought by this new birth ! "[1]

Between the years 1521 and 1595 the *Common-places* passed through sixty-seven editions, without including translations. Next to the Bible, this is the book that has possibly contributed most to the establishment of the evangelical doctrine.

CHAPTER X.

Opposition—Henry VIII.—Wolsey—The Queen—Fisher—Sir Thomas More—Luther's Books burnt—Henry's attack on Luther—Presented to the Pope—Its Effect on Luther—Energy and Violence—Luther's Reply—Answer by the Bishop of Rochester—Reply of Sir Thomas More—Henry's Proceedings.

WHILE the " grammarian " Melancthon was contributing by these gentle strains a powerful support to Luther, men of authority, enemies to the reformer, were turning violently against him. He had escaped from the Wartburg and reappeared on the stage of the world ; and at this news the rage of his former adversaries was revived.

Luther had been three months and a half at Wittemberg when a rumour, increased by the thousand tongues of fame, brought intelligence that one of the greatest kings of Christendom had risen against him. Henry VIII., the head of the house of Tudor, a prince descended from the families of York and Lancaster, and in whose person, after so much bloodshed, the white and red roses were at length united, the mighty king of England, who claimed to re-establish on the continent, and especially in France, the former influence of his crown,—had just written a book against the poor monk of Wittemberg. " There is much boasting about a little book by the King of England," wrote

---

[1] Quandoquidem omnia quæ eveniunt, necessario eveniunt juxta divinam prædestinationem, nulla est voluntatis nostræ libertas. Loc. Com. Theol. Basle, 1521, p. 35.
[2] See the edition of 1561, reprinted in 1829, p. 14-44, the several chapters :—De tribus personis ;—De divinitate Filii ;—De duabus naturis in Christo ;—Testimonia quod Filius sit persona ;—Testimonia refutantia Arianos ;—De discernendis proprietatibus humanæ et divinæ naturæ Christi ;—De Spiritu Sancto, &c. &c.
[3] Hoc est Christum cognoscere, beneficia ejus cognoscere. Ibid.

[1] Heu ! Infelicem hoc novo partu Germaniam ! Cochlœus

Luther to Lange on the 26th of June 1522.[1]

Henry was then thirty-one years old; "he was tall, strong-built and proportioned, and had an air of authority and empire."[2] His countenance expressed the vivacity of his mind; vehement, presuming to make every thing give way to the violence of his passions, and thirsting for glory, he at first concealed his faults under a certain impetuosity that is peculiar to youth, and flatterers were not wanting to encourage them. He would often visit, in company with his courtiers, the house of his chaplain, Thomas Wolsey, the son of an Ipswich butcher. Endowed with great skill, of overweening ambition, and of unbounded audacity, this man, protected by the Bishop of Winchester, chancellor of the kingdom, had rapidly advanced in his master's favour, and allured him to his residence by the attractions of pleasures and disorders, in which the young prince would not have ventured to indulge in his own palace. This is recorded by Polydore Virgil, at that time papal sub-collector in England.[3] In these dissolute meetings, the chaplain surpassed the licentiousness of the young courtiers who attended Henry VIII. Forgetful of the decorum befitting a minister of the Church, he would sing, dance, laugh, play the fool, fence, and indulge in obscene conversation.[4] By these means he succeeded in obtaining the first place in the king's councils, and, as sole minister, all the princes of Christendom were forced to purchase his favour.

Henry lived in the midst of balls, banquets, and jousting, and riotously squandered the treasures his father had slowly accumulated. Magnificent tournaments succeeded each other without interval. In these sports the king, who was distinguished above all the combatants by his manly beauty, played the chief part.[5] If the contest appeared for a moment doubtful, the strength and address of the young monarch, or the artful policy of his opponents, gave him the victory, and the lists resounded with shouts and applause in his honour. The vanity of the youthful prince was inflated by these easy triumphs, and there was no success in the world to which he thought he might not aspire. The queen was often seen among the spectators.

Her serious features and sad look, her absent and dejected air, formed a striking contrast with the noise and glitter of these festivities. Shortly after his accession to the throne, and for reasons of state, Henry VIII. had espoused Catherine of Aragon, his senior by eight years: she was his brother Arthur's widow, and aunt to Charles V. While her husband followed his pleasures, the virtuous Catherine, whose piety was truly Spanish, would leave her bed in the middle of the night to take a silent part in the prayers of the monks,[1] at which she would kneel down without cushion or carpet. At five in the morning, after taking a little rest, she would again rise, and putting on the Franciscan dress, for she had been admitted into the tertiary order of St. Francis, and hastily throwing the royal garments around her,[2] would repair to church at six o'clock to join in the service.

Two beings, living in such different spheres, could not long continue together.

Romish piety had other representatives besides Catherine in the court of Henry VIII. John Fisher, bishop of Rochester, then nearly seventy years of age, as distinguished for learning as for the austerity of his manners, was the object of universal veneration. He had been the oldest councillor of Henry VII., and the Duchess of Richmond, grandmother to Henry VIII., calling him to her bedside, had commended to his care the youth and inexperience of her grandson. The king, in the midst of his irregularities, long continued to revere the aged bishop as a father.

A man much younger than Fisher, a layman and a lawyer, had prior to this attracted general attention by his genius and noble character. His name was Thomas More, son of one of the judges of the King's Bench. He was poor, austere, and diligent. At the age of twenty he had endeavoured to quench the passions of youth by wearing a shirt of haircloth, and by self-scourging. On one occasion, being summoned by Henry VIII. while he was attending mass, he replied, that God's service was before the king's. Wolsey introduced him to Henry, who employed him on various embassies, and showed him much kindness. He would often send for him, and converse with him on astronomy, about Wolsey, or on divinity.

In truth, the king himself was not unacquainted with the Romish doctrines. It would appear, that if Arthur had lived, Henry was destined for the archiepiscopal see of Canterbury. Thomas Aquinas,[3] St. Bonaventure, tournaments, banquets, Elizabeth Blunt and others of his mistresses—all were mixed up in the mind and life of this

---

[1] Jactant libellum regis Angliæ; sed *eum* illum suspicor sub pelle tectum;—an allusion to Leo, the king's chaplain, and a pun on the word *leo*, a lion. L. Epp. ii. 213.
[2] Collier, Eccl. Hist. of Great Britain, fol. ii. 1.
[3] Domi suæ voluptatum omnium sacrarium fecit, quo regem frequenter ducebat. Polyd. Virgilius, Angl. Hist., Basle, 1570, fol. p. 633. Polydore appears to have suffered from Wolsey's pride, and to be rather inclined to exaggerate the minister's faults.
[4] Cum illis adolescentibus una psallebat, saltabat, sermones leporis plenos habebat, ridebat, jocabatur, &c. Ibid.
[5] Eximia corporis forma præditus, in qua etiam regiæ majestatis augusta quædam species elucebat. Sanderus de Schismate Anglicano, p. 4. This work of Sanders, papal nuncio in Ireland, should be read very cautiously; for it abounds in false and calumnious assertions, as has been remarked by Cardinal Quirini and the Roman-catholic Doctor Lingard. See the History of England by the latter, vol. vi. 173.

[1] Surgebat media nocte ut nocturnis religiosorum precibus interesset. Sanderus de Schismate Anglicano, p. 5.
[2] Sub regio vestitu *Divi Francisci* habitu utebatur. Ibid.
[3] Legebat studiose libros divi Thomæ Aquinatis. Pol. Virg. p. 634.

prince, who had masses of his own composition sung in his chapel.

As soon as Henry had heard talk of Luther, he became indignant against him, and hardly was the decree of the Diet of Worms known in England, before he ordered the pontiff's bull against the reformer's works to be put into execution. [1] On the 12th of May 1521, Thomas Wolsey, who, together with the office of chancellor of England, combined those of cardinal and legate of Rome, went in solemn procession to St. Paul's. This man, whose pride had attained the highest pitch, thought himself the equal of kings. He used to sit in a chair of gold, sleep in a golden bed, and a cover of cloth of gold was spread on the table during his meals. [2] On this occasion he displayed great magnificence. His household, consisting of 800 persons, among whom were barons, knights, and sons of the most distinguished families, who hoped by serving him to obtain public office, surrounded this haughty prelate. Silk and gold glittered not only on his garments (he was the first ecclesiastic who ventured to dress so sumptuously), [3] but even on the housings and harness of the horses. Before him walked a tall priest bearing a silver column terminated by a cross; behind him, another ecclesiastic of similar height carried the archiepiscopal crosier of York; a nobleman at his side held the cardinal's hat. [4] Lords, prelates, ambassadors from the pope and emperor, accompanied him, followed by a long line of mules bearing chests covered with the richest and most brilliant hangings. It was this magnificent procession that was carrying to the burning pile the writings of the poor monk of Wittemberg. When they reached the cathedral, the insolent priest placed his cardinal's hat on the altar. The virtuous Bishop of Rochester stationed himself at the foot of the cross, and with agitated voice preached earnestly against the heresy. After this the impious books of the heresiarch were brought together and devoutly burned in the presence of an immense crowd. Such was the first intelligence that England received of the Reformation.

Henry would not stop here. This prince, whose hand was ever upraised against his adversaries, his wives, or his favourites, wrote to the elector-palatine: "It is the devil, who, by Luther's means, has kindled this immense conflagration. If Luther will not be converted, let him and his writings be burnt together!" [5]

This was not enough. Having been convinced that the progress of heresy was owing to the extreme ignorance of the German princes, Henry thought the moment had arrived for showing his learning. The victories of his battle-axe did not permit him to doubt of those that were reserved for his pen. But another passion, vanity, ever greatest in the smallest minds, spurred the king onward. He was humiliated at having no title to oppose to that of "Catholic" and "Most Christian," borne by the kings of Spain and France, and he had been long begging a similar distinction from the court of Rome. What would be more likely to procure it than an attack upon heresy? Henry therefore threw aside the kingly purple, and descended from his throne into the arena of theological discussion. He enlisted Thomas Aquinas, Peter Lombard, Alexander Hales, and Bonaventure into his service; and the world beheld the publication of the *Defence of the Seven Sacraments, against Martin Luther, by the most invincible King of England and France, Lord of Ireland, Henry the eighth of that name.*

"I will rush in front of the Church to save her," said the King of England in this treatise; "I will receive in my bosom the poisoned arrows of her assailants. [1] The present state of things calls me to do so. Every servant of Christ, whatever be his age, sex, or rank, should rise up against the common enemy of Christendom. [2]

"Let us put on a twofold breastplate; the heavenly breastplate, to conquer by the weapons of truth him who combats with those of error; but also an earthly breastplate, that if he shows himself obstinate in his malice, the hand of the executioner may constrain him to be silent, and that once at least he may be useful to the world, by the terrible example of his death. [3]

Henry VIII. was unable to hide the contempt he felt towards his feeble adversary. "This man," said the crowned theologian, "seems to be in the pangs of childbirth; after a travail without precedent, he produces nothing but wind.[4] Remove the daring envelope of the insolent verbiage with which he clothes his absurdities, as an ape is clothed in purple, and what remains?...... a wretched and empty sophism."

The king defends, successively, the mass, penance, confirmation, marriage, orders, and extreme unction; he is not sparing of abusive language towards his opponent; he calls him by turns a wolf of hell, a poisonous viper, a limb of the devil. Even Luther's sincerity is attacked. Henry VIII. crushes the mendicant monk with his royal anger, "and writes as 'twere with his sceptre," says an historian.[5]

---

[1] Primum libros Lutheranos, quorum magnus jam numerus pervenerat in manus suorum Anglorum, comburendos curavit. Pol. Virg. p. 664.
[2] Uti sella aurea, uti pulvino aureo, uti velo aureo ad mensam. Ibid.
[3] Primus episcoporum et cardinalium, vestitum exteriorem sericum sibi induit. Ibid. p. 633.
[4] Galerum cardinalium, ordinis insignem, sublime a ministro præferebat....super altare collocabat Ibid. p. 645.
[5] Knapp's Nachlese, ii. 458.

[1] Meque adversus venenata jacula hostis eam oppugnantes objicerem. Assertio septem sacramentorum adv. M. Lutherum, in prologo.
[2] Omnis Christi servus, omnis ætas, omnis sexus, omnis ordo consurgat. Ibid.
[3] Et qui nocuit verbo malitiæ, supplicii prosit exemplo. Ibid.
[4] Mirum est quanto nixu parturiens, quam nihil peperit, nisi merum ventum. Ibid.
[5] Collyer, Eccl. Hist. p. 17.

And yet it must be confessed that his work was not bad, considering the author and his age. The style is not altogether without force; but the public of the day did not confine themselves to paying it due justice. The theological treatise of the powerful King of England was received with a torrent of adulation. "It is the most learned work the sun ever saw," cried some.[1]—"We can only compare it," re-echoed others, "to the works of Augustine. He is a Constantine, a Charlemagne!"—He is more," said others, "he is a second Solomon!"

These flatteries soon extended beyond the limits of England. Henry desired John Clarke, dean of Windsor, his ambassador at Rome, to present his book to the sovereign pontiff. Leo X. received the envoy in full consistory, and Clarke laid the royal work before him, saying: "The king my master assures you that, having now refuted Luther's errors with the pen, he is ready to combat his adherents with t..e sword." Leo, touched with this promise, replied, that the king's book could not have been written without the aid of the Holy Ghost, and conferred upon Henry the title of *Defender of the Faith*, which is still borne by the sovereigns of England.

The reception which this volume met with at Rome contributed greatly to increase the number of its readers. In a few months many thousand copies issued from different presses.[2] "The whole christian world," says Cochlœus, "was filled with admiration and joy."[3]

Such extravagant panegyrics augmented the insufferable vanity of this chief of the Tudors. He himself seemed to have no doubt that he was inspired by the Holy Ghost.[4] From that time he would suffer no contradiction. His papacy was no longer at Rome, but at Greenwich; infallibility reposed on his shoulders: at a subsequent period this contributed greatly to the Reformation of England.

Luther read Henry's book with a smile mingled with disdain, impatience, and indignation. The falsehood and the abuse it contained, but especially the air of contempt and compassion which the king assumed, irritated the Wittemberg doctor to the highest degree. The thought that the pope had crowned this work, and that on all sides the enemies of the Gospel were triumphing over the Reformation and the reformer as already overthrown and vanquished, increased his indignation. Besides, what reason had he to temporize? Was he not fighting in the cause of a King greater than all the kings of the earth? The meekness of the Gospel appeared to him unseasonable. An eye for an eye, a tooth for a tooth. He went beyond all bounds. Persecuted, insulted, hunted down, and wounded, the furious lion turned round, and proudly roused himself to crush his enemy. The elector, Spalatin, Melancthon, and Bugenhagen, strove in vain to pacify him. They would have prevented his replying; but nothing could stop him. "I will not be gentle towards the king of England," said he. "I know that it is vain for me to humble myself, to give way, to entreat, to try peaceful methods. At length I will show myself more terrible towards these furious beasts, who goad me every day with their horns. I will turn mine upon them. I will provoke Satan until he falls down lifeless and exhausted.[1] If this heretic does not recant, says Henry VIII. the new Thomas, he must be burnt alive! Such are the weapons they are now employing against me: the fury of stupid asses and swine of the brood of Thomas Aquinas; and then the stake.[2] Well then, be it so! Let these hogs advance if they dare, and let them burn me! Here I am waiting for them. After my death, though my ashes should be thrown into a thousand seas, they will rise, pursue, and swallow up this abominable herd. Living, I shall be the enemy of the papacy; burnt, I shall be its destruction. Go then, swine of St. Thomas, do what seemeth good to you. You will ever find Luther like a bear upon your road, and as a lion in your path. He will spring upon you whithersoever you go, and will never leave you at peace, until he has broken your iron heads, and ground your brazen foreheads into dust."

Luther first reproaches Henry VIII. with having supported his doctrines solely by the decrees and opinions of men. "As for me," says he, "I never cease crying the Gospel, the Gospel! Christ, Christ!—And my adversaries continue to reply: Custom, custom! Ordinances, ordinances! Fathers, fathers! —St. Paul says: *Let not your faith stand in the wisdom of men, but in the power of God* (1 Cor. ii. 5.) And the apostle by this thunderclap from heaven overthrows and disperses all the hobgoblins of this Henry, as the wind scatters the dust. Frightened and confounded, these Thomists, Papists, and Henrys fall prostrate before the thunder of these words."[3]

He then refutes the king's book in detail, and overturns his arguments one after the other, with a perspicuity, spirit, and know-

---

[1] Burnet, Hist. Ref. of England, i. 30.
[2] Intra paucos menses, liber ejus a multis chalcographis in multa millia multiplicatus. Cochlœus, p. 44.
[3] Ut totum orbem christianum et gaudio et admiratione repleverit. Ibid.
[4] He was brought to fancy it was written with some degree of inspiration. Burnet, Preface.

[1] Mea in ipsos exercebo cornua, irritaturus Satanam, donec effusis viribus et conatibus corruat in se ipso. L. Epp. ii. 236.
[2] Ignis et furor insulsissimorum asinorum et Thomisticorum porcorum. Contra Henricum Regem, Opp. Lat. ii. 331. This language reminds us of the Irish Agitator. There is, however, greater force and nobility in the orator of the 16th than in him of the 19th century. See *Revue Britannique* for November 1835. *Le Règne d'O'Connel.* "Soaped swine of civilized society," &c. p. 30.
[3] Confusi et prostrati jacent a facie verborum istius tonitrui. Contra Henricum reg. Opp. Lat. ii. 336.

ledge of the Holy Scriptures and history of the Church, but also with an assurance, disdain, and sometimes violence, that ought not to surprise us.

Having reached the end of his confutation, Luther again becomes indignant that his opponent should derive his arguments from the Fathers only: this was the basis of the whole controversy. "To all the words of the Fathers and of men, of angels and of devils," said he, "I oppose, not old customs, not the multitude of men, but the Word of the Eternal Majesty,—the Gospel, which even my adversaries are obliged to recognise. To this I hold fast, on this I repose, in this I boast, in this I exult and triumph over the papists, the Thomists, the Henrys, the sophists, and all the swine of hell.[1] The King of heaven is with me; for this reason I fear nothing, although a thousand Augustines, a thousand Cyprians, and a thousand of these churches which Henry defends, should rise up against me. It is a small matter that I should despise and revile a king of the earth, since he himself does not fear in his writings to blaspheme the King of heaven, and to profane His holy name by the most impudent falsehoods."[2]

"Papists!" exclaimed he in conclusion, "will ye never cease from your idle attacks? Do what you please. Nevertheless, before that Gospel which I preach down must come popes, bishops, priests, monks, princes, devils, death, sin, and all that is not Christ or in Christ."[3]

Thus spoke the poor monk. His violence certainly cannot be excused, if we judge it by the rule to which he himself appealed,—by the Word of God. It cannot even be justified by alleging either the grossness of the age (for Melancthon knew how to observe decorum in his writings), or the energy of his character, for if this energy had any influence over his language, passion also exerted more. It is better, then, that we should condemn it. And yet it is but right to observe that in the sixteenth century this violence did not appear so strange as it would in our days. The learned were then an estate, as well as the princes. By becoming a writer, Henry had attacked Luther. Luther replied according to an established law in the republic of letters, that we must consider the truth of what is said, and not the quality of him that says it. Let us add also, that when this same king turned against the pope, the abuse which the Romish writers and the pope himself poured upon him, far exceeded all that Luther had ever said.

Besides, if Luther called Dr. Eck an ass and Henry VIII. a hog, he indignantly rejected the intervention of the secular arm; while Eck was writing a dissertation to prove that heretics ought to be burned, and Henry was erecting scaffolds that he might conform with the precepts of the chancellor of Ingolstadt.

Great was the emotion at the king's court; Surrey, Wolsey, and the crowd of courtiers, put a stop to the festivities and pageantry at Greenwich to vent their indignation in abuse and sarcasm. The venerable Bishop of Rochester, who had been delighted to see the young prince, formerly confided to his care, breaking a lance in defence of the Church, was deeply wounded by the attack of the monk. He replied to it immediately. His words distinctly characterize the age and the Church. "Take us the foxes, the little foxes, that spoil the vines, says Christ in the Song of Songs. This teaches us," said Fisher, "that we must take the heretics before they grow big. Now Luther is become a big fox, so old, so cunning, and so sly, that he is very difficult to catch, What do I say? ......a fox? He is a mad dog, a ravening wolf, a cruel bear; or rather all those animals in one; for the monster includes many beasts within him."[1]

Sir Thomas More also descended into the arena to contend with the monk of Wittemberg. Although a layman, his zeal against the Reformation amounted to fanaticism, if it did not even urge him to shed blood. When young nobles undertake the defence of the papacy, their violence often exceeds even that of the ecclesiastics. "Reverend brother, father, tippler, Luther, runagate of the order of St. Augustine, mis-shapen bacchanal of either faculty, unlearned doctor of theology."[2] Such is the language addressed to the reformer by one of the most illustrious men of his age. He then proceeds to explain in what manner Luther had composed his book against Henry VIII.: "He called his companions together, and desired them to go each his own way and pick up all sorts of abuse and scurrility. One frequented the public carriages and boats; another the baths and gambling-houses; a third the taverns and barbers' shops; a fourth the mills and brothels. They noted down in their tablets all the most insolent, filthy, and infamous things they heard; and bringing back these abominations and impurities, discharged them all into that filthy kennel which is called Luther's mind. If he retracts his falsehoods and calumnies," continues More, "if he lays aside his folly and his madness, if he swallows his own filth[3]......he will find one who will seriously discuss with him. But if he proceeds as he has begun, joking, teasing, fooling, calumniating, vomiting sewers and cesspools[4]......let others do what they please;

---

[1] Hic sto, hic sedeo, hic maneo, hic glorior, hic triumphor, hic insulto papistis....Opp. Lat. ii. 342.
[2] Nec magnum si ego regem terræ contemno. Ibid. 344, verso.
[3] L. Opp. Leips. xviii. 209.

[1] Canem dixissem rabidum, imo lupum rapacissimum, aut sævissimam quandam ursam. Cochlœus, p. 60.
[2] Reverendus frater, pater, potator, Lutherus. Ibid. p. 61.
[3] Si....suas resorbeat et sua relingat stercora. Ibid. p. 62.
[4] Sentinas, cloacas, latrinas,....stercora. Ibid. p. 63.

as for me, I should prefer leaving the little friar to his own fury and filth."[1] More would have done better to have restrained his own. Luther never degraded his style to so low a degree. He made no reply.

This writing still further increased Henry's attachment to More. He would often visit him in his humble dwelling at Chelsea. After dinner, the king, leaning on his favourite's shoulder, would walk in the garden, while Mistress More and her children, concealed behind a window, could not turn away their astonished eyes. After one of these walks, More, who knew his man well, said to his wife: " If my head could win him a single castle in France, he would not hesitate to cut it off."

The king, thus defended by the Bishop of Rochester and by his future chancellor, had no need to resume his pen. Confounded at finding himself treated in the face of Europe as a common writer, Henry VIII. abandoned the dangerous position he had taken, and throwing away the pen of the theologian, had recourse to the more effectual means of diplomacy.

An ambassador was despatched from the court of Greenwich with a letter for the elector and dukes of Saxony. " Luther, the real serpent fallen from heaven," wrote he, " is pouring out his floods of venom upon the earth. He is stirring up revolts in the Church of Jesus Christ, abolishing laws, insulting the powers that be, inflaming the laity against the priests, laymen and priests against the pope, and subjects against their sovereigns, and he desires nothing better than to see Christians fighting and destroying one another, and the enemies of our faith hailing this scene of carnage with a frightful grin.[2]

" What is this doctrine which he calls evangelical, if it be not Wickliffe's? Now, most honoured uncles, I know what your ancestors have done to destroy it. In Bohemia, they hunted it down like a wild beast, and driving it into a pit, they shut it up and kept it fast. You will not allow it to escape through your negligence, lest, creeping into Saxony, and becoming master of the whole of Germany, its smoking nostrils should pour forth the flames of hell, spreading that conflagration far and wide which your nation hath so often wished to extinguish in its blood.[3]

" For this reason, most worthy princes, I feel obliged to exhort you and even to entreat you in the name of all that is most sacred, promptly to extinguish the cursed sect of Luther: put no one to death, if that can be avoided; but if this heretical obstinacy continues, then shed blood without hesitation, in order that the abominable heresy may disappear from under heaven."[1]

The elector and his brother referred the king to the approaching council. Thus Henry VIII. was far from attaining his end. " So great a name mixed up in the dispute," said Paul Sarpi, " served to render it more curious, and to conciliate general favour towards Luther, as usually happens in combats and tournaments, where the spectators have always a leaning towards the weaker party, and take delight in exaggerating the merit of his actions."[2]

CHAPTER XI.

General Movement — The Monks — How the Reformation was carried on—Unlearned Believer—The Old and the New Doctors—Printing and Literature—Bookselling and Colportage.

A GREAT movement was going on. The Reformation, which, after the Diet of Worms, had been thought to be confined with its first teacher in the narrow chamber of a strong castle, was breaking forth in every part of the empire, and, so to speak, throughout Christendom. The two classes, hitherto mixed up together, were now beginning to separate; and the partisans of a monk, whose only defence was his tongue, now took their stand fearlessly in the face of the servants of Charles V. and Leo X. Luther had scarcely left the walls of the Wartburg, the pope had excommunicated all his adherents, the imperial diet had just condemned his doctrine, the princes were endeavouring to crush it in most of the German states, the ministers of Rome were lowering it in the eyes of the people by their violent invectives, and the other states of Christendom were calling upon Germany to sacrifice a man whose assaults they feared even at a distance; and yet this new sect, few in numbers, and among whose members there was no organization, no bond of union, nothing in short that concentrated their common power, was already frightening the vast, ancient, and powerful sovereignty of Rome by the energy of its faith and the rapidity of its conquests. On all sides, as in the first warm days of spring, the seed was bursting from the earth spontaneously and without effort. Every day showed some new progress. Individuals, villages, towns, whole cities, joined in this new confession of the name of Jesus Christ. There was unpitying

---

[1] Cum suis....et stercoribus....relinquere. Cochlæus, p. 63. Cochlæus is delighted at quoting these passages, selecting what according to his taste are the finest parts in More's reply. M. Nisard, on the contrary, confesses in his article on More, whom he defends with great warmth and erudition, that in this writing " the impurities dictated by the anger of the Catholic are such that all attempt at translation is impossible." Revue des deux Mondes, v. 592.
[2] So ergiest er, gleich wie eine Schlang vom Himmel geworfen. L. Opp. xviii. 212. The original is in Latin: Velut e cœlo dejectus serpens, virus effundit in terras.
[3] Und durch sein schädlich Anblasen das höllische Feuer ausspruhe. Ibid. 213.

[1] Oder aber auch mit Blut vergiessen. L. Opp. xviii. 212.
[2] Hist. Council of Trent, pp. 15, 16.

opposition, there were terrible persecutions, but the mysterious power that urged all these people onward was irresistible ; and the persecuted, quickening their steps, going forward through exile, imprisonment, and the burning pile, every where prevailed over their persecutors.

The monastic orders that Rome had spread over Christendom, like a net intended to catch souls and keep them prisoners, were the first to break their bonds, and rapidly to propagate the new doctrine throughout the Church. The Augustines of Saxony had walked with Luther, and felt that inward experience of the Holy Word which, by putting them in possession of God himself, dethroned Rome and her lofty assumptions. But in the other convents of the order, evangelical light had dawned in like manner. Sometimes they were old men, who, like Staupitz, had preserved the sound doctrines of truth in the midst of deluded Christendom, and who now besought God to permit them to depart in peace, for their eyes had seen his salvation. At other times, they were young men, who had received Luther's teaching with the eagerness peculiar to their age. The Augustine convents at Nuremberg, Osnabruck, Dillingen, Ratisbon, Strasburg, and Antwerp, with those in Hesse and Wurtemberg, turned towards Jesus Christ, and by their courage excited the wrath of Rome.

But this movement was not confined to the Augustines only. High-spirited men imitated them in the monasteries of other orders, and notwithstanding the clamours of the monks, who would not abandon their carnal observances, notwithstanding the anger, contempt, sentences, discipline, and imprisonments of the cloister, they fearlessly raised their voices in behalf of that holy and precious truth, which they had found at last after so many painful inquiries, such despair and doubt, and such inward struggle. In the majority of the cloisters, the most spiritual, pious, and learned monks declared for the Reformation. In the Franciscan convent at Ulm, Eberlin and Kettenbach attacked the slavish works of monasticism, and the superstitious observances of the Church, with an eloquence capable of moving the whole nation ; and they called for the immediate abolition of the monasteries and houses of ill-fame. Another Franciscan, Stephen Kempe, preached the Gospel at Hamburg, and, alone, presented a firm front to the hatred, envy, menaces, snares, and attacks of the priests, who were irritated at seeing the crowd abandon their altars, and flock with enthusiasm to hear his sermons.[1]

Frequently the superiors of the convents were the first led away in the path of reform. At Halberstadt, Neuenwerk, Halle, and Sagan, the priors set the example to their monks, or at least declared that if a monk

felt his conscience burdened by the weight of monastic vows, far from detaining him in the convent, they would take him by the shoulders and thrust him out of doors.[1]

Indeed throughout all Germany the monks were seen laying down their frocks and cowls at the gates of the monasteries. Some were expelled by the violence of the brethren or the abbots ; others, of mild and pacific character, could no longer endure the continual disputes, abuse, clamour, and hatred which pursued them even in their slumbers ; the majority were convinced that the monastic life was opposed to the will of God and to a christian life ; some had arrived at this conviction by degrees ; and others suddenly, by reading a passage in the Bible. The sloth, grossness, ignorance, and degradation that constituted the very nature of the mendicant orders, inspired with indescribable disgust all men of elevated mind, who could no longer support the society of their vulgar associates. One day, a Franciscan going his rounds, stopped with the box in his hand begging alms at a blacksmith's forge in Nuremberg : " Why," said the smith, " do you not gain your bread by the work of your own hands ? " At these words the sturdy monk threw away his staff, and seizing the hammer plied it vigorously on the anvil. The useless mendicant had become an honest workman. His box and frock were sent back to the monastery.[2]

The monks were not the only persons who rallied round the standard of the Gospel ; priests in still greater numbers began to preach the new doctrines. But preachers were not required for its propagation ; it frequently acted on men's minds, and aroused them from their deep slumber without any one having spoken.

Luther's writings were read in cities, towns, and even villages; at night by the fireside the schoolmaster would often read them aloud to an attentive audience. Some of the hearers were affected by their perusal ; they would take up the Scriptures to clear away their doubts, and were struck with surprise at the astonishing contrast between the Christianity of the Bible and their own. After oscillating between Rome and Scripture, they soon took refuge with that living Word which shed so new and sweet a radiance on their hearts. While they were in this state, some evangelical preacher, probably a priest or a monk, would arrive. Speaking eloquently and with conviction, [3] he announced that Christ had made full atonement for the sins of his people, and demonstrated by Holy Scripture the vanity of works and human penances. A terrible opposition would then break out ; the clergy, and sometimes the magistrates, would strain

---

[1] Der übrigen Prediger Feindschafft, Neid, Nachstellungen, Praticken, und Schrecken. Seckendorff, p. 559.

[1] Seckendorff, p. 811 ; Stentzel, Script. Rer. Siles, i. 457.
[2] Ranke, Deutsche Geschichte. ii. 70.
[3] Eaque omnia prompte, alacriter, eloquenter. Cochlœus, p. 52.

every nerve to bring back the souls they were about to lose. But there was in the new preaching a harmony with Scripture and a hidden force that won all hearts, and subdued even the most rebellious. At the peril of their goods, and of their life if need be, they ranged themselves on the side of the Gospel, and forsook the barren and fanatical orators of the papacy.[1] Sometimes the people, incensed at being so long misled, compelled them to retire; more frequently the priests, deserted by their flocks, without tithes or offerings, departed voluntarily and in sadness to seek a livelihood elsewhere.[2] And while the supporters of the ancient hierarchy retired from these places sorrowful and dejected, and sometimes bidding farewell to their old flocks in the language of anathema, the people, whom truth and liberty transported with joy, surrounded the new preachers with acclamations, and, thirsting for the Word of God, carried them as it were in triumph into the church and into the pulpit.[3]

A word of power, proceeding from God, was at that time regenerating society. The people, or their leaders, would frequently invite some man celebrated for his faith to come and enlighten them; and he for love of the Gospel, would immediately abandon his interests and his family, his country and friends.[4] Persecution often compelled the partisans of the Reformation to leave their homes: they reached some spot where it was as yet unknown; there they would find some house that offered an asylum to poor travellers; there they would speak of the Gospel, read a chapter to the attentive hearers, and perhaps, by the intercession of their new friends, obtain permission to preach once publicly in the church......Then indeed a fierce fire would break out in the city, and the greatest exertions were ineffectual to quench it.[5] If they could not preach in the church, they found some other spot. Every place became a temple. At Husum in Holstein, Hermann Tast, who was returning from Wittemberg, and against whom the clergy of the parish had closed the church doors, preached to an immense crowd in the cemetery, beneath the shade of two large trees, not far from the spot where, seven centuries before, Anschar had proclaimed the Gospel to the heathen. At Arnstadt, Gaspard Güttel, an Augustine monk, preached in the market-place. At Dantzic, the Gospel was announced on a little hill without the city. At Gosslar, a Wittemberg student taught the new doctrines in a meadow planted with lime-trees; whence the evangelical

Christians were denominated the *Lime-tree Brethren.*

While the priests were exhibiting their sordid covetousness before the eyes of the people, the new preachers said to them, "Freely we have received, freely do we give."[1] The idea often expressed by the new preachers from the pulpit, that Rome had formerly sent the Germans a corrupted Gospel, so that now for the first time Germany heard the Word of Christ in its heavenly and primal beauty, produced a deep impression on men's minds.[2] And the noble thought of the equality of all men, of a universal brotherhood in Jesus Christ, laid strong hold upon those souls which for so long a period had groaned beneath the yoke of feudalism and of the papacy of the Middle Ages.[3]

Often would unlearned Christians, with the New Testament in their hands, undertake to justify the doctrine of the Reformation. The catholics who remained faithful to Rome withdrew in affright; for to priests and monks alone had been assigned the task of studying sacred literature. The latter were therefore compelled to come forward; the conference began; but erelong, overwhelmed by the declarations of Holy Scripture cited by these laymen, the priests and monks knew not how to reply.[4].........." Unhappily," says Cochlœus, "Luther had persuaded his followers to put no faith in any other oracle than the Holy Scriptures." A shout was raised in the assembly, denouncing the scandalous ignorance of these old theologians, who had hitherto been reputed such great scholars by their own party.[5]

Men of the lowest station, and even the weaker sex, with the aid of God's Word, persuaded and led away men's hearts. Extraordinary works are the result of extraordinary times. At Ingolstadt, under the eyes of Dr. Eck, a young weaver read Luther's works to the assembled crowd. In this very city, the university having resolved to compel a disciple of Melancthon to retract, a woman, named Argula de Staufen, undertook his defence, and challenged the doctors to a public disputation. Women and children, artisans and soldiers, knew more of the Bible than the doctors of the schools or the priests of the altars.

Christendom was divided into two hostile bodies, and their aspects were strikingly contrasted. Opposed to the old champions of the hierarchy, who had neglected the study of languages and the cultivation of literature (as one of their own body informs us), were generous-minded youths, devoted to study, investigating Scripture, and familiarizing themselves with the masterpieces of anti-

---

[1] Populo odibiles catholici concionatores. Cochlœus, p. 52.
[2] Ad extremam redacti inopiam, aliunde sibi victum quærere cogerentur. Ibid. p. 53.
[3] Triumphantibus novis prædicatoribus qui sequacem populum verbo novi Evangelii sui ducebant. Ibid.
[4] Multi, omissa re domestica, in speciem veri Evangelii, parentes et amicos relinquebant. Ibid.
[5] Ubi vero aliquos nacti fuissent amicos in ea civitate.... Ibid. 54.

[1] Mira eis erat liberalitas. Cochlœus, p. 53.
[2] Eam usque diem nunquam Germane prædicatam. Ibid.
[3] Omnes æquales et fratres in Christo. Ibid.
[4] A laicis Lutheranis, plures Scripturæ locos, quam a monachis et presbyteris. Ibid. p. 54.
[5] Reputabantur catholici ab illis ignari Scripturarum. Ibid.

quity.[1] Possessing an active mind, an elevated soul, and intrepid heart, these young men soon acquired such knowledge, that for a long period none could compete with them. It was not only the vitality of their faith which rendered them superior to their contemporaries, but an elegance of style, a perfume of antiquity, a sound philosophy, a knowledge of the world, completely foreign to the theologians " of the old leaven," as Cochlœus himself terms them.[2] Accordingly, when these youthful defenders of the Reformation met the Romish doctors in any assembly, they attacked them with such ease and confidence, that these ignorant men hesitated, became embarrassed, and fell into a contempt merited in the eyes of all.

The ancient edifice was crumbling under the load of superstition and ignorance; the new one was rising on the foundations of faith and learning. New elements entered deep into the lives of the people. Torpor and dulness were in all parts succeeded by a spirit of inquiry and a thirst for instruction. An active, enlightened, and living faith took the place of superstitious devotion and ascetic meditations. Works of piety succeeded bigoted observances and penances. The pulpit prevailed over the ceremonies of the altar; and the ancient and sovereign authority of God's Word was at length restored in the Church.

The printing-press, that powerful machine discovered in the fifteenth century, came to the support of all these exertions, and its terrible missiles were continually battering the walls of the enemy.

The impulse which the Reformation gave to popular literature in Germany was immense. Whilst in the year 1513 only thirty-five publications had appeared, and thirty-seven in 1517, the number of books increased with astonishing rapidity after the appearance of Luther's theses. In 1518 we find seventy-one different works; in 1519, one hundred and eleven; in 1520, two hundred and eight; in 1521, two hundred and eleven; in 1522, three hundred and forty-seven; and in 1523, four hundred and ninety-eight...... And where were all these published? For the most part at Wittemberg. And who were their authors? Generally Luther and his friends. In 1522 one hundred and thirty of the reformer's writings were published; and in the year following, one hundred and eighty-three. In this same year only twenty Roman-catholic publications appeared.[3] The literature of Germany thus saw the light in the midst of struggles, contemporaneously with her religion. Already it appeared, as later times have seen it, learned, profound, full of boldness and activity. The national spirit showed itself for the first time without alloy, and at the very moment of its birth received the baptism of fire from christian enthusiasm.

What Luther and his friends composed, others circulated. Monks, convinced of the unlawfulness of monastic obligations, and desirous of exchanging a long life of slothfulness for one of active exertion, but too ignorant to proclaim the Word of God, travelled through the provinces, visiting hamlets and cottages, where they sold the books of Luther and his friends. Germany soon swarmed[1] with these bold colporteurs.[2] Printers and booksellers eagerly welcomed every writing in defence of the Reformation; but they rejected the books of the opposite party, as generally full of ignorance and barbarism.[3] If any one of them ventured to sell a book in favour of the papacy, and offered it for sale in the fairs at Frankfort or elsewhere, merchants, purchasers, and men of letters overwhelmed him with ridicule and sarcasm.[4] It was in vain that the emperor and princes had published severe edicts against the writings of the reformers. As soon as an inquisitorial visit was to be paid, the dealers, who had received secret intimation, concealed the books that it was intended to proscribe; and the multitude, ever eager for what is prohibited, immediately bought them up, and read them with the greater avidity. It was not only in Germany that such scenes were passing; Luther's writings were translated into French, Spanish, English, and Italian, and circulated among these nations.

CHAPTER XII.

Luther at Zwickau—The Castle of Freyberg—Worms—Frankfort—Universal Movement—Wittemberg the Centre of the Reformation—Luther's Sentiments.

If the most puny instruments inflicted such terrible blows on Rome, what was it when the voice of the monk of Wittemberg was heard? Shortly after the discomfiture of the new prophets, Luther, in a layman's attire, traversed the territories of Duke George in a waggon. His gown was hidden, and the reformer seemed to be a plain country gentleman. If he had been recognised, if he had fallen into the hands of the exasperated duke, perhaps his fate would have been sealed. He was going to preach at Zwickau,

---

[1] Totam vero juventutem, eloquentiæ litteris, linguarumque studio deditam....in partem suam traxit. Cochlœus, p. 54.
[2] Veteris farinæ.
[3] Panzer's Annalen der Deutsch. Litt.; Ranke's Deutsch. Gesch. ii. 79.

[1] Apostatarum, monasteriis relictis, infinitus jam erat numerus, in speciem bibliopolarum. Cochlœus, p. 54.
[2] We have ventured to employ the words *colporteur* and *colportage* to express the title and trade of those itinerant booksellers. Besides the inadequacy of our English equivalents, these words appear to be making their way into our vocabulary. (*Translator*.)
[3] Catholicorum, velut indocta et veteris barbarici trivialia scripta, contemnebant. Cochlœus, p. 54.
[4] In publicis mercatibus Francofordiæ et alibi, vexabantur ac ridebantur. Ibid.

the birthplace of the pretended prophets. It was no sooner known at Schneeberg, Annaberg, and the surrounding places, than the people crowded around him. Fourteen thousand persons flocked into the city, and as there was no church that could contain such numbers, Luther went into the balcony of the town-hall, and preached before an audience of twenty-five thousand persons who thronged the market-place, some of whom had mounted on heaps of cut stones piled up near the building.[1] The servant of God was dilating with fervour on the election of grace, when suddenly cries were heard from the midst of the audience. An old woman of haggard mien, who had taken her station on a pile of stones, stretched out her emaciated arms, and seemed as though she would restrain with her fleshless hands the crowd that was about to fall prostrate at the feet of Jesus. Her wild yells interrupted the preacher. " It was the devil," said Seckendorff, " who had taken the form of an old woman in order to excite a disturbance."[2] But it was all in vain; the reformer's words silenced the wicked spirit, enthusiasm seized these listening thousands; glances of admiration were exchanged; hands were warmly grasped, and erelong the monks, confounded and unable to avert the storm, found it necessary to leave Zwickau.

In the castle of Freyberg dwelt Henry, brother of Duke George. His wife, a princess of Mecklenburg, had the preceding year borne him a son who had been named Maurice. With a fondness for the table and for pleasure, Duke Henry combined the rudeness and coarse manners of a soldier. In other respects, he was pious after the fashion of the times, had gone to the Holy Land, and made a pilgrimage to St. Iago of Compostella. He would often say: " At Compostella I placed a hundred golden florins on the altar of the saint, and said to him: O St. Iago, to please thee I came hither; I make thee a present of this money; but if these knaves (the priests) take it from thee, I cannot help it; so be on your guard."[3]

A Franciscan and a Dominican, both disciples of Luther, had been for some time preaching the Gospel at Freyberg. The duchess, whose piety had inspired her with a horror of heresy, listened to their sermons in astonishment to find that this gentle message of a Saviour was the object she had been taught to fear. Gradually her eyes were opened, and she found peace in Christ Jesus. No sooner had Duke George learnt that the Gospel was preached at Freyberg, than he entreated his brother to oppose these novelties. Chancellor Strehlin and the canons seconded his prayer with their fanaticism. A violent explosion took place in the court of Freyberg. Duke Henry harshly reprimanded and reproached his wife, and more than once the pious duchess watered her child's cradle with her tears. Yet by degrees her prayers and gentleness won the heart of her husband; the rough man was softened; harmony was restored between the married pair, and they were enabled to join in prayer beside their sleeping babe. Great destinies were hovering over that child; and from that cradle, where a christian mother had so often poured forth her sorrows, God was one day to bring forth the liberator of the Reformation.

Luther's intrepidity had excited the inhabitants of Worms. The imperial decree terrified the magistrates; all the churches were closed; but in a public place, filled by an immense crowd, a preacher ascended a rudely constructed pulpit, and proclaimed the Gospel with persuasive accents. If the authorities showed a disposition to interfere, the hearers dispersed in a moment, and stealthily carried away the pulpit; but the storm was no sooner passed, than it was immediately set up in some more secluded spot, to which the crowd again flocked to hear the Word of Christ. This temporary pulpit was every day carried from one place to another, and served to encourage the people, who were still agitated by the emotions of the great drama lately performed in their city.[1]

At Frankfort on the Maine, one of the principal free cities of the empire, all was in commotion. A courageous evangelist, Ibach, preached salvation by Jesus Christ. The clergy, among whom was Cochlœus, so notorious by his writings and his opposition, were irritated against this audacious colleague, and denounced him to the Archbishop of Mentz. The council undertook his defence, although with timidity, but to no purpose, for the clergy discharged the evangelical minister, and compelled him to leave the town. Rome triumphed; every thing seemed lost; the poor believers fancied themselves for ever deprived of the Word; but at the very moment when the citizens appeared inclined to yield to these tyrannical priests, many nobles declared for the Gospel. Max of Molnheim, Harmuth of Cronberg, George of Stockheim, and Emeric of Reiffenstein, whose estates lay near Frankfort, wrote to the council: " We are constrained to rise up against these spiritual wolves." And addressing the clergy, they said: " Embrace the evangelical doctrine, recall Ibach, or else we will refuse to pay our tithes!"

The people, who listened gladly to the Reformation, being encouraged by the language of the nobles, began to put themselves in motion; and one day, just as Peter Mayer, the persecutor of Ibach and the most determined enemy of the reform, was going to

[1] Von dem Rathhaus unter einem Zulauf von 25,000 Menschen. Seck. p. 539.
[2] Der Teufel indem er sich in Gestalt eines alten Weibes. Ibid.
[3] Lasst du dir's die Buben nehmen....Ibid. p. 430.

[1] So liessen sie eine Canzel machen, die man von einem Ort zum andern....Seck. p. 436.

preach against the heretics, a great uproar was heard. Mayer was alarmed, and hastily quitted the church. This movement decided the council. All the preachers were enjoined by proclamation to preach the pure Word of God, or to leave the city.

The light which proceeded from Wittemberg, as from the heart of the nation, was thus shedding its rays through the whole empire. In the west,—Berg, Cleves, Lippstadt, Munster, Wesel, Miltenberg, Mentz, Deux Ponts, and Strasburg, listened to the Gospel; on the south,—Hoff, Schlesstadt, Bamberg, Esslingen, Halle in Swabia, Heilbrunn, Augsburg, Ulm, and many other places, received it with joy. In the east,—Pomerania, Prussia, and the duchy of Liegnitz, opened their gates to it; and in the north.—Brunswick, Halberstadt, Gosslar, Zell, Friesland, Bremen, Hamburg, Holstein, and even Denmark, with other neighbouring countries, were moved at the sounds of this new doctrine.

The Elector Frederick had declared that he would allow the bishops to preach freely in his states, but that he would deliver no one into their hands. Accordingly, the evangelical teachers, persecuted in other countries, soon took refuge in Saxony. Ibach of Frankfort, Eberlin of Ulm, Kauxdorf of Magdeburg, Valentine Mustœus, whom the canons of Halberstadt had horribly mutilated,[1] and other faithful ministers, coming from all parts of Germany, fled to Wittemberg, as the only asylum in which they could be secure. Here they conversed with the reformers; at their feet they strengthened themselves in the faith; and communicated to them their own experience and the knowledge they had acquired. It is thus the waters of the rivers return by the clouds from the vast expanse of the ocean, to feed the glaciers whence they first descended to the plains.

The work which was evolving at Wittemberg, and formed in this manner of many different elements, became more and more the work of the nation, of Europe, and of Christendom. This school, founded by Frederick, and quickened by Luther, was the centre of an immense revolution which regenerated the Church, and impressed on it a real and living unity far superior to the apparent unity of Rome. The Bible reigned at Wittemberg, and its oracles were heard on all sides. This academy, the most recent of all, had acquired that rank and influence in Christendom which had hitherto belonged to the ancient university of Paris. The crowds that flocked thither from every part of Europe made known the wants of the Church and of the nations; and as they quitted these walls, now become holy to them, they

carried back with them to the Church and the people the Word of Grace appointed to heal and to save the nations.

Luther, as he witnessed this success, felt his confidence increase. He beheld this feeble undertaking, begun in the midst of so many fears and struggles, changing the aspect of the christian world, and was astonished at the result. He had foreseen nothing of the kind, when first he rose up against Tetzel. Prostrate before the God whom he adored, he confessed the work to be His, and exulted in the assurance of a victory that could not be torn from him. "Our enemies threaten us with death," said he to Harmuth of Cronberg; "if they had as much wisdom as foolishness, they would, on the contrary, threaten us with life. What an absurdity and insult to presume to threaten death to Christ and Christians, who are themselves lords and conquerors of death![1].....
It is as if I would seek to frighten a man by saddling his horse and helping him to mount. Do they not know that Christ is risen from the dead? In their eyes he is still lying in the sepulchre; nay more—in hell. But we know that He lives." He was grieved at the thought that he was regarded as the author of a work, in whose minutest details he beheld the hand of God. "Many believe because of me," said he. "But those alone truly believe, who would continue faithful even should they hear (which God forbid!) that I had denied Jesus Christ. True disciples believe not in Luther, but in Jesus Christ. As for myself, I do not care about Luther.[2] Whether he is a saint or a knave, what matters it? It is not he that I preach; but Christ. If the devil can take him, let him do so! But let Christ abide with us, and we shall abide also."

And vainly, indeed, would men endeavour to explain this great movement by mere human circumstances. Men of letters, it is true, sharpened their wits and discharged their keen-pointed arrows against the pope and the monks; the shout of liberty, which Germany had so often raised against the tyranny of the Italians, again resounded in the castles and provinces; the people were delighted with the song of "the nightingale of Wittemberg," a herald of the spring that was everywhere bursting forth.[3] But it was not a mere outward movement, similar to that effected by a longing for earthly liberty, that was then accomplishing. Those who assert that the Reformation was brought about by bribing the princes with the wealth of the convents,—the priests with permission to marry,—and the people with the prospect of freedom, are strangely mistaken in its nature. No doubt a useful employment of the funds that had hitherto supported the sloth of the monks; no doubt marriage and

<hr>

[1] Aliquot ministri canonicorum, capiunt D. Valentinum Mustæum et vinctum manibus pedibusque, injecto in ejus os freno, deferunt per trabes in inferiores cœnobii partes, ibique in cella cerevisiaria eum castrant. Hamelmann, Historia renati Evangelii, p. 880.

[1] Herren und Seigmänner des Todes. L. Epp. ii. 164.
[2] Ich kenne auch selbst nicht den Luther. Ibid. 168.
[3] Wittemberger Nachtigall, a poem by Hans Sachs, 1523.

liberty, gifts that proceed direct from God, might have favoured the development of the Reformation; but the mainspring was not there. An interior revolution was then going on in the depths of the human heart. Christians were again learning to love, to pardon, to pray, to suffer, and even to die for a truth that offered no repose save in heaven. The Church was passing through a state of transformation. Christianity was bursting the bonds in which it had been so long confined, and returning in life and vigour into a world that had forgotten its ancient power. The hand that made the world was turned towards it again; and the Gospel, reappearing in the midst of the nations, accelerated its course, notwithstanding the violent and repeated efforts of priests and kings; like the ocean which, when the hand of God presses on its surface, rises calm and majestic along its shores, so that no human power is able to resist its progress.

BOOK X.

AGITATION, REVERSES, AND PROGRESS. 1522—1526.

CHAPTER I.

Political Element—Want of Enthusiasm at Rome—Siege of Pampeluna—Courage of Ignatius—Transition—Luther and Loyola—Visions—Two Principles.

THE Reformation, which at first had existed in the hearts of a few pious men, had entered into the worship and the life of the Church; it was natural that it would take a new step, and penetrate into civil relationships and the life of nations. Its progress was always from the interior to the exterior. We are about to see this great revolution taking possession of the political life of the world.

For eight centuries past, Europe had formed one vast sacerdotal state. Emperors and kings had been under the patronage of popes. Whenever any energetic resistance had been offered to her audacious pretensions, particularly in Germany and France, Rome had eventually prevailed, and princes, docile agents of her terrible decrees, had been seen fighting to secure her dominion against private believers obedient to their rule, and profusely shedding in her behalf the blood of their people's children.

No injury could be inflicted on this vast ecclesiastical state, of which the pope was the head, without affecting the political relations.

Two great ideas then agitated Germany. On the one hand, a desire for a revival of faith; and on the other, a longing for a national government, in which the German states might be represented, and thus serve as a counterpoise to the power of the emperors. [1]

The Elector Frederick had insisted on this latter point at the election of Maximilian's successor; and the youthful Charles had submitted. A national government had been framed in consequence, consisting of the imperial governor and representatives of the electors and circles.

Thus Luther reformed the Church, and Frederick of Saxony reformed the State.

But while, simultaneously with the religious reform, important political modifications were introduced by the leaders of the nation, it was to be feared that the commonalty would also put itself in motion, and by its excesses, both in politics and religion, compromise both reforms.

This violent and fanatical intrusion of the people and of certain ringleaders, which seems inevitable where society is shaken and in a state of transition, did not fail to take place in Germany at the period of which we are now treating.

There were other circumstances also that contributed to give rise to such disorders.

The emperor and the pope had combined against the Reformation, and it seemed on the point of falling beneath the blows of two such powerful enemies. Policy, ambition, and interest compelled Charles V. and Leo X. to attempt its destruction. But these are poor champions to contend against the truth. Devotedness to a cause which is looked upon as sacred can only be conquered by a similar devotedness. But the Romans, yielding to the impulses of a Leo X., were enthusiastic about a sonnet or a melody, but insensible to the religion of Jesus Christ; and if any less futile thought came across their minds, instead of purifying and tempering their hearts anew in the Christianity of the apostles, they were busied with alliances, wars conquests, and treaties, which gained new provinces, and with cold disdain left the Reformation to awaken on all sides a religious enthusiasm, and to march triumphantly

[1] Pfeffel Droit publ. de l'Allemagne, 590. Robertson, Charles V. iii. 114. Ranke, Deutsche Gesch.

to more noble conquests. The enemy that had been doomed to destruction in the cathedral of Worms, reappeared full of confidence and strength; the contest must be severe; and blood must flow.

Yet some of the most imminent dangers that threatened the Reformation seemed at this time to be disappearing. It is true that shortly before the publication of the edict of Worms, the youthful Charles, standing one day at a window of his palace with his confessor, had said, laying his hand on his heart: "I swear to hang up at this very window the first man who shall declare himself a Lutheran after the publication of my edict."[1] But it was not long before his zeal abated considerably. His project for reviving the ancient glory of the holy empire, that is to say, of increasing his own power, had been coldly received.[2] Dissatisfied with Germany, he left the banks of the Rhine, repaired to the Netherlands, and availed himself of his residence there to afford the monks those gratifications that he found himself unable to give them in the empire. At Ghent Luther's works were burnt by the hangman with all possible solemnity. More than fifty thousand spectators were present at this auto-da-fé, the emperor himself looking on with an approving smile.[3] He thence proceeded to Spain, where wars and internal dissensions compelled him, for a time at least, to leave Germany at peace. Since he has been refused in the empire the power to which he lays claim, others if they pleased, might hunt down the heretic of Wittemberg. More anxious thoughts engrossed his attention.

In effect, Francis I., impatient to try his strength with his rival, had thrown down the gauntlet. Under the pretence of restoring the children of Jean d'Albret, king of Navarre, to their patrimony, he had commenced a bloody struggle, destined to last all his life, by sending into that kingdom an army under the command of Lesparre, whose rapid conquests were only stopped before the fortress of Pampeluna.

On these strong walls was to be kindled an enthusiasm destined afterwards to oppose the enthusiasm of the reformer, and to breathe into the papacy a new spirit of energy, devotedness, and control. Pampeluna was destined to be the cradle, as it were, of the rival of the Wittemberg monk.

The chivalrous spirit that had so long animated the christian world survived in Spain alone. The wars against the Moors, scarcely terminated in the Peninsula, and continually breaking out in Africa, with distant and adventurous expeditions beyond the seas, fostered in the Castilian youths that enthusiastic and unaffected valour of which Amadis formed the ideal model.

Among the defenders of Pampeluna was a young gentleman, Inigo Lopez of Recalda, the youngest of a family of thirteen children. Recalda, better known as Ignatius Loyola, had been brought up in the court of Ferdinand the Catholic. He was graceful in person,[1] expert in handling the sword and the lance, and ardent in the pursuit of chivalrous renown. To array himself in glittering arms, to ride a noble steed,[2] to expose himself to the brilliant dangers of the tournament, to engage in hazardous exploits, to share in the envenomed struggles of faction,[3] and to display as much devotion for Saint Peter as for his lady-love—such was the life of this young chevalier.

The governor of Navarre, having gone into Spain to procure succours, had left the defence of Pampeluna to Inigo and a few nobles. The latter, perceiving the superiority of the French troops, resolved to withdraw. Inigo conjured them to make a stand against Lesparre, but finding them resolute in their intention, he looked at them with indignation, accused them of cowardice and perfidy, and then flung himself alone into the citadel, determined to hold it at the peril of his life.[4]

The French, who were enthusiastically received into Pampeluna, having summoned the commander of the fortress to capitulate: "Let us suffer every thing," said Inigo impetuously to his companions, "rather than surrender."[5] Upon this the French began to batter the walls with their powerful machines, and soon attempted an assault. Inigo's courage and exhortations inspirited the Spaniards, who repelled the assailants with arrows, swords, and battle-axes. Inigo fought at their head: standing on the ramparts, his eyes glistening with rage, the young cavalier brandished his sword, and the enemy fell beneath his blows. Suddenly a ball struck the wall close by him; a splinter from the stone wounded him severely in the right leg, and the ball recoiling with the violence of the blow, broke his left leg. Inigo fell senseless.[6] The garrison surrendered immediately; and the French, admiring the courage of their youthful opponent, had him conveyed in a litter to his parents in the castle of Loyola. In this lordly mansion, from which he afterwards derived his name, Inigo had been born, eight years after Luther, of one of the most illustrious families of that district.

---

[1] Sancte juro....eum ex hac fenestra meo jussu suspensum iri. Pallav. i. 130.
[2] Essendo tornato dalla Dieta che sua Maestà haveva fatta in Wormatia, escluso d'ogni conclusion buona d'ajuti e di favori che si fussi proposto d'ottenere in essa. Instructions to Cardinal Farnese. MS. in the Corsini library, published by Ranke.
[3] Ipso Cæsare, ore subridenti, spectaculo plausit. Pallav. L. 130.

[1] Cum esset in corporis ornatu elegantissimus. Maffei Vita Loyolæ. 1586, p. 3.
[2] Equorumque et armorum usu præcelleret. Ibid.
[3] Partim in factionum rixarumque periculis, partim in amatoria vesania....tempus consumeret. Ibid.
[4] Ardentibus oculis, detestatus ignaviam perfidiamque, spectantibus omnibus, in arcem solus introit. Ibid. p. 6.
[5] Tam acri ac vehementi oratione commilitonibus dissuasit. Ibid.
[6] Ut e vestigio semianimis alienata mente corruerit. Ibid. p. 7.

A painful operation had become necessary. Under the most acute sufferings, Inigo firmly clenched his hands, but did not utter a single groan.[1]

Confined to a wearisome inactivity, he found it necessary to employ his active imagination. In the absence of the romances of chivalry, which had hitherto been his only mental food, he took up the life of Jesus Christ, and the legends or *Flowers of the Saints*. This kind of reading, in his state of solitude and sickness, produced an extraordinary impression on his mind. The noisy life of tournaments and battles, which had hitherto exclusively occupied his thoughts, appeared to recede, to fade and vanish from his sight; and at the same time a more glorious career seemed opening before his astonished eyes. The humble actions of the saints and their heroic sufferings appeared far more worthy of praise than all the high feats of arms and chivalry. Stretched upon his bed, a prey to fever, he indulged in the most conflicting thoughts. The world that he was forsaking, the world whose holy mortifications lay before him, appeared together, the one with its pleasures, the other with its austerities; and these two antagonists contended in deadly struggle within his bosom. "What if I were to act like St. Francis or St. Dominick?" said he.[2] Then the image of the lady to whom he had pledged his heart rose before him: "She is not a countess," exclaimed he with artless vanity, "nor a duchess; but her condition is much loftier than either."[3] Such thoughts as these filled his mind with distress and *ennui*, while his plan of imitating the saints inspired him with peace and joy.

From this period his choice was made. As soon as his health was restored, he determined to bid adieu to the world. After having, like Luther, partaken of one more repast with his old companions in arms, he departed alone, in great secrecy,[4] for the solitary dwellings that the hermits of St. Benedict had hewn out of the rocks of Montserrat. Impelled not by a sense of sin or his need of Divine grace, but by a desire to become a "knight of the Virgin," and of obtaining renown by mortifications and pious works, after the example of the whole army of saints, he confessed for three days together, gave his rich attire to a beggar, put on sackcloth, and girt himself with a rope.[5] Then, remembering the celebrated armed vigils of Amadis of Gaul, he suspended his sword before an image of Mary, passed the night in watching in his new and strange costume, and sometimes on his knees, sometimes upright, but always in prayer and with the pilgrim's staff in his hand, he repeated all the devout practices that the illustrious Amadis had observed before him. "It was thus," says his biographer, the Jesuit Maffei, "that while Satan was arming Luther against all laws human and divine, and while that infamous heresiarch was appearing at Worms, and impiously declaring war against the apostolic see, Christ, by a call of his heavenly providence, was awakening this new champion, and binding him, and those who were to follow in his steps, to the service of the Roman pontiff, and setting him up to oppose the licentiousness and fury of heretical depravity."[1]

Loyola, although still lame in one of his legs, dragged himself by winding and lonely paths to Manresa, where he entered a Dominican convent, in order to devote himself in this secluded spot to the severest mortifications. Like Luther, he daily begged his bread from door to door.[2] He passed seven hours upon his knees, and scourged himself three times a-day; at midnight he rose to pray; he allowed his hair and nails to grow, and in the thin pale face of the monk of Manresa it would have been impossible to recognise the young and brilliant knight of Pampeluna.

Yet the hour had come when religious ideas, which hitherto had been to Inigo a mere chivalrous amusement, were to be evolved in him with greater depth, and make him sensible of a power to which he was as yet a stranger. Suddenly, without any thing to give him warning, the joy he had felt disappeared.[3] In vain he had recourse to prayer and singing hymns; he could find no rest.[4] His imagination had ceased to call up pleasing illusions; he was left alone with his conscience. A state so new to him was beyond his comprehension, and he fearfully asked himself whether God, after all the sacrifices he had made, was still angry with him. Night and day gloomy terrors agitated his soul; he shed bitter tears; with loud cries he called for the peace of mind which he had lost......but all was in vain.[5] He then recommenced the long confession he had made at Montserrat. "Perhaps," thought he, "I have forgotten something." But this confession only increased his anguish, for it reminded him of all his errors. He wandered about gloomy and dejected; his conscience accused him of having done nothing all his life but add sin to sin; and

---

[1] Nullum aliud indicium dedit doloris, nisi ut coactos in pugnum digitos valde constringeret. Maffei Vita Loyolæ, 1586, p. 8.
[2] Quid si ego hoc agerem quod fecit beatus Franciscus, quid si hoc quod beatus Dominicus? Acta Sanct. vii. 634.
[3] Non era condessa, ni duquessa, mas era su estado mas alto. Ibid.
[4] Ibi duce amicisque ita salutatis, ut arcana consiliorum suorum quam accuratissime tegeret. Maffei, p. 16.
[5] Pretiosa vestimenta quibus erat ornatus, pannoso cuidam largitus, sacco sese alacer induit ac fune præcinxit. Ibid. p. 20.

[1] Furori ac libidini hæreticæ pravitatis opponeret. Maffei, p. 21.
[2] Victum osteatim precibus, infimis emendicare quotidie. Ibid. p. 23.
[3] Tunc subito, nulla præcedente significatione, prorsus exui nudarique se omni gaudio sentiret. Ibid. p. 27.
[4] Nec jam in precibus, neque in psalmis....ullam invenit ret delectationem aut requiem. Ibid.
[5] Vanis agitari terroribus, dies noctesque fletibus jungere. Ibid. p. 28.

the wretched man, a prey to overwhelming terrors, filled the cloister with his groans.

Strange thoughts then entered into his heart. Finding no consolation in confession or in the various ordinances of the Church,[1] he began, like Luther, to doubt their efficacy. But instead of forsaking the works of men, and seeking the all-sufficient work of Christ, he asked himself whether he should not again pursue the pleasures of time. His soul sprang eagerly towards the delights of the world he had renounced,[2] but immediately recoiled with affright.

Was there, at that time, any difference between the monk of Manresa and the monk of Erfurth? Unquestionably,—in secondary points: but the state of their souls was the same. Both were deeply sensible of the multitude of their sins. Both were seeking for reconciliation with God, and longed to have the assurance in their hearts. If a Staupitz with the Bible in his hand had appeared in the convent of Manresa, possibly Inigo might have become the Luther of the Peninsula. These two great men of the sixteenth century, these founders of two spiritual powers which for three centuries have been warring together, were at this moment brothers; and perhaps, if they had met, Luther and Loyola would have embraced, and mingled their tears and their prayers.

But from this hour the two monks were destined to follow entirely different paths. Inigo, instead of feeling that his remorse was sent to drive him to the foot of the cross, persuaded himself that these inward reproaches proceeded not from God, but from the devil; and he resolved never more to think of his sins, to erase them from his memory, and bury them in eternal oblivion.[3] Luther turned towards Christ; Loyola only fell back upon himself.

Visions came erelong to confirm Inigo in the conviction at which he had arrived. His own resolves had become a substitute for the grace of the Lord; his own imaginings supplied the place of God's Word. He had looked upon the voice of God in his conscience as the voice of the devil; and accordingly then the remainder of his history represents him as given up to the inspirations of the spirit of darkness.

One day Loyola met an old woman, as Luther in the hour of his trial was visited by an old man. But the Spanish crone, instead of proclaiming remission of sins to the penitent of Manresa, predicted visitations from Jesus. Such was the Christianity to which Loyola, like the prophets of Zwickau, had

recourse. Inigo did not seek truth in the Holy Scriptures; but imagined in their place immediate communication with the world of spirits. He soon lived entirely in ecstasies and contemplation.

One day, as he was going to the church of St. Paul, outside the city, he walked along the banks of the Llobregat, and sat down absorbed in meditation. His eyes were fixed on the river, which rolled its deep waters silently before him. He was lost in thought. Suddenly he fell into an ecstasy: he saw with his bodily eyes what men can with difficulty understand after much reading, long vigils, and study.[1] He rose, and as he stood on the brink of the river, he appeared to have become another man; he then knelt down at the foot of a cross which was close at hand, ready to sacrifice his life in the service of that cause whose mysteries had just been revealed to him.

From this time his visions became more frequent. Sitting one day on the steps of St. Dominick's church at Manresa, he was singing a hymn to the Holy Virgin, when on a sudden his soul was wrapt in ecstasy; he remained motionless, and absorbed in contemplation; the mystery of the most Holy Trinity was revealed to his sight under magnificent symbols;[2] he shed tears, filled the church with his sobs, and all day long did not but speak of this ineffable vision.

These numerous apparitions had removed all his doubts; he believed, not like Luther because the things of faith were written in the Word of God, but because of the visions he had seen. " Even had there been no Bible," say his apologists, " even had these mysteries never been revealed in Scripture,[3] he would have believed them, for God had appeared to him."[4] Luther, on taking his doctor's degree, had pledged his oath to Holy Scripture,[5] and the only infallible authority of the Word of God had become the fundamental principle of the Reformation. Loyola, at this time, bound himself to dreams and visions; and chimerical apparitions became the principle of his life and of his faith.

Luther's sojourn in the convent of Erfurth and that of Loyola in the convent of Manresa explain to us—the one, the Reformation; the other, modern Popery. The monk who was to reanimate the exhausted vigour of Rome repaired to Jerusalem after quitting the cloister. We will not follow him on this pilgrimage, as we shall meet with him again in the course of this history.

[1] Ut nulla jam res mitigare dolorem posse videretur. Maff. p. 29.
[2] Et sæculi commodis repetendis magno quodam impetu cogitaverit. Ibid. p. 30.
[3] Sine ulla dubitatione constitut præteritæ vitæ labes perpetua oblivione conterere. Ibid. p. 31.

[1] Quæ vix demum solent homines intelligentia comprehendere. Maff. p. 32.
[2] En figuras de tres teclas.
[3] Quod etsi nulla scriptura, mysteria illa fidei doceret Acta Sancti.
[4] Quæ Deo sibi aperiente cognoverant. Maff. p. 34.
[5] Vol. i. p. 72.

CHAPTER II.

Victory of the Pope—Death of Leo X.—The Oratory of Divine Love—Adrian VI.—Plan of Reform—Opposition.

WHILE these events were taking place in Spain, Rome herself appeared to be assuming a more serious character. The great patron of music, hunting, and festivities disappeared from the pontifical throne, and was succeeded by a pious and grave monk.

Leo X. had been greatly delighted at hearing of the edict of Worms and of Luther's captivity; and immediately, in testimony of his victory, he had consigned the effigy and writings of the reformer to the flames.[1] It was the second or third time that Rome had indulged in this innocent enjoyment. At the same time Leo X., wishing to testify his gratitude to Charles V., united his army with the emperor's. The French were compelled to evacuate Parma, Piacenza, and Milan; and Giulio de Medici, the pope's cousin, entered the latter city. The pope was thus approaching the summit of earthly power.

These events took place at the beginning of the winter of 1521. Leo X. was accustomed to spend the autumn in the country. At such times he would leave Rome without surplice, and, what was considered still more scandalous, wearing boots.[2] At Viterbo he amused himself with hawking; at Corneti in hunting the stag: the lake of Bolsena afforded him the pleasure of fishing; thence he passed to his favourite villa at Malliana, where he spent his time in the midst of festivities. Musicians, improvisatori, and all the artists whose talents could enliven this delightful abode, were gathered round the pontiff. He was residing there when he received intelligence of the capture of Milan. A great excitement immediately ensued in the villa. The courtiers and officers could not restrain their exultation, the Swiss discharged their carbines, and Leo, in excess of joy, walked up and down his room all night, from time to time looking out of the window at the rejoicings of the soldiers and of the people. He returned to Rome fatigued, but intoxicated with success. He had scarcely reached the Vatican when he felt suddenly indisposed. "Pray for me," said he to his attendants. He had not even time to receive the holy sacrament, and died in the prime of life, at the age of forty-five, in the hour of victory, and amid the noise of rejoicing.

The crowd followed the pontiff to the grave, loading him with abuse. They could not forgive him for having died without the sacrament, and for leaving his debts unpaid, the result of his enormous expenses. "You gained your pontificate like a fox," said the Romans; "you held it like a lion, and left it like a dog."

Such was the funeral oration with which Rome honoured the pope who excommunicated the Reformation, and whose name serves to designate one of the great epochs in history.

Meantime a feeble reaction against the spirit of Leo and of Rome was already beginning in Rome itself. Some pious men had there established an oratory for their common edification,[1] near the spot which tradition assigns as the place where the early Christians used to meet. Contarini, who had heard Luther at Worms, was the leader in these prayer-meetings. Thus a species of reformation was beginning at Rome almost at the same time as at Wittemberg. It has been said with truth, that wherever the seeds of piety exist, there also are the germs of reformation. But these good intentions were soon to be frustrated.

In other times, a Gregory VII. or an Innocent III. would have been chosen to succeed Leo X., could such men have been found; but the interest of the Empire was now superior to that of the Church, and Charles V. required a pope devoted to his service. The Cardinal de Medici, afterwards Clement VII., seeing that he had no chance at present of obtaining the tiara, exclaimed: "Elect the Cardinal of Tortosa, a man in years, and whom every one regards as a saint." This prelate, who was a native of Utrecht, and sprung from the middle classes, was chosen, and reigned under the title of Adrian VI. He had been professor at Louvain, and afterwards tutor to Charles V., by whose influence he was invested with the Roman purple in 1517. Cardinal de Vio supported his nomination. "Adrian," said he, "had a great share in procuring Luther's condemnation by the Louvain doctors."[2] The cardinals, tired out and taken by surprise, elected this foreigner; but as soon as they came to their senses (says a chronicler), they almost died of fright. The thought that the austere Netherlander would not accept the tiara, at first gave them some little consolation; but this hope was not of long duration. Pasquin represented the pontiff elect under the character of a schoolmaster, and the cardinals as little boys under the rod. The citizens were so exasperated that the members of the conclave thought themselves fortunate to have escaped being thrown into the river.[3] In Holland, on the contrary, the people testified by general rejoicings their

---

[1] Comburi jussit alteram vultus in ejus statua, alteram animi ejus in libris. Pallav. i. 128.
[2] Paris de Grassis, his master of the ceremonies, has this entry in his diary. "Thursday, 10th Jan., after breakfast, the pope went to Toscanello and its neighbourhood. He went without his stole, and, worse than that, without his rochet, and worse than all, wore boots. Diar. inedit.

[1] Si unirono in un oratorio, chiamato del divino amore, circa sessanta di loro. Caracciolo, Vita da Paolo IV. MS. Ranke.
[2] Doctores Lovanienses accepisse consilium a tam conspicuo alumno. Pallav. p. 136.
[3] Sleidan, Hist. de la Réf. i. 124.

delight at giving a pope to the Church. "Utrecht planted; Louvain watered; the Emperor gave the increase," was the inscription on the hangings suspended from the fronts of the houses. A wag wrote below these words: "And God had nothing to do with it."

Notwithstanding the dissatisfaction at first manifested by the people of Rome, Adrian VI. repaired to that city in the month of August 1522, and was well received. It was reported that he had more than five thousand benefices in his gift, and every man reckoned on having his share. For many years the papal throne had not been filled by such a pontiff. Just, active, learned, pious, sincere, and of irreproachable morals, he permitted himself to be blinded neither by favour nor passion.

He followed the middle course traced out by Erasmus, and in a book reprinted at Rome during his pontificate, he said, "It is certain that the pope may err in matters of faith, in defending heresy by his opinions or decretals."[1] This is indeed a remarkable assertion for a pope to make; and if the ultra-montanists reply that Adrian was mistaken on this point, by this very circumstance they affirm what they deny, viz. the fallibility of the popes.

Adrian arrived at the Vatican with his old housekeeper, whom he charged to continue providing frugally for his moderate wants in that magnificent palace which Leo X. had filled with luxury and dissipation. He had not a single taste in common with his predecessor. When he was shown the magnificent group of Laocoon, discovered a few years before, and purchased at an enormous price by Julius II., he turned coldly away, observing: "They are the idols of the heathen!" "I would rather serve God," said he, "in my deanery of Louvain, than be pope at Rome." Alarmed at the dangers with which the Reformation threatened the religion of the Middle Ages, and not, like the Italians, at those to which Rome and her hierarchy were exposed, it was his earnest desire to combat and check it; and he judged the best means to this end would be a reform of the Church carried out by the Church itself. "The Church needs a reform," said he; "but we must go step by step."—"The pope means," says Luther, "that a few centuries should intervene between each step." In truth, for ages the Church had been moving towards a reformation. But there was no longer room for temporizing: it was necessary to act.

Faithful to his plan, Adrian set about banishing from the city all perjurers, profane persons, and usurers; a task by no means easy, since they formed a considerable portion of the inhabitants.

At first the Romans ridiculed him; soon they began to hate him. The sacerdotal rule, the immense profits it brought, the power of Rome, the sports, festivals, and luxury that filled it,—all would be irretrievably lost, if there was a return to apostolic manners.

The restoration of discipline, in particular, met with a strong opposition. "To succeed in this," said the cardinal high-penitentiary, "we must first revive the zeal of Christians. The remedy is more than the patient can bear, and will cause his death. Beware lest, by wishing to preserve Germany, you should lose Italy."[1] In effect, Adrian had soon greater cause to fear Romanism than Lutheranism itself.

Exertions were made to bring him back into the path he was desirous of quitting. The old and crafty Cardinal Soderini of Volterra, the familiar friend of Alexander VI., Julius II., and Leo X.,[2] often let fall hints well adapted to prepare the worthy Adrian for that character, so strange to him, which he was called upon to fill. "The heretics," remarked Soderini one day, "have in all ages spoken of the corrupt manners of the court of Rome, and yet the popes have never changed them."—"It has never been by reform," said he on another occasion, "that heresies have been put down, but by crusades."—"Alas," replied the pontiff with a deep sigh, "how unhappy is the fate of a pope, since he has not even liberty to do what is right!"[3]

CHAPTER III.

Diet of Nuremberg—Soliman's Invasion—The Nuncio calls for Luther's Death—The Nuremberg Preachers—Promise of Reform—The Nuncio's Alarm—Grievances of the Nation—Decree of the Diet—Fulminating Letter of the Pope—Luther's Advice.

On the 23d March 1522, before Adrian had reached Rome, the diet assembled at Nuremberg. Prior to this date the Bishops of Mersburg and Misnia had asked permission of the Elector of Saxony to make a visitation of the convents and churches in his states. Frederick, thinking that truth would be strong enough to resist error, had given a favourable reply to this request, and the visitation took place. The bishops and their doctors preached violently against the Reformation, exhorting, threatening, and entreating; but their arguments seemed useless; and when, desirous of having recourse to more effectual weapons, they called upon the secular authority to carry out their decrees,

[1] Certum est quod (Pontifex) potuit errare in iis quæ tangunt fidem, heresim per suam determinationem aut decretalem asserendo. Comm. in lib. 4. Sententiarum Quest. de Sacr. Confirm. Romæ, 1522, folio.

[1] Sarpi, Hist. Council of Trent, p. 20.
[2] Per longa esperienza delle cose del mundo, molto prudente e accorto. Nardi. Hist. Hist. Fior. lib. vii.
[3] Sarpi, Hist. Council of Trent, p. 21.

the elector's ministers replied, that the business was one that required to be examined according to the Bible, and that the elector in his advanced age could not begin to study divinity. These efforts of the bishops did not lead one soul back to the fold of Rome; and Luther, who passed through these districts shortly after, and preached in his usual powerful strain, erased the feeble impressions that had been here and there produced.

It might be feared that the emperor's brother, the Archduke Ferdinand, would do what Frederick had refused. This young prince, who presided during part of the sittings of the diet, gradually acquiring more firmness, might in his zeal rashly draw the sword which his more prudent and politic brother wisely left in the scabbard. In fact, he had already begun a cruel persecution of the partisans of the Reformation in his hereditary states of Austria. But God on several occasions made use of the same instrument for the deliverance of reviving Christianity that he had employed in the destruction of corrupt Christianity. The crescent appeared in the terrified provinces of Hungary. On the 9th of August, after a six weeks' siege, Belgrade, the bulwark of this kingdom and of the empire, fell before Soliman's attack. The followers of Mahomet, after having evacuated Spain, seemed bent on entering Europe by the East. The Diet of Nuremberg forgot the monk of Worms, to think only of the Sultan of Constantinople. But Charles V. kept both these adversaries in mind. On the 31st of October, he wrote to the pope from Valladolid: "We must check the Turks, and punish the abettors of Luther's poisonous doctrines with the sword."[1]

The storm which seemed to be passing away from the Reformation, and turning towards the east, soon gathered anew over the head of the reformer. His return to Wittemberg, and the zeal he had there displayed, rekindled animosity. "Now that we know where to catch him," said Duke George, "let us execute the decree of Worms!" It was even asserted in Germany that Charles V. and Adrian would meet at Nuremberg to concert their plans.[2] "Satan feels the wound that has been inflicted on him," says Luther; "and this is why he is so furious. But Christ has already stretched out his hand, and will soon trample him under foot in spite of the gates of hell."[3]

In the month of December 1522, the diet again assembled at Nuremberg. Every thing seemed to indicate, that if Soliman had been the great enemy that had engaged its attention in the spring session, Luther would be that of the winter meeting. Adrian VI.,

in consequence of his German descent, flattered himself with the hope of a more favourable reception from his nation than any pope of Italian origin could expect.[1] He therefore commissioned Chieregati, whom he had known in Spain, to repair to Nuremberg.

As soon as the diet had opened, several princes spoke strongly against Luther. The Cardinal-archbishop of Salzburg, who enjoyed the full confidence of the emperor, desired that prompt and decisive measures should be taken before the arrival of the Elector of Saxony. The Elector Joachim of Brandenburg, always inflexible in his proceedings, and the Chancellor of Treves, alike pressed for the execution of the edict of Worms. The other princes were in a great measure undecided and divided in opinion. The state of confusion in which the Church was placed filled its most faithful servants with anguish. The Bishop of Strasburg exclaimed, in a full meeting of the diet, " I would give one of my fingers not to be a priest."[2]

Chieregati, jointly with the Cardinal of Salzburg, called for Luther's death. "We must," said he in the pope's name, and holding the pontiff's brief in his hands, "we must cut off this gangrened member from the body.[3] Your fathers put John Huss and Jerome of Prague to death at Constance; but they live again in Luther. Follow the glorious example of your ancestors, and, with the aid of God and St. Peter, gain a signal victory over the infernal dragon."

On hearing the brief of the pious and moderate Adrian, most of the princes were awe-stricken.[4] Many were beginning to understand Luther more clearly, and had hoped better things of the pope. Thus then Rome, under an Adrian, will not acknowledge her faults; she still hurls her thunderbolts, and the provinces of Germany are about to be laid waste and drowned in blood. While the princes remained sad and silent, the prelates and members of the diet in the interest of Rome became tumultuous. "Let him be put to death,"[5] cried they, according to the report of the Saxon envoy, who was present at the sitting.

Very different language was heard in the churches of Nuremberg. The people crowded into the chapel attached to the hospital, and to the churches of the Augustines, of St. Sebaldus, and St. Lawrence, to listen to the preaching of the Gospel. Andrew Osiander was preaching powerfully in the latter temple. Several princes, and especially Albert, margrave of Brandenburg, who, in his quality of grand-master of the Teutonic Order,

[1] Das man die Nachfolger derselben vergiften Lehre, mit dem Schwert strafen mag. L. Opp. xvii. 321.
[2] Cum fama sit fortis et Cæsarem et papam Nurnbergam conventuros. L. Epp. ii. 214.
[3] Sed Christus qui cœpit conteret eum. Ibid. 215.

[1] Quod ex ea regione venirent, unde nobis secundum carnem origo est. Papal Brief. L. Opp. Lat. ii. 352.
[2] Er wollte einen Finger drum geben....Seck. p. 568.
[3] Resecandos uti membra jam putrida a sano corpore. Pallavicini, i. 158.
[4] Einen grossen Schrecken eingejagt. Seck. p. 552.
[5] Nicht anders geschrien denn : Crucifige! crucifige! (they cried out, Crucify him! crucify him!) L. Opp. xviii. 367.

took rank immediately after the archbishops, frequently attended these. Monks, abandoning the convents in the city, were learning trades in order to gain a livelihood by their labour.

Chieregati could not endure such audacity. He insisted that the priests and rebellious monks should be thrown into prison. The diet, notwithstanding the resolute opposition of the envoys of the Elector of Saxony and of the Margrave Casimir, determined on seizing the monks, but consented to make a previous communication of the nuncio's complaint to Osiander and his colleagues. This duty was in committee, of which the fanatical Cardinal of Salzburg was president. The danger was threatening; the struggle was about to begin, and it was the council of the nation that provoked it.

The people, however, anticipated them. While the diet was deliberating what should be done with these ministers, the town-council of Nuremberg were considering how they should proceed with regard to the decision of the diet. They resolved, without exceeding their jurisdiction, that if attempts were made to lay violent hands on the city preachers, they should be set at liberty by main force. Such a determination was very significant. The astonished diet replied to the nuncio, that it was not lawful to arrest the preachers of the free city of Nuremberg, unless previously convicted of heresy.

Chieregati was deeply moved at this new insult to the omnipotence of the papacy. "Well then," said he haughtily to Ferdinand, "do nothing, but let me act. I will have these preachers seized in the pope's name."[1] As soon as the Cardinal-archbishop Albert of Mentz and the Margrave Casimir were informed of this extravagant design, they hastened to the legate, entreating him to renounce his intentions. The nuncio was immovable, affirming that in the bosom of Christendom obedience to the pope was of the first importance. The two princes quitted the legate, saying: "If you persist in your design, we desire that you will give us warning; for we will leave the city before you venture to lay hands on these preachers."[2] The legate abandoned his project.

Despairing of success by measures of authority, he resolved to have recourse to other expedients, and with this view, he made the diet acquainted with the intentions and mandates of the pontiff, which he had hitherto kept secret.

But the worthy Adrian, a stranger to the ways of the world, injured by his very frankness the cause he so heartily desired to serve. "We are well aware," said he in the resolutions intrusted to his legate, "that for many years certain abuses and abominations have

crept into the holy city.[1] The contagion has spread from the head to the members; it has descended from the popes to the other ecclesiastics. It is our desire to reform this Roman court, whence proceed so many evils; the whole world is craving after it, and to effect this we submitted to ascend the papal chair."

The partisans of Rome blushed for shame as they heard this extraordinary language. They thought, with Pallavicini, that these avowals were too sincere.[2] The friends of the Reformation, on the contrary, were delighted at seeing Rome proclaim her own corruption. They no longer doubted that Luther was right, since the pope himself declared it.

The reply of the diet showed how much the authority of the sovereign pontiff had fallen in the empire. Luther's spirit seemed to have entered into the hearts of the representatives of the nation. The moment was favourable: Adrian's ear seemed open; the emperor was absent; the diet resolved to collect into one body all the grievances that for ages Germany had endured from Rome, and forward them to the pope.

The legate was frightened at this determination. He entreated and threatened by turns. He insinuated that under a purely religious exterior, the reformer concealed great political dangers; he asserted, like Adrian, that these children of iniquity had no other end in view than to destroy all obedience, and lead every man to do as he pleased. "Will those men keep your laws," said he, "who not only despise the holy canons of the Father, but still further, tear them in pieces and burn them in their diabolical fury? Will they spare your lives who do not fear to insult, to strike, to kill the anointed of the Lord? It is your persons, your goods, your houses, your wives, your children, your domains, your states, your temples, and all that you adore, that are threatened by this frightful calamity."[3]

All these declamations proved of no avail. The diet, although commending the promises of the pope, required for their speedy fulfilment that a free and christian council should be assembled as soon as possible at Strasburg, Mentz, Cologne, or Metz, in which laymen should be present. Laymen in a council! Laymen regulating the affairs of the Church in concert with priests! It is more than we can see even now in many protestant states. The diet added, that every man should have liberty to speak freely for the glory of God, the salvation of souls, and the good of the christian common-

<hr>

[1] Sese auctoritate pontifica curaturum ut isti caperentur. Corp. Ref. i. 606.
[2] Priusquam illi caperentur, se urbe cessuros esse. Ibid.

[1] In eam sedem aliquot jam annos quædam vitia irrepsisse, abusus in rebus sacris, in legibus violationes, in cunctis denique perversionem. Pallav. i. 160. See also Sarpi, p. 25; L. Opp. xviii. 329, &c.
[2] Liberioris tamen, quam par erat, sinceritatis fuisse visum est, ea conventui patefacere. Ibid. 162.
[3] In eos, in vestras res, domos, uxores, liberos, ditiones, dominatus, templa quæ colitis. L. Opp. Lat. ii. 536.

wealth. [1] It then proceeded to draw up a catalogue of grievances, which amounted to the number of eighty. The abuses and arts of the popes and the Roman court to extort money from Germany; the scandals and profanations of the clergy; the disorders and simony of the ecclesiastical tribunals; the encroachments on the secular power for the enslaving of consciences; were all set forth with as much frankness as energy. The states gave the pope to understand that the traditions of men were the source of all this corruption, and concluded by saying: "If these grievances are not redressed within a limited time, we shall seek other means of deliverance from so many oppressions and sufferings." [2] Chieregati, foreseeing the formidable *recess* (report) that the diet would draw up, hastily left Nuremberg, that he might not be the bearer of this sad and insolent message.

And yet, was it not to be feared that the diet would seek to make amends for its boldness by sacrificing Luther? People thought so at first; but a spirit of justice and truth had descended on this assembly. It demanded, as Luther had done, the convocation of a free council in the empire, and added, that in the meanwhile the pure Gospel alone should be preached, and nothing should be printed without the approbation of a certain number of pious and learned men. [3] These resolutions furnish us with the means of calculating the immense progress the Reformation had made subsequently to the Diet of Worms; and yet the knight of Feilitsch, the Saxon envoy, solemnly protested against this censorship, moderate as it was, which the diet prescribed. This decree was regarded as the first triumph of the Reformation, to be followed by other more decisive victories. The Swiss themselves, in the midst of their mountains, thrilled with delight. "The Roman pontiff is vanquished in Germany," said Zwingle. "We have nothing more to do than deprive him of his weapons. This is the battle we have now to fight, and a furious one it will be. But Christ is the umpire of the conflict." [4] Luther said publicly that God himself had inspired the princes to draw up this edict. [5]

The indignation at the Vatican among the papal ministers was very great. What! is it not enough to have a pope who disappoints all the expectations of the Romans, and in whose palace there is neither singing nor playing; but, more than this, secular princes are allowed to hold a language that Rome detests, and refuse to put the Wittemberg heretic to death!

Adrian himself was filled with indignation at the events in Germany, and it was on the head of the Elector of Saxony that he discharged his anger. Never had the Roman pontiffs uttered a cry of alarm more energetic, more sincere, and perhaps more affecting.

"We have waited long—and perhaps too long," said the pious Adrian in the brief he addressed to the elector; "we were anxious to see whether God would visit thy soul, and if thou wouldst not at last escape from the snares of Satan. But where we looked to gather grapes, we found nothing but sour grapes. The blower hath blown in vain; thy wickedness is not melted. Open, then, thine eyes to see the greatness of thy fall!......

"If the unity of the Church is broken; if the simple have been turned aside from that faith which they had imbibed at their mothers' breasts; if the churches are deserted; if the people are without priests; if the priests receive not the honour that is due to them; if Christians are without Christ: to whom is it owing, but to thee? [1]......If Christian peace has vanished from the earth; if the world is full of discord, rebellion, robbery, murder, and conflagration; if the cry of war is heard from east to west; if a universal conflict is at hand: it is thou—thou who art the author of these things!

"Seest thou not this sacrilegious man (Luther) rending with his wicked hands and trampling under his impure feet the images of the saints and even the holy cross of Christ?......Dost thou not behold him, in his ungodly wrath, instigating laymen to imbrue their hands in the blood of the priests, and overturning the churches of our Lord?

"And what matters it, if the priests he assails are wicked priests? Has not the Lord said: *Whatsoever they bid you observe, that observe and do; but do not ye after their works;* thus showing the honour that belongs to them, even when their lives are blame-worthy. [2]

"Rebellious apostate! he is not ashamed to defile the vessels consecrated to God; he drags from their sanctuaries the holy virgins dedicated to Christ, and gives them over to the devil; he takes the priests of the Lord, and delivers them up to infamous harlots...…Awful profanation! which even the heathen would have condemned with horror in the priests of their idols!

"What punishment, what torments dost thou think we judge thee to deserve?...... Have pity on thyself; have pity on thy wretched Saxons; for if you do not all return into the fold, God will pour out his vengeance upon you.

"In the name of the Almighty God, and

[1] Quod in tali concilio eis qui interesse deberent vel ecclesiastici vel laicalis ordinis libere liceret loqui. Geldart, Constit. Imper. i. 452.
- Wie sie solcher Beschwerung und Drangsaal entladen werden. L. Opp. xviii. 354.
[3] Ut pie placideque purum Evangelium prædicaretur. Pall. i. 166; Sleidan, i. 135.
[4] Victus est ac ferme profligatus e Germania Romanus pontifex. Zw. Epp. 313.—11th October 1523.
[5] Gott habe solches E. G. eingeben. L. Opp. xviii. 476.

[1] Dass die Kirchen ohne Volk sind, dass die Völker ohne Priester sind, dass die Priester ohne Ehre sind, und dass die Christen ohne Christo sind. L. Opp. xviii. 371.
[2] Wen sie gleich eines verdammten Lebens sind. Ibid 379.

of our Lord Jesus Christ, whose representative I am upon earth, I declare that thou shalt be punished in this world, and plunged into everlasting fire in that which is to come. Repent and be converted!......Both swords are suspended over thy head,—the sword of the Empire and the sword of the Church."

The pious Frederick shuddered as he read this threatening brief. He had written to the emperor shortly before, to the effect that old age and sickness rendered him incapable of taking any part in these affairs; and he had been answered by the most insolent letter that a sovereign prince had ever received. Although bowed down by age, he cast his eyes on that sword which he had worn at the holy sepulchre in the days of his manly strength. He began to think that he would have to unsheathe it in defence of the conscience of his subjects, and that, already on the brink of the tomb, he would not be allowed to go down to it in peace. He immediately wrote to Wittemberg to hear the opinion of the fathers of the Reformation.

There also troubles and persecutions were apprehended. "What shall I say?" exclaimed the gentle Melancthon; "whither shall I turn? Hatred overwhelms us, and the world is transported with fury against us."[1] Luther, Linck, Melancthon, Bugenhagen, and Amsdorff consulted together on the reply they should make to the elector. Their answer was almost entirely to the same purport, and the advice they gave him is very remarkable.

"No prince," said they, "can undertake a war without the consent of the people, from whose hands he has received his authority.[2] Now, the people have no desire to fight for the Gospel, for they do not believe. Let not princes, therefore, take up arms; they are rulers of the nations, that is to say, of unbelievers." Thus, it was the impetuous Luther who counselled the discreet Frederick to restore his sword to its sheath. He could not have returned a better answer to the reproach of the pope, that he excited the laity to imbrue their hands in the blood of the clergy. Few characters have been more misunderstood than his. This advice was dated the 8th of February. Frederick restrained himself.

The pope's wrath soon bore fruit. The princes who had set forth their grievances against Rome, alarmed at their own daring, were now desirous of making amends by their compliance. Many, besides, thought that the victory would remain with the Roman pontiff, as he appeared to be the stronger party. "In our days," said Luther, "princes are content to say three times three make nine; or else, twice seven make

fourteen: The reckoning is correct; the affair will succeed. Then our Lord God arises and says: How many do you reckon me?......For a cipher perhaps?......He then turns their calculations topsy-turvy, and their reckonings prove false."[1]

CHAPTER IV.

Persecution—Exertions of Duke George—The Convent at Antwerp—Miltenberg—The Three Monks of Antwerp—The Scaffold—The Martyrs of Brussels.

THE torrent of fire poured forth by the humble and meek Adrian kindled a conflagration; and his emotion caused an immense agitation in the whole of Christendom. Persecution, which had been for some time relaxed, broke out afresh. Luther trembled for Germany, and endeavoured to avert the storm. "If the princes," said he, "oppose the truth, the result will be a confusion that will destroy princes and magistrates, priests and people. I fear to see all Germany erelong deluged with blood.[2] Let us rise up as a wall and preserve our people from the wrath of our God. Nations are not such now as they have hitherto been.[3] The sword of civil war is impending over the heads of kings. They are resolved to destroy Luther; but Luther is bent on saving them. Christ lives and reigns; and I shall live and reign with him."[4]

These words produced no effect; Rome was hastening onward to scaffolds and to bloodshed. The Reformation, like Jesus Christ, did not come to bring peace, but a sword. Persecution was necessary in God's purposes. As certain substances are hardened in the fire, to protect them from the influence of the atmosphere, so the fiery trial was intended to protect the evangelical truth from the influence of the world. But the fire did still more than this: it served, as in the primitive times of Christianity, to kindle in men's hearts a universal enthusiasm for a cause so furiously persecuted. There is in man, when he begins to know the truth, a holy indignation against injustice and violence. A heaven-descended instinct impels him to the side of the oppressed; and at the same time the faith of the martyrs exalts, wins, and leads him to that saving doctrine which imparts such courage and tranquillity.

Duke George took the lead in the persecution. But it was a little thing to carry it on in his own states only; he desired, above all,

---

[1] Quid dicam? quo me vertam? Corp. Ref. 1. 627.
[2] Principi nullum licet suscipere bellum. nisi consentiente populo, a quo accepit imperium. Ibid. 601.

[1] So kehrt er ihnen auch die Rechnung gar um. L. Opp. xxii. 1831.
[2] Ut videar mihi videre Germaniam in sanguine natare. L. Epp. ii. 156.
[3] Cogitent populos non esse tales modo, quales hactenus fuerunt. Ibid. 157.
[4] Christus meus vivit et regnat, et ego vivam et regnabc. Ibid. 158.

that it should devastate electoral Saxony, that focus of heresy, and he spared no labour to move the Elector Frederick and Duke John. " Certain merchants from Saxony," he wrote to them from Nuremberg, " relate strange things about that country, and such as are opposed to the honour of God and of the saints : the sacrament of the Lord's Supper is there received in the hand !.........
The bread and wine are consecrated *in the language of the people ;* Christ's blood is put into common vessels ; and at Eulenburg, a man to insult the priest entered the church riding on an ass !......Accordingly, what is the consequence ? The mines with which God had enriched Saxony have become less productive since the innovating sermons of Luther. Would to God that those who boast of having uplifted the Gospel in the electorate had rather carried it to Constantinople. Luther's strain is sweet and pleasing, but it has a poisoned tail, that stings like a scorpion's. Let us now prepare for the conflict! Let us imprison these apostate monks and impious priests ; and that too without delay, for our hair is turning gray as well as our beards, and shows us that we have but short time left for action."[1]

Thus wrote Duke George to the elector. The latter replied firmly but mildly, that any one who committed a crime in his states would meet with due punishment; but that matters of conscience must be left to God.[2]

George, unable to persuade Frederick, hastened to persecute the followers of the work he detested. He imprisoned the monks and priests who followed Luther ; he recalled the students belonging to his states from the universities which the Reformation had reached ; and ordered that all the copies of the New Testament in the vulgar tongue should be given up to the magistrates. The same measures were enforced in Austria, Wurtemberg, and the duchy of Brunswick.

But it was in the Low Countries, under the immediate authority of Charles V., that the persecution broke out with greatest violence. The Augustine convent at Antwerp was filled with monks who had welcomed the truths of the Gospel. Many of the brethren had passed some time at Wittemberg, and since 1519, salvation by grace had been preached in their church with great energy. The prior, James Probst, a man of ardent temperament, and Melchior Mirisch, who was remarkable, on the other hand, for his ability and prudence, were arrested and taken to Brussels about the close of the year 1521. They were brought before Aleander, Glapio, and several other prelates. Taken by surprise, confounded, and alarmed, Probst retracted. Melchior Mirisch found means to pacify his judges ; he escaped both from recantation and condemnation.

These persecutions did not alarm the

monks who remained in the convent at Antwerp. They continued to preach the Gospel with power. The people crowded to hear them, and the church of the Augustines in that city was found too small, as had been the case at Wittemberg. In October 1522, the storm that was muttering over their heads burst forth ; the convent was closed, and the monks thrown into prison and condemned to death.[1] A few of them managed to escape. Some women, forgetting the timidity of their sex, dragged one of them (Henry Zuphten) from the hands of the executioners.[2] Three young monks, Henry Voes, John Esch, and Lambert Thorn, escaped for a time the search of the inquisitors. All the sacred vessels of the convent were sold ; the gates were barricaded; the holy sacrament was removed, as if from a polluted spot ; Margaret, the governor of the Low Countries, solemnly received it into the church of the Holy Virgin ;[3] orders were given that not one stone should be left upon another of that heretical monastery ; and many citizens and women who had joyfully listened to the Gospel were thrown into prison.[4]

Luther was filled with sorrow on hearing this news. "The cause that we defend," said he, "is no longer a mere game ; it will have blood, it calls for our lives."[5]

Mirisch and Probst were to meet with very different fates. The prudent Mirisch soon became the docile instrument of Rome, and the agent of the imperial decrees against the partisans of the Reformation.[6] Probst, on the contrary, having escaped from the hands of the inquisitors, wept over his backsliding ; he retracted his recantation, and boldly preached at Bruges in Flanders the doctrines he had abjured. Being again arrested and thrown into prison at Brussels, his death seemed inevitable.[7] A Franciscan took pity on him, and assisted his escape ; and Probst, "preserved by a miracle of God," says Luther, reached Wittemberg, where his twofold deliverance filled the hearts of the friends to the Reformation with joy.[8]

On all sides the Roman priests were under arms. The city of Miltenberg on the Maine, which belonged to the Archbishop of Mentz, was one of the German towns that had re-

---

[1] Wie ihre Bärt und Haare ausweisen. Seckend. p. 482.
[2] Müsse man solche Dinge Gott überlassen. Ibid. p. 485.

[1] Zum Tode verurtheilet. Seck. p. 548.
[2] Quomodo mulieres vi Henricum liberarint. L. Epp. ii. 265.
[3] Susceptum honorifice a domina Margareta. Ibid.
[4] Cives aliquos, et mulieres vexatæ et punitæ. Ibid.
[5] Et vitam exiget et sanguinem. Ibid. 181.
[6] Est executor Cæsaris contra nostros. Ibid. 207.
[7] Domo captum, exustum credimus. Ibid. 214.
[8] Jacobus, Dei miraculo liberatus, qui nunc agit nobiscum. L. Epp. ii. 182. This letter, placed in M. de Wette's collection, under the date of April 14, must be posterior to the month of June ; since on the 26th of June Luther writes that Probst has been taken a second time and is going to be burnt. We cannot admit that Probst visited Wittemberg between his two imprisonments, for Luther would not have said of a Christian, who had saved his life by a recantation, that he had been delivered by a miracle of God. Perhaps we should read in the date of the letter *in die S. Turiaf*, instead of *in die S. Tiburtii*, which would bring it down to the 13th of July,—a far more probable date in my opinion.

ceived the Word of God with the greatest eagerness. The inhabitants were much attached to their pastor John Draco, one of the most enlightened men of his times. He was compelled to leave the city; but the Roman ecclesiastics were frightened, and withdrew at the same time, fearing the vengeance of the people. An evangelical deacon alone remained to comfort their hearts. At the same time troops from Mentz marched into the city and spread through the streets, uttering blasphemies, brandishing their swords, and giving themselves up to debauchery.[1]

Some evangelical Christians fell beneath their blows;[2] others were seized and thrown into dungeons; the Romish rites were restored; the reading of the Bible was prohibited; and the inhabitants were forbidden to speak of the Gospel, even in the most private meetings. On the entrance of the troops, the deacon had taken refuge in the house of a poor widow. He was denounced to their commanders, who sent a soldier to apprehend him. The humble deacon, hearing the hasty steps of the soldier who sought his life, quietly waited for him, and just as the door of the chamber was abruptly opened, he went forward meekly, and cordially embracing him, said; "I welcome thee, brother; here I am; plunge thy sword into my bosom."[3] The fierce soldier, in astonishment, let his sword fall from his hand, and protected the pious evangelist from any further harm.

Meantime, the inquisitors of the Low Countries, thirsting for blood, scoured the country, searching every where for the young Augustines who had escaped from the Antwerp persecution. Esch, Voes, and Lambert were at last discovered, put in chains, and led to Brussels. Egmondanus, Hochstraten, and several other inquisitors, summoned them into their presence. "Do you retract your assertion," asked Hochstraten, "that the priest has not power to forgive sins, and that it belongs to God alone?" He then proceeded to enumerate other evangelical doctrines which they were called upon to abjure. "No! we will retract nothing," exclaimed Esch and Voes firmly; "we will not deny the Word of God; we will rather die for the faith."

THE INQUISITOR.—"Confess that you have been led astray by Luther."

THE YOUNG AUGUSTINES.—"As the apostles were led astray by Jesus Christ."

THE INQUISITORS.—"We declare you to be heretics, worthy of being burnt alive, and we give you over to the secular arm."

Lambert kept silence; the prospect of death terrified him; distress and doubt tormented his soul. "I beg four days' respite,"

said he with a stifled voice. He was led back to prison. As soon as this delay had expired, Esch and Voes were solemnly deprived of their sacerdotal character, and given over to the council of the governor of the Low Countries. The council delivered them, fettered, to the executioner. Hochstraten and three other inquisitors accompanied them to the stake.[1]

When they came near the scaffold, the youthful martyrs looked at it calmly; their firmness, their piety, their youth,[2] drew tears even from the inquisitors. When they were bound, the confessors approached them: "Once more we ask you if you will receive the christian faith."

THE MARTYRS.—"We believe in the Christian Church, but not in your Church."

Half an hour elapsed: the inquisitors hesitated, and hoped that the prospect of so terrible a death would intimidate these youths. But alone tranquil in the midst of the turbulent crowd in the square, they sang psalms, stopping from time to time to declare boldly: "We will die for the name of Jesus Christ."

"Be converted—be converted," cried the inquisitors, "or you will die in the name of the devil."—"No," replied the martyrs, "we will die like Christians, and for the truth of the Gospel."

The pile was lighted. While the flames were ascending slowly, a heavenly peace filled their hearts, and one of them went so far as to say: "I seem to be lying on a bed of roses."[3] The solemn hour was come; death was near: the two martyrs cried with a loud voice: "O Domine Jesu! Fili David! miserere nostri! O Lord Jesus, Son of David, have mercy on us!" They then began solemnly to repeat the Apostle's Creed.[4] At last the flames reached them, burning the cords that fastened them to the stake, before their breath was gone. One of them, taking advantage of this liberty, fell on his knees in the midst of the fire,[5] and thus worshipping his Master, exclaimed, clasping his hands: "Lord Jesus, Son of David, have mercy on us!" The flames now surrounded their bodies: they sang the Te Deum; soon their voices were stifled, and nothing but their ashes remained.

This execution had lasted four hours. It was on the 1st of July 1523 that the first martyrs of the Reformation thus laid down their lives for the Gospel.

All good men shuddered when they heard of it. The future filled them with the keenest apprehension. "The executions have begun," said Erasmus.[6]—"At last,"

---

[1] So sie doch schändlicher leben denn Huren und Buben. L. Epp. ii. 482.
[2] Schlug etliche Todt. Seck. p. 604.
[3] Sey gegrüsst, mein Bruder. Scultet. Ann. i. 173.

[1] Facta est hæc res Bruxellæ in publico foro. L. Epp. ii. 361.
[2] Nondum triginta annorum. Ibid.
[3] Dit schijnen mij als roosen te zijn. Brandt, Hist. der Reformatie, i. 79.
[4] Admoto igne, canere cœperunt symbolum fidei, says Erasmus. Epp. i. 1278.
[5] Da ist der eine im Feuer auf die Knie gefallen. L. Opp. xviii. 481.
[6] Cœpta est carnificina. Epp. i. 1429.

exclaimed Luther, "Christ is gathering some fruits of our preaching, and is creating new martyrs."

But the joy Luther felt at the constancy of these two young Christians was troubled by the thought of Lambert. The latter was the most learned of the three; he had succeeded to Probst's station as preacher at Antwerp. Agitated in his dungeon, and alarmed at the prospect of death, he was still more terrified by his conscience, which reproached him with cowardice, and urged him to confess the Gospel. He was soon delivered from his fears, and after boldly proclaiming the truth, died like his brethren. [1]

A rich harvest sprang from the blood of these martyrs. Brussels turned towards the Gospel. [2] "Wherever Aleander raises a pile," said Erasmus, "there he seems to have been sowing heretics." [3]

"Your bonds are mine," said Luther; "your dungeons and your burning piles are mine! [4].........We are all with you, and the Lord is at our head!" He then commemorated the death of these young monks in a beautiful hymn, and soon, in Germany and in the Netherlands, in city and country, these strains were heard communicating in every direction an enthusiasm for the faith of these martyrs.

> No! no! their ashes shall not die!
> But, borne to every land,
> Where'er their sainted dust shall fall
> Up springs a holy band.
>
> Though Satan by his might may kill,
> And stop their powerful voice,
> They triumph o'er him in their death,
> And still in Christ rejoice.

CHAPTER V.

The New Pope, Clement VII.—The Legate Campeggio—Diet of Nuremberg—Demand of the Legate—Reply of the Diet —A Secular Council projected—Alarm and Exertions of the Pope—Bavaria—League of Ratisbon—Campeggio's Dishonesty—Severity and Reforms—Political Schism— Opposition—Intrigues of Rome—Decree of Burgos—Rupture.

ADRIAN would doubtless have persisted in these violent measures; the inutility of his exertions to arrest the reform, his orthodoxy, his zeal, his austerity, and even his conscientiousness, would have made him a cruel persecutor. But this Providence did not permit. He died on the 14th of September 1523, and the Romans, overjoyed at being delivered from this stern foreigner, crowned his physician's door with flowers, and set this inscription over it: "To the saviour of his country."

Giulio de Medici, cousin to Leo X., succeeded Adrian VI., under the name of Clement VII. From the day of his election there was no more question of religious reform. The new pope, like many of his predecessors, thought only of upholding the privileges of the papacy, and of employing its resources for his own aggrandizement.

Anxious to repair Adrian's blunders, Clement sent to Nuremberg a legate of his own character, one of the most skilful prelates of his court, a man of great experience in public business, and acquainted with almost all the princes of Germany. Cardinal Campeggio, for such was his name, after a magnificent reception in the Italian cities on his road, soon perceived the change that had taken place in the empire. When he entered Augsburg, he desired, as was usual, to give his benediction to the people, but they burst into laughter. This was enough: he entered Nuremberg privately, without going to the church of St. Sebaldus, where the clergy awaited him. No priests in sacerdotal ornaments came out to meet him; no cross was solemnly borne before him; [1] one would have thought him some private individual passing through the streets of the city. Every thing betokened that the reign of the papacy was drawing to an end.

The Diet of Nuremberg resumed its sittings in the month of January 1524. A storm threatened the national government, which the country owed to the firmness of Frederick. The Swabian league, the wealthiest cities of the empire, and particularly Charles V., had sworn his destruction. He was accused of favouring the new heresy. Accordingly it was resolved to remodify this administration without retaining one of its former members. Frederick, overwhelmed with grief, immediately quitted Nuremberg.

The festival of Easter was approaching. Osiander and the evangelical preachers redoubled their zeal. The former openly declared in his sermons that Antichrist entered Rome the very day when Constantine left it to fix his residence at Constantinople. The consecration of the palm-branches and many other ceremonies of this feast were omitted: four thousand persons received the sacrament in both kinds, and the Queen of Denmark, the emperor's sister, received it publicly, in like manner, at the castle. "Ah!" exclaimed the Archduke Frederick, losing his temper, "would that you were not my sister!"—"The same womb bore us," replied the queen, "and I will sacrifice every thing to please you, except the Word of God." [2]

---

[1] Quarta post exustus est tertius frater Lambertus. L. Epp. ii. 351.
[2] Ea mors multos fecit Lutheranos. Er. Epp. p. 952; Tum demum cœpit civitas favere Luthero. Ibid. p. 1676. Erasmus to Duke George; Ea civitas antea purissima. Ibid. p. 1430.
[3] Ubicumque fumos excitavit nuntius, ibi diceres fuisse factam hereseôn sementem. Ibid.
[4] Vestra vincula mea sunt, vestri carceres et ignes mei sunt. L. Epp. ii. 464.

[1] Communi habitu, quod per sylvas et campos ierat per mediam urbem....sine clero, sine prævia cruce. Cochl. p. 82.
[2] Wolle sich des Wortes Gottes halten. Seckend. p. 611.

Campeggio shuddered as he witnessed such audacity; but affecting to despise the laughter of the populace and the discourses of the preachers, and resting on the authority of the emperor and of the pope, he reminded the diet of the edict of Worms, and called upon them to put down the Reformation by force. At this language many of the princes and deputies gave vent to their indignation: "What has become of the list of grievances presented to the pope by the German nation?" said they to Campeggio. The legate, following his instructions, assumed an air of candour and surprise, and answered, " Three copies of that list reached Rome; but we have received no official communication of it,[1] and neither the pope nor the college of cardinals could believe that such a paper could have emanated from your lordships. We thought that it came from some private individuals who had published it out of hatred to the court of Rome. In consequence of this I have no instructions on the matter."

The diet was incensed at this reply. If it is thus the pope receives their representations, they will also know how to listen to those he addresses to them. "The people," said many deputies, "are thirsting for the Word of God; and to take it away, as the edict of Worms enjoins, would cause torrents of blood to flow."

The diet immediately made preparations for replying to the pope. As they could not repeal the edict of Worms, a clause was added to it rendering it ineffectual. They said, " The people must conform with it *as far as possible.*"[2] Now many states had declared it impossible to enforce it. At the same time, raising up the importunate shade of the councils of Constance and of Basle, the diet demanded the convocation of a general council of Christendom to be held in Germany.

The friends of the Reformation did not confine themselves to this. What could they expect from a council which perhaps would never be convoked, and which, under all circumstances, would be composed of bishops from every nation? Will Germany submit her anti-Romish inclinations to prelates from France, Spain, Italy, and England? The government of the nation had already been abolished; for it a national assembly should be substituted to protect the interests of the people.

In vain did Hannaart, the Spanish envoy from Charles V., and all the partisans of Rome and the emperor, endeavour to oppose this suggestion; the majority of the diet was immovable. It was agreed that a diet, a secular assembly, should meet at Spires, in the month of November, to regulate all religious questions, and that the states should immediately instruct their theologians to draw up a list of the controverted points to be laid before that august assembly.

They forthwith applied to their task. Each province drew up its memorial, and never had Rome been threatened with a more terrible explosion. Franconia, Brandenburg, Henneburg, Windsheim, Wertheim, and Nuremberg, declared in favour of the Gospel, and against the seven sacraments, the abuses of the mass, the adoration of saints, and the papal supremacy. " Here is coin of the right stamp," said Luther. Not one of the questions that were agitating the popular mind was to be passed over in this national council. The majority would succeed in carrying general measures. The unity, independence, and reformation of Germany would be saved.

On being apprized of this, the pope could not restrain his wrath. What! dare they set up a secular tribunal to decide on religious questions in direct opposition to his authority![1] If this extraordinary resolution should be carried out, Germany would doubtless be saved, but Rome would be lost. A consistory was hastily convened, and from the alarm of the senators one might have thought the Germans were marching against the Capitol. " We must take the electoral hat from Frederick's head," said Aleander. " The kings of England and Spain must threaten to break off all commercial intercourse with the free cities," said another cardinal. The congregation at last decided that the only means of safety would be in moving heaven and earth to prevent the meeting at Spires.

The pope immediately wrote to the emperor: " If I am the first to make head against the storm, it is not because I am the only one the tempest threatens; but because I am at the helm. The rights of the empire are yet more invaded than the dignity of the court of Rome."

While the pope was sending this letter to Castile, he was endeavouring to procure allies in Germany. He soon gained over one of the most powerful houses in the empire, that of the dukes of Bavaria. The edict of Worms had not been more strictly enforced there than elsewhere, and the evangelical doctrine had made great progress. But about the close of the year 1521, the princes of that country, put in motion by Doctor Eck, chancellor in the university of Ingolstadt, had drawn nearer to Rome, and had published a decree enjoining all their subjects to remain faithful to the religion of their ancestors.[2]

The Bavarian bishops were alarmed at this encroachment of the secular power. Eck set out for Rome to solicit the pope for an extension of authority in behalf of the princes.

[1] Tria solum exemplaria fuisse perlata Romam, ad quosdam privatim, ex iis unum sibi contigisse. Sleidan. lib. iv.
[2] Quantum eis possibile sit. Cochlœus, p. 84.

[1] Pontifex ægerrime tulit....intelligens novum de religione tribunal eo pacto excitari citra ipsius auctoritatem Pallav. i. 182.
[2] Erstes baierisches Religions mandat. Winter, Gesch. der Evang. Lehre in Baiern, i. 310.

The pope granted every thing, and even conferred on the dukes a fifth of the ecclesiastical revenues of their country.

Thus, at a time when the Reformation possessed no organization, Roman-catholicism already had recourse to powerful institutions for its support; and catholic princes, aided by the pope, laid their hands on the revenues of the Church, long before the Reformation ventured to touch them. What must we think of the reproaches the Roman-catholics have so often made in this respect?

Clement VII. might reckon upon Bavaria to avert the formidable assembly at Spires. Erelong the Archduke Ferdinand, the Bishop of Salzburg, and other princes, were gained in their turn.

But Campeggio desired to go still further: Germany must be divided into two hostile camps; Germans must be opposed to Germans.

Some time before, during his residence at Stuttgard, the legate had concerted with Ferdinand the plan of a league against the Reformation. " There is every thing to be feared in an assembly where the voice of the people is heard," said he. " The Diet of Spires may destroy Rome and save Wittemberg. Let us close our ranks; let us come to an understanding for the day of battle."[1] Ratisbon was fixed upon as the place of meeting.

Notwithstanding the jealousy between the houses of Bavaria and Austria, Campeggio succeeded in bringing the Dukes of Bavaria and the Archduke Ferdinand to this city, at the end of June 1524. They were joined by the Archbishop of Salzburg and the Bishops of Trent and Ratisbon. The Bishops of Spires, Bamberg, Augsburg, Strasburg, Basle, Constance, Freisingen, Passau, and Brixen, were present by deputy.

The legate opened the sittings, describing in forcible language the dangers threatened by the Reformation both to princes and clergy. " Let us extirpate heresy and save the Church," exclaimed he.

The conference lasted fifteen days in the town-hall of Ratisbon. A grand ball, that continued till daylight, served to enliven this first Catholic assembly held by the papacy against the dawning Reformation.[2] After this, measures were resolved upon for the destruction of the heretics.

The legate thought that, according to the notorious axiom of the Council of Constance, no faith should be kept with heretics,[3] and in the mean time he carried out this great principle on a small scale. During the sittings of the diet at Nuremberg, Campeggio had taken a globe and a book from a poor vendor of astronomical instruments: these

he kept, and refused to make any compensation, because the man was a Lutheran. Our authority for this incident is the celebrated Pirckheimer, one of the chief magistrates of Nuremberg.[1]

The princes and bishops bound themselves to enforce the edicts of Worms and Nuremberg; to permit no change in public worship; to tolerate no married priest in their states; to recall all their subjects who might be studying at Wittemberg; and to employ every means in their power for the extirpation of heresy. They enjoined the preachers, in the interpretation of difficult passages, to rely on the fathers of the Latin Church, Ambrose, Jerome, Augustine, and Gregory. Not venturing, in the face of the Reformation, to appeal to the authority of the schoolmen, they were content to lay the first foundations of Roman orthodoxy.

But, on the other hand, as they could not close their eyes against the scandals and corrupt morals of the priests,[2] they agreed on a project of reform, in which they endeavoured to embrace those German grievances which least concerned the court of Rome. The priests were forbidden to trade, to haunt the taverns, " to frequent dances," and to dispute over their cups about articles of faith.

Such was the result of the confederation of Ratisbon.[3] Even while taking up arms against the Reformation, Rome conceded something; and in these decrees we may observe the first influence of the Reformation of the sixteenth century to effect an inward renovation of catholicism. The Gospel cannot display its strength without its enemies endeavouring to imitate it in some way or another. Emser had published a translation of the Bible in opposition to Luther's; Eck his *Common-places*, by way of counterpoise to Melancthon's;[4] and now Rome was opposing to the Reformation those partial essays of reform to which modern Romanism is owing. But all these works were in reality subtle expedients to escape from impending danger; branches plucked indeed from the tree of the Reformation, but planted in a soil which killed them; there was no vitality, and never will there be any vitality in such attempts.

Another fact here occurs to us. The Roman party formed at Ratisbon the first league that infringed the unity of Germany. The signal for battle was given from the pope's camp. Ratisbon was the cradle of this division, this political rending of their native land, which so many Germans deplore to this hour. The national assembly of Spires, by sanctioning and generalizing the reform of the Church, would have secured

---

[1] Winter, Gesch. der Evang. Lehre in Baiern, i. 156.
[2] Ranke, Deutsche Gesch. ii. 159.
[3] Non est frangere fidem in eo, qui Deo fidem frangit. Decret. Conc. Sess. gen. 19. September 23, 1415.

[1] Strobel's Verm. Beyträge zur Geech. der Litt. Nurnberg. 1775, p. 96.
[2] Improbis clericorum abusibus et perditis moribus. Cochlœus, p. 91.
[3] Ut Lutheranæ factioni efficacius resistere possint, ultronea confederatione sese constrixerunt. Ibid.
[4] Enchiridion, seu loci communes contra hæreticos. 1526.

the unity of the empire. The conventicle of separatists at Ratisbon for ever divided the nation into two parties.[1]

Yet Campeggio's plans did not at first succeed as had been expected. Few princes answered this appeal. Luther's most decided adversaries, Duke George of Saxony, the Elector Joachim of Brandenburg, the ecclesiastical electors, and the imperial cities, took no part in it. It was felt that the pope's legate was forming a Romish party in Germany against the nation itself. Popular sympathies counterbalanced religious antipathies, and in a short time the *Ratisbon reformation* became the laughing-stock of the people. But the first step had been taken, the example given. It was imagined that it would be no difficult task eventually to strengthen and enlarge this Roman league. Those who still hesitated would necessarily be drawn into it by the progress of events. To the legate Campeggio belongs the glory of having dug the mine which was most seriously to endanger the liberties of Germany, the existence of the empire, and of the Reformation. Henceforward Luther's cause ceased to be a mere religious affair ; the dispute with the monk of Wittemberg ranked among the political events of Europe. Luther is about to be eclipsed ; and Charles V., the pope, and the princes, will be the principal actors on the stage where the grand drama of the sixteenth century is to be performed.

Yet the assembly at Spires was still kept in view ; it might repair the mischief that Campeggio had effected at Ratisbon. Rome made every exertion to prevent it. " What !" said the papal deputies, not only to Charles V. but also to Henry VIII. and other princes of Christendom, " What ! do these insolent Germans pretend to decide points of faith in a national assembly ? It would seem that kings, the imperial authority, all Christendom, and the whole world, ought to submit to their decrees !"

The moment was well chosen to act upon the emperor. The war between this prince and Francis I. was at its height. Pescara and the Constable of Bourbon had quitted Italy, and entering France in the month of May, had laid siege to Marseilles. The pope, who looked with an evil eye on this attack, might make a powerful diversion in the rear of the imperial army. Charles, who must have feared to displease him, did not hesitate, and immediately sacrificed the independence of the empire to the favour of Rome and the success of his struggle with France.

On the 15th of July, Charles issued an edict from Burgos in Castile, wherein he declared, with an imperious and angry tone, " that the pope alone had the right of convoking a council, and the emperor of demanding one ; that the meeting appointed to take place at Spires could not, and ought not to be tolerated ; that it was strange the German nation should undertake a task which all the other nations in the universe, even with the pope's guidance, would not have the right of doing ; and that no time should be lost in enforcing the decree of Worms against the new Mahomet."

Thus came from Spain and Italy the blow that arrested the development of the Gospel in Germany. Charles was not yet satisfied. In 1519, he had proposed to unite his sister, the Archduchess Catherine, to John Frederick, son of Duke John, the elector's brother, and heir to the electorate. But was it not this Saxon house that supported in Germany those principles of religious and political independence which Charles hated ? He decided on breaking off entirely with the troublesome and guilty representative of the evangelical and national ideas, and gave his sister in marriage to John III., king of Portugal. Frederick, who in 1519 had shown his indifference to the overtures of the King of Spain, was able in 1524 to suppress the indignation he felt at the emperor's conduct ; but Duke John haughtily intimated that this proceeding had wounded his feelings very deeply.

Thus the two hostile camps that were destined to rend the empire for so long a period became daily more distinct.

CHAPTER VI.

Persecution—Gaspard Tauber—A Bookseller—Cruelties in Wurtemberg, Salzburg, and Bavaria—Pomerania—Henry of Zuphten.

THE Roman party was not satisfied with this. The alliance of Ratisbon was not to be a mere form ; it must be sealed with blood. Ferdinand and Campeggio descended the Danube together from Ratisbon to Vienna, and during their journey bound each other by cruel promises. A persecution immediately broke out in the Austrian states.

One Gaspar Tauber, a citizen of Vienna, had circulated Luther's writings, and had even written against the invocation of saints, purgatory, and transubstantiation.[1] Being thrown into prison, he was summoned by his judges, both theologians and lawyers, to retract his errors. It was thought that he had consented, and every preparation was made in Vienna to gratify the people with this solemn spectacle. On the festival of St. Mary's nativity, two pulpits were erected in St. Stephen's cemetery, one for the leader of the choir, who was to extol by his chants the repentance of the heretic ; and the other

Ranke, Deutsche Gesch. ii. 163.

[1] Atque etiam proprios ipse tractatus perscripserim. Cochlæus, p. 92. verso.

366

for Tauber himself. The formula of recantation was placed in his hands;[1] the people and choristers waited in silence. Either because Tauber had made no promise, or that at the moment of abjuration his faith suddenly revived with fresh energy, he exclaimed, "I am not convinced, and I appeal to the holy Roman empire!" Clergy, choristers, and people were seized with astonishment and alarm. But Tauber continued to call for death rather than that he should deny the Gospel. He was decapitated, and his body burnt;[2] and his courage made an indelible impression on the inhabitants of Vienna.

At Buda in Hungary, an evangelical bookseller, named John, had circulated Luther's New Testament and other of his writings throughout that country. He was bound to a stake; his persecutors then piled his books around him, enclosing him as if in a tower, and set fire to them. John manifested unshaken courage, exclaiming from the midst of the flames, that he was delighted to suffer in the cause of the Lord.[3] "Blood follows blood," cried Luther, when informed of this martyrdom, "but that generous blood, which Rome loves to shed, will at last suffocate the pope with his kings and their kingdoms."[4]

Fanaticism grew fiercer every day; evangelical ministers were expelled from their churches; magistrates were banished; and at times the most horrible punishments were inflicted. In Wurtemberg, an inquisitor named Reichler caused the Lutherans, and above all the preachers, to be hanged upon trees. Barbarous ruffians were found who unfeelingly nailed the pastors to a post by their tongues; so that these unhappy victims, tearing themselves violently from the wood to which they were fastened, were horribly mutilated in attempting to recover their liberty, and thus deprived of that gift which they had long used to proclaim the Gospel.[5]

Similar persecutions took place in the other states of the catholic league. An evangelical minister in the neighbourhood of Salzburg was led to prison, where he was to pass the rest of his days; whilst the police who had him in charge were drinking at an alehouse on the road, two young peasants, moved with compassion, eluded their vigilance, and liberated the pastor. The anger of the archbishop was inflamed against these poor people, and without any form of trial ordered them to be beheaded. They were secretly led outside the town early in the morning; and when they arrived on the plain where

they were to die, the executioner himself hesitated, "for (said he) they have not been tried."—"Do what I command you," harshly replied the archbishop's emissary, "and leave the responsibility to the prince!" and the heads of these youthful liberators immediately fell beneath the sword.[1]

The persecution was most violent in the states of the Duke of Bavaria: priests were deprived of their office; nobles driven from their castles; spies filled the whole country; and in every heart reigned mistrust and alarm. As Bernard Fichtel, a magistrate, was going to Nuremberg on the duke's business, on the high-road he fell in with Francis Burkhardt, professor at Ingolstadt, and one of Dr. Eck's friends. Burkhardt accosted him, and they travelled together. After supper the professor began to talk of religion; Fichtel, who was no stranger to his fellow-traveller, reminded him that the new edict prohibited such conversations. "Between us," replied Burkhardt, "there is nothing to fear."—Upon this Fichtel remarked: "I do not think this edict can ever be enforced." He then proceeded to express himself in an ambiguous manner on purgatory, and said it was a horrible thing to punish religious differences with death. At these words Burkhardt could not contain himself: "What is more just," said he, "than to cut off the heads of all these Lutheran rascals!" He took a friendly leave of Fichtel, but immediately denounced him. Fichtel was thrown into prison, and the wretched man, who had never thought of becoming a martyr, and whose religious convictions were not very deep, only escaped death by a shameful retractation. There was no security in any place, not even in the bosom of a friend.

But others met with that death from which Fichtel escaped. In vain was the Gospel preached in secret;[2] the dukes tracked it in its obscurity and mystery,—beneath the domestic roof and in the lonely fields.

"The cross and persecution reign in Bavaria," said Luther; "these wild beasts are lashing themselves into madness."[3]

Even the north of Germany was not free from these cruelties. Bogislaus, duke of Pomerania, being dead, his son, who had been brought up at Duke George's court, persecuted the Gospel; Suaven and Knipstrow were compelled to flee.

But it was in Holstein that one of the most extraordinary instances of fanaticism occurred.

Henry von Zuphten, who had escaped, as we have seen, from the convent at Antwerp, was preaching the Gospel at Bremen; Nicholas Boye, pastor of Mehldorf in the Dittmarsh, and several pious men of that dis-

[1] See Cochl., ibid.; Cum igitur ego Casparus Tauber, etc.
[2] Credo te vidisse Casparis Tauber historiam martyris novi Viennæ, quem cæsum capite scribunt et igne exustum pro verbo Dei. Luther to Hausmann, 12th November 1524, ii. 563.
[3] Idem accidit Budæ in Ungaria bibliopolæ cuidam Johanni, simul cum libris circa eum positis exusto, fortissimeque passo pro Domino. Luther to Hausmann, ii. 563.
[4] Sanguis sanguinem tangit, qui suffocabit papam cum regibus et regnis suis. Ibid.
[5] Ranke, Deutsche Gesch. ii. 174.

[1] Zauner, Salzburger Chronik. iv. 381.
[2] Verbi non palam seminati. L. Epp. ii. 559.
[3] In Bavaria multum regnat crux et persecutio. Ibid.

trict, invited him to come and proclaim Jesus Christ among them. He complied with their wishes. Immediately the prior of the Dominicans and the vicar of the official of Hamburg consulted together. " If he preaches and the people listen to him," said they, " all is lost ! " The prior, after passing an agitated night, rose early and repaired to the barren and uncultivated heath where the forty-eight regents of the country were wont to hold their meetings. " The monk of Bremen is come to ruin all the Dittmarshers," said he to them. These forty-eight simple-minded and ignorant men, being persuaded that they would acquire great renown by delivering the world from the heretical monk, resolved on putting him to death, without having either seen or heard him.

This was on Saturday, and the prior wished to prevent Henry from preaching on the following day. He arrived at the pastor Boye's dwelling in the middle of the night with the letter of the forty-eight regents. " If it be God's will that I should die among the Dittmarshers," said Henry von Zuphten, " heaven is as near me there as elsewhere;[1] I will preach."

He went up into the pulpit and preached with great energy. His hearers, moved and excited by his christian eloquence, had scarcely left the church when the prior handed them the letter of the forty-eight regents, forbidding the monk to preach. They immediately sent their representatives to the heath ; and, after a long discussion, the Dittmarshers agreed that, considering their great ignorance, they would wait until Easter. But the incensed prior went up to some of the regents and inflamed their zeal afresh. " We will write to him," said they. —" Mind what you are about," replied the prior; " if he begins to speak, we shall be able to do nothing with him. We must seize him during the night, and burn him before he can open his mouth."

They determined to adopt this course. At nightfall on the day after the Festival of the Conception, the *Ave Maria* bell was rung. At this signal, all the neighbouring villagers assembled, to the number of five hundred, and their leaders having broached three butts of Hamburg beer, by this means inspired them with great courage. It was striking midnight when they reached Mehldorf;—the peasants were armed ;—the monks carried torches ;—all marched in disorder, exchanging shouts of fury. As they entered the village, they kept deep silence for fear Henry should escape.

On a sudden the gates of the parsonage were burst open; the drunken peasants rushed in, striking every thing they saw ; dishes, kettles, flagons, clothing, were tossed about pell-mell ; they seized on all the gold and silver they could find, and falling on the poor

pastor, beat him, with loud cries of " Kill him ! kill him !" and then flung him into the mud. But it was Henry they were seeking; they pulled him out of bed, tied his hands behind his back, and dragged him after them, without clothing, and in a piercing cold night. " Why did you come here," said they. And as Henry answered mildly, they cried out, " Down with him ! down with him ! if we listen to him we shall become heretics also !" They had dragged him naked through the ice and snow ; his feet were bleeding ; he entreated to be set on horseback. " Yes, indeed," replied they, mocking him, " we will find horses for heretics !......March !"—And they continued hurrying him towards the heath. A woman, standing at the door of her cottage as the servant of God was passing, began to weep. " My good woman," said Henry, " do not weep for me." The bailiff pronounced his condemnation. Upon this one of the madmen who had dragged him thither struck the preacher of Jesus Christ on the head with a sword; another gave him a blow with a club; after which they brought him a poor monk to receive his confession. " Brother," said Henry, " have I ever done you any wrong ?"—" None," replied the monk.—" In that case I have nothing to confess to you," resumed Henry, " and you have nothing to forgive me." The monk retired in confusion. Several ineffectual attempts were made to kindle the pile ; the logs would not catch fire. For two hours the martyr remained thus before the furious peasantry,—calm, and raising his eyes to heaven. While they were binding him to throw him into the flames, he began the confession of his faith. " Burn first," said a peasant, striking him on the mouth with his fist, " and then you may speak !" They tried to fling him on the pile, but he fell on one side. John Holme, seizing a club, struck him upon the breast, and he was laid dead on the burning heap. " Such is the true history of the sufferings of the holy martyr, Henry von Zuphten."[1]

CHAPTER VII.

Divisions—The Lord's Supper—Two Extremes—Hoen's Discovery—Wessel on the Lord's Supper—Carlstadt—Luther —Mysticism of the Anabaptists—Carlstadt at Orlamund —Luther's Mission—Interview at Table—The Conference of Orlamund—Carlstadt banished.

WHILE the Roman party was every where drawing the sword against the Reformation, this work underwent new developments. It is not at Zurich or at Geneva, but in Wittemberg, the focus of the Lutheran revival, that

---

[1] Der Himmel wäre da so nahe als anderswo. L. Opp. xix. 330.

[1] Das ist die wahre Historie, &c. L. Opp. L. xix. 333.

we should look for the commencement of that reformed Church, of which Calvin became the chief doctor. These two great families had slept in the same cradle. Union ought in like manner to have crowned their mature age. But when the question of the Lord's Supper was once started, Luther violently rejected the reformed element, and bound himself and his Church in an exclusive Lutheranism. The vexation he felt at this rival doctrine caused him to lose much of his natural kindness of disposition, and aroused in him a mistrust, an habitual discontent and irritation, to which he had hitherto been a stranger.

The controversy broke out between the two old friends, the two champions who had fought side by side at Leipsic against Rome, —between Carlstadt and Luther. In each of them their attachment to contrary doctrines originated in a turn of mind that merits our esteem. In fact, there are two extremes in questions of religion; the one materializes, the other spiritualizes every thing. The former of these two extremes is that of Rome; the latter, of the Mystics. Religion, like man himself, is compounded of body and soul; the pure idealists as well as the materialists, in religious views no less than in philosophical systems, are equally mistaken.

Such is the great question hidden under the discussion about the Lord's Supper. While on a superficial glance we see nothing but a trivial dispute about words, a deeper observation discloses to us one of the most important controversies that can occupy the human mind.

Here the reformers divide into two parties; but each carries away with it a portion of the truth. Luther and his followers oppose an exaggerated spiritualism; Carlstadt and the reformed attack a hateful materialism. Each of them arraigns the error which in his view appears the most fatal, and, in assailing it, possibly goes beyond the truth. But this is of no importance; each of them is true in his general tendency, and although belonging to two different hosts, these two illustrious teachers both take their stand under one common banner,—that of Jesus Christ, who alone is Truth in its infinite extent.

Carlstadt thought that nothing could be more injurious to real piety than confidence in outward ceremonies and in a certain magical influence of the sacraments. The outward participation in the Lord's Supper, according to Rome, was sufficient for salvation, and this principle had materialized religion. Carlstadt saw no better way of restoring its spirituality than by denying all presence of Christ's body: and he taught that this holy feast was to believers simply a pledge of their redemption.

Did Carlstadt arrive at these opinions unaided? No: all things are bound together

in the Church; and the historical filiation of the reformed doctrine, so long overlooked, now appears clearly established. Unquestionably we cannot fail to see in this doctrine the sentiments of several of the Fathers; but if we search in the long chain of ages for the link which more immediately connects that of Carlstadt and the Swiss reformers, we shall find it in John Wessel, the most illustrious doctor of the fifteenth century. [1]

A christian lawyer of Holland, Cornelius Hoen (Honius), a friend of Erasmus, and who had been thrown into prison in 1523 for his attachment to the Gospel, found among the papers of James Hoek, dean of Naeldwik, and a great friend of Wessel, several treatises by this illustrious doctor, touching the Lord's Supper. [2] Hoen, convinced of the truth of the spiritual sense ascribed by Wessel to this sacrament, thought it his duty to communicate to the reformers these papers written by his fellow-countryman. He therefore transmitted them to two of his friends, John Rhodius, president of the brethren of the Common-life at Utrecht, and George Sagarus or Saganus, together with a letter on the same subject, and desired them to lay all of them before Luther.

About the close of the year 1520, the two Dutchmen arrived at Wittemberg, where they seem to have been favourably received by Carlstadt from the first moment; while Luther, as was his custom, invited these foreign friends to meet some of his colleagues at dinner. The conversation naturally fell on the treasure these Netherlanders had brought with them, and particularly on the writings of Wessel concerning the Lord's Supper.

Rhodius invited Luther to receive the doctrine that the great doctor of the fifteenth century had so clearly set forth, and Carlstadt entreated his friend to acknowledge the spiritual signification of the Eucharist, and even to write against the carnal eating of Christ's body. Luther shook his head and refused, upon which Carlstadt exclaimed warmly: "Well, then, if you will not do it, I will, although far less fitted than yourself." Such was the beginning of the division that afterwards occurred between these two colleagues. [3] The two Netherlanders, being rejected in Saxony, resolved to turn their steps towards Switzerland, where we shall meet with them again.

Luther henceforward took a diametrically opposite direction. At first, he had apparently contended in favour of the opinion we have just pointed out. In his treatise on the

[1] See vol. l. p. 33.
[2] See Hardenberg *Vita Wesseli*; Gerdes. *Hist. Evang. renov.* l. 228-230; Gieseler, Kirchen G. iii. 190; Ulman Joh. Wessel (2d edit.), p. 564.
[3] Hardenberg, Vita Wesseli; W. Opp. Amsterdam, p. 13. Hardenberg refers to Rhodius, Goswin, Melancthon, and Th. Blaurer, from whom he says that he received his account, and adds: Interim velim illis credi, ut viris bonis; mihi saltem, ut fideli relatori.

mass, which appeared in 1520, he said: " I can every day partake of the sacraments, if I only call to mind the words and promises of Christ, and if I nourish and strengthen my faith with them." Neither Carlstadt, Zwingle, nor Calvin, have ever used stronger language than this. It would even appear that the idea frequently occurred to him at this period, that a symbolical explanation of the Lord's Supper would be the most powerful weapon to overturn the papal system from top to bottom ; for he said in 1525, that five years previously he had undergone many severe temptations for this doctrine,[1] and that the man who could have proved to him that there was only bread and wine in the eucharist, would have done him the greatest of services.

But new circumstances threw him into an opposition, at times not unmingled with violence, against those very opinions to which he had made so near an approach. The fanaticism of the Anabaptists explains the direction Luther now took. These enthusiasts were not content with undervaluing what they called the external Word, that is, the Bible, and with pretending to special revelations from the Holy Ghost ; they went so far as to despise the sacrament of the Lord's Supper, as something outward, and to speak of an inward communion as being the only true communion. From that time, in every attempt made to explain the doctrine of the Lord's Supper in a symbolical manner, Luther saw only the danger of weakening the authority of the Holy Scriptures ; of substituting arbitrary allegories for their real meaning ; of spiritualizing every thing in religion ; of making it consist, not in the gifts of God, but in the impressions of men : and of substituting by this means for the true Christianity a mysticism, a theosophy, a fanaticism, that would infallibly become its grave. We must acknowledge that, had it not been for Luther's violent opposition, the mystical, enthusiastic, and subjective tendency would then perhaps have made rapid progress, and would have turned back the tide of blessings that the Reformation was to spread over the world.

Carlstadt, impatient at being prevented from explaining his doctrine freely in Wittemberg, and urged by his conscience to combat a system which in his " opinion lowered Christ's death and destroyed his righteousness," resolved " to give a public testimony for the love of poor and cruelly deceived Christendom." He left Wittemberg at the beginning of 1524, without informing either the university or the chapter of his intentions, and repaired to the small town of Orlamund, the church of which was placed under his superintendence. He had the incumbent dismissed, got himself nominated pastor in his stead, and in despite of

the chapter, the university, and the elector, established himself in this new post.

He soon began to propagate his doctrine. " It is impossible," said he, " to find in the real presence any advantage that does not proceed from faith ; it is therefore useless." In explaining Christ's words at the institution of the Lord's Supper, he had recourse to an interpretation which is not admitted by the reformed Churches. Luther, in the disputation at Leipsic, had explained these words : *Thou art Peter, and on this rock I will build my Church*, by separating the two propositions, and applying the latter to our Saviour's person. " In like manner," said Carlstadt, " the words, *take, eat*, refer to the bread ; but *this is my body* relates to Jesus Christ, who then pointed to himself, and intimated by the symbol of breaking the bread, that his body was soon to be broken."

Carlstadt did not stop here. He was scarcely emancipated from the guardianship of Luther, before he felt his zeal revive against the images. It was easy for his imprudent discourses and his enthusiastic language to inflame men's minds in these agitated times. The people, imagining they heard a second Elijah, broke the idols of Baal. The excitement soon spread to the surrounding villages. The elector would have interfered ; but the peasants replied that they ought to obey God rather than man. Upon this, the prince determined to send Luther to Orlamund to restore peace. Luther regarded Carlstadt as a man eaten up by a love of notoriety,[1]—a fanatic who might be so far carried away as to make war on Christ himself. Frederick might perhaps have made a wiser choice. Luther departed, and Carlstadt was fated to see this troublesome rival once more come and disturb his plans of reform, and check his soaring flight.

Jena was on the road to Orlamund. Luther reached this city on the 23d of August, and on the 24th went into the pulpit at seven in the morning ; he spoke for an hour and a half in the presence of a numerous auditory against fanaticism, rebellion, the breaking of images, and the contempt of the real presence, inveighing most energetically against the innovations of Orlamund. He did not mention Carlstadt by name, but every one could see whom he had in view.

Carlstadt, either by accident or design, was at Jena, and among the number of Luther's hearers. He did not hesitate to seek an explanation of this sermon. Luther was dining with the prior of Wittemberg, the burgomaster, the town-clerk, the pastor of Jena, and several officers of the emperor and the margrave, when he received a note from Carlstadt demanding an interview ; he handed it to his neighbours, and replied to the bearer : " If Doctor Carlstadt wishes to come to me, let him come ; if not, I can do

---

[1] Ich habe wohl so harte Anfechtungen da erlitten. L. Epp. ii. 577.

[1] Huc perpulit eum insana gloriæ et laudis libido. L. Epp. ii. 551.

without him." Carlstadt came. His visit produced a lively sensation in the whole party. The majority, eager to see the two lions battling, suspended their repast and looked on, while the more timid turned pale with alarm.

Carlstadt, on Luther's invitation, took a seat in front of him and said: " Doctor, in your sermon of this morning you classed me with those who inculcate rebellion and assassination. Such a charge I declare to be false."

LUTHER.—" I did not name you ; but since the cap fits, you may wear it."

After a brief pause Carlstadt resumed : " I will undertake to prove that on the doctrine of the sacrament you have contradicted yourself, and that no one, since the days of the apostles, has taught it so purely as myself."

LUTHER.—" Write! combat my opinions!"

CARLSTADT.—" I challenge you to a public disputation at Wittemberg or at Erfurth, if you will procure me a safe-conduct."

LUTHER.—" Fear nothing, doctor."

CARLSTADT.—" You bind me hand and foot, and when you have rendered me unable to defend myself, you strike me."[1]

There was another brief silence, when Luther resumed :—

" Write against me,—but openly and not in secret."

CARLSTADT.—" I would do so, if I knew that you were speaking sincerely."

LUTHER.—" Do so, and I will give you a florin."

CARLSTADT.—" Give it me ; I accept the challenge."

At these words Luther took a gold florin out of his pocket, and giving it to Carlstadt, said : " There is the money: now strike boldly."

Carlstadt holding the florin in his hand, turned towards the assembly and said : " Dear brethren, this is my earnest-money, a warrant that I have authority to write against Doctor Luther; be you all witnesses to this."

Then bending the florin that it might be known again, he put it in his purse and shook hands with Luther, who drank his health, to which Carlstadt responded. " The more vigorous your attack, the better I shall like it," resumed Luther.

" If I miss you," replied Carlstadt, " it shall be through no fault of mine."

They once more shook hands, and Carlstadt returned to his dwelling.

Thus, says an historian, as from a single spark often proceeds the conflagration of a whole forest, so from this small beginning a great division arose in the Church.[2]

Luther set out for Orlamund, and arrived there very ill prepared by the scene at Jena.

[1] Ihr bandet mir Hände und Füsse, darnach schlugt ihr mich. L. Opp. xix. 150.
[2] Sicut una scintilla sæpe totam sylvam comburit. M. Adami Vita Carlst. p. 83. Our narrative is mostly taken from the Acts of Reinhardt, pastor of Jena, an eye-witness, but a friend of Carlstadt, and whom Luther charged with inaccuracy.

He assembled the council and the church, and said : " Neither the elector nor the university will acknowledge Carlstadt as your pastor."—" If Carlstadt is not our pastor," replied the treasurer of the town-council, " St. Paul is a false teacher, and your books are full of falsehoods, for we have elected him."

As he said this, Carlstadt entered the room. Some of those who were near Luther beckoned him to sit down, but Carlstadt, going straight up to Luther, said : " Dear doctor, if you will allow me, I will entertain you."

LUTHER.—" You are my opponent. I gave you a gold florin for that purpose."

CARLSTADT.—" I will be your opponent so long as you remain the enemy of God and of his truth."

LUTHER.—" Leave the room : I cannot allow you to be present here."

CARLSTADT.—" This is a public meeting. If your cause is good, why should you fear me ? "

LUTHER to his servant.—" Go and put the horses to ; I have nothing to do with Carlstadt, and since he will not leave, I must."[1]

At the same time Luther rose from his seat, upon which Carlstadt quitted the room.

After a short pause, Luther resumed :— " Prove by Scripture that we ought to destroy the images."

A COUNCILLOR, opening a Bible.—" Doctor, you will grant me, however, that Moses knew God's commandments ? Well, then, here are his words: Thou shalt not make unto thee any graven image, or any likeness."

LUTHER.—" This passage refers only to idolatrous images. If I have a crucifix hung up in my chamber, and do not worship it, what harm can it do me ? "

A SHOEMAKER.—" I have frequently taken off my hat before an image that I have seen in a room or in the streets. It is an idolatrous act that deprives God of the glory that is due to him alone."

LUTHER.—" Must we then, because of their abuse, put our women to death, and throw our wine into the streets ? "[2]

ANOTHER MEMBER OF THE CHURCH.—" No ! these are God's creatures, which we are not commanded to destroy."

After the conference had lasted some time longer, Luther and his friends returned to their carriage, astonished at what they had seen, and without having succeeded in convincing the inhabitants, who claimed for themselves the right of freely interpreting and explaining the Scriptures. The excitement was very great in Orlamund ; the people insulted Luther, and some of them shouted out : " Begone, in the name of all the devils ! May you break your neck before you get out of our city ! "[3] Never had the reformer undergone such humiliation.

[1] Spann an, spann an. L. Opp. xix. 154.
[2] So muss du dess Missbrauchs halber auch. Ibid. 155.
[3] Two of the most distinguished contemporary historians

He proceeded thence to Kale, where the pastor had also embraced the doctrines of Carlstadt, and resolved to preach there. But when he entered the pulpit, he found in it the fragments of a crucifix. At first his emotion was very great; but recovering himself, he gathered up the pieces into a corner, and delivered a sermon without a single allusion to this circumstance. He said at a later period : " I determined to revenge myself on the devil by contempt."

The nearer the elector approached the end of his days, the more he feared lest men should go too far in the Reformation. He gave orders that Carlstadt should be deprived of his offices, and that he should not only leave Orlamund, but the electoral states also. In vain did the church of this place intercede in his favour ; in vain did they ask that he might be allowed to remain among them as a private citizen, with permission to preach occasionally; in vain did they represent that they valued God's truth more than the whole world, or even a thousand worlds,[1] if God had created as many : Frederick was inflexible, and he even went so far as to refuse Carlstadt the funds necessary for his journey. Luther had nothing to do with these severe measures of the prince ; they were far from his disposition, as he showed at a later period. But Carlstadt looked upon him as the author of all his misfortunes, and filled Germany with his complaints and lamentations. He wrote a farewell address to his friends at Orlamund. The people were called together by the ringing of the bells ; and the letter, which was read to the assembled church, drew tears from every eye.[2] It was signed, " Andrew Bodenstein, expelled by Luther, unheard and unconvicted."

We cannot but feel pain at seeing the contest between these two men, who once were friends, and who were both so excellent. A feeling of sadness took possession of all the disciples of the Reformation. What would become of it, now that its most illustrious defenders thus opposed each other ? Luther noticed these fears, and endeavoured to allay them. "Let us fight," said he, "as if fighting for another. The cause is God's, the care is God's, the work is God's, the victory is God's, and to God belongs the glory![3] He will contend and conquer without us. Let that fall which ought to fall; let that stand which ought to stand. It is not our own cause that is at stake, nor our own glory that we seek."

Carlstadt took refuge at Strasburg, where

he published several works. He was a sound Latin, Greek, and Hebrew scholar, says Dr. Scheur ; and Luther acknowledged his superior erudition. Endowed with an elevated mind, he sacrificed his reputation, his rank, his home, his very bread, to his convictions. He afterwards proceeded to Switzerland; it is there he should have commenced his teaching : his independence needed the free air in which Zwingle and Œcolampadius breathed. His doctrine soon awakened almost as much attention as that obtained by Luther's first theses. Switzerland appeared to be won ; Bucer and Capito seemed to be carried away by it.

Luther's indignation was then at its height, and he published one of the most powerful, but at the same time one of his most violent controversial works—his book "*Against the Celestial Prophets.*"

Thus the Reformation, attacked by the pope, the emperor, and the princes, was beginning to tear its own vitals. It seemed that it must fall under the weight of so many evils ; and assuredly it would have fallen had it been a work of man. But soon from the very brink of destruction it rose up with renewed energy.

CHAPTER VIII.

Progress—Resistance against the Ratisbon Leaguers—Meeting between Philip of Hesse and Melancthon—The Landgrave converted to the Gospel—The Palatinate—Luneburg—Holstein—The Grand-Master at Wittemberg.

The Catholic League of Ratisbon and the persecutions that followed it, created a powerful reaction among the German people. They did not feel disposed to suffer themselves to be deprived of that Word of God which had been restored to them at last; and to the orders of Charles V., to the bulls of the pope, to the menaces and burning piles of Ferdinand and the other Roman-catholic princes, they replied: " We will keep it ! "

No sooner had the members of the league quitted Ratisbon, than the deputies of the towns, whose bishops had taken part in this alliance, in surprise and indignation met at Spires, and declared that their ministers, in despite of the prohibition of the bishops, should preach the Gospel, and nothing but the Gospel, conformably to the doctrine of the prophets and apostles. They then proceeded to draw up a memorial in firm and consistent language, to be laid before the national assembly.

The imperial letter from Burgos, it is true, came to disturb their minds. Nevertheless, about the close of the year, the deputies of these cities, with many nobles, met at Ulm, and swore to assist one another in case of attack.

---

of Germany (Dr. **Markelneke, Ref. Gesch. II.** 139, and Fred. von Raumer, Gesch. Europ. i. 371), add, that the people of Orlamund flung mud and stones at Luther; but he asserts the very contrary : " Dass ich froh ward, dass ich nit mit Steinen und Dreck ausgeworffen ward." I was glad to escape without being pelted with stones and mud. L. Epp. ii. 579.

[1] Höher als tausend Welten. Seck. p. 628.

[2] Quæ publice vocatis per campanas lectæ sunt omnibus simul flentibus. L. Epp. ii. 558.

[3] Causa Dei est, cura Dei est, opus Dei est, victoria Dei est, gloria Dei est ! Ibid. 556.

Thus to the camp formed by Austria, Bavaria, and the bishops, the free cities immediately opposed another in which they planted the standard of the Gospel and of the national liberties.

While the cities were thus placing themselves in the van of the Reformation, many princes were gained over to its cause. In the beginning of the month of June 1524, as Melancthon was returning on horseback from a visit to his mother, accompanied by Camerarius and some other friends, he met a brilliant train near Frankfort. It was Philip, landgrave of Hesse, who three years before had called on Luther at Worms, and who was then on his road to the tournament at Heidelberg, where all the princes of Germany would be present.

Thus did Providence bring Philip successively into contact with the two reformers. As it was known that the celebrated doctor had gone to his native place, one of the landgrave's attendants said: " It is Philip Melancthon, I think." The young prince, immediately clapped spurs to his horse, and coming near the doctor said : " Is your name Philip ?"—" It is," replied the scholar a little intimidated, and respectfully preparing to alight. [1] " Keep your seat," said the prince ; "turn round, and come and pass the night with me; there are some matters on which I desire to have a little talk with you; fear nothing."—" What can I fear from such a prince as you ?" replied the doctor.—"Ah! ah !" said the landgrave with a laugh, "if I were to carry you off and give you up to Campeggio, he would not be offended, I think." The two Philips rode on together, side by side, the prince asking questions and the doctor replying. The landgrave was delighted with the clear and impressive views set before him by Melancthon. The latter at length begged permission to continue his journey, and Philip of Hesse parted from him with reluctance. " On one condition," said he, "that on your return home you will carefully examine the questions we have been discussing, and send me the result in writing." [2] Melancthon gave his promise. " Go, then," said Philip, " and pass through my states."

Melancthon drew up with his usual talent an *Abridgment of the Revived Doctrine of Christianity ;* [3] a forcible and concise treatise, that made a decided impression on the landgrave's mind. Shortly after his return from the tournament at Heidelberg, this prince, without joining the free cities, published an edict by which, in opposition to the league of Ratisbon, he ordered the Gospel to be preached in all its purity. He embraced it himself with the energy peculiar to his character. " Rather would I give up my body and life, my subjects, and my states," said he, " than the Word of God." A Minorite friar, named Ferber, perceiving this prince's leaning towards the Reformation, wrote him a letter full of reproach, in which he conjured him to remain faithful to Rome. " I will remain faithful to the old doctrine," replied Philip, " but such as it is contained in Scripture." He then proved very forcibly that man is justified solely by faith. Astonishment kept the monk silent. [1] The landgrave was commonly styled " Melancthon's disciple." [2]

Other princes followed in the same direction. The elector-palatine refused to lend himself to any persecution ; the Duke of Luneburg, nephew to the Elector of Saxony, began to reform his own states; and the King of Denmark gave orders that in Sleswick and Holstein every one should be free to serve God as his conscience suggested.

The Reformation gained a still more important victory. A prince, whose conversion to the Gospel was destined to exert the greatest influence, even in our days, began about this time to turn aside from Rome. One day about the end of June, shortly after Melancthon's return to Wittemberg, Albert, margrave of Brandenburg and grand-master of the Teutonic order, entered Luther's chamber. This chief of the military monks of Germany, who then possessed Prussia, had gone to the Diet of Nuremberg to invoke the aid of the empire against Poland. He returned in the deepest distress. On the one hand, the preaching of Osiander and the reading of the Bible had convinced him that his monastic profession was contrary to the Word of God ; and on the other the fall of the national government in Germany had deprived him of all hope of obtaining the succour he had gone to solicit. What can he do then ?......The Saxon councillor Von Planitz, with whom he had quitted Nuremberg, advised him to see the reformer. " What do you think of the regulations of my order ?" said the restless and agitated prince. Luther felt no hesitation : he saw that a line of conduct in conformity with the Gospel was the only thing that could save Prussia. " Invoke the aid of God," said he to the grand-master ; " throw off the senseless and confused rules of your order ; put an end to that abominable principality, a veritable hermaphrodite, which is neither religious nor secular ; [3] relinquish that false chastity, and seek the true one ; take a wife, and instead of that nameless monster, found a legitimate sovereignty." [4] These words placed distinctly before the mind of the grand-master a state of things that he had

---

[1] Honoris causa de equo descensurus. Camerarius, p. 94.
[2] Ut de questionibus quas audisset moveri, aliquid diligenter conscriptum curaret. Ibid. p. 94.
[3] Epitome renovatæ ecclesiasticæ doctrinæ.

[1] Seckendorf, p. 738.
[2] Princeps ille discipulus Philippi fuit a quibusdam appellatus. Camer. p. 95.
[3] Ut loco illius abominabilis principatus, qui hermaphrodita quidem. L. Epp. ii. 527.
[4] Ut contempta ista stulta confusaque regula, uxorem duceret. Ibid.

as yet conceived but vaguely. A smile lit up his features; but as he had too much prudence to declare himself, he remained silent.[1] Melancthon, who was present, spoke to the same effect as Luther, and the prince returned to his states, leaving the reformers under the conviction that the seed they had sown in his heart would one day bear fruit.

Thus Charles V. and the pope had opposed the national assembly at Spires for fear the Word of God should gain over all who might be present; but the Word of God cannot be bound; they refused to let it be heard in one of the halls of a town in the Lower Palatinate; it avenged itself by spreading over all the provinces; it stirred the hearts of the people, enlightened the princes, and manifested in every part of the empire that Divine power which neither bulls nor edicts can ever take away.

CHAPTER IX.

Reforms—All-Saints Church—Fall of the Mass—Learning—Christian Schools—Learning extended to the Laity—The Arts—Moral Religion—Esthetical Religion—Music—Poetry—Painting.

WHILE the nations and their rulers were thus hastening forward to the light, the reformers were endeavouring to regenerate every thing, to interpenetrate every thing with the principles of Christianity. The state of public worship first engaged their attention. The time fixed by the reformer, on his return from the Wartburg, had arrived. "Now," said he, "that men's hearts have been strengthened by Divine grace, we must put an end to the scandals that pollute the kingdom of the Lord, and dare something in the name of Jesus." He required that men should communicate in both kinds (the bread and wine); that every thing should be retrenched from the ceremony of the eucharist that tended to make it a sacrifice;[2] that Christians should never assemble together without having the Gospel preached;[3] that believers, or at least the priests and scholars, should meet every morning at five or six o'clock to read the Old Testament; and at a corresponding hour in the evening to read the New Testament; that every Sunday, the whole Church should assemble in the morning and afternoon, and that the great object of their worship should be to sound abroad the Word of God.[4]

The church of All Saints at Wittemberg especially excited Luther's indignation. Seckendorf informs us that 9901 masses were there celebrated yearly, and 35,570 pounds of wax annually burnt. Luther called it "a sacrilegious Tophet." "There are only three or four lazy-bellies," said he, "who still worship this shameful mammon, and if I had not restrained the people, this house of All Saints, or rather of all devils, would have made such a noise in the world as has never before been heard."

The struggle began around this church. It resembled those ancient sanctuaries of paganism in Egypt, Gaul, and Germany, which were destined to fall that Christianity might be established.

Luther, desiring that the mass should be abolished in this cathedral, addressed a petition to the chapter to this effect on the 1st of March 1523, and a second on the 11th of July.[1] The canons having pleaded the elector's orders, Luther replied, "What is the prince's order to us in this case? He is a secular prince; the sword, and not the preaching of the Gospel, belongs to him."[2] Here Luther clearly marks the distinction between the State and the Church. "There is but one sacrifice that taketh away sins," said he again, "Christ, who offered himself up once for all; and in this we are partakers, not by works or by sacrifices, but solely by faith in the Word of God."

The elector, who felt his end drawing near, was opposed to new reforms.

But fresh entreaties were added to those of Luther. "It is time to act," said Jonas, provost of the cathedral, to the elector. "A manifestation of the Gospel, so striking as that which we now have, does not ordinarily last longer than a sunbeam. Let us make haste then."[3]

As the letter of Jonas did not change the elector's views, Luther lost all patience; he thought the moment had come for striking a decisive blow, and addressed a threatening letter to the chapter: "I entreat you amicably, and urge you seriously, to put an end to all this sectarian worship. If you refuse, you will receive (with God's help) the reward that you have deserved. I mention this for your guidance, and require a positive and immediate answer,—yes or no,—before Sunday next, that I may know what I have to do. May God give you grace to follow his light.

"Thursday, 8th December 1524.

"MARTIN LUTHER,
"Preacher at Wittemberg."[4]

At the same time the rector, two burgomasters, and ten councillors, waited on the dean, and entreated him in the name of the university, the council, and the township of

---

[1] Ille tum arrisit, sed nihil respondit. L. Epp. ii. 527.
[2] Weise christliche Messe zu halten. L. Opp. (L.) xxii. 232.
[3] Die christliche Gemeine nimmer soll zusammen kommen, es werde denn daselbst Gottes Wort geprediget. Ibid. 226.
[4] Dass das Wort im Schwange gehe (to ring out the Word in full peal.) Ibid. 227.

[1] L. Epp. ii. pp. 308, 354.
[2] Welchem gebührt das Schwerd, nicht das Predigtamt zu versorgen. L. Opp. xviii. p. 497.
[3] Corp. Ref. i. 636.
[4] L. Epp. ii. 565.

Wittemberg, " to abolish the great and horrible impiety committed in the mass against the majesty of God."

The chapter was forced to give way; they declared that, being enlightened by the holy Word of God,[1] they acknowledged the abuses that had been pointed out, and published a new order of church-service, which began to be observed on Christmas-day 1524.

Thus fell the mass in this renowned sanctuary, where it had so long resisted the reiterated attacks of the reformers. The Elector Frederick, suffering from the gout, and rapidly drawing near his end, could not, in spite of all his exertions, prevent this great victory of the Reformation. He saw in it a manifestation of the Divine will, and gave way. The fall of the Romish observances in the church of All Saints hastened their abolition in a great number of churches throughout Christendom; every where the same resistance was offered,—every where there was the same triumph. In vain did the priests, and even the princes in many places, try to interpose obstacles; they could not succeed.

It was not the public worship alone that the Reformation was ordained to change. The school was early placed beside the Church; and these two great institutions, so powerful to regenerate the nations, were equally reanimated by it. It was by a close alliance with learning that the Reformation entered into the world; in the hour of its triumph, it did not forget its ally.

Christianity is not a simple development of Judaism. Unlike the papacy, it does not aim at confining man again in the close swaddling bands of outward ordinances and human doctrines. Christianity is a new creation; it lays hold of the inner man, and transforms him in the inmost principles of his human nature, so that man no longer requires other men to impose rules upon him; but, aided by God, he can of himself and by himself distinguish what is true, and do what is right.[2]

To lead mankind to that ripe age which Christ has purchased for them, and to free them from that tutelage in which Rome had held them so long, the Reformation had to develop the whole man; and while regenerating his heart and his will by the Word of God, to enlighten his understanding by the study of profane and sacred learning.

Luther saw this; he felt that to strengthen the Reformation, it was requisite to work on the young, to improve the schools, and to propagate throughout Christendom the knowledge necessary for a profound study of the Holy Scriptures. This, accordingly, was one of the objects of his life. He saw it in particular at the period which we have reached, and wrote to the councillors of all the cities of Germany, calling upon them to

found christian schools. " Dear sirs," said he, " we annually expend so much money on arquebuses, roads, and dikes, why should we not spend a little to give one or two schoolmasters to our poor children ? God stands at the door and knocks; blessed are we if we open to him ! Now the Word of God abounds. O my dear Germans, buy, buy, while the market is open before your houses. The Word of God and his grace are like a shower that falls and passes away. It was among the Jews ; but it passed away, and now they have it no longer. Paul carried it into Greece ; but in that country also it has passed away, and the Turk reigns there now. It came to Rome and the Latin empire; but there also it has passed away, and Rome now has the pope.[1] O Germans, do not expect to have this Word for ever. The contempt that is shown to it will drive it away. For this reason, let him who desires to possess it lay hold of it and keep it !

" Busy yourselves with the children," continues Luther, still addressing the magistrates ; " for many parents are like ostriches ; they are hardened towards their little ones, and, satisfied with having laid the egg, they care nothing for it afterwards. The prosperity of a city does not consist merely in heaping up great treasures, in building strong walls, in erecting splendid mansions, in possessing glittering arms. If madmen fall upon it, its ruin will only be the greater. The true wealth of a city, its safety, and its strength, is to have many learned, serious, worthy, well educated citizens. And whom must we blame, because there are so few at present, except your magistrates, who have allowed our youth to grow up like trees in a forest ? "

Luther particularly insisted on the necessity of studying literature and languages : " What use is there, it may be asked, in learning Latin, Greek, and Hebrew? We can read the Bible very well in German. Without languages," replies he, " we could not have received the Gospel......Languages are the scabbard that contains the sword of the Spirit ;[2] they are the casket that guards the jewels: they are the vessel that holds the wine ; and, as the Gospel says, they are the baskets in which the loaves and fishes are kept to feed the multitude. If we neglect the languages, we shall not only eventually lose the Gospel, but be unable to speak or write in Latin or in German. No sooner did men cease to cultivate them than Christendom declined, even until it fell under the power of the pope. But now that languages are again honoured, they shed such light that all the world is astonished, and every one is forced to acknowledge that our Gospel is almost as pure as that of the apostles

---

[1] Durch das Licht des heiligen göttlichen Wortes....L. Opp. xviii. 502.
[2] Hebrews viii. 11.

[1] Aber hin ist hin (*but lost is lost*); sie haben nun den Pabst. L. Opp. W. x. 535.
[2] Die Sprachen sind die Scheide, darinnen dies Messer des Geistes stecket. Ibid.

themselves. In former times the holy Fathers were frequently mistaken, because they were ignorant of languages; and in our days there are some who, like the Waldenses, do not think the languages to be of any use; but although their doctrine be good, they have often erred in the real meaning of the sacred text; they are without arms against error, and I fear very much that their faith will not remain pure.[1] If the languages had not made me positive as to the meaning of the Word, I might have been a pious monk, and quietly preached the truth in the obscurity of a cloister; but I should have left the pope, the sophists, and their anti-christian empire still unshaken."[2]

Luther did not concern himself about the education of the clergy only; it was his desire that knowledge should not be confined to the Church; he proposed extending it to the laity, who hitherto had been deprived of it. He called for the establishment of libraries, which should comprise not only editions and commentaries of the schoolmen and of the fathers of the Church, but also the works of orators and poets, even were they heathens, as well as writings devoted to the fine arts, law, medicine, and history. "These productions," said he, "serve to make known the works and the wonders of God."

This effort on the part of Luther is one of the most important produced by the Reformation. He emancipated learning from the hands of the priests, who had monopolized it, like those of Egypt in times of old, and put it within the reach of all. From this impulse given by the Reformation have proceeded the greatest developments of modern times. Those laymen, whether men of letters or scholars, who now revile the Reformation, forget that they themselves are its offspring, and that, without it, they would still be, like ignorant children, under the rod of the clergy. The Reformation perceived the close tie that connected all the sciences: it saw that, as all knowledge is derived from God, it leads man back to God. It desired that all men should learn, and that they should learn every thing. "Those who despise profane literature," said Melancthon, "hold theology in no greater estimation. Their contempt is a mere pretext, with which they seek to conceal their idleness."[3]

The Reformation was not satisfied with merely giving a strong impulse to letters; it gave also a fresh impulse to the arts. Protestantism has often been reproached as their enemy, and many Protestants willingly accept this reproach. We will not inquire whether the Reformation ought to glory in it or not: we shall be content to observe that impartial history does not confirm the fact on which this accusation is founded. Let Roman-catholicism pride itself in being more favourable to the arts than Protestantism; be it so: paganism was still more favourable, and Protestantism places its glory elsewhere. There are some religions in which the esthetic tendencies of man hold a more important place than his moral nature. Christianity is distinct from these religions, inasmuch as the moral element is its essence. The christian sentiment is manifested not by the productions of the fine arts, but by the works of a christian life. Every sect that should abandon this moral tendency of Christianity, would by that very circumstance forfeit its claims to the name of christian. Rome has not entirely abandoned it, but Protestantism cherishes this essential characteristic with much greater purity. It places its glory in examining into all that concerns the moral being, in judging of religious actions, not by their external beauty and the manner in which they strike the imagination, but according to their internal worth, and the connexion they have with the conscience; so that if the papacy is above all an esthetical religion, as a celebrated writer has proved it to be,[1] Protestantism is above all a moral religion.

And yet, although the Reformation at first addressed man as a moral being, it addressed the whole man. We have just seen how it spoke to his understanding and what it did for literature; it also spoke to his sensibility, to his imagination, and contributed to the development of the arts. The Church was no longer composed exclusively of monks and priests; it was the assembly of the faithful. All were to take part in its public worship; and the chanting of the clergy was to be succeeded by the singing of the people. Accordingly Luther, in translating the Psalms, thought of adapting them to congregational singing. Thus a taste for music was spread among the nation.

"Next to theology," said Luther, "I give the first place and the highest honour to music.[2] A schoolmaster should know how to sing," said he at another time, "or else I would not so much as look at him."

One day, as certain of his friends were singing some beautiful hymns at his house, he exclaimed with enthusiasm: "If our Lord God has scattered such admirable gifts on this earth, which is but a dark corner, what will it not be in the life eternal, in which all will be perfection!"......Since Luther's time, the people have sung; the Bible inspired their songs, and the impulse given at the epoch of the Reformation produced in later years those noble oratorios which seem to be the summit of this art.

Poetry shared in the general movement. In singing the praises of God, men could not

---

[1] Es sey oder werde nicht lauter bleiben. L. Opp. W. x. 535.
[2] Ich hätte wohl auch können fromm seyn und in der stille recht predigen. Ibid.
[3] Hunc titulum ignaviæ suæ prætextunt. Corp. Ref. 1. 612.

[1] Chateaubriand, Génie du Christianisme.
[2] Ich gebe nach der Theologie, der Musica den nähesten Locum und höchste Ehre. L. Opp. W. xxii. p. 2253.

confine themselves to mere translations of the ancient hymns. The souls of Luther and many of his contemporaries, elevated by faith to the sublimest ideas, excited to enthusiasm by the conflicts and dangers that continually threatened the infant Church, and inspired by the poetic genius of the Old Testament, and by the faith of the New, soon poured forth their feelings in religious songs, in which poetry and music united and blended their most heavenly features. Thus in the sixteenth century the canticle was revived which in the first century had consoled the pangs of the martyrs. In 1523, Luther, as we have already seen, consecrated it to the memory of the Brussels martyrs, and other children of the Reformation imitated his example. These hymns increased in number, and were circulated rapidly among the people, and contributed powerfully to awaken them from their slumbers. It was in the same year that Hans Sachs composed *The Nightingale of Wittemberg.* The doctrine that for the last four centuries had prevailed in the Church was as the moonlight, during which men had lost their way in the wilderness. Now the nightingale proclaimed the dawn, and, soaring above the mists of the morning, celebrates the brightness of the coming day.

Whilst lyric poetry thus owed its birth to the loftiest inspirations of the Reformation, satirical verses and dramas from the pen of Hütten and Manuel attacked the most crying abuses.

It is to the Reformation that the greatest poets of England, Germany, and perhaps of France, are indebted for their highest flights.

Of all the arts, painting is that on which the Reformation had the least influence. Nevertheless, it was renovated, and as it were sanctified, by the universal movement which at that time agitated all the powers of man. Lucas Cranach, the great master of that age, settled at Wittemberg, lived on intimate terms with Luther, and became the painter of the Reformation. We have seen how he represented the contrast between Christ and Antichrist (the pope),[1] and thus ranked among the most influential organs of the revolution that was transforming the nations. As soon as he had received new convictions, he consecrated his chaste pencil solely to paintings in harmony with christian sentiments, and spread over groups of children, blessed by our Saviour, those graces with which he had previously adorned legendary saints. Albert Durer also was gained over by the Word of the Gospel, and his genius received a fresh impulse. His masterpieces date from this period. We see from the touches with which he henceforward depicted the evangelists and apostles, that the Bible was restored to the people,

and that the painter thence derived a depth, power, life, and sublimity, which he could never have found in himself.[1]

And yet we must confess that of all the arts painting is that whose religious influence is most exposed to well-founded and strong objections. Poetry and music come from heaven, and will be found again in heaven; but we continually see painting connected with serious immoralities or mournful errors. After a man has studied history or visited Italy, he expects nothing beneficial to humanity from this art. Whatever may be the value of this exception which we think it our duty to make, our general remark still holds good.

The Reformation of Germany, while it primarily addressed man's moral nature, gave an impulse to the arts that they had not yet received from Roman-catholicism.

Thus every thing advanced : arts, literature, spirituality of worship, and the minds of princes and of people. But this noble harmony which the Gospel at its revival every where called forth, was about to be disturbed. The songs of the Wittemberg nightingale were to be interrupted by the howling of the tempest and the roaring of lions. In a moment a cloud overspread all Germany, and a glorious day was followed by the deepest darkness.

CHAPTER X.

Political Ferment — Luther against Rebellion — Thomas Munzer—Agitation—The Black Forest—The Twelve Articles—Luther's Opinion — Helfenstein — March of the Peasants—March of the Imperial Army—Defeat of the Peasants—Cruelty of the Princes.

A POLITICAL ferment, very different from that produced by the Gospel, had long been at work in the empire. The people, bowed down by civil and ecclesiastical oppression, bound in many countries to the seigneurial estates, and transferred from hand to hand along with them, threatened to rise with fury and to break their chains. This agitation had shown itself long before the Reformation by many symptoms, and even then the religious element was blended with the political; in the sixteenth century it was impossible to separate these two principles, which were so closely associated in the existence of nations. In Holland, at the close of the preceding century, the peasants had revolted, placing on their banners, by way of arms, a loaf and a cheese, the two great blessings of these poor people. "The Alliance of the Shoes" had shown itself in the neighbourhood of Spires in 1502.[2] In 1513,

---

[1] See vol. II. p. 216.

[1] Ranke, Deutsche Geschichte, ii. 85.   [2] See vol. I. p. 26.

it appeared again in Brisgau, being encouraged by the priests. In 1514, Wurtemberg had seen the "League of Poor Conrad," whose aim was to maintain by rebellion "the right of God." In 1515, Carinthia and Hungary had been the theatre of terrible agitations. These seditions had been quenched in torrents of blood; but no relief had been accorded to the people. A political reform, therefore, was not less necessary than a religious reform. The people were entitled to this; but we must acknowledge that they were not ripe for its enjoyment.

Since the commencement of the Reformation, these popular disturbances had not been renewed; men's minds were occupied by other thoughts. Luther, whose piercing glance had discerned the condition of the people, had already from the summit of the Wartburg addressed them in serious exhortations calculated to restrain their agitated minds:—

"Rebellion," he had said, "never produces the amelioration we desire, and God condemns it. What is it to rebel, if it be not to avenge oneself? The devil is striving to excite to revolt those who embrace the Gospel, in order to cover it with opprobrium; but those who have rightly understood my doctrine do not revolt."[1]

Every thing gave cause to fear that the popular agitation could not be restrained much longer. The government that Frederick of Saxony had taken such pains to form, and which possessed the confidence of the nation, was dissolved. The emperor, whose energy might have been an efficient substitute for the influence of this national administration, was absent; the princes whose union had always constituted the strength of Germany were divided; and the new declarations of Charles V. against Luther, by removing every hope of future harmony, deprived the reformer of part of the moral influence by which in 1522 he had succeeded in calming the storm. The chief barriers that hitherto had confined the torrent being broken, nothing could any longer restrain its fury.

It was not the religious movement that gave birth to political agitations; but in many places it was carried away by their impetuous waves. Perhaps we might even go further, and acknowledge that the movement communicated to the people by the Reformation gave fresh strength to the discontent fermenting in the nation. The violence of Luther's writings, the intrepidity of his actions and language, the harsh truths that he spoke, not only to the pope and prelates, but also to the princes themselves, must all have contributed to inflame minds that were already in a state of excitement. Accordingly, Erasmus did not fail to tell him: "We are now reaping the fruits that you have

sown."[1] And further, the cheering truths of the Gospel at last brought to light, stirred all hearts, and filled them with anticipation and hope. But many unregenerated souls were not prepared by repentance for the faith and liberty of Christians. They were very willing to throw off the papal yoke, but they would not take up the yoke of Christ. And hence, when princes devoted to the cause of Rome endeavoured in their wrath to stifle the Reformation, real Christians patiently endured these cruel persecutions; but the multitude resisted and broke out, and seeing their desires checked in one direction, gave vent to them in another. "Why," said they, "should slavery be perpetuated in the state, while the Church invites all men to a glorious liberty? Why should governments rule only by force, when the Gospel preaches nothing but gentleness?" Unhappily at a time when the religious reform was received with equal joy both by princes and people, the political reform, on the contrary, had the most powerful part of the nation against it; and while the former had the Gospel for its rule and support, the latter had soon no other principles than violence and despotism. Accordingly, while the one was confined within the bounds of truth, the other rapidly, like an impetuous torrent, overstepped all limits of justice. But to shut one's eyes against the indirect influence of the Reformation on the troubles that broke out in the empire, would betoken partiality. A fire had been kindled in Germany by religious discussions, from which it was impossible to prevent the escape of a few sparks calculated to inflame the passions of the people.

The claims of a few fanatics to Divine inspiration increased the evil. While the Reformation had continually appealed from the pretended authority of the Church to the real authority of the Holy Scriptures, these enthusiasts not only rejected the authority of the Church, but of Scripture also; they spoke only of an inner Word, of an internal revelation from God; and overlooking the natural corruption of their hearts, gave way to all the intoxication of spiritual pride, and fancied they were saints.

"To them the Holy Scriptures were but a dead letter," said Luther, "and they all began to cry, *The Spirit! the Spirit!* But most assuredly I will not follow where their spirit leads them. May God of his mercy preserve me from a Church in which there are none but saints.[2] I desire to dwell with the humble, the feeble, the sick, who know and feel their sins, and who groan and cry continually to God from the bottom of their hearts to obtain his consolation and support." These words of Luther's have great depth of meaning, and point out the change that was taking

---

[1] Luther's treue Ermahnung an alle Christen sich vor Aufruhr und Empörung zu hüten. Opp. xviii. 288.

[1] Habemus fructum tui spiritus. Erasm. Hyperasp. b. iv.
[2] Der barmherzige Gott behüte mich ja für der christlichen Kirche, darin eitel Heilige sind. On John i. 2. L. Opp. (W.) vii. 1469.

place in his views as to the nature of the Church. They indicate at the same time how contrary were the religious opinions of the rebels to those of the Reformation.

The most notorious of these enthusiasts was Thomas Munzer; he was not devoid of talent, had read his Bible, was zealous, and might have done good, if he had been able to collect his agitated thoughts and find peace of heart. But as he did not know himself, and was wanting in true humility, he was possessed with a desire of reforming the world, and forgot, as all enthusiasts do, that the reformation should begin with himself. Some mystical writings that he had read in his youth had given a false direction to his mind. He first appeared at Zwickau, quitted Wittemberg after Luther's return, dissatisfied with the inferior part he was playing, and became pastor of the small town of Alstadt in Thuringia. He could not long remain quiet, and accused the reformers of founding, by their adherence to the letter, a new popery, and of forming churches which were not pure and holy.

"Luther," said he, "has delivered men's consciences from the yoke of the pope, but he has left them in a carnal liberty, and not led them in spirit towards God."[1]

He considered himself as called of God to remedy this great evil. The revelations of the *Spirit* were in his eyes the means by which his reform was to be effected. "He who possesses this Spirit," said he, "possesses the true faith, although he should never see the Scriptures in his life. Heathens and Turks are better fitted to receive it than many Christians who style us enthusiasts." It was Luther whom he here had in view. "To receive this Spirit we must mortify the flesh," said he at another time, "wear tattered clothing, let the beard grow, be of a sad countenance, keep silence,[2] retire into desert places, and supplicate God to give us a sign of his favour. Then God will come and speak with us, as formerly He spoke with Abraham, Isaac, and Jacob. If He were not to do so, He would not deserve our attention.[3] I have received from God the commission to gather together his elect into a holy and eternal alliance."

The agitation and ferment at work in men's minds were but too favourable to the dissemination of these enthusiastic ideas. Man loves the marvellous, and whatever flatters his pride. Munzer, having persuaded a part of his flock to adopt his views, abolished congregational singing and all other ceremonies. He maintained that obedience to princes "void of understanding," was at once to serve God and Belial. Then marching out at the head of his parishioners to a

chapel in the vicinity of Alstadt, whither pilgrims from all quarters were accustomed to resort, he pulled it down. After this exploit, being compelled to leave that neighbourhood, he wandered about Germany, and went as far as Switzerland, carrying with him, and communicating to all who would listen to him, the plan of a general revolution. Every where he found men's minds prepared; he threw gunpowder on the burning coals, and the explosion forthwith took place.

Luther, who had rejected the warlike enterprises of Sickengen,[1] could not be led away by the tumultuous movements of the peasantry. Fortunately for social order, the Gospel preserved him; for what would have happened had he carried his extensive influence into their camp?......He ever firmly maintained the distinction between secular and spiritual things; he continually repeated that it was immortal souls which Christ emancipated by his Word; and if, with one hand, he attacked the authority of the Church, with the other he upheld with equal power the authority of princes. "A Christian," said he, "should endure a hundred deaths, rather than meddle in the slightest degree with the revolt of the peasants." He wrote to the elector: "It causes me especial joy that these enthusiasts themselves boast, to all who are willing to listen to them, that they do not belong to us. The Spirit urges them on, say they; and I reply, it is an evil spirit, for he bears no other fruit than the pillage of convents and churches; the greatest highway robbers upon earth might do as much."

At the same time, Luther, who desired that others should enjoy the liberty he claimed for himself, dissuaded the prince from all measures of severity: "Let them preach what they please, and against whom they please," said he; "for it is the Word of God that must march in front of the battle and fight against them. If their spirit be the true Spirit, he will not fear our severity; if ours is the true one, he will not fear their violence. Let us leave the spirits to struggle and contend with one another.[2] Perhaps some persons may be led astray; there is no battle without wounds; but he who fighteth faithfully shall be crowned. Nevertheless, if they desire to take up the sword, let your highness forbid it, and order them to quit the country."

The insurrection began in the Black Forest, and near the sources of the Danube, so frequently the theatre of popular commotions. On the 19th of July 1524, some Thurgovian peasants rose against the Abbot of Reichenau, who would not accord them an evangelical preacher. Erelong thousands were collected round the small town of Tengen,

---

[1] Führete sie nicht weiter in Geist und zu Gott. L. Opp. xix. 294.
[2] Saur sehen, den Bart nicht abschneiden. Ibid.
[3] Munzer's language is low and impious: Er wollt in Gott scheissen wenn er nicht mit ihm redet, wie mit Abraham. Hist. of Munzer by Melancthon. Ibid. 295.

[1] See vol. i. p. 47.
[2] Man lasse die Geister auf einander platzen und treffen. L. Epp. ii. 547.

to liberate an ecclesiastic who was there imprisoned. The revolt spread with inconceivable rapidity from Swabia as far as the Rhenish provinces, Franconia, Thuringia, and Saxony. In the month of January 1525, all these countries were in a state of rebellion.

About the end of this month, the peasants published a declaration in twelve articles, in which they claimed the liberty of choosing their own pastors, the abolition of small tithes, of slavery, and of fines on inheritance, the right to hunt, fish, and cut wood, &c. Each demand was backed by a passage from Holy Writ, and they said in conclusion, "If we are deceived, let Luther correct us by Scripture."

The opinions of the Wittemberg divines were consulted. Luther and Melancthon delivered theirs separately, and they both gave evidence of the difference of their characters. Melancthon, who thought every kind of disturbance a crime, overstepped the limits of his usual gentleness, and could not find language strong enough to express his indignation. The peasants were criminals, against whom he invoked all laws human and Divine. If friendly negotiation was unavailing, the magistrates ought to hunt them down, as if they were robbers and assassins. "And yet," he added (and we require at least one feature to remind us of Melancthon), "let them take pity on the orphans when having recourse to the penalty of death!"

Luther's opinion of the revolt was the same as Melancthon's; but he had a heart that beat for the miseries of the people. On this occasion he manifested a dignified impartiality, and spoke the truth frankly to both parties. He first addressed the princes, and more especially the bishops :—

"It is you," said he, "who are the cause of this revolt; it is your clamours against the Gospel, your guilty oppressions of the poor, that have driven the people to despair. It is not the peasants, my dear Lords, that rise up against you,—it is God himself who opposes your madness.[1] The peasants are but the instruments he employs to humble you. Do not imagine you can escape the punishment he is preparing for you. Even should you have succeeded in destroying all these peasants, God is able from the very stones to raise up others to chastise your pride. If I desired revenge, I might laugh in my sleeve, and look on while the peasants were carrying on their work, or even increase their fury; but may God preserve me from such thoughts!......My dear Lords, put away your indignation, treat these poor peasants as a man of sense treats people who are drunk or insane. Quiet these commotions by mildness, lest a conflagration should arise and burn all Germany. Among these twelve articles there are certain demands which are just and equitable."

This prologue was calculated to conciliate the peasants' confidence in Luther, and to make them listen patiently to the truths he had to tell them. He represented to them that most of their demands were well founded; but that to revolt was to act like heathens; that the duty of a Christian is to be patient, and not to fight; that if they persisted in revolting against the Gospel in the name of the Gospel, he should look upon them as more dangerous enemies than the pope. "The pope and the emperor," continued he, "combined against me; but the more they blustered the more did the Gospel gain ground......And why was this? Because I never drew the sword or called for vengeance; because I never had recourse to tumult or insurrection: I relied wholly upon God, and placed every thing in His almighty hands. Christians fight not with swords or arquebuses, but with sufferings and with the cross. Christ, their Captain, handled not the sword......he was hung upon a tree."

But to no purpose did Luther employ this christian language. The people were too much excited by the fanatical speeches of the leaders of the insurrection, to listen, as of old, to the words of the reformer. "He is playing the hypocrite," said they; "he flatters the nobles. He has declared war against the pope, and yet wishes us to submit to our oppressors."

The revolt, instead of dying away, became more formidable. At Weinsberg, Count Louis of Helfenstein and the seventy men under his orders were condemned to death by the rebels. A body of peasants drew up with their pikes lowered, whilst others drove the count and his soldiers against this wall of steel.[1] The wife of the wretched Helfenstein, a natural daughter of the Emperor Maximilian, holding an infant two years old in her arms, knelt before them, and with loud cries begged for her husband's life, and vainly endeavoured to avert this barbarous murder. A boy who had been in the count's service, and had joined the rebels, capered gaily before him, and played the dead march upon his fife, as if he had been leading his victims in a dance. All perished; the child was wounded in its mother's arms; and she herself thrown upon a dung-cart, and thus conveyed to Heilbrunn.

At the news of these cruelties, a cry of horror was heard from the friends of the Reformation, and Luther's feeling heart underwent a terrible conflict. On the one hand the peasants, ridiculing his advice, pretended to have received revelations from heaven, made an impious use of the threatenings of the Old Testament, proclaimed an equality of ranks and a community of goods, defended

---

[1] Gott ist's selber der setzt sich wider euch. L. Opp. xix. 254.

[1] Und jechten ein Grafen durch die Spiesse. Mathesiu : p. 46.

their cause with fire and sword, and indulged in barbarous atrocities. On the other hand, the enemies of the Reformation asked the reformer, with a malicious sneer, if he did not know that it was easier to kindle a fire than to extinguish it. Shocked at these excesses, and alarmed at the thought that they might check the progress of the Gospel, Luther hesitated no longer, no longer temporized; he inveighed against the insurgents with all the energy of his character, and perhaps overstepped the just bounds within which he should have contained himself.

" The peasants," said he, " commit three horrible sins against God and man, and thus deserve the death of body and soul. First, they revolt against their magistrates to whom they have sworn fidelity; next, they rob and plunder convents and castles; and lastly, they veil their crimes with the cloak of the Gospel. If you do not put a mad dog to death, you will perish, and all the country with you. Whoever is killed fighting for the magistrates will be a true martyr, if he has fought with a good conscience." Luther then gives a powerful description of the guilty violence of the peasants who force simple and peaceable men to join their alliance, and thus drag them to the same condemnation. He then adds: " For this reason, my dear Lords, help, save, deliver, have pity on these poor people. Let every one strike, pierce, and kill, who is able.........If thou diest, thou canst not meet a happier death; for thou diest in the service of God, and to save thy neighbour from hell." [1]

Neither gentleness nor violence could arrest the popular torrent. The church-bells were no longer rung for divine service; whenever their deep and prolonged sounds were heard in the fields, it was the tocsin, and all ran to arms. The people of the Black Forest had rallied round John Muller of Bulgenbach. With an imposing aspect, wrapped up in a red cloak, and wearing a red cap, this leader boldly advanced from village to village followed by the peasantry. Behind him, on a waggon decorated with ribands and branches of trees, was raised the tricolor flag, black, red, and white,—the signal of revolt. A herald, dressed in the same colours, read the twelve articles, and invited the people to join in the rebellion. Whoever refused was banished from the community.

Erelong this march, which at first was peaceable, became more disquieting. " We must compel the lords to submit to our alliance," exclaimed they. And to induce them to do so, they plundered the granaries, emptied the cellars, drew the seigneurial fish-ponds, demolished the castles of the nobles who resisted, and burnt the convents. Opposition had inflamed the passions of those rude men; equality no longer satisfied

them; they thirsted for blood, and swore to put to death every man who wore a spur.

At the approach of the peasants, the cities that were unable to resist them opened their gates and joined them. In whatever place they entered, they pulled down the images and broke the crucifixes; armed women paraded the streets and threatened the monks. If they were defeated in one quarter, they assembled again in another, and braved the most formidable forces. A committee of peasants was established at Heilbrunn. The Counts of Lowenstein were taken prisoners, dressed in a smock-frock, and a white staff having been placed in their hands, were compelled to swear to the twelve articles. " Brother George, and thou, brother Albert," said a tinker of Ohringen to the Counts of Hohenlohe, who had gone to their camp, " swear to conduct yourselves as our brethren; for you also are now peasants; you are no longer lords." Equality of rank, the dream of many democrats, was established in aristocratic Germany.

Many nobles, some through fear, others from ambition, then joined the insurgents. The famous Goetz von Berlichingen, finding his vassals refuse to obey him, desired to flee to the Elector of Saxony; but his wife, who was lying-in, wishing to keep him near her, concealed the elector's answer. Goetz, being closely pursued, was compelled to put himself at the head of the rebel army. On the 7th of May the peasants entered Wurtzburg, where the citizens received them with acclamations. The forces of the princes and knights of Swabia and Franconia, which had assembled in that city, evacuated it, and retired in confusion to the citadel, the last bulwark of the nobility.

But the movement had already extended to other parts of Germany. Spires, the Palatinate, Alsace, and Hesse, accepted the twelve articles, and the peasants threatened Bavaria, Westphalia, the Tyrol, Saxony, and Lorraine. The Margrave of Baden, having rejected the articles, was compelled to flee. The coadjutor of Fulda acceded to them with a smile. The smaller towns said, they had no lances with which to oppose the insurgents. Mentz, Treves, and Frankfort obtained the liberties which they had claimed.

An immense revolution was preparing in all the empire. The ecclesiastical and secular privileges, that bore so heavily on the peasants, were to be suppressed; the possessions of the clergy were to be secularized, to indemnify the princes and provide for the wants of the empire; taxes were to be abolished, with the exception of a tribute payable every ten years; the imperial power alone was to subsist, as being recognised by the New Testament; all the other princes were to cease to reign; sixty-four free tribunals were to be established, in which men of all classes should have a seat; all ranks were to return to their primitive condition; the clergy

---

[1] Deinen Nehesten zu retten aus der Hölle. L. Opp. xix. 266.

were to be henceforward merely the pastors of the churches; princes and knights were to be simply the defenders of the weak; uniformity in weights and measures was to be introduced; and only one kind of money was to be coined throughout the empire.

Meanwhile the princes had shaken off their first lethargy, and George von Truchsess, commander-in-chief of the imperial army, was advancing on the side of the Lake of Constance. On the 2d of May he defeated the peasants at Beblingen, marched on the town of Weinsberg, where the unhappy Count of Helfenstein had perished, burnt and razed it to the ground, giving orders that the ruins should be left as an eternal monument of the treason of its inhabitants. At Fürfeld he united with the Elector Palatine and the Elector of Treves, and all three moved towards Franconia.

The Frauenburg, the citadel of Wurtzburg, held out for the princes, and the main army of the peasants still lay before its walls. As soon as they heard of Truchsess' march, they resolved on an assault, and at nine o'clock at night on the 15th of May, the trumpets sounded, the tricolor flag was unfurled, and the peasants rushed to the attack with horrible shouts. Sebastian von Rotenham, one of the warmest partisans of the Reformation, was governor of the castle. He had put the fortress in a formidable state of defence, and having exhorted the garrison to repel the assault with courage, the soldiers, holding up three fingers, had all sworn to hold out till the last. A most terrible conflict then took place. To the vigour and despair of the insurgents the fortress replied from its walls and towers by petards, showers of sulphur and boiling pitch, and the discharges of artillery. The peasants, thus struck by their unseen enemies, were staggered for a moment; but in an instant their fury grew more violent. The struggle was prolonged as the night advanced. The fortress, lit up by a thousand battle-fires, appeared in the darkness like a towering giant, who, vomiting flames, struggled alone amidst the roar of thunder for the salvation of the empire against the ferocious valour of these furious hordes. Two hours after midnight the peasants withdrew, having failed in all their efforts.

They now tried to enter into negotiations, either with the garrison or with Truchsess, who was advancing at the head of his army. But this was going out of their line; violence and victory alone could save them. After some little hesitation, they resolved to march against the imperial forces, but the cavalry and artillery made terrible havoc in their ranks. At Königshofen, and afterwards at Engelstadt, those unfortunate creatures were totally defeated. The princes, nobles, and bishops, abusing their victory, indulged in most unprecedented cruelties. The prisoners were hung on the trees by the

wayside. The Bishop of Wurtzburg, who had run away, now returned, traversed his diocese accompanied by executioners, and watered it alike with the blood of the rebels and of the peaceful friends of the Word of God. Goetz von Berlichingen was sentenced to imprisonment for life. The Margrave Casimir of Anspach put out the eyes of eighty-five insurgents, who had sworn that their eyes should never look upon that prince again; and he cast this troop of blinded individuals upon the world, who wandered up and down, holding each other by the hand, groping along, and begging their bread. The wretched boy, who had played the dead-march on his fife at the murder of Helfenstein, was chained to a post; a fire was kindled around him, and the knights looked on laughing at his horrible contortions.

Public worship was every where restored in its ancient forms. The most flourishing and populous districts of the empire exhibited to those who travelled through them nothing but heaps of dead bodies and smoking ruins. Fifty thousand men had perished, and the people lost nearly every where the little liberty they had hitherto enjoyed. Such was the horrible termination of this revolt in the south of Germany.

CHAPTER XI.

Munzer at Mulhausen—Appeal to the People—March of the Princes—End of the Revolt—Influence of the Reformers—Sufferings—Changes—Two Results.

BUT the evil was not confined to the south and west of Germany. Munzer, after having traversed a part of Switzerland, Alsace, and Swabia, had again directed his steps towards Saxony. A few citizens of Mulhausen, in Thuringia, had invited him to their city, and elected him their pastor. The town-council having resisted, Munzer deposed it and nominated another, consisting of his friends, with himself at their head. Full of contempt for that Christ, "sweet as honey," whom Luther preached, and being resolved to employ the most energetic measures, he exclaimed: "Like Joshua, we must put all the Canaanites to the sword." He established a community of goods, and pillaged the convents.[1] "Munzer," wrote Luther to Amsdorff on the 11th of April 1525, "Munzer is not only pastor, but king and emperor of Mulhausen." The poor no longer worked; if any one needed corn or cloth, he went and demanded it of some rich man; if the latter refused, the poor man took it by force; if he resisted, he was hung. As Mulhausen was an independent city, Munzer was able

[1] Omnia simul communia. L. Opp. xix. 292.

to exercise his power for nearly a year without opposition. The revolt in the south of Germany led him to imagine that it was time to extend his new kingdom. He had a number of heavy guns cast in the Franciscan convent, and endeavoured to raise the peasantry and miners of Mansfeldt. "How long will you sleep?" said he to them in a fanatical proclamation. "Arise and fight the battle of the Lord! The time is come. France, Germany, and Italy are moving. On, on, on!—Dran, Dran, Dran!......Heed not. the groans of the impious ones. They will implore you like children; but be pitiless.—Dran, Dran, Dran!......The fire is burning: let your sword be ever warm with blood. [1]—Dran, Dran, Dran!......Work while it is yet day." The letter was signed "MUNZER, servant of God against the wicked."

The country people. thirsting for plunder, flocked round his standard. Throughout all the districts of Mansfeldt, Stolberg, Schwartzburg in Hesse, and the duchy of Brunswick, the peasantry rose in insurrection. The convents of Michelstein, Ilsenburg, Walkenried, Rossleben, and many others in the neighbourhood of the Hartz, or in the plains of Thuringia, were devastated. At Reinhardsbrunn, which Luther had visited, the tombs of the ancient landgraves were profaned, and the library destroyed.

Terror spread far and wide. Even at Wittemberg some anxiety began to be felt. Those doctors, who had feared neither the emperor nor the pope, trembled in the presence of a madman. They were always on the watch for news, and every step in the progress of the rebels was counted. "We are here in great danger," said Melancthon. "If Munzer succeeds, it is all over with us, unless Christ should rescue us. Munzer advances with a worse than Scythian cruelty, [2] and it is impossible to repeat the dreadful threats he utters."

The pious elector had long hesitated what he should do. Munzer had exhorted him and all the princes to be converted, because (said he) their hour was come; and he had signed these letters: "MUNZER, armed with the sword of Gideon." Frederick would have desired to reclaim these misguided men by gentle measures. On the 14th of April, when he was dangerously ill, he had written to his brother John: "We may have given these wretched people more than one cause for insurrection. Alas! the poor are oppressed in many ways by their spiritual and temporal lords." And when his attention was directed to the humiliation, the revolutions, and the dangers to which he would expose himself, unless he promptly stifled the rebellion, he replied: "Hitherto I have been a mighty elector, having chariots and

horses in abundance; if it be God's pleasure to take them from me now, I will go on foot."[1]

The youthful Philip, landgrave of Hesse, was the first of the princes who took up arms. His knights and soldiers swore to live and die with him. After pacifying his own states, he directed his march towards Saxony. On their side, Duke John, the elector's brother, Duke George of Saxony, and Duke Henry of Brunswick, advanced and united their troops with those of Hesse. The peasants, terrified at the sight of this army, fled to a small hill, where, without any discipline, without arms, and for the most part without courage, they formed a rampart with their waggons. Munzer had not even prepared ammunition for his large guns. No succours appeared; the rebels were hemmed in by the army; they lost all confidence. The princes, taking pity on them, proposed a capitulation, which they appeared willing to accept. Upon this Munzer had recourse to the most powerful lever that enthusiasm can put in motion. "To-day we shall behold the arm of the Lord," said he, "and all our enemies shall be destroyed." At this moment a rainbow appeared over their heads; the fanatical host, who carried a rainbow on their flags, regarded it as a sure prognostic of the Divine protection. Munzer took advantage of it: "Fear nothing," said he to the citizens and peasants; "I will catch all their balls in my sleeve."[2] At the same time he cruelly put to death a young gentleman, Maternus von Geholfen, an envoy from the princes, in order to deprive the insurgents of all hope of pardon.

The landgrave, having assembled his horsemen, said to them: "I well know that we princes are often in fault, for we are but men; but God commands all men to honour the powers that be. Let us save our wives and children from the fury of these murderers. The Lord will give us the victory, for he has said: *Whosoever resisteth the power, resisteth the ordinance of God.*" Philip then gave the signal of attack. It was the 15th of May 1525. The army was put in motion; but the peasant host stood immovable, singing the hymn, "Come, Holy Ghost," and waiting for heaven to declare in their favour. The artillery soon broke down their rude rampart, carrying dismay and death into the midst of the insurgents. Their fanaticism and courage at once forsook them; they were seized with a panic-terror, and ran away in disorder. Five thousand perished in the flight.

After the battle the princes and their victorious troops entered Frankenhausen. A soldier, who had gone into a loft in the house where he was quartered, found a man in bed. [3]

---

[1] Lasset euer Schwerdt nicht kalt warden von Blut. L. Opp. xix. 289.
[2] Moncerus plus quam Scythicam crudelitatem præ se fert. Corp. Ref. i. 741.

[1] So wolle er hinkünftig zu fuss gehen. Seck. p. 685.
[2] Ihr sollt sehen dass ich alle Büchsensteine in Ermel fassen will. L. Opp. xix. 297.
[3] So findet er einem am Bett.

" Who art thou ? " asked he ; " art thou one of the rebels ? " Then observing a pocket-book, he took it up, and found several letters addressed to Thomas Munzer. "Art thou Munzer ? " demanded the trooper. The sick man answered " No." But as the soldier uttered dreadful threats, Munzer, for it was really he, confessed who he was. "Thou art my prisoner," said the horseman. When Munzer was taken before Duke George and the landgrave, he persevered in saying that he was right to chastise the princes, since they opposed the Gospel. " Wretched man!" replied they, "think of all those of whose death you have been the cause." But he answered, smiling in the midst of his anguish: " They would have it so ! " He took the sacrament under one kind, and was beheaded at the same time with Pfeiffer, his lieutenant. Mulhausen was taken, and the peasants were loaded with chains.

A nobleman having observed among the crowd of prisoners a peasant of favourable appearance, went up and said to him : " Well, my man, which government do you like best —that of the peasants or of the princes ? " The poor fellow made answer with a deep sigh : "Ah, my lord, no knife cuts so deep as the rule of peasant over his fellows." [1]

The remains of the insurrection were quenched in blood ; Duke George, in particular, acted with the greatest severity. In the states of the elector, there were neither executions nor punishment. [2] The Word of God, preached in all its purity, had shown its power to restrain the tumultuous passions of the people.

From the very beginning, indeed, Luther had not ceased to struggle against the rebellion, which was, in his opinion, the forerunner of the judgment-day. Advice, prayers, and even irony, had not been spared. At the end of the articles drawn up at Erfurth by the rebels, he had subjoined, as a supplementary article: " *Item*, The following article has been omitted. Henceforward the honourable council shall have no power ; it shall do nothing ; it shall sit like an idol or a log of wood ; the commonalty shall chew its food, and it shall govern with its hands and feet tied ; henceforth the waggon shall guide the horses, the horses shall hold the reins, and we shall go on admirably, in conformity with the glorious system set forth in these articles."

Luther did not confine himself to writing. While the disturbance was still at its height, he quitted Wittemberg and went through some of the districts where the agitation was greatest. He preached, he laboured to soften his hearers' hearts, and his hand, to which God had given power, turned aside, calmed, and brought back the impetuous and overflowing torrents into their natural channels.

In every quarter the doctors of the Reformation exerted a similar influence. At Halle, Brentz had revived the drooping spirits of the citizens by the promises of God's Word, and four thousand peasants had fled before six hundred citizens. [1] At Ichterhausen, a mob of peasants having assembled with an intent to demolish several castles and put their lords to death, Frederick Myconius went out to them alone, and such was the power of his words, that they immediately abandoned their design. [2]

Such was the part taken by the reformers and the Reformation in the midst of this revolt ; they contended against it with all their might, with the sword of the Word, and boldly maintained those principles which alone, in every age, can preserve order and subjection among the nations. Accordingly, Luther asserted that if the power of sound doctrine had not checked the fury of the people, the revolt would have extended its ravages far more widely, and have overthrown both Church and State. Every thing leads us to believe that these melancholy prognostics would have been realized.

If the reformers thus contended against sedition, it was not without receiving grievous wounds. That moral agony which Luther had first suffered in his cell at Erfurth, became still more serious after the insurrection of the peasants. No great change takes place among men without suffering on the part of those who are its instruments. The birth of Christianity was effected by the agony of the cross ; but He who hung upon that cross addressed these words to each of his disciples : *Are ye able to drink of the cup that I shall drink of, and to be baptized with the same baptism that I am baptized with ?*

On the side of the princes, it was continually repeated that Luther and his doctrine were the cause of the revolt, and, however absurd this idea may be, the reformer could not see it so generally entertained without experiencing the deepest grief. On the side of the people, Munzer and all the leaders of the insurrection represented him as a vile hypocrite, and a flatterer of the great,[3] and their calumnies easily obtained belief. The violence with which Luther had declared against the rebels had displeased even moderate men. The friends of Rome exulted ;[4] all were against him, and bore heavily upon him the anger of his contemporaries. But his greatest affliction was to behold the work of heaven thus dragged in the mire, and classed with the most fanatical projects. Here he felt was his Gethsemane : he saw the bitter cup that was presented to him ; and foreboding that he would be forsaken by

<hr>

[1] Kein Messer scherpfer schirrt denn wenn ein Baur des andern Herr wird. Mathes. p. 48.
[2] Hic nulla carnificina, nullum supplicium. Corp. Ref. i. 752.

[1] Eorum animos fractos et perturbatos verbo Dei erexit. M. Adami Vit. Brentii, p. 441.
[2] Agmen rusticorum qui convenerant ad demoliendas arces, unica oratione sic compescuit. M. Adami Vita Fred Myconii, p. 178.
[3] Quod adulator principum vocer. L. Epp. II. 671.
[4] Gaudent papistæ de nostro dissidio. Ibid. 612.

all, he exclaimed: "Soon, perhaps, I also shall be able to say: *All ye shall be offended because of me this night.*"[1]

Yet in the midst of this deep bitterness, he preserved his faith: "He who has given me power to trample the enemy under foot," said he, "when he rose up against me like a cruel dragon or a furious lion, will not permit this enemy to crush me, now that he appears before me with the treacherous glance of the basilisk.[2] I groan as I contemplate these calamities. Often have I asked myself, whether it would not have been better to have allowed the papacy to go on quietly, rather than to witness the occurrence of so many troubles and seditions in the world. But no! it is better to have snatched a few souls from the jaws of the devil, than to have left them all between his murderous fangs."[3]

Now terminated the revolution in Luther's mind that had begun at the period of his return from the Wartburg. The inner life no longer satisfied him: the Church and her institutions now became most important in his eyes. The boldness with which he had thrown down every thing was checked at the sight of still more sweeping destructions; he felt it his duty to preserve, govern, and build up; and from the midst of the blood-stained ruins with which the peasant war had covered all Germany, the edifice of the new Church began slowly to arise.

These disturbances left a lasting and deep impression on men's minds. The nations had been struck with dismay. The masses, who had sought in the Reformation nothing but political reform, withdrew from it of their own accord, when they saw it offered them spiritual liberty only. Luther's opposition to the peasants was his renunciation of the ephemeral favour of the people. A seeming tranquillity was soon established, and the noise of enthusiasm and sedition was followed in all Germany by a silence inspired by terror.[4]

Thus the popular passions, the cause of revolution, and the interests of a radical equality, were quelled in the empire; but the Reformation did not yield. These two movements, which many have confounded with each other, were clearly marked out by the difference of their results. The insurrection was from below; the Reformation from above. A few horsemen and cannons were sufficient to put down the one; but the other never ceased to rise in strength and vigour, in despite of the reiterated assaults of the empire and the Church.

---

[1] Matt. xxvi. 31. L. Epp. ii. 671.
[2] Qui cum toties hactenus sub pedibus meis calcavit et contrivit leonem et draconem, non sinet etiam basiliscum super me calcare. Ibid.
[3] Es ist besser einige aus dem Rachen des Teufels herausreissen. L. Opp. H. Ed. ix. 961.
[4] Ea res incussit....vulgo terrorem, ut nihil usquam moveatur. Corp. Ref. i. 752.

CHAPTER XII.

Death of the Elector Frederick—The Prince and the Reformer—Roman-catholic Alliance—Plans of Charles the Fifth—Dangers.

MEANWHILE the cause of the Reformation itself appeared as if it would perish in the gulf that had swallowed up the liberties of the people. A melancholy event seemed destined to accelerate its fall. At the moment when the princes were marching against Munzer, and ten days before his defeat, the aged Elector of Saxony, that man whom God had raised up to defend the Reformation against all dangers from without, descended to the tomb.

His strength diminished day by day; the horrors that accompanied the peasant war wrung his feeling heart. "Alas!" exclaimed he with a deep sigh, "if it were God's will, I should die with joy. I see neither love, nor truth, nor faith, nor any good remaining upon earth."[1]

Averting his eyes from the struggles then prevailing throughout Germany, this pious prince, who was at that time residing in the castle of Lochau, tranquilly prepared to depart. On the 4th of May he called for his chaplain, the faithful Spalatin: "You do right to come and see me," said he mildly, as the chaplain entered: "for it is good to visit the sick." Then ordering his couch to be wheeled towards the table near which Spalatin was sitting, he bade his attendants leave the room, and then affectionately taking his friend's hand, spoke with him familiarly about Luther, the peasants, and his approaching departure. Spalatin came again at eight in the evening; the aged prince then unburdened his soul, and confessed his sins in the presence of God. On the morrow (it was the 5th of May), he received the communion under both kinds. No member of his family was near him; his brother and his nephew were gone with the army; but his domestics stood around him, according to the ancient custom of those times. As they gazed on that venerable prince, whom it had been so sweet a task to serve, they all burst into tears.[2] "My little children," said he tenderly, "if I have offended any one of you, forgive me for the love of God; for we princes often give offence to the poor, and that is wrong." Thus did Frederick obey the injunction of the apostle: *Let him that is rich rejoice in that he is made low; because as the flower of the grass he shall pass away.*[3]

Spalatin did not leave him again; he set before him the rich promises of the Gospel, and the pious elector drank in its powerful consolations with indescribable peace. The doctrine of the Gospel was no longer to him

---

[1] Noch etwas gutes mehr in der Welt. Seckend. p. 702.
[2] Dass alle Umstehende zum weinen bewegt. Ibid.
[3] James, i. 10.

that sword which attacks error, following it up wherever it may be found, and after a vigorous contest triumphing over it at last; it fell upon his heart like the dew, or the gentle rain, filling it with hope and joy. Frederick had forgotten the present world: he saw nothing but God and eternity.

Feeling the rapid approach of death, he destroyed a will that he had made some years before, and in which he had commended his soul to "the mother of God;" and dictated another, in which he called upon the holy and the sole merits of Jesus Christ "for the forgiveness of his sins," and declared his firm assurance "that he was redeemed by the precious blood of his beloved Saviour."[1] He then added: "I am quite exhausted!" and that evening, at five o'clock, he quietly fell asleep. "He was a child of peace," exclaimed his physician, "and in peace he has departed."—"O bitter death to all whom he has left behind him!" said Luther.[2]

Luther, who was then travelling through Thuringia to allay the excitement, had never seen the elector, except at a distance, as at Worms by the side of Charles the Fifth. But these two men had met in spirit from the very moment the reformer appeared. Frederick laboured for nationality and independence, as Luther did for truth and reformation. Unquestionably the Reformation was above all things a spiritual work; but it was perhaps necessary for its early success that it should be linked with some national interest. Accordingly Luther had no sooner risen up against indulgences than the alliance between the prince and the monk was tacitly concluded:—an alliance that was purely moral, without contract or writing, or even words, and in which the strong man lent no aid to the weak, but only allowed him to act. But now that the vigorous oak was cut down under whose shelter the Reformation had gradually grown up,—now that the enemies of the Gospel were every where manifesting fresh force and hatred, and that its supporters were compelled to hide themselves or remain silent, nothing seemed able to defend them any longer against the sword of those who were pursuing it with such violence.

The confederates of Ratisbon, who had conquered the peasants in the south and west of the empire, were in all parts attacking the Reformation and the revolt alike. At Wurtzburg and at Bamberg they put to death many of the most peaceable citizens, and even some of those who had resisted the peasants. "What matters it?" said they openly; "these people were attached to the Gospel." This was enough to make their heads fall on the scaffold.[3]

Duke George hoped to impart his hatred and his antipathies to the landgrave and Duke John. "See,", said he to them after the defeat of the peasants, as he pointed to the field of battle, "see what miseries Luther has occasioned!" John and Philip appeared to give him hopes that they would adopt his ideas. "Duke George," said the reformer, "imagines he shall triumph, now that Frederick is dead; but Christ reigns in the midst of His enemies: in vain do they gnash their teeth,......their desire shall perish."[1]

George lost no time in forming a confederation in the north of Germany, similar to that of Ratisbon. The Electors of Mentz and Brandenburg, Dukes Henry and Erick of Brunswick, and Duke George, met at Dessau and concluded a Romish alliance in the month of July.[2] George urged the new elector and his son-in-law the landgrave to join it. And then, as if to intimate what might be expected of it, he beheaded two citizens of Leipsic in whose houses some of the reformer's writings had been found.

At the same time letters from Charles V., dated from Toledo, arrived in Germany, by which another diet was convoked at Augsburg. Charles wished to give the empire a constitution that would enable him to dispose of the forces of Germany at his good pleasure. Religious differences offered him the means; he had only to let loose the Catholics against the followers of the Gospel, and when they had exhausted their strength, he would easily triumph over both. Down with the Lutherans! was therefore the cry of the emperor.[3]

Thus all things combined against the Reformation. Never had Luther's spirit been overwhelmed by so many fears. The remnants of Munzer's party had sworn to take his life; his sole protector was no more; Duke George, he was informed, intended to have him arrested in Wittemberg itself;[4] the princes who might have defended him bowed their heads, and seemed to have forsaken the Gospel; it was rumoured that the university, the number of whose students was already diminished by these troubles, was about to be suppressed by the new elector; and Charles, victorious at Pavia, was assembling a new diet with the intention of giving a deathblow to the Reformation. What dangers must not Luther have foreboded!......This anguish, these inward struggles, that had so often tortured him to groans, now wrung his soul. How can he resist so many enemies? In the midst of these agitations, in the face of so many dangers, beside the corpse of Frederick that was scarcely cold, and the dead bodies of the peasants that yet strewed the plains of Germany, Luther—none could certainly have imagined such a thing—Luther married.

[1] Durch das theure Blut meines allerliebsten Heylandes erlöset. Seck. p. 703.
[2] O mors amara! L. Epp. ii. 659.
[3] Ranke, Deutsche Gesch. ii. 226.

[1] Dux Georgius, mortuo Frederico, putat se omnia posse. L. Epp. iii. 22.
[2] Habito conciliabulo conjuraverunt restituros sese esse omnia.....Ibid.
[3] Sleidan. Hist. de la Réf. i. 214.
[4] Keil, Luther's Leben, p. 160.

CHAPTER XIII.

The Nuns of Nimptsch—Luther's Sentiments—The Convent dissolved—Luther's Marriage—Domestic Happiness.

In the monastery of Nimptsch, near Grimma in Saxony, dwelt in the year 1523 nine nuns, who were diligent in reading the Word of God, and who had discovered the contrast that exists between a christian and a cloistered life. Their names were Magdalen Staupitz, Eliza Canitz, Ava Grossen, Ava and Margaret Schonfeldt, Laneta Golis, Margaret and Catherine Zeschau, and Catherine Bora. The first impulse of these young women, after they were delivered from the superstitions of the monastery, was to write to their parents. "The salvation of our souls," said they, "will not permit us to remain any longer in a cloister."[1] Their parents, fearing the trouble likely to arise from such a resolution, harshly rejected their prayers. The poor nuns were dismayed. How can they leave the monastery? Their timidity was alarmed at so desperate a step. At last, the horror caused by the papal services prevailed, and they promised not to leave one another, but to repair in a body to some respectable place, with order and decency.[2] Two worthy and pious citizens of Torgau, Leonard Koppe and Wolff Tomitzsch, offered their assistance,[3] which was accepted as coming from God himself, and they left the convent of Nimptsch without any opposition, and as if the hand of the Lord had opened the doors to them.[4] Koppe and Tomitzsch received them in their waggon; and on the 7th of April 1523, the nine nuns, amazed at their own boldness, stopped in great emotion before the gate of the old Augustine convent in which Luther resided.

" This is not my doing," said Luther, as he received them; " but would to God that I could thus rescue all captive consciences, and empty all the cloisters![5]—the breach is made!" Many persons offered to receive these nuns into their houses, and Catherine Bora found a welcome in the family of the burgomaster of Wittemberg.

If Luther at that time thought of preparing for any solemn event, it was to ascend the scaffold, and not to approach the altar. Many months after this, he still replied to those who spoke to him of marriage: "God may change my heart, if it be his pleasure; but now at least I have no thought of taking a wife; not that I do not feel any attractions in that estate; I am neither a stock nor a stone; but every day I expect the death and the punishment of a heretic."[6]

Yet every thing in the Church was advancing. The habits of a monastic life, the invention of man, were giving way in every quarter to those of domestic life, appointed by God. On Sunday the 9th of October 1524, Luther, having risen as usual, laid aside the frock of the Augustine monk, and put on the dress of a secular priest; he then made his appearance in the church, where this change caused a lively satisfaction. Renovated Christendom hailed with transport every thing that announced that the old things were passed away.

Shortly after this, the last monk quitted the convent; but Luther remained; his footsteps alone re-echoed through the long galleries; he sat silent and solitary in the refectory that had so lately resounded with the babbling of the monks. An eloquent silence, attesting the triumphs of the Word of God! The convent had ceased to exist. About the end of December 1524, Luther sent the keys of the monastery to the elector, informing him that he should see where it might please God to feed him.[1] The elector gave the convent to the university, and invited Luther to continue his residence in it. The abode of the monks was destined erelong to be the sanctuary of a christian family.

Luther, whose heart was formed to taste the sweets of domestic life, honoured and loved the marriage state; it is even probable that he had some liking for Catherine Bora. For a long while his scruples and the thought of the calumnies which such a step would occasion had prevented his thinking of her; and he had offered the poor Catherine, first to Baumgartner of Nuremberg,[2] and then to Dr. Glatz of Orlamund. But when he saw Baumgartner refuse to take her, and when she had declined to accept Glatz, he asked himself seriously whether he ought not to think of marrying her himself.

His aged father, who had been so grieved when he embraced a monastic life, was urging him to enter the conjugal state.[3] But one idea above all was daily present before Luther's conscience, and with greater energy: marriage is an institution of God, —celibacy an institution of man. He had a horror of every thing that emanated from Rome. He would say to his friends, " I desire to retain nothing of my papistical life."[4] Day and night he prayed and entreated the Lord to deliver him from his uncertainty. At last a single thought broke the last links that still held him captive. To all the motives of propriety and personal obedience which led him to apply to himself this declaration of God, *It is not good that man should*

---

[1] Der Seelen Seligkeit halber. L. Epp. ii. 323.
[2] Mit aller Zucht und Ehre an redliche Stätte und Orte kommen. Ibid. 322.
[3] Per honestos cives Torgavienses adductæ. Ibid. 319.
[4] Mirabiliter evaserunt. Ibid.
[5] Und alle Klöster ledig machen. Ibid. 322.
[6] Cum expectem quotidie mortem et meritum hæretici

supplicium. L. Epp. ii. 570. Letter to Spalatin, 30th November 1524.
[1] Muss und will Ich sehen wo mich Gott ernähret. L. Epp. ii. 582.
[2] Si vis Ketam tuam a Bora tenere. Ibid. 553.
[3] Aus Begehren meines lieben Vaters. Ibid. iii. 2.
[4] Ibid. 1.

be alone,[1] was added a motive of a higher and more powerful nature. He saw that if he was called to the marriage-state as a man, he was also called to it as a reformer ; this decided him.

"If this monk should marry," said his friend Schurff the lawyer, "he will make all the world and the devil himself burst with laughter, and will destroy the work that he has begun."[2] This remark made a very different impression on Luther from what might have been supposed. To brave the world, the devil, and his enemies, and, by an action which they thought calculated to ruin the cause of the Reformation, prevent its success being in any measure ascribed to him—this was all he desired. Accordingly, boldly raising his head, he replied, "Well, then, I will do it ; I will play the devil and the world this trick ; I will content my father, and marry Catherine!" Luther, by his marriage, broke off still more completely from the institutions of the Papacy ; he confirmed the doctrine he had preached, by his own example, and encouraged timid men to an entire renunciation of their errors.[3] Rome appeared to be recovering here and there the ground she had lost ; she flattered herself with the hope of victory ; and now a loud explosion scattered terror and surprise through her ranks, and still more fully disclosed to her the courage of the enemy she fancied she had crushed. "I will bear witness to the Gospel," said Luther, "not by my words only, but also by my works. I am determined, in the face of my enemies who already exult and raise the shout of victory, to marry a nun, that they may see and know that they have not conquered me.[4] I do not take a wife that I may live long with her ; but seeing the nations and the princes letting loose their fury against me, foreseeing that my end is near, and that after my death they will again trample my doctrine under foot, I am resolved, for the edification of the weak, to bear a striking testimony to what I teach here below."[5]

On the 11th of June 1525, Luther went to the house of his friend and colleague Amsdorff. He desired Pomeranus, whom he styled emphatically *The Pastor*, to bless his union. The celebrated painter Lucas Cranach and Doctor John Apella witnessed the marriage. Melancthon was not present.

No sooner was Luther married than all Europe was disturbed. He was overwhelmed with accusations and calumnies from every quarter. "It is incest," exclaimed Henry VIII. "A monk has married a vestal,"

said some.[1]—"Antichrist will be the offspring of such a union," said others ; "for a prophecy announces that he will be born of a monk and a nun." To this Erasmus replied with a sarcastic smile : "If the prophecy is true, what thousands of antichrists already exist in the world!"[2] But while Luther was thus assailed, many wise and moderate men, whom the Roman Church still counted among her members, undertook his defence. "Luther," said Erasmus, "has taken a wife from the noble family of Bora, but she has no dowry."[3] A more valuable testimony was now given in his favour. The master of Germany, Philip Melancthon, whom this bold step had at first alarmed, said with that grave voice to which even his enemies listened with respect : "It is false and slanderous to mantain that there is anything unbecoming in Luther's marriage.[4] I think that in marrying he must have done violence to himself. A married life is one of humility, but it is also a holy state, if there be any such in the world, and the Scriptures every where represent it as honourable in the eyes of God."

Luther was troubled at first when he saw such floods of anger and contempt poured out upon him ; Melancthon became more earnest in friendship and kindness towards him ;[5] and it was not long before the reformer could see a mark of God's approbation in this opposition of man. "If I did not offend the world," said he, "I should have cause to fear that what I have done is displeasing to God."[6]

Eight years had elapsed between the time when Luther had attacked the indulgences and his marriage with Catherine Bora. It would be difficult to ascribe, as is still done, his zeal against the abuses of the Church to an "impatient desire" for wedlock. He was then forty-two years old, and Catherine Bora had already been two years in Wittemberg.

Luther was happy in this union. "The best gift of God," said he, "is a pious and amiable wife, who fears God, loves her family, with whom a man may live in peace, and in whom he may safely confide." Some months after his marriage he informed one of his friends of Catherine's pregnancy,[7] and a year after they came together she gave birth to a son.[8] The sweets of domestic life

---

[1] Genesis ii. 18.
[2] Risuros mundum universum et diabolum ipsum. M. Adami Vita Luth. p. 130.
[3] Ut confirmem facto quæ docui, tam multos invenio pusillanimes in tanta luce Evangelii. L. Epp. iii. 13.
[4] Nonna ducta uxore in despectum triumphantium et clamantium Jo! Jo! hostium. Ibid. 21.
[5] Non duxi uxorem ut diu viverem, sed quod nunc propiorem finem meum suspicarer. Ibid. 32.

[1] Monachus cum vestali copularetur. M. Ad. Vit. Luth. p. 131.
[2] Quot Antichristorum millia jam olim habet mundus. Er. Epp. p. 789.
[3] Erasmus adds, alluding to reports spread by Luther's enemies that he had not been married more than a fortnight when his wife was already brought to bed of a son ; "Partu maturo sponsæ vanus erat rumor." Ibid. pp. 788, 789.
[4] "Οτι ψευδος τουτο και διαβολη εστι. Corp. Ref. i. 753, ad Camerarius.
[5] Πασα σπουδη και ευνοια. Ibid.
[6] And he adds : Offenditur etiam in carne ipsius divinitatis et creatoris. L. Epp. iii. 32.
[7] This letter is dated October 21, 1525. Catena mea simulat vel vere implet illud Genes. 3. Tu dolore gravida eris. Ibid. 35.
[8] Mir meine liebe Kethe einen Hansen Luther bracht hat, gestern um zwei. Ibid. 116. June 8, 1526.

soon dispersed the storms that the exasperation of his enemies had at first gathered over him. His Ketha, as he styled her, manifested the tenderest affection towards him, consoled him in his dejection by repeating passages from the Bible, exonerated him from all household cares, sat near him during his leisure moments, worked his portrait in embroidery, reminded him of the friends to whom he had forgotten to write, and often amused him by the simplicity of her questions. A certain dignity appears to have marked her character, for Luther would sometimes call her, *My Lord Ketha.* One day he said playfully, that if he were to marry again, he would carve an obedient wife for himself out of a block of stone, for, added he, " it is impossible to find such a one in reality." His letters overflowed with tenderness for Catherine; he called her " his dear and gracious wife, his dear and amiable Ketha." Luther's character became more cheerful in Catherine's society, and this happy frame of mind never deserted him afterwards, even in the midst of his greatest trials.

The almost universal corruption of the clergy had brought the priesthood into general contempt, from which the isolated virtues of a few faithful servants of God had been unable to extricate it. Domestic peace and conjugal fidelity, those surest foundations of happiness here below, were continually disturbed in town and country by the gross passions of the priests and monks. No one was secure from those attempts at seduction. They took advantage of the access allowed them into every family, and some times even of the confidence of the confessional, to instil a deadly poison into the souls of their penitents, and to satisfy their guilty desires. The Reformation, by abolishing the celibacy of the ecclesiastics, restored the sanctity of the conjugal state. The marriage of the clergy put an end to an immense number of secret crimes. The reformers became the models of their flocks in the most intimate and important relations of life; and the people were not slow in rejoicing to see the ministers of religion once more husbands and fathers.

CHAPTER XIV.

The Landgrave—The Elector—Prussia—Reformation—Secularization—The Archbishop of Mentz—Conference at Friedwalt—Diet—Alliance of Torgau—Resistance of the Reformers—Alliance of Magdeburg—The Catholics redouble their Exertions—The Emperor's Marriage—Threatening Letters—The Two Parties.

At the first glance, Luther's marriage had, in truth, seemed to add to the difficulties of the Reformation. It was still suffering from the blow inflicted on it by the revolt of the peasants; the sword of the emperor and of the princes was yet unsheathed against it; and its friends, the Landgrave Philip and the new Elector John, appeared discouraged and silenced.

This state of things did not, however, last long. The youthful landgrave in a short time boldly raised his head. Ardent and courageous as Luther, the noble character of the reformer had won his esteem. He threw himself into the Reformation with all the enthusiasm of a young man, and at the same time studied it with all the gravity of a superior mind.

In Saxony, Frederick's place could not be supplied either in discretion or in influence; but his brother, the Elector John, instead of confining himself to the passive part of a protector, interposed more directly and with greater courage in religious affairs. As he was leaving Weimar on the 16th of August 1525, he said to the assembled clergy, " I desire that you will in future preach the pure Word of God, without any additions of man." Some aged ecclesiastics, who were puzzled how to obey his directions, replied artlessly, " But we are not forbidden to say mass for the dead, or to bless the water and salt ?"— " Every thing," said the elector, " ceremonies as well as sermons, must be conformed to God's Word."

Erelong the landgrave formed the extraordinary project of converting his father-in-law, Duke George. At one time he would establish the sufficiency of Scripture; at another, he would attack the mass, the papacy, and compulsory vows. Letter followed letter, and all the declarations of the Word of God were in turns opposed to the faith of the aged duke.[1]

These efforts did not prove unavailing. The son of Duke George was won to the new doctrine. But Philip did not succeed with the father. "A hundred years hence we shall see who is right," said the latter. "A terrible saying," observed the Elector of Saxony; "what can that faith be which requires such long experience?[2] Poor duke! ......he will wait long enough. I fear God has hardened his heart, as he did Pharaoh's of old."

In Philip the evangelical party found a bold and intelligent leader, capable of making head against the terrible attacks the enemy were planning against them. But have we not cause to regret that the chief of the Reformation should have been from this moment a man of the sword, and not simply a disciple of the Word of God? The human element expanded in the Reformation, and the spiritual element declined. This was injurious to the work; for every work should develop itself in accordance with the laws of its own

---

[1] Rommel's Urkundenbuch, i. 2.
[2] Was das für ein Glaube sey, der eine solche Erfahrung erfordert. Seck. p. 739.

nature, and the Reformation was of a nature essentially spiritual.

God was adding to the number of its supporters. Prussia, that powerful state on the frontiers of Germany, had already taken its station with joy under the banner of the Gospel. The chivalrous and religious spirit which had founded the Teutonic order gradually faded away with the ages in which it had arisen. The knights, consulting their own interests alone, had dissatisfied the people under their rule. Poland had taken advantage of this in 1466 to compel the order to recognise her supremacy. The people, the knights, the grand-master, and the Polish domination, were so many contrary powers ever in collision and rendering the prosperity of the country impossible.

Then came the Reformation, and it was perceived that this was the only means of salvation remaining for the unhappy people. Brismann, Speratus, Poliander who had been Dr. Eck's secretary at the Leipsic dispute, and many others, preached the Gospel in Prussia.

One day a mendicant from the country under the rule of the Teutonic knights, arrived at Wittemberg, and stopping before Luther's house, sang with a solemn voice the beautiful hymn by Poliander :—

"To us at last salvation's come!"[1]

The reformer, who had never heard this christian strain, listened in astonishment and rapture; the foreign accent of the singer added to his delight: "Again, again," said he when the mendicant had finished. He then asked where he had learned the hymn; and his tears began to flow when the poor man informed him that a cry of deliverance was sounding from the shores of the Baltic even to Wittemberg. Luther clasped his hands and thanked God.[2]

In truth the tidings of salvation had gone thither.

"Have pity on our wretched state," said the people of Prussia to the grand-master, "and give us preachers who teach the pure doctrine of the Gospel." Albert at first made no reply; but entered into correspondence with Sigismund, king of Poland, his uncle and lord-suzerain.

The latter recognised him as hereditary duke of Prussia,[3] and the new prince made a public entry into his capital of Konigsberg with the ringing of bells and the acclamations of the people; all the houses were splendidly decorated, and the streets strewn with flowers. "There is but one order," said Albert, "and that is Christianity." The monastic orders were disappearing, and this Divine order was re-established.

The bishops resigned their secular rights to the new duke; the convents were changed into hospitals, the Gospel was preached in the meanest villages, and in the following year Albert married Dorothea, daughter of the King of Denmark, whose "faith in the one only Saviour" was not to be shaken.

The pope called upon the emperor to take severe measures against this "apostate" monk, and Charles laid Albert under an interdict.

Another prince of the family of Brandenburg, the Cardinal-archbishop of Mentz, was then on the point of following his cousin's example. The peasant-wars more especially threatened the ecclesiastical states ; the elector, Luther, and all Germany imagined they were on the eve of a great revolution. The archbishop, thinking the only way of preserving his principality would be to secularize it, secretly invited Luther to prepare the people for this daring step,[1] which the latter did by a letter addressed to the archbishop and intended to be made public: "God," said he, "has laid his heavy hand upon the clergy; they must fall, nothing can save them."[2] But the peasant-war having come to an end more speedily than had been anticipated, the cardinal kept his temporal possessions; his anxiety disappeared, and he renounced his plans of secularization.

While John of Saxony, Philip of Hesse, and Albert of Prussia were taking so prominent a part in the Reformation, and instead of the prudent Frederick three princes were found full of resolution and courage, the holy work was advancing in the Church and among the nations. Luther entreated the elector to establish the evangelical ministry instead of the Roman priesthood, and to direct a general visitation of the churches.[3] About the same time they were beginning at Wittemberg to exercise the episcopal functions and to ordain ministers. "Let not the pope, the bishops, the monks, and the priests exclaim : 'We are the Church; whosoever separates from us, separates from the Church!' There is no other Church than the assembly of those who have the Word of God, and who are purified by it."[4] Such was the language of Melancthon.

All this could not be said and done without occasioning a strong reaction. Rome had thought the Reformation extinguished in the blood of the rebellious peasants : but its flames burst forth again in every quarter with greater power and brightness. She resolved on making another effort. The pope and the emperor wrote threatening letters,—the one from Rome, the other from Spain. The imperial government prepared to set matters on their old footing ; and the idea was seriously entertained of effectually

---

1 Es ist das Heyl uns kommen her.
2 Dankte Gott met Freuden. Seck. p. 668.
3 Sleidan, Hist. Ref. p. 220.

1 Seckend. p. 712.
2 Er muss herunter. L. Epp. II. 674.
3 L. Epp. iii. 28, 38, 51, &c.
4 Dass Kirche sey allein diejenige, so Gottes Wort haben und damit gereiniget werden. Corp. Ref. i. 766.

crushing the Reformation in the approaching diet.

On the 7th of November, the electoral prince of Saxony and the landgrave met in alarm at the castle of Friedewalt, and agreed that their deputies at the diet should act in concert. Thus in the forest of Sullingen, were created the first elements of an evangelical alliance, in opposition to the leagues of Ratisbon and Dessau.

The diet opened at Augsburg on the 11th of December. The evangelical princes were not present in person. From the very first the deputies of Saxony and Hesse spoke out boldly : " The insurrection of the peasants," said they, " was owing to an impolitic severity. It is neither by fire nor sword that God's truth can be torn from the heart. If you determine to employ violent measures against the Reformation, more terrible calamities will befall you than those from which you have so recently and so narrowly escaped."

It was felt that whatever resolution was adopted, its results would be of the greatest importance. Every one desired to put off the decisive moment, in order to increase his own strength. They therefore determined to assemble again at Spires, in the month of May following ; and that in the meanwhile the *recess* of Nuremberg should continue in force. Then, said they, we will enter thoroughly into the subject " of the holy faith, of justice, and of peace."

The landgrave persevered in his plan. He had a conference with the elector at Gotha at the end of February 1526. These two princes agreed that if they were attacked on account of the Word of God, they should unite their forces to resist their adversaries. This alliance was ratified at Torgau, and was destined to produce important results.

The alliance of Torgau did not satisfy the landgrave. Convinced that Charles V. was endeavouring to form a league " against Christ and his holy Word," he wrote letter after letter to the elector, representing to him the necessity of combining with other states. " As for me," wrote he, " I would rather die than renounce the Word of God and allow myself to be driven from my throne."[1]

There was great uncertainty at the electoral court. In fact, a serious obstacle stood in the way of any union between the evangelical princes, and this obstacle was Luther and Melancthon. Luther desired that the evangelical doctrine should be defended by God alone. He thought that the less men interfered with it, the more striking would be God's interposition. It seemed to him that whatever measures they desired to take, they must be ascribed to an unworthy timidity or a blamable mistrust. Melancthon feared that the alliance of the evangelical

princes would precipitate that very struggle which they were desirous of avoiding.

The landgrave was not to be checked by these considerations, and he endeavoured to bring the neighbouring states into the alliance ; but his exertions were not crowned with success. Frankfort refused to enter it. The Elector of Treves abandoned his opposition and accepted a pension from the emperor. Even the elector-palatine, whose evangelical disposition was well known, rejected Philip's proposals.

Thus the landgrave failed on the side of the Rhine ; but the elector, notwithstanding the opinions of the theologians of the Reformation, entered into negotiations with the princes who had at all times rallied round the powerful house of Saxony. On the 12th of June, the elector and his son, the Dukes Philip, Ernest, Otho, and Francis of Brunswick and Luneburg, Duke Henry of Mecklenburg, Prince Wolff of Anhalt, Counts Albert and Gebhard of Mansfeldt, assembled at Magdeburg ; and there, under the presidence of the elector, formed an alliance similar to that of Torgau.

" Almighty God," said these princes, " having in his unspeakable mercy revived among men his holy and eternal Word, the food of our souls, and our greatest treasure here below ; and great exertions having been made on the part of the clergy and their adherents to suppress and extirpate it, we, being firmly assured that He who hath sent it to glorify His name upon earth, will also know how to maintain it, bind ourselves to preserve that blessed Word for our people, and to that end to employ our goods, our lives, our states, our subjects, and all that we possess ; putting our trust, not in our armies, but solely in the omnipotence of the Lord, whose instruments we desire to be."[1] Such was the language of the princes.

Two days after, the city of Magdeburg was received into the alliance, and the new duke of Prussia, Albert of Brandenburg, acceded to it by a separate treaty.

The evangelical alliance was thus formed ; but the perils that it was intended to avert became every day more threatening. The clergy and the princes friendly to Rome had seen the Reformation, which they had thought stifled, suddenly growing up before them in a formidable shape. Already the partisans of the Reformation were almost as powerful as those of the pope. If they had a majority in the diet, the consequences to the ecclesiastical states might easily be imagined. Now or never ! It is no longer a question of refuting a heresy ; they have to contend against a powerful party. Other victories than those of Dr. Eck are required to save Christendom.

Effectual precautions had already been

1 Seckendorf, p. 768.

1 Allein auf Gott den Allmächtigen, als dessen Werkzeuge sie handeln. Hortleber, Ursache des Deutschen Krieges. i. 1490.

taken. The metropolitan chapter of the collegiate church at Mentz had called a meeting of all its suffragans, and decided on sending a deputation to the emperor and the pope, calling on them to preserve the Church.

At the same time, Duke George of Saxony, Duke Henry of Brunswick, and the Cardinal-elector Albert, had met at Halle, and resolved to address a memorial to Charles V. " The detestable doctrine of Luther," said they, " is making rapid progress. Every day attempts are made to gain over even us ; and as they cannot succeed by gentle measures, they are striving to compel us, by exciting our subjects to revolt. We implore the assistance of the emperor."[1] Immediately after this conference, Brunswick himself set out for Spain in order to influence Charles's determination.

He could not have arrived at a more favourable moment ; the emperor had just concluded the famous treaty of Madrid with France ; he seemed to have nothing more to fear in that quarter, and his eyes were now turned solely towards Germany. Francis I. had offered to defray a moiety of the expenses of a war, either against the heretics or against the Turks.

The emperor was at Seville, where he was about to marry a princess of Portugal, and the banks of the Guadalquivir re-echoed with the noise of his festivities. A glittering train of nobles and a vast concourse of people crowded that ancient capital of the Moors. Under the arched roof of its magnificent cathedral were displayed all the pompous ceremonies of the Church; a legate from the pope officiated, and never, even under the dominion of the Arabs, had Andalusia witnessed a spectacle of greater splendour and solemnity.

At this very moment Henry of Brunswick arrived from Germany, and besought Charles to rescue the empire and the Church from the attacks of the monk of Wittemberg. His request was immediately favoured with consideration, and the emperor decided on adopting vigorous measures.

On the 23d of March 1526, he wrote to several of the princes and cities that had remained faithful to Rome. At the same time he gave Henry of Brunswick a special commission to inform them verbally that he had been seriously grieved to learn that the continual progress of the Lutheran heresy threatened to fill Germany with sacrilege, devastation, and bloodshed; that on the contrary he beheld with extreme pleasure the fidelity of the majority of the states ; that, laying aside all other occupations, he was about to leave Spain and repair to Rome, to come to an understanding with the pope, and from thence proceed to Germany to fight against the abominable pest of Wittemberg ;

that, on their parts, it was their duty to adhere to their faith ; and if the Lutherans sought to lead them into error by stratagem or force, they should form a close alliance and boldly resist them ; and that he would soon arrive and support them with all his power.[1]

When Brunswick returned to Germany, the Romish party were transported with joy and proudly lifted up their heads. The Dukes of Brunswick and Pomerania, Albert of Mecklenburg, John of Juliers, George of Saxony, the Dukes of Bavaria, and all the princes of the Church, thought themselves secure of victory, as they read the menacing letters of the conqueror of Francis I. They resolved to attend the approaching diet, to humble the heretical princes, and if they did not submit, to compel them by the sword. Duke George is reported to have said, " I may be Elector of Saxony whenever I please ;"[2] he subsequently, however, endeavoured to give another meaning to these words. " Luther's cause will not last long : let him look to it!" said the duke's chancellor one day at Torgau with an air of triumph.

Luther, indeed, was looking to it, but not as the chancellor understood the expression ; he was attentively watching the motions of the enemies of God's Word, and, like Melancthon, imagined he saw thousands of swords unsheathed against the Gospel. But he sought for other and higher strength than that of man. " Satan," wrote he to Frederick Myconius, " is putting forth his fury ; ungodly pontiffs are conspiring ; and we are threatened with war. Exhort the people to contend valiantly before the throne of the Lord by faith and prayer, so that our enemies, vanquished by the Spirit of God, may be constrained to peace. Our chief want, our chief labour is prayer; let the people know that they are now exposed to the edge of the sword and to the rage of Satan, and let them pray."[3]

Thus were all things tending towards a decisive struggle. The Reformation had on its side the prayers of Christians, the sympathy of the people, and an increasing influence over men's minds that no power could check. The papacy had in its favour the ancient order of things, the strength of old custom, the zeal and hatred of formidable princes, and the power of that mighty emperor who reigned over two worlds, and who had just before given so rude a check to the ambition of Francis the First.

Such was the state of affairs when the Diet of Spires was opened. Now let us return to Switzerland.

---

[1] Schmidt. Deutsche Gesch. viii. 202.

[1] Weimar State-papers, Seckendorff, p. 768.
[2] Ranke, Deutsch Gesch. ii. p. 349; Rommel Urkunden, p. 22.
[3] Ut in mediis gladiis et furoribus Satanæ posito et periclitanti. L. Epp. iii. 100.

BOOK XI.

DIVISIONS.

SWITZERLAND—GERMANY. 1523—1527.

CHAPTER I.

Unity in Diversity—Primitive Fidelity and Liberty—Formation of Romish Unity—Leo Juda and the Monk—Zwingle's Theses—The Disputation of January.

WE are about to contemplate the diversities, or, as they have been called, the *variations* of the Reformation. These diversities are one of its most essential characteristics.

Unity in diversity and diversity in unity, is a law of nature as well as of the Church.

Truth is like the light of the sun: it descends from heaven one and ever the same; and yet it assumes different colours upon earth, according to the objects on which it falls. In like manner, formularies somewhat different may sometimes express the same christian idea considered under different aspects.

How dull would creation be if this boundless variety of forms and colours, which gives it beauty, were replaced by an absolute uniformity! But how melancholy also would be its appearance, if all created beings did not form a magnificent unity!

Divine unity has its rights, so also has human diversity. In religion we must suppress neither God nor man. If you have not unity, your religion is not of God; if you have not diversity, the religion is not of man; but it ought to be of both. Would you erase from creation one of the laws that God himself has imposed on it,—that of infinite diversity? *And even things without life giving sound, whether pipe or harp, except they give a distinction in the sounds, how shall it be known what is piped or harped?* [1] But if there is a diversity in religion arising from the difference of individuality, and which consequently must subsist even in heaven, there is one that proceeds from man's rebellion, and this is indeed a great calamity.

There are two tendencies which equally lead us into error. The one exaggerates diversity, the other exaggerates unity. The essential doctrines of salvation are the limit between these two courses. To require more than these doctrines, is to infringe this diversity; to require less, is to infringe unity.

The latter excess is that of rash and rebellious minds, who look beyond Jesus Christ to form systems and doctrines of men.

The former exists in various exclusive sects, and particularly in that of Rome.

The Church should reject error, and, unless this be done, Christianity cannot be maintained. But if this idea were carried to extremes, it would follow that the Church should take arms against the least deviation, and put herself in motion for mere verbal disputes. Faith would thus be fettered, and the feelings of Christians reduced to bondage. Such was not the condition of the Church in the times of real catholicity,—the catholicity of the primitive ages. It rejected the sects that attacked the fundamental truths of the Gospel; but these truths once received, it left full liberty to faith. Rome soon departed from this wise course; and in proportion as the dominion and teaching of men arose in the Church, there sprung up by their side a unity of man.

When a merely human system had been once invented, coercion increased from age to age. The christian liberty, respected by the catholicism of the earlier ages, was at first limited, then enslaved, and finally stifled. Conviction, which according to the laws of human nature and of the Word of God should be freely formed in the heart and understanding of man, was imposed from without, completely formed and symmetrically arranged by the masters of mankind. Reflection, will, feeling, all the faculties of the human being, which, subjected to the Word and Spirit of God, should work and bear fruit freely, were deprived of their liberty, and constrained to expand in shapes that had been determined upon beforehand. The mind of man became as a mirror on which extraneous objects are reflected, but which possesses nothing by itself. Doubtless there still existed many souls that had been taught direct of God. But the great majority of Christians from that time received the convictions of others only; a faith peculiar to the individual was rare; it was the Reformation alone that restored this treasure to the Church.

And yet for some time there was a space within which the human mind was permitted to move; there were certain opinions that might be received or rejected at will. But as a hostile army day by day presses closer to a besieged city, compels the garrison to move only within the narrow boundary of its ramparts, and at last forces it to surren-

[1] 1 Corinthians xiv. 7.

der; so the hierarchy, from age to age, and almost from year to year, contracted the space that it had temporarily granted to the human mind, until at last this space, from continual encroachments, had ceased to exist. All that man ought to love, believe, or do, was regulated and decreed in the offices of the Roman chancery. The faithful were relieved of the fatigue of examining, of reflecting, of contending; all that they had to do was to repeat the formularies they had been taught.

From that time, if there appeared in the bosom of Roman-catholicism any one who had inherited the catholicism of the apostolic ages, such a man feeling his inability to expand in the bonds in which he was confined, was compelled to snap them asunder, and display again to the astonished world the unfettered bearing of a Christian, who acknowledges no law save that of God.

The Reformation, by restoring liberty to the Church, was destined also to restore its original diversity, and to people it with families united by the great features of resemblance they derive from their common parent; but different in their secondary features, and reminding us of the varieties inherent in human nature. Perhaps it would have been desirable for this diversity to exist in the universal Church without leading to sectarian divisions. Nevertheless, we must not forget that these sects are but the expression of this diversity.

Switzerland and Germany, which had till this time developed themselves independently of each other, began to come in contact in the years whose history we are about to retrace, and realized the diversity of which we have been speaking, and which was to be one of the characteristics of Protestantism. We shall there behold men perfectly agreed on all the great doctrines of faith, and yet differing on certain secondary points. Passion, indeed, entered into these discussions; but while deploring such a melancholy intermixture, Protestantism, far from seeking to conceal her diversity, publishes and proclaims it. Its path to unity is long and difficult, but this unity is the real unity.

Zwingle was advancing in the christian life. While the Gospel had freed Luther from that profound melancholy to which he had formerly given way in the convent of Erfurth, and had developed in him a serenity which often amounted to gaiety, and of which the reformer afterwards gave so many proofs, even in the face of great dangers, Christianity had produced the very opposite effect on the joyous child of the Tockenburg mountains. Tearing Zwingle from his thoughtless and worldly life, it had imprinted a seriousness on his character that was not natural to him. This seriousness was very necessary to him. We have seen how towards the close of the year 1522 numerous enemies appeared rising up against the Re-

formation.[1] Zwingle was overwhelmed with reproaches from every quarter, and disputes would often take place even in the churches.

Leo Juda, who (says an historian) was a man of small stature,[2] but full of love for the poor, and zeal against false teachers, had arrived at Zurich about the end of the year 1522 to occupy the station of pastor of St. Peter's church. He had been replaced at Einsidlen by Oswald Myconius.[3] This was a valuable acquisition for Zwingle and for the Reformation.

One day, not long after his arrival, as he was in the church of which he had been appointed pastor, he heard an Augustine monk asserting forcibly that man is able of himself to satisfy the righteousness of God. "Reverend father prior," said Leo, "listen to me for an instant; and you, my dear citizens, keep still; I will speak as becomes a Christian." He then proved to the people the falseness of the doctrine to which he had just been listening.[4] Upon this a great disturbance arose in the church; and immediately several persons angrily fell upon "the little priest" from Einsidlen. Zwingle appeared before the great council, requiring permission to give an account of his doctrine in the presence of the deputies of the bishop; and the council, desirous of putting an end to these disturbances, convened a conference for the 29th of January 1523. The news spread rapidly through the whole of Switzerland. His adversaries exclaimed in their vexation: "A *diet* of vagabonds is to be held at Zurich; all the beggars from the highways will be there."

Zwingle, desiring to prepare for the struggle, published sixty-seven theses. The mountaineer of the Tockenburg boldly assailed the pope in the eyes of all Switzerland.

"All those (said he) who maintain that the Gospel is nothing without the confirmation of the Church, blaspheme God.

"Jesus Christ is the only way of salvation for all those who have been, who are, or who shall be.

"All Christians are Christ's brethren, and brethren of one another, and they have no father upon earth: thus orders, sects, and parties fall to the ground.

"We should not constrain those who will not acknowledge their error, unless they disturb the public peace by their seditious behaviour."

Such were some of Zwingle's propositions.

Early in the morning of Thursday the 29th of January, more than six hundred persons had collected in the hall of the Great Council at Zurich. Citizens and strangers, scholars, men of rank and the clergy, had responded to the call of the council. "What

1 See vol. ii. book viii. near the end.
2 Er war ein kurzer Mann. Füsslin Beyträge, iv. 44.
3 Ut post abitum Leonis, monachis aliquid legam. Zw. Epp. 253.
4 J. J. Hottinger, Helv. Kirch. Gesch. iii. 605.

will be the end of all this?" asked they of one another.[1] No one ventured to reply; but the attention, emotion, and agitation prevailing in this assembly, clearly manifested that they were expecting some extraordinary result.

The burgomaster Roust, who had fought at Marignan, presided at the conference. The chevalier James d'Anwyl, grand-master of the episcopal court at Constance, the vicar-general Faber, and many other doctors, were present as the bishop's representatives. Sebastian Hofmeister had been sent by Schaffhausen, and he was the only deputy from the cantons : such was still the weakness of the Reformation in Switzerland. On a table in the middle of the hall lay a Bible ; in front of it sat Zwingle : " I am agitated and tormented on every side," he had said, " and yet I stand firm, relying not on my own strength, but on Christ the rock, with whose help I can do all things."[2]

Zwingle stood up and said : " I have preached that salvation is found in Jesus Christ alone, and for this reason I am stigmatized throughout Switzerland as a heretic, a seducer of the people, a rebel.........Now, then, in the name of God, here I stand!"[3]

Upon this all eyes were turned towards Faber, who rose and made answer : " I was not sent here to dispute, but merely to listen!" The assembly in surprise began to laugh. " The Diet of Nuremberg," continued Faber, " has promised a council within a year ; we must wait until it meets."

" What!" said Zwingle, " is not this vast and learned meeting as good as any council?" Then turning to the presidents, he added : " My gracious lords, defend the Word of God."

A deep silence followed this appeal ; it was interrupted by the burgomaster, who said : " If there is any one here who desires to speak, let him do so." There was another pause. " I call upon all those who have accused me, and I know that there are several here," said Zwingle, " to come forward and reprove me for the love of truth." No one said a word. Zwingle repeated his request a second and a third time, but to no purpose. Faber, thus closely pressed, dropped for an instant the reserve he had imposed on himself, to declare that the pastor of Filispach, whom he had convinced of his error, was now confined in prison ; but immediately after resumed his character as a spectator. But vainly was he urged to set forth the reasons by which he had convinced this pastor : he obstinately refused. This silence on the part of the Romish doctors exhausted the patience of the meeting. A voice was heard exclaiming from the farther part of the hall :

" Where are now these valiant fellows,[1] who talk so loudly in the streets ? Come along, step forward, there's your man!" No one moved. Upon this the burgomaster said with a smile : " It would appear that this famous sword with which you smote the pastor of Filispach will not come out of its sheath to-day ;" and he then broke up the meeting.

When the assembly met again in the afternoon, the council declared that Master Ulrich Zwingle, not being reproved by any one, might continue to preach the holy Gospel, and that the rest of the clergy in the canton should teach nothing that they could not substantiate by Scripture.

" Praised be God, who will cause his holy Word to prevail in heaven and earth!" exclaimed Zwingle. Upon this Faber could not restrain his indignation. " The theses of Master Ulrich," said he, " are contrary to the honour of the Church and the doctrine of Christ ; and I will prove it." " Do so," replied Zwingle. But Faber declined his challenge, except it should be at Paris, Cologne, or Friburg. " I will have no other judge than the Gospel," said Zwingle. " Sooner than you can shake one of its words, the earth will open before you."[2] " The Gospel!" sneered Faber, " always the Gospel!......Men might live in holiness, peace, and charity, though there were no Gospel."[3]

At these words the spectators rose indignantly from their seats, and thus terminated the disputation.

CHAPTER II.

Papal Temptations—Progress of the Reformation—The Idol at Stadelhofen — Sacrilege — The Ornaments of the Saints.

THE Reformation had gained the day ; it was now to accelerate its conquests. After this battle of Zurich, in which the most skilful champions of the papacy were dumb, who would be bold enough to oppose the new doctrine? But weapons of a different kind were tried. Zwingle's firmness and republican bearing overawed his adversaries ; accordingly they had recourse to peculiar measures to subdue him. While Rome was pursuing Luther with her anathemas, she endeavoured to win over the reformer of Zurich by gentleness. The dispute was scarcely ended when Zwingle received a visit from the captain of the pope's guard— the son of the burgomaster Roust. He was

---

[1] Ein grosses Verwunderen, was doch uss der Sach werden wollte. Bullinger Chronik. i. 97.
[2] Immotus tamen maneo, non meis nervis nixus, sed petra Christo, in quo omnia possum. Zw. Epp. p. 261.
[3] Nun wohlan in dem Namen Gottes, hie bin ich. Bullinger Chronik. p. 98.

[1] Sc. the monks. Wo sind nun die grossen Hansen.....
Zw. Opp. i. 124.
[2] Ee müss das Erdrych brechen. Ibid. 148.
[3] Man möcht denocht früntlich, fridlich und tugendlich läben, wenn glich kein Evangelium were. Bull. Chron. p. 107 ; Zw. Opp. i. 152.

accompanied by the legate Einsius, the bearer of a papal brief, in which Adrian VI. called Zwingle his beloved son, and assured him of "his special favour."[1] At the same time the pope urged Zink to gain over Zwingle. "And what has the pope commissioned you to offer him?" asked Oswald Myconius. "Every thing," replied Zink, "except the papal chair."[2]

There was no mitre, or crozier, or cardinal's hat, that the pope would not have given to bribe the reformer of Zurich. But Rome was strangely mistaken in this respect; all her proposals were unavailing. In Zwingle, the Romish Church had a still more pitiless enemy than Luther. He cared far less than the Saxon reformer for the ideas and ceremonies of former ages; it was enough for him that any custom, however innocent in itself, was connected with some abuse; he fell violently upon it. The Word of God (thought he) should stand alone.

But if Rome understood so imperfectly what was then taking place in Christendom, she found councillors who endeavoured to put her in the way.

Faber, exasperated at seeing the pope thus humble himself before his adversary, hastened to enlighten him. He was a courtier with a constant smile upon his lips and honied words in his mouth; to judge from his own language, he was everybody's friend, even of those whom he accused of heresy. But his hatred was mortal. Accordingly, the reformer, playing on his name (Faber, a smith), used to say, "the Vicar of Constance is a lie-smith. Let him openly take up arms, and see how Christ defends us."[3]

These words were no mere idle boasting; for while the pope was complimenting Zwingle on his eminent virtues, and the special confidence he placed in him, the enemies of the reformer were increasing in number throughout Switzerland. The veteran soldiers, the great families, and the herdsmen of the mountains combined their hatred against this doctrine which thwarted their tastes. At Lucerne, the magnificent representation of Zwingle's *passion* was announced; in effect, the people dragged the reformer's effigy to the scaffold, shouting out that they were going to put the heretic to death; and laying hands on some Zurichers who happened to be at Lucerne, compelled them to be spectators of this mock execution. "They shall not trouble my repose," said Zwingle; "Christ will never be wanting to his followers."[4] Even the diet re-echoed with threats against him. "My dear confederates," said the councillor of Mullinen to the cantons, "make a timely resistance

to the Lutheran cause......At Zurich a man is no longer master in his own house!"

This agitation among the enemy announced what was passing in Zurich more loudly than any proclamations could have done. The victory was indeed bearing fruit; the conquerors were gradually taking possession of the country, and every day the Gospel made fresh progress. Twenty-four canons and a great number of chaplains voluntarily petitioned the council to reform their statutes. It was decided to replace these sluggish priests by pious and learned men, with commission to give the Zurich youth a christian and liberal education, and to establish in the place of their vespers and Latin masses, a daily explanation of a chapter in the Bible, according to the Hebrew and Greek texts, first for the learned, and afterwards for the people.

There are unfortunately in every army a number of those desperate heroes who leave their ranks and make unseasonable attacks on points that ought still to be respected. A young priest, Louis Hetzer, had published a treatise in German, entitled, *The judgment of God against Images*, which produced a great sensation, and the question of images wholly engrossed the thoughts of a part of the people. It is only to the detriment of those essentials that ought to occupy his mind, that man can fix his attention on secondary matters. At a place called Stadelhofen, outside the city gates, stood a crucifix elaborately carved and richly ornamented. The most zealous partisans of the Reformation, shocked at the superstitions to which this image gave rise, could not pass by without giving vent to their indignation. A citizen named Claude Hottinger, "a worthy man," says Bullinger, "and well read in the Holy Scriptures," having fallen in with the miller of Stadelhofen, to whom the crucifix belonged, asked him when he intended to throw down his idols. "No one compels you to worship them," replied the miller.—"But do you not know," retorted Hottinger, "that the Word of God forbids us to have any graven images?"—"Well, then," said the miller, "if you are authorized to remove them, I abandon them to you." Hottinger thought himself empowered to act, and shortly after, about the end of September, he was seen passing the gates with a body of citizens. On arriving at the crucifix, they deliberately dug round it, until the image, yielding to their efforts, fell to the earth with a loud crash.

This daring action spread dismay on every side: one might have thought that religion itself had fallen with the crucifix of Stadelhofen. "They are guilty of sacrilege! They deserve to be put to death!" exclaimed the friends of Rome. The council caused the image-breakers to be apprehended.

"No!" cried Zwingle and his colleagues from their pulpits: "Hottinger and his friends

[1] Cum de tua egregia virtute specialiter nobis sit cognitum. Zw. Epp. p. 266.
[2] Serio respondit: Omnia certe præter sedem papalem. Vita Zwinglii, per Osw. Myc.
[3] Prodeant volo, palamque arma capiant. Zw. Epp. p. 292.
[4] Christum suis nunquam defecturum. Ibid. p. 278.

are not guilty in the sight of God and worthy of death.[1] But they may be punished for having acted with violence and without the sanction of the magistrates."[2]

Meantime acts of a similar nature were continually taking place. A curate of Saint Peter's, one day remarking in front of the church a number of poor people ill fed and with tattered garments, said to one of his colleagues, as he turned his eyes on the costly ornaments of the saints: "I should like to strip those idols of wood to procure clothing for these poor members of Jesus Christ." A few days later, at three o'clock in the morning, the saints and all their ornaments disappeared. The council flung the curate into prison, notwithstanding he protested his innocence of this proceeding. "What!" exclaimed the people, "is it these logs of wood that Jesus ordered us to clothe? Is it on account of these images that he will say to the righteous: *I was naked, and ye clothed me?*"

Thus, the greater the resistance, the higher soared the Reformation; and the more it was compressed, the more energetically did it spring forward, and threaten to overthrow all that withstood it.

CHAPTER III.

The Disputation of October—Zwingle on the Church—The Church—Commencement of Presbyterianism—Discussion on the Mass—Enthusiasts—The Language of Discretion—Victory—A Characteristic of the Swiss Reformation—Moderation—Oswald Myconius at Zurich—Revival of Literature—Thomas Plater of the Valais.

Even these excesses were destined to be salutary; a new combat was needed to secure fresh triumphs; for in the things of the Spirit, as in the affairs of the world, there is no conquest without a struggle; and as the soldiers of Rome stood motionless, the conflict was to be brought on by the undisciplined sons of the Reformation. In fact, the magistrates were embarrassed and agitated; they felt the necessity of having their consciences enlightened, and with this view they resolved to appoint another public disputation in the German language, in which the question of idols should be examined according to Scripture.

The Bishops of Coire, Constance, and Basle, the university of the latter city, and the twelve cantons, were accordingly requested to send deputies to Zurich. But the bishops declined the invitation, and calling to mind the wretched figure their deputies had made

at the former disputation, they had little inclination to repeat such humiliating scenes. Let the evangelicals dispute if they please, but let them dispute alone. On the first occasion, the Romish party had kept silence; on the second they were resolved not to appear. Rome may possibly have imagined that the great combat would cease for want of combatants. The bishops were not alone in refusing to attend. The men of Unterwalden replied that they had no scholars among them, but only worthy and pious priests, who explained the Gospel as their fathers had done; that they would send no deputy to Zwingle "and his fellows;" but that, if he fell into their hands, they would treat him in such a manner as to deprive him of all wish to relapse into the same faults.[1] Schaffhausen and St. Gall alone sent representatives.

On the 26th of October, after the sermon, an assembly of more than nine hundred persons, composed of members of the Great Council and of three hundred and fifty priests, filled the large hall of the town-house. Zwingle and Leo Juda were seated at a table, on which lay the Old and New Testaments in the original languages. Zwingle spoke first, and overthrowing with a vigorous arm the authority of the hierarchy and of its councils, established the rights of every Christian Church, and claimed the liberty of the primitive ages—of those times when the Church knew neither general nor provincial councils. "The universal Church," said he, "is spread over the whole world, wherever there is faith in Christ, in India as well as at Zurich...... And as for particular churches, we have them at Berne, at Schaffhausen, and even here. But the popes, with their cardinals and their councils, form neither the universal Church nor a particular Church.[2] The assembly before which I now speak," continued he with energy, "is the Church of Zurich; it desires to hear the Word of God, and it has the right of ordering all that may appear to it conformable with the Holy Scriptures."

Thus did Zwingle rely on the Church, but on the true Church; not on the clergy alone, but on the assembly of Christians,—on the people. All that the Scriptures say of the Church in general, he applied to particular churches. He did not think that any church could err which listened with docility to the Word of God. In his eyes, the Church was represented politically and ecclesiastically by the Great Council.[3] At first he explained every question from the pulpit; and when his hearers' minds were convinced of the truth, he carried the matter before the Great Council, who, in harmony with the ministers

[1] An exposition of the same principles may be seen in the speeches of MM. de Broglie and Royer-Collard, at the period of the famous debates on the law of sacrilege in France, 1824.

[2] Dorum habend ir unser Herren kein rächt zu inen, sy zu töden. Bull. Chron. p. 127.

[1] So wollten wir ihm den Lohn geben, dass er's nimmer mehr thäte. Simmler Samml. MS. ix.

[2] Der Päbste, Cardinäle und Bischöffe Concilia sind nich die christliche Kirche. Fussl. Beytr. iii. 20.

[3] Diacosian Senatus summa est potestas Ecclesiæ vice. Zw. Opp. iii. 339.

of the Church, formed such decisions as the Church called for.[1]

In the absence of the bishop's deputies, Conrad Hoffmann, the same aged canon who had procured Zwingle's election to Zurich, undertook the defence of the pope. He maintained that the Church, the flock, the "third estate," had no right to discuss such matters. "I was thirteen years at Heidelberg," said he, "living in the house of a very great scholar, whose name was Doctor Joss, a worthy and pious man, with whom I long ate and drank and led a merry life; but I always heard him say that it was not proper to discuss such matters; so you see......" All were ready to burst into laughter; but the burgomaster checked them. "Let us therefore wait for a council," continued Hoffmann. "For the present, I shall not dispute, but obey the bishop's orders, even should he be a knave!"

"Wait for a council!" replied Zwingle. "And who will attend a council? The pope with a pack of sluggish and ignorant bishops who will do nothing but what suits their fancy. No! the Church is not there! Höng and Küssnacht, (these were two Zurich villages) are certainly more of a church than all the bishops and popes put together!"

Thus did Zwingle vindicate the rights of the christian people, whom Rome had deprived of their privileges. The assembly before which he was speaking was not, in his judgment, the Church of Zurich, but its first representative. This is the beginning of the Presbyterian system in the age of the Reformation. Zwingle was withdrawing Zurich from the jurisdiction of the Bishop of Constance, separating it from the Latin hierarchy, and founding on this idea of the flock, of the christian assembly, a new ecclesiastical constitution, to which other countries were afterwards to adhere.

The disputation continued. Many priests having risen to defend the images, but without having recourse to Holy Writ, Zwingle and the other reformers confuted them by the Bible. "If no one stands forward to defend the use of images by arguments derived from Scripture," said one of the presidents, "we shall call upon some of their advocates by name." As no one arose, the priest of Wadischwyl was called. "He is asleep," answered one of the spectators. The priest of Horgen was next called. "He has sent me in his place," replied his curate, "but I will not answer for him." Evidently the power of God's Word was making itself felt in this assembly. The partisans of the Reformation were full of energy, liberty, and joy; their adversaries appeared speechless, uneasy, and dejected. They summoned, one after another, the parish-priests of Laufen, Glattfel-

den, Wetzikon, the rector and priest of Pfaffikon, the dean of Elgg, the priest of Bäretschwyl, with the Dominicans and Gray-friars, notorious for their preaching in defence of images, the virgin, the saints, and the mass; but all made answer that they could say nothing in their favour, and that henceforward they would apply themselves to the study of the truth. "Hitherto," said one of them, "I have put my trust in the old doctors; now, I will believe in the new."—"You should believe not in us, but in God's Word," exclaimed Zwingle. "It is Scripture alone that can never err!" The sitting had been long, and night was approaching. The president, Hofmeister of Schaffhausen, stood up and said: "Blessed be the Almighty and Everlasting God for that in all things he has vouchsafed us the victory;" and he then exhorted the councillors of Zurich to pull down all the images.

On Tuesday the assembly met again in order to discuss the doctrine of the mass. Vadian was in the chair. "My brethren in Christ," said Zwingle, "far from us be the thought that there is any deception or falsehood in the body and blood of Christ.[1] Our only aim is to show that the mass is not a sacrifice that one man can offer to God for another, unless any one should maintain also that a man can eat and drink for his friend."

Vadian having twice demanded if any there present desired to uphold by Scripture the doctrine impugned, and no one having replied, the canons of Zurich, the chaplains, and many other ecclesiastics, declared that they agreed with Zwingle.

But scarcely had the reformers thus vanquished the partisans of the old doctrines, than they had to contend against those impatient spirits who call for sudden and violent innovations, and not for wise and gradual reforms. The wretched Conrad Grebel rose and said: "It is not enough to have disputed about the mass, we must put an end to its abuses."—"The council will draw up an edict on the subject," replied Zwingle. Upon this Simon Stumpf exclaimed: "The Spirit of God has already decided: why refer to the decision of the council?"[2]

The commander Schmidt of Küssnacht arose gravely, and in language full of wisdom said, "Let us teach Christians to receive Christ in their hearts.[3] Until this hour, ye have all gone after idols. The dwellers in the plain have run to the mountains, and those of the mountains have gone to the plain; the French to Germany, and the Germans to France. Now ye know whither ye ought to go. God has combined all things in Christ. Ye noble citizens of Zurich! go to the true source; and may Christ at length

[1] Ante omnia multitudinem de quæstione probe docere Ita factum est, ut quidquid diacosii (the great council of two hundred), cum verbi ministris ordinarent, jamdudum in animis fidelium ordinatum esset. Zw. Opp. iii. 339.

[1] Dass einigerley Betrug oder Falschsyg in dem reinen Blut und Fleisch Christi. Zw. Opp. i. 498.
[2] Der Geist Gottes urtheilet. Ibid. 529.
[3] Wie sy Christum in iren Herzen sollind bilden und machen. Ibid. 534.

re-enter your territory, and there resume his ancient empire."

This discourse made a deep impression, and no one stood up to reply to it. Zwingle rose with emotion and said, " Gracious lords, God is with us......He will defend his cause. Now, then, forward in the name of God." Here Zwingle's agitation became so great that he could not proceed. He wept, and many joined their tears with his.[1]

Thus ended the disputation. The presidents rose ; the burgomaster thanked them ; and the aged warrior, turning to the council, said gravely, with that voice which had so often been heard on the field of battle, " Now, then,...... let us grasp the sword of God's Word, and may the Lord prosper his work."

This dispute, which took place in the month of October 1523, was decisive. The majority of the priests, who had been present at it, returned full of zeal to the different parts of the canton, and the effect of these two days was felt throughout Switzerland. The Church of Zurich, that had always preserved a certain independence with respect to the see of Constance, was then entirely emancipated. Instead of resting on the pope through the bishop, it rested henceforward through the people on the Word of God. Zurich recovered the privileges that Rome had taken from her. Town and country vied with each other in interest for the work of the Reformation, and the Great Council did but follow the movements of the people. On all important occasions the city and the villages made known their opinions. Luther had restored the Bible to the christian world; Zwingle went farther, he restored their rights. This is a characteristic feature of the Swiss Reformation. The maintenance of sound doctrine was thus confided, under God, to the people ; and recent events have shown that a christian people can guard this precious deposit better than priests and pontiffs.[2]

Zwingle did not allow himself to be elated by victory ; on the contrary, the Reformation, according to his wish, was carried on with great moderation. " God knows my heart," said he, when the council asked his advice ; " He knows that I am inclined to build up, and not to throw down. I am aware that there are timid souls who ought to be conciliated ; let the mass, therefore, for some time longer be read on Sunday in all the churches, and let us avoid insulting the priests who celebrate it."[3]

The council drew up an edict to this purport. Hottinger and Hochrutiner, one of his friends, were banished from the canton for two years, and forbidden to return without permission.

The Reformation at Zurich followed a prudent and christian course. Daily raising this city more and more, it surrounded her with glory in the eyes of all the friends of the Word of God. Accordingly those in Switzerland who had saluted the new light that was dawning upon the Church felt themselves powerfully attracted towards Zurich. Oswald Myconius, expelled from Lucerne, had been residing for six months at Einsidlen, when, as he was returning one day from a journey he had made to Glaris,[1] oppressed by fatigue and by the heat of the sun, he saw his little boy Felix running to meet him, and to tell him that he had been invited to Zurich to superintend one of the schools. Oswald could not believe such joyful tidings : he hesitated between fear and hope.[2] " I am thine," wrote he at last to Zwingle. Geroldsek saw him depart with regret ; gloomy thoughts filled his mind. " Alas ! " said he to Oswald, " all those who confess Christ are going to Zurich ; I fear that one day we shall all perish there together."[3] A melancholy presentiment, which by the death of Geroldsek himself and of so many other friends of the Gospel, was but too soon fulfilled on the plains of Cappel.

At Zurich, Myconius found at last a safe retreat. His predecessor, who from his stature had been nicknamed at Paris " the great devil," had neglected his duties ; Oswald devoted all his heart and strength to their fulfilment. He explained the Greek and Latin classics, taught rhetoric and logic, and the youth of the city listened to him with delight.[4] Myconius was destined to become for the rising generation what Zwingle was to those of riper years.

At first Myconius was alarmed at the advanced age of the scholars under his care ; but he had gradually resumed his courage, and was not long in distinguishing among his pupils a young man, twenty-four years of age, from whose eyes beamed forth a love of study. Thomas Plater, for such was his name, was a native of the Valais. In that beautiful valley, where the torrent of the Viége rolls its noisy waters, after issuing from the sea of ice and snow which encircles Mount Rosa, between St. Nicholas and Stalden, on the lofty hill that rises on the right bank of the river, may still be seen the village of Grächen. This was Plater's birthplace. From the neighbourhood of these colossal Alps was to proceed one of the most original of all the characters that appeared in the great drama of the sixteenth century. At the age of nine years, he had been placed under the care of a priest who was his relation, by whom the little peasant was often

---

[1] Dass er sich selbst mit vil andren bewegt zu weinen. Zw. Opp. i. 537.
[2] In 1839, the celebrated pantheist and unbeliever, Strauss, having been nominated professor of dogmatical theology in the university of Zurich, the people of all the canton resisted the appointment, and raised a new government into power.
[3] Ohne dass jemand sich unterstehe die Messpriester zu beschimpfen. Wirtz. II. K. G., v. 208.

[1] Inesperato nuntio excepit me filius redeuntem ex Glareana. Zw. Epp. p. 322.
[2] Inter spem et metum. Ibid.
[3] Ac deinde omnes simul pereamus. Ibid. p. 323.
[4] Juventus illum lubens audit. Ibid. p. 264.

so cruelly beaten that he cried (as he tells us himself) like a kid under the knife. He was taken by one of his cousins to attend the German schools. But he had already attained the age of twenty years, and yet, through running from school to school, he scarcely knew how to read. [1] When he arrived at Zurich, he came to the determination of gaining knowledge ; and having taken his place in Oswald's school, he said to himself, "There shalt thou learn or die." The light of the Gospel shone into his heart. One very cold morning, when he had no fuel for the school-room stove, which it was his duty to keep up, he thought to himself: "Why should you want wood, while there are many idols in the church!" There was no one as yet in the church, although Zwingle was to preach, and the bells were already summoning the congregation. Plater entered very softly, laid hold of an image of St. John that stood upon an altar, and thrust it into the stove, saying: "Down with you, for in you must go." Most assuredly neither Myconius nor Zwingle would have sanctioned such a proceeding.

It was in truth by better arms than these that incredulity and superstition were to be combated. Zwingle and his colleagues had given the hand of fellowship to Myconius ; and the latter daily expounded the New Testament in the church of Our Lady before an eager and attentive crowd.[2] Another public disputation, held on the 13th and 14th of January 1524, had again proved fatal to Rome ; and in vain did the canon Koch exclaim : "Popes, cardinals, bishops, councils —these are my church!"

Every thing was making progress in Zurich ; men's minds were becoming more enlightened, their hearts more decided, and the Reformation was increasing in strength. Zurich was a fortress gained by the new doctrine, and from her walls it was about to spread over the whole confederation.

CHAPTER IV.

Diet of Lucerne—Hottinger arrested—His Death—Deputation from the Diet to Zurich—Abolition of Religious Processions—Abolition of Images—The Two Reformations—Appeal to the People.

THE adversaries were aware of what might be the consequences of these changes in Zurich. They felt that they must now decide upon striking a vigorous blow. They had been silent spectators long enough. The iron-clad warriors of Switzerland determined to rise at last ; and whenever they

[1] See his Autobiography.
[2] Weise, Füsslin Beyt. iv. 66.

arose, the field of battle had been dyed with blood.

The diet had met at Lucerne ; the clergy were endeavouring to excite the chief council of the nation in their favour. Friburg and the Forest Cantons proved their docile instruments ; Berne, Basle, Soleure, Glaris, and Appenzel were undecided. Schaffhausen was inclining towards the Gospel; but Zurich alone stood forward boldly in its defence. The partisans of Rome urged the assembly to yield to their demands and prejudices. "Let the people be forbidden," said they, "to preach or repeat any new or Lutheran doctrine in private or in public, and to talk or dispute about such things in taverns and over their wine."[1] Such was the ecclesiastical law they were desirous of establishing in the confederation.

Nineteen articles were drawn up to this effect, approved of by all the states, except Zurich, on the 26th of January 1523, and sent to all the bailiffs with orders to see that they were strictly observed : "which caused great joy among the priests," says Bullinger, "and great sorrow among believers." A persecution, regularly organized by the supreme authority of the confederation, was about to begin.

One of the first who received the mandate of the diet was Henry Flackenstein of Lucerne, bailiff of Baden. Hottinger, when banished from Zurich for pulling down the crucifix of Stadelhofen, had retired to this bailiwick, where he had not concealed his opinions. One day, as he chanced to be dining at the Angel tavern in Zurzach, he had said that the priests wrongly interpreted Holy Scripture, and that man should put his trust in God alone. [2] The landlord, who was continually going in and out to bring bread or wine, listened to what appeared to him very extraordinary language. Another day, Hottinger paid a visit to his friend John Schutz of Schneyssingen. After they had eaten and drunk together, Schutz asked him : "What is this new faith that the Zurich pastors are preaching?" "They preach," replied Hottinger, "that Christ was sacrificed once for all Christians ; that by this one sacrifice he has purified and redeemed them from their sins ; and they show by Holy Scripture that the mass is a lie."

After this (in February 1523), Hottinger had quitted Switzerland, and gone on business to Waldshut, on the other side of the Rhine. Measures were taken to seize his person, and about the end of the same month the poor unsuspecting Zuricher, having recrossed the river, had scarcely reached Coblentz, a village on the left bank of the Rhine, before he was arrested. He was taken to Klingenau, and as he there frankly confessed

[1] Es soll nieman in den Wirtzhüseren, oder sunst hinterdem Wyn von Lutherischen, oder newen Sachen uzid reden. Bull. Chr. p. 144.
[2] Wie wir unser pitt Hoffnung und Trost allein uf Gott. Ibid. p. 146.

his faith, the exasperated Flackenstein said: "I will take you to a place where you will find people to make you a suitable answer."

In effect, the bailiff conducted him successively before the judges of Klingenau, before the superior tribunal of Baden, and, since he could find no one who would declare him guilty, before the diet sitting at Lucerne. He was firmly resolved to seek judges who would condemn his prisoner.

The diet lost no time, and condemned Hottinger to be beheaded. When informed of his sentence, he gave glory to God: "That will do," said James Troger, one of his judges, "we do not sit here to listen to sermons. You can have your talk some other time." "He must have his head taken off this once," said the bailiff Am Ort, with a laugh; "if he should ever get it on again, we will all embrace his faith." "May God forgive all those who have condemned me," said the prisoner. A monk then presented a crucifix to his lips, but he put it away, saying: "It is in the heart that we must receive Jesus Christ."

When he was led out to execution, many of the spectators could not refrain from tears. "I am going to eternal happiness," said he, turning towards them. On reaching the place where he was to die, he raised his hands to heaven, exclaiming: "Into thy hands, O my Redeemer, I commit my spirit!" In another minute his head rolled upon the scaffold.

The blood of Hottinger was hardly cold before the enemies of the Reformation seized the opportunity of still further inflaming the anger of the confederates. It was in Zurich itself that the mischief should be crushed. The terrible example that had just been given must have filled Zwingle and his partisans with terror. Another vigorous effort, and the death of Hottinger would be followed by that of the Reform......The diet immediately resolved that a deputation should be sent to Zurich, calling upon the councils and the citizens to renounce their faith.

The deputation received an audience on the 21st of March. "The ancient christian unity is broken," said the deputies; "the disease is gaining ground; already have the clergy of the four Forest Cantons declared, that unless the magistrates come to their aid, they must discontinue their functions. Confederates of Zurich, join your efforts to ours; stifle this new faith;[1] dismiss Zwingle and his disciples, and then let us all unite to remedy the injuries that have been inflicted on the popes and their courtiers."

Thus spoke the adversaries: and what would the citizens of Zurich do? Would their hearts fail them? Had their courage cooled with the blood of their fellow-citizen?

Zurich did not leave her friends or enemies long in suspense. The council announced calmly and nobly that they could make no concessions in what concerned the Word of God; and then proceeded to make a still more forcible reply.

Ever since the year 1351, it had been customary for a numerous procession, each member of which bore a cross, to go on Whitmonday on a pilgrimage to Einsidlen to worship the Virgin. This festival, which had been established in commemoration of the battle of Tatwyll, was attended with great disorders.[1] The procession should have taken place on the 7th of May. On the petition of the three pastors it was prohibited by the council, and all the other processions were reformed in their turn.

They did not stop here. The relics, that source of innumerable superstitions, were honourably interred;[2] and then, at the request of the three pastors, the council published a decree, to the effect that honour being due to God alone, the images should be removed from all the churches of the canton, and their ornaments sold for the benefit of the poor. Twelve councillors, one from each guild, the three pastors, the city-architect, blacksmiths, carpenters, builders, and masons, went into the various churches, and having closed the doors,[3] took down the crosses, defaced the frescoes, whitewashed the walls, and took away the images, to the great delight of the believers, who regarded this proceeding (says Bullinger) as a striking homage paid to the true God. In some of the country churches, the ornaments were burnt "to the honour and glory of God." Erelong the organs were taken down, on account of their connexion with many superstitious practices; and a baptismal service was drawn up, from which every thing unscriptural was excluded.

The burgomaster Roust and his colleague, with their dying eyes joyfully hailed the triumph of the Reformation. They had lived long enough, and they died at the very time of this great renovation of public worship.

The Swiss Reformation here presents itself under an aspect somewhat different from that of the German Reformation. Luther had risen up against the excesses of those who had broken the images in the churches of Wittemberg; and in Zwingle's presence the idols fell in the temples of Zurich. This difference is explained by the different lights in which the two reformers viewed the same object. Luther desired to maintain in the Church all that was not expressly contrary to the Scriptures, and Zwingle to abolish all that could not be proved by them. The German reformer wished to remain united to the Church of the preceding ages, and was content to purify it of all that was opposed

---

[1] Zurich selbigen ausreuten und untertrucken helfe. Hott. Helv. K. G. iii. 170.

[1] Uff einen Creitzgang, sieben unehelicher kinden überkommen wurdend. Bull. Chr. p. 160.
[2] Und es eerlich bestattet hat. Ibid. 161.
[3] Habend die nach inen zu beschlossen. Ibid. 175.

to the Word of God. The Zurich reformer passed over these ages, returned to the apostolic times, and, carrying out an entire transformation of the Church, endeavoured to restore it to its primitive condition.

Zwingle's reformation was therefore the more complete. The work that Providence had confided to Luther, the restoration of the doctrine of justification by faith, was doubtless the great work of the Reformation; but when this was accomplished, others remained to be done, which, although secondary, were still important; and to these Zwingle's exertions were more especially directed.

In fact, two mighty tasks had been imposed on the reformers. Christian catholicism, born in the midst of Jewish pharisaism and Greek paganism, had gradually felt the influence of these two religions, which had transformed it into Roman-catholicism. The Reformation that was called to purify the Church, was destined to purge it alike from the Jewish and the pagan element.

The Jewish element prevailed chiefly in that part of the christian doctrine which relates to man. Catholicism had received from Judaism the pharisaical ideas of self-righteousness, of salvation by human strength or works.

The pagan element prevailed especially in that part of the christian doctrine which relates to God. Paganism had corrupted in the catholic church the idea of an infinite Deity, whose power, being perfectly all-sufficient, is at work in all times and in all places. It had established in the Church the reign of symbols, images, and ceremonies; and the saints had become the demigods of popery.

Luther's reform was directed essentially against the Jewish element. It was against this element that he had been compelled to struggle, when an impudent monk on behalf of the pope was making a trade of the salvation of souls.

Zwingle's reform was particularly directed against the pagan element. It was this element with which he had come in contact at the temple of our Lady of Einsidlen, when a crowd, gathered together from every side, fell down blindly before a gilded idol, as of old in the temple of the Ephesian Diana.

The German reformer proclaimed the great doctrine of justification by faith, and with it inflicted a death-blow on the pharisaical righteousness of Rome. The reformer of Switzerland unquestionably did the same; the inability of man to save himself forms the basis of the work of all the reformers. But Zwingle did something more: he established the sovereign, universal, and exclusive agency of God, and thus inflicted a deadly blow on the pagan worship of Rome.

Roman-catholicism had exalted man and lowered God. Luther lowered man, and Zwingle exalted God.

These two tasks, which were specially but not exclusively theirs, were the complement of each other. Luther laid the foundation of the building; Zwingle raised its crowning stone.

It was reserved for a still more capacious genius to impress, from the banks of the Leman lake, these two characters conjointly upon the Reformation. [1]

But while Zwingle was thus advancing with mighty strides to the head of the confederation, the disposition of the cantons became daily more hostile. The Zurich government felt the necessity of relying on the people. The people, moreover, that is to say the assembly of believers, was, according to Zwingle's principles, the highest power to which there could be any appeal on earth. It was resolved to test the state of public opinion, and the bailiffs were enjoined to demand of all the parishes whether they were ready to suffer every thing for our Lord Jesus Christ, "who," said the council, "gave his life and his blood for us sinners."[2] The whole canton had carefully followed the progress of the Reformation in the city; and in many places, the cottages of the peasants had become christian schools, wherein the Holy Scriptures were read.

The proclamation of the council was read and enthusiastically received in every parish. "Let our lords," answered they, "remain fearlessly attached to the Word of God: we will aid them in upholding it;[3] and if any one seeks to molest them, we will come to their support like brave and loyal fellow-citizens." The peasantry of Zurich showed then, that the strength of the Church is in the christian people.

But the people were not alone. The man whom God had placed at their head answered worthily to the call. Zwingle appeared to multiply himself for the service of God. All that were enduring persecution in the Helvetic cantons for the cause of the Gospel addressed themselves to him.[4] The responsibility of public affairs, the care of the churches, the anxieties of the glorious conflict that was going on in every valley of Switzerland, weighed heavily upon the evangelist of Zurich.[5] At Wittemberg, the news of his courageous proceedings was received with joy. Luther and Zwingle were two great lights, placed in Upper and Lower Germany; and the doctrine of salvation, so powerfully proclaimed by both, filled the vast tracts that extend from the summit of the Alps to the shores of the Baltic and of the North Sea.

1 Litterarischer Anzeiger, 1840, No. 27.
2 Der sin rosenfarw Blüt alein fur uns arme Sünder vergossen hat. Bull. Chron. p. 180.
3 Meine Herrn sollten auch nur dapfer bey dem Gottsworte verbleiben. Füsslin Beytr. iv. p. 107, which contains the replies given by all the parishes.
4 Scribunt ex Helvetiis ferme omnes qui propter Christum premuntur. Zw. Epp. p. 348.
5 Negotiorum strepitus et ecclesiarum curæ ita me undique quatiunt. Ibid.

CHAPTER V.

New Opposition—Abduction of Œxlin—The Family of the Wirths—The Populace at the Convent of Ittingen—The Diet of Zug—The Wirths apprehended and given up to the Diet—Their Condemnation.

THE Word of God could not thus invade extensive countries, without its triumphs exasperating the pope in his palace, the priest in his presbytery, and the Swiss magistrates in their councils. Their terror increased from day to day. The people had been consulted; the christian people became of consequence in the Christian Church, and appeals were made to their sympathy and faith and not to the decrees of the Roman chancery! So formidable an attack required a still more formidable resistance. On the 18th of April, the pope addressed a brief to the confederates, and the diet, which met at Zug in the month of July, yielding to the urgent exhortations of the pontiff, sent a deputation to Zurich, Schaffhausen, and Appenzel, commissioned to acquaint these states with the firm resolve of the diet to crush the new doctrine, and to prosecute its adherents to the forfeiture of their goods, their honours, and even of their lives. Zurich did not hear this warning without emotion; but a firm reply was made, that, in matters of faith, the Word of God alone must be obeyed. On receiving this answer, Lucerne, Schwytz, Uri, Unterwalden, Friburg, and Zug, trembled with rage; and, unmindful of the reputation and strength the accession of Zurich had formerly given to the infant confederation, forgetting the precedence that had been immediately accorded to her, the simple and solemn oaths that had been made to her, and the many victories and reverses they had shared with her,—these states declared that they would no longer sit in diet with Zurich. Thus in Switzerland, as in Germany, the partisans of Rome were the first to break the federal unity. But threats and the rupture of alliances were not enough. The fanaticism of the cantons called for blood; and it was soon seen with what arms Rome intended combating the Word of God.

One of Zwingle's friends, the worthy Œxlin,[1] was pastor of Burg upon the Rhine, in the neighbourhood of Stein. The bailiff Am-Berg, who had appeared to listen to the Gospel with delight,[2] being desirous of obtaining that bailiwick, had promised the leading men of Schwytz to root out the new faith. Œxlin, although not within his jurisdiction, was the first upon whom he exercised his severity.

About midnight, on the 7th of July 1524, some persons knocked at the pastor's door; they were the bailiff's soldiers, who entered the house, seized Œxlin, and carried him away prisoner, in defiance of his cries. Thinking they meant to assassinate him, he cried " Murder;" the inhabitants started from their beds in affright, and the village soon became the scene of a frightful tumult, which was heard as far as Stein. The sentinel on guard at the castle of Hohenklingen fired the alarm-gun; the tocsin was rung, and the inhabitants of Stein, Stammheim, and the adjoining places, were soon a-foot, and inquiring of one another in the darkness what was the matter.

At Stammheim lived the deputy-bailiff Wirth, whose two eldest sons, Adrian and John, both young priests full of piety and courage, were preaching the Gospel with great unction. John especially abounded in faith, and was ready to sacrifice his life for his Saviour. This was truly a patriarchal family. Hannah, the mother, who had borne the bailiff many children, and brought them up in the fear of the Lord, was revered for her virtues throughout the whole district. At the noise of the tumult in Burg, the father and the two eldest sons went out like their neighbours. The father was indignant that the bailiff of Frauenfeld should have exercised his authority in a manner contrary to the laws of the country. The sons learned with sorrow that their brother, their friend, the man whose good example they were delighted to follow, had been dragged away like a criminal. Each of them seized a halberd, and in spite of the fears of a tender wife and mother, the father and his two sons joined the band of citizens of Stein with the determination of rescuing their pastor. Unhappily, a number of those miscreants who make their appearance in every disorder, had joined the expedition; they pursued the bailiff's officers; the latter, hearing the tocsin and the shouts of alarm, redoubled their speed, dragging their victim after them, and soon placed the river Thur between themselves and their pursuers.

When the people of Stein and Stammheim reached the bank of the river, and found no means of crossing, they halted, and resolved to send a deputation to Frauenfeld. "The pastor of Stein is so dear to us," said the bailiff Wirth, "that for his sake I would willingly sacrifice my goods, my liberty, and my life."[1] The populace, finding themselves near the Carthusian convent of Ittingen, whose inmates were believed to have encouraged the tyranny of the bailiff Am-Berg, entered the building and took possession of the refectory. These miserable wretches soon became intoxicated, and shameful disorders were the consequence. Wirth vainly entreated them to leave the convent;[2] he was in danger of being maltreated by them. His son Adrian

---

[1] See vol. ii. p. 269.
[2] Der war anfangs dem Evangelio günstig. Bull. Chr. p. 180.

[1] Sunder die Kuttlen im Buch fur Im wagen. Bull. Chr. p. 193.
[2] Und badt sy um Gootes willen uss dem Kloster zu gand, Ibid. p. 183.

remained outside the cloister. John entered, but soon came out again, distressed at what he had seen.[1] The drunken peasants proceeded to ransack the wine-cellars and the storerooms, to break the furniture, and burn the books.

When the news of these disorders reached Zurich, some deputies from the council hastened to the spot, and ordered all persons under the jurisdiction of the canton to return to their homes. They did so immediately. But a body of Thurgovians, attracted by the disturbance, established themselves in the convent, for the sake of its good cheer. On a sudden a fire broke out, no one knew how, and the monastery was burnt to the ground.

Five days after this, the deputies of the cantons met at Zug. Nothing was heard in the assembly but threats of vengeance and of death. "Let us march with banners flying on Stein and Stammheim," said they, "and put the inhabitants to the sword." The deputy-bailiff and his two sons had long been objects of especial dislike on account of their faith. "If any one is guilty," said the deputy of Zurich, "he must be punished, but according to the laws of justice, and not by violence." Vadian, deputy of St. Gall, supported this opinion. Upon this the avoyer John Hug of Lucerne, unable to contain himself any longer, exclaimed with frightful imprecations:[2] "The heretic Zwingle is the father of all these insurrections; and you too, doctor of St. Gall, are favourable to his infamous cause, and aid him in securing its triumphs......You ought no longer to have a seat among us." The deputy of Zug endeavoured to restore peace, but in vain. Vadian left the hall, and as the populace had designs upon his life, he quitted the town secretly, and reached the convent of Cappel by a circuitous route.

Zurich, intent on suppressing every disorder, resolved to apprehend provisionally those persons who were marked out by the rage of the confederates. Wirth and his two sons were living quietly at Stammheim. "Never will the enemies of God be able to vanquish His friends," said Adrian Wirth from the pulpit. The father was warned of the fate impending over him, and was entreated to flee with his two sons. "No," answered he; "I will wait for the officers, putting my trust in God." And when the soldiers made their appearance at his house, he said: "My lords of Zurich might have spared themselves all this trouble: if they had only sent a child I should have obeyed their summons."[3] The three Wirths were taken to Zurich and put in prison. Rutiman, bailiff of Nussbaum, shared their fate. They were strictly examined, but nothing reprehensible was found in their conduct.

As soon as the deputies of the cantons had heard of the imprisonment of these four citizens, they required them to be sent to Baden, and ordered that in case of refusal their troops should march upon Zurich and carry them off by force. "To Zurich belongs the right of ascertaining whether these men are guilty or not," said the deputies of that state; "and we have found no fault in them." On this the deputies of the cantons exclaimed: "Will you surrender them to us? Answer yes or no, and not a word more." Two deputies of Zurich mounted their horses, and rode off with all haste to their constituents.

On their arrival the whole town was in agitation. If the prisoners were refused, the confederates would come and seek them with an armed force; to give them up was consenting to their death. Opinions were divided: Zwingle declared for their refusal. "Zurich," said he, "ought to remain faithful to its constitution." At last it was supposed a middle course had been found. "We will deliver the prisoners into your hands," said they to the diet, "but on condition that you will examine them solely with regard to the affair of Ittingen, and not on their faith." The diet acceded to this proposition, and on the Friday before St. Bartholomew's day (18th August 1524) the three Wirths and their friend, accompanied by four councillors of state and several armed men, quitted Zurich.

A deep concern was felt by all the city at the prospect of the fate which awaited the two youths and their aged companions. Sobbing alone was heard as they passed along. "Alas!" exclaims a contemporary, "what a mournful procession!"[1] The churches were all filled. "God will punish us!" cried Zwingle. "Let us at least pray him to impart his grace to these poor prisoners, and to strengthen them in the faith."[2]

On Friday evening the accused arrived at Baden, where an immense crowd was waiting for them. At first they were taken to an inn, and thence to prison. They could scarcely advance, the crowd so pressed around to catch a sight of them. The father, who walked in front, turned towards his two sons, and observed to them meekly; "See, my dear children, we are (as the apostle says) men appointed to death; for we are made a spectacle unto the world, and to angels, and to men" (1 Cor. iv, 9). Then, as he saw among the crowd his deadly enemy, Am-Berg, the cause of all his misfortunes, he went up to him and held out his hand, although the bailiff would have turned away: "There is a God in heaven who knows all things," said he calmly, as he grasped his adversary's hand.

The examination began on the following day: the bailiff Wirth was first brought in.

---

[1] Dan es Im leid was. Bull. Chr. p. 195.
[2] Mit Fluchen und Wüten. Ibid. p. 184.
[3] Dann hättind sy mir ein Kind geschikt. Ibid. p. 186.

[1] O weh! was elender Fahrt war das! Bern. Weyss. Fussl. Beyt. iv. p. 56.
[2] Sy troste und in warem glouben starckte. Bull. Chr. p. 188.

He was put to the torture, without any regard to his character or his age; but he persisted in declaring his innocence of the pillage and burning of Ittingen. He was then accused of having destroyed an image representing St. Anne. Nothing could be substantiated against the other prisoners, except that Adrian Wirth was married, and preached after the manner of Zwingle and Luther; and that John Wirth had given the sacrament to a sick man without bell and taper. [1]

But the more apparent their innocence, the greater was the fury of their adversaries. From morning until noon they inflicted the cruelest tortures on the old man. His tears could not soften his judges. John Wirth was treated with still greater barbarity. "Tell us," they said to him in the midst of his anguish, "whence did you learn this heretical faith? From Zwingle or from any other person?" And when he exclaimed, "O merciful and everlasting God, help and comfort me!" "Where is your Christ now?" asked one of the deputies. When Adrian appeared, Sebastian of Stein, the Bernese deputy, said to him: "Young man, tell us the truth; for if you refuse to do so, I swear by the knighthood that I gained on the very spot where the Lord suffered martyrdom, that we will open your veins one after another." They then fastened the young man to a rope, and hoisted him into the air: "There, my little master," said Stein with a devilish sneer, "there is your wedding present;" [2] alluding to the marriage of this youthful servant of the Lord.

When the examination was ended, the deputies returned to their cantons to deliver their report, and did not meet again till four weeks after. The bailiff's wife, the mother of the two priests, repaired to Baden, carrying an infant child in her arms, to intercede with the judges. John Escher of Zurich accompanied her as her advocate. Among the judges he saw Jerome Stocker, landamman of Zug, who had been twice bailiff of Frauenfeld: "Landamman!" said he, "you know the bailiff Wirth; you know that he has always been an upright man."—"You say the truth, my dear Escher," replied Stocker, "he has never injured anybody; fellow-citizens and strangers were always kindly welcomed to his table: his house was a convent, an inn, and an hospital; [3] and so, if he had committed robbery or murder, I would have made every exertion to obtain his pardon. But seeing that he has burnt Saint Anne, Christ's grandmother, he must die!" —"The Lord have mercy upon us," exclaimed Escher.

The gates were now shut: it was the 28th September, and the deputies of Berne, Lucerne, Uri, Schwytz, Unterwalden, Zug, Glaris, Friburg, and Soleure, having proceeded to deliberate on their judgment with closed doors, as was customary, passed sentence of death on the bailiff Wirth, on his son John, who was the firmest in his faith, and who appeared to have led away the others, and on the bailiff Rutiman. Adrian, the second son, was granted to his mother's tears.

The officers proceeded to the tower to fetch the prisoners. "My son," said the father to Adrian, "never avenge our death, although we have not deserved punishment." Adrian burst into tears. "Brother," said John, "the cross of Christ must always follow his Word." [1]

After the sentence was read, the three Christians were led back to prison; John Wirth walking first, the two vice-bailiffs next, and a priest behind them. As they were crossing the castle bridge, on which was a chapel dedicated to St. Joseph, the priest called out to the two old men, "Fall down and call upon the saints." John Wirth, who was in front, turned round at these words and said, "Father, be firm. You know that there is only one Mediator between God and man, the Lord Jesus Christ." —"Assuredly, my son," replied the old man, "and by the help of His grace I will continue faithful even to the end." Upon this they all three began to repeat the Lord's Prayer, "Our Father which art in heaven," and so crossed the bridge.

They were next conducted to the scaffold John Wirth, whose heart was filled with the tenderest anxiety for his parent, bade him farewell. "My dearly beloved father," said he, "henceforward thou art no longer my father, and I am no longer thy son, but we are brothers in Christ our Lord, for whose name we must suffer death. [2] To-day, if it be God's pleasure, my beloved brother, we shall go to Him who is the Father of us all. Fear nothing." "Amen!" replied the old man, "and may God Almighty bless thee, my beloved son and brother in Christ!"

Thus, on the threshold of eternity, did father and son take leave of each other, hailing the new mansions in which they should be united by everlasting ties. The greater part of those around them shed floods of tears. [3] The bailiff Rutiman prayed in silence.

All three then knelt down, "in Christ's name," and their heads rolled upon the scaffold.

The crowd, observing the marks of torture upon their bodies, gave loud utterance to their grief. The two bailiffs left twenty-two children, and forty-five grandchildren.

---

[1] On Kerzen, Schellen und anders so bisshar geüpt ist. Bull. Chr. p. 196.
[2] Alls man inn am folter seyl uffzog, sagt der zum Stein: Herrli, das ist die Gaab die wir üch zu üwer Hussfrowen schänckend. Ibid, p. 190.
[3] Sin Huss ist alwey gsin wie ein Kloster, Wirtshuss und Pitall. Ibid. p. 196.

[1] Doch allwäg das Crütz darbey. Bull. Chr. p. 198.
[2] Furohin bist du nitt me min Vatter und ich din Sun, sondern wir sind Brüdern in Christo. Ibid. p. 204.
[3] Des gnadens weyneten vil Lüthen herzlich. Ibid.

Hannah was obliged to pay twelve golden crowns to the executioner who had deprived her husband and her son of life.

Thus blood, innocent blood, had been shed. Switzerland and the Reformation were baptized with the blood of the martyrs. The great enemy of the Gospel had done his work; but in doing it, his power was broken. The death of the Wirths was to accelerate the triumphs of the Reformation.

CHAPTER VI.

Abolition of the Mass—Zwingle's Dream—Celebration of the Lord's Supper—Fraternal Charity—Original Sin—The Oligarchs opposed to the Reform—Various Attacks.

IT was not thought desirable to proceed to the abolition of the mass in Zurich immediately after the suppression of images; but now the proper moment seemed to have arrived.

Not only had the light of the Gospel been diffused among the people; but the violence of the blows struck by the enemy called upon the friends of God to reply to them by some impressive demonstration of their unalterable fidelity. Every time that Rome erects a scaffold, and that heads fall upon it, the Reformation will exalt the holy Word of the Lord, and throw down some abuses. When Hottinger was executed, Zurich suppressed images; and now that the heads of the Wirths have rolled on the ground, Zurich will reply by the abolition of the mass. The more Rome increases her cruelties, the more will the Reformation increase in strength.

On the 11th of April 1525, the three pastors of Zurich, accompanied by Megander and Oswald Myconius, appeared before the Great Council, and demanded the re-establishment of the Lord's Supper. Their language was solemn;[1] all minds were absorbed in meditation; every man felt the importance of the resolution which the council was called upon to take. The mass, that mystery which for more than three centuries had been the very soul of the religious service of the Latin Church, was to be abolished, the corporeal presence of Christ to be declared an illusion, and the illusion itself removed from the minds of the people. Courage was needed to arrive at such a resolution, and there were men in the council who shuddered at this daring thought. Joachim Am-Grütt, undersecretary of state, alarmed at the bold demand of the pastors, opposed it with all his might. "These words, *This is my body*," said he, "unquestionably prove that the bread is the body of Christ himself." Zwingle observed that ἐστὶ (is) is the proper word in the Greek language to express *signifies*, and he quoted several instances in which this word is employed in a figurative sense. The Great Council were convinced and did not hesitate; the Gospel doctrines had penetrated their hearts; besides, as they were separating from the Church of Rome, there was a certain satisfaction in making that separation as complete as possible, and in digging a gulf between it and the Reformation. The council, therefore, ordered the mass to be suppressed, and decreed that on the next day, Holy Thursday, the Lord's Supper should be celebrated in conformity with the apostolical usages.

Zwingle was seriously engrossed by these thoughts, and when he closed his eyes at night, was still seeking for arguments with which to oppose his adversaries. The subjects that had so strongly occupied his mind during the day presented themselves before him in a dream. He fancied that he was disputing with Am-Grütt, and that he could not reply to his principal objection. Suddenly a figure stood before him and said: "Why do you not quote the 11th verse of the 12th chapter of Exodus: *Ye shall eat it* (the lamb) *in haste: it is the Lord's passover?*" Zwingle awoke, sprung out of bed, took up the Septuagint translation, and there found the same word ἐστὶ (is), which all are agreed is synonymous with *signifies* in this passage.

Here then, in the institution of the paschal feast under the old covenant, is the very meaning that Zwingle defends. How can he avoid concluding that the two passages are parallel?

On the following day Zwingle preached a sermon on this text, and spoke so forcibly that he removed every doubt.

This circumstance, which admits of so simple an explanation, and the very expression Zwingle employs to show that he could not recall the appearance of the figure he had seen in his dream,[1] have given rise to the assertion that Zwingle received this doctrine from the devil.

The altars had disappeared; plain tables bearing the sacramental bread and wine were substituted in their place, and an attentive crowd pressed round them. There was something particularly solemn in this multitude. On Holy Thursday, the young people,—on Friday, the day of the Passion, the adult men and women,—and on Easter Sunday, the aged, celebrated in turn the death of the Lord.[2]

The deacons read aloud the passages of Scripture that relate to this sacrament; the pastors addressed the flock in an earnest exhortation, calling upon all to retire from this sacred feast who, by persevering in their sin,

[1] Und vermantend die ernstlich. Bull. Chron. p. 263.

[1] Ater fuerit an albus nihil memini, *I do not remember whether he was white or black* (a phrase very expressive of indistinctness and uncertainty.—Tr.); somnium enim narro.
[2] Fusslin Beyträge, iv. 64.

would pollute the body of Jesus Christ. The people knelt down, the bread was carried round on large platters or wooden plates, and each one broke off a morsel; the wine was next distributed in wooden goblets: in this manner it was thought they made a nearer approach to the simplicity of the primitive Supper. Emotions of surprise or joy filled every heart.[1]

Thus was the Reform carried on in Zurich. The simple celebration of the Lord's Supper appeared to have shed anew over the Church the love of God and of the brethren. The words of Jesus Christ were once more spirit and life. While the different orders and parties in the Church of Rome were incessantly disputing among themselves, the first effect of the Gospel was to restore charity among the brethren. The love of the first ages was then revived in Christendom. Enemies were seen renouncing their long-cherished and inveterate enmities, and embracing one another after having partaken of the sacramental bread. Zwingle, delighted at these affecting manifestations, returned thanks to God that the Lord's Supper was again working those miracles of charity which the sacrifice of the mass had long ceased to accomplish.[2]

"Peace dwells in our city," exclaimed he; "among us there is no fraud, no dissension, no envying, no strife. Whence can proceed such harmony except from the Lord, and that the doctrine we preach inclines us to innocence and peace?"[3]

Charity and unity then prevailed, although there was no uniformity. Zwingle in his *Commentary on True and False Religion*,[4] which he dedicated to Francis I. in March 1525, the year of the battle of Pavia, had put forward some truths in the manner best calculated to procure their reception by human reason, following in this respect the example of several of the most distinguished scholastic divines. In this way he had given the name of *disease* to our original corruption, and reserved the appellation of *sin* for the actual transgression of the law.[5] But these statements, which called forth some objections, did not however interrupt brotherly love; for Zwingle, even when he persisted in calling original sin a disease, added, that all men were lost by this disease, and that Jesus Christ was the only remedy.[6] In this position there is no error of Pelagianism.

But while the celebration of the Lord's Supper at Zurich was attended by a return to christian brotherhood, Zwingle and his friends had to support a severer struggle against their adversaries from without. Zwingle was not only a christian teacher, he was also a true patriot; and we know how zealously he contended against the foreign capitulations, pensions, and alliances. He felt convinced that these external influences must tend to destroy piety, blind the reason, and scatter discord on every side. But his bold protests were destined to prejudice the advancement of the Reformation. In almost every canton, the chiefs who received the pensions of the foreigner, and the officers who led the youth of Helvetia to battle, formed powerful factions, formidable oligarchies, that attacked the Reformation, not so much on behalf of the Church as on account of the injury it would inflict on their interests and honours. They had already gained the victory in Schwytz; and that canton, where Zwingle, Leo Juda, and Oswald Myconius had taught, and which seemed as if it would walk in the footsteps of Zurich, had suddenly reverted to the mercenary capitulations, and shut its gates against the Reformation.

Even in Zurich, some wretches, instigated by foreign intrigues, attacked Zwingle during the night, flung stones at his house, broke the windows, and called with loud cries for "the red haired Uli, the vulture of Glaris;" so that Zwingle awoke from his sleep and ran to his sword.[1] This action is very characteristic of the man.

But these isolated attacks could not paralyze the movement by which Zurich was carried onward, and which was beginning to shake all Switzerland. They were pebbles thrown into a torrent to check its course. Every where its waters were swelling, threatening to sweep away the most formidable obstacles.

The Bernese having informed the people of Zurich that several states had refused to sit with them in future in the diet: "Well, then," replied these men of Zurich with calmness, and raising their hands towards heaven, as the heroes of Rutli in old time, "we have the firm assurance that God, the Father, Son, and Holy Ghost, in whose name the confederation was formed, will not desert us, and will at last, of his great mercy, make us sit at the right hand of his sovereign majesty."[2] Possessing such faith the Reformation had nothing to fear. But would it gain similar victories in the other states of the confederation? Would not Zurich remain alone on the side of God's Word? Would Berne, Basle, and other cantons remain subject to the power of Rome? This we shall soon see. Let us therefore turn towards Berne, and study the progress of the Refor

---

[1] Mit grossen verwundern viler Lüthen und noch mit vil grössern fröuden der Glöubigen. Bull. Chron. p. 264.
[2] Expositio fidei. Zw. Opp. ii. 241.
[3] Ut tranquillitatis et innocentiæ studiosos reddat. Zw. Epp. p. 390.
[4] De vera et falsa religione commentarius. Zw. Opp. iii. 145-325.
[5] Peccatum ergo *morbus* est cognatus nobis, quo fugimus aspera et gravia, sectamur jucunda et voluptuosa : secundo loco accipitur *peccatum* pro eo quod contra legem fit. Ibid. 204.
[6] Originali morbo perdimur omnes; remedio vero quod contra ipsum invenit Deus, incolumitati restituimur. De pecc. orig. declaratio ad Urbanum Rhegium. Ibid. i. 632.

[1] Interea surgere Zwinglius ad ensem suum. Zw. Opp. iii. 411.—Uli is an abridgment of Ulrich. Zwingle had been priest at Glaris.
[2] Bey Ihm zuletzt sitzen. Kirchhofer Ref. v. Bern. p. 55.

mation in the most influential state of the confederation.

CHAPTER VII.

Berne—The Provost Watteville—First Successes of the Reformed Doctrines—Haller at the Convent—Accusation and Deliverance—The Monastery of Königsfeldt—Margaret Watteville to Zwingle—The Convent opened—Two Champions—Clara May and the Provost Watteville.

NOWHERE was the struggle likely to be so severe as at Berne, for there the Gospel counted both powerful friends and formidable adversaries. At the head of the reforming party were the banneret John Weingarten, Bartholomew May, member of the Smaller Council, his sons Wolfgang and Claudius, his grandsons James and Benedict, and above all, the family of the Wattevilles. The avoyer James Watteville, who since 1512 had occupied the first station in the republic, had early read the writings of Luther and Zwingle, and had often conversed about the Gospel with John Haller, pastor of Anseltingen, whom he had protected against his persecutors.

His son Nicholas, then thirty-one years of age, had been for two years provost of the church of Berne, and as such, by virtue of the papal ordinances, enjoyed great privileges; accordingly Berthold Haller used to call him " our bishop." [1]

The prelates and the pope spared no endeavours to bind him to the interests of Rome; [2] and it seemed as if every thing would keep him from a knowledge of the Gospel; but the ways of God are more powerful than the flatteries of man. Watteville was turned from darkness to the mild light of the Gospel, says Zwingle. [3] As a friend of Berthold Haller, he read all the letters which the latter received from Zwingle, and could not find language to express his admiration. [4]

The influence of the two Wattevilles, one of whom was at the head of the state, and the other of the church, would apparently draw after it the whole republic. But the opposite party was not less powerful. Amongst its leaders were the schulthess of Erlach, the banneret Willading, and many patricians whose interests were identical with those of the convents under their administration. Behind these influential men were an ignorant and corrupted clergy, who called the evangelical doctrine " an invention of hell."—" My dear confederates," said the

councillor Mullinen before a full assembly in the month of July, " take care that this Reformation does not come here; at Zurich a man is not safe in his own house, and he is obliged to have a guard to protect him." Accordingly they invited to Berne the reader of the Dominicans of Mentz, one John Hein, who went into the pulpit and declaimed against the Reformation with all the eloquence of Saint Thomas. [1]

Thus were the two parties drawn up in battle-array against each other; a struggle seemed inevitable, and already the result did not appear doubtful. In fact, one common faith united a part of the people to the most distinguished families of the state. Berthold Haller exclaimed, full of confidence in the future: " Unless God's anger be turned against us, it is not possible for the Word of God to be banished from this city, for the Bernese are hungering after it ! " [2]

Shortly after this two acts of the government appeared to incline the balance to the side of the Reformation. The Bishop of Lausanne having announced an episcopal visitation, the council intimated to him through the provost Watteville, that he had better refrain from so doing. [3] And at the same time the councils of Berne issued an ordinance which, whilst in appearance it conceded something to the enemies of the Reformation, sanctioned the principles of the new doctrines. They decreed that the Gospel and the doctrine of God, as it is laid down by the books of the Old and New Testaments, should be preached exclusively, freely, and openly; and that the ministers should abstain from every doctrine, discussion, or writing, proceeding from Luther or other teachers. [4] Great was the surprise of the adversaries of the Reformation when they saw the evangelical preachers boldly appealing to this ordinance. This decree, which was the basis of all those that succeeded, was the legal commencement of the Reformation in Berne. From that time the progress of this canton was more decided, and Zwingle, whose attentive eyes watched every thing that was passing in Switzerland, was able to write to the provost Watteville: " All Christians are overjoyed, on account of the faith which the pious city of Berne has just received." [5]—" The cause is the cause of Christ," exclaimed the friends of the Gospel; [6] and they devoted themselves to it with an increase of courage.

The enemies of the Reformation, alarmed at these first advantages, closed their ranks, and resolved to strike a blow that would se-

---

[1] Episcopus noster *Vadiviliius.* Zw. Epp. p. 285.
[2] Tantum favoris et amicitiæ quæ tibi cum tanto summorum pontificum et potentissimorum episcoporum cœtu hactenus intercessit. Zw. Opp. i. anc. ed. lat. 305.
[3] Ex obscuris ignorantiæ tenebris in amœnam Evangelii lucem productum. Ibid.
[4] Epistolas tuæ et eruditionis et humanitatis testes locupletissimas. Zw. Epp. p. 287.

[1] Suo Thomistico Marte omnia invertere. Zw. Epp. p. 287.
[2] Famem verbi Bernates habent. Ibid. 295.
[3] Ut nec oppidum, nec pagos Bernatum visitare prætendat omnino. Ibid.
[4] Alein das heilig Evangellum und die leer Gottes frey, offentlich und unverborgen. Bull. Chr. p. 111.
[5] Alle Christen sich allenthalben fröuwend des glaubens. Zw. Opp. i. 426.
[6] Christi negotium agitur. Zw. Epp. 9th May 1523.

cure their victory. They conceived the project of getting rid of these ministers whose bold discourses were overthrowing the most time honoured customs ; and it was not long before a favourable opportunity occurred. There existed in Berne, on the spot now occupied by the hospital of the Island, a convent of nuns of St. Dominic, consecrated to St. Michael. The anniversary of the archangel (29th September) was a great festival at the monastery. Many of the clergy were present this year, and among others Wittenbach of Bienne, Sebastian Meyer, and Berthold Haller. Having entered into conversation with the nuns, among whom was Clara, daughter of Claudius May, a supporter of the Reformation, Haller said to her, in the presence of her grandmother : " The merits of the conventual life are imaginary, whilst marriage is an honourable state, instituted by God himself." Some of the nuns to whom Clara repeated Berthold's words were horrified at them. "Haller maintains," was the rumour in the city, " that all nuns are children of the devil." The opportunity which the enemies of the Reformation were looking for was found. Going before the Smaller Council, they referred to an ancient law which enacted that whoever carried off a nun from her convent should lose his head, but asked for a mitigation of the penalty, and that, without giving the three ministers a hearing, they should be banished for life. The Smaller Council acceded to their prayer, and the matter was immediately carried before the Great Council.

Thus was Berne about to be deprived of her reformers : the intrigues of the papal party were successful. But Rome, who triumphed when she addressed herself to the oligarchs, was beaten before the people or their representatives. Scarcely had they heard the names of Haller, Meyer, and Wittembach, men whom all Switzerland venerated, than an energetic opposition was manifested by the Great Council against the Smaller Council and the clergy. " We cannot condemn the accused unheard," exclaimed Tillmann ; " their testimony is surely as good as that of a few women." The ministers were called before them : the affair was embarrassing. At length John Weingarten said : " Let us give credit to both parties." They did so : the ministers were discharged, with an intimation to confine themselves to their pulpits, and not to meddle with the cloisters. But the pulpit was sufficient for them. The efforts of their adversaries had redounded to their own disgrace. It was a great victory for the Reformation. Accordingly one of the patricians exclaimed : " It is all over now : Luther's affair must go forward."[1]

And it did in fact go forward, and in the very places where they expected it the least.

At Königsfeldt, on the Aar, near the castle of Hapsburg, stood a monastery adorned with all the conventual magnificence of the Middle Ages, and where reposed the ashes of several members of that illustrious house which had given so many emperors to Germany. Here the daughters of the greatest families of Switzerland and Swabia used to take the veil. It was not far from the spot where, on the 1st of May 1308, the Emperor Albert had fallen by the hand of his nephew John of Swabia : and the beautiful painted windows of the church of Königsfeldt represented the horrible punishments that had been inflicted on the relations and vassals of the murderer. Catherine of Waldburg-Truchsess, abbess of the convent at the period of the Reformation, numbered among her nuns Beatrice of Landenberg, sister to the Bishop of Constance, Agnes of Mullinen, Catherine of Bonstetten, and Margaret of Watteville, the provost's sister. The liberty enjoyed in this convent, which in former times had given room for scandalous disorders, now permitted the Holy Scriptures with the writings of Zwingle and Luther to be introduced ; and soon a new life entirely changed its aspect. Near that cell to which Queen Agnes, Albert's daughter, had retired, after having bathed in torrents of blood as in "maydew," and where, plying the distaff or embroidering ornaments for the church, she had mingled exercises of devotion with thoughts of vengeance,—Margaret Watteville had only thoughts of peace, and divided her time between reading the Scriptures and compounding salutary ingredients to form an excellent electuary. Retiring to her cell, this youthful nun had the boldness to write to the doctor of Switzerland. Her letter displays to us, better than any reflections could do, the christian spirit that existed in those pious women, who are still so grievously calumniated even in our own days.

" May grace and peace in the Lord Jesus be given and multiplied towards you always by God our heavenly Father," wrote the nun of Königsfeldt to Zwingle. " Most learned, reverend, and dear Sir, I entreat you to take in good part the letter I now address to you. The love which is in Christ constrains me to do so, especially since I have learnt that the doctrine of salvation is spreading day by day through your preaching of the Word of God. For this reason I give praise to the everlasting God for enlightening us anew, and sending us by his Holy Spirit so many heralds of His blessed Word ; and at the same time I offer up my ardent prayers that he will clothe with his strength both you and all those who proclaim His glad tidings, and that, arming you against all the enemies of the truth, He will cause his Divine Word to grow in all men. Very learned Sir, I venture to send your reverence this trifling mark of my affection ; do not despise it ; it is an

[1] Es ist nun gethan. Der Lutherische Handel muss vorgehen. Anshelm, Wirtz. K. G. v. 290. .

offering of christian charity. If this electuary does you good, and you should desire more, pray let me know ; for it would be a great pleasure to me to do any thing that was agreeable to you ; and it is not I only who think thus, but all those who love the Gospel in our convent of Königsfeldt. They salute your reverence in Jesus Christ, and we all commend you without ceasing to His almighty protection.[1]

" Saturday before *Lætare*, 1523."

Such was the pious letter that the nun of Königsfeldt wrote to the doctor of Switzerland.

A convent into which the light of the Gospel had thus penetrated could not persevere in the observances of a monastic life. Margaret Watteville and her sisters, convinced that they could better serve God in the bosom of their families than in the cloister, asked permission to leave it. The council of Berne in alarm endeavoured at first to bring these nuns to reason, and the provincial and abbess employed threats and promises by turns ; but the sisters Margaret, Agnes, Catherine, and their friends were not to be shaken. Upon this the discipline of the convent was relaxed, the nuns were exempted from fasting and matins, and their allowance was increased. " It is not the liberty of the flesh that we require," said they to the council ; " it is that of the spirit. We, your poor and innocent prisoners, entreat you to have pity on us !"—" *Our prisoners ! our prisoners !*" exclaimed the banneret Krauchthaler, " they shall be no prisoners of mine !" This language from one of the firmest supporters of the convents decided the council ; the convent gates were opened, and shortly after, Catherine Bonstetten was married to William of Diesbach.

And yet Berne, far from siding openly with the reformers, held a middle course, and endeavoured to pursue a see-saw system. An opportunity soon occurred for showing this vacillating procedure. Sebastian Meyer, reader of the Franciscans, published a retractation of his Romish errors, which created a great sensation, and in which, describing a conventual life, he said : " In the convents the monks live more impurely, fall more frequently, recover themselves more tardily, walk more unsteadily, rest more dangerously, are pitied more rarely, are cleansed more slowly, die more despairingly, and are condemned more severely."[2] At the very time Meyer was thus denouncing the cloisters, John Heim, reader of the Dominicans, was exclaiming from the pulpit : " No ! Christ has not, as the evangelists teach, made satisfaction to his Father once for all. It is further necessary that God should every day be reconciled to man by the sacrifice of the mass and by good works." Two citizens who chanced to be present, interrupted him by saying : " It is not true." There was immediately a great disturbance in the church ; Heim remained silent ; many persons urged him to continue, but he left the pulpit without finishing his sermon. On the morrow, the Great Council struck a blow at once against Rome and the Reformation ; they turned the two great controversialists, Meyer and Heim, out of the city. It was said of the Bernese, " they are neither muddy nor clear,"[1]—a play on the word *Luther*, which in old German signifies *clear*.[2]

But in vain did they seek to stifle the Reformation in Berne. It was advancing on every side. The sisters of the convent of the Island had not forgotten Haller's visit. Clara May and several of her friends, anxiously pondering on what they ought to do, wrote to the learned Henry Bullinger. " St. Paul," replied he, " enjoins young women not to make vows, but to marry, and not to live in idleness under a false show of piety. (1 Timothy v. 13, 14.) Follow Jesus Christ in humility, charity, patience, purity, and kindness."[3] Clara, praying for help from on high, resolved to adopt this advice, and renounce a life so contrary to the Word of God, invented by men, and fraught with temptation and sin. Her father Bartholomew, who had spent fifty years on the battle-field or in the council-chamber, heard

[1] Dass sie weder luther noch trüb seyen. Kirchhofer, Reform. v. Bern. p. 50.
[2] Romish writers, and M. de Haller in particular, following Salat and Tschudi, both enemies of the Reformation, quote a pretended letter of Zwingle's, addressed about this time to Kolb at Berne. It is as follows :—

" Health and blessing from God our Lord. Dear Francis, proceed gently in the affair ; at first throw the bear only one sour pear among many sweet ones ; then two, and afterwards three ; and when he has begun to eat them, throw him more and more—sour and sweet altogether ; at last empty the sack entirely, hard and soft, sweet, sour, and unripe ; he will eat them all, and will no longer allow them to be taken away, or himself to be driven from them.—Zurich, Monday before St. George's day, 1525.

" Your servant in Christ, ULRICH ZWINGLE."

There are decisive reasons against the authenticity of this letter.—I. In 1525, Kolb was pastor at Wertheimer ; he did not remove to Berne until 1527. (See Zw. Epp. p. 526.) —M. de Haller, indeed, very arbitrarily substitutes 1527 for 1525 : this correction was no doubt very well meant ; but here, unfortunately, Haller is at variance with Salat and Tschudi, who, although they do not agree as to the day on which this letter was alluded to in the diet, are unanimous as to the year, which with both is clearly 1525.—II. There is a difference as to the manner in which this letter was divulged ; according to one version, it was intercepted ; according to another, some of Kolb's parishioners communicated it to an inhabitant of the smaller cantons who chanced to be at Berne.—III. The original is in German ; but Zwingle always wrote in Latin to his learned friends ; and besides he saluted them as their *brother*, and not as their *servant*.—IV. If we read Zwingle's letters, we shall see that it is impossible to find two styles more unlike than that of the pretended letter and his. Zwingle would never have written a letter to say so little ; his epistles are generally long and full of news. To call the paltry jest preserved by Salat *a letter*, is mere mockery.—V. As an historian Salat deserves little confidence, and Tschudi appears to have copied him with a few variations. It is possible that a man of the smaller cantons may have had communication from some Bernese of Zwingle's letter to Haller, which we have mentioned in our second volume (p. 207). where Zwingle employs this same comparison of the bears with much dignity, which moreover occurs in all the authors of that time. This may have suggested to some wag the idea of inventing this spurious letter as addressed by Zwingle to Kolb.
[3] Euerem Herrn Jesu nachfolget in Demuth. Kirchh. Ref. v. B. 60.

[1] Cujus præsidio auxilioque præsentissimo, nos vestram dignitatem assidue commendamus. Zw. Epp, p. 280.
[2] Langsamer gereiniget, verzweifelter stirbt, härter verdammet. Kirchhofer, Reform. v. Bern. p. 48.

of his daughter's resolution with delight. Clara left the convent.

The provost Nicholas Watteville, whose whole interest bound him to the Roman hierarchy, and who was to be raised to the first vacant bishopric in Switzerland, also renounced his titles, his revenues, and his expectations, that he might preserve an unspotted conscience; and snapping all the bonds by which the popes had endeavoured to entangle him, he entered into the marriage state,—a state established by God from the creation of the world. Nicholas Watteville married Clara May; and about the same time, her sister Margaret, the nun of Königsfeldt, was united to Lucius Tscharner of Coire.[1]

CHAPTER VIII.

Basle—Œcolampadius—He visits Augsburg—Enters a Convent—Retires to Sickingen's Castle—Returns to Basle—Ulrich Hütten—His Plans—Last Effort of Chivalry—Hütten dies at Ufnau.

THUS every thing announced the triumphs that the Reformation would soon obtain at Berne. Basle, a city of no less importance, and which was then the Athens of Switzerland, was also arming herself for the great combat that has distinguished the sixteenth century.

Each of the cities of the confederation had its peculiar character. Berne was the city of the great families, and it seemed that the question would be decided by the part adopted by certain of the leading men. At Zurich, the ministers of the Word,—Zwingle, Leo Juda, Myconius, and Schmidt,—carried with them a powerful class of citizens. Lucerne was the city of arms and military capitulations; Basle, of learning and the printing-press. Here Erasmus, the head of the literary republic in the sixteenth century, had taken up his abode; and preferring the liberty he enjoyed in this capital to the flattering invitations of popes and kings, he had become the centre of a numerous concourse of men of letters.

But an humble, meek, and pious man, though in genius far inferior to Erasmus, was destined erelong to exercise in this very city a more powerful influence than that of the prince of the schools. Christopher of Utenheim, bishop of Basle, in concert with Erasmus, was endeavouring to surround himself with men fitted to accomplish a kind of half-way Reformation. With this view he had invited Capito and Œcolampadius to his court. In the latter person there was a taint of monasticism that often annoyed the illustrious philosopher. But Œcolampadius soon became enthusiastically attached to him; and perhaps would have lost all independence in this close intimacy, if Providence had not separated him from his idol. In 1517, he returned to Weinsberg, his native place, where he was soon disgusted with the disorders and profane jests of the priests. He has left us a noble monument of the serious spirit which then animated him, in his celebrated work on *The Easter Revels*, which appears to have been written about that time.[1]

Having been invited to Augsburg about the end of 1518, as cathedral preacher, he found that city still agitated by the famous conference held there in the month of May between Luther and the papal legate. He had to decide between one party and the other; Œcolampadius did not hesitate, and declared in favour of the reformer. This frankness soon gave rise to a violent opposition against him; and feeling convinced that his timidity and the weakness of his voice would be prejudicial to his success in the world, he looked around him, and fixed his eyes on a convent of monks of Saint Bridget, near Augsburg, celebrated for their piety and their profound and liberal studies. Feeling the need of repose, of leisure, of study, and of prayer, he turned towards these friars, and inquired: "Can I live among you according to the Word of God?" The latter having replied in the affirmative, Œcolampadius entered the monastery on the 23d of April 1520, with the express condition that he should be free, if ever the service of God's Word should call him elsewhere.

It was well that the future reformer of Basle should, like Luther, become acquainted with that monastic life which is the highest expression of Roman-catholicism. But here he found no repose; his friends blamed the step; and he himself openly declared that Luther was nearer the truth than his adversaries. Accordingly, Eck and the other Romish doctors pursued him with their menaces, even in his calm retreat.

At this time Œcolampadius was neither reformed nor a follower of Rome; he desired a certain purified catholicism, which is nowhere to be found in history, but the idea of which has often bridged the way to many minds. He began to correct the rules of his order in conformity with the Word of God. "Do not, I beseech you," said he to his brethren, "set a higher value upon your statutes than on the ordinances of God!"— "We desire no other law," replied the brothers, "than that of our Saviour. Take our books, and mark, as if in the presence of Christ himself, whatever you find contrary to His Word." Œcolampadius applied himself to the task, but was almost wearied by the labour. "O Almighty God!" exclaimed he, "what abominations has not Rome approved of in these statutes!"

As soon as he pointed out some of them,

[1] Zw. Epp. annotatio, p. 451. The Tscharners of Berne are descended from this marriage.

[1] Herzog, Studien und Kritiken, 1840, p, 334.

the anger of the monks was aroused. "Heretic!" exclaimed they, "apostate! you deserve to be thrown into a dungeon for the rest of your days!" They excluded him from public prayers. But the danger from without was still greater. Eck and his party had not relinquished their projects. "In three days," he was told, "they will be here to arrest you." He went to the brethren and said, "Will you give me up to assassins?" The monks were silent and undetermined; they had no desire either to save or to destroy him. At this moment some friends of Œcolampadius arrived near the cloister with horses to carry him to a place of safety. On being informed of this, the monks resolved to allow the departure of a brother who had brought trouble into their convent. "Farewell," said he, and was free. He had remained nearly two years in the cloister of Saint Bridget.

Œcolampadius was saved; at last he began to breathe. "I have sacrificed the monk," wrote he to a friend, "and have regained the Christian." But his flight from the convent and his heretical writings were known every where, and every where people shrank back at his approach. He knew not what would become of him, when, in the spring of 1522, Sickingen offered him an asylum, which he accepted.

His mind, oppressed by monastic servitude, took a new flight in the midst of the noble warriors of Ebernburg. "Christ is our liberty," exclaimed he, "and death, which men consider their greatest misfortune, is a real gain to us." He directly began reading the Gospels and Epistles in German to the people. "As soon as these trumpets sound," said he, "the walls of Jericho will fall down."

Thus, in a fortress on the banks of the Rhine, and in the midst of illiterate warriors, the most humble man of his age was preparing for that change of worship which Christianity was shortly to undergo. But Ebernburg was too confined for him, and he felt the need of other society than these armed men. The bookseller Cratander invited him to Basle; Sickingen allowed him to depart, and Œcolampadius, delighted at the thought of seeing his old friends again, arrived in that city on the 16th of November 1522. After having lived there some time, simply as a man of learning without any public occupation, he was nominated curate of Saint Martin's church, and it was this call to an humble and obscure employment[1] that possibly decided the Reformation of Basle. An immense crowd filled the church whenever Œcolampadius went into the pulpit.[2] At the same time the public lectures delivered by himself and Pellican were crowned with such success that even Erasmus was forced to exclaim, "Œcolampadius triumphs."[1]

In effect, this mild yet firm man (says Zwingle) spread around him the sweet savour of Christ, and all those who crowded about him grew in truth.[2] Often, indeed, a rumour was circulated that he would be forced to leave Basle and recommence his perilous pilgrimage. His friends, and Zwingle in particular, were alarmed; but erelong the tidings of fresh victories gained by Œcolampadius scattered their fears and raised their hopes. The renown of his lectures extended even to Wittemberg, and delighted Luther, who talked with Melancthon about him every day. And yet the Saxon reformer was not without anxiety. Erasmus was at Basle, and Erasmus was the friend of Œcolampadius......Luther thought it his duty to put the man whom he loved on his guard. "I much fear," wrote he, "that Erasmus, like Moses, will die in the country of Moab, and never lead us into the land of promise."[3]

Erasmus had taken refuge at Basle, as in a quiet city, lying in the centre of the literary movement, and from the bosom of which he could, by means of the press of Frobenius, act upon France, Germany, Switzerland, Italy, and England. But he did not like men to come and trouble him there; and if he looked upon Œcolampadius with suspicion, another man inspired him with still greater apprehension. Ulrich Hütten had followed Œcolampadius to Basle. For a long while he had been attacking the pope, as one knight engages with another. "The axe," said he, "is already laid at the root of the tree. Germans! faint not in the heat of the battle; the die is cast; the work is begun......Liberty for ever!" He had abandoned Latin, and now wrote only in German; for it was the people he wished to address.

His views were noble and generous. It was his idea that there should be an annual meeting of the bishops to regulate the interests of the Church. A christian constitution, and above all a christian spirit, were to go forth from Germany, as from Judea in other times, and spread through the whole world. Charles V. was to be the youthful hero appointed to realise this golden age; but Hütten having seen the failure of his hopes in this quarter, had turned towards Sickingen, and sought from knighthood what the empire had refused him. Sickingen, at the head of the feudal nobility, had played a distinguished part in Germany; but the princes had besieged him in his castle of Landstein, and the new invention of cannons

---

[1] Meis sumtibus non sine contemptu et invidia. Œcol. ad Pirckh. de Eucharistia.
[2] Das er kein Predigt thate, er hatte ein mächtig Volk darinn, says his contemporary Peter Ryf. Wirtz. v. 350.

[1] Œcolampadius apud nos triumphat. Eras. ad Zwing. Zw. Epp. p. 312.
[2] Illi magis ac magis in omni bono augescunt. Ibid.
[3] Et in terram promissionis ducere non potest. L. Epp. ii. 353.

had crushed those aged walls, intended for resisting other kinds of attack.[1] The taking of Landstein had proved the final defeat of chivalry,—the decisive victory of artillery over shields and lances,—the triumph of modern times over the middle ages. Thus the last exploit of the knights was destined to be in favour of the Reformation ; the first effort of these new arms and this new system of warfare was to be against it. The mailed warriors that fell beneath the unlooked-for storm of balls, and lay among the ruins of Landstein, gave way to other soldiers. Other conflicts were about to begin ; a spiritual chivalry succeeded to that of the Du Guesclins and Bayards. And those old and ruined battlements, those battered walls, those dying heroes, proclaimed with greater energy than even Luther could have done, that not by such allies or by such arms would the Gospel of the Prince of peace obtain the victory.

The fall of Landstein and of chivalry had blasted all Hütten's hopes. Standing beside the corpse of Sickingen, he bade farewell to those brighter days which his imagination had conjured up before him, and losing all confidence in man, he sought only for seclusion and repose. In search of these he visited Erasmus in Switzerland. These two men had long been friends ; but the unpolished and turbulent knight, braving the opinions of others, ever ready to lay his hand upon the sword, dealing his blows right and left on all whom he met, could scarcely live in harmony with the squeamish and timid Dutchman, with his refined manners, his mild and polished language, his love of approbation, and his readiness to sacrifice every thing for its sake, and fearing nothing in the world so much as a dispute. On arriving at Basle, Hütten, poor, sick, and a fugitive, immediately inquired for his old friend. But Erasmus trembled at the thought of receiving at his table a person under the ban of the pope and the emperor, who would spare no one, who would borrow money of him, and who would no doubt be dragging after him a crowd of those " Gospellers" whom Erasmus dreaded more and more.[2] He refused to see him, and shortly after, the magistrates of Basle desired Hütten to leave the city. Wounded to the quick, and exasperated against his timid friend, Hütten repaired to Mulhausen, and there published a violent pamphlet against Erasmus, to which the latter replied in a paper overflowing with wit. The knight had grasped his sword with both hands, and aimed a crushing blow at his antagonist ; the scholar adroitly stepping aside, stung the soldier smartly in return.[3]

Hütten was again compelled to flee ; he reached Zurich, and there met with a generous reception from the noble-hearted Zwingle. But intrigues again compelled him to leave that city ; and after passing some time at the baths of Pfeffers, he repaired with a letter from the Swiss reformer to the pastor John Schnepp, who inhabited the small island of Ufnau in the lake of Zurich. This poor minister entertained the sick and fugitive knight with the most touching charity. It was in this peaceful and unknown retreat that Ulrich Hütten, one of the most remarkable men of the sixteenth century, died obscurely about the end of August 1523, after a most agitated life, expelled by one party, persecuted by another, deserted by nearly all, and having always contended against superstition, but, as it would seem, without having ever possessed the truth. The poor pastor, who had some skill in the healing art, had vainly lavished on him all his care. With him chivalry expired. He left neither money, nor furniture, nor books ;—nothing in the world but a pen.[1] Thus was broken the arm of iron that had presumed to support the ark of God.

CHAPTER IX.

Erasmus and Luther—Vacillations of Erasmus—Luther to Erasmus—Erasmus's Treatise against Luther on Free Will—Three Opinions—Effect upon Luther—Luther on Free Will—The Jansenists and the Reformers—Homage to Erasmus—His Anger—The Three Days.

THERE was in Germany a man more formidable to Erasmus than the ill-fated Hütten : this was Luther. The moment had now arrived when these two great champions of the age were to measure their strength hand to hand. The two reformations at which they arrived were very different. While Luther desired a thorough reform, Erasmus, a friend to half-measures, was endeavouring to obtain concessions from the hierarchy that would unite the extreme parties. The vacillations and inconsistency of Erasmus disgusted Luther. " You desire to walk upon eggs without crushing them," said the latter, " and among glasses without breaking them."[2]

At the same time he met the vacillations of Erasmus with absolute decision. " We Christians," said he, " ought to be sure of our doctrine, and able to say yes or no without hesitation. To presume to hinder us from affirming our belief with full conviction, is depriving us of faith itself. The Holy Ghost is no sceptic ;[3] and He has written in our hearts a firm and strong assurance, which

---

[1] Vol. i. p. 47.
[2] " Ille egens et omnibus rebus destitutus quærebat nidum aliquem ubi moveretur. Erat mihi gloriosus ille miles cum sua scabie in ædes recipiendus, simulque recipiendus ille chorus titulo *Evangelicorum*," writes Erasmus to Melancthon, in a letter in which he endeavours to excuse himself. Er. Epp. p. 949.
[3] Expostulatio Hutteni.—Erasmi Spongia.

[1] Libros nullos habuit, supellectilem nullam, præter calamum. Zw. Epp. p. 313.
[2] Auf Eyern gehen und keines zutreten. L. Opp. xix. 11.
[3] Der heilige Geist ist kein Scepticus. Ibid. 8.

makes us as certain of our faith as we are of life itself."

These words alone suffice to show us on which side strength was to be found. To accomplish a religious transformation, there is need of a firm and living faith. A salutary revolution in the Church will never proceed from philosophical views and mere human opinions. To fertilize the earth after a long drought, the lightning must cleave the cloud, and the windows of heaven must be opened. Criticism, philosophy, and even history may prepare the way for the true faith, but cannot supply its place. In vain would you clear the water-courses and repair the dikes, so long as the rain does not come down from heaven. All human learning without faith is but an aqueduct without water.

Whatever might have been the essential difference between Luther and Erasmus, the friends of Luther, and even the reformer himself, had long hoped to see Erasmus unite with them against Rome. Many sayings which his caustic humour let fall were quoted, as showing his disagreement with the most zealous defenders of Romanism. One day, for instance, when he was in England, he had a keen discussion with Thomas More on transubstantiation : " Believe that you have the body of Christ," said the latter, " and you have it really." Erasmus made no reply. Shortly after, when leaving England, More lent him a horse to carry him to the seaside ; but Erasmus took it with him to the Continent. As soon as More was informed of this, he wrote very severely to him about it. Erasmus, by way of reply, sent him these lines :—

> " You said of the bodily presence of Christ :
> Believe that you have, and you have him !
> Of the nag that I took my reply is the same :
> Believe that you have, and you have him !" [1]

It was not only in England and Germany that Erasmus had thus become known. It was said at Paris that Luther had only opened the door, after Erasmus had picked the lock.[2]

The position taken by Erasmus was by no means easy : " I shall not be unfaithful to the cause of Christ," wrote he to Zwingle, " at least so far as the age will permit me."[3] In proportion as he beheld Rome rising up against the friends of the Reformation, he prudently retreated. He was applied to from all quarters ; the pope, the emperor, kings, princes, scholars, and even his most intimate friends, entreated him to write against the reformer.[4] " No work," wrote the pope,

" can be more acceptable to God, and worthier of yourself and of your genius." [1]

Erasmus long resisted these solicitations ; he could not conceal from himself that the cause of the reformers was the cause of religion as well as of letters. Besides, Luther was an adversary with whom every one feared to try his strength, and Erasmus already imagined he felt the quick and vigorous blows of the Wittemberg champion. " It is very easy to say, Write against Luther," replied he to a Romish theologian ; " but it is a matter full of peril."[2] Thus he would—and yet he would not.

This irresolution on the part of Erasmus drew on him the attacks of the most violent men of both parties. Luther himself knew not how to reconcile the respect he felt for Erasmus's learning with the indignation he felt at his timidity. Resolving to free himself from so painful a dilemma, he wrote him a letter in April 1524, which he intrusted to Camerarius. " You have not yet received from the Lord," said Luther, " the courage necessary to walk with us against the papists. We put up with your weakness. If learning flourishes : if by its means the treasures of Scripture are opened to all ; this is a gift which God has bestowed on us through you ; a noble gift, and for which our thanksgivings ascend to heaven ! But do not forsake the task that has been imposed upon you, and pass over to our camp. No doubt your eloquence and genius might be very useful to us ; but since you are wanting in courage, remain where you are. I could wish that our people would allow your old age to fall asleep peacefully in the Lord. The greatness of our cause has long since gone beyond your strength. But on the other hand, my dear Erasmus, refrain from scattering over us with such profusion that pungent salt which you know so well how to conceal under the flowers of rhetoric ; for it is more dangerous to be slightly wounded by Erasmus than to be ground to powder by all the papists put together. Be satisfied to remain a spectator of our tragedy ;[3] and publish no books against me ; and for my part, I will write none against you."

Thus did Luther, the man of strife, ask for peace ; it was Erasmus, the man of peace, who began the conflict.

Erasmus received this communication from the reformer as the bitterest of insults ; and if he had not yet determined to write against Luther, he probably did so then. " It is possible," he replied, " that Erasmus by writing against you will be of more service to the Gospel than certain dunces who write for you,[4] and who do not permit him to be a simple spectator of this tragedy."

---

[1] Quod mihi dixisti nuper de corpore Christi :
  Crede quod habes, et habes ;
  Hoc tibi rescribo tantum de tuo caballo :
  Crede quod habes, et habes.
        Paravicini Singularia, p. 71.
[2] Histoire Cathol. de notre temps, par S. Fontaine, de l'ordre de St. François, Paris, 1562.
[3] Quantum hoc seculum patitur. Zw. Epp. p. 221.
[4] A pontifice, a Cæsare, a regibus, et principibus, a doctissimis etiam et carissimis amicis huc provocor. Erasm. Zw. Epp. p. 308.

[1] Nulla te et ingenio, eruditione, eloquentiaque tua dignior esse potest. Adrianus Papa, Epp. Er. p. 1202.
[2] Res est periculi plena. Er. Epp. p. 758.
[3] Spectator tantum sis tragœdiæ nostræ. L. Epp. ii. 50L
[4] Quidam stolidi scribentes pro te. Unschuldige Nachricht, p. 545.

But he had other motives besides.

Henry VIII. of England, and the nobility of that kingdom, earnestly pressed him to declare himself openly against the Reformation. Erasmus, in a moment of courage, suffered the promise to be wrung from him. His equivocal position had become a source of constant trouble to him; he loved repose, and the necessity he felt of continually justifying his conduct disturbed his existence; he was fond of glory, and already men were accusing him of fearing Luther, and of being too weak to answer him; he was accustomed to the highest seat, and the little monk of Wittemberg had dethroned the mighty philosopher of Rotterdam. He must then, by some bold step, recover the position he had lost. All Christendom that adhered to the old worship implored him to do so. A capacious genius and the greatest reputation of the age were wanted to oppose the Reformation. Erasmus answered the call.

But what weapons will he employ? Will he hurl the thunders of the Vatican? Will he defend the abuses that disgrace the papacy? Erasmus could not act thus. The great movement that agitated men's minds after the lethargy of so many centuries filled him with joy, and he would have feared to trammel it. Unable to be the champion of Romanism in what it has added to Christianity, he undertook to defend it in what it had taken away. In attacking Luther, Erasmus selected the point where Romanism is lost in Rationalism,—the doctrine of free will, or the natural power of man. Thus, while undertaking the defence of the Church, Erasmus gratified the men of the world, and while battling for the popes, he contended also on behalf of the philosophers. It has been said that he had injudiciously confined himself to an obscure and unprofitable question.[1] Luther, the reformers, and their age, judged very differently; and we agree with them. " I must acknowledge," said Luther, " that in this controversy you are the only man that has gone to the root of the matter. I thank you for it with all my heart; for I would rather be occupied with this subject than with all those secondary questions about the pope, purgatory, and indulgences, with which the enemies of the Gospel have hitherto pestered me."[2]

His own experience and an attentive study of the Holy Scriptures and of St. Augustine, had convinced Luther that the natural powers of man are so inclined to evil, that he cannot, of himself, reach any farther than a certain outward rectitude, altogether insufficient in the eyes of the Deity. He had at the same time recognised that it was God who gives true righteousness, by carrying on freely the work of faith in man by his Holy Spirit. This doctrine had become the mainspring of his religion, the predominant idea in his theology, and the point on which the whole Reformation turned.

While Luther maintained that every good thing in man came down from God, Erasmus sided with those who thought that this good proceeded from man himself. God or man, —good or evil,—these are certainly no paltry questions; and if " trivialities " exist, they must be looked for elsewhere.

It was in the autumn of 1524 that Erasmus published his famous treatise entitled *Dissertation on the Freedom of the Will;* and it had no sooner appeared, than the philosopher could hardly believe his own boldness. With eyes fixed on the arena, he looked tremblingly at the gauntlet he had flung to his adversary. " The die is cast," wrote he with emotion to Henry VIII.; " the book on *free will* has appeared.—Trust me, this is a daring act. I expect to be stoned for it.— But I console myself by the example of your majesty, whom the rage of these people has not spared."[1]

His alarm soon increased to such a degree that he bitterly regretted the step he had taken. " Why was I not permitted to grow old in the garden of the Muses?" exclaimed he. " Here am I, at sixty, driven into the arena, and holding the cestus and the net of the gladiator, instead of the lyre!—I am aware," wrote he to the Bishop of Rochester, " that in writing upon free will, I have gone beyond my sphere......You congratulate me upon my triumphs! Ah! I know not that I triumph. The faction (*i. e.* the Reformation) is spreading daily.[2] Was it then fated, that at my time of life I should be transformed from a friend of the Muses into a wretched gladiator! "

It was no doubt an important matter for the timid Erasmus to have stood up against Luther; he was, however, far from showing any very great boldness. In his book he seems to ascribe but little to man's will, and to leave the greater portion to Divine grace; but at the same time he chose his arguments in a manner to make it be believed that man does every thing, and God nothing. Not daring openly to express his thoughts, he affirms one thing and proves another; and hence we may be allowed to suppose that he believed what he proved and not what he affirmed.

He distinguishes three several opinions, opposed in three different degrees to Pelagianism. " Some think," said he, " that man can neither will, nor commence, and still less perform, any good work, without the special and continual aid of Divine grace; and this opinion seems probable enough.

---

[1] On this subject, M. Nisard says (Erasme, Revue des deux mondes, iii. 411), " We are grieved for our kind, when we see men capable of grappling with eternal truths, fencing all their lives against trivialities, like gladiators fighting against flies."
[2] L. Opp. xix. 146.

[1] Jacta est alea....audax, mihi crede, facinus....expecto lapidationem. Er. Epp. p. 811.
[2] Quomodo triumphans nescio....Factio crescit in dies latius. Ibid. 809.

Others teach that man's will is powerless except for evil, and that it is grace alone which works in us any good; and finally, there are some who assert that there has never been any free will either in angels, or in Adam, or in us, either before or after grace, but that God works in man both good and evil, and that every thing happens from an absolute necessity."[1]

Erasmus, while seeming to admit the former of these opinions, makes use of arguments that confute it, and which the most decided Pelagian might employ. In this manner, quoting the passages of Scripture in which God offers man the choice between good and evil, he adds: "Man must therefore have the power to will and to choose; for it would be ridiculous to say to any one, Choose! when it was not in his power to do so."

Luther did not fear Erasmus. "Truth," said he, "is mightier than eloquence. The victory remains with him who lisps out the truth, and not with him who puts forth a lie in flowing language."[2] But when he received Erasmus's treatise in the month of October 1524, he found it so weak that he hesitated to reply to it. "What! so much eloquence in so bad a cause!" said he; "it is as if a man were to serve up mud and dung on dishes of silver and gold.[3] One cannot lay hold of you. You are like an eel that slips through the fingers; or like the fabulous Proteus who changes his form in the very arms of those who wish to grasp him."

But as Luther did not reply, the monks and scholastic divines began to utter shouts of victory: "Well, where is your Luther now? Where is the great Maccabeus? Let him come down into the lists! let him come forth! Ah, ah! he has met with his match at last! He has learnt now to remain in the back-ground; he has found out how to hold his tongue."[4]

Luther saw that he must write an answer; but it was not until the end of the year 1525 that he prepared to do so; and Melancthon having informed Erasmus that Luther would be moderate, the philosopher was greatly alarmed. "If I have written with moderation," said he, "it is my disposition; but Luther possesses the wrath of Peleus' son (Achilles). And how can it be otherwise? When a vessel braves a storm such as that which has burst upon Luther, what anchor, what ballast, what helm does it not require to prevent it from being driven out of its course! If therefore he replies to me in a manner not in accordance with his character, these sycophants will cry out that we are in collusion."[5] We shall see that Eras-

mus was soon relieved from this apprehension.

The doctrine of God's election as the sole cause of man's salvation had always been dear to the reformer; but hitherto he had considered it in a practical light only. In his reply to Erasmus, he investigated it particularly in a speculative point of view, and endeavoured to establish by such arguments as appeared to him most conclusive, that God works every thing in man's conversion, and that our hearts are so alienated from the love of God that they cannot have a sincere desire for righteousness, except by the regenerating influence of the Holy Spirit.

"To call our will a free will," said he, "is to imitate those princes who accumulate long titles, styling themselves lords of sundry kingdoms, principalities, and distant islands (of Rhodes, Cyprus, and Jerusalem, &c.), while they have not the least power over them." Here, however, Luther makes an important distinction, clearly showing that he by no means participated in the third opinion that Erasmus had pointed out and imputed to him. "Man's will may be called a free will, not in relation to that which is above him, that is to say, to God; but with respect to that which is below, that is, to the things of the earth.[1] As regards my property, my fields, my house, my farm, I can act, do, and manage freely. But in the things of salvation, man is a captive; he is subjected to the will of God, or rather of the devil.[2] Show me but one of all these advocates of free will (he exclaims) that has found in himself sufficient strength to endure a trifling injury, a fit of anger, or merely a look from his enemy, and bear it with joy; then—without even asking him to be ready to give up his body, his life, his wealth, his honour, and all things—I acknowledge you have gained your cause."[3]

Luther's glance was too penetrating not to discover the contradictions into which his opponent had fallen. And accordingly, in his reply, he endeavours to fasten the philosopher in the net in which he had entangled himself. "If the passages you quote," said he, "establish that it is easy for us to do good, why do we dispute? What need have we of Christ and of the Holy Ghost? Christ would then have acted foolishly in shedding his blood to acquire for us a power that we already possessed by nature." In truth, the passages cited by Erasmus must be taken in quite a different sense. This much debated question is clearer than it appears to be at first sight. When the Bible says to man, Choose, it presupposes the assistance of God's grace, by which alone he can do what it commands. God, in giving the commandment, also gives the strength to fulfil it. If Christ said to Lazarus, Come forth, it was not that Lazarus had power to restore him-

[1] De libero arbitrio Diatribe. Eras. Opp. ix. 1215, sqq.
[2] Victoria est penes balbutientem veritatem, non apud mendacem eloquentiam. L. Epp. ii. 200.
[3] Als wenn einer in silbern oder guldern Schusseln wolte Mist und Unflath auftragen. L. Opp. xix. 4.
[4] Sehet, sehet nun da zu! wo ist nun Luther. Ibid. 3.
[5] Ille si hic multum sui dissimilis fuerit, clamabunt sycophantæ colludere nos. Erasm. Epp. p. 819.

[1] Der Wille des Menschen mag....L. Opp. xix. 29.
[2] Ibid. 33.   [3] Ibid.

self; but that Christ, by commanding him to leave the sepulchre, gave him also the strength to do so, and accompanied His words with His creative power. He spoke, and it was done. Moreover, it is very true that the man to whom God speaks, must will; it is he who wills, and not another; he can receive this will but from God alone; but it is in him that this will must be, and the very commandment that God addresses to him, and which, according to Erasmus, establishes the ability of man, is so reconcilable with the workings of God, that it is precisely by these means that the working is effected. It is by saying to the man "Be converted," that God converts him.

But the idea on which Luther principally dwelt in his reply is, that the passages quoted by Erasmus are intended to teach man their duty, and their inability to perform it, but in no way to make known to them the pretended power ascribed to them. "How frequently it happens," says Luther, "a father calls his feeble child to him, and says: 'Will you come, my son! come then, come!' in order that the child may learn to call for his assistance, and allow himself to be carried."[1]

After combating Erasmus's arguments in favour of free will, Luther defends his own against the attacks of his opponent. "Dear Dissertation," says he ironically, "mighty heroine, who pridest thyself in having overthrown these words of our Lord in St. John: *Without me ye can do* NOTHING, which thou regardest nevertheless as the prop of my argument, and callest *Luther's Achilles*, listen to me. Unless thou canst prove that this word *nothing*, not only may, but must, signify *little*, all thy high-sounding phrases, thy splendid examples, have no more effect than if a man were to attempt to quench an extensive conflagration with a handful of straw. What are such assertions as these to us: *This may mean; that may be understood......* whilst it was thy duty to show us that it *must* be so understood......Unless thou doest so, we take this declaration in its literal meaning, and laugh at all thy examples, thy great preparations, and thy pompous triumphs."[2]

Finally, in a concluding part, Luther shows, and always from Scripture, that the grace of God does every thing. "In short," says he at the end, "since Scripture every where contrasts Christ with that which has not the spirit of Christ; since it declares that all which is not Christ and in Christ is under the power of error, darkness, the devil, death, sin, and the wrath of God, it follows that all these passages of the Bible that speak of Christ are opposed to free will. Now such passages are numberless; the Holy Scriptures are full of them."[3]

We perceive that the discussion which arose between Luther and Erasmus is the same as that which a century after took place between the Jansenists and Jesuits, between Pascal and Molina.[1] How is it that, while the results of the Reformation were so immense, Jansenism, though adorned by the noblest geniuses, wasted and died away? It is because Jansenism went back to Augustine and relied on the Fathers; while the Reformation went back to the Bible and leant upon the Word of God. It is because Jansenism entered into a compromise with Rome, and wished to establish a middle course between truth and error, while the Reformation, relying upon God alone, cleared the soil, swept away all the rubbish of past ages, and laid bare the primitive rock. To stop half way is a useless work; in all things we should persevere to the end. Accordingly, while Jansenism has passed away, the destinies of the world are bound up with evangelical Christianity.

Further, after having keenly refuted error, Luther paid a brilliant, but perhaps a somewhat sarcastic, homage to Erasmus himself. "I confess," said he, "that you are a great man; where have we ever met with more learning, intelligence, or ability, both in speaking and writing? As for me, I possess nothing of the kind; there is only one thing from which I can derive any glory—I am a Christian. May God raise you infinitely above me in the knowledge of the Gospel, so that you may surpass me as much in this respect as you do already in every other."[2]

Erasmus was beside himself when he read Luther's reply; and would see nothing in his encomiums but the honey of a poisoned cup, or the embrace of a serpent at the moment he darts his envenomed sting. He immediately wrote to the Elector of Saxony, demanding justice; and Luther having desired to appease him, he lost his usual temper, and, in the words of one of his most zealous apologists, began "to pour forth invectives with a broken voice and hoary hair."[3]

Erasmus was vanquished. Hitherto, moderation had been his strength,—and he had lost it. Passion was his only weapon against Luther's energy. The wise man was wanting in wisdom. He replied publicly in his *Hyperaspistes*, accusing the reformer of barbarism, lying, and blasphemy. The philosopher even ventured on prophesying. "I prophesy," said he, "that no name under the sun will be held in greater execration than Luther's." The jubilee of 1817 has replied to this prophecy, after a lapse of three hundred years, by the enthusiasm and acclamations of the whole Protestant world.

Thus, while Luther with the Bible was setting himself at the head of his age, Eras-

[1] L. Opp. xix. 55. [2] Ibid 116. [3] Ibid. 143.

[1] It is unnecessary to state that I do not speak of personal discussions between these two men, one of whom died in 1600, and the other was not born until 1623.
[2] L. Opp. xix. pp. 146, 147.
[3] M. Nisard, Erasme, p. 419.

mus, standing up against him, wished to occupy the same place with philosophy. Which of these two leaders has been followed? Both undoubtedly. Nevertheless Luther's influence on the nations of Christendom has been infinitely greater than that of Erasmus. Even those who did not thoroughly understand the grounds of the dispute, seeing the conviction of one antagonist and the doubts of the other, could not refrain from believing that the first was right and the second wrong. It has been said that the three last centuries, the sixteenth, the seventeenth, and the eighteenth, may be conceived as an immense battle of three days' duration.[1] We willingly adopt this beautiful comparison, but not the part that is assigned to each of the days. The same struggle has been ascribed to the sixteenth and to the eighteenth century. On the first day, as on the last, it is philosophy that breaks the ranks. The sixteenth century philosophical!......Strange error! No: each of these days has its marked and distinct character. On the first day of the conflict, it was the Word of God, the Gospel of Christ, that triumphed ; and then Rome was defeated, as well as human philosophy, in the person of Erasmus and her other representatives. On the second day, we grant that Rome, her authority, her discipline, her doctrine, reappeared and were about to triumph by the intrigues of a celebrated society and the power of the scaffold, aided by men of noble character and sublime genius. On the third day, human philosophy arose in all its pride, and finding on the field of battle, not the Gospel, but Rome, made short work, and soon carried every intrenchment. The first day was the battle of God, the second the battle of the priest, the third the battle of reason. What will be the fourth ?......In our opinion, the confused strife, the deadly contest of all these powers together, to end in the victory of Him to whom triumph belongs.

CHAPTER X.

The Three Adversaries—Source of Truth—Anabaptism—Anabaptism and Zwingle—Constitution of the Church—Prison—The Prophet Blaurock — Anabaptism at Saint Gall—An Anabaptist Family—Discussion at Zurich—The Limits of the Reformation—Punishment of the Anabaptists.

THE battle fought by the Reformation in the great day of the sixteenth century, under the standard of the Word of God, was not one and single but manifold. The Reformation had many enemies to contend with at once ; and after having first protested against the decretals and the supremacy of the pope, and then against the cold apophthegms of the rationalists, philosophers, or schoolmen,

[1] Port Royal, by M. Sainte Beuve, i. 20.

it had equally to struggle with the reveries of enthusiasm and the hallucinations of mysticism ; opposing alike to these three powers the shield and the sword of Divine revelation.

It must be admitted that there is a great similarity, a striking unity, between these three powerful adversaries. The false systems that in every age have been the most opposed to evangelical Christianity, have always been distinguished by their making religious knowledge proceed from within the man himself. Rationalism makes it proceed from reason ; mysticism from certain inner lights ; and Romanism from an illumination of the pope. These three errors look for truth in man : evangelical Christianity looks for it wholly in God : and while mysticism, rationalism, and Romanism, admit a permanent inspiration in certain of our fellow-men, and thus open a door to every extravagance and diversity, evangelical Christianity recognises this inspiration solely in the writings of the apostles and prophets, and alone presents that great, beautiful, and living unity which is ever the same in all ages.

The task of the Reformation has been to re-establish the rights of the Word of God, in opposition not only to Romanism, but also to mysticism and rationalism.

The fanaticism of the anabaptists, extinguished in Germany by Luther's return to Wittemberg, reappeared in full vigour in Switzerland, and threatened the edifice that Zwingle, Haller, and Œcolampadius had built on the Word of God. Thomas Munzer, having been forced to quit Saxony in 1521, had reached the frontiers of Switzerland. Conrad Grebel, whose restless and ardent disposition we have already noticed,[1] had become connected with him, as had also Felix Manz, a canon's son, and several other Zurichers ; and Grebel had immediately endeavoured to gain over Zwingle. In vain had the latter gone farther than Luther ; he saw a party springing up which desired to proceed farther still. " Let us form a community of true believers," said Grebel to him ; " for to them alone the promise belongs, and let us found a church in which there shall be no sin."[2]—" We cannot make a heaven upon earth," replied Zwingle ; " and Christ has taught us that we must let the tares grow up along with the wheat."[3]

Grebel having failed with the reformer, would have desired to appeal to the people. " The whole community of Zurich," said he, " ought to have the final decision in matters of faith." But Zwingle feared the influence these radical enthusiasts might exercise over a large assembly. He thought that, except on extraordinary occasions when the people

[1] Vol. ii. p. 279.
[2] Vermeintend ein Kilchen ze versammlen die one Sünd wär. Zw. Opp. ii. 231.
[3] Ibid. iii. 362.

might be called upon to express their assent, it was better to confide the interests of religion to a college, which might be considered the chosen representatives of the Church. Accordingly the Council of Two Hundred, which exercised the supreme political authority in Zurich, was also intrusted with the ecclesiastical power, on the express condition that they should conform in all things to the Holy Scriptures. No doubt it would have been better to have thoroughly organized the Church, and called on it to appoint its own representatives, who should be intrusted solely with the religious interests of the people; for a man may be very capable of administering the interests of the State, and yet very unskilful in those of the Church; just as the reverse of this is true also. Nevertheless the inconvenience was not then so serious as it would be in our days, since the members of the Great Council had frankly entered into the religious movement. But, however this may be, Zwingle, while appealing to the Church, was careful not to make it too prominent, and preferred the representative system to the actual sovereignty of the people. This is what, after three centuries, the states of Europe have been doing in the political world for the last fifty years.

Being rejected by Zwingle, Grebel turned to another quarter. Rubli, formerly pastor at Basle, Brödtlein, pastor at Zollikon, and Louis Herzer, received him with eagerness. They resolved to form an independent congregation in the midst of the great congregation, a church within the Church. A new baptism was to be their means of assembling their congregation, consisting exclusively of true believers. "Infant baptism," said they, "is a horrible abomination, a flagrant impiety, invented by the wicked spirit, and by Nicholas II., pope of Rome."[1]

The council of Zurich was alarmed, and ordered a public discussion to be held; and as the anabaptists still refused to abjure their errors, some of the Zurichers among their number were thrown into prison, and several foreigners were banished. But persecution only inflamed their zeal: "Not by words alone," cried they, "but with our blood, are we ready to bear testimony to the truth of our cause." Some of them, girding themselves with cords or ozier twigs, ran through the streets, exclaiming: "Yet a few days, and Zurich will be destroyed! Woe to thee, Zurich! Woe! woe!"—Many uttered blasphemies: "Baptism," said they, "is but the washing of a dog; it is of no more avail to baptize a child than to baptize a cat."[2] The simple-minded and pious were agitated and alarmed. Fourteen men, among whom was Felix Mantz, and seven women, were appre-

hended, in despite of Zwingle's intercession, and put on bread and water in the heretic's tower. After being confined a fortnight, they managed to loosen some planks in the night, and aiding one another, effected their escape. "An angel," said they, "had opened the prison and led them forth."[1]

A monk, who had escaped from his convent, George Jacob of Coire, surnamed Blaurock, as it would seem, from the blue dress he constantly wore, joined their sect, and from his eloquence was denominated a second Paul. This daring monk travelled from place to place, constraining many, by his imposing fervour, to receive his baptism. One Sunday, when at Zollikon, the impetuous anabaptist interrupted the deacon as he was preaching, calling out in a voice of thunder: "It is written, My house is a house of prayer, but ye have made it a den of thieves.' Then raising the staff he carried in his hand, he struck four violent blows.

"I am a door," exclaimed he; "whosoever entereth by me shall find pasture. I am a good shepherd. My body I give to the prison; my life I give to the sword, the stake, or the wheel. I am the beginning of the baptism and of the Lord's bread."[2]

While Zwingle was opposing the torrent of anabaptism in Zurich, Saint Gall was soon inundated with it. Grebel arrived there, and was received by the brethren with acclamations; and on Palm Sunday he proceeded to the banks of the Sitter with a great number of his adherents, whom he there baptized.

The news quickly spread through the adjoining cantons; and a great crowd flocked from Zurich, Appenzel, and several other places to the "Little Jerusalem."

Zwingle's heart was wrung at the sight of this agitation. He saw a storm bursting on these districts where the seed of the Gospel was just beginning to spring up.[3] He resolved to oppose these disorders, and wrote a treatise On Baptism,[4] which the council of Saint Gall, to whom it was addressed, ordered to be read in the church before all the people.

"My dear brethren in the Lord," said Zwingle, "the water of the torrents that issue from our rocks carries with it everything within its reach. At first it is only small stones; but these dash violently against larger ones, until at last the torrent becomes so strong that it carries away all it meets, and leaves in its track wailing and vain regrets, and fertile meadows changed into a wilderness. The spirit of strife and self-righteousness acts in a similar manner: it excites discord, destroys charity, and where it found beautiful and flourishing churches,

---

[1] Impietatem manifestissimam, a cacodæmone, a Nicolao II. esse. Hottinger, iii. 219.
[2] Nützete eben so viel als wenn man eine Katze taufet. Fus. Beyt. i. 243.

[1] Wie die Apostel von dem Engel Gottes gelediget, Bull. Chr. p. 261.
[2] Ich bin ein Anfänger der Taufe und des Herrn Brodes. Füssl. Beytr. i. 264.
[3] Mich beduret seer das ungewitter. Zw. to Council of St. Gall, ii. 230.
[4] Vom Touf, vom Widertouf, und vom Kindertouf. Ibid.

leaves behind it nothing but flocks plunged into mourning and desolation."

Thus spoke Zwingle, the child of the Tockenburg mountains. "Give us the Word of God," exclaimed an anabaptist, who was present in the church; "and not the word of Zwingle." Immediately confused voices were heard: "Away with the book! away with the book!" shouted the anabaptists. After this they rose and quitted the church, crying out: "You may keep the doctrine of Zwingle; as for us. we will keep the Word of God."[1]

This fanaticism now broke forth into the most lamentable disorders. Maintaining that the Lord had exhorted us to become like children, these unhappy creatures began to clap their hands, and skip about in the streets, to dance in a ring, sit on the ground, and tumble each other about in the dust. Some burnt the New Testament, saying: "The letter killeth, the Spirit giveth life." Others, falling into convulsions, pretended to have revelations from the Holy Ghost.

In a solitary house on the Müllegg near St. Gall, lived an aged farmer, John Schucker, with his five sons. They had all of them, including the domestics, received the new baptism; and two of the sons, Thomas and Leonard, were distinguished for their fanaticism. On Shrove Tuesday (7th February 1526), they invited a large party of anabaptists to their house, and their father killed a calf for the feast. The viands, the wine, and this numerous assembly, heated their imaginations; the whole night was passed in fanatical conversation and gesticulations, convulsions, visions, and revelations.[2]

In the morning, Thomas, still agitated by this night of disorder, and having, as it would seem, lost his reason, took the calf's bladder, and placing in it part of the gall, intending thus to imitate the symbolical language of the prophets, approached his brother Leonard, saying with a gloomy voice: "Thus bitter is the death thou art to suffer!" He then added: "Brother Leonard, kneel down!" Leonard fell on his knees; shortly after, "Brother Leonard, arise!" Leonard stood up. The father, brothers, and the other anabaptists looked on with astonishment, asking themselves what God would do. Thomas soon resumed: "Leonard, kneel down again!" He did so. The spectators, alarmed at the gloomy countenance of the wretched man, said to him: "Think of what you are about, and take care that no mischief happens."—"Fear not," replied Thomas, "nothing will happen but the will of the Father." At the same time he hastily caught up a sword, and striking a violent blow at his brother, kneeling before him as a

criminal before the executioner, he cut off his head, exclaiming: "Now the will of the Father is accomplished." All the bystanders recoiled with horror at the deed; and the farm resounded with groans and lamentations. Thomas, who had nothing on but a shirt and trousers, rushed barefooted and bareheaded out of the house, ran to St. Gall with frenzied gestures, entered the house of the burgomaster Joachim Vadian, and said to him with haggard looks and wild cries: "I proclaim to thee the day of the Lord!" The frightful news soon spread through Saint Gall. "He has slain his brother, as Cain slew Abel," said the people.[2] The culprit was seized. "It is true I did it," he continually repeated; "but it is God who did it through me." On the 16th of February, this unhappy creature lost his head by the sword of the executioner. Fanaticism had made its last effort. The eyes of all were opened, and, in the words of an old historian, the same blow cut off the heads of Thomas Schucker and of anabaptism in Saint Gall.

It still prevailed at Zurich. On the 6th of November in the preceding year, a public discussion had taken place, in order to satisfy the anabaptists, who were constantly exclaiming that the innocent were condemned unheard. The three following theses were proposed by Zwingle and his friends, as the subject of the conference, and vigorously maintained by them in the council hall:—

"Children born of believing parents are children of God, like those who were born under the Old Testament, and consequently may receive baptism.

"Baptism under the New Testament is what circumcision was under the Old; consequently, baptism ought now to be administered to children, as circumcision was formerly.

"We cannot prove the custom of re-baptizing either by examples, texts, or arguments drawn from Scripture; and those who are re-baptized crucify Jesus Christ afresh."

But the anabaptists did not confine themselves exclusively to religious questions; they called for the abolition of tithes, on the ground that they were not of Divine appointment. Zwingle replied, that the maintenance of the schools and churches depended on the tithes. He desired a complete religious reform; but was decided not to permit the public order or political institutions to be in the least degree shaken. This was the limit at which he perceived that word from heaven, written by the hand of God, "Hitherto shalt thou come, and no farther."[2] It was necessary to stop somewhere, and here Zwingle and the reformers halted, in spite of those headstrong men who endeavoured to hurry them farther still.

But if the reformers halted, they could not

[1] So wollen wir Gottes Wort haben. Zw. to Council of St. Gall, ii. 237.
[2] Mit wunderbaren geperden und gesprächen, verzucken, gesichten und offenbarungen. Bull. Chr. i. 324.

[1] Glych wie Kain den Abel sinen Bruder ermort hat Bull. Chron. i. 324.
[2] Job xxxviii. 11.

stop the enthusiasts, who seemed placed at their sides as if in contrast with their discretion and prudence. The anabaptists were not content with having formed a church; this church in their eyes was the state. When they were summoned before the tribunals, they declared they did not recognise the civil authority, that it was only a remnant of paganism, and that they would obey no other power than God. They taught that it was not lawful for Christians to fill public offices, or to carry the sword; and resembling in this respect certain irreligious enthusiasts that have sprung up in our days, they looked upon a community of goods as the perfection of humanity.[1]

Thus the danger was increasing; the existence of civil society was threatened. It rose up to reject from its bosom these destructive elements. The government, in alarm, suffered itself to be hurried into strange measures. Being resolved to make an example, it condemned Mantz to be drowned. On the 5th of January 1527, he was placed in a boat; his mother (the aged concubine of the canon) and his brother were among the crowd that followed him to the water's edge. "Persevere unto the end," exclaimed they. When the executioner prepared to throw Mantz into the lake, his brother burst into tears; but his mother, calm and resolute, witnessed with dry and burning eyes the martyrdom of her son.[2]

On the same day Blaurock was scourged with rods. As they were leading him outside of the city, he shook his blue cloak and the dust from off his feet against the state of Zurich.[3] It would appear that two years later this unhappy man was burnt alive by the Roman-catholics of the Tyrol.

Undoubtedly a spirit of rebellion existed among the anabaptists; no doubt the old ecclesiastical law, condemning heretics to death, still existed, and the Reformation could not in one or two years reform every error; and further, there is no question that the Romish states would have accused the Protestant states of encouraging disorder if they had not punished these enthusiasts: but these considerations may explain, although they cannot justify, the severity of the magistrates. They might have taken measures against every thing that infringed the civil authority; but religious errors, being combated by the teachers, should have enjoyed complete liberty before the civil tribunals. Such opinions are not to be expelled by the scourge; they are not drowned by throwing their professors into the water: they float up again from the depth of the abyss; and fire but serves to kindle in their adherents a fiercer enthusiasm and thirst for

martyrdom. Zwingle, with whose sentiments on this subject we are acquainted, took no part in these severities.[1]

CHAPTER XI.

Progression and Immobility—Zwingle and Luther—The Netherlanders at Zurich—Result of Zwingle's inquiries—Luther's Return to Scholasticism—Respect for Tradition—Occam—Contrary Tendency in Zwingle—Beginning of the Controversy—Œcolampadius and the Swabian Syngramma—Strasburg mediates.

It was not, however, on baptism alone that diversities were to prevail; more serious differences were to arise on the doctrine of the Lord's Supper.

The human mind, freed from the yoke that had pressed upon it for so many ages, made use of its liberty; and if Roman-catholicism has to fear the shoals of despotism, Protestantism is equally exposed to those of anarchy. Progression is the character of Protestantism, as immobility is that of Romanism.

Roman-catholicism, which possesses in the papacy a means of continually establishing new doctrines, appears at first sight, indeed, to contain a principle eminently favourable to variations. It has in truth largely availed itself of it, and from age to age we see Rome bringing forward or ratifying new doctrines. But its system once complete, Roman-catholicism has declared itself the champion of immobility. In this its safety lies; it resembles those buildings which tremble at the least motion, and from which nothing can be taken without bringing them wholly to the ground. Permit the Romish priests to marry, or aim a blow at the doctrine of transubstantiation, and the whole system is shaken, the whole edifice crumbles into dust.

It is not thus with evangelical Christianity. Its principle is much less favourable to variations, and much more so to progression and to life. In fact, on the one hand it recognises Scripture only as the source of truth, one and always the same, from the beginning of the Church to the end: how then should it vary as Popery has done? But, on the other hand, each Christian is to go and draw for himself from this fountain; and hence proceed action and liberty. Accordingly, evangelical Christianity, while it is the same in the nineteenth as in the sixteenth century, and as in the first, is in every age full of spontaneity and motion, and is now filling the world with its researches, its labours, bibles, missionaries, light, salvation, and life.

It is a great error to classify together and almost to confound evangelical Christianity with mysticism and rationalism, and to im-

[1] Füssli Beyträge, i. 229-258; ii. 263.
[2] Ohne das er oder die Mutter, sondern nur der Bruder, geweinet. Hott. Helv. K. Gesch. iii. 385.
[3] Und schüttlet sinen blauen Rock und sine Schüh über die Statt Zurich. Bull. Chr. i. 382.

[1] Quod homines seditiosi, reipublicæ turbatores, magistratuum hostes, justa Senatus sententia, damnati sunt, num id Zwinglio fraudi esse poterit? Rod. Gualteri Ep. ad lectorem, Opp. 1544. ii.

pute their irregularities to it. Motion is in the very nature of Christian Protestantism; it is directly opposed to immobility and lethargy; but it is the motion of health and life that characterizes it, and not the aberrations of man deprived of reason, or the convulsions of disease. We shall see this characteristic manifested in the doctrine of the Lord's Supper.

Such a result might have been expected. This doctrine had been understood in very different manners in the former ages of the Church, and this diversity existed until the time when the doctrine of transubstantiation and the scholastic theology began simultaneously to rule over the middle ages. But when this dominion was shaken, the old diversities were destined to reappear.

Zwingle and Luther, who had each been developed separately, the one in Switzerland and the other in Saxony, were however one day to meet face to face. The same spirit, and in many respects the same character, animated both. Both alike were filled with love for the truth and hatred of injustice; both were naturally violent; and this violence was moderated in each by a sincere piety. But there was one feature in Zwingle's character destined to carry him farther than Luther. It was not only as a man that he loved liberty, but also as a republican and fellow-countryman of Tell. Accustomed to the decision of a free state, he did not permit himself to be stopped by those considerations before which Luther recoiled. He had moreover studied less profoundly the scholastic theology, and thus found his motions less fettered. Both were ardently attached to their own convictions; both resolved to defend them; and, little habituated to yield to the convictions of another, they were now to meet, like two proud war-horses, which, rushing through the contending ranks, suddenly encounter each other in the hottest of the strife.

A practical tendency predominated in the character of Zwingle and in the Reformation of which he was the author, and this tendency was directed to two great objects, simplicity of worship and sanctification of life. To harmonize the worship with the necessities of the mind, that seeks not external pomp but invisible things—this was Zwingle's first aim. The idea of the corporeal presence of Christ in the Lord's Supper, the origin of so many ceremonies and superstitions of the Church, must therefore be abolished. But another desire of the Swiss reformer led to the same results. He found that the Roman doctrine of the eucharist, and even that of Luther, presupposed a certain magical influence prejudicial to sanctification; he feared lest Christians, imagining they received Jesus Christ in the consecrated bread, should henceforward less earnestly seek to be united to him by faith in the heart. "Faith," said he, "is not knowledge, opinion, imagination;

it is a reality.[1] It leads to a real union with Divine things." Thus, whatever Zwingle's adversaries may have asserted, it was not a leaning to rationalism, but a profoundly religious view, that led him to his peculiar doctrines.

But there was another element in Zwingle's convictions: he was subject to those historical influences which we must every where recognise in the annals of the Church as in that of the world. It has been long supposed that he was acquainted with the sentiments of Ratram, Wickliffe, and Peter Waldo; but we possess a much safer historical clue to the convictions of the Swiss reformer.

The two Netherlanders, Rhodius and Sagarus, whom we have seen arrive at Wittemberg, and there occasion the first difference between Luther and Carlstadt, had turned their steps towards Switzerland, carrying with them Wessel's manuscripts, and had reached Basle, where Luther himself had commended them to Œcolampadius. The latter person, who was of timid character, finding that Luther did not approve of the opinions which these brethren from Holland were endeavouring to propagate, did not venture to declare his sentiments, and sent them to Zwingle. They arrived at Zurich in 1521, and having waited on the reformer, immediately turned the conversation on the doctrine of the Lord's Supper.[2]

Rhodius and his friend did not at first make known their opinions, but after listening to Zwingle, they gave thanks to God for having delivered them from so great an error.[3] They then presented the letter from Cornelius Hoen, which Zwingle read, and published shortly after.

This letter had an incalculable influence on the destinies of the Reformation. Hoen, resting his arguments on Christ's words in the sixth chapter of Saint John, said: "Christ gives himself to us by means of the bread:[4] but let us distinguish between the bread we receive by the mouth, and Christ whom we receive by faith. Whoever thinks that he receives only what he takes into his mouth, does not discern the body of the Lord, and eats and drinks his own condemnation, because by eating and drinking he bears testimony to the presence of Christ, whilst by his unbelief he remains far from Him."—At the same time the Netherlanders laid Wessel's theses before Zwingle.[5] These writings made a deep impression on the reformer's mind.

1 Fidem rem esse, non scientiam, non opinionem vel imaginationem. Comment. de vera relig. Zw. Opp. iii. 230.
2 Factum est ut Johannes Rhodius et Georgius Sagarus, pii et docti viri, Tigurum venirent, ut de Eucharistia cum Zwinglio conferrent. Lavateri Hist. de origine controv. sacram. Tiguri, 1564, p. 1.
3 Qui cum ejus sententiam audivissent dissimulantes suam, gratias egerunt Deo, quod a tanto errore liberati essent atque Honii Batavi epistolam protulerunt. Ibid.
4 Dominus per panem se ipsum tradit nobis. Epist. Christiana per Honnium Batavum Hist. Ev. i. 231-260.
5 Propositiones ex evangelio de corpore et sanguine Christi sumendo, &c. It is uncertain whether Zwingle had, at this time, received Wessel's treatise de Eucharistia.

The result of Zwingle's inquiries corresponded with his tendencies. By studying Scripture as a whole, which was his custom, and not in detached passages, and by having recourse to classical antiquity for the solution of the difficulties of language, he arrived at the conviction that the word *is*, employed in the formula of the institution of the Lord's Supper, ought to be taken (as Hoen said) in the meaning of *signifies*, and as early as 1523 he wrote to his friend Wittembach that the bread and wine are in the Eucharist what the water is in baptism. " It would be in vain," added he, " for us to plunge a man a thousand times in water, if he does not believe. Faith is the one thing needful."[1]

It would appear, besides, that Zwingle had been prepared,[2] indirectly at least, for these views by Erasmus. Melancthon says : " Zwingle confessed to me (at Marburg) that it was originally from the writings of Erasmus that he had derived his opinions on the Lord's Supper." In fact Erasmus wrote in 1526 : " The sentiments of Œcolampadius would not displease me if the testimony of the Church were not against them. I do not see what an insensible body can do, or what utility would be derived from it, even if we could feel it ; it is enough that spiritual grace be found in the symbols."[3]

Luther at first set out, in appearance at least. from principles very similar to those of the Zurich doctor. " It is not the sacrament that sanctifieth," said he, " but faith in the sacrament." But the extravagances of the anabaptists, whose mysticism spiritualized every thing, led to a great change in his views. When he saw enthusiasts who pretended to a particular inspiration, breaking images, rejecting baptism, and denying the presence of Christ in the Lord's Supper, he was alarmed ; he had a sort of prophetic presentiment of the dangers that would threaten the Church if this ultra-spiritual tendency should get the upper hand, and he accordingly threw himself into the very opposite course ; as a pilot who, seeing his boat lean too much on one side and near foundering, throws himself on the other to restore the equilibrium.

From that time Luther attached a higher importance to the sacraments. He maintained that they were not only signs, by means of which Christians were outwardly distinguished, as Zwingle said, but testimonials of the Divine will, calculated to strengthen our faith. More than this, Christ, in his view, had determined to give believers a full assurance of their salvation, and in order to seal this promise in the most effec-

tual manner, he had added his real body to the bread and wine. " Just as iron and fire," continued he, " which are nevertheless two distinct substances, are confounded together in a heated mass of iron, so that in each of its parts there is at once iron and fire ; in like manner, and with much greater reason, the glorified body of Christ is found in all the parts of the bread."

Thus at this period there seems to have been some return on the part of Luther towards the scholastic theology. In his doctrine of justification by faith he had entirely renounced it ; but in that of the sacrament he abandoned one point only, transubstantiation, and preserved the other, the corporeal presence. He even went so far as to say, that he would rather receive the blood only with the pope, than the wine only with Zwingle.

Luther's great principle was never to depart from the doctrine and customs of the Church, except when the language of Scripture rendered it absolutely necessary. " Where has Christ commanded us to elevate the host and exhibit it to the people ? " Carlstadt had demanded.—" And where has Christ forbidden it," was Luther's reply. In this answer lies the principle of the two Reformations. Ecclesiastical traditions were dear to the Saxon reformer. If he separated from them on several points, it was not until after terrible struggles, and because, above all, it was necessary to obey the Scriptures. But when the letter of the Word of God appeared in harmony with the tradition and usages of the Church, he adhered to it with immovable firmness. Now this was what happened in the question of the eucharist. He did not deny that the word *is* might be taken in the sense indicated by Zwingle. He acknowledged, for instance, that in the words, *That rock was Christ*,[1] it must be so understood ; but he denied that this word must have the same meaning in the institution of the Lord's Supper.

He found in one of the later schoolmen, Occam,[2] whom he preferred to all others, an opinion which he embraced. Like Occam, he gave up the continually repeated miracle, by virtue of which, according to the Roman Church, the body and blood of Christ takes the place of the bread and wine after every consecration by the priest ; and following this doctor, he substituted a universal miracle, worked once for all,—that of the ubiquity and omnipresence of the body of Jesus Christ. " Christ," said he, " is present in the bread and wine, because he is present every where, and above all, wherever he wills to be."[3]

The turn of Zwingle's mind was very different from Luther's. He was less inclined

---

[1] Haud aliter hic panem et vinum esse puto quam aqua est in baptismo. Ad Wittenbachium Ep. 15th June 1523.
[2] Zwinglius mihi confessus est, se ex Erasmi scriptis primum hausisse opinionem suam de cœna Domini. Corp. Ref. iv. 97C.
[3] Nec enim video quid agat corpus insensibile, nec utilitatem allaturum si sentiretur, modo adsit in Symbolis gratia spiritualis. Er. Opp. iii. 941.

[1] 1 Cor. x. 4.
[2] Diu multumque legit scripta Occami cujus acumen an teferebat Thomæ et Scoto. Melancth. Vita Luth.
[3] Occam und Luther, *Studien und Kritiken*, 1839, p. 69.

to preserve a certain union with the universal Church and to maintain his connexion with the traditions of past ages. As a theologian, he looked at Scripture alone, and thence only would he receive his faith freely and immediately, without troubling himself about what others had thought before him. As a republican, he looked to his *commune of* Zurich. It was the idea of the present Church that engrossed his thoughts, and not that of the Church of former times. He clung particularly to these words of St. Paul : *For we being many are one bread, and one body;* and he saw in the Lord's Supper the sign of a spiritual communion between Christ and all Christians. "Whoever acts unworthily," said he, "is guilty of sin against the body of Christ of which he is a member." This thought had a great practical influence over men's minds ; and the effects it produced in the lives of many confirmed Zwingle in it.

Thus Luther and Zwingle had insensibly separated from each other. It is probable however that peace might have subsisted longer between them, if the turbulent Carlstadt, who kept passing to and fro between Switzerland and Germany, had not inflamed these contrary opinions.

A step taken with a view to maintain peace led to the explosion. The council of Zurich, desirous of preventing all controversy, forbade the sale of Carlstadt's works. Zwingle, who disapproved of his violence, and blamed his mystical and obscure expressions,[1] thought himself now called upon to defend his doctrine, both in the pulpit and before the council ; and shortly after wrote a letter to Albert, pastor of Reutlingen, in which he said : "Whether or not Christ speaks of the sacrament in the sixth chapter of St. John, it is very evident that he there inculcates a manner of eating his flesh and drinking his blood, in which there is nothing corporeal."[2] He then proceeded to prove that the Lord's Supper, by reminding the faithful, according to Christ's intention, of his body which was broken for them, procured for them that spiritual eating which alone is truly salutary.

Yet Zwingle shrunk from a rupture with Luther ; he trembled at the thought that these unhappy disputes might tear in pieces that new society which was then forming in the midst of fallen Christendom. But it was not so with Luther. He did not hesitate to class Zwingle with those enthusiasts against whom he had already broken so many lances. He did not reflect that if the images had been taken down at Zurich, it was done legally and by order of the public authority. Accustomed to the forms of the German principalities, he knew but little of the proceedings of the Swiss republics ; and he inveighed against the grave divines of Helvetia, as he had done against the Munzers and the Carlstadts.

Luther having published his *Treatise against the Celestial Prophets*, Zwingle no longer hesitated, and at nearly the same time he gave to the world his *Letter to Albert*, and his *Commentary on True and False Religion*, dedicated to Francis I. In this last he said : "Since Christ, in the sixth chapter of St. John, ascribes to faith the power of imparting eternal life, and of uniting the believer to Him in the closest union, what need have we of more ? Why should He afterwards have ascribed this virtue to His flesh, whilst He himself declares that His flesh profiteth nothing ? The flesh of Christ, so far as it suffered death for us, is of incalculable utility, for it saves us from perdition ; so far as it is eaten by us, it is of no use whatever."

The struggle began. Pomeranus, Luther's friend, rushed into the conflict, and attacked the evangelist of Zurich somewhat too contemptuously. Œcolampadius then began to blush at having so long combated his doubts, and of having preached doctrines that already began to give way in his mind. He took courage, and wrote from Basle to Zwingle : "The dogma of the real presence is the fortress and safeguard of their impiety. So long as they preserve this idol, no one can conquer them." He then entered into the lists, by publishing a book on the meaning of our Lord's words : *This is my body.*[1]

The mere fact that Œcolampadius had joined the reformer of Zurich excited an immense sensation, not only in Basle but in all Germany. Luther was deeply affected by it. Brenz, Schnepff, and twelve other pastors of Swabia, to whom Œcolampadius had dedicated his book, and most of whom had been his pupils, experienced the keenest sorrow. "At this very moment when I am separating from him in a just cause," said Brenz, taking up the pen to reply to him, "I honour and admire him as much as it is possible for a man to do. The bonds of love are not broken between us because we are not of one opinion." He then published, conjointly with his friends, the famous *Swabian Syngramma*, in which he replied to Œcolampadius with firmness but with charity and respect. "If an emperor," said the authors, "give a wand to a judge, saying : 'Take ; this is the power of judging ;' the wand no doubt is a mere sign ; but the words being added, the judge has not only the symbol but the power itself." The true members of the reformed churches may admit this illustration. The *Syngramma* was received with acclamations ; its authors were looked upon as the champions of truth ; many theologians, and even laymen, desirous of sharing in their glory, began to defend the doc-

---

[1] Quod morosior est (Carlstadius) in cæremoniis non ferendis, non admodum probo. Zw. Epp. p. 369.
[2] A manducatione cibi, qui ventrem implet, transilit ad verbi manducationem, quam cibum vocat cœlestem, qui mundum vivificet. Zw. Opp. iii. 573.

[1] He took the word *is* in its usual acceptation, but by *body* he understood a symbol of the body.

trine attacked, and fell upon Œcolampadius.

Strasburg then came forward to mediate between Switzerland and Germany. Capito and Bucer were the friends of peace, and the question in debate was, in their opinion, of secondary consequence; they therefore placed themselves between the two parties, sent one of their colleagues, George Cassel, to Luther, and conjured him to beware of snapping the ties of fraternity which united him with the Swiss divines.

Nowhere did Luther's character shine forth more strikingly than in this controversy on the Lord's Supper. Never were more clearly displayed that firmness with which he clung to a conviction which he believed to be christian, his faithfulness in seeking for no other foundation than Scripture, the sagacity of his defence, his animated eloquence, and often overwhelming powers of argumentation. But never also were more clearly shown the obstinacy with which he adhered to his own opinions, the little attention he paid to the reasons of his opponents, and the uncharitable haste with which he ascribed their errors to the wickedness of their hearts, or to the wiles of the devil. " One or other of us," said he to the Strasburg mediator, " must be ministers of Satan—the Swiss or ourselves."

This was what Capito styled " the frenzies of the Saxon Orestes;" and these frenzies were followed by exhaustion. Luther's health was affected by them; one day he fainted in the arms of his wife and friends; he was a whole week as if in " death and hell."[1]—" He had lost Jesus Christ," he said, " and was tossed to and fro by the tempests of despair. The world was passing away, and announcing by prodigies that the last day was at hand."

But the divisions among the friends of the Reformation were destined to have still more fatal consequences. The Romish theologians exulted, particularly in Switzerland, at being able to oppose Luther to Zwingle. And yet, if after three centuries, the recollection of these divisions should convey to evangelical Christians the precious fruits of unity in diversity and of charity in liberty, they will not have been in vain. Even then, the reformers, by opposing one another, showed that they were not governed by a blind hatred of Rome, and that truth was the primary object of their inquiries. Herein we must acknowledge there is something generous; and conduct so disinterested did not fail to bear fruit, and to extort, even from enemies, a feeling of interest and esteem.

And further than this, we may here again recognise that sovereign hand which directs all things, and permits nothing without the wisest design. Luther, notwithstanding his opposition to the Papacy, was in an eminent degree conservative. Zwingle, on the contrary, was inclined to a radical reform. These two opposite tendencies were necessary. If Luther and his friends had stood alone at the time of the Reformation, the work would have been stopped too soon, and the reforming principle would not have accomplished its prescribed task. If, on the contrary, Zwingle had been alone, the thread would have been snapped too abruptly, and the Reformation would have been isolated from the ages that had gone before.

These two tendencies, which to a superficial observer might seem to have existed only to combat each other, were ordained to complete each other ; and after a lapse of three centuries we can say that they have fulfilled their mission.

CHAPTER XII.

The Tockenburg—An Assembly of the People—Reformation —The Grisons—Disputation at Ilantz—Results—Reformation at Zurich.

THUS the Reformation had struggles to maintain in every quarter, and after having contended with the rationalist philosophy of Erasmus, and the fanatical enthusiasm of the anabaptists, it had still to endure an intestine war. But its great conflict had always been with popery ; and the attack begun in the cities of the plain was now carried on among the most distant mountains.

The mountains of the Tockenburg had heard the sound of the Gospel, and three ecclesiastics were there persecuted by order of the bishop, as inclining to heresy. " Convince us by the Word of God," said Militus, Döring, and Farer, " and we will submit not only to the chapter, but even to the least of our brethren in Christ; otherwise we will obey no one, not even the mightiest among men."[1]

This was truly the spirit of Zwingle and of the Reformation. A circumstance occurred shortly after that inflamed the minds of the inhabitants of these lofty valleys. A meeting of the people took place on Saint Catherine's day; the citizens were assembled, and two men of Schwytz, having come to the Tockenburg on business, were seated at one of the tables; they entered into conversation. " Ulrich Zwingle," said one of them, " is a heretic and a robber !" Steiger, the secretary of state, undertook Zwingle's defence. Their noise attracted the attention of the whole meeting. George Bruggmann, Zwingle's uncle, who was at an adjoining table, sprung angrily from his seat, exclaiming: " Surely they are speaking of Master Ulrich !" All the guests rose and followed

---

[1] In morte et in inferno jactatus. L. Epp. iii. 132.

[1] Ne potentissimo quidem, sed soli Deo ejusque verbo. Zw. Epp. p. 370.

him, fearing a brawl.[1] As the tumult kept increasing, the bailiff hastily assembled the council in the street, and prayed Bruggmann, for the sake of peace, to be content with saying to these men: " If you do not retract your words, it is you who are guilty of lying and thieving."—" Recollect what you have just said," replied the men of Schwytz; " be sure we shall remember them." They then mounted their horses, and galloped off on the road to Schwytz.[2]

The government of Schwytz then addressed a threatening letter to the inhabitants of the Tockenburg, which spread dismay among them. " Be bold and fearless,"[3] wrote Zwingle to the council of his native place. " Be not concerned at the lies they utter against me! Any brawler can call me a heretic; but do you refrain from insults, disorders, debauchery, and mercenary wars; relieve the poor, protect those who are oppressed, and whatever abuse may be heaped upon you, preserve an unshaken confidence in Almighty God."[4]

Zwingle's exhortations produced the desired effect. The council still hesitated, but the people, meeting in their respective parishes, unanimously decreed that the mass should be abolished, and that they would be faithful to the Word of God.[5]

The conquests were not less important in Rhætia, which Salandronius had been compelled to leave, but where Comander was boldly proclaiming the Gospel. The anabaptists, indeed, by preaching their fanatical doctrines in the Grisons, had at first done great mischief to the Reformation. The people were divided into three parties. Some had embraced the views of these new prophets; others, amazed and confounded, regarded this schism with anxiety; and lastly, the partisans of Rome were loud in their exultation.[6]

A meeting was held at Ilantz, in the Gray League, for a public disputation; the supporters of the papacy, on the one hand, the friends of the Reformation on the other, collected their forces. The bishop's vicar at first sought how to evade the combat. " These disputes lead to great expense," said he; " I am ready to lay down ten thousand florins in order to meet them; but I require the opposite party to do as much."—" If the bishop has ten thousand florins at his disposal," exclaimed the rough voice of a peasant in the crowd, " it is from us he has wrung them; to give as much more to these poor priests would be too bad."—" We are poor

people with empty purses," said Comander, pastor of Coire; " we have hardly the means of buying food: where then can we find ten thousand florins?"[1] Every one laughed at this expedient, and the business proceeded.

Among the spectators were Sebastian Hofmeister and James Amman of Zurich; they held in their hands the Holy Bible in Greek and Hebrew. The bishop's vicar desired that all strangers should be excluded. Hofmeister understood this to be directed against him. " We have come provided with a Greek and Hebrew Bible," said he, " in order that no violence may be done in any manner to Scripture. Yet sooner than prevent the conference, we are willing to withdraw."— " Ah!" exclaimed the priest of Dintzen, looking at the books of the Zurichers, " if the Greek and Hebrew languages had never entered our country, there would have been fewer heresies!"[2]—" St. Jerome," said another, " has translated the Bible for us; we do not want the books of the Jews!"—" If the Zurichers are turned out," said the banneret of Ilantz, " the *commune* will interfere."—" Well then," replied others, " let them listen, but be silent." The Zurichers remained accordingly, and their Bible with them.

After this Comander stood up and read the first of the theses he had published; it ran thus: " The christian Church is born of the Word of God; it must abide by this Word, and listen to no other voice." He then proved what he had advanced by numerous passages from Scripture. " He trod with a firm step," said an eye-witness,[3] " each time setting down his foot with the firmness of an ox."— " This is too long," said the vicar.—" When he is at table with his friends listening to the pipers," said Hofmeister, " he does not find the time too long."[4]

Presently a man arose and advanced from the midst of the crowd, tossing his arms about, knitting his brows, blinking his eyes,[5] and who appeared to have lost his senses; he rushed towards the reformer, and many thought he was about to strike him. He was a schoolmaster of Coire. " I have committed several questions to writing," said he to Comander; " answer them instantly."— " I am here," said the reformer of the Grisons, " to defend my doctrine: attack it, and I will defend it; or else return to your place. I will answer you when I have done." The schoolmaster remained a moment in suspense. " Very well," said he at last, and returned to his seat.

It was proposed to pass on to the doctrine of the sacraments. The Abbot of St. Luke's declared that he could not approach such a

---

[1] Totumque convivium sequi, grandem conflictum timentes. Zw. Epp. p. 371.
[2] Auf solches, ritten sie wieder heim. Ibid. p. 374.
[3] Macti animo este et interriti. Ibid. p. 351.
[4] Verbis diris abstinete....opem ferte egenis....spem certissimam in Deo reponatis omnipotente. Zw. Epp. p. 351. There must be a mistake in the dates of one of the letters, 14th and 23d (anno 1524), or else one of Zwingle's letters to his fellow-countrymen is lost.
[5] Parochiæ uno consensu statuerunt in verbo Dei manere. Ibid. p. 423.
[6] Pars tertia papistarum est in immensum gloriantium de schismate inter nos facto. Ibid. p. 400.

[1] Sie wären gute arme Gesellen mit lehren Secklen. Füssl. Beytr. i. 358.
[2] Wäre die Griechische und Hebraische Sprache nicht in das Land gekommen. Ibid. 360.
[3] Satzte den Fuss wie ein milder Ochs. Ibid. 362.
[4] Den Pfeiffern zuzuhören, die....wie dem Fürsten hofierten. Ibid.
[5] Blintzete mit den Augen, rumfete die Stirne. Ibid. 368

subject without awe, and the horrified curate in alarm made the sign of the cross.

The schoolmaster of Coire, who had already made one attempt to attack Comander, began with much volubility to argue in favour of the doctrine of the sacrament according to the text, "This *is* my body."—"My dear Berre," said Comander, "how do you understand these words, John is Elias?"—"I understand," replied Berre, who saw what Comander was aiming at, "that he was really and essentially Elias."—"Why then," continued Comander, "did John the Baptist himself say to the Pharisees that he was not Elias?" The schoolmaster was silent: at last he replied, "It is true." Everybody began to laugh, even those who had urged him to speak.

The Abbot of St. Luke's made a long speech on the eucharist, which closed the conference. Seven priests embraced the evangelical doctrine; complete religious liberty was proclaimed, and the Romish worship was abolished in several churches. "Christ," to use the language of Salandronius, "grew up every where in these mountains, as the tender grass of spring; and the pastors were like living fountains, watering these lofty valleys."[1]

The Reform made still more rapid strides at Zurich. The Dominicans, the Augustines, the Capuchins, so long at enmity, were reduced to the necessity of living together; a foretaste of hell for these poor monks. In the place of these corrupted institutions were founded schools, an hospital, a theological college: learning and charity every where supplanted indolence and selfishness.

CHAPTER XIII.

The Oligarchs—Deputation to Berne—Bernese Mandate of 1526 in favour of the Papacy—Discussion at Baden—Regulations of the Discussion—Riches and Poverty—Eck and Œcolampadius—Discussion—Zwingle's Share in the Discussion—Vaunts of the Romanists—Abusive Language of a Monk—Close of the Disputation.

THESE victories of the Reformation could not remain unnoticed. Monks, priests, and prelates, in distraction, felt that the ground was every where slipping from beneath their feet, and that the Romish Church was on the point of sinking under unprecedented dangers. The oligarchs of the cantons, the advocates of foreign pensions and capitulations, saw that they could delay no longer, if they wished to preserve their privileges; and at the very moment when the Church was frightened and beginning to sink, they stretched out their mailed hands to save it. A Stein and a John Hug of Lucerne united with a John Faber; and the civil authority rushed to the support of that hierarchical

power which openeth its mouth to blaspheme and maketh war upon the saints.[1]

Their first efforts were directed against Berne. The seven Roman-catholic cantons, in collusion with the Bernese oligarchs, sent a deputation to that city, who laid their complaints before the council on Whitmonday 1526. "All order is destroyed in the Church," said the schulthess (chief magistrate) of Lucerne; "God is blasphemed, the sacraments, the mother of God, and the saints, are despised, and imminent and terrible calamities threaten to dissolve our praiseworthy confederation." At the same time the Bernese partisans of Rome, in harmony with the Forest cantons, had summoned to Berne the deputies of the country, chosen from those who were devoted to the papacy. Some of them had the courage to pronounce in favour of the Gospel. The sitting was stormy. "Berne must renounce the evangelical faith and walk with us," said the Forest cantons. The Bernese councils decreed that they would maintain "the ancient christian faith, the holy sacraments, the mother of God, the saints, and the ornaments of the churches."[2] Thus Rome triumphed, and the mandate of 1526 was about to annul that of 1523. In effect, all the married priests not born in the canton were compelled to leave it; they drove from their borders all who were suspected of Lutheranism; they exercised a vigilant censorship over every work sold by the booksellers, and certain books were publicly burnt. Even John Faber, with audacious falsehood, said publicly that Haller had bound himself before the council to perform mass again, and to preach the doctrine of Rome. It was resolved to take advantage of so favourable an opportunity to crush the new faith.

For a long while public opinion had been demanding a discussion; this was the only means left of quieting the people.[3] "Convince us by the Holy Scriptures," said the council of Zurich to the diet, "and we will comply with your wishes."—"The Zurichers," it was every where said, "have made you a promise; if you can convince them by the Bible, why not do so; if you cannot, why do you not conform to the Bible?"

The conferences held at Zurich had exercised an immense influence, and it was felt necessary to oppose them by a conference held in a Romish city, with all necessary precautions to secure the victory to the pope's party.

True, these discussions had been pronounced unlawful, but means were found to evade this difficulty. "It is only intended," said they, "to check and condemn the pestilent doctrines of Zwingle."[4] This being settled, they looked about for a vigorous cham-

---

[1] Vita, moribus et doctrina herbescenti Christo apud Rhætos fons irrigans. Zw. Epp. p. 485.

[1] Revelation xiii. 5, 6, 7.
[2] Actum uff den heil. Pfingsel Montag, 1526. Tschudi.
[3] Das der gmein man, one eine offne Disputation, nit zu stillen was. Bull. Chr. i. 331.
[4] Diet of Lucerne, 13th March 1526.

pion, and Doctor Eck offered himself. He feared nothing. "Zwingle no doubt has milked more cows than he has read books," said he, according to Hofmeister's account.[1]

The Great Council of Zurich sent Dr. Eck a safe-conduct to go direct to Zurich; but Eck replied that he would wait for the answer of the confederation. Zwingle then offered to dispute at Saint Gall or Schaffhausen; but the council, acting on an article of the federal compact, which provided "that every accused person should be tried in the place of his abode," ordered Zwingle to withdraw his offer.

At last the diet decided that the conference should take place at Baden on the 16th of May 1526. This meeting promised to be important; for it was the result and the seal of the alliance which had just been concluded between the clergy and the oligarchs of the confederation. "See," said Zwingle to Vadian, "what Faber and the oligarchs now venture to attempt."[2]

Accordingly, the decision of the diet produced a great sensation in Switzerland. It was not doubted that a conference held under such auspices would be favourable to the Reformation. Are not the five cantons the most devoted to the pope supreme in Baden? said the Zurichers. Have they not already declared Zwingle's doctrine heretical, and pursued it with fire and sword? Was not Zwingle burnt in effigy at Lucerne, with every mark of ignominy? At Friburg, were not his writings committed to the flames? Do they not every where call for his death? Have not the cantons that exercise sovereign rights in Baden declared, that in whatever part of their territory Zwingle made his appearance, he should be apprehended?[3] Did not Uberlinger, one of their chiefs, say that the only thing in the world that he desired was to hang Zwingle, though he should be called a hangman all the rest of his days?[4] And has not Doctor Eck himself, for years past, been crying out that the heretics must be attacked with fire and sword? What then will be the end of this conference? what other result can it have, but the death of the reformer?

Such were the fears that agitated the commission appointed at Zurich to examine into the affair. Zwingle, an eye-witness of their agitation, rose and said: "You know what happened at Baden to the valiant men of Stammheim, and how the blood of the Wirths dyed the scaffold......and it is to the very place of their execution that they challenge us!......Let Zurich, Berne, Saint Gall or even Basle, Constance, or Schaffhausen, be selected for the conference; let it be agreed to dis-

cuss essential points only, employing nothing else than the Word of God; let no judge be set above it; and then I am ready to appear."[1]

Meanwhile, fanaticism was already bestirring itself and striking down its victims. On the 10th of May 1526, about a week before the discussion at Baden, a consistory, headed by that same Faber who had challenged Zwingle, condemned to the flames, as a heretic, an evangelical minister named John Hügel, pastor of Lindau,[2] who walked to the place of execution singing the *Te Deum.* At the same time, another minister, Peter Spengler, was drowned at Friburg by order of the Bishop of Constance.

Sinister rumours reached Zwingle from all quarters. His brother-in-law, Leonard Tremp, wrote to him from Berne: "I entreat you, as you regard your life, not to repair to Baden. I know that they will not respect your safe-conduct."[3]

It was affirmed that a plan had been formed to seize and gag him, throw him into a boat, and carry him off to some secret place.[4] With these threats and persecutions before them, the council of Zurich decreed that Zwingle should not go to Baden.[5]

The discussion being fixed for the 19th of May, the disputants and the representatives of the cantons and bishops began to arrive gradually. On the side of the Roman-catholics appeared in the foremost place the warlike and vain-glorious Doctor Eck; on the side of the Protestants, the retiring and gentle Œcolampadius. The latter was well aware of the perils attending this discussion. "He had long hesitated, like a timid stag worried by furious dogs," says an old historian; at length he decided on going to Baden, previously making this solemn declaration, "I acknowledge no other standard of judgment than the Word of God." At first, he had earnestly desired that Zwingle should share his danger;[6] but he soon became convinced that, if the intrepid doctor had appeared in that fanatical city, the anger of the Romanists, kindling at his sight, would have caused the death of both of them.

The first step was to determine the regulations of the conference. Doctor Eck proposed that the deputies of the Forest Cantons should be empowered to pronounce the final judgment; which was, in truth, anticipating the condemnation of the reformed doctrines. Thomas Plater, who had come from Zurich to attend the colloquy, was despatched by Œcolampadius to ask Zwingle's advice. Arriving during the night, he was with dif-

---

[1] Er habe wohl mehr Kühe gemolken, als Bücher gelesen. Zw. Opp. ii. 405.
[2] Vide nunc quid audeant oligarchi atque Faber. Zw. Epp. p. 484.
[3] Zwingli in ihrem Gebiet, wo er betreten werde, gefangen zu nehmen. Zw. Opp. ii. 422.
[4] Da wollte er gern all sein Lebtag ein Henker genannt werden. Ibid. 454.

[1] Wellend wir ganz geneigt syn ze erschynen. Zw. Opp. ii. 423.
[2] Hunc hominem hæreticum damnamus, projicimus et conculcamus. Hotting. Helv. K. Gesch. iii. 300.
[3] Caveatis per caput vestrum....Zw. Epp. p. 483.
[4] Navigio captum, ore mox obturato, clam fuisse deportandum. Osw. Myc. Vit. Zw.
[5] Zwinglium Senatus Tigurinus Badenam dimittere recusavit. Ibid.
[6] Si periclitaberis, periclitabimur omnes tecum. Zw. Epp. p. 312.

ficulty admitted into the reformer's house. "Unlucky disturber," said Zwingle to him, as he rubbed his eyes, "for six weeks I have not gone to bed, owing to this discussion.[1] ......What are your tidings?" Plater stated Eck's demands. "And who can make those peasants understand such things?" replied Zwingle; "they would be much more at home in milking their cows."[2]

On the 21st of May the conference opened. Eck and Faber, accompanied by prelates, magistrates, and doctors, robed in garments of damask and silk, and adorned with rings, chains, and crosses,[3] repaired to the church. Eck haughtily ascended a pulpit splendidly decorated, while the humble Œcolampadius, meanly clothed, was forced to take his seat in front of his opponent on a rudely carved stool. "All the time the conference lasted," said the chronicler Bullinger, "Eck and his friends were lodged at the Baden parsonage, faring sumptuously, living gaily and scandalously, and drinking much wine, with which the abbot of Wettingen provided them.[4] Eck took the baths at Baden (it was said) but......in wine. The evangelicals, on the contrary, made a sorry appearance, and the people laughed at them, as at a troop of mendicants. Their way of living was in strong contrast to that of the papal champions. The landlord of the *Pike*, the inn at which Œcolampadius lodged, being curious to know what the latter did in his room, reported that every time he peeped in, he found him reading or praying. "It must be confessed (said he) that he is a very pious heretic."

The disputation lasted eighteen days, and during the whole time the clergy walked daily in solemn procession, chanting litanies in order to ensure victory. Eck alone spoke in defence of the Romish doctrines. He was still the champion of the Leipsic disputation, with the same German accent, broad shoulders, and strong lungs,—an excellent town-crier, and in outward appearance having more resemblance to a butcher than a theologian. According to his usual custom he disputed with great violence, seeking to gall his adversaries by sarcasm, and from time to time slipping out an oath.[5] But the president never called him to order.

> Eck stamps with his feet, and thumps with his hands,
> He blusters, he swears, and he scolds;
> Whatever the pope and the cardinals teach,
> Is the faith, he declares, that he holds.[6]

Œcolampadius, on the contrary, with his calm features and noble and patriarchal air, spoke with so much mildness, and at the same time with such courage and ability,

that even his adversaries, affected and impressed, said one to another: "Oh! that the tall sallow man were on our side."[1]......At times, however, he was moved when he saw the hatred and violence of his auditors: "How impatiently they listen to me!" said he; "but God will not forsake his glory; and that is all we seek."[2]

Œcolampadius having combated Dr. Eck's first thesis on the real presence, Haller, who had come to Baden after the opening of the conference, entered the lists against the second. But little used to such conferences, of a timid character, tied down by the orders of his government, and embarrassed by the looks of his avoyer, Gaspard de Mullinen, a great enemy to the Reformation, Haller possessed not the haughty confidence of his opponent; but he had more real strength. When Haller had finished, Œcolampadius returned to the combat, and pressed Eck so closely, that the latter was compelled to fall back on the customs of the Church. "Custom," replied Œcolampadius, "has no force in our Switzerland, unless it be according to the constitution; now, in matters of faith, the Bible is our constitution."

The third thesis on the invocation of saints; the fourth on images; the fifth on purgatory, were successively discussed. No one rose to contest the truth of the two last, which turned on original sin and baptism.

Zwingle took an active part in the whole of the discussion. The Romish party, which had appointed four secretaries, had forbidden all other persons to take notes under pain of death.[3] But Jerome Walsch, a student from the Valais, who possessed an excellent memory, impressed on his mind all that he heard, and on returning home, hastened to commit it to writing. Thomas Plater and Zimmerman of Winterthur carried these notes to Zwingle every day, with letters from Œcolampadius, and brought back the reformer's answers. Soldiers armed with halberds were posted at all the gates of Baden, and it was only by inventing different excuses that these two messengers evaded the inquiries of the sentinels, who could not understand why they were so frequently passing to and fro.[4] Thus Zwingle, though absent from Baden in body, was present in spirit.

He advised and strengthened his friends, and refuted his adversaries. "Zwingle," said Oswald Myconius, "has laboured more by his meditations, his sleepless nights, and the advice which he transmitted to Baden,

[1] Ich bin in sechs Wochen nie in das Beth Kommen. Plater's Leben, p. 263.
[2] Sie verstunden sich bas auf Kuh mälken. Ibid.
[3] Mit Syden, Damast und Sammet bekleydet. Bull. Chr. i. 351.
[4] Verbruchten vil wyn. Ibid. i. 351.
[5] So entwuscht imm ettwan ein Schwür. Ibid.
[6] Egg zablet mit fussen und henden
Fing au schelken und schenden. &c.
Contemporary Poems by Nicholas Manuel of Berne.

[1] O were der lange gäl man uff unser syten. Bull. Chr. i. 353.
[2] Domino suam gloriam, quam salvam cupimus ne utiquam deserturo. Zw. Epp. p. 511.
[3] Man sollte einem ohne aller weiter Urtheilen, den Kopf abhauen. Thom. Plateri Lebens Beschreib. p. 262.
[4] When they asked me: "What are you going to do?" I replied: "I am carrying chickens to sell to the gentlemen at the baths;" for they gave me some chickens at Zurich, and the sentries could not make out how I procured them always, and in so short a time. Plater's Autobiography. p 262. Leben's Beschrieb.

than he would have done by discussing in person in the midst of his enemies."[1]

During the whole conference, the Roman-catholics were in commotion, sending letters in every direction and loudly boasting of their victory. "Œcolampadius," exclaimed they, "vanquished by Dr. Eck and laid prostrate in the lists, has sung his recantation ;[2] the dominion of the pope will be every where restored."[3] These statements were circulated through the cantons, and the people, prompt to believe every thing they heard, gave credit to all the vaunts of the Romish partisans.

When the dispute was finished, the monk Murner of Lucerne, nicknamed "the tom-cat," stepped forward, and read forty charges against Zwingle. " I thought," said he, that the coward would come and reply to them ; but he has not appeared. Well, then, by every law, both human and divine, I declare forty times that the tyrant of Zurich and all his partisans are traitors, liars, per-jurers, adulterers, infidels, robbers, sacrile-gers, gallows-birds, and such that every honest man must blush at having any inter-course whatever with them." Such was the abuse which at this time was honoured with the name of " christian controversy," by doctors whom the Romish church should herself disavow.

Great agitation prevailed in Baden ; the general impression was, that the Roman champions had talked the loudest, but argued the weakest.[4] Only Œcolampadius and ten of his friends voted against Eck's theses ; while eighty persons, including the presi-dents of the debate and all the monks of Wittingen, adopted them. Haller had quitted Baden before the end of the conference.

The majority of the diet then decreed that, as Zwingle, the chief of this pestilent doctrine, had refused to appear, and as the ministers who had come to Baden had re-sisted all conviction, they were all together cast out from the bosom of the catholic church.[5]

CHAPTER XIV.

Consequences at Basle, Berne, Saint Gall, and other Places —Diet at Zurich—The small Cantons—Threats against Berne—Foreign Support.

But this famous conference, owing to the zeal of the oligarchs and clergy, was destined to be fatal to both. Those who had com-bated for the Gospel were, on their return home, to fill their countrymen with enthu-siasm for the cause they had defended, and two of the most important cantons in the Helvetic alliance, Berne and Basle, were thenceforth to begin their separation from the papacy.

The first blows were to fall on Œcolampa-dius, a stranger in Switzerland ; and he did not return to Basle without apprehension. But his anxiety was soon dissipated. The mildness of his language had struck all im-partial witnesses, much more than the cla-mours of Dr. Eck, and all pious men received him with acclamation. The adversaries made, in truth, every exertion to drive him from the pulpit, but in vain ; he taught and preached with greater energy than before, and the people had never shown such thirst for the Word.[1]

Similar results followed at Berne. The conference at Baden, intended to crush the Reformation, gave it a new impulse in this canton, the most powerful of all the Swiss league. Haller had no sooner arrived in the capital, than the Smaller Council summoned him before them, and ordered him to cele-brate the mass. Haller demanded permis-sion to reply before the Great Council, and the people, thinking it their duty to defend their pastor, hastened to the spot. Haller in alarm declared that he would rather leave the city than be the occasion of any distur-bance. Upon this, tranquillity being re-stored : " If I am required to perform this ceremony," said the reformer, " I must re-sign my office ; the honour of God and the truth of his Holy Word are dearer to me than any care about what I shall eat or wherewithal I shall be clothed." Haller uttered these words with emotion ; the mem-bers of the council were affected ; even some of his opponents burst into tears.[2] Once more it was found that moderation was stronger than force. To satisfy Rome in some degree, Haller was deprived of his canonry, but nominated preacher. His most violent enemies, Lewis and Anthony Dies-bach, and Anthony d'Erlach, incensed at this resolution, immediately withdrew from the council and the city, and renounced their citizenship. " Berne stumbled," said Haller, " but has risen up again with greater strength than ever." This firmness in the Bernese made a deep impression in Switzerland.[3]

But the results of the conference at Baden were not limited to Basle and Berne. While these events were taking place in these powerful cities, a movement, more or less similar, was going on in several other states of the confederation. The preachers of St. Gall, on their return from Baden, proclaimed

---

[1] Quam laborasset disputando vel inter medios hostes. Osw. Myc. Vita Zw.—See also Zwingle's several writings having reference to the Baden disputation. Opp. ii. pp. 394-520.
[2] Œcolampadius victus jacet in arena prostratus ab Ec-cio, herbam porrexit. Zw. Epp. p. 514.
[3] Spem concipiunt lætam fore ut regnum ipsorum resti-tuatur. Ibid. 513.
[4] Die Evangelische weren wol *uberschryen*, nicht aber *uberdisputiert* worden. Hotting. Helv. K. Gesch. iii. 320.
[5] Von gemeiner Kylchen ussgestossen. Bull. Chr. p. 355

[1] Plebe Verbi Domini admodum sitiente. Zw. Epp. p. 518.
[2] Tiliier. Gesch. v. Bern., iii. 242.
[3] Profuit hic nobis Bernates tam dextre in servando Berchtoldo suo egisse. Ecol. ad Zw. Epp. p. 518.

the Gospel;[1] the images were removed from the parochial church of St. Lawrence after a conference, and the inhabitants sold their costly garments, their jewels, rings, and gold chains, to found almshouses. The Reformation despoiled, but it was to clothe the poor; and the spoils were those of the reformed themselves.[2]

At Mulhausen the Gospel was preached with fresh courage; Thurgovia and the Rheinthal daily approximated more and more to Zurich. Immediately after the disputation, Zurzach removed the images from its churches, and almost the whole district of Baden received the Gospel.

Nothing was better calculated to show which party had really triumphed; and hence Zwingle, as he looked around him, gave glory to God. "We have been attacked in many ways," said he, "but the Lord is not only above their threats, but also above the wars themselves. In the city and canton of Zurich there is an admirable agreement in favour of the Gospel. We shall overcome all things by prayer offered up with faith."[3] And shortly after, addressing Haller, Zwingle said: "Every thing here below has its course. The rude north wind is followed by the gentle breeze. After the scorching heat of summer, autumn pours forth its treasures. And now, after severe contests, the Creator of all things, whom we serve, has opened a way for us into the camp of our adversaries. At last we may welcome among us the christian doctrine, that dove so long repulsed, and which ceased not to watch for the hour of her return. Be thou the Noah to receive and save her."

This same year, Zurich had made an important acquisition. Conrad Pellican, superior of the Franciscans at Basle, professor of divinity at the age of twenty-four, had been invited, through Zwingle's exertions, to be Hebrew professor at Zurich. "I have long since renounced the pope," said he on arriving, "and desired to live to Jesus Christ."[4] Pellican, by his critical talents, became one of the most useful labourers in the work of the Reformation.

Zurich, still excluded from the diet by the Romish cantons, wishing to take advantage of the more favourable disposition manifested by some of the confederates, convened, in the beginning of 1527, a diet to be held in Zurich itself. The deputies of Berne, Basle, Schaffhausen, Appenzell, and St. Gall, attended it. "We desire, said the deputies of Zurich, "that the Word of God, which leads us solely to Christ crucified, should be the only thing preached, taught, and exalted. We abandon all human doctrines, whatever may have been the custom of our forefathers; being assured that had they possessed this light of the Divine Word which we enjoy, they would have embraced it with more reverence than we their feeble descendants have done."[1] The deputies present promised to take the representations of Zurich into consideration.

Thus the breach in the walls of Rome was widened daily. The discussion at Baden had been intended to repair it; and from that time, on the contrary, the wavering cantons seemed willing to walk with Zurich. Already the inhabitants of the plain inclined towards the Reformation; already it was hemming in the mountains; already it was invading them, and the primitive cantons, which were as the cradle, and are still the citadel, of Switzerland, shut up in their higher Alps, seemed alone to adhere firmly to the doctrine of their sires. These mountaineers, continually exposed to violent storms, to avalanches, to overflowing torrents and rivers, are compelled all their lives to struggle against these formidable enemies, and to sacrifice every thing to preserve the meadow in which their herds graze, and the cottage where they shelter themselves from the storms, and which the first inundation sweeps away. Accordingly the conservative principle is strongly developed in them, and transmitted from age to age, from generation to generation. To preserve what they have received from their fathers constitutes the whole wisdom of these mountains. These rude Helvetians were then struggling against the Reformation, which aimed at changing their faith and their worship, as they struggle to this day against the torrents that fall in thunder from their snowy peaks, or against the new political ideas that have been established at their very doors in the surrounding cantons. They will be the last to lay down their arms before that twofold power which already raises its banners on all the hills around, and threatens daily and more nearly these conservative districts.

Accordingly these cantons, at the period which I am recording, still more irritated against Berne than against Zurich, and trembling lest this powerful state should desert them, assembled their deputies in Berne itself a week after the conference at Zurich. They called on the council to depose the new teachers, to prosecute their doctrines, and to maintain the ancient and true christian faith, as confirmed by past ages, and confessed by the martyrs. "Convoke all the bailiwicks of the canton," added they; "if you refuse, we will take it upon ourselves." The Bernese replied with irritation: "We have power enough ourselves to speak to those under our jurisdiction."

This reply only increased the anger of the Forest Cantons, and these cantons, which

[1] San Gallenses officiis suis restitutos. Zw. Epp. p. 518.
[2] Kostbare Kleider, Kleinodien, Ring, Ketten, &c. freywillig verkauft. Hott. iii. p. 338.
[3] Fideli enim oratione omnia superabimus. Zw. Epp. p. 519.
[4] Jamdudum papæ renuntiavi et Christo vivere concupivi. Ibid. 455.

[1] Mit höherem Werth und mehr Dankbarkeit dann wir angenommen. Zurich. Archiv. Absch. Sonntag nach Lichtmesse.

had been the cradle of the political freedom of Switzerland, alarmed at the progress of religious liberty, began to seek, even from without, for allies to destroy it. To combat the enemies of foreign service, that foreign service might reasonably be resorted to; and if the oligarchy of Switzerland could not suffice alone, was it not natural to have recourse to the princes, their allies ? In fact, Austria, who had found it impossible to maintain her own authority in the confederation, was ready to interfere to strengthen the power of Rome. Berne learnt with dismay that Ferdinand, brother of Charles V., was making preparations against Zurich and all those who adhered to the Reformation.[1] Circumstances were becoming more critical. A succession of events, more or less unfortunate, the excesses of the anabaptists, the disputes with Luther on the Eucharist, and others besides, appear to have seriously compromised the Reformation in Switzerland. The discussion at Baden had disappointed the hopes of the papal party, and the sword they had brandished against their adversaries had broken in their hands ; but this had only increased their vexation and anger, and they were preparing for a fresh effort. Already the imperial power itself was beginning to move ; and the Austrian

[1] Berne to Zurich, Monday after *Misericorde*. Kirchhoff. B. Haller, p. 85.

bands which had been routed in the defiles of Morgarten and on the heights of Sempach, were ready to enter Switzerland with colours flying to re-establish the tottering power of Rome. The moment was critical ; it was no longer possible to halt between two opinions, and be neither " muddy nor clear." Berne and other cantons, which had long hesitated, were now to come to a decision. They must either promptly return to the papacy, or take their stand with fresh courage under the banners of Christ.

A Frenchman from the mountains of Dauphiny, William Farel by name, at this time gave a powerful impulse to Switzerland, decided the Reformation of Roman Helvetia, still immersed in deep slumber, and thus turned the balance throughout the whole confederation in favour of the new doctrines. Farel arrived on the field of battle like those fresh troops which, when the issue of the contest hangs in the balance, rush into the thickest of the fight and decide the victory. He prepared the way in Switzerland for another Frenchman, whose austere faith and commanding genius were to put a finishing hand to the Reformation, and make the work complete. By means of these illustrious men, France took her part in that vast commotion which agitated christian society. It is now time that we should turn our eyes towards that country.

BOOK XII.

THE FRENCH. 1500—1526.

CHAPTER I.

Universality of Christianity—Enemies of the Reform in France—Heresy and Persecution in Dauphiny—A country Mansion—The Farel Family—Pilgrimage to the Holy Cross—Immorality and Superstition—William desires to become a Student.

UNIVERSALITY is one of the essential characteristics of Christianity. It is not so with human religions. They are adapted to certain nations, and to the degree of cultivation at which they have arrived ; they keep these nations stationary, or if by any extraordinary circumstance the people attain a fuller growth, their religion is left behind, and by that means becomes useless to them.

There has been an Egyptian, a Grecian, a Latin, and even a Jewish religion ; Christianity is the only religion of mankind.

Its starting point in man is sin ; and this is a characteristic not peculiar to any one **race**, but is the heritage of every human

being. Hence the Gospel, as satisfying the universal and most elevated wants of our nature, is received as coming from God by the most barbarous and by the most civilized nations. It does not, like the religions of antiquity, deify national peculiarities ; but it does not destroy them as modern cosmopolitism would do. It does better; it sanctifies, ennobles, and raises them to a holy unity by the new and living principle it communicates to them.

The introduction of Christianity into the world has wrought a great revolution in history. Until then, there had only been a history of nations ; now there is a history of mankind ; and the idea of a universal education of the human race, accomplished by Jesus Christ, has become the historian's compass, the clue to history, and the hope of the nations.

But Christianity exerts its influence not

only on all nations, but also on every period of their history.

At the moment of its appearance, the world was like a torch about to become extinct, and Christianity rekindled it with fire from heaven.

Subsequently, the barbarian tribes, having rushed upon the Roman empire, had shattered and confounded every thing; and Christianity, stemming that desolating torrent with the cross, subdued by it the savage children of the north, and gave society a new form.

Yet an element of corruption already lay hid in the religion carried by courageous missionaries to those barbarous tribes. Their faith came from Rome almost as much as from the Bible. This element soon gathered strength; man every where substituted himself for God,—the essential characteristic of the Romish church; and a renovation of religion became necessary. This Christianity accomplished at the epoch of which we are treating.

The history of the Reformation in the countries that we have hitherto surveyed has shown us the new doctrine rejecting the extravagances and of the new prophets; but in the country towards which we now turn our attention, infidelity is the shoal which it has to encounter. Nowhere had bolder protests been made against the superstitions and abuses of the Church: nowhere had there been a more striking development of a certain love of learning, independent of Christianity, which often ends in irreligion. France carried in her bosom two reformations at the same time,—the one of man, the other of God. "Two nations were in her womb, and two manner of people were to be separated from her bowels."[1]

In France, the Reformation had to combat not only with infidelity as well as superstition, but there was a third antagonist which it had not yet encountered, at least in such force, among the people of German origin: this was immorality. The scandals in the Church were very great; debauchery sat on the throne of Francis I. and Catherine de Medicis; and the austere virtues of the reformers irritated these "Sardanapaluses."[2] Every where, no doubt, but especially in France, the Reformation was of necessity not only doctrinal and ecclesiastical, but moral also.

Those violent enemies which the Reformation encountered simultaneously in France, gave it a character altogether peculiar. Nowhere did it so often dwell in dungeons, or so much resemble primitive Christianity in faith, in charity, and in the number of its martyrs. If, in the countries of which we have hitherto spoken, the Reformation was

more glorious by its triumphs, in that which is now to engage our attention, it was still more so by its defeats. If elsewhere it could point to thrones and sovereign councils, here it might point to scaffolds and "hill-side" meetings. Whoever knows what constitutes the true glory of Christianity upon earth, and the features that assimilate it to its Head, will study with a livelier feeling of respect and love the often blood-stained history that we now proceed to relate.

The majority of the men who have afterwards glittered on the stage of the world were born in the provinces where their minds first began to expand. Paris is a tree that presents many flowers and fruits to the eye, but whose roots spread far and wide into the bosom of the earth, to draw from thence the nutritious juices which they transform. The Reformation also followed this law.

The Alps, which beheld bold and christian men spring up in every canton and almost in every valley of Switzerland, were destined in France also to cover with their lengthened shadows the infancy of some of the first reformers. For ages they had guarded the treasure more or less pure in their high valleys, among the inhabitants of the Piedmontese districts of Luzerne, Angrogne, and La Peyrouse. The truth, which Rome could not reach there, had spread from these valleys to the other side of these mountains, and along their base to Provence and Dauphiny.

The year after the accession of Charles VIII., son of Louis XI., a sickly and timid child, Innocent VIII. had assumed the pontifical tiara (1484). He had seven or eight sons by different mothers; and hence, according to an epigram of the times, Rome unanimously saluted him with the name of Father.[1]

There was at that time on all the slopes of the Dauphinese Alps, and along the banks of the Durance, a new growth of the old Waldensian opinions. "The roots," says an old chronicler, "were continually putting forth new shoots in every direction."[2] Bold men called the Roman Church the church of devils, and maintained that it was as profitable to pray in a stable as in a church.

The priests, the bishops, and the Roman legates uttered a cry of alarm, and on the 5th kalends of May (27th April) 1487, Innocent VIII., the father of the Romans, issued a bull against these humble Christians. "To arms," said the pontiff, "and trample these heretics under foot as venomous serpents."[3]

At the approach of the legate, followed by an army of eighteen thousand men and a

---

[1] Genesis xxv. 23.
[2] Sardanapalus (Henry II.) inter scorta. Calvin's Epp. MS.

[1] Octo nocens pueros genuit totidemque puellas.
Hunc merito poterit dicere Roma Patrem.
[2] In Ebredunensi archiepiscopatu veteres Waldensium. hæreticorum fibræ repullularunt. Raynald, Annales Eccles. ad ann. 1487.
[3] Armis insurgant, eosque veluti aspides venenosos......conculcent. Bull of Innocent VIII. preserved at Cambridge. Leger, ii. 8.

number of volunteers, who wished to share the spoils of the Waldenses, the latter abandoned their houses and took refuge in the mountains, caverns, and clefts of the rocks, as the birds flee for shelter when the storm begins to lower. Not a valley, nor a wood, nor a rock, escaped their persecutors; every where in this part of the Alps, and particularly on the Italian side, these poor disciples of Christ were hunted down like beasts of prey. At last the pope's satellites were worn out: their strength was exhausted, their feet could no longer scale the steep retreats of the "heretics," and their arms refused to strike.

In these alpine districts, then disturbed by Romish fanaticism, three leagues from the ancient town of Gap,[1] in the direction of Grenoble, not far from the flowery turf that clothes the table-land of Bayard's mountain, at the foot of the Aiguille and near the pass of Glaize, towards the place where the Buzon takes its rise, stood and still stands a group of houses, half hidden by the surrounding trees, and which bears the name of Farel,— or, in the dialect of the country, Fareau.[2] On an extensive terrace raised above the neighbouring cottages might be seen a house of that class which is denominated *Gentii-hommière*, a manor-house. It was surrounded by an orchard which led to the village. Here, in these days of trouble, dwelt a noble family of established piety, known by the name of Farel.[3] In 1489, the very year in which the papacy was employing its severest measures in Dauphiny, was born in this modest mansion a son who received the name of William. Three brothers, Daniel, Walter, and Claude, and one sister, grew up with William, and shared his sports on the banks of the Buzon and at the foot of the Bayard.

There William's childhood and early youth were passed. His parents were among the most devoted servants of the papacy. "My father and mother believed every thing," he tells us himself;[4] "and accordingly they brought up their children in all the observances of Romish devotion."

God had bestowed rare qualities on William Farel, such as were fitted to give him a great ascendancy over his fellows. Possessing a penetrating mind and lively imagination, sincere and upright, having a greatness of soul that never allowed him, at whatever risk, to betray the convictions of his heart, he was remarkable also for ardour, fire, in-

domitable courage, and daring, which never shrunk from any obstacle. But, at the same time, he had all the defects allied to these qualities; and his parents were often compelled to check his impetuosity.

William threw himself with his whole soul into the superstitious habits of his credulous family. "I am horror-struck," said he, "when I consider the hours, the prayers, and the divine honours, which I myself have offered and caused others to offer to the cross and other such things."[1]

Four leagues to the south of Gap, near Tallard, on a hill that rises above the impetuous stream of the Durance, was a place in great repute, named Sainte Croix (the holy cross). William was only seven or eight years old when his father and mother resolved to take him thither on a pilgrimage.[2] "The cross in that place," they told him, "is made of the very wood on which Christ was crucified."

The family began their journey, and at last reached the highly venerated cross, before which they all fell prostrate. After gazing for a time on the sacred wood and the copper of the cross, the latter being made (as the priest told them) of the basin in which Christ washed his apostles' feet, the pilgrims turned their eyes to a small crucifix attached to the cross: "When the devil sends us hail and thunder," continued the priest, "this crucifix moves about so violently, that it seems to get loose from the cross, as if desirous of running at the devil, and it continues throwing out sparks of fire against the storm; if it were not for this, nothing would be left upon earth."[3]

The pious pilgrims were deeply moved by the account of these wonderful prodigies. "No one," continued the priest, "sees or knows aught of these things except myself and this man." The pilgrims turned their heads, and saw a strange-looking person standing near them. "It was frightful to look at him," said Farel.[4] White scales covered the pupils of his eyes, "whether they were there in reality, or Satan only made them appear so." This extraordinary man, whom the incredulous denominated "the priest's wizard," on being appealed to by the latter, immediately replied that the prodigy was true.[5]

A new episode completed the picture by mingling a suspicion of criminal disorders with these superstitions. "There came up a young woman, intent on other devotion than that of the cross, carrying her infant wrapped in a cloth. Then the priest went up, took hold of the woman and child, and led them into the chapel. I may safely assert, that never did dancer take a woman and lead her out more lovingly than he did.

1 Chief town of the Hautes Alpes.
2 Revue du Dauphiné, July 1837, p. 35. As you go from Grenoble to Gap, a quarter of an hour's journey beyond the last post-house, and about a stone's throw to the right of the high-road, may be seen the village of the Farels. The site of the house inhabited by Farel's father is still shown. It is now occupied only by a cottage, but from its dimensions it may be seen that it could not have belonged to an ordinary house. The present inhabitant bears the name of Farel. I am indebted for this information to M. Blanc, pastor of Mens.
3 Gulielmum Farellum, Delphinatem, nobili familia ortum. Bezæ Icones.—Calvin, writing to Cardinal Sadolet, sets off Farel's disinterestedness—*sorti de si noble maison* (sprung from so noble a family). Opuscula, p. 148.
4 Du vray usage de la croix, par Guillaume Farel, p. 237.

1 Du vray usage de la croix, by W. Farel, p. 239
2 J'estoye fort petit et à peine je savoye lire. Ibid. p. 237. Le premier pèlerinage auquel j'ay esté a esté à la saincte croix. Ibid. p. 233.
3 Ibid. p. 235-239.   4 Ibid. p. 237.   5 Ibid. p. 238.

But such was our blindness, that neither their looks nor their gestures, even when they had behaved in an unseemly manner before us, appeared otherwise than good and holy. It was clear that the woman and my gallant of a priest understood the miracle thoroughly, and made it a cover to their intercourse."[1]

Such is a faithful picture of religion and morals in France at the commencement of the Reformation. Morality and belief were alike poisoned, and both required a powerful renovation. The greater the value attached to external works, the farther men were removed from sanctification of heart ; dead ordinances had been every where substituted for a christian life, and a strange but not unnatural union had taken place between the most scandalous debauchery and the most superstitious devotion. Theft had been committed before the altar, seduction practised in the confessional, poison mingled with the consecrated elements, adultery perpetrated at the foot of the cross. Superstition, by destroying belief, had destroyed morality.

There were, however, numerous exceptions in the Christianity of the middle ages. Even a superstitious faith might be sincere, and of this William Farel is an example. The same zeal that afterwards urged him to travel to so many different places to spread the knowledge of Jesus Christ was at this time attracting him wherever the Church exhibited a miracle or claimed any adoration. Dauphiny had its seven wonders, which long possessed the power of striking the imagination of the people.[2] But the beauties of nature that surrounded him had also their influence in raising his soul to the Creator. The magnificent chain of the Alps, those summits covered with eternal snow,—those vast rocks, here rearing their sharp peaks to heaven, there stretching their immense and jagged ridges high above the clouds, as if an island was suspended in the air ;—all these wonders of creation, which were at this time elevating the soul of Ulrich Zwingle in the Tockenburg, were appealing also in mute but powerful language to the heart of William Farel among the mountains of Dauphiny. He thirsted for life, for knowledge, and for light ; —he aspired to be something great ;—he asked permission to study.

This was a great blow to his father, who thought that a young noble ought to know nothing beyond his rosary and his sword. At this time fame was trumpeting the prowess of a youthful countryman of William Farel's, a Dauphinese like himself, named Du Terrail, but better known as Bayard, who at the battle of the Tar, on the other side of the Alps, had just given a signal display of courage. "Such sons," it was observed, "are like arrows in the hand of a strong man. Blessed is the man that hath his quiver full of them !" Accordingly, Farel's father opposed the taste which William manifested for learning. But the young man was not to be shaken. God destined him for nobler conquests than those of Bayard. He persevered in his entreaties, and the old gentleman gave way at last.[1]

Farel immediately applied to study with surprising ardour. The masters whom he found in Dauphiny were of little help to him, and he had to contend with bad methods and the incapability of his teachers.[2] These difficulties excited instead of discouraging him, and he soon surmounted these obstacles. His brothers followed his example. Daniel afterwards entered on the career of politics, and was employed in important negotiations concerning religion.[3] Walter gained the entire confidence of the Count of Furstemberg.

Farel, eager in the pursuit of knowledge, having learnt all that could be acquired in his province, turned his eyes elsewhere. The renown of the university of Paris had long filled the christian world. He desired to see "that mother of all learning, that true lamp of the Church which never knew eclipse, that clear and polished mirror of the faith, dimmed by no cloud, and spotted by no touch."[4] He obtained the permission of his parents, and set out for the capital of France.

CHAPTER II.

Louis XII. and the Assembly of Tours—Francis and Margaret—Learned Men—Lefevre—His Courses at the University—Meeting between Lefevre and Farel—Farel's Hesitation and Researches—First Awakening—Lefevre's Prophecy—Teaches Justification by Faith—Objections—Disorder of the Colleges—Effects on Farel—Election—Sanctification of Life.

ONE day in the year 1510, or shortly after, the young Dauphinese arrived in Paris. The province had made him an ardent follower of the papacy ; the capital was to make him something very different. In France the Reformation was not destined to go forth, as in Germany, from a small city. All the movements that agitate the people proceed from the metropolis. A concurrence of providential circumstances made Paris, at the beginning of the sixteenth century, a focus whence a spark of life might easily escape. The young man from the neighbourhood of Gap, who arrived there humble and ignorant, was to receive that spark in his heart, and share it with many others.

---

1 Du vray usage de la croix, par Guillaume Farel, p. 235.
2 The burning spring, the cisterns of Sassenage, the manna of Briançon, &c.

1 Cum a parentibus vix impetrassem ad literas concessum. (Farel, Natali Galeoto, 1527. MS. letters belonging to the consistory of Neufchatel.)
2 A præceptoribus præcipue in Latina lingua ineptissimis institutus. Farelli Epist.
3 Vie de Farel. MS. at Geneva.
4 Universitatem Parisiensem matrem omnium scientiarum....speculum fidei torsum et politum....Prima Apellat. Universit. an. 1396. Bulœus. iv. p. 806.

Louis XII., the father of his people, had just convoked the representatives of the French clergy to meet at Tours. This prince seems to have anticipated the times of the Reformation; so that had this great revolution taken place during his reign, the whole of France might have become protestant. The assembly of Tours had declared that the king possessed the right of waging war on the pope, and of enforcing the decrees of the Council of Basle. These measures were the object of general conversation in the colleges, the city, and the court; and must have made a deep impression on the mind of young Farel.

Two children were then growing up in the court of Louis XII. One was a prince of tall stature and striking features, who showed little moderation in his character, and followed blindly wherever his passions led him; so that the king was in the habit of saying: "That great boy will spoil all."[1] This was Francis of Angoulème, duke of Valois, and cousin to the king. Boisy, his tutor, had taught him, however, to honour literature.

By the side of Francis was his sister Margaret, his senior by two years, "a princess," says Brantôme, "of great mind and ability, both natural and acquired."[2] Accordingly, Louis had spared no pains in her education, and the most learned men in the kingdom hastened to acknowledge her as their patroness.

Already, indeed, a group of illustrious men surrounded these two Valois. William Budœus, a man giving the run to his passions, fond of the chase, living only for his hawks, his horses, and his hounds, on a sudden, at the age of twenty-three, had stopped short, sold his hunting train, and applied himself to study with the zeal he had formerly displayed in scouring the fields and forests with his dogs;[3] the physician Cop; Francis Vatable, whose knowledge of Hebrew was admired by the Jews themselves; James Tusan, a celebrated Hellenist; and many others, encouraged by Stephen Poncher, bishop of Paris, by Louis Ruzé, the civil lieutenant, and by Francis de Luynes, and already protected by the two young Valois, resisted the violent attacks of the Sorbonne, who looked upon the study of Greek and Hebrew as the most deadly heresy. At Paris, as in Germany and Switzerland, the restoration of sound doctrine was to be preceded by the revival of letters. But in France the hands that thus prepared the materials were not destined to construct the edifice.

Among all the doctors who then adorned the capital, was observed a man of very diminutive stature, of mean appearance, and humble origin,[4] whose intellect, learning, and powerful eloquence had an indefinable

attraction for all who heard him. His name was Lefevre; and he was born about 1455 at Etaples, a village in Picardy. He had received a rude, or as Theodore Beza calls it, a barbarous education; but his genius had supplied the want of masters; and his piety, learning, and nobility of soul, shone out with so much the brighter lustre. He had travelled much, and it would appear that his desire of acquiring knowledge had led him into Asia and Africa.[1] As early as 1493, Lefevre, then doctor of divinity, was professor in the university of Paris. He immediately occupied a distinguished rank, and, in the estimation of Erasmus, was the first.[2]

Lefevere saw that he had a task to perform. Although attached to the practices of the Romish Church, he resolved to attack the barbarism then prevailing in the university;[3] he began to teach the various branches of philosophy with a clearness hitherto unknown. He endeavoured to revive the study of languages and learned antiquity. He went farther than this; he perceived that, as regards a work of regeneration, philosophy and learning are insufficient. Abandoning, therefore, scholasticism, which for so many ages had reigned supreme in the schools, he returned to the Bible, and revived in Christendom the study of the Holy Scriptures and evangelical learning. He did not devote his time to dry researches, he went to the marrow of the Bible. His eloquence, his candour, his amiability captivated all hearts. Serious and fervent in the pulpit, he indulged in a sweet familiarity with his pupils. "He loves me exceedingly," wrote Glarean, one of their number, to his friend Zwingle. "Full of candour and kindness, he often sings, prays, disputes, and laughs at the follies of the world with me."[4] Accordingly, a great number of disciples from every country sat at his feet.

This man, with all his learning, submitted with the simplicity of a child to every observance of the Church. He passed as much time in the churches as in his study, so that a close union seemed destined to unite the aged doctor of Picardy and the young scholar of Dauphiny. When two natures so similar as these meet together, though it be within the wide circuit of a capital, they tend to draw near each other. In his pious pilgrimages, young Farel soon noticed an aged man, and was struck by his devotion. He prostrated himself before the images, and remained long on his knees, praying with fervour and devoutly repeating his hours. "Never," said Farel, "never had I seen a chanter of the mass sing it with greater re-

---

[1] Mezeray, vol. iv. 127.
[2] Brant., Dames illustres, p. 331.
[3] His wife and sons came to Geneva in 1540, after his death.
[4] Homunculi unius neque genere insignis. Bezæ Icones.

[1] In his Commentary on 2 Thessalonians ii. will be found a curious account of Mecca and its temple, furnished to him by some traveller.
[2] Fabro, viro quo vix in multis millibus reperias vel integriorem vel humaniorem, says Erasmus. Epp. p. 174.
[3] Barbariem nobilissimæ academiæ....incumbentem detrudi. Beza Icones.
[4] Supra modum me amat totus integer et candidus, mecum cantillat, ludit, disputat, ridet mecum. Zw. Epp. p. 26.

verence."[1] This man was Lefevre. William Farel immediately desired to become acquainted with him; and could not restrain his joy when he found himself kindly received by this celebrated man. William had gained his object in coming to the capital. From that time his greatest pleasure was to converse with the doctor of Etaples, to listen to him, to hear his admirable lessons, and to kneel with him devoutly before the same shrines. Often might the aged Lefevre and his young disciple be seen adorning an image of the Virgin with flowers; and alone, far from all Paris, far from its scholars and its doctors, they murmured in concert the fervent prayers they offered up to Mary.[2]

Farel's attachment to Lefevre was noticed by many. The respect felt towards the old doctor was reflected on his young disciple. This illustrious friendship drew the Dauphinese from his obscurity. He soon acquired a reputation for zeal; and many devout rich persons in Paris intrusted him with various sums of money intended for the support of the poorer students.[3]

Some time elapsed ere Lefevre and his disciple arrived at a clear perception of the truth. It was not the hope of a rich benefice or a propensity to a dissolute life which bound Farel to the pope; those vulgar ties were not made for souls like his. To him the pope was the visible head of the Church, a sort of deity, by whose commandments souls might be saved. Whenever he heard any one speaking against this highly venerated pontiff, he would gnash his teeth like a furious wolf, and would have called down lightning from heaven "to overwhelm the guilty wretch with utter ruin and confusion."—"I believe," said he, "in the cross, in pilgrimages, images, vows and relics. What the priest holds in his hands, puts into the box, and there shuts up, eats, and gives others to eat, is my only true God, and to me there is no other, either in heaven or upon earth."[4] —"Satan," says he in another place, "had so lodged the pope, the papacy, and all that is his in my heart, that even the pope had not so much of it in himself."

Thus, the more Farel appeared to seek God, the more his piety decayed and superstition increased in his soul; every thing was going from bad to worse. He has himself described this condition in energetic language:[5] "Alas! how I shudder at myself and at my faults," said he, "when I think upon it; and how great and wonderful a work of God it is, that man should ever have been dragged from such an abyss!"

From this abyss he emerged only by degrees. He had at first studied the profane authors; his piety finding no food there, he began to meditate on the lives of the saints; infatuated as he was before, these legends only made him still more so.[1] He then attached himself to several doctors of the age; but as he had gone to them in wretchedness, he left them more wretched still. At last he began to study the ancient philosophers, and expected to learn from Aristotle how to be a Christian; again his hopes were disappointed. Books, images, relics, Aristotle, Mary, and the saints—all proved unavailing. His ardent soul wandered from one human wisdom to another, without finding the means of allaying its burning thirst.

Meantime the pope, allowing the writings of the Old and New Testaments to be called *The Holy Bible*, Farel began to read them, as Luther had done in the cloister at Erfurth; he was amazed[2] at seeing that every thing upon earth was different from what is taught in the Scriptures. Perhaps he was on the point of reaching the truth, but on a sudden a thicker darkness plunged him into another abyss. "Satan came suddenly upon me," said he, "that he might not lose his prize, and dealt with me according to his custom."[3] A terrible struggle between the Word of God and the word of the Church then took place in his heart. If he met with any passages of Scripture opposed to the Romish practices, he cast down his eyes, blushed, and dared not believe what he read.[4] "Alas!" said he, fearing to keep his looks fixed on the Bible, "I do not well understand these things; I must give a very different meaning to the Scriptures from that which they seem to have. I must keep to the interpretation of the Church, and indeed of the pope."

One day, as he was reading the Bible, a doctor who happened to come in rebuked him sharply. "No man," said he, "ought to read the Holy Scriptures before he has learnt philosophy and taken his degree in arts." This was a preparation the apostles had not required; but Farel believed him. "I was," says he, "the most wretched of men, shutting my eyes lest I should see."[5]

From that time the young Dauphinese had a return to his Romish fervour. The legends of the saints inflamed his imagination. The greater the severity of the monastic rules, the greater was the attraction he felt towards them. In the midst of the woods near Paris, some Carthusians inhabited a group of gloomy cells; he visited them with reverence, and shared in their austerities. "I was wholly employed, day

---

[1] Ep. de Farel à tous seigneurs, peuples et pasteurs.
[2] Floribus jubebat Marianum idolum, dum una soli murmuraremus preces Marianas ad idolum, ornari. Farel to Pellican, anno 1556.
[3] Geneva MS.
[4] Ep. de Farel. A tous seigneurs, &c.
[5] Quo plus pergere et promovere adnitebar, eo amplius retrocedebam. Farellus Galeoto, MS. Letters at Neufchatel.

[1] Quæ de sanctis conscripta öffendebam, verum ex stulto insanum faciebant. Farellus Galeoto, MS. Letters at Neufchatel.
[2] Farel. A tous seigneurs, &c.
[3] Ibid.
[4] Oculos demittens, visis non credebam. Farellus Natali Galeoto.
[5] Oculos a luce avertebam. Ibid.

and night, in serving the devil," said he, "after the fashion of that man of sin, the pope. I had my Pantheon in my heart, and such a troop of mediators, saviours, and gods, that I might well have passed for a papal register."

The darkness could not grow deeper; the morning star was soon to arise, and it was destined to appear at Lefevre's voice. There were already some gleams of light in the doctor of Etaples; an inward conviction told him that the Church could not long remain in its actual position; and often, at the very moment of his return from saying mass, or of rising from before some image, the old man would turn towards his youthful disciple, and grasping him by the hand would say in a serious tone of voice: "My dear William, God will renew the world, and you will see it!"[1] Farel did not thoroughly understand these words. Yet Lefevre did not confine himself to this mysterious language; a great change which was then wrought in him, was destined to produce a similar effect on his disciple.

The old doctor was engaged in a laborious task; he was carefully collecting the legends of the saints and martyrs, and arranging them according to the order in which their names are found in the calendar. Two months had already been printed, when one of those beams of light which come from heaven, suddenly illuminated his soul. He could not resist the disgust which such puerile superstitions must ever cause in the heart of a Christian. The sublimity of the Word of God made him perceive the paltry nature of these fables. They now appeared to him no better than "brimstone fit to kindle the fire of idolatry."[2] He abandoned his work, and throwing these legends aside, turned ardently towards the Holy Scriptures. At the moment when Lefevre, quitting the wondrous tales of the saints, laid his hand on the Word of God, a new era began in France, and was the commencement of the Reformation.

In effect, Lefevre, weaned from the fables of the Breviary, began to study the Epistles of St. Paul; the light increased rapidly in his heart, and he immediately imparted to his disciples that knowledge of the truth which we find in his commentaries.[3] Strange doctrines were those for the school and for the age, which were then first heard in Paris, and disseminated by the press throughout the christian world. We may easily understand that the young disciples who listened to

them were aroused, impressed, and changed by them; and that thus, prior to the year 1512, the dawn of a brighter day was preparing for France.

The doctrine of justification by faith, which overthrew by a single blow the subtleties of the schoolmen and the observances of popery, was boldly proclaimed in the bosom of the Sorbonne. "It is God alone," said the doctor, and the vaulted roofs of the university must have been astonished as they re-echoed such strange sounds, "it is God alone, who by his grace, through faith, justifies unto everlasting life.[1] There is a righteousness of works, there is a righteousness of grace; the one cometh from man, the other from God; one is earthly and passeth away, the other is heavenly and eternal; one is the shadow and the sign, the other the light and the truth; one makes sin known to us that we may escape death, the other reveals grace that we may obtain life."[2]

"What then!" asked his hearers, as they listened to this teaching, which contradicted that of four centuries; "has any one man been ever justified without works?" "One!" answered Lefevre, "they are innumerable. How many people of disorderly lives, who have ardently prayed for the grace of baptism, possessing faith alone in Christ, and who, if they died the moment after, have entered into the life of the blessed without works!"—"If, therefore, we are not justified by works, it is in vain that we perform them," replied some. The Paris doctor answered, and the other reformers would not perhaps have altogether approved of this reply: "Certainly not! they are not in vain. If I hold a mirror to the sun, its image is reflected; the more I polish and clear it, the brighter is the reflection; but if we allow it to become tarnished, the splendour of the sun is dimmed. It is the same with justification in those who lead an impure life." In this passage, Lefevre, like Augustine in many, does not perhaps make a sufficient distinction between sanctification and justification. The doctor of Etaples reminds us strongly of the Bishop of Hippona. Those who lead an unholy life have never received justification, and therefore cannot lose it. But Lefevre may have intended to say that the Christian, when he has fallen into any sin, loses the assurance of salvation, and not salvation itself. If so, there is no objection to be made against his doctrine.

Thus a new life and a new teaching had penetrated into the university of Paris. The doctrine of faith, formerly preached in Gaul by Pothinus and Irenæus, was heard there again. From this time there were two parties, two people in this great school of Christendom. Lefevre's lessons and the zeal

---

[1] A tous seigneurs.—See also his letter to Pellican. Ante annos plus minus quadraginta, me manu apprehensum ita alloquebatur: "Gulielme, oportet orbem immutari et tu videbis!"
[2] A tous seigneurs, peuples et pasteurs.
[3] The first edition of his Commentary on the Epistles of St. Paul is, if I mistake not, that of 1512. A copy is extant in the Bibliothèque Royale of Paris. The second edition is that from which I quote. The learned Simon says (Observations on the New Testament), that "James Lefevre deserves to be ranked among the most skilful commentators of the age." We should give him greater praise than this.

[1] Solus enim Deus est qui hanc justitiam per fidem tradit, qui sola gratia ad vitam justificat æternam. Fabri Comm. in Epp. Pauli, p. 70.
[2] Illa umbratile vestigium atque signum, hæc lux et veritas est. Fabri Comm. in Epp. Pauli, p. 70.

of his disciples formed the most striking contrast to the scholastic teaching of the majority of the doctors, and the irregular and frivolous lives of most of the students. In the colleges, they were far more busily engaged in learning their parts in comedies, in masquerading, and in mountebank farces, than in studying the oracles of God. In these plays the honour of the great, of the princes, of the king himself, was frequently attacked. The parliament interfered about this period; and summoning the principals of several colleges before them, forbade those indulgent masters to permit such dramas to be represented in their houses.[1]

But a more powerful diversion than the decrees of parliament suddenly came to correct these disorders. Jesus Christ was preached. Great was the uproar on the benches of the university, and the students began to occupy themselves almost as much with the evangelical doctrines as with the quibbles of the school or with comedies. Many of those whose lives were the least irreproachable, adhered however to the doctrine of works; and feeling that the doctrine of faith condemned their way of living, they pretended that St. James was opposed to St. Paul. Lefevre, resolving to defend the treasure he had discovered, showed the agreement of these two apostles: "Does not St. James in his first chapter declare that every good and perfect gift cometh down *from above?* Now, who will deny that justification is the good and perfect gift?......If we see a man moving, the respiration that we perceive is to us a sign of life. Thus works are necessary, but only as signs of a living faith, which is accompanied by justification.[2] Do eye-salves or lotions give light to the eye?......No! it is the influence of the sun. Well, then, these lotions and these eye-salves are our works. The ray that the sun darts from above is justification itself."[3]

Farel listened earnestly to this teaching. These words of salvation by grace had immediately an indescribable charm for him. Every objection fell: every struggle ceased. No sooner had Lefevre put forward this doctrine than Farel embraced it with all the ardour of his soul. He had undergone labour and conflicts enough to be aware that he could not save himself. Accordingly, immediately he saw in the Word that God saves freely, he believed. "Lefevre," said he, "extricated me from the false opinion of human merits, and taught me that every thing came from grace: which I believed as soon as it was spoken."[4] Thus by a conversion as prompt and decisive as that of St.

Paul was Farel led to the faith,—that Farel who (as Theodore Beza says) undismayed by difficulties, threats, abuse, or blows, won over to Jesus Christ Montbelliard, Neufchatel, Lausanne, Aigle, and finally Geneva.[1]

Meanwhile Lefevre, continuing his lessons, and delighting, as Luther did, in employing contrasts and paradoxes containing weighty truths, extolled the greatness of the mysteries of redemption: "Ineffable exchange," exclaimed he, "the innocent One is condemned and the criminal acquitted; the Blessing is cursed, and he who was cursed is blessed; the Life dies, and the dead live; the Glory is covered with shame, and He who was put to shame is covered with glory."[2] The pious doctor, going still deeper acknowledged that all salvation proceeds from the sovereignty of God's love. "Those who are saved," said he, "are saved by election, by grace, by the will of God, not by their own. Our own election, will, and works are of no avail: the election of God alone is profitable. When we are converted, it is not our conversion that makes us the elect of God, but the grace, will, and election of God which convert us."[3]

But Lefevre did not confine himself to doctrines alone: if he gave to God the glory, he required obedience from man, and urged the obligations which proceed from the great privileges of the Christian. "If thou art a member of Christ's Church, thou art also a member of his body," said he; "and if thou art a member of Christ's body, thou art full of the Divinity; for in him dwelleth the fulness of the Godhead bodily. Oh! if men could but understand this privilege, how chastely, purely, and holily would they live, and they would look upon all the glory of this world as disgrace, in comparison with that inner glory which is hidden from the eyes of the flesh."[4]

Lefevre perceived that the office of a teacher of the Word is a lofty station; and he exercised it with unshaken fidelity. The corruption of the times, and particularly that of the clergy, excited his indignation, and became the subject of severe rebuke. "How scandalous it is," said he, "to see a bishop asking persons to drink with him, gambling, rattling the dice, spending his time with hawks and dogs, and in hunting, hallooing after rooks and deer, and frequenting houses of ill-fame![5].........O men deserving a severer punishment than Sardanapalus himself!"

[1] Nullis difficultatibus fractus, nullis minis, convitiis, verberibus denique inflictis territus. Bezæ Icones.
[2] O ineffabile commercium!....Fabri Comm. 145, verso.
[3] Inefficax est ad hoc ipsum nostra voluntas, nostra electio: Dei autem electio efficacissima et potentissima est, &c. Ibid. p. 89, verso.
[4] Si de corpore Christi, divinitate repletus es. Ibid. p. 176, verso.
[5] Et virgunculas gremio tenentem, cum suaviis sermones miscentem. Ibid. p. 208.

[1] Crévier, Hist. de l'Université, v. 95.
[2] Opera signa vivæ fidei, quam justificatio sequitur. Fabri Comm. in Epp. Pauli, p. 73.
[3] Sed radius desuper a sole vibratus, justificatio est. Ibid.
[4] Farel. A tous seigneurs.

CHAPTER III.

Farel and the Saints—The University—Farel's Conversion —Farel and Luther—Other Disciples—Date of the Reform in France—Spontaneous Rise of the different Reforms—Which was the first ?—Lefevre's Place.

THUS taught Lefevre. Farel listened, trembling with emotion; he received all, and rushed suddenly into the new path that was opening before him. There was, however, one point of his ancient faith which he could not as yet entirely renounce; this was the invocation of saints. The best spirits often have these relics of darkness, which they cling to after their illumination. Farel was astonished as he heard the illustrious doctor declare that Christ alone should be invoked. " Religion has but one foundation," said Lefevre, " one object, one Head, Jesus Christ, blessed for evermore: alone hath He trodden the wine-press. Let us not then call ourselves after St. Paul, or Apollos, or St. Peter. The cross of Christ alone openeth the gates of heaven, and shutteth the gates of hell." When he heard these words, a fierce conflict took place in Farel's soul. On the one hand, he beheld the multitude of saints with the Church; on the other, Jesus Christ alone with his master. Now he inclined to one side, now to another; it was his last error and his last battle. He hesitated, he still clung to those venerable men and women at whose feet Rome falls in adoration. At length the decisive blow was struck from above. The scales fell from his eyes. Jesus alone appeared deserving of his worship. " Then," said he, " popery was utterly overthrown; I began to detest it as devilish, and the holy Word of God had the chief place in my heart."[1]

Public events accelerated the course of Farel and his friends. Thomas de Vio, who afterwards contended with Luther at Augsburg and at Leipsic, having advanced in one of his works that the pope was the absolute monarch of the Church, Louis XII. laid the book before the university in the month of February 1512. James Allmain, one of the youngest doctors, a man of profound genius and indefatigable application, read before the faculty of theology a refutation of the cardinal's assertions, which was received with the greatest applause.[2]

What impression must not such discourses have produced on the minds of Lefevre's young disciples! Could they hesitate when the university seemed impatient under the papal yoke? If the main body itself was in motion, ought not they to rush forward as skirmishers and clear the way? " It was necessary," said Farel, " that popery should have fallen little by little from my heart; for it did not tumble down at the first shock."[3]

He contemplated the abyss of superstitions in which he had been plunged. Standing on the brink, he once more surveyed its depth with an anxious eye, and shrunk back with a feeling of terror. " Oh! what horror do I feel at myself and my sins, when I think of these things!" exclaimed he.[1] " O Lord," he continued, " would that my soul had served thee with a living faith, as thy obedient servants have done; would that it had prayed to and honoured thee as much as I have given my heart to the mass and to serve that enchanted wafer, giving it all honour!" In such terms did the youthful Dauphinese deplore his past life, and repeat in tears, as St. Augustine had done before: " I have known Thee too late; too late have I loved Thee!"

Farel had found Jesus Christ; and having reached the port, he was delighted to find repose after such terrible storms.[2] " Now,' said he, " every thing appears to me under a fresh aspect.[3] Scripture is cleared up; prophecy is opened; the apostle shed a strong light upon my soul.[4] A voice, till now unknown, the voice of Christ, my Shepherd, my Master, my Teacher, speaks to me with power."[5] He was so changed that, " instead of the murderous heart of a ravening wolf, he came back," he tells us, " quietly, like a meek and harmless lamb, having his heart entirely withdrawn from the pope, and given to Jesus Christ."[6]

Having escaped from so great an evil, he turned towards the Bible,[7] and began to study Greek and Hebrew with much earnestness.[8] He read the Scriptures constantly, with ever increasing affection, and God enlightened him from day to day. He still continued to attend the churches of the established worship; but what found he there? loud voices, interminable chantings, and words spoken without understanding.[9] Accordingly, when standing in the midst of a crowd that was passing near an image or an altar, he would exclaim, " Thou alone art God! thou alone art wise! thou alone art good![10] Nothing must be taken away from thy holy law, and nothing added. For thou alone art the Lord, and thou alone wilt and must command."

Thus fell in his eyes all men and all teachers from the height to which his imagination had raised them, and he now saw nothing in the world but God and his Word. The other doctors of Paris, by their persecutions of Lefevre had already fallen

---

1 Farel. A tous seigneurs.
2 Crévier, Hist. de l'Université de Paris, v. 81.
3 Farel. A tous seigneurs.

1 Farel. A tous seigneurs.
2 Animus per varia jactatus, verum nactus portum, soli hæsit. Farel Galeoto.
3 Jam rerum nova facies. Ibid.
4 Notior scriptura, apertiores prophetæ, lucidiores apostoli. Ibid.
5 Agnita pastoris, magistri, et præceptoris Christi vox. Ibid.
6 Farel. A tous seigneurs.
7 Lego sacra ut causam inveniam. Farel Galeoto.
8 Life of Farel, Geneva and Choupard MSS.
9 Clamores multi, cantiones innumeræ. Farel Galeoto. Neufchatel MS.
10 Vere tu solus Deus. Ibid.

in his esteem; but erelong Lefevre himself, his beloved guide, was no more than a man like himself. He loved and venerated him still; but God alone became his master.

Of all the reformers, Farel and Luther are perhaps those whose early spiritual developments are best known to us, and who had to pass through the greatest struggles. Quick and ardent, men of conflict and strife, they underwent the severest trials before attaining peace. Farel is the pioneer of the Reformation in France and Switzerland; he rushes into the wood, and hews down the aged giants of the forest with his axe. Calvin came after, like Melancthon, from whom he differs indeed in character, but whom he resembles in his part as theologian and organizer. These two men, who have something in common with the legislators of antiquity, —the one in its graceful, the other in its severe style,—built up, settled, and gave laws to the territory conquered by the first two reformers. If, however, Luther and Farel approximate in some of their features, we must acknowledge that the latter resembles the Saxon reformer in one aspect only. Besides his superior genius, Luther had, in all that concerned the Church, a moderation and wisdom, an acquaintance with the past, a comprehensive judgment, and even an organizing faculty, that did not exist to the same degree in the Dauphinese reformer.

Farel was not the only young Frenchman into whose mind the new light beamed. The doctrines that fell from the lips of the illustrious doctor of Etaples fermented among the crowd who listened to his lectures, and in his school were trained the daring soldiers who, in the hour of battle, were to contend even to the foot of the scaffold. They listened, compared, discussed, and keenly argued on both sides. It is probable that among the small number of scholars who defended the truth was young Peter Robert Oliveton, born at Noyon about the close of the fifteenth century, who afterwards translated the Bible into French from Lefevre's version, and who seems to have been the first to draw the attention of a youth of his family, also a native of Noyon, to the Gospel, and who became the most illustrious chief of the Reformation.[1]

Thus in 1512, at a time when Luther had made no impression on the world, and was going to Rome on some trifling monkish business,—at an epoch when Zwingle had not yet begun to apply himself earnestly to sacred learning, and was crossing the Alps with the confederates to fight for the pope,—Paris and France were listening to the teaching of those vital truths from which the Reformation was ordained to issue; and souls prepared to disseminate them were drinking them in with holy thirst. Hence Theodore

Beza, speaking of Lefevre, hails him as the man " who boldly began the revival of the pure religion of Jesus Christ;"[1] and remarks that, " as in ancient times the school of Isocrates sent forth the best orators, so from the lecture-room of the doctor of Etaples issued many of the best men of the age and of the Church."[2]

The Reformation was not, therefore, in France a foreign importation. It was born on French soil; it germinated in Paris; it put forth its first shoots in the university itself, that second authority in Romish Christendom. God planted the seeds of this work in the simple hearts of a Picard and a Dauphinese, before they had begun to bud forth in any other country upon earth. The Swiss Reformation, as we have seen,[3] was independent of the German Reformation; and in its turn the Reformation in France was independent of that of Switzerland and of Germany. The work commenced at the same time in different countries, without any communication one with the other; as in a battle all the divisions begin to move at the same moment, although one has not told the other to march, but because one and the same command, issuing from a higher power, has been heard by all. The time had come, the nations were prepared, and God was every where beginning the revival of his Church at the same time. Such facts demonstrate that the great revolution of the sixteenth century was a work of God.

If we look only to dates, we must acknowledge that neither to Switzerland nor to Germany belongs the honour of having begun this work, although, hitherto, these two countries alone have contended for it. This honour belongs to France. This is a truth, a fact that we are anxious to establish, because until now it may possibly have been overlooked. Without dwelling on the influence that Lefevre exercised directly or indirectly on many individuals, and in particular on Calvin himself, as we conjecture, let us reflect on that which he had on one only of his disciples,—on Farel, and on the energetic activity which this servant of God manifested ever afterwards. Can we, after that, resist the conviction, that if Zwingle and Luther had never appeared, there would still have been a reforming movement in France? It is impossible, no doubt, to calculate what might have been its extent; we must even acknowledge that the report of what was taking place on the other side of the Rhine and the Jura afterwards animated and accelerated the progress of the French reformers. But they were the first awakened by the trumpet that sounded from heaven in the sixteenth century, and they were the first on foot and under arms upon the field of battle.

[1] Et purioris religionis instaurationem fortiter aggressus. Beza Icones.
[2] Sic ex Stapulensis auditorio praestantissimi viri plurimi prodierunt. Ibid.
[3] See vol. ii. p. 257.

[1] Biogr. Univ., art. *Olivetan.* Hist. du Calvinisme by Maimbourg, p. 53.

Nevertheless Luther is the great workman of the sixteenth century, and in the fullest sense the first reformer. Lefevre is not so complete as Calvin, Farel, and Luther. He is of Wittemberg and Geneva, but there is still a tinge of the Sorbonne; he is the first catholic in the reform movement, and the last of the reformers in the catholic movement. He is to the end a sort of go-between, a mediator not altogether free from mystery, destined to remind us of the connexion between the old things and the new, which seemed for ever separated by an impassable gulf. Though rejected and persecuted by Rome, he still clings to Rome by a slender thread which he has no desire to break. Lefevre of Etaples has a station apart in the theology of the sixteenth century: he is the link connecting the ancient times with the modern, and the man in whom the transition is made from the theology of the middle ages to the theology of the Reformation.

CHAPTER IV.

Character of Francis I.—Commencement of Modern Times —Liberty and Obedience—Margaret of Valois—The Court —Briçonnet, Count of Montbrun—Lefevre commends him to the Bible—Francis I. and "his Children"—The Gospel brought to Margaret—Conversion—Adoration—Margaret's Character.

Thus the whole university was in a state of restlessness. But the Reformation in France was not to be a work of the learned only. It was to take its place among the great ones of the world, and even in the court of the sovereign.

The youthful Francis I. of Angoulême had succeeded his father-in-law and cousin Louis XII. His beauty and address, his courage and love of pleasure, made him the first knight of his time. He aspired, however, at being something more: he desired to be a great and even a good king, provided every thing would bend to his sovereign pleasure. Valour, a taste for letters, and a love of gallantry, are three terms that will express the character of Francis and the spirit of his age. Two other illustrious kings, Henry IV. and especially Louis XIV., presented the same features in after-years. But these princes wanted what the Gospel communicates; and although there had always existed in the nation elements of holiness and christian elevation, we may say that these three great monarchs of modern France have in some measure stamped upon their subjects the impress of their own peculiarities, or rather that they themselves were the faithful images of the character of their people. If the Gospel had entered France with the most illustrious of the Valois family, it would have brought the nation what it does not possess,—a spiritual tendency, a christian holiness, a knowledge of divine things, and

would thus have perfected it in what constitutes the real strength and greatness of a people.

It was in the reign of Francis I. that France and Europe passed from the middle ages to modern times. The new world, which was then in the bud, grew up and entered into possession. Two classes of men imposed their influence on the new state of society. On the one hand were the men of faith, men also of wisdom and holiness; and by their side were the courtly writers, friends of the world and of vice, who by the freedom of their principles, contributed as much to the depravation of morals as the former to their reformation.

If Europe in the days of Francis I. had not witnessed the rise of the reformers, and had been handed over by the severe judgment of Providence to the unbelieving innovators, her fate and that of Christianity would have been decided. The danger was great. For some time these two classes of combatants, the antagonists of the pope and the opponents of the Gospel, were mixed up together; and as they both claimed liberty, they appeared to employ the same arms against the same enemies. An unpractised eye could not distinguish between them amid the dust and clouds of the battle-field. If the former had allowed themselves to be carried away by the latter, all would have been lost. The enemies of the hierarchy were passing rapidly to the extremes of impiety, and urging christian society into a frightful abyss; the papacy itself was helping towards this terrible catastrophe, and accelerating by its ambition and its disorders the destruction of the remnants of truth and life still surviving in the Church. But God raised up the Reformation, and Christianity was saved. The reformers who had shouted liberty, soon called for obedience. The very men who had cast down the throne whence the Roman pontiff issued his oracles, fell prostrate before the Word of God. Then a clear and definite separation took place; nay more, the two bodies engaged in war against each other. The one party had desired liberty only for themselves, the others had claimed it for the Word of God. The Reformation became the most formidable enemy of that incredulity towards which Rome is often so lenient. After restoring liberty to the Church, the reformers restored religion to the world. Of these two gifts, the latter was the most needed.

The friends of infidelity hoped, for a while, to reckon among their number Margaret of Valois, duchess of Alençon, whom Francis tenderly loved, and always called "*sa mignonne*," his darling, as we learn from Brantôme.[1] The same tastes, the same acquirements, distinguished both brother and sister. Possessing, like Francis, a handsome person,

[1] Vie des Dames Illustres, p. 333. La Haye, 1740

442

Margaret combined with those eminent qualities that make great characters those gentler virtues that win the affections. In the world, in the gay entertainments at the court of the king and of the emperor, she shone like a queen, charming, surprising, and captivating all hearts. Passionately fond of letters, and endowed with a rare genius, she would retire to her closet, and there indulge in the sweet pleasures of thought, study, and learning. But her ruling passion was to do good and prevent evil. When ambassadors had been received by the king, they went and paid their respects to Margaret. " They were mightily enchanted with her," says Brantôme, " and made a glowing report of her to their own countrymen." And the king would often refer matters of importance to her, " leaving them solely to her decision."[1]

This celebrated princess was distinguished for the strictness of her morals ; but while many confine this austerity to their lips, and are lax in their behaviour, Margaret did the contrary. Irreproachable in conduct, she was not altogether free from censure in her writings. Instead of being surprised at this, we might rather wonder that a woman so dissolute as Louisa of Savoy should have a daughter so pure as Margaret. While visiting different parts of the country with the court, she amused herself with describing the manners of the time, and particularly the disorders of the priests and monks. " I have heard her," says Brantôme, " thus narrating tales to my grandmother, who always accompanied her in her litter, as lady-in-waiting, and who had charge of her ink-horn."[2]

This Margaret, so beautiful, so full of wit, and living in the atmosphere of a corrupted court, was one of the first to be carried away by the religious movement then beginning in France. But how could the Duchess of Alençon be reached by the Reformation in the midst of so profane a court, and of the licentious tales by which it was amused ? Her elevated soul felt wants that the Gospel alone could satisfy ; grace works every where ; and Christianity, which even before an apostle had appeared in Rome, already counted followers in the house of Narcissus and in the court of Nero,[3] penetrated rapidly, at the period of its renovation, into the court of Francis I. High-bred dames and noble lords addressed the princes in the language of faith ; and that sun, then rising upon France, shed its earliest beams upon an illustrious head, by which they were immediately reflected on the Duchess of Alençon.

Among the most distinguished noblemen at the court was William of Montbrun, son of Cardinal Briconnet of St. Malo, who had entered the church after the decease of his wife. Count William, who was fond of study, took holy orders, and became successively bishop of Lodève and of Meaux. Being twice sent ambassador to Rome, he returned to Paris, unseduced by the flattery and pomps of Leo X.

At the period of his return to France, the sap was every where beginning to move. Farel, then master of arts, was lecturing in the celebrated college of the Cardinal Lemoine, one of the four principal colleges of the theological faculty in Paris, equal in rank to the Sorbonne. Two fellow-countrymen of Lefevre, Arnaud and Gerard Roussel, with several others, increased the circle of liberal and generous minds. Briçonnet, fresh from the gay entertainments and festivities of Rome, was astonished at what had taken place in Paris during his absence. Thirsting for the truth, he renewed his ancient relations with Lefevre, and passed many precious hours with the doctor of the Sorbonne, with Farel, the two Roussels and their friends.[1] This illustrious but humble-minded prelate was willing to be instructed by the lowliest Christians, but particularly by the Lord himself. " I am in darkness," said he, " awaiting the grace of the Divine benevolence, from which I am exiled by my demerits." His mind was dazzled, as it were, by the brilliancy of the Gospel. His eyelids drooped before its unequalled brightness. " The eyes of all men," added he, " are insufficient to receive the whole light of this great luminary."[2]

Lefevre had recommended the Bishop to the Bible ; he had pointed to it as the clue which ever leads men back to the primitive truth of Christianity,—to what it was when schools, sects, ordinances, and traditions were unknown, and as the powerful medium by which the religion of Jesus Christ is renovated. Briçonnet read the Bible. " Such is the sweetness of this Divine food," said he, " that it makes the mind insatiable ; the more we taste of it, the more we long for it."[3] The simple and mighty truth of salvation charmed him : he found Christ,—he found God himself. ' What vessel," said he, " is able to receive the exceeding fulness of this inexhaustible sweetness ? But the dwelling extends according to our desire to entertain the good guest. Faith is the quartermaster who alone can find room for him, or, more truly, who makes us dwell in him." But at the same time the good bishop, afflicted at seeing this doctrine of life, which the Reformation restored to the world, held in so little estimation at court, in the city, and among the people, exclaimed : " Oh singular and

---

[1] Vie des Dames illustres, p. 337.
[2] Ibid. p. 346.
[3] Romans xvi. 11 ; Philip. iv. 22.

[1] Histoire de la Révocat. de l'édit. de Nantes, i. 7. Maimbourg, Hist. du Calv. p. 12.
[2] This passage is taken from a manuscript in the Bibliothèque Royale at Paris, entitled Lettres de Marguerite, reine de Navarre, and marked S. F. 337. I shall have frequent occasion to quote the manuscript, which I had great difficulty in deciphering.
[3] Ibid.

most worthy innovation, and yet to my fellow-men most unacceptable!"

It is in this way that evangelical opinions made their way into the midst of the frivolous, dissolute, and literary court of Francis I. Many of the men who composed it, and who enjoyed the entire confidence of the king, as John du Bellay, Budæus, Cop the court physician, and even Petit the king's confessor, appeared favourably disposed towards the sentiments of Briçonnet and Lefevre. Francis, who loved learning, who invited into his states learned men inclined to Lutheranism, and who thought (as Erasmus says) "in this manner to adorn and illustrate his age in a more magnificent manner than he could have done by trophies, pyramids, or by the most pompous structures," was himself carried away by his sister, by Briçonnet, and by the literary men of his court and universities. He would often be present at the discussions of the learned, listening with delight to their conversation at table, and calling them "his children." He prepared the way for the Word of God by founding Hebrew and Greek professorships. And hence Theodore Beza, when placing his portrait at the head of the reformers, says: "Pious spectator! do not shudder at the sight of this adversary! Ought he not to have a part in this honour, who expelled barbarism from the world, and with firm hand substituted in its stead three languages and sound learning, to be as it were the portals to the new building that was shortly to be erected?"[1]

But there was at the court of Francis I. one soul in particular, which seemed prepared to receive the evangelical influence of the doctor of Etaples and the bishop of Meaux. Margaret, yet hesitating and wavering, in the midst of the depraved society that surrounded her, looked for support, and found it in the Gospel. She turned towards this fresh breath that was reanimating the world, and inhaled it with delight as an emanation from heaven. From some of the ladies of her court she learnt what the new doctors were teaching; they lent her their writings, their little books, called in the language of the time, "tracts;" and spoke to her of the "primitive Church, of the pure Word of God, of worshipping in spirit and in truth, and of christian liberty which shakes off the yoke of superstition and traditions of men to bind them closer to God alone."[2] Erelong this princess conversed with Lefevre, Farel, and Roussel; their zeal, their piety, their purity of morals,—all in them struck her imagination; but it was the Bishop of Meaux in particular, who had long enjoyed her friendship, that became her guide in the path of faith.

Thus, in the midst of the brilliant court of Francis I. and of the profligate household of Louisa of Savoy, was accomplished one of those conversions of the heart which, although not thoroughly evangelical, are not the fruit of a mere æsthetical religion. Margaret subsequently recorded in her poems the different movements of her soul at this important period of her life; and in them we may trace the path she then trod. We find that the sense of sin had taken strong hold of her, and that she wept over the levity with which she had treated the scandals of the world. She exclaimed:

> Is there a gulf of ill, so deep and wide
> That can suffice but e'en a tenth to hide
> Of my vile sins?

This corruption, of which she had so long been ignorant, she discovered every where, now that her eyes were opened.

> Well do I feel within me is the root,
> Without are branch and foliage, flower and fruit.[1]

Yet amidst the alarm caused by the state of her soul, she felt that a God of peace had appeared to her:

> My God, thou hast come down on earth to me,—
> To me, although a naked worm I be.[2]

And ere long a sense of the love of God in Christ was shed abroad in her heart. Margaret had found faith, and her enraptured soul indulged in holy transports.[3]

> Word Divine. Jesus the Salvator,
> Only Son of the eternal Pater,
> The first, the last; of all things renovator,
> Bishop and king, and mighty triumphator,
> From death by death our liberator.
> By faith we're made the sons of the Creator.

From this time a great change took place in the Duchess of Alençon:—

> Though poor, and weak, and ignorant I be,
> How rich, how strong, how wise I am in Thee![4]

But the power of sin was not yet subdued in her. She found a struggle, a discord in her soul that alarmed her:[5]

> In spirit noble,—but in nature slave;
> Immortal am I,—tending to the grave;
> Essence of heaven,—and yet of earthly birth;
> God's dwelling place,—and yet how little worth.

Margaret, seeking in nature the symbols that might express the wants and affections of her soul, chose for her emblem (says Brantôme) the marigold, "which by its rays and leaves has more affinity with the sun, and turns wherever he goes."[6]—She added this device:—

> *Non inferiora secutus,*
> I seek not things below.

"as a sign," adds the courtly writer, "that

---

[1] Neque rex potentissime pudeat....quasi atrienses hujus ædia futuras. Bezæ Icones.—Disputationibus eorum ipse interfuit. Flor. Ræmundi Hist. de ortu hæresum, vii. 2.
[2] Maimbourg, Hist. du Calvinisme, p. 17.

[1] Marguerites de la Marguerite des princesses. Lyon. 1547, tome i. Miroir de l'âme pécheresse, p. 15. The copy I have used appears to have belonged to the Queen of Navarre herself, and some notes that it contains are said to be in her own handwriting. It is now in the possession of a friend of the author's.
[2] Ibid. pp. 18, 19.
[3] Marguerites, &c. Discord de l'esprit et de la chair, p. 73. (The translator has endeavoured to preserve the quaintness of the original, both in rhyme and rhythm.)
[4] Ibid. Miroir de l'Ame, p. 22.
[5] Ibid. Discord de l'esprit, p. 71.
[6] Vie des Femmes illustres, p. 33.

she directed all her actions, thoughts, desires, and affections, to that great sun which is God ; and hence she was suspected of being attached to the Lutheran religion." [1]

In fact, the princess experienced, not long after, the truth of the saying, that *all who will live godly in Jesus Christ shall suffer persecution.* At the court, they talked of Margaret's new opinions, and the surprise was great. What! even the sister of the king takes part with these people ! For a moment it might have been thought that Margaret's ruin was certain. She was denounced to Francis I. But the king, who was tenderly attached to his sister, pretended to think that it was untrue. Margaret's character gradually lessened the opposition. Every one loved her, says Brantôme : " she was very kind, mild, gracious, charitable, affable, a great alms-giver, despising nobody, and winning all hearts by her excellent qualities." [2]

In the midst of the corruption and frivolity of that age, the mind reposes with delight on this chosen soul, which the grace of God had seized from beneath such a load of vanities and grandeur. But her feminine character held her back. If Francis I. had felt his sister's convictions, he would no doubt have followed them out. The timid heart of the princess trembled before the anger of the king. She was constantly wavering between her brother and her Saviour, and could not resolve to sacrifice either. We cannot recognise her as a Christian who has reached the perfect liberty of the children of God : she is a correct type of those elevated souls, so numerous in every age, particularly among women, who, powerfully attracted towards heaven, have not sufficient strength to detach themselves entirely from the earth.

However, such as she is, she is a pleasing character on the stage of history. Neither Germany nor England present her parallel. She is a star, slightly clouded no doubt, but shedding an indescribable and gentle radiance, and, at the time of which I am treating, her rays shine out still more brightly. It is not until later years, when the angry looks of Francis I. denounce a mortal hatred against the Reformation, that his frightened sister will screen her holy faith from the light of day. But now she raises her head in the midst of this corrupted court, and appears a bride of Christ. The respect paid to her, the high opinion entertained of her understanding and of her heart, plead the cause of the Gospel at the court of France much better than any preacher could have done. The gentle influence of woman gained admission for the new doctrine. It is perhaps to this period we should trace the inclination of the French nobility to embrace Protestantism. If Francis had followed his

sister, if all the nation had opened its gates to Christianity, Margaret's conversion might have been the saving of France. But while the nobles welcomed the Gospel, the king and the people remained faithful to Rome ; and there came a time when it was a cause of serious misfortune to the Reformation to count a Navarre and a Condé among its ranks.

CHAPTER V.

Enemies of the Reformation—Louisa—Duprat—Concordat of Bologna—Opposition of the Parliament and the University—The Sorbonne—Beda—His Character—His Tyranny—Berquin, the most learned of the Nobility—The Intriguers of the Sorbonne—Heresy of the three Magdalens—Luther condemned at Paris—Address of the Sorbonne to the King—Lefevre quits Paris for Meaux.

THUS already had the Gospel made illustrious conquests in France, Lefevre, Briçonnet, Farel, and Margaret joyfully yielded in Paris to the movement that was already beginning to shake the world. Francis I. himself seemed at that time more attracted by the splendour of literature, than repelled by the severity of the Gospel. The friends of the Word of God were entertaining the most pleasing expectations ; they thought that the heavenly doctrine would be disseminated without obstacle over their country, at the very moment when a formidable opposition was organizing at court and in the Sorbonne. France, which was to signalize itself among Roman-catholic states for nearly three centuries by its persecutions, rose with pitiless severity against the Reformation. If the seventeenth century was the age of a bloody victory, the sixteenth was that of a cruel struggle. Probably in no place did the reformed Christians meet with more merciless adversaries on the very spot where they raised the standard of the Gospel. In Germany, it was in the Romish states that their enemies were found ; in Switzerland, in the Romish cantons ; but in France, it was face to face. A dissolute woman and a rapacious minister then headed the long list of the enemies of the Reformation.

Louisa of Savoy, mother of the king and of Margaret, notorious for her gallantries, absolute in her will, and surrounded by a train of ladies of honour whose licentiousness began at the court of France a long series of immorality and scandal, naturally took part against the Word of God ; she was the more to be feared as she had always preserved an almost unbounded influence over her son. But the Gospel met with a still more formidable adversary in Louisa's favourite, Anthony Duprat, who by her influence was nominated chancellor of the kingdom. This man, whom a contemporary historian calls the most vicious of all bipeds,[1] was more rapacious

---

[1] Vie des Femmes illustres, p. 33. [2] Ibid. p. 341. | [1] Bipedum omnium nequissimus. Belcarius, xv. 436.

than Louisa was dissolute. Having first enriched himself at the expense of justice, he desired subsequently to increase his wealth at the expense of religion, and entered holy orders to gain possession of the richest livings.

Lust and avarice thus characterized these two persons, who, being both devoted to the pope, endeavoured to conceal the disorders of their lives by shedding the blood of the heretics.[1]

One of their first acts was to deliver up the kingdom to the ecclesiastical dominion of the pope. The king, after the battle of Marignan, met Leo X. at Bologna, and there was sealed the famous *concordat*, in virtue of which these two princes divided the spoils of the Church between them. They annulled the supremacy of councils to give it to the pope; and depriving the churches of their right to fill up the vacant bishoprics and livings, conferred it on the king. After this, Francis I., supporting the pontiff's train, proceeded to the minster-church of Bologna to ratify this negotiation. He was sensible of the injustice of the concordat, and turning to Duprat, whispered in his ear: "It is enough to damn us both."[2] But what was salvation to him? Money and the pope's alliance were what he wanted.

The parliament vigorously resisted the concordat. The king made its deputies wait several weeks at Amboise, and then calling them before him one day, as he rose from table, he said: "There is a king in France, and I will not have a Venetian senate formed in my dominions." He then commanded them to depart before sunset. Evangelical liberty had nothing to hope from such a prince. Three days after, the high-chamberlain La Tremouille appeared in parliament, and ordered the concordat to be registered.

Upon this the university put itself in motion. On the 18th of March 1518, a solemn procession, at which all the students and the bachelors with their hoods were present, repaired to the Church of Saint Catherine of the Scholars, to implore God to preserve the liberties of the Church and of the kingdom.[3] "The colleges were closed, strong bodies of the students went armed through the city, threatening and sometimes maltreating the exalted personages who were publishing and carrying out the said concordat by the king's orders."[4] The university eventually tolerated the execution of this edict: but without revoking the resolutions on which it had declared its opposition; and from that time, says the Venetian ambassador Correro, "the king began to give away the bishoprics with a liberal hand at the solicitation of the court ladies, and to bestow abbeys on his soldiers; so that at the court of France a trade was

carried on in bishoprics and abbeys, as at Venice in pepper and cinnamon."[1]

While Louisa and Duprat were preparing to destroy the Gospel by the destruction of the liberties of the Gallican Church, a fanatical and powerful party was forming against the Bible. Christian truth has always had to encounter two powerful adversaries, the depravity of the world and the fanaticism of the priests. The scholastic Sorbonne and a profligate court were now to march forward hand in hand against the confessors of Jesus Christ. In the early days of the Church, the unbelieving Sadducees and the hypocritical Pharisees were the fiercest enemies of Christianity: and so they have remained through every age. Erelong from the darkness of the schools emerged the most pitiless adversaries of the Gospel. At their head was Noel Bédier, commonly called Beda, a native of Picardy and syndic of the Sorbonne, reputed to be the greatest brawler and most factious spirit of his day. Educated in the dry maxims of scholasticism, matured in the theses and antitheses of the Sorbonne, having a greater veneration for the distinctions of the school than for the Word of God, he was transported with anger against those whose daring mouths ventured to put forth other doctrines. Of a restless disposition, unable to enjoy any repose, always requiring new pursuits, he was a torment to all around him: confusion was his native element; he seemed born for contention; and when he had no adversaries he fell foul of his friends. This impetuous quack filled the university with stupid and violent declamations against literature, against the innovations of the age, and against all those who were not, in his opinion, sufficiently earnest in repressing them. Many smiled as they listened to him, but others gave credit to the invectives of the blustering orator, and the violence of his character secured him a tyrannical sway in the Sorbonne. He must always have some new enemy to fight, some victim to drag to the scaffold; and accordingly he had created heretics before any existed, and had called for the burning of Merlin, vicar-general of Paris, for having endeavoured to justify Origen. But when he saw the new doctors appear, he bounded like a wild beast that suddenly perceives an easy prey within its reach. "There are three thousand monks in one Beda," said the cautious Erasmus.[2]

These excesses, however, were prejudicial to his cause. "What!" said the wisest men of the age, "does the Roman Church rest on the shoulders of such an Atlas as this?[3] Whence comes all this disturbance, except from the absurdities of Beda himself?"

In effect, the very invectives that frightened weak minds, disgusted more generous

[1] Sismondi, Hist. des Français, xvi. 387.
[2] Mathieu, i. 16.
[3] Crévier, v. 110.
[4] Fontaine, Hist. Cathol., Paris, 1562, p. 16.

[1] Raumer, Gesch. Europ. i. 270.
[2] In uno Beda sunt tria millia monachorum. Erasm. Epp. p. 373.
[3] Talibus Atlantibus nititur Ecclesia Romana. Ibid. p. 1113.

spirits. At the court of Francis I. was a gentleman of Artois, named Louis de Berquin, then about thirty years of age, and who was never married. The purity of his life,[1] his profound knowledge, which procured him the title of "the most learned of the nobles,"[2] the openness of his disposition, his tender care for the poor, and his unbounded attachment to his friends, distinguished him above his equals.[3] There was not a more devout observer of the ceremonies of the Church, fasts, festivals, and masses;[4] and he held in the greatest horror all that was denominated heretical. It was a matter of astonishment to witness so much devotion at the court.

It seemed as if nothing could make such a man incline to the side of the Reformation; there were, however, one or two features in his character that might lead him to the Gospel. He abhorred every kind of dissimulation, and, as he never desired to injure any himself, he could not bear to see them injured by others. The tyranny of Beda and other fanatics, their bickerings and persecutions, filled his generous soul with indignation; and as he never did things by halves, he was accustomed wherever he went, in the city or at the court, "even among the highest personages in the kingdom,"[5] to inveigh with the utmost vehemence against the tyranny of these doctors, and attack "in their very nests," says Theodore Beza, "those odious hornets who were then the terror of the world."[6]

He did not stop here: opposition to injustice led Berquin to inquire after truth. He desired to know that holy Scripture, so dear to the men against whom Beda and his creatures were raging; and he had scarcely begun to read the book, before it won his heart. Berquin immediately joined Margaret, Lefevre, Briçonnet, and all those who loved the Word, and in their society tasted of the purest joys. He felt that he had something more to do besides opposing the Sorbonne, and would have loved to communicate the convictions of his soul to all France. He immediately began to write and translate several christian books into French. It seemed to him that every man ought to acknowledge and embrace the truth as promptly as he had done himself. That impetuosity which Beda had exerted in the service of human traditions, Berquin employed in the service of the Word of God. Although younger than the syndic of the Sorbonne, less prudent, and less skilful, he had in his favour the noble enthusiasm of truth. They were two strong wrestlers

about to try which should throw the other. But Berquin had another object in view than a triumph over Beda: he would have desired to pour forth floods of truth over all his countrymen. And hence Theodore Beza says, that France might have found a second Luther in Berquin, if he had found a second elector in Francis I.[1]

Numerous obstacles were destined to impede his efforts. Fanaticism finds disciples every where; it is a fire that spreads far and near. The monks and ignorant priests took part with the syndic of the Sorbonne. A party-spirit pervaded the whole troop, which was governed by a few intriguing and fanatical leaders, who cleverly took advantage of the insignificance or vanity of their colleagues, to infect them with their own prejudices. At all their meetings these chiefs were the only speakers: they domineered over their party by their violence, and reduced the moderate and weak-minded to silence. Hardly had they made any proposition, before these ringleaders exclaimed: "We shall soon see now who are of the Lutheran faction."[2] Did any one give utterance to a reasonable sentiment, a shuddering fell upon Beda, Lecouturier, Duchesne, and the whole band; and all cried out at once: "He is worse than Luther." This manœuvre was successful; the timid minds that prefer peace to disputation, those who are ready to give up their own opinions for their own advantage, those who do not understand the simplest questions, and, lastly, those who are always carried away by the clamour of others,—all became the willing tools of Beda and his satellites. Some were silent, others shouted, all submitted to that influence which a proud and tyrannical mind exercises over vulgar souls. Such was the state of this association, which was regarded as so venerable, and which was at that time the most violent enemy of evangelical Christianity. It would often be sufficient to cast a single glance upon the most celebrated bodies to estimate at its just value the war they wage upon truth.

Thus the university which, under Louis XII., had applauded Allmain's aspirations after independence, abruptly plunged once more, under Duprat and Louisa of Savoy, into fanaticism and servility. If we except the Jansenists and a few other doctors, a noble and real independence has never existed among the Gallican clergy. They have never done more than oscillate between servility to the court and servility to the pope. If under Louis XII. or Louis XIV. they had some appearance of liberty, it was because their master in Paris was at strife with their master at Rome. And thus we have an explanation of the change we have pointed out.

---

[1] Ut ne rumusculus quidem impudicitiæ sit unquam in illum exortus. Er. Epp. p. 1278.
[2] Gaillard, Hist. de François I.
[3] Mirere benignus in egenos et amicos. Er. Epp. p. 1238.
[4] Constitutionum ac rituum ecclesiasticorum observantissimus. Ibid.
[5] Actes des Martyrs de Crespin, p. 103.
[6] Ut maxime omnium tunc metuendos crabrones in ipsis eorum cavis....Bezæ Icones.

[1] Gallia fortassis alterum esset Luterum nacta. Bezæ Icones.
[2] Hic, inquiunt, apparebit qui sint Lutheranæ factionis. Er. Epp. p. 889

The university and the bishops forgot their rights and duties as soon as the king ceased to enjoin their observance.

For a long period Beda had been incensed against Lefevre; the renown of the Picard doctor's lectures irritated his compatriot and ruffled his pride; he would gladly have silenced him. Once already Beda had attacked the doctor of Etaples, and as yet little able to distinguish the evangelical doctrines, he had assailed his colleague on a point which, however strange it may appear, was near sending Lefevre to the scaffold.[1] This doctor had asserted that Mary, the sister of Lazarus, Mary Magdalen, and the "woman which was a sinner," of whom Saint Luke speaks in the seventh chapter of his Gospel, were three distinct persons. The Greek fathers had distinguished them: the Latin fathers had confounded them together. This terrible *heresy* of the three Magdalens set Beda and all his host in motion; Christendom was roused; Fisher, bishop of Rochester, one of the most distinguished prelates of the age, wrote against Lefevre, and the whole Church then declared against an opinion now admitted by every Roman-catholic. Already Lefevre, condemned by the Sorbonne, was prosecuted by the parliament as a heretic, when Francis I., pleased at the opportunity of striking a blow at the Sorbonne, and of humbling the monks, rescued him from the hands of his persecutors.

Beda, enraged at seeing his victim snatched from his grasp, resolved to take better aim another time. The name of Luther was beginning to be heard in France. The reformer, after the dispute with Dr. Eck at Leipsic, had agreed to acknowledge the universities of Erfurth and Paris as his judges. The zeal displayed by the latter university against the concordat, no doubt led him to hope that he should find impartial judges in its members. But the times were changed, and the more decided the theological faculty had been against the encroachments of Rome, the more it was bent on showing its orthodoxy. Beda accordingly found it quite disposed to enter into his views.

On the 20th of January 1520, the treasurer of the French nation[2] bought twenty copies of the conference between Luther and Eck for distribution among the members of the commission who were to make a report on the matter. More than a year was employed in this investigation. The German Reformation was beginning to create a strong sensation in France. The universities, which were then truly catholic institutions, to which students resorted from every country in Christendom, brought Germany, France, Switzerland, and England, into closer and speedier relation with each other, as regards

theology and philosophy, than those of the present day. The reports prevailing in Paris of Luther's success strengthened the hands of such men as Lefevre, Briçonnet, and Farel. Each of his victories increased their courage. Many of the Sorbonne doctors were struck by the admirable truths they found in the writings of the Wittemberg monk. There had already been many a bold confession; but there had also been a terrible resistance. "All Europe," says Crévier, "was waiting for the decision of the university of Paris." The contest appeared doubtful. At length Beda prevailed; and in April 1521, the university decreed that Luther's works should be publicly burnt, and the author compelled to retract.

This was not enough. In fact Luther's disciples had crossed the Rhine more speedily even than his writings. "In a short time," says the Jesuit Maimbourg, "the university was filled with foreigners, who, because they knew a little Hebrew and more Greek, acquired a reputation, insinuated themselves into the houses of persons of quality, and claimed an insolent liberty of interpreting the Bible."[1] The faculty, therefore, appointed a deputation to bear their remonstrances to the king.

Francis I., caring little for the quarrels of theologians, was continuing his career of pleasure; and passing from castle to castle, with his gentlemen and the ladies composing his mother's and his sister's court, he indulged in every species of disorder, far from the troublesome observation of the citizens of the capital. He thus made his progresses through Brittany, Anjou, Guienne, Angoumois, and Poitou, leading the same sumptuous life in villages and forests, as if he had been at Paris in his palace of Tournelles. It was one round of tournaments, sham-fights, masquerades, costly entertainments, and banquets, which even those of Lucullus (as Brantôme says) could not equal.[2]

For a moment, however, he interrupted the course of his pleasures to receive the grave deputies of the Sorbonne; but he saw only men of learning in those whom the faculty pointed out as heretics. Could a prince who boasted of having put the kings of France *hors de page* (out of leading-strings), bend his head before a few fanatical doctors? He replied: "I will not have these people molested. To persecute those who teach us, would prevent able scholars from coming into our country."[3]

The deputation left the king's presence in great wrath. What will be the consequence? The disease grows stronger every day; already the heretical opinions are denominated "the sentiments of men of genius;" the devouring flame is stealing into the most

[1] Gaillard, Hist. de François I. iv. 228.
[2] It was formerly the custom in the university of Paris to classify its members into four nations, viz.: France, Picardy, Normandy, and Germany.—Tr.

[1] Hist. du Calvinisme, p. 10.
[2] Vie des Hommes illustres, i. 326.
[3] Maimbourg, p. 11.

secret recesses; erelong the conflagration will burst forth, and throughout France the edifice of faith will fall with a terrible crash.

Beda and his party, failing to obtain the king's permission to erect their scaffolds, resort to persecutions of a more invidious nature. There was no kind of annoyance to which the evangelical teachers were not subjected. Fresh reports and fresh denunciations followed each other daily. The aged Lefevre, tormented by these ignorant zealots, longed for repose. The pious Briçonnet, who was unremitting in his veneration for the doctor of Etaples,[1] offered him an asylum. Lefevre quitted Paris and retired to Meaux. This was the first victory gained over the Gospel, and it was then seen that if the Romish party cannot succeed in engaging the civil power on its side, there is a secret and fanatical police, by means of which it is enabled to obtain its end.

CHAPTER VI.

Briçonnet visits his Diocese—Reform—The Doctors persecuted in Paris—Philiberta of Savoy—Correspondence between Margaret and Briçonnet.

THUS Paris was beginning to rise against the Reformation. and to trace the outlines of that circumvallation which was destined for more than three centuries to bar the entrance of the reformed worship. It had been God's will that the first beams of light should shine upon the capital; but men immediately arose to extinguish them; the spirit of the *Sixteen*[2] was already fermenting in the metropolis, and other cities were about to receive the light which Paris rejected.

Briçonnet, on returning to his diocese, had manifested the zeal of a Christian and of a bishop. He had visited every parish, and, assembling the deans, the incumbents, and their curates, with the church-wardens and principal parishioners, had inquired into the doctrine and lives of the preachers. At collection time (they answered) the Franciscans of Meaux begin their rounds; a single preacher will visit four or five parishes in a day, always delivering the same sermon, not to feed the souls of his hearers, but to fill his belly, his purse, and his convent.[3] Their wallets once replenished, their end is gained, the sermons are over, and the monks do not appear again in the churches until the time for another collection has arrived. The only

business of these shepherds is to shear their sheep.[1]

The majority of the parish priests spent their stipends at Paris. " Alas!" exclaimed the pious bishop, finding a presbytery deserted that he had gone to visit, " are they not traitors who thus desert the service of Jesus Christ?"[2] Briçonnet resolved to apply a remedy to these evils, and convoked a synod of all his clergy for the 13th of October 1519. But these worldly priests, who troubled themselves but little about the remonstrances of their bishop, and for whom Paris had so many charms, took advantage of a custom in virtue of which they might substitute one or more curates to tend their flocks in their absence. Out of one hundred and twenty-seven of these curates, there were only fourteen of whom Briçonnet could approve upon examination.

Worldly-minded priests, imbecile curates, monks who thought only of their belly;—such was then the condition of the Church. Briçonnet interdicted the Franciscans from entering the pulpit;[3] published a mandate on the 27th of October 1520, in which he declared " traitors and deserters all those pastors who, by abandoning their flocks, show plainly that what they love is their fleece and their wool; selected others who were found to be capable, and gave them to the poor sheep, ransomed by the most holy blood of Jesus Christ;"[4] and feeling convinced that the only means of providing able ministers for his diocese was to train them himself, he determined to establish a theological school at Meaux, under the direction of pious and learned doctors. It was necessary to find them, and Beda soon provided them.

This fanatic and his band did not relax their exertions; and, bitterly complaining of the toleration of their government, declared that they would make war on the new doctrines with it, without it, and against it. In vain had Lefevre quitted the capital; did not Farel and his friends remain behind? Farel, it is true, did not preach, for he was not in holy orders; but at the university and in the city, with professors and priests, students and citizens, he boldly maintained the cause of the Reformation. Others, inspirited by his example, were inculcating the Gospel more openly. A celebrated preacher, Martial Mazurier, president of St. Michael's college, threw aside all reserve, depicted the disorders of the age in the darkest and yet truest colours, and it seemed impossible to resist the torrent of his eloquence.[5] The

---

[1] Pro innumeris beneficiis, pro tantis ad studia commodis. Epist. dedicatoria Epp. Pauli.
[2] About this time (1579) a popular society, more violent in its principles, was formed among the Leaguers, and which was called the *Sixteen* (Seize), from the number of its directing committee, each of whom became a religious agitator in as many quarters of Paris. White's Universal History, p. 459.
[3] Ea solum doceri quæ ad cœnobium illorum ac ventrem explendum pertinerent. Acta Mart. p. 334.

[1] MS. of Meaux. I am indebted to the kindness of M. Ladevèze, pastor at Meaux, for a copy of this manuscript, which is preserved in that city.
[2] MS. of Meaux.
[3] Eis in universa diocesi sua prædicationem interdixit. Act. Mart. p. 334.
[4] Histoire Généalogique de la maison des Briçonnets, by Eug. Britonneau, published in 1621, and quoted in the *Semeur* of 4th May 1842.
[5] Frequentissimas de reformandis hominum moribus conciones habuit. Lannoi, Navarræ gymnasii Hist. p. 261.

anger of Beda and his theological friends was at its height. "If we tolerate these innovators," said he, "they will invade the whole body, and all will be over with our teaching, our traditions, our places, and the respect felt towards us by France and the whole of Christendom!"

The divines of the Sorbonne were the stronger party. Farel, Mazurier, Gerard Roussel, and his brother Arnold, soon found their active exertions every where thwarted. The Bishop of Meaux entreated his friends to come and join Lefevre; and these excellent men, hunted down by the Sorbonne, and hoping to form, under Briçonnet's protection, a sacred phalanx for the triumph of the truth, accepted the bishop's invitation, and repaired to Meaux.[1] Thus the light of the Gospel was gradually withdrawn from the capital, where Providence had kindled its earliest sparks. *And this is the condemnation, that light is come into the world, and men loved darkness rather than light, because their deeds were evil.*[2] It is impossible not to discover that Paris then drew down upon its walls the judgment of God pointed out in these words of Jesus Christ.

Margaret of Valois, successively deprived of Briçonnet, Lefevre, and their friends, felt anxious at her lonely position in the midst of Paris and the licentious court of Francis I. A young princess, Philiberta of Savoy, her mother's sister, lived in close intimacy with her. Philiberta, whom the King of France had given in marriage to Julian the Magnificent, brother to Leo X., in confirmation of the concordat, had repaired to Rome after her nuptials, when the pope, delighted at so illustrious an alliance, had expended 150,000 ducats in sumptuous festivities on the occasion.[3] Julian, who then commanded the papal army, died, leaving his widow only eighteen years of age. She became attached to Margaret, who by her talents and virtues exercised a great influence over all around her. Philiberta's grief opened her heart to the voice of religion. Margaret imparted to her all she read; and the widow of the lieutenant-general of the Church began to taste the sweets of the doctrine of salvation. But Philiberta was too inexperienced to support her friend. Margaret often trembled as she thought of her exceeding weakness. If the love she bore the king and the fear she had of displeasing him led her to any action contrary to her conscience, trouble immediately entered into her soul, and turning sorrowfully towards the Lord, she found in him a brother and a master more compassionate and dearer to her heart than Francis himself. It was then she said to Jesus Christ:—[4]

Sweet brother, who, when thou might'st justly chide
Thy foolish sister, tak'st her to thy side;
And grace and love giv'st her in recompense
Of murmurings, injury, and great offence.
Too much, too much, dear brother, thou hast done,
Too much, alas! for such a worthless one.

Margaret seeing all her friends retiring to Meaux, looked sadly after them from the midst of the festivities of the court. Every thing appeared to be deserting her again. Her husband, the Duke of Alençon, was setting out for the army; her youthful aunt Philiberta was going to Savoy. The duchess turned to Briçonnet.

"Monsieur de Meaux," wrote she, "knowing that One alone is necessary, I apply to you, entreating you to be, by prayer, the means that He will be pleased to guide according to His holy will, M. d'Alençon, who by command of the king is setting out as lieutenant-general in his army, which I fear will not be disbanded without a war. And thinking that, besides the public weal of the kingdom, you have a good title in whatsoever concerns his salvation and mine, I pray for your spiritual aid. To-morrow, my aunt of Nemours departs for Savoy. I am obliged to meddle with many things that cause me much fear. Wherefore, if you should know that master Michael could undertake a journey hither, it would be a consolation to me, which I beseech only for the honour of God."[1]

Michael of Aranda, whose aid Margaret sought, was one of the members of the evangelical society of Meaux, who subsequently exposed himself to many dangers in preaching the Gospel.

This pious princess beheld with alarm the opposition against truth becoming more formidable every day. Duprat and the creatures of the government, Beda and those of the Sorbonne, filled her with terror. Briçonnet, to encourage her, replied: "It is the war which the gentle Jesus told us in the Gospel he came to send on earth......and also the fire......the great fire that transformeth earthliness into heavenliness. I desire with all my heart to aid you, madam, but from my own nothingness expect nothing but the will. Whoso hath faith, hope, and love, hath all he requires, and needeth not aid or support......God alone is all in all, and out of him can nothing be found. To fight, take with you that great giant......love unspeakable......The war is led on by love. Jesus demandeth the presence of the heart: wretched is the man who withdraws from him. Whoso fighteth in person is sure of victory. He often faileth who fighteth by others."[2]

The Bishop of Meaux was beginning to know by personal experience what it is to fight for the Word of God. The theologians and monks, irritated by the asylum he gave to the friends of the Reformation, accused him with such violence that his brother, the

[1] Ce fut la persécution qui se suscita contre eux à Paris en 1521, qui les obliges à quitter cette ville. Vie de Farel, par Choupard.
John iii. 19.
Guichemon, Hist. gén. de Savoie, ii. 180.
[4] Miroir de l'âme pécheresse. Marguerites de la Marguerite, i. 36.

[1] Letters of Margaret, Queen of Navarre, in the Royal Library at Paris, S. F. 337 (1521).
[2] Lettres de Marguerite, MS. S. F. 12th June 1521.

Bishop of St. Malo, came to Paris to inquire into the matter.[1] Hence Margaret was the more touched by the consolations that Briçonnet addressed to her, and she replied with offers of assistance.

"If in any thing," she wrote, "you think that I can pleasure you or yours, I pray you believe that every trouble will turn to my comfort. May everlasting peace be yours after these long wars you are waging for the faith, in which battle you desire to die......
"Wholly your daughter,
"MARGARET."[2]

It is to be lamented that Briçonnet did not die in the contest. Yet he was then full of zeal. Philiberta of Nemours, respected by all for her sincere devotion, her liberality towards the poor, and the great purity of her life, read with increasing interest the evangelical writings transmitted to her by the Bishop of Meaux. "I have all the tracts that you have sent me," wrote Margaret to Briçonnet, "of which my aunt of Nemours has her part, and I will forward her the last; for she is in Savoy at her brother's wedding, which is no slight loss to me ; wherefore I beseech you have pity on my loneliness." Unhappily Philiberta did not live long enough to declare herself openly in favour of the Reformation. She died in 1524 at the castle of Virieu le Grand, in Bugey, at the age of twenty-six.[3] This was a severe blow to Margaret. Her friend, her sister, she who could fully comprehend her, was taken from her. There was perhaps only one individual, her brother, whose death would have occasioned her more sorrow than this:

Such floods of tears fall from my eyes,
They hide from view both earth and skies.[4]

Margaret, feeling her inability to resist her grief and the seductions of the court, entreated Briçonnet to exhort her to the love of God, and the humble bishop replied :—

"May the mild and gentle Jesus, who wills, and who alone is able to effect what he mightily wills, in his infinite mercy visit your heart, exhorting you to love him with your whole being. Other him, madam, none has the power to do this ; you must not seek light from darkness, or warmth from cold. By attracting he kindles ; and by warmth he attracts to follow him, enlarging the heart. Madam, you write to me to have pity on you, because you are alone. I do not understand that word. Whoso lives in the world and has his heart there, is alone ; for many and evil go together. But she whose heart sleeps to the world, and is awake to the meek and gentle Jesus, her true and loyal husband, is truly alone, for she lives on the one thing needful ; and yet she is not alone, not being forsaken by him who fills and preserves all things. Pity I cannot, and must not, such loneliness, which is more to be esteemed than the whole world, from which I am persuaded that the love of God has saved you, and that you are no longer its child......Abide, madam, alone in your only One......who has been pleased to suffer a painful and ignominious death and passion.

"Madam, in commending myself to your good graces, I entreat you not to use any more such words as in your last letters. Of God alone you are the daughter and bride : other father you should not seek......I exhort and admonish you, that you will be such and as good a daughter to him, as he is a good Father to you......and forasmuch as you cannot attain to this, because the finite cannot correspond to infinity, I pray that he will vouchsafe to increase your strength, that you may love and serve him with your whole heart."[1]

Notwithstanding these exhortations, Margaret was not consoled. She bitterly regretted the spiritual guides whom she had lost ; the new pastors forced upon her to bring her back did not possess her confidence, and whatever the bishop might say, she felt herself alone in the midst of the court, and all around her appeared dark and desolate. "As a sheep in a strange country," wrote she to Briçonnet, " wandering about, not knowing where to find its pasture, through lack of knowing its new shepherds, naturally lifts its head to catch the breeze from that quarter where the chief shepherd was once accustomed to give her sweet nourishment, in such sort am I constrained to pray for your charity......Come down from the high mountain, and in pity regard, among this benighted people, the blindest of all thy fold. "MARGARET."[2]

The Bishop of Meaux, in his reply, taking up the image of the stray sheep under which Margaret had depicted herself, uses it to describe the mysteries of salvation under the figure of a wood : " The sheep entering the forest, led by the Holy Ghost," said he, " is immediately enchanted by the goodness, beauty, straightness, length, breadth, depth, and height, and the fragrant and invigorating sweetness of this forest......and when it has looked all around, has seen only Him in all, and all in Him ;[3] and moving rapidly through its depths, finds it so pleasant, that the way is life, and joy, and consolation."[4] The bishop then shows her the sheep searching in vain for the limits of the forest (an image of the soul that would fathom the mysteries of God), meeting with lofty mountains, which it endeavours to scale, finding every where " inaccessible and in-

1 MS. de Meaux.
2 MS. S. F. 227, de la Bibl. Royale.
3 Guichemon, Hist. de la maison de Savoie, ii. 181.
4 Chanson spirituelle après la mort du Roi. Marguerites, i. 473.

1 MS. Bibl. Roy. S. F. 337, dated 10th July.
2 Ibid.   3 All in Christ.
4 MS. S. F. 337. Bibl. Roy.

comprehensible infinity." He then teaches her the road by which the soul, inquiring after God, surmounts all these difficulties; he shows how the sheep in the midst of the hirelings finds "the cabin of the great Shepherd," and "enters on the wing of meditation by faith ;" all is made smooth, all is explained ; and she begins to sing : "I have found him whom my soul loveth."

Thus wrote the Bishop of Meaux. At that period he was burning with zeal, and would gladly have seen all France regenerated by the Gospel.[1] Often would his mind dwell especially on those three great individuals who seemed to preside over the destinies of its people,—the king, his mother, and his sister. He thought that if the royal family were enlightened, all the people would be so, and the priests, stirred to rivalry, would at last awaken from their lethargy. "Madam," wrote he to Margaret, "I humbly entreat Almighty God, that he will be pleased of his goodness to kindle a fire in the hearts of the king, of his mother, and in your own ......so that from you there may go forth a light burning and shining on the rest of the nation ; and particularly on that class by whose coldness all others are frozen."

Margaret did not share these hopes. She speaks neither of her brother nor of her mother ; they were subjects she dared not touch upon ; but, replying to the bishop in January 1522, with a heart wrung by the indifference and worldliness of those around her, she said : "The times are so cold, my heart so icy ;" and signs her letter, "your frozen, thirsty, and hungry daughter.

"MARGARET."

This letter did not discourage Briçonnet, but it made him ponder ; and feeling how much he, who desired to re-animate others, required to be animated himself, he commended himself to the prayers of Margaret and of Madam de Nemours. "Madam," wrote he, with great simplicity, "I beseech you to awaken the poor slumberer with your prayers."[2]

Such in 1521 were the sentiments interchanged at the court of France. A strange correspondence, no doubt, and one which, after more than three centuries, a manuscript in the Royal Library has revealed to us. Was this influence of the Reformation in such high places a benefit to it or a misfortune? The sting of truth penetrated the court ; but perhaps it only served to arouse the drowsy beast, and exciting his rage, caused it to spring with deadlier fury on the humblest of the flock.

[1] Studio veritatis aliis declarandæ inflammatus. Act. Martyrum, p. 334.
[2] MS. Bibl. Royale.

CHAPTER VII.

Beginning of the Church at Meaux—The Scriptures in French—The Artisans and the Bishop—Evangelical Harvest—The Epistles of St. Paul sent to the King—Lefevre and Roma—The Monks before the Bishop—The Monks before the Parliament—Briçonnet's first fall—Lefevre and Farel—Persecution—Francis Lambert—His Noviciate and Apostolic Labours—His Early Struggles—He quits Avignon.

THE time was indeed approaching when the storm should burst upon the Reformation ; but it was first to scatter a few more seeds and to gather in a few more sheaves. This city of Meaux, renowned a century and a half later by the sublime defender[1] of the Gallican system against the autocratic pretensions of Rome, was called to be the first town of France where regenerated Christianity should establish its dominion. It was then the field on which the labourers were prodigal of their exertions and their seed, and where already the ears were falling before the reapers. Briçonnet, less sunk in slumber than he had said, was animating, inspecting, and directing all. His fortune equalled his zeal ; never did man devote his wealth to nobler uses, and never did such noble devotedness promise at first to bear such glorious fruits. The most pious teachers, transferred from Paris to Meaux, from that time acted with more liberty. There was freedom of speech, and great was the stride then taken by the Reformation in France. Lefevre energetically expounded that Gospel with which he would have rejoiced to fill the world. He exclaimed : "Kings, princes, nobles, people, all nations should think and aspire after Christ alone.[2] Every priest should resemble that archangel whom John saw in the Apocalypse, flying through the air, holding the everlasting Gospel in his hand, and carrying it to every people, nation, tongue, and king. Come near ye pontiffs, come ye kings, come ye generous hearts !......Nations, awake to the light of the Gospel, and inhale the heavenly life.[3] The Word of God is all-sufficient."[4]

Such in truth was the motto of that school : THE WORD OF GOD IS ALL-SUFFICIENT. In this device the whole Reformation is embodied. "To know Christ and his Word," said Lefevre, Roussel, and Farel, "is tl only living and universal theology......H who knows that, knows every thing."[5]

The truth was making a deep impression at Meaux. Private meetings took place at first ; then conferences ; and at last the Gospel was preached in the churches. But a new effort inflicted a still more formidable blow against Rome.

[1] Bossuet.
[2] Reges, principes, magnates omnes et subinde omnium nationum populi, ut nihil aliud cogitent....ac Christum. Fabri. Comm. in Evang. Præf.
[3] Ubivis gentium expergiscimini ad Evangelii lucem. Ibid.
[4] Verbum Dei sufficit. Ibid.
[5] Hæc est universa et sola vivifica Theologia....Christum et verbum ejus esse omnia. Ibid. in Ev. Johan. p. 271.

Lefevre desired to enable the Christians of France to read the Holy Scriptures. On the 30th October 1522, he published a French translation of the four Gospels; on the 6th November, the remaining books of the New Testament; on the 12th October 1524, all these books together, at the house of Collin in Meaux; and in 1525, a French version of the Psalms.[1] Thus was begun in France, almost at the same time as in Germany, that printing and dissemination of the Scriptures in the vulgar tongue which, three centuries later, was to be so wonderfully developed throughout the world. In France, as on the other side of the Rhine, the Bible had a decisive influence. Experience had taught many Frenchmen, that when they sought to know Divine things, doubt and obscurity encompassed them on every side. In how many moments and perhaps years in their lives had they been tempted to regard the most certain truths as mere delusions! We need a ray from heaven to enlighten our darkness. Such was the ejaculation of many a soul at the epoch of the Reformation. With longings such as these, numbers received the sacred writings from the hands of Lefevre; they were read in their families and in private; conversations on the Bible became frequent; Christ appeared to those souls so long misled, as the centre and the sun of all revelation. No longer did they require demonstrations to prove that Scripture was from God; they knew it, for by it they had been transported from darkness to light.

Such was the course by which so many distinguished persons in France attained a knowledge of God. But there were yet simpler and more common paths, if such can be, by which many of the lower classes were brought to the truth. The city of Meaux was almost wholly inhabited by artisans and dealers in wool. "There was engendered in many," says a chronicler of the sixteenth century, "so ardent a desire of knowing the way of salvation, that artisans, fullers, and wool-combers took no other recreation, as they worked with their hands, than conversation with each other on the Word of God, and comforting themselves with the same. Sundays and holidays especially were devoted to the reading of Scripture, and inquiring into the good pleasure of the Lord."[2]

Briçonnet rejoiced to see piety take the place of superstition in his diocese. "Lefevre, aided by the renown of his great learning," says a contemporary historian, "contrived so to cajole and circumvent Messire Guillaume Briçonnet with his plausible talk, that he caused him to turn aside grievously, so that it has been impossible up to this day to free the city and diocese of Meaux from that pestilent doctrine, where it has so marvellously increased. The misleading that good

bishop was a great injury, as until then he had been so devoted to God and to the Virgin Mary."[1]

Yet all were not so grievously turned aside as the Franciscan says, whom we have just quoted. The city was divided into two parties. On the one side were the monks of St. Francis and the friends of the Romish doctrine; on the other, Briçonnet, Lefevre, Farel, and all those who loved the new preaching. A man of the poorer classes, by name Leclerc, was one of the most servile adherents of the monks; but his wife and two sons, Peter and John, had received the Gospel with eagerness, and John, who was a wool-carder, soon distinguished himself among the new Christians. James Pavanne, a learned and youthful Picard, "a man of great sincerity and uprightness," whom Briçonnet had invited to Meaux, showed an ardent zeal for the Reformation. Meaux had become a focus of light. Persons called thither by business heard the Gospel, and carried it back to their homes. It was not in the city alone that men were examining the Scriptures; "many of the villages did the same," says a chronicle, "so that in this diocese an image of the renovated Church was seen to shine forth."

The environs of Meaux were covered with rich crops, and at harvest season a crowd of labourers flocked thither from the surrounding countries. Resting from their toils in the middle of the day, they conversed with the people of the place, who spoke to them of other seed-times and other harvests. Many peasants from Thierache, and particularly from Landouzy, persevered, on their return home, in the doctrines they had heard, and erelong an evangelical church was formed in this district, which is one of the oldest churches in the kingdom.[2] "The renown of this great blessing spread through France," says the chronicler.[3] Briçonnet himself proclaimed the Gospel from the pulpit, and endeavoured to scatter around him "that infinite, sweet, mild, true, and only light (to use his own words) which dazzles and enlightens every creature capable of receiving it, and which, while it enlightens him, raises him by adoption to the dignity of a son of God."[4] He besought his flock to lend no ear to those who would turn them aside from the Word. "Though an angel from heaven," said he, "should preach any other Gospel, do not listen to him." Sometimes gloomy thoughts would prey upon his soul. He was not sure of himself: he shrunk back in alarm, as he dwelt upon the fatal consequences of his unfaithfulness; and forewarning his hearers, he said to them:

[1] Le Long. Biblioth. sacrée, 2d edit. p. 42.
[2] Act. des Mart. p. 182.

[1] Histoire Catholique de notre temps. par Fontaine, de l'ordre de St. François. Paris, 1562.
[2] These particulars are derived from some old and much discoloured papers, found in the church of Landouzy-la-Ville, in the department of Aisne, by M. Colany, while pastor of that place.
[3] Act Mort. p. 182.
[4] MS. Bibl. Roy. S. F. No. 337.

"Even should I, your bishop, change my language and my doctrine, beware of changing like me."[1] At that moment nothing seemed to indicate the possibility of such a misfortune. "Not only was the Word of God preached," says the chronicle, "but it was followed; all works of charity and love were practised there; the morals were reformed and superstitions laid low."[2]

Still clinging to the idea of gaining over the king and his mother, the bishop sent to Margaret "the epistles of St. Paul, translated and splendidly illuminated, most humbly entreating her to present them to the king; which cannot but be most pleasing from your hands," added the good bishop. "They are a royal dish," continued he, "fattening without corruption, and healing all manner of sickness. The more we taste them, the more we hunger after them with desire unsatiable, and that never cloys."[3]

What more welcome message could Margaret receive? The moment seemed favourable. Michael Aranda was at Paris, detained by order of the king's mother, for whom he was translating portions of the Holy Scripture.[4] But Margaret would have preferred that Briçonnet should present this book himself to her brother. "You would do well to come here," wrote she, "for you know the confidence that Madam and the king place in you "[5]

Thus, probably, was the Word of God placed at that time (in 1522 and 1523) under the eyes of Francis I. and Louisa of Savoy. They came into contact with that Gospel which they were afterwards to persecute. We do not find that this Word produced any salutary effect upon them. An impulse of curiosity led them to open that Bible which was then making so much noise; but they closed it as soon as they had opened it.

Margaret herself found it hard to contend against the worldliness by which she was every where surrounded. Her tender affection towards her brother, the obedience she owed to her mother, and the flatteries lavished on her by the court, all seemed to conspire against the love she had vowed to Christ. Christ was alone against many. Sometimes Margaret's soul, assailed by so many adversaries, and stunned by the noise of the world, turned aside from its Master. Then, becoming sensible of her faults, the princess would shut herself up in her apartments, and giving way to her sorrow, utter cries very different from the joyous sounds with which Francis and the young lords, the companions of his debauchery, filled the royal palaces in the midst of their entertainments and festivities :—

Left you I have, to follow pleasure's voice,
Left you I have, and for an evil choice,
Left you I have, and whither am I come?....[1]

Then turning towards Meaux, Margaret would exclaim in her anguish: "I return to you, to M. Fabry (Lefevre) and all your gentlemen, beseeching you, by your prayers, to obtain of the unspeakable Mercy an alarum for the poor weak and sleepy one, to arouse her from her heavy and deadly slumber."[2]

Thus had Meaux become a focus whence the light of the Gospel emanated. The friends of the Reformation indulged in flattering illusions. Who could resist the Gospel if the power of Francis cleared the way? The corrupting influence of the court would then be changed into a holy influence, and France would acquire a moral strength that would render her the benefactress of the world.

But, on their side, the friends of Rome had taken the alarm. Among those at Meaux was a Jacobin monk named Roma. One day, as Lefevre, Farel, and their friends were talking with him and some other of the papal partisans, Lefevre could not suppress his anticipations. "The Gospel is already gaining the hearts of the great and of the people," said he, "and in a short time, spreading all over France, it will every where throw down the inventions of men." The aged doctor was animated; his eyes sparkled; his worn-out voice grew sonorous; one might have compared him to the aged Simeon returning thanks to the Lord, because his eyes had seen His salvation. Lefevre's friends shared in his emotion: their amazed opponents were dumb. On a sudden Roma started up impetuously, and exclaimed in the tone of a popular tribune: "Then I and all the other religioners will preach a crusade; we will raise the people; and if the king permits the preaching of your Gospel, we will expel him from his kingdom by his own subjects."[3]

Thus did a monk venture to rise up against the knightly monarch. The Franciscans applauded this language. They must not allow the doctor's prophecy to be fulfilled. Already the friars were returning daily with diminished offerings. The Franciscans in alarm went about among private families. "These new preachers are heretics," said they; "they attack the holiest observances, and deny the most sacred mysteries." Then growing bolder, the most incensed among them issued from their cloister, and proceeded to the bishop's residence. On being admitted, they said to the prelate: "Crush this heresy, or else the pestilence, which is already desolating the city of Meaux, will spread over the whole kingdom."

Briçonnet was moved, and for an instant disturbed by this attack, but he did not give

1 Hist. Catholique de Fontaine.
2 Act. Mart. p. 182.
3 MS. Bibl. Roy. S. F. No. 337.
4 Par le commandement de Madame à qui il a lyvré quelque chose de la saincte Escripture qu'elle désire parfaire. Ibid.
5 Ibid.

1 Les Marguerites. i. 40.
2 MS. Bibl. Roy. S. F. No. 337.
3 Farel, Epître au Duc de Lorraine, Gen. 1634.

way; he felt too much contempt for these ignorant monks and their interested clamours. He went into the pulpit, justified Lefevre, and called the monks pharisees and hypocrites. Still this opposition had already excited trouble and conflict in his soul; he sought to encourage himself by the persuasion that such spiritual combats were necessary. "By this warfare," said he, in his somewhat mystical language, "we arrive at a vivifying death, and by continually mortifying life, we die living, and live dying."[1] The way would have been surer if, casting himself upon the Saviour, as the apostles when tossed by the winds and waves, he had exclaimed: "Lord, help me! or I perish."

The monks of Meaux, enraged at their unfavourable reception by the bishop, resolved to carry their complaints before a higher tribunal. An appeal lay open to them. If the bishop will not give way, he may be reduced to compliance. Their leaders set out for Paris, and concerted measures with Beda and Duchesne. They hastened before the parliament, and denounced the bishop and the heretical teachers. "The city and all the neighbourhood," said they, "are infected with heresy, and its polluted waters flow from the episcopal palace."

Thus did France begin to hear the cry of persecution raised against the Gospel. The sacerdotal and the civil power, the Sorbonne and the parliament, grasped their arms,—arms that were to be stained with blood. Christianity had taught mankind that there are duties and rights anterior to all civil associations; it had emancipated the religious mind, promoted liberty of conscience, and worked a great change in society; for antiquity, which contemplated the citizen every where and the man no where, had made religion a mere matter of state. But these ideas of liberty had scarcely been given to the world, ere the papacy corrupted them; for the despotism of the prince it had substituted the despotism of the priest; and not unfrequently it had raised both prince and priest against the christian people. A new emancipation was needed; it took place in the sixteenth century. Wherever the Reformation established itself, it broke the yoke of Rome, and the religious mind was again enfranchised. But so rooted in the nature of man is the disposition to tyrannize over truth, that among many protestant nations, the Church, liberated from the arbitrary power of the priest, has again in our days fallen under the yoke of the civil power; destined, like its founder, to be bandied from one despotism to another, to pass from Caiaphas to Pilate, and from Pilate to Caiaphas.

Briçonnet had not the courage necessary for resistance. He would not yield every thing, but what he did concede satisfied Rome. "We may well do without Luther's

writings," he thought, "if we keep the Gospel; we may easily accede to a certain invocation of the Virgin, if we add that it is only by the mediation of Jesus Christ that she possesses any influence." If beside the truth we place the power of error, the papacy is satisfied. But the sacrifice which Briçonnet felt the deepest, and which yet was required of him, was the loss of his friends. If the bishop would escape, he must sacrifice his brethren. Of timid character, but little prepared to give up his riches and his station for Christ's sake, already alarmed, shaken, and cast down, he was still further led astray by treacherous advisers: if the evangelical doctors should quit Meaux (said some), they will carry the Reformation elsewhere. His heart was torn by a painful struggle. At last the wisdom of this world prevailed; he gave way, and on the 15th of October 1523, published three mandates, the first of which enjoined prayers for the dead, and the invocation of the Virgin and of the saints; the second forbade any one to buy, borrow, read, possess, or carry about with him Luther's works, and ordered them to be torn in pieces, to be scattered to the winds, or to be burnt; and the last established in express terms the doctrine of purgatory. Then, on the 13th of November in the same year, Briçonnet forbade the parish priests and their curates to permit the "Lutherans" to preach.[1] This was not all. The first president of the Parliament of Paris, and Andrew Verjus, councillor in the same court, and before whom Briçonnet had shortly afterwards to appear, arrived at Meaux during Lent 1524, no doubt to satisfy themselves of the bishop's proceedings. The poor prelate did all he could to please them. Already on the 29th of January he had taken the images of the saints under his especial protection; he now began to visit his churches, to preach, and to struggle hard in the presence of the first president and of councillor Verjus to "weed out the heresies that were there shooting up."[2] The deputies of the Parliament returned to Paris fully satisfied. This was Briçonnet's first fall.

Lefevre was the special object of hostility. His commentary on the four Gospels, and particularly the "Epistle to Christian Readers," prefixed to it, had inflamed the anger of Beda and his allies. They denounced this writing to the faculty. "Does he not dare recommend all the faithful to read the Scriptures?" said the fiery syndic. "Does he not say therein that whoever loves not Christ's Word is not a Christian;[3] and that the Word of God is sufficient to lead to eternal life?"

But Francis I. looked on this accusation as a mere theological squabble. He appointed a commission: and Lefevre, having justified

---

[1] MS. Bibl. Roy. S. F. No. 337.

[1] Hist. Généalogique de Briçonnet, ad annum.
[2] MS. Bibl. Roy. S. F. No. 337.
[3] Qui verbum ejus hoc modo non diligunt, quo pacto hi Christiani essent. Præf. Comm. in Evang.

himself before it, came off from this attack with all the honours of war.

Farel, who had not so many protectors at court, was compelled to leave Meaux. It would appear that he first repaired to Paris ;[1] and that, having unsparingly attacked the errors of Rome, he could remain there no longer, and was forced to retire to Dauphiny, whither he was eager to carry the Gospel.

At the time of the dispersion of the Christians at Meaux, another Frenchman, quitting his native country, crossed the threshold of the Augustine convent at Wittemberg, where Luther resided. This was in January 1523.

Farel was not the only man in the south of France whom God had prepared for his work. A little further to the south than Gap, on the banks of the Rhone, in that city of Avignon called by Petrarch " the third Babylon," may still be seen the walls of the " apostolic palace," which the popes and cardinals had long filled with their luxury and debauchery, and which a Roman legate now inhabited, lonely and dejected in the midst of this deserted city, whose narrow filthy streets were seldom trod but by the feet of monks and priests.

The little court of the legate was, however, sometimes enlivened by a beautiful, amiable, and laughing boy, who gambolled about its halls.[2] This was Francis Lambert, son of the secretary of the apostolic palace, born in 1487, two years before Farel. The child was at first astonished at the irreligion and crimes of these prelates,—" crimes so numerous and so enormous," says he, " that I cannot describe them."[3] He became habituated to them, however, by degrees, and it would appear that he was himself seduced by bad example.[4] Yet God had implanted in his heart a desire for holiness. His father being dead, his mother had the charge of his education, and, according to the custom of the times, intrusted him to the care of the Franciscans. The sanctified air of these monks imposed on Francis, and his timid looks followed them respectfully, as he saw them clad in coarse garments, barefoot, or with rude sandals only, moving to and fro, begging in the city and calling on his mother ; and if at any time they chanced to smile upon him, he fancied himself (he tells us) almost in heaven.[5] The monks worked upon this disposition, and Francis, attracted by them, assumed the cowl at the age of fifteen. " It was God's pleasure," said he in after-years, " that I should make known to the world the impurity of these whited sepulchres."

During the year of his noviciate every thing went on smoothly ; he was studiously kept in the dark ; but no sooner had he pronounced his vows, than the monks showed themselves in all their deformity, and the halo of sanctity that he had discovered around their heads faded away, and he remained incensed, alarmed, and dejected. Francis soon began to feel a secret strength within him, that drove him forcibly towards the Holy Scriptures,[1] and bound him to believe and to teach the Word of God. In 1517, he was nominated apostolical preacher of the convent, and instead of running about like his colleagues after " fat presents and well-stored tables," he employed himself in travelling afoot through the deserted country, and calling those ignorant people to conversion whom the fire and sincerity of his language drew in crowds around him. But when, after spending several months in passing through the Comtat Venaissin and the surrounding districts, he returned exhausted to his convent on a mule that had been given him to carry his weakened frame, and went to seek a brief repose in his poor cell, some of the monks received him with coldness, others with raillery, and a third party with anger; and they hastened to sell the animal, which they all agreed in saying was the only profit of these evangelical journeys.

One day, as brother Francis was preaching in a certain town, with a gravity quite apostolic and the vivacity of a native of the south : " Kindle a fire," exclaimed he, " before this sacred porch, and there consume the spoils of your luxury, your worldlymindedness, and your debauchery." Immediately the whole assembly was in commotion ; some lighted up a fire ; others ran into their houses and returned with dice, playing-cards, and obscene pictures ; and then, like the Christians of Ephesus at the preaching of St. Paul, cast all into the flames. A great crowd was gathered round the fire, and among them some Franciscans, who perceiving an indecent drawing of a young female, cunningly drew it away, and hid it under one of their frocks, " to add fuel to their own flames," says Lambert. This did not escape the eye of brother Francis ; a holy indignation kindled within him, and boldly addressing the monks, he inveighed against their lubricity and theft. Abashed at being discovered, they sunk their heads, gave up the picture, but swore to be revenged.[2]

Lambert, surrounded with debauchery, and become an object of hatred to the monks, felt from time to time an ardent desire to return into the world, which appeared to him infinitely more holy than the cloister : but he found something still better. Luther's

[1] Farel, après avoir subsisté tant qu'il put à Paris. Beza, Hist. Eccl. i. 6.
[2] In palatio sæpe versatus, quod genitor meus legationis ejus secretarius esset. Lamb. Epistola ad Galliæ Regem.
[3] Impietates et horrenda scelera tam multa et enormia. Ibid.
[4] Olim seductus et peccator. Ibid.
[5] Rationes propter quas minoritarum conversationem, habitumque rejecerit. Wittenberg, 1522.

[1] Urgebat me vehementer latens quædam vis (confido non aliena a Domini spiritu) ad sacrarum studia literarum. Exegesis in S. Johannis Apocalypsia, præf.
[2] Lambert von Avignon, by Professor Baum.

works, carried to the fairs of Lyons, descended the Rhone and reached his cell. They were soon taken from him and burnt; but it was too late. The spirit that animated the Augustine of Wittemberg had passed into the Franciscan of Avignon: he was saved. Vainly until then had he resorted to frequent fasting; vainly had he slept sitting on a stool;[1] vainly had he shunned the looks of woman, worn haircloth next his skin, scourged himself, and so weakened his body that he could scarcely hold himself upright, and sometimes even fainted in the churches and fields as he was preaching to the people. All this, he tells us, could not extinguish the desires and banish the thoughts that preyed upon him, and it was only in faith on the free grace of God and in the sanctity of a married life that he found purity and peace.[2] This is one of those numerous examples which prove that marriage, being of Divine appointment, is a means of grace and holiness, and that the celibacy of priests and monks, the invention of man, is one of the most effectual agents to foster impurity, sully the imagination, disturb the peace of families, and fill society with innumerable disorders.

At last the friar had made up his mind; he will quit the convent, he will abandon popery, he will leave France. He will go where the streams of the Gospel flow abundant and pure, and he will there plunge into them, and quench the fires that are consuming him.[3] Since all his efforts are unavailing, he will go to Wittemberg, to that great servant of God, whose name alone conjures and affrights the devil, in order that he may find peace.[4] He took advantage of some letters that were to be carried to one of the superiors of the order, and having donned his frock, quitted the Franciscan convent of Avignon in the spring of 1522, after twenty years of struggle. He ascended the Rhone, traversed Lyons, and crossed the forests that cover the lower ridges of the Jura. This tall, thin, ungraceful monk still wore the habit of his order, and rode on an ass, his bare feet almost touching the ground. We have already seen him pass through Geneva, Lausanne, Berne, and Zurich.[5] In the beginning of 1523, he was at Wittemberg, and embraced Luther. But let us return to France and to the Church of Meaux.

[1] Non aliter dormuisse multo tempore quam in scamno nudo sedentem. Lamb. de sacro conjugio.
[2] Donec secundum altissimi jussionem conjux factus est. Ibid.
[3] Urebar tamen etiamsi nescirent alii. Ibid.
[4] Tametsi non habeam scorta et multis modis niterer ad continentiam, nunquam pacem habui. Ibid.
[5] Vol. ii. p. 295.

CHAPTER VIII.

Lefevre and Farel persecuted—Difference between the Lutheran and Reformed Churches—Leclerc posts up his Placards—Leclerc branded—Berquin's Zeal—Berquin before the Parliament—Rescued by Francis I.—Mazurier's Apostacy—Fall and Remorse of Pavanne—Metz—Agrippa and Chatelain—Lambert at Wittemberg—Evangelical Press at Hamburg—Lambert marries—He longs to return to France—The Lots—Peter Toussaint becomes attentive—Leclerc breaks the Images—Leclerc's Condemnation and Torture—Martyrdom of Chatelain—Flight.

LEFEVRE intimidated, Briçonnet drawing back, Farel compelled to fly—here was a beginning of victory. They already imagined at the Sorbonne that they had mastered the movement; the doctors and monks congratulated each other on their triumphs. But this was not enough; blood had not flowed. They set to work again; and blood, since it must be so, was erelong to gratify the fanaticism of Rome.

The evangelical Christians of Meaux, seeing their leaders dispersed, sought to edify one another. The wool-carder, John Leclerc, whom the lessons of the doctors, the reading of the Bible, and some tracts, had instructed in the christian doctrine,[1] signalized himself by his zeal and facility in expounding Scripture. He was one of those men whom the Spirit of God fills with courage,[2] and soon places at the head of a religious movement. It was not long before the Church of Meaux regarded him as its minister.

The idea of a universal priesthood, such a living principle among the first Christians, had been re-established by Luther in the sixteenth century.[3] But this idea seems then to have existed only in theory in the Lutheran church, and to have been really acted upon solely among the reformed Christians. The Lutheran Churches (and here they agree with the Anglican Church) perhaps took a middle course between the Romish and the Reformed Churches. Among the Lutherans, every thing proceeded from the pastor or the priest; and nothing was counted valid in the Church that did not flow regularly through its chiefs. But the Reformed Churches, while they maintained the Divine appointment of the ministry, which some sects deny, approached nearer to the primitive condition of the apostolical communities. From the times of which we are speaking, they recognised and proclaimed that the christian flocks ought not simply to receive what the pastor gives; that the members of the Church as well as its leaders, possess the key of that treasure whence they derive their instruction, for the Bible is in the hands of all; that the graces of God, the spirit of faith, of wisdom, of consolation, of light, are not bestowed on the pastor only; that every man is called upon to employ the gift he has

[1] Aliis pauculis libellis diligenter lectis. Bezæ Icones.
[2] Animosæ fidei plenus. Ibid.
[3] See vol. ii. p. 188.

received for the good of all; and that a certain gift, necessary to the edification of the Church, may be refused to a minister, and yet granted to one of his flock. Thus the passive state of the Church was then changed into a state of general activity; and in France, especially, this revolution was accomplished. In other countries, the reformers were almost exclusively pastors and doctors; but in France men of learning had from the very beginning pious men of the people for their allies. In that country God selected for his first workmen a doctor of the Sorbonne and a wool-comber.

The wool-comber Leclerc began to visit from house to house, confirming the disciples. But not stopping short at these ordinary cares, he would fain have seen the edifice of popery overthrown, and France, from the midst of these ruins, turning with a cry of joy towards the Gospel. His unguarded zeal may remind us of that of Hottinger at Zurich, and of Carlstadt at Wittemberg. He wrote a proclamation against the Antichrist of Rome, announcing that the Lord was about to destroy it by the breath of his mouth. He then boldly posted his "placards" on the gates of the cathedral.[1] Presently all was in confusion around that ancient edifice. The faithful were amazed; the priests exasperated. What! a fellow whose employment is wool-combing dares measure himself with the pope! The Franciscans were outrageous, and demanded that this once at least a terrible example should be made. Leclerc was thrown into prison.

His trial was finished in a few days, under the eyes of Briçonnet himself, who was now to witness and tolerate all that was done. The carder was condemned to be whipped three days successively through the city, and on the third to be branded on the forehead. This sad spectacle soon began. Leclerc was led through the streets with his hands bound, his back bare, and the executioners inflicted on him the blows he had drawn upon himself by rising up against the Bishop of Rome. An immense crowd followed in the track marked by the martyr's blood. Some yelled with rage against the heretic; others by their silence gave him no unequivocal marks of their tender compassion. One woman encouraged the unhappy man by her looks and words: she was his mother.

At last, on the third day, when the blood-stained procession was ended, they halted with Leclerc at the usual place of execution. The hangman prepared the fire, heated the iron that was to stamp its burning mark on the evangelist, and approaching him, branded him on the forehead as a heretic. A shriek was heard, but it did not proceed from the martyr. His mother, a spectator of the dreadful scene, and wrung with anguish, endured a bitter strife: it was the enthusiasm of faith struggling in her heart with maternal love; faith prevailed at last, and she exclaimed with a voice that made the adversaries tremble: "Glory to Jesus Christ and to his witnesses!"[1] Thus did that Frenchwoman of the sixteenth century fulfil the commandment of the Son of God: "He that loveth his son more than me is not worthy of me." Such boldness, and at such a moment, merited signal punishment; but this christian mother had appalled the hearts both of priests and soldiers. All their fury was controlled by a stronger arm than theirs. The crowd, respectfully making way, allowed the martyr's mother slowly to regain her humble dwelling. The monks, and even the town-sergeants, gazed on her without moving. "Not one of her enemies dared lay hands upon her," said Theodore Beza. After this execution, Leclerc, being set at liberty, retired to Rosay in Brie, a small town about six leagues from Meaux, and subsequently to Metz, where we shall meet with him again.

The adversaries were triumphant. "The Cordeliers having re-captured the pulpits, propagated their lies and trumpery as usual."[2] But the poor workmen of the city, prevented from hearing the Word in regular assemblies, "began to meet in secret," says our chronicler, "after the manner of the sons of the prophets in the time of Ahab, and of the Christians of the primitive Church; and, as opportunity offered, they assembled at one time in a house, at another in some cave, sometimes also in a vineyard or in a wood. There, he amongst them who was most versed in the Holy Scriptures exhorted the rest; and this done, they all prayed together with great courage, supporting each other by the hope that the Gospel would be revived in France, and that the tyranny of Antichrist would come to an end."[3] There is no power that can arrest the progress of truth.

But one victim only was not enough; and if the first against whom the persecution was let loose was a wool-comber, the second was a gentleman of the court. It was necessary to frighten the nobles as well as the people. Their reverences of the Sorbonne of Paris could not think of being outstripped by the Franciscans of Meaux. Berquin, "the most learned of the nobles," had derived fresh courage from the Holy Scriptures, and after having attacked "the hornets of the Sorbonne" in certain epigrams, had openly accused them of impiety.[4]

Beda and Duchesne, who had not ventured to reply in their usual manner to the witti-

---

[1] Cet hérétique écrivit des pancartes qu'il attacha aux portes de la grande église de Meaux (MS. de Meaux). See also Bezæ Icones; Crespin Actes des Martyrs, &c.

[1] Hist. Eccles. de Th. de Bèze, p. 4. Hist. des Martyrs de Crespin, p. 92.
[2] Actes des Martyrs, p. 183.
[3] Ibid.
[4] Impietatis etiam accusatos, tum voce, tum scriptis Bezæ Icones.

cisms of the king's gentleman, changed their mind, as soon as they discovered that beneath serious convictions lay these attacks. Berquin had become a Christian: his ruin was determined on. Beda and Duchesne, having seized some of his translations, found in them sufficient to burn more heretics than one. "He maintains," said they, "that it is wrong to invoke the Virgin Mary in place of the Holy Ghost, and to call her the source of all grace.[1] He inveighs against the practice of calling her *our hope, our life,* and says that these titles belong only to the Son of God." There were other matters besides these. Berquin's study was like a bookseller's shop, whence works of corruption were circulated through the whole kingdom. The *Commonplaces* of Melancthon, in particular, served, by the elegance of their style, to shake the faith of the literary men in France. This pious noble, living only amidst his folios and his *tracts*, had become, out of christian charity, translator, corrector, printer, and bookseller......It was essential to check this formidable torrent at its very source.

One day, as Berquin was quietly seated at his studies, among his beloved books, his house was suddenly surrounded by the sergeants-at-arms, who knocked violently at the door. They were the Sorbonne and its agents, who, furnished with authority from the parliament, were making a domiciliary visit. Beda, the formidable syndic, was at their head, and never did inquisitor perform his duty better; accompanied by his satellites, he entered Berquin's library, told him his business, ordered a watchful eye to be kept upon him, and began his search. Not a book escaped his piercing glance, and an exact inventory of the whole was drawn up by his orders. Here was a treatise by Melancthon, there a book by Carlstadt; farther on, a work of Luther's. Here were heretical books translated from Latin into French by Berquin himself; there, others of his own composition. All the works that Beda seized, except two, were filled with Lutheran errors. He left the house, carrying off his booty, and more elated than ever was general laden with the spoils of vanquished nations.[2]

Berquin saw that a great storm had burst upon him; but his courage did not falter. He despised his enemies too much to fear them. Meanwhile Beda lost no time. On the 13th of May 1523, the parliament issued a decree that all the books seized in Berquin's house should be laid before the faculty of theology. The opinion of the Sorbonne was soon pronounced; on the 25th of June it condemned all the works, with the exception of the two already mentioned, to be burnt as heretical, and ordered that Berquin should abjure his errors. The parliament ratified this decision.

The nobleman appeared before this formidable body. He knew that the next step might be to the scaffold; but, like Luther at Worms, he remained firm. Vainly did the parliament order him to retract. Berquin was not one of those *who fall away after having been made partakers of the Holy Ghost. Whosoever is begotten of God, keepeth himself, and that wicked one toucheth him not.*[1] Every fall proves that the previous conversion has been only apparent or partial; but Berquin's conversion was real. He replied with firmness to the court before which he stood. The parliament, more severe than the Diet of Worms had been, ordered its officers to seize the accused, and take him to the prison of the Conciergerie. This was on the 1st of August 1523. On the 5th the parliament handed over the heretic to the Bishop of Paris, in order that this prelate might take cognizance of the affair, and that, assisted by the doctors and councillors, he should pronounce sentence on the culprit. He was transferred to the episcopal prison.[2]

Thus was Berquin passed from court to court, and from one prison to another. Beda, Duchesne, and their cabal had their victim in their grasp; but the court still cherished a grudge against the Sorbonne, and Francis was more powerful than Beda. This transaction excited great indignation among the nobles. Do these monks and priests forget what the sword of a gentleman is worth? "Of what is he accused?" said they to Francis I.; "of blaming the custom of invoking the Virgin in place of the Holy Ghost? But Erasmus and many others blame it likewise. Is it for such trifles that they imprison a king's officer?[3] This attack is aimed at literature, true religion, the nobility, chivalry, nay the crown itself." The king was glad to have another opportunity of vexing the whole company. He issued letters transferring the cause to the royal council, and on the 8th of August an usher appeared at the bishop's prison with an order from the king to set Berquin at liberty.

The question now was whether the monks would give way. Francis I., who had anticipated some resistance, said to the agent commissioned to execute his orders: "If you meet with any resistance, I authorize you to break open the gates." This language was clear. The monks and the Sorbonne submitted to the affront, and Berquin being restored to liberty appeared before the king's council, by which he was acquitted.[4]

Thus did Francis I. humiliate the Church. Berquin imagined that France, under his reign, might emancipate herself from the papacy, and had thoughts of renewing the

---

[1] Incongrue beatam Virginem invocari pro Spiritu Sancto. Erasm. Epp. 1279.
[2] Gaillard Hist. de François I. iv. 241. Crévier, Univ. de Paris, v. 171.

[1] Hebrews vi. 4; 1 John v. 18.
[2] Ductus est in carcerem, reus hæreseos periclitatus. Erasmi Epp. 1279; Crévier; Gaillard; loc. cit.
[3] Ob hujusmodi nœnias. Erasm. Epp. 1279.
[4] At judices, ubi viderunt causam esse nullius momenti absolverunt hominem. Ibid.

war. For this purpose he entered into communication with Erasmus, who at once recognised him as a man of worth.[1] But, ever timid and temporizing, the philosopher said to him: " Beware of treading on a hornet's nest, and pursue your studies in peace.[2] Above all, do not mix me up with your affair; that would serve neither you nor me."[3]

This rebuff did not discourage Berquin; if the mightiest genius of the age draws back, he will put his trust in God who never falters. God's work will be done either with or without the aid of man. " Berquin," said Erasmus, " had some resemblance to the palm-tree; he rose up again, and became proud and towering against those who sought to alarm him."[4]

Such were not all who had embraced the evangelical doctrine. Martial Mazurier had been one of the most zealous preachers. He was accused of teaching very erroneous opinions,[5] and even of having committed certain acts of violence while at Meaux. " This Martial Mazurier, being at Meaux," says a manuscript of that city, which we have already quoted, " going to the church of the reverend Grayfriars, and seeing the image of St. Francis, with the five wounds, outside the convent-gate, where that of St. Roch now stands, threw it down and broke it in pieces." Mazurier was apprehended, and sent to the Conciergerie,[6] where he suddenly fell into deep reflection and severe anguish. It was the morality rather than the doctrine of the Gospel that had attracted him to the ranks of the reformers; and morality left him without strength. Alarmed at the prospect of the stake, and decidedly of opinion that in France the victory would remain on the side of Rome, he easily persuaded himself that he would enjoy more influence and honour by returning to the papacy. Accordingly he retracted what he had taught, and caused doctrines the very opposite of those he had previously held to be preached in his parish;[7] and subsequently joining the most fanatical doctors, and particularly the celebrated Ignatius Loyola, he became from that time the most zealous supporter of the papal cause.[8] From the days of the Emperor Julian, apostates, after their infidelity, have always become the most merciless persecutors of the doctrines they had once professed.

Mazurier soon found an opportunity of showing his zeal. The youthful James Pavanne had also been thrown into prison. Martial hoped that by making him fall like himself, he might cover his own shame. The youth, amiability, learning, and uprightness of Pavanne, created a general interest in his favour, and Mazurier imagined that he would himself be less culpable, if he could persuade Master James to follow his example. He visited him in prison, and began his manoeuvres by pretending that he had advanced further than Pavanne in the knowledge of the truth: " You are mistaken, James," he often repeated to him; " you have not gone to the depths of the sea; you only know the surface of the waters."[1] Nothing was spared, neither sophistry, promises, nor threats. The unhappy youth, seduced, agitated, and shaken, sunk at last under these perfidious attacks, and publicly retracted his pretended errors on the morrow of Christmas-day 1524. But from that hour a spirit of dejection and remorse was sent on Pavanne by the Almighty. A deep sadness preyed upon him, and he was continually sighing. " Alas!" repeated he, " there is nothing but bitterness for me in life." Sad wages of unbelief!

Nevertheless, among those who had received the Word of God in France, were men of more intrepid spirit than Mazurier and Pavanne. About the end of the year 1523, Leclerc had withdrawn to Metz in Lorraine, and there, says Theodore Beza, he had followed the example of Saint Paul at Corinth, who, while working at his trade as a tentmaker, persuaded the Jews and the Greeks.[2] Leclerc, still pursuing his occupation as a wool-carder, instructed the people of his own condition; and many of them had been really converted. Thus did the humble artisan lay the foundation of a church which afterwards became celebrated.

Leclerc was not the first individual who had endeavoured to shed the new light of the Gospel over Metz. A scholar, renowned in that age for his skill in the occult sciences, Master Agrippa of Nettesheim, " a marvellously learned clerk, of small stature, who had spent much time in travel, who spoke every language, and had studied every science,"[3] had fixed his residence at Metz, and had even become syndic of the city. Agrippa had procured Luther's works, and communicated them to his friends,[4] and among others to Master John, priest of Sainte-Croix, himself a great clerk, and with whom Master Agrippa was very intimate. Many of the clergy, nobility, and citizens, stirred by the courage Luther had shown at Worms, were gained over to his cause,[5] and already in March 1522, an evangelical placard extolling what Luther had done was posted in large letters on a corner of the

[1] Ex epistola visus est mihi vir bonus. Erasm. Epp. 1279.
[2] Sineret crabrones et suis se studiis oblectaret. Ibid.
[3] Deinde ne me involveret suæ causæ. Ibid.
[4] Ille, ut habebat quiddam cum palma commune, adversus deterrentem tollebat animos. Ibid. There is probably an allusion to Pliny's Natural History, xvi. 42.
[5] Hist. de l'Université, par Crévier, v. 203.
[6] Gaillard, Hist. de François I. v. 234.
[7] " Comme il était homme adroit, il esquiva la condamnation," says Crévier, v. 203.
[8] Cum Ignatio Loyola init amicitiam. Launoi, Navarræ gymnasii historia, p. 621.

[1] Actes des Martyrs, p. 99.
[2] Acts of the Apostles, xviii. 3, 4.—Apostoli apud Corinthios exemplum secutus. Bezæ Icones.
[3] Les chroniques de la ville de Metz. Metz, 1838.
[4] Apud Metenses mihi nonnulla Lutherana communicare dignatus sis. Amicus ad Agrippam, Epp. lib. iii. ep. 10.
[5] Lambert von Avignon, by Prof. Baum, p. 59.

episcopal palace, and excited much public attention. But when Leclerc arrived, the flames, for an instant overpowered, sprung up with renewed energy. In the council-room, in the hall of the chapter, and in the homes of the citizens, the conversation turned perpetually on the Lutheran business. "Many great clerks and learned persons were daily questioning, discussing, and debating this matter, and for the most part taking Luther's side, and already preaching and proclaiming that accursed sect."[1]

Erelong the evangelical cause received a powerful reinforcement. "About this same time (1524)," says the chronicle, "there came to Metz an Augustine friar named John Chaistellain (Chatelain), a man declining in years, and of agreeable manners, a great preacher and very eloquent, a wondrous comforter to the poorer sort. By which means he gained the good-will of most of the people (not of all), especially of the majority of the priests and great rabbins, against whom the said friar John preached daily, setting forth their vices and their sins, saying that they abused the poor people, by which great animosity was stirred up."[2]

John Chatelain, an Augustine monk of Tournay, and doctor of divinity, had been brought to the knowledge of God[3] by his intercourse with the Augustines of Antwerp. The doctrine of Christ, when preached by him attired in chasuble and stole, appeared less extraordinary to the inhabitants of Metz, than when it fell from the lips of a poor artizan, who laid aside the comb with which he carded his wool, to explain a French version of the Gospel.

Every thing was fermenting in Metz during that famous Lent of 1524, when a new character appeared on the stage, a priest, a doctor, an ex-friar, and (what had never yet been seen in France or Lorraine) having a wife with him.[4] This was Lambert of Avignon.

On Lambert's arrival at Wittemberg, which had been the object of his journey on leaving the convent, he was well received by Luther, and the reformer had hastened to recommend to Spalatin and to the elector this friar, who "on account of persecution, had chosen poverty and exile......He pleases me in all respects," added Luther.[5] Lambert had begun to lecture on the prophet Hosea at the university, before an auditory who could not conceal their surprise at hearing such things from the mouth of a Gaul.[6] And then, with eyes ever turned towards his native land, he had begun to translate into French and Italian several evangelical pamphlets published by Luther and other doctors. He was not the only Frenchman at Wittemberg: he there met with counts, knights, nobles, and others come from France to see the elector and to converse with Luther, "the overseer of the works that were accomplishing in the world."[1] These Frenchmen mutually encouraged each other, and, as is usual with emigrants, exaggerated the state of affairs, imagining that a speedy revolution would lead to the triumph in their own country of the cause which they had so much at heart. "Almost the whole of Gaul is stirring," wrote Lambert to the Elector of Saxony. "Although in France the truth has no master and no leader, its friends are very numerous."[2]

One thing alone checked these Frenchmen at Wittemberg: the printing of the pamphlets intended for their countrymen. "Would that I could find some one," exclaimed Lambert, "that could print not only in Latin, but in French and even in Italian."[3] This was the posture of affairs when certain strangers appeared: they were from Hamburg. "We come to ask you for some French treatises," said they to Lambert; "for we have some one in Hamburg who will print them carefully."[4] It would appear that there were also a number of French emigrants at Hamburg, and a printer among the rest. Lambert could not restrain his joy; but there was still another difficulty: "And how," said he, "can we convey these books into France from the banks of the Elbe?"— "By sea; by the vessels that sail to and fro," replied the Hamburgers.[5] "Every necessary arrangement has been made." Thus the Gospel had hardly been restored to the Church, before the ocean became an instrument of its dissemination. *The Lord maketh a way in the sea.*[6]

Yet this could not suffice; every Frenchman returning into France was to carry a few books with him. although the scaffold might be the reward of his enterprise. *Now* there is more talking, *then* there was more action. A young French nobleman. Claude of Taureau, who left Wittemberg in May 1523, took with him a great number of evangelical treatises and letters which Lambert had written to many of the most conspicuous men of France and Savoy.[7]

On the 13th of July 1523, Lambert, then at the age of thirty-six, "determined (in his

[1] Chroniques de Metz, anno 1523.
[2] Ibid. p. 808.
[3] Vocatus ad cognitionem Dei. Act. Mart. p. 180.
[4] Y vient ung, se disant docteur, qui premier avait esté religieulx et à présent estait marié. Chroniques de Metz, p. 807.
[5] Ob persecutionem exul atque pauper factus; mihi per omnia placet vir. L. Epp. ii. 302.
[6] Aliquid nostri Martini consilio exordiar, vel Oseam Prophetam, vel Psalmos, vel Lucam, vel aliquid tale. Schelhorn, Amœnitates Litt. iv. 336.

[1] Veniunt passim Wittembergam Comites, Equites, Nobiles, et alii etiam e Gallia nostra ut te inclytum Ducem (the Elector) videant, et Præfectum Operum, M. Lutherum. Comment. in Oseam præf.
[2] Gallia pene omnis commota est, et absque magistro sinceros habet veritatis dilectores. Schelhorn, Amœn. iv.
[3] Si inveniatur qui imprimat non tantum Latine sed Gallice et Italice, hæc atque alia tradam. Ibid.
[4] Quod ad me ex Amburgo nuntii advenerint tractatus Gallicos postulantes; aiunt enim quod illic sit qui ea lingua elimatissimos posset cudere libros. Ibid. p. 343.
[5] Quos demum navigio in Galliam mittit. Ibid.
[6] Isaiah xliii. 16.
[7] Occupatus multis scriptis potissimum quæ pluribus in Gallia misi. Junior quippe nobilis Claudius de Tauro abiit Ibid.

own words) to flee the paths of impurity as he had always done," entered into the holy bonds of wedlock, two years before Luther, and the first of the French monks or priests. When married, he called to mind that he ought not to think " how he might please his wife, but how he might please the Lord." Christina, the daughter of a worthy citizen of Herzberg, was ready to be the companion of his sufferings. Lambert told his Wittemberg friends that he intended returning to France.

Luther and Melancthon were terrified at the thought. " It is rather from France to Germany," said Luther, "than from Germany to France, that you should go."[1] Lambert, all whose thoughts were in France, paid no attention to the reformer's advice.[2]

And yet Luther's sentiments could not fail to make some impression on him. Should he go to Zurich, whither Luther urges him? or to France or Lorraine, where Farel and, as he believes, Christ himself are calling him? He was in great perplexity.[3] At Zurich he would find peace and safety; in France peril and death.[4] His rest was broken, he could find no repose;[5] he wandered through the streets of Wittemberg with downcast eyes, and his wife could not restore him to serenity. At last he fell on his knees, and called upon the Lord to put an end to his struggle, by making known His will in the casting of lots.[6] He took two slips of paper; on one he wrote *France*, on the other *Switzerland;* he closed his eyes and drew; the lot had fallen on France.[7] Again he fell on his knees: " O God," said he, " if thou wilt not close these lips that desire to utter thy praise, deign to make known thy pleasure."[8] Again he tried, and the answer still was *France.* And some hours after, recollecting (said he) that Gideon, when called to march against the Midianites, had thrice asked for a sign from heaven near the oak of Ophrah,[9] he prayed God a third time, and a third time the lot replied *France.* From that hour he hesitated no longer, and Luther, who could not put such confidence in the lot, for the sake of peace, ceased urging his objections, and Lambert, in the month of February or March 1524, taking his wife with him, departed for Strasburg, whence he repaired to Metz.

He soon became intimate with Chatelain, whom he called " his Jonathan," and appearing before a meeting commissioned to inquire into his doctrines: " Suffer me to preach in public," said the man of Avignon, "and I will forthwith publish one hundred and sixteen theses explanatory of my doctrine, which I will defend against all manner of persons."

The Chamber of XIII., messieurs the clerks, and messeigneurs of justice, before whom Lambert had been called, were frightened at such a request, and refused permission; and shortly after, the whole troop of Antichrist was in commotion, said Lambert; canons, monks, inquisitors, the bishop's officials, and all their partisans, endeavoured to seize and throw him into the dungeon of some cloister.[1] The magistrates protected Lambert, but intimated that he had better leave the city. Lambert obeyed. " I will flee," said he to his Master, "but will still confess thy name! Whenever it be thy good pleasure, I will endure death. I am in thy hands; I flee, and yet I flee not; it is the flight which becometh all those who are made perfect."[2] Lambert had not been a fortnight in Metz. He was to learn that God makes known his will by other means than the drawing of lots. It was not for France that this monk from the banks of the Rhone was destined; we shall soon behold him playing an important part in Germany, as reformer of Hesse. He returned to Strasburg, leaving Chatelain and Leclerc at Metz.

Owing to the zeal of these two men the light of the Gospel spread more and more through the whole city. A very devout woman, named Toussaint, of the middle rank, had a son called Peter, with whom, in the midst of his sports, she would often converse in a serious strain. Every where, even in the homes of the townspeople, something extraordinary was expected. One day the child, indulging in the amusements natural to his age, was riding on a stick in his mother's room, when the latter, conversing with her friends on the things of God, said to them with an agitated voice: " Antichrist will soon come with great power, and destroy those who have been converted at the preaching of Elias."[3] These words being frequently repeated attracted the child's attention, and he recollected them long after. Peter Toussaint was no longer a child when the doctor of theology and the wool-comber were preaching the Gospel at Metz. His relations and friends, surprised at his youthful genius, hoped to see him one day filling an eminent station in the Church. One of

[1] Potius ad nos illinc, quam ad vos hinc, cuiquam migrandum esse. L. Epp. ad Gerbellium Strasburg, ii. 438.
[2] Nec audit meum consilium, sic occupatus suo proprio. Ibid. 437.
[3] In gravissima perplexitate. Lambert de Fidelium vocatione, cap. 22.
[4] In priore vocatione erat pax et serenitas; in alia vero multa et eadem gravissima, etiam mortis pericula erant.
[5] Nulla erat misero requies, ut quidem vixdum somnium caperet. Ibid.
[6] Oravit Dominum, ut hanc contradictionem sorte dirimeret. Ibid.
[7] Et sors cecidit super vocatione secunda. Ibid.
[8] Ut non clauderetur omnino os Deum laudare volentis. Ibid. I agree with Professor Baum in thinking that Lambert's narrative refers to this circumstance.
[9] Judges vi. 20-40.

[1] Sed mox insanavit tota Antichristi cohors, nempe canonici, monachi, inquisitor, officialis, et reliqui qui sunt ex parte eorum et me capere voluerunt. Epistola ad Franciscum regem.
[2] In manu tua sum, sic fugio quasi non fugiam. Hæc est fuga omnibus perfectissimis conveniens. De vocatione fidelium, cap. 15.
[3] Cum equitabam in arundine longa, memini sæpe audisse mea a matre venturum Antichristum cum potentia magna, perditurumque eos qui essent ad Eliæ prædicationem conversi. Tossanus Farello, 4th September 1525, MS. in the conclave of Neufchatel.

his uncles, his father's brother, was dean of Metz; it was the highest dignity in the chapter.[1] The Cardinal John of Lorraine, son of Duke René, who maintained a large establishment, testified much regard for the dean and his nephew. The latter, notwithstanding his youth, had just obtained a prebend, when he began to lend an attentive ear to the Gospel. Might not the preaching of Chatelain and Leclerc be that of Elias? It is true, Antichrist is already arming against it in every quarter. But it matters not. " Let us lift up our heads to the Lord," said he, " for he will come and will not tarry."[2]

The evangelical doctrine was making its way into the first families of Metz. The chevalier D'Esch, a man highly respected, and the dean's intimate friend, had just been converted.[3] The friends of the Gospel rejoiced. " The knight, our worthy master," ......repeated Peter, adding with noble candour; " if, however, we are permitted to have a master upon earth."[4]

Thus Metz was about to become a focus of light, when the imprudent zeal of Leclerc suddenly arrested this slow but sure progress, and aroused a storm that threatened utter ruin to the rising church. The common people of Metz continued walking in their old superstitions, and Leclerc's heart was vexed at seeing this great city plunged in " idolatry." One of their great festivals was approaching. About a league from the city stood a chapel containing images of the Virgin and of the most celebrated saints of the country, and whither all the inhabitants of Metz were in the habit of making a pilgrimage on a certain day in the year, to worship the images and to obtain the pardon of their sins.

The eve of the festival had arrived: Leclerc's pious and courageous soul was violently agitated. Has not God said: *Thou shalt not bow down to their gods; but thou shalt utterly overthrow them, and quite break down their images?*[5] Leclerc thought that this command was addressed to him, and without consulting either Chatelain, Esch, or any of those who he might have suspected would have dissuaded him, quitted the city in the evening, just as night was coming on, and approached the chapel. There he pondered a while sitting silently before the statues. He still had it in his power to withdraw: but......to-morrow, in a few hours, the whole city that should worship God alone will be kneeling down before these blocks of wood and stone. A struggle ensued in the wool-comber's bosom, like that which we trace in so many Christians of the primitive ages of the Church. What matters it to him

that what he sees are the images of saints, and not of heathen gods and goddesses? Does not the worship which the people pay to these images belong to God alone? Like Polyeucte before the idols in the temple, his heart shudders, his courage revives:

Ne perdons plus de temps, le sacrifice est prêt,
Allons y du vrai Dieu soutenir l'intérêt ;
Allons fouler aux pieds ce foudre ridicule,
Dont arme un bois pourri ce peuple trop crédule ;
Allons en éclairer l'aveuglement fatal,
Allons briser ces dieux de pierre et de métal ;
Abandonnons nos jours à cette ardeur céleste—
Faisons triompher Dieu ;—qu'il dispose du reste.[1]
Corneille, Polyeucte.

Leclerc arose, approached the images, took them down and broke them in pieces, indignantly scattering their fragments before the altar. He doubted not that the Spirit of the Lord had excited him to this action, and Theodore Beza thought the same.[2] After this, Leclerc returned to Metz, which he entered at daybreak, unnoticed save by a few persons as he was entering the gates.[3]

Meanwhile all were in motion in the ancient city; bells were ringing ; the brotherhoods were assembling ; and the whole population of Metz, headed by the canons, priests, and monks, went forth in solemn procession ; they recited prayers or sung hymns to the saints they were going to adore ; crosses and banners moved on in due order, and instruments of music or drums responded to the voices of the faithful. At length, after nearly an hour's march, the procession reached the place of pilgrimage. But what was the astonishment of the priests, when advancing, censer in hand, they discovered the images they had come to worship mutilated and covering the earth with their fragments. They recoiled with horror, and announced this sacrilegious act to the crowd. Suddenly the chanting ceased, the instruments were silent, the banners lowered, and the whole multitude was in a state of indescribable agitation. The canons, priests, and monks endeavoured to inflame their minds, and excited the people to search for the criminal, and demand his death.[4] But one cry burst from every lip: " Death, death to the sacrilegious wretch!" They returned to Metz in haste and in disorder.

Leclerc was known to all ; many times he had called the images idols. Besides, had he not been seen at daybreak returning from the direction of the chapel? He was seized ; he immediately confessed his crime, and conjured the people to worship God alone. But this language still further exasperated the fury of the multitude, who would have dragged him to instant death. When led before his judges, he boldly declared that Jesus Christ, God manifest in the flesh, should alone be adored. He was sentenced to be

---

[1] Tossanus Farello, 21st July 1525.
[2] Levemus interim capita nostra ad Dominum qui veniet et non tardabit. Ibid. 4th September 1525.
[3] Clarissimum illum equitem....cui multum familiaritatis et amicitiæ, cum primicerio Metensi, patruo meo. Ibid. 2d Aug. 1524.
[4] Ibid. 21st July 1525. MS. of Neufchatel.
[5] Exodus xx. 4; xxiii. 24.

[1] What many admire in verse they condemn in history.
[2] Divini spiritus afflatu impulsus. Bezæ Icones.
[3] Mane apud urbis portas deprehensus.
[4] Totam civitatem concitarunt ad auctorem ejus facinoris quærendum. Act. Mart. Lat. p. 189.

burnt alive, and taken out to the place of execution.

Here a fearful scene awaited him. The cruelty of his persecutors had been contriving all that could render his punishment more horrible. Near the scaffold men were heating pincers that were to serve as the instruments of their rage. Leclerc, firm and calm, heard unmoved the wild yells of the monks and people. They began by cutting off his right hand; then taking up the burning pincers, they tore off his nose; after this, they lacerated his arms, and when they had thus mangled them in several places, they concluded by burning his breasts.[1] While his enemies were in this manner wreaking their vengeance on his body, Leclerc's mind was at rest. He recited solemnly and with a loud voice[2] these words of David: *Their idols are silver and gold, the work of men's hands. They have mouths, but they speak not; eyes have they, but they see not; they have ears, but they hear not; noses have they, but they smell not; they have hands, but they handle not; feet have they, but they walk not; neither speak they through their throat. They that make them are like unto them; so is every one that trusteth in them. O Israel, trust thou in the Lord; he is their help and their shield.* (Psalm cxv. 4–9.) The sight of such fortitude daunted the enemies, and strengthened the faithful;[3] the people, who had before shown so much anger, were astonished and touched with compassion.[4] After these tortures Leclerc was burnt by a slow fire. in conformity with his sentence. Such was the death of the first martyr of the Gospel in France.

But the priests of Metz were not satisfied. In vain had they endeavoured to shake the constancy of Chatelain. "He is deaf as an adder," said they, "and refuses to hear the truth."[5] He was seized by the creatures of the Cardinal of Lorraine and carried to the castle of Nommeny.

He was then degraded by the bishop's officers, who stripped him of his priestly vestments, and scraped his fingers with a piece of glass, saying: "By this scraping, we deprive thee of the power to sacrifice, consecrate, and bless, which thou receivedst by the anointing of hands."[6] Then, throwing over him a layman's dress, they surrendered him to the secular power, which condemned him to be burnt alive. The pile was soon erected, and the minister of Christ consumed by the flames. "Lutheranism spread not the less through the whole district of Metz," says the authors of the history of the Galli-can Church, who in other respects highly approve of this severity.

As soon as this storm began to beat upon the Church at Metz, tribulation had entered into Toussaint's family. His uncle, the dean, without taking an active part in the measures directed against Leclerc and Chatelain, shuddered at the thought that his nephew was one of their party. His mother's alarm was greater still. There was not a moment to lose; the liberty and life of all who had lent their ear to the Gospel were endangered. The blood that the inquisitors had shed had only increased their thirst: more scaffolds would erelong be raised. Peter Toussaint, the knight Esch, and many others, hastily quitted Metz, and sought refuge at Basle.

CHAPTER IX.

Farel and his Brothers—Farel expelled from Gap—He preaches in the Fields—The Knight Anemond of Coct—The Minorite—Anemond quits France—Luther to the Duke of Savoy—Farel quits France.

THUS violently did the storm of persecution rage at Meaux and at Metz. The north of France rejected the Gospel: the Gospel for a while gave way. But the Reformation only changed its ground; and the provinces of the south-east became the scene of action.

Farel, who had taken refuge at the foot of the Alps, was there labouring with great activity. It was of little moment to him to enjoy the sweets of domestic life in the bosom of his family. The rumour of what had taken place at Meaux and at Paris had filled his brothers with a certain degree of terror; but an unknown power was drawing them towards the new and admirable things on which William conversed with them. The latter besought them with all the impetuosity of his zeal to be converted to the Gospel;[1] and Daniel, Walter, and Claude were at last won over to that God whom their brother announced. They did not at first abandon the religious worship of their forefathers; but, when persecution arose, they courageously sacrificed their friends, their property, and their country, to worship Jesus Christ in freedom.[2] The brothers of Luther and of Zwingle do not appear to have been so decidedly converted to the Gospel; the French Reform from its very commencement had a more tender and domestic character.

Farel did not confine his exhortations to his brethren; he proclaimed the truth to his relations and friends at Gap and in the neighbourhood. It would even appear, if we may credit a manuscript, that, profiting by the

---

[1] Naso candentibus forcipibus abrepto, iisdemque brachio utroque ipsisque mammis crudelissime perustis. Bezæ Icones ; MS. de Meaux Crespin, &c.
[2] Altissima voce recitans. Bezæ Icones.
[3] Adversariis territis, piis magnopere confirmatis. Ibid.
[4] Nemo qui non commoveretur, attonitus. Act. Mart. Lat. p. 189.
[5] Instar aspidis serpentis aures omni surditate affecta. Ibid. p. 183.
[6] Utriusque manus digitos lamina vitrea erasit. Ibid. p. 86.

[1] Choupard MS.
[2] Farel, gentilhomme de condition, doué de bons moyens, lesquels il perdit tous pour sa religion, aussi bien que trois autres siens frères. Geneva MS.

friendship of certain clergymen, he began to preach the Gospel in several churches;[1] but other authorities positively declare that he did not at this time ascend the pulpit. However this may be, the doctrine he professed caused great agitation. The multitude and the clergy desired to silence him. " What new and strange heresy is this?" said they; " must all the practices of piety be counted vain? He is neither monk nor priest: he has no business to preach."[2]

Erelong all the civil and ecclesiastical powers of Gap combined against Farel. He was evidently an agent of that sect which the whole country is opposing. " Let us cast this firebrand of discord far from us," they exclaimed. Farel was summoned to appear, harshly treated, and violently expelled from the city.[3]

He did not, however, abandon his native country: were there not in the fields, the villages, the banks of the Durance, of the Guisanne, and of the Isère, many souls that stood in need of the Gospel? and if he incurred any danger, could he not find an asylum in those forests, caverns, and steep rocks that he had so often traversed in his youth? He began, therefore, to go through the country preaching in private houses and in solitary fields, and seeking an asylum in the woods and on the brink of torrents.[4] This was a school in which God trained him for other labours. " The crosses, persecutions, and machinations of Satan, of which I was forewarned, have not been wanting," said he; " they are even much severer than I could have borne of myself; but God is my father; He has provided and always will provide me the strength which I require."[5] A great number of the inhabitants of these rural districts received the truth from his lips. Thus the persecution that had driven Farel from Paris and from Meaux, contributed to the spread of the Reformation in the provinces of the Saone, of the Rhone, and of the Alps. Every age has witnessed the fulfilment of the saying of Scripture: *They that were scattered abroad went every where preaching the Word.*[6]

Among the Frenchmen who were at that time gained over to the Gospel was a gentleman of Dauphiny, the chevalier Anemond de Coct, younger son of the auditor of Coct, lord of Châtelard. He was active, ardent, and lively, sincerely pious, and a foe to relics, processions, and the clergy; he received the evangelical doctrine with great alacrity, and was soon entirely devoted to it. He could not endure forms in religion, and would gladly have abolished all the ceremonies of the Church. The religion of the heart, the inward worship, was in his view the only true one. " Never," said he, " has my spirit found any rest in externals. The sum of Christianity is comprised in these words: *John truly baptized with water, but ye shall be baptized with the Holy Ghost; ye must put on the new man.*"[1]

Coct, endued with all the vivacity of a Frenchman, spoke and wrote at one time in Latin, at another in French. He read and quoted Donatus, Thomas Aquinas, Juvenal, and the Bible! His style was abrupt, passing suddenly from one idea to another. Ever in motion, he presented himself wherever a door seemed open to the Gospel, or a celebrated doctor was to be heard. By his cordiality he won the hearts of all his acquaintances. " He is distinguished by rank and learning," said Zwingle at a later period, " but more distinguished still for piety and affability."[2] Anemond is the type of many of the reformed Frenchmen. Vivacity, simple-heartedness, zeal sometimes carried even to imprudence, are the qualities often found in those of his fellow-countrymen who embraced the Gospel. But at the opposite extreme of the French character we find the serious features of Calvin, a weighty counterpoise to the levity of Coct. Calvin and Anemond are the two poles between which revolves the whole religious world in France.

No sooner had Anemond received the knowledge of Jesus Christ from Farel,[3] than he sought himself to gain converts to that doctrine of spirit and of life. His father was dead; his elder brother, of harsh and haughty temper, disdainfully repelled him. Lawrence, the youngest of the family, and who loved him sincerely, seemed but half to understand him. Anemond, finding himself rejected by his own kindred, turned his activity to another quarter.

Hitherto the awakening in Dauphiny had been confined solely to the laity. Farel, Anemond, and their friends, desired to see a priest at the head of this movement, which seemed as if it would shake the provinces of the Alps. There dwelt at Grenoble a minorite priest, Peter Sebville by name, a preacher of great eloquence, of an honest and good heart, not taking counsel with flesh and blood, whom God was gradually attracting to him.[4] Sebville soon became aware that there is no infallible teacher but the Word of God; and, abandoning the doctrines that are supported on human testimony alone, he determined in his own mind to preach the Word " purely, clearly, and holily.'[5] In

[1] Il prêcha l'évangile publiquement avec une grande liberté. Choupard MS.
[2] Ibid.; Hist. des Evêques de Nismes, 1738.
[3] Il fut chassé, voire fort rudement, tant par l'évêque que par ceux de la ville. Choupard MS.
[4] Olim errabundus in silvis, in nemoribus, in aquis vagatus sum. Farel ad Capit de Bucer. Basil, 25th Oct. 1526. MS. letter at Neufchatel.
[5] Non defuere cruces, persecutio, et Satanæ machinamenta. Farel Galeoto.
[6] Acts viii. 4.

[1] Nunquam in externis quievit spiritus meus. Coctus Farello MS. in the conclave of Neufchatel.
[2] Virum esse genere, doctrinaque clarum, ita pietate humanitateque longe clariorem. Zw. Epp. p. 319.
[3] In a letter to Farel he subscribes himself: *Filius tuus humilis.* 2d September 1524.
[4] Pater cœlestis animum sic tuum ad se traxit. Zwinglius Sebvillæ, Epp. p. 320.
[5] Nitide, pure, sancteque prædicare in animum inducis. Ibid.

these three words the whole of the Reformation is summed up. Coct and Farel were delighted as they heard this new preacher of grace raising his eloquent voice in their province, and thought that their own presence would henceforward be less necessary.

The more the awakening spread, the more violent became the opposition. Anemond, desirous of becoming acquainted with Luther and Zwingle, and of visiting those countries where the Reformation had originated, and indignant at the rejection of the Gospel by his fellow-countrymen, resolved to bid farewell to his home and his family. He made his will, disposing of his property, at that time in the hands of his elder brother, the lord of Châtelard, in favour of his brother Lawrence ;[1] and then quitting Dauphiny and France, he made his way with all the impetuosity of the south, through countries which it was no easy matter in that age to traverse, and passing through Switzerland, hardly stopping at Basle, he arrived at Wittemberg, where Luther was residing. This was shortly after the second Diet of Nuremberg. The French gentleman accosted the Saxon doctor with his usual vivacity ; talked with him enthusiastically about the Gospel, and eagerly laid before him the plans he had formed for the propagation of the truth. The gravity of the Saxon smiled at the southern imagination of the chevalier ;[2] and Luther, notwithstanding certain prejudices against the French character, was fascinated and carried away by Anemond. He was affected by the thought that this gentleman had come from France to Wittemberg for the sake of the Gospel.[3] "Assuredly," said the reformer to his friends, "this French knight is an excellent, learned, and pious man."[4] The young noble produced the same impression on Zwingle and on Luther.

Anemond, seeing what Luther and Zwingle had done, thought that if they would turn their attention to France and Savoy, nothing could resist them. Accordingly, as he could not prevail on them to go thither, he begged them at least to write. In particular, he requested Luther to address a letter to Duke Charles of Savoy, brother to Louisa and Philiberta, and uncle to Francis I. and Margaret. "This prince," said he to the doctor, "feels great attraction towards piety and true religion,[5] and loves to converse on the Reformation with some of the persons about his court. He is just the man to understand you ; for his motto is this : *Nihil deest timentibus Deum*,[6] and this device is yours also.

Injured in turns by the empire and by France, humiliated, vexed, and always in danger, his heart stands in need of God and of his grace: all that he wants is a powerful impulse. If he were won to the Gospel, he would have an immense influence on Switzerland, Savoy, and France. Write to him, I beseech you."

Luther was wholly German in character, and would have found himself ill at ease out of Germany ; yet, animated by a true catholicism, he stretched out his hands as soon as he saw brethren, and in every place, when there was any word of exhortation to be given, he took care that it should be heard. He sometimes wrote on the same day to the farthest parts of Europe, to the Low Countries, to Savoy, and to Livonia.

"Assuredly," replied he to Anemond's request, "a love for the Gospel is a rare gift, and an inestimable jewel in a prince."[1] And he addressed a letter to the duke, which Anemond probably carried as far as Switzerland.

"May your highness pardon me," wrote Luther, "if I, a weak and despised man, presume to address you ; or rather, ascribe this boldness to the glory of the Gospel ; for I cannot see that glorious light rising and shining in any quarter without exulting at the joyful sight......It is my desire that my Lord Jesus Christ should gain many souls by the example of your most serene highness. And for this reason I desire to set our doctrine before you......We believe that the commencement of salvation and the sum of Christianity is faith in Christ, who by his blood alone, and not by our works, has made atonement for sin, and put an end to the dominion of death. We believe that this faith is a gift of God, and that it is created by the Holy Ghost in our hearts, and not found by our own labours. For faith is a living thing,[2] which spiritually begetteth the man, and maketh him a new creature."

Luther then proceeded to the consequences of faith, and showed how it could not be possessed without sweeping away the whole scaffolding of false doctrines and human works that the Church had so laboriously raised. "If grace," said he, "is obtained by Christ's blood, it is not by our own works. This is the reason why all the labours of all the cloisters are unavailing, and these institutions should be abolished, as being contrary to the blood of Jesus Christ, and leading men to trust in their own good works. Ingrafted in Christ, nothing remains for us but to do good, for having become good trees, we should bear witness to it by good fruits.

"Gracious prince and lord," said Luther in conclusion, "may your highness, who has made so happy a beginning, help to propa-

---

[1] Mon frère Annemond Coct, chevalier, au partir du pays me feist son heritier. MS. letters in the library at Neufchatel.
[2] Mire ardens in Evangelium, says Luther to Spalatin. Epp. ii. 340 ; Sehr brünstig in der Herrlichkeit des Evangelii, said he to the Duke of Savoy. Ibid. 401.
[3] Evangelii gratia huc profectus e Gallia. L. Epp. ii. 340.
[4] Hic Gallus eques....optimus vir est, eruditus ac pius. Ibid.
[5] Ein grosser Liebhaber der wahren Religion und Gottseligkeit. Ibid. 401.
[6] Nothing is wanting to those who fear God. Hist. Gén. de la Maison de Savoie, par Guichenon, ii. 228.

[1] Eine seltsame Gabe und hohes Kleinod unter den Fürsten. L. Epp. ii. 401.
[2] Der Glaube ist ein lebendig Ding. Ibid 402. The Latin is wanting.

gate this doctrine, not by the power of the sword, which would injure the Gospel, but by inviting into your states learned doctors who may preach the Word. It is by the breath of his mouth that Jesus will destroy Antichrist, in order that, as Daniel says (chap. viii. ver. 25), he may be broken without hand. For this reason, most serene prince, may your highness fan the spark that has been kindled in your heart; may a flame go forth from the house of Savoy, as in former times from the house of Joseph;[1] may all France be consumed like stubble before that fire; may it burn, blaze, and purify, so that this illustrious kingdom may truly be called *most christian*, for which it is indebted, up to this hour, solely to the rivers of blood shed in the service of Antichrist."

Thus did Luther endeavour to diffuse the Gospel in France. We are ignorant of the effect produced on the prince by this letter; but we do not learn that he ever showed any desire to separate from Rome. In 1522, he requested Adrian VI. to stand godfather to his eldest son; and, shortly after, the pope promised a cardinal's hat for his second son. Anemond, after making an effort to see the court and the Elector of Saxony, and having received a letter from Luther for this purpose,[2] returned to Basle, more decided than ever to expose his life for the Gospel. In his ardour, he would have rejoiced to possess the power of rousing the whole of France. "All that I am," said he, "all that I shall be, all that I have, all that I shall have, I am determined to consecrate to the glory of God."[3]

Anemond found his compatriot Farel at Basle. Anemond's letters had excited in him a great desire to see the reformers of Switzerland and Germany. Moreover, Farel required a sphere of activity in which he could more freely exert his strength. He therefore quitted that France which already offered nothing but scaffolds and the stake for the preachers of the unadulterated Gospel. Following byroads and concealing himself in the woods, he escaped, although with difficulty, from the hands of his enemies. Often did he lose his way. At last he reached Switzerland in the beginning of 1524. There he was destined to spend his life in the service of the Gospel, and it was then that France began to send into Helvetia those noble-minded evangelists who were to establish the Reformation in Switzerland *Romande*,[4] and to give it a new and powerful impulse in other parts of the confederation and in the whole world.

[1] Dass ein Feuer von dem Hause Sophoy ausgehe. L. Epp. ii. 406.
[2] Vult videre aulam et faciem Principis nostri. Ibid. 340.
[3] Quidquid sum, habeo, ero, habebove, ad Dei gloriam insumere mens est. Coct. Epp. MS. of Neufchatel.
[4] The French part of Switzerland, comprising the cantons of Geneva, Vaud, Neufchatel, and part of those of Friburg, Berne, and Valois.

CHAPTER X.

Catholicity of the Reformation—Friendship between Farel and Œcolampadius—Farel and Erasmus—Altercation—Farel demands a Disputation—Theses—Scripture and Faith—Discussion.

THE catholicity of the Reformation is a noble feature in its character. The Germans pass into Switzerland; the French into Germany; in latter times men from England and Scotland pass over to the continent, and doctors from the continent into Great Britain. The reformers in the different countries spring up almost independently of one another; but no sooner are they born than they hold out the hand of fellowship. There is among them one sole faith, one spirit, one Lord. It has been an error, in our opinion, to write, as hitherto, the history of the Reformation for a single country; the work is one, and from their very origin the Protestant Churches form "a whole body, fitly jointed together."[1]

Many refugees from France and Lorraine at this time formed at Basle a French Church, whose members had escaped from the scaffold. They had spoken there of Farel, of Lefevre, and of the occurrences at Meaux; and when the former arrived in Switzerland, he was already known as one of the most devoted champions of the Gospel.

He was immediately taken to Œcolampadius, who had returned to Basle some time before. Rarely does it happen that two men of more opposite character are brought together. Œcolampadius charmed by his mildness, Farel carried away his hearers by his impetuosity: but from the first moment these two men felt themselves united for ever.[2] It was another meeting of a Luther and Melancthon. Œcolampadius received Farel into his house, gave him an humble chamber, a frugal table, and introduced him to his friends; and it was not long before the learning, piety, and courage of the young Frenchman gained every heart. Pellican, Imeli, Wolfhard, and other ministers of Basle felt themselves strengthened in the faith by his energetic language. Œcolampadius was at that time much depressed in spirit: "Alas!" said he to Zwingle, "I speak in vain, and see not the least reason to hope. Perhaps among the Turks I might meet with greater success![3].........Alas!" added he with a deep sigh, "I lay the blame on myself alone." But the more he saw of Farel, the more his heart was cheered, and the courage he received from the Dauphinese became the ground-work of an undying affection. "O my dear Farel," said he, "I hope that the Lord will make our friendship immortal, and if we cannot live together here below, our joy will only be the greater when

[1] Ephes. iv. 16.
[2] Amicum semper habui a primo colloquio. Farel to Bulling. 27th May 1556.
[3] Fortasse in mediis Turcis felicius docuissem. Zw. et Ecol. Epp. p. 200.

we shall be united at Christ's right hand in heaven."[1] Pious and affecting thoughts! ......Farel's arrival was for Switzerland evidently a succour from on high.

But while this Frenchman was delighted with Œcolampadius, he shrank coldly and with noble pride from a man at whose feet all the nations of Christendom fell prostrate. The prince of the schools, he from whom every one coveted a word or a look, the master of the age—Erasmus—was neglected by Farel. The young Dauphinese had refused to go and pay homage to the old sage of Rotterdam, despising those men who are only by halves on the side of the truth, and who, though clearly aware of the consequences of error, are full of forbearance towards those who propagate it. Thus we witness in Farel that decision which has become one of the distinctive characters of the Reformation in France and French Switzerland, and which some have called stiffness, exclusiveness, and intolerance. A controversy, arising out of the commentaries of the doctor of Etaples, had begun between the two great doctors of the age, and at every entertainment the guests would take part with Erasmus against Lefevre, and Lefevre against Erasmus.[2] Farel hesitated not to take his master's side. But what had especially annoyed him was the cowardice of the philosopher of Rotterdam with regard to the evangelical Christians. Erasmus shut his door against them. Good! Farel will not go and beg for admission. This was a trifling sacrifice to him, as he felt that Erasmus possessed not that piety of heart which is the foundation of all true theology. "Frobenius's wife knows more of theology than he does," said Farel; and indignant at the conduct of Erasmus, who had written to the pope advising him how to set about extinguishing the Lutheran conflagration, he boldly affirmed that Erasmus desired to stifle the Gospel.[3]

This independence in young Farel exasperated the illustrious scholar. Princes, kings, doctors, bishops, popes, reformers, priests, men of the world—all were ready to pay him their tribute of admiration; even Luther had treated him with a certain forbearance; and this Dauphinese, unknown to fame and an exile, dared brave his power. Such insolent freedom caused Erasmus more annoyance than the homage of the whole world could give him pleasure; and accordingly he neglected no opportunity of venting his ill humour on Farel; besides, by attacking so notorious a heretic, he was clearing himself in the eyes of the Romanists from all suspicion of heresy. "I have never met with any thing more false, more violent, and more seditious than this man,"[1] said he; "his heart is full of vanity, his tongue overflowing with malice."[2] But the anger of Erasmus was not confined to Farel; it was directed against all the French refugees in Basle, whose frankness and decision offended him. They had little respect to persons; and if the truth was not openly professed, they cared not for the man, however exalted might be his genius. They were possibly wanting in some measure in the sauvity of the Gospel; but their fidelity reminds us of the vigour of the ancient prophets; and it is gratifying to meet with men who do not bow down before what the world adores. Erasmus, amazed at this lofty disdain, complained of it to every one. "What!" wrote he to Melancthon, "shall we reject pontiffs and bishops, to have more cruel, scurvy, and furious tyrants in their place;......for such it is that France has sent us."[3]—"Some Frenchmen," wrote he to the pope's secretary, in a letter accompanying his book on *Free Will*, "are still more out of their wits than even the Germans. They have five expressions always in their mouths: *Gospel, Word of God, Faith, Christ, Holy Ghost;* and yet I doubt whether they be not urged on by the spirit of Satan."[4] Instead of Farellus he would often write *Fallicus*, thus designating one of the frankest men of his day with the epithets of cheat and deceiver.

The vexation and anger of Erasmus were at their height, when it was reported to him that Farel had called him a *Balaam*. Farel believed that Erasmus, like this prophet, allowed himself (perhaps unconsciously) to be swayed by presents to curse the people of God. The learned Dutchman, unable longer to contain himself, resolved to chastise the impudent Dauphinese; and one day, as Farel was talking with several friends on the doctrines of Christianity in the presence of Erasmus, the latter, rudely interrupting him, said: "Why do you call me Balaam?"[5] Farel, at first astonished by so abrupt a question, soon recovered himself and answered, that it was not he who had given him that title. On being pressed to name the offender, he said it was Du Blet of Lyons, a refugee at Basle like himself.[6] "It may be he who made use of the word," replied Erasmus, "but it was you who taught him." And then, ashamed of having lost his temper, he quickly turned the conversation to another subject. "Why," said he to Farel, "do you assert that we ought not to invoke the saints? Is it because it is not enjoined in Holy Scripture?"—"Yes!" replied the Frenchman.—"Well then!" resumed Erasmus, "I call

[1] Mi Farelle, spero Dominum conservaturum amicitiam nostram immortalem; et si hic conjungi nequimus, tanto beatius alibi apud Christum erit contubernium. Zw. et Ecol. Epp. p. 201.
[2] Nullum est pene convivium. Er. Epp. p. 179.
[3] Consilium quo sic extinguatur incendium Lutheranum. Ibid.
[1] Quo nihil vidi mendacius, virulentius, et seditiosius. Er. Epp. p. 798.
[2] Acidæ linguæ et vanissimus. Ibid. 2129.
[3] Scabiosos....rabiosos....nam nuper nobis misit Gallia. Ibid. 350.
[4] Non dubitem quin agantur spiritu Satanæ. Ibid.
[5] Diremi disputationem. Ibid. p. 404.
[6] Ut diceret negotiatorem quemdam Dupletum hoc dixisse. Ibid. p. 2129.

upon you to prove by Scripture that we ought to invoke the Holy Ghost." Farel made this simple and true reply: "If He is God, we must invoke Him."[1]—" I dropt the conversation," says Erasmus, "for night was coming on."[2] From that hour, whenever the name of Farel fell from his pen, he represented him as a hateful person, who ought by all means to be shunned. The reformer's letters, on the contrary, are full of moderation as regards Erasmus. The Gospel is milder than philosophy, even in the most fiery temper.

The evangelical doctrine already counted many friends in Basle, both in the council and among the people; but the doctors of the university opposed it to the utmost of their power. Œcolampadius, and Stör pastor of Liestal, had maintained some theses against them. Farel thought it his duty also to profess in Switzerland the great principle of the evangelical school of Paris and of Meaux: *The Word of God is all-sufficient.* He requested permission of the university to maintain certain theses, " the rather to be reproved," added he, " if I am in error, than to teach others ; "[3] but the university refused.

Upon this Farel addressed the council; and the council issued a public notice that a christian man, named William Farel, having by the inspiration of the Holy Ghost drawn up certain articles in conformity with the Gospel,[4] they had given him leave to maintain them in Latin. The university forbade all priests and students to be present at the disputation; but the council sent out a proclamation to the contrary effect.

The following are some of the thirteen propositions put forth by Farel:

" Christ has given us the most perfect rule of life : no one has the right to take any thing from it, or to add any thing thereto.

" To live according to any other precepts than those of Christ, leads directly to impiety.

" The real ministry of priests is to attend to the ministering of the Word; and for them there is no higher dignity.

" To deprive the glad-tidings of Christ of their certainty, is to destroy them.

" He who hopes to be justified by his own power, and by his own merits, and not by faith, sets himself up as God.

" Jesus Christ, whom all things obey, is our polestar, and the only star that we ought to follow."[5]

Thus did this " Frenchman stand up in Basle.[6] It was a child of the mountains of Dauphiny, brought up in Paris at the feet of Lefevre, who thus boldly set forth in that illustrious university of Switzerland, and in the presence of Erasmus, the great principles of the Reformation. Two leading ideas pervaded Farel's theses : one, that of a return to Holy Scripture ; the other, of a return to faith : two things which the Papacy at the beginning of the 18th century distinctly condemned as impious and heretical in the famous constitution *Unigenitus*, and which, closely connected with each other, do in fact subvert the whole of the papal system. If faith in Christ is the beginning and end of Christianity, it follows that we must cleave to the Word of Christ, and not to the voice of the Church. Nay more : if faith in Christ unites souls, where is the necessity of an external bond ? Is it with croziers, bulls, and tiaras, that their holy unity is formed ? Faith joins in spiritual and true unity all those in whose hearts it takes up its abode. Thus vanished at a single blow the triple delusion of meritorious works, human traditions, and false unity; and these are the sum of Roman-catholicism.

The disputation began in Latin.[1] Farel and Œcolampadius set forth and proved their articles, calling repeatedly on their adversaries to reply; but not one of them appeared. These sophists, as Œcolampadius terms them, acted the braggart,—but in dark holes and corners.[2] The people, therefore, began to despise the cowardice of the priests, and to detest their tyranny.[3]

Thus Farel took his stand among the defenders of the Reformation. They were greatly delighted to see a Frenchman combine so much learning and piety, and already began to anticipate the noblest triumphs. " He is strong enough," said they, " to destroy the whole Sorbonne single-handed."[4] His candour, sincerity, and frankness captivated every heart.[5] But amidst all his activity, he did not forget that every mission should begin with our own souls. The gentle Œcolampadius made a compact with the ardent Farel, by which they mutually engaged to practise humility and meekness in their familiar conversations. These bold men, even on the field of battle, were fitting themselves for the duties of peace. It should be observed, however, that the impetuosity of a Luther and a Farel were necessary virtues. Some effort is required when the world is to be moved and the Church renovated. In our days we are too apt to forget this truth, which the meekest men then acknowledged. " There are certain men," wrote Œcolampadius to Luther when intro-

[1] Si Deus est, inquit, invocandus est. Er. Epp. p. 804.
[2] Omissa disputatione, nam imminebat nox. Ibid. p. 804. We have only Erasmus's account of this conversation ; he himself informs us that Farel reported it very differently.
[3] Damit er gelehrt werde, ob er irre. Fussli Beytr. iv. 244.
[4] Aus Eingiessung des heiligen Geistes ein christlicher Mensch und Bruder. Ibid.
[5] Gulielmus Farellus Christianis lectoribus, die Martis post Reminiscere. Füssli Beytr. iv. 247. Füssli does not give the Latin text.
[6] Schedam conclusionum a Gallo illo. Zw. Epp. p. 333.

[1] Schedam conclusionum, Latine apud nos disputatam. Zw. Epp. p. 333.
[2] Agunt tamen magnos interim thrasones sed in angulis lucifugæ. Ibid.
[3] Incipit tamen plebs paulatim illorum ignaviam et tyrannidem verbo Dei agnoscere. Ibid.
[4] Ad totam Sorbonicam affligendam si non et perdendam. Œcol. Luthero, Epp. p. 200.
[5] Farello nihil candidius est. Ibid.

ducing Farel to him, "who would have his zeal against the enemies of the truth more moderate ; but I cannot help seeing in this same zeal an admirable virtue, which, if seasonably exerted, is no less needed than gentleness itself."[1] Posterity has ratified the judgment of Œcolampadius.

In the month of May 1524, Farel, with some friends from Lyons, visited Schaffhausen, Zurich, and Constance. Zwingle and Myconius gladly welcomed this exile from France, and Farel remembered their kindness all his life. But on his return to Basle he found Erasmus and his other enemies at work, and received orders to quit the city. In vain did his friends loudly give utterance to their displeasure at such an abuse of authority; he was compelled to quit the territory of Switzerland, already, at this early period, the asylum and refuge of the persecuted. "It is thus we exercise hospitality," said the indignant Œcolampadius, "we true children of Sodom!"[2]

At Basle, Farel had contracted a close friendship with the Chevalier Esch, who resolved to bear him company, and they set out with letters for Luther and Capito from Œcolampadius, to whom the doctor of Basle commended Farel as "that William who had toiled so much in the work of God."[3] At Strasburg, Farel formed an intimacy with Capito, Bucer, and Hedio ; but it does not appear that he went so far as Wittemberg.

CHAPTER XI.

New Campaign—Farel's Call to the Ministry—An Outpost —Lyons—Sebville at Grenoble—Conventicles—Preaching at Lyons—Maigret in Prison—Margaret intimidated.

GOD usually withdraws his servants from the field of battle, only to bring them back stronger and better armed. Farel and his friends of Meaux, Metz, Lyons, and Dauphiny, driven from France by persecution, had been retempered in Switzerland and Germany among the elder reformers ; and now, like an army at first dispersed by the enemy, but immediately rallied, they were turning round and marching forward in the name of the Lord. It was not only on the frontiers that these friends of the Gospel were assembling ; in France also they were regaining courage, and preparing to renew the attack. The bugles were already sounding the reveillé ; the soldiers were girding on their arms, and gathering together to multiply their attacks ; their leaders were planning the order of battle ; the signal,

"Jesus, his Word, and his grace," more potent in the hour of battle than the sound of warlike music, filled all hearts with the same enthusiasm ; and every thing was preparing in France for a second campaign, to be signalized by new victories, and new and greater reverses.

Montbeliard was then calling for a labourer in the Gospel. The youthful Duke Ulrich of Wurtemberg, a violent and cruel prince, having been dispossessed of his states by the Swabian league in 1519, had taken refuge in this earldom, his only remaining possession. In Switzerland he became acquainted with the reformers ; his misfortunes had proved salutary to him ; and he took delight in the Gospel.[1] Œcolampadius intimated to Farel that a door was opened at Montbeliard, and the latter secretly repaired to Basle.

Farel had not regularly entered on the ministry of the Word ; but we find in him, at this period of his life, all that is necessary to constitute a minister of the Lord. He did not lightly and of his own prompting enter the service of the Church. "Considering my weakness," said he, "I should not have dared preach, waiting for the Lord to send more suitable persons."[2] But God at this time addressed him in a threefold call. As soon as he had reached Basle, Œcolampadius, touched with the wants of France, entreated him to devote himself to it. "Behold," said he, "how little is Jesus Christ known to all those who speak the French language. Will you not give them some instruction in their own tongue, that they may better understand the Scriptures ?"[3] At the same time, the people of Montbeliard invited him among them, and the prince gave his consent to this call.[4] Was not this a triple call from God? ......"I did not think," said he, "that it was lawful for me to resist. I obeyed in God's name."[5] Concealed in the house of Œcolampadius, struggling against the responsibility offered to him, and yet obliged to submit to so clear a manifestation of the will of God, Farel accepted this charge, and Œcolampadius set him apart, calling upon the name of the Lord,[6] and addressing his friend in language full of wisdom. "The more you are inclined to violence," said he, "the more should you practise gentleness; temper your lion's courage with the meekness of the dove."[7] Farel responded to this appeal with all his soul.

Thus Farel, once the zealous follower of the old Church, was about to become a servant of God in the new. If Rome imperatively requires in a valid ordination the

[1] Verum ego virtutem illam admirabilem et non minus placiditate, si tempestive fuerit, necessariam. Œcol. Luthero, Epp. p. 200.
[2] Adeo hospitum habemus rationem, veri Sodomitæ. Zw. Epp. p. 434.
[3] Gulielmus ille qui tam probe navavit operam. Zw. et Œcol. Epp. p. 175.

[1] Le prince qui avoit cognoissance de l'Evangile. Farel, Summaire, c'est à dire, briève déclaration de G. Farel, in the concluding part.
[2] Ibid. [3] Ibid.
[4] Etant requis et demandé du peuple et du consentement du prince. Summaire.
[5] Farel, Summaire.
[6] Avec l'Invocation du nom de Dieu. Ibid.
[7] Leoninam magnanimitatem columbina modestia frangas. Œcol. Epp. p. 198.

imposition of the hands of a bishop who descends from the apostles in uninterrupted succession, it is because she places human traditions above the Word of God. In every church where the authority of the Word is not absolute, some other authority must needs be sought. And then, what is more natural than to ask of the most venerated of God's ministers, that which they cannot find in God himself? If we do not speak in the name of Jesus Christ, is it not something at least to speak in the name of Saint John or of Saint Paul? He who speaks in the name of antiquity is stronger than the rationalist who speaks only in his own name. But the christian minister has a still higher authority: he preaches, not because he descends from St. Chrysostom or St. Peter, but because the Word that he proclaims comes down from God himself. The idea of succession, venerable as it may appear, is not the less a human system, substituted for the system of God. In Farel's ordination there was no human succession. Nay more: we do not see in it that which is necessary in the Lord's fold, where every thing should be done *decently and in order*, and whose God *is not a God of confusion.* He was not regularly ordained by the Church: but extraordinary times justify extraordinary measures. At this memorable epoch God himself interposed. He consecrated by marvellous dispensations those whom he called to the regeneration of the world; and this consecration is quite as valid as that of the Church. In Farel's ordination we see the infallible Word of God, given to a man of God, that he might bear it to the world,—the call of God and of the people,—the consecration of the heart; and perhaps no minister of Rome or of Geneva was ever more legitimately set apart for the holy ministry. Farel took his departure for Montbeliard in company with Esch.

Farel thus found himself stationed as it were at an advanced post. Behind him, Basle and Strasburg supported him with their advice and their printing-presses; before him lay the provinces of Franche Comté, Burgundy, Lorraine, the Lyonnais, and the rest of France, where men of God were beginning to struggle against error in the midst of profound darkness. He immediately began to preach Jesus Christ, and to exhort the faithful not to permit themselves to be turned aside from the Holy Scriptures either by threats or stratagems. Beginning, long before Calvin, the work that this reformer was to accomplish on a much larger scale, Farel was at Montbeliard, like a general on a hill, whose piercing eye glances over the field of battle, who cheers those who are actively engaged with the enemy, rallies the ranks which the impetuosity of the charge has broken, and animates by his courage those who hang back.[1] Erasmus immediately

wrote to his Roman-catholic friends, that a Frenchman, escaped from France, was making a great disturbance in these regions.[1] Farel's labours were not unfruitful. " On every side," wrote he to a fellow-countryman, " men are springing up who devote all their powers and their lives to extend Christ's kingdom as widely as possible."[2] The friends of the Gospel gave thanks to God that his blessed Word shone brighter every day in all parts of France.[3] The adversaries were astounded. " The *faction*," wrote Erasmus to the Bishop of Rochester, " is spreading daily, and is penetrating Savoy, Lorraine, and France."[4]

For some time Lyons appeared to be the centre of evangelical action within the kingdom, as Basle was without. Francis I., marching towards the south on an expedition against Charles V., had arrived in this city with his mother, his sister, and the court. Margaret brought with her many gentlemen devoted to the Gospel. " All other people she had removed from about her person," says a letter written at this time.[5] While Francis I. was hurrying through Lyons an army composed of 14,000 Swiss, 6000 French, and 1500 lances of the nobility, to repel the invasion of the imperialists into Provence; while this great city re-echoed with the noise of arms, the tramp of horses, and the sound of the trumpet, the friends of the Gospel were marching to more peaceful conquests. They desired to attempt in Lyons what they had been unable to do in Paris. Perhaps, at a distance from the Sorbonne and from the parliament, the Word of God might have freer course. Perhaps the second city in the kingdom was destined to become the first for the Gospel. Was it not there that about four centuries previously the excellent Peter Waldo had begun to proclaim the Divine Word? Even then he had shaken all France. And now that God had prepared every thing for the emancipation of his Church, might there not be hopes of more extended and more decisive success? Thus the people of Lyons, who were not generally, indeed, " poor men," as in the twelfth century, were beginning more courageously to handle " the sword of the Spirit, which is the Word of God."

Among those who surrounded Margaret was her almoner, Michael d'Arande. The duchess caused the Gospel to be publicly preached at Lyons; and Master Michael

[1] This comparison is employed by one of Farel's friends

during his stay at Montbeliard. Strenuum et oculatum imperatorem, qui iis etiam animum facias qui in acie versantur. Tossanus Farello, MS. in the conclave of Neufchatel, 2d September 1524.
[1] Tumultuatur et Burgundia nobis proxima, per Phallicum quemdam Gallum qui e Gallia profugus. Er. Epp. p. 809.
[2] Suppullulare qui omnes conatus afferant, quo possit Christi regnum quam latissime patere. Neufchatel MS., 2d August 1524.
[3] Quod in Galliis omnibus sacrosanctum Dei verbum in dies magis ac magis elucescat. Ibid.
[4] Factio crescit in dies latius, propagata in Sabaudiam, Lothoringiam, Franciam. Erasm. Epp. p. 809.
[5] De Sebville to Coct, 28th December 1524. Neufchatel MS.

471

proclaimed the Word of God with courage and purity before a great number of hearers, attracted partly by the charm that attends the glad tidings wherever they are published, and partly also by the favour in which the preaching and the preacher were held by the king's beloved sister.[1]

Anthony Papillon, a man of highly cultivated mind, an elegant Latin scholar, a friend of Erasmus, " the first in France for knowledge of the Gospel,"[2] accompanied the princess also. At Margaret's request he had translated Luther's work on monastic vows, " in consequence of which he had much ado with those Parisian vermin," says Sebville;[3] but Margaret had protected him against the attacks of the Sorbonne, and procured him the appointment of head-master of requests to the dauphin, with a seat in the Great Council.[4] He was not less useful to the Gospel by his devotedness than by his prudence. A merchant, named Vaugris, and especially a gentleman named Anthony du Blet, a friend of Farel's, took the lead in the Reformation at Lyons. The latter person, a man of great activity, served as a bond of union between the Christians scattered throughout those countries, and placed them in communication with Basle. While the armed hosts of Francis I. had merely passed through Lyons, the spiritual soldiers of Jesus Christ halted there with Margaret; and leaving the former to carry the war into Provence and the plains of Italy, they began the fight of the Gospel in Lyons itself.

But they did not confine their efforts to the city. They looked all around them; the campaign was opened on several points at the same time; and the Christians of Lyons encouraged by their exertions and their labours all those who confessed Christ in the surrounding provinces. They did more: they went and proclaimed it in places where it was as yet unknown. The new doctrine ascended the Saone, and an evangelist passed through the narrow and irregular streets of Macon. Michael d'Arande himself visited that place in 1524, and, aided by Margaret's name, obtained permission to preach in this city,[5] which was destined at a later period to be filled with blood, and become for ever memorable for its *sauteries*.[6]

After exploring the districts of the Saone, the Christians of Lyons, ever on the watch, extended their incursions in the direction of the Alps. There was at Lyons a Dominican named Maigret, who had been compelled to quit Dauphiny, where he had boldly preached the new doctrine, and who earnestly requested that some one would go and encourage his brethren of Grenoble and Gap. Papillon and Du Blet repaired thither.[1] A violent storm had just broken out there against Sebville and his preaching. The Dominicans had moved heaven and earth; and maddened at seeing so many evangelists escape them (as Farel, Anemond, and Maigret), they would fain have crushed those who remained within their reach.[2] They therefore called for Sebville's arrest.[3]

The friends of the Gospel in Grenoble were alarmed; must Sebville also be taken from them!......Margaret interceded with her brother; many of the most distinguished personages at Grenoble, the king's advocate among others, open or secret friends to the Gospel, exerted themselves in behalf of the evangelical grayfriar, and at length their united efforts rescued him from the fury of his adversaries.[4]

But if Sebville's life was saved, his mouth was stopped. " Remain silent," said they, " or you will be led to the scaffold."— " Silence has been imposed on me," he wrote to Anemond de Coct, " under pain of death."[5] These threats alarmed even those of whom the most favourable hopes had been entertained. The king's advocate and other friends of the Gospel now showed nothing but coldness.[6] Many returned to the Romish worship, pretending to adore God secretly in their hearts, and to give a spiritual signification to the outward observances of Romanism —a melancholy delusion, leading from infidelity to infidelity. There is no hypocrisy that cannot be justified in the same manner. The unbeliever, by means of his systems of myths and allegories, will preach Christ from the christian pulpit; and a philosopher will be able, by a little ingenuity, to find in an abominable superstition among the pagans, the type of a pure and elevated idea. In religion the first thing is truth. Some of the Grenoble Christians, among whom were Amadeus Galbert, and a cousin of Anemond's, still clung fast to their faith.[7] These pious men would meet secretly with Sebville at each other's houses, and *talk* together about the Gospel. They repaired to some secluded spot; they visited some brother by night; or met in secret to pray to Christ, as thieves lurking for a guilty purpose. Often would

---

[1] Elle a ung docteur de Paris appelé maître Michel, Eleymosinarius, lequel ne prêche devant elle que purement l'évangile. Neufchatel MS.
[2] Ibid.   [3] Ibid.   [4] Ibid.
[5] Arandius prêche à Mascon. Coct to Farel, December 1524, Ibid.
[6] After the taking of Macon in 1562, the governor, St. Pont, amused the dissolute women who were invited to his table, by taking several Huguenots from prison, and compelling them to *leap* (sauter) from the bridge over the Saone into the river. It is added that he did not confine his savage cruelty to the Huguenots, but would seize other persons, untainted with heresy, and put them to the same inhuman death.

[1] Il y a eu deux grands personages à Grenoble. Neufchatel MS. The title of *Messire*, given to Du Blet in Coct's letter, indicates a person of rank. I am inclined to think that the epithet *negotiator*, elsewhere applied to him, refers to his activity; it is possible, however, that he may have been a great merchant of Lyons.
[2] Conjicere potes ut post Macretum et me in Sebvillam exarserint. Anemond to Farel, 7th September 1524. Neufchatel MS.
[3] Les Thomistes ont voulu procéder contre moi par inquisition et caption de personne. Letter from Sebville. Ibid.
[4] Si ce ne fut certains amis secrets, je estois mis entre les mains des Pharisiens. Letter from Sebville, Neufchatel MS.
[5] Ibid.
[6] Non solum tepidi sed frigidi. Neufchatel MS.
[7] Tuo cognato, Amedeo Galberto exceptis. Ibid.

a false alarm disturb the humble assembly. The adversaries consented to wink at these secret conventicles; but they had sworn that the stake should be the lot of any one who ventured to speak of the Word of God in public.[1]

Such was the state of affairs when Du Blet and Papillon arrived at Grenoble. Finding that Sebville had been silenced, they exhorted him to go and preach the Gospel at Lyons. The Lent of the following year would present a favourable opportunity for proclaiming the Gospel to a numerous crowd. Michael d'Arande, Maigret, and Sebville, proposed to fight at the head of the Gospel army. Every thing was thus preparing for a striking manifestation of evangelical truth in the second city of France. The rumour of this evangelical Lent extended as far as Switzerland. "Sebville is free, and will preach the Lent sermons at Saint Paul's in Lyons," wrote Anemond to Farel.[2] But a great disaster, which threw all France into confusion, intervened and prevented this spiritual combat. It is during peace that the conquests of the Gospel are achieved. The defeat of Pavia, which took place in the month of February, disconcerted the daring project of the reformers.

Meantime, without waiting for Sebville, Maigret had begun early in the winter to preach salvation by Jesus Christ alone, in despite of the strenuous opposition of the priests and monks of Lyons.[3] In these sermons there was not a word of the worship of the creature, of saints, of the virgin, of the power of the priesthood. The great mystery of godliness, "God manifest in the flesh," was alone proclaimed. The old heresies of the poor men of Lyons are reappearing, it was said, and in a more dangerous form than ever! But notwithstanding this opposition, Maigret continued his ministry; the faith that animated his soul found utterance in words of power: it is in the nature of truth to embolden the hearts of those who have received it. Yet Rome was destined to prevail at Lyons as at Grenoble. Maigret was arrested, notwithstanding Margaret's protection, dragged through the streets, and cast into prison. The merchant Vaugris, who then quitted the city on his road to Switzerland, spread his news every where on his passage. All were astonished and depressed. One thought, however, gave confidence to the friends of the Reformation: "Maigret is taken," said they, "but *Madame d'Alençon is there; praised be God!*"[4]

It was not long before they were compelled to renounce even this hope. The Sorbonne had condemned several of this faithful minister's propositions.[5] Margaret, whose position became daily more difficult, found the boldness of the partisans of the Reformation and the hatred of the powerful increasing side by side. Francis I. began to grow impatient at the zeal of these evangelists: he looked upon them as mere fanatics whom it was good policy to repress. Margaret, thus fluctuating between desire to serve her brethren and her inability to protect them, sent them word to avoid running into fresh dangers, as she could no longer intercede with the king in their favour. The friends of the Gospel believed that this determination was not irrevocable. "God has given her grace," said they, "to say and write only what is necessary to poor souls."[1] But if this human support is taken away, Christ still remains. It is well that the soul should be stripped of all other protection, that it may rely upon God alone.

CHAPTER XII.

The French at Basle—Encouragement of the Swiss—Fears of Discord—Translating and Printing at Basle—Bibles and Tracts disseminated in France.

THE exertions of the friends of the Gospel in France were paralyzed. The men in power were beginning to show their hostility to Christianity; Margaret was growing alarmed; terrible news would soon be coming across the Alps and plunging the nation into mourning, filling it with one thought only—of saving the king, of saving France. But if the Christians of Lyons were checked in their labours, were there not soldiers at Basle who had escaped from the battle, and who were ready to begin the fight again. The exiles from France have never forgotten her. Driven from their country for nearly three centuries by the fanaticism of Rome, their latest descendants have been seen carrying to the cities and fields of their ancestors those treasures of which the pope still deprives them.[2] At the very moment when the soldiers of Christ in France were mournfully laying down their arms, the refugees at Basle were preparing for the combat. As they saw the monarchy of Saint Louis and of Charlemagne falling from the hands of Francis I., shall they not feel urged to lay hold of *a kingdom which cannot be moved.*"[3]

Farel, Anemond, Esch, Toussaint, and their friends formed an evangelical society in Switzerland with the view of rescuing their country from its spiritual darkness. Intelligence reached them from every quarter, that there was an increasing thirst for God's

---

[1] Mais de en parler publiquement, il n'y pend que le feu. Neufchatel MS.
[2] Le samedi des Quatre-Temps. Dec. 1524. Ibid.
[3] Pour vray Maigret a prêché à Lion, maulgré les prêtres et moines. Ibid.
[4] Ibid.
[5] Histoire de François I. par Gaillard, iv. 233.

[1] Peter Toussaint to Farel, Basle, 17th December 1524. Neufchatel MS.
[2] The General Committee of the Evangelical Society of Geneva, which sends a hundred missionaries and *colporteurs* into France, is composed almost entirely of the descendants of French refugees.
[3] Hebrews xii. 28.

Word in France;[1] it was desirable to take advantage of this, and to sow and water while it was yet seedtime. Œcolampadius, Zwingle, and Oswald Myconius, were continually exhorting them to do this, giving the right hand of fellowship, and communicating to them a portion of their own faith. In January 1525, the Swiss schoolmaster wrote to the French chevalier: "Banished as you are from your country by the tyranny of Antichrist, even your presence among us proves that you have acted boldly in the cause of the Gospel. The tyranny of christian bishops will at length induce the people to look upon them as deceivers. Stand firm; the time is not far distant when we shall enter the haven of repose, whether we be struck down by our tyrants, or they themselves be struck down;[2] all then will be well for us, provided we have been faithful to Christ Jesus."

These encouragements were of great value to the French refugees; but a blow inflicted by these very Christians of Switzerland and Germany, who sought to cheer them, cruelly wrung their hearts. Recently escaped from the scaffold or the burning pile, they saw with dismay the evangelical Christians on the other side of the Rhine disturbing by their lamentable differences the repose they enjoyed. The discussions on the Lord's Supper had begun. Deeply moved and agitated, and feeling strongly the necessity of brotherly unity, the French would have made every sacrifice to conciliate these divided sentiments. This became their leading idea. At the epoch of the Reformation, none had greater need than they of christian unity; of this Calvin was afterwards a proof. "Would to God," said Peter Toussaint, "that I might purchase peace, concord, and union in Jesus Christ at the cost of my life, which in truth is of little worth."[3] The French, whose discernment was correct and prompt, saw immediately that these rising dissensions would check the work of the Reformation. "All things would go on more prosperously than many persons imagine, if we were but agreed among ourselves. Numbers would gladly come to the light; but when they see these divisions among the learned, they stand hesitating and confused."[4]

The French were the first to suggest conciliatory advances. "Why," wrote they from Strasburg, "is not Bucer or some other learned man sent to Luther? The longer we wait the greater will these dissensions become." Their fears grew stronger every day.[5] At length, finding all their exertions of no avail, these Christians mournfully

turned their eyes away from Germany and fixed them solely upon France.

France—the conversion of France, thenceforth exclusively occupied the hearts of these generous men whom history, that has inscribed on her pages the names of so many individuals vainly puffed up with their own glory, has for three centuries passed over in silence. Thrown on a foreign land, they fell on their knees, and daily, in silence and obscurity, invoked God in behalf of the country of their forefathers.[1] Prayer was the power by which the Gospel spread through the kingdom, and the great instrument by which the conquests of the Reformation were gained.

But these Frenchmen were not merely men of prayer: never has the evangelical army contained combatants more ready to sacrifice their lives in the day of battle. They felt the importance of scattering the Holy Scriptures and pious books in their country, still overshadowed with the gloom of superstition. A spirit of inquiry was breathing over the whole kingdom: it seemed necessary on all sides to spread the sails to the wind. Anemond, ever prompt in action, and Michael Bentin, a refugee like himself, resolved to unite their zeal, their talents, their resources, and their labours. Bentin wished to establish a printing press at Basle, and the chevalier, to profit by the little German he knew, to translate the best works of the Reformers into French. "Oh," said they, rejoicing in their plans, "would to God that France were filled with evangelical volumes, so that every where, in the cottages of the poor, in the palaces of the nobles, in cloisters and presbyteries, nay, in the inmost sanctuary of the heart, a powerful testimony might be borne to the grace of Jesus Christ."[2]

Funds were necessary for such an undertaking, and the refugees had none. Vaugris was then at Basle; on his departure Anemond gave him a letter for the brethren of Lyons, many of whom abounded in the riches of this world, and who, although oppressed, were faithful to the Gospel; he requested them to send him some assistance;[3] but that did not suffice; the French wished to establish several presses at Basle, that should be worked night and day, so as to inundate France with the Word of God.[4] At Meaux, at Metz, and in other places, were men rich and powerful enough to support this enterprise. No one could address Frenchmen with so much authority as Farel himself, and it was to him that Anemond applied.

It does not appear that the chevalier's project was realized, but the work was done

[1] Gallis verborum Dei sitientibus. Coct to Farel, 2d Sept. 1524, Neufchatel MS.
[2] Non longe abest enim, quo in portum tranquillum perveniamus, &c. Osw. Myc. to Coct. Ibid.
[3] Ibid. 21st December 1525.
[4] Ibid.
[5] Multis jam christianis Gallis dolet, quod a Zwinglii aliorumque de Eucharistia sententia dissentiat Lutherus. Toussaint to Farel, 14th July 1525.

[1] Quam sollicite quotidianis precibus commendem. Tous saint to Farel, 2d Sept. 1524, Neufchatel MS.
[2] Opto enim Galliam Evangelicis voluminibus abundare. Coct to Farel, Neufchatel MS.
[3] Ut pecuniæ aliquid ad me mittant. Ibid.
[4] Ut præla multa erigere possimus. Ibid.
[5] An censes inveniri posse Lugdunæ, Meldæ, aut alibi in Galliis qui nos ad hæc juvare velint. Ibid.

by others. The presses of Basle were constantly occupied in printing French works; they were forwarded to Farel, and by him introduced into France with unceasing activity. One of the first writings sent by this Religious Tract Society was Luther's *Explanation of the Lord's Prayer.* "We are retailing the *Pater* at four deniers of Basle each," wrote Vaugris to Farel, "but we sell them wholesale at the rate of two florins the two hundred, which comes to something less."[1]

Anemond sent to Farel from Basle all the useful books that appeared or that arrived from Germany; at one time a work on the appointment of Gospel ministers, at another a treatise on the education of children.[2] Farel examined these works; he composed, translated or got others to translate them into French, and seemed at one and the same time entirely devoted to active exertions and to the labours of the study. Anemond urged on and superintended the printing; and these epistles, prayers, books, and broadsheets, were the means of the regeneration of the age. While profligacy descended from the throne, and darkness from the steps of the altar, these unnoticed writings alone diffused throughout the nation beams of light and seeds of holiness.

But it was especially God's Word that the evangelical merchant of Lyons was calling for in the name of his fellow-countrymen. These people of the sixteenth century, so hungering for intellectual food, were to receive in their own tongue those ancient monuments of the first ages of the world, in which the new breath of primitive humanity respires, and those holy oracles of the Gospel times in which shines forth the fulness of the revelation of Christ. Vaugris wrote to Farel: "I beseech you, if possible, to have the New Testament translated by some person who can do it efficiently: it would be a great blessing for France, Burgundy, and Savoy. And if you want proper type, I will have some brought from Paris or Lyons; but if there be any good types at Basle, it will be all the better."

Lefevre had already published at Meaux, but in detached portions, the books of the New Testament in French. Vaugris wished for some one to revise it thoroughly, and to superintend a complete edition. Lefevre undertook to do so, and he published it, as we have already seen, on the 12th of October 1524. An uncle of Vaugris, named Conrard, also a refugee at Basle, immediately procured a copy. The Chevalier Coct happening to be at a friend's house on the 18th of November, there saw the book, and was filled with joy. "Lose no time in reprinting it," said

he, "for I doubt not a great number will be called for."[1]

Thus was the Word of God offered to France in opposition to the traditions of the Church, which Rome still continues to present to her. "How can we distinguish what is of man in your traditions, and what is of God," said the reformers, "except by the Scriptures of God? The maxims of the Fathers, the decretals of the pontiffs, cannot be the rule of our faith. They show us what was the opinion of these old doctors; but the Word alone teaches us what is the judgment of God. We must submit every thing to the rule of Scripture."

Such were the principal means by which these writings were circulated. Farel and his friends consigned the books to certain pedlars or *colporteurs,* simple and pious men, who, laden with their precious burden, passed from town to town, from village to village, and from house to house, in Franche Comté, Lorraine, Burgundy, and the adjoining provinces, knocking at every door. They procured the books at a low rate, "that they might be the more eager to sell them."[2] Thus as early as 1524 there existed in Basle a Bible society, a tract society, and an association of colporteurs, for the benefit of France. It is a mistake to conceive that these efforts date only from our own age; they go back in essentials not only to the times of the Reformation, but still farther to the primitive ages of the Church.

CHAPTER XIII.

Progress at Montbeliard—Resistance and Commotion—Toussaint leaves Œcolampadius—The Image of Saint Anthony—Death of Anemond—Strasburg—Lambert's Letter to Francis I.—Successive Defeats.

THE attention which Farel bestowed on France did not divert his attention from the place where he was residing. Arriving at Montbeliard about the end of July 1524, he had hardly sown the seed, before the first fruits of the harvest (to use the words of Œcolampadius) began to appear. Farel wrote to his friend with great exultation. "It is an easy thing," replied the doctor of Basle, "to instil a few dogmas into the ears of our auditors; but to change their hearts is in the power of God alone."[3]

The Chevalier de Coct, delighted with this intelligence, ran with his usual vivacity to Peter Toussaint. "I shall set off to-morrow to visit Farel," said he hastily. Toussaint, more calm, was writing to the evangelist of Montbeliard: "Be careful," said he to Farel; "you are engaged in an important cause; it

---

1 Vaugris to Farel, Basle, 29th August 1524. Neufchatel MS.—The value of the florin is about 1s. 9d. sterling.
2 Mitto tibi librum de instituendis ministris ecclesiæ cum libro de instituendis pueris. Coct to Farel, 2d September 1524. Ibid.

1 Neufchatel MS.
2 Vaugris to Farel. Ibid.
3 Animum autem immutare, divinum opus est. Œcol. Epp. p. 200.

must not be polluted by the councils of men. The mighty ones promise you their favour, their support, and heaps of gold......But to put your trust in these things, is deserting Christ and walking in darkness."[1] Toussaint was finishing this letter when the chevalier entered; the latter took it, and departed for Montbeliard.

He found the city in great commotion. Many of the nobles were alarmed, and said as they looked contemptuously at Farel: "What does this sorry fellow want with us? Would to God he had never come! He cannot stay here, for he will ruin us all, as well as himself." The lords who had taken refuge with the duke at Montbeliard, feared that the disturbance, which every where accompanied the Reformation, would attract the attention of Ferdinand and Charles V., and that they would be expelled from their last asylum. But it was the clergy in particular who resisted Farel. The superior of the Franciscans of Besançon had hastened to Montbeliard, and formed a plan of defence in conjunction with the clergy of the place. On the following Sunday, Farel had hardly begun to preach, before they interrupted him, calling him liar and heretic. In an instant the whole assembly was in an uproar. The audience rose up, and called for silence. The duke hurried to the spot, seized both Farel and the superior, and ordered the latter either to prove or to retract his charges. The Franciscan adopted the last alternative, and an official account of the whole affair was published.[2]

This attack excited Farel all the more; he thought it was now his duty to unmask without scruple those interested priests; and drawing the sword of the Word, he wielded it vigorously. He was more inclined to imitate Jesus when he expelled the money-changers from the temple and overthrew their tables, than when the spirit of prophecy declared of him: *He shall neither strive nor cry, neither shall any man hear his voice in the streets.* Œcolampadius was affrighted. These two men were perfect types of two characters diametrically opposed to each other, and yet both worthy of admiration. "You were sent," wrote Œcolampadius to Farel, "to draw men gently to the truth, and not to drag them with violence; to spread the Gospel, and not to curse them. Physicians resort to amputation only when other means have failed. Act the part of a physician, and not of an executioner. It is not enough, in my opinion, to be gentle towards the friends of the Gospel; you must likewise gain over the adversaries. If the wolves are driven from the sheepfold, let the sheep at least hear the voice of the shepherd. Pour oil and wine into the wounds, and con-

duct yourself as an evangelist, not as a judge or a tyrant."[1]

The report of these labours spread into France and Lorraine, and the Sorbonne and the Cardinal Guise were beginning to be alarmed at this meeting of refugees at Basle and Montbeliard. They would willingly have broken up a troublesome alliance; for error knows no greater triumph than when attracting some deserter to its standard. Already had Martial Mazurier and others given the papal party in France an opportunity of rejoicing over shameful defections; but if they could succeed in seducing one of these confessors of Christ, who had taken refuge on the banks of the Rhine, and who had suffered so much for the name of the Lord, how great would be the victory for the Roman hierarchy! They therefore planted their batteries, and the youngest of these refugees was the object of their attack.

The dean, the Cardinal of Lorraine, and all those who joined the crowded meetings held in this prelate's mansion, deplored the sad fate of Peter Toussaint, who had once promised so fair. He is at Basle, said they, in the house of Œcolampadius, living with one of the leaders of this heresy! They wrote to him with fervour, and as if they would rescue him from eternal condemnation. These letters were the more painful to the young man, because he could not help recognising in them the marks of sincere affection.[2] One of his relations, probably the dean himself, urged him to remove to Paris, to Metz, or to any other place in the world, provided it were far away from these Lutherans. This relation, bearing in mind all that Toussaint owed to him, doubted not that he would immediately comply; but when he found his efforts useless, his affection changed into violent hatred. At the same time this resistance exasperated the whole family and all his friends against the young refugee. They went to his mother, who was "under the power of the monks;"[3] the priests crowded round her, frightening and persuading her that her son had committed crimes that they could not mention without shuddering. Upon this the afflicted mother wrote a touching letter to her son, "full of weeping" (said he), in which she described her misery in heart-rending language. "Oh! wretched mother!" said she, "Oh! unnatural son! cursed be the breasts that suckled thee, and the knees that bare thee!"[4]

The unhappy Toussaint was distracted: What should he do? He could not return into France. By leaving Basle and going to Zurich or Wittemberg, beyond the reach of

---

[1] A quibus si pendemus, jam a Christo defecimus. Neufchatel MS.
[2] Der Christliche Handel zu Mümpelgard, verloffen mit gründlichen Wahrheit.

[1] Quod Evangelistam, non tyrannicum legislatorem præstes. Œcol. Epp. p. 206.
[2] Me in dies divexari legendis amicorum literis qui me.. ..ab instituto remorari nituntur. Toussaint to Farel. 2d Sept. 1524, Neufchatel MS.
[3] Jam capulo proxima. Ibid.
[4] Literas ad me dedit plenas lacrymis quibus maledicit et uberibus quæ me lactarunt, &c. Ibid.

his family, he would only add to their sorrow. Œcolampadius advised a middle course: Leave my house," said he.[1] With a heart full of sadness, he adopted the suggestion, and went to live with an ignorant and obscure priest,[2] one well adapted to reassure his relations. What a change for Toussaint! He never met his host save at meals, at which times they were continually discussing matters of faith; and as soon as the repast was over, Toussaint retired to his chamber, where alone, far from noise and controversy, he carefully studied the Word of God. "The Lord is my witness," said he, " that in this valley of tears I have but one desire, that of seeing Christ's kingdom extended, so that all with one mouth may glorify God."[3]

One circumstance occurred which consoled Toussaint. The enemies of the Gospel were daily growing stronger in Metz. At his entreaty, the Chevalier d'Esch departed in the month of January 1525, to encourage the evangelical Christians in this city. He traversed the forests of the Vosges, and reached the place where Leclerc had laid down his life, carrying with him several books with which Farel had provided him.[4]

It was not only to Lorraine that these Frenchmen turned their eyes. The Chevalier de Coct received letters from one of Farel's brothers, depicting the state of Dauphiny in the gloomiest colours. He carefully avoided showing them lest he should alarm the weak-hearted, and was content with ardently seeking from God the support of his almighty hands.[5] In December 1524, Peter Verrier, a Dauphinese messenger, arrived on horseback at Montbeliard with commissions for Anemond and Farel. The chevalier, with his usual vivacity, immediately resolved on returning to France. " If Peter has brought any money," wrote he to Farel, " keep it; if he has brought any letters, open and copy them, and then forward them to me. Do not, however, sell the horse, but take care of it, for perchance I may need it. I am inclined to enter France secretly, and go to Jacobus Faber (Lefevre) and Arandius. Write and tell me what you think of it."[6]

Such was the confidence and open-heartedness that existed between these refugees. The one opened the other's letters, and received his money. It is true that de Coct was already indebted thirty-six crowns to Farel, whose purse was always open to his friends. There was more zeal than discretion in the chevalier's desire to re-enter France. He was of too imprudent a character not to expose himself to certain death. This Farel no doubt explained to him. He left Basle, and withdrew to a small town, where he had " great hopes of acquiring the German language, God willing."[1]

Farel continued preaching the Gospel in Montbeliard. His soul was vexed as he beheld the majority of the people in this city entirely given up to the worship of images. It was, in his opinion, a revival of the old pagan idolatry.

Yet the exhortations of Œcolampadius, and the fear of compromising the truth, would perhaps have long restrained him, but for an unforeseen circumstance. One day about the end of February (it was the feast of Saint Anthony) Farel was walking on the banks of a little river that runs through the city, beneath a lofty rock on which the citadel is built, when, on reaching the bridge, he met a procession, which was crossing it, reciting prayers to St. Anthony, and headed by two priests bearing the image of this saint. Farel suddenly found himself face to face with these superstitions, without, however, having sought for them. A violent struggle took place in his soul. Shall he give way? shall he hide himself? Would not this be a cowardly act of unbelief? These lifeless images, borne on the shoulders of ignorant priests, made his blood boil. Farel boldly advanced, snatched the shrine of the holy hermit from the priest's arms, and threw it over the bridge into the river. And then, turning to the awe-stricken crowd, he exclaimed: " Poor idolaters, will ye never forsake your idolatry !"[2]

The priests and people stood motionless with astonishment. A religious fear seemed to rivet them to the spot. But they soon recovered from their stupor. " The image is drowning," exclaimed one of the crowd; and transports and shouts of rage succeeded their death-like silence. The multitude would have rushed on the sacrilegious wretch who had just thrown the object of their adoration into the water. But Farel, we know not how, escaped their violence.[3]

There is reason, we are aware, to regret that the reformer should have been hurried into the commission of an act that tended rather to check the progress of the truth. No one should think himself authorized to attack with violence any institution sanctioned by the public authority. There is, however, in the zeal of the reformer something more noble than that cold prudence so common among men, which shrinks before the least danger, and fears to make the least sacrifice for the advancement of God's kingdom. Farel was not ignorant that by this

---

[1] Visum est Œcolampadio consultum....ut a se secedere. Neufchatel MS.
[2] Utor domo cujusdam sacrificuli. Ibid.
[3] Ut Christi regnum quam latissime pateat. Ibid.
[4] Qu'il s'en retourne à Metz, là ou les ennemis de Dieu s'élèvent journellement contre l'Evangile. Toussaint to Farel, 17th Dec. 1524. Ibid.
[5] Accepi ante horam a fratre tuo epistolam quam hic nulli manifestavi, terrerentur enim infirmi. Coct to Farel, 2d Sept. 1524.
[6] Coct to Farel, Dec. 1525, Neufchatel MS.

[1] Coct to Farel, Jan. 1525.
[2] Revue du Dauphiné, ii. p. 38; Choupard MS.
[3] M. Kirchhofer, in his Life of Farel, gives this circumstance as an uncertain tradition; but it is related by Protestant writers, and it appears to me quite in harmony with Farel's character and the fears of Œcolampadius. We must not be blind to the weaknesses of the reformers.

proceeding he was exposing himself to the fate of Leclerc. But his own conscience bore witness that he desired only to promote the glory of God, and this made him superior to all fear.

After this affair of the bridge, which is a characteristic feature in Farel's history, the reformer was obliged to hide himself, and he quitted the town soon after. He took refuge at Basle with Œcolampadius ; but ever preserved that attachment for Montbeliard which a servant of God never ceases to entertain for the first fruits of his ministry.[1]

Sad tidings awaited Farel at Basle. If he was a fugitive, his friend Anemond de Coct was seriously ill. Farel immediately sent him four gold crowns ; but a letter written by Oswald Myconius on the 25th of March, announced the death of the chevalier. " Let us so live," said Oswald, " that we may enter into that rest into which we hope the soul of Anemond has already entered."[2]

Thus did Anemond descend to a premature grave ; still young, full of activity and strength, willing to undertake every labour to evangelize France, and in himself a host. *God's ways are not our ways.* Not long before, and in the neighbourhood of Zurich, another chevalier, Ulrich Hütten, had breathed his last. There is some similarity in the characters of the German and French knights, but the piety and christian virtues of the Dauphinese place him far above the witty and intrepid enemy of the pope and of the monks.

Shortly after Anemond's death, Farel, unable to remain in Basle, whence he had been once banished, joined his friends Capito and Bucer at Strasburg.

Strasburg, an imperial city, at whose head was Sturm, one of the most distinguished men in Germany, and which contained many celebrated doctors within its walls, was as it were an advanced post of the Reformation, thrown beyond the Rhine, in which the persecuted Christians of France and Lorraine took refuge, and whence they hoped to win these countries to the Gospel of Jesus Christ. Lambert's pious ambition was to become for France what Luther was for Germany, and accordingly he had no sooner reached Strasburg after quitting Metz, than he made his preparations, waiting for the moment when he should be enabled to carry the sword of the Gospel into the very heart of that country which he loved so tenderly.[3]

He first appealed to Francis I. " The pope," said he, " if he had his way, would change every king into a beggar. Lend your ear to the truth, most excellent prince, and God will make you great among the princes of the earth. Woe be to all the nations whose master is the pope. Oh, Avignon, city of my birth, art thou not the wretched daughter of Babylon ? Given over to a legate, not of holiness, but of impiety and heresy ;[1]—thou seest lewd sports, immodest dances, and adultery multiply within thy walls, and all around thy fields are laid waste by daily hunting parties, and thy poor labourers oppressed.

" O most christian king, thy people thirst for the Word of God." At the same time addressing the pope, he said, " Erelong that powerful France which thou art wont to call thy arm will separate from thee."[2] Such were Lambert's illusions !

Finding that his epistle had produced no effect, he wrote a second in a still more earnest tone. " What," said he, " the Arabians, Chaldeans, Greeks, and Jews possess the Word of God in their own language, and the French, Germans, Italians, and Spaniards cannot have it in theirs ! Let God but speak to the nations in the language of the people, and the empire of pride will crumble into dust."[3]

These anticipations were not realised. At Montbeliard and Basle, as at Lyons, the ranks of the reformers had suffered. Some of the most devoted combatants had been taken off by death, others by persecution and exile. In vain did the warriors of the Gospel mount every where to the assault ; every where they were beaten back. But if the forces they had concentrated, first at Meaux, then at Lyons, and afterwards at Basle, were dispersed in succession, there still remained combatants here and there, who in Lorraine, at Meaux, and even in Paris, struggled more or less openly to uphold the Word of God in France. Though the Reformation saw its columns broken, it still had its isolated champions. Against these the Sorbonne and the Parliament were about to turn their anger. They would not have remaining on the soil of France, a single one of these noble minded men who had undertaken to plant in it the standard of Jesus Christ ; and unheard of misfortunes seemed now to be conspiring with the enemies of the Reformation, and to aid them in the accomplishment of their task.

---

[1] Ingens affectus, qui me cogit Mumpelgardum amare. Farelli Epp.
[2] Quo Anemundi spiritum jam pervenisse speramus. Myconius to Farel, Neufchatel MS.
[3] Hic operior donec ad ipsos Metenses aut in aliquam urbem Galliæ revoces. Ad Franc. Reg. Comment. in Cantic.

[1] Ab hæresis et impietatis latere legatum. Epistola ad Franciscum G. R. præf. Comm. de Sacra conjugis.
[2] Est autem in proximo ut aliena fiat a te potens Gallia quam brachium tuum appellare solebas. De Causis Excusationis, p. 76.
[3] Epist. ad Franc. R. Præf. Comment. in Cantic. Cantic.

CHAPTER XIV.

Francis made Prisoner at Pavia—Margaret's anxiety for her Brother—Allegorical Letter—Reaction against the Reformation—Louisa consults the Sorbonne—Commission against the Heretics—Charges against Briçonnet—The Faculty of Paris—The Bishop's Alarm—Appeals to the Parliament—Temptation—His second fall—Consequences —Recantation—Briçonnet and Fénelon—Lefevre accused —Condemnation and Flight—Lefevre at Strasburg—Louis Berquin imprisoned—Erasmus attacked—He appeals to the King and the Emperor—Esch imprisoned—Schuch at Nancy—His Martyrdom—Beda's Struggle with Caroli— Sorrow of Pavanne—His Martyrdom—A Christian Hermit —Concourse at Notre Dame.

DURING the latter period of Farel's sojourn at Montbeliard, great events were passing on the theatre of the world. Lannoy and Pescara, Charles's generals, having quitted France on the approach of Francis I., this prince had crossed the Alps, and blockaded Pavia. On the 24th of February 1525, he was attacked by Pescara. Bonnivet, La Trémouille, Palisse, and Lescure died fighting round their sovereign. The Duke of Alençon, Margaret's husband, the first prince of the blood, had fled with the rear-guard, and gone to die of shame and grief at Lyons; and Francis, thrown from his horse, had surrendered his sword to Charles Lannoy, viceroy of Naples, who received it kneeling. The King of France was prisoner to the emperor. His captivity seemed the greatest of misfortunes. "Nothing is left me but honour and life," wrote the king to his mother. But no one felt a keener sorrow than Margaret. The glory of her country tarnished, France without a monarch and exposed to the greatest dangers, her beloved brother the captive of his haughty enemy, her husband dishonoured and dead......What bitter thoughts were these !......But she had a comforter; and while her brother to console himself repeated: "*Tout est perdu, fors l'honneur,* all is lost save honour !" she was able to say :—

Fors Jésus seul, mon frère, fils de Dieu ! [1]
Save Christ alone, dear brother, Son of God !

Margaret thought that in the hour of trial Francis might receive the Word of God. A few months before, the king had already betrayed religious sentiments on the death of his daughter the Princess Charlotte. The Duchess of Alençon, having concealed the child's sickness from him, Francis, who no doubt suspected something, dreamed three several times that his daughter said to him : "Farewell, my king, I am going to paradise." He guessed that she was dead, and gave way to "extreme grief," but wrote to his sister that "he would rather die than desire to have her in this world contrary to the will of God, whose name be blessed." [2]

Margaret thought that the terrible disaster of Pavia would complete what the first trial had begun; and most earnestly desiring that the Word of God might be with Francis in his prison, she wrote a very touching letter, which deserves to be preserved, to Marshal Montmorency, who had been taken prisoner along with the king. It is very probable that she speaks of herself and Bishop Briçonnet in the graceful allegory which serves as an introduction to her request :—

"Dear cousin, there is a certain very devout hermit who for these three years past has been constantly urging a man whom I know to pray to God for the king, which he has done; and he is assured that if it pleases the king by way of devotion, daily, when in his closet, to read the epistles of St. Paul, he will be delivered to the glory of God; for He promises in His Gospel, that whosoever loveth the truth, *the truth shall make him free.* And forasmuch as I think he has them not, I send you mine, begging you to entreat him on my part that he will read them, and I firmly believe that the Holy Ghost, which abideth in the letter, will do by him as great things as he has done by those who wrote them; for God is not less powerful or good than He has been, and his promises never deceive. He has humbled you by captivity, but he has not forsaken you, giving you patience and hope in his goodness, which is always accompanied by consolation and a more perfect knowledge of Him, which I am sure is better than the king ever knows, having his mind less at liberty, on account of the imprisonment of the body.

"Your good Cousin,
"MARGARET."

In such language did Margaret of Valois, full of anxiety for the salvation of her brother's soul, address the king after the battle of Pavia. It is unfortunate that her letter and the Epistles of St. Paul were not sent direct to Francis; she could not have selected a worse medium than Montmorency.

The letters which the king wrote from the Castle of Pizzighitone, where he was confined, afforded his sister some little consolation. At the beginning of April she wrote to him: "After the sorrow of the Passion this has been a Holy Ghost (*i. e.* a Pentecost), seeing the grace that our Lord has shown you."[1] But unhappily the prisoner did not find in the Word of God that *truth which maketh free,* and which Margaret so earnestly desired he might possess.

All France, princes, parliament, and people, were overwhelmed with consternation. Erelong, as in the first three ages of the Church, the calamity that had befallen the country was imputed to the Christians; and fanatical cries were heard on every side calling for blood, as a means of averting still greater disasters. The moment, therefore, was favourable; it was not enough to have dislodged the evangelical Christians from the

1 Les Marguerites de la Marguerite, i. 29.
2 Lettres inedites de la reine de Navarre, p. 170.

1 Lettres de la reine de Navarre à François, i. p. 27.

three strong positions they had taken; it was necessary to take advantage of the general panic, to strike while the iron was hot, and to sweep the whole kingdom clear of that opposition which had become so formidable to the papacy.

At the head of this conspiracy and of these clamours were Beda, Duchesne, and Lecouturier. These irreconcilable enemies of the Gospel flattered themselves they might easily obtain from public terror the victims that had been hitherto refused them. They instantly employed every device; conversations, fanatical harangues, lamentations, threats, defamatory writings, to excite the anger of the nation, and particularly of their governors. They vomited fire and flame against their adversaries, and covered them with the most scurrilous abuse.[1] All means were good in their eyes; they picked out a few words here and there, neglecting the context that might explain the passage quoted; substituted expressions of their own for those of the doctors they criminated, and omitted or added, according as it was necessary to blacken their adversaries' characters.[2] We have this on the testimony of Erasmus himself.

Nothing excited their wrath so much as the fundamental doctrine of Christianity and of the Reformation,—salvation by grace. "When I see these three men," said Beda, "Lefevre, Erasmus, and Luther, in other respects endowed with so penetrating a genius, uniting and conspiring against meritorious works, and resting all the weight of salvation on faith alone,[3] I am no longer astonished that thousands of men, seduced by these doctrines, have learned to say: 'Why should I fast and mortify my body?' Let us banish from France this hateful doctrine of grace. This neglect of good works is a fatal delusion from the devil."

In such language did the Syndic of the Sorbonne endeavour to fight against the faith. He was destined to find supporters in a debauched court, and also in another part of the nation, more respectable, but not less opposed to the Gospel; I mean those grave men, those rigid moralists, who, devoted to the study of laws and forms of jurisprudence, regard Christianity as no more than a system of legislation; the Church as a moral police; and who, unable to adapt to those principles of jurisprudence which absorb their whole thoughts the doctrines of the spiritual inability of man, of the new birth, and of justification by faith, look upon them as fanciful dreams, dangerous to public morals and to the prosperity of the state. This hostile tendency to the doctrine of grace was manifested in the sixteenth century by two very different excesses; in Italy and Poland by the doctrine of Socinus, the descendant of an illustrious family of lawyers at Sienna; and in France by the persecuting decrees and burning piles of the parliament.

The parliament, in fact, despising the great truths of the Gospel which the reformers announced, and thinking themselves called upon to do something in so overwhelming a catastrophe, presented an address to Louisa of Savoy, full of strong remonstrances on the conduct of the government with regard to the new doctrine. " Heresy," said they, " has raised its head among us, and the king, by neglecting to bring the heretics to the scaffold, has drawn down the wrath of heaven upon the nation."

At the same time the pulpits resounded with lamentations, threats, and maledictions; prompt and exemplary punishments were loudly called for. Martial Mazurier was particularly distinguished among the preachers of Paris; and endeavouring by his violence to efface the recollection of his former connexion with the partisans of the Reformation, he declaimed against the " secret disciples of Luther." " Do you know the rapid operation of this poison?" exclaimed he. " Do you know its potency? Well may we tremble for France; as it works with inconceivable activity, and in a short time may destroy thousands of souls."[1]

It was not difficult to excite the regent against the partisans of the Reformation. Her daughter Margaret, the first personage of the court, Louisa of Savoy herself, who had always been so devoted to the Roman pontiff, were pointed at by certain fanatics as countenancing Lefevre, Berquin, and the other innovators. Had she not read their tracts and their translations of the Bible? The queen-mother desired to clear herself of such outrageous suspicions. Already she had despatched her confessor to the Sorbonne to consult that body on the means of extirpating this heresy. " The damnable doctrine of Luther," said she to the faculty, " is every day gaining new adherents." The faculty smiled on the receipt of this message. Till then, its representations had not been listened to, and now their advice was humbly solicited in the matter. At length they held within their grasp that heresy they had so long desired to stifle. They commissioned Noel Beda to return an immediate answer to the regent. " Seeing that the sermons, the discussions, the books with which we have so often opposed heresy, have failed in destroying it," said the fanatical syndic, " all the writings of the heretics should be prohibited by a royal proclamation; and if this means does not suffice, we must employ force and constraint against the *persons* of these false doctors; for those who resist the

---

[1] Plus quam scurrilibus conviciis debacchantes. Er. Francisco Reig, p. 1108.
[2] Pro meis verbis supponit sua, prætermittit, addit. Ibid. 887.
[3] Cum itaque cerneram tres istos....uno animo in opera meritoria conspirasse. Natalias Bedæ Apologia adversus clandestinos Lutheranos, fol. 41.

[1] Mazurius contra occultos Lutheri discipulos declamat, ac recentis veneni celeritatem vimque denunciat. Lannoi, regii Navarræ gymnasii historia, p. 621.

light must be subdued by *torture* and by *terror*."[1]

But Louisa had not waited for this reply. Francis had scarcely fallen into the hands of the emperor when she wrote to the pope to know his pleasure concerning the heretics. It was of great importance to Louisa's policy to secure the favour of a pontiff who could raise all Italy against the victor of Pavia, and she was ready to conciliate him at the cost of a little French blood. The pope, delighted that he could wreak his vengeance in the "most christian kingdom" against a heresy that he could not destroy either in Switzerland or Germany, gave immediate orders for the introduction of the Inquisition into France, and addressed a brief to the parliament. At the same time Duprat, whom the pontiff had created cardinal, and on whom he had conferred the archbishopric of Sens, and a rich abbey, laboured to respond to the favours of the court of Rome by the display of indefatigable animosity against the heretics. Thus the pope, the regent, the doctors of the Sorbonne, the parliament, and the chancellor, with the most ignorant and fanatical part of the nation, were conspiring together to ruin the Gospel and put its confessors to death.

The parliament took the lead. Nothing less than the first body in the kingdom was required to begin the campaign against this doctrine ; and moreover, was it not their peculiar business, since the public safety was at stake ? Accordingly the parliament, "influenced by a holy zeal and fervour against these novelties,[2] issued a decree to the effect that the Bishop of Paris and the other prelates should be bound to commission Messieurs Philip Pot, president of requests, and Andrew Verjus, councillor, and Messieurs William Duchesne and Nicholas Leclerc, doctors of divinity, to institute and conduct the trial of those who should be tainted with the Lutheran doctrine.

"And that it might appear that these commissioners were acting rather under the authority of the Church than of the parliament, it has pleased his holiness to send his brief of the 20th of May 1525, approving of the appointment of the said commissioners :

"In consequence of which, all those who were declared Lutherans by the bishop or ecclesiastical judges to these deputies, were delivered over to the secular arm, that is to say, to the aforesaid parliament, which thereupon condemned them to be burnt alive."[3]

This is the language of a manuscript of the time.

Such was the terrible commission of inquiry appointed during the captivity of Francis I. against the evangelical Christians

of France on the ground of public safety. It was composed of two laymen and two ecclesiastics, and one of the latter was Duchesne, after Beda, the most fanatical doctor of the Sorbonne. They had sufficient modesty not to place him at their head, but his influence was only the more secure on that account.

Thus the machine was wound up : its springs were well prepared ; death would be the result of each of its blows. It now became a question on whom they should make their first attack. Beda, Duchesne, and Leclerc, assisted by Philip Pot the president, and Andrew Verjus the councillor, met to deliberate on this important point. Was there not the Count of Montbrun, the old friend of Louis XII., and formerly ambassador at Rome,—Briçonnet, bishop of Meaux ? The committee of public safety, assembled in Paris in 1525, thought that by commencing with a man in so exalted a station, they would be sure to spread dismay throughout the kingdom. This was a sufficient reason, and the venerable bishop was impeached.

It is true that Briçonnet had given guarantees of submission to Rome, to the parliament, and to the popular superstitions ; but it was strongly suspected that he had done so merely to ward off the blow about to fall upon him, and that he was still countenancing heresy in secret. It would appear that, after giving way, he had partly regained his courage ;—a circumstance quite in harmony with these irresolute characters, who are tossed about and driven to and fro, as the waves of the sea by the wind. Several acts were ascribed to him in different places that would have been the most signal retractation of his unhappy decrees of 1523 and 1524. The more eminent his rank in the Church and in the State, the more fatal was his example, and the more necessary also was it to obtain from him a striking recantation of his errors, or to inflict upon him a still more notorious punishment. The commission of inquiry eagerly collected the evidence against him. They took account of the kindly reception the bishop had given to the heretics ; they stated that, a week after the superior of the Cordeliers had preached in St. Martin's Church at Meaux, conformably to the instructions of the Sorbonne, to restore sound doctrine, Briçonnet himself had gone into the pulpit, and publicly refuted the orator, calling him and the other Grayfriars bigots, hypocrites, and false prophets : and that, not content with this public affront, he had, through his official, summoned the superior to appear before him in person.[1] It would even appear from a manuscript of the times that the bishop had gone much farther, and that in the autumn of 1524, accompanied by Lefevre of Etaples, he had spent three months in travelling through his diocese, and had burnt all the images, save the crucifix alone. Such daring conduct, which would

[1] Histoire de l'Université, par Crévier, v. 196.
[2] De la religion catholique en France, par de Lezeau. MS. in the library of St. Geneviève, Paris.
[3] The manuscript in the library of Ste. Geneviève at Paris, from which I have quoted this passage, bears the name of Lezeau, but that of Lefèbre in the catalogue.

[1] Hist. de l'Univ. par. Crévier, v. 204.

prove Briçonnet to have possessed great boldness combined with much timidity, cannot, if it be true, fix upon him the blame attached to other image-breakers; for he was at the head of that Church whose superstitions he was reforming, and was acting in the sphere of his rights and duties.[1]

Be that as it may, Briçonnet could not fail of being guilty in the eyes of the enemies of the Gospel. He had not only attacked the Church in general; he had grappled with the Sorbonne itself, that body whose supreme law was its own glory and preservation. Accordingly it was delighted on hearing of the examination instituted against its adversary; and John Bochart, one of the most celebrated advocates of the times, supporting the charge against Briçonnet before the parliament, cried out, elevating his voice: " Against the Faculty, neither the Bishop of Meaux nor any private individual may raise his head or open his mouth. Nor is the Faculty called upon to enter into discussion, to produce and set forth its reasons before the said bishop, who ought not to resist the wisdom of that holy society, which he should regard as aided of God."[2]

In consequence of this requisition, the parliament issued a decree on the 3d October 1525, by which, after authorizing the arrest of all those who had been informed against, it ordered that the bishop should be interrogated by James Menager and Andrew Verjus, councillors of the court, touching the facts of which he was accused.[3]

This decree of the parliament amazed the bishop. Briçonnet, the ambassador of two kings—Briçonnet, a bishop and a prince, the friend of Louis XII. and Francis I.—to submit to an examination by two councillors of the court!......He who had hoped that God would kindle in the heart of the king, of his mother, and of his sister, a fire that would spread over the whole nation, now saw the nation turning against him to extinguish the flame which he had received from heaven. The king is a prisoner, his mother is at the head of the enemies of the Gospel, and Margaret, alarmed at the misfortunes that burst upon France, dares not ward off the blows that are about to fall on her dearest friends, and directed first against that spiritual father who has so often consoled her; or, if she dares, she cannot. Quite recently she had written to Briçonnet a letter full of pious outpourings: " Oh! that my poor, lifeless

heart could feel some spark of love, with which I desire it were burnt to ashes."[1] But now it was a question of literal burning. This mystic language was no longer in season; and whoever now desired to confess his faith, must brave the scaffold. The poor bishop, who had so earnestly hoped to see an evangelical reform gradually and gently making its way into every heart, was frightened, and trembled as he saw that he must now purchase it at the cost of his life. Never perhaps had this terrible thought occurred to him, and he recoiled from it in agony and affright.

Yet Briçonnet had still one hope: if he were permitted to appear before the assembled chambers of parliament, as became a person of his rank, in that august and numerous court, he would be sure to find generous hearts responding to his appeal, and undertaking his defence. He therefore entreated the court to grant him this favour; but his enemies had equally reckoned on the issue of such a hearing. Had they not seen Luther appearing before the German diet, and shaking the most determined hearts! On the watch to remove every chance of safety, they exerted themselves to such effect that the parliament refused Briçonnet this favour by a decree dated the 25th of October 1525, in confirmation of the one previously issued.[2]

Here then was the Bishop of Meaux referred like the humblest priest to the jurisdiction of James Menager and Andrew Verjus. These two lawyers, docile instruments in the hands of the Sorbonne, would not be moved by those higher considerations to which the whole chamber might have been sensible; they were matter-of-fact men: had the bishop differed from that society, or had he not? This is all they desire to know. Briçonnet's conviction was therefore secured.

While the parliament was thus holding the sword over the head of the bishop, the monks, priests, and doctors were not idle; they saw that Briçonnet's retractation would be of more service to them than his punishment. His death would only inflame the zeal of all those who held the same faith with him; but his apostacy would plunge them into the deepest discouragement. They went to work accordingly. They visited and entreated him, Martial Mazurier in particular endeavouring to make him fall, as he had done himself. There was no lack of arguments which might appear specious to Briçonnet. Would he like to be deprived of his functions? Could he not, by remaining in the church, employ his influence with the king and the court to effect an incalculable amount of good? What would become of his old friends, when he was no longer in power? Might not his resistance compromise a reform, which, to be salutary and durable, should be carried out by the legiti-

[1] In the library of the pastors at Neufchatel there is a letter from Sebville, in which the following passage occurs : " Je te notifie que l'évêque de Meaux en Brie près Paris, cum Jacobo Fabro Stapulensi, depuis trois mois, en visitant l'évêché, ont brûlé actu toutes les images, réservé le crucifix, et sont personellement ajournés à Paris, à ce mois de Mars venant, pour répondre coram suprema curia et universitate." I am inclined to believe this fact authentic, although Sebville was not on the spot, and neither Mezeray, Daniel, nor Maimbourg alludes to it. These Romanist authors, who are very brief, might have had reasons for passing it over in silence, considering the issue of the trial; and Sebville's report agrees in other respects with all the known facts. The matter is, however, doubtful.
[2] Hist. de l'Univ. par Crévier, v. 204.
[3] Maimbourg, Hist. du Calv. p. 14.

[1] MS. in the Royal Library (Paris) S. F. No. 337.
[2] Maimbourg, Hist. du Calv. p. 15.

mate influence of the clergy? How many souls he would offend by resisting the Church; how many souls he would attract, on the contrary, by giving way!......They, like himself, were anxious for a reform. All is advancing insensibly; at the court and in the city and provinces, every thing is moving forward......and would he in mere recklessness of heart destroy so fair a prospect! ......After all, they did not call upon him to sacrifice his opinions, but only to submit to the established order of the Church. Was it well in him, when France was labouring under so many reverses, to stir up new confusions? "In the name of religion, of your country, of your friends, and of the Reformation itself, be persuaded," said they. By such sophisms are the noblest causes ruined.

Yet every one of these considerations had its influence on the mind of the bishop. The tempter, who desired to make our Saviour fall in the wilderness, thus presented himself to Briçonnet in specious colours, but instead of saying with his Master: "Get thee behind me, Satan!" he listened, welcomed and pondered on these suggestions. From that hour his fidelity was at an end.

Briçonnet had never embarked with his whole heart, like Luther or Farel, in the movement that was then regenerating the Church; there was in him a certain mystical tendency which weakens men's minds, and deprives them of that firmness and courage which proceed from faith alone based on the Word of God. The cross that he was called to take up that he might follow Christ was too heavy.[1] Shaken, alarmed, stupified, and distracted,[2] he stumbled against the stone which had been artfully placed in his path ......he fell, and instead of throwing himself into the arms of Jesus, he threw himself into those of Mazurier,[3] and by a shameful recantation sullied the glory of a noble faithfulness.[4]

Thus fell Briçonnet, the friend of Lefevre and of Margaret; thus the earliest supporter of the Gospel in France denied the glad tidings of grace, in the guilty thought, that, if he remained faithful, he would lose his influence over the Church, the court, and France. But what was represented to him as the salvation of his country, perhaps became its ruin. What would have been the result if Briçonnet had possessed the courage of Luther? If one of the first bishops of France, beloved by the king and by the people, had ascended the scaffold, and had, like the little ones of the world, sealed the truth of the Gospel by a bold confession and a christian death, would not France herself have been moved; and the blood of the bishop becoming, like that of Polycarp and Cyprian, the

seed of the Church, might we not have seen that country, so illustrious in many respects, emerging in the sixteenth century from that spiritual darkness with which it is still clouded?

Briçonnet underwent a mere formal examination before James Menager and Andrew Verjus, who declared that he had sufficiently vindicated himself of the crime imputed to him. He was then subjected to penance, and assembled a synod in which he condemned Luther's books, retracted all that he had taught contrary to the doctrine of the Church, restored the invocation of saints, endeavoured to bring back those who had forsaken the Romish worship, and wishing to leave no doubt of his reconciliation with the pope and the Sorbonne, kept a solemn fast on the eve of Corpus Christi, and gave orders for pompous processions, in which he appeared personally, still further testifying his faith by his magnificence and by every kind of devout observance.[1] In his will he commended his soul to the Virgin Mary and to the heavenly choir of paradise, and desired that, after his death (which happened in 1533), twelve hundred masses should be said for the repose of his soul.

The fall of Briçonnet is perhaps the most memorable in the history of the Reformation. Nowhere else do we find a man so sincerely pious and so deeply engaged in the reform turning round so suddenly against it: yet we must clearly understand his character and his fall. Briçonnet was, as regards Rome, what Lefevre was with respect to the Reformation. They were both persons of half-measures, properly belonging to neither party. The doctor of Etaples inclined towards the Word, while the Bishop of Meaux leaned to the hierarchy; and, when these two men who touch each other were called upon to decide, the one ranged himself under the banner of Rome, and the other under that of Jesus Christ. We cannot, however, be sure that Briçonnet was wholly untrue to the convictions of his faith; at no period after his recantation did the Romish doctors place entire confidence in him. But he acted, perhaps, as the Archbishop of Cambray afterwards did, and whom he resembled in many points; he thought he might submit outwardly to the pope, while remaining inwardly subject to his old convictions. Such weakness is incompatible with the principles of the Reformation. Briçonnet was one of the chiefs of the mystic or quietest school in France, and we know that one of its leading maxims has ever been to accommodate itself to the church in which it exists, whatever that church may be.

Briçonnet's guilty fall went to the hearts of his old friends, and was the sad forerunner of those lamentable apostacies

---

[1] Crucis statim oblatæ terrore perculsus. Bezæ Icones.
[2] Dementatus. Ibid.
[3] Ut Episcopus etiam desisteret suis consiliis effecit. Launoi, regii Navarræ gymnasii hist. p. 621.
[4] Nisi turpi palinodia gloriam hanc omnem ipse sibi invidisset. Bezæ Icones.

[1] Mezeray, ii. 981; Daniel, vi. 544; Moreri, art. Briçonnet

which the spirit of the world so often obtained in France in another age. The man who seemed to hold the reins of the Reformation in his hand was suddenly thrown from his seat; and the Reformation was thenceforward destined to pursue its course in France, without a human leader, without a chief, in humility and in obscurity. But the disciples of the Gospel raised their heads, and from that time looked with a firmer faith towards that heavenly Guide, whose faithfulness they knew could not be shaken.

The Sorbonne triumphed; this was a great stride towards the destruction of the Reform in France; and it was important to achieve another victory without delay. Lefevre stood next after Briçonnet. Accordingly Beda had immediately turned the attack against him, by publishing a book against this illustrious doctor, full of such gross calumnies, that Erasmus says, "even smiths and cobblers could have pointed them out." His fury was particularly excited by the doctrine of justification through faith, which Lefevre was the first to preach to Christendom in the sixteenth century. To this point Beda continually recurred, as an article which, according to him, overturned the Church. "What!" said he, "Lefevre affirms that whoever places his salvation in himself will surely perish; while the man that lays aside all strength of his own, and throws himself entirely into the arms of Jesus Christ, will be saved!......Oh, what heresy! to teach the inefficacy of meritorious works! ......What a hellish error! what a deceitful snare of the devil! Let us oppose it with all our might!"[1]

That engine of persecution which produces either retractation or death, was immediately turned against the doctor of Etaples; and hopes were already entertained of seeing Lefevre share the fate of the poor woolcomber or of the illustrious Briçonnet. His accusation was soon drawn up; and a decree of the parliament (dated 28th August 1525) condemned nine propositions extracted from his commentaries on the Gospels, and placed his translation of the Scriptures in the list of prohibited books.[2]

This was only the prelude; and that the learned doctor knew. Upon the first symptoms of persecution, he had felt that, in the absence of Francis I., he must fall under the assault of his enemies, and that the moment was now come to obey the Lord's commandment: *When they persecute you in one city, flee ye into another.*[3] Lefevre quitted Meaux, where, after the bishop's apostacy, he had drunk nothing but the cup of bitterness, and saw all his activity paralyzed; and as he withdrew from his persecutors, he shook the dust from off his feet against them, "not to call

down evil upon them, but as a sign of the evils that were in store for them; for (says he in one place) just as this dust is shaken from off our feet, are they cast off from the face of the Lord."[1]

The persecutors had missed their victim; but they consoled themselves with the thought that France was at least delivered from the father of the heretics.

The fugitive Lefevre arrived at Strasburg under a borrowed name: there he immediately united with the friends of the Reformation; and what must have been his joy at hearing that Gospel publicly taught which he had been the first to bring forward in the Church! Lo, there was his faith! this was exactly what he had intended to teach! He seemed to have been born a second time to the christian life. Gerard Roussel, one of those evangelical men who, like the doctor of Etaples, did not attain complete emancipation, had also been compelled to quit France. Together they followed the teaching of Capito and Bucer;[2] they had frequent private conversations with these faithful doctors,[3] and a report was circulated that they had even been commissioned to do so by Margaret, the king's sister.[4] But Lefevre was more occupied in contemplating the ways of God than with polemics. Casting his eyes over Christendom, filled with astonishment on beholding the great events that were taking place, moved with thankfulness, and his heart full of anticipation, he fell on his knees and prayed the Lord "to perfect that which he saw then beginning."[5]

One pleasure in particular awaited him in Strasburg; Farel his disciple, his son, from whom he had been separated by persecution for nearly three years, had arrived there before him. The aged doctor of the Sorbonne found in his young pupil a man in the vigour of life, a Christian in all the energy of faith. Farel affectionately clasped that wrinkled hand which had guided his first steps, and experienced an indescribable joy at again meeting with his father in an evangelical city, and in seeing him surrounded with faithful men. Together they listened to the pure instructions of illustrious teachers; together they partook of the Lord's Supper in conformity with Christ's institution; together they received touching proofs of the love of their brethren. "Do you remember," said Farel, "what you once observed to me when we were both sunk in darkness: William, God will renew the world, and you will see it!......Here is the beginning of what you then told me."—"Yes:" answered the pious old man, "God is renewing the world......

---

[1] Perpendens perniciosissimam dæmonis fallaciam...... Occurri quantum valui. Nat. Bedæ Apolog. Adv. Lutheranos, fol. 42.
[2] J. Lelong, Biblioth. sacrée, 2d partie, p. 44.
[3] Matthew x. 14, 23.

[1] Quod excussi sunt a facie Domini sicut pulvis ille ex cussus est a pedibus. Faber in Ev. Ma??h. p. 40.
[2] Faber stapulensis et Gerardus Rufus, clam e Gallia profecti, Capitonem et Bucerum audierunt. Melch. Adam. Vita Capitonis. p. 90.
[3] De omnibus doctrinæ præcipuis locis cum ipsis disseruerint. Ibid.
[4] Missi a Margaretha, regis Francisci sorore. Ibid.
[5] Farel à tous seigneurs, peuples, et pasteurs.

My dear son, continue to preach boldly the holy Gospel of Jesus Christ."[1]

Lefevre, from excess of caution doubtless, wished to live unknown at Strasburg, and had taken the name of Anthony Pilgrim, while Roussel assumed that of Solnin. But the illustrious doctor could not remain hidden; in a short time the whole city and the very children saluted the aged Frenchman with respect.[2] He did not dwell alone; but resided in Capito's house with Farel, Roussel, Vedastus who was eulogized for his diffidence, and with a certain Simon, a converted Jew. The houses of Capito, Œcolampadius, Zwingle, and Luther, were then like inns. Such was at that time the strength of brotherly love. Many other Frenchmen were living in this city on the banks of the Rhine, and they founded a church in which Farel often preached the doctrine of salvation. This christian society soothed the pain of exile.

While these brethren were thus enjoying the asylum offered them by fraternal affection, those in Paris and in other parts of France were exposed to great dangers. Briçonnet had retracted; Lefevre had quitted France; this was no doubt something for the Sorbonne; but it had still to wait for the punishments that it had advised. Beda and his party had found no victims......one man exasperated them still more than Briçonnet and Lefevre; this was Louis Berquin. The gentleman of Artois, of a more decided character than his two masters, omitted no opportunity of tormenting the monks and theologians, and of unmasking their fanaticism. Living by turns at Paris and in the provinces, he collected and translated the writings of Luther and Erasmus:[3] he himself would compose controversial works, and defend and propagate the new doctrine with all the zeal of a new convert. The Bishop of Amiens denounced him; Beda seconded the charge; and the parliament had him thrown into prison. "This one," said they, "shall not escape us like Briçonnet or Lefevre." In effect, they kept him in close confinement. In vain did the superior of the Carthusians and others entreat him to apologize; he boldly declared that he would not give way on a single point. "There seemed no way left," says a chronicler, "but to lead him to the stake."[4]

Margaret, in consternation at what had happened to Briçonnet, dreaded to see Berquin dragged to that scaffold which the bishop had so shamefully escaped. Not daring to visit him in prison, she endeavoured to convey a few words of consolation to him; and it was perhaps for him that the princess composed this touching complaint of the prisoner, in which the latter, addressing the Lord, exclaims;—[1]

> But yet, where'er my prison be,
> Its gates can never keep out Thee;
> For where I am, Thou instant art with me.

But Margaret did not stop here; she instantly wrote to her brother, soliciting this gentleman's pardon. Happy would she be if she could deliver him in time from the hatred of his enemies.

While waiting for this victim, Beda resolved to intimidate the enemies of the Sorbonne and of the monks by crushing the most celebrated of them. Erasmus had taken up the pen against Luther; but that was of little consequence. If they can succeed in destroying Erasmus, with much stronger reason would the ruin of Farel, of Luther. and of their associates be inevitable. The surest way to reach the mark is to aim beyond it. When once Rome has placed her foot upon the neck of the philosopher of Rotterdam, where is the heretical doctor that can escape its vengeance? Lecouturier, commonly known by his Latin name *Sutor* (cobbler), had already begun the attack, by launching from his solitary Carthusian cell a treatise overflowing with violence, in which he called his opponents theologasters and jackasses, charging them with scandalous crimes, heresy, and blasphemy. Treating of subjects which he did not understand. he reminded his readers of the old proverb: *Ne sutor ultra crepidam*, Let the cobbler stick to his last.

Beda hastened to the assistance of his brother. He ordered Erasmus to write no more;[2] and taking up that pen which he had commanded the greatest writer of the age to lay down, he made a collection of all the calumnies that the monks had invented against the illustrious philosopher, translated them into French, and composed a book that he circulated in the city and at court, striving to raise all France against him.[3] This work was the signal of attack; Erasmus was assailed from every quarter. An old Carmelite of Louvain, Nicholas Ecmond, exclaimed every time he went into the pulpit, "There is no difference between Luther and Erasmus, except that Erasmus is the greater heretic;[4] and wherever the Carmelite might be, at table, in coach, or in boat, he called Erasmus a heresiarch and forger.[5] The faculty of Paris, excited by these clamours, prepared a censure against the illustrious writer.

Erasmus was astounded. This, then, is the end of all his forbearance, and of even his hostility against Luther. He had mounted to the breach with greater courage than any man; and now they want to make

---

[1] Quod et plus senex fatebatur; meque hortabatur pergerem in annuntiatione sacri evangelii. Farel to Pellican. Hotting. H. L. vi. 17.
[2] Nam latere cupiunt et tamen pueris noti sunt. Capito to Zwingle, Epp. p. 439.
[3] Erasmus, Epp. p. 923.
[4] Actes des Martyrs, p. 103.

[1] Marguerites de la Marguerite des Princesses, i. 445.
[2] Primum jubet ut desinam scribere. Erasm. Epp. 921.
[3] Ut totam Galliam in me concitaret. Ibid. 866.
[4] Nisi quod Erasmus esset major hæreticus. Ibid. 915.
[5] Quoties in conviviis, in vehiculis, in navibus. Ibid.

him a stepping stone, and trample him under foot, that they may the more securely attack the common enemy. This idea disgusted him: he turned round immediately, and almost before he had ceased his attack upon Luther, fell upon these fanatical doctors, who had assailed him from behind. Never was his correspondence more active than now. He glances all around him, and his piercing eye soon discovers in whose hands depends his fate. He does not hesitate: he will lay his complaints and remonstrances at the feet of the Sorbonne, of the parliament, of the king, and of the emperor himself. "What is it that has kindled this immense Lutheran conflagration?" wrote he to those theologians of the Sorbonne, from whom he still expected some little impartiality; "what has fanned it, if not the virulence of Beda and his fellows?[1] In war, a soldier who has done his duty receives a reward from his general; and all the recompense I shall receive from you, the leaders in this war, is to be delivered up to the calumnies of such as Beda and Lecouturier."

"What!" wrote he to the parliament, "when I was contending with these Lutherans, and while I was maintaining a severe struggle by order of the emperor, the pope, and other princes, even at the peril of my life, Beda and Lecouturier attacked me from behind with their foul libels! Ah, if fortune had not deprived us of King Francis, I should have invoked this avenger of the muses against this new invasion of the barbarians.[2] But now it is your duty to put an end to such injustice!"

As soon as he found the possibility of conveying a letter to the king, he wrote to him immediately. His penetrating eye detected in these fanatical doctors of the Sorbonne the germs of the league, the predecessors of those three priests who were one day to set up the *Sixteen* against the last of the Valois; his genius forewarned the king of the crimes and misfortunes which his descendants were destined to know but too well. "Religion is their pretext," said he, "but they aspire to tyranny even over princes. They move with a sure step, though their path is under ground. Should the prince be disinclined to submit to them in every thing, they will declare that he may be deposed by the Church; that is to say, by a few false monks and theologians who conspire against the public peace."[3] Erasmus, in writing to Francis I., could not have touched a tenderer point.

Finally, to be more certain of escape from his enemies, Erasmus invoked the protection of Charles V. "Invincible emperor," said he, "certain individuals who, under the pretence of religion, wish to establish their own gluttony and despotism, are raising a horrible outcry against me.[1] I am fighting under your banners and those of Jesus Christ. May your wisdom and power restore peace to the christian world."

Thus did the prince of letters address the great ones of the age. The danger was averted; the powers of the world interposed; the vultures were compelled to abandon a prey which they fancied already in their talons. Upon this they turned their eyes to another quarter, seeking fresh victims, which were soon found.

Lorraine was the first place in which blood was again to flow. From the earliest days of the Reform there had been a fanatical alliance between Paris and the country of the Guises. When Paris was quiet, Lorraine applied to the task; and then Paris resumed her labour, while Metz and Nancy were recovering their strength. In June 1525, Peter Toussaint returned to Metz, in company with Farel. They desired a hearing before their lordships *the Thirteen;* and this being refused, they appealed to the *eschevin.* Plans were already laid for throwing them into prison, when, fearful of danger, they quickly left the city, travelling all night lest they should be overtaken.[2]

The first blows were destined apparently to fall on an excellent man, one of the Basle refugees, a friend of Farel and Toussaint. The Chevalier d'Esch had not been able to escape the suspicions of the priests in Metz. They discovered that he kept up a communication with the evangelical Christians, and he was imprisoned at Pont-a-Mousson, about five miles from Metz on the banks of the Moselle.[3] These tidings overwhelmed the French refugees and the Swiss themselves with sorrow. "O heart full of innocence!" exclaimed Œcolampadius. "I have confidence in the Lord," added he, "that he will preserve this man to us, either in life as a preacher of righteousness, to announce His name, or as a martyr to confess him in death."[4] But at the same time Œcolampadius disapproved of the impetuosity, enthusiasm, and imprudent zeal which distinguished the French refugees. "I wish," said he, "that my very dear lords of France would not be so hasty in returning into their own country, before they have duly examined all things;[5] for the devil is spreading his snares on every side. Nevertheless let them obey the Spirit of Christ, and may this Spirit never abandon them."

There was, in truth, reason to fear for the chevalier. The fury of the enemy had broken

[1] Hoc gravissimum Lutheri incendium, unde natum, unde huc progressum, nisi ex Beddaicis intemperiis. Er. Epp. p. 887.
[2] Musarum vindicem adversus barbarorum incursiones. Ibid. p. 2070.
[3] Nisi princeps ipsorum voluntati per omnia paruerit, dicetur fautor hæreticorum et destitui poterit per ecclesiam. Ibid. p. 1108.

[1] Simulato religionis prætextu, ventris tyrannidisque suæ negotium agentes. Er. Epp. p. 962.
[2] Chroniques de Metz, p. 823.
[3] Noster captus detinetur in Bundamosa quinque millibus a Metis. Œcol. to Farel, Epp. 201.
[4] Vel vivum confessorem, vel mortuum martyrem servabit. Ibid.
[5] Nollem carissimos dominos meos Galles properare in Galliam, &c. Ibid.

out in Lorraine with redoubled violence. The provincial of the Cordeliers, Bonaventure Renel, confessor to Duke Anthony the Good, a man devoid of shame, and not very commendable on the score of morals, gave this weak prince, who reigned from 1508 to 1544, great licence in his pleasures, and persuaded him, almost by way of penance, to destroy the innovators without mercy. "It is enough for every one to know his *Pater* and his *Ave*," this prince, so well tutored by Renel, would say; "the greater the doctor, the greater the disturbance."[1]

Towards the end of 1524 the duke's court was informed that a pastor named Schuch was preaching some new doctrine in the town of St. Hippolyte, at the foot of the Vosges. "Let them return to their duty," said Anthony *the Good*, "or else I will march against the city, and destroy it by fire and sword."[2]

Upon this the faithful pastor resolved to give himself up for his flock, and repaired to Nancy, where the prince was residing. As soon as he arrived he was thrown into a filthy prison, under the guard of brutal and cruel men; and Friar Bonaventure at last saw the heretic in his power. It was he who presided at the trial. "Heretic! Judas! devil!" exclaimed he. Schuch, calm and collected, made no reply to this abuse; but holding in his hands a Bible, all covered with notes, he meekly yet forcibly confessed Christ crucified. On a sudden he became animated; he stood up boldly, and raising his voice, as if filled by the Spirit from on high, looked his judges in the face, and threatened them with the terrible judgments of God.

Brother Bonaventure and his companions, amazed and transported with rage, rushed upon him with violent cries, tore away the Bible from which he was reading this menacing language, "and like mad dogs," says the chronicler, "unable to bite his doctrine, they burnt it in their convent."[3]

All the court of Lorraine resounded with the obstinacy and impudence of the minister of St. Hippolyte, and the prince, curious to hear the heretic, desired to be present at his last interrogatory, but in secret, however, and concealed from every eye. As the examination took place in Latin, he could not understand a word; but he was struck with the firm countenance of the minister, who seemed neither vanquished nor confounded. Exasperated at such obstinacy, Anthony the Good rose up, and said as he withdrew: "Why do you still dispute? He denies the sacrament of the mass; let them proceed to execution against him."[4] Schuch was instantly condemned to be burnt alive. When the sentence was made known to him, he raised his eyes to heaven, saying mildly:

"I was glad when they said unto me, let us go into the house of the Lord."[1]

On the 19th August 1525 the whole city of Nancy was in motion. The bells were tolling for the death of a heretic. The mournful procession set out. It was necessary to pass before the convent of the Cordeliers, who, rejoicing and expectant, had assembled before the gate. At the moment that Schuch appeared, Father Bonaventure, pointing to the carved images over the portals of the convent, exclaimed: "Heretic! pay honour to God, to his mother, and to the saints."— "Ye hypocrites!" replied Schuch, standing erect before these blocks of wood and stone, "God will destroy you, and bring your deceits to light!"

When the martyr reached the place of execution, his books were burnt before his face; he was then called upon to retract; but he refused, saying: "It is thou, O God, who hast called me, and thou wilt give me strength unto the end."[2] After this he began to repeat aloud the fifty-first psalm: "Have mercy upon me, O Lord, according to thy loving kindness." Having mounted the pile, he continued to recite the psalm until the smoke and the flames stifled his voice.

Thus the persecutors of France and Lorraine beheld a renewal of their victories; at length men paid attention to their advice. The ashes of a heretic had been scattered to the winds at Nancy; it was a challenge to the capital of France. What! shall Beda and Lecouturier be the last to show their zeal for the pope! Let flames reply to flames, and heresy, swept from the soil of the kingdom, would soon be entirely driven back beyond the Rhine.

But before he could succeed, Beda had to sustain a combat, half serious, half ludicrous, against one of those men with whom the struggle against the Papacy is merely an intellectual pastime and not an earnest purpose of the heart.

Among the scholars whom Briçonnet had attracted to his diocese, was a doctor of the Sorbonne, named Peter Caroli, a vain and frivolous man, not less quarrelsome and litigious than Beda himself. In the new doctrine Caroli saw the means of vexing Beda, whose ascendancy he could not endure. Accordingly, on his return from Meaux to Paris, he made a great sensation by carrying into the pulpit what was called, "the new way of preaching." Then began an indefatigable struggle between the two doctors; it was blow for blow, and trick for trick. Beda summoned Caroli before the Sorbonne, and Caroli summoned him before the bishop's court by way of reparation. The faculty continued the examination, and Caroli gave notice of an appeal to the parliament. He was provisionally forbidden to enter the

1 Actes des Martyrs, p. 97.   2 Ibid. p. 95.
3 Actes des Martyrs, recueillis par Crespin, en Français, p. 97.
4 Hist. de François I. par Gaillard. iv. 233.

1 Psalm cxii. 1.
2 Eum auctorem vocationis suæ atque conservatorem, ad extremum usque spiritum recognovit. Acta Mart. p. 202.

pulpit, and he preached in all the churches of Paris. Being positively forbidden to preach at all, he publicly lectured on the Psalms in the College of Cambray. The faculty forbade him to continue his course, and he begged permission to finish the explanation of the 22d Psalm, which he had just begun. Finally, on the refusal of his request, he posted the following placard on the college gates: " *Peter Caroli, desirous of obeying the orders of the sacred faculty, has ceased to lecture; he will resume his lectures (whenever it shall please God) at the verse where he left off:* THEY HAVE PIERCED MY HANDS AND MY FEET." Thus Beda at last found his match. If Caroli had seriously defended the truth, the burning pile would soon have been his reward; but he was of too profane a spirit to be put to death. How could the judges capitally punish a man who made them lose their gravity. Neither the bishop's court, nor the parliament, nor the council, could ever come to a definite decision in his cause. Two men such as Caroli would have wearied out the activity of Beda himself; but the Reformation did not produce his parallel.[1]

As soon as this unseasonable contest was ended, Beda applied to more serious matters. Happily for the syndic of the Sorbonne, there were men who gave persecution a better hold of them than Caroli. Briçonnet, Erasmus, Lefevre, and Farel had escaped him; but since he cannot reach these distinguished individuals, he will content himself with meaner persons. The poor youth, James Pavanne, after his abjuration at Christmas 1524, had done nothing but weep and sigh. He might be seen with a melancholy air, his eyes fixed on the earth, groaning inwardly, and severely reproaching himself for having denied his Saviour and his God.[2]

Pavanne was undoubtedly the most diffident and inoffensive of men: but what mattered that! he had been at Meaux, and in those days that was sufficient. "Pavanne has relapsed," was the cry; " *the dog is turned to his own vomit again, and the sow that was washed to her wallowing in the mire.*" He was immediately arrested, thrown into prison, and taken before his judges. This was all that the youthful James required. He felt comforted as soon as he was in chains, and found strength sufficient to confess Jesus Christ with boldness.[3] The cruel persecutors smiled as they saw that, this time at least, nothing could save their victim; there was no recantation, no flight, no powerful patronage. The young man's mildness, his candour and courage, failed to soften his adversaries.

He regarded them with love; for by casting him into prison, they had restored him to tranquillity and joy; but his tender looks only served to harden their hearts. His trial was soon concluded: a pile was erected on the Grève, where Pavanne died rejoicing, strengthening by his example all those who in that large city believed openly or secretly in the Gospel of Christ.

This was not enough for the Sorbonne. If they are compelled to sacrifice the little ones of the world, their number must at least make amends for their quality. The flames of the Grève struck terror into Paris and the whole of France; but a new pile, kindled on another spot, will redouble that terror. It will be talked of at court, in the colleges, and in the workshops of the people; and such proofs will show more clearly than any edicts, that Louisa of Savoy, the Sorbonne, and the parliament, are resolved to sacrifice the very last heretic to the anathemas of Rome.

In the forest of Livry, three leagues from Paris, and not far from the spot where once stood the ancient abbey of the Augustines, dwelt a hermit, who having in his excursions met with some men of Meaux, had received the evangelical doctrine into his heart.[1] The poor hermit had felt himself rich in his retreat, when one day, returning with the scanty food that public charity bestowed on him, he carried back Jesus Christ and his grace. From that time he found that it was better to give than to receive. He went from house to house in the surrounding villages, and as soon as he had opened the doors of the poor peasants whom he visited in their humble huts, he spoke to them of the Gospel, of the perfect pardon that it offers to the burdened soul, and which is far better than absolutions.[2] Erelong the good hermit of Livry was known in the environs of Paris; people went to visit him in his lowly cell, and he became a mild and fervent missionary for the simple souls of that district.

The rumour of the doings of this new evangelist did not fail to reach the ears of the Sorbonne and of the magistrates of Paris. The hermit was seized, dragged from his hermitage, from his forest, from those fields through which he used to wander daily, thrown into a prison in that great city which he had ever shunned, and condemned " to suffer the exemplary punishment of the slow fire."[3]

In order to render the example more striking, it was determined that he should be burnt alive in the front of Notre-Dame, before that splendid cathedral, that majestic

---

[1] Gerdesius, Hist. seculi xvi. renovati, p. 52; D'Argentré, Collectio judiciorum de novis erroribus, ii. 21; Gaillard, Hist. de François I. iv. 233.
[2] Animi factum suum destestantis dolorem, sæpe declaraverit. Acta Mart. p. 203.
[3] Puram religionis Christianæ confessionem addit. Ibid.

[1] Cette semence de Faber et de ses disciples, prise au grenier de Luther, germa dans le sot esprit d'un ermite, qui se tenait près la ville de Paris. Hist. cath. de notre temps, par S. Fontaine, Paris, 1562.
[2] Lequel par les villages qu'il fréquentait, sous couleur de faire ses quêtes, tenait propos hérétiques. Hist. cath. de notre-temps, par S. Fontaine, Paris, 1562.
[3] Ibid.

symbol of Roman-catholicism. All the clergy were convoked, and as much pomp was displayed as on the most solemn festivals.[1] They would, if possible, have attracted all Paris round the stake, "the great bell of the church of Notre-Dame (says an historian) tolling solemnly to arouse the citizens."[2] The people flocked in crowds through all the streets that led into the square. The deep tones of the bell drew the workman from his toil, the scholar from his books, the merchant from his traffic, the soldier from his idleness, and already the wide space was covered by an immense crowd which still kept increasing. The hermit, clad in the garments assigned to obstinate heretics, with head and feet bare, had been led before the gates of the cathedral. Calm, firm, and collected, he made no reply to the exhortations of the confessors who presented a crucifix to him, save by declaring that his sole hope was in the pardon of God. The doctors of the Sorbonne, in the front ranks of the spectators, seeing his constancy, and the effect it was producing on the people, cried aloud: "He is damned: they are leading him to hell-fire!"[3] The great bell still continued tolling, and its loud notes, by stunning the ears of the crowd, increased the solemnity of this mournful spectacle. At length the bell was silent, and the martyr having replied to the last questions of his enemies, that he was resolved to die in the faith of his Lord Jesus Christ, was burnt by a slow fire, according to the tenor of his sentence. And thus, in front of Notre-Dame, amid the shouts and emotion of a whole people, under the shadow of the towers raised by the piety of Louis the younger, peacefully died a man, whose name history has not transmitted to us, except as the "Hermit of Livry."

CHAPTER XV.

A Student of Noyon—Character of young Calvin—Early Education—Consecrated to Theology—The Bishop gives him the Tonsure—He leaves Noyon on Account of the Plague—The Two Calvins—Slanders—The Reformation creates new Languages—Persecution and Terror—Margaret's Letter to her Brother—Toussaint put in Prison—The Persecution more furious—Death of Du Blet, Moulin, and Papillon—God saves the Church—Margaret's Project—Her Departure for Spain.

WHILE men were thus putting to death the first confessors of Jesus Christ in France, God was preparing mightier ones to fill their places. Beda hurried to the stake an unassuming scholar, an humble hermit, and thought he was dragging almost the whole of the Reform along with them. But Providence has resources that are unknown to the world. The Gospel, like the fabulous phœnix, contains a principle of life within itself,

which the flames cannot consume, and it springs up again from its own ashes. It is often at the moment when the storm is at its height, when the thunderbolt seems to have struck down the truth, and when thick darkness hides it from our view, that a sudden glimmering appears, the forerunner of a great deliverance. At this time, when all human powers in France were arming against the Gospel for the complete destruction of the Reformation, God was preparing an instrument, weak to all appearance, who should one day support His rights and defend His cause with more than mortal intrepidity. In the midst of the persecutions and blazing piles that followed each other in close succession after Francis became Charles's prisoner, let us fix our eyes on a youth, one day to be called to the head of a great army in the holy warfare of Israel.

Among the inhabitants of the city and colleges of Paris who heard the sound of the great bell was a young scholar of sixteen, a native of Noyon in Picardy, of middle stature, sallow features, and with piercing eye and animated looks that announced a mind of no common sagacity.[1] His dress, extremely neat but of perfect simplicity, betokened order and moderation.[2] This young man, by name John Cauvin or Calvin, was then studying at the college of La Marche, under Mathurin Cordier, a rector celebrated for his probity, erudition, and peculiar fitness for the instruction of youth. Brought up in all the superstitions of popery, the scholar of Noyon was blindly submissive to the Church, cheerfully complying with all her observances,[3] and persuaded that the heretics had richly deserved their fate. The blood which was then flowing in Paris aggravated the crime of heresy in his eyes. But although naturally of a timid and fearful disposition, which he himself has styled soft and pusillanimous,[4] he possessed that uprightness and generosity of heart which lead a man to sacrifice every thing to his convictions. Accordingly, in vain had his youth been appalled by those frightful spectacles, in vain had murderous flames consumed the faithful disciples of the Gospel on the Grève and in front of Notre-Dame; the recollection of these horrors could not prevent him from one day entering on the new path, which seemed to lead only to the prison or the stake. Moreover, there were already perceptible in the character of young Calvin certain traits that announced what he would become. Strictness of morals in him led the way to strictness of doctrine, and the scholar of sixteen already gave promise of a man who

---

[1] Avec une grande cérémonie. Hist. des Egl. Réf. par Theod. de Bèze, i. 4.   [2] Ibid.
[3] Beza, Histoire des Eglises Réf. i. 4.

[1] Statura fuit mediocri, colore subpallido et nigricante, oculis ad mortem usque limpidis, quique ingenii sagacitatem testarentur. Bezæ Vita Calvini.
[2] Cultu corporis neque culto neque sordido sed qui singularem modestiam deceret. Ibid.
[3] Primo quidem quum superstitionibus Papatus magis pertinaciter addictus essem. Calv. Præf. ad Psalm.
[4] Ego qui natura timido, molli et pusillo animo me esse fateor. Ibid.

would deal seriously with every principle he embraced, and who would firmly require in others what he himself found it so easy to perform. Quiet and serious during his lessons, never sharing in the amusements or follies of his schoolfellows during the hours of recreation, holding himself aloof,[1] and filled with horror at sin, he would often reprimand their disorders with severity and even bitterness.[2] And hence, as a canon of Noyon informs us, his fellow-students nicknamed him the *accusative case.*[3] Among them he was the representative of conscience and of duty, so far was he from being as some of his calumniators have depicted him. The pale features and the piercing eyes of the scholar of sixteen had already inspired his comrades with more respect than the black gowns of their masters; and this Picard youth, of a timid air, who daily took his seat on the benches in the college of La Marche, was even then, by the seriousness of his conversation and life, an unconscious minister and reformer.

It was not in these particulars alone that the youth of Noyon was already far above his schoolfellows. His great timidity sometimes prevented him from manifesting all the horror he felt at vanity and vice; but he already consecrated to study the whole force of his genius and of his will, and to look at him one might see he was a man who would spend his life in toil. He comprehended every thing with inconceivable facility; he ran in his studies while his companions were lazily creeping along, and he impressed deeply on his profound genius what others spend much time in learning superficially. Accordingly, his master was compelled to take him out of the classes, and introduce him singly to fresh studies.[4]

Among his fellow-students were the young De Mommors, belonging to the first nobility of Picardy. John Calvin was very intimate with them, especially with Claude, who afterwards became abbot of Saint Eloi, and to whom he dedicated his commentary on Seneca. It was in the company of these young nobles that Calvin had come to Paris. His father, Gerard Calvin, apostolic notary, procurator-fiscal of the county of Noyon, secretary of the diocese, and proctor of the chapter,[5] was a man of judgment and ability, whose talents had raised him to offices sought after by the best families, and who had gained the esteem of all the gentry in the province, and in particular of the noble

family of Mommor.[1] Gerard resided at Noyon;[2] he had married a young woman of Cambray, of remarkable beauty and unassuming piety, by name Jane Lefranq, who had already borne him a son named Charles, when on the 10th of July 1509 she gave birth to a second son, who received the name of John, and who was christened in the church of St. Godeberte.[3] A third son, Anthony, who died young, and two daughters, made up the family of the procurator-fiscal of Noyon.

Gerard Calvin, living in familiar intercourse with the heads of the clergy and the chief persons in the province, desired that his children should receive the same education as those of the best families. John, whose precocious habits he had observed, was brought up with the sons of the Mommor family; he lived in their house as one of themselves, and studied the same lessons as Claude. In this family he learnt the first elements of literature and of life, and thus received a higher polish than he appeared destined to acquire.[4] He was afterwards sent to the college of the Capettes, founded in the city of Noyon.[5] The child enjoyed but little recreation. The austerity, that was one of the characteristic features of the son, was found also in the father. Gerard brought him up strictly; from his earliest years, John was compelled to bend to the inflexible rule of duty, which soon became habitual to him, and the influence of the father counteracted that of the Mommor family. Calvin, who was of a timid and somewhat rustic character (as he says himself),[6] and rendered still more timid by his father's severity, shrunk from the splendid apartments of his protectors, and loved to remain alone and in obscurity.[7] Thus in retirement his young mind formed itself to great thoughts. It would appear that he sometimes went to the village of Pont l'Evêque, near Noyon, where his grandfather resided in a small cottage,[8] and where other relatives also, who at a later period changed their name from detestation of the heresiarch, kindly received the son of the procurator-

---

[1] Summam in moribus affectabat gravitatem et paucorum hominum consuetudine utebatur. Ræmundi Hist. Hæres. vii. 10.
[2] Severus omnium in suis sodalibus censor. Bezæ Vita Calv.
[3] Annales de l'Eglise de Noyon, par Levasseur, chanoine, p. 1158.
[4] Exculto ipsius ingenio quod ei jam tum erat acerrimum, ita profecit ut cæteris sodalibus in grammatices curriculo relictis, ad dialecticos et aliarum quas vocant artium studium promoveretur. Beza.
[5] Levasseur, doctor of the Sorbonne, Annales de l'Eglise Cathédrale de Noyon, p. 1151. Drelincourt, Défense de Calvin, p. 193.

[1] Erat is Gerardus non parvi judicii et concilii homo, ideoque nobilibus ejus regionis plerisque carus. Beza.
[2] Dans la place où est bastie maintenant la maison du Cerf. Desmay, docteur de la Sorbonne, Vie de Jean Calvin, hérésiarque, p. 30. Levasseur, Ann. de Noyon, p. 1157.
[3] The calumnies and extravagant tales about Calvin began early. J. Levasseur, afterwards dean of the canons at Noyon, relates that when Calvin's mother was in labour, "before the child was born, there came forth a swarm of large flies, an indubitable presage that he would one day be an evil speaker and a calumniator." Ann. de la Cath. de Noyon, p. 1157. These absurdities and many others of the same kind refute themselves, without our taking upon ourselves to do so. In our days, those Romish doctors who are not ashamed to employ the weapons of calumny, make a selection from these low and ridiculous stories, not daring to cite them all; but they are all equally worthless.
[4] Domi vestræ puer educatus, iisdem tecum studiis initiatus, primam vitæ et literarum disciplinam familiæ vestræ nobilissimæ acceptam refero. Calv. Præf. in Senecam ad Claudium.
[5] Desmay, Remarques, p. 31; Drélincourt, Défense, p. 158
[6] Ego qui natura subrusticus. Præf. ad Psalm.
[7] Umbram et otium semper amavi....latebras captare. Ibid.
[8] Le bruit est que son grand-père était tonnelier. Drélincourt, p. 30; Levasseur, Ann. de Noyon, p. 1151.

fiscal. But it was to study chiefly that young Calvin devoted his time. While Luther, who was to act upon the people, was brought up like a child of the people, Calvin, who was to act especially as a theologian and profound reasoner, and become the legislator of the renovated Church, received even in childhood a more liberal education.[1] A spirit of piety early showed itself in the child's heart. One author relates that he was accustomed, when very young, to pray in the open air, under the vault of heaven; a habit which contributed to awaken in his heart the feeling of God's omnipresence.[2] But although Calvin might, even in infancy, have heard the voice of God in his heart, no one at Noyon was so rigid as he in the observance of ecclesiastical regulations. And hence Gerard, remarking this disposition, conceived the design of devoting his son to theology.[3] This prospect no doubt contributed to impress on his soul that serious form, that theological stamp, by which it was subsequently distinguished. His spirit was of a nature to receive a strong impression in early years, and to familiarize itself from childhood with the most elevated thoughts. The report that he was at this time a chorister has no foundation, as even his adversaries admit. But they assure us that, when a child, he was seen joining the religious processions, and carrying a sword with a cross-shaped hilt by way of a crucifix.[4] "A presage," add they, "of what he was one day to become!" "The Lord hath made my mouth like a sharp sword," says the servant of Jehovah in Isaiah. The same may be said of Calvin.

Gerard was poor; his son's education had cost him much, and he wished to attach him irrevocably to the Church. The Cardinal of Lorraine had been coadjutor of the Bishop of Metz at the age of four years. It was then a common practice to confer ecclesiastical titles and revenues on children. Alphonso of Portugal was made cardinal by Leo X. at the age of eight, and Odet of Châtillon by Clement VII. at eleven; and subsequent to Calvin's day, the celebrated Mère Angélique of Port Royal was appointed coadjutrix of that nunnery at the age of seven years. Gerard, who died a good catholic, was regarded with favour by Messire Charles de Hangest, bishop of Noyon, and by his vicars-general. Accordingly, when the chaplain of La Gésine resigned, the bishop, on the 21st May 1521, conferred this benefice on John Calvin, who was then nearly twelve years old. The appointment was communicated to the chapter twelve days after. On the eve of Corpus Christi, the bishop solemnly

cut off the child's hair;[1] and by this ceremony of the tonsure, John became a member of the clergy, and capable of entering into holy orders, and of holding a benefice without residing on the spot.

Thus was Calvin called to make trial in his own person of the abuses of the Romish Church. Of all who wore the tonsure in France, there was none more serious in his piety than the chaplain of La Gésine, and the serious child was probably astonished himself at the work of the bishop and his vicars-general. But in his simplicity he felt too much veneration towards these exalted personages to indulge in the least suspicion on the lawfulness of his tonsure. He had held the title about two years when Noyon was visited by a dreadful pestilence. Several of the canons petitioned the chapter that they might be allowed to quit the city. Already many of the inhabitants had been carried off by the *great death*, and Gerard was beginning to fear that his son John, the hope of his life, might in a moment be snatched from his tenderness by the scourge of God. The young de Mommors were going to Paris to continue their studies; this was what the procurator-fiscal had always desired for his son. Why should he separate John from his fellow-students? On the 5th of August 1523, he petitioned the chapter to procure the young chaplain " liberty to go wherever he pleased during the plague, without loss of his allowance ; which was granted him until the feast of Saint Remy."[2] John Calvin quitted his father's house at the age of fourteen. It requires great audacity in calumny to ascribe his departure to other causes, and in mere wantonness to challenge that disgrace which justly recoils on those who circulate charges the falsehood of which has been so authentically demonstrated. It appears that in Paris, Calvin lodged at the house of one of his uncles, Richard Cauvin, who resided near the church of St. Germain l'Auxerrois. " Thus flying from the pestilence," says the canon of Noyon, " he went to catch it elsewhere."

Some years after Calvin had quitted Noyon, another individual of the same name arrived in that city.[3] John Cauvin was a young man of corrupt principles, but as he came from another part of France, and was a stranger (*or unknown*) in Noyon, he was received among the priests who chanted in the choir, and in a short time a chapel was given him, as in the case of the first Calvin. As this took place at a time when the latter had already " turned to heresy," the good canons

---

[1] Henry, Das Leben Calvins, p. 29.
[2] Calvin's Leben von Fischer, Leipzig, 1794. The author does not quote his authority for this fact.
[3] Destinarat autem eum pater ab initio theologiæ studiis, quod in illa etiam tenera ætate mirum in modum religiosus esset. Bezæ Vita Calv.
[4] Levasseur, Ann. de Noyon, pp. 1159, 1173.

[1] Vie de Calvin, par Desmay, p. 31; Levasseur, p. 1158.
[2] This is what the priest and the vicar-general Desmay (Jean Calvin, hérésiarque, p. 32), and the canon Levasseur (Ann. de Noyon, p. 1160), declare they found in the registers of the chapter of Noyon. Thus these Romanist authors refute the inventions or mistakes of Richelieu and other writers.
[3] Annales de l'Eglise de Noyon, at the chapter entitled *D'un autre Jean Cauvin*, chapelain, vicaire de la même église de Noyon, non hérétique, by Jacques Levasseur, canon and dean of that city.

looked upon Cauvin's arrival as a sort of recompense and consolation; but it was not long before the disorderly life of this wretched man excited alarm among his protectors. He was reprimanded, punished, and even deprived of his stipend : but to this he paid no attention,[1] continually lapsing again into incontinence. " Seeing then," says the canon, " his hardness of heart, which made him neglect every kind of remonstrance," the canons deprived John Cauvin of his chapel and expelled him from the choir. James Desmay, a priest and doctor of divinity, who had studied at Noyon every thing that concerned this church, adds, that he was privately scourged in 1552, and then driven from the town.[2] This is indeed a disgraceful end for a priest! The canon Levasseur disputes the scourging, but admits all the rest.

In the following year the same circumstances happened again, for the history of popery abounds in such adventures. A certain Baldwin the younger, also chaplain at Noyon, having taken to live scandalously with him certain women of suspicious character,[3] was condemned to attend every service in the church during a month, and to be scourged.[4]

While these two Romanist authors agree in relating the disorders and punishments inflicted on these young ecclesiastics, they likewise agree in declaring that they had found nothing at Noyon or in its registers against the morals of the great French reformer, and are content to execrate his error ; " for to call a man a heretic, is to call him by the most opprobrious of names."[5]

The Dean of Noyon goes even farther in his zeal for the papacy, and relates that John Cauvin, who had been expelled in 1552 for incontinence, died a *good catholic*. " Thanks be to God," adds he, " that he never turned his coat, nor changed his religion, to which his libertine life and the example of his namesake Calvin seemed to incline him." The dean concludes his strange narrative, the discovery of which is highly valuable to the history of the Reformation, in these words : " I thought it my duty to add this chapter to the history of the first Calvin the reformer, *ad diluendam homonymiam* (to guard against the similarity of names), for fear one should be taken for the other, the catholic for the heretic."[6]

Never was fear better founded. We know what the popish writers are accustomed to do. They take advantage of the misdeeds of John Cauvin at Noyon, and ascribe them

to the reformer. They tell their readers gravely that he was driven from his native town for misconduct, after having been condemned to be scourged and even branded. In spite of all the pains taken by the Dean of Noyon to add a chapter *for fear one should be taken for the other, the catholic for the heretic*, the apologists of Rome fail not to ascribe to the reformer the debaucheries of his namesake. What engrossed the thoughts of the canon of Noyon was the glory of John Cauvin who died a good catholic, and he feared lest Calvin's heresy should be laid to his charge. And, accordingly, he clearly assigns *incontinence* to the one, and *heresy* to the other. There have indeed been *equivocations*, as he says, but in a contrary direction. Let us now return to Calvin at Paris.

A new world opened before the young man in the metropolis of letters. He profited by it, applied to his studies, and made great progress in Latin literature. He became familiar with Cicero, and learned from this great master to employ the language of the Romans with a facility, purity, and ease that excite the admiration even of his enemies. But at the same time, he found riches in this language which he afterwards transferred to his own.

Up to this time Latin had been the only language of the learned ; and to our own days it has remained the language of the Roman Church. The Reformation created or at least emancipated the vulgar tongue. The exclusive office of the priest had ceased ; the people were called to learn and know for themselves. In this one fact was involved the ruin of the language of the priest, and the inauguration of the language of the people. It is no longer to the Sorbonne alone, to a few monks, or ecclesiastics, or literary men, that the new ideas are to be addressed ; but to the noble, the citizen, and the labourer. All men are now to be preached to ; nay more, all are to become preachers—wool-combers and knights, as well as doctors and parish-priests. A new language is wanted, or, at the least, the language of the people must undergo an immense transformation, a great enfranchisement, and, drawn from the common uses of life, must receive its patent of nobility from renovated Christianity. The Gospel, so long slumbering, has awoke ; it speaks and addresses whole nations, every where kindling generous affections ; it opens the treasures of heaven to a generation that was thinking only of the mean things on earth ; it shakes the masses; it talks to them of God, of man, of good and evil, of the pope and the Bible, of a crown in heaven, and perhaps a scaffold upon earth. The popular tongue, which hitherto had been the language of chroniclers and troubadours only, was called by the Reformation to act a new part, and consequently to new developments. A new world is opening upon society, and for a new world there

---

[1] Annales l'Eglise de Noyon, at the chapter entitled, *D'un autre Jean Cauvin*, chapelain, vicaire de la même église de Noyon, non hérétique, by Jacques Levasseur, canon and dean of that city.
[2] Vie de Jean Calvin, par T. Desmay, imprimée à Rouen, chez Richard l'Allement, 1621.
[3] Scandalose vivendo cum quibusdam mulieribus suspectis. Annales de l'Eglise de Noyon, p. 1171.
[4] Præfati Domini ordinarunt ipsum cædi virgis. Ibid.
[5] Ann. de l'Egl. de Noyon, 1162.
[6] Ibid. 1171.

must be new languages. The Reformation removed the French dialect from the swaddling bands in which it had hitherto been bound, and reared it to its majority. From that time the language has had full possession of those exalted privileges that belong to the operations of the mind and the treasures of heaven, of which it had been deprived under the guardianship of Rome. No doubt the language is formed by the people themselves : they invent those happy words, those energetic and figurative expressions, that impart to language such colouring and life. But there are resources beyond their reach, which can only proceed from men of intellect. Calvin, when called upon to discuss and to prove, enriched his mother-tongue with modes of connexion and dependence, with shadows, transitions, and dialectic forms, that it did not as yet possess.

These elements were already beginning to ferment in the head of the young student at the college of La Marche. This lad, who was destined to exercise so powerful a mastery over the human heart, was also to subjugate the language he would have to use as his weapon. Protestant France subsequently habituated itself to the French of Calvin, and Protestant France comprehends the most cultivated portion of the nation ; from it issued those families of scholars and dignified magistrates who exerted so powerful an influence over the refinement of the people ; out of it sprang the Port-Royal,[1] one of the greatest instruments that have ever contributed to form the prose and even the poetry of France, and who, after endeavouring to transfer to the Gallican catholicism the doctrine and language of the Reformation, failed in one of his projects, but succeeded in the other ; for Roman-catholic France was forced to go and learn of her Jansenist and reformed adversaries how to wield those weapons of language without which it cannot contend against them.[2]

While the future reformer of religion and language was thus growing to maturity in the college of La Marche, every thing was in commotion around the young and serious scholar, who took no part as yet in the great movements that were agitating society. The flames that consumed the hermit and Pavanne had spread terror through Paris. But the persecutors were not satisfied ; a system of terror was set on foot throughout France. The friends of the Reformation no longer dared correspond with one another, for fear their intercepted letters should betray to the vengeance of the tribunals both those who wrote them and those to whom they were addressed.[3] One man, however,

ventured to carry intelligence from Paris and France to the refugees at Basle, by sewing a letter that bore no signature under his doublet. He escaped the squadrons of arquebusiers, the maréchaussée of the several districts, the examinations of the provosts and lieutenants, and reached Basle without the mysterious doublet being searched. His tidings filled Toussaint and his friends with alarm. " It is frightful," said Toussaint, " to hear of the great cruelties there inflicted !"[1] Shortly before this, two Franciscan monks had arrived at Basle, closely pursued by the officers of justice. One of them named John Prévost had preached at Meaux, and had afterwards been thrown into prison at Paris.[2] All that they told of Paris and Lyons, through which they had passed, excited the compassion of these refugees. " May our Lord send his grace thither," wrote Toussaint to Farel : " I assure you that I am sometimes in great anxiety and tribulation."

These excellent men still kept up their courage ; in vain were all the parliaments on the watch ; in vain did the spies of the Sorbonne and of the monks creep into churches, colleges, and even private families, to catch up any word of evangelical doctrine that might there be uttered ; in vain did the king's soldiers arrest on the highways every thing that seemed to bear the stamp of the Reformation : those Frenchmen whom Rome and her satellites were hunting down and treading under foot, had faith in better days to come, and already perceived afar off the end of this Babylonish captivity, as they called it. " The seventieth year, the year of deliverance, will come at last," said they, " and liberty of spirit and of conscience will be given to us."[3] But the seventy years were destined to last nearly three centuries, and it was only after calamities without a parallel that these hopes were to be realized. It was not in man, however, that the refugees placed any hope. " Those who have begun the dance," said Toussaint, " will not stop on the road." But they believed that the Lord " knew those whom he had chosen, and would deliver his people with a mighty hand."[4]

The Chevalier d'Esch had in effect been delivered. Escaping from the prison at Pont à Mousson, he had hastened to Strasburg ; but he did not remain there long. " For the honour of God," immediately wrote Toussaint to Farel, " endeavour to prevail on the knight, our worthy master,[5] to return as speedily as possible ; for our brethren have great need of such a leader ! " In truth, the

---

[1] M. A. Arnauld, grandfather of the Mère Angélique, and of all the Arnaulds of Port-Royal, was a Protestant. See Port-Royal, by Sainte Beuve.
[2] Etude littéraire sur Calvin, par M. A. Sayous, Genève, 1839, art. iv. It has been followed by others on Farel, Viret, and Beza.
[3] Il n'y a personne qui ose m'écrire. Toussaint to Farel, 4th September 1525. Neufchatel M.S.

[1] Neufchatel MS.
[2] Ibid. 21st July 1525.
[3] Sane venit annus septuagesimus, et tempus appetit ut tandem vindicemur in libertatem spiritus et conscientiæ. Toussaint to Farel, 21st July 1525.
[4] Sed novit Dominus quos elegerit. Ibid.
[5] Si nos magistrum in terris habere deceat (if it becomes us to have any master upon earth) he adds. Ibid. Neufchatel MS.

French refugees had new cause of alarm. They trembled lest that dispute about the Lord's Supper, which had so much distressed them in Germany, should pass the Rhine, and cause fresh troubles in France. Francis Lambert, the monk of Avignon, after visiting Zurich and Wittemberg, had been in Metz; but they did not place entire confidence in him; they feared lest he should have imbibed Luther's sentiments, and lest by controversies, both useless and "monstrous" (as Toussaint calls them), he should check the progress of the Reformation.[1] Esch therefore returned to Lorraine; but it was to be again exposed to great dangers, "along with all those who were seeking the glory of Jesus Christ."[2]

Yet Toussaint was not of a disposition to send others to the battle without joining in it himself. Deprived of his daily intercourse with Œcolampadius, and reduced to associate with an ignorant priest, he had sought communion with Christ, and felt his courage augmented. If he could not return to Metz, might he not at least go to Paris? True, the piles of Pavanne and the hermit of Livry were smoking still, and seemed to repel from the capital all those who held the same faith as they did. But if the colleges and the streets of Paris were struck with terror, so that no one dared even name the Gospel and the Reformation, was not that a reason why he should go thither? Toussaint quitted Basle, and entered those walls where fanaticism had taken the place of riot and debauchery. While advancing in christian studies, he endeavoured to form a connexion with those brethren who were in the colleges, and especially in that of the Cardinal Lemoine, where Lefevre and Farel had taught.[3] But he could not long do so freely. The tyranny of the parliamentary commissioners and of the theologians reigned supreme in the capital, and whoever displeased them was accused of heresy.[4] A duke and an abbot, whose names are unknown to us, denounced Toussaint as a heretic; and one day the king's sergeants arrested the youth from Lorraine and put him in prison. Separated from all his friends, and treated like a criminal, Toussaint felt his wretchedness the more keenly. "O Lord," exclaimed he, "withdraw not thou thy Spirit from me! for without it I am but flesh and a sink of iniquity." While his body was in chains, he turned in heart to those who were still combating freely for the Gospel. There was Œcolampadius, his father, and "whose work I am in the Lord," said he.[5] There was Leclerc,

whom he no doubt believed, on account of his age, "unable to bear the weight of the Gospel;"[1] Vaugris, who had displayed all the zeal "of the most affectionate brother" to rescue him from the hands of his enemies;[2] Roussel, "by whom he hoped the Lord would bring great things to pass;"[3] and lastly, Farel, to whom he wrote, "I commend myself to your prayers, for fear that I should fall in this warfare."[4] How must the names of all these men have softened the bitterness of his imprisonment, for he showed no signs of falling. Death, it is true, seemed hanging over him in this city where the blood of a number of his brethren was to be poured out like water;[5] the friends of his mother, of his uncle the Dean of Metz, and the Cardinal of Lorraine, made him the most lavish offers.[6]......" I despise them," answered he; " I know that they are a temptation of the devil. I would rather suffer hunger, I would rather be a slave in the house of the Lord, than dwell with riches in the palaces of the wicked."[7] At the same time he made a bold confession of his faith. " It is my glory," exclaimed he, " to be called a heretic by those whose lives and doctrines are opposed to Jesus Christ."[8] And this interesting and bold young man subscribed his letters, "Peter Toussaint, unworthy to be called a Christian."

Thus, in the absence of the king, new blows were continually aimed against the Reformation. Berquin, Toussaint, and many others, were in prison; Schuch, Pavanne, and the hermit of Livry, had been put to death; Farel. Lefevre, Roussel, and many other defenders of the holy doctrine, were in exile; the mouths of the mighty ones were dumb. The light of the Gospel day was growing dim; the storm was roaring incessantly, bending and shaking as if it would uproot the young tree that the hand of God had so recently planted in France.

Nor was this all. The humble victims who had already fallen were to be succeeded by more illustrious martyrs. The enemies of the Reform in France, having failed when they began with persons of rank, had submitted to begin at the bottom, but with the hope of rising gradually until they procured the condemnation and death of the most exalted personages. The inverse progress succeeded with them. Scarcely had the ashes with which the persecution had covered the Grève and the avenues of Notre-Dame been dispersed by the wind, before fresh

saint's deliverance, and shows the thoughts that then filled his mind.
1 Faber impar est oneri evangelico ferendo. Toussaint to Farel. Neuf. MS.
2 Fidelissimi fratris officio functum. Ibid.
3 Per Rufum magna operabitur Dominus. Ibid.
4 Commendo me vestris precibus ne succumbam in nac militia. Ibid.
5 Me periclitari de vita. Ibid.
6 Offerebantur hic mihi conditiones amplissimæ. Ibid.
7 Malo esurire et abjectus esse in domo Domini......Ibid.
8 Hæc, hæc gloria mea quod habeor hæreticus ab his quorum vitam et doctrinam video pugnare cum Christo. Ibid.

1 Vereor ne aliquid monstri alat. Toussaint to Farel, 27th Sept. 1525.
2 Audio etiam equitem periclitari, simul et omnes qui illic Christi gloriæ favent. Ibid. 27th December 1525.
3 Fratres qui in collegio Cardinalis Monachi sunt te salutant. Toussaint to Farel, Neufchatel MS.
4 Regnante hic tyrannide commissariorum et theologorum. Ibid.
5 Patrem nostrum cujus nos opus sumus in Domino. Toussaint to Farel, Neufchatel MS. This letter is undated, but it would seem to have been written shortly after Tous-

attacks were commenced. Messire Anthony Du Blet, that excellent man, the Lyons merchant, sank under the persecutions of these enemies of the truth, in company with another disciple, Francis Moulin, of whose fate no details have been handed down.[1] They went further still; they now took a higher aim; there was an illustrious person whom they could not reach, but whom they could strike through those who were dear to her. This was the Duchess of Alençon. Michael d'Arande, chaplain to the king's sister, for whose sake Margaret had dismissed her other preachers, and who proclaimed the pure doctrine of the Gospel in her presence, became the object of attack, and was threatened with imprisonment and death.[2] About the same time Anthony Papillon, for whom the princess had obtained the office of chief master of requests to the Dauphin, died suddenly, and the general report, even among the enemies, was that he had been poisoned.[3]

Thus the persecution spread over the kingdom, and daily drew nearer to the person of Margaret. After the forces of the Reform, concentrated at Meaux, at Lyons, and at Basle, had been dispersed, they brought down one after another those isolated combatants who here and there stood up for it. Yet a few more efforts, and the soil of France will be free from heresy. Underhanded contrivances and secret practices took the place of clamour and the stake. They will make war in open day, but they will also carry it on in darkness. If fanaticism employs the tribunal and the scaffold for the meaner sort, poison and the dagger are in reserve for the great. The doctors of a célebrated society have made too good a use of these means, and even kings have fallen under the dagger of the assassins. But justice demands that we should remember that, if Rome has had in every age its fanatical assassins, it has also had men like Vincent de Paul and Fenelon. These blows struck in darkness and silence were well adapted to spread terror on every side.

To this perfidious policy and fanatical persecution from within were added the fatal reverses from without. A veil of mourning hung over the whole nation. There was not a family, particularly among the nobles, whose tears did not flow for the loss of a father, a husband, or a son, left on the fields of Italy,[4] or whose hearts did not tremble for the liberty and even the life of one of its members. The great reverses that had fallen upon the nation diffused a leaven of hatred against the heretics. People and parliament, church and throne, joined hand in hand.

Was it not enough for the Duchess of Alençon that the defeat of Pavia should have deprived her of a husband, and made her brother a prisoner? Must the torch of the Gospel, in whose mild light she so rejoiced, be extinguished perhaps for ever? In May 1525, she had felt increase of sorrow. Charles of Lannoy had received orders to take his prisoner into Spain. Margaret had recourse to the consolations of faith, and having found them, immediately communicated them to her brother. "My lord," she wrote, "the farther you are removed from us, the stronger is my hope of your deliverance: for when the reason of man is troubled and fails, then the Lord performs his mighty works.—And now, if he makes you partaker of the pains he has borne for you, I beseech you, my lord, to believe that it is only to try how much you love him, and to afford you space to learn how he loves you; for he will have your whole heart, as he through love hath given his own. After having united you to himself by tribulation, he will deliver you to his glory and your consolation, by the merits of his victorious resurrection. in order that by you his name may be known and sanctified, not only in your kingdom, but in all Christendom, until the conversion of the unbelievers. Oh! how blessed will be your brief captivity, by which God will deliver so many souls from unbelief and eternal condemnation!"[1] Francis I. deceived the hopes of his pious sister.

The news from Spain soon increased the general sorrow. Mortification and illness endangered the life of the haughty Francis. If the king remains a prisoner, if he dies. or if his mother's regency is prolonged for many years, will not the Reformation be crushed for ever? "But when all seems lost," said the young scholar of Noyon at a later period. "God saves his Church in a marvellous way."[2] The Church of France, which was as if in the travail of birth, was to have an interval of ease before her pains returned: and to this end God made use of a weak woman, who never openly declared in favour of the Reformation. At that time she thought more of saving the king and the kingdom, than of delivering obscure Christians, who nevertheless rested great hopes in her.[3] But under the splendour of worldly affairs God often conceals the mysterious ways by which he governs his people. A noble project arose in the mind of the Duchess of Alençon. To cross the sea or the Pyrenees, and rescue Francis from the power of Charles V., was now the object of her life.

Margaret of Valois announced her intention, which was suggested by her mother, and all France hailed it with shouts of gra-

---

[1] Periit Franciscus Molinus ac Dubletus. Erasm. Epp. p, 1109. In this letter, addressed to Francis I. in July 1526, Erasmus gives the names of all those who, during the king's captivity, had fallen victims to these Roman fanatics.
[2] Periclitatus est Michael Arantius. Ibid.
[3] Periit Papilio non sine gravi suspicione veneni. Ibid.
[4] Gaillard, François I. vol. ii. 255.

[1] Letters de la Reine de Navarre à François I. p. 32.
[2] Nam habet Deus modum, quo electos suos mirabiliter custodiat, ubi omnia perdita videntur. Calvin, in Epp. ad Rom. xi. 2.
[3] Beneficio illustrissimæ Ducis Alanconiæ. Toussaint to Farel.

titude. Her great genius, the reputation she had acquired, the love she felt for her brother, and that of Francis towards her, were a great counterpoise in the eyes of Louisa and Duprat to her attachment to the new doctrine. All eyes were turned upon her, as the only person capable of extricating the kingdom from its perilous position. Let Margaret visit Spain, let her speak to the powerful emperor and to his ministers, and let her employ that admirable genius which Providence has bestowed on her, for the deliverance of her brother and her king!

Yet very different sentiments filled the hearts of the nobles and of the people, as they saw the Duchess of Alençon going into the midst of the enemy's councils, and among the fierce soldiery of the catholic king.

All admired the courage and devotion of this young woman, but did not share it. The friends of the princess had fears on her behalf, which were but too near being realized. The evangelical Christians were full of hope. The captivity of Francis I. had brought unheard-of severities on the friends of the Reform; his liberation, they thought, might bring them to an end. To open the gates of Spain to the king, would be to close those of the prisons into which the servants of the Word of God had been thrown. Margaret encouraged herself in a project towards which her soul felt attracted by so many different motives:

Heaven's height cannot my passage stay,
Nor powers of hell can bar my way,
My Saviour holds the keys of both.

Her woman's heart was strengthened by that faith which overcomes the world, and her resolution was irrevocable. Every preparation was made for this important and dangerous journey.

The Archbishop of Embrun, afterwards Cardinal of Tournon, and the president Selves, were already at Madrid, treating for the king's deliverance. They were placed under Margaret's orders, as was also the Bishop of Tarbes, afterwards Cardinal of Grammont; full powers being given to the princess alone. At the same time Montmorency, afterwards so hostile to the Reform, was sent in all haste to Spain to procure a safe-conduct for the king's sister.[1] The emperor objected at first, and said that it was the duty of his ministers alone to arrange this affair. "One hour's conference," exclaimed Selves, "between your majesty, the

[1] Mémoires de Du Bellay, p. 124.

king my master, and the Duchess of Alençon, would forward the treaty more than a month's discussion between diplomatists."[1]

Margaret, impatient to arrive in consequence of the king's illness, set off without a safe-conduct, accompanied by a splendid train.[2] She quitted the court, moving towards the Mediterranean; but while she was on the road, Montmorency returned with letters from Charles guaranteeing her liberty for three months only. That matters not; she will not be stopped. The eagerness for this journey was such that the Duchess had been compelled to ask the king whom she should select to accompany her. "Your good servants have so great a desire to see you, that each one prays to be allowed to go with me," she wrote to her brother.

Margaret had scarcely reached the shores of the Mediterranean when the fears of those about her on the insufficiency of the safe-conduct, but especially the bad weather and the tempest, made her halt. "The seamen themselves (wrote she to Montmorency) are alarmed." On the 27th August she made up her mind. "The bearer," she wrote to the king on the very day, "the bearer will tell you how the heavens, the sea, and the opinions of men have retarded my departure. But He alone to whom all things pay obedience, hath given such favourable weather that every difficulty is solved......I will not delay either on account of my own security or of the sea, which is unsettled at this season, to hasten towards the place where I may see you; for the fear of death, imprisonment, and every sort of evil are now so habitual to me, that I hold lightly my life, health, glory, and honour, thinking by this means to share your fortune, which I would desire to bear alone."[3] Nothing therefore could detain this princess at Aigues-Mortes,[4] and in this port Margaret embarked on board the ship prepared for her. Led by Providence into Spain, rather for the deliverance of humble and oppressed Christians, than to free the mighty King of France from his captivity, she confided herself to the waves of that sea which had borne her brother a captive after the disastrous battle of Pavia.

[1] Histoire de France, par Garnier, tome xxiv.
[2] Pour taster au vif la voulunté de l'esleu empereur.... madame Marguerite, duchesse d'Alençon, très-notablement accompaignée de plusieurs ambassadeurs....Les gestes de Françoise de Valois, par E. Dolet, 1540.
[3] Lettres de la reine de Navarre à François I. pp. 39, 40.
[4] Jam in itinere erat Margarita, Francisci soror....e fossis Marianis solvens, Barcinonem primum, deinde Cæsar Augustam appulerat. Belcarius, Rerum Gallic. Comm. p. 565.

PREFACE TO VOLUME FOURTH.

WHEN a foreigner visits certain countries, as England, Scotland, or America, he is sometimes presented with the rights of citizenship. Such has been the privilege of the " History of the Reformation of the Sixteenth Century." From 150,000 to 200,000 copies are in circulation, in the English language, in the countries I have just mentioned ; while in France the number hardly exceeds 4000. This is a real adoption,—naturalizing my Work in the countries that have received it with so much favour.

I accept this honour. Accordingly, while the former Volumes of my History were originally published in France ; now that, after a lapse of five years, I think of issuing a continuation of it, I do so In Great Britain.

This is not the only change in the mode of publication. I did not think it right to leave to translators, as in the cases of the former Volumes, the task of expressing my ideas in English. The best translations are always faulty ; and the Author alone can have the certainty of conveying his idea, his whole idea, and nothing but his idea. Without overlooking the merit that the several existing translations may possess, even the best of them is not free from inaccuracies, more or less important, of which I have given a specimen in my Preface to the First Volume of this Edition. These inaccuracies, no doubt most involuntary, gave rise to a very severe contest in America, on the subject of this Work, between the Episcopalians and the Baptists on the one hand, and the Presbyterians on the other,—a contest that I hope is now terminated, but in which (as a New York correspondent informed me) one of the most beneficial and powerful Christian Societies of the United States had been on the brink of dissolution.

With such facts before me, I could no longer hesitate. It became necessary for me to publish, myself, in English ; and this I accordingly do. But although that language is familiar to me, I was desirous of securing, to a certain extent, the co-operation of an English literary gentleman. Dr. HENRY WHITE, of Croydon, has had the great kindness to visit Switzerland for this purpose, although such a step exposed him to much inconvenience, and to pass with me at Geneva the time necessary for this labour. I could not have had a more enlightened coadjutor ; and I here express my obligations to him for his very able assistance.

I therefore publish in English this Continuation of the History of the Reformation. I do not think that, as I publish, myself, in this language, any one will have the power, or will entertain the idea, of attempting another publication. It would be a very bad speculation on the part of any bookseller ; for where is the reader that would not prefer the original text, as published by the Author himself, to a translation made by a stranger ?

But there is a higher question—a question of morality. Of all property that a man can possess, there is none so essentially his own as the labours of his mind. He acquires the fruits of his fields by the sweat of his servants and of his beasts of burden ; and the produce of his manufactures by the labour of his workmen and the movement of his machines; but it is by his own toils, by the exercise of his most exalted faculties, that he creates the productions of his mind. Accordingly, in putting this History under the protection of the laws, I place it at the same time under a no less secure safe-guard,—that of justice. I know that it is written in the consciences on the other side of the Channel and of the Atlantic : *Ye shall have one manner of law, as well for the stranger as for one of your own country : for I am the Lord your God.*[1] To English honour I confide this work.

The first two Books of this Volume contain the most important epochs of the Reformation—the Protest of Spires, and the Confession of Augsburg. The last two describe the establishment of the Reform in most of the Swiss cantons, and the instructive and deplorable events that are connected with the catastrophe of Cappel.

It was my desire to narrate also the beginnings of the English Reformation ; but my Volume is filled, and I am compelled to

[1] Levit. xxiv. 22.

defer this subject to the next. It is true I might have omitted some matters here treated of, but I had strong reasons for doing the contrary. The Reformation in Great Britain is not very important before the period described in this volume ; the order of time compelled me, therefore, to remain on the Continent ; for whatever may be the historian's desire, he cannot change dates and the sequence that God has assigned to the events of the world. Besides, before turning more especially towards England, Scotland, France, and other countries, I determined on bringing the Reformation of Germany and German Switzerland to the decisive epochs of 1530 and 1531. The History of the Reformation, properly so called, is then, in my opinion, almost complete in those countries. The work of Faith has there attained its apogee : that of conferences, of interims, of diplomacy begins. I do not, however, entirely abandon Germany and German Switzerland, but henceforward they will occupy me less : the movement of the sixteenth century has there made its effort. I said from the very first : It is the History of the Reformation and not of Protestantism that I am relating.

I cannot, however, approach the History of the Reformation in England without some portion of fear ; it is perhaps more difficult there than elsewhere. I have received communications from some of the most respectable men of the different ecclesiastical parties, each of whom feeling convinced that his own point of view is the true one, desires me to present the history in this light. I hope to execute my task with impartiality and truth ; and I thought it would be advantageous to study for some time longer the principles and the facts. In this task I am at present occupied, and shall consecrate to it, with God's assistance, the first part of my next volume.

Should it be thought that I might have described the Reformation in Switzerland with greater brevity, I beg my readers will call to mind that, independently of the intrinsic importance of this history, Switzerland is the Author's birth-place.

I had at first thought of making arrangements for the present publication with the English and Scotch booksellers who had translated the former portions. Relations that I had maintained with some of these publishers, and which had gained my esteem for them, induced me to adopt this course. They were consequently informed by letter of my purpose, and several months later I had an interview with some of them at Glasgow. From circumstances which it is unnecessary to explain, no arrangement was entered into with these gentlemen. But at the same time, one of the first houses in Great Britain, Messrs OLIVER & BOYD of Edinburgh, who were introduced to me by my highly respected friend Dr. CHALMERS, made me a suitable and precise offer. I could wait no longer ; and on the very eve of my departure from London for the Continent, after a sojourn of three months in Scotland and in England, I made arrangements with them, which have since been definitively settled, and the Work is now their property.

The French laws are positive to protect literary property in France, even if it belongs to a foreigner. I am less familiar with the English laws ; but I will not do England the injustice of believing that its legislation is surpassed by that of France in justice and in morality.

EAUX-VIVES, GENEVA, }
January 1846. }

498

HISTORY OF THE REFORMATION.

VOLUME FOURTH.

~~~~~~~~~~~~~~~

BOOK XIII.

THE PROTEST AND THE CONFERENCE. 1526—1529.

CHAPTER I.

Twofold Movement of Reform—Reform the Work of God—
First Diet of Spires—Palladium of Reform—Firmness of
the Reformers—Proceedings of the Diet—Report of the
Commissioners—The Papacy painted and described by
Luther—The Destruction of Jerusalem—Instructions of
Seville—Change of Policy—Holy League—Religious Liber-
ty proposed—Crisis of the Reformation.

WE have witnessed the commencement, the struggles, the reverses, and the progress of the Reformation; but the conflicts hitherto described have been only partial; we are entering upon a new period,—that of general battles. Spires (1529) and Augsburg (1530) are names that shine forth with more surpassing glory than Marathon, Pavia, or Marengo. Forces that up to the present time were separate, are now uniting into one energetic band; and the power of God is at work in those brilliant actions, which open a new era in the history of nations, and communicate an irresistible impulse to mankind. The passage from the middle ages to modern times has arrived.

A great protest is about to be accomplished; and although there have been protestants in the Church from the very beginning of Christianity, since liberty and truth could not be maintained here below, save by protesting continually against despotism and error, Protestantism is about to take a new step. It is about to become a body, and thus attack with greater energy that "mystery of iniquity" which for ages has taken a bodily shape at Rome, in the very temple of God.[1]

But although we have to treat of protests, it must not however be imagined that the Reformation is a negative work. In every sphere in which any thing great is evolved, whether in nature or society, there is a principle of life at work,—a seed that God fertilizes. The Reformation, when it appeared in the sixteenth century, did not, indeed, perform a new work, for a reformation is not a formation; but it turned its face toward the beginnings of Christianity; it seized upon them with affection, and embraced them with adoration. Yet it was not satisfied with this return to primitive times. Laden with its precious burden, it again crossed the interval of ages, and brought back to fallen and lifeless Christendom the sacred fire that was destined to restore it to light and life. In this twofold movement consisted its action and its strength. Afterwards, no doubt, it rejected superannuated forms, and combated error; but this was, so to speak, only the least of its works, and its third movement. Even the protest of which we have to speak had for its end and aim the re-establishment of truth and of life, and was essentially a positive act.

This powerful and rapid twofold action of reform, by which the apostolic times were re-established at the opening of modern history, proceeded not from man. A reformation is not arbitrarily made, as charters and revolutions are in some countries. A real reformation, prepared during many ages, is the work of the Spirit of God. Before the appointed hour, the greatest geniuses and even the most faithful of God's servants cannot produce it: but when the reforming time is come, when it is God's pleasure to renovate the affairs of the world, the divine life must clear a passage, and it is able to create of itself the humble instruments by which this life is communicated to the human race. Then, if men are silent, the very stones will cry out.[1]

---

[1] 2 Thess. ii.

[1] Luke xix. 40.

It is to the protest of Spires (1529) that we are now about to turn our eyes; but the way to this protest was prepared by years of peace, and followed by attempts at concord that we shall have also to describe. Nevertheless the formal establishment of Protestantism remains the great fact that prevails in the history of the Reformation from 1526 to 1529.

The Duke of Brunswick had brought into Germany the threatening message of Charles the Fifth. That emperor was about to repair from Spain to Rome to come to an understanding with the pope, and thence to pass into Germany to constrain the heretics. The last summons was to be addressed to them by the Diet of Spires, 1526.[1] The decisive hour for the Reformation was on the point of striking.

On the 25th June 1526, the diet opened. In the instructions, dated at Seville, 23d March, the emperor ordered that the Church customs should be maintained entire, and called upon the diet to punish those who refused to carry out the edict of Worms.[2] Ferdinand himself was at Spires, and his presence rendered these orders more formidable. Never had the hostility which the Romish partisans entertained against the evangelical princes, appeared in so striking a manner. "The Pharisees," said Spalatin, "are inveterate in their hatred against Jesus Christ."[3]

Never also had the evangelical princes showed so much hope. Instead of coming forward frightened and trembling, like guilty men, they were seen advancing, surrounded by the ministers of the Word, with uplifted heads and cheerful looks. Their first step was to ask for a place of worship. The Bishop of Spires, count-palatine of the Rhine, having indignantly refused this strange request,[4] the princes complained of it as an act of injustice, and ordered their ministers to preach daily in the halls of their palaces, which were immediately filled by an immense crowd from the city and the country, amounting to many thousands.[5] In vain on the feast days did Ferdinand, the ultra-montane princes, and the bishops, assist in the pomps of the Roman worship in the beautiful cathedral of Spires; the unadorned Word of God, preached in the protestant vestibules, engrossed all hearers, and the mass was celebrated in an empty church.[6]

It was not only the ministers, but knights and grooms, "mere idiots," who, unable to control their zeal, every where eagerly extolled the Word of the Lord.[7] All the followers of the evangelical princes wore these letters embroidered on their right sleeves: V. D. M. I. Æ., that is to say, "The Word of the Lord endureth for ever."[1] The same inscription might be read on the escutcheons of the princes, suspended over their hotels. The Word of God—such from this moment was the palladium of the Reformation.

This was not all. The Protestants knew that mere worship would not suffice: the landgrave had therefore called upon the elector to abolish certain "court customs" which dishonoured the Gospel. These two princes had consequently drawn up an order of living, forbidding drunkenness, debauchery, and other vicious customs prevalent during a diet.[2]

Perhaps the protestant princes some times put forward their dissent beyond what prudence would have required. Not only they did not go to mass, and did not observe the prescribed fasts, but still farther, on the fast days, their attendants were seen, says Cochlœus, carrying dishes of meat and game, destined for their masters' tables, across the halls in which the worship was celebrating, in the presence of the whole auditory. "It was," says this writer, "with the intent of attracting the catholics by the savour of the meats and of the wines."[3]

The elector in effect had a numerous court: seven hundred persons formed his retinue. One day he gave a banquet at which twenty-six princes with their gentlemen and councillors were present. They continued playing until a very late hour—ten at night. Every thing in Duke John announced the most powerful prince of the empire. The youthful landgrave of Hesse, full of zeal and knowledge, and in the strength of a first christian love, made a still deeper impression on those who approached him. He would frequently dispute with the bishops, and owing to his acquaintance with the Holy Scriptures, easily stopped their mouths.[4]

This firmness in the friends of the Reformation produced results that surpassed their expectation. It was no longer possible to be deceived: the spirit that was manifested in these men was the spirit of the Bible. Every where the sceptre was falling from the hands of Rome. "The leaven of Luther," said a zealous papist, "sets all the people of Germany in a ferment, and foreign nations themselves are agitated by formidable movements."[5]

It was immediately seen how great is the strength of deep convictions. The states that were well disposed towards the reform, but which had not ventured to give their

---

[1] See vol. iii. book x. chap. xiv. The Diet of Spires, held in 1526, must not be confounded with that of 1529, at which the protest took place.
[2] Sleidan, Hist. Ref. book vi.
[3] Christum pharisæis vehementer fuisse invisum. Seckend. ii. 46.
[4] Fortiter interdixit. Cochlœus, p. 138.
[5] Ingens concursus plebis et rusticorum. Cochlœus. Multis millibus hominum accurrentibus. Seckend. ii. 48.
[6] Populum a sacris avertebant. Cochlœus, p. 138.
[7] Ministri eorum, equites et stabularii, idiotæ, petulanter jactabant verbum Domini. Ibid.

[1] Verbum Domini manet in æternum. Cochlœus, p. 138.
[2] Adversus inveteratos illos et impios usus nitendum esse. Seck. ii. 46.
[3] Ut complures allicerentur ad eorum sectam, in ferculis portabantur carnes coctæ in diebus jejunii, aperte in conspectu totius auditorii. Cochlœus, p. 138.
[4] Annales Spalatini.
[5] Germaniæ populi Lutherico fermento inescati, et in externis quoque nationibus, gravissimi erant motus. Cochlœus, p. 138.

adhesion publicly, became emboldened. The neutral states, demanding the repose of the empire, formed the resolution of opposing the edict of Worms, the execution of which would have spread trouble through all Germany; and the papist states lost their boldness. The bow of the mighty was broken.[1]

Ferdinand did not think proper, at so critical a moment, to communicate to the diet the severe instructions he had received from Seville.[2] He substituted a proposition calculated to satisfy both parties.

The laymen immediately recovered the influence of which the clergy had dispossessed them. The ecclesiastics resisted a proposal in the college of princes that the diet should occupy itself with church abuses, but their exertions were unavailing. Undoubtedly a non-political assembly would have been preferable to the diet, but it was already a point gained that religious matters were no longer to be regulated solely by the priests.

As soon as this resolution was communicated to the deputies from the cities, they called for the abolition of every usage contrary to the faith in Jesus Christ. In vain did the bishops exclaim that, instead of doing away with pretended abuses, they would do much better to burn all the books with which Germany had been inundated during the last eight years. "You desire," was the reply, "to destroy all wisdom and knowledge."[3] The request of the cities was agreed to,[4] and the diet was divided into committees for the abolition of abuses.

Then was manifested the profound disgust inspired by the priests of Rome. "The clergy," said the deputy for Frankfort, "make a jest of the public good, and look after their own interests only." "The laymen," said the deputy from Duke George, "have the salvation of Christendom much more at heart than the clergy."

The commissioners made their report: people were astonished at it. Never had men spoken out so freely against the pope and the bishops. The commission of the princes, in which the ecclesiastics and laymen were in equal numbers, proposed a fusion of popery and reform. "The priests would do better to marry," said they, "than to keep women of ill fame in their houses; every man should be at liberty to communicate under one or both forms; German and Latin may be equally employed in the Lord's Supper and in Baptism; as for the other sacraments, let them be preserved, but let them be administered gratuitously. Finally, let the Word of God be preached according to the interpretation of the Church (this was the demand of Rome), but always explaining Scripture by Scripture" (this was the great principle of the Reformation). Thus the first step was taken towards a national union. Yet a few efforts more, and the whole German race will be walking in the direction of the Gospel.

The evangelical Christians, at the sight of this glorious prospect, redoubled their exertions. "Stand fast in the doctrine," said the Elector of Saxony to his councillors.[1] At the same time in every part of the city hawkers were selling Christian pamphlets, short and easy to read, written in Latin and in German, and ornamented with engravings, in which the errors of Rome were vigorously attacked.[2] One of these books was entitled, *The Papacy with its Members painted and described by Doctor Luther*. In it figured the pope, the cardinals, and all the religious orders, exceeding sixty, each with their costumes and description in verse. Under the picture of one of these orders were the following lines:

Greedy priests, see, roll in gold,
Fergetful of the humble Jesu :

under another:

We forbid you to behold
The Bible, lest it should mislead you![3]

and under a third:

We can fast and pray the harder
With an overflowing larder.[4]

"Not one of these orders," said Luther to the reader, "thinks either of faith or charity. This one wears the tonsure, the other a hood; this a cloak, that a robe. One is white, another black, a third gray, and a fourth blue. Here is one holding a looking-glass, there one with a pair of scissars. Each has his playthings......Ah! these are the palmerworms, the locusts, the canker-worms, and the caterpillars, which, as Joel saith, have eaten up all the earth."[5]

But if Luther employed the scourge of sarcasm, he also blew the trumpet of the prophets; and this he did in a work entitled *The Destruction of Jerusalem*. Shedding tears like Jeremiah, he denounced to the German people a ruin similar to that of the holy city, if like it they rejected the Gospel.[6] "God has imparted to us all his treasures," exclaimed he; "he became man, he has served us,[7] he died for us, he has risen again, and he has so opened the gates of heaven, that

---

[1] 1 Samuel ii. 4.
[2] Some historians appear to think that these instructions were really communicated at the opening of the diet. Ranke shows that this was not the case; but adds, that he sees no reason why the commissaries should have thought themselves authorized to make any other proposition. The motives that I have assigned appear to me the true ones. I shall state below why the commissaries afterwards returned to the imperial instructions.
[3] Omnes libros esse comburendos. Sed rejectum est quia sic omnis doctrina et eruditio theologica interitura esset. Seckend. ii. 45.
[4] Civitatum suffragia multum valuerunt. Ibid.

[1] Elector Saxoniæ conciliarios suos exhortatus est, in doctrina evangelica firmi. Seckend. ii. 48.
[2] Circumferebantur item libri Lutherani venales per totam civitatem. Cochlœus, p. 138.
[3] Dass die Schrift sie nicht verführe,
Durft ihr keinen nicht studir. L. Opp. xix. p. 536.
[4] Doch war ihr küch nimmer leer. Ibid.
[5] Ibid. 535. Joel i. 4.
[6] Libelli, parvuli quidem mole, sed virulentia perquam grandes, sermo Lutheri Teuthonicus de destructione Jerusalem. Cochlœus, p. 138.
[7] Wird Mensch, dienet uns, stirbt fur uns. Luth. Opp. xiv. (L.) 226.

all may enter......The hour of grace is come ......The glad tidings are proclaimed...... But where is the city, where is the prince that has received them? They insult the Gospel: they draw the sword, and daringly seize God by the beard.[1]......But wait......He will turn round; with one blow will he break their jaws, and all Germany will be one wide ruin."

These works had a very great sale.[2] They were read not only by the peasants and townspeople, but also by the nobles and princes. Leaving the priests alone at the foot of the altar, they threw themselves into the arms of the new Gospel.[3] The necessity of a reform of abuses was proclaimed on the 1st of August by a general committee.

Then Rome, which had appeared to slumber, awoke. Fanatical priests, monks, ecclesiastical princes, all gathered round Ferdinand. Cunning, bribery, nothing was spared. Did not Ferdinand possess the instructions of Seville? To refuse their publication was to effect the ruin of the Church and of the empire. Let the voice of Charles, said they, oppose its powerful *veto* to the dizziness that is hurrying Germany along, and the empire will be saved! Ferdinand made up his mind, and at length, on the 3d August, published the decree drawn up more than four months previously in favour of the edict of Worms.[4]

The persecution was about to begin; the reformers would be thrown into dungeons, and the sword drawn on the banks of the Guadalquivir would at last pierce the bosom of the Reformation.

The effect of the imperial ordinance was immense. The breaking of an axletree does not more violently arrest the velocity of a railway train. The elector and the landgrave announced that they were about to quit the diet, and ordered their attendants to prepare for their departure. At the same time the deputies from the cities drew towards these two princes, and the Reformation appeared as if it would enter immediately upon a contest with the pope and Charles the Fifth.

But it was not yet prepared for a general struggle. The tree was destined to strike its roots deeper, before the Almighty unchained the stormy winds against it. A spirit of blindness, similar to that which in former times was sent out upon Saul and Herod,[5] then seized upon the great enemy of the Gospel; and thus was it that Divine Providence saved the Reformation in its cradle.

The first movement of trouble being over, the friends of the Gospel began to consider the date of the imperial instructions, and to

weigh the new political combinations which seemed to announce to the world the most unlooked-for events. "When the emperor wrote these letters," said the cities of Upper Germany, "he was on good terms with the pope, but now every thing is changed. It is even asserted that he told Margaret, his vicegerent in the Low Countries, to proceed *gently* with respect to the Gospel. Let us send him a deputation." That was not necessary. Charles had not waited until now to form a different resolution. The course of public affairs, taking a sudden turn, had rushed into an entirely new path. Years of peace were about to be granted to the Reformation.

Clement VII., whom Charles was about to visit, according to the instructions of Seville, in order to receive the imperial crown in Rome itself and from his sacred hands, and in return to surrender the Gospel and the Reformation to the pontiff,—Clement VII., seized with a strange infatuation, had suddenly turned against this powerful monarch. The emperor, unwilling to favour his ambition in every point, had opposed his claims on the states of the Duke of Ferrara. Clement immediately became exasperated, and exclaimed that Charles wished to enslave the peninsula, but that the time was come for re-establishing the independence of Italy. This great idea of Italian independence, entertained at that period by a few literary men, had not, as in our days, penetrated the mass of the nation. Clement therefore hastened to have recourse to political combinations. The pope, the Venetians, and the King of France, who had scarcely recovered his liberty, formed a *holy league*, of which the King of England was by a bull nominated the preserver and protector.[1] In June 1526, the emperor caused the most favourable propositions to be laid before the pope; but his advances were ineffectual, and the Duke of Sessa, Charles's ambassador at Rome, returning on horseback from his last audience, placed a court-fool behind him, who, by a thousand monkey tricks, gave the Roman people to understand how little they cared for the pope and his projects. Clement responded to these bravadoes by a brief, in which he threatened the emperor with excommunication, and without loss of time pushed his troops into Lombardy, whilst Milan, Florence, and Piedmont declared for the holy league. Thus was Europe preparing to be avenged for the triumph of Pavia.

Charles did not hesitate. He wheeled to the right as quickly as the pope had done to the left, and turned abruptly towards the evangelical princes. "Let us suspend the edict of Worms," wrote he to his brother; "let us bring back Luther's partisans by mildness, and by a good council cause the triumph of evangelical truth." At the

[1] Greiffen Gott zu frech in den Bart. Ibid. Deo nimis ferociter barbam vellicant. Cochlœus.
[2] Perquam plurima vendebantur exemplaria. Ibid. p. 139.
[3] Non solum plebs et rustica turba, verum etiam plerique optimatum et nobilium trahebantur in favorem novi Evangelii, atque in odium antiquæ religionis. Ibid. p. 160.
[4] Sleidan, Hist. de la Ref. vi. 229.
[5] 1 Sam. xvi. 14-23; Matth. ii.

[1] Sleidan, Hist. de la Ref. vi.; Bullar. Mag. roman. x.

same time he required that the elector, the landgrave, and their allies should march with him against the Turks—or against Italy, for the common good of Christendom.

Ferdinand hesitated. To gain the friendship of the Lutherans was to forfeit that of the other princes, who were already beginning to utter violent threats.[1] The Protestants themselves were not very eager to take the emperor's hand. "It is God, God himself," they said, "who will save his churches." [2]

What was to be done? The edict of Worms could neither be repealed nor carried into execution.

So strange a situation led of necessity to the desired solution: religious liberty. The first idea of this occurred to the deputies of the cities. "In one place," said they, "the ancient ceremonies have been preserved; in another they have been abolished; and both parties think they are right. Let us allow every man to do as he thinks fit, until a council shall re-establish the desired unity by the Word of God." This idea gained favour, and the *recess* of the diet, dated the 27th August, decreed that a universal or at the least a national free council should be convoked within a year; that they should request the emperor to return speedily to Germany; and that, until then, each state should behave in its own territory in such a manner as to be able to render an account to God and to the emperor.[3]

Thus they escaped from their difficulty by a middle course; and this time it was really the true path. Each one maintained his own rights, while recognising another's. The diet of 1526 forms an important epoch in history: an ancient power, that of the middle ages, is shaken; a new power, that of modern times, is advancing; religious liberty boldly takes its stand in front of Romish despotism; a lay spirit prevails over the sacerdotal spirit. In this single step there is a complete victory: the cause of the reform is won.

Yet it was little suspected. Luther, on the morrow of the day on which the *recess* was published, wrote to a friend: "The diet is sitting at Spires in the German fashion. They drink and gamble, and that is all."[4] "Le congrès danse et ne marche pas,"[5] has been said in our days. Great things are often transacted under an appearance of frivolity, and God accomplishes his designs unknown even to those whom he employs as his instruments. In this diet a gravity and a love of liberty of conscience were manifested, which are the fruits of Christianity,

and which in the sixteenth century had their earliest, if not their most energetic development among the German nations.

Yet Ferdinand still hesitated. Mahomet himself came to the aid of the Gospel. Louis, king of Hungary and Bohemia, drowned at Mohacz on the 29th August 1526, as he was fleeing from before Soliman II., had bequeathed the crown of these two kingdoms to Ferdinand. But the Duke of Bavaria, the Waywode of Transylvania, and, above all, the terrible Soliman, contested it against him. This was sufficient to occupy Charles's brother: he left Luther, and hastened to dispute two thrones.

CHAPTER II.

Italian War—The Emperor's Manifesto—March on Rome—Revolt of the Troops—The Sack of Rome—German Humours—Violence of the Spaniards—Clement VII. capitulates.

THE emperor immediately reaped the fruits of his new policy. No longer having his hands tied by Germany, he turned them against Rome. The Reformation was to be exalted and the Papacy abased. The blows aimed at its pitiless enemy were about to open a new career to the evangelical work.

Ferdinand, who was detained by his Hungarian affairs, gave the charge of the Italian expedition to Freundsberg, that old general who had in so friendly a manner patted Luther on the shoulder, as the reformer was about to appear before the Diet of Worms.[1] This veteran, who, as a contemporary observes,[2] "bore in his chivalrous heart God's holy Gospel well fortified and flanked by a strong wall," pledged his wife's jewels, sent recruiting parties into all the towns of Upper Germany, and, owing to the magic idea of a war against the pope, soon witnessed crowds of soldiers flocking to his standard. "Announce," Charles had said to his brother,—"announce that the army is to march against the Turks; every one will know which Turks are meant."

Thus the puissant Charles, instead of marching with the pope against the Reformation, as he had threatened at Seville, marched with the Reformation against the pope. A few days had sufficed to produce this change of direction: there are few periods in history in which the hand of God is more plainly manifested. Charles immediately assumed all the airs of a reformer. On the 17th September, he addressed a manifesto to the pope,[3] in which he reproached him for behaving not like the father of the faithful, but like an insolent and haughty man;[4] and declared his astonishment that

[1] Ferdinandus, ut audio, graviter minatur. Corp. Ref. i. 801.
[2] Imperator pollicetur....sed nemo his promissis movetur. Spero Deum defensurum esse suas Ecclesias. Ibid.
[3] Unusquisque in sua ditione ita se gereret ut rationem Deo et imperatori reddere posset. Seckend. ii. 41.
[4] Potatur et luditur, praeterea nihil. L. Epp. iii. 126.
[5] The congress dances but does not advance.

[1] See vol. ii. book vii. chap. viii.
[2] Haug marschalk, surnamed Zeller.
[3] Caroli Imperat. Rescriptum ad Clementis Septimi criminationes. Goldasti, Constitut. Imperiales, i. 479.
[4] Non jam pastoris seu communis patris laudem, sed superbi et insolentis nomen. Ibid. 487.

he, Christ's vicar, should dare shed blood to acquire earthly possessions, "which," added he, "is quite contrary to the evangelical doctrine."[1] Luther could not have spoken better. "Let your holiness," continued Charles the Fifth, "return the sword of St. Peter into the scabbard, and convoke a holy and universal council." But the sword was much more to the pontiff's taste than the council. Is not the papacy, according to the Romish doctors, the source of the two powers? Can it not depose kings, and consequently fight against them?[2] Charles prepared to requite "eye for eye, and tooth for tooth."[3]

Now began that terrible campaign during which the storm that had been destined to fall on Germany and the Gospel burst on Rome and on the Papacy. By the violence of the blows inflicted on the pontifical city, we may judge of the severity of those that would have dashed in pieces the reformed churches. While retracing such scenes of horror, we have constant need of calling to mind that the chastisement of the seven-hilled city had been predicted by the Holy Scriptures.[4]

In the month of November, Freundsberg at the head of fifteen thousand men was at the foot of the Alps. The old general, avoiding the military roads, that were well guarded by the enemy, flung himself into a narrow path over frightful precipices, that a few blows of the mattock would have rendered impassable. The soldiers were forbidden to look behind them; nevertheless their heads turned, their feet slipped, and horse and foot rolled from time to time into the abyss. In the most difficult passes, the surest-footed of the infantry lowered their long pikes to the right and left of their aged chief, by way of barrier, and Freundsberg advanced clinging to the lansquenet in front, and pushed on by the one behind. In three days the Alps were crossed, and on the 19th November the army reached the territory of Brescia.

The Constable of Bourbon, who succeeded to the chief command of the imperial army after the death of Pescara, had just taken possession of the duchy of Milan. The emperor having promised him this conquest for a recompense, Bourbon was compelled to remain there some time to consolidate his power. At length, on the 12th February, he and his Spanish troops joined the army of Freundsberg which was becoming impatient at his delays. The constable had many men, but no money; he resolved therefore to follow the advice of the Duke of Ferrara, that inveterate enemy of the princes

of the Church, and proceed straight to Rome.[1] The whole army received this news with a shout of joy. The Spaniards were filled with the desire of avenging Charles the Fifth, and the Germans were overflowing with hatred against the pope: all exulted in the hope of receiving their pay and of having their labours richly repaid at last by those treasures of Christendom that Rome had been accumulating for ages. Their shouts re-echoed beyond the Alps. Every man in Germany thought that the last hour of the papacy had arrived, and prepared to contemplate its fall. "The emperor's forces are triumphing in Italy," wrote Luther; "the pope is visited from every quarter. His destruction draweth nigh: his hour and his end are come."[2]

A few slight advantages gained by the papal soldiers in the kingdom of Naples led to the conclusion of a truce that was to be ratified by the pope and by the emperor. As soon as this was known, a frightful tumult broke out in the constable's army. The Spanish troops revolted, compelled him to flee, and pillaged his tent. Then approaching the lansquenets, they began to shout as loudly as they could, the only German words they knew: *Lance! lance! money! money!*[3] Such cries found an echo in the bosoms of the imperialists: they were moved in their turn, and also began to shout with all their might: *Lance! lance! money! money!* Freundsberg beat to muster, and having drawn up the soldiers around him and his principal officers, calmly demanded if he had ever deserted them. All was useless. The old affection which the lansquenets bore to their leader seemed extinct. One chord alone vibrated in their hearts: they must have pay and war. Accordingly, lowering their lances, they presented them, as if they would slay their officers, and again began to shout, "Lance! lance! money! money!" When Freundsberg, whom no army however large had ever frightened,—Freundsberg, who was accustomed to say, "the more enemies, the greater the honour," saw these lansquenets, at whose head he had grown gray, aiming their murderous steel against him, he lost all power of utterance, and fell senseless upon a drum, as if struck with a thunderbolt.[4] The strength of the veteran general was broken for ever. But the sight of their dying captain produced on the lansquenets an effect that no speech could have made. All the lances were upraised, and the agitated soldiers retired with downcast eyes. Four days later, Freundsberg recovered his speech.

[1] Cum id ab evangelica doctrina, prorsus alienum videtur. Goldasti, Constitut. Imperiales, i. 489.
[2] Utriusque potestatis apicem Papa tenet. Turrecremata de Potestate Papali.
[3] Exod. xxi. 24.
[4] Revel. xviii. We should not however restrict this prediction to the incomplete sack of 1527, from which the city recovered.

[1] Guicciardini, History of the Wars in Italy, xviii. 698.
[2] Papa ubique visitatur, ut destruatur: venit enim finis et hora ejus. Luther to Haussmann, 10th January 1527. Epp. iii. 156.
[3] Lanz, lanz, gelt, gelt.
[4] Cum vero hastas ducibus obverterent indignatione et ægritudine animi oppressus, Fronsbergius subito in deliquium incidit, ita ut in tympano quod adstabat desidere cogeretur, nullumque verbum proloqui amplius posset. Seckend. ii. 79.

"Forward," said he to the Constable; "God himself will bring us to the mark." "Forward! forward!" repeated the lansquenets. Bourbon had no alternative: besides, neither Charles nor Clement would listen to any proposals of peace. Freundsberg was carried to Ferrara, and afterwards to his castle of Mindelheim, where he died after an illness of eighteen months; and on the 18th April, Bourbon took that high road to Rome, which so many formidable armies coming from the north had already trodden.

Whilst the storm descending from the Alps was approaching the eternal city, the pope lost his presence of mind, sent away his troops, and kept only his body-guard. More than thirty thousand Romans, capable of bearing arms, paraded their bravery in the streets, dragging their long swords after them, quarrelling and fighting; but these citizens, eager in the pursuit of gain, had little thought of defending the pope; and on the contrary hoping to derive great profit from his stay, they wished that the magnificent Charles would come and settle in Rome.

On the evening of the 5th May, Bourbon arrived under the walls of the capital; and he would have begun the assault at that very moment had he been provided with ladders. On the morning of the 6th, the army, concealed by a thick fog, which hid its movements,[1] was put in motion, the Spaniards marching to their station above the gate of the Holy Ghost, and the Germans below.[2] The Constable, wishing to encourage his soldiers, seized a scaling-ladder, mounted the wall, and called on them to follow him. At this moment a ball struck him: he fell, and expired an hour after. Such was the end of this unhappy man, a traitor to his king and to his country, and suspected even by his new friends.

His death, far from checking, served only to excite the army. Claudius Seidenstucker, grasping his long sword, first cleared the wall; he was followed by Michael Hartmann, and these two reformed Germans exclaimed that God himself was marching before them in the clouds. The gates were opened, the army poured in, the suburbs were taken, and the pope, attended by thirteen cardinals, fled to the castle of St. Angelo. The Imperialists, at whose head was now the Prince of Orange, offered him peace on condition of his paying three hundred thousand crowns. But Clement, who thought that the holy league was on the point of delivering him, and fancied he already saw their leading horsemen, rejected every proposition. After four hours' repose the attack was renewed, and by sunset the army was master of all the city. It remained under arms and in good order until midnight, the Spaniards in the Piazza Navona, and the Germans in the Campofiore. At last, seeing no demonstrations either of war or of peace, the soldiers disbanded and ran to pillage.

Then began the famous "Sack of Rome." The papacy had for centuries put Christendom in the press. Prebends, annates, jubilees, pilgrimages, ecclesiastical graces,—she had made money of them all. These greedy troops, that for months had lived in wretchedness, determined to make her disgorge. No one was spared, the imperialists not more than the ultramontane party, the Ghibellines not more than the Guelfs. Churches, palaces, convents, private houses, basilics, banks, tombs—every thing was pillaged, even to the golden ring that the corpse of Julius II. still wore on its finger. The Spaniards displayed the greatest skill, scenting out and discovering treasures in the most mysterious hiding-places; but the Neapolitans were the most outrageous.[1] "On every side were heard," says Guicciardini, "the piteous shrieks of the Roman women and of the nuns whom the soldiers dragged away by companies to satiate their lust."[2]

At first the Germans found a certain pleasure in making the papists feel the weight of their swords. But erelong, happy at procuring victuals and drink, they were more pacific than their allies. It was upon those things which the Romans called "holy" that the anger of the Lutherans was especially discharged. They took away the chalices, pyxes, and silver remonstrances, and clothed their servants and camp-boys with the sacerdotal garments.[3] The Campofiore was changed into an immense gambling-house. Here the soldiers brought golden vessels and bags full of crowns, staked them upon one throw of the dice, and after losing them, went in search of others. A certain Simon Baptista, who had foretold the sack of the city, had been thrown into prison by the pope; the Germans liberated him, and made him drink with them. But, like Jeremiah, he prophesied against all. "Rob, plunder," cried he to his liberators; "you shall however give back all; the money of the soldiers and the gold of the priests will follow the same road."

Nothing pleased the Germans more than to mock the papal court. "Many prelates," says Guicciardini, "were paraded on asses throughout the city."[4] After this procession, the bishops paid their ransom; but they fell into the hands of the Spaniards, who made them pay it a second time.[5]

One day a lansquenet named Guillaume de

---

[1] Guicciardini, ii. 721.
[2] Since the new wall built by Urban VIII. on the top of the Janiculum, the gates of the Holy Ghost and of Settimiana have become useless.

[1] Jovius Vita Pompeii Colonnæ, p. 191; Ranke, Deutsche Gesch. ii. 398.
[2] Guicciardini, ii. 724.
[3] Sacras vestes profanis induebant lixis. Cochlœus, p. 156.
[4] Wars of Italy, ii. 723.
[5] Eundem civem seu curialem haud raro, nunc ab Hispanis, nunc a Germanis ære mutuato redimi. Cochlœus, p. 156.

Sainte Célle put on the pope's robes, and placed the triple crown upon his head; others gathered round him, adorning themselves with the red hats and long robes of the cardinals; and going in procession upon asses through the streets of the city, they all arrived at last before the castle of St. Angelo, to which Clement VII. had retired. Here the soldier-cardinals alighted, and lifting up the front of their robes, kissed the feet of the pretended pontiff. The latter drank to the health of Clement VII., the cardinals kneeling did the same, and exclaimed that henceforward they would be pious popes and good cardinals, careful not to excite wars as their predecessors had done. They then formed a conclave, and the pope having announced to his consistory that it was his intention to resign the papacy, all hands were immediately raised for the election, and they cried out, "Luther is pope! Luther is pope!" [1] Never had pontiff been proclaimed with such perfect unanimity. Such were the humours of the Germans.

The Spaniards did not let the Romans off so easily. Clement VII. had called them "Moors," and had published a plenary indulgence for whoever should kill any of them. Nothing, therefore, could restrain their fury. These faithful Catholics put the prelates to death in the midst of horrible cruelties, devised to extort their treasures from them: they spared neither rank, sex, nor age. It was not until the sack had lasted ten days, and a booty of ten millions of golden crowns had been collected, and from five to eight thousand victims had perished, that quiet began to be in some degree restored.

Thus did the pontifical city decline in the midst of a long and cruel pillage, and that splendour with which Rome from the beginning of the sixteenth century had filled the world faded in a few hours. Nothing could preserve this haughty capital from chastisement, not even the prayers of its enemies. "I would not have Rome burnt," Luther had exclaimed; "it would be a monstrous deed." [2] The fears of Melancthon were still keener: "I tremble for the libraries," said he: "we know how hateful books are to Mars." [3] But in despite of these wishes of the reformers, the city of Leo X. fell under the judgment of God.

Clement VII., who was besieged in the castle of Saint Angelo, and who feared that the enemy would blow his asylum into the air with their mines, at last capitulated. He renounced every alliance against Charles the Fifth, and bound himself to remain a prisoner until he had paid the army four hundred thousand ducats. The evangelical Christians gazed with astonishment on this judgment of the Lord. "Such," said they, "is the

empire of Jesus Christ, that the emperor, persecuting Luther on behalf of the pope, is constrained to ruin the pope instead of Luther. All things minister unto the Lord, and turn against his adversaries." [1]

CHAPTER III.

Profitable Calm—Constitution of the Church—Philip of Hesse—The Monk of Marburg—Lambert's Paradoxes—Friar Boniface—Disputation at Hamburg—Triumph of the Gospel in Hesse—Constitution of the Church—Bishops—Synods—Two Elements of the Church—Luther on the Ministry—Organization of the Church—Luther's Contradictions on State Interference—Luther to the Elector—German Mass—Melancthon's Instructions—Disaffection—Visitation of the Reformed Churches—Results—The Reformation advances—Elizabeth of Brandenburg.

THE Reformation needed some years of repose that it might increase and gain strength; and it could not enjoy peace unless its greatest enemies were at war with each other. The madness of Clement VII. was as it were the *lightning-conductor* of the Reformation, and the ruins of Rome built up the Gospel. It was not only a few months' gain; from 1526 to 1529 there was a calm in Germany, by which the Reformation profited to organize and extend itself. A constitution was now to be given to the renovated Church.

As the papal yoke had been broken, the ecclesiastical order required to be re-established. It was impossible to restore to the bishops their ancient jurisdiction; for these continental prelates maintained that they were, in an especial manner, the pope's servants. A new state of things was therefore called for, under pain of seeing the Church fall into anarchy. This was immediately provided against. It was then that the evangelical nations separated definitely from that despotic dominion which had for ages kept all the West in bondage.

The diet had already on two occasions wished to make the reform of the Church a national work; the emperor, the pope, and a few princes were opposed to it; the diet of Spires had therefore resigned to each state the task that it could not accomplish itself.

But what constitution were they about to substitute for the papal hierarchy?

They could, while suppressing the pope, preserve the Episcopal order: it was the form nearest approximating that which was on the point of being destroyed. This was done in England, where there is an Episcopalian Church; but as we have just observed, it could not be realized on the continent. There were no Latimers, no Cranmers among the continental bishops.

They might, on the contrary, reconstruct the ecclesiastical order, by having recourse to the sovereignty of God's Word, and by re-establishing the rights of the christian

---

[1] Milites itaque levasse manum ac exclamasse: Lutherus Papa! Lutherus Papa! Cochlœus, p. 156.
[2] Romam nollem exustam, magnum enim portentum esset. Epp. iii. 221.
[3] Metuo bibliothecis. Corp. Ref. i. 869.

[1] Ut Cæsar pro Papa Lutherum persequens, pro Luthero papam cogatur vastare. L. Epp. iii. 188.

people. This form was the most remote from the Roman hierarchy. Between these two extremes there were several middle courses.

The latter plan was Zwingle's: but the reformer of Zurich had not fully carried it out. He had not called upon the christian people to exercise the sovereignty, and had stopped at the Council of Two Hundred as representing the Church.[1]

The step before which Zwingle had hesitated, might be taken, and it was so. A prince did not shrink from what had alarmed even republicans. Evangelical Germany, at the moment when she began to try her hand on ecclesiastical constitutions, began with that which trenched deepest on the papal monarchy.

It was not, however, from Germany that such a system could proceed. If aristocratic England was destined to cling to the episcopal form, docile Germany was destined rather to stop in a governmental medium. The democratic extreme issued from Switzerland and France. One of Calvin's predecessors now hoisted that flag which the powerful arm of the Genevese Reformer was to lift again in after-years and plant in France, Switzerland, Holland, Scotland, and even in England, whence it was a century later to cross the Atlantic and summon North America to take its rank among the nations.

Philip of Hesse, who has been compared to Philip of Macedon in subtlety, and to his son Alexander in courage, was the most enterprising of all the evangelical princes. He comprehended that religion was at length acquiring its due importance; and far from opposing the great development that was agitating the people, put himself in harmony with the new ideas.

The morning-star had risen for Hesse almost at the same time as for Saxony. In 1517, when Luther in Wittemberg was preaching the gratuitous remission of sins, men and women in Marburg were seen repairing secretly to one of the ditches of the city, and there, collected round a solitary loophole, listening eagerly to the words of consolation that issued from within. It was the voice of the Franciscan, James Limburg, who having declared that for fifteen centuries the priests had falsified the Gospel of Christ, had been thrown into this gloomy dungeon. These mysterious assemblies lasted a fortnight. On a sudden the voice was silent; these lonely meetings had been discovered, and the Franciscan, torn from his cell, had been hurried away across the Lahnberg towards some unknown spot. Not far from the Ziegenberg, some weeping citizens of Marburg came up with him, and hastily pulling aside the awning that covered his car, asked him, " Whither are you going ? "—" Where God wills," calmly replied the friar.[2] He was never heard of again, and

it is not known what became of him. These disappearances are usual in the papacy.

No sooner had Philip prevailed in the Diet of Spires, than he resolved on devoting himself to the reformation of his hereditary states.

His resolute character made him incline towards the Swiss reform : it was not therefore one of the moderates that he wanted. He had formed a connexion at Spires with James Sturm, the deputy from Strasburg, who spoke to him of Francis Lambert of Avignon, who was then at Strasburg. Of a pleasing exterior and decided character, Lambert combined with the fire of the south all the perseverance of the north. He was the first in France to throw off the cowl, and from that time he had never ceased to call for a thorough reform in the Church. " Formerly," said he, " when I was a hypocrite, I lived in abundance ; now I consume frugally my daily bread with my small family ;[1] but I had rather be poor in Christ's kingdom, than possess abundance of gold in the dissolute dwellings of the pope." The landgrave saw that Lambert was just the man he required, and invited him to his court.

Lambert, desiring to clear the way for the Reformation of Hesse, drew up one hundred and fifty-eight theses, which he entitled " paradoxes," and posted them, according to the custom of the times, on the church doors.

Friends and enemies immediately crowded round them. Some Roman-catholics would have torn them down, but the reformed townspeople kept watch, and holding a synod in the public square, discussed, developed, and proved these propositions, ridiculing at the same time the anger of the papists.

Boniface Dornemann, a young priest, full of self-conceit, whom the bishop, on the day of his consecration, had extolled above Paul for his learning, and above the Virgin for his chastity, finding himself too short to reach Lambert's placard, borrowed a stool, and, surrounded by a numerous audience, began to read the propositions aloud.[2]

" All that is deformed ought to be reformed. The Word of God alone teaches us what ought to be so, and all reform that is effected otherwise is vain."[3]

This was the first thesis. " Hem ! " said the young priest, " I shall not attack that." He continued.

" It belongs to the Church to decide in matters of faith. Now the Church is the congregation of those who are united by the same

---

[1] Nunc cum familiola mea panem manduco et potum capio in mensura. Lamberti Commentarii de Sacro Conjugio.
[2] Cum statura hominis hujusmodi esset ut inter Pygmæos internosci difficulter posset, scabellum sibi dari postulabat, eoque conscenso, cœpit, &c. Othon. Meiandri Jocorum Cent.
[3] Vana est omnis Reformatio quæ alioqui fit. Paradoxa Lamberti : Sculteti Annal.

---

[1] Supra, vol. iii. b. xi. ch. x.
[2] Rommel, Phil. von. Hesse, i. 128.

spirit, the same faith, the same God, the same Mediator, and the same Word, by which alone they are governed, and in which alone they have life."[1]

" I cannot attack that proposition," said the priest.[2] He continued reading from his stool.

" The Word is the true key. The kingdom of heaven is open to him who believes the Word, and shut against him who believes it not. Whoever, therefore, truly possesses the Word of God, has the power of the keys. All other keys, all the decrees of the councils and popes, and all the rules of the monks, are valueless."

Friar Boniface shook his head and continued.

" Since the priesthood of the Law has been abolished, Christ is the only immortal and eternal priest, and he does not, like men, need a successor. Neither the Bishop of Rome nor any other person in the world is his representative here below. But all Christians, since the commencement of the Church, have been and are participators in his priesthood."

This proposition smelt of heresy. Dornemann, however, was not discouraged; and whether it was from weakness of mind, or from the dawning of light, at each proposition that did not too much shock his prejudices, he repeated : " Certainly, I shall not attack that one !" The people listened in astonishment, when one of them—whether he was a fanatical Romanist, an enthusiastic reformer, or a mischievous wag, I cannot tell—tired with these continual repetitions, exclaimed : " Get down, you knave, who cannot find a word to impugn." Then rudely pulling away the stool, he threw the unfortunate clerk flat in the mud.[3]

On the 21st October, at seven in the morning, the gates of the principal church at Homburg were thrown open, and prelates, abbots, priests, counts, knights, and deputies of the towns, entered in succession, and among them was Philip, in his quality of first member of the church.

After Lambert had explained and proved his theses, he added : " Let him stand forth who has any thing to say against them." At first there was a profound silence; but at length Nicholas Ferber, superior of the Franciscans of Marburg, who in 1524, applying to Rome's favourite argument, had entreated the Landgrave to employ the sword against the heretics, began to speak with drooping head and downcast eyes. As he invoked Augustin, Peter Lombard, and other doctors to his assistance, the landgrave observed to him : " Do not put forward the wavering

opinions of men, but the Word of God. which alone fortifies and strengthens our hearts." The Franciscan sat down in confusion, saying, " This is not the place for replying." The disputation, however, recommenced, and Lambert, showing all the power of truth, so astonished his adversary, that the superior, alarmed at what he called thunders of blasphemy and lightnings of impiety,"[1] sat down again, observing a second time, " This is not the place for replying."

In vain did the Chancellor Feige declare to him that each man had the right of maintaining his opinion with full liberty ; in vain did the landgrave himself exclaim that the Church was sighing after truth : silence had become Rome's refuge. " I will defend the doctrine of purgatory," a priest had said prior to the discussion ; " I will attack the paradoxes under the sixth head (on the true priesthood)," had said another ;[2] and a third had exclaimed, " I will overthrow those under the tenth head (on images) ;" but now they were all dumb.

Upon this Lambert, clasping his hands, exclaimed with Zacharias ; *Blessed be the Lord God of Israel; for he hath visited and redeemed his people.*

After three days of discussion, which had been a continual triumph for the evangelical doctrine, men were selected and commissioned to constitute the churches of Hesse in accordance with the Word of God. They were more than three days occupied in the task, and their new constitution was then published in the name of the synod.

The first ecclesiastical constitution produced by the Reformation should have a place in history, and the more so as it was then put forward as a model for the new churches of Christendom.[3]

The autonomy or self-government of the Church is its fundamental principle: it is from the Church, from its representatives assembled in the name of the Lord, that this legislation emanates ; there is no mention in the prologue either of state or of landgrave.[4] Philip, content with having broken for himself and for his people the yoke of a foreign priest, had no desire to put himself in his place, and was satisfied with that external superintendence which is necessary for the maintenance of order.

A second distinctive feature in this constitution is its simplicity both of government and worship. The assembly conjures all future synods not to load the churches with a multitude of ordinances, " seeing that where orders abound, disorder superabounds." They would not even continue the organs in

---

[1] Ecclesia est congregatio eorum quos unit idem spiritus. Paradoxa Lamberti: Sculteti Annal.
[2] Hanc equidem haud impugnaverim. Illam ne quidem attigerim. Othon. Mil. Joc. Cent.
[3] Apagesis, nebulo! qui quod impugnes infirmesque invenire haud possis! hisque dictis scabellum ei mox subtrahit, ut miser ille præceps in lutum ageretur. Ibid.

[1] Fulgura impietatum, tonitrua blasphemiarum.
[2] Erant enim prius qui dicerent : Ego asseram purgatorium ; alius, Ego impugnabo paradoxa tituli sexti, etc. Lamberti Epistola ad Colon.
[3] This constitution will be found in Schminke, Monumenta Hassiaca, vol. ii. p. 588 : " Pro Hassiæ Ecclesia, et si deinde nonnullæ *aliæ* ad idem *nostro exemplo* provocarentur."
[4] Synodus *in nomine Domini* congregata. Ibid.

the churches, because, said they, "men should understand what they hear."[1] The more the human mind has been bent in one direction, the more violent is the reaction when it is unbent. The Church passed at that time from the extreme of symbols to the extreme of simplicity. These are the principal features of this constitution :—

"The Church can be taught and governed by the Word of its Sovereign Pastor alone. Whoever has recourse to any other word shall be deposed and excommunicated.[2]

"Every pious man, learned in the Word of God, whatever be his condition, may be elected bishop if he desire it, for he is called inwardly of God.[3]

"Let no one believe that by a bishop we understand any thing else than a simple minister of the Word of God.[4]

"The ministers are servants, and consequently they ought not to be lords, princes, or governors.

"Let the faithful assemble and choose their bishops and deacons. Each church should elect its own pastor.[5]

"Let those who are elected bishops be consecrated to their office by the imposition of the hands of three bishops; and as for the deacons, if there are no ministers present, let them receive the laying on of hands from the elders of the Church.[6]

"If a bishop causes any scandal to the Church by his effeminacy, by the splendour of his garments, or by levity of conduct, and if, on being warned, he persists, let him be deposed by the Church.[7]

"Let each church place its bishop in a condition to live with his family, and to be hospitable, as St. Paul enjoins ; but let the bishops exact nothing for their casual duties.[8]

"On every Sunday let there be in some suitable place an assembly of all the men who are in the number of the saints, to regulate with the bishop, according to God's Word, all the affairs of the Church, and to excommunicate whoever gives occasion of scandal to the Church ; for the Church of Christ has never existed without exercising the power of excommunication.[9]

"As a weekly assembly is necessary for the direction of the particular churches, so a general synod should be held annually

for the direction of all the churches in the country.[1]

"All the pastors are its natural members ; but each church shall further elect from its body a man full of the Spirit and of faith, to whom it shall intrust its powers for all that is in the jurisdiction of the synod.[2]

"Three visitors shall be elected yearly, with commission to go through all the churches, to examine those who have been elected bishops, to confirm those who have been approved of, and to provide for the execution of the decrees of the synod."

It will no doubt be found that this first evangelical constitution went in some points to the extreme of ecclesiastical democracy ; but certain institutions had crept in that were capable of increase and of changing its nature. Six superintendents for life were afterwards substituted for the three annual visitors (who, according to the primitive institution, might be simple members of the church) ; and, as has been remarked,[3] the encroachments, whether of these superintendents or of the state, gradually paralyzed the activity and independence of the churches of Hesse. This constitution fared like that of the Abbé Sièyes, in the year 8 (A. D. 1799), which although intended to be republican, served through the influence of Napoleon Bonaparte to establish the despotism of the empire.

It was not the less a remarkable work. Romish doctors have reproached the Reformation for making the Church a too interior institution.[4] In effect, the Reformation and Popery recognise two elements in the Church, —the one exterior, the other interior ; but while Popery gives precedence to the former, the Reformation assigns it to the latter. If however it be a reproach against the Reformation for having an inward Church only, and for not creating an external one, the remarkable constitution of which we have just exhibited a few features, will save us the trouble of replying. The exterior ecclesiastical order, which then sprang from the very heart of the Reformation, is far more perfect than that of Popery.

One great question presented itself : Would these principles be adopted by all the Churches of the Reformation ?

Every thing seemed to indicate that they would. At that time the most pious men were of opinion, that the ecclesiastical power proceeded from the members of the Church. On withdrawing from the hierarchical extreme, they flung themselves into a democratical one. Luther himself had professed this doctrine as early as 1523. When the

---

[1] Ne homines non intelligant. Monumenta Hassiaca, cap. 3.
[2] Non admittimus verbum aliud quam ipsius pastoris nostri. Ibid. cap. 2.
[3] Si quis pius, in verbo sancto et exercitatus, docere petit verbum sanctum, non repellatur, a Deo enim interne mittitur. Ibid. cap. 23.
[4] Ne quis putet, nos hic per episcopos, alios intelligere, quam ministros Dei verbi. Ibid.
[5] Eligat quævis ecclesia episcopum suum. Ibid.
[6] Manus imponant duo ex senioribus, nisi alii episcopi intersint. Ibid. cap. 21.
[7] Deponat ecclesia episcopum suum, quod ad eam spectet judicare de voce pastorum. Ibid. cap. 23.
[8] Alat quævis ecclesia episcopum suum sicque illi administret ut cum sua familia vivere possit. Ibid.
[9] Fiat conventus fidelium in congruo loco, ad quem quotquot ex viris in sanctorum numero habentur......Christi ecclesiam nunquam fuisse sine excommunicatione. Ibid. cap. 15.

[1] Ut semel pro toto Hessia celebretur synodus apud Marpurgum tertia dominica post pascha. Monumenta Hassiaca, cap. 18.
[2] Universi episcopi....Quælibet ecclesia congregetur et eligat ex se ipsa unum plenum fide et Spiritu Dei. Ibid.
[3] Rettig, Die Freie Kirche.
[4] This is the opinion set forth in the *Symbolik* of Dr. Möhler, the most celebrated defender of the Romish doctrine among our contemporaries.

Calixtins of Bohemia found that the bishops of their country refused them ministers, they had gone so far as to take the first vagabond priest. "If you have no other means of procuring pastors," wrote Luther to them, "rather do without them, and let each head of a family read the Gospel in his own house, and baptize his children, sighing after the sacrament of the altar, as the Jews at Babylon did for Jerusalem."[1] The consecration of the pope creates priests—not of God, but of the devil, ordained solely to trample Jesus Christ under foot, to bring his sacrifice to naught, and to sell imaginary holocausts to the world in his name.[2] Men become ministers only by election and calling, and that ought to be effected in the following manner :—

" First, seek God by prayer ;[3] then being assembled together with all those whose hearts God has touched, choose in the Lord's name him or them whom you shall have acknowledged to be fitted for this ministry. After that, let the chief men among you lay their hands on them, and recommend them to the people and to the Church."[4]

Luther, in thus calling upon the people alone to nominate their pastors, submitted to the necessities of the times in Bohemia. It was requisite to constitute the ministry ; and as the ministry had no existence, it could not then have the legitimate part that belongs to it in the choice of God's ministers.

But another necessity, proceeding in like manner from the state of affairs, was to incline Luther to deviate in Saxony from the principles he had formerly laid down.

It can hardly be said that the German Reformation began with the lower classes, as in Switzerland and France ; and Luther had difficulty in finding any where that christian people, which should have played so great a part in his new constitution. Ignorant men, conceited townspeople, who would not even maintain their ministers— these were the members of the Church. Now what could be done with such elements ?

But if the people were indifferent, the princes were not so. They stood in the foremost rank of the great battle of the Reformation, and sat on the first bench in the council. The democratic organization was therefore compelled to give way to an organization conformable to the civil government. The Church is composed of Christians, and they are taken wherever they are found—high or low. It was particularly in high stations that Luther found them. He admitted the princes (as Zwingle did the Council of Two Hundred) as representatives of the people, and henceforward the influence of the State

became one of the principal elements in the constitution of the evangelical Church in Germany.

Thus Luther, setting out in principle from the democratic, arrived in fact at the Erastian extreme. Never perhaps was there so immense a space between the premises laid down by any man, and the conduct he adopted. If Luther crossed that wide interval without hesitation, it was not from mere inconsistency on his part ; he yielded to the necessities of the times. The rules of Church government are not, like the doctrines of the Gospel, of an absolute nature ; their application depends in a measure on the state of the Church. Nevertheless there was some inconsistency in Luther : he often expressed himself in a contradictory manner on what princes ought and ought not to do in the Church. This is a point upon which the reformer and his age had no very settled opinions : there were other questions to be cleared up.

In the mind of the reformer the tutelage of the princes was only to be provisional. The faithful being still in their minority, they had need of a guardian : but the era of the Church's majority might arrive, and then would come its emancipation.

As we said in another place,[1] we will not decide on this great controversy of Church and State. But there are certain ideas which can never be forgotten. God is the principle from which every being emanates, and who ought to govern the whole world—societies as well as individuals—the State not less than the Church. God has to do with governments, and governments with God. The great truths of which the Church is the depository are given from above to exert their influence on the whole nation,—on him who is seated on the throne, as well as on the peasant in his cottage : and it is not only as an individual that the prince must be partaker of this heavenly light ; it is also that he may receive a Divine wisdom as governor of his people. God must be in the State. To place nations, governments, social and political life on one side,—and God, his Word, and his Church on the other, as if there were a great gulf between them, and that these two orders of things should never meet,— would be at once high treason against man and against God.

But if there ought to be a close union between these two spheres (the Church and State), we ought to seek the means best calculated to obtain it. Now, if the direction of the Church is intrusted to the civil government, as was the case in Saxony, there is great reason to fear lest the reality of this union should be compromised, and the infiltration of heavenly strength into the body of the nation be obstructed. The Church administered by a civil department will often

---

[1] Tutius enim et salubrius esset, quemlibet patrem-familias suæ domui legere Evangelium. L. Opp. Lat. ii. 363.
[2] Per ordines papisticos non sacerdotes Dei sed sacerdotes Satanæ, tantum ut Christum conculcent. Ibid. 364.
[3] Orationibus tum privatis tum publicis. Ibid. 370.
[4] Eligite quem et quos volueritis. Tum impositis super eos manibus, sint hoc ipso vestri episcopi, vestri ministri, seu pastores. Ibid.

[1] Vol. ii. p. 286.

be sacrificed to political ends, and, gradually becoming secularized, will lose its pristine vigour. This at least has taken place in Germany, where in some places religion has sunk to the rank of a temporal administration. In order that any created being may exercise all the influence of which it is capable, it ought to have a free development. Let a tree grow unconfined in the open fields, you will better enjoy its cool shade, and gather more abundant fruits, than if you planted it in a vase and shut it up in your chamber. Such a tree is the Church of Christ.

The recourse to the civil power, which was perhaps at that time necessary in Germany, had still another consequence : when Protestantism became an affair of governments, it ceased to be universal. The new spirit was capable of creating a new earth. But instead of opening new roads and of purposing the regeneration of all Christendom and the conversion of the whole world, Protestantism shrank back, and Protestants sought to settle themselves as comfortably as possible in a few German duchies. This timidity, which has been called prudence, did immense injury to the Reformation.

The organizing power being once discovered in the councils of princes, the reformers thought of organization, and Luther applied to the task : for although he was in an especial manner an assailant and Calvin an organizer, these two qualities, as necessary to the reformers of the Church as to the founders of empires, were not wanting in either of these great servants of God.

It was necessary to compose a new ministry, for most of the priests who had quitted the papacy were content to receive the watchword of Reform without having personally experienced the sanctifying power of the truth. There was even one parish in which the priest preached the Gospel in his principal church, and sang mass in its succursal.[1]

But something more was wanting: a christian people had to be created. " Alas !" said Luther of some of the adherents of the Reform, " they have abandoned their Romish doctrines and rites, and they scoff at ours."[2]

Luther did not shrink from before this double necessity ; and he made provision for it. Convinced that a general visitation of the churches was necessary, he addressed the elector on this subject, on the 22d October 1526. " Your highness, in your quality of guardian of youth, and of all those who know not how to take care of themselves," said he, " should compel the inhabitants, who desire neither pastors nor schools, to receive these means of grace, as they are compelled to work on the roads, on bridges,

and such like services.[1] The papal order being abolished, it is your duty to regulate these things: no other person cares about them, no other can, and no other ought to do so. Commission, therefore, four persons to visit all the country; let two of them inquire into the tithes and church property; and let two take charge of the doctrine, schools, churches, and pastors." It may be asked, on reading these words, whether the Church which was formed in the first century without the support of princes, could not in the sixteenth be reformed without them ?

Luther was not content with soliciting in writing the intervention of the prince. He was indignant at seeing the courtiers, who in the time of the Elector Frederick had shown themselves the inveterate enemies of the Reformation, now rushing, " sporting, laughing, skipping," as he said, on the spoils of the Church. Accordingly, at the end of this year, the elector having come to Wittemberg, the reformer repaired immediately to the palace, made his complaint to the prince-electoral, whom he met at the gate, and then, without caring about those who would have stopped his way, forced his way into the elector's bedchamber, and addressing this prince, who was surprised at so unexpected a visit, begged him to remedy the evils of the Church. The visitation of the churches was resolved upon, and Melancthon was commissioned to draw up the necessary instructions.

In 1526, Luther published his " German Mass," by which he signified the order of church service in general. " The real evangelical assemblies," he said, " do not take place publicly, pell-mell, admitting people of every sort;[2] but they are formed of serious Christians, who confess the Gospel by their words and by their lives,[3] and in the midst of whom we may reprove and excommunicate those who do not live according to the rule of Christ Jesus.[4] I cannot institute such assemblies, for I have no one to place in them ;[5] but if the thing becomes possible, I shall not be wanting in this duty."

It was with a conviction that he must give the Church, not the best form of worship imaginable, but the best possible, that Melancthon, like Luther, laboured at his Instructions.

The German Reformation at that time tacked about, as it were. If Lambert in Hesse had gone to the extreme of a democratical system, Melancthon in Saxony was approximating the contrary extreme of traditional principles. A conservative principle was substituted for a reforming one.

---

[1] In æde parochiali evangelico more docebat, in filiali missificabat. Seck. p. 102.
[2] Sic enim sua papistica neglexerunt, et nostra contemnunt. L. Epp. iii. 224.

[1] Als oberster vormund der Jugend und aller die es be durfen, soll sie mit Gewalt dazu halten. L. Epp. iii. 136.
[2] Non publice, sive promiscue et admissa omnis generis plebe. De Missa Germ.
[3] Qui nomina sua in catalogum referrent, adds he. Ibid
[4] Excommunicari qui Christiano more se non gererent. Ibid.
[5] Neque enim habeo qui sint idonei. Ibid.

Melancthon wrote to one of the inspectors:[1] "All the old ceremonies that you can preserve, pray do so.[2] Do not innovate much, for every innovation is injurious to the people."[3]

They retained, therefore, the Latin liturgy, a few German hymns being mingled with it;[4] the communion in one kind for those only who scrupled from habit to take it in both; a confession made to the priest without being in any way obligatory; many saints' days, the sacred vestments,[5] and other rites, "in which," said Melancthon, "there is no harm, whatever Zwingle may say."[6] And at the same time they set forth with reserve the doctrines of the Reformation.

It is but right to confess the dominion of facts and circumstances upon these ecclesiastical organizations; but there is a dominion which rises higher still—that of the Word of God.

Perhaps Melancthon did all that could be effected at that time; but it was necessary for the work to be one day resumed and re-established on its primitive plan, and this was Calvin's glory.

A cry of astonishment was heard both from the camp of Rome and from that of the Reformation. "Our cause is betrayed," exclaimed some of the evangelical Christians: "the liberty is taken away that Jesus Christ had given us."[7]

On their part the Ultramontanists triumphed in Melancthon's moderation: they called it a retractation, and took advantage of it to insult the Reform. Cochlœus published a "horrible" engraving, as he styles it himself, in which, from beneath the same hood, was seen issuing a seven-headed monster representing Luther. Each of these heads had different features, and all, uttering together the most frightful and contradictory words, kept disputing, tearing, and devouring each other.[8]

The astonished Elector resolved to communicate Melancthon's paper to Luther. But never did the reformer's respect for his friend show itself in a more striking manner. He made only one or two unimportant additions to this plan, and sent it back accompanied with the highest eulogiums. The Romanists said that the tiger caught in a net was licking the hands that clipped his talons. But it was not so. Luther knew that the aim of Melancthon's labours was to strengthen the very soul of the Reformation in all the churches of Saxony. That was sufficient for him. He thought besides, that in every thing there must be a transition; and being justly convinced that his friend was more than himself a man of transition, he frankly accepted his views.

The general visitation began. Luther in Saxony, Spalatin in the districts of Altenburg and Zwickau, Melancthon in Thuringia, and Thuring in Franconia, with ecclesiastical deputies and several lay colleagues, commenced the work in October and November 1528.

They purified the clergy by dismissing every priest of scandalous life;[1] assigned a portion of the church property to the maintenance of public worship, and placed the remainder beyond the reach of plunder. They continued the suppression of the convents, and every where established unity of instruction. "Luther's greater and smaller catechisms," which appeared in 1529, contributed more perhaps than any other writings to propagate throughout the new churches the ancient faith of the apostles. The visiters commissioned the pastors of the great towns under the title of superintendents, to watch over the churches and the schools; they maintained the abolition of celibacy; and the ministers of the Word, become husbands and fathers, formed the germ of a third estate, whence in after-years were diffused in all ranks of society learning, activity, and light. This is one of the true causes of that intellectual and moral superiority which indisputably distinguishes the evangelical nations.

The organization of the churches in Saxony, notwithstanding its imperfections, produced for a time at least the most important results. It was because the Word of God prevailed; and because, wherever this Word exercises its power, secondary errors and abuses are paralyzed. The very discretion that was employed really originated in a good principle. The reformers, unlike the enthusiasts, did not utterly reject an institution because it was corrupted. They did not say, for example, "The sacraments are disfigured, let us do without them! the ministry is corrupt, let us reject it!"—but they rejected the abuse, and restored the use. This prudence is the mark of a work of God; and if Luther sometimes permitted the chaff to remain along with the wheat, Calvin appeared later, and more thoroughly purged the christian threshing-floor.

The organization which was at that time going on in Saxony, exerted a strong reaction on all the German empire, and the doctrine of the Gospel advanced with gigantic strides. God's design in turning aside from the reformed states of Germany the thunderbolt

---

[1] Dr. Dewette thinks this letter is Luther's, L. Epp. iii. 352. It appears clear to me, as also to Dr. Bretschneider, that it is Melancthon's. Luther never went so far in the way of concession.
[2] Observo quantum ex veteribus cæremoniis retineri potest, retineas. Corp. Ref. ii. 990.
[3] Omnis novitas nocet in vulgo. Ibid.
[4] Non aboleas eam totam (the Latin mass): satis est alicubi miscere Germanicas cautationes. Ibid.
[5] Ut retineantur vestes usitatæ in sacris. Corp. Ref. ad Jonam, 26th December 1527.
[6] Vel si Zwinglius ipse prædicaturus sit. Corp. Ref. ii. 910.
[7] Alii dicerent prodi causam. Camer. Vita Melancthon, p. 107.
[8] Monstrosus ille Germaniæ partus, Lutherus septiceps. Cochlœus, p. 169.

[1] Viginti fere rudes et inepti, multique concubinarii et potatores deprehensi sunt. Seckend. p. 102.

that he caused to fall upon the seven-hilled city, was clearly manifest. Never were years more usefully employed; and it was not only to framing a constitution that the Reformation devoted itself, it was also to the extension of its doctrine.

The duchies of Luneburg and Brunswick, many of the most important imperial cities, as Nuremberg, Augsburg, Ulm, Strasburg, Gottingen, Gosslar, Nordhausen, Lubeck, Bremen, and Hamburg, removed the tapers from the chapels, and substituted in their place the brighter torch of the Word of God.

In vain did the frightened canons allege the authority of the Church. "The authority of the Church," replied Kempe and Zechenhagen, the reformer of Hamburg, " cannot be acknowledged unless the Church herself obeys her pastor Jesus Christ."[1] Pomeranus visited many places to put a finishing hand to the Reform.

In Franconia, the Margrave George of Brandenburg, having reformed Anspach and Bayreuth, wrote to his ancient protector, Ferdinand of Austria, who had knit his brows on being informed of these proceedings: " I have acted thus by God's order; for he commands princes to take care not only of the bodies of their subjects, but also of their souls."[2]

In East Friesland, on new-year's day 1527, a Dominican named Resius, having put on his hood,[3] ascended the pulpit at Noorden, and declared himself ready to maintain certain theses according to the tenor of the Gospel. After silencing the Abbot of Noorden by the soundness of his arguments, Resius took off his cowl, left it on the pulpit, and was received in the nave by the acclamations of the faithful. Erelong the whole of Friesland laid aside the uniform of popery, as Resius had done.

At Berlin, Elizabeth, electress of Brandenburg, having read Luther's works, felt a desire to receive the Lord's Supper in conformity with Christ's institution. A minister secretly administered it at the festival of Easter, 1528; but one of her children informed the elector. Joachim was greatly exasperated, and ordered his wife to keep her room for several days;[4] it was even rumoured that he intended shutting her up.[5] This princess, being deprived of all religious support, and mistrusting the perfidious manœuvres of the Romish priests, resolved to escape by flight, and claim the assistance of her brother, Christian II. of Denmark, then residing at Torgau. Taking advantage of a dark night, she quitted the castle in a

peasant's dress. and got into a rude country-waggon that was waiting for her at the gate of the city. Elizabeth urged on the driver, when, in a bad road, the wain broke down. The electress, hastily unfastening a handkerchief she wore round her head, flung it to the man, who employed it in repairing the damage, and erelong Elizabeth arrived at Torgau. " If I should expose you to any risk," said she to her uncle, the Elector of Saxony, "I am ready to go wherever Providence may lead me." But John assigned her a residence in the castle of Lichtenberg, on the Elbe, near Wittemberg. Without taking upon us to approve of Elizabeth's flight, let us acknowledge the good that God's Providence derived from it. This amiable lady, who lived at Lichtenberg in the study of His Word, seldom appearing at court, frequently going to hear Luther's sermons, and exercising a salutary influence over her children, who sometimes had permission to see her, was the first of those pious princesses whom the house of Brandenburg has counted, and even still counts, among its members.

At the same time, Holstein, Sleswick, and Silesia decided in favour of the Reformation: and Hungary, as well as Bohemia, saw the number of its adherents increase.

In every place, instead of a hierarchy seeking its righteousness in the works of man, its glory in external pomp, its strength in a material power, the Church of the Apostles reappeared, humble as in primitive times, and like the ancient Christians, looking for its righteousness, its glory, and its power solely in the blood of the Lamb and in the Word of God.[1]

CHAPTER IV.

Edict of Ofen—Persecutions—Winchler, Carpenter, and Keyser—Alarm in Germany—Pack's Forgery—League of the Reformed Princes—Advice of the Reformers—Luther's Pacific Council—Surprise of the Papist Princes—Pack's Scheme not improbable—Vigour of the Reformation.

THESE triumphs of the Gospel could not pass unperceived; there was a powerful reaction, and until political circumstances should permit a grand attack upon the Reformation on the very soil where it was established, and of fighting against it by means of diets, and if necessary by armies, the adversaries began to persecute it in detail in the Romish countries with tortures and the scaffold.

On the 20th August 1527, King Ferdinand, by the Edict of Ofen in Hungary, published a tariff of crimes and penalties, in which he threatened death by the sword, by fire, or by water,[2] against any who should say that Mary was like other women; or partake of the sacrament in an heretical

---

[1] Evangelici auctoritatem Ecclesiæ non aliter agnoscendam esse contendebant quam si vocem pastoris Christi sequeretur. Seckend. i. 245.
[2] Non modo quoad corpus, sed etiam quoad animam. Ibid. ii. 121.
[3] Resius, cucullum indutus, suggestum ascendit. Scultet. Ann. p. 98.
[4] Aliquot diebus a marito in cubiculo detenta fuisse. Seckend. ii. 122.
[5] Marchio statuerat eam immurare. L. Epp. ad Lenkium, iii. 296.

[1] Revelation xii. 11.
[2] Die sollen mit den Feuer, Schwerdt oder Wasser gestraft werden. Ferd. Mandat. L. Opp. xix. 596.

manner; or consecrate the bread and wine, not being a Romish priest; and further, in the second case, the house in which the sacrament should have been administered was to be confiscated or rased to the ground.

Such was not the legislation of Luther. Link having asked him if it were lawful for the magistrate to put the false prophets to death, meaning the Sacramentarians, whose doctrines Luther had so violently attacked,[1] the reformer replied : "I am slow whenever life is concerned, even if the offender is exceedingly guilty.[2] I can by no means admit that the false teachers should be put to death :[3] it is sufficient to remove them." For ages the Romish Church has bathed in blood. Luther was the first to profess the great principles of humanity and religious liberty.

Recourse was sometimes had to more expeditious means than the scaffold itself. George Winkler, pastor of Halle, having been summoned before Archbishop Albert in the spring of 1527, for having administered the sacrament in both kinds, had been acquitted. As this minister was returning home along an unfrequented road in the midst of the woods, he was suddenly attacked by a number of horsemen, who murdered him, and immediately fled through the thickets without taking anything from his person.[4] "The world," exclaimed Luther, "is a cavern of assassins under the command of the devil; an inn, whose landlord is a brigand, and which bears this sign, *Lies and Murder :* and none are more readily put to death therein than those who proclaim Jesus Christ."

At Munich, George Carpenter was led to the scaffold for having denied that the baptism of water is able by its own virtue to save a man. " When you are thrown into the fire," said some of his brethren, " give us a sign by which we may know that you persevere in the faith."—" As long as I can open my mouth, I will confess the name of the Lord Jesus."[5] The executioner stretched him on a ladder, tied a small bag of gunpowder round his neck, and then flung him into the flames. Carpenter immediately cried out " Jesus ! Jesus !" and while the executioner was turning him again and again with his hooks, the martyr several times repeated the same word Jesus, and expired.

At Landsberg nine persons were consigned to the flames, and at Munich twenty-nine were thrown into the water. At Scherding, Leonard Keyser, a friend and disciple of Luther, having been condemned by the bishop, had his head shaved, and being dressed in a smock-frock, was placed on horseback. As the executioners were cursing and swearing, because they could not disentangle the ropes with which his limbs were to be tied, he said to them mildly : " Dear friends, your bonds are not necessary ; my Lord Christ has already bound me." When he drew near the stake, Keyser looked at the crowd and exclaimed : " Behold the harvest ! O Master, send forth thy labourers !" And then ascending the scaffold he cried : " O Jesu, save me ! I am thine." These were his last words.[1] " What am I, a wordy preacher," said Luther when he received the news of his death, " in comparison with this great doer of the word !"[2]

Thus the Reformation manifested by such striking works the truth that it had come to re-establish ; namely, that faith is not, as Rome maintains, an historical, vain, dead knowledge,[3] but a lively faith, the work of the Holy Ghost, the channel by which Christ fills the heart with new desires and with new affections,—the true worship of the living God.

These martyrdoms filled Germany with horror, and gloomy forebodings descended from the throne into the ranks of the people. Around the domestic hearth, in the long winter evenings, the conversation wholly turned on prisons, tortures, scaffolds, and martyrs; the slightest noise alarmed the old men, women, and children. Such narratives gathered strength as they passed from mouth to mouth : the rumour of a universal conspiracy against the Gospel spread throughout the empire. Its adversaries, taking advantage of this terror, announced with a mysterious air that they must look during this year (1528) for some decisive measure against the reform.[4] One scoundrel (Pack) resolved to profit by this state of mind to satisfy his avarice.

No blows are more terrible to a cause than those which it inflicts upon itself. The Reformation, seized with a dizziness, was on the verge of self-destruction. There is a spirit of error that conspires against the cause of truth, beguiling by subtlety ;[5] the Reformation was about to experience its attacks, and to stagger under the most formidable assault,—perturbation of thought, and estrangement from the ways of wisdom and of truth.

Otho Pack, vice-chancellor to Duke George of Saxony, was a crafty and dissipated man,[6] who took advantage of his office, and had recourse to all sorts of practices to procure

---

[1] Contra hostes sacramentarios strenue nobiscum certare. Epp. to Lenk, July 14, 1528.
[2] Ego ad judicium sanguinis tardus sum, etiam ubi meritum abundat. Ibid.
[3] Nullo modo possum admittere falsos doctores occidi. Ibid.
[4] Mox enim ut interfecerunt, aufugerunt per avia loca, nihil prædæ aut pecuniæ capientes. Cochl. p. 152.
[5] Dum os aperire licebit, servatoris nostri nomen profiteri nunquam intermittam. Scultet. ii. 110.

[1] Incenso jam igne, clara voce proclamavit : *Tuus sum, Jesu ! Salva me !* Seckend. ii. 85.
[2] Tam impar verbosus prædicator, illi tam potenti verbi operator. L. Epp. iii. 1214.
[3] Si quis dixerit fidem non esse veram fidem, licet non fit viva, aut eum qui fidem sine charitate habet, non esse christianum, anathema sit. Conc. Frid. Sess. 6, p. 28.
[4] Nescio quid mirari quod hoc anno contra reformationem expentandum sit. Seckend. ii. 101.
[5] 2 Corinthians xi. 3.
[6] Homo erat versutus, et præterea prodigus, quo vitio ad alia inductus est. Seckend. ii. 94.

money. The duke having on one occasion sent him to the Diet of Nuremberg as his representative, the Bishop of Merseburg confided to him his contribution towards the imperial government. The bishop having been afterwards called upon for the money, Pack declared that he had paid it to a citizen of Nuremberg, whose seal and signature he produced. This paper was a forgery, and Pack himself was the author of it.[1] The wretch, however, put an impudent face on the matter, and having escaped conviction, preserved the confidence of his master. Erelong an opportunity presented itself of exercising his criminal talents on a larger scale.

No one entertained greater suspicions with regard to the papists than the Landgrave of Hesse. Young, susceptible, and restless, he was always on the alert. In the month of February 1528, Pack happening to be at Cassel to assist Philip in some difficult business, the landgrave imparted to him his fears. If any one could have had any knowledge of the designs of the papists, it must have been the vice-chancellor of one of the greatest enemies to the Reformation. The crafty Pack heaved a sigh, bent down his eyes, and was silent. Philip immediately became uneasy, entreated him, and promised to do nothing that would injure the duke. Pack, as if he had allowed an important secret to be torn from him with regret, then confessed that a league against the Lutherans had been concluded at Breslau on the Wednesday following *Jubilate* Sunday (12th May 1527); and engaged to procure the original of this act for the landgrave, who offered him a remuneration of ten thousand florins for this service. This was the greatest transaction that the wretched man had ever undertaken; but it tended to nothing less than the utter overthrow of the empire.

The landgrave was amazed: he restrained himself, however, wishing to see the act with his own eyes before informing his allies. He therefore repaired to Dresden. "I cannot," said Pack, "furnish you with the original: the duke always carries it about his person to read it to other princes whom he hopes to gain over. Quite recently at Leipsic, he showed it to Duke Henry of Brunswick. But here is a copy made by his highness's order." The landgrave took the document, which bore all the marks of the most perfect authenticity. It was crossed by a cord of black silk, and fastened at both ends by the seal of the ducal chancery.[2] Above was an impression from the ring Duke George always wore on his finger, with the three quarterings that Philip had so often seen; at the top, the coronet, and at the bottom, the two lions. He had no more doubts as to its authenticity. But how can we describe his indignation as he read this guilty document? King Ferdinand, the Electors of Mentz and of Brandenburg, Duke George of Saxony, the Dukes of Bavaria, the Bishops of Salzburg, Wurtzburg, and Bamberg, had entered into a coalition to call upon the Elector of Saxony to deliver up the arch-heretic Luther, with all the apostate priests, monks, and nuns, and to re-establish the ancient worship. If he made default, his states were to be invaded, and this prince and his descendants for ever dispossessed. The same measure was next to be applied to the landgrave, only ("it was your father-in-law, Duke George," said Pack to Philip, "who got this clause inserted") his states were to be restored to him in consideration of his youth, if he became fully reconciled to the holy Church. The document stated moreover the contingents of men and money to be provided by the confederates, and the share they were to have in the spoils of the two heretical princes.[1]

Many circumstances tended to confirm the authenticity of this paper. Ferdinand, Joachim of Brandenburg, and George of Saxony, had in fact met at Breslau on the day indicated, and an evangelical prince, the Margrave George, had seen Joachim leave Ferdinand's apartments, holding in his hand a large parchment, to which several seals were attached. The agitated landgrave caused a copy to be taken of this document, promised secrecy for a time, paid Pack four thousand florins, and engaged to make up the sum agreed upon, if he would procure him the original. And then, wishing to prevent the storm, he hastened to Weimar to inform the elector of this unprecedented conspiracy.

"I have seen," said he to John and his son, "nay more—I have had in my hands a duplicate of this horrible treaty. Signatures, seals—nothing was wanting.[2] Here is a copy, and I bind myself to place the original before your eyes. The most frightful danger threatens us—ourselves, our faithful subjects, and the Word of God."

The elector had no reason to doubt the account the landgrave had just given him: he was stunned, confounded, and overpowered. The promptest measures alone could avert such unprecedented disasters: every thing must be risked to extricate them from certain destruction. The impetuous Philip breathed fire and flames;[3] his plan of defence was already prepared. He presented it, and in the first moment of consternation carried the consent of his ally, as it were by assault. On the 9th March 1528, the two princes agreed to employ all their forces to defend themselves, and even to take the offensive, and sacrifice life, honour, rank, subjects, and states, that they might preserve the Word of God. The Dukes of Prussia, Mecklen-

---

1 It is still to be seen in the records at Dresden.
2 Cui filum sericum circumligatum, et sigillum cancellariæ impressum erat. Seck. ii. 94.

1 Hortleber, De Bello Germanico. ii. 579.
2 Nam is affirmabat se archetypon vidisse, commemorabat σφράγιδας. Corp. Ref. i. 986.
3 Mirabiliter incensus erat. Ibid.

burg, Luneburg, and Pomerania, the Kings of Denmark and Poland, and the Margrave of Brandenburg, were to be invited to enter into this alliance. Six hundred thousand florins were destined for the expenses of the war; and to procure them, they would raise loans, pledge their cities, and sell the offerings in the churches.[1] They had already begun to raise a powerful army.[2] The landgrave set out in person for Nuremberg and Anspach. The alarm was general in those countries; the commotion was felt throughout all Germany,[3] and even beyond it. John Zapolya, king of Hungary, at that time a refugee at Cracow, promised a hundred thousand florins to raise an army, and twenty thousand florins a month for its maintenance. Thus a spirit of error was misleading the princes; if it should carry away the Reformers also, the destruction of the Reformation would not be far distant.

But God was watching over them. Supported on the rock of the Word, Melancthon and Luther replied: "It is written, Thou shalt not tempt the Lord thy God." As soon as these two men whom the danger threatened (for it was they who were to be delivered up to the papal power) saw the youthful landgrave drawing the sword, and the aged elector himself putting his hand on the hilt, they uttered a cry, and this cry, which was heard in heaven, saved the Reformation.

Luther, Pomeranus, and Melancthon immediately forwarded the following advice to the elector: "Above all things, let not the attack proceed from our side, and let no blood be shed through our fault. Let us wait for the enemy, and seek after peace. Send an ambassador to the emperor to make him acquainted with this hateful plot."

Thus it was that the faith of the children of God, which is so despised by politicians, conducted them aright, at the very moment when the diplomatists were going astray. The elector and his son declared to the landgrave that they would not assume the offensive. Philip was amazed. "Are not the preparations of the papists worthy an attack?" asked he.[4] "What! we will threaten war, and yet not make it! We will inflame the hatred of our antagonists, and leave them time to prepare their forces! No, no; forward! It is thus we shall secure the means of an honourable peace."——"If the landgrave desires to begin the war," replied the reformer, "the elector is not obliged to observe the treaty; for we must obey God rather than men. God and the right are above every alliance. Let us beware of painting the devil on our doors, and inviting him as godfather.[5] But if the landgrave is

attacked, the elector ought to go to his assistance; for it is God's will that we preserve our faith." This advice, which the reformers gave, cost them dear. Never did man, condemned to the torture, endure a punishment like theirs. The fears excited by the landgrave were succeeded by the terrors inspired by the papist princes. This cruel trial left them in great distress. "I am worn away with sorrow," cried Melancthon; "and this anguish puts me to the most horrible torture.[1] The issue," added he, "will be found on our knees before God."[2]

The elector, drawn in different directions by the theologians and the politicians, at last took a middle course: he resolved to assemble an army, "but only," said he, "to obtain peace." Philip of Hesse at length gave way, and forthwith sent copies of the famous treaty to Duke George, to the dukes of Bavaria, and to the emperor's representatives, calling upon them to renounce such cruel designs. "I would rather have a limb cut off," said he to his father-in-law, "than know you to be a member of such an alliance."

The surprise of the German courts, when they read this document, is beyond description. Duke George immediately replied to the landgrave, that he had allowed himself to be deceived by unmeaning absurdities; that he who pretended to have seen the original of this act was an infamous liar, and an incorrigible scoundrel; and called upon the landgrave to give up his authority, or else it might well be thought that he was himself the inventor of this impudent fabrication. King Ferdinand, the Elector of Brandenburg, and all the pretended conspirators, made similar replies.

Philip of Hesse saw that he had been deceived;[1] his confusion was only exceeded by his anger. He had in this affair justified the accusations of his adversaries, who called him a hot-headed young man, and had compromised to the highest degree the cause of the Reformation and that of his people. He said afterwards, "If that business had not happened, it could not happen now. Nothing that I have done in my whole life has caused me greater vexation."

Pack fled in alarm to the landgrave, who caused him to be arrested; and envoys from the several princes whom this scoundrel had compromised met at Cassel, and proceeded to examine him. He maintained that the original act of the alliance had really existed in the Dresden archives. In the following year the landgrave banished him from Hesse, proving by this action that he did not fear him. Pack was afterwards discovered in Belgium; and at the demand of Duke George, who had never shown any pity to-

---

[1] Venditisque templorum donariis. Seckend. ii. 95.
[2] Magno studio validum comparaverunt ambo exercitum. Cochlœus, p. 171.
[3] Non leviter commotos esse nostrorum animos. Corp. Ref. ii. 986.
[4] Landgravius præparamenta adversariorum pro aggressione habebat. Seck. ii. 95.
[5] Man darf den Teufel nicht über die Thür malen, noch ihn zu gevattern bitten. L. Epp. iii. 321.

[1] Curæ vehementer cruciarunt. Corp. Ref. i. 968.
[2] Εν γουναοι θεου. Ibid.
[3] Wir fühlten dass wir betrogen waren. Hortleber. iv. 567.

wards him, he was seized, tortured, and finally beheaded.

The landgrave was unwilling to have taken up arms to no purpose. The Archbishop-elector of Mentz was compelled, on the 11th June 1520, to renounce in the camp of Herzkirchen, all spiritual jurisdiction in Saxony and Hesse.[1] This was no small advantage.

Scarcely had the arms been laid aside before Luther took up his pen and began a war of another kind. "Impious princes may deny this alliance as long as they please," wrote he to Link ; " I am very certain that it is not a chimera. These insatiable leeches will take no repose until they see the whole of Germany flowing with blood."[2] This idea of Luther's was the one generally entertained. " The document presented to the landgrave may be Pack's invention," it was said, " but all this fabric of lies is founded on some truth. If the alliance has not been concluded, it has been conceived."[3]

Melancholy were the results of this affair. It inspired division in the bosom of the Reformation, and fanned the hatred between the two parties.[4] The sparks from the piles of Keyser, Winkler, Carpenter, and so many other martyrs, added strength to the fire that was already threatening to set the empire in flames. It was under such critical circumstances, and with such menacing dispositions, that the famous Diet of Spires was opened in March 1529. The Empire and the Papacy were in reality preparing to annihilate the Reformation, although in a manner different from what Pack had pretended. It was still to be learnt whether more vital strength would be found in the revived Church than in so many sects that Rome had easily crushed. Happily faith had increased, and the constitution given to the Church had imparted greater power to its adherents. All were resolved on defending a doctrine so pure, and a church government so superior to that of Popery. During three years of tranquillity, the Gospel tree had struck its roots deep ; and if the storm should burst, it would now be able to brave it.

CHAPTER V.

Alliance between Charles and Clement VII.—Omens—Hostility of the Papists—Arbitrary Proposition of Charles—Resolutions of the Diet—The Reformation in Danger—Decision of the Princes—Violence of Ferdinand—The Schism completed.

THE sack of Rome, by exasperating the adherents of the Papacy, had given arms to all the enemies of Charles V. The French army under Lautrec had forced the imperial army, enervated by the delights of a new Capua,

to hide itself within the walls of Naples. Doria, at the head of his Genoese galleys, had destroyed the Spanish fleet, and the imperial power seemed drawing to an end in Italy. But Doria suddenly declared for the emperor ; pestilence carried off Lautrec and half of his troops ; and Charles, suffering only from alarm, had again assumed the superiority with a firm resolution to unite henceforward closely with the pontiff, whose humiliation had nearly cost him so dear. On his side, Clement VII., hearing the Italians reproach him for his illegitimate birth, and even refuse him the title of pope, said aloud, that he would rather be the emperor's groom than the sport of his people. On the 29th June 1528, a peace between the heads of the Empire and of the Church was concluded at Barcelona, based on the destruction of heresy ; and in November a diet was convoked to meet at Spires on the 21st February 1529. Charles was resolved to endeavour at first to destroy the Reform by a federal vote ; and if this means did not suffice, to employ his whole power against it. The road being thus traced out, they were about to commence operations.

Germany felt the seriousness of the position. Mournful omens filled every mind. About the middle of January, a great brightness in the sky had suddenly dispersed the darkness of the night.[1] " What that forebodes," exclaimed Luther, " God only knows!" At the beginning of April there was a rumour of an earthquake that had engulphed castles, cities, and whole districts in Carinthia and Istria, and split the tower of St. Mark at Venice into four parts. " If that is true," said the reformer, " these prodigies are the forerunners of the day of Jesus Christ."[2] Astrologers declared that the aspect of the quartiles of Saturn and Jupiter, and the general position of the stars, were ominous.[3] The waters of the Elbe rolled thick and stormy, and stones fell from the roofs of churches. " All these things," exclaimed the terrified Melancthon, " excite me in no trifling degree."[4]

The letters of convocation issued by the imperial government agreed but too well with these prodigies. The emperor, writing from Toledo to the elector, accused him of sedition and revolt. Alarming whispers passed from mouth to mouth that were sufficient to cause the fall of the weak. Duke Henry of Mecklenburg and the elector-palatine hastily returned to the side of popery.

Never had the sacerdotal party appeared in the diet in such numbers, or so powerful and decided.[5] On the 5th March, Ferdinand,

---

[1] Kopp. Hess. Gerichts.—Verf. i. 107.
[2] Sanguisugæ insatiabiles quiescere nolunt, nisi Germaniam sanguine madere sentiant. 14th June 1528.
[3] Non enim prorsus conficta res. Corp. Ref. i. 988.
[4] Hæc minæ apud inimicos odia auxerint. Ibid. 985.

[1] An aurora borealis. " Magnum chasma, quo nox tota illuminabatur." L. Epp. iii. 420.
[2] Si vera sunt, diem Christi præcurrunt hæc monstra. Ibid. 438.
[3] Adspectum τιτραγόνων Saturni et Jovis. Corp. Ref. i. 1075.
[4] Ego non leviter commoveor his rebus. Ibid. 1076.
[5] Nunquam fuit tanta frequentia ullis conciliis ἀρχιερέων quanta in his est. Ibid. 1039.

the president of the diet, the Dukes of Bavaria, and lastly the ecclesiastical electors of Mentz and Treves, had entered the gates of Spires surrounded by a numerous armed escort.[1] On the 13th March, the Elector of Saxony arrived, attended only by Melancthon and Agricola. But Philip of Hesse, faithful to his character, entered the city on the 18th March to the sound of trumpets, and with two hundred horsemen.

The divergence of men's minds soon became manifest. A papist did not meet an evangelical in the street without casting angry glances at him, and secretly threatening him with perfidious machinations.[2] The elector-palatine passed the Saxons without appearing to know them;[3] and although John of Saxony was the most important of the electors, none of the chiefs of the opposite party visited him. Grouped around their tables, the Roman-catholic princes seemed absorbed in games of hazard.[4]

But erelong they gave positive marks of their hostile disposition. The elector and the landgrave were prohibited from having the Gospel preached in their mansions. It was asserted, even at this early period, that John was about to be turned out of Spires, and deprived of his electorate.[5] "We are the execration and the sweepings of the earth," said Melancthon; "but Christ will look down on his poor people, and will preserve them."[6] In truth, God was with the witnesses to his Word. The people of Spires thirsted for the Gospel, and the elector wrote to his son on Palm Sunday : "About eight thousand persons were present to-day in my chapel at morning and evening worship."

The Roman party now quickened their proceedings : their plan was simple but energetic. It was necessary to put down the religious liberty that had existed for more than three years, and for this purpose they must abrogate the decree of 1526, and revive that of 1521.

On the 15th March the imperial commissioners announced to the diet that as the last resolution of Spires, which left all the states free to act in conformity with the inspirations of their consciences, had given rise to great disorders, the emperor had annulled it by virtue of his supreme power. This arbitrary act, which had no precedent in the empire, as well as the despotic tone in which it was notified, filled the evangelical Christians with indignation and alarm. "Christ," exclaimed Sturm, "has again fallen into the hands of Caiaphas and Pilate."[7]

A commission was appointed to examine the imperial proposition. The Archbishop of Salzburg, with Faber and Eck, that is to say, the most violent enemies of the Reformation, were among its members. "The Turks are better than the Lutherans," said Faber, "for the Turks observe fast-days, and the Lutherans violate them.[1] If we must choose between the Holy Scriptures of God and the old errors of the Church, we should reject the former."[2] "Every day in full assembly Faber casts some new stone at us Gospellers," says Melancthon.[3] "Oh, what an Iliad I should have to compose," added he, "if I were to report all these blasphemies !"

The priests called for the execution of the edict of Worms, 1521, and the evangelical members of the commission, among whom were the Elector of Saxony and Sturm, demanded, on the contrary, the maintenance of the edict of Spires, 1526. The latter thus remained within the bounds of legality, whilst their adversaries were driven to *coups d'état*. In fact, a new order of things had been legally established in the empire, no one could infringe it; and if the diet presumed to destroy by force what had been constitutionally established three years before, the evangelical states had the right of opposing it. The majority of the commission felt that the re-establishment of the ancient order of things would be a revolution no less complete than the Reformation itself. How could they subject anew to Rome and to her clergy those nations in whose bosom the Word of God had been so richly spread abroad ? For this reason, equally rejecting the demands of the priests and of the evangelicals, the majority came to a resolution on the 24th March that every religious innovation should continue to be interdicted in the places where the edict of Worms had been carried out ; and that in those where the people had deviated from it, and where they could not conform to it without danger of revolt, they should at least effect no new reform, they should touch upon no controverted point, they should not oppose the celebration of the mass, they should permit no Roman-catholic to embrace Lutheranism,[4] they should not decline the Episcopal jurisdiction, and should tolerate no anabaptists or sacramentarians. The *status-quo* and no proselytism—such were the essentials of this resolution.

The majority no longer voted as in 1526: the wind had turned against the Gospel. Accordingly this proposition, after having been delayed a few days by the festival of

---

[1] Mogantinum et Trevirensem cum comitatu armato. Seckend. ii. 129.
[2] Vultu significant quantum nos oderint, et quid machinentur. Corp. Ref. i. 1040.
[3] Pfalz kennt kein Sachsen mehr. Epp. Alberti Mansfeld.
[4] Adversæ partes procerea alea tempus perdere. L. Epp. iii. 436.
[5] Alii exclusum Spiræ, alii ademtum electoratum. Ibid.
[6] Sed Christus respiciet et salvabit populum pauperem. Corp. Ref. i. 1040.
[7] Christus est denuo in manibus Caiaphi et Pilati. Jung Beyträge, 4.

[1] Vociferatus est Turcos Lutheranis meliores esse. Corp. Ref. p. 1041.
[2] Malle abjicere scripturam quam veteres errores Ecclesiæ. Ibid. p. 1046.
[3] Faber lapidat nos quotidie pro concione. Ibid.
[4] Nec catholicos a libero religionis exercitio impediri debere, neque cuiquam ex his licere Lutheranismum amplecti Seckend. ii. 127.

Easter, was laid before the diet on the 6th April, and passed on the 7th.[1]

If it became a law, the Reformation could neither be extended into those places where as yet it was unknown, nor be established on solid foundations in those where it already existed. The re-establishment of the Romish hierarchy, stipulated in the proposition, would infallibly bring back the ancient abuses ; and the least deviation from so vexatious an ordinance would easily furnish the Romanists with a pretext for completing the destruction of a work already so violently shaken.

The Elector, the Landgrave, the Margrave of Brandenburg, the Prince of Anhalt, and the Chancellor of Luneburg on one side, and the deputies for the cities on the other, consulted together. An entirely new order of things was to proceed from this council. If they had been animated by selfishness, they would perhaps have accepted this decree. In fact they were left free, in appearance at least, to profess their faith : ought they to demand more ? could they do so ? Were they bound to constitute themselves the champions of liberty of conscience in all the world ? Never, perhaps, had there been a more critical situation ; but these noble-minded men came victorious out of the trial. What ! should they legalize by anticipation the scaffold and the torture ? Should they oppose the Holy Ghost in its work of converting souls to Christ ? Should they forget their Master's command : " *Go ye into all the world and preach the Gospel to every creature ?*" If one of the states of the empire desired some day to follow their example and be reformed, should they take away its power of doing so ? Having themselves entered the kingdom of heaven, should they shut the door after them ? No ! rather endure every thing, sacrifice every thing, even their states, their crowns, and their lives.

" Let us reject this decree," said the princes. " In matters of conscience the majority has no power."—" It is to the decree of 1526," added the cities, " that we are indebted for the peace that the empire enjoys : its abolition would fill Germany with troubles and divisions. The diet is incompetent to do more than preserve religious liberty until a council meets." Such in fact is the grand attribute of the state, and if, in our days, the protestant powers desire to influence the Romish governments, they should strive solely at obtaining for the subjects of the latter that religious liberty which the pope confiscates to his own advantage wherever he reigns alone, and by which he profits greatly in every evangelical state. Some of the deputies proposed refusing all assistance against the Turks, hoping thus to force the emperor to interfere in this reli-

gious question. But Sturm called upon them not to mix up political matters with the salvation of souls. They resolved therefore to reject the proposition, but without holding out any threats. It was this noble resolution that gained for modern times liberty of thought and independence of faith.

Ferdinand and the priests, who were no less resolute, determined, however, on vanquishing what they called a daring obstinacy ; and they commenced with the weaker states. They began to frighten and divide the cities, which had hitherto pursued a common course. On the 12th April they were summoned before the diet : in vain did they allege the absence of some of their number, and ask for delay. It was refused, and the call was hurried on. Twenty-one free cities accepted the proposition of the diet, and fourteen rejected it. It was a bold act on the part of the latter, and was accomplished in the midst of the most painful sufferings. " This is the first trial," said Pfarrer, second deputy of Strasburg ; " now will come the second : we must either deny the Word of God or—be burnt."[1]

A violent proceeding of Ferdinand's immediately commenced the series of humiliations that were reserved for the evangelical cities. A deputy of Strasburg should, in conformity with the decree of Worms, have been a member of the imperial government from the commencement of April. He was declared excluded from his rights until the re-establishment of the mass in Strasburg. All the cities united in protesting against this arbitrary act.

At the same time, the elector-palatine and King Ferdinand himself begged the princes to accept the decree, assuring them that the emperor would be exceedingly pleased with them. " We will obey the emperor," replied they calmly, " in every thing that may contribute to maintain peace and the honour of God."

It was time to put an end to this struggle. On the 18th April it was decreed that the evangelical states should not be heard again ; and Ferdinand prepared to inflict the decisive blow on the morrow.

When the day came, the king appeared in the diet, surrounded by the other commissioners of the empire, and by several bishops. He thanked the Roman-catholics for their fidelity, and declared that the resolution having been definitively agreed to, it was about to be drawn up in the form of an imperial decree. He then announced to the elector and his friends, that their only remaining course was to submit to the majority.

The evangelical princes, who had not expected so positive a declaration, were excited at this summons, and passed, according to custom, into an adjoining chamber to deliberate. But Ferdinand was not in a humour

[1] Sleidan, i. 261.

[1] Das wort Gottes zu wiederrufen oder aber brennen. Jung Beyträge, p. 37.

519

to wait for their answer. He rose, and the imperial commissioners with him. Vain were all endeavours to stop him. "I have received an order from his imperial majesty," replied he; "I have executed it. All is over."

Thus did Charles's brother notify an order to the christian princes, and then retire without even caring if there was any reply to be made! To no purpose did they send a deputation entreating the king to return. "It is a settled affair," repeated Ferdinand; "submission is all that remains."[1] This refusal completed the schism: it separated Rome from the Gospel. Perhaps more justice on the part of the empire and of the papacy might have prevented the rupture that since then has divided the Western Church.

CHAPTER VI.

The Protest—Principles of the Protest—Supremacy of the Gospel—Christian Union—Ferdinand rejects the Protest —Attempt at Conciliation—Exultation of the Papists— Evangelical Appeal—Christian Unity a Reality—Dangers of the Protestants—The Protestants leave Spires—The Princes the True Reformers—Germany and Reform.

IF the imperial party displayed such contempt, it was not without a cause. They felt that weakness was on the side of the Reformation, and strength with Charles and the pope. But the weak have also their strength; and of this the evangelical princes were aware. As Ferdinand paid no attention to their complaints, they ought to pay none to his absence, to appeal from the report of the diet to the Word of God, and from the Emperor Charles to Jesus Christ, the King of kings and Lord of lords.

They resolved upon this step. A declaration was drawn up to that effect, and this was the famous *Protest* that henceforward gave the name of *Protestant* to the renovated Church. The elector and his allies, having returned to the common hall of the diet, thus addressed the assembled states:[2]—

"Dear Lords, Cousins, Uncles, and Friends! Having repaired to this diet at the summons of his majesty, and for the common good of the empire and of Christendom, we have heard and learnt that the decisions of the last diet concerning our holy Christian faith are to be repealed, and that it is proposed to substitute for them certain restrictive and onerous resolutions.

"King Ferdinand and the other imperial commissioners, by affixing their seals to the last *Recess* of Spires, had promised, however, in the name of the emperor, to carry out sincerely and inviolably all that it contained, and to permit nothing that was contrary to

it. In like manner, also, you and we, electors, princes, prelates, lords, and deputies of the empire, bound ourselves to maintain always and with our whole might every article of that decree.

"We cannot therefore consent to its repeal:—

"Firstly, because we believe that his imperial majesty (as well as you and we), is called upon to maintain firmly what has been unanimously and solemnly resolved.

"Secondly, because it concerns the glory of God and the salvation of our souls, and that in such matters we ought to have regard, above all, to the commandments of God, who is King of kings and Lord of lords; each of us rendering him account for himself, without caring the least in the world about majority or minority.[1]

"We form no judgment on that which concerns you, most dear lords; and we are content to pray God daily that he will bring us all to unity of faith, in truth, charity, and holiness through Jesus Christ, our throne of grace and our only mediator.

"But in what concerns ourselves, adhesion to your resolution (and let every honest man be judge!) would be acting against our conscience, condemning a doctrine that we maintain to be christian, and pronouncing that it ought to be abolished in our states, if we could do so without trouble.

"This would be to deny our Lord Jesus Christ, to reject his holy Word, and thus give him just reason to deny us in turn before his Father, as he has threatened.

"What! we ratify this edict! We assert that when Almighty God calls a man to His knowledge, this man cannot however receive the knowledge of God! Oh! of what deadly backslidings should we not thus become the accomplices, not only among our own subjects, but also among yours!

"For this reason we reject the yoke that is imposed on us. And although it is universally known that in our states the holy sacrament of the body and blood of our Lord is becomingly administered, we cannot adhere to what the edict proposes against the sacramentarians, seeing that the imperial edict did not speak of them, that they have not been heard, and that we cannot resolve upon such important points before the next council.

"Moreover"—and this is the essential part of the protest—"as the new edict declares that the ministers shall preach the Gospel, explaining it according to the writings accepted by the holy Christian Church; we think that, for this regulation to have any value, we should first agree on what is meant by the true and holy Church. Now, seeing that there is great diversity of opinion in this respect; that there is no sure doctrine but such as is conformable to the Word of God;

---

[1] Die artikel weren beschlossen. Jung Beytr. p. 90.
[2] There are two copies of this act; one of them is brief, and the other, which is longer, was transmitted in writing to the imperial commissioners. It is from the latter we extract the passages in the text. They will both be found in Jung Beyträge, p. 91-105. See also Müller's *Historie der Protestation*, p. 52.

[1] Ein jeglicher fur sich selbt vor Gott stehen. Jung Beyträge, p. 96.

that the Lord forbids the teaching of any other doctrine; that each text of the Holy Scriptures ought to be explained by other and clearer texts; and that this holy book is in all things necessary for the Christian, easy of understanding, and calculated to scatter the darkness: we are resolved, with the grace of God, to maintain the pure and exclusive preaching of his only Word, such as it is contained in the biblical books of the Old and New Testament, without adding any thing thereto that may be contrary to it.[1] This Word is the only truth; it is the sure rule of all doctrine and of all life, and can never fail or deceive us. He who builds on this foundation shall stand against all the powers of hell, whilst all the human vanities that are set up against it shall fall before the face of God.

"For these reasons, most dear lords, uncles, cousins, and friends, we earnestly entreat you to weigh carefully our grievances and our motives. If you do not yield to our request, we PROTEST by these presents, before God, our only Creator, Preserver, Redeemer, and Saviour, and who will one day be our judge, as well as before all men and all creatures, that we, for us and for our people, neither consent nor adhere in any manner whatsoever to the proposed decree, in any thing that is contrary to God, to his holy Word, to our right conscience, to the salvation of our souls, and to the last decree of Spires.

"At the same time we are in expectation that his imperial majesty will behave towards us like a christian prince who loves God above all things; and we declare ourselves ready to pay unto him, as well as unto you, gracious lords, all the affection and obedience that are our just and legitimate duty."

Thus, in presence of the diet, spoke out those courageous men whom Christendom will henceforward denominate THE PRO-TESTANTS.

They had barely finished when they announced their intention of quitting Spires on the morrow.[2]

This protest and declaration produced a deep impression. The diet was rudely interrupted and broken into two hostile parties,—thus preluding war. The majority became the prey of the liveliest fears. As for the Protestants, relying *jure humano*, upon the edict of Spires, and, *jure divino*, upon the Bible, they were full of courage and firmness.

The principles contained in this celebrated protest of the 19th April 1529, constitute the very essence of Protestantism. Now this protest opposes two abuses of man in matters of faith: the first is the intrusion of the civil magistrate, and the second the arbitrary autho-

rity of the Church. Instead of these abuses, Protestantism sets the power of conscience above the magistrate; and the authority of the Word of God above the visible church. In the first place, it rejects the civil power in divine things, and says with the prophets and apostles: *We must obey God rather than man.* In presence of the crown of Charles the Fifth, it uplifts the crown of Jesus Christ. But it goes farther: it lays down the principle, that all human teaching should be subordinate to the oracles of God. Even the primitive Church, by recognising the writings of the apostles, had performed an act of submission to this supreme authority, and not an act of authority, as Rome maintains; and the establishment of a tribunal charged with the interpretation of the Bible, had terminated only in slavishly subjecting man to man in what should be most unfettered—conscience and faith. In this celebrated act of Spires no doctor appears, and the Word of God reigns alone. Never has man exalted himself like the pope; never have men kept in the back ground like the reformers.

A Romish historian maintains that the word *Protestant* signifies *enemy of the emperor and of the pope.*[1] If he means that Protestantism, in matters of faith, rejects the intervention both of the empire and of the papacy, it is well. But even this explanation does not exhaust the signification of the word, for Protestantism threw off man's authority solely to place Jesus Christ on the throne of the Church, and his Word in the pulpit. There has never been any thing more positive, and at the same time more aggressive, than the position of the Protestants at Spires. By maintaining that their faith is alone capable of saving the world, they defended with intrepid courage the rights of christian proselytism. We cannot abandon this proselytism without deserting the protestant principle.

The Protestants of Spires were not content to exalt the truth; they defended charity. Faber and the other papal partisans had endeavoured to separate the princes, who in general walked with Luther, from the cities that ranged themselves rather on the side of Zwingle. Œcolampadius had immediately written to Melancthon, and enlightened him on the doctrines of the Zurich reformer. He had indignantly rejected the idea that Christ was banished into a corner of heaven, and had energetically declared that, according to the Swiss Christians, Christ was in every place upholding all things by the Word of his power.[2] "With the visible symbols," he added, "we give and we receive the invisible grace, like all the faithful."[3]

---

[1] Allein Gottes wort, lauter und rein, und nichts das dawieder ist. Jung Beyträge, p. 101.
[2] Also zu verritten urlaub genommen. Jung Beyträge, p. 52.

[1] Perduelles in Pontificem ac Cæsarem. Pallavicini, O. T. I. p. 217.
[2] Ubique ut et portet omnia verbo virtutis suæ. Hospin. Hist. Sacr. ii. 112.
[3] Χάριν γὰρ τὴν ἀόρατον μιτὰ τῶν συμβόλων ὁράτων. Ibid.

These declarations were not useless. There were at Spires two men who from different motives opposed the efforts of Faber, and seconded those of Œcolampadius. The landgrave, ever revolving projects of alliance in his mind, felt clearly that if the Christians of Saxony and of Hesse allowed the condemnation of the churches of Switzerland and of Upper Germany, they would by that very means deprive themselves of powerful auxiliaries.[1] Melancthon, who unlike the landgrave was far from desiring a diplomatic alliance, lest it should hasten on a war, defended the great principles of justice, and exclaimed: "To what just reproaches should we not be exposed, were we to recognise in our adversaries the right of condemning a doctrine without having heard those who defend it!" The union of all evangelical Christians is therefore a principle of primitive Protestantism.

As Ferdinand had not heard the protest of the 19th April, a deputation of the evangelical states went the next day to present it to him. The brother of Charles the Fifth received it at first, but immediately after desired to return it. Then was witnessed a strange scene—the king refusing to keep the protest, and the deputies to take it back. At last the latter, out of respect, received it from Ferdinand's hands; but they laid it boldly upon a table, and directly quitted the hall.

The king and the imperial commissaries remained in presence of this formidable writing. It was there—before their eyes—a significant monument of the courage and faith of the Protestants. Irritated against this silent but mighty witness, which accused his tyranny, and left him the responsibility of all the evils that were about to burst upon the empire, the brother of Charles the Fifth called some of his councillors, and ordered them instantly to carry the important document back to the Protestants.

All this was unavailing; the protest had been registered in the annals of the world, and nothing could erase it. Liberty of thought and of conscience had been secured for ages to come. Thus all evangelical Germany, foreseeing these things, was moved at this courageous act, and adopted it as the expression of its will and of its faith. Men in every quarter beheld in it not a mere political event, but a christian action, and the youthful electoral prince, John Frederick, in this respect the organ of his age, cried to the Protestants of Spires: "May the Almighty, who has given you grace to confess energetically, freely, and fearlessly, preserve you in that christian firmness until the day of eternity!"[2]

While the Christians were filled with joy, their enemies were frightened at their own work. The very day on which Ferdinand had declined to receive the protest (Tuesday 20th April), at one in the afternoon, Henry of Brunswick and Philip of Baden presented themselves as mediators, announcing, however, that they were acting solely of their own authority. They proposed that there should be no more mention of the decree of Worms, and that the first decree of Spires should be maintained, but with a few modifications; that the two parties, while remaining free until the next council, should oppose every new sect, and tolerate no doctrine contrary to the sacrament of the Lord's body.[1]

On Wednesday, 21st April, the evangelical states did not appear adverse to these propositions; and even those who had embraced the doctrines of Zwingle declared boldly that such a proposal would not compromise their existence. "Only let us call to mind," said they, "that in such difficult matters we must act, not with the sword, but with the sure Word of God.[2] For, as Saint Paul says: *What is not of faith is sin.* If therefore we constrain Christians to do what they believe unjust, instead of leading them by God's Word to acknowledge what is good, we force them to sin and incur a terrible responsibility."

The fanatics of the Roman party trembled as they saw the victory nearly escaping from them; they rejected all compromise, and desired purely and simply the re-establishment of the papacy. Their zeal overcame every thing, and the negotiations were broken off.

On Thursday, 22d April, the diet reassembled at seven in the morning, and the *Recess* was read precisely as it had been previously drawn up, without even mentioning the attempt at conciliation which had just failed.

Faber triumphed. Proud of having the ear of kings, he tossed himself furiously about, and, to look at him, one would have said (according to an eye-witness) that he was a Cyclops forging in his cavern the monstrous chains with which he was about to bind the Reformation and the reformers.[3] The papist princes, carried away by the tumult, gave the spur, says Melancthon, and flung themselves headlong into a path filled with dangers.[4] Nothing was left for the evangelical Christians but to fall on their knees and cry to the Lord. "All that remains for us to do," repeated Melancthon, "is to call upon the Son of God."[5]

The last sitting of the diet took place on the 24th April. The princes renewed their protest, in which fourteen free and imperial

---

1 Omni studio laborabat ut illos uniret. Seck. ii. 127.
2 In eo mansuros esse, nec passuros ut ulla hominum machinatione ab ea sententia divellerentur. Ibid. 121.

1 Vergleich artikel. Jung Beyträge, p. 55.
2 In diesen Schweren Sachen, nichts mit Gewalt noch Schwerdt, sondern mit Gottes gewissem wort. Ibid. p. 59. This document is from the pen of Sturm.
3 Cyclops ille nunc ferocem se facit. Corp. Ref. i. 1062.
4 Ut ingrediantur lubricum isti iter, impingendo stimulis calces. Ibid.
5 De quo reliquum est ut invocemus Filium Dei. Ibid.

cities joined; and they next thought of giving their appeal a legal form.

On Sunday, 25th April, two notaries, Leonard Stetner of Freysingen and Pangrace Saltzmann of Bamberg, were seated at a small table in a narrow chamber on the ground-floor of a house situated in St. John's Lane, near the church of the same name in Spires, and around them were the chancellors of the princes and of the evangelical cities, with several witnesses.[1]

This little house belonged to an humble pastor, Peter Muterstatt, deacon of St. John's, who, taking the place of the elector or of the landgrave, had offered a domicile for the important act that was preparing. His name is worthy in consequence of being transmitted to posterity. The document having been definitively drawn up, one of the notaries began reading it. "Since there is a natural communion between all men," said the Protestants, "and since even persons condemned to death are permitted to unite and appeal against their condemnation; how much more are we, who are members of the same spiritual body, the Church of the Son of God, children of the same Heavenly Father, and consequently brothers in the Spirit,[2] authorized to unite when our salvation and eternal condemnation are concerned?"

After reviewing all that had passed in the diet, and after intercalating in their appeal the principal documents that had reference to it, the Protestants ended by saying: "We therefore appeal for ourselves, for our subjects, and for all who receive or who shall hereafter receive the Word of God, from all past, present, or future vexatious measures, to his Imperial Majesty, and to a free and universal assembly of holy Christendom." This document filled twelve sheets of parchment; the signatures and seals were affixed to the thirteenth.

Thus in the obscure dwelling of the chaplain of St. John's was made the first confession of the true christian union. In presence of the wholly mechanical unity of the pope, these confessors of Jesus raised the banner of the living unity of Christ; and, as in the days of our Saviour, if there were many synagogues in Israel, there was at least but one temple. The Christians of Electoral Saxony, of Luneburg, of Anhalt, of Hesse and the Margravate, of Strasburg, Nuremberg, Ulm, Constance, Lindau, Memmingen, Kempten, Nordlingen, Heilbronn, Reutlingen, Isny, Saint Gall, Weissemburg, and Windsheim, took each other's hands on the 25th April, near the church of St. John, in the face of threatening persecutions. Among them might be found those who, like Zwingle, acknowledged in the Lord's Supper the entirely spiritual presence of Jesus Christ, as well as those who, with Luther, admitted his corporeal presence. There existed not at that time in the evangelical body any sects, hatred, or schism; christian unity was a reality. That upper chamber in which during the early days of Christianity, the apostles with the women and the brethren " continued with one accord in prayer and supplication,"[1] and that lower chamber where, in the first days of the Reformation, the renewed disciples of Jesus Christ presented themselves to the pope and the emperor, to the world and to the scaffold, as forming but one body, are the two cradles of the Church; and it is in this its hour of weakness and humiliation that it shines forth with the brightest glory.

After this appeal each one returned in silence to his dwelling. Several tokens excited alarm for the safety of the Protestants. A short time previously Melancthon hastily conducted through the streets of Spires toward the Rhine his friend Simon Grynæus, pressing him to cross the river. The latter was astonished at such precipitation.[2] "An old man of grave and solemn air, but who is unknown to me," said Melancthon, " appeared before me and said: In a minute the officers of justice will be sent by Ferdinand to arrest Grynæus." As he was intimate with Faber, and had been scandalized at one of his sermons, Grynæus went to him, and begged him no longer to make war against the truth. Faber dissembled his anger, but immediately after repaired to the king, from whom he had obtained an order against the importunate professor of Heidelberg.[3] Melancthon doubted not that God had saved his friend by sending one of His holy angels to forewarn him. Motionless on the banks of the Rhine, he waited until the waters of that stream had rescued Grynæus from his persecutors. "At last," cried Melancthon, as he saw him on the opposite side, " at last he is torn from the cruel jaws of those who thirst for innocent blood."[4] When he returned to his house, Melancthon was informed that officers in search of Grynæus had ransacked it from top to bottom.[5]

There was nothing to detain the Protestants any longer in Spires, and accordingly, on the morning after their appeal (Monday, 26th April), the elector, the landgrave, and the Dukes of Luneburg, quitted the city, reached Worms, and then returned by Hesse into their own states. The appeal of Spires was published by the landgrave on the 5th, and by the elector on the 13th of May.

---

[1] Untem in einem Kleinen Stüblein. Jung Beyträge, p. 78. Instrumentum Appellationis.
[2] Membra unius corporis spiritualis Jesu Christi et filii unius patris cœlestis, ideoque fratres spirituales. Seckend. ii. 130.

[1] Acts i. 14.
[2] Miranti quæ esset tantæ festinationis causa. Camerarius Vita Mel. p. 113.
[3] Faber qui valde offenderetur orationi tali, dissimulare tamen omnia. Ibid.
[4] Ereptus quasi e faucibus eorum qui sitiunt sanguinem innocentium. Mel. ad Camer. 23d April, Corp. Ref. i. 1062.
[5] Affluit armata quædam manus ad comprehendum Grynæum missa. Camer. Vit. Mel. p. 113.

Melancthon had returned to Wittemberg on the 6th of May, persuaded that the two parties were about to draw the sword. His friends were alarmed at seeing him agitated, exhausted, and like one dead.[1] "It is a great event that has just taken place at Spires," said he; "an event pregnant with dangers, not only to the empire, but to religion itself.[2] All the pains of hell oppress me."[3]

It was Melancthon's greatest affliction that these evils were attributed to him, as indeed he ascribed them himself. "One single thing has injured us," said he; "our not having approved, as was required of us, the edict against the Zwinglians." Luther did not take this gloomy view of affairs; but he was far from comprehending the force of the protest. "The diet," said he, "has come to an end almost without results, except that those who scourge Jesus Christ were not able to satisfy their fury."[4]

Posterity has not ratified this decision, and, on the contrary, dating from this epoch the definitive formation of Protestantism, it has hailed in the Protest of Spires one of the greatest movements recorded in history. Let us see to whom the chief glory of this act belongs. The part taken by the princes, and especially by the Elector of Saxony, in the German Reformation, must strike every impartial observer. These are the true reformers—the true martyrs. The Holy Ghost, that bloweth where it listeth, had inspired them with the courage of the ancient confessors of the Church; and the God of Election was glorified in them. Somewhat later, perhaps, this great part played by the princes produced deplorable consequences: there is no grace of God that man cannot pervert. But nothing should prevent us from rendering honour to whom honour is due, and from adoring the work of the eternal Spirit in these eminent men who, under God, were in the sixteenth century the liberators of Christendom.

The Reformation had taken a bodily form. It was Luther alone who had said No at the Diet of Worms: but churches and ministers, princes and people, said No at the Diet of Spires.

In no country had superstition, scholasticism, hierarchy, and popery, been so powerful as among the Germanic nations. These simple and candid people had humbly bent their neck to the yoke that came from the banks of the Tiber. But there was in them a depth, a life, a need of interior liberty, which, sanctified by the Word of God, might render them the most energetic organs of christian truth. It was from them that was

destined to emanate the reaction against that material, external, and legal system, which had taken the place of Christianity; it was they who were called to shatter in pieces the skeleton which had been substituted for the spirit and the life, and restore to the heart of Christendom, ossified by the hierarchy, the generous beatings of which it had been deprived for so many ages. The universal Church will never forget the debt it owes to the princes of Spires and to Luther.

CHAPTER VII.

Union necessary to Reform—Luther's Doctrine on the Lord's Supper—A Lutheran Warning—Proposed Conference at Marburg—Melancthon and Zwingle—Zwingle leaves Zurich—Rumours in Zurich—The Reformers at Marburg—Carlstadt's Petition—Preliminary Discussions—Holy Ghost—Original Sin—Baptism—Luther, Melancthon, and Zwingle—Opening of the Conference—The Prayer of the Church—Hoc est Corpus Meum—Syllogism of OEcolampadius—The Flesh profiteth nothing—Lambert convinced—Luther's Old Song—Agitation in the Conference—Arrival of new Deputies—Christ's Humanity finite—Mathematics and Popery—Testimony of the Fathers—Testimony of Augustine—Argument of the Velvet Cover—End of the Conference—The Landgrave mediates—Necessity of Union—Luther rejects Zwingle's Hand—Sectarian Spirit of the Germans—Bucer's Dilemma—Christian Charity prevails—Luther's Report—Unity of Doctrine—Unity in Diversity—Signatures—Two Extremes—Three Views—Germ of Popery—Departure—Luther's Dejection—Turks before Vienna—Luther's Battle-Sermon and Agony—Luther's Firmness—Victory—Exasperation of the Papists—Threatening Prospects.

THE Protest of Spires had still further increased the indignation of the papal adherents; and Charles the Fifth, according to the oath he had made at Barcelona, set about preparing "a suitable antidote for the pestilential disease with which the Germans were attacked, and avenging in a striking manner the insult offered to Jesus Christ."[1] The pope, on his part, endeavoured to combine all the other princes of Christendom in this crusade; and the peace of Cambray, concluded on the 5th August, tended to the accomplishment of his cruel designs. It left the emperor's hands free against the heretics. After having entered their protest at Spires, it was necessary for the evangelicals to think of maintaining it.

The protestant states that had already laid the foundations of an evangelical alliance at Spires, had agreed to send deputies to Rothach; but the elector, staggered by the representations of Luther, who was continually repeating to him, "In returning and rest shall ye be saved; in quietness and in confidence shall be your strength,"[2] ordered his deputies to listen to the proposals of his allies, but to decide upon nothing. They adjourned to a new conference, which never took place. Luther triumphed; for human alliances failed. "Christ the Lord will know how to deliver us without the landgrave, and even against the landgrave," said he to his friends.[3]

---

[1] Ita fult perturbatus ut primis diebus pene extinctus sit. Corp. Ref. i. 1067.
[2] Non enim tantum imperium, sed religio etiam periclitantur. Ibid.
[3] Omnes dolores inferni oppresserant me. Ibid. 1067, 1069.
[4] Christo-mastiges et Psycho-tyranni suum furorem non potuerunt explere. L. Epp. Linco, 6th May 1529.

[1] Illatamque Christo injuriam pro viribus ulciscentur. Dumont, Corp. Univ. Diplomatique, iv. 1, 5.
[2] Isaiah xxx. 15. L. Epp. iii. 454.
[3] Unser Herr Christus, &c. Ibid. This confidence of Luther shocks a Lutheran historian.—Plank, ii. 454.

Philip of Hesse, who was vexed at Luther's obstinacy, was convinced that it arose from a dispute about words. "They will hear no mention of alliances because of the Zwinglians," said he; "well then, let us put an end to the contradictions that separate them from Luther."

The union of all the disciples of the Word of God seemed in fact a necessary condition to the success of the Reformation. How could the Protestants resist the power of Rome and of the empire, if they were divided? The landgrave no doubt wished to unite their minds, that he might afterwards be able to unite their arms; but the cause of Christ was not to triumph by the sword. If they should succeed in uniting their hearts and prayers, the Reformation would then find such strength in the faith of its children, that Philip's spearmen would no longer be necessary.

Unfortunately this union of minds, that was now to be sought after above all things, was a very difficult task. Luther in 1519 had at first appeared not only to reform, but entirely renovate the doctrine of the Lord's Supper, as the Swiss did somewhat later. "I go to the sacrament of the Lord's Supper," he had said, "and I there receive a sign from God that Christ's righteousness and passion justify me: such is the use of the sacrament."[1] This discourse, which had gone through several impressions in the cities of Upper Germany, had prepared men's minds for the doctrine of Zwingle. Accordingly Luther, astonished at the reputation he had gained, published this solemn declaration in 1527: "I protest before God and before the whole world that I have never walked with the sacramentarians."

Luther in fact was never Zwinglian as regards the Communion. Far from that, in 1519, he still believed in Transubstantiation. Why then should he speak of a sign? It was for this reason: While, according to Zwingle, the bread and wine are signs of the body and blood of Christ; according to Luther, the very body and blood of Jesus Christ are signs of God's grace. These opinions are widely different from one another.

Erelong this disagreement declared itself. In 1527 Zwingle, in his *Friendly Exposition*,[2] refuted Luther's opinion with mildness and respect. Unluckily the pamphlet of the Saxon reformer "against the enthusiasts," was then issuing from the press, and in it Luther expressed his indignation that his adversaries should dare speak of christian unity and peace. "Well!" exclaimed he, "since they thus insult all reason, I will give them a Lutheran warning."[3] Cursed be

this concord! cursed be this charity! down, down with it, to the bottomless pit of hell! If I should murder your father, your mother, your wife, your child, and then, wishing to murder you, I should say to you, 'Let us be at peace, my dear friend!' what answer would you make?—It is thus that the enthusiasts, who murder Jesus Christ my Lord, God the Father, and Christendom my mother, wish to murder me also; and then they say, Let us be friends!"

Zwingle wrote two replies "to the excellent Martin Luther," in a cold tone and with a haughty calmness more difficult to pardon than the invectives of the Saxon doctor. "We ought to esteem you a vessel of honour," said he, "and we do so with joy, notwithstanding your faults." Pamphlet followed pamphlet, Luther always writing with the same impetuosity, and Zwingle with unalterable coolness and irony.

Such were the doctors whom the landgrave undertook to reconcile. Already, during the sitting of the Diet of Spires, Philip of Hesse, who was afflicted at hearing the papists continually repeating "You boast of your attachment to the pure Word of God, and yet you are nevertheless disunited,"[1] had made overtures to Zwingle in writing. He now went farther, and invited the theologians of the different parties to meet at Marburg. These invitations met with various receptions. Zwingle, whose heart was large and fraternal, answered the landgrave's call; but it was rejected by Luther, who discovered leagues and battles behind this pretended concord.

It seemed, however, that great difficulties would detain Zwingle. The road from Zurich to Marburg lay through the territories of the emperor and of other enemies to the Reformation; the landgrave himself did not conceal the dangers of the journey;[2] but in order to obviate these difficulties, he promised an escort from Strasburg to Hesse, and for the rest "the protection of God."[3] These precautions were not of a nature to reassure the Zurichers.

Reasons of another kind detained Luther and Melancthon. "It is not right," said they, "that the landgrave should have so much to do with the Zwinglians. Their error is of such a nature that people of acute minds are easily tainted by it. Reason loves what it understands, particularly when learned men clothe their ideas in a scriptural dress."

Melancthon did not stop here, but put forth the very extraordinary notion of selecting papists as judges of the discussion. "If there were no impartial judges," said he, "the Zwinglians would have a good chance of

[1] In the writing entitled, *Dass diese Worte noch feste Stehen.* L. Opp. xix.
[2] *Amica exegesis,* id est, Expositio Eucharistiæ negotii ad M. Lutherum. Zw. Opp.
[3] Eine Lutherische Warnung. L. Opp. xix. 391. Wider die Schwärmgeister.

[1] Inter nos ipsos de religionis doctrina non consentire. Zw. Epp. ii. 287.
[2] Viam Francofurdi capias, quam autem hac periculosio rem esse putamus. Ibid. p. 312.
[3] Juvante Deo tuti. Ibid. p. 329.

boasting of victory."[1] Thus, according to Melancthon, papists would be impartial judges when the real presence was the subject of discussion! He went still farther. "Let the Elector," he wrote on the 14th May to the Prince Electoral, "refuse to permit our journey to Marburg, so that we may be able to allege this excuse." The elector would not lend himself to so disgraceful a proceeding; and the reformers of Wittemberg found themselves compelled to accede to the request of Philip of Hesse. But they did so with these words : "If the Swiss do not yield to us, all your trouble will be lost;" and they wrote to the theologians among their friends who were convoked by the prince : "Stay away if you can ; your absence will be very useful to us."[2]

Zwingle, on the contrary, who would have gone to the end of the world, made every exertion to obtain permission from the magistrates of Zurich to visit Marburg. "I am convinced," said he to the secret council, "that if we doctors meet face to face, the splendour of truth will illuminate our eyes."[3] But the council, that had only just signed the first religious peace,[4] and who feared to see war burst out afresh, positively refused to allow the reformer's departure.

Upon this Zwingle decided for himself. He felt that his presence was necessary for the maintenance of peace in Zurich ; but the welfare of all Christendom summoned him to Marburg. Accordingly, raising his eyes towards heaven, he resolved to depart, exclaiming, "O God! Thou hast never abandoned us ; Thou wilt perform thy will for thine own glory."[5] During the night of the 31st of August, Zwingle, who was unwilling to wait for the landgrave's safe-conduct, prepared for his journey. Rodolph Collins, the Greek professor, was alone to accompany him. The reformer wrote to the Smaller and to the Great Council : "If I leave without informing you, it is not, most wise lords, because I despise your authority ; but knowing the love you bear towards me, I foresee that your anxiety will oppose my going."

As he was writing these words, a fourth message arrived from the landgrave, more pressing still than the preceding ones. The reformer sent the prince's letter to the burgomaster with his own, and then quitted his house privily by night,[6] concealing his departure both from friends, whose importunity he feared, and from enemies, whose snares he had good cause to dread. He did not even tell his wife where he was going, lest it should distress her. He and Collins then mounted two horses that had been hired for the purpose,[1] and rode off rapidly in the direction of Basle.

During the day the rumour of Zwingle's absence spread through Zurich, and his enemies were elated. "He has fled the country," said they ; "he has run away with a pack of scoundrels !" "As he was crossing the river at Bruck," said others, "the boat upset and he was drowned." "The devil," affirmed many with a malicious smile, "appeared to him bodily and carried him off."[2] —"There was no end to their stories," says Bullinger. But the council immediately resolved on acceding to the wish of the reformer. On the very day of his departure they appointed one of the councillors, Ulrich Funck, to accompany him to Marburg, and he forthwith set out with one domestic and an arquebusier. Strasburg and Basle in like manner sent statesmen in company with their theologians, under the idea that this conference would doubtless have, also, a political object.

Zwingle arrived safely at Basle,[3] and embarked on the river on the 6th September with Œcolampadius and several merchants.[4] In thirteen hours they reached Strasburg, where the two reformers lodged in the house of Matthew Zell, the cathedral preacher. Catherine, the pastor's wife, prepared the dishes in the kitchen, waited at table, according to the ancient German manners,[5] and then sitting down near Zwingle, listened attentively, and spoke with so much piety and knowledge, that the latter soon ranked her above many doctors.

After discussing with the magistrates the means of resisting the Romish league, and the organization to be given to the christian confederacy,[6] Zwingle quitted Strasburg : and he and his friends, conducted along byroads, through forests, over mountains and valleys, by secret but sure paths, at length reached Marburg, escorted by forty Hessian cavaliers.[7]

Luther, on his side, accompanied by Melancthon, Cruciger, and Jonas, had stopped on the Hessian frontier, declaring that nothing should induce him to cross it without a safe-conduct from the landgrave. This document being obtained, Luther arrived at Alsfeld, where the scholars, kneeling under the reformer's windows, chanted their pious hymns. He entered Marburg on the 30th September, a day after the arrival of the Swiss. Both parties went to inns ; but they had scarcely alighted before the landgrave invited them to come and lodge in the castle, thinking by this means to bring these op-

1 Papistische als unparteische. Corp. Ref. i. 1066.
2 Si potes, noli adesse. L. Epp. iii. 501.
3 Ut veritatis splendor oculos nostros feriat. Zw. Epp. ii. 321.
4 See below. Book xvi. chap. ii. anno 1529.
5 Dei nunquam fallentis, qui nos numquam deseruit, gratiam reputavi. Zw. Epp. ii. 356.
6 Sabbati die, mane ante lucem, 1 Septembris. Ibid.

1 Equis conductoriis. Zw. Epp. ii. 361.
2 Der Tufel vere by imm gesin. Bulling. ii. 224.
3 Integer et sanus Basiliam pervenit. Zw. Epp. ii. 361.
4 Aliquos mercatorum fide dignos, comites. Ibid.
5 Ich bin 14 Tag magd und Köchin gewesen. Füssl. Beytr. v. 313. See her remarkable correspondence with the superintendent Rabus. Ibid. 191-354.
6 De jure præsidendi conciliis civitatum christianarum Zw. Epp. ii. 364. See book xvi. of this History.
7 Per devia et sylvas, montes et valles, tutissimos et occultos. Ibid. 368.

posing bodies closer together. Philip entertained them in a manner truly royal.[1] "Ah!" said the pious Jonas, as he wandered through the halls of the palace, "it is not in honour of the Muses, but in honour of God and of his Christ, that we are so munificently treated in these forests of Hesse!" After dinner, on the first day, Œcolampadius, Hedio, and Bucer, desirous of entering into the prince's views, went and saluted Luther. The latter conversed affectionately with Œcolampadius in the castle-court; but Bucer, with whom he had once been very intimate, and who was now on Zwingle's side, having approached him, Luther said to him, smiling and shaking his hand: "As for you, you are a good-for-nothing fellow and a knave!"[2]

The unhappy Carlstadt, who had begun this dispute, was at that time in Friesland, preaching the spiritual presence of Christ, and living in such destitution that he had been forced to sell his Hebrew Bible to procure bread. The trial had crushed his pride, and he wrote to the landgrave: "We are but one body, one house, one people, one sacerdotal race; we live and die by one and the same Saviour. For this reason, I, poor and in exile, humbly pray your highness, by the blood of Jesus Christ, to allow me to be present at the disputation."[3]

But how bring Luther and Carlstadt face to face? and yet how repel the unhappy man? The landgrave, to extricate himself from this difficulty, referred him to the Saxon reformer. Carlstadt did not appear.

Philip of Hesse desired that, previously to the public conference, the theologians should have a private interview. It was however considered dangerous, says a contemporary, for Zwingle and Luther, who were both naturally violent, to contend with one another at the very beginning; and as Œcolampadius and Melancthon were the mildest, they were apportioned to the roughest champions.[4] On Friday the 1st of October, after divine service, Luther and Œcolampadius were conducted into one chamber, and Zwingle and Melancthon into another. The combatants were then left to struggle two and two.

The principal contest took place in the room of Zwingle and Melancthon. "It is affirmed," said Melancthon to Zwingle, "that some among you speak of God after the manner of the Jews, as if Christ was not essentially God." "I think on the Holy Trinity," replied Zwingle, "with the Council of Nice and the Athanasian creed." "Councils! creeds! What does that mean?" asked Melancthon. "Have you not continually repeated that you recognise no other authority than that of Scripture?" "We have

never rejected the councils," replied the Swiss reformer, "when they are based on the authority of the Word of God.[1] The four first councils are truly sacred as regards doctrine, and none of the faithful have ever rejected them." This important declaration, handed down to us by Œcolampadius, characterizes the reformed theology.[2]

"But you teach," resumed Melancthon, "like Thomas Munzer, that the Holy Ghost acts quite alone, independently of the sacraments and of the Word of God." "The Holy Ghost," replied Zwingle, "works in us justification by the Word, but by the Word preached and understood, by the soul and the marrow of the Word, by the mind and will of God clothed in human language."[3]

"At least," continued Melancthon, "you deny original sin, and make sin consist only in actual and external works, like the Pelagians, the philosophers, and the Papists." This was the principal difficulty. "Since man naturally loves himself," replied Zwingle, "instead of loving God; in that there is a crime, a sin that condemns him."[4] He had more than once before expressed the same opinion;[5] and yet Melancthon exulted on hearing him: "Our adversaries," said he afterwards, "have given way on all these points!"

Luther had pursued the same method with Œcolampadius, as Melancthon with Zwingle. The discussion had in particular turned on baptism. Luther complained that the Swiss would not acknowledge that by this simple sacrament a man became a member of the Church. "It is true," said Œcolampadius, "that we require faith—either an actual or a future faith. Why should we deny it? Who is a Christian, if it be not he who believes in Christ? However, I should be unwilling to deny that the water of baptism is, in a certain sense, a water of regeneration; for by it he, whom the Church knew not, becomes its child."[6]

These four theologians were in the very heat of their discussions, when domestics came to inform them that the prince's dinner was on the table. They immediately arose, and Zwingle and Melancthon meeting Luther and Œcolampadius, who were also quitting their chamber, the latter approached Zwingle, and whispered mournfully in his ear: "I have fallen a second time into the hands of Dr. Eck."[7] In the language of the reformers nothing stronger could be said.

It does not appear that the conference

---

[1] Excepit in arce hospitio et mensa regali. Corp. Ref. i. 1096.
[2] Subridens aliquantulum respondit: *tu es nequam et nebulo.* Sculteti Annal. ad. 1529.
[3] State Papers of Cassel.
[4] Abgetheilt zu den rühren. Bull. ii. 225.

[1] Ubi unquam concilia rejicimus, verbi divini auctoritati suffulta? Zw. Opp. iv. 191.
[2] The word *Reformed* is used to distinguish the doctrine and the church of Zwingle and Calvin from those of Luther
[3] Mens et medulla verbi, mens et voluntas Dei amicta tamen humanis verbis. Zw. Epp. iv. 173.
[4] Malum, peccatum. Ibid. 172.
[5] De peccato originali ad Urb. Rhegium. Ibid. iii. 632.
[6] Atque adeo ipse non negarim, aquam baptismi esse aquam regenerantem: fit enim puer ecclesiæ, qui dudum ab ecclesia non agnoscebatur. Zw. Opp. iv. 193.
[7] Lutherum Œcolampadem ita excepit, ut ad me veniens clam queratur, se denuo in Eccium incidisse. Zw. Epp. ii. 369.

between Luther and Œcolampadius was resumed after dinner. Luther's manner held out very little hope; but Melancthon and Zwingle returned to the discussion, and the Zurich doctor finding the Wittemberg professor escape him like an eel, as he said, and take " like Proteus a thousand different forms," seized a pen in order to fix his antagonist. Zwingle committed to writing whatever Melancthon dictated, and then wrote his reply, giving it to the other to read.[1] In this manner they spent six hours, three in the morning and three in the afternoon.[2] They prepared for the general conference.

Zwingle requested that it should be an open one; this Luther resisted. It was eventually resolved that the princes, nobles, deputies, and theologians, should be admitted; but a great crowd of citizens, and even many scholars and gentlemen, who had come from Frankfort, from the Rhine districts, from Strasburg, from Basle and other Swiss towns, were excluded. Brentz speaks of fifty or sixty hearers; Zwingle of twenty-four only.[3]

On a gentle elevation, watered by the Lahn, is situated an old castle, overlooking the city of Marburg; in the distance may be seen the beautiful valley of the Lahn, and beyond the mountain-tops rising one above another, until they are lost in the horizon. It was beneath the vaults and Gothic arches of an antique chamber in this castle, known as the Knight's Hall, that the conference was to take place.

On Saturday morning (2d October) the landgrave took his seat in the hall, surrounded by his court, but in so plain a dress that no one would have taken him for a prince. He wished to avoid all appearance of acting the part of a Constantine in the affairs of the Church. Before him was a table which Luther, Zwingle, Melancthon, and Œcolampadius approached. Luther, taking a piece of chalk, bent over the velvet cloth which covered it, and steadily wrote four words in large characters. All eyes followed the movement of his hand, and soon they read Hoc EST CORPUS MEUM.[4] Luther wished to have this declaration continually before him, that it might strengthen his own faith, and be a sign to his adversaries.

Behind these four theologians were seated their friends,—Hedio, Sturm, Funck, Frey, Eberhard, Than, Jonas, Cruciger, and others besides. Jonas cast an inquiring glance upon the Swiss: " Zwingle," said he, " has a certain rusticity and arrogance;[5] if he is

well versed in letters, it is in spite of Minerva and of the muses. In Œcolampadius there is a natural goodness and admirable meekness. Hedio seems to have as much liberality as kindness; but Bucer possesses the cunning of a fox, that knows how to give himself an air of sense and prudence." Men of moderate sentiments often meet with worse treatment than those of the extreme parties.

Other feelings animated those who contemplated this assembly from a distance. The great men who had led the people in their footsteps on the plains of Saxony, on the banks of the Rhine, and in the lofty valleys of Switzerland, were there met face to face: the chiefs of that part of Christendom which had separated from Rome, were come together to see if they could remain one. Accordingly, from all parts of Germany, prayers and anxious looks were directed towards Marburg. " Illustrious princes of the Word,"[1] cried the evangelical Church through the mouth of the poet Cordus, " penetrating Luther, mild Œcolampadius, magnanimous Zwingle, pious Snepf, eloquent Melancthon, courageous Bucer, candid Hedio, excellent Osiander, valiant Brentz, amiable Jonas, fiery Craton, Mænus, whose soul is stronger than his body, great Dionysius, and you Myconius—all you whom Prince Philip, that illustrious hero, has summoned, ministers and bishops, whom the christian cities have sent to terminate the schism, and to show us the way of truth; the suppliant Church falls weeping at your feet, and begs you by the bowels of Jesus Christ to bring this matter to a happy issue, that the world may acknowledge in your resolution the work of the Holy Ghost himself."[2]

The landgrave's chancellor, John Feige, having reminded them in the prince's name that the object of this colloquy was the re-establishment of union, " I protest," said Luther, " that I differ from my adversaries with regard to the doctrine of the Lord's Supper, and that I shall always differ from them. Christ has said, *This is my body*. Let them show me that a body is not a body. I reject reason, common sense, carnal arguments, and mathematical proofs. God is above mathematics.[3] We have the Word of God; we must adore it and perform it!"

" It cannot be denied, said Œcolampadius, " that there are figures of speech in the Word of God; as *John is Elias, the rock was Christ, I am the vine*. The expression *This is my body*, is a figure of the same kind." Luther granted that there were figures in the Bible, but denied that this last expression was figurative.

All the various parties, however, of which the Christian Church is composed, see a

---

[1] At Melancthon, cum nimis lubricus esset et Protei in morem se in omnia transformaret, me compulit, ut sumpto calamo manu armarem. Zw. Epp. ii. 369.
[2] Istud colloquium sex in horas traximus. Ibid. 370.
[3] Quinquaginta aut sexaginta colloquio præsentes. Zw. Opp. iv. 201. Pauci arbitri ad summum quatuor et viginti. Epp. ii. 370.
[4] This is my body. Zw. Opp. iv. 175.
[5] In Zwinglio agreste quiddam est et arrogantulum. Corp. Ref. i. p. 1097.

[1] Insignes verbi proceres. Bull. ii. 236.
[2] Et cupido supplex vobis Ecclesia voto Vestros cadit flens ad pedes. Ibid.
[3] Deum esse supra mathematicam. Zw. Opp. iv. 176.

figure in these words. In fact, the Romanists declare that *This is my body* signifies not only "my body," but also "my blood," "my soul," and even "my Divinity," and "Christ wholly."[1] These words, therefore, according to Rome, are a synecdoche, a figure by which a part is taken for the whole. And, as regards the Lutherans, the figure is still more evident.[2] Whether it be synecdoche, metaphor, or metonymy, there is still a figure.

In order to prove it, Œcolampadius employed this syllogism :—

"What Christ rejected in the sixth chapter of St. John, he could not admit in the words of the Eucharist.

"Now Christ, who said to the people of Capernaum, *The flesh profiteth nothing*, rejected by those very words the oral manducation of his body.

"Therefore he did not establish it at the institution of his Supper."

LUTHER.—"I deny the minor (the second of these propositions) ; Christ has not rejected all oral manducation, but only a material manducation, like that of the flesh of oxen or of swine."[3]

ŒCOLAMPADIUS.—"There is danger in attributing too much to mere matter."

LUTHER.—"Every thing that God commands becomes spirit and life. If we lift up a straw, by the Lord's order, in that very action we perform a spiritual work. We must pay attention to him who speaks, and not to what he says. God speaks: Men, worms, listen !—God commands : let the world obey ! and let us all together fall down and humbly kiss the Word."[4]

ŒCOLAMPADIUS.—"But since we have the spiritual eating, what need of the bodily one ?"

LUTHER.—"I do not ask what need we have of it ; but I see it written, *Eat, this is my body*. We must therefore believe and do. We must do—we must do![5]—If God should order me to eat dung, I would do it, with the assurance that it would be salutary."[6]

At this point Zwingle interfered in the discussion.

"We must explain Scripture by Scripture," said he. "We cannot admit two kinds of corporeal manducation, as if Jesus had spoken of eating, and the Capernaites of tearing in pieces, for the same word is employed in both cases. Jesus says that to eat his flesh corporeally profiteth nothing (John vi. 63) ; whence it would result that he had given us in the Supper a thing that would be useless to us.—Besides, there are

certain words that seem to me rather childish,—the dung, for instance. The oracles of the demons were obscure, not so are those of Jesus Christ."

LUTHER.—"When Christ says the flesh profiteth nothing, he speaks not of his own flesh, but of ours."

ZWINGLE. — "The soul is fed with the Spirit and not with the flesh."

LUTHER.—"It is with the mouth that we eat the body ; the soul does not eat it."[1]

ZWINGLE.—"Christ's body is therefore a corporeal nourishment, and not a spiritual."

LUTHER.—"You are captious."

ZWINGLE—"Not so ; but you utter contradictory things."

LUTHER.—"If God should present me wild apples, I should eat them spiritually. In the Eucharist, the mouth receives the body of Christ, and the soul believes in his words."

Zwingle then quoted a great number of passages from the Holy Scriptures, in which the sign is described by the very thing signified ; and thence concluded that, considering our Lord's declaration in St. John, *The flesh profiteth nothing*, we must explain the words of the Eucharist in a similar manner.

Many hearers were struck by these arguments. Among the Marburg professors sat the Frenchman Lambert ; his tall and spare frame was violently agitated. He had been at first of Luther's opinion,[2] and was then hesitating between the two reformers. As he went to the conference, he said : "I desire to be a sheet of blank paper, on which the finger of God may write his truth." Erelong he exclaimed, after hearing Zwingle and Œcolampadius : "Yes ! the Spirit, 'tis that which vivifies !"[3] When this conversion was known, the Wittembergers, shrugging their shoulders, called it "Gallic fickleness." "What !" replied Lambert, "was St. Paul fickle because he was converted from Pharasaism ? And have we ourselves been fickle in abandoning the lost sects of popery ?"

Luther was, however, by no means shaken. "*This is my body*," repeated he, pointing with his finger to the words written before him. "*This is my body*. The devil himself shall not drive me from that. To seek to understand it, is to fall away from the faith."[4]

"But, doctor," said Zwingle, "St. John explains how Christ's body is eaten, and you will be obliged at last to leave off singing always the same song."

"You make use of unmannerly expressions," replied Luther.[5] The Wittembergers themselves called Zwingle's argument "his old song."[6] Zwingle continued without be-

---

[1] If any one denies that the body and blood of our Saviour Jesus Christ, with his soul and his divinity, and consequently the whole Jesus Christ (totum Christum), is contained in the sacrament of the Eucharist, let him be anathema. Council of Trent, sess. 13.
[2] Tota Christi persona. Form. concord. viii.
[3] Qualis est carnis bovillæ aut suillæ. Scult. p. 217.
[4] Quum præcipit quid, pareat mundus ; et omnes osculemur verbum. Zw. Opp. iv. 176.
[5] *Man mus es thun* sæpe inculcabat. Ibid.
[6] Si juberet fimum comedere, facerem. Ibid.

[1] Anima non edit ipsum (corpus) corporaliter. Zw. Epp. ii. 370.
[2] See his commentary on St. Luke xxii. 19, 20.
[3] He added, that the body of Christ was in the Eucharist neither mathematically or commensurably, nor really (neque mathematice nec commensurative, neque re ipsa). Epist. Lamb. de Marb. col.
[4] Si interrogo, excido a fide. Zw. Epp. ii. 177.
[5] Invidiose loqueris. Bull. ii. 228.
[6] Veterem suam cantilenam. Zw. Opp. iv. 221.

ing disconcerted: " I ask you, doctor, whether Christ in the sixth chapter of St. John did not wish to reply to the question that had been put to him?"

LUTHER.—" Master Zwingle, you wish to stop my mouth by the arrogancy of your language. That passage has nothing to do here."

ZWINGLE, *hastily.*—" Pardon me, doctor, that passage breaks your neck."

LUTHER.—" Do not boast so much! You are in Hesse, and not in Switzerland. In this country we do not break people's necks."

Then turning towards his friends, Luther complained bitterly of Zwingle; as if the latter had really wished to break his neck. " He makes use of camp terms and blood-stained words," said he.[1] Luther forgot that he had employed a similar expression in speaking of Carlstadt.

ZWINGLE resumed: " In Switzerland also there is strict justice, and we break no man's neck without trial. That expression signifies merely that your cause is lost and hopeless."

Great agitation prevailed in the Knight's Hall. The roughness of the Swiss and the obstinacy of the Saxon had come into collision. The landgrave, fearing to behold the failure of his project of conciliation, nodded assent to Zwingle's explanation. " Doctor," said he to Luther, " you should not be offended at such common expressions." It was in vain: the agitated sea could not again be calmed. The prince, therefore, arose, and they all repaired to the banqueting hall. After dinner they resumed their tasks.

" I believe," said Luther, " that Christ's body is in heaven, but I also believe that it is in the sacrament. It concerns me little whether it be against nature, provided that it be not against faith.[2] Christ is substantially in the sacrament, such as he was born of the Virgin."

ŒCOLAMPADIUS, *quoting a passage from St. Paul*: " We know not Jesus Christ after the flesh."[3]

LUTHER.—" After the flesh means, in this passage, after our carnal affections."[4]

ŒCOLAMPADIUS.—" You will not allow that there is a metaphor in these words, *This is my body*, and yet you admit a synecdoche."

LUTHER.—" Metaphor permits the existence of a sign only; but it is not so with synecdoche. If a man says he wishes to drink a bottle, we understand that he means the beer in the bottle. Christ's body is in the bread, as a sword in the scabbard,[5] or as the Holy Ghost in the dove."

The discussion was proceeding in this manner, when Osiander, pastor of Nurem-

berg, Stephen Agricola, pastor of Augsburg, and Brentz, pastor of Halle in Swabia, author of the famous Syngramma, entered the hall. These also had been invited by the landgrave. But Brentz, to whom Luther had written that he should take care not to appear, had no doubt by his indecision retarded his own departure as well as that of his friends. Places were assigned them near Luther and Melancthon. " Listen, and speak if necessary," they were told. They took but little advantage of this permission. " All of us, except Luther," said Melancthon, " were silent personages."[1]

The struggle continued.

When Zwingle saw that exegesis was not sufficient for Luther, he added dogmatical theology to it, and, subsidiarily, natural philosophy.

" I oppose you," said he, " with this article of our faith: *Ascendit in cœlum*—he ascended into heaven. If Christ is in heaven, as regards his body, how can he be in the bread? The Word of God teaches us that he was like his brethren in all things (Heb. ii. 17). He therefore cannot be in several places at once."

LUTHER.—" Were I desirous of reasoning thus, I would undertake to prove that Jesus Christ had a wife; that he had black eyes,[2] and lived in our good country of Germany.[3] I care little about mathematics."

" There is no question of mathematics here," said Zwingle, " but of St. Paul, who writes to the Philippians, μοϱφὴν δούλου λαβὼν."[4]

LUTHER, *interrupting him.*—" Read it to us in Latin or in German, not in Greek."

ZWINGLE (*in Latin*).—" Pardon me: for twelve years past I have made use of the Greek Testament only." Then continuing to read the passage, he concluded from it, that Christ's humanity is of a finite nature like our own.

LUTHER, *pointing to the words written before him.*—" Most dear sirs, since my Lord Jesus Christ says, *Hoc est corpus meum*, I believe that his body is really there."

Here the scene grew animated. Zwingle started from his chair, sprung towards Luther, and said, striking the table before him:[5]

" You maintain then, doctor, that Christ's body is locally in the Eucharist; for you say Christ's body is really *there—there—there*," repeated Zwingle. " *There* is an adverb of place.[6] Christ's body is then of such a nature as to exist in a place. If it is in a place, it is in heaven, whence it follows that it is not in the bread."

---

[1] Verbum istud, tanquam castrense et cruentum. Hospin. p. 131.
[2] Non curo quod sit contra naturam, modo non contra fidem. Zw. Opp. iv. 178.
[3] 2 Cor. v. 16.
[4] Pro carnalibus affectibus. Zw. Opp. iv. p. 202.
[5] Corpus est in pane sicut gladius in vagina. Ibid.

[1] Fuimus κῶφα πϱόσωπα. Corp. Ref. i. 1098.
[2] Quod uxorem et nigros oculos habuisset. Scultet. p. 225.
[3] In Germania diuturnum contubernium egisse. Zw. Opp. iv. 202.
[4] Having taken the form of a servant. Phil. ii. 7.
[5] Ibi Zwinglius illico prosiliens. Scultet. p. 225.
[6] Da, da, da. *Ibi* est adverbium loci. Ibid.

LUTHER.—" I repeat that I have nothing to do with mathematical proofs. As soon as the words of consecration are pronounced over the bread, the body is there, however wicked be the priest who pronounces them."

ZWINGLE.—" You are thus re-establishing Popery."[1]

LUTHER.—" This is not done through the priest's merits, but because of Christ's ordinance. I will not, when Christ's body is in question, hear speak of a particular place. I absolutely will not."

ZWINGLE.—" Must every thing, then, exist precisely as you will it?"

The landgrave perceived that the discussion was growing hot; and as the repast was waiting, he broke off the contest.[2]

The conference was continued on the next day, Sunday, the 3d October, perhaps because of an epidemic (the Sweating Sickness) that had just broken out at Marburg, and which did not allow any great prolongation of the colloquy. Luther, returning to the discussion of the previous evening, said:

" Christ's body is in the sacrament, but it is not there as in a place."

ZWINGLE.—" Then it is not there at all."

LUTHER.—" Sophists say, that a body may very well be in several places at once. The universe is a body, and yet we cannot assert that it is in a particular place."

ZWINGLE.—" Ah! you speak of sophists, doctor; are you really after all obliged to return to the onions and fleshpots of Egypt?[3] As for what you say, that the universe is in no particular place, I beg all intelligent men to weigh this proof." Then Zwingle, who, whatever Luther may have said, had more than one arrow in his quiver, after establishing his proposition by exegesis and philosophy, resolved on confirming it by the testimony of the Fathers of the Church.

" Listen," said he, " to what Fulgentius, bishop of Ruspa, in Numidia, said, in the fifth century, to Trasamond, king of the Vandals: " The Son of God took the attributes of true humanity, and did not lose those of true divinity. Born in time, according to his mother, he lives in eternity according to the divinity that he holds from the Father: coming from man, he is man, and consequently in a place; proceeding from the Father, he is God, and consequently present in every place. According to his human nature, he was absent from heaven while he was upon earth, and quitted the earth when he ascended into heaven; but, according to his divine nature, he remained in heaven, when he came down thence, and did not abandon the earth when he returned thither."[4]

But Luther still replied: " It is written,

This is my body." Zwingle, becoming impatient, said, " All that is idle wrangling. An obstinate disputant might also maintain this expression of our Saviour to his mother, *Behold thy son,* pointing to St. John. Vain would be every explanation, he would continue crying No, no! He said *Ecce filius tuus.* Behold thy son, behold thy son! Listen to new testimony; it is from the great Augustine: ' Let us not think,' says he, ' that Christ, according to his human form, is present in every place; let us beware, in our endeavour to establish his divinity, of taking away his truth from his body. Christ is now every where present, like God; and yet, in consequence of his real body, he is in a definite part of heaven."[1]

" St. Augustine," replied Luther, " is not here speaking of the Eucharist. Christ's body is not in the Eucharist, as in a place."

Œcolampadius saw that he might take advantage of this assertion of Luther's. " The body of Christ," said he, " is not locally in the Eucharist, therefore no real body is there; for every one knows that the essence of a body is its existence in a place."

Here finished the morning's discussion.

Œcolampadius, upon reflection, felt convinced that Luther's assertion might be looked upon as an approximation. " I remember," said he after dinner, " that the doctor conceded this morning, that Christ's body was not in the sacrament as in a place. Let us therefore inquire amicably what is the nature of Christ's bodily presence."

" You will not make me take a step further," exclaimed Luther, who saw where they wished to drag him; " you have Fulgentius and Augustine on your side, but all the other Fathers are on ours."

Œcolampadius, who seemed to the Wittembergers to be vexatiously precise,[2] then said, " Name these doctors. We will take upon ourselves to prove that they are of our opinion."

" We will not name them to you,"[3] said Luther. " It was in his youth," added he, " that Augustine wrote what you have quoted; and, besides, he is an obscure author." Then, retreating to the ground which he had resolved never to quit, he was no longer content to point his finger at the inscription, *Hoc est corpus meum,* but seized the velvet cover on which the words were written, tore it off the table, held it up in front of Zwingle and Œcolampadius, and placing it before their eyes,[4] " See!" said he, " see! This is our text: you have not yet driven us from it, as you had boasted, and we care for no other proofs."

---

1 Damit richtend ir das papstum uf. Zw. Opp. iii. 57.
2 Cœna instabat et diremit certamen. Ibid. iv. 179.
3 Ad cæpas et ollas Ægyptiacas. Ibid. ii. part 3, 57.
4 Secundum humanam substantiam, absens cœlo, cum esset in terra, et derelinquens terram cum ascendisset in cœlum. Fulgentius to King Trasamond, lib. ii.

1 In loco aliquo cœli propter veri corporis modum. Aug. Ep. p. 57.
2 Quem omnes sperassemus mitiorem, interdum videbatur paulo moro sior, sed citra contumeliam. Zw. Opp. iv. 201.
3 Non nominabimus illos. Scultet. p. 228.
4 Da hub Luther die Sammatendeck auf, und Zeigt ihm den Spruch, den er mit kreyden hett für sich geschrieben Oslander; Niederer's Nachrichten. ii. 114

"If this be the case," said Œcolampadius, "we had better leave off the discussion. But I will first declare, that, if we quote the Fathers, it is only to free our doctrine from the reproach of novelty, and not to support our cause by their authority." No better definition can be given of the legitimate use of the doctors of the Church.

There was no reason, in fact, for prolonging the conference. "As Luther was of an intractable and imperious disposition," says one of those papists whom Melancthon wished to be judges, "he did not cease from calling upon the Swiss to submit simply to his opinion."[1]

The chancellor, alarmed at such a termination of the colloquy, exhorted the theologians to come to some understanding. "I know but one means for that," said Luther; "and this it is: Let our adversaries believe as we do." "We cannot," answered the Swiss. "Well then," rejoined Luther, "I abandon you to God's judgment, and pray that he will enlighten you." "We will do the same," added Œcolampadius.

While these words were passing, Zwingle sat silent, motionless, and deeply moved; and the liveliness of his affections, of which he had given more than one proof during the conference, was then manifested in a very different manner. He burst into tears in the presence of all.

The conference was ended. It had been in reality more tranquil than the documents seem to show, or perhaps the chroniclers appreciated such matters differently from ourselves. "With the exception of a few sallies, all had passed off quietly, in a courteous manner, and with very great gentleness," says an eye-witness.[2] "During the colloquy no other words than these were heard: 'Sir, and very dear friend, your charity,' or other similar expressions. Not a word of schism or of heresy. It might have been said that Luther and Zwingle were brothers, and not adversaries."[3] This is the testimony of Brentz. But these flowers concealed an abyss, and Jonas, also an eye-witness, styles the conference "a very sharp contest."[4]

The contagion that had suddenly broken out in Marburg was creating frightful ravages, and filling everybody with alarm.[5] All were anxious to leave the city. "Sirs," remarked the landgrave, "you cannot separate thus." And desirous of giving the doctors an opportunity of meeting one another with minds unoccupied by theological debates, he invited them to his table. This was Sunday night.

Philip of Hesse had all along shown the most constant attention, and each one ima-

gined him to be on his side. "I would rather place my trust in the simple words of Christ than in the subtle thoughts of man," was a remark he made, according to Jonas:[1] but Zwingle affirmed that this prince entertained the same opinions as himself, although with regard to certain persons he dissembled the change. Luther, sensible of the weakness of his defence as to the declarations of the Fathers, transmitted a note to Philip, in which several passages were pointed out from Hilary, Chrysostom, Cyprian, Irenæus, and Ambrose, which he thought were in his favour.

The time of departure drew near, and nothing had been done. The landgrave toiled earnestly at the union, as Luther wrote to his wife.[2] He invited the theologians one after another into his closet;[3] he pressed, entreated, warned, exhorted, and conjured them. "Think," said he, "of the salvation of the christian republic, and remove all discord from its bosom."[4] Never had general at the head of an army taken such pains to win a battle.

A final meeting took place, and undoubtedly the Church has seldom witnessed one of greater solemnity. Luther and Zwingle, Saxony and Switzerland, met for the last time. The sweating sickness was carrying off men around them by thousands;[5] Charles the Fifth and the pope were uniting in Italy; Ferdinand and the Roman-catholic princes were preparing to tear the Protest of Spires in pieces; the thunder-cloud became more threatening every day; union alone seemed capable of saving the Protestants, and the hour of departure was about to strike —an hour that would separate them perhaps for ever.

"Let us confess our union in all things in which we agree," said Zwingle; "and as for the rest, let us remember that we are brothers. There will never be peace between the churches, if, while we maintain the grand doctrine of salvation by faith, we cannot differ on secondary points."[6] Such is, in fact, the true principle of christian union. The sixteenth century was still too deeply sunk in scholasticism to understand this: let us hope that the nineteenth century will comprehend it better.

"Yes, yes!" exclaimed the landgrave; "you agree! Give then a testimony of your unity, and recognise one another as brothers." —"There is no one upon earth with whom I more earnestly desire to be united, than with you," said Zwingle, approaching the

---

[1] Maimbourg in Seck. p. 136.
[2] Omnia humanissime et summa cum mansuetudine transigebantur. Zw. Opp. iv. 201.
[3] Amicissime Domine, Vestra charitas, et id genus...... Dixisses Lutherum et Zwinglium non adversarios. Ibid.
[4] Acerrimo certamine. Corp. Ref. i. 1096.
[5] Nisi *Sudor Anglicus* subito Marburgum invasisset et terrore omnium animos percutisset. Hospin. p. 131.

[1] Dicitur palam proclamasse. Corp. Ref. p. 1097.
[2] Da arbeit der Landgraf heftig. L. Epp. iii. 512.
[3] Unumquemque nostrum seorsim absque arbitris. Zw. Opp. iv. 203.
[4] Compellans, rogans, monens, exhortans, postulans ut Reipublicæ Christianæ rationem haberemus, et discordiam e medio tolleremus. Ibid.,
[5] Multa perierunt millia. Hospin. p. 131.
[6] Quod nulla unquam Ecclesiarum pax constituta sit, si non in multis aliis dissentiendi a se facultatem faciant. Scultet. p. 207.

Wittemberg doctors.[1] Œcolampadius, Bucer, and Hedio said the same.

"Acknowledge them! acknowledge them as brothers!" continued the landgrave.[2] Their hearts were moved; they were on the eve of unity: Zwingle, bursting into tears, in the presence of the prince, the courtiers, and divines (it is Luther himself who records this),[3] approached Luther, and held out his hand. The two families of the Reformation were about to be united: long quarrels were about to be stifled in their cradle; but Luther rejected the hand that was offered him: "You have a different spirit from ours," said he. These words communicated to the Swiss, as it were, an electric shock. Their hearts sunk each time Luther repeated them, and he did so frequently. He himself is our informant.

A brief consultation took place among the Wittemberg doctors. Luther, Melancthon, Agricola, Brentz, Jonas, and Osiander conferred together. Convinced that their peculiar doctrine on the eucharist was essential to salvation, they considered all those who rejected it as without the pale of the faith. "What folly!"[4] said Melancthon, who afterwards nearly coincided with Zwingle's sentiments; "they condemn us, and yet they desire we should consider them as our brothers!" "What versatility!" added Brentz: "they accused us but lately of worshipping a bread-god, and they now ask for communion with us!"[5] Then, turning towards Zwingle and his friends, the Wittembergers said: "You do not belong to the communion of the Christian Church; we cannot acknowledge you as brethren!"[6]

The Swiss were far from partaking of this sectarian spirit. "We think," said Bucer, "that your doctrine strikes at the glory of Jesus Christ, who now reigns at the right hand of the Father. But seeing that in all things you acknowledge your dependence on the Lord, we look at your conscience, which compels you to receive the doctrine you profess, and we do not doubt that you belong to Christ."

"And we," said Luther—"we declare to you once more that our conscience opposes our receiving you as brethren."—"If such is the case,' replied Bucer, "it would be folly to ask it."

"I am exceedingly astonished that you wish to consider me as your brother," pursued Luther. "It shows clearly that you do not attach much importance to your own doctrine."

"Take your choice," said Bucer, proposing a dilemma to the reformer: "either you should not acknowledge as brethren those who differ from you in any point—and if so, you will not find a single brother in your own ranks[1]—or else you will receive some of those who differ from you, and then you ought to receive us."

The Swiss had exhausted their solicitations. "We are conscious," said they, "of having acted as if in the presence of God. Posterity will be our witness."[2] They were on the point of retiring: Luther remained like a rock, to the landgrave's great indignation.[3] The Hessian divines, Kraft, Lambert, Snepf, Lonicer, and Melander, united their exertions to those of the prince.

Luther was staggered, and conferred anew with his colleagues. "Let us beware," said he to his friends, "of wiping our noses too roughly, lest blood should come."[4]

Then turning to Zwingle and Œcolampadius, they said: "We acknowledge you as friends; we do not consider you as brothers and members of Christ's Church.[5] But we do not exclude you from that universal charity which we owe even to our enemies."[6]

The hearts of Zwingle, Œcolampadius, and Bucer, were ready to burst,[7] for this concession was almost a new insult. "Let us carefully avoid all harsh and violent words and writings," said they; "and let each one defend himself without railing."[8]

Luther then advanced towards the Swiss, and said: "We consent, and I offer you the hand of peace and charity." The Swiss rushed in great emotion towards the Wittembergers, and all shook hands.[9] Luther himself was softened: christian charity resumed her rights in his heart. "Assuredly," said he, "a great portion of the scandal is taken away by the suppression of our fierce debates; we could not have hoped for so much. May Christ's hand remove the last obstacle that separates us.[10] There is now a friendly concord between us, and if we persevere in prayer, brotherhood will come."

It was desirable to confirm this important result by a report. "We must let the christian world know," said the landgrave, "that, except the manner of the presence of the body and blood in the eucharist, you are agreed in all the articles of faith."[11] This was resolved on; but who should be charged with drawing up the paper? All eyes were turned upon Luther. The Swiss themselves appealed to his impartiality.

1 Nemo alteri vel inter ipsos frater erit. Zw. Opp. iv. 194.
2 Id testabitur posteritas. Ibid.
3 Principi illud durum videbatur. Ibid. 203.
4 Ne nimis mungendo, sanguinem eliceremus. L. Epp. in his letter written to Gerbellius on the same day—Monday.
5 Agnoscere quidem velimus tanquam amicos, sed non tanquam fratres. Zw. Opp. iv. 203.
6 Charitate quæ etiam hosti debetur. Ibid. 190.
7 Indignissime affecti sunt. Ibid.
8 Quisque suam sententiam doceat absque invectivis. L. Epp. iii. 514.
9 Dedimus tamen manus pacis et caritatis. Ibid. 513.
10 Utinam et ille reliquus scrupulus per Christum tandem tollatur,—in his letter written to Gerbellius after leaving this meeting.
11 Ut orbi Christiano notum fieret eos in omnibus fidei capitibus consentire. Hospin. p. 127.

1 Es werendt keine lüth uff Erden. Bull. ii. 225.
2 Idque Princeps valde urgebat. L. Epp. iii. 513.
3 Zwinglius palam lacrymans coram Langravio et omnibus. Hospin. p. 136.
4 Vide eorum stultitiam! Corp. Ref. i. 1108.
5 Nos tanquam adoratores panifici Dei traduxerant. Zw. Opp. iv. 203.
6 Eos a communione Ecclesiæ Christianæ alienos esse. Ibid.

Luther retired to his closet, lost in thought, uneasy, and finding the task very difficult. "On the one hand," said he, "I should like to spare their weakness;[1] but, on the other, I would not in the least degree strike at the holy doctrine of Christ." He did not know how to set about it, and his anguish increased. He got free at last. "I will draw up the articles," said he, "in the most accurate manner. Do I not know that whatever I may write, they will never sign them?"[2] Erelong fifteen articles were committed to paper, and Luther, holding them in his hand, repaired to the theologians of the two parties.

These articles are of importance. The two doctrines that were evolved in Switzerland and in Saxony, independently of each other, were brought together and compared. If they were of man, there would be found in them a servile uniformity, or a remarkable opposition. This was not the case. A great unity was found between the German and the Swiss Reformations, for they both proceeded from the same Divine teaching; and a diversity on secondary points, for it was by man's instrumentality that God had effected them.

Luther took his paper, and reading the first article, said:

"First, we believe that there is one sole, true, and natural God, creator of heaven and earth, and of all creatures; and that this same God, one in essence and in nature, is threefold in person, that is to say, Father, Son, and Holy Ghost, as was declared in the Nicene Council, and as all the Christian Church professes."

To this the Swiss gave their assent.

They were agreed also on the divinity and humanity of Jesus Christ; on his death and resurrection, on original sin, justification by faith, the operation of the Holy Ghost and of the Word of God, baptism, good works, confession, civil order, and tradition.

Thus far all were united. The Wittembergers could not recover from their astonishment.[3] The two parties had rejected, on the one hand, the errors of the papists, who make religion little more than an outward form; and, on the other, those of the Enthusiasts, who speak exclusively of internal feelings; and they were found drawn up under the same banners between these two camps. But the moment was come that would separate them. Luther had kept till the last the article on the Eucharist.

The reformer resumed:

"We all believe with regard to the Lord's Supper, that it ought to be celebrated in both kinds, according to the primitive institution; that the mass is not a work by which a Christian obtains pardon for another man,

whether dead or alive; that the sacrament of the altar is the sacrament of the very body and very blood of Jesus Christ; and that the spiritual manducation of this body and blood is specially necessary to every true Christian."[1]

It was now the turn of the Swiss to be astonished. Luther continued:

"In like manner, as to the use of the sacrament, we are agreed that, like the Word, it was ordained of Almighty God, in order that weak consciences might be excited by the Holy Ghost to faith and charity."

The joy of the Swiss was redoubled. Luther continued: "And although at present we are not agreed on the question whether the real body and blood of Christ are corporeally present in the bread and wine, yet both the interested parties shall cherish more and more a truly christian charity for one another, so far as conscience permits; and we will all earnestly implore the Lord to condescend by his Spirit to confirm us in the sound doctrine."[2]

The Swiss obtained what they had asked: unity in diversity. It was immediately resolved to hold a solemn meeting for the signature of the articles.

They were read over again. Œcolampadius, Zwingle, Bucer, and Hedio, signed them first on one copy; while Luther, Melancthon, Jonas, Osiander, Brentz, and Agricola, wrote their names on the other; both parties then subscribed the copy of their adversaries, and this important document was sent to the press.[3]

Thus the Reformation had made a sensible step at Marburg. The opinion of Zwingle on the spiritual presence, and of Luther on the bodily presence, are both found in christian antiquity; but the two extreme doctrines have always been rejected: that of the Rationalists, on the one hand, who behold in the Eucharist nothing but a simple commemoration; and of the Papists, on the other, who adore in it a transubstantiation. These are both errors; while the doctrines of Luther and Zwingle, and the medium taken by Calvin, already maintained by some of the Fathers, were considered in ancient times as different views of the same truth. If Luther had yielded, it might have been feared that the Church would fall into the extreme of rationalism; if Zwingle, that it would rush into the extreme of popery. It is a salutary thing for the Church that these different views should be entertained; but it is a pernicious thing for individuals to attach themselves to one of them in such a manner as to

---

[1] Het gern ihrer Schwachheit verschont. Niederer Nachr. ll. 120.
[2] Doch zuletz sprach er Ich will die artikel auf aller pesste stellen, sy werdens doch nicht annemen. Ibid.
[3] Quod mirari non satis potuimus. Brentius. Zw. Opp. w. 203.

[1] Quod spiritualis manducatio hujus corporis et sanguinis unicuique Christiano præcipue necessaria sit. Scultet. p. 232.
[2] Osiander (a Lutheran) employs the accusative, "in den rechten Verstand," which would indicate a movement towards an object that we do not possess; Bullinger and Scultet (both Reformed divines) have the dative.
[3] Bullinger and others indicate the 3d October as the day on which the articles were signed; Osiander, an eye-witness, and whose narrative is very exact, says it was the 4th, which agrees with all the other data.

anathematize the other. "There is only this little stumbling-block," wrote Melancthon, "that embarrasses the Church of our Lord."[1]

All,—Romanists and Evangelicals, Saxons and Swiss,—admitted the presence, and even the real presence of Christ; but here was the essential point of separation: Is this presence effected by the faith of the communicant, or by the *opus operatum* of the priest? The germs of Popery, Sacerdotalism, and Puseyism, are inevitably contained in this latter thesis. If it is maintained that a wicked priest (as has been said) operates this real presence of Christ by three words, we enter the church of the pope. Luther appeared sometimes to admit this doctrine, but he has often spoken in a more spiritual manner; and taking this great man in his best moments, we behold merely an essential unity and a secondary diversity in the two parties of the Reformation. Undoubtedly the Lord has left his Church outward seals of his grace; but he has not attached salvation to these signs. The essential point is the connexion of the faithful with the Word, with the Holy Ghost, with the Head of the Church. This is the great truth which the Swiss Reform proclaims, and which Lutheranism itself recognises. After the Marburg conference, the controversy became more moderate.

There was another advantage. The evangelical divines at Marburg marked with one accord their separation from the Papacy. Zwingle was not without fears (unfounded, no doubt) with regard to Luther: these fears were dispersed. "Now that we are agreed," said he, "the Papists will no longer hope that Luther will ever be one of them."[2] The Marburg articles were the first bulwark erected in common by the reformers against Rome.

It was not, then, in vain that, after the Protest of Spires, Philip of Hesse endeavoured, at Marburg, to bring together the friends of the Gospel. But, if the religious object was partially attained, the political object almost entirely failed. They could not arrive at a confederation of Switzerland and Germany. Nevertheless, Philip of Hesse and Zwingle, with a view to this, had numerous secret conversations, which made the Saxons uneasy, as they were not less opposed to Zwingle's politics than to his theology. "When you have reformed the peasant's cap," said Jonas to him, "you will also claim to reform the princes' sable hat."

The landgrave collected all the doctors at his table on the last day, when they shook hands in a friendly manner,[3] and each one thought of leaving the town.

On Tuesday the 5th October, Philip of Hesse quitted Marburg early, and in the afternoon of the same day Luther departed, accompanied by his colleagues; but he did not go forth as a conqueror. A spirit of dejection and alarm had taken possession of his mind.[1] He writhed in the dust, like a worm, according to his own expression. He fancied he should never see his wife and children again, and cried out that he, "the consoler of so many tortured souls, was now without consolation!"[2]

This state might partly arise from Luther's want of brotherly feeling; but it had other causes also. Soliman had come to fulfil a promise made to King Ferdinand. The latter having demanded, in 1528, the surrender of Belgrade, the sultan had haughtily replied, that he would bring the keys himself to Vienna. In fact, the Grand Turk, crossing the frontiers of Germany, had invaded countries "on which the hoofs of the Mussulman war-horses had never trod," and eight days before the conference at Marburg, he had covered with his innumerable tents the plain and the fertile hills in the midst of which rise the walls of Vienna. The struggle had begun under ground, the two parties having dug deep galleries beneath the ramparts. Three different times the Turkish mines were exploded; the walls were thrown down;[3] "the balls flew through the air like a flight of small birds," says a Turkish historian; "and there was a horrible banquet, at which the genii of death joyously drained their glasses."[4]

Luther did not keep in the background. He had already written against the Turks, and now he published a *Battle-Sermon*. "Mahomet," said he, "exalts Christ as being without sin; but he denies that he was the true God; he is therefore His enemy. Alas! to this hour the world is such that it seems every where to rain disciples of Mahomet. Two men ought to oppose the Turks: the first is Christian, that is to say, Prayer; the second is Charles, that is to say, The sword." And in another place, "I know my dear Germans well, fat and well-fed swine as they are; no sooner is the danger removed, than they think only of eating and sleeping. Wretched man! if thou dost not take up arms, the Turk will come; he will carry thee away into his Turkey; he will there sell thee like a dog; and thou shalt serve him night and day, under the rod and the cudgel, for a glass of water and a morsel of bread. Think on this; be converted, and implore the Lord not to give thee the Turk for thy schoolmaster."[5]

The two arms pointed out by Luther were, in reality, vigorously employed; and Soliman, perceiving at last that he was not the "soul of the universe," as his poets had styled him,

[1] Hic unus in Ecclesia hæret scrupulus. Corp. Ref. i. 1106.
[2] Pontifici non ultra possunt sperare Lutherum suum fore. Zw. Opp. ii. 370.
[3] Die Händ einander fründtlich gebotten. Bull. ii. 236.

[1] Ego vix et ægre domum reversus sum. L. Epp. iii. 520.
[2] Sic me vexante Angelo Satanæ, ut desperarim me vivum et salvum visurum meos. Ibid.
[3] Ipsam urbem in tribus locis, suffosso solo et pulvere supposito dis'cut et patefecit. Ibid. 518.
[4] Dschelalsade, quoted by Ranke.
[5] Heer predigt wider die Türken. L. Opp. (W.) xx. 2691.

but that there was a strength in the world superior to his own, raised the siege of Vienna on the 16th October ; and "the shadow of God over the two worlds," as he called himself, "disappeared and vanished in the Bosphorus."

But Luther imagined that, when retiring from before the walls of Vienna, "the Turk, or at least his God, who is the devil," had rushed upon him ; and that it was this enemy of Christ and of Christ's servants that he was destined to combat and vanquish in his frightful agony.[1] There is an immediate re-action of the violated law upon him who violates it. Now Luther had transgressed the royal law, which is charity, and he suffered the penalty. At last he re-entered Wittemberg, and flung himself into the arms of his friends, "tormented by the angel of death."[2]

Let us not, however, overlook the essential qualities of a reformer that Luther manifested at Marburg. There are in God's work, as in a drama, different parts. What various characters we see among the Apostles and among the Reformers! It has been said that the same characters and the same parts were assigned to St. Peter and to Luther, at the times of the Formation and of the Reformation of the Church.[3] They were both in fact men of the initiative, who start forward alone, but around whom an army soon collects at the sight of the standard which they wave. But there was perhaps in the reformer a characteristic not existing to the same degree in the apostle : this was firmness.

As for Zwingle, he quitted Marburg in alarm at Luther's intolerance. "Lutheranism," wrote he to the landgrave, "will lie as heavy upon us as popery."[4] He reached Zurich on the 19th October. "The truth," said he to his friends, "has prevailed so manifestly, that if ever any one has been defeated before all the world, it is Luther, although he constantly exclaimed that he was invincible."[5] On his side, Luther spoke in a similar strain. "It is through fear of their fellow-citizens," added he, " that the Swiss, although vanquished, are unwilling to retract."[6]

[1] Forte ipsum Turcam partim in isto agone cogor ferre et vincere, saltem ejus Deum, diabolum. L. Epp. iii. 520.
[2] Angelus Satanæ, vel quisquis est diabolus mortis ita me fatigat Ibid. 515.
[3] Dr. Vinet.
[4] Das Lutherthum werde so schwer, als das Papsthum. Zw. Epp. p. 374.
[5] Lutherus impudens et contumax aperte est victus. Ibid. p. 370.
[6] Metuebant plebem suam ad quam non licuisset reverti. Zw. Opp. ii. 19.

If it should be asked, on which side the victory really was, perhaps we ought to say that Luther assumed the air of a conqueror, but Zwingle was so in reality. The conference propagated through all Germany the doctrine of the Swiss, which had been little known there until then, and it was adopted by an immense number of persons. Among these were Laffards, first rector of St. Martin's school at Brunswick, Dionysius Melander, Justus Lening, Hartmann, Ibach, and many others. The landgrave himself, a short time before his death, declared that this conference had induced him to renounce the oral manducation of Christ.[1]

Still the dominant principle at this celebrated epoch was unity. The adversaries are the best judges. The Roman-catholics were exasperated that the Lutherans and Zwinglians had agreed on all the essential points of faith. "They have a fellow-feeling against the Catholic Church," said they, " as Herod and Pilate against Jesus Christ." The enthusiastic sects said the same,[2] and the extreme hierarchical as well as the extreme radical party deprecated alike the unity of Marburg.

Erelong a greater agitation eclipsed all these rumours, and events which threatened the whole evangelical body, proclaimed its great and intimate union with new force. The emperor, it was every where said, exasperated by the Protest of Spires, had landed at Genoa with the pomp of a conqueror. After having sworn at Barcelona to reduce the heretics under the power of the pope, he was going to visit this pontiff, humbly to bend the knee before him ; and he would rise only to cross the Alps and accomplish his terrible designs. "The Emperor Charles," said Luther, a few days after the landing of this prince, "has determined to show himself more cruel against us than the Turk himself, and he has already uttered the most horrible threats. Behold the hour of Christ's agony and weakness. Let us pray for all those who will soon have to endure captivity and death."[3]

Such was the news that then agitated all Germany. The grand question was, whether the Protest of Spires could be maintained against the power of the emperor and of the pope. This was seen in the year 1530.

[1] Rommels Anmerkungen, p. 227-229.
[2] Pontificiis et catabaptistis multum displicuit consensus Marpurgi. Scultet. p. 208.
[3] Carolus Cæsar multo atrocius minatur et sævire statuit in nos, quam Turca. L. Epp. iii. 324.

BOOK XIV

THE AUGSBURG CONFESSION.—1530

CHAPTER I.

Two striking Lessons—Charles V. in Italy—The German Envoys—Their Boldness—The Landgrave's Present—The Envoys under Arrest—Their Release and Departure—Meeting of Charles and Clement—Gattinara's Proposition—Clement's Arms—War imminent—Luther's Objections—The Saviour is coming—Charles's Conciliatory Language—The Emperor's Motives.

THE Reformation was accomplished in the name of a spiritual principle. It had proclaimed for its teacher the Word of God; for salvation, Faith; for king, Jesus Christ; for arms, the Holy Ghost; and had by these very means rejected all worldly elements. Rome had been established by *the law of a carnal commandment;* the Reformation, by *the power of an endless life.*[1]

If there is any doctrine that distinguishes Christianity from every other religion, it is its spirituality. A heavenly life brought down to man—such is its work; thus the opposition of the spirit of the Gospel to the spirit of the world, was the great fact which signalized the entrance of Christianity among the nations. But what its Founder had separated, had soon come together again; the Church had fallen into the arms of the world; and by this criminal union it had been reduced to the deplorable condition in which we find it at the era of the Reformation.

Thus one of the greatest tasks of the sixteenth century was to restore the spiritual element to its rights. The Gospel of the reformers had nothing to do with the world and with politics. While the Roman hierarchy had become a matter of diplomacy and a court intrigue, the Reformation was destined to exercise no other influence over princes and people than that which proceeds from the Gospel of peace.

If the Reformation, having attained a certain point, became untrue to its nature, began to parley and temporize with the world, and thus ceased to follow up the spiritual principle that it had so loudly proclaimed, it was faithless to God and to itself.

Henceforward its decline was at hand.

It is impossible for a society to prosper if it be unfaithful to the principles it lays down. Having abandoned what constituted its life, it can find naught but death.

It was God's will that this great truth should be inscribed on the very threshold of the temple He was then raising in the world; and a striking contrast was to make this truth stand gloriously prominent.

One portion of the reform was to seek the alliance of the world, and in this alliance find a destruction full of desolation.

Another portion, looking up to God, was haughtily to reject the arm of the flesh, and by this very act of faith secure a noble victory.

If three centuries have gone astray, it is because they were unable to comprehend so holy and so solemn a lesson.

It was in the beginning of September 1529 that Charles V., the victor by battles or by treaties over the pope and the King of France, landed at Genoa. The shouts of the Spaniards had saluted him as he quitted the Iberian peninsula; but the dejected eyes, the bended heads, the silent lips of the Italians given over to his hands, alone welcomed him to the foot of the Apennines. Everything led to the belief that Charles would indemnify himself on them for the apparent generosity with which he had treated the pope.

They were deceived. Instead of those barbarous chiefs of the Goths and Huns,—instead of those proud and fierce emperors, who more than once had crossed the Alps and rushed upon Italy sword in hand and with cries of vengeance, the Italians saw among them a young and graceful prince, with pale features, a delicate frame, and weak voice, of winning manners, having more the air of a courtier than of a warrior, scrupulously performing all the duties of the Romish religion, and leading in his train no terrible cohorts of German barbarians, but a brilliant retinue of Spanish grandees, who condescendingly paraded the pride of their race and the splendour of their nation. This prince, the victor of Europe, spoke only of peace and amnesty; and even the Duke of Ferrara, who of all the Italian princes had most cause of fear, having at Modena placed the keys of the city in his hands, heard from his friendly lips the most unexpected encouragements.

Whence did this strange conduct proceed? Charles had shown plainly enough, at the time of the captivity of Francis I., that generosity towards his enemies was not his dominant virtue. It was not long before this mystery was explained.

Almost at the same time with Charles there arrived in Italy, by way of Lyons and Genoa, three German burgesses, whose whole equipage consisted of six horses.[1] These

[1] Hebrews vii. 16.

[1] Legatis attribuerunt equos sex. Seckend. ii. 134.

were John Ehinger, burgomaster of Memmingen, who carried his head high, scattered money around him, and who was not remarkable for great sobriety; Michael Caden, syndic of Nuremberg, a worthy, pious, and brave man, but detested by the Count of Nassau, the most influential of Charles's ministers; and, lastly, Alexis Frauentraut, secretary to the Margrave of Brandenburg, who, having married a nun, was in very bad odour among the Roman-catholics. Such were the three men whom the Protestant princes, assembled at Nuremberg, commissioned to bear to the emperor the famous Protest of Spires. They had purposely chosen these deputies from a middle station, under the impression that they would incur less danger.[1] To carry such a message to Charles V. was, to say the truth, a task that few persons cared to execute. Accordingly a pension had been secured to the widows of these envoys in case of misfortune.

Charles was on his way from Genoa to Bologna, and staying at Piacenza, when the three Protestant deputies overtook him. These plain Germans presented a singular contrast to that Spanish pomp and Romish fervour by which the young prince was surrounded. Cardinal Gattinara, the emperor's chancellor, who sincerely desired a reform of the Church, procured them an audience of Charles V. on the 22d of September; but they were recommended to be sparing in their words, for there was nothing the emperor disliked so much as a Protestant sermon.

The deputies were not to be checked by these intimations; and after handing the protest to Charles, Frauentraut began to speak: "It is to the Supreme Judge that each one of us must render an account," said he, "and not to creatures who turn at every wind. It is better to fall into the most cruel necessity, than to incur the anger of God. Our nation will obey no decrees that are based on any other foundation than the Holy Scriptures."[2]

Such was the proud tone held by these German citizens to the emperor of the west. Charles said not a word—it would have been doing them too much honour; but he charged one of his secretaries to announce an answer at some future time.

There was no hurry to send back these paltry ambassadors. In vain did they renew their solicitations daily. Gattinara treated them with kindness, but Nassau sent them away with bitter words. A workman, the armourer to the court, having to visit Augsburg to purchase arms, begged the Count of Nassau to despatch the Protestant deputies. "You may tell them," replied the minister of Charles V., "that we will terminate their business in order that you may have travelling companions." But the armourer

having found other company, they were compelled to wait.[1]

These envoys endeavoured, at least, to make a good use of their time. "Take this book," said the landgrave to Caden at the very moment of departure, giving him a French work bound in velvet, and richly ornamented, "and deliver it to the emperor."[2] It was a summary of the Christian Faith which the landgrave had received from Francis Lambert, and which had probably been written by that doctor. Caden sought an opportunity of presenting this treatise; and did so one day, as Charles was going publicly to mass. The emperor took the book, and passed it immediately to a Spanish bishop. The Spaniard began to read,[3] and lighted upon that passage of Scripture in which Christ enjoins his apostles *not to exercise lordship*.[4] The author took advantage of it to maintain that the minister, charged with spiritual matters, should not interfere with those which are temporal. The papist prelate bit his lips, and Charles, who perceived it, having asked, "Well, what is the matter?" the bishop in confusion had recourse to a falsehood.[5] "This treatise," replied he, "takes the sword from the christian magistrate, and grants it only to nations that are strangers to the faith." Immediately there was a great uproar: the Spaniards above all were beside themselves. "The wretches that have endeavoured to mislead so young a prince," said they, "deserve to be hung on the first tree by the wayside!" Charles swore, in fact, that the bearer should suffer the penalty of his audacity.

At length, on the 12th October, Alexander Schweiss, imperial secretary, transmitted the emperor's reply to the deputies. It said that the minority ought to submit to the decrees passed in diet, and that if the Duke of Saxony and his allies were contumacious, means would not be wanting to compel them.[6]

Upon this Ehinger and Caden read aloud the appeal to the emperor drawn up at Spires, whilst Frauentraut, who had renounced his quality of deputy and assumed that of a notary,[7] took notes of what was passing. When the reading was finished, the deputies advanced towards Schweiss, and presented the appeal. The imperial secretary rejected the document with amazement; the deputies insisted; Schweiss continued firm. They then laid the appeal on the table. Schweiss was staggered; he took the paper, and carried it to the emperor.

After dinner, just as one of the deputies (Caden) had gone out, a tumult in the hotel announced some catastrophe. It was the

---

[1] Ut essent tutiores. Seckend. ii. 133.
[2] Neque suarum esse virium aut officii, ut eos ad impossibilia et noxia adigant. Ibid. 134.

[1] Hortleben, von den Ursachen des deutschen Kriegs, p. 50.
[2] Libellum eleganter ornatum. Scultet. p. 253.
[3] Cum obiter legisset. Ibid.
[4] Luke xxii. 26.
[5] Falso et maligne relatum esset. Seckend. ii. 133.
[6] Sibi non defore media quibus ad id compellerentur. Ibid.
[7] Tabellionis sive notarii officium. Ibid.

imperial secretary who returned duly accompanied. " The emperor is exceedingly irritated against you on account of this appeal," said he to the Protestants; " and he forbids you, under pain of confiscation and death, to leave your hotel, to write to Germany, or to send any message whatsoever."[1] Thus Charles put ambassadors under arrest, as he would the officers of his guard, desirous in this manner of showing his contempt, and of frightening the princes.

Caden's servant slipped in alarm out of the hotel, and ran to his master. The latter, still considering himself free, wrote a hasty account of the whole business to the senate of Nuremberg, sent off his letters by express, and returned to share in the arrest of his colleagues.[2]

On the 23d of October, the emperor left Piacenza, carrying the three Germans with him. But on the 30th he released Ehinger and Frauentraut, who mounting their horses in the middle of the night, rushed at full speed along a road thronged with soldiers and robbers. " As for you," said Granvelle to Caden, " you will stay under pain of death. The emperor is waiting to show the pope the book you presented to him."[3] Perhaps Charles thought it a good joke to lay before the Roman pontiff this prohibition issued against the ministers of God to mingle in the government of nations. But Caden, profiting by the confusion of the court, secretly procured a horse, and fled to Ferrara, and thence to Venice, from which place he returned to Nuremberg.[4]

The more Charles appeared irritated against Germany, the greater moderation he showed towards the Italians: heavy pecuniary contributions were all that he required. It was beyond the Alps, in the centre of Christendom, by means of these very religious controversies, that he desired to establish his power. He pressed on, and required only two things: behind him,—peace; with him,—money.

On the 5th of November he entered Bologna. Every thing about him was impressive: the crowd of nobles, the splendour of the equipages, the haughtiness of the Spanish troops, the four thousand ducats that were scattered by handfuls among the people;[5] but above all, the majesty and magnificence of the young emperor. The two chiefs of Romish Christendom were about to meet. The pope quitted his palace with all his court; and Charles, at the head of an army which would have conquered the whole of Italy in a few days, affecting the humility of a child, fell on his knees, and kissed the pontiff's feet.

The emperor and the pope resided at Bologna in two adjoining palaces, separated by a single wall, through which a doorway had been opened, of which each had a key; and the young and politic emperor, with papers in his hand, was often seen visiting the old and crafty pontiff.

Clement obtained Sforza's forgiveness, who appeared before the emperor sick and leaning on a staff. Venice also was forgiven: a million of crowns arranged these two matters. But Charles could not obtain from the pope the pardon of Florence. That illustrious city was sacrificed to the Medici, " considering," it was said, " that it is impossible for Christ's vicar to demand anything that is unjust."

The most important affair was the Reformation. Some represented to the emperor that, victor over all his enemies, he ought to carry matters with a high hand, and constrain the Protestants by force of arms.[1] Charles was more moderate: he preferred weakening the Protestants by the Papists, and then the Papists by the Protestants, and by this means raising his power above them both.

A wiser course was nevertheless proposed in a solemn conference. " The Church is torn in pieces," said Chancellor Gattinara. " You (Charles) are the head of the empire; you (the pope) the head of the Church. It is your duty to provide by common accord against unprecedented wants. Assemble the pious men of all nations, and let a free council deduce from the Word of God a scheme of doctrine such as may be received by every people."[2]

A thunderbolt falling at Clement's feet could not have startled him more. The offspring of an illegitimate union, and having obtained the papacy by means far from honourable, and squandered the treasures of the Church in an unjust war, this pontiff had a thousand personal motives for dreading an assembly of Christendom. " Large congregations," replied he, " serve only to introduce popular opinions. It is not by the decrees of councils, but with the edge of the sword, that we should decide controversies."[3]

As Gattinara still persisted: " What!" said the pope, angrily interrupting him, " you dare contradict me, and excite your master against me!" Charles rose up; all the assembly preserved profound silence, and the prince resuming his seat, seconded his chancellor's request. Clement was content to say that he would reflect upon it. He then began to work upon the young emperor in their private conferences, and Charles

---

[1] Sub capitis pœna, ne pedem a diversario moveant. Seckend. ii. 133.
[2] A famulo certior factus, rem omnem senatui aperuit. Ibid.
[3] Ut idem scriptum exhibeat quoque Pontifici. Scultet. p. 254.
[4] Silentio conscendit equum. Ibid.
[5] In vulgus sparsum aurum quatuor millia ducatorum. L. Epp. iii. 565.

[1] Armis cogendos. Seckend. ii. 112; Maimbourg, ii. 194.
[2] Oratio *de Congressu Bononiensi,* in *Melancthonis Orationum,* iv. 87, and Cælestinus Hist. Concil. 1830, Augustæ, i. 10. Respectable authors, Walsh, Muller, and Beausobre, incorrectly quote at full length the speeches delivered at this conference. They are amplifications; but to deny that they have some historical foundation would be flying to the opposite extreme.
[3] Non concilii decretis, sed armis controversias dirimendas. Scultet. p. 245; Maimbourg the Jesuit, ii. 177.

promised at last to constrain the heretics by violence, while the pope should summon all other princes to his aid.[1] "To overcome Germany by force, and then erase it from the surface of the earth, is the sole object of the Italians," wrote a correspondent from Venice to the elector.[2]

Such was the sinister news which, by spreading alarm among the Protestants, should also have united them. Unfortunately a contrary movement was then taking place. Luther and some of his friends had revised the Marburg articles in a sense exclusively Lutheran, and the ministers of the Elector of Saxony had presented them to the conference at Schwabach. The reformed deputies from Ulm and Strasburg had immediately withdrawn, and the conference was broken up.

But new conferences had erelong become necessary. The express that Caden had forwarded from Piacenza had reached Nuremberg. Every one in Germany understood that the arrest of the princes' deputies was a declaration of war. The elector was staggered, and ordered his chancellor to consult the theologians of Wittemberg.

"We cannot on our conscience," replied Luther on the 18th November, "approve of the proposed alliance. We would rather die ten times than see our Gospel cause one drop of blood to be shed.[3] Our part is to be like lambs of the slaughter. The cross of Christ must be borne. Let your highness be without fear. We shall do more by our prayers than all our enemies by their boastings. Only let not your hands be stained with the blood of your brethren! If the emperor requires us to be given up to his tribunals, we are ready to appear. You cannot defend our faith: each one should believe at his own risk and peril."[4]

On the 29th November an evangelical congress was opened at Smalkald, and an unexpected event rendered this meeting still more important. Ehinger, Caden, and Frauentraut, who had escaped from the grasp of Charles V., appeared before them.[5] The landgrave had no further doubts of the success of his plan.

He was deceived. No agreement between contrary doctrines, no alliance between politics and religion—were Luther's two principles, and they still prevailed. It was agreed that those who felt disposed to sign the articles of Schwabach, and those only, should meet at Nuremberg on the 6th of January.

The horizon became hourly more threatening. The papists of Germany wrote one to another these few but significant words:

"The Saviour is coming."[1] "Alas" exclaimed Luther, "what a pitiless saviour! He will devour them all, as well as us." In effect, two Italian bishops, authorized by Charles V., demanded in the pope's name all the gold and silver from the churches, and a third part of the ecclesiastical revenues: a proceeding which caused an immense sensation. "Let the pope go to the devil," replied a canon of Paderborn, a little too freely.[2] "Yes, yes!" archly replied Luther, "this is your saviour that is coming!" The people already began to talk of frightful omens. It was not only the living who were agitated: a child still in its mother's womb had uttered horrible shrieks.[3] "All is accomplished," said Luther; "the Turk has reached the highest degree of his power, the glory of the papacy is declining, and the world is splitting on every side."[4] The reformer, dreading lest the end of the world should arrive before he had translated all the Bible, published the prophecies of Daniel separately,—"a work," said he, "for these latter times." "Historians tell us," he added, "that Alexander the Great always placed Homer under his pillow: the prophet Daniel is worthy not only that kings and princes should lay him under their heads, but carry him in their hearts; for he will teach them that the government of nations proceeds from the power of God. We are balanced in the hand of the Lord, as a ship upon the sea, or a cloud in the sky."[5]

Yet the frightful phantom that Philip of Hesse had not ceased pointing out to his allies, and whose threatening jaws seemed already opening, suddenly vanished, and they discovered in its place the graceful image of the most amiable of princes.

On the 21st January, Charles had summoned all the states of the empire to Augsburg, and had endeavoured to employ the most conciliatory language. "Let us put an end to all discord," he said, "let us renounce our antipathies, let us offer to our Saviour the sacrifice of all our errors, and let us make it our business to comprehend and weigh with meekness the opinions of others. Let us annihilate all that has been said or done on both sides contrary to right, and let us seek after christian truth. Let us all fight under one and the same leader, Jesus Christ, and let us strive thus to meet in one communion, one church, and one unity."[6]

What language! How was it that this prince, who hitherto had spoken only of the sword, should now speak only of peace? Some may say that the wise Gattinara had a share in it; that the act of convocation was

[1] Pontifex, ut cæteri Christiani principes, ipsos pro viribus iuvent. Guicciardini, xix. 908.
[2] Ut Germania vi et armis opprimatur, funditus deleatur et eradicetur. Cælestin. i. 42.
[3] Lieber zehn mal todt seyn. Epp. iii. 526.
[4] Auf sein eigen Fahr glauben. Ibid. 527.
[5] Advenerant et gesta referebant. Seckend. ii. 140; Sleidan. i. 235.

[1] Invicem scriptitant, dicentes: Salvator venit. L. Epp iii. 540.
[2] Dat de Duwel dem Bawst int Lieff fare. Ibid.
[3] Infans in utero, audiente tota familia, bis vociferatus est. Ibid.
[4] Dedication of Daniel to John Frederick. Ibid. 555.
[5] Schwebt in seiner Macht, wie ein Schiff auf dem Meer, Ja wie eine Wolke unter dem Himmel. L. Epp. iii. 555.
[6] Wie wir alle unter einem Christo seyn und streiten Forstenmann's Urkundenbuch, i. 1.

drawn up under the impression of the terror caused by the Turkish invasion ; that the emperor already saw with how little eagerness the Roman-catholics of Germany seconded his views ; that he wished to intimidate the pope ; that this language, so full of graciousness, was but a mask which Charles employed to deceive his enemies ; that he wished to manage religion in true imperial fashion, like Theodosius and Constantine, and seek first to unite both parties by the influence of his wisdom and of his favours, reserving to himself, if kindness should fail, to employ force afterwards. It is possible that each of these motives may have exercised a certain influence on Charles, but the latter appears to us nearer the truth, and more conformable to the character of this prince.

If Charles, however. showed any inclination to mildness, the fanatical Ferdinand was at hand to bring him back. " I will continue negotiating without coming to any conclusion," wrote he to his brother ; " and should I even be reduced to that, do not fear ; pretexts will not be wanting to chastise these rebels, and you will find men enough who will be happy to aid you in your revenge."[1]

CHAPTER II.

The Coronation—The Emperor made a Deacon—The Romish Church and the State—Alarm of the Protestants——Luther advocates Passive Resistance—Bruck's noble Advice—Articles of Faith prepared—Luther's Strong Tower—Luther at Coburg—Charles at Innspruck—Two Parties at Court—Gattinara—The King of Denmark won over by Charles—Piety of the Elector—Wiles of the Romanists.

CHARLES, like Charlemagne in former times, and Napoleon in later days, desired to be crowned by the pope, and had at first thought of visiting Rome for that purpose ; but Ferdinand's pressing letters compelled him to choose Bologna.[2] He appointed the 22d February for receiving the iron crown as king of Lombardy, and resolved to assume the golden crown, as emperor of the Romans, on the 24th of the same month—his birthday and the anniversary of the battle of Pavia—a day which he thought always fortunate to him.[3]

The offices of honour that belonged to the electors of the empire were given to strangers ; in the coronation of the Emperor of Germany all was Spanish or Italian. The sceptre was carried by the Marquis of Montferrat, the sword by the Duke of Urbino, and the golden crown by the Duke of Savoy. One single German prince of little importance, the Count-palatine Philip, was present : he carried the orb. After these lords came the emperor himself between two cardinals ; then

the members of his council. All this procession defiled across a magnificent temporary bridge erected between the palace and the church. At the very moment the emperor drew near the church of San Petronio, where the coronation was to take place, the scaffolding cracked behind him and gave way : many of his train were wounded, and the multitude fled in alarm. Charles calmly turned back and smiled, not doubting that his lucky star had saved him.

At length Charles V. arrived in front of the throne on which Clement was seated. But before being made emperor, it was necessary that he should be promoted to the sacred orders. The pope presented him with the surplice and the amice to make him a canon of St. Peter's and of St. John Lateranus, and the canons of these two churches immediately stripped him of his royal ornaments, and robed him with the sacerdotal garments. The pope went to the altar and began mass, the new canon drawing near to wait upon him. After the offertory, the imperial deacon presented the water to the pontiff; and then kneeling down between two cardinals, communicated from the pope's hand. The emperor now returned to his throne, where the princes robed him with the imperial mantle brought from Constantinople, all sparkling with diamonds, and Charles humbly bent the knee before Clement VII.

The pontiff, having anointed him with oil and given him the sceptre, presented him with a naked sword, saying : " Make use of it in defence of the Church against the enemies of the faith !" Next taking the golden orb, studded with jewels, which the count-palatine held, he said : " Govern the world with piety and firmness !" Last came the Duke of Savoy, who carried the golden crown enriched with diamonds. The prince bent down, and Clement put the diadem on his head, saying : " Charles, emperor invincible, receive this crown which we place on your head, as a sign to all the earth of the authority that is conferred upon you."

The emperor then kissed the white cross embroidered on the pope's red slipper, and exclaimed : " I swear to be, with all my powers and resources, the perpetual defender of the pontifical dignity and of the Church of Rome."[1]

The two princes now took their seats under the same canopy, but on thrones of unequal height, the emperor's being half a foot lower than the pontiff's, and the cardinal-deacon proclaimed to the people " The invincible emperor, Defender of the Faith." For the next half-hour nothing was heard but the noise of musketry, trumpets, drums, and fifes, all the bells of the city, and the shouts of the multitude. Thus was proclaimed anew the close union of politics with religion. The

---

[1] Bucholz Geschichte Ferdinands. iii. 432.
[2] Sopravennero lettere di Germania che lo sollicittavano à transferirsi in quella provincia. Guicciardini, L. xx.
[3] Natali suo quem semper felicem habuit. Seckend. ii. 150.

[1] Omnibus viribus, ingenio, et facultatibus suis Pontificiæ dignitatis et Romanæ Ecclesiæ perpetuum fore defensorem. Cœlestin. Hist. Commit. Aug. 16.

mighty emperor, transformed to a Roman deacon and humbly serving mass, like a canon of St. Peter's, had typified and declared the indissoluble union of the Romish Church with the State. This is one of the essential doctrines of Popery, and one of the most striking characteristics that distinguish it from the evangelical and the Christian Church.

Nevertheless, during the whole of the ceremony the pope seemed ill at ease, and sighed as soon as the eyes of the spectators were turned away from him. Accordingly, the French ambassador wrote to his court that these four months which the emperor and pope had spent together at Bologna, would bear fruit of which the King of France would assuredly have no cause to complain.[1]

Scarcely had Charles V. risen from before the altar of San Petronio, ere he turned his face towards Germany, and appeared on the Alps as the anointed of the Papacy. The letter of convocation, so indulgent and benign, seemed forgotten : all things were made new since the pope's blessings: there was but one thought in the imperial train, the necessity of rigorous measures; and the legate Campeggio continued to insinuate irritating words into Charles's ear. " At the first rumour of the storm that threatens them," said Granvelle, " we shall see the Protestants flying on every side, like timid doves upon which the Alpine eagle pounces."[2]

Great indeed was the alarm throughout the empire; the affrighted people, apprehensive of the greatest disasters, repeated every where that Luther and Melancthon were dead. " Alas !" said Melancthon, consumed by sorrow, when he heard these reports, " the rumour is but too true, for I die daily."[3] But Luther, on the contrary, boldly raising the eye of faith towards heaven, exclaimed : " Our enemies triumph,—but erelong to perish." In truth the councils of the elector displayed an unprecedented boldness. " Let us collect our troops," said they ; " let us march on the Tyrol, and close the passage of the Alps against the emperor."[4] Philip of Hesse uttered a cry of joy when he heard of this. The sword of Charles had aroused his indolent allies at last. Immediately fresh couriers from Ferdinand were sent to hasten the arrival of Charles, and all Germany was in expectation.

Before carrying out this gigantic design, the elector desired to consult Luther once more. The emperor in the midst of the electors was only the first among his equals ; and independent princes were allowed to resist another prince, even if he were of higher rank than themselves. But Luther, dreading above all things the intervention of the secular arm in church affairs, was led to reply on the 6th March in this extraordinary manner : " Our princes' subjects are also the emperor's subjects, and even more so than princes are. To protect by arms the emperor's subjects against the emperor, would be as if the burgomaster of Torgau wished to protect by force his citizens against the elector."

" What must be done then ?"—" Listen," replied Luther. " If the emperor desires to march against us, let no prince undertake our defence. God is faithful : he will not abandon us." All preparations for war were immediately suspended, the landgrave received a polite refusal, and the confederation was dissolved. It was the will of God that his cause should appear before the emperor without league and without soldiers, having faith alone for its shield.

Never perhaps has such boldness been witnessed in feeble and unarmed men ; but never, although under an appearance of blindness, was there so much wisdom and understanding.

The question next discussed in the elector's council was, whether he should go to the diet. The majority of the councillors opposed it. " Is it not risking every thing," said they, " to go and shut oneself up within the walls of a city with a powerful enemy ?" Bruck and the prince-electoral were of a different opinion. Duty in their eyes was a better councillor than fear. " What !" said they, " would the emperor insist so much on the presence of the princes at Augsburg only to draw them into a snare? We cannot impute such perfidy to him." The landgrave, on the contrary, seconded the opinion of the majority. " Remember Piacenza," said he. " Some unforeseen circumstance may lead the emperor to take all his enemies in one cast of the net."

The chancellor stood firm. " Let the princes only comport themselves with courage," said he, " and God's cause is saved." The decision was in favour of the nobler plan.

This diet was to be a lay council, or at the very least a national convention.[1] The Protestants foresaw that a few unimportant concessions would be made to them at first, and then that they would be required to sacrifice their faith. It was therefore necessary to settle what were the essential articles of christian truth, in order to know whether, by what means, and how far they might come to an understanding with their adversaries. The elector accordingly had letters sent on the 14th March to the four principal theologians of Wittemberg, setting them this task before all other business.[2] Thus, in-

[1] Letter to M. L'Admiral, 25th February. Legrand, Histoire du Divorce, iii. 386.
[2] Tanquam columbæ, adveniente aquila, dispergentur. Rommel Anmerkungen, p. 236.
[3] Ego famam de qua scribis intelligo nimis veram esse, morior enim quotidie. Corp. Ref. ii. 122.
[4] Cum copiis quas habitant per Tyrolensem ditionem incedenti occurrere et Alpium transitum impedire. Seckend. ii. 150.

[1] Cum hæc comitia pro concilio aut conventu nationali haberi videantur. Seckend. ii. 17. Letter to the Elector. Corp. Ref. ii. 26.
[2] Omnibus sepositis aliis rebus. L. Epp. iii. 564.

stead of collecting soldiers, this prince drew up articles : they were the best armament.

Luther, Jonas, and Melancthon (Pomeranus remaining at Wittemberg), arrived at Torgau in Easter week, asking leave to deliver their articles in person to Charles the Fifth.[1] " God forbid ! " replied the elector, " I also desire to confess my Lord."

John having then confided to Melancthon the definitive arrangement of the confession, and ordered general prayers to be offered up, began his journey on the 3d April, with one hundred and sixty horsemen, clad in rich scarlet cloaks embroidered with gold.

Every man was aware of the dangers that threatened the elector, and hence many in his escort marched with downcast eyes and sinking hearts. But Luther, full of faith, revived the courage of his friends, by composing and singing with his fine voice that beautiful hymn, since become so famous : *Ein' veste Burg ist unser Gott*, Our God is a strong tower.[2] Never did soul that knew its own weakness, but which, looking to God, despised every fear, find such noble accents.

> With our own strength we nought can do,
> Destruction yawns on every side :
> He fights for us, our champion true,
> Elect of God to be our guide.
> What is his name? The anointed One,
> The God of armies he ;
> Of earth and heaven the Lord alone—
> With him, on field of battle won,
> Abideth victory.

This hymn was sung during the diet, not only at Augsburg, but in all the churches of Saxony, and its energetic strains often revived and inspirited the most dejected minds.[3]

On Easter-eve the troop reached Coburg, and on the 23d April the elector resumed his journey ; but at the very moment of departure Luther received an order to remain. " Some one has said, ' Hold your tongue, you have a harsh voice,'" wrote he to a friend.[4] He submitted, however, without hesitation, setting an example of that passive obedience which he so boldly advocated. The elector feared that Luther's presence would still further exasperate his adversaries, and drive Charles to extreme measures : the city of Augsburg had also written to him to that effect. But at the same time John was anxious to keep the reformer within reach, that he might be able to consult him. He was therefore left at Coburg, in the castle overlooking the town and the

river Itz, in the upper story on the south side. It was from this place he wrote those numerous letters dated from the *region of birds ;* and it was there that for many months he had to maintain with his old enemy of the Wartburg, Satan, a struggle full of darkness and of anguish.

On the 2d May the elector reached Augsburg ; it had been expected that he would stay away, and, to the great astonishment of all, he was the first at the rendezvous.[1] He immediately sent Dolzig, marshal of the court, to meet the emperor and to compliment him. On the 12th May Philip of Hesse, who had at last resolved on not separating himself from his ally, arrived with an escort of one hundred and ninety horsemen : and almost at the same time the emperor entered Innspruck, in the Tyrol, accompanied by his brother, the queens of Hungary and Bohemia, the ambassadors of France, England, and Portugal, Campeggio, the papal legate, and other cardinals, with many princes and nobles of Germany, Spain, and Italy.

How to bring back the heretics to obedience to the Church was the great topic of conversation in this brilliant court among nobles and priests, ladies and soldiers, councillors and ambassadors. They, or Charles at least, were not for making them ascend the scaffold, but they wished to act in such a manner that, untrue to their faith, they should bend the knee to the pope. Charles stopped at Innspruck to study the situation of Germany, and ensure the success of his schemes.

Scarcely was his arrival known ere a crowd of people, high and low, flocked round him on every side, and more than 270,000 crowns, previously raised in Italy, served to make the Germans understand the justice of Rome's cause. " All these heretics," was the cry, " will fall to the ground and crawl to the feet of the pope."[2]

Charles did not think so. He was, on the contrary, astonished to see what power the Reformation had gained. He momentarily even entertained the idea of passing by Augsburg, and of going straight to Cologne, and there proclaim his brother King of the Romans.[3] Thus, religious interests would have given way to dynastic interests, at least so ran the report. But Charles the Fifth did not stop at this idea. The question of the Reformation was there before him, increasing hourly in strength, and it could not be eluded.

Two parties divided the imperial court. The one, numerous and active, called upon the emperor to revive simply the edict of Worms, and, without hearing the Protestants, condemn their cause.[4] The legate

---

[1] Different projects will be found in *Forstenmann's Urkundenbuch*, i. p. 63-108, and in the Corp. Ref. iv. p. 973, sqq. Those that were presented were doubtless the *Articuli non concedendi, Articles not to be conceded.* They treat of the communion in both kinds, of celibacy, the mass, orders, the pope, convents, confession, distinction of meats, and of the sacraments. Corp. Ref. iv. 981.

[2] We have attempted a very feeble translation of the second stanza.

[3] Qui tristem etiam et abjectum animum erigere et exhilarare, et velut ἐνθοσιάζειν possent. Scult. p. 270.

[4] Sed erat qui diceret : Tace tu, habes malam vocem. L. Epp. iv. 2.

[1] Mirantibus hominibus. Seck. ii. 153.
[2] Zum kreutz kriechen werden. Mathesius Pred. p. 91. The allusion is to the cross embroidered on the pope's slipper.
[3] Iter Coloniam versus decrevisse. Epp. Zw. May 13.
[4] Alii censent Cæsarem debere, edicto proposito, sine ulla cogitatione damnare causam nostram. Corp. Ref. ii. 57.

was at the head of this party. "Do not hesitate," said he to Charles; "confiscate their property, establish the inquisition, and punish these obstinate heretics with fire and sword."[1] The Spaniards, who strongly seconded these exhortations, gave way to their accustomed debauchery, and many of them were arrested for seduction.[2] This was a sad specimen of the faith they wished to impose on Germany. Rome has always thought lightly of morality.

Gattinara, although sick, had painfully followed in Charles's train to neutralize the influence of the legate. A determined adversary of the Roman policy, he thought that the Protestants might render important services to Christendom. "There is nothing I desire so much," said he, "as to see the Elector of Saxony and his allies persevere courageously in the profession of the Gospel, and call for a free religious council. If they allow themselves to be checked by promises or threats, I hesitate myself, I stagger, and I doubt of the means of salvation."[3] The enlightened and honest members of the Papal Church (and of whom there is always a small number) necessarily sympathize with the Reformation.

Charles V., exposed to these contrary influences, desired to restore Germany to religious unity by his personal intervention: for a moment he thought himself on the eve of success.

Amongst the persons who crowded to Innspruck was the unfortunate Christian, king of Denmark, Charles's brother-in-law. In vain had he proposed to his subjects undertaking a pilgrimage to Rome in expiation of the cruelties of which he was accused: his people had expelled him. Having repaired to Saxony, to his uncle the elector, he had there heard Luther, and had embraced the evangelical doctrines, as far at least as external profession goes. This poor dethroned monarch could not resist the eloquence of the powerful ruler of two worlds, and Christian, won over by Charles the Fifth, publicly placed himself again under the sceptre of the Roman hierarchy. All the papal party uttered a shout of triumph. Nothing equals their credulity, and the importance they attach to such worthless accessions. "I cannot describe the emotion with which this news has filled me," wrote Clement VII. to Charles, his hand trembling with joy; "the brightness of your majesty's virtues begins at last to scatter the darkness: this example will lead to conversions beyond number."

Things were in this state when Duke George of Saxony, Duke William of Bavaria, and the Elector Joachim of Brandenburg, the three German princes who were the greatest enemies to the Reformation, hastily arrived at Innspruck.

The tranquillity of the elector, whom they had seen at Augsburg, had alarmed them, for they knew not the source whence John derived his courage: they fancied he was meditating some perfidious design. "It is not without reason," said they to Charles, "that the Elector John has repaired the first to Augsburg, and that he appeared there with a considerable train: he wishes to seize your person. Act then with energy, and allow us to offer your majesty a guard of six thousand horse."[1] Conference upon conference immediately took place. The Protestants were affrighted. "They are holding a diet at Innspruck," said Melancthon, "on the best means of having our heads."[2] But Gattinara prevailed on Charles to preserve his neutrality.

While this agitation prevailed in the Tyrol, the evangelical Christians, instead of mustering in arms, as they were accused, sent up their prayers to heaven, and the Protestant princes were preparing to render an account of their faith.

The Elector of Saxony held the first rank among them. Sincere, upright, and pure from his youth, early disgusted with the brilliant tourneys in which he had at first taken part, John of Saxony had joyfully hailed the day of the Reformation, and the Gospel light had gradually penetrated his serious and reflective mind. His great pleasure was to have the Holy Scriptures read to him during the latter hours of the day. It is true that, having arrived at an advanced age, the pious elector sometimes fell asleep, but he would soon awake with a start, and repeat the last passage aloud. Although moderate and a friend of peace, he yet possessed an energy that was powerfully aroused by the great interests of faith. There is no prince in the sixteenth century, and none perhaps since the primitive times of the Church, who has done so much as John of Saxony for the cause of the Gospel. Accordingly it was against him that the first efforts of the Papists were directed.

In order to gain him over, they wished to put in operation very different tactics from those which had been previously employed. At Spires the evangelicals had met with angry looks in every quarter; at Augsburg, on the contrary, the Papists gave them a hearty welcome; they represented the distance that separated the two parties as very trifling, and in their private conversations made use of the mildest language, "seeking thus to entice the credulous Protestants to take the bait," says an historian.[3] The latter yielded with simplicity to these skilful manœuvres.

<hr />

[1] *Instructio data Cæsari* dal Reverendissimo Campeggio. Ranke, iii. 288.
[2] Sich die Spanier zu Inspruck unfläthig gehalten. Corp. Ref. ii. 56.
[3] Semper vacillaturum de vera et certa salutis adipiscendæ ratione. Seck. ii. 57.

[1] Ut mascule ageret, sex mille equitum præsidium ei offerentes. Seck. ii. 156.
[2] Ibi habentur de nostris cervicibus comitia. Corp. Ref. ii. 45.
[3] Seckendorf.

Charles the Fifth was convinced that the simple Germans would not be able to resist his star. "The King of Denmark has been converted," said his courtiers to him, "why should not the elector follow his example? Let us draw him into the imperial atmosphere." John was immediately invited to come and converse familiarly with the emperor at Innspruck, with an assurance that he might reckon on Charles's particular favour.

The prince-electoral, John Frederick, who, on seeing the advances of the Papists, had at first exclaimed: "We conduct our affairs with such awkwardness, that it is quite pitiable!" allowed himself to be caught by this stratagem. "The Papist princes," said he to his father, "exert every means of blackening our characters. Go to Innspruck in order to put a stop to these underhand practices; or if you are unwilling, send me in your place."

This time the prudent elector moderated his son's precipitancy, and replied to Charles's ministers, that it was not proper to treat of the affairs of the diet in any other place than that which the emperor had himself appointed, and begged, in consequence, that his majesty would hasten his arrival. This was the first check that Charles met with.

CHAPTER III.

Augsburg—The Gospel Preached—The Emperor's Message—The Sermons prohibited—Firmness of the Elector—The Elector's Reply—Preparation of the Confession—Luther's Sinai—His Son and his Father—Luther's Merriment—Luther's Diet at Coburg—Saxony, a Paradise below—To the Bishops—Travail of the Church—Charles—The Pope's Letter—Melancthon on Fasting—The Church, the Judge—The Landgrave's catholic Spirit.

MEANTIME Augsburg was filling more and more every day. Princes, bishops, deputies, gentlemen, cavaliers, soldiers in rich uniforms, entered by every gate, and thronged the streets, the public places, inns, churches, and palaces. All that was most magnificent in Germany was there about to be collected. The critical circumstances in which the empire and Christendom were placed, the presence of Charles V. and his kindly manners, the love of novelty, of grand shows, and of lively emotions, tore the Germans from their homes. All those who had great interests to discuss, without reckoning a crowd of idlers, flocked from the various provinces of the empire, and hastily made their way towards this illustrious city.[1]

In the midst of this crowd the elector and the landgrave were resolved to confess Jesus Christ, and to take advantage of this convocation in order to convert the empire. Scarcely had John arrived when he ordered one of his theologians to preach daily with open doors in the church of the Dominicans. On Sunday the 8th May, the same was done in the church of St. Catherine; on the 13th, Philip of Hesse opened the gates of the cathedral, and his chaplain Snepff there proclaimed the Word of salvation; and on the following Sunday (May 15) this prince ordered Cellarius, minister of Augsburg and a follower of Zwingle, to preach in the same temple. Somewhat later the landgrave firmly settled himself in the church of St. Ulric, and the elector in that of St. Catherine. These were the two positions taken up by these illustrious princes. Every day the Gospel was announced in these places to an immense and attentive crowd.[2]

The partisans of Rome were amazed. They expected to see criminals endeavouring to dissemble their faults, and they met with confessors of Christ with uplifted heads and words of power. Desirous of counterbalancing these sermons, the Bishop of Augsburg ordered his suffragan and his chaplain to ascend the pulpit. But the Romish priests understood better how to say mass than to preach the Gospel. "They only shout and bawl," said some. "They are stupid fellows," added all their hearers, shrugging their shoulders.[3]

The Romanists, ashamed of their own priests, began to grow angry,[4] and unable to hold their ground by preaching, had recourse to the secular power. "The priests are setting wondrous machines at work to gain Cæsar's mind," said Melancthon.[5] They succeeded, and Charles made known his displeasure at the hardihood of the princes. The friends of the pope then drew near the Protestants, and whispered into their ears, "that the emperor, victor over the King of France and the Roman pontiff, would appear in Germany to crush all the Gospellers."[6] The anxious elector demanded the advice of his theologians.

Before the answer was ready, Charles's orders arrived, brought by two of his most influential ministers, the Counts of Nassau and of Nuenar. A more skilful choice could not have been made. These two nobles, although devoted to Charles, were favourable to the Gospel, which they professed not long after. The elector was therefore fully disposed to listen to their counsel.

On the 24th May, the two counts delivered their letters to John of Saxony, and declared to him the emperor's exceeding grief that religious controversies should disturb the good understanding which had for so many years united the houses of Saxony

---

[1] Omnes alliciebat. Cochlœus, p. 191.

[1] Rogantibus Augustanis publice in templum Dominicorum. Seck. Lat. p. 193.
[2] Täglig in den kirchen, unverstört; dazu kommt schr viel Volks. Corp. Ref. ii. 53.
[3] Clamant et vociferantur. Audires homines stupidissimos atque etiam sensu communi carentes. Ibid. 56.
[4] Urebat hoc pontifices. Scultet. p. 271.
[5] Ὁι ἀρχιερεῖς miris machinis oppugnant. Corp. Ref. ii. 70.
[6] Evangelicos omnes obtriturum. Scultet. p. 269.

and Austria;[1] that he was astonished at seeing the elector oppose an edict (that of Worms) which had been unanimously passed by all the states of the empire; and that the alliances he had made tended to tear asunder the unity of Germany, and might inundate it with blood. They required, finally, that the elector would immediately put a stop to the evangelical preachings, and added, in a confidential tone, that they trembled at the thought of the immediate and deplorable consequences which would certainly follow the elector's refusal. "This," said they, "is only the expression of our own personal sentiments." It was a diplomatic manœuvre, the emperor having enjoined them to give utterance to a few threats, but solely as if proceeding from themselves.[2]

The elector was greatly agitated. "If his majesty forbids the preaching of the Gospel," exclaimed he, "I shall immediately return home."[3] He waited however for the advice of his theologians.

Luther's answer was ready first. "The emperor is our master," said he; "the town and all that is in it belong to him. If your highness should give orders at Torgau for this to be done, and for that to be left undone, the people ought not to resist. I should prefer endeavouring to change his majesty's decision by humble and respectful solicitation; but if he persists, might makes right; we have but done our duty."[4] Thus spoke the man who has often been represented as a rebel.

Melancthon and the others were nearly of the same opinion, except that they insisted more on the necessity of representing to the emperor, "that in their sermons nothing controversial was introduced, but they were content simply to teach the doctrine of Christ the Saviour.[5] Let us beware, above all," continued they, "of leaving the city. Let your highness with an intrepid heart confess in presence of his majesty by what wonderful ways you have attained to a right understanding of the truth,[6] and do not allow yourself to be alarmed at these thunder-claps that fall from the lips of our enemies." To confess the truth—such was the object to which, according to the Reformers, every thing else should be subordinate.

Will the elector yield to this first demand of Charles, and thus begin, even before the emperor's arrival, that list of sacrifices, the end of which cannot be foreseen!

No one in Augsburg was firmer than John. In vain did the reformers represent that they were in the emperor's city, and only strang-

ers:[1] the elector shook his head. Melancthon in despair wrote to Luther: "Alas! how untractable is our old man!"[2] Nevertheless he again returned to the charge. Fortunately there was an intrepid man at the elector's right hand, the chancellor Bruck, who feeling convinced that policy, honour, and above all, duty, bound the friends of the Reformation to resist the menaces of Charles, said to the elector: "The emperor's demand is but a worthy beginning to bring about the definitive abolition of the Gospel.[3] If we yield at present, they will crush us by and by. Let us therefore humbly beg his majesty to permit the continuance of the sermons." Thus, at that time, a statesman stood in the foremost rank of the confessors of Jesus Christ. This is one of the characteristic features of this great age, and it must not be forgotten, if we would understand its history aright.

On the 31st May, the elector sent his answer in writing to Charles's ministers. "It is not true," it bore, "that the edict of Worms was approved of by the six electors. How could the elector, my brother, and myself, by approving it, have opposed the everlasting Word of Almighty God? Accordingly, succeeding diets have declared this edict impossible to be executed. As for the relations of friendship that I have formed, their only aim is to protect me against acts of violence. Let my accusers lay before the eyes of his majesty the alliances they have made; I am ready to produce mine, and the emperor shall decide between us.—Finally, As to the demand to suspend our preachings, nothing is proclaimed in them but the glorious truth of God, and never was it so necessary to us. We cannot therefore do without it!"[4]

This reply must necessarily hasten the arrival of Charles; and it was urgent they should be prepared to receive him. To proclaim their belief, and then be silent, was the whole plan of the protestant campaign. A Confession was therefore necessary. One man, of small stature, frail, timid, and in great alarm, was commissioned to prepare this instrument of war. Philip Melancthon worked at it night and day: he weighed every expression, softened it down, changed it, and then frequently returned to his first idea. He was wasting away his strength; his friends trembled lest he should die over his task; and Luther enjoined him, as early as the 12th of May, under pain of anathema, to take measures for the preservation of "his little body," and not "to commit suicide for the love of God."[5] "God is as usefully served by repose," added he, "and indeed man never

---

[1] These instructions may be found in Cœlestin, i. 50, and Forstemann Urk. i. 220.
[2] Quidquid duri Electori denuntiabant suo veluti nomine et injussi dicebant. Seck. ii. 156.
[3] Den nächsten heim zu reiten. Corp. Ref. ii. 88.
[4] L. Epp. iv. 18.
[5] Nullas materias disputabiles a nobis doceri. Corp. Ref. ii. 72.
[6] Quo modo plane inenarrabili atque mirifico. Ibid. 74.

[1] In cujus urbe jam sumus hospites. Corp. Ref. ii. 46.
[2] Sed noster senex difficilis est. Ibid.
[3] Ein fügsamer Anfang der Niderbrengung des Evangelii. Ibid. 76.
[4] Quo carere non possit. Seck. p. 156; Muller, Hist. Prot. p. 506.
[5] Ut sub anathemate cogam te in regulas servandi corpusculi tui. L. Epp. iv. 16.

serves him better than by keeping himself tranquil. It is for this reason God willed that the Sabbath should be so strictly observed."[1]

Notwithstanding these solicitations, Melancthon's application augmented, and he set about an exposition of the christian faith, at once mild, moderate, and as little removed as possible from the doctrine of the Latin Church. At Coburg he had already put his hand to the task, and traced out in the first part the doctrines of the faith, according to the articles of Schwabach; and in the second, the abuses of the Church, according to the articles of Torgau, making altogether quite a new work. At Augsburg he gave a more correct and elegant form to this Confession.[2]

The Apology, as it was then called, was completed on the 11th May; and the elector sent it to Luther, begging him to mark what ought to be changed. "I have said what I thought most useful," added Melancthon, who feared that his friend would find the Confession too weak; for Eck is always circulating the most diabolical calumnies against us, and I have endeavoured to oppose an antidote to his poisons."[3]

Luther replied to the elector on the 15th May: "I have read Master Philip's Apology; I like it well enough, and have no corrections to make. Besides, that would hardly suit me, for I cannot walk so meekly and so silently. May Christ our Lord grant that this work may produce much and great fruit."

Each day, however, the elector's councillors and theologians, in concert with Melancthon, improved the Confession, and endeavoured to render it such that the charmed diet should, in its own despite, hear it to the very end.[4]

While the struggle was thus preparing at Augsburg, Luther at Coburg, on the summit of the hill, "on his Sinai," as he called it, raised his hands, like Moses towards heaven.[5] He was the real general of the spiritual war that was then waging; his letters were continually bearing to the combatants the directions which they needed, and numerous pamphlets issuing from his stronghold, like discharges of musketry, spread confusion in the enemy's camp.

The place where he had been left was, by its solitude, favourable to study and to meditation.[6] "I shall make a Zion of this Sinai," said he on the 22d April, "and I shall build here three tabernacles; one to the Psalms, another to the Prophets, and a third ——

to Esop!" This last word may well startle us. The association belongs neither to the language nor the spirit of the Apostles. It is true that Esop was not to be his principal study; the fables were soon laid aside, and truth alone engaged Luther. "I shall weep, I shall pray, I shall never be silent," wrote he, "until I know that my cry has been heard in heaven."[1]

Besides, by way of relaxation, he had something better than Esop; he had those domestic joys whose precious treasures the Reformation had opened to the ministers of the Word. It was at this time he wrote that charming letter to his infant son, in which he describes a delightful garden where children dressed in gold are sporting about, picking up apples, pears, cherries, and plums; they sing, dance, and enjoy themselves, and ride pretty little horses, with golden bridles and silver saddles.[2]

But the reformer was soon drawn away from these pleasing images. About this time he learnt that his father had gently fallen asleep in the faith which is in Jesus Christ. "Alas!" exclaimed he, shedding tears of filial love, "it is by the sweat of his brow that he made me what I am."[3] Other trials assailed him; and to bodily pains were added the phantoms of his imagination. One night in particular he saw three torches pass rapidly before his eyes, and at the same moment heard claps of thunder in his head, which he ascribed to the devil. His servant ran in at the moment he fainted, and after having restored him to animation, read to him the Epistle to the Galatians. Luther, who had fallen asleep, said as he awoke: "Come, and despite of the devil let us sing the Psalm, *Out of the depths have I cried unto thee, O Lord!*" They both sang the hymn. While Luther was thus tormented by these internal noises, he translated the prophet Jeremiah, and yet he often deplored his idleness.

He soon devoted himself to other studies, and poured out the floods of his irony on the mundane practices of courts. He saw Venice, the pope, and the King of France, giving their hands to Charles V. to crush the Gospel. Then, alone in his chamber in the old castle, he burst into irresistible laughter. "Mr. *Par-ma-foy* (it was thus he designated Francis I.), *In-nomine-Domini* (the pope), and the republic of Venice, pledge their goods and their bodies to the emperor......... *Sanctissimum fœdus.* A most holy alliance truly! This league between these four powers belongs to the chapter *Non-credimus.* Venice, the pope, and France become *imperialists!*......But these are three persons in one substance, filled with unspeakable hatred

[1] Ideo enim Sabbatum voluit tam rigide præ cæteris servari. L. Epp. iv. 16.
[2] More rhetorically. Feci aliquando ρητορικώτερον quam Coburgæ scripseram. Corp. Ref. ii. 40.
[3] Quia Ecklus addidit διαβολικωτάτας διαβολὰς contra nos. Ibid. 45.
[4] In Apologia quotidie multa mutamus. Ibid. 60.
[5] Mathesius Predigten, p. 92.
[6] Longe amœnissimus et studiis commodissimus. L. Epp. iv. 2.

[1] Orabo igitur et plorabo, non quieturus donec, &c. L. Epp. iv. 2.
[2] This letter, which is a masterpiece of its kind, may be found in Luther's Epp. iv. 41, and also in Riddle's "Luther and his Times," p. 268.
[3] Per ejus sudores aluit et finxit qualis sum. Epp. iv. 33.

against the emperor. Mr. *Par-ma-foy* cannot forget his defeat at Pavia; Mr. *In-nomine-Domini* is, 1st, an Italian, which is already too much; 2d, a Florentine, which is worse; 3d, a bastard—that is to say, a child of the devil; 4th, he will never forget the disgrace of the sack of Rome. As for the Venetians, they are Venetians: that is quite enough; and they have good reason to avenge themselves on the posterity of Maximilian. All this belongs to the chapter *Firmiter-credimus*. But God will help the pious Charles, who is a sheep among wolves. Amen."[1] The ex-monk of Erfurth had a surer political foresight than many diplomatists of his age.

Impatient at seeing the diet put off from day to day, Luther formed his resolution, and ended by convoking it even at Coburg. "We are already in full assembly," wrote he on the 28th April and the 9th May. "You might here see kings, dukes, and other grandees, deliberating on the affairs of their kingdom, and with indefatigable voice publishing their dogmas and decrees in the air. They dwell not in those caverns which you decorate with the name of palaces: the heavens are their canopy; the leafy trees form a floor of a thousand colours, and their walls are the ends of the earth. They have a horror of all the unmeaning luxury of silk and gold; they ask neither coursers nor armour, and have all the same clothing and the same colour. I have not seen or heard their emperor; but if I can understand them, they have determined this year to make a pitiless war upon——the most excellent fruits of the earth.—Ah! my dear friends," said he to his colleagues,[2] to whom he was writing, "these are the sophists, the papists, who are assembled before me from all quarters of the world to make me hear their sermons and their cries." These two letters, dated from the "*empire of ravens and crows*," finish in the following mournful strain, which shows us the reformer descending into himself after this play of his imagination: "Enough of jesting!—jesting which is, however, sometimes necessary to dispel the gloomy thoughts that overwhelm me."[3]

Luther soon returned to real life, and thrilled with joy at beholding the fruits that the Reformation was already bearing, and which were for him a more powerful "apology" than even the Confession of Melancthon. "Is there in the whole world a single country to be compared to your highness's states," wrote he to the elector, "and which possesses preachers of so pure a doctrine, or pastors so fitted to bring about the reign of peace? Where do we see, as in Saxony, boys and girls well instructed in the Holy Scriptures and in the Catechism, increasing in wisdom and in stature, praying, believing,

talking of God and of Christ better than has been done hitherto by all the universities, convents, and chapters of Christendom?"[1] —"My dear Duke John, says the Lord to you, I commend this paradise to thee, the most beautiful that exists in the world, that thou mayst be its gardener." And then he added: "Alas! the madness of the papist princes changes this paradise of God into a dirty slough, and corrupting the youth, daily peoples with real devils their states, their tables, and their palaces."

Luther, not content with encouraging his prince, desired also to frighten his adversaries. It was with this intent that he wrote at that time an address to the members of the clergy assembled at Augsburg. A crowd of thoughts, like lansquenets armed cap-a-pié. "rushed in to fatigue and bewilder him;"[2] and in fact there is no want of barbed words in the discourse he addresses to the bishops. "In short," said he to them in conclusion, "we know and you know that we have the Word of God, and that you have it not. O pope! if I live I shall be a pestilence to thee; and if I die, I shall be thy death!"[3]

Thus was Luther present at Augsburg, although invisible; and he effected more by his words and by his prayers than Agricola, Brentz, or Melancthon. These were the days of travail for the Gospel truth. It was about to appear in the world with a might destined to eclipse all that had been done since the time of St. Paul; but Luther only announced and manifested the things that God was effecting: he did not execute them himself. He was, as regards the events of the Church, what Socrates was to philosophy: "I imitate my mother (she was a midwife)," this philosopher was in the habit of saying; "she does not travail herself, but she aids others." Luther—and he never ceased repeating it—has created nothing; but he has brought to light the precious seed, hidden for ages in the bosom of the Church. The man of God is not he who seeks to form his age according to his own peculiar ideas; but he who, distinctly perceiving God's truth, such as it is found in his Word, and as it is hidden in his Church, brings it to his contemporaries with courage and decision.

Never had these qualities been more necessary, for matters were taking an alarming aspect. On the 4th June died Chancellor Gattinara, who was to Charles the Fifth "what Ulpian was to Alexander Severus," says Melancthon, and with him all the human hopes of the Protestants vanished. "It is God," Luther had said, "who has raised up for us a Naaman in the court of the King of Syria." In truth Gattinara alone resisted the pope. When Charles brought to him the

[1] To Gasp. of Teutleben, 19th June. L. Epp. iv. 37.
[2] An seine Tischgesellen, messmates or table-companions. Ibid. 7.
[3] Sed serio et necessario joco qui mihi irruentes cogitationes repelleret. Ibid. 14.

[1] Es wächst jetzt daher die zart Jugend von Knäblin un Maidlin. L. Epp. iv. 21.
[2] Ut plurimos Lansknecktos, prorsus vi repellere cogar, qui insalutati non cessant obstrepere. Ibid. 10.
[3] Pestis eram vivus, moriens ero mors tua, Papa. L. Opp. xx. 164.

objections of Rome: " Remember," said the chancellor, " that you are master !" Henceforward every thing seemed to take a new direction. The pope required that Charles should be satisfied with being his " lictor," as Luther says, to carry out his judgments against the heretics.[1] Eck, whose name (according to Melancthon) was no bad imitation of the cry of Luther's crows, heaped one upon another[2] a multitude of pretended heretical propositions, extracted from the reformer's writings. They amounted to *four hundred and four*, and yet he made excuse that, being taken unawares, he was forced to restrict himself to so small a number, and he called loudly for a disputation with the Lutherans. They retorted on these propositions by a number of ironical and biting theses on " wine, Venus, and baths, against John Eck ;" and the poor doctor became the general laughing-stock.

But others went to work more skilfully than he. Cochlœus, who became chaplain to Duke George of Saxony in 1527, begged an interview with Melancthon, " for," added he, " I cannot converse with your married ministers."[3] Melancthon, who was looked upon with an evil eye at Augsburg, and who had complained of being more solitary there than Luther in his castle,[4] was touched by this courtesy, and was still more fully penetrated with the idea that things should be ordered in the mildest manner possible.

The Romish priests and laymen made a great uproar, because on fast days meat was usually eaten at the elector's court. Melancthon advised his prince to restrict the liberty of his attendants in this respect. " This disorder," said he, " far from leading the simpleminded to the Gospel, scandalizes them." He added, in his ill-humour: " A fine holiness truly, to make it a matter of conscience to fast, and yet to be night and day given up to wine and folly !"[5] The elector did not yield to Melancthon's advice ; it would have been a mark of weakness of which his adversaries would have known how to take advantage.

On the 31st May, the Saxon Confession was at length communicated to the other Protestant states, who required that it should be presented in common in the name of them all.[6] But at the same time they desired to make their reservations with regard to the influence of the state. " We appeal to a council," said Melancthon ; " we will not

receive the emperor as our judge ; the ecclesiastical constitutions themselves forbid him to pronounce in spiritual matters.[1] Moses declares that it is not the civil magistrate who decides, but the sons of Levi. St. Paul also says (1 Cor. xiv.), ' *let the others judge*,' which cannot be understood except of an entire christian assembly ; and the Saviour himself gives us this commandment : ' *Tell it unto the Church.*' We pledge, therefore, our obedience to the emperor in all civil matters ; but as for the Word of God, we demand liberty."

All were agreed on this point ; but the dissent came from another quarter. The Lutherans feared to compromise their cause if they went hand in hand with the Zwinglians. " This is Lutheran madness," replied Bucer : " it will perish of its own weight."[2] But, far from allowing this madness " to perish," the reformed augmented the disunion by exaggerated complaints. " In Saxony they are beginning to sing Latin hymns again," said they ; " the sacred vestments are resumed, and oblations are called for anew.[3] We would rather be led to slaughter, than be Christians after that fashion."

The afflicted landgrave, says Bucer, was " between the hammer and the anvil ;" and his allies caused him more uneasiness than his enemies.[4] He applied to Rhegius, to Brentz, to Melancthon, declaring that it was his most earnest wish to see concord prevail among all the evangelical doctors. " If these fatal doctrines are not opposed," replied Melancthon, " there will be rents in the Church that will last to the end of the world. Do not the Zwinglians boast of their full coffers, of having soldiers prepared, and of foreign nations disposed to aid them? Do they not talk of sharing among them the rights and the property of the bishops, and of proclaiming liberty?....Good God ! shall we not think of posterity, which, if we do not repress these guilty seditions, will be at once without throne and without altar?"[5]—" No, no ! we are one," replied this generous prince, who was so much in advance of his age ; " we all confess the same Christ, we all profess that we must eat Jesus Christ, by faith, in the eucharist. Let us unite." All was unavailing. The time in which true catholicity was to replace this sectarian spirit, of which Rome is the most perfect expression, had not yet arrived.

1 Tantum lictorem suum in hæreticos. Epp. iv. 10.
2 Magnum acervum conclusionum congessit. Corp. Ref. p. 39.
3 Cum uxoratis presbyteris tuis privatim colloqui non intendimus. Ibid. p. 82.
4 Nos non minus sumus monachi quam vos in illa arce vestra. Ibid. p. 46.
5 Und dennoch Tag und Nacht voll und toll seyn. Ibid. ii. p. 79.
6 In gemein in aller Fürsten und Stadte Nämen. Ibid. ii. p. 88.

1 Die *constitutiones canonicæ* den Kaysern verbieten zu richten und sprechen in geistlichen sachen. Corp. Ref. ii. p. 66.
2 De Lutheranis furoribus....sua ipsi mole ruent. Zw Epp. ii. 432.
3 Hinc Latinæ resumuntur cantiones, repetuntur sanctæ vestes. Ibid. p. 457.
4 Cattus inter sacrum et saxum stat, et de sociis magis quam hostibus solicitus est. Ibid.
5 Keine Kirche und kein Regiment. Corp. Ref. ii. 95.

CHAPTER IV.

Agitation in Augsburg—Violence of the Imperialists—Charles at Munich—Charles's Arrival—The Nuncio's Blessing—The Imperial Procession—Charles's Appearance—Enters Augsburg—Te Deum—The Benediction—Charles desires the Sermons to be discontinued—Brandenburg offers his Head—The Emperor's Request for Corpus Christi—Refusal of the Princes—Agitation of Charles—The Princes oppose Tradition—Procession of Corpus Christi—Exasperation of Charles.

In proportion as the emperor drew near Augsburg, the anxieties of the Protestants increased. The burghers of this imperial city expected to see it become the theatre of strange events. Accordingly they said that if the elector, the landgrave, and other friends of the Reformation were not in the midst of them, they would all desert it.[1] " A great destruction threatens us," was repeated on every side.[2] One of Charles's haughty expressions above all disquieted the Protestants. " What do these electors want with me ?" he had said impatiently ; " I shall do what I please !"[3] Thus arbitrary rule was the imperial law destined to prevail in the diet.

To this agitation of men's minds was added the agitation of the streets, or rather one led to the other. Masons and locksmiths were at work in all the public places and crossings, laboriously fastening barriers and chains to the walls, that might be closed or stretched at the first cry of alarm.[4] At the same time about eight hundred foot and horse soldiers, whom the magistrates had enrolled in order to receive the emperor with magnificence, were seen patrolling the streets, dressed in velvet and silk.[5]

Matters were in this state, and it was about the middle of May, when a number of insolent Spanish quartermasters arrived, who, looking with contemptuous eyes on these wretched burghers, entered their houses, conducted themselves with violence, and even rudely tore down the arms of some of the princes.[6] The magistrates having delegated councillors to treat with them, the Spaniards made an impudent reply. " Alas ! " said the citizens, " if the servants are so, what will their master be ? " The ministers of Charles were grieved at their impertinence, and sent a German quartermaster who employed the forms of German politeness to make them forget this Spanish haughtiness.

That did not last long, and they soon felt more serious alarm. The Council of Augsburg were asked what was the meaning of these chains and soldiers, and they were ordered, in the emperor's name, to take down the one and disband the other. The magistrates of the city answered in alarm, " For more than ten years past we have intended putting up these chains ;[1] and as for the soldiers, our object is simply to pay due honour to his majesty." After many parleys it was agreed to dismiss the troops, and that the imperial commanders should select afresh a thousand men, who should make oath to the emperor, but be paid by the city of Augsburg.

The imperial quartermasters then resumed all their insolence : and no longer giving themselves the trouble of entering the houses and the shops, they tore down the signboards of the Augsburg citizens, and wrote in their place how many men and horses the latter would be required to lodge.[2]

Such were the preludes to the work of conciliation that Charles V. had announced, and that he was so slow in beginning. Accordingly his delay, attributed by some to the crowds of people who surrounded him with their acclamations ; by others to the solicitations of the priests, who opposed his entry into Augsburg until he had imposed silence on the ministers ; and by others, finally, to the lessons the pope had given him in the arts of policy and stratagem,[3] still more estranged the elector and his allies.

At last Charles, having quitted Innspruck two days after Gattinara's death, arrived at Munich on the 10th June. His reception was magnificent. About two miles from the town a temporary fortress had been erected, around which a sham-fight took place. Soldiers mounted to the assault, mines were exploded ; discharges of artillery, clouds of smoke, the clash of arms, the shouts of the combatants, delighted the eyes and ears of the emperor ;[4] within the city, theatres had been raised in the open air, in which *the Jewess Esther*, the *Persian Cambyses*, and other pieces not less famous, were represented ; and the whole, combined with splendid fireworks, formed the welcome given by the adherents of the pope to him whom they styled their saviour.

Charles was not far distant from Augsburg. As early as the 11th June, every day and every hour, members of the imperial household, carriages, waggons, and baggage entered the city, to the sound of the clacking whip and of the horn ;[5] and the burghers in amazement gazed with dejected eyes on all this insolent train, that fell upon their city like a flight of locusts.[6]

At five o'clock in the morning of the 15th June,[7] the elector, the princes, and their councillors, assembled at the town-hall, and erelong arrived the imperial commissaries.

[1] Wo Sachsen, Hessen, und andere Lutherische nit hie wären. Corp. Ref. ii. 89.
[2] Minatur nobis Satan grande exitium. Ibid. 92.
[3] Er wolte es machen, wie es Ihm eben wäre. Ibid. 88.
[4] Neu aufgerichte Ketten und Stöck. Ibid. 66.
[5] Mit samment und seide auf's kostlichst ausgestrichen. Ibid.
[6] Den jungen Fürsten zu Neuburg ihre wappen abgerissen. Ibid. 55.

[1] Vor zehn Jahren in Sinn gehalt. Corp. Ref. ii. 66.
[2] Gehen nicht mehr in die Häuser und schrieben an die Thür. Ibid. 89.
[3] Cæsarem instructum arte pontificum quærere causae moræ. L. Epp. iv. 31.
[4] Das hat Kais. Maj. wohl gefallen. Forstemann, Urkunden, i. 246.
[5] Alle stund die Wagen, der Tross und viel gesinds nach einander herein. Corp. Ref. ii. 90.
[6] Finden aber wenig Freuden feuer. Ibid.
[7] Zu morgens, um fünf Uhr. F. Urkunden, i. 263.

with orders for them to go out and meet Charles. At three in the afternoon the princes and deputies quitted the city, and, having reached a little bridge across the river Lech, they halted and waited for the emperor. The eyes of every member of the brilliant assemblage, thus stopping on the smiling banks of an alpine torrent, were directed along the road to Munich. At length, after waiting two or three hours, clouds of dust and a loud noise announced the emperor. Two thousand of the imperial guard marched first; and as soon as Charles had come to within fifty paces of the river, the electors and princes alighted. Their sons, who had advanced beyond the bridge, perceiving the emperor preparing to do the same, ran to him and begged him to remain on horseback;[1] but Charles dismounted without hesitation,[2] and approaching the princes with an amiable smile, cordially shook hands with them. Albert of Mentz, in his quality of arch-chancellor of the empire, now welcomed the emperor, and the Count-palatine Frederick replied in behalf of Charles.

While this was passing, three individuals remained apart on a little elevation;[3] these were the Roman legate, proudly seated on a mule, glittering with purple, and accompanied by two other cardinals, the Archbishop of Salzburg and the Bishop of Trent. The Nuncio, beholding all these great personages on the road, raised his hands, and gave them his blessing. Immediately the emperor, the king, and the princes who submitted to the pope, fell on their knees; the Spaniards, Italians, Netherlanders, and Germans in their train, imitated their movements, casting however a side glance on the Protestants, who, in the midst of this humbly prostrate crowd, alone remained standing.[4] Charles did not appear to notice this, but he doubtless understood what it meant. The Elector of Brandenburg then delivered a Latin speech to the legate. He had been selected because he spoke this language better than the princes of the Church; and accordingly, Charles, when praising his eloquence, slily put in a word about the negligence of the prelates.[5] The emperor now prepared to remount his horse; the Prince-electoral of Saxony, and the young princes of Luneburg, Mecklenburg, Brandenburg, and Anhalt, rushed towards him to aid him in getting into his saddle: one held the bridle, another the stirrup, and all were charmed at the magnificent appearance of their powerful sovereign.[6] The procession began to move on.

First came two companies of lansquenets, commanded by Simon Seitz, a citizen of Augsburg, who had made the campaign of Italy, and was returning home laden with gold.[1] Next advanced the households of the six electors, composed of princes, counts, councillors, gentlemen, and soldiers; the household of the Dukes of Bavaria had slipped into their ranks, and the four hundred and fifty horsemen that composed it marched five abreast, covered with bright cuirasses, and wearing red doublets, while over their heads floated handsome many-coloured plumes. Bavaria was already in this age the main support of Rome in Germany.

Immediately after came the households of the emperor and of his brother, in striking contrast with this warlike show. They were composed of Turkish, Polish, Arabian, and other led horses; then followed a multitude of young pages, clad in yellow or red velvet, with Spanish, Bohemian, and Austrian nobles in robes of silk and velvet;[2] among these the Bohemians had the most martial air, and gracefully rode their superb and prancing coursers. Last the trumpeters, drummers, heralds, grooms, footmen, and the legate's cross-bearers, announced the approach of the princes.

In fact these powerful lords, whose contentions had so often filled Germany with confusion and war, now advanced riding peacefully side by side. After the princes appeared the electors; and the Elector of Saxony, according to custom, carried the naked and glittering imperial sword immediately before the emperor.[3]

Last came the prince, on whom all eyes were fixed.[4] Thirty years of age, of distinguished port and pleasing features, robed in golden garments that glittered all over with precious stones,[5] wearing a small Spanish hat on the crown of his head,[6] mounted on a beautiful Polish hackney of the most brilliant whiteness, riding beneath a rich canopy of red, white, and green damask borne by six senators of Augsburg, and casting around him looks in which gentleness was mingled with gravity, Charles excited the liveliest enthusiasm, and every one exclaimed that he was the handsomest man in the empire, as well as the mightiest prince in the world.

He had at first desired to place his brother and the legate at his side; but the Elector of Mentz, attended by two hundred guards arrayed in silk, had claimed the emperor's right hand; and the Elector of Cologne, with a hundred well-armed attendants, had taken his station on the left. King Ferdinand and the legate followed after, and next came cardinals, ambassadors, and prelates, among whom was remarked the haughty

---

[1] Ab Electorum filiis qui procurrerant rogatus. Seck. ii. 101.
[2] Mox ab equis descenderunt. Cochlœus.
[3] Auf ein Ort geruckt. F. Urkunden, i. 256.
[4] Primum constantiæ specimen. Seck. ii. 101.
[5] Prelatorum autem negligentiam accusaret. Ibid.
[6] Conscendentem juniores principes adjuverunt. Ibid. and F. Urkunden, i. 258.

[1] Bekleit von gold. Lit. clothed with gold. F. Urkunden, i. 258.
[2] Viel sammete unde seiden Röcke. L. Opp. xx. 201.
[3] Noster princeps de more prætulit ensem. Corp. Ref. ii. 118.
[4] Omnium oculos in se convertit. Seck. ii. 160.
[5] Totus gemmis coruscabat. Ibid.
[6] Ein klein Spanisch Hütlein. F. Urkunden, i. 260.

Bishop of Osma, the emperor's confessor. The imperial cavalry and the troops of Augsburg closed the procession.

Never, according to the historians, had anything so magnificent been seen in the empire;[1] but they advanced slowly, and it was between eight and nine o'clock in the evening before they reached the gates of Augsburg.[2] Here they met the burgomaster and councillors, who prostrated themselves before Charles, and at the same time the cannon from the ramparts, the bells from all the steeples in full peal, the noise of trumpets and kettle-drums, and the joyful acclamations of the people, re-echoed with loud din. Stadion, bishop of Augsburg, and his clergy robed in white, struck up the *Advenisti desirabilis;* and six canons, advancing with a magnificent canopy, prepared to conduct the emperor to the cathedral, when Charles's horse, startled at this unusual sight, suddenly reared,[3] and the emperor had some difficulty in mastering him. At length Charles entered the minster, which was ornamented with garlands and flowers, and suddenly illuminated by a thousand torches. The emperor went up to the altar, and, falling on his knees, raised his hands towards heaven.[4] During the *Te Deum*, the Protestants observed with anxiety that Charles kept conversing in a low tone with the Archbishop of Mentz; that he bent his ear to the legate who approached to speak to him, and nodded in a friendly manner to Duke George. All this appeared to them of evil omen; but at the moment when the priests sang the *Te ergo quæsumus*, Charles, breaking off his conversations, suddenly rose, and one of the acolytes running to him with a gold embroidered cushion, the emperor put it aside, and knelt on the bare stones of the church. All the assembly knelt down with him; the elector and the landgrave alone remained standing. Duke George, astonished at such boldness, cast a threatening glance at his cousin. The Margrave of Brandenburg, carried away by the crowd, had fallen on his knees: but having seen his two allies standing, he hastily rose up again. The Cardinal-archbishop of Salzburg then proceeded to pronounce the benediction; but Campeggio, impatient at having as yet taken no part in the ceremony, hastened to the altar, and rudely thrusting the archbishop aside, said sharply to him:[5] "This office belongs to me, and not to you." The other gave way, the emperor bent down, and the landgrave, with difficulty concealing a smile, hid himself behind a candelabrum. The bells now rang out anew, the procession recommenced its march, and the princes conducted the emperor to the palatinate (the name given to the bishop's palace), which had been prepared for him. The crowd now dispersed: it was after ten at night.

The hour was come in which the partisans of the papacy flattered themselves with the prospect of rendering the Protestants untrue to their faith. The arrival of the emperor, the procession of the holy sacrament that was preparing, the late hour,—all had been calculated beforehand; "the nocturns of treason were about to begin," said Spalatin.

A few minutes of general conversation took place in the emperor's apartments; the princes of the Romish party were then allowed to retire; but Charles had given a sign to the Elector of Saxony, to the Landgrave of Hesse, to George, margrave of Brandenburg, to the Prince of Anhalt, and to the Duke of Luneburg, to follow him into his private chamber.[1] His brother Ferdinand, who was to serve as interpreter, alone went in with them. Charles thought that so long as the Protestant princes were before the world, they would not yield; but that in a private and friendly interview, he might obtain all he desired of them.

"His majesty requests you to discontinue the sermons," said Ferdinand. On hearing these words the two elder princes (the elector and the margrave) turned pale, and did not speak:[2] there was a long silence. At last, the landgrave said: "We entreat your majesty to withdraw your request, for our ministers preach only the pure Word of God, as did the ancient doctors of the Church, St. Augustine, St. Hilary, and so many others. Of this your majesty may easily convince yourself. We cannot deprive ourselves of the food of the Word of God, and deny his Gospel."[3]

Ferdinand, resuming the conversation in French[4] (for it was in this language that he conversed with his brother), informed the emperor of the landgrave's answer. Nothing was more displeasing to Charles than these citations of Hilary and Augustine; the colour mounted to his cheeks, and he was nearly giving way to his anger.[5] "His majesty," said Ferdinand in a more positive tone, "cannot desist from his demand."— "Your conscience," quickly replied the landgrave, "has no right to command ours."[6] As Ferdinand still persisted, the margrave, who had been silent until then, could contain himself no longer; and without caring for interpreters, stretched out his neck towards Charles, exclaiming in deep emotion: "Rather than allow the Word of the Lord to be taken from me, rather than deny my God, I would kneel down before your majesty and

---

[1] Antea in imperio non erat visa. Seck. ii. 160.
[2] Ingressus est in urbem intra octavam et nonam. Ibid. 114.
[3] Da entsetzt sich K. M. Hengst für solchem Himel. F. Urkunden, i. 26.
[4] Ihr hand aufgehebt. Ibid.
[5] Cardinalem legatus castigatum abegit. Seck. ii. 161.

[1] Ad conclave suum. Corp. Ref. pp. 106, 114.
[2] Die beede alte Fürsten zum höchsten entsetz. Ibid.
[3] Se non posse cibo verbi Dei carere, nec sana conscientia Evangelium negare. Ibid. 115.
[4] In Französischer Sprache. Ibid. 107.
[5] Sich darob etwas angeröt und erhitzt. Ibid. 115.
[6] K. M. gewissen sey aber kein Herr und meyster uber ihr gewisson. Ibid.

have my head cut off!" As he uttered these simple and magnanimous words, says a contemporary,[1] the prince accompanied them with a significant gesture, and let his hands fall on his neck like the headsman's axe. The excitement of the princes was at its height: had it been necessary, they would all four have instantly walked to the scaffold. Charles was moved; surprised and agitated, he hastily cried out in his bad German, making a show of checking the landgrave: "Dear prince, not the head! not the head!" But he had scarcely uttered these few words, when he checked himself.

These were the only words that Charles pronounced before the princes during all the diet. His ignorance of the German language, and sometimes also the etiquette of the Escurial, compelled him to speak only by the mouth of his brother or of the count-palatine. As he was in the habit of consecrating four hours daily to divine worship, the people said: "He talks more with God than with men." This habitual silence was not favourable to his plans. They required activity and eloquence; but instead of that the Germans saw in the dumb countenance of their youthful emperor, a mere puppet, nodding his head and winking his eyes. Charles sometimes felt very keenly the faults of this position: "To be able to speak German," said he, "I would willingly sacrifice any other language, even were it Spanish or French, and more than that, one of my states."[2]

Ferdinand saw that it was useless to insist on the cessation of these meetings; but he had another arrow in his quiver. The next day was the festival of *Corpus Christi*, and by a custom that had never as yet been infringed, all the princes and deputies present at the diet were expected to take part in the procession. Would the Protestants refuse this act of courtesy at the very opening of a diet to which each one came in a conciliatory spirit? Have they not declared that the body and blood of Christ are really in the Host? Do they not boast of their opposition to Zwingle, and can they stand aloof, without being tainted with heresy? Now, if they share in the pomp that surrounds "the Lord's body;" if they mingle with that crowd of clergy, glittering in luxury and swelling with pride, who carry about the God whom they have created; if they are present when the people bow down; will they not irrevocably compromise their faith? The machine is well prepared; its movements cannot fail; there is no more doubt! The craft of the Italians is about to triumph over the simplicity of these German boors.

Ferdinand therefore resumes, and making a weapon of the very refusal that he had just met with: "Since the emperor," said

he, "cannot obtain from you the suspension of your assemblies, he begs at least that you will accompany him to-morrow, according to custom, in the procession of the Holy Sacrament. Do so, if not from regard to him, at least for the honour of Almighty God."[7]

The princes were still more irritated and alarmed. "Christ," said they, "did not institute his sacrament to be worshipped." Charles persevered in his demand, and the Protestants in their refusal.[2] Upon this the emperor declared that he would not accept their excuse, that he would give them time for reflection, and that they must be prepared to reply early on the morrow.

They separated in the greatest agitation. The prince-electoral, who had waited for his father in the first hall along with other lords, sought, at the moment the princes issued from the emperor's chamber, to read on their countenance what had taken place. Judging from the emotion depicted on their features that the struggle had been severe, he thought that his father was incurring the greatest dangers, and accordingly, grasping him by the hand, dragged him to the staircase of the palace, exclaiming in affright, as if Charles's satellites were already at his heels, "Come, come quickly!"

Charles, who had expected no such resistance, was, in truth, confounded, and the legate endeavoured to exasperate him still more.[3] Agitated, filled with anger and vexation, and uttering the most terrible threats,[4] the young emperor paced hastily to and fro the halls of his palace; and unable to wait for the answer until the morrow, he sent in the middle of the night to demand the elector's final decision. "At present we require sleep," replied the latter; "to-morrow we will let you know our determination."[5] As for the landgrave, he could not rest any more than Charles. Scarcely had he returned home, when he sent his chancellor to the Nuremberg deputies, and had them awoke to make them acquainted with what had taken place.[6]

At the same time Charles's demand was laid before the theologians, and Spalatin, taking the pen, drew up their opinion during the night. "The sacrament," it bore, "was not instituted to be worshipped, as the Jews worshipped the brazen image.[7] We are here to confess the truth, and not for the confirmation of abuses. Let us therefore stay away!" This opinion confirmed the evangelical princes in their determination; and the day of the 16th June began to dawn.

---

[1] Ut simpliciter, ita magnanimiter, says Brentz. Corp. Ref. p. 115.
[2] Es wäre Spanisch oder Französisch und dazu eines Landes minder. Ibid. ii. 114.

[1] Et saltem in honorem Dei illud facerent. Corp. Ref. ii. 116.
[2] Persistit Cæsar in postulatione, perstiterunt illi in recusatione. Ibid. 115.
[3] A sævitia Legati Romanensium captivi. Ibid. 116.
[4] Hinc secutæ sunt gravissimæ minæ, jactatæ sævissimæ Cæsaris indignationes. Ibid.
[5] Quiete sibi opus esse dicens, responsum in diem alterum distulit. Seck. ii. 162.
[6] Hat nächten uns aufwecken lassen. Corp. Ref. ii. 106.
[7] Wie die Juden die Schlange haben angebethet. Ibid. 111.

The elector of Saxony, feeling indisposed during the night, commissioned his son to represent him ; and at seven o'clock the princes and councillors repaired on horseback to the emperor's palace.[1]

The Margrave of Brandenburg was their spokesman. " You know," said he to Charles, " how, at the risk of our lives, my ancestors and myself have supported your august house. But, in the things of God, the commands of God himself oblige me to put aside all commandment of man. We are told that death awaits those who shall persevere in the sound doctrine: I am ready to suffer it." He then presented the declaration of the evangelical princes to the emperor. "We will not countenance by our presence," said they, " these impious human traditions, which are opposed to the Word of God. We declare, on the contrary, without hesitation, and with one accord, that we must expel them from the Church, lest those of its members that are still sound should be infected by this deadly poison."[2] " If you will not accompany his majesty for the love of God," said Ferdinand, " do so at least for love of the emperor, and as vassals of the empire.[3] His majesty commands you." " An act of worship is in question," replied the princes, " our conscience forbids it." Then Ferdinand and Charles having conversed together in a low tone: "His majesty desires to see," said the king, " whether you will obey him or not."[4] At the same time the emperor and his brother quitted the room ; but the princes, instead of following him, as Charles had hoped, returned full of joy to their palaces.

The procession did not begin till noon. Immediately behind the canopy under which the Elector of Mentz carried the host, came the emperor alone, with a devout air, bearing a taper in his hand, his head bare and shorn like a priest's, although the noon-day sun darted on him its most ardent rays.[5] By exposing himself to these fatigues, Charles desired to profess aloud his faith in what constitutes the essence of Roman-catholicism. In proportion as the spirit and the life had escaped from the primitive churches, they had striven to replace them by forms, shows, and ceremonies. The essential cause of the Romish worship is found in that decline of charity and faith which the Catholic Christians of the first ages have often deplored ; and the history of Rome is summed up in this expression of St. Paul, *Having a form of godliness, but denying the power thereof.*[6] But as the *power* was then beginning to revive in the Church, the *form* began also to decline. Barely a hundred citizens of

Augsburg had joined in the procession of the 16th June. It was no longer the pomp of former times: the christian people had learned anew to love and to believe.

Charles, however, under an air of devotion concealed a wounded heart. The legate was less able to command himself, and said aloud that this obstinacy of the princes would be the cause of great mischief to the pope.[1] When the procession was over (it had lasted an hour), Charles could no longer master his extreme irritation; and he had scarcely returned to his palace, when he declared that he would give the Protestant princes a safeconduct, and that on the very next day these obstinate and rebellious men should quit Augsburg ;[2] the diet would then take such resolutions as were required for the safety of the Church and of the Empire. It was no doubt the legate who had given Charles this idea, which, if executed, would infallibly have led to a religious war. But some of the princes of the Roman party, desirous of preserving peace, succeeded, though not without difficulty, in getting the emperor to withdraw his threatening order.[3]

<hr>

CHAPTER V.

The Sermons prohibited—Compromise proposed and accepted—The Herald—Curiosity of the Citizens—The new Preachers—The Medley of Popery—Luther encourages the Princes—Veni Spiritus—Mass of the Holy Ghost—The Sermon—Opening of the Diet—The Elector's Prayer—Insidious Plan of the Romanists—Valdez and Melancthon—No Public Discussion—Evangelical firmness prevails.

CHARLES, being defeated on the subject of the procession, resolved to take his revenge on the assemblies, for nothing galled him like these sermons. A crowd continually filled the vast church of the Franciscans, where a Zwinglian minister of lively and penetrating eloquence was preaching on the Book of Joshua.[4] He placed the kings of Canaan and the children of Israel before them : his congregation heard them speak and saw them act, and every one recognized in the kings of Canaan the emperor and the ultramontane princes, and in the people of God the adherents of the Reformation. In consequence, his hearers quitted the church enthusiastic in their faith, and filled with the desire of seeing the abominations of the idolaters fall to the ground. On the 16th June, the Protestants deliberated on Charles's demand, and it was rejected by the majority. " It is but a scarecrow," said they; " the Papists only desire to see if the nail shakes in the wall, and if they can start the hare from the thicket."

The next morning (17th June) before

<hr>

[1] Heute zu sieben Uhren sind gemeldete Fürsten. Corp. Ref. iii. 107.
[2] Cælestin. i. 82.
[3] Ut vassalli et principes imperii. Cochlœus, p. 192.
[4] Sie wolle sehen, ob sie I. M. gehorchsam leisten oder nicht. Corp. Ref. ii. 108.
[5] Clericaliter, detonso capillo. Zw. Epp. ii. 471. Nudo capite sub meridiani solis ardoribus. Pallavicini, i. 228.
[6] 2 Timothy iii. 5.

[1] Sarpi, Council of Trent, i. 99.
[2] Ut mox altera die, cum salvo-conductu, Lutherani abi rent domum. Cochl. p. 193.
[3] Pacis et concordiæ avidi, supplicarunt ejus majestati ut sedata ira. Ibid.
[4] Maximus populi concursus amplissima æde. Ibid.

breakfast, the princes replied to the emperor. "To forbid our ministers to preach purely the holy Gospel would be rebellion against God who wills not that his Word be bound. Poor sinners that we are, we need this Divine Word to surmount our troubles.[1] Moreover, his majesty has declared, that in this diet each doctrine should be examined with impartiality. Now, to order us henceforward to suspend the sermons, would be to condemn ours beforehand."

Charles immediately convoked the other temporal and spiritual princes, who arrived at mid-day at the palatine palace, and remained sitting until the evening;[2] the discussion was exceedingly animated. "This very morning," said some of the speakers, "the Protestant princes, as they quitted the emperor, had sermons delivered in public."[3] Exasperated at this new affront, Charles with difficulty contained himself. Some of the princes, however, entreated him to accept their mediation, to which he consented; but the Protestants were immovable. Did these heretics, whom they imagined to reduce so easily, appear in Augsburg only to humiliate Charles? The honour of the chief of the empire must be saved at any cost. "Let us ourselves renounce our preachers," said the princes; "the Protestants will not then persist in keeping theirs!"

The committee accordingly proposed that the emperor should set aside both Papist and Lutheran preachers, and nominate a few chaplains, with authority to announce the pure Word of God, without attacking either of the two parties.[4] "They shall be neutral men," said they to the Protestants; "neither Faber nor his partisans shall be admitted."—"But they will condemn our doctrine."— "By no means. The preacher shall do nothing but read the text of the Gospels, Epistles, and a general confession of sins."[5] The evangelical states required time to reflect upon it.

"We must accept it," said Melancthon; "for if our obstinacy should lead the emperor to refuse hearing our Confession, the evil would be greater still."

"We are called to Augsburg," said Agricola, "to give an account of our doctrine, and not to preach."[6]

"There is no little disorder in the city," remarked Spalatin. "The sacramentarians and enthusiasts preach here as well as we: we must get out of this confusion."

"What do the Papists propose?" said other theologians; "to read the Gospels and Epistles without explanation. But is not that a victory? What! we protest against the interpretations of the Church; and lo! the priests are to read the Word of God without notes or commentaries, that is to say, transforming themselves into Protestant ministers!" "O! admirable wisdom of the courtiers!" exclaimed Melancthon, smiling.[1]

To these motives were added the opinions of the lawyers. As the emperor ought to be considered the rightful magistrate of an imperial city, so long as he made it his residence, all jurisdiction in Augsburg really belonged to him.

"Well, then," said the Protestant princes, "we agree to silence our preachers, in the hope that we shall hear nothing offensive to our consciences. If it were otherwise, we should feel ourselves constrained to repel so serious an insult.[2] Besides," added the elector, as he withdrew, "we expect that if at any time we desire to hear one of our chaplains in our own palace, we shall be free to do so."[3]

They hastened to the emperor, who desired nothing better than to come to an understanding with the Protestants on this subject, and who ratified every thing.

This was Saturday. An imperial herald was immediately sent out, who, parading the streets of the city at seven in the evening to the sound of trumpets,[4] made the following proclamation:—"O yes, O Yes![5] Thus ordains his imperial majesty, our most gracious lord: no one shall be allowed to preach in Augsburg except by his majesty's nomination, under penalty of incurring his majesty's displeasure and punishment."

A thousand different remarks were exchanged in the houses of the citizens of Augsburg. "We are very impatient," said they, "to see the preachers appointed by the emperor, and who will preach (O! unprecedented wonder!) neither against the evangelical doctrine nor against the doctrine of the pope!"[6] "We must expect," added another, "to behold some Tragelaph or some chimera with the head of a lion, a goat's body, and a dragon's tail."[7] The Spaniards appeared well satisfied with this agreement, for many of them had never heard a single sermon in their lives; it was not the custom in Spain; but Zwingle's friends were filled with indignation and alarm.[8]

At length Sunday the 19th of June arrived;

[1] Nec se illo animæ nutrimento carere. Cælestinus, Hist. Comit. i. 88; Forst. Urkunden, i. 283.
[2] Cæsar a meridie. Seck. 165. Den gangen Tag. Corp. Ref. ii. 113.
[3] Eo ipso die conciones continuatæ. Seckend. p. 165.
[4] Cæsare omnes tam papistarum quam evangelicorum conciones. Corp. Ref. ii. 116.
[5] Qui tantum recitent Evangelium et epistolam $\gamma\rho\alpha\mu\mu\alpha\tau\iota\kappa\tilde\omega\varsigma$. Ibid. 119.
[6] Non sumus parochi Augustanorum, added he. Ibid.

[1] Vide miram sapientiam Aulicorum. Corp. Ref. ii. 119
[2] Ut de remediis propulsandæ injuriæ cogitent. Seck. ii. 105.
[3] Ob je einer einen Prediger in seiner Herberg fur sich predigen liess. Corp. Ref. ii. 113.
[4] Per tubicines et heraldum. Sturmius, Zw. Epp. p. 466.
[5] Hört, Hört. Corp. Ref. ii. 124.
[6] Omnes hunc avidissime expectant. Ibid. 116.
[7] Chimæram aut Tragelaphum aliquem expectamus. Ibid. The *Tragelaph* is a fabulous animal partaking of the nature of a goat and a stag. Representations of it were common on drinking-bowls and goblets among the ancient Greeks.
[8] Multos deterreat. Sturm to Zwingle, Epp. p. 466.

every one hastened to the churches, and the people who filled them, with eyes fixed on the priest and with attentive ears,[1] prepared to listen to what these new and strange preachers would say.[2] It was generally believed that their task would be to make an evangelico-papistical discourse, and they were very impatient to hear this marvel. But

"The mountain in labour gave birth to a mouse!"

The preacher first read the common prayer; he then added the Gospel of the day, finished with a general confession of sins, and dismissed his congregation. People looked at one another in surprise: "Verily," said they, "here is a preacher that is neither Gospeller nor Papist, but strictly textual."[3] At last all burst into laughter; "and truly," adds Brentz, "there was reason enough."[4] In some churches, however, the chaplains, after reading the Gospel, added a few puerile words, void of Christianity and of consolation, and in no way founded on the Holy Scripture.[5]

After the so-called sermon, they proceeded to the mass. That in the cathedral was particularly noisy. The emperor was not present, for he was accustomed to sleep until nine or ten o'clock,[6] and a late mass was performed for him; but Ferdinand and many of the princes were present. The pealing notes of the organ, the resounding voices of the choir echoed through the minster, and a numerous and motley crowd, rushing in at all the doors, filled the aisles of the temple. One might have said that every nation in the world had agreed to meet in the cathedral of Augsburg. Here were Frenchmen, there Spaniards, Moors in one place, Moriscos in another, on one side Italians, on the other Turks, and even, says Brentz, those who are called Stratiots.[7] This crowd was no bad representation of the medley of popery.

One priest alone, a fervent Romanist, dared offer an apology for the mass in the church of the Holy Cross. Charles, wishing to maintain his authority, had him thrown into the Grayfriars' prison, whence he contrived to escape. As for the evangelical pastors of Augsburg, almost all left the city to hear the Gospel elsewhere. The Protestant princes were anxious to secure for their churches the assistance of such distinguished men. Discouragement and alarm followed close upon this step, and even the firmest were moved. The elector was inconsolable

at the privation imposed upon him by the emperor. "Our Lord God," said he, heaving a deep sigh, "has received an order to be silent at the Diet of Augsburg."[1] From that time forward Luther lost the good opinion he had previously entertained of Charles, and foreboded the stormiest future. "See what will be the end of all this," said he. "The emperor, who has ordered the elector to renounce the assemblies, will afterwards command him to renounce the doctrine; the diet will enter upon its paroxysm, and nothing will remain for us but to rely upon the arm of the Lord." Then giving way to all his indignation, he added: "The Papists, abandoned to devils, are transported with rage; and to live they must drink blood.[2] They wish to give themselves an air of justice, by giving us one of obstinacy. At Augsburg you have not to deal with men, but with the very gates of hell." Melancthon himself saw his hopes vanish. "All, except the emperor," said he, "hate us with the most violent hatred. The danger is great, very great.[3]......Pray to Christ that he may save us!" But Luther, however full of sorrow he might be, far from being cast down, raised his head and endeavoured to reanimate the courage of his brethren. "Be assured and doubt not," wrote he to them, "that you are the confessors of Jesus Christ, and the ambassadors of the Great King."[4]

They had need of these reflections, for their adversaries, elated by this first success, neglected nothing that might destroy the Protestants; and taking another step forward, proposed forcing them to be present at the Romish ceremonies.[5] "The Elector of Saxony," said the legate to Charles, "ought in virtue of his office of grand-marshal of the empire to carry the sword before you in all the ceremonies of the diet. Order him therefore to perform his duty at the mass of the Holy Ghost, which is to open the sittings." The emperor did so immediately, and the elector, uneasy at this message, called together his theologians. If he refused, his dignity would be taken away; and if he obeyed, he would trample his faith under foot (thought he), and would do dishonour to the Gospel.

But the Lutheran divines removed the scruples of their prince. "It is for a ceremony of the empire," said they, "as grand-marshal, and not as a Christian, that you are summoned; the Word of God itself, in the history of Naaman, authorizes you to comply with this invitation."[6] The friends of Zwingle did not think so; their walk was more de-

---

[1] Arrectis auribus. Corp. Ref. ii. 116.
[2] Quid novi novus concionator allaturus sit. Ibid. 117. 117.
[3] Sic habes concionatorem neque evangelicum neque papisticum, sed nudum textualem. Ibid.
[4] Rident omnes, et certe res valde ridicula est. Ibid.
[5] Pancula quædam, eaque puerilia et inepta, nec Christiane, absque fundamento verbi Divini et consolatione. Seck. ii. 165.
[6] Dormire solet usque ad nonam aut decimam. Corp. Ref. ii. 117.
[7] Ibi videas hic Gallos, hic Hispanos, hic Ethiopes, illic etiam Ethiopissas, hic Italos, illic etiam Turcas, aut quos vocant Stratiotas. Ibid.

[1] Hac ratione, Deo-ejusque verbo silentium est impositum. Seck. ii. 165.
[2] Ut nisi sanguinem biberint, vivere non possint. Ibid.
[3] Magnum omnino periculum est. Corp. Ref. ii. 118.
[4] Ea fides vivificabit et consolabitur vos, quia Magni Regis estis legati. L. Epp. iv. 59.
[5] Sarpi, Hist. Council of Trent, book i. 99.
[6] 2 Kings v. 18. Exemplo Naamanis, Seck. ii. 167; Sarpi. p. 99.

cided than that of Wittemberg. "The martyrs allowed themselves to be put to death," said they, "rather than burn a grain of incense before the idols." Even some of the Protestants, hearing that the *Veni Spiritus* was to be sung, said, wagging their heads: "We are very much afraid that the chariot of the Spirit, which is the Word of God, having been taken away by the papists, the Holy Ghost, despite their mass, will never reach Augsburg."[1] Neither these fears nor these objections were listened to.

On Monday the 20th June, the emperor and his brother, with the electors and princes of the empire, having entered the cathedral, took their seats on the right side of the choir; on the left were placed the legate, the archbishops, and bishops; in the middle were the ambassadors. Without the choir, in a gallery that overlooked it, were ranged the landgrave and other Protestants, who preferred being at a distance from the host.[2] The elector, bearing the sword, remained upright near the altar at the moment of the adoration. The acolytes having closed the gates of the choir immediately after,[3] Vincent Pompinello, archbishop of Bassano, preached the sermon. He commenced with the Turks and their ravages, and then, by an unexpected turn, began suddenly to exalt the Turks even above the Germans. "The Turks," said he, "have but one prince whom they all obey; but the Germans have many who obey no one. The Turks live under one sole law, one only custom, one only religion; but among the Germans there are some who are always wishing for new laws, new customs, new religions. They tear the seamless coat of Christ; they abolish by devilish inspirations the sacred doctrines established by unanimous consent, and substitute for them, alas! buffoonery and obscenity.[4] Magnanimous emperor, powerful king!" said he, turning towards Charles and his brother, "sharpen your swords, wield them against these perfidious disturbers of religion, and thus bring them back into the fold of the Church.[5] There is no peace for Germany so long as the sword shall not have entirely eradicated this heresy.[6] O St. Peter and St. Paul! I call upon you; upon you, St. Peter, in order that you may open the stony hearts of these princes with your keys; and upon you, St. Paul, that if they show themselves too rebellious, you may come with your sword, and cut in pieces this unexampled hardness!"

This discourse, intermingled with panegyrics of Aristides, Themistocles, Scipio,

Cato, the Curtii and Scævola, being concluded, the emperor and princes arose to make their offerings. Pappenheim returned the sword to the elector, who had intrusted it to him; and the grand-marshal, as well as the margrave, went to the offertory, but with a smile, as it is reported.[1] This fact is but little in harmony with the character of these princes.

At length they quitted the cathedral. No one, except the friends of the nuncio, was pleased with the sermon. Even the Archbishop of Mentz was offended at it. "What does he mean," exclaimed he, "by calling on St. Paul to cut the Germans with his sword?" As nothing more than a few inarticulate sounds had been heard in the nave, the Protestants eagerly questioned those of their party who had been present in the choir. "The more these priests inflame people's minds, and the more they urge their princes to bloody wars," said Brentz at that time, "the more we must hinder ours from giving way to violence."[2] Thus spoke a minister of the Gospel of peace after the sermon of the priests of Rome.

After the mass of the Holy Ghost, the emperor entered his carriage,[3] and having reached the town-hall, where the sittings of the diet were to take place, took his seat on a throne covered with cloth of gold, while his brother placed himself on a bench in front of him; then all around them were ranged the electors, forty-two sovereign princes, the deputies from the cities, the bishops, and ambassadors, forming, indeed, that illustrious assembly which Luther, six weeks before, had imagined he saw sitting in the air.[4]

The count-palatine read the imperial proposition. It referred to two points; the war against the Turks, and the religious controversy. "Sacrificing my private injuries and interests to the common good," said the emperor, "I have quitted my hereditary kingdoms, to pass, not without great danger, into Italy, and from thence to Germany. I have heard with sorrow of the divisions that have broken out here, and which, striking not only at the imperial majesty, but still more at the commandments of Almighty God, must engender pillage, conflagration, war, and death."[5] At one o'clock the emperor, accompanied by all the princes, returned to his palace.

On the same day the elector gathered around him all his co-religionists, whom the emperor's speech had greatly excited, and exhorted them not to be turned aside by any

---

[1] Ne ablato Spiritus vehiculo, quod est verbum Dei, Spiritus Sanctus ad Augustam præ pedum imbecillitate pervenire non possit. Corp. Ref. ii. 116.
[2] Abstinendo ab adoratione hostiæ. Seck. ii. 119.
[3] Erant enim chori fores clausæ, nec quisquam orationi interfuit. Corp. Ref. ii. 120.
[4] Diabolica persuasione eliminant, et ad scurrilia ac impudica quæque deducunt. Pallavicini, Hist. Trid. C. i. 23.
[5] Exacuant gladios quos in perversos illos perturbatores. Corp. Ref. ii. 120.
[6] Nisi eradicata funditus per gladium hæresi illa. Ibid.

[1] Protestantes etiam ad offerandum munuscula in altari, ut moris erat, accessisse, sed cum risu. Spalat. Seck. ii. 167.
[2] Ut nostros principes ab importuna violentia retineamus. Corp. Ref. ii. 120.
[3] Imperator cum omnibus in curiam vectus est. Sturm to Zw. Epp. ii. 430.
[4] Ex volucrum monedularumque regno. L. Epp. iv. 13.
[5] Nicht anders dann zu Raub, Brandt, und Krieg. F. Urkunden, i. 307.

threats from a cause which was that of God himself.[1] All seemed penetrated with this expression of Scripture : " Speak the word, and it shall not stand ; for God is with us."[2]

The elector had a heavy burden to bear. Not only had he to take the lead among the princes, but he had further to defend himself against the enervating influence of Melancthon. Throughout the whole of the diet this prince offers to our notice no mere abstraction of the state, but the noblest individuality. Early on Tuesday morning, feeling the necessity of that invisible strength which, according to a beautiful figure in the Holy Scriptures, causes us to ride upon the high places of the earth ; and seeing, as was usual, his domestics, his councillors, and his son assembled around him, John begged them affectionately to withdraw.[3] He knew that it was only by kneeling humbly before God that he could stand with courage before Charles. Alone in his chamber, he opened and read the Psalms ; then falling on his knees, he offered up the most fervent prayer to God ;[4] and afterwards, wishing to confirm himself in the immovable fidelity that he had just vowed to the Lord, he went to his desk, and there committed his resolutions to writing. Dolzig and Melancthon afterwards saw these lines, and were filled with admiration as they read them.[5]

Being thus tempered anew in heavenly thoughts, John took up the imperial proposition and meditated over it ; then having called in his son and the chancellor Brück, and Melancthon shortly after, they all agreed that the deliberations of the diet ought to commence with the affairs of religion; and his allies, who were consulted, concurred in this advice.

The legate had conceived a plan diametrically opposed to this. He desired to stifle the religious question, and for this end required that the princes should examine it in a secret committee.[6] The evangelical Christians entertained no doubt that if the truth was proclaimed in the great council of the nation, it would gain the victory ; but the more they desired a public confession, the more it was dreaded by the pope's friends. The latter wished to take their adversaries by silence, without confession, without discussion, as a city is taken by famine without fighting and without a storm : to gag the Reformation, and thus reduce it to powerlessness and death, were their tactics. To have silenced the preachers was not enough : the princes must be silenced also. They wished to shut up the Reformation as in a dungeon,

and there leave it to die, thinking they would thus get rid of it more surely than by leading it to the scaffold.

This plan was well conceived : it now remained to be put in execution, and for that purpose it was necessary to persuade the Protestants that such a method would be the surest for them. The person selected for this intrigue was Alphonso Valdez, secretary to Charles V., a Spanish gentleman, a worthy individual, and who afterwards showed a leaning towards the Reformation. Policy often makes use of good men for the most perfidious designs. It was decided that Valdez should address the most timid of the Protestants—Melancthon.

On the 16th or 17th of June, immediately after the arrival of Charles, Valdez begged Melancthon to call on him. " The Spaniards," said he, "imagine that the Lutherans teach impious doctrines on the Holy Trinity, on Jesus Christ, on the blessed Mother of God.[1] Accordingly, they think they do a more meritorious work in killing a Lutheran than in slaying a Turk."

" I know it," replied Melancthon, " and I have not yet been able to succeed in making your fellow-countrymen abandon that idea."

" But what, pray, do the Lutherans desire ? "

" The Lutheran question is not so complicated and so unseemly as his majesty fancies. We do not attack the Catholic Church, as is commonly believed;[2] and the whole controversy is reducible to these three points. The two kinds in the sacrament of the Lord's Supper, the marriage of pastors, and the abolition of private masses. If we could agree on these articles, it would be easy to come to an understanding on the others."

" Well, I will report this to his majesty."

Charles V. was charmed at this communication. " Go," said he to Valdez, " and impart these things to the legate, and ask Master Philip to transmit to you in writing a short exposition of what they believe and what they deny."

Valdez hastened to Campeggio. " What you relate pleases me tolerably," said the latter. " As for the two kinds in the sacrament, and the marriage of priests, there will be means of accommodation :[3] but we cannot consent to the abolition of private masses." This would have been in fact cutting off one of the greatest revenues of the Church.

On Saturday, June 18, Valdez saw Melancthon again. " The emperor begs of you a moderate and concise exposition," said he, " and he is persuaded that it will be more advantageous to treat of this matter briefly

[1] Cohortatus est ad intrepidam causæ Dei assentionem. Seck. ii. 108.
[2] Isaiah viii. 10.
[3] Mane remotis omnibus consiliariis et ministris. Seck. ii. 169.
[4] Precibus ardentissimis a Deo successum negotii petiisset. Ibid.
[5] Quæ cum admiratione legisse dicuntur. Ibid.
[6] Si acturi sunt secreto et inter sese, nulla publica disputatione vel audientia. L. Epp. iv. 43.

[1] Hispanis persuasum esse Lutheranos impie de Sanctissima Trinitate. Ex relatione Spalati in Seck. ii. 165.
[2] Non adeo per eos Ecclesiam Catholicam oppugnari, quam vulgo putaretur. Ibid. 100.
[3] Mit beider Gestalt sacraments oder des Pfaffen und Mönch Ehe. Corp. Ref. ii. 123.

and privately,[1] avoiding all public hearing and all prolix discussion, which would only engender anger and division."— "Well," said Melancthon, "I will reflect upon it."

Melancthon was almost won over: a secret conference agreed better with his disposition. Had he not often repeated that peace should be sought after above all things? Thus every thing induced the legate to hope that a public struggle would be avoided, and that he might be content, as it were, to send mutes against the Reform, and strangle it in a dungeon.[2]

Fortunately the chancellor and the Elector John did not think fit to entertain the propositions with which Charles had commissioned the worthy Valdez. The resolution of these lay members of the Church saved it from the false step its doctors were about to take; and the wiles of the Italians failed against evangelical firmness. Melancthon was only permitted to lay the Confession before the Spaniard, that he might look into it, and in despite of the moderation employed in it, Valdez exclaimed: "These words are too bitter, and your adversaries will never put up with them!"[3] Thus finished the legate's manœuvre.

CHAPTER VI.

The Elector's Zeal—The Signing of the Confession—Courage of the Princes—Melancthon's Weakness—The Legate's Speech—Delays—The Confession in Danger—The Protestants are firm — Melancthon's Despondency — Luther's Prayer and Anxiety—Luther's Texts—His Letter to Melancthon—Faith.

CHARLES, compelled to resign himself to a public sitting, ordered on Wednesday, 22d June, that the elector and his allies should have their Confession ready for the ensuing Friday. The Roman party were also invited to present a confession of faith; but they excused themselves, saying that they were satisfied with the Edict of Worms.

The emperor's order took the Protestants by surprise, for the negotiations between Valdez and Melancthon had prevented the latter from putting the finishing stroke to the Confession. It was not copied out fair; and the conclusions, as well as the exordium, were not definitively drawn up. In consequence of this, the Protestants begged the Archbishop of Mentz to obtain for them the delay of a day; but their petition was refused.[4] They therefore laboured incessantly, even during the night, to correct and transcribe the Confession.

On Thursday, 23d June, all the Protestant princes, deputies, councillors, and theologians met early at the elector's. The Confession was read in German, and all gave their adhesion to it, except the landgrave and the Strasburgers, who required a change in the article on the sacrament.[1] The princes rejected their demand.

The Elector of Saxony was already preparing to sign it, when Melancthon stopped him: he feared giving too political a colouring to this religious business. In his idea it was the Church that should appear, and not the State. "It is for the theologians and ministers to propose these things," said he;[2] "let us reserve for other matters the authority of the mighty ones of the earth."— "God forbid that you should exclude me," replied the elector; "I am resolved to do what is right without troubling myself about my crown. I desire to confess the Lord. My electoral hat and my ermine are not so precious to me as the cross of Jesus Christ. I shall leave on earth these marks of my greatness; but my Master's cross will accompany me to heaven."

How resist such christian language! Melancthon gave way.

The elector then approached, signed, and handed the pen to the landgrave, who at first made some objections; however the enemy was at the door; was this a time for disunion? At last he signed, but with a declaration that the doctrine of the Eucharist did not please him.[3]

The margrave and Luneburg having joyfully subscribed their names, Anhalt took the pen in his turn, and said: "I have tilted more than once to please others; now, if the honour of my Lord Jesus Christ requires it, I am ready to saddle my horse, to leave my goods and life behind, and rush into eternity, towards an everlasting crown." Then, having signed, this youthful prince said, turning to the theologians, "I would rather renounce my subjects and my states, rather quit the country of my fathers staff in hand, rather gain my bread by cleaning the shoes of the foreigner, than receive any other doctrine than that which is contained in this Confession." Nuremberg and Reutlingen alone of the cities subscribed their signatures;[4] and all resolved on demanding of the emperor that the Confession should be read publicly.[5]

The courage of the princes surprised every one. Rome had crushed the members of the Church, and had reduced them to a herd of slaves, whom she dragged silent and humiliated behind her: the Reformation enfranchised them, and with their rights it restored

---

[1] Die Sache in einer Enge und Stille vorzu nehmen. Corp. Ref. ii. 123.
[2] Cælestin, Hist. Comit. August. p. 193. Intelligo hoc τους αρχιεσας moliri, ut omnino nihil agatur de negotiis ecclesiasticis. Ibid. 57.
[3] Ac plane putarit πικρότερον esse quam ut ferre possent adversarii. Ibid. 140.
[4] Dasselbige abgeschlagen. Ibid. 127.

[1] Argentinenses ambierunt aliquid ut excepto articulo sacramenti susciperentur. Corp. Ref. ii. 155.
[2] Non principum nomine edi sed docentium, qui theologi vocantur. Camer. p. 120.
[3] Landgravius subscribit nobiscum, sed tamen dicit sibi, de sacramento, a nostris non satisfieri. Corp. Ref. ii. 155.
[4] Confessioni tantum subscripserunt Nuremberga et Reutlingen. Ibid.
[5] Decretum est ut publicæ recitandæ concessio ab Imperatore peteretur. Seck. ii. 169.

to them their duties. The priest no longer enjoyed the monopoly of religion : each head of a family again became priest in his own house, and all the members of the Church of God were thenceforward called to the rank of confessors. The laymen are nothing, or almost nothing, in the sect of Rome, but they are the essential portion of the Church of Jesus Christ. Wherever the priestly spirit is established, the Church dies ; wherever laymen, as these Augsburg princes, understand their duty and their immediate dependence on Christ, the Church lives.

The evangelical theologians were moved by the devotedness of the princes. "When I consider their firmness in the confession of the Gospel," said Brentz, "the colour mounts to my cheeks. What a disgrace that we, who are only beggars beside them, are so afraid of confessing Christ!"[1] Brentz was then thinking of certain towns, particularly of Halle, of which he was pastor, but no doubt also of the theologians.

The latter in truth, without being deficient in devotedness, were sometimes wanting in courage. Melancthon was in constant agitation ; he ran to and fro, slipping in every where (says Cochlœus in his Philippics), visiting not only the houses and mansions of private persons, but also insinuating himself into the palaces of cardinals and princes, nay, even into the court of the emperor ; and, whether at table or in conversation, he spared no means of persuading every person, that nothing was more easy than to restore peace between the two parties.[2]

One day he was with the Archbishop of Salzburg, who, in a long discourse, gave an eloquent description of the troubles produced, as he said, by the Reformation, and ended with a peroration "written in blood," as Melancthon characterized it.[3] Philip in agony had ventured during the conversation to slip in the word conscience. "Conscience!" hastily interrupted the archbishop, "Conscience!—What does that mean ? I tell you plainly that the emperor will not allow confusion to be thus brought upon the empire."—"Had I been in Melancthon's place," said Luther, "I should have immediately replied to the archbishop : And our emperor,—ours, —will not tolerate such blasphemy."— "Alas," said Melancthon, "they are all as full of assurance as if there was no God."[4]

Another day Melancthon was with Campeggio, and conjured him to persevere in the moderate sentiments he appeared to entertain. And at another time, as it would seem, he was with the emperor himself.[5] "Alas!" said the alarmed Zwinglians, "after having qualified one-half of the Gospel, Melancthon is sacrificing the other."[1]

The wiles of the Ultramontanists were added to Philip's dejection, in order to arrest the courageous proceedings of the princes. Friday, 24th June, was the day fixed for reading the Confession, but measures were taken to prevent it. The sitting of the diet did not begin till three in the afternoon ; the legate was then announced ; Charles went to meet him as far as the top of the grand staircase, and Campeggio, taking his seat in front of the emperor, in King Ferdinand's place, delivered a harangue in Ciceronian style. "Never," said he, "has St. Peter's bark been so violently tossed by such various waves, whirlwinds, and abysses.[2] The Holy Father has learnt these things with pain, and desires to drag the Church from these frightful gulfs. For the love of Jesus Christ, for the safety of your country and for your own, O mighty Prince! get rid of these errors, deliver Germany, and save Christendom!"

After a temperate reply from Albert of Mentz, the legate quitted the town-hall, and the evangelical princes stood up ; but a fresh obstacle had been provided. Deputies from Austria, Carinthia, and Carniola, first received a hearing.[3]

Much time had thus elapsed. The evangelical princes, however, rose up again, and the Chancellor Brück said : "It is pretended that new doctrines not based on Scripture, that heresies and schisms, are spread among the people by us. Considering that such accusations compromise not only our good name, but also the safety of our souls,[4] we beg his majesty will have the goodness to hear what are the doctrines we profess."

The emperor, no doubt by arrangement with the legate, made reply that it was too late ; besides, that this reading would be useless ; and that the princes should be satisfied with putting in their Confession in writing. Thus the mine, so skilfully prepared, worked admirably ; the Confession, once handed to the emperor, would be thrown aside, and the Reformation would be forced to retire, without the Papists having even condescended to hear it, without defence, and overwhelmed with contumely.

The Protestant princes, uneasy and agitated, insisted. "Our honour is at stake." said they ; "our souls are endangered.[5] We are accused publicly ; publicly we ought to answer." Charles was shaken ; Ferdinand leant towards him, and whispered a few words in his ear ;[6] the emperor refused a second time.

[1] Rubore suffundor non mediocri, quod nos, præ illis mendici, &c. Corp. Ref. ii. 125.
[2] Cursitabat hinc inde, perreptans ac penetrans. Cochl. Phil. 4. in Apol.
[3] Addebat Epilogum plane sanguine scriptum. Corp. Ref. ii. 126.
[4] Securi sunt quasi nullus sit Deus. Ibid. 156.
[5] Melancthon a Cæsare, Salisburgensi et Campegio vocatus est. Zw. Epp. ii. 473.

[1] Ut cum mitigarit tam multa, cedat et reliqua. Zw. Epp. ii. 473.
[2] Neque unquam tam variis sectarum turbinibus navicula Petri fluctuaverit. Seck. ii. 169.
[3] Oratio valde lugubris et miserabilis contra Turcas. Corp. Ref. ii. 154.
[4] Verum etiam ad animæ dispendium aut salutem æternam. Seck. ii. 189.
[5] Ihre Seele, Ehre und Glimpf belunget. Corp. Ref. ii. 128
[6] Viderant enim eum subinde aliquid illi in aurem in susurrare. Seck. ii. 169.

Upon this the elector and princes, in still greater alarm, said for the third time, with emotion and earnestness :[1] " For the love of God, let us read our Confession! No person is insulted in it." Thus were seen, on the one hand, a few faithful men, desiring with loud cries to confess their faith ; and on the other, the great emperor of the west, surrounded by a crowd of cardinals, prelates, and princes, endeavouring to stifle the manifestation of the truth.[2] It was a serious, violent, and decisive struggle, in which the holiest interests were discussed !

At last Charles appeared to yield : " His majesty grants your request," was the reply to the princes ; " but as it is now too late, he begs you to transmit him your written Confession, and to-morrow, at two o'clock, the diet will be prepared to hear it read at the Palatine Palace."

The princes were struck by these words, which, seeming to grant them every thing, in reality granted nothing. In the first place, it was not in a public sitting at the town-hall, but privately in his own palace, that the emperor was willing to hear them ;[3] then they had no doubt that if the Confession left their hands it was all over with the public reading. They therefore remained firm. " The work has been done in great haste," said they, and it was the truth ; " pray leave it with us to-night, that we may revise it." The emperor was obliged to yield, and the Protestants returned to their hotels full of joy ; while the legate and his friends, perceiving that the Confession was inevitable, saw the morrow approach with continually increasing anxiety.

Among those who prepared to confess the evangelical truth, was one, however, whose heart was filled with sadness :—it was Melancthon. Placed between two fires, he saw the reformed, and many even of his own friends, reproach his weakness ; while the opposite party detested what they called his hypocrisy. His friend Camerarius, who visited Augsburg about this time, often found him plunged in thought, uttering deep sighs, and shedding bitter tears.[4] Brentz, moved with compassion, coming to the unhappy Philip, would sit down by his side and weep with him ;[5] and Jonas endeavoured to console him in another manner, by exhorting him to take the book of Psalms, and cry to God with all his heart, making use of David's words rather than of his own.

One day intelligence arrived which formed a general topic of conversation in Augsburg, and which, by spreading terror among the partisans of the pope, gave a momentary relief to Melancthon. It was said that a mule in Rome had given birth to a colt with crane's feet. " This prodigy," said Melancthon thoughtfully, "announces that Rome is near its end ;"[1] perhaps because the crane is a bird of passage, and that the pope's mule thus gave signs of departure. Melancthon immediately wrote to Luther, who replied that he was exceedingly rejoiced that God had given the pope so striking a sign of his approaching fall.[2] It is good to recall to memory these puerilities of the age of the reformers, that we may better understand the high range of these men of God in matters of faith.

These idle Roman stories did not long console Melancthon. On the eve of the 25th of June, he was present in imagination at the reading of that Confession which he had drawn up, which was about to be proclaimed before the world, and in which one word too many or too few might decide on the approbation or the hatred of the princes, on the safety or ruin of the Reformation and of the empire. He could bear up no longer, and the feeble Atlas, crushed under the burden of the world upon his shoulders, gave utterance to a cry of anguish. " All my time here is spent in tears and mourning," wrote he to Vitus Diedrich, Luther's secretary in the castle of Coburg ;[3] and on the morrow he wrote to Luther himself · " My dwelling is in perpetual tears.[4] My consternation is indescribable.[5] O my father ! I do not wish my words to exaggerate my sorrows ; but without your consolations, it is impossible for me to enjoy here the least peace."

Nothing in fact presented so strong a contrast to Melancthon's distrust and dejection, as the faith, calmness, and exultation of Luther. It was of advantage to him that he was not then in the midst of the Augsburg vortex, and that he was able from his stronghold to set his foot with tranquillity upon the rock of God's promises. He was sensible himself of the value of this peaceful hermitage, as he called it.[6] " I cannot sufficiently admire," said Vitus Diedrich, " the firmness, cheerfulness, and faith of this man, so astonishing in such cruel times."

Luther, besides his constant reading of the Word of God,[7] did not pass a day without devoting three hours at least to prayer, and they were hours selected from those the most favourable to study.[8] One day, as Diedrich approached the reformer's chamber, he

---

1 Zum dritten mal heftig angehalten. Corp. Ref. ii. 128.
2 Circumsistebant Cæsarem magno numero cardinales et prælati ecclesiastici. Seck. ii. 169.
3 Non quidem publice in prætorio, sed privatim in palatio suo. Corp. Ref. ii. 124.
4 Non modo suspirantem sed profundentem lacrymas conspexi. Camer. p. 121.
5 Brentius assidebat hæc scribenti, una lacrymans. Corp. Ref il. 126.

1 Romæ quædam mula peperit, et partus habuit pedes gruis. Vides significari exitium Romæ per schismata. Corp. Ref. ii. 126.
2 Gaudeo Papæ signum datum in mula puerpera, ut citius pereat. L. Epp. iv. 4.
3 Hic consumitur omne mihi tempus in lacrymis et luctu. Corp. Ref. ii. 126.
4 Versamur hic in miserrimis curis et plane perpetuis lacrymis. Ibid. p. 140.
5 Mira consternatio animorum nostrorum. Ibid.
6 Ex eremo tacita. L. Epp. iv. 51. It is thus he dates his letter.
7 Assidue autem illa diligentiore verbi Dei tractatione alit. Corp. Ref. ii. 159.
8 Nullus abit dies, quin ut minimum tres horas easque studiis optimas in orationibus ponat. Ibid.

heard his voice,[1] and remained motionless, holding his breath, a few steps from the door. Luther was praying, and his prayer (said the secretary) was full of adoration, fear, and hope, as when one speaks to a friend or to a father.[2] " I know that thou art our Father and our God," said the reformer, alone in his chamber, " and that thou wilt scatter the persecutors of thy children, for thou art thyself endangered with us. All this matter is thine, and it is only by thy constraint that we have put our hands to it. Defend us then, O Father ! " The secretary, motionless as a statue, in the long gallery of the castle, lost not one of the words that the clear and resounding voice of Luther bore to his ears.[3] The reformer was earnest with God, and called upon him with such unction to accomplish his promises, that Diedrich felt his heart glow within him.[4] " Oh!" exclaimed he, as he retired, " how could these prayers do otherwise than prevail in the desperate struggle at Augsburg ! "

Luther might also have allowed himself to be overcome with fear, for he was left in complete ignorance of what was taking place in the diet. A Wittemberg messenger, who should have brought him forests of letters (according to his own expression), having presented himself : " Do you bring any letters ? " asked Luther. " No ! " " How are those gentlemen ? " " Well ! " Luther, grieved at such silence, returned and shut himself up in his chamber.

Erelong there appeared a courier on horseback carrying despatches from the elector to Torgau. " Do you bring me any letters ? " asked Luther. " No ! " " How are those gentlemen ? " continued he fearfully. " Well ! " " This is strange," thought the reformer. As a waggon had left Coburg laden with flour (for they were almost in want of provisions at Augsburg), Luther impatiently awaited the return of the driver; but he returned empty. Luther then began to revolve the gloomiest thoughts in his mind, not doubting that they were concealing some misfortune from him.[5] At last another individual, Jobst Nymptzen, having arrived from Augsburg, Luther rushed anew towards him, with his usual question : " Do you bring me any letters ? " He waited trembling for the reply. " No ! " " And how are those gentlemen ? " " Well ! " The reformer withdrew, a prey to anger and to fear.

Then Luther opened his Bible, and to console himself for the silence of men, conversed with God. There were some passages of Scripture in particular that he read continu-

ally. We point them out below.[1] He did more; he wrote with his own hand many declarations of Scripture over the doors and windows, and on the walls of the castle. In one place were these words from the 118th Psalm : *I shall not die, but live, and declare the works of the Lord.* In another, those of the 12th chapter of Proverbs : *The way of the wicked seduceth them ;* and over his bed, this passage from the 4th Psalm : *I will both lay me down in peace and sleep ; for thou, Lord, only makest me dwell in safety.* Never perhaps did man so environ himself with the promises of the Lord, or so dwell in the atmosphere of his Word and live by his breath, as Luther at Coburg.

At length letters came. " If the times in which we live were not opposed to it, I should have imagined some revenge," wrote Luther to Jonas ; " but the hour of prayer prevented my growing angry, and anger prevented my praying.[2] I am delighted at that tranquil mind which God gives our prince. As for Melancthon, it is his philosophy that tortures him, and nothing else. For our cause is in the very hands of Him who can say with unspeakable dignity ; *No one shall pluck it out of my hands.* I would not have it in our hands, and it would not be desirable that it were so.[3] I have had many things in my hands, and I have lost them all; but whatever I have been able to place in God's, I still possess."

On learning that Melancthon's anguish still continued, Luther wrote to him ; and these are words that should be preserved :—

" Grace and peace in Christ ! in Christ, I say, and not in the world, Amen. I hate with exceeding hatred those extreme cares which consume you. If the cause is unjust, abandon it ; if the cause is just, why should we belie the promises of Him who commands us to sleep without fear ? Can the devil do more than kill us ? Christ will not be wanting to the work of justice and of truth. He lives ; he reigns ; what fear, then, can we have ? God is powerful to upraise his cause if it is overthrown, to make it proceed if it remains motionless, and if we are not worthy of it, he will do it by others.

" I have received your Apology,[4] and I cannot understand what you mean, when you ask what we must concede to the papists. We have already conceded too much. Night and day I meditate on this affair, turning it over and over, diligently searching the Scriptures, and the conviction of the truth of our

---

[1] Semel mihi contigit ut orantem eum audirem. Corp. Ref. ii. 159.
[2] Tanta spe et fide ut cum patre et amico colloqui sentiat. Ibid.
[3] Tum orantem clara voce, procul stans, audivi. Ibid.
[4] Ardebat mihi quoque animus singulari quodam impetu. Ibid.
[5] Hic cœpi cogitare tristia, suspirans, vos aliquid mali me celare velle. L. Epp. iv. 60.

[1] 2 Tim. iii. 12 ; Philip. ii. 12, 13 ; John x. 17, 18 ; Matth. xvi. 18 ; Psalm xlvi. 1, 2 ; 1 John iv. 4 ; Psalm lv. 23 ; xxvii. 14 ; John xvi. 33 ; Luke xvii. 5 ; Psalm xxxii. 11 ; cxlv. 18, 19 ; xci. 14, 15 ; Sirach. ii. 11 ; 1 Maccab. ii. 61 ; Matth. vi. 31 ; 1 Peter v. 6, 7 ; Matth. x. 28 ; Rom. iv. and vi. ; Heb. v. and xi. ; 1 Sam. iv. 18 ; xxxi. 4-8 ; ii. 30 ; 2 Tim. ii. 17, 18, 19 ; i. 12 ; Eph. iii. 20, 21. Among these passages will be observed two verses taken from the Apocrypha, but whose equivalents might easily be found in the Word of God.
[2] Sed orandi tempus non sinebat irasci, et ira non sinebat orare. L. Epp. iv. 46.
[3] Nec vellem, nec consultum esset, in nostra manu esse. Ibid.
[4] The Confession revised and corrected.

doctrine every day becomes stronger in my mind. With the help of God, I will not permit a single letter of all that we have said to be torn from us.

"The issue of this affair torments you, because you cannot understand it. But if you could, I would not have the least share in it. God has put it in a 'common place,' that you will not find either in your rhetoric or in your philosophy: that place is called Faith.[1] It is that in which subsist all things that we can neither understand nor see. Whoever wishes to touch them, as you do, will have tears for his sole reward.

"If Christ is not with us, where is he in the whole universe? If we are not the Church, where, I pray, is the Church? Is it the Dukes of Bavaria, is it Ferdinand, is it the pope, is it the Turk, who is the Church? If we have not the Word of God, who is it that possesses it?

"Only we must have faith, lest the cause of faith should be found to be without faith.[2]

"If we fall, Christ, that is to say, the Master of the world, falls with us. I would rather fall with Christ, than remain standing with Cæsar."

Thus wrote Luther. The faith which animated him flowed from him like torrents of living water. He was indefatigable: in a single day he wrote to Melancthon, Spalatin, Brentz, Agricola, and John Frederick, and they were letters full of life. He was not alone in praying, speaking, and believing. At the same moment the evangelical Christians exhorted one another every where to prayer.[3] Such was the arsenal in which the weapons were forged that the confessors of Christ wielded before the Diet of Augsburg.

CHAPTER VII.

The 25th June 1530—The Palatine Chapel—Recollections and Contrast—The Confession—Prologue—Justification—The Church—Free Will and Works—Faith—Interest of the Hearers—The Princes become Preachers—The Confession—Abuses—Church and State—The two Governments—Epilogue—Argumentation—Prudence—Church and State—The Sword—Moderate Tone of the Confession—Its Defects—A new Baptism.

At length the 25th June arrived. This was destined to be the greatest day of the Reformation, and one of the most glorious in the history of Christianity and of mankind.

As the chapel of the Palatine Palace, where the emperor had resolved to hear the Confession, would contain only about two hundred persons,[4] before three o'clock a great crowd was to be seen around the building and thronging the court, hoping by this means to catch a few words: and many hav-

ing gained entrance to the chapel, all were turned out except those who were, at the least, councillors to the princes.

Charles took his seat on the throne. The electors or their representatives were on his right and left hand; next to them, the other princes and states of the empire. The legate had refused to appear in this solemnity, lest he should seem by his presence to authorize the reading of the Confession.[1]

Then stood up John elector of Saxony, with his son John Frederick, Philip landgrave of Hesse, the Margrave George of Brandenburg, Wolfgang prince of Anhalt, Ernest duke of Brunswick-Luneburg, and his brother Francis, and last of all the deputies of Nuremberg and Reutlingen. Their air was animated and their features were radiant with joy.[2] The apologies of the early Christians, of Tertullian and Justin Martyr, hardly reached in writing the sovereigns to whom they were addressed. But now, to hear the new apology of resuscitated Christianity, behold that puissant emperor, whose sceptre, stretching far beyond the Columns of Hercules, reaches the utmost limits of the world, his brother the King of the Romans, with electors, princes, prelates, deputies, ambassadors, all of whom desire to destroy the Gospel, but who are constrained by an invisible power to listen, and, by that very listening, to honour the Confession!

One thought was involuntarily present in the minds of the spectators,—the recollection of the Diet of Worms.[3] Only nine years before, a poor monk stood alone for this same cause in a hall of the town-house at Worms, in presence of the empire. And now in his stead behold the foremost of the electors, princes, and cities! What a victory is declared by this simple fact! No doubt Charles himself cannot escape from this recollection.

The emperor, seeing the Protestants stand up, motioned them to sit down; and then the two chancellors of the elector, Brück and Bayer, advanced to the middle of the chapel, and stood before the throne, holding in their hands, the former the Latin and the other the German copy of the Confession. The emperor required the Latin copy to be read.[4] "We are Germans," said the Elector of Saxony, "and on German soil; I hope therefore your majesty will allow us to speak German." If the Confession had been read in Latin, a language unknown to most of the princes, the general effect would have been lost. This was another means of shutting the mouth of the Gospel. The emperor complied with the elector's demand.

Bayer then began to read the evangelical Confession, slowly, seriously, distinctly, with a clear, strong, and sonorous voice, which re-echoed under the arched roof of the chapel,

---

[1] Deus posuit eam in *locum* quendam *communem*, quem in tua rhetorica non habes nec in philosophia tua; is vocatur *fides.* L. Epp. iv. 53.
[2] Tantum est opus fide, ne causa fidei sit sine fide. Ibid. 61.
[3] Wittembergæ scribunt, tam diligenter ibi Ecclesiam orare. Ibid. 69.
[4] Capiebat forsan ducentos. Jonas, Corp. Ref. ii. 157.

[1] Sarpi, Hist. Council Trent, i. 101.
[2] Læto et alacri animo et vultu Scultet. i. 273.
[3] Ante decennium in conventu Wormatensi. Corp. Ref. ii. 153.
[4] Cæsar Latinum prelegi volebat. Seck. ii. 170.

and carried even to the outside this great testimony paid to the truth.[1]

" Most serene, most mighty, and invincible emperor and most gracious lord," said he, " we who appear in your presence, declare ourselves ready to confer amicably with you on the fittest means of restoring one sole, true, and same faith, since it is for one sole and same Christ that we fight.[2] And in case that these religious dissensions cannot be settled amicably, we then offer to your majesty to explain our cause in a general, free, and christian council."[3]

This prologue being ended, Bayer confessed the Holy Trinity, conformably with the Nicene Council,[4] original and hereditary sin, " which bringeth eternal death to all who are not born again,"[5] and the incarnation of the Son, " very God and very man."[6]

" We teach, moreover," continued he, " that we cannot be justified before God by our own strength, our merits, or our works ; but that we are justified freely for Christ's sake through faith,[7] when we believe that our sins are forgiven in virtue of Christ, who by his death has made satisfaction for our sins : this faith is the righteousness that God imputeth to the sinner.

" But we teach, at the same time, that this faith ought to bear good fruits, and that we must do all the good works commanded by God, for the love of God, and not by their means to gain the grace of God."

The Protestants next declared their faith in the Christian Church, " which is," said they, " the assembly of all true believers and all the saints,"[8] in the midst of whom there are, nevertheless, in this life, many false Christians, hypocrites even, and manifest sinners ; and they added, " that it is sufficient for the real unity of the Church that they agree on the doctrine of the Gospel and the administration of the sacraments, without the rites and ceremonies instituted by men being every where the same."[9] They proclaimed the necessity of baptism, and declared " that the body and blood of Christ are really present and administered in the Lord's Supper to those who partake of it."[10]

The chancellor then successively confessed the faith of the evangelical Christians touching confession, penance, the nature of the sacraments, the government of the Church, ecclesiastical ordinances, political government, and the last judgment. " As regards free will," continued he, " we confess that man's will has a certain liberty of accomplishing civil justice, and of loving the things that reason comprehends ; that man can do the good that is within the sphere of nature —plough his fields, eat, drink, have a friend, put on a coat, build a house, take a wife, feed cattle, exercise a calling ; as also he can, of his own movement, do evil, kneel before an idol, and commit murder. But we maintain that without the Holy Ghost he cannot do what is righteous in the sight of God."

Then, returning to the grand doctrine of the Reformation, and recalling to mind that the doctors of the pope " have never ceased impelling the faithful to puerile and useless works, as the custom of chaplets, invocations of saints, monastic vows, processions, fasts, feast-days, brotherhoods," the Protestants added, that as for themselves, while urging the practice of truly christian works, of which little had been said before their time,[1] " they taught that man is justified by faith alone ; not by that faith which is a simple knowledge of the history, and which wicked men and even devils possess, but by a faith which believes not only the history, but also the effect of the history ;[2] which believes that through Christ we obtain grace ; which sees that in Christ we have a merciful Father ; which knows this God ; which calls upon him ; in a word, which is not without God, as the heathen are."

" Such," said Bayer, " is a summary of the doctrine professed in our churches, by which it may be seen that this doctrine is by no means opposed to Scripture, to the universal Church, nor even to the Romish Church, such as the doctors describe it to us ;[3] and since it is so, to reject us as heretics is an offence against unity and charity."

Here terminated the first part of the Confession, the aim of which was to explain the evangelical doctrine. The chancellor read with so distinct a voice, that the crowd which was unable to enter the hall, and which filled the court and all the approaches of the episcopal palace, did not lose a word.[4] This reading produced the most marvellous effect on the princes who thronged the chapel. Jonas watched every change in their countenances,[5] and there beheld interest, asto-

[1] Qui clare, distincte, tarde et voce adeo grandi et sonora eam pronunciavit. Scultet. p. 276.
[2] Ad unam veram concordem religionem, sicut omnes sub uno Christo sumus et militamus. Confessio, Præfatio. Urkund. i. 474.
[3] Causam dicturos in tali generali, libero, et Christiano concilio. Ibid. 479.
[4] Et tamen tres sunt personæ ejusdem essentiæ. Ibid. 682.
[5] Vitium originis, afferns æternam mortem his qui non renascuntur. Ibid. 483.
[6] Unus Christus, vere Deus, et vere homo. Ibid.
[7] Quod homines non possint justificari coram Deo, propriis viribus, meritis, aut operibus, sed gratis, propter Christum, per fidem. Ibid. 484.
[8] Congregatio sanctorum et vere credentium. Ibid. 487.
[9] Ad veram unitatem Ecclesiæ, satis est consentire de doctrina Evangelii et administratione sacramentorum, nec necesse est, &c. Ibid. 486.
[10] Quod corpus et sanguis Christi vere adsint et distribuantur vescentibus in cœna Domini. F. Urkund. i. 488.

[1] De quibus rebus olim parum docebant concionatores; tantum puerilia et non necessaria opera urgebant. F. Urkund. i. 495.
[2] Non tantum historiæ notitiam, sed fidem quæ credit non tantum historiam, sed etiam effectum historiæ. Ibid. 496.
[3] Nihil inesse quod discrepat a Scripturis vel ab Ecclesia Catholica, vel ab Ecclesia Romana, quatenus ex Scripturibus nota est. Ibid. 501.
[4] Verum etiam in area inferiori et vicinis locis exaudiri potuerit. Scultet. p. 274.
[5] Jonas scribit vidisse se vultus omnium de quo mihi spondet narrationem coram. L. Epp. iv. 71.

nishment, and even approbation depicted by turns. "The adversaries imagine they have done a wonderful thing by forbidding the preaching of the Gospel," wrote Luther to the elector; "and they do not see, poor creatures! that by the reading of the Confession in the presence of the diet, there has been more preaching than in the sermons of ten doctors. Exquisite subtlety! admirable expedient! Master Agricola and the other ministers are reduced to silence; but in their places appear the Elector of Saxony and the other princes and lords, who preach before his imperial majesty and the members of the whole empire, freely, to their beard, and before their noses. Yes, Christ is in the diet, and he does not keep silence: *the Word of God cannot be bound.* They forbid it in the pulpit, and are forced to hear it in the palace; poor ministers cannot announce it, and great princes proclaim it; the servants are forbidden to listen to it, and their masters are compelled to hear it; they will have nothing to do with it during the whole course of the diet, and they are forced to submit to hear more in one day than is heard ordinarily in a whole year......When all else is silent, the very stones cry out, as says our Lord Jesus Christ."[1]

That part of the Confession destined to point out errors and abuses still remained. Bayer continued: he explained and demonstrated the doctrine of the two kinds; he attacked the compulsory celibacy of priests, maintained that the Lord's Supper had been changed into a regular fair, in which it was merely a question of buying and selling, and that it had been re-established in its primitive purity by the Reformation, and was celebrated in the evangelical churches with entirely new devotion and gravity. He declared that the sacrament was administered to no one who had not first made confession of his faults, and he quoted this expression of Chrysostom: "Confess thyself to God the Lord, thy real Judge; tell thy sin, not with the tongue, but in thy conscience and in thy heart."

Bayer next came to the precepts on the distinction of meats and other Roman usages. "Celebrate such a festival," said he; "repeat such a prayer, or keep such a fast; be dressed in such a manner, and so many other ordinances of men—this is what is now styled a spiritual and christian life; while the good works prescribed by God, as those of a father of a family who toils to support his wife, his sons, and his daughters—of a mother who brings children into the world, and takes care of them—of a prince or of a magistrate who governs his subjects, are looked upon as secular things, and of an imperfect nature." As for monastic vows in particular, he represented that, as the pope could give a dispensation from them, those vows ought therefore to be abolished.

[1] L. Epp. iv. 32.

The last article of the Confession treated of the authority of the bishops: powerful princes crowned with the episcopal mitre were there; the Archbishops of Mentz, Cologne, Salzburg, and Bremen, with the Bishops of Bamberg, Wurzburg, Eichstadt, Worms, Spires, Strasburg, Augsburg, Constance, Coire, Passau, Liege, Trent, Brixen, and of Lebus and Ratzburg, fixed their eyes on the humble confessor. He fearlessly continued, and energetically protesting against that confusion of Church and State which had characterized the Middle Ages, he called for the distinction and independence of the two societies.

"Many," said he, "have unskilfully confounded the episcopal and the temporal power; and from this confusion have resulted great wars, revolts, and seditions.[1] It is for this reason, and to reassure men's consciences, that we find ourselves constrained to establish the difference which exists between the power of the Church and the power of the sword.[2]

"We therefore teach that the power of the keys or of the bishops is, conformably with the Word of the Lord, a commandment emanating from God, to preach the Gospel, to remit or retain sins, and to administer the Sacraments. This power has reference only to eternal goods, is exercised only by the minister of the Word, and does not trouble itself with political administration. The political administration, on the other hand, is busied with every thing else but the Gospel. The magistrate protects, not souls, but bodies and temporal possessions. He defends them against all attacks from without, and, by making use of the sword and of punishment, compels men to observe civil justice and peace.[3]

"For this reason we must take particular care not to mingle the power of the Church with the power of the State.[4] The power of the Church ought never to invade an office that is foreign to it; for Christ himself said: *My kingdom is not of this world.* And again: *Who made me a judge over you?* St. Paul said to the Philippians: *Our citizenship is in heaven.*[5] And to the Corinthians: *The weapons of our warfare are not carnal, but mighty through God.*

"It is thus that we distinguish the two governments and the two powers, and that we honour both as the most excellent gifts that God has given us here on earth.

"The duty of the bishops is therefore to

[1] Nonnulli incommode commiscuerunt potestatem ecclesiasticam et potestatem gladii; et ex hac confusione, &c. Urkund. Confess. Augs. i. 539.
[2] Coacti sunt ostendere discrimen ecclesiasticæ potestatis et potestatis gladii. Ibid.
[3] Politica administratio versatur enim circa alias res quam Evangelium; magistratus defendit non mentes sed corpora —— et coercet hominēs gladio. Ibid. 541.
[4] Non igitur commiscendæ sunt potestates ecclesiasticæ et civiles. Ibid.
[5] Greek, πολιτευμα. Philip. iii. 20. Scott and Henry Comment.

preach the Gospel, to forgive sins, and to exclude from the Christian Church all who rebel against the Lord, but without human power, and solely by the Word of God.[1] If the bishops act thus, the churches ought to be obedient to them, according to this declaration of Christ: *Whoever heareth you, heareth me.*

" But if the bishops teach any thing that is contrary to the Gospel, then the churches have an order from God which forbids them to obey (Matth. vii. 15; Galatians i. 8; 2 Cor. xiii. 8, 10). And St. Augustine himself, in his letter against Pertilian, writes: ' We must not obey the catholic bishops, if they go astray, and teach any thing contrary to the canonical Scriptures of God.'"[2]

After some remarks on the ordinances and traditions of the Church, Bayer came to the epilogue of the Confession.

" It is not from hatred that we have spoken," added he, " nor to insult any one; but we have explained the doctrines that we maintain to be essential, in order that it may be understood that we admit of neither dogma nor ceremony which is contrary to the Holy Scriptures, and to the usage of the universal Church."

Bayer then ceased to read. He had spoken for two hours: the silence and serious attention of the assembly were not once disturbed.[3]

This Confession of Augsburg will ever remain one of the masterpieces of the human mind enlightened by the Spirit of God.

The language that had been adopted, while it was perfectly natural, was the result of a profound study of character. These princes, these warriors, these politicians who were sitting in the Palatine Palace, entirely ignorant as they were of divinity, easily understood the Protestant doctrine; for it was explained to them not in the style of the schools, but in that of everyday life, and with a simplicity and clearness that rendered all misunderstanding impossible.

At the same time the power of argumentation was so much the more remarkable, as it was the more concealed. At one time Melancthon (for it was really he who spoke through the mouth of Bayer) was content to quote a single passage of Scripture or of the Fathers in favour of the doctrine he maintained; and at another he proved his thesis so much the more strongly, that he appeared only to be declaring it. With a single stroke he pointed out the sad consequences that would follow the rejection of the faith he professed, or with one word showed its importance for the prosperity of the Church; so that, while listening to him, the most violent enemies were obliged to acknowledge to themselves that there was really something to say in favour of the new sect.

To this force of reasoning the apology added a prudence no less remarkable. Melancthon, while declining with firmness the errors attributed to his party, did not even appear to feel the injustice of these erroneous imputations; and while pointing out those of Popery, he did not say expressly they were those of his adversaries; thus carefully avoiding every thing that might irritate their minds. In this he showed himself wise as a serpent and harmless as a dove.

But the most admirable thing of all is the fidelity with which the Confession explains the doctrines most essential to salvation. Rome is accustomed to represent the reformers as the creators of the Protestant doctrines; but it is not in the sixteenth century that we must look for the days of that creation. A bright track of light, of which Wickliffe and Augustine mark the most salient points, carries us back to the apostolic age: it was then that shone in all their brilliancy the creative days of evangelical truth. Yet it is true (and if this is what Rome means, we fully concur in the idea), never since the time of St. Paul had the Christian doctrine appeared with so much beauty, depth, and life, as in the days of the Reformation.

Among these doctrines, that of the Church, which had been so long disfigured, appeared at this time in all its native purity. With what wisdom, in particular, the confessors of Augsburg protest against that confusion of religion and politics which, since the deplorable epoch of Constantine, had changed the kingdom of God into an earthly and carnal institution! Undoubtedly what the Confession stigmatizes with the greatest energy is the intrusion of the Church into the affairs of the State; but can it be thought that it was to approve the intrusion of the State in Church affairs? The evil of the Middle Ages was the having enslaved the State to the Church, and the confessors of Augsburg rose like one man to combat it. The evil of the three centuries which have passed away since then, is to have subjected the Church to the State; and we may believe that Luther and Melancthon would have found equally powerful thunders against this disorder. What they attack in a general sense, is the confusion of the two societies; what they demand, is their independence, I do not say their separation, for separation of Church and State was quite unknown to the reformers. If the Augsburg confessors were unwilling that things from above should monopolize those of the earth, they would have been still less willing for things of the earth to oppress those from heaven.

There is a particular application of this principle, which the Confession points out.

---

[1] Excludere a communione Ecclesiæ, sine vi humana sed verbo. Urkund. Confes. Augs. i. 544.
[2] Nec catholicis episcopis consentiendum est, sicuti forte falluntur, aut contra canonicas Dei scripturas aliquid sentiunt. Ibid.
[3] Mit grosser Stille und Ernst. Brück's Apologie, p. 59.

It wills the bishops should reprimand those who obey wickedness, "but without human power, and solely by the Word of God." It therefore rejects the use of the sword in the chastisement of heretics. This we see is a primitive principle, fundamental and essential to the Reformation, as the contrary doctrine is a primitive principle, fundamental and essential to the Papacy. If among Protestants we find any treatise, or even any example opposed to this, it is but an isolated fact, which cannot invalidate the official principles of the reform—it is one of those exceptions which always serve to confirm the rule.

Finally, the Augsburg Confession does not usurp the rights of the Word of God; it desires to be its handmaid and not its rival; it does not found, it does not regulate the faith, but simply professes it. "Our churches teach," it says; and it will be remembered that Luther considered it only as a sermon preached by princes and kings. Had it desired more, as has since been maintained, by that very circumstance it would have been nullified.

Was, however, the Confession able to follow in all things the exact path of truth? We may be permitted to doubt it.

It professes not to separate from the teaching of the Catholic Church, and even from that of the Romish Church—by which is no doubt signified the ancient Roman Church—and rejects the popish particularism which, for about eight centuries, imprisoned men's consciences. The Confession, however, seems overlaid with superstitious fears when there is any question of deviating from the views entertained by some of the Fathers of the Church, of breaking the toils of the hierarchy, and of acting, as regards Rome, without blamable forbearance. This, at least, is what its author, Melancthon, professes. "We do not put forward any dogma," said he, "which is not founded on the Gospel, or on the teaching of the Catholic Church; we are prepared to concede every thing that is necessary for the episcopal dignity;[1] and provided the bishops do not condemn the Gospel, we preserve all the rites that appear indifferent to us. In a word, there is no burden that we reject, if we can bear it without guilt."[2]

Many will think, no doubt, that a little more independence would have been proper in this matter, and that it would have been better to have passed over the ages that have followed the times of the apostles, and have frankly put in practice the grand principle which the Reformation had proclaimed: "There is no other foundation for articles of faith than the Word of God."[3]

Melancthon's moderation has been admired; and, in truth, while pointing out the abuses

of Rome, he was silent on what is most revolting in them, on their disgraceful origin, their scandalous consequences, and is content to show that they are in contradiction to the Scripture. But he does more; he is silent on the divine right claimed by the pope, on the number of the sacraments, and on several other points. His great business is to justify the renovated, and not to attack the deformed Church. "Peace, peace!" was his cry. But if, instead of all this circumspection, the Reformation had advanced with courage, had wholly unveiled the Word of God, and had made an energetic appeal to the sympathies of reform then spread in men's hearts, would it not have taken a stronger and more honourable position, and would it not have secured more extensive conquests?

The interest that Charles the Fifth showed in listening to the Confession seems doubtful. According to some, he endeavoured to understand that foreign language;[1] according to others, he fell asleep.[2] It is easy to reconcile these contradictory testimonies.

When the reading was finished, Chancellor Brück, with the two copies in his hand, advanced towards the emperor's secretary and presented them to him. Charles the Fifth, who was wide awake at this moment, himself took the two Confessions, handed the German copy, considered as official, to the Elector of Mentz, and kept the Latin one for himself.[3] He then made reply to the Elector of Saxony and to his allies, that he had graciously heard their Confession;[4] but as this affair was one of extreme importance, he required time to deliberate upon it.

The joy with which the Protestants were filled shone in their eyes.[5] God had been with them; and they saw that the striking act which had so recently been accomplished imposed on them the obligation of confessing the truth with immovable perseverance. "I am overjoyed," wrote Luther, "that I have lived until this hour, in which Christ has been publicly exalted by such illustrious confessors and in so glorious an assembly."[6] The whole evangelical church, excited and renovated by this public confession of its representatives, was then more intimately united to its Divine Chief, and baptized with a new baptism. "Since the apostolic age," said they (these are the words of a contemporary), "there has never been a greater work or a more magnificent confession."[7]

The emperor, having descended from his throne, approached the Protestant princes,

---

1 Concessuros omnia quæ ad dignitatem Episcoporum stabiliendam pertinent. Corp. Ref. ii. 431.
2 Nullum detractavimus onus, quod sine scelere suscipi vosset. Ibid.
3 Solum verbum Dei condit articulos fidei.

1 Satis attentus erat Cæsar. Jonas in Corp. Ref. ii. 184.
2 Cum nostra confessio legeretur, obdormivit. Brentius in Corp. Ref. ii. 245.
3 The Latin copy, deposited in the archives of the imperial house, should be found at Brussels; and the German copy, sent afterwards to the Council of Trent, ought to be in the Vatican.
4 Gnedichlich vernehmen. F. Urkund. ii. 3.
5 Cum incredibili protestantium gaudio. Seck. ii. 170.
6 Mihi vehementer placet vixisse in hanc horam. L. Epp. iv. 71.
7 Grösser und höher Werk. Mathesius, Hist. p. 93-98.

and begged them in a low tone not to publish the Confession ;[1] they acceded to his request, and every one withdrew.

CHAPTER VIII.

Effect on the Romanists—Luther demands Religious Liberty—His dominant Idea—Song of Triumph—Ingenuous Confessions—Hopes of the Protestants—Failure of the Popish Intrigues—The Emperor's Council—Violent Discussions—A Refutation proposed—Its Authors—Rome and the Civil Power—Perils of the Confessors—Melancthon's Minimum—The Emperor's Sister—Melancthon's Fall—Luther opposes Concession—The Legate repels Melancthon—The Pope's Decision—Question—Melancthon's School-matters—Answer.

THE Romanists had expected nothing like this. Instead of a hateful controversy, they had heard a striking confession of Jesus Christ; the most hostile minds were consequently disarmed. "We would not for a great deal," was the remark on every side, "have missed being present at this reading."[2] The effect was so prompt, that for an instant the cause was thought to be definitively gained. The bishops themselves imposed silence on the sophisms and clamours of the Fabers and the Ecks.[3] "All that the Lutherans have said is true," exclaimed the Bishop of Augsburg; "we cannot deny it."[4] — "Well, doctor," said the Duke of Bavaria to Eck, in a reproachful tone, "you had given me a very different idea of this doctrine and of this affair."[5] This was the general cry; accordingly the sophists, as they called them, were embarrassed. "But, after all," said the Duke of Bavaria to them, "can you refute by sound reasons the Confession made by the elector and his allies?" —"With the writings of the apostles and prophets—no!" replied Eck; "but with those of the Fathers and of the councils—yes!"[6] "I understand," quickly replied the duke; "I understand. The Lutherans, according to you, are in Scripture; and we are outside."

The Archbishop Hermann, elector of Cologne, the Count-palatine Frederick, Duke Erick of Brunswick-Luneburg, Duke Henry of Mecklenburg, and the Dukes of Pomerania, were gained over to the truth; and Hermann sought erelong to establish it in his electorate.

The impression produced in other countries by the Confession was perhaps still greater. Charles sent copies to all the courts; it was translated into French, Italian,[7] and even into Spanish and Portuguese; it circulated through all Europe, and thus accomplished what Luther had said: "Our Confession will penetrate into every court, and the sound thereof will spread through the whole earth."[1] It destroyed the prejudices that had been entertained, gave Europe a sounder idea of the Reformation, and prepared the most distant countries to receive the seeds of the Gospel.

Then Luther's voice began to be heard again. He saw that it was a decisive moment, and that he ought now to give the impulse that would gain religious liberty. He boldly demanded this liberty of the Roman-catholic princes of the diet ;[2] and at the same time endeavoured to make his friends quit Augsburg. Jesus Christ had been boldly confessed. Instead of that long series of quarrels and discussions which was about to become connected with this courageous act, Luther would have wished for a striking rupture, even should he seal with his blood the testimony rendered to the Gospel. The stake, in his idea, would have been the real catastrophe of this tragedy. "I absolve you from this diet, in the name of the Lord,"[3] wrote he to his friends. "Now home, return home, again I say home! Would to God that I were the sacrifice offered to this new council, as John Huss at Constance !"[4]

But Luther did not expect so glorious a conclusion : he compared the diet to a drama. First, there had been the exposition, then the prologue, afterwards the action, and now he waited for the tragic catastrophe, according to some, but which, in his opinion, would be merely comic.[5] Every thing, he thought, would be sacrificed to political peace, and dogmas would be set aside. This proceeding, which, even in our own days, would be in the eyes of the world the height of wisdom, was in Luther's eyes the height of folly.

He was especially alarmed at the thought of Charles's intervention. To withdraw the Church from all secular influence, and the governments from all clerical influence, was then one of the dominant ideas of the great reformer. "You see," wrote he to Melancthon, "that they oppose to our cause the same argument as at Worms, to wit, still and for ever the judgment of the emperor. Thus Satan is always harping on the same string, and that emaciated strength[6] of the civil power is the only one which this myriad-willed spirit is able to find against Jesus Christ." But Luther took courage, and boldly raised his head. "Christ is coming," continued he ; "he is coming, sitting at the

[1] In still angeredet und gebethen. Corp. Ref. ii. 143.
[2] Brücks Geschichte der Handl. in den Sachen des Glaubens zu Augsbourg. Förstemann Archiv. p. 50.
[3] Multi episcopi ad pacem sunt inclinati. L. Epp, iv. 70.
[4] Illa quæ recitata vera sunt, sunt pura veritas ; non possumus inficiari. Corp. Ref. ii. 154.
[5] So habman Im vor nicht gesagt. Mathes. Hist. p. 99.
[6] Mit Propheten und Aposteln schriften——nicht. Mathes. Hist. p. 99.
[7] Cæsar sibi fecit nostram confessionem reddi Italica et Gallica lingua. Corp. Ref. ii. 155. The French translation will be found in *Forstemann's Urkunden.* i. 357.—*Articles primitveaulx de la foy.*

[1] Perrumpet in omnes aulas Principum et Regum. L Epp. iv. 96.
[2] Epistle to the Elector of Mentz. Ibid. 74.
[3] Igitur absolvo vos in nomine Domini ab isto conventu Ibid. 96.
[4] Vellem ego sacrificium esse hujus novissimi concilii, sicut Johannes Huss Contantiæ. Ibid. 110.
[5] Sed catastrophen illi tragicam, nos comicam expectamus. Ibid. 85.
[6] Sic Satan chorda semper oberrat eadem, et mille-artifex ille non habet contra Christum, nisi unum illud elumbe robur. Ibid. 100.

right hand......Of whom? not of the emperor, or we should long ago have been lost, but of God himself: let us fear nothing. Christ is the King of kings, and the Lord of lords. If he loses this title at Augsburg, he must also lose it in all the earth, and in all the heavens."

Thus a song of triumph was, on the part of the confessors of Augsburg, the first movement that followed this courageous act, unique doubtless in the annals of the Church. Some of their adversaries at first shared in their triumph, and the others were silent; but a powerful reaction took place erelong.

On the following morning, Charles having risen in ill-humour and tired for want of sleep, the first of his ministers who appeared in the imperial apartments was the count-palatine, as wearied and embarrassed as his master. "We must yield something," said he to Charles; "and I would remind your majesty that the Emperor Maximilian was willing to grant the two kinds in the Eucharist, the marriage of priests, and liberty with respect to the fasts." Charles the Fifth eagerly seized at this proposition as a means of safety. But Granvelle and Campeggio soon arrived, and induced him to withdraw it.

Rome, bewildered for a moment by the blow that had struck her, rose up again with energy. "I stay with the mother," exclaimed the Bishop of Wartzburg, meaning by it the Church of Rome; "the mother, the mother!" "My lord," wittily replied Brentz, "pray, do not, for the mother, forget either the Father or the Son!"—"Well! I grant it," replied the Archbishop of Salzburg to one of his friends, "I also should desire the communion in both kinds, the marriage of priests, the reformation of the mass, and liberty as regards food and other traditions.........But that it should be a monk, a poor monk, who presumes to reform us all, is what we cannot tolerate."[1]—"I should have no objection," said another bishop, "for Divine worship to be celebrated every where as it is at Wittemberg; but we can never consent that this new doctrine should issue from such a corner."[2] And as Melancthon insisted with the Archbishop of Salzburg on the necessity of a reform of the clergy: "Well! and how can you wish to reform us?" said the latter abruptly: "we priests have always been good for nothing." This is one of the most ingenuous confessions that the Reformation has extorted from the priests. Every day fanatical monks and doctors, brimful of sophisms, were seen arriving at Augsburg, and endeavouring to inflame the hatred of the emperor and of the princes.[3] "If we formerly had friends," said Melancthon on the morrow of the Confession, "now we possess them no longer. We are here alone, abandoned by all, and contending against measureless dangers."[1]

Charles, impelled by these contrary parties, affected great indifference. But without permitting it to be seen, he endeavoured, meanwhile, to examine this affair thoroughly. "Let there not be a word wanting," he had said to his secretary, when requiring from him a French translation of the Confession. "He does not allow any thing to be observed," whispered the Protestants one to another, convinced that Charles was gained; "for if it were known, he would lose his Spanish states: let us maintain the most profound secrecy." But the emperor's courtiers, who perceived these strange hopes, smiled and shook their heads. "If you have money," said Schepper, one of the secretaries of state, to Jonas and Melancthon, "it will be easy for you to buy from the Italians whatever religion you please;[2] but if your purse is empty, your cause is lost." Then assuming a more serious tone: "It is impossible," said he, "for the emperor, surrounded as he is by bishops and cardinals, to approve of any other religion than that of the pope." This was soon evident. On the day after the Confession (Sunday, 26th June), before the breakfast hour,[3] all the deputations from the imperial cities were collected in the emperor's antechamber. Charles, desirous of bringing back the states of the empire to unity, began with the weakest. "Some of the cities," said the count-palatine, "have not adhered to the last Diet of Spires: the emperor calls upon them to submit to it."

Strasburg, Nuremberg, Constance, Ulm, Reutlingen, Heilbronn, Memmingen, Lindau, Kempten, Windsheim, Isny, and Weissemburg, which were thus summoned to renounce the famous protest, thought the moment curiously chosen. They asked for time.

The position was complicated: discord had been thrown into the midst of the cities, and intrigue was labouring daily to increase it.[4] It was not only between the popish and the evangelical cities that disagreement existed; but also between the Zwinglian and the Lutheran cities, and even among the latter, those which had not adhered to the Confession of Augsburg manifested great ill-humour towards the deputies of Reutlingen and Nuremberg. This proceeding of Charles the Fifth was therefore skilfully calculated, for it was based on the old axiom, *Divide et impera*.

But the enthusiasm of faith overcame all these stratagems, and on the next day (27th June), the deputies from the cities transmitted a reply to the emperor, in which

---

[1] Sed quod unus monachus debeat nos reformare omnes. Corp. Ref. ii. 155.
[2] Aus dem Loch und Winckel. L. Opp. xx. 307.
[3] Quotidie confluunt huc sophistæ ac monachi. Corp. Ref. ii. 141.

[1] Nos hic soli ac deserti. Corp. Ref. ii. 141.
[2] Nos, si pecuniam haberemus, facile religionem quam vellemus emturos ab Italis. Ibid. 156.
[3] Heute vor dem morgenessen. Ibid. 143.
[4] Es sind unter uns Städten, viel practica und Seltsames wesens. Ibid. 151.

they declared that they could not adhere to the *Recess* of Spires " without disobeying God, and without compromising the salvation of their souls."[1]

Charles, who desired to observe a just medium, more from policy than from equity, wavered between so many contrary convictions. Desirous nevertheless of essaying his mediating influence, he convoked the states faithful to Rome, on Sunday, 26th June, shortly after his conference with the cities.

All the princes were present : even the pope's legate and the most influential Roman divines appeared at this council, to the great scandal of the Protestants. " What reply should be made to the Confession ? " was the question set by Charles the Fifth to the senate that surrounded him.[2]

Three different opinions were proposed. " Let us beware," said the men of the papacy, " of discussing our adversaries' reasons, and let us be content with executing the edict of Worms against the Lutherans, and with constraining them by arms."[3]—" Let us submit the Confession to the examination of impartial judges," said the men of the empire, "and refer the final decision to the emperor. Is not even the reading of the Confession an appeal of the Protestants to the imperial power?" Others, in the last place (and these were the men of tradition and of ecclesiastical doctrine), were desirous of commissioning certain doctors to compose a refutation, which should be read to the Protestants and ratified by Charles.

The debate was very animated : the mild and the violent, the politic and the fanatical, took a decided course in the assembly. George of Saxony and Joachim of Brandenburg showed themselves the most inveterate, and surpassed in this respect even the ecclesiastical princes.[4] " A certain clown, whom you know well, is pushing them all from behind,"[5] wrote Melancthon to Luther; " and certain hypocritical theologians hold the torch and lead the whole band." This clown was doubtless Duke George. Even the princes of Bavaria, whom the Confession had staggered at first, immediately rallied around the chiefs of the Roman party. The Elector of Mentz, the Bishop of Augsburg, and the Duke of Brunswick, showed themselves the least unfavourable to the evangelical cause. " I can by no means advise his majesty to employ force," said Albert. " If his majesty should constrain their consciences, and should afterwards quit the empire, the first victims sacrificed would be the priests ; and who knows whether, in the midst of these discords, the Turks would not suddenly fall upon

us ? " But this somewhat interested wisdom of the archbishop did not find many supporters, and the men of war immediately plunged into the discussion with their harsh voices. " If there is any fighting against the Lutherans," said Count Felix of Werdenberg, " I gratuitously offer my sword, and I swear never to return it to its scabbard until it has overthrown the stronghold of Luther." This nobleman died suddenly a few days after, from the consequences of his intemperance. Then the moderate men again interfered : " The Lutherans attack no one article of the faith," said the Bishop of Augsburg; " let us come to an arrangement with them; and to obtain peace, let us concede to them the sacrament in both kinds and the marriage of priests. I would even yield more, if it were necessary." Upon this loud cries arose : " He is a Lutheran," they exclaimed, " and you will see that he is fully prepared to sacrifice even the private masses!"—" The masses! we must not even think of it," remarked some with an ironical smile; " Rome will never give them up, for it is they which maintain her cardinals and her courtiers, with their luxury and their kitchens."[1] The Archbishop of Salzburg and the Elector of Brandenburg replied with great violence to the motion of the Bishop of Augsburg. " The Lutherans," said they abruptly, " have laid before us a Confession written with black ink on white paper. Well : If I were emperor, I would answer them with *red ink*."[2]—" Sirs," quickly replied the Bishop of Augsburg, " take care then that the red letters do not fly in your faces !" The Elector of Mentz was compelled to interfere and calm the speakers.

The emperor, desirous of playing the character of an umpire, would have wished the Roman party at least to have placed in his hands an act of accusation against the Reform : but all was now altered ; the majority, becoming daily more compact since the Diet of Spires, no longer sided with Charles. Full of the sentiment of their own strength, they refused to assume the title of a party, and to take the emperor as a judge. " What are you saying," cried they, " of diversity between the members of the empire ? There is but one legitimate party. It is not a question of deciding between two opinions whose rights are equal, but of crushing rebels, and of aiding those who have remained faithful to the constitution of the empire."

This haughty language enlightened Charles : he found they had outstripped him, and that, abandoning his lofty position of arbiter, he must submit merely to be the agent of the orders of the majority. It was this majority which henceforward commanded in Augsburg. They excluded the imperial councillors who advocated more equi-

---

[1] Ohne Verletzung der gewissen gegen Gott. F. Urkund. ii. 6.
[2] Adversarii nostri jam deliberant quid velint respondere. Corp. Ref. ii. 26th June.
[3] Rom agendam esse vi, non audiendam causam. Ibid. 154.
[4] Hi sunt duces, et quidem acerrimi alterius partis. Ibid.
[5] Omnes unus gubernat rusticus. Ibid. 26th June, 176.

[1] Cardinel, Churstusanen, Pracht und Küchen. Brück Apol. p. 63.
[2] Wir wokten antvorten mit einer Schrift mit Rubricken geschrieben. Corp. Ref. ii. 147.

table views, and the Archbishop of Mentz himself ceased for a time to appear in the diet.[1]

The majority ordered that a refutation of the Evangelical doctrine should be immediately drawn up by Romish theologians. If they had selected for this purpose moderate men, like the Bishop of Augsburg, the Reformation would still have had some chance of success with the great principles of Christianity; but it was to the enemies of the Reform, to the old champions of Rome and of Aristotle, exasperated by so many defeats, that they resolved to intrust this task.

They were numerous at Augsburg, and not held in very great esteem. "The princes," said Jonas, "have brought their learned men with them, and some even their *unlearned* and their *fools*."[2] Provost Faber and Doctor Eck led the troop; behind them was drawn up a cohort of monks, and above all of Dominicans, tools of the Inquisition, and impatient to recompense themselves for the opprobrium they had so long endured. There was the provincial of the Dominicans, Paul Hugo, their vicar John Bourkard, one of their priors Conrad Koelein, who had written against Luther's marriage; with a number of Carthusians, Augustines, Franciscans, and the vicars of several bishops. Such were the men who, to the number of twenty, were commissioned to refute Melancthon.

One might beforehand have augured of the work by the workmen. Each one understood that it was a question, not of refuting the Confession, but of branding it. Campeggio, who doubtless suggested this ill-omened list to Charles, was well aware that these doctors were incapable of measuring themselves with Melancthon; but their names formed the most decided standard of popery, and announced to the world clearly and immediately what the diet proposed doing. This was the essential point. Rome would not leave Christendom even hope.

It was, however, requisite to know whether the diet, and the emperor who was its organ, had the right of pronouncing in this purely religious matter. Charles put the question both to the Evangelicals and to the Romanists.[3]

"Your highness," said Luther, who was consulted by the elector, "may reply with all assurance: Yes, if the emperor wish it, let him be judge! I will bear every thing on his part; but let him decide nothing contrary to the Word of God. Your highness cannot put the emperor above God himself.[4] Does not the first commandment say, *Thou shalt have no other Gods before me?*"

The reply of the papal adherents was quite as positive in a contrary sense. "We think," said they, "that his majesty, in accord with the electors, princes, and states of the empire, has the right to proceed in this affair, as Roman Emperor, guardian, advocate, and sovereign protector of the Church and of our most holy faith."[1] Thus, in the first days of the Reformation, the Evangelical Church frankly ranged itself under the throne of Jesus Christ, and the Roman Church under the sceptre of kings. Enlightened men, even among Protestants, have misunderstood this double nature of Protestantism and Popery.

The philosophy of Aristotle and the hierarchy of Rome, thanks to this alliance with the civil power, were at length about to see the day of their long-expected triumph arrive. So long as the schoolmen had been left to the force of their syllogisms and of their abuse, they had been defeated; but now Charles the Fifth and the diet held out their hands to them; the reasonings of Faber, Eck, and Wimpina were about to be countersigned by the German chancellor, and confirmed by the great seals of the empire. Who could resist them? The Romish error has never had any strength except by its union with the secular arm; and its victories in the Old and in the New World are owing, even in our days, to state patronage.[2]

These things did not escape the piercing eye of Luther. He saw at once the weakness of the argument of the papist doctors and the power of Charles's arm. "You are waiting for your adversaries' answer," wrote he to his friends in Augsburg; "it is already written, and here it is: The Fathers, the Fathers, the Fathers; the Church, the Church, the Church; usage, custom; but of the Scriptures——nothing![3] Then the emperor, supported by the testimony of these arbiters, will pronounce against you;[4] and then will you hear boastings from all sides that will ascend to heaven, and threats that will descend even to hell."

Thus changed the situation of the Reform. Charles was obliged to acknowledge his weakness; and to save the appearance of his power, he took a decisive part with the enemies of Luther. The emperor's impartiality disappeared: the state turned against the Gospel, and there remained for it no other saviour than God.

At first many gave way to extreme dejection: above all, Melancthon, who had a nearer view of the cabals of the adversaries, exhausted moreover by long vigils, fell almost into despair.[5] "In the presence of these formidable evils," cried he, "I see no more hope."[6] And then, however, he added—"Except the help of God."

1 Non venit in senatum. Corp. Ref. ii. 175.
2 Quidem etiam suos ineruditos et ineptos.
3 See the document extracted from the archives of Bavaria in F. Urkund. ii. 9
4 Konnen den Kaiser nicht uber Gott setzen. L. Epp. iv. 83.

1 Romischen Kaiser, Vogt, Advocaten und Obristen Beschirmer der kirken. F. Urkund. ii. 10.
2 Otaheite for instance.
3 Patres, Patres, Patres; Ecclesia, Ecclesia; usus, consuetudo, præterea e Scriptura nihil. L. Epp. iv. 96.
4 Pronuntiabit Cæsar contra vos. Ibid.
5 Quadam tristitia et quasi desesperatione vexatur. Corp. Ref. ii. 163.
6 Quid nobis sit sperandum in tantis odiis inimicorum. Ibid. 145.

The legate immediately set all his batteries to work. Already had Charles several times sent for the elector and the landgrave, and had used every exertion to detach them from the Evangelical Confession.[1] Melancthon, uneasy at these secret conferences, reduced the Confession to its *minimum*, and entreated the elector to demand only the two kinds in the Eucharist and the marriage of priests. "To interdict the former of these points," said he, "would be to alienate a great number of Christians from the communion; and to forbid the second would be depriving the Church of all the pastors capable of edifying it. Will they destroy religion and kindle civil war, rather than apply to these purely ecclesiastical constitutions a mitigation that is neither contrary to sound morals nor to faith?"[2] The Protestant princes begged Melanethon to go himself and make these proposals to the legate.[3]

Melancthon agreed; he began to flatter himself with success; and, in truth, there were, even among the papists, individuals who were favourable to the Reformation. There had recently arrived at Augsburg, from beyond the Alps, certain propositions tolerably Lutheran,[4] and one of the emperor's confessors boldly professed the doctrine of justification by faith, cursing "those asses of Germans," as he called them, "who are incessantly braying against this truth."[5] One of Charles's chaplains approved of even the whole of the Confession. There was something farther still: Charles the Fifth having consulted the grandees of Spain, who were famous for their orthodoxy: "If the opinions of the Protestants are contrary to the articles of the faith," they had replied, "let your majesty employ all his power to destroy this faction; but if it is a question merely of certain changes in human ordinances and external usages, let all violence be avoided."[6] "Admirable reply!" exclaimed Melancthon, who persuaded himself that the Romish doctrine was at the bottom in accordance with the Gospel.

The Reformation found defenders in even still higher stations. Mary, sister of Charles the Fifth, and widow of King Louis of Hungary, arriving at Augsburg three days after the reading of the Confession, with her sister-in-law the Queen of Bohemia, Ferdinand's wife, assiduously studied the Holy Scriptures; she carried them with her to the hunting parties, in which she found little pleasure, and had discovered therein the jewel of the Reform,—the doctrine of gratuitous salvation. This pious princess made her chaplain read evangelical sermons to her,

and often endeavoured, although with prudence, to appease her brother Charles with regard to the Protestants.[1]

Melancthon, encouraged by these demonstrations, and at the same time alarmed by the threats of war that the adversaries were continually uttering, thought it his duty to purchase peace at any cost, and resolved in consequence to descend in his propositions as low as possible. He therefore demanded an interview with the legate in a letter whose authenticity has been unreasonably doubted.[2] At the decisive moment the heart of the reform champion fails,—his head turns—he staggers—he falls; and in his fall he runs the risk of dragging with him the cause which martyrs have already watered with their blood.

Thus speaks the representative of the Reformation to the representative of the papacy:—

"There is no doctrine in which we differ from the Roman Church;[3] we venerate the universal authority of the Roman Pontiff, and are ready to obey him, provided he does not reject us, and that of his clemency, which he is accustomed to show towards all nations, he will kindly pardon or approve certain little things that it is no longer possible for us to change......Now then, will you reject those who appear as suppliants before you? Will you pursue them with fire and sword? ......Alas! nothing draws upon us in Germany so much hatred, as the unshaken firmness with which we maintain the doctrines of the Roman Church.[4] But with the aid of God, we will remain faithful, even unto death, to Christ and to the Roman Church, although you should reject us."[5]

Thus did Melancthon humble himself. God permitted this fall, that future ages might clearly see how low the Reformation was willing to descend in order to maintain unity, and that no one might doubt that the schism had come from Rome; but also, assuredly, that they might learn how great, in every important work, is the weakness of the noblest instruments.

Fortunately there was then another man who upheld the honour of the Reformation. At this very time Luther wrote to Melancthon: "There can be no concord between Christ and Belial. As far as regards me, I will not yield a hair's breadth.[6] Sooner than yield, I should prefer suffering everything, even the most terrible evils. Concede so much the less, as your adversaries require the more. God will not aid us until we are abandoned by all."[7] And fearing some weak-

---

[1] Legati Norinberg ad Senatum. Corp. Ref. ii. 161.
[2] Melancthon ad Duc. Sax. Elect. Ibid. 162.
[3] Principes nostri miserunt nos ad R. D. V. Ibid. 171.
[4] Pervenerunt ad nos propositiones quædam Italicæ satis Lutheranæ. Ibid. 163.
[5] Istis Germanis asinis, nobis in hac parte obgannientibus. Ibid.
[6] Hispanici proceres præclare et sapienter responderunt Cæsari. Ibid. 179.

[1] "Η ἀδελφὴ ἀυτοκρα]ορος studet nobis placare fratrem. Corp. Ref. ii. 178.
[2] See the Corp. Ref. ii. 168.
[3] Dogma nullum habemus diversum ab Ecclesia Romana. Ibid. 170.
[4] Quam quia Ecclesiæ Romanæ dogmata summa constantia defendimus. Ibid.
[5] Vel si recusabitis nos in gratiam recipere. Ibid.
[6] At certe pro mea persona, ne pilum quidem cedam. L. Epp. iv. 88.
[7] Neque enim juvabimur ni deserti prius simus Ibid 91.

ness on the part of his friends, Luther added: "If it were not tempting God, you would long ago have seen me at your side!"[1]

Never, in fact, had Luther's presence been so necessary, for the legate had consented to an interview, and Melancthon was about to pay court to Campeggio.[2]

The 8th of July was the day appointed by the legate. His letter inspired Philip with the most sanguine hopes. "The cardinal assures me that he will accede the usage of the two kinds, and the marriage of priests," said he; "I am eager to visit him!"[3]

This visit might decide the destiny of the Church. If the legate accepted Philip's *ultimatum*, the evangelical countries would be replaced under the power of the Romish bishops, and all would have been over with the Reformation; but it was saved through the pride and blindness of Rome. The Papists, believing it on the brink of the abyss, thought that a last blow would settle it, and resolved, like Luther, to concede nothing, "not even a hair's breadth." The legate, however, even while refusing, assumed an air of kindness, and of yielding to foreign influence. "I might have the power of making certain concessions, but it would not be prudent to use it without the consent of the German princes;[4] their will must be done; one of them in particular conjures the emperor to prevent us from yielding the least thing. I can grant nothing." The Roman prince, with the most amiable smile, then did all he could to gain the chief of the Protestant teachers. Melancthon retired filled with shame at the advances he had made, but still deceived by Campeggio. "No doubt," said he, "Eck and Cochlœus have been beforehand with me at the legate's."[5] Luther entertained a different opinion. "I do not trust to any of these Italians," said he; "they are scoundrels. When an Italian is good, he is very good; but then he is a black swan."

It was truly the Italians who were concerned. Shortly after the 12th of July arrived the pope's instructions. He had received the Confession by express,[6] and sixteen days had sufficed for the transmission, the deliberation, and the return. Clement would hear no mention either of discussions or of council. Charles was to march straight to the mark, to send an army into Germany, and stifle the Reformation by force. At Augsburg, however, it was thought best not to go so quickly to work, and recourse was had to other means.

"Be quiet; we have them," said the Romish doctors. Sensible of the reproach that had been made against them, of having misrepresented the Reformation, they accused the Protestants themselves of being the cause. "These it is," they said, "who, to give themselves an air of being in accord with us, now dissemble their heresy; but we will catch them in their own nets. If they confess to not having inserted in their Confession all that they reject, it will be proved that they are trifling with us. If, on the contrary, they pretend to have said everthing, they will by that very circumstance be compelled to admit all that they have not condemned." The Protestant princes were therefore called together, and they were asked if the Reformation was confined to the doctrines indicated in the Apology, or if there was something more.[1]

The snare was skilfully laid. The papacy had not even been mentioned in Melancthon's Confession; other errors besides had been omitted, and Luther himself complained of it aloud. "Satan sees clearly," said he, "that your Apology has passed lightly over the articles of purgatory, the worship of saints, and, above all, of the Pope and of Antichrist." The princes requested to confer with their allies of the towns; and all the Protestants assembled to deliberate on this momentous incident.

They looked for Melancthon's explanation, who did not decline the responsibility of the affair. Easily dejected through his own anxiety, he became bold whenever he was directly attacked. "All the essential doctrines," said he, "have been set forth in the Confession, and every error and abuse that is opposed to them has been pointed out. But was it necessary to plunge into all those questions so full of contention and animosity, that are discussed in our universities? Was it necessary to ask if all Christians are priests, if the primacy of the pope is of right divine, if there can be indulgences, if every good work is a deadly sin, if there are more than seven sacraments, if they may be administered by a layman, if divine election has any foundation in our own merits, if sacerdotal consecration impresses an indelible character, if auricular confession is necessary to salvation?......No, no! all these things are in the province of the schools, and by no means essential to faith."[2]

It cannot be denied that in the questions thus pointed out by Melancthon there were important points. However that may be, the evangelical committee were soon agreed, and on the morrow they gave an answer to Charles's ministers, drawn up with as much frankness as firmness, in which they said "that the Protestants, desirous of arriving at a cordial understanding, had not wished to complicate their situation, and had proposed, not to specify all the errors that

---

[1] Certe jamdudum coram vidissetis me. L. Epp. iv. 98.
[2] Ego multos prehensare soleo et Campegium etiam. Corp. Ref. ii. 193.
[3] Propero enim ad Campegium. Ibid. 174.
[4] Se nihil posse decernere, nisi de voluntate principum Germaniæ. Ibid.
[5] Forte ad legatum veniebant Eccius et Cochlœus. Ibid. 175.
[6] Nostra Confessio ad Romam per veredarios missa est. Ibid. 166, 219

---

[1] An plura velimus Cæsari præponere controversa quam fecerimus. Corp. Ref. ii. 188.
[2] Melancthonis Judicium. Ibid. 182.

had been introduced into the Church, but to confess all the doctrines that were essential to salvation; that if, nevertheless, the adverse party felt itself urged to maintain certain abuses, or to put forward any point not mentioned in the Confession, the Protestants declared themselves ready to reply in conformity with the Word of God."[1] The tone of this answer showed pretty clearly that the evangelical Christians did not fear to follow their adversaries wherever the latter should call them. Accordingly the Roman party said no more on this business.

CHAPTER IX.

The Refutation—Charles's Dissatisfaction—Interview with the Princes—The Swiss at Augsburg—Tetrapolitan Confession—Zwingle's Confession—Afflicting Divisions—The Elector's Faith—His Peace—The Lion's Skin—The Refutation—one Concession—Scripture and the Hierarchy—Imperial Commands—Interview between Melancthon and Campeggio—Policy of Charles—Stormy Meeting—Resolutions of the Consistory—The Prayers of the Church—Two Miracles—The Emperor's Menace—The Prince's Courage—The Mask—Negotiations—The Spectres at Spires—Tumult in Augsburg.

THE commission charged to refute the Confession met twice a-day,[2] and each of the theologians who composed it added to it his refutations and his hatred.

On the 13th July the work was finished. "Eck with his band,"[3] said Melancthon, "transmitted it to the emperor." Great was the astonishment of this prince and of his ministers at seeing a work of two hundred and eighty pages filled with abuse.[4] "Bad workmen waste much wood," said Luther, "and impious writers soil much paper." This was not all; to the Refutation were subjoined eight appendices on the heresies that Melancthon had dissembled (as they said), and wherein they exposed the contradictions and "the horrible sects" to which Lutheranism had given birth. Lastly, not confining themselves to this official answer, the Romish theologians, who saw the sun of power shining upon them, filled Augsburg with insolent and abusive pamphlets.

There was but one opinion on the Papist Refutation; it was found confused, violent, and blood-thirsty.[5] Charles the Fifth had too much good taste not to perceive the difference that existed between this coarse work and the noble dignity of Melancthon's Confession. He rolled, handled, crushed, and so damaged the two hundred and eighty pages of his doctors, that when he returned them two days after, says Spalatin, there were not more than twelve entire. Charles would have been ashamed to have such a pamphlet read in the diet, and he required, in conse-

quence, that it should be drawn up anew, shorter, and in more moderate language.[1] That was not easy, "for the adversaries, confused and stupified," says Brentz, "by the noble simplicity of the Evangelical Confession, neither knew where to begin, nor where to end ; they accordingly took nearly three weeks to do their work over again."[2]

Charles and his ministers had great doubts of its success ; leaving, therefore, the theologians for a moment, they imagined another manœuvre. "Let us take each of the Protestant princes separately," said they : "isolated, they will not resist." Accordingly, on the 15th July, the Margrave of Brandenburg was visited by his two cousins, the Electors of Mentz and of Brandenburg, and by his two brothers the Margraves Frederick and John Albert. "Abandon this new faith," said they to him, "and return to that which existed a century ago. If you do so, there are no favours that you may not expect from the emperor; if not, dread his anger."[3]

Shortly after, Duke Frederick of Bavaria, the Count of Nassau, De Rogendorf, and Truchses were announced to the Elector on the part of Charles. "You have solicited the emperor," said they, "to confirm the marriage of your son with the Princess of Juliers, and to invest you with the electoral dignity ; but his majesty declares, that if you do not renounce the heresy of Luther, of which you are the principal abettor, he cannot accede to your demand." At the same time the Duke of Bavaria, employing the most urgent solicitations, accompanied with the most animated gestures[4] and the most sinister threats,[5] called upon the elector to abandon his faith. "It is asserted," added Charles's envoys, "that you have made an alliance with the Swiss. The emperor cannot believe it ; and he orders you to let him know the truth."

The Swiss ! it was the same thing as rebellion. This alliance was the phantom incessantly invoked at Augsburg to alarm Charles the Fifth. And in reality deputies, or at least friends of the Swiss, had already appeared in that city, and thus rendered the position still more serious.

Bucer had arrived two days before the reading of the Confession, and Capito on the day subsequent to it.[6] There was even a report that Zwingle would join them.[7] But for a long time all in Augsburg, except the Strasburg deputation, were ignorant of the

[1] Aus Gottes Wort, weiter bericht zu thun. F. Urkundenbuch, ii. 19.
[2] Bis die convenire dicuntur. Zw. Epp. ii. 472.
[3] Eccius cum sua commanipulatione. Corp. Ref. ii. 193.
[4] Longum et plenum conviciis scriptum. Ibid.
[5] Adeo confusa, incondita, violenta, sanguinolenta et crudelis ut puduerint. Ibid. 198.

[1] Hodie auctoribus ipsis Sophistis, a Cæsare rursus esse redditam ut emendetur et civilius componatur. Corp. Ref. ii. 198.
[2] Nostra confessioneita stupidos, attonitos, et confusos. Ibid.
[3] Ibid. 206 ; F. Urkund. ii. 93.
[4] Mit reden und Gebehrden prächtig erzeigt. Ibid. 207.
[5] Minas diras promissis ingentibus adjiciens. Zw. Epp. ii. 484.
[6] Venimus huc, ego pridie solemnitatis Divi Johannis, Capito die dominica sequente. Ibid. 472.
[7] Rumor apud nos est, et te cum tuis Helvetiis comitia advolaturum. Ibid. 431, 467.

presence of these doctors.[1] It was only twenty-one days after their arrival that Melancthon learnt it positively,[2] so great was the mystery in which the Zwinglians were forced to enshroud themselves. This was not without reason : a conference with Melancthon having been requested by them. "Let them write," replied he; "I should compromise our cause by an interview with them."

Bucer and Capito in their retreat, which was like a prison to them, had taken advantage of their leisure to draw up the *Tetrapolitan Confession*, or the confession of the four cities. The deputies of Strasburg, Constance, Memmingen, and Lindau, presented it to the emperor.[3] These cities purged themselves from the reproach of war and revolt that had been continually objected against them. They declared that their only motive was Christ's glory, and professed the truth "freely, boldly, but without insolence and without scurrility."[4]

Zwingle about the same time caused a private confession to be communicated to Charles,[5] which excited a general uproar. "Does he not dare to say," exclaimed the Romanists, "that the *mitred and withered race* (by which he means the bishops) is in the Church what hump-backs and the scrofula are in the body?"[6]—"Does he not insinuate," said the Lutherans; "that we are beginning to look back after the onions and garlic of Egypt?"—"One might say with great truth that he had lost his senses," exclaimed Melancthon.[7] "All ceremonies, according to him, ought to be abolished; all the bishops ought to be suppressed. In a word, all is perfectly *Helvetic*, that is to say, supremely barbarous."

One man formed an exception to this concert of reproaches, and this was Luther. "Zwingle pleases me tolerably, and so does Bucer," wrote he to Jonas.[8] By Bucer, he meant no doubt the Tetrapolitan Confession: this expression should be noted.

Thus three Confessions, laid at the feet of Charles the Fifth, attested the divisions that were rending Protestantism. In vain did Bucer and Capito endeavour to come to an understanding with Melancthon, and write to him: "We will meet where you will, and when you will; we will bring Sturm only with us, and if you desire it, we will not even bring him."[9] All was unavailing. It

is not enough for a Christian to confess Christ ; one disciple should confess another disciple, even if the latter lies under the shame of the world ; but they did not then comprehend this duty. "Schism is in the schism," said the Romanists, and the emperor flattered himself with an easy victory. "Return to the Church," was the cry from every side, "which means," interrupted the Strasburgers, "let us put the bit in your mouths, that we may lead you as we please."[1]

All these things deeply afflicted the elector, who was besides still under the burden of Charles's demands and threats. The emperor had not once spoken to him,[2] and it was every where said that his cousin George of Saxony would be proclaimed elector in his stead.

On the 28th July, there was a great festival at the court. Charles, robed in his imperial garments, whose value was said to exceed 200,000 gold ducats, and displaying an air of majesty which impressed respect and fear,[3] conferred on many princes the investiture of their dignities ; the elector alone was excluded from these favours. Erelong he was made to understand more plainly what was reserved for him, and it was insinuated, that if he did not submit, the emperor would expel him from his states, and inflict upon him the severest punishment."[4]

The elector turned pale, for he doubted not that such would certainly be the termination. How with his small territory could he resist that powerful monarch who had just vanquished France and Italy, and now saw Germany at his feet? And besides, if he could do it, had he the right? Frightful nightmares pursued John in his dreams. He beheld himself stretched beneath an immense mountain under which he lay painfully struggling, while his cousin George of Saxony stood on the summit and seemed to brave him.

John at length came forth from this furnace. "I must either renounce God or the world," said he. "Well! my choice is not doubtful. It is God who made me elector,— me, who was not worthy of it. I fling myself into his arms, and let him do with me what shall seem good to him." Thus the elector by faith stopped the mouths of lions and subdued kingdoms."[5]

All evangelical Christendom had taken part in the struggle of John the Persevering. It was seen that if he should now fall, all would fall with him ; and they endeavoured to support him. "Fear not," cried the Christians of Magdeburg, "for your highness is under Christ's banner."[6] "Italy is in expec-

---

[1] Ita latent ut non quibuslibet sui copiam faciant. Corp. Ref. p. 196.
[2] Capito et Bucerus adsunt. Id hodie certo comperi. Ibid.
[3] Cinglianæ civitates propriam Confessionem obtulerunt Cæsari. Corp. Ref. p. 187. This Confession will be found in *Niemeyer*, Collectio Confessionum, p. 740.
[4] Ingenue ac fortiter ; citra procaciam tamen et sannas, id fateri et dicere quod res est. Zw. Epp. ii. 485.
[5] See Niemeyer Coll. Conf. p. 16.
[6] Pedatum et mitratum genus Episcoporum. id esset in Ecclesia, quod gibbi et strumata in corpore. Ibid. Zwingle compares the bishops to the dry and fruitless props that support the vines.
[7] Dicas simpliciter mente captum esse. Corp. Ref. p. 193.
[8] Zwinglius mihi sane placet, et Bucerus. L. Epp. iv. 110.
[9] Veniemus quo et quando tu voles. Corp. Ref. ii. 208.

[1] Una tamen omnium vox : *Revertimini ad Ecclesiam.* Zw. Epp. ii. 484.
[2] Colloquium ejus nondum frui potuisse. Seck. ii. 154.
[3] Apparuit Cæsar majestate......insignitus vestibus suis imperialibus. Corp. Ref. ii. 242.
[4] Müller, Gesch. der Protestation, p. 715.
[5] Hebrews xi. 33, 34.
[6] Unter dem Heerpannyr Jesu Christi. Ibid. p. 131.

tation," wrote they from Venice; "if for Christ's glory you must die, fear nothing."[1] But it was from a higher source that John's courage was derived. "I beheld Satan as lightning fall from heaven," said his Master.[2] The elector, in like manner, beheld in his dreams George fall from the top of the mountain, and lie dashed in pieces at its feet.

Once resolved to lose every thing, John, free, happy, and tranquil, assembled his theologians. These generous men desired to save their master. "Gracious lord," said Spalatin, "recollect that the Word of God, being the sword of the Spirit, must be upheld, not by the secular power, but by the hand of the Almighty."[3]—"Yes!" said all the doctors, "we do not wish that, to save us, you should risk your children, your subjects, your states, your crown......We will rather give ourselves into the hands of the enemy, and conjure him to be satisfied with our blood."[4] John, touched by this language, refused, however, their solicitations, and firmly repeated these words, which had become his device: "I also desire to confess my Saviour."

It was on the 20th July that he replied to the pressing arguments by which Charles had endeavoured to shake him. He proved to the emperor that, being his brother's legitimate heir, he could not refuse him the investiture, which, besides, the Diet of Worms had secured to him. He added, that he did not blindly believe what his doctors said, but that, having recognized the Word of God to be the foundation of their teaching, he confessed anew, and without any hesitation, all the articles of the Apology. "I therefore entreat your majesty," continued he, "to permit me and mine to render an account to God alone of what concerns the salvation of our souls."[5] The Margrave of Brandenburg made the same reply. Thus failed this skilful manœuvre by which the Romanists had hoped to break the strength of the Reformation.

Six weeks had elapsed since the Confession, and as yet there was no reply. "The Papists, from the moment they heard the Apology," it was said, suddenly became dumb."[6] At length the Romish theologians handed their revised and corrected performance to the emperor, and persuaded this prince to present it in his own name. The mantle of the state seemed to them admirably adapted to the movements of Rome. "These sycophants," said Melancthon, "have desired to clothe themselves with the lion's skin, to appear to us so much

the more terrible."[1] All the states of the empire were convoked for the next day but one.

On Wednesday, 3d August, at two o'clock in the afternoon, the emperor took his seat on the throne in the chapel of the Palatinate Palace, attended by his brother, the electors, princes, and deputies. When the Elector of Saxony and his allies were introduced, the count-palatine, who was called "Charles's mouthpiece;" said to them: "His majesty having handed your Confession to several doctors of different nations, illustrious by their knowledge, their morals, and their impartiality, has read their reply with the greatest care, and submits it to you as his own."[2]

Alexander Schweiss then took the papers and read the Refutation. The Roman party approved some articles of the Confession, condemned others, and in certain less salient passages, it distinguished between what must be rejected and what accepted.

It gave way on an important point; the *opus operatum*. The Protestants having said in their 13th Article that faith was necessary in the sacrament, the Romish party assented to it; thus abandoning an error which the papacy had so earnestly defended against Luther in that very city of Augsburg by the mouth of Cajetan.

Moreover, they recognized as truly christian the evangelical doctrine on the Trinity, on Christ, on baptism, on eternal punishment, and on the origin of evil.

But on all the other points, Charles, his princes, and his theologians, declared themselves immovable. They maintained that men are born with the fear of God, that good works are meritorious, and that they justify in union with faith. They upheld the seven sacraments, the mass, transubstantiation, the withdrawal of the cup, the celibacy of priests, the invocation of saints, and denied that the Church was an assembly of the saints.

This Refutation was skilful in some respects, and, above all, in what concerned the doctrine of works and of faith. But on other points, in particular on the withdrawal of the cup and the celibacy of priests, its arguments were lamentably weak, and contrary to the well known facts of history.

While the Protestants had taken their stand on the Scriptures, their adversaries supported the divine origin of the hierarchy, and laid down absolute submission to its laws. Thus, the essential character, which still distinguishes Rome from the Reformation, stood prominently forth in this first combat.

Among the auditors who filled the chapel of the Palatinate Palace, concealed in the midst of the deputies of Nuremberg, was Joa-

[1] Etiamsi mors subeunda tibi foret ob Christi gloriam. Corp. Ref. ii. 228. L. P. Roselli.
[2] Luke x. 18.
[3] Gottes Wort keines wegs durch weltlich Schwert. F. Urkund. ii. 82.
[4] Sie wollen ihnen an ihrem Blüte genügen lassen. Ibid. 80.
[5] Forstemann's Urkundenbuch, pp. 80-92, 113-119.
[6] Papistas obmutuisse ad ipsorum Confessionem. Cochl. p. 195.

[1] Voluerunt sycophantæ theologi λεον͡ζην illam sibi circumdare, ut essent nobis formidabiliores. Corp. Ref. p. 252.
[2] Velut suam suaque publica auctoritate roboratam. Urkundenbuch ii. 144.

chim Camerarius, who, while Schweiss was reading, leant over his tablets and carefully noted down all he could collect. At the same time others of the Protestants, speaking to one another, were indignant, and even laughed, as one of their opponents assures us.[1] " Really," said they with one consent, " the whole of this Refutation is worthy of Eck, Faber, and Cochlœus !"

As for Charles, little pleased with these theological dissertations, he slept during the reading;[2] but he awoke when Schweiss had finished, and his awakening was that of a lion.

The count-palatine then declared that his majesty found the articles of this Refutation orthodox, catholic, and conformable to the Gospel; that he therefore required the Protestants to abandon their Confession, now refuted, and to adhere to all the articles which had just been set forth;[3] that, if they refused, the emperor would remember his office, and would know how to show himself the advocate and defender of the Roman Church.

This language was clear enough : the adversaries imagined they had refuted the Protestants by commanding the latter to consider themselves beaten. Violence—arms—war—were all contained in these cruel words of Charles's minister.[4] The princes represented that, as the Refutation adopted some of their articles and rejected others, it required a careful examination, and they consequently begged a copy should be given them.

The Romish party had a long conference on this demand : night was at hand ; the count-palatine replied that, considering the late hour and the importance of this affair, the emperor would make known his pleasure somewhat later. The diet separated, and Charles the Fifth, exasperated at the audacity of the evangelical princes, says Cochlœus, returned in ill-humour to his apartments.[5]

The Protestants, on the contrary, withdrew full of peace ; the reading of the Refutation having given them as much confidence as that of the Confession itself.[6] They saw in their adversaries a strong attachment to the hierarchy, but a great ignorance of the Gospel—a characteristic feature of the Romish party ; and this thought encouraged them. " Certainly," said they, " the Church cannot be where there is no knowledge of Christ."[7]

Melancthon alone was still alarmed : he walked by sight and not by faith, and, re-

membering the legate's smiles, he had another interview with him, as early as the 4th August, still demanding the cup for the laity, and lawful wives for the priests. " Then," said he, " our pastors will place themselves again under the government of the bishops, and we shall be able to prevent those innumerable sects with which posterity is threatened."[1] Melancthon's glance into the future is remarkable : it does not, however, mean that he, like many others, preferred a dead unity to a living diversity.

Campeggio, now certain of triumphing by the sword, disdainfully handed this paper to Cochlœus, who hastened to refute it. It is hard to say whether Melancthon or Campeggio was the more infatuated. God did not permit an arrangement that would have enslaved his Church.

Charles passed the whole of the 4th and the morning of the 5th of August in consultation with the Ultramontane party. " It will never be by discussion that we shall come to an understanding," said some ; " and if the Protestants do not submit voluntarily, it only remains for us to compel them." They nevertheless decided, on account of the Refutation, on adopting a middle course. During the whole of the diet Charles pursued a skilful policy. At first he refused every thing, hoping to lead away the princes by violence; then he conceded a few unimportant points, under the impression that the Protestants, having lost all hope, would esteem so much the more the little he did yield. This was what he did again under the present circumstances. In the afternoon of the 5th, the count-palatine announced that the emperor would give them a copy of the Refutation, but on these conditions ; namely, that the Protestants should not reply, that they should speedily agree with the emperor, and that they should not print or communicate to any one the Refutation that should be confided to them.[2]

This communication excited murmurs among the Protestants. " These conditions," said they all, " are inadmissible."—" The Papists present us with their paper," added the Chancellor Brück, " as the fox offered a thin broth to his gossip the stork."

The savoury broth upon a plate by Reynard was served up, But Mistress Stork, with her long beak, she could not get a sup.[3]

" If the Refutation," continued he, " should become known without our participation (and how can we prevent it ?), we shall be charged with it as a crime. Let us beware of accepting so perfidious an offer.[4] We already possess in the notes of Camerarius several articles of this paper, and if we omit

---

1 Multi e Lutheranis inepte cachinnabantur. Cochlœus, v. 695.
2 Imperator iterum obdormivit. Corp. Ref. ii. 245.
3 Petiit Cæsar ut omnes in illos articulos consentiant. Ibid.
4 Orationis summa atrox. Ibid. 253.
5 Cæsar non æquo animo ferebat eorum contumaciam. Cochl. p. 195.
6 Facti sunt erectiore animo. Corp. Ref. ii. 259.
7 Ecclesiam ibi non esse, ubi ignoratur Christus.

1 Quod nisi fiet, quid in tot sectis ad posteros futurum sit. Corp. Ref. ii. 148.
2 F. Urkund. ii. 179 ; Corp. Ref. ii. 256 ; Brück. Apol. 72.
3 Gluck wie der Fuchs brauchet, da er den Storch zu gast lud. Brück, Apol. 74.
4 Quando exemplum per alios in vulgus exire poterat, Corp. Ref. ii. 76.

any point, no one will have the right to reproach us with it."

On the next day (6th August), the Protestants declared to the diet that they preferred declining the copy thus offered to them, and appealed to God and to his majesty.[1] They thus rejected all that the emperor proposed to them, even what he considered as a favour.

Agitation, anger, and affright were manifested on every bench of that august assembly.[2] This reply of the evangelicals was war—was rebellion. George of Saxony, the Princes of Bavaria, all the violent adherents of Rome, trembled with indignation; there was a sudden, an impetuous movement, an explosion of murmurs and of hatred; and it might have been feared that the two parties would have come to blows in the very presence of the emperor, if Archbishop Albert, the Elector of Brandenburg, and the Dukes of Brunswick, Pomerania, and Mecklenburg, rushing between them, had not conjured the Protestants to put an end to this deplorable combat, and not drive the emperor to extremities.[3] The diet separated, their hearts filled with emotion, apprehension, and trouble.

Never had the diet proposed such fatal alternatives. The hopes of agreement, set forth in the edict of convocation, had only been a deceitful lure: now the mask was thrown aside; submission or the sword—such was the dilemma offered to the Reformation. All announced that the day of tentatives was passed, and that they were beginning one of violence.

In truth, on the 6th July, the pope had assembled the consistory of cardinals in his palace at Rome, and had made known to them the Protestant ultimatum; namely, the cup for the laity, the marriage of priests, the omission of the invocation of saints in the sacrifice of the mass, the use of ecclesiastical property already secularized, and for the rest, the convocation of a council. "These concessions," said the cardinals, "are opposed to the religion, discipline, and laws of the Church.[4] We reject them, and vote our thanks to the emperor for the zeal which he employs in bringing back the deserters." The pope having thus decided, every attempt at conciliation became useless.

Campeggio, on his side, redoubled in zeal. He spoke as if in his person the pope himself were present at Augsburg.[5] "Let the emperor and the right-thinking princes form a league," said he to Charles; "and if these rebels, equally insensible to threats and promises, obstinately persist in their diabolical course, then let his majesty seize fire and sword, let him take possession of all the property of the heretics, and utterly eradicate these venomous plants.[1] Then let him appoint holy inquisitors, who shall go on the track of the remnants of the Reformation, and proceed against them, as in Spain against the Moors. Let him put the university of Wittemberg under ban, burn all heretical books, and send back the fugitive monks to their convents. But this plan must be executed with courage."

Thus the jurisprudence of Rome consisted, according to a prophecy uttered against the city which *is seated on seven hills*, in adorning itself with pearls that it had stolen, and in becoming drunk with the blood of the saints.[2]

While Charles was thus urged on with blind fury by the diet and the pope, the Protestant princes, restrained by a mute indignation, did not open their mouths,[3] and hence they seemed to betray a weakness of which the emperor was eager to profit. But there was also strength concealed beneath this weakness. "We have nothing left," exclaimed Melancthon, "but to embrace our Saviour's knees." In this they laboured earnestly. Melancthon begged for Luther's prayers; Brentz for those of his own church: a general cry of distress and of faith ran through evangelical Germany. "You shall have sheep," said Brentz, "if you will send us sheep: you know what I mean."[4] The sheep that were to be offered in sacrifice were the prayers of the saints.

The Church was not wanting to itself. "Assembled every day," wrote certain cities to the electors, "we beg for you strength, grace, and victory,—victory full of joy." But the man of prayer and faith was especially Luther. A calm and sublime courage, in which firmness shines at the side of joy—a courage that rises and exults in proportion as the danger increases—is what Luther's letters at this time present in every line. The most poetical images are pale beside those energetic expressions which issue in a boiling torrent from the reformer's soul. "I have recently witnessed two miracles," wrote he on the 5th August to Chancellor Brück; "this is the first. As I was at my window, I saw the stars, and the sky, and that vast and magnificent firmament in which the Lord has placed them. I could nowhere discover the columns on which the Master has supported this immense vault, and yet the heavens did not fall......

"And here is the second. I beheld thick clouds hanging above us like a vast sea. I

[1] Das Sie es Gott und Kays. Maj. beschlen muften. Urkund. i. 181.
[2] Und darob wie man Spüren mag, ein Entzet zen gehabt. Ibid.
[3] Hi accedunt ad nostros principes et jubent omittere hoc certamen, ne Cæsar vehementius commoveatur. Corp. Ref. ii. 254.
[4] Oppositas religioni, disciplinæ, legibusque Ecclesiæ. Pallav. i. 234.
[5] Als were der Papst selbst gegenwärtig gewest. Brück, Apol. 62.

[1] Se alcuni......perseverassero in questa diabolica via quella S. M. potrà mettere la mano al ferro e al foco et radicitus extirpare questa venenata pianta. Instructio data Cæsari a reverendissimo Campeggi in dieta Augustana, 1530.
[2] Revelation xvii. and xviii.
[3] Tacita indignatio. Corp. Ref. ii. 254.
[4] Habebitis oves, si oves ad nos mittatis: intelligitis quæ volo. Ibid. 246.

could neither perceive ground on which they reposed, nor cords by which they were suspended; and yet they did not fall upon us, but saluted us rapidly and fled away.

"God," continued he, "will choose the manner, the time, and the place suitable for deliverance, and he will not linger. What the men of blood have begun, they have not yet finished......Our rainbow is faint......their clouds are threatening......the enemy comes against us with frightful machines......But at last it will be seen to whom belong the ballistæ, and from what hands the javelins are launched.[1] It is no matter if Luther perishes: if Christ is conqueror, Luther is conqueror also."[2]

The Roman party, who did not know what was the victory of faith, imagined themselves certain of success.

As the doctors had refuted the Confession, the Protestants ought, they imagined, to declare themselves convinced, and all would then be restored to its ancient footing: such was the plan of the emperor's campaign. He therefore urged and called upon the Protestants; but instead of submitting, they announced a refutation of the Refutation. Upon this Charles looked at his sword, and all the princes who surrounded him did the same.

John of Saxony understood what that meant, but he remained firm. "The straight line," said he (the axiom was familiar to him), "is the shortest road." It is this indomitable firmness that has secured for him in history the name of John the Persevering. He was not alone: all those Protestant princes who had grown up in the midst of courts, and who were habituated to pay an humble obedience to the emperor, at that time found in their faith a noble independence that confounded Charles the Fifth.

With the design of gaining the Marquis of Brandenburg, they opened to him the possibility of accórding him some possessions in Silesia on which he had claims. "If Christ is Christ," replied he, "the doctrine that I have confessed is truth."—"But do you know," quickly replied his cousin the Elector Joachim, "what is your stake?"—"Certainly," replied the margrave, "it is said I shall be expelled from this country. Well! may God protect me!" One day Prince Wolfgang of Anhalt met Doctor Eck. "Doctor," said he, "you are exciting to war, but you will find those who will not be behindhand with you. I have broken many a lance for my friends in my time. My Lord Jesus Christ is assuredly worthy that I should do as much for him."

At the sight of this resolution, each one asked himself whether Charles, instead of curing the disease, was not augmenting it. Reflections, criticisms, and jests passed between the citizens; and the good sense of the people manifested in its own fashion what they thought of the folly of their chiefs. We will adduce one instance.

It is said that one day, as the emperor was at table with several Roman-catholic princes, he was informed that some comedians begged permission (according to custom) to amuse their lordships. First appeared an old man wearing a mask, and dressed in a doctor's robe, who advanced with difficulty, carrying a bundle of sticks in his arms, some straight and some crooked. He approached the wide fire-place of the Gothic hall, threw down his load in disorder, and immediately withdrew.[1] Charles and the courtiers read on his back the inscription—JOHN REUCHLIN. Next came another mask with an intelligent look, who made every exertion to pair the straight and the crooked pieces;[2] but finding his labour useless, he shook his head, turned to the door, and disappeared. They read—ERASMUS OF ROTTERDAM. Almost immediately after advanced a monk with bright eye and decided gait, carrying a brasier of lighted coals.[3] He put the wood in order, set fire to it, and blew and stirred it up, so that the flame rose bright and sparkling into the air. He then retired, and on his back were the words—MARTIN LUTHER.

Next approached a magnificent personage, covered with all the imperial insignia, who, seeing the fire so bright, drew his sword, and endeavoured by violent thrusts to extinguish it; but the more he struck, the fiercer burnt the flames, and at last he quitted the hall in indignation. His name, as it would seem, was not made known to the spectators, but all divined it. The general attention was soon attracted by a new character. A man, wearing a surplice and a mantle of red velvet, with an alb of white wool reaching to his heels, and having a stole around his neck, the ends ornamented with pearls, advanced majestically. On beholding the flames that already filled the hearth, he wrung his hands in terror, and looked around for something to extinguish them. Seeing two vessels at the very extremity of the hall, one filled with water, and the other with oil, he rushed towards them, seized unwittingly on that containing the oil, and threw it on the fire.[4] The flame then spread with such violence that the mask fled in alarm, raising his hands to heaven; on his back was read the name of LEO X.

The mystery was finished; but instead of claiming their remuneration, the pretended actors had disappeared. No one asked the moral of this drama.

The lesson, however, proved useless; and the majority of the diet, assuming at the

---

[1] In fine videbitur cujus toni......L. Epp. iv. 130.
[2] Vincat Christus modo, nihil refert si pereat Lutherus, quia victore Christo victor erit. Ibid. 139.

[1] Persona larva contecta, habitu doctorali portabat struem lignorum. T. L. Fabricius. opp. omnia, ii. 231.
[2] Hic conabatur curva rectis exequare lignis. Ibid.
[3] In azula ferens ignem et prunas. Ibid.
[4] Currens in amphoram oleo plenam. Ibid. 232.

same time the part assigned to the emperor and the pope, began to prepare the means necessary for extinguishing the fire kindled by Luther. They negotiated in Italy with the Duke of Mantua, who engaged to send a few regiments of light cavalry across the Alps;[1] and in England with Henry VIII., who had not forgotten Luther's reply, and who promised Charles, through his ambassador, an immense subsidy to destroy the heretics.[2]

At the same time frightful prodigies announced the gloomy future which threatened the Reform. At Spires fearful spectres, in the shape of monks with angry eyes and hasty steps, had appeared during the night. " What do you want ? " they had been asked.—" We are going to the Diet of Augsburg ! " they replied. The circumstance had been carefully investigated, and was found perfectly trustworthy.[3] " The interpretation is not difficult," exclaimed Melancthon : " Evil spirits are coming to Augsburg to counteract our exertions, and to destroy peace. They forebode horrible troubles to us."[4] No one doubted this. " Every thing is advancing towards war," said Erasmus.[5] " The diet will not terminate," wrote Brentz, " except by the destruction of all Germany."[6] " There will be a slaughter of the saints," exclaimed Bucer, " which will be such that the massacres of Diocletian will scarcely come up to it."[7] War and blood !—this was the general cry.

Suddenly, on the night of Saturday, 6th August, a great disturbance broke out in the city of Augsburg.[8] There was running to and fro in the streets ; messengers from the emperor were galloping in every direction ; the senate was called together and received an order to allow no one to pass the city gates.[9] All were afoot in the imperial barracks ; the soldiers got ready their arms ; the regiments were drawn up, and at daybreak (about three o'clock on Sunday morning) the emperor's troops, in opposition to the custom always observed in the diet, relieved the garrison of the city and took possession of the gates. At the same time it was reported that they would not be opened, and that Charles had given orders to keep a strict watch upon the elector and his allies.[10]

A terrible awakening for those who still flattered themselves with seeing the religious debates conclude peacefully ! Might not these unheard-of measures be the commencement of war and the signal of a frightful massacre ?

CHAPTER X.

Philip of Hesse—Temptation—Union resisted—The Landgrave's Dissimulation—The Emperor's Order to the Protestants—Brandenburg's threatening Speeches—Resolution of Philip of Hesse—Flight from Augsburg—Discovery—Charles's Emotion—Revolution in the Diet—Metamorphosis—Unusual Moderation—Peace ! Peace !

TROUBLE and anger prevailed in the imperial palace, and it was the landgrave who had caused them. Firm as a rock in the midst of the tempest with which he was surrounded, Philip of Hesse had never bent his head to the blast. One day, in a public assembly, addressing the bishops, he had said to them, " My lords, give peace to the empire ; we beg it of you. If you will not do so, and if I must fall, be sure that I will drag one or two of you along with me." They saw it was necessary to employ milder means with him, and the emperor endeavoured to gain him by showing a favourable disposition with respect to the county of Katzenellenbogen, about which he was at variance with Nassau, and to Wurtemberg, which he claimed for his cousin Ulric. On his side Duke George of Saxony, his father-in-law, had assured him that he would make him his heir if he would submit to the pope. " They carried him to an exceeding high mountain, whence they showed him all the kingdoms of the world and the glory thereof,"[1] says a chronicler, but the landgrave resisted the temptation.

One day he heard that the emperor had manifested a desire to speak to him. He leapt instantly on his horse and appeared before Charles.[2] The latter, who had with him his secretary Schweiss and the Bishop of Constance, represented that he had four complaints against him ; namely, of having violated the edict of Worms, of despising the mass, of having, during his absence, excited all kinds of revolt, and finally, of having transmitted to him a book in which his sovereign rights were attacked. The landgrave justified himself ; and the emperor said that he accepted his replies, except with regard to the faith, and begged him to show himself in that respect entirely submissive to his majesty. " What would you say," added Charles, in a winning tone, " if I elevated you to the regal dignity ?[3] But, if you show yourself rebellious to my orders, then I shall behave as becomes a Roman emperor."

---

1 Che tentano col Duca di Mantova d' avere il modo di condurre 1000 cavalli leggieri d' Italia in caso si facesse guerra in Germania. Nic. Tiefolo Relat.
2 Cui (Cæsari) ingentem vim pecuniæ in hoc sacrum bellum contra hæreticos Anglus promisisse fertur. Zw. Epp. ii. 484.
3 Res et diligenter inquisita et explorata maximeque αξιοπιστος. Corp. Ref. ii. 259.
4 Monachorum Spirensium φάσμα plane significat horribilem tumultum. Ibid. 260.
5 Vides rem plane tendere ad bellum. Corp. Ref. Aug. 12, p. 268.
6 Comitia non finientur nisi totius Germaniæ malo et exitio. Corp. Ref. ii. 216.
7 Laniena sanctorum qualis vix Diocletiani tempore fuit. Buc. Ep. Aug. 14, 1530.
8 Tumultum magnum fuisse in civitate. Corp. Ref. ii. 277.
9 Facto autem intempesta nocte Cæsar senatui mandavit, ne quenquam per portas urbis suæ emittant. Ibid.
10 Daß man auf den Churfurst zu Sachsen aufschen haben soll. Brück, Apol. p. 80.

1 Auf den hohen berg gefuhrt. Lanze's Chronik.
2 Von ihr selbst gen Hof geritten. Corp. Ref. ii. 165.
3 Quin et in regem te evehendum curabimus. Rommel, Philip der Gr. i. 268.

These words exasperated the landgrave, but they did not move him. " I am in the flower of my age," replied he, " and I do not pretend to despise the joys of life and the favour of the great ; but to the deceitful goods of this world I shall always prefer the ineffable grace of my God." Charles was stupified ; he could not understand Philip.

From this time the landgrave had redoubled his exertions to unite the adherents of the Reformation. The Zwinglian cities felt that, whatever was the issue of the diet, they would be the first victims, unless the Saxons should give them their hand. But this there was some difficulty in obtaining. " It does not appear to me useful for the public weal, or safe for the conscience," wrote Melancthon to Bucer, "to load our princes with all the hatred your doctrine inspires."[1] The Strasburgers replied that the real cause of the Papists' hatred was not so much the doctrine of the eucharist as that of justification by faith. " All we, who desire to belong to Christ," said they, " are one, and have nothing to expect but death."[2]

This was true ; but another motive besides checked Melancthon. If all the Protestants united, they would feel their strength, and war would be inevitable. Therefore, then, no union !

The landgrave, threatened by the emperor, rejected by the theologians, began to ask himself what he did at Augsburg. The cup was full. Charles's refusal to communicate the Romish Refutation, except on inadmissible conditions, made it run over. Philip of Hesse saw but one course to take— to quit the city.

Scarcely had the emperor made known the conditions which he placed on the communication of the reply, than on Friday evening, 5th August, the landgrave, going alone to the count-palatine, Charles's minister, had begged for an immediate audience with his majesty. Charles, who did not care to see him, pretended to be busy, and had put off Philip until the following Sunday.[3] But the latter answered that he could not wait ; that his wife, who was dangerously ill, entreated him to return to Hesse without delay ; and that, being one of the youngest princes, the meanest in understanding, and useless to Charles, he humbly begged his majesty would permit him to leave on the morrow. The emperor refused.

We may well understand the storms this refusal excited in Philip's mind : but he knew how to contain himself ; never had he appeared more tranquil. During the whole of Saturday (6th August), he seemed occupied only with a magnificent tourney in honour of the emperor and of his brother Ferdinand.[1] He prepared for it publicly ; his servants went to and fro, but under that din of horses and of armour, Philip concealed very different designs. " The landgrave conducts himself with very great moderation," wrote Melancthon to Luther the same day.[2] " He told me openly that, to preserve peace, he would submit to conditions still harder than those which the emperor imposes on us, and accept all that he could without dishonouring the Gospel."

Yet Charles was not at ease. The landgrave's demand annoyed him ; all the Protestants might do the same, and even quit Augsburg unexpectedly. The clue, that he had hitherto so skilfully held in his hands, was perhaps about to be broken : it was better to be violent than ridiculous. The emperor therefore resolved on striking a decisive blow. The elector, the princes, the deputies, were still in Augsburg : and he must at every risk prevent their leaving it. Such were the heavy thoughts that on the night of the 6th August, while the Protestants were calmly sleeping,[3] banished repose from Charles's eyes ; and which made him hastily arouse the councillors of Augsburg, and send his messengers and soldiers through the streets of the city.

The Protestant princes were still slumbering, when they received, on the part of the emperor, the unexpected order to repair immediately to the Hall of the Chapter.[4]

It was eight o'clock when they arrived. They found there the Electors of Brandenburg and Mentz, the Dukes of Saxony, Brunswick, and Mecklenburg, the Bishops of Salzburg, Spires, and Strasburg, George Truchses, the Margrave of Baden's representative, Count Martin of Œlting, the Abbot of Weingarten, and the Provost of Bamberg. These were the commissioners nominated by Charles to terminate this great affair.

It was the most decided among them, Joachim of Brandenburg, who began to speak. " You know," said he to the Protestants, " with what mildness the emperor has endeavoured to re-establish unity. If some abuses have crept into the Christian Church, he is ready to correct them, in conjunction with the pope. But how contrary to the Gospel are the sentiments you have adopted ! Abandon your errors, do not any longer remain separate from the Church, and sign the Refutation without delay.[5] If you refuse, then, through your fault, how many souls will be lost, how much blood shed, what countries laid waste, what trouble in all the empire ! And you," said he, turning

---

[1] Nostros principes onerare invidia vestri dogmatis. Corp. Ref. ii. 221.
[2] Arctissime quoque inter nos conjuncti essemus, quotquot Christi esse volumus. Ibid. p. 236.
[3] Cum imperator dilationem respondendi astu quodam accepisset. Ibid. pp. 254, 276.

[1] Ad ludos equestres in honorem Cæsaris instituendos publice sese apparavit. Seck. ii. 172.
[2] Landgravius valde moderate se gerit. Corp. Ref. ii. 254.
[3] Ego vero somno sopitus dulciter quiescebam. Ibid. 273.
[4] Mane facto Cæsar......convocavit nostros principes. Ibid. 277; Brück, Apol. p. 79.
[5] Ut sententiis quam in refutatione audivissent subscribant. Corp. Ref. ii. 277.

towards the elector, "your electorate, your life, all will be torn from you, and certain ruin will fall upon your subjects, and even upon their wives and children."

The elector remained motionless. At any time this language would have been alarming: it was still more so now that the city was almost in a state of siege. "We now understand," said the Protestants to one another, "why the imperial guards occupy the gates of the city."[1] It was evident, indeed, that the emperor intended violence.[2]

The Protestants were unanimous: surrounded with soldiers, at the very gates of the prison, and beneath the thousand swords of Charles, they remained firm. All these threats did not make them take one step backwards.[3] It was important for them, however, to consider their reply. They begged for a few minutes' delay, and retired.

To submit voluntarily, or to be reduced by force, was the dilemma proposed by Charles to the evangelical Christians.

At the moment when each was anxious about the issue of this struggle, in which the destinies of Christianity were contending, an alarming rumour suddenly raised the agitation of all minds to its height.

The landgrave, in the midst of his preparations for the tournament, meditated the most serious resolution. Excluded by Charles from every important deliberation, irritated at the treatment the Protestants had undergone during this diet,[4] convinced that they had no more chance of peace,[5] not doubting that their liberty was greatly endangered in Augsburg, and feeling unable to conceal under the appearance of moderation the indignation with which his soul was filled, being besides of a quick, prompt, and resolute character, Philip had decided on quitting the city and repairing to his states, in order to act freely, and to serve as a support to the Reformation.

But what mystery was required! If the landgrave was taken in the act, no doubt he would be put under arrest. This daring step might therefore become the signal of those extreme measures from which he longed to escape.

It was Saturday, the 6th August, the day for which Philip had requested the emperor's leave of absence. He waited until the commencement of the night, and then, about eight o'clock, disguised in a foreign dress, without bidding farewell to any of his friends,[6] and taking every imaginable precaution,[7] he made for the gates of the city, about the time when they are usually closed. Five or six

cavaliers followed him singly, and at a little distance.[1] In so critical a moment might not these men-at-arms attract attention? Philip traversed the streets without danger, approached the gate,[2] passed with a careless air through the midst of the guard, between the scattered soldiers; no one moved, all remained idly seated, as if nothing extraordinary was going on. Philip had passed without being recognized.[3] His five or six horsemen came through in like manner. Behold them all at last in the open country. The little troop immediately spurred their horses, and fled with headlong speed far from the walls of the imperial city.

Yet Philip had taken his measures so well, that no one as yet suspected his departure. When during the night Charles occupied the gates with his own guards, he thought the landgrave still in the city.[4] When the Protestants assembled at eight in the morning in the Chapter-hall, the princes of both parties were a little astonished at the absence of Philip of Hesse. They were accustomed, however, to see him keep aloof, and thought he might be out of humour. No one imagined he was between twelve and fifteen leagues from Augsburg.

After the termination of the conference, and as all were returning to their hotels (the Elector of Brandenburg and his friends on the one hand, elated at the speech they had delivered, the Elector of Saxony and his allies on the other, resolved to sacrifice everything), inquiries were made at the landgrave's lodgings as to the reason of his absence; they closely questioned Saltz, Nuszbicker, Mayer, and Schnepf. At last the Hessian councillors could no longer keep the secret. "The landgrave," said they, "has returned to Hesse."

This news circulated immediately through all the city, and shook it like the explosion of a mine. Charles especially, who found himself mocked and frustrated in his expectations—Charles, who had not had the least suspicion,[5] trembled, and was enraged.[6] The Protestants, whom the landgrave had not admitted to his secret,[7] were as much astonished as the Roman-catholics themselves, and feared that this inconsiderate departure might be the immediate signal for a terrible persecution. There was only Luther, who, the moment he heard of Philip's proceeding, highly approved of it, and exclaimed: "Of a truth, all these delays and indignities are

[1] Intelligis nunc cur portæ munitæ fuerunt. Corp. Ref. ii. 277.
[2] Quia volebat Cæsar nostros violentia ad suam sententiam cogere. Ibid.
[3] Sed hæ minæ nostros nihil commoverunt: perstant in sententia, nec vel tantillum recedunt. Ibid. 260.
[4] Commotus indignitate actionum. Ibid. 260.
[5] Spem pacis abjecisse. Ibid.
[6] Clam omnibus abit. Ibid.
[7] Multa cum cautela. Seck. ii. 172.

[1] Clam cum paucis equitibus. Corp. Ref. ii. 277; Mit 5 oder 6 pferden. Ibid. 263.
[2] Seckendorf, and M. de Rommel no doubt after him, say that the landgrave went out through a secret gate (porta urbis secretiori, Seck. ii. 172; Rommel, i. 270). I prefer the contemporary evidence, particularly that of Brentz, which says: Vesperi priusquam portæ urbis clauderentur, urbe elapsus est. Corp. Ref. ii. 277. The chief magistrate of Augsburg, who alone had the keys of the wicket, would never have dared favour the departure of the landgrave.
[3] Abierat ille ignotus. Corp. Ref. 261.
[4] Existimabat enim Cæsar adhuc præsto adesse. Ibid.
[5] Cæsare nihil suspicante. Ibid. 277.
[6] Imperator re insperata commotus. Seck. ii. 172.
[7] Unwissend des Churfursten von Sachsen und unserer. Corp. Ref. ii. 263.

enough to fatigue more than one landgrave."[1]

The Chancellor of Hesse gave the Elector of Saxony a letter that his master had left for him. Philip spoke in this ostensible document of his wife's health; but he had charged his ministers to inform the elector in private of the real causes of his departure. He announced, moreover, that he had given orders to his ministers to assist the Protestants in all things, and exhorted his allies to permit themselves in no manner to be turned aside from the Word of God.[2] "As for me," said he, "I shall fight for the Word of God, at the risk of my goods, my states, my subjects, and my life."

The effect of the landgrave's departure was instantaneous: a real revolution was then effected in the diet. The Elector of Mentz and the Bishops of Franconia, Philip's near neighbours, imagined they already saw him on their frontiers at the head of a powerful army, and replied to the Archbishop of Salzburg, who expressed astonishment at their alarm: "Ah! if you were in our place you would do the same." Ferdinand, knowing the intimate relations of Philip with the Duke of Wurtemberg, trembled for the estates of this prince, at that time usurped by Austria; and Charles the Fifth, undeceived with regard to those princes whom he had believed so timid, and whom he had treated with so much arrogance, felt no doubt that this sudden step of Philip's had been maturely deliberated in the common council of the Protestants. All saw a declaration of war in the landgrave's hasty departure. They called to mind that at the moment when they thought the least about it, they might see him appear at the head of his soldiers, on the frontiers of his enemies, and no one was ready; no one even wished to be ready. A thunderbolt had fallen in the midst of the diet. They repeated the news to one another, with troubled eyes and affrighted looks. All was confusion in Augsburg; and couriers bore afar, in every direction, astonishment and consternation.

This alarm immediately converted the enemies of the reform. The violence of Charles and of the princes was broken in this memorable night as if by enchantment; and the furious wolves were suddenly transformed into meek and docile lambs.[3]

It was still Sunday morning: Charles the Fifth immediately convoked the diet for the afternoon.[4] "The landgrave has quitted Augsburg," said Count Frederick from the emperor; "his majesty flatters himself that even the friends of that prince were ignorant of his departure. It is without the emperor's

knowledge, and even in defiance of his express prohibition, that Philip of Hesse has left, thus failing in all his duties. He has wished to put the diet out of joint.[1] But the emperor conjures you not to permit yourselves to be led astray by him, and to contribute rather to the happy issue of this national assembly. You will thus be secure of his majesty's gratitude."

The Protestants replied, that the departure of the landgrave had taken place without their knowledge; that they had heard of it with pain, and that they would have dissuaded him. Nevertheless they did not doubt that this prince had solid reasons for such a step; besides he had left his councillors with full powers, and that, as for them, they were ready to do every thing to conclude the diet in a becoming manner. Then, confident in their rights, and being determined to resist Charles's arbitrary acts, they continued: "It is pretended that the gates were closed on our account. We beg your majesty to revoke this order, and to prevent any similar orders being given in future."

Never was Charles the Fifth less at ease; he had just spoken as a father, and they reminded him that a few hours back he had acted like a tyrant. Some subterfuge was requisite. "It is not on your account," replied the count-palatine, "that the emperor's soldiers occupy the gates......Do not believe those who tell you so......Yesterday there was a quarrel between two soldiers,[2] and a mob was collected......This is why the emperor took this step. Besides, such things will not be done again without the Elector of Saxony, in his quality of marshal of the empire, being first informed of them." An order was given immediately to reopen the gates.

No exertions were now spared by the Roman party to convince the Protestants of their good will: there was an unaccustomed mildness in the language of the count-palatine and in the looks of Charles.[3] The princes of the papal party, once so terrible, were similarly transformed. They had been hastily forced to speak out; if they desired war, they must begin it instantly.

But they shrank back at this frightful prospect. How, with the enthusiasm that animated the Protestants, take up arms against them! Were not the abuses of the Church every where acknowledged, and could the Roman princes be sure of their own subjects? Besides, what would be the issue of a war but the increase of the emperor's power? The Roman-catholic states, and the Duke of Bavaria in particular, would have been glad to see Charles at war with the Protestants, in the hope that he would

---

1 Es möchte wohl *ista mora et indignitas* nocheinen landgraven müde machen. L. Epp. iv. 134.
2 Ut nullo modo a verbo Dei abstrahi aut terreri se patiantur. Seck. ii. 172.
3 Sed hanc violentiam abitus Landgravii interrupit. Corp. Ref. p. 277.
4 Nam cum paucis post horis resciscunt Landgravium elapsum, convocant iterum nostros. Ibid.

1 Zertrennung dieses Reichstags zu verursachen. Corp. Ref. p. 264.
2 Es habe ein Trabant mit einem andern ein Unwill gehabt. Ibid. ii. 265.
3 Nullo alio tempore mitius et benignius quam tunc cum protestantibus egerit. Seck. ii. 172.

thus consume his strength; but it was, on the contrary, with their own soldiers that the emperor designed attacking the heretics. Henceforth they rejected the instrumentality of arms, as eagerly as they had at first desired it.

Every thing had thus changed in Augsburg; the Romish party was paralyzed, disheartened, and even broken up. The sword, already drawn, was hastily thrust back into the sheath. Peace! peace! was the cry of all.

CHAPTER XI.

The Mixed Commission—The Three Points—Romish Dissimulation—Abuses—Concessions—The Main Question—Bishops and Pope conceded—Danger of Concession—Opposition to the pretended Concord—Luther's opposing Letters—The Word above the Church—Melancthon's Blindness—Papist Infatuation—A new Commission—Be Men and not Women—The Two Phantoms—Concessions—The Three Points—The great Antithesis—Failure of Conciliation—The Gordian Knot—A Council granted—Charles's Summons—Menaces—Altercations—Peace or War—Romanism concedes—Protestantism resists—Luther recalls his Friends.

THE diet now entered upon its third phasis, and as the time of tentatives had been followed by that of menaces; now that of arrangements was to succeed the period of threatenings. New and more formidable dangers were now to be encountered by the Reformation. Rome, beholding the sword torn from its grasp, had seized the net, and enlacing her adversaries with "cords of humanity and bands of love," was endeavouring to drag them gently into the abyss.

At eight o'clock in the morning of the 16th August, a mixed commission was framed, which counted on each side two princes, two lawyers, and three theologians. In the Romish party, there were Duke Henry of Brunswick, the Bishop of Augsburg, the Chancellors of Baden and Cologne, with Eck, Cochlœus, and Wimpina; on the part of the Protestants, were the Margrave George of Brandenburg, the Prince Electoral of Saxony, the Chancellors Brück and Heller, with Melancthon, Brentz, and Schnepf.[1]

They agreed to take as basis the Confession of the evangelical states, and began to read it article by article. The Romish theologians displayed an unexpected condescension. Out of twenty-one dogmatical articles, there were only six or seven to which they made any objection. Original Sin stopped them some time, but at length they came to an understanding, the Protestants admitting that Baptism removed the guilt of the sin, and the Papists agreeing that it did not wash away concupiscence. As for the Church, they granted that it contained sanctified men and sinners; and they coincided also on Confession. The Protestants rejected especially as impossible the enumeration of

all the sins prescribed by Rome. Dr. Eck yielded this point.[1]

There remained three doctrines only on which they differed.

The first was that of Penance. The Romish doctors taught that it contained three parts: contrition, confession, and satisfaction. The Protestants rejected the latter, and the Romanists clearly perceiving that with satisfaction would fall indulgences, purgatory, and other of their doctrines and profits, vigorously maintained it. "We agree." said they, "that the penance imposed by the priest does not procure remission of the guilt of sin: but we maintain that it is necessary to obtain remission of the penalty."

The second controverted point was the Invocation of Saints; and the third, and principal one, Justification by Faith. It was of the greatest importance for the Romanists to maintain the meritorious influence of works: all their system in reality was based on that. Eck therefore haughtily declared war on the assertion that faith alone justifies. "That word *sole*," said he, " we cannot tolerate. It generates scandals, and renders men brutal and impious. Let us send back the *sole* to the cobbler."[2]

But the Protestants would not listen to such reasoning; and even when they put the question to each other, Shall we maintain that faith alone justifies us gratuitously? " Undoubtedly, undoubtedly," exclaimed one of them with exaggeration, " *gratuitously and uselessly.*"[3] They even adduced strange authorities: " Plato," said they, " declares that it is not by external works, but by virtue that God is to be adored; and every one knows these verses of Cato's:

Si deus est animus, nobis ut carmina dicunt,
Hic tibi præcipue pura sit mente colendus."[4]

" Certainly," resumed the Romish theologians: " it is only of works performed with grace that we speak; but we say that in such works there is something meritorious." The Protestants declared they could not grant it.

They had approximated however beyond all hope. The Roman theologians, clearly understanding their position, had purposed to appear agreed, rather than be so in reality. Every one knew, for instance, that the Protestants rejected transubstantiation: but as the article of the Confession on this point might be taken in the Romish sense, the Papists had admitted it. Their triumph was only deferred. The general expressions that were used on the controverted points, would permit somewhat later a Romish interpreta-

---

[1] F. Urkundenbuch, ii. 219.

[1] Die Sünd die man nicht wisse, die durff man nicht beichten. F. Urkunden. ii. 228.
[2] Man soll die *Sole* ein weil zum Schuster Schicken. Urkund. ii. 225. This wretched pun of Eck's requires no comment.
[3] Omnino, omnino, addendum etiam *frustra*. Scultet. p. 289.
[4] If God is a spirit, as the poets teach, he should be worshipped with a pure mind.

tion to be given to the Confession; ecclesiastical authority would declare this the only true one; and Rome, thanks to a few moments of dissimulation, would thus reascend the throne. Have we not seen in our own days the Thirty-nine Articles of the Anglican Church interpreted in accordance with the Council of Trent? There are causes in which falsehood is never awanting. This plot was as skilfully executed, as it was profoundly conceived.

The commissioners were on the best terms with one another, and concord seemed restored. One single uneasiness disturbed that happy moment: the idea of the landgrave: "Ignorant that we are almost agreed," said they, "this young madbrain is doubtless already assembling his army; we must bring him back, and make him a witness of our cordial union." On the morning of the 13th, one of the members of the Commission (Duke Henry of Brunswick), accompanied by a councillor of the emperor, set out to discharge this difficult mission.[1] Duke George of Saxony supplied his place as arbitrator.

They now passed from the first part of the Confession to the second: from doctrines to abuses. Here the Romish theologians could not yield so easily, for if they appeared to agree with the Protestants, it was all over with the honour and power of the hierarchy. It was accordingly for this period of the combat that they had reserved their cunning and their strength.

They began by approaching the Protestants as near as they could, for the more they granted, the more they might draw the Reform to them and stifle it. "We think," said they, "that with the permission of his holiness, and the approbation of his majesty, we shall be able to allow, until the next council, the communion in both kinds, wherever it is practised already; only, your ministers should preach at Easter that it is not of divine institution, and that Christ is wholly in each kind.[2]

"Moreover, as for the married priests," continued they, "desirous of sparing the poor women whom they have seduced, of providing for the maintenance of their innocent children, and of preventing every kind of scandal, we will tolerate them until the next council, and we shall then see if it will not be right to decree that married men may be admitted to holy orders, as was the case in the primitive Church for many centuries.[3]

"Finally, we acknowledge that the sacrifice of the mass is a mystery, a representation, a sacrifice of commemoration, a memorial of the sufferings and death of Christ, accomplished on the cross."[1]

This was yielding much: but the turn of the Protestants was come; for if Rome appeared to give, it was only to take in return.

The grand question was the Church, its maintenance and government: who should provide for it? They could see only two means: princes or bishops. If they feared the bishops, they must decide for the princes: if they feared the princes, they must decide for the bishops. They were at that time too distant from the normal state to discover a third solution, and to perceive that the Church ought to be maintained by the Church itself—by the christian people. "Secular princes in the long-run will be defaulters to the government of the Church," said the Saxon divines in the opinion they presented on the 18th August; "they are not fit to execute it, and besides it would cost them too dear:[2] the bishops, on the contrary, have property destined to provide for this charge."

Thus the presumed incapacity of the state, and the fear they entertained of its indifference, threw the Protestants into the arms of the hierarchy.

They proposed, therefore, to restore to the bishops their jurisdiction, the maintenance of discipline, and the superintendence of the priests, provided they did not persecute the evangelical doctrine, or oppress the pastors with impious vows and burdens. "We may not," added they, "without strong reasons rend that order by which bishops are over priests, and which existed in the Church from the beginning. It is dangerous before the Lord to change the order of governments." Their argument is not founded upon the Bible, as may be seen, but upon ecclesiastical history.

The Protestant divines went even farther, and, taking a last step that seemed decisive, they consented to acknowledge the pope as being (but of human right) supreme bishop of Christendom. "Although the pope is Antichrist, we may be under his government, as the Jews were under Pharaoh, and in later days under Caiaphas." We must confess these two comparisons were not flattering to the pope. "Only," added the doctors, "let sound doctrine be fully accorded to us."

The chancellor Brück alone appears to have been conscious of the truth: he wrote on the margin with a firm hand: "We cannot acknowledge the pope, because we say he is Antichrist, and because he claims the primacy by divine right."[3]

Finally, the Protestant theologians consented to agree with Rome as regards in-

---

[1] Brunswigus coactus est abire πρὸς τὸν μαχίδονα quem timent contrahere exercitum. Scultet. p 279.
[2] Vorschläge des Anschlusses der Sieben des Gegentheils. Urk. ii. 251.
[3] Wie von alters in der ersten Kirche etliche Hundert Jahre, in Gebrauch gewesen. Ibid. 254.

[1] Zu Errinnerung und Gedächtniss. Urk. ii. 253.
[2] Ist Ihnen auch nicht möglich. Dazu Kostet es zu viel. Ibid. 247.
[3] Cum dicimus eum Antichristum. Ibid. 247.

different ceremonies, fasts, and forms of worship; and the elector engaged to put under sequestration the ecclesiastical property already secularized, until the decision of the next council.

Never was the conservative spirit of Lutheranism more clearly manifested. "We have promised our adversaries to concede to them certain points of church government, that may be granted without wounding the conscience," wrote Melancthon.[1] But it began to be very doubtful whether ecclesiastical concessions would not drag with them doctrinal concessions also. The Reform was drifting away......still a few more fathoms, and it would be lost. Already disunion, trouble, and affright were spreading among its ranks. "Melancthon has become more childish than a child," said one of his friends;[2] and yet he was so excited, that the Chancellor of Luneburg having made some objections to these unprecedented concessions, the little master of arts proudly raised his head, and said with a sharp, harsh tone of voice: "He who dares assert that the means indicated are not christian is a liar and a scoundrel."[3] On which the chancellor immediately repaid him in his own coin. These expressions, however, cannot detract from Melancthon's reputation for mildness. After so many useless efforts, he was exhausted, irritated, and his words cut the deeper, as they were the less expected from him. He was not the only one demoralized. Brentz appeared clumsy, rude, and uncivil; Chancellor Heller had misled the pious Margrave of Brandenburg, and transformed the courage of this prince into pusillanimity: no other human support remained tc the elector than his chancellor Brück. And even this firm man began to grow alarmed at his isolation.

But he was not alone: the most earnest protests were received from without. "If it is true that you are making such concessions," said their affrighted friends to the Saxon divines, "christian liberty is at an end.[4] What is your pretended concord? a thick cloud that you raise in the air to eclipse the sun that was beginning to illumine the Church.[5] Never will the christian people accept conditions so opposed to the Word of God; and your only gain will be furnishing the enemies of the Gospel with a specious pretext to butcher those who remain faithful to it." Among the laymen these convictions were general. "Better die with Jesus Christ," said all Augsburg,[6] "than gain the favour of the whole world without him!"

No one felt so much alarm as Luther when he saw the glorious edifice that God had raised by his hands on the point of falling to ruin in those of Melancthon. The day on which this news arrived, he wrote five letters, —to the elector, to Melancthon, to Spalatin. to Jonas, and to Brentz, all equally filled with courage and with faith.

"I learn," said he, "that you have begun a marvellous work, namely, to reconcile Luther and the pope; but the pope will not be reconciled, and Luther begs to be excused.[1] And if, in despite of them, you succeed in this affair, then after your example I will bring together Christ and Belial.

"The world I know is full of wranglers who obscure the doctrine of justification by faith, and of fanatics who persecute it. Do not be astonished at it, but continue to defend it with courage, for it is the heel of the seed of the woman that shall bruise the head of the serpent.[2]

"Beware also of the jurisdiction of the bishops, for fear we should soon have to recommence a more terrible struggle than the first. They will take our concessions widely, very widely, always more widely, and will give us theirs narrowly, very narrowly, and always more narrowly.[3] All these negotiations are impossible, unless the pope should renounce his papacy.

"A pretty motive indeed our adversaries assign! They cannot, say they, restrain their subjects, if we do not publish every where that they have the truth on their side: as if God only taught his Word, that our enemies might at pleasure tyrannize over their people.

"They cry out that we condemn all the Church. No, we do not condemn it; but as for them, they condemn all the Word of God, and the Word of God is more than the Church."[4]

This important declaration of the reformers decides the controversy between the evangelical Christians and the Papacy: unfortunately we have often seen Protestants return, on this fundamental point, to the error of Rome, and set the visible Church above the Word of God.

"I write to you now," continues Luther, "to believe with all of us (and that through obedience to Jesus Christ), that Campeggio is a famous demon.[5] I cannot tell how violently I am agitated by the conditions which you propose. The plan of Campeggio and the pope has been to try us first by threats, and then, if these do not succeed, by stratagems; you have triumphed over the first attack, and sustained the terrible coming of Cæsar: now, then, for the second. Act with courage, and yield nothing to the ad-

---

[1] Nos politica quædam concessuros ;quæ sine offensione conscientiæ. Corp. Ref. il. 302.
[2] Philippus ist kindischer denn ein Kind worden. Baumgartner, Ibid. 363.
[3] Der Lüge als ein Bösewichst. Ibid. 364.
[4] Actum est de christiana libertate. Ibid. 295.
[5] Quid ea concordia aliud esset quam natæ jam et divulgatæ luci obducere nubem. Ibid. 296.
[6] Die ganze Stadt sagt. Ibid. 297.

[1] Sed Papa nolet et Lutherus deprecatur. L. Epp. iv. 144.
[2] Nam hic est ille unicus calcaneus seminis antiquo serpenti adversantis. Ibid. 151.
[3] Ipsi enim nostras concessiones large, largius, largissime, suas vero, stricte, strictius, strictissime. Ibid. 145.
[4] Sed ab ipsis totum verbum Dei, quod plus quam ecclesia est, damnari. Ibid. 145.
[5] Quod Campeggius est unus magnus et insignis diabolus. Ibid. 147.

versaries, except what can be proved with evidence from the very Word of God.

"But if, which Christ forbid! you do not put forward all the Gospel; if, on the contrary, you shut up that glorious eagle in a sack; Luther—doubt it not!—Luther will come and gloriously deliver the eagle.[1] As certainly as Christ lives, that shall be done!"

Thus spoke Luther, but in vain: every thing in Augsburg was tending towards approaching ruin; Melancthon had a bandage over his eyes that nothing could tear off. He no longer listened to Luther, and cared not for popularity. "It does not become us," said he, "to be moved by the clamours of the vulgar:[2] we must think of peace and of posterity. If we repeal the episcopal jurisdiction, what will be the consequence to our descendants? The secular powers care nothing about the interests of religion.[3] Besides, too much dissimilarity in the churches is injurious to peace: we must unite with the bishops, lest the infamy of schism should overwhelm us for ever."[4]

The evangelicals too readily listened to Melancthon, and vigorously laboured to bind to the papacy by the bonds of the hierarchy that Church which God had so wonderfully emancipated. Protestantism rushed blindfold into the nets of its enemies. Already serious voices announced the return of the Lutherans into the bosom of the Romish Church. "They are preparing their defection, and are passing over to the Papists," said Zwingle.[5] The politic Charles the Fifth acted in such a manner that no haughty word should compromise the victory; but the Roman clergy could not master themselves: their pride and insolence increased every day. "One would never believe," said Melancthon, "the airs of triumph which the Papists give themselves." There was good reason! the agreement was on the verge of conclusion: yet one or two steps......and then, woe to the Reformation!

Who could prevent this desolating ruin? It was Luther who pronounced the name towards which all eyes should be turned: "Christ lives," said he, and He by whom the violence of our enemies has been conquered will give us strength to surmount their wiles." This, which was in truth the only resource, did not disappoint the Reformation.

If the Roman hierarchy had been willing, under certain admissible conditions, to receive the Protestants who were ready to capitulate, all would have been over with them. When once it held them in its arms, it would have stifled them; but God blinded the Papacy, and thus saved his Church. "No concessions," had declared the Romish senate; and Campeggio, elated with his victory, repeated, "No concessions!" He moved heaven and earth to inflame the Catholic zeal of Charles in this decisive moment. From the emperor he passed to the princes. "Celibacy, confession, the withdrawal of the cup, private masses!" exclaimed he: "all these are obligatory: we must have all." This was saying to the evangelical Christians, as the Samnites to the ancient Romans: "Here are the Caudine Forks; pass through them!"

The Protestants saw the yoke, and shuddered. God revived the courage of confessors in their weakened hearts. They raised their heads, and rejected this humiliating capitulation. The commission was immediately dissolved.

This was a great deliverance; but soon appeared a fresh danger. The evangelical Christians ought immediately to have quitted Augsburg; but, said one of them,[1] "Satan, disguised as an angel of light, blinded the eyes of their understanding." They remained.

All was not yet lost for Rome, and the spirit of falsehood and of cunning might again renew its attacks.

It was believed at court that this disagreeable termination of the commission was to be ascribed to some wrong-headed individuals, and particularly to Duke George. They therefore resolved to name another, composed of six members only: on the one side, Eck, with the Chancellors of Cologne and Baden; on the other, Melancthon, with the Chancellors Brück and Heller. The Protestants consented, and all was begun anew.

The alarm then increased among the most decided followers of the Reformation. "If we expose ourselves unceasingly to new dangers, must we not succumb at last?"[2] The deputies of Nuremberg in particular declared that their city would never place itself again under the detested yoke of the bishops. "It is the advice of the undecided Erasmus that Melancthon follows," said they. "Say rather of Ahithophel" (2 Sam. xv.), replied others. "However it may be," added they; "if the pope had bought Melancthon, the latter could have done nothing better to secure the victory for him."[3]

The landgrave was especially indignant at this cowardice. "Melancthon," wrote he to Zwingle, "walks backwards like a crab."[4] From Friedwald, whether he had repaired after his flight from Augsburg, Philip of Hesse endeavoured to check the fall of Protestantism. "When we begin to yield, we

---

[1] Veniet, ne dubita, veniet Lutterus, hanc aquilam liberaturus magnifice. L. Epp. iv. 155.
[2] Sed nos nihil decet vulgi clamoribus moveri. Corp. Ref. ii. 303.
[3] Profani jurisdictionem ecclesiasticam et similia negotia religionem non curent. Ibid.
[4] Ne schismatis infamia perpetuo laboremus. Ibid.
[5] Lutherani defectionem parant ad Papistas. Zw. Epp. ii. 461.

[1] Baumgartner to Spengler. Corp. Ref. ii. 363.
[2] Fremunt et alii socii ac indignantur regnum Episcoporum restitui. Ibid. 328.
[3] Si conductus quanta ipse voluisset pecunia a Papa esset. Ibid. 333.
[4] Retro it, ut cancer. Zw. Epp. ii. 506.

always yield more," wrote he to his ministers at Augsburg. "Declare therefore to my allies that I reject these perfidious conciliations. If we are Christians, what we should pursue is, not our own advantage, but the consolation of so many weary and afflicted consciences, for whom there is no salvation if we take away the Word of God. The bishops are not real bishops, for they speak not according to the Holy Scriptures. If we acknowledge them, what would follow? They would remove our ministers, silence the Gospel, re-establish ancient abuses, and the last state would be worse than the first. If the Papists will permit the free preaching of the pure Gospel, let us come to an understanding with them; for the truth will be the strongest, and will root out all the rest. But if not!—No. This is not the moment to yield, but to remain firm even to death. Baffle these fearful combinations of Melancthon, and tell the deputies of the cities, from me, to be men, and not women.[1] Let us fear nothing: God is with us."

Melancthon and his friends, thus attacked, sought to justify themselves: on the one hand, they maintained, that if they preserved the doctrine it would finally overthrow the hierarchy. But why then restore it? Was it not more than doubtful whether a doctrine so enfeebled would still retain strength sufficient to shake the Papacy? On the other hand, Melancthon and his friends pointed out two phantoms before which they shrank in affright. The first was *war*, which, in their opinion, was imminent. "It will not only," said they, "bring numberless temporal evils with it,—the devastation of Germany, murder, violation, sacrilege, rapine; but it will produce spiritual evils more frightful still, and inevitably bring on the perturbation of all religion."[2] The second phantom was the supremacy of the state. Melancthon and his friends foresaw the dependence to which the princes would reduce the Church, the increasing secularization of its institutions and of its instruments, and the spiritual death that would result, and shrank back with terror from the frightful prospect. "Good men do not think that the court should regulate the ministry of the Church,"[3] said Brentz. "Have you not yourselves experienced," added he ironically, "with what wisdom and mildness these boors ('tis thus I denominate the officials and prefects of the princes) treat the ministers of the Church, and the Church itself. I would rather die seven times!"—"I see," exclaimed Melancthon, "what a Church we shall have, if the ecclesiastical government is abolished. I behold in the future a tyranny far more intolerable than that which has existed to

this day."[1] Then, bowed down by the accusations that poured upon him from every side, the unhappy Philip exclaimed: "If it is I who have aroused this tempest, I pray his majesty to throw me, like Jonas, into the sea, and to drag me out only to give me up to torture and to the stake."[2]

If the Romish episcopacy were once recognized, all seemed easy. In the Commission of Six, they conceded the cup to the laity, marriage to the pastors, and the article of prayer to saints appeared of little importance. But they stopped at three doctrines which the evangelicals could not yield. The first was the necessity of human satisfaction for the remission of the penalties of sin; the second, the idea of something meritorious in every good work; the third, the utility of private masses. "Ah!" quickly replied Campeggio to Charles the Fifth, "I would rather be cut in pieces than concede any thing about masses."[3]

"What!" replied the politicians, "when you agree on all the great doctrines of salvation, will you rend the unity of the Church for ever for three such trivial articles? Let the theologians make a last effort, and we shall see the two parties unite, and Rome embrace Wittemberg."

It was not so: under these three points was concealed a whole system. On the Roman side, they entertained the idea that certain works gain the Divine favour, independently of the disposition of him who performs them, and by virtue of the will of the Church. On the evangelical side, on the contrary, they felt a conviction that these external ordinances were mere human traditions, and that the only thing which procured man the Divine favour was the work that God accomplished by Christ on the cross; while the only thing that put him in possession of this favour was the work of regeneration that Christ accomplishes by his Spirit in the heart of the sinner. The Romanists, by maintaining their three articles, said: "The Church saves," which is the essential doctrine of Rome; the evangelicals, by rejecting them, said: "Jesus Christ alone saves," which is Christianity itself. This is the great antithesis which then existed, and which still separates the two Churches. With these three points, which placed souls under her dependence, Rome justly expected to recover every thing; and she showed by her perseverance that she understood her position. But the evangelicals were not disposed to abandon theirs. The christian principle was maintained against the ecclesiastical principle which aspired to swallow it up: Jesus Christ stood firm in presence of

---

[1] Das sie nicht weyber seyen sondern männer. Corp. Ref. ii. 327.
[2] Confusio et perturbatio religionum. Ibid. 382.
[3] Ut asla ministerium in ecclesia ordinet bonis non detivur consultum. Ibid. 362.

[1] Video postea multo intolerabiliorem futuram tyrannidem quam unquam antea fuisse. Corp. Ref. ii. 334.
[2] Si mea causa hæc tempestas coacta est, me statim velut Jonam in mare ejiciat. Ibid. 382.
[3] Er wollte sich ehe auf Stücker Zureissen lassen. L. Opp. xx. 328.

the Church, and it was seen that henceforward all conferences were superfluous.

Time pressed: for two months and a half Charles the Fifth had been labouring in Augsburg, and his pride suffered because four or five theologians checked the triumphal progress of the conqueror of Pavia. "What!" said they to him, "a few days sufficed to overthrow the King of France and the pope, and you cannot succeed with these gospellers!" They determined on breaking off the conferences. Eck, irritated because neither stratagem nor terror had been effectual, could not master himself in the presence of the Protestants. "Ah!" exclaimed he, at the moment of separation, "why did not the emperor, when he entered Germany, make a general inquest about the Lutherans? He would then have heard arrogant answers, witnessed monsters of heresy, and his zeal suddenly taking fire, would have led him to destroy all this faction.[1] But now Brück's mild language and Melancthon's concessions prevent him from getting as angry as the cause requires." Eck said these words with a smile; but they expressed all his thoughts. The colloquy terminated on the 30th August.

The Romish states made their report to the emperor. They were face to face, three steps only from each other, without either side being able to approach nearer, even by a hair's breadth.

Thus, then, Melancthon had failed; and his enormous concessions were found useless. From a false love of peace, he had set his heart on an impossibility. Melancthon was at the bottom a really christian soul. God preserved him from his great weakness, and broke the clue that was about to lead him to destruction. Nothing could have been more fortunate for the Reformation than Melancthon's failure; but nothing could, at the same time, have been more fortunate for himself. His friends saw that though he was willing to yield much, he could not go so far as to yield Christ himself, and his defeat justified him in the eyes of the Protestants.

The Elector of Saxony and the Margrave of Brandenburg sent to beg Charles's leave to depart. The latter refused at first rather rudely, but at last he began to conjure the princes not to create by their departure new obstacles to the arrangements they soon hoped to be able to conclude.[2] We shall see what was the nature of these arrangements.

The Romanists appeared to redouble their exertions. If they let the clue slip now, it would be lost for ever: they laboured accordingly to reunite the two ends. There were conferences in the gardens, conferences in the churches, at St. George's, at St. Maurice's, between the Duke of Brunswick and John Frederick the elector's son, the Chancellors of Baden and of Saxony, the Chancellor of Liege and Melancthon; but all these attempts were unavailing. It was to other means they were going to have recourse.

Charles the Fifth had resolved to take the affair in hand, and to cut the Gordian knot, which neither doctors nor princes could untie. Irritated at seeing his advances spurned and his authority compromised, he thought that the moment was come for drawing the sword. On the 4th September, the members of the Roman party, who were still endeavouring to gain over the Protestants, whispered these frightful intentions in Melancthon's ears. "We scarcely dare mention it," said they: "the sword is already in the emperor's hands, and certain people exasperate him more and more. He is not easily enraged, but once angry, it is impossible to quiet him."[1]

Charles had reason to appear exacting and terrible. He had at length obtained from Rome an unexpected concession—a council. Clement VII. had laid the emperor's request before a congregation: "How will men who reject the ancient councils submit to a new one?" they had replied. Clement himself had no wish for an assembly, which he dreaded alike on account of his birth and conduct.[2] However, his promises at the Castle of St. Angelo and at Bologna rendered it impossible for him to give a decided refusal. He answered, therefore, that "the remedy would be worse than the disease:[3] but that if the emperor, who was so good a Catholic, judged a council absolutely necessary, he would consent to it, under the express condition, however, that the Protestants should submit in the meanwhile to the doctrines and rites of the Church." Then for the place of meeting he appointed Rome!

Scarcely had the news of this concession spread abroad, than the fear of a Reformation froze the papal court. The public charges of the Papacy, which were altogether venal, immediately fell, says a cardinal, and were offered at the lowest price,[4] without even being able to find purchasers.[5] The Papacy was compromised; its merchandise was endangered; and the *price current* immediately declined on the Roman exchange.

On Wednesday (7th September), at two in the afternoon, the Protestant princes and deputies having been introduced into the chamber of Charles the Fifth, the countpalatine said to them, "that the emperor, considering their small number, had not

1 Hæc inflammassent Imperatorem ad totam hanc factionem delendam. Corp. Ref. ii. 335.
2 Antwort des Kaisers, &c. Urkund. ii. 313.

1 Nescio an ausim dicere, jam ferrum in manu Cæsaris esse. Corp. Ref. ii. 342.
2 In eam (concilii celebrationem) Pontificis animus haud propendebatur. Pallavicini, i. 251.
3 Al contrario, remedio e piu pericoloso e per partorir maggiori mali. Lettere de Principe, ii. 197.
4 Evulgatus concilii rumor....publica Romæ munera.... jam in vilissimum pretium decidissent. Pallav. i. 251.
5 Che non se non trovano danari. Lett. di Prin. iii. 5.

589

expected they would uphold new sects against the ancient usages of the Universal Church; that, nevertheless, being desirous of appearing full of kindness to the last, he would require of his holiness the convocation of a council; but that in the meanwhile they should return immediately into the bosom of the Catholic Church, and restore every thing to its ancient footing."[1]

The Protestants replied on the morrow, the 8th of September, that they had not stirred up new sects contrary to the Holy Scriptures;[2] that, quite the reverse, if they had not agreed with their adversaries, it was because they had desired to remain faithful to the Word of God; that, by convoking in Germany a general, free, and christian council, it would only be doing what preceding diets had promised; and that nothing should compel them to re-establish in their churches an order of things opposed to the commandments of God."

It was eight in the evening when, after a long deliberation, the Protestants were again called in. "His majesty," said George Truschses to them, "is equally astonished, both that the catholic members of the commissions have accorded so much, and that the Protestant members have refused every thing. What is your party in the presence of his imperial majesty, of his papal holiness, of the electors, princes, estates of the empire, and other kings, rulers, and potentates of Christendom? It is but just that the minority should yield to the majority. Do you desire the means of conciliation to be protracted, or do you persist in your answer? Speak frankly; for if you persist, the emperor will immediately see to the defence of the Church. To-morrow at one o'clock you will bring your final decision."

Never had such threatening words issued from Charles's mouth. It was evident he wished to subdue the Protestants by terror; but this end was not attained. They replied the next day but one—a day more having been accorded them—that new attempts at conciliation would only fatigue the emperor and the diet; that they only required regulations to maintain political peace until the assembling of the council.[3] "Enough," replied the redoubtable emperor; "I will reflect upon it; but in the meantime let no one quit Augsburg."

Charles the Fifth was embarrassed in a labyrinth from which he knew not how to escape. The State had resolved to interfere with the Church, and saw itself compelled to have immediate recourse to its *ultima ratio*—the sword. Charles did not desire war, and yet how could he now avoid it? If he did not execute his threats, his dignity was com-

promised, and his authority rendered contemptible. He sought an outlet on one side or the other, but could find none. It therefore only remained for him to close his eyes, and rush forward heedless of the consequences. These thoughts disturbed him: these cares preyed upon him; he was utterly confounded.

It was now that the elector sent to beg Charles would not be offended if he left Augsburg. "Let him await my answer," abruptly replied the emperor: and the elector having rejoined that he would send his ministers to explain his motives to his majesty: "Not so many speeches," resumed Charles, with irritation; "let the elector say whether he will stay or not!"[1]

A rumour of the altercation between these two powerful princes having spread abroad, the alarm became universal; it was thought war would break out immediately, and there was a great disturbance in Augsburg.[2] It was evening: men were running to and fro, they rushed into the hotels of the princes and of the Protestant deputies, and addressed them with the severest reproaches. "His imperial majesty," said they, "is about to have recourse to the most energetic measures!" They even declared that hostilities had begun: it was whispered that the commander of Horneck (Walter of Kronberg), elected by the emperor grand-master of the Teutonic order, was about to enter Prussia with an army, and dispossess Duke Albert, who had been converted by Luther.[3] Two nights successively the same tumult was repeated. They shouted, quarrelled, and fought, particularly in and before the mansions of the princes: the war was nearly commencing in Augsburg.

At that crisis (12th September), John Frederick, prince-electoral of Saxony, quitted the city.

On the same day, or on the morrow, Jerome Wehe, chancellor of Baden, and Count Truschses on the one side; Chancellor Brück and Melancthon on the other, met at six in the morning in the church of St. Maurice.[4]

Charles, notwithstanding his threats, could not decide on employing force. He might no doubt by a single word to his Spanish bands or to his German lansquenets have seized on these inflexible men, and treated them like Moors. But how could Charles, a Netherlander, a Spaniard, who had been ten years absent from the empire, dare, without raising all Germany, offer violence to the favourites of the nation? Would not the Roman-catholic princes themselves see in this act an infringement of their privileges?

---

[1] Interim restitui debere omnia Papistis. Corp. Ref. ii. 355. See also *Erklarung des Kaisers Karl. v.* Urkunden. ii. 391.
[2] Nit neue, Secten wieder die heilige Schrifft. Brück, Apol. p. 136.
[3] Urkunden. ii. 410; Brück, Apol. p. 139.

[1] Kurtz mit Solchen worten ob er erwarten wolte oder nicht? Brück, Apol. p. 143.
[2] Ein beschwerlich Geschrey zu Augsbourg den selben abend ausge-brochen. Ibid. p. 145.
[3] Man würde ein Kriegs-volk in Preussen Schicken. Ibid. p. 143.
[4] Ibid. p. 155-160.

War was unseasonable. " Lutheranism is extending already from the Baltic to the Alps," wrote Erasmus to the legate : " You have but one thing to do: tolerate it."[1]

The negotiation begun in the church of St. Maurice was continued between the Margrave of Brandenburg and Count Truchses. The Roman party only sought to save appearances, and did not hesitate, besides, to sacrifice every thing. It asked merely for a few theatrical decorations—that the mass should be celebrated in the sacerdotal garment, with chanting, reading, ceremonies, and its two canons.[2] All the rest was referred to the next council, and the Protestants, till then, were to conduct themselves so as to render an account to God, to the council, and to his majesty.

But on the side of the Protestants the wind had also changed. Now they no longer desired peace with Rome : the scales had at last fallen from their eyes, and they discovered with affright the abyss into which they had so nearly plunged. Jonas, Spalatin, and even Melancthon were agreed. " We have hitherto obeyed the commandment of St. Paul, *Be at peace with all men*," said they; " now we must obey this commandment of Christ, *Beware ye of the leaven of the Pharisees, which is hypocrisy*. On the one side of our adversaries is nothing but cunning and perfidy, and their only aim is to stifle our doctrine, which is truth itself.[3] They hope to save the abominable articles of purgatory, indulgences, and the Papacy, because we have passed them by in silence.[4] Let us beware of betraying Christ and his Word in order to please Antichrist and the devil."[5]

Luther at the same time redoubled his entreaties to withdraw his friends from Augsburg. " Return, return," cried he to them ; " return, even if it must be so, cursed by the pope and the emperor.[6] You have confessed Jesus Christ, offered peace, obeyed Charles, supported insults, and endured blasphemies. I will canonize you, I, as faithful members of Jesus Christ. You have done enough, and more than enough : now it is for the Lord to act, and he will act ! They have our Confession, they have the Gospel ; let them receive it, if they will ; and if they will not, let them go——. If a war should come, let it come ! We have prayed enough ; we have discussed enough. The Lord is preparing our adversaries as the victim for the sacrifice ; he will destroy their magnificence, and deliver his people. Yes ! he will preserve us even from Babylon, and from her burning walls."

[1] A mare Baltico ad Helvetios. Eras. Epp. xiv. 1.
[2] In gewöhnlichen Kleidungen mit Gesang und Lesen. Urk. ii. 418. The canon was a frame of card-board placed on the altar before the priest, and which contained the Apostles' Creed with various prayers.
[3] Eitel List, gefährliche Tücke, &c. Jonas. Urkund. ii. 423.
[4] Die gräuliche artikel. Spalat. Ibid. 428. De Primatu Papæ, de Purgatorio, de Indulgentiis. Melancthon, Corp. Ref. ii. 374.
[5] Dem Teufel und Antichrist zu gefallen. Urk. ii. 431.
[6] Vel maledicti a Papa et Cæsare. L. Epp. iv. 162-171.

CHAPTER XII.

The Elector's Preparatives and Indignation—Recess of Augsburg—Irritating Language—Apology of the Confession—Intimidation—Final Interview—Messages of Peace—Exasperation of the Papists—Restoration of Popery—Tumult in the Church—Union of the Churches—The Pope and the Emperor—Close of the Diet—Armaments—Attack on Geneva—Joy of the Evangelicals—Establishment of Protestantism.

THUS Luther gave the signal of departure. They replied to the reformer's appeal, and all prepared to quit Augsburg. On Saturday, the 17th of September, at ten at night, Duke Ernest of Luneburg assembled the deputies of Nuremberg and the ministers of the landgrave in his hotel, and announced to them that the elector was determined to leave the next morning, without informing any one, and that he would accompany him. " Keep the secret," said he to them, " and know that if peace cannot be preserved, it will be a trifling matter for me to lose, combating with you, all that God has given me."[1]

The elector's preparations betrayed his intentions. In the middle of the night Duke Henry of Brunswick arrived hastily at his hotel, beseeching him to wait :[2] and towards morning Counts Truchses and Mansfeldt announced that, on the morrow between seven and eight, the emperor would give him his congé.

On Monday, the 19th of September, the elector purposing to leave Augsburg immediately after his audience with Charles, breakfasted at seven o'clock, then sent off his baggage and his cooks,[3] and ordered his officers to be ready at ten o'clock. At the moment when John quitted the hotel to wait upon the emperor, all the members of his household were drawn up on each side booted and spurred ;[4] but, having been introduced to Charles, he was requested to wait two, four, or six days longer.

As soon as the elector was alone with his allies, his indignation burst forth, and he even became violent. " This new delay will end in nothing,"[5] he said ; " I am resolved to set out, happen what may. It seems to me, from the manner in which things are arranged, that I have now completely the air of a prisoner." The Margrave of Brandenburg begged him to be calm. " I shall go," the elector still replied. At last he yielded, and having appeared again before Charles the Fifth, he said, " I will wait until Friday next; and, if nothing is done by that time, I shall leave forthwith."

Great was the anxiety of the Protestants during these four days of expectation. Most of them doubted not that, by acceding to

[1] Alles das, so Ihm Gott geben hätt, darob zu verlieren ein geringes wäre. Corp. Ref. ii. 379.
[2] In der selben Nacht. Ibid.
[3] Præmissis fere omnibus impedimentis una cum cocis. Ibid. 385.
[4] Gestiefelt und gespornt. Ibid. 380.
[5] Etwas darob schwermütig und hitzig erzeight. Ibid.

Charles's prayers, they had delivered themselves into the hands of their enemies. " The emperor is deliberating whether he ought to hang us or let us live," wrote Brentz.[1] Fresh negotiations of Truchses were without success. [2]

The emperor now had nothing more to do than draw up, in common with the Romish states, the *recess* of the diet. This was done; and that the Protestants might not complain of its having been prepared without their knowledge, he assembled them in his palace on Thursday (22d September), the day previous to that fixed for the elector's departure, and had his project read to them by the count-palatine. This project was insult and war. The emperor granted to the elector, the five princes, and the six cities,[3] a delay of six months (until the 15th of April in the next year), to come to an arrangement with the Church, the Pope, the Emperor, and all the princes and monarchs of Christendom. This was clearly announcing to them that the Romanists were very willing to delay until the usual period for bringing armies into the field.

Nor was this all : the delay was granted only on the express condition that the Protestants should immediately join the emperor in reducing the Anabaptists, and all those who opposed the holy sacrament, by which were meant the Zwinglian cities. He wished by this means to tie the hands of the Protestants, and prevent the two families of the Reformation from uniting during the winter.

Finally, the Protestants were forbidden to make any innovations, to print or sell anything on the objects of faith, or to draw any one whatever to their *sect*, " since the Confession had been soundly refuted by the Holy Scriptures." Thus the Reformation was officially proclaimed a *sect*, and a sect contrary to the Word of God.

Nothing was better calculated to displease the friends of the Gospel, who remained in Charles's presence astonished, alarmed, and indignant.[4] This had been foreseen ; and, at the moment when the Protestants were about to enter the emperor's chamber, Truchses and Wehe, making signs to them, mysteriously slipped a paper into their hands, containing a promise that if, on the 15th April, the Protestants required a prolongation of the delay, their request would certainly be granted.[5] But Brück, to whom the paper was given, was not deceived. A subtle ambuscade," said he ; " a masterpiece of knavery ! God will save his own, and will not permit them to fall into the snare."[6]

This trick, in fact, served only still more to increase the courage of the Protestants.

Brück, without discussing the *recess* in a political point of view, confined himself to what was principally at stake; the Word of God. " We maintain," said he, " that our Confession is so based on the holy Word of God, that it is impossible to refute it. We consider it as the very truth of God, and we hope by it to stand one day before the judgment-seat of the Lord." He then announced that the Protestants had refuted the Refutation of the Romish theologians, and holding in his hand the famous Apology of the Confession of Augsburg written by Melancthon, he stepped forward, and offered it to Charles the Fifth. The count-palatine took it, and the emperor was already stretching out his hand, when Ferdinand having whispered a few words, he beckoned to the count, who immediately returned the Apology to Doctor Brück.[1] This paper, and the " Commonplaces," are the reformer's masterpieces. The embarrassed emperor told the Protestants to come again at eight the next morning.

Charles the Fifth, resolving to employ every means to get his decree accepted, began by entreaties ; and scarcely was the Margrave of Brandenburg seated to take his evening repast, when Truchses and Wehe appeared before him, using every kind of discourse and argument, but without success.[2]

The next day (Friday, 23d September), the evangelical princes and the deputies of the cities assembled at five in the morning at the margrave's hotel, where the *recess* was again read in the presence of Truchses and Wehe, Chancellor Brück assigning seven reasons for its rejection. " I undertake," said Wehe, " to translate the *recess* into German in such a manner as you can accept it. As for the word *sect*, in particular, it is the clerk who placed it there by mistake."[3] The mediators retired in haste to communicate to Charles the complaints of the Protestants.

Charles and his ministers gave up every idea of reconciliation, and hoped for nothing except through fear. The Protestants reached the imperial palace at eight o'clock, but were made wait an hour : the Elector of Brandenburg than said to them in Charles's name : " His majesty is astonished beyond measure that you still maintain your doctrine to be based on the Holy Scriptures. If you say the truth, his majesty's ancestors, so many kings and emperors, and even the ancestors of the Elector of Saxony, were heretics ! There is no Gospel, there is no Scripture, that imposes on us the obligation

---

[1] Adhuc deliberat Cæsar pendendum ne nobis sit, an diutius vivendum. Corp. Ref. ii.
[2] Urkund. ii. 455-472.
[3] Nuremberg and Reutlingen, to which were added the cities of Kempten, Heilbronn, Windsheim, and Weissemburg. Ibid. 474-478.
[4] Protestantes vehementer hoc decreto minime expectato territi. Seck. ii. 200. [5] Brück, Apologie, p. 182.
[6] Betrüge, meisterstuck, aber Gott errettet die seinen. Ibid.

[1] Auf König Ferdinandus wincke wieder geben. Apologie, p. 184.
[2] Nach essen allerley Rede Disputation und Persuasion furgewendt. Urk. ii. 601.
[3] Sondern vom Schreiber gesetzt, der dis nicht geacht. Ibid. 606.

of seizing by violence the goods of another, and of then saying that we cannot conscientiously restore them. "It is for this reason," added Joachim, after these words, which he accompanied with a sardonic smile, "I am commissioned to inform you, that if you refuse the *recess*, all the Germanic states will place their lives and property at the emperor's disposal, and his majesty himself will employ the resources of all his kingdoms to complete this affair before leaving the empire."

"We do not accept it," replied the Protestants firmly.—"His majesty also has a conscience," then resumed the Elector of Brandenburg, in a harsh tone; "and if you do not submit, he will concert with the pope and the other potentates on the best means of extirpating this sect and its new errors." But in vain did they add threat to threat: the Protestants remained calm, respectful, and unshaken. "Our enemies, destitute of all confidence in God," said they, "would shake like a reed in presence of the emperor's anger, and they imagine that we should tremble in like manner; but we have called unto God, and he will keep us faithful to his truth."

The Protestants then prepared to take their final leave of the emperor. This prince, whose patience had been put to a severe trial, approached to shake hands according to custom; and beginning with the Elector of Saxony, he said to him in a low voice: "Uncle, uncle! I should never have expected this of you." The elector was deeply affected: his eyes filled with tears: but, firm and resolute, he bent his head and quitted Charles without reply. It was now two in the afternoon.

While the Protestants were returning to their hotels, calm and happy, the Romish princes retired to theirs, confused and dispirited, uneasy and divided. They doubted not that the *congé* which had just been granted to the Protestants would be regarded by them as a declaration of war, and that on quitting Augsburg, they would rush to arms. This thought terrified them. Accordingly, the Elector of Saxony had hardly reached his palace, when he saw Dr. Ruhel, councillor of the Elector of Mentz, hastening towards him, commissioned by his master to deliver this message: "Although my brother the elector (Joachim of Brandenburg) has declared that the states of the empire are ready to support the emperor against you, know that both myself and the ministers of the elector-palatine and of the Elector of Treves immediately declared to his majesty that we did not adhere to this declaration, seeing that we thought very favourably of you.[1] I intended saying this to the emperor in your presence, but you left so precipitately, that I was unable."

Thus spoke the primate of the German Church, and even the choice of his messenger

was significant: Dr. Ruhel was Luther's brother-in-law. John begged him to thank his master.

As this envoy retired, there arrived one of the gentlemen of Duke Henry of Brunswick, a zealous Romanist. He was at first refused admittance on account of the departure, but returned hastily, just as Brück's carriage was leaving the courtyard of the hotel. Approaching the carriage-door, he said: "The duke informs the elector that he will endeavour to put things in a better train, and will come this winter to kill a wild boar with him."[1] Shortly after this, the terrible Ferdinand himself declared that he would seek every means of preventing an outbreak.[2] All these manifestations of the affrighted Roman-catholics showed on which side was the real strength.

At three o'clock in the afternoon the Elector of Saxony, accompanied by the Dukes of Luneburg and the Princes of Anhalt, quitted the walls of Augsburg. "God be praised," said Luther, "that our dear prince is at last out of hell!"[3]

As he saw these intrepid princes thus escaping from his hands, Charles the Fifth gave way to a violence that was not usual with him.[4] "They want to teach me a new faith," cried he; "but it is not with the doctrine that we shall finish this matter: we must draw the sword, and then shall we see who is the strongest."[5] All around him gave way to their indignation. They were astonished at the audacity of Brück, who had dared call the Romanists—heretics![6] But nothing irritated them so much as the spirit of proselytism which in those glorious days characterized evangelical Germany; and the anger of the Papists was particularly directed against the Chancellor of Luneburg, "who," said they, "had sent more than a hundred ministers to different places to preach the new doctrine, and had even publicly boasted of it."[7]—The deputies of Nuremberg, who remained almost alone at Augsburg, wrote, as they heard these complaints, "Our adversaries are thirsting for our blood."

On the 4th October, Charles the Fifth wrote to the pope, for it was from Rome that the new crusade was to set out: "The negotiations are broken off: our adversaries are more obstinate than ever; and I am resolved to employ my strength and my person in combating them. For this reason I beg your holiness will demand the support of all christian princes."

The enterprise began in Augsburg itself. The day on which he wrote to the pope,

---

[1] Wüssten auch nicht anders denn wohl und gut. Urk. p. 210.

[1] Ein Sawe fahen helfen. Urk. p. 211.
[2] Corp. Ref. ii. 397.
[3] Ein mal aus der Hölle los ist. L. Epp. iv. 175.
[4] Der Kaiser ist fast hitzig im Handel. Corp. Ref. ii. 591.
[5] Es gehören die Fauste dar zu. Ibid. 592; Urkund. ii. 710.
[6] Für Ketzer angezogen. Ibid.
[7] Bis in die Hundert Prediger in andere Lande Schiken helfen daselbst die neue Lehre zu predigen. Urkund. ii. 646.

Charles, in honour of St. Francis of Assisi, whose feast it was, re-established the Cordeliers in that city, and a monk ascending the pulpit said : " All those who preach that Jesus Christ alone has made satisfaction for our sins, and that God saves us without regard to our works, are thorough scoundrels. There are, on the contrary, two roads to salvation ; the common road, namely, the observance of the commandments ; and the perfect road, namely, the ecclesiastical state." Scarcely was the sermon finished ere the congregation began to remove the benches placed in the church for the evangelical preaching, breaking them violently (for they were fixed with chains), and throwing them one upon another. Within these consecrated walls two monks, in particular, armed with hammers and pincers, tossed their arms, and shouted like men possessed. " From their frightful uproar," exclaimed some, " one would imagine they were pulling down a house." [1] It was in truth the house of God they wished to begin destroying.

After the tumult was appeased, they sang mass. As soon as this was concluded, a Spaniard desired to recommence breaking the benches, and on being prevented by one of the citizens, they began to hurl chairs at each other ; one of the monks, leaving the choir, ran up to them, and was soon dragged into the fray ; at length the captain of police arrived with his men, who distributed their well directed blows on every side. Thus began in Germany the restoration of Roman-catholicism : popular violence has often been one of its most powerful allies.

On the 13th October the *recess* was read to all the Romish states, and on the same day they concluded a Roman league. [2]

Two cities had signed the Confession, and four others had assented to it ; the imperialists hoped, however, that these powerless municipalities, affrighted at the imperial authority, would withdraw from the Protestant union. But on the 17th October, instead of six cities, sixteen imperial towns, among which were the most important in Germany, declared it was impossible to grant any support against the Turks, so long as public peace was not secured in Germany itself. [3]

An event more formidable to Charles had just taken place. The unity of the Reformation had prevailed. " We are *one* in the fundamental articles of faith," the Zwinglian cities had said, " and in particular (notwithstanding some disputes about words among our theologians), we are *one* in the doctrine of the communion in the body and blood of our Lord. Receive us." The Saxon deputies immediately gave their hands. Nothing unites the children of God so much as the violence of their adversaries. " Let us unite," said all, " for the consolation of our brethren and the terror of our enemies." [1]

In vain did Charles, who was intent on keeping up division among the Protestants, convoke the deputies of the Zwinglian cities : in vain, desiring to render them odious, had he accused them of fastening a consecrated wafer to a wall and firing bullets at it ; [2] in vain did he overwhelm them with fierce threats ;—all his efforts were useless. At length the evangelical party was one.

The alarm increased among the Roman party, who resolved on fresh concessions. " The Protestants call for public peace," said they ; " well then, let us draw up articles of peace." But, on the 29th October, the Protestants refused these offers, because the emperor enjoined peace to all the world. without binding himself. " An emperor has the right to command peace to his subjects," haughtily answered Charles : " but it has never been heard that he commanded it to himself." [3]

Nothing remained but to draw the sword ; and for that Charles made every preparation. On the 25th October, he wrote to the cardinals at Rome : " We inform you that we shall spare neither kingdoms nor lordships ; and that we shall venture even our soul and our body to complete such necessary matters."

Scarcely had Charles's letter been received before his major-domo, Pedro de la Cueva, arrived in Rome by express. " The season is now too far advanced to attack the Lutherans immediately," said he to the pope ; " but prepare every thing for this enterprise. His majesty thinks it his duty to prefer before all things the accomplishment of your designs." Thus Clement and the emperor were also united, and both sides began to concentrate their forces.

On the evening of the 11th November, the *recess* was read to the Protestant deputies, and on the 12th they rejected it, declaring that they did not acknowledge the emperor's power to command in matters of faith. [4] The deputies of Hesse and of Saxony departed immediately after, and on the 19th November the *recess* was solemnly read in the presence of Charles the Fifth, and of the princes and deputies who were still in Augsburg. This report was more hostile than the project communicated to the Protestants. It bore, among other things (and this is only a sample of the urbanity of this official document), that " to deny free will was the error not of man, but of a brute."—" We beg his majesty," said the Elector Joachim, after it was read, " not to leave Germany, until by his cares one and the same faith be re-established in all the empire."

1 Ein alt Haus abbrechen. Corp. Ref. II. 400.
2 Ratschlag, &c. Urkund. ii. 737-740.
3 Wo sie nicht einen gemeinen Friedens versichert. Corp. Ref. ii. 411, 416.

1 Diesem Theil desto mehr Freude und Trost und dem gegentheil Erschrecken. Urkund. ii. 728.
2 An eine Wand geheftet und dazu geschossen. Corp. Ref. ii. 423.
3 These negotiations will be found in Forstermann's Urkunden. p. 750-793.
4 Urkunden. ii. 823 ; Corp. Ref. ii. 437.

The emperor replied, that he would not go farther than his states of the Low Countries. They desired that deeds should follow close upon words. It was then nearly seven in the evening; a few torches were lighted up here and there by the ushers, and their feeble light alone illuminated this assembly: they separated without seeing each other; and thus ended, as it were by stealth, that diet so pompously announced to the christian world.

On the 22d November, the *recess* was made public, and two days after Charles the Fifth set out for Cologne. The ruler of two worlds had seen all his influence baffled by a few Christians; and he who had entered the imperial city in triumph, now quitted it gloomy, silent, and dispirited. The mightiest power of the earth was broken against the power of God.

But the emperor's ministers and officers, excited by the pope, displayed so much the more energy. The states of the empire were bound to furnish Charles, for three years, 40,000 foot, 8000 horse, and a considerable sum of money;[1] the Margrave Henry of Zenete, the Count of Nassau, and other nobles, made considerable levies on the side of the Rhine; a captain going through the Black Forest called its rude inhabitants to his standard, and enrolled six companies of lansquenets; King Ferdinand had written to all the knights of the Tyrol and of Wurtemberg to gird on their cuirasses and take down their swords; Joachim of Talheim collected the Spanish bands in the Low Countries, and ordered them towards the Rhine; Peter Scher solicited from the Duke of Lorraine the aid of his arms; and another chief hastily moved the Spanish army of Florence in the direction of the Alps. There was every reason to fear that the Germans, even the Roman-catholics, would take Luther's part; and hence principally foreign troops were levied.[2] Nothing but war was talked of in Augsburg.

On a sudden a strange rumour was heard.[3] The signal is given, said every one. A free city, lying on the confines of the Germanic and Roman world,—a city at war with its bishop, in alliance with the Protestants, and which passed for reformed even before really being so, had been suddenly attacked. A courier from Strasburg brought this news to Augsburg, and it circulated through the town with the rapidity of lightning. Three days after Michaelmas, some armed men, sent by the Duke of Savoy, pillaged the suburbs of Geneva, and threatened to take possession of the city, and put all to the edge of the sword. Every one in Augsburg was amazed. "Ho!" exclaimed Charles the Fifth, in French, "the Duke of Savoy has

begun too soon."[1] It was reported that Margaret, governor of the Low Countries, the pope, the Dukes of Lorraine and Gueldres, and even the King of France, were directing their troops against Geneva. It was there that the army of Rome intended fixing its *point d'appui*. The avalanche was gathering on the first slopes of the Alps, whence it would rush over all Switzerland, and then roll into Germany, burying the Gospel and the Reformation under its huge mass.[2]

This sacred cause appeared to be in great danger, and never in reality had it gained so noble a triumph. The *coup de main* attempted on those hills, where six years later Calvin was to take his station, and plant the standard of Augsburg and of Nazareth, having failed, all fears were dispelled, and the victory of the confessors of Christ, for an instant obscured, shone forth anew in all its splendour.

While the Emperor Charles, surrounded by a numerous train of princes, was approaching the banks of the Rhine sad and dispirited, the evangelical Christians were returning in triumph to their homes. Luther was the herald of the victory gained at Augsburg by Faith. "Though our enemies should have around them, beside them, with them, not only that puissant Roman emperor, Charles, but still more the emperor of the Turks and his Mahomet," said he, "they could not intimidate, they could not frighten me. It is I who in the strength of God am resolved to frighten and overthrow them. They shall yield to me—they shall fall! and I shall remain upright and firm. My life shall be their headsman, and my death their hell![3] ......God blinds them and hardens their hearts; he is driving them towards the Red Sea: all the horses of Pharaoh, his chariots and his horsemen, cannot escape their inevitable destiny. Let them go then, let them perish, since they will it so![4] As for us, the Lord is with us."

Thus the Diet of Augsburg, destined to crush the Reformation, was what strengthened it for ever. It has been usual to consider the peace of Augsburg (1555) as the period when the Reform was definitively established. That is the date of legal Protestantism; evangelical Christianity has another—the autumn of 1530. In 1555 was the victory of the sword and of diplomacy; in 1530 was that of the Word of God and of Faith; and this latter victory is in our eyes the truest and the surest. The evangelical history of the Reformation in Germany is nearly finished at the epoch we have reached, and the diplomatic history of legal Protestantism begins. Whatever may now be done, whatever may be said, the Church of the first ages has re-

---

[1] 40,000 zu Tuss und 8000 zu Ross. Corp. Ref. ii. 399.
[2] Legati Norinb. ad Senatum, 11th October. Ioid. 402; Legati Sax. ad Electorem, 10th October. Urkund. ii. 711.
[3] Shortly before the close of the diet.

[1] Hatt der Kayser unter andern in Franzosisch geredet. Urk. ii. 421.
[2] Geneva expugnata, bellum etiam urbibus Germaniæ Superioris inferretur. Corp. Ref. ii. 402.
[3] Mein leben soll ihr Henker seyn. L. Opp. xx. 304.
[4] Vadant igitur et pereant, quomodo sic volunt. L. Epp iv. 167.

appeared; and it has reappeared strong enough to show that it will live. There will still be conferences and discussions; there will still be leagues and combats; there will even be deplorable defeats; but all these are a secondary movement. The great move-ment is accomplished: the cause of faith is won by faith. The effort has been made: the evangelical doctrine has taken root in the world, and neither the storms of men, nor the powers of hell, will ever be able to tear it up.

BOOK XV.

SWITZERLAND—CONQUESTS. 1526—1530.

CHAPTER I.

Originality of the Swiss Reform—Change—Three Periods of Reform—Switzerland Romande—The two Movements in the Church—Aggressive Spirit—The Schoolmaster—Farel's new Baptism—Mysticism and Scholasticism—A Door is opened—Opposition—Lausanne—Manners of the Clergy—Farel to Galeotto—Farel and the Monk—The Tribunal—The Monk cries for Pardon—Opposition of the Ormonds—A false Convert—Christian Unity.

THE divisions which the Reformation disclosed within its bosom, on its appearance before the Diet of Augsburg, humbled it and compromised its existence; but we must not forget that the cause of these divisions was one of the conditions of the existence of the regenerated Church. No doubt it would have been desirable for Germany and Switzerland to have agreed; but it was of still greater importance that Germany and Switzerland should have each its original Reform. If the Swiss Reformation had been only a feeble copy of the German, there would have been uniformity, but no duration. The tree, transplanted into Switzerland, without having taken deep root, would soon have been torn up by the vigorous hand that was erelong about to seize upon it. The regeneration of Christianity in these mountains proceeded from forces peculiar to the Helvetic Church, and received an organization in conformity with the ecclesiastical and political condition of that country. By this very originality it communicated a particular energy to the principles of the Reformation, of much greater consequence to the common cause than a servile uniformity. The strength of an army arises in great measure from its being composed of soldiers of different arms.

The military and political influence of Switzerland was declining. The new developments of the European nations, subsequent to the sixteenth century, were about to banish to their native mountains those proud Helvetians, who for so long a period had placed their two-handed swords in the balance in which the destinies of nations were weighed. The Reformation communicated a new influence in exchange for that which was departing. Switzerland, where the Gospel appeared in its simplest and purest form, was destined to give in these new times to many nations of the two worlds a more salutary and glorious impulse than that which had hitherto proceeded from its halberds and its arequebuses.

The history of the Swiss Reformation is divided into three periods, in which the light of the Gospel is seen spreading successively over three different zones. From 1519 to 1526 Zurich was the centre of the Reformation, which was then entirely German, and was propagated in the eastern and northern parts of the confederation. Between 1526 and 1532 the movement was communicated from Berne: it was at once German and French, and extended to the centre of Switzerland from the gorges of the Jura to the deepest valleys of the Alps. In 1532 Geneva became the focus of the light; and the Reformation, which was here essentially French, was established on the shores of the Leman lake, and gained strength in every quarter. It is of the second of these periods—that of Berne—of which we are now to treat.

Although the Swiss Reformation is not yet essentially French, still the most active part in it is taken by Frenchmen. Switzerland *Romande*[1] is yoked to the chariot of Reform, and communicates to it an accelerated motion. In the period we are about to treat of, there is a mixture of races, of forces, and of characters from which proceeds a greater commotion. In no part of the christian world will the resistance be so stubborn; but no where will the assailants display so much courage. This petty country of Switzerland Romande, enclosed within the colossal arms of the Jura and the Alps, was for centuries one of the strongest fortresses of the Papacy. It is about to be carried by storm; it is going to turn its arms against its ancient masters; and from these few hillocks, scattered at the foot of the highest

[1] The French part of Switzerland, comprising the cantons of Geneva, Vaud, Neufchatel, and part of those of Friburg Berne, and Valais.

mountains in Europe, will proceed the reiterated shocks that will overthrow, even in the most distant countries, the sanctuaries of Rome, their images and their altars.

There are two movements in the Church: one is effected inwardly, and its object is its preservation; the other is effected outwardly, and the object aimed at is its propagation. There is thus a doctrinal Church and a missionary Church. These two movements ought never to be separated, and whenever they are disunited, it is because the spirit of man, and not the Spirit of God prevails. In the apostolic ages these two tendencies were evolved at the same time and with equal power. In the second and third centuries the external tendency prevailed; after the Council of Nice (325) the doctrinal movement resumed the superiority; at the epoch of the irruption of the northern tribes the missionary spirit revived; but erelong came the times of the hierarchy and of the schoolmen, in which all doctrinal powers warred within the Church to found therein a despotic government and an impure doctrine—the Papacy. The revival of Christianity in the sixteenth century, which emanated from God, was destined to renovate these two movements, but by purifying them. Then indeed the Spirit of God acted at once externally and internally. In the days of the Reformation there were tranquil and internal developments; but there was also a more powerful and aggressive action. Men of God had for ages studied the Word, and had peacefully explained its salutary lessons. Such had been the work of Vesalia Goch, Groot, Radewin, Ruysbrook, Tauler, Thomas à Kempis, and John Wessel; now, something more was required. The power of action was to be combined with the power of thought. The Papacy had been allowed all necessary time for laying aside its errors; for ages men had been in expectation; it had been warned, it had been entreated; all had been unavailing. Popery being unwilling to reform itself, it became necessary for men of God to take its accomplishment upon themselves. The calm and moderate influence of the precursors of the Reform was succeeded by the heroic and holy revolutionary work of the Reformers; and the revolution they effected consisted in overthrowing the usurping power to re-establish the legitimate authority. "To every thing there is a season," says the preacher, "and a time to every purpose under heaven: a time to plant, and a time to pluck up that which is planted; a time to break down, and a time to build up."[1] Of all Reformers, those who carried the aggressive spirit to its highest degree were the men who came from France, and more especially Farel, whose labours we have now to consider.

Never were such mighty effects accomplished by so puny a force. In the government of God we pass in an instant from the greatest to the least of things. We now quit the haughty Charles V. and all that court of princes over which he presides, to follow the steps of a schoolmaster; and leave the palaces of Augsburg to take our seats in the lowly cottages of Switzerland.

The Rhone, after issuing, near St. Gothard, from the mountains of the Furka, from beneath an immense sea of eternal ice, rolls its noisy waters through a rugged valley separating the two great chains of the Alps; then issuing from the gorge of St. Maurice, it wanders through a more smiling and fertile country. The sublime Dent du Midi on the south, the proud Dent de Morcles on the north, picturesquely situated opposite each other, point out from afar to the traveller's eye the beginning of this latter basin. On the tops of these mountains are vast glaciers and threatening peaks, near which the shepherds in the midst of summer lead their numerous flocks to pasture: while, in the plain, the flowers and fruits of southern climes grow luxuriantly, and the laurel blooms beside the most exquisite grapes.

At the opening of one of the lateral valleys that lead into the Northern Alps, on the banks of the Grande Eau that falls in thunder from the glaciers of the Diablerets, is situated the small town of Aigle, one of the most southern in Switzerland. For about fifty years it had belonged to Berne, with the four parishes (*mandemens*) which are under its jurisdiction, namely, Aigle, Bex, Ollon, and the chalets scattered in the lofty valleys of the Ormonds. It is in this country that the second epoch of the Swiss Reformation was destined to begin.

In the winter of 1526–1527, a foreign schoolmaster, named Ursinus, arrived in this humble district. He was a man of middle stature, with red beard and quick eyes, and with a voice of thunder (says Beza) combined the feelings of a hero: his modest lessons were intermingled with new and strange doctrines. As the benefices had been abandoned by their titularies to ignorant curates, the people, who were naturally of rude and turbulent habits, had remained without any cultivation. Thus did this stranger, who was no other than Farel, meet with new obstacles at every step.

Whilst Lefevre and most of his friends had quitted Strasburg to re-enter France, after the deliverance of Francis I., Farel had turned his steps towards Switzerland; and on the very first day of his journey, he received a lesson that he frequently called to mind.

He was on foot, accompanied by a single friend. Night had closed around them, the rain fell in torrents, and the travellers, in despair of finding their road, had sat down midway, drenched with rain.[1] " Ah !" said

---

[1] Eccles. iii. 1, 2, 3.

[1] Gravabat nox, opprimebat pluvia........coegit viæ diffi-

Farel, " God, by showing me my helplessness in these little things, has willed to teach me how weak I am in the greatest, without Jesus Christ!" [1] At last, Farel springing up, plunged into the marshes, waded through the waters, crossed vineyards, fields, hills, forests, and valleys, and at length reached his destination covered with mud and soaked to the skin.

In this night of desolation, Farel had received a new baptism. His natural energy had been quelled ; he became, for some time at least, wise as a serpent, and harmless as a dove ; and, as not unfrequently happens to men of such a disposition, he at first overstepped his aim. Believing that he was following the example of the apostles, he sought, in the words of Œcolampadius, " by pious frauds to circumvent the old serpent that was hissing around him." [2] He represented himself to be a schoolmaster, and waited until a door should be opened to him to appear as a reformer.[3]

Magister Ursinus had no sooner quitted the schoolroom and his primers, than, taking refuge in his modest chamber, he became absorbed in the Greek and Hebrew Scriptures, and the most learned treatises of the theologians. The struggle between Luther and Zwingle was then commencing. To which of these two chiefs should the French Reform attach itself ? Luther had been known in France for a much longer time than Zwingle ; yet Farel decided in favour of the latter. Mysticism had characterized the Germanic nations during the Middle Ages, and scholasticism those of Roman descent. The French were in closer relation with the dialectician Zwingle than with the mystic Luther ; or rather they were the mediators between the two great tendencies of the Middle Ages ; and, while giving to the christian thought that correct form which seems to be the province of southern nations, they became the instruments of God to spread through the Church the fulness of life and of the Spirit of Christ.

It was in his little chamber at Aigle that Farel read the first publication addressed to the German by the Swiss reformer.[4] " With what learning," cries he, " does Zwingle scatter the darkness ! with what holy ingenuity he gains over the wise, and what captivating meekness he unites with deep erudition ! Oh, that by the grace of God this work may win over Luther, so that the Church of Christ, trembling from such violent shocks, may at length find peace !" [5]

The schoolmaster Ursinus, excited by so noble an example, gradually set about instructing the parents as well as the children. He at first attacked the doctrine of purgatory, and next the Invocation of Saints. " As for the pope, he is nothing," said he, " or almost nothing, in these parts ; [1] and as for the priests, provided they annoy the people with all that nonsense, which Erasmus knows so well how to turn into ridicule, that is enough for them."

Ursinus had been some months at Aigle : a door was opened to him ; a flock had been collected there, and he believed the looked-for moment had arrived.

Accordingly one day the prudent schoolmaster disappeared. " I am William Farel," said he, " minister of the Word of God." The terror of the priests and magistrates was great, when they saw in the midst of them that very man whose name had already become so formidable. The schoolmaster quitted his humble study ; he ascended the pulpit, and openly preached Jesus Christ to the astonished multitude. The work of Ursinus was over : Farel was himself again.[2] It was then about the month of March or April 1527, and in that beautiful valley, whose slopes were brightening in the warm rays of the sun, all was fermenting at the same time, the flowers, the vineyards, and the hearts of this sensible but rude people.

Yet the rocks that the torrent meets as it issues from the Diablerets, and against which it dashes at every step as it falls from the eternal snows, are more trifling obstacles than the prejudice and hatred that were shown erelong in this populous valley to the Word of God.

The Council of Berne, by a license of the 9th of March, had commissioned Farel to explain the Holy Scriptures to the people of Aigle and its neighbourhood. But the arm of the civil magistrate, by thus mingling in religious affairs, served only to increase the irritation of men's minds. The rich and lazy incumbents, the poor and ignorant curates, were the first to cry out. " If this man," said they one to another, " continues preaching, it is all over with our benefices and our Church."[3]

In the midst of this agitation, the bailiff of Aigle and the governor of the four mandemens, Jacques de Roverea, instead of supporting the minister of their excellencies of Berne, eagerly embraced the cause of the priests. " The emperor," said they, " is about to declare war against all innovators. A great army will shortly arrive from Spain to assist the Archduke Ferdinand."[4] Farel stood firm. Upon this the bailiff and Rove-

cultas in media sedere via sub pluvia. Farel to Capito and Bucer. Neufchatel MS.

[1] Voluit Dominus per infirma hæc, docere quid possit homo in majoribus. Coct. Epp. MS. of Neufchatel.
[2] Piis artibus et apostolicis versatiis ad circumveniendum illum opus est. Œcol. to Farel, 27th December 1526. Neufchatel MS.
[3] Ubi ostium patuerit, tunc adversariis liberius obsistetur. Ibid.
[4] Pia et amica ad Lutheri sermonem apologia. Opp. vol. ii. t. 2. p. 1.
[5] Ut Christi succussa undique Ecclesia, pacis non nihil sentiat. Zw. Epp. ii. 26.

[1] Papa aut nullus aut modicus hic est. Zw. Epp. ii. 36.
[2] The name of Ursinus was doubtless taken from the bear (ursa) which was on the shield of Berne. Ursinus meant Bernese.
[3] J. J. Hottinger, H. K. G., iii. 364.
[4] Ferdinando adventurum esse ingentem ex Hispania exercitum. Zwinglius, Epp. ii. 64 ; dated 11th May 1527.

rea, exasperated by such boldness, interdicted the heretic from every kind of instruction, whether as minister or schoolmaster. But Berne caused to be posted on the doors of all the churches in the four mandemens a new decree, dated the 3d of July, in which their excellencies, manifesting great displeasure at this interdiction " of the very learned Farel from the propagation of the Divine Word,[1] ordered all the officers of the state to allow him to preach publicly the doctrines of the Lord."

This new proclamation was the signal of revolt. On the 25th July, great crowds assembled at Aigle, at Bex, at Ollon, and in the Ormonds, crying out, " No more submission to Berne ! down with Farel !" From words they soon proceeded to actions. At Aigle the insurgents, headed by the fiery syndic, tore down the edict, and prepared to fall upon the reformed. These promptly united and, surrounding Farel, resolved to defend him. The two parties met face to face, and blood was near flowing. The firm countenance of the friends of the Gospel checked the partisans of the priests, who dispersed, and Farel, quitting Aigle for a few days, carried his views farther.

In the middle of the beautiful valley of the Leman, on hills which overlook the lake. stands Lausanne, the city of the bishop and of the Virgin, placed under the patronage of the Dukes of Savoy. A host of pilgrims, assembling from all the surrounding places, knelt devoutly before the image of Our Lady, and made costly purchases at the great fair of indulgences that was held within its precincts. Lausanne, extending its episcopal crosier from its lofty towers, pretended to keep the whole country at the feet of the pope. But owing to the dissolute life of the canons and priests, the eyes of many began to be opened. The ministers of the Virgin were seen in public playing at games of chance, which they seasoned with mockery and blasphemy. They fought in the churches; disguised as soldiers, they descended by night from the cathedral hill, and roaming through the streets, sword in hand and in liquor, surprised, wounded, and sometimes even killed the worthy citizens; they debauched married women, seduced young girls, changed their residences into houses of ill-fame, and heartlessly turned out their young children to beg their bread.[2] Nowhere, perhaps, was better exemplified the description of the clergy given us by one of the most venerable prelates at the beginning of the fifteenth century : " Instead of training up youth by their learning and holiness of life, the priests train birds and dogs; instead of books they have children; they sit with topers in the taverns, and give way to drunkenness."[3]

Among the theologians in the court of the Bishop Sebastian of Montfaucon, was Natalis Galeotto, a man of elevated rank and great urbanity, fond of the society of scholars, and himself a man of learning,[1] but nevertheless very zealous about fasts and all the ordinances of the Church. Farel thought that, if this man could be gained over to the Gospel, Lausanne, "slumbering at the foot of its steeples," would perhaps awaken, and all the country with it. He therefore addressed himself to him. " Alas ! alas !" said Farel, " religion is now little better than an empty mockery, since people who think only of their appetites are the kings of the Church. Christian people, instead of celebrating in the sacrament the death of the Lord, live as if they commemorated Mercury, the god of fraud. Instead of imitating the love of Christ, they emulate the lewdness of Venus ; and, when they do evil, they fear more the presence of a wretched swineherd than of God Almighty."[2]

But Galeotto made no reply, and Farel persevered. " Knock ; cry out with all your might," wrote he in a second letter ; redouble your attacks upon our Lord."[3] Still there was no answer. Farel returned to the charge a third time, and Natalis, fearing perhaps to reply in person, commissioned his secretary, who forwarded a letter to Farel full of abusive language.[4] For a season Lausanne was inaccessible.

After having thus contended with a priest, Farel was destined to struggle with a monk. The two arms of the hierarchy by which the Middle Ages had been governed were chivalry and monachism. The latter still remained for the service of the Papacy, although falling into decay. " Alas !" exclaimed a celebrated Carthusian, " what an obstinate devil would fear to do, a reprobate and arrogant monk will commit without hesitation."[5]

A mendicant friar, who dared not oppose the reformer in a direct manner at Aigle, ventured into the village of Noville, situated on the low grounds deposited by the Rhone, as it falls into the Lake of Geneva. The friar, ascending the pulpit, exclaimed, " It is the devil himself who preaches by the mouth of the minister, and all those who listen to him will be damned." Then, taking courage, he slunk along the bank of the Rhone, and arrived at Aigle with a meek and humble look, not to appear there against Farel, whose powerful eloquence terribly alarmed him, but to beg in behalf of his convent a few barrels

[1] Inhibita verbi divini propagatio. Choupard MS.
[2] Histoire de la Reformation Suisse by Ruchat, i. 35.
[*] Pro *libros* sibi *liberos* comparant, pro studio concubinas

amant. Tritheim Instit. Vitæ Sacerdotalis, p. 765. The play upon *libros* and *liberos* (books and children) cannot be conveyed in English.
[1] Urbanus, doctus, magnus, consuetudine doctorum obligatus. Farel to Galeotto. Neufchatel MS.
[2] Pluris faciunt miserrimi subulci aspectum quam omnipotentis Dei. Farel to Galeotto. Ibid.
[3] Pulsare, vociferari perge, nec prius cessa quam, &c. Ibid.
[4] Næniis totas implevit et conviciis. Ibid.
[5] Quod agere veretur obstinatus diabolus, intrepide agit reprobus et contumax monachus. Jacob von Juterbock: de Negligentia Prelatorum.

of the most exquisite wine in all Switzerland. He had not advanced many steps into the town before he met the minister. At this sight he trembled in every limb. "Why did you preach in such a manner at Noville?" demanded Farel. The monk, fearful that the dispute would attract public attention, and yet desirous of replying to the point, whispered in his ear, "I have heard say that you are a heretic and misleader of the people." "Prove it," said Farel. Then the monk "began to storm," says Farel,[1] and, hastening down the street, endeavoured to shake off his disagreeable companion, "turning now this way, now that, like a troubled conscience."[2] A few citizens beginning to collect around them, Farel said to them, pointing to the monk, "You see this fine father; he has said from the pulpit that I preach nothing but lies." Upon this the monk, blushing and stammering, began to speak of the offerings of the faithful (the precious wine of Yvorne, for which he had come begging, and accused Farel of opposing them. The crowd had now increased in number, and Farel, who only sought an opportunity of proclaiming the true worship of God, exclaimed with a loud voice, "It is no man's business to ordain any other way of serving God than that which He has commanded. We must keep his commandments without swerving either to the right hand or to the left.[3] Let us worship God alone in spirit and in truth, offering to him a broken and a contrite heart."

The eyes of all the spectators were fixed on the two actors in this scene, the monk with his wallet, and the reformer with his glistening eye. Confounded by Farel's daring to speak of any other worship than that which the holy Roman Church prescribed, the friar "was out of his senses; he trembled, and was agitated, becoming pale and red by turns. At last, taking his cap off his head, from under his hood, he flung it on the ground, trampling it under foot and crying: 'I am surprised that the earth does not gape and swallow us up!'"[4].........Farel wished to reply, but in vain. The friar with downcast eyes kept stamping on his cap, "bawling like one out of his wits:" and his cries resounding through the streets of Aigle, drowned the voice of the reformer. At length one of the spectators, who stood beside him, plucked him by the sleeve, and said, "listen to the minister, as he is listening to you." The affrighted monk, believing himself already half-dead, started violently

and cried out: "Oh, thou excommunicate! layest thou thy hand upon me?"

The little town was in an uproar; the friar at once furious and trembling, Farel following up his attack with vigour, and the people confused and amazed. At length the magistrate appeared, ordered the monk and Farel to follow him, and shut them up, "one in one tower and one in another."[1]

On the Saturday morning Farel was liberated from his prison, and conducted to the castle before the officers of justice, where the monk had preceded him. The minister began to address them: "My lords, to whom our Saviour enjoins obedience without any exception, this friar has said that the doctrine which I preach is against God. Let him make good his words, or, if he cannot, permit your people to be edified." The violence of the monk was over. The tribunal before which he was standing, the courage of his adversary, the power of the movement which he could not resist, the weakness of his cause, —all alarmed him, and he was now ready to make matters up. "Then the friar fell upon his knees saying: My lords, I entreat forgiveness of you and of God. Next turning to Farel: And also, Magister, what I preached against you was grounded on false reports. I have found you to be a good man, and your doctrine good, and I am prepared to recall my words."[2]

Farel was touched by this appeal, and said: "My friend, do not ask forgiveness of me, for I am a poor sinner like other men, putting my trust not in my own righteousness, but in the death of Jesus."[3]

One of the lords of Berne coming up at this time, the friar, who already imagined himself on the brink of martyrdom, began to wring his hands, and to turn now towards the Bernese councillors, now towards the tribunal, and then to Farel, crying, "Pardon, pardon!"—"Ask pardon of our Saviour," replied Farel. The lord of Berne added; "Come to-morrow and hear the minister's sermon; if he appears to you to preach the truth, you shall confess it openly before all; if not, you will declare your opinion: this promise in my hand." The monk held out his hand, and the judges retired. "Then the friar went away, and I have not seen him since, and no promises or oaths were able to make him stay."[4] Thus the Reformation advanced in Switzerland Romande.

But violent storms threatened to destroy the work that was hardly begun. Romish agents from the Valais and from Savoy had crossed the Rhone at St. Maurice, and were exciting the people to energetic resistance. Tumultuous assemblages took place, in which

---

[1] Commença de se tempester; in the narrative he gives of this adventure to the nuns of Vevay. Neufchatel MS.
[2] Tournant maintenant he ça, maintenant de là, comme fait la conscience mal assurée. Ibid.
[3] Il n'appartient à personne vivante d'ordonner autre manière de faire service à Dieu, que celle qu'il a commandée. Nous devons garder ses commandemens, sans tirer ni à la dextre, ni à la senestre. Ibid.
[4] Hors de sens, trembloit, s'agitoit, palissoit et rougissoit tour à tour. Enfin tirant son bonnet de sa tête, hors du chaperon, il le rua à terre, jettant et mettant son pied sus, en s'écriant: "Je suis esbahi comme la terre ne nous abyme!" Ibid.

[1] L'un en une tour, et l'autre en l'autre. Neufchatel MS.
[2] Lors le frère se jeta à genoux disant: Messeigneurs, je demande merci à Dieu et à vous......Et aussi, Magister, ce que j'ai prêché contre vous a été par de faux rapports, &c. Ibid.
[3] Je suis pauvre pécheur comme les autres, ayant ma fiance, non en ma justice, mais à la mort de Jesus. Ibid.
[4] Puis quand le frère fut parti, depuis ne l'ai vu, et nulles promesses ni sermens ne l'ont pu faire demeurer. Ibid.

dangerous projects were discussed; the proclamations of the government were torn down from the church-doors; troops of citizens paraded the town; the drum beat in the streets to excite the populace against the reformer: every where prevailed riot and sedition. And hence, when Farel ascended the pulpit on the 16th February, for the first time after a short absence, some papist bands collected round the gate of the church, raised their hands in tumult, uttered savage cries, and compelled the minister to break off in his sermon.

The council of Berne thereupon decreed that the parishioners of the four mandemens should assemble. Those of Bex declared for the Reform; Aigle followed their example, but with indecision; and in the mountains above Ollon, the peasants, not daring to maltreat Farel, excited their wives, who rushed upon him with their fulling-clubs. But it was especially the parish of the Ormonds which, calm and proud at the foot of its glaciers, signalized itself by its resistance. A companion of Farel's labours, named Claude (probably Claude de Gloutinis), when preaching there one day with great animation, was suddenly interrupted by the ringing of the bells, whose noise was such that one might have said all hell was busy pulling them. "In fact," says another herald of the Gospel, Jacques Camralis, who chanced to be present, "it was Satan himself, who, breathing his anger into some of his agents, filled the ears of the auditors with all this uproar."[1] At another time, some zealous reformers having, according to the language of the times, thrown down the altars of Baal, the evil spirit began to blow with violence in all the chalets scattered over the sides of the mountains; the shepherds issued precipitously, like avalanches, and fell upon the church and the evangelicals. "Let us only find these sacrilegious wretches," cried the furious Ormondines; "we will hang them,—we will cut off their heads,—we will burn them,—we will throw their ashes into the Great Water."[2] Thus were these mountaineers agitated, like the wind that roars in their lofty valleys with a fury unknown to the inhabitants of the plains.

Other difficulties overwhelmed Farel. His fellow-labourers were not all of them blameless. One Christopher Ballista, formerly a monk of Paris, had written to Zwingle: "I am but a Gaul, a barbarian,[3] but you will find me pure as snow, without any guile, of open heart, through whose windows all the world may see."[1] Zwingle sent Ballista to Farel, who was loudly calling for labourers in Christ's vineyard. The fine language of the Parisian at first charmed the multitude; but it was soon found necessary to beware of these priests and monks disgusted with popery. "Brought up in the slothfulness of the cloister, gluttonous and lazy," says Farel, "Ballista could not conform to the abstemiousness and rude labours of the evangelists, and soon began to regret his monk's hood. When he perceived the people beginning to distrust him, he became like a furious monster, vomiting waggon-loads of threats."[2] Thus ended his labours.

Notwithstanding all these trials, Farel was not discouraged. The greater the difficulties, the more his energy increased. "Let us scatter the seed every where," said he, "and let civilized France, provoked to jealousy by this barbarous nation, embrace piety at last. Let there not be in Christ's body either fingers, or hands, or feet, or eyes, or ears, or arms, existing separately, and working each for itself, but let there be only one heart that nothing can divide. Let not variety in secondary things divide into many separate members that vital principle which is one and simple.[3] Alas! the pastures of the Church are trodden under foot, and its waters are troubled! Let us set our minds to concord and peace. When the Lord shall have opened heaven, there will not be so many disputes about bread and water.[4] A fervent charity is the powerful battering-ram with which we shall beat down those proud walls, those material elements, within which men would confine us."[5]

Thus wrote the most impetuous of the reformers. These words of Farel, preserved for three centuries in the city where he died, disclose to us more clearly the intimate nature of the great Revolution of the sixteenth century, than all the venturesome assertions of its popish interpreters. Christian unity thus from these earliest moments found a zealous apostle. The nineteenth century is called to resume the work which the sixteenth century was unable to accomplish.

[1] Sed Sathan per ejus servos, voluit aures auditorum ejus sono cymbali implere. Neufchatel MS.
[2] Quo invento suspenderetur primum, deinde dignus comburi, ulterius capitis obtruncatione, novissime in aquis mergeretur. Ibid.
[3] Me quantumvis Gallum et barbarum. Zw. Epp. ii. 205.

[1] Absque ullo fuco, niveum, et aperti fenestratique pectoris. Zw. Epp. ii. 205.
[2] Quam beatus hic venter incanduit! quot minarum plaustra! Solent tales belluæ, &c. Neufchatel MS.
[3] Ne in digitos, manus, pedes, oculos, nares, aures, brachia, cor quod unum est discindatur, et quæ in rebus est varietas, principium non faciat multiplex. Ibid.
[4] An allusion to the controversies on anabaptism and the real presence. Non tanta erit super aqua et pane contentio, nec super gramine, solutaque obsidione. Ibid. The sense of these latter words is obscure.
[5] Charitas fortissimus aries. Farel to Bucer, 10th May 1529.

CHAPTER II.

State—Religion in Berne—Irresolution of Berne—Almanack of Heretics—Evangelical Majority—Haller—Zwingle's Signal—Anabaptists in Berne—Victory of the Gospel—Papist Provocations—The City Companies—Proposed Disputation—Objections of the Forest Cantons—The Church, the Judge of Controversies—Unequal Contest—Zwingle—A Christian Band—The Cordeliers' Church—Opening of the Conference—The sole Head—Unity of Error—A Priest converted at the Altar—St. Vincent's Day—The Butchers—A strange Argument—Papist Bitterness—Necessity of Reform—Zwingle's Sermon—Visit of the King of Kings—Edict of Reform—Was the Reformation Political?

OF all the Swiss cantons, Berne appeared the least disposed to the Reformation. A military state may be zealous for religion, but it will be for an external and a disciplined religion: it requires an ecclesiastical organization that it can see, and touch, and manage at its will. It fears the innovations and the free movements of the Word of God: it loves the form and not the life. Napoleon, by restoring religion in France in the *Concordat*, has given us a memorable example of this truth. Such, also, was the case with Berne. Its government, besides, was absorbed in political interests, and although it had little regard for the pope, it cared still less to see a reformer put himself, as Zwingle did, at the head of public affairs. As for the people, feasting on the "butter of their kine and milk of their sheep, with fat of lambs,"[1] they remained closely shut up within the narrow circle of their material wants. Religious questions were not to the taste either of the rulers or of their fellow-citizens.

The Bernese government, being without experience in religious matters, had proposed to check the movement of the Reform by its edict of 1523. As soon as it discovered its mistake, it moved towards the cantons that adhered to the ancient faith; and while that portion of the people whence the Great Council was recruited, listened to the voice of the reformers, most of the patrician families, who composed the Smaller Council, believing their power, their interests, and their honour menaced, attached themselves to the old order of things. From this opposition of the two councils there arose a general uneasiness, but no violent shocks. Sudden movements, repeated starts, announced from time to time that incongruous matters were fermenting in the nation; it was like an indistinct earthquake, which raises the whole surface without causing any rents: then anon all returns to apparent tranquillity.[2] Berne, which was always decided in its politics, turned in religious matters at one time to the right, and at another to the left; and declared that it would be neither popish nor reformed. To gain time was, for the new faith, to gain every thing.

What was done to turn aside Berne from the Reformation, was the very cause of precipitating it into the new way. The haugh-

tiness with which the five primitive cantons arrogated the guardianship of their confederates, the secret conferences to which Berne was not even invited, and the threat of addressing the people in a direct manner, deeply offended the Bernese oligarchs. Thomas Murner, a Carmelite of Lucerne, one of those rude men who act upon the populace, but who inspire disgust in elevated minds, made the cup run over. Furious against the Zurich calendar, in which the names of the saints had been purposely omitted, he published in opposition to it the "Almanack of Heretics and Church-robbers," a tract filled with lampoons and invectives, in which the portraits of the reformers and of their adherents, among whom were many of the most considerable men of Berne, were coupled with the most brutal inscriptions.[1] Zurich and Berne in conjunction demanded satisfaction, and from this time the union of these two states daily became closer.

This change was soon perceived at Berne. The elections of 1527 placed a considerable number of friends of the Reform in the Great Council; and this body, forthwith resuming its right to nominate the members of the Smaller Council, which had been usurped for twenty years by the Bannerets and the Sixteen, removed from the government the most decided partisans of the Roman hierarchy, and among others Gaspard de Mulinen and Sebastian de Stein,[2] and filled the vacancies with members of the evangelical majority. The union of Church and State, which had hitherto checked the progress of the Reform in Switzerland, was now about to accelerate its movements.

The reformer Haller was not alone in Berne. Kolb had quitted the Carthusian monastery at Nuremberg, in which he had been compelled to take refuge, and had appeared before his compatriots, demanding no other stipend than the liberty of preaching Jesus Christ. Already bending under the weight of years, his head crowned with hoary locks, Kolb, young in heart, full of fire, and of indomitable courage, presented boldly before the chiefs of the nation that Gospel which had saved him. Haller, on the contrary, although only thirty-five years old, moved with a measured step, spoke with gravity, and proclaimed the new doctrines with unusual circumspection. The old man had taken the young man's part, and the youth that of the graybeard.

Zwingle, whose eye nothing escaped, saw that a favourable hour for Berne was coming, and immediately gave the signal. "The dove commissioned to examine the state of the waters is returning with an olive-branch into the ark," wrote he to Haller; "come forth now, thou second Noah, and take pos-

[1] Deut. xxxii. 14.
[2] Hundeshagen, Conflikte der Bernischen Kirche, p. 19.

[1] Quum nudus-tertius *Murneri* Calendarium legissem, partim ridendo hominis stultissimam impudentiam. Œcolamp. to Zwingle, Febr. 1527, Epp. ii. 26.
[2] Mullinen e Senatoria dignitate protrusus est. Lapides quoque. Haller to Zwingle, April 25, 1527.

session of the land. Enforce, be earnest, and fix deeply in the hearts of men the hooks and grapnels of the Word of God, so that they can never again be rid of them."[1]—" Your bears," wrote he to Thomas ab Hofen, "have again put forth their claws. Please God that they do not draw them back until they have torn every thing in pieces that opposes Jesus Christ."

Haller and his friends were on the point of replying to this appeal, when their situation became complicated. Some anabaptists, who formed every where the extreme party, arriving at Berne in 1527, led away the people from the evangelical preachers "on account of the presence of idols."[2] Haller had a useless conference with them. "To what dangers is not Christianity exposed," cried he, " wherever these furies have crept in!"[3] There has never been any revival in the Church, which the hierarchical or radical sects have not immediately endeavoured to disturb. Haller, although alarmed, still maintained his unalterable meekness. "The magistrates are desirous of banishing them," said he; "but it is our duty to drive out their errors, and not their persons. Let us employ no other weapons than the sword of the Spirit."[4] It was not from popery that the Reformers had learnt these principles. A public disputation took place. Six anabaptists declared themselves convinced, and two others were sent out of the country.

The decisive moment was drawing near. The two great powers of the age, the Gospel and the Papacy, were stirring with equal energy; the Bernese councils were to speak out. They saw on the one hand the five primitive cantons taking daily a more threatening attitude, and announcing that the Austrian would soon reappear in Helvetia, to reduce it once more into subjection to Rome; and on the other they beheld the Gospel every day gaining ground in the confederation. Which was destined to prevail in Switzerland—the lances of Austria or the Word of God? In the uncertainty in which the councils were placed, they resolved to side with the majority. Where could they discover a firm footing, if not there? *Vox populi, vox Dei.* " No one," said they, " can make any change of his own private authority: the consent of all is necessary."[5]

The government of Berne had to decide between two mandates, both emanating from its authority: that of 1523, in favour of the free preaching of the Gospel, and that of 1526, in favour " of the sacraments, the saints, the mother of God, and the ornaments of the churches." State messengers set out and traversed every parish: the people gave their votes against every law contrary to liberty, and the councils, supported by the nation, decreed that " the Word of God should be preached publicly and freely, even if it should be in opposition to the statutes and doctrines of men." Such was the victory of the Gospel and of the people over the oligarchy and the priests.

Contentions immediately arose throughout the canton, and every parish became a battle-field. The peasants began to dispute with the priests and monks, in reliance on the Holy Scriptures. " If the mandate of our lords," said many, accords to our pastors the liberty of preaching, why should it not grant the flock the liberty of acting?"—" Peace, peace!" cried the councils, alarmed at their own boldness. But the flocks resolutely declared that they would send away the mass, and keep their pastors and the Bible.[1] Upon this the papal partisans grew violent. The banneret Kuttler called the good people of Emmenthal, " heretics, rascals, and wantons;" but the peasants obliged him to make an apology.[2] The bailiff of Trachselwald was more cunning. Seeing the inhabitants of Rudersweil listening with eagerness to the Word of God, which a pious minister was preaching to them, he came with fifers and trumpeters, and interrupted the sermon, inviting the village girls by words and by lively tunes to quit the church for the dance.

These singular provocations did not check the Reform. Six of the city companies (the shoemakers, weavers, merchants, bakers, stone-masons, and carpenters) abolished in the churches and convents of their district all masses, anniversaries, advowsons, and prebends. Three others (the tanners, smiths, and tailors) prepared to imitate them;[3] the seven remaining companies were undecided, except the butchers, who were enthusiastic for the pope. Thus the majority of the citizens had embraced the Gospel. Many parishes throughout the canton had done the same; and the avoyer d'Erlach, that great adversary of the Reformation, could no longer keep the torrent within bounds.

Yet the attempt was made: the bailiffs were ordered to note the irregularities and dissolute lives of the monks and nuns; all women of loose morals were even turned out of the cloisters.[4] But it was not against these abuses alone that the Reformation was levelled; it was against the institutions themselves, and against popery on which they were founded. The people ought therefore to decide.—" The Bernese clergy," said they, " must be convoked, as at Zurich, and let the two doctrines be discussed in a solemn conference. We will proceed afterwards in conformity with the result."

---

[1] Aculeos ac hamos, sic in mortalium pectora dimitte, ut etiam si velint, non possint. Zw. Epp. ii. 10.
[2] Ne plebem dehortentur ab auditione concionum nostrarum ob idolorum præsentiam. Ibid. 49.
[3] Consideravimus omnes periculum urbis nostræ et totius Christianismi, ubi illæ furiæ irrepserint. Ibid. 50.
[4] Nostrum est, omnia gladio spiritus refellere. Ibid.
[5] Ut privata auctoritate nemo quippiam immutare præsumat. Haller to Vadian.

[1] Incolas vallis Emmenthal Senatum adiisse, *missamque missam fecisse.* Zw. Epp. ii. 104.
[2] Pueros, hereticos, et homines lascivos. Ibid. 106.
[3] Haller to Zwingle, 4th November 1527. Epp. ii. 105.
[4] J. J. Hottinger, H. Kirchen. viii. 394.

On the Sunday following the festival of Saint Martin (11th November), the council and citizens unanimously resolved that a public disputation should take place at the beginning of the succeeding year. " The glory of God and his Word," said they, " will at length appear ! " Bernese and strangers, priests and laymen, all were invited by letter or by printed notice to come and discuss the controverted points, but by Scripture alone, without the glosses of the ancients, and renouncing all subtleties and abusive language.[1] Who knows, said they, whether all the members of the ancient Swiss confederation may not thus be brought to unity of faith ?

Thus, within the walls of Berne, the struggle was about to take place that would decide the fate of Switzerland ; for the example of the Bernese must necessarily lead with it a great part of the confederation.

The Five Cantons, alarmed at this intelligence, met at Lucerne, where they were joined by Friburg, Soleure, and Glaris. There was nothing either in the letter or in the spirit of the federal compact to obstruct religious liberty. " Every state," said Zurich, " is free to choose the doctrine that it desires to profess." The Waldstettes,[2] on the contrary, wished to deprive the cantons of this independence, and to subject them to the federal majority and to the pope. They protested, therefore, in the name of the confederation, against the proposed discussion. " Your ministers," wrote they to Berne, " dazzled and confounded at Baden by the brightness of truth, would desire by this new discussion to hide their shame ; but we entreat you to desist from a plan so contrary to our ancient alliances."—" It is not we who have infringed them," replied Berne ; " it is much rather your haughty missive that has destroyed them. We will not abandon the Word of our Lord Jesus Christ." Upon this the Roman Cantons decided on refusing a safe-conduct to those who should proceed to Berne. This was giving token of sinister intentions.

The Bishops of Lausanne, Constance, Basle, and Sion, being invited to the conference under pain of forfeiting all their privileges in the canton of Berne, replied that, since it was to be a disputation according to the Scriptures, they had nothing to do with it. Thus did these priests forget the words of one of the most illustrious Roman doctors of the fifteenth century : " In heavenly things man should be independent of his fellows, and trust in God alone."[3]

The Romanist doctors followed the example of the bishops. Eck, Murner, Cochlœus, and many others, said wherever they

went : " We have received the letter of this leper, of this accursed heretic, Zwingle.[1] They want to take the Bible for their judge ; but has the Bible a voice against those who do it violence ? We will not go to Berne ; we will not crawl into that obscure corner of the world ; we will not go and combat in that gloomy cavern, in that school of heretics. Let these villains come out into the open air, and contend with us on level ground, if they have the Bible on their side, as they say." The emperor ordered the discussion to be adjourned ; but on the very day of its opening, the council of Berne replied, that as every one was already assembled, delay would be impossible.

Then, in despite of the doctors and bishops, the Helvetic Church assembled to decide upon its doctrines. Had it a right to do so ? No ;—not if priests and bishops were appointed, as Rome pretends, to form a mystic bond between the Church and our Lord ; Yes—if they were established, as the Bible declares, only to satisfy that law of order by virtue of which all society should have a directing power. The opinions of the Swiss reformers in this respect were not doubtful. The grace which creates the minister comes from the Lord, thought they ; but the Church examines this grace, acknowledges it, proclaims it by the elders, and in every act in which faith is concerned, it can always appeal from the minister to the Word of God. *Try the spirits —prove all things*, it says to the faithful. The Church is the judge of controversies ;[2] and it is this duty, in which it should never be found wanting, that it was now about to fulfil in the disputation at Berne.

The contest seemed unequal. On one side appeared the Roman hierarchy, a giant which had increased in strength during many centuries ; and on the other, there was at first but one weak and timid man, the modest Berthold Haller. " I cannot wield the sword of the Word," said he in alarm to his friends. " If you do not stretch out your hands to me, all is over." He then threw himself trembling at the feet of the Lord, and soon arose enlightened and exclaiming, " Faith in the Saviour gives me courage, and scatters all my fears."[3]

Yet he could not remain alone : all his looks were turned towards Zwingle : " It was I who took the bath at Baden," wrote Œcolampadius to Haller, " and now it is Zwingle who should lead off the bear-dance in Berne."[4]—" We are between the hammer and the anvil," wrote Haller to Zwingle ; " we hold the wolf by the ears, and know not how to let him go.[5] The houses of De Watteville, Noll, Tremp, and Berthold are open to

[1] Solam sacram Scripturam, absque veterum glossematis. Haller to Zwingle, 19th November 1527. Epp. ii. 113.
[2] The inhabitants of the primitive democratic cantons, Schwytz, Uri, Underwald, and Lucerne, to which Zug may be added.
[3] John Goch, Dialogus de quatuor erroribus, p. 237.

[1] Epistolam leprosi, damnati, hæretici Zwinglii accepi. Eck to G. A. Zell, Zw. Epp. ii. 126.
[2] *Judex controversiarum*—1 John iv. 1 ; 1 Thess. v. 21.
[3] Fides in Dominum me animat, ut nihil verear. Zw. Epp. ii. 123.
[4] An allusion to the dispute at Baden, a celebrated bathing-place, and to the arms of Berne. Ibid. 118.
[5] Lupum auribus tenemus. Zurich MS.

604

you. Come, then, and command the battle in person."

Zwingle did not hesitate. He demanded permission of the Council of Zurich to visit Berne, in order to show there "that his teaching was full of the fear of God, and not blasphemous; mighty to spread concord through Switzerland, and not to cause troubles and dissension."[1] At the very time that Haller received news of Zwingle's coming, Œcolampadius wrote to him: "I am ready, if it be necessary, to sacrifice my life. Let us inaugurate the new year by embracing one another to the glory of Jesus Christ." Other doctors wrote to the same effect. "These, then," cried Haller with emotion, "these are the auxiliaries that the Lord sends to my infirmity, to aid me in fighting this rude battle!"

It was necessary to proceed with circumspection, for the violence of the oligarchs and of the Five Cantons was well known.[2] The doctors of Glaris, Schaffhausen, St. Gall, Constance, Ulm, Lindau, and Augsburg assembled at Zurich, to proceed under the same escort as Zwingle, Pellican, Collin, Megander, Grossman, the commander Schmidt, Bullinger, and a great number of the rural clergy, selected to accompany the reformer. "When all this game traverses the country," said the pensioners, "we will go a-hunting, and see if we cannot kill some, or at least catch them and put them into a cage."

Three hundred chosen men, selected from the companies of Zurich and from the parishes within its precincts, donned their breastplates and shouldered their arquebuses; but in order not to give the journey of these doctors the appearance of a military expedition, they took neither colours, fife, nor drum; and the trumpeter of the city, a civil officer, rode alone at the head of the company.

On Tuesday the 2d of January they set out. Never had Zwingle appeared more cheerful. "Glory be to the Lord," said he, "my courage increases every day."[3] The burgomaster Roust, the town-clerk of Mangoldt, with Funck and Jaëkli, both masters of arts, and all four delegated by the council, were on horseback near him. They reached Berne on the 4th of January, having had only one or two unimportant alarms.

The Cordeliers' Church was to serve as the place of Conference. Tillmann, the city architect, had made arrangements according to a plan furnished by Zwingle.[4] A large platform had been erected, on which were placed two tables, and around them sat the champions of the two parties. On the evangelical side were remarked, besides Haller, Zwingle, and Œcolampadius, many distinguished men of the Reformed Church, stran-

gers to Switzerland, as Bucer, Capito, and Ambrose Blarer. On the side of the Papacy, Dr. Treger of Friburg, who enjoyed a high reputation, appeared to keep up the fire of the combat. As for the rest, whether through fear or contempt, the most famous Roman doctors were absent.

The first act was to publish the regulations of the conference. "No proof shall be proposed that is not drawn from the Holy Scriptures, and no explanation shall be given of those Scriptures that does not come from Scripture itself, explaining obscure texts by such as are clear." After this, one of the secretaries, rising to call over the roll, shouted with a loud voice that re-echoed through the church,—The Bishop of Constance! No one replied. He did the same for the Bishops of Sion, Basle, and Lausanne. Neither of these prelates was present at this meeting, either in person or by deputy. The Word of God being destined to reign alone, the Roman hierarchy did not appear. These two powers cannot walk together. There were present about three hundred and fifty Swiss and German ecclesiastics.

On Tuesday, 7th January 1528, the burgomaster Vadian of St. Gaul, one of the presidents, opened the disputation. After him the aged Kolb stood up and said: "God is at this moment agitating the whole world; let us, therefore, humble ourselves before him;" and he pronounced with fervour a confession of sins.

This being ended, the first thesis was read. It ran thus: "The holy christian Church, of which Christ is the sole head, is born of the Word of God, abideth in it, and listeneth not to the voice of a stranger."

ALEXIS GRAT, a Dominican monk.—"The word sole is not in Scripture. Christ has left a vicar here below."

HALLER.—"The vicar that Christ left is the Holy Ghost."

TREGER.—"See then to what a pass things have come these last ten years. This man calls himself a Lutheran, that a Zwinglian; a third, a Carlstadtian; a fourth, an Œcolampadist; a fifth, an Anabaptist......"

BUCER.—"Whosoever preaches Jesus as the only Saviour, we recognise as our brother. Neither Luther, nor Zwingle, nor Œcolampadius, desires the faithful to bear his name. Besides, you should not boast so much of a mere external unity. When Antichrist gained the upperhand throughout the world, in the east by Mahomet, in the west by the pope, he was able to keep the people in unity of error. God permits divisions, in order that those who belong to him may learn to look not to men, but to the testimony of the Word, and to the assurance of the Holy Ghost in their hearts. Thus then, dearly beloved brethren, to the Scriptures, the Scriptures![1] O Church of Berne, hold fast to the

---

[1] Neque ad perturbationem nostræ almæ Helvetiæ. Zw. Epp. ii. 120.
[2] Oligarchæ in angulis obmurmurent. Ibid. 123.
[3] Crescit Domino gloria, mihi animus in hac pugna. Zw. Epp. Vadiano.
[4] Tillmannus urbis architectus locum juxta tuam deformationem operabit. Ibid. ii. 123.

[1] Darum fromme Christen! Zur Schrift, zur Schrift. Acta Zw. ii. 92.

teaching of Him who said, *Come unto me*, and not, *Come unto my vicar!*"

The disputation then turned successively on Tradition, the Merits of Christ, Transubstantiation, the Mass, Prayer to the Saints, Purgatory, Images, Celibacy, and the Disorders of the Clergy. Rome found numerous defenders, and among others, Murer, priest of Rapperswyl, who had said: "If they wish to burn the two ministers of Berne, I will undertake to carry them both to the stake."

On Sunday the 19th of January, the day on which the doctrine of the mass was attacked, Zwingle, desirous of acting on the people also, went into the pulpit, and reciting the Apostles' Creed, made a pause after these words : " He ascended into heaven, and sitteth at the right hand of God the Father Almighty ; from thence he shall come to judge the quick and the dead." " These three articles," said he, " are in contradiction to the mass." All his hearers redoubled their attention ; and a priest, clothed in his sacerdotal vestments, who was preparing to celebrate the holy sacrifice in one of the chapels, stopped in astonishment at Zwingle's words. Erect before the consecrated altar on which lay the chalice and the body of the Saviour, with eyes fixed upon the reformer, whose words electrified the people, a prey to the most violent struggles, and beaten down by the weight of truth, the agitated priest resolved to give up every thing for it. In the presence of the whole assembly, he stripped off his priestly ornaments, and throwing them on the altar, exclaimed: " Unless the mass reposes on a more solid foundation, I can celebrate it no longer !" The noise of this conversion, effected at the very foot of the altar, immediately spread through the city,[1] and it was regarded as an important omen. So long as the mass remains, Rome has gained every thing: as soon as the mass falls, Rome has lost all. The mass is the creative principle of the whole system of Popery.

Three days later, on the 22d January, was the feast of St. Vincent, the patron of the city. The disputation that had been continued during Sunday was suspended on that day. The canons asked the council what they were to do. " Such of you," replied the council, " as receive the doctrine of the theses ought not to say mass ; the others may perform divine worship as usual."[2] Every preparation was accordingly made for the solemnity. On St. Vincent's eve the bells from every steeple announced the festival to the inhabitants of Berne. On the morrow the sacristans lit up the tapers ; incense filled the temple, but no one appeared. No priests to say mass, no faithful to hear it ! Already there was a vast chasm in the Roman sanctuary, a deep silence, as on the field of battle, where none but the dead are lying.

In the evening it was the custom for the canons to chant vespers with great pomp. The organist was at his post, but no one else appeared. The poor man left thus alone, beholding with sorrow the fall of that worship by which he gained his bread, gave utterance to his grief by playing a mourning-hymn instead of the majestic *Magnificat:* " Oh, wretched Judas, what hast thou done, that thou hast betrayed our Lord ? " After this sad farewell, he rose and went out. Almost immediately after, some men, excited by the passions of the moment, fell upon his beloved organ, an accomplice in their eyes of so many superstitious rites, and violently broke it to pieces. No more mass, no more organ, no more anthems ! A new Supper and new hymns shall succeed the rites of popery.

On the next day there was the same silence. Suddenly, however, a band of men with loud voices and hasty steps was heard. It was the Butchers' Company that, at this moment so fatal to Rome, desired to support it. They advanced, carrying small fir-trees and green branches, for the decoration of their chapel. In the midst of them was a foreign priest, behind whom walked a few poor scholars. The priest officiated ; the sweet voices of the scholars supplied the place of the mute organ, and the butchers retired proud of their victory.

The discussion was drawing to a close; the combatants had dealt vigorous blows, Burgauer, pastor of St. Gall, had maintained the real presence in the host ; but on the 19th January he declared himself convinced by the reasonings of Zwingle, Œcolampadius, and Bucer ; and Matthias, minister of Saengen, had done the same.

A conference in Latin afterwards took place between Farel and a Parisian doctor. The latter advanced a strange argument. " Christians," said he, " are enjoined to obey the devil ;[1] for it is said, *Submit unto thine adversary* (Matt. v. 25) ; now, our adversary is the devil. How much more, then, should we submit to the Church !" Loud bursts of laughter greeted this remarkable syllogism. A discussion with the anabaptists terminated the conference.

The two councils decreed that the mass should be abolished, and that every one might remove from the churches the ornaments he had placed there.

Immediately twenty-five altars and a great number of images were destroyed in the cathedral, yet without disorder or bloodshed;

---

[1] Das lachet menklich und ward durch die gantzen Stadt kundt. Bulling. i. 436. In this and other quotations, we preserve the orthography of the times.
[2] Bullinger says, on the contrary, that the council positively forbade the mass. But Bullinger, who is a very animated writer, is not always exact in diplomatic matters. The council would not have come to such a resolution before the close of the discussion. Other contemporary historians and official documents leave no room for doubt on this point. Stettler, in his Chronicle, pars ii. 6, ad annum 1528, details these proceedings as in the text.

[1] Nos tenemur obedire diabolo. J. J. Hottinger, iii. 406.

and the children began to sing in the streets (as Luther informs us) :[1]

By the Word at length we're saved
From a God in a mortar brayed.

The hearts of the adherents of the Papacy were filled with bitterness as they heard the objects of their adoration fall one after another. "Should any man," said John Schneider, "take away the altar of the Butchers' Company, I will take away his life." Peter Thorman compared the cathedral stripped of its ornaments to a stable. "When the good folks of the Oberland come to market," added he, "they will be happy to put up their cattle in it." And John Zehender, member of the Great Council, to show the little value he set on such a place of worship, entered it riding on an ass, insulting and cursing the Reform. A Bernese, who chanced to be there, having said to him, "It is by God's will that these images have been pulled down."—"Say rather by the devil's," replied Zehender ; "when have you ever been with God so as to learn his will?" He was fined twenty livres, and expelled from the council.[2] "What times! what manners!" exclaimed many Romanists ; "what culpable neglect! How easy would it have been to prevent so great a misfortune! Oh! if our bishops had only been willing to occupy themselves more with learning, and a little less with their mistresses!"[3]

This Reform was necessary. When Christianity in the fourth century had seen the favour of princes succeed to persecution, a crowd of heathens rushing into the church had brought with them the images, pomps, statues, and demigods of paganism, and a likeness of the mysteries of Greece and Asia, and above all of Egypt, had banished the Word of Jesus Christ from the christian oratories. This Word returning in the sixteenth century, a purification must necessarily take place; but it could not be done without grievous rents.

The departure of the strangers was drawing near. On the 28th of January, the day after that on which the images and altars had been thrown down, while their piled fragments still encumbered here and there the porches and aisles of the cathedral, Zwingle crossed these eloquent ruins, and once more ascended the pulpit in the midst of an immense crowd. In great emotion, directing his eyes by turns on these fragments and on the people, he said: "Victory has declared for the truth, but perseverance alone can complete the triumph. Christ persevered even until death. *Ferendo vincitur fortuna.* Cornelius Scipio, after the disaster at Cannæ, having learnt that the generals

surviving the slaughter meditated quitting Italy, entered the senate-house, although not yet of senatorial age, and drawing his sword, constrained the affrighted chiefs to swear that they would not abandon Rome. Citizens of Berne, to you I address the same demand : do not abandon Jesus Christ."

We may easily imagine the effect produced on the people by such words, pronounced with Zwingle's energetic eloquence.

Then, turning towards the fragments that lay near him : "Behold," said he, "behold these idols! Behold them conquered, mute, and shattered before us! These corpses must be dragged to the shambles, and the gold you have spent upon such foolish images must henceforward be devoted to comforting in their misery the living images of God. Feeble souls, ye shed tears over these sad idols; do ye not see that they break, do ye not hear that they crack like any other wood, or like any other stone? Look! here is one deprived of its head...... (Zwingle pointed to the image, and all the people fixed their eyes upon it); here is another maimed of its arms.[1] If this ill usage had done any harm to the saints that are in heaven, and if they had the power ascribed to them, would you have been able, I pray, to cut off their arms and their heads?"

"Now, then," said the powerful orator in conclusion, "stand fast in the liberty wherewith Christ has made you free, and be not entangled again with the yoke of bondage (Gal. v. 1). Fear not! That God who has enlightened you, will enlighten your confederates also, and Switzerland, regenerated by the Holy Ghost, shall flourish in righteousness and peace."

The words of Zwingle were not lost. The mercy of God called forth that of man. Some persons condemned to die for sedition were pardoned, and all the exiles were recalled. "Should we not have done so," said the council, "had a great prince visited us? Shall we not much more do so, now that the King of kings and the Redeemer of our souls has made his entry among us, bearing an everlasting amnesty?"[2]

The Romish cantons, exasperated at the result of the discussion, sought to harass the return of the doctors. On arriving before Bremgarten, they found the gates closed. The bailiff Schutz, who had accompanied them with two hundred men-at-arms, placed two halberdiers before Zwingle's horse, two behind him, and one on each side ; then putting himself at the reformer's left hand, while the burgomaster Roust stationed himself on the right, he ordered the escort to proceed, lance in rest.[3] The avoyers of the town, being intimidated, came to a parley ; the

---

[1] Pueri in plateis cantant : se esse a Deo pisto liberatos. L. Epp. iii. 290.
[2] History of Berne, by Tillier, iii. 257.
[3] Si studiorum quam scortorum nostri episcopi amantiores essent. Ruchat, i. 576. Letter of J. de Munster, priest at Soleure.

[1] Hie lüt einer, dem ist's houpt ab, dem andern ein arm. &c. Zw. Opp. ii. 228.
[2] Da der König aller Könige....Haller, by Kirchhofer, p. 439.
[3] Mit iren Spyessen für den hauffen. Bull. Chr. i. 439.

gates were opened; the escort traversed Bremgarten amidst an immense crowd, and on the 1st of February reached Zurich without accident, which Zwingle re-entered, says Luther, like a conqueror.[1]

The Roman-catholic party did not dissemble the check they had received. " Our cause is falling," said the friends of Rome.[2] " Oh ! that we had had men skilled in the Bible! The impetuosity of Zwingle supported our adversaries ; his ardour was never relaxed. That brute has more knowledge than was imagined.[3] Alas ! alas ! the greater party has vanquished the better."[4]

The Council of Berne, desirous of separating from the pope, relied upon the people. On the 30th of January, messengers going from house to house convoked the citizens ; and on the 2d of February, the burgesses and inhabitants, masters and servants, uniting in the cathedral, and forming but one family, with hands upraised to heaven, swore to defend the two councils in all they should undertake for the good of the State or of the Church.

On the 7th of February 1528, the council published a general edict of Reform, and " threw for ever from the necks of the Bernese the yoke of the four bishops, who," said they, " know well how to shear their sheep, but not how to feed them."[5]

At the same time the reformed doctrines were spreading among the people. In every quarter might be heard earnest and keen dialogues, written in rhyme by Manuel, in which the mass, pale and expiring, and stretched on her deathbed, was loudly calling for all her physicians, and finding their advice useless, at length dictating with a broken voice her last will and testament, which the people received with loud bursts of laughter.

The Reformation generally, and that of Berne in particular, has been reproached as being brought about by political motives. But, on the contrary, Berne, which of all the Helvetic states was the greatest favourite of the court of Rome—which had in its canton neither bishop to dismiss nor powerful clergy to humiliate—Berne, whose most influential families, the Weingartens, Manuels, Mays, were reluctant to sacrifice the pay and the service of the foreigner, and all whose traditions were conservative, ought to have opposed the movement. The Word of God was the power that overcame this political tendency.[6]

At Berne, as elsewhere, it was neither a learned, nor a democratic, nor a sectarian spirit that gave birth to the Reformation. Undoubtedly the men of letters, the liberals,

the sectarian enthusiasts, rushed into the great struggle of the sixteenth century ; but the duration of the Reform would not have been long had it received its life from them. The primitive strength of Christianity, reviving after ages of long and complete prostration, was the creative principle of the Reformation ; and it was erelong seen separating distinctly from the false allies that had presented themselves, rejecting an incredulous learning by elevating the study of the classics, checking all demagogic anarchy by upholding the principles of true liberty, and repudiating the enthusiastic sects by consecrating the rights of the Word and of the christian people.

But while we maintain that the Reformation was at Berne, as elsewhere, a truly christian work, we are far from saying that it was not useful to the canton in a political sense. All the European states that have embraced the Reformation have been elevated, while those which have combated it have been lowered.

CHAPTER III.

The Reform accepted by the People—Faith, Purity, and Charity—First Evangelical Communion—Bernese Proposition to the Diet—Cavern, and Head of Beatus—Threatening Storm from the Mountains—Revolt—Confusion in Berne—Unterwalden crosses the Brunig—Energy of Berne—Victory—Political Advantages.

IT now became a question of propagating throughout all the canton the Reform accomplished in the city. On the 17th February, the council invited the rural parishes to assemble on the following Sunday to receive and deliberate upon a communication. The whole Church, according to the ancient usage of Christendom, was about to decide for itself on its dearest interests.

The assemblies were crowded ; all conditions and ages were present. Beside the hoary and the trembling head of the aged man might be seen the sparkling eye of the youthful herdsman. The messengers of the council first read the edict of the Reformation. They next proclaimed that those who accepted it should remain, and that those who rejected it should withdraw.

Almost all the assembled parishioners remained in their places. An immense majority of the people chose the Bible. In some few parishes this decision was accompanied with energetic demonstrations. At Arberg, Zofingen, Brugg, Arau, and Buren, the images were burnt. " At Stauffberg," it was said, " idols were seen carrying idols, and throwing one another into the flames."[1]

The images and the mass had disappeared

[1] Zwingel triumphator et imperator gloriosus. L. Epp. iii. 290.
[2] Ruunt res nostræ. Letter of the priest J. de Muller, an eyewitness of the discussion. Ruchat, i. 575.
[3] Doctior tamen hæc bellua est quam putabam. Ibid.
[4] Vicitque pars major meliorem. Ibid.
[5] Bull. Chron. i. 466.
[6] Hundeshagen, Conflikte der Bernischen Kirche, p. 22.

[1] Da tregt ein Götz den andern in das fhüwr. Bull. Chron. ii. 1. A man whose business it was to shear the flocks. and who had been nicknamed Götz-scherer (idol-snearer), had made himself very distinguished among those who carried the images to the fire. Such was the origin o this popular legend, and it is the key to many others.

from this vast canton. "A great cry resounded far and wide," writes Bullinger.[1] In one day Rome had fallen throughout the country, without treachery, violence, or seduction, by the strength of truth alone. In some places, however, in the Hasli, at Frutigen, Unterseen, and Grindewald, the malcontents were heard to say: "If they abolish the mass, they should also abolish tithes." The Roman form of worship was preserved in the Upper Simmenthal, a proof that there was no compulsion on the part of the state.

The wishes of the canton being thus manifested, Berne completed the Reformation. All excesses in gambling, drinking, and dancing, and all unbecoming dress, were forbidden by proclamation. The houses of ill-fame were destroyed, and their wretched inhabitants expelled from the city.[2] A consistory was appointed to watch over the public morals.

Seven days after the edict, the poor were received into the Dominican cloister, and a little later the convent of the Island was changed into an hospital; the princely monastery of Königsfield was also devoted to the same useful purpose. Charity followed every where in the steps of faith. "We will show," said the council, "that we do not use the property of the convents to our own advantage;" and they kept their word. The poor were clothed with the priests' garments; the orphans decorated with the ornaments of the church. So strict were they in these distributions, that the state was forced to borrow money to pay the annuities of the monks and nuns; and for eight days there was not a crown in the public treasury.[3] Thus it was that the State, as it has been continually asserted, grew rich with the spoils of the Church! At the same time they invited from Zurich the ministers Hofmeister, Megander, and Rhellican, to spread throughout the canton the knowledge of the classics and of the Holy Scriptures.

At Easter the Lord's Supper was celebrated for the first time according to the evangelical rites. The two councils and all the people, with few exceptions, partook of it. Strangers were struck with the solemnity of this first communion. The citizens of Berne and their wives, dressed in decent garments, which recalled the ancient Swiss simplicity, approached Christ's table with gravity and fervour;[4] the heads of the state showed the same holy devotion as the people, and piously received the bread from the hands of Berthold Haller. Each one felt that the Lord was among them; and hence Hofmeister, charmed at this solemn service, exclaimed: "How can the adversaries of the Word re-

fuse to embrace the truth at last, seeing that God himself renders it so striking a testimony!"[1]

Yet every thing was not changed. The friends of the Gospel witnessed with pain the sons of the chief families of the republic parading the streets in costly garments, inhabiting sumptuous houses in the city, dwelling in magnificent mansions in the country, — true seignorial abodes, — following the chase with hound and horn, sitting down to luxurious banquets, conversing in licentious language, or talking with enthusiasm of foreign wars and of the French party. "Ah!" said the pious people, "could we but see old Switzerland revive with its ancient virtues!"

There was soon a powerful reaction. The annual renewal of the magistracy being about to take place, the councillor Butschelbach, a violent adversary of the Gospel, was ejected for adultery; four other senators and twenty members of the Great Council were also replaced by friends of the Reformation and of public morality. Emboldened by this victory, the evangelical Bernese proposed in the diet that every Swiss should renounce foreign service. At these words the warriors of Lucerne started under their weighty armour, and replied with a haughty smile: "When you have returned to the ancient faith we will listen to your homilies." All the members of the Government, assembled at Berne in sovereign council, resolved to set the example, and solemnly abjured the pay of foreign princes. Thus the Reformation showed its faith by its works.

Another struggle took place. Above the lake of Thun rises a chain of steep rocks, in the midst of which is situated a deep cavern, where, if we may believe tradition, the pious Breton, Beatus, came in ancient times to devote himself to all the austerities of an ascetic life; but especially to the conversion of the surrounding district that was still heathen. It was affirmed that the head of this saint, who had died in Gaul, was preserved in this cavern; and hence pilgrims resorted thither from every quarter. The pious citizens of Zug, Schwytz, Uri, and Argovia, groaned, as they thought that the holy head of the apostle of Switzerland would hereafter remain in a land of heretics. The abbot of the celebrated convent of Muri in Argovia and some of his friends set out, as in ancient times the Argonauts went in quest of the golden fleece. They arrived in the humble guise of poor pilgrims, and entered the cavern; one skilfully took away the head, another placed it mysteriously in his hood, and they disappeared. The head of a dead man!—and this was all that Rome saved from the shipwreck. But even this conquest was more than doubtful. The Bernese, who had gained information of the procession, sent three deputies on

---

[1] Das wyt und breit ein gross geschrey und wunder gepar. Bull. Chron. ii. 1.
[2] J. J. Hottinger, iii. 414.
[3] Hoc unum tibi dico secretissime. Haller to Zwingle, 31st January 1530.
[4] Relucet enim in illorum vestitu et habitu nescio quid veteris illius Helvetiæ simplicitatis. Hofmeister to Zwingle. Zw. Epp. ii. 167.

[1] Ea res magnam spem mihi injecit de illis lucrandis qui hactenu fuerunt male morigeri verbo. Zw. Epp. ii. 167.

the 18th of May, who, according to their report, found this famous head, and caused it to be decently interred before their eyes in the cemetery belonging to the convent of Interlaken. This contest about a skull characterizes the Church that had just given way in Berne before the vivifying breath of the Gospel. *Let the dead bury their dead.*

The Reformation had triumphed in Berne; but a storm was gathering unperceived in the mountains, which threatened to overthrow it. The State in union with the Church recalled its ancient renown. Seeing itself attacked by arms, it took up arms in its turn, and acted with that decision which had formerly saved Rome in similar dangers.

A secret discontent was fermenting among the people of the valleys and mountains. Some were still attached to the ancient faith; others had only quitted the mass because they thought they would be exempted from tithes. Ancient ties of neighbourhood, a common origin, and similarity of manners, had united the inhabitants of the Obwald (Unterwalden) to those of the Hasli and of the Bernese Oberland, which were separated only by Mount Brunig and the high pass of the Yoke. A rumour had been set afloat that the government of Berne had profaned the spot where the precious remains of Beatus, the apostle of these mountains, were preserved, and indignation immediately filled these pastoral people, who adhere firmer than others to the customs and superstitions of their forefathers.

But while some were excited by attachment to Rome, others were aroused by a desire for liberty. The subjects of the monastery of Interlaken, oppressed by the monkish rule, began to cry out, " We desire to become our own masters, and no longer pay rent or tithes." The provost of the convent in affright ceded all his rights to Berne for the sum of one hundred thousand florins;[1] and a bailiff accompanied by several councillors, went and took possession of the monastery. A report was soon spread that they were about to transfer all the property of the convent to Berne; and on the 21st April bands of men from Grindelwald, Lauterbrunnen, Ringelberg, Brienz, and other places, crossed the lake, or issued from their lofty valleys, and taking forcible possession of the cloister, swore they would go even to Berne in quest of the goods which the citizens had dared take from them.

They were quieted for a time; but in the beginning of June, the people, at the instigation of Unterwalden, again arose in all the Hasli. The *Landsgemeinde*[2] having been convoked, it decided by a majority of forty voices for the re-establishment of the mass. The pastor Jaëkli was immediately expelled; a few men crossed the Brunig, and brought

back some priests from Unterwalden, to the sound of fifes and trumpets. They were seen from afar descending the mountain, and shouts, both loud and long, replied to them from the bottom of the valley. At last they arrived:—all embraced one another, and the people celebrated the mass anew with great demonstrations of joy. At the same time, the people of Frutigen and of the fertile valley of Adelboden assailed the castellan Reuter, carried off his flocks, and established a Roman-catholic priest in the place of their pastor. At Aeschi even the women took up arms, drove out the pastor from the church, and brought back the images in triumph. The revolt spread from hamlet to hamlet and from valley to valley, and again took possession of Interlaken. All the malcontents assembled there on the 22d October, and swore, with hands upraised to heaven, boldly to defend their rights and liberty.

The republic was in great danger. All the kings of Europe, and almost all the cantons of Switzerland, were opposed to the Gospel. The report of an army from Austria, destined to interpose in favour of the pope, spread through the reformed cantons.[1] Seditious meetings took place every day,[2] and the people refused to pay their magistrates either quit-rent, service, tithes, or even obedience, unless they shut their eyes to the designs of the Roman-catholics. The council became confused. Amazed and confounded, exposed to the mistrust of some and to the insults of others, they had the cowardice to separate under the pretext of gathering the vintage, and folding their arms, in the presence of this great danger, they waited until a Messiah should descend from heaven (says a reformer) to save the republic.[3] The ministers pointed out the danger, forewarned and conjured them; but they all turned a deaf ear. " Christ languishes in Berne," said Haller, " and appears nigh perishing."[4] The people were in commotion : they assembled, made speeches, murmured, and shed tears ! Every where—in all their tumultuous meetings—might be heard this complaint of Manuel on Papists and the Papacy :[5]

With rage our foes their hateful threats denounce,
Because, O Lord, we love Thee best of all ;
Because at sight of Thee the idols fall ;
And war and bloodshed, shuddering, we renounce.

Berne was like a troubled sea, and Haller, who listened to the roaring of the waves, wrote in the deepest anguish : " Wisdom has forsaken the wise, counsel has departed from the councillors, and energy from the chiefs and from the people. The number of the seditious augments every day. Alas ! what

---

[1] Totum regnum suum tradiderunt in manus magistratus nostri. Haller to Zwingle, 31st March.
[2] The assembly of all the people.

[1] Audisti nimirum quam se apparent *Austriaci* ad bellum, adversus quos ignoratur. Suspicantur quidam in Helvetios. Œcol. to Zw. Epp. ii. 161.
[2] Seditiosorum concursus sunt quotidiani. Zw. Epp. ii. 227.
[3] Nunc, nunc suum Messiam advenisse sperantes. Ibid.
[4] Ita languet Christus apud nos. Ibid.
[5] Dass wir hand d' Gotzen geworfen hin. Hymn and Prayer.

can the Bear, oppressed with sleep, oppose to so many and to such sturdy hunters?[1] If Christ withdraw himself, we shall all perish."

These fears were on the point of being realized. The smaller cantons claimed to have the power of interfering in matters of faith without infringing the federal compact. While six hundred men of Uri kept themselves ready to depart, eight hundred men of Unterwalden, bearing pine-branches in their hats, symbols of the old faith, with haughty heads, and gloomy, threatening looks, crossed the Brunig under the ancient banner of the country, which was carried by Gaspard de Flue, a very unworthy grandson of the great Nicholas.[2] This was the first violation of the national peace for many a year. Uniting at Brienz with the men of Hasli, this little army crossed the lake passed under the cascades of Giesbach, and arrived at Unterseen, thirteen hundred strong, and ready to march on Berne to re-establish the pope, the idols, and the mass in that rebellious city. In Switzerland, as in Germany, the Reformation at its outset met with a peasant war. At the first success, new combatants would arrive and pour through the passes of the Brunig upon the unfaithful republic. The army was only six leagues from Berne, and already the sons of Unterwalden were proudly brandishing their swords on the banks of the lake of Thun.

Thus were federal alliances trodden under foot by those very persons who aspired to the name of conservatives. Berne had the right to repel this criminal attack by force. Suddenly calling to mind her ancient virtues, the city roused herself, and vowed to perish rather than tolerate the intervention of Unterwalden, the restoration of the mass, and the fiery violence of the peasants.[3] There was at that moment in the hearts of the Bernese one of those inspirations that come from above, and which save nations as well as individuals. "Let the strength of the city of Berne," exclaimed the avoyer d'Erlach, "be in God alone, and in the loyalty of its people." All the council and the whole body of the citizens replied by noisy acclamations. The great banner was hastily brought forth, the townspeople ran to arms, the companies assembled, and the troops of the republic marched out with the valiant avoyer at their head.

Scarcely had the Bernese government acted thus energetically, before it saw the confidence of its friends increase, and the courage of its adversaries diminish. God never abandons a people who are true to themselves. Many of the Oberlanders became intimidated, and deserted the ranks of the revolt. At the same time deputies from Basle and Lucerne represented to Unterwalden that it was trampling the ancient alliances under foot. The rebels, disheartened by the firmness of the republic, abandoned Unterseen, and retired to the convent of Interlaken. And soon after, when they beheld the decision of their adversaries, distressed besides by the cold rains that fell incessantly, and fearing that the snow, by covering the mountains, would prevent their return to their homes, the men of Unterwalden evacuated Interlaken during the night. The Bernese, to the number of five thousand men, entered it immediately, and summoned the inhabitants of the Hasli and of the bailiwick of Interlaken to assemble on the 4th November in the plain that surrounds the convent.[1] The day being arrived, the Bernese army drew up in order of battle, and then formed a circle within which D'Erlach ordered the peasants to enter. Hardly had he placed the rebels on the left, and the loyal citizens on the right, before the muskets and artillery fired a general discharge, whose report re-echoing among the mountains filled the insurgents with terror. They thought it the signal of their death. But the avoyer only intended to show that they were in the power of the republic. D'Erlach, who addressed them immediately after this strange exordium, had not finished his speech, before they all fell on their knees, and, confessing their crime, begged for pardon. The republic was satisfied: the rebellion was over. The banners of the district were carried to Berne, and the Eagle of Interlaken, in union with the Wildgoat of Hasli, hung for a time beneath the Bear, as a trophy of this victory. Four of the chiefs were put to death, and an amnesty was granted to the remainder of the rebels. "The Bernese," said Zwingle, "as Alexander of Macedon in times of old, have cut the Gordian knot with courage and with glory."[2] Thus thought the reformer of Zurich; but experience was one day to teach him, that to cut such knots requires a different sword from that of Alexander and of D'Erlach. However that may be, peace was restored, and in the valleys of the Hasli no other noise was heard than the sublime tumult borne afar by the Reichenbach and the surrounding torrents, as they pour from the mountaintops their multitudinous and foaming waters.

While we repudiate on behalf of the Church the swords of the Helvetic bands, it would be unwise not to acknowledge the political advantages of this victory. The nobles had imagined that the Reformation of the Church would endanger the very existence of the State. They now had a proof to the contrary: they saw that when a nation receives the Gospel, its strength is doubled. The

---

[1] Quid hæc inter tot et tantos venatores robustos. Zw. Epp. ii. 223.
[2] A celebrated hermit who prevented a civil war in Switzerland in 1481.
[3] Quam missam reducem aut violentiam villanorum pati. Haller to Zwingle, 26th October.

[1] Tradition says that it was on the spot where the hotel of Interlaken now stands.
[2] Bernenses pro sua dignitate nodum hunc, quemadmodum Alexander Macedo, Gordium dissectari. Zw. Epp. ii. 243.

generous confidence with which, in the hour of danger, they had placed some of the adversaries of the Reformation, at the head of affairs and of the army, produced the happiest results. All were now convinced that the Reformation would not trample old recollections under foot: prejudices were removed, hatred was appeased, the Gospel gradually rallied all hearts around it, and then was verified the ancient and remarkable saying, so often repeated by the friends and enemies of that powerful republic—" God is become a citizen of Berne."

CHAPTER IV.

Reformation of St. Gall—Nuns of St. Catherine—Reformation of Glaris, Berne, Appenzell, the Grisons, Schaffhausen, and the Rhine District—A Popish Miracle—Obstacles in Basle—Zeal of the Citizens—Œcolampadius marries—Witticism of Erasmus—First Action—Half Measures—Petition of the Reformed.

THE reformation of Berne was decisive for several cantons. The same wind that had blown from on high with so much power on the country of De Watteville and Haller, threw down " the idols " in a great part of Switzerland. In many places the people were indignant at seeing the Reformation checked by the timid prudence of diplomatists; but when diplomacy was put to flight at Berne, the torrent so long restrained poured violently onwards.

Vadian, burgomaster of St. Gall, who presided at the Bernese disputation, had scarcely returned home, when the citizens, with the authority of the magistrates, removed the images from the church of St. Magnus, carried to the mint a hand of the patron saint in silver, with other articles of plate, and distributed among the poor the money they received in exchange ; thus, like Mary, pouring their precious ointment on the head of Christ.[1] The people of St. Gall, being curious to unveil the ancient mysteries, laid their hands on the abbey itself, on the shrines and crosses which had so long been presented to their adoration ; but instead of saintly relics, they found, to their great surprise, nothing but some resin, a few pieces of money, several paltry wooden images, some old rags, a skull, a large tooth, and a snail's shell ! Rome, instead of that noble fall which marks the ends of great characters, sunk in the midst of stupid superstitions, shameful frauds, and the ironical laughter of a whole nation.

Such discoveries unfortunately excited the passions of the multitude. One evening some evil-disposed persons, wishing to alarm the poor nuns of St. Catherine, who had obstinately resisted the Reform, surrounded the convent with loud cries. In vain did the nuns barricade the doors: the walls were soon scaled, and the good wine, meat, con-

fectionaries, and all the far from ascetic delicacies of the cloister became the prey of these rude jesters. Another persecution awaited them. Doctor Schappeler having been appointed their catechist, they were recommended to lay aside their monastic dress, and to attend his heretical sermons " clothed like all the world," said the sister Wiborath. Some of them embraced the Reform, but thirty others preferred exile.[1] On the 5th February of 1528, a numerous synod framed the constitution of the church of St. Gall.

The struggle was more violent at Glaris. The seeds of the Gospel truth, which Zwingle had scattered there, prospered but little. The men in power anxiously rejected every innovation, and the people loved better " to leap and dance, and work miracles, *glass in hand*," as an old chronicle says, " than to busy themselves about the Gospel." The Landsgemeinde having pronounced, on the 15th May of 1528, in favour of the mass by a majority of thirty-three voices, the two parties were marked out with greater distinctness : the images were broken at Matt, Elm, and Bettschwanden, and as each man remained aloof in his own house and village, there was no longer in the canton either council of state or tribunal of justice. At Schwanden, the minister Peter Rumelin, having invited the Roman-catholics to a disputation with him in the church, the latter, instead of discussing, marched in procession to the sound of drums round the place of worship in which the Reformed were assembled, and then rushing into the pastor's house, which was situated in the middle of the city, destroyed the stoves and the windows: the irritated Reformed took their revenge and broke the images. On the 15th of April 1529, an agreement was concluded by virtue of which every man was free to choose between the mass and the sermon.

At Wesen, where Schwytz exercised sovereignty conjointly with Glaris, the deputies of the former canton threatened the people. Upon this the young men took the images out of the churches, carried them to an open place near the banks of the picturesque lake of Wallenstadt, above which soar the mountains of the Ammon and of the Seven Electors, and cried : " Look ! this road (that by the lake) leads to Coire and to Rome ; that (to the south) to Glaris ; this other (to the west) to Schwytz; and the fourth (by the Ammon) to St. Gall. Take which you please ! But if you do not move off, you shall be burnt !" After waiting a few moments, these young people flung the motionless images into the fire, and the Schwytz deputies, eye-witnesses of this execution, withdrew in consternation, and filled the whole canton with projects of vengeance that were but too soon realized.

In the canton of Appenzell, where a con-

---

[1] War gemünzet und den Armen ausgetheilt. J. J. Hottinger, iii. 415. St. Matthew xxvi. 7.

[1] Arx. Gesch. St. Gall, ii. 529. J. J. Hottinger, 416. Müller; Hottinger, ii. 91.

ference had been opened, there suddenly appeared a band of Roman-catholics, armed with whips and clubs, and crying out: " Where are these preachers? we are resolved to put them out of the village." These strange doctors wounded the ministers and dispersed the assembly with their whips. Out of the eight parishes of the canton, six embraced the Reform, and Apenzell became finally divided into two little sections, the one Romanist and the other Reformed.

In the Grisons religious liberty was proclaimed; the parishes had the election of their pastors, several castles were rased to the ground to render all return to arbitrary government impossible, and the affrighted bishop went and hid in the Tyrol his anger and his desire for vengeance. "The Grisons," said Zwingle, " advance daily. It is a nation that by its courage reminds us of the ancient Tuscans, and by its candour of the ancient Swiss."[1]

Schaffhausen, after having long " halted between two opinions," at the summons of Zurich and of Berne removed the images from its churches without tumult or disorder. At the same time the Reformation invaded Thurgovia, the valley of the Rhine, and other bailiwicks subordinate to these cantons. In vain did the Roman-catholic cantons, that were in the majority, protest against it. " When temporal affairs are concerned," replied Zurich and Berne, " we will not oppose a plurality of votes; but the Word of God cannot be subjected to the suffrages of men." All the districts that lie along the banks of the Thur, of the Lake of Constance, and of the Upper Rhine, embraced the Gospel. The inhabitants of Mammeren, near the place where the Rhine issues from the lake, flung their images into the water. But the statue of St. Blaise, after remaining some time upright, and contemplating the ungrateful spot whence it was banished, swam across the lake to Catahorn, situated on the opposite shore, if we may believe the account of a monk named Lang.[2] Even while running away, Popery worked its miracles.

Thus were the popular superstitions overthrown in Switzerland, and sometimes not without violence. Every great development in human affairs brings with it an energetic opposition to that which has existed. It necessarily contains an aggressive element, which ought to act freely, and by that means open the new path. In the times of the Reformation the doctors attacked the pope, and the people the images. The movement almost always exceeded a just moderation. In order that human nature may make one step in advance, its pioneers must take many. Every superfluous step should be condemned, and yet we must acknowledge

their necessity. Let us not forget this in the history of the Reformation, and especially in that of Switzerland.

Zurich was reformed; Berne had just become so; Basle still remained, before the great cities of the Confederation were gained over to the evangelical faith. The reformation of this learned city was the most important consequence resulting from that of the warlike Berne.

For six years the Gospel had been preached in Basle. The meek and pious Œcolampadius was always waiting for happier times. " The darkness," said he, " is about to retire before the rays of truth."[1] But his expectation was vain. A triple aristocracy—the superior clergy, the nobles, and the university—checked the free expansion of christian convictions. It was the middle classes who were destined to effect the triumph of the Reformation in Basle.[2] Unhappily the popular wave invades nothing without tossing up some foul scum.

It is true that the Gospel had many friends in the councils: but being men of a middle party, they tacked backwards and forwards like Erasmus, instead of sailing straight to the port. They ordered " the pure preaching of the Word of God;" but stipulated at the same time that it should be " without Lutheranism." The aged and pious Bishop Utenheim, who was living in retirement at Bruntrut, tottered daily into the church, supported by two domestics, to celebrate mass with a broken voice. Gundelsheim, an enemy of the Reformation, succeeded him erelong; and on the 23d September, followed by many exiles and with a train of forty horses, he made his triumphal entry into Basle, proposing to restore every thing to its ancient footing. This made Œcolampadius write in alarm to Zwingle: " Our cause hangs upon a thread."

But in the citizens the Reform found a compensation for the disdain of the great, and for the terrors inspired by the new bishop. They organized repasts for fifty and a hundred guests each; Œcolampadius and his colleagues took their seats at these tables with the people, where energetic acclamations and reiterated cheers greeted the work of the Reformation. In a short time even the council appeared to incline to the side of the Gospel. Twenty feast-days were retrench- and the priests were permitted to ref.. brating the mass. " It is all ove.. .... Rome," was now the cry. But Œcolampadius, shaking his head, replied : " I am afraid that, by wishing to sit on two stools, Basle will at last fall to the ground."[3]

This was at the period of his return from the discussion at Berne. He arrived in time

1 Gens animo veteres Tuscos referens, candore veteres Helvetios. Zw. Epp.
2 J. J. Hottinger, iii. 426.

1 Sperabam enim tenebras veritatis radio cessuras tandem. Zw. Epp. ii. 136.
2 Major pars civitatis quæ toto corde dolet tantis nos disidiis laborare. Ibid. 36.
3 Vereorque ne dum semper utraque sella sedere velit, utraque extrudatur aliquando. Ibid. 157.

to close the eyes of his pious mother; and then the reformer found himself alone, succumbing under the weight of public and domestic cares; for his house was like an inn for all fugitive Christians. "I shall marry a Monica,"[1] he had often said, " or else I shall remain a bachelor." He thought he had now discovered the "christian sister" of whom he was in search. This was Wilibrandis, daughter of one of the Emperor Maximilian's knights, and widow of a master of arts named Keller,—a woman already proved by many trials. He married her, saying: " I look to the ordinances of God, and not to the scowling faces of men." This did not prevent the sly Erasmus from exclaiming: " Luther's affair is called a tragedy, but I maintain it is a comedy, for each act of the drama ends in a wedding." This witticism has been often repeated. For a long time it was the fashion to account for the Reformation by the desire of the princes for the church-property, and of the priests for marriage. This vulgar method is now stigmatized by the best Roman controversialists as " a proof of a singularly narrow mind.— The Reformation originated," add they, " in a true and christian, although unenlightened zeal."[2]

The return of Œcolampadius had still more important consequences for Basle than it had for himself. The discussion at Berne caused a great sensation there. " Berne, the powerful Berne, is reforming!" was passed from mouth to mouth. "How, then!" said the people one to another, "the fierce Bear has come out of his den......he is groping about for the rays of the sun......and Basle, the city of learning—Basle, the adopted city of Erasmus and of Œcolampadius, remains in darkness!"

On Good Friday (10th April 1528), without the knowledge of the council and Œcolampadius, five workmen of the Spinners' Company entered the church of St. Martin, which was that of the reformer, and where the mass was already abolished, and carried away all the "idols." On Easter Monday, after the evening sermon, thirty-four citizens removed all the images from the church of the Augustines.

This was going too far. Were they desirous, then, of drawing Basle and its councils from that just medium in which they had till this moment so wisely halted? The council met hastily on Tuesday morning, and sent the five men to prison; but, on the intercession of the burghers, they were released, and the images suppressed in five other churches. These half-measures sufficed for a time.

On a sudden the flame burst out anew with greater violence. Sermons were preached at St. Martin's and St. Leonard's against the abominations of the cathedral; and at the cathedral the reformers were called " heretics, knaves, and profligates."[1] The papists celebrated mass upon mass. The burgomaster Meyer, a friend of the Reform, had with him the majority of the people; the burgomaster Meltinger, an intrepid leader of the partisans of Rome, prevailed in the councils: a collision became inevitable. " The fatal hour approaches," says Œcolampadius, " terrible for the enemies of God!"[2]

On Wednesday the 23d December, two days before Christmas, three hundred citizens from all the companies, pious and worthy men, assembled in the hall of the Gardeners' Company, and there drew up a petition to the senate. During this time the friends of popery, who resided for the most part in Little Basle and the suburb of St. Paul, took up arms, and brandished their swords and lances against the reformed citizens at the very moment that the latter were bearing their petition to the council, and endeavoured, although ineffectually, to bar their road. Meltinger haughtily refused to receive the petition, and charged the burghers, on the faith of their civic oath, to return to their homes. The burgomaster Meyer, however, took the address, and the senate ordered it to be read.

" Honoured, wise, and gracious Lords," it ran, " we, your dutiful fellow-citizens of the companies, address you as well-beloved fathers, whom we are ready to obey at the cost of our goods and of our lives. Take God's glory to heart; restore peace to the city; and oblige all the pope's preachers to discuss freely with the ministers. If the mass be true, we desire to have it in our churches; but if it is an abomination before God, why, through love for the priests, should we draw down His terrible anger upon ourselves and upon our children?"

Thus spoke the citizens of Basle. There was nothing revolutionary either in their language or in their proceedings. They desired what was right with decision, but also with calmness. All might still proceed with order and decorum. But here begins a new period: the vessel of reform is about to enter the port, but not until it has passed through violent storms.

CHAPTER V.

Crisis in Basle—Half-measures rejected—Reformed Propositions—A Night of Terror—Idols broken in the Cathedral—The Hour of Madness—Idols broken in all the Churches—Reform legalized—Erasmus in Basle—A great Transformation—Revolution and Reformation.

THE bishop's partisans first departed from the legal course. Filled with terror on learn-

1 The name of St. Augustine's mother.
2 See Möhler's *Symbolik*, both in the preface and in the body of the work. This is one of the most important writings produced by Rome since the time of Bossuet.

1 Ketzer, schelmen, und büben. Bulling. ii. 36.
2 Maturatur fatalis hora et tremenda hostibus Dei. Zw. Epp. ii. 213.

ing that mediators were expected from Zurich and Berne, they ran into the city, crying that an Austrian army was coming to their aid, and collected stones in their houses. The reformed did the same. The disturbance increased hourly, and in the night of the 25th December the Papists met under arms : priests with arquebuse in hand were numbered among their ranks.

Scarcely had the reformed learnt this, when some of them running hastily from house to house, knocked at the doors and awoke their friends, who, starting out of bed, seized their muskets and repaired to the Gardeners' Hall, the rendezvous of their party. They soon amounted to three thousand.

Both parties passed the night under arms. At every moment a civil war, and what is worse, " a war of hearths," might break out. It was at last agreed that each party should nominate delegates to treat with the senate on this matter. The reformed chose thirty men of respectability, courage, faith, and experience, who took up their quarters at the Gardeners' Hall. The partisans of the ancient faith chose also a commission, but less numerous and less respectable : their station was at the Fishmongers' Hall. The council was constantly sitting. All the gates of the city, except two, were closed ; strong guards were posted in every quarter. Deputies from Lucerne, Uri, Schaffhausen, Zug, Schwytz, Mulhausen, and Strasburg, arrived successively. The agitation and tumult increased from hour to hour.

It was necessary to put an end to so violent a crisis. The senate, faithful to its ideas of half-measures, decreed that the priests should continue to celebrate the mass ; but that all, priests and ministers alike, should preach the Word of God, and for this purpose should meet once a-week to confer upon the Holy Scriptures. They then called the Lutherans together in the Franciscan church, and the Papists in that belonging to the Dominicans. The senate first repaired to the former church, where they found two thousand five hundred citizens assembled. The secretary had hardly read the ordinance before a great agitation arose. " That shall not be," cried one of the people,[1] " We will not put up with the mass, not even a single one ! " exclaimed another ; and all repeated, " No mass,—no mass,—we will die sooner ! "[2]

The senate having next visited the Dominican church, all the Romanists, to the number of six hundred, among whom were many foreign servants, cried out : " We are ready to sacrifice our lives for the mass. We swear it, we swear it !" repeated they with uplifted hands. " If they reject the mass— to arms ! to arms ! "[3]

The senate withdrew more embarrassed than ever.

The two parties again assembled three days after. Œcolampadius was in the pulpit. " Be meek and tractable," said he ; and he preached with such unction that many were ready to burst into tears.[1] The assembly offered up prayers, and then decreed that it would accept a new ordinance, by virtue of which, fifteen days after Pentecost, there should be a public disputation, in which no arguments should be employed but such as were drawn from the Word of God : after this a general vote should take place upon the mass, that the majority should decide the question, and that in the meanwhile the mass should be celebrated in three churches only ; it being however understood, that nothing should be taught there that was in opposition to the Holy Scriptures.

The Romanist minority rejected these propositions : " Basle," said they, " is not like Berne and Zurich. Its revenues are derived in great measure from countries opposed to the Reformation ! " The priests having refused to resort to the weekly conferences, they were suspended ; and during a fortnight there was neither sermon nor mass at the cathedral, or in the churches of St. Ulric, St. Peter, and St. Theodore.

Those who remained faithful to Rome resolved upon an intrepid defence. Meltinger placed Sebastian Muller in the pulpit at St. Peter's, from which he had been interdicted, and this hot-headed priest vented such abusive sarcasms against the Reform, that several of the evangelicals, who were listening to the sermon, were insulted and nearly torn in pieces.

It was necessary to arouse Basle from this nightmare, and strike a decisive blow. " Let us remember our liberty," said the reformed citizens, " and what we owe to the glory of Christ, to public justice, and to our posterity."[2] They then demanded that the enemies of the Reformation, friends and relations of the priests, who were the cause of all these delays and troubles, should no longer sit in the councils until peace was re-established. This was on the 8th of February. The council notified that they would return an answer on the morrow.

At six o'clock in the evening, twelve hundred citizens were assembled in the corn-market. They began to fear that the delay required by the senate concealed some evil design. " We must have a reply this very night," they said. The senate was convoked in great haste.

From that period affairs assumed a more threatening attitude in Basle. Strong guards were posted by the burghers in the halls of the different guilds ; armed men patrolled

---

[1] Quidam e plebe clamitabat : Hoc non fiet ! Zw. Epp. ii. 255.
[2] Nos plane ea non feremus, aut moriemur omnes. Ibid.
[3] At altera pars minitabat prælia si missam rejicerent. Ibid.

[1] Ut nemo non commoveretur et profecto fere mihi lacrymas excussisset. Zw. Epp. ii. 255.
[2] Cogitans quid gloriæ Christi, quid justitiæ publicæ, quidque posteritati suæ deberet. Œcol. Zurich MS.

the city, and bivouacked in the public places, to anticipate the machinations of their adversaries;[1] the chains were stretched across the streets; torches were lighted, and resinous trees, whose flickering light scattered the darkness, were placed at intervals through the town; six pieces of artillery were planted before the town-hall; and the gates of the city, as well as the arsenal and the ramparts, were occupied. Basle was in a state of siege.

There was no longer any hope for the Romish party. The burgomaster, Meltinger, an intrepid soldier and one of the heroes of Marignan, where he had led eight hundred men into battle, lost courage. In the darkness he gained the banks of the Rhine with his son-in-law, the councillor Eglof d'Offenburgh, embarked unnoticed in a small boat, and rapidly descended the stream amid the fogs of the night.[2] Other members of the council escaped in a similar manner.

This gave rise to new alarms. "Let us beware of their secret manœuvres," said the people. "Perhaps they are gone to fetch the Austrians, with whom they have so often threatened us!" The affrighted citizens collected arms from every quarter, and at break of day they had two thousand men on foot. The beams of the rising sun fell on this resolute but calm assembly.

It was mid-day. The senate had come to no decision: the impatience of the burghers could be restrained no longer. Forty men were detached to visit the posts. As this patrol was passing the cathedral, they entered it, and one of the citizens, impelled by curiosity, opened a closet with his halberd, in which some images had been hidden. One of them fell out, and was broken into a thousand pieces against the stone pavement.[3] The sight of these fragments powerfully moved the spectators, who began throwing down one after another all the images that were concealed in this place. None of them offered any resistance: heads, feet, and hands—all were heaped in confusion before the halberdiers. "I am much surprised," said Erasmus, "that they performed no miracle to save themselves; formerly the saints worked frequent prodigies for much smaller offences."[4] Some priests ran to the spot, and the patrol withdrew.

A rumour, however, having spread that a disturbance had taken place in this church, three hundred men came to the support of the forty. "Why," said they, "should we spare the idols that light up the flames of discord?" The priests in alarm had closed the gates of the sanctuary, drawn the bolts, raised barricades, and prepared every thing for maintaining a siege. But the townspeople, whose patience had been exhausted by the delays of the council, dashed against one of the doors of the church: it yielded to their blows, and they rushed into the cathedral. The hour of madness had arrived. These men were no longer recognizable, as they brandished their swords, rattled their pikes, and uttered formidable cries: were they Goths, or fervent worshippers of God, animated by the zeal which in times of yore inflamed the prophets and the kings of Israel? However that may have been, these proceedings were disorderly, since public authority alone can interfere in public reforms. Images, altars, pictures—all were thrown down and destroyed. The priests who had fled into the vestry and there concealed themselves, trembled in every limb at the terrible noise made by the fall of their holy decorations. The work of destruction was completed without one of them venturing to save the objects of his worship, or to make the slightest remonstrance. The people next piled up the fragments in the squares and set fire to them; and during the chilly night the armed burghers stood round and warmed themselves at the crackling flame.[1]

The senate collected in amazement, and desired to interpose their authority and appease the tumult; but they might as well have striven to command the winds. The enthusiastic citizens replied to their magistrates in these haughty words: "What you have not been able to effect in three years, we will complete in one hour."[2]

In truth the anger of the people was no longer confined to the cathedral. They respected all kinds of private property;[3] but they attacked the churches of St. Peter, St. Ulric, St. Alban, and of the Dominicans; and in all these temples "the idols" fell[1] under the blows of these good citizens of Basle, who were inflamed by an extraordinary zeal. Already they were making preparations to cross the bridge and enter Little Basle, which was devoted to the cause of popery, when the alarmed inhabitants begged to be allowed to remove the images themselves, and with heavy hearts they hastily carried them into the upper chambers of the church, whence they hoped to be able after a time to restore them to their old position.

They did not stop at these energetic demonstrations: the most excited talked of going to the town-hall, and of constraining the senate to accede to the wishes of the people; but the good sense of the majority treated these brawlers as they deserved, and checked their guilty thoughts.

The senators now perceived the necessity of giving a legal character to this popular

---

[1] Ne quid forte ab adversariis insidiarum strueretur. Œcol. Zurich MS.
[2] Clam conscensa navicula fuga, nescio senatu, elapsus est. Ibid.
[3] Cum halpardis quasi per ludum aperirent armarium idolorum, unumque idolum educerent. Ibid.
[4] Erasm. Opp. p. 291.

[1] Lignis imaginum usi sunt vigiles, pro arcendo frigore nocturno. Zurich MS.
[2] De quo vos per triennium deliberâstis, nihil efficientes, nos intra horam omnem absolvemus. Œcol. Capitoni, Basle MS.
[3] Nulli enim vel obolum abstulerunt. Ibid.

movement, and of thus changing a tumultuous revolution into a durable reformation.[1] Democracy and the Gospel were thus established simultaneously in Basle. The senate, after an hour's deliberation, granted that in future the burghers should participate in the election of the two councils; that from this day the mass and images should be abolished throughout all the canton, and that in every deliberation which concerned the glory of God or the good of the state the opinion of the guilds should be taken. The people, delighted at having obtained these conditions, which secured their political and religious liberty, returned joyful to their houses. It was now the close of day.[2]

On the morrow, Ash-Wednesday, it was intended to distribute the ruins of the church altars and other ornaments of the church among the poor, to serve them for firewood. But these unhappy creatures, in their eagerness for the fragments, having begun to dispute about them, great piles were constructed in the cathedral close and set on fire. "The idols," said some wags, "are really keeping their Ash-Wednesday to-day!" The friends of popery turned away their horror-stricken eyes from the sacrilegious sight, says Œcolampadius, and shed tears of blood. "Thus severely did they treat the idols," continues the reformer, "and the mass died of grief in consequence."[3] On the following Sunday hymns in German were sung at every church; and on the 18th February a general amnesty was published. Every thing was changed in Basle. The last had become first, and the first last. While Œcolampadius, who a few years before had entered the city as a stranger, without resources and without power, found himself raised to the first station in the Church, Erasmus, disturbed in the quiet study whence during so long a period he had issued his absolute commands to the world of letters, saw himself compelled to descend into the arena. But this king of the schools had no desire to lay down his sceptre before the sovereign people. For a long time he used to turn aside his head when he met his friend Œcolampadius. Besides, he feared by remaining at Basle to compromise himself with his protectors. "The torrent," said he, "which was hidden underground has burst forth with violence, and committed frightful ravages.[4] My life is in danger: Œcolampadius possesses all the churches. People are continually bawling in my ears; I am besieged with letters, caricatures, and pamphlets. It is all over: I am resolved to leave Basle. Only shall I or shall I not depart by stealth? The one is more becoming, the other more secure."

Wishing as much as possible to make his honour and his prudence agree, Erasmus desired the boatman with whom he was to descend the Rhine to depart from an unfrequented spot. This was opposed by the senate, and the timid philosopher was compelled to enter the boat as it lay near the bridge, at that time covered with a crowd of people. He floated down the river, sadly bade adieu to the city he had so much loved, and retired to Friburg in Brisgau with several other learned men.

New professors were invited to fill the vacant chairs in the university, and in particular Oswald Myconius, Phrygio, Sebastian Munster, and Simon Grynæus. At the same time was published an ecclesiastical order and confession of faith, one of the most precious documents of this epoch.

Thus had a great transformation been effected without the loss of a single drop of blood. Popery had fallen in Basle in despite of the secular and spiritual power. "The wedge of the Lord," says Œcolampadius, "has split this hard knot."[1]

We cannot, however, help acknowledging that the Basle Reformation may afford ground for some objections. Luther had opposed himself to the power of the many. "When the people prick up their ears, do not whistle too loud. It is better to suffer at the hand of one tyrant, that is to say, of a king, than of a thousand tyrants, that is to say, of the people." On this account the German Reformer has been reproached for acknowledging no other policy than servilism.

Perhaps when the Swiss Reformation is canvassed, a contrary objection will be made against it, and the Reform at Basle in particular, will be looked upon as a revolution.

The Reformation must of necessity bear the stamp of the country in which it is accomplished: it will be monarchical in Germany, republican in Switzerland. Nevertheless, in religion as in politics, there is a great difference between reformation and revolution.

In no sphere does Christianity desire either despotism, servitude, stagnation, retrogression, or death. But while looking for progress, it seeks to accomplish it by reformation and not by revolution.

Reformation works by the power of the Word, of doctrine, cultivation, and truth, while revolution, or rather revolt, operates by the power of riot, of the sword, and of the club.

Christianity proceeds by the inner man, and charters themselves, if they stand alone, cannot satisfy it. No doubt political constitutions are one of the blessings of our age; but it is not sufficient for these securities to be committed to parchment; they must be

---

[1] Cedendum plebi. Œcol. Capitoni, Basle MS.
[2] His conditionibus plebs læta domum rediit, sub ipsum noctis crepusculum. Ibid. Zurich MS.
[3] Ita sævitum est in idola, ac missa præ dolore expiravit. Ibid.
[4] Basilica torrens quidem, qui sub terra labebatur, subito erumpens, &c. Err. Epp. ad Pirkheimer, July 1529.

[1] Malo nodo suus cuneus obvenit. Œcol. Capit.

written in the heart, and guaranteed by the manners of the people.

Such were the principles of the Swiss Reformers ; such were those of the Reform at Basle, and by these it is distinguished from a revolution.

There were, it is true, some excesses. Never perhaps has a reformation been accomplished among men without some mixture of revolution. But it was doctrines, however, that were in question at Basle : these doctrines had acted powerfully on the moral convictions and on the lives of the people ; the movement had taken place within before it showed itself without. But more than this : the Reformation was not satisfied with taking away ; it gave more than it took ; and, far from confining itself to the work of destruction, it scattered rich blessings over all the people.[1]

CHAPTER VI.

Farel's Commission—Farel at Lausanne and Morat—Neufchatel—Farel preaches at Serrière—Enters Neufchatel—Sermon—The Monks—Farel's Preaching—Popery in Neufchatel—Canons and Monks unite—Farel at Morat and in the Vuilly—Reformation of the Bishopric of Basle—Farel again in Neufchatel—Placards—The Hospital Chapel—Civil Power invoked by the Romanists.

THE recoil of the discussion at Berne had overthrown Popery in a considerable part of German Switzerland. It was also felt in many of the churches of French Switzerland, lying at the foot of the Jura, or scattered amid the pine-forests of its elevated valleys, and which up to this time had shown the most absolute devotion to the Roman pontiff.

Farel, seeing the Gospel established in the places where the Rhone mingles its sandy waters with the crystal Leman, turned his eyes to another quarter. He was supported by Berne. This state, which possessed jointly with Friburg the bailiwicks of Morat, Orbe, and Granson, and which had alliances with Lausanne, Avenches, Payerne, Neufchatel, and Geneva, saw that both its interest and its duty alike called it to have the Gospel preached to its allies and subjects. Farel was empowered to carry it among them, provided he obtained the consent of the respective governments.

One day, therefore, journeying towards Morat, Farel arrived and preached the Gospel at the foot of those towers and battlements that had been attacked at three different periods by the armies of Conrad the Salic, Rodolph of Hapsburg, and Charles the Bold. Erelong the friends of the Reform amounted to a great number. A general vote having nevertheless declared in favour of the pope, Farel proceeded to Lausanne.

He was at first driven away by the bishop and the clergy, but soon reappeared provided

with a letter from the lords of Berne. " We send him to you," said their excellencies to the authorities of the city, " to defend his own cause and ours. Allow him to preach the Word of God, and beware that you touch not a hair of his head."

There was great confusion in the councils. Placed between Berne and the bishop, what could they do ? The Council of Twenty-four, finding the matter very serious, convoked the Council of Sixty ; and this body excusing itself, they convoked the Council of Two Hundred, on the 14th November 1529. But these in their turn referred the business to the Smaller Council. No one would have any thing to do with it. The inhabitants of Lausanne, it is true, complained loudly of the holy members of their chapters, whose lives (they said) were one long train of excesses ; but when their eyes turned on the austere countenance of the Reform, they were still more terrified. Besides, how deprive Lausanne of her bishop, her court, and her dignitaries ? What ! no more pilgrims in the churches,—no more suitors in the ecclesiastical courts, —no more purchasers in the markets, or boon companions in the taverns ! —The widowed and desolate Lausanne would no longer behold the noisy throng of people, that were at once her wealth and her glory ! —Better far a disorder that enriches, than a reform that impoverishes ! Farel was compelled to depart a second time.

He returned to Morat, and soon the Word gained over the hearts of the people. On feast-days the roads from Payerne and Avenches were covered with merry bands, who laughingly said to one another, " Let us go to Morat and hear the preachers ! " and exhorted each other slily, as they went along the road, " not to fall into the nets of the heretics." But at night, all was changed. Grasped by the strong hand of truth, these very people returned,—some in deep thought, others discussing with animation the doctrines they had heard. The fire was sparkling throughout all this district, and spreading in every direction its long rays of light. This was enough for Farel : he required new conquests.

At a short distance from Morat lay one of the strongholds of Popery—the earldom of Neufchatel. Joan of Hochberg, who had inherited this principality from her ancestors, had married, in 1504, Louis of Orleans, duke of Longueville. This French nobleman having supported the King of France in 1512, in a war against the Swiss, the cantons had taken possession of Neufchatel, but had restored it to his widow in 1529.

Few countries could have presented greater difficulties to the daring reformer. The Princess of Longueville, residing in France in the suite of Francis I., a woman of courtly habits, vain, extravagant, always in debt, and thinking of Neufchatel only as a farm that should bring her in a large revenue, was

[1] Hagenbach, Vorlesungen, ii. 125, 200.

devoted to the Pope and Popery. Twelve canons with several priests and chaplains formed a powerful clergy, at whose head was the provost Oliver of Hochberg, natural brother to the princess. Auxiliaries full of zeal flanked this main army. On the one side there was the abbey of the Premonstrantes of Fontaine-André, three quarters of a league beyond the town, the monks of which, after having in the twelfth century cleared the ground with their own hands,[1] had gradually become powerful lords; and, on the other side, the Benedictines of the Island of St. John, whose abbot, having been deposed by the Bernese, had taken refuge, burning with hatred and vengeance, in his priory at Corcelles.

The people of Neufchatel had a great respect for ancient rights, and it was easy to take advantage of this state of feeling, considering the general ignorance, to maintain the innovations of Popery. The canons improved the opportunity. For the instructions of the Gospel they substituted pomps and shows. The church, situated on a steep rock, was filled with altars, chapels, and images of saints; and religion, descending from this sanctuary, ran up and down the streets, and was travestied in dramas and mysteries, mingled with indulgences, miracles and debauchery.[2]

The soldiers of Neufchatel, however, who had made the campaign of 1529 with the Bernese army brought back to their homes the liveliest enthusiasm for the evangelical cause. It was at this period that a frail boat, quitting the southern bank of the lake, on the side opposite Morat, and carrying a Frenchman of mean appearance, steered towards the Neufchatel shore. Farel, for it was he, had learnt that the village of Serrière, situated at the gates of Neufchatel, depended as to spiritualities on the evangelical city of Bienne, and that Emer Beynon, the priest of the place, "had some liking for the Gospel." The plan of his campaign was immediately drawn up. He appeared before parson Emer, who received him with joy; but what could be done? for Farel had been interdicted from preaching in any church whatever in the earldom. The poor priest thought to reconcile every thing by permitting Farel to mount on a stone in the cemetery, and thus preach to the people, turning his back upon the church.[3]

A great disturbance arose in Neufchatel. On one side the government, the canons, and the priests, cried, "Heresy!" but on the other, "some inhabitants of Neufchatel, to whom God had given a knowledge of the truth,"[4] flocked to Serrière. In a short time these last could not contain themselves: "Come," said they to Farel, "and preach to us in the town."

This was at the beginning of December. They entered by the gate of the castle, and leaving the church on the hill to the left, they passed in front of the canons' houses, and descended to the narrow streets inhabited by the citizens. On reaching the market-cross, Farel ascended a platform and addressed the crowd, which gathered together from all the neighbourhood,—weavers, vine-dressers, and husbandmen,—a worthy race, possessing more feeling than imagination. The preacher's exterior was grave, his discourse energetic, his voice like thunder: his eyes, his features, his gestures, all showed him a man of intrepidity. The citizens, accustomed to run about the streets after the mountebanks, were touched by his powerful language. "Farel preached a sermon of such great efficacy," says a manuscript, "that he gained over much people."[1]

Some monks, however, with shaven crowns[2] glided among his hearers, seeking to excite them against the heretical minister. "Let us beat out his brains," said some. "Duck him, duck him!" cried others, advancing to throw Farel into a fountain, which may still be seen near the spot where he preached. But the reformer stood firm.

This first preaching was succeeded by others. To this Gospel missionary every place was a church; every stone, every bench, every platform was a pulpit. Already the cutting winds and the snows of December should have kept the Neufchatelans around their firesides; "the canons made a vigorous defence;"[3] and in every quarter "the shorn crowns" were in agitation, supplicating, menacing, shouting, and threatening,—but all was useless. No sooner did this man of small stature rise up in any place, with his pale yet sunburnt complexion, with red and uncombed beard, with sparkling eye and expressive mouth, than the monks' labour was lost: the people collected around him, for it was the Word of God that fell from his lips.[4] All eyes were fixed on him: with open mouth and attentive ears they hung upon his words.[5] And scarcely did he begin to speak, when—Oh! wonderful work of God! he himself exclaims—this multitude believed as if it had but one soul.

The Word of God carried the town, as it were, at the first assault: and throwing down the devices Rome had taken ages to compose, established itself in triumph on the ruins of human traditions. Farel saw in imagination Jesus Christ himself walking in spirit through the midst of this crowd, open-

[1] Propriis manibus. Hist. of Neufchatel, by F. de Chambrier, p. 13.
[2] Mémoires sur l'Eglise collégiale de Neufchatel, p. 240.
[3] M. de Perrot, ex-pastor of Serrière, and author of a work entitled "L'Eglise et la Réformation," has shown me the stone on which Farel stood.
[4] "Aucuns de Neufchatel, auxquels Dieu avaient donné connoissance de la vérité," &c. Choupard MS.

[1] Quoted in the Choupard MS.
[2] Rasorum remoramenta. Farellus Molano, Neufchatel MS.
[3] Contra tyrannica præcepta. Ibid.
[4] Ad verbum festinarent. Ibid.
[5] Avide audientes. Ibid.

ing the eyes of the blind, softening the hard heart, and working miracles[1].........so that scarcely had he returned to his humble residence before he wrote to his friends with a heart full of emotion : " Render thanks with me to the Father of mercies, in that he has shown his favour to those bowed down by a weighty tyranny ;" and falling on his knees, he worshipped God.[2]

But during this time what were the adherents of the pope doing in Neufchatel ?

The canons, members of the General Audiences, of which they formed the first estate, treated both priests and laymen with intolerable haughtiness. Laying the burden of their offices on poor curates, they publicly kept dissolute women, clothed them sumptuously, endowed their children by public acts, fought in the church, haunted the streets by night, or went into a foreign country to enjoy in secret the produce of their avarice and of their intrigues. Some poor lepers placed in a house near the city were maintained by the produce of certain offerings. The rich canons, in the midst of their banquets, dared take away the bread of charity from these unhappy wretches.

The Abbey of Fontaine-André was at a little distance from the town. Now the canons of Neufchatel and the monks of Fontaine were at open war. These hostile powers, encamped on their two hills, disputed each other's property, wrested away each other's privileges, launched at one another the coarsest insults, and even came to blows. " Debaucher of women !" said the canons to the Abbot of Fontaine-André, who returned the compliment in the same coin. It is the Reformation which, through faith, has re-established the moral law in Christendom,—a law that Popery had trodden under foot.

For a long time these conventual wars had disturbed the country. On a sudden they ceased. A strange event was passing in Neufchatel,—the Word of God was preached there. The canons, seized with affright in the midst of their disorders, looked down from their lofty dwellings on this new movement. The report reached Fontaine-André. The monks and priests suspended their orgies and their quarrels. The heathen sensualism that had invaded the Church was put to the rout ; Christian spiritualism had reappeared.

Immediately the monks and canons, so long at war, embraced and united against the reformer. " We must save religion," said they, meaning their tithes, banquets, scandals, and privileges. Not one of them could oppose a doctrine to the doctrine preached by Farel: to insult him was their sole weapon. At Corcelles, however, they went farther. As

the minister was proclaiming the Gospel near the priory, the monks fell upon him ; in the midst of them was the prior Rodolph de Benoit, storming, exciting, and striving to augment the tempest. He even had a dagger in his hand, according to one writer.[1] Farel escaped with difficulty.

This was not enough. Popery, as it has always done, had recourse to the civil power. The canons, the abbot, and the prior, solicited the governor George de Rive at the same time. Farel stood firm. " The glory of Jesus Christ," said he, " and the lively affection his sheep bear to his Word, constrain me to endure sufferings greater than tongue can describe."[2] Erelong, however, he was compelled to yield. Farel again crossed the lake ; but this passage was very different from the former. The fire was kindled !—On the 22d December he was at Morat ; and shortly after at Aigle.

He was recalled thence. On the 7th January, religion was put to the vote at Morat. and the majority was in favour of the Gospel. But the Romish minority, supported by Friburg, immediately undertook to recover its ancient position by insults and bad treatment. " Farel ! Farel !" cried the reformed party.[3]

A few days after this, Farel, accompanied by a Bernese messenger, scaled that magnificent amphitheatre of mountains above Vevay, whence the eye plunges into the waters of the Leman ; and soon he crossed the estates of Count John of Gruyère, who was in the habit of saying, " We must burn this French Luther !"[4] Scarcely had Farel reached the heights of Saint Martin de Vaud,[5] when he saw the vicar of the place with two priests running to meet him. " Heretic ! devil !" cried they ; but the knight, through fear of Berne, remained behind his walls, and Farel passed on.

The reformer, not allowing himself to be stopped by the necessity of defending himself in Morat, or by the inclemency of the season, immediately carried the Gospel to those beautiful hills that soar between the smiling waters of lakes Morat and Neufchatel into the villages of the Vully. This manœuvre was crowned with the most complete success. On the 15th February four deputies from the Vully came to Morat to demand permission to embrace the Reform, which was immediately granted them. " Let our ministers preach the Gospel," said their excellencies of Berne to the Friburgers, " and we will let your priests play their monkey tricks. We desire to force no man."[6] The Reform restored freedom of will to the christian people. It was about this time that Farel wrote his

[1] Rosselet in Annotat. Farel Leben von Kirchofer.
[2] At levia facit omnia Christus, added he. Farel to Dumoulin, 15th December. Neufchatel MS.
[3] Choupard MS. Chambrier, Hist. de Neufchatel, p. 293.
[4] Missive of Berne to the Count of Gruyère, 5th and 16th January 1530.
[5] To the left of the modern road from Vevay to Friburg.
[6] Missive of Berne, Choupard MS.

[1] Quid Christus in suis egerit. Farellus Molano, Neufshatel MS.
[2] Gratias ergo, Fratres, mecum agite Patri misericordiarum, quod sit propitius gravi pressis tirannide. Ibid.

beautiful letter " To all lords, people, and pastors," which we have so often quoted.[1]

The indefatigable reformer now went forward to new conquests. A chain of rocks separates the Juran valley of Erguel, already evangelized by Farel, from the country of the ancient Rauraci, and a passage cut through the rock serves as a communication between the two districts. It was the end of April when Farel, passing through the Pierre-Pertuis,[2] descended to the village of Tavannes, and entered the church just as the priest was saying mass. Farel went into the pulpit: the astonished priest stopped, —the minister filled his hearers with emotion, and seemed to be an angel come down from heaven. Immediately the images and the altars fell, and " the poor priest who was chanting the mass could not finish it."[3] To put down Popery had required less time than the priest had spent at the altar.

A great part of the bishopric of Basle was in a few weeks gained over to the Reformation.

During this time the Gospel was fermenting in Neufchatel. The young men who had marched with Berne to deliver Geneva from the attacks of Savoy, recounted in their jovial meetings the exploits of the campaign, and related how the soldiers of Berne, feeling cold, had taken the images from the Dominican church at Geneva, saying : " Idols of wood are of no use but to make a fire with in winter."

Farel reappeared in Neufchatel.[4] Being master of the lower part of the town, he raised his eyes to the lofty rocks on which soared the cathedral and the castle. The best plan, thought he, is to bring these proud priests down to us. One morning his young friends spread themselves in the streets, and posted up large placards bearing these words : " *All those who say mass are robbers, murderers, and seducers of the people.*"[5] Great was the uproar in Neufchatel. The canons summoned their people, called together the clerks, and marching at the head of a large troop, armed with swords and clubs, descended into the town, tore down the sacrilegious placards, and cited Farel before the tribunal as a slanderer, demanding ten thousand crowns damages.

The two parties appeared in court, and this was all that Farel desired. " I confess the fact," said he, " but I am justified in what I have done. Where are there to be found more horrible murderers than these seducers who sell paradise, and thus nullify the merits of our Lord Jesus Christ ? I will prove my assertion by the Gospel." And he prepared to open it, when the canons, flushed with anger, cried out : " The common law of Neufchatel, and not the Gospel, is in question here ! Where are the witnesses ? " But Farel, constantly reverting to that fearful assertion, proved by the Word of God that the canons were really guilty of murder and robbery. To plead such a cause was to ruin Popery. The court of Neufchatel, that had never heard a similar case, resolved according to ancient custom to lay it before the council of Besançon,[1] which not daring to pronounce the first estate of the General Audiences guilty of murder and robbery referred the matter to the emperor and to a general council. Bad causes gain nothing by making a disturbance.

At every step they wished to drive him back, Farel made one in advance. The streets and the houses were still his temple. One day when the people of Neufchatel were around him, " Why," cried they, " should not the Word of God be proclaimed in a church ? " They then hurried Farel along with them, opened the doors of the Hospital Chapel, set the minister in the pulpit, and a numerous crowd stood silent before him. " In like manner as Jesus Christ, appearing in a state of poverty and humility, was born in a stable at Bethlehem," said the reformer ; " so this hospital, this abode of the sick and of the poor, is to-day become his birthplace in the town of Neufchatel." Then feeling ill at ease in the presence of the painted and carved figures that decorated the chapel, he laid his hands on these objects of idolatry, removed them, and broke them in pieces.[2]

Popery, which anger had blinded, now took a step that it undoubtedly had a right to take, but which destroyed it : it had recourse to the secular arm, and the governor sent a deputation to the Bernese council, praying the removal of Farel and his companions.

But almost at the same time deputies from the townspeople arrived at Berne. " Did not these hands bear arms at Interlaken and at Bremgarten to support your Reformation ? " said they, " and will you abandon us in ours ? "

Berne hesitated. A public calamity was at that time filling the whole city with mourning. One of the most illustrious citizens of the republic, the Banneret of Weingarten, attacked by the plague, was expiring amid the tears of his sons and of his fellow-citizens. Being informed of the arrival of the Neufchatelans, he rallied his waning strength : " Go," said he, " and beg the senate in my name to ask for a general assembly of the people of Neufchatel for Sunday next."[3] This message of the dying banneret decided the council.

The deputies from Berne arrived in Neufchatel on the 7th August. Farel thought

---

[1] A tous seigneurs, peuples, et pasteurs. See above, vol. iii. book xii.
[2] Petra Pertusa.
[3] Donc le pauvre prêtre qui chantoit sa messe ne la peut pas achever. Old MS. quoted in the Choupard MS.
[4] Farellus suo more magna fortitudine jam-jam agit. Mexander to Zwingle, 6th Aug. 1530.
[5] De Chambrier, Hist. de Neufchatel, i. 293.

[1] Prendre les *entraives*.
[2] Choupard MS.
[3] Wingarterus iste infectus peste apud senatum nostrum. pia legatione. Megander to Zwingle.

that during the debates he had time to make a new conquest, and quitted the city. His zeal can be compared only to St. Paul's. His body was small and feeble, but his activity was wholly apostolic: danger and bad treatment wasted him every day, but he had within him a divine power that rendered him victorious.

CHAPTER VII.

Valangin—Guillemette de Vergy—Farel goes to the Val de Ruz—The Mass interrupted—Farel dragged to the River —Farel in Prison—Apostles and Reformers compared— Farel preaching at Neufchatel—Installed in the Cathedral —A Whirlwind sweeps over the People—The Idols destroyed—Interposition of the Governor—Triumph of the Reformed.

At the distance of a league from Neufchatel, beyond the mountain, extends the Val de Ruz, and near its entrance, in a precipitous situation, where roars an impetuous torrent surrounded by steep crags, stands the town of Valangin. An old castle, built on a rock, raises its vast walls into the air, overlooking the humble dwellings of the townspeople, and extending its jurisdiction over five valleys of these lofty and severe mountains, at that time covered with forests of pine, but now peopled by the most active industry.[1]

In this castle dwelt Guillemette de Vergy, dowager-countess of Valangin, strongly attached to the Romish religion and full of respect for the memory of her husband. A hundred priests had chanted high mass at the count's burial; when many penitent young women had been married, and large alms distributed; the curate of Locle had been sent to Jerusalem, and Guillemette herself had made a pilgrimage for the repose of the soul of her departed lord.

Sometimes, however, the Countess of Gruyère and other ladies would come and visit the widow of Vergy, who assembled in the castle a number of young lords. The fife and tambourine re-echoed under its vaulted roofs, chattering groups collected in the immense recesses of its Gothic windows, and merry dances followed hard upon a long silence and gloomy devotion.[2] There was but one sentiment that never left Guillemette —this was her hatred against the Reformation, in which she was warmly seconded by her intendant, the Sieur of Bellegarde.

Guillemette and the priests had in fact reason to tremble. The 15th August was a great Romish festival—Our Lady of August, or the Assumption, which all the faithful of the Val de Ruz were preparing to keep. This was the very day Farel selected. Animated by the fire and courage of Elijah, he set out for Valangin, and a young man, his fellow-countryman, and, as it would appear,

[1] Here are situated Chaux de Fonds, Locle, &c.
[2] Chambrier, Hist. de Neufchatel, p. 276.

a distant relation, Anthony Boyve, an ardent Christian and a man of decided character, accompanied him.[1] The two missionaries climbed the mountain, plunged into the pine forest, and then descending again into the valley, traversed Valangin, where the vicinity of the castle did not give them much encouragement to pause, and arrived at a village, probably Boudevilliers, proposing to preach the Gospel there.[2]

Already on all sides the people were thronging to the church : Farel and his companion entered also with a small number of the inhabitants who had heard him at Neufchatel. The reformer immediately ascended the pulpit, and the priest prepared to celebrate mass. The combat began. While Farel was preaching Jesus Christ and his promises, the priest and the choir were chanting the missal. The solemn moment approached : the ineffable transubstantiation was about to take place : the priest pronounced the sacred words over the elements. At this instant the people hesitate no longer ancient habits, an irresistible influence, draw them towards the altar ; the preacher is deserted ; the kneeling crowd has recovered its old worship ; Rome is triumphant.........Suddenly a young man springs from the throng, —traverses the choir,—rushes to the altar, —snatches the host from the hands of the priest, and cries, as he turns towards the people : "This is not the God whom you should worship. He is above,—in heaven, in the majesty of the Father, and not, as you believe, in the hands of a priest."[3] This man was Anthony Boyve.

Such a daring act at first produced the desired effect. The mass was interrupted, the chanting ceased, and the crowd, as if struck by a supernatural intervention, remained silent and motionless. Farel, who was still in the pulpit, immediately took advantage of this calm, and proclaimed that Christ "whom the heaven must receive until the times of restitution of all things."[4] Upon this the priests and choristers with their adherents rushed to the towers, ran up into the belfry, and sounded the tocsin.

These means succeeded : a crowd was collected, and if Farel had not retired, his death and Boyve's would have been inevitable. "But God," says the chronicle, "delivered them." They crossed the interval that separates Boudevilliers from Valangin, and drew near the steep gorges of the torrent of the Seyon. But how traverse that town which the tocsin had already alarmed ?

Leaving Chaumont and its dark forests to the left, these two heralds of the Gospel took

[1] Annals of Boyve and a family MS.—This family has since given several pastors to the Church of Neufchatel.
[2] There are two original manuscripts (both quoted in the Choupard MS.) which give an account of this transaction. One says that Farel preached at Valangin, the other indicates a village near Valangin. Ruchat has adopted the former version ; I think the latter preferable. The second MS. appears to me older and more correct than the first.
[3] Choupard MS.
[4] Acts iii. 21.

a narrow path that wound beneath the castle : they were stealing cautiously along, when suddenly a shower of stones assailed them, and at the same time a score of individuals,— priests, men, and women,—armed with clubs, fell furiously upon them. " The priests had not the gout either in their feet or arms," says a chronicler ; " the ministers were so beaten, that they nearly lost their lives."[1]

Madame de Vergy, who descended to the terrace, far from moderating the anger of the priests, cried out : " Drown them—drown them ! throw them into the Seyon—these Lutheran dogs, who have despised the host !"[2] In fact, the priests were beginning to drag the two heretics towards the bridge. Never was Farel nearer death.

On a sudden, from behind the last rock that hides Valangin in the direction of the mountain, there appeared " certain good persons of the Val de Ruz, coming from Neufchatel,"[3] and descending into the valley. " What are you doing ? " asked they of the priests, with the intention no doubt of saving Farel ; " put them rather in a place of safety, that they may answer for their proceedings. Would you deprive yourselves of the only means in your power of discovering those infected by the poison of heresy ? "

The priests left off at these words, and conducted the prisoners to the castle. As they were passing before a little chapel, which contained an image of the virgin, " Kneel down," said they to Farel and Boyve, showing them the statue ; " prostrate yourselves before Our Lady !" Farel began to admonish them : " Worship one God alone in spirit and in truth," said he to them, " and not dumb images without life or power." But they, continues the chronicle, " greatly vexed at his words and his firmness, inflicted on him so many blows, that he was covered with blood, which even spirted on the walls of the chapel. For a long time after the traces of it might still be seen."[4]

They resumed their march—they entered the town—they climbed the steep road that led to the esplanade where Guillemette de Vergy and her attendants waited for the " Lutherans ; " so that, continues the chronicle, " from beating them thus continually, they were conducted all covered with filth and blood to the prisons, and let down almost lifeless into the dungeon (croton) of the castle of Valangin." Thus had Paul at Lystra been stoned by the Jews, drawn out of the city, and left for dead.[5] The apostles and

the reformers preached the same doctrine and suffered the same treatment.

It may perhaps be said that Farel and Boyve were too violent in their attack ; but the Church of the Middle Ages, which had fallen back into the legal spirit of Judaism, and into all the corruptions that flow from it, needed an energetic opposition to lead it again to the principle of grace. Augustine and St. Paul reappeared in the Church of the sixteenth century ; and when we read of Boyve rushing in great emotion on those who were about to worship the bread of the mass, may we not recall to mind the action of St. Paul, rending his clothes, and running in among the people, who were desirous of worshipping " men of like passions with themselves ? "[1]

Farel and Boyve, thrust into the dungeons of the castle, could, like Paul and Silas in the prison at Philippi, " sing praises unto God." Messire de Bellegarde, ever ready to persecute the Gospel, was preparing for them a cruel end, when some townsmen of Neufchatel arrived to claim them. Madame de Valangin dared not refuse, and at the demand of the Bernese even instituted an inquiry, " to put a good face on the matter," says a manuscript. " Nevertheless the priest who had beaten Farel most, never after failed to eat daily at the lady's table, by way of recompense."[2] But this was of little consequence : the seed of truth had been sown in the Val de Ruz.

At Neufchatel the Bernese supported the evangelical citizens. The governor, whose resources were exhausted sent deputies to the princess, " begging her to cross the mountains, to appease her people, who were in terrible trouble in consequence of this Lutheran religion."[3]

Meantime the ferment increased. The townspeople prayed the canons to give up the mass : they refused ; whereupon the citizens presented them their reasons in writing, and begged them to discuss the question with Farel. Still the same refusal !— " But, for goodness' sake, speak either for or against ! " It was all of no use !

On Sunday, the 23d of October, Farel, who had returned to Neufchatel, was preaching at the hospital. He knew that the magistrates of the city had deliberated on the expediency of consecrating the cathedral itself to the evangelical worship. " What then," said he, " will you not pay as much honour to the Gospel as the other party does to the mass ? ......And if this superstitious act is celebrated in the high church, shall not the Gospel be proclaimed there also?" At these words all his hearers arose. " To the church !" cried they ; " to the church !" Impetuous men are desirous of putting their hands to the work, to accomplish what the prudence of the bur-

---

[1] Les prêtres n'avoient pas la goutte aux pieds et aux bras, et ils les battirent tellement que peu s'en fallut qu'ils ne perdissent la vie. Choupard MS.
[2] A l'eau ! à l'eau ! jettez les dans le Seyon ces chiens de Luthériens qui ont méprisé le bon Dieu ! Ibid.
[3] Ibid.
[4] Choupard MS. Mais eux, rudement fachés de ses propos et constance, lui donnèrent tant de coups, qu'ils le mirent tout en sang, jusques là que son sang jaillissoit sur les murailles de la chapelle. On en voyoit long temps après encore les marques.
[5] Acts xiv. 19.

[1] Acts xiv. 14.
[2] Choupard MS.
[3] Letter from the Governor to the Princess.

gesses had proposed.[1] They leave the hospital, and take Farel with them. They climb the steep street of the castle: in vain would the canons and their frightened followers stop the crowd: they force a passage. Convinced that they are advancing for God's glory, nothing can check them. Insults and shouts assail them from every side, but in the name of the truth they are defending, they proceed: they open the gates of the Church of our Lady; they enter, and here a fresh struggle begins. The canons and their friends assembled around the pulpit endeavour to stop Farel; but all is useless. They have not to deal with a band of rioters. God has pronounced in his Word, and the magistrates themselves have passed a definitive resolution. The townspeople advance, therefore, against the sacerdotal coterie; they form a close battalion, in the centre of which they place the reformer. They succeed in making their way through the opposing crowd, and at last place the minister in the pulpit without any harm befalling him.[2]

Immediately all is calm within the church and without; even the adversaries are silent, and Farel delivers " one of the most effective sermons he had hitherto preached." Their eyes are opened; their emotion increases; their hearts are melted; the most obstinate appear converted; and from every part of the old church these cries resound: " We will follow the evangelical religion, both we and our children, and in it will we live and die."[3]

Suddenly a whirlwind, as it were, sweeps over this multitude, and stirs it up like a vast sea. Farel's hearers desire to imitate the pious King Josiah.[4] " If we take away these idols from before our eyes, will it not be aiding us," said they, " in taking them from our own hearts? Once these idols broken, how many souls among our fellow-citizens, now disturbed and hesitating, will be decided by this striking manifestation of the truth! We must save them as it were by fire."[5]

This latter motive decided them, and then began a scene that filled the Romanists with horror, and which must, according to them, bring down the terrible judgment of God on the city.

The very spot where this took place would seem to add to its solemnity. To the north, the castle-walls rise above the pointed crags of the gloomy but picturesque valley of the Seyon, and the mountain in front of the castle presents to the observer's eye little more than bare rocks, vines, and black firs. But to the south, beneath the terrace on which this tumultuous scene was passing, lay the wide and tranquil waters of the lake, with its fertile and picturesque shores; and in the distance the continuous summits of the higher Alps with their dazzling snows, their immense glaciers, and gigantic peaks, stretch far away before the enraptured eye.

On this platform the people of Neufchatel were in commotion, paying little attention to these noble scenes of nature. The governor, whose castle adjoined the church, was compelled to remain an idle spectator of the excesses that he could not prevent; he was content to leave us a description of them. " These daring fellows," says he, " seize mattocks, hatchets, and hammers, and thus march against the images of the saints." They advance—they strike the statues and the altars—they dash them to pieces. The figures carved in the fourteenth century by the " imagers " of Count Louis are not spared; and scarcely do the statues of the counts themselves, which were mistaken for idols, escape destruction. The townspeople collect all these fragments of an idolatrous worship, and carrying them out of the church, throw them from the top of the rock. The paintings meet with no better treatment. " It is the devil," thought they with the early Christians, " who taught the world this art of statues, images, and all sorts of likenesses."[1] They tear out the eyes in the pictures of the saints, and cut off their noses. The crucifix itself is thrown down, for this wooden figure usurps the homage that Jesus Christ claims in the heart. One image, the most venerated of all, still remains: it is our Lady of Mercy, which Mary of Savoy had presented to the collegiate church; but Our Lady herself is not spared. A hand more daring than the rest strikes it, as in the fourth century the colossal statue of Serapis was struck.[2] " They have even bored out the eyes of Our Lady of Mercy, which the departed lady your mother had caused to be made," wrote the governor to the Duchess of Longueville.

The reformed went still further: they seized the patens in which lay the *corpus Domini*, and flung them from the top of the rock into the torrent; after which, being desirous of showing that the consecrated wafers are mere bread, and not God himself, they distributed them one to another and ate them.........At this sight the canons and chaplains could no longer remain quiet. A cry of horror was heard; they ran up with their adherents, and opposed force to force. At length began the struggle that had been so much dreaded.

The provost Oliver of Hochberg, the canons Simon of Neufchatel and Pontus of Soleilant,

---

1 This is the conclusion I draw from various papers, and in particular from the report of the meeting held at Neufchatel by the Bernese deputies, in which the heads of the burgesses declare, *that it appeared to them a very good matter to take down the altars, &c.* Hitherto only one phasis of this action has been seen,—the popular movement; and the other, namely, the legal resolution of the magistrates of the city, appears to have been overlooked.
2 Choupard MS.
3 Ibid.
4 2 Chron. xxxiv. 7.
5 Choupard MS.

1 Diabolum sæculo intulisse artifices statuarum et imaginum et omnis generis simulacrorum. Tertullian, de idolatria, cap. 3.
2 Socrates v. 16.

all three members of the privy council, had repaired hastily to the castle, as well as the other councillors of the princess. Until this moment they had remained silent spectators of the scene; but when they saw the two parties coming to blows, they ordered all "the supporters of the evangelical doctrine" to appear before the governor. This was like trying to chain the winds. Besides, why should the reformers stop? They were not acting without legitimate authority.[1] "Tell the governor," replied the townspeople haughtily, "that in the concerns of God and of our souls he has no command over us."[2]

George de Rive then discovered that his authority failed against a power superior to his own. He must yield, and save at least some remnants. He hastened therefore to remove the images that still remained, and to shut them up in secret chambers. The citizens of Neufchatel allowed him to execute this measure. "Save your gods," thought they, "preserve them under strong bars, lest perchance a robber should deprive you of the objects of your adoration!"[3] By degrees the tumult died away, the popular torrent returned within its channel, and a short time after, in commemoration of this great day, these words were inscribed on a pillar of the church:—

L'AN 1530, LE 23 OCTOBRE, FUT OTEE ET ABATTUE L'IDOLATRIE DE CEANT PAR LES BOURGEOIS.[4]

An immense revolution had been effected. Doubtless it would have been better if the images had been taken away, and the Gospel substituted in their place with calmness, as at Zurich; but we must take into consideration the difficulties that so profound and contested a change brings with it, and make allowance for the inexperience and excesses inseparable from a first explosion. He who should see in this revolution its excesses only, would betray a singularly narrow mind. It is the Gospel that triumphed on the esplanade of the castle. It was no longer a few pictures or legends that were to speak to the imagination of the Neufchatelans: the revelation of Christ and of the apostles, as it had been preserved in the Holy Scriptures, was restored to them. In place of the mysteries, symbols, and miracles of Popery, the Reformation brought them sublime tenets, powerful doctrines, holy and eternal truths. Instead of a mass, void of God, and filled with human puerilities, it restored to them the Supper of our Lord Jesus Christ, his invisible yet real and mighty presence, his promises giving peace to the soul, and his Spirit, which changes the heart, and is a sure pledge of a glorious resurrection. All is gain in such an exchange.

CHAPTER VIII.

The Romanists demand a Ballot—The Bernese in Favour of the Reform—Both Parties come to the Poll—The Prud-hommes of Neufchatel—Proposed Delay—The Romanists grasp the Sword—The Voting—Majority for Reform—Protestantism perpetual—The Image of Saint John—A Miracle—Retreat of the Canons—Popery and the Gospel.

THE governor and his trusty friends had not, however, lost all hope. "It is only a minority," said they at the castle, "which has taken part in the destruction of the images; the majority of the nation still obeys the ancient doctrine." M. de Rive had yet to learn that if, in a popular movement, the minority only appears, it is in some cases because the majority, being of the same mind with it, prefers leaving the action to others. However that may be, the governor, thinking himself upon sure ground, resolved to put the preservation of the mass to the vote. If the majority were doubtful, the combined influence of the government and clergy would make it incline to the side of Rome. The friends of the Reformation perceiving this trick, and feeling the necessity of securing the integrity of the votes, demanded the presence of Bernese commissioners. This was at first refused. But Neufchatel, divided into two hostile parties, might at any time see her streets run blood: De Rive therefore called Berne to his aid.

Anthony Noll and Sulpice Archer, both members of the council, with Jacques Tribolet, bailiff of the Isle of St. John, all three devoted to the Reform, made their entry into Neufchatel on the 4th November,—an eventful day for the principality, and one which would decide its reformation. The deputies proceeded to the castle, where they spoke with great haughtiness.[1] "Their excellencies of Berne," said they to the governor, "are much astonished that you should oppose the true and pure Word of God. Desist immediately, or else your state and lordship may suffer for it."[2]

George de Rive was amazed; he had thought to summon helpers, and he had found masters. He made, however, an attempt to escape from the strait in which he was caught. The Roman-catholic cantons of Lucerne, Friburg, and Soleure, were also allies of the state. The governor insinuated to the Bernese deputies, that he might well claim their intervention. At these words the deputies indignantly arose, and declared to M. de Rive, that if he did so, he might be the cause of his sovereign's losing Neufchatel.

[1] "Par les quatre du dit Neufchatel," by the Four (the municipal authorities) of the said Neufchatel, remarks the priest Besancenet. See also the *recess* of the council held at Neufchatel by MM. of Berne, 4th November 1530.
[2] The Governor's letter to the Princess.
[3] Cur vos sub validissimis clavibus, ingentibusque sub claustris conservatis, ne forte fur aliquis irreptat? Arnobius contra gentes, vi. 257.
[4] On the 23d of October 1530, idolatry was overthrown and removed from this church by the citizens.

[1] Trois ambassadeurs qui me tinrent assez gros et rudes propos. The Governor to the Princess.
[2] Ibid.

The governor saw the impossibility of escaping from the net into which he had fallen. There remained no alternative but submission, and to watch the current of events which it was impossible for him to direct.

It was not thus with the canons and the nobles. Not considering themselves beaten, they surrounded the Bernese; and mingling religion and politics, as is their wont in similar cases, endeavoured to shake them. "Do you not see," said they, "that unless we support the spiritual power, we shall compromise the civil power? The surest bulwark of the throne is the altar! These men, whose defenders you have become, are but a handful of mischief-makers: the majority are for the mass!"—"Turn which way you like," replied one of the stubborn Bernese, "even though the majority should be on your side, still you must go that way; never will our lordships abandon the defenders of the evangelical faith."[1]

The people assembled at the castle for the definitive vote. The destiny of Neufchatel was about to be decided. On one hand were crowded around the governor the privy council, the canons, and the most zealous of the Romanists; on the other were to be seen the four aldermen, the town-council, and a great number of the citizens, gravely ascending the steep avenue leading to the government-house, and drawing up in front of their adversaries. On both sides there was the same attachment to their faith and the same decision; but around the canons were many anxious minds, troubled hearts, and downcast eyes, while the friends of the Reform advanced with uplifted heads, firm looks, and hearts full of hope.

George de Rive, wishing to gain over their minds, began to address them. He described the violence with which the reformed had broken the images and thrown down the altars; "And yet," continued he, "who founded this church? It was the princess's predecessors, and not the citizens. For which reason, I demand that all those who have violently infringed our sovereign's authority, be obliged to restore what they have taken away, so that the holy mass and the canonical hours may be celebrated anew."[2]

Upon this the *prudhommes* of Neufchatel advanced. They were not a troop of young and giddy persons, as the Papists had pretended, but were grave citizens, whose liberties were guaranteed, and who had weighed what they had to say. "By the illumination of the Holy Ghost," replied they, "and by the holy doctrines of the Gospel, which are taught us in the pure Word of God, we will show that the mass is an abuse, without any utility, and which conduces much more

to the damnation than to the salvation of souls. And we are ready to prove, that by taking away the altars, we have done nothing that was not right and acceptable to God."[1]

Thus the two parties met face to face with "great hatred and division," says the Bernese report. The arbitrators consulted together. The governor persisted, feeling that this movement would decide the future. A few votes would suffice for the triumph of Rome, and he reckoned on gaining them by his assurance. "You should understand," said he, "that the majority of this town, men and women, adhere firmly to the ancient faith. The others are hot-headed young soldiers, vain of their persons, and puffed up with the new doctrine."[2]—"Well!" replied the Bernese deputies, "to prevent all mischief, let us settle this difference by the plurality of suffrages, in accordance with the treaty of peace made at Bremgarten between the cantons."

This was what the reformed desired. "The vote! the vote!" cried they, according to the expression consecrated to such cases.[3] But the lord of Prangins and the priests, who had desired it when they were alone, shrunk back in the presence of Berne. "We ask for time," said they. If the reformed allowed themselves to be cheated by these dilatory measures, all was over. When once the Bernese had quitted Neufchatel, the governor and the clergy would easily have the upper hand. They therefore remained firm. "No, no!" said they, "now!—no delay!—not a day! not an hour!" But the governor, in the face of a proceeding that would decide the legal fall of Popery, trembled, and obstinately opposed the cries of the people. The magistrates were already indignant, the burghers murmured, and the most violent looked at their swords. "They were resolved to compel us, sword in hand," wrote the governor to the princess. A fresh storm was gathering over Neufchatel. Yet a few more minutes' resistance, and it would burst forth upon the church, the town, and the castle, destroying not only statues, images, and altars, but "there would have remained dead men," said the lord of Rive.[4] He gave way in trouble and affright.

At the news of this concession, the partisans of Rome saw all their danger. They conferred, they concerted their measures, and in an instant their resolution was taken: they were resolved to fight.[5] "My lord," said they, turning to M. de Rive, and touching the hilt of their swords, "all of us who adhere to the holy Sacrament are resolved to die martyrs for our holy faith."[6] This de-

---

[1] Chambrier, Hist. de Neufchatel, p. 296. The Governor's letter. Quand bien *le plus* sera des votres, si passerez vous par là, &c.
[2] Choupard MS.; Reces du MM. de Berne.

[1] Choupard MS.; Reces du MM. de Berne.
[2] Devez entendre que la pluspart de cette ville, hommes et femmes, tiennent fermement à l'ancienne foi. Les autres sont jeunes gens de guerre, forts de leurs personnes, remplis de la nouvelle doctrine, ayants le feu à la tête. Ibid.
[3] *Le plus*, the majority.
[4] The Governor's letter to the Princess.
[5] Ibid. [6] Ibid.

monstration did not escape the notice of the young soldiers who had returned from the Genevese war. One minute more and the swords would have been drawn, and the platform changed into a battlefield.

Monseigneur de Prangins, more wily than orthodox, shuddered at the thought. " I cannot suffer it," said he to the most violent of his party; " such an enterprize would forfeit my mistress's state and lordship."[1]—" I consent," said he to the Bernese, " to take the votes, with reserve nevertheless of the sovereignty, rights, and lordship of Madame."— " And we," replied the townspeople, "with the reserve of our liberties and privileges."

The Romanists, seeing the political power they had invoked now failing them, felt that all was lost. They will save their honour at least in this great shipwreck; they will subscribe their names, that posterity may know who had remained faithful to Rome. These proud supporters of the hierarchy advanced towards the governor; tears coursed down their rough cheeks, betraying thus their stifled anger. They wrote their signatures as witnesses at the foot of the solemn testament that Popery was now drawing up in Neufchatel, in the presence of the Bernese deputies. They then asked, with tears in their eyes, " that the names and surnames of the good and of the perverse should be written in perpetual memory, and declared that they were still good and faithful burghers of Madame, and would do her service into death!"[2]

The reformed burgesses were convinced that it was only by frankly bearing testimony to their religious convictions that they could discharge their duty before God, their sovereign, and their fellow-citizens. So that the Catholics had scarcely protested their fidelity towards their lady, when, turning towards the governor, the reformed cried out: " We say the same in every other thing in which it shall please our Mistress to command us, save and except the evangelical faith, in which we will live and die."[3]

Every thing was then prepared for taking the votes. The Church of Our Lady was opened, and the two parties advanced between the shattered altars, torn pictures, mutilated statues, and all those ruins of Popery, which clearly foretold to its partisans the last and irrevocable defeat it was about to undergo. The three lords of Berne took their station beside the governor as arbitrators of the proceedings and presidents of the assembly, and the voting began.

George de Rive, notwithstanding the despondency of his friends, was not altogether without hope. All the partisans of the ancient worship in Neufchatel had been forewarned; and but a few days previously the reformed themselves, by refusing a poll, had acknowledged the numerical superiority of their adversaries. But the friends of the Gospel in Neufchatel had a courage and hope that seemed to repose on a firmer basis. Were they not the victorious party, and could they be vanquished in the midst of their triumph?

The two parties, however, moved forward, confounded with one another, and each man gave his vote in silence. They counted each other: the result appeared uncertain; fear froze each party by turns. At length the majority seemed to declare itself;—they took out the votes,—the result was proclaimed. A majority of eighteen voices gave the victory to the Reformation, and the last blow to the Papacy!

The Bernese lords immediately hastened to profit by this advantage. " Live henceforth," said they, " in good understanding with one another; let the mass be no longer celebrated; let no injury be done to the priests; and pay to your Lady, or to whomsoever they may be justly due, all tithes, quit-rent, cense, and revenues." These different points were proclaimed by the assembly, and a report was immediately drawn up, to which the deputies, the governors, and the magistrates of the city of Neufchatel affixed their respective seals.[1]

Farel did not appear in all this business: one might have said that the reformer was not at Neufchatel: the citizens appealed only to the Word of God; and the governor himself, in his long report to the princess, does not once mention him. It was the apostles of our Lord, St. Peter, St. John, St. Paul, and St. James, who by their divine writings re-established the true foundations of the Church in the midst of the people of Neufchatel. The Word of God was the law of the *prudhommes*. In vain will the Roman Church say, " But these very Scriptures,— it is I who give them to you; you cannot therefore believe in them without believing in me." It is *not* from the Church of Rome that the Protestant Church receives the Bible. Protestantism has always existed in the Church. It has existed alone in every place where men have been engaged in the study of the Holy Scriptures, of their Divine origin, of their interpretation, and in their dissemination. The Protestantism of the sixteenth century received the Bible from the Protestantism of every age. When Rome speaks of the hierarchy, she is on her own ground: as soon as she speaks of the Scriptures, she is on ours. If Farel had been put forward in Neufchatel, he would not perhaps have been able to stand against the

---

[1] The Governor's letter to the Princess.
[2] Alors iceux dirent en pleurant que les noms et les surnoms des bons et des pervers fussent écrits en perpétuelle mémoire, et qu'ils protestoient être bons et fidèles bourgeois de Madame, et lui faire service jusqu'à la mort.
[3] Governor's letter. Nous disons le semblable en toute autre chose où il plaira à Madame nous commander, sauf et reserve icelle foi évangelique, dans laquelle nous voulons vivre et mourir.

[1] Reces de MM. de Berne, MS. Et que l'on paie à Madame ou à qui il sera dû justement dimes, cens, rentes et revenus

pope; but the Word of Christ alone was concerned, and Rome must fall before Jesus.

Thus terminated, by a mutual contract, that day at first so threatening. If the reformed had sacrificed any of their convictions to a false peace, disorder would have been perpetuated in Neufchatel. A bold manifestation of the truth, and the inevitable shocks that accompanied it, far from destroying society, preserved it. This manifestation is the wind that lifts the vessel from the rocks and brings it into the harbour.

The Lord of Prangins felt that, between fellow-citizens, "it is better to touch one another, even if it be by collision, than to avoid each other continually." The free explanation that had taken place had rendered the opposition of the two parties less irritating. "I give my promise," said the governor, "to undertake nothing against the vote of this day, for I am myself a witness that it has been honest, upright, without danger, and without coercion."[1]

It was necessary to dispose of the spoils of the vanquished party: the governor opened the castle to them. Thither were transported the relics, the ornaments of the altars, the church papers, and even the organ; and the mass, expelled from the city, was there mournfully chanted every day.

All the ornaments, however, did not take this road. Some days after, as two citizens, named Fauche and Sauge, were going out together to their vineyards, they passed a little chapel, in which the latter had set up a wooden figure of St. John. He said to his companion, "There is an image I shall heat my stove with to-morrow." And, in fact, as he returned, he carried away the saint and laid it down in front of his house.

The next morning he took the image and put it on the fire. Immediately a horrible explosion spread dismay through this humble family. The trembling Fauche doubted not that it was a miracle of the saint, and hastened to return to the mass. In vain did his neighbour Sauge protest to him upon oath that, during the night, he had made a hole in the statue, filled it with gunpowder, and closed it up again. Fauche would listen to nothing, and resolved to flee from the vengeance of the saints. He went and settled with his family at Morteau in Franche Comté.[2] Such are the miracles upon which the divinity of Rome reposes!

By degrees every thing became settled: some of the canons, as Jacques Baillod, William de Pury, and Benedict Chambrier, embraced the Reformation. Others were recommended by the governor to the priory of Motiers, in the Val de Travers; and, in the middle of November, at the time when the winds began to rage among the mountains, several canons, surrounded by a few

singing-boys,—sad relics of the ancient powerful, rich, voluptuous, and haughty chapter of Neufchatel,—painfully climbed the gorges of the Jura, and went to conceal in these lofty and picturesque valleys the disgrace of a defeat, which their long disorders and their insupportable tyranny had but too justly provoked.

During this time the new worship was organized. In room of the high-altar were substituted two marble tables to receive the bread and wine: and the Word of God was preached from a pulpit stripped of every ornament. The pre-eminence of the Word, which characterizes the evangelical worship, replaced in the church of Neufchatel the pre-eminence of the sacrament, which characterizes Popery. Towards the end of the second century, Rome, that ancient metropolis of all religions, after having welcomed the christian worship in its primitive purity, had gradually transformed it into mysteries: a magic power had been ascribed to certain forms; and the reign of the sacrifice offered by the priest had succeeded to the reign of the Word of God. The preaching of Farel had restored the Word to the rights which belonged to it; and those vaulted roofs, which the piety of Count Ulric II. had, on his return from Jerusalem, dedicated to the worship of the Virgin, served at last, after four centuries, to nourish the faithful, as in the time of the apostles, "in the words of faith and of good doctrine."[1]

CHAPTER IX.

Reaction preparing—Failure of the Plot—Farel in Valangin and near the Lake—De Bély at Fontaine—Farel's Sufferings—Marcourt at Valangin—Disgraceful Expedient—Vengeance—The Reform established—French Switzerland characterized—Gathering Tempest.

THE convention, drawn up under the mediation of Berne, stipulated that "the change should take place only in the city and parish of Neufchatel." Must the rest of the country remain in darkness? This was not Farel's wish, and the zeal of the citizens, in its first fervour, effectually seconded him. They visited the surrounding villages, exhorting some, combating others. Those who were compelled to labour with their hands during the day went thither at night. "Now, I am informed," writes the governor to the princess, "that they are working at a reformation night and day."

George de Rive, in alarm, convoked the magistrates of all the districts in the earldom. These good folks believed that their consciences, as well as their places, depended upon Madame de Longueville. Affrighted at the thought of freely receiving a new conviction from the Word of God, they were quite ready to accept it from the countess as

---

[1] Ungefährlich, ungezwringen, aufrecht und redlich. Berne to the Governor, 17th Dec. 1530.
[2] Boyve Annals, MS.

[1] 1 Tim. iv. 6.

they would a new impost;—a sad helotism, in which religion springs from the soil, instead of descending from heaven! " We desire to live and die under the protection of our lady," said the magistrates to the Lord of Rive, " without changing the ancient faith, *until it be so ordered by her.*"[1] Rome, even after her fall, could not receive a deeper insult.

These assurances of fidelity and the absence of the Bernese restored De Rive's confidence, and he secretly prepared a reaction among the nobles and the lower classes. There is in every historical catastrophe, in the fall of great establishments, and in the spectacle of their ruins, something which excites and improves the mind. This was what happened at the period in question. Some were more zealous for Popery after its fall than in its day of power. The clergy gliding into the houses said mass to a few friends mysteriously called together around a temporary altar. If a child was born, the priest noiselessly arrived, breathed on the infant, made the sign of the cross on its forehead and breast, and baptized it according to the Roman ritual.[2] Thus they were rebuilding in secret what had been overthrown in the light of day. At length a counter-revolution was agreed upon; and Christmas-day was selected for the restoration of Roman Catholicism. While the Christians' songs of joy should be rising to heaven, the partisans of Rome were to rush into the church, expel the heretical assembly, overthrow the pulpit and the holy table, restore the images, and celebrate the mass in triumph. Such was the plan of the Neufchatelan vespers.[3]

The plot got wind. Deputies from Berne arrived at Neufchatel on the very eve of the festival. " You must see to this," said they to the governor: " if the reformed are attacked, we, their co-burghers, will protect them with all our power." The conspirators laid down their arms, and the Christmas hymns were not disturbed.

This signal deliverance augmented the devotion and zeal of the friends of the Gospel. Already Emer Beynon of Serrière, where Farel had one day landed from a small boat, ascending the pulpit, had said to his parishioners : " If I have been a good priest, I desire by the grace of God to be a still better pastor." It was necessary that these words should be heard from ever pulpit. Farel recommenced a career of labours, fatigues, and struggles, which the actions of the apostles and missionaries alone can equal.

Towards the end of the year 1530, he crossed the mountain in the middle of winter, entered the church of Valangin, went into the pulpit, and began to preach at the very moment that Guillemette de Vergy was coming to mass. She endeavoured to shut the reformer's mouth, but in vain, and the aged and noble dowager retired precipitately saying : " I do not think this is according to the old Gospels ; if there are any new ones that encourage it, I am quite amazed at them."[1] The people of Valangin embraced the Gospel. The affrighted lieutenant ran to Neufchatel, thence to Berne, and on the 11th February 1531 laid his complaint before the council ; but all was useless. " Why," said their excellencies of Berne to him, " why should you disturb the water of the river? let it flow freely on."

Farel immediately turned to the parishes on the slopes between the lake and Mount Jura. At Corcelles a fanatic crowd, well armed and led on by the curate of Neufchatel, rushed into the church where the minister was preaching, and he did not escape without a wound. At Bevay, the abbot John of Livron and his monks collected a numerous body of friends, surrounded the church, and having thus completed the blockade, entered the building, dragged the minister from the pulpit, and drove him out with blows and insults. Each time he reappeared, they pursued him as far as Auvernier with stones and gun-shots.

While Farel was thus preaching in the plain, he sent one of his brethren into the valley ; it was John de Bély, a man of good family from Crest in Dauphiny. Beyond Valangin, at a little distance from Fontaine, on the left side of the road to Cernier, was a stone that remains to this day. Here in the open air, as if in a magnificent temple, this herald of the Gospel began to proclaim salvation by grace.[2] Before him stretched the declivity of Chaumont, dotted with the pretty villages of Fenin, Villars, Sole, and Savagnier, and beyond, where the mountains fell away, might be seen the distant and picturesque chain of the Alps. The most zealous of his hearers entreated him to enter the church. He did so; but suddenly the priest and his curate " arrived with great noise." They proceeded to the pulpit, dragged Bély down ; and then turning to the women and young persons of the place, " excited them to beat him and drive him away."[3]

John de Bély returned to Neufchatel, hooted and bruised, like his friend after the affair at Valangin ; but these evangelists followed the traces of the Apostle Paul, whom neither whips nor scourges could arrest.[4] De Bély often returned to Fontaine. The mass was abolished erelong in this village ; Bély was its pastor for twenty-seven years ;

---

[1] Chaupard **MS**. Nous voulons vivre et mourir sous la protection de Madame, sans changer l'ancienne foi, *jusqu' à ce que par elle en soit ordonné*.
[2] Berne to Neufchatel, 17th December.
[3] Berne to the Governor. 23d December.

[1] Chambrier. Hist. de Neufchatel et Valangin, p. 299. Je ne crois pas que ce soit selon les vieux évangiles ; s'il y en a de nouveaux qui fassent cela faire, j'en suis esbahie.
[2] It does not appear that Bély could have stood and preached on this stone, as is generally said, unless what now remains is but a fragment of the original.
[3] MS. AA. in the Choupard MS.
[4] 2 Cor. xi. 24, 25.

his descendants have more than once exercised the ministry there, and now they form the most numerous family of agriculturists in the place.

Farel, after evangelizing the shores of the lake to the south of Neufchatel, had gone to the north and preached at St. Blaise. The populace, stirred up by the priests and the lieutenant, had fallen upon him, and Farel escaped from their hands, severely beaten, spitting blood, and scarcely to be recognised. His friends had thrown him hurriedly into a boat, and conveyed him to Morat, where his wounds detained him for some time.[1]

At the report of this violence the reformed Neufchatelans felt their blood boil. If the lieutenant, the priest, and his flock have bruised the body of Christ's servant, which is truly the altar of the living God, why should they spare dead idols? Immediately they rushed to St. Blaise, threw down the images, and did the same at the abbey of Fontaine-André,—a sanctuary of the ancient worship.

The images still existed at Valangin, but their last hour was about to strike. A Frenchman, Anthony Marcourt, had been nominated pastor of Neufchatel. Treading in Farel's footsteps, he repaired with a few of the citizens to Valangin on the 14th June, a great holiday in that town.[2] Scarcely had they arrived when a numerous crowd pressed around the minister, listening to his words. The canons, who were on the watch in their houses, and Madame de Vergy and M. de Bellegarde from their towers, sought how they could make a diversion against this heretical preaching. They could not employ force because of Berne. They had recourse to a brutal expedient, worthy of the darkest days of Popery, and which, by insulting the minister, might divert (they imagined) the attention of the people, and change it into shouts and laughter. A canon,[3] assisted by the countess's coachman, went to the stables and took thence two animals, which they led to the spot where Marcourt was preaching. We will throw a veil over this scene: it is one of those disgraceful subjects that the pen of history refuses to transcribe.[4] But never did punishment follow closer upon crime. The conscience of the hearers was aroused at the sight of this infamous spectacle. The torrent, that such a proceeding was intended to check, rushed out of its channel. The indignant people, undertaking the defence of that religion which their opponents had wished to insult, entered the church like an avenging wave; the ancient windows were broken, the shields of the lords were demo-

lished, the relics scattered about, the books torn, the images thrown down, and the altar overturned. But this was not enough: the popular wave, after sweeping out the church, flowed back again, and dashed against the canons' houses. Their inhabitants fled in consternation into the forests, and every thing was destroyed in their dwellings.

Guillemette de Vergy and M. de Bellegarde, agitated and trembling behind their battlements, repented, but too late, of their monstrous expedient. They were the only ones who had not yet felt the popular vengeance. Their restless eyes watched the motions of the indignant townspeople. The work is completed: the last house is sacked! The burghers consult together.—O horror! —they turn towards the castle,—they ascend the hill,—they draw near. Is then the abode of the noble counts of Arberg about to be laid waste? But no!—"We come," said the delegates standing near the gate of the castle, "we are come to demand justice for the outrage committed against religion and its minister." They were permitted to enter, and the trembling countess ordered the poor wretches to be punished who had acted solely by her orders. But at the same time she sent deputies to Berne, complaining of the "great insults that had been offered her."[1] Berne declared that the reformed should pay for the damage; but that the countess should grant them the free exercise of their worship. Jacques Veluzat, a native of Champagne, was the first pastor of Valangin. A little later we shall see new struggles at the foot of Mount Jura.

Thus was the Reformation established at Valangin, as it had been at Neufchatel: the two capitals of these mountains were gained to the Gospel. Erelong it received a legal sanction. Francis, marquis of Rothelin, son of the Duchess of Longueville, arrived in the principality in March 1531, with the intention of playing on this small theatre the part of a Francis I. But he soon found out that there are revolutions which an irresistible hand has accomplished, and that must be submitted to. Rothelin excluded from the estates of the earldom the canons who had hitherto formed the first power, and replaced them by four bannerets and four burgesses. Then, availing himself of the principle that all abandoned property falls to the state, he laid his hands upon their rich heritage, and proclaimed freedom of conscience throughout the whole country. All the necessary forms having been observed with Madame, the politic M. de Rive became reformed also. Such was the support Rome received from the state, to which she had looked for her deliverance.

A great energy characterized the Reformation of French Switzerland; and this is

---

[1] De Perrot: L'Eglise et la Réformation, ii. 233.
[2] This incident is generally attributed to Farel, but Choupard, following an older manuscript, says, *le ministre de Neufchatel*, by which title he always means Marcourt, and never Farel.
[3] Some historians say "the coachman of the countess;" but Choupard, on three different occasions, writes *a canon*. The latter is no doubt more revolting; but there is nothing incredible in it.
[4] De equo admissario loquitur qui equam init.

[1] Curate of Bexancenet's Chronicle. Des grands vitupères qu'on lui avait faits.

shown by the events we have just witnessed. Men have attributed to Farel this distinctive feature of his work; but no man has ever created his own times; it is always, on the contrary, the times that create the man. The greater the epoch, the less do individualities prevail in it. All the good contained in the events we have just related came from that Almighty Spirit, of which the strongest men are but weak instruments. All the evil proceeded from the character of the people; and, indeed, it was almost always Popery that began these scenes of violence. Farel submitted to the influence of his times, rather than the times received his. A great man may be the personification and the type of the epoch for which God destines him: he is never its creator.

But it is time to quit the Jura and its beautiful valleys, brightened by the vernal sun, to direct our steps towards the Alps of German Switzerland, along which thick clouds and horrible tempests are gathering. The free and courageous people, who dwell there below the eternal glaciers, or on the smiling banks of the lakes, daily assume a fiercer aspect, and the collision threatens to be sudden, violent, and terrible. We have just been witnessing a glorious conquest: a dreadful catastrophe awaits us.

BOOK XVI.

SWITZERLAND—CATASTROPHE. 1528—1531.

CHAPTER I.

Two great Lessons—Christian Warfare—Zwingle, Pastor, Statesman, and General—His noble Character—Persecutions—Swiss Catholics seek an Alliance with Austria—Great Dissatisfaction—Deputation to the Forest Cantons—Zwingle's Proposal—Moderation of Berne—Keyser's Martyrdom—Zwingle and War—Zwingle's Error.

It was the will of God that at the very gates of his revived Church there should be two great examples to serve as lessons for future generations. Luther and the German Reformation, declining the aid of the temporal power, rejecting the force of arms, and looking for victory only in the confession of the truth, were destined to see their faith crowned with the most brilliant success; while Zwingle and the Swiss Reformation, stretching out their hands to the mighty ones of the earth, and grasping the sword, were fated to witness a horrible, cruel, and bloody catastrophe fall upon the Word of God—a catastrophe which threatened to engulf the evangelical cause in the most furious whirlpool. God is a jealous God, and gives not his glory to another; he claims to perform his own work himself, and to attain his ends sets other springs in motion than those of a skilful diplomacy.

We are far from forgetting that we are called upon to relate facts and not to discuss theories; but there is a principle which the history we are narrating sets forth in capital letters: it is that professed in the Gospel, where it says: THE WEAPONS OF OUR WARFARE ARE NOT CARNAL, BUT MIGHTY THROUGH GOD! In maintaining this truth we do not place ourselves on the ground of any particular school, but on that of universal conscience and of the Word of God.

Of all carnal support that religion can invoke, there is none more injurious to it than arms and diplomacy. The latter throws it into tortuous ways; the former hurries it into paths of bloodshed; and religion, from whose brow has been torn the double wreath of truth and meekness, presents but a degraded and humiliated countenance that no person can, that no person desires to recognise.

It was the very extension of the Reform in Switzerland that exposed it to the dangers under which it sunk. So long as it was concentrated at Zurich, it continued a religious matter; but when it had gained Berne, Basle, Schaffhausen, St. Gall, Glaris, Appenzell, and numerous bailiwicks, it formed inter-cantonal relations; and—here was the error and misfortune—while the connexion should have taken place between church and church, it was formed between state and state.

As soon as spiritual and political matters became mingled together, the latter took the upperhand. Zwingle erelong thought it his duty to examine not only doctrinal, but also federal questions; and the illustrious reformer might be seen, unconscious of the snares beneath his feet, precipitating himself into a course strewn with rocks, at the end of which a cruel death awaited him.

The primitive Swiss cantons had resigned the right of forming new alliances without the consent of all; but Zurich and Berne had reserved the power. Zwingle thought himself therefore quite at liberty to promote an alliance with the evangelical states. Constance was the first city that gave her adhesion. But this christian co-burghery, which might become the germ of a new confederation, immediately raised up numerous adversaries against Zwingle, even among the partisans of the Reformation.

There was yet time: Zwingle might withdraw from public affairs, and occupy himself entirely with those of the Gospel. But no one in Zurich had, like him, that application to labour, that correct, keen, and sure eye, so necessary for politicians. If he retired, the vessel of the state would be left without a pilot. Besides, he was convinced, that political acts alone could save the Reform. He resolved, therefore, to be at one and the same time the man of the State and of the Church. The registers prove that in his later years he took part in the most important deliberations; and he was commissioned by the councils of his canton to write letters, compose proclamations, and draw up opinions. Already, before the dispute with Berne, looking upon war as possible, he had traced out a very detailed plan of defence, the manuscript of which is still in existence.[1] In 1528 he did still more; he showed in a remarkable paper, how the republic should act with regard to the empire, France, and other European states, and with respect to the several cantons and bailiwicks. Then, as if he had grown gray at the head of the Helvetic troops (and it is but just to remark that he had long lived among soldiers), he explained the advantages there would be in surprising the enemy; and described even the nature of the arms, and the manner of employing them. In truth, an important revolution was then taking place in the art of war. The pastor of Zurich is at once the head of the state and general of the army: this double—this triple part of the reformer was the ruin of the Reformation and of himself. Undoubtedly we must make allowances for the men of this age, who, being accustomed to see Rome wield two swords for so many centuries, did not understand that they must take up one and leave the other. We must admire the strength of that superior genius, which, while pursuing a political course, in which the greatest minds would have been absorbed, ceased not however to display an indefatigable activity as pastor, preacher, divine, and author. We must acknowledge that the republican education of Zwingle had taught him to confound his country with his religion, and that there was in this great man enough to fill up many lives. We must appreciate that indomitable courage which, relying upon justice, feared not, at a time when Zurich had but one or two weak cities for allies, to confront the redoubtable forces of the empire and of the confederation; but we should also see in the great and terrible lesson that God gave him, a precept for all times and for every

[1] Escher et Hottinger, Archives ii. 263.

nation; and finally, understand what is so often forgotten, "that the kingdom of Christ is not of this world."

The Roman-catholic cantons, on hearing of the new alliances of the reformed, felt a violent indignation. William of Diesbach, deputy from Berne at the diet, was forced to submit to the keenest reproaches. The sitting, for a while interrupted, was resumed immediately after his departure. "They may try to patch up the old faith," said the Bernese, as he withdrew, "it cannot, however, last any longer."[1] In truth, they patched away with all their might, but with a sharp and envenomed needle that drew blood. Joseph Am Berg of Schwytz and Jacques Stocker of Zug, bailiffs of Thurgovia, behaved with cruelty towards all who were attached to the Gospel. They enforced against them fines, imprisonment, torture, the scourge, confiscation, and banishment: they cut out the ministers' tongues, beheaded them, or condemned them to be burnt.[2] At the same time they took away the Bibles and all the evangelical books; and if any poor Lutherans, fleeing from Austria, crossed the Rhine and that low valley where its calm waters flow between the Alps of the Tyrol and of Appenzell,—if these poor creatures, tracked by the lansquenets, came to seek a refuge in Switzerland, they were cruelly given up to their persecutors.

The heavier lay the hands of the bailiffs on Thurgovia and the Rheinthal, the greater conquests did the Gospel make. The Bishop of Constance wrote to the Five Cantons, that if they did not act with firmness, all the country would embrace the Reform. In consequence of this, the cantons convoked at Frauenfeld all the prelates, nobles, judges, and persons of note in the district; and a second meeting taking place six days after (6th December 1528) at Weinfeld, deputies from Berne and Zurich entreated the assembly to consider the honour of God above all things, and in no respect to care for the threats of the world.[3] A great agitation followed upon this discourse. At last a majority called for the preaching of the Word of God; the people came to the same decision; and the Rheinthal, as well as Bremgarten, followed this example.

What was to be done? The flood had become hourly more encroaching. Must then the Forest Cantons open their valleys to it at last? Religious antipathies put an end to national antipathies; and these proud mountaineers, directing their looks beyond the Rhine, thought of invoking the succour of Austria, which they had vanquished at Morgarten and at Sempach.[4] The fanatical

[1] Mögen sie blätzen am alten Glauben. Hottinger, Zwingli, p. 389.
[2] Die Zungen geschlitzt, mit dem Schwerdt richten und verbrännt. Bull. ii. 31.
[3] Die Eer Gottes, uwer Seelen Heil. Bulling. Chron. ii. 28.
[4] Bulling. Chron. ii. 48.

German party that had crushed the revolted Swabian peasants was all-powerful on the frontiers. Letters were exchanged ; messengers passed to and fro across the river ; at last they took advantage of a wedding in high rank that was to take place at Feldkirch in Swabia, six leagues from Appenzell. On the 16th February 1529, the marriage-party, forming a brilliant cavalcade, in the midst of which the deputies of the Five Cantons were concealed, made their entry into Feldkirch, and Am Berg had an immediate interview with the Austrian governor. "The power of the enemies of our ancient faith has so increased," said the Swiss, "that the friends of the Church can resist them no longer. We therefore turn our eyes to that illustrious prince who has saved in Germany the faith of our fathers."

This alliance was so very unnatural, that the Austrians had some difficulty in believing it to be sincere. "Take hostages," said the Waldstettes, "write the articles of the treaty with your own hands ; command and we will obey !"—"Very good !" replied the Austrians ; "in two months you will find us again at Waldshut, and we will let you know our conditions."

A rumour of these negotiations which spread abroad excited great dissatisfaction, even in the partisans of Rome. In no place did it burst out with greater force than in the council of Zug. The opposing parties were violently agitated ; they stamped their feet, they started from their seats, and were nearly coming to blows ; but hatred prevailed over patriotism. The deputies of the Forest Cantons appeared at Waldshut ; they suspended the arms of their cantons by the side of those of the oppressors of Switzerland ; decorated their hats with peacocks' feathers (the badge of Austria), and laughed, drank, and chattered with the Imperialists. This strange alliance was at last concluded.[1] "Whoever shall form new sects among the people," it ran, "shall be punished with death ; and, if need be, with the help of Austria. This power, in case of emergency, shall send into Switzerland six thousand foot soldiers, and four hundred horse, with all requisite artillery. If necessary, the reformed cantons shall be blockaded, and all provisions intercepted." To the Romish cantons, then, belongs the initiative of this measure so much decried. Finally, Austria guaranteed to the Waldstettes the possession, not only of the common bailiwicks, but of all the *conquests* that might be made on the left bank of the Rhine.

Dejection and consternation immediately pervaded all Switzerland. This national complaint, which Bullinger has preserved, was sung in every direction :—

[1] Bullinger gives the treaty at full length. Chron. ii. 49-59.

Wail, Helvetians, wail,
For the peacock's plume of pride
To the forest cantons' savage bull
In friendship is allied.

All the cantons not included in this alliance, with the exception of Friburg, assembled in diet at Zurich, and resolved to send a deputation to their mountain confederates, with a view to reconciliation. The deputation, admitted at Schwytz in the presence of the people, was able to execute its mission without tumult. At Zug there was a cry of "No sermon ! no sermon !" At Altorf the answer was : "Would to God that your new faith was buried for ever !" At Lucerne they received this haughty reply : "We shall know how to defend ourselves, our children, and our children's children, from the poison of your rebellious priests." It was at Unterwalden that the deputation met with the worst reception. "We declare our alliance at an end," said they. "It is we,— it is the other Waldstettes who are the real Swiss. We graciously admitted you into our confederation, and now you claim to become our masters !—The emperor, Austria, France, Savoy, and Valais will assist us !" The deputies retired in astonishment, shuddering as they passed before the house of the secretary of state, where they saw the arms of Zurich, Berne, Basle, and Strasburg hanging from a lofty gibbet.

The deputation had scarcely returned to Zurich and made their report, when men's minds were inflamed. Zwingle proposed to grant no peace to Unterwalden, if it would not renounce foreign service, the alliance with Austria, and the government of the common bailiwicks. "No ! no !" said Berne, that had just stifled a civil war in its own canton, "let us not be so hasty. When the rays of the sun shine forth, each one wishes to set out ; but as soon as it begins to rain, every man loses heart ! The Word of God enjoins peace. It is not with pikes and lances that faith is made to enter the heart. For this reason, in the name of our Lord's sufferings, we entreat you to moderate your anger."

This christian exhortation would have succeeded, if the fearful news that reached Zurich, on the very day when the Bernese delivered their moderate speech, had not rendered it unavailing.

On Saturday the 22d May, Jacques Keyser, a pastor and father of a family in the neighbourhood of the Greiffensee, after coasting the fertile shores of this little lake, crossed the rich pastures of the bailiwick of Gruningen, passed near the Teutonic house of Bubikon and the convent of Ruti, and reached that simple and wild district bathed by the upper part of Lake Zurich. Making his way to Oberkirk, a parish in the Gaster district, between the two lakes of Zurich and Wallenstadt, of which he had been nominated pastor, and where he was to preach on the morrow, he crossed on foot the lengthened and rounded flanks of the Buchberg, fronting the picturesque heights of the Ammon. He was confidently advancing into those woods which for many weeks he had often traversed without obstruction, when he was suddenly seized by six men, posted there to surprise him, and carried off to Schwytz. " The bailiffs," said they to the magistrates, " have ordered all innovating ministers to be brought before the tribunals : here is one that we bring you." Although Zurich and Glaris interposed ; although the government of Gaster, where Keyser had been taken, did not then belong to Schwytz ; the landsgemeinde desired a victim, and on the 29th May they condemned the minister to be burnt alive. On being informed of his sentence, Keyser burst into tears.[1] But when the hour of execution arrived, he walked cheerfully to death, freely confessed his faith, and gave thanks to the Lord even with his latest breath. " Go and tell them at Zurich how he thanks us !" said one of the Schwytz magistrates to the Zurich deputies with a sarcastic smile. Thus had a fresh martyr fallen under the hands of that formidable power that is " drunk with the blood of the saints."[2]

The cup was full. The flames of Keyser's pile became the signal of war. Exasperated Zurich uttered a cry that resounded through all the confederation. Zwingle above all called for energetic measures. Every where, —in the streets, in the councils, and even in the pulpits,—he surpassed in daring even the most valiant captains. He spoke at Zurich,—he wrote to Berne. " Let us be firm, and fear not to take up arms," said he. " This peace, which some desire so much, is not peace, but war : while the war that we call for is not war but peace.[3] We thirst for no man's blood, but we will clip the wings of the oligarchy.[4] If we shun it, the truth of the Gospel and the ministers' lives will never be secure among us."

Thus spoke Zwingle. In every part of Europe he beheld the mighty ones of the earth aiding one another to stifle the reviving animation of the Church ; and he thought that without some decisive and energetic movement, Christianity, overwhelmed by so many blows, would soon fall back into its ancient slavery. Luther under similar circumstances arrested the swords ready to be crossed, and demanded that the Word of God alone should appear on the field of battle. Zwingle thought not thus. In his opinion war was not revolt, for Switzerland had no master. " Undoubtedly," said he, " we must trust in God alone ; but when He gives us a just cause, we must also know how to defend

it, and, like Joshua and Gideon, shed blood in behalf of our country and our God."

If we adopt the principles of justice which govern the rulers of nations, the advice of Zwingle was judicious and irreproachable. It was the duty of the Swiss magistrates to defend the oppressed against the oppressor. But is not language, which might have been suitable in the mouth of a magistrate, blamable in a minister of Christ? Perhaps Zwingle forgot his quality of pastor, and considered himself only as a citizen, consulted by his fellow-citizens ; perhaps he wished to defend Switzerland, and not the Church, by his counsels ; but it is a question, if he ought ever to have forgotten the Church and his ministry. We think we may go even further ; and while granting all that may be urged in favour of the contrary supposition, we may deny that the secular power ought ever to interfere with the sword to protect the faith.

To accomplish his designs, the reformer needed even in Zurich the greatest unity. But there were many men in that city devoted to interests and superstitions which were opposed to him. " How long," he had exclaimed in the pulpit on the 1st December 1528, " how long will you support in the council these unbelievers, these impious men, who oppose the Word of God?"[1] They had decided upon purging the council, as required by the reformer : they had examined the citizens individually ; and then had excluded all the hostile members.

CHAPTER II.

Free Preaching of the Gospel in Switzerland—Zwingle supports the common Bailiwicks—War—Zwingle joins the Army—The Zurich Army threatens Zug—The Landamman Aebli—Bernese Interposition—Zwingle's Opposition —Swiss Cordiality—Order in the Zurich Camp—A Conference—Peace restored—Austrian Treaty torn—Zwingle's Hymn—Nuns of Saint Catherine.

ON Saturday the 15th of June 1529, seven days after Keyser's martyrdom, all Zurich was in commotion. The moment was come when Unterwalden should send a governor to the common bailiwicks ; and the images, having been burnt in those districts, Unterwalden had sworn to take a signal revenge.[2] Thus the consternation had become general. " Keyser's pile," thought they, " will be rekindled in all our villages." Many of the inhabitants flocked to Zurich, and on their alarmed and agitated features, one might, in imagination, have seen reflected the flames that had just consumed the martyr.

These unhappy people found a powerful advocate in Zwingle. The reformer imagined that he had at last attained the object he never ceased to pursue—the free preaching of the Gospel in Switzerland. To inflict a final blow would, in his opinion, suffice to

---

[1] Weinet häfftig. Bull. ii. 149.
[2] Rev. xvii. 6.
[3] Bellum cui nos instamus pax est, non bellum. Vita Zwinglii, per O. Myconium.
[4] Oligarchiæ nervi succidantur. Ibid.

[1] Den rath reinigen. Füssli Beyträge, iv. 91.
[2] Den götzen brand, an inen mitt der Hand zu rächen. Bull. Chron. ii. 193.

bring this enterprise to a favourable issue. " Greedy pensioners," said Zwingle to the Zurichers, " profit by the ignorance of the mountaineers to stir up these simple souls against the friends of the Gospel. Let us therefore be severe upon these haughty chiefs. The mildness of the lamb would only serve to render the wolf more ferocious.[1] Let us propose to the Five Cantons to allow the free preaching of the Word of the Lord, to renounce their wicked alliances, and to punish the abettors of foreign service. As for the mass, idols, rites, and superstitions, let no one be forced to abandon them. It is for the Word of God alone to scatter with its powerful breath all this idle dust.[2] Be firm, noble lords, and in despite of certain black horses, as black at Zurich as they are at Lucerne,[3] but whose malice will never succeed in overturning the chariot of Reform, we shall clear this difficult pass, and arrive at the unity of Switzerland and at unity of faith." Thus Zwingle, while calling for force against political abuses, asked only liberty for the Gospel; but he desired a prompt intervention, in order that this liberty might be secured to it. Œcolampadius thought the same: " It is not a time for delay," said he; " it is not a time for parsimony and pusillanimity ! So long as the venom shall not be utterly removed from this adder in our bosoms we shall be exposed to the greatest dangers."[4]

The council of Zurich, led away by the reformer, promised the bailiwicks to support religious liberty among them ; and no sooner had they learnt that Anthony ab Acker of Unterwalden was proceeding to Baden with an army, than they ordered five hundred men to set out for Bremgarten with four pieces of artillery. This was the 5th June, and on the same evening the standard of Zurich waved over the convent of Mouri.

The war of religion had begun. The horn of the Waldstettes re-echoed afar in the mountains : men were arming in every direction, and messengers were sent off in haste to invoke the assistance of the Valais and of Austria. Three days later (Tuesday the 8th June), six hundred Zurichers, under the command of Jacques Werdmüller, set out for Rapperschwyl and the district of Gaster ; and, on the morrow, four thousand men repaired to Cappel, under the command of the valiant Captain George Berguer, to whom Conrad Schmidt, pastor of Kussnacht, had been appointed chaplain. " We do not wish you to go to the war," said Burgomaster Roust to Zwingle ; " for the pope, the Archduke Ferdinand, the Romish cantons, the bishops, the abbots, and the prelates, hate

you mortally. Stay with the council : we have need of you."—" No !" replied Zwingle, who was unwilling to confide so important an enterprise to any one : " when my brethren expose their lives I will not remain quietly at home by my fireside. Besides, the army also requires a watchful eye, that looks continually around it." Then, taking down his glittering halberd, which he had carried (as it is said) at Marignan, and placing it on his shoulder, the reformer mounted his horse, and set out with the army.[1] The walls, towers, and battlements were covered with a crowd of old men, children, and women, among whom was Anna, Zwingle's wife.

Zurich had called for the aid of Berne ; but that city, whose inhabitants showed little disposition for a religious war, and which besides was not pleased at seeing the increasing influence of Zurich, replied, "Since Zurich has begun the war without us, let her finish it in like manner." The evangelical states were disunited at the very moment of struggle.

The Romish cantons did not act thus. It was Zug that issued the first summons ; and the men of Uri, of Schwytz, and of Unterwalden had immediately begun to march. On the 8th June, the great banner floated before the townhouse of Lucerne, and on the next day the army set out to the sound of the antique horns that Lucerne pretended to have received from the Emperor Charlemagne.

On the 10th June, the Zurichers, who were posted at Cappel, sent a herald at daybreak to Zug, who was commissioned, according to custom, to denounce to the Five Cantons the rupture of the alliance. Immediately Zug was filled with cries and alarm. This canton, the smallest in Switzerland, not having yet received all the confederate contingents, was not in a condition to defend itself. The people ran to and fro, sent off messengers, and hastily prepared for battle ; the warriors fitted on their armour, the women shed tears, and the children shrieked.

Already the first division of the Zurich army, amounting to two thousand men, under the command of William Thöming, and stationed near the frontier below Cappel, was preparing to march, when they observed, in the direction of Baar, a horseman pressing the flanks of his steed, and galloping up as fast as the mountain which he had to ascend would permit. It was Aebli, landamman of Glaris. " The Five Cantons are prepared," said he, as he arrived, " but I have prevailed upon them to halt, if you will do the same. For this reason I entreat my lords and the people of Zurich, for the love of God and the safety of the confederation, to suspend their march at the present moment." As he uttered these words, the brave Helvetian

---

[1] Lupus lenitate agni, magis magisque vorax fit. Zw. Epp. ii. 296.
[2] Dei verbum enim hos pulveres omnes facile flatu suo disperget. Ibid.
[3] The Pensioners.—Exceptis aliquot nigris equis. Ibid. 298.
[4] Venenum a domestico illo colubro. Ibid.

[1] Sondern sass auf ein Ross, und führte eine hubsche Helparten auf den Achseln. Füssli Beytr. iv. 103.

shed tears.[1] "In a few hours," continued he, "I shall be back again. I hope, with God's grace, to obtain an honourable peace, and to prevent our cottages from being filled with widows and orphans."

Aebli was known to be an honourable man, friendly to the Gospel, and opposed to foreign service: his words, therefore, moved the Zurich captains, who resolved to halt. Zwingle alone, motionless and uneasy, beheld in his friend's intervention the machinations of the adversary. Austria, occupied in repelling the Turks, and unable to succour the Five Cantons, had exhorted them to peace. This, in Zwingle's opinion, was the cause of the propositions brought to them by the Landamman of Glaris. So at the moment Aebli turned round to return to Zug,[2] Zwingle, approaching him, said with earnestness, "Gossip landamman, you will render to God an account of all this. Our adversaries are caught in a sack: and hence they give you sweet words. By and by they will fall upon us unawares, and there will be none to deliver us." Prophetic words, whose fulfilment went beyond all foresight! "Dear gossip!" replied the landamman, "I have confidence in God that all will go well. Let each one do his best." And he departed.

The army, instead of advancing upon Zug, now began to erect tents along the edge of the forest and the brink of the torrent, a few paces from the sentinels of the Five Cantons; while Zwingle, seated in his tent, silent, sad, and in deep thought, anticipated some distressing news from hour to hour.

He had not long to wait. The deputies of the Zurich council came to give reality to his fears. Berne, maintaining the character that it had so often filled as representative of the federal policy, declared that if Zurich or the cantons would not make peace, they would find means to compel them: this state at the same time convoked a diet at Arau, and sent five thousand men into the field, under the command of Sebastian Diesbach. Zwingle was struck with consternation.

Aebli's message, supported by that of Berne, was sent back by the council to the army; for, according to the principles of the time, "wherever the banner waves, there is Zurich."—"Let us not be staggered," cried the reformer, ever decided and firm; "our destiny depends upon our courage; to-day they beg and entreat, and in a month, when we have laid down our arms, they will crush us. Let us stand firm in God. Before all things, let us be just; peace will come after that." But Zwingle, transformed to a statesman, began to lose the influence which he had gained as a servant of God. Many could not understand him, and asked if what they had heard was really the language of a minis-

ter of the Lord. "Ah!" said Oswald Myconius, one of his friends, who perhaps knew him best, "Zwingle certainly was an intrepid man in the midst of danger; but he always had a horror of blood, even of that of his most deadly enemies. The freedom of his country, the virtues of our forefathers, and, above all, the glory of Christ, were the sole end of all his designs.[1]—I speak the truth, as if in the presence of God," adds he.

While Zurich was sending deputies to Arau, the two armies received reinforcements. The men of Thurgovia and St. Gall joined their banners to that of Zurich: the Valaisans and the men of St. Gothard united with the Romanist cantons. The advanced posts were in sight of each other at Thun, Leematt, and Goldesbrunnen, on the delightful slopes of the Albis.

Never, perhaps, did Swiss cordiality shine forth brighter with its ancient lustre. The soldiers called to one another in a friendly manner, and shook hands, styling themselves confederates and brothers. "We shall not fight," said they. "A storm is passing over our heads, but we will pray to God, and he will preserve us from every harm." Scarcity afflicted the army of the Five Cantons, while abundance reigned in the camp of Zurich.[2] Some young famishing Waldstettes one day passed the outposts: the Zurichers made them prisoners, conducted them to the camp, and then sent them back laden with provisions, with still greater good-nature than was shown by Henry IV. at the siege of Paris. At another time, some warriors of the Five Cantons, having placed a bucket filled with milk on the frontier-line, cried out to the Zurichers that they had no bread. The latter came down immediately, and cut their bread into the enemies' milk, upon which the soldiers of the two parties began with jokes to eat out of the same dish—some on this side, some on that. The Zurichers were delighted that, notwithstanding the prohibition of their priests, the Waldstettes ate with heretics. When one of the troop took a morsel that was on the side of his adversaries, the latter sportively struck him with their spoons, and said: "Do not cross the frontier!" Thus did these good Helvetians make war upon one another; and hence it was that the Burgomaster Sturm of Strasburg, one of the mediators, exclaimed: "You confederates are a singular people! When you are disunited, you still, live in harmony with one another, and your ancient friendship never slumbers."[3]

The most perfect order reigned in the camp of Zurich. Every day Zwingle, the commander Schmidt, Zink abbot of Cappel, or some other minister, preached among the soldiers. No oath or dispute was heard; all

---

[1] Das redt er mitt weynenden Ougen. Bull. ii. 169.
[2] Alls nun der Amman wiederumn zu den 5 orten ryten wollt. Bull. Chron. ii. 170. Zwingle was godfather to one of Aebli's children.

[1] Libertas patriæ, virtutes avitæ, et imprimis gloria Christi. Osw. Myc. De vita Zw.
[2] A measure of corn was sold for a florin, and one of wine for a half-batz, about three half-pence. Bull. Chron. ii. 182.
[3] Wenn ihr schon uneins sind, so sind ir eins. Ibid. 183.

disorderly women were turned out of the camp; prayers were offered up before and after every meal; and each man obeyed his chiefs. There were no dice, no cards, no games calculated to excite quarrels; but psalms, hymns, national songs, bodily exercise, wrestling, or pitching the stone, were the military recreations of the Zurichers.[1] The spirit that animated the reformer had passed into the army.

The assembly at Arau, transported to Steinhausen in the neighbourhood of the two camps, decreed that each army should hear the complaints of the opposite party. The reception of the deputies of the Five Cantons by the Zurichers was tolerably calm; it was not so in the other camp.

On the 15th June, fifty Zurichers, surrounded by a crowd of peasants, proceeded on horseback to the Waldstettes. The sound of the trumpet, the roll of the drum, and repeated salvos of artillery announced their arrival. Nearly twelve thousand men of the smaller cantons, in good order, with uplifted heads and arrogant looks, were under arms. Escher of Zurich spoke first, and many persons from the rural districts enumerated their grievances after him, which the Waldstettes thought exaggerated. "When have we ever refused you the federal right?" asked they. "Yes, yes!" replied Funk, Zwingle's friend; "we know how you exercise it. That pastor (Keyser) appealed to it, and you referred him—to the executioner!" "Funk, you would have done better to have held your tongue," said one of his friends. But the words had slipped out: a dreadful tumult suddenly arose; all the army of the Waldstettes was in agitation; the most prudent begged the Zurichers to retire promptly, and protected their departure.

At length the treaty was concluded on the 26th June 1529. Zwingle did not obtain all he desired. Instead of the free preaching of the Word of God, the treaty stipulated only liberty of conscience; it declared that the common bailiwicks should pronounce for or against the Reform by a majority of votes. Without decreeing the abolition of foreign pensions, it was recommended to the Romish cantons. The alliance with Austria was broken; the Five Cantons were to pay the expenses of the war, Murner to retract his insulting words, and an indemnity was secured to Keyser's family.[2]

An incontrovertible success had just crowned the warlike demonstration of Zurich. The Five Cantons felt it. Gloomy, irritated, silently champing the bit that had been placed in their mouths, their chiefs could not decide upon giving up the deed of their alliance with Austria. Zurich immediately recalled her troops, the mediators redoubled

their solicitations, and the Bernese exclaimed: "If you do not deliver up this document, we will ourselves go in procession and tear it from your archives." At last it was brought to Cappel on the 26th June, two hours after midnight. All the army was drawn out at eleven in the forenoon, and they began to read the treaty. The Zurichers looked with astonishment at its breadth and excessive length, and the nine seals which had been affixed, one of which was in gold. But scarcely had a few words been read, when Aebli, snatching the parchment, cried out: "Enough, enough!"—"Read it, read it!" said the Zurichers; "we desire to learn their treason!" But the Landamman of Glaris replied boldly: "I would rather be cut in a thousand pieces than permit it." Then dashing his dagger into the parchment, he cut it in pieces in the presence of Zwingle and the soldiers,[1] and threw the fragments to the secretary, who committed them to the flames. "The paper was not Swiss," says Bullinger, with sublime simplicity.

The banners were immediately struck. The men of Unterwalden retired in anger; those of Schwytz swore they would for ever preserve their ancient faith; while the troops of Zurich returned in triumph to their homes. But the most opposite thoughts agitated Zwingle's mind. "I hope," said he, doing violence to his feelings, "that we bring back an honourable peace to our dwellings. It was not to shed blood that we set out.[2] God has once again shown the great ones of the earth that they can do nothing against us." Whenever he gave way to his natural disposition, a very different order of thoughts took possession of his mind. He was seen walking apart in deep dejection, and anticipating the most gloomy future. In vain did the people surround him with joyful shouts. "This peace," said he, "which you consider a triumph, you will soon repent of, striking your breasts." It was at this time that, venting his sorrow, he composed, as he was descending the Albis, a celebrated hymn often repeated to the sound of music in the fields of Switzerland, among the burghers of the confederate cities, and even in the palaces of kings. The hymns of Luther and of Zwingle play the same part in the German and Swiss Reformation as the Psalms in that of France.

Do thou direct thy chariot, Lord,
  And guide it at thy will;
Without thy aid our strength is vain,
  And useless all our skill.
Look down upon thy saints brought low,
And prostrate laid beneath the foe.

Beloved Pastor, who hast saved
  Our souls from death and sin,
Uplift thy voice, awake thy sheep
  That slumbering lie within
Thy fold, and curb with thy right hand
The rage of Satan's furious band.

---

[1] Sondern sang, sprang, wurf und Stiess die Steine. Füssli Beyt. iv. 108.
[2] Supra, p. 603. The treaty is given entire in Bullinger. V. 185, and Ruchat, ii.

[1] Tabellæ fœderis a prætore Pagi Glaronensis gladio concisæ et deletæ, id quod ipse vidi. Zw. Epp. ii. 310.
[2] Cum non cædem factum profecti sumus. Ibid.

Send down thy peace, and banish strife,
  Let bitterness depart ;
Revive the spirit of the past
  In every Switzer's heart :
Then shall thy Church for ever sing
  The praises of her heavenly King.

An edict, published in the name of the confederates, ordered the revival every where of the old friendship and brotherly concord ; but decrees are powerless to work such miracles.

This treaty of peace was nevertheless favourable to the Reform. Undoubtedly it met with a violent opposition in some places. The nuns of the vale of St. Catherine in Thurgovia, deserted by their priests and excited by some noblemen beyond the Rhine, who styled them in their letters, " Chivalrous women of the house of God," sang mass themselves, and appointed one of their number preacher to the convent. Certain deputies from the Protestant cantons having had an interview with them, the abbess and three of the nuns secretly crossed the river by night, carrying with them the papers of the monastery and the ornaments of the church. But such isolated resistance as this was unavailing. Already in 1529 Zwingle was able to hold a synod in Thurgovia, which organized the church there, and decreed that the property of the convents should be consecrated to the instruction of pious young men in sacred learning. Thus concord and peace seemed at last to be re-established in the confederation.

CHAPTER III.

Conquests of Reform in Schaffhausen and Zurzack—Reform in Glaris—To-day the Cowl, To-morrow the Reverse—Italian Bailiwicks—The Monk of Como—Egidio's Hope for Italy—Call of the Monk of Locarno—Hopes of reforming Italy—The Monks of Wettingen—Abbey of Saint Gall—Kilian Kouffi—Saint Gall recovers its Liberty—The Reform in Soleure—Miracle of Saint Ours—Popery triumphs—The Grisons invaded by the Spaniards—Address of the Ministers to the Romish Cantons—God's Word the Means of Unity—Œcolampadius for Spiritual Influence—Autonomy of the Church.

WHENEVER a conqueror abandons himself to his triumph, in that very confidence he often finds destruction. Zurich and Zwingle were to exemplify this mournful lesson of history. Taking advantage of the national peace, they redoubled their exertions for the triumph of the Gospel. This was a legitimate zeal, but it was not always wisely directed. To attain the unity of Switzerland by unity of faith was the object of the Zurichers ; but they forgot that, by desiring to force on a unity, it is broken to pieces, and that freedom is the only medium in which contrary elements can be dissolved, and a salutary union established. While Rome aims at unity by anathemas, imprisonment, and the stake, christian truth demands unity through liberty. And let us not fear that liberty, expanding each individuality beyond measure, will produce by this means an infinite multiplicity. While we urge every mind to attach itself to the Word of God, we give it up to a power capable of restoring its diverging opinions to a wholesome unity.

Zwingle at first signalized his victory by legitimate conquests. He advanced with courage. " His eye and his arm were every where." " A few wretched mischief-makers," says Salat, a Romanist chronicler, " penetrating into the Five Cantons, troubled men's souls, distributed their frippery, scattered every where little poems, tracts, and testaments, and were continually repeating that the people ought not to believe the priests."[1] This was not all : while the Reform was destined to be confined around the lake of the Waldstettes to a few fruitless efforts, it made brilliant conquests among the cantons,—the allies and subjects of Switzerland ; and all the blows there inflicted on the Papacy re-echoed among the lofty valleys of the primitive cantons, and filled them with affright. Nowhere had Popery shown itself more determined than in the Swiss mountains. A mixture of Romish despotism and Helvetian roughness existed there. Rome was resolved to conquer all Switzerland, and yet she beheld her most important positions successively wrested from her.

On the 29th September 1529, the citizens of Schaffhausen removed the " great God"[2] from the cathedral, to the deep regret of a small number of devotees whom the Roman worship still counted in this city ; then they abolished the mass, and stretched out their hands to Zurich and to Berne.

At Zurzack, near the confluence of the Rhine and the Aar, at the very moment when the priest of the place, a man devoted to the ancient worship, was preaching with zeal, a person named Tüfel (devil), raising his head, observed to him : " Sir, you are heaping insults on good men, and loading the pope and the saints of the Roman calendar with honour ; pray where do we find that in the Holy Scriptures ?" This question, put in a serious tone of voice, raised a sly smile on many faces, and the congregation with their eyes fixed on the pulpit awaited the reply. The priest in astonishment and at his wit's end answered with a trembling voice : " Devil is thy name ; thou actest like the devil, and thou art the devil ! For this reason I will have nothing to do with thee." He then hastily left the pulpit, and ran away as if Satan had been behind him. Immediately the images were torn down, and the mass abolished. The Roman-catholics sought to console themselves by repeating every where " At Zurzack it was the devil who introduced the Reformation."[3]

[1] Die sectischen haltend vil elenda Hüdel volk gefunden. &c. Salat, Chron.
[2] Le bon Dieu, probably the patron saint. W.
[3] That der Tüffel den ersten Angriff.

The priests and warriors of the Forest Cantons beheld the overthrow of the Romish faith in countries that lay nearer to them. In the canton of Glaris, whence by the steep passes of the Klaus and the Pragel,[1] the Reform might suddenly fall upon Uri and Schwytz, two men met face to face. At Mollis, Fridolin Brunner who questioned himself every day by what means he could advance the cause of Christ,[2] attacked the abuses of the Church with the energy of his friend Zwingle,[3] and endeavoured to spread among the people, who were passionately fond of war, the peace and charity of the Gospel. At Glaris, on the contrary, Valentine Tschudi studied with all the circumspection of his friend Erasmus to preserve a just medium between Rome and the Reform. And although, in consequence of Fridolin's preaching, the doctrines of purgatory, indulgences, meritorious works, and intercession of the saints, were looked at by the Glaronais as mere follies and fables,[4] they still believed with Tschudi that the body and blood of Christ were substantially in the bread of the Lord's Supper.

At the same time a movement in opposition to the Reform was taking place in that high and savage valley, where the Linth, roaring at the foot of vast rocks with jagged crests—enormous citadels which seem built in the air,—bathes the villages of Schwanden and Ruti with its waters. The Roman-catholics, alarmed at the progress of the Gospel, and wishing to save these mountains at least, had scattered with liberal hands the money they derived from their foreign pensions; and from that time violent hostility divided old friends, and men who appeared to have been won over to the Gospel basely sought for a pretext to conceal a disgraceful flight.[5] "Peter[6] and I," wrote Rasdorfer, pastor of Ruti, in despair, "are labouring in the vineyard, but alas! the grapes we gather are not employed for the sacrifice, and the very birds do not eat them. We fish, but after having toiled all night, we find that we have only caught leeches.[7] Alas! we are casting pearls before dogs, and roses before swine!" The spirit of revolt against the Gospel soon descended from these valleys with the noisy waters of the Linth as far as Glaris and Mollis. "The council, as if it had been composed only of silly women, shifted its sails every day," said Rasdorfer;[8] "one day it

will have the cowl, on the next it will not."[1] Glaris, like a leaf carried along on the bosom of one of its torrents, and which the waves and eddies drive in different directions, wavered, wheeled about, and was nearly swallowed up.

But this crisis came to an end: the Gospel suddenly regained strength, and on Easter Monday 1530, a general assembly of the people "put the mass and the altars to the vote." A powerful party that relied upon the Five Cantons vainly opposed the Reform. It was proclaimed, and its vanquished and disconcerted enemies were forced to content themselves, says Bullinger, with mysteriously concealing a few idols, which they reserved for better days.

In the meanwhile, the reform advanced in the exterior *Rhodes* of Appenzell,[2] and in the district of Sargans. But what most exasperated the cantons that remained faithful to the Romish doctrines, was to see it pass the Alps and appear in Italy, in those beautiful districts round Lake Maggiore, where, near the embouchure of the Maggia, within the walls of Locarno, in the midst of laurels, pomegranates, and cypresses, flourished the noble families of Orelli, Muralto, Magoria, and Duni, and where floated since 1512 the sovereign standard of the cantons. "What!" said the Waldstettes, "is it not enough that Zurich and Zwingle infest Switzerland! They have the impudence to carry their pretended reform even into Italy,—even into the country of the pope!"

Great irregularities prevailed there among the clergy: "Whoever wishes to be damned must become a priest," was a common saying.[3] But the Gospel succeeded in making its way even into that district. A monk of Como, Egidio à Porta, who had taken the cowl in 1511, against the wishes of his family,[4] struggled for years in the Augustine convent, and nowhere found peace for his soul. Motionless, environed, as it appeared to him, with profound night, he cried aloud: "Lord, what wilt thou that I should do?" Erelong the monk of Como thought he heard these words in his heart: "Go to Ulrich Zwingle and he will tell thee." He rose trembling with emotion. "It is you," wrote he to Zwingle immediately, "but no! it is not you, it is God who, through you, will deliver me from the nets of the hunters." "Translate the New Testament into Italian," replied Zwingle; "I will undertake to get it printed at Zurich." This is what the Reform did for Italy more than three centuries ago.

Egidio therefore remained. He commenced translating the Gospel; but at one

[1] This is the road by which the army of Suwaroff escaped in 1799.
[2] Nam quotidie cogitare soleo quanam re Christianum adjuvem profectum. Zw. Epp. ii. 13.
[3] Audeo ego intrepide omnem ecclesiæ abusum et omnia humana præcepta in enunciatione verbi Dei damnare. Ibid.
[4] Nugas esse et fabulas. Ibid.
[5] Jam ære convicti palinodi..m canunt. Ibid. 292.
[6] Pierre Rumelin, pastor of Schwanden.
[7] Tota enim nocte piscantes, sanguisugas, aspendios cepimus. Zw. Epp. ii. 13. Rasdorfer evidently alludes to what Pliny says of a kind of vine termed *Aspendios:* Ediverso aspendios, damnata aris. Ferunt eam nec ab alite ulla attingi. Hist. Nat. lib. xiv. cap. xviii. § 22.
[8] Vertit vela indies senatus noster muliercularum more. Zw. Epp. ii. 13.

[1] Vult jam cucullum, post non vult. Zw. Epp. ii. 13. That is, at one time it recognises, at another rejects, the Abbot of Saint Gall.
[2] See Benedict Noll's Letter to Zwingle, Epp. ii. 635.
[3] St. Chorles Barromeo, archbishop of Milan, suppressed somewhat later several convents in this district: "Monialium non dicam collegia, sed amantium contubernia," said he. Die evangel Gem. in Locarno von F. Meyer, i. 109.
[4] Subduxi memet a parentum patrocinio, cucullumque nigrum ex animo suscepi. Zw. Epp. i. 448.

time he had to beg for the convent, at another to repeat his "hours," and then to accompany one of the fathers on his journeys.[1] Every thing that surrounded him increased his distress. He saw his country reduced to the greatest misery by desolating wars,—men formerly rich, holding out their hands for alms,—crowds of women driven by want to the most shameful degradation. He imagined that a great political deliverance could alone bring about the religious independence of his fellow-countrymen.

On a sudden he thought that this happy hour was arrived. He perceived a band of Lutheran lansquenets descending the Alps. Their serried phalanxes, their threatening looks, were directed towards the banks of the Tiber. At their head marched Freundsberg, wearing a chain of gold around his neck, and saying: "If I reach Rome I will make use of it to hang the pope."—"God wills to save us," wrote Egidio to Zwingle: "write to the constable;[2] entreat him to deliver the people over whom he rules,—to take from the shaven crowns, whose God is their belly, the wealth which renders them so proud,—and to distribute it among the people who are dying of hunger. Then let each one preach without fear the pure Word of the Lord.—The strength of Antichrist is near its fall!"

Thus, about the end of 1526, Egidio already dreamt of the Reformation of Italy. From that time his letters cease: the monk disappeared. There can be no doubt that the arm of Rome was able to reach him, and that, like so many others, he was plunged into the gloomy dungeon of some convent.

In the spring of 1530, a new epoch commenced for the Italian bailiwicks. Zurich appointed Jacques Werdmüller bailiff of Locarno; he was a grave man, respected by all, and who even in 1524 had kissed the feet of the pope; he had since then been won over to the Gospel, and had sat down at the feet of the Saviour.[3] "Go," said Zurich, "and bear yourself like a Christian, and in all that concerns the Word of God conform to the ordinances." Werdmüller met with nothing but darkness in every quarter. Yet, in the midst of this gloom, a feeble glimmering seemed to issue from a convent situated on the delightful shores of Lake Maggiore. Among the Carmelites at Locarno was a monk named Fontana, skilled in the Holy Scriptures, and animated with the same spirit that had enlightened the monk of Como. The doctrine of salvation, "without money and without price," which God proclaims in the Gospel, filled him with love and joy. "As long as I live," said he, "I will preach upon the Epistles of St. Paul;"[4] for it was

particularly in these epistles that he had found the truth. Two monks, of whose names we are ignorant, shared his sentiments. Fontana wrote a letter "to all the Church of Christ in Germany," which was forwarded to Zwingle. We may imagine we hear that man of Macedonia, who appeared in a vision to Paul in the night, calling him to Europe, and saying, "Come over and help us."[1]—"O, trusty and well-beloved of Christ Jesus," cried the monk of Locarno to Germany, "remember Lazarus, the beggar, in the Gospel,—remember that humble Canaanitish woman, longing for the crumbs that fell from the Lord's table! hungry as David, I have recourse to the shewbread placed upon the altar. A poor traveller devoured by thirst, I rush to the springs of living water.[2] Plunged in darkness, bathed in tears, we cry to you who know the mysteries of God to send us by the hands of the munificent J. Werdmüller all the writings of the divine Zwingle, of the famous Luther, of the skilful Melancthon, of the mild Œcolampadius, of the ingenious Pomeranus, of the learned Lambert, of the elegant Brentz, of the penetrating Bucer, of the studious Leo, of the vigilant Hütten, and of the other illustrious doctors, if there are any more. Excellent princes, pivots of the Church, our holy mother, make haste to deliver from the slavery of Babylon a city of Lombardy that has not yet known the Gospel of Jesus Christ. We are but three who have combined together to fight on behalf of the truth;[3] but it was beneath the blows of a small body of men, chosen by God, and not by the thousands of Gideon, that Midian fell. Who knows if, from a small spark, God may not cause a great conflagration?"

Thus three men on the banks of the Maggia hoped at that time to reform Italy. They uttered a call to which, for three centuries, the evangelical world has not replied. Zurich, however, in these days of its strength and of its faith, displayed a holy boldness, and dared extend her heretical arms beyond the Alps. Hence, Uri, Schwytz, Unterwalden, and all the Romanists of Switzerland gave vent to loud and terrible threats, swearing to arrest even in Zurich itself the course of these presumptuous invasions.

But the Zurichers did not confine themselves to this: they gave the confederates more serious cause of fear by waging incessant war against the convents,—those centres of ultra-montane fanaticism. The extensive monastery of Wettingen, around which roll the waters of the Limmat, and which, by its proximity to Zurich, was exposed more than any other to the breath of reform, was in violent commotion. On the 23d August

[1] Confratres nonnulli viri certe et pietate et eruditione nequaquam contemptibiles. Zw. Epp. i. 533.
[2] Bourbon, who commanded in Italy on behalf of the emperor. Supra, book xiii. p. 504.
[3] Luke x. 39.
[4] Se dum vivat satis de Epistolis Pauli concionaturum esse. Zw. Epp. ii. 497.

[1] Acts xvi. 9.
[2] Debilis et infirmus apud piscinam, salutem mei et patriæ toto mentis affectu citissime expecto. Hottinger, sæcul. 16, pars 2, p. 619.
[3] Confederati conjunctique in expeditionem veritatis tres tantum numero sumus. Ibid. 620.

1529, a great change took place; the monks ceased to sing mass; they cut off each other's beards, not without shedding a few tears; they laid down their frocks and their hoods, and clothed themselves in becoming secular dresses.[1] Then, in astonishment at this metamorphosis, they listened devoutly to the sermon which Sebastian Benli of Zurich came and preached to them, and erelong employed themselves in propagating the Gospel, and in singing psalms in German. Thus Wettingen fell into the current of that river which seemed to be every where reviving the confederation. The cloister, ceasing to be a house for gaming, gluttony, and drunkenness, was changed into a school. Two monks alone in all the monastery remained faithful to the cowl.

The commander of Mulinen, without troubling himself about the threats of the Romish cantons, earnestly pressed the commandery of St. John at Hitzkirch towards the Reformation. The question was put to the vote, and the majority declared in favour of the Word of God. " Ah !" said the commander, " I have been long pushing behind the chariot."[2] On the 4th September the commandery was reformed. It was the same with that of Wadenswyl, with the convent of Pfeffers, and others besides. Even at Mury the majority declared for the Gospel; but the minority prevailed through the support of the Five Cantons.[3] A new triumph, and one of greater value, was destined to indemnify the reform, and to raise the indignation of the Waldstettes to the highest pitch.

The Abbot of St. Gall, by his wealth, by the number of his subjects, and the influence which he exercised in Switzerland, was one of the most formidable adversaries of the Gospel. In 1529, therefore, at the moment when the army of Zurich took the field against the Five Cantons, the Abbot Francis of Geisberg, in alarm and at the brink of death, caused himself to be hastily removed into the strong castle of Rohrschach, not thinking himself secure except within its walls. Four days after this, the illustrious Vadian, burgomaster of St. Gaul, entered the convent, and announced the intention of the people to resume the use of their cathedral-church, and to remove the images. The monks were astonished at such audacity, and having in vain protested and cried for help, put their most precious effects in a place of safety, and fled to Einsidlen.

Among these was Kilian Kouffi, headsteward of the abbey, a cunning and active monk, and, like Zwingle, a native of the Tockenburg. Knowing how important it was to find a successor to the abbot, before the news of his death was bruited abroad, he came to an understanding with those who waited on the prelate; and the latter dying on Tuesday in Holy Week, the meals were carried as usual into his chamber, and with downcast eyes and low voice the attendants answered every inquiry about his health. While this farce was going on round a dead body, the monks who had assembled at Einsidlen repaired in all haste to Rapperschwyl, in the territory of St. Gall, and there elected Kilian, who had so skilfully managed the affair. The new abbot went immediately to Rohrschach, and on Good Friday he there proclaimed his own election and the death of his predecessor. Zurich and Glaris declared they would not recognise him, unless he could prove by the Holy Scriptures that a monkish life was in conformity with the Gospel. " We are ready to protect the house of God," said they; " and for this reason we require that it be consecrated anew to the Lord. But we do not forget that it is our duty also to protect the people. The free Church of Christ should raise its head in the bosom of a free people." At the same time the ministers of St. Gall published forty-two theses, in which they asserted that convents were not " houses of God, but houses of the devil."[1] The abbot, supported by Lucerne and Schwytz, which with Zurich and Glaris exercised sovereign power in St. Gall, replied that he could not dispute about rights which he held from popes and emperors. The two natives of the Tockenburg, Zwingle and Kilian, were thus struggling around St. Gall,—the one claiming the people for the abbey, and the other the abbey for the people. The army of Zurich having approached Wyl, Kilian seized upon the treasures and muniments of the convent, and fled precipitately beyond the Rhine. As soon as peace was concluded, the crafty monk put on a secular dress, and crept mysteriously as far as Einsidlen, whence on a sudden he made all Switzerland re-echo with his cries. Zurich in conjunction with Glaris replied by publishing a constitution, according to which a governor, " confirmed in the evangelical faith," should preside over the district, with a council of twelve members, while the election of pastors was left to the parishes.[2] Not long afterwards, the abbot, expelled and a fugitive, while crossing a river near Bregentz, fell from his horse, got entangled in his frock, and was drowned. Of the two combatants from the Tockenburg, it was Zwingle who gained the victory.

The convent was put up to sale, and was purchased by the town of St. Gall, " with the exception," says Bullinger, " of a detached building, called *Hell*, where the monks were left who had not embraced the Reform."[3] The time having arrived when the governor sent by Zurich was to give place

1 Bekleitend sich in erbare gemeine Landskleyder. Bull. Chron. ii. 21.
2 Diu me in hoc curru promovendo laborasse, priusquam tam longe processit. Zw. Epp. ii. 334.
3 Das das minder müst das meer sin. Bull. ii. 241.

1 Thesis 8. Bull. ii. 115.
2 Die Pfarer soll den Gmeinden irs gfallens zu erkiessen Zugestelt syn. Ibid. 268.
3 Alein was ein gebuw die *Hell* genampt, das liess man den Munchen blyten. Ibid. 271.

to one from Lucerne, the people of St. Gall called upon the latter to swear to their constitution. " A governor has never been known," replied he, " to make an oath to peasants; it is the peasants who should make oath to the governor ! " Upon this he retired : the Zurich governor remained, and the indignation of the Five Cantons against Zurich, which so daringly assisted the people of St: Gall in recovering their ancient liberties, rose to the higest paroxysm of anger.

A few victories, however, consoled in some degree the partisans of Rome. Soleure was for a long time one of the most contested battle-fields. The citizens and the learned were in favour of Reform : the patricians and canons for Popery. Philip Grotz of Zug was preaching the Gospel there, and when the council desired to compel him to say mass, one hundred of the reformed appeared in the hall of assembly on the 13th September 1529, and with energy called for liberty of conscience. As Zurich and Berne supported this demand, their prayer was granted.

Upon this the most fanatical of the Roman-catholics exasperated at the concession, closed the gates of the city, pointed the guns, and made a show of expelling the friends of the Reform. The council prepared to punish these agitators, when the reformed, willing to set an example of christian moderation, declared they would forgive them.[1] The Great Council then published throughout the canton that the dominion of conscience belonging to God alone, and faith being the free gift of His grace, each one might follow the religion which he thought best. Thirty-four parishes declared for the Reformation, and only ten for the mass. Almost all the rural districts were in favour of the Gospel; but the majority in the city sided with the pope.[2] Haller, whom the reformed of Soleure had sent for, arrived, and it was a day of triumph for them. It was in the middle of winter : " To-day," ironically observed one of the evangelical Christians, " the patron saint (St. Ours) will sweat ! " And in truth—oh! wonderful !—drops of moisture fell from the holy image ! It was simply a little holy water that had frozen and then thawed. But the Romanists would listen to no raillery on so illustrious a prodigy, which may remind us of the blood of St. Januarius at Naples. All the city resounded with piteous cries,—the bells were tolled,—a general procession moved through the streets, —and high mass was sung in honour of the heavenly prince who had shown in so marvellous a manner the pangs he felt for his dearly beloved. " It is the fat minister of Berne (Haller) who is the cause of the saint's alarm," said the devout old women. One of them declared that she would thrust a knife

into his body ; and certain Roman-catholics threatened to go to the Cordeliers' church and murder the pastors who preached there. Upon this the reformed rushed to that church and demanded a public discussion : two hundred of their adversaries posted themselves at the same time in the church of St. Ours, and refused all inquiry. Neither of the two parties was willing to be the first to abandon the camp in which it was entrenched. The senate, wishing to clear the two churches thus in a manner transformed into citadels, announced that at Martinmas, i. e. nine months later, a public disputation should take place. But as the reformed found the delay too long, both parties remained for a whole week more under arms. Commerce was interrupted,—the public offices were closed,— messengers ran to and fro,—arrangements were proposed ;—but the people were so stiff-necked,[1] that no one would give way. The city was in a state of siege. At last all were agreed about the discussion, and the ministers committed four theses to writing, which the canons immediately attempted to refute.

Nevertheless they judged it a still better plan to elude them. Nothing alarmed the Romanists so much as a disputation. "What need have we of any ?" said they. " Do not the writings of the two parties declare their sentiments ?" The conference was, therefore, put off until the following year. Many of the reformed, indignant at these delays, imprudently quitted the city ; and the councils, charmed at this result, which they were far from expecting, hastily declared that the people should be free in the canton, but that in the city no one should attack the mass. From that time the reformed were compelled every Sunday to leave Soleure and repair to the village of Zuchswyl to hear the Word of God. Thus Popery, defeated in so many places, triumphed in Soleure.

Zurich and the other reformed cantons attentively watched these successes of their adversaries, and lent a fearful ear to the threats of the Roman-catholics, who were continually announcing the intervention of the emperor : when on a sudden a report was heard that nine hundred Spaniards had entered the Grisons ; that they were led by the Chatelain of Musso, recently invested with the title of marquis by Charles the Fifth ; that the chatelain's brother-in-law, Didier d'Embs, was also marching against the Swiss at the head of three thousand imperial lansquenets ; and that the emperor himself was ready to support them with all his forces. The Grisons uttered a cry of alarm. The Waldstettes remained motionless ; but all the reformed cantons assembled their troops, and eleven thousand men began their march.[2] The emperor and the Duke of Milan having soon after declared that they

---

[1] Ruchat, ii. 139.
[2] Major pars agri abolita superstitione a parte nostra stat. Major et potior pars urbis a papistis. Zw. Epp. ii. 489.

[1] Tam duræ cervicis populus est. Zw. Epp. ii. 489.
[2] Bull. Chron. ii. 357.

would not support the chatelain, this adventurer beheld his castle razed to the ground, and was compelled to retire to the banks of the Sesia, giving guarantees of future tranquillity; while the Swiss soldiers returned to their homes, fired with indignation against the Five Cantons, who by their inactivity had infringed the federal alliance.[1] " Our prompt and energetic resistance," said they, " has undoubtedly baffled their perfidious designs; but the reaction is only adjourned. Although the parchment of the Austrian alliance has been torn in pieces, the alliance itself still exists. The truth has freed us, but soon the imperial lansquenets will come and try to place us again under the yoke of slavery."

Thus in consequence of so many violent shocks, the two parties that divided Switzerland had attained the highest degree of irritation. The gulf that separated them widened daily. The clouds—the forerunners of the tempest—drove swiftly along the mountains, and gathered threateningly above the valleys. Under these circumstances Zwingle and his friends thought it their duty to raise their voices, and if possible to avert the storm. In like manner, Nicholas de Flue had in former days thrown himself between the hostile parties.

On the 5th September 1530, the principal ministers of Zurich, Berne, Basle, and Strasburg,—Œcolampadius, Capito, Megander, Leo Juda, and Myconius,—were assembled at Zurich in Zwingle's house. Desirous of taking a solemn step with the Five Cantons, they drew up an address that was presented to the Confederates at the meeting of the diet at Baden. However unfavourable the deputies were, as a body, to these heretical ministers, they nevertheless listened to this epistle, but not without signs of impatience and weariness.[2] " You are aware, gracious lords, that concord increases the power of states, and that discord overthrows them.[3] You are yourselves a proof of the first of these truths. Setting out from a small beginning, you have, by a good understanding one with another, arrived at a great end. May God condescend to prevent you also from giving a striking proof of the second! Whence comes disunion, if not from selfishness? and how can we destroy this fatal passion, except by receiving from God the love of the common weal? For this reason we conjure you to allow the Word of God to be freely preached among you, as did your pious ancestors. When has there ever existed a government, even among the heathens, which saw not that the hand of God alone upholds a nation? Do not two drops of quicksilver unite so soon as you remove

that which separates them? Away then with that which separates you from our cities, that is, the absence of the Word of God; and immediately the Almighty will unite us, as our fathers were united. Then placed in your mountains, as in the centre of Christendom, you will be an example to it, its protection and its refuge; and after having passed through this vale of tears, being the terror of the wicked and the consolation of the faithful, you will at last be established in eternal happiness."

Thus frankly did these men of God address their brothers, the Waldstettes. But their voice was not attended to. " The ministers' sermon is rather long,"[1] said some of the deputies yawning and stretching their arms, while others pretended to find in it new cause of complaint against the cities.

This proceeding of the ministers was useless: the Waldstettes rejected the Word of God, which they had been entreated to admit; they rejected the hands that were extended towards them in the name of Jesus Christ. They called for the pope and not for the Gospel. All hope of reconciliation appeared lost.

Some persons, however, had at that time a glimpse of what might have saved Switzerland and the Reformation,—the *autonomy* (self-government) of the Church, and its independence of political interests. Had they been wise enough to decline the secular power to secure the triumph of the Gospel, it is probable that harmony might have been gradually established in the Helvetic cantons, and that the Gospel would have conquered by its Divine strength. The power of the Word of God presented chances of success that were not afforded by pikes and muskets. The energy of faith, the influence of charity, would have proved a securer protection to Christians against the burning piles of the Waldstettes than diplomatists and men-at-arms. None of the reformers understood this so clearly as Œcolampadius. His handsome countenance, the serenity of his features, the mild expression of his eyes, his long and venerable beard, the spirituality of his expression, and a certain dignity that inspired confidence and respect, gave him rather the air of an apostle than of a reformer. It was the power of the inner word that he particularly extolled; perhaps he even went too far in spiritualism. But, however that may be, if any man could have saved Reform from the misfortunes that were about to befall it—that man was he. In separating from the Papacy, he desired not to set up the magistracy in its stead. " The magistrate who should take away from the churches the authority that belongs to them," wrote he to Zwingle, " would be more intolerable than

---

[1] Ward ein grosser Unwill wieder sie. Bull. Chron. ii. 361.
[2] Lecta est epistola nostra in comitiis Badensibus. Œcol. to Bucer. 28th December 1530
[3] Wie mit einhelligkeit kleine Ding gross werdend. Zw. Opp. ii. 78.

[1] Libellum supplicem ad quinque pagos breviorem vellent. Zw. Epp. ii. 511. Fastidiunt tam sancta. Œcol.

Antichrist himself (*i. e.* the pope)."[1]—" The hand of the magistrate strikes with the sword, but the hand of Christ heals. Christ has not said,—If thy brother will not hear thee, tell it to the magistrate, but—*tell it to the Church.* The functions of the State are distinct from those of the Church. The State is free to do many things which the purity of the Gospel condemns."[2] Œcolampadius saw how important it was that his convictions should prevail among the reformed. This man, so mild and so spiritual, feared not to stand forth boldly in defence of doctrines then so novel. He expounded them before a synodal assembly, and next developed them before the senate of Basle.[3] It is a strange circumstance that these ideas, for a moment at least, were acceptable to Zwingle;[4] but they displeased an assembly of the brethren to whom he communicated them; the politic Bucer above all feared that this independence of the Church would in some measure check the exercise of the civil power.[5] The exertions of Œcolampadius to constitute the Church were not, however, entirely unsuccessful. In February 1531, a diet of four reformed cantons (Basle, Zurich, Berne, and St. Gall), was held at Basle, in which it was agreed, that whenever any difficulty should arise with regard to doctrine or worship, an assembly of divines and laymen should be convoked, which should examine what the Word of God said on the matter.[6] This resolution, by giving greater unity to the renovated Church, gave it also fresh strength.

CHAPTER IV.

Zwingle and the Christian State—Zwingle's double Part—Zwingle and Luther in Relation to Politics—Philip of Hesse and the Free Cities—Projected Union between Zwingle and Luther—Zwingle's political Action—Project of Alliance against the Emperor—Zwingle advocates active Resistance—He destines the Imperial Crown for Philip—Faults of the Reformation—Embassy to Venice—Giddiness of the Reformation—Projected Alliance with France—Zwingle's Plan of Alliance—Approaching Ruin—Slanders in the Five Cantons—Violence—Mysterious Paper—Berne and Basle vote for Peace—General Diet at Baden—Evangelical Diet at Zurich—Political Reformation of Switzerland—Activity of Zurich.

BUT it was too late to tread in this path which would have prevented so many disasters. The Reformation had already entered with all her sails set upon the stormy ocean of politics, and terrible misfortunes were gathering over her. The impulse communicated to the Reform came from another than Œcolampadius. Zwingle's proud and piercing eyes,—his harsh features,—his bold step,

[1] Intolerabilior enim Antichristo ipso magistratus, qui Ecclesiis auctoritatem suam adimit. Zw. Epp. ii. 510.
[2] Ipsorum functio alia est et ecclesiastica, multaque ferre et facere potest quæ puritas evangelica non agnoscit. Ibid.
[3] Orationis meæ quam, fratrum nomine, coram senatu habui. Ibid.
[4] Ut mihi magis ac magis arridet. Ibid. 518.
[5] Ut non impediat alicubi magistratum Christianum. Bucer to Zw. p. 836.
[6] J. J. Hottinger, iii. 554.

—all proclaimed in him a resolute mind and the man of action. Nurtured in the exploits of the heroes of antiquity, he threw himself, to save Reform, in the footsteps of Demosthenes and Cato, rather than in those of St. John and St. Paul. His prompt and penetrating looks were turned to the right and to the left,—to the cabinets of kings and the councils of the people, whilst they should have been directed solely to God. We have already seen, that as early as 1527, Zwingle, observing how all the powers were rising against the Reformation, had conceived the plan of a *co-burghery* or Christian State,[1] which should unite all the friends of the Word of God in one holy and powerful league. This was so much the easier as Zwingle's reformation had won over Strasburg, Augsburg, Ulm, Reutlingen, Lindau, Memmingen, and other towns of Upper Germany. Constance in December 1527, Berne in June 1528, St. Gall in November of the same year, Bienne in January 1529, Mulhausen in February, Basle in March, Schaffhausen in September, and Strasburg in December, entered into this alliance. This political phasis of Zwingle's character is in the eyes of some persons his highest claim to glory; we do not hesitate to acknowledge it as his greatest fault. The reformer, deserting the paths of the apostles, allowed himself to be led astray by the perverse example of Popery. The primitive Church never opposed their persecutors but with the sentiments derived from the Gospel of peace. Faith was the only sword by which it vanquished the mighty ones of the earth. Zwingle felt clearly that by entering into the ways of worldly politicians, he was leaving those of a minister of Christ; he therefore sought to justify himself. " No doubt, it is not by human strength," said he, " it is by the strength of God alone that the Word of the Lord should be upheld. But God often makes use of men as instruments to succour men. Let us therefore unite, and from the sources of the Rhine to Strasburg let us form but one people and one alliance."[2]

Zwingle played two parts at once—he was a reformer and a magistrate. But these are two characters that ought not more to be united than those of a minister and of a soldier. We will not altogether blame the soldiers and the magistrates; in forming leagues and drawing the sword, even for the sake of religion, they act according to their point of view, although it is not the same as ours; but we must decidedly blame the christian minister who becomes a diplomatist or a general.

In October 1529, as we have already observed, Zwingle repaired to Marburg, whither he had been invited by Philip of Hesse; and while neither of them had been able to

[1] Civitas Christiana.
[2] Dass von oben hinab hie dises Rhyns, bis gen Strasbourg ein Volk und Bundniss würde. Zw. Opp. ii. 28.

come to an understanding with Luther, the landgrave and the Swiss reformer, animated by the same bold and enterprising spirit, soon agreed together.

The two reformers differed not less in their political than in their religious system. Luther, brought up in the cloister and in monastic submission, was imbued in youth with the writings of the fathers of the Church; Zwingle, on the other hand, reared in the midst of Swiss liberty, had, during those early years which decide the course of all the rest, imbibed the history of the ancient republics. Thus, while Luther was in favour of a passive obedience, Zwingle advocated resistance against tyrants.

These two men were the faithful representatives of their respective nations. In the north of Germany, the princes and nobility were the essential part of the nation, and the people—strangers to all political liberty—had only to obey. Thus, at the epoch of the Reformation they were content to follow the voice of their doctors and chiefs. In Switzerland, in the south of Germany, and on the Rhine, on the contrary, many cities, after long and violent struggles, had won civil liberty; and hence we find in almost every place the people taking a decided part in the Reform of the Church. There was good in this; but evil was close at hand. The reformers, themselves men of the people, who dared not act upon princes, might be tempted to hurry away the people. It was easier for the Reformation to unite with republics than with kings. This facility nearly proved its ruin. The Gospel was thus to learn that its alliance is in heaven.

There was, however, one prince with whom the reformed party of the free states desired to be in union: this was Philip of Hesse. It was he who in great measure prompted Zwingle's warlike projects. Zwingle desired to make him some return, and to introduce his new friend into the evangelical league. But Berne, watchful to avert any thing that might irritate the emperor and its ancient confederates, rejected this proposal, and thus excited a lively discontent in the "Christian State."—"What!" cried they, "do the Bernese refuse an alliance that would be honourable for us, acceptable to Jesus Christ, and terrible to our adversaries?"[1]—"The Bear," said the high-spirited Zwingle, "is jealous of the Lion (Zurich); but there will be an end to all these artifices, and victory will remain with the bold." It would appear, indeed, according to a letter in cipher, that the Bernese at last sided with Zwingle, requiring only that this alliance with a prince of the empire should not be made public.[2]

Still Œcolampadius had not given way, and his meekness contended, although mo-

destly, with the boldness of his impetuous friend. He was convinced that faith was destined to triumph only by the cordial union of all believers. A valuable relief occurred to reanimate his exertions. The deputies of the christian co-burghery having assembled at Basle in 1530, the envoys from Strasburg endeavoured to reconcile Luther and Zwingle. Œcolampadius wrote to Zwingle on the subject, begging him to hasten to Basle,[1] and not show himself too unyielding. "To say that the body and blood of Christ are really in the Lord's Supper, may appear to many too hard an expression," said he, "but is it not softened, when it is added—spiritually and not bodily?"[2]

Zwingle was immovable. "It is to flatter Luther that you hold such language, and not to defend the truth.[3] *Edere est credere.*"[4] Nevertheless there were men present at the meeting, who were resolved upon energetic measures. Brotherly love was on the eve of triumphing: peace was to be obtained by union. The Elector of Saxony himself proposed a concord of all evangelical christians, to which the Swiss cities were invited by the landgrave to accede. A report spread that Luther and Zwingle were about to make the same confession of faith. Zwingle, calling to mind the early professions of the Saxon reformer, said one day at table before many witnesses, that Luther would not think so erroneously about the Eucharist, if he were not misled by Melancthon.[5] The union of the whole of the Reformation seemed about to be concluded: it would have vanquished by its own weapons. But Luther soon proved that Zwingle was mistaken in his expectations. He required a written engagement by which Zwingle and Œcolampadius should adhere to his sentiments, and the negotiations were broken off in consequence. Concord having failed, there remained nothing but war. Œcolampadius must be silent, and Zwingle must act.

And in truth from that hour Zwingle advanced more and more along that fatal path into which he was led by his character, his patriotism, and his early habits. Stunned by so many violent shocks, attacked by his enemies and by his brethren, he staggered, and his head grew dizzy. From this period the reformer almost entirely disappears, and we see in his place the politician, the great citizen, who beholding a formidable coalition preparing its chains for every nation, stands up energetically against it. The emperor had just formed a close alliance with the pope. If his deadly schemes were not opposed it

---

[1] Ipsis et nobis honestius, ob religionis et caritatis causam, Christo gratius, ob conjunctas vires utilius, hostibusque terribilius. Zw. Epp. ii. 481.
[2] Tantum recusaverunt aperte agere. Ibid. 487. This cipher 3 appears to indicate the Bernese.

[1] Si potes, mox advola. Zw. Epp. ii. 547.
[2] Christi corpus et sanguinem adesse vero in cœna for tasse cuipiam durius sonat, sed mitigatur dum adjungitur animo non corpore. Ibid.
[3] Hæc omnia fieri pro Luthero neque pro veritate propugnandi causa. Ibid. 550.
[4] To eat is to believe. Ibid.
[5] Memini dudum Tiguri te dicentem cum convivio me exciperes, Lutherum non adeo perperam de Eucharistia sentire, nisi quod Melancthon ex alio eum cogeret. Ibid. 562.

would be all over, in Zwingle's opinion, with the Reformation, with religious and political liberty, and even with the confederation itself. "The emperor," said he, "is stirring up friend against friend, enemy against enemy: and then he endeavours to raise out of this confusion the glory of the Papacy, and, above all, his own power. He excites the Chatelain of Musso against the Grisons—Duke George of Saxony against Duke John—the Bishop of Constance against the city—the Duke of Savoy against Berne—the Five Cantons against Zurich—and the bishops of the Rhine against the landgrave; then, when the confusion shall have become general, he will fall upon Germany, will offer himself as a mediator, and ensnare princes and cities by fine speeches, until he has them all under his feet. Alas! what discord, what disasters, under the pretence of re-establishing the empire and restoring religion!"[1] Zwingle went farther. The reformer of a small town in Switzerland, rising to the most astonishing political conceptions, called for a European alliance against such fatal designs. The son of a peasant of the Tockenburg held up his head against the heir of so many crowns. "That man must either be a traitor or a coward," wrote he to a senator of Constance, "who is content to stretch and yawn, when he ought to be collecting men and arms on every side, to convince the emperor that in vain he strives to re-establish the Romish faith, to enslave the free cities, and to subdue the Helvetians.[2] He showed us only six months ago how he would proceed. To-day he will take one city in hand, to-morrow another; and so, step by step, until they are all reduced. Then their arms will be taken away, their treasures, their machines of war, and all their power......Arouse Lindau and all your neighbours; if they do not awake, public liberty will perish under the pretext of religion. We must place no confidence in the friendship of tyrants. Demosthenes teaches us that there is nothing so hateful in their eyes as την των πολιων ιλιυθιριαν.[3] The emperor with one hand offers us bread, but in the other he conceals a stone."[4] And a few months later Zwingle wrote to his friends in Constance: "Be bold; fear not the schemes of Charles. The razor will cut him who is sharpening it."[5]

Away, then, with delay! Should they wait until Charles the Fifth claimed the ancient castle of Hapsburg? The papacy and the empire, it was said at Zurich, are so confounded together,[6] that one cannot exist or perish without the other. Whoever rejects Popery should reject the empire, and whoever rejects the emperor should reject the pope.

It appears that Zwingle's thoughts even went beyond a simple resistance. When once the Gospel had ceased to be his principal study, there was nothing that could arrest him. "A single individual," said he, "must not take it into his head to dethrone a tyrant; this would be a revolt, and the kingdom of God commands peace, righteousness, and joy. But if a whole people with common accord, or if the majority at least, rejects him, without committing any excess, it is God himself who acts."[1] Charles V. was at that time a tyrant in Zwingle's eyes; and the reformer hoped that Europe, awakening at length from its long slumber, would be the hand of God to hurl him from his throne.

Never since the time of Demosthenes and of the two Catos had the world seen a more energetic resistance to the power of its oppressors. Zwingle in a political point of view is one of the greatest characters of modern times: we must pay him this honour, which is, perhaps, for a minister of God, the greatest reproach. Every thing was prepared in his mind to bring about a revolution that would have changed the history of Europe. He knew what he desired to substitute in place of the power he wished to overthrow. He had already cast his eyes upon the prince who was to wear the imperial crown instead of Charles. It was his friend the landgrave. "Most gracious prince," wrote he on the 2d November 1529, "if I write to you as a child to a father, it is because I hope that God has chosen you for great events.......I dare think, but I dare not speak of them[2]......However, we must bell the cat at last.[3]......All that I can do with my feeble means to manifest the truth, to save the universal Church, to augment your power and the power of those who love God—with God's help, I will do." Thus was this great man led astray. It is the will of God that there be spots even in those who shine brightest in the eyes of the world, and that only one upon earth shall say—"Which of you convinceth me of sin?" We are now viewing the faults of the Reformation: they arise from the union of religion with politics. I could not take upon myself to pass them by; the recollection of the errors of our predecessors is perhaps the most useful legacy they have bequeathed to us.

It appears that already at Marburg, Zwingle and the landgrave had drawn out the first sketch of a general alliance against Charles V. The landgrave had undertaken to bring over the princes, Zwingle the free cities of Southern Germany and Switzerland. He went still further, and formed a plan of gaining over to this league the republics of

---

[1] Quæ dissidia, quas turbas, quæ mala, quas clades! Zw. Epp. ii. 429.
[2] Romanam fidem restituere, urbes liberas capere, Helvetios in ordinem cogere. Ibid. March 153C.
[2] "The freedom of cities." These words are in Greek in the original.
[4] Cæsar altera manu panem ostentat, altera lapidem celat. Ibid.
[5] Incidet in cotem aliquando novacula. Ibid. 544.
[6] Bapst und Keyserthumen habend sich dermassen in einandern geflickt. Bull. ii. 343.

[1] So ist es mit Gott. Zw. Opp.
[2] Spero Deum te ad magnas res....quas quidem cogitare sed non dicere licet. Zw. Epp. ii. 666.
[3] Sed fieri non potest quin tintinnabulum aliquando feli adnectatur. Ibid.

Italy—the powerful Venice at least—that she might detain the emperor beyond the Alps, and prevent him from leading all his forces into Germany. Zwingle, who had earnestly pleaded against all foreign alliances, and proclaimed on so many occasions that the only ally of the Swiss should be the arm of the Almighty, began now to look around for what he had condemned, and thus prepared the way for the terrible judgment that was about to strike his family, his country, and his Church.

He had hardly returned from Marburg, and had made no official communication to the Great Council, when he obtained from the senate the nomination of an ambassador to Venice. Great men, after their first success, easily imagine that they can do every thing. It was not a statesman who was charged with this mission, but one of Zwingle's friends, who had accompanied him into Germany, to the court of the future chief of the new empire—the Greek professor, Rodolph Collins, a bold and skilful man, and who knew Italian. Thus the Reform stretched its hands to the Doge and the Procurator of St. Marc. The Bible was not enough for it —it must have the *Golden Book :* never did a greater humiliation befall God's work. The opinion which Protestants then entertained of Venice may, however, partly excuse Zwingle. There was in that city more independence of the pope, more freedom of thought, than in all the rest of Italy. Luther himself about this time wrote to Gabriel Zwilling, pastor at Torgau : " With what joy do I learn what you write to me concerning the Venetians. God be praised and glorified, for that they have received his Word ! " [1]

Collins was admitted, on the 26th December, to an audience with the doge and senate, who looked with an air of astonishment at this schoolmaster, this strange ambassador, without attendants and without parade. They could not even understand his credentials, in so singular a style were they drawn up, and Collins was forced to explain their meaning. " I am come to you," said he, " in the name of the council of Zurich and of the cities of the christian co-burghery— free cities like Venice, and to which common interests should unite you. The power of the emperor is formidable to republics ; he is aiming at a universal monarchy in Europe ; if he succeeds, all the free states will perish. We must therefore check him." [2] The doge replied that the republic had just concluded an alliance with the emperor, and betrayed the distrust that so mysterious a mission excited in the Venetian senate. But afterwards, in a private conference,[3] the doge, wishing to preserve a retreat on both sides,

added, that Venice gratefully received the message from Zurich, and that a Venetian regiment, armed and paid by the republic itself, should be always ready to support the evangelical Swiss. The chancellor, covered with his purple robe, attended Collins to the door, and, at the very gates of the ducal palace, confirmed the promise of support. The moment the Reformation passed the magnificent porticos of St. Marc it was seized with giddiness ; it could but stagger onwards to the abyss. They dismissed poor Collins by placing in his hands a present of twenty crowns. The rumour of these negotiations soon spread abroad, and the less suspicious, Capito for example, shook their heads, and could see in this pretended agreement nothing but the accustomed perfidy of Venice.[1]

This was not enough. The cause of the Reform was fated to drink the cup of degradation to the very dregs. Zwingle, seeing that his adversaries in the empire increased daily in numbers and in power, gradually lost his ancient aversion for France : and, although there was now a greater obstacle than before between him and Francis I.,— the blood of his brethren shed by that monarch,—he showed himself favourably disposed to a union that he had once so forcibly condemned.

Lambert Maigret, a French general, who appears to have had some leaning to the Gospel—which is a slight excuse for Zwingle —entered into correspondence with the reformer, giving him to understand that the secret designs of Charles V. called for an alliance between the King of France and the Swiss republics. " Apply yourself," said this diplomatist to him in 1530, " to a work so agreeable to our Creator, and which, by God's grace, will be very easy to your mightiness." [2] Zwingle was at first astonished at these overtures. " The King of France," thought he, " cannot know which way to turn." [3] Twice he took no heed of this prayer ; but the envoy of Francis I. insisted that the reformer should communicate to him a plan of alliance. At the third attempt of the ambassador, the simple child of the Tockenburg mountains could no longer resist his advances. If Charles V. must fall, it cannot be without French assistance ; and why should not the Reformation contract an alliance with Francis I., the object of which would be to establish a power in the empire that should in its turn oblige the king to tolerate the Reform in his own dominions ? Every thing seemed to meet the wishes of Zwingle ; the fall of the tyrant was at hand, and he would drag the pope along with him. He communicated the general's

---

[1] Lætus audio de Venetis quæ scribis, quod verbum Dei receperint, Deo gratia ac gloria. 7th March 1528. L. Epp. iii. 289.
[2] Formidandam rebus-publicis potentiam Cæsaris, quæ omnino ad Europæ monarchiam vergit. Zw. Epp. ii. 445.
[3] Postea privatim alia respondisse. Ibid.

[1] Perfidiam adversus Cæsarem, fidem videri volunt. Capito, Zw. Epp. ii. 445.
[2] Operi Creatori nostro acceptissimo, Dominationi tuæ facillimo, media gratia Dei. Zw. Epp. ii. 413.
[3] Regem admodum desesperare et inopem concilii esse, ut nesciat quo se vertat. Ibid. 414.

overtures to the secret council, and Collins set out, commissioned to bear the required project to the French ambassador.[1] "In ancient times," it ran, "no kings or people ever resisted the Roman empire with such firmness as those of France and Switzerland. Let us not degenerate from the virtues of our ancestors. His most Christian Majesty—all whose wishes are that the purity of the Gospel may remain undefiled[2]—engages therefore to conclude an alliance with the christian co-burghery that shall be in accordance with the Divine law, and that shall be submitted to the censure of the evangelical theologians of Switzerland." Then followed an outline of the different articles of the treaty.

Lanzerant, another of the king's envoys, replied the same day (27th February) to this astonishing project of alliance about to be concluded between the reformed Swiss and the persecutor of the French reformed, *under reserve of the censure of the theologians* ......This was not what France desired: it was Lombardy, and not the Gospel that the king wanted. For that purpose, he needed the support of all the Swiss. But an alliance which ranged the Roman-catholic cantons against him, would not suit him. Being satisfied, therefore, for the present with knowing the sentiments of Zurich, the French envoys began to look coolly upon the reformer's scheme. "The matters you have submitted to us are admirably drawn up," said Lanzerant to the Swiss commissioner, "but I can scarcely understand them, no doubt because of the weakness of my mind ......We must not put seed into the ground, unless the soil be properly prepared for it."

Thus, the Reform acquired nothing but shame from these propositions. Since it had forgotten these precepts of the Word of God: "Be ye not unequally yoked together with unbelievers!"[3] how could it fail to meet with striking reverses? Already, Zwingle's friends began to abandon him. The landgrave, who had pushed him into this diplomatic career, drew towards Luther, and sought to check the Swiss reformer, particularly after this saying of Erasmus had sounded in the ears of the great: "They ask us to open our gates, crying aloud—the Gospel! the Gospel!......Raise the cloak, and under its mysterious folds you will find —democracy."

While the Reform, by its culpable proceedings, was calling down the chastisement of Heaven, the Five Cantons, that were to be the instruments of its punishment, accelerated with all their might those fatal days of anger and of vengeance. They were irritated at the progress of the Gospel throughout the confederation, while the peace they

had signed became every day more irksome to them. "We shall have no repose," said they, "until we have broken these bonds and regained our former liberty."[1] A general diet was convoked at Baden for the 8th January 1531. The Five Cantons then declared that if justice was not done to their grievances, particularly with respect to the abbey of St. Gall, they would no more appear in diet. "Confederates of Glaris, Schaffhausen, Friburg, Soleure, and Appenzell," cried they, "aid us in making our ancient alliances respected, or we will ourselves contrive the means of checking this guilty violence: and may the Holy Trinity assist us in this work!"[2]

They did not confine themselves to threats. The treaty of peace had expressly forbidden all insulting language—"for fear," it said, "that by insults and calumnies, discord should again be excited, and greater troubles than the former should arise." Thus was concealed in the treaty itself the spark whence the conflagration was to proceed. In fact, to restrain the rude tongues of the Waldstettes was impossible. Two Zurichers, the aged prior Ravensbühler, and the pensioner Gaspard Gödli, who had been compelled to renounce, the one his convent, and the other his pension, especially aroused the anger of the people against their native city. They used to say every where in these valleys, and with impunity, that the Zurichers were heretics; that there was not one of them who did not indulge in unnatural sins, and who was not a robber at the very least;[3] that Zwingle was a thief, a murderer, and an arch-heretic; and that, on one occasion at Paris (where he had never been), he had committed a horrible offence, in which Leo Juda had been his pander.[4] "I shall have no rest," said a pensioner, "until I have thrust my sword up to the hilt in the heart of this impious wretch." Old commanders of troops, who were feared by all on account of their unruly character; the satellites who followed in their train; insolent young people, sons of the first persons in the state, who thought every thing lawful against miserable preachers and their stupid flocks; priests inflamed with hatred, and treading in the footsteps of these old captains and giddy young men, who seemed to take the pulpit of a church for the bench of a pot-house: all poured torrents of insults on the Reform and its adherents. "The townspeople," exclaimed with one accord these drunken soldiers and fanatic priests, "are heretics, soul-stealers, conscience-slayers, and Zwingle—that horrible man, who commits infamous sins—is the *Lutheran God.*"[5]

---

[1] Bis negavi, at tertio misi, non sine conscientia Probu-latarum. Zw. Epp. ii. 422.
[2] Nihil enim æqui esse in votis Christianissimi Regis, atque ut Evangelii puritas illibata permaneat. Ibid. 417.
[3] 2 Cor. vi. 14.

[1] Nitt ruwen biss sy der banden ledig. Bull. ii. 324.
[2] Darzu helfe uns die helig dryfaltikeit. Ibid. 330.
[3] Es were kein Zurycher er hätte chuy und merchen gehygt. Ibid. 336.
[4] Alls der zu Parys ein Esel gehygt; und habe imm Leo Jud denselben gehept. Ibid.
[5] Der lutherischen Gott. Ibid. 337.

They went still further. Passing from words to deeds, the Five Cantons persecuted the poor people among them who loved the Word of God, flung them into prison, imposed fines upon them, brutally tormented them, and mercilessly expelled them from their country. The people of Schwytz did even worse. Not fearing to announce their sinister designs, they appeared at a landsgemeinde wearing pine-branches in their hats, in sign of war, and no one opposed them. "The Abbot of St. Gall," said they, "is a prince of the empire, and holds his investiture from the emperor. Do they imagine that Charles V. will not avenge him?"—"Have not these heretics," said others, "dared to form a *christian fraternity*, as if old Switzerland was a heathen country?" Secret councils were continually held in one place or another.[1] New alliances were sought with the Valais, the pope, and the emperor[2]—blamable alliances no doubt, but such as might at least be justified by the proverb: "Birds of a feather go together;" which Zurich and Venice could not say.

The Valaisans at first refused their support: they preferred remaining neuter; but on a sudden their fanaticism was inflamed. A sheet of paper was found on an altar—such at least was the report circulated in their valleys—in which Zurich and Berne were accused of preaching that to commit an offence against nature is a smaller crime than to hear mass![3] Who had placed this mysterious paper on the altar? Came it from man? Did it fall from heaven?...... They know not; but however that might be, it was copied, circulated, and read every where; and the effects of this fable, invented by some villain, says Zwingle,[4] was such that Valais immediately granted the support it had at first refused. The Waldstettes, proud of their strength, then closed their ranks; their fierce eyes menaced the heretical cantons; and the winds bore from their mountains to their neighbours of the towns a formidable clang of arms.

At the sight of these alarming manifestations the evangelical cities were in commotion. They first assembled at Basle in February 1531, then at Zurich in March. 'What is to be done?" said the deputies from Zurich, after setting forth their grievances; "how can we punish these infamous calumnies, and force these threatening arms to fall?"—"We understand," replied Berne, "that you would have recourse to violence; but think of these secret and formidable alliances that are forming with the pope, the emperor, the King of France, with so many

princes, in a word with all the priests' party, to accelerate our ruin;—think on the innocence of so many pious souls in the Five Cantons, who deplore these perfidious machinations;—think how easy it is to begin a war, but that no one can tell when it will end."[1] Sad foreboding! which a catastrophe, beyond all human foresight, accomplished but too soon. "Let us therefore send a deputation to the Five Cantons," continued Berne; "let us call upon them to punish these infamous calumnies in accordance with the treaty; and if they refuse, let us break off all intercourse with them."—"What will be the use of this mission?" asked Basle. "Do we not know the brutality of this people? And is it not to be feared that the rough treatment to which our deputies will be exposed may make the matter worse? Let us rather convoke a general diet." Schaffhausen and St. Gall having concurred in this opinion, Berne summoned a diet at Baden for the 10th April, at which deputies from all the cantons were assembled.

Many of the principal men among the Waldstettes disapproved of the violence of the retired soldiers and of the monks. They saw that these continually repeated insults would injure their cause. "The insults of which you complain," said they to the diet, "afflict us no less than you. We shall know how to punish them, and we have already done so. But there are violent men on both sides. The other day a man of Basle having met on the high road a person who was coming from Berne, and having learnt that he was going to Lucerne:—'To go from Berne to Lucerne,' exclaimed he, 'is passing from a father to an arrant knave!'" The mediating cantons invited the two parties to banish every cause of discord.

But the war of the Chatelain of Musso having then broken out, Zwingle and Zurich, who saw in it the first act of a vast conspiracy, destined to stifle the Reform in every place, called their allies together. "We must waver no longer," said Zwingle; "the rupture of the alliance on the part of the Five Cantons, and the unheard-of insults with which they load us, impose upon us the obligation of marching against our enemies,[1] before the emperor, who is still detained by the Turks, shall have expelled the landgrave, seized upon Strasburg, and subjugated even ourselves." All the blood of the ancient Swiss seemed to boil in this man's veins; and while Uri, Schwytz, and Unterwalden basely kissed the hand of Austria, this Zuricher—the greatest Helvetian of the age—faithful to the memory of old Switzerland, but not so to still holier traditions, followed in the glorious steps of Stauffacher and Winkelried.

The warlike tone of Zurich alarmed its

[1] Radtschlagtend und tagentend heymlich v. c. Bull. ii. 336.
[2] Nüwe fründschaften, by den Walliseren, dem Bapst, und den Keysserischen. Ibid.
[3] Ut si quis rem obscænam cum jumento eive bove habeat, minus peccare quam si missam inaudiat. Zw. Epp. p 510.
[4] Perfidorum ac sceleratorum hominum commentum. Ibid.

[1] Aber sin end und ussgang möchte nieman bald wüssen. Bull. ii. 346
[2] Sy gwaltig ze überziehen. Ibid. 366.

confederates. Basle proposed a summons, and then, in case of refusal, the rupture of the alliance. Schaffhausen and St. Gall were frightened even at this step: " The mountaineers, so proud, indomitable, and exasperated," said they, " will accept with joy the dissolution of the confederation, and then shall we be more advanced." Such was the posture of affairs, when, to the great astonishment of all, deputies from Uri and Schwytz made their appearance. They were coldly received; the cup of honour was not offered to them; and they had to walk, according to their own account, in the midst of the insulting cries of the people. They unsuccessfully endeavoured to excuse their conduct. " We have long been waiting," was the cold reply of the diet, " to see your actions and your words agree."[1] The men of Schwytz and of Uri returned in sadness to their homes; and the assembly broke up, full of sorrow and distress.

Zwingle beheld with pain the deputies of the evangelical towns separating without having come to any decision. He no longer desired only a reformation of the Church; he wished for a transformation in the confederacy; and it was this latter reform that he now was preaching from the pulpit, according to what we learn from Bullinger.[2] He was not the only person who desired it. For a long time the inhabitants of the most populous and powerful towns of Switzerland had complained that the Waldstettes, whose contingent of men and money was much below theirs, had an equal share in the deliberations of the diet, and in the fruits of their victories. This had been the cause of division after the Burgundian war. The Five Cantons, by means of their adherents, had the majority. Now Zwingle thought that the reins of Switzerland should be placed in the hands of the great cities, and, above all, in those of the powerful cantons of Berne and Zurich. New times, in his opinion, called for new forms. It was not sufficient to dismiss from every public office the pensioners of foreign princes, and substitute pious men in their place; the federal compact must be remodelled, and settled upon a more equitable basis. A national constituent assembly would doubtless have responded to his wishes. These discourses, which were rather those of a tribune of the people than of a minister of Jesus Christ, hastened on the terrible catastrophe.

And indeed the animated words of the patriot reformer passed from the church where they had been delivered into the councils and the halls of the guilds, into the streets and the fields. The burning words that fell from this man's lips kindled the hearts of his fellow-citizens. The electric spark, escaping with noise and commotion, was felt even in the most distant cottage. The ancient traditions of wisdom and prudence seemed forgotten. Public opinion declared itself energetically. On the 29th and 30th April, a number of horsemen rode hastily out of Zurich; they were envoys from the council, commissioned to remind all the allied cities of the encroachment of the Five Cantons, and to call for a prompt and definitive decision. Reaching their several destinations, the messengers recapitulated the grievances.[1] Take care," said they in conclusion; " great dangers are impending over all of us. The emperor and King Ferdinand are making vast preparations; they are about to enter Switzerland with large sums of money, and with a numerous army."

Zurich joined actions to words. This state, being resolved to make every exertion to establish the free preaching of the Gospel in those bailiwicks where it shared the sovereignty with the Roman-catholic cantons, desired to interfere by force wherever negotiations could not prevail. The federal rights, it must be confessed, were trampled under foot at St. Gall, in Thurgovia, in the Rheinthal; and Zurich substituted arbitrary decisions in their place, that excited the indignation of the Waldstettes to the highest degree. Thus the number of enemies to the Reform kept increasing; the tone of the Five Cantons became daily more threatening, and the inhabitants of the canton of Zurich, whom business called into the mountains, were loaded with insults, and sometimes badly treated. These violent proceedings excited in turn the anger of the reformed cantons. Zwingle traversed Thurgovia, St. Gall, and the Tockenburg, every where organizing synods, taking part in their proceedings, and preaching before excited and enthusiastic crowds. In all parts he met with confidence and respect. At St. Gall an immense crowd assembled under his windows, and a concert of voices and instruments expressed the public gratitude in harmonious songs. " Let us not abandon ourselves," he repeated continually, " and all will go well." It was resolved that a meeting should be held at Arau on the 12th May, to deliberate on a posture of affairs that daily became more critical. This meeting was to be the beginning of sorrows.

They are to be found in Bullinger, ii. 368-376.

[1] Und wortt und werk mit einandern gangen werind. Bull. ii. 367.
[2] Trang gar häfftig uff eine gemeine Reformation gemeiner Eydgenoschaft. Ibid. 365.

CHAPTER V.

Diet of Arau—Helvetic Unity—Berne proposes to close the Markets—Opposition of Zurich—Proposition agreed to and published—Zwingle's War Sermon—Blockade of the Waldstettes—No Bread, no Wine, no Salt—Indignation of the Forest Cantons—The Roads blockaded—Processions —Cry of Despair—France tries to conciliate—Diet at Bremgarten — Hope — The Cantons inflexible — The Strength of Zurich broken—Discontent—Zwingle's false Position—Zwingle demands his Dismission—The Council remonstrate—He remains—Zwingle at Bremgarten— Zwingle's Farewell to Bullinger—Zwingle's Agony—The Forest Cantons reject all Conciliation—Frightful Omens —The Comet—Zwingle's Tranquillity.

ZWINGLE'S scheme with regard to the establishment of a new Helvetian constitution did not prevail in the diet of Arau. Perhaps it was thought better to see the result of the crisis. Perhaps a more christian, a more federal view—the hope of procuring the unity of Switzerland by unity of faith—occupied men's minds more than the pre-eminence of the cities. In truth, if a certain number of cantons remained with the pope, the unity of the confederation was destroyed, it might be for ever. But if all the confederation was brought over to the same faith, the ancient Helvetic unity would be established on the strongest and surest foundation. Now was the time for acting—or never; and there must be no fear of employing a violent remedy to restore the whole body to health.

Nevertheless, the allies shrank back at the thought of restoring religious liberty or political unity by means of arms; and to escape from the difficulties in which the confederation was placed, they sought a middle course between war and peace. "There is no doubt," said the deputies from Berne, "that the behaviour of the cantons with regard to the Word of God fully authorizes an armed intervention; but the perils that threaten us on the side of Italy and the empire—the danger of arousing the lion from his slumber—the general want and misery that afflict our people—the rich harvests that will soon cover our fields, and which the war would infallibly destroy—the great number of pious men among the Waldstettes, and whose innocent blood would flow along with that of the guilty :—all these motives enjoin us to leave the sword in the scabbard. Let us rather close our markets against the Five Cantons ; let us refuse them corn, salt, wine, steel, and iron ; we shall thus impart authority to the friends of peace among them, and innocent blood will be spared."[1] The meeting separated forthwith to carry this intermediate proposition to the different evangelical cantons ; and on the 15th May again assembled at Zurich.

Convinced that the means apparently the most violent were nevertheless both the surest and the most humane, Zurich resisted the Bernese proposition with all its might. "By accepting this proposition," said they,

"we sacrifice the advantages that we now possess, and we give the Five Cantons time to arm themselves, and to fall upon us first. Let us take care that the emperor does not then assail us on one side, while our ancient confederates attack us on the other ; a just war is not in opposition to it—taking the bread from the mouths of the innocent as well as the guilty ; straitening by hunger the sick, the aged, pregnant women, children, and all who are deeply afflicted by the injustice of the Waldstettes.[1] We should beware of exciting by this means the anger of the poor, and transforming into enemies many who at the present time are our friends and our brothers !"

We must acknowledge that this language, which was Zwingle's, contained much truth. But the other cantons, and Berne in particular, were immovable. "When we have once shed the blood of our brothers," said they, "we shall never be able to restore life to those who have lost it ; while, from the moment the Waldstettes have given us satisfaction, we shall be able to put an end to all these severe measures. We are resolved not to begin the war." There were no means of running counter to such a declaration. The Zurichers consented to refuse supplies to the Waldstettes ; but it was with hearts full of anguish, as if they had foreseen all that this deplorable measure would cost them.[2] It was agreed that the severe step that was now about to be taken should not be suspended except by common consent, and that, as it would create great exasperation, each one should hold himself prepared to repel the attacks of the enemy. Zurich and Berne were commissioned to notify this determination to the Five Cantons ; and Zurich, discharging its task with promptitude, immediately forwarded an order to every bailiwick to suspend all communication with the Waldstettes, commanding them at the same time to abstain from ill-usage and hostile language. Thus the Reformation, becoming imprudently mixed up with political combinations, marched from fault to fault ; it pretended to preach the Gospel to the poor, and was now about to refuse them bread !

On the Sunday following—it was Whitsunday—the resolution was published from the pulpits. Zwingle walked towards his, where an immense crowd was waiting for him. The piercing eye of this great man easily discovered the dangers of the measure in a political point of view, and his christian heart deeply felt all its cruelty. His soul was overburdened, his eyes downcast. If at this moment the true character of a minister of the Gospel had awoke within him ;—if Zwingle with his powerful voice had called on the people to humiliation before God, to

---

[1] Und dadurch unshuldiez Blüt erspart wurde. Bull.·ii. 383.

[1] Kranke, alte, shwangere wyber, kinder und sunst tetrubte. Bull. ii. 384.
[2] Schmerzlich und kummersachlich. Ibid. 386.

forgiveness of trespasses, and to prayer; safety might yet have dawned on "broken-hearted" Switzerland. But it was not so. More and more the Christian disappeared in the reformer, and the citizen alone remained; but in that character he soared far above all, and his policy was undoubtedly the most skilful. He saw clearly that every delay might ruin Zurich; and after having made his way through the congregation, and closed the book of the Prince of Peace, he hesitated not to attack the resolution which he had just communicated to the people, and on the very festival of the Holy Ghost to preach war. "He who fears not to call his adversary a criminal," said he in his usual forcible language, "must be ready to follow the word with a blow.[1] If he does not strike, he will be stricken. Men of Zurich! you deny food to the Five Cantons, as to evil doers: well! let the blow follow the threat, rather than reduce poor innocent creatures to starvation. If, by not taking the offensive, you appear to believe that there is not sufficient reason for punishing the Waldstettes, and yet you refuse them food and drink, you will force them by this line of conduct to take up arms, to raise their hands, and to inflict punishment upon you. This is the fate that awaits you."

These words of the eloquent reformer moved the whole assembly. Zwingle's politic mind already so influenced and misled all the people, that there were few souls christian enough to feel how strange it was, that on the very day when they were celebrating the outpouring of the Spirit of peace and love upon the Christian Church, the mouth of a minister of God should utter a provocation to war. They looked at this sermon only in a political point of view: "It is a seditious discourse; it is an excitement to civil war!" said some. "No," replied others, "it is the language that the safety of the state requires!" All Zurich was agitated. "Zurich has too much fire," said Berne. "Berne has too much cunning," replied Zurich.[2] Zwingle's gloomy prophecy was too soon to be fulfilled!

No sooner had the reformed cantons communicated this pitiless decree to the Waldstettes than they hastened its execution; and Zurich showed the greatest strictness respecting it. Not only the markets of Zurich and of Berne, but also those of the free bailiwicks of St. Gall, of the Tockenburg, of the district of Sargans and of the valley of the Rhine, a country partly under the sovereignty of the Waldstettes, were shut against the Five Cantons. A formidable power had suddenly encompassed with barrenness, famine, and death the noble founders of Helvetian liberty. Uri, Schwytz, Unterwalden,

Zug, and Lucerne, were, as it seemed, in the midst of a vast desert. Their own subjects, at least they thought the communes that have taken the oath of allegiance to them, would range themselves on their side! But no; Bremgarten, and even Mellingen, refused all succour. Their last hope was in Wesen and the Gastal. Neither Berne nor Zurich had any thing to do there; Schwytz and Glaris alone ruled over them; but the power of their enemies had penetrated every where. A majority of thirteen votes had declared in favour of Zurich at the landsgemeinde of Glaris; and Glaris closed the gates of Wesen and of the Gastal against Schwytz. In vain did Berne itself cry out: "How can you compel subjects to refuse supplies to their lords?" In vain did Schwytz raise its voice in indignation; Zurich immediately sent to Wesen—gunpowder and bullets. It was upon Zurich, therefore, that fell all the odium of a measure which that city had at first so earnestly combated. At Arau, at Bremgarten, at Mellingen, in the free bailiwicks, were several carriages laden with provisions for the Waldstettes. They were stopped, unloaded, and upset: with them barricades were erected on the roads leading to Lucerne, Schwytz, and Zug. Already a year of dearth had made provisions scarce in the Five Cantons;—already had a frightful epidemic, the *Sweating Sickness*, scattered every where despondency and death: but now the hand of man was joined to the hand of God; the evil increased, and the poor inhabitants of these mountains beheld unheard-of calamities approach with hasty steps. No more bread for their children—no more wine to revive their exhausted strength—no more salt for their flocks and herds! Every thing failed them that man requires for subsistence.[1] One could not see such things, and be a man, without feeling his heart wrung. In the confederate cities, and out of Switzerland, numerous voices were raised against this implacable measure. What good can result from it? Did not St. Paul write to the Romans: "If thine enemy hunger, feed him; if he thirst, give him drink: for in so doing thou shalt heap coals of fire on his head?"[2] And when the magistrates wished to convince certain refractory communes of the utility of the measure: "We desire no religious war," cried they. "If the Waldstettes will not believe in God, let them stick to the devil!"

But it was especially in the Five Cantons that earnest complaints were heard. The most pacific individuals, and even the secret partisans of the Reform, seeing famine invade their habitations, felt the deepest indignation. The enemies of Zurich skilfully took advantage of this disposition; they fostered these murmurs; and soon the cry of

---

[1] Das er wortt und faust mitt einander gan lasse. Bull. ii. 388.
[2] It was Zwingle who thus characterized the two cities:—Bern: klage Zurich wäre zu hitzig; Zurich: Bern wäre zu witzig.—Stettler.

[1] Deshalb sy bald grossen mangel erlittend an allem dem das der Mensh geläben soll. Bull. ii. 396.
[2] Ibid. Romans xii. 20.

anger and distress re-echoed from all the mountains. In vain did Berne represent to the Waldstettes that it is more cruel to refuse men the nourishment of the soul than to cut off that of the body. "God," replied these mountaineers in their despair, "God causes the fruits of the earth to grow freely for all men!"[1] They were not content with groaning in their cottages, and venting their indignation in the councils; they filled all Switzerland with complaints and menaces.[2] "They wish to employ famine to tear us from our ancient faith; they wish to deprive our wives and our children of bread, that they may take from us the liberty we derive from our forefathers. When did such things ever take place in the bosom of the confederation? Did we not see, in the last war, the confederates with arms in their hands, and who were ready to draw the sword, eating together from the same dish? They tear in pieces old friendships—they trample our ancient manners under foot——they violate treaties—they break alliances ......We invoke the charters of our ancestors. Help! help!......Wise men of our people give us your advice, and all you who know how to handle the sling and the sword, come and maintain with us the sacred possessions for which our fathers, delivered from the yoke of the stranger, united their arms and their hearts."

At the same time the Five Cantons sent into Alsace, Brisgau, and Swabia, to obtain salt, wine, and bread; but the administration of the cities was implacable; the orders were every where given and every where strictly executed. Zurich and the other allied cantons intercepted all communication, and sent back to Germany the supplies that had been forwarded to their brethren. The Five Cantons were like a vast fortress, all the issues from which were closely guarded by watchful sentinels. The afflicted Waldstettes, on beholding themselves alone with famine between their lakes and their mountains, had recourse to the observances of their worship. All sports, dances, and every kind of amusement were interdicted;[3] prayers were directed to be offered up; and long processions covered the roads to Einsidlen and other resorts of pilgrims. They assumed the belt, and staff, and arms of the brotherhood to which they each belonged; each man carried a chaplet in his hands, and repeated paternosters; the mountains and the valleys re-echoed with their plaintive hymns. But the Waldstettes did still more: they grasped their swords—they sharpened the points of their halberds—they brandished their weapons in the direction of Zurich and of Berne, and exclaimed with rage: "They block up their roads, but we will open them with our right arms!"[1] No one replied to this cry of despair; but there is a just Judge in heaven to whom vengeance belongs, and who will soon reply in a terrible manner, by punishing those misguided persons, who, forgetful of christian mercy, and making an impious mixture of political and religious matters, pretend to secure the triumph of the Gospel by famine and by armed men.

Some attempts, however, were made to arrange matters; but these very efforts proved a great humiliation for Switzerland and for the Reform. It was not the ministers of the Gospel, it was France—more than once an occasion of discord to Switzerland—that offered to restore peace. Every proceeding calculated to increase its influence among the cantons was of service to its policy. On the 14th May, Maigret and Dangertin (the latter of whom had received the Gospel truth, and consequently did not dare return to France),[2] after some allusions to the spirit which Zurich had shown in this affair—a spirit little in accordance with the Gospel—said to the council: "The king our master has sent you two gentlemen to consult on the means of preserving concord among you. If war and tumult invade Switzerland, the whole society of the Helvetians will be destroyed,[3] and whichever party is the conqueror, he will be as much ruined as the other." Zurich having replied that if the Five Cantons would allow the free preaching of the Word of God, the reconciliation would be easy, the French secretly sounded the Waldstettes, whose answer was: "We will never permit the preaching of the Word of God, as the people of Zurich understand it."[4]

These more or less interested exertions o. the foreigners having failed, a general diet became the only chance of safety that remained for Switzerland. One was accordingly convoked at Bremgarten. It was opened in presence of deputies from France, from the Duke of Milan, from the Countess of Neufchatel, from the Grisons, Valais, Thurgovia, and the district of Sargans; and met on five different occasions,—on the 14th and 20th June, on the 9th July, and the 10th and 23d August. The chronicler Bullinger, who was pastor of Bremgarten, delivered an oration at the opening, in which he earnestly exhorted the confederates to union and peace.

A gleam of hope for a moment cheered Switzerland. The blockade had become less strict; friendship and good neighbourhood had prevailed in many places over the de-

---

[1] Hartmann von Hallwyll to Albert of Mulinen, 7th August.
[2] Klagtend sich allent halben wyt und breit. Bull. ii. 397.
[3] Stelltent ab Spielen, Tanzen.—Tschudi der Capeller krieg, 1531. This MS. is attributed to Egidius Tschudi, who must have written it in 1533, in favour of the Five Cantons; it was printed in the "Helvetia," vol. ii. 165.

[1] Trotwend auch die Straassen uff zu thun mit gwalt. Bull. ii. 397.
[2] Ep. Rugeri ad Bulling., 12th November 1560.
[3] Universa societas *Helvetiorum* dilabetur, si tumultus et bellum inter eam eruperit. Zw. Epp. ii. 604.
[4] Responderunt verbi Dei predicationem non laturos, quomodo nos intelligimus. Ibid. 607.

crees of the state. Unusual roads had been opened across the wildest mountains to convey supplies to the Waldstettes. Provisions were concealed in bales of merchandise; and while Lucerne imprisoned and tortured its own citizens, who were found with the pamphlets of the Zurichers,[1] Berne punished but slightly the peasants who had been discovered bearing food for Unterwalden and Lucerne; and Glaris shut its eyes on the frequent violation of its orders. The voice of charity, that had been momentarily stifled, pleaded with fresh energy the cause of their confederates before the reformed cantons.

But the Five Cantons were inflexible. "We will not listen to any proposition before the raising of the blockade," said they. "We will not raise it," replied Berne and Zurich, "before the Gospel is allowed to be freely preached, not only in the common bailiwicks, but also in the Five Cantons." This was undoubtedly going too far, even according to the natural law and the principles of the confederation. The councils of Zurich might consider it their duty to have recourse to war for maintaining liberty of conscience in the common bailiwicks; but it was unjust—it was a usurpation, to constrain the Five Cantons in a matter that concerned their own territory. Nevertheless the mediators succeeded, not without much trouble, in drawing up a plan of conciliation that seemed to harmonize with the wishes of both parties. The conference was broken up, and this project was hastily transmitted to the different states for their ratification.

The diet met again a few days after; but the Five Cantons persisted in their demand, without yielding in any one point. In vain did Zurich and Berne represent to them, that, by persecuting the reformed, the cantons violated the treaty of peace; in vain did the mediators exhaust their strength in warnings and entreaties. The parties appeared at one time to approximate, and then on a sudden they were more distant and more irritated than ever. The Waldstettes at last broke up the third conference by declaring, that far from opposing the evangelical truth, they would maintain it, as it had been taught by the Redeemer, by his holy apostles, by the four doctors, and by their holy mother, the Church—a declaration that seemed a bitter irony to the deputies from Zurich and Berne. Nevertheless Berne, turning towards Zurich as they were separating, observed : " Beware of too much violence, even should they attack you !"

This exhortation was unnecessary. The strength of Zurich had passed away. The first appearance of the Reformation and of the reformers had been greeted with joy. The people, who groaned under a twofold slavery, believed they saw the dawn of liberty. But their minds, abandoned for ages to superstition and ignorance, being unable immediately to realize the hopes they had conceived, a spirit of discontent soon spread among the masses. The change by which Zwingle, ceasing to be a man of the Gospel, became the man of the State, took away from the people the enthusiasm necessary to resist the terrible attacks they would have to sustain. The enemies of the Reform had a fair chance against it so soon as its friends abandoned the position that gave them strength. Besides, Christians could not have recourse to famine and to war to secure the triumph of the Gospel, without their consciences becoming troubled. The Zurichers " walked not in the Spirit, but in the flesh; now, the works of the flesh are hatred, variance, emulations, wrath, strife, seditions."[1] The danger without was increasing, while within, hope, union, and courage were far from being augmented : men saw on the contrary the gradual disappearance of that harmony and lively faith which had been the strength of the Reform. The Reformation had grasped the sword, and that very sword pierced its heart.

Occasions of discord were multiplied in Zurich. By the advice of Zwingle, the number of nobles was diminished in the two councils, because of their opposition to the Gospel; and this measure spread discontent among the most honourable families of the canton. The millers and bakers were placed under certain regulations, which the dearth rendered necessary, and a great part of the townspeople attributed this proceeding to the sermons of the reformer, and became irritated against him. Rodolph Lavater, bailiff of Kibourg, was appointed captain-general, and the officers who were of longer standing than he were offended. Many who had been formerly the most distinguished by their zeal for the Reform, now openly opposed the cause they had supported. The ardour with which the ministers of peace demanded war spread in every quarter a smothered dissatisfaction, and many persons gave vent to their indignation. This unnatural confusion of Church and State, which had corrupted Christianity after the age of Constantine, was hurrying on the ruin of the Reformation. The majority of the Great Council, ever ready to adopt important and salutary resolutions, was destroyed. The old magistrates, who were still at the head of affairs, allowed themselves to be carried away by feelings of jealousy against men whose non-official influence prevailed over theirs. All those who hated the doctrine of the Gospel, whether from love of the world or from love to the pope, boldly raised their heads in Zurich. The partisans of the monks, the friends of foreign service, the malcontents of every class, coalesced in pointing out Zwingle as the author of all the sufferings of the people.

---

[1] Warf sie in Gefängniss. Bull. iii. 30.

[1] Galatians v. 19, 20.

Zwingle was heart-broken. He saw that Zurich and the Reformation were hastening to their ruin, and he could not check them. How could he do so, since, without suspecting it, he had been the principal accomplice in these disasters? What was to be done? Should the pilot remain in the ship which he is no longer permitted to save? There was but one means of safety for Zurich and for Zwingle. He should have retired from the political stage, and fallen back on that *kingdom which is not of this world*; he should, like Moses, have kept his hands and his heart night and day raised towards heaven, and energetically preached repentance, faith, and peace. But religious and political matters were united in the mind of this great man by such old and dear ties, that it was impossible for him to distinguish their line of separation. This confusion had become his dominant idea; the Christian and the citizen were for him one and the same character; and hence it resulted, that all resources of the state — even cannons and arquebuses — were to be placed at the service of the Truth. When one peculiar idea thus seizes upon a man, we see a false conscience formed within him, which approves of many things condemned by the Word of the Lord. This was now Zwingle's condition. War appeared to him legitimate and desirable; and if that was refused, he had only to withdraw from public life: he was for every thing or nothing. He therefore, on the 26th July, appeared before the Great Council with dimmed eyes and disconsolate heart: "For eleven years," said he, "I have been preaching the Gospel among you, and have warned you faithfully and paternally of the woes that are hanging over you; but no attention has been paid to my words; the friends of foreign alliances, the enemies of the Gospel, are elected to the Council, and while you refuse to follow my advice, I am made responsible for every misfortune. I cannot accept such a position, and I ask for my dismissal." The reformer retired bathed in tears.

The council shuddered as they heard these words. All the old feelings of respect which they had so long entertained for Zwingle were revived; to lose him now was to ruin Zurich. The burgomaster and the other magistrates received orders to persuade him to recall his fatal resolution. The conference took place on the same day; Zwingle asked time for consideration. For three days and three nights he sought the road that he should follow. Seeing the dark storm that was gathering from every quarter, he considered whether he ought to quit Zurich and seek refuge on the lofty hills of the Tockenburg, where he had been reared, at a time when his country and his Church were on the point of being assailed and beaten down by their enemies, like corn by the hail-storm. He groaned and cried to the

Lord. He would have put away the cup of bitterness that was presented to his soul, but could not gather up the resolution. At length the sacrifice was accomplished, and the victim was placed shuddering upon the altar. Three days after the first conference, Zwingle reappeared in the council: "I will stay with you," said he, "and I will labour for the public safety—until death!"

From this moment he displayed new zeal. On the one hand, he endeavoured to revive harmony and courage in Zurich; on the other, he set about arousing and exciting the allied cities to increase and concentrate all the forces of the Reformation. Faithful to the political vocation he imagined to have received from God himself—persuaded that it was in the doubts and want of energy of the Bernese that he must look for the cause of all the evil, the reformer repaired to Bremgarten with Collins and Steiner, during the fourth conference of the diet, although he incurred great danger in the attempt. He arrived secretly by night, and having entered the house of his friend and disciple, Bullinger, he invited the deputies of Berne (J. J. de Watteville and Im Hag) to meet him there with the greatest secrecy, and prayed them in the most solemn tone earnestly to reflect upon the dangers of the Reform. "I fear," said he, "that in consequence of our unbelief this business will not succeed. By refusing supplies to the Five Cantons, we have begun a work that will be fatal to us. What is to be done? Withdraw the prohibition? The cantons will then be more insolent and haughty than ever. Enforce it? They will take the offensive, and if their attack succeed you will behold our fields red with the blood of the believers, the doctrine of truth cast down, the Church of Christ laid waste, all social relations overthrown, our adversaries more hardened and irritated against the Gospel, and crowds of priests and monks again filling our rural districts, streets, and temples......And yet," added Zwingle, after a few instants of emotion and silence, "that also will have an end." The Bernese were filled with agitation by the solemn voice of the reformer. "We see," replied they, "all that is to be feared for our common cause, and we will employ every care to prevent such great disasters." —"I who write these things was present and heard them," adds Bullinger.[1]

It was feared that if the presence of Zwingle at Bremgarten became known to the deputies of the Five Cantons, they would not restrain their violence. During this nocturnal conference three of the town-councillors were stationed as sentinels in front of Bullinger's house. Before daybreak, the reformer and his two friends, accompanied by Bullinger and the three councillors, passed through the deserted streets leading

[1] These words are in Latin: Hæc ipse, qui hæc scribo, at illis audivi, præsens colloquio. Bul. iii. 49.

to the gate on the road to Zurich. Three different times Zwingle took leave of Bullinger, who was erelong to be his successor. His mind was filled with a presentiment of his approaching death; he could not tear himself from that young friend whose face he was never to see again; he blessed him amidst floods of tears. "O my dear Henry!" said he, "may God protect you! Be faithful to our Lord Jesus Christ and to his Church." At length they separated; but at that very moment, says Bullinger, a mysterious personage, clad in a robe as white as snow, suddenly appeared, and after frightening the soldiers who guarded the gate, plunged suddenly into the water, and vanished. Bullinger, Zwingle, and their friends did not perceive it; Bullinger himself sought for it all around, but to no purpose;[1] still the sentinels persisted in the reality of this frightful apparition. Bullinger greatly agitated returned in darkness and in silence to his house. His mind involuntarily compared the departure of Zwingle and the white phantom; and he shuddered at the frightful omen which the thought of this spectre impressed upon his mind.

Sufferings of another kind pursued Zwingle to Zurich. He had thought that by consenting to remain at the head of affairs, he would recover all his ancient influence. But he was deceived: the people desired to see him there, and yet they would not follow him. The Zurichers daily became more and more indisposed towards the war which they had at first demanded, and identified themselves with the passive system of Berne. Zwingle remained for some time stupified and motionless before this inert mass, which his most vigorous exertions could not move. But soon discovering in every quarter of the horizon the prophetic signs, precursors of the storm about to burst upon the ship of which he was the pilot, he uttered cries of anguish, and showed the signal of distress. "I see," exclaimed he one day to the people from the pulpit, whither he had gone to give utterance to his gloomy forebodings,—"I see that the most faithful warnings cannot save you; you will not punish the pensioners of the foreigner......They have too firm a support among us! A chain is prepared—behold it entire—it unrolls link after link,—soon will they bind me to it, and more than one pious Zuricher with me......It is against me they are enraged! I am ready; I submit to the Lord's will. But these people shall never be my masters......As for thee, O Zurich, they will give thee thy reward; they will strike thee on the head. Thou willest it. Thou refusest to punish them; well! it is they who will punish thee.[2] But God will not the less preserve his Word, and their haughtiness shall come to an end." Such was Zwin-

gle's cry of agony; but the immobility of death alone replied. The hearts of the Zurichers were so hardened that the sharpest arrows of the reformer could not pierce them, and they fell at his feet blunted and useless.

But events were pressing on, which justified all his fears. The Five Cantons had rejected every proposition that had been made to them. "Why do you talk of punishing a few wrongs?" they had replied to the mediators: "it is a question of quite another kind. Do you not require that we should receive back among us the heretics whom we have banished, and tolerate no other priests than those who preach conformably to the Word of God? We know what that means. No —no—we will not abandon the religion of our fathers; and if we must see our wives and our children deprived of food, our hands will know how to conquer what is refused to us: to that we pledge our bodies—our goods —our lives." It was with this threatening language that the deputies quitted the diet of Bremgarten. They had proudly shaken the folds of their mantles, and war had fallen from them.

The terror was general, and the alarmed citizens beheld every where frightful portents, terrific signs, apparently foreboding the most horrible events. It was not only the white phantom that had appeared at Bremgarten at Zwingle's side: the most fearful omens, passing from mouth to mouth, filled the people with the gloomiest presentiments. The history of these phenomena, however strange it may appear, characterizes the period of which we write. We do not create the times: it is our simple duty to paint them as they really were.

On the 26th July, a widow chancing to be alone before her house, in the village of Castelenschloss, suddenly beholds a frightful spectacle—blood springing from the earth all around her.[1] She rushes in alarm into the cottage......but, oh horrible! blood is flowing every where—from the wainscot and from the stones;[2]—it falls in a stream from a basin on a shelf, and even the child's cradle overflows with it. The woman imagines that the invisible hand of an assassin has been at work, and rushes in distraction out of doors, crying murder! murder![3] The villagers and the monks of a neighbouring convent assemble at the noise—they partly succeed in effacing the bloody stains; but a little later in the day, the other inhabitants of the house, sitting down in terror to eat their evening meal under the projecting eaves, suddenly discover blood bubbling up in a pond—blood flowing from the loft— blood covering all the walls of the house. Blood—blood—every where blood! The bailiff of Schenkenberg and the pastor of

---

[1] Ein menschen in ein schneeweissen Kleid. Bull. iii. 49.
[2] Straafen willt sy nitt, des werden sy dich straafen. Ibid. 52.

[1] Ante et post eam purus sanguis ita acriter ex dura terra effluxit, ut ex vena incisa. Zw. Epp. ii. 627.
[2] Sed etiam sanguis ex terra, lignis, et lapidibus effluxit. Ibid. 627.
[3] Ut eadem excurreret cædem clamitans. Ibid.

Dalheim arrive—inquire into the matter—and immediately report it to the lords of Berne and to Zwingle.

Scarcely had this horrible recital—the particulars of which are faithfully preserved in Latin and in German—filled all minds with the idea of a horrible butchery, than in the western quarter of the heavens there appeared a frightful comet,[1] whose immense train of a pale yellow colour turned towards the south. At the time of its setting, this apparition shone in the sky like the fire of a furnace.[2] One night—on the 15th August as it would appear[3]—Zwingle and George Müller, formerly abbot of Wettingen, being together in the cemetery of the cathedral, both fixed their eyes upon this terrific meteor. "This ominous globe," said Zwingle, "is come to light the path that leads to my grave. It will be at the cost of my life and of many good men with me. Although I am rather shortsighted, I foresee great calamities in the future.[4] The truth and the Church will mourn; but Christ will never forsake us." It was not only at Zurich that this flaming star spread consternation. Vadian being one night on an eminence in the neighbourhood of St. Gall, surrounded by his friends and disciples, after having explained to them the names of the stars and the miracles of the Creator, stopped before this comet, which denounced the anger of God; and the famous Theophrastus declared that it foreboded not only great bloodshed, but most especially the death of learned and illustrious men. This mysterious phenomenon prolonged its frightful visitation until the 3d September.

When once the noise of these omens was spread abroad, men could no longer contain themselves. Their imaginations were excited; they heaped fright upon fright: each place had its terrors. Two banners waving in the clouds had been seen on the mountain of the Brunig; at Zug a buckler had appeared in the heavens; on the banks of the Reuss, reiterated explosions were heard during the night; on the lake of the Four Cantons, ships with aërial combatants careered about in every direction. War—war;—blood—blood!—these were the general cries.

In the midst of all this agitation, Zwingle alone seemed tranquil. He rejected none of these presentiments, but contemplated them with calmness. "A heart that fears God," said he, "cares not for the threats of the world. To forward the designs of God, whatever may happen,—this is his task. A carrier who has a long road to go must make

up his mind to wear his waggon and his gear during the journey. If he carry his merchandise to the appointed spot, that is enough for him. We are the waggon and the gear of God. There is not one of the articles that is not worn, twisted, or broken; but our great Driver will not the less accomplish by our means his vast designs. Is it not to those who fall upon the field of battle that the noblest crown belongs? Take courage, then, in the midst of all these dangers, through which the cause of Jesus Christ must pass. Be of good cheer! although we should never here below see its triumphs with our own eyes. The Judge of the combat beholds us, and it is he who confers the crown. Others will enjoy upon earth the fruits of our labours; while we, already in heaven, shall enjoy an eternal reward."[1]

Thus spoke Zwingle, as he advanced calmly towards the threatening noise of the tempest, which, by its repeated flashes and sudden explosions, foreboded death.

CHAPTER VI.

The Five Cantons decide for War—Deceitful Calm—Fatal Inactivity—Zurich forewarned—Banner of Lucerne planted—Manifesto—The Bailiwicks pillaged—The Monastery of Cappel—Letter—Infatuation of Zurich—New Warnings—The War begins—The Tocsin—A fearful Night—The War—Banner and Army of Zurich—Zwingle's Departure—Zwingle's Horse—Anna Zwingle.

THE Five Cantons, assembled in diet at Lucerne, appeared full of determination, and war was decided upon. "We will call upon the cities to respect our alliances," said they, "and if they refuse, we will enter the common bailiwicks by force to procure provisions, and unite our banners in Zug to attack the enemy." The Waldstettes were not alone. The nuncio, being solicited by his Lucerne friends, had required that auxiliary troops, paid by the pope, should be put in motion towards Switzerland, and he announced their near arrival.

These resolutions carried terror into Switzerland; the mediating cantons met again at Arau, and drew up a plan that should leave the religious question just as it had been settled by the treaty of 1529. Deputies immediately bore these propositions to the different councils. Lucerne haughtily rejected them. "Tell those who sent you," was the reply, "that we do not acknowledge them as our schoolmasters. We would rather die than yield the least thing to the prejudice of our faith." The mediators returned to Arau, trembling and discouraged. This useless attempt increased the disagreement among the reformed, and gave the Waldstettes still greater confidence. Zurich, so decided for the reception of the Gospel, now became daily more irresolute! The mem-

[1] Ein gar eschrocklicher comet. Bull. ii. 46. It was Halley's comet, that returns about every 76 years. It appeared last in 1835.
[2] Wie ein fhuwr in einer ess. Ibid. Perhaps Bullinger alludes in this way to the phenomenon remarked by Appian, astronomer to Charles V., who observed this comet at Ingolstadt, and who says that the tail disappeared as the nucleus approached the horizon. In 1456, its appearance had already excited great terror.
[3] Cometam jam tribus noctibus viderunt apud nos alii, ego una tantum, puto 15 Augusti. Zw. Epp. p. 634.
[4] Ego cæculus non unam calamitatem expecto. Ibid. p. 626.

[1] Zw. Opp. Comment. in Jeremiam. This work was composed the very year of Zwingle's death.

657

bers of the council distrusted each other; the people felt no interest in this war; and Zwingle, notwithstanding his unshaken faith in the justice of his cause, had no hope for the struggle that was about to take place. Berne, on its side, did not cease to entreat Zurich to avoid precipitation. "Do not let us expose ourselves to the reproach of too much haste, as in 1529," was the general remark in Zurich. "We have sure friends in the midst of the Waldstettes; let us wait until they announce to us, as they have promised, some real danger."

It was soon believed that these temporizers were right. In fact the alarming news ceased. That constant rumour of war, which incessantly came from the Waldstettes, was discontinued. There were no more alarms—no more fears! Deceitful omen! Over the mountains and valleys of Switzerland hangs a gloomy and mysterious silence, the forerunner of the tempest.

Whilst the Zurichers were sleeping, the Waldstettes were preparing to conquer their rights by force of arms. The chiefs, closely united to each other by common interests and dangers, found a powerful support in the indignation of the people. In a diet of the Five Cantons, held at Brunnen on the banks of the Lake of Lucerne, opposite Grutli, the alliances of the confederation were read; and the deputies, having been summoned to declare by their votes whether they thought the war just and lawful, all hands were raised with a shudder. The Waldstettes had immediately prepared their attack with the profoundest mystery. All the passes had been guarded—all communication between Zurich and the Five Cantons had been rendered impossible. The friends upon whom the Zurichers had reckoned on the banks of the Lakes Lucerne and Zug, and who had promised them intelligence, were like prisoners in their mountains. The terrible avalanche was about to slip from the icy summits of the mountain, and to roll into the valleys, even to the gates of Zurich, overthrowing every thing in its passage, without the least forewarning of its fall. The mediators had returned discouraged to their cantons. A spirit of imprudence and of error—sad forerunner of the fall of republics as well as of kings—had spread over the whole city of Zurich. The council had at first given orders to call out the militia; then, deceived by the silence of the Waldstettes, it had imprudently revoked the decree, and Lavater, the commander of the army, had retired in discontent to Rybourg, and indignantly thrown far from him that sword which they had commanded him to leave in the scabbard. Thus the winds were about to be unchained from the mountains; the waters of the great deep, aroused by a terrible earthquake, were about to open; and yet the vessel of the state, sadly abandoned, sported up and down with indifference over a frightful gulf,—its yards

struck, its sails loose and motionless—without compass or crew—without pilot, watch, or helm.

Whatever were the exertions of the Waldstettes, they could not entirely stifle the rumour of war, which from chalet to chalet called all their citizens to arms. God permitted a cry of alarm—a single one, it is true—to resound in the ears of the people of Zurich. On the 4th October, a little boy, who knew not what he was doing, succeeded in crossing the frontier of Zug, and presented himself with two loaves at the gate of the reformed monastery of Cappel, situated in the farthest limits of the canton of Zurich. He was led to the abbot, to whom the child gave the loaves without saying a word. The superior, with whom there chanced to be at that time a councillor from Zurich, Henry Peyer, sent by his government, turned pale at the sight. "If the Five Cantons intend entering by force of arms into the free bailiwicks," had said these two Zurichers to one of their friends in Zug, "you will send your son to us with one loaf; but you will give him two if they are marching at once upon the bailiwicks and upon Zurich." The abbot and the councillor wrote with all speed to Zurich. "Be upon your guard! take up arms," said they; but no credit was attached to this information. The council were at that time occupied in taking measures to prevent the supplies that had arrived from Alsace from entering the cantons. Zwingle himself, who had never ceased to announce war, did not believe it. "These pensioners are really clever fellows," said the reformer. "Their preparations may be after all nothing but a French manœuvre."[1]

He was deceived—they were a reality. Four days were to accomplish the ruin of Zurich. Let us retrace in succession the history of these disastrous moments.

On Sunday, 8th October, a messenger appeared at Zurich, and demanded in the name of the Five Cantons, letters of perpetual alliance.[2] The majority saw in this step nothing but a trick; but Zwingle began to discern the thunderbolt in the black cloud that was drawing near. He was in the pulpit: it was the last time he was destined to appear there; and as if he had seen the formidable spectre of Rome rise frightfully above the Alps, calling upon him and upon his people to abandon the faith:— "No—no!" cried he, "never will I deny my Redeemer!"

At the same moment a messenger arrived in haste from Mulinen, commander of the Knights-hospitallers of St. John at Hitzkylch. "On Friday, 6th October," said he to the councils of Zurich, "the people of Lucerne planted their banner in the Great

[1] Dise ire Rustung mochte woll eine französische prattik sein. Bull. iii. 86.
[2] Die ewige Bünd abgefordert. J. J Hottinger, iii. 577. According to Bullinger, this did not take place until Monday.

Square.[1] Two men that I sent to Lucerne have been thrown into prison. To-morrow morning, Monday, 9th October, the Five Cantons will enter the bailiwicks. Already the country-people, frightened and fugitive, are running to us in crowds."—"It is an idle story," said the councils.[2] Nevertheless they recalled the commander-in-chief Lavater, who sent off a trusty man, nephew of James Winckler, with orders to repair to Cappel, and if possible as far as Zug, to reconnoitre the arrangements of the cantons.

The Waldstettes were in reality assembling round the banner of Lucerne. The people of this canton; the men of Schwytz, Uri, Zug, and Unterwalden; refugees from Zurich and Berne, with a few Italians, formed the main body of the army, which had been raised to invade the free bailiwicks. Two manifestoes were published—one addressed to the cantons, the other to foreign princes and nations.

The Five Cantons energetically set forth the attacks made upon the treaties, the discord sown throughout the confederation, and finally the refusal to sell them provisions—a refusal whose only aim was (according to them) to excite the people against the magistrates, and to establish the Reform by force. "It is not true," added they, "that— as they are continually crying out—we oppose the preaching of the truth and the reading of the Bible. As obedient members of the Church, we desire to receive all that our holy mother receives. But we reject the books and the innovations of Zwingle and his companions."[3]

Hardly had the messengers charged with these manifestoes departed, before the first division of the army began to march, and arrived in the evening in the free bailiwicks. The soldiers having entered the deserted churches, and seen the images of the saints removed and the altars broken, their anger was kindled; they spread like a torrent over the whole country, pillaged every thing they met with, and were particularly enraged against the houses of the pastors, where they destroyed the furniture with oaths and maledictions. At the same time the division that was to form the main army marched upon Zug, thence to move upon Zurich.

Cappel, at three leagues from Zurich, and about a league from Zug, was the first place they would reach in the Zurich territory, after crossing the frontier of the Five Cantons. Near the Albis, between two hills of similar height, the Granges on the north, and the Ifelsberg on the south, in the midst of delightful pastures, stood the ancient and wealthy convent of the Cistercians, in whose church were the tombs of many ancient and noble families of these districts. The Abbot

Wolfgang Joner, a just and pious man, a great friend of the arts and letters, and a distinguished preacher, had reformed his convent in 1527. Full of compassion, and rich in good works, particularly towards the poor of the canton of Zug and the free bailiwicks, he was held in great honour throughout the whole country.[1] He predicted what would be the termination of the war; yet as soon as danger approached, he spared no labour to serve his country.

It was on Sunday night that the abbot received positive intelligence of the preparations at Zug. He paced up and down his cell with hasty steps; sleep fled from his eyes; he drew near his lamp, and addressing his intimate friend, Peter Simmler, who succeeded him, and who was then residing at Kylchberg, a village on the borders of the lake, and about a league from the town, he hastily wrote these words: "The great anxiety and trouble which agitate me prevent me from busying myself with the management of the house, and induce me to write to you all that is preparing. The time is come......the scourge of God appears.[2]......After many journeys and inquiries, we have learnt that the Five Cantons will march to-day (Monday) to seize upon Hitzkylch, while the main army assembles its banners at Baar, between Zug and Cappel. Those from the valley of the Adige and the Italians will arrive to-day or to-morrow." This letter, through some unforeseen circumstance, did not reach Zurich till the evening.

Meanwhile the messenger whom Lavater had sent—the nephew of J. Winckler— creeping on his belly, gliding unperceived past the sentinels, and clinging to the shrubs that overhung the precipices, had succeeded in making his way where no road had been cleared. On arriving near Zug, he had discovered with alarm the banner and the militia hastening from all sides at beat of drum: then traversing again these unknown passes, he had returned to Zurich with this information.[3]

It was high time that the bandage should fall from the eyes of the Zurichers; but the delusion was to endure until the end. The council which was called together met in small number. "The Five Cantons," said they, "are making a little noise to frighten us, and to make us raise the blockade."[4] The council, however, decided on sending Colonel Rodolph Dumysen and Ulrich Funck to Cappel, to see what was going on; and each one, tranquillized by this unmeaning step, retired to rest.

They did not slumber long. Every hour brought fresh messengers of alarm to Zurich.

---

1 Ire paner in den Brunnen gesteckt. Bull. iii. 86.
2 Ein gepöch und prögerey und unt darauff setzend. Ibid.
3 Als wir vertruwen Gott und der Welt antwurt zu geben. Ibid. 101.

1 That armen lüten vil guts....und by aller Erbarkeit in grossern ansähen. Bull. iii. 151.
2 Die Zyt ist hie, das die rüt gottes sich wil erzeigen Ibid. 87.
3 Naben den Wachten, durch umwäg und gestrupp Ibid.
4 Sy machtend alein ein geprög. Ibid. 103.

"The banners of four cantons are assembled at Zug," said they. "They are only waiting for Uri. The people of the free bailiwicks are flocking to Cappel, and demanding arms ......Help! help!"

Before the break of day the council was again assembled, and it ordered the convocation of the Two Hundred. An old man, whose hair had grown gray on the battle-field and in the council of the state—the banneret John Schweitzer—raising his head enfeebled by age, and darting the last beam, as it were, from his eyes, exclaimed, "Now —at this very moment, in God's name, send an advanced-guard to Cappel, and let the army, promptly collecting round the banner, follow it immediately." He said no more; but the charm was not yet broken. "The peasants of the free bailiwicks," said some, "we know to be hasty, and easily carried away. They make the matter greater than it really is. The wisest plan is to wait for the report of the councillors." In Zurich there was no longer either arm to defend or head to advise.

It was seven in the morning, and the assembly was still sitting, when Rodolph Gwerb, pastor of Rifferschwyl, near Cappel, arrived in haste. "The people of the lordship of Knonau," said he, "are crowding round the convent, and loudly calling for chiefs and for aid. The enemy is approaching. Will our lords of Zurich (say they) abandon themselves, and us with them? Do they wish to give us up to slaughter?" The pastor, who had witnessed these mournful scenes, spoke with animation. The councillors, whose infatuation was to be prolonged to the last, were offended at his message. "They want to make us act imprudently," replied they, turning in their arm-chairs.

They had scarcely ceased speaking before a new messenger appeared, wearing on his features the marks of the greatest terror: it was Schwytzer, landlord of the "Beech Tree" on Mount Albis. "My lords Dumysen and Funck," said he, "have sent me to you with all speed to announce to the council that the Five Cantons have seized upon Hitzkylch, and that they are now collecting all their troops at Baar. My lords remain in the bailiwicks to aid the frightened inhabitants."

This time the most confident turned pale. Terror, so long restrained, passed like a flash of lightning through every heart.[1] Hitzkylch was in the power of the enemy, and the war was begun.

It was resolved to expedite to Cappel a flying camp of six hundred men with six guns; but the command was intrusted to George Güdli, whose brother was in the army of the Five Cantons, and he was enjoined to keep on the defensive. Güdli and his troops had just left the city, when the captain-general Lavater, summoning into the hall of the Smaller Council the old banneret Schweitzer, William Toning, captain of the arquebusiers, J. Dennikon, captain of the artillery. Zwingle, and some others, said to them, "Let us deliberate promptly on the means of saving the canton and the city. Let the tocsin immediately call out all the citizens." The captain-general feared that the councils would shrink at this proceeding, and he wished to raise the landsturm by the simple advice of the chiefs of the army and of Zwingle. "We cannot take it upon ourselves," said they; "the two councils are still sitting; let us lay this proposition before them." They hastened towards the place of meeting; but, fatal mischance! there were only a few members of the Smaller Council on the benches. "The consent of the Two Hundred is necessary," said they. Again a new delay, and the enemy were on their march. Two hours after noon the Great Council met again, but only to make long and useless speeches.[1] At length the resolution was taken, and at seven in the evening the tocsin began to sound in all the country districts. Treason united with this dilatoriness, and persons who pretended to be envoys from Zurich stopped the landsturm in many places, as being contrary to the opinion of the council. A great number of citizens went to sleep again.

It was a fearful night. The thick darkness—a violent storm—the alarm-bell ringing from every steeple—the people running to arms—the noise of swords and guns—the sound of trumpets and of drums, combined with the roaring of the tempest,—the distrust, discontent, and even treason, which spread affliction in every quarter—the sobs of women and of children—the cries which accompanied many a heart-rending adieu—an earthquake which occurred about nine o'clock at night, as if nature herself had shuddered at the blood that was about to be spilt, and which violently shook the mountains and the valleys:[2] all increased the terrors of this fatal night,—a night to be followed by a still more fatal day.

While these events were passing, the Zurichers encamped on the heights of Cappel to the number of about one thousand men, fixed their eyes on Zug and upon the lake, attentively watching every movement. On a sudden, a little before night, they perceived a few barks filled with soldiers coming from the side of Arth, and rowing across the lake towards Zug. Their number increases —one boat follows another—soon they distinctly hear the bellowing of the Bull (the horn) of Uri,[3] and discern the banner. The barks draw near Zug; they are moored to the shore, which is lined with an immense crowd. The warriors of Uri and the arque-

[1] Dieser Bottschaft erschrack menklich übel. Bull. iii. 104.

[1] Ward so vil und lang darin geradschlagt. Bull. iii. 104.
[2] Ein startrer Erdbidem, der das Land, auch Berg und Thal gwaltiglich ershütt. Tschudi, Helvetia, ii. 186.
[3] Vil schiffen uff Zug faren, und hort man luyen den Uri Stier. Bull. iii. 109.

busiers of the Adige spring up and leap on shore, where they are received with acclamations, and take up their quarters for the night : behold the enemies assembled ! The council are informed with all speed.

The agitation was still greater at Zurich than at Cappel : the confusion was increased by uncertainty. The enemy attacking them on different sides at once, they knew not where to carry assistance. Two hours after midnight five hundred men with four guns quitted the city for Bremgarten, and three or four hundred men with five guns for Wadenschwyl. They turned to the right and to the left, while the enemy was in front.

Alarmed at its own weakness, the council resolved to apply without delay to the cities of the christian co-burghery. " As this revolt," wrote they, " has no other origin than the Word of God, we entreat you once—twice—thrice, as loudly, as seriously, as firmly, and as earnestly, as our ancient alliances and our christian co-burghery permit and command us to do—to set forth without delay with all your forces. Haste ! haste ! haste ! Act as promptly as possible[1]—the danger is yours as well as ours." Thus spake Zurich ; but it was already too late.

At break of day the banner was raised before the town-house ; instead of flaunting proudly in the wind, it hung drooping down the staff—a sad omen that filled many minds with fear. Lavater took up his station under this standard ; but a long period elapsed before a few hundred soldiers could be got together.[2] In the square and in all the city disorder and confusion prevailed. The troops, fatigued by a hasty march or by long waiting, were faint and discouraged.

At ten o'clock, only 700 men were under arms. The selfish, the lukewarm, the friends of Rome and of the foreign pensioners, had remained at home. A few old men who had more courage than strength—several members of the two councils who were devoted to the holy cause of God's Word—many ministers of the Church who desired to live and die with the Reform—the boldest of the townspeople and a few peasants, especially those from the neighbourhood of the city—such were the defenders who, wanting that moral force so necessary for victory, incompletely armed, and without uniform, crowded in disorder around the banner of Zurich.

The army should have numbered at least 4000 men ; they waited still ; the usual oath had not been administered ; and yet courier after courier arrived, breathless and in disorder, announcing the terrible danger that threatened Zurich. All this disorderly crowd was violently agitated—they no longer waited for the commands of their chiefs, and many without taking the oath rushed through the

gates. About 200 men thus set out in confusion. All those who remained prepared to depart.

Zwingle was now seen issuing from a house before which a caparisoned horse was stamping impatiently : it was his own. His look was firm, but dimmed by sorrow. He parted from his wife, his children, and his numerous friends, without deceiving himself, and with a bruised heart.[1] He observed the thick waterspout, which, driven by a terrible wind, advanced whirling towards him. Alas ! he had himself called up this hurricane by quitting the atmosphere of the Gospel of peace, and throwing himself into the midst of political passions. He was convinced that he would be its first victim. Fifteen days before the attack of the Waldstettes, he had said from the pulpit : " I know the meaning of all this : I am the person specially pointed at. All this comes to pass—in order that I may die."[2] The council, according to an ancient custom, had called upon him to accompany the army as its chaplain. Zwingle did not hesitate. He prepared himself without surprise and without anger,—with the calmness of a Christian who places himself confidently in the hands of his God. If the cause of Reform was doomed to perish, he was ready to perish with it. Surrounded by his weeping wife and friends—by his children who clung to his garments to detain him, he quitted that house where he had tasted so much happiness. At the moment that his hand was upon his horse, just as he was about to mount, the animal violently started back several paces, and when he was at last in the saddle, it refused for a time to move, rearing and prancing backwards, like that horse which the greatest captain of modern times had mounted as he was about to cross the Niemen. Many in Zurich at that time thought with the soldier of the Grand Army when he saw Napoleon on the ground : " It is a bad omen ! a Roman would go back ! "[3] Zwingle having at last mastered his horse, gave the reins, applied the spur, started forward, and disappeared.

At eleven o'clock the flag was struck, and all who remained in the square—about 500 men—began their march along with it. The greater part were torn with difficulty from the arms of their families, and walked sad and silent, as if they were going to the scaffold instead of battle. There was no order—no plan ; the men were isolated and scattered, some running before, some after the colours, their extreme confusion presenting a fearful appearance ;[4] so much so, that those who remained behind—the women, the children, and the old men, filled with gloomy fore-

---

1 Ylentz, ylentz, ylentz, uffs aller schnellist. Bull. iii. 10.
2 Sammlet sich doch das volck gmachsam. Ibid. 112.

1 Anna Rheinhard par G. Meyer of Knonau, and Bull. iii. 33.
2 Ut ego tollar fiunt omnia. De vita et obitu Zwinglii, Myconius.
3 Ségur : Hist. de Napoléon et de la Grande Armée, i. 142.
4 Nullus ordo, nulla consilia, nullæ mentes, tanta animorum dissonantia, tam horrenda facies ante et post signa sparsim currentium hominum. De vita et ob. Zwinglii.

bodings, beat their breasts as they saw them pass, and many years after, the remembrance of this day of tumult and sadness drew this groan from Oswald Myconius: " Whenever I recall it to mind, it is as if a sword pierced my heart." Zwingle, armed according to the usage of the chaplains of the confederation, rode mournfully behind this distracted multitude. Myconius, when he saw him, was nigh fainting.[1] Zwingle disappeared, and Oswald remained behind to weep.

He did not shed tears alone; in all quarters were heard lamentations, and every house was changed into a house of prayer.[2] In the midst of this universal sorrow, one woman remained silent; her only cry was a bitter heart, her only language the mild and suppliant eye of faith:—this was Anna, Zwingle's wife. She had seen her husband depart— her son, her brother, a great number of intimate friends and near relations, whose approaching death she foreboded. But her soul, strong as that of her husband, offered to God the sacrifice of her holiest affections. Gradually the defenders of Zurich precipitated their march, and the tumult died away in the distance.

CHAPTER VII.

The Scene of War—The Enemy at Zug—Declaration of War —Council—Army of the Forest Cantons appears—The first Gun fired—Zwingle's Gravity and Sorrow—Zurich Army ascending the Albis—Halt and Council at the Beech Tree—They quicken their March—Jauch's Reconnaissance—His Appeal—Ambuscade.

THIS night, which was so stormy in Zurich, had not been calmer among the inhabitants of Cappel. They had received the most alarming reports one after another. It was necessary to take up a position that would allow the troops assembled round the convent to resist the enemy's attack until the arrival of the reinforcements that were expected from the city. They cast their eyes on a small hill, which lying to the north towards Zurich, and traversed by the highroad, presented an uneven but sufficiently extensive surface. A deep ditch that surrounded it on three sides defended the approaches; but a small bridge, that was the only issue on the side of Zurich, rendered a precipitate retreat very dangerous. On the south-west was a wood of beech-trees; on the south, in the direction of Zug, was the highroad and a marshy valley. " Lead us to the Granges," cried all the soldiers. They were conducted thither. The artillery was stationed near some ruins. The line of battle was drawn up on the side of the monastery and of Zug, and sentinels were placed at the foot of the slope.

Meantime, the signal was given at Zug

[1] Quem ut vidi repentino dolore cordis vix consistebam. De vita et ob. Zwinglii.
[2] Manebamus non certe sine jugibus suspiriis, non sine precibus ad Deum. Ibid.

and Baar; the drums beat: the soldiers of the Five Cantons took up their arms. A universal feeling of joy animated them. The churches were opened, the bells rang, and the serried ranks of the cantons entered the cathedral of St. Oswald, where mass was celebrated and the Host offered up for the sins of the people. All the army began their march at nine o'clock, with banners flying. The avoyer John Golder commanded the contingent of Lucerne ; the landamman James Troguer that of Uri ; the landamman Rychmuth, a mortal enemy of the Reformation, that of Schwytz ; the landamman Zellger, that of Unterwalden ; and Oswald Dooss that of Zug. Eight thousand men marched in order of battle : all the picked men of the Five Cantons were there. Fresh and active after a quiet night, and having only one short league to cross before reaching the enemy, these haughty Waldstettes advanced with a firm and regular step under the command of their chiefs.

On reaching the common meadow of Zug, they halted to take the oath : every hand was upraised to heaven, and all swore to avenge themselves. They were about to resume their march, when some aged men made signs to them to stop. " Comrades," said they, " we have long offended God. Our blasphemies, our oaths, our wars, our revenge, our pride, our drunkenness, our adulteries, the gold of the stranger to whom our hands have been extended, and all the disorders in which we have indulged, have so provoked his anger, that if he should punish us to-day, we should only receive the desert of our crimes." The emotion of the chiefs had passed into the ranks. All the army bent the knee in the midst of the plain; deep silence prevailed, and every soldier, with bended head, crossed himself devoutly, and repeated in a low voice five paters, as many aves, and the credo. One might have said that they were for a time in the midst of a vast and stilly desert. Suddenly the noise of an immense crowd was again heard. The army rose up. " Soldiers," said the captains, " you know the cause of this war. Bear your wives and your children continually before your eyes."

The chief usher (*grand sautier*) of Lucerne, wearing the colours of the canton, now approached the chiefs of the army : they placed in his hands the declaration of war, dated on that very day, and sealed with the arms of Zug. He then set off on horseback, preceded by a trumpeter, to carry this paper to the commander of the Zurichers.

It was eleven in the morning. The Zurichers soon discovered the enemy's army, and cast a sorrowful glance on the small force they were able to oppose to it. Every minute the danger increased. All bent their knees, their eyes were raised to heaven, and every Zuricher uttered a cry from the bottom of his heart, praying for deliverance from God. As soon as the prayer was ended, they got ready for battle. There were at that time about twelve hundred men under arms.

At noon the trumpet of the Five Cantons sounded not far from the advanced posts. Gödli, having collected the members of the two councils who happened to be with the army, as well as the commissioned and non-commissioned officers, and having ranged them in a circle, ordered the secretary Rheinhard to read the declaration of which the Sautier of Lucerne was the bearer. After the reading, Gödli opened a council of war. "We are few in number, and the forces of our adversaries are great," said Landolt, bailiff of Marpac, "but I will here await the enemy in the name of God." "Wait!" cried the captain of the halberdiers, Rodolph Zigler; "impossible! let us rather take advantage of the ditch that cuts the road to effect our retreat, and let us every where raise a levée en masse." This was in truth the only means of safety. But Rudi Gallmann, considering every step backwards as an act of cowardice, cried out, stamping his feet forcibly on the earth, and casting a fiery glance around him, "Here—here shall be my grave!"[1]—"It is now too late to retire with honour," said other officers. "This day is in the hands of God. Let us suffer whatever he lays upon us." It was put to the vote.

The members of the council had scarcely raised their hands in token of assent, when a great noise was heard around them. "The captain! the captain!" cried a soldier from the outposts who arrived in haste. "Silence, silence!" replied the ushers driving him back; "they are holding a council!"—"It is no longer time to hold a council," replied the soldier. "Conduct me immediately to the captain.".....—"Our sentinels are falling back," cried he with an agitated voice, as he arrived before Gödli. "The enemy is there—they are advancing through the forest with all their forces and with great tumult." He had not ceased speaking before the sentinels, who were in truth retiring on all sides, ran up, and the army of the Five Cantons was soon seen climbing the slope of Ifelsberg in face of the Granges, and pointing their guns. The leaders of the Waldstettes were examining the position, and seeking to discover by what means their army could reach that of Zurich. The Zurichers were asking themselves the same question. The nature of the ground prevented the Waldstettes from passing below the convent, but they could arrive by another quarter. Ulrich Brüder, under-bailiff of Husen, in the canton of Zurich, fixed his anxious look on the beech-wood. "It is thence that the enemy will fall upon us!" "Axes—axes!" immediately cried several voices: "let us cut down the trees!"[2]

Gödli, the abbot, and several others were opposed to this: "If we stop up the wood, by throwing down the trees, we shall ourselves be unable to work our guns in that direction," said they.—"Well! at least let us place some arquebusiers in that quarter."—"We are already so small a number," replied the captain, "that it will be imprudent to divide the forces." Neither wisdom nor courage were to save Zurich. They once more invoked the help of God, and waited in expectation.

At one o'clock the Five Cantons fired the first gun: the ball passing over the convent fell below the Granges; a second passed over the line of battle; a third struck a hedge close to the ruins. The Zurichers, seeing the battle was begun, replied with courage; but the slowness and awkwardness with which the artillery was served in those days prevented any great loss being inflicted on either side. When the enemy perceived this, they ordered their advanced guard to descend from Ifelsberg to reach the Granges through the meadow; and soon the whole army of the cantons advanced in this direction, but with difficulty and over bad roads. Some arquebusiers of Zurich came and announced the disorder of the cantons. "Brave Zurichers," cried Rudi Gallmann, "if we attack them now, it is all over with them." At these words some of the soldiers prepared to enter the wood on the left, to fall upon the disheartened Waldstettes. But Gödli perceiving this movement, cried out: "Where are you going?—do you not know that we have agreed not to separate?" He then ordered the skirmishers to be recalled, so that the wood remained entirely open to the enemy. They were satisfied with discharging a few random shots from time to time to prevent the cantons from establishing themselves there. The firing of the artillery continued until three o'clock, and announced far and wide, even to Bremgarten and Zurich, that the battle had commenced.

In the meanwhile the great banner of Zurich and all those who surrounded it, among whom was Zwingle, came advancing in disorder towards the Albis. For a year past the gaiety of the reformer had entirely disappeared: he was grave, melancholy, easily moved, having a weight on his heart that seemed to crush it. Often would he throw himself weeping at the feet of his Master, and seek in prayer the strength of which he stood in need. No one had ever observed in him any irritation; on the contrary, he had received with mildness the counsels that had been offered, and had remained tenderly attached to men whose convictions were not the same as his own. He was now advancing mournfully along the road to Cappel; and John Maaler of Winterthour, who was riding a few paces behind him, heard his groans and sighs, intermingled with fervent prayers. If any one spoke to him, he was

[1] Da, da mus min Kirchhof sin. Bull. III. 118.
[2] Ettliche schrüwend nach Achsen das man das Wäldi verhallte. Ibid.

found firm and strong in the peace that proceeds from faith; but he did not conceal his conviction that he should never see his family or church again. Thus advanced the forces of Zurich. A woful march! resembling rather a funeral procession than an army going to battle.

As they approached they saw express after express galloping along the road from Cappel, begging the Zurichers to hasten to the defence of their brothers.[1]

At Adliswyl, having passed the bridge under which flow the impetuous waters of the Sihl, and traversed the village through the midst of women, children and old men, who, standing before their cottages, looked with sadness on this disorderly troop, they began to ascend the Albis. They were about half-way from Cappel when the first cannon-shot was heard. They stop, they listen: a second, a third succeeds.........There is no longer any doubt. The glory, the very existence of the republic are endangered, and they are not present to defend it! The blood curdles in their veins. On a sudden they arouse, and each one begins to run to the support of his brothers. But the road over the Albis was much steeper than it is in our days. The badly harnessed artillery could not ascend it; the old men and citizens, little habituated to marching, and covered with weighty armour, advanced with difficulty: and yet they formed the greater portion of the troops. They were seen stopping one after another, panting and exhausted, along the sides of the road near the thickets and ravines of the Albis, leaning against a beech or an ash tree, and looking with dispirited eyes to the summit of the mountain covered with thick pines.

They resumed their march, however; the horsemen and the most intrepid of the foot-soldiers hastened onwards, and having reached the "Beech Tree," on the top of the mountain, halted to take council.

What a prospect then extended before their eyes! Zurich, the lake and its smiling shores—those orchards, those fertile fields, those vine-clad hills, almost the whole of the canton, alas! soon, perhaps, to be devastated by the forest-bands.

Scarcely had these noble-minded men begun to deliberate, when fresh messengers from Cappel appeared before them, exclaiming, "Hasten forwards!" At these words many of the Zurichers prepared to gallop towards the enemy.[2] Toning, the captain of the arquebusiers, stopt them. "My good friends," cried he to them, "against such great forces what can we do alone? Let us wait here until our people are assembled, and then let us fall upon the enemy with the whole army."—"Yes, if we had an army," bitterly replied the captain-general, who, in despair of

saving the republic, thought only of dying with glory; "but we have merely a banner and no soldiers."—"How can we stay calmly upon these heights," said Zwingle, "while we hear the shots that are fired at our fellow-citizens? In the name of God I will march towards my brother warriors, prepared to die in order to save them."[1]—"And I too," added the aged banneret Schweitzer. "As for you," continued he, turning with a contemptuous look towards Toning, "wait till you are a little recovered."—"I am quite as much refreshed as you," replied Toning, the colour mantling on his face, "and you shall soon see whether I cannot fight." All hastened their steps towards the field of battle.

The descent was rapid; they plunged into the woods, passed through the village of Husen, and at length arrived near the Granges. It was three o'clock when the banner crossed the narrow bridge that led thither; and there were so few soldiers round it that every one trembled as he beheld this venerated standard thus exposed to the attacks of so formidable an enemy. The army of the Cantons was at that moment deploying before the eyes of the new comers. Zwingle gazed upon this terrible spectacle. Behold, then, these phalanxes of soldiers!—a few minutes more, and the labours of eleven years will be destroyed perhaps for ever!...

A citizen of Zurich, one Leonard Bourkhard, who was ill-disposed towards the reformer, said to him in a harsh tone, "Well, Master Ulrich, what do you say about this business? Are the radishes salt enough?... who will eat them now?"[2] "I," replied Zwingle, "and many a brave man who is here in the hands of God; for we are his in life and in death."—"And I too—I will help to eat them," resumed Bourkhard immediately, ashamed of his brutality; "I will risk my life for them." And he did so, and many others with him, adds the chronicle.

It was four o'clock; the sun was sinking rapidly; the Waldstettes did not advance, and the Zurichers began to think that the attack would be put off till the morrow. In fact, the chiefs of the Five Cantons seeing the great banner of Zurich arrive, the night near at hand, and the impossibility of crossing under the fire of the Zurichers the marsh and the ditch that separated the combatants, were looking for a place in which their troops might pass the night. "If at this moment any mediators had appeared," says Bullinger, "their proposals would have been accepted."

The soldiers, observing the hesitation of their chiefs, began to murmur loudly. "The big ones abandon us," said one. "The captains fear to bite the fox's tail," said another. "Not to attack them," cried they all, "is to ruin our cause." During this time a daring

---

[1] Dan ein Manung uff die ander, von Cappel kamm. Bull. lii. 113.
[2] Uff rossen häftig ylttend zum augriff. Ibid.

[1] Ich will rächt, in den namen Gotts, zu den biderben luten und willig mitt und under inen sterben. Bull. lii. 123.
[2] Sind die Rüben gesaltzen? wer will sie ausessen. J. J. Hott. iii. 383.

man was preparing the skilful manœuvre that was to decide the fate of the day. A warrior of Uri, John Jauch, formerly bailiff of Sargans, a good marksman and experienced soldier, having taken a few men with him, moved towards the right of the army of the Five Cantons, crept into the midst of the clump of beech-trees that, by forming a semi-circle to the east, unites the hill of Ifelsberg to that of the Granges, found the wood empty, arrived to within a few paces of the Zurichers, and there, hidden behind the trees, remarked unperceived the smallness of their numbers, and their want of caution. Then, stealthily retiring, he went to the chiefs at the very moment the discontent was on the point of bursting out. " Now is the time to attack the enemy," cried he. " Dear gossip," replied Troguer, captain-in-chief of Uri, " you do not mean to say that we should set to work at so late an hour; besides, the men are preparing their quarters, and every body knows what it cost our fathers at Naples and Marignan for having commenced the attack a little before night. And then it is Innocent's day, and our ancestors have never given battle on a feast-day." [1]—" Don't think about the Innocents of the calendar," replied Jauch, " but let us rather remember the innocents that we have left in our cottages." Gaspard Gödli of Zurich, brother of the commander of the Granges, added his entreaties to those of the warrior of Uri. " We must either beat the Zurichers to-night," said he, " or be beaten by them to-morrow. Take your choice."

All was unavailing; the chiefs were inflexible, and the army prepared to take up its quarters. Upon this the warrior of Uri, understanding, like his fellow-countryman, Tell, that great evils require great remedies, drew his sword and cried: " Let all true confederates follow me." [2] Then hastily leaping to his saddle, he spurred his horse into the forest; [3] and immediately arquebusiers, soldiers from the Adige, and many other warriors of the Five Cantons, especially from Unterwalden—in all about 300 men, rushed into the wood after him. At this sight Jauch no longer doubted of the victory of the Waldstettes. He dismounted and fell upon his knees, " for," says Tschudi, " he was a man who feared God." All his followers did the same, and together invoked the aid of God, of His holy mother, and of all the heavenly host. They then advanced; but soon the warrior of Uri, wishing to expose no one but himself, halted his troops, and glided from tree to tree to the verge of the wood. Observing that the enemy was incautious as ever, he rejoined his arquebusiers, led them stealthily forward, and posted them silently behind the trees of the forest,[1] enjoining them to take their aim so as not to miss their men. During this time the chiefs of the Five Cantons, foreseeing that this rash man was about to bring on the action, decided against their will, and collected their soldiers around the banners.

CHAPTER VIII.

Unforeseen Change—The whole Army advances—Universal Disorder—The Banneret's Death—The Banner in Danger—The Banner saved—Terrible Slaughter—Slaughter of the Pastors—Zwingle's last Words—Barbarity of the Victors—The Furnace of Trial—Zwingle's dying Moments—Day after the Battle—Homage and Outrage.

THE Zurichers, fearing that the enemy would seize upon the road that led to their capital, were then directing part of their troops and their guns to a low hill by which it was commanded. At the very moment that the invisible arquebusiers stationed among the beech-trees were taking their aim, this detachment passed near the little wood. The deepest silence prevailed in this solitude: each one posted there picked out the man he desired to bring down, and Jauch exclaimed: " In the name of the Holy Trinity—of God the Father, the Son, and the Holy Ghost—of the Holy Mother of God, and of all the heavenly host—fire !" At the word the deadly balls issued from the wood, and a murderous carnage in the ranks of Zurich followed this terrible discharge. The battle, which had begun four hours ago, and which had never appeared to be a serious attack, now underwent an unforeseen change. The sword was not again to be returned to the scabbard until it had been bathed in torrents of blood. Those of the Zurichers who had not fallen at this first discharge lay flat on the ground, so that the balls passed over their heads; but they soon sprang up, saying: " Shall we allow ourselves to be butchered? No! let us rather attack the enemy!" Lavater seized a lance, and rushing into the foremost rank exclaimed: " Soldiers, uphold the honour of God and of our lords, and behave like brave men !" Zwingle, silent and collected, like nature before the bursting of the tempest, was there also halberd in hand. " Master Ulrich," said Bernard Sprungli, " speak to the people and encourage them." " Warriors!" said Zwingle, " fear nothing. If we are this day to be defeated, still our cause is good. Commend yourselves to God !"

The Zurichers quickly turned the artillery they were dragging to another quarter, and pointed it against the wood: but their bullets, instead of striking the enemy, only

[1] Au einem solchen Tag Blut ze vergiessen. Tschudi, Helv. ii. 189.
[2] Welche redlicher Eidgnossen würt sind, die louffind uns nach. Bull. iii. 125.
[3] Sass ylends wiederum uff sin Ross. Tschudi, Helv. ii. 191.

[1] Zertheilt die Hagken hinter die Bäum im Wald in grosser Stille. Tschudi, Helv. ii. 191.

reached the top of the trees, and tore off a few branches that fell upon the skirmishers.[1]

Rychmuth, the landamman of Schwytz, came up at a gallop to recall the volunteers; but seeing the battle begun, he ordered the whole army to advance. Immediately the five banners moved forward.

But already Jauch's skirmishers, rushing from among the trees, had fallen impetuously upon the Zurichers, charging with their long and pointed halberds. " Heretics! sacrilegists! " cried they, " we have you at last! " —" Man-sellers, idolaters, impious papists! " replied the Zurichers, " is it really you? " At first a shower of stones fell from both parties and wounded several; immediately they came to close quarters. The resistance of the Zurichers was terrible.[2] Each struck with the sword or with the halberd: at last the soldiers of the Five Cantons were driven back in disorder. The Zurichers advanced, but in so doing lost the advantages of their position, and got entangled in the marsh. Some Roman-catholic historians pretend that this flight of their troops was a stratagem to draw the Zurichers into the snare.[3]

In the mean time the army of the Five Cantons hastened through the wood. Burning with courage and with anger, they eagerly quickened their steps; from the midst of the beech-trees there resounded a confused and savage noise — a frightful murmur; the ground shook; one might have imagined the forest was uttering a horrible roar, or that witches were holding their nocturnal revels in its dark recesses.[4] In vain did the bravest of the Zurichers offer an intrepid resistance: the Waldstettes had the advantage in every quarter. " They are surrounding us," cried some. " Our men are fleeing," said others. A man from the canton of Zug, mingling with the Zurichers, and pretending to be of their party, exclaimed: " Fly, fly, brave Zurichers, you are betrayed! " Thus every thing was against Zurich. Even the hand of Him who is the disposer of battles turned against this people. Thus was it also in times of old that God frequently chastised his own people of Israel by the Assyrian sword. A panic-terror seized upon the bravest, and the disorder spread every where with frightful rapidity.

In the mean while the aged Schweitzer had raised the great banner with a firm hand, and all the picked men of Zurich were drawn up around it; but soon their ranks were thinned. John Kammli, charged with the defence of the standard, having observed the small number of combatants that remained upon the field of battle, said to the banneret: " Let us lower the banner, my lord, and save

it, for our people are flying shamefully."— " Warriors, remain firm," replied the aged banneret, whom no danger had ever shaken. The disorder augmented—the number of fugitives increased every minute; the old man stood fast, amazed and immovable as an aged oak beaten by a frightful hurricane. He received unflinchingly the blows that fell upon him, and alone resisted the terrible storm. Kammli seized him by the arm: " My lord," said he again, " lower the banner, or else we shall lose it : there is no more glory to be reaped here! " The banneret, who was already mortally wounded, exclaimed : " Alas! must the city of Zurich be so punished! " Then, dragged off by Kammli, who held him by the arm, he retreated as far as the ditch. The weight of years, and the wounds with which he was covered, did not permit him to cross it. He fell in the mire at the bottom, still holding the glorious standard, whose folds dropped on the other bank.

The enemy ran up with loud shouts, being attracted by the colours of Zurich, as the bull by the gladiator's flag. Kammli seeing this, unhesitatingly leapt to the bottom of the ditch, and laid hold of the stiff and dying hands of his chief, in order to preserve the precious ensign, which they tightly grasped. But it was in vain: the hands of the aged Schweitzer would not loose the standard. " My lord banneret! " cried this faithful servant, " it is no longer in your power to defend it." The hands of the banneret, already stiffened in death, still refused; upon which Kammli violently tore away the sacred standard, leapt upon the other bank, and rushed with his treasure far from the steps of the enemy. The last Zurichers at this moment reached the ditch : they fell one after another upon the expiring banneret, and thus hastened his death.

Kammli, however, having received a wound from a gun-shot, his march was retarded, and the Waldstettes soon surrounded him with their swords. The Zuricher, holding the banner in one hand, and his sword in the other, defended himself bravely. One of the Waldstettes caught hold of the staff—another seized the flag itself and tore it. Kammli with one blow of his sword cut down the former, and striking around him, called out: " To the rescue, brave Zurichers! save the honour and the banner of our lords." The assailants increased in number, and the warrior was about to fall, when Adam Naeff of Wollenwyd rushed up sword in hand, and the head of the Waldstette who had torn the colours rolled upon the plain, and his blood gushed out upon the flag of Zurich. Dumysen, member of the Smaller Council, supported Naeff with his halberd, and both dealt such lusty blows, that they succeeded in disengaging the standard-bearer. He, although dangerously wounded, sprang forward, holding the blood-stained folds of the banner in

---

[1] Denn das die Aest auf sie fielent. Tschudi, p. 182.
[2] Der angriff war hart und währt der Wiederstand ein gute Wyl. Ibid. 192.
[3] Catholici autem, positis insidiis, retrocesserunt, fugam simulantes. Cochlœus, Acta Luth. p. 214.
[4] Der Boden erzittert ; und nit anders war, denn als ob der Wald lut bruelete. Tschudi, p. 122.

666

one hand, which he carried off hastily, dragging the staff behind him. With fierce look and fiery eye, he thus passed, sword in hand, through the midst of friends and enemies: he crossed plains, woods, and marshes, every where leaving traces of his blood, which flowed from numerous wounds. Two of the enemy, one from Schwytz, the other from Zug—were particularly eager in his pursuit. "Heretic! villain!" cried they, "surrender and give us the banner."—"You shall have my life first," replied the Zuricher. Then the two hostile soldiers, who were embarrassed by their cuirasses, stopped a moment to take them off. Kammli took advantage of this to get in advance: he ran; Huber, Dumysen, and Dantzler of Naenikon were at his side. They all four thus arrived near Husen, half-way up the Albis. They had still to climb the steepest part of the mountain. Huber fell covered with wounds. Dumysen, the colonel-general, who had fought as a private soldier, almost reached the church of Husen, and there he dropt lifeless; and two of his sons, in the flower of youth, soon lay stretched on the battle-field that had drunk their father's blood. Kammli took a few steps farther; but halted erelong, exhausted and panting, near a hedge that he would have to clear, and discovered his two enemies and other Waldstettes running from all sides, like birds of prey, towards the wavering standard of Zurich. The strength of Kammli was sinking rapidly, his eyes grew dim, thick darkness surrounded him: a hand of lead fastened him to the ground, as, mustering all his expiring strength, he flung the standard on the other side of the hedge, exclaiming: "Is there any brave Zuricher near me? Let him preserve the banner and the honour of our lords! As for me, I can do no more!" Then turning a last look to heaven, he added: "May God be my helper!" He fell exhausted by this effort. Dantzler, who came up, flung away his sword, sprang over the hedge, seized the banner, and cried, "With the aid of God, I will carry it off." He then rapidly climbed the Albis, and at last placed the ancient standard of Zurich in safety. God, on whom these warriors fixed all their hopes, had heard their prayers, but the noblest blood of the republic had been spilt.

The enemy were victorious at all points. The soldiers of the Five Cantons, and particularly those of Unterwalden, long hardened in the wars of the Milanese, showed themselves more merciless towards their confederates than they had ever been towards foreigners. At the beginning of the battle, Gödli had taken flight, and soon after he quitted Zurich for ever. Lavater, the captain-general, after having fought valiantly, had fallen into the ditch. He was dragged out by a soldier and escaped.

The most distinguished men of Zurich fell one after another under the blows of the Waldstettes.[1] Rudi Gallman found the glorious tomb he had wished for, and his two brothers stretched beside him left their father's house desolate. Toning, captain of the arquebusiers, died for his country as he had foretold. All the pride of the population of Zurich, seven members of the Smaller Council, nineteen members of the Two Hundred, sixty-five citizens of the town, four hundred and seventeen, from the rural districts: the father in the midst of his children,—the son surrounded by his brothers,—lay on the field.

Gerold Meyer of Knonau, son of Anna Zwingle, at that time twenty-two years of age, and already a member of the council of Two Hundred,—a husband and a father,—had rushed into the foremost ranks with all the impetuosity of youth. "Surrender, and your life shall be spared," cried some of the warriors of the Five Cantons, who desired to save him. "It is better for me to die with honour, than to yield with disgrace," replied the son of Anna, and immediately, struck by a mortal blow, he fell and expired not far from the castle of his ancestors.

The ministers were those who paid proportionally the greatest tribute on this bloody day. The sword that was at work on the heights of Cappel thirsted for their blood: twenty-five of them fell beneath its stroke. The Waldstettes trembled with rage whenever they discovered one of these heretical preachers, and sacrificed him with enthusiasm, as a chosen victim to the Virgin and the saints. There has, perhaps, never been any battle in which so many men of the Word of God have bitten the dust. Almost every where the pastors had marched at the head of their flocks. One might have said that Cappel was an assembly of christian churches rather than an army of Swiss companies. The abbot Joner, receiving a mortal wound near the ditch, expired in sight of his own monastery. The people of Zug, in pursuit of the enemy, uttered a cry of anguish as they passed his body, remembering all the good he had done them.[2] Schmidt of Kussnacht, stationed on the field of battle in the midst of his parishioners, fell surrounded by forty of their bodies.[3] Geroldsek, John Haller, and many other pastors, at the head of their flocks, suddenly met, in a terrible and unforeseen manner, the Lord whom they had preached.

But the death of one individual far surpassed all others. Zwingle was at the post of danger, the helmet on his head, the sword hanging at his side, the battle-axe in his hand.[4] The action had scarcely begun, when, stooping to console a dying man, says J. J.

1 Optimi et docti viri, quos necessitas traxerat in commune periculum patriæ et ecclesiæ veritatisque defensandæ, quam et suo sanguine redemerunt. Pell. Vit. MS. p. 6.
2 Es klagtend inn insonders die Züger. Bull. lit. 151.
3 Uff der Walstett ward er funden, under und by sinen Kussnachern. Ibid. 147.
4 The chaplains of the Swiss troops still wear a sword. Zwingle did not make use of his arms.

Hottinger, a stone hurled by the vigorous arm of a Waldstette struck him on the head and closed his lips. Yet Zwingle arose, when two other blows which hit him successively on the leg,[1] threw him down again. Twice more he stands up; but a fourth time he receives a thrust from a lance; he staggers, and sinking beneath so many wounds, falls on his knees. Does not the darkness that is spreading around him announce a still thicker darkness that is about to cover the Church? Zwingle turns away from such sad thoughts; once more he uplifts that head which had been so bold, and gazing with calm eye upon the trickling blood, exclaims: "What matters this misfortune? They may indeed kill the body, but they cannot kill the soul!"[2] These were his last words.

He had scarcely uttered them ere he fell backwards. There, under a tree (Zwingle's Pear-tree), in a meadow, he remained lying on his back, with clasped hands, and eyes upturned to heaven.[3]

While the bravest were pursuing the scattered soldiers of Zurich, the stragglers of the Five Cantons had pounced like hungry ravens on the field of battle. Torch in hand, these wretches prowled among the dead, casting looks of irritation around them, and lighting up the features of their expiring victims by the dull glimmering of these funereal torches. They turned over the bodies of the wounded and the dead; they tortured and stripped them.[4] If they found any who were still sensible, they cried out, "Call upon the saints and confess to our priests!" If the Zurichers, faithful to their creed, rejected these cruel invitations, these men, who were as cowardly as they were fanatical, pierced them with their lances, or dashed out their brains with the but-ends of their arquebuses. The Roman-catholic historian, Salat of Lucerne, makes a boast of this. "They were left to die like infidel dogs, or were slain with the sword or the spear, that they might go so much the quicker to the devil, with whose help they had fought so desperately."[5] If any of the soldiers of the Five Cantons recognised a Zuricher against whom they had any grudge, with dry eyes, disdainful mouth, and features distorted by anger, they drew near the unhappy creature, writhing in the agonies of death, and said: "Well! has your heretical faith preserved you? Ah ha! it was pretty clearly seen to-day who had the true faith......To-day we have dragged your Gospel in the mud, and you too, even you are covered with your own blood. God, the

Virgin, and the saints have punished you." They had scarcely uttered these words before they plunged their swords into their enemy's bosom. "Mass or death!" was their watchword.

Thus triumphed the Waldstettes; but the pious Zurichers who expired on the field of battle called to mind that they had for God one who has said: "*If ye endure chastening, God dealeth with you as with sons; for what son is he whom the father chasteneth not?*"—"*Though he slay me, yet will I trust in him.*" It is in the furnace of trial that the God of the Gospel conceals the pure gold of his most precious blessings. This punishment was necessary to turn aside the Church of Zurich from the "broad ways" of the world, and lead it back to the "narrow ways" of the Spirit and the life. In a political history, a defeat like that of Cappel would be styled a great misfortune; but in a history of the Church of Jesus Christ, such a blow, inflicted by the hand of the Father himself, ought rather to be called a great blessing.

Meanwhile Zwingle lay extended under the tree, near the road by which the mass of the people was passing. The shouts of the victors, the groans of the dying, those flickering torches borne from corpse to corpse, Zurich humbled, the cause of Reform lost,—all cried aloud to him that God punishes his servants when they have recourse to the arm of man. If the German reformer had been able to approach Zwingle at this solemn moment, and to pronounce those oft-repeated words: "Christians fight not with sword and arquebuse, but with sufferings and with the cross,"[1] Zwingle would have stretched out his dying hand, and said, "Amen!"

Two of the soldiers who were prowling over the field of battle, having come near the reformer without recognising him, "Do you wish for a priest to confess yourself?" asked they. Zwingle, without speaking (for he had not strength), made signs in the negative. "If you cannot speak," replied the soldiers, "at least think in thy heart of the Mother of God, and call upon the saints!" Zwingle again shook his head, and kept his eyes still fixed on heaven.[2] Upon this the irritated soldiers began to curse him. "No doubt," said they, "you are one of the heretics of the city!" One of them, being curious to know who it was, stooped down and turned Zwingle's head in the direction of a fire that had been lighted near the spot.[3] The soldier immediately let him fall to the ground. "I think," said he, surprised and amazed, "I think it is Zwingle!" At this moment Captain Fockinger of Unterwalden, a veteran and a pensioner, drew near: he had heard the last words of the soldier. "Zwingle!" exclaimed he; "that vile heretic Zwingle!

---

[1] Hatt auch in den Schenklen zween Stiche. Tschudi, Helv. ii. 194.
[2] In genua prolapsum dixisse: "Ecquid hoc infortunii! Age! corpus quidem occidere possunt, animam non possunt." Osw. Myconius, Vit. Zw.
[3] Was er nach lebend, lag an dem Ruggen und hat seine beide händ zamen gethan, wie die betenden, sach mit synem angen obsich in hymel. B. iii. 136.
[4] Ein gross plünderen, ein ersuchen und usgiessen der todten und der wunden. Bull. iii. 135.
[5] Damit sie desto eher zum Teufel, damit sie mit allen vieren fechtend, geführt würdend. Salat.

[1] Christen sind nicht die für sich selbst mit dem Schwerdt oder Büchsen streiten, sondern mit dem Kreuz und Leyden. Luth. Opp.
[2] Und sach uber sich in Hymel. Bull. iii. 136.
[3] Beym Fuwr besach. Tschudi, Helv. ii 194.

that rascal, that traitor!" Then raising his sword, so long sold to the stranger, he struck the dying Christian on the throat, exclaiming in a violent passion, " Die, obstinate heretic!" Yielding under this last blow, the reformer gave up the ghost: he was doomed to perish by the sword of a mercenary. " Precious in the sight of the Lord is the death of his saints." The soldiers ran to other victims. All did not show the same barbarity. The night was cold; a thick hoar-frost covered the fields and the bodies of the dying. The Protestant historian, Bullinger, informs us that some of the Waldstettes gently raised the wounded in their arms, bound up their wounds, and carried them to the fires lighted on the field of battle. " Ah!" cried they, " why have the Swiss thus slaughtered one another!"

The main body of the army had remained on the field of battle near the standards. The soldiers conversed around the fires, interrupted from time to time by the cries of the dying. During this time the chiefs assembled in the convent sent messengers to carry the news of their signal victory to the confederate cantons, and to the Roman-catholic powers of Germany.

At length the day appeared. The Waldstettes spread over the field of battle, running here and there, stopping, contemplating, struck with surprise at the sight of their most formidable enemies stretched lifeless on the plain ; but sometimes also shedding tears as they gazed on corpses which reminded them of old and sacred ties of friendship. At length they reached the pear-tree under which Zwingle lay dead, and an immense crowd collected around it. His countenance still beamed with expression and with life. " He has the look," said Bartholomew Stocker of Zug, who had loved him, " he has the look of a living rather than of a dead man.[1] Such was he when he kindled the people by the fire of his eloquence." All eyes were fixed upon the corpse. John Schönbrunner, formerly canon of Zurich, who had retired to Zug at the epoch of the Reformation, could not restrain his tears: " Whatever may have been thy creed," said he, " I know, Zwingle, that thou hast been a loyal confederate ! May thy soul rest with God ! "

But the pensioners of the foreigner, on whom Zwingle had never ceased to make war, required that the body of the heretic should be dismembered, and a portion sent to each of the Five Cantons. " Peace be to the dead ! and God alone be their judge ! " exclaimed the avoyer Golder and the landamman Thoss of Zug. Cries of fury answered their appeal, and compelled them to retire. Immediately the drums beat to muster ; the dead body was tried, and it was decreed that it should be quartered for treason against the confederation, and then burnt for heresy.

[1] Nicht einem Todten sondern einem Lebenden gleich. Zwingli fur das Volk von J. J. Hottinger.

The executioner of Lucerne carried out the sentence. Flames consumed Zwingle's disjointed members ; the ashes of swine were mingled with his ; and a lawless multitude rushing upon his remains flung them to the four winds of heaven.[1]

Zwingle was dead. A great light had been extinguished in the Church of God. Mighty by the Word as were the other reformers, he had been still mightier than they in action ; but this very power had been his weakness, and he had fallen under the weight of his own strength. Zwingle was not forty-eight years old when he died. If the might of God always accompanied the might of man, what would he not have done for the Reformation in Switzerland, and even in the empire ! But he had wielded an arm that God had forbidden ; the helmet had covered his head, and he had grasped the halberd. His more devoted friends were themselves astonished, and exclaimed : " We know not what to say !......a bishop in arms ! "[2] The bolt had furrowed the cloud, the blow had reached the reformer, and his body was no more than a handful of dust in the palm of a soldier.

CHAPTER IX.

Consternation in Zurich—Violence of the Populace—Grief and Distress—Zwingle is dead !—Funeral Oration—Arms of Zurich—Another Reverse on the Goubel—Inactivity of the Bernese—Hopes and Plan of Charles V.—End of the War—Treaty of Peace.

FRIGHTFUL darkness hung over Zurich during the night that followed the afflicting day of Cappel. It was seven in the evening when the first news of the disaster arrived...... Vague but alarming reports spread at first with the rapidity of lightning. It was known that a terrible blow had been inflicted, but not of what kind ; soon a few wounded men, who arrived from the field of battle, cleared up the frightful mystery. " Then," said Bullinger, whom we shall allow to speak, " there arose suddenly a loud and horrible cry of lamentation and tears, bewailing and groaning." The consternation was so much the greater as no one had expected such a disaster. " There is not enough for a breakfast," had said some haughty worldly men ; " With one blow we shall be masters of the Five Chalets," had said another ; and an old soldier added with disdainful sneer, " We shall soon have scattered these five dung-hills." The christian portion, convinced that Zurich was fighting in a good cause, had not doubted that victory would be on the side of truth......Thus their first stupefaction was succeeded by a violent outburst

[1] Tschudi Helvet. II. 195. " Cadaver Zwinglii.....in quatuor partes secatur, in ignem conjicitur, in cinerem resolvitur." Myc. de Vit. Zw.
[2] Ego nihil certe apud me possum statuere, maxime de Episcopo in armis. Zuickius Ecolampadio, 8th November 1531, Zurich MS.

of rage. With blind fury the mob accused all their chiefs, and loaded with insults even those who had defended their country at the price of their blood. An immense crowd—agitated, pale, and bewildered, filled all the streets of the city. They met, questioned each other, and replied; they questioned again, and the answer could not be heard, for the shouts of the people interrupted or drowned the voices of the speakers. The councillors who had remained in Zurich repaired in haste to the town-hall. The people, who had already assembled there in crowds, looked on with threatening eyes. Accusations of treason burst from every mouth, and the patricians were pointed out to the general indignation. They must have victims. "Before going to fight against the enemy on the frontiers," said the mob, "we should defend ourselves against those who are within our walls." Sorrow and fear excited the minds of all. That savage instinct of the populace, which in great calamities leads them, like a wild beast, to thirst for blood, was violently aroused. A hand from the midst of the crowd pointed out the councilhall, and a harsh and piercing voice exclaimed: "Let us chop off the heads of some of the men who sit in these halls, and let their blood ascend to heaven, to beg for mercy in behalf of those whom they have slain."

But this fury was nothing in comparison with that which broke out against the ministers, against Zwingle, and all those Christians who were the cause (as they said) of the ruin of the country. Fortunately the sword of the Waldstettes had withdrawn them from the rage of their fellow-citizens; nevertheless, there still remained some who could pay for the others. Leo Juda, whom Zwingle's death was about to raise to the head of religious affairs, had scarcely recovered from a serious illness; it was on him they rushed. They threatened, they pursued him; a few worthy citizens carried him off and hid him in their houses. The rage of these madmen was not appeased: they continued shouting that atonement must be made for the slaughter at Cappel, by a still more frightful slaughter within the very walls of the city. But God placed a curb in the mouths of these infuriate beasts of prey, and subdued them.

On a sudden, grief succeeded to rage, and sobs choked the utterance of the most furious. All those whose relatives had marched to Cappel imagined that they were among the number of the victims. Old men, women, and children, went forth in the darkness by the glimmering light of torches, with haggard eyes and hurried steps; and as soon as some wounded man arrived, they questioned him with trembling voice about those whom they were seeking. Some replied: "I saw him fall close by my side."— "He was surrounded by so many enemies," said others, "that there was no chance of

safety for him."[1] At these words the distracted family dropt their torches, and filled the air with shrieks and groans.

Anna Zwingle had heard from her house the repeated discharges of artillery. As wife and mother, she had passed in expectation many long hours of anguish, offering fervent prayers to heaven. At length the most terrible accounts, one after another, burst upon her.

In the midst of those whose cries of despair re-echoed along the road to Cappel, was Oswald Myconius, who inquired with anxiety what had become of his friend. Soon he heard one of the unfortunate wretches who had escaped from the massacre, relating to those around him that Zwingle had fallen![2] ...... "Zwingle is no more! Zwingle is dead!" The cry was repeated: it ran through Zurich with the rapidity of lightning, and at length reached the unhappy widow. Anna fell on her knees. But the loss of her husband was not enough: God had inflicted other blows. Messengers following each other at short intervals announced to her the death of her son Gerold of Knonau, of her brother the bailiff of Reinhard, of her son-in-law Antony Wirz, of John Lutschi the husband of her dear sister, as well as of all her most intimate friends. This woman remained alone—alone with her God; alone with her young children, who, as they saw her tears, wept also, and threw themselves disconsolate into their mother's arms.

On a sudden the alarm-bell rang. The council, distracted by the most contrary opinions, had at last resolved to summon all the citizens towards the Albis. But the sound of the tocsin re-echoing through the darkness, the lamentable stories of the wounded, and the distressful groans of bereaved families, still further increased the tumult. A numerous and disorderly troop of citizens rushed along the road to Cappel. Among them was the Valaisan, Thomas Plater. Here he met with a man that had but one hand,[3]—there with others who supported their wounded and bleeding heads with both hands;—further still was a soldier whose bowels protruded from his body. In front of these unhappy creatures peasants were walking with lighted torches, for the night was very dark. Plater wished to return; but he could not, for sentinels placed on the bridge over the Sihl allowed persons to quit Zurich, but permitted no one to re-enter.

On the morrow the news of the disgraceful treatment of Zwingle's corpse aroused all the anger of Zurich; and his friends, uplifting their tear-bedimmed eyes, exclaimed:

[1] Dermassen umbgäben mit 'Fygenden, dass kein Hoffnung der rettung uberig. Bull. iii. 163.
[2] Ut igitur mane videram exeuntem, ita sub noctem audio nuntium, pugnatum quidem acriter, tamen infeliciter, et Zwinglium nobis perlisse. Myc. Vit. Zw.
[3] Ettlich kamen, hatten nur eine hand. Lebensbeschreibung Plateri, p. 297.

"These men may fall upon his body; they may kindle their piles, and brand his innocent life......but he lives—this invincible hero lives in eternity, and leaves behind him an immortal monument of glory that no flames can destroy.[1] God, for whose honour he has laboured, even at the price of his blood, will make his memory eternal."—"And I," adds Leo Juda, "I, upon whom he has heaped so many blessings, will endeavour, after so many others, to defend his renown and to extol his virtues." Thus Zurich consecrated to Zwingle a funeral oration of tears and sighs, of gratitude and cries of anguish. Never was funeral speech more eloquent!

Zurich rallied her forces. John Steiner had collected on the Albis some scattered fragments of the army for the defence of the pass: they bivouacked around their fires on the summit of the mountain, and all were in disorder. Plater, benumbed with cold (it is himself who gives us the account), had drawn off his boots to warm his feet at the watchfire. On a sudden an alarm was given, the troop was hastily drawn up, and, while Plater was getting ready, a trumpeter, who had escaped from the battle, seized his halberd. Plater took it back, and stationed himself in the ranks; before him stood the trumpeter, without hat or shoes, and armed with a long pole. Such was the army of Zurich.

The chief captain Lavater rejoined the army at daybreak. Gradually the allies came up; 1500 Grisons, under the orders of the captain-general Frey of Zurich, 1500 Thurgovians, 600 Tockenburgers, and other auxiliaries besides, soon formed an army of 12,000 men. All, even children, ran to arms. The council gave orders that these young folks[2] should be sent back to share in the domestic duties with the women.

Another reverse erelong augmented the desolation of the Reformed party. While the troops of Berne, Zurich, Basle, and Bienne, amounting to 24,000 men, were assembling at Bremgarten, the Five Cantons intrenched themselves at Baar, near Zug. But Zwingle was wanting to the Reformed army, and he would have been the only man capable of inspiring them with courage. A gust of wind having thrown down a few firtrees in the forests where the Zurichers were encamped, and caused the death of some of their soldiers, they failed not to see in this the signal of fresh reverses.

Nevertheless, Frey called loudly for battle; but the Bernese commandant Diesbach refused. Upon this the Zurich captain set off in the night of the 23d October at the head of 4000 men of Zurich, Schaffhausen, Basle, and St. Gall; and, while the Bernese

were sleeping quietly, he turned the Waldstettes, drove their outposts beyond the Sihl, and took his station on the heights that overlook the Goubel. His imprudent soldiers, believing victory to be certain, proudly waved their banners, and then sunk into a heavy sleep. The Waldstettes had observed all. On the 24th October, at two in the morning, by a bright moonlight, they quitted their camp in profound silence, leaving their fires burning, and wearing white shirts over their dresses that they might recognise one another in the obscurity. Their watchword was "Mary, the mother of God." They glided stealthily into a pine forest, near which the Reformed troops were encamped. The men stationed at the advanced guard of the Zurichers having perceived the enemy, ran up to the fires to arouse their friends, but they had scarcely reached the third fire before the Waldstettes appeared, uttering frightful shouts.[1] "Har...Har...Har...Har! ...Where are these impious heretics?......... Har...Har...Har...Har!" The army of the cities at first made a vigorous resistance, and many of the white shirts fell covered with blood; but this did not continue long. The bravest, with the valiant Frey at their head, having bitten the dust, the rout became general, and 800 men were left on the field of battle.

In the midst of these afflictions the Bernese remained stubborn and motionless. Francis Kolb, who, notwithstanding his advanced age, had accompanied the Bernese contingent as chaplain, reproached in a sermon the negligence and cowardice of his party. "Your ancestors," said he, "would have swum across the Rhine, and you—this little stream stops you! They went to battle for a word, and you, even the Gospel cannot move. For us it only remains to commit our cause to God." Many voices were raised against the imprudent old man, but others took up his defence; and the captain, James May, being as indignant as the aged chaplain at the delays of his fellow-citizens, drew his sword, and thrusting it into the folds of the Bernese banner, pricked the bear that was represented on it, and cried out in the presence of the whole army, "You knave, will you not show your claws?"[2] But the bear remained motionless.

The whole of the Reformation was compromised. Scarcely had Ferdinand received intelligence of the death of the arch-heretic Zwingle, and of the defeat at Cappel, than with an exclamation of joy, he forwarded these good news to his brother the Emperor Charles the Fifth, saying, "this is the first of the victories destined to restore the faith." After the defeat at the Goubel, he wrote again, saying that if the emperor were not so near at hand, he would not hesitate, how-

---

[1] Vivit adhunc, et æternum vivit fortissimus heros. Leonis Judæ exhort. ad Chr. Sect. Enchiridio Psalm. Zwinglii præmissa.
[2] Jungen fasels, young brood. Bull. Chr. iii. 176.

[1] Mit einem grossen grusamen geschrey. Bull. iii. 201.
[2] Bötz, Bötz, willt dan nicht kretzen! Ibid. 215.

ever weak he might be, to rush forward in person, sword in hand, to terminate so righteous an enterprise. " Remember," said he, that you are the first prince in Christendom, and that you will never have a better opportunity of covering yourself with glory. Assist the cantons with your troops; the German sects will perish, when they are no longer supported by heretical Switzerland."[1] —" The more I reflect," replied Charles, " the more I am pleased with your advice. The imperial dignity with which I am invested, the protection that I owe to Christendom and to public order, in a word, the safety of the house of Austria,—every thing appeals to me ! "

Already about two thousand Italian soldiers, sent by the pope and commanded by the Genoese De l'Isola, had unfolded their seven standards, and united near Zug with the army of the Five Cantons. Auxiliary troops, diplomatic negotiations, and even missionaries to convert the heretics, were not spared. The Bishop of Veroli arrived in Switzerland in order to bring back the Lutherans to the Roman faith by means of his friends and of his money.[2] The Roman politicians hailed the victory at Cappel as the signal of the restoration of the papal authority, not only in Switzerland, but throughout the whole of Christendom.[3] At last this presumptuous Reformation was about to be repressed. Instead of the great deliverance of which Zwingle had dreamt, the imperial eagle let loose by the Papacy was about to pounce on all Europe, and strangle it in its talons. The cause of liberty had perished on the Albis.

But the hopes of the Papists were vain: the cause of the Gospel, although humbled at this moment, was destined finally to gain a glorious victory. A cloud may hide the sun for a time; but the cloud passes and the sun reappears. Jesus Christ is always the same, and the gates of hell may triumph on the battle-field, but cannot prevail against his Church.

Nevertheless every thing seemed advancing towards a grand catastrophe. The Tockenburgers made peace and retired. The Thurgovians followed them; and next the people of Gaster. The evangelical army was thus gradually disbanded. The severity of the season combined with these dissensions; continual storms of wind and rain drove the soldiers to their homes.

Upon this the Five Cantons with the un-

disciplined bands of the Italian general Isola threw themselves on the left bank of the Lake of Zurich. The alarm-bell was wrung on every side; the peasants retired in crowds into the city, with their weeping wives, their frightened children, and their cattle that filled the air with sullen lowings. A report too was circulated that the enemy intended laying siege to Zurich. The country-people in alarm declared that if the city refused to make terms, they would treat on their own account.

The peace party prevailed in the council; deputies were elected to negotiate. " Above all things, preserve the Gospel, and then our honour, as far as may be possible !" Such were their instructions. On the 16th November, the deputies from Zurich arrived in a meadow situated near the frontier, on the banks of the Sihl, in which the representatives of the Five Cantons awaited them. They proceeded to the deliberations. " In the name of the most honourable, holy, and divine Trinity," began the treaty, " Firstly. we the people of Zurich bind ourselves and agree to leave our trusty and well-beloved confederates of the Five Cantons, their well-beloved co-burghers of the Valais, and all their adherents lay and ecclesiastic, in their true and indubitable christian faith,[1] renouncing all evil intention, wiles, and stratagems. And, on our side, we of the Five Cantons, agree to leave our confederates of Zurich and their allies in possession of their faith."[2] At the same time, Rapperschwyl, Gaster, Wesen, Bremgarten, Mellingen, and the common bailiwicks, were abandoned to the Five Cantons.

Zurich had preserved its faith; and that was all. The treaty having been read and approved of, the plenipotentiaries got off their horses, fell upon their knees, and called upon the name of God.[3] Then the new captain-general of the Zurichers, Escher, a hasty and eloquent old man, rising up, said as he turned towards the Waldstettes : " God be praised that I can again call you my well - beloved confederates !" and approaching them, he shook hands successively with Golder, Hug, Troguer, Rychmuth, Marquart, Zellger, and Thoss, the terrible victors at Cappel. All eyes were filled with tears.[4] Each took with trembling hand the bottle suspended at his side, and offered a draught to one of the chiefs of the opposite party. Shortly after a similar treaty was concluded with Berne.

---

1 Que se perdo deslar ! camino para remediar las quiebras de nuestra fé y ser Va. Md. Senor de Allemana. Ferdinand to Charles V. 11th November 1531.
2 Con proposita di rimòver Lutheriani dalla loro mala opinione, con mezzo di alcuni suoi amici e con denari. Report of Basadonna, Archbishop of Venice.
4 Ranke, Deutshe Geschichte, iii. 867.

1 By ihren wahren ungezwyflłten christenlichen glauben. Tschudi, p. 247.
2 By ihren Glauben. Ibid.
3 Knuwet mencklich wider und bättet. Bull. iii. 253.
4 Und luffend ihnen allen die Augen über. Tschudi, p. 245.

CHAPTER X.

Restoration of Popery at Bremgarten and Rapperschwyl—Priests and Monks every where—Sorrow of Œcolampadius—A tranquil Scene—Peaceful Death of Œcolampadius—Henry Bullinger at Zurich—Contrition and Exultation—The great Lesson—Conclusion.

THE restoration of Popery immediately commenced in Switzerland, and Rome showed herself every where proud, exacting, and ambitious.

After the battle of Cappel, the Romish minority at Glaris had resumed the upperhand. It marched with Schwytz against Wesen and the district of the Gaster. On the eve of the invasion, at midnight, twelve deputies came and threw themselves at the feet of the Schwytzer chiefs, who were satisfied with confiscating the national banners of these two districts, with suppressing their tribunals, annulling their ancient liberties, and condemning some to banishment, and others to pay a heavy fine. Next the mass, the altars, and images were every where reestablished, and they are maintained until the present day.[1] Such was the pardon of Schwytz!

It was especially on Bremgarten, Mellingen, and the free bailiwicks that the cantons proposed inflicting a terrible vengeance. Berne having recalled its army, Mutschli, the avoyer of Bremgarten, followed Diesbach as far as Arau. In vain did the former remind the Bernese that it was only according to the orders of Berne and Zurich that Bremgarten had blockaded the Five Cantons. "Bend to circumstances," replied the general. On this the wretched Mutschli, turning away from the pitiless Bernese, exclaimed, " The prophet Jeremiah has well said,—*Cursed be he that trusteth in man!*" The Swiss and Italian bands entered furiously into these flourishing districts, brandishing their weapons, inflicting heavy fines on all the inhabitants, compelling the Gospel ministers to flee, and restoring every where at the point of the sword, mass, idols, and altars.

On the other side of the lake the misfortune was still greater. On the 18th November, while the Reformed of Rapperschwyl were sleeping peacefully in reliance on the treaties, an army from Schwytz silently passed the wooden bridge nearly 2000 feet long which crosses the lake, and was admitted into the city by the Romish party. On a sudden the Reformed awoke at the loud pealing of the bells, and the tumultuous voices of the Catholics : the greater part quitted the city. One of them, however, by name Michael Wohlgemuth, barricaded his house, placed arquebuses at every window, and repelled the attack. The exasperated enemy brought up some heavy pieces of artillery, besieged this extemporaneous citadel in regular form, and Wohlgemuth was soon

taken and put to death in the midst of horrible tortures.

Nowhere had the struggle been more violent than at Soleure ; the two parties were drawn up in battle-array on each side of the Aar, and the Romanists had already discharged one ball against the opposite bank, another was about to follow, when the avoyer Wenge, throwing himself on the mouth of the cannon, cried out earnestly : " Fellow-citizens, let there be no bloodshed, or else let me be your first victim !" The astonished multitude dropped their arms : but seventy evangelical families were obliged to emigrate, and Soleure returned under the papal yoke.

The deserted cells of St. Gall, Muri, Einsidlen, Wettingen, Rheinau, St. Catherine, Hermetschwyll, and Guadenthal witnessed the triumphant return of Benedictines, Franciscans, Dominicans, and all the Romish militia; priests and monks, intoxicated with their victory, overran country and town, and prepared for new conquests.

The wind of adversity was furiously raging : the evangelical churches fell one after another, like the pines in the forest whose fall before the battle of the Goubel had raised such gloomy presentiments. The Five Cantons, full of gratitude to the Virgin, made a solemn pilgrimage to her temple at Einsidlen. In this desolated sanctuary the chaplains celebrated their mysteries anew ; the abbot, who had no monks, sent a number of youths into Swabia to be trained up in the rules of the order ; and this famous chapel, which Zwingle's voice had converted into a sanctuary for the Word, became for Switzerland, what it has remained until this day, the centre of the power and of the intrigues of the Papacy.

But this was not enough. At the very time that these flourishing churches were falling to the ground, the Reform witnessed the extinction of its brightest lights. A blow from a stone had slain the energetic Zwingle on the field of battle, and the rebound reached the pacific Œcolampadius at Basle, in the midst of a life that was wholly evangelical. The death of his friend, the severe judgments with which his memory was persecuted, the terror that had suddenly taken the place of the hopes he had entertained of the future—all these sorrows rent the heart of Œcolampadius, and his head and his life soon inclined sadly to the tomb. " Alas !" cried he, " that Zwingle, whom I have so long regarded as my right arm, has fallen under the blows of cruel enemies !"[1] He recovered, however, sufficient energy to defend the memory of his brother. " It was not," said he, " on the heads of the most guilty that the wrath of Pilate and the tower of Siloam fell. The judgment began in the house of God; our presumption has been

---

[1] Es würdent mäss, altâr und götzen vieder uff gericht. Bull. iii. 277.

[1] Zwinglium nostrum, quem pro manu altera nunc multo tempore habui. Zurich MS.

punished; let our trust now be placed on the Lord alone, and this will be an inestimable gain. Œcolampadius declined the call of Zurich to take Zwingle's place. " My post is here," said he, as he looked upon Basle.

He was not destined to hold it long. Illness fell upon him in addition to so many afflictions; the plague was in the city; a violent inflammation attacked him,[1] and erelong a tranquil scene succeeded the tumult of Cappel. A peaceful death calmed the agitated hearts of the faithful, and replaced by sweet and heavenly emotions the terror and distress with which a horrible disaster had filled them.

On hearing of the danger of Œcolampadius, all the city was plunged into mourning; a crowd of men of every age and of every rank rushed to his house. " Rejoice," said the reformer with a meek look; " I am going to a place of everlasting joy." He then commemorated the death of our Lord with his wife, his relations, and domestics, who shed floods of tears. " This supper," said the dying man, " is a sign of my real faith in Jesus Christ my Redeemer."

On the morrow he sent for his colleagues: " My brethren," said he, " the Lord is there; he calls me away. Oh! my brethren, what a black cloud is appearing on the horizon— what a tempest is approaching! Be steadfast: the Lord will preserve his own." He then held out his hand, which all these faithful ministers clasped with veneration.

On the 23d November he called his children around him, the eldest of whom was barely three years old. " Eusebius, Irene, Alethea," said he to them, as he took their little hands, " love God who is your Father." Their mother having promised for them, the children retired with the blessing of the dying servant of the Lord. The night that followed this scene was his last. All the pastors were around his bed: " What is the news?" asked Œcolampadius of a friend who came in. " Nothing," was the reply. " Well," said the faithful disciple of Jesus, " I will tell you something new." His friends awaited in astonishment. " In a short time I shall be with the Lord Jesus." One of his friends now asking him if he was incommoded by the light, he replied, putting his hand on his heart: " There is light enough here." As the day began to break, he repeated in a feeble voice the 51st Psalm: *Have mercy upon me, O Lord, according to thy loving kindness.* Then remaining silent, as if he wished to recover strength, he said, " Lord Jesus, help me!" The ten pastors with uplifted hands fell on their knees around his bed; at this moment the sun rose, and darted his earliest rays on a scene of sorrow so great and so afflicting with which the Church of God was again stricken.[2]

The death of this servant of the Lord was like his life, full of light and peace. Œcolampadius was in an especial degree the christian spiritualist and biblical divine. The importance he attached to the study of the books of the Old Testament imprinted one of its most essential characters on the reformed theology.[1] Considered as a man of action, his moderation and meekness placed him in the second rank. Had he been able to exert more of this peaceful spirit over Zwingle, great misfortunes might perhaps have been avoided. But like all men of meek disposition, his peaceful character yielded too much to the energetic will of the minister of Zurich; and he thus renounced, in part at least, the legitimate influence that he might have exercised over the Reformer of Switzerland and of the Church.

Zwingle and Œcolampadius had fallen. There was a great void and a great sorrow in the Church of Christ. Dissensions vanished before these two graves, and nothing could be seen but tears. Luther himself was moved. On receiving the news of these two deaths, he called to mind the days he had passed with Zwingle and Œcolampadius at Marburg; and the blow inflicted on him by their sudden decease was such, that many years after he said to Bullinger: " Their death filled me with such intense sorrow, that I was near dying myself."[2]

The youthful Henry Bullinger, threatened with the scaffold, had been compelled to flee from Bremgarten, his native town, with his aged father, his colleagues, and sixty of the principal inhabitants, who abandoned their houses to be pillaged by the Waldstettes.[3] Three days after this, he was preaching in the cathedral of Zurich: " No! Zwingle is not dead!" exclaimed Myconius; " or, like the phœnix, he has risen again from his ashes." Bullinger was unanimously chosen to succeed the great Reformer. He adopted Zwingle's orphan children, Wilhelm, Regula, and Ulrich, and endeavoured to supply the place of their father. This young man, scarcely twenty-eight years of age, and who presided forty years with wisdom and blessing over this church, was every where greeted as the apostle of Switzerland.[4]

Yet as the sea roars long after the violent tempest has subsided, so the people of Zurich were still in commotion. Many were agitated from on high. They came to themselves; they acknowledged their error; the weapons of their warfare had been carnal; they were now of a contrite and humble

[1] Ater carbunculus quovis carbunculo in domo Dei splendidiorem perdidit. J. J. Hottinger, iii. 634.
[2] De Joannis Œcolampadis obitu, per Simonem Gryneum. Epp. Œcol. et Zwinglii, libri iv.

[1] See his Commentaries on Isaiah (1525), 1st chapter; on Ezekiel (1527); Haggai, Zachariah, Malachi (1527); Daniel (1530); and the commentaries published after his death, with interpretations on Jeremiah, Ezekiel, Hosea, Joel, Amos, Obadiah, Jonah, and the 1st and 2d chapters of Micah.
[2] De cujus morte dolorem concepi......ita ut eorum casus me pene exanimaverit. L. Epp. v. 112.
[3] Ne a quinque pagis aut obtruncarer aut comburerer. Bull. ad Myc. November 1531.
[4] Haller ad Bulling. 1536.

spirit; they arose and went to their Father and confessed their sin. In those days there was great mourning in Zurich. Some, however, stood up with pride, protested by the mouth of their ministers against the work of the diplomatists, and boldly stigmatized the shameful compact. "If the shepherds sleep, the dogs must bark," exclaimed Leo Juda in the cathedral of Zurich. "My duty is to give warning of the evil they are about to do to my Master's house."[1]

Nothing could equal the sorrow of this city, except the exultation of the Waldstettes. The noise of drums and fifes, the firing of guns, the ringing of bells, had long resounded on the banks of their lakes, and even to their highest valleys. Now the noise was less, but the effect greater. The Five Cantons, in close alliance with Friburg and Soleure, formed a perpetual league for the defence of the ancient christian faith with the Bishop of Sion and the tithings of the Valais; and henceforward carried their measures in the federal affairs with boldness. But a deep conviction was formed at that period in the hearts of the Swiss Reformed. "Faith comes from God," said they; "its success does not depend on the life or death of one man. Let our adversaries boast of our ruin, we will boast only in the Cross."[2]—"God reigns," wrote Berne to Zurich, "and he will not permit the bark to founder." This conviction was of more avail than the victory of Cappel.

Thus the Reformation that had deviated from the right path, was driven back by the very violence of the assault into its primitive course, having no other power than the Word of God. An inconceivable infatuation had taken possession of the friends of the Bible. They had forgotten that our warfare is not carnal; and had appealed to arms and to battle. But God reigns; he punishes the churches and the people who turn aside from his ways. We have taken a few stones, and piled them as a monument on the battle-field of Cappel, in order to remind the Church of the great lesson which this terrible catastrophe teaches. As we bid farewell to this sad scene, we inscribe on these monumental stones, on the one side, these words from God's Book: "*Some trust in chariots, and some in horses: but we will remember the name of the Lord our God. They are brought down and fallen: but we are risen and stand upright.*" And on the other, this declaration of the Head of the Church: "*My kingdom is not of this world.*" If, from the ashes of the martyrs at Cappel, a voice could be heard, it would be in these very words of the Bible that these noble confessors would, after three centuries, address the Christians of our days. That the Church has no other king than Jesus Christ; that she ought not to meddle with the policy of the world, derive from it her inspiration, and call for its swords, its prisons, or its treasures; that she will conquer by the spiritual powers which God has deposited in her bosom, and, above all, by the reign of her adorable Head; that she must not expect upon earth thrones and mortal triumphs; but that her march resembles that of her King, from the manger to the cross, and from the cross to the crown:—such is the lesson to be read on the blood-stained page that has crept into our simple and evangelical narrative.[1]

But if God teaches his people great lessons, he also gives them great deliverances. The bolt had fallen from heaven. The Reformation seemed to be little better than a lifeless body cumbering the ground, and whose dissevered limbs were about to be reduced to ashes. But God raises up the dead. New and more glorious destinies were awaiting the Gospel of Jesus Christ at the foot of the Alps. At the south-western extremity of Switzerland, in a great valley which the white giant of the mountains points out from afar; on the banks of the Leman lake, at the spot where the Rhone, clear and blue as the sky above it, rolls its majestic waters; on a small hill that the foot of Cæsar had once trod, and on which the steps of another conqueror, of a Gaul, of a Picardine,[2] were destined erelong to leave their ineffaceable and glorious traces, stood an ancient city, as yet covered with the dense shadows of Popery; but which God was about to raise to be a beacon to the Church, and a bulwark to Christendom.

---

1 Ich mus bellen. Bull. iii. 321.
2 Gloriantibus adversariis in ruinam, nos in cruce gloriemur. Ad Œcolamp. 29th November 1531. Zurich MS.

1 Zwingle's *Pear Tree* having perished, a rock has been placed over the spot where this illustrious reformer died; and on it are engraved suitable inscriptions, different, however, from those in the text.
2 John Calvin of Noyon.

PREFACE TO VOLUME FIFTH.

In the four previous volumes the author has described the origin and essential development of the Reformation of the Sixteenth Century on the Continent; he has now to relate the history of the Reformation in England.

The notes will direct the reader to the principal sources whence the author has derived his information. Most of them are well known; some, however, had not been previously explored, among which are the later volumes of the State Papers published by order of Government, by a commission of which the illustrious Sir Robert Peel was the first president. Three successive Home Secretaries, Sir James Graham, Sir George Grey, and the honourable Mr S. H. Walpole, have presented the author with copies of the several volumes of this great and important collection; in some instances they were communicated to him as soon as printed, which was the case in particular with the seventh volume, of which he has made much use. He takes this opportunity of expressing his sincere gratitude to these noble friends of literature.

The History of the Reformation of the Sixteenth Century was received with cordiality on the Continent, but it has had a far greater number of readers in the British dominions and in the United States. The author looks upon the relations which this work has established between him and many distant Christians, as a precious reward for his labours. Will the present volume be received in those countries as favourably as the others? A foreigner relating to the Anglo-Saxon race the history of their reformation is at a certain disadvantage; and although the author would rather have referred his readers to works, whether of old or recent date, by native writers, all of them more competent than himself to accomplish this task, he did not think it becoming him to shrink from the undertaking.

At no period is it possible to omit the history of the Reformation in England from a general history of the Reformation of the Sixteenth Century; at the present crisis it is less possible than ever.

In the first place, the English Reformation has been, and still is, calumniated by writers of different parties, who look upon it as nothing more than an external political transformation, and who thus ignore its spiritual nature. History has taught the author that it was essentially a religious transformation, and that we must seek for it in men of faith, and not, as is usually done, solely in the caprices of the prince, the ambition of the nobility, and the servility of the prelates. A faithful recital of this great renovation will perhaps show us that beyond and without the measures of Henry VIII. there was something—everything, so to speak—for therein was the essence of the Reformation, that which makes it a divine and imperishable work.

A second motive forced the author to acknowledge the necessity of a true History of the English Reformation. An active party in the Episcopalian Church is reviving with zeal, perseverance, and talent, the principles of Roman-catholicism, and striving to impose them on the Reformed Church of England, and incessantly attacking the foundations of evangelical Christianity. A number of young men in the universities, seduced by that deceitful *mirage* which some of their teachers have placed before their eyes, are launching out into clerical and superstitious theories, and running the risk of falling, sooner or later, as so many have done already, into the ever yawning gulf of Popery. We must therefore call to mind the reforming principles which were proclaimed from the very commencement of this great transformation.

The new position which the Romish court is taking in England, and its insolent aggressions, are a third consideration which seems to demonstrate to us the present importance of this history. It is good to call to mind that the primitive Christianity of Great Britain perseveringly repelled the invasion of the popedom, and that after the definitive victory of this foreign power, the noblest voices among kings, lords, priests, and people, boldly protested against it. It is good to show that, while the word of God recovered its inalienable rights in Britain, in the sixteenth century, the popedom, agitated by wholly political interests, broke of itself the chain with which it had so long bound England.—We shall see in this volume the English government fortifying itself, for instance under Edward III., against the invasions of Rome. It has been pretended in our days, and by others besides ultramontanists, that the papacy is a purely spiritual power, and ought to be opposed by spiritual arms only. If the first part of this argument were true, no one would be readier than ourselves to adopt the conclusion. God forbid that any protestant state should ever refuse the completest liberty to the Roman-catholic doctrines. We certainly wish for reciprocity; we desire that ultramontanism should no longer throw into prison the humble believers who seek consolation for themselves, and for their friends, in holy Scripture. But though a deplorable fanaticism should still continue to transplant into the nineteenth century the mournful tragedies of the Middle Ages, we should persist in demanding the fullest liberty, not only of conscience, but of worship, for Roman-catholics in protestant states. We should ask it in the name of justice, whose immutable laws the injustice of our adversaries can never make us forget; we should ask it, on behalf of the final triumph of truth; for if our demands proved unavailing, perhaps with God's help it might be otherwise with our example. When two worlds meet face to face, in one of which light abounds, and in the other darkness, it is the darkness that should disappear before the light, and not the light fly from before the darkness. We might go farther than this: far from constraining the English catholics in anything, we would rather desire to help them to be freer than they are, and to aid them in recovering the rights of which the Roman bishop robbed them in times posterior to the establishment of the papacy; for instance, the election of bishops and pastors, which belongs to the clergy and the people. Indeed, Cyprian, writing to a bishop of Rome (Cornelius) demanded three elements to secure the legitimacy of episcopal election: "The call of God, the voice of the people, and the consent of the co-bishops."[1] And the council of Rome, in 1080, said: "Let the clergy and the *people*, with the consent of the apostolic see or of their *metropolitan*, elect their bishop."[2] In our days,—days distinguished by great liberty, — shall the church be less free than it was in the Middle Ages?

But if we do not fear to claim for Roman-catholics the rights of the church of the first ages, and a greater liberty than what they now possess, even in the very seat of the popedom, are we therefore to say that the

state, whether under Edward III. or in later times, should oppose no barrier against Romish aggressions? If it is the very life and soul of popery to pass beyond the boundaries of religion, and enter into the field of policy, why should it be thought strange for the state to defend itself, when attacked upon its own ground? Can the state have no need of precautions against a power which has pretended to be paramount over England, which gave its crown to a French monarch, which obtained an oath of vassalage from an English king, and which lays down as its first dogma its infallibility and immutability?

And it was not only under Edward III. and throughout the Middle Ages that Rome encroached on royalty; it has happened in modern times also. M. Mignet has recently brought to light some remarkable facts. On the 28th of June 1570 a letter from Saint Pius V. was presented to the catholic king Philip II. by an agent just arrived from Rome. "Our dear son, Robert Ridolfi," says the writer, "will explain (God willing) to your majesty certain matters which concern not a little the honour of Almighty God...... We conjure your majesty to take into your serious consideration the matter which he will lay before you, and to furnish him with all the means your majesty may judge most proper for its execution." The pope's "dear son," accordingly, explained to the duke of Feria, who was commissioned by Philip to receive his communication, "that it was proposed to *kill* queen Elizabeth; that the attempt would not be made in London, because it was the seat of heresy, but during one of her journeys; and that a certain James G—— would undertake it." The same day the council met and deliberated on Elizabeth's assassination. Philip declared his willingness to undertake the foul deed recommended by his holiness; but as it would be an expensive business, his ministers hinted to the nuncio that the pope ought to furnish the money. This horrible but instructive recital will be found with all its details in the *Histoire de Marie Stuart*, by M. Mignet, vol. ii. p. 159, etc. It true is that these things took place in the sixteenth century; but the Romish church has canonized this priestly murderer, an honour conferred on a very small number of popes, and the canonization took place in the eighteenth century.[1] This is not a very distant date.

And these theories, so calculated to trouble nations, are still to be met with in the nineteenth century. At this very moment there are writers asserting principles under cover of which the pope may interfere in affairs of state. The kings of Europe, terrified by the deplorable outbreaks of 1848, appear almost everywhere ready to support the court of Rome by arms; and ultra-montanism takes advantage of this to proclaim once more,

---

[1] Divinum judicium, populi suffragium, co-episcoporum consensus. Epist. 55.
[2] Clerus et populus, apostolicæ sedis, vel metropolitani sui consensu, pastorem sibi eligat. Mansi, xx. p. 533.

[3] Acta canonisationis S. Pii. V. Romæ, 1720, folio.

"that the popedom is above the monarchy: that it is the duty of the inferior (the king) to obey the superior; that it is the duty of the superior (the pope) to depose the sovereigns who abuse their power, and to condemn the subjects who resist it; and, finally, that this public law of Christian Europe, abolished by the ambition of sovereigns or the insubordination of peoples, should be revived." Such are the theories now professed not only by priests but by influential laymen.[1] To this opinion belong, at the present hour, all the zeal and enthusiasm of Romanism, and this alone we are bound to acknowledge is consistent with the principles of popery. And accordingly it is to be feared that this party will triumph, unless we oppose it with all the forces of the human understanding, of religious and political liberty, and above all, of the word of God. The most distinguished organ of public opinion in France, alarmed by the progress of these ultramontane doctrines, said not long ago of this party: " In its eyes there exists but one real authority in the world, that of the pope. All questions, not only religious but moral and political, are amenable to one tribunal, supreme and infallible, the pope's. The pope has the right to absolve subjects of their oath of fidelity; subjects have the right to take up arms against their prince when he rebels against the decisions of the holy see. This is the social and political theory of the Middle Ages."[2]

Since the popedom asserts claims both spiritual and temporal, the church and the state ought to resist it, each in its own sphere, and with its peculiar arms: the church (by which I mean the believers), solely with holy Scripture; the state with such institutions as are calculated to secure its independence. What! the church is bound to defend what belongs to the church, and the state is not to defend what belongs to the state? If robbers should endeavour to plunder two houses, would it be just and charitable for one neighbour to say to the other, " I must defend my house, but you must let yours be stripped?" If the pope desires to have the immaculate conception of the Virgin, or any other religious doctrine preached, let the fullest liberty be granted him, and let him build as many churches as he pleases to do it in: we claim this in the plainest language. But if the pope, like Saint Pius, desires to kill the Queen of England, or at least (for no pope in our days, were he even saint enough to be canonized would conceive such an idea), if the pope desires to infringe in any way on the rights of the state, then let the state resist him with tried wisdom and unshaken firmness. Let us beware of an ultra-spiritualism which forgets the lessons of history, and overlooks the rights of kings and peoples. When it is found among theologians, it is an error in statesmen, it is a danger.

Finally, and this consideration revives our hopes, there is a fourth motive which gives at this time a particular importance to the history we are about to relate. The Reformation is now entering upon a new phasis. The movement of the sixteenth century had died away during the seventeenth and eighteenth, and it was often to churches which had lost every spark of life that the historian had then to recount the narrative of this great revival. This is the case no longer. After three centuries a new and a greater movement is succeeding that which we describe in these volumes. The principles of the religious regeneration, which God accomplished three hundred years ago, are now carried to the end of the world with the greatest energy. The task of the sixteenth century lives again in the nineteenth, but more emancipated from the temporal power, more spiritual, more general; and it is the Anglo-Saxon race that God chiefly employs for the accomplishment of this universal work. The English Reformation acquires therefore, in our days, a special importance. If the Reformation of Germany was the foundation of the building, that of England was its crowning stone.

The work begun in the age of the apostles, renewed in the times of the reformers, should be resumed in our days with a holy enthusiasm: and this work is very simple and very beautiful, for it consists in establishing the throne of Jesus Christ both in the church and on earth.

Evangelical faith does not place on the throne of the church either human reason or religious conscientiousness, as some would have it; but it sets thereon Jesus Christ, who is both the knowledge taught and the doctor who teaches it; who explains his word by the word, and by the light of his Holy Spirit; who, by it bears witness to the truth, that is to say, to his redemption, and teaches the essential laws which should regulate the inner life of his disciples. Evangelical faith appeals to the understanding, to the heart, and to the will of every Christian, only to impose on them the duty to submit to the divine authority of Christ, to listen, believe, love, comprehend, and act, as God requires.

Evangelical faith does not place on the throne of the church the civil power, or the secular magistrate; but it sets thereon Jesus Christ, who has said, *I am King;* who imparts to his subjects the principle of life, who establishes his kingdom here on earth, and preserves and develops it; and who, directing all mortal events, is now making the progressive conquest of the world, until he shall exercise in person his divine authority in the kingdom of his glory.

Finally, evangelical faith does not place

[1] See in particular *Le Catholicisme, le Libéralisme et le Socialisme*, and other writings of Donoso Cortès, marquis of Valdegamas, one of the most distinguished members of the constitutional party in Spain.
[2] Journal des Débats, 15th January 1853.

on the throne of the church priests, councils, doctors, or their traditions,—or that vice-God (*veri Dei vicem gerit in terris,* as the Romish gloss has it), that *infallible* pontiff, who reviving the errors of the pagans, ascribes salvation to the forms of worship and to the meritorious works of men. It sets thereon Jesus Christ, the great High-priest of his people, the God-man, who, by an act of his free love, bore in our stead, in his atoning sacrifice, the penalty of sin;—who has taken away the curse from our heads, and thus become the creator of a new race.

Such is the essential work of that Christianity, which the apostolic age transmitted to the reformers, and which it now transmits to the Christians of the nineteenth century.

While the thoughts of great numbers are led astray in the midst of ceremonies, priests, human lucubrations, pontifical fables and philosophic reveries, and are driven to and fro in the dust of this world, evangelical faith rises even to heaven, and falls prostrate before Him who sitteth on the throne.

The Reformation is Jesus Christ.

" Lord, to whom shall we go, if not unto thee ? " Let others follow the devices of their imaginations, or prostrate themselves before traditional superstitions, or kiss the feet of a sinful man......O King of glory, we desire but Thee alone!

Eaux-Vives, Geneva, *March* 1853.

HISTORY OF THE REFORMATION.

VOLUME FIFTH.

BOOK XVII.

ENGLAND BEFORE THE REFORMATION.

CHAPTER I.

Introduction—Work of the Sixteenth Century—Unity and Diversity—Necessity of considering the entire Religious History of England—Establishment of Christianity in Great Britain—Formation of Ecclesiastical Catholicism in the Roman Empire—Spiritual Christianity received by Britain—Slavery and Conversion of Succat—His Mission to Ireland—Anglo-Saxons re-establish Paganism in England—Columba at Iona—Evangelical Teaching—Presbytery and Episcopacy in Great Britain—Continental Missions of the Britons—An Omission.

THOSE heavenly powers which had lain dormant in the church since the first ages of Christianity, awoke from their slumber in the sixteenth century, and this awakening called the modern times into existence. The church was created anew, and from that regeneration have flowed the great developments of literature and science, of morality, liberty, and industry, which at present characterize the nations of Christendom. None of these things would have existed without the Reformation. Whenever society enters upon a new era, it requires the baptism of faith. In the sixteenth century God gave to man this consecration from on high by leading him back from mere outward profession and the mechanism of works to an inward and lively faith.

This transformation was not effected without struggles—struggles which presented at first a remarkable unity. On the day of battle one and the same feeling animated every bosom : after the victory they became divided. Unity of faith indeed remained, but the difference of nationalities brought into the church a diversity of forms. Of this we are about to witness a striking example. The Reformation, which had begun its triumphal march in Germany, Switzerland, France, and several other parts of the continent, was destined to receive new strength by the conversion of a celebrated country, long known as the *Isle of Saints.* This island was to add its banner to the trophy of Protestantism, but that banner preserved its distinctive colours. When England became reformed, a puissant individualism joined its might to the great unity.

If we search for the characteristics of the British Reformation, we shall find that, beyond any other, they were social, national, and truly human. There is no people among whom the Reformation has produced to the same degree that morality and order, that liberty, public spirit, and activity, which are the very essence of a nation's greatness. Just as the papacy has degraded the Spanish peninsula, has the gospel exalted the British islands. Hence the study upon which we are entering possesses an interest peculiar to itself.

In order that this study may be useful, it should have a character of universality. To confine the history of a people within the space of a few years, or even of a century, would deprive that history of both truth and life. We might indeed have traditions, chronicles, and legends, but there would be no history. History is a wonderful organization, no part of which can be retrenched. To understand the present, we must know the past. Society, like man himself, has its infancy, youth, maturity, and old age. Ancient or Pagan society, which had spent its infancy in the East in the midst of the antihellenic races, had its youth in the animated epoch of the Greeks, its manhood in the stern period of Roman greatness, and its old age under the decline of the empire. Modern society has passed through analogous stages : at the time of the Reformation it attained that of the full-grown man. We shall now proceed to trace the destinies of the church in England, from the earliest times of Christianity. These long and distant preparations are one of the distinctive characteristics of its reformation.

Before the sixteenth century this church had passed through two great phases.

The first was that of its formation—the second that of its corruption.

In its formation it was oriento-apostolical.

In its corruption it was successively national-papistical and royal-papistical.

After these two degrees of decline came the last and great phasis of the Reformation.

In the second century of the Christian era vessels were frequently sailing to the savage shores of Britain from the ports of Asia Minor, Greece, Alexandria, or the Greek colonies in Gaul. Among the merchants busied in calculating the profits they could make upon the produce of the East with which their ships were laden, would occasionally be found a few pious men from the banks of the Meander or the Hermus, conversing peacefully with one another about the birth, life, death, and resurrection of Jesus of Nazareth, and rejoicing at the prospect of saving by these glad tidings the pagans towards whom they were steering. It would appear that some British prisoners of war, having learnt to know Christ during their captivity, bore also to their fellow-countrymen the knowledge of this Saviour. It may be, too, that some Christian soldiers, the Corneliuses of those imperial armies whose advanced posts reached the southern parts of Scotland, desirous of more lasting conquests, may have read to the people whom they had subdued, the writings of Matthew, John, and Paul. It is of little consequence to know whether one of these first converts was, according to tradition, a prince named Lucius. It is certain that the tidings of the Son of man, crucified and raised again, under Tiberius, spread through these islands more rapidly than the dominion of the emperors, and that before the end of the second century many churches worshipped Christ beyond the walls of Adrian; in those mountains, forests, and western isles, which for centuries past the Druids had filled with their mysteries and their sacrifices, and on which even the Roman eagles had never stooped.[1] These churches were formed after the eastern type: the Britons would have refused to receive the type of that Rome whose yoke they detested.

The first thing which the British Christians received from the capital of the empire was persecution. But Diocletian, by striking the disciples of Jesus Christ in Britain only increased their number.[1] Many Christians from the southern part of the island took refuge in Scotland, where they raised their humble roofs, and under the name of *Culdees* prayed for the salvation of their protectors. When the surrounding pagans saw the holiness of these men of God, they abandoned in great numbers their sacred oaks, their mysterious caverns, and their blood-stained altars, and obeyed the gentle voice of the Gospel. After the death of these pious refugees, their cells were transformed into houses of prayer.[2] In 305, Constantius Chlorus succeeded to the throne of the Cæsars, and put an end to the persecution.

The Christianity which was brought to these people by merchants, soldiers, or missionaries, although not the ecclesiastical catholicism already creeping into life in the Roman empire, was not the primitive evangelism of the apostles. The East and the South could only give to the North of what they possessed. The mere human period had succeeded to the creative and miraculous period of the church. After the extraordinary manifestations of the Holy Ghost, which had produced the apostolic age, the church had been left to the inward power of the word and of the Comforter. But Christians did not generally comprehend the spiritual life to which they were called. God had been pleased to give them a divine religion; and this they gradually assimilated more and more to the religions of human origin. Instead of saying, in the spirit of the gospel, the word of God first, and through it the doctrine and the life — the doctrine and the life, and through them the forms; they said, forms first, and salvation by these forms. They ascribed to bishops a power which belongs only to Holy Scripture. Instead of ministers of the word, they desired to have priests; instead of an inward sacrifice, a sacrifice offered on the altar; and costly temples instead of a living church. They began to seek in men, in ceremonies, and in holy places, what they could find only in the Word and in the lively faith of the children of God. In this manner evangelical religion gave place to catholicism, and by gradual degeneration in after-years catholicism gave birth to popery.

This grievous transformation took place more particularly in the East, in Africa, and in Italy. Britain was at first comparatively exempt. At the very time that the savage Picts and Scots, rushing from their heathen homes, were devastating the country, spreading terror on all sides, and reducing the

[1] Britannorum inaccessa Romanis loca Christo vero subdita. (Tertullian contra Judæos, lfb. vii.) This work, from its bearing no traces of Montanism, seems to belong to the first part of Tertullian's life. See also Origen in Lucam, cap. i. homil. 6.

[1] Lactantius, de mortibus persecutorum, cap. xii.
[2] Multi ex Brittonibus Christiani sævitiam Diocletiani timentes ad eos confugerant....ut vita functorum cellæ in templa commutarentur. Buchanan, iv. c. xxxv.

people to slavery, we discover here and there some humble Christian receiving salvation not by a clerical sentimentalism, but by the work of the Holy Ghost in the heart. At the end of the fourth century we meet with an illustrious example of such conversions.

On the picturesque banks of the Clyde, not far from Glasgow, in the Christian village of Bonavern, now Kilpatrick, a little boy, of tender heart, lively temperament, and indefatigable activity, passed the earlier days of his life. He was born about the year 372 A.D., of a British family, and was named Succat.[1] His father, Calpurnius, deacon of the church of Bonavern, a simple-hearted pious man, and his mother, Conchessa, sister to the celebrated Martin, archbishop of Tours,[2] and a woman superior to the majority of her sex, had endeavoured to instil into his heart the doctrines of Christianity; but Succat did not understand them. He was fond of pleasure, and delighted to be the leader of his youthful companions. In the midst of his frivolities, he committed a serious fault.

Some few years later, his parents having quitted Scotland and settled in Armorica (Bretagne), a terrible calamity befell them. One day as Succat was playing near the seashore with two of his sisters, some Irish pirates, commanded by O'Neal, carried them all three off to their boats, and sold them in Ireland to the petty chieftain of some pagan clan. Succat was sent into the fields to keep swine.[3] It was while alone in these solitary pastures, without priest and without temple, that the young slave called to mind the divine lessons which his pious mother had so often read to him. The fault which he had committed pressed heavily night and day upon his soul: he groaned in heart, and wept. He turned repenting towards that meek Saviour of whom Conchessa had so often spoken; he fell at His knees in that heathen land, and imagined he felt the arms of a father uplifting the prodigal son. Succat was then born from on high, but by an agent so spiritual, so internal, that he knew not " whence it cometh or whither it goeth." The gospel was written with the finger of God on the tablets of his heart. " I was sixteen years old," said he, " and knew not the true God; but in that strange land the Lord opened my unbelieving eyes, and, although late, I called my sins to mind, and was converted with my whole heart to the Lord my God, who regarded my low estate, had pity on my youth and ignorance, and consoled me as a father consoles his children."[4]

Such words as these from the lips of a swineherd in the green pastures of Ireland set clearly before us the Christianity which in the fourth and fifth centuries converted many souls in the British isles. In after-years, Rome established the dominion of the priest and salvation by forms, independently of the dispositions of the heart; but the primitive religion of these celebrated islands was that living Christianity whose substance is the grace of Jesus Christ, and whose power is the grace of the Holy Ghost. The herdsman from the banks of the Clyde was then undergoing those experiences which so many evangelical Christians in those countries have subsequently undergone. " The love of God increased more and more in me," said he, " with faith and the fear of His name. The Spirit urged me to such a degree that I poured forth as many as a hundred prayers in one day. And even during the night, in the forests and on the mountains where I kept my flock, the rain, and snow, and frost, and sufferings which I endured, excited me to seek after God. At that time, I felt not the indifference which now I feel: The Spirit fermented in my heart."[1] Evangelical faith even then existed in the British islands in the person of this slave, and of some few Christians born again, like him, from on high.

Twice a captive and twice rescued, Succat, after returning to his family, felt an irresistible appeal in his heart. It was his duty to carry the gospel to those Irish pagans among whom he had found Jesus Christ. His parents and his friends endeavoured in vain to detain him; the same ardent desire pursued him in his dreams. During the silent watches of the night he fancied he heard voices calling to him from the dark forests of Erin : " Come, holy child, and walk once more among us." He awoke in tears, his breast filled with the keenest emotion.[2] He tore himself from the arms of his parents, and rushed forth—not as heretofore with his playfellows, when he would climb the summit of some lofty hill —but with a heart full of charity in Christ. He departed : " It was not done of my own strength " said he ; " it was God who overcame all."

Succat, afterwards known as Saint Patrick, and to which name, as to that of St Peter and other servants of God, many superstitions have been attached, returned to Ireland, but without visiting Rome, as an historian of the twelfth century has asserted.[3] Ever active, prompt, and ingenious, he collected the pagan tribes in the fields

[1] In baptismo haud Patricium sed Succat a parentibus fuisse dictum. Usser. Brit. Eccl. Antiq. p. 428.
[2] Martini Turonum archiepiscopi consanguineam. Ibid.
[3] Cujus porcorum pastor erat. Ibid. p. 431.
[4] Et ibi Dominus aperuit sensum incredulitatis meæ, ut vel sero remorarem delicta mea, et ut converterer toto corde ad Dominum Deum meum. Patr. Confess. Usser, 431.

[1] Ut etiam in sylvis et monte manebam, et ante lucem excitabar ad orationem per nivem. per gelu, per pluviam.. ..quia tunc Spiritus in me fervebat. Patr. Confess. Usser. 432.
[2] Valde compunctus sum corde et sic expergefactus. Ibid. p. 433.
[3] Jocelinus, Vita in Acta Sanctorum.

by beat of drum, and then narrated to them in their own tongue the history of the Son of God. Erelong his simple recitals exercised a divine power over their rude hearts, and many souls were converted, not by external sacraments or by the worship of images, but by the preaching of the word of God. The son of a chieftain, whom Patrick calls Benignus, learnt from him to proclaim the Gospel, and was destined to succeed him. The court bard, Dubrach Mac Valubair, no longer sang druidical hymns, but canticles addressed to Jesus Christ. Patrick was not entirely free from the errors of the time ; perhaps he believed in pious miracles ; but generally speaking we meet with nothing but the gospel in the earlier days of the British church. The time no doubt will come when Ireland will again feel the power of the Holy Ghost, which had once converted it by the ministrations of a Scotchman.

Shortly before the evangelization of Patrick in Ireland, a Briton named Pelagius, having visited Italy, Africa, and Palestine, began to teach a strange doctrine. Desirous of making head against the moral indifference into which most of the Christians in those countries had fallen, and which would appear to have been in strong contrast with the British austerity, he denied the doctrine of original sin, extolled free-will, and maintained that, if man made use of all the powers of his nature, he would attain perfection. We do not find that he taught these opinions in his own country ; but from the continent, where he disseminated them, they soon reached Britain. The British churches refused to receive this " perverse doctrine," their historian tells us, " and to blaspheme the grace of Jesus Christ." [1] They do not appear to have held the strict doctrine of Saint Augustine : they believed indeed that man has need of an inward change, and that this the divine power alone can effect ; but like the churches of Asia, from which they had sprung, they seem to have conceded something to our natural strength in the work of conversion ; and Pelagius, with a good intention it would appear, went still further. However that may be, these churches, strangers to the controversy, were unacquainted with all its subtleties. Two Gaulish bishops, Germanus and Lupus, came to their aid, and those who had been perverted returned into the way of truth. [2]

Shortly after this, events of great importance took place in Great Britain, and the light of faith disappeared in profound night. In 449, Hengist and Horsa, with their Saxon followers, being invited by the wretched inhabitants to aid them against the cruel ravages of the Picts and Scots, soon turned their swords against the people they had come to assist. Christianity was driven back with the Britons into the mountains of Wales and the wild moors of Northumberland and Cornwall. Many British families remained in the midst of the conquerors, but without exercising any religious influence over them. While the conquering races, settled at Paris, Ravenna, or Toledo, gradually laid aside their paganism and savage manners, the barbarous customs of the Saxons prevailed unmoderated throughout the kingdoms of the Heptarchy, and in every quarter temples to Thor rose above the churches in which Jesus Christ had been worshipped. Gaul and the south of Europe, which still exhibited to the eyes of the barbarians the last vestiges of Roman grandeur, alone had the power of inspiring some degree of respect in the formidable Germans, and of transforming their faith. From this period, the Greeks and Latins, and even the converted Goths, looked at this island with unutterable dread. The soil, said they, is covered with serpents ; the air is thick with deadly exhalations ; the souls of the departed are transported thither at midnight from the shores of Gaul. Ferrymen, sons of Erebus and Night, admit these invisible shades into their boats, and listen, with a shudder, to their mysterious whisperings. England, whence light was one day to be shed over the habitable globe, was then the trysting-place of the dead. And yet the Christianity of the British isles was not to be annihilated by these barbarian invasions ; it possessed a strength which rendered it capable of energetic resistance.

In one of the churches formed by Succat's preaching, there arose about two centuries after him a pious man named Columba, son of Feidlimyd, the son of Fergus. Valuing the cross of Christ more highly than the royal blood that flowed in his veins, he resolved to devote himself to the King of heaven. Shall he not repay to the country of Succat what Succat had imparted to his? " I will go," said he, " and preach the word of God in Scotland ;" [1] for the word of God and not an ecclesiastical hierarchism was then the converting agency. The grandson of Fergus communicated the zeal which animated him to the hearts of several fellow-christians. They repaired to the seashore, and cutting down the pliant branches of the osier, constructed a frail bark, which they covered with the skins of beasts. In this rude boat they embarked in the year 565, and after being driven to and fro on the ocean, the little missionary band reached the waters of the Hebrides. Columba landed near the barren rocks of Mull, to the south of the basaltic caverns of Staffa,

[1] Verum Britanni cum neque suscipere dogma perversum, gratiam Christi blasphemando nullatenus vellent. Beda, Hist. Angl. lib. i. cap. xvii et xxi.
[2] Depravati viam correctionis agnoscerent. Ibid.

[1] Prædicaturus verbum Dei. Usser. Antiq. p. 359.

and fixed his abode in a small island, afterwards known as Iona or Icolmkill, " the island of Columba's cell." Some Christian Culdees, driven out by the dissensions of the Picts and Scots, had already found a refuge in the same retired spot. Here the missionaries erected a chapel, whose walls, it is said, still exist among the stately ruins of a later age.[1] Some authors have placed Columba in the first rank after the apostles.[2] True, we do not find in him the faith of a Paul or a John; but he lived as in the sight of God; he mortified the flesh, and slept on the ground with a stone for his pillow. Amid this solemn scenery, and among customs so rude, the form of the missionary, illumined by a light from heaven, shone with love, and manifested the joy and serenity of his heart.[3] Although subject to the same passions as ourselves, he wrestled against his weakness, and would not have one moment lost for the glory of God. He prayed and read, he wrote and taught, he preached and redeemed the time. With indefatigable activity he went from house to house, and from kingdom to kingdom. The king of the Picts was converted, as were also many of his people; precious manuscripts were conveyed to Iona; a school of theology was founded there, in which the Word was studied; and many received through faith the salvation which is in Christ Jesus. Erelong a missionary spirit breathed over this ocean rock, so justly named " the light of the western world."

The Judaical sacerdotalism which was beginning to extend in the Christian church found no support in Iona. They had forms, but not to them did they look for life. It was the Holy Ghost, Columba maintained, that made a servant of God. When the youth of Caledonia assembled around the elders on these savage shores, or in their humble chapel, these ministers of the Lord would say to them : " The Holy Scriptures are the only rule of faith.[4] Throw aside all merit of works, and look for salvation to the grace of God alone.[5] Beware of a religion which consists of outward observances : it is better to keep your heart pure before God than to abstain from meats.[6] One alone is your head, Jesus Christ. Bishops and presbyters are equal;[7] they should be the husbands of one wife, and have their children in subjection."[8]

The sages of Iona knew nothing of transubstantiation or of the withdrawal of the cup in the Lord's Supper, or of auricular confession, or of prayers to the dead, or tapers, or incense; they celebrated Easter on a different day from Rome;[1] synodal assemblies regulated the affairs of the church, and the papal supremacy was unknown.[2] The sun of the gospel shone upon these wild and distant shores. In after-years, it was the privilege of Great Britain to recover with a purer lustre the same sun and the same gospel.

Iona, governed by a simple elder,[3] had become a missionary college. It has been sometimes called a monastery, but the dwelling of the grandson of Fergus in nowise resembled the popish convents. When its youthful inmates desired to spread the knowledge of Jesus Christ, they thought not of going elsewhere in quest of episcopal ordination. Kneeling in the chapel of Icolmkill, they were set apart by the laying on of the hands of the elders : they were called *bishops*, but remained obedient to the *elder* or presbyter of Iona. They even consecrated other bishops : thus Finan laid hands upon Diuma, bishop of Middlesex. These British Christians attached great importance to the ministry; but not to one form in preference to another. Presbytery and episcopacy were with them, as with the primitive church, almost identical.[4] Somewhat later we find that neither the venerable Bede, nor Lanfranc, nor Anselm—the two last were archbishops of Canterbury—made any objection to the ordination of British bishops by plain presbyters.[5] The religious and moral element that belongs to Christianity still predominated; the sacerdotal element, which characterizes human religions, whether among the Brahmins or elsewhere, was beginning to show itself, but in Great Britain at least it held a very subordinate station. Christianity was still a religion and not a caste. They did not require of the servant of God, as a warrant of his capacity, a long list of names succeeding one another like the beads of a rosary; they entertained serious, noble, and holy ideas of the ministry; its

[1] I visited Iona in 1845 with Dr Patrick M'Farlan, and saw these ruins. One portion of the building seems to be of primitive architecture.
[2] Nulli post apostolos secundus. Notker.
[3] Qui de prosapia regali claruit. Sed morum gratia magis emicuit. Usser. Antiq. p. 360.
[4] Prolatis Sanctæ Scripturæ testimoniis. Adomn. l. i. c. 22.
[5] Bishop Munter, Altbritische Kirche. Stud. und Krit. vi. 745.
[6] Meliores sunt ergo qui non magno opere jejunant, cor intrinsecus nitidum coram Deo sollicite servantes. Gildas in ejusd. Synod. Append.
[7] In Hibernia episcopi et presbyteri unum sunt. Ekkehardi liber. Arx. Geschichte von S. Gall. i. 267.
[8] Patrem habui Calpornium diaconum filium quondam

Potiti Presbyteri. Patricii Confessio. Even as late as the twelfth century we meet with married Irish bishops. Bernard, Vita Malachiæ, cap. x.
[1] In die quidem dominica alia tamen quam dicebat hebdomade celebrabant. Beda. lib. iii. cap. iv.
[2] Augustinus *novam* religionem docet.....dum ad unius episcopi romani dominatum omnia revocat. Buchan. lib. v. cap. xxxvi.
[3] Habere autem solet ipsa insula rectorem semper abbatem *presbyterum* cujus juri et omnis provincia et *ipsi etiam episcopi*, ordine inusitato, debeant esse subjecti, juxta exemplum primi doctoris illius qui non episcopus sed *presbyter* exstitit et monachus. Beda, Hist. Eccl. iii. cap. iv.
[4] Idem est ergo presbyter qui episcopus, et antequam diaboli instinctu studia in religione fierent... communi presbyterorum concilio Ecclesiæ gubernabantur. Indifferenter de episcopo quasi de presbytero est loquutus (Paulus) ....sciant episcopi se, magis consuetudine quam dispositionis dominicæ veritate, presbyteris esse majores. Hieronymus ad Titum, i. 5.
[5] Bishop Munter makes this remark in his dissertation *On the Ancient British Church*, about the primitive identity of bishops and priests, and episcopal consecration. *Stud. und Krit.* an. 1833.

authority proceeded wholly from Jesus Christ its head.

The missionary fire, which the grandson of Fergus had kindled in a solitary island, soon spread over Great Britain. Not in Iona alone, but at Bangor and other places, the spirit of evangelization burst out. A fondness for travelling had already become a second nature in this people.[1] Men of God, burning with zeal, resolved to carry the evangelical torch to the continent—to the vast wildernesses sprinkled here and there with barbarous and heathen tribes. They did not set forth as antagonists of Rome, for at that epoch there was no place for such antagonism; but Iona and Bangor, less illustrious than Rome in the history of nations, possessed a more lively faith than the city of the Cæsars; and that faith,—unerring sign of the presence of Jesus Christ,—gave those whom it inspired a right to evangelize the world, which Rome could not gainsay.

The missionary bishops[2] of Britain accordingly set forth and traversed the Low Countries, Gaul, Switzerland, Germany, and even Italy.[3] The free church of the Scots and Britons did more for the conversion of central Europe than the half-enslaved church of the Romans. These missionaries were not haughty and insolent like the priests of Italy; but supported themselves by the work of their hands. Columbanus (whom we must not confound with Columba),[4] "feeling in his heart the burning of the fire which the Lord had kindled upon earth,"[5] quitted Bangor in 590 with twelve other missionaries, and carried the gospel to the Burgundians, Franks, and Swiss. He continued to preach amidst frequent persecutions, left his disciple Gall in Helvetia, and retired to Bobbio, where he died, honouring Christian Rome, but placing the church of Jerusalem above it,[6]—exhorting it to beware of corruption, and declaring that the power would remain with it so long only as it retained the true doctrine (recta ratio). Thus was Britain faithful in planting the standard of Christ in the heart of Europe. We might almost imagine this unknown people to be a new Israel, and Icolmkill and Bangor to have inherited the virtues of Zion.

Yet they should have done more: they should have preached—not only to the continental heathens, to those in the north of Scotland and the distant Ireland, but also to the still pagan Saxons of England. It is true that they made several attempts; but while the Britons considered their conquerors as the enemies of God and man, and shuddered while they pronounced their name,[1] the Saxons refused to be converted by the voice of their slaves. By neglecting this field, the Britons left room for other workmen, and thus it was that England yielded to a foreign power, beneath whose heavy yoke it long groaned in vain.

CHAPTER II.

Pope Gregory the Great—Desires to reduce Britain—Policy of Gregory and Augustine—Arrival of the Mission—Appreciation—Britain superior to Rome—Dionoth at Bangor—First and Second Romish Aggressions—Anguish of the Britons—Pride of Rome—Rome has recourse to the Sword—Massacre—Saint Peter scourges an Archbishop—Oswald—His Victory—Corman—Mission of Oswald and Aidan—Death of Oswald.

It is matter of fact that the spiritual life had waned in Italian catholicism; and in proportion as the heavenly spirit had become weak, the lust of dominion had grown strong. The Roman metropolitans and their delegates soon became impatient to mould all Christendom to their peculiar forms.

About the end of the sixth century an eminent man filled the see of Rome. Gregory was born of senatorial family, and already on the high road to honour, when he suddenly renounced the world, and transformed the palace of his fathers into a convent. But his ambition had only changed its object. In his views, the whole church should submit to the ecclesiastical jurisdiction of Rome. True, he rejected the title of *universal bishop* assumed by the patriarch of Constantinople; but if he desired not the name, he was not the less eager for the substance.[2] On the borders of the West, in the island of Great Britain, was a Christian church independent of Rome: this must be conquered, and a favourable opportunity soon occurred.

Before his elevation to the primacy, and while he was as yet only the monk Gregory, he chanced one day to cross a market in Rome where certain foreign dealers were exposing their wares for sale. Among them he perceived some fair-haired youthful slaves, whose noble bearing attracted his attention. On drawing near them, he learned that the Anglo-Saxon nation to which they belonged had refused to receive the gospel from the Britons. When he afterwards became bishop of Rome, this crafty and energetic pontiff, "the last of the good and the

---

[1] Natio Scotorum quibus consuetudo peregrinandi jam pæne in naturam conversa est. Vita S. Galli, s. 47.
[2] They were called *episcopi regionarii*, because they had no settled diocese.
[3] Antiquo tempore doctissimi solebant magistri de Hibernia Britanniam, Galliam, Italiam venire, et multos per ecclesias Christi fecisse profectus. Alcuin, Epp. ccxxi.
[4] Thierry, in his *Hist. de la Conquête de l' Angleterre*, makes Columba and Columbanus one personage. Columba preached the Gospel in Scotland about 560, and died in 597; Columbanus preached among the Burgundians in 600, and died in 615.
[5] Ignitum igne Domini desiderium. Mabillon, Acta, p. 9.
[6] Salva loci dominicæ resurrectionis *singulari prærogativa*. Columb. Vita, s. 10.

[1] Nefandi nominis Saxoni Deo hominibusque invisi. Gildas, De excidio Britanniæ.
[2] He says (Epp. lib. ix. ep. xii.): De Constantinopolitana ecclesia quis eam dubitet apostolicæ sedi esse subjectam?

first of the bad," as he has been called, determined to convert these proud conquerors, and make use of them in subduing the British church to the papacy, as he had already made use of the Frank monarchs to reduce the Gauls. Rome has often shown herself more eager to bring Christians rather than idolaters to the pope.[1] Was it thus with Gregory? We must leave the question unanswered.

Ethelbert, king of Kent, having married a Christian princess of Frank descent, the Roman bishop thought the conjuncture favourable for his design, and despatched a mission under the direction of one of his friends named Augustine, A.D. 596. At first the missionaries recoiled from the task appointed them; but Gregory was firm. Desirous of gaining the assistance of the Frank kings, Theodoric and Theodebert, he affected to consider them as the lords paramount of England, and commended to them the conversion of *their subjects*.[2] Nor was this all. He claimed also the support of the powerful Brunehilda, grandmother of these two kings, and equally notorious for her treachery, her irregularities, and her crimes; and did not scruple to extol the *good works* and *godly fear* of this modern Jezebel.[3] Under such auspices the Romish mission arrived in England. The pope had made a skilful choice of his delegate. Augustine possessed even to a greater extent than Gregory himself a mixture of ambition and devotedness, of superstition and piety, of cunning and zeal. He thought that faith and holiness were less essential to the church than authority and power; and that its prerogative was not so much to save souls as to collect all the human race under the sceptre of Rome.[4] Gregory himself was distressed at Augustine's spiritual pride, and often exhorted him to humility.

Success of that kind which popery desires soon crowned the labours of its servants. The forty-one missionaries having landed in the isle of Thanet, in the year 597, the king of Kent consented to receive them, but in the open air, for fear of magic. They drew up in such a manner as to produce an effect on the rude islanders. The procession was opened by a monk bearing a huge cross on which the figure of Christ was represented: his colleagues followed chanting their Latin hymns, and thus they approached the oak appointed for the place of conference. They inspired sufficient confidence in Ethelbert to gain permission to celebrate their worship in an old ruinous chapel at Durovern (Canterbury), where British Christians had in former times

adored the Saviour Christ. The king and thousands of his subjects received not long after, with certain forms, and certain Christian doctrines, the errors of the Roman pontiffs—as purgatory, for instance, which Gregory was advocating with the aid of the most absurd fables.[1] Augustine baptized ten thousand pagans in one day. As yet Rome had only set her foot in Great Britain, she did not fail erelong to establish her kingdom there.

We should be unwilling to undervalue the religious element now placed before the Anglo-Saxons, and we can readily believe that many of the missionaries sent from Italy desired to work a Christian work. We think, too, that the Middle Ages ought to be appreciated with more equitable sentiments than have always been found in the persons who have written on that period. Man's conscience lived, spoke, and groaned during the long dominion of popery; and like a plant growing among thorns, it often succeeded in forcing a passage through the obstacles of traditionalism and hierarchy, to blossom in the quickening sun of God's grace. The Christian element is even strongly marked in some of the most eminent men of the theocracy—in Anselm for instance.

Yet as it is our task to relate the history of the struggles which took place between primitive Christianity and Roman-catholicism, we cannot forbear pointing out the superiority of the former in a religious light, while we acknowledge the superiority of the latter in a political point of view. We believe (and we shall presently have a proof of it)[2] that a visit to Iona would have taught the Anglo-Saxons much more than their frequent pilgrimages to the banks of the Tiber. Doubtless, as has been remarked, these pilgrims contemplated at Rome "the noble monuments of antiquity," but there existed at that time in the British islands—and it has been too often overlooked—a Christianity which, if not perfectly pure, was at least better than that of popery. The British church, which at the beginning of the seventh century carried faith and civilisation into Burgundy, the Vosges mountains, and Switzerland, might well have spread them both over Britain. The influence of the arts, whose civilizing influence we are far from depreciating, would have come later.

But so far was the Christianity of the Britons from converting the Saxon heptarchy, that it was, alas! the Romanism of the heptarchy which was destined to conquer Britain. These struggles between the Roman and British churches, which fill all the seventh century, are of the highest importance to the English church, for they

---

[1] We know the history of Tahiti and of other modern missions of the Romish church.
[2] Subjectos vestros. Opp. Gregorii, tom. iv. p. 334.
[3] Prona in bonis operibus....in omnipotentis Dei timore. Ibid. tom. ii. p. 635.
[4] We find the same idea in Wiseman, Lect. ix., On the principal doctrines and practices of the Catholic Church. Lond. 1836.

[1] Hoepfner, De origine dogmatis de purgatorio. Halle 1792.
[2] In the history of Oswald, king of Northumberland.

establish clearly its primitive liberty. They possess also great interest for the other churches of the West, as showing in the most striking characters the usurping acts by which the papacy eventually reduced them beneath its yoke.

Augustine, appointed archbishop not only of the Saxons, but of the free Britons, was settled by papal ordinance, first at London and afterwards at Canterbury. Being at the head of a hierarchy composed of twelve bishops, he soon attempted to bring all the Christians of Britain under the Roman jurisdiction. At that time there existed at Bangor,[1] in North Wales, a large Christian society, amounting to nearly three thousand individuals, collected together to work with their own hands,[2] to study, and to pray, and from whose bosom numerous missionaries (Columbanus was among the number) had from time to time gone forth. The president of this church was Dionoth, a faithful teacher, ready to serve all men in charity, yet firmly convinced that no one should have supremacy in the Lord's vineyard. Although one of the most influential men in the British church, he was somewhat timid and hesitating; he would yield to a certain point for the love of peace; but would never flinch from his duty. He was another apostle John, full of mildness, and yet condemning the Diotrephes, *who love to have pre-eminence among the brethren.* Augustine thus addressed him : " Acknowledge the authority of the Bishop of Rome." These are the first words of the papacy to the ancient Christians of Britain. " We desire to love all men," meekly replied the venerable Briton ; " and what we do for you, we will do for him also whom you call the pope. But he is not entitled to call himself the *father of fathers,* and the only submission we can render him is that which we owe to every Christian."[3] This was not what Augustine asked.

He was not discouraged by this first check. Proud of the pallium which Rome had sent him, and relying on the swords of the Anglo-Saxons, he convoked in 601 a general assembly of British and Saxon bishops. The meeting took place in the open air, beneath a venerable oak, near Wigornia (Worcester or Hereford), and here occurred the second Romish aggression. Dionoth resisted with firmness the extravagant pretensions of Augustine, who again summoned him to recognise the authority of Rome.[4] Another Briton protested against the presumption of the Romans, who ascribed to their consecration a virtue which they refused to that of Iona or of the Asiatic churches.[1] The Britons, exclaimed a third, " cannot submit either to the haughtiness of the Romans or the tyranny of the Saxons."[2] To no purpose did the archbishop lavish his arguments, prayers, censures, and miracles even; the Britons were firm. Some of them who had eaten with the Saxons while they were as yet heathens, refused to do so now that they had submitted to the pope.[3] The Scotch were particularly inflexible; for one of their number, by name Dagam, would not only take no food at the same table with the Romans, but not even under the same roof.[4] Thus did Augustine fail a second time, and the independence of Britain appeared secure.

And yet the formidable power of the popes, aided by the sword of the conquerors, alarmed the Britons. They imagined they saw a mysterious decree once more yoking the nations of the earth to the triumphal car of Rome, and many left Wigornia uneasy and sad at heart. How is it possible to save a cause, when even its defenders begin to despair? It was not long before they were summoned to a new council. " What is to be done?" they exclaimed with sorrowful forebodings. Popery was not yet thoroughly known : it was hardly formed. The half-enlightened consciences of these believers were a prey to the most violent agitation. They asked themselves whether, in rejecting this new power, they might not be rejecting God himself. A pious Christian, who led a solitary life, had acquired a great reputation in the surrounding district. Some of the Britons visited him, and inquired whether they should resist Augustine or follow him.[5] " If he is a man of God, follow him," replied the hermit. —" And how shall we know that?"—"If he is meek and humble of heart, he bears Christ's yoke ; but if he is violent and proud, he is not of God."—" What sign shall we have of his humility?"—" If he rises from his seat when you enter the room." Thus spoke the oracle of Britain : it would have been better to have consulted the Holy Scriptures.

But humility is not a virtue that flourishes among Romish pontiffs and legates : they love to remain seated while others court and worship them. The British bishops entered the council-hall, and the archbishop, desirous of indicating his superiority, proudly kept his seat.[6] Astonished

---

[1] Bann-cor, the choir on the steep hill. Carlisle, Top. Dict. Wales.

[2] Ars unicuique dabatur, ut ex opere manuum quotidiano se posset in victu necessario continere. Preuves de l'hist. de Bretagne, ii. 25.

[3] Istam obedientiam nos sumus parati dare et solvere ei et *cuique Christiano* continuo. Wilkins, Conc. M. Brit. i. 26.

[4] Dionothus de non approbanda apud eos Romanorum auctoritate disputabat. Ibid. 24.

[1] Ordinationesque more asiatico eisdem contulisse. Wilkins, Conc. M. Brit. i. 24.

[2] In communionem admittere vel Romanorum fastum vel Saxonum tyrannidem. Ibid. 26.

[3] According to the apostolic precept, 1 Cor. v. 9-11.

[4] Dagamus ad nos veniens, non solum cibum nobiscum, sed nec in eodem hospitio quo vescebamur, sumere noluit. Beda, lib. ii. cap. iv.

[5] Ad quendam virum sanctum et prudentem qui apud eos anachoreticam ducere vitam solebat, consulentes an ad prædicationem Augustini suas deserere traditiones deberent. Ibid. lib. ii. cap. ii.

[6] Factumque est ut venientibus illis sederet Augustinus in sella. Ibid.

at this sight, the Britons would hear no more of the authority of Rome. For the third time they said No—they knew *no other master but Christ.* Augustine, who expected to see these bishops prostrate their churches at his feet, was surprised and indignant. He had reckoned on the immediate submission of Britain, and the pope had now to learn that his missionary had deceived him.........Animated by that insolent spirit which is found too often in the ministers of the Romish Church, Augustine exclaimed: " If you will not receive brethren who bring you peace, you shall receive enemies who will bring you war. If you will not unite with us in showing the Saxons the way of life, you shall receive from them the stroke of death."[1] Having thus spoken, the haughty archbishop withdrew, and occupied his last days in preparing the accomplishment of his ill-omened prophecy.[2] Argument had failed: now for the sword!

Shortly after the death of Augustine, Edelfrid, one of the Anglo-Saxon kings, and who was still a heathen, collected a numerous army, and advanced towards Bangor, the centre of British Christianity. Alarm spread through those feeble churches. They wept and prayed. The sword of Edelfrid drew nearer. To whom can they apply, or where shall they find help? The magnitude of the danger seemed to recall the Britons to their pristine piety: not to men, but to the Lord himself will they turn their thoughts. Twelve hundred and fifty servants of the living God, calling to mind what are the arms of Christian warfare, after preparing themselves by fasting, met together in a retired spot to send up their prayers to God.[3] A British chief, named Brocmail, moved by tender compassion, stationed himself near them with a few soldiers; but the cruel Edelfrid, observing from a distance this band of kneeling Christians, demanded: " Who are these people, and what are they doing?" On being informed, he added: " They are fighting then against us, although unarmed;" and immediately he ordered his soldiers to fall upon the prostrate crowd. Twelve hundred of them were slain.[4] They prayed and they died. The Saxons forthwith proceeded to Bangor, the chief seat of Christian learning, and razed it to the ground. Romanism was triumphant in England. The news of these massacres filled the country *with weeping and great mourning;* but the priests of Romish consecration (and

the venerable Bede shared their sentiments) beheld in this cruel slaughter the accomplishment of the prophecy of the *holy pontiff* Augustine;[1] and a national tradition among the Welsh for many ages pointed to him as the instigator of this cowardly butchery. Thus did Rome loose the savage Pagan against the primitive church of Britain, and fastened it all dripping with blood to her triumphal car. A great mystery of iniquity was accomplishing.

But while the Saxon sword appeared to have swept everything from before the papacy, the ground trembled under its feet, and seemed about to swallow it up. The hierarchical rather than Christian conversions effected by the priests of Rome were so unreal that a vast number of neophytes suddenly returned to the worship of their idols. Eadbald, king of Kent, was himself among the number of apostates. Such reversions to paganism are not unfrequent in the history of the Romish missions. The bishops fled into Gaul: Mellitus and Justus had already reached the continent in safety, and Lawrence, Augustine's successor, was about to follow them. While lying in the church where he had desired to pass the night before leaving England, he groaned in spirit as he saw the work founded by Augustine perishing in his hands. He saved it by a miracle. The next morning he presented himself before the king with his clothes all disordered and his body covered with wounds. " Saint Peter," he said, " appeared to me during the night and scourged me severely because I was about to forsake his flock."[2] The *scourge* was a means of moral persuasion which Peter had forgotten in his epistles. Did Lawrence cause these blows to be inflicted by others— or did he inflict them himself—or is the whole account an idle dream? We should prefer adopting the latter hypothesis. The superstitious prince, excited at the news of this supernatural intervention, eagerly acknowledged the authority of the pope, the vicar of an apostle who so mercilessly scourged those who had the misfortune to displease him. If the dominion of Rome had then disappeared from England, it is probable that the Britons, regaining their courage, and favoured in other respects by the wants which would have been felt by the Saxons, would have recovered from their defeat, and would have imparted their free Christianity to their conquerors. But now the Roman bishop seemed to remain master of England, and the faith of the Britons to be crushed for ever. But it was not so. A young man, sprung from the energetic race of the conquerors, was about

---

[1] Si pacem cum fructibus accipere nollent, bellum ab hostibus forent accepturi.... Beda, Hist. Eccl. ii. cap. ii.
[2] Ipsum Augustinum hujus belli non modo conscium sed et *impulsorem* exstitisse. Wilkins adds, that the expression found in Bede, concerning the death of Augustine, is a parenthesis foisted in by Romanist writers, and not found in the Saxon manuscripts. Conc. Brit. p. 26.
[3] Ad memoratam aciem, peracto jejunio triduano, cum aliis orandi causa convenerant. Beda, lib. ii. cap. ii.
[4] Extinctos in ea pugna ferunt de his qui ad orandum venerunt viros circiter mille ducentos. Ibid.

[1] Sic completum est presagium sancti pontificis Augustini. Beda, lib. ii. cap. ii.
[2] Apparuit ei beatissimus apostolorum princeps, et multo illum tempore secretæ noctis flagellis acrioribus afficiens. Ibid. cap. vi.

to become the champion of truth and liberty, and almost the whole island to be freed from the Roman yoke.

Oswald, an Anglo-Saxon Prince, son of the heathen and cruel Edelfrid, had been compelled by family reverses to take refuge in Scotland, when very young, accompanied by his brother Oswy and several other youthful chiefs. He had acquired the language of the country, been instructed in the truths of Holy Writ, converted by the grace of God, and baptized into the Scottish church.[1] He loved to sit at the feet of the elders of Iona and listen to their words. They showed him Jesus Christ going from place to place doing good, and he desired to do so likewise; they told him that Christ was the only head of the church, and he promised never to acknowledge any other. Being a single-hearted generous man, he was especially animated with tender compassion towards the poor, and would take off his own cloak to cover the nakedness of one of his brethren. Often, while mingling in the quiet assemblies of the Scottish Christians, he had desired to go as a missionary to the Anglo-Saxons. It was not long before he conceived the bold design of leading the people of Northumberland to the Saviour; but being a prince as well as a Christian, he determined to begin by reconquering the throne of his fathers. There was in this young Englishman the love of a disciple and the courage of a hero. At the head of an army, small indeed, but strong by faith in Christ,[2] he entered Northumberland, knelt with his troops in prayer on the field of battle, and gained a signal victory over a powerful enemy, 634 A. D.

To recover the kingdom of his ancestors was only a part of his task. Oswald desired to give his people the benefits of the true faith.[3] The Christianity taught in 625 to King Edwin and the Northumbrians by Pendin of York had disappeared amidst the ravages of the pagan armies. Oswald requested a missionary from the Scots who had given him an asylum, and they accordingly sent one of the brethren named Corman, a pious but uncultivated and austere man. He soon returned dispirited to Iona: "The people to whom you sent me," he told the elders of that island, "are so obstinate that we must renounce all idea of changing their manners." As Aidan, one of their number, listened to this report, he said to himself: "If thy love had been offered to this people, oh, my Saviour, many hearts would have been touched!......I will go and make Thee known—Thee who breaketh not the bruised reed!" Then, turning to the

missionary with a look of mild reproach, he added: "Brother, you have been too severe towards hearers so dull of heart. You should have given them spiritual milk to drink until they were able to receive more solid food." All eyes were fixed on the man who spoke so wisely. "Aidan is worthy of the episcopate," exclaimed the brethren of Iona; and, like Timothy, he was consecrated by the laying on of the hands of the company of elders.[1]

Oswald received Aidan as an angel from heaven, and as the missionary was ignorant of the Saxon language, the king accompanied him everywhere, standing by his side, and interpreting his gentle discourses.[2] The people crowded joyfully around Oswald, Aidan, and other missionaries from Scotland and Ireland, listening eagerly to the *Word of God*.[3] The king preached by his works still more than by his words. One day during Easter, as he was about to take his seat at table, he was informed that a crowd of his subjects, driven by hunger, had collected before his palace gates. Instantly he ordered the food prepared for himself to be carried out and distributed among them; and taking the silver vessels which stood before him, he broke them in pieces and commanded his servants to divide them among the poor. He also introduced the knowledge of the Saviour to the people of Wessex, whither he had gone to marry the king's daughter; and after a reign of nine years, he died at the head of his army while repelling an invasion of the idolatrous Mercians, headed by the cruel Penda (5th August 642 A.D.) As he fell he exclaimed: "Lord, have mercy on the souls of my people!" This youthful prince has left a name dear to the churches of Great Britain.

His death did not interrupt the labours of the missionaries. Their meekness and the recollection of Oswald endeared them to all. As soon as the villagers caught sight of one on the high-road, they would throng round him, begging him to teach them the *Word of life*.[4] The faith which the terrible Edelfrid thought he had washed away in the blood of the worshippers of God, was re-appearing in every direction; and Rome, which once already in the days of Honorius had been forced to leave Britain, might be perhaps a second time compelled to flee to its ships from before the face of a people who asserted their liberty.

---

[1] Cum magna nobilium juventute apud Scotos sive Pictos exulabant, ibique ad doctrinam Scottorum cathechisati et baptismatis gratia sunt recreati. Beda, lib. iii. cap. i.
[2] Superveniente cum parvo exercitu, sed fide Christi munito. Ibid.
[3] Desiderans totam cui præesse cœpit gentem fidei Christianæ gratia imbui. Ibid. cap. iii.

[1] Aydanus accepto gradu *episcopatus*, quo tempore eodem monasterio Segenius abbas et *presbyter* præfuit. Beda, lib. iii. cap. v. When Bede tells us that a plain priest was president, he excludes the idea that there were bishops in the assembly. See 1 Timothy, iv. 14.
[2] Evangelisante antistite, ipse Rex suis ducibus ac ministris interpres verbi existeret cœlestis. Beda, lib. iii. cap. iii.
[3] Confluebant *ad audiendum verbum Dei* populi gaudentes. Ibid.
[4] Mox congregati in unum vicani, *verbum vitæ* ab illo expetere curabant. Ibid. cap. xxvi.

CHAPTER III.

Character of Oswy—Death of Aidan—Wilfrid at Rome—At Oswald's Court—Finan and Colman—Independence of the Church attacked—Oswy's Conquests and Troubles—*Synodus Pharensis*—Cedda—Degeneration — The Disputation—Peter, the Gatekeeper—Triumph of Rome—Grief of the Britons—Popedom organized in England—Papal Exultation—Archbishop Theodore — Cedda re-ordained—Discord in the Church — Disgrace and Treachery of Wilfrid—His end—Scotland attacked—Adamnan—Iona resists—A King converted by Architects — The Monk Egbert at Iona—His History—Monkish Visions — Fall of Iona.

THEN uprose the papacy. If victory remained with the Britons, their church, becoming entirely free, might even in these early times head a strong opposition against the papal monarchy. If, on the contrary, the last champions of liberty are defeated, centuries of slavery awaited the Christian church. We shall have to witness the struggle that took place erelong in the very palace of the Northumbrian kings.

Oswald was succeeded by his brother Oswy, a prince instructed in the free doctrine of the Britons, but whose religion was all external. His heart overflowed with ambition, and he shrank from no crime that might increase his power. The throne of Deira was filled by his relative Oswin, an amiable king, much beloved by his people. Oswy, conceiving a deadly jealousy towards him, marched against him at the head of an army, and Oswin, desirous of avoiding bloodshed, took shelter with a chief whom he had loaded with favours. But the latter offered to lead Oswy's soldiers to his hiding-place; and at dead of night the fugitive king was basely assassinated, one only of his servants fighting in his defence. The gentle Aidan died of sorrow at his cruel fate.[1] Such was the first exploit of that monarch who surrendered England to the papacy. Various circumstances tended to draw Oswy nearer Rome. He looked upon the Christian religion as a means of combining the Christian princes against the heathen Penda, and such a religion, in which expediency predominated, was not very unlike popery. And further, Oswy's wife, the proud Eanfeld, was of the Romish communion. The private chaplain of this bigoted princess was a priest named Romanus, a man worthy of the name. He zealously maintained the rites of the Latin church, and accordingly the festival of Easter was celebrated at court twice in the year; for while the king, following the eastern rule, was joyfully commemorating the resurrection of our Lord, the queen, who adopted the Roman ritual, was keeping Palm Sunday with fasting and humiliation.[2] Eanfeld and Romanus would often converse together on the means of winning over Northumberland to the papacy. But the first step was to increase the number of its partisans, and the opportunity soon occurred.

A young Northumbrian, named Wilfrid, was one day admitted to an audience of the queen. He was a comely man, of extensive knowledge, keen wit, and enterprising character, of indefatigable activity, and insatiable ambition.[1] In this interview he remarked to Eanfeld: "The way which the Scotch teach us is not perfect; I will go to Rome and learn in the very temples of the apostles." She approved of his project, and with her assistance and directions he set out for Italy. Alas! he was destined at no very distant day to chain the whole British church to the Roman see. After a short stay at Lyons, where the bishop, delighted at his talents, would have desired to keep him, he arrived at Rome, and immediately became on the most friendly footing with archdeacon Boniface, the pope's favourite councillor. He soon discovered that the priests of France and Italy possessed more power both in ecclesiastical and secular matters than the humble missionaries of Iona; and his thirst for honours was inflamed at the court of the pontiffs. If he should succeed in making England submit to the papacy, there was no dignity to which he might not aspire. Henceforward this was his only thought, and he had hardly returned to Northumberland before Eanfeld eagerly summoned him to court. A fanatical queen, from whom he might hope everything—a king with no religious convictions, and enslaved by political interests—a pious and zealous prince, Alfred, the king's son, who was desirous of imitating his noble uncle Oswald, and converting the pagans, but who had neither the discernment nor the piety of the illustrious disciple of Iona: such were the materials Wilfrid had to work upon. He saw clearly that if Rome had gained her first victory by the sword of Edelfrid, she could only expect to gain a second by craft and management. He came to an understanding on the subject with the queen and Romanus, and having been placed about the person of the young prince, by adroit flattery he soon gained over Alfred's mind. Then finding himself secure of two members of the royal family, he turned all his attention to Oswy.

The elders of Iona could not shut their eyes to the dangers which threatened Northumberland. They had sent Finan to supply Aidan's place, and this bishop, consecrated by the presbyters of Iona, had witnessed the progress of popery at the court; at first humble and inoffensive, and then increasing year by year in ambition and audacity. He had openly opposed the pon-

---

[1] Aydanus duodecimo post occisionem regis quem amabat die, de seculo ablatus. Beda, lib. iii. cap. xiv.
[2] Cum rex pascha dominicum solutis jejuniis faceret, tunc regina cum suis persistens adhuc in jejunio diem Palmarum celebraret. Ibid. cap. xxv.

[1] Acris erat ingenii....gratia venusti vultus, alacritate actionis. Beda, lib. v. p. 135.

tiff's agents, and his frequent contests had confirmed him in the truth.[1] He was dead, and the presbyters of the Western Isles, seeing more clearly than ever the wants of Northumbria, had sent thither bishop Colman, a simple-minded but stout-hearted man, —one determined to oppose a front of adamant to the wiles of the seducers.

Yet Eanfeld, Wilfrid, and Romanus were skilfully digging the mine that was to destroy the apostolic church of Britain. At first Wilfrid prepared his attack by adroit insinuations ; and next declared himself openly in the king's presence. If Oswy withdrew into his domestic circle, he there found the bigoted Eanfeld, who zealously continued the work of the Roman missionary. No opportunities were neglected; in the midst of the diversions of the court, at table, and even during the chase, discussions were perpetually raised on the controverted doctrines. Men's minds became excited : the Romanists already assumed the air of conquerors ; and the Britons often withdrew full of anxiety and fear. The king, placed between his wife and his faith, and wearied by these disputes, inclined first to one side, and then to the other, as if he would soon fall altogether.

The papacy had more powerful motives than ever for coveting Northumberland. Oswy had not only usurped the throne of Deira, but after the death of the cruel Penda, who fell in battle in 654, he had conquered his states with the exception of a portion governed by his son-in-law Peada, the son of Penda. But Peada himself having fallen in a conspiracy said to have been got up by his wife, the daughter of Oswy, the latter completed the conquest of Mercia, and thus united the greatest part of England under his sceptre. Kent alone at that time acknowledged the jurisdiction of Rome : in every other province, free ministers, protected by the kings of Northumberland, preached the gospel. This wonderfully simplified the question. If Rome gained over Oswy, she would soon gain England : if she failed, she must sooner or later leave that island altogether.

This was not all. The blood of Oswyn, the premature death of Aidan, and other things besides, troubled the king's breast. He desired to appease the Deity he had offended, and not knowing that *Christ is the door*, as holy scripture tells us, he sought among men for a *doorkeeper* who would open to him the kingdom of heaven. He was far from being the last of those kings whom the necessity of expiating their crimes impelled towards Romish practices. The crafty Wilfrid, keeping alive both the hopes and fears of the prince, often spoke to him of Rome, and of the grace to be found

[1] Apertum veritatis adversarium reddidit, says the Romanist Bede, lib. v. p. 135.

there. He thought that the fruit was ripe, and that now he had only to shake the tree. "We must have a public disputation, in which the question may be settled once for all," said the queen and her advisers ; "but Rome must take her part in it with as much pomp as her adversaries. Let us oppose bishop to bishop." A Saxon bishop named Agilbert, a friend of Wilfrid's, who had won the affection of the young prince Alfred, was invited by Eanfeld to the conference, and he arrived in Northumberland attended by a priest named Agathon. Alas! poor British church, the earthen vessel is about to be dashed against the vase of iron. Britain must yield before the invading march of Rome.

On the coast of Yorkshire, at the farther extremity of a quiet bay, was situated the monastery of Strenæshalh, or Whitby, of which Hilda, the pious daughter of king Edwin, was abbess. She, too, was desirous of seeing a termination of the violent disputes which had agitated the church since Wilfrid's return. On the shores of the North Sea[1] the struggle was to be decided between Britain and Rome, between the East and the West, or, as they said then, between Saint John and Saint Peter. It was not a mere question about Easter, or certain rules of discipline, but of the great doctrine of the freedom of the church under Jesus Christ, or its enslavement under the papacy. Rome, ever domineering, desired for the second time to hold England in its grasp, not by means of the sword, but by her dogmas. With her usual cunning she concealed her enormous pretensions under secondary questions, and many superficial thinkers were deceived by this manœuvre.

The meeting took place in the convent of Whitby. The king and his son entered first ; then, on the one side, Colman, with the bishops and elders of the Britons ; and on the other bishop Agilbert, Agathon, Wilfrid, Romanus, a deacon named James, and several other priests of the Latin confession. Last of all came Hilda with her attendants, among whom was an English bishop named Cedda, one of the most active missionaries of the age.[2] He had at first preached the Gospel in the midland districts, whence he turned his footsteps towards the Anglo-Saxons of the East, and after converting a great number of these pagans, he had returned to Finan, and, although an Englishman, had received Episcopal consecration from a bishop, who had been himself ordained by the elders of Iona. Then proceeding westwards, the indefatigable evangelist founded churches, and appointed

[1] This conference is generally known as the *Synodus Pharensis* (from *Strenæshalh*, sinus Phari). "Hodie Whitbie dicitur (White bay), et est villa in Eboracensi littore satis nota." Wilkins, Concil. p. 37, note.
[2] Presbyteri Cedda et Adda et Berti et Duina. quorum ultimus natione Scotus, cæteri fuere Angli. Beda, lib. iii. cap. xxi.

elders and deacons wherever he went.[1] By birth an Englishman, by ordination a Scotchman, everywhere treated with respect and consideration, he appeared to be set apart as mediator in this solemn conference. His intervention could not, however, retard the victory of Rome. Alas! the primitive evangelism had gradually given way to an ecclesiasticism, coarse and rude in one place, subtle and insinuating in another. Whenever the priests were called upon to justify certain doctrines or ceremonies, instead of referring solely to the word of God, that fountain of all light, they maintained that thus St James did at Jerusalem, St Mark at Alexandria, St John at Ephesus, or St Peter at Rome. They gave the name of *apostolical canons* to rules which the apostles had never known. They even went further than this: at Rome and in the East, ecclesiasticism represented itself to be a law of God, and from a state of weakness, it thus became a state of sin. Some marks of this error were already beginning to appear in the Christianity of the Britons.

King Oswy was the first to speak: "As servants of one and the same God, we hope all to enjoy the same inheritance in heaven; why then should we not have the same rule of life here below? Let us inquire which is the true one, and follow it." ......"Those who sent me hither as bishop," said Colman, "and who gave me the rule which I observe, are the beloved of God. Let us beware how we despise their teaching, for it is the teaching of Columba, of the blessed evangelist John,[2] and of the churches over which that apostle presided."

"As for us," boldly rejoined Wilfrid, for to him as to the most skilful had bishop Agilbert intrusted the defence of their cause, "our custom is that of Rome, where the holy apostles Peter and Paul taught; we found it in Italy and Gaul, nay, it is spread over every nation. Shall the Picts and Britons, cast on these two islands, on the very confines of the ocean, dare to contend against the whole world?[3] However holy your Columba may have been, will you prefer him to the prince of the apostles, to whom Christ said, *Thou art Peter, and I will give unto thee the keys of the kingdom of heaven?*"

Wilfrid spoke with animation, and his words being skilfully adapted to his audience, began to make them waver. He had artfully substituted Columba for the apostle John, from whom the British church claimed descent, and opposed to Saint Peter a plain elder of Iona. Oswy, whose idol was power, could not hesitate between paltry

bishops, and that pope of Rome who commanded the whole world. Already imagining he saw Peter at the gates of paradise, with the keys in his hand, he exclaimed with emotion: "Is it true, Colman, that these words were addressed by our Lord to Saint Peter?"—"It is true." "Can you prove that similar powers were given to your Columba?"—The bishop replied, "We cannot;" but he might have told the king: "John, whose doctrine we follow, and indeed every disciple, has received in the same sense as St Peter the power to remit sins, to bind and to loose on earth and in heaven."[1] But the knowledge of the Holy Scriptures was fading away in Iona, and the unsuspecting Colman had not observed Wilfrid's stratagem in substituting Columba for Saint John. Upon this Oswy, delighted to yield to the continual solicitations of the queen, and above all, to find some one who would admit him into the kingdom of heaven, exclaimed: "Peter is the doorkeeper, I will obey him, lest when I appear at the gate there should be no one to open it to me."[2] The spectators, carried away by this royal confession, hastened to give in their submission to the vicar of St Peter.

Thus did Rome triumph at the Whitby conference. Oswy forgot that the Lord had said: *I am he that openeth, and no man shutteth; and shutteth, and no man openeth.*[3] It was by ascribing to Peter the servant, what belongs to Jesus Christ the master, that the papacy reduced Britain. Oswy stretched out his hands, Rome riveted the chains, and the liberty which Oswald had given his church seemed at the last gasp.

Colman saw with grief and consternation Oswy and his subjects bending their knees before the foreign priests. He did not, however, despair of the ultimate triumph of the truth. The apostolic faith could still find shelter in the old sanctuaries of the British church in Scotland and Ireland. Immovable in the doctrine he had received, and resolute to uphold Christian liberty, Colman withdrew with those who would not bend beneath the yoke of Rome, and returned to Scotland. Thirty Anglo-Saxons, and a great number of Britons, shook off the dust of their feet against the tents of the Romish priests. The hatred of popery became more intense day by day among the remainder of the Britons. Determined to repel its erroneous dogmas and its illegitimate dominion, they maintained their communion with the Eastern Church, which was more ancient than that of Rome. They shuddered as they saw the red dragon of the Celts gradually retiring towards the western sea from before the white dragon of the Saxons.

---

[1] Qui accepto gradu episcopatus et majore auctoritate cœptum opus explens, fecit per tuam ecclesias, presbyteros et diaconos ordinavit. Beda, lib. iii. cap. xxii.
[2] Ipsum est quod beatus evangelista Johannes, discipulus specialiter Domino dilectus. Ibid. cap. xxv.
[3] Pictos dico ac Brittones, cum quibus de duabus ultimis oceani insulis, contra totum orbem stulto labore pugnant. Ibid.

[1] John xx. 23; Matth. xviii. 18.
[2] Ne forte adveniente ad fores regni cœlorum, non sit qui reseret. Beda, lib. iii. cap. xxv.
[3] John x. 9; Rev. iii. 7.

They ascribed their misfortunes to a horrible conspiracy planned by the iniquitous ambition of the foreign monks, and the bards in their chants cursed the negligent ministers who defended not the flock of the Lord against the wolves of Rome.[1] But vain were their lamentations!

The Romish priests, aided by the queen, lost no time. Wilfrid, whom Oswy desired to reward for his triumph, was named bishop of Northumberland, and he immediately visited Paris to receive episcopal consecration in due form. He soon returned, and proceeded with singular activity to establish the Romish doctrine in all the churches.[2] Bishop of a diocese extending from Edinburgh to Northampton, enriched with the goods which had belonged to divers monasteries, surrounded by a numerous train, served upon gold and silver plate, Wilfrid congratulated himself on having espoused the cause of the papacy; he offended every one who approached him by his insolence, and taught England how wide was the difference between the humble ministers of Iona and a Romish priest. At the same time Oswy, coming to an understanding with the king of Kent, sent another priest named Wighard to Rome to learn the pope's intentions respecting the church in England, and to receive consecration as archbishop of Canterbury. There was no episcopal ordination in England worthy of a priest! In the meanwhile Oswy, with all the zeal of a new convert, ceased not to repeat that "the Roman Church was the catholic and apostolic church," and thought night and day on the means of converting his subjects, hoping thus (says a pope) to redeem his own soul![3]

The arrival of this news at Rome created a great sensation. Vitalian, who then filled the episcopal chair, and was as insolent to his bishops as he was fawning and servile to the emperor, exclaimed with transport: "Who would not be overjoyed![4] a king converted to the true apostolic faith, a people that believes at last in Christ the Almighty God!" For many long years this people had believed in Christ, but they were now beginning to believe in the pope, and the pope will soon make them forget Jesus the Saviour. Vitalian wrote to Oswy, and sent him—not copies of the Holy Scriptures (which were already becoming scarce at Rome), but—relics of the Saints, Peter, John, Lawrence, Gregory, and Pancratius; and being in an especial manner desirous of rewarding Queen Eanfeld, to whom with Wilfrid belonged the glory of this work, he offered her a cross, made, as he assured her,

out of the chains of St Peter and St Paul.[1] "Delay not," said the pope in conclusion, "to reduce all your island under Jesus Christ"—or, in other words, under the bishop of Rome.

The essential thing, however, was to send an archbishop from Rome to Britain; but Wighard was dead, and no one seemed willing to undertake so long a journey.[2]

There was not much zeal in the city of the pontiffs; and the pope was compelled to look out for a stranger. There happened at that time to be in Rome a man of great reputation for learning, who had come from the east, and adopted the rites and doctrines of the Latins in exchange for the knowledge he had brought them. He was pointed out to Vitalian as well qualified to be the metropolitan of England. Theodore, for such was his name, belonged by birth to the churches of Asia Minor, would be listened to by the Britons in preference to any other, when he solicited them to abandon their oriental customs. The Roman pontiff, however, fearful perhaps that he might yet entertain some leaven of his former Greek doctrines, gave him as companion, or rather as overseer, a zealous African monk named Adrian.[3]

Theodore began the great crusade against British Christianity, and endeavouring to show the sincerity of his conversion by his zeal, he traversed all England in company with Adrian,[4] everywhere imposing on the people that ecclesiastical supremacy to which Rome is indebted for her political supremacy. The superiority of character which distinguished Saint Peter, Theodore transformed into a superiority of office. For the jurisdiction of Christ and his word, he substituted that of the bishop of Rome and of his decrees. He insisted on the necessity of ordination by bishops who, in an unbroken chain, could trace back their authority to the apostles themselves. The British still maintained the validity of their consecration; but the number was small of those who understood that pretended successors of the apostles, who sometimes carry Satan in their hearts, are not true ministers of Christ; that the one thing needful for the church is, that the apostles themselves (and not their successors only) should dwell in its bosom by their word, by their teaching, and by the Divine Comforter who shall be with it for ever and ever.

The grand defection now began: the best were sometimes the first to yield. When Theodore met Cedda, who had been conse-

1 Horæ Britannicæ, b. ii. p. 277.
2 Ipse perplura catholicæ observationis moderamina ecclesiis Anglorum sua doctrina contulit. Beda, lib. iii. cap. xxviii.
3 Omnes subjectos suos meditatur die ac nocte ad fidem catholicam atque apostolicam pro suæ animæ redemptione converti. Ibid. xxix.
4 Quis enim audiens hæc suavia non lætetur? Ibid.

1 Conjugi, nostræ spirituali filiæ, crucem.... Beda, lib. iii. cap. xxix.
2 Minime volumus nunc reperire pro longinquitate itineris. Ibid.
3 Ut diligenter attenderet, ne quid ille contrarium veritati fidei Græcorum more, in ecclesiam cui præesset introduceret. Ibid. lib. iv. cap. i.
4 Peragrata insula tota, rectum vivendi ordinem disseminabat. Ibid. cap. ii.

crated by a bishop who had himself received ordination from the elders of Iona, he said to him : " You have not been regularly ordained." Cedda, instead of standing up boldly for the truth, gave way to a carnal modesty, and replied : " I never thought myself worthy of the episcopate, and am ready to lay it down."—" No," said Theodore, "you shall remain a bishop, but I will consecrate you anew according to the catholic ritual."[1] The British minister submitted. Rome triumphant felt herself strong enough to deny the imposition of hands of the elders of Iona, which she had hitherto recognised. The most stedfast believers took refuge in Scotland.

In this manner a church in some respects deficient, but still a church in which the religious element held the foremost place, was succeeded by another in which the clerical element predominated. This was soon apparent : questions of authority and precedence, hitherto unknown among the British Christians, were now of daily occurrence. Wilfrid, who had fixed his residence at York, thought that no one deserved better than he to be primate of all England ; and Theodore on his part was irritated at the haughty tone assumed by this bishop. During the life of Oswy, peace was maintained, for Wilfrid was his favourite ; but erelong that prince fell ill ; and, terrified by the near approach of death, he vowed that if he recovered he would make a pilgrimage to Rome and there end his days.[2] " If you will be my guide to the city of the apostles," he said to Wilfrid, " I will give you a large sum of money." But his vow was of no avail : Oswy died in the spring of the year 670 A.D.

The *Witan* set aside Prince Alfred, and raised his youngest brother Egfrid to the throne. The new monarch, who had often been offended by Wilfrid's insolence, denounced this haughty prelate to the archbishop. Nothing could be more agreeable to Theodore. He assembled a council at Hertford, before which the chief of his converts were first summoned, and presenting to them, not the holy scripture but the *canons of the Romish church*,[3] he received their solemn oaths : such was the religion then taught in England. But this was not all. " The diocese of our brother Wilfrid is so extensive," said the primate, "that there is room in it for four bishops." They were appointed accordingly. Wilfrid indignantly appealed from the primate and the king to the pope. " Who converted England, who, if not I?......and it is thus I am rewarded ?"......Not allowing himself to be checked

by the difficulties of the journey, he set out for Rome, attended by a few monks, and Pope Agathon assembling a council (679), the Englishman presented his complaint, and the pontiff declared the destitution to be illegal. Wilfrid immediately returned to England, and haughtily presented the pope's decree to the king. But Egfrid, who was not of a disposition to tolerate these transalpine manners, far from restoring the see, cast the prelate into prison, and did not release him until the end of the year, and then only on condition that he would immediately quit Northumbria.

Wilfrid—for we must follow even to the end of his life that remarkable man, who exercised so great an influence over the destinies of the English church—Wilfrid was determined to be a bishop at any cost. The kingdom of Sussex was still pagan ; and the deposed prelate, whose indefatigable activity we cannot but acknowledge, formed the resolution of winning a bishopric, as other men plan the conquest of a kingdom. He arrived in Sussex during a period of famine, and having brought with him a number of nets, he taught the people the art of fishing, and thus gained their affections. Their king Edilwalch had been baptized, his subjects now followed his example, and Wilfrid was placed at the head of the church. But he soon manifested the disposition by which he was animated : he furnished supplies of men and money to Ceadwalla, king of Wessex, and this cruel chieftain made a fierce inroad into Sussex, laying it waste, and putting to death Edilwalch, the prelate's benefactor. The career of the turbulent bishop was not ended. King Egfrid died, and was succeeded by his brother Alfred, whom Wilfrid had brought up, a prince fond of learning and religion, and emulous of the glory of his uncle Oswald. The ambitious Wilfrid hastened to claim his see of York, by acquiescing in the partition ; it was restored to him, and he forthwith began to plunder others to enrich himself. A council begged him to submit to the decrees of the church of England : he refused, and having lost the esteem of the king, his former pupil, he undertook, notwithstanding his advanced years, a third journey to Rome. Knowing how popes are won, he threw himself at the pontiff's feet, exclaiming that " the suppliant bishop Wilfrid, the humble slave of the servant of God, implored the favour of our most blessed lord, the pope universal." The bishop could not restore his creature to his see, and the short remainder of Wilfrid's life was spent in the midst of the riches his cupidity had so unworthily accumulated.

Yet he had accomplished the task of his life : all England was subservient to the papacy. The names of *Oswy* and of *Wilfrid* should be inscribed in letters of mourning in the annals of Great Britain. Posterity

---

[1] Cum Ceadda Episcopum argueret non fuisse rite consecratum, ipse (Theodorus) ordinationem ejus denuo catholica ratione consummavit. Beda, lib. iv. cap. ii.
[2] Ut si ab infirmitate salvaretur, etiam Romam venire, ibique ad loca sancta vitam finire. Ibid.
[3] Quibus statim protuli eundem *librum canonum*. Ibid. cap. v.

has erred in permitting them to sink into oblivion; for they were two of the most influential and energetic men that ever flourished in England. Still this very forgetfulness is not wanting in generosity. The grave in which the liberty of the church lay buried for nine centuries is the only monument—a mournful one indeed—that should perpetuate their memory.

But Scotland was still free, and to secure the definitive triumph of Rome, it was necessary to invade that virgin soil, over which the standard of the faith had floated for so many years.

Adamnan was then at the head of the church of Iona, the first elder of that religious house. He was virtuous and learned, but weak and somewhat vain, and his religion had little spirituality. To gain him was in the eyes of Rome to gain Scotland. A singular circumstance favoured the plans of those who desired to draw him into the papal communion. One day during a violent tempest, a ship coming from the Holy Land, and on board of which was a Gaulish bishop named Arculf, was wrecked in the neighbourhood of Iona.[1] Arculf eagerly sought an asylum among the pious inhabitants of that island. Adamnan never grew tired of hearing the stranger's descriptions of Bethlehem, Jerusalem, and Golgotha, of the sun-burnt plains over which our Lord had wandered, and the cleft stone which still lay before the door of the sepulchre.[2] The elder of Iona, who prided himself on his learning, noted down Arculf's conversation, and from it composed a description of the Holy Land. As soon as his book was completed, the desire of making these wondrous things more widely known, combined with a little vanity, and perhaps other motives, urged him to visit the court of Northumberland, where he presented his work to the pious King Alfred,[3] who, being fond of learning and of the Christian traditions, caused a number of copies of it to be made.

Nor was this all: the Romish clergy perceived the advantage they might derive from this imprudent journey. They crowded round the elder; they showed him all the pomp of their worship, and said to him: "Will you and your friends, who live at the very extremity of the world, set yourselves in opposition to the observances of the universal church?"[4] The nobles of the court flattered the author's self-love, and invited him to their festivities, while the king loaded him with presents. The free presbyter of Britain became a priest of Rome,

and Adamnan returned to Iona to betray his church to his new masters. But it was all to no purpose: Iona would not give way.[1] He then went to hide his shame in Ireland, where having brought a few individuals to the Romish uniformity, he took courage and revisited Scotland. But that country, still inflexible, repelled him with indignation.[2]

When Rome found herself unable to conquer by the priest, she had recourse to the prince, and her eyes were turned to Naitam, king of the Picts. "How much more glorious it would be for you" urged the Latin priests, "to belong to the powerful church of the universal pontiff of Rome, than to a congregation superintended by miserable elders! The Romish church is a monarchy, and ought to be the church of every monarch. The Roman ceremonial accords with the pomp of royalty, and its temples are palaces." The prince was convinced by the last argument. He despatched messengers to Ceolfrid, the abbot of an English convent, begging him to send him *architects* capable of building a church *after the Roman pattern*[3]—of stone and not of wood. Architects, majestic porches, lofty columns, vaulted roofs, gilded altars, have often proved the most influential of Rome's missionaries. The builder's art, though in its earliest and simplest days, was more powerful than the Bible. Naitam, who, by submitting to the pope, thought himself the equal of Clovis and Clotaire, assembled the nobles of his court and the pastors of his church, and thus addressed them: "I recommend all the clergy of my kingdom to receive the tonsure of Saint Peter."[4] Then without delay (as Bede informs us) this important revolution was accomplished by royal authority.[5] He sent agents and letters into every province, and caused all the ministers and monks to receive the circular tonsure according to the Roman fashion.[6] It was the mark that popery stamped, not on the forehead, but on the crown. A royal proclamation and a few clips of the scissors placed the Scotch, like a flock of sheep, beneath the crook of the shepherd of the Tiber.

Iona still held out. The orders of the Pictish king, the example of his subjects, the sight of that Italian power which was devouring the earth, had shaken some few minds; but the Church still resisted the innovation. Iona was the last citadel of liberty in the western world, and popery was filled with anger at that miserable

---

[1] Vi tempestatis in occidentalia Britanniæ littora delatus est. Beda, lib. v. cap. xvi.
[2] Lapis qui ad ostium monumenti positus erat, fissus est. Ibid. cap. xvii.
[3] Porrexit autem librum tunc Adamnanus Alfrido regi. Ibid. cap. xvi.
[4] Ne contra universalem ecclesiæ morem, cum suis paucissimis et in extremo mundi angulo positis, vivere præsumeret. Ibid.

[1] Curavit suos ad eum veritatis calcem producere, nec voluit. Beda, lib. v. cap. xvi.
[2] Nec tamen perficere quod conabatur posset. Ibid. The conversions of which abbot Ceolfrid speaks in chap. xxii. are probably those effected in Ireland, the word Scotia being at this period frequently applied to that country.
[3] Architectos sibi mitti petiit qui juxta morem Romanorum ecclesiam facerent. Ibid. lib. v. cap. xxii.
[4] Et hanc accipere tonsuram, omnes qui in meo regno sunt clericos decerno. Ibid.
[5] Nec mora, quæ dixerat regia auctoritate perfecti. Ibid.
[6] Per universas Pictorum provincias....tondebantur omnes in coronam ministri altaris ac monachi. Ibid.

band which in its remote corner refused to bend before it. Human means appeared insufficient to conquer this rock: something more was needed, visions and miracles for example; and these Rome always finds when she wants them. One day towards the end of the seventh century, an English monk, named Egbert, arriving from Ireland, appeared before the elders of Iona, who received him with their accustomed hospitality. He was a man in whom enthusiastic devotion was combined with great gentleness of heart, and he soon won upon the minds of these simple believers. He spoke to them of an external unity, urging that a universality manifested under different forms was unsuited to the church of Christ. He advocated the special form of Rome, and for the truly catholic element which the Christians of Iona had thus far possessed, substituted a sectarian element. He attacked the traditions of the British church,[1] and lavishly distributing the rich presents confided to him by the lords of Ireland and of England,[2] he soon had reason to acknowledge the truth of the saying of the wise man: *A gift is as a precious stone in the eyes of him that hath it: whithersoever it turneth it prospereth.*

Some pious souls, however, still held out in Iona. The enthusiast Egbert—for such he appears to have been rather than an impostor—had recourse to other means. He represented himself to be a messenger from heaven: the saints themselves, said he, have commissioned me to convert Iona; and then he told the following history to the elders who stood round him. "About thirty years ago I entered the monastery of Rathmelfig in Ireland, when a terrible pestilence fell upon it, and of all the brethren the monk Edelhun and myself were left alone. Attacked by the plague, and fearing my last hour was come, I rose from my bed and crept into the chapel.[3] There my whole body trembled at the recollection of my sins, and my face was bathed with tears. 'O God,' I exclaimed, 'suffer me not to die until I have redeemed my debt to thee by an abundance of good works.'[4] I returned staggering to the infirmary, got into bed, and fell asleep. When I awoke, I saw Edelhun with his eyes fixed on mine. 'Brother Egbert,' said he, 'it has been revealed to me in a vision that thou shalt receive what thou hast asked.' On the following night Edelhun died and I recovered. "Many years passed away: my repentance and my vigils did not satisfy me, and

wishing to pay my debt, I resolved to go with a company of monks and preach the blessings of the gospel to the heathens of Germany. But during the night a blessed saint from heaven appeared to one of the brethren and said: 'Tell Egbert that he must go to the monasteries of Columba, for their ploughs do not plough straight, and he must put them into the right furrow.'[1] I forbade this brother to speak of his vision, and went on board a ship bound for Germany. We were waiting for a favourable wind, when, of a sudden, in the middle of the night, a frightful tempest burst upon the vessel, and drove us on the shoals. 'For my sake this tempest is upon us,' I exclaimed in terror; 'God speaks to me as He did to Jonah;' and I ran to take refuge in my cell. At last I determined to obey the command which the holy man had brought me. I left Ireland, and came among you, in order to pay my debt by converting you. And now," continued Egbert, "make answer to the voice of heaven, and submit to Rome."

A ship thrown on shore by a storm was a frequent occurrence on those coasts, and the dream of a monk, absorbed in the plans of his brother, was nothing very unnatural. But in those times of darkness, everything appeared miraculous; phantoms and apparitions had more weight than the word of God. Instead of detecting the emptiness of these visions by the falseness of the religion they were brought to support, the elders of Iona listened seriously to Egbert's narrative. The primitive faith planted on the rock of Icolmkill was now like a pine-tree tossed by the winds: but one gust, and it would be uprooted and blown into the sea. Egbert, perceiving the elders to be shaken, redoubled his prayers, and even had recourse to threats. "All the west," said he, "bends the knee to Rome: alone against all, what can you do?" The Scotch still resisted: obscure and unknown, the last British Christians contended in behalf of expiring liberty. At length bewildered — they stumbled and fell. The scissors were brought; they received the Latin tonsure[2]—they were the pope's.

Thus fell Scotland. Yet there still remained some sparks of grace, and the mountains of Caledonia long concealed the hidden fire which after many ages burst forth with such power and might. Here and there a few independent spirits were to be found who testified against the tyranny of Rome. In the time of Bede they might be seen "halting in their paths," (to use the words of the Romish historian,) refusing to join in the holidays of the pontifical adherents, and pushing away the hands that

---

[1] Sedulis exhortationibus inveteratam illam traditionem parentum eorum. Beda, lib. v. cap. xxiii.
[2] Pietate largiendi de his quæ a divitibus acceperat, multum profuit. Ibid. cap. xxvii.
[3] Cum se existimaret esse moriturum, egressus est tempore matutino de cubiculo, et residens solus.... Ibid. lib. iii. cap. xxvii.
[4] Precabatur ne adhuc mori deberet priusquam vel præteritas negligentias perfectim ex tempore castigaret, vel in bonis se operibus abundantius exerceret. Ibid.

[1] Quia aratra eorum non recte incedunt; oportet autem eum ad rectum hæc tramitem revocare. Beda, lib. iii. cap. xxvii.
[2] Ad ritum tonsuræ canonicum sub figura coronæ perpetuæ. Ibid. lib. v. cap. xxiii.

were eager to shave their crowns.[1] But the leaders of the state and of the church had laid down their arms. The contest was over, after lasting more than a century. British Christianity had in some degree prepared its own fall, by substituting too often the form for the faith. The foreign superstition took advantage of this weakness, and triumphed in these islands by means of royal decrees, church ornaments, monkish phantoms, and conventual apparitions. At the beginning of the eighth century the British Church became the serf of Rome; but an internal struggle was commencing, which did not cease until the period of the Reformation.

CHAPTER IV.

Clement—Struggle between a Scotchman and an Englishman—Word of God only—Clement's Success—His Condemnation—Virgil and the Antipodes—John Scotus and Philosophical Religion—Alfred and the Bible—Darkness and Popery—William the Conqueror—Wulston at Edward's Tomb—Struggle between William and Hildebrand—The Pope yields—Cæsaropapia.

The independent Christians of Scotland, who subordinated the authority of man to that of God, were filled with sorrow as they beheld these backslidings: and it was this no doubt which induced many to leave their homes and fight in the very heart of Europe in behalf of that Christian liberty which had just expired among themselves.

At the commencement of the eighth century a great idea took possession of a pious doctor of the Scottish church named Clement.[2] The *work of God* is the very essence of Christianity, thought he, and this work must be defended against all the encroachments of man. To human traditionalism he opposed the sole authority of the word of God; to clerical materialism, a church which is the assembly of the saints; and to Pelagianism, the sovereignty of grace. He was a man of decided character and firm faith, but without fanaticism; his heart was open to the holiest emotions of our nature; he was a husband and a father. He quitted Scotland and travelled among the Franks, everywhere scattering the seeds of the faith. It happened unfortunately that a man of kindred energy, Winifrid or Boniface of Wessex, was planting the pontifical Christianity in the same regions. This great missionary, who possessed in an essential degree the faculty of organization, aimed at external unity above all things, and when he had taken the oath of fidelity to Gregory II., he had received

from that pope a collection of the Roman laws. Boniface, henceforth a docile disciple or rather a fanatical champion of Rome, supported on the one hand by the pontiff, and on the other by Charles Martel, had preached to the people of Germany, among some undoubted Christian truths,— the doctrine of tithes and of papal supremacy. The Englishman and the Scotchman, representatives of two great systems, were about to engage in deadly combat in the heart of Europe — in a combat whose consequences might be incalculable.

Alarmed at the progress made by Clement's evangelical doctrines, Boniface, archbishop of the German churches, undertook to oppose them. At first he confronted the Scotchman with the laws of the Roman church; but the latter denied the authority of these ecclesiastical canons, and refuted their contents.[1] Boniface then put forward the decisions of various councils; but Clement replied that if the decisions of the councils are contrary to holy Scripture, they have no authority over Christians.[2] The archbishop, astonished at such audacity, next had recourse to the writings of the most illustrious fathers of the Latin church, quoting Jerome, Augustine, and Gregory; but the Scotchman told him, that instead of submitting to the word of men, he would obey the word of God alone.[3] Boniface with indignation now introduced the Catholic church which, by its priests and bishops, all united to the pope, forms an invincible unity; but to his great surprise his opponent maintained that there only, where the Holy Spirit dwells, can be found the spouse of Jesus Christ.[4] Vainly did the archbishop express his horror; Clement was not to be turned aside from his great idea, either by the clamours of the followers of Rome, or by the imprudent attacks made on the papacy by other Christian ministers.

Rome had, indeed, other adversaries. A Gallic bishop named Adalbert, with whom Boniface affected to associate Clement, one day saw the archbishop complacently exhibiting to the people some relics of St Peter which he had brought from Rome; and being desirous of showing the ridiculous character of these Romish practices, he distributed among the bystanders his own hair and nails, praying them to pay these the same honours as Boniface claimed for the relics of the papacy. Clement smiled, like many others, at Adalbert's singular argument; but it was not with such arms that he was wont to fight. Gifted with profound discernment, he had remarked that the authority of man substituted

---

[1] Sicut e contra Brittones, inveterati et claudicantes a semitis suis, et capita ferre sine corona prætendunt. Beda, lib. v. cap. xxiii.
[2] Alter qui dicitur Clemens, genere *Scotus* est. Bonifacii epistola ad Papam, Labbei concilia ad ann. 745.

[1] Canones ecclesiarum Christi abnegat et refutat. Bonifacii epistola ad Papam, Labbei concilia ad ann. 745.
[2] Synodalia jura spernens. Ibid.
[3] Tractatus et sermones sanctorum patrum, Hieronymi, Augustini, Gregorii recusat. Ibid.
[4] Clemens contra catholicam contendit ecclesiam. Ibid.

for the authority of God was the source of all the errors of Romanism. At the same time he maintained on predestination what the archbishop called "horrible doctrines, contrary to the Catholic faith."[1] Clement's character inclines us to believe that he was favourable to the doctrine of predestination. A century later the pious Gottschalk was persecuted by one of Boniface's successors for holding this very doctrine of Augustine's. Thus then did a Scotchman, the representative of the ancient faith of his country, withstand almost unaided in the centre of Europe the invasion of the Romans. But he was not long alone : the great especially, more enlightened than the common people, thronged around him. If Clement had succeeded, a Christian church would have been founded on the continent independent of the papacy.

Boniface was confounded. He wished to do in central Europe what his fellow-countryman Wilfrid had done in England; and at the very moment he fancied he was advancing from triumph to triumph, victory escaped from his hands. He turned against this new enemy, and applying to Charles Martel's sons, Pepin and Carloman, he obtained their consent to the assembling of a council before which he summoned Clement to appear.

The bishops, counts, and other notabilities having met at Soissons on the 2d March 744, Boniface accused the Scotchman of despising the laws of Rome, the councils, and the fathers ; attacked his marriage, which he called an adulterous union, and called in question some secondary points of doctrine. Clement was accordingly excommunicated by Boniface, at once his adversary, accuser, and judge, and thrown into prison, with the approbation of the pope and the king of the Franks.[2]

The Scotchman's cause was everywhere taken up ; accusations were brought against the German primate, his persecuting spirit was severely condemned, and his exertions for the triumph of the papacy were resisted.[3] Carloman yielded to this unanimous movement. The prison doors were opened, and Clement had hardly crossed the threshold before he began to protest boldly against human authority in matters of faith : the word of God is the only rule. Upon this Boniface applied to Rome for the heretic's condemnation, and accompanied his request by a silver cup and a garment of delicate texture.[4] The pope decided in synod that if Clement did not retract his errors, he

should be delivered up to everlasting damnation, and then requested Boniface to send him to Rome under a sure guard. We here lose all traces of the Scotchman, but it is easy to conjecture what must have been his fate.

Clement was not the only Briton who became distinguished in this contest. Two fellow-countrymen, Sampson and Virgil, who preached in central Europe, were in like manner persecuted by the Church of Rome. Virgil, anticipating Galileo, dared maintain that there were other men and another world beneath our feet.[1] He was denounced by Boniface for this *heresy*, and condemned by the pope, as were other Britons, for the apostolical simplicity of their lives. In 813, certain Scotchmen who called themselves bishops, says a canon, having appeared before a council of the Roman church at Châlons, were rejected by the French prelates, because, like St Paul, *they worked with their own hands.* Those enlightened and faithful men were superior to their time : Boniface and his ecclesiastical materialism were better fitted for an age in which clerical forms were regarded as the substance of religion.

Even Great Britain, although its light was not so pure, was not altogether plunged in darkness. The Anglo-Saxons imprinted on their church certain characteristics which distinguished it from that of Rome ; several books of the Bible were translated into their tongue, and daring spirits on the one hand, with some pious souls on the other, laboured in a direction hostile to popery.

At first we see the dawning of that philosophic rationalism, which gives out a certain degree of brightness, but which can neither conquer error nor still less establish truth. In the ninth century there was a learned scholar in Ireland, who afterwards settled at the court of Charles the Bald. He was a strange mysterious man, of profound thought, and as much raised above the doctors of his age by the boldness of his ideas, as Charlemagne above the princes of his day by the force of his will. John Scot Erigena—that is, a native of Ireland and not of Ayr, as some have supposed—was a meteor in the theological heavens. With a great philosophic genius he combined a cheerful jesting disposition. One day, while seated at table opposite to Charles the Bald, the latter archly inquired of him : " What is the distance between a *Scot* and a *sot* ?" " The width of the table," was his ready answer, which drew a smile from the king. While the doctrine of Bede, Boniface, and even Alcuin was traditional, servile, and, in one word, Romanist, that of Scot was mystical, philosophic, free, and daring. He sought for the truth not in the word or in

---

[1] Multa alia horribilia de prædestinatione Dei contraria fidei catholicæ affirmat. Bonifacii epistola ad Papam. Labbei concilia ad ann. 745.
[2] Sacerdotio privans, reduci facit in custodiam. Concilium Romanum. Ibid.
[3] Propter istas enim, persecutiones et inimicitias et maledictiones multorum populorum patior. Ibid.
[4] Poculum argenteum et sindonem unam. Gemuli Ep. Ibid.

[1] Perversa doctrina....quod alius mundus et alii homines sub terra sint. Zachariæ papæ Ep. ad Bonif. Labbei concilia, vi. p. 152.

the Church, but in himself:—" The knowledge of ourselves is the true source of religious wisdom. Every creature is a theophany—a manifestation of God ; since revelation presupposes the existence of truth, it is this truth, which is above revelation, with which man must set himself in immediate relation, leaving him at liberty to show afterwards its harmony with scripture, and the other theophanies. We must first employ reason, and then authority. Authority proceeds from reason, and not reason from anthority."[1] Yet this bold thinker, when on his knees, could give way to aspirations full of piety: " O Lord Jesus," exclaimed he, " I ask no other happiness of Thee, but to understand, unmixed with deceitful theories, the word that Thou hast inspired by thy Holy Spirit! Show thyself to those who ask for Thee alone!" But while Scot rejected on the one hand certain traditional errors, and in particular the doctrine of transubstantiation which was creeping into the church, he was near falling as regards God and the world into other errors savouring of pantheism.[2] The philosophic rationalism of the contemporary of Charles the Bald—the strange product of one of the obscurest periods of history (850) —was destined after the lapse of many centuries to be taught once more in Great Britain as a modern invention of the most enlightened age.

While Scot was thus plumbing the depths of philosophy, others were examining their Bibles ; and if thick darkness had not spread over these first glimpses of the dawn, perhaps the Church of Great Britain might even then have begun to labour for the regeneration of Christendom. A youthful prince, thirsting for intellectual enjoyments, for domestic happiness, and for the word of God, and who sought, by frequent prayer, for deliverance from the bondage of sin, had ascended the throne of Wessex, in the year 871. Alfred being convinced that Christianity alone could rightly mould a nation, assembled round him the most learned men from all parts of Europe, and was anxious that the English, like the Hebrews, Greeks, and Latins, should possess the holy scripture in their own language. He is the real patron of the biblical work,—a title far more glorious than that of founder of the university of Oxford. After having fought more than fifty battles by land and sea, he died while translating the Psalms of David for his subjects.[3]

After this gleam of light thick darkness once more settled upon Great Britain. Nine Anglo-Saxon kings ended their days in monasteries ; there was a seminary in Rome from which every year fresh scholars bore to England the new forms of popery ; the celibacy of priests, that cement of the Romish hierarchy, was established by a bull about the close of the tenth century ; convents were multiplied, considerable possessions were bestowed on the Church, and the tax of *Peter's pence*, laid at the pontiff's feet, proclaimed the triumph of the papal system. But a reaction soon took place : England collected her forces for a war against the papacy—a war at one time secular and at another spiritual. William of Normandy, Edward III., Wickliffe, and the Reformation, are the four ascending steps of protestantism in England.

A proud, enterprising, and far-sighted prince, the illegitimate son of a peasant girl of Falaise and Robert the Devil, duke of Normandy, began a contest with the papacy which lasted until the Reformation. William the Conqueror, having defeated the Saxons at Hastings in 1066 A. D., took possession of England, under the benediction of the Roman pontiff. But the conquered country was destined to conquer its master. William, who had invaded England in the pope's name, had no sooner touched the soil of his new kingdom, than he learned to resist Rome, as if the ancient liberty of the British Church had revived in him. Being firmly resolved to allow no foreign prince or prelate to possess in his dominions a jurisdiction independent of his own, he made preparations for a conquest far more difficult than that of the Anglo-Saxon kingdom. The papacy itself furnished him with weapons. The Roman legates prevailed on the king to dispossess the English episcopacy in a mass, and this was exactly what he wished. To resist the papacy, William desired to be sure of the submission of the priests of England. Stigand, archbishop of Canterbury, was removed, and Lanfranc of Pavia, who had been summoned from Bec in Normandy to fill his place, was commissioned by the Conqueror to bend the clergy to obedience. This prelate, who was regular in his life, abundant in almsgiving, a learned disputant, a prudent politician, and a skilful mediator, finding that he had to choose between his master King William and his friend the pontiff Hildebrand, gave the prince the preference. He refused to go to Rome, notwithstanding the threats of the pope, and applied himself resolutely to the work the king had intrusted to him. The Saxons sometimes resisted the Normans, as the Britons had resisted the Saxons : but the second struggle was less glorious than the first A synod at which the king was present having met in the abbey of Westminster, William commanded Wulston, bishop of Worcester, to give up his crosier to him. The old man rose, animated with holy fervour : " O king," he said, " from a better man than you I re-

[1] Prius ratione utendum ac deinde auctoritate. Auctoritas ex vera ratione processit, ratio vero nequaquam ex auctoritate. De div. prædestin.
[2] Deum in omnibus esse. De divisione naturæ, b. 74.
[3] A portion of the law of God translated by Alfred may be found in Wilkins, Concilia, i. p. 186 et seq.

ceived it, and to him only will I return it." [1] Unhapily this "better man" was not Jesus Christ. Then approaching the tomb of Edward the Confessor, he continued : "O my master, it was you who compelled me to assume this office; but now behold a new king and a new primate who promulgate new laws. Not unto them, O master, but unto you, do I resign my crosier and the care of my flock." With these words Wulston laid his pastoral staff on Edward's tomb. On the sepulchre of the confessor perished the liberty of the Anglo-Saxon hierarchy. The deprived Saxon bishops were consigned to fortresses or shut up in convents.

The Conqueror being thus assured of the obedience of the bishops, put forward the supremacy of the sword in opposition to that of the pope. He nominated directly to all vacant ecclesiastical offices, filled his treasury with the riches of the churches, required that all priests should make oath to him, forbade them to excommunicate his officers without his consent, not even for incest, and declared that all synodal decisions must be countersigned by him. "I claim," said he to the archbishop one day, raising his arms towards heaven, "I claim to hold in this hand all the pastoral staffs in my kingdom." [2] Lanfranc was astonished at this daring speech, but prudently kept silent,[3] for a time at least. Episcopacy connived at the royal pretensions.

Will Hildebrand, the most inflexible of popes, bend before William ? The king was earnest in his desire to enslave the Church to the state; the pope to enslave the State to the Church : the collision of these two mighty champions threatened to be terrible. But the haughtiest of pontiffs was seen to yield as soon as he felt the mail-clad hand of the Conqueror, and to shrink unresistingly before it. The pope filled all Christendom with confusion, that he might deprive princes of the right of investiture to ecclesiastical dignities : William would not permit him to interfere with that question in England, and Hildebrand submitted. The king went even farther : the pope, wishing to enslave the clergy, deprived the priests of their lawful wives; William got a decree passed by the council of Winchester in 1076 to the effect that the married priests living in castles and towns should not be compelled to put away their wives.[4] This was too much : Hildebrand summoned Lanfranc to Rome, but William forbade him to go. "Never did king, not even a pagan," ex-

claimed Gregory, "attempt against the holy see what this man does not fear to carry out!" [1]......To console himself, he demanded payment of the *Peter's pence*, and an oath of fidelity. William sent the money, but refused the homage; and when Hildebrand saw the tribute which the king had paid, he said bitterly : "What value can I set on money which is contributed with so little honour!" [2] William forbade his clergy to recognise the pope, or to publish a bull without the royal approbation, which did not prevent Hildebrand from styling him the "pearl of princes." [3] "It is true," said he to his legate, "that the English king does not behave in certain matters so religiously as we could desire......Yet beware of exasperating him......We shall win him over to God and St Peter more surely by mildness and reason than by strictness or severity." [4] In this manner the pope acted like the archbishop—*siluit :* he was silent. It is for feeble governments that Rome reserves her energies.

The Norman kings, desirous of strengthening their work, constructed Gothic cathedrals in the room of wooden churches, in which they installed their soldier-bishops, as if they were strong fortresses. Instead of the moral power and the humble crook of the shepherd, they gave them secular power and a staff. The religious episcopate was succeeded by a political one. William Rufus went even to greater lengths than his father. Taking advantage of the schism which divided the papacy, he did without a pope for ten years, leaving abbeys, bishoprics, and even Canterbury vacant, and scandalously squandering their revenues. Cæsaropapia (which transforms a king into a pope) having thus attained its greatest excess, a sacerdotal reaction could not fail to take place.

The papacy is about to rise up again in England, and royalty to decline—two movements which are always found combined in Great Britain.

CHAPTER V.

Anselm's Firmness—Becket's Austerity—The King scourged —John becomes the Pope's Vassal—Collision between Popery and Liberty—The Vassal King ravages his Kingdom—Religion of the Senses and Superstition.

WE are now entering upon a new phase of history. Romanism is on the point of triumphing by the exertions of learned men.

[1] Divino animi ardore repente inflammatus, regi inquit: Melior te his me ornavit cui et reddam. Wilkins, Concilia, i. 367.
[2] Respondit rex et dixit se velle omnes baculos pastorales Angliæ in manu sua tenere. Script. Anglic. Lond. 1652, fol. p. 1327.
[3] Lanfranc ad hæc miratus est, sed propter majores ecclesiæ Christi utilitates, quas sine rege perficere non potuit, ad tempus *siluit*. Ibid.
[4] Sacerdotes vero in castellis vel in vicis habitantes habentes uxores, non cogantur ut dimittant. Wilkins, Concilia, i. p. 367.

[1] Nemo enim omnium regum, etiam paganorum.... Greg. lib. vii. Ep. i. ad Hubert.
[2] Pecunias sine honore tributas, quanti pretii habeam. Ibid.
[3] Gemma principum esse meruisti. Ibid. Epp. xxiii. ad Gulielm.
[4] Facilius lenitatis dulcedine ac rationis ostensione, quam austeritate vel rigore justitiæ. Ibid. Ep. v ad Hugonem.

energetic prelates, and princes in whom extreme imprudence was joined with extreme servility. This is the era of the dominion of popery, and we shall see it unscrupulously employing the despotism by which it is characterized.

A malady having occasioned some degree of remorse in the king, he consented to fill up the vacancy in the archiepiscopal see. And now Anselm first appears in England. He was born in an Alpine valley, at the town of Aosta in Piedmont. Imbibing the instructions of his pious mother Ermenberga, and believing that God's throne was placed on the summit of the gigantic mountains he saw rising around him, the child Anselm climbed them in his dreams, and received the bread of heaven from the hands of the Lord. Unhappily in after-years he recognised another throne in the church of Christ, and bowed his head before the chair of St Peter. This was the man whom William II. summoned in 1093 to fill the primacy of Canterbury. Anselm, who was then sixty years old, and engaged in teaching at Bec, refused at first: the character of Rufus terrified him. "The Church of England," said he, "is a plough that ought to be drawn by two oxen of equal strength. How can you yoke together an old and timid sheep like me and that wild bull?" At length he accepted, and concealing a mind of great power under an appearance of humility, he had hardly arrived in England before he recognised Pope Urban II., demanded the estates of his see which the treasury had seized upon, refused to pay the king the sums he demanded, contested the right of investiture against Henry I., forbade all ecclesiastics to take the feudal oath, and determined that the priests should forthwith put away their wives. Scholasticism, of which Anselm was the first representative, freed the church from the yoke of royalty, but only to chain it to the papal chair. The fetters were about to be riveted by a still more energetic hand; and what this great theologian had begun, a great worldling was to carry on.

At the hunting-parties of Henry II. a man attracted the attention of his sovereign by his air of frankness, agreeable manners, witty conversation, and exuberant vivacity. This was Thomas Becket, the son of an Anglo-Saxon and a Syrian woman. Being both priest and soldier, he was appointed at the same time by the king prebend of Hastings and governor of the Tower. When nominated chancellor of England, he shewed himself no less expert than Wilfrid in misappropriating the wealth of the minors in his charge, and of the abbeys and bishoprics, and indulged in the most extravagant luxury. Henry, the first of the Plantagenets, a man of undecided character, having noticed Becket's zeal in upholding the prerogatives of the crown, appointed him archbishop of Canterbury. "Now, sire," remarked the primate, with a smile, "when I shall have to choose between God's favour and yours, remember it is yours that I shall sacrifice."

Becket, who, as keeper of the seals, had been the most magnificent of courtiers, affected as archbishop to be the most venerable of saints. He sent back the seals to the king, assumed the robe of a monk, wore sackcloth filled with vermin, lived on the plainest food, every day knelt down to wash the feet of the poor, paced the cloisters of his cathedral with tearful eyes, and spent hours in prayer before the altar. As champion of the priests, even in their crimes, he took under his protection one who to the crime of seduction had added the murder of his victim's father.

The judges having represented to Henry that during the first eight years of his reign a hundred murders had been committed by ecclesiastics, the king in 1164 summoned a council at Clarendon, in which certain regulations or *constitutions* were drawn up, with the object of preventing the encroachments of the hierarchy. Becket at first refused to sign them, but at length consented, and then withdrew into solitary retirement to mourn over his fault. Pope Alexander III. released him from his oath; and then began a fierce and long struggle between the king and the primate. Four knights of the court, catching up a hasty expression of their master's, barbarously murdered the archbishop at the foot of the altar in his own cathedral church (A.D. 1170). The people looked upon Becket as a saint: immense crowds came to pray at his tomb, at which many miracles were worked.[1] "Even from his grave," said Becket's partisans, "he rendered his testimony in behalf of the papacy."

Henry now passed from one extreme to the other. He entered Canterbury barefooted, and prostrated himself before the martyr's tomb: the bishops, priests, and monks, to the number of eighty, passed before him, each bearing a scourge, and struck three or five blows according to their rank on the naked shoulders of the king. In former ages, so the priestly fable ran, Saint Peter had scourged an archbishop of Canterbury: now Rome in sober reality scourges the back of royalty, and nothing can henceforward check her victorious career. A Plantagenet surrendered England to the pope, and the pope gave him authority to subdue Ireland.[2]

Rome, who had set her foot on the neck of a king, was destined under one of the sons of Henry II. to set it on the neck of

[1] In loco passionis et ubi sepultus est, paralytici curantur, cœci vident, surdi audiunt. Johan. Salisb. Epp. 286.
[2] Significasti si quidem nobis, fili carissime, te Hiberniæ insulam ad subdendum illum populum velle intrare. nos itaque gratum et acceptum habemus ut pro dilatandis ecclesiæ terminis insulam ingrediaris. Adrian IV., Bulla 1154 in Rymer, Acta Publica.

England. John being unwilling to acknowledge an archbishop of Canterbury illegally nominated by Pope Innocent III., the latter, more daring than Hildebrand, laid the kingdom under an interdict. Upon this John ordered all the prelates and abbots to leave England, and sent a monk to Spain as ambassador to Mahomet-el-Nasir, offering to turn Mahometan and to become his vassal. But as Philip Augustus was preparing to dethrone him, John made up his mind to become a vassal of Innocent, and not of Mahomet—which was about the same thing to him. On the 15th May 1213, he laid his crown at the legate's feet, declared that he surrendered his kingdom of England to the pope, and made oath to him as to his lord paramount.[1]

A national protest then boldly claimed the ancient liberties of the people. Forty-five barons armed in complete mail, and mounted on their noble war-horses, surrounded by their knights and servants and about two thousand soldiers, met at Brackley during the festival of Easter in 1215, and sent a deputation to Oxford, where the court then resided. "Here," said they to the king, "is the charter which consecrates the liberties confirmed by Henry II., and which you also have solemnly sworn to observe." ......" Why do they not demand my crown also?" said the king in a furious passion, and then with an oath,[2] he added: "I will not grant them liberties which will make me a slave." This is the usual language of weak and absolute kings. Neither would the nation submit to be enslaved. The barons occupied London, and on the 15th June 1215, the king signed the famous *Magna Charta* at Runnymede. The political protestantism of the thirteenth century would have done but little, however, for the greatness of the nation, without the religious protestantism of the sixteenth.

This was the first time that the papacy came into collision with modern liberty. It shuddered in alarm, and the shock was violent. Innocent swore (as was his custom), and then declared the Great Charter null and void, forbade the king under pain of anathema to respect the liberties which he had confirmed,[3] ascribed the conduct of the barons to the instigation of Satan, and ordered them to make apology to the king, and to send a deputation to Rome to learn from the mouth of the pope himself what should be the government of England. This was the way in which the papacy welcomed the first manifestations of liberty among the nations, and made known the model system under which it claimed to govern the whole world.

The priests of England supported the ana-

themas pronounced by their chief. They indulged in a thousand jeers and sarcasms against John about the charter he had accepted:—"This is the twenty-fifth king of England—not a king, not even a kingling —but the disgrace of kings—a king without a kingdom—the fifth wheel of a waggon —the last of kings, and the disgrace of his people!—I would not give a straw for him ......*Fuisti rex, nunc fex* (once a king, but now a clown)." John, unable to support his disgrace, groaned and gnashed his teeth and rolled his eyes, tore sticks from the hedges and gnawed them like a maniac, or dashed them into fragments on the ground.[1]

The barons, unmoved alike by the insolence of the pope and the despair of the king, replied that they would maintain the charter. Innocent excommunicated them. "Is it the pope's business to regulate temporal matters?" asked they. "By what right do vile usurers and foul simoniacs domineer over our country and excommunicate the whole world?"

The pope soon triumphed throughout England. His vassal John having hired some bands of adventurers from the continent, traversed at their head the whole country from the Channel to the Forth. These mercenaries carried desolation in their track: they extorted money, made prisoners, burnt the barons' castles, laid waste their parks, and dishonoured their wives and daughters.[2] The king would sleep in a house, and the next morning set fire to it. Blood-stained assassins scoured the country during the night, the sword in one hand and the torch in the other, marking their progress by murder and conflagration.[3] Such was the enthronization of popery in England. At this sight the barons, overcome by emotion, denounced both the king and the pope: "Alas! poor country!" they exclaimed. "Wretched England!........And thou, O pope, a curse light upon thee!"[4]

The curse was not long delayed. As the king was returning from some more than usually successful foray, and as the royal waggons were crossing the sands of the Wash, the tide rose and all sank in the abyss.[5] This accident filled John with terror: it seemed to him that the earth was about to open and swallow him up; he fled to a convent, where he drank copiously of cider, and died of drunkenness and fright.[6]

Such was the end of the pope's vassal—of his armed missionary in Great Britain. Never had so vile a prince been the invo-

---

[1] Resignavit coronam suam in manus domini papæ. Matth. Paris, 198 et 207.
[2] Cum juramento furibundus. Ibid. 213.
[3] Sub intimatione anathematis prohibentes ne dictus rex eam observare præsumat. Ibid. 224.

[1] Arreptos baculos et stipites more furiosi nunc corrodere, nunc corrosos confringere. Matth. Paris, 222.
[2] Uxores et filias suas ludibrio expositas. Ibid. 231.
[3] Discurrebant sicarii cæde humana cruentati, noctivagi, incendiarii, strictis ensibus. Ibid.
[4] Sic barones lacrymantes et lamentantes regem et papam maledixerunt. Ibid. 234.
[5] Aperta est in mediis fluctibus terra et voraginis abyssus, quæ absorbuerunt universa cum hominibus et equis. Ibid. 242.
[6] Novi ciceris potatione nimis repletus. Ibid. ad ann. 1216.

luntary occasion to his people of such great benefits. From his reign England may date her enthusiasm for liberty and her dread of popery.

During this time a great transformation had been accomplished. Magnificent churches and the marvels of religious art, with ceremonies and a multitude of prayers and chantings dazzled the eyes, charmed the ears, and captivated the senses; but testified also to the absence of every strong moral and Christian disposition, and the predominance of worldliness in the church. At the same time the adoration of images and relics, saints, angels, and Mary the mother of God, the worships of *latria, doulia,* and *hyperdoulia,*[1] the real Mediator transported from the throne of mercy to the seat of vengeance, at once indicated and kept up among the people that ignorance of truth and absence of grace which characterize popery. All these errors tended to bring about a reaction: and in fact the march of the Reformation may now be said to begin.

England had been brought low by the papacy: it rose up again by resisting Rome. Grostête, Bradwardine, and Edward III. prepared the way for Wickliffe, and Wickliffe for the Reformation.

CHAPTER VI.

Reaction—Grostête—Principles of Reform—Contest with the Pope—Sewal—Progress of the Nation—Opposition to the Papacy—Conversion of Bradwardine—Grace is Supreme—Edward III.—Statutes of *Provisors* and *Pramunire.*

In the reign of Henry III. son of John, while the king was conniving at the usurpations of Rome, and the pope ridiculing the complaints of the barons, a pious and energetic man, of comprehensive understanding, was occupied in the study of the Holy Scriptures in their original languages, and bowing to their sovereign authority. Robert Grostête (Greathead or *Capito*) was born of poor parents in the county of Lincolnshire, and being raised to the see of Lincoln in 1235, when he was sixty years of age, he boldly undertook to reform his diocese, one of the largest in England. Nor was this all. At the very time when the Roman pontiff, who had hitherto been content to be called the vicar of St Peter, proclaimed himself the vicar of God,[2] and was ordering the English bishops to find benefices for *three hundred Romans,*[3] Grostête was declaring that "to follow a pope who rebels against the will of

Christ, is to separate from Christ and his body; and if ever the time should come when all men follow an erring pontiff, then will be the great apostasy. Then will true Christians refuse to obey, and Rome will be the cause of an unprecedented schism."[1] Thus did he predict the Reformation. Disgusted at the avarice of the monks and priests, he visited Rome to demand a reform. "Brother," said Innocent IV. to him with some irritation, "*Is thine eye evil, because I am good?*" The English bishop exclaimed with a sigh: "O money, money! how great is thy power—especially in this court of Rome!"

A year had scarcely elapsed before Innocent commanded the bishop to give a canonry in Lincoln cathedral to his infant nephew. Grostête replied: "After the sin of Lucifer there is none more opposed to the gospel than that which ruins souls by giving them a faithless minister. Bad pastors are the cause of unbelief, heresy, and disorder. Those who introduce them into the church are little better than antichrists, and their culpability is in proportion to their dignity. Although the chief of the angels should order me to commit such a sin, I would refuse. My obedience forbids me to obey; and therefore I rebel."[2]

Thus spoke a bishop to his pontiff: his obedience to the word of God forbade him to obey the pope. This was the principle of the Reformation. "Who is this old driveller that in his dotage dares to judge of my conduct?" exclaimed Innocent, whose wrath was appeased by the intervention of certain cardinals. Grostête on his dying bed professed still more clearly the principles of the reformers; he declared that a heresy was "an opinion conceived by carnal motives, *contrary to Scripture,* openly taught and obstinately defended," thus asserting the authority of Scripture instead of the authority of the church. He died in peace, and the public voice proclaimed him "a searcher of the Scriptures, an adversary of the pope, and despiser of the Romans."[3] Innocent, desiring to take vengeance on his bones, meditated the exhumation of his body, when one night (says Matthew of Paris) the bishop appeared before him. Drawing near the pontiff's bed, he struck him with his crosier, and thus addressed him with terrible voice and threatening look:[4] "Wretch! the Lord doth not permit thee to have any power over me. Woe be to thee!" The vision disappeared, and the pope, uttering a cry as if he had been struck by some sharp weapon, lay senseless on his couch. Never after did he

---

[1] The Romish church distinguishes three kinds of worship: *latria,* that paid to God; *doulia,* to saints; and *hyperdoulia,* to the Virgin Mary.
[2] Non puri hominis sed veri Dei vicem gerit in terris. Innocent III. Epp. lib. vi. l. 335.
[3] Ut trecentis Romanis in primis beneficiis vacantibus providerent. Matth. Paris, ann. 1240.

[1] Absit et quod....hæc sedes et in ea præsidentes causa sint schismatis apparentis. Ortinnus Gratius, ed. Brown, fol. 251.
[2] Obedienter non obedio sed contradico et rebello. Matth. Paris, ad ann. 1252.
[3] Scripturarum sedulus perscrutator diversarum, Romanorum malleus et contemptor. Matth. Paris, vol. ii. p. 876, fol. Lond. 1640. Sixteen of his writings (Sermones et epistolæ) will be found in *Brown, app. ad Fasciculum.*
[4] Nocte apparuit ei episcopus vultu severo, intuitu austero, ac voce terribili. Ibid. 883.

pass a quiet night, and pursued by the phantoms of his troubled imagination, he expired while the palace re-echoed with his lamentable groans.

Grostête was not single in his opposition to the pope. Sewal, archbishop of York, did the same, and " the more the pope cursed him, the more the people blessed him." [1]— " Moderate your tyranny," said the archbishop to the pontiff, " for the Lord said to Peter, *Feed* my sheep, and not *shear them, flay them,* or *devour them.*" [2] The pope smiled and let the bishop speak, because the king allowed the pope to act. The power of England, which was constantly increasing, was soon able to give more force to these protests.

The nation was indeed growing in greatness. The madness of John, which had caused the English people to lose their continental possessions, had given them more unity and power. The Norman kings, being compelled to renounce entirely the country which had been their cradle, had at length made up their minds to look upon England as their home. The two races, so long hostile, melted one into the other. Free institutions were formed ; the laws were studied ; and colleges were founded. The language began to assume a regular form, and the ships of England were already formidable at sea. For more than a century the most brilliant victories attended the British armies. A king of France was brought captive to London : an English king was crowned at Paris. Even Spain and Italy felt the valour of these proud islanders. The English people took their station in the foremost rank. Now the character of a nation is never raised by halves. When the mighty ones of the earth were seen to fall before her, England could no longer crawl at the feet of an Italian priest.

At no period did her laws attack the papacy with so much energy. At the beginning of the fourteenth century an Englishman having brought to London one of the pope's bulls—a bull of an entirely spiritual character, it was an excommunication—was prosecuted as a traitor to the crown, and would have been hanged, had not the sentence, at the chancellor's intercession, been changed to perpetual banishment. [3] The *common law* was the weapon the government then opposed to the papal bulls. Shortly afterwards, in 1307, King Edward ordered the sheriffs to resist the arrogant pretensions of the Romish agents. But it is to two great men in the fourteenth century equally illustrious, the one in the state, and the other in the church, that England is indebted for the development of the protestant element in England.

In 1346, an English army, 34,000 strong, met face to face at Crecy a French army of 100,000 fighting men. Two individuals of very different characters were in the English host. One of them was King Edward III., a brave and ambitious prince, who, being resolved to recover for the royal authority all its power, and for England all her glory, had undertaken the conquest of France. The other was his chaplain Bradwardine, a man of so humble a character that his meekness was often taken for stupidity. And thus it was that on his receiving the pallium at Avignon from the hands of the pope on his elevation to the see of Canterbury, a jester mounted on an ass rode into the hall and petitioned the pontiff to make him *primate* instead of that imbecile priest.

Bradwardine was one of the most pious men of the age, and to his prayers his sovereign's victories were ascribed. He was also one of the greatest geniuses of his time, and occupied the first rank amongst astronomers, philosophers, and mathematicians. [1] The pride of science had at first alienated him from the doctrine of the cross. But one day while in the house of God and listening to the reading of the Holy Scriptures, these words struck his ear : *It is not of him that willeth, nor of him that runneth, but of God that showeth mercy.* His ungrateful heart, he tells us, at first rejected this humiliating doctrine with aversion. Yet the word of God had laid its powerful hold upon him ; he was converted to the truths he had despised, and immediately began to set forth the doctrines of eternal grace at Merton College, Oxford. He had drunk so deep at the fountain of Scripture that the traditions of men concerned him but little, and he was so absorbed in adoration in spirit and in truth, that he remarked not outward susperstitions. His lectures were eagerly listened to and circulated through all Europe. The grace of God was their very essence, as it was of the Reformation. With sorrow Bradwardine beheld Pelagianism everywhere substituting a mere religion of externals for inward Christianity, and on his knees he struggled for the salvation of the church. " As in the times of old four hundred and fifty prophets of Baal strove against a single prophet of God ; so now, O Lord," he exclaimed, " the number of those who strive with Pelagius against thy free grace cannot be counted. [2] They pretend not to receive grace freely, but to buy it. [3] The will of men (they say) should precede, and thine should follow : theirs is the mistress, and thine the servant. [4] ......Alas ! nearly the whole world is walking in error in the steps of Pelagius. [5] Arise, O Lord, and judge thy

---

[1] Quanto magis a papa maledicebatur, tanto plus a populo benedicebatur. Matth. Paris, ad ann. 1257.
[2] *Pasce* oves meas, non *tonde*, non *excoria*, non *eviscera*, vel devorando *consume*. Ibid. ad ann. 1258.
[3] Fuller's Church History, cent. xiv. p. 90, fol. Lond. 1655.

[1] His Arithmetic and Geometry have been published ; but I am not aware if that is the case with his Astronomical Tables.
[2] Quot, Domine, hodie cum Pelagio pro libero arbitrio contra gratuitam gratiam tuam pugnant ! De causa Dei adversus Pelagium, libri tres. Lond. 1618.
[3] Nequaquam gratuita sed vendita. Ibid.
[4] Suam voluntatem præire ut dominam, tuam subsequi ut ancillam. Ibid.
[5] Totus pæne mundus post Pelagium abiit in errorem. Ibid.

cause." And the Lord did arise, but not until after the death of this pious archbishop—in the days of Wickliffe, who, when a youth, listened to the lectures at Merton College—and especially in the days of Luther and of Calvin. His contemporaries gave him the name of the *profound doctor*.

If Bradwardine walked truthfully in the path of faith, his illustrious patron Edward advanced triumphantly in the field of policy. Pope Clement IV. having decreed that the first two vacancies in the Anglican church should be conferred on two of his cardinals: "France is becoming *English*," said the courtiers to the king; "and by way of compensation, England is becoming *Italian*." Edward, desirous of guaranteeing the religious liberties of England, passed with the consent of parliament in 1350 the statute of *provisors*, which made void every ecclesiastical appointment contrary to the rights of the king, the chapters, or the patrons. Thus the privileges of the chapters and the liberty of the English Catholics, as well as the independence of the crown, were protected against the invasion of foreigners; and imprisonment or banishment for life was denounced upon all offenders against the law.

This bold step alarmed the pontiff. Accordingly, three years after, the king having nominated one of his secretaries to the see of Durham—a man without any of the qualities becoming a bishop—the pope readily confirmed the appointment. When some one expressed his astonishment at this, the pope made answer: "If the king of England had nominated an ass, I would have accepted him." This may remind us of the *ass* of Avignon; and it would seem that this humble animal at that time played a significant part in the elections to the papacy. But be that as it may, the pope withdrew his pretensions. "Empires have their term," observes an historian at this place; "when once they have reached it, they halt, they retrograde, they fall."[1]

The term seemed to be drawing nearer every day. In the reign of Edward III., between 1343 and 1353, again in 1364, and finally under Richard II. in 1393, those stringent laws were passed which interdicted all appeal to the court of Rome, all bulls from the Roman bishop, all excommunications, &c., in a word, every act infringing on the rights of the crown: and declared that whoever should bring such documents into England, or receive, publish, or execute them, should be put out of the king's protection, deprived of their property, attached in their persons, and brought before the king in council to undergo their trial according to the terms of the act. Such was the statute of *Præmunire*.[2]

Great was the indignation of the Romans at the news of this law: "If the statute of *mortmain* put the pope into a sweat," says Fuller, "this of *præmunire* gave him a fit of fever." One pope called it an "execrable statute,"—"a horrible crime."[1] Such are the terms applied by the pontiffs to all that thwarts their ambition.

Of the two wars carried on by Edward—the one against the King of France, and the other against popery—the latter was the most righteous and important. The benefits which this prince had hoped to derive from his brilliant victories at Crecy and Poitiers dwindled away almost entirely before his death; while his struggles with the papacy, founded as they were on truth, have exerted even to our own days an indisputable influence on the destinies of Great Britain. Yet the prayers and the conquests of Bradwardine, who proclaimed in that fallen age the doctrine of grace, produced effects still greater, not only for the salvation of many souls, but for the liberty, moral force, and greatness of England.

CHAPTER VII.

The Mendicant Friars—Their Disorders and Popular Indignation—Wickliffe—His Success—Speeches of the Peers against the Papal Tribute—Agreement of Bruges—Courtenay and Lancaster—Wickliffe before the Convocation—Altercation between Lancaster and Courtenay—Riot—Three Briefs against Wickliffe—Wickliffe at Lambeth—Mission of the *Poor Priests*—Their Preachings and Persecutions—Wickliffe and the Four Regents.

Thus in the first half of the fourteenth century, nearly two hundred years before the Reformation, England appeared weary of the yoke of Rome. Bradwardine was no more; but a man who had been his disciple was about to succeed him, and without attaining to the highest functions, to exhibit in his person the past and future tendencies of the church of Christ in Great Britain. The English Reformation did not begin with Henry VIII: the revival of the sixteenth century is but a link in the chain commencing with the apostles and reaching to us.

The resistance of Edward III. to the papacy *without* had not suppressed the papacy *within*. The mendicant friars, and particularly the Franciscans, those fanatical soldiers of the pope, were endeavouring by pious frauds to monopolize the wealth of the country. "Every year," said they, "Saint Francis descends from heaven to purgatory, and delivers the souls of all those who were buried in the dress of his order." These friars used to kidnap children from their parents and shut them up in monasteries.

---

[1] Habent imperia suos terminos; huc cum venerint, sistant, retrocedunt, ruunt. Fuller's Hist. cent. xiv. p. 116.
[2] The most natural meaning of the word *præmunire* (given more particularly to the act of 1393) seems to be that suggested by Fuller, cent. xiv. (p. 148): to fence and fortify the regal power from foreign assault. See the whole bill, *ibid.* p. 145-147.
[1] Execrabile statutum....fœdum et turpe facinus. Martin V. to the Duke of Bedford, Fuller, cent. xiv. p. 148.

They affected to be poor, and with a wallet on their back, begged with a piteous air from both high and low; but at the same time they dwelt in palaces, heaped up treasures, dressed in costly garments, and wasted their time in luxurious entertainments.[1] The least of them looked upon themselves as *lords*, and those who wore the doctor's cap considered themselves *kings*. While they diverted themselves, eating and drinking at their well-spread tables, they used to send ignorant uneducated persons in their place to preach fables and legends to amuse and plunder the people.[2] If any rich man talked of giving alms to the poor and not to the monks, they exclaimed loudly against such impiety, and declared with threatening voice : " If you do so we will leave the country, and return accompanied by a legion of glittering helmets."[3] Public indignation was at its height. " The monks and priests of Rome," was the cry, " are eating us away like a cancer. God must deliver us or the people will perish......Woe be to them ! the cup of wrath will run over. Men of holy church shall be despised as carrion, as dogs shall they be cast out in open places."[4]

The arrogance of Rome made the cup run over. Pope Urban V., heedless of the laurels won by the conqueror at Crecy and Poitiers, summoned Edward III. to recognise him as legitimate sovereign of England, and to pay as feudal tribute the annual rent of one thousand marcs. In case of refusal the king was to appear before him at Rome. For thirty-three years the popes had never mentioned the tribute accorded by John to Innocent III., and which had always been paid very irregularly. The conqueror of the Valois was irritated by this insolence on the part of an Italian bishop, and called on God to avenge England. From Oxford came forth the avenger.

John Wickliffe, born in 1324, in a little village in Yorkshire, was one of the students who attended the lectures of the pious Bradwardine at Merton College. He was in the flower of his age, and produced a great sensation in the university. In 1348, a terrible pestilence, which is said to have carried off half the human race, appeared in England after successively devastating Asia and the continent of Europe. This visitation of the Almighty sounded like the trumpet of the judgment-day in the heart of Wickliffe. Alarmed at the thoughts of eternity, the young man—for he was then only twenty-four years old—passed days and nights in his cell groaning and sighing, and calling upon God to show him the path he ought to follow.[5] He found it in the Holy Scriptures,

and resolved to make it known to others. He commenced with prudence ; but being elected in 1361 warden of Balliol, and in 1365 warden of Canterbury College also, he began to set forth the doctrine of faith in a more energetic manner. His biblical and philosophical studies, his knowledge of theology, his penetrating mind, the purity of his manners, and his unbending courage, rendered him the object of general admiration. A profound teacher, like his master, and an eloquent preacher, he demonstrated to the learned during the course of the week what he intended to preach, and on Sunday he preached to the people what he had previously demonstrated. His disputations gave strength to his sermons, and his sermons shed light upon his disputations. He accused the clergy of having banished the Holy Scriptures, and required that the authority of the word of God should be re-established in the church. Loud acclamations crowned these discussions, and the crowd of vulgar minds trembled with indignation when they heard these shouts of applause.

Wickliffe was forty years old when the papal arrogance stirred England to its depths. Being at once an able politician and a fervent Christian, he vigorously defended the rights of the crown against the Romish aggression, and by his arguments not only enlightened his fellow-countrymen generally, but stirred up the zeal of several members of both houses of parliament.

The parliament assembled, and never perhaps had it been summoned on a question which excited to so high a degree the emotions of England, and indeed of Christendom. The debates in the House of Lords were especially remarkable : all the arguments of Wickliffe were reproduced. " Feudal *tribute* is due," said one, " only to him who can grant feudal *protection* in return. Now how can the pope wage war to protect his fiefs ?" —" Is it as vassal of the crown or as feudal superior," asked another, " that the pope demands part of our property ? Urban V. will not accept the first of these titles. ....Well and good ! but the English people will not acknowledge the second."— " Why," said a third, " was this tribute originally granted ? To pay the pope for absolving John.........His demand, then, is mere simony, a kind of clerical swindling, which the lords spiritual and temporal should indignantly oppose."—" No," said another speaker, " England belongs not to the pope. The pope is but a man subject to sin ; but Christ is the Lord of lords, and this kingdom is held directly and solely of Christ alone."[1] Thus spoke the lords inspired by Wickliffe.

---

[1] When they have overmuch riches, both in great waste houses and precious clothes. in great feasts and many jewels and treasures. Wickliffe's Tracts and Treatises, edited by the Wickliffe Society, p. 224. [2] Ibid. 240.
[3] Come again with bright heads. Ibid.
[4] Wickliffe. The Last Age of the Church.
[5] Long debating and deliberating with himself, with many

secret sighs. Fox, Acts and Monuments, i. p. 485, fol. Lond. 1684.
[1] These opinions are reported by Wickliffe, in a treatise preserved in the *Selden MSS.* and printed by Mr J. Lewis, in his History of Wickliffe, App. No. 30, p. 349. He was present during the debate : *quam audivi in quodam concilio a dominis secularibus.*

Parliament decided unanimously that no prince had the right to alienate the sovereignty of the kingdom without the consent of the other two estates, and that if the pontiff should attempt to proceed against the king of England as his vassal, the nation should rise in a body to maintain the independence of the crown.

To no purpose did this generous resolution excite the wrath of the partisans of Rome: to no purpose did they assert that, by the canon law, the king ought to be deprived of his fief, and that England now belonged to the pope: "No," replied Wickliffe, "the canon law has no force when it is opposed to the word of God." Edward III. made Wickliffe one of his chaplains, and the papacy has ceased from that hour to lay claim—in explicit terms at least—to the sovereignty of England.

When the pope gave up his temporal he was desirous, at the very least, of keeping up his ecclesiastical pretensions, and to procure the repeal of the statutes of *Præmunire* and *Provisors*. It was accordingly resolved to hold a conference at Bruges to treat of this question, and Wickliffe, who had been created doctor of theology two years before, proceeded thither with the other commissioners in April 1374. They came to an arrangement in 1375 that the king should bind himself to repeal the penalties denounced against the pontifical agents, and that the pope should confirm the king's ecclesiastical presentations.[1] But the nation was not pleased with this compromise. "The clerks sent from Rome," said the Commons, are more dangerous for the kingdom than Jews or Saracens: every papal agent resident in England, and every Englishman living at the court of Rome, should be punished with death." Such was the language of the *Good Parliament*. In the fourteenth century the English nation called a parliament *good* which did not yield to the papacy.

Wickliffe, after his return to England, was presented to the rectory of Lutterworth, and from that time a practical activity was added to his academic influence. At Oxford he spoke as a master to the young theologians; in his parish he addressed the people as a preacher and as a pastor. "The Gospel," said he, "is the only source of religion. The Roman pontiff is a mere cut-purse,[2] and, far from having the right to reprimand the whole world, he may be lawfully reproved by his inferiors, and even by laymen."

The papacy grew alarmed. Courtenay, son of the Earl of Devonshire, an imperious but grave priest, and full of zeal for what he believed to be the truth, had recently been appointed to the see of London. In parliament he had resisted Wickliffe's patron, John of Gaunt, duke of Lancaster, third son of Edward III., and head of the house of that name. The bishop, observing that the doctrines of the reformer were spreading among the people, both high and low, charged him with heresy, and summoned him to appear before the convocation assembled in St Paul's Cathedral.

On the 19th February, 1377, an immense crowd, heated with fanaticism, thronged the approaches to the church and filled its aisles, while the citizens favourable to the reform remained concealed in their houses. Wickliffe moved forward, preceded by Lord Percy, marshal of England, and supported by the Duke of Lancaster, who defended him from purely political motives. He was followed by four bachelors of divinity, his counsel, and passed through the hostile multitude who looked upon Lancaster as the enemy of their liberties, and upon himself as the enemy of the church. "Let not the sight of these bishops make you shrink a hair's-breadth in your profession of faith," said the prince to the doctor. "They are unlearned; and as for this concourse of people, fear nothing, we are here to defend you."[1] When the reformer had crossed the threshold of the cathedral, the crowd within appeared like a solid wall; and, notwithstanding the efforts of the earl-marshal, Wickliffe and Lancaster could not advance. The people swayed to and fro, hands were raised in violence, and loud hootings re-echoed through the building. At length Percy made an opening in the dense multitude, and Wickliffe passed on.

The haughty Courtenay, who had been commissioned by the archbishop to preside over the assembly, watched these strange movements with anxiety, and beheld with displeasure the learned doctor accompanied by the two most powerful men in England. He said nothing to the Duke of Lancaster, who at that time administered the kingdom, but turning towards Percy observed sharply: "If I had known, my lord, that you claimed to be master in this church, I would have taken measures to prevent your entrance." Lancaster coldly rejoined: "He shall keep such mastery here, though you say nay." Percy now turned to Wickliffe, who had remained standing and said: "Sit down and rest yourself." At this Courtenay gave way to his anger, and exclaimed in a loud tone: "He must not sit down; criminals stand before their judges." Lancaster, indignant that a learned doctor of England should be refused a favour to which his age alone entitled him (for he was between fifty and sixty) made answer to the bishop: "My lord, you are very arrogant; take care......or I may bring down your pride, and not yours only, but that of all the prelacy in England."[2]— "Do me all the harm you can," was Cour-

[1] Rymer. vii. p. 33, 63–68.
[2] The proud worldly priest of Rome, and the most cursed of clippers and purse-kervers. Lewis, History of Wickliffe, p. 37. Oxford, 1820.

[1] Fox, Acts, i. p. 487. fol. Lond. 1684.
[2] Fuller, Church Hist. cent. xiv. p. 136.

tenay's haughty reply. The prince rejoined with some emotion : " You are insolent, my lord. You think, no doubt, you can trust on your family......but your relations will have trouble enough to protect themselves." To this the bishop nobly replied : " My confidence is not in my parents nor in any man ; but only in God, in whom I trust, and by whose assistance I will be bold to speak the truth." Lancaster, who saw hypocrisy only in these words, turned to one of his attendants, and whispered in his ear, but so loud as to be heard by the bystanders : " I would rather pluck the bishop by the hair of his head out of his chair, than take this at his hands." Every impartial reader must confess that the prelate spoke with greater dignity than the prince. Lancaster had hardly uttered these imprudent words before the bishop's partisans fell upon him and Percy, and even upon Wickliffe, who alone had remained calm.[1] The two noblemen resisted, their friends and servants defended them, the uproar became extreme, and there was no hope of restoring tranquillity. The two lords escaped with difficulty, and the assembly broke up in great confusion.

On the following day the earl-marshal having called upon parliament to apprehend the disturbers of the public peace, the clerical party uniting with the enemies of Lancaster, filled the streets with their clamour ; and while the duke and the earl escaped by the Thames, the mob collected before Percy's house, broke down the doors, searched every chamber, and thrust their swords into every dark corner. When they found that he had escaped, the rioters, imagining that he was concealed in Lancaster's palace, rushed to the Savoy, at that time the most magnificent building in the kingdom. They killed a priest who endeavoured to stay them, tore down the ducal arms, and hung them on the gallows like those of a traitor. They would have gone still farther if the bishop had not very opportunely reminded them that they were *in Lent*. As for Wickliffe, he was dismissed with an injunction against preaching his doctrines.

But this decision of the priests was not ratified by the people of England. Public opinion declared in favour of Wickliffe. " If he is guilty," said they, " why is he not punished ? If he is innocent, why is he ordered to be silent ? If he is the weakest in power, he is the strongest in truth ! " And so indeed he was, and never had he spoken with such energy. He openly attacked the pretended apostolical chair, and declared that the *two* antipopes who sat at Rome and Avignon together made *one* antichrist. Being now in opposition to the pope, Wickliffe was soon to confess that Christ alone was king of the church ; and that it is not possible for a man to be excommunicated, unless first and principally he be excommunicated by himself.[1]

Rome could not close her ears. Wickliffe's enemies sent thither nineteen propositions which they ascribed to him, and in the month of June 1377, just as Richard II., son of the Black Prince, a child eleven years old, was ascending the throne, three letters from Gregory XI., addressed to the king, the archbishop of Canterbury, and the university of Oxford, denounced Wickliffe as a heretic, and called upon them to proceed against him as against a common thief. The archbishop issued the citation : the crown and the university were silent.

On the appointed day, Wickliffe, unaccompanied by either Lancaster or Percy, proceeded to the archiepiscopal chapel at Lambeth. " Men expected he should be devoured," says an historian ; " being brought into the lion's den."[2] But the burgesses had taken the prince's place. The assault of Rome had aroused the friends of liberty and truth in England. " The pope's briefs," said they, " ought to have no effect in the realm without the king's consent. Every man is master in his own house."

The archbishop had scarcely opened the sitting, when Sir Louis Clifford entered the chapel, and forbade the court, on the part of the queen-mother, to proceed against the reformer. The bishops were struck with a panic-fear : " they bent their heads," says a Roman-catholic historian, " like a reed before the wind."[3] Wickliffe retired after handing in a protest. " In the first place," said he, " I resolve with my whole heart, and by the grace of God, to be a sincere Christian ; and, while my life shall last, to profess and defend the law of Christ so far as I have power."[4] Wickliffe's enemies attacked this protest, and one of them eagerly maintained that whatever the pope ordered should be looked upon as right. " What ! " answered the reformer ; " the pope may then exclude from the canon of the scriptures any book that displeases him, and alter the Bible at pleasure ?" Wickliffe thought that Rome, unsettling the grounds of infallibility, had transferred it from the Scriptures to the pope, and was desirous of restoring it to its true place, and re-establishing authority in the church on a truly divine foundation.

A great change was now taking place in the reformer. Busying himself less about the kingdom of England, he occupied himself more about the kingdom of Christ. In him the political phasis was followed by the religious. To carry the glad tidings of the gospel into the remotest hamlets, was now the great idea which possessed Wickliffe. If begging friars (said he) stroll over the coun-

1 Vaughan's Wickliffe. Appendix, vol. i. p. 434.
2 Fuller's Church Hist. cent. xiv. p. 137.
3 Walsingham, Hist. Angliæ Major, p. 203.
4 Propono et volo esse ex integro Christianus, et quamdiu manserit in me halitus, profitens verbo et opere legem Christi. Vaughan's Wickliffe, i. p. 426.

1 Fell furiously on the lords. Fuller, Church Hist. cent. xiv. p. 134.

try, preaching the legends of saints and the history of the Trojan war, we must do for God's glory what they do to fill their wallets, and form a vast itinerant evangelization to convert souls to Jesus Christ. Turning to the most pious of his disciples, he said to them : "Go and preach, it is the sublimest work ; but imitate not the priests whom we see after the sermon sitting in the ale-houses, or at the gaming-table, or wasting their time in hunting. After your sermon is ended, do you visit the sick, the aged, the poor, the blind, and the lame, and succour them according to your ability." Such was the new practical theology which Wickliffe inaugurated—it was that of Christ himself.

The "poor priests," as they were called, set off barefoot, a staff in their hands, clothed in a coarse robe, living on alms, and satisfied with the plainest food. They stopped in the fields near some village, in the churchyards, in the market-places of the towns, and sometimes in the churches even.[1] The people, among whom they were favourites, thronged around them, as the men of Northumbria had done at Aidan's preaching. They spoke with a popular eloquence that entirely won over those who listened to them. Of these missionaries none was more beloved than John Ashton. He might be seen wandering over the country in every direction, or seated at some cottage hearth, or alone in some retired crossway, preaching to an attentive crowd. Missions of this kind have been constantly revived in England at the great epochs of the church.

The "poor priests" were not content with mere polemics : they preached the great mystery of godliness. "An angel could have made no propitiation for man," one day exclaimed their master Wickliffe ; "for the nature which has sinned is not that of the angels. The mediator must needs be a man ; but every man being indebted to God for every thing that he is able to do, this man must needs have infinite merit, and be at the same time God." [2]

The clergy became alarmed, and a law was passed commanding every king's officer to commit the preachers and their followers to prison.[3] In consequence of this, as soon as the humble missionary began to preach, the monks set themselves in motion. They watched him from the windows of their cells, at the street corners, or from behind a hedge, and then hastened off to procure assistance. But when the constables approached, a body of stout bold men stood forth, with arms in their hands, who surrounded the preacher, and zealously protected him against the attacks of the clergy. Carnal weapons were thus mingled with the preachings of the word of peace. The poor priests returned to their master : Wickliffe comforted them, advised with them, and then they departed

once more. Every day this evangelization reached some new spot, and the light was thus penetrating into every quarter of England, when the reformer was suddenly stopped in his work.

Wickliffe was at Oxford in the year 1379, busied in the discharge of his duties as professor of divinity, when he fell dangerously ill. His was not a strong constitution ; and work, age, and above all persecution, had weakened him. Great was the joy in the monasteries ; but for that joy to be complete, the *heretic* must recant. Every effort was made to bring this about in his last moments.

The four regents, who represented the four religious orders, accompanied by four aldermen, hastened to the bedside of the dying man, hoping to frighten him by threatening him with the vengeance of Heaven. They found him calm and serene. "You have death on your lips," said they ; "be touched by your faults, and retract in our presence all that you have said to our injury." Wickliffe remained silent, and the monks flattered themselves with an easy victory. But the nearer the reformer approached eternity, the greater was his horror of monkery. The consolation he had found in Jesus Christ had given him fresh energy. He begged his servant to raise him on his couch. Then feeble and pale, and scarcely able to support himself, he turned towards the friars, who were waiting for his recantation, and opening his livid lips, and fixing on them a piercing look, he said with emphasis : "I shall not die but live ; and again declared the evil deeds of the friars." We might almost picture to ourselves the spirit of Elijah threatening the priests of Baal. The regents and their companions looked at each other with astonishment. They left the room in confusion, and the reformer recovered to put the finishing touch to the most important of his works against the monks and against the pope.[1]

CHAPTER VIII.

The Bible—Wickliffe's Translation—Effects of its Publication—Opposition of the Clergy—Wickliffe's Fourth Phasis—Transubstantiation—Excommunication—Wickliffe's Firmness—Wat Tyler—The Synod—The Condemned Propositions—Wickliffe's Petition—Wickliffe before the Primate at Oxford—Wickliffe summoned to Rome—His Answer—The Trialogue—His Death—And Character—His Teaching—His Ecclesiastical Views—A Prophecy.

WICKLIFFE's ministry had followed a progressive course. At first he had attacked the papacy ; next he preached the gospel to the poor ; he could take one more step and put the people in permanent possession of the word of God. This was the third phase of his activity.

---

[1] A private statute made by the clergy. Fox, Acts, i. 503.
[2] Exposition of the Decalogue.
[3] Fox, Acts, i. p. 503.

[1] Petrie's Church History, i. p. 504.

Scholasticism had banished the Scriptures into a mysterious obscurity. It is true that Bede had translated the Gospel of St John; that the learned men at Alfred's court had translated the four evangelists: that Elfric in the reign of Ethelred had translated some books of the Old Testament; that an Anglo-Norman priest had paraphrased the Gospels and the Acts; that Richard Rolle, "the hermit of Hampole," and some pious clerks in the fourteenth century, had produced a version of the Psalms, the Gospels, and Epistles :—but these rare volumes were hidden, like theological curiosities, in the libraries of a few convents. It was then a maxim that the reading of the Bible was injurious to the laity; and accordingly the priests forbade it, just as the Brahmins forbid the Shasters to the Hindoos. Oral tradition alone preserved among the people the histories of the Holy Scriptures, mingled with legends of the saints. The time appeared ripe for the publication of a Bible. The increase of population, the attention the English were beginning to devote to their own language, the development which the system of representative government had received, the awakening of the human mind :—all these circumstances favoured the reformer's design.

Wickliffe was ignorant indeed of Greek and Hebrew; but was it nothing to shake off the dust which for ages had covered the Latin Bible, and to translate it into English? He was a good Latin scholar, of sound understanding and great penetration; but above all he loved the Bible, he understood it, and desired to communicate this treasure to others. Let us imagine him in his quiet study: on his table is the Vulgate text, corrected after the best manuscripts; and lying open around him are the commentaries of the doctors of the church, especially those of St Jerome and Nicholas Lyrensis. Between ten and fifteen years he steadily prosecuted his task; learned men aided him with their advice, and one of them, Nicholas Hereford, appears to have translated a few chapters for him. At last in 1380 it was completed. This was a great event in the religious history of England, who, outstripping the nations on the continent, took her station in the foremost rank in the great work of disseminating the Scriptures.

As soon as the translation was finished, the labour of the copyists began, and the Bible was erelong widely circulated either wholly or in portions. The reception of the work surpassed Wickliffe's expectations. The Holy Scriptures exercised a reviving influence over men's hearts; minds were enlightened; souls were converted; the voices of the "poor priests" had done little in comparison with this voice; something new had entered into the world. Citizens, soldiers, and the lower classes welcomed this new era with acclamations; the high-born curiously examined the unknown book; and

even Anne of Luxemburg, wife of Richard II., having learnt English, began to read the Gospels diligently. She did more than this: she made them known to Arundel, archbishop of York and chancellor, and afterwards a persecutor, but who now, struck at the sight of a foreign lady—of a queen, humbly devoting her leisure to the study of *such virtuous books*,[1] commenced reading them himself, and rebuked the prelates who neglected this holy pursuit. "You could not meet two persons on the highway," says a contemporary writer, "but one of them was Wickliffe's disciple."

Yet all in England did not equally rejoice: the lower clergy opposed this enthusiasm with complaints and maledictions. "Master John Wickliffe, by translating the gospel into English," said the monks, "has rendered it more acceptable and more intelligible to laymen and even to women, than it had hitherto been to learned and intelligent clerks !......The gospel pearl is everywhere cast out and trodden under foot of swine." [2] New contests arose for the reformer. Wherever he bent his steps, he was violently attacked. "It is heresy," cried the monks, "to speak of Holy Scripture in English." [3] —" Since the church has approved of the four Gospels, she would have been just as able to reject them and admit others ! The church sanctions and condemns what she pleases...... Learn to believe in the church rather than in the gospel." These clamours did not alarm Wickliffe. "Many nations have had the Bible in their own language. The Bible is the faith of the church. Though the pope and all his clerks should disappear from the face of the earth," said he, " our faith would not fail, for it is founded on Jesus alone, our Master and our God." But Wickliffe did not stand alone: in the palace as in the cottage, and even in parliament, the rights of Holy Scripture found defenders. A motion having been made in the Upper House (1390) to seize all the copies of the Bible, the Duke of Lancaster exclaimed: "Are we then the very dregs of humanity, that we cannot possess the laws of our religion in our own tongue ?" [4]

Having given his fellow-countrymen the Bible, Wickliffe began to reflect on its contents. This was a new step in his onward path. There comes a moment when the Christian, saved by a lively faith, feels the need of giving an account to himself of this faith, and this originates the science of theology. This is a natural movement: if the child, who at first possesses sensations and affections only, feels the want, as he grows up, of reflection and knowledge, why should it not be the same with the Christian? Politics—home missions—Holy Scripture—had

[1] Fox, Acts, i. p. 578.
[2] Evangelica margarita spargitur et a porcis conculcatur. Knyghton, De eventibus Angliæ, p. 264.
[3] It is heresy to speak of the Holy Scripture in English Wickliffe's Wicket, p. 4. Oxford. 1612, quarto.
[4] Weber, Akatholische Kirchen, i. p. 81.

engaged Wickliffe in succession; theology had its turn, and this was the fourth phase of his life. Yet he did not penetrate to the same degree as the men of the sixteenth century into the depths of the Christian doctrine; and he attached himself in a more especial manner to those ecclesiastical dogmas which were more closely connected with the presumptuous hierarchy and the simoniacal gains of Rome,—such as transubstantiation. The Anglo-Saxon church had not professed this doctrine. "The host is the body of Christ, not bodily but spiritually," said Elfric in the tenth century in a letter addressed to the archbishop of York; but Lanfranc, the opponent of Berengarius, had taught England that at the word of a priest God quitted heaven and descended on the altar. Wickliffe undertook to overthrow the pedestal on which the pride of the priesthood was founded. "The eucharist is naturally bread and wine," he taught at Oxford in 1381; "but by virtue of the sacramental words it contains in every part the real body and blood of Christ." He did not stop here. "The consecrated wafer which we see on the altar," said he, "is not Christ, nor any part of him, but his efficient sign."[1] He oscillated between these two shades of doctrine; but to the first he more habitually attached himself. He denied the sacrifice of the mass offered by the priest, because it was substituted for the sacrifice of the cross offered up by Jesus Christ; and rejected transubstantiation, because it nullified the spiritual and living presence of the Lord.

When Wickliffe's enemies heard these propositions, they appeared horror-stricken, and yet in secret they were delighted at the prospect of destroying him. They met together, examined twelve theses he had published, and pronounced against him suspension from all teaching, imprisonment, and the greater excommunication. At the same time his friends became alarmed, their zeal cooled, and many of them forsook him. The Duke of Lancaster, in particular, could not follow him into this new sphere. That prince had no objection to an ecclesiastical opposition which might aid the political power, and for that purpose he had tried to enlist the reformer's talents and courage; but he feared a dogmatic opposition that might compromise him. The sky was heavy with clouds; Wickliffe was alone.

The storm soon burst upon him. One day, while seated in his doctoral chair in the Augustine school, and calmly explaining the nature of the eucharist, an officer entered the hall, and read the sentence of condemnation. It was the design of his enemies to humble the professor in the eyes of his disciples. Lancaster immediately became alarmed, and hastening to his old friend begged him—ordered him even—to trouble himself no more

about this matter. Attacked on every side, Wickliffe for a time remained silent Shall he sacrifice the truth to save his reputation—his repose—perhaps his life? Shall expediency get the better of faith,—Lancaster prevail over Wickliffe? No: his courage was invincible. "Since the year of our Lord 1000," said he, "all the doctors have been in error about the sacrament of the altar—except, perhaps, it may be Berengarius. How canst thou, O priest, who art but a man, make thy Maker? What! the thing that groweth in the fields—that ear which thou pluckest to-day, shall be God to-morrow! ....As you cannot make the works which he made, how shall ye make Him who made the works?[1] Woe to the adulterous generation that believeth the testimony of Innocent rather than of the Gospel."[2] Wickliffe called upon his adversaries to refute the opinions they had condemned, and finding that they threatened him with a civil penalty (imprisonment), he appealed to the king.

The time was not favourable for such an appeal. A fatal circumstance increased Wickliffe's danger. Wat Tyler and a dissolute priest named Ball, taking advantage of the ill-will excited by the rapacity and brutality of the royal tax-gatherers, had occupied London with 100,000 men. John Ball kept up the spirits of the insurgents, not by expositions of the gospel, like Wickliffe's *poor priests*, but by fiery comments on the distich they had chosen for their device:—

When Adam delved and Eve span,
Who was then the gentleman?

There were many who felt no scruple in ascribing these disorders to the reformer, who was quite innocent of them; and Courtenay, bishop of London, having been translated to the see of Canterbury, lost no time in convoking a synod to pronounce on this matter of Wickliffe's. They met in the middle of May, about two o'clock in the afternoon, and were proceeding to pronounce sentence when an an earthquake, which shook the city of London and all Britain, so alarmed the members of the council that they unanimously demanded the adjournment of a decision which appeared so manifestly rebuked by God. But the archbishop skilfully turned this strange phenomenon to his own purposes: "Know you not," said he, "that the noxious vapours which catch fire in the bosom of the earth, and give rise to these phenomena which alarm you, lose all their force when they burst forth? Well, in like manner, by rejecting the wicked from our community, we shall put an end to the convulsions of the church." The bishops regained their courage; and one of the primate's officers read ten propositions, said to be Wickliffe's, but

[1] Efficax ejus signum. Conclusio 1ma. Vaughan, ii. p. 436, App.

[1] Wycleff's Wyckett, Tracts. pp. 276, 279.
[2] Væ generationi-adulteræ quæ plus credit testimonio Innocentii quam sensui Evangelii. Confessio, Vaughan, ii. 453, App.

ascribing to him certain errors of which he was quite innocent. The following most excited the anger of the priests: "God must obey the devil.[1] After Urban VI. we must receive no one as pope, but live according to the manner of the *Greeks*." The ten propositions were condemned as heretical, and the archbishop enjoined all persons to shun, as they would a venomous serpent, all who should preach the aforesaid errors. "If we permit this heretic to appeal continually to the passions of the people," said the primate to the king, "our destruction is inevitable. We must silence these *lollards*—these psalm-singers."[2] The king gave authority "to confine in the prisons of the state any who should maintain the condemned propositions."

Day by day the circle contracted around Wickliffe. The prudent Repingdon, the learned Hereford, and even the eloquent Ashton, the firmest of the three, departed from him. The veteran champion of the truth which had once gathered a whole nation round it, had reached the days when "strong men shall bow themselves," and now, when harassed by persecution, he found himself alone. But boldly he uplifted his hoary head and exclaimed: "The doctrine of the gospel shall never perish; and if the earth once quaked, it was because they condemned Jesus Christ."

He did not stop here. In proportion as his physical strength decreased, his moral strength increased. Instead of parrying the blows aimed at him, he resolved on dealing more terrible ones still. He knew that if the king and the nobility were for the priests, the lower house and the citizens were for liberty and truth. He therefore presented a bold petition to the Commons in the month of November 1382. "Since Jesus Christ shed his blood to free his church, I demand its freedom. I demand that every one may leave those gloomy walls [the convents], within which a tyrannical law prevails, and embrace a simple and peaceful life under the open vault of heaven. I demand that the poor inhabitants of our towns and villages be not constrained to furnish a worldly priest, often a vicious man and a heretic, with the means of satisfying his ostentation, his gluttony, and his licentiousness—of buying a showy horse, costly saddles, bridles with tinkling bells, rich garments, and soft furs, while they see their wives, children, and neighbours, dying of hunger."[3] The House of Commons, recollecting that they had not given their consent to the persecuting statute drawn up by the clergy and approved by the king and the lords, demanded its repeal. Was the Reformation about to begin by the will of the people?

Courtenay, indignant at this intervention of the Commons, and ever stimulated by a zeal for his church, which would have been better directed towards the word of God, visited Oxford in November 1382, and having gathered round him a number of bishops, doctors, priests, students, and laymen, summoned Wickliffe before him. Forty years ago the reformer had come up to the university: Oxford had become his home......and now it was turning against him! Weakened by labours, by trials, by that ardent soul which preyed upon his feeble body, he might have refused to appear. But Wickliffe, who never feared the face of man, came before them with a good conscience. We may conjecture that there were among the crowd some disciples who felt their hearts burn at the sight of their master; but no outward sign indicated their emotion. The solemn silence of a court of justice had succeeded the shouts of enthusiastic youths. Yet Wickliffe did not despair: he raised his venerable head, and turned to Courtenay with that confident look which had made the regents of Oxford shrink away. Growing wroth against the *priests of Baal*, he reproached them with disseminating error in order to sell their masses. Then he stopped, and uttered these simple and energetic words: "The truth shall prevail!"[1] Having thus spoken he prepared to leave the court: his enemies dared not say a word; and, like his divine master at Nazareth, he passed through the midst of them, and no man ventured to stop him. He then withdrew to his cure at Lutterworth.

He had not yet reached the harbour. He was living peacefully among his books and his parishioners, and the priests seemed inclined to leave him alone, when another blow was aimed at him. A papal brief summoned him to Rome, to appear before that tribunal which had so often shed the blood of its adversaries. His bodily infirmities convinced him that he could not obey this summons. But if Wickliffe refused to hear Urban, Urban could not choose but hear Wickliffe. The church was at that time divided between two chiefs: France, Scotland, Savoy, Lorraine, Castile, and Arragon acknowledged Clement VII.; while Italy, England, Germany, Sweden, Poland, and Hungary acknowledged Urban VI. Wickliffe shall tell us who is the true head of the church universal. And while the two popes were excommunicating and abusing each other, and selling heaven and earth for their own gain, the reformer was confessing that incorruptible Word, which establishes real unity in the church. "I believe," said he, "that the gospel of Christ is the whole body of God's law. I believe that Christ, who gave it to us, is very God and very man, and that this gospel re-

---

[1] Quod Deus debet obedire diabolo. Mansi. xxvi. p. 695. Wickliffe denied having written or spoken the sentiment here ascribed to him.
[2] From *lollen*, to sing; as *beggards* (beggars) from *beggen*.
[3] A complaint of John Wycleff. Tracts and Treatises edited by the Wickliffe Society, p. 268.

[1] Finaliter veritas vincet eos. Vaughan, Appendix, ii. p. 453.

velation is, accordingly, superior to all other parts of Holy Scripture.[1] I believe that the bishop of Rome is bound more than all other men to submit to it, for the greatness among Christ's disciples did not consist in worldly dignity or honours, but in the exact following of Christ in his life and manners. No faithful man ought to follow the pope, but in such points as he hath followed Jesus Christ. The pope ought to leave unto the secular power all temporal dominion and rule; and thereunto effectually more and more exhort his whole clergy......If I could labour according to my desire in mine own person, I would surely present myself before the bishop of Rome, but the Lord hath otherwise visited me to the contrary, and hath taught me rather to obey God than men." [2]

Urban, who at that moment chanced to be very busied in his contest with Clement, did not think it prudent to begin another with Wickliffe, and so let the matter rest there.

From this time the doctor passed the remainder of his days in peace in the company of three personages, two of whom were his particular friends, and the third his constant adversary: these were *Aletheia, Phronesis,* and *Pseudes. 'Aletheia* (truth) proposed questions; *Pseudes* (falsehood) urged objections; and *Phronesis* (understanding) laid down the sound doctrine. These three characters carried on a conversation (*trialogue*) in which great truths were boldly professed. The opposition between the pope and Christ—between the canons of Romanism and the Bible—was painted in striking colours. This is one of the primary truths which the church must never forget. "The church has fallen," said one of the interlocutors in the work in question, "because she has abandoned the gospel, and preferred the laws of the pope. Although there should be a hundred popes in the world at once, and all the friars living should be transformed into cardinals, we must withhold our confidence unless so far as they are founded in Holy Scripture." [3]

These words were the last flicker of the torch. Wickliffe looked upon his end as near, and entertained no idea that it would come in peace. A dungeon on one of the seven hills, or a burning pile in London, was all he expected. "Why do you talk of seeking the crown of martyrdom afar?" asked he. "Preach the gospel of Christ to haughty prelates, and martyrdom will not fail you. What! I should live and be silent?.........never! Let the blow fall, I await its coming." [4]

The stroke was spared him. The war between two wicked priests, Urban and Clement, left the disciples of our Lord in peace. And besides, was it worth while cutting short a life that was drawing to a close? Wickliffe, therefore, continued tranquilly to preach Jesus Christ; and on the 29th December 1384, as he was in his church at Lutterworth, in the midst of his flock, at the very moment that he stood before the altar, and was elevating the host with trembling hands, he fell upon the pavement struck with paralysis. He was carried to his house by the affectionate friends around him, and after lingering forty-eight hours resigned his soul to God on the last day of the year.

Thus was removed from the church one of the boldest witnesses to the truth. The seriousness of his language, the holiness of his life, and the energy of his faith, had intimidated the popedom. Travellers relate that if a lion is met in the desert, it is sufficient to look steadily at him, and the beast turns away roaring from the eye of man. Wickliffe had fixed the eye of a Christian on the papacy, and the affrighted papacy had left him in peace. Hunted down unceasingly while living, he died in quiet, at the very moment when by faith he was eating the flesh and drinking the blood which give eternal life. A glorious end to a glorious life.

The Reformation of England had begun.

Wickliffe is the greatest English reformer: he was in truth the first reformer of Christendom, and to him, under God, Britain is indebted for the honour of being the foremost in the attack upon the theocratic system of Gregory VII. The work of the Waldenses, excellent as it was, cannot be compared to his. If Luther and Calvin are the fathers of the Reformation, Wickliffe is its grandfather.

Wickliffe, like most great men, possessed qualities which are not generally found together. While his understanding was eminently speculative—his treatise on the *Reality of universal Ideas* [1] made a sensation in philosophy—he possessed that practical and active mind which characterizes the Anglo-Saxon race. As a divine, he was at once scriptural and spiritual, soundly orthodox, and possessed of an inward and lively faith. With a boldness that impelled him to rush into the midst of danger, he combined a logical and consistent mind, which constantly led him forward in knowledge, and caused him to maintain with perseverance the truths he had once proclaimed. First of all, as a Christian, he had devoted his strength to the cause of the church; but he was at the same time a citizen, and the realm, his nation, and his king, had also a great share in his unwearied activity. He was a man complete.

---

[1] This is the reading of the Bodleian manuscript—" and be [by] this it passes all other laws." In Fox, Wickliffe appears to ascribe to Christ himself this superiority over all Scripture,—a distinction hardly in the mind of the reformer or of his age.
[2] An Epistle of J. Wickliffe to Pope Urban VI. Fox, Acts, i. p. 5u7, fol. Lond. 1684; also Lewis, Wickliffe, p. 333, Append.
[3] Ideo si essent centum papæ, et omnes fratres essent versi in cardinales, non deberet concedi sententiæ suæ in materia fidei, nisi de quanto se fundaverint in Scriptura, Trialogus. lib. iv. cap. vii.
[4] Vaughan's Life of Wickliffe, ii. p. 215, 257.

[1] De universalibus realibus.

If the man is admirable, his teaching is no less so. Scripture, which is the rule of truth, should be (according to his views) the rule of Reformation, and we must reject every doctrine and every precept which does not rest on that foundation.[1] To believe in the power of man in the work of regeneration is the great heresy of Rome, and from that error has come the ruin of the church. Conversion proceeds from the grace of God alone, and the system which ascribes it partly to man and partly to God is worse than Pelagianism.[2] Christ is everything in Christianity; whosoever abandons that fountain which is ever ready to impart life, and turns to muddy and stagnant waters, is a madman.[3] Faith is a gift of God; it puts aside all merit, and should banish all fear from the mind.[4] The one thing needful in the Christian life and in the Lord's Supper is not a vain formalism and superstitious rites, but communion with Christ according to the power of the spiritual life.[5] Let Christians submit not to the word of a priest but to the word of God. In the primitive church there were but two orders, the deacon and the priest: the presbyter and the bishop were one.[6] The sublimest calling which man can attain on earth is that of preaching the word of God. The true church is the assembly of the righteous for whom Christ shed his blood. So long as Christ is in heaven, in Him the church possesses the best pope. It is possible for a pope to be condemned at the last day because of his sins. Would men compel us to recognise as our head "a devil of hell?"[7] Such were the essential points of Wickliffe's doctrine. It was the echo of the doctrine of the apostles —the prelude to that of the reformers.

In many respects Wickliffe is the Luther of England; but the times of revival had not yet come, and the English reformer could not gain such striking victories over Rome as the German reformer. While Luther was surrounded by an ever-increasing number of scholars and princes, who confessed the same faith as himself, Wickliffe shone almost alone in the firmament of the church. The boldness with which he substituted a living spirituality for a superstitious formalism, caused those to shrink back in affright who had gone with him against friars, priests, and popes. Erelong the Roman pontiff ordered him to be thrown into prison, and the monks threatened his life;[1] but God protected him, and he remained calm amidst the machinations of his adversaries. "Antichrist," said he, "can only kill the body." Having one foot in the grave already, he foretold that, from the very bosom of monkery, would some day proceed the regeneration of the church. "If the friars, whom God condescends to teach, shall be converted to the primitive religion of Christ," said he, "we shall see them abandoning their unbelief, returning freely, with or without the permission of Antichrist, to the primitive religion of the Lord, and building up the church, as did St Paul."[2]

Thus did Wickliffe's piercing glance discover, at the distance of nearly a century and a half, the young monk Luther in the Augustine convent at Erfurth, converted by the Epistle to the Romans, and returning to the spirit of St Paul and the religion of Jesus Christ. Time was hastening on to the fulfilment of this prophecy. "The rising sun of the Reformation," for so has Wickliffe been called, had appeared above the horizon, and its beams were no more to be extinguished. In vain will thick clouds veil it at times; the distant hill-tops of Eastern Europe will soon reflect its rays;[3] and its piercing light, increasing in brightness, will pour over all the world, at the hour of the church's renovation, floods of knowledge and of life.

CHAPTER IX.

The Wickliffites—Call for Reform—Richard II.—The first Martyr—Lord Cobham—Appears before Henry V.—Before the Archbishop—His Confession and Death—The Lollards.

Wickliffe's death manifested the power of his teaching. The master being removed, his disciples set their hands to the plough, and England was almost won over to the reformer's doctrines. The Wickliffites recognised a ministry independent of Rome, and deriving authority from the word of God alone. "Every minister," said they, "can administer the sacraments and confer the cure of souls as well as the pope." To the licentious wealth of the clergy they opposed a Christian poverty, and to the degenerate asceticism of the mendicant orders, a spiritual and free life. The townsfolk crowded around these humble preachers; the soldiers listened to them, armed with sword and buckler to defend them;[4] the nobility took down the

---

[1] Auctoritas Scripturæ sacræ, quæ est lex Christi, infinitum excedit quam libet scripturam aliam. Dialog. [Trialogus] lib. iii. cap. xxx.; see in particular, chap. xxxi.
[2] Ibid. de prædestinatione, de peccato, de gratia, &c.
[3] Ibid. lib. iii. cap. xxx.
[4] Fidem a Deo infusam sine aliqua trepidatione fidei contraria. Ibid. lib. iii. cap. ii.
[5] Secundum rationem spiritualis et virtualis existentiæ. Ibid. lib. iv. cap. viii.
[6] Fuit idem presbyter atque episcopus. Ibid. lib. iv. cap. xv.
[7] Vaughan's Life of Wickliffe, ii. 307. The Christian public is much indebted to Dr Vaughan for his biography of this reformer.

[1] Multitudo fratrum mortem tuam multipliciter machinantur. Dialog. lib. iv. cap. iv.
[2] Aliqui fratres quos Deus docere dignatur....relicta sua perfidia....redibunt libere ad religionem Christi primævam, et tunc ædificabunt ecclesiam, sicut Paulus. Ibid. lib. iv. cap. xxx.
[3] John Huss in Bohemia.
[4] Assistere solent gladio et pelta stipati ad eorum defensionem. Knyghton, lib. v. p. 2660.

images from their baronial chapels;[1] and even the royal family was partly won over to the Reformation. England was like a tree cut down to the ground, from whose roots fresh buds are shooting out on every side, erelong to cover all the earth beneath their shade.[2]

This augmented the courage of Wickliffe's disciples, and in many places the people took the initiative in the reform. The walls of St Paul's, and other cathedrals were hung with placards aimed at the priests and friars, and the abuses of which they were the defenders; and in 1395 the friends of the Gospel petitioned parliament for a general reform. "The essence of the worship which comes from Rome," said they, "consists in signs and ceremonies, and not in the efficacity of the Holy Ghost: and therefore it is not that which Christ has ordained. Temporal things are distinct from spiritual things : a king and a bishop ought not to be one and the same person."[3] And then, from not clearly understanding the principle of the separation of the functions which they proclaimed, they called upon parliament to "abolish celibacy, transubstantiation, prayers for the dead, offerings to images, auricular confession, war, the arts unnecessary to life, the practice of blessing oil, salt, wax, incense, stones, mitres, and pilgrims' staffs. All these pertain to necromancy and not to theology." Emboldened by the absence of the king in Ireland, they fixed their *Twelve Conclusions* on the gates of St Paul's and Westminster Abbey. This became the signal for persecution.

As soon as Arundel, archbishop of York, and Braybrooke, bishop of London, had read these propositions, they hastily crossed St George's channel, and conjured the king to return to England. The prince hesitated not to comply, for his wife, the pious Anne of Luxemburg, was dead. Richard, during childhood and youth, had been committed in succession to the charge of several guardians, and like children (says an historian), whose nurses have been often changed, he thrived none the better for it. He did good or evil, according to the influence of those around him, and had no decided inclinations except for ostentation and licentiousness. The clergy were not mistaken in calculating on such a prince. On his return to London he forbade the parliament to take the Wickliffite petition into consideration; and having summoned before him the most distinguished of its supporters, such as Story, Clifford, Latimer, and Montacute, he threatened them with death if they continued to defend their abominable opinions. Thus was the work of the reformer about to be destroyed.

But Richard had hardly withdrawn his hand from the gospel, when God (says the annalist) withdrew his hand from him.[1] His cousin, Henry of Hereford, son of the famous Duke of Lancaster, and who had been banished from England, suddenly sailed from the continent, landed in Yorkshire, gathered all the malcontents around him, and was acknowledged king. The unhappy Richard, after being formally deposed, was confined in Pontefract castle, where he soon terminated his earthly career.

The son of Wickliffe's old defender was now king : a reform of the church seemed imminent; but the primate Arundel had foreseen the danger. This cunning priest and skilful politician had observed which way the wind blew, and deserted Richard in good time. Taking Lancaster by the hand, he put the crown on his head, saying to him : "To consolidate your throne, conciliate the clergy, and sacrifice the Lollards."—"I will be the protector of the church," replied Henry IV., and from that hour the power of the priests was greater than the power of the nobility. Rome has ever been adroit in profiting by revolutions.

Lancaster, in his eagerness to show his gratitude to the priests, ordered that every incorrigible heretic should be burnt alive, to terrify his companions.[2] Practice followed close upon the theory. A pious priest named William Sawtre had presumed to say : "Instead of adoring the cross on which Christ suffered, I adore Christ who suffered on it."[3] He was dragged to St Paul's ; his hair was shaved off; a layman's cap was placed on his head; and the primate handed him over to the *mercy* of the earl-marshal of England. This *mercy* was shown him—he was burnt alive at Smithfield in the beginning of March 1401. Sawtre was the first martyr to protestantism.

Encouraged by this act of faith—this *auto da fé*—the clergy drew up the articles known as the "Constitutions of Arundel," which forbade the reading of the Bible, and styled the pope, "not a mere man, but a true God."[4] The Lollards' tower, in the archiepiscopal palace of Lambeth, was soon filled with pretended heretics, many of whom carved on the walls of their dungeons the expression of their sorrow and their hopes : *Jesus amor meus*, wrote one of them.[5]

To crush the lowly was not enough : the gospel must be driven from the more exalted stations. The priests, who were sincere in their belief, regarded those noblemen as misleaders, who set the word of God above the laws of Rome ; and accordingly they girded themselves for the work. A few miles from Rochester stood Cowling Castle, in the midst

[1] Milites cum ducibus et comitibus erant præcipue eis adhærentes. Knyghton, lib. v, p. 2660.
[2] Quasi germinantes multiplicati sunt nimis et implevirunt ubique orbem regni. Ibid. These "*Conclusiones*" are reprinted by Lewis (Wickliffe). p. 337.
[3] Rex et episcopus in una persona, &c. Ibid.

[1] Fox, Acts, i. p. 584, fol. Lond. 1684.
[2] Ibid. p. 586. This is the statute known as 2 Henry IV. c. 15, the first actual law in England against heresy.
[3] Ibid. p. 589.
[4] Not of pure man but of true God, here in earth. Ibid. p. 596.
[5] "Jesus is my love." These words are still to be read in the tower.

of the fertile pastures watered by the Med-way,

> The fair Medways that with wanton pride
> Forms silver mazes with her crooked tide.[1]

In the beginning of the fifteenth century it was inhabited by Sir John Oldcastle, Lord Cobham, a man in high favour with the king. The "poor priests" thronged to Cowling in quest of Wickliffe's writings, of which Cobham had caused numerous copies to be made, and whence they were circulated through the dioceses of Canterbury, Rochester, London, and Hertford. Cobham attended their preaching, and if any enemies ventured to interrupt them, he threatened them with his sword.[2] "I would sooner risk my life," said he, "than submit to such unjust decrees as dishonour the everlasting Testament." The king would not permit the clergy to lay hands on his favourite.

But Henry V. having succeeded his father in 1413, and passed from the house of ill-fame he had hitherto frequented, to the foot of the altars and the head of the armies, the archbishop immediately denounced Cobham to him, and he was summoned to appear before the king. Sir John had understood Wickliffe's doctrine, and experienced in his own person the might of the divine Word. "As touching the pope and his spirituality," he said to the king, "I owe them neither suit nor service, forasmuch as I know him by the Scriptures to be the great antichrist."[3] Henry thrust aside Cobham's hand as he presented his confession of faith: "I will not receive this paper, lay it before your judges." When he saw his profession refused, Cobham had recourse to the only arm which he knew of out of the gospel. The differences which we now settle by pamphlets were then very commonly settled by the sword:—"I offer in defence of my faith to fight for life or death with any man living, Christian or pagan, always excepting your majesty."[4] Cobham was led to the Tower.

On the 23d September 1413, he was taken before the ecclesiastical tribunal then sitting at St Paul's. "We must believe," said the primate to him, "what the holy church of Rome teaches, without demanding Christ's authority."—"Believe!" shouted the priests, "believe!"—"I am willing to believe all that God desires," said Sir John; "but that the pope should have authority to teach what is contrary to Scripture—that I can never believe." He was led back to the Tower. The word of God was to have its martyr.

On Monday, 25th September, a crowd of priests, canons, friars, clerks, and indulgence-sellers, thronged the large hall of the Dominican convent, and attacked Lord Cobham

with abusive language. These insults, the importance of the moment for the Reformation of England, the catastrophe that must needs close the scene: all agitated his soul to its very depths. When the archbishop called upon him to confess his offence, he fell on his knees, and lifting up his hands to heaven, exclaimed: "I confess to Thee, O God! and acknowledge that in my frail youth I seriously offended Thee by my pride, anger, intemperance, and impurity: for these offences I implore thy mercy!" Then standing up, his face still wet with tears, he said: "I ask not your absolution: it is God's only that I need."[1] The clergy did not despair, however, of reducing this high-spirited gentleman: they knew that spiritual strength is not always conjoined with bodily vigour, and they hoped to vanquish by priestly sophisms the man who dared challenge the papal champions to single combat. "Sir John," said the primate at last, "you have said some very strange things; we have spent much time in endeavours to convince you, but all to no effect. The day passeth away: you must either submit yourself to the ordinance of the most holy church......" "I will none otherwise believe than what I have told you. Do with me what you will." —"Well then, we must needs do the law," the archbishop made answer.

Arundel stood up; all the priests and people rose with him and uncovered their heads. Then holding the sentence of death in his hand, he read it with a loud clear voice. "It is well," said Sir John; "though you condemn my body, you can do no harm to my soul, by the grace of my eternal God." He was again led back to the Tower whence he escaped one night, and took refuge in Wales. He was retaken in December 1417, carried to London, dragged on a hurdle to Saint Giles's fields, and there suspended by chains over a slow fire, and cruelly burned to death. Thus died a Christian, illustrious after the fashion of his age—a champion of the Word of God. The London prisons were filled with Wickliffites, and it was decreed that they should be hung on the king's account, and burnt for God's.[2]

The intimidated Lollards were compelled to hide themselves in the humblest ranks of the people, and to hold their meetings in secret. The work of redemption was proceeding noiselessly among the elect of God. Of these Lollards, there were many who had been redeemed by Jesus Christ; but in general they knew not, to the same extent as the evangelical Christians of the sixteenth century, the quickening and justifying power of faith. They were plain, meek, and often timid folks, attracted by the word of God, affected at the condemnation it pronounces

1 Blackmore.
2 Eorum prædicationibus nefariis interfuit, et contradictores, si quos repererat, minis et terroribus et gladii secularis potentia compescuit. Rymer, Fœdera, tom. iv. pars 2, p. 50.
3 Fox, vol. i. p. 636, fol.   4 Ibid. p. 637.

1 Quod nullam absolutionem in hac parte peteret a nobis, sed a solo Deo. Rymer, Fœdera, p. 51.
2 Incendio propter Deum, suspendio propter regem, Thom. Waldensis in proemio. Raynald, ann. 1414. No. 16.

against the errors of Rome, and desirous of living according to its commandments. God had assigned them a part—and an important part too—in the great transformation of Christianity. Their humble piety, their passive resistance, the shameful treatment which they bore with resignation, the penitent's robes with which they were covered, the tapers they were compelled to hold at the church door—all these things betrayed the pride of the priests, and filled the most generous minds with doubts and vague desires. By a baptism of suffering, God was then preparing the way to a glorious reformation.

CHAPTER X.

Learning at Florence—The Tudors—Erasmus visits England—Sir Thomas More—Dean Colet—Erasmus and young Henry—Prince Arthur and Catherine—Marriage and Death—Catherine betrothed to Henry—Accession of Henry VIII.—Enthusiasm of the Learned—Erasmus recalled to England—Cromwell before the Pope—Catherine proposed to Henry—Their Marriage and Court—Tournaments—Henry's Danger.

THIS reformation was to be the result of two distinct forces—the revival of learning and the resurrection of the word of God. The latter was the principal cause, but the former was necessary as a means. Without it the living waters of the gospel would probably have traversed the age, like summer streams which soon dry up, such as those which had burst forth here and there during the middle ages; it would not have become that majestic river, which, by its inundations, fertilized all the earth. It was necessary to discover and examine the original fountains, and for this end the study of Greek and Hebrew was indispensable. Lollardism and humanism (the study of the classics) were the two laboratories of the reform. We have seen the preparations of the one, we must now trace the commencement of the other; and as we have discovered the light in the lowly valleys, we shall discern it also on the lofty mountain tops.

About the end of the fifteenth century, several young Englishmen chanced to be at Florence, attracted thither by the literary glory which environed the city of the Medici. Cosmo had collected together a great number of works of antiquity, and his palace was thronged with learned men. William Selling, a young English ecclesiastic, afterwards distinguished at Canterbury by his zeal in collecting valuable manuscripts; his fellow-countrymen, Grocyn, Lilly, and Latimer " more bashful than a maiden; "[1] and, above all, Linacre, whom Erasmus ranked before all the scholars of Italy,—used to meet in the delicious villa of the Medici with

[1] Pudorem plus quam virgineum. Erasm. Ep. ɪ. p. 525.

Politian, Chalcondyles, and other men of learning; and there, in the calm evenings of summer, under that glorious Tuscan sky, they dreamt romantic visions of the Platonic philosophy. When they returned to England, these learned men laid before the youth of Oxford the marvellous treasures of the Greek language. Some Italians even, attracted by the desire to enlighten the barbarians, and a little, it may be, by the brilliant offers made them, quitted their beloved country for the distant Britain. Cornelius Vitelli taught at Oxford, and Caius Amberino at Cambridge. Caxton imported the art of printing from Germany, and the nation hailed with enthusiasm the brilliant dawn which was breaking at last in their cloudy sky.

While learning was reviving in England, a new dynasty succeeded to the throne, bringing with it that energy of character which of itself was able to effect great revolutions; the Tudors succeeded the Plantagenets. That inflexible intrepidity by which the reformers of Germany, Switzerland, France, and Scotland were distinguished, did not exist so generally in those of England; but it was found in the character of her kings, who often stretched it even to violence. It may be that to this preponderance of energy in its rulers, the church owes the preponderance of the state in its affairs.

Henry Tudor, the Louis XI. of England, was a clever prince, of decided but suspicious character, avaricious and narrow-minded. Being descended from a Welsh family, he belonged to that ancient race of Celts, who had so long contended against the papacy. Henry had extinguished faction at home, and taught foreign nations to respect his power. A good genius seemed to exercise a salutary influence over his court as well as over himself: this was his mother the Countess of Richmond. From her closet, where she consecrated the first five hours of the day to reading, meditation, and prayer, she moved to another part of the palace to dress the wounds of some of the lowest mendicants; thence she passed into the gay saloons, where she would converse with the scholars, whom she encouraged by her munificence. This noble lady's passion for study, of which her son inherited but little, was not without its influence in her family. Arthur and Henry, the king's eldest sons, trembled in their father's presence; but, captivated by the affection of their pious grandmother, they began to find a pleasure in the society of learned men. An important circumstance gave a new impulse to one of them.

Among the countess's friends was Montjoy, who had known Erasmus at Paris, and heard his cutting sarcasms upon the schoolmen and friars. He invited the illustrious Dutchman to England, and Erasmus, who was fearful of catching the plague, gladly accepted the invitation, and set out for what he believed to be the kingdom of darkness.

But he had not been long in England before he discovered unexpected light.

Shortly after his arrival, happening to dine with the lord-mayor, Erasmus noticed on the other side of the table a young man of nineteen, slender, fresh-coloured, with blue eyes, coarse hands, and the right shoulder somewhat higher than the other. His features indicated affability and gaiety, and pleasant jests were continually dropping from his lips. If he could not find a joke in English, he would in French, and even in Latin or Greek. A literary contest soon ensued between Erasmus and the English youth. The former, astonished at meeting with any one that could hold his own against him, exclaimed: *Aut tu es Morus aut nullus!* (you are either More or nobody); and his companion, who had not learnt the stranger's name, quickly replied: *Aut tu es Erasmus aut diabolus!* (you are either the devil or Erasmus).[1] More flung himself into the arms of Erasmus, and they became inseparable friends. More was continually joking, even with women, teasing the young maidens, and making fun of the dull, though without any tinge of ill-nature in his jests.[2] But under this sportive exterior he concealed a deep understanding. He was at that time lecturing on Augustine's *City of God* before a numerous audience composed of priests and aged men. The thought of eternity had seized him: and being ignorant of that internal discipline of the Holy Ghost, which is the only true discipline, he had recourse to the scourge on every Friday. Thomas More is the ideal of the catholicism of this period. He had, like the Romish system, two poles —worldliness and asceticism; which, although contrary, often meet together. In fact, asceticism makes a sacrifice of *self*, only to preserve it; just as a traveller attacked by robbers will readily give up a portion of his treasures to save the rest. This was the case with More, if we rightly understand his character. He sacrificed the accessories of his fallen nature to save that same nature. He submitted to fasts and vigils, wore a shirt of hair-cloth, mortified his body by small chains next his skin—in a word, he immolated everything in order to preserve that *self* which a real regeneration alone can sacrifice.

From London Erasmus went to Oxford, where he met with John Colet, a friend of More's, but older, and of very dissimilar character. Colet, the scion of an ancient family, was a very portly man, of imposing aspect, great fortune, and elegance of manners, to which Erasmus had not been accustomed. Order, cleanliness, and decorum prevailed in his person and in his house. He kept an excellent table, which was open to all the friends of learning, and at which the Dutchman, no great admirer of the colleges of Paris with their sour wine and stale eggs, was glad to take a seat.[1] He there met also most of the classical scholars of England, especially Grocyn, Linacre, Thomas Wolsey, bursar of Magdalene College, Halsey, and some others. "I cannot tell you how I am delighted with your England," he wrote to Lord Montjoy from Oxford. "With such men I could willingly live in the farthest coasts of Scythia."[2]

But if Erasmus on the banks of the Thames found a Mæcenas in Lord Montjoy, a Labeo and perhaps a Virgil in More, he nowhere found an Augustus. One day as he was expressing his regrets and his fears to More, the latter said: "Come, let us go to Eltham, perhaps we shall find there what you are looking for." They set out, More jesting all the way, inwardly resolving to expiate his gaiety by a severe scourging at night. On their arrival they were heartily welcomed by Lord and Lady Montjoy, the governor and governess of the king's children. As the two friends entered the hall, a pleasing and unexpected sight greeted Erasmus. The whole of the family were assembled, and they found themselves surrounded not only by some of the royal household, but by the domestics of Lord Montjoy also. On the right stood the Princess Margaret, a girl of eleven years, whose great-grandson under the name of Stuart was to continue the Tudor line in England; on the left was Mary, a child four years of age; Edmund was in his nurse's arms; and in the middle of the circle, stood a boy, at that time only nine years old, whose handsome features, royal carriage, intelligent eye, and exquisite courtesy, had an extraordinary charm for Erasmus.[3] That boy was Henry, Duke of York, the king's second son, born on the 28th June 1491. More, advancing towards the young prince, presented to him some piece of his own writing; and from that hour Erasmus kept up a friendly intercourse with Henry, which in all probability exercised a certain influence over the destinies of England. The scholar of Rotterdam was delighted to see the prince excel in all the manly sports of the day. He sat his horse with perfect grace and rare intrepidity, could hurl a javelin farther than any of his companions, and having an excellent taste for music, he was already a performer on several instruments. The king took care that he should receive a learned education, for he destined him to fill the see of Canterbury; and the illustrious Erasmus, noticing his aptitude for every thing he undertook, did his best to cut and polish this English diamond that it might glitter with the greater brilliancy. "He will

[1] Life of More by his Great-grandson (1828), p. 93.
[2] Cum mulieribus fere atque etiam cum uxore nonnisi lusus jocosque tractat. Erasm. Ep. i. p. 536.

[1] Quantum ibi devorabatur ovorum putrium, quantum vini putris hauriebatur. Erasm. Colloq. p. 564.
[2] Dici non potest quam mihi dulcescat Anglia tua....vel in extrema Scythia vivere non recusem. Erasm. Ep. i. p. 311.
[3] Erasm. Ep. ad Botzhem. Jortin. Appendix, p. 108.

begin nothing that he will not finish," said the scholar. And it is but too true, that this prince always attained his end, even if it were necessary to tread on the bleeding bodies of those he had loved. Flattered by the attentions of the young Henry, attracted by his winning grace, charmed by his wit, Erasmus on his return to the continent everywhere proclaimed that England at last had found its Octavius.

As for Henry VII. he thought of everything but Virgil or Augustus. Avarice and ambition were his predominant tastes, which he gratified by the marriage of his eldest son in 1501. Burgundy, Artois, Provence, and Brittany having been recently united to France, the European powers felt the necessity of combining against that encroaching state. It was in consequence of this that Ferdinand of Aragon had given his daughter Joanna to Philip of Austria, and that Henry VII. asked the hand of his daughter Catherine, then in her sixteenth year and the richest princess in Europe, for Arthur prince of Wales, a youth about ten months younger. The catholic king made one condition to the marriage of his daughter. Warwick, the last of the Plantagenets and a pretender to the crown, was confined in the Tower. Ferdinand, to secure the certainty that Catherine would really ascend the English throne, required that the unhappy prince should be put to death. Nor did this alone satisfy the king of Spain. Henry VII., who was not a cruel man, might conceal Warwick, and say that he was no more. Ferdinand demanded that the chancellor of Castile should be present at the execution. The blood of Warwick was shed ; his head rolled duly on the scaffold ; the Castilian chancellor verified and registered the murder, and on the 14th November the marriage was solemnized at St Paul's. At midnight the prince and princess were conducted with great pomp to the bridal-chamber.[1] These were ill-omened nuptials—fated to set the kings and nations of Christendom in battle against each other, and to serve as a pretext for the external and political discussions of the English Reformation. The marriage of Catherine the Catholic was a marriage of blood.

In the early part of 1502 Prince Arthur fell ill, and on the 2d of April he died. The necessary time was taken to be sure that Catherine had no hope of becoming a mother, after which the friend of Erasmus, the youthful Henry, was declared heir to the crown, to the great joy of all the learned. This prince did not forsake his studies: he spoke and wrote in French, German, and Spanish with the facility of a native; and England hoped to behold one day the most learned of Christian kings upon the throne of Alfred the Great.

A very different question, however filled the mind of the covetous Henry VII. Must he restore to Spain the two hundred thousand ducats which formed Catherine's dowry? Shall this rich heiress be permitted to marry some rival of England? To prevent so great a misfortune the king conceived the project of uniting Henry to Arthur's widow. The most serious objections were urged against it. "It is not only inconsistent with propriety," said Warham, the primate, "but the will of God himself is against it. It is declared in His law that *if a man shall take his brother's wife, it is an unclean thing*, (Lev. xx. 21); and in the Gospel John Baptist says to Herod: *It is not lawful for thee to have thy brother's wife*," (Mark vi. 18.) Fox, bishop of Winchester, suggested that a dispensation might be procured from the pope, and in December 1503 Julius II. granted a bull declaring that for the sake of preserving union between the catholic princes he authorized Catherine's marriage with the brother of her first husband, *accedente forsan copula carnali*. These four words, it is said, were inserted in the bull at the express desire of the princess. All these details will be of importance in the course of our history. The two parties were betrothed, but not married, in consideration of the youth of the prince of Wales.

The second marriage projected by Henry VII. was ushered in with auspices still less promising than the first. The king having fallen sick and lost his queen, looked upon these visitations as a divine judgment.[1] The nation murmured, and demanded whether it was in the pope's power to permit what God had forbidden.[2] The young prince, being informed of his father's scruples and of the people's discontent, declared, just before attaining his majority (27th June 1505), in the presence of the bishop of Winchester and several royal counsellors, that he protested against the engagement entered into during his minority, and that he would never make Catherine his wife.

His father's death, which made him free, made him also recall this virtuous decision. In 1509, the hopes of the learned seemed about to be realized. On the 9th of May, a hearse decorated with regal pomp, bearing on a rich pall of cloth of gold the mortal remains of Henry VII., with his sceptre and his crown, entered London, followed by a long procession. The great officers of state, assembled round the coffin, broke their staves and cast them into the vault, and the heralds cried with a loud voice: "God send the noble King Henry VIII. long life."[3] Such a cry perhaps had never on any previous occasion been so joyfully repeated by the people. The young king gratified the wishes of the nation by ordering the arrest of Emp-

---

[1] Principes summa nocte ad thalamum solemni ritu deducti sunt. Sanderus, de schismate Angl. p. 2.

[1] Morysin's Apomaxis.
[2] Herbert, Life of Henry VIII. p. 18.
[3] Leland's Collectanea, vol. iv. p. 309.

son and Dudley, who were charged with extortion ; and he conformed to the enlightened counsels of his grandmother, by choosing the most able ministers, and placing the archbishop of Canterbury as lord-chancellor at their head. Warham was a man of great capacity. The day was not too short for him to hear mass, receive ambassadors, consult with the king in the royal closet, entertain as many as two hundred guests at his table, take his seat on the woolsack, and find time for his private devotions. The joy of the learned surpassed that of the people. The old king wanted none of their praises or congratulations, for fear he should have to pay for them ; but now they could give free course to their enthusiasm. Montjoy pronounced the young king "divine ;" the Venetian ambassador likened his port to Apollo's, and his noble chest to the torso of Mars ; he was lauded both in Greek and Latin ; he was hailed as the founder of a new era, and Henry seemed desirous of meriting these eulogiums. Far from permitting himself to be intoxicated by so much adulation, he said to Montjoy : "Ah ! how I should like to be a scholar !"—"Sire," replied the courtier, "it is enough that you show your regard for those who possess the learning you desire for yourself."—"How can I do otherwise," he replied with earnestness ; "without them we hardly exist !" Montjoy immediately communicated this to Erasmus.

Erasmus !—Erasmus !—the walls of Eltham, Oxford, and London resounded with the name. The king could not live without the learned ; nor the learned without Erasmus. This scholar, who was an enthusiast for the young king, was not long in answering to the call. When Richard Pace, one of the most accomplished men of that age, met the learned Dutchman at Ferrara, the latter took from his pocket a little box which he always carried with him : "You don't know," he said, "what a treasure you have in England : I will just show you ;" and he took from the box a letter of Henry's expressing in Latin of considerable purity the tenderest regard for his correspondent.[1] Immediately after the coronation Montjoy wrote to Erasmus : "Our Henry *Octavus*, or rather *Octavius*, is on the throne. Come and behold the new star.[2] The heavens smile, the earth leaps for joy, and all is flowing with milk, nectar, and honey.[3] Avarice has fled away, liberality has descended, scattering on every side with gracious hand her bounteous largesses. Our king desires not gold or precious stones, but virtue, glory, and immortality."

In such glowing terms was the young king described by a man who had seen him closely. Erasmus could resist no longer : he bade the pope farewell, and hastened to London, where he met with a hearty welcome from Henry. Science and power embraced each other : England was about to have its Medici ; and the friends of learning no longer doubted of the regeneration of Britain.

Julius II., who had permitted Erasmus to exchange the white frock of the monks for the black dress of the seculars,[1] allowed him to depart without much regret. This pontiff had little taste for letters, but was fond of war, hunting, and the pleasures of the table. The English sent him a dish to his taste in exchange for the scholar. Sometime after Erasmus had left, as the pope was one day reposing from the fatigues of the chase, he heard voices near him singing a strange song. He asked with surprise what it meant.[2] "It is some Englishmen," was the answer, and three foreigners entered the room, each bearing a closely covered jar, which the youngest presented on his knees. This was Thomas Cromwell, who appears here for the first time on the historic scene. He was the son of a blacksmith of Putney ; but he possessed a mind so penetrating, a judgment so sound, a heart so bold, ability so consummate, such easy elocution, such an accurate memory, such great activity, and so able a pen, that the most brilliant career was foreboded him. At the age of twenty he left England, being desirous to see the world, and began life as a clerk in the English factory at Antwerp. Shortly after this two fellow-countrymen from Boston came to him in their embarrassment. "What do you want?" he asked them. "Our townsmen have sent us to the pope," they told him, "to get the renewal of the *greater* and *lesser pardons*, whose term is nearly run, and which are necessary for the repair of our harbour. But we do not know how to appear before him." Cromwell, prompt to undertake every thing, and knowing a little Italian, replied, "I will go with you." Then slapping his forehead he muttered to himself : "What fish can I throw out as a bait to these greedy cormorants ?" A friend informed him that the pope was very fond of dainties. Cromwell immediately ordered some exquisite jelly to be prepared, after the English fashion, and set out for Italy with his provisions and his two companions.

This was the man who appeared before Julius after his return from the chase. "Kings and princes alone eat of this preserve in England," said Cromwell to the pope. One cardinal, who was a greedier "cormorant" than his master, eagerly tasted the delicacy. "Try it," he exclaimed, and the pope, relishing this new confectionary, immediately signed the pardons, on condition however that the receipt for the jelly should

---

[1] Scripsit ad me suapte manu litteras amantissimas. Erasm. vita ad Ep.
[2] Ut hoc novum sidus aspicias. Ibid. p. 277 ; an expression of Virgil, speaking of the deified Augustus.
[3] Ridet æther, exultat terra, omnia lactis, omnia mellis, omnia nectaris sunt plena. Ibid.

[1] Vestem albam commutavit in nigram. Epp. ad Servat.
[2] The pope suddenly marvelling at the strangeness of the song. Fox, Acts, v. 364, ed. Lond. 1838.

be left with him. "And thus were the *jelly-pardons* obtained," says the annalist. It was Cromwell's first exploit, and the man who began his busy career by presenting jars of confectionary to the pope was also the man destined to separate England from Rome.

The court of the pontiff was not the only one in Europe devoted to gaiety. Hunting parties were as common in London as at Rome. The young king and his companions were at that time absorbed in balls, banquets, and the other festivities inseparable from a new reign. He recollected however that he must give a queen to his people : Catherine of Aragon was still in England, and the council recommended her for his wife. He admired her piety without caring to imitate it ; [1] he was pleased with her love for literature, and even felt some inclination towards her. [2] His advisers represented to him that " Catherine, daughter of the illustrious Isabella of Castile, was the image of her mother. Like her, she possessed that wisdom and greatness of mind which win the respect of nations ; and that if she carried to any of his rivals her marriage-portion and the Spanish alliance, the long-contested crown of England would soon fall from his head......We have the pope's dispensation : will you be more scrupulous than he is ?" [3] The archbishop of Canterbury opposed in vain : Henry gave way, and on the eleventh of June, about seven weeks after his father's death, the nuptials were privately celebrated. On the twenty-third the king and queen went in state through the city, the bride wearing a white satin dress with her hair hanging down her back nearly to her feet. On the next day they were crowned at Westminster with great magnificence.

Then followed a series of expensive entertainments. The treasures which the nobility had long concealed from fear of the old king, were now brought out ; the ladies glittered with gold and diamonds ; and the king and queen, whom the people never grew tired of admiring, amused themselves like children with the splendour of their royal robes. Henry VIII. was the forerunner of Louis XIV. Naturally inclined to pomp and pleasure, the idol of his people, a devoted admirer of female beauty, and the husband of almost as many wives as Louis had adulterous mistresses, he made the court of England what the son of Anne of Austria made the court of France,—one constant scene of amusements. He thought he could never get to the end of the riches amassed by his prudent father. His youth—for he was only eighteen—the gaiety of his disposition, the grace he displayed in all bodily exercises,

the tales of chivalry in which he delighted. and which even the clergy recommended to their high-born hearers, the flattery of his courtiers [1]—all these combined to set his young imagination in a ferment. Wherever he appeared, all were filled with admiration of his handsome countenance and graceful figure : such is the portrait bequeathed to us by his greatest enemy. [2] "His brow was made to wear the crown, and his majestic port the kingly mantle," adds Noryson. [3]

Henry resolved to realize without delay the chivalrous combats and fabulous splendours of the heroes of the Round Table, as if to prepare himself for those more real struggles which he would one day have to maintain against the papacy. At the sound of the trumpet the youthful monarch would enter the lists, clad in costly armour, and wearing a plume that fell gracefully down to the saddle of his vigorous courser ; "like an untamed bull," says an historian, "which breaks away from its yoke and rushes into the arena." On one occasion, at the celebration of the queen's churching, Catherine with her ladies was seated in a tent of purple and gold, in the midst of an artificial forest, strewn with rocks and variegated with flowers. On a sudden a monk stepped forward, wearing a long brown robe, and kneeling before her, begged permission to run a course. It was granted, and rising up he threw aside his coarse frock, and appeared gorgeously armed for the tourney. He was Charles Brandon, afterwards Duke of Suffolk, one of the handsomest and strongest men in the kingdom, and the first after Henry in military exercises. He was followed by a number of others dressed in black velvet, with wide-brimmed hats on their heads, staffs in their hands, and scarfs across their shoulders ornamented with cockle shells, like pilgrims from St James of Compostella. These also threw off their disguise, and stood forth in complete armour. At their head was Sir Thomas Boleyn, whose daughter was fated to surpass in beauty, greatness, and misfortune, all the women of England. The tournament began. Henry, who has been compared to Amadis in boldness, to the lion-hearted Richard in courage, and to Edward III. in courtesy, did not always escape danger in these chivalrous contests. One day the king had forgotten to lower his vizor, and Brandon, his opponent, setting off at full gollop, the spectators noticed the oversight, and cried out in alarm. But nothing could stop their horses : the two cavaliers met. Suffolk's lance was shivered against Henry, and the fragments struck him in the face. Every one thought the king was dead, and some were running to arrest Brandon, when Henry, recovering from the blow which

---

[1] Admirabatur quidem uxoris sanctitatem. Sanders, p. 5.
[2] Ut amor plus apud regem posset. Moryson Apom. p. 14.
[3] Herbert's Henry VIII. p. 7. Fuller's Church Hist. Book V. p. 165. Erasm. Ep. ad Amerb. p. 19.

[1] Tyndale, Obedience of a Christian Man (1528).
[2] Eximiâ corporis forma præditus, in qua etiam regiæ majestatis augusta quædam species elucebat. Sanderus de Schism. p. 4.
[3] Turner, Hist. Engl. i. p. 28.

had fallen on his helmet, recommenced the combat, and ran six new courses amid the admiring cries of his subjects. This intrepid courage changed as he grew older into unsparing cruelty; and it was this young tiger, whose movements were then so graceful, that at no distant day tore with his bloody fangs the mother of his children.

CHAPTER XI.

The Pope excites to War—Colet's Sermon at St Paul's—The Flemish Campaign—Marriage of Louis XII. and Princess Mary—Letter from Anne Boleyn—Marriage of Brandon and Mary—Oxford—Sir Thomas More at Court—Attack upon the Monasteries—Colet's Household—He preaches Reform—The Greeks and Trojans.

A MESSAGE from the pope stopped Henry in the midst of these amusements. In Scotland, Spain, France, and Italy, the young king had nothing but friends; a harmony which the papacy was intent on disturbing. One day, immediately after high mass had been celebrated, the archbishop of Canterbury, on behalf of Julius II. laid at his feet a golden rose, which had been blessed by the pope, anointed with holy oil, and perfumed with musk.[1] It was accompanied by a letter saluting him as head of the Italian league. The warlike pontiff having reduced the Venetians, desired to humble France, and to employ Henry as the instrument of his vengeance. Henry, only a short time before, had renewed his alliance with Louis XII.; but the pope was not to be baffled by such a trifle as that, and the young king soon began to dream of rivalling the glories of Crecy, Poitiers, and Agincourt. To no purpose did his wisest councillors represent to him that England, in the most favourable times, had never been able to hold her ground in France, and that the sea was the true field open to her conquests. Julius, knowing his vanity, had promised to deprive Louis of the title of Most Christian king, and confer it upon him. "His holiness hopes that your Grace will utterly exterminate the king of France," wrote the king's agent.[2] Henry saw nothing objectionable in this very unapostolic mission, and decided on substituting the terrible game of war for the gentler sports of peace.

In the spring of 1511, after some unsuccessful attempts by his generals, Henry determined to invade France in person. He was in the midst of his preparations when the festival of Easter arrived. Dean Colet had been appointed to preach before Henry on Good Friday, and in the course of his sermon he showed more courage than could have been expected in a scholar, for a spark of the Christian spirit was glowing in his bosom. He chose for the subject of his discourse Christ's victory over death and the grave. "Whoever takes up arms from ambition," said he, "fights not under the standard of Christ, but of Satan. If you desire to contend against your enemies, follow Jesus Christ as your prince and captain, rather than Cæsar or Alexander." His hearers looked at each other with astonishment; the friends of polite literature became alarmed; and the priests, who were getting uneasy at the uprising of the human mind, hoped to profit by this opportunity of inflicting a deadly blow on their antagonists. There were among them men whose opinions we must condemn, while we cannot forbear respecting the zeal for what they believed to be the truth: of this number were Bricot, Fitzjames, and above all Standish. Their zeal, however, went a little too far on this occasion: they even talked of *burning* the dean.[1] After the sermon, Colet was informed that the king requested his attendance in the garden of the Franciscan monastery, and immediately the priests and monks crowded round the gate, hoping to see their adversary led forth as a criminal. "Let us be alone," said Henry; "put on your cap, Mr Dean, and we will take a walk. Cheer up," he continued, "you have nothing to fear. You have spoken admirably of Christian charity, and have almost reconciled me to the king of France; yet, as the contest is not one of choice, but of necessity, I must beg of you in some future sermon to explain this to my people. Unless you do so, I fear my soldiers may misunderstand your meaning." Colet was not a John Baptist, and, affected by the king's condescension, he gave the required explanation. The king was satisfied and exclaimed: "Let every man have his doctor as he pleases; this man is my doctor, and I will drink his health!" Henry was then young: very different was the fashion with which in after-years he treated those who opposed him.

At heart the king cared little more about the victories of Alexander than of Jesus Christ. Having fitted out his army, he embarked at the end of June, accompanied by his almoner, Wolsey, who was rising into favour, and set out for the war as if for a tournament. Shortly after this, he went, all glittering with jewels, to meet the Emperor Maximilian, who received him in a plain doublet and cloak of black serge. After his victory at the battle of Spurs, Henry, instead of pressing forward to the conquest of France, returned to the siege of Terouenne, wasted his time in jousts and entertainments, conferred on Wolsey the bishopric of Tournay which he had just captured, and then returned to England, delighted at having made so pleasant an excursion.

---

[1] Odorifico musco aspersam. Wilkins, Concilia, III. p. 652.
[2] Letter of Cardinal Bembridge. Cotton MSS. Vitell. B. 2, p. 8.

[1] Dr Colet was in trouble and should have been burnt. Latimer's Sermons. Parker edition. p. 440.

Louis XII. was a widower in his 53d year, and bowed down by the infirmities of a premature old age; but being desirous of preventing, at any cost, the renewal of the war, he sought the hand of Henry's sister, the Princess Mary, then in her 16th year. Her affections were already fixed on Charles Brandon, and for him she would have sacrificed the splendour of a throne. But reasons of state opposed their union. "The princess," remarked Wolsey, "will soon return to England a widow with a royal dowry." This decided the question. The disconsolate Mary, who was an object of universal pity, embarked at Dover with a numerous train, and from Boulogne, where she was received by the duke of Angoulême, she was conducted to the king, elated at the idea of marrying the handsomest princess in Europe.

Among Mary's attendants was the youthful Anne Boleyn. Her father, Sir Thomas Boleyn, had been charged by Henry, conjointly with the bishop of Ely, with the diplomatic negotiations preliminary to this marriage. Anne had passed her childhood at Hever Castle, surrounded by all that could heat the imagination. Her maternal grandfather, the earl of Surrey, whose eldest son had married the sister of Henry the Seventh's queen, had filled, as did his sons also, the most important offices of state. At the age probably of fourteen, when summoned by her father to court, she wrote him the following letter in French, which appears to refer to her departure for France:—

"Sir,—I find by your letter that you wish me to appear at court in a manner becoming a respectable female, and likewise that the queen will condescend to enter into conversation with me; at this I rejoice, as I do to think, that conversing with so sensible and elegant a princess will make me even more desirous of continuing to speak and to write good French; the more as it is by your earnest advice, which (I acquaint you by this present writing) I shall follow to the best of my ability..........As to myself, rest assured that I shall not ungratefully look upon this fatherly office as one that might be dispensed with; nor will it tend to diminish my affection, quest [wish], and deliberation to lead as holy a life as you may please to desire of me; indeed my love for you is founded on so firm a basis that it can never be impaired. I put an end to this my lucubration after having very humbly craved your good will and affection. Written at Hever, by

"Your very humble and obedient daughter,
"ANNA DE BOULLAN."[1]

Such were the feelings under which this

[1] The French original is preserved among Archbishop Parker's MSS. at Corpus Christi College, Cambridge. The translation in the text is (with a slight variation) from Sir H. Ellis's Collection of royal and other letters, vol. ii. second series.

young and interesting lady, so calumniated by papistical writers, appeared at court.

The marriage was celebrated at Abbeville on the 9th of October 1514, and after a sumptuous banquet, the king of France distributed his royal largesses among the English lords, who were charmed by his courtesy. But the morrow was a day of trial to the young queen. Louis XII. had dismissed the numerous train which had accompanied her, and even Lady Guildford, to whom Henry had specially confided her. Three only were left,—of whom the youthful Anne Boleyn was one. At this separation, Mary gave way to the keenest sorrow. To cheer her spirits, Louis proclaimed a grand tournament. Brandon hastened to France at its first announcement, and carried off all the prizes; while the king, languidly reclining on a couch, could with difficulty look upon the brilliant spectacle over which his queen presided, sick at heart yet radiant with youth and beauty. Mary was unable to conceal her emotion, and Louisa of Savoy, who was watching her, divined her secret. But Louis, if he experienced the tortures of jealousy, did not feel them long, for his death took place on the first January 1515.

Even before her husband's funeral was over, Mary's heart beat high with hope. Francis I., impatient to see her wedded to some unimportant political personage, encouraged her love for Brandon. The latter, who had been commissioned by Henry to convey to her his letters of condolence, feared his master's anger if he should dare aspire to the hand of the princess. But the widowed queen, who was resolved to brave everything, told her lover: "Either you marry me in four days or you see me no more." The choice the king had made of his ambassador announced that he would not behave very harshly. The marriage was celebrated in the abbey of Clugny, and Henry pardoned them.

While Mary returned to England, as Wolsey had predicted, Anne Boleyn remained in France. Her father, desiring his daughter to become an accomplished woman, intrusted her to the care of the virtuous Claude of France, *the good queen*, at whose court the daughters of the first families of the kingdom were trained. Margaret, duchess of Alençon, the sister of Francis, and afterwards queen of Navarre, often charmed the queen's circle by her lively conversation. She soon became deeply attached to the young Englishwoman, and on the death of Claude took her into her own family. Anne Boleyn was destined at no very remote period to be at the court of London a reflection of the graceful Margaret, and her relations with that princess were not without influence on the English Reformation.

And indeed the literary movement which had passed from Italy into France appeared at that time as if it would cross from France into Britain. Oxford exercises over England as great an influence as the metropolis; and it is almost always within its walls that a movement commences whether for good or evil. At this period of our history, an enthusiastic youth hailed with joy the first beams of the new sun, and attacked with their sarcasms the idleness of the monks, the immorality of the clergy, and the superstition of the people. Disgusted with the priestcraft of the middle ages, and captivated by the writers of antiquity and the purity of the Gospel, Oxford boldly called for a reform which should burst the bonds of clerical domination and emancipate the human mind. Men of letters thought for a while that they had found the most powerful man in England in Wolsey, the ally that would give them the victory.

He possessed little taste for learning, but seeing the wind of public favour blow in that direction, he readily spread his sails before it. He got the reputation of a profound divine, by quoting a few words of Thomas Aquinas, and the fame of a Mæcenas and Ptolemy, by inviting the learned to his gorgeous entertainments. "O happy cardinal," exclaimed Erasmus, "who can surround his table with such torches!"[1]

At that time the king felt the same ambition as his minister, and having tasted in turn the pleasures of war and diplomacy, he now bent his mind to literature. He desired Wolsey to present Sir Thomas More to him. —"What shall I do at court?" replied the latter. "I shall be as awkward as a man that never rode sitteth in a saddle." Happy in his family circle, where his father, mother, and children, gathering round the same table, formed a pleasing group, which the pencil of Holbein has transmitted to us, More had no desire to leave it. But Henry was not a man to put up with a refusal; he employed force almost to draw More from his retirement, and in a short time he could not live without the society of the man of letters. On calm and starlight nights they would walk together upon the leads at the top of the palace, discoursing on the motions of the heavenly bodies. If More did not appear at court, Henry would go to Chelsea and share the frugal dinner of the family with some of their simple neighbours. "Where," asked Erasmus, "where is the Athens, the Porch, or the Academe, that can be compared with the court of England? ......It is a seat of the muses rather than a palace......The golden age is reviving, and I congratulate the world."

But the friends of classical learning were not content with the cardinal's banquets or the king's favours. They wanted victories, and their keenest darts were aimed at the cloisters, those strong fortresses of the hier-

archy and of uncleanness.[1] The abbot of Saint Albans, having taken a married woman for his concubine, and placed her at the head of a nunnery, his monks had followed his example, and indulged in the most scandalous debauchery. Public indignation was so far aroused, that Wolsey himself—Wolsey, the father of several illegitimate children, and who was suffering the penalty of his irregularities[2]—was carried away by the spirit of the age, and demanded of the pope a general reform of manners. When they heard of this request, the priests and friars were loud in their outcries. "What are you about?" said they to Wolsey. "You are giving the victory to the enemies of the church, and your only reward will be the hatred of the whole world." As this was not the cardinal's game, he abandoned his project, and conceived one more easily executed. Wishing to deserve the name of "Ptolemy" conferred on him by Erasmus, he undertook to build two large colleges, one at Ipswich, his native town, the other at Oxford; and found it convenient to take the money necessary for their endowment, not from his own purse, but from the purses of the monks. He pointed out to the pope twenty-two monasteries in which (he said) vice and impiety had taken up their abode.[3] The pope granted their secularization, and Wolsey having thus procured a revenue of £2000 sterling, laid the foundations of his college, traced out various courts, and constructed spacious kitchens. He fell into disgrace before he had completed his work, which led Gualter to say with a sneer: "He began a college and built a cook's shop."[4] But a great example had been set: the monasteries had been attacked, and the first breach made in them by a cardinal. Cromwell, Wolsey's secretary, remarked how his master had set about his work, and in after-years profited by the lesson.

It was fortunate for letters that they had sincerer friends in London than Wolsey. Of these were Colet, dean of St Paul's, whose house was the centre of the literary movement which preceded the Reformation, and his friend and guest Erasmus. The latter was the hardy pioneer who opened the road of antiquity to modern Europe. One day he would entertain Colet's guests with the account of a new manuscript; on another, with a discussion on the forms of ancient literature; and at other times he would attack the schoolmen and monks, when Colet would take the same side. The only antagonist who dared measure his strength with him was Sir Thomas More, who, although a lay-

---

[1] Cujus mensa talibus luminibus cingitur. Erasm. Ep. 725.

[1] Loca sacra etiam ipsa Dei templa monialium stupro et sanguinis et seminis effusione profanare non verentur. Papal bull. Wilkins, Concilia, p. 632.
[2] Morbus venereus. Burnet.
[3] Wherein much vice and wickedness was harboured. Strype. i. 169. The names of the monasteries are given. Ibid. ii. 132.
[4] Instituit collegium et absolvit popinam. Fuller, cent. xvi. p. 169.

man, stoutly defended the ordinances of the church.

But mere table-talk could not satisfy the dean: a numerous audience attended his sermons at St Paul's. The spirituality of Christ's words, the authority which characterizes them, their admirable simplicity and mysterious depth, had deeply charmed him: "I admire the writings of the apostles," he would say, "but I forget them almost, when I contemplate the wonderful majesty of Jesus Christ."[1] Setting aside the texts prescribed by the church, he explained, like Zwingle, the Gospel of St Matthew. Nor did he stop here. Taking advantage of the Convocation, he delivered a sermon on *conformation* and *reformation*, which was one of the numerous forerunners of the great reform of the sixteenth century. "We see strange and heretical ideas appear in our days, and no wonder," said he. "But you must know there is no heresy more dangerous to the church than the vicious lives of its priests. A reformation is needed; and that reformation must begin with the bishops and be extended to the priests. The clergy once reformed, we shall proceed to the reformation of the people."[2] Thus spoke Colet, while the citizens of London listened to him with rapture, and called him a new Saint Paul.[3]

Such discourses could not be allowed to pass unpunished. Fitzjames, bishop of London, was a superstitious obstinate old man of eighty, fond of money, excessively irritable, a poor theologian, and a slave to Duns Scotus, the *subtle doctor.* Calling to his aid two other bishops as zealous as himself for the preservation of abuses, namely, Bricot and Standish, he denounced the dean of St Paul's to Warham. The archbishop having inquired what he had done: "What has he done?" rejoined the bishop of London. "He teaches that we must not worship images; he translates the Lord's Prayer into English; he pretends that the text *Feed my sheep*, does not include the temporal supplies the clergy draw from their flock. And besides all this," he continued with some embarrassment, "he has spoken against those who carry their manuscripts into the pulpit and read their sermons!" As this was the bishop's practice, the primate could not refrain from smiling; and since Colet refused to justify himself, Warham did so for him.

From that time Colet laboured with fresh zeal to scatter the darkness. He devoted the larger portion of his fortune to found the celebrated school of St Paul, of which the learned Lilly was the first master. Two parties, the *Greeks* and the *Trojans*, entered the lists, not to contend with sword and spear, as in the ancient epic, but with the tongue, the pen, and sometimes the fist. If the *Trojans* (the obscurants) were defeated in the public disputations, they had their revenge in the secret of the confessional. *Cave a Græcis ne fias hereticus,*[1] was the watchword of the priests—their daily lesson to the youths under their care. They looked on the school founded by Colet as the monstrous horse of the perjured Sinon, and announced that from its bosom would inevitably issue the destruction of the people. Colet and Erasmus replied to the monks by inflicting fresh blows. Linacre, a thorough literary enthusiast,—Grocyn, a man of sarcastic humour but generous heart,—and many others, reinforced the *Grecian* phalanx. Henry himself used to take one of them with him during his journeys, and if any unlucky *Trojan* ventured in his presence to attack the tongue of Plato and of Saint Paul, the young king would set his Hellenian on him. Not more numerous were the contests witnessed in times of yore on the classic banks of Xanthus and Simois.

CHAPTER XII.

Wolsey—His first Commission—His Complaisance and Dioceses—Cardinal, Chancellor, and Legate—Ostentation and Necromancy—His Spies and Enmity—Pretensions of the Clergy.

JUST as everything seemed tending to a reformation, a powerful priest rendered the way more difficult.

One of the most striking personages of the age was then making his appearance on the stage of the world. It was the destiny of that man, in the reign of Henry VIII., to combine extreme ability with extreme immorality; and to be a new and striking example of the wholesome truth that immorality is more effectual to destroy a man than ability to save him. Wolsey was the last highpriest of Rome in England, and when his fall startled the nation, it was the signal of a still more striking fall—the fall of popery.

Thomas Wolsey, the son of a wealthy butcher of Ipswich, according to the common story, which is sanctioned by high authority, had attained under Henry VII. the post of almoner, at the recommendation of Sir Richard Nanfan, treasurer of Calais and an old patron of his. But Wolsey was not at all desirous of passing his life in saying mass. As soon as he had discharged the regular duties of his office, instead of spending the rest of the day in idleness, as his colleagues did, he strove to win the good graces of the persons round the king.

Fox, Bishop of Winchester, keeper of the privy-seal under Henry VII., uneasy at the

---

[1] Ita suspiciebat admirabilem illam Christi majestatem. Erasm. Epp. 707.
[2] Colet, Sermon to the Convocation.
[3] Pene apostolus Paulus habitus est. Polyd. Virg. p. 618.

[1] Beware of the Greeks, lest you should become a heretic.

growing power of the earl of Surrey, looked about for a man to counterbalance them. He thought he had found such a one in Wolsey. It was to oppose the Surreys, the grandfather and uncles of Anne Boleyn, that the son of the Ipswich butcher was drawn from his obscurity. This is not an unimportant circumstance in our narrative. Fox began to praise Wolsey in the king's hearing, and at the same time he encouraged the almoner to give himself to public affairs. The latter was not deaf,[1] and soon found an opportunity of winning his sovereign's favour.

The king having business of importance with the emperor, who was then in Flanders, sent for Wolsey, explained his wishes, and ordered him to prepare to set out. The chaplain determined to show Henry VII. how capable he was of serving him. It was long past noon when for the king at Richmond—at four o'clock he was in London, at seven at Gravesend. By travelling all night he reached Dover just as the packet-boat was about to sail. After a passage of three hours he reached Calais, whence he travelled post, and the same evening appeared before Maximilian. Having obtained what he desired, he set off again by night, and on the next day but one reached Richmond, three days and some few hours after his departure. The king, catching sight of him just as he was going to mass, sharply inquired why he had not set out. "Sire, I am just returned," answered Wolsey, placing the emperor's letters in his master's hands. Henry was delighted, and Wolsey saw that his fortune was made.

The courtiers hoped at first that Wolsey, like an inexperienced pilot, would run his vessel on some hidden rock; but never did helmsman manage his ship with more skill. Although twenty years older than Henry VIII. the almoner danced, and sang, and laughed with the prince's companions, and amused his new master with tales of scandal and quotations from Thomas Aquinas. The young king found his house a temple of paganism, a shrine of voluptuousness;[2] and while Henry's councillors were entreating him to leave his pleasures and attend to business, Wolsey was continually reminding him that he ought to devote his youth to learning and amusement, and leave the toils of government to others. Wolsey was created bishop of Tournay during the campaign in Flanders, and on his return to England, was raised to the sees of Lincoln and of York. Three mitres had been placed on his head in one year. He found at last the vein he so ardently sought for.

And yet he was not satisfied. The archbishop of Canterbury had insisted, as primate, that the cross of York should be

lowered to his. Wolsey was not of a disposition to concede this, and when he found that Warham was not content with being his equal, he resolved to make him his inferior. Francis I., who desired to conciliate England, demanded the purple for Wolsey, and the archbishop of York received the title of Cardinal St Cecilia beyond the Tiber. In November 1515, his hat was brought by the envoy of the pope: "It would have been better to have given him a Tyburn tippet," said some indignant Englishmen; "these Romish hats never brought good into England"[1]—a saying that has become proverbial.

This was not enough for Wolsey: he desired secular greatness above all things. Warham, tired of contending with so arrogant a rival, resigned the seals, and the king immediately transferred them to the cardinal. At length a bull appointed him legate *a latere* of the holy see, and placed under his jurisdiction all the colleges, monasteries, spiritual courts, bishops, and the primate himself (1519). From that time, as lord-chancellor of England and legate, Wolsey administered everything in church and state. He filled his coffers with money procured both at home and from abroad, and yielded without restraint to his dominant vices, ostentation and pride. Whenever he appeared in public, two priests, the tallest and comeliest that could be found, carried before him two huge silver crosses, one to mark his dignity as archbishop, the other as papal legate. Chamberlains, gentlemen, pages, sergeants, chaplains, choristers, clerks, cupbearers, cooks, and other domestics, to the number of more than 500, among whom were nine or ten lords and the stateliest yeomen of the country, filled his palace. He generally wore a dress of scarlet velvet and silk, with hat and gloves of the same colour. His shoes were embroidered with gold and silver, inlaid with pearls and precious stones. A kind of papacy was thus forming in England; for wherever pride flourishes there popery is developed.

One thing occupied Wolsey more than all the pomp with which he was surrounded: his desire, namely, to captivate the king. For this purpose he cast Henry's nativity, and procured an amulet which he wore constantly, in order to charm his master by its magic properties.[2] Then having recourse to a still more effectual necromancy, he selected from among the licentious companions of the young monarch those of the keenest discernment and most ambitious character; and after binding them to him by a solemn oath, he placed them at court to be as eyes and ears to him. Accordingly not a word was said in the presence of the monarch, particu-

---

[1] Hæc Wolseius non surdis audierit auribus. Polyd. Virg. 622.
[2] Domi suæ voluptatum omnium sacrarium fec't. Ibid. 623.

[1] Latimer's Sermons (Parker Society), p. 119.
[2] He caiked [calculated] the king's nativity....he made by craft of necromancy graven imagery to bear upon him, wherewith he bewitched the king's mind. Tyndale's Expositions (Parker Soc.), p. 308.

larly against Wolsey, of which he was not informed an hour afterwards. If the culprit was not in favour, he was expelled without mercy; in the contrary case, the minister sent him on some distant mission. The queen's ladies, the king's chaplains, and even their confessors, were the cardinal's spies. He pretended to omnipresence, as the pope to infallibility.

Wolsey was not devoid of certain showy virtues, for he was liberal to the poor even to affectation, and as chancellor inexorable to every kind of irregularity, and strove particularly to make the rich and high-born bend beneath his power. Men of learning alone obtained from him some little attention, and hence Erasmus calls him "the Achates of a new Æneas." But the nation was not to be carried away by the eulogies of a few scholars. Wolsey—a man of more than suspected morals, double-hearted, faithless to his promises, oppressing the people with heavy taxes, and exceedingly arrogant to everybody—Wolsey soon became hated by the people of England.

The elevation of a prince of the Roman church could not be favourable to the Reformation. The priests, encouraged by it, determined to make a stand against the triple attack of the learned, the reformers, and the state: and they soon had an opportunity of trying their strength. Holy orders had become during the middle ages a warrant for every sort of crime. Parliament, desirous of correcting this abuse and checking the encroachments of the church, declared in the year 1513 that any ecclesiastic, accused of theft or murder, should be tried before the secular tribunals. Exceptions, however, were made in favour of bishops, priests, and deacons—that is to say, nearly all the clergy. Notwithstanding this timid precaution, an insolent clerk, the abbot of Winchelcomb, began the battle by exclaiming at St Paul's: "Touch not mine anointed, said the Lord." At the same time Wolsey, accompanied by a long train of priests and prelates, had an audience of the king, at which he said with hands upraised to heaven: "Sire, to try a clerk, is a violation of God's laws." This time, however, Henry did not give way. "By God's will, we are king of England," he replied, "and the kings of England in times past had never any superior but God only. Therefore know you well that we will maintain the right of our crown." He saw distinctly that to put the clergy above the laws was to put them above the throne. The priests were beaten, but not disheartened: perseverance is a characteristic feature of every hierarchical order. Not walking by faith, they walk all the more by sight; and skilful combinations supply the place of the holy aspirations of the Christian. Humble disciples of the gospel were soon to experience this, for the clergy by a few isolated attacks were

about to flesh themselves for the great struggles of the Reformation.

CHAPTER XIII.

The Wolves—Richard Hun—A Murder—Verdict of the Jury—Hun condemned, and his Character vindicated—The Gravesend Passage-boat—A Festival disturbed—Brown tortured—Visit from his Wife—A Martyr—Character of Erasmus—1516 and 1517—Erasmus goes to Basle.

It is occasionally necessary to soften down the somewhat exaggerated colours in which contemporary writers describe the Romish clergy; but there are certain appellations which history is bound to accept. The wolves, for so the priests were called, by attacking the Lords and Commons had attempted a work beyond their reach. They turned their wrath on others. There were many shepherds endeavouring to gather together the sheep of the Lord beside the peaceful waters: these must be frightened, and the sheep driven into the howling wilderness. "The wolves" determined to fall upon the Lollards.

There lived in London an honest tradesman named Richard Hun, one of those witnesses of the truth who, sincere though unenlightened, have been often found in the bosom of Catholicism. It was his practice to retire to his closet and spend a portion of each day in the study of the Bible. At the death of one of his children, the priest required of him an exorbitant fee, which Hun refused to pay, and for which he was summoned before the legate's court. Animated by that public spirit, which characterizes the people of England, he felt indignant that an Englishman should be cited before a foreign tribunal, and laid an information against the priest and his counsel under the act of præmunire. Such boldness—most extraordinary at that time—exasperated the clergy beyond all bounds. "If these proud citizens are allowed to have their way," exclaimed the monks, "every layman will dare to resist a priest."

Exertions were accordingly made to snare the pretended rebel in the trap of heresy;[1] he was thrown into the Lollards' tower at St Paul's, and an iron collar was fastened round his neck, attached to which was a chain so heavy that neither man nor beast (says Foxe) would have been able to bear it long. When taken before his judges, they could not convict him of heresy, and it was observed with astonishment "that he had his beads in prison with him."[2] They would have set him at liberty, after inflicting on him perhaps some trifling penance — but then, what a bad example it would be, and

---

[1] Foxe, Acts and Mon. ii. p. 8. Folio, 1684, London.
[2] Ibid.

who could stop the reformers, if it was so easy to resist the papacy? Unable to triumph by justice, certain fanatics resolved to triumph by crime.

At midnight on the 2d December—the day of his examination—three men stealthily ascended the stairs of the Lollards' tower: the bellringer went first carrying a torch; a sergeant named Charles Joseph followed, and last came the bishop's chancellor. Having entered the cell, they went up to the bed on which Hun was lying, and finding that he was asleep, the chancellor said: "Lay hands on the thief." Charles Joseph and the bellringer fell upon the prisoner, who, awaking with a start, saw at a glance what this midnight visit meant. He resisted the assassins at first, but was soon overpowered and strangled. Charles Joseph then fixed the dead man's belt round his neck, the bellringer helped to raise his lifeless body, and the chancellor slipped the other end of the belt through a ring fixed in the wall. They then placed his cap on his head, and hastily quitted the cell.[1] Immediately after, the conscience-stricken Charles Joseph got on horseback and rode from the city; the bellringer left the cathedral and hid himself: the crime dispersed the criminals. The chancellor alone kept his ground, and he was at prayers when the news was brought him that the turnkey had found Hun hanging. "He must have killed himself in despair," said the hypocrite. But every one knew poor Hun's Christian feelings. "It is the priests who have murdered him," was the general cry in London, and an inquest was ordered to be held on his body.

On Tuesday, the 5th of December, William Barnwell, the city coroner, the two sheriffs, and twenty-four jurymen, proceeded to the Lollards' tower. They remarked that the belt was so short that the head could not be got out of it, and that consequently it had never been placed in it voluntarily, and hence the jury concluded that the suspension was an after-thought of some other persons. Moreover they found that the ring was too high for the poor victim to reach it,—that the body bore marks of violence—and that traces of blood were to be seen in the cell: "Wherefore all we find by God and all our consciences (runs the verdict), that Richard Hun was murdered. Also we acquit the said Richard Hun of his own death."[2]

It was but too true, and the criminals themselves confessed it. The miserable Charles Joseph having returned home on the evening of the 6th December, said to his maid-servant: "If you will swear to keep my secret, I will tell you all." — "Yes, master," she replied, "if it is neither felony nor treason."—Joseph took a book, swore the

girl on it, and then said to her "I have killed Richard Hun!"—"O master! how? he was called a worthy man."—"I would lever [rather] than a hundred pounds it were not done," he made answer; "but what is done cannot be undone." He then rushed out of the house.

The clergy foresaw what a serious blow this unhappy affair would be to them, and to justify themselves they examined Hun's Bible (it was Wickliffe's version), and having read in the preface that "poor men and idiots [simple folks] have the truth of the holy Scriptures more than a thousand prelates and religious men and clerks of the school," and further, that "the pope ought to be called Antichrist," the bishop of London, assisted by the bishops of Durham and Lincoln, declared Hun guilty of heresy, and on the 20th December his dead body was burnt at Smithfield. "Hun's bones have been burnt, and therefore he was a heretic," said the priests; "he was a heretic, and therefore he committed suicide."

The triumph of the clergy was of short duration; for almost at the same time William Horsey, the bishop's chancellor, Charles Joseph, and John Spalding the bellringer, were convicted of the murder. A bill passed the Commons restoring Hun's property to his family and vindicating his character; the Lords accepted the bill, and the king himself said to the priests: "Restore to these wretched children the property of their father whom you so cruelly murdered to our great and just horror."[1]—"If the clerical theocracy should gain the mastery of the state," was the general remark in London, "it would not only be a very great lie, but the most frightful tyranny!" England has never gone back since that time, and a theocratic rule has always inspired the sound portion of the nation with a just and insurmountable antipathy. Such were the events taking place in England shortly before the Reformation. This was not all.

The clergy had not been fortunate in Hun's affair, but they were not for that reason unwilling to attempt a new one.

In the spring of 1517—the year in which Luther posted up his *theses*—a priest, whose manners announced a man swollen with pride, happened to be on board the passage-boat from London to Gravesend with an intelligent and pious Christian of Ashford, by name John Brown. The passengers, as they floated down the stream, were amusing themselves by watching the banks glide away from them, when the priest, turning towards Brown, said to him insolently: "You are too near me, get farther off. Do you know who I am?"—"No, sir," answered Brown.— "Well, then, you must know that I am a priest."—"Indeed, sir; are you a parson, or vicar, or a lady's chaplain?"—"No; I am a

---

[1] Foxe, Acts and Mon. ii. p. 13. "And so all we murdered Hun....and so Hun was hanged." (Evidence of Charles Joseph.)
[2] For particulars of the inquest, see Ibid. ii. 14.

[1] Verdict on the Inquest. Foxe. 12.

soul-priest," he haughtily replied; " I sing mass to save souls."—" Do you, sir," rejoined Brown somewhat ironically ; " that is well done: and can you tell me where you find the soul when you begin the mass ? "—" I cannot," said the priest.—" And where you leave it when the mass is ended ? "—" I do not know."—" What !" continued Brown with marks of astonishment, " you do not know where you find the soul or where you leave it......and yet you say that you save it ! "—" Go thy ways," said the priest angrily, " thou art a heretic, and I will be even with thee." Thenceforward the priest and his neighbour conversed no more together. At last they reached Gravesend and the boat anchored.

As soon as the priest had landed, he hastened to two of his friends, Walter and William More, and all three mounting their horses set off for Canterbury, and denounced Brown to the archbishop.

In the meantime John Brown had reached home. Three days later, his wife, Elizabeth, who had just left her chamber, went to church, dressed all in white, to return thanks to God for delivering her in the perils of childbirth. Her husband, assisted by her daughter Alice and the maid-servant, were preparing for their friends the feast usual on such occasions, and they had all of them taken their seats at table, joy beaming on every face, when the street-door was abruptly opened, and Chilton, the constable, a cruel and savage man, accompanied by several of the archbishop's apparitors, seized upon the worthy townsman. All sprang from their seats in alarm; Elizabeth and Alice uttered the most heart-rending cries ; but the primate's officers, without showing any emotion, pulled Brown out of the house, and placed him on horseback, tying his feet under the animal's belly.[1] It is a serious matter to jest with a priest. The cavalcade rode off quickly, and Brown was thrown into prison, and there left forty days.

At the end of this time, the archbishop of Canterbury and the bishop of Rochester called before them the impudent fellow who doubted whether a priest's mass could save souls, and required him to retract this " blasphemy." But Brown, if he did not believe in the mass, believed in the Gospel: " Christ was once offered," he said, " to take away the sins of many. It is by this sacrifice we are saved, and not by the repetitions of the priests." At this reply the archbishop made a sign to the executioners, one of whom took off the shoes and stockings of this pious Christian, while the other brought in a pan of burning coals, upon which they set the martyr's feet.[2] The English laws in truth forbade torture to be inflicted on any subject of the crown, but the clergy thought themselves above the laws. " Confess the efficacity of the mass," cried the two bishops to poor Brown. " If I deny my Lord upon earth," he replied, " He will deny me before his Father in heaven." The flesh was burnt off the soles of the feet even to the bones, and still John Brown remained unshaken. The bishops therefore ordered him to be given over to the secular arm that he might be burnt alive.

On the Saturday preceding the festival of Pentecost, in the year 1517, the martyr was led back to Ashford, where he arrived just as the day was drawing to a close. A number of idle persons were collected in the street, and among them was Brown's maid-servant, who ran off crying to the house, and told her mistress : " I have seen him !...... He was bound, and they were taking him to prison."[1] Elizabeth hastened to her husband and found him sitting with his feet in the stocks, his features changed by suffering, and expecting to be burnt alive on the morrow. The poor woman sat down beside him, weeping most bitterly, while he, being hindered by his chains, could not so much as bend towards her. " I cannot set my feet to the ground," said he, " for bishops have burnt them to the bones ; but they could not burn my tongue and prevent my confessing the Lord......O Elizabeth !......continue to love him for He is good ; and bring up our children in his fear."

On the following morning—it was Whitsunday—the brutal Chilton and his assistants led Brown to the place of execution, and fastened him to the stake. Elizabeth and Alice, with his other children and his friends, desirous of receiving his last sigh, surrounded the pile, uttering cries of anguish. The fagots were set on fire, while Brown, calm and collected, and full of confidence in the blood of the Saviour, clasped his hands, and repeated this hymn, which Foxe has preserved :—[2]

O Lord, I yield me to thy grace,
Grant me mercy for my trespass;
Let never the fiend my soul chase.
Lord, I will bow, and thou shalt beat,
Let never my soul come in hell-heat.

The martyr was silent: the flames had consumed their victim. Then redoubled cries of anguish rent the air. His wife and daughter seemed as if they would lose their senses. The bystanders showed them the tenderest compassion, and turned with a movement of indignation towards the executioners. The brutal Chilton perceiving this, cried out :—" Come along ; let us toss the heretic's children into the flames, lest they should one day spring from their father's

---

[1] Foxe, Acts. ii. p. 7. His feet bound under his own horse.
[2] His bare feet were set upon hot burning coals. The Lollards (edit. Tract. Soc.), p. 149.

[1] A young maid of his house coming by saw her master; she ran home. The Lollards, p. 50.
[2] Foxe, Acts and Mon. ii. p. 8 (folio 1684), iv. p. 132 (Lond. 1838). We shall in future refer to the latter edition, as being more accessible.

ashes."[1] He rushed towards Alice, and was about to lay hold of her, when the maiden shrank back screaming with horror. To the end of her life, she recollected the fearful moment, and to her we are indebted for the particulars. The fury of the monster was checked. Such were the scenes passing in England shortly before the Reformation.

The priests were not yet satisfied, for the scholars still remained in England : if they could not be burnt, they should at least be banished. They set to work accordingly. Standish, bishop of St Asaph, a sincere man, as it would seem, but fanatical, was inveterate in his hatred of Erasmus, who had irritated him by an idle sarcasm. When speaking of *St Asaph's* it was very common to abbreviate it into *St As's ;* and as Standish was a theologian of no great learning, Erasmus, in his jesting way, would sometimes call him *Episcopus a Sancto Asino.* As the bishop could not destroy Colet, the disciple, he flattered himself that he should triumph over the master.

Erasmus knew Standish's intentions. Should he commence in England that struggle with the papacy which Luther was about to begin in Germany ? It was no longer possible to steer a middle course : he must either fight or leave. The Dutchman was faithful to his nature—we may even say, to his vocation : he left the country.

Erasmus was, in his time, the head of the great literary community. By means of his connexions and his correspondence, which extended over all Europe, he established between those countries where learning was reviving, an interchange of ideas and manuscripts. The pioneer of antiquity, an eminent critic, a witty satirist, the advocate of correct taste, and a restorer of literature, one only glory was wanting : he had not the creative spirit, the heroic soul of a Luther. He calculated with no little skill, could detect the smile on the lips or the knitting of the brows ; but he had not that self-abandonment, that enthusiasm for the truth, that firm confidence in God, without which nothing great can be done in the world, and least of all in the church. " Erasmus *had* much, but *was* little," said one of his biographers.[2]

In the year 1517 a crisis had arrived : the period of the revival was over, that of the Reformation was beginning. The restoration of letters was succeeded by the regeneration of religion : the days of criticism and neutrality by those of courage and action. Erasmus was then only forty-nine years old ; but he had finished his career. From being first, he must now be second : the monk of Wittemberg dethroned him. He looked around himself in vain : placed in a new country, he had lost his road. A hero was needed to inaugurate the great movement of modern times : Erasmus was a mere man of letters.

When attacked by Standish in 1516, the literary king determined to quit the court of England, and take refuge in a printing-office. But before laying down his sceptre at the foot of a Saxon monk, he signalized the end of his reign by the most brilliant of his publications. The epoch of 1516-17, memorable for the theses of Luther, was destined to be equally remarkable by a work which was to imprint on the new times their essential character. What distinguishes the Reformation from all anterior revivals is the union of learning with piety, and a faith more profound, more enlightened, and based on the word of God. The Christian people was then emancipated from the tutelage of the schools and the popes, and its charter of enfranchisement was the Bible. The sixteenth century did more than its predecessors : it went straight to the fountain (the Holy Scriptures), cleared it of weeds and brambles, plumbed its depths, and caused its abundant streams to pour forth on all around. The Reformation age studied the Greek Testament, which the clerical age had almost forgotten,—and this is its greatest glory. Now the first explorer of this divine source was Erasmus. When attacked by the hierarchy, the leader of the schools withdrew from the splendid halls of Henry VIII. It seemed to him that the new era which he had announced to the world was rudely interrupted : he could do nothing more by his conversation for the country of the Tudors. But he carried with him those precious leaves, the fruit of his labours —a book which would do more than he desired. He hastened to Basle, and took up his quarters in Frobenius's printing-office,[1] where he not only laboured himself, but made others labour. England will soon receive the seed of the new life, and the Reformation is about to begin.

---

[1] Bade cast in his children also, for they would spring of his ashes. Foxe, Acts and Mon. iv. p. 132.
[2] Ad. Muller.

[1] Frobenio, ut nullius officinæ plus debeant sacrarum studia literarum. Erasm. Ep. p. 330.

BOOK XVIII.

THE REVIVAL OF THE CHURCH.

CHAPTER I.

Four reforming Powers—Which reformed England?—Papal Reform?—Episcopal Reform?—Royal Reform?—What is required in a legitimate Reform—The Share of the Kingly Power—Share of the Episcopal Authority—High and Low Church—Political Events—The Greek and Latin New Testament—Thoughts of Erasmus—Enthusiasm and Anger—Desire of Erasmus—Clamours of the Priests—Their Attack at Court—Astonishment of Erasmus—His Labours for this Work—Edward Lee; his Character—Lee's *Tragedy*—Conspiracy.

IT was within the province of four powers in the sixteenth century to effect a reformation of the church : these were the papacy, the episcopate, the monarchy, and Holy Scripture.

The Reformation in England was essentially the work of Scripture.

The only true reformation is that which emanates from the word of God. The Holy Scriptures, by bearing witness to the incarnation, death, and resurrection of the Son of God, create in man by the Holy Ghost a faith which justifies him. That faith which produces in him a new life, unites him to Christ, without his requiring a chain of bishops or a Roman mediator, who would separate him from the Saviour instead of drawing him nearer. This Reformation *by the word* restores that spiritual Christianity which the outward and hierarchical religion had destroyed ; and from the regeneration of individuals naturally results the regeneration of the church.

The Reformation of England, perhaps to a greater extent than that of the continent, was effected by the word of God. This statement may appear paradoxical, but it is not the less true. Those great individualities we meet with in Germany, Switzerland, and France — men like Luther, Zwingle, and Calvin—do not appear in England ; but Holy Scripture is widely circulated. What brought light into the British isles subsequently to the year 1517, and on a more extended scale after the year 1526, was the word—the invisible power of the invisible God. The religion of the Anglo-Saxon race—a race called more than any other to circulate the oracles of God throughout the world—is particularly distinguished by its biblical character.

The Reformation of England could not be papal. No reform can be hoped from that which ought to be not only reformed but abolished ; and besides, no monarch dethrones himself. We may even affirm that the popedom has always felt a peculiar affection for its conquests in Britain, and that they would have been the last it would have renounced.

A serious voice had declared in the middle of the fifteenth century : " A reform is neither in the will nor in the power of the popes." [1]

The Reformation of England was not episcopal. Roman hierarchism will never be abolished by Roman bishops. An episcopal assembly may perhaps, as at Constance, depose three competing popes, but then it will be to save the papacy. And if the bishops could not abolish the papacy, still less could they reform themselves. The then existing episcopal power being at enmity with the word of God, and the slave of its own abuses, was incapable of renovating the church. On the contrary, it exerted all its influence to prevent such a renovation.

The Reformation in England was not royal. Samuel, David, and Josiah were able to do something for the raising up of church, when God again turned his face towards it ; but a king cannot rob his people of their religion, and still less can he give them one. It has often been repeated that " the English Reformation derives its origin from the monarch :" but the assertion is incorrect. The work of God, here as elsewhere, cannot be put in comparison with the work of the king ; and if the latter was infinitely surpassed in importance, it was also preceded in time by many years. The monarch was still keeping up a vigorous resistance behind his intrenchments, when God had already decided the victory along the whole line of operations.

Shall we be told that a reform effected by any other principle than the established authorities, both in *church* and *state*, would have been a revolution ? But has God, the lawful sovereign of the church, forbidden all revolution in a sinful world ? A *revolution* is not a revolt. The fall of the first man was a great revolution : the restoration of man by Jesus Christ was a counter-revolution. The corruption occasioned by popery was allied to the fall : the reformation accomplished in the sixteenth century was connected therefore with the restoration. There will be no doubt be other interventions of the Deity, which will be revolutions in the same direction as the Reformation. When God creates a new heaven and a new earth, will not that be one of the most glorious of revolutions ? The Reformation by the word alone gives truth, alone gives unity ; but more than that, it alone bears the marks of true *legitimacy ;*

[1] James of Juterbock, prior of the Carthusians: De sep. tem ecclesiæ statibus opusculum.

for the church belongs not unto men, even though they be priests. God alone is its lawful sovereign.

And yet the human elements which we have enumerated were not wholly foreign to the work that was accomplishing in England. Besides the word of God, other principles were in operation, and although less radical and less primitive, they still retain the sympathy of eminent men of that nation.

And in the first place, the intervention of the king's authority was necessary to a certain point. Since the supremacy of Rome had been established in England by several usages which had the force of law, the intervention of the temporal power was necessary to break the bonds which it had previously sanctioned. But it was requisite for the monarchy, while adopting a negative and political action, to leave the positive, doctrinal, and creative action to the word of God.

Besides the Reformation *in the name of the Scriptures*, there was then in England another *in the name of the king.* The word of God began, the kingly power followed ; and ever since, these two forces have sometimes gone together against the authority of the Roman pontiffs — sometimes in opposition to each other, like those troops which march side by side in the same army, against the same enemy, and which have occasionally been seen, even on the field of battle, to turn their swords against each other.

Finally, the episcopate, which had begun by opposing the Reformation, was compelled to accept it in despite of its convictions. The majority of the bishops were opposed to it ; but the better portion were found to incline, some to the side of outward reform, of which separation from the papacy was the very essence, and others to the side of internal reform, whose mainspring was union with Jesus Christ. Lastly, the episcopate took up its ground on its own account, and soon two great parties alone existed in England : the scriptural party and the clerical party.

These two parties have survived even to our days, and their colours are still distinguishable in the river of the church, like the muddy Arve and the limpid Rhone after their confluence. The royal supremacy, from which many Christians, preferring the paths of independence, have withdrawn since the end of the 16th century, is recognised by both parties in the establishment, with some few exceptions. But whilst the High Church is essentially hierarchical, the Low Church is essentially biblical. In the one, the Church is above and the Word below ; in the other, the Church is below and the Word above. These two principles, evangelism and hierarchism, are found in the Christianity of the first centuries, but with a signal difference. Hierarchism then almost entirely effaced evangelism ; in the age of protestantism, on the contrary, evangelism continued to exist by the side of hierarchism, and it has remained *de jure*, if not always *de facto*, the only legitimate opinion of the church.

Thus there is in England a complication of influences and contests, which render the work more difficult to describe ; but it is on that very account more worthy the attention of the philosopher and the Christian.

Great events had just occurred in Europe. Francis I. had crossed the Alps, gained a signal victory at Marignano, and conquered the north of Italy. The affrighted Maximilian knew of none who could save him but Henry VIII. "I will adopt you ; you shall be my successor in the empire," he intimated to him in May 1516. " Your army shall invade France ; and then we will march together to Rome, where the sovereign pontiff shall crown you king of the Romans." The king of France, anxious to effect a diversion, had formed a league with Denmark and Scotland, and had made preparations for invading England to place on the throne the " white rose,"—the pretender Pole, heir to the claims of the house of York.[1] Henry now showed his prudence ; he declined Maximilian's offer, and turned his whole attention to the security of his kingdom. But while he refused to bear arms in France and Italy, a war of quite another kind broke out in England.

The great work of the 16th century was about to begin. A volume fresh from the presses of Basle had just crossed the Channel. Being transmitted to London, Oxford, and Cambridge, this book, the fruit of Erasmus's vigils, soon found its way wherever there were friends of learning. It was the *New Testament* of our Lord Jesus Christ, published for the first time in Greek with a new Latin translation—an event more important for the world than would have been the landing of the pretender in England, or the appearance of the chief of the Tudors in Italy. This book, in which God has deposited for man's salvation the seeds of life, was about to effect alone, without patrons and without interpreters, the most astonishing revolution in Britain.

When Erasmus published this work, at the dawn, so to say, of modern times, he did not see all its scope. Had he foreseen it, he would perhaps have recoiled in alarm. He saw indeed that there was a great work to be done, but he believed that all good men would unite to do it with common accord. " A spiritual temple must be raised in desolated Christendom," said he. " The mighty of this world will contribute towards it their marble, their ivory, and their gold ; I who am poor and humble offer the foundation stone," and he laid down before the world his edition of the Greek Testament. Then

---

1 A private combination, &c. Strype's Memorials, i. part ii. p. 16.

glancing disdainfully at the traditions of men, he said : " It is not from human reservoirs, fetid with stagnant waters, that we should draw the doctrine of salvation ; but from the pure and abundant streams that flow from the heart of God." And when some of his suspicious friends spoke to him of the difficulties of the times, he replied : " If the ship of the church is to be saved from being swallowed up by the tempest, there is only one anchor that can save it : it is the heavenly word, which, issuing from the bosom of the Father, lives, speaks, and works still in the gospel." [1] These noble sentiments served as an introduction to those blessed pages which were to reform England. Erasmus, like Caiaphas, prophesied without being aware of it.

The New Testament in Greek and Latin had hardly appeared when it was received by all men of upright mind with unprecedented enthusiasm. Never had any book produced such a sensation. It was in every hand : men struggled to procure it, read it eagerly, and would even kiss it. [2] The words it contained enlightened every heart. But a reaction soon took place. Traditional catholicism uttered a cry from the depths of its noisome pools, (to use Erasmus's figure). Franciscans and Dominicans, priests and bishops, not daring to attack the educated and well-born, went among the ignorant populace, and endeavoured by their tales and clamours to stir up susceptible women and credulous men. " Here are horrible heresies," they exclaimed, " here are frightful antichrists ! If this book be tolerated it will be the death of the papacy !"—" We must drive this man from the university," said one. " We must turn him out of the church," added another. " The public places re-echoed with their howlings," said Erasmus. [3] The firebrands tossed by their furious hands were raising fires in every quarter ; and the flames kindled in a few obscure convents threatened to spread over the whole country.

This irritation was not without a cause. The book, indeed, contained nothing but Latin and Greek : but this first step seemed to augur another—the translation of the Bible into the vulgar tongue. Erasmus loudly called for it. [4] " Perhaps it may be necessary to conceal the secrets of kings," he remarked, " but we must publish the mysteries of Christ. The Holy Scriptures, translated into all languages, should be read not only by the Scotch and Irish, but even by Turks and Saracens. The husbandman should sing them as he holds the handle of his plough, the weaver repeat them as he plies his shuttle, and the wearied traveller, halting on his journey, refresh him under some shady tree by these

godly narratives." These words prefigured a golden age after the iron age of popery. A number of Christian families in Britain and on the continent were soon to realize these evangelical forebodings, and England after three centuries was to endeavour to carry them out for the benefit of all the nations on the face of the earth.

The priests saw the danger, and by a skilful manœuvre, instead of finding fault with the Greek Testament, attacked the translation and the translator. " He has corrected the Vulgate," they said, " and puts himself in the place of Saint Jerome. He sets aside a work authorized by the consent of ages and inspired by the Holy Ghost. What audacity !" And then, turning over the pages, they pointed out the most odious passages: " Look here ! this book calls upon men to *repent*, instead of requiring them, as the Vulgate does, *to do penance !*" (Matt. iv. 17.) The priests thundered against him from their pulpits : [1] " This man has committed the unpardonable sin," they asserted ; " for he maintains that there is nothing in common between the Holy Ghost and the monks—that they are logs rather than men !" These simple remarks were received with a general laugh ; but the priests, in no wise disconcerted, cried out all the louder : " He 's a heretic, an heresiarch, a forger ! he's a goose [2]......what do I say ? he 's a very antichrist ! "

It was not sufficient for the papal janissaries to make war in the plain, they must carry it to the higher ground. Was not the king a friend of Erasmus ? If he should declare himself a patron of the Greek and Latin Testament, what an awful calamity !...... After having agitated the cloisters, towns, and universities, they resolved to protest against it boldly, even in Henry's presence. They thought : " If he is won, all is won." It happened one day that a certain theologian (whose name is not given) having to preach in his turn before the king, he declaimed violently against the *Greek* language and its new interpreters. Pace, the king's secretary, was present, and turning his eyes on Henry, observed him smiling good-humouredly. [3] On leaving the church, every one began to exclaim against the preacher. " Bring the priest to me," said the king ; and then turning to More, he added : " You shall defend the Greek cause against him, and I will listen to the disputation." The literary tribunal was soon formed, but the sovereign's order had taken away all the priest's courage. He came forward trembling, fell on his knees, and with clasped hands exclaimed : " I know not what spirit impelled me." " A spirit of madness," said the king, " and not the spirit

---

[1] In evangelicis litteris, sermo ille cœlestis, quondam e corde Patris ad nos profectus. Erasm. Leoni, Ep. p. 1843.
[2] Opus avidissime rapitur... amatur, manibus teritur. Er. Ep. 557.
[3] Obiatrabant sycophantæ. Ibid. p. 329.
[4] Paraclesis ad lectorem pium.

[1] Quam stolide debacchati sunt quidam e suggestis ad populum. Erasm. Ep. p. 1193.
[2] Nos clamitans esse grues (*cranes*) et bestias. Ibid. p. 914.
[3] Pacæus in regem conjecit oculos....Is mox Pacæo suaviter arrisit. Ibid.

of Jesus Christ."[1] He then added: "Have you ever read Erasmus?" "No, Sire." "Away with you then, you are a blockhead." "And yet," said the preacher in confusion, "I remember to have read something about *Moria*," (Erasmus's treatise on *Folly*).—"A subject, your majesty, that ought to be very familiar to him," wickedly interrupted Pace. The *obscurant* could say nothing in his justification. "I am not altogether opposed to the Greek," he added at last, "seeing that it is derived from the Hebrew."[2] This was greeted with a general laugh, and the king impatiently ordered the monk to leave the room, and never appear before him again.

Erasmus was astonished at these discussions. He had imagined the season to be most favourable. "Every thing looks peaceful," he had said to himself: "now is the time to launch my Greek Testament into the learned world."[3] As well might the sun rise upon the earth, and no one see it! At that very hour God was raising up a monk at Wittemberg who would lift the trumpet to his lips, and proclaim the new day. "Wretch that I am!" exclaimed the timid scholar, beating his breast, "who could have foreseen this horrible tempest!"[4]

Nothing was more important at the dawn of the Reformation than the publication of the Testament of Jesus Christ in the original language. Never had Erasmus worked so carefully. "If I told what sweat it cost me, no one would believe me."[5] He had collated many Greek MSS. of the New Testament,[6] and was surrounded by all the commentaries and translations, by the writings of Origen, Cyprian, Ambrose, Basil, Chrysostom, Cyril, Jerome, and Augustine. *Hic sum in campo meo!* he exclaimed as he sat in the midst of his books. He had investigated the texts according to the principles of sacred criticism. When a knowledge of Hebrew was necessary, he had consulted Capito and more particularly Œcolampadius. *Nothing without Theseus*, said he of the latter, making use of a Greek proverb. He had corrected the amphibologies, obscurities, hebraisms, and barbarisms of the Vulgate; and had caused a list to be printed of the errors in that version.

"We must restore the pure text of the word of God," he had said; and when he heard the maledictions of the priests, he had exclaimed: "I call God to witness I thought I was doing a work acceptable to the Lord and necessary to the cause of Christ."[7] Nor in this was he deceived.

At the head of his adversaries was Edward Lee, successively king's almoner, archdeacon of Colchester, and archbishop of York. Lee, at that time but little known, was a man of talent and activity, but also vain and loquacious, and determined to make his way at any cost. Even when a schoolboy he looked down on all his companions.[1] As child, youth, man, and in mature years, he was always the same, Erasmus tells us;[2] that is to say, vain, envious, jealous, boasting, passionate, and revengeful. We must bear in mind, however, that when Erasmus describes the character of his opponents, he is far from being an impartial judge. In the bosom of Roman-catholicism, there have always existed well-meaning, though ill-informed men, who, not knowing the interior power of the word of God, have thought that if its authority were substituted for that of the Romish church, the only foundation of truth and of Christian society would be shaken. Yet while we judge Lee less severely than Erasmus does, we cannot close our eyes to his faults. His memory was richly furnished, but his heart was a stranger to divine truth: he was a schoolman, and not a believer. He wanted the people to obey the church and not trouble themselves about the Scriptures. He was the Doctor Eck of England, but with more of outward appearance and morality than Luther's adversary. Yet he was by no means a rigid moralist. On one occasion, when preaching at the palace, he introduced ballads into his sermon, one of which began thus:—

"Pass time with good company."

And the other:—

"I love unloved."

We are indebted to Secretary Pace for this characteristic trait.[3]

During the sojourn of Erasmus in England, Lee, observing his influence, had sought his friendship, and Erasmus, with his usual courtesy, had solicited his advice upon his work. But Lee, jealous of his great reputation, only waited for an opportunity to injure it, which he seized upon as soon as it occurred. The New Testament had not been long published, when Lee turned round abruptly, and from being Erasmus's friend became his implacable adversary.[4] "If we do not stop this leak," said he, when he heard of the New Testament, "it will sink the ship." Nothing terrifies the defenders of human traditions so much as the word of God.

Lee immediately leagued himself with all those in England who abhorred the study of Scripture, says Erasmus. Although exceedingly conceited, he showed himself the most amiable of men, in order to accomplish his

---

[1] Tum rex: ut qui inquit, spiritus iste non erat Christi sed stultitiæ. Erasm. Ep. p. 614.
[2] Græcis, inquit, literis non perinde sum infensus, quod originem habeant ex lingua hebraica. Ibid. p. 347.
[3] Erant tempora tranquilla. Ibid. 911.
[4] Quis enim suspicaturus erat hanc fatalem tempestatem exorituram in orbe? Ibid.
[5] Quantis mihi constiterit sudoribus. Ibid. 329.
[6] Collatis multis Græcorum exemplaribus. Ibid.
[7] Deum testor simpliciter existimabam me rem facere Deo gratam ac rei christianæ necessariam. Ibid. p. 911.

[1] Solus haberi in pretio volebat. Erasm. Ep. p. 593.
[2] Talis erat puer, talis adolescens, talis juvenis, talis nunc etiam vir est. Ibid. 594.
[3] State Papers, Henry VIII. etc. i. p. 10, pub. 1830.
[4] Subito factus est inimicus. Erasm. Ep. 746.

designs. He invited Englishmen to his house, welcomed strangers, and gained many recruits by the excellence of his dinners.[1] While seated at table among his guests, he hinted perfidious charges against Erasmus, and his company left him "loaded with lies."[2] —" In this New Testament," said he, " there are three hundred dangerous, frightful passages......three hundred did I say ?......there are more than a thousand ! " Not satisfied with using his tongue, Lee wrote scores of letters, and employed several secretaries. Was there any convent in the odour of sanctity, he "forwarded to it instantly wine, choice viands, and other presents." To each one he assigned his part, and over all England they were rehearsing what Erasmus calls *Lee's Tragedy*.[3] In this manner they were preparing the catastrophe : a prison for Erasmus, the fire for the Holy Scriptures.

When all was arranged, Lee issued his manifesto. Although a poor Greek scholar,[4] he drew up some *Annotations* on Erasmus's book, which the latter called " mere abuse and blasphemy ;" but which the members of the league regarded as *oracles*. They passed them secretly from hand to hand, and these obscure sheets, by many indirect channels, found their way into every part of England, and met with numerous readers.[5] There was to be no publication—such was the watchword ; Lee was too much afraid. " Why did you not publish your work," asked Erasmus, with cutting irony. " Who knows whether the holy father, appointing you the Aristarchus of letters, might not have sent you a birch to keep the whole world in order !"[6]

The *Annotations* having triumphed in the convents, the *conspiracy* took a new flight. In every place of public resort, at fairs and markets, at the dinner-table and in the council-chamber, in shops, and taverns, and houses of ill-fame, in churches and in the universities, in cottages and in palaces, the league blattered against Erasmus and the Greek Testament.[7] Carmelites, Dominicans, and Sophists, invoked heaven and conjured hell. What need was there of Scripture ? Had they not the apostolical succession of the clergy ? No hostile landing in England could, in their eyes, be more fatal than that of the New Testament. The whole nation must rise to repel this impudent invasion. There is, perhaps, no country in Europe, where the Reformation was received by so unexpected a storm.

1 Excipiebat advenas, præsertim Anglos, eos conviviis faciebat suos. Erasm. Ep. 593.
2 Abeuntes omni mendaciorum genere dimittebat onustos. Ibid.
3 Donec Leus ordiretur suam *tragœdiam*. Ibid. 913.
4 Simon, Hist. crit. du. N. Test. p. 246.
5 Liber volitat inter manus conjuratorum. Erasm. Ep. p. 746.
6 Tibi tradita virgula totius orbis censuram fuerit mandaturus. Ibid. p. 742.
7 Ut nusquam non blaterent in Erasmum, in compotationibus, in foris, in conciliabulis, in pharmacopoliis, in curribus, in tonstrinis, in fornicibus.... Ibid. p. 746.

CHAPTER II.

Effects of the New Testament in the Universities—Conversations—A Cambridge Fellow—Bilney buys the New Testament—The first Passage—His Conversion—Protestantism, the Pruit of the Gospel—The Vale of the Severn—William Tyndale—Evangelization at Oxford—Bilney teaches at Cambridge—Fryth—Is Conversion Possible ?—True Consecration—The Reformation has begun.

WHILE this rude blast was rushing over England, and roaring in the long galleries of its convents, the still small voice of the Word was making its way into the peaceful homes of praying men and the ancient halls of Oxford and Cambridge. In private chambers, in the lecture-rooms and refectories, students, and even masters of arts, were to be seen reading the Greek and Latin Testament. Animated groups were discussing the principles of the Reformation. When Christ came on earth (said some) He gave the word, and when He ascended up into heaven He gave the Holy Spirit. These are the two forces which created the church—and these are the forces that must regenerate it.—No (replied the partisans of Rome), it was the teaching of the apostles at first, and it is the teaching of the priests now.— The apostles (rejoined the friends of the Testament of Erasmus)—yes, it is true—the apostles were during their ministry a living scripture ; but their oral teaching would infallibly have been altered by passing from mouth to mouth. God willed, therefore, that these precious lessons should be preserved to us in their writings, and thus become the ever-undefiled source of truth and salvation. To set the Scriptures in the foremost place, as your pretended reformers are doing (replied the schoolmen of Oxford and Cambridge), is to propagate heresy ! And what are the reformers doing (asked their apologists) except what Christ did before them ? The sayings of the prophets existed in the time of Jesus only as *Scripture*, and it was to this written Word that our Lord appealed when he founded his kingdom.[1] And now in like manner the teaching of the apostles exists only as Scripture, and it is to this written word that we appeal in order to re-establish the kingdom of our Lord in its primitive condition. The night is far spent, the day is at hand ; all is in motion—in the lofty halls of our colleges, in the mansions of the rich and noble, and in the lowly dwellings of the poor. If we want to scatter the darkness, must we light the shrivelled wick of some old lamp ? Ought we not rather to open the doors and shutters and admit freely into the house the great light which God has placed in the heavens ?

There was, in Trinity Hall, Cambridge, a young doctor much given to the study of the canon law, of serious turn of mind and bashful disposition, and whose tender con-

1 Matth. xxii. 29 ; xxvi. 24. 54 ; Mark. xiv. 49 ; Luke, xviii. 31 ; xxiv. 27, 44, 45 ; John, v. 39, 46 ; x. 35 ; xvii. 12, &c.

science strove, although ineffectually, to fulfil the commandments of God. Anxious about his salvation, Thomas Bilney applied to the priests, whom he looked upon as physicians of the soul. Kneeling before his confessor, with humble look and pale face, he told him all his sins, and even those of which he doubted.[1] The priest prescribed at one time fasting, at another prolonged vigils, and then masses and indulgences which cost him dearly.[2] The poor doctor went through all these practices with great devotion, but found no consolation in them. Being weak and slender, his body wasted away by degrees;[3] his understanding grew weaker, his imagination faded, and his purse became empty. "Alas!" said he with anguish, "my last state is worse than the first." From time to time an idea crossed his mind: "May not the priests be seeking their own interest, and not the salvation of my soul."[4] But immediately rejecting the rash doubt, he fell back under the iron hand of the clergy.

One day Bilney heard his friends talking about a new book: it was the Greek Testament printed with a translation which was highly praised for its elegant Latinity.[5] Attracted by the beauty of the style rather than by the divinity of the subject,[6] he stretched out his hand; but just as he was going to take the volume, fear came upon him and he withdrew it hastily. In fact the confessors strictly prohibited Greek and Hebrew books, "the sources of all heresies;" and Erasmus's Testament was particularly forbidden. Yet Bilney regretted so great a sacrifice; was it not the Testament of Jesus Christ? Might not God have placed therein some word which perhaps might heal his soul? He stepped forward, and then again shrank back ......At last he took courage. Urged, said he, by the hand of God, he walked out of the college, slipped into the house where the volume was sold in secret, bought it with fear and trembling, and then hastened back and shut himself up in his room.[7]

He opened it—his eyes caught these words: *This is a faithful saying, and worthy of all acceptation, that Christ Jesus came into the world to save sinners; of whom I am chief.*[8] He laid down the book, and meditated on the astonishing declaration. "What! St Paul the chief of sinners, and yet St Paul is sure of being saved!" He read the verse again and again. "O assertion of St Paul, how sweet art thou to my soul!" he exclaimed.[9] This declaration continually haunted him,

and in this manner God instructed him in the secret of his heart.[1] He could not tell what had happened to him;[2] it seemed as if a refreshing wind were blowing over his soul, or as if a rich treasure had been placed in his hands. The Holy Spirit took what was Christ's, and announced it to him. "I also am like Paul," exclaimed he with emotion, "and more than Paul, the greatest of sinners!......But Christ saves sinners. At last I have heard of Jesus."[3]

His doubts were ended—he was saved. Then took place in him a wonderful transformation. An unknown joy pervaded him;[4] his conscience until then sore with the wounds of sin was healed;[5] instead of despair he felt an inward peace passing all understanding.[6] "Jesus Christ," exclaimed he, "Yes, Jesus Christ saves!"......Such is the character of the Reformation: it is Jesus Christ who saves and not the church. "I see it all," said Bilney; "my vigils, my fasts, my pilgrimages, my purchase of masses and indulgences, were destroying instead of saving me.[7] All these efforts were, as St Augustine says, a hasty running out of the right way."[8]

Bilney never grew tired of reading his New Testament. He no longer lent an attentive ear to the teaching of the schoolmen; he heard Jesus at Capernaum, Peter in the temple, Paul on Mars' hill, and felt within himself that Christ possesses the words of eternal life. A witness to Jesus Christ had just been born by the same power which had transformed Paul, Apollos, and Timothy. The Reformation of England was beginning. Bilney was united to the Son of God, not by a remote succession, but by an immediate generation. Leaving to the disciples of the pope the entangled chain of their imaginary succession, whose links it is impossible to disengage, he attached himself closely to Christ. The word of the first century gave birth to the sixteenth. Protestantism does not descend from the gospel in the fiftieth generation like the Romish church of the Council of Trent, or in the sixtieth like some modern doctors: it is the direct legitimate son—the son of the master.

God's action was not limited to one spot. The first rays of the sun from on high gilded with their fires at once the gothic colleges of Oxford and the antique schools of Cambridge.

Along the banks of the Severn extends a picturesque country, bounded by the forest of Dean, and sprinkled with villages, steeples, and ancient castles. In the sixteenth century it was particularly admired by priests and friars, and a familiar oath among them

---

[1] In ignaros medicos, indoctos confessionum auditores. Th. Bilnæus Tonstallo Episcopo; Foxe, iv. p. 633.
[2] Indicebant enim mihi jejunia, vigilias, indulgentiarum et missarum emptiones. Ibid.
[3] Ut parum mihi virium (alioqui natura imbecilli) reliquum fuerit. Ibid.
[4] Sua potius quærebant quam salutem animæ meæ languentis. Ibid.
[5] Cum ab eo latinius redditum accepi. Ibid.
[6] Latinitate potius quam verbo Dei, allectus. Ibid.
[7] Emebam providentiâ (sine dubio) divinâ. Ibid.
[8] 1 Tim. i. 15.
[9] O mihi suavissimam Pauli sententiam! Foxe, iv. p. 633.

[1] Hac una sententia, Deo intus in corde meo docente. Foxe, iv. p. 633.
[2] Quod tunc fieri ignorabam. Ibid.
[3] Tandem de Jesu audiebam. Ibid.
[4] Sic exhilaravit pectus meum. Ibid.
[5] Peccatorum conscientia saucium ac pene desperabundum. Ibid.
[6] Nescio quantam intus tranquillitatem sentire. Ibid.
[7] Didici omnes meos conatus, etc. Ibid.
[8] Quod ait Augustinus, celerem cursum extra viam. Ibid.

was: "As sure as God's in Glo'ster!" The papal birds of prey had swooped upon it. For fifty years, from 1484 to 1534, four Italian bishops, placed in succession over the diocese, had surrendered it to the pope, to the monks, and to immorality. Thieves in particular were the objects of the tenderest favours of the hierarchy. John de Giglis, collector of the apostolical chamber, had received from the sovereign pontiff authority to pardon murder and theft, on condition that the criminal shared his profits with the pontifical commissioners.[1]

In this valley, at the foot of Stinchcomb hill, to the south-west of Gloucester, there dwelt, during the latter half of the fifteenth century, a family which had taken refuge there during the wars of the Roses, and assumed the name of Hutchins. In the reign of Henry VII. the Lancasterian party having the upper hand, they resumed their name of Tyndale, which had been borne of yore by many noble barons.[2] In 1484, about a year after the birth of Luther, and about the time that Zwingle first saw light in the mountains of the Tockenburg, these partisans of the *red rose* were blessed with a son, whom they called William. His youth was passed in the fields surrounding his native village of North Nibley, beneath the shadows of Berkeley Castle, or beside the rapid waters of the Severn, and in the midst of friars and pontifical collectors. He was sent very early to Oxford,[3] where he learnt grammar and philosophy in the school of St Mary Magdalene, adjoining the college of that name. He made rapid progress, particularly in languages, under the first classical scholars in England—Grocyn, W. Latimer, and Linacre—and took his degrees.[4] A more excellent master than these doctors—the Holy Spirit speaking in Scripture—was soon to teach him a science which it is not in the power of man to impart.

Oxford, where Erasmus had so many friends, was the city in which his New Testament met with the warmest welcome. The young Gloucestershire student, inwardly impelled towards the study of sacred literature, read the celebrated book which was then attracting the attention of Christendom. At first he regarded it only as a work of learning, or at most as a manual of piety, whose beauties were calculated to excite religious feelings; but erelong he found it to be something more. The more he read it, the more was he struck by the truth and energy of the word. This strange book spoke to him of God, of Christ, and of regeneration, with a simplicity and authority which completely subdued him. William had found a master whom he had not sought at Oxford—this was God himself. The pages he held in his hand

were the divine revelation so long mislaid. Possessing a noble soul, a bold spirit, and indefatigable activity, he did not keep this treasure to himself. He uttered that cry, more suited to a Christian than to Archimedes: εὕρηκα, *I have found it.* It was not long before several of the younger members of the university, attracted by the purity of his life and the charms of his conversation,[1] gathered round him, and read with him the Greek and Latin gospels of Erasmus.[2] "A certain well-informed young man," wrote Erasmus in a letter wherein he speaks of the publication of his New Testament, "began to lecture with success on Greek Literature at Oxford."[3] He was probably speaking of Tyndale.

The monks took the alarm. "*A barbarian,*" continues Erasmus, "entered the pulpit and violently abused the Greek language."— "These folk," said Tyndale, "wished to extinguish the light which exposed their trickery, and they have been laying their plans these dozen years."[4] This observation was made in 1531, and refers therefore to the proceedings of 1517. Germany and England were beginning the struggle at nearly the same time, and Oxford perhaps before Wittemberg. Tyndale, bearing in mind the injunction: "When they persecute you in one city, flee ye into another," left Oxford and proceeded to Cambridge. It must needs be that souls whom God has brought to his knowledge should meet and enlighten one another: live coals, when separated, go out; when gathered together, they brighten up, so as even to purify silver and gold. The Romish hierarchy, not knowing what they did, were collecting the scattered brands of the Reformation.

Bilney was not inactive at Cambridge. Not long had the "sublime lesson of Jesus Christ" filled him with joy, before he fell on his knees and exclaimed: "O Thou who art the truth, give me strength that I may teach it; and convert the ungodly by means of one who has been ungodly himself."[5] After this prayer his eyes gleamed with new fire; he had assembled his friends, and opening Erasmus's Testament, had placed his finger on the words that had reached his soul, and these words had touched many. The arrival of Tyndale gave him fresh courage, and the light burnt brighter in Cambridge.

John Fryth, a young man of eighteen, the son of an innkeeper of Sevenoaks in Kent, was distinguished among the students of King's College, by the promptitude of his understanding and the integrity of his life. He was as deeply read in the mathematics as Tyndale in the classics, and Bilney in canon

[1] Annals of the English Bible, i. p. 12.
[2] Bigland's Glo'ster, p. 293. Annals of the English Bible. p. 19.
[3] From a child. Foxe, Acts and Mon. v. p. 115. Proceeding in degrees of the schools. Ibid.

[1] His manners and conversation being correspondent to the Scriptures. Foxe, Acts and Mon. v. p. 115.
[2] Read privily to certain students and fellows, instructing them in the knowledge and truth of the Scriptures. Ibid.
[3] Oxoniæ cum juvenis quidam non vulgariter doctus. Erasm. Ep. p. 346.
[4] Which they have been in brewing as I hear this dozen years. Tyndale's Expositions (Park Soc.) p. 225.
[5] Ut impii ad ipsum per me olim impium converterentur. Foxe, Acts, iv. p. 633.

law. Although of an exact turn of mind, yet his soul was elevated, and he recognised in Holy Scripture a learning of a new kind. "These things are not demonstrated like a proposition of Euclid," he said; "mere study is sufficient to impress the theories of mathematics on our minds; but this science of God meets with a resistance in man that necessitates the intervention of a divine power. Christianity is a regeneration." The heavenly seed soon grew up in Fryth's heart.[1]

These three young scholars set to work with enthusiasm. They declared that neither priestly absolution nor any other religious rite could give remission of sins; that the assurance of pardon is obtained by faith alone; and that faith purifies the heart. Then they addressed to all men that saying of Christ's at which the monks were so offended: *Repent and be converted!*

Ideas so new produced a great clamour. A famous orator undertook one day at Cambridge to show that it was useless to preach conversion to the sinner. "Thou, who, for sixty years past," said he, "hast wallowed in thy lusts, like a sow in her mire,[2] dost thou think that thou canst in one year take as many steps towards heaven, and that in thine age, as thou hast done towards hell?" Bilney left the church with indignation. "Is that preaching repentance in the name of Jesus?" he asked. "Does not this priest tell us: Christ will not save thee.[3] Alas! for so many years that this deadly doctrine has been taught in Christendom, not one man has dared open his mouth against it!" Many of the Cambridge fellows were scandalized at Bilney's language: was not the preacher whose words he condemned duly *ordained* by the bishop? He replied: "What would be the use of being a hundred times consecrated, were it even by a thousand papal bulls, if the inward calling is wanting?[4] To no purpose hath the bishop breathed on our heads if we have never felt the breath of the Holy Ghost in our hearts!" Thus, at the very beginning of the Reformation, England, rejecting the Romish superstitions, discerned with extreme nicety what constitutes the essence of consecration to the service of the Lord.

After pronouncing these noble words, Bilney, who longed for an outpouring of the Holy Ghost, shut himself up in his room, fell on his knees, and called upon God to come to the assistance of his church. Then rising up, he exclaimed, as if animated by a prophetic spirit: "A new time is beginning. The Christian assembly is about to be renewed......Some one is coming unto us, I see him,

I hear him—it is Jesus Christ.[1]......He is the king, and it is he who will call the true ministers commissioned to evangelize his people."

Tyndale, full of the same hopes as Bilney, left Cambridge in the course of the year 1519.

Thus the English Reformation began independently of those of Luther and Zwingle —deriving its origin from God alone. In every province of Christendom there was a simultaneous action of the divine word. The principle of the Reformation at Oxford, Cambridge, and London was the *Greek New Testament,* published by Erasmus. England, in course of time learnt to be proud of this origin of its Reformation.

CHAPTER III.

Alarm of the Clergy—The Two Days—Thomas Man's Preaching—True real Presence—Persecutions at Coventry —Standish Preaches at St Paul's—His Petition to the King and Queen—His Arguments and Defeat—Wolsey's Ambition—First Overtures—Henry and Francis Candidates for the Empire—Conference between Francis I. and Sir T. Boleyn—The Tiara promised to Wolsey—The Cardinal's Intrigues with Charles and Francis.

THIS revival caused great alarm throughout the Roman hierarchy. Content with the baptism they administered, they feared the baptism of the Holy Ghost perfected by faith in the word of God. Some of the clergy, who were full of zeal, but of zeal without knowledge, prepared for the struggle, and the cries raised by the prelates were repeated by all the inferior orders.

The first blows did not fall on the members of the universities, but on those humble Christians, the relics of Wickliffe's ministry, to whom the reform movement among the learned had imparted a new life. The awakening of the fourteenth century was about to be succeeded by that of the sixteenth, and the last gleams of the closing day were almost lost in the first rays of that which was commencing. The young doctors of Oxford and Cambridge aroused the attention of the alarmed hierarchy, and attracted their eyes to the humble Lollards, who here and there still recalled the days of Wickliffe.

An artisan named Thomas Man, sometimes called Doctor Man, from his knowledge of Holy Scripture, had been imprisoned for his faith in the priory of Frideswide at Oxford (1511 A. D.) Tormented by the remembrance of a recantation which had been extorted from him, he had escaped from this monastery and fled into the eastern parts of England, where he had preached the Word, supplying his daily wants by the labour of his hands.[2]

---

[1] Through Tyndale's instructions he first received into his heart the seed of the Gospel. Foxe, Acts, v. p. 4.
[2] Even as a beast in his own dung. Bilnæus Tonstallo episcopo; Foxe. Acts, iv. p. 640.
[3] He will not be thy Jesus or Saviour. Ibid.
[4] Without this inward calling it helpeth nothing before God to be a hundred times elect and consecrated. Ibid. p. 638.

[1] If it be Christ, him that cometh unto us. Foxe, Acts, iv. p. 637.
[2] Work thereby to sustain his poor life. Ibid. p. 209.

This "champion of God" afterwards drew near the capital, and assisted by his wife, the new Priscilla of this new Aquila, he proclaimed the doctrine of Christ to the crowd collected around him in some "upper chamber" of London, or in some lonely meadow watered by the Thames, or under the aged oaks of Windsor Forest. He thought with Chrysostom of old, that "all priests are not saints, but all saints are priests."[1] "He that receiveth the word of God," said he, "receiveth God himself: that is the true *real presence*. The vendors of masses are not the high-priests of this mystery;[2] but the men whom God hath *anointed with his Spirit* to be kings and priests." From six to seven hundred persons were converted by his preaching.[3]

The monks who dared not as yet attack the universities, resolved to fall upon those preachers who made their temple on the banks of the Thames, or in some remote corner of the city. Man was seized, condemned, and burnt alive on the 29th March 1519.

And this was not all. There lived at Coventry a little band of serious Christians—four shoemakers, a glover, a hosier, and a widow named Smith—who gave their children a pious education. The Franciscans were annoyed that *laymen*, and even a *woman*, should dare meddle with religious instruction. On Ash Wednesday (1519) Simon Morton, the bishop's sumner, apprehended them all, men, women, and children. On the following Friday, the parents were taken to the abbey of Mackstock, about six miles from Coventry, and the children to the Grey Friars' convent. "Let us see what heresies you have been taught?" said Friar Stafford to the intimidated little ones. The poor children confessed they had been taught in English the Lord's prayer, the apostles' creed, and the ten commandments. On hearing this, Stafford told them angrily: "I forbid you (unless you wish to be burnt as your parents will be) to have any thing to do with the *Pater*, the *credo*, or the ten commandments *in English*."

Five weeks after this, the men were condemned to be burnt alive, but the judges had compassion on the widow, because of her young family (for she was their only support,) and let her go. It was night: Morton offered to see Dame Smith home: she took his arm, and they threaded the dark and narrow streets of Coventry. "Eh, eh!" said the apparitor on a sudden, "what have we here?" He heard in fact the noise of paper rubbing against something. "What have you got there?" he continued, dropping her arm, and putting his hand up her sleeve, from which he drew out a parchment. Approaching a window whence issued the faint rays of a lamp, he examined the mysterious scroll,

and found it to contain the Lord's prayer, the apostles' creed, and the ten commandments *in English*. "Oh, oh! sirrah!" said he; "come along. As good now as another time!"[2] Then seizing the poor widow by the arm, he dragged her before the bishop. Sentence of death was immediately pronounced on her, and on the 4th of April, Dame Smith, Robert Hatchets, Archer, Hawkins, Thomas Bond, Wrigsham, and Lansdale, were burnt alive at Coventry in the Little Park, for the crime of teaching their children the Lord's prayer, the apostles' creed, and the commandments of God.

But what availed it to silence these obscure lips, so long as the Testament of Erasmus could speak? Lee's conspiracy must be revived. Standish, bishop of St Asaph, was a narrow-minded man, rather fanatical, but probably sincere, of great courage, and not without some degree of piety. This prelate, being determined to preach a crusade against the New Testament, began at London, in St Paul's cathedral, before the mayor and corporation. "Away with these new translations," he said, "or else the religion of Jesus Christ is threatened with utter ruin."[2] But Standish was deficient in tact, and instead of confining himself to general statements, like most of his party, he endeavoured to show how far Erasmus had corrupted the gospel, and continued thus in a whining voice: "Must I who for so many years have been a doctor of the Holy Scriptures, and who have always read in my Bible: *In principio erat* VERBUM,—must I now be obliged to read: *In principio erat* SERMO," for thus had Erasmus translated the opening words of St John's Gospel. *Risum teneatis*, whispered one to another, when they heard this puerile charge: "My lord," proceeded the bishop, turning to the mayor, "magistrates of the city, and citizens all, fly to the succour of religion!" Standish continued his pathetic appeals, but his oratory was all in vain; some stood unmoved, others shrugged their shoulders, and others grew impatient. The citizens of London seemed determined to support liberty and the Bible.

Standish, seeing the failure of his attack in the city, sighed and groaned and prayed, and repeated mass against the so much dreaded book. But he also made up his mind to do more. One day, during the rejoicings at court for the betrothal of the Princess Mary, then two years old, with a French prince who was just born, St Asaph, absorbed and absent in the midst of the gay crowd, meditated a bold step. Suddenly he made his way through the crowd, and threw himself at the feet of the king and queen. All were thunderstruck, and asked one another what the old bishop could mean.

---

[1] Chrysostom, 43 Homily on Matth.
[2] He called them *pilled knaves*. Foxe, iv. p. 209.
[3] Ibid. p. 211.

[1] Foxe, Acts, iv. p. 357.
[2] Imminere christianæ religionis πανολιτρείαν, nisi novæ translationes omnes subito de medio tollerentur. Erasm. Ep. p. 596.

" Great king," said he, " your ancestors who have reigned over this island,—and yours, O great queen, who have governed Aragon, were always distinguished by their zeal for the church. Show yourselves worthy of your forefathers. Times full of danger are come upon us,[1] a book has just appeared, and been published too, by Erasmus! It is such a book that, if you close not your kingdom against it, it is all over with the religion of Christ among us."

The bishop ceased, and a dead silence ensued. The devout Standish, fearing lest Henry's well-known love of learning should be an obstacle to his prayer, raised his eyes and his hands toward heaven, and kneeling in the midst of the courtly assembly, exclaimed in a sorrowful tone : " O Christ! O Son of God! save thy spouse !....for no man cometh to her help."[2]

Having thus spoken, the prelate, whose courage was worthy of a better cause, rose up and waited. Every one strove to guess at the king's thoughts. Sir Thomas More was present, and he could not forsake his friend Erasmus. " What are the heresies this book is likely to engender ? " he inquired. After the sublime came the ridiculous. With the forefinger of his right hand, touching successively the fingers of his left,[3] Standish replied: First, this book destroys *the resurrection;* secondly, it annuls the *sacrament of marriage;* thirdly, it abolishes *the mass.*" Then uplifting his thumb and two fingers, he showed them to the assembly with a look of triumph. The bigoted Catherine shuddered as she saw Standish's three fingers,—signs of the three heresies of Erasmus; and Henry himself, an admirer of Aquinas, was embarrassed. It was a critical moment : the Greek Testament was on the point of being banished from England. " The proof, the proof," exclaimed the friends of literature. " I will give it," rejoined the impetuous Standish, and then once more touching his left thumb : " Firstly," he said,......But he brought forward such foolish reasons, that even the women and the unlearned were ashamed of them. The more he endeavoured to justify his assertions, the more confused he became : he affirmed among other things that the Epistles of St Paul were written in *Hebrew.* " There is not a schoolboy that does not know that Paul's epistles were written in *Greek,*" said a doctor of divinity kneeling before the king. Henry, blushing for the bishop, turned the conversation, and Standish, ashamed at having made a Greek write to the Greeks in Hebrew, would have withdrawn unobserved. " The beetle must not attack the eagle,"[4] was whispered in his

ear. Thus did the book of God remain in England the standard of a faithful band, who found in its pages the motto, which the church of Rome had usurped : *The truth is in me alone.*

A more formidable adversary than Standish aspired to combat the Reformation, not only in England, but in all the West. One of those ambitious designs, which easily germinate in the human heart, developed itself in the soul of the chief minister of Henry VIII. ; and if this project succeeded, it promised to secure for ever the empire of the papacy on the banks of the Thames, and perhaps in the whole of Christendom.

Wolsey, as chancellor and legate, governed both in state and in church, and could, without an untruth, utter his famous *Ego et rex meus.* Having reached so great a height, he desired to soar still higher. The favourite of Henry VIII., almost his master, treated as a brother by the emperor, by the king of France, and by other crowned heads, invested with the title of Majesty, the peculiar property of sovereigns,[1] the cardinal, sincere in his faith in the popedom, aspired to fill the throne of the pontiffs, and thus become *Deus in terris.* He thought, that if God permitted a Luther to appear in the world, it was because he had a Wolsey to oppose to him.

It would be difficult to fix the precise moment when this immoderate desire entered his mind : it was about the end of 1518 that it began to show itself. The bishop of Ely, ambassador at the court of Francis I., being in conference with that prince on the 18th of December in that year, said to him mysteriously: " The cardinal has an idea in his mind......on which he can unbosom himself to nobody......except it be to your majesty." Francis understood him.

An event occurred to facilitate the cardinal's plans. If Wolsey desired to be the first priest, Henry desired to be the first king. The imperial crown, vacant by the death of Maximilian, was sought by two princes:—by Charles of Austria, a cold and calculating man, caring little about the pleasures and even the pomp of power, but forming great designs, and knowing how to pursue them with energy ; and by Francis I., a man of less penetrating glance and less indefatigable activity, but more daring and impetuous. Henry VIII., inferior to both, passionate, capricious, and selfish, thought himself strong enough to contend with such puissant competitors, and secretly strove to win " the monarchy of all Christendom."[2] Wolsey flattered himself that, hidden under the cloak of his master's ambition, he might satisfy his own. If he procured the crown of the Cæsars for Henry, he might easily obtain the tiara of the popes for himself; if he failed, the least

---

[1] Adesse tempora longe periculosissima. Erasm. Ep. p. 597.
[2] Cœpit obsecrare Christum dignaretur ipse suæ sponsæ opitulari. Ibid. p. 598.
[3] Et rem in digitos porrectos dispartiens. Ibid.
[4] Scarabæus ille qui maximo suo malo aquilam quæsivit. Ibid. p. 555.

[1] Consultissima tua Majestas. Vestra sublimis et longe reverendissima Majestas, etc. Fiddes, Bodleian Papers, p. 178.
[2] Cotton MSS. Brit. Mus. Calig. D. 7, p. 88.

that could be done to compensate England for the loss of the empire, would be to give the sovereignty of the church to her prime minister.

Henry first sounded the king of France. Sir Thomas Boleyn appeared one day before Francis I. just as the latter was returning from mass. The king, desirous to anticipate a confidence that might be embarrassing, took the ambassador aside to the window and whispered to him: "Some of the electors have offered me the empire; I hope your master will be favourable to me." Sir Thomas, in confusion, made some vague reply, and the chivalrous king, following up his idea, took the ambassador firmly by one hand, and laying the other on his breast,[1] exclaimed: "By my faith, if I become emperor, in three years I shall be in Constantinople, or I shall die on the road!" This was not what Henry wanted; but dissembling his wishes, he took care to inform Francis that he would support his candidature. Upon hearing this Francis raised his hat and exclaimed: "I desire to see the king of England; I will see him, I tell you, even if I go to London with only one page and one lackey."

Francis was well aware that if he threatened the king's ambition, he must flatter the minister's, and recollecting the hint given by the bishop of Ely, he said one day to Boleyn: "It seems to me that my brother of England and I could do, indeed ought to do......something for the cardinal. He was prepared by God for the good of Christendom......one of the greatest men in the church......and on the word of a king, if he consents, I will do it." A few minutes after he continued: "Write and tell the cardinal, that if he aspires to be the head of the church, and if anything should happen to the reigning pope, I will promise him fourteen cardinals on my part.[2] Let us only act in concert, your master and me, and I promise you, Mr Ambassador, that neither pope nor emperor shall be created in Europe without our consent."

But Henry did not act in concert with the king of France. At Wolsey's instigation he supported three candidates at once: at Paris he was for Francis I.; at Madrid for Charles V.; and at Frankfort for himself. The kings of France and England failed, and on the 10th August, Pace, Henry's envoy at Frankfort, having returned to England, desired to console the king by mentioning the sums of money which Charles had spent. "By the mass!"[3] exclaimed the king, congratulating himself at not having obtained the crown at so dear a rate. Wolsey proposed to sing a *Te Deum* in St Paul's, and bonfires were lighted in the city.

The cardinal's rejoicings were not misplaced. Charles had scarcely ascended the im-

perial throne, in despite of the king of France, when these two princes swore eternal hatred of each other, and each was anxious to win over Henry VIII. At one time Charles, under the pretence of seeing his uncle and aunt, visited England; at another, Francis had an interview with the king in the neighbourhood of Calais. The cardinal shared in the flattering attentions of the two monarchs. "It is easy for the king of Spain, who has become the head of the empire, to raise whomsoever he pleases to the supreme pontificate," said the young emperor to him, and at these words the ambitious cardinal surrendered himself to Maximilian's successor. But erelong Francis I. flattered him in his turn, and Wolsey replied also to his advances. The king of France gave Henry tournaments and banquets of Asiatic luxury; and Wolsey, whose countenance yet bore the marks of the graceful smile with which he had taken leave of Charles, smiled also on Francis, and sang mass in his honour. He engaged the hand of the Princess Mary to the Dauphin of France and to Charles V., leaving the care of unravelling the matter to futurity. Then proud of his skilful practices he returned to London full of hope. By walking in falsehood he hoped to attain the tiara: and if it was yet too far above him, there were certain *gospellers* in England who might serve as a ladder to reach it. Murder might serve as the complement to fraud.

CHAPTER IV.

Tyndale—Sodbury Hall—Sir John and Lady Walsh—Table-Talk—The Holy Scriptures—The Images—The Anchor of Faith—A Roman Camp—Preaching of Faith and Works—Tyndale accused by the Priests—They tear up what he has planted—Tyndale resolves to translate the Bible—His first Triumph—The Priests in the Taverns—Tyndale summoned before the Chancellor of Worcester—Consoled by an aged Doctor—Attacked by a Schoolman—His Secret becomes known—He leaves Sodbury Hall.

WHILST this ambitious prelate was thinking of nothing but his own glory and that of the Roman pontificate, a great desire, but of a very different nature, was springing up in the heart of one of the humble "gospellers" of England. If Wolsey had his eyes fixed on the throne of the popedom in order to seat himself there, Tyndale thought of raising up the true throne of the church by re-establishing the legitimate sovereignty of the word of God. The Greek Testament of Erasmus had been one step; and it now became necessary to place before the simple what the king of the schools had given to the learned. This idea, which pursued the young Oxford doctor everywhere, was to be the mighty mainspring of the English reformation.

On the slope of Sodbury hill there stood a plain but large mansion commanding an extensive view over the beautiful vale of the

---

[1] He took me hard by the wrist with one hand, and laid the other upon his breast. Cott. MSS. Calig. D. 8, p. 93.
[2] He will assure you full fourteen cardinals for him. Ibid. D. F. p. 98.
[3] Bi the messe! State Papers, i. 9.

Severn where Tyndale was born. It was inhabited by a family of gentle birth: Sir John Walsh had shone in the tournaments of the court, and by this means conciliated the favour of his prince. He kept open table; and gentlemen, deans, abbots, archdeacons, doctors of divinity, and fat rectors, charmed by Sir John's cordial welcome and by his good dinners, were ever at his house. The former brother at arms of Henry VIII. felt an interest in the questions then discussing throughout Christendom. Lady Walsh herself, a sensible and generous woman, lost not a word of the animated conversation of her guests, and discreetly tried to incline the balance to the side of truth.[1]

Tyndale after leaving Oxford and Cambridge had returned to the home of his fathers. Sir John had requested him to educate his children, and he had accepted. William was then in the prime of life (he was about thirty-six), well instructed in Scripture, and full of desire to show forth the light which God had given him. Opportunities were not wanting. Seated at table with all the doctors welcomed by Sir John,[2] Tyndale entered into conversation with them. They talked of the learned men of the day—of Erasmus much, and sometimes of Luther, who was beginning to astonish England.[3] They discussed several questions touching the Holy Scriptures, and sundry points of theology. Tyndale expressed his convictions with admirable clearness, supported them with great learning, and kept his ground against all with unbending courage. These animated conversations in the vale of the Severn are one of the essential features of the picture presented by the Reformation in this country. The historians of antiquity invented the speeches which they have put into the mouths of their heroes. In our times history, without inventing, should make us acquainted with the sentiments of the persons of whom it treats. It is sufficient to read Tyndale's works to form some idea of these conversations. It is from his writings that the following discussion has been drawn.

In the dining-room of the old hall a varied group was assembled round the hospitable table. There were Sir John and Lady Walsh, a few gentlemen of the neighbourhood, with several abbots, deans, monks, and doctors, in their respective costumes. Tyndale occupied the humblest place, and generally kept Erasmus's New Testament within reach in order to prove what he advanced.[4] Numerous domestics were moving about engaged in waiting on the guests; and at length the conversation, after wandering a little, took a more precise direction. The priests grew impatient when they saw the terrible volume appear. "Your Scriptures only serve to make heretics," they exclaimed. "On the contrary," replied Tyndale, "the source of all heresies is *pride;* now the word of God strips man of everything, and leaves him as bare as Job."[1]—"*The word of God!* why even *we* don't understand your word, how can the *vulgar* understand it?"—"You do not understand it," rejoined Tyndale, "because you look into it only for foolish questions, as you would into *our Lady's Matins* or *Merlin's Prophecies.*[2] Now the Scriptures are a clue which we must follow, without turning aside, until we arrive at Christ;[3] for Christ is the end."—"And I tell you," shouted out a priest, "that the Scriptures are a Dædalian labyrinth, rather than Ariadne's clue—a conjuring book wherein everybody finds what he wants."—"Alas!" replied Tyndale; "you read them without Jesus Christ; that's why they are an obscure book to you. What do I say? a den of thorns where you only escape from the briers to be caught by the brambles."[4] "No!" exclaimed another clerk, heedless of contradicting his colleague, "nothing is obscure to us; it is we who give the Scriptures, and we who explain them to you."—"You would lose both your time and your trouble," said Tyndale; "do you know who taught the eagles to find their prey?[5] Well, that same God teaches his hungry children to find their Father in his word. Far from having given us the Scriptures, it is you who have hidden them from us; it is you who burn those who teach them, and if you could, you would burn the Scriptures themselves."

Tyndale was not satisfied with merely laying down the great principles of faith: he always sought after what he calls "the sweet marrow within;" but to the divine unction he added no little humour, and unmercifully ridiculed the superstitions of his adversaries. "You set candles before images," he said to them; "and since you give them *light,* why don't you give them *food?* Why don't you make their bellies hollow, and put victuals and drink inside?[6] To serve God by such mummeries is treating him like a spoilt child, whom you pacify with a toy or with a horse made of a stick."[7]

But the learned Christian soon returned to more serious thoughts; and when his adversaries extolled the papacy as the power that would save the church in the tempest, he re-

---

[1] Lady Walsh, a stout and wise woman. Foxe, Acts, v. p. 115.
[2] Who were together with Master Tyndale sitting at the same table. Ibid.
[3] Talk of learned men, as of Luther and Erasmus, &c. Ibid.
[4] When they at any time did vary from Tyndale in opinions and judgment, he would show them in the book. Ibid.

[1] Tyndale, Expositions (Park. Soc.) p. 140.
[2] Ibid. p. 141.
[3] So along by the Scripture as by a line until thou come at Christ. Tynd Works. i. 354 (ed. Russell).
[4] A grave of briers; if thou loose thyself in one place thou art caught in another. Tyndale. Expositions, p. 5.
[5] Ibid. Answer to More (Park. Soc.), p. 49.
[6] Make a hollow belly in the image. Tyndale, Answer to More (Park. Soc.), p. 81.
[7] Make him a horse of a stick. Tyndale's Wks. (ed. Russell), ii. 475.

plied: "Let us only take on board the anchor of faith, after having dipped it in the blood of Christ,[1] and when the storm bursts upon us, let us boldly cast the anchor into the sea; then you may be sure the ship will remain safe on the great waters." And, in fine, if his opponents rejected any doctrine of the truth, Tyndale (says the chronicler) opening his Testament would set his finger on the verse which refuted the Romish error, and exclaim: "Look and read."[2]

The beginnings of the English Reformation are not to be found, as we have seen, in a material ecclesiasticism, which has been decorated with the name of *English Catholicism*: they are essentially spiritual. The Divine Word, the creator of the new life in the individual, is also the founder and reformer of the church. The reformed churches, and particularly the reformed churches of Great Britain, belong to evangelism.

The contemplation of God's works refreshed Tyndale after the discussions he had to maintain at his patron's table. He would often ramble to the top of Sodbury hill, and there repose amidst the ruins of an ancient Roman camp which crowned the summit. It was here that Queen Margaret of Anjou halted; and here too rested Edward IV., who pursued her, before the fatal battle of Tewkesbury, which caused this princess to fall into the hands of the White Rose. Amidst these ruins, monuments of the Roman invasion and of the civil dissensions of England, Tyndale meditated upon other battles, which were to restore liberty and truth to Christendom. Then rousing himself he would descend the hill, and courageously resume his task.

Behind the mansion stood a little church, overshadowed by two large yew trees, and dedicated to Saint Adeline. On Sundays Tyndale used to preach there, Sir John and Lady Walsh, with the eldest of the children, occupying the manorial pew. This humble sanctuary was filled by their household and tenantry, listening attentively to the words of their teacher, which fell from his lips like *the waters of Shiloah that go softly.* Tyndale was very lively in conversation; but he explained the Scriptures with so much unction, says the chronicler, "that his hearers thought they heard St John himself." If he resembled John in the mildness of his language, he resembled Paul in the strength of his doctrine. "According to the pope," he said, "we must first be good after his doctrine, and compel God to be good again for our goodness. Nay, verily, God's goodness is the root of all goodness. Antichrist turneth the tree of salvation topsy-turvy:[3] he planteth the branches, and setteth the roots upwards. We must put

it straight......As the husband marrieth the wife, before he can have any lawful children by her; even so faith justifieth us to make us fruitful in good works.[1] But neither the one nor the other should remain barren. Faith is the only candle wherewith we must bless ourselves at the last hour; without it you will go astray in the valley of the shadow of death, though you had a thousand tapers lighted around your bed."[2]

The priests, irritated at such observations, determined to ruin Tyndale, and some of them invited Sir John and his lady to an entertainment, at which he was not present. During dinner, they so abused the young doctor and his New Testament, that his patrons retired greatly annoyed that their tutor should have made so many enemies. They told him all they had heard, and Tyndale successfully refuted his adversaries' arguments. "What!" exclaimed Lady Walsh, "There are some of these doctors worth one hundred, some two hundred, and some three hundred pounds[3]......and were it reason, think you, Master William, that we should believe you before them?" Tyndale, opening the New Testament, replied: "No! it is not me you should believe. That is what the priests have told you; but look here, St Peter, St Paul, and the Lord himself say quite the contrary."[4] The Word of God was there, positive and supreme: the sword of the spirit cut the difficulty.

Before long the manor-house and St Adeline's church became too narrow for Tyndale's zeal. He preached every Sunday, sometimes in a village, sometimes in a town. The inhabitants of Bristol assembled to hear him in a large meadow, called St Austin's Green.[5] But no sooner had he preached in any place than the priests hastened thither, tore up what he had planted,[6] called him a heretic, and threatened to expel from the church every one who dared listen to him. When Tyndale returned he found the field laid waste by the enemy; and looking sadly upon it, as the husbandman who sees his corn beaten down by the hail, and his rich furrows turned into a barren waste, he exclaimed: "What is to be done? While I am sowing in one place, the enemy ravages the field I have just left. I cannot be everywhere. Oh! if Christians possessed the Holy Scriptures in their own tongue, they could of themselves withstand these sophists. Without the Bible it is impossible to establish the laity in the truth."[7]

[1] Tyndale, Parable of the Wicked Mammon. Park. Soc. p. 126.
[2] Though thou hadst a thousand holy candles about thee. Ibid. p. 48.
[3] Well, there was such a doctor who may dispend a hundred pounds. Foxe, Acts, v. p. 115.
[4] Answering by the Scriptures maintained the truth. Ibid.
[5] Ibid. p. 117.
[6] Whatsoever truth is taught them, these enemies of all truth quench it again. Tynd. Doct. Tr. p. 394.
[7] Impossible to establish the lay people in any truth, except the Scripture were plainly laid before their eyes in their mother-tongue. Ibid.

[1] Tyndale's Expositions (Park. Soc.), p. 15.
[2] And lay plainly before them the open and manifest places of the Scriptures, to confute their errors and confirm his sayings. Foxe, Acts, v. p. 115.
[3] Antichrist turneth the roots of the trees upward. Tyndale, Doctrinal Treatises (Park. Soc.), p. 296.

Then a great idea sprang up in Tyndale's heart: "It was in the language of Israel," said he, "that the Psalms were sung in the temple of Jehovah; and shall not the gospel speak the language of England among us? ......Ought the church to have less light at noonday than at the dawn?......Christians must read the New Testament in their mother-tongue." Tyndale believed that this idea proceeded from God. The new sun would lead to the discovery of a new world, and the infallible rule would make all human diversities give way to a divine unity. "One holdeth this doctor, another that," said Tyndale, "one followeth Duns Scotus, another St Thomas, another Bonaventure, Alexander Hales, Raymond of Penaford, Lyra, Gorram, Hugh de Sancto Victore, and so many others besides......Now, each of these authors contradicts the other. How then can we distinguish him who says right from him who says wrong?......How?......Verily, by God's word."[1] Tyndale hesitated no longer...... While Wolsey sought to win the papal tiara, the humble tutor of Sodbury undertook to place the torch of heaven in the midst of his fellow-countrymen. The translation of the Bible shall be the work of his life.

The first triumph of the word was a revolution in the manor-house. In proportion as Sir John and Lady Walsh acquired a taste for the gospel, they became disgusted with the priests. The clergy were not so often invited to Sodbury, nor did they meet with the same welcome.[2] They soon discontinued their visits, and thought of nothing but how they could drive Tyndale from the mansion and from the diocese.

Unwilling to compromise themselves in this warfare, they sent forward some of those light troops which the church has always at her disposal. Mendicant friars and poor curates, who could hardly understand their missal, and the most learned of whom made *Albertus de secretis mulierum* their habitual study, fell upon Tyndale like a pack of hungry hounds. They trooped to the alehouses,[3] and calling for a jug of beer, took their seats, one at one table, another at another. They invited the peasantry to drink with them, and entering into conversation with them, poured forth a thousand curses upon the daring reformer: "He's a hypocrite," said one; "he's a heretic," said another. The most skilful among them would mount upon a stool, and turning the tavern into a temple, deliver, for the first time in his life, an extemporaneous discourse. They reported words that Tyndale had never uttered, and actions that he had never committed.[4] Rushing upon the poor tutor (he himself informs us) "like unclean swine that follow their carnal lusts,"[1] they tore his good name to very tatters, and shared the spoil among them; while the audience, excited by their calumnies and heated by the beer, departed overflowing with rage and hatred against the heretic of Sodbury.

After the monks came the dignitaries. The deans and abbots, Sir John's former guests, accused Tyndale to the chancellor of the diocese,[2] and the storm which had begun in the tavern burst forth in the episcopal palace.

The titular bishop of Worcester (an appanage of the Italian prelates) was Giulio de' Medici, a learned man, great politician, and crafty priest, who already governed the popedom without being pope.[3] Wolsey, who administered the diocese for his absent colleague, had appointed Thomas Parker chancellor, a man devoted to the Roman church. It was to him the churchmen made their complaint. A judicial inquiry had its difficulties; the king's companion-at-arms was the patron of the pretended heretic, and Sir Anthony Poyntz, Lady Walsh's brother, was sheriff of the county. The chancellor was therefore content to convoke a general conference of the clergy. Tyndale obeyed the summons, but foreseeing what awaited him, he cried heartily to God, as he pursued his way up the banks of the Severn, "to give him strength to stand fast in the truth of his word."[4]

When they were assembled, the abbots and deans, and other ecclesiastics of the diocese, with haughty heads and threatening looks, crowded round the humble but unbending Tyndale. When his turn arrived, he stood forward, and the chancellor administered him a severe reprimand, to which he made a calm reply. This so exasperated the chancellor, that, giving way to his passion, he treated Tyndale as if he had been a dog.[5] "Where are your witnesses?" demanded the latter. "Let them come forward, and I will answer them." Not one of them dared support the charge—they looked another way. The chancellor waited, one witness at least he must have, but he could not get that.[6] Annoyed at this desertion of the priests, the representative of the Medici became more equitable, and let the accusation drop. Tyndale quietly returned to Sodbury, blessing God who had saved him from the cruel hands of his adversaries,[7] and entertaining nothing but the tenderest charity towards them. "Take away my goods," he said to them one

---

1 Tynd. Doct. Tr. p. 149.
2 Neither had they the cheer and countenance when they came, as before they had. Foxe, Acts, v. p. 116.
3 Come together to the alehouse, which is their preaching place. Tynd. Doct. Tr. 394.
4 They add too of their own heads what I never spake. Ibid. p. 395.

1 Tyndale, Expositions, p. 10.
2 Ibid. Doctr. Tr. 395.
3 Governava il papato e havia piu zente a la sua audien zia che il papa. (He governed the popedom, and had more people at his audiences than the pope.) Relazione di Marco Foscari, 1526.
4 Foxe, Acts, v. p. 116.
5 He threatened me grievously and reviled me, and rated me as though I had been a dog. Tynd. Doct. Tr. p. 395.
6 And laid to my charge whereof there would be none accuser brought forth. Ibid.
7 Escaping out of their hands. Foxe, Acts, v. p. 116.

day, " take away my good name! yet so long as Christ dwelleth in my heart, so long shall I love you not a whit the less."[1] Here indeed is the Saint John to whom Tyndale has been compared.

In this violent warfare, however, he could not fail to receive some heavy blows; and where could he find consolation? Fryth and Bilney were far from him. Tyndale recollected an *aged doctor* who lived near Sodbury, and who had shewn him great affection. He went to see him, and opened his heart to him.[2] The old man looked at him for a while as if he hesitated to disclose some great mystery. " Do you not know," said he, lowering his voice, " that *the pope is very Antichrist* whom the Scripture speaketh of?......But beware what you say......That knowledge may cost you your life."[3] This doctrine of Antichrist, which Luther was at that moment enunciating so boldly, struck Tyndale. Strengthened by it, as was the Saxon reformer, he felt fresh energy in his heart, and the aged doctor was to him what the aged friar had been to Luther.

When the priests saw that their plot had failed, they commissioned a celebrated divine to undertake his conversion. The reformer replied with his Greek Testament to the schoolman's arguments. The theologian was speechless: at last he exclaimed: "Well then! it were better to be without God's laws than the pope's."[4] Tyndale, who did not expect so plain and blasphemous a confession, made answer: " And I defy the pope and all his laws!" and then, as if unable to keep his secret, he added: " If God spares my life, I will take care that a ploughboy shall know more of the Scriptures than you do."[5]

All his thoughts were now directed to the means of carrying out his plans; and desirous of avoiding conversations that might compromise them, he thenceforth passed the greater portion of his time in the library.[6] He prayed, he read, he began his translation of the Bible, and in all probability communicated portions of it to Sir John and Lady Walsh.

All his precautions were useless: the scholastic divine had betrayed him, and the priests had sworn to stop him in his translation of the Bible. One day he fell in with a troop of monks and curates, who abused him in the grossest manner. " It's the favour of the gentry of the county that makes you so proud," said they; " but notwithstanding your patrons, there will be a talk about you before long, and in a pretty fashion too!.... You shall not always live in a manor-house!"

" Banish me to the obscurest corner of England," replied Tyndale ; " provided you will permit me to teach children and preach the gospel, and give me ten pounds a-year for my support[1].... I shall be satisfied!" The priests left him, but with the intention of preparing him a very different fate.

Tyndale indulged in his pleasant dreams no longer. He saw that he was on the point of being arrested. condemned, and interrupted in his great work. He must seek a retreat where he can discharge in peace the task God has allotted him. "You cannot save me from the hands of the priests," said he to Sir John, " and God knows to what troubles you would expose yourself by keeping me in your family. Permit me to leave you." Having said this, he gathered up his papers, took his Testament, pressed the hands of his benefactors, kissed the children, and then descending the hill, bade farewell to the smiling banks of the Severn, and departed alone—alone with his faith. What shall he do? What will become of him? Where shall he go? He went forth like Abraham, one thing alone engrossing his mind :—the Scriptures shall be translated into the vulgar tongue, and he will deposit the oracles of God in the midst of his countrymen.

CHAPTER V.

Luther's Works in England—Consultation of the Bishops—The Bull of Leo X. published in England—Luther's Books burnt—Letter of Henry VIII.—He undertakes to write against Luther—Cry of Alarm—Tradition and Sacramentalism—Prudence of Sir T. More—The Book presented to the Pope—*Defender of the Faith*—Exultation of the King.

WHILST a plain minister was commencing the Reformation in a tranquil valley in the west of England, powerful reinforcements were landing on the shores of Kent. The writings and actions of Luther excited a lively sensation in Great Britain. His appearance before the diet of Worms was a common subject of conversation. Ships from the harbours of the Low Countries brought his books to London,[2] and the German printers had made answer to the nuncio Aleander, who was prohibiting the Lutheran works in the empire: "Very well! we shall send them *to England!*" One might almost say that England was destined to be the asylum of truth. And in fact, the *Theses* of 1517, the *Explanation of the Lord's Prayer*, the books *against Emser, against the papacy of Rome, against the bull of Antichrist*, the *Epistle to the Galatians*, the *Appeal to the German nobility*, and above all, the *Babylonish Captivity of the Church*—all crossed the sea, were translated, and circulated

---

[1] Tynd. Doctr. Tr. p. 298.
[2] For to him he durst be bold to disclose his heart. Foxe, Acts, v. p. 117.
[3] Ibid.   [4] Ibid.
[5] Cause a boy that driveth the plough to know more of the Scriptures than he did. Ibid.
[6] This part of the house was standing in 1839, but has since been pulled down. Anderson, Bible Annals, i. p. 37. We cannot but unite in the wish expressed in that volume, that the remainder of the building, now tenanted by a farmer, may be carefully preserved.

[1] Binding him to no more but to teach children and to preach. Foxe, Acts, v. p. 117.
[2] Burnet, Hist. of the Reformation (Lond. 1841, Oct.) i. p. 21.

throughout the kingdom.[1] The German and English nations, having a common origin and being sufficiently alike at that time in character and civilization, the works intended for one might be read by the other with advantage. The monk in his cell, the country gentleman in his hall, the doctor in his college, the tradesman in his shop, and even the bishop in his palace, studied these extraordinary writings. The laity in particular, who had been prepared by Wickliffe and disgusted by the avarice and disorderly lives of the priests, read with enthusiasm the eloquent pages of the Saxon monk. They strengthened all hearts.

The papacy was not inactive in presence of all these efforts. The times of Gregory VII. and of Innocent III., it is true, were passed; and weakness and irresolution had succeeded to the former energy and activity of the Roman pontificate. The spiritual power had resigned the dominion of Europe to the secular powers, and it was doubtful whether faith in the papacy could be found in the papacy itself. Yet a German (Dr Eck), by the most indefatigable exertions, had extorted a bull from the profane Leo X.,[2] and this bull had just reached England. The pope himself sent it to Henry, calling upon him to extirpate the Lutheran heresy.[3] The king handed it to Wolsey, and the latter transmitted it to the bishops, who, after reading *the heretic's* books, met together to discuss the matter.[4] There was more Romish faith in London than in the Vatican. " This false friar," exclaimed Wolsey, " attacks submission to the clergy—that fountain of all virtues." The humanist prelates were the most annoyed; the road they had taken ended in an abyss, and they shrank back in alarm. Tonstall, the friend of Erasmus, afterwards bishop of London, and who had just returned from his embassy to Germany where Luther had been painted to him in the darkest colours, was particularly violent: " This monk is a *Proteus*......I mean an *atheist*.[5] If you allow the heresies to grow up which he is scattering with both hands, they will choke the faith and the church will perish.[6] Had we not enough of the Wickliffites—here are new legions of the same kind!......To-day Luther calls for the abolition of the mass; to-morrow he will ask for the abolition of Jesus Christ.[7] He rejects every thing, and puts nothing in its place. What? if barbarians plunder our frontiers, we punish them ......and shall we bear with heretics who plunder our altars?......No! by the mortal agony that Christ endured, I entreat you......

What am I saying? the whole church conjures you to combat against this devouring *dragon*......to punish this *hell-dog*, to silence his sinister howlings, and to drive him shamefully back into his den."[1] Thus spoke the eloquent Tonstall; nor was Wolsey far behind him. The only attachment at all respectable in this man was that which he entertained for the church; it may perhaps be called respectable, for it was the only one that did not exclusively regard himself. On the 14th May 1521, this English pope, in imitation of the Italian pope, issued his bull against Luther.

It was read (probably on the first Sunday in June) in all the churches during high mass, when the congregation was most numerous.[2] A priest exclaimed : " For every book of Martin Luther's found in your possession within fifteen days after this injunction, you will incur the greater excommunication." Then a public notary, holding the pope's bull in his hand, with a description of Luther's *perverse opinions*, proceeded towards the principal door of the church and fastened up the document.[3] The people gathered round it ; the most competent person read it aloud, while the rest listened ; and the following are some of the sentences which, by the pope's order, resounded in the porches of all the cathedral, conventual, collegiate, and parish churches of every county in England :

" 11. Sins are not pardoned to any, unless, the priest remitting them, he believe they are remitted to him.

" 13. If by reason of some impossibility, the *contrite* be not confessed, or the priest absolve him, not in earnest, but in jest; yet if he believe that he is absolved, he is most truly absolved.

" 14. In the sacrament of *penance* and the remission of a fault, the pope or bishop doth not more than the lowest priest; yea, where there is not a priest, then any Christian will do; yea, if it were a woman or a child.

" 26. The pope, the successor of Peter, is not Christ's vicar.

" 28. It is not at all in the hand of the church or the pope to decree articles of faith, no, nor to decree the laws of manners or of good works."

The cardinal-legate, accompanied by the nuncio, by the ambassador of Charles V., and by several bishops, proceeded in great pomp to St Paul's, where the bishop of Rochester preached, and Wolsey burnt Luther's books.[5] But they were hardly reduced to ashes, before sarcasms and jests were heard in every direction. " *Fire* is not a theological argument," said one. " The papists,

---

[1] Libros Lutheranos quorum magnus jam numerus per. venerat in manus Anglorum. Polyd. Virg. Angl. Hist. (Basil, 1570, fol.) p. 664.
[2] See above, Book VI. chap. iv.
[3] Ab hoc regno extirpandum et abolendum. Cardinal. Ebor. Commissio. Strype, M. I. v. p. 22.
[4] Habitoque super hac re diligenti tractatu. Ibid.
[5] Cum illo *Proteo*....Imo *Atheo*. Erasm. Ep. 1158.
[6] Tota ruet Ecclesia. Ibid. p. 1159.
[7] Nisi de abolendo Christo scribere destinavit. Ibid. p. 1160.

[1] Gladio Spiritus abactum in antrum suum coges. Erasm. Ep. p. 1160.
[2] Cum major convenerit multitudo. Ibid.
[3] In valvis seu locis publicis ecclesiæ vestræ. Ibid. p. 24.
[4] Strype, M. I. p. 57 (Oxf. ed.), or Luther, xvii. p. 306.
[5] See above, Book IX. chap. x.

who accuse Martin Luther of slaying and murdering Christians," added another, " are like the pickpocket, who began to cry *stop thief*, as soon as he saw himself in danger of being caught." " The bishop of Rochester," said a third, " concludes that because Luther has thrown the pope's decretals into the fire, he would throw in the pope himself......We may hence deduce another syllogism, quite as sound: The popes have burnt the New Testament, therefore, if they could, they would burn Christ himself."[1] These jests were rapidly circulated from mouth to mouth. It was not enough that Luther's writings were in England, they must needs be known, and the priests took upon themselves to advertise them. The Reformation was advancing, and Rome herself pushed behind the car.

The cardinal saw that something more was required than these paper *autos-da-fé*, and the activity he displayed may indicate what he would have done in Europe, if ever he had reached the pontifical chair. " The spirit of Satan left him no repose," says the papist Sanders.[2] Some action out of the ordinary course is needful, thought Wolsey. Kings have hitherto been the enemies of the popes: a king shall now undertake their defence. Princes are not very anxious about learning, a prince shall publish a book !...... " Sire," said he to the king, to get Henry in the vein, " you ought to write to the princes of Germany on the subject of this heresy." He did so. Writing to the Archduke Palatine, he said : " This fire, which has been kindled by Luther, and fanned by the arts of the devil, is raging everywhere. If Luther does not repent, deliver him and his audacious treatises to the flames. I offer you my royal co-operation, and even, if necessary, my life."[3] This was the first time Henry showed that cruel thirst, which was in after-days to be quenched in the blood of his wives and friends.

The king having taken the first step, it was not difficult for Wolsey to induce him to take another. To defend the honour of Thomas Aquinas, to stand forward as the champion of the church and to obtain from the pope a title equivalent to that of *Christianissimus*, most Christian king, were more than sufficient motives to induce Henry to break a lance with Luther. " I will combat with the pen this Cerberus, sprung from the depths of hell,"[4] said he, " and if he refuses to retract, the fire shall consume the heretic and his heresies together."[5]

The king shut himself up in his library; all the scholastic tastes with which his youth had been imbued were revived; he worked

as if he were archbishop of Canterbury, and not king of England; with the pope's permission he read Luther's writings ; he ransacked Thomas Aquinas; forged, with infinite labour, the arrows with which he hoped to pierce the heretic ; called several learned men to his aid, and at last published his book. His first words were a cry of alarm. " Beware of the track of this serpent," said he to his Christian readers ; " walk on tiptoe ; fear the thickets and caves in which he lies concealed, and whence he will dart his poison on you. If he licks you, be careful ! the cunning viper caresses only that he may bite !"[1] After that Henry sounded a charge : " Be of good cheer ! Filled with the same valour that you would display against Turks, Saracens, and other infidels, march now against this *little friar*,—a fellow apparently weak, but more formidable through the spirit that animates him than all infidels, Saracens, and Turks put together."[2] Thus did Henry VIII., the *Peter the Hermit* of the sixteenth century, preach a crusade against Luther, in order to save the papacy.

He had skilfully chosen the ground on which he gave battle : sacramentalism and tradition are in fact the two essential features of the papal religion ; just as a lively faith and Holy Scripture are of the religion of the gospel. Henry did a service to the Reformation, by pointing out the principles it would mainly have to combat ; and by furnishing Luther with an opportunity of establishing the authority of the Bible, he made him take a most important step in the path of reform. " If a teaching is opposed to Scripture," said the Reformer, " whatever be its origin—traditions, custom, kings, Thomists, sophists, Satan, or even an angel from heaven,—all from whom it proceeds must be accursed. *Nothing can exist contrary to Scripture*, and everything must exist for it."

Henry's book being terminated by the aid of the bishop of Rochester, the king showed it to Sir Thomas More, who begged him to pronounce less decidedly in favour of the papal supremacy. " I will not change a word," replied the king, full of servile devotion to the popedom. " Besides, I have my reasons," and he whispered them in More's ear.

Doctor Clarke, ambassador from England at the court of Rome, was commissioned to present the pope with a magnificently bound copy of the king's work. " The glory of England," said he, " is to be in the foremost rank among the nations in obedience to the papacy."[3] Happily Britain was erelong to know a glory of a very different kind. The ambassador added that his master, after having refuted Luther's errors with the *pen*, was

---

[1] They would have burnt Christ himself. Tynd. Doct. Tr. Obedience, &c. (Park. Soc.) p. 221.
[2] Satanæ spiritu actus. De Schism. Angl. p. 8.
[3] Kapp's Urkunden, ii. p. 458.
[4] Velut Cerberum ex inferis producit in lucem. Regis ad lectorem. Epist. p. 94.
[5] Ut errores ejus eumque ipsum ignis exurat. Ibid. p. 95.

[1] Qui tantum ideo lambit ut mordeat. Assertio Sept. Sacram.
[2] Sed animo Turcis omnibus Sarracenis omnibus usquam infidelibus nocentiorem fraterculum. Ibid. p. 147.
[3] Fiddes' Life of Wolsey, p. 249.

ready to combat his adherents with the sword.[1] The pope, touched with this offer, gave him his foot, and then his cheek to kiss, and said to him : " I will do for your master's book as much as the church has done for the works of St Jerome and St Augustine."

The enfeebled papacy had neither the power of intelligence, nor even of fanaticism. It still maintained its pretensions and its pomp, but it resembled the corpses of the mighty ones of the earth that lie in state, clad in their most magnificent robes : splendour above, death and corruption below. The thunderbolts of a Hildebrand ceasing to produce their effect, Rome gratefully accepted the defence of laymen, such as Henry VIII. and Sir Thomas More, without disdaining their judicial sentences and their scaffolds. " We must honour those noble champions," said the pope to his cardinals, " who show themselves prepared to cut off with the sword the rotten members of Jesus Christ.[2] What title shall we give to the virtuous king of England ?"—*Protector of the Roman church,* suggested one ; *Apostolic king,* said another ; and finally, but not without some opposition, Henry VIII. was proclaimed *Defender of the Faith.* At the same time the pope promised ten years' indulgence to all readers of the king's book. This was a lure after the fashion of the middle ages, and which never failed in its effect. The clergy compared its author to the wisest of kings ; and the book, of which many thousand copies were printed, filled the Christian world (Cochlœus tells us) with admiration and delight.

Nothing could equal Henry's joy. " His majesty," said the vicar of Croydon, " would not exchange that name for all London and twenty miles round."[3] The king's fool, entering the room just as his master had received the bull, asked him the cause of his transports. " The pope has just named me *Defender of the Faith!*"—" Ho ! ho ! good Harry," replied the fool, " let you and me defend one another ; but......take my word for it......*let the faith alone to defend itself.*"[4] An entire modern system was found in those words. In the midst of the general intoxication, the fool was the only sensible person. But Henry could listen to nothing. Seated on an elevated throne, with the cardinal at his right hand, he caused the pope's letter to be read in public. The trumpets sounded : Wolsey said mass ; the king and his court took their seats around a sumptuous table, and the heralds at arms proclaimed : *Henricus Dei gratia Rex Angliæ et Franciæ, Defensor Fidei et Dominus Hiberniæ!*

Thus was the king of England more than ever united to the pope : whoever brings the Holy Scriptures into his kingdom shall there encounter that material sword, *ferrum et materialem gladium,* in which the papacy so much delighted.

CHAPTER VI.

Wolsey's Machinations to obtain the Tiara — He gains Charles V —Alliance between Henry and Charles—Wolsey offers to command the Troops—Treaty of Bruges—Henry believes himself King of France—Victories of Francis I.—Death of Leo X.

ONE thing only was wanting to check more surely the progress of the gospel : Wolsey's accession to the pontifical throne. Consumed by the desire of reaching " the summit of sacerdotal unity,"[1] he formed, to attain this end, one of the most perfidious schemes ambition ever engendered. He thought with others : " The end justifies the means."

The cardinal could only attain the popedom through the emperor or the king of France ; for then, as now, it was the secular powers that really elected the chief of catholicity. After carefully weighing the influence of these two princes, Wolsey found that the balance inclined to the side of Charles, and his choice was made. A close intimacy of long standing united him to Francis I., but that mattered little ; he must betray his friend to gain his friend's rival.

But this was no easy matter. Henry was dissatisfied with Charles the Fifth.[2] Wolsey was therefore obliged to employ every imaginable delicacy in his manœuvres. First he sent Sir Richard Wingfield to the emperor ; then he wrote a flattering letter in Henry's name to the princess-regent of the Low Countries. The difficulty was to get the king to sign it. " Have the goodness to put your name," said Wolsey, " even if it should annoy your Highness......You know very well......that women like to be pleased."[3] This argument prevailed with the king, who still possessed a spirit of gallantry. Lastly, Wolsey being named arbitrator between Charles and Francis, resolved to depart for Calais, apparently to hear the complaints of the two princes ; but in reality to betray one of them. Wolsey felt as much pleasure in such practices, as Francis in giving battle.

The king of France rejected his arbitration : he had a sharp eye, and his mother one still sharper. " Your master loves me not," said he to Charles's ambassador, " and I do not love him any more, and am determined to be his enemy."[4] It was impossible to speak more plainly. Far from imitating this frankness, the politic Charles endeavoured to gain Wolsey, and Wolsey, who was eager to sell

---

[1] Totius regni sui viribus et armis. Rymer, Fœdera, vi. p. 199.
[2] Putida membra....ferro et materiali gladio abscindere. Ibid.
[3] Foxe, Acts, iv. p. 596.   [4] Fuller, book v. p. 168.

[1] Unitatis sacerdotalis fastigium conscendere. Sanders, De Schism. Ang. 8.
[2] Hys owne affayris doith not succede with th' Emperour. State Papers, vol. i. p. 10.   [3] Ibid. p. 12.
[4] He was utterly determined to be his enemy. Cotton MSS. Galba, B. 7, p. 35.

himself, adroitly hinted at what price he might be bought. " If the king of England sides with me," Charles informed the cardinal, " you shall be elected pope at the death of Leo X." [1] Francis, betrayed by Wolsey, abandoned by the pope, and threatened by the emperor, determined at last to accept Henry's mediation.

But Charles was now thinking of very different matters. Instead of a mediation, he demanded of the king of England 4000 of his famous bowmen. Henry smiled as he read the despatch, and looking at Pace his secretary, and Marney the captain of his guards, he said : " *Beati qui audiunt et non intelligunt !* " thus forbidding them to understand, and above all to bruit abroad this strange request. It was agreed to raise the number of archers to 6000 ; and the cardinal, having the tiara continually before his eyes, departed to perform at Calais the odious comedy of a hypocritical arbitration. Being detained at Dover by contrary winds, the mediator took advantage of this delay to draw up a list of the 6000 archers and their captains, not forgetting to insert in it, " certain obstinate deer," as Henry had said, " that must of necessity be hunted down." [2] These were some gentlemen whom the king desired to get rid of.

While the ambassadors of the king of France were received at Calais on the 4th of August with great honours, by the lord high chamberlain of England, the cardinal signed a convention with Charles's ministers that Henry should withdraw his promise of the Princess Mary's hand to the dauphin, and give her to the emperor. At the same time he issued orders to destroy the French navy, and to invade France.[3] And finally he procured by way of compensating England for the pension of 16,000 pounds hitherto received from the court of St Germains, that the emperor should pay henceforward the annual sum of 40,000 marks. Without ready money the bargain would not have been a good one.

This was not all. While Wolsey was waiting to be elected pope, he conceived the idea of becoming a soldier. A commander was wanted for the 6000 archers Henry was sending against the king of France ; and why should he not be the cardinal himself ? He immediately intrigued to get the noblemen set aside who had been proposed as generals in chief. " Shrewsbury," he said to the king, " is wanted for Scotland— Worcester by his experience is worthy that ......you should keep him near you. As for Dorset......he will be very dear." Then the priest added : " Sire, if during my sojourn on the other side of the sea, you have good

reason to send your archers......I hasten to inform you that whenever the emperor takes the command of his soldiers, I am ready, although an ecclesiastic,[1] to put myself at the head of yours." What devotedness ! Wolsey would cause his cross of cardinal *a latere* to be carried before him (he said) : and neither Francis nor Bayard would be able to resist him. To command at the same time the state, the church, and the army, while awaiting the tiara,—to surround his head with laurels : such was this man's ambition. Unfortunately for him, they were not of that opinion at court. The king made the earl of Essex commander-in-chief.

As Wolsey could not be general, he turned to diplomacy. He hastened to Bruges ; and as he entered at the emperor's side, a voice was heard above the crowd, exclaiming : *Salve, Rex regis tui atque regni sui !* [2]—a sound most pleasing to his ears. People were very much astonished at Bruges by the intimacy existing between the cardinal and the emperor. " There is some mystery beneath it all," they said.[3] Wolsey desired to place the crown of France on Henry's head, and the tiara on his own. Such was the mystery, which was well worth a few civilities to the mighty Charles V. The alliance was concluded, and the contracting parties agreed " to avenge the insults offered to the throne of Jesus Christ," or in other words, to the popedom.

Wolsey, in order to drag Henry into the intrigues which were to procure him the tiara, had reminded him that he was *king of France*, and the suggestion had been eagerly caught at. At midnight on the 7th of August, the king dictated to his secretary a letter for Wolsey containing this strange expression : *Si ibitis parare regi locum in regno ejus hereditario, Majestas ejus quum tempus erit opportunam, sequetur.* [4] The theologian who had corrected the famous latin book of the king's against Luther, most certainly had not revised this phrase. According to Henry, France was his hereditary kingdom, and Wolsey was going to prepare the throne for him.......The king could not restrain his joy at the mere idea, and already he surpassed in imagination both Edward III. and the Black Prince. " I am about to attain a glory superior to that which my ancestors have gained by so many wars and battles."[5] Wolsey traced out for him the road to his palace on the banks of the Seine : " Mezières is about to fall ; afterwards there is only Rheims, which is not a strong city ; and thus your grace will very easily reach

---

[1] Ut Wolseus mortuo Leone decimo fieret summus pontifex.
[2] Saying that certayne hartes were so toggidde for hym, that he must neadys hunte them. State Papers, i. p. 26.
[3] Ibid. i. p. 23.

[1] Though I be a spiritual man. State Papers, i. p. 31.
[2] Hail, both king of thy king and also of his kingdom. Tynd. Expos. p. 314.
[3] There was a certain secret whereof all men knew not. Ibid. 315.
[4] If you go to prepare a place for the king in his hereditary kingdom, his Majesty will follow you at a fitting season. State Papers. i. 36.
[5] Majora assequi quam omnes ipsius progenitores tot bellis et prӕliis. Ibid. 45.

Paris."[1] Henry followed on the map the route he would have to take: "Affairs are going on well," wrote the cardinal, "the Lord be praised." In him this Christian language was a mere official formality. Wolsey was mistaken : things were going on badly. On the 20th of October 1522, Francis I. whom so much perfidy had been unable to deceive,—Francis, ambitious and turbulent, but honest in this matter at least, and confiding in the strength of his arms, had suddenly appeared between Cambray and Valenciennes. The emperor fled to Flanders in alarm, and Wolsey, instead of putting himself at the head of the army, had shielded himself under his arbitrator's cloak. Writing to Henry, who, a fortnight before, had by his advice excited Charles to attack France, he said : " I am confident that your *virtuous mediation* will greatly increase your reputation and honour throughout Christendom."[2] Francis rejected Wolsey's offers, but the object of the latter was attained. The negotiations had gained time for Charles, and bad weather soon stopped the French army. Wolsey returned satisfied to London about the middle of December. It was true that Henry's triumphant entry into Paris became very difficult ; but the cardinal was sure of the emperor's favour, and through it (he imagined) of the tiara. Wolsey had done, therefore, what he desired. He had hardly arrived in England, when there came news which raised him to the height of happiness : Leo X. was dead. His joy surpassed what Henry had felt at the thought of his *hereditary kingdom.* Protected by the powerful Charles V., to whom he had sacrificed everything, the English cardinal was at last on the point of receiving that pontifical crown which would permit him to crush heresy, and which was, in his eyes, the just reward of so many infamous transactions.

CHAPTER VII.

The Just Men of Lincolnshire—Their Assemblies and Teaching—Agnes and Morden—Itinerant Libraries—Polemical Conversations—Sarcasm—Royal Decree and Terror—Depositions and Condemnations—Four Martyrs—A Conclave—Charles consoles Wolsey.

WOLSEY did not stay until he was pope, before persecuting the disciples of the word of God. Desirous of carrying out the stipulations of the convention at Bruges, he had broken out against " the king's subjects who disturbed the apostolic see." Henry had to vindicate the title conferred on him by the pope ; the cardinal had to gain the popedom ;

and both could satisfy their desires by the erection of a few scaffolds.

In the county of Lincoln on the shores of the North Sea, along the fertile banks of the Humber, Trent, and Witham, and on the slopes of the smiling hills, dwelt many peaceful Christians—labourers, artificers, and shepherds—who spent their days in toil, in keeping their flocks, in doing good, and in reading the Bible.[1] The more the gospel-light increased in England, the greater was the increase in the number of these children of peace.[2] These " just men," as they were called, were devoid of human knowledge, but they thirsted for the knowledge of God. Thinking they were alone the true disciples of the Lord, they married only among themselves.[3] They appeared occasionally at church ; but instead of repeating their prayers like the rest, they sat, said their enemies, " mum like beasts."[4] On Sundays and holidays, they assembled in each other's houses, and sometimes passed a whole night in reading a portion of Scripture. If there chanced to be few books among them, one of the brethren, who had learnt by heart the Epistle of St James, the beginning of St Luke's gospel, the sermon on the mount, or an epistle of St Paul's, would recite a few verses in a loud and calm voice ; then all would piously converse about the holy truths of the faith, and exhort one another to put them in practice. But if any person joined their meetings, who did not belong to their body, they would all keep silent.[5] Speaking much among each other, they were speechless before those from without: fear of the priests and of the fagot made them dumb. There was no family rejoicing without the Scriptures. At the marriage of a daughter of the aged Durdant, one of their patriarchs, the wedding party met secretly in a barn, and read the whole of one of St Paul's epistles. Marriages are rarely celebrated with such pastimes as this !

Although they were dumb before enemies or suspected persons, these poor people did not keep silence in the presence of the humble : a glowing proselytism characterized them all. " Come to my house," said the pious Agnes Ashford to James Morden, " and I will teach you some verses of Scripture." Agnes was an educated woman ; she could read ; Morden came, and the poor woman's chamber was transformed into a school of theology. Agnes began : " Ye are the salt of the earth," and then recited the following verses.[6] Five times did Morden return to Agnes before he knew that beautiful discourse. " We are spread like salt

[1] Your grace shall have but a leyve wey to Parys. State Papers, i. 46.
[2] Cotton MSS. Calig. D. 8, p. 85.

[1] Being simple labourers and artificers. Foxe, Acts, iv. p. 240.
[2] As the light of the gospel began more to appear, and the number of professors to grow. Ibid. p. 2l7.
[3] Did contract matrimony only with themselves. Ibid. p. 223.   [4] Ibid. p. 225.
[5] If any came in among them that were not of their side, then they would keep all silent. Ibid. p. 222.
[6] Matth. v. 13-16.

over the various parts of the kingdom," said this Christian woman to the neophyte, " in order that we may check the progress of superstition by our doctrine and our life. But," added she in alarm, " keep this secret in your heart, as a man would keep a thief in prison."[1]

As books were rare these pious Christians had established a kind of itinerant library, and one John Scrivener was continually engaged in carrying the precious volumes from one to another.[2] But at times, as he was proceeding along the banks of the river or through the forest glades, he observed that he was followed. He would quicken his pace and run into some barn where the friendly peasants promptly hid him beneath the straw, or, like the spies of Israel, under the stalks of flax.[3] The bloodhounds arrived, sought and found nothing; and more than once those who so generously harboured these evangelists cruelly expiated the crime of charity.

The disappointed officers had scarcely retired from the neighbourhood when these friends of the word of God came out of their hiding-place, and profited by the moment of liberty to assemble the brethren. The persecutions they suffered irritated them against the priests. They worshipped God, read, and sang with a low voice; but when the conversation became general, they gave free course to their indignation. " Would you know the use of the pope's pardons ? " said one of them ; " they are to blind the eyes and empty the purse." — " True pilgrimages," said the tailor Geoffrey of Uxbridge, " consist in visiting the poor and sick—barefoot, if so it please you—for these are the little ones that are God's true image."—" Money spent in pilgrimages," added a third, " serves only to maintain thieves and harlots."[4]—The women were often the most animated in the controversy. " What need is there to go to the *feet*," said Agnes Ward, who disbelieved in saints, " when we may go to the *head?*"[5] —" The clergy of the good old times," said the wife of David Lewis, " used to lead the people as a hen leadeth her chickens;[6] but now if our priests lead their flocks anywhere, it is to the devil assuredly."

Erelong there was a general panic throughout this district. The king's confessor John Longland was bishop of Lincoln. This fanatic priest, Wolsey's creature, took advantage of his position to petition Henry for a severe persecution : this was the ordinary use in England, France, and elsewhere, of the confessors of princes. It was unfortunate that among these pious disciples of the word, men of a cynical turn were now and then met with, whose biting sarcasms went beyond all bounds. Wolsey and Longland

knew how to employ these expressions in arousing the king's anger. " As one of these fellows," they said, " was busy beating out his corn in his barn, a man chanced to pass by. ' Good morrow, neighbour,' (said the latter), ' you are hard at it !'—' Yes,' replied the old heretic, thinking of transubstantiation, ' I am thrashing the corn out of which the priests make God Almighty.'"[1] Henry hesitated no longer.

On the 20th October 1521, nine days after the bull on the *Defender of the Faith* had been signed at Rome, the king, who was at Windsor, summoned his secretary, and dictated an order commanding all his subjects to assist the bishop of Lincoln against the heretics. " You will obey it at the peril of your lives," added he. The order was transmitted to Longland, and the bishop immediately issued his warrants, and his officers spread terror far and wide. When they beheld them, these peaceful but timid Christians were troubled. Isabella Bartlet, hearing them approach her cottage, screamed out to her husband : " You are a lost man ! and I am a dead woman !"[2] This cry was re-echoed from all the cottages of Lincolnshire. The bishop, on his judgment-seat, skilfully played upon these poor unhappy beings to make them accuse one another. Alas ! according to the ancient prophecy : " the brother delivered up the brother to death." Robert Bartlet deposed against his brother Richard and his own wife ; Jane Bernard accused her own father, and Tredway his mother. It was not until after the most cruel anguish that these poor creatures were driven to such frightful extremities ; but the bishop and death terrified them : a small number alone remained firm. As regards heroism, Wickliffe's Reformation brought but a feeble aid to the Reformation of the sixteenth century ; still, if it did not furnish many heroes, it prepared the English people to love God's word above all things. Of these humble people, some were condemned to do penance in different monasteries ; others to carry a faggot on their shoulders thrice round the market-place, and then to stand some time exposed to the jeers of the populace ; others were fastened to a post while the executioner branded them on the cheek with a red-hot iron. They also had their martyrs. Wickliffe's revival had never been without them. Four of these brethren were chosen to be put to death, and among them the pious evangelical *colporteur* Scrivener. By burning him to ashes, the clergy desired to make sure that he would no longer circulate the word of God ; and by a horrible refinement of cruelty his children were compelled to set fire to the pile that was to consume their father.[3] They stretched

1 Foxe, Acts. iv. p. 225.
2 Carrying about books from one to another. Ibid. p. 224.
3 Hiding others in their barns. Ibid. p. 243.
4 Ibid.   5 Ibid. p. 229.   6 Ibid. p. 224.

1 I thresh God Almighty out of the straw. Foxe, Acts.
iv. p. 222.
2 Alas ! now are you an undone man, and I but a dead woman. Ibid. p. 224.
3 Ibid. p. 245.

forth their trembling hands, held in the strong grasp of the executioners......Poor children!......But it is easier to burn the limbs of Christians than to quench the Spirit of Heaven. These cruel fires could not destroy among the Lincolnshire peasantry that love of the Bible which in all ages has been England's strength, far more than the wisdom of her senators or the bravery of her generals.

Having by these exploits gained indisputable claims to the tiara, Wolsey turned his efforts towards Rome. Leo X. as we have seen, was just dead (1522). The cardinal sent Pace to Rome, instructing him to " Represent to the cardinals that by choosing a partisan of Charles or Francis, they will incur the enmity of one or the other of these princes, and that if they elect some feeble Italian priest, the apostolical see must become the prey of the strongest. Luther's revolt and the emperor's ambition endanger the papacy. There is only one means of preventing the threatening dangers.........It is to choose me.........Now go and exert yourself."[1] The conclave opened at Rome on the 27th December, and Wolsey was proposed; but the cardinals were not generally favourable to his election. " He is too young," said one; " too firm," said another. " He will fix the seat of the papacy in England and not in Rome," urged many. He did not receive twenty votes. " The cardinals," wrote the English ambassador, " snarled and quarrelled with each other; and their bad faith and hatred increased every day." On the sixth day, only one dish was sent them; and then in despair they chose Adrian, who had been tutor to the emperor, and the cry was raised; *Papam habemus!*

During all this time Wolsey was in London, consumed by ambition, and counting the days and hours. At length a despatch from Ghent, dated the 22d January, reached him with these words: " On the 9th of January, the cardinal of Tortosa was elected!"...... Wolsey was almost distracted. To gain Charles, he had sacrificed the alliance of Francis I.; there was no stratagem that he had not employed, and yet Charles, in spite of his engagements, had procured the election of his tutor!......The emperor knew what must be the cardinal's anger, and endeavoured to appease it: " The new pope," he wrote, " is old and sickly;[2] he cannot hold his office long ......Beg the cardinal of York for my sake to *take great care of his health.*"

Charles did more than this: he visited London in person, under pretence of his betrothal with Mary of England, and, in the treaty then drawn up, he consented to the insertion of an article by virtue of which Henry VIII. and the mighty emperor bound themselves, if either should infringe the treaty, to appear

before Wolsey and to submit to his decisions.[1] The cardinal, gratified by such condescension, grew calm; and at the same time he was soothed with the most flattering hopes. " Charles's imbecile preceptor," they told him, " has arrived at the Vatican, attended only by his female cook; you shall soon make your entrance there surrounded by all your grandeur." To be certain of his game, Wolsey made secret approaches to Francis I., and then waited for the death of the pope.[2]

CHAPTER VIII.

Character of Tyndale—He arrives in London—He preaches —The Cloth and the Ell—The Bishop of London gives Audience to Tyndale—He is dismissed—A Christian Merchant of London—Spirit of Love in the Reformation— Tyndale in Monmouth's House—Fryth helps him to translate the New Testament—Importunities of the Bishop of Lincoln—Persecution in London—Tyndale's resolution— He departs—His Indignation against the Prelates—His Hopes.

WHILE the cardinal was intriguing to attain his selfish ends, Tyndale was humbly carrying out the great idea of giving the Scriptures of God to England.

After bidding a sad farewell to the manor-house of Sodbury, the learned tutor had departed for London. This occurred about the end of 1522 or the beginning of 1523. He had left the university—he had forsaken the house of his protector; his wandering career was about to commence; but a thick veil hid from him all its sorrows. Tyndale, a man simple in his habits, sober, daring, and generous, fearing neither fatigue nor danger, inflexible in his duty, anointed with the Spirit of God, overflowing with love for his brethren, emancipated from human traditions, the servant of God alone, and loving nought but Jesus Christ, imaginative, quick at repartee, and of touching eloquence—such a man might have shone in the foremost ranks; but he preferred a retired life in some poor corner, provided he could give his countrymen the Scriptures of God. Where could he find this calm retreat? was the question he put to himself as he was making his solitary way to London. The metropolitan see was then filled by Cuthbert Tonstall, who was more of a statesman and a scholar than of a churchman, " the first of English men in Greek and Latin literature," said Erasmus. This eulogy of the learned Dutchman occurred in Tyndale's memory.[3] It was the Greek Testament of Erasmus that led me to Christ, said he to himself; why should not the house of Erasmus's friend offer me a shelter that I may translate it......At last he reached London, and, a stranger in that crowded city, he

---

[1] The sole way....was to chuse him. Herbert, p. 110.
[2] The new elect is both old, sickly....so that he shall not have the office long. Cotton MSS. Galba, B. vii. p. 6.

[1] Both princes appearing before the cardinal of York as Judge. Art. xiii. Herbert, p. 118.
[2] Mortem etiam Adriani expectat. Sanders, p. 5.
[3] As I thus thought, the Bishop of London came to my remembrance. Tyndale, Doctr. Tr. p. 395.

wandered along the streets, a prey by turns to hope and fear.

Being recommended by Sir John Walsh to Sir Harry Guildford, the king's comptroller, and by him to several priests, Tyndale began to preach almost immediately, especially at St Dunstan's, and bore into the heart of the capital the truth which had been banished from the banks of the Severn. The *word* of God was with him the basis of salvation, and the *grace* of God its essence. His inventive mind presented the truths he proclaimed in a striking manner. He said on one occasion :—" It is the blood of Christ that opens the gates of heaven, and not thy works. I am wrong .....Yes, if thou wilt have it so, by thy good works shalt thou be saved.—Yet, understand me well,—not by those which thou hast done, but by those which Christ has done for thee. Christ is in thee and thou in him, knit together inseparably. Thou canst not be damned, except Christ be damned with thee ; neither can Christ be saved except thou be saved with him."[1] This lucid view of justification by faith places Tyndale among the reformers. He did not take his seat on a bishop's throne, or wear a silken cope ; but he mounted the scaffold, and was clothed with a garment of flames. In the service of a crucified Saviour this latter distinction is higher than the former.

Yet the translation was his chief business ; he spoke to his acquaintance about it, and some of them opposed his project. " The teachings of the doctors," said some of the city tradesmen, " can alone make us understand Scripture." " That is to say," replied Tyndale, " I must measure the *yard* by the *cloth*.[2] Look here," continued he, using a practical argument, " here are in your shop twenty pieces of stuff of different lengths...... Do you measure the yard by these pieces, or the pieces by the yard ?......The universal standard is Scripture." This comparison was easily fixed in the minds of the petty tradesmen of the capital.

Desirous of carrying out his project, Tyndale aspired to become the bishop's chaplain ;[3] his ambition was more modest than Wolsey's. The hellenist possessed qualities which could not fail to please the most learned of Englishmen in Greek literature : Tonstall and Tyndale both liked and read the same authors. The ex-tutor determined to plead his cause through the elegant and harmonious disciple of Radicus and Gorgias: "Here is one of Isocrates' orations that I have translated into Latin," said he to Sir Harry Guildford: " I should be pleased to become chaplain to his lordship the bishop of London ; will you beg him to accept this trifle. Isocrates ought to be an excellent recommendation to a scholar ; will you be good enough to add yours." Guildford spoke to the bishop,

placed the translation in his hands, and Tonstall replied with that benevolence which he showed to every one. " Your business is in a fair way," said the comptroller to Tyndale ; " write a letter to his lordship, and deliver it yourself."[1]

Tyndale's hopes now began to be realized. He wrote his letter in the best style, and then, commending himself to God, proceeded to the episcopal palace. He fortunately knew one of the bishop's officers, William Hebilthwayte, to whom he gave the letter. Hebilthwayte carried it to his lordship, while Tyndale waited. His heart throbbed with anxiety : shall he find at last the long hoped for asylum ? The bishop's answer might decide the whole course of his life. If the door is opened,—if the translator of the Scriptures should be settled in the episcopal palace, why should not his London patron receive the truth like his patron at Sodbury ? and, in that case, what a future for the church and for the kingdom !......The Reformation was knocking at the door of the hierarchy of England, and the latter was about to utter its yea or its nay. After a few moments' absence Hebilthwayte returned : " I am going to conduct you to his lordship." Tyndale fancied himself that he had attained his wishes.

The bishop was too kind-hearted to refuse an audience to a man who called upon him with the triple recommendation of Isocrates, of the comptroller, and of the king's old companion in arms. He received Tyndale with kindness, a little tempered however with coldness, as if he were a man whose acquaintanceship might compromise him. Tyndale having made known his wishes, the bishop hastened to reply : " Alas ! my house is full ; I have now more people than I can employ."[2] Tyndale was discomfited by this answer. The bishop of London was a learned man, but wanting in courage and consistency ; he gave his right hand to the friends of letters and of the gospel, and his left hand to the friends of the priests ; and then endeavoured to walk with both. But when he had to choose between the two parties, clerical interests prevailed. There was no lack of bishops, priests, and laymen about him, who intimidated him by their clamours. After taking a few steps forward, he suddenly recoiled. Still Tyndale ventured to hazard a word; but the prelate was cold as before. The humanists, who laughed at the ignorance of the monks, hesitated to touch an ecclesiastical system which lavished on them such rich sinecures. They accepted the new ideas in theory, but not in practice. They were very willing to discuss them at table, but not to proclaim them from the pulpit; and covering the Greek Testament

---

[1] Tyndal, Doctr. Tr. p. 79,   [2] Ibid. p. 153.
[3] He laboured to be his chaplain. Foxe, Acts, iv. p. 617.

[1] He willed me to write an epistle to my lord, and to go to him myself. Foxe, Acts, iv. p. 617.
[2] My Lord answered me, his house was full. Tyndale, Doctr. Tr. p. 395.

with applause, they tore it in pieces when rendered into the vulgar tongue. " If you will look well about London," said Tonstall coldly to the poor priest; " you will not fail to meet with some suitable employment." This was all Tyndale could obtain. Hebilthwayte waited on him to the door, and the hellenist departed sad and desponding.

His expectations were disappointed. Driven from the banks of the Severn, without a home in the capital, what would become of the translation of the Scriptures? " Alas!" he said ; " I was deceived......[1] there is nothing to be looked for from the bishops......Christ was smitten on the cheek before the bishop, Paul was buffeted before the bishop [2]...and a bishop has just turned me away." His dejection did not last long : there was an elastic principle in his soul. " I hunger for the word of God," said he, " I will translate it, whatever they may say or do. God will not suffer me to perish. He never made a mouth but he made food for it, nor a body, but he made raiment also." [3]

This trustfulness was not misplaced. It was the privilege of a layman to give what the bishop refused. Among Tyndale's hearers at St Dunstan's was a rich merchant named Humphrey Monmouth, who had visited Rome, and to whom (as well as to his companions) the pope had been so kind as to give certain Roman curiosities, such as indulgences, a culpâ et a pœnâ. Ships laden with his manufactures every year quitted London for foreign countries. He had formerly attended Colet's preaching at St Paul's, and from the year 1515 he had known the word of God.[4] He was one of the gentlest and most obliging men in England ; he kept open house for the friends of learning and of the Gospel, and his library contained the newest publications. In putting on Jesus Christ, Monmouth had particularly striven to put on his character ; he helped generously with his purse both priests and men of letters ; he gave forty pounds sterling to the chaplain of the bishop of London, the same to the king's, to the provincial of the Augustines, and to others besides. Latimer, who sometimes dined with him, once related in the pulpit an anecdote characteristic of the friends of the Reformation in England. Among the regular guests at Monmouth's table was one of his poorest neighbours, a zealous Romanist, to whom his generous host often used to lend money. One day when the pious merchant was extolling Scripture and blaming popery, his neighbour turned pale, rose from the table, and left the room. " I will never set foot in his house again," he said to his friends, " and I will never borrow another shilling of him." [5] He next went

to the bishop and laid an information against his benefactor. Monmouth forgave him, and tried to bring him back ; but the neighbour constantly turned out of his way. Once, however, they met in a street so narrow that he could not escape. " I will pass by without looking at him," said the Romanist turning away his head. But Monmouth went straight to him, took him by the hand, and said affectionately : " Neighbour, what wrong have I done you? " and he continued to speak to him with so much love, that the poor man fell on his knees, burst into tears, and begged his forgiveness.[1] Such was the spirit which, at the very outset, animated the work of the Reformation in England : it was acceptable to God, and found favour with the people.

Monmouth being edified by Tyndale's sermons, inquired into his means of living. " I have none," [2] replied he, " but I hope to enter into the bishop's service." This was before his visit to Tonstall. When Tyndale saw all his hopes frustrated, he went to Monmouth and told him everything. " Come and live with me," said the wealthy merchant, " and there labour." God did' to Tyndale according to his faith. Simple, frugal, devoted to work, he studied night and day ;[3] and wishing to guard his mind against " being overcharged with surfeiting," he refused the delicacies of his patron's table, and would take nothing but sodden meat and small beer.[4] It would even seem that he carried simplicity in dress almost too far.[5] By his conversation and his works, he shed over the house of his patron the mild light of the Christian virtues, and Monmouth loved him more and more every day.

Tyndale was advancing in his work when John Fryth, the mathematician of King's College, Cambridge, arrived in London. It is probable that Tyndale, feeling the want of an associate, had invited him. United like Luther and Melancthon, the two friends held many precious conversations together. " I will consecrate my life wholly to the church of Jesus Christ," said Fryth.[6] " To be a good man, you must give great part of yourself to your parents, a greater part to your country ; but the greatest of all to the church of the Lord." " The people should know the word of God," [7] they said both. " The interpretation of the gospel without the intervention of councils or popes, is sufficient to create a saving faith in the heart." They shut themselves up in the little room in Monmouth's house, and translated chapter after chapter from the Greek into plain English. The bishop of London knew nothing of the work going on a few yards from him, and every-

1 I was beguiled. Tyndale, Doctr. Tr. p. 395.
2 Expositions, p. 59.
3 Tynd. and Fryth's Works, ii. p. 349.
4 The rich man began to be a Scripture man. Latimer's Sermons. p. 440 (Park. Soc).
5 Latimer's Works, i. p. 441. He would borrow no [more] money of him.

1 Latimer's Works. i. p. 441.   2 Foxe, Acts, iv p. 617.
3 Strype, Records, i. p. 664.
4 Ibid. He would eat but sodden meat and drink but small single beer.
5 He was never seen in that house to wear linen about him. Ibid.
6 Tyndale and Fryth's Works, iii. p. 73, 74.
7 That the poor people might also read and see the simple plain word of God. Foxe, Acts, v. p. 118.

thing was succeeding to Tyndale's wishes when it was interrupted by an unforeseen circumstance.

Longland, the persecutor of the Lincolnshire Christians, did not confine his activity within the limits of his diocese; he besieged the king, the cardinal, and the queen with his cruel importunities, using Wolsey's influence with Henry, and Henry's with Wolsey. "His majesty," he wrote to the cardinal, "shows in this holy dispute as much goodness as zeal......yet, be pleased to urge him to overthrow God's enemies." And then turning to the king, the confessor said, to spur him on: "The cardinal is about to fulminate the greater excommunication against all who possess Luther's Works or hold his opinions, and to make the booksellers sign a bond before the magistrates, not to sell *heretical* books." "Wonderful!" replied Henry with a sneer. "they will fear the *magisterial* bond, I think, more than the *clerical* excommunication." And yet the consequences of the "clerical" excommunication were to be very positive; whosoever persevered in his offence was to be pursued by the law *ad ignem*, even to the fire.[1] At last the confessor applied to the queen : "We cannot be sure of restraining the press," he said to her. "These wretched books come to us from Germany, France, and the Low Countries ; and are even printed in the very midst of us. Madam, we must train and prepare skilful men, such as are able to discuss the controverted points, so that the laity, struck on the one hand by well developed arguments, and frightened by the fear of punishment on the other, may be kept in obedience."[2] In the bishop's system, "fire" was to be the complement of Roman learning. The essential idea of Jesuitism is already visible in this conception of Henry the Eighth's confessor. That system is the natural development of Romanism.

Toustall, urged forward by Longland, and desirous of showing himself as holy a churchman as he had once been a skilful statesman and elegant scholar—Tonstall, the friend of Erasmus, began to persecute. He would have feared to shed blood, like Longland ; but there are measures which torture the mind and not the body, and which the most moderate men fear not to make use of. John Higgins, Henry Chambers, Thomas Eaglestone, a priest named Edmund Spilman, and some other Christians in London, used to meet and read portions of the Bible in English, and even asserted publicly that "Luther had more learning in his little finger than all the doctors in England."[3] The bishop ordered these rebels to be arrested : he flattered and alarmed them, threatening them with a cruel death (which he would hardly

have inflicted on them), and by these skilful practices reduced them to silence.

Tyndale, who witnessed this persecution, feared lest the stake should interrupt his labour. If those who read a few fragments of Scripture are threatened with death, what will he not have to endure who is translating the whole? His friends entreated him to withdraw from the bishop's pursuit. "Alas!" he exclaimed, "is there then no place where I can translate the Bible?......It is not the bishop's house alone that is closed against me, but all England."[1]

He then made a great sacrifice. Since there is no place in his own country where he can translate the word of God, he will go and seek one among the nations of the continent. It is true the people are unknown to him ; he is without resources ; perhaps persecution and even death await him there...... It matters not! some time must elapse before it is known what he is doing, and perhaps he will have been able to translate the Bible. He turned his eyes towards Germany. "God does not destine us to a quiet life here below," he said.[2] "If he calls us to peace on the part of Jesus Christ, he calls us to war on the part of the world."

There lay at that moment in the river Thames a vessel loading for Hamburg. Monmouth gave Tyndale ten pounds sterling for his voyage, and other friends contributed a like amount. He left the half of this sum in the hands of his benefactor to provide for his future wants, and prepared to quit London, where he had spent a year. Rejected by his fellow countrymen, persecuted by the clergy, and carrying with him only his New Testament and his ten pounds, he went on board the ship, shaking off the dust of his feet, according to his Master's precept, and that dust fell back on the priests of England. He was indignant (says the chronicler) against those coarse monks, covetous priests, and pompous prelates,[3] who were waging an impious war against God. "What a trade is that of the priests!" he said in one of his later writings ; "they want money for every thing; money for baptism, money for churchings, for weddings, for buryings, for images, brotherhoods, penances, soul masses, bells, organs, chalices, copes, surplices, ewers, censers, and all manner of ornaments. Poor sheep! The parson shears, the vicar shaves, the parish priest polls, the friar scrapes, the indulgence seller pares......all that you want is a butcher to flay you and take away your skin.[4] He will not leave you long. Why are your prelates dressed in red? Because they are ready to shed the blood of whomsoever seeketh the word of God.[5] Scourge of states, devastators of kingdoms, the priests take away not only

---

1 Anderson's Annals of the Bible, i. p. 42.
2 Ibid. i. p, 42, 43. Herbert says (p. 147) " to suspend the laity betwixt fear and controversies."
3 Foxe, Acts. v. p. 179.

1 But also that there was no place to do it in all England, Tynd. Doctr. Tr. 396.
2 We be not called to a soft living. Ibid. ii. p. 249.
3 Marking especially the demeanour of the preachers, and beholding the pomp of the prelates. Foxe, Acts, v. p. 1i8.
4 Doct. Tr. p. 238. Obedience of a Chr. Man.
5 Ibid. p. 251.

Holy Scripture, but also prosperity and peace; but of their councils is no layman; reigning over all, they obey nobody; and making all concur to their own greatness, they conspire against every kingdom."[1]

No kingdom was to be more familiar than England with the conspiracies of the papacy of which Tyndale spoke; and yet none was to free itself more irrevocably from the power of Rome.

Yet Tyndale was leaving the shores of his native land, and as he turned his eyes towards the new countries, hope revived in his heart. He was going to be free, and he would use his liberty to deliver the word of God, so long held captive. "The priests," he said one day, "when they had slain Christ, set pole-axes to keep him in his sepulchre, that he should not rise again; even so have our priests buried the testament of God, and all their study is to keep it down, that it rise not again.[2] But the hour of the Lord is come, and nothing can hinder the word of God, as nothing could hinder Jesus Christ of old from issuing from the tomb." Indeed that poor man, then sailing towards Germany, was to send back, even from the banks of the Elbe, the eternal gospel to his countrymen.

CHAPTER IX.

Bilney at Cambridge—Conversions—The University Cross-Bearer—A Leicestershire Farmer—A Party of Students—Superstitious Practices—An obstinate Papist—The Sophists—Latimer attacks Stafford—Bilney's Resolution—Latimer hears Bilney's Confession—Confessor converted—New Life in Latimer—Bilney preaches Grace—Nature of the Ministry—Latimer's Character and Teaching—Works of Charity—Three Classes of Adversaries—Clark and Dalaber.

This ship did not bear away all the hopes of England. A society of Christians had been formed at Cambridge, of which Bilney was the centre. He now knew no other canon law than Scripture, and had found a new master, "the Holy Spirit of Christ," says an historian. Although he was naturally timid, and often suffered from the exhaustion brought on by his fasts and vigils, there was in his language a life, liberty, and strength, strikingly in contrast with his sickly appearance. He desired to draw to the knowledge of God,[3] all who came nigh him; and by degrees, the rays of the gospel sun, which was then rising in the firmament of Christendom, pierced the ancient windows of the colleges, and illuminated the solitary chambers of certain of the masters and fellows. Master Arthur, Master Thistle of Pembroke Hall, and Master Stafford, were among the first to join Bilney. George Stafford, professor of divinity, was a man of deep learning and holy

life, clear and precise in his teaching. He was admired by every one in Cambridge, so that his conversion, like that of his friends, spread alarm among the partisans of the schoolmen. But a conversion still more striking than this was destined to give the English Reformation a champion more illustrious than either Stafford or Bilney.

There was in Cambridge, at that time, a priest notorious for his ardent fanaticism. In the processions, amidst the pomp, prayers, and chanting of the train, none could fail to notice a master of arts, about thirty years of age, who, with erect head, carried proudly the university cross. Hugh Latimer, for such was his name, combined a biting humour with an impetuous disposition and indefatigable zeal, and was very quick in ridiculing the faults of his adversaries. There was more wit and raillery in his fanaticism than can often be found in such characters. He followed the friends of the word of God into the colleges and houses where they used to meet, debated with them, and pressed them to abandon their faith. He was a second Saul, and was soon to resemble the apostle of the Gentiles in another respect.

He first saw light in the year 1491, in the county of Leicester. Hugh's father was an honest yeoman; and, accompanied by one of his six sisters, the little boy had often tended in the pastures the five score sheep belonging to the farm, or driven home to his mother the thirty cows it was her business to milk.[1] In 1497, the Cornish rebels, under Lord Audley, having encamped at Blackheath, our farmer had donned his rusty armour, and, mounting his horse, responded to the summons of the crown. Hugh, then only six years old, was present at his departure, and as if he had wished to take his little part in the battle, he had buckled the straps of his father's armour.[2] Fifty-two years afterwards he recalled this circumstance to mind in a sermon preached before king Edward. His father's house was always open to the neighbours; and no poor man ever turned away from the door without having received alms. The old man brought up his family in the love of men and in the fear of God, and having remarked with joy the precocious understanding of his son, he had him educated in the country schools, and then sent to Cambridge at the age of fourteen. This was in 1505, just as Luther was entering the Augustine convent.

The son of the Leicestershire yeoman was lively, fond of pleasure, and of cheerful conversation, and mingled frequently in the amusements of his fellow-students. One day, as they were dining together, one of the party exclaimed: *Nil melius quam lætari et facere bene!*—"There is nothing better than to be merry and to do well."[3]—"A vengeance on

------

[1] Doctr. Tr. p. 191.
[2] Tyndale, ibid. p. 251.
[3] So was in his heart an incredible desire to allure many. Foxe, Acts, iv. p. 620.

[1] My mother milked thirty kine. Latimer's Sermons, (Parker ed.) p. 101.
[2] I can remember that I buckled his harness. Ibid.
[3] Eccles. iii. 12.

that *bene!*" replied a monk of impudent mien; "I wish it were beyond the sea;[1] it mars all the rest." Young Latimer was much surprised at the remark: "I understand it now," said he, "that will be a heavy *bene* to these monks when they have to render God an account of their lives."

Latimer having become more serious, threw himself heart and soul into the practices of superstition, and a very bigoted old cousin undertook to instruct him in them. One day, when one of their relations lay dead, she said to him: "We must drive out the devil. Take this holy taper, my child, and pass it over the body, first long ways and then athwart, so as always to make the sign of the cross."

But the scholar performing this exorcism very awkwardly, his aged cousin snatched the candle from his hand, exclaiming angrily: "It's a great pity your father spends so much money on your studies: he will never make anything of you."[2]

This prophecy was not fulfilled. He became Fellow of Clare Hall in 1509, and took his master's degree in 1514. His classical studies being ended, he began to study divinity. Duns Scotus, Aquinas, and Hugo de Sancto Victore were his favourite authors. The practical side of things, however, engaged him more than the speculative; and he was more distinguished in Cambridge for his ascetism and enthusiasm than for his learning. He attached importance to the merest trifles. As the missal directs that water should be mingled with the sacramental wine, often while saying mass he would be troubled in his conscience for fear he had not put *sufficient water*.[3] This remorse never left him a moment's tranquillity during the service. In him, as in many others, attachment to puerile ordinances occupied in his heart the place of faith in the great truths. With him, the cause of the church was the cause of God, and he respected Thomas à Becket at least as much as St Paul. "I was then," said he, "as obstinate a papist as any in England."[4] Luther said the same thing of himself.

The fervent Latimer soon observed that everybody around him was not equally zealous with himself for the ceremonies of the church. He watched with surprise certain young members of the university, who, forsaking the doctors of the School, met daily to read and search into the Holy Scriptures. People sneered at them in Cambridge: "It is only the *sophists*," was the cry; but raillery was not enough for Latimer. One day he entered the room where these *sophists* were assembled, and begged them to cease studying the Bible. All his entreaties were useless. Can we be astonished at it? said La-

timer to himself. Don't we see even the tutors setting an example to these stray sheep? There is Master Stafford, the most illustrious professor in English universities, devoting his time *ad Biblia*, like Luther at Wittemberg, and explaining the Scriptures according to the Hebrew and Greek texts! and the delighted students celebrate in bad verse the doctor,

Qui Paulum explicuit rite et evangelium,[1]

That young people should occupy themselves with these new doctrines was conceivable, but that a doctor of divinity should do so—what a disgrace! Latimer therefore determined to attack Stafford. He insulted him;[2] he entreated the youth of Cambridge to abandon the professor and his heretical teaching; he attended the hall in which the doctor taught, made signs of impatience during the lesson, and cavilled at it after leaving the school. He even preached in public against the learned doctor. But it seemed to him that Cambridge and England were struck blind: true, the clergy approved of Latimer's proceedings—nay, praised them; and yet they did nothing. To console him, however, he was named cross-bearer to the university, and we have already seen him discharging this duty.

Latimer desired to show himself worthy of such an honour. He had left the students to attack Stafford; and he now left Stafford for a more illustrious adversary. But this attack led him to some one *that was stronger than he*. At the occasion of receiving the degree of bachelor of divinity he had to deliver a Latin discourse in the presence of the university; Latimer chose for his subject *Philip Melancthon and his doctrines*. Had not this daring heretic presumed to say quite recently that the fathers of the church have altered the sense of Scripture? Had he not asserted that, like those rocks whose various colours are imparted to the polypus which clings to them,[3] so the doctors of the church give each their own opinion in the passages they explain? And finally had he not discovered a new *touchstone* (it is thus he styles the Holy Scripture) by which we must test the sentences even of St Thomas?

Latimer's discourse made a great impression. At last (said his hearers) England, nay Cambridge, will furnish a champion for the church that will confront the Wittemberg doctors, and save the vessel of our Lord. But very different was to be the result. There was among the hearers one man almost hidden through his small stature: it was Bilney. For some time he had been watching Latimer's movements, and his zeal interested

---

[1] I would that *bene* had been banished beyond the sea. Latimer's Sermons, p. 153.   [2] Ibid. p. 499.
[3] He thought he had never sufficiently mingled his massing wine with water. Foxe, Acts, viii. p. 433.
[4] Ibid, p. 334.

[1] Who has explained to us the true sense of St Paul and of the gospel. Strype's Mem. i. p. 74.
[2] Most spitefully railing against him. Foxe, Acts, viii. p. 437.
[3] Ut polypus cuicunque petræ adhæserit, ejus colorem imitatur. Corp. Ref. i. p. 114.

him, though it was a zeal without knowledge. His energy was not great, but he possessed a delicate tact, a skilful discernment of character which enabled him to distinguish error, and to select the fittest method for combating it. Accordingly, a chronicler styles him "a trier of Satan's subtleties, appointed by God to detect the bad money that the enemy was circulating throughout the church." [1] Bilney easily detected Latimer's sophisms, but at the same time loved his person, and conceived the design of winning him to the gospel. But how to manage it? The prejudiced Latimer would not even listen to the evangelical Bilney. The latter reflected, prayed, and at last planned a very candid and very strange plot, which led to one of the most astonishing conversions recorded in history.

He went to the college where Latimer resided. "For the love of God," he said to him, "be pleased to hear my confession." [2] The *heretic* prayed to make confession to the *catholic:* what a singular fact! My discourse against Melancthon has no doubt converted him, said Latimer to himself. Had not Bilney once been among the number of the most pious zealots? His pale face, his wasted frame, and his humble look are clear signs that he ought to belong to the ascetics of catholicism. If he turns back, all will turn back with him, and the reaction will be complete at Cambridge. The ardent Latimer eagerly yielded to Bilney's request, and the latter, kneeling before the cross-bearer, related to him with touching simplicity the anguish he had once felt in his soul, the efforts he had made to remove it; their unprofitableness so long as he determined to follow the precepts of the church, and lastly, the peace he had felt when he believed that Jesus Christ is *the Lamb of God that taketh away the sins of the world.* He described to Latimer the spirit of adoption he had received, and the happiness he experienced in being able now to call God his father.......Latimer, who expected to receive a confession, listened without mistrust. His heart was opened, and the voice of the pious Bilney penetrated it without obstacle. From time to time the confessor would have chased away the new thoughts which came crowding into his bosom; but the penitent continued. His language, at once so simple and so lively, entered like a two-edged sword. Bilney was not without assistance in his work. A new, a strange witness,—the Holy Ghost, [3]—was speaking in Latimer's soul. He learned from God to know God: he received a new heart. At length grace prevailed: the penitent rose up, but Latimer remained seated, absorbed in thought. The strong cross-bearer contended in vain against the words of the feeble Bilney. Like Saul on the way to Damascus, he was conquered, and his conversion, like the apostle's, was instantaneous. He stammered out a few words; Bilney drew near him with love, and God scattered the darkness which still obscured his mind. He saw Jesus Christ as the only Saviour given to man: he contemplated and adored him. "I learnt more by this confession," he said afterwards, "than by much reading and in many years before [1]......I now tasted the word of God, [2] and forsook the doctors of the school and all their fooleries." [3] It was not the penitent but the confessor who received absolution. Latimer viewed with horror the obstinate war he had waged against God; he wept bitterly; but Bilney consoled him. "Brother," said he, "though your sins be as scarlet, they shall be white as snow." These two young men, then locked in their solitary chamber at Cambridge, were one day to mount the scaffold for that divine Master whose spirit was teaching them. But one of them before going to the stake was first to sit on an episcopal throne.

Latimer was changed. The energy of his character was tempered by a divine unction. Becoming a believer, he had ceased to be superstitious. Instead of persecuting Jesus Christ, he became a zealous seeker after him. [4] Instead of cavilling and railing, he showed himself meek and gentle; [5] instead of frequenting company, he sought solitude, studying the scriptures and advancing in true theology. He threw off the old man and put on the new. He waited upon Stafford, begged forgiveness for the insult he had offered him, and then regularly attended his lectures, being subjugated more by this doctor's angelic conversation [6] than by his learning. But it was Bilney's society Latimer cultivated most. They conversed together daily, took frequent walks together into the country, and occasionally rested at a place, long known as "the heretic's hill." [7]

So striking a conversion gave fresh vigour to the evangelical movement. Hitherto Bilney and Latimer had been the most zealous champions of the two opposite causes; the one despised, the other honoured; the weak man had conquered the strong. This action of the Spirit of God was not thrown away upon Cambridge. Latimer's conversion, as of old the miracles of the apostles, struck men's minds; and was it not in truth a miracle? All the youth of the university ran to hear Bilney preach. He proclaimed "Jesus Christ as He who, having tasted death, has delivered his people from the penalty of sin." [8] While the doctors of the

[1] Foxe, Acts, vii. p. 438.
[2] He came to me afterwards in my study, and desired me for God's sake to hear his confession. Latimer's Sermons, p. 334.
[3] He was through the good Spirit of God so touched. Foxe, viii. p. 436.

[1] Latimer's Sermons. p. 334.
[2] From that time forward I began to smell the word of God. Ibid.   [3] Ibid. p. 335.
[4] Whereas ̇ ̇ efore he was an enemy and almost a persecutor of Christ, he was now a zealous seeker after him. Foxe, Acts, vii. p. 338.   [5] Ibid.
[6] A man of a very perfect life and angelic conversation. Becon's Works (Parker Soc.) p. 425.
[7] Foxe, viii. p. 452.
[8] Christus quem pro virili doceo....denique et satisfactionem. Ep. ad Tonstallum episcop. Ibid. Acts, iv. p. 633.

school (even the most pious of them) laid most stress upon *man's* part in the work of redemption, Bilney on the contrary emphasized the other term, namely, *God's* part. This doctrine of grace, said his adversaries, annuls the sacraments, and contradicts baptismal regeneration. The selfishness which forms the essence of fallen humanity rejected the evangelical doctrine, and felt that to accept it was to be lost. "Many listened with *the left ear,*" to use an expression of Bilney's; "like Malchus, having their *right* ear cut off;" and they filled the university with their complaints.

But Bilney did not allow himself to be stopped. The idea of eternity had seized on his mind, and perhaps he still retained some feeble relic of the exaggerations of asceticism. He condemned every kind of recreation, even when innocent. Music in the churches seemed to him a mockery of God;[1] and when Thurlby, who was afterwards a bishop, and who lived at Cambridge in the room below his, used to begin playing on the recorder, Bilney would fall on his knees and pour out his soul in prayer: to him prayer was the sweetest melody. He prayed that the lively faith of the children of God might in all England be substituted for the vanity and pride of the priests. He believed — he prayed — he waited. His waiting was not to be in vain.

Latimer trod in his footsteps: the transformation of his soul was going on; and the more fanaticism he had shown for the sacerdotal system, which places salvation in the hands of the priest, the more zeal he now showed for the evangelical system, which placed it in the hands of Christ. He saw that if the churches must needs have ministers, it is not because they require a human mediation, but from the necessity of a regular preaching of the gospel and a steady direction of the flock; and accordingly he would have wished to call the servant of the Lord minister (ὑπηρέτης or διάκοyος τοῦ λόyου), and not *priest²* (ἱερεύς or *sacerdos*.) In his view, it was not the imposition of hands by the bishop that gave grace, but grace which authorized the imposition of hands. He considered activity to be one of the essential features of the gospel ministry. "Would you know," said he, "why the Lord chose *fishermen* to be his apostles?......See how they watch day and night at their nets to take all such fishes that they can get and come in their way....... So all our bishops, and curates, and vicars should be as painful in casting their nets, that is to say, in preaching God's word."[3] He regarded all confidence in human strength as a remnant of paganism. "Let us not do," he said, "as the haughty Ajax, who said to his father as he went to battle: Without the

help of God I am able to fight, and I will get the victory with mine own strength."[1]

The Reformation had gained in Latimer a very different man from Bilney. He had not so much discernment and prudence perhaps, but he had more energy and eloquence. What Tyndale was to be for England by his writings, Latimer was to be by his discourses. The tenderness of his conscience, the warmth of his zeal, and the vivacity of his understanding, were enlisted in the service of Jesus Christ; and if at times he was carried too far by the liveliness of his wit, it only shows that the reformers were not *saints*, but sanctified men. "He was one of the first," says an historian, "who, in the days of King Henry VIII., set himself to preach the gospel in the truth and simplicity of it."[2] He preached in Latin *ad clerum*, and in English *ad populum*. He boldly placed the law with its curses before his hearers, and then conjured them to flee towards the Saviour of the world.[3] The same zeal which he had employed in saying mass, he now employed in preaching the true sacrifice of Christ. He said one day:— "If one man had committed all the sins since Adam, you may be sure he should be punished with the same horror of death, in such a sort as all men in the world should have suffered.......Such was the pain Christ endured......If our Saviour had committed all the sins of the world; all that I for my part have done, all that you for your part have done, and that any man else hath done; if he had done all this himself, his agony that he suffered should have been no greater nor grievouser than it was......Believe in Jesus Christ, and you shall overcome death. ......But, alas!" said he at another time, "the devil, by the help of that Italian bishop, his chaplain, has laboured by all means that he might frustrate the death of Christ and the merits of his passion."[4]

Thus began in British Christendom the preaching of the Cross. The Reformation was not the substitution of the catholicism of the first ages for the popery of the middle ages: it was a revival of the preaching of St Paul, and thus it was that on hearing Latimer every one exclaimed with rapture: "Of a *Saul*, God has made him a very *Paul*."[5]

To the inward power of faith, the Cambridge evangelists added the outward power of the life. Saul become Paul, the strong, the ardent Latimer, had need of action; and Bilney, the weak and humble Bilney, in delicate health, observing a severe diet, taking ordinarily but one meal a-day, and never sleeping more than four hours, absorbed in prayer and in the study of the

---

[1] Foxe, Acts, iv. p. 621.
[2] Minister is a more fit name for that office. Latimer's Remains, p. 264.
[3] Ibid. p. 24.

[1] Latimer's Sermons. p. 491. Sophocles, Ajax, 783, et. seq.
[2] Strype's Mem. iii. part i. p. 378.
[3] Flying to him by an evangelical faith. Ibid.
[4] Lat. Ser. p. 74.
[5] This was said by Ralph Morice, afterwards Cranmer's secretary. Strype, Eccl. Mem. iii. part i. p. 368.

word displayed at that time all the energy of charity. These two friends devoted themselves not merely to the easy labours of Christian beneficence; but caring little for that formal Christianity so often met with among the easy classes, they explored the gloomy cells of the madhouse to bear the sweet and subtle voice of the gospel to the infuriate maniacs. They visited the miserable lazar-house without the town, in which several poor lepers were dwelling; they carefully tended them, wrapped them in clean sheets, and wooed them to be converted to Christ.[1] The gates of the jail at Cambridge were opened to them,[2] and they announced to the poor prisoners that word which giveth liberty. Some were converted by it, and longed for the day of their execution.[3] Latimer, afterwards bishop of Worcester, was one of the most beautiful types of the Reformation in England.

He was opposed by numerous adversaries. In the front rank were the priests, who spared no endeavours to retain souls. "Beware," said Latimer to the new converts, "lest robbers overtake you, and plunge you into the pope's prison of purgatory."[4] After these came the sons and favourites of the aristocracy, worldly and frivolous students, who felt little disposition to listen to the gospel. "By yeomen's sons the faith of Christ is and hath been chiefly maintained in the church,"[5] said Latimer. "Is this realm taught by rich men's sons? No, no; read the chronicles; ye shall find sometime noblemen's sons which have been unpreaching bishops and prelates, but ye shall find none of them learned men." He would have desired a mode of election which placed in the Christian pulpit, not the richest and most fashionable men, but the ablest and most pious. This important reform was reserved for other days. Lastly, the evangelists of Cambridge came into collision with the *brutality* of many, to use Latimer's own expression. "What need have we of universities and schools?" said the students of this class. The Holy Ghost "will give us always what to say."—"We must trust in the Holy Ghost," replied Latimer, "but not presume on it. If you will not maintain universities, you shall have a *brutality*."[6] In this manner the Reformation restored to Cambridge gravity and knowledge, along with truth and charity.

Yet Bilney and Latimer often turned their eyes towards Oxford, and wondered how the light would be able to penetrate there. Wolsey provided for that. A Cambridge master of arts, John Clark, a conscientious man, of tender heart, great prudence, and unbounded devotion to his duty, had been enlightened by the word of God. Wolsey, who since 1523 had been seeking everywhere for distinguished scholars to adorn his new college, invited Clark among the first. This doctor, desirous of bearing to Oxford the light which God had given Cambridge, immediately began to deliver a course of divinity lectures, to hold conferences, and to preach in his eloquent manner. He taught every day.[1] Among the graduates and students who followed him was Anthony Dalaber, a young man of simple but profound feeling, who while listening to him had experienced in his heart the regenerating power of the gospel. Overflowing with happiness which the knowledge of Jesus Christ imparted to him, he went to the Cardinal's college, knocked at Clark's door, and said: "Father, allow me never to quit you more!" The teacher, beholding the young disciple's enthusiasm, loved him, but thought it his duty to try him: "Anthony," said he, "you know not what you ask. My teaching is now pleasant to you, but the time will come when God will lay the cross of persecution on you; you will be dragged before bishops; your name will be covered with shame in the world, and all who love you will be heart-broken on account of you. ......Then, my friend, you will regret that you ever knew me."

Anthony believing himself rejected, and unable to bear the idea of returning to the barren instructions of the priests, fell on his knees, and weeping bitterly,[2] exclaimed: "For the tender mercy of God, turn me not away." Touched by his sorrow, Clark folded him in his arms, kissed him, and with tears in his eyes exclaimed: "The Lord give thee what thou askest!......Take me for thy father, I take thee for my son." From that hour Anthony, all joy, was like Timothy at the feet of Paul. He united a quick understanding with tender affections. When any of the students had not attended Clark's conferences, the master commissioned his disciple to visit them, to inquire into their doubts, and to impart to them his instructions. "This exercise did me much good," said Dalaber, "and I made great progress in the knowledge of Scripture."

Thus the kingdom of God, which consists not in forms, but in the power of the Spirit, was set up in Cambridge and Oxford. The alarmed schoolmen, beholding their most pious scholars escaping one after another from their teaching, called the bishops to their aid, and the latter determined to send agents to Cambridge, the focus of the heresy, to apprehend the leaders. This took place in 1523 or the beginning of 1524. The episcopal officers had arrived, and were proceeding to business. The most timid began

---

[1] Preaching at the lazar cots, wrapping them in sheets. Foxe, Acts, vol. iv. p. 620. Lond. 1846.
[2] Latimer's Sermons, p. 335 (Park. Soc.)
[3] She had such a savour, such a sweetness, and feeling, that she thought it long to the day of execution. Latimer's Sermons, p. 180.
[4] Strype's Eccles. Memorials, vol. iii. pt. i. p. 378.
[5] Latimer's Sermons, p. 102.   [6] Ibid. p. 269.

[1] Teach or preach, which he did daily. Foxe, Acts, v. p. 496.   [2] Ibid.

to feel alarm, but Latimer was full of courage; when suddenly the agents of the clergy were forbidden to go on, and this prohibition, strange to say, originated with Wolsey; "upon what ground I cannot imagine," says Burnet.[1] Certain events were taking place at Rome of a nature to exercise great influence over the priestly councils, and which may perhaps explain what Burnet could not understand.

CHAPTER X.

Wolsey seeks the Tiara—Clement VII. is elected—Wolsey's Dissimulation—Charles offers France to Henry—Pace's Mission on this Subject—Wolsey reforms the Convents—His secret Alliances—Treaty between France and England —Taxation and Insurrection—False Charges against the Reformers—Latimer's Defence—Tenterden Steeple.

ADRIAN VI. died on the 14th September 1523, before the end of the second year of his pontificate. Wolsey thought himself pope. At length he would no longer be the favourite only, but the arbiter of the kings of the earth; and his genius, for which England was too narrow, would have Europe and the world for its stage. Already revolving gigantic projects in his mind, the future pope dreamt of the destruction of heresy in the west, and in the east the cessation of the Greek schism, and new crusades to replant the cross on the walls of Constantinople. There is nothing that Wolsey would not have dared undertake when once seated on the throne of catholicism, and the pontificates of Gregory VII. and Innocent III. would have been eclipsed by that of the Ipswich butcher's son. The cardinal reminded Henry of his promise, and the very next day the king signed a letter addressed to Charles the Fifth.

Believing himself sure of the emperor, Wolsey turned all his exertions to the side of Rome. "The legate of England," said Henry's ambassadors to the cardinals, "is the very man for the present time. He is the only one thoroughly acquainted with the interests and wants of Christendom, and strong enough to provide for them. He is all kindness, and will share his dignities and wealth among all the prelates who support him."

But Julio de' Medici himself aspired to the papacy, and as eighteen cardinals were devoted to him, the election could not take place without his support. "Rather than yield," said he in the conclave, "I would die in this prison." A month passed away, and nothing was done. New intrigues were then resorted to: there were cabals for Wolsey, cabals for Medici. The cardinals were besieged:

Into their midst, by many a secret path,
Creeps sly intrigue.[1]

At length, on the 19th November 1523, the people collected under their windows, shouting: "No foreign pope." After forty-nine days debating, Julio was elected, and according to his own expression, "bent his head beneath the yoke of apostolic servitude."[2] He took the name of Clement VII.

Wolsey was exasperated. It was in vain that he presented himself before St Peter's chair at each vacancy: a more active or more fortunate rival always reached it before him. Master of England, and the most influential of European diplomatists, he saw men preferred to him who were his inferiors. This election was an event for the Reformation. Wolsey as pope would, humanly speaking, have tightened the cords which already bound England so closely to Rome; but Wolsey, rejected, could hardly fail to throw himself into tortuous paths which would perhaps contribute to the emancipation of the Church. He became more crafty than ever; declared to Henry that the new election was quite in conformity with his wishes,[3] and hastened to congratulate the new pope. He wrote to his agents at Rome: "This election, I assure you, is as much to the king's and my rejoicing, consolation, and gladness, as possibly may be devised or imagined...... Ye shall show unto his holiness what joy, comfort, and gladness it is both to the king's highness and me to perceive that once in our lives it hath pleased God of his great goodness to provide such a pastor unto his church, as his grace and I have long inwardly desired; who for his virtue, wisdom, and other high and notable qualities, we have always reputed the most able and worthy person to be called to that dignity."[4] But the pope, divining his competitor's vexation, sent the king a golden rose, and a ring to Wolsey. "I am sorry," he said as he drew it from his finger, "that I cannot present it to his eminence in person." Clement moreover conferred on him the quality of legate *for life*—an office which had hitherto been temporary only. Thus the popedom and England embraced each other, and nothing appeared more distant than that Christian revolution which was destined very shortly to emancipate Britain from the tutelage of the Vatican.

Wolsey's disappointed ambition made him suspend the proceedings of the clergy at Cambridge. He had revenge in his heart, and cared not to persecute his fellow-countrymen merely to please his rival; and besides, like several popes, he had a certain

[1] History of the Reformation, vol. i. p. 25. Lond. 1841.

[1] Un conclave, by C. Delavigne.
[2] Colla subjecimus jugo apostolicæ servitutis. Rymer, Fœdera, vi. 2, p. 7.
[3] I take God to witness, I am more joyous thereof, than if it had fortuned upon my person. Wolsey to Henry VIII. Burnet, Records, p. cccxxviii. (Lond. 1841.)
[4] Wolsey to Secretary Pace. Galt's Wolsey, p. 381, Appendix. (Lond. 1846.)

fondness for learning. To send a few Lollards to prison was a matter of no difficulty; but learned doctors.......,this required a closer examination. Hence he gave Rome a sign of independence. And yet it was not specially against the pope that he began to entertain sinister designs : Clement had been more fortunate than himself; but that was no reason why he should be angry with him......Charles V. was the offender, and Wolsey swore a deadly hatred against him. Resolved to strike, he sought only the place where he could inflict the severest blow. To obtain his end, he resolved to dissemble his passion, and to distil drop by drop into Henry's mind that mortal hatred against Charles, which gave fresh energy to his activity.

Charles discovered the indignation that lay hid under Wolsey's apparent mildness, and wishing to retain Henry's alliance, he made more pressing advances to the king. Having deprived the minister of a tiara, he resolved to offer the king a crown : this was, indeed, a noble compensation ! " You are king of France," the emperor said, " and I undertake to win your kingdom for you.[1] Only send an ambassador to Italy to negotiate the matter." Wolsey, who could hardly contain his vexation, was forced to comply, in appearance at least, with the emperor's views. The king, indeed, seemed to think of nothing but his arrival at St Germain's, and commissioned Pace to visit Italy for this important business. Wolsey hoped that he would be unable to execute his commission : it was impossible to cross the Alps, for the French troops blockaded every passage. But Pace, who was one of those adventurous characters whom nothing can stop, spurred on by the thought that the king himself had sent him, determined to cross the *Col di Tenda*. On the 27th July, he entered the mountains, traversed precipitous passes, sometimes climbing them on all-fours,[2] and often falling during the descent. In some places he could ride on horseback ; " but in the most part thereof I durst not either turn my horse traverse (he wrote to the king) for all the worldly riches, nor in manner look on my left hand, for the pronite and deepness to the valley." After this passage, which lasted six days, Pace arrived in Italy worn out by fatigue. " If the king of England will enter France immediately by way of Normandy," said the constable of Bourbon to him, " I will give him leave to pluck out both my eyes[3] if he is not master of Paris before All-Saints ; and when Paris is taken, he will be master of the whole kingdom." But Wolsey, to whom these remarks were transmitted by the ambassador, slighted them, delayed furnishing the subsidies, and required certain conditions

which were calculated to thwart the project. Pace, who was ardent and ever imprudent, but plain and straightforward, forgot himself, and in a moment of vexation wrote to Wolsey : " To speak frankly, if you do not attend to these things, I shall impute to your grace the loss of the crown of France." These words ruined Henry's envoy in the cardinal's mind. Was this man, who owed everything to him, trying to supplant him ?... Pace in vain assured Wolsey that he should not take seriously what he had said, but the bolt had hit. Pace was associated with Charles in the cruel enmity of the minister, and he was one day to feel its terrible effects. It was not long before Wolsey was able to satisfy himself that the service Charles had desired to render the king of England was beyond the emperor's strength.

No sooner at ease on one side, than Wolsey found himself attacked on another. This man, the most powerful among kings' favourites, felt at this time the first breath of disfavour blow over him. On the pontifical throne, he would no doubt have attempted a reform after the manner of Sixtus V. : and wishing to rehearse on a smaller stage, and regenerate after his own fashion the catholic church in England, he submitted the monasteries to a strict inquisition, patronized the instruction of youth, and was the first to set a great example, by suppressing certain religious houses whose revenues he applied to his college in Oxford. Thomas Cromwell, his solicitor, displayed much skill and industry in this business,[1] and thus, under the orders of a cardinal of the Roman church, made his first campaign in a war of which he was in later days to hold the chief command. Wolsey and Cromwell, by their reforms, drew down the hatred of certain monks, priests, and noblemen, always the very humble servants of the clerical party. The latter accused the cardinal of not having estimated the monasteries at their just value, and of having, in certain cases, encroached on the royal jurisdiction. Henry, whom the loss of the crown of France had put in a bad humour, resolved, for the first time, not to spare his minister: " There are loud murmurs throughout this kingdom," he said to him : " it is asserted that your new college at Oxford is only a convenient cloak to hide your malversations."[2] " God forbid," replied the cardinal, " that this virtuous foundation at Oxford, undertaken for the good of my poor soul, should be raised *ex rapinis!* But, above all, God forbid that I should ever encroach upon your royal authority." He then cunningly insinuated, that by his will he left all his property to the king. Henry was satisfied : he had a share in the business.

Events of very different importance drew the king's attention to another quarter. The

---

[1] Ellis' Letters, Second Series, p. 326, 327.
[2] It made us creep of all-four. Pace to the king, Strype, vol. i. part ii. p. 27.
[3] Cotton MSS. Vitellius, B. 6, p. 87.

[1] Very forward and industrious. Foxe, Acts, v. p. 366.
[2] Collier's Eccles. Hist. x. p. 20.

two armies, of the empire and of France, were in presence before Pavia. Wolsey, who openly gave his right hand to Charles V., and secretly his left to Francis, repeated to his master: " If the emperor gains the victory, are you not his ally ? and if Francis, am I not in secret communication with him ? [1] Thus," added the cardinal, " whatever happens, your Highness will have great cause to give thanks to Almighty God."

On the 24th of February 1525, the battle of Pavia was fought, and the imperialists found in the French king's tent several of Wolsey's letters, and in his military chest and in the pockets of his soldiers the cardinal's corrupting gold. This alliance had been contrived by Giovanni Gioacchino, a Genoese master of the household to Louisa, regent of France, who passed for a merchant of Bologna, and lived in concealment at Blackfriars. Charles now saw what he had to trust to ; but the news of the battle of Pavia had scarcely reached England, when, faithful in perfidy, Wolsey gave utterance to a feigned pleasure. The people rejoiced also, but they were in earnest. Bonfires were lighted in the streets of London : the fountains ran wine, and the lord-mayor, attended by the aldermen, passed through the city on horseback to the sound of the trumpet.

The cardinal's joy was not altogether false. He would have been pleased at his enemy's defeat ; but his victory was perhaps still more useful to him.

He said to Henry : " The emperor is a liar, observing neither faith nor promise : the Archduchess Margaret is a woman of evil life ;[2] Don Ferdinand is a child, and Bourbon a traitor. Sire, you have other things to do with your money than to squander it on these four individuals. Charles is aiming at universal monarchy ; Pavia is the first step of this throne, and if England does not oppose him, he will attain it." Joachim having come privily to London, Wolsey prevailed upon Henry to conclude between England and France an " *indissoluble peace* by land and sea." [3] At last then he was in a position to prove to Charles that it is a dangerous thing to oppose the ambition of a priest.

This was not the only advantage Wolsey derived from the triumph of his enemy. The citizens of London imagined that the king of England would be in a few weeks in Paris ; Wolsey, rancorous and grasping, determined to make them pay dearly for their enthusiasm. " You desire to conquer France," said he ; " you are right. Give me then for that purpose the sixth part of your property ; that is a trifle to gratify so noble an inclination." England did not think so : this illegal demand aroused universal com-

plaint. " We are English and not French, freemen and not slaves,"[1] was the universal cry. Henry might tyrannize over his court, but not lay hands on his subjects' property.

The eastern counties rose in insurrection : four thousand men were under arms in a moment ; and Henry was guarded in his own palace by only a few servants. It was necessary to break down the bridges to stop the insurgents.[2] The courtiers complained to the king ; the king threw the blame on the cardinal ; the cardinal laid it on the clergy, who had encouraged him to impose this tax by quoting to him the example of Joseph demanding of the Egyptians the fifth part of their goods ; and the clergy in their turn ascribed the insurrection to the gospellers, who (said they) were stirring up a peasant war in England, as they had done in Germany. Reformation produces revolution : this is the favourite text of the followers of the pope. Violent hands must be laid upon the heretics. *Non pluit Deus, duc ad christianos.*[3]

The charge of the priests was absurd ; but the people are blind whenever the gospel is concerned, and occasionally the governors are blind also. Serious reasoning was not necessary to confute this invention. " Here, by the way, I will tell you a merry toy," said Latimer one day in the pulpit. " Master More was once sent in commission into Kent to help to try out, if it might be, what was the cause of Goodwin Sands and the shelf that stopped up Sandwich haven. He calleth the country afore him, such as were thought to be men of experience, and among others came in an old man with a white head, and one that was thought to be little less than one hundred years old. So Master More called the old aged man unto him, and said : Father, tell me if you can, what is the cause of this great arising of the sands and shelves hereabout, that stop up Sandwich haven ? Forsooth, Sir (quoth he) I am an old man, for I am well-nigh an hundred, and I think that Tenterden steeple is the cause of the Goodwin Sands. For I am an old man, Sir, and I may remember the building of Tenterden steeple, and before that steeple was in building, there was no manner of flats or sands." After relating this anecdote, Latimer slyly added : " Even so, to my purpose, is preaching of God's word the cause of rebellion, as Tenterden steeple was the cause Sandwich haven is decayed." [4]

There was no persecution : there was something else to be done. Wolsey, feeling certain that Charles had obstructed his accession to the popedom, thought only in what manner he might take his revenge. But during this time Tyndale also was pursuing

---

[1] By such communications as he set forth with France apart. State Papers, i. p. 156.
[2] Milady Margaret was a ribaud. Cotton MSS. Vesp. C. 3. p. 55.
[3] Sincera fidelis, firma et indissolubilis pax. Rymer, Fœdera, p. 32, 33.

[1] Hall's Chronicle, p. 696. If men should give their goods by a commission, then were it worse than the taxes of France ; and so England would be bond and not free.
[2] Ibid.
[3] " God sends no rain....lead us against the Christians." A cry ascribed by Augustine to the pagans of the first ages.
[4] Latimer's Sermons, vol. i. p. 251.

his aim; and the year 1525, memorable for the battle of Pavia, was destined to be no less so in the British isles, by a still more important victory.

CHAPTER XI.

Tyndale at Hamburg—First two Gospels—Embarrassment—Tyndale at Wittemberg—At Cologne—The New Testament at Press—Sudden Interruption—Cochlœus at Cologne—Rupert's Manuscripts—Discovery of Cochlœus—His inquiries—His Alarm—Rincke and the Senate's Prohibition—Consternation and Decision of Tyndale—Cochlœus writes to England—Tyndale ascends the Rhine—Prints two Editions at Worms—Tyndale's Prayer.

THE ship which carried Tyndale and his MSS. cast anchor at Hamburg, where, since the year 1521, the gospel had counted numerous friends. Encouraged by the presence of his brethren, the Oxford fellow had taken a quiet lodging in one of the narrow winding streets of that old city, and had immediately resumed his task. A secretary, whom he terms his "faithful companion,"[1] aided him in collating texts; but it was not long before this brother, whose name is unknown to us, thinking himself called to preach Christ in places where He had as yet never been proclaimed, left Tyndale. A former friar-observant of the Franciscan order at Greenwich, having abandoned the cloister, and being at this time without resources, offered his services to the Hellenist. William Roye was one of those men (and they are always pretty numerous) whom impatience of the yoke alienates from Rome without their being attracted by the Spirit of God to Christ. Acute, insinuating, crafty, and yet of pleasing manners, he charmed all those who had mere casual relations with him. Tyndale banished to the distant shores of the Elbe, surrounded by strange customs, and hearing only a foreign tongue, often thought of England, and was impatient that his country should enjoy the result of his labours: he accepted Roye's aid. The Gospels of Matthew and Mark, translated and printed at Hamburg, became, it would seem, the first fruits to England of his great task.

But Tyndale was soon overwhelmed by annoyances. Roye, who was pretty manageable while he had no money, had become intractable now that his purse was less empty.[2] What was to be done? The reformer having spent the ten pounds he had brought from England, could not satisfy the demands of his assistant, pay his own debts, and remove to another city. He became still more sparing and economical. The Wartburg, in which Luther had translated the New Testament, was a palace in comparison with the lodging in which the reformer of wealthy England endured hunger and cold, while toiling day and night to give the gospel to the English Christians.

About the end of 1524, Tyndale sent the two Gospels to Monmouth; and a merchant named John Collenbeke, having brought him the ten pounds he had left in the hands of his old patron, he prepared to depart immediately.

Where should he go? Not to England; he must complete his task before all things. Could he be in Luther's neighbourhood and not desire to see him? He needed not the Saxon reformer either to find the truth, which he had already known at Oxford, or to undertake the translation of the Scriptures, which he had already begun in the vale of the Severn. But did not all evangelical foreigners flock to Wittemberg? To remove all doubt as to the interview of the reformers, it would be desirable perhaps to find some trace at Wittemberg[1] either in the university registers or in the writings of the Saxon reformers. Yet several contemporaneous testimonies seem to give a sufficient degree of probability to this conference. Foxe tells us: "He had an interview with Luther and other learned men of that country."[2] This must have been in the spring of 1525.

Tyndale, desirous of drawing nearer to his native country, turned his eyes towards the Rhine. There were at Cologne some celebrated printers well known in England, and among others Quentel and the Byrckmans. Francis Byrckman had warehouses in St Paul's churchyard in London,—a circumstance that might facilitate the introduction and sale of the Testament printed on the banks of the Rhine. This providential circumstance decided Tyndale in favour of Cologne, and thither he repaired with Roye and his MSS. Arrived in the gloomy streets of the city of Agrippina, he contemplated its innumerable churches, and above all its ancient cathedral re-echoing to the voices of its canons, and was oppressed with sorrow as he beheld the priests and monks and mendicants and pilgrims who, from all parts of Europe, poured in to adore the pretended relics of the *three wise men* and of the *eleven thousand virgins*. And then Tyndale asked himself whether it was really in this superstitious city that the New Testa-

---

[1] Tyndale's Doctr. Treatises, p. 37.
[2] Anderson's Annals of the Bible, i. 49.

[1] I requested a German divine to investigate this matter, but his researches were unsuccessful.
[2] Mr Anderson, in his excellent work (Annals of the English Bible, vol. i. p. 47) disputes the interview between these two reformers, but his arguments do not convince me. We can understand how Luther, at that time busily engaged in his dispute with Carlstadt, does not mention Tyndale's visit in his letters. But, besides Foxe, there are other contemporaneous authorities in favour of this fact. Cochlœus, a German well informed on all the movements of the reformers, and whom we shall presently see on Tyndale's traces, says of him and Roye : " Duo Angli apostatæ, *qui aliquamdiu fuerant Vuitenbergæ*" (p. 123). And Sir Thomas More, having said that Tyndale had gone to see Luther, Tyndale was content to reply : " When Mr More saith Tyndale was confederate with Luther, that is not truth." Answer to Sir Thos. More's Dialogue, p. 147 (Park. Soc.) He denied the *confederation*, but not the *visit*. If Tyndale had not *seen* Luther, he would have been more explicit, and would probably have said that he had never even met him.

ment was to be printed in English. This was not all. The reform movement then at work in Germany had broken out at Cologne during the feast of Whitsuntide, and the archbishop had just forbidden all evangelical worship. Yet Tyndale persevered, and submitting to the most minute precautions, not to compromise his work, he took an obscure lodging where he kept himself closely hidden.

Soon however, trusting in God, he called on the printer, presented his manuscripts to him, ordered six thousand copies, and then, upon reflection, sank down to three thousand for fear of a seizure.[1] The printing went on; one sheet followed another; gradually the gospel unfolded its mysteries in the English tongue, and Tyndale could not contain himself for very joy.[2] He saw in his mind's eye the triumphs of the Scriptures over all the kingdom, and exclaimed with transport: "Whether the king wills it or not, erelong all the people of England, enlightened by the New Testament, will obey the gospel."[3]

But on a sudden that sun whose earliest beams he had hailed with songs of joy, was hidden by thick clouds. One day, just as the tenth sheet had been thrown off, the printer hastened to Tyndale, and informed him that the senate of Cologne forbade him to continue the work. Everything was discovered then. No doubt Henry VIII., who has burnt Luther's books, wishes to burn the New Testament also, to destroy Tyndale's manuscripts, and deliver him up to death. Who had betrayed him? He was lost in unavailing conjectures, and one thing only appeared certain; alas! his vessel, which was moving onwards in full sail, had struck upon a reef! The following is the explanation of this unexpected incident.

A man whom we have often met with in the course of this history,[4] one of the most violent enemies of the Reformation — we mean Cochlœus—had arrived in Cologne. The wave of popular agitation which had stirred this city during the Whitsuntide holidays, had previously swept over Frankfort during the festival of Easter; and the dean of Notre-Dame, taking advantage of a moment when the gates of the city were open, had escaped a few minutes before the burghers entered his house to arrest him. On arriving at Cologne, where he hoped to live unknown under the shadow of the powerful elector, he had gone to lodge with George Lauer, a canon in the church of the Apostles.

By a singular destiny the two most opposite men, Tyndale and Cochlœus, were in hiding in the same city; they could not long remain there without coming into collision. On the right bank of the Rhine, and oppo-

site Cologne, stood the monastery of Deutz, one of whose abbots, Rupert, who lived in the twelfth century, had said: "To be ignorant of Scripture is to be ignorant of Jesus Christ. This is *the scripture of nations!*[1] This book of God, which is not pompous in words and poor in meaning like Plato, ought to be set before every people, and to proclaim aloud to the whole world the salvation of all." One day, when Cochlœus and his host were talking of Rupert, the canon informed the dean that the *heretic* Osiander of Nuremberg was in treaty with the abbot of Deutz about publishing the writings of this ancient doctor. Cochlœus guessed that Osiander was desirous of bringing forward the contemporary of Saint Bernard as a witness in defence of the Reformation. Hastening to the monastery he alarmed the abbot: "Intrust to me the manuscripts of your celebrated predecessor," he said; "I will undertake to print them and prove that he was one of us." The monks placed them in his hands, stipulating for an early publication, from which they expected no little renown.[2] Cochlœus immediately went to Peter Quentel and Arnold Byrckman to make the necessary arrangements. They were Tyndale's printers.

There Cochlœus made a more important discovery than that of Rupert's manuscripts. Byrckman and Quentel having invited him one day to meet several of their colleagues at dinner, a printer, somewhat elevated by wine, declared in his cups, (to borrow the words of Cochlœus):[3] "Whether the king and the cardinal of York wish it or not, all England will soon be Lutheran."[4] Cochlœus listened and grew alarmed; he made inquiry, and was informed that *two Englishmen*, learned men and skilled in the languages, were concealed at Cologne.[5] But all his efforts to discover more proved unavailing.

There was no more repose for the dean of Frankfort; his imagination fermented, his mind became alarmed. "What," said he, "shall England, that faithful servant of the popedom, be perverted like Germany? Shall the English, the most religious people of Christendom,[6] and whose king once ennobled himself by writing against Luther,—shall they be invaded by heresy?......Shall the mighty cardinal-legate of York be compelled to flee from his palace, as I was from Frankfort?" Cochlœus continued his search; he paid frequent visits to the printers, spoke to them in a friendly tone, flattered them, invited them to visit him at the canon's; but as yet he dared not hazard the important

---

[1] Sex millia sub prælum dari. Cochlæus. p. 123.
[2] Tanta ex ea spe lætitia Lutheranos invasit. Ibid. p. 124.
[3] Cunctos Anglix populos, volente nolente rege. Ibid 123.
[4] Book ix. chapter xii. etc.

[1] Scripturæ populorum. Opp. i. p. 641.
[2] Cum monachi quieturi non erant, nisi ederentur opera illa. Cochl. p. 124.
[3] Audivit eos aliquando inter pocula fiducialiter jactitare. Ibid. p. 125.
[4] Velint nolint rex et cardinalis Angliæ, totam Angliam brevi fore Lutheranam. Ibid.
[5] Duos ibi latitare Anglos eruditos, linguarumque peritos. Ibid.
[6] In gente illa religiosissima vereque Christiana. Ibid. p. 131.

question; it was sufficient for the moment to have won the good graces of the depositaries of the secret. He soon took a new step; he was careful not to question them before one another; but he procured a private interview with one of them,[1] and supplied him plentifully with Rhine wine:—he himself is our informant.[2] Artful questions embarrassed the unwary printer, and at last the secret was disclosed. "The New Testament," Cochlœus learnt, "is translated into English; three thousand copies are in the press; fourscore pages in quarto are ready; the expense is fully supplied by English merchants, who are secretly to convey the work when printed, and to disperse it widely through all England, before the king or the cardinal can discover or prohibit it.[3] ...... Thus will Britain be converted to the opinions of Luther."[4]

The surprise of Cochlœus equalled his alarm;[5] he dissembled; he wished to learn, however, where the two Englishmen lay concealed; but all his exertions proved ineffectual, and he returned to his lodgings filled with emotion. The danger was very great. A stranger and an exile, what can he do to oppose this impious undertaking? Where shall he find a friend to England, prepared to show his zeal in warding off the threatened blow? ......He was bewildered.

A flash of light suddenly dispelled the darkness. A person of some consequence at Cologne, Herman Rincke, a patrician and imperial councillor, had been sent on important business by the Emperor Maximilian to Henry VII., and from that time he had always shown a great attachment to England. Cochlœus determined to reveal the fatal secret to him; but, being still alarmed by the scenes at Frankfort, he was afraid to conspire openly against the Reformation. He had left an aged mother and a little niece at home, and was unwilling to do anything which might compromise them. He therefore crept stealthily towards Rincke's house (as he tells us himself),[6] slipped in secretly, and unfolded the whole matter to him. Rincke could not believe that the New Testament in English was printing at Cologne; however, he sent a confidential person to make inquiries, who reported to him that Cochlœus's information was correct, and that he had found in the printing office a large supply of paper intended for the edition.[7] The patrician immediately proceeded to the senate, and spoke of Wolsey, of Henry VIII., and of the preservation of the Romish church in England; and that body which, under the influence of the arch-

bishop, had long since forgotten the rights of liberty, forbade the printer to continue the work. Thus then there were to be no New Testaments for England! A practised hand had warded off the blow aimed at Roman-catholicism; Tyndale would perhaps be thrown into prison, and Cochlœus enjoy a complete triumph.

Tyndale was at first confounded. Were so many years of toil lost, then, for ever? His trial seemed beyond his strength.[1] "They are ravening wolves," he exclaimed, "they preach to others, Steal not, and yet they have robbed the soul of man of the bread of life, and fed her with the shales [shells?] and cods of the hope in their merits and confidence in their good works."[2] Yet Tyndale did not long remain cast down; for his faith was of that kind which would remove mountains. Is it not the word of God that is imperilled? If he does not abandon himself, God will not abandon him. He must anticipate the senate of Cologne. Daring and prompt in all his movements, Tyndale bade Roye follow him, hastened to the printing office, collected the sheets, jumped into a boat, and rapidly ascended the river, carrying with him the hope of England.[3]

When Cochlœus and Rincke, accompanied by the officers of the senate, reached the printing office, they were surprised beyond measure. The apostate had secured the abominable papers! ......Their enemy had escaped like a bird from the net of the fowler. Where was he to be found now? He would no doubt go and place himself under the protection of some *Lutheran* prince, whither Cochlœus would take good care not to pursue him; but there was one resource left. These English books can do no harm in Germany; they must be prevented reaching London. He wrote to Henry VIII., to Wolsey, and to the bishop of Rochester. "Two Englishmen," said he to the king, "like the two eunuchs who desired to lay hands on Ahasuerus, are plotting wickedly against the peace of your kingdom: but I, like the faithful Mordecai,[4] will lay open their designs to you. They wish to send the New Testament in English to your people. Give orders at every seaport to prevent the introduction of this most baneful merchandise."[5] Such was the name given by this zealous follower of the pope to the word of God. An unexpected ally soon restored peace to the soul of Cochlœus. The celebrated Dr Eck, a champion of popery far more formidable than he was, had arrived at Cologne on his way to Lon-

---

[1] Unus eorum in secretiori colloquio revelavit illi arcanum. Cochlæus, p. 131.
[2] Rem omnem ut acceperat *vini beneficio*. Ibid.
[3] Opus excussum clam invecturi per totam Angliam latenter dispergere vellent. Ibid.
[4] Ad Lutheri partes trahenda est Anglia. Ibid.
[5] Metu et admiratione affectus. Ibid.
[6] Abiit igitur clam ad H. Rincke. Ibid.
[7] Ingentem papyri copiam ibi existere. Ibid.

Necessity and combrance (God is record) *above strength.* Tynd. Doctr. Tr. p. 390.
[2] Tyndale, Expositions, p. 123, (Parker Society).
[3] Arreptis secum quaternionibus impressis aufugerunt navigio per Rhenum ascendentes. Cochl. p. 126.
[4] He was indebted to me no less than Ahasuerus was indebted to Mordecai. Annals of the Bible. i. p. 61.
[5] Ut quam diligentissime præcaverint in omnibus Angliæ portubus, ne merx illa perniciosissima inveheretur. Cochl. p. 126.

don, and he undertook to arouse the anger of the bishops and of the king.[1] The eyes of the greatest opponents of the Reformation seemed now to be fixed on England. Eck, who boasted of having gained the most signal triumphs over Luther, would easily get the better of the humble tutor and his New Testament.

During this time, Tyndale, guarding his precious bales, ascended the rapid river as quickly as he could. He passed before the antique cities and the smiling villages scattered along the banks of the Rhine amidst scenes of picturesque beauty. The mountains, glens, and rocks, the dark forests, the ruined fortresses, the gothic churches, the boats that passed and repassed each other, the birds of prey that soared over his head, as if they bore a mission from Cochlœus—nothing could turn his eyes from the treasure he was carrying with him. At last, after a voyage of five or six days, he reached Worms, where Luther, four years before, had exclaimed: " Here I stand, I can do no other; may God help me!"[2] These words of the German reformer, so well known to Tyndale, were the star that had guided him to Worms. He knew that the gospel was preached in that ancient city. " The citizens are subject to fits of Lutheranism," said Cochlœus.[3] Tyndale arrived there, not as Luther did, surrounded by an immense crowd, but unknown, and imagining himself pursued by the myrmidons of Charles and of Henry. As he landed from the boat he cast an uneasy glance around him, and laid down his precious burden on the bank of the river.

He had had time to reflect on the dangers which threatened his work. As his enemies would have marked the edition, some few sheets of it having fallen into their hands, he took steps to mislead the inquisitors, and began a new edition, striking out the prologue and the notes, and substituting the more portable *octavo* form for the original *quarto.* Peter Schæffer, the grandson of Fust, one of the inventors of printing, lent his presses for this important work. The two editions were quietly completed about the end of the year 1525.[4]

Thus were the wicked deceived : they would have deprived the English people of the oracles of God, and *two* editions were now ready to enter England. " Give diligence," said Tyndale to his fellow-countrymen, as he sent from Worms the Testament he had just translated, " unto the words of eternal life, by the which, if we repent and believe them, we are born anew, created

afresh, and enjoy the fruits of the blood of Christ."[1] In the beginning of 1526, these books crossed the sea by way of Antwerp or Rotterdam. Tyndale was happy ; but he knew that the unction of the Holy Ghost alone could enable the people of England to understand these sacred pages ; and accordingly he followed them night and day with his prayers. " The scribes and pharisees," said he, " had thrust up the sword of the word of God in a scabbard or sheath of glosses, and therein had knit it fast, so that it could neither stick nor cut.[2] Now, O God, draw this sharp sword from the scabbard. Strike, wound, cut asunder, the soul and the flesh, so that man being divided in two, and set at variance with himself, may be in peace with thee to all eternity ! "

CHAPTER XII.

Worms and Cambridge—St Paul resuscitated—Latimer's Preaching—Never Man spake like this Man—Joy and Vexation at Cambridge—Sermon by Prior Buckingham—Irony—Latimer's Reply to Buckingham—The Students threatened—Latimer preaches before the Bishop—He is forbidden to preach—The most zealous of Bishops—Barnes the Restorer of Letters—Bilney undertakes to convert him—Barnes offers his Pulpit to Latimer—Fryth's Thirst for God—Christmas Eve, 1525—Storm against Barnes—Ferment in the Colleges—Germany at Cambridge—Meetings at Oxford—General Expectation.

WHILE these works were accomplishing at Cologne and Worms, others were going on at Cambridge and Oxford. On the banks of the Rhine they were preparing the seed ; in England they were drawing the furrows to receive it. The gospel produced a great agitation at Cambridge. Bilney, whom we may call the father of the English Reformation, since, being the first converted by the New Testament, he had brought to the knowledge of God the energetic Latimer, and so many other witnesses of the truth,—Bilney did not at that time put himself forward, like many of those who had listened to him : his vocation was prayer. Timid before men, he was full of boldness before God, and day and night called upon him for souls. But while he was kneeling in his closet, others were at work in the world. Among these Stafford was particularly remarkable. " Paul is risen from the dead," said many as they heard him. And in fact Stafford explained with so much life the true meaning of the words of the apostle and of the four evangelists,[3] that these holy men, whose faces had been so long hidden under the dense traditions of the schools,[4] reappeared before the youth of the university such as the apostolic times had beheld them. But it was not only their *persons* (for that

---

[1] Ad quem Doctor Eckius venit, dum in Angliam tenderet. Cochlæus, p. 109.
[2] See above, book vii. chapter viii.
[3] Ascendentes Wormatiam ubi plebes pleno furore lutherisabat. Cochlœus, p. 126.
[4] A copy of the *octavo* edition exists in the Museum of the Baptist College at Bristol. If it is compared with the *quarto* edition, a sensible progress will be found in the orthography. Thus we read in the latter : *prophettes, synners, mooste, sekynge ;* in the octavo we find, *prophets, sinners, most, seking.* Annals of the Bible, i. p. 70.

[1] Epistle. in init.
[2] Tyndale's Works, ii. p. 378; or expositions (Matthew), p. 131. (Park. Soc.)
[3] He set forth in his lectures the native sense. Thomas Becon, ii. p. 426.
[4] Obscured through the darkness and mists of the papists. Ibid.

would have been a trifling matter), it was their *doctrine* which Stafford laid before his hearers. While the schoolmen of Cambridge were declaring to their pupils a reconciliation which was not yet worked out, and telling them that pardon must be purchased by the works prescribed by the church, Stafford taught that redemption was *accomplished*, that the satisfaction offered by Jesus Christ was *perfect;* and he added, that popery having revived the *kingdom of the law*, God, by the Reformation, was now reviving the *kingdom of grace*. The Cambridge students, charmed by their master's teaching, greeted him with applause, and, indulging a little too far in their enthusiasm, said to one another as they left the lecture-room: "Which is the most indebted to the other? Stafford to Paul, who left him the holy epistles; or Paul to Stafford, who has resuscitated that apostle and his holy doctrines, which the middle ages had obscured?"

Above Bilney and Stafford rose Latimer, who, by the power of the Holy Ghost, transfused into other hearts the learned lessons of his master.[1] Being informed of the work that Tyndale was preparing, he maintained from the Cambridge pulpits that the Bible ought to be read in the vulgar tongue.[2] "The author of Holy Scripture," said he, "is the Mighty One, the Everlasting......*God himself!*.........and this Scripture partakes of the might and eternity of its author. There is neither king nor emperor that is not bound to obey it. Let us beware of those bypaths of human tradition, filled of stones, brambles, and uprooted trees. Let us follow the straight road of the word. It does not concern us what the Fathers have done, but what they should have done."[3]

A numerous congregation crowded to Latimer's preaching, and his hearers hung listening to his lips. One in particular attracted attention. He was a Norfolk youth, sixteen years of age, whose features were lighted up with understanding and piety. This poor scholar had received with eagerness the truth announced by the former cross-bearer. He did not miss one of his sermons; with a sheet of paper on his knees, and a pencil in his hand, he took down part of the discourse, trusting the remainder to his memory.[4] This was Thomas Becon, afterwards chaplain to Cranmer, archbishop of Canterbury. "If I possess the knowledge of God," said he, "I owe it (under God) to Latimer."

Latimer had hearers of many sorts. By the side of those who gave way to their enthusiasm stood men "swelling, blown full, and puffed up like unto Esop's frog, with

envy and malice against him," said Becon;[1] these were the partisans of traditional catholicism, whom curiosity had attracted, or whom their evangelical friends had dragged to the church. But as Latimer spoke, a marvellous transformation was worked in them; by degrees their angry features relaxed, their fierce looks grew softer; and if these friends of the priests were asked, after their return home, what they thought of the heretic preacher, they replied in the exaggeration of their surprise and rapture: "*Nunquam sic locutus est homo, sicut hic homo!*" (John vii. 46.)

When he descended from the pulpit, Latimer hastened to practise what he had taught. He visited the narrow chambers of the poor scholars, and the dark rooms of the working classes: "he watered with good deeds whatsoever he had before planted with godly words,"[2] said the student who collected his discourses. The disciples conversed together with joy and simplicity of heart; everywhere the breath of a new life was felt; as yet no external reforms had been effected, and yet the spiritual church of the gospel and of the Reformation was already there. And thus the recollection of these happy times was long commemorated in the adage:

> When Master Stafford read,
> And Master Latimer preached,
> Then was Cambridge blessed.[3]

The priests could not remain inactive: they heard speak of grace and liberty, and would have nothing to do with either. If *grace* is tolerated, will it not take from the hands of the clergy the manipulation of salvation, indulgences, penance, and all the rubrics of the canon law? If *liberty* is conceded, will not the hierarchy, with all its degrees, pomps, violence, and scaffolds, be shaken? Rome desires no other liberty than that of free-will, which, exalting the natural strength of fallen man, dries up as regards mankind the springs of divine life, withers Christianity, and changes that heavenly religion into a human moralism and legal observances.

The friends of popery, therefore, collected their forces to oppose the new religion. "Satan, who never sleeps," says the simple chronicler, "called up his familiar spirits, and sent them forth against the reformers." Meetings were held in the convents, but particularly in that belonging to the Greyfriars. They mustered all their forces. *An eye for an eye, and a tooth for a tooth*, said they. Latimer extols in his sermons the *blessings* of Scripture; we must deliver a sermon also to shew its *dangers*. But where was the orator to be found who could cope with him? This was a very embarrassing question to the clerical party. Among the Greyfriars there was a haughty monk, adroit and skilful in little matters, and full at once of ignorance and

---

[1] A private instructor to the rest of his brethren within the university. Foxe, Acts, vii. p. 438.
[2] He proved in his sermons that the Holy Scriptures ought to be read in the English tongue of all Christian people. Becon, vol. ii. p. 424. (Park. Soc.)
[3] We find his opinions upon that subject in a later sermon. Latimer's Sermons, p. 96, 97, (Park. Soc.)
[4] A poor scholar of Cambridge....but a child of sixteen years. Becon's Works, ii. p. 424.

[1] Becon's Works, ii. p. 425. [2] Ibid. [3] Ibid.

pride: it was the prior Buckingham. No one had shown more hatred against the evangelical Christians, and no one was in truth a greater stranger to the gospel. This was the man commissioned to set forth the dangers of the word of God. He was by no means familiar with the New Testament; he opened it however, picked out a few passages here and there which seemed to favour his thesis; and then, arrayed in his costliest robes, with head erect and solemn step, already sure of victory, he went into the pulpit, combated the heretic, and with pompous voice stormed against the reading of the Bible;[1] it was in his eyes the fountain of all heresies and misfortunes. "If that heresy should prevail," he exclaimed, "there will be an end of everything useful among us. The ploughman, reading in the gospel that *no man having put his hand to the plough should look back*, would soon lay aside his labour......The baker, reading that *a little leaven leaveneth the whole lump*, will in future make us nothing but very insipid bread ; and the simple man finding himself commanded *to pluck out the right eye and cast it from thee*, England, after a few years, will be a frightful spectacle ; it will be little better than a nation of blind and one-eyed men, sadly begging their bread from door to door."[2]

This discourse moved that part of the audience for which it was intended. "The heretic is silenced," said the monks and clerks ; but sensible people smiled, and Latimer was delighted that they had given him such an adversary. Being of a lively disposition and inclined to irony, he resolved to lash the platitudes of the pompous friar. There are some absurdities, he thought, which can only be refuted by showing how foolish they are. Does not even the grave Tertullian speak of things which are only to be laughed at, for fear of giving them importance by a serious refutation?[3] "Next Sunday I will reply to him," said Latimer.

The church was crowded when Buckingham, with the hood of St Francis on his shoulders and with a vain-glorious air, took his place solemnly in front of the preacher. Latimer began by recapitulating the least weak of his adversary's arguments; then taking them up one by one, he turned them over and over, and pointed out all their absurdity with so much wit, that the poor prior was buried in his own nonsense. Then turning towards the listening crowd, he exclaimed with warmth: "This is how your skilful guides abuse your understanding. They look upon you as children that must be for ever kept in leading-strings. Now, the hour of your majority has arrived; boldly examine the Scriptures, and you will easily discover

the absurdity of the teaching of your doctors." And then desirous, as Solomon has it, of *answering a fool according to his folly*, he added : "As for the comparisons drawn from the *plough*, the *leaven*, and the *eye*, of which the reverend prior has made so singular a use, is it necessary to justify these passages of Scripture? Must I tell you what *plough*, what *leaven*, what *eye* is here meant. Is not our Lord's teaching distinguished by those expressions which, under a popular form, conceal a spiritual and profound meaning? Do not we know that in all languages and in all speeches, it is not on the *image* that we must fix our eyes, but on the *thing* which the image represents ?......For instance," he continued, and as he said these words he cast a piercing glance on the prior, "if we see a fox painted preaching in a friar's hood, nobody imagines that a fox is meant, but that craft and hypocrisy are described, which are so often found disguised in that garb."[1] At these words the poor prior, on whom the eyes of all the congregation were turned, rose and left the church hastily, and ran off to his convent to hide his rage and confusion among his brethren. The monks and their creatures uttered loud cries against Latimer. It was unpardonable (they said) to have been thus wanting in respect to the coul of St Francis. But his friends replied : "Do we not whip children ? and he who treats Scripture worse than a child, does he not deserve to be well flogged ? "

The Romish party did not consider themselves beaten. The heads of colleges and the priests held frequent conferences. The professors were desired to watch carefully over their pupils, and to lead them back to the teaching of the church by flattery and by threats. "We are putting our lance in rest," they told the students; "if you become evangelicals, your advancement is at an end." But these open-hearted generous youths loved rather to be poor with Christ than rich with the priests. Stafford continued to teach, Latimer to preach, and Bilney to visit the poor: the doctrine of Christ ceased not to be spread abroad, and souls to be converted.

One weapon only was left to the schoolmen ; this was persecution, the favourite arm of Rome. "Our enterprise has not succeeded," said they ; "Buckingham is a fool. The best way of answering these *gospellers* is to prevent their speaking." Dr West, bishop of Ely, was ordinary of Cambridge; they called for his intervention, and he ordered one of the doctors to inform him the next time Latimer was to preach; "but," added he, "do not say a word to any one. I wish to come without being expected."

One day as Latimer was preaching in Latin *ad clerum*, the bishop suddenly entered the university church, attended by a number of priests. Latimer stopped, waiting respectfully

---

[1] With great pomp and prolixity. Gilpin's Life of Latimer, p. 8.
[2] The nation full of blind beggars. Ibid.
[3] Si et ridebitur alicubi materiis ipsis satisfiet. Multa sunt sic digna revinci, ne gravitate adorentur. Contra Valentin. c. vi. See also Pascal's Provincials, Letter xi.

[1] Gilpin's Life of Latimer, p. 10.

until West and his train had taken their places. "A new audience," thought he; "and besides, an audience worthy of greater honour calls for a new theme. Leaving, therefore, the subject I had proposed, I will take up one that relates to the episcopal charge, and will preach on these words: *Christus existens Pontifex futurorum bonorum.*" (Hebrews ix. 11.) Then describing Jesus Christ, Latimer represented him as the "true and perfect pattern unto all other bishops."[1] There was not a single virtue pointed out in the divine bishop that did not correspond with some defect in the Romish bishops. Latimer's caustic wit had a free course at their expense; but there was so much gravity in his sallies, and so lively a Christianity in his descriptions, that every one must have felt them to be the cries of a Christian conscience rather than the sarcasms of an ill-natured disposition. Never had bishop been taught by one of his priests like this man. "Alas!" said many, "our bishops are not of that breed: they are descended from Annas and Caiaphas." West was not more at his ease than Buckingham had been formerly. He stifled his anger, however; and after the sermon, said to Latimer with a gracious accent: "You have excellent talents, and if you would do one thing I should be ready to kiss your feet."[2]......What humility in a bishop!...... "Preach in this same church," continued West, "a sermon......against Martin Luther. That is the best way of checking heresy." Latimer understood the prelate's meaning, and replied calmly: "If Luther preaches the word of God, I cannot oppose him. But if he teaches the contrary, I am ready to attack him."—"Well, well, Master Latimer," exclaimed the bishop, "I perceive that you smell somewhat of the pan.[3]......One day or another you will repent of that merchandise."

West having left Cambridge in great irritation against that rebellious clerk, hastened to convoke his chapter, and forbade Latimer to preach either in the university or in the diocese. "All that will live godly shall suffer persecution," Saint Paul had said; Latimer was now experiencing the truth of the saying. It was not enough that the name of heretic had been given him by the priests and their friends, and that the passers-by insulted him in the streets;......the work of God was violently checked. "Behold then," he exclaimed with a bitter sigh, "the use of the episcopal office......to hinder the preaching of Jesus Christ!" Some few years later he sketched, with his usual caustic irony, the portrait of a certain bishop, of whom Luther also used frequently to speak: "Do you know," said Latimer, "who is the most diligentest bishop and prelate in all England? ......I see you listening and hearkening that

I should name him......I will tell you......It is the devil. He is never out of his diocese; ye shall never find him out of the way; call for him when you will, he's ever at home. He is ever at his plough. Ye shall never find him idle, I warrant you. Where the devil is resident—there away with books and up with candles; away with bibles and up with beads; away with the light of the gospel and up with the light of candles, yea at noondays; down with Christ's cross, up with purgatory pickpurse; away with clothing the naked, the poor, and impotent, up with decking of images and gay garnishing of stocks and stones; down with God's traditions and his most holy word......Oh! that our prelates would be as diligent to sow the corn of good doctrine as Satan is to sow cockle and darnel!"[1] Truly may it be said, "There was never such a preacher in England as he is."[2]

The reformer was not satisfied with merely speaking: he acted. "Neither the menacing words of his adversaries nor their cruel imprisonments," says one of his contemporaries,[3] "could hinder him from proclaiming God's truth." Forbidden to preach in the churches, he went about from house to house. He longed for a pulpit however, and this he obtained. A haughty prelate had in vain interdicted his preaching; Jesus Christ, who is above all bishops, is able, when one door is shut, to open another. Instead of one great preacher there were soon two at Cambridge.

An Augustine monk named Robert Barnes, a native of the county of Norfolk, and a great scholar, had gone to Louvain to prosecute his studies. Here he received the degree of doctor of divinity, and having returned to Cambridge, was nominated prior of his monastery in 1523. It was his fortune to reconcile learning and the gospel in the university; but by leaning too much to learning he diminished the force of the word of God. A great crowd collected every day in the Augustine convent to hear his lectures upon Terence, and in particular upon Cicero. Many of those who were offended by the simple Christianity of Bilney and Latimer, were attracted by this reformer of another kind. Coleman, Coverdale, Field, Cambridge, Barley, and many other young men of the university, gathered round Barnes, and proclaimed him "the restorer of letters."[4]

But the classics were only a preparatory teaching. The masterpieces of antiquity having aided Barnes to clear the soil, he opened before his class the epistles of St Paul. He did not understand their divine depth, like Stafford; he was not, like him, anointed with the Holy Ghost; he differed

[1] Strype's Eccles. Mem. III. p. 369.
[2] I will kneel down and kiss your foot. Ibid.
[3] Ibid. 370.

[1] Latimer's Sermons (Park. Soc.) vol. i. p. 70. Sermon of the Plough.   [2] Ibid. p. 72.
[3] He adds: Whatsoever he had once preached, he valiantly defended the same. Becon, vol. ii. p. 424.
[4] The great restorer of good learning. Strype, i. p. 568; Foxe, Acts, v. p. 415.

from him on several of the apostle's doctrines, on justification by faith, and on the new creature; but Barnes was an enlightened and liberal man, not without some degree of piety, and desirous, like Stafford, of substituting the teaching of Scripture for the barren disputations of the school. But they soon came into collision, and Cambridge long remembered that celebrated discussion in which Barnes and Stafford contended with so much renown, employing no other weapons than the word of God, to the great astonishment of the blind doctors, and the great joy of the clear-sighted, says the chronicler.[1]

Barnes was not as yet thoroughly enlightened, and the friends of the gospel were astonished that a man, a stranger to the truth, should deal such heavy blows against error. Bilney, whom we continually meet with when any secret work, a work of irresistible charity, is in hand,—Bilney, who had converted Latimer, undertook to convert Barnes; and Stafford, Arthur, Thistel of Pembroke, and Fooke of Benet's, earnestly prayed God to grant his assistance. The experiment was difficult: Barnes had reached that *juste milieu*, that "golden mean" of the humanists, that intoxication of learning and glory, which render conversion more difficult. Besides, could a man like Bilney really dare to instruct the restorer of antiquity? But the humble bachelor of arts, so simple in appearance, knew, like David of old, a secret power by which the Goliath of the university might be vanquished. He passed days and nights in prayer; and then urged Barnes openly to manifest his convictions without fearing the reproaches of the world. After many conversations and prayers, Barnes was converted to the gospel of Jesus Christ.[2] Still, the prior retained something undecided in his character, and only half relinquished that middle state with which he had begun. For instance, he appears to have always believed in the efficacy of sacerdotal consecration to transform the bread and wine into the body and blood of Christ. His eye was not single, and his mind was often agitated and driven to and fro by contrary thoughts: " Alas!" said this divided character one day, " I confess that my cogitations are innumerable."[3]

Barnes, having come to a knowledge of the truth, immediately displayed a zeal that was somewhat imprudent. Men of the least decided character, and even those who are destined to make a signal fall, are often those who begin their course with the greatest ardour. Barnes seemed prepared at this time to withstand all England. Being now united to Latimer by a tender Christian affection, he was indignant that the powerful voice of his friend should be lost to the church. "The

bishop has forbidden you to preach," he said to him, "but my monastery is not under episcopal jurisdiction. You can preach there." Latimer went into the pulpit at the Augustine's, and the church could not contain the crowd that flocked to it. At Cambridge, as at Wittemberg, the chapel of the Augustine monks was used for the first struggles of the gospel. It was here that Latimer delivered some of his best sermons.

A very different man from Latimer, and particularly from Barnes, was daily growing in influence among the English reformers: this was Fryth. No one was more humble than he, and on that very account no one was stronger. He was less brilliant than Barnes, but more solid. He might have penetrated into the highest departments of science, but he was drawn away by the deep mysteries of God's word; the call of conscience prevailed over that of the understanding.[1] He did not devote the energy of his soul to difficult questions; he thirsted for God, for his truth, and for his love. Instead of propagating his particular opinions and forming divisions, he clung only to the faith which saves, and advanced the dominion of true unity. This is the mark of the great servants of God. Humble before the Lord, mild before men, and even in appearance somewhat timid, Fryth in the face of danger displayed an intrepid courage. "My learning is small," he said, "but the little I have I am determined to give to Jesus Christ for the building of his temple."[2]

Latimer's sermons, Barnes's ardour, and Fryth's firmness, excited fresh zeal at Cambridge. They knew what was going on in Germany and Switzerland; shall the English, ever in front, now remain in the rear? Shall not Latimer, Bilney, Stafford, Barnes, and Fryth do what the servants of God are doing in other places?

A secret ferment announced an approaching crisis: every one expected some change for better or for worse. The evangelicals, confident in the truth, and thinking themselves sure of victory, resolved to fall upon the enemy simultaneously on several points. The Sunday before Christmas, in the year 1525, was chosen for this great attack. While Latimer should address the crowds that continued to fill the Augustine chapel, and others were preaching in other places, Barnes was to deliver a sermon in one of the churches in the town. But nothing compromises the gospel so much as a disposition turned towards outward things. God, who grants his blessing only to undivided hearts, permitted this general assault, of which Barnes was to be the hero, to be marked by a defeat. The prior, as he went into the pulpit, thought only of Wolsey. As the representative of the popedom in England, the

[1] Marvellous in the sight of the great blind doctors. Foxe. Acts, v. p. 415.
[2] Bilney converted Dr Barnes to the gospel of Jesus Christ. Ibid. iv. p. 620. [3] Ibid. v. p. 434.

[1] Notwithstanding his other manifold and singular gifts and ornaments of the mind, in him most oregnant. Tyndale and Fryth's Works. iii. p. 73.
[2] That is very small, nevertheless that little. Ibid. p. 83.

cardinal was the great obstacle to the Reformation. Barnes preached from the epistle for the day : *Rejoice in the Lord alway.*[1] But instead of announcing Christ and the joy of the Christian, he imprudently declaimed against the luxury, pride, and diversions of the churchmen, and everybody understood that he aimed at the cardinal. He described those magnificent palaces, that brilliant suite, those scarlet robes, and pearls, and gold, and precious stones, and the prelate's ostentation, so little in keeping (said he) with the stable of Bethlehem. Two fellows of King's College, Robert Ridley and Walter Preston, relations of Tonstall, bishop of London, who were intentionally among the congregation, noted down in their tablets the prior's imprudent expressions.

The sermon was scarcely over when the storm broke out. " These people are not satisfied with propagating monstrous heresies," exclaimed their enemies, " but they must find fault with the powers that be. To-day they attack the cardinal, to-morrow they will attack the king !" Ridley and Preston accused Barnes to the vice-chancellor. All Cambridge was in commotion. What ! Barnes the Augustine prior, the restorer of letters, accused as a Lollard !......The gospel was threatened with a danger more formidable than a prison or a scaffold. The friends of the priests, knowing Barnes's weakness, and even his vanity, hoped to obtain of him a disavowal that would cover the evangelical party with shame. " What ! " said these dangerous counsellors to him, " the noblest career was open to you, and would you close it ?......Do, pray, explain away your sermon." They alarmed, they flattered him ; and the poor prior was near yielding to their solicitations. " Next Sunday you will read this declaration," they said to him. Barnes ran over the paper put into his hands, and saw no great harm in it. However he desired to show it to Bilney and Stafford. " Beware of such weakness," said these faithful men. Barnes then recalled his promise, and for a season the enemies of the gospel were silent.

Its friends worked with increased energy. The fall from which one of their companions had so narrowly escaped inspired them with fresh zeal. The more indecision and weakness Barnes had shown, the more did his brethren flee to God for courage and firmness. It was reported, moreover, that a powerful ally was coming across the sea, and that the Holy Scriptures, translated into the vulgar tongue, were at last to be given to the people. Wherever the word was preached, there the congregation was largest. It was the seed-time of the church ; all were busy in the fields to prepare the soil and trace the furrows. Seven colleges at least were in full ferment : Pembroke, St John's,

Queens', King's, Caius, Benet's and Peterhouse. The gospel was preached at the Augustine's, at Saint Mary's, (the University church,) and in other places, and when the bells rang to prayers, the streets were alive with students issuing from the colleges, and hastening to the sermon.[1]

There was at Cambridge a house called the White Horse, so situated as to permit the most timid members of King's, Queens', and St John's Colleges, to enter at the rear without being perceived. In every age Nicodemus has had his followers. Here those persons used to assemble who desired to read the Bible and the works of the German reformers. The priests, looking upon Wittemberg as the focus of the Reformation, named this house Germany : the people will always have their bywords. At first the frequenters of the White Horse were called sophists ; and now, whenever a group of " fellows " was seen walking in that direction, the cry was, " There are the Germans going to Germany." —" We are not Germans," was the reply, " neither are we Romans." The Greek New Testament had made them Christians. The gospel-meetings had never been more fervent. Some attended them to communicate the new life they possessed ; others to receive what God had given to the more advanced brethren. The Holy Spirit united them all, and thus, by the fellowship of the saints, were real churches created. To these young Christians the word of God was the source of so much light, that they imagined themselves transported to that heavenly city of which the Scriptures speak, *which had no need of the sun, for the glory of God did lighten it.* " So oft as I was in the company of these brethren," said a youthful student of St John's, " methought I was quietly placed in the new glorious Jerusalem."[2]

Similar things were taking place at Oxford. In 1524 and 1525, Wolsey had successively invited thither several Cambridge fellows, and although only seeking the most able, he found that he had taken some of the most pious. Besides John Clark, there were Richard Cox, John Fryer, Godfrey Harman, W. Betts, Henry Sumner, W. Baily, Michael Drumm, Th. Lawny, and, lastly, the excellent John Fryth. These Christians, associating with Clark, with his faithful Dalaber, and with other evangelicals of Oxford, held meetings, like their Cambridge brethren, at which God manifested his presence. The bishops made war upon the gospel ; the king supported them with all his power ; but the word had gained the victory ; there was no longer any doubt. The church was born again in England.

The great movement of the sixteenth century had begun more particularly among the younger doctors and students at Oxford and Cambridge. From them it was necessary that

---

[1] Philippians iv. 4-7.

[1] Flocked together in open street. Strype, Mem. i. p. 568.
[2] Becon, ii. p. 426.

it should be extended to the people, and for that end the New Testament, hitherto read in Latin and in Greek, must be circulated in English. The voices of these youthful evangelists were heard, indeed, in London and in the provinces; but their exhortations would have been insufficient, if the mighty hand which directs all things had not made this Christian activity coincide with that holy work for which it had set Tyndale apart. While all was agitation in England, the waves of ocean were bearing from the continent to the banks of the Thames those Scriptures of God, which, three centuries later, multiplied by thousands and by millions, and translated into a hundred and fifty tongues, were to be wafted from the same banks to the ends of the world. If in the fifteenth century, and even in the early years of the sixteenth, the English New Testament had been brought to London, it would only have fallen into the hands of a few Lollards. Now, in every place, in the parsonages, the universities, and the palaces, as well as in the cottages of the husbandmen and the shops of the tradesmen, there was an ardent desire to possess the Holy Scriptures. The *fiat lux* was about to be uttered over the chaos of the church, and light to be separated from darkness by the word of God.

BOOK XIX.

THE ENGLISH NEW TESTAMENT AND THE COURT OF ROME.

CHAPTER I.

Church and State essentially distinct—Their fundamental Principles—What restores Life to the Church—Separation from Rome necessary—Reform and Liberty—The New Testament crosses the Sea—Is hidden in London—Garret's Preaching and Zeal—Dissemination of Scripture—What the People find in it—The Effects it produces—Tyndale's Explanations—Roper, More's Son-in-law—Garret carries Tyndale's Testament to Oxford—Henry and his Valet—The Supplication of the Beggars—Two Sorts of Beggars—Evils caused by Priests—More's Supplications of the Souls in Purgatory.

THE Church and the State are essentially distinct. They both receive their task from God, but that task is different in each. The task of the church is to lead men to God; the task of the state is to secure the earthly development of a people in conformity with its peculiar character. There are certain bounds, traced by the particular spirit of each nation within which the state should confine itself; while the church, whose limits are co-extensive with the human race, has a universal character, which raises it above all national differences. These two distinctive features should be maintained. A state which aims at universality loses itself; a church whose mind and aim are sectarian falls away. Nevertheless, the church and the state, the two poles of social life, while they are in many respects opposed to one another, are far from excluding each other absolutely. The church has need of that justice, order, and liberty, which the state is bound to maintain; but the state has especial need of the church. If Jesus can do without kings to establish his kingdom, kings cannot do without Jesus, if they would have their kingdoms prosper. Justice, which is the fundamental principle of the state, is continually fettered in its progress by the internal power of sin; and as force can do nothing against this power, the state requires the gospel in order to overcome it. That country will always be the most prosperous where the church is the most evangelical. These two communities having thus need one of the other, we must be prepared, whenever a great religious manifestation takes place in the world, to witness the appearance on the scene not only of the little ones, but of the great ones also, of the state. We must not then be surprised to meet with Henry VIII., but let us endeavour to appreciate accurately the part he played.

If the Reformation, particularly in England, happened necessarily to be mixed up with the state, with the world even, it originated neither in the state nor in the world. There was much worldliness in the age of Henry VIII., passions, violence, festivities, a trial, a divorce; and some historians call that *the history of the Reformation in England.* We shall not pass by in silence these manifestations of the worldly life; opposed as they are to the Christian life, they are in history, and it is not our business to tear them out. But most assuredly they are not the Reformation. From a very different quarter proceeded the divine light which then rose upon the human race.

To say that Henry VIII. was the reformer of his people is to betray our ignorance of history. The kingly power in England by turns opposed and favoured the reform in the church; but it opposed before it favoured, and much more than it favoured. This great transformation was begun and extended by its own strength, by the Spirit from on high.

When the church has lost the life that is peculiar to it, it must again put itself in communication with its creative principle, that is, with the word of God. Just as the buckets of a wheel employed in irrigating the meadows have no sooner discharged their reviving waters, than they dip again into the stream to be re-filled, so every generation, void of the Spirit of Christ, must return to the divine source to be again filled up. The primitive words which created the church have been preserved for us in the Gospels, the Acts, and the Epistles; and the humble reading of these divine writings will create in every age the communion of saints. God was the father of the Reformation, not Henry VIII. The visible world which then glittered with such brightness; those princes and sports, those noblemen, and trials and laws, far from effecting a reform, were calculated to stifle it. But the light and the warmth came from heaven, and the new creation was completed.

In the reign of Henry VIII. a great number of citizens, priests, and noblemen possessed that degree of cultivation which favours the action of the holy books. It was sufficient for this divine seed to be scattered on the well-prepared soil for the work of germination to be accomplished.

A time not less important also was approaching—that in which the action of the popedom was to come to an end. The hour had not yet struck. God was first creating within by his word a spiritual church, before he broke without by his dispensations the bonds which had so long fastened England to the power of Rome. It was his good pleasure first to give truth and life, and then liberty. It has been said that if the pope had consented to a reform of abuses and doctrines, on condition of his keeping his position, the religious revolution would not have been satisfied at that price, and that after demanding *reform*, the next demand would have been for *liberty*. The only reproach that can be made to this assertion is, that it is superabundantly true. Liberty was an integral part of the Reformation, and one of the changes imperatively required was to withdraw religious authority from the pope, and restore it to the word of God. In the sixteenth century there was a great outpouring of the Christian life in France, Italy, and Spain; it is attested by martyrs without number, and history shows that to transform these three great nations, all that the gospel wanted was liberty.[1] " If we had set to work two months later," said a grand inquisitor of Spain who had dyed himself in the blood of the saints, " it would have been too late: Spain would have been lost to the Roman church." We may therefore believe that if Italy, France, and Spain had had some generous king to check the myrmidons of the

pope, those three countries, carried along by the renovating power of the gospel, would have entered upon an era of liberty and faith.

The struggles of England with the popedom began shortly after the dissemination of the English New Testament by Tyndale. The epoch at which we are arrived accordingly brings in one view before our eyes both the Testament of Jesus Christ and the court of Rome. We can thus study the men (the reformers and the Romanists) and the works they produce, and arrive at a just valuation of the two great principles which dispute the possession of authority in the church.

It was about the close of the year 1525; the English New Testament was crossing the sea; five pious Hanseatic merchants had taken charge of the books. Captivated by the Holy Scriptures they had taken them on board their ships, hidden them among their merchandise; and then made sail from Antwerp for London.

Thus those precious pages were approaching England, which were to become its light and the source of its greatness. The merchants, whose zeal unhappily cost them dear, were not without alarm. Had not Cochlœus caused orders to be sent to every port to prevent the entrance of the precious cargo they were bringing to England? They arrived and cast anchor; they lowered the boat to reach the shore; what were they likely to meet there? Tonstall's agents, no doubt, and Wolsey's, and Henry's, ready to take away their New Testaments! They landed and soon again returned to the ship; boats passed to and fro, and the vessel was unloaded. No enemy appeared; and no one seemed to imagine that these ships contained so great a treasure.

Just at the time this invaluable cargo was ascending the river, an invisible hand had dispersed the preventive guard. Tonstall, bishop of London, had been sent to Spain; Wolsey was occupied in political combinations with Scotland, France, and the Empire; Henry VIII., driven from his capital by an unhealthy winter, was passing the Christmas holidays at Eltham; and even the courts of justice, alarmed by an extraordinary mortality, had suspended their sittings. God, if we may so speak, had sent his angel to remove the guards.

Seeing nothing that could stop them, the five merchants, whose establishment was at the Steelyard in Thames Street, hastened to conceal their precious charge in their warehouses. But who will receive them? Who will undertake to distribute these Holy Scriptures in London, Oxford, Cambridge, and all England? It is a little matter that they have crossed the sea. The principal instrument God was about to use for their dissemination was an humble servant of Christ.

In Honey Lane, a narrow thoroughfare

[1] Geddes's Martyrology. Gonsalvi, Mart. Hisp. Llorente. Inquis. M'Crie, Ref. in Spain.

adjoining Cheapside, stood the old church of All Hallows, of which Robert Forman was rector. His curate was a plain man of lively imagination, delicate conscience, and timid disposition, but rendered bold by his faith, to which he was to become a martyr. Thomas Garret, for that was his name, having believed in the gospel, earnestly called his hearers to repentance;[1] he urged upon them that works, however good they might be in appearance, were by no means capable of justifying the sinner, and that faith alone could save him.[2] He maintained that every man had the right to preach the word of God;[3] and called those bishops pharisees, who persecuted christian men. Garret's discourses, at once so quickening and so gentle, attracted great crowds; and to many of his hearers, the street in which he preached was rightly named Honey Lane, for there they found the *honey out of the rock*.[4] But Garret was about to commit a fault still more heinous in the eyes of the priests than preaching faith. The Hanse merchants were seeking some sure place where they might store up the New Testaments and other books sent from Germany; the curate offered his house, stealthily transported the holy deposit thither, hid them in the most secret corners, and kept a faithful watch over this sacred library.[5] He did not confine himself to this. Night and day he studied the holy books; he held gospel meetings, read the word and explained its doctrines to the citizens of London. At last, not satisfied with being at once student, librarian, and preacher, he became a trader, and sold the New Testament to laymen, and even to priests and monks, so that the Holy Scriptures were dispersed over the whole realm.[6] This humble and timid priest was then performing alone the biblical work of England.

And thus the word of God, presented by Erasmus to the learned in 1517 was given to the people by Tyndale in 1526. In the parsonages and in the convent cells, but particularly in shops and cottages, a crowd of persons were studying the New Testament. The clearness of the Holy Scriptures struck each reader. None of the systematic or aphoristic forms of the school were to be found there: it was the language of human life which they discovered in those divine writings: here a conversation, there a discourse; here a narrative, and there a comparison; here a command, and there an argument; here a parable, and there a prayer. It was not all doctrine or all history;

but these two elements mingled together made an admirable whole. Above all, the life of our Saviour, so divine and so human, had an inexpressible charm which captivated the simple. One work of Jesus Christ explained another, and the great facts of the redemption, birth, death, and resurrection of the Son of God, and the sending of the Holy Ghost, followed and completed each other. The authority of Christ's teaching, so strongly contrasting with the doubts of the schools, increased the clearness of his discourses to his readers; for the more certain a truth is, the more distinctly it strikes the mind. Academical explanations were not necessary to those noblemen, farmers, and citizens. It is to me, for me, and of me that this book speaks, said each one. It is I whom all these promises and teachings concern. This *fall* and this *restoration*......they are mine. That old *death* and this new *life*......I have passed through them. That *flesh* and that *spirit*......I know them. This *law* and this *grace*, this *faith*, these *works*, this *slavery*, this *glory*, this *Christ* and this *Belial*......all are familiar to me. It is my own history that I find in this book. Thus by the aid of the Holy Ghost each one had in his own experience a key to the mysteries of the Bible. To understand certain authors and certain philosophers, the intellectual life of the reader must be in harmony with theirs; so must there be an intimate affinity with the holy books to penetrate their mysteries. "The man that has not the Spirit of God," said a reformer, "does not understand one jot or tittle of the Scripture."[1] Now that this condition was fulfilled, the Spirit of God moved upon the face of the waters.

Such at that period were the hermeneutics of England. Tyndale had set the example himself by explaining many of the words which might stop the reader. "The *New Testament!*" we may suppose some farmer saying, as he took up the book; "what *Testament* is that?" "Christ," replied Tyndale in his prologue, "commanded his disciples before his death to publish over all the world *his last will*, which is to give all his goods unto all that repent and believe.[2] He bequeaths them his righteousness to blot out their sins—his salvation to overcome their condemnation; and this is why that document is called the *Testament* of Jesus Christ."

"The *law* and the *gospel*," said a citizen of London, in his shop; "what is that?" "They are two *keys*," answered Tyndale. "The *law* is the key which shuts up all men under condemnation, and the *gospel* is the key which opens the door and lets them out.

---

[1] Earnestly laboured to call us to repentance. Becon, iii. p. 11.
[2] Quod opera nostra quantumvis bona in specie nihil conducunt ad justificationem nec ad meritum, sed sola fides. Foxe, Acts. v. p. 428.
[3] Every man may preach the word of God. Ibid.
[4] Psalm lxxxi. 16.
[5] Having the said books in his custody. Foxe, Acts, v. p. 428.
[6] Dispersing abroad of the said books within this realm. Ibid. p. 428. See also Strype, *Cranmer's Mem.* p. 81.

[1] Nullus homo unum iota in Scripturis sacris videt, nisi qui spiritum Dei habet. Luther, de servo arbitrio, Witt. ii. p. 424.
[2] Tyndale and Fryth's Works (ed. Russell), vol. ii. p. 491. The "Pathway unto the Holy Scripture" is the prologue to the quarto Testament, with a few changes of little importance.

Or, if you like it, they are two salves. The law, sharp and biting, driveth out the disease and killeth it; while the gospel, soothing and soft, softens the wound and brings life."[1] Every one understood and read, or rather devoured the inspired pages.; and the hearts of the elect (to use Tyndale's words), warmed by the love of Jesus Christ, began to melt like wax.[2]

This transformation was observed to take place even in the most catholic families. Roper, More's son-in-law, having read the New Testament, received the truth. "I have no more need," said he, "of auricular confession, of vigils, or of the invocation of saints. The ears of God are always open to hear us. Faith alone is necessary to salvation. I believe......and I am saved......Nothing can deprive me of God's favour."[3]

The amiable and zealous young man desired to do more. "Father," said he one day to Sir Thomas, "procure for me from the king, who is very fond of you, a license to preach. God hath sent me to instruct the world." More was uneasy. Must this new doctrine, which he detests, spread even to his children? He exerted all his authority to destroy the work begun in Roper's heart. "What," said he with a smile, "is it not sufficient that we that are your friends should know that you are a fool, but you would proclaim your folly to the world? Hold your tongue; I will debate with you no longer." The young man's imagination was struck, but his heart had not been changed. The discussions having ceased, the father's authority being restored, Roper became less fervent in his faith, and gradually he returned to popery, of which he was afterwards a zealous champion.

The humble curate of All Hallows having sold the New Testament to persons living in London and its neighbourhood, and to many pious men who would carry it to the farthest parts of England, formed the resolution to introduce it into the University of Oxford, that citadel of traditional catholicism. It was there he had studied, and he felt towards that school the affection which a son bears to his mother: he set out with his books.[4] Terror occasionally seized him, for he knew that the word of God had many deadly enemies at Oxford: but his inexhaustible zeal overcame his timidity. In concert with Dalaber, he stealthily offered the mysterious book for sale; many students bought it, and Garret carefully entered their names in his register. This was in January 1526; an incident disturbed this Christian activity.

One morning when Edmund Moddis, one of Henry's valets-de-chambre, was in attendance on his master, the prince, who was much attached to him, spoke to him of the new books come from beyond the sea. "If your grace," said Moddis, "would promise to pardon me and certain individuals, I would present you a wonderful book which is dedicated to your majesty."[1] "Who is the author?" "A lawyer of Gray's Inn, named Simon Fish, at present on the continent." "What is he doing there?" "About three years ago, Mr Kow, a fellow-student of Gray's Inn, composed for a private theatre a drama against my lord the cardinal." The king smiled; when his minister was attacked, his own yoke seemed lighter. "As no one was willing to represent the character employed to give the cardinal his lesson," continued the valet, "Master Fish boldly accepted it. The piece produced a great effect; and my lord being informed of this impertinence, sent the police one night to arrest Fish. The latter managed to escape, crossed the sea, joined one Tyndale, the author of some of the books so much talked of; and, carried away by his friend's example, he composed the book of which I was speaking to your grace." "What's the name of it?" "The Supplication of the Beggars."— "Where did you see it?"—"At two of your tradespeople's, George Elyot and George Robinson;[2] if your grace desires it, they shall bring it you." The king appointed the day and the hour.

The book was written for the king, and everybody read it but the king himself. At the appointed day, Moddis appeared with Elyot and Robinson, who were not entirely without fear, as they might be accused of proselytism even in the royal palace. The king received them in his private apartments.[3] "What do you want," he said to them. "Sir," replied one of the merchants, "we are come about an extraordinary book that is addressed to you." "Can one of you read it to me?"—"Yes, if it so please your grace," replied Elyot. "You may repeat the contents from memory," rejoined the king......"but, no, read it all; that will be better. I am ready." Elyot began,

"THE SUPPLICATION OF THE BEGGARS."

"To the king our sovereign lord,—

"Most lamentably complaineth of their woeful misery, unto your highness, your poor daily bedesmen, the wretched hideous monsters, on whom scarcely, for horror, any eye dare look; the foul unhappy sort of lepers and other sore people, needy, impotent, blind, lame, and sick, that live only by alms; how that their number is daily sore increased, that all the alms of all the well-disposed people of this your realm are not half enough to sustain them, but that for very constraint they die for hunger.

"And this most pestilent mischief is come

---

[1] Tyndale and Fryth's Works (ed. Russell), vol. ii. p. 503.
[2] Ibid. p. 500.
[3] More's Life, p. 184.
[4] And brought with him Tyndale's first translation of the New Testament in English. Foxe, Acts, v. p. 421.

[1] His grace should see such a book as it was a marvel to hear of. Foxe, Acts. iv. p. 658.
[2] Ibid. [3] Ibid.

upon your said poor bedesmen, by the reason that there hath, in the time of your noble predecessors, craftily crept into this your realm, another sort, not of impotent, but of strong, puissant, and counterfeit, holy and idle beggars and vagabonds, who by all the craft and wiliness of Satan are now increased not only into a great number, but also into a kingdom."

Henry was very attentive: Elyot continued:

" These are not the shepherds, but the ravenous wolves going in shepherds' clothing, devouring the flock : bishops, abbots, priors, deacons, archdeacons, suffragans, priests, monks, canons, friars, pardoners, and sumners......The goodliest lordships, manors, lands, and territories are theirs. Besides this, they have the tenth part of all the corn, meadow, pasture, grass, wood, colts, calves, lambs, pigs, geese, and chickens. Over and besides, the tenth part of every servant's wages, the tenth part of wool, milk, honey, wax, cheese, and butter. The poor wives must be accountable to them for every tenth egg, or else she getteth not her rights [i. e. absolution] at Easter......Finally what get they in a year? Summa totalis: L.430,333, 6s. 8d. sterling, whereof not four hundred years past they had not a penny......

" What subjects shall be able to help their prince, that be after this fashion yearly polled ? What good Christian people can be able to succour us poor lepers, blind, sore, and lame, that be thus yearly oppressed ?......The ancient Romans had never been able to have put all the whole world under their obeisance, if they had had at home such an idle sort of cormorants."

No subject could have been found more likely to captivate the king's attention. " And what doth all this greedy sort of sturdy idle holy thieves with their yearly exactions that they take of the people ? Truly nothing, but translate all rule, power, lordship, authority, obedience, and dignity, from your grace unto them. Nothing, but that all your subjects should fall into disobedience and rebellion.......Priests and doves make foul houses ; and if you will ruin a state, set up in it the pope with his monks and clergy......Send these sturdy loobies abroad in the world to take them wives of their own, and to get their living with their labour in the sweat of their faces......Then shall your commons increase in riches ; then shall matrimony be much better kept ; then shall not your sword, power, crown, dignity, and obedience of your people be translated from you."

When Elyot had finished reading, the king was silent, sunk in thought. The true cause of the ruin of the state had been laid before him : but Henry's mind was not ripe for these important truths. At last he said, with an uneasy manner: " If a man who desires to pull down an old wall, begins at the bottom, I fear the upper part may chance to fall on his head." [1] Thus then, in the king's eyes, Fish by attacking the priests was disturbing the foundations of religion and society. After this royal verdict, Henry rose, took the book, locked it up in his desk, and forbade the two merchants to reveal to any one the fact of their having read it to him.

Shortly after the king had received this copy, on Wednesday the 2d of February, the feast of Candlemas, a number of persons, including the king himself, were to take part in the procession, bearing wax tapers in their hands. During the night this famous invective was scattered about all the streets through which the procession had to pass. The cardinal ordered the pamphlet to be seized, and immediately waited upon the king. The latter put his hand under his robe, and with a smile took out the so much dreaded work, and then, as if satisfied with this proof of independence. he gave it up to the cardinal.

While Wolsey replied to Fish by confiscation, Sir Thomas More with greater liberality, desiring that press should reply to press, published *The Supplications of the Souls in Purgatory.* " Suppress," said they, " the pious stipends paid to the monks, and then Luther's gospel will come in, Tyndale's testament will be read, heresy will preach, fasts will be neglected, the saints will be blasphemed, God will be offended, virtue will be mocked of, vice will run riot, and England will be peopled with beggars and thieves." [2] The Souls in Purgatory then call the author of the Beggars' Supplication " a goose, an ass, a mad dog." Thus did superstition degrade More's noble genius. Notwithstanding the abuse of the souls in purgatory, the New Testament was daily read more and more in England.

CHAPTER II.

The two Authorities—Commencement of the Search—Garret at Oxford—His Flight—His Return and Imprisonment—Escapes and takes refuge with Dalaber—Garret and Dalaber at Prayer—The *Magnificat*—Surprise among the Doctors—Clark's Advice—Fraternal Love at Oxford—Alarm of Dalaber—His Arrest and Examination—He is tortured—Garret and twenty Fellows imprisoned—The Cellar—Condemnation and Humiliation.

WOLSEY did not stop with Fish's book. It was not that " miserable pamphlet " only that it was necessary to hunt down ; the New Testament in English had entered the kingdom by surprise ; there was the danger. The gospellers, who presumed to emancipate man from the priests, and put him in absolute dependence on God, did precisely the reverse of what Rome demands.[3] The cardinal hastened to assemble the bishops, and these (parti-

---

1 The upper part thereof might chance to fall upon his head. Foxe, Acts. iv. p. 658.
2 Supplication of the Souls in Purgatory. More's Works.
3 Actus meritorius est in potestate hominis. Duns Scotus in Sentent. lib. i. diss. 17.

cularly Warham and Tonstall, who had long enjoyed the jests launched against superstition) took the matter seriously when they were shown that the New Testament was circulating throughout England. These priests believed with Wolsey, that the authority of the pope and of the clergy was a dogma to which all others were subordinate. They saw in the reform an uprising of the human mind, a desire of thinking for themselves, of judging freely the doctrines and institutions, which the nations had hitherto received humbly from the hands of the priests. The new doctors justified their attempt at enfranchisement by substituting a new authority for the old. It was the New Testament that compromised the absolute power of Rome. It must be seized and destroyed, said the bishops. London, Oxford, and above all Cambridge, those three haunts of heresy, must be carefully searched. Definitive orders were issued on Saturday, 3d February 1526, and the work began immediately.

The first visit of the inquisitors was to Honey Lane, to the house of the curate of All Hallows. They did not find Garret: they sought after him at Monmouth's, and throughout the city, but he could not be met with.[1] " He is gone to Oxford to sell his detestable wares," the inquisitors were informed, and they set off after him immediately, determined to burn the evangelist and his books ; " so burning hot," says an historian, " was the charity of these holy fathers." [2]

On Tuesday, the 6th of February, Garret was quietly selling his books at Oxford, and carefully noting down his sales in his register, when two of his friends ran to him exclaiming, " Fly ! or else you will be taken before the cardinal, and thence......to the Tower." The poor curate was greatly agitated. " From whom did you learn that ? " —" From Master Cole, the clerk of the assembly, who is deep in the cardinal's favour." Garret, who saw at once that the affair was serious, hastened to Anthony Dalaber, who held the stock of the Holy Scriptures at Oxford ; others followed him ; the news had spread rapidly, and those who had bought the book were seized with alarm, for they knew by the history of the Lollards what the Romish clergy could do. They took counsel together. The brethren, " for so did we not only call one another, but were in deed one to another," says Dalaber,[3] decided that Garret should change his name ; that Dalaber should give him a letter for his brother, the rector of Stalbridge, in Dorsetshire, who was in want of a curate ; and that, once in this parish, he should seek the first opportunity of crossing the sea. The rector was in truth a " mad papist " (it is Dalaber's expression), but that did not alter their resolution. They knew of no other resource. Anthony wrote to him hurriedly ; and, on the morning of the

7th of February, Garret left Oxford without being observed.

Having provided for Garret's safety, Dalaber next thought of his own. He carefully concealed in a secret recess of his chamber, at St Alban's Hall, Tyndale's Testament, and the works of Luther, Œcolampadius, and others, on the word of God. Then, disgusted with the scholastic sophisms which he heard in that college, he took with him the New Testament and the Commentary on the Gospel of St Luke, by Lambert of Avignon, the second edition of which had just been published at Strasburg,[1] and went to Gloucester college, where he intended to study the civil law, not caring to have anything more to do with the church.

During this time, poor Garret was making his way into Dorsetshire. His conscience could not bear the idea of being, although for a short time only, the curate of a bigoted priest,—of concealing his faith, his desires, and even his name. He felt more wretched, although at liberty, than he could have been in Wolsey's prisons. It is better, he said within himself, to confess Christ before the judgment seat, than to seem to approve of the superstitious practices I detest. He went forward a little, then stopped—and then resumed his course. There was a fierce struggle between his fears and his conscience. At length, after a day and a half spent in doubt, his conscience prevailed ; unable to endure any longer the anguish that he felt, he retraced his steps, returned to Oxford, which he entered on Friday evening, and lay down calmly in his bed. It was barely past midnight when Wolsey's agents, who had received information of his return, arrived, and dragged him from his bed,[2] and delivered him up to Dr Cottisford, the commissary of the university. The latter locked him up in one of his rooms, while London and Higdon, dean of Frideswide, " two arch papists " (as the chronicler terms them), announced this important capture to the cardinal. They thought popery was saved, because a poor curate had been taken.

Dalaber, engaged in preparing his new room at Gloucester college, had not perceived all this commotion.[3] On Saturday, at noon, having finished his arrangements, he double-locked his door, and began to read the Gospel according to St Luke. All of a sudden he hears a knock. Dalaber made no reply ; it is no doubt the commissary's officers. A louder knock was given ; but he still remained silent. Immediately after, there was a third knock, as if the door would be beaten in. " Perhaps somebody wants me," thought Dalaber. He laid his book aside, opened the door, and to his great surprise saw Garret, who, with alarm in every feature, exclaimed, " I am a lost man ! They have caught me ! "

---

[1] He was searched for through all London. Foxe, Acts, v. p. 421. [2] Ibid. [3] Ibid.

[1] In Lucæ Evangelium Commentarii, nunc secundo recogniti et locupletati. Argentorati, 1595. [2] Foxe, v. p. 422. [3] Ibid.

Dalaber, who thought his friend was with his brother at Stalbridge, could not conceal his astonishment, and at the same time he cast an uneasy glance on a stranger who accompanied Garret. He was one of the college servants who had led the fugitive curate to Dalaber's new room. As soon as this man had gone away, Garret told Anthony everything: " Observing that Dr Cottisford and his household had gone to prayers, I put back the bolt of the lock with my finger.........and here I am.".......'' Alas ! Master Garret," replied Dalaber, " the imprudence you committed in speaking to me before that young man has ruined us both!" At these words, Garret, who had resumed his fear of the priests, now that his conscience was satisfied, exclaimed with a voice interrupted by sighs and tears:[1] " For mercy's sake, help me! Save me!" Without waiting for an answer, he threw off his frock and hood, begged Anthony to give him a sleeved coat, and thus disguised, he said : " I will escape into Wales, and from there, if possible, to Germany and Luther."

Garret checked himself ; there was something to be done before he left. The two friends fell on their knees and prayed together ; they called upon God to lead his servant to a secure retreat. That done, they embraced each other, their faces bathed with tears, and unable to utter a word.[2]

Silent on the threshold of his door, Dalaber followed both with eyes and ears his friend's retreating footsteps. Having heard him reach the bottom of the stairs, he returned to his room, locked the door, took out his New Testament, and placing it before him, read on his knees the tenth chapter of the Gospel of St Matthew, breathing many a heavy sigh :......Ye shall be brought before governors and kings for my sake......but fear them not ; the very hairs of your head are all numbered. This reading having revived his courage, Anthony, still on his knees, prayed fervently for the fugitive and for all his brethren: " O God, by thy Holy Spirit endue with heavenly strength this tender and new-born little flock in Oxford.[3] Christ's heavy cross is about to be laid on the weak shoulders of thy poor sheep. Grant that they may bear it with godly patience and unflinching zeal !"

Rising from his knees, Dalaber put away his book, folded up Garret's hood and frock, placed them among his own clothes, locked his room door, and proceeded to the Cardinal's College (now Christ Church,) to tell Clark and the other brethren what had happened.[4] They were in chapel : the evening service had begun ; the dean and canons, in full costume, were chanting in the choir. Dalaber stopped at the door listening to the majestic sounds of the organ at which Taverner presided, and to the harmonious strains of the choristers. They were singing

the *Magnificat : My soul doth magnify the Lord.......He hath holpen his servant Israel.* It seemed to Dalaber that they were singing Garret's deliverance. But his voice could not join in their song of praise. " Alas !" he exclaimed, " all my singing and music is turned into sighing and musing."[1]

As he listened, leaning against the entrance into the choir, Dr Cottisford, the university commissary, arrived with hasty step, " bare headed, and as pale as ashes." He passed Anthony without noticing him, and going straight to the dean appeared to announce some important and unpleasant news. " I know well the cause of his sorrow," thought Dalaber as he watched every gesture. The commissary had scarcely finished his report when the dean arose, and both left the choir with undisguised confusion. They had only reached the middle of the anti-chapel when Dr London ran in, puffing and chafing and stamping, " like a hungry and greedy lion seeking his prey."[2] All three stopped, questioned each other, and deplored their misfortune. Their rapid and eager movements indicated the liveliest emotion ; London above all could not restrain himself. He attacked the commissary, and blamed him for his negligence, so that at last Cottisford burst into tears. " Deeds, not tears," said the fanatical London ; and forthwith they despatched officers and spies along every road.

Anthony having left the chapel hurried to Clark's to tell him of the escape of his friend. " We are walking in the midst of wolves and tigers," replied Clark ; " prepare for persecution. *Prudentia serpentina et simplicitas columbina* (the wisdom of serpents and the harmlessness of doves) must be our motto. O God, give us the courage these evil times require." All in the little flock were delighted at Garret's deliverance. Sumner and Betts, who had come in, ran off to tell it to the other brethren in the college,[3] and Dalaber hastened to Corpus Christi. All these pious young men felt themselves to be soldiers in the same army, travellers in the same company, brothers in the same family. Fraternal love nowhere shone so brightly in the days of the Reformation as among the Christians of Great Britain. This is a feature worthy of notice.

Fitzjames, Udal, and Diet were met together in the rooms of the latter, at Corpus Christi college, when Dalaber arrived. They ate their frugal meal, with downcast eyes and broken voices, conversing of Oxford, of England, and of the perils hanging over them.[4] Then rising from table they fell on their knees, called upon God for aid, and separated, Fitzjames taking Dalaber with him to St Alban's Hall. They were afraid that

---

[1] With deep sighs and plenty of tears. Foxe. v. p. 422.
[2] That we all bewet both our faces. Ibid. 423.
[3] Ibid.   [4] Ibid.
[1] Foxe, v. p. 423.   [2] Ibid. p. 424.
[3] To tell unto our other brethren ; (for there were divers else in that college.) Ibid.
[4] Considering our state and peril at hand. Ibid.

the servant of Gloucester college had be-trayed him.

The disciples of the gospel at Oxford passed the night in great anxiety. Garret's flight, the rage of the priests, the dangers of the rising church, the roaring of a storm that filled the air and re-echoed through the long cloisters—all impressed them with terror. On Sunday the 11th of February, Dalaber, who was stirring at five in the morning, set out for his room in Gloucester college. Find-ing the gates shut, he walked up and down beneath the walls in the mud, for it had rained all night. As he paced to and fro along the solitary street in the obscure dawn, a thousand thoughts alarmed his mind. It was known, he said to himself, that he had taken part in Garret's flight; he would be arrested, and his friend's escape would be revenged on him.[1] He was weighed down by sorrow and alarm; he sighed heavily;[2] he imagined he saw Wolsey's commissioners demanding the names of his accomplices, and pretending to draw up a proscription list at his dictation; he recollected that on more than one occasion cruel priests had extorted from the Lollards the names of their brethren, and terrified at the possibility of such a crime, he exclaimed; "O God, I swear to thee that I will accuse no man,......I will tell nothing but what is perfectly well known."[3]

At last, after an hour of anguish, he was able to enter the college. He hastened in, but when he tried to open his door, he found that the lock had been picked. The door gave way to a strong push, and what a sight met his eyes! his bedstead overturned, the blankets scattered on the floor, his clothes all confusion in his wardrobe, his study broken into and left open. He doubted not that Garret's dress had betrayed him; and he was gazing at this sad spectacle in alarm, when a monk who occupied the adjoining rooms came and told him what had taken place: "The commissary and two proctors, armed with swords and bills, broke open your door in the middle of the night. They pierced your bed-straw through and through to make sure Garret was not hidden there;[4] they carefully searched every nook and corner, but were not able to discover any traces of the fugitive." At these words Dalaber breathed again......but the monk had not ended. "I have orders," he added, "to send you to the prior." Anthony Dunstan, the prior, was a fanatical and avaricious monk; and the con-fusion into which this message threw Da-laber was so great, that he went just as he was, all bespattered with mud, to the rooms of his superior.

The prior, who was standing with his face towards the door, looked at Dalaber from head to foot as he came in. "Where did you pass the night?" he asked. "At St Alban's Hall with Fitzjames." The prior with a gesture of incredulity continued: "Was not Master Garret with you yesterday?"—"Yes."—"Where is he now?"—"I do not know." During this examination, the prior had remarked a large double gilt silver ring on Anthony's finger, with the initials A. D.[1] "Show me that," said the prior. Dalaber gave him the ring, and the prior believing it to be of solid gold, put it on his own finger, adding with a cunning leer: "This ring is mine: it bears my name. A is for Anthony, and D for Dunstan." "Would to God," thought Dalaber, "that I were as well deli-vered from his company, as I am sure of being delivered of my ring."

At this moment the chief beadle, with two or three of the commissary's men, entered and conducted Dalaber to the chapel of Lincoln college, where three ill-omened figures were standing beside the altar: they were Cottis-ford, London, and Higdon. "Where is Gar-ret?" asked London; and pointing to his disordered dress, he continued: "Your shoes and garments covered with mud prove that you have been out all night with him. If you do not say where you have taken him, you will be sent to the Tower."—"Yes," added Higdon, "to Little-ease [one of the most horrible dungeons in the prison], and you will be put to the torture, do you hear?" Then the three doctors spent two hours at-tempting to shake the young man by flatter-ing promises and frightful threats; but all was useless. The commissary then gave a sign, the officers stepped forward, and the judges ascended a narrow staircase leading to a large room situated above the commis-sary's chamber. Here Dalaber was deprived of his purse and girdle, and his legs were placed in the stocks, so that his feet were almost as high as his head.[2] When that was done, the three doctors devoutly went to mass.

Poor Anthony, left alone in this frightful position, recollected the warning Clark had given him two years before. He groaned heavily and cried to God:[3] "O Father! that my suffering may be for thy glory, and for the consolation of my brethren! Happen what may, I will never accuse one of them." After this noble protest, Anthony felt an in-crease of peace in his heart; but a new sor-row was reserved for him.

Garret, who had directed his course west-wards, with the intention of going to Wales, had been caught at Hinksey, a short dis-tance from Oxford. He was brought back, and thrown into the dungeon in which Dala-ber had been placed after the torture. Their gloomy presentiments were to be more than fulfilled.

In fact Wolsey was deeply irritated at seeing the college [Christ Church], which

[1] My musing head being full of forecasting cares. Foxe, v. p. 424.
[2] My sorrowful heart flowing with doleful sighs. Ibid.
[3] I fully determined in my conscience before God that I would accuse no man. Ibid.
[4] With bills and swords thrusted through my bed-straw. Ibid. p. 425.

[1] Then had he spied on my fore-finger a big ring of silver, very well double-gilted. Foxe, v. p. 425.   [2] Ibid. p. 426.
[3] Ibid. p. 427.

he had intended should be "the most glorious in the world," made the haunt of heresy, and the young men, whom he had so carefully chosen, become distributors of the New Testament. By favouring literature, he had had in view the triumph of the clergy, and literature had on the contrary served to the triumph of the gospel. He issued his orders without delay, and the university was filled with terror. John Clark, John Fryth, Henry Sumner, William Betts, Richard Taverner, Richard Cox, Michael Drumm, Godfrey Harman, Thomas Lawney, Radley, and others besides of Cardinal's College: Udal, Diet, and others of Corpus Christi; Eden and several of his friends of Magdalene; Goodman, William Bayley, Robert Ferrar, John Salisbury of Gloucester, Barnard, and St Mary's Colleges; were seized and thrown into prison. Wolsey had promised them glory; he gave them a dungeon, hoping in this manner to save the power of the priests, and to repress that awakening of truth and liberty which was spreading from the continent to England.

Under Cardinal's College there was a deep cellar sunk in the earth, in which the butler kept his salt fish. Into this hole these young men, the choice of England, were thrust. The dampness of this cave, the corrupted air they breathed, the horrible smell given out by the fish, seriously affected the prisoners, already weakend by study. Their hearts were bursting with groans, their faith was shaken, and the most mournful scenes followed each other in this foul dungeon. The wretched captives gazed on one another, wept, and prayed. This trial was destined to be a salutary one to them: "Alas!" said Fryth on a subsequent occasion, "I see that besides the word of God, there is indeed a second purgatory......but it is not that invented by Rome; it is the cross of tribulation to which God has nailed us."[1]

At last the prisoners were taken out one by one and brought before their judges; two only were released. The first was Betts, afterwards chaplain to Anne Boleyn: they had not been able to find any prohibited books in his room, and he pleaded his cause with great talent. The other was Taverner; he had hidden Clark's books under his school-room floor, where they had been discovered; but his love for the arts saved him: "Pshaw! he is only a musician," said the cardinal.

All the rest were condemned. A great fire was kindled at the top of the market-place;[2] a long procession was marshalled, and these unfortunate men were led out, each bearing a fagot. When they came near the fire, they were compelled to throw into it the heretical books that had been found in their

rooms, after which they were taken back to their noisome prison. There seemed to be a barbarous pleasure in treating these young and generous men so vilely. In other countries also, Rome was preparing to stifle in the flames the noblest geniuses of France, Spain, and Italy. Such was the reception letters and the gospel met with from popery in the sixteenth century. Every plant of God's must be beaten by the wind even at the risk of its being uprooted: if it receives only the gentle rays of the sun, there is reason to fear that it will dry up and wither before it produces fruit. *Except a corn of wheat fall into the ground and die, it abideth alone.* There was to arise one day a real church in England, for the persecution had begun.

We have to contemplate still further trials.

CHAPTER III.

Persecution at Cambridge—Barnes arrested—A grand Search—Barnes at Wolsey's Palace—Interrogated by the Cardinal—Conversation between Wolsey and Barnes—Barnes threatened with the Stake—His Fall and public Penance—Richard Bayfield—His Faith and Imprisonment—Visits Cambridge—Joins Tyndale—The Confessors in the Cellar at Oxford—Four of them die—The rest liberated.

CAMBRIDGE, which had produced Latimer, Bilney, Stafford, and Barnes, had at first appeared to occupy the front rank in the English reformation. Oxford by receiving the crown of persecution seemed now to have outstripped the sister university. And yet Cambridge was to have its share of suffering. The investigation had begun at Oxford on Monday the 5th of February, and on the very same day two of Wolsey's creatures, Dr Capon, one of his chaplains, and Gibson, a sergeant-at-arms, notorious for his arrogance, left London for Cambridge. Submission was the pass-word of popery. "Yes, submission," was responded from every part of Christendom by men of sincere piety and profound understanding; "submission to the legitimate authority against which Roman-catholicism has rebelled." According to their views the traditionalism and pelagianism of the Romish church had set up the supremacy of fallen reason in opposition to the divine supremacy of the word and of grace. The external and apparent sacrifice of self which Roman-catholicism imposes,—obedience to a confessor or to the pope, arbitrary penance, ascetic practices, and celibacy,—only served to create, and so to strengthen and perpetuate, a delusion as to the egotistic preservation of a sinful personality. When the Reformation proclaimed liberty, so far as regarded ordinances of human invention, it was with the view of bringing man's heart and life into subjection to their real Sovereign. The reign of God was commencing; that of the

---

[1] God naileth us to the cross to heal our infirmities. Tyndale and Fryth's Works, iii. p. 91 (ed. Russell).
[2] There was made a great fire upon the top of Carfax. Foxe, v. p. 428.

priests must needs come to an end. No man can serve two masters. Such were the important truths which gradually dawned upon the world, and which it became necessary to extinguish without delay.

On the day after their arrival in Cambridge, on Tuesday the 6th of February, Capon and Gibson went to the convocation house, where several of the doctors were talking together. Their appearance caused some anxiety among the spectators, who looked upon the strangers with distrust. On a sudden Gibson moved forward, put his hand on Barnes, and arrested him in the presence of his friends.[1] The latter were frightened, and this was what the sergeant wanted. "What!" said they, "the prior of the Augustines, the restorer of letters in Cambridge, arrested by a sergeant!" This was not all. Wolsey's agents were to seize the books come from Germany, and their owners; Bilney, Latimer, Stafford, Arthur, and their friends, were all to be imprisoned, for they possessed the New Testament. Thirty members of the university were pointed out as suspected; and some miserable wretches, who had been bribed by the inquisitors, offered to show the place in every room where the prohibited books were hidden. But while the necessary preparations were making for this search, Bilney, Latimer, and their colleagues, being warned in time, got the books removed; they were taken away not only by the doors but by the windows, even by the roofs, and anxious inquiry was made for sure places in which they could be concealed.

This work was hardly ended, when the vice-chancellor of the university, the sergeant-at-arms, Wolsey's chaplain, the proctors, and the informers began their rounds. They opened the first room, entered, searched, and found nothing. They passed on to the second, there was nothing. The sergeant was astonished, and grew angry. On reaching the third room, he ran directly to the place that had been pointed out,—still there was nothing. The same thing occurred everywhere; never was inquisitor more mortified. He dared not lay hands on the persons of the evangelical doctors: his orders bore that he was to seize the books and *their owners.* But as no books were found, there could be no prisoners. Luckily there was one man (the prior of the Augustines) against whom there were particular charges. The sergeant promised to compensate himself at Barnes's expense for his useless labours.

The next day Gibson and Capon set out for London with Barnes. During this mournful journey the prior, in great agitation, at one time determined to brave all England, and at another trembled like a leaf. At last their journey was ended; the chaplain left his prisoner at Parnell's house, close by

the stocks.[1] Three students (Coverdale, Goodwin, and Field) had followed their master to cheer him with their tender affection.

On Thursday (8th February) the sergeant conducted Barnes to the cardinal's palace at Westminster; the wretched prior, whose enthusiasm had given way to dejection, waited all day before he could be admitted. What a day! Will no one come to his assistance? Doctor Gardiner, Wolsey's secretary, and Fox, his steward, both old friends of Barnes, passed through the gallery in the evening, and went up to the prisoner, who begged them to procure him an audience with the cardinal. When night had come, these officers introduced the prior into the room, where their master was sitting, and Barnes, as was customary, fell on his knees before him. "Is this the Doctor Barnes who is accused of heresy?" asked Wolsey, in a haughty tone, of Fox and Gardiner. They replied in the affirmative. The cardinal then turning to Barnes, who was still kneeling, said to him ironically, and not without reason : "What, master doctor, had you not sufficient scope in the Scriptures to teach the people; but my golden shoes, my poleaxes, my pillars, my golden cushions, my crosses, did so sore offend you, that you must make us a laughing-stock, *ridiculum caput,* amongst the people? We were jollily that day laughed to scorn. Verily it was a sermon more fit to be preached on a stage than in a pulpit; for at the last you said I wore a pair of *red* gloves— I should say *bloody* gloves (quoth you)...... Eh! what think you, master doctor?" Barnes, wishing to elude these embarrassing questions, answered vaguely : "I spoke nothing but the truth out of the Scriptures, according to my conscience and according to the old doctors." He then presented to the cardinal a statement of his teaching.

Wolsey received the papers with a smile : "Oh, ho!" said he as he counted the six sheets, "I perceive you intend to stand to your articles and to show your learning." "With the grace of God," said Barnes. Wolsey then began to read them, and stopped at the sixth article, which ran thus : "I will never believe that one man may, by the law of God, be bishop of two or three cities, yea, of a whole country, for it is contrary to St Paul, who saith : *I have left thee behind, to set in every city a bishop.*" Barnes did not quote correctly, for the apostle says ; "*to ordain elders in every city.*"[2] Wolsey was displeased at this thesis : "Ah! this touches me," he said : "Do you think it wrong (seeing the ordinance of the church) that one bishop should have so many cities underneath him?" "I know of no ordinance of the church," Barnes replied, "as concerning this thing, but Paul's saying only."

Although this controversy interested the

[1] Suddenly arrested Barnes openly in the convocation house to make all others afraid. Foxe, v. p. 416.

[1] Foxe, v. p. 416.
[2] Καὶ καταστήσῃς κατὰ πόλιν πρισβυτέρους. Titus i. 5.

cardinal, the personal attack of which he had to complain touched him more keenly. " Good," said Wolsey ; and then with a condescension hardly to be expected from so proud a man, he deigned almost to justify himself. "You charge me with displaying a royal pomp ; but do you not understand that, being called to represent his majesty, I must strive by these means to strike terror into the wicked ?"—" It is not your pomp or your poleaxes," Barnes courageously answered, " that will save the king's person...... God will save him, who said : *Per me reges regnant.*" Barnes, instead of profiting by the cardinal's kindness to present an humble justification, as Dean Colet had formerly done to Henry VIII., dared preach him a second sermon to his face. Wolsey felt the colour mount to his cheeks. " Well, gentlemen," said he, turning.to Fox and Gardiner, " you hear him ! Is this the wise and learned man of whom you spoke to me ? "

At these words both steward and secretary fell on their knees, saying : " My lord, pardon him for mercy's sake."—" Can you find ten or even six doctors of divinity willing to swear that you are free from heresy ?" asked Wolsey. Barnes offered twenty honest men, quite as learned as himself, or even more so. " I must have doctors in divinity, men as old as yourself." " That is impossible," said the prior. " In that case you must be burnt," continued the cardinal. " Let him be taken to the Tower." Gardiner and Fox offering to become his sureties, Wolsey permitted him to pass the night at Parnell's.

" It is no time to think of sleeping," said Barnes as he entered the house, " we must write." Those harsh and terrible words, *you must be burnt,* resounded continually in his ears. He dictated all night to his three young friends a defence of his articles.

The next day he was taken before the chapter, at which Clarke, bishop of Bath, Standish, and other doctors were present. His judges laid before him a long statement, and said to him : " Promise to read this paper in public, without omitting or adding a single word." It was then read to him. " I would die first," was his reply. " Will you abjure or be burnt alive ? " said his judges ; " take your choice." The alternative was dreadful. Poor Barnes, a prey to the deepest agony, shrank at the thought of the stake ; then, suddenly his courage revived, and he exclaimed : " I would rather be burnt than abjure." Gardiner and Fox did all they could to persuade him. " Listen to reason," said they craftily : " your articles are true ; that is not the question. We want to know whether by your death you will let error triumph, or whether you would rather remain to defend the truth, when better days may come."

They entreated him ; they put forward the most plausible motives ; from time to time they uttered the terrible words, *burnt alive !*

His blood froze in his veins ; he knew not what he said or did......they placed a paper before him—they put a pen in his hand—his head was bewildered, he signed his name with a deep sigh. This unhappy man was destined at a later period to be a faithful martyr of Jesus Christ ; but he had not yet learnt to " resist even unto blood." Barnes had fallen.

On the following morning (Sunday, 11th February) a solemn spectacle was preparing at St Paul's. Before daybreak, all were astir in the prison of the poor prior ; and at eight o'clock, the knight-marshal with his tipstaves, and the warden of the Fleet prison, with his billmen, conducted Barnes to St Paul's, along with four of the Hanse merchants who had first brought to London the New Testament of Jesus Christ in English. The fifth of these pious merchants held an immense taper in his hands. A persevering search had discovered that it was these men to whom England was indebted for the so much dreaded book ; their warehouses were surrounded and their persons arrested. On the top of St Paul's steps was a platform, and on the platform a throne, and on the throne the cardinal, dressed in scarlet—like a " bloody antichrist," says the chronicler. On his head glittered the hat of which Barnes had spoken so ill ; around him were thirty-six bishops, abbots, priors, and all his doctors, dressed in damask and satin ; the vast cathedral was full. The bishop of Rochester having gone into a pulpit placed at the top of the steps, Barnes and the merchants, each bearing a fagot, were compelled to kneel and listen to a sermon intended to cure these poor creatures of that taste for insurrection against popery which was beginning to spread in every quarter. The sermon ended, the cardinal mounted his mule, took his station under a magnificent canopy, and rode off. After this Barnes and his five companions walked three times round a fire, lighted before the cross at the north gate of the cathedral. The dejected prior, with downcast head, dragged himself along, rather than walked. After the third turn. the prisoners threw their fagots into the flames ; some " heretical " books also were flung in ; and the bishop of Rochester having given absolution to the six penitents, they were led back to prison to be kept there during the lord cardinal's pleasure. Barnes could not weep now ; the thought of his relapse, and of the effects so guilty an example might produce, had deprived him of all moral energy. In the month of August, he was led out of prison and confined in the Augustine convent.

Barnes was not the only man at Cambridge upon whom the blow had fallen. Since the year 1520, a monk named Richard Bayfield had been an inmate of the abbey of Bury St Edmunds. His affability delighted every traveller. One day, when engaged as chamberlain in receiving Barnes, who had come to visit Dr Ruffam, his fellow-student at Louvain, two men entered the convent. They were pious persons, and of great consideration in London, where they carried on the occupation of brick-making, and had risen to be wardens of their guild. Their names were Maxwell and Stacy, men " well grafted in the doctrine of Christ," says the historian, who had led many to the Saviour by their conversation and exemplary life. Being accustomed to travel once a-year through the counties to visit their brethren, and extend a knowledge of the gospel, they used to lodge, according to the usages of the time, in the convents and abbeys. A conversation soon arose between Barnes, Stacy, and Maxwell, which struck the lay-brother. Barnes, who had observed his attention, gave him, as he was leaving the convent, a New Testament in Latin, and the two brick-makers added a New Testament in English, with *The Wicked Mammon* and *The Obedience of a Christian Man.* The lay-brother ran and hid the books in his cell, and for two years read them constantly. At last he was discovered, and reprimanded; but he boldly confessed his faith. Upon this the monks threw him into prison, set him in the stocks, put a gag in his mouth, and cruelly whipped him, to prevent his speaking of grace.[1] The unhappy Bayfield remained nine months in this condition.

When Barnes repeated his visit to Bury at a later period, he did not find the amiable chamberlain at the gates of the abbey. Upon inquiry he learnt his condition, and immediately took steps to procure his deliverance. Dr Ruffam came to his aid: " Give him to me," said Barnes, " I will take him to Cambridge." The prior of the Augustines was at that time held in high esteem; his request was granted, in the hope that he would lead back Bayfield to the doctrines of the church. But the very reverse took place: intercourse with the Cambridge brethren strengthened the young monk's faith. On a sudden his happiness vanished. Barnes, his friend and benefactor, was carried to London, and the monks of Bury St Edmonds, alarmed at the noise this affair created, summoned him to return to the abbey. But Bayfield, resolving to submit to their yoke no longer, went to London, and lay concealed at Maxwell and Stacy's. One day, having left his hiding-place, he was crossing Lombard Street, when he met a priest named Pierson and two other religious of his order, with whom he entered into a conversation which greatly scandalized them. " You must depart forthwith," said Maxwell and Stacy to him on his return. Bayfield received a small sum of money from them, went on board a ship, and as soon as he reached the continent, hastened to find Tyndale. During this time scenes of a very different nature from those which had taken place at Cambridge, but not less heart-rending, were passing at Oxford.

[1] Foxe, iv. p. 681.

The storm of persecution was raging there with more violence than at Cambridge. Clark and the other confessors of the name of Christ were still confined in their underground prison. The air they breathed, the food they took (and they ate nothing but salt fish[1]), the burning thirst this created, the thoughts by which they were agitated, all together combined to crush these noble-hearted men. Their bodies wasted day by day: they wandered like spectres up and down their gloomy cellar. Those animated discussions in which the deep questions then convulsing Christendom were so eloquently debated were at an end; they were like shadow meeting shadow. Their hollow eyes cast a vague and haggard glance on one another, and after gazing for a moment, they passed on without speaking. Clark, Sumner, Bayley, and Goodman, consumed by fever, feebly crawled along, leaning against their dungeon walls. The first, who was also the eldest, could not walk without the support of one of his fellow-prisoners. Soon he was quite unable to move, and lay stretched upon the damp floor. The brethren gathered round him, sought to discover in his features whether death was not about to cut short the days of him who had brought many of them to the knowledge of Christ. They repeated to him slowly the words of Scripture, and then knelt down by his side and uttered a fervent prayer.

Clark, feeling his end draw near, asked for the communion. The jailers conveyed his request to their master; the noise of the bolts was soon heard, and a turnkey, stepping into the midst of the disconsolate band, pronounced a cruel *no!*[2] On hearing this, Clark looked towards heaven, and exclaimed with a father of the church: *Crede et manducasti*, Believe, and thou hast eaten.[3] He was lost in thought: he contemplated the crucified Son of God; by faith he ate and drank the flesh and blood of Christ, and experienced in his inner life the strengthening action of the Redeemer. Men might refuse him the host, but Jesus had given him his body; and from that hour he felt strengthened by a living union with the King of heaven.

Not alone did Clark descend into the shadowy valley: Sumner, Bayley, and Goodman were sinking rapidly. Death, the gloomy inhabitant of this foul prison, had taken possession of these four friends.[4] Their brethren addressed fresh solicitations to the cardinal, at that time closely occupied in negotiations with France, Rome, and Venice.[5] He found means, however, to give a moment to the Oxford martyrs; and just as these Christians were praying over their four dying compa-

[1] Foxe, v. p. 5.
[2] Not be suffered to receive the communion, being in prison. Ibid. p. 428.
[3] Ibid. Habe fidem et tecum est quem non vides, says Augustine in another place. See Serm. 235, 272. Tract. 26, Evang. Joh.
[4] Taking their death in the same prison. Foxe, v. p. 5.
[5] State Papers, i. p. 169.

nions, the commissioner came and informed them, that "his lordship, of his great goodness, permitted the sick persons to be removed to their own chambers." Litters were brought, on which the dying men were placed and carried to their rooms ;[1] the doors were closed again upon those whose lives this frightful dungeon had not yet attacked.

It was the middle of August. The wretched men who had passed six months in the cellar were transported in vain to their chambers and their beds ; several members of the university ineffectually tried by their cares and their tender charity to recall them to life. It was too late. The severities of popery had killed these noble witnesses. The approach of death soon betrayed itself; their blood grew cold, their limbs stiff, and their bedimmed eyes sought only Jesus Christ, their everlasting hope. Clark, Sumner, and Bayley died in the same week. Goodman followed close upon them.[2]

This unexpected catastrophe softened Wolsey. He was cruel only as far as his interest and the safety of the church required. He feared that the death of so many young men would raise public opinion against him, or that these catastrophes would damage his college ; perhaps even some sentiment of humanity may have touched his heart. "Set the rest at liberty," he wrote to his agents, "but upon condition that they do not go above ten miles from Oxford." The university beheld these young men issue from their living tomb pale, wasted, weak, and with faltering steps. At that time they were not men of mark ; it was their youth that touched the spectators' hearts ; but in after-years they all occupied an important place in the church. They were Cox, who became Bishop of Ely, and tutor to Edward the Prince Royal ; Drumm, who under Cranmer became one of the six preachers at Canterbury ; Udal, afterwards master of Westminster and Eton schools Salisbury, dean of Norwich, and then bishop of Sodor and Man, who in all his wealth and greatness often recalled his frightful prison at Oxford as a title to glory ; Ferrar, afterwards Cranmer's chaplain, bishop of St David's, and a martyr even unto death, after an interval of thirty years ; Fryth, Tyndale's friend, to whom this deliverance proved only a delay ; and several others. When they came forth from their terrible dungeon, their friends ran up to them, supported their faltering steps, and embraced them amidst floods of tears. Fryth quitted the university not long after and went to Flanders.[3] Thus was the tempest stayed which had so fearfully ravaged Oxford. But the calm was of no long duration ; an unexpected circumstance became perilous to the cause of the Reformation.

CHAPTER IV.

Luther's Letter to the King—Henry's Anger—His Reply— Luther's Resolution—Persecutions—Barnes escapes—Proclamations against the New Testament—W. Roy to Caiaphas—Third Edition of the New Testament—The Triumph of Law and Liberty—Hackett attacks the Printer—Hackett's Complaints—A Seizure—The Year 1526 in England.

HENRY was still under the impression of the famous *Supplication of the Beggars*, when Luther's interference increased his anger. The letter which, at the advice of Christiern, king of Denmark, this reformer had written to him in September 1525, had miscarried. The Wittemberg doctor hearing nothing of it, had boldly printed it, and sent a copy to the king. "I am informed," said Luther, "that your Majesty is beginning to favour the gospel,[1] and to be disgusted with the perverse race that fights against it in your noble kingdom......It is true that, according to Scripture, *the kings of the earth take counsel[2] together against the Lord*, and we cannot, consequently, expect to see them favourable to the truth. How fervently do I wish that this miracle may be accomplished in the person of your Majesty."[2]

We may imagine Henry's wrath as he read this letter. "What !" said he, "does this apostate monk dare print a letter addressed to us, without having even sent it, or at the least without knowing if we have ever received it?......And as if that were not enough, he insinuates that we are among his partisans.........He wins over also one or two wretches, born in our kingdom, and engages them to translate the New Testament into English, adding thereto certain prefaces and poisonous glosses." Thus spoke Henry. The idea that his name should be associated with that of the Wittemberg monk called all the blood into his face. He will reply right royally to such unblushing impudence. He summoned Wolsey forthwith. "Here !" said he, pointing to a passage concerning the prelate, "here ! read what is said of you !" And then he read aloud : *Illud monstrum et publicum odium Dei et hominum, cardinalis Eboracensis, pestis illa regni tui.* You see, my lord, you are a *monster*, an object of *hatred*, both to God and man, the *scourge* of my kingdom !" The king had hitherto allowed the bishops to do as they pleased, and observed a sort of neutrality. He now determined to lay it aside and begin a crusade against the gospel of Jesus Christ, but he must first answer this impertinent letter. He consulted Sir Thomas More, shut himself in his closet, and dictated to his secretary a reply to the reformer : "You are ashamed of the book you have written against me," he said, "I would counsel you to be ashamed of all that you have written. They are full of disgusting errors and frantic heresies ; and are sup-

---

[1] Foxe, v. p. 5.
[2] Ibid.
[3] Tyndale and Fryth's Works, iii. p. 75 (edit. Russell).

[1] Majestatem tuam cæpisse favere Evangelio. Cochlœus. p. 136.
[2] Huic miraculo in Majestate tua quam opto ex totis medullis. Ibid. p. 127.

ported by the most audacious obstinacy. Your venomous pen mocks the church, insults the fathers, abuses the saints, despises the apostles, dishonours the holy virgin, and blasphemes God, by making him the author of evil......And after all that, you claim to be an author whose like does not exist in the world!"[1]

" You offer to publish a book in my praise ......I thank you!......You will praise me most by abusing me ; you will dishonour me beyond measure if you praise me. I say with Seneca : *Tam turpe tibi sit laudari a turpibus, quam si lauderis ob turpia.*"[2]

This letter, written by the *king of the English to the king of the heretics*,[3] was immediately circulated throughout England bound up with Luther's epistle. Henry, by publishing it, put his subjects on their guard against the *unfaithful* translations of the New Testament, which were besides about to be burnt everywhere. " The grapes seem beautiful," he said, " but beware how you wet your lips with the wine made from them, for the adversary hath mingled poison with it."

Luther, agitated by this rude lesson, tried to excuse himself. " I said to myself, *There are twelve hours in the day.* Who knows? perhaps I may find one lucky hour to gain the King of England. I therefore laid my humble epistle at his feet; but alas! the swine have torn it. I am willing to be silent...... but as regards my doctrine, I cannot impose silence on it. It must cry aloud, it must bite. If any king imagines he can make me retract my faith, he is a dreamer. So long as one drop of blood remains in my body, I shall say NO. Emperors, kings, the devil, and even the whole universe, cannot frighten me when faith is concerned. I claim to be proud, very proud, exceedingly proud. If my doctrine had no other enemies than the king of England, Duke George, the pope and their allies, all these soap-bubbles......one little prayer would long ago have worsted them all. Where are Pilate, Herod, and Caiaphas now? Where are Nero, Domitian, and Maximilian? Where are Arius, Pelagius, and Manes?—Where are they?......Where all our scribes and all our tyrants will soon be.—But Christ? Christ is the same always.

" For a thousand years the Holy Scriptures have not shone in the world with so much brightness as now.[4] I wait in peace for my last hour ; I have done what I could. O princes, my hands are clean from your blood ; it will fall on your own heads."

Bowing before the supreme royalty of Jesus Christ, Luther spoke thus boldly to King Henry, who contested the rights of the word of God.

A letter written against the reformer was not enough for the bishops. Profiting by the wound Luther had inflicted on Henry's self-esteem, they urged him to put down this revolt of the human understanding, which threatened (as they averred) both the popedom and the monarchy. They commenced the persecution. Latimer was summoned before Wolsey, but his learning and presence of mind procured his dismissal. Bilney also, who had been ordered to London, received an injunction not to preach *Luther's doctrines.* " I will not preach Luther's doctrines, if there are any peculiar to him," he said ; "but I can and I must preach the doctrine of Jesus Christ, although Luther should preach it too." And finally Garret, led into the presence of his judges, was seized with terror, and fell before the cruel threats of the bishop. When restored to liberty, he fled from place to place,[1] endeavouring to hide his sorrow, and to escape from the despotism of the priests, awaiting the moment when he should give his life for Jesus Christ.

The adversaries of the Reformation were not yet satisfied. The New Testament continued to circulate, and depots were formed in several convents. Barnes, a prisoner in the Augustine monastery in London, had regained his courage, and loved his Bible more and more. One day about the end of September, as three or four friends were reading in his chamber, two simple peasants, John Tyball and Thomas Hilles, natives of Bumpstead in Essex, came in. " How did you come to a knowledge of the truth?" asked Barnes. They drew from their pockets some old volumes containing the Gospels, and a few of the Epistles in English. Barnes returned them with a smile. " They are nothing," he told them, " in comparison with the new edition of the New Testament,"[2] a copy of which the two peasants bought for three shillings and two-pence. " Hide it carefully," said Barnes. When this came to the ears of the clergy, Barnes was removed to Northampton to be burnt at the stake ; but he managed to escape ; his friends reported that he was drowned; and while strict search was making for him during a whole week along the sea-coast, he secretly went on board a ship, and was carried to Germany. " The cardinal will catch him even now," said the bishop of London, "whatever amount of money it may cost him." When Barnes was told of this, he remarked : " I am a poor simple wretch, not worth the tenth penny they will give for me. Besides, if they burn me, what will they gain by it?......The sun and the moon, fire and water, the stars and the elements—yea, and also stones shall defend this cause against them, *rather than the*

1 Tantus autor haberi postulas, quantus nec hodie quisquam sit. Cochlœus. p. 127.
2 Let it be as disgraceful to you to be praised by the vile, as if you were praised for vile deeds.
3 Rex Anglorum Regi hæreticorum scribit. Strype, Mem. i. p. 91. The title of the pamphlet was *Litterarum quibus invictus Pr. Henricus VIII. etc. etc. respondit ad quandam Epistolam M. Lutheri ad se missam.*
4 Als in tausend Jahren nicht gewesen ist. Luth. Opp. xix. p. 501.

1 Foxe, v. p. 428.
2 Which books he did little regard, and made a twit of it. Tybull's Confession in Bible Annals, i. p. 184.

truth should perish." Faith had returned to Barnes's feeble heart.

His escape added fuel to the wrath of the clergy. They proclaimed, throughout the length and breadth of England, that the Holy Scriptures contained an *infectious poison*,[1] and ordered a general search after the word of God. On the 24th of October 1526, the bishop of London enjoined on his archdeacons to seize all translations of the New Testament in English with or without glosses; and, a few days later, the archbishop of Canterbury issued a mandate against all the books which should contain "any particle of the New Testament."[2] The primate remembered that a spark was sufficient to kindle a large fire.

On hearing of this order, William Roy, a sarcastic writer, published a violent satire, in which figured *Judas* (Standish), *Pilate* (Wolsey), and *Caiaphas* (Tonstall.) The author exclaimed with energy:

> God, of his goodness, grudged not to die,
> Man to deliver from deadly damnation;
> Whose will is, that we should know perfectly
> What he here hath done for our salvation.
> O cruel Caiaphas! full of crafty conspiration,
> How durst thou give them false judgment
> To burn God's word—the Holy Testament.[3]

The efforts of Caiaphas and his colleagues were indeed useless: the priests were undertaking a work beyond their strength. If by some terrible revolution all social forms should be destroyed in the world, the living church of the elect, a divine institution in the midst of human institutions, would still exist by the power of God, like a rock in the midst of the tempest, and would transmit to future generations the seeds of Christian life and civilisation. It is the same with the word, the creative principle of the church. It cannot perish here below. The priests of England had something to learn on this matter.

While the agents of the clergy were carrying out the archiepiscopal mandate, and a merciless search was making everywhere for the New Testaments from Worms, a new edition was discovered, fresh from the press, of a smaller and more portable, and consequently more dangerous size. It was printed by Christopher Eyndhoven of Antwerp, who had consigned it to his correspondents in London. The annoyance of the priests was extreme, and Hackett, the agent of Henry VIII. in the low Countries, immediately received orders to get this man punished. "We cannot deliver judgment without inquiry into the matter," said the lords of Antwerp; "we will therefore have the book translated into Flemish." "God forbid," said Hackett in alarm, "What! would you also on your side of the ocean translate this book into the

language of the people?" "Well then," said one of the judges, less conscientious than his colleagues, "let the king of England send us a copy of each of the books he has burnt, and we will burn them likewise." Hackett wrote to Wolsey for them, and as soon as they arrived the court met again. Eyndhoven's counsel called upon the prosecutor to point out the *heresies* contained in the volume. The margrave (an officer of the imperial government) shrank from the task, and said to Hackett, "I give up the business!" The charge against Eyndhoven was dismissed.

Thus did the Reformation awaken in Europe the slumbering spirit of law and liberty. By enfranchising thought from the yoke of popery, it prepared the way for other enfranchisements; and by restoring the authority of the word of God, it brought back the reign of the law among nations long the prey of turbulent passions and arbitrary power. Then, as at all times, religious society forestalled civil society, and gave it those two great principles of order and liberty, which popery compromises or annuls. It was not in vain that the magistrates of a Flemish city, enlightened by the first dawn of the Reformation, set so noble an example; the English, who were very numerous in the Hanse Towns, thus learnt once more the value of that civil and religious liberty which is the time-honoured right of England, and of which they were in after-years to give other nations so much needed lessons.

"Well then," said Hackett, who was annoyed at their setting the law above his master's will, "I will go and buy all these books, and send them to the cardinal, that he may burn them." With these words he left the court. But his anger evaporating,[1] he set off for Malines to complain to the regent and her council of the Antwerp decision. "What!" said he, "you punish those who circulate false money, and you will not punish still more severely the man who coins it?—in this case, he is the printer." "But that is just the point in dispute," they replied: "we are not sure the money is *false*." —"How can it be otherwise?" answered Henry's agent, "since the bishops of England have declared it so?" The imperial government, which was not very favourably disposed towards England, ratified Eyndhoven's acquittal, but permitted Hackett to burn all the copies of the New Testament he could seize. He hastened to profit by this concession, and began hunting after the Holy Scriptures, while the priests eagerly came to his assistance. In their view, as well as in that of their English colleagues, the supreme decision in matter of faith rested not with the word of God but with the pope; and the best means of securing this privilege to the pontiff was to reduce the Bible to ashes.

[1] Libri pestiferum virus in se continentes, in promiscuam provinciæ Cant. multitudinem sunt dispersi. Wilkins, Concilia, iii. p. 706.

[2] Vel aliquam ejus particulam. Ibid.

[3] Satyre of W. Roy, printed in the Harl. Misc., vol. ix. p. 77, (ed. 18.9).

[1] My choler was descended. Anderson's Annals of the Bible, i. p. 129.

Notwithstanding these trials, the year 1526 was a memorable one for England. The English New Testament had been circulated from the shores of the Channel to the borders of Scotland, and the Reformation had begun in that island by the word of God. The revival of the sixteenth century was in no country less than in England the emanation of a royal mandate. But God, who had disseminated the Scriptures over Britain, in defiance of the rulers of the nation, was about to make use of their passions to remove the difficulties which opposed the final triumph of his plans. We here enter upon a new phasis in the history of the Reformation ; and having studied the work of God in the faith of the little ones, we proceed to contemplate the work of man in the intrigues of the great ones of the earth.

CHAPTER V.

Wolsey desires to be revenged—The Divorce suggested—Henry's Sentiments towards the Queen—Wolsey's first Steps—Longland's Proceedings—Refusal of Margaret of Valois—Objection of the Bishop of Tarbes—Henry's Uneasiness—Catherine's Alarm—Mission to Spain.

WOLSEY, mortified at not being able to obtain the pontifical throne, to which he had so ardently aspired, and being especially irritated by the ill-will of Charles V., meditated a plan which, entirely unsuspected by him, was to lead to the enfranchisement of England from the papal yoke. " They laugh at me, and thrust me into the second rank," he had exclaimed. " So be it ! I will create such a confusion in the world as has not been seen for ages......I will do it, even should England be swallowed up in the tempest ! "[1] Desirous of exciting imperishable hatred between Henry VIII. and Charles V., he had undertaken to break the marriage which Henry VII. and Ferdinand the Catholic had planned to unite for ever their families and their crowns. His hatred of Charles was not his only motive. Catherine had reproached him for his dissolute life,[2] and he had sworn to be revenged. There can be no doubt about Wolsey's share in the matter. " The *first terms* of the divorce were put forward by me," he told the French ambassador. " I did it," he added, " to cause a lasting separation between the houses of England and Burgundy."[3] The best informed writers of the sixteenth century, men of the most opposite parties, Pole, Polydore Virgil, Tyndale, Meteren, Pallavicini, Sanders, and Roper, More's son-in-law, all agree in pointing to Wolsey as the instigator of that divorce, which has be-

come so famous.[1] He desired to go still farther, and after inducing the king to put away his queen, he hoped to prevail on the pope to depose the emperor.[2] It was not his passion for Anne Boleyn, as so many of the Romish fabulists have repeated ; but the passion of a cardinal for the triple crown which gave the signal of England's emancipation. Offended pride is one of the most active principles of human nature.

Wolsey's design was a strange one, and difficult of execution, but not impossible. Henry was living apparently on the best terms with Catherine ; on more than one occasion Erasmus had spoken of the royal family of England as the pattern of the domestic virtues. But the most ardent of Henry's desires was not satisfied ; he had no son ; those whom the queen had borne him had died in their infancy, and Mary alone survived. The deaths of these little children, at all times so heart-rending, were particularly so in the palace of Greenwich. It appeared to Catherine that the shade of the last Plantagenet, immolated on her marriage altar, came forth to seize one after another the heirs she gave to the throne of England, and to carry them away to his tomb. The queen shed tears almost unceasingly, and implored the divine mercy, while the king cursed his unhappy fate. The people seemed to share in the royal sorrow ; and men of learning and piety (Longland was among their number)[3] declared against the validity of the marriage. They said that "the papal dispensations had no force even in opposition to the law of God." Yet hitherto Henry had rejected every idea of a divorce.[4]

The times had changed since 1509. The king had loved Catherine : her reserve, mildness, and dignity, had charmed him. Greedy of pleasure and applause, he was delighted to see his wife content to be the quiet witness of his joys and of his triumphs. But gradually the queen had grown older, her Spanish gravity had increased, her devout practices were multiplied, and her infirmities, become more frequent, had left the king no hope of having a son. From that hour, even while continuing to praise her virtues, Henry grew cold towards her person, and his love by degrees changed into repugnance. And then he thought that the death of his children might be a sign of God's anger. This idea had taken hold of him, and induced him to occupy apartments separate from the queen's.[5]

----

[1] Instigator et auctor concilii existimabatur (Pole, Apology). He was furious mad, and imagined this divorcement between the king and the queen (Tyndale's Works, i. p. 465. See also Sanderus, 7 and 9 ; Polyd. Virg. p. 685 ; Meteren, Hist. of the Low Countries, p. 20 ; Pallavicini, Conc. Trident. i. p. 203, etc. A contrary assertion of Wolsey's has been adduced against these authorities in the *Pamphleteer*, No. 42, p. 336 ; but a slight acquaintance with his history soon teaches us that veracity was the least of his virtues.
[2] Le Grand, Hist. du divorce, Preuves, p. 65, 69.
[3] Jampridem conjugium regium, veluti infirmum. Polyd. Virg. p. 685.
[4] That matrimony which the king at first seemed not disposed to annul. Strype, i. p. 135.
[5] Burnet. vol. i. p. 20 (London, 1841), Letter from Grynæus to Bucer. Strype, i. p. 135.

----

[1] Sandoval, i. p. 358. Ranke, Deutsche Gesch. iii. p. 17.
[2] Malos oderat mores. Polyd. Virg. p. 685.
[3] Le Grand, Hist. du divorce, Preuves, p. 186.

Wolsey judged the moment favourable for beginning the attack. It was in the latter months of 1526, when calling Longland, the king's confessor, to him, and concealing his principal motive, he said : " You know his majesty's anguish. The stability of his crown and his everlasting salvation seem to be compromised alike. To whom can I unbosom myself, if not to you, who must know the inmost secrets of his soul ? " The two bishops resolved to awaken Henry to the perils incurred by his union with Catherine;[1] but Longland insisted that Wolsey should take the first steps.

The cardinal waited upon the king, and reminded him of his scruples before the betrothal ; he exaggerated those entertained by the nation, and speaking with unusual warmth, he entreated the king to remain no longer in such danger :[2] " The holiness of your life and the legitimacy of your succession are at stake."—" My good father," said Henry, " you would do well to consider the weight of the stone that you have undertaken to move.[3] The queen is a woman of such exemplary life that I have no motive for separating from her."

The cardinal did not consider himself beaten ; three days later he appeared before the king accompanied by the bishop of Lincoln. " Most mighty prince," said the confessor, who felt bold enough to speak after the cardinal, " you cannot, like Herod, have your brother's wife.[4] I exhort and conjure you, as having the care of your soul,[5] to submit the matter to competent judges." Henry consented, and perhaps not unwillingly.

It was not enough for Wolsey to separate Henry from the emperor; he must, for greater security, unite him to Francis I. The King of England shall repudiate the aunt of Charles V., and then marry the sister of the French king. Proud of the success he had obtained in the first part of his plan, Wolsey entered upon the second. " There is a princess," he told the king, " whose birth, graces, and talents charm all Europe. Margaret of Valois, sister of King Francis, is superior to all of her sex, and no one is worthier of your alliance."[6] Henry made answer that it was a serious matter, requiring deliberate examination. Wolsey, however, placed in the king's hands a portrait of Margaret, and it has been imagined that he even privily caused her sentiments to be sounded. Be that as it may, the sister of Francis I. having learnt that she was pointed at as the future queen of England, rebelled at the idea of taking from an innocent woman a crown she had worn so nobly. " The

French king's sister knows too much of Christ to consent unto such wickedness," said Tyndale.[1] Margaret of Valois replied : " Let me hear no more of a marriage that can be effected only at the expense of Catherine of Aragon's happiness and life."[2] The woman who was destined in future years to fill the throne of England was then residing at Margaret's court. Shortly after this, on the 24th of January 1527, the sister of Francis I. married Henry d'Albret, king of Navarre.

Henry VIII., desirous of information with regard to his favourite's suggestion, commissioned Fox, his almoner, Pace, dean of St Paul's, and Wakefield, professor of Hebrew at Oxford, to study the passages of Leviticus and Deuteronomy which related to marriage with a brother's wife. Wakefield, who had no wish to commit himself, asked whether Henry was *for* or *against* the divorce.[3] Pace replied to this servile hebraist that the king wanted nothing but the truth.

But who would take the first public step in an undertaking so hazardous ? Every one shrank back ; the terrible emperor alarmed them all. It was a French bishop that hazarded the step ; bishops meet us at every turn in this affair of the divorce, with which bishops have so violently reproached the Reformation. Henry, desirous of excusing Wolsey, pretended afterwards that the objections of the French prelate had preceded those of Longland and the cardinal. In February 1527, Francis I. had sent an embassy to London, at the head of which was Gabriel de Grammont, bishop of Tarbes, with the intention to procure the hand of Mary of England. Henry's ministers having inquired whether the engagement of Francis with the queen dowager of Portugal did not oppose the commission with which the French bishop was charged, the latter answered : " I will ask you in turn what has been done to remove the impediments which opposed the marriage of which the Princess Mary is issue."[4] They laid before the ambassador the dispensation of Julius II., which he returned, saying, that the bull was not *sufficient*, seeing that such a marriage was forbidden *jure divino* ;[5] and he added : " Have you English a different gospel from ours ?[6]

The king, when he heard these words (as he informs us himself), was filled with fear

[1] Quamprimum regi patefaciendum. Polyd. Virg. p. 685.
[2] Vehementer orat ne se patiatur in tanto versari discrimine. Ibid.
[3] Bone pater, vide bene quale saxum suo loco jacens movere coneris. Ibid.
[4] Like another Herodes. More's Life, p 129.
[5] Ipse cui de salute animæ tuæ cura est, *hortor, rogo, persuadeo.* Polyd. Virg. p. 686.
[6] Mulier præter cæteras digna matrimonio tuo. Ibid.

[1] Works (ed. Russell), vol. i. p. 464.
[2] Princeps illa, mulier optima, noluerit quicquam audire de nuptiis, quæ nuptiæ non possunt conjungi sine miserabili Catharinæ casu atque adeo interitu. Polyd. Virg. p. 687.
[3] Utrum staret ad te an contra te? Le Grand, Preuves, p. 2.
[4] What had been here provided for taking away the impediment of that marriage. (State Papers, i. p. 199.) Le Grand (vol. i. p. 17.) discredits the objections of the bishop of Tarbes ; but this letter from Wolsey to Henry VIII. establishes them incontrovertibly. And besides, Du Bellay, in a letter afterwards quoted by Le Grand himself, states the matter still more strongly than Wolsey.
[5] Wherewith the pope could not dispense, *nisi ex urgentissima causa.* Wolsey to Henry VIII., dated 6th July. State Papers, vol. i. p. 199.
[6] Anglos, qui tuo imperio subsunt, hoc idem evangelium colere quod nos colimus. Sanders, 12.

and horror.[1] Three of the most respected bishops of Christendom united to accuse him of incest! He began to speak of it to certain individuals : "The scruples of my conscience have been terribly increased (he said) since the bishop spoke of this matter before my council in exceedingly plain words."[2] There is no reason to believe that these *terrible* troubles of which the king speaks were a mere invention on his part. A disputed succession might again plunge England into civil war. Even if no pretenders should spring up, might they not see a rival house, a French prince for instance, wedded to Henry's daughter, reigning over England ? The king, in his anxiety, had recourse to his favourite author, Thomas Aquinas, and this *angel of the schools* declared his marriage unlawful. Henry next opened the Bible, and found this threat against the man who took his brother's wife: " He shall be *childless !* " The denunciation increased his trouble, for he had no heir. In the midst of this darkness a new perspective opened before him. His conscience might be unbound ; his desire to have a younger wife might be gratified ; he might have a son ! ......The king resolved to lay the matter before a commission of lawyers, and this commission soon wrote volumes.[3]

During all this time Catherine, suspecting no evil, was occupied in her devotions. Her heart, bruised by the death of her children and by the king's coldness, sought consolation in prayer both privately and in the royal chapel. She would rise at midnight and kneel down upon the cold stones, and never missed any of the canonical services. But one day (probably in May or June 1527) some officious person informed her of the rumours circulating in the city and at court. Bursting with anger and alarm, and all in tears, she hastened to the king, and addressed him with the bitterest complaints.[4] Henry was content to calm her by vague assurances ; but the unfeeling Wolsey, troubling himself still less than his master about Catherine's emotion, called it, with a smile, " a short tragedy."

The offended wife lost no time : it was necessary that the emperor should be informed promptly, surely, and accurately of this unprecedented insult. A letter would be insufficient, even were it not intercepted. Catherine therefore determined to send her servant Francis Philip, a Spaniard, to her nephew ; and to conceal the object of his journey, they proceeded, after the *tragedy*, to play a *comedy* in the Spanish style. " My mother is sick and desires to see me," said Philip. Catherine begged the king to refuse her servant's

prayer; and Henry, divining the stratagem, resolved to employ trick against trick.[1] " Philip's request is very proper," he made answer, and Catherine, *from regard to her husband*, consented to his departure. Henry meantime had given orders that, " notwithstanding any safe conduct, the said Philip should be arrested and detained at Calais, in such a manner, however, that no one should know whence the stoppage proceeded."

It was to no purpose that the queen indulged in a culpable dissimulation ; a poisoned arrow had pierced her heart, and her words, her manners, her complaints, her tears, the numerous messages she sent, now to one and now to another, betrayed the secret which the king wished still to conceal.[2] Her friends blamed her for this publicity ; men wondered what Charles would say when he heard of his aunt's distress ; they feared that peace would be broken ; but Catherine, whose heart was " rent in twain," was not to be moved by diplomatic considerations. Her sorrow did not check Henry ; with the two motives which made him eager for a divorce—the scruples of his conscience and the desire of an heir— was now combined a third still more forcible. A woman was about to play an important part in the destinies of England.

CHAPTER VI.

Anne Boleyn appointed Maid of Honour to Catherine— Lord Percy becomes attached to her—Wolsey separates them—Anne enters Margaret's Household—Siege of Rome ; Cromwell—Wolsey's Intercession for the Popedom —He demands the Hand of Renée of France for Henry— Failure—Anne reappears at Court—Repels the King's Advances—Henry's Letter—He resolves to accelerate the Divorce—Two Motives which induce Anne to refuse the Crown—Wolsey's Opposition.

ANNE BOLEYN, who had been placed by her father at the court of France, had returned to England with Sir Thomas, then ambassador at Paris, at the time that an English army made an incursion into Normandy (1522). It would appear that she was presented to the queen about this period, and appointed one of Catherine's maids of honour. The following year was a memorable one to her from her first sorrow.

Among the young noblemen in the cardinal's household was Lord Percy, eldest son of the Earl of Northumberland. While Wolsey was closeted with the king, Percy was accustomed to resort to the queen's apartments, where he passed the time among her ladies. He soon felt a sincere passion for Anne, and the young maid of honour, who had been cold to the addresses of the gentle-

[1] Quæ oratio quanto metu ac horrore animum nostrum turbaverit. Henry's speech to the Lord Mayor and common council at his palace of Bridewell, 8th November 1528. Hall, p. 754 ; Wilkins, Concili. iii. p. 714.
[2] Du Bellay's letter in Le Grand. Preuves, p. 218.
[3] So as the books excrescunt in magna volumina. Wolsey to Henry VIII. State Papers, vol. i. p. 200.
[4] The queen hath broken with your grace thereof. Ibid.

[1] The king's highness knowing great collusion and dissimulation between them, doth also dissemble. Knight to Wolsey. State Papers, vol. i. p. 215.
[2] By her behaviour, manner, words, and messages sent to diverse, hath published, divulged, &c. Ibid. p. 280.

men at the court of Francis, replied to the affections of the heir of Northumberland. The two young people already indulged in day-dreams of a quiet, elegant, and happy life in their noble castles of the north; but such dreams were fated to be of short duration.

Wolsey hated the Norfolks, and consequently the Boleyns. It was to counterbalance their influence that he had been first introduced at court. He became angry, therefore, when he saw one of his household suing for the hand of the daughter and niece of his enemies. Besides, certain partisans of the clergy accused Anne of being friendly to the Reformation.[1]......It is generally believed that even at this period Wolsey had discovered Henry's eyes turned complacently on the young maid of honour, and that this induced him to thwart Percy's love; but this seems improbable. Of all the women in England, Anne was the one whose influence Wolsey would have had most cause to fear, and he really did fear it; and he would have been but too happy to see her married to Percy. It has been asserted that Henry prevailed on the cardinal to thwart the affection of the two young people; but in that case did he confide to Wolsey the real motive of his opposition? Did the latter entertain criminal intentions? Did he undertake to yield up to dishonour the daughter and niece of his political adversaries? This would be horrible, but it is possible, and may even be deduced from Cavendish's narrative; yet we will hope that it was not so. If it were, Anne's virtue successfully baffled the infamous plot.

But be that as it may, one day when Percy was in attendance upon the cardinal, the latter rudely addressed him: "I marvel at your folly, that you should attempt to contract yourself with that girl without your father's or the king's consent. I command you to break with her." Percy burst into tears, and besought the cardinal to plead his cause. "I charge you to resort no more into her company," was Wolsey's cold reply,[2] after which he rose up and left the room. Anne received an order at the same time to leave the court. Proud and bold, and ascribing her misfortune to Wolsey's hatred, she exclaimed as she quitted the palace, "I will be revenged for this insult." But she had scarcely taken up her abode in the gothic halls of Hever Castle, when news still more distressing overwhelmed her. Percy was married to Lady Mary Talbot. She wept long and bitterly, and vowed against the young nobleman who had deserted her a contempt equal to her hatred of the cardinal. Anne was reserved for a more illustrious, but more unhappy fate.

This event necessarily rendered her residence in this country far from attractive to Anne Boleyn. "She did not stay long in England," says Burnet, following Camden; "she served queen Claude of France till her death, and after that she was taken into service by King Francis' sister." Anne Boleyn, lady-in-waiting to Margaret of Valois, was consoled at last. She indulged in gaieties with all the vivacity of her age, and glittered among the youngest and the fairest at all the court festivities.

In Margaret's house she met the most enlightened men of the age, and her understanding and heart were developed simultaneously with the graces. She began to read, without thoroughly understanding it, the holy book in which her mistress (as Brantome informs us) found consolation and repose, and to direct a few light and passing thoughts to that "mild Emmanuel" to whom Margaret addressed such beautiful verses.

At last Anne returned definitively to England. It has been asserted that the queen-regent, fearing that Henry after the battle of Pavia would invade France, had sent Anne to London to dissuade him from it. But it was a stronger voice than hers which stopped the king of England. "Remain quiet," wrote Charles V. to him: "I have the stag in my net, and we have only to think of sharing the spoils." Margaret of Valois having married the king of Navarre at the end of January 1527, and quitted Paris and her brother's court, it is supposed that Sir Thomas Boleyn, who was unwilling that his daughter should take up her abode in the Pyrenees, recalled her to England probably in the winter or spring of the same year. "There is not the least evidence that she came to it earlier," says a modern author.[1] She appeared once more at court, and the niece of the Duke of Norfolk soon eclipsed her companions, "by her excellent gesture and behaviour,"[2] as we learn from a contemporary unfriendly to the Boleyns. All the court was struck by the regularity of her features, the expression of her eyes, the gentleness of her manners, and the majesty of her carriage.[3] "She was a beautiful creature," says an old historian, "well proportioned, courteous, amiable, very agreeable, and a skilful musician."[4]

While entertainments were following close upon each other at the court of Henry VIII., a strange rumour filled all England with surprise. It was reported that the imperialist soldiers had taken Rome by assault, and that some Englishmen were among those who had mounted the breach. One Thomas Cromwell was specially named[5]—the man who nearly twenty years before had obtained certain indulgences from Julius II., by offering

[1] Meteren's Hist of the Low Countries, folio. 2).
[2] Cavendish's Wolsey, p. 123. Cavendish was present at this conversation.

[1] Turner. Hist. Henry VIII. ii. p. 185.
[2] Cavendish's Life of Wolsey, p. 120.
[3] Memoirs of Sir Thomas Wyatt, in Cavendish's Life of Wolsey, p. 424.
[4] Meteren's Hist. of the Low Countries, folio, 20.
[5] Foxe, vol. v. p. 365.

him some jars of English confectionary. This soldier carried with him the New Testament of Erasmus, and he is said to have learned it by heart during the campaign. Being gay, brave, and intelligent, he entertained, from reading the gospel and seeing Rome, a great aversion for the policy, superstitions, and disorders of the popedom. The day of the 7th May 1527 decided the tenor of his life. To destroy the papal power became his dominant idea. On returning to England he entered the cardinal's household.

However, the captive pope and cardinals wrote letters "filled with tears and groans."[1] Full of zeal for the papacy, Wolsey ordered a public fast. "The Emperor will never release the pope, unless he be compelled," he told the king. "Sir, God has made you *defender of the faith;* save the church and its head!"—"My Lord," answered the king with a smile, "I assure you that this war between the emperor and the pope is not for the faith, but for temporal possessions and dominions."

But Wolsey would not be discouraged; and, on the 3d of July, he passed through the streets of London, riding a richly caparisoned mule, and resting his feet on gilt stirrups, while twelve hundred gentlemen accompanied him on horseback. He was going to entreat Francis to aid his master in saving Clement VII. He had found no difficulty in prevailing upon Henry; Charles talked of carrying the pope to Spain, and of permanently establishing the apostolic see in that country.[2] Now, how could they obtain the divorce from a *Spanish* pope? During the procession, Wolsey seemed oppressed with grief, and even shed tears;[3] but he soon raised his head and exclaimed: My heart is inflamed, and I wish that it may be said of the pope *per secula sempiterna.*

"Rediit Henrici octavi virtute serena."

Desirous of forming a close union between France and England for the accomplishment of his designs, he had cast his eyes on the princess Renée, daughter of Louis XII., and sister-in-law to Francis I., as the future wife of Henry VIII. Accordingly the treaty of alliance between the two crowns having been signed at Amiens on the 18th of August (1527), Francis, with his mother and the cardinal, proceeded to Compiègne, and there Wolsey, styling Charles the most obstinate defender of Lutheranism,[4] promising "perpetual *conjunction* on the one hand [between France and England], and perpetual *disjunction* on the other" [between England and Germany],[5] demanded Renée's hand for King

Henry. Staffileo, dean of Rota, affirmed that the pope had been able to permit the marriage between Henry and Catherine only by an error of the keys of St Peter.[1] This avowal, so remarkable on the part of the dean of one of the first jurisdictions of Rome, induced Francis' mother to listen favourably to the cardinal's demand. But whether this proposal was displeasing to Renée, who was destined on a future day to profess the pure faith of the Gospel with greater earnestness than Margaret of Valois, or whether Francis was not over-anxious for a union that would have given Henry rights over the duchy of Brittany, she was promised to the son of the Duke of Ferrara. It was a check to the cardinal; but it was his ill fortune to receive one still more severe on his return to England.

The daughter of Sir Thomas Boleyn, (who had been created Viscount Rochford in 1525,) was constantly at court, "where she flourished in great estimation and favour,"says Cavendish, "having always a private indignation against the cardinal for breaking off the precontract made between Lord Percy and her," little suspecting that Henry had had any share in it.[2] Her beauty, her graceful carriage, her black hair, oval face, and bright eyes, her sweet voice in singing, her skill and dignity in the dance, her desire to please which was not entirely devoid of coquetry, her sprightliness, the readiness of her repartees, and above all the amiability of her character, won every heart. She brought to Greenwich and to London the polished manners of the court of Francis I. Every day (it was reported) she invented a new style of dress, and set the fashion in England. But to all these qualities, she added modesty, and even imposed it on others by her example. The ladies of the court, who had hitherto adopted a different fashion (says her greatest enemy), covered the neck and bosom as she did;[3] and the malicious, unable to appreciate Anne's motives, ascribed this modesty on the young lady's part to a desire to hide a secret deformity.[4] Numerous admirers once more crowded round Anne Boleyn, and among others, one of the most illustrious noblemen and poets of England, Sir Thomas Wyatt, a follower of Wickliffe. He, however, was not the man destined to replace the son of the Percies.

Henry, absorbed in anxiety about his divorce from Catherine, had become low-spirited and melancholy. The laughter, songs, repartees, and beauty of Anne Boleyn struck

---

1 Plenas lacrymarum et miseriæ. State Papers, vol. i.
2 The see apostolic should perpetually remain in Spain. Ibid. p. 227.
3 I saw the lord cardinal weep very tenderly. Cavendish, p. 151.
4 Omnium maxime dolosus et hæresis Lutheranæ fautor acerrimus. State Papers, i. p. 274.
5 Du Bellay to Montmorency. Le Grand, Preuves, i. p. 186.

1 Nisi clave errante. State Papers, i. p. 272.
2 For all this while she knew nothing of the king's intended purpose, said one of his adversaries. Cavendish's Wolsey, p. 129.
3 Ad illius imitationem reliquæ regiæ ancillæ colli et pectoris superiora, quæ antea · nuda gestabant, operire cœperunt. Sanders, p. 16.
4 See Sanders, ibid. It is useless to refute Sanders' stories. We refer our readers to Burnet's Hist. of the Reformation, to Lord Herbert's Life of Henry VIII., to Wyatt, and others. We need only read Sanders to estimate at their true value *the foul calumnies*, as these writers term them, of the man whom they style *the Roman legendary.*

and captivated him, and his eyes were soon fixed complacently on the young maid of honour. Catherine was more than forty years old, and it was hardly to be expected that so susceptible a man as Henry would have made, as Job says, *a covenant with his eyes not to think upon a maid.* Desirous of showing his admiration, he presented Anne, according to usage, with a costly jewel; she accepted and wore it, and continued to dance, laugh, and chatter as before, without attaching particular importance to the royal present. Henry's attentions became more continuous; and he took advantage of a moment when he found Anne alone to declare his sentiments. With mingled emotion and alarm, the young lady fell trembling at the king's feet, and exclaimed, bursting into tears: "I think, most noble and worthy king, your majesty speaks these words in mirth to prove me......I will rather lose my life than my virtue."[1] Henry gracefully replied, that he should at least continue to hope. But Anne, rising up, proudly made answer: "I understand not, most mighty king, how you should retain any such hope; your wife I cannot be, both in respect of mine own unworthiness, and also because you have a queen already. Your mistress I will not be." Anne kept her word. She continued to show the king, even after this interview, all the respect that was due to him; but on several occasions she proudly, violently even, repelled his advances.[2] In this age of gallantry, we find her resisting for nearly six years all the seductions Henry scattered round her. Such an example is not often met with in the history of courts. The books she had read in Margaret's palace gave her a secret strength. All looked upon her with respect; and even the queen treated her with politeness. Catherine showed, however, that she had remarked the king's preference. One day, as she was playing at cards with her maid of honour, while Henry was in the room, Anne frequently holding the *king*, she said: "My Lady Anne, you have good hap to stop ever at a *king;* but you are not like others, you will have all or none." Anne blushed: from that moment Henry's attentions acquired more importance; she resolved to withdraw from them, and quitted the court with Lady Rochford.

The king, who was not accustomed to resistance, was extremely grieved: and having learnt that Anne would not return to the court either with or without her mother, sent a courier to Hever with a message and a letter for her. If we recollect the manners of the age of Henry VIII. and how far the men, in their relations with the gentler sex, were strangers to that reserve which society now imposes upon them, we cannot but be struck by the king's respectful tone: He writes thus in French:—

"As the time seems to me very long since I heard from you or concerning your health, the great love I have for you has constrained me to send this bearer to be better informed both of your health and pleasure; particularly, because since my last parting with you, I have been told that you have entirely changed the mind in which I left you, and that you neither mean to come to court with your mother nor any other way, which report, if true, I cannot enough marvel at, being persuaded in my own mind that I have never committed any offence against you; and it seems hard, in return for the great love I bear you, to be kept at a distance from the person and presence of the woman in the world that I value the most. And if you love me with as much affection as I hope you do, I am sure the distance of our two persons would be equally irksome to you, though this does not belong so much to the mistress as to the servant.

"Consider well, my mistress, how greatly your absence afflicts me. I hope it is not your will that it should be so; but if I heard for certain that you yourself desired it, I could but mourn my ill-fortune, and strive by degrees to abate of my great folly.

"And so for lack of time I make an end of this rude letter, beseeching you to give the bearer credence in all he will tell you from me. Written by the hand of your entire servant,

"H. R."[1]

The word *servant* (serviteur) employed in this letter explains the sense in which Henry used the word *mistress.* In the language of chivalry, the latter term expressed a person to whom the lover had surrendered his heart.

It would seem that Anne's reply to this letter was the same she had made to the king from the very first; and Cardinal Pole mentions more than once her obstinate refusal of an adulterous love.[2] At last Henry understood Anne's virtue; but he was far from *abating of his great folly,* as he had promised. That tyrannical selfishness, which the prince often displayed in his life, was shown particularly in his amours. Seeing that he could not attain his end by illegitimate means, he determined to break, as quickly as possible, the bonds which united him to the queen. Anne's virtue was the third cause of Henry's divorce.

His resolution being once taken, it must needs be carried out. Henry having succeeded in bringing Anne back to court, pro-

---

[1] Sloane MSS., No. 2495; Turner's Hist. Eng. ii. p. 196.
[2] Tanto vehementius preces regias illa repulit. Sanders, p. 17.

[1] Pamphleteer, No. 42, p. 347. It is difficult to fix the order and chronology of Henry's letters to Anne Boleyn. This is the second in the Vatican Collection, but it appears to us to be of older date. It is considered as written in May 1528; we are inclined to place it in the autumn of 1527. The originals of these letters, chiefly in old French, are still preserved in the Vatican, having been stolen from the royal cabinet and conveyed thither.
[2] Concubina enim tua fieri pudica mulier nolebat, uxor volebat. Illa cujus amore rex deperibat, pertinacissime negabat sui corporis potestatem. Polus ad Regem, p. 176. Cardinal Pole is a far more trustworthy authority than Sanders.

cured a private interview with her, offered her his crown, and seizing her hand, took off one of her rings. But Anne, who would not be the king's mistress, refused also to be his wife. The glory of a crown could not dazzle her, said Wyatt, and two motives in particular counterbalanced all the prospects of greatness which were set before her eyes. The first was her respect for the queen : "How could I injure a princess of such great virtue ? " she exclaimed.[1] The second was the fear that a union with " one that was her lord and her king," would not give her that freedom of heart and that liberty which she would enjoy by marrying a man of the same rank with herself.[2]

Yet the noblemen and ladies of Henry's court whispered to one another that Anne would certainly become queen of England. Some were tormented by jealousy : others, her friends, were delighted at the prospect of a rapid advancement. Wolsey's enemies in particular were charmed at the thought of ruining the favourite. It was at the very moment when all these emotions were so variously agitating the court that the cardinal, returning from his embassy to Francis, reappeared in London, where an unexpected blow struck him.

Wolsey was expressing his grief to Henry at having failed in obtaining either Margaret or Renée for him, when the king interrupted him : " Console yourself, I shall marry Anne Boleyn." The cardinal remained speechless for a moment. What would become of him, if the king placed the crown of England on the head of the daughter and niece of his greatest enemies? What would become of the church, if a second Anne of Bohemia should ascend the throne? Wolsey threw himself at the feet of his master, and entreated him to renounce so fatal a project.[3] It was then no doubt that he remained (as he afterwards said) an hour or two on his knees before the king in his privy chamber,[4] but without prevailing on Henry to give up his design. Wolsey, persuaded that if he continued openly to oppose Henry's will, he would for ever lose his confidence, dissembled his vexation, waiting an opportunity to get rid of this unfortunate rival by some intrigue. He began by writing to the pope, informing him that a young lady, brought up by the queen of Navarre, and consequently tainted by the Lutheran heresy, had captivated the king's heart ; [5] and from that hour Anne Boleyn became the object of the hatred and calumnies of Rome. But at the same time, to conceal his intentions, Wolsey received Henry at a series of splendid entertainments, at which Anne outshone all the ladies of the court.

CHAPTER VII.

Bilney's Preaching—His Arrest—Arthur's Preaching and Imprisonment—Bilney's Examination—Contest between the Judge and the Prisoner—Bilney's Weakness and Fall —His Terrors—Two Wants—Arrival of the Fourth Edition of the New Testament—Joy among the Believers.

WHILE these passions were agitating Henry's palace. the most moving scenes, produced by Christian faith, were stirring the nation. Bilney, animated by that courage which God sometimes gives to the weakest men, seemed to have lost his natural timidity, and preached for a time with an energy quite apostolic. He taught that all men should first acknowledge their sins and condemn them, and then hunger and thirst after that righteousness which Jesus Christ gives.[1] To this testimony borne to the truth. he added his testimony against error. " These five hundred years," he added, " there hath been no good pope ; and in all the times past we can find but fifty : for they have neither preached nor lived well, nor conformably to their dignity ; wherefore, unto this day, they have borne the keys of simony."[2]

As soon as he descended from the pulpit, this pious scholar, with his friend Arthur, visited the neighbouring towns and villages. " The Jews and Saracens would long ago have become believers," he once said at Wilsdon, " had it not been for the idolatry of Christian men in offering candles, wax, and money to stocks and stones." One day when he visited Ipswich, where there was a Franciscan convent, he exclaimed : " The cowl of St Francis wrapped round a dead body hath no power to take away sins...... *Ecce agnus Dei qui tollit peccata mundi.*" (John i. 29.) The poor monks, who were little versed in Scripture, had recourse to the *Almanac* to convict the *Bible* of error. " St Paul did rightly affirm," said Friar John Brusierd, " that there is but one mediator of God and man, because as yet there was no *saint* canonized or put into the calendar."— " Let us ask of the Father in the name of the Son," rejoined Bilney, " and he will give unto us."—" You are always speaking of the Father and never of the *saints*," replied the friar ; " you are like a man who has been looking so long upon the sun, that he can see nothing else."[3] As he uttered these words the monk seemed bursting with anger. " If I did not know that the *saints* would take everlasting vengeance upon you, I would surely with these nails of mine be your death."[4] Twice in fact did two monks pull him out of his pulpit. He was arrested and taken to London.

Arthur, instead of fleeing, began to visit the flocks which his friend had converted. " Good people," said he, " if I should suffer persecution for the preaching of the gospel,

[1] The love she bare even to the queen whom she served. that was also a personage of great virtue. Wyatt, Mem. of A. B. p. 428.   [2] Ibid.
[3] Whose persuasion to the contrary, made to the king upon his knees. Cavendish, p. 204.   [4] Ibid p. 388.
[5] Meteren, Hist. of the Low Countries, folio, 20.

[1] Ut omnes primum peccata sua agnoscant et damnent, deinde esuirant et sitiant justitiam illam. Foxe, iv. p. 634.   [2] Ibid. p. 627.   [3] Ibid. p. 629.   [4] Ibid. p. 630.

there are seven thousand more that would preach it as I do now. Therefore, good people! good people!" (and he repeated these words several times in a sorrowful voice) "think not that if these tyrants and persecutors put a man to death, the preaching of the gospel therefore is to be forsaken. Every Christian man, yea every layman, is a priest. Let our adversaries preach by the authority of the cardinal; others by the authority of the university; others by the pope's; we will preach by the authority of God. It is not the man who brings the word that saves the soul, but the word which the man brings. Neither bishops nor popes have the right to forbid any man to preach the gospel;[1] and if they kill him he is not a heretic but a martyr."[2] The priests were horrified at such doctrines. In their opinion, there was no God out of their church, no salvation out of their sacrifices. Arthur was thrown into the same prison as Bilney.

On the 27th of November 1527 the cardinal and the archbishop of Canterbury, with a great number of bishops, divines, and lawyers, met in the chapter-house of Westminster, when Bilney and Arthur were brought before them. But the king's prime minister thought it beneath his dignity to occupy his time with miserable heretics. Wolsey had hardly commenced the examination, when he rose, saying: "The affairs of the realm call me away; all such as are found guilty, you will compel them to abjure, and those who rebel you will deliver over to the secular power." After a few questions proposed by the bishop of London, the two accused men were led back to prison.

Abjuration or death—that was Wolsey's order. But the conduct of the trial was confided to Tonstall; Bilney conceived some hope.[3] "Is it possible," he said to himself, "that the bishop of London, the friend of Erasmus, will gratify the monks?......I must tell him that it was the Greek Testament of his learned master that led me to the faith." Upon which the humble evangelist having obtained paper and ink, set about writing to the bishop from his gloomy prison those admirable letters which have been transmitted to posterity. Tonstall, who was not a cruel man, was deeply moved, and then a strange struggle took place: a judge wishing to save the prisoner, the prisoner desiring to give up his life. Tonstall, by acquitting Bilney, had no desire to compromise himself. "Submit to the church," said the bishop, "for God speaks only through it." But Bilney, who knew that God speaks in the Scriptures, remained inflexible. "Very well, then," said Tonstall, taking up the prisoner's eloquent letters, "in discharge of my conscience I shall lay these letters before the court." He hoped,

perhaps, that they would touch his colleagues, but he was deceived. He determined, therefore, to make a fresh attempt. On the 4th of December, Bilney was brought again before the court. "Abjure your errors," said Tonstall. Bilney refusing by a shake of the head, the bishop continued: "Retire into the next room and consider." Bilney withdrew, and returning shortly after with joy beaming in his eyes, Tonstall thought he had gained the victory. "You will return to the church, then?" said he........ The doctor answered calmly: "Fiat judicium in nomine Domini."[1] "Be quick," continued the bishop, "this is the last moment, and you will be condemned." "Hæc est dies quam fecit Dominus," answered Bilney, "exultemus et lætemur in ea!" (Ps. cxviii. 24). Upon this Tonstall took off his cap, and said: "In nomine Patris et Filii et Spiritus Sancti......Exsurgat Deus et dissipentur inimici ejus!" (Ps. lxviii. 1). Then making the sign of the cross on his forehead and on his breast, he gave judgment: "Thomas Bilney, I pronounce thee convicted of heresy." He was about to name the penalty......a last hope restrained him; he stopped: "For the rest of the sentence we take deliberation until to-morrow." Thus was the struggle prolonged between two men, one of whom desired to walk to the stake, the other to bar the way as it were with his own body.

"Will you return to the unity of the church?" asked Tonstall the next day. "I hope I was never separated from the church," answered Bilney. "Go and consult with some of your friends," said the bishop, who was resolved to save his life; "I will give you till one o'clock in the afternoon." In the afternoon Bilney made the same answer. "I will give you two nights' respite to deliberate," said the bishop; "on Saturday at nine o'clock in the forenoon, the court will expect a plain definitive answer." Tonstall reckoned on the night with its dreams, its anguish, and its terrors, to bring about Bilney's recantation.

This extrordinary struggle occupied many minds both in court and city. Anne Boleyn and Henry VIII. watched with interest the various phases of this tragic history. What will happen? was the general question. Will he give way? Shall we see him live or die? One day and two nights still remained; everything was tried to shake the Cambridge doctor. His friends crowded to his prison; he was overwhelmed with arguments and examples; but an inward struggle, far more terrible than those without, agitated the pious Bilney. "Whoever will save his soul shall lose it," Christ had said. That selfish love of his soul, which is found even in the advanced Christian,—that self, which after his conversion had been not absorbed, but overruled by the Spirit of God, gradually recovered strength in his heart, in the presence of

[1] Foxe, iv. p 623.
[2] Collyer's Church History, vol. ii. p. 26.
[3] In talem nunc me judicem incidisse gratulor. Foxe, iv. p. 633.

[1] Let judgment be done in the name of the Lord.

disgrace and death. His friends who wished to save him, not understanding that the fallen Bilney would be Bilney no longer, conjured him with tears to have pity on himself; and by these means his firmness was overcome. The bishop pressed him, and Bilney asked himself: " Can a young soldier like me know the rules of war better than an old soldier like Tonstall? Or can a poor silly sheep know his way to the fold better than the chief pastor of London?"[1] His friends quitted him neither night nor day, and entangled by their fatal affection, he believed at last that he had found a compromise which would set his conscience at rest. "I will preserve my life," he said, " to dedicate it to the Lord." This delusion had scarcely laid hold of his mind before his views were confused, his faith was veiled, the Holy Ghost departed from him, God gave him over to his carnal thoughts, and under the pretext of being useful to Jesus Christ for many years, Bilney disobeyed him at the present moment. Being led before the bishops on the morning of Saturday the 7th of December, at nine o'clock, he fell......(Arthur had fallen before him), and whilst the false friends who had misled him hardly dared raise their eyes, the living church of Christ in England uttered a cry of anguish. " If ever you come in danger," said Latimer, " for God's quarrel, I would advise you, above all things, to abjure all your friendships; leave not one unabjured. It is they that shall undo you, and not your enemies. It was his very friends that brought Bilney to it."[2]

On the following day (Sunday, 8th December) Bilney was placed at the head of a procession, and the fallen disciple, bareheaded, with a fagot on his shoulders, stood in front of St Paul's cross, while a priest from the pulpit exhorted him to repentance; after which he was led back to prison.

What a solitude for the wretched man! At one time the cold darkness of his cell appeared to him as a burning fire; at another he fancied he heard accusing voices crying to him in the silence of the night. Death, the very enemy he had wished to avoid, fixed his icy glance upon him and filled him with fear. He strove to escape from the horrible spectre, but in vain. Then the friends who had dragged him into this abyss, crowded round and endeavoured to console him; but if they gave utterance to any of Christ's gentle promises, Bilney started back with affright and shrank to the farthest part of the dungeon, with a cry "as though a man had run him through the heart with a sword."[3] Having denied the word of God, he could no longer endure to hear it. The curse of the Apocalypse : *Ye mountains, hide me from the wrath of the Lamb!* was the only passage of Scripture in harmony with his soul. His mind wandered, the blood froze in his veins, he

sank under his terrors; he lost all sense, and almost his life, and lay motionless in the arms of his astonished friends " God," exclaimed those unhappy individuals who had caused his fall, " God, by a just judgment, delivers up to the tempests of their conscience all who deny his truth."

This was not the only sorrow of the church. As soon as Richard Bayfield, the late chamberlain of Bury, had joined Tyndale and Fryth, he said to them : " 1 am at your disposal; you shall be my head and I will be your hand; I will sell your books and those of the German reformers in the Low Countries, France, and England." It was not long indeed before he returned to London. But Pierson, the priest whom he had formerly met in Lombard Street, found him again, and accused him to the bishop. The unhappy man was brought before Tonstall. " You are charged," said the prelate, " with having asserted that praise is due to God alone, and not to saints or creatures."[1] Bayfield acknowledged the charge to be true. " You are accused of maintaining that every priest may preach the word of God by the authority of the gospel without the license of the pope or cardinals." This also Bayfield acknowledged. A penance was imposed on him ; and then he was sent back to his monastery with orders to show himself there on the 25th of April. But he crossed the sea once more, and hastened to join Tyndale.

The New Testaments, however, sold by him and others remained in England. At that time the bishops subscribed to suppress the Scriptures, as so many persons have since done to circulate them ; and, accordingly, a great number of the copies brought over by Bayfield and his friends were bought up.[2] A scarcity of food was erelong added to the scarcity of the word of God ; for as the cardinal was endeavouring to foment a war between Henry and the emperor, the Flemish ships ceased to enter the English ports. It was in consequence of this that the lord mayor and aldermen of London hastened to express their apprehensions to Wolsey almost before he had recovered from the fatigues of his return from France. " Fear nothing," he told them ; " the king of France assured me, that if he had three bushels of wheat, England should have two of them." But none arrived, and the people were on the point of breaking out into violence, when a fleet of ships suddenly appeared off the mouth of the Thames. They were German and Flemish vessels laden with corn, in which the worthy people of the Low Countries had also concealed the New Testament. An Antwerp bookseller, named John Raimond or Ruremond, from his birthplace, had printed a fourth edition more beautiful than the previous ones. It was enriched with references and engravings on wood, and each page bordered with

[1] Foxe, iv. p. 638.
[2] Latimer's Sermons (Parker Society), p. 222.   [3] Ibid.
[1] That all laud and praise should be given to God alone, Foxe. iv. p. 682.
[2] Anderson, Annals of the Bible, i. p. 158.

red lines. Raimond himself had embarked on board one of the ships with five hundred copies of his New Testament.[1] About Christmas 1527, the book of God was circulated in England along with the bread that nourishes the body. But certain priests and monks having discovered the Scriptures among the sacks of corn, they carried several copies to the bishop of London, who threw Raimond into prison. The greater part, however, of the new edition escaped him. The New Testament was read everywhere, and even the court did not escape the contagion. Anne Boleyn, notwithstanding her smiling face, often withdrew to her closet at Greenwich or at Hampton Court, to study the gospel. Frank, courageous, and proud, she did not conceal the pleasure she found in such reading; her boldness astonished the courtiers, and exasperated the clergy. In the city things went still farther: the New Testament was explained in frequent conventicles, particularly in the house of one Russell, and great was the joy among the faithful. "It is sufficient only to enter London," said the priests, "to become a heretic!" The Reformation was taking root among the people before it arrived at the upper classes.

CHAPTER VIII.

The Papacy intercepts the Gospel—The King consults Sir Thomas More—Ecclesiastical Conferences about the Divorce—The Universities—Clark—The Nun of Kent—Wolsey decides to do the King's Will—Mission to the Pope—Four Documents—Embarrassment of Charles V.—Francis Philip at Madrid—Distress and Resolution of Charles—He turns away from the Reformation—Conference at the Castle of St Angelo—Knight arrives in Italy—His Flight—Treaty between the Pope and the Emperor—Escape of the Pope—Confusion of Henry VIII.— Wolsey's Orders —His Entreaties.

THE sun of the word of God, which daily grew brighter in the sky of the sixteenth century, was sufficient to scatter all the darkness in England; but popery, like an immense wall, intercepted its rays. Britain had hardly received the Scriptures in Greek and Latin, and then in English, before the priests began to make war upon them with indefatigable zeal. It was necessary that the wall should be thrown down in order that the sun might penetrate freely among the Anglo-Saxon people. And now events were ripening in England, destined to make a great breach in popery. The negotiations of Henry VIII. with Clement VII. play an important part in the Reformation. By showing up the Court of Rome, they destroyed the respect which the people felt for it; they took away that *power and strength*, as Scripture says, which the monarchy had given it; and the throne of the pope once fallen in England, Jesus Christ uplifted and strengthened his own.

Henry, ardently desiring an heir, and thinking that he had found the woman that

[1] Foxe, v. p. 27.

would ensure his own and England's happiness, conceived the design of severing the ties that united him to the queen, and with this view he consulted his most favourite councillors about the divorce. There was one in particular whose approval he coveted: this was Sir Thomas More. One day as Erasmus's friend was walking with his master in the beautiful gallery at Hampton Court, giving him an account of a mission he had just executed on the continent, the king suddenly interrupted him: "My marriage with the queen," he said, "is contrary to the laws of God, of the church, and of nature." He then took up the Bible, and pointed out the passages in his favour.[1] "I am not a theologian," said More, somewhat embarrassed; "your majesty should consult a council of doctors."

Accordingly, by Henry's order, Warham assembled the most learned canonists at Hampton Court; but weeks passed away before they could agree.[2] Most of them quoted in the king's favour those passages in Leviticus (xviii. 16; xx. 21,) that forbid a man to take *his brother's wife*.[3] But Fisher, bishop of Rochester, and the other opponents of the divorce, replied that, according to Deuteronomy (xxv. 5,) when a woman is left a widow without children, her brother-in-law ought to take her to wife, to perpetuate his brother's name in Israel. "This law concerned the Jews only," replied the partisans of the divorce; they added that its object was "to maintain the inheritances distinct, and the genealogies intact, until the coming of Christ. The Judaical dispensation has passed away; but the law of Leviticus, which is a moral law, is binding upon all men in all ages."

To free themselves from their embarrassment, the bishops demanded that the most eminent universities should be consulted; and commissioners were forthwith despatched to Oxford, Cambridge, Paris, Orleans, Toulouse, Louvain, Padua, and Bologna, furnished with money to reward the foreign doctors for the time and trouble this question would cost them. This caused some little delay, and every means was now to be tried to divert the king from his purpose.

Wolsey, who was the first to suggest the idea of a divorce, was now thoroughly alarmed. It appeared to him that a nod from the daughter of the Boleyns would hurl him from the post he had so laboriously won; and this made him vent his ill-humour on all about him, at one time threatening Warham, and at another persecuting Pace. But fearing to oppose Henry openly, he summoned from Paris, Clarke, bishop of Bath and Wells, at that time ambassador to the French court.

[1] Laid the Bible open before me, and showed me the words. More to Cromwell, Strype, i. 2d part, p. 197.
[2] Consulting from day to day, and time to time. Cavendish, p. 209.
[3] Ex his doctoribus asseritur quod Papa non potest dispensare in primo gradu affinitatis. Burnet's Reform., ii. Records, p. 8 (Lond. 1841.)

The latter entered into his views, and after cautiously preparing the way, he ventured to say to the king: "The progress of the inquiry will be so slow, your majesty, that it will take more than seven years to bring it to an end!" — "Since my patience has already held out for *eighteen* years," the king replied coldly, "I am willing to wait *four or five* more."[1]

As the political party had failed, the clerical party set in motion a scheme of another kind. A young woman, Elizabeth Barton, known as *the holy maid of Kent*, had been subject from childhood to epileptic fits. The priest of her parish, named Masters, had persuaded her that she was inspired of God, and confederating with one Bocking, a monk of Canterbury, he turned the weakness of the prophetess to account. Elizabeth wandered over the country, passing from house to house, and from convent to convent; on a sudden her limbs would become rigid, her features distorted; violent convulsions shook her body, and strange unintelligible sounds fell from her lips, which the amazed bystanders received as revelations from the Virgin and the saints. Fisher, bishop of Rochester, Abel, the queen's ecclesiastical agent, and even Sir Thomas More, were among the number of Elizabeth's partisans. Rumours of the divorce having reached the *saint's* ears, an angel commanded her to appear before the cardinal. As soon as she stood in his presence, the colour fled from her cheeks, her limbs trembled, and falling into an ecstasy, she exclaimed: "Cardinal of York, God has placed three swords in your hand: the spiritual sword, to range the church under the authority of the pope: the civil sword, to govern the realm; and the sword of justice, to prevent the divorce of the king......If you do not wield these three swords faithfully, God will lay it sore to your charge."[2] After these words the prophetess withdrew.

But other influences were then dividing Wolsey's breast: hatred, which induced him to oppose the divorce; and ambition, which foreboded his ruin in this opposition. At last ambition prevailed, and he resolved to make his objections forgotten by the energy of his zeal.

Henry hastened to profit by this change. "Declare the divorce yourself," said he to Wolsey; "has not the pope named you his vicar-general?"[3] The cardinal was not anxious to raise himself so high. "If I were to decide the affair," said he, "the queen would appeal to the pope; we must therefore either apply to the holy father for special powers, or persuade the queen to retire to a nunnery. And if we fail in either of these expedients, we will obey the voice of conscience, even in despite of the pope."[1] It was arranged to begin with the more regular attempt, and Gregory Da Casale, secretary Knight, and the prothonotary Gambara, were appointed to an extraordinary mission at the pontifical court. Casale was Wolsey's man, and Knight was Henry's. Wolsey told the envoys: "You will demand of the pope, 1stly, a *commission* authorizing me to inquire into this matter; 2dly, his promise to pronounce the nullity of Catherine's marriage with Henry, if we should find that her marriage with Arthur was consummated; and 3dly, a *dispensation* permitting the king to marry again." In this manner Wolsey hoped to make sure of the divorce without damaging the papal authority. It was insinuated that false representations, with regard to the consummation of the first marriage, had been sent from England to Julius II., which had induced the pontiff to permit the second. The pope being deceived as to the *fact*, his infallibility was untouched. Wolsey desired something more; knowing that no confidence could be put in the good faith of the pontiff, he demanded a fourth instrument by which the pope should bind himself *never to recall the other three;* he only forgot to take precautions in case Clement should withdraw *the fourth.* "With these four snares, skilfully combined," said the cardinal, "I shall catch the hare; if he escapes from one, he will fall into the other." The courtiers anticipated a speedy termination of the affair. Was not the emperor the declared enemy of the pontiff? Had not Henry, on the contrary, made himself *protector of the Clementine league?* Could Clement hesitate, when called upon, to choose between his jailer and his benefactor?

Indeed, Charles V., at this moment, was in a very embarrassing position. It is true, his guards were posted at the gates of the castle of St Angelo, where Clement was a prisoner, and people in Rome said to one another with a smile: "Now indeed it is true, *Papa non potest errare.*"[2] But it was not possible to keep the pope a prisoner in Rome; and then what was to be done with him? The viceroy of Naples proposed to Alercon, the governor of St Angelo, to remove Clement to Gaeta; but the affrighted colonel exclaimed: "Heaven forbid that I should drag after me the very body of God!" Charles thought one time of transporting the pontiff to Spain; but might not an enemy's fleet carry him off on the road? The pope in prison was far more embarrassing to Charles than the pope at liberty.

It was at this critical time that Francis Philip, Queen Catherine's servant, having

---

[1] Since his patience had already held out for eighteen years. Collyer, ii. p. 24.
[2] Strype. vol. i. part i. p. 19.
[3] When Napoleon, from similar motives, desired to separate from Josephine, fearing the unwillingness of the pope (as Henry did), he entertained, like him, the design of doing without the pontiff, and of getting his marriage annulled by the French bishops. As he was more powerful, he succeeded.

[1] Quid possit clam fieri quoad forum conscientiæ. Collyer, ii. p. 24.
[2] The pope cannot err,—a play upon the double meaning of the word *errare.*

escaped the snares laid by Henry VIII. and Wolsey, arrived at Madrid, where he passed a whole day in conference with Charles V. This prince was at first astonished, shocked even, by the designs of the king of England. The curse of God seemed to hang over his house. His mother was a lunatic; his sister of Denmark expelled from her dominions; his sister of Hungary made a widow by the battle of Mohacz; the Turks were encroaching upon his territories; Lautrec was victorious in Italy, and the catholics, irritated by the pope's captivity, detested his ambition. This was not enough. Henry VIII. was striving to divorce his aunt, and the pope would naturally give his aid to this criminal design. Charles must choose between the pontiff and the king. The friendship of the king of England might aid him in breaking the league formed to expel him from Italy, and by sacrificing Catherine he would be sure to obtain his support; but placed between reasons of state and his aunt's honour, the emperor did not hesitate; he even renounced certain projects of reform that he had at heart. He suddenly decided for the pope, and from that very hour followed a new course.

Charles, who possessed great discernment, had understood his age: he had seen that concessions were called for by the movement of the human mind, and would have desired to carry out the change from the middle ages to modern times by a carefully managed transition. He had consequently demanded a council to reform the church and weaken the Romish dominion in Europe. But very different was the result. If Charles turned away from Henry, he was obliged to turn towards Clement; and after having compelled the head of the church to enter a prison, it was necessary to place him once more upon the throne. Charles V. sacrificed the interests of Christian society to the interests of his own family. This divorce, which in England has been looked upon as the ruin of the popedom, was what saved it in continental Europe.

But how could the emperor win the heart of the pontiff, filled as it was with bitterness and anger? He selected for this difficult mission a friar of great ability, De Angelis, general of the Spanish Observance, and ordered him to proceed to the castle of St Angelo under the pretext of negotiating the liberation of the holy father. The cordelier was conducted to the strongest part of the fortress, called the Rock, where Clement was lodged; and the two priests brought all their craft to bear on each other. The monk, assisted by the artful Moncade, adroitly mingled together the pope's deliverance and Catherine's marriage. He affirmed that the emperor wished to open the gates of the pontiff's prison, and had already given the order; [1]

and then he added immediately: " The emperor is determined to maintain the rights of his aunt, and will never consent to the divorce."[1]—" If you are a *good shepherd* to me," wrote Charles to the pope with his own hand on the 22d of November, " I will be a *good sheep* to you." Clement smiled as he read these words; he understood his position; the emperor had need of the priest, Charles was at his captive's feet; Clement was saved! The divorce was a rope fallen from the skies, which could not fail to drag him out of the pit; he had only to cling to it quietly in order to reascend his throne. Accordingly from that hour Clement appeared less eager to quit the castle than Charles to liberate him. " So long as the divorce is in suspense," thought the crafty De' Medici, " I have two great friends; but as soon as I declare for one, I shall have a mortal enemy in the other." He promised the monk to come to no decision in the matter without informing the emperor.

Meantime Knight, the envoy of the impatient monarch, having heard, as he crossed the Alps, that the pope was at liberty, hastened on to Parma, where he met Gambara: " He is not free yet," replied the prothonotary; " but the general of the Franciscans hopes to terminate his captivity in a few days.[2] Continue your journey," he added. Knight could not do so without great danger. He was told at Foligno, sixty miles from the metropolis, that if he had not a safe-conduct he could not reach Rome without exposing his life; Knight halted. Just then a messenger from Henry brought him despatches more pressing than ever; Knight started again with one servant and a guide. At Monte Rotondo he was nearly murdered by the inhabitants; but on the next day (25th November), protected by a violent storm of wind and rain,[3] Henry's envoy entered Rome at ten o'clock without being observed, and kept himself concealed.

It was impossible to speak with Clement, for the emperor's orders were positive. Knight, therefore, began to *practise* upon the cardinals; he gained over the Cardinal of Pisa, by whose means his despatches were laid before the pontiff. Clement after reading them laid them down with a smile of satisfaction.[4] " Good! " said he, " here is *the other* coming to me now!" But night had hardly closed in before the Cardinal of Pisa's secretary hastened to Knight and told him: " Don Alercon is informed of your arrival; and the pope entreats you to depart immediately." This officer had scarcely left him, when the prothonotary Gambara arrived in great agitation: " His holiness presses you to leave; as soon as he is at liberty, he will

[1] That in anywise he should not consent to the same. State Papers, vol. vii. p. 29.
[2] Quod sperabat intra paucos dies auferre suæ Sanctitati squalorem et tenebras. State Papers, vol. vii. p. 13.
[3] Veari trobelous with wynde and rayne, and therefore more mete for our voyage. Ibid. p. 16.
[4] Reponed the same saufly, as Gambara showed unto me. Ibid. p. 17.

[1] La Cæsarea Majesta si come grandamente desidera la liberatione de nostro signor, cosi efficacemente la manda. Capituli, etc. Le Grand, iii. p. 48.

attend to your master's request." Two hours after this, two hundred Spanish soldiers arrived, surrounded the house in which Knight had concealed himself, and searched it from top to bottom, but to no purpose ; the English agent had escaped.[1]

Knight's safety was not the true motive which induced Clement to urge his departure. The very day on which the pope received the message from the king of England, he signed a treaty with Charles V., restoring him, under certain conditions, to both his powers. At the same time the pontiff, for greater security, pressed the French general Lautrec to hasten his march to Rome in order to save him from the hands of the emperor. Clement, a disciple of Machiavelli, thus gave the right hand to Charles and the left to Francis ; and as he had not another for Henry, he made him the most positive promises. Each of the three princes could reckon on the pope's friendship, and on the same grounds.

The 10th of December (1527) was the day on which Clement's imprisonment would terminate ; but he preferred owing his freedom to intrigue rather than to the emperor's generosity. He therefore procured the dress of a tradesman, and, on the evening before the day fixed for his deliverance, his ward being already much relaxed, he escaped from the castle, and, accompanied only by Louis of Gonzago in his flight, he made his way to Orvieto.

While Clement was experiencing all the joy of a man just escaped from prison, Henry was a prey to the most violent agitation. Having ceased to love Catherine, he persuaded himself that he was the victim of his father's ambition, a martyr to duty, and the champion of conjugal sanctity. His very gait betrayed his vexation, and even among the gay conversation of the court, deep sighs would escape from his bosom. He had frequent interviews with Wolsey. "I regard the safety of my soul above all things,"[2] he said ; "but I am concerned also for the peace of my kingdom. For a long while an unceasing remorse has been gnawing at my conscience,[3] and my thoughts dwell upon my marriage with unutterable sorrow.[4] God, in his wrath, has taken away my sons, and if I persevere in this unlawful union, he will visit me with still more terrible chastisements.[5] My only hope is in the holy father." Wolsey replied with a low bow : " Please your majesty, I am occupied with this business, as if it were my only means of winning heaven."

And indeed he redoubled his exertions.

He wrote to Sir Gregory Da Casale on the 5th of December (1527) : " You will procure an audience of the pope at any price. Disguise yourself, appear before him as the servant of some nobleman,[1] or as a messenger from the duke of Ferrara. Scatter money plentifully ; sacrifice everything, provided you procure a secret interview with his holiness ; ten thousand ducats are at your disposal. You will explain to Clement the king's scruples, and the necessity of providing for the continuance of his house and the peace of his kingdom. You will tell him that in order to restore him to liberty, the king is ready to declare war against the emperor, and thus show himself to all the world to be a true son of the church."

Wolsey saw clearly that it was essential to represent the divorce to Clement VII. as a means likely to secure the safety of the popedom. The cardinal, therefore, wrote again to Da Casale on the 6th of December : " Night and day, I revolve in my mind the actual condition of the church,[2] and seek the means best calculated to extricate the pope from the gulf into which he has fallen. While I was turning these thoughts over in my mind during a sleepless night......one way suddenly occurred to me. I said to myself, the king must be prevailed upon to undertake the defence of the holy father. This was no easy matter, for his majesty is strongly attached to the emperor ;[3] however, I set about my task. I told the king that his holiness was ready to satisfy him ; I staked my honour ; I succeeded......To save the pope, my master will sacrifice his treasures, subjects, kingdom, and even his life[4]......I therefore conjure his holiness to entertain our just demand."

Never before had such pressing entreaties been made to a pope.

CHAPTER IX.

The English Envoys at Orvieto—Their Oration to the Pope—Clement gains time—The Envoys and Cardinal Sanctorum Quatuor—Stratagem of the Pope—Knight discovers it and returns—The Transformations of Antichrist—The English obtain a new Document—Fresh Stratagem—Demand of a second Cardinal-legate—The Pope's new Expedient—End of the Campaign.

THE envoys of the king of England appeared in the character of the saviours of Rome. This was doubtless no stratagem ; and Wolsey probably regarded that thought as coming from heaven, which had visited him during the weary sleepless night. The zeal of his agents increased. The pope was hardly set at liberty, before Knight and Da Casale

---

[1] I was not passed out of Rome, by the space of two hours, ere two hundred Spaniards invaded and searched the house. Burnet, Records, ii. p. 12.
[2] Deumque primo et ante omnia ac animæ suæ quietem et salutem respiciens. Burnet's Reformation, ii. Records, p. vii.
[3] Longo jam temoore intimo suæ conscientiæ remorsu. Ibid.
[4] Ingenti cum molestia cordisque perturbatione. Ibid.
[5] Graviusque a Deo supplicium expavescit. Ibid. p. viii.

[1] Mutato habitu et tanquam alicujus minister. Burnet's Reformation, ii. Records. p. viii.
[2] Diuque ac noctu mente volvens quo facto. State Papers, vol. vii. p. 18.
[3] Adeo tenaciter Cæsari adhærebat. Ibid.
[4] Usque ad mortem. Ibid. p. 19.

appeared at the foot of the precipitous rock on which Orvieto is built, and demanded to be introduced to Clement VII. Nothing could be more compromising to the pontiff than such a visit. How could he appear on good terms with England, when Rome and all his states were still in the hands of Catherine's nephew? The pope's mind was utterly bewildered by the demand of the two envoys. He recovered however; to reject the powerful hand extended to him by England, was not without its danger; and as he knew well how to bring a difficult negotiation to a successful conclusion, Clement regained confidence in his skill, and gave orders to introduce Henry's ambassadors.

Their discourse was not without eloquence. "Never was the church in a more critical position," said they. "The unmeasured ambition of the kings who claim to dispose of spiritual affairs at their own pleasure (this was aimed at Charles V.) holds the apostolical bark suspended over an abyss. The only port open to it in the tempest is the favour of the august prince whom we represent, and who has always been the shield of the faith. But, alas! this monarch, the impregnable bulwark of your holiness, is himself the prey of tribulations almost equal to your own. His conscience torn by remorse, his crown without an heir, his kingdom without security, his people exposed once more to perpetual disorders......Nay, the whole Christian world given up to the most cruel discord.[1]......Such are the consequences of a fatal union which God has marked with his displeasure......There are also," they added in a lower tone, "certain things of which his majesty cannot speak in his letter......certain incurable disorders under which the queen suffers, which will never permit the king to look upon her again as his wife.[2] If your holiness puts an end to such wretchedness by annulling his unlawful marriage, you will attach his majesty by an indissoluble bond. Assistance, riches, armies, crown, and even life—the king our master is ready to employ all in the service of Rome. He stretches out his hand to you, most holy father......stretch out yours to him; by your union the church will be saved, and Europe will be saved with it."

Clement was cruelly embarrassed. His policy consisted in holding the balance between the two princes, and he was now called upon to decide in favour of one of them. He began to regret that he had ever received Henry's ambassadors. "Consider my position," he said to them, "and entreat the king to wait until more favourable events leave me at liberty to act."—"What!" replied Knight proudly, "has not your holiness promised to consider his majesty's

prayer? If you fail in your promise now, how can I persuade the king that you will keep it some future day?"[1] Da Casale thought the time had come to strike a decisive blow. "What evils," he exclaimed, "what inevitable misfortunes your refusal will create!......The emperor thinks only of depriving the church of its power, and the king of England alone has sworn to maintain it." Then speaking lower, more slowly, and dwelling upon every word, he continued: "We fear that his majesty, reduced to such extremities......of the two evils will choose the *least*,[2] and supported by the purity of his intentions, will do *of his own authority*...... what he now so respectfully demands...... What should we see then?......I shudder at the thought......Let not your holiness indulge in a false security which will inevitably drag you into the abyss......Read all ......remark all......divine all......take note of all[3]......Most holy father, this is a question of life and death." And Da Casale's tone said more than his words.

Clement understood that a positive refusal would expose him to lose England. Placed between Henry and Charles, as between the hammer and the forge, he resolved to gain time. "Well then," he said to Knight and Da Casale, "I will do what you ask; but I am not familiar with the *forms* these dispensations require......I will consult the Cardinal *Sanctorum Quatuor* on the subject ......and then will inform you."

Knight and Da Casale, wishing to anticipate Clement VII., hastened to Lorenzo Pucci, cardinal Sanctorum Quatuor, and intimated to him that their master would know how to be grateful. The cardinal assured the deputies of his affection for Henry VIII., and they, in the fulness of their gratitude, laid before him the four documents which they were anxious to get executed. But the cardinal had hardly looked at the first—the proposal that Wolsey should decide the matter of the divorce in England — when he exclaimed: "Impossible!......a bull in such terms would cover with eternal disgrace not only his holiness and the king, but even the cardinal of York himself." The deputies were confounded, for Wolsey had ordered them to ask the pope for nothing but his signature.[4] Recovering themselves, they rejoined: "All that we require is a *competent* commission." On his part, the pope wrote Henry a letter, in which he managed to say nothing.[5]

Of the four required documents there were two on whose immediate despatch Knight and Da Casale insisted: these were the

---

[1] Discordiæ crudelissimæ per omnem christianum orbem. State Papers, vol. vii. p. 19.
[2] Nonnulla sunt secreta S.D.N. secreto exponenda et non credenda scriptis....ob morbos nonnullos quibus absque remedio regina laborat. Ibid.

[1] Perform the promise once broken. Burnet's Ref. ii. Records. p. xiii.
[2] Ex duobus malis minus malum eligat. State Papers, vii. p. 20.
[3] Ut non gravetur, cuncta legere, et bene notare. Ibid. p. 18.
[4] Alia nulla re esset opus, præterquam ejus Sanctitatis signatura. Ibid. p. 29.
[5] Charissime in Christo fili, &c., dated 7th December 1527. Ibid. p. 27.

commission to pronounce the divorce, and the *dispensation* to contract a second marriage. The *dispensation* without the *commission* was of no value; this the pope knew well; accordingly he resolved to give the *dispensation* only. It was as if Charles had granted Clement when in prison permission to visit his cardinals, but denied him liberty to leave the castle of St Angelo. It is in such a manner as this that a religious system transformed into a political system has recourse, when it is without power, to stratagem. "The *commission*," said the artful Medici to Knight, "must be corrected according to the style of our court; but here is the *dispensation*." Knight took the document; it was addressed to Henry VIII. and ran thus: "We accord to you, in case your marriage with Catherine shall be declared null,[1] free liberty to take another wife, provided she have not been the wife of your brother. ......" The Englishman was duped by the Italian. "To my poor judgment," he said, "this document will be of use to us." After this Clement appeared to concern himself solely about Knight's health, and suddenly manifested the greatest interest for him. "It is proper that you should hasten your departure," said he, "for it is necessary that you should travel *at your ease.* Gambara will follow you post, and bring the commission." Knight thus mystified, took leave of the pope, who got rid of Da Casale and Gambara in a similar manner. He then began to breathe once more. There was no diplomacy in Europe which Rome, even in its greatest weakness, could not easily dupe.

It had now become necessary to elude the commission. While the king's envoys were departing in good spirits, reckoning on the document that was to follow them, the general of the Spanish Observance reiterated to the pontiff in every tone : "Be careful to give no document authorizing the divorce, and above all, do not permit this affair to be judged in Henry's states." The cardinals drew up the document under the influence of De Angelis, and made it a masterpiece of insignificance. If good theology ennobles the heart, bad theology, so fertile in subtleties, imparts to the mind a skill by no means common; and hence the most celebrated diplomatists have often been churchmen. The act being thus drawn up, the pope despatched three copies, to Knight, to Da Casale, and to Gambara. Knight was near Bologna when the courier overtook him. He was stupified, and taking post-horses returned with all haste to Orvieto.[2] Gambara proceeded through France to England with the useless *dispensation* which the pope had granted.

Knight had thought to meet with more good faith at the court of the pope than with kings, and he had been outwitted. What would Wolsey and Henry say of his folly? His wounded self-esteem began to make him believe all that Tyndale and Luther said of the popedom. The former had just published the *Obedience of a Christian Man,* and the *Parable of the Wicked Mammon,* in which he represented Rome as one of the transformations of Antichrist. "Antichrist," said he in the latter treatise, "is not a man that should suddenly appear with wonders; he is a spiritual thing, who was in the Old Testament, and also in the time of Christ and the apostles, and is now, and shall (I doubt not) endure till the world's end. His nature is (when he is overcome with the word of God) to go out of the play for a season, and to disguise himself, and then to come in again with a new name and new raiment. The Scribes and Pharisees in the gospel were very Antichrists; popes, cardinals, and bishops have gotten their new names, but the thing is all one. Even so now, when we have uttered [detected] him, *he will change himself once more,* and turn himself into an angel of light. Already *the beast,* seeing himself now to be sought for, roareth and seeketh new holes to hide himself in, and changeth himself into a thousand fashions."[1] This idea, paradoxical at first, gradually made its way into men's minds. The Romans, by their practices, familiarized the English to the somewhat coarse descriptions of the reformers. England was to have many such lessons, and thus by degrees learn to set Rome aside for the sake of her own glory and prosperity.

Knight and Da Casale reached Orvieto about the same time. Clement replied with sighs, "Alas! I am the emperor's prisoner. The imperialists are every day pillaging towns and castles in our neighbourhood.[2]..... Wretch that I am! I have not a friend except the king your master, and he is far away. ......If I should do anything now to displease Charles, I am a lost man.....To sign the commission would be to sign an eternal rupture with him." But Knight and Da Casale pleaded so effectually with Cardinal Sanctorum Quatuor, and so pressed Clement, that the pontiff, without the knowledge of the Spaniard De Angelis, gave them a more satisfactory document, but not such as Wolsey required. "In giving you this commission," said the pope, "I am giving away my liberty, and perhaps my life. I listen not to the voice of prudence, but to that of affection only. I confide in the generosity of the king of England, he is the master of my destiny." He then began to weep,[3] and seemed ready to faint. Knight, forgetting his vexation, promised Clement that the king would do everything to save him.—"Ah!" said the pope, "there is one effectual

---

[1] Matrimonium cum Catharina nullum fuisse et esse declarari. Herbert's Henry VIII. p. 280.
[2] Burnet's Reformation, Records, ii. p. xiii.

[1] Tyndale, Doctr. Tr. p. 42, 43.
[2] The imperialists do daily spoil castles and towns about Rome....they have taken within three days two castles lying within six miles of this. Burnet's Ref. vol. ii. Records, p. xiii.
[3] Cum suspiriis et lacrymis. Ibid. p. xii.

means."—" What is that ?" inquired Henry's agents.—" M. Lautrec, who says daily that he will come, but never does," replied Clement, "has only to bring the French army promptly before the gates of Orvieto; then I could excuse myself by saying that he constrained me to sign the commission." [1]— "Nothing is easier," replied the envoys, "we will go and hasten his arrival."

Clement was not even now at ease. The safety of the Roman church troubled him not less than his own......Charles might discover the trick and make the popedom suffer for it. There was danger on all sides. If the English spoke of *independence*, did not the emperor threaten a *reform ?*......The catholic princes, said the papal councillors, are capable, without perhaps a single exception, of supporting the cause of Luther to gratify a criminal ambition.[2] The pope reflected, and withdrawing his word, promised to give the commission when Lautrec was under the walls of Orvieto; but the English agents insisted on having it immediately. To conciliate all, it was agreed that the pope should give the required document at once, but as soon as the French army arrived, he should send another copy bearing the date of the day on which he saw Lautrec. " Beseech the king to keep secret the commission I give you," [3] said Clement VII. to Knight; "if he begins the process immediately he receives it, I am undone for ever." [4] The pope thus gave permission to act, on condition of not acting at all. Knight took leave on the 1st of January 1528; he promised all the pontiff desired, and then, as if fearing some fresh difficulty, he departed the same day. Da Casale, on his side, after having offered the Cardinal Sanctorum Quatuor a gift of 4000 crowns, which he refused, repaired to Lautrec, to beg him to *constrain* the pope to sign a document which was already on its way to England.

But while the business seemed to be clearing at Rome, it was becoming more complicated at London. The king's project got wind, and Catherine gave way to the liveliest sorrow. " I shall protest," said she, " against the commission given to the cardinal of York. Is he not the king's subject, the vile flatterer of his pleasures?" Catherine did not resist alone; the people, who hated the cardinal, could not with pleasure see him invested with such authority. To obviate this inconvenience, Henry resolved to ask the pope for another cardinal, who should be empowered to terminate the affair in London with or without Wolsey.

The latter agreed to the measure: it is even possible that he was the first to suggest it, for he feared to bear alone the responsibi-

lity of so hateful an inquiry. Accordingly, on the 27th of December, he wrote to the king's agents at Rome : " Procure the envoy of a legate, and particularly of an able, easy, *manageable* legate......desirous of meriting the king's favour,[1] Campeggio for instance. You will earnestly request the cardinal who may be selected, to travel with all diligence, and you will assure him that the king will behave liberally towards him." [2]

Knight reached Asti on the 10th of January, where he found letters with fresh orders. This was another check : at one time it is the pope who compels him to retrograde, at another it is the king. Henry's unlucky valetudinarian secretary, a man very susceptible of fatigue, and already wearied and exhausted by ten painful journeys, was in a very bad humour. He determined to permit Gambara to carry the two documents to England ; to commission Da Casale, who had not left the pope's neighbourhood, to solicit the despatch of the legate ; and as regarded himself, to go and wait for further orders at Turin :—" If it be thought good unto the king's highness that I do return unto Orvieto, I shall do as much as *my poor carcass* may endure." [3]

When Da Casale reached Bologna, he pressed Lautrec to go and constrain the pontiff to sign the act which Gambara was already bearing to England. On receiving the new despatches he returned in all haste to Orvieto, and the pope was very much alarmed when he heard of his arrival. He had feared to grant a simple paper, destined to remain *secret;* and now he is required to send a prince of the church ! Will Henry never be satisfied ? " The mission you desire would be full of dangers," he replied ; " but we have discovered another means, alone calculated to finish this business. Mind you do not say that I pointed it out to you," added the pope in a mysterious tone ; " but that it was suggested by Cardinal Sanctorum Quatuor and Simonetta." Da Casale was all attention. " There is not a doctor in the world who can better decide on this matter, and on its most private circumstances, than the king himself.[4] If therefore he sincerely believes that Catherine had really become his brother's wife, let him empower the cardinal of York to pronounce the divorce, and let him take another wife without any further ceremony;[5] he can then afterwards demand the confirmation of the consistory. The affair being concluded in this way, I will take the rest upon myself."—" But," said Da Casale, somewhat dissatisfied with this new intrigue. " I must fulfil my mission, and the king demands a legate."—" And whom shall I send," asked

<hr>

[1] And by this colour he would cover the matter. Burnet's Ref., vol. ii. Records, p. xii.
[2] Non potest Sua Sanctitas sibi persuadere ipsos principes (ut forte aliqui jactant) assumpturos sectam Lutheranam contra ecclesiam. State Papers, vii. p. 47.   [3] Ibid. p. 36.
[4] Is fully in your puissance with publishing of the commission to destroy for ever. Ibid.

[1] Eruditus, indifferens, tractabilis, de regia majestate bene merendi cupidus. State Papers, vii. p. 33.
[2] Regia majestas sumptus, labores, atque molestias liberalissime compenset. Ibid. p. 34.
[3] Burnet's Ref., vol. ii. Records, p. xiii.
[4] Nullus doctor in mundo est, qui de hac re melius decernere possit quam ipse rex. Burnet, ii., Records, p. xiv.
[5] Aliam uxorem ducat. Ibid.

Clement. "Da Monte? he cannot move. De Cæsis? he is at Naples. Ara Cœli? he has the gout. Piccolomini? he is of the imperial party......Campeggio would be the best, but he is at Rome, where he supplies my place, and cannot leave without peril to the church."......And then with some emotion he added, " I throw myself into his majesty's arms. The emperor will never forgive what I am doing. If he hears of it he will summon me before *his council; I shall* have no rest until he has deprived me of my throne and my life."[1]

Da Casale hastened to forward to London the result of the conference. Clement being unable to untie the knot, requested Henry to cut it. Will this prince hesitate to employ so easy a means, the pope (Clement declared it himself) being willing to ratify everything?

Here closes Henry's first campaign in the territories of the popedom. We shall now see the results of so many efforts.

CHAPTER X.

Disappointment in England—War declared against Charles V.—Wolsey desires to get him deposed by the Pope—A new Scheme—Embassy of Fox and Gardiner—Their Arrival at Orvieto—Their first Interview with Clement—The Pope reads a Treatise by Henry—Gardiner's Threats and ?lement's Promise—The Modern Fabius—Fresh Interview and Menaces—The Pope has not *the Key*—Gardiner's Proposition—Difficulties and Delays of the Cardinals—Gardiner's last Blows—Reverses of Charles V. in Italy—The Pope's Terror and Concession—The *Commission* granted—Wolsey demands the *Engagement*—A Loophole—The Pope's Distress.

NEVER was disappointment more complete than that felt by Henry and Wolsey after the arrival of Gambara with the commission; the king was angry, the cardinal vexed. What Clement called the *sacrifice of his life* was in reality but a sheet of paper fit only to be thrown into the fire. " This commission is of no value,"[2] said Wolsey.—" And even to put it into execution," added Henry, " we must wait until the imperialists have quitted Italy! The pope is putting us off to the Greek calends."—" His holiness," observed the cardinal, " does not bind himself to pronounce the divorce; the queen will therefore appeal from our judgment."—" And even if the pope had bound himself," added the king, " it would be sufficient for the emperor to smile upon him, to make him retract what he had promised."—" It is all a cheat and a mockery," concluded both king and minister.

What was to be done next? The only way to make Clement ours, thought Wolsey, is to get rid of Charles; it is time his pride was brought down. Accordingly, on the 21st of January 1528, France and England declared hostilities against the emperor. When Charles heard of this proceeding he exclaimed: " I know the hand that has flung the torch of war into the midst of Europe. My crime is not having placed the cardinal of York on St Peter's throne."

A mere declaration of war was not enough for Wolsey; the bishop of Bayonne, ambassador from France, seeing him one day somewhat excited,[1] whispered in his ear: " In former times popes have deposed emperors for smaller offences." Charles's deposition would have delivered the king of France from a troublesome rival; but Du Bellay, fearing to take the initiative in so bold an enterprise, suggested the idea to the cardinal. Wolsey reflected: such a thought had never before occurred to him. Taking the ambassador aside to a window, he there swore *stoutly,* said Du Bellay, that he should be delighted to use all his influence to get Charles deposed by the pope. " No one is more likely than yourself," replied the bishop, " to induce Clement to do it."—" I will use all my credit," rejoined Wolsey, and the two priests separated. This bright idea the cardinal never forgot. Charles had robbed him of the tiara; he will retaliate by depriving Charles of his crown. *An eye for an eye, and a tooth for a tooth.* Staffileo, dean of the Rota, was then in London, and still burning with resentment against the author of the Sack of Rome, he favourably received the suggestions Wolsey made to him; and, finally, the envoy from John Zapolya, king-elect of Hungary, supported the project. But the kings of France and England were not so easily induced to put the thrones of kings at the disposal of the priests. It appears, however, that the pope was sounded on the subject; and if the emperor had been beaten in Italy, it is probable that the bull would have been fulminated against him. His sword preserved his crown, and the plot of the two bishops failed.

The king's councillors began to seek for less heroic means. " We must prosecute the affair at *Rome*," said some.—" No," said others, " in *England*. The pope is too much afraid of the emperor to pronounce the divorce in person."—" If the pope fears the emperor more than the king of England," exclaimed the proud Tudor, " we shall find some other way to set him at ease."[2] Thus, at the first contradiction, Henry placed his hand on his sword, and threatened to sever the ties which bound his kingdom to the throne of the Italian pontiff.

" I have hit it !" said Wolsey at length ; " we must combine the two plans—judge the affair in London, and at the same time bind the pontiff at Rome." And then the able cardinal proposed the draft of a bull, by which

---

[1] Vocabit eum ad concilium, vel nihil aliud quæret, nisi ut eum omni statu et vita privet. Burnet, ii. Records, p. xxvi.
[2] Nullius sit roboris vel effectus. State Papers, vii. p. 50.

[1] Du Bellay to Francis 1. Le Grand, Preuves, p. 64.
[2] Burnet's Reformation, i. p. 50.

the pope, delegating his authority to two legates, should declare that the acts of that delegation should have a perpetual effect, notwithstanding any contrary decrees that might subsequently emanate from his infallible authority.[1] A new mission was decided upon for the accomplishment of this bold design.

Wolsey, annoyed by the folly of Knight and his colleagues, desired men of another stamp. He therefore cast his eyes on his own secretary, Stephen Gardiner, an active man, intelligent, supple, and crafty, a learned canonist, desirous of the king's favour, and, above all, a good Romanist, which at Rome was not without its advantage. Gardiner was in small the living image of his master; and hence the cardinal sometimes styled him *the half of himself*.[2] Edward Fox, the chief almoner, was joined with him—a moderate, influential man, a particular friend of Henry's, and a zealous advocate of the divorce. Fox was named first in the commission; but it was agreed that Gardiner should be the real head of the embassy. "Repeat without ceasing," Wolsey told them, "that his majesty cannot do otherwise than separate from the queen. Attack each one on his weak side. Declare to the pope that the king promises to defend him against the emperor; and to the cardinals that their services will be nobly rewarded.[3] If that does not suffice, let the energy of your words be such as to excite a wholesome fear in the pontiff."

Fox and Gardiner, after a gracious reception at Paris (23d February), by Francis I., arrived at Orvieto on the 20th of March, after many perils, and with their dress in such disorder, that no one could have taken them for the ambassadors of Henry VIII. "What a city!" they exclaimed, as they passed through its streets; "what ruins, what misery! It is indeed truly called Orvieto (*urbs vetus*)!" The state of the town gave them no very grand idea of the state of the popedom, and they imagined that with a pontiff so poorly lodged, their negotiation could not be otherwise than easy. "I give you my house," said Da Casale, to whom they went, "my room and my own bed;" and as they made some objections, he added: "It is not possible to lodge you elsewhere; I have even been forced to borrow what was necessary to receive you."[4] Da Casale, pressing them to change their clothes, which were still dripping (they had just crossed a river on their mules), they replied, that being obliged to travel post, they had not been able to bring a change of raiment. "Alas!" said Casale, "what is to be done? there are few persons in Orvieto who have more garments than one;[5] even the shopkeepers have no cloth for sale; this town is quite a prison. People

say the pope is at liberty here. A pretty liberty indeed! Want, impure air, wretched lodging, and a thousand other inconveniences keep the holy father closer than when he was in the Castle of St Angelo. Accordingly, he told me the other day, it was better to be in captivity at Rome than at liberty here."[1]

In two days, however, they managed to procure some new clothing; and being now in a condition to show themselves, Henry's agents were admitted to an after-dinner audience on Monday the 22d of March (1528).

Da Casale conducted them to an old building in ruins. "This is where his holiness lives," he said. They looked at one another with astonishment, and crossing the rubbish lying about, passed through three chambers whose ceilings had fallen in, whose windows were curtainless, and in which thirty persons " *riff-raff* were standing against the bare walls for a garnishment."[2] This was the pope's court.

At length the ambassadors reached the pontiff's room, and placed Henry's letters in his hands. "Your holiness," said Gardiner, " when sending the king a dispensation, was pleased to add, that if this document were not sufficient, you would willingly give a better. It is that favour the king now desires." The pope with embarrassment strove to soften his refusal. " I am informed," he said, " that the king is led on in this affair by a secret inclination, and that the lady he loves is far from being worthy of him." Gardiner replied with firmness: " The king truly desires to marry again after the divorce, that he may have an heir to the crown; but the woman he proposes to take is animated by the noblest sentiments: the cardinal of York and all England do homage to her virtues."[3] The pope appeared convinced. " Besides," continued Gardiner, " the king has written a book on the motives of his divorce."—" Good! come and read it to me to-morrow," rejoined Clement.

The next day the English envoys had hardly appeared, before Clement took Henry's book, ran over it as he walked up and down the room, and then seating himself on a long bench covered with an old carpet, " not worth twenty pence," says an annalist, he read the book aloud. He counted the number of arguments, made objections as if Henry were present, and piled them one upon another without waiting for an answer. " The marriages forbidden in Leviticus," said he, in a short and quick tone of voice, " are permitted in Deuteronomy; now Deuteronomy coming after Leviticus, we are bound by the latter. The honour of Catherine and the emperor is at stake, and the divorce would give rise to a terrible war."[4] The pope continued speaking, and whenever the Englishmen attempted to reply, he bade them be silent, and kept

---

[1] Non obstantibus quibuscunque decretis revocatoriis præsentis concessionis nostræ. Burnet, Records, ii. p. xvii.
[2] Mei dimidium. Ibid. p. xv.
[3] Money to present the cardinals. Strype's Mem. i. p. 137.
[4] Borrowing of divers men so much as might furnish three beds. Ibid. p. 139.
[5] Ibid.

[1] State Papers, vii. p. 63.   [2] Strype, 1. p. 139.
[3] The cardinal's judgment as to the good qualities of the gentlewoman. Ibid. p. 141.
[4] Quis præstabit ne hoc divortium magni alicujus belli causam præbeat. Sanderus, p. 26.

on reading. "It is an excellent book," said he, however, in a courteous tone, when he had ended; "I shall keep it to read over again at my leisure." Gardiner then presenting a draft of the commission which Henry required, Clement made answer: "It is too late to look at it now; leave it with me."— "But we are in haste," added Gardiner.— "Yes, yes, I know it," said the pope. All his efforts tended to protract the business.

On the 28th of March, the ambassadors were conducted to the room in which the pope slept; the cardinals Sanctorum Quatuor and De Monte, as well as the councillor of the Rota, Simonetta, were then with him. Chairs were arranged in a semicircle. "Be seated," said Clement, who stood in the middle,[1] "Master Gardiner, now tell me what you want."—"There is no question between us but one of *time*. You promised to ratify the divorce, as soon as it was pronounced; and we require you to do *before* what you engage to do *after*. What is right on one day must be right on another." Then, raising his voice, the Englishman added: "If his majesty perceives that no more respect is paid to him than to a common man,[2] he will have recourse to a *remedy* which I will not name, but which will not fail in its effect."

The pope and his councillors looked at one another in silence;[3] they had understood him. The imperious Gardiner, remarking the effect which he had produced, then added in an absolute tone: "We have our instructions, and are determined to keep to them."— "I am ready to do every thing compatible with my honour," exclaimed Clement, in alarm.—"What your honour would not permit you to grant," said the proud ambassador, "the honour of the king, my master, would not permit him to ask." Gardiner's language became more imperative every minute. "Well, then," said Clement, driven to extremity, "I will do what the king demands, and if the emperor is angry, I cannot help it." The interview, which had commenced with a storm, finished with a gleam of sunshine.

That bright gleam soon disappeared: Clement, who imagined he saw in Henry a Hannibal at war with Rome, wished to play the temporizer, the *Fabius Cunctator*. "*Bis dat qui cito dat*,"[4] said Gardiner sharply, who observed this manœuvre.—"It is a question of law," replied the pope, "and as I am very ignorant in these matters, I must give the doctors of the canon law the necessary time to make it all clear."—"By his delays Fabius Maximus saved Rome," rejoined Gardiner: "you will destroy it by yours."[5]— "Alas!" exclaimed the pope, "if I say the king is right, I shall have to go back to prison."[6]—"When truth is concerned," said

the ambassador, "of what consequence are the opinions of men?" Gardiner was speaking at his ease, but Clement found that the castle of St Angelo was not without weight in the balance. "You may be sure that I shall do everything for the best," replied the modern Fabius. With these words the conference terminated.

Such were the struggles of England with the popedom—struggles which were to end in a definitive rupture. Gardiner knew that he had a skilful adversary to deal with; too cunning to allow himself to be irritated, he coolly resolved to frighten the pontiff: that was in his instructions. On the Friday before Palm Sunday, he was ushered into the pope's closet; there he found Clement attended by De Monte, Sanctorum Quatuor, Simonetta, Staffileo, Paul, auditor of the Rota, and Gambara. "It is impossible," said the cardinals, "to grant a decretal commission in which the pope pronounces *de jure* in favour of the divorce, with a promise of confirmation *de facto*." Gardiner insisted; but no persuasion, "neither dulce nor poynante,"[1] could move the pontiff. The envoy judged the moment had come to discharge his strongest battery. "O perverse race," said he to the pontiff's ministers, "instead of being harmless as doves, you are as full of dissimulation and malice as serpents; promising every thing but performing nothing.[2] England will be driven to believe that God has taken from you the key of knowledge, and that the laws of the popes, ambiguous to the popes themselves, are only fit to be cast into the fire.[3] The king has hitherto restrained his people, impatient of the Romish yoke; but he will now give them the rein." A long and gloomy silence followed. Then the Englishman, suddenly changing his tone, softly approached Clement, who had left his seat, and conjured him in a low voice to consider carefully what justice required of him. "Alas!" replied Clement, "I tell you again, I am ignorant in these matters. According to the maxims of the canon law *the pope carries all laws in the tablets of his heart*,[4] but unfortunately God has never given me *the key* that opens them." As he could not escape by silence, Clement retreated under cover of a jest, and heedlessly pronounced the condemnation of the popedom. If he had never received the famous *key*, there was no reason why other pontiffs should have possessed it. The next day he found another loophole; for when the ambassadors told him that the king would carry on the matter without him, he sighed, drew out his handkerchief, and said as he wiped his eyes:[5] "Would to God that I were dead!" Clement employed tears as a political engine.

[1] In medio semicircull. Strype, Records, i. p. 81.
[2] Promiscuæ plebis. Ibid. p. 82.
[3] Every man looked on other and so stayed. Ibid.
[4] He gives twice who gives quickly.
[5] In Fabio Maximo qui rem Romanam cunctando restituit. Strype, p 99.
[6] Materia novæ captivitatis. Ibid. p. 86.

[1] Strype, Records, p. 114.
[2] Pleni omni dolo et versatione et dissimulatione. Verbis, omnia pollicentur, reipsa nihil præstant. Ibid. p. 98.
[3] Digna esse quæ mandentur flammis pontificia jura. Ibid.
[4] Pontifex habet omnia jura in scrinio pectoris. Ibid. p. 99.   [5] Ibid. p. 100.

" We shall not get the *decretal* commission," (that which pronounced the divorce) said Fox and Gardiner after this, " and it is not really necessary. Let us demand the *general* commission (authorizing the legates to pronounce it), and exact a promise that shall supply the place of the act which is denied us." Clement, who was ready to make all the promises in the world, swore to ratify the sentence of the legates without delay. Fox and Gardiner then presented to Simonetta a draft of the act required. The dean, after reading it, returned it to the envoys, saying, " It is very well, I think, except *the end*;[1] show it to Sanctorum Quatuor." The next morning they carried the draft to that cardinal : " How long has it been the rule for the patient to write the prescription ? I always thought it was the physician's business."—" No one knows the disease so well as the patient," replied Gardiner : " and this disease may be of such a nature that the doctor cannot prescribe the remedy without taking the patient's advice." Sanctorum Quatuor read the prescription, and then returned it, saying : " It is not bad, with the exception of *the beginning*.[2] Take the draft to De Monte and the other councillors." The latter liked neither beginning, middle, nor end. " We will send for you this evening," said De Monte.

Three or four days having elapsed, Henry's envoys again waited on the pope, who showed them the draft prepared by his councillors. Gardiner remarking in it additions, retrenchments, and corrections, threw it disdainfully from him, and said coldly : " Your holiness is deceiving us ; you have selected these men to be the instruments of your duplicity." Clement, in alarm, sent for Simonetta ; and after a warm discussion,[3] the envoys, more discontented than ever, quitted the pope at one in the morning.

The night brings wisdom. " I only desire two little words more in the commission," said Gardiner next day to Clement and Simonetta. The pope requested Simonetta to wait upon the cardinals immediately ; the latter sent word that they were at dinner, and adjourned the business until the morrow.

When Gardiner heard of this epicurean message, he thought the time had come for striking a decisive blow. A new tragedy began. " We are deceived," exclaimed he, " you are laughing at us. This is not the way to gain the favour of princes. Water mixed with wine spoils it ;[5] your corrections nullify our document. These ignorant and suspicious priests have spelled over our draft as if a scorpion was hidden under every word.[6]—You made us come to Italy," said he to Staffileo and Gambara, " like hawks

which the fowler lures by holding out to them a piece of meat ;[1] and now that we are here, the bait has disappeared, and, instead of giving us what we sought, you pretend to lull us to sleep by the sweet voice of the sirens." [2] Then, turning to Clement, the English envoy added, " Your holiness will have to answer for this." The pope sighed and wiped away his tears. " It was God's pleasure," continued Gardiner, whose tone became more threatening every minute, " that we should see with our own eyes the disposition of the people here. It is time to have done. Henry is not an ordinary prince— bear in mind that you are insulting *the defender of the faith*......You are going to lose the favour of the only monarch who protects you, and the apostolical chair, already tottering, will fall into dust, and disappear entirely amidst the applause of all Christendom."

Gardiner paused. The pope was moved. The state of Italy seemed to confirm but too strongly the sinister predictions of the envoy of Henry VIII. The imperial troops, terrified and pursued by Lautrec, had abandoned Rome and retired on Naples. The French general was following up this wretched army of Charles V., decimated by pestilence and debauchery ; Doria, at the head of his galleys, had destroyed the Spanish fleet ; Gaeta and Naples only were left to the imperialists ; and Lautrec, who was besieging the latter place, wrote to Henry on the 26th of August that all would soon be over. The timid Clement VII. had attentively watched all these catastrophes. Accordingly, Gardiner had hardly denounced the danger which threatened the popedom, before he turned pale with affright, rose from his seat, stretched out his arms in terror, as if he had desired to repel some monster ready to devour him, and exclaimed, " Write, write ! Insert whatever words you please." As he said this, he paced up and down the room, raising his hands to heaven and sighing deeply, while Fox and Gardiner, standing motionless, looked on in silence. A tempestuous wind seemed to be stirring the depths of the abyss ; the ambassadors waited until the storm was abated. At last Clement recovered himself,[3] made a few trivial excuses, and dismissed Henry's ministers. It was an hour past midnight.

It was neither morality, nor religion, nor even the laws of the church which led Clement to refuse the divorce ; ambition and fear were his only motives. He would have desired that Henry should first constrain the emperor to restore him his territories. But the king of England, who felt himself unable to protect the pope against Charles, required, however, this unhappy pontiff to provoke the emperor's anger. Clement reaped the fruits of that fatal system which had transformed

---

[1] The matter was good saving in the latter end. Strype, p. 102.
[2] The beginning pleased him not. Ibid. p. 103.
[3] Incalescente disputatione. Ibid. p. 104.
[4] Here began a new tragedy. Ibid. p. 105.
[5] Vinum conspurcat infusa aqua. Ibid.
[6] Putantes sub omni verbo latere scorpionem. Ibid.

[1] Praetendere pugno carnem. Strype, p. 105.
[2] Dulcibus sirenum vocibus incantare. Ibid.
[3] Compositis affectibus. Ibid. p. 106.

the church of Jesus Christ into a pitiful combination of policy and cunning.

On the next day, the tempest having thoroughly abated,[1] Sanctorum Quatuor corrected the commission. It was signed, completed by a leaden seal attached to a piece of string, and then handed to Gardiner, who read it. The bull was addressed to Wolsey, and " authorized him, in case he should acknowledge the nullity of Henry's marriage, to pronounce judicially the sentence of divorce, but without noise or display of judgment;[2] for that purpose he might take any English bishop for his colleague. "—" All that we can do, you can do," said the pope. " We are very doubtful," said the importunate Gardiner after reading the bull, " whether this commission, without the clauses of *confirmation* and *revocation*, will satisfy his majesty : but we will do all in our power to get him to accept it."—" Above all, do not speak of our altercations," said the pope. Gardiner, like a discreet diplomatist, did not scruple to note down every particular in cipher in the letters whence these details are procured. " Tell the king," continued the pontiff, " that this commission is on my part a declaration of war against the emperor, and that I now place myself under his majesty's protection." The chief-almoner of England departed for London with the precious document.

But one storm followed close upon another. Fox had not long quitted Orvieto when new letters arrived from Wolsey, demanding the fourth of the acts previously requested, namely, the *engagement* to ratify at Rome whatever the commissioners might decide in England. Gardiner was to set about it *in season and out of season;* the verbal promise of the pope counted for nothing; this document must be had, whether the pope was ill, dying, or dead.[3] "*Ego et Rex meus*," his majesty and I command you ; " said Wolsey; " This divorce is of more consequence to us than twenty popedoms."[4] The English envoy renewed their demand. " Since you refuse the decretal," he said, " there is the greater reason why you should not refuse *the engagement*." This application led to fresh discussion and fresh tears. Clement gave way once more ; but the Italians, more crafty than Gardiner, reserved a loophole in the document through which the pontiff might escape. The messenger Thaddeus carried it to London ; and Gardiner left Orvieto for Rome to confer with Campeggio.

Clement was a man of penetrating mind, and although he knew as well as any how to deliver a clever speech, he was irresolute and timid ; and accordingly the commission had not long been despatched before he repented. Full of distress, he paced the ruined chambers of his old palace, and imagined he saw hanging over his head that terrible sword of Charles the Fifth, whose edge he had already felt. " Wretch that I am," said he ; " cruel wolves surround me ; they open their jaws to swallow me up.........I see none but enemies around me. At their head is the emperor.........What will he do ? Alas ! I have yielded that fatal commission which the general of the Spanish observance had enjoined me to refuse. Behind Charles come the Venetians, the Florentines, the duke of Ferrara......They have cast lots upon my vesture.[1]......Next comes the king of France, who promises nothing, but looks on with folded arms ; or rather, what perfidy ! calls upon me at this critical moment to deprive Charles V. of his crown......And last, but not least, Henry VIII., *the defender of the faith,* indulges in frightful menaces against me...... The emperor desires to maintain the queen on the throne of England ; the latter, to put her away......Would to God that Catherine were in her grave ! But, alas ! she lives...... to be the apple of discord dividing the two greatest monarchies, and the inevitable cause of the ruin of the popedom......Wretched man that I am ! how cruel is my perplexity, and around me I can see nothing but horrible confusion."[2]

CHAPTER XI.

Fox's Report to Henry and Anne—Wolsey's Impression—He demands the Decretal—One of the Cardinal's petty Manœuvres—He sets his Conscience at Rest—Gardiner fails at Rome—Wolsey's new Perfidy—The King's Anger against the Pope—Sir T. More predicts Religious Liberty —Immorality of Ultramontane Socialism—Erasmus invited—Wolsey's last Flight—Energetic Efforts at Rome—Clement grants all—Wolsey triumphs—Union of Rome and England.

DURING this time Fox was making his way to England. On the 27th of April he reached Paris ; on the 2d of May he landed at Sandwich, and hastened to Greenwich, where he arrived the next day at five in the evening, just as Wolsey had left for London. Fox's arrival was an event of great importance. " Let him go to Lady Anne's apartments," said the king, " and wait for me there." Fox told Anne Boleyn of his and Gardiner's exertions, and the success of their mission, at which she expressed her very great satisfaction. Indeed, more than a year had elapsed since her return to England, and she no longer resisted Henry's project. " Mistress Anne always called me Master Stephen," wrote Fox to Gardiner, " her thoughts were so full of you." The king appeared and Anne withdrew.

---

[1] The divers tempests passed over. Strype, Records, l. p. 106.
[2] Sine strepitu et figura judicii sententiam divortii judicialiter proferendam. Rymer, Fœdera, vi. pars. ii. p. 95.
[3] In casu mortis pontificis, quod Deus avertat. Burnet, Records, p. xxviii.
[4] The thing which the king's highness and I more esteem than twenty papalities. Ibid. p. xxv.

[1] Novo fœdere inito super vestem suam miserunt sortem. Strype, Records, l. p. 109.
[2] His holiness findeth himself in a marvellous perplexity and confusion. Ibid. p. 106.

"Tell me as briefly as possible what you have done," said Henry. Fox placed in the king's hands the pope's insignificant letter, which he bade his almoner read; then that from Staffileo, which was put on one side; and lastly Gardiner's letter, which Henry took hastily and read himself. "The pope has promised us," said Fox, as he terminated his report, "to confirm the sentence of the divorce, as soon as it has been pronounced by the commissioners."—"Excellent!" exclaimed Henry; and then he ordered Anne to be called in. "Repeat before this lady," he said to Fox, "what you have just told me." The almoner did so. "The pope is convinced of the justice of your cause," he said in conclusion, "and the cardinal's letter has convinced him that my lady is worthy of the throne of England."—"Make your report to Wolsey this very night," said the king.

It was ten o'clock when the chief almoner reached the cardinal's palace; he had gone to bed, but immediate orders were given that Fox should be conducted to his room. Being a churchman, Wolsey could understand the pope's artifices better than Henry; accordingly, as soon as he learnt that Fox had brought the commission only, he became alarmed at the task imposed upon him. "What a misfortune!" he exclaimed; "your commission is no better than Gambara's...... However, go and rest yourself; I will examine these papers to-morrow." Fox withdrew in confusion. "It is not bad," said Wolsey the next day, "but the whole business still falls on me alone!—Never mind, I must wear a contented look, or else......" In the afternoon he summoned into his closet Fox, Dr Bell, and Viscount Rochford: "Master Gardiner has surpassed himself," said the crafty supple cardinal; "What a man! what an inestimable treasure! what a jewel in our kingdom!"[1]

He did not mean a word he was saying. Wolsey was dissatisfied with everything,—with the refusal of the *decretal*, and with the drawing up of the *commission*, as well as of the *engagement* (which arrived soon after in good condition, so far as the outside was concerned). But the king's ill humour would infallibly recoil on Wolsey; so putting a good face on a bad matter, he ruminated in secret on the means of obtaining what had been refused him. "Write to Gardiner," said he to Fox, "that everything makes me desire the pope's *decretal*—the need of unburdening my conscience, of being able to reply to the calumniators who will attack my judgment,[2] and the thought of the accidents to which the life of man is exposed. Let his holiness, then, pronounce the divorce himself; we engage on our part to keep his

resolution secret. But order Master Stephen to employ every kind of persuasion that his *rhetoric* can imagine." In case the pope should positively refuse the decretal, Wolsey required that at least Campeggio should share the responsibility of the divorce with him.

This was not all: while reading the engagement, Wolsey discovered the loophole which had escaped Gardiner, and this is what he contrived:—"The *engagement* which the pope has sent us," he wrote to Gardiner, "is drawn up in such terms that he can retract it at pleasure: we must therefore find some *good way* to obtain another. You may do it under this pretence. You will appear before his holiness with a dejected air, and tell him that the courier, to whom the conveyance of the said engagement was intrusted, fell into the water with his despatches, so that the rescripts were totally defaced and illegible: that I have not dared deliver it into the king's hands, and unless his holiness will grant you a duplicate, some notable blame will be imputed unto you for not taking better care in its transmission. And further, you will continue: I remember the expressions of the former document, and to save your holiness trouble, I will dictate them to your secretary. Then, added Wolsey, "while the secretary is writing, you will find means to introduce, without its being perceived, as many *fat, pregnant,* and available words as possible, to bind the pope and enlarge my powers, the politic handling of which the king's highness and I commit unto your good discretion."[1]

Such was the expedient invented by Wolsey. The papal secretary, imagining he was making a fresh copy of the original document (which was, by the way, in perfect condition), was at the dictation of the ambassador to draw up another of a different tenor. The "politic handling" of the cardinal-legate, which was not very unlike forgery, throws a disgraceful light on the policy of the sixteenth century.

Wolsey read this letter to the chief-almoner; and then, to set his conscience at rest, he added piously: "In an affair of such high importance, on which depends the glory or the ruin of the realm,—my honour or my disgrace—the condemnation of my soul or my everlasting merit—I will listen solely to the voice of my conscience,[2] and I shall act in such a manner as to be able to render an account to God without fear."

Wolsey did more; it seems that the boldness of his declarations reassured him with regard to the baseness of his works. Being at Greenwich on the following Sunday, he said to the king in the presence of Fox, Bell, Wolman, and Tuke: "I am bound to your royal person more than any subject was ever bound to his prince. I am ready to sacrifice my goods, my blood, my life for you.....

---

[1] O non æstimandum thesaurum margaritamque regni nostri. Strype, Records, i. p. 119.
[2] Justissime obstruere ora calumniantium et temere dissertientium. Ibid. p. 120.

[1] Burnet, Records, p. xxx.
[2] Reclamante conscientia. Strype, Records, i. p. 124.

But my obligations towards God are greater still. For that cause, rather than act against his will, I would endure the extremest evils.[1] I would suffer your royal indignation, and, if necessary, deliver my body to the executioners that they may cut it in pieces." What could be the spirit then impelling Wolsey? Was it blindness or impudence? He may have been sincere in the words he addressed to Henry; at the bottom of his heart he may have desired to set the pope above the king, and the church of Rome above the kingdom of England: and this desire may have appeared to him a sublime virtue, such as would hide a multitude of sins. What the public conscience would have called treason, was heroism to the Romish priest. This zeal for the papacy is sometimes met with in conjunction with the most flagrant immorality. If Wolsey deceived the pope, it was to save popery in the realm of England. Fox, Bell, Wolman, and Tuke listened to him with astonishment.[2] Henry, who thought he knew his man, received these holy declarations without alarm, and the cardinal having thus eased his conscience, proceeded boldly in his iniquities. It seems, however, that the inward reproaches which he silenced in public, had their revenge in secret. One of his officers entering his closet shortly afterwards, presented a letter addressed to Campeggio for his signature. It ended thus: "I hope all things shall be done according to the will of God, the desire of the king, the quiet of the kingdom, and to our honour *with a good conscience.*" The cardinal having read the letter, dashed out the four last words.[3] Conscience has a sting from which none can escape, not even a Wolsey.

However, Gardiner lost no time in Italy. When he met Campeggio (to whom Henry VIII. had given a palace at Rome, and a bishopric in England), he entreated him to go to London and pronounce the divorce. This prelate, who was to be empowered in 1530 with authority to crush Protestantism in Germany, seemed bound to undertake a mission that would save Romanism in Britain. But proud of his position at Rome, where he acted as the pope's representative, he cared not for a charge that would undoubtedly draw upon him either Henry's hatred or the emperor's anger. He begged to be excused. The pope spoke in a similar tone. When he was informed of this, the terrible Tudor, beginning to believe that Clement desired to entangle him, as the hunter entangles the lion in his toils, gave vent to his anger on Tuke, Fox, and Gardiner, but particularly on Wolsey. Nor were reasons wanting for this explosion. The cardinal, perceiving that his hatred against Charles had carried him too far, pretended

that it was without his orders that Clarencieux, bribed by France, had combined with the French ambassador to declare war against the emperor; and added that he would have the English king-at-arms put to death as he passed through Calais. This was an infallible means of preventing disagreeable revelations. But the herald, who had been forewarned, crossed by way of Boulogne, and, without the cardinal's knowledge, obtained an interview with Henry, before whom he placed the *orders* he had received from Wolsey in *three* consecutive letters. The king, astonished at his minister's impudence, exclaimed profanely: "O Lord Jesu, the man in whom I had most confidence told me quite the contrary." He then summoned Wolsey before him, and reproached him severely for his falsehoods. The wretched man shook like a leaf. Henry appeared to pardon him, but the season of his favour had passed away. Henceforward he kept the cardinal as one of those instruments we make use of for a time, and then throw away when we have no further need of them.

The king's anger against the pope far exceeded that against Wolsey; he trembled from head to foot, rose from his seat, then sat down again, and vented his wrath in the most violent language:—"What!" he exclaimed, "I shall exhaust my political combinations, empty my treasury, make war upon my friends, consume my forces......and for whom?......for a heartless priest who, considering neither the exigencies of my honour, nor the peace of my conscience, nor the prosperity of my kingdom, nor the numerous benefits which I have lavished on him, refuses me a favour, which he ought, as the common father of the faithful, to grant even to an enemy......Hypocrite!......You cover yourself with the cloak of friendship, you flatter us by crafty practices,[1] but you give us only a bastard document, and you say like Pilate: It matters little to me if this king perishes, and all his kingdom with him; take him and judge him according to your law!......I understand you......you wish to entangle us in the briers,[2] to catch us in a trap, to lure us into a pitfall......But we have discovered the snare; we shall escape from your ambuscade, and brave your power."

Such was the language then heard at the court of England, says an historian.[3] The monks and priests began to grow alarmed, while the most enlightened minds already saw in the distance the first gleams of religious liberty. One day, at a time when Henry was proving himself a zealous follower of the Romish doctrines, Sir Thomas More was sitting in the midst of his family, when his son-in-law, Roper, now become a warm

---

Extrema quæque....contra conscientiam suam. Strype. Records, i. p. 126.
[2] To my great mervail and no less joy and comfort. Ibid.
[3] Burnet's Ref. vol. i. p. 41.

[1] By crafty means and under the face and visage of entire amity. Strype, vol. i. p. 166.
[2] To involve and cast us so in the briers and fetters. Ibid.
[3] Strype.

papist, exclaimed: " Happy kingdom of England, where no heretic dares show his face!"—" That is true, son Roper," said More; " we seem to sit now upon the mountains, treading the heretics under our feet like ants; but I pray God that some of us do not live to see the day when we gladly would wish to be at league with them, to suffer them to have their churches quietly to themselves, so that they would be content to let us have ours peaceably to ourselves." Roper angrily replied:[1] " By my word, sir, that is very desperately spoken!" More, however, was in the right; genius is sometimes a great diviner. The Reformation was on the point of inaugurating religious liberty, and by that means placing civil liberty on an immovable foundation.

Henry himself grew wiser by degrees. He began to have doubts about the Roman hierarchy, and to ask himself, whether a priest-king, embarrassed in all the political complications of Europe, could be the head of the church of Jesus Christ. Pious individuals in his kingdom recognised in Scripture and in conscience a law superior to the law of Rome, and refused to sacrifice at the command of the church their moral convictions, sanctioned by the revelation of God. The hierarchical system, which claims to absorb man in the papacy, had oppressed the consciences of Christians for centuries. When the Romish Church had required from such as Berengarius, John Huss, Savonarola, John Wesel, and Luther, the denial of their consciences enlightened by the word, that is to say, by the voice of God, it had shown most clearly how great is the immorality of ultramontane socialism. " If the Christian consents to this enormous demand of the hierarchy," said the most enlightened men; "if he renounces his own notions of good and evil in favour of the clergy; if he reserves not his right to obey God, who speaks to him in the Bible, rather than men, even if their agreement were universal; if Henry VIII., for instance, should silence his conscience, which condemns his union with his brother's widow, to obey the clerical voice which approves of it; by that very act he renounces truth, duty, and even God himself." But we must add, that if the rights of conscience were beginning to be understood in England, it was not about such holy matters as these that the pope and Henry were contending. They were both intriguers—both dissatisfied, the one desirous of love, the other of power.

Be that as it may, a feeling of disgust for Rome then took root in the king's heart, and nothing could afterwards eradicate it. He immediately made every exertion to attract Erasmus to London. Indeed, if Henry separated from the pope, his old friends, the humanists, must be his auxiliaries, and not the heretical doctors. But Erasmus. in a letter dated 1st June, alleged the weak state of his health, the robbers who infested the roads, the wars and rumours of wars then afloat. " Our destiny leads us," he said; " let us yield to it."[1] It is a fortunate thing for England that Erasmus was not its reformer.

Wolsey noted this movement of his master's, and resolved to make a strenuous effort to reconcile Clement and Henry; his own safety was at stake. He wrote to the pope. to Campeggio, to Da Casale, to all Italy. He declared that if he was ruined, the popedom would be ruined too, so far at least as England was concerned : " I would obtain the *decretal* bull with my own blood, if possible,"[2] he added. " Assure the holy father on my life that no mortal eye shall see it." Finally, he ordered the chief-almoner to write to Gardiner : " If Campeggio does not come, *you shall never return* to England;"[3] an infallible means of stimulating the secretary's zeal.

This was the last effort of Henry VIII. Bourbon and the Prince of Orange had not employed more zeal a year before in scaling the walls of Rome. Wolsey's fire had inflamed his agents : they argued, entreated, stormed, and threatened. The alarmed cardinals and theologians, assembling at the pope's call, discussed the matter, mixing political interests with the affairs of the church.[4] At last they understood what Wolsey now communicated to them. " Henry is the most energetic defender of the faith," they said. " It is only by acceding to his demand that we can preserve the kingdom of England to the popedom. The army of Charles is in full flight, and that of Francis triumphs." The last of these arguments decided the question; the pope suddenly felt a great sympathy for Wolsey and for the English Church; the emperor was beaten; therefore he was wrong. Clement granted everything.

First, Campeggio was desired to go to London. The pontiff knew that he might reckon on his intelligence and inflexible adhesion to the interests of the hierarchy; even the cardinal's gout was of use, for it might help to innumerable delays. Next, on the 8th of June, the pope, then at Viterbo, gave a new commission, by which he conferred on Wolsey and Campeggio the power to declare null and void the marriage between Henry and Catherine, with liberty for the king and queen to form new matrimonial ties.[5] A few days later he signed the famous *decretal* by which he himself annulled the marriage between Henry and Catherine; but instead of intrusting it to Gardiner, he gave it to Campeggio, with orders not to let it go out of his hands. Clement was not sure of the course of events :

---

[1] My uncle said in a rage. More's life, p. 132.

[1] Fatis agimur, fatis cedendum. Erasm. Epp. p. 1032.
[2] Ut vel proprio sanguine id vellemus posse a S. D. N. impetrare. Burnet, Records. ii. p. 19.
[3] Neither should Gardiner ever return. Strype, i. p. 167.
[4] Negotia ecclesiastica politicis rationibus interpolantes. Sand. p. 27.
[5] Ad alia vota commigrandi. Herbert, p. 262.

if Charles should decidedly lose his power, the bull would be published in the face of Christendom : if he should recover it, the bull would be burnt.[1] In fact the flames did actually consume some time afterwards this decree which Clement had wetted with his tears as he put his name to it. Finally, on the 23d of July, the pope signed a valid *engagement*, by which he declared beforehand that all retractation of these acts should be *null and void*.[2] Campeggio and Gardiner departed. Charles's defeat was as complete at Rome as at Naples ; the justice of his cause had vanished with his army.

Nothing, therefore, was wanting to Henry's desires. He had Campeggio, the commission, the decretal bull of divorce signed by the pope, and the engagement giving an irrevocable value to all these acts. Wolsey was conqueror,—the conqueror of Clement !......He had often wished to mount the restive courser of the popedom and to guide it at his will,

but each time the unruly steed had thrown him from the saddle. Now he was firm in his seat, and held the horse in hand. Thanks to Charles's reverses, he was master at Rome. The popedom, whether it was pleased or not, must take the road he had chosen, and before which it had so long recoiled. The king's joy was unbounded, and equalled only by Wolsey's. The cardinal, in the fulness of his heart, wishing to shew his gratitude to the officers of the Roman court, made them presents of carpets, horses, and vessels of gold.[1] All near Henry felt the effects of his good humour. Anne smiled ; the court indulged in amusements ; the *great affair* was about to be accomplished ; the New Testament to be delivered to the flames. The union between England and the popedom appeared confirmed for ever, and the victory which Rome seemed about to gain in the British isles might secure her triumph in the west. Vain omens ! far different were the events in the womb of the future.

[1] State Papers, vol. vii. p. 78. Dr Lingard acknowledges the existence of this bull and the order to burn it.
[2] Si (quod absit) aliquid contra præmissa faciamus, illud pro casso, irrito, inani et vacuo omnino haberi volumus. Herbert, p. 250.

[1] Num illi, aulæa, vas aureum aut equi maxime probentur. Burnet, Records, i. p. xv.

BOOK XX.

THE TWO DIVORCES.

CHAPTER I.

Progress of the Reformation—The two Divorces—Entreaties to Anne Boleyn—The Letters in the Vatican—Henry to Anne—Henry's Second Letter—Third—Fourth—Wolsey's Alarm—His fruitless Proceedings—He turns—The Sweating Sickness—Henry's Fears—New Letters to Anne—Anne falls sick; her Peace—Henry writes to her—Wolsey's Terror—Campeggio does not arrive—All dissemble at Court.

WHILE England seemed binding herself to the court of Rome, the general course of the church and of the world gave stronger presage every day of the approaching emancipation of Christendom. The respect which for so many centuries had hedged in the Roman pontiff was everywhere shaken ; the Reform, already firmly established in several states of Germany and Switzerland, was extending in France, the Low Countries, and Hungary, and beginning in Sweden, Denmark, and Scotland. The South of Europe appeared indeed submissive to the Romish church ; but Spain, at heart, cared little for the pontifical infallibility ; and even Italy began to inquire whether the papal dominion was not an obstacle to her prosperity. England, notwithstanding appearances, was also going to throw off the yoke of the bishops of the Tiber,

and many faithful voices might already be heard demanding that the word of God should be acknowledged the supreme authority in the church.

The conquest of Christian Britain by the papacy occupied all the seventh century, as we have seen. The sixteenth was the counterpart of the seventh. The struggle which England then had to sustain, in order to free herself from the power that had enslaved her during nine hundred years, was full of sudden changes ; like those of the times of Augustine and Oswy. This struggle indeed took place in each of the countries where the church was reformed ; but nowhere can it be traced in all its diverse phases so distinctly as in Great Britain. The positive work of the Reformation—that which consisted in recovering the truth and life so long lost—was nearly the same everywhere ; but as regards the negative work—the struggle with the popedom—we might almost say that other nations committed to England the task by which they were all to profit. An unenlightened piety may perhaps look upon the relations of the court of London with the court of Rome, at the period of the Reformation, as void of interest to the faith; but history will not think the same. It has been too often forgotten that the main point in this contest was not the divorce (which was only the occasion), but the contest itself and its important consequences. The divorce of Henry Tudor and Catherine of Aragon is a secondary event; but the divorce of England and the popedom is a primary event, one of the great evolutions of history, a creative act (so to speak) which still exercises a normal influence over the destinies of mankind. And accordingly every thing connected with it is full of instruction for us. Already a great number of pious men had attached themselves to the authority of God; but the king, and with him that part of the nation, strangers to the evangelical faith, clung to Rome, which Henry had so valiantly defended. The word of God had spiritually separated England from the papacy; the *great matter* separated it materially. There is a close relationship between these two divorces, which gives extreme importance to the process between Henry and Catherine. When a great revolution is to be effected in the bosom of a people (we have the Reformation particularly in view), God instructs the minority by the Holy Scriptures, and the majority by the dispensations of the divine government. Facts undertake to push forward those whom the more spiritual voice of the word leaves behind. England, profiting by this great teaching of facts, has thought it her duty ever since to avoid all contact with a power that had deceived her; she has thought that popery could not have the dominion over a people without infringing on its vitality, and that it was only by emancipating themselves from this priestly dictatorship that modern nations could advance safely in the paths of liberty, order, and greatness.

For more than a year, as Henry's complaints testify, Anne continued deaf to his homage. The despairing king saw that he must set other springs to work, and taking Lord Rochford aside, he unfolded his plans to him. The ambitious father promised to do all in his power to influence his daughter. "The divorce is a settled thing," he said to her; "you have no control over it. The only question is, whether it shall be you or another who shall give an heir to the crown. Bear in mind that terrible revolutions threaten England if the king has no son." Thus did everything combine to weaken Anne's resolution. The voice of her father, the interests of her country, the king's love, and doubtless some secret ambition, influenced her to grasp the proffered sceptre. These thoughts haunted her in society, in solitude, and even in her dreams. At one time she imagined herself on the throne, distributing to the people her charities and the word of God; at another, in some obscure exile, leading a useless life, in tears and ignominy. When, in the sports of her imagination, the crown of England appeared all glittering before her, she at first rejected it; but afterwards that regal ornament seemed so beautiful, and the power it conferred so enviable, that she repelled it less energetically. Anne still refused, however, to give the so ardently solicited assent.

Henry, vexed by her hesitation, wrote to her frequently, and almost always in French. As the court of Rome makes use of these letters, which are kept in the Vatican, to abuse the Reformation, we think it our duty to quote them. The theft committed and cardinal has preserved them for us; and we shall see that, far from supporting the calumnies that have been spread abroad, they tend, on the contrary, to refute them. We are far from approving their contents as a whole: but we cannot deny to the young lady, to whom they are addressed, the possession of noble and generous sentiments.

Henry, unable to support the anguish caused by Anne's refusal wrote to her, as it is generally supposed, in May 1528 :[1]

" By revolving in my mind the contents of your last letters, I have put myself into great agony, not knowing how to interpret them, whether to my disadvantage, as I understand some passages, or not, as I conclude from others. I beseech you earnestly to let me know your real mind as to the love between us two. It is needful for me to obtain this answer of you, having been for a whole year wounded with the dart of love, and not yet assured whether I shall succeed in finding a place in your heart and affection. This uncertainty has hindered me of late from declaring you my mistress, lest it should prove that you only entertain for me an ordinary regard. But if you please to do the duty of a true and loyal mistress, I promise you that not only the name shall be given to you, but also that I will take you for my mistress, casting off all others that are in competition with you out of my thoughts and affection, and serving you only. I beg you to give an entire answer to this my rude letter, that I may know on what and how far I may depend. But if it does not please you to answer me in writing, let me know some place where I may have it by word of mouth, and I will go thither with all my heart. No more for fear of tiring you. Written by the hand of him, who would willingly remain yours, " H. REX."

Such were the affectionate, and we may add (if we think of the time and the man) the respectful terms employed by Henry in writing to Anne Boleyn. The latter, without making any promises, betrayed some little affection for the king, and added to her reply an emblematical jewel, representing " a soli-

---

[1] Vatican Letters. Pamphleteer, No. 43, p. 114. The date in the text is that assigned by the editor; we are inclined to place it somewhat earlier.

tary damsel in a boat tossed by the tempest," wishing thus to make the prince understand the dangers to which his love exposed her. Henry was ravished, and immediately replied :—

" For a present so valuable, that nothing could be more (considering the whole of it), I return you my most hearty thanks, not only on account of the costly diamond, and the ship in which the solitary damsel is tossed about, but chiefly for the fine interpretation, and the too humble submission which your goodness hath made to me. Your favour I will always seek to preserve, and this is my firm intention and hope, according to the matter, *aut illic aut nullibi.*

" The demonstrations of your affections are such, the fine thoughts of your letter so cordially expressed, that they oblige me for ever to honour, love, and serve you sincerely. I beseech you to continue in the same firm and constant purpose, and assuring you that, on my part, I will not only make you a suitable return, but outdo you, so great is the loyalty of the heart that desires to please you. I desire, also, that if, at any time before this, I have in any way offended you, that you would give me the same absolution that you ask, assuring you, that hereafter my heart shall be dedicated to you alone. I wish my person were so too. God can do it, if he pleases, *to whom I pray once a-day* for that end, hoping that at length *my prayers will be heard.* I wish the time may be short, but I shall think it long till we see one another. Written by the hand of that secretary, who in heart, body, and will, is

" Your loyal and most faithful Servant,
" H. T. Rex."[1]

Henry was a passionate lover, and history is not called upon to vindicate that cruel prince ; but in the preceding letter we cannot discover the language of a seducer. It is impossible to imagine the king praying to God *once a-day* for anything but a lawful union. These daily prayers seem to present the matter in a different light from that which Romanist writers have imagined.

Henry thought himself more advanced than he really was. Anne then shrank back ; embarrassed by the position she held at court, she begged for one less elevated : the king submitted, although very vexed at first :

" Nevertheless that it belongeth not to a gentleman," he wrote to her, to put his *mistress* in the situation of a *servant*, yet, by following your wishes, I would willingly concede it, if by that means you are less uncom-

fortable in the place you shall choose than in that where you have been placed by me. I thank you most cordially that you are pleased still to bear me in your remembrance.
" H. T."

Anne, having retired in May to Hever castle, her father's residence, the king wrote to her as follows :—

" My Mistress and my Friend,
" My heart and I surrender ourselves into your hands, and we supplicate to be commended to your good graces, and that by absence your affections may not be diminished to us. For that would be to augment our pain, which would be a great pity, since absence gives enough, and more than I ever thought could be felt. This brings to my mind a fact in astronomy, which is, that the longer the days are, the farther off is the sun, and yet the more scorching is his heat. Thus is it with our love ; absence has placed distance between us, nevertheless fervour increases, at least on my part. I hope the same from you, assuring you that in my case the anguish of absence is so great that it would be intolerable were it not for the firm hope I have of your indissoluble affection towards me. In order to remind you of it, and because I cannot in person be in your presence, I send you the thing which comes nearest that is possible, that is to say, my picture, and the whole device, which you already know of,[1] set in bracelets ; wishing myself in their place when it pleases you. This is from the hand of
" Your Servant and Friend,
" H. T. Rex."

Pressed by her father, her uncles, and by Henry, Anne's firmness was shaken. That crown, rejected by Renée and by Margaret, dazzled the young Englishwoman ; every day she found some new charm in it : and gradually familiarizing herself with her new future, she said at last : " If the king becomes free, I shall be willing to marry him." This was a great fault ; but Henry was at the height of joy.

The courtiers watched with observant eyes these developments of the king's affection, and were already preparing the homage which they proposed to lay at Anne Boleyn's feet. But there was one man at court whom Henry's resolution filled with sorrow ; this was Wolsey. He had been the first to suggest to the king the idea of separating from Catherine ; but if Anne is to succeed her, there must be no divorce. He had first alienated Catherine's party ; he was now going to irritate that of the Boleyns ; accordingly he began to fear that whatever might be the issue of this affair, it would cause his ruin. He took frequent walks in his park

---

[1] Pamphleteer. No. 43, p. 115. After the signature comes the following device :

 Nulle autre que A B *ne cherche H.T.*

[1] Doubtless the *aut illic aut nullibi.* For this letter see the Pamphleteer, No. 42, p. 346.

at Hampton Court, accompanied by the French ambassador, the confidant of his sorrows : " I would willingly lose one of my fingers," he said, " if I could only have two hours' conversation with the king of France." At another time, fancying all England was pursuing him, he said with alarm, " The king my master and all his subjects will cry murder against me ; they will fall upon me more fiercely than on a Turk, and all Christendom will rise against me ! " The next day Wolsey, to gain the French ambassador, gave him a long history of what he had done for France *against the wishes of all England :* " I need much dexterity in my affairs," he added, " and must use a terrible *alchymy*." [1] But alchymy could not save him. Rarely has so much anguish been veiled beneath such grandeur. Du Bellay was moved with pity at the sight of the unhappy man's sufferings. " When he gives way," he wrote to Montmorency, " it lasts a day together ;— he is continually sighing.—You have never seen a man in such anguish of mind." [2]

In truth Wolsey's reason was tottering. That fatal idea of the divorce was the cause of all his woes, and to be able to recall it, he would have given, not a *finger* only, but an arm, and perhaps more. It was too late ; Henry had started his car down the steep, and whoever attempted to stop it would have been crushed beneath its wheels. However, the cardinal tried to obtain something. Francis I. had intercepted a letter from Charles V. in which the emperor spoke of the divorce as likely to raise the English nation in revolt. Wolsey caused this letter to be read to the king, in the hope that it would excite his serious apprehensions ; but Henry only *frowned*, and Du Bellay, to whom the monarch ascribed the report on these troubles foreboded by Charles, received " a gentle lash." [3] This was the sole result of the manœuvre.

Wolsey now resolved to broach this important subject in a straightforward manner. The step might prove his ruin ; but if he succeeded he was saved and the popedom with him. Accordingly one day (shortly before the sweating sickness broke out, says Du Bellay, probably in June 1528) Wolsey openly prayed the king to renounce his design ; his own reputation, he told him, the prosperity of England, the peace of Europe, the safety of the church,—all required it ; besides the pope would never grant the divorce. While the cardinal was speaking, Henry's face grew black ; and before he had concluded the king's anger broke out. " The king used terrible words," said Du Bellay. He would have given a thousand Wolseys for one Anne Boleyn. " No other than God shall take her from me," was his most decided resolution.

Wolsey, now no longer doubting of his disgrace, began to take his measures accordingly. He commenced building in several places, in order to win the affections of the common people ; he took great care of his bishoprics, in order that they might ensure him an easy retreat ; he was affable to the courtiers ; and thus covered the earth with flowers to deaden his fall. Then he would sigh as if he were disgusted with honours, and would celebrate the charms of solitude.[1] He did more than this. Seeing plainly that the best way of recovering the king's favour would be to conciliate Anne Boleyn, he made her the most handsome presents,[2] and assured her that all his efforts would now be directed to raise her to the throne of England. Anne believing these declarations replied, that she would help him in her turn, " As long as any breath was in her body." [3] Even Henry had no doubt that the cardinal had profited by his lesson.

Thus were all parties restless and uneasy —Henry desiring to marry Lady Anne, the courtiers to get rid of Wolsey, and the latter to remain in power—when a serious event appeared to put every one in harmony with his neighbour. About the middle of June, the terrible sweating sickness (*sudor anglicus*) broke out in England. The citizens of London, " thick as flies," said Du Bellay,[4] suddenly feeling pains in the head and heart, rushed from the streets or shops to their chambers, began to sweat, and took to their beds. The disease made frightful and rapid progress, a burning heat preyed on their limbs ; if they chanced to uncover themselves, the perspiration ceased, delirium came on, and in four hours the victim was dead and " stiff as a wall," [5] says the French ambassador. Every family was in mourning. Sir Thomas More, kneeling by his daughter's bedside, burst into tears, and called upon God to save his beloved Margaret.[6] Wolsey, who was at Hampton Court, suspecting nothing amiss, arrived in London as usual to preside in the Court of Chancery ; but he ordered his horses to be saddled again immediately and rode back. In four days, 2000 persons died in London.

The court was at first safe from the contagion ; but on the fourth day one of Anne Boleyn's ladies was attacked ; it was as if a thunderbolt had fallen on the palace. The king removed with all haste, and staid at a place twelve miles off, for he was not prepared to die. He ordered Anne to return to her father, invited the queen to join him, and took up his residence at Waltham. His real conscience awoke only in the presence of death. Four of his attendants and a friar,

[1] Une terrible Alquemie. Le Grand, Preuves, p. 157.
[2] 26th April, 1528. Ibid. p. 93.
[3] *Quelque petit coup de fouet.* 24th May, 1528. Du Bellay to Montmorency. Le Grand, Preuves, p. 102.

[1] 20th August 1528. Du Bellay to Montmorency. Le Grand. Preuves, p. 165.
[2] Pamphleteer, No. 43, p. 150.   [3] Ibid.
[4] Dru comme mouches. Le Grand, Preuves, p. 138.
[5] Raide comme un pan de mur. Ibid.
[6] More's Life, p. 136.

Anne's confessor, as it would appear,[1] falling ill, the king departed for Hunsdon. He had been there two days only when Powis, Carew, Carton, and others of his court, were carried off in two or three hours. Henry had met an enemy whom he could not vanquish. He quitted the place attacked by the disease; he removed to another quarter; and when the sickness laid hold of any of his attendants in his new retreat, he again left that for a new asylum. Terror froze his blood; he wandered about pursued by that terrible scythe whose sweep might perhaps reach him; he cut off all communication, even with his servants; shut himself up in a room at the top of an isolated tower; ate all alone, and would see no one but his physician:[2] he prayed, fasted, confessed, became reconciled with the queen; took the sacrament every Sunday and feast day; received *his Maker*,[3] to use the words of a gentleman of his chamber; and the queen and Wolsey did the same. Nor was that all: his councillor, Sir Brian Tuke, was sick in Essex; but that mattered not; the king ordered him to come to him, even in his litter; and on the 20th of June, Henry after hearing three masses (he had never done so much before in one day) said to Tuke: "I want you to write *my will*." He was not the only one who took that precaution. "There were *a hundred thousand* made," says Du Bellay.

During this time, Anne in her retirement at Hever was calm and collected; she prayed much, particularly for the king and for Wolsey.[4] But Henry, far less submissive, was very anxious. "The uneasiness my doubts about your health gave me," he wrote to her, "disturbed and frightened me exceedingly; but now, since you have as yet felt nothing, I hope it is with you as it is with us......I beg you, my entirely beloved, not to frighten yourself, or be too uneasy at our absence, for wherever I am, I am yours. And yet we must sometimes submit to our misfortunes, for whoever will struggle against fate, is generally but so much the farther from gaining his end. Wherefore, comfort yourself and take courage, and make this misfortune as easy to you as you can."[5]

As he received no news, Henry's uneasiness increased; he sent to Anne a messenger and a letter: "To acquit myself of the duty of a true servant, I send you this letter, beseeching you to apprize me of your welfare, which I pray may continue as long as I desire mine own."

Henry's fears were well founded; the malady became more severe; in four hours eighteen persons died at the archbishop of Canterbury's; Anne Boleyn herself and her brother also caught the infection. The king was exceedingly agitated; Anne alone appeared calm; the strength of her character raised her above exaggerated fears; but her enemies ascribed her calmness to other motives. "Her ambition is stronger than death," they said. "The king, queen, and cardinal tremble for their lives, but she...... she would die content if she died a queen." Henry once more changed his residence. All the gentlemen of his privy-chamber were attacked with one exception; "he remained alone, keeping himself apart," says Du Bellay, and confessed every day. He wrote again to Anne, sending her his physician, Dr Butts:[1] "The most displeasing news that could occur came to me suddenly at night. On three accounts I must lament it. One, to hear of the illness of my mistress, whom I esteem more than all the world, and whose health I desire as I do my own. I would willingly bear half of what you suffer to cure you. The second, from the fear that I shall have to endure that wearisome absence much longer, which has hitherto given me all the vexation that was possible; and when gloomy thoughts fill my mind, then I pray God to remove far from me such troublesome and rebellious ideas. The third, because my physician, in whom I have most confidence, is absent. Yet, from the want of him, I send you my second, and hope that he will soon make you well. I shall then love him more than ever. I beseech you to be guided by his advice in your illness. By your doing this, I hope soon to see you again, which will be to me a greater comfort than all the precious jewels in the world."

The pestilence soon broke out with more violence around Henry; he fled in alarm to Hatfield, taking with him only the gentlemen of his chamber; he next quitted this place for Tittenhanger, a house belonging to Wolsey, whence he commanded general processions throughout the kingdom in order to avert this scourge of God.[2] At the same time he wrote to Wolsey: "As soon as any one falls ill in the place where you are, fly to another; and go thus from place to place." The poor cardinal was still more alarmed than Henry. As soon as he felt the slightest perspiration, he fancied himself a dead man. "I entreat your highness," he wrote trembling to the king on the 5th of July, "to show yourself full of pity for my soul; these are perhaps the last words I shall address to you......the whole world will see by my last testament that you have not bestowed your favour upon an ungrateful man." The king, perceiving that Wolsey's mind was affected, bade him "put apart fear and fantasies,"[3] and wear a cheerful humour in the midst of death.

At last the sickness began to diminish, and immediately the desire to see Anne revived in Henry's bosom. On the 18th of August

[1] Votre père maître Jesonère est tombé malade. Henry to Anne. Pamphleteer, No. 42, p. 347
[2] With his physician in a chamber within a tower to sup apart. State Papers, vol. i. p. 296. [3] Ibid. p. 294.
[4] I thank our Lord that them that I desired and prayed for are escaped, and that is the king's grace and you. Anne to Wolsey. Pamphleteer, No 43, p. 154.
[5] Ibid. No. 42, p. 347.

[1] Pamphleteer, No. 43, p. 120.
[2] State Papers, i. p. 308.   [3] Ibid. p. 314.

she re-appeared at court, and all the king's thoughts were now bent on the divorce.

But this business seemed to proceed in inverse ratio to his desires. There was no news of Campeggio; was he lost in the Alps or at sea? Did his gout detain him in some village, or was the announcement of his departure only a feint? Anne Boleyn herself was uneasy, for she attached great importance to Campeggio's coming. If the church annulled the king's first marriage, Anne seeing the principal obstacle removed, thought she might accept Henry's hand. She therefore wrote to Wolsey: " I long to hear from you news of the legate, for I do hope (an' they come from you) they shall be very good." The king added in a postscript: "The not hearing of the legate's arrival in France causeth us somewhat to muse. Notwithstanding we trust by your diligence and vigilancy (with the assistance of Almighty God) shortly to be eased out of that trouble."[1]

But still there was no news. While waiting for the long-desired ambassador, every one at the English court played his part as well as he could. Anne, whether from conscience, prudence, or modesty, refused the honours which the king would have showered upon her, and never approached Catherine but with marks of profound respect. Wolsey had the look of desiring the divorce, while in reality he dreaded it, as fated to cause his ruin and that of the popedom. Henry strove to conceal the motives which impelled him to separate from the queen; to the bishops, he spoke of his *conscience*, to the nobility *of an heir*, and to all of the sad obligation which compelled him to put away so justly beloved a princess. In the meanwhile, he seemed to live on the best terms with her, from what Du Bellay says.[2] But Catherine was the one who best dissembled her sentiments; she lived with the king as during their happiest days, treated Anne with every kindness, adopted an elegant costume, encouraged music and dancing in her apartments, often appeared in public, and seemed desirous of captivating by her gracious smiles the good-will of England. This was a mournful comedy, destined to end in tragedy full of tears and agony.

CHAPTER II.

Coverdale and Inspiration—He undertakes to translate the Scriptures—His Joy and Spiritual Songs—Tyball and the Laymen—Coverdale preaches at Brumstead—Revival at Colchester—Incomplete Societies and the New Testament —Persecution—Monmouth arrested and released.

WHILE these scenes were acting in the royal palaces, far different discussions were going on among the people. After having dwelt for some time on the agitations of the court, we gladly return to the lowly disciples of the divine word. The Reformation of England (and this is its characteristic) brings before us by turns the king upon his throne, and the laborious artizan in his humble cottage: between these two extremes we meet with the doctor in his college, and the priest in his pulpit.

Among the young men trained at Cambridge under Barnes's instruction, and who had aided him at the time of his trial, was Miles Coverdale, afterwards bishop of Exeter, a man distinguished by his zeal for the gospel of Jesus Christ. Some time after the prior's fall, on Easter Eve, 1527, Coverdale and Cromwell met at the house of Sir Thomas More, when the former exhorted the Cambridge student to apply himself to the study of sacred learning.[1] The lapse of his unhappy master had alarmed Coverdale, and he felt the necessity of withdrawing from that outward activity which had proved so fatal to Barnes. He therefore turned to the Scriptures, read them again and again, and perceived, like Tyndale, that the reformation of the church must be effected by the word of God. The inspiration of that word, the only foundation of its sovereign authority, had struck Coverdale. " Wherever the Scripture is known it reformeth all things. And why? Because it is given *by the inspiration of God.*"[2] This fundamental principle of the Reformation in England must, in every age, be that of the church.

Coverdale found happiness in his studies: " Now," he said, " I begin to taste of Holy Scriptures! Now, honour be to God! I am set to the most sweet smell of holy letters."[3] He did not stop there, but thought it his duty to attempt in England the work which Tyndale was prosecuting in Germany. The Bible was so important in the eyes of these Christians, that two translations were undertaken simultaneously. " Why should other nations," said Coverdale, " be more plenteously provided for with the Scriptures in their mother-tongue than we?"[4]—" Beware of translating the Bible!" exclaimed the partisans of the schoolmen; " your labour will only make divisions in the faith and in the people of God."[5]—" God has now given his church," replied Coverdale, " the gifts of translating and of printing; we must improve them." And if any friends spoke of Tyndale's translation, he answered: " Do not you know that when many are starting together, every one doth his best to be nighest the mark?"[6]— " But Scripture ought to exist in Latin only," objected the priests.—" No," replied Coverdale again, " the Holy Ghost is as much the author of it in the Hebrew, Greek, French,

[1] Pamphleteer, No. 48, p. 149.
[2] 16th October 1528. Du Bellay to Montmorency. Le Grand, Preuves, p. 170.

[1] Coverdale's Remains (Park. Soc.), p. 490. The authority for this statement is a letter from Coverdale to Cromwell, which the editor of the " Remains" assigns to the year 1527. Mr Anderson (Annals of the Bible, i. p. 239), places it four years later, in 1531. Foxe asserts that Cromwell was at the siege of Rome in May 1527, on the authority of Cranmer and Cromwell himself (Acts and Mon. v. p. 365). If so, the letter cannot belong to that year; but 1531 is improbable. I am inclined to think it was written in 1528; but any way there is a difficulty with the date.   [2] Coverdale's Remains, p. 10.   [3] Ibid. p. 490.
[4] Ibid. p. 12.   [5] Ibid.   [6] Ibid. p. 14.

Dutch, and English, as in Latin.......The word of God is of like authority, in what language soever the Holy Ghost speaketh it."[1] This does not mean that translations of Holy Scripture are inspired, but that the word of God, faithfully translated, always possesses a divine authority.

Coverdale determined, therefore, to translate the Bible, and, to procure the necessary books, he wrote to Cromwell, who, during his travels, had made a collection of these precious writings. "Nothing in the world I desire but books," he wrote; "like Jacob, you have drunk of the dew of heaven......I ask to drink of your waters."[2] Cromwell did not refuse Coverdale his treasures. "Since the Holy Ghost moves you to bear the cost of this work," exclaimed the latter, "God gives me boldness to labour in the same."[3] He commenced without delay, saying: "Whosoever believeth not the Scripture, believeth not Christ; and whoso refuseth it, refuseth God also."[4] Such were the foundations of the reformed church in England.

Coverdale did not undertake to translate the Scriptures as a mere literary task: the Spirit which had inspired them spoke to his heart; and tasting their life-giving promises, he expressed his happiness in pious songs:—

> Be glad now, all ye christen men,
>   And let us rejoyce unfaynedly.
> The kindnesse cannot be written with penne,
>   That we have receaved of God's mercy;
> Whose love towarde us hath never ende:
> He hath done for us as a frende;
>   Now let us thanke him hartely.
>
> These lovynge wordes he spake to me:
>   I wyll delyver thy soule from payne;
> I am desposed to do for thee,
>   And to myne owne selfe thee to retayne.
> Thou shalt be with me, for thou art myne;
> And I with thee, for I am thyne;
>   Such is my love, I can not layne.
>
> They wyll shed out my precyous bloude,
>   And take away my lyfe also;
> Which I wyll suffre all for thy good:
>   Beleve this sure, where ever thou go.
> For I will yet ryse up agayne;
> Thy synnes I beare, though it be payne,
>   To make thee safe and free from wo.

Coverdale did not remain long in the solitude he desired. The study of the Bible, which had attracted him to it, soon drew him out of it. A revival was going on in Essex; John Tyball, an inhabitant of Bumpstead, having learnt to find in Jesus Christ the *true bread from heaven*, did not stop there. One day as he was reading the first epistle to the Corinthians, these words: "eat of this *bread*," and "drink of this *cup*," repeated four times within a few verses, convinced him that there was no transubstantiation. "A priest has no power to create the body of the Lord," said he; "Christ truly is present in the Eucharist, but he is there only *for him*

that believeth, and by a spiritual presence and action only." Tyball, disgusted with the Romish clergy and worship, and convinced that Christians are called to a universal priesthood, soon thought that men could do without a special ministry, and without denying the offices mentioned in Scripture, as some Christians have done since, he attached no importance to them. "Priesthood is not necessary,"[1] he said: "every layman may administer the sacraments as well as a priest." The minister of Bumpstead, one Richard Foxe, and next a greyfriar of Colchester named Meadow, were successively converted by Tyball's energetic preaching.

Coverdale, who was living not far from these parts, having heard of this religious revival, came to Bumpstead, and went into the pulpit in the spring of 1528, to proclaim the treasures contained in Scripture. Among his hearers was an Augustine monk, named Topley, who was supplying Foxe's place during his absence. This monk, while staying at the parsonage, had found a copy of Wickliffe's *Wicket*, which he read eagerly. His conscience was wounded by it, and all seemed to totter about him.[2] He had gone to church full of doubt, and after divine service he waited upon the preacher, exclaiming: "O my sins, my sins!" "Confess yourself to God," said Coverdale, "and not to a priest. God accepteth the confession which cometh from the heart, and blotteth out all your sins."[3] The monk believed in the forgiveness of God, and became a zealous evangelist for the surrounding country.

The divine word had hardly lighted one torch, before that kindled another. At Colchester, in the same county, a worthy man named Pykas, had received a copy of the Epistles of Saint Paul from his mother, with this advice: "My son, live according to these writings, and not according to the teaching of the clergy." Some time after, Pykas having bought a New Testament, and "read it thoroughly many times,"[4] a total change took place in him. "We must be baptized by the Holy Ghost," he said, and these words passed like a breath of life over his simple-minded hearers. One day, Pykas having learnt that Bilney, the first of the Cambridge doctors who had known the power of God's word, was preaching at Ipswich, he proceeded thither, for he never refused to listen to a priest, when that priest proclaimed the truth. "O, what a sermon! how full of the Holy Ghost!" exclaimed Pykas.

From that period meetings of the brothers in Christ (for thus they were called) increased in number. They read the New Testament, and each imparted to the others what he had

---

[1] Coverdale's Remains, p. 26.
[2] De tuo ipso torrente maxime potare exopto. Ibid. p. 491.
[3] Ibid. p. 10.   [4] Ibid. p. 19.

[1] Strype, Records, i. p. 51.
[2] I felt in my conscience a great wavering. Anderson's Annals of the Bible, vol. i. p. 185.
[3] Coverdale's Remains, p. 481.
[4] Strype, vol. i. ch. i. p. 121.

received for the instruction of all.' One day when the twenty-fourth chapter of Matthew had been read, Pykas, who was sometimes wrong in the spiritual interpretation of Scripture, remarked : " When the Lord declares that *not one stone of the temple shall be left upon another*, he speaks of those haughty priests who persecute those whom they call heretics, and who pretend to be the temple of God. God will destroy them all." After protesting against the priest, he protested against the host : " The real body of Jesus Christ is in the Word," he said ; " God is in the Word, the Word is in God.[1] God and the Word cannot be separated. Christ is the living Word that nourishes the soul." These humble preachers increased. Even women knew the Epistles and Gospels by heart ; Marion Matthew, Dorothy Long, Catherine Swain, Alice Gardiner, and above all, Gyrling's wife, who had been in service with a priest lately burnt for heresy, took part in these gospel meetings. And it was not in cottages only that the glad tidings were then proclaimed ; Bower Hall, the residence of the squires of Bumpstead, was open to Foxe, Topley, and Tyball, who often read the Holy Scriptures in the great hall of the mansion, in the presence of the master and all their household : a humble Reformation more real than that effected by Henry VIII.

There was, however, some diversity of opinion among these brethren. " All who have begun to believe," said Tyball, Pykas, and others, " ought to meet together to hear the word and increase in faith. We pray in common .....and that constitutes a church." Coverdale, Bilney, and Latimer willingly recognised these incomplete societies, in which the members met simply as *disciples ;* they believed them necessary at a period when the church was forming. These societies (in the reformers' views) proved that organization has not the priority in the Christian church, as Rome maintains, and that this priority belongs to the faith and the life. But this imperfect form they also regarded as provisional. To prevent numerous dangers, it was necessary that this society should be succeeded by another, the church of the New Testament, with its elders or bishops, and deacons. The word, they thought, rendered a ministry of the word necessary ; and for its proper exercise not only piety was required, but a knowledge of the sacred languages, the gift of eloquence, its exercise and perfection. However, there was no division among these Christians upon secondary matters.

For some time the bishop of London watched this movement with uneasiness. He caused Hacker to be arrested, who, for six years past, had gone from house to house reading the Bible in London and Essex ; examined and threatened him, inquired carefully after the names of those who had shewn him hospitality ; and the poor man in alarm had given up about forty of his brethren. Sebastian Harris, priest of Kensington, Forman, rector of All Hallows, John and William Pykas, and many others, were summoned before the bishop. They were taken to prison ; they were led before the judges ; they were put in the stocks ; they were tormented in a thousand ways. Their minds became confused ; their thoughts wandered ; and many made the confessions required by their persecutors.

The adversaries of the gospel, proud of this success, now desired a more glorious victory. If they could not reach Tyndale, had they not in London the patron of his work, Monmouth, the most influential of the merchants, and a follower of the true faith ? The clergy had made religion their business, and the Reformation restored it to the people. Nothing offended the priests so much, as that laymen should claim the right to believe without their intervention, and even to propagate the faith. Sir Thomas More, one of the most amiable men of the sixteenth century, participated in their hatred. He wrote to Cochlœus ! " Germany now daily bringeth forth monsters more deadly than what Africa was wont to do ;[1] but, alas ! she is not alone. Numbers of Englishmen, who would not a few years ago even hear Luther's name mentioned, are now publishing his praises ! England is now like the sea, which swells and heaves before a great storm, without any wind stirring it."[2] More felt particularly irritated, because the boldness of the gospellers had succeeded to the timidity of the Lollards " The heretics," he said, " have put off hypocrisy, and put on impudence." He therefore resolved to set his hand to the work.

On the 14th of May 1529, Monmouth was in his shop, when an usher came and summoned him to appear before Sir J. Dauncies. one of the privy council. The pious merchant obeyed, striving to persuade himself that he was wanted on some matter of business ; but in this he was deceived, as he soon found out. " What letters and books have you lately received from abroad ?"[3] asked, with some severity, Sir Thomas More, who, with Sir William Kingston, was Sir John's colleague. " None," replied Monmouth. " What aid have you given to any persons living on the continent ?"—" None for these last three years. William Tyndale abode with me six months," he continued, " and his life was what a good priest's ought to be. I gave him ten pounds at the period of his departure, but nothing since. Besides, he is not the only one I have helped ; the bishop of London's chaplain, for instance, has received of me more than L.50."—" What books have you in your possession ?" The merchant named the New Testament and some other works. " All these books have lain more than two years on my table, and I never heard that

[1] Strype, vol. i. ch. i. p. 130.

[1] More's Life, p. 82.   [2] Ibid. p. 117.
[3] Strype's Records, p. 363.

either priests, friars, or laymen learnt any great errors from them."[1] More tossed his head. "It is a hard matter," he used to say, "to put a dry stick in the fire without its burning, or to nourish a snake in our bosom and not be stung by it.[2] That is enough," he continued, "we shall go and search your house." Not a paper escaped their curiosity; but they found nothing to compromise Monmouth; he was, however, sent to the Tower.

After some interval the merchant was again brought before his judges. "You are accused," said More, "of having bought Martin Luther's tracts; of maintaining those who are translating the Scriptures into English; of subscribing to get the New Testament printed in English, with or without glosses; of having imported it into the kingdom; and, lastly, of having said that faith alone is sufficient to save a man."[3]

There was matter enough to burn several men. Monmouth, feeling convinced that Wolsey alone had power to deliver him, resolved to apply to him. "What will become of my poor workmen in London and in the country during my imprisonment?" he wrote to the cardinal. "They must have their money every week; who will give it them? ......Besides, I make considerable sales in foreign countries, which bring large returns to his majesty's customs.[4] If I remain in prison, this commerce is stopped, and of course all the proceeds for the exchequer." Wolsey, who was as much a statesman as a churchman, began to melt; on the eve of a struggle with the pope and the emperor, he feared, besides, to make the people discontented. Monmouth was released from prison. As alderman, and then as sheriff of London, he was faithful until death, and ordered in his last will that thirty sermons should be preached by the most evangelical ministers in England, "to make known the holy word of Jesus Christ."—"That is better," he thought, "than founding masses." The Reformation shewed, in the sixteenth century, that great activity in commerce might be allied to great piety."

CHAPTER III.

Political Changes—Fresh Instructions from the Pope to Campeggio—His Delays—He unbosoms himself to Francis—A Prediction—Arrival of Campeggio—Wolsey's Uneasiness—Henry's Satisfaction—The Cardinal's Project—Campeggio's Reception—First Interview with the Queen and with the King—Useless Efforts to make Campeggio part with the Decretal—The Nuncio's Conscience—Public Opinion—Measures taken by the King—His Speech to the Lords and Aldermen—Festivities—Wolsey seeks French Support—Contrariety.

WHILE these persecutions were agitating the fields and the capital of England, all had changed in the ecclesiastical world, because all had changed in the political. The pope pressed by Henry VIII. and intimidated by the armies of Francis I., had granted the decretal and despatched Campeggio. But, on a sudden, there was a new evolution; a change of events brought a change of counsels. Doria had gone over to the emperor; his fleet had restored abundance to Naples; the army of Francis I., ravaged by famine and pestilence, had capitulated, and Charles V., triumphant in Italy, had said proudly to the pope: "We are determined to defend the queen of England against King Henry's injustice."[1]

Charles having recovered his superiority, the affrighted pope opened his eyes to the justice of Catherine's cause. "Send four messengers after Campeggio," said he to his officers; "and let each take a different road; bid them travel with all speed and deliver our despatches to him."[2] They overtook the legate, who opened the pope's letters. "In the first place," said Clement VII. to him, "protract your journey. In the second place, when you reach England, use every endeavour to reconcile the king and queen. In the third place, if you do not succeed, persuade the queen to take the veil. And in the last place, if she refuses, do not pronounce any sentence favourable to the divorce without a new and express order from me. This is the essential: *Summum et maximum mandatum.*" The ambassador of the sovereign pontiff had a mission to do nothing. This instruction is sometimes as effective as any.

Campeggio, the youngest of the cardinals, was the most intelligent and the slowest; and this slowness caused his selection by the pope. He understood his master. If Wolsey was Henry's spur to urge on Campeggio, the latter was Clement's bridle to check Wolsey.[3] One of the judges of the divorce was about to pull forwards, the other backwards; thus the business stood a chance of not advancing at all, which was just what the pope required.

The legate, very eager to relax his speed, spent three months on his journey from Italy to England. He should have embarked for France on the 23d of July; but the end of August was approaching, and no one knew in that country what had become of him.[4] At length they learnt that he had reached Lyons on the 22d of August. The English ambassador in France sent him horses, carriages, plate, and money, in order to hasten his progress; the legate complained of the *gout*, and Gardiner found the greatest difficulty in getting him to move. Henry wrote every day to Anne Boleyn, complaining of the slow progress of the nuncio. "He arrived in Paris last Sunday or Monday," he

[1] Strype's Records, p. 345.   [2] Strype's Mem. i. p. 490.
[3] More's Life, p. 116.   [4] Strype, Records, i. p. 367.

[1] Cum Cæsar materteræ suæ causam contra injurias Henrici propugnaverit. Sanders, p. 28.
[2] Quatuor nuncios celerrimo cursu diversis itineribus ad Campegium misit. Ibid. et Herbert, p. 253.
[3] Fuller, book v. p. 172.   [4] State Papers, vii. p. 91, 92.

says at the beginning of September; "Monday next we shall hear of his arrival in Calais, and then I shall obtain what I have so longed for, to God's pleasure and both our comforts."[1]

At the same time this impatient prince sent message after message to accelerate the legate's rate of travelling.

Anne began to desire a future which surpassed all that her youthful imagination had conceived, and her agitated heart expanded to the breath of hope. She wrote to Wolsey:

"This shall be to give unto your grace, as I am most bound, my humble thanks for the great pain and travail that your grace doth take in studying, by your wisdom and great diligence, how to bring to pass honourably the greatest wealth [well-being] that is possible to come to any creature living; and in especial remembering how wretched and unworthy I am in comparison to his highness. ......Now, good my lord, your discretion may consider as yet how little it is in my power to recompense you but alonely [only] with my good will; the which I assure you, look what thing in this world I can imagine to do you pleasure in, you shall find me the gladdest woman in the world to do it."[2]

But the impatience of the king of England and of Anne seemed as if it would never be satisfied. Campeggio, on his way through Paris, told Francis I. that the divorce would never take place, and that he should soon go to *Spain* to see Charles V......This was significative. "The king of England ought to know," said the indignant Francis to the duke of Suffolk, "that Campeggio is *imperialist* at heart, and that his mission in England will be a mere mockery."[3]

In truth, the Spanish and Roman factions tried every manœuvre to prevent a union they detested. Anne Boleyn, queen of England, signified not only Catherine humbled, but Charles offended; the clerical party weakened, perhaps destroyed, and the evangelical party put in its place. The Romish faction found accomplices even in Anne's own family. Her brother George's wife, a proud and passionate woman, and a rigid Roman catholic, had sworn an implacable hatred against her young sister. By this means wounds might be inflicted, even in the domestic sanctuary, which would not be the less deep because they were the work of her own kindred. One day we are told that Anne found in her chamber a book of pretended prophecies, in which was a picture representing a king, a queen shedding tears, and at their feet a young lady headless. Anne turned away her eyes with disgust. She desired, however, to know what this

emblem signified, and officious friends brought to her one of those pretended wise men, so numerous at all times, who abuse the credulity of the ignorant by professing to interpret such mysteries. "This prophetic picture," he said, "represents the history of the king and his wife." Anne was not credulous, but she understood what her enemies meant to insinuate, and dismissed the mock interpreter without betraying any signs of fear; then turning to her favourite attendant, Anne Saville, "Come hither, Nan," said she, "look at this book of prophecies; this is the king, this is the queen wringing her hands and mourning, and this (putting her finger on the bleeding body) is *myself*, with my head cut off."—The young lady answered with a shudder: "If I thought it were true, I would not myself have him were he an emperor."—"Tut, Nan," replied Anne Boleyn with a sweet smile, "I think the book a bauble, and am resolved to have him, that my issue may be royal, whatever may become of me."[1] This story is based on good authority, and there were so many predictions of this kind afloat that it is very possible one of them might come true: people afterwards recollected only the prophecies confirmed by the events. But, be that as it may, this young lady, so severely chastised in after-days, found in her God an abundant consolation.

At length Campeggio embarked at Calais on the 29th of September, and unfortunately for him he had an excellent passage across the channel. A storm to drive him back to the French coast would have suited him admirably. But on the 1st of October he was at Canterbury, whence he announced his arrival to the king. At this news, Henry forgot all the delays which had so irritated him. "His majesty can never be sufficiently grateful to your holiness for so great a favour," wrote Wolsey to the pope; "but he will employ his riches, his kingdom, his life even, and deserve the name of *Restorer of the Church* as justly as he has gained that of *Defender of the Faith*." This zeal alarmed Campeggio, for the pope wrote to him that any proceeding which might irritate Charles would inevitably cause the ruin of the church.[2] The nuncio became more dilatory than ever, and although he reached Canterbury on the 1st of October, he did not arrive at Dartford un til the 5th, thus taking four days for a journey of about thirty miles.[3]

Meanwhile preparations were making to receive him in London. Wolsey, feeling contempt for the poverty of the Roman cardinals, and very uneasy about the equipage with which his colleague was likely to make his entrance into the capital, sent a number of showy chests, rich carpets, litters hung with

1 Pamphleteer, No. 43, p. 117.   2 Ibid. p. 154.
3 The cardinal intended not that your Grace's matter should take effect, but only to use dissimulation with your Grace, for he is entirely imperial. Suffolk to Henry, State Papers, vii. p. 183.

1 Wyatt, p. 430.
2 Sanga to Campeggio. from Viterbo, 27th September Ranke. Deutsche Gesch. iii. p. 135.
3 State Papers, vii. p. 94, 95.

drapery, and harnessed mules. On the other hand Campeggio, whose secret mission was to keep in the back-ground, and above all to do nothing, feared these banners, and trappings, and all the parade of a triumphal entry. Alleging therefore an attack of gout in order to escape from the pomps his colleague had prepared for him, he quietly took a boat, and thus reached the palace of the bishop of Bath, where he was to lodge.

While the nuncio was thus proceeding unnoticed up the Thames, the equipages sent by Wolsey entered London through the midst of a gaping crowd, who looked on them with curiosity as if they had come from the banks of the Tiber. Some of the mules however took fright and ran away. the coffers fell off and burst open, when there was a general rush to see their contents; but to the surprise of all they were empty. This was an excellent jest for the citizens of London. "Fine outside, empty inside; a just emblem of the popedom, its embassy, and foolish pomps," they said; "a sham legate, a procession of masks, and the whole a farce!"

Campeggio was come at last, and now what he dreaded most was an audience. "I cannot move," he said, "or endure the motion of a litter."[1] Never had an attack of gout been more seasonable. Wolsey, who paid him frequent visits, soon found him to be his equal in cunning. To no purpose did he treat him with every mark of respect, shaking his hand and making much of him;[2] it was labour lost, the Roman nuncio would say nothing, and Wolsey began to despair. The king, on the contrary, was full of hope, and fancied he already had the act of divorce in his portfolio, because he had the nuncio in his kingdom.

The greatest effect of the nuncio's arrival was the putting an end to Anne Boleyn's indecision. She had several relapses: the trials which she foresaw, and the grief Catherine must necessarily feel, had agitated her imagination and disturbed her mind. But when she saw the church and her own enemies prepared to pronounce the king's divorce, her doubts were removed, and she regarded as legitimate the position that was offered her. The king, who suffered from her scruples, was delighted at this change. "I desire to inform you," he wrote to her in English, "what joy it is to me to understand of your conformableness with reason, and of the suppressing of your inutile and vain thoughts and fantasies with the bridle of reason. I assure you all the greatness of this world could not counterpoise for my satisfaction the knowledge and certainty thereof......The unfeigned sickness of this well-willing legate doth somewhat retard his

access to your person."[1] It was therefore the determination of the pope that made Anne Boleyn resolve to accept Henry's hand; this is an important lesson for which we are indebted to the *Vatican letters*. We should be grateful to the papacy for having so carefully preserved them.

But the more Henry rejoiced, the more Wolsey despaired; he would have desired to penetrate into Clement's thoughts, but could not succeed. Imagining that De Angelis, the general of the Spanish Observance, knew all the secrets of the pope and of the emperor, he conceived the plan of kidnapping him. "If he goes to Spain by sea," said he to Du Bellay, "a good brigantine or two would do the business; and if by land, it will be easier still." Du Bellay failed not (as he informs us himself) "to tell him plainly that by such proceedings he would entirely forfeit the pope's good will."—"What matter?" replied Wolsey, "I have nothing to lose." As he said this, tears started to his eyes.[2] At last he made up his mind to remain ignorant of the pontiff's designs, and wiped his eyes, awaiting, not without fear, the interview between Henry and Campeggio.

On the 22d of October, a month after his arrival, the nuncio, borne in a sedan chair of red velvet, was carried to court. He was placed on the right of the throne, and his secretary in his name delivered a high-sounding speech, saluting Henry with the name of Saviour of Rome, *Liberator urbis*. "His majesty," replied Fox in the king's name, "has only performed the duties incumbent on a Christian prince, and he hopes that the holy see will bear them in mind."—"Well attacked, well defended," said Du Bellay. For the moment, a few Latin declamations got the papal nuncio out of his difficulties.

Campeggio did not deceive himself: if the divorce were refused, he foresaw the reformation of England. Yet he hoped still, for he was assured that Catherine would submit to the judgment of the church; and being fully persuaded that the queen would refuse the holy father nothing, the nuncio began "his approaches," as Du Bellay calls them. On the 27th of October, the two cardinals waited on Catherine, and in flattering terms insinuated that she might prevent the blow which threatened her by voluntary retirement into a convent. And then, to end all indecision in the queen's mind, Campeggio put on a severe look and exclaimed: "How is it, madam, explain the mystery to us? From the moment the holy father appointed us to examine the question of your divorce, you have been seen not only at court, but in public, wearing the most magnificent ornaments, participating with an appearance of gaiety and satisfaction at amusements and festivities which you had never tolerated before......

---

[1] Despatch from the bishop of Bayonne, 16th October 1529. Le Grand, Preuves, p. 169.
[2] Quem sæpius visitavi et amantissime sum complexus. State Papers, vii. p. 103.

[1] Pamphleteer, No. 43, p. 123.
[2] Du Bellay to Montmorency, 21st October. Le Grand. Preuves, p. 185.

The church is in the most cruel embarrassment with regard to you ; the king, your husband, is in the greatest perplexity : the princess, your daughter, is taken from you ......and instead of shedding tears, you give yourself up to vanity. Renounce the world, madam ; enter a nunnery. Our holy father himself requires this of you."[1]

The agitated queen was almost fainting ; stifling her emotion, however, she said mildly but firmly : " Alas ! my lords, is it now a question whether I am the king's lawful wife or not, when I have been married to him almost twenty years and no objection raised before ?......Divers prelates and lords are yet alive who then adjudged our marriage good and lawful,—and now to say it is detestable ! this is a great marvel to me, especially when I consider what a wise prince the king's father was, and also the natural love and affection my father, King Ferdinand, bare unto me. I think that neither of these illustrious princes would have made me contract an illicit union." At these words, Catherine's emotion compelled her to stop.—" If I weep, my lords," she continued almost immediately, " it is not for myself, it is for a person dearer to me than my life. What ! I should consent to an act which deprives my daughter of a crown? No, I will not sacrifice my child. I know what dangers threaten me. I am only a weak woman, a stranger, without learning, advisers, or friends......and my enemies are skilful, learned in the laws, and desirous to merit their master's favour...... and more than that, even my judges are my enemies. Can I receive as such," she said as she looked at Campeggio, " a man extorted from the pope by manifest lying ?......And as for you," added she, turning haughtily to Wolsey, "having failed in attaining the tiara, you have sworn to revenge yourself on my nephew the emperor......and you have kept him true promise ; for of all his wars and vexations he may only thank you. One victim was not enough for you. Forging abominable suppositions, you desire to plunge his aunt into a frightful abyss......But my cause is just, and I trust it in the Lord's hand." After this bold language, the unhappy Catherine withdrew to her apartments. The imminence of the danger effected a salutary revolution in her ; she laid aside her brilliant ornaments, assumed the sober garments in which she is usually represented, and passed days and nights in mourning and in tears.[2]

Thus Campeggio saw his hopes deceived ; he had thought to find a nun, and had met a queen and a mother......He now proceeded to set every imaginable spring at work ; as Catherine would not renounce Henry, he must try and prevail upon Henry to renounce his idea of separating from the queen. The Roman legate therefore changed his batteries, and turned them against the king.

Henry, always impatient, went one day unannounced to Campeggio's lodging, accompanied by Wolsey only :[1] " As we are without witnesses," he said, taking his seat familiarly between the two cardinals, " let us speak freely of our affairs.[2]—How shall you proceed ? " But to his great astonishment and grief,[3] the nuncio prayed him, with all imaginable delicacy, to renounce the divorce.[4] At these words the fiery Tudor burst out : " Is this how the pope keeps his word ? He sends me an ambassador to annul my marriage, but in reality to confirm it." He made a pause. Campeggio knew not what to say. Henry and Catherine being equally persuaded of the justice of their cause, the nuncio was in a dilemma. Wolsey himself suffered a martyrdom.[5] The king's anger grew fiercer ; he had thought the legate would hasten to withdraw an imprudent expression, but Campeggio was dumb. " I see that you have chosen your part," said Henry to the nuncio ; " mine, you may be sure, will soon be taken also. Let the pope only persevere in this way of acting, and the apostolical see, covered with perpetual infamy, will be visited with a frightful destruction."[6] The lion had thrown off the lamb's skin which he had momentarily assumed. Campeggio felt that he must appease the monarch. " Craft and delay" were his orders from Rome ; and with that view the pope had provided him with the necessary arms. He hastened to produce the famous *decretal* which pronounced the divorce. " The holy father," he told the king, " ardently desires that this matter should be terminated by a happy reconciliation between you and the queen ; but if that is impossible, you shall judge yourself whether or not his holiness can keep his promises." He then read the bull, and even shewed it to Henry, without permitting it, however, to leave his hands. This exhibition produced the desired effect : Henry grew calm. " Now I am at ease again," he said ; " this miraculous talisman revives all my courage. This decretal is the efficacious remedy that will restore peace to my oppressed conscience, and joy to my bruised heart.[7] Write to his holiness, that this immense benefit binds me to him so closely, that he may expect from me more than his imagination can conceive."

And yet a few clouds gathered shortly after in the king's mind.

Campeggio having shewn the bull had has-

[1] Du Bellay to Montmorency, 1st November. Le Grand, Preuves, p. 195.
[2] Regina in luctu et lacrymis noctes diesque egit. Sanders, p. 29.

[1] Regia majestas et ego ad eum crebro accessimus. State Papers, vii. p. 103.
[2] Rex et duo cardinales, remotis arbitris, de suis rebus multum et diu collocuti. Sanders, p. 29.
[3] Incredibili utriusque nostrum animi mœrore. State Papers, vii. p. 104.
[4] Conatus est omne divortium inter regiam majestatem et reginam dissuadere. Ibid.
[5] Non absque ingenti cruciatu. Ibid.
[6] Ingemiscendum excidium, perpetua infamia. Ibid.
[7] Remedium levamenque afflictæ oppressæque conscientiæ. Ibid.

tened to lock it up again. Would he presume to keep it in his own hands? Henry and Wolsey will leave no means untried to get possession of it; that point gained, and victory is theirs.

Wolsey having returned to the nuncio, he asked him for the decretal with an air of candour as if it was the most natural thing in the world. He desired, he said, to shew it to the king's privy-councillors. " The pope," replied Campeggio, " has granted this bull not to be used, but to be kept secret;[1] he simply desired to shew the king the good feeling by which he was animated." Wolsey having failed, Henry tried his skill. " Have the goodness to hand me the bull which you shewed me," said he. The nuncio respectfully refused. " For a single moment," he said. Campeggio still refused. The haughty Tudor retired, stifling his anger. Then Wolsey made another attempt, and founded his demand on justice. " Like you, I am delegated by his holiness to decide this affair," he said, " and I wish to study the important document which is to regulate our proceedings."—This was met by a new refusal. " What!" exclaimed the minister of Henry VIII. " am I not, like you, a cardinal?...... like you, a judge? your colleague?" It mattered not, the nuncio would not, by any means, let the decretal go.[2] Clement was not deceived in the choice he had made of Campeggio; the ambassador was worthy of his master.

It was evident that the pope in granting the bull had been acting a part: this trick revolted the king. It was no longer anger that he felt, but disgust. Wolsey knew that Henry's contempt was more to be feared than his wrath. He grew alarmed, and paid the nuncio another visit. " The *general* commission," he said, " is insufficient, the *decretal* commission alone can be of service, and you do not permit us to read a word of it.[3]...... The king and I place the greatest confidence in the good intentions of his holiness, and yet we find our expectations frustrated.[4] Where is that paternal affection with which we had flattered ourselves? What prince has ever been trifled with as the king of England is now? If this is the way in which the *Defender of the Faith* is rewarded, Christendom will know what those who serve Rome will have to expect from her, and every power will withdraw its support. Do not deceive yourselves: the foundation on which the holy see is placed is so very insecure, that the least movement will suffice to precipitate it into everlasting ruin.[5] What a sad futurity!......what inexpressible torture! ......whether I wake or sleep, gloomy thoughts

continually pursue me like a frightful nightmare."[1] This time Wolsey spoke the truth.

But all his eloquence was useless; Campeggio refused to give up the so much desired bull. When sending him, Rome had told him: " Above all, do not succeed!" This means having failed, there remained for Wolsey one other way of effecting the divorce. " Well, then," he said to Campeggio, " let us pronounce it ourselves."—" Far be it from us," replied the nuncio; " the anger of the emperor will be so great, that the peace of Europe will be broken for ever."—" I know how to arrange all that," replied the English cardinal; " in political matters you may trust to me."[2] The nuncio then took another tone, and proudly wrapping himself up in his morality, he said: " I shall follow the voice of my conscience; if I see that the divorce is possible, I shall leap the ditch; if otherwise, I shall not."—" Your conscience! that may be easily satisfied," rejoined Wolsey. " Holy Scripture forbids a man to marry his brother's widow; now no pope can grant what is forbidden by the law of God."—" The Lord preserve us from such a principle," exclaimed the Roman prelate; " the power of the pope is unlimited."—The nuncio had hardly put his conscience forward before it stumbled; it bound him to Rome and not to heaven. But for that matter, neither public opinion nor Campeggio's own friends had any great idea of his morality; they thought that to make him *leap the ditch*, it was only requisite to know the price at which he might be bought. The bishop of Bayonne wrote to Montmorency: " Put at the close of a letter which I can shew Campeggio something *promissory*, that he shall have *benefices*......That will cost you nothing, and may serve in this matter of the marriage; for I know that he is longing for something of the sort."—" What is to be done then," said Wolsey at last, astonished at meeting with a resistance to which he was unaccustomed. " I shall inform the pope of what I have seen and heard," replied Campeggio, " and I shall wait for his instructions." Henry was forced to consent to this new course, for the nuncio hinted, that if it were opposed he would go in person to Rome to ask the pontiff's orders, and he never would have returned. By this means several months were gained.

During this time men's minds were troubled. The prospect of a divorce between the king and queen had stirred the nation; and the majority, particularly among the women, declared against the king. " Whatever may be done," the people said boldly, " whoever marries the princess Mary will be king of England."[3] Wolsey's spies informed him that Catherine and Charles V. had many de-

---

[1] Non ut ea uteremur, sed ut secreta haberetur. State Papers, vii. p. 104.
[2] Nullo pacto adduci vult, ut mihi, *suo collega*, commissionem hanc decretalem e suis manibus credat. Ibid. p. 105.
[3] Nec ullum verbum nec mentionem ullam. Ibid.
[4] Esse omni spe frustratos quam in præfata Sanctitate tam ingenue reposueramus. Ibid.
[5] A fundamento tam levi, incertaque statera pendeat, ut in sempiternam ruinam. Ibid. p. 106.

[1] Quanto animi cruciatu....vigilans dormiensque. State Papers, vii. p. 106.
[2] Du Bellay to Montmorency. Le Grand, Preuves, p. 266.
[3] Du Bellay to Montmorency, 8th November 1528. Ibid 204.

voted partisans even at the court. He wished to make sure of this. " It is pretended," he said one day in an indifferent tone, " that the emperor has boasted that he will get the king driven from his realm, and that by his majesty's own subjects..... What do you think of it, my lords?"—"Tough against the spur," says Du Bellay, the lords remained silent. At length, however, one of them more imprudent than the rest, exclaimed : " Such a boast will make the emperor lose more than a hundred thousand Englishmen." This was enough for Wolsey. To *lose* them, he thought, Charles must *have* them. If Catherine thought of levying war against her husband, following the example of former queens of England, she would have, then, a party ready to support her ; this became dangerous.

The king and the cardinal immediately took their measures. More than 15,000 of Charles's subjects were ordered to leave London ; the arms of the citizens were seized, " in order that they might have no worse weapon than the tongue ;"[1] the Flemish councillors accorded to Catherine were dismissed, after they had been heard by the king and Campeggio, " for they had no commission to speak to *the other* [Wolsey]"—and finally, they kept " a great and constant watch" upon the country. Men feared an invasion of England, and Henry was not of a humour to subject his kingdom to the pope.

This was not enough ; the alarmed king thought it his duty to come to an explanation with his people ; and having summoned the lords spiritual and temporal, the judges, the members of the privy-council, the mayor and aldermen of the city, and many of the gentry, to meet him at his palace of Bridewell on the 13th of November,[2] he said to them with a very condescending air : " You know, my lords and gentlemen, that for these twenty years past divine Providence has granted our country such prosperity as it had never known before. But in the midst of all the glory that surrounds me, the thought of my last hour often occurs to me,[3] and I fear that if I should die without an heir, my death would cause more damage to my people than my life has done them good. God forbid, that for want of a legitimate king England should be again plunged into the horrors of civil war !" Then calling to mind the illegalities invalidating his marriage with Catherine, the king continued : " These thoughts have filled my mind with anxiety, and are continually pricking my conscience. This is the only motive, and God is my witness,[4] which has made me lay this matter before the pontiff. As touching the queen, she is a woman incomparable in gentleness, humility, and buxomness, as I these twenty years have had experiment of ;

so that if I were to marry again, if the marriage might be good, I would surely choose her above all other women. But if it be determined by judgment that our marriage was against God's law, and surely void, then I shall not only sorrow in departing from so good a lady and loving companion, but much more lament and bewail my unfortunate chance, that I have so long lived in adultery, to God's great displeasure, and have no true heir of my body to inherit this realm....Therefore I require of you all to pray with us that the very truth may be known, for the discharging of our conscience and the saving of our soul."[1] These words, though wanting in sincerity, were well calculated to soothe men's minds. Unfortunately, it appears that after this *speech from the crown,* the official copy of which has been preserved, Henry added a few words of his own. " If, however," he said, according to Du Bellay, casting a threatening glance around him, " there should be any man whatsoever who speaks of his prince in other than becoming terms, I will shew him that I am the master, and there is no head so high that I will not roll it from his shoulders."[2] This was a speech in Henry's style ; but we cannot give unlimited credit to Du Bellay's assertions, this diplomatist being very fond, like others of his class, of " seasoning " his despatches. But whatever may be the fact as regards the postscript, the speech on the divorce produced an effect. From that time there were no more jests, not even on the part of the Boleyns' enemies. Some supported the king, others were content to pity the queen in secret ; the majority prepared to take advantage of a court-revolution which every one foresaw. " The king so *plainly* gave them to understand his pleasure," says the French ambassador, " that they speak more soberly than they have done hitherto."

Henry wishing to silence the clamours of the people, and to allay the fears felt by the higher classes, gave several magnificent entertainments at one time in London, at another at Greenwich, now at Hampton Court, and then at Richmond. The queen accompanied him, but Anne generally remained " in a very handsome lodging which Henry had furnished for her," says Du Bellay. The cardinal, following his master's example, gave representations of French plays with great magnificence. All his hope was in France. " I desire nothing in England, neither in word nor in deed, which is not French," [3] he said to the bishop of Bayonne. At length Anne Boleyn had accepted the brilliant position she had at first refused, and every day her stately mansion (Suffolk House) was filled with a numerous court,—" more than ever had crowded to the queen."— " Yes, yes," said Du Bellay, as he saw the

[1] Le Grand, Preuves, p. 232.
[2] This act is dated Idibus Novembris. Wilkins, Concilia, iii. p. 714. Herbert and Collyer say the 8th November.
[3] In mentem una venit et concurrit mortis cogitatio. Ibid.
[4] Hæc una res quod Deo teste et in regis oraculo affirmamus. Ibid.

[1] Hall, p. 754.
[2] Du Bellay to Montmorency, 17th November 1528. Le Grand, Preuves, p. 218.
[3] Du Bellay to Montmorency, 1st January. Ibid. p. 268.

crowd turning towards the *rising sun*, "they wish by these *little* things to accustom the people to endure her, that when *great* ones are attempted, they may not be found so strange."

In the midst of these festivities the grand business did not slumber. When the French ambassador solicited the subsidy intended for the ransom of the sons of Francis I., the cardinal required of him in exchange a paper proving that the marriage had never been valid. Du Bellay excused himself on the ground of his age and want of learning; but being given to understand that he could not have the subsidy without it, he wrote the memoir in a single day. The enraptured cardinal and king entreated him to speak with Campeggio.[1] The ambassador consented, and succeeded beyond all expectation. The nuncio, fully aware that a bow too much bent will break, made Henry by turns become the sport of hope and fear. "Take care how you assert that the pope had not the right to grant a dispensation to the king," said he to the French bishop, "this would be denying *his power, which is infinite.* But," added he in a mysterious tone, "I will point out a road that will infallibly lead you to the mark. Show that the holy father has been deceived by false information. *Push me hard on that*," he continued, "so as to force me to declare that the dispensation was granted on erroneous grounds."[2] Thus did the legate himself reveal the breach by which the fortress might be surprised. "Victory!" exclaimed Henry, as he entered Anne's apartments all beaming with joy.

But this confidence on the part of Campeggio was only a new trick. "There is a great rumour at court," wrote Du Bellay soon after, "that the emperor and the king of France are coming together, and leaving Henry alone, so that all will fall on his shoulders."[3] Wolsey, finding that the intrigues of diplomacy had failed, thought it his duty to put fresh springs in motion, "and by all good and honest means to gain the pope's favour."[4] He saw, besides, to his great sorrow, the new catholicity then forming in the world, and uniting, by the closest bonds, the Christians of England to those of the continent. To strike down one of the leaders of this evangelical movement might incline the court of Rome in Henry's favour. The cardinal undertook, therefore, to persecute Tyndale; and this resolution will now transport us to Germany.

[1] Du Bellay to Montmorency, 1st January. Le Grand, p. 200.
[2] Poussez-moi cela raide. Du Bellay to Montmorency. Ibid. p. 217.   [3] Ibid. p. 219.   [4] Ibid. p. 225.

CHAPTER IV.

True Catholicity—Wolsey—Harman's Matter—West sent to Cologne—Labours of Tyndale and Fryth—Rincke at Frankfort—He makes a Discovery—Tyndale at Marburg—West returns to England—His Tortures in the Monastery.

THE residence of Tyndale and his friends in foreign countries, and the connexions there formed with pious Christians, testify to the fraternal spirit which the Reformation then restored to the church. It is in protestantism that true catholicity is to be found. The Romish church is not a catholic church. Separated from the churches of the east, which are the oldest in Christendom, and from the reformed churches, which are the purest, it is nothing but a sect, and that a degenerate one. A church which should profess to believe in an episcopal unity, but which kept itself separate from the episcopacy of Rome and of the East, and from the evangelical churches, would be no longer a catholic church; it would be a sect more sectarian still than that of the Vatican, a fragment of a fragment. The church of the Saviour requires a truer, a diviner unity than that of priests, who condemn one another. It was the reformers, and particularly Tyndale,[1] who proclaimed throughout Christendom the existence of a *body of Christ*, of which all the children of God are members. The disciples of the Reformation are the true catholics.

It was a catholicity of another sort that Wolsey desired to uphold. He did not reject certain reforms in the church, particularly such as brought him any profit; but, before all, he wished to preserve for the hierarchy their privileges and uniformity. The Romish Church in England was then personified in him, and if he fell, its ruin would be near. His political talents and multiplied relations with the continent, caused him to discern more clearly than others the dangers which threatened the popedom. The publication of the Scriptures of God in English appeared to some a cloud without importance, which would soon disappear from the horizon; but to the foreseeing glance of Wolsey, it be tokened a mighty tempest. Besides, he loved not the fraternal relations then forming between the evangelical Christians of Great Britain and of other nations. Annoyed by this spiritual catholicity, he resolved to procure the arrest of Tyndale, who was its principal organ.

Already had Hackett, Henry's envoy to the Low Countries, caused the imprisonment of Harman, an Antwerp merchant, one of the principal supporters of the English reformer. But Hackett had in vain asked Wolsey for such documents as would convict him of *treason* (for the crime of loving the Bible was not sufficient to procure Har-

[1] The Church of Christ is the multitude of all them that believe in Christ, &c. Exposition of Matthew, Prologue.

man's condemnation in Brabant); the envoy had remained without letters from England, and the last term fixed by the law having expired, Harman and his wife were liberated after seven months' imprisonment.

And yet Wolsey had not been inactive. The cardinal hoped to find elsewhere the co-operation which Margaret of Austria refused. It was Tyndale that he wanted, and every-thing seemed to indicate that he was then hidden at Cologne or in its neighbourhood. Wolsey, recollecting senator Rincke and the services he had already performed, deter-mined to send to him one John West, a friar of the Franciscan convent at Greenwich. West, a somewhat narrow-minded but ener-getic man, was very desirous of distinguish-ing himself, and he had already gained some notoriety in England among the adversaries of the Reformation. Flattered by his mis-sion, this vain monk immediately set off for Antwerp, accompanied by another friar, in order to seize Tyndale, and even Roy, once his colleague at Greenwich, and against whom he had there ineffectually contended in argument.

While these men were conspiring his ruin, Tyndale composed several works, got them printed, and sent to England, and prayed God night and day to enlighten his fellow-country-men. "Why do you give yourself so much trouble," said some of his friends. "They will burn your books as they have burnt the Gospel." "They will only do what I expect," replied he, "if they burn me also." Already he beheld his own burning pile in the dis-tance; but it was a sight which only served to increase his zeal. Hidden, like Luther at the Wartburg, not however in a castle, but in a humble lodging, Tyndale, like the Saxon reformer, spent his days and nights translat-ing the Bible. But not having an elector of Saxony to protect him, he was forced to change his residence from time to time.

At this epoch, Fryth, who had escaped from the prisons of Oxford, rejoined Tyndale, and the sweets of friendship softened the bitter-ness of their exile. Tyndale having finished the New Testament, and begun the translation of the Old, the learned Fryth was of great use to him. The more they studied the word of God, the more they admired it. In the be-ginning of 1529, they published the books of Genesis and Deuteronomy, and addressing their fellow-countrymen, they said: "As thou readest, think that every syllable pertaineth to thine own self, and suck out the pith of the Scripture."[1] Then denying that visible signs naturally impart grace, as the schoolmen had pretended, Tyndale maintained that the sa-craments are effectual only when the Holy Ghost sheds his influence upon them. "The ceremonies of the law," he wrote, "stood the Israelites in the same stead as the sacraments do us. We are saved not by the power of the sacrifice or the deed itself, but by virtue of *faith in the promise*, whereof the sacrifice or ceremony was a token or sign. The Holy Ghost is no dumb God, no God that goeth a mumming. Wherever the word is proclaim-ed, this inward witness worketh. If baptism preach me the washing in Christ's blood, so doth the Holy Ghost accompany it; and that deed of preaching through faith doth put away my sins. The ark of Noah saved them in the water through faith."[1]

The man who dared address England in language so contrary to the teaching of the middle ages must be imprisoned. John West, who had been sent with this object, arrived at Antwerp; Hackett procured for him as interpreter a friar of English descent, made him assume a secular dress, and gave him "three pounds" on the cardinal's account; the less attention the embassy attracted, the more likely it would be to succeed. But great was West's vexation, on reaching Cologne, to learn that Rincke was at Frankfort. But that mattered not; the Greenwich monk could search for Tyndale at Cologne, and desire Rincke to do the same at Frankfort; thus there would be two searches instead of one. West procured a "swift" messenger, (he too was a monk,) and gave him the letter Wol-sey had addressed to Rincke.

It was fair-time at Frankfort, and the city was filled with merchants and their wares. As soon as Rincke had finished reading Wol-sey's letter, he hastened to the burgomasters, and required them to confiscate the English translations of the Scriptures, and, above all, to seize "the heretic who was troubling Eng-land as Luther troubled Germany." "Tyn-dale and his friends have not appeared in our fairs since the month of March 1528," replied the magistrates, "and we know not whether they are dead or alive."

Rincke was not discouraged. John Schoot of Strasburg, who was said to have printed Tyndale's books, and who cared less about the works he published than the money he drew from them, happened to be at Frankfort. "Where is Tyndale?" Rincke asked him. "I do not know," replied the printer: but he confessed that he had printed a thousand vo-lumes at the request of Tyndale and Roy. "Bring them to me," continued the senator of Cologne. "If a fair price is paid me, I will give them up to you." Rincke paid all that was demanded.

Wolsey would now be gratified, for the New Testament annoyed him almost as much as the divorce; this book, so dangerous in his eyes, seemed on the point of raising a confla-gration which would infallibly consume the edifice of Roman traditionalism. Rincke, who participated in his patron's fears, impatiently opened the volumes made over to him; but there was a sad mistake, they were not the New Testament, not even a work of Tyn-

---

[1] Prologue to the Book of Genesis (Doct., Tr.) p. 400.

[1] Prologue to the Book of Leviticus (Doctr. Tr.) v. 423, 424, 426.

dale's but one written by William Roy, a changeable and violent man, whom the reformer had employed for some time at Hamburg, and who had followed him to Cologne, but with whom he had soon become disgusted. " I bade him farewell for our two lives," said Tyndale, " and a day longer." Roy, on quitting the reformer, had gone to Strasburg, where he boasted of his relations with him, and had got a satire in that city printed against Wolsey and the monastic orders, entitled *The Burial of the Mass* : this was the book delivered to Rincke. The monk's sarcastic spirit had exceeded the ligitimate bounds of controversy, and the senator accordingly dared not send the volumes to England. He did not, however, discontinue his inquiries, but searched every place where he thought he could discover the New Testament, and having seized all the suspected volumes, set off for Cologne.[1]

Yet he was not satisfied. He wanted Tyndale, and went about asking every one if they knew where to find him. But the reformer, whom he was seeking in so many places, and especially at Frankfort and Cologne, chanced to be residing at about equal distances from these two towns, so that Rincke, while travelling from one to the other, might have met him face to face, as Ahab's messenger met Elijah.[2] Tyndale was at Marburg, whither he had been drawn by several motives. Prince Philip of Hesse was the great protector of the evangelical doctrines. The university had attracted attention in the Reform by the paradoxes of Lambert of Avignon. Here a young Scotsman named Hamilton, afterwards illustrious as a martyr, had studied shortly before, and here too the celebrated printer, John Luft, had his presses. In this city Tyndale and Fryth had taken up their abode, in September 1528, and, hidden on the quiet banks of the Lahn, were translating the Old Testament. If Rincke had searched this place he could not have failed to discover them. But either he thought not of it, or was afraid of the terrible landgrave. The direct road by the Rhine was that which he followed, and Tyndale escaped.

When he arrived at Cologne, Rincke had an immediate interview with West. Their investigations having failed, they must have recourse to more vigorous measures. The senator, therefore, sent the monk back to England, accompanied by his son Hermann, charging them to tell Wolsey : " To seize Tyndale we require fuller powers, ratified by the emperor. The traitors who conspire against the life of the king of England are not tolerated in the empire, much less Tyndale and all those who conspire against Christendom. He must be put to death : nothing but some striking example can check the Lutheran heresy.—And as to ourselves," they

were told to add, " by the favour of God there may possibly be an opportunity for his royal highness and your grace to recompense us."[1] Rincke had not forgotten the subsidy of ten thousand pounds which he had received from Henry VII. for the Turkish war, when he had gone to London as Maximilian's envoy.

West returned to England sorely vexed that he had failed in his mission. What would they say at court and in his monastery? A fresh humiliation was in reserve for him. Roy, whom West had gone to look for on the banks of the Rhine, had paid a visit to his mother on the banks of the Thames ; and to crown all, the new doctrines had penetrated into his own convent. The warden, father Robinson, had embraced them, and night and day the Greenwich monks read that New Testament which West had gone to Cologne to burn. The Antwerp friar, who had accompanied him on his journey, was the only person to whom he could confide his sorrows ; but the Franciscans sent him back again to the continent, and then amused themselves at poor West's expense. If he desired to tell of his adventures on the banks of the Rhine, he was laughed at ; if he boasted of the names of Wolsey and Henry VIII., they jeered him still more. He desired to speak to Roy's mother, hoping to gain some useful information from her ; this the monks prevented. " It is in my commission," he said. They ridiculed him more and more. Robinson, perceiving that the commission made West assume unbecoming airs of independence, requested Wolsey to withdraw it ; and West, fancying he was about to be thrown into prison, exclaimed in alarm : " I am weary of my life !" and conjured a friend whom he had at court to procure him before Christmas an *obedience* under his lordship's hand and seal, enabling him to leave the monastery ; " What you pay him for it," he added, " I shall see you be reimbursed." Thus did West expiate the fanatical zeal which had urged him to pursue the translator of the oracles of God. What became of him, we know not : he is never heard of more.

At that time Wolsey had other matters to engage him than this " obedience." While West's complaints were going to London, those of the king were travelling to Rome. The great business in the cardinal's eyes was to maintain harmony between Henry and the church. There was no more thought about investigations in Germany, and for a time Tyndale was saved.

[1] Cotton MSS., Vitellius, B. xxI. fol. 43. Bible Annals, L p. 204.

[1] Anderson, Annals of the Bible, i. p. 203 : " I gathered together and packed up all the books from every quarter."
[2] 1 Kings xviii. 7.

CHAPTER V.

Necessity of the Reformation—Wolsey's Earnestness with Da Casale—An Audience with Clement VII.—Cruel Position of the Pope—A Judas' Kiss—A new Brief—Bryan and Vannes sent to Rome—Henry and Du Bellay—Wolsey's Reasons against the Brief—Excitement in London—Metamorphosis—Wolsey's Decline—His Anguish.

THE king and a part of his people still adhered to the popedom, and so long as these bonds were not broken the word of God could not have free course. But to induce England to renounce Rome, there must indeed be powerful motives : and these were not wanting.

Wolsey had never given such pressing orders to any of Henry's ambassadors : " The king," he wrote to Da Casale on the 1st of November 1528, "commits this business to your prudence, dexterity, and fidelity ; and I conjure you to employ all the powers of your genius, and even to surpass them. Be very sure that you have done nothing and can do nothing that will be more agreeable to the king, more desirable by me, and more useful and glorious for you and your family."[1]

Da Casale possessed a tenacity which justified the cardinal's confidence, and an active, excitable mind : trembling at the thought of seeing Rome lose England, he immediately requested an audience of Clement VII. " What ! " said he to the pope, " just as it was proposed to go on with the divorce, your nuncio endeavours to dissuade the king !...... There is no hope that Catherine of Aragon will ever give an heir to the crown. Holy father, there must be an end of this. Order Campeggio to place the *decretal* in his majesty's hands."—" What say you ? " exclaimed the pope. " I would gladly lose one of my fingers to recover it again, and you ask me to make it public......it would be my ruin."[2] Da Casale insisted : " We have a duty to perform," he said ; " we remind you at this last hour of the perils threatening the relations which unite Rome and England. The crisis is at hand. We knock at your door, we cry, we urge, we entreat, we lay before you the present and future dangers which threaten the papacy.[3]......The world shall know that the king at least has fulfilled the duty of a devoted son of the church. If your holiness desires to keep England in St Peter's fold, I repeat......now is the time......now is the time."[4] At these words, Da Casale, unable to restrain his emotion, fell down at the pope's feet, and begged him to save the church in Great Britain. The pope was moved. " Rise," said he, with marks of unwonted grief, [5] " I grant you all that is in

my power ; I am willing to confirm the judgment which the legates may think it their duty to pass ; but I acquit myself of all responsibility as to the untold evils which this matter may bring with it......If the king, after having defended the faith and the church, desires to ruin both, on him alone will rest the responsibility of so great a disaster." Clement granted nothing. Da Casale withdrew disheartened, and feeling convinced that the pontiff was about to treat with Charles V.

Wolsey desired to save the popedom ; but the popedom resisted. Clement VII. was about to lose that island which Gregory the Great had won with such difficulty. The pope was in the most cruel position. The English envoy had hardly left the palace before the emperor's ambassador entered breathing threats. The unhappy pontiff escaped the assaults of Henry only to be exposed to those of Charles ; he was thrown backwards and forwards like a ball. " I shall assemble a general council," said the emperor through his ambassador, " and if you are found to have infringed the canons of the church in any point, you shall be proceeded against with every rigour. Do not forget," added his agent in a low tone, " that your birth is *illegitimate*, and consequently excludes you from the pontificate." The timid Clement, imagining that he saw the tiara falling from his head, swore to refuse Henry everything. " Alas ! " he said to one of his dearest confidants, " I repent in dust and ashes that I ever granted this decretal bull. If the king of England so earnestly desires it to be given him, certainly it cannot be merely to know its contents. He is but too familiar with them. It is only to tie my hands in this matter of the divorce ; I would rather die a thousand deaths." Clement, to calm his agitation, sent one of his ablest gentlemen of the bed-chamber, Francis Campana, apparently to feed the king with fresh promises, but in reality to cut the only thread on which Henry's hopes still hung. " We embrace your majesty," wrote the pope in the letter given to Campana, " with the paternal love your numerous merits deserve."[1] Now Campana was sent to England to burn clandestinely the famous decretal ;[2] Clement concealed his blows by an embrace. Rome had granted many divorces not so well founded as that of Henry VIII. ; but a very different matter from a divorce was in question here ; the pope, desirous of upraising in Italy his shattered power, was about to sacrifice the Tudor, and to prepare the triumph of the Reformation. Rome was separating herself from England.

All Clement's fear was, that Campana would arrive too late to burn the bull ; he

---

[1] Vobis westræque familiæ utilius aut honorificentius. State Papers, vii. p. 114.
[2] Burnet, Records, ii. p. 20. Unius digiti jactura....quod factum fuit revocarem.
[3] Admonere, exclamare, rogare, instare, urgere, pulsare, pericula præsentia et futura demonstrare. State Papers, vii. p. 112.
[4] Tempus jam in promptu adest. Ibid.
[5] Burnet's Ref. i. p. 44. Records, p. xx.

[1] Nos illum paterna charitate complecti, ut sua erga nos atque hanc sedem plurima merita requirunt. State Papers, vii. 116.
[2] To charge Campegius to burn the decretal. Herbert, p. 250. Burnet's Ref. i. 47.

was soon reassured ; a dead calm prevented the *great matter* from advancing. Campeggio, who took care to be in no hurry about his mission, gave himself up, like a skilful diplomatist, to his worldly tastes ; and when he could not, due respect being had to the state of his legs, indulge in the chase, of which he was very fond, he passed his time in gambling, to which he was much addicted. Respectable historians assert that he indulged in still more illicit pleasures.[1] But this could not last for ever, and the nuncio sought some new means of delay, which offered itself in the most unexpected manner. One day an officer of the queen's presented to the Roman legate a *brief* of Julius II., bearing the same date as the *bull* of dispensation, signed too, like that, by the secretary Sigismond, and in which the pope expressed himself in such a manner, that Henry's objections fell of themselves. "The emperor," said Catherine's messenger, "has discovered this brief among the papers of Puebla, the Spanish ambassador in England, at the time of the marriage."—"It is impossible to go on," said Campeggio to Wolsey ; "all your reasoning is now cut from under you. *We must wait for fresh instructions.*" This was the cardinal's conclusion at every new incident, and the journey from London to the Vatican being very long (without reckoning the Roman dilatoriness), the expedient was infallible.

Thus there existed two acts of the same pope, signed on the same day—the one secret, the other public, in contradiction to each other. Henry determined to send a new mission to Rome. Anne proposed for this embassy one of the most accomplished gentlemen of the court, her cousin, Sir Francis Bryan. With him was joined an Italian, Peter Vannes, Henry's Latin secretary. "You will search all the registers of the time of Julius II.," said Wolsey to them ; "you will study the hand-writing of secretary Sigismond, and you will attentively examine the ring of the fisherman used by that pontiff.[2]—Moreover you will inform the pope that it is proposed to set a certain greyfriar, named De Angelis, in his place, to whom Charles would give the *spiritual* authority, reserving the *temporal* for himself. You will manage so that Clement takes alarm at the project, and you will then offer him a guard of 2000 men to protect him. You will ask whether, in case the queen should desire to embrace a religious life, on condition of the king's doing the same, and Henry should yield to this wish,[3] he could have the assurance that the pope would afterwards release him from his vows. And, finally, you will enquire whether, in case the queen should refuse to enter a convent, the pope would

permit the king to have *two wives*, as we see in the Old Testament."[1] The idea which has brought so much reproach on the landgrave of Hesse was not a new one ; the honour of it belongs to a cardinal and legate of Rome, whatever Bossuet may say. "Lastly," continued Wolsey, "as the pope is of a timid disposition, you will not fail to season your remonstrances with threats. You, Peter, will take him aside and tell him that, as an Italian, having more at heart than any one the glory of the holy see, it is your duty to warn him, that if he persists, the king, his realm, and many other princes, will for ever separate from the papacy."

It was not on the mind of the pope alone that it was necessary to act ; the rumour that the emperor and the king of France were treating together disturbed Henry. Wolsey had vainly tried to sound Du Bellay ; these two priests tried craft against craft. Besides, the Frenchman was not always seasonably informed by his court, letters taking *ten days* to come from Paris to London.[2] Henry resolved to have a conference with the ambassador. He began by speaking to him of *his matter*, says Du Bellay, "and I promise you," he added, "that he needs no advocate, he understands the whole business so well." Henry next touched upon the *wrongs* of Francis I., "recalling so many things that the envoy knew not what to say."—"I pray you, Master Ambassador," said Henry in conclusion, "to beg the king, my brother, to give up a little of his amusements during a year only for the prompt despatch of his affairs. Warn those whom it concerns." Having given this spur to the king of France, Henry turned his thoughts towards Rome.

In truth, the fatal brief from Spain tormented him day and night, and the cardinal tortured his mind to find proofs of its nonauthenticity ; if he could do so, he would acquit the papacy of the charge of duplicity, and accuse the emperor of forgery. At last he thought he had succeeded. "In the first place," he said to the king, "the brief has the same date as the bull. Now, if the errors in the latter had been found out on the day it was drawn up, it would have been more natural to make another than to append a brief pointing out the errors. What! the same pope, the same day, at the petition of the same persons, give out two rescripts for one effect,[3] one of which contradicts the other! Either the bull was good, and then, why the brief? or the bull was bad, and then, why deceive princes by a worthless bull? Many names are found in the brief incorrectly spelt, and these are faults which the pontifi-

[1] Hunting and gaming all the day long, and following harlots all the night. Burnet, i. p. 52.
[2] State Papers, vii. p. 126, note.
[3] Only thereby to conduce the queen thereunto. Ibid. p. 136, note.

[1] De duabus uxoribus. Henry's Instructions to Knight in the middle of December 1528. State Papers, vii. p. 137. Some great reasons and precedents of the Old Testament appear. Instructions to same, 1st Dec. Ibid. p. 136, note.
[2] La dite lettre du roi, combien qu'elle fût du 3, je l'ai reçue sinon le 13 ; le pareil m'advint quasi de toutes autres. Du Bellay to Montmorency, 20 Dec. Le Grand, Preuves.
[3] State Papers, vol. vii. p. 130.

cal secretary, whose accuracy is so well known, could not have committed.[1] Lastly, no one in England ever heard mention of this brief; and yet it is here that it ought to be found." Henry charged Knight, his principal secretary, to join the other envoys with all speed, in order to prove to the pope the supposititious character of the document.

This important paper revived the irritation felt in England against Charles V., and it was resolved to come to extremities. Every one discontented with Austria took refuge in London, particularly the Hungarians. The ambassador from Hungary proposed to Wolsey to adjudge the imperial crown of Germany to the elector of Saxony or the landgrave of Hesse, the two chiefs of protestantism.[2] Wolsey exclaimed in alarm: "It will be an inconvenience to Christendom, *they are so Lutheran.*" But the Hungarian ambassador so satisfied him that in the end he did not find the matter quite so inconvenient. These schemes were prospering in London, when suddenly a new metamorphosis took place under the eyes of Du Bellay. The king, the cardinal, and the ministers appeared in strange consternation. Vincent da Casale had just arrived from Rome with a letter from his cousin the prothonotary, informing Henry that the pope, seeing the triumph of Charles V., the indecision of Francis I., the isolation of the king of England, and the distress of his cardinal, had flung himself into the arms of the emperor. At Rome they went so far as to jest about Wolsey, and to say that since he could not be St Peter they would make him St Paul.

While they were ridiculing Wolsey at Rome, at St Germain's they were joking about Henry. "I will make him get rid of the notions he has in his head," said Francis; and the Flemings, who were again sent out of the country, said as they left London, 'that this year they would carry on the war so vigorously, that it would be really a sight worth seeing."

Besides these public griefs, Wolsey had his private ones. Anne Boleyn, who had already begun to use her influence on behalf of the despotic cardinal's victims, gave herself no rest until Cheyney, a courtier disgraced by Wolsey, had been restored to the king's favour. Anne even gave utterance to several biting sarcasms against the cardinal, and the Duke of Norfolk and his party began "to speak big," says Du Bellay. At the moment when the pope, scared by Charles V., was separating from England, Wolsey himself was tottering. Who shall uphold the papacy?......After Wolsey, nobody! Rome was on the point of losing the power which for nine centuries she had exercised in the

bosom of this illustrious nation. The cardinal's anguish cannot be described; unceasingly pursued by gloomy images, he saw Anne on the throne causing the triumph of the Reformation: this nightmare was stifling him. "His grace, the legate, is in great trouble," wrote the bishop of Bayonne. "However......he is more cunning than they are."[1]

To still the tempest Wolsey had only one resource left: this was to render Clement favourable to his master's designs. The crafty Campana, who had burnt the decretal, conjured him not to believe all the reports transmitted to him concerning Rome. "To satisfy the king," said he to the cardinal, "the holy father will, if necessary, descend from the pontifical throne."[2] Wolsey therefore resolved to send to Rome a more energetic agent than Vannes, Bryan, or Knight, and cast his eyes on Gardiner. His courage began to revive, when an unexpected event fanned once more his loftiest hopes.

CHAPTER VI.

The Pope's Illness—Wolsey's Desire—Conference about the Members of the Conclave—Wolsey's Instructions—The Pope recovers—Speech of the English Envoys to the Pope—Clement willing to abandon England—The English demand the Pope's Denial of the Brief—Wolsey's Alarm—Intrigues—Bryan's Clearsightedness—Henry's Threats—Wolsey's new Efforts—He calls for an Appeal to Rome, and retracts—Wolsey and Du Bellay at Richmond—The Ship of the State.

On the 6th of January 1529, the feast of Epiphany, just as the pope was performing mass, he was attacked by a sudden illness; he was taken to his room, apparently in a dying state. When this news reached London, the cardinal resolved to hasten to abandon England, where the soil trembled under his feet, and to climb boldly to the throne of the pontiffs. Bryan and Vannes, then at Florence, hurried on to Rome through roads infested with robbers. At Orvieto they were informed the pope was better: at Viterbo, no one knew whether he was alive or dead; at Ronciglione, they were assured that he had expired: and, finally, when they reached the metropolis of the popedom, they learnt that Clement could not survive, and that the imperialists, supported by the Colonnas, were striving to have a pope devoted to Charles V.[3]

But great as might be the agitation at Rome, it was greater still at Whitehall. If God caused De' Medici to descend from the pontifical throne, it could only be, thought Wolsey, to make him mount it. "It is expedient to have such a pope as may save the realm," said he to Gardiner. "And although it cannot but be incommodious to me in this mine old age to be the common father, yet,

---

[1] Queen *Isabella* was called *Elisabeth* in the brief; but I have seen a document from the court of Madrid in which Queen Elizabeth of England was called Isabella; it is not therefore an error without a parallel.
[2] Du Bellay to Montmorency, 12 Jan. 1529. Le Grand, Preuves, p. 279.

[1] Le Grand, Preuves, p. 295, 296.
[2] Burnet. Hist. Ref. vol. i. p. 60.
[3] State Papers, vii. p. 148-150.

when all things be well pondered, the qualities of all the cardinals well considered, I am the only one, without boasting, that can and will remedy the king's secret matter. And were it not for the redintegration of the state of the church, and especially to relieve the king and his realm from their calamities, all the riches and honour of the world should not cause me to accept the said dignity. Nevertheless I conform myself to the necessities of the times. Wherefore, Master Stephen, that this matter may succeed, I pray you to apply all your ingenuity, spare neither money nor labour. I give you the amplest powers, without restriction or limitation."[1] Gardiner departed to win for his master the coveted tiara.

Henry VIII. and Wolsey, who could hardly restrain their impatience, soon heard of the pontiff's death from different quarters.[2] "The emperor has taken away Clement's life,"[3] said Wolsey, blinded by hatred. "Charles," rejoined the king, "will endeavour to obtain by force or fraud a pope according to his desires." "Yes, to make him his chaplain," replied Wolsey, "and to put an end by degrees both to pope and popedom."[4] "We must fly to the defence of the church," resumed Henry, "and with that view, my lord, make up your mind to be pope."—"That alone," answered the cardinal, "can bring your Majesty's weighty matter to a happy termination, and by saving you, save the church.........and myself also," he thought in his heart.—"Let us see, let us count the voters."

Henry and his minister then wrote down on a strip of parchment the names of all the cardinals, marking with the letter *A* those who were on the side of the kings of England and France, and with the letter *B* all who favoured the emperor. "There was no *C*," says a chronicler sarcastically, "to signify any on *Christ's* side." The letter *N* designated the neutrals. "The cardinals present," said Wolsey, "will not exceed thirty-nine, and we must have two-thirds, that is, twenty-six. Now, there are twenty upon whom we can reckon; we must, therefore, at any price, gain six of the neutrals."

Wolsey, deeply sensible of the importance of an election that would decide whether England was to be reformed or not, carefully drew up the instructions, which Henry signed, and which history must register. "We desire and ordain," the ambassadors were informed in them, "that you secure the election of the cardinal of York; not forgetting that next to the salvation of his own soul, there is nothing the king desires more earnestly.

"To gain over the neutral cardinals you will employ two methods in particular. The first is, the cardinals being present, and having God and the Holy Ghost before them, you shall remind them that the cardinal of York alone can save Christendom.

"The second is, because human fragility suffereth not all things to be pondered and weighed in a just balance, it appertaineth in matter of so high importance, to the comfort and relief of all Christendom, to succour the infirmity that may chance......not for corruption, you will understand......but rather to help the lacks and defaults of human nature. And, therefore, it shall be expedient that you promise spiritual offices, dignities, rewards of money, or other things which shall seem meet to the purpose.

"Then shall you, with good dexterity, combine and knit those favourable to us in a perfect fastness and indissoluble knot. And that they may be the better animated to finish the election to the king's desire, you shall offer them a guard of 2000 or 3000 men from the kings of England and France, from the viscount of Turin, and the republic of Venice.

"If, notwithstanding all your exertions, the election should fail, then the cardinals of the king's shall repair to some sure place, and there proceed to such an election as may be to God's pleasure.

"And to win more friends for the king, you shall promise, on the one hand, to the Cardinal de' Medici and his party our special favour; and the Florentines, on the other hand, you shall put in comfort of the exclusion of the said family De' Medici. Likewise you shall put the cardinals in perfect hope of recovering the patrimony of the church; and you shall contain the Venetians in good trust of a reasonable way to be taken for Cervia and Ravenna (which formed part of the patrimony) to their contentment."[1]

Such were the means by which the cardinal hoped to win the papal throne. To the right he said *yes*, to the left he said *no*. What would it matter that these perfidies were one day discovered, provided it were after the election. Christendom might be very certain that the choice of the future pontiff would be the work of the Holy Ghost. Alexander VI. had been a poisoner; Julius II. had given way to ambition, anger, and vice; the liberal Leo X. had passed his life in worldly pursuits; the unhappy Clement VII. had lived on stratagems and lies; Wolsey would be their worthy successor:

"All the seven deadly sins have worn the triple crown."[2]

Wolsey found his excuse in the thought, that if he succeeded, the divorce was secured, and England enslaved for ever to the court of Rome.

Success at first appeared probable. Many

[1] Foxe, Acts, iv. p. 601.
[2] By sundry ways hath been advertised of the death of our holy father. Ibid. The king's Instructions.
[3] By some detestable act committed for the late pope's destruction. Ibid. 603.
[4] By little and little utterly to exclude and extinguish him and his authority. Ibid.

[1] Foxe, iv. p. 604-608.
[2] Les sept péchés mortels ont porté la tiare. Casimir Delavigne, Derniers chaāts, le Conclave.

cardinals spoke openly in favour of the English prelate; one of them asked for a detailed account of his life, in order to present it as a model to the church; another worshipped him (so he said) as a divinity......... Among the gods and popes adored at Rome there were some no better than he. But erelong alarming news reached England. What grief! the pope was getting better. "Conceal your instructions," wrote the cardinal, "and reserve them *in omnem eventum.*"

Wolsey not having obtained the tiara, it was necessary at least to gain the divorce. "God declares," said the English ambassadors to the pope, "*except the Lord build the house, they labour in vain that build it.*[1] Therefore, the king, taking God alone for his guide, requests of you, in the first place, an engagement to pronounce the divorce in the space of three months, and in the second the avocation to Rome."—"The promise first, and only after that the avocation," Wolsey had said, "for I fear that if the pope begins with the avocation, he will never pronounce the divorce."—"Besides," added the envoys, "the king's second marriage admits of no refusal, whatever bulls or briefs there may be.[2] The only issue of this matter is the divorce; the divorce in one way or another must be procured."

Wolsey had instructed his envoys to pronounce these words with a certain air of familiarity, and at the same time with a gravity calculated to produce an effect.[3] His expectations were deceived: Clement was colder than ever. He had determined to abandon England in order that he might secure the States of the Church, of which Charles was then master, thus sacrificing the spiritual to the temporal. "The pope will not do the least thing for your majesty," wrote Bryan to the king; "your matter may well be in his *Pater noster,* but it certainly is not in his *Credo.*"[4] "Increase in importunity," answered the king; "the cardinal of Verona should remain about the pope's person and counterbalance the influence of De Angelis and the archbishop of Capua. I would rather lose my two crowns than be beaten by these two friars."

Thus was the struggle about to become keener than ever, when Clement's relapse once more threw doubt on everything. He was always between life and death; and this perpetual alternation agitated the king and the impatient cardinal in every way. The latter considered that the pope had need of *merits* to enter the kingdom of heaven. "Procure an interview with the pope," he wrote to the envoys, "even though he be in the very agony of death;[5] and represent to

him that nothing will be more likely *to save his soul* than the bill of divorce." Henry's commissioners were not admitted; but towards the end of March, the deputies appearing in a body,[1] the pope promised to examine the letter from Spain. Vannes began to fear this document; he represented that those who had fabricated it would have been able to give it an appearance of authenticity. "Rather declare immediately that this brief is not a brief," said he to the pope. "The king of England, who is your holiness's son, is not so like the rest of the world. We cannot put the same shoe on every foot."[2] This rather vulgar argument did not touch Clement. "If to content your master in this business," said he, "I cannot employ my head, at least I will my finger."[3]—"Be pleased to explain yourself," replied Vannes, who found the *finger* a very little matter.— "I mean," resumed the pontiff, "that I shall employ every means, provided they are *honourable.*" Vannes withdrew disheartened.

He immediately conferred with his colleagues, and all together, alarmed at the idea of Henry's anger, returned to the pontiff; they thrust aside the lackeys, who endeavoured to stop them, and made their way into his bed chamber. Clement opposed them with that resistance of inertia by which the popedom has gained its greatest victories: *siluit,* he remained silent. Of what consequence to the pontiff were Tudor, his island, and his church, when Charles of Austria was threatening him with his armies? Clement, less proud than Hildebrand, submitted willingly to the emperor's power, provided the emperor would protect him. "I had rather," he said, "be Cæsar's servant, not only in a temple, but in a stable if necessary, than be exposed to the insults of rebels and vagabonds."[4] At the same time he wrote to Campeggio: "Do not irritate the king, but spin out this matter as much as possible;[5] the Spanish brief gives us the means."

In fact, Charles V. had twice shown Lee the original document, and Wolsey, after this ambassador's report, began to believe that it was not Charles who had forged the brief, but that Pope Julius II. had really given two contradictory documents on the same day. Accordingly the cardinal now feared to see this letter in the pontiff's hands. "Do all you can to dissuade the pope from seeking the original in Spain," wrote he to one of his ambassadors; "it may exasperate the emperor." We know how cautious the cardinal was towards Charles. Intrigue attained its highest point at this epoch, and

---

[1] Where Christ is not the foundation, surely no building can be of good work. State Papers, vii. p. 122.
[2] Convolare ad secundas nuptias non patitur negativum. Ibid. p. 138.
[3] Which words, fashioned with a familiarity and somewhat with earnestness and gravity. Ibid.
[4] State Papers, vol. i. p. 330.
[5] Burnet's Ref. i. p. 49.

[1] Postquam conjunctim omnes. State Papers, vii. p. 154.
[2] Uno eodemque calceo omnium pedes velle vestire. Ibid. p. 156.
[3] Quod forsan non licebit toto capite assequi, in eo digitum imponam. Ibid. p. 157.
[4] Malle Cæsari a stabulo nedum a sacris inservire, quam inferiorum hominum subditorum, vassalorum, rebellium injurias sustinere. Herbert, vol. i. p. 261.
[5] Le Grand, vol. i. p. 131.

Englishmen and Romans encountered craft with craft. "In such ticklish negotiations," says Burnet, (who had had some little experience in diplomacy) "ministers must say and unsay as they are instructed, which goes of course as a part of their business."[1] Henry's envoys to the pope intercepted the letters sent from Rome, and had Campeggio's seized.[2] On his part the pope indulged in flattering smiles and perfidious equivocations. Bryan wrote to Henry VIII.: "Always your grace hath done for him in deeds, and he hath recompensed you with fair *words* and fair *writings*, of which both I think your grace shall lack none; but as for the *deeds*, I never believe to see them, and especially at this time."[3] Bryan had comprehended the court of Rome better perhaps than many politicians. Finally, Clement himself, wishing to prepare the king for the blow he was about to inflict, wrote to him: "We have been able to find nothing that would satisfy your ambassadors."[4]

Henry thought he knew what this message meant: that he had found nothing, and would find nothing; and accordingly this prince, who, if we may believe Wolsey, had hitherto shown incredible patience and gentleness,[5] gave way to all his violence. "Very well then," said he; "my lords and I well know how to withdraw ourselves from the authority of the Roman see." Wolsey turned pale, and conjured his master not to rush into that fearful abyss;[6] Campeggio, too, endeavoured to revive the king's hopes. But it was all of no use. Henry recalled his ambassadors.

Henry, it is true, had not yet reached the age when violent characters become inflexible from the habit they have encouraged of yielding to their passions. But the cardinal, who knew his master, knew also that his inflexibility did not depend upon the number of his years; he thought Rome's power in England was lost, and placed between Henry and Clement, he exclaimed: "How shall I avoid Scylla, and not fall into Charybdis?"[7] He begged the king to make one last effort by sending Dr Bennet to the pope with orders to support the avocation to Rome, and he gave him a letter in which he displayed all the resources of his eloquence. "How can it be imagined," he wrote, "that the persuasions of sense urge the king to break a union in which the ardent years of his youth were passed with such purity?[8] ......The matter is very different. I am on the spot, I know the state of men's minds.

......Pray, believe me......The divorce is the secondary question; the primary one is *the fidelity of this realm* to the papal see. The nobility, gentry, and citizens all exclaim with indignation: Must our fortunes, and even our lives, depend upon the nod of a foreigner? We must abolish, or at the very least diminish, the authority of the Roman pontiff.[1]......Most holy father, we cannot mention such things without a shudder." ......This new attempt was also unavailing. The pope demanded of Henry how he could doubt his good will, seeing that the king of England had done so much for the apostolic see.[2] This appeared a cruel irony to Tudor; the king requested a favour of the pope, and the pope replied by calling to mind those which the papacy had received from his hands. "Is this the way," men asked in England, "in which Rome pays her debts?"

Wolsey had not reached the term of his misfortunes. Gardiner and Brian had just returned to London: they declared that to demand an avocation to Rome was to lose their cause. Accordingly Wolsey, who turned to every wind, ordered Da Casale, in case Clement should pronounce the avocation, to appeal from the pope, the false head of the church, *to the true vicar of Jesus Christ*.[3] This was almost in Luther's style. Who was this true vicar? Probably a pope nominated by the influence of England.

But this proceeding did not assure the cardinal: he was losing his judgment. A short time before this Du Bellay, who had just returned from Paris, whither he had gone to retain France on the side of England, had been invited to Richmond by Wolsey. As the two prelates were walking in the park, on that hill whence the eye ranges over the fertile and undulating fields through which the winding Thames pours its tranquil waters, the unhappy cardinal observed to the bishop: "My trouble is the greatest that ever was!......I have excited and carried on this matter of the divorce, to dissolve the union between the two houses of Spain and England, by sowing misunderstanding between them, as if I had no part in it.[4] You know it was in the interest of France; I therefore entreat the king your master and her majesty to do everything that may forward the divorce. I shall esteem such a favour more than if they made me pope; but if they refuse me, my ruin is inevitable." And then giving way to despair, he exclaimed: "Alas! would that I were going to be buried to-morrow!"

The wretched man was drinking the bitter cup his perfidies had prepared for him. All seemed to conspire against Henry, and

[1] Burnet's Ref. vol. i. p. 54.
[2] De intercipiendis literis. State Papers, vol. vii. p. 185.
[3] Ibid. p. 167.
[4] He added: Tametsi noctes ac dies per nos ipsi, ac per juris-peritissimos viros omnes vias tentemus. Ibid. p. 165.
[5] Incredibili patientia et humanitate. Burnet, Records, p. xxxii.
[6] Ne præceps huc vel illuc rex hic ruat curamus. Ibid. p. xxxiii.
[7] Hanc Charybdin et hos scopulos evitasse. Ibid. p xxxii.
[8] Sensuum suadela eam abrumpere cupit consuetudinem. Ibid. p. xxxiii.

[1] Qui nullam aut certe diminutam hic Romani pontificis auctoritatem. Burnet, Records, p. xxxiii.
[2] Dubitare non debes si quidem volueris recordare tua erga nos merita. State Papers, vii. p. 178.
[3] A non vicario ad verum vicarium Jesu Christi. Ibid. p. 191.
[4] Du Bellay to Montmorency, 22d May. Le Grand Preuves, p. 319.

Bennet was recalled shortly after. It was said at court and in the city: " Since the pope sacrifices us to the emperor, let us sacrifice the pope." Clement VII., intimidated by the threats of Charles V., and tottering upon his throne, madly repelled with his foot the bark of England. Europe was all attention, and began to think that the proud vessel of Albion, cutting the cable that bound her to the pontiffs, would boldly spread. her canvass to the winds, and ever after sail the sea alone, wafted onwards by the breeze that comes from heaven.

The influence of Rome over Europe is in great measure political. It loses a kingdom by a royal quarrel, and might in this same way lose ten.

CHAPTER VII.

Discussion between the Evangelicals and the Catholics—Union of Learning and Life—The Laity ; Tewkesbury—His Appearance before the Bishop's Court—He is tortured—Two Classes of Opponents—A Theological Duel—Scripture and the Church—Emancipation of the Mind—Mission to the Low Countries—Tyndale's Embarrassment—Tonstall wishes to buy the Books—Packington's Stratagem—Tyndale departs for Antwerp—His Shipwreck—Arrival at Hamburg—Meets Coverdale.

OTHER circumstances from day to day rendered the emancipation of the church more necessary. If behind these political debates there had not been found a Christian people, resolved never to temporize with error, it is probable that England, after a few years of independence, would have fallen back into the bosom of Rome. The affair of the divorce was not the only one agitating men's minds ; the religious controversies, which for some years filled the continent, were always more animated at Oxford and Cambridge. The *Evangelicals* and the *Catholics* (not very catholic indeed) warmly discussed the great questions which the progress of events brought before the world. The former maintained that the primitive church of the apostles and the actual church of the papacy were not identical ; the latter affirmed, on the contrary, the identity of popery and apostolic Christianity. Other Romish doctors in later times, finding this position somewhat embarrassing, have asserted that Catholicism existed only *in the germ* in the apostolic church, and had subsequently developed itself. But a thousand abuses, a thousand errors may creep into a church under cover of this theory. A plant springs from the seed and grows up in accordance with immutable laws ; whilst a doctrine cannot be transformed in the mind of man without falling under the influence of sin. It is true that the disciples of popery have supposed a constant action of the divine Spirit in the Catholic church, which excludes every influence of error. To stamp on the development of the church the character of

truth, they have stamped on the church itself the character of infallibility ; *quod erat demonstrandum.* Their reasoning is a mere begging of the question. To know whether the Romish development is identical with the gospel, we must examine it by Scripture.

It was not university men alone who occupied themselves with Christian truth. The separation which has been remarked in other times between the opinions of the people and of the learned, did not now exist. What the doctors taught, the citizens practised ; Oxford and London embraced each other. The theologians knew that learning has need of life, and the citizens believed that life has need of that learning which derives its doctrine from the wells of the Scriptures of God. It was the harmony between these two elements, the one theological, the other practical, which constituted the strength of the English reformation.

The evangelical life in the capital alarmed the clergy more than the evangelical doctrine in the colleges. Since Monmouth had escaped, they must strike another. Among the London merchants was John Tewkesbury, one of the oldest friends of the Scriptures in England. As early as 1512 he had become possessor of a manuscript copy of the Bible, and had attentively studied it ; when Tyndale's New Testament appeared, he read it with avidity ; and, finally, *The Wicked Mammon* had completed the work of his conversion. Being a man of heart and understanding, clever in all he undertook, a ready and fluent speaker, and liking to get to the bottom of everything, Tewkesbury like Monmouth became very influential in the city, and one of the most learned in Scripture of any of the evangelicals. These generous Christians, being determined to consecrate to God the good things they had received from him, were the first among that long series of laymen who were destined to be more useful to the truth than many ministers and bishops. They found time to interest themselves about the most trifling. details of the kingdom of God ; and in the history of the Reformation in Britain their names should be inscribed beside those of Latimer and Tyndale.

The activity of these laymen could not escape the cardinal's notice. Clement VII. was abandoning England : it was necessary for the English bishops, by crushing the heretics, to show that they would not abandon the popedom. We can understand the zeal of these prelates, and without excusing their persecutions, we are disposed to extenuate their crime. The bishops determined to ruin Tewkesbury. One day in April 1529, as he was busy among his peltries, the officers entered his warehouse, arrested him, and led him away to the bishop of London's chapel, where, besides the ordinary (Tonstall), the bishops of Ely, St Asaph, Bath, and Lincoln, with the abbot of Westminster, were on the bench. The composition of this tribunal indicated the importance of his case. The emancipation of the laity, thought these judges, is perhaps a more dangerous heresy than justification by faith.

"John Tewkesbury," said the bishop of London, "I exhort you to trust less to your own wit and learning, and more unto the doctrine of the holy mother the church." Tewkesbury made answer, that in his judgment he held no other doctrine than that of the church of Christ. Tonstall then broached the principal charge, that of having read the Wicked Mammon, and after quoting several passages, he exclaimed: "Renounce these errors."—"I find no fault in the book," replied Tewkesbury. "It has enlightened my conscience and consoled my heart. But it is not my gospel. I have studied the Holy Scriptures these seventeen years, and as a man sees the spots of his face in a glass, so by reading them I have learnt the faults of my soul.[1] If there is a disagreement between you and the New Testament, put yourselves in harmony with it, rather than desire to put that in accord with you." The bishops were surprised that a leather-seller should speak so well, and quote Scripture so happily, that they were unable to resist him.[2] Annoyed at being catechised by a layman, the bishops of Bath, St Asaph, and Lincoln thought they could conquer him more easily by the rack than by their arguments. He was taken to the Tower, where they ordered him to be put to the torture. His limbs were crushed, which was contrary to the laws of England, and the violence of the rack tore from him a cry of agony to which the priests replied by a shout of exultation. The inflexible merchant had promised at last to renounce Tyndale's Wicked Mammon. Tewkesbury left the Tower almost "a cripple,"[3] and returned to his house to lament the fatal word which the question had extorted from him, and to prepare in the silence of faith to confess in the burning pile the precious name of Christ Jesus.

We must, however, acknowledge that the "question" was not Rome's only argument. The gospel had two classes of opponents in the sixteenth century, as in the first ages of the church. Some attacked it with the torture, others with their writings. Sir Thomas More, a few years later, was to have recourse to the first of these arguments; but for the moment he took up his pen. He had first studied the writings of the Fathers of the church and of the Reformers, but rather as an advocate than as a theologian; and then, armed at all points, he rushed into the arena of polemics, and in his attacks dealt those "technical convictions and that malevolent subtlety," says one of his greatest admirers,[4] "from which the honestest men of his profession are not free." Jests and sarcasms

had fallen from his pen in his discussion with Tyndale, as in his controversy with Luther. Shortly after Tewkesbury's affair (in June, 1529) there appeared *A Dialogue of Sir Thomas More, Knt., touching the pestilent Sect of Luther and Tyndale, by the one begun in Saxony, and by the other laboured to be brought into England.*[1]

Tyndale soon became informed of More's publication, and a remarkable combat ensued between these two representatives of the two doctrines that were destined to divide Christendom—Tyndale the champion of Scripture, and More the champion of the church. More having called his book a *dialogue*, Tyndale adopted this form in his reply,[2] and the two combatants valiantly crossed their swords, though wide seas lay between them. This theological duel is not without importance in the history of the Reformation. The struggles of diplomacy, of sacerdotalism, and of royalty were not enough; there must be struggles of doctrine. Rome had set the hierarchy above the faith; the Reformation was to restore faith to its place above the hierarchy.

MORE. Christ said not, the Holy Ghost shall *write*, but shall *teach*. Whatsoever the church says, it is the word of God, though it be not in Scripture.

TYNDALE. What! Christ and the apostles not spoken of *Scriptures!......These are written,* says St John, *that ye believe and through belief have life.* (1 John ii. 1; Rom. xv. 4; Matthew xxii. 29.)[3]

MORE. The apostles have taught by *mouth* many things they did not *write*, because they should not come into the hands of the heathen for mocking.

TYNDALE. I pray you what thing more to be mocked by the heathen could they teach than the resurrection; and that Christ was God and man, and died between two thieves? And yet all these things the apostles *wrote*. And again, purgatory, penance, and satisfaction for sin, and praying to saints, are marvellous agreeable unto the superstition of the heathen people, so that they need not to abstain from writing of them for fear lest the heathen should have mocked them.[4]

MORE. We must not examine the teaching of the church by Scripture, but understand Scripture by means of what the church says.

TYNDALE. What! Does the air give light to the sun, or the sun to the air? Is the church before the gospel, or the gospel before the church? Is not the father older than the son? *God begat us with his own will, with the word of truth,* says St James (i. 18.) If he who begetteth is before him who is begotten, the *word* is before the *church,*

---

1 Foxe, iv. p. 690.   2 Ibid. p. 689.   3 Ibid.
4 Nisard, Hommes illustres de la renaissance. *Revue des Deux Mondes.*

1 The Dialogue consisted of 250 pages, and was printed by John Rastell, More's brother-in-law. Tyndale's answer did not appear until later; we have thought it our duty to introduce it here.
2 Answer to Sir Thomas More's Dialogue.
3 Ibid. p. 101.
4 Ibid. p. 28, 29.

or, to speak more correctly, before the *congregation*.

MORE. Why do you say *congregation* and not *church?*

TYNDALE. Because by that word *church,* you understand nothing but a multitude of shorn and oiled, which we now call the spirituality or clergy; while the word of right is common unto all the congregation of them that believe in Christ.[1]

MORE. The church is the pope and his sect or followers.

TYNDALE. The pope teacheth us to trust in holy works for salvation, as penance, saints' merits, and friars' coats.[2] Now, he that hath no faith to be saved through Christ, is not of Christ's church.[3]

MORE. The Romish church from which Lutherans came out, was before them, and therefore is the right one.

TYNDALE. In like manner you may say, the church of the Pharisees, whence Christ and his apostles came out, was before them, and was therefore the right church, and consequently Christ and his disciples are heretics.

MORE. No: the apostles came out from the church of the Pharisees because they found not Christ there; but your priests in Germany and elsewhere, have come out of our church, because they wanted wives.

TYNDALE. Wrong:............these priests were at first attached to what you call *heresies,* and then they took wives; but yours were first attached to the *holy* doctrine of the pope, and then they took harlots.[4]

MORE. Luther's books be open, if ye will not believe us.

TYNDALE. Nay, ye have shut them up, and have even burnt them.[5]......

MORE. I marvel that you deny *purgatory,* Sir William, except it be a plain point with you to go straight to hell.[6]

TYNDALE. I know no other purging but faith in the cross of Christ; while you, for a groat or a sixpence, buy some secret pills [indulgences] which you take to purge yourselves of your sins.[7]

MORE. Faith, then, is your purgatory, you say: there is no need, therefore, of works—a most immoral doctrine!

TYNDALE. It is faith *alone* that saves us, but not a *bare faith.* When a horse beareth a saddle and a man thereon, we may well say that the horse only and alone beareth the saddle, but we do not mean the saddle empty, and no man thereon.[8]

In this manner did the catholic and the evangelical carry on the discussion. According to Tyndale, what constitutes the true church is the work of the Holy Ghost within; according to More, the constitution of the papacy without. The spiritual character of the gospel is thus put in opposition to the formalist character of the Roman church. The Reformation restored to our belief the solid foundation of the word of God; for the sand it substituted the rock. In the discussion to which we have just been listening, the advantage remained not with the catholic. Erasmus, a friend of More's, embarrassed by the course the latter was taking, wrote to Tonstall: " I cannot heartily congratulate More."[1]

Henry interrupted the celebrated knight in these contests to send him to Cambray, where a peace was negotiating between France and the empire. Wolsey would have been pleased to go himself; but his enemies suggested to the king, " that it was only that he might not expedite the matter of the divorce." Henry, therefore, despatched More, Knight, and Tonstall; but Wolsey had created so many delays that they did not arrive until after the conclusion of the *Ladies' Peace* (August, 1529). The king's vexation was extreme. Du Bellay had in vain helped him to spend a *good preparatory July* to make him *swallow the dose.*[2] Henry was angry with Wolsey, Wolsey threw the blame on the ambassador, and the ambassador defended himself, he tells us, " with tooth and nail."[3]

By way of compensation, the English envoys concluded with the emperor a treaty prohibiting on both sides the printing and sale of " any Lutheran books."[4] Some of them could have wished for a good persecution, for a few burning piles, it may be. A singular opportunity occurred. In the spring of 1529, Tyndale and Fryth had left Marburg for Antwerp, and were thus in the vicinity of the English envoys. What West had been unable to effect, it was thought the two most intelligent men in Britain could not fail to accomplish. " Tyndale must be captured," said More and Tonstall.—" You do not know what sort of a country you are in," replied Hackett. " Will you believe that on the 7th of April, Harman arrested me at Antwerp for damages, caused by his imprisonment? If you can lay anything to my charge as a private individual, I said to the officer, I am ready to answer for myself; but if you arrest me as ambassador, I know no judge but the emperor. Upon which the procurator had the audacity to reply, that I was arrested *as ambassador;* and the lords of Antwerp only set me at liberty on condition that I should appear again at the first summons.[5] These merchants are so proud of their franchises, that they would resist even Charles himself." This anecdote was not at all calculated to encourage More; and not caring about a pursuit, which promised to be of little use, he returned to England. But

---

[1] Answer to Sir Thomas More's Dialogue. p. 12, 13.
[2] Ibid. p. 40.   [4] Ibid. p. 104.   [6] Ibid. p. 214.   [8] Ibid. p. 197.
[3] Ibid. p. 39.   [5] Ibid. p. 189.   [7] It id.

[1] Thomæ Moro non admodum gratulor. Erasm. Epp. p. 1478.
[2] Juillet préparatoire pour lui faire avaler la médecine.
[3] Du hec et des ongles. Du Bellay to Montmorency Le Grand, iii. p. 328.   [4] Herbert, p. 316.
[5] Hackett to Wolsey, Brussels, 13th April, 1529. Bible Annals, vol. i. p. 199.

judge without fear or favour, and would admit of neither recusation nor appeal.[1] Then the usher cried: "Henry, king of England, come into court." The king, cited in his own capital to accept as judges two priests, his subjects, repressed the throbbing of his proud heart, and replied, in the hope that this strange trial would have a favourable issue: "Here I am." The usher continued: "Catherine, queen of England, come into court." The queen handed the cardinals a paper in which she protested against the legality of the court, as the judges were the subjects of her opponent,[2] and appealed to Rome. The cardinals declared they could not admit this paper, and consequently Catherine was again called into court. At this second summons she rose, devoutly crossed herself, made the circuit of the court to where the king sat, bending with dignity as she passed in front of the legates, and fell on her knees before her husband. Every eye was turned upon her. Then speaking in English, but with a Spanish accent, which by recalling the distance she was from her native home, pleaded eloquently for her, Catherine said with tears in her eyes, and in a tone at once dignified and impassioned:

"Sir,—I beseech you, for all the love that hath been between us, and for the love of God, let me have justice and right; take some pity on me, for I am a poor woman and a stranger, born out of your dominions. I have here no assured friend, much less impartial counsel, and I flee to you as to the head of justice within this realm. Alas! Sir, wherein have I offended you, or what occasion given you of displeasure, that you should wish to put me from you? I take God and all the world to witness, that I have been to you a true, humble, and obedient wife, ever conformable to your will and pleasure. Never have I said or done aught contrary thereto, being always well pleased and content with all things wherein you had delight; neither did I ever grudge in word or countenance, or show a visage or spark of discontent. I loved all those whom you loved, only for your sake. This twenty years I have been your true wife, and by me ye have had divers children, although it hath pleased God to call them out of this world, which yet hath been no default in me."

The judges, and even the most servile of the courtiers, were touched when they heard these simple and eloquent words, and the queen's sorrow moved them almost to tears. Catherine continued:—

"Sir,—When ye married me at the first, I take God to be my judge I was a true maid: and whether it be true or not, I put it to your conscience......If there be any just cause that ye can allege against me, I am contented to depart from your kingdom, albeit to my great shame and dishonour; and if there be none, then let me remain in my former estate until death. Who united us? The king, your father, who was called the second Solomon; and my father, Ferdinand, who was esteemed one of the wisest princes that, for many years before, had reigned in Spain. It is not, therefore, to be doubted that the marriage between you and me is good and lawful. Who are my judges? Is not one the man that has put sorrow between you and me?[1]......a judge whom I refuse and abhor!—Who are the councillors assigned me? Are they not officers of the crown, who have made oath to you in your own council?...... Sir, I conjure you not to call me before a court so formed. Yet, if you refuse me this favour......your will be done......I shall be silent, I shall repress the emotions of my soul, and remit my just cause to the hands of God."

Thus spoke Catherine through her tears:[2] humbly bending, she seemed to embrace Henry's knees. She rose and made a low obeisance to the king. It was expected that she would return to her seat; but leaning on the arm of Griffiths, her receiver-general, she moved towards the door. The king, observing this, ordered her to be recalled; and the usher following her, thrice cried aloud: "Catherine, queen of England, come into court."—"Madam," said Griffiths, "you are called back."—"I hear it well enough," replied the queen, "but go you on, for this is no court wherein I can have justice: let us proceed." Catherine returned to the palace, and never again appeared before the court either by proxy or in person.[3]

She had gained her cause in the minds of many. The dignity of her person, the quaint simplicity of her speech, the propriety with which, relying upon her innocence, she had spoken of the most delicate subjects, and the tears which betrayed her emotion, had created a deep impression. But "the sting in her speech," as an historian says,[4] was her appeal to the king's conscience, and to the judgment of Almighty God, on the capital point in the cause. "How could a person so modest, so sober in her language," said many, "dare utter such a falsehood? Besides, the king did not contradict her."

Henry was greatly embarrassed: Catherine's words had moved him. Catherine's defence, one of the most touching in history, had gained over the accuser himself. He therefore felt constrained to render this testimony to the accused: "Since the queen has withdrawn, I will, in her absence, declare to

---

[1] The king's letter to his ambassadors at Rome, 23d June. Burnet's Ref., Records, p. liv.
[2] Personas judicum non solum regi devinctas verum et subjectas esse. Sanders, p. 35.

[1] Qui dissensionem inter ipsam et virum suum. Polyd Virg. p. 688.
[2] Hæc illa flebiliter dicente. Ibid. p. 686, and Cavendish
[3] Burnet, Records, p. 36. In this letter the king says, Both we and the queen appeared in person.
[4] Fuller, p. 173.

you all present, that she has been to me as true and obedient a wife as I could desire. She has all the virtues and good qualities that belong to a woman. She is as noble in character as in birth."

But Wolsey was the most embarrassed of all. When the queen had said, without naming him, that one of her judges was the cause of all her misfortunes, looks of indignation were turned upon him.[1] He was unwilling to remain under the weight of this accusation. As soon as the king had finished speaking, he said : " Sir, I humbly beg your majesty to declare before this audience, whether I was the first or chief mover in this business." Wolsey had formerly boasted to Du Bellay, " that the first project of the divorce was set on foot by himself, to create a perpetual separation between the houses of England and Spain ;[2] but now it suited him to affirm the contrary. The king, who needed his services, took care not to contradict him. " My lord cardinal," he said, " I can well excuse you herein. Marry, so far from being a mover, ye have been rather against me in attempting thereof. It was the bishop of Tarbes, the French ambassador, who begot the first scruples in my conscience by his doubts on the legitimacy of the princess Mary." This was not correct. The bishop of Tarbes was not in England before the year 1527, and we have proofs that the king was meditating a divorce in 1526.[3] " From that hour," he continued, " I was much troubled, and thought myself in danger of God's heavy displeasure, who, wishing to punish my incestuous marriage, had taken away all the sons my wife had borne me. I laid my grief before you, my lord of Lincoln, then being my ghostly father; and by your advice I asked counsel of the rest of the bishops, and you all informed me under your seals, that you shared in my scruples."—" That is the truth," said the archbishop of Canterbury.— " No, Sir, not so, under correction," quoth the bishop of Rochester, " you have not my hand and seal."—" No?" exclaimed the king, showing him a paper which he held in his hand; " is not this your hand and seal?"— " No, forsooth," he answered. Henry's surprise increased, and turning with a frown to the archbishop of Canterbury, he asked him : " What say you to that?" " Sir, it is his hand and seal," replied Warham."—" It is not," rejoined Rochester; " I told you I would never consent to any such act."— " You say the truth," responded the archbishop, " but you were fully resolved at the last, that I should subscribe your name and put your seal."—" All which is untrue," added

Rochester, in a passion. The bishop was not very respectful to his primate. " Well, well," said the king, wishing to end the dispute, " we will not stand in argument with you ; for you are but one man."[1] The court adjourned. The day had been better for Catherine than for the prelates.

In proportion as the first sitting had been pathetic, so the discussions in the second between the lawyers and bishops were calculated to revolt a delicate mind. The advocates of the two parties vigorously debated *pro* and *con* respecting the consummation of Arthur's marriage with Catherine. " It is a very difficult question," said one of the counsel ; "none can know the truth."—" But I know it," replied the bishop of Rochester.— " What do you mean ?" asked Wolsey.— " My lord," he answered, " he was the very Truth who said : *What God hath joined together, let not man put asunder :* that is enough for me."—" So every body thinks," rejoined Wolsey ; " but whether it was God who united Henry of England and Catherine of Aragon, *hoc restat probandum*, that remains to be proved. The king's council decides that the marriage is unlawful, and consequently it was not *God who joined them together.*" The two bishops then exchanged a few words less edifying than those of the preceding day. Several of the hearers expressed a sentiment of disgust. " It is a disgrace to the court," said Dr Ridley with no little indignation, " that you dare discuss questions which fill every right-minded man with horror." This sharp reprimand put an end to the debate.

The agitations of the court spread to the convents ; priests, monks, and nuns were everywhere in commotion. It was not long before astonishing revelations began to circulate through the cloisters. There was no talk then of an old portrait of the Virgin that winked its eyes ; but other miracles were invented. " An angel," it was rumoured, " has appeared to Elizabeth Barton, the maid of Kent, as he did formerly to Adam, to the patriarchs, and to Jesus Christ." At the epochs of the creation and of the redemption. and in the times which lead from one to the other, miracles are natural ; God then appeared, and his coming without any signs of power, would be as surprising as the rising of the sun unattended by its rays of light. But the Romish Church does not stop there ; it claims in every age, for its saints, the privilege of miraculous powers, and the miracles are multiplied in proportion to the ignorance of the people. And accordingly the angel said to the epileptic maid of Kent: " Go to the unfaithful king of England, and tell him there are three things he desires, which I forbid now and for ever. The first is the power of the pope ; the second the new doctrine ; the third Anne Boleyn. If he takes her for his wife, God will visit him."

[1] Vidisses Wolseum infestis fere omnium oculis conspici. Polyd. Virg. p. 688.
[2] Du Bellay to Montmorency. Le Grand, Preuves, p. 186, 319.
[3] See Pace's letter to Henry in 1526. Le Grand, Preuves, p. 1. Pace there shows that it is incorrect to say : *Deuteronomium abrogare Leviticum* (Deuteronomy abrogates Leviticus,) so far as concerns the prohibition to take the wife of a deceased brother.

[1] Cavendish's Wolsey, p. 223.

The vision-seeing maid delivered the message to the king,[1] whom nothing could now stop.

On the contrary, he began to find out that Wolsey proceeded too slowly, and the idea sometimes crossed his mind that he was betrayed by this minister. One fine summer's morning, Henry as soon as he rose summoned the cardinal to him at Bridewell. Wolsey hastened thither, and remained closeted with the king from eleven till twelve. The latter gave way to all the fury of his passion and the violence of his despotism. "We must finish this matter promptly," he said, "we must positively." Wolsey retired very uneasy, and returned by the Thames to Westminster. The sun darted his bright rays on the water. The bishop of Carlisle, who sat by the cardinal's side, remarked, as he wiped his forehead: "A very warm day, my lord." —"Yes," replied the unhappy Wolsey, "if you had been *chafed* for an hour as I have been, you would say it was a *hot* day." When he reached his palace, the cardinal lay down on his bed to seek repose; he was not quiet long.

Catherine had grown in Henry's eyes, as well as in those of the nation. The king shrank from a judgment; he even began to doubt of his success. He wished that the queen would consent to a separation. This idea occurred to his mind after Wolsey's departure, and the cardinal had hardly closed his eyes before the Earl of Wiltshire (Anne Boleyn's father) was announced to him with a message from the king. "It is his majesty's pleasure," said Wiltshire, "that you represent to the queen the shame that will accrue to her from a judicial condemnation, and persuade her to confide in his wisdom." Wolsey, commissioned to execute a task he knew to be impossible, exclaimed: "Why do you put such fancies in the king's head?" and then he spoke so reproachfully that Wiltshire, with tears in his eyes, fell on his knees beside the cardinal's bed.[2] Boleyn, desirous of seeing his daughter queen of England, feared perhaps that he had taken a wrong course. "It is well," said the cardinal, recollecting that the message came from Henry VIII., "I am ready to do everything to please his majesty." He rose, went to Bath-Place to fetch Campeggio, and together they waited on the queen.

The two legates found Catherine quietly at work with her maids of honour. Wolsey addressed the queen in Latin: "Nay, my lord," she said, "speak to me in English; I wish all the world could hear you."—"We desire, madam, to communicate to *you alone* our counsel and opinion."—"My lord," said the queen. "you are come to speak of things beyond my capacity;" and then, with noble simplicity, showing a skein of red silk hanging about her neck, she continued: "These are my occupations, and all that I am capable of. I am a poor woman, without friends in this foreign country, and lacking wit to answer persons of wisdom as ye be; and yet, my lords, to please you, let us go to my withdrawing room."

At these words the queen rose, and Wolsey gave her his hand. Catherine earnestly maintained her rights as a woman and a queen. "We who were in the outer chamber," says Cavendish, "from time to time could hear the queen speaking very loud, but could not understand what she said." Catherine, instead of justifying herself, boldly accused her judge. "I know, Sir Cardinal," she said with noble candour, "I know who has given the king the advice he is following: it is you. I have not ministered to your pride —I have blamed your conduct—I have complained of your tyranny, and my nephew the emperor has not made you pope......Hence all my misfortunes. To revenge yourself you have kindled a war in Europe, and have stirred up against me this most wicked matter. God will be my judge....and yours!" Wolsey would have replied, but Catherine haughtily refused to hear him, and while treating Campeggio with great civility, declared that she would not acknowledge either of them as her judge. The cardinals withdrew, Wolsey full of vexation, and Campeggio beaming with joy, for the business was getting more complicated. Every hope of accommodation was lost: nothing remained now but to proceed judicially.

CHAPTER IX.

The Trial resumed—Catherine summoned—Twelve Articles—The Witnesses' Evidence—Arthur and Catherine really married—Campeggio opposes the argument of Divine Right—Other Arguments—The Legates required to deliver Judgment—Their Tergiversations—Change in Men's Minds—Final Session—General Expectation—Adjournment during Harvest—Campeggio excuses this Impertinence—The King's Indignation—Suffolk's Violence—Wolsey's Reply—He is ruined—General Accusations—The Cardinal turns to an Episcopal Life.

THE trial was resumed. The bishop of Bath and Wells waited upon the queen at Greenwich, and peremptorily summoned her to appear in the parliament-chamber.[1] On the day appointed Catherine limited herself to sending an appeal to the pope. She was declared contumacious, and the legates proceeded with the cause.

Twelve articles were prepared, which were to serve for the examination of the witnesses, and the summary of which was, that the marriage of Henry with Catherine, being forbidden both by the law of God and of the church, was null and void.[2]

---

[1] She showed this unto the king. Letter to Cromwell in Strype, vol. i. p. 272.
[2] Cavendish, p. 226.

[1] In quadam superiori camera: *the queen's dining-chamber*, nuncupata, 26 die mensis Junii. Rymer, Acta, p. 119.
[2] Divino, ecclesiastico jure....nullo omnino et invalidum. Herbert, p. 263.

The hearing of the witnesses began, and Dr Taylor, archdeacon of Buckingham, conducted the examination. Their evidence, which would now be taken only with closed doors, may be found in Lord Herbert of Cherbury's History of Henry VIII. The duke of Norfolk, high-treasurer of England, the duke of Suffolk, Maurice St John, gentleman-carver to Prince Arthur, the viscount Fitzwalter and Anthony Willoughby, his cup-bearers, testified to their being present on the morrow of the wedding at the breakfast of the prince, then in sound health, and reported the conversation that took place.[1] The old duchess of Norfolk, the earl of Shrewsbury, and the marquis of Dorset, confirmed these declarations, which proved that Arthur and Catherine were really married. It was also called to mind that, at the time of Arthur's death, Henry was not permitted to take the title of prince of Wales, because Catherine hoped to give an heir to the crown of England.[2]

"If Arthur and Catherine were really married," said the king's counsellors after these extraordinary depositions, "the marriage of this princess with Henry, Arthur's brother, was forbidden by the divine law, by an express command of God contained in Leviticus, and no dispensation could permit what God had forbidden." Campeggio would never concede this argument, which limited the right of the popes; it was necessary therefore to abandon the *divine right* (which was in reality to lose the cause), and to seek in the bull of Julius II. and in his famous brief for flaws that would invalidate them both;[3] and this the king's counsel did, although they did not conceal the weakness of their position. "The motive alleged in the dispensation," they said, "is the necessity of preserving a cordial relation between Spain and England; now, there was nothing that threatened their harmony. Moreover, it is said in this document that the pope grants it at the prayer of Henry, prince of Wales. Now as this prince was only thirteen years old, he was not of age to make such a request. As for the brief, it is found neither in England nor in Rome; we cannot therefore admit its authenticity." It was not difficult for Catherine's friends to invalidate these objections. "Besides," they added, "a union that has lasted twenty years, sufficiently establishes its own lawfulness. And will you declare the Princess Mary illegitimate, to the great injury of this realm?"

The king's advocates then changed their course. Was not the Roman legate provided with a decretal pronouncing the divorce, in case it should be proved that Arthur's marriage had been really consummated? Now, this fact had been proved by the depositions. "This is the moment for delivering judgment," said Henry and his counsellors to Campeggio. "Publish the pope's decretal." But the pope feared the sword of Charles V., then hanging over his head; and accordingly, whenever the king advanced one step, the Romish prelate took several in an opposite direction. "I will deliver judgment in *five* days," said he; and when the five days were expired, he bound himself to deliver it in six. "Restore peace to my troubled conscience," exclaimed Henry. The legate replied in courtly phrase: he had gained a few days' delay, and that was all he desired.

Such conduct on the part of the Roman legate produced an unfavourable effect in England, and a change took place in the public mind. The first movement had been for Catherine; the second was for Henry. Clement's endless delays and Campeggio's stratagems exasperated the nation. The king's argument was simple and popular: "The pope cannot dispense with the laws of God;" while the queen, by appealing to the authority of the Roman pontiff, displeased both high and low. "No precedent," said the lawyers, "can justify the king's marriage with his brother's widow."

There were, however, some evangelical Christians who thought Henry was "troubled" more by his passions than by his conscience; and they asked how it happened that a prince, who represented himself to be so disturbed by the possible transgression of a law of doubtful interpretation, could desire, after twenty years, to violate the indisputable law which forbade the divorce?...... On the 21st of July, the day fixed *ad concludendum*, the cause was adjourned until the Friday following, and no one doubted that the matter would then be terminated.

All prepared for this important day. The king ordered the dukes of Norfolk and Suffolk to be present at the sitting of the court; and being himself impatient to hear the so much coveted judgment, he stole into a gallery of the parliament-chamber facing the judges.

The legates of the holy see having taken their seats, the attorney general signified to them, "that everything necessary for the information of their conscience having been judicially laid before them, that day had been fixed for the conclusion of the trial." There was a pause; every one feeling the importance of this judgment, waited for it with impatience. "Either the papacy pronounces my divorce from Catherine," the king had said, "or I shall divorce myself from the papacy." That was the way Henry put the question. All eyes, and particularly the king's, were turned on the judges; Campeggio could not retreat; he must now say *yes* or *no*. For some time he was silent. He knew for certain that the queen's appeal had been admitted by Clement VII. and that the latter had concluded an alliance with the emperor. It was no

[1] Quoad Arthurus mane postridie potum flagitaret, idque nt, aiebant, quoniam diceret se illa nocte in calida Hispaniarum regione peregrinatum fuisse. Sanders, p. 43.
[2] Foxe, v. p. 51.
[3] Herbert gives them at length, p. 264-267.

840

longer in his power to grant the king's request. Clearly foreseeing that a *no* would perhaps forfeit the power of Rome in England, while a *yes* might put an end to the plans of religious emancipation which alarmed him so much, he could not make up his mind to say either *yes* or *no*.

At last the nuncio rose slowly from his chair, and all the assembly listened with emotion to the oracular decision which for so many years the powerful king of England had sought from the Roman pontiff. "The general vacation of the harvest and vintage," he said, "being observed every year by the court of Rome, dating from to-morrow the 24th of July, the beginning of the dog-days, we adjourn, to some future period, the conclusion of these pleadings."[1]

The auditors were thunderstruck. "What! because the *malaria* renders the air of Rome dangerous at the end of July, and compels the Romans to close their courts, must a trial be broken off on the banks of the Thames, when its conclusion is looked for so impatiently?" The people hoped for a judicial sentence, and they were answered with a jest; it was thus Rome made sport of Christendom. Campeggio, to disarm Henry's wrath, gave utterance to some noble sentiments; but his whole line of conduct raises legitimate doubts as to his sincerity. "The queen," he said, "denies the competency of the court; I must therefore make my report to the pope, who is the source of life and honour, and wait his sovereign orders. I have not come so far to please any man, be he king or subject. I am an old man, feeble and sickly, and fear none but the Supreme Judge, before whom I must soon appear. I therefore adjourn this court until the 1st of October."

It was evident that this adjournment was only a formality intended to signify the definitive rejection of Henry's demand. The same custom prevails in the British legislature.

The king, who from his place of concealment had heard Campeggio's speech, could scarcely control his indignation. He wanted a regular judgment; he clung to forms; he desired that his cause should pass successfully through all the windings of ecclesiastical procedure, and yet here it is wrecked upon the vacations of the Romish court. Henry was silent, however, either from prudence, or because surprise deprived him of the power of speech, and he hastily left the gallery.

Norfolk, Suffolk, and the other courtiers, did not follow him. The king and his ministers, the peers and the people, and even the clergy, were almost unanimous, and yet the pope pronounced his *veto*. He humbled the Defender of the Faith to flatter the author of the sack of Rome. This was too much.

The impetuous Suffolk started from his seat, struck his hand violently on the table in front of him, cast a threatening look upon the judges and exclaimed: "By the mass, the old saying is confirmed to-day, that no cardinal has ever brought good to England."[1] —"Sir, of all men in this realm," replied Wolsey, "you have the least cause to disparage cardinals, for if I, poor cardinal, had not been, you would not have had a head on your shoulders."[2] It would seem that Wolsey pacified Henry, at the time of the duke's marriage with the Princess Mary. "I cannot pronounce sentence," continued Wolsey, "without knowing the good pleasure of his holiness." The two dukes and the other noblemen left the hall in anger, and hastened to the palace.[3] The legates, remaining with their officers, looked at each other for a few moments. At last Campeggio, who alone had remained calm during this scene of violence, arose, and the audience dispersed.

Henry did not allow himself to be crushed by this blow. Rome, by her strange proceedings, aroused in him that suspicious and despotic spirit, of which he gave such tragic proofs in after-years. The papacy was making sport of him. Clement and Wolsey tossed his divorce from one to the other like a ball which, now at Rome and now at London, seemed fated to remain perpetually in the air. The king thought he had been long enough the plaything of his holiness and of the crafty cardinal; his patience was exhausted, and he resolved to show his adversaries that Henry VIII. was more than a match for these bishops. We shall find him seizing this favourable opportunity, and giving an unexpected solution to the matter.

Wolsey sorrowfully hung his head; by taking part with the nuncio and the pope, he had signed the warrant of his own destruction. So long as Henry had a single ray of hope, he thought proper still to dissemble with Clement VII.; but he might vent all his anger on Wolsey. From the period of the *Roman Vacations* the cardinal was ruined in his master's mind. Wolsey's enemies seeing his favour decline, hastened to attack him. Suffolk and Norfolk in particular, impatient to get rid of an insolent priest who had so long chafed their pride, told Henry that Wolsey had been continually playing false; they went over all his negotiations month by month and day by day, and drew the most overwhelming conclusions from them. Sir William Kingston and Lord Manners laid before the king one of the cardinal's letters which Sir Francis Bryan had obtained from the papal archives. In it the cardinal desired Clement to spin out the

[1] Feriæ generales messium et vindemiarum. Herbert, p. 278; Cavendish, p. 229.

[1] Mensam quæ proponebatur magno ictu concutiens: Per sacram, inquit, missam, nemo unquam legatorum aut cardinalium quicquam boni ad Angliam apportavit. Sanders, p. 49.
[2] Cavendish, p. 233.
[3] Duces ex judicio discedentes, ut ipsi omnibus iracundiæ flammis urebantur. Sanders, p. 49.

divorce question, and finally to oppose it, see-ing (he added) that if Henry was separated from Catherine, a friend to the reformers would become queen of England.[1] This letter clearly expressed Wolsey's inmost thoughts : Rome at any price......and perish England and Henry rather than the popedom! We can imagine the king's anger.

Anne Boleyn's friends were not working alone. There was not a person at court whom Wolsey's haughtiness and tyranny had not offended ; no one in the king's coun-cil in whom his continual intrigues had not raised serious suspicions. He had (they said) betrayed in France the cause of England ; kept up in time of peace and war secret in-telligence with Madam, mother of Francis I.; received great presents from her ;[2] oppressed the nation, and trodden under foot the laws of the kingdom. The people called him *Frenchman* and *traitor*, and all England seem-ed to vie in throwing burning brands at the superb edifice which the pride of this prelate had so laboriously erected.[3]

Wolsey was too clearsighted not to dis-cern the signs of his approaching fall. " Both the rising and the setting sun (for thus an historian calls Anne Boleyn and Catherine of Aragon) frowned upon him,"[4] and the sky, growing darker around him, gave token of the storm that was to overwhelm him. If the *cause* failed, Wolsey incurred the ven-geance of the king; if it succeeded, he would be delivered up to the vengeance of the Boleyns, without speaking of Catherine's, the emperor's, and the pope's. Happy Campeg-gio ! thought the cardinal, he has nothing to fear. If Henry's favour is withdrawn from him, Charles and Clement will make him compensation. But Wolsey lost everything when he lost the king's good graces. De-tested by his fellow-citizens, despised and hated by all Europe, he saw to whatever side he turned nothing but the just reward of his avarice and falseness. He strove in vain, as on other occasions, to lean on the ambassador of France ; Du Bellay was solicited on the other side. " I am exposed here to such a heavy and continual fire that I am half dead," exclaimed the bishop of Bayonne ;[5] and the cardinal met with an unusual reserve in his former confidant.

Yet the crisis approached. Like a skilful but affrighted pilot, Wolsey cast his eyes around him to discover a port in which he could take refuge. He could find none but his see of York. He therefore began once more to complain of the fatigues of power, of the weariness of the diplomatic career, and to extol the sweetness of an episcopal life. On a sudden he felt a great interest about the flock of whom he had never thought be-

fore. Those around him shook their heads, well knowing that such a retreat would be to Wolsey the bitterest of disgraces. One single idea supported him ; if he fell, it would be because he had clung more to the pope than to the king : he would be the martyr of his faith.—What a faith, what a martyr !

CHAPTER X.

Anne Boleyn at Hever—She Reads the Obedience of a Chris-tian Man—Is recalled to Court—Miss Gainsford and George Zouch—Tyndale's Book converts Zouch—Zouch in the Chapel-Royal—The Book seized—Anne applies to Henry—The King reads the Book—Pretended Influence of the Book on Henry—The Court at Woodstock—The Park and its Goblins—Henry's Esteem for Anne.

WHILE these things were taking place Anne was living at Hever Castle in retirement and sadness. Scruples from time to time still alarmed her conscience. It is true, the king represented to her unceasingly that his sal-vation and the safety of his people demanded the dissolution of a union condemned by the divine law, and that what he solicited several popes had granted. Had not Alexander VI. annulled, after ten years, the marriage of Ladislaus and Beatrice of Naples ? Had not Louis XII., the father of his people, been di-vorced from Joan of France ? Nothing was more common, he said, than to see the divorce of a prince authorized by a pope; the security of the state must be provided for before everything else. Carried away by these arguments and dazzled by the splendour of a throne, Anne Boleyn consented to usurp at Henry's side the rank belonging to another. Yet, if she was imprudent and ambitious, she was feeling and generous, and the misfor-tunes of a queen whom she respected soon made her reject with terror the idea of taking her place. The fertile pastures of Kent and the gothic halls of Hever Castle were by turns the witnesses of the mental conflicts this young lady experienced. The fear she entertained of seeing the queen again, and the idea that the two cardinals, her enemies, were plotting her ruin, made her adopt the resolution of not returning to court, and she shut herself up in her solitary chamber.

Anne had neither the deep piety of a Bil-ney, nor the somewhat vague and mystic spirituality observable in Margaret of Valois ; it was not feeling which prevailed in her religion, it was knowledge, and a horror of superstition and pharisaism. Her mind re-quired light and activity, and at that time she sought in reading the consolations so necessary to her position. One day she opened one of the books prohibited in Eng-land, which a friend of the Reformation had given her : *The Obedience of a Christian Man.* Its author was William Tyndale, that invisi-ble man whom Wolsey's agents were hunting for in Brabant and Germany, and this was a

---

[1] Edm. Campion *De divortio.* Herbert, p. 289.
[2] Du Bellay's Letters. Le Grand, Preuves, p. 374.
[3] Novis etiam furoris et insaniæ facibus incenderunt. Sanders, p. 49. [4] Fuller, p. 176.
[5] Du Bellay to Montmorency, 15th June. Le Grand, Preuves, p. 324.

recommendation to Anne. "If thou believe the promises," she read, "then God's truth justifieth thee; that is, forgiveth thy sins and sealeth thee with his Holy Spirit. If thou have true faith, so seest thou the exceeding and infinite love and mercy which God hath shown thee freely in Christ: then must thou needs love again: and love cannot but compel thee to work. If when tyrants oppose thee thou have power to confess, then art thou sure that thou art safe.[1] If thou be fallen from the way of truth, come thereto again and thou art safe. Yea, Christ shall save thee, and the angels of heaven shall rejoice at thy coming."[2] These words did not change Anne's heart, but she marked with her nail, as was her custom,[3] other passages which struck her more, and which she desired to point out to the king if, as she hoped, she was ever to meet him again. She believed that the truth was there, and took a lively interest in those whom Wolsey, Henry, and the pope were at that time persecuting.

Anne was soon dragged from these pious lessons, and launched into the midst of a world full of dangers. Henry, convinced that he had nothing to expect henceforward from Campeggio, neglected those proprieties which he had hitherto observed, and immediately after the adjournment ordered Anne Boleyn to return to court; he restored her to the place she had formerly occupied, and even surrounded her with increased splendour. Every one saw that Anne, in the king's mind, was queen of England; and a powerful party was formed around her, which proposed to accomplish the definitive ruin of the cardinal.

After her return to court, Anne read much less frequently *The Obedience of a Christian Man* and the *Testament of Jesus Christ*. Henry's homage, her friends' intrigues, and the whirl of festivities, bade fair to stifle the thoughts which solitude had aroused in her heart. One day having left Tyndale's book in a window, Miss Gainsford, a fair young gentlewoman[4] attached to her person, took it up and read it. A gentleman of handsome mien, cheerful temper, and extreme mildness, named George Zouch, also belonging to Anne's household, and betrothed to Miss Gainsford, profiting by the liberty his position gave him, indulged sometimes in "love tricks."[5] On one occasion when George desired to have a little talk with her, he was annoyed to find her absorbed by a book of whose contents he knew nothing; and taking advantage of a moment when the young lady had turned away her head, he laughingly snatched it from her. Miss Gainsford ran after Zouch to recover her book; but just at that moment she heard her mistress calling her, and she

left George, threatening him with her finger.

As she did not return immediately, George withdrew to his room, and opened the volume; it was the *Obedience of a Christian Man*. He glanced over a few lines, then a few pages, and at last read the book through more than once. He seemed to hear the voice of God. "I feel the Spirit of God," he said, "speaking in my heart as he has spoken in the heart of him who wrote the book."[1] The words which had only made a temporary impression on the preoccupied mind of Anne Boleyn, penetrated to the heart of her equerry and converted him. Miss Gainsford, fearing that Anne would ask for her book, entreated George to restore it to her; but he positively refused, and even the young lady's tears failed to make him give up a volume in which he had found the life of his soul. Becoming more serious, he no longer jested as before; and when Miss Gainsford peremptorily demanded the book, he was, says the chronicler, "ready to weep himself."

Zouch, finding in this volume an edification which empty forms and ceremonies could not give, used to carry it with him to the king's chapel. Dr Sampson, the dean, generally officiated; and while the choir chanted the service, George would be absorbed in his book, where he read: "If when thou seest the celebration of the sacrament of the Lord's Supper, thou believest in this promise of Christ: *This is my body that is broken for you,* and if thou have this promise fast in thine heart, thou art saved and justified thereby; thou eatest his body and drinkest his blood. If not, so helpeth it thee not, though thou hearest a thousand masses in a day: no more than it should help thee in a dead thirst to behold a bush at a tavern door, if thou knewest not thereby that there was wine within to be sold."[2] The young man dwelt upon these words: by faith he ate the body and drank the blood of the Son of God. This was what was passing in the palaces of Henry VIII.; there were saints in the household of Cæsar.

Wolsey, desirous of removing from the court everything that might favour the Reformation, had recommended extreme vigilance to Dr Sampson so as to prevent the circulation of the innovating books. Accordingly, one day when George was in the chapel absorbed in his book, the dean, who, even while officiating, had not lost sight of the young man, called him to him after the service, and rudely taking the book from his hands, demanded: "What is your name, and in whose service are you?" Zouch having replied, the dean withdrew with a very angry look, and carried his prey to the cardinal.

When Miss Gainsford heard of this mishap, her grief was extreme; she trembled at

[1] Tyndale and Fryth's Works, vol. i. p. 295.
[2] Tyndale's Works, vol. i. p. 300.
[3] Wyatt's Memoirs, p. 438.
[4] Strype, i. p. 171.
[5] Ibid. p. 172.

[1] Strype, p. 172.
[2] Tyndale and Fryth's Works, vol. i. p. 286.

the thought that the *Obedience of a Christian Man* was in Wolsey's hands. Not long after this, Anne having asked for her book, the young lady fell on her knees, confessed all, and begged to be forgiven.[1] Anne uttered not a word of reproach; her quick mind saw immediately the advantage she might derive from this affair. " Well," said she, " it shall be the dearest book to them that ever the dean or cardinal took away."

" The noble lady," as the chronicler styles her, immediately demanded an interview of the king, and on reaching his presence she fell at his feet,[2] and begged his assistance. " What is the matter, Anne," said the astonished monarch. She told him what had happened, and Henry promised that the book should not remain in Wolsey's hands.

Anne had scarcely quitted the royal apartments, when the cardinal arrived with the famous volume, with the intention of complaining to Henry of certain passages which he knew could not fail to irritate him, and to take advantage of it even to attack Anne, if the king should be offended.[3] Henry's icy reception closed his mouth; the king confined himself to taking the book, and bowing out the cardinal. This was precisely what Anne had hoped for. She begged the king to read the book, which he promised to do.

And Henry accordingly shut himself up in his closet, and read the *Obedience of a Christian Man*. There were few works better calculated to enlighten him, and none, after the Bible, that has had more influence upon the Reformation in England. Tyndale treated of *obedience*, " the essential principle," as he terms it, " of every political or religious community." He declaimed against the unlawful power of the popes, who usurped the lawful authority of Christ and of his Word. He professed political doctrines too favourable doubtless to absolute power, but calculated to show that the reformers were not, as had been asserted, instigators of rebellion. Henry read as follows :—

" The king is in the room of God in this world. He that resisteth the king, resisteth God; he that judgeth the king, judgeth God. He is the minister of God to defend thee from a thousand inconveniences; though he be the greatest tyrant in the world, yet is he unto thee a great benefit of God; for it is better to pay the tenth than to lose all, and to suffer wrong of one man than of every man."[4]

These are indeed strange doctrines for *rebels* to hold, thought the king; and he continued :—

" Let kings, if they had lever [rather] be Christians in deed than so to be called, give themselves altogether to the wealth [wellbeing] of their realms after the ensample of Jesus Christ; remembering that the people are God's, and not theirs; yea, are Christ's inheritance, bought with his blood. The most despised person in his realm (if he is a Christian) is equal with him in the kingdom of God and of Christ. Let the king put off all pride, and become a brother to the poorest of his subjects."[1]

It is probable that these words were less satisfactory to the king. He kept on reading :—

" Emperors and kings are nothing now-a-days, but even hangmen unto the pope and bishops, to kill whomsoever they condemn, as Pilate was unto the scribes and pharisees and high bishops to hang Christ."[2]

This seemed to Henry rather strong language.

" The pope hath received no other authority of Christ than to preach God's word. Now, this word should rule only, and not bishops' decrees or the pope's pleasure. *In præsentia majoris cessat potestas minoris*, in the presence of the greater, the less hath no power.[3] The pope, against all the doctrine of Christ, which saith, *My kingdom is not of this world*, hath usurped the right of the emperor. Kings must make account of their doings only to God.[4] No person may be exempt from this ordinance of God; neither can the profession of monks and friars, or anything that the popes or bishops can lay for themselves, except them from the sword of the emperor or king, if they break the laws. For it is written, (Rom. xiii.) Let every soul submit himself unto the authority of the higher powers."[5]

" What excellent reading!" exclaimed Henry, when he had finished; " this is truly a book for all kings to read, and for me particularly."[6]

Captivated by Tyndale's work, the king began to converse with Anne about the church and the pope; and she who had seen Margaret of Valois unassumingly endeavour to instruct Francis I. strove in like manner to enlighten Henry VIII. She did not possess the influence over him she desired; this unhappy prince was, to the very end of his life, opposed to the evangelical reformation; protestants and catholics have been equally mistaken when they have regarded him as being favourable to it. " In a short time," says the annalist quoted by Strype at the end of his narrative, " the king, by the help of this virtuous lady, had his eyes opened to the truth. He learned to seek after that truth, to advance God's religion and glory, to detest the pope's doctrine, his lies, his pomp, and pride, and to deliver his subjects from the Egyptian darkness and Babylonian bonds that the pope had brought him and his subjects under. Despising the rebellions of his subjects and the rage of so many mighty po-

---

[1] She on her knees told it all. Strype, vol. i. p. 172.
[2] Upon her knees she desireth the king's help for her book. Ibid.
[3] Wyatt's Memoirs, p. 441.
[3] Tyndale's Works, edited by Russell, vol. i. p. 212.

[1] Tyndale's Works, p. 233.   [3] Ibid. p. 243.   [5] Ibid. p. 213.
[2] Ibid. p. 274.   [4] Ibid. p. 220.   [6] Strype, i. p. 172.

tentates abroad, he set forward a religious reformation, which, beginning with the triple-crowned head, came down to all the members of the hierarchy." History has rarely delivered a more erroneous judgment. Henry's eyes were never opened to the truth, and it was not he who made the Reformation. It was accomplished first of all by Scripture, and then by the ministry of simple and faithful men baptized of the Holy Ghost.

Yet Tyndale's book and the conduct of the legates had given rise in the king's mind to new thoughts which he sought time to mature. He desired also to conceal his anger from Wolsey and Campeggio, and dissipate his *spleen*, says the historian Collyer; he therefore gave orders to remove the court to the palace of Woodstock. The magnificent park attached to this royal residence, in which was the celebrated bower constructed (it is said) by Henry II. to conceal the fair Rosamond, offered all the charms of the promenade, the chase, and solitude.[1] Hence he could easily repair to Langley, Grafton, and other country seats. It was not long before the entertainments, horseraces, and other rural sports began. The world with its pleasures and its grandeur, were at the bottom the idols of Anne Boleyn's heart; but yet she felt a certain attraction for the new doctrine, which was confounded in her mind with the great cause of all knowledge, perhaps even with her own. More enlightened than the generality of women, she was distinguished by the superiority of her understanding not only over her own sex, but even over many of the gentlemen of the court. While Catherine, a member of the third order of St Francis, indulged in trifling practices, the more intelligent, if not more pious Anne, cared but little for amulets which the friars had blessed, for apparitions, or visions of angels. Woodstock furnished her with an opportunity of curing Henry VIII. of the superstitious ideas natural to him. There was a place in the forest said to be haunted by evil spirits; not a priest or a courtier dared approach it. A tradition ran that if a king ventured to cross the boundary, he would fall dead. Anne resolved to take Henry there. Accordingly, one morning she led the way in the direction of the place where these mysterious powers manifested their presence (as it was said) by strange apparitions; they entered the wood; they arrived at the so much dreaded spot; all hesitated; but Anne's calmness reassured her companions; they advanced; they found......nothing but trees and turf, and, laughing at their former terrors, they explored every corner of this mysterious resort of the evil spirits. Anne returned to the palace, congratulating herself on the triumph Henry had gained over

his imaginary fears.[1] This prince, who could as yet bear with superiority in others, was struck with Anne Boleyn's.

> Never too gay nor yet too melancholy,
> A heavenly mind is hers, like angels holy.
> None purer ever soared above the sky.
> O mighty marvel, thus may every eye
> See of what monster strange the humble serf am I;
> Monster indeed, for in her frame divine
> A woman's form, man's heart, and angel's head combine.[2]

These verses of Clement Marot, written in honour of Margaret of Valois, faithfully express what Henry then felt for Anne, who had been with Marot in the household of that princess. Henry's love may perhaps have deceived him as to Anne's excellencies.

CHAPTER XI.

Embarrassment of the Pope—The Triumphs of Charles decide him—He traverses the Cause to Rome—Wolsey's Dejection—Henry's Wrath—His Fears—Wolsey obtains Comfort—Arrival of the two Legates at Grafton—Wolsey's Reception by Henry—Wolsey and Norfolk at Dinner—Henry with Anne—Conference between the King and the Cardinal—Wolsey's Joy and Grief—The Supper at Euston—Campeggio's Farewell Audience—Wolsey's Disgrace—Campeggio at Dover—He is accused by the Courtiers—Leaves England—Wolsey foresees his own Fall and that of the Papacy.

WHILE the court was thus taking its pleasure at Woodstock, Wolsey remained in London, a prey to the acutest anguish. "This avocation to Rome," wrote he to Gregory Da Casale, "will not only completely alienate the king and his realm from the apostolic see, but will ruin me utterly."[3] This message had hardly reached the pope, before the imperial ambassadors handed to him the queen's protest, and added in a very significant tone : " If your holiness does not call this cause before you, the emperor, who is determined to bring it to an end, will have recourse to *other arguments*." The same perplexity always agitated Clement : Which of the two must be sacrificed, Henry or Charles? Anthony de Leyva, who commanded the imperial forces, having routed the French army, the pope no longer doubted that Charles was the elect of Heaven. It was not Europe alone which acknowledged this prince's authority; a new world had just laid its power and its gold at his feet. The formidable priest-king of the Aztecs had been unable to withstand Cortez; could the priest-king of Rome withstand Charles V. ?

---

[1] The letters from the king's secretaries Gardiner and Tuke to Wolsey, dated Woodstock, run from 4th August to 6th September. State Papers, i. p. 335-347.

[1] Foxe, v. p. 136; Miss Benger's Life of Anne Boleyn, p. 299.

> [2] Jamais trop gay, ne trop mélancolique,
> Elle a au chef un esprit angélique,
> Le plus subtil qui onc au ciel vola.
> O grand' merveille ! on peut voir par cela
> Que je suis serf d'un monstre fort étrange :
> Monstre je dy, car pour tout vray elle a
> Corps féminin, cœur d'homme et tête d'ange.

[3] Non solum regium animum et totum hoc regnum a sedis apostolicæ devotione penitus abalienabit, ac me omnino perdet et funditus destruet. State Papers, vii. p. 189.

Cortez had returned from Mexico, bringing with him Mexican chiefs in all their barbarous splendour, with thousands of *pesos*, with gold and silver and emeralds of extraordinary size, with magnificent tissues and birds of brilliant plumage. He had accompanied Charles, who was then going to Italy, to the place of embarkation, and had sent to Clement VII. costly gifts of the precious metals, valuable jewels, and a troop of Mexican dancers, buffoons, and jugglers, who charmed the pope and the cardinal above all things.[1]

Clement, even while refusing Henry's prayer, had not as yet granted the emperor's. He thought he could now resist no longer the star of a monarch victorious over two worlds, and hastened to enter into negotiations with him. Sudden terrors still assailed him from time to time: My refusal (he said to himself) may perhaps cause me to lose England. But Charles, holding him in his powerful grasp, compelled him to submit. Henry's antecedents were rather encouraging to the pontiff. How could he imagine that a prince, who alone of all the monarchs of Europe had once contended against the great reformer, would now separate from the popedom? On the 6th of July Clement declared to the English envoys that he *avoked to Rome* the cause between Henry VIII. and Catherine of Aragon. In other words, this was refusing the divorce. "There are twenty-three points in this case," said the courtiers, "and the debate on the first has lasted a year; before the end of the trial, the king will be not only past marrying but past living."[2]

When he learned that the fatal blow had been struck, Bennett in a tone of sadness exclaimed: "Alas! most holy father, by this act the Church in England will be utterly destroyed; the king declared it to me with tears in his eyes."[3]—"Why is it my fortune to live in such evil days?" replied the pope, who, in his turn, began to weep;[4] "but I am encircled by the emperor's forces, and if I were to please the king, I should draw a fearful ruin upon myself and upon the church......God will be my judge."

On the 15th of July Da Casale sent the fatal news to the English minister. The king was cited before the pope, and in case of refusal condemned in a fine of 10,000 ducats. On the 18th of July peace was proclaimed at Rome between the pontiff and the emperor, and on the next day (these dates are important) Clement, wishing still to make one more attempt to ward off the blow with which the papacy was threatened, wrote to Cardinal Wolsey: "My dear son, how can I describe to you my affliction? Show in this matter the prudence which so distinguishes you, and preserve the king in those kindly feelings which he has ever manifested towards me."[1] A useless attempt! Far from saving the papacy, Wolsey was to be wrecked along with it.

Wolsey was thunderstruck. At the very time he was assuring Henry of the attachment of Clement and Francis, both were deserting him. The "politic handling" failed, which the cardinal had thought so skilful, and which had been so tortuous. Henry now had none but enemies on the continent of Europe, and the reformation was daily spreading over his kingdom. Wolsey's anguish cannot be described. His power, his pomp, his palaces were all threatened; who could tell whether he would even preserve his liberty and his life?—A just reward for so much duplicity.

But the king's wrath was to be greater than even the minister's alarm. His terrified servants wondered how they should announce the pontiff's decision. Gardiner, who, after his return from Rome, had been named secretary of state, went down to Langley on the 3d of August to communicate it to him. What news for the proud Tudor! The decision on the divorce was forbidden in England; the cause avoked to Rome, there to be buried and unjustly lost; Francis I. treating with the emperor; Charles and Clement on the point of exchanging at Bologna the most striking signs of their unchangeable alliance; the services rendered by the king to the popedom repaid with the blackest ingratitude; his hope of giving an heir to the crown disgracefully frustrated; and last, but not least, Henry VIII., the proudest monarch of Christendom, summoned to Rome to appear before an ecclesiastical tribunal......It was too much for Henry. His wrath, a moment restrained, burst forth like a clap of thunder,[2] and all trembled around him. "Do they presume," he exclaimed, "to try my cause elsewhere than in my own dominions? I, the king of England, summoned before an Italian tribunal!......Yes,......I will go to Rome, but it shall be with such a mighty army that the pope, and his priests, and all Italy shall be struck with terror.[3]— I forbid the letters of citation to be executed," he continued; "I forbid the commission to consider its functions at an end." Henry would have desired to tear off Campeggio's purple robes, and throw this prince of the Roman church into prison in order to frighten Clement; but the very magnitude of the insult compelled him to restrain himself. He feared above all things to appear humbled in the eyes of England, and he hoped, by showing moderation, to hide the

---

[1] Prescott's Conquest of Mexico, book vii. chap. iv. [2] Fuller, p. 178. [3] Burnet, Records, ii. p. xxxvii. [4] Ibid.

[4] Ut dictum regem in solita erga nos benevolentia retinere velis. Burnet, Records, ii. p. xxxviii.
[2] He became much incensed. Herbert, p. 287. Supra quam dici potest excanduit. Sanders, p. 50.
[2] He would do the same with such a mayn [great] and army royal, as should be formidable to the pope and all Italy. State Papers, vii. p. 154; Burnet, Records, p. xxxvii.

affront he had received. " Let everything be done," he told Gardiner, " to conceal from my subjects these letters of citation, which are so hurtful to my glory. Write to Wolsey that I have the greatest confidence in his dexterity, and that he ought, by good handling, to win over Campeggio [1] and the queen's counsellors, and, above all, prevail upon them at any price not to serve these citatory letters on me." But Henry had hardly given his instructions when the insult of which he had been the object recurred to his imagination ; the thought of Clement haunted him night and day, and he swore to exact a striking vengeance from the pontiff. Rome desires to have no more to do with England......England in her turn will cast off Rome. Henry will sacrifice Wolsey, Clement, and the church ; nothing shall stop his fury. The crafty pontiff has concealed his game, the king shall beat him openly ; and from age to age the popedom shall shed tears over the imprudent folly of a Medici.

Thus after insupportable delays which had fatigued the nation, a thunderbolt fell upon England. Court, clergy, and people, from whom it was impossible to conceal these great events, were deeply stirred, and the whole kingdom was in commotion. Wolsey, still hoping to ward off the ruin impending over both himself and the papacy. immediately put in play all that dexterity which Henry had spoken of ; he so far prevailed that the letters citatorial were not served on the king, but only the brief addressed to Wolsey by Clement VII. [2] The cardinal, all radiant with this trivial success, and desirous of profiting by it to raise his credit, resolved to accompany Campeggio, who was going down to Grafton to take leave of the king. When the coming of the two legates was heard of at court, the agitation was very great. The dukes of Norfolk and Suffolk regarded this proceeding as the last effort of their enemy, and entreated Henry not to receive him. " The king will receive him," said some. " The king will not receive him," answered others. At length one Sunday morning it was announced that the prelates were at the gates of the mansion. Wolsey looked round with an anxious eye for the great officers who were accustomed to introduce him. They appeared and desired Campeggio to follow them. When the legate had been taken to his apartments, Wolsey waited his turn ; but great was his consternation on being informed that there was no chamber appointed for him in the palace. Sir Henry Norris, groom of the stole, offered Wolsey the use of his own room, and the cardinal followed him, almost sinking beneath the humiliation he had undergone. [3] He made ready to appear before the

king, and summoning up his courage, proceeded to the presence-chamber.

The lords of the council were standing in a row according to their rank ; Wolsey, taking off his hat, passed along saluting each of them with affected civility. A great number of courtiers arrived, impatient to see how Henry would receive his old favourite : and most of them were already exulting in the striking disgrace of which they hoped to be witnesses. At last the king was announced.

Henry stood under the cloth of state ; and Wolsey advanced and knelt before him. Deep silence prevailed throughout the chamber......To the surprise of all, Henry stooped down and raised him up with both hands...... Then, with a pleasing smile, he took Wolsey to the window, desired him to put on his hat, and talked familiarly with him. " Then," says Cavendish, the cardinal's gentleman usher, " it would have made you smile to behold the countenances of those who had laid wagers that the king would not speak with him."

But this was the last ray of evening which then lighted up the darkening fortunes of Wolsey : the star of his favour was about to set for ever......The silence continued, for every one desired to catch a few words of the conversation. The king seemed to be accusing Wolsey, and Wolsey to be justifying himself. On a sudden Henry pulled a letter out of his bosom, and showing it to the cardinal, said in a loud voice : " How can that be ? is not this your hand ?" It was no doubt the letter which Bryan had intercepted. Wolsey replied in an under-tone, and seemed to have appeased his master. The dinner hour having arrived, the king left the room telling Wolsey that he would not fail to see him again ; the courtiers were eager to make their profoundest reverences to the cardinal, but he haughtily traversed the chamber, and the dukes hastened to carry to Anne Boleyn the news of this astonishing reception.

Wolsey, Campeggio, and the lords of the council sat down to dinner. The cardinal, well aware that the terrible letter would be his utter ruin, and that Henry's good graces had no other object than to prepare his fall, began to hint at his retirement. " Truly," said he with a devout air, " the king would do well to send his bishops and chaplains home to their cures and benefices." The company looked at one another with astonishment. " Yea, marry," said the duke of Norfolk somewhat rudely, " and so it were meet for you to do also."—" I should be very well contented therewith," answered Wolsey, " if it were the king's pleasure to license me with leave to go to my cure at Winchester."— " Nay, to your benefice at York, where your greatest honour and charge is," replied Norfolk, who was not willing that Wolsey should be living so near Henry.—" Even as it shall please the king," added Wolsey, and changed the subject of conversation.

Henry had caused himself to be announced

[1] Your grace's dexterity....by good handling of the cardinal Campeggio. State Papers, vol. i. p. 336.
[2] Ibid. p. 343.   [3] Cavendish, p. 237-245.

to Anne Boleyn, who (says Cavendish) "kept state at Grafton more like a queen than a simple maid." Possessing extreme sensibility, and an ardent imagination, Anne, who felt the slightest insult with all the sensibility of her woman's heart, was very dissatisfied with the king after the report of the dukes. Accordingly, heedless of the presence of the attendants, she said to him: "Sir, is it not a marvellous thing to see into what great danger the cardinal hath brought you with all your subjects?"—"How so. sweetheart?" asked Henry, Anne continued: "Are you ignorant of the hatred his exactions have drawn upon you? There is not a man in your whole realm of England worth one hundred pounds, but he hath made you his debtor." Anne here alluded to the loan the king had raised among his subjects. "Well, well," said Henry, who was not pleased with these remarks, "I know that matter better than you."—"If my lord of Norfolk, my lord of Suffolk, my uncle, or my father had done much less than the cardinal hath done," continued Anne, "they would have lost their heads ere this." "Then I perceive," said Henry, "you are none of his friends."—"No, sir, I have no cause, nor any that love you," she replied. The dinner was ended; the king, without appearing at all touched, proceeded to the presence-chamber where Wolsey expected him.

After a long conversation, carried on in a low tone, the king took Wolsey by the hand and led him into his private chamber. The courtiers awaited impatiently the termination of an interview which might decide the fate of England; they walked up and down the gallery, often passing before the door of the closet, in the hope of catching from Wolsey's looks, when he opened it, the result of this secret conference; but one quarter of an hour followed another, these became hours, and still the cardinal did not appear. Henry having resolved that this conversation should be the last, was no doubt collecting from his minister all the information necessary to him. But the courtiers imagined he was returning into his master's favour; Norfolk, Suffolk, Wiltshire, and the other enemies of the prime minister, began to grow alarmed, and hastened off to Anne Boleyn, who was their last hope.

It was night when the king and Wolsey quitted the royal closet: the former appeared gracious, the latter satisfied; it was always Henry's custom to smile on those he intended to sacrifice. "I shall see you in the morning," he said to the cardinal with a friendly air. Wolsey made a low bow, and turning round to the courtiers, saw the king's smile reflected on their faces. Wiltshire, Tuke, and even Suffolk, were full of civility. "Well," thought he, "the motion of such weathercocks as these shows me from what quarter the wind of favour is blowing."[1]

But a moment after the wind began to change. Men with torches waited for the cardinal at the gates of the palace to conduct him to the place where he would have to pass the night. Thus he was not to sleep beneath the same roof with Henry. He was to lie at Euston, one of Empson's houses, about three miles off. Wolsey, repressing his vexation, mounted his horse, the footmen preceded him with their links, and after an hour's riding along very bad roads, he reached the lodging assigned him.

He had sat down to supper, to which some of his most intimate friends had been invited, when suddenly Gardiner was announced. Gardiner owed everything to the cardinal, and yet he had not appeared before him since his return from Rome. He comes no doubt to play the hypocrite and the spy, thought Wolsey. But as soon as the secretary entered, Wolsey rose, made him a graceful compliment, and prayed him to take a seat. "Master Secretary," he asked, "where have you been since your return from Rome?"—"I have been following the court from place to place."—"You have been hunting then? Have you any dogs?" asked the prime minister, who knew very well what Gardiner had been doing in the king's closet. "A few," replied Gardiner. Wolsey thought that even the secretary was a bloodhound on his track. And yet after supper he took Gardiner aside, and conversed with him until midnight. He thought it prudent to neglect nothing that might clear up his position; and Wolsey sounded Gardiner, just as he himself had been sounded by Henry not long before.

The same night at Grafton the king gave Campeggio a farewell audience, and treated him very kindly, "by giving him presents and other matters," says Du Bellay. Henry then returned to Anne Boleyn. The dukes had pointed out to her the importance of the present moment; she therefore asked and obtained of Henry, without any great difficulty, his promise never to speak to his minister again.[1] The insults of the papacy had exasperated the king of England, and as he could not punish Clement, he toook his revenge on the cardinal.

The next morning, Wolsey, impatient to have the interview which Henry had promised, rode back early to Grafton. But as he came near, he met a numerous train of servants and sumpter-horses; and presently afterwards Henry, with Anne Boleyn and many lords and ladies of the court, came riding up. "What does all this mean?" thought the cardinal in dismay. "My lord," said the king, as he drew near, "I cannot stay with you now. You will return to London with cardinal Campeggio." Then striking the spurs into his horse, Henry galloped off

[1] Burnet's Ref. vol. i. p. 59.

[1] Du Bellay to the Grand Master. Le Grand, Preuves, p. 375; also Cavendish.

848

with a friendly salutation. After him came Anne Boleyn, who rode past Wolsey with head erect, and casting on him a proud look. The court proceeded to Hartwell Park, where Anne had determined to keep the king all day. Wolsey was confounded. There was no room for doubt; his disgrace was certain. His head swam, he remained immovable for an instant, and then recovered himself; but the blow he had received had not been unobserved by the courtiers, and the cardinal's fall became the general topic of conversation.

After dinner, the legates departed, and on the second day reached Moor Park, a mansion built by Archbishop Neville, one of Wolsey's predecessors, who for high treason had been first imprisoned at Calais, and afterwards at Ham. These recollections were by no means agreeable to Wolsey. The next morning the two cardinals separated, Campeggio proceeded to Dover and Wolsey to London.

Campeggio was impatient to get out of England, and great was his annoyance, on reaching Dover, to find that the wind was contrary. But a still greater vexation was in reserve. He had hardly lain down to rest himself, before his door was opened, and a band of sergeants entered the room. The cardinal, who knew what scenes of this kind meant in Italy, thought he was a dead man,[1] and fell trembling at his chaplain's feet begging for absolution. Meantime the officers opened his luggage, broke into his chests, scattered his property about the floor, and even shook out his clothes.[2]

Henry's tranquillity had not been of long duration. "Campeggio is the bearer of letters from Wolsey to Rome," whispered some of the courtiers; "who knows but they contain treasonable matter?" "There is, too, among his papers the famous *decretal* pronouncing the divorce," said one; "if we had but that document it would finish the business." Another affirmed that Campeggio "had large treasure with him of my lord's (Wolsey's) to be conveyed in great tuns to Rome,"[3] whither it was surmised the cardinal of York would escape to enjoy the fruits of his treason. "It is certain," added a third, "that Campeggio, assisted by Wolsey, has been able to procure your majesty's correspondence with Anne Boleyn, and is carrying it away with him." Henry, therefore, sent a messenger after the nuncio, with orders that his baggage should be thoroughly searched.

Nothing was found, neither letters, nor bull, nor treasures. The bull had been destroyed; the treasures Wolsey had never thought of entrusting to his colleague; and the letters of Anne and Henry, Campeggio had sent on before by his son Rodolph, and the pope was stretching out his hands to receive them, proud, like his successors, of the robbery committed by two of his legates.

Campeggio being reassured, and seeing that he was neither to be killed nor robbed, made a great noise at this act of violence, and at the insulting remarks which had given rise to it. "I will not leave England," he caused Henry to be informed, "until I have received satisfaction." "My lord forgets that he is legate no longer," replied the king, "since the pope has withdrawn his powers; he forgets, besides, that, as bishop of Salisbury, he is my subject; as for the remarks against him and the cardinal of York, it is a liberty the people of England are accustomed to take, and which I cannot put down." Campeggio, anxious to reach France, was satisfied with these reasons, and soon forgot all his sorrows at the sumptuous table of cardinal Duprat.

Wolsey was not so fortunate. He had seen Campeggio go away, and remained like a wrecked seaman thrown on a desert isle, who has seen depart the only friends capable of giving him any help. His necromancy had forewarned him that this would be a fatal year.[1] The angel of the maid of Kent had said: "Go to the cardinal and announce his fall, because he has not done what you had commanded him to do."[2] Other voices besides hers made themselves heard: the hatred of the nation, the contempt of Europe, and, above all, Henry's anger, told him that his hour was come. It was true the pope said, that he would do all in his power to save him;[3] but Clement's good offices would only accelerate his ruin. Du Bellay, whom the people believed to be the cardinal's accomplice, bore witness to the change that had taken place in men's minds. While passing on foot through the streets of the capital, followed by two valets, "his ears were so filled with coarse jests as he went along," he said, "that he knew not which way to turn."[4] "The cardinal is utterly undone," he wrote, "and I see not how he can escape." The idea occurred to Wolsey, from time to time, to pronounce the divorce himself; but it was too late. He was even told that his life was in danger. Fortune, blind and bald, her foot on the wheel, fled rapidly from him, nor was it in his power to stop her. And this was not all: after him (he thought) there was no one who could uphold the church of the pontiffs in England. The ship of Rome was sailing on a stormy sea among rocks and shoals; Wolsey at the helm looked in vain for a port of refuge; the vessel leaked on every side; it was rapidly sinking, and the cardinal uttered a cry of distress. Alas! he had desired to save Rome, but Rome would not have it so.

---

[1] Le Grand, vol. II. p. 156. Life of Campeggio, by Sigonius.
[2] Sarcinas excuti jussit. Sanders. p. 51.
[3] Cavendish, p. 246. See also Le Grand, II. p. 258.

[1] He had learnt of his necromancy that this would be a jeopardous year for him. Tyndale's Works, i. p. 480.
[2] Strype, i. p. 373.   [3] Herbert, p. 289.
[4] Du Bellay to Montmorency, 12th October. Le Grand, Preuves, p. 365.

CHAPTER XII.

A Meeting at Waltham—Youth of Thomas Cranmer—His early Education—Studies Scripture for three Years—His Functions as Examiner—The Supper at Waltham—New View of the Divorce—Fox communicates it to Henry—Cranmer's Vexation—Conference with the King—Cranmer at the Boleyns.

As Wolsey's star was disappearing in the West in the midst of stormy clouds, another was rising in the East, to point out the way to save Britain. Men, like stars, appear on the horizon at the command of God.

On his return from Woodstock to Greenwich, Henry stopped full of anxiety at Waltham in Essex. His attendants were lodged in the houses of the neighbourhood. Fox, the almoner, and Secretary Gardiner, were quartered on a gentleman named Cressy, at Waltham Abbey. When supper was announced, Gardiner and Fox were surprised to see an old friend enter the room. It was Thomas Cranmer, a Cambridge doctor. "What! is it you?" they said, "and how came you here?" "Our host's wife is my relation," replied Cranmer, "and as the epidemic is raging at Cambridge, I brought home my friend's sons, who are under my care." As this new personage is destined to play an important part in the history of the Reformation, it may be worth our while to interrupt our narrative, and give a particular account of him.

Cranmer was descended from an ancient family, which came into England, as is generally believed, with the Conqueror. He was born at Aslacton in Nottinghamshire on the 2d July 1489, six years after Luther. His early education had been very much neglected; his tutor, an ignorant and severe priest, had taught him little else than patiently to endure severe chastisement—a knowledge destined to be very useful to him in after-life. His father was an honest country gentleman, who cared for little besides hunting, racing, and military sports. At this school, the son learnt to ride, to handle the bow and the sword, to fish, and to hawk; and he never entirely neglected these exercises, which he thought essential to his health. Thomas Cranmer was fond of walking, of the charms of nature, and of solitary meditations; and a hill, near his father's mansion, used often to be shown where he was wont to sit, gazing on the fertile country at his feet, fixing his eyes on the distant spires, listening with melancholy pleasure to the chime of the bells, and indulging in sweet contemplations. About 1504, he was sent to Cambridge, where "barbarism still prevailed," says an historian.[1] His plain, noble, and modest air conciliated the affections of many, and, in 1510, he was elected fellow of Jesus College. Possessing a tender heart, he became attached, at the age of twenty-three, to a young person of good birth (says

[1] Fæda barbaries. Melch. Adam. Vitæ Theol. i.

Foxe,) or of inferior rank, as other writers assert. Cranmer was unwilling to imitate the disorderly lives of his fellow-students, and although marriage would necessarily close the career of honours, he married the young lady, resigned his fellowship (in conformity with the regulations), and took a modest lodging at the Dolphin. He then began to study earnestly the most remarkable writings of the times, polishing, it has been said, his old asperity on the productions of Erasmus, of Lefevre of Etaples, and other great authors; every day his crude understanding received new brilliancy.[1] He then began to teach in Buckingham (afterwards Magdalene) College, and thus provided for his wants.

His lessons excited the admiration of enlightened men, and the anger of obscure ones, who disdainfully called him (because of the inn at which he lodged) *the hostler*. "This name became him well," said Fuller, for in his lessons he roughly rubbed the backs of the friars, **and** famously curried the hides of the lazy priests." His wife dying a year after his marriage, Cranmer was re-elected fellow of his old college, and the first writing of Luther's having appeared, he said: "I must know on which side the truth lies. There is only one infallible source, the Scriptures; in them I will seek for God's truth."[2] And for three years he constantly studied the holy books,[3] without commentary, without human theology, and hence he gained the name of the *Scripturist*. At last his eyes were opened; he saw the mysterious bond which unites all biblical revelations, and understood the completeness of God's design. Then without forsaking the Scriptures, he studied all kinds of authors.[4] He was a slow reader, but a close observer:[5] he never opened a book without having a pen in his hand.[6] He did not take up with any particular party or age; but possessing a free and philosophic mind, he weighed all opinions in the balance of his judgment,[7] taking the Bible for his standard.

Honours soon came upon him; he was made successively doctor of divinity, professor, university preacher, and examiner. He used to say to the candidates for the ministry: "Christ sendeth his hearers to the Scriptures, and not to the church."[8]—"But," replied the monks, "they are so difficult."—"Explain the obscure passages by those which are clear," rejoined the professor, "Scripture by Scripture. Seek, pray, *and he who has the key of David* will open them to you." The

[1] Ad eos non aliter quam ad cotem, quotidie priscam detergebat scabritiem. Melch. Adam. Vitæ Theol. i.
[2] Behold the very fountains. Foxe, viii. p. 4.
[3] Totum triennium Sacræ Scripturæ monumentis perlegendis impendit. M. Adam. p. 1.
[4] Like a merchant greedy of all good things. Foxe, viii. p. 4.
[5] Tardus quidem lector sed vehemens observator. M. Adam. p. 1.
[6] Sine calamo nunquam ad scriptoris cujusquam librum accessit. Ibid.
[7] Omnes omnium opiniones tacito seoum judicio trutinabat. Ibid.
[8] Cranmer's Works, p. 17, 18.

monks, affrighted at this task, withdrew bursting with anger; and erelong Cranmer's name was a name of dread in every convent. Some, however, submitted to the labour, and one of them, Doctor Barrett, blessed God that the examiner had turned him back; "for," said he, "I found the knowledge of God in the holy book he compelled me to study." Cranmer toiled at the same work as Latimer, Stafford, and Bilney.

Fox and Gardiner having renewed acquaintance with their old friend at Waltham Abbey, they sat down to table, and both the almoner and the secretary asked the doctor what he thought of the divorce. It was the usual topic of conversation, and not long before, Cranmer had been named member of a commission appointed to give their opinion on this affair. "You are not in the right path," said Cranmer to his friends; "you should not cling to the decisions of the church. There is a surer and a shorter way which alone can give peace to the king's conscience."—"What is that?" they both asked. —"The true question is this," replied Cranmer: "*What says the word of God?* If God has declared a marriage of this nature *bad*, the pope cannot make it *good*. Discontinue these interminable Roman negotiations. When God has spoken man must obey."— "But how shall we know what God has said?"—"Consult the universities: they will discern it more surely than Rome."

This was a new view. The idea of consulting the universities had been acted upon before; but then their own opinions only had been demanded: now, the question was simply to know *what God says in his word.* "The word of God is above the church," was the principle laid down by Cranmer, and in that principle consisted the whole of the Reformation. The conversation at the supper-table of Waltham was destined to be one of those secret springs which an invisible Hand sets in motion for the accomplishment of his great designs. The Cambridge doctor, suddenly transported from his study to the foot of the throne, was on the point of becoming one of the principal instruments of Divine wisdom.

The day after this conversation, Fox and Gardiner arrived at Greenwich, and the king summoned them into his presence the same evening. "Well, gentlemen," he said to them, "our holidays are over; what shall we do now? If we still have recourse to Rome, God knows when we shall see the end of this matter."[1]—"It will not be necessary to take so long a journey," said Fox; "we know a shorter and surer way."—"What is it?" asked the king eagerly.—"Doctor Cranmer, whom we met yesterday at Waltham, thinks that the Bible should be the sole judge in your cause." Gardiner, vexed at his colleague's frankness, desired to claim all the

honour of this luminous idea for himself; but Henry did not listen to him. "Where is Doctor Cranmer?" said he, much affected.[1] "Send, and fetch him immediately. Mother of God! (this was his customary oath) this man has the right sow by the ear.[2] If this had only been suggested to me two years ago, what expense and trouble I should have been spared."

Cranmer had gone into Nottinghamshire; a messenger followed and brought him back. "Why have you entangled me in this affair?" he said to Fox and Gardiner. "Pray make my excuses to the king." Gardiner, who wished for nothing better, promised to do all he could; but it was of no use. "I will have no excuses," said Henry. The wily courtier was obliged to make up his mind to introduce the ingenuous and upright man, to whom that station, which he himself had so coveted, was one day to belong. Cranmer and Gardiner went down to Greenwich, both alike dissatisfied.

Cranmer was then forty years of age, with pleasing features, and mild and winning eyes, in which the candour of his soul seemed to be reflected. Sensible to the pains as well as to the pleasures of the heart, he was destined to be more exposed than other men to anxieties and falls; a peaceful life in some remote parsonage would have been more to his taste than the court of Henry VIII. Blessed with a generous mind, unhappily he did not possess the firmness necessary in a public man; a little stone sufficed to make him stumble. His excellent understanding showed him the better way; but his great timidity made him fear the more dangerous. He was rather too fond of relying upon the power of men, and made them unhappy concessions with too great facility. If the king had questioned him, he would never have dared advise so bold a course as that he had pointed out; the advice had slipped from him at table during the intimacy of familiar conversation. Yet he was sincere, and after doing everything to escape from the consequences of his frankness, he was ready to maintain the opinion he had given.

Henry, perceiving Cranmer's timidity, graciously approached him. "What is your name," said the king, endeavouring to put him at his ease? "Did you not meet my secretary and my almoner at Waltham?" And then he added: "Did you not speak to them of my great affair?"—repeating the words ascribed to Cranmer. The latter could not retreat: "Sir, it is true, I did say so."— "I see," replied the king with animation, "that you have found the breach through which we must storm the fortress. Now, sir doctor, I beg you, and as you are my subject I command you, to lay aside every other occupation, and to bring my cause to a conclusion in conformity with the ideas you have

: God knows, and not I. Foxe, viii. 7.   1 Burnet, vol. i. p. 60   2 Ibid.

851

put forth. All that I desire to know is, whether my marriage is contrary to the laws of God or not. Employ all your skill in investigating the subject, and thus bring comfort to my conscience as well as to the queen's.[1]

Cranmer was confounded; he recoiled from the idea of deciding an affair on which depended, it might be, the destinies of the nation, and sighed after the lonely fields of Aslacton. But grasped by the vigorous hand of Henry, he was compelled to advance. "Sir," said he, "pray intrust this matter to doctors more learned than I am."—"I am very willing," answered the king, "but I desire that you will also give me your opinion in writing." And then summoning the earl of Wiltshire to his presence, he said to him: "My lord, you will receive Doctor Cranmer into your house at Durham Place, and let him have all necessary quiet to compose a report for which I have asked him." After this precise command, which admitted of no refusal, Henry withdrew.

In this manner was Cranmer introduced by the king to Anne Boleyn's father, and not, as some Romanist authors have asserted, by Sir Thomas Boleyn to the king.[2] Wiltshire conducted Cranmer to Durham House (now the Adelphi in the Strand), and the pious doctor on whom Henry had imposed these quarters, soon contracted a close friendship with Anne and her father, and took advantage of it to teach them the value of the divine Word, as *the pearl of great price*.[3] Henry, while profiting by the address of a Wolsey and a Gardiner, paid little regard to the men; but he respected Cranmer, even when opposed to him in opinion, and until his death placed the learned doctor above all his courtiers and all his clerks. The pious man often succeeds better, even with the great ones of this world, than the ambitious and the intriguing.

CHAPTER XIII.

Wolsey in the Court of Chancery—Accused by the Dukes—Refuses to give up the Great Seal—His Despair—He gives up the Seal—Order to depart—His Inventory—Alarm—The Scene of Departure—Favourable Message from the King—Wolsey's Joy—His Fool—Arrival at Esher.

WHILE Cranmer was rising notwithstanding his humility, Wolsey was falling in despite of his stratagems. The cardinal still governed the kingdom, gave instructions to ambassadors, negotiated with princes, and filled his sumptuous palaces with his haughtiness. The king could not make up his mind to turn him off; the force of habit, the need he

had of him, the recollection of the services Henry had received from him, pleaded in his favour. Wolsey without the seals appeared almost as inconceivable as the king without his crown. Yet the fall of one of the most powerful favourites recorded in history was inevitably approaching, and we must now describe it.

On the 9th of October, after the Michaelmas vacation, Wolsey, desirous of showing a bold face, went and opened the high court of chancery with his accustomed pomp; but he noticed, with uneasiness, that none of the king's servants walked before him, as they had been accustomed to do. He presided on the bench with an inexpressible depression of spirits, and the various members of the court sat before him with an absent air; there was something gloomy and solemn in this sitting, as if all were taking part in a funeral: it was destined indeed to be the last act of the cardinal's power. Some days before (Foxe says on the 1st of October) the dukes of Norfolk and Suffolk, with other lords of the privy-council, had gone down to Windsor, and denounced to the king Wolsey's unconstitutional relations with the pope, his usurpations, "his robberies, and the discords sown by his means between Christian princes."[1] Such motives would not have sufficed; but Henry had stronger. Wolsey had not kept any of his promises in the matter of the divorce; it would even appear that he had advised the pope to excommunicate the king, and thus raise his people against him.[2] This enormity was not at that time known by the prince; it is even probable that it did not take place until later. But Henry knew enough, and he gave his attorney-general, Sir Christopher Hales, orders to prosecute Wolsey.

Whilst the heart-broken cardinal was displaying his authority for the last time in the court of chancery, the attorney-general was accusing him in the King's Bench for having obtained papal bulls conferring on him a jurisdiction which encroached on the royal power; and calling for the application of the penalties of *præmunire*. The two dukes received orders to demand the seals from Wolsey; and the latter, informed of what had taken place, did not quit his palace on the 10th, expecting every moment the arrival of the messengers of the king's anger; but no one appeared.

The next day the two dukes arrived: "It is the king's good pleasure," said they to the cardinal, who remained seated in his armchair, "that you give up the broad seal to us and retire to Esher" (a country-seat near Hampton Court). Wolsey, whose presence of mind never failed him, demanded to see the commission under which they were acting. "We have our orders from his

---

[1] For the discharging of both our consciences. Foxe, viii. p. 8.
[2] Sanders. p. 57; Lingard, vol. vi. chap. iii. Compare Foxe, vol. viii. p. 8.
[3] Teque nobilis illius margaritæ desiderio teneri. Erasm. Epp. p. 1751.

[1] Du Bellay to Montmorency, 22d October. Le Grand. Preuves. p. 377.
[2] Ranke, Deutsche Geschichte, iii. p. 140.

majesty's mouth," said they.—" That may be sufficient for you," replied the cardinal, " but not for me. The great seal of England was delivered to me by the hands of my sovereign ; I may not deliver it at the simple word of any lord, unless you can show me your commission." Suffolk broke out into a passion, but Wolsey remained calm, and the two dukes returned to Windsor. This was the cardinal's last triumph.

The rumour of his disgrace created an immense sensation at court, in the city, and among the foreign ambassadors. Du Bellay hastened to York Place (Whitehall) to contemplate this great ruin and console his unhappy friend. He found Wolsey, with dejected countenance and lustreless eyes, " shrunk to half his wonted size," wrote the ambassador to Montmorency, " the greatest example of fortune which was ever beheld." Wolsey desired " to set forth his case " to him ; but his thoughts were confused, his language broken, " for heart and tongue both failed him entirely ;" he burst into tears. The ambassador regarded him with compassion: " Alas !" thought he, " his enemies cannot but feel pity for him." At last the unhappy cardinal recovered his speech, but only to give way to despair. " I desire no more authority," he exclaimed, " nor the pope's legation, nor the broad seal of England ......I am ready to give up everything, even to my shirt.[1]......I can live in a hermitage, provided the king does not hold me in disgrace." The ambassador " did all he could to comfort him," when Wolsey, catching at the plank thrown out to him, exclaimed : " Would that the king of France and Madame might pray the king to moderate his anger against me. But above all," he added in alarm, " take care the king never knows that I have solicited this of you." Du Bellay wrote indeed to France, that the king and Madame alone could " withdraw their affectionate servant from the gates of hell," and Wolsey being informed of these despatches, his hopes recovered a little. But this bright gleam did not last long.

On Sunday the 17th of October, Norfolk and Suffolk reappeared at Whitehall, accompanied by Fitzwilliam, Taylor, and Gardiner, Wolsey's former dependant. It was six in the evening ; they found the cardinal in an upper chamber, near the great gallery, and presented the king's orders to him. Having read them he said : " I am happy to obey his majesty's commands ;" then having ordered the great seal to be brought him, he took it out of the white leather case in which ne kept it, and handed it to the dukes, who placed it in a box, covered with crimson velvet, and ornamented with the arms of England, [2] ordered Gardiner to seal it up with red wax, and gave it to Taylor to convey to the king.

Wolsey was thunderstruck ; he was to drink the bitter cup even to the dregs : he was ordered to leave his palace forthwith, taking with him neither clothes, linen, nor plate ; the dukes had feared that he would convey away his treasures. Wolsey comprehended the greatness of his misery ; he found strength however to say : " Since it is the king's good pleasure to take my house and all it contains, I am content to retire to Esher." The dukes left him.

Wolsey remained alone. This astonishing man, who had risen from a butcher's shop to the summit of earthly greatness—who, for a word that displeased him, sent his master's most faithful servants (Pace for instance) to the Tower—and who had governed England as if he had been its monarch, and even more, for he had governed without a parliament : was driven out, and thrown, as it were, upon a dunghill. A sudden hope flashed like lightning through his mind ; perhaps the magnificence of the spoils would appease Henry. Was not Esau pacified by Jacob's present ? Wolsey summoned his officers : " Set tables in the great gallery," he said to them, " and place on them all I have intrusted to your care, in order to render me an account." These orders were executed immediately. The tables were covered with an immense quantity of rich stuffs, silks and velvets of all colours, costly furs, rich copes and other ecclesiastical vestures ; the walls were hung with cloth of gold and silver, and webs of a valuable stuff named baudykin,[1] from the looms of Damascus, and with tapestry, representing scriptural subjects or stories from the old romances of chivalry. The gilt chamber and the council chamber, adjoining the gallery, were both filled with plate, in which the gold and silver were set with pearls and precious stones : these articles of luxury were so abundant that basketfuls of costly plate, which had fallen out of fashion, were stowed away under the tables. On every table was an exact list of the treasures with which it was loaded, for the most perfect order and regularity prevailed in the cardinal's household. Wolsey cast a glance of hope upon this wealth, and ordered his officers to deliver the whole to his majesty.

He then prepared to leave his magnificent palace. That moment of itself so sad, was made sadder still by an act of affectionate indiscretion. " Ah, my lord," said his treasurer, Sir William Gascoigne, moved even to tears, " your grace will be sent to the Tower." This was too much for Wolsey : to go and join his victims !.....He grew angry, and exclaimed : " Is this the best comfort you can give your master in adversity ? I would have

---

[1] Du Bellay to Montmorency. Le Grand, Preuves, p. 371.
[2] In quadam theca de veluto crimisino. Rymer, Act. p. 138.

[1] Baldekinum, pannus omnium ditissimus cujus utpote stamen ex filo auri, subtegmen ex serico texitur, plumaric opere intertextus. Ducange's Glossary.

you and all such blasphemous reporters know that it is untrue."

It was necessary to depart; he put round his neck a chain of gold, from which hung a pretended relic of the true cross; this was all he took. "Would to God," he exclaimed, as he placed it on, "that I had never had any other." This he said alluding to the legate's cross which used to be carried before him with so much pomp. He descended the back stairs, followed by his servants, some silent and dejected, others weeping bitterly, and proceeded to the river's brink, where a barge awaited him. But, alas! it was not alone. The Thames was covered with innumerable boats full of men and women. The inhabitants of London, expecting to see the cardinal led to the Tower, desired to be present at his humiliation, and prepared to accompany him. Cries of joy hailing his fall were heard from every side; nor were the cruellest sarcasms wanting. "The butcher's dog will bite no more," said some; "look, how he hangs his head." In truth, the unhappy man, distressed by a sight so new to him, lowered those eyes which were once so proud, but now were filled with bitter tears. This man, who had made all England tremble, was then like a withered leaf carried along the stream. All his servants were moved; even his fool, William Patch, sobbed like the rest. "O wavering and newfangled multitude," exclaimed Cavendish, his gentleman usher.[1] The hopes of the citizens were disappointed; the barge, instead of descending the river, proceeded upwards in the direction of Hampton Court; gradually the shouts died away, and the flotilla dispersed.

The silence of the river permitted Wolsey to indulge in less bitter thoughts, but it seemed as if invisible furies were pursuing him, now that the people had left him. He left his barge at Putney, and mounting his mule, though with difficulty, proceeded slowly with downcast looks. Shortly after, upon lifting his eyes, he saw a horseman riding rapidly down the hill towards them. "Whom do you think it can be?" he asked of his attendants. "My lord," replied one of them, "I think it is Sir Henry Norris." A flash of joy passed through Wolsey's heart. Was it not Norris, who, of all the king's officers, had shown him the most respect during his visit to Grafton? Norris came up with them, saluted him respectfully, and said: "The king bids me declare that he still entertains the same kindly feelings towards you, and sends you this ring as a token of his confidence." Wolsey received it with a trembling hand: it was that which the king was in the habit of sending on important occasions. The cardinal immediately alighted from his mule, and kneeling down in the road, raised his hands to heaven with an indescribable expression of happiness. The fallen man would have pulled off his velvet under-cap,

but unable to undo the strings, he broke them, and threw it on the ground. He remained on his knees bareheaded praying fervently amidst profound silence. God's forgiveness had never caused Wolsey so much pleasure as Henry's.

Having finished his prayer, the cardinal put on his cap, and remounted his mule. "Gentle Norris," said he to the king's messenger, "if I were lord of a kingdom, the half of it would scarcely be enough to reward you for your happy tidings; but I have nothing left except the clothes on my back." Then taking off his gold chain: "Take this," he said; "it contains a piece of the true cross. In my happier days I would not have parted with it for a thousand pounds." The cardinal and Norris separated: but Wolsey soon stopped, and the whole troop halted on the heath. The thought troubled him greatly that he had nothing to send to the king; he called Norris back, and looking round him saw mounted on a sorry horse poor William Patch, who had lost all his gaiety since his master's misfortune. "Present this poor jester to the king from me," said Wolsey to Norris; "his buffooneries are a pleasure fit for a prince; he is worth a thousand pounds." Patch, offended at being treated thus, burst into a violent passion, his eyes flashed fire, he foamed at the mouth, he kicked and fought, and bit all who approached him;[1] but the inexorable Wolsey, who looked upon him merely as a toy, ordered six of his tallest yeomen to lay hold of him. They carried off the unfortunate creature, who long continued to utter his piercing cries. At the very moment when his master had had pity on him, Wolsey, like the servant in the parable, had no pity on his poor companion in misfortune.

At last they reached Esher. What a residence compared with Whitehall!......It was little more than four bare walls. The most urgent necessaries were procured from the neighbouring houses, but Wolsey could not adapt himself to this cruel contrast. Besides, he knew Henry VIII.; he knew that he might send Norris one day with a gold ring, and the executioner the next with a rope. Gloomy and dejected, he remained seated in his lonely apartments. On a sudden he would rise from his seat, walk hurriedly up and down, speak aloud to himself, and then falling back in his chair, he would weep like a child. This man who formerly had shaken kingdoms, had been overthrown in the twinkling of an eye, and was now atoning for his perfidies in humiliation and terror,—a striking example of God's judgment.

[1] The poor fool took on, and fired so in such a rage. Cavendish, p. 257.

---

[1] Cavendish, Wolsey, p. 251.

CHAPTER XIV.

Thomas More elected Chancellor—A Lay Government one of the great facts of the Reformation—Wolsey accused of subordinating England to the Pope—He implores the King's Clemency—His Condemnation—Cromwell at Esher—His Character—He sets out for London—Sir Christopher Hales recommends him to the King—Cromwell's Interview with Henry in the Park—A new Theory—Cromwell elected Member of Parliament—Opened by Sir Thomas More—Attack on Ecclesiastical Abuses—Reforms pronounced by the Convocation—Three Bills—Rochester attacks them—Resistance of the House of Commons—Struggles—Henry Sanctions the Three Bills—Alarm of the Clergy and Disturbances.

DURING all this time everybody was in commotion at court. Norfolk and Suffolk, at the head of the council, had informed the Star Chamber of the cardinal's disgrace. Henry knew not how to supply his place. Some suggested the archbishop of Canterbury; the king would not hear of him. "Wolsey," says a French writer, "had disgusted the king and all England with those subjects of two masters who, almost always, sold one to the other. They preferred a lay minister." "I verily believe the priests will never more obtain it," wrote Du Bellay. The name of Sir Thomas More was pronounced. He was a layman, and that quality, which a few years before would, perhaps, have excluded him, was now a recommendation. A breath of Protestantism wafted to the summit of honours one of its greatest enemies. Henry thought that More, placed between the pope and his sovereign, would decide in favour of the interests of the throne, and of the independence of England. His choice was made.

More knew that the cardinal had been thrown aside because he was not a sufficiently docile instrument in the matter of the divorce: the work required of him was contrary to his convictions; but the honour conferred on him was almost unprecedented; very seldom indeed had the seals been intrusted to a mere knight.[1] He followed the path of ambition and not of duty; he showed, however, in after days that his ambition was of no common sort. It is even probable that, foreseeing the dangers which threatened to destroy the papal power in England, More wished to make an effort to save it. Norfolk installed the new chancellor in the Star Chamber. "His majesty," said the duke, "has not cast his eyes upon the nobility of the blood, but on the worth of the person. He desires to show by this choice that there are among the laity and gentlemen of England, men worthy to fill the highest offices in the kingdom, to which, until this hour, bishops and noblemen alone think they have a right."[2] The Reformation which restored religion to the general body of the church, took away at the same time political power

from the clergy. The priests had deprived the people of Christian activity, and the governments of power; the gospel restored to both what the priests had usurped. This result could not but be favourable to the interests of religion; the less cause kings and their subjects have to fear the intrusion of clerical power into the affairs of the world, the more will they yield themselves to the vivifying influence of faith.

More lost no time; never had lord-chancellor displayed such activity. He rapidly cleared off the cases which were in arrear, and having been installed on the 26th of October he called on Wolsey's cause on the 28th or 29th. "The crown of England," said the attorney-general, "has never acknowledged any superior but God.[1] Now, the said Thomas Wolsey, legate a latere, has obtained from the pope certain bulls, by virtue of which he has exercised since the 28th of August 1523 an authority derogatory to his majesty's power, and to the rights of his courts of justice. The crown of England cannot be put under the pope; and we therefore accuse the said legate of having incurred the penalties of præmunire."

There can be no doubt that Henry had other reasons for Wolsey's disgrace than those pointed out by the attorney-general; but England had convictions of a higher nature than her sovereign's. Wolsey was regarded as the pope's accomplice, and this was the cause of the great severity of the public officer and of the people. The cardinal was generally excused by alleging that both king and parliament had ratified the unconstitutional authority with which Rome had invested him; but had not the powers conferred on him by the pope produced unjustifiable results in a constitutional monarchy? Wolsey, as papal legate, had governed England without a parliament; and, as if the nation had gone back to the reign of John, he had substituted de facto, if not in theory, the monstrous system of the famous bull Unam Sanctam[2] for the institution of Magna Charta. The king, and even the lords and commons, had connived in vain at these illegalities; the rights of the constitution of England remained not the less inviolable, and the best of the people had protested against their infringement. And hence it was that Wolsey, conscious of his crime, "put himself wholly to the mercy and grace of the king,"[3] and his council declared his ignorance of the statutes he was said to have infringed. We cannot here allege, as some have done, the prostration of Wolsey's moral powers; he could, even after his fall, reply with energy to Henry VIII. When, for instance, the

[1] It has been often asserted that Sir Thomas More was the first layman to whom the office of chancellor was intrusted; but there were no less than six between A.D. 1342 and 1410; viz. Sir Robert Boucher, knight; Sir Robert de Thorp, knight; Sir R. de la Scrope, knight; Sir M. de la Pole; R. Neville, Earl of Salisbury, and Sir T. Beaufort, knight.
[2] More's Life, p. 172.

[1] The crown of England, free at all times, has been in no earthly subjection, but immediately subject to God in all things. Herbert, p. 251. See also Articles of Impeachment, sec. 1.
[2] Since the 13th of Nov. 1302. Raynold ad ann. Uterque ergo gladius est in potestate ecclesiæ, spiritualis scilicet et materialis.
[3] Cavendish, p. 276.

king sent to demand for the crown his palace of Whitehall, which belonged to the see of York, the cardinal answered: "Show his majesty from me that I must desire him to call to his most gracious remembrance that there is both a heaven and a hell;" and when other charges besides those of complicity with the papal aggression were brought against him, he defended himself courageously, as will be afterwards seen. If therefore the cardinal did not attempt to justify himself for infringing the rights of the crown, it was because his conscience bade him be silent. He had committed one of the gravest faults of which a statesman can be guilty. Those who have sought to excuse him have not sufficiently borne in mind that, since the Great Charter, opposition to Romish aggression has always characterized the constitution and government of England. Wolsey perfectly recollected this; and this explanation is more honourable to him than that which ascribes his silence to weakness or to cunning.

The cardinal was pronounced guilty, and the court passed judgment, that by the statute of *præmunire* his property was forfeited, and that he might be taken before the king in council. England, by sacrificing a churchman who had placed himself above kings, gave a memorable example of her inflexible opposition to the encroachments of the papacy. Wolsey was confounded, and his troubled imagination conjured up nothing but perils on every side.

While More was lending himself to the condemnation of his predecessor, whose friend he had been, another layman of still humbler origin was preparing to defend the cardinal, and by that very act to become the appointed instrument to throw down the convents in England, and to shatter the secular bonds which united this country to the Roman pontiff.

On the 1st of November, two days after Wolsey's condemnation, one of his officers, with a prayer-book in his hand, was leaning against the window in the great hall, apparently absorbed in his devotions. "Good morrow," said Cavendish as he passed him, on his way to the cardinal for his usual morning duties. The person thus addressed raised his head, and the gentleman-usher, seeing that his eyes were filled with tears, asked him: "Master Cromwell, is my lord in any danger?"—"I think not," replied Cromwell, "but it is hard to lose in a moment the labour of a life. In his master's fall Cromwell foreboded his own. Cavendish endeavoured to console him. "God willing, this is my resolution," replied Wolsey's ambitious solicitor; "I intend this afternoon, as soon as my lord has dined, to ride to London, and so go to court, where I will either make or mar before I come back again." At

<hr>

1 Cavendish, p. 280.

this moment Cavendish was summoned, and he entered the cardinal's chamber.

Cromwell, devoured by ambition, had clung to Wolsey's robe in order to attain power; but Wolsey had fallen, and the solicitor, dragged along with him, strove to reach by other means the object of his desires. Cromwell was one of those earnest and vigorous men whom God prepares for critical times. Blessed with a solid judgment and intrepid firmness, he possessed a quality rare in every age, and particularly under Henry VIII.,—fidelity in misfortune. The ability by which he was distinguished, was not at all times without reproach: success seems to have been his first thought.

After dinner Cromwell followed Wolsey into his private room: "My lord, permit me to go to London, I will endeavour to save you." A gleam passed over the cardinal's saddened features.—"Leave the room," he said to his attendants. He then had a long private conversation with Cromwell,[1] at the end of which the latter mounted his horse and set out for the capital, riding to the assault of power with the same activity as he had marched to the attack of Rome. He did not hide from himself that it would be difficult to procure access to the king; for certain ecclesiastics, jealous of Wolsey, had spoken against his solicitor at the time of the secularization of the convents, and Henry could not endure him. But Cromwell knew that fortune favours the bold, and, carried away by his ambitious dreams, he galloped on, saying to himself: "One foot in the stirrup, and my fortune is made!"

Sir Christopher Hales, a zealous Roman-catholic, entertained a sincere friendship for him; and to this friend Cromwell applied. Hales proceeded immediately to the palace (2d November) where he found a numerous company talking about the cardinal's ruin. "There was one of his officers," said Hales, "who would serve your majesty well."—"Who is he?" asked Henry.—"Cromwell.—"Do not speak to me of that man, I hate him," replied the king angrily;[2] and upon that all the courtiers chimed in with his majesty's opinion. This opening was not very encouraging; but Lord Russell, earl of Bedford, advancing to the midst of the group around the king, said boldly:[3] "Permit me, Sir, to defend a man to whom I am indebted for my life. When you sent me privately into Italy, your majesty's enemies, having discovered me at Bologna, would have put me to death, had not Thomas Cromwell saved me. Sir, since you have now to do with the pope, there is no man (I think) in all England who will be fitter for your purpose."—"Indeed," said the king; and after a little reflection, he said to Hales: "Very

<hr>

1 Long communication with my lord in secret. Cavendish, p. 270.
2 The king began to detest the mention of him. Foxe, v. p. 366.
3 In a vehement boldness. Ibid. p. 367.

well then, let your client meet me in White-hall gardens." The courtiers and the priests withdrew in great discomfiture.

The interview took place the same day at the appointed spot. "Sir," said Cromwell to his majesty, " the pope refuses your divorce... But why do you ask his consent? Every Englishman is master in his own house, and why should not you be so in England? Ought a foreign prelate to share your power with you? It is true, the bishops make oath to your majesty, but they make another to the pope immediately after, which absolves them from the former. Sir, you are but half a king, and we are but half your subjects.[1] This kingdom is a two-headed monster. Will you bear with such an anomaly any longer? What! are you not living in an age when Frederick the Wise and other German princes have thrown off the yoke of Rome? Do likewise; become once more a king; govern your kingdom in concert with your lords and commons. Henceforward let Englishmen alone have any thing to say in England; let not your subjects' money be cast any more into the yawning gulf of the Tiber; instead of imposing new taxes on the nation, convert to the general good those treasures which have hitherto only served to fatten proud priests and lazy friars. Now is the moment for action. Rely upon your parliament; proclaim yourself the head of the church in England. Then shall you see an increase of glory to your name, and of prosperity to your people."

Never before had such language been addressed to a king of England. It was not only on account of the divorce that it was necessary to break with Rome; it was, in Cromwell's view, on account of the independence, glory, and prosperity of the monarchy. These considerations appeared more important to Henry than those which had hitherto been laid before him; none of the kings of England had been so well placed as he was to understand them. When a Tudor had succeeded the Saxon, Norman, and Plantagenet kings, a man of the free race of the Celts had taken on the throne of England the place of princes submissive to the Roman pontiffs. The ancient British church, independent of the papacy, was about to rise again with this new dynasty, and the Celtic race, after eleven centuries of humiliation, to recover its ancient heritage. Undoubtedly, Henry had no recollection of this kind: but he worked in conformity with the peculiar character of his race, without being aware of the instinct which compelled him to act. He felt that a sovereign, who submits to the pope, becomes, like King John, his vassal; and now, after having been the second in his realm, he desired to be the first.

The king reflected on what Cromwell had said; astonished and surprised, he sought to understand the new position which his bold adviser had made for him. " Your proposal pleases me much," he said; " but can you prove what you assert?" " Certainly," replied this able politician, " I have with me a copy of the oath the bishops make to the Roman pontiff." With these words he drew a paper from his pocket, and placed the oath before the king's eyes. Henry, jealous of his authority even to despotism, was filled with indignation, and felt the necessity of bringing down that foreign authority which dared dispute the power with him, even in his own kingdom. He drew off his ring and gave it to Cromwell, declaring that he took him into his service, and soon after made him a member of his privy council. England, we may say, was now virtually emancipated from the papacy.

Cromwell had laid the first foundations of his greatness. He had remarked the path his master had followed, and which had led to his ruin,—complicity with the pope; and he hoped to succeed by following the contrary course, namely, by opposing the papacy. He had the king's support, but he wanted more. Possessing a clear and easy style of eloquence, he saw what influence a seat in the great council of the nation would give him. It was somewhat late, for the session began on the next day, (3d November,) but to Cromwell nothing was impossible. The son of his friend, Sir Thomas Rush, had been returned to parliament; but the young member resigned his seat, and Cromwell was elected in his place.

Parliament had not met for seven years, the kingdom having been governed by a prince of the Roman church. The reformation of the church, whose regenerating influence began to be felt already, was about to restore to the nation those ancient liberties of which a cardinal had robbed it; and Henry being on the point of taking very important resolutions, felt the necessity of drawing nearer to his people. Everything betokened that a good feeling would prevail between the parliament and the crown, and that " the priests would have a terrible fright."[1]

While Henry was preparing to attack the Roman church in the papal supremacy, the commons were getting ready to war against the numerous abuses with which it had covered England. " Some even thought," says Tyndale, " that this assembly would reform the church, and that the golden age would come again.[2] But it was not from acts of parliament that the Reformation was destined to proceed, but solely from the word of God. And yet the commons, without touching upon doctrine, were going to do their duty manfully in things within their province, and the parliament of 1529 may be regarded (Lord Herbert of Cherbury observes)

[1] Foxe, v. p. 366. See also Apol. Regin. Poll ad Car. 1. pp. 120, 121.

[1] Du Bellay to Montmorency. Le Grand, Preuves, p. 378, 380. [2] Works 1. p. 481.

857

as the first Protestant parliament of England.[1] " The bishops require excessive fines for the probates of wills," said Tyndale's old friend, Sir Henry Guilford. " As testamentary executor to Sir William Compton I had to pay a thousand marks sterling."—" The spiritual men," said another member, " would rather see the poor orphans die of hunger than give them the lean cow, the only thing their father left them."[2] " Priests," said another, " have farms, tanneries, and warehouses, all over the country. In short, the clerks take everything from their flocks, and not only give them nothing, but even deny them the word of God."

The clergy were in utter consternation. The power of the nation seemed to awaken in this parliament for the sole purpose of attacking the power of the priest. It was important to ward off these blows. The convocation of the province of Canterbury, assembling at Westminster on the 5th of November, thought it their duty, in self-defence, to reform the most crying abuses. It was therefore decreed, on the 12th of November, that the priests should no longer keep shops or taverns, play at dice or other forbidden games, pass the night in suspected places, be present at disreputable shows,[3] go about with sporting dogs, or with hawks, falcons, or other birds of prey, on their fist;[4] or, finally, hold suspicious intercourse with women.[5] Penalties were denounced against these various disorders; they were doubled in case of adultery; and still further increased in the case of more abominable impurities.[6] Such were the laws rendered necessary by the manners of the clergy.

These measures did not satisfy the Commons. Three bills were introduced having reference to the fees on the probate of wills, mortuaries, pluralities, non-residence, and the exercise of secular professions. " The destruction of the church is aimed at," exclaimed Bishop Fisher, when these bills were carried to the Lords, " and if the church falls, the glory of the kingdom will perish. Lutheranism is making great progress amongst us, and the savage cry that has already echoed in Bohemia, *Down with the church*, is now uttered by the Commons......How does that come about? Solely from want of faith.— My lords, save your country! save the church!" Sir Thomas Audley, the speaker, with a deputation of thirty members, immediately went to Whitehall. " Sir," they said to the king, " we are accused of being with-

out faith, and of being almost as bad as the *Turks*. We demand an apology for such offensive language." Fisher pretended that he only meant to speak of the *Bohemians*; and the Commons, by no means satisfied, zealously went on with their reforms.

These the king was resolved to concede; but he determined to take advantage of them to present a bill making over to him all the money borrowed of his subjects. John Petit, one of the members for the city, boldly opposed this demand. " I do not know other persons' affairs," he said, " and I cannot give what does not belong to me. But as regards myself personally, I give without reserve all that I have lent the king." The royal bill passed, and the satisfied Henry gave his consent to the bills of the Commons. Every dispensation coming from Rome, which might be contrary to the statutes, was strictly forbidden. The bishops exclaimed that the Commons were becoming schismatical; disturbances were excited by certain priests; but the clerical agitators were punished, and the people, when they heard of it, were delighted beyond measure.

CHAPTER XV.

The Last Hour—More's Fanaticism—Debates in Convocation—Royal Proclamation—The Bishop of Norwich—Sentences condemned—Latimer's Opposition—The New Testament Burnt—The Persecution begins—Hitton—Bayfield—Tonstall and Packington—Bayfield arrested—The Rector Patmore—Lollards' Tower—Tyndale and Patmore—A Musician—Freese the Painter—Placards and Martyrdom of Bennet—Thomas More and John Petit—Bilney.

THE moment when Henry aimed his first blows at Rome was also that in which he began to shed the blood of the disciples of the gospel. Although ready to throw off the authority of the pope, he would not recognise the authority of Christ: obedience to the Scriptures is, however, the very soul of the Reformation.

The king's contest with Rome had filled the friends of Scripture with hope. The artizans and tradesmen, particularly those who lived near the sea, were almost wholly won over to the gospel. " The king is one of us," they used to boast; " he wishes his subjects to read the New Testament. Our faith, which is the true one, will circulate through the kingdom, and by Michaelmas next those who believe as we do will be more numerous than those of a contrary opinion. We are ready, if needs be, to die in the struggle."[1] This was indeed to be the fate of many.

Language such as this aroused the clergy: " The last hour has come," said Stokesley, who had been raised to the see of London

---

[1] It was the first step, a great and bold sally towards that reformation. Herbert, p. 320.
[2] Rather than give to them the silly cow, if he had but only one. Foxe, iv. p. 611.
[3] Quod non exerceant tabernas, nec ludant taxillis vel aliis ludis prohibitis; quod non pernoctent in locis suspectis; quod non intersint inhonestis spectaculis, &c. Convocatio prælatorum. Wilkins, Concilia, iii. p. 717.
[4] Canes venaticos loris ducere ac accipitres manibus. Ibid. p. 723.
[5] Mulierum colloquia suspecta nullatenus habeant. Ibid. p. 722.
[6] Et in cæteris carnis spurcitiis pœna crescat. Ibid. p. 721.

[1] The bishop of Norwich to Primate Warham, 14th May 1530. Cotton MSS. Cleopatra, E. v. folio 360; Bible Annals, i. p. 256.

after Tonstall's translation to Durham; "if we would not have Luther's heresy pervade the whole of England, we must hasten to throw it in the sea." Henry was fully disposed to do so; but as he was not on very good terms with the clergy, a man was wanted to serve as mediator between him and the bishops. He was soon found.

Sir Thomas More's noble understanding was then passing from ascetic practices to fanaticism, and the humanist turning into an inquisitor. In his opinion, the burning of heretics was just and necessary.[1] He has even been reproached with binding evangelical Christians to a tree in his garden, which he called "the tree of truth," and of having flogged them with his own hand.[2] More has declared that he never gave "stripe nor stroke, nor so much as a fillip on the forehead," to any of his religious adversaries;[3] and we willingly credit his denial. All must be pleased to think that if the author of the *Utopia* was a severe judge, the hand which held one of the most famous pens of the sixteenth century never discharged the duties of an executioner.

The bishops led the attack. "We must clear the Lord's field of the thorns which choke it," said the archbishop of Canterbury to Convocation on the 29th of November 1529; immediately after which the bishop of Bath read to his colleagues the list of books that he desired to have condemned. There were a number of works by Tyndale, Luther, Melanchthon, Zwingle, Œcolampadius, Pomeranus, Brentius, Bucer, Jonas, Francis Lambert, Fryth, and Fish.[4] The Bible in particular was set down. "It is impossible to translate the Scripture into English," said one of the prelates.[5]—"It is not lawful for the laity to read it in their mother tongue," said another.—"If you tolerate the Bible," added a third, "you will make us all heretics."—"By circulating the Scriptures," exclaimed several, "you will raise the nation against the king." Sir T. More laid the bishops' petition before the king, and some time after, Henry gave up orders by proclamation that "no one should preach, or write any book, or keep any school without his bishop's license;—that no one should keep any heretical book in his house;—that the bishops should detain the offenders in prison at their discretion, and then proceed to the execution of the guilty; —and, finally, that the chancellor, the justices of the peace, and other magistrates, should aid and assist the bishops."[6] Such was the cruel proclamation of Henry VIII., "the *father* of the English Reformation."

The clergy were not yet satisfied. The blind and octogenarian bishop of Norwich, being more ardent than the youngest of his priests, recommenced his complaints. "My diocese is *accumbered* with such as read the Bible," said he to the archbishop of Canterbury, "and there is not a clerk from Cambridge but *savoureth of the frying-pan*. If this continues any time, they will undo us all. We must have greater authority to punish them, than we have."

Consequently, on the 24th of May 1530, More, Warham, Tonstall, and Gardiner having been admitted into St Edward's chamber at Westminster, to make a report to the king concerning heresy, they proposed forbidding, in the most positive manner, the New Testament and certain other books in which the following doctrines were taught: "That Christ has shed his blood for our iniquities, as a sacrifice to the Father.—Faith only doth justify us.—Faith without good works is no little or weak faith, it is no faith.—Labouring in good works to come to heaven, thou dost shame Christ's blood."[1]

Whilst nearly every one in the audience-chamber supported the prayer of the petition, there were three or four doctors who kept silence. At last one of them, it was Latimer, opposed the proposition. Bilney's friend was more decided than ever to listen to no other voice than God's. "Christ's sheep hear no man's voice but Christ's," he answered Dr Redman, who had called upon him to submit to the church; "trouble me no more from the talking with the Lord my God."[2] The church, in Latimer's opinion, presumed to set up its own voice in the place of Christ's, and the Reformation did the contrary; this was his abridgment of the controversy. Being called upon to preach during Christmas tide, he had censured his hearers because they celebrated that festival by playing at cards, like mere worldlings, and then proceeded to lay before their eyes Christ's *cards*, that is to say, his laws.[3] Being placed on the Cambridge commission to examine into the question of the king's marriage, he had conciliated the esteem of Henry's deputy, Doctor Butts, the court physician who had presented him to his master, by whose orders he preached at Windsor.

Henry felt disposed at first to yield something to Latimer. "Many of my subjects," said he to the prelates assembled in St Edward's hall, "think that it is my duty to cause the Scriptures to be translated and given to the people." The discussion immediately began between the two parties;[4] and Latimer concluded by asking "that the Bible should be permitted to circulate freely in English."[5]—"But the most part overcame the better," he tells us.[6] Henry declared that

[1] More's Works; A Dialogue concerning Heresies, p. 274.
[2] Strype's Mem. vol. i. p. 315; Foxe, iv. p. 698.
[3] Apology, ch. xxxvi. pp. 901-902.
[4] See the catalogue in Wilkins' Concilia, pp. 713 to 720. Wilkins is of opinion (p. 717, note) that this document belongs to the year 1529. There are, however, some portions of these *statuta* which have evident reference to the year following.
[5] Tyndale's Works, vol. i. p. 1.   [6] Foxe, iv. pp. 677, 678.

[1] Wilkins. Concilia, iii. p. 728-731.
[2] Latimer's Remains, p. 297.
[3] Sermons, p. 8.
[4] Wilkins, Concilia, iii. p. 736.
[5] Latimer's Remains, p. 306.   [6] Ibid.

the teaching of the priests was sufficient for the people, and was content to add, " that he would give the Bible to his subjects when they renounced the arrogant pretension of interpreting it according to their own fancies."—" Shun these books," cried the priests from the pulpit, " detest them, keep them not in your hands, deliver them up to your superiors."[1] Or if you do not, your prince, who has received from God the sword of justice, will use it to punish you." Rome had every reason to be satisfied with Henry VIII. Tonstall, who still kept under lock and key the Testaments purchased at Antwerp through Packington's assistance, had them carried to St Paul's churchyard, where they were publicly burnt. The spectators retired shaking the head, and saying : " The teaching of the priests and of Scriptures must be in contradiction to each other, since the priests destroy them." Latimer did more : " You have promised us the word of God," he wrote courageously to the king, " perform your promise now rather than to-morrow! The day is at hand when you shall give an account of your office, and of the blood that hath been shed with your sword."[2] Latimer well knew that by such language he hazarded his life; but that he was ready to sacrifice, as he tells us himself.[3]

Persecution soon came. Just as the sun appeared to be rising on the Reformation, the storm burst forth. " There was not a stone the bishops left unremoved," says the chronicler, " any corner unsearched, for the diligent execution of the king's proclamation; whereupon ensued a grievous persecution and slaughter of the faithful."[4]

Thomas Hitton, a poor and pious minister of Kent, used to go frequently to Antwerp to purchase New Testaments. As he was returning from one of these expeditions, in 1529, the bishop of Rochester caused him to be arrested at Gravesend, and put to the cruellest tortures, to make him deny his faith.[5] But the martyr repeated with holy enthusiasm : " Salvation cometh by faith and not by works, and Christ giveth it to whomsoever he willeth."[6] On the 20th of February 1530 he was tied to the stake and there burned to death.[7]

Scarcely were Hitton's sufferings ended for bringing the Scriptures into England, when a vessel laden with New Testaments arrived at Colchester. The indefatigable Bayfield, who accompanied these books, sold them in London, went back to the continent, and returned to England in November; but this time the Scriptures fell into the hands of Sir Thomas More. Bayfield, undismayed, again visited the Low Countries, and soon reappear-

ed, bringing with him the New Testament and the works of almost all the Reformers. " How cometh it it that there are so many New Testaments from abroad?" asked Tonstall of Packington ; " you promised me that you would buy them all."—" They have printed more since," replied the wily merchant ; " and it will never be better so long as they have letters and stamps [type and dies.] My lord, you had better buy the stamps too, and so you shall be sure."[1]

Instead of the stamps, the priests sought after Bayfield. The bishop of London could not endure this godly man. Having one day asked Bainham, (who afterwards suffered martyrdom) whether he knew a single individual who, since the days of the apostles, had lived according to the true faith in Jesus Christ, the latter answered : " Yes, I know Bayfield."[2] Being tracked from place to place, he fled from the house of his pious hostess, and hid himself at his binder's, where he was discovered, and thrown into the Lollards' tower.[3]

As he entered the prison Bayfield noticed a priest named Patmore, pale, weakened by suffering, and ready to sink under the ill-treatment of his jailers. Patmore, won over by Bayfield's piety, soon opened his heart to him. When rector of Haddam, he had found the truth in Wickliffe's writings. " They have burnt his bones," he said, " but from his ashes shall burst forth a well-spring of life."[4] Delighting in good works, he used to fill his granaries with wheat, and when the markets were high, he would send his corn to them in such abundance as to bring down the prices.[5] " It is contrary to the law of God to burn heretics," he said ; and growing bolder, he added : " I care no more for the pope's curse than for a bundle of hay."[6]

His curate, Simon Smith, unwilling to imitate the disorderly lives of the priests, and finding Joan Bennore, the rector's servant, to be a discreet and pious person, desired to marry her. " God," said Patmore, " has declared marriage lawful for all men ; and accordingly it is permitted to the priests in foreign parts."[7] The rector alluded to Wittemberg, where he had visited Luther. After his marriage Smith and his wife quitted England for a season, and Patmore accompanied them as far as London.

The news of this marriage of a priest—a fact without precedent in England—made Stokesley throw Patmore into the Lollards' tower, and although he was ill, neither fire, light, nor any other comfort was granted him. The bishop and his vicar-general visited him alone in his prison, and endeavoured by their threats to make him deny his faith.

It was during these circumstances that Bayfield was thrust into the tower. By his

1 Wilkins, Concilia, iii. p. 736.
2 Latimer's Remains, p. 308.
3 I had rather suffer extreme punishment. Ibid. p. 298.
4 Foxe, vol. iv. p. 679.
5 Dieted and tormented him secretly. Tyndale's Works, vol. i. p. 485.
6 For the constant and manifest testimony of Jesus Christ and of his free grace and salvation. Foxe, vol. iv. p. 619.
7 The bishops murdered him most cruelly. Tyndale, vol. i. p. 485.

1 Foxe, vol. iv. p. 670.   4 Foxe, vol. v. p. 34.
2 Ibid. p. 699.   5 Ibid. vol. iv. p. 681.
3 Ibid. p. 681.   6 Ibid.
7 Yet it was in other countries beyond sea. Ibid.

Christian words he revived Patmore's languishing faith,[1] and the latter complained to the king that the bishop of London prevented his feeding the flock which God had committed to his charge. Stokesley, comprehending whence Patmore derived his new courage,[2] removed Bayfield from the Lollards' tower and shut him up in the coal-house, where he was fastened upright to the wall by the neck, middle, and legs.[3] The unfortunate gospeller of Bury passed his time in continual darkness, never lying down, never seated, but nailed as it were to the wall, and never hearing the sound of human voice. We shall see him hereafter issuing from this horrible prison to die on the scaffold.

Patmore was not the only one in his family who suffered persecution; he had in London a brother named Thomas, a friend of John Tyndale, the younger brother of the celebrated reformer. Thomas had said that the truth of Scripture was at last reappearing in the world, after being hidden for many ages;[4] and John Tyndale had sent five marks to his brother William, and received letters from him. Moreover, the two friends (who were both tradesmen) had distributed a great number of Testaments and other works. But their faith was not deeply rooted, and it was more out of sympathy for their brothers that they had believed; accordingly, Stokesley, so completely entangled them, that they confessed their "crime." More, delighted at the opportunity which offered to cover the name of Tyndale with shame, was not satisfied with condemning the two friends to pay a fine of L.100 each; he invented a new disgrace. He sewed on their dress some sheets of the New Testament which they had circulated, placed the two penitents on horseback with their faces towards the tail, and thus paraded them through the streets of London, exposed to the jeers and laughter of the populace. In this, More succeeded better than in his refutation of the reformer's writings.

From that time the persecution became more violent. Husbandmen, artists, tradespeople, and even noblemen, felt the cruel fangs of the clergy and of Sir Thomas More. They sent to jail a pious musician who used to wander from town to town, singing to his harp a hymn in commendation of Martin Luther and of the Reformation.[5] A painter, named Edward Freese, a young man of ready wit, having been engaged to paint some hangings in a house, wrote on the borders certain sentences of the Scripture. For this he was seized and taken to the bishop of London's palace at Fulham, and there imprisoned, where his chief nourishment was bread made out of sawdust.[6] His poor wife, who was

pregnant, went down to Fulham to see her husband; but the bishop's porter had orders to admit no one, and the brute gave her so violent a kick, as to kill her unborn infant, and cause the mother's death not long after. The unhappy Freese was removed to the Lollards' tower, where he was put into chains, his hands only being left free. With these he took a piece of coal, and wrote some pious sentences on the wall; upon this he was manacled, but his wrists were so severely pinched, that the flesh grew up higher than the irons. His intellect became disturbed; his hair in wild disorder soon covered his face, through which his eyes glared fierce and haggard. The want of proper food, bad treatment, his wife's death, and his lengthened imprisonment, entirely undermined his reason; when brought to St Paul's, he was kept three days without meat; and when he appeared before the consistory the poor prisoner, silent and scarce able to stand, looked around and gazed upon the spectators, "like a wild man." The examination was begun, but to every question put to him, Freese made the same answer: "My Lord is a good man." They could get nothing from him but this affecting reply. Alas! the light shone no more upon his understanding, but the love of Jesus was still in his heart. He was sent back to Bearsy Abbey, where he did not remain long; but he never entirely recovered his reason.[1] Henry VIII. and his priests inflicted punishments still more cruel even than the stake.

Terror began to spread far and wide. The most active evangelists had been compelled to flee to a foreign land; some of the most godly were in prison; and among those in high station there were many, and perhaps Latimer was one, who seemed willing to shelter themselves under an exaggerated moderation. But just as the persecution in London had succeeded in silencing the most timid, other voices more courageous were raised in the provinces. The city of Exeter was at that time in great agitation; placards had been discovered on the gates of the cathedral containing some of the principles "of the new doctrine." While the mayor and his officers were seeking after the author of these "blasphemies," the bishop and all his doctors, "as hot as coals," says the chronicler,[2] were preaching in the most fiery style. On the following Sunday, during the sermon, two men who had been the busiest of all the city in searching for the author of the bills were struck by the appearance of a person seated near them. "Surely, this fellow is the heretic," they said. But their neighbour's devotion, for he did not take his eyes off his book, quite put them out: they did not perceive that he was reading the New Testament in Latin.

This man, Thomas Bennet, was indeed the

---

[1] Confirmed by him in the doctrine. Foxe, vol. iv. p. 681.
[2] Confirmed him in the doctrine. Ibid. iv. p. 68.
[3] Ibid. [4] Ibid. v. p. 34.
[5] His name was Robert Lambe. Ibid.
[6] Fed with fine manchet made of sawdust, or at least a great part thereof. Ibid. iv. p. 695.

[1] Foxe, iv. p. 695. [2] Ibid. v. p. 19.

offender. Being converted at Cambridge by the preaching of Bilney, whose friend he was, he had gone to Torrington for fear of the persecution, and thence to Exeter, and after marrying to avoid unchastity (as he says)[1] he became schoolmaster. Quiet, humble, courteous to every body, and somewhat timid, Bennet had lived six years in that city without his faith being discovered. At last his conscience being awakened he resolved to fasten by night to the cathedral gates certain evangelical placards. " Everybody will read the writing," he thought, " and nobody will know the writer." He did as he had proposed.

Not long after the Sunday on which he had been so nearly discovered, the priests prepared a great pageant, and made ready to pronounce against the unknown heretic the great curse " with book, bell, and candle." The cathedral was crowded, and Bennet himself was among the spectators. In the middle stood a great cross on which lighted tapers were placed, and around it were gathered all the Franciscans and Dominicans of Exeter. One of the priests having delivered a sermon on the words: *There is an accursed thing in the midst of thee, O Israel,*[2] the bishop drew near the cross and pronounced the curse against the offender. He took one of the tapers and said: " Let the soul of the unknown heretic, if he be dead already, be quenched this night in the pains of hell-fire, as this candle is now quenched and put out ;" and with that he put out the candle. Then taking off a second, he continued : " and let us pray to God, if he be yet alive, that his eyes be put out, and that all the senses of his body may fail him, as now the light of this candle is gone ;" extinguishing the second candle. After this, one of the priests went up to the cross and struck it, when the noise it made in falling re-echoing along the roof so frightened the spectators that they uttered a shriek of terror, and held up their hands to heaven, as if to pray that the divine curse might not fall on them. Bennet, a witness of this comedy, could not forbear smiling. " What are you laughing at ?" asked his neighbours ; " here is the heretic, here is the heretic, hold him fast." This created great confusion among the crowd, some shouting, some clapping their hands, others running to and fro ; but, owing to the tumult, Bennet succeeded in making his escape.

The excommunication did but increase his desire to attack the Romish superstitions ; and accordingly, before five o'clock the next morning (it was in the month of October 1530), his servant-boy fastened up again by his orders on the cathedral gates some placards similar to those which had been torn down. It chanced that a citizen going to early mass saw the boy, and running up to

him, caught hold of him and pulled down the papers ; and then dragging the boy with one hand, and with the placards in the other, he went to the mayor of the city. Bennet's servant was recognised ; his master was immediately arrested, and put in the stocks, " with as much favour as a dog would find," says Foxe.

Exeter seemed determined to make itself the champion of sacerdotalism in England. For a whole week, not only the bishop, but all the priests and friars of the city, visited Bennet night and day. But they tried in vain to prove to him that the Roman church was the true one. " God has given me grace to be of a better church," he said.—" Do you not know that ours is built upon St Peter ? " —" The church that is built upon a man," he replied, " is the devil's church and not God's." His cell was continually thronged with visitors ; and, in default of arguments, the most ignorant of the friars called the prisoner a heretic, and spat upon him. At length they brought to him a learned doctor of theology, who, they supposed, would infallibly convert him. " Our ways are God's ways," said the doctor gravely. But he soon discovered that theologians can do nothing against the word of the Lord. " He only is my way," replied Bennet, " who saith, *I am the way, the truth, and the life.* In his *way* will I walk ;—his *truth* will I embrace ;—his everlasting *life* will I seek."

He was condemned to be burnt ; and More having transmitted the order *de comburendo* with the utmost speed, the priests placed Bennet in the hands of the sheriff on the 15th of January 1531, by whom he was conducted to the Liverydole, a field without the city, where the stake was prepared. When Bennet arrived at the place of execution, he briefly exhorted the people, but with such unction, that the sheriff's clerk, as he heard him, exclaimed : " Truly this is a servant of God." Two persons, however, seemed unmoved : they were Thomas Carew, and John Barnehouse, both holding the station of gentlemen. Going up to the martyr, they exclaimed in a threatening voice : " Say *Precor sanctam Mariam et omnes sanctos Dei.*"—" I know no other advocate but Jesus Christ," replied Bennet. Barnehouse was so enraged at these words, that he took a furze-bush upon a pike, and setting it on fire, thrust it into the martyr's face, exclaiming : " Accursed heretic, pray to our Lady, or I will make you do it."—" Alas ! " replied Bennet patiently, " trouble me not ;" and then holding up his hands, he prayed : " Father, forgive them ! " The executioners immediately set fire to the wood, and the most fanatical of the spectators, both men and women, seized with an indescribable fury, tore up stakes and bushes, and whatever they could lay their hands on, and flung them all into the flames to increase their violence. Bennet, lifting up his eyes to heaven, exclaimed·

[1] Ut ne scortator aut immundus essem, uxorem duxi. Foxe, v. p. 19.   [2] Joshua, vii. 13.

"Lord, receive my spirit." Thus died, in the sixteenth century, the disciples of the Reformation sacrificed by Henry VIII.

The priests, thanks to the king's sword, began to count on victory; yet schoolmasters, musicians, tradesmen, and even ecclesiastics, were not enough for them. They wanted nobler victims, and these were to be looked for in London. More himself, accompanied by the lieutenant of the Tower,[1] searched many of the suspected houses. Few citizens were more esteemed in London than John Petit, the same who, in the house of Commons, had so nobly resisted the king's demand about the loan. Petit was learned in history and in Latin literature: he spoke with eloquence, and for twenty years had worthily represented the city. Whenever any important affair was debated in parliament, the king feeling uneasy, was in the habit of inquiring, which side he took? This political independence, very rare in Henry's parliaments, gave umbrage to the prince and his ministers. Petit, the friend of Bilney, Fryth, and Tyndale, had been one of the first in England to taste the sweetness of God's word,[2] and had immediately manifested that beautiful characteristic by which the gospel faith makes itself known, namely, charity. He abounded in almsgiving, supported a great number of poor preachers of the gospel in his own country and beyond the seas; and whenever he noted down these generous aids in his books, he wrote merely the words: "Lent unto Christ."[3] He moreover forbade his testamentary executors to call in these debts.

Petit was tranquilly enjoying the sweets of domestic life in his modest home in the society of his wife and two daughters, Blanche and Audrey, when he received an unexpected visit. One day, as he was praying in his closet, a loud knock was heard at the street door. His wife ran to open it, but seeing Lord-chancellor More, she returned hurriedly to her husband, and told him that the lord-chancellor wanted him. More, who followed her, entered the closet, and with inquisitive eye ran over the shelves of the library, but could find nothing suspicious. Presently he made as if he would retire, and Petit accompanied him. The chancellor stopped at the door and said to him: "You assert that you have none of these new books?"—"You have seen my library," replied Petit.—"I am informed, however," replied More, "that you not only read them, but pay for the printing." And then he added in a severe tone: "Follow the lieutenant." In spite of the tears of his wife and daughters this independent member of parliament was conducted to the Tower, and shut up in a damp dungeon where he had nothing but straw to lie upon. His wife went thither each day in vain, asking with tears permission to see him, or at least to send him a bed; the jailers refused her everything; and it was only when Petit fell dangerously ill that the latter favour was granted him. This took place in 1530, sentence was passed in 1531:[1] we shall see Petit again in his prison. He left it, indeed, but only to sink under the cruel treatment he had there experienced.

Thus were the witnesses to the truth struck down by the priests, by Sir Thomas More, and by Henry VIII. A new victim was to be the cause of many tears. A meek and humble man, one dear to all the friends of the gospel, and whom we may regard as the spiritual father of the Reformation in England, was on the point of mounting the burning pile raised by his persecutors. Some time prior to Petit's appearance before his judges, which took place in 1531, an unusual noise was heard in the cell above him; it was Thomas Bilney, whom they were conducting to the tower.[2] We left him at the end of 1528 after his fall. Bilney had returned to Cambridge tormented by remorse; his friends in vain crowded round him by night and by day; they could not console him, and even the Scriptures seemed to utter no voice but that of condemnation.[3] Fear made him tremble constantly, and he could scarcely eat or drink. At length a heavenly and unexpected light dawned in the heart of the fallen disciple; a witness whom he had vexed—the Holy Spirit—spoke once more in his heart. Bilney fell at the foot of the cross, shedding floods of tears, and there he found peace. But the more God comforted him, the greater seemed his crime. One only thought possessed him, that of giving his life for the truth. He had shrunk from before the burning pile; its flames must now consume him. Neither the weakness of his body, which his long anguish had much increased, nor the cruelty of his enemies, nor his natural timidity, nothing could stop him he strove for the martyr's crown. At ten o'clock one night, when every person in Trinity Hall was retiring to rest, Bilney called his friends round him, reminded them of his fall, and added: "You shall see me no more......Do not stay me: my decision is formed and I shall carry it out. My face is set to go to Jerusalem."[4] Bilney repeated the words used by the Evangelist, when he describes Jesus going up to the city where he was to be put to death. Having shaken hands with his brethren, this venerable man, the foremost of the evangelists of England in order of time, left Cambridge under cover of the night, and proceeded to Norfolk, to confirm in the faith those who had believed, and to invite the ignorant multitude to the Saviour. We shall not follow him in this last and solemn minis-

---

[1] Strype, i. p. 312.   Ibid.   [2] Ibid. p. 314.

[1] Strype, p. 312.   [3] Ibid. p. 313.
[3] He thought that all the while the Scriptures were against him. Latimer's Sermons, p. 52.
[4] Foxe, iv. p. 642. See Luke ix. 51.

try; these facts and others of the same kind belong to a later date. Before the year 1531 closed in, Bilney, Bainham, Bayfield, Tewkesbury, and many others, struck by Henry's sword, sealed by their blood the testimony rendered by them to the perfect grace of Christ.

— —

CHAPTER XVI.

Wolsey's Terror—Impeachment by the Peers—Cromwell saves him—The Cardinal's illness—Ambition returns to him—His practices in Yorkshire—He is arrested by Northumberland—His departure—Arrival of the Constable of the Tower—Wolsey at Leicester Abbey—Persecuting language—He dies—Three Movements: Supremacy, Scripture, and Faith.

WHILE many pious Christians were languishing in the prisons of England, the great antagonist of the Reformation was disappearing from the stage of this world. We must return to Wolsey, who was still detained at Esher.[1]

The cardinal, fallen from the summit of honours, was seized with those panic terrors usually felt after their disgrace by those who have made a whole nation tremble, and he fancied he saw an assassin lay hid behind every door. "This very night," he wrote to Cromwell on one occasion, "I was as one that should have died. If I might, I would not fail to come on foot to you, rather than this my speaking with you shall be put over and delayed. If the displeasure of my Lady Anne be somewhat assuaged, as I pray God the same may be, then I pray you exert all possible means of attaining her favour."[2]

In consequence of this, Cromwell hastened down to Esher two or three days after taking his seat in Parliament, and Wolsey, all trembling, recounted his fears to him. "Norfolk, Suffolk, and Lady Anne perhaps, desire my death.[3] Did not Thomas à Becket, an archbishop like me, stain the altar with his blood?"......Cromwell reassured him, and, moved by the old man's fears, asked and obtained of Henry an order of protection.

Wolsey's enemies most certainly desired his death; but it was from the justice of the three estates, and not by the assassin's dagger that they sought it. The House of Peers authorized Sir Thomas More, the dukes of Norfolk and Suffolk, and fourteen other lords, to impeach the cardinal-legate of high treason. They forgot nothing: that haughty formula, *Ego et rex meus*, I and my king, which Wolsey had often employed; his infringement of the laws of the kingdom; his

[1] Burnet and some more modern historians are, in my opinion, mistaken when they state that Wolsey was present in Parliament at the close of 1529. See State Papers, i. pp. 347 to 354.
[2] Ibid. p. 351, mutilated by fire.
[3] Timebat sibi damnum et periculum de corpore suo per quosdam suos æmulos. Rymer, Fœdera, p. 139.

monopolizing the church revenues; the crying injustice of which he had been guilty,—as for instance, in the case of Sir John Stanley, who was sent to prison until he gave up a lease to the son of a woman who had borne the cardinal two children; many families ruined to satisfy his avarice; treaties concluded with foreign powers without the king's order; his exactions, which had impoverished England; and the foul diseases and infectious breath with which he had polluted his majesty's presence.[1] These were some of the forty-four grievances presented by the peers to the king, and which Henry sent down to the Lower House for their consideration.

It was at first thought that nobody in the Commons would undertake Wolsey's defence, and it was generally expected that he would be given up to the vengeance of the law (as the bill of impeachment prayed) or in other words, to the axe of the executioner. But one man stood up, and prepared, though alone, to defend the cardinal: this was Cromwell. The members asked of each other, who the unknown man was; he soon made himself known. His knowledge of facts, his familiarity with the laws, the force of his eloquence, and the moderation of his language, surprised the house. Wolsey's adversaries had hardly aimed a blow, before the defender had already parried it. If any charge was brought forward to which he could not reply, he proposed an adjournment until the next day, departed for Esher at the end of the sitting, conferred with Wolsey, returned during the night, and next morning reappeared in the Commons with fresh arms. Cromwell carried the house with him; the impeachment failed, and Wolsey's defender took his station among the statesmen of England. This victory, one of the greatest triumphs of parliamentary eloquence at that period, satisfied both the ambition and the gratitude of Cromwell. He was now firmly fixed in the king's favour, esteemed by the Commons, and admired by the people: circumstances which furnished him with the means of bringing to a favourable conclusion the emancipation of the church of England.

The ministry, composed of Wolsey's enemies, was annoyed at the decision of the Lower House, and appointed a commission to examine into the matter. When the cardinal was informed of this he fell into new terrors. He lost all appetite and desire of sleep,[2] and a fever attacked him at Christmas. "The cardinal will be dead in four days," said his physician to Henry, "if he receives no comfort shortly from you and Lady Anne."—"I would not lose him for twenty thousand pounds," exclaimed the king. He desired to preserve Wolsey in case his old minister's consummate ability should become

[1] Article vi. Herbert, p. 295.
[2] Cum prostratione appetitus et continuo insomnio. Wolsey to Gardiner; Cavendish, Appendix, p. 474.

necessary, which was by no means unlikely. Henry gave the doctor his portrait in a ring, and Anne, at the king's desire, added the tablet of gold that hung at her girdle. The delighted cardinal placed the presents on his bed, and as he gazed on them he felt his strength return. He was removed from his miserable dwelling at Esher to the royal palace at Richmond, and before long he was able to go into the park, where every night he read his breviary.

Ambition and hope returned with life. If the king desired to destroy the papal power in England, could not the proud cardinal preserve it? Might not Thomas Wolsey do under Henry VIII. what Thomas à Becket had done under Henry II. His see of York, the ignorance of the priests, the superstition of the people, the discontent of the great,—all would be of service to him; and indeed, six years later, 40,000 men were under arms in a moment in Yorkshire to defend the cause of Rome. Wolsey, strong in England by the support of the nation (such at least was his opinion), aided without by the pope and the continental powers, might give the law to Henry and crush the Reformation.

The king having permitted him to go to York, Wolsey prayed for an increase to his archiepiscopal revenues, which amounted, however, to four thousand pounds sterling.[1] Henry granted him a thousand marks, and the cardinal, shortly before Easter 1530, departed with a train of 160 persons. He thought it was the beginning of his triumph.

Wolsey took up his abode at Cawood Castle, Yorkshire, one of his archiepiscopal residences, and strove to win the affections of the people. This prelate, once "the haughtiest of men," says George Cavendish, the man who knew him, and served him best, became quite a pattern of affability. He kept an open table, distributed bounteous alms at his gate, said mass in the village churches, went and dined with the neighbouring gentry, gave splendid entertainments, and wrote to several princes imploring their help. We are assured that he even requested the pope to excommunicate Henry VIII.[2] All being thus prepared, he thought he might make his solemn entry into York, preparatory to his enthronization, which was fixed for Monday the 5th of November.

Every movement of his was known at court; every action was canvassed, and its importance exaggerated. "We thought we had brought him down," some said, "and here he is rising up again." Henry himself was alarmed. "The cardinal, by his detestable intrigues," he said, "is conspiring against my crown, and plotting both at home and abroad;" the king even added *where* and

how.[1] Wolsey's destruction was resolved upon.

The morning after All Saints day (Friday, 2d November) the earl of Northumberland, attended by a numerous escort, arrived at Cawood, where the cardinal was still residing. He was the same Percy whose affection for Anne Boleyn had been thwarted by Wolsey; and there may have been design in Henry's choice. The cardinal eagerly moved forward to meet this unexpected guest, and impatient to know the object of his mission, took him into his bed-chamber, under the pretence of changing his travelling dress.[2] They both remained some time standing at a window without uttering a word: the earl looked confused and agitated, whilst Wolsey endeavoured to repress his emotion. But at last, with a strong effort, Northumberland laid his hand upon the arm of his former master, and with a low voice said: "My lord, I arrest you for high treason." The cardinal remained speechless, as if stunned. He was kept a prisoner in his room.

It is doubtful whether Wolsey was guilty of the crime with which he was charged. We may believe that he entertained the idea of some day bringing about the triumph of the popedom in England, even should it cause Henry's ruin; but perhaps this was all. But, an idea is not a conspiracy, although it may rapidly expand into one.

More than three thousand persons attracted (not by hatred, like the Londoners, when Wolsey departed from Whitehall) but by enthusiasm, collected the next day before the castle to salute the cardinal. "God save your grace," they shouted on every side, and a numerous crowd escorted him at night; some carried torches in their hands, and all made the air re-echo with their cries. The unhappy prelate was conducted to Sheffield Park, the residence of the earl of Shrewsbury. Some days after his arrival, the faithful Cavendish ran to him, exclaiming: "Good news, my lord! Sir William Kingston and twenty-four of the guard are come to escort you to his majesty." — "Kingston!" exclaimed the cardinal, turning pale, "Kingston!" and then slapping his hand on his thigh, he heaved a deep sigh. This news had crushed his mind. One day a fortune-teller, whom he consulted, had told him: *You shall have your end at Kingston;* and from that time the cardinal had carefully avoided the town of Kingston on Thames. But now he thought he understood the prophecy......Kingston, constable of the Tower, was about to cause his death. They left Sheffield park; but fright had given Wolsey his death-blow. Several times he was near falling from his mule, and on the third day, when they reached Leicester abbey, he said

---

[1] State Papers, vol. i. p. 354.
[2] Hall, p. 773.

[1] Cosi mi disse el Re, che contra de S. M. el machinava nel regno le fuori, et m'a dètto dove e come. Le Grand, Preuves, p. 529.
[2] And there you may shift your apparel. Cavendish, p. 347.

as he entered: "Father abbot, I am come hither to leave my bones among you;" and immediately took to his bed. This was on Saturday the 26th of November.

On Monday morning, tormented by gloomy forebodings, Wolsey asked what was the time of day. "Past eight o'clock," replied Cavendish.—"That cannot be," said the cardinal, "eight o'clock......No! for by eight o'clock you shall lose your master." At six on Tuesday, Kingston having come to inquire about his health, Wolsey said to him: "I shall not live long."—"Be of good cheer," rejoined the governor of the Tower.—"Alas, Master Kingston," exclaimed the cardinal, "if I had served God as diligently as I have served the king, he would not have given me over in my grey hairs!" and then he added with downcast head: "This is my just reward." What a judgment upon his own life!

On the very threshold of eternity (for he had but a few minutes more to live) the cardinal summoned all his hatred against the Reformation, and made a last effort. The persecution was too slow to please him: "Master Kingston," he said, "attend to my last request: tell the king that I conjure him in God's name to destroy this new pernicious sect of Lutherans." And then, with astonishing presence of mind in this his last hour, Wolsey described the misfortunes which the Hussites had, in his opinion, brought upon Bohemia; and then, coming to England, he recalled the times of Wickliffe and Sir John Oldcastle. He grew animated; his dying eyes yet shot forth fiery glances. He trembled lest Henry VIII., unfaithful to the pope, should hold out his hand to the Reformers. "Master Kingston," said he, in conclusion, "the king should know that if he tolerates heresy, God will take away his power, and we shall then have mischief upon mischief ......barrenness, scarcity, and disorder to the utter destruction of this realm."

Wolsey was exhausted by the effort; after a momentary silence, he resumed with a dying voice: "Master Kingston, farewell! My time draweth on fast. Forget not what I have said and charged you withal; for when I am dead ye shall peradventure understand my words better." It was with difficulty he uttered these words; his tongue began to falter, his eyes became fixed, his sight failed him; he breathed his last. At the same minute the clock struck *eight*, and the attendants standing round his bed looked at each other in affright. It was the 29th of November, 1530.

Thus died the man once so much feared. Power had been his idol; to obtain it in the state, he had sacrificed the liberties of England; and to win it or to preserve it in the church, he had fought against the Reformation. If he encouraged the nobility in the luxuries and pleasures of life, it was only to render them more supple and more servile;

if he supported learning, it was only that he might have a clergy fitted to keep the laity in their leading-strings. Ambitious, intriguing, and impure of life, he had been as zealous for the sacerdotal prerogative as the austere Becket; and by a singular contrast, a shirt of hair was found on the body of this voluptuous man. The aim of his life had been to raise the papal power higher than it had ever been before, at the very moment when the Reformation was attempting to bring it down; and to take his seat on the pontifical throne with more than the authority of a Hildebrand. Wolsey, as pope, would have been the man of his age, and in the political world he would have done for the Roman primacy what the celebrated Loyola did for it soon after by his fanaticism. Obliged to renounce this idea, worthy only of the middle ages, he had desired at least to save the popedom in his own country; but here again he had failed. The pilot who had stood in England at the helm of the Romish church was thrown overboard, and the ship, left to itself, was about to founder. And yet, even in death, he did not lose his courage. The last throbs of his heart had called for victims; the last words from his failing lips, the last message to his master, his last testament had been......Persecution. This testament was to be only too faithfully executed.

The epoch of the fall and death of cardinal Wolsey, which is the point at which we halt, was not only important, because it ended the life of a man who had presided over the destinies of England, and had endeavoured to grasp the sceptre of the world; but it is of especial consequence, because then three movements were accomplished, from which the great transformation of the sixteenth century was to proceed. Each of these movements has its characteristic result.

The first is represented by Cromwell. The supremacy of the pope in England was about to be wrested from him, as it was in all the reformed churches. But a step further was taken in England. That supremacy was transferred to the person of the king. Wolsey had exercised as vicar-general a power till then unknown. Unable to become pope at the Vatican, he had made himself a pope at Whitehall. Henry had permitted his minister to raise this hierarchical throne by the side of his own. But he had soon discovered that there ought not to be two thrones in England, or at least not two kings. He had dethroned Wolsey; and resolutely seating himself in his place, he was about to assume at Whitehall that tiara which the ambitious prelate had prepared for himself. Some persons, when they saw this, exclaimed, that if the papal supremacy were abolished, that of the word of God ought alone to be substituted. And, indeed, the true Reformation is not to be found in this first movement.

The second, which was essential to the renewal of the church, was represented by Cranmer, and consisted particularly in re-establishing the authority of holy Scripture. Wolsey did not fall alone, nor did Cranmer rise alone: each of these two men carried with him the systems he represented. The fabric of Roman traditions fell with the first; the foundations of the holy Scriptures were laid by the second; and yet, while we render all justice to the sincerity of the Cambridge doctor, we must not be blind to his weaknesses, his subserviency, and even a certain degree of negligence, which, by allowing parasite plants to shoot up here and there, permitted them to spread over the living rock of God's word. Not in this movement, then, was found the Reformation with all its energy and all its purity.

The third movement was represented by the martyrs. When the church takes a new life, it is fertilized by the blood of its confessors: and being continually exposed to corruption, it has constant need to be purified by suffering.[1] Not in the palaces of Henry VIII., nor even in the councils where the question of throwing off the papal supremacy was discussed, must we look for the true children of the Reformation; we must go to the Tower of London, to the Lollards' towers of St Paul's and of Lambeth, to the other prisons of England, to the bishops' cellars, to the fetters, the stocks, the rack, and the stake. The godly men who invoked the sole intercession of Christ Jesus, the only head of his people, who wandered up and down, deprived of everything, gagged, scoffed at, scourged, and tortured, and who, in the midst of all their tribulations, preserved their Christian patience, and turned, like their Master, the eyes of their faith towards Jerusalem :—these were the disciples of the Reformation in England. The purest church is the church under the cross.

The father of this church in England was not Henry VIII. When the king cast into prison or gave to the flames men like Hitton, Bennet, Patmore, Petit, Bayfield, Bilney, and so many others, he was not " the father of the Reformation of England," as some have so falsely asserted ; he was its executioner.

The church of England was foredoomed to be in its renovation a church of martyrs ; and the true father of this church is our Father which is in heaven.

---

[1] 1 Peter iv. 1⁷.—Plerumque ecclesia est cœtus exiguus sustinens varias et ingentes ærumnas. Melancthon, Loci.

INDEX.

ABEL, secretary to Catherine of Aragon, 795
Absolution, real, 215
Abstemius, Botzhemus, 185
Acker, Anthony ab, 635
Adalbert, Bishop, 694
Adamnan of Iona, 692
Adelmann, Bernard, Canon of Augsburg, 102, 205
Adolphus, Bishop of Merseburg 163
Adrian VI., Pope, 355, 357, 359, 363, 749, 758
Adrian, Professor of Hebrew at Wittemberg, 206
Aebli, landamman of Glaris, 635, 636, 637
Agathon, 688
Agilbert, 688
Agrippa of Nettesheim, 460
Aidan, missionary from Iona to Northumberland, 686, 687
Aigle, 597, 598, 599
Aix-la-Chapelle, coronation of Charles V. at, 211
Albert, Archbishop of Mentz and Magdeburg, 92; Luther's letter to, 97; endeavours to prevent Luther's journey to Worms, 237; attempt to conciliate Luther, 248; gives way to the enthusiasm for Luther, 312; his policy attacked by Luther, 317–318; seeks to secularize his principality, 392; memorial to Charles V., 392; at Augsburg, 551; offended at Pompinello's sermon, 557; replies to Campeggio, 556
Aleander, appointed colleague to Dr Eck, 202; his demands from Charles V., 211; terror at spread of Lutheran doctrines, 220; his activity, 224; at Worms, 225; endeavours to prevent Luther's appearance at the Diet, 228; induces Charles V. to act with vigour, 246; sends Cochleus to the Archbishop of Treves, 249; his plot exposed, 250; triumphant, 254; effect of his persecutions, 363
Alexander III., Pope, 698
Alexander VI. (Rodrigo Borgia), 19
Alfred, son of Oswy, 687, 688, 691
Alfred the Great, 696
Allmain, James, 440
All-Saints' Festival at Wittemberg (1517), 96
Alva, Duke of, 229
Am-Berg, Bailiff, 403, 632
Amberino, Caius, 714
Am-Grütt, Joachim, 406
Amsdorff, Nicholas, 164, 213, 233, 255, 321, 388
Anabaptism, 418, 603

Andrew, Cardinal, 31
Anemond de Coct, preaches the gospel, 465, 466; his activity in France and Switzerland, 472, 473, 474, 475, 477. 478
Angelis, De, 793, 819
Anhalt, George of, 176, 559
Anhorn, Christian, 298
Anne of Luxembourg, 707, 712
Anselm of Canterbury, 31, 698
Antichrist, 215
Antiquity, study of, in Italy, 35
Antwerp, Augustine convent at, 361; New Testament at, 784
Appenzel, 297, 612, 639
Aranda, Michael of, 450, 454, 471, 495
Arau, 636, 651, 652, 657
Areulf, 692
Arthur, Master, 753, 791
Arthur, Prince, marriage of, 716
Arundel, 707, 712
Ashford, Agnes, 747
Ashton, John, 706, 709
Audley, Sir Thomas, 858
Auerbach, 317
Augsburg, Bishop of, 568, 570
Augsburg Diet, 126; Papal Legate at, 135; diets convoked by Charles V., 385, 391, 541, 543; confession of faith, 563; refutation of, 574
Augustine, 683, 684
Augustine monks, 322, 324, 346, 361, 387, 768
Austria, 633

BADEN, discussion at, 428
Bainham, 860
Ball, John, 708
Bangor, 682, 684, 685
Baptism, Luther on, 198
Barbarians, influence of, in establishing the Primacy, 11
Barnes, Robert, the Restorer of Letters, 767–769; arrested, 779; relapse, 780; in the Bury St Edmunds convent, 781; his escape, 783
Barton, Elizabeth, the Maid of Kent, 795, 838, 849
Basle, Zwingle at, 259, 261, 282; Œcolampadius at, 266; Hedio at, 282; Rubli at, 289; reformers at, 411; effect of Baden discussion at, 430; Anemond de Coct at, 467; French exiles at, 473; Reformation struggle in, 613–617; attempt to reconcile Luther and Zwingle at, 645; vote for peace at, 649; New Testament issued from, 729
Battli, Melchior. 291
Bavaria, Duke of, 364, 365, 367, 568, 574, 577

Bayard, 435
Bayer, Chancellor, 563
Bayfield, Richard, 780, 793, 860
Bayley, 781
Beatus, cavern and head of, 609
Becket, Thomas, 698
Becon, Thomas, 765
Beda, syndic of the Sorbonne, 446, 450, 458, 480, 481, 484, 485, 487
Bede, Venerable, 685, 692, 693, 695, 707
" Beggars, the Supplication of the," 773
Bell, Dr, 806, 807
Bellay, Du, 807, 812, 813, 819, 821, 828, 831, 848, 849, 853
Bellegarde, M. de, 630
Bély, John de, 629
Benedict IX., Pope, 12
Benignus, 680
Bennet, Dr, 831, 846
Bennet, Thomas, 861, 862
Bentin, Michael, 474
Bergner, George, 635
Berne, Zwingle at, 260; carnival at, 296; Reformation struggle at, 408; deputation from Papal cantons to, 427; consequences of Baden discussion at, 430; religion in, 602; disputation at, 604–607; Edict of Reform at, 608; triumph of Reformation at, 609–611; interposes between Zurich and the Forest Cantons, 636; fanatics at, 642; disagreement with Zurich, 645; vote for peace, 649; proposal to close markets against the Five Cantons, 651, 652, 654; treaty with the Five Cantons, 672; faith of, 675
Berquin, 447, 453, 485
Berweger, Bartholomew, 298
Betts, William, 778
Bevay, 629
Beza, Theodore, 444, 447, 457
Bible, Luther's translation, 319; Wickliffe's, 707; Coverdale's, 814
Bibra, on Luther, 101; meets Luther at Wurzburg, 118
Bicocca, 294
Bilney, Thomas, at Cambridge, 732, 753; buys New Testament, 733; readings, 734; friendship with Latimer, 753–757: father of the English Reformation, 764; seeks to convert Barnes, 768; avoids arrest, 779; injunction as to preaching, 783; arrest and fall, 791–793; recognition of incomplete religious societies, 816; his remorse and martyrdom, 863.
Binzli, Gregory, 259, 282

Black Forest, revolt in, 379
Blarer, Ambrose, 605
Blaurock, 419, 421
Blet, Anthony du, 472, 495
Bohemia, 28
Bohemian brethren, 33, 178
Boleyn, Anne, Letter from, 720; appointed Maid of Honour to Catherine, 787; enters household of Margaret of Valois, 788; reappears at Court, 789; resists Henry's advances, 790; hatred of Wolsey to, 791; receives Fox's report, 805; letters from Henry to, 810, 811; letter from, to Wolsey, 818; her change of position, 819; uses her influence against Wolsey, 828; reads *The Obedience of a Christian Man*, 842; returns to Court, 843; causes Henry to read Tyndale's book, 844; at Woodstock, 845; influence over Henry, 848
Boleyn, Sir Thomas (Earl of Wiltshire), 718, 720, 738, 787, 806, 839, 852
Bologna, Concordat of, 446
Bonavern (Kilpatrick), 679
Boniface of Wessex, 694
Bora, Catherine, Luther's wife, 387
Borgia, Cæsar, 19
Borgia, Rodrigo (Alexander VI.), 19
Boschenstein, John, 288
Bourbon, Constable of, 504
Bourkhard, Leonard, 664
Boye, Nicholas, 368
Boyne, Anthony, 622
Brackley, 699
Bradwardine, 701
Brandenburg, Albert, Margrave of, 373, 390, 552, 554, 574, 576, 589, 591
Brandenburg, Bishop of, 100, 102; Luther's letter to, 123
Brandenburg, Elector of, 319, 338, 357, 366, 513, 551, 570, 581, 593
Brawn, John, 64, 65
Braybrooke, Bishop of London, 712
Bremgarten, 607, 635, 652-655, 673
Brendi, Doctor, 291
Brentz, John, 120, 384, 424, 533, 556, 557, 560, 561, 569, 574, 578, 587, 588, 592
Briçonnet, 443, 449-455, 481-483
Bricot, 719
Britain, Augustine's mission to, 683
Brown, John, of Ashford, 725
Brück, Chancellor, 560, 563, 577, 585, 592
Brunner, Fridolin, 639
Brunswick, Eric, Duke of, 246, 500, 570
Bursierd, Friar John, 791
Bryan, Sir Francis, 827, 830, 831
Bucer, Martin, 120, 237, 372, 527, 533, 549, 574, 605
Buckingham, Prior, 766
Budaeus, 436
Bugenhagen, 232, 388, 424
Bull, Papal, on indulgences, 153; excommunicating Luther, 194; burnt by Luther, 207; re-issue of, against Luther, 221; bull for Henry's marriage with Catherine, 716; bull for their divorce, 820
Bullinger, Dean, 277
Bullinger, Henry, 278, 288, 301, 304, 396, 400, 410, 429, 605, 637, 639, 641, 652, 655, 664, 669, 674
Burgdorff, Dean of, 301
Burgos, decree of, 366
Burkhardt, 367
Burkli, Jacques, 298

Butcher's Company at Berne, 603, 606
Butts, Dr, 813, 859
Byrckman, Francis, 761

CADEN, MICHAEL, 538
Caesaropapia, 697
Cajetan (*see* Vio, De)
Calpurnius, 679
Calvin, Gerard, 490
Calvin, John, 489, 491, 492
Cambridge, 714, 732, 734, 753, 764, 778, 781, 832, 845
Camerarius, 195, 561, 577
Campana, Francis, 826, 828
Campeggio, Papal nuncio, at Nuremberg Diet, 363-365; at Augsburg Diet, 552, 558; speech, 560; visited by Melancthon, 573, 577; advises persecution, 578; sent to England by Clement VII., 807; receives fresh instructions from the Pope, 817; hears the Flemish commissioners, 822; his letters seized, 831; his deceit, 836; opposes argument of Divine Right, 840; his tergiversations, 841; farewell audiences on leaving England, 847, 848, 849
Canterbury, 683, 684, 859
Cantons, meeting of the, at Lucerne, 604
Cantons, the Five Forest, 635-638; slanders and violence in, 649; blockade of, 652-654; war, 657-672; league with Friburg and Soleure, 675
Capito, chaplain to Archbishop of Mentz, 239, 248; at Einsidlen, 269; at Basle, 282; called to Mentz, 283; sent to Wittemberg, 317, 335; leans to Carlstadt's doctrines, 372, 425; at Augsburg, 574; at Berne, 605; at Zurich, 643-645
Capon, 778
Cappel, 635, 659, 660, 665
Carloman, 695
Carlstadt, A. Bodenstein of, (A. B. C.), Dean of Theological Faculty, Wittemberg, 72; disputation with Eck, 162-170; named in Papal bull by Eck, 205; attack on Leo X., 299; views on marriage of priests, 315; his character, 324; on images, 328; disappointment, 336; controversy with Luther on transubstantiation, 369-372, 423, 424, 527
Carnival at Berne, 296; at Wittemberg, 216
Caroli, Peter, 695
Carpenter, George, 514
Carracioli, 202, 211
Casale, Gregory da, Wolsey's emissary to the Papal Court, 795-802, 808, 826, 831, 845, 846
Castelenschloss, 656
Catherine of Aragon, 341; marriage with Henry, 716, 718; dislike of Wolsey, 785; her alarm, 787; her sorrow, 800; her protest, 836; her speech, 837; summoned before the legates, 839; evidence taken as to her marriage with Arthur, 840
Catholicity, true, 823
Catholics and Evangelicals in England, 832
Cauvin, John, 491
Cavendish, 856, 865
Caxton, 714
Cedda, 688, 690
Celibacy, 13, 189, 298

Cellarius, 173
Cellarius, Wittemberg schoolmaster, 327, 336
Ceolfrid, 692
Chalcondyles, 714
Chambers, Henry, 752
Charlemagne, 11
Charles of Spain and Burgundy, candidate for the imperial crown, 182, 737; elected as Charles V., 183; receives a letter from Luther, 183; coronation, 211; his "see-saw" policy, 214; demands the production of Luther at Worms, 219; Elector's reply, 220; yields to the Pope (Adrian VI.), 224; appealed to against Luther, 226; grants safe conduct to Luther, 230; letter from Hütten to, 233; his council, 239; presides at Diet of Worms, 240; his message to the Diet, 247; condemnation of Luther, 254; his wars, 322; threat against Lutherans, 352; issues the Burgos Edict, 366; convokes Augsburg Diet, 385; marriage, 392; rupture with the Pope (Clement VII.), 502; his manifesto, 503; alliance with Clement, 517; annuls the last resolution of the Spires Diet, 518; in Italy, 537; coronation as Emperor of the Romans, 541; at Munich, 550; at Augsburg, 551-595; gained over by Wolsey, 746; consoles Wolsey on loss of the tiara, 749; offers France to Henry VIII., 759; jailor of Clement, 795; war declared against him by France and England, 801; his reverses in Italy, 804; his triumphs, 845
Charles the Bald, 695
Chatelain, 461
Chieregati, 357
Chilton, 726
Chlorus, Constantius, 678
Christianity, appearance of, 7; distinctive principles of, 7; the Papacy, 16; imperishable nature of, 20; universality of, 432
Christians, all, are priests, 188
Church, formation of, at Rome, 8; condition before the Reformation, 17; constitution of, 506, 509; and State, 510, 565, 770
Churches, metropolitan, 10; visitation of reformed, 512; High and Low in England, 728
Clarencieux, 807
Clarendon, council at, 698
Clark, John, 756, 776, 781
Clarke, Doctor, 744, 794
Clement, doctor of Scottish Church, 694
Clement IV., 702
Clement VII., sends Campeggio to Nuremberg, 363; rupture with Charles, 503-506; alliance with Charles, 517; objects to a council, 539; concession, 539; disappointment of Wolsey at Clement's election, 758; negotiations for divorce of Henry and Catherine, 795-804; his embarrassment, 826; illness, 829, 830; submits to demands of Charles, 845, 846
Clergy, ignorance of, 20; should be subject to the magistracy in secular things, 187
Clifford, Sir Louis, 705
Cobham, Lord (Sir John Oldcastle), 713
Cochleus, 59, 226, 237, 239, 249, 250

252, 314, 347, 349, 512, 549, 577, 604, 762, 763
Coleman, 767
Colet, Dean, 715, 719, 721, 722
Collins, Rodolph, 526, 605, 647, 648
Colman, 688, 689
Cologne, 761
Colporteurs, 475
Columba, 680
Columbanus, 682
Comander, 426
Commission, mixed, on Augsburg confession, 584
Como, monk of, 639
Conchessa, 679
Conecte, Thomas, 31
Confession, Luther on, 215, 314; of faith, at Augsburg, 559
Constance, 303, 304
Conventicles, 472
Corcellus, 629
Cordeliers re-established in Augsburg, 594
Cotta, Conrad and Ursula, 52
Cottisford, Dr, 775, 776, 777
Courtenay, Bishop of London, 704, 708, 709
Coventry, 736
Coverdale, 767, 779, 814–816, 835
Cowling, Castle, 712
Cox, 782
Cranach, Lucas, 216, 253, 377, 388
Cranmer, Thomas, 850, 851, 852, 867
Cromwell, Thomas, 717, 721, 759, 788, 814, 835, 856, 857, 864, 866
Cruciger, Gaspard, 176, 207
Crusades, 13
Culdees, 678

DALABER, ANTHONY, 757, 773, 775, 776
Dangertin, 653
Dante, 35
Dantzler, 667
Dauphiny, 433
Decretals, false, of Isidore, 11
Deira, 687, 688
Denmark, 28
D'Erlach, 611
Dessaw, 386
Didymus, Gabriel, 336
Diedrich, Vitus, 561
Diesbach, Sebastian, 636, 671, 673
Diet, 776
Diocletian, 678
Dionoth, 684
Divorce of Henry VIII. from Catherine of Aragon, proceedings for, 785, 794–807, 837–839, 846–851
Dominicans, 260, 730, 862
Dornemann, Boniface, 506
Dresden, Luther at, 78, 81
Drumm, 782
Duchesne, 458, 480
Dumysen, Colonel Rodolph, 660, 666
Dunstan, Anthony, 777
Duprat, Anthony, 445, 480
Durer, Albert, 134, 377
Durovern, 683

EADBAD, king of Kent, 685
Eaglestone, Thomas, 752
Eanfield, 687, 688, 690
Easter revels, 17, 411
Ebernburg, 237
Eck, Doctor (John Meyer), of Ingolstadt, 84; attacks Luther's theses on indulgences, 114; disputation at Leipsic, 164–177; attacks Melancthon, 178; attacked by Œcolampadius and others, 180; at Rome, 191; brings the Papal bull to Saxony, 202;

adds six names to the bull, 205; his insolence, 206; activity against the Reformers, 364, 365, 411; disputation with Œcolampadius at Baden, 428; his propositions, 549; reproached by the Duke of Bavaria, 568; at Augsburg, 571, 584, 589; abuses Zwingle, 604; resolves to circumvent Tyndale, 763
Eck, John ab, 241, 242, 250
Edelfrid, 685
Edilwalch, 691
Edward III., 696, 701
Egbert, 693
Egfrid, 691
Egidio, 639, 640
Egranus, 205
Ehinger, John, 538
Einsidlen, 268, 273, 299, 641, 673
Eisenach, Luther at, 52, 253
Eisleben, Luther born at, 50; chapter of Augustines at, 198
Elector Frederick, his dream, 95; uneasiness, 103; Luther's letter to, 150; his refusal to give up Luther, 151; encourages him, 180; declines the Imperial crown, 182; sends Luther to Lichtemberg, 199; gives audience to the nuncios, 212; letter to Charles, 220; demands safe conduct for Luther, 230; after Luther's speech at Worms, 246; fears for Luther, 248; leaves Worms, 254; endeavours to suppress monastic dissensions at Wittemberg, 322; views regarding the prophets, 327; his pacific nature, 328; Luther's letter to, 332; protects his people from the bishops, 350; reforms the State, 351; letter from Pope Adrian VI. to, 359; consults the Wittemberg Reformers, 360; banishes Carlstadt, 372; death, 385
Elector John (see John, Duke of Saxony), declares in favour of the Reformation, 389; his court, 500; instruction to his councillors, 501; address by Luther to, 511; sends Melancthon's propositions to Luther, 512; receives false information of a conspiracy, 515; pacific nature, 516; at Spires, 518, 524; his councils, 542; at Augsburg, 545–593
Elfric, 707–708
Elyot, George, 773
Emeric of Reiffenstein, 349
Emser, Jerome, 81, 178, 365
Engelhard, 291
England, attitude of, to the Reformation, 27; before the Reformation, 677
Ennius, 270
Erasmus, parentage of, 40; his influence on the Reformation, 41; his Praise of Folly, 41; translation of Greek Testament, 42; his failings, 43; loss of influence, 44; Luther on, 76; on Luther's ninety-five theses, 101; defends Luther, 185; at Cologne, 213; advice to the Elector of Saxony, 214; reception of Melancthon's work, 339; on the persecutions, 362; sarcasm on Henry VIII., 388; at Basle, 412; controversy with Luther, 413; answer to More on transubstantiation, 414; on the Bodily Presence, 422; altercation with Farel, 468; attacked by Beda, 485; on the marriage of Œcolampadius, 614; departure from Basle, 617; in-

vited to England by Lord Montjoy, 714; meets Sir Thomas More, 715; recalled to England on accession of Henry VIII., 717; on learning in England, 721; attacks the monks, 722; leaves England, 727; publishes the New Testament at Basle, 729; his dismay at its reception, 731; on Lee's Tragedy, 732; opinion of Lonstall, 749; invited again to England by Henry VIII., 808
Erfurth, 53, 78, 203, 235
Esch, Chevalier, 464, 470, 471, 477, 486, 493
Esch, John, 361, 362
Escher, John, 405, 637, 672
Esher, 854, 864
Ethelbert, 683
Evangelicals and Catholics in England, 832
Exeter, 861
Eyndhoven, Christopher, 784

FABER, 261, 271, 276, 278, 281, 290, 293, 294, 395, 396, 427, 518, 522, 523, 571
Fable, Lawrence, 272
Faith, justification by, 29, 438; Luther's confession of, 70; the first of good works, 186; defender of the, title of, 843; confession of, at Augsburg, 559, 563; tetrapolitan, 575
Farel, William, 432; his parentage, 434; on superstitions, 435; goes to University of Paris, 435; meets Lefevre, 436; reads the Scriptures, 437; his conversion, 440; comparison with Luther, 441; goes to Meaux, 450; retires to Dauphiny, 456; his brothers, 464; expelled from Gap, 465; leaves France, 467; meeting with Œcolampadius, 467; with Erasmus, 468; expelled from Basle, 470; called to Montbeliard, 470; introduces religious works into France, 474; attacked by Franciscans, 476; sees the image of St Anthony, 477; goes to Aigle, Switzerland, 597; becomes schoolmaster Ursinus, 598; letter to Natalis Galeotto, 599; altercation with a monk, 600; at the Berne disputation, 606; commission from Berne, 618; at Neufchatel, 619; at Valangin 622, 628; at St Blaise, 630
Feldkirchen, Bernard of, 78, 205 315, 322
Ferdinand, Archduke, 357, 500, 501 503, 513, 518, 519, 522, 541, 551 552, 583, 592, 671
Ferrar, 782
Festivals, Luther's demand for abolition of, 189
Fichtel, 367
Field, 767, 779
Finan, 687
Fish, Simon, 773
Fisher, Bishop of Rochester, 341 344, 794, 795, 836, 838, 858, 860
Fitzjames, 776
Fitzjames, Bishop of London, 715 722
Flagellations, 15
Flek on Luther's theses, 101
Florence, Englishmen at, 714
Flue, Gaspard de, 611
Flue, Nicholas de, 295
Fockinger, 668
Fontaine, 629
Fontaine, André Abbey, 620, 630
Fox, Bishop of Winchester, 71 722, 779, 780, 786

Fox, Edward, ambassador to Rome, 802–807, 850, 851
Foxe, Richard, 815
France, Reformation in, 27, 433, 441, 445
Francis I., 182, 289, 322, 352, 442, 444, 446, 448, 455, 459, 479, 495, 720, 723, 729, 738, 745, 747, 756
Franciscans, 179, 260, 346, 449, 454, 456, 476, 702, 730, 736, 791, 825, 862
Frankfort, 25, 108, 182, 237, 349
Franks, aid of, invoked by Rome, 11
Fraubrunn, 301
Frauentraut, Alexis, 538
Frederick of Saxony (see Elector Frederick)
Frederick of Thun, 250
Freese, Edward, 861
Freundsberg, George of, 240, 503, 504, 640
Frey, Captain-General, 671
Frey, Felix, 272, 274
Freyberg, Castle, 349
Friars, mendicant, 702
Friburg, 302
Frobenius, 160
Frosch, John, 137
Fryth, John, 734, 751, 768, 782, 824, 834.
Fugger, "King of Crowns," 192, 202
Funck, Ulrich, 660
Funk, 605, 637
Füsslein, 275

Gainsford, Miss, 843
Galatians, Luther's Commentary on, 179
Galeotto, Natalis, 599
Gallman, Rudi, 663, 667
Galster, 286
Gambara, English envoy, 795, 796; at Rome, 799–801, 803
Gardiner, ambassador to Rome, 779, 780, 802–807, 817, 829, 846, 848, 850, 851, 859
Garret, Thomas, 772, 775, 776, 782
Gastral, 652
Gattinara, Cardinal, 538, 544, 548
Gaunt, John of, Duke of Lancaster, 704, 707, 708
Geneva, 595
Geoffrey of Uxbridge, 748
George, Duke, of Saxony, 80, 163, 170, 173, 206, 227, 247, 329, 338, 349, 357, 360, 366; at the Peasant's War, 383, 384, 386; attempt of Philip of Hesse to convert him, 389; forgery practised on him, 515; at Augsburg, 570, 575, 578
George of Stockheim, 349
German nobility and the Reformation, 45, 184
Germany, the centre of Christendom, 24; commencement of learning in, 36
Geroldsek, Baron Theobald of, 269, 399, 667
Ghent, 352
Gibson, 778
Giglio, John de, 734
Glapio, John, 222, 237, 242
Glaris, Reformation in, 612, 639, 641, 652, 654, 673
Goch, John of, 33
Gödli, Gaspard, 648
Gödli, George, 660, 663, 666
Goodman, 781
Goodwin, 779
Gottschalk, 695
Goubel, defeat of Frey at, 671
Grace, doctrine of salvation by, 14, 309

Grammont, Gabriel de, 786
Granges, 662, 664
Grat, Alexis, 605
Grebel, Conrad, 283, 301, 398, 418
Gregory the Great, 682
Gregory VII., 12, 696, 697
Gregory XI., 705
Grenoble, 472
Greyfriars' convent, 765
Grisons, 298, 426, 613, 642
Grocyn, 714, 715, 722, 734
Grostête, 700
Grotz, Philip, 642
Grynæus, Simon, 523, 617
Guildford, Sir Harry, 750
Gundelsheim, 613
Gwerb, Rodolph, 660

Hacket, 784, 823, 834
Hag, Im, 655
Hales, Sir Christopher, 852, 856
Halle, idol of, 317
Haller, Berthold, 287, 302, 408, 409, 429, 430, 602, 604, 609, 610, 642
Halsey, 715
Hamburg, 461
Hampton Court, meeting of Canonists at, 794
Harman, 823, 834
Harmut of Cronberg, 47, 185, 349
Hasli, 610, 611
Hausmann, Nicholas, 327
Hausschein (see Œcolampadius)
Hebilthwaite, William, 750
Hedio, Gaspard, 185, 239, 270, 281, 282, 289, 527
Helfenstein, Count Louis of, 380
Henry, Duke, 349, 383, 392
Henry I., 698
Henry II., 698
Henry IV., 712
Henry V., 713
Henry VII., 714, 715, 716
Henry VIII., candidate for imperial crown, 182, 738; writes against Luther, 340, 744; his court, 341; his book, 342, 343; answered by Luther, 344, 345, 782; on Luther's marriage, 388; meets Erasmus, 715; accession, 716; marriage, 718; incited to war with France, 719; Sir Thomas More presented to, 721; petition of Standish to, 737; receives title of D. F., 745; alliance with Charles V., 746; decree against heretics, 748; offered France by Charles, 759; not a Reformer, 770; reads The Supplication of Beggars, 773; divorce from Catherine suggested to him, 785; his advances to Anne Boleyn, 790; consults Sir Thomas More on the legality of his marriage, 794; ecclesiastical conferences ordered, 794, 795; negotiations with Clement VII. for divorce, 795–807; letters to Anne Boleyn, 810, 811; audience to Campeggio, 819; the Papal bull shown him, 820; speech to Lords and aldermen, 822; summoned before the legates, 837; declaration regarding Catherine, 837; chafes Wolsey, 839; indignation at Campeggio, 841; shown Wolsey's letter, 842; reads The Obedience of a Christian Man, 844; at Woodstock, 845; wrath on being summoned to Rome, 846; his reception of Wolsey and Campeggio at Grafton, 847; meets Thomas Cranmer, 851; orders prosecution of Wolsey, 852; sends him a ring, 854;

elects More chancellor, 855; sanctions bills aimed at clerical abuses, 858; proclamation, 859
Hereford, Nicholas, 707, 709
"Heretics, Almanac of," 602
Hertenstein, 302
Hesse, Philip of, at Worms, 214, 248; meets Melancthon, 373; marches against the peasants, 383; attempts to convert Duke George, 389; at Spires, 500; his position in the Reformation, 507; deceived by Pack, 515; the protest, 520–522; presides at Marburg Conference, 526–535; at Augsburg, 545, 549, 552, 559, 580, 587; relations with the Free Cities, 645, 646.
Hetzer, Louis, 396
Higdon, 777
Higgins, John, 752
Hilda, Abbess of Whitby, 688
Hildebrand (see Gregory VII.)
Hilten, John, prophecy of, 34
Hirschfeldt, 253
Hitton, Thomas, 860
Hitzkirch, 641
Hitzkylch, 658, 660
Hochstratten, James, 39, 114, 183, 362
Hoen, Cornelius, 369
Hoffman, 274, 280, 292, 398
Hofmeister, 398, 427, 609
Hollard, 302
Horse, the White, 769
Horsey, William, 725
Hottinger, Claus, 301, 396, 399, 401
Humanists, 35
Hun, Richard, 724
Hungary, 28, 513
Huss, John, 30
Hütten, Ulrich von, 45, 185, 206, 216, 233, 239, 311, 412

Ibach, 349
Icolmkill (Iona), 681, 686, 692, 693
Ilantz, 426
Indulgences, 15; Tetzel's sale of, 87; farmed by Albert of Brandenburg, 93; in Switzerland, 271, 276
Ingentinus, Philip, 279
Ingoldstadt, 347
Innocent III., 699
Innocent IV., 700
Innspruck, 543, 544
Inquisition ordered into France, 481
Interlaken, 610, 611
Ireland, 679
Isidore, false decretals of, 11
Italy, the European apple of discord, 22; attitude of, to the Reformation, 26; infidelity in, 36; Gospel in, 197
Ittingen convent, 403

Jaekli, 605, 610
Jansenism, 417
Jauch, John, 665
Jelly-pardons, the, 718
Jetzer, John, 260
Jodocus, 121
John, Duke of Saxony, 184, 186, 212 (see Elector John)
John Frederick, 212
John, King, 699
John, the bookseller, 367
Jonas, Justus, 235, 317, 374, 561, 564
Joner, Wolfgang, 659, 667
Joseph, Charles, 725
Juda, Leo, 262, 269, 273, 394, 397, 643, 671, 675

Julius II., Pope, 68, 717, 719, 795

Kammli, John, 666
Kent, the Holy Maid of, 795
Kessler, John, 331
Kestner, John, 134
Keyser, Jacques, 633
Keyser, Leonard, 514, 637
Kilchmeyer, Canon, 302, 303
Kingston, Sir William, 865
Klarer, Walter, 297
Knight, Secretary, 795–801
Knipstrow, John, 109, 367
Knonau, Meyer v., 288
Kolb, 602, 605, 671
Konigsfeldt monastery, 409, 609
Kouffi, Kilian, 641

Lallier, John, 32
Lambert, Francis, 298, 456, 461, 462, 478, 494, 507, 529
Landenberg, Hugo, 271, 294
Landstein, 412
Lanfranc, 696, 708
Langer, 234
Lanzerant, 648
Latimer, Hugh, at Cambridge, 753–758; story of More, 760; his sermons and controversy, 764–770; escape from arrest, 779; summoned before Wolsey, 783; recognition of incomplete societies, 816; asks for free circulation of the Bible, 859, 860
Latomus, 314
Lausanne, 599, 618
Lautrec, 800, 804
Lavater, Rodolph, 654, 658, 665, 671
Lawrence, Archbishop, 685
League of the Reformed Princes, 516
"League of the Shoes," 25
Leclerc, 457, 458, 460, 463, 464
Lee, Edward, 731
Lefevre, 436, 448, 452, 453, 454, 455, 484
Legate, Luther before, at Augsburg, 139
Leipsic, disputation between Luther and Eck at, 164–177; Papal bull at, 203
Leo X., 87, 92; on Luther's theses, 102; Luther's letter to, 124; brief, 128; letter to the Elector, 129; bull on indulgences, 153; change of policy, 155; gives way to Eck, 192; Luther's letter to, 200; his duplicity, 247; on Emperor's side, 289; death of, 355; his bull published in England, 743
Lichtemberg, Luther and Mititz at, 199
Lilly, 714, 722
Limburg, James, 507
Lime-tree Brethren, 347
Linacre, 714, 715, 722, 734
Lincolnshire, Just Men of, 747
Link, Wenceslas, 134, 147, 198
Lisighaus, 258
Literæ Virorum Obscurorum, 46
Literature, 348
Livry, Hermit of, 488
Locarno, 640
Lollards, 712, 713, 735
London, Dr. 775, 776, 777
Longland, Bishop of Lincoln, 748, 752, 786
Louis XII., 436, 720
Louisa of Savoy, 445, 480
Louvain, 206
Loyola, Ignatius, 352
Lucerne, 287, 296, 301, 303, 396, 400, 604, 635, 641, 652, 659
Luneburg, 373, 559, 591, 593

Lupulus, 260
Luther, descent, 49; birth at Eisleben, 50; education, 51; sent to Magdeburg, 51; at Eisenach, 52; at Erfurth University, 53; discovery of the Bible, 54; admitted M.A., 55; effect of thunder-storm on him, 55; enters the Augustinian convent, 56; life in the cloister, 57; reads the chained Bible, 58; meeting with Staupitz, 61; the forgiveness of sins, 63; ordained priest, 64; at the festival of Corpus Christi, 64; becomes professor at Wittemberg, 65; Biblical lecturer, 65; preaches, 66; journey to Rome, 67; on Pilate's staircase, 70; his confession of faith, 70; return to Wittemberg, 70; made Doctor of Divinity, 71; his oath, 72; his *Popular Declamations*, 74; letter to Spenlein, 76; on Erasmus, 76; first thesis, 78; discharges functions of Vicar-General, 78; relations with the Elector, 80; with Duke George of Saxony, 80; sermon at Dresden, 81; evening with Emser, 81; Wittemberg theses, 82; in the confessional, 94; sermon against indulgences, 95; posts ninety-five theses on church door in Wittemberg, 96; letter to Albert, 99; attacked by Tetzel, replies, 105; letters to Spalatin, 106; reply to Prierio, 113; reply to Hochstratten, 114; reply to Eck, 115; popular writings, 116; journey to Heidelberg, 118; his *Paradoxes*, 119; his *Resolutions*, 122; letters to Bishop of Brandenburg and to Leo X., 123, 124; sermon on excommunication, 125; summoned to Rome, 127; goes to Augsburg, 134; conversation with Serra Longa, 136; letter to Melancthon from Augsburg, 138; appears before the legate, 139; letter to the legate, 147; appeals to the Pope, 148; flight from Augsburg, 149; letter to the Elector, 150; protest and appeal to a general council of the Church, 154; meeting with Militz, 157; letter to the Pope, 159; spread of his writings, 160; disputation with Eck, 162–177; his emancipation, 177; letter to Staupitz, 179; his commentary on Galatians, 179; his earliest ideas on the Lord's Supper, 180; declared a Bohemian, 180; letter to Charles, 183; offered protection by German nobles, 185; publishes his *Appeal to the German Nobility*, 187; attack on Papacy, 188; excommunicated, 194; his sermon on the Mass, 197; publishes his *Babylonish Captivity of the Church*, 197; conference with Militz, 199; letter to the Pope, 200; his opinion of the bull, 204, 205; appeals to a General Council, 207; burns the bull, 207; protected by the Elector, 212; on confession, 215, 314; letter to the Elector at Worms, 221; receives a safe conduct to Worms, 230; answers to Papal bull, 231; departs for Worms, 234; preaches at Erfurth, 235; enters Worms, 238; appears before the Diet, 240; letter to Cuspianus, 242; his prayer, 242; his speech, 243; conference with the Archbishop

of Treves, 249; ordered to leave Worms, 252; letter to Cranach, 253; letter to Charles, 253; condemned by Charles, 254; made prisoner in Thuringia, 255; captivity in the Wartburg fortress. 310; his tract against monachism, 316; tract against the new idol of Halle, 317; letter to Archbishop of Mentz, 318; his translation of the Bible, 319; conflict with Satan, 321; visits Wittemberg, 321; on the new teachers, 328–329; leaves Wartburg, 330; letter to the Elector, 332; return to Wittemberg, 333; on faith and Scripture, 337; answer to Henry VIII., 343; at Zwickau, 348; letter to Harmut, 350; his death demanded, 357; his advice to the Elector, 360; on the persecutions, 363, 367; controversy with Carlstadt on the Lord's Supper, 369; sent to Orlamund, 370; at Kale, 372; advice to the Margrave of Brandenburg, 373; on All Saints' church, 374; letter to the Elector, 374; letter to German magistrates, 375; on rebellion, 378; on the revolt in the Black Forest, 380; marries Catherine Bora, 388; letter to Myconius, 392; controversy with Erasmus, 413; comparison with Farel, 441; condemned at Paris, 448; letter to the Duke of Savoy, 466; sarcasms on the Papacy, 501; on the ministry, 510; letter to the Elector, 511; his toleration, 514; desire for peace, 524; his doctrine on the Lord's Supper, 525; altercation with Zwingle, 525; conference at Marburg, 525–535; his *Battle Sermon*, 535; objections to war on behalf of the Reformed States, 540, 542; at Coburg, 543; his opinion of Charles V., 556; his firmness, 561; letter to Melancthon, 562; letter to the Elector, 565; demands religious liberty, 568; letter to Melancthon, 572; letter to Brück, 578; rejects Melancthon's concessions, 586; recalls his friends from Augsburg, 591; his relation to politics, 645; his works in England, 742; his letter to Henry VIII., 782; his *Parable of the Wicked Mammon*, 799
Luther, James, 255
Luther, John, 49, 50, 52, 56, 316, 387
Luti, 286, 290
Lutterworth, 704, 709, 710
Lyons, 471

Macchiavelli, 69
Macrinus, 301
Magdeburg, 51, 391
Magna Charta, 699
Maigret, 472, 473
Maigret, Lambert, 647, 653
Man, Thomas, 735
Mansfeldt, Luther's family at, 50
Mantz, Felix, 418, 421
Manuel, Nicholas, author of *The Eaters of the Dead*, 296, 608, 610
Marburg, 507, 525, 646, 825
Marcourt, Anthony, 630
Margaret of Valois (*see* Valois)
Marriage of priests, 315
Martin, Friar, 31
Mary, Princess, 715, 720
Marys, heresy of the three, 448

Mass, Luther's sermon on the, 197; fall of the, 325, 374; in Zurich, 406; German, 511
Max of Molnheim, 349
Maximilian, 101, 181, 719, 729
Maxwell, 781
May, Clara, 409
May, James, 671
Mayer, Peter, 349
Mazurier, Martial, 449, 460, 481, 482
Meaux, 443, 449, 452, 453, 457
Megander, 609, 643
Mehldorf, 367
Melancthon, birth, 129; called to Wittemberg, 131; with Luther at Leipsic, 164, 169; devotes himself to theology, 176; reply to Eck, 178; his fears for Luther, 184; his marriage and domestic life, 195; new work by, 209; on the nobility, 213; letter to Hess, 216; admiration for Luther, 233; grief because of Luther's abduction, 311; letter to, 313; views on clerical marriages, 315; attack on the Sorbonne, 321; propositions regarding mass, 323; alarm at the new prophets, 327; assists in translation of New Testament, 337; on the commonplaces of theology, 338; meets Philip of Hesse, 373; on profane literature, 375; on the revolt in the Black Forest, 380; on Munzer, 383; on Luther's marriage, 388; on the church, 390; instructions for visitation of churches, 512; terror of omens, 517; at Spires, 518; desire for Christian union, 522; saves Grynæus, 523; his fears, 524; controversy on transubstantiation, 525; his Apology, 547; interview with Cochleus, 549; interview with Valdez, 558; draws up the Augsburg Confession, 559; his weakness, 560, 561; his minimum, 572; refuses to meet Swiss deputies at Augsburg, 575; concessions, 586; failure, 589
Mellingen, 652, 673
Meltinger, burgomaster of Basle, 614, 615, 616
Metz, 460, 462
Meyer, burgomaster of Basle, 614
Meyer, Gerald, 667
Meyer, Sebastian, 409, 410
Miltenberg, 361
Miltitz, Pope's chamberlain, 155, 160, 179, 198, 203
Mirisch, Melchior, 361
Moddis, Henry, 773
Mommors, De, 490, 491
Monachism, Luther's tract against, 316
Monks, outcry of, against Luther, 109; emancipation of, 323, 346
Monmouth, Humphrey, 751, 816
Montanus, 321
Montbelliard, 470, 475
Monte, De, 803, 804
Montjoy, Lord, 714, 715, 717
Montmorency, 496
Morals of Pre-Reformation period, 18
Morat, 618
Morden, James, 747
More, Sir Thomas, his austerity, 341; attack on Luther, 344; meets Erasmus, 715; intimacy with Henry, 721; defends Erasmus, 737; prevents his son-in-law from preaching, 773; consulted by Henry on his marriage, 794; partisan of Maid of Kent, 795; his prophetic saving, 808;

hatred of gospellers, 816; dialogue with Tyndale, 833; elected Chancellor, 855; his fanaticism, 859; ridicule of Patmore and Tyndale, 861; orders the burning of Bennet, 862; searches house of John Petit, 863; ordered to impeach Wolsey, 864
Mosellanus, 162, 164
Moulin, Francis, 495
Mulhausen, 382, 384
Muller, Sebastian, 615
Mulliner, 408, 641, 658
Munich, 514, 550
Munster, Sebastian, 617
Munzer, Thomas, 326, 379, 382, 384
Murner, Monk, of Lucerne, 430, 602, 604, 637
Mury, 641
Music, 376
Muterstatt, Peter, 523
Mutschli, 673
Myconius, Frederick, 17, 90, 102, 236, 384
Myconius, Oswald, 265, 272, 275, 281, 285, 287, 296, 301, 302, 399, 429, 474, 478, 617, 636, 643, 662, 674
Mystery-play at Berne, 296
Mysticism and scholasticism, 598
Mystics, 29

Naeff, Adam, 666
Naitam, King of the Picts, 692
Nancy, 487
Nesse, 293
Netherlands, attitude of, to the Reformation, 27
Neufchatel, 618, 621, 623, 624, 625, 626, 627
Nimptsch, nuns of, 387
Norfolk, Duke of, 847, 852, 855, 864
Norris, Sir Henry, 854
Northumberland, 686
Norway, 28
Norwich, Bishop of, 859
Noyon, 489
Nuns of Nimptsch, 387
Nuremberg deputies, 591
Nuremberg, diet at, 356, 363

Obedience of a Christian Man, Tyndale's, 843, 843
Œcolampadius, 47, 178, 180, 266, 411, 424, 428, 467, 474, 520, 527, 604, 605, 613, 614, 615, 617, 635, 643, 645, 673, 731
Œtenbach, nuns of, 294
Œxlin, 403
Ofen, Edict of, 513
Oldcastle, Sir John (see Lord Cobham)
Oliveton, 441
Omens, 517, 561, 656, 708
Organ destroyed at Berne, 606
Orlamund, 370
Orvieto, 798, 799, 802
Osiander, Andrew, 357, 363
Oswald, John, 236
Oswald, Prince, 686
Oswin, 687
Oswy, 687, 688, 689, 690, 691
Oxford, 696, 699, 701, 703, 705, 709, 714, 715, 721, 732, 734, 757, 764, 773, 775, 778, 782, 832

Pace, Richard, 717, 730, 738, 746, 759, 786
Pack, Otho, 514
Packington, 835, 860
Painting, 377
Pallavicini, Roman historian, quoted, 161, 166, 202, 224, 225, 238, 247, 251, 254, 358
Pampeluna, 352

Papacy, establishment of the, 11; shameful orgies of the, 12; exaltation of the, 12; relation to Christianity, 16; attack on, 188
Papillon, Anthony, 472, 495
Paradoxes, Luther's, 119
Paris, University of, 440, 447
Parker, Thomas, 741
Parliament, English, 703, 709, 724, 857
Patmore, 860
Pavanne, 460, 488
Pavia, 479, 760
Pelagianism, 14, 701
Pelagius, 680
Pellican, Conrad, 431, 605
Penances, 15
Pepin, defender of the "Republic of God," 11, 695
Percy, Lord, 704, 787, 865
Persecution, 360, 366
Peter, primacy of St, 10
Petit, John, 858, 863
Peutinger, 251
Pfeffers, 279, 280, 641
Philiberta of Savoy, 450
Philip, Francis, servant to Catherine of Aragon, 787, 795
Phrygio, 617
Pilate's staircase, Luther on, 70
Pirckheimer, 204, 365
Plague in Zurich, 280
Planitz, 373
Plater, Thomas, 399, 428, 670, 671
Platonic philosophy, 36
Poetry, 376
Poland, 28
Poliander, 164, 176, 390
Politian, 714
Pomerania, Duke of, 164, 166, 170, 367
Pomeranus (see Bugenhagen)
Pompinello, Vincent, 557
Pontanus, 222, 322
Popes, deposition of, by Henry III., 12
Præmunire statute, 702, 704
Prangins, Mons. de, 626, 627, 628
Presbyterianism, commencement of, 398
Presbyters, ordination of British bishops by, 681
Preston, Walter, 769
Prierio, 111, 192
Priests, salvation at the hands of the, 15; marriage of, 189
"Priests, the Poor," 706, 713
Primacy of St Peter, 10
Probst, James, 361
Proles, prophecy of, 34
Protest of Spires, the, 520, 538
Protestantism before the Reformation, 30, 33
Pucci, 270
Purgatory, 16, 774
Pykas, 815, 816

Quatuor, Cardinal Sanctorum, 799, 800, 803, 804, 805
Quentel, Peter, 762

Rapperschwyl, 641, 673
Rasdorfer, 639
Ratisbon, League at, 365
Rausberg, 298
Räuschlin, 275
Ravensbühler, 648
Rechberg, Conrad, 268
Reformation, state of Church before the, 17; providential preparations for the, 23; nature of, 159; spread of, 350; political element in, 351; catholicity of, 467; reaction against, 480; in England, the work of Scripture, 728
Reformed churches, 457

Reichler, 367
Reinhardt, Anna, 288, 298
Relics, 17
Religion, moral and æsthetic, 376
Renée, Princess, 789
Repingdon, 709
Reuchlin, John, 37; his contest with the Dominicans, 39, 45, 74; receives Luther's ninety-five theses, 101
Rheinthal, 632, 650, 652
Rhellican, 609
Rhenanus, 276
Rhodius, John, 369, 422
Richard II., 712
Richmond, Countess of, 714
Ridley, Robert, 769, 836, 838
Rive, George de, 625, 626, 627, 628
Rincke, Herman, 763, 824
Robinson, George, 773
Rœschli, 291
Rohrschach, 641
Rolle, Richard, 707
Roma, 454
Roman bishops, encroachments of, 9; declared "Rectors of whole Church," 10; invoke aid of the Franks, 11
Roman censor and Luther's theses, 111
Roman dissimulation, 585
Roman scandals, 68
Roman theology, 28
Romanus, 687, 688
Rome, formation of church at, 8; apparent strength of, 21; loss of ancient credit, 22; Luther at, 67; Holy Thursday at, 230; sack of, 505
Roper, son-in-law of More, 773, 807
Rothelin, Marquis of, 630
Roust, burgomaster of Zurich, 301, 395, 401, 605, 607, 635
Roye, William, 761, 784, 824
Rubli, William, 289
Rufus, William, 697
Ruhel, Dr, 593
Runnymede, 699
Russell, Lord, 856
Russia, 28
Ruti, 639
Rutiman, 404

Sachs, Hans, of Nuremberg, 48, 377
Sagarus, George, 369, 422
St Blaise, 630
St Catherine, nuns of, 638
St Dunstan's, 750
St Gall, 419, 430, 612, 636, 641, 649, 650, 652
St Gothard, 636
St Patrick, 679, 680
St Paul's Cathedral, London, 704, 713
St Peter, primacy of, 10
Salat, Roman chronicler, 638
Salisbury, 782
Saltzmann, 523
Salzburg, 367, 560
Sampson, Dr, 843
Samson, Franciscan monk, 271, 276
Sanctification, 440
Sargans, 652
Savonarola, Jerome, 32; his portrait, 234
Sawtre, William, 712
Saxony, Elector Frederick of (see Elector Frederick)
Saxony, Elector John of (see Elector John)
Saxony, George, Duke of (see George, Duke of Saxony)
Schæffer, Peter, 764
Schaffhausen, 613, 638, 649
Schaumberg, Sylvester von, 185

Schepper, 569
Scheurl, Christopher, 106
Schinner, Matthew, Bishop of Sion, 262, 270
Schleswig-Holstein, 373
Schmidt, Conrad, 296, 635, 667
Scholasticism and mysticism, 598
Schönbrunner, John, 669
Schools, 375
Schoot, John, 824
Schuch, 487
Schucker family, 420
Schurff, Jerome, 233, 335, 388
Schutz, 607
Schwanden, 639
Schwartzerd (see Melancthon)
Schweiss, Alex., 538, 576
Schweitzer, John, 660, 662, 666
Schwytz canton leads in war with Zurich, 635–673
Scotland, 28, 692
Scotus, John, 695
Scrivener, John, 748
Sebville, Peter, 465, 472
Seidler, 315
Serra Longa, 136–138, 183
Severn, vale of, 733
Sewal, Archbishop of York, 701
Shunamite, the Eisenach, 52
Sickingen, Francis von, 47, 185, 237, 247
Simmler, 659
Simonetta, 800, 803, 804
Sin, original, Melancthon on, 339
Smith, Simon, 860
Sneff, Ehrhard, 120
Sodbury Hall, 739
Soderini, 356
Soissons, 695
Soleure, 642, 673
Soliman, 357
Sorbonne, the, 321, 446, 448, 450, 457, 458, 473, 480, 484, 487
Spain, 26
Spalatin, George, 73; Luther's letters to, 106, 141, 147, 151, 159, 163, 206, 212, 229, 237, 238, 312, 316, 317; and the Elector, 385, 553, 574
Spalding, John, 725
Spanish grandees at Worms, 229
Spengler, 205
Spenlein, George, 76
Spilman, Edmund, 752
Spires, 372, 500, 517
Stacy, 781
Stadelhofen, crucifix of, 396
Staffileo, dean of the Rota, 789, 800, 803
Stafford, Master, 753, 754, 764
Stäheli, 286, 293
Stammheim, 403
Standish, 719, 722, 727, 736, 836
Stapfer, 271
Staufen, Argula de, 347
Staupitz, 60, 78, 124, 133, 141, 145, 179, 191, 198, 209, 217
Stein, 403
Steiner, 671
Steinhausen, 637
Stetner, 523
Stigand, 696
Stokesley, Bishop of London, 858, 860
Storch, Nicholas, 326, 336
Strasburg, 478, 575, 645
Stubner, Mark, 326, 336
Sturm, Gaspari, 232, 249, 252, 253, 575, 636
Suaven, 233, 367
Succat, 679
Suffolk, Duke of (Charles Brandon), 718, 720, 841, 847, 852, 855, 864
Sumner, 781
Supper, Luther's earliest ideas on

the Sacrament of the, 180; controversy on, 369; re-establishment of, in Zurich, 406; doctrine of, 525–536
Surrey, Earl of, 723
Sweden, 28
Sweating sickness, the, 652, 812
Swiss Reformation, originality of, 596
Switzerland before the Reformation, 25; Reformation in, 257
Sylvester III., 12

Taurer, Gaspar, 366
Taverner, 778
Testament, the New, translation of, 337; publication of, at Basle, 729; printing of Tyndal's translation in Cologne, 761–763; introduced into England, 771; Raimond's edition, 793
Testament, the Old, translation of, 824
Tetrapolitan Confession, 575
Tetzel, 85; his sermon, 86; conversation with Myconius, 90; tricked by a nobleman, 91; at Interbock, 93; attack on Luther, 105; his theses, 108; burns Luther's, 109; his own burned by Wittemburg students, 110; refuses to obey the legate's summons to Altenburg, 157; reproached by the legate, 159
Teutleben, Valentine, 183
Tewkesbury, John, 832, 833
Theodore, Archbishop, 690
Theses, the ninety-five, 97; burnt at Frankfort, 109
Thistle, Master, 753
Thomas, Mark, 326
Thöming, William, 635
Thorn, Lambert, 361
Thurgovia, 613, 632, 636, 638, 650
Tockenburg, 258, 423, 650, 652
Toning, 622
Tonstall, Bishop of London, 743, 749, 750, 752, 771, 775, 783, 792, 816, 832, 835, 859, 860
Topley, 815
Torgau, 391
Tours, Assembly at, 436
Toussaint, Peter, 462, 474, 475, 476, 493, 494
Transubstantiation, 422, 525–536, 708
Trebonius, John, 53
Treger, Dr, 605
Treves, Archbishop of, 249
Trialogue, Wickliffe's, 710
Truchsess, George Von, 382, 590, 592
Tschudi, Valentine, 265, 639, 665
Tudor, Henry, 714
Tuke, Sir Brian, 806, 813
Tyball, John, 815, 816
Tyler, Wat, 708
Tyndale, John, 861
Tyndale, William, birth and education, 734; at Sodbury Hall, 738–742; in London, 749–753; prints New Testament translation at Cologne, 761–764; introduction of the translation into England, 772; at Marburg, 824, 825; dialogue with More, 833, 834; sells the New Testament to Packington, 835; his Obedience of a Christian Man, 842–844

Udal, 776, 782
Ufnau, 413
Unity in diversity, 393
Unterwalden, 610, 611, 634, 635, 637, 640, 652, 659
Urban V. 708

Urban VI., 708, 709
Urban Regius, 84
Uri, 611, 635, 640, 650, 652, 659
Ursinus (Farel), 597

VADIAN, 283, 398, 404, 605, 612, 641
Valais, 635, 636, 649
Valangin, 622, 628
Valdez, Alphonso, 255, 558
Valdo, Pierre, 30
Valla, Laurentius, 35
Valois, Francis, Duke of, 436 (see Francis I.)
Valois, Margaret of, 436, 442, 444, 451, 454, 471, 472, 473, 479, 495, 786
Vanner, John, 291, 293
Vannes, Peter, 827, 830
Vaugris, 472, 473, 475
Venice, 197, 647
Vergy, Guillemette de, 622, 630
Vienna, 366
Vio, De, 135, 160, 194, 355
Virgil, 695
Virgil, Polydore, 341
Vitalian, 690
Vitrarius, 32
Voes, Henry, 361, 362
Voït, John, 235

WADENSWYL, 641
Wakefield, 786
Waldenses, 29
Waldstettes (see Cantons, the Five)
Walsh, Sir John, 739, 750
Waltham, 850
Warham, Primate of England, 716, 717, 722, 723, 775, 794, 838, 859
Wartburg, Luther at the, 256, 312–330
Warwick, execution of, 716
Watteville, J. J. de, 655
Watteville, Margaret de, letter of, to Zwingle, 409
Watteville, Nicholas de, 408
Watzdorf, Vollrat v., 250
Wehe, Jerome, 249, 251, 592
Weimar, Luther at, 234
Weinsberg, 380, 382
Weiss, Urban, 303
Werdmuller, Jacques, 635, 640
Wesalia, 32
Wesen, 612, 652, 673
Wessel, John, 33, 369, 422
Wessex, 686
West, Bishop of Ely, 767, 836
West, John, 824
Wettingen monastery, 640
Whitby, 688
Wickliffe, 30, 696, 702–711
Wickliffites, 711, 712
Wighard, 690
Wigornia, 684
Wildhaus, 258
Wilfrid, 687, 688, 689, 690, 691
William the Conqueror, 696
Wimpana, 108
Winifred of Wessex, 694
Winkler, George, 514
Wirth family, 403
Wissemburger, Wolfgang, 289
Witan, the, 691
Wittembach, Thomas, 262, 409

Wittemberg, 61, 65, 79, 96, 110, 151, 196, 203, 216, 323, 325, 327, 333, 350
Wolman, 806
Wolsey, Thomas, 341, 344, 715; almoner to Henry, 719; attack on monasteries, 721; cardinal, chancellor, legate, 723, 724; his ambition, 737; his intrigues, 738; calls a conference of the clergy, 741; attacks and burns Luther's works, 743; incites Henry to write against Luther, 744; his machinations to obtain the tiara, 745, 746; his persecutions, 747, 748; loses the tiara, 749; seeks it again, and loses it, 758; reforms the convents, 759; his secret alliances, 760; causes the arrest of Barnes, 779, 780; satirized by W. Roy, 784; suggests divorce to Henry, 785; separates Lord Percy and Anne Boleyn, 787; his intercession for the Pope, 789; opposition to Henry's proposed marriage with Anne Boleyn, 791; demands abjuration or death of Bilney, 792; sends a mission to the Pope, 795; letter to Clement VII.; seeks deposition of Charles V. 801; his new perfidy, 806, 807; attempts to reconcile Clement and Henry, 808; his alarm, 812, 813; refused decretal by Campeggio, 821; attempts to save Romish Church in England, 826; sends Peter Vannes to Rome, 827; decline of his influence, 828; attempts to gain the tiara, 829; his alarm at the Pope's conduct, 831; sits with Campeggio to decide on Henry's divorce, 836; attempts to attack Anne Boleyn, 844; at Grafton, 847; ordered to return to London, 848; in Chancery, 852; ordered to give up Great Seal, 853; at Esher, 854; impeached, 864; in Yorkshire, 865; arrested by Northumberland, 865; death at Leicester Abbey, 866
Woodstock, 845
Worms, Diet of, 218; Reformation at, 349; edict of, rendered ineffectual, 364; Tyndale at, 764
Wulston, Bishop of Worcester, 696
Würtemberg, 367
Wyatt, Sir Thomas, 789

XYLOCTEET, 281, 287, 302

ZAPOLYA, JOHN, King of Hungary, 516, 801
Zehender, John, 607
Zink, 636
Zouch, George, 843
Zuchswyl, 642
Zug, 403, 404, 635, 659, 662
Zurich, Zwingle called to, 272; preaches in cathedral, 275; plague at, 280; truth triumphant at, 288, 289; Council of, 291;

conference at, 394; disputation at, 397; answer to deputation from Lucerne Diet, 401; abolition of mass at, 406; discussion on baptism at, 420; Diet at, 431; controversy and war with the Forest Cantons, 634–675
Zurzack, 638
Zutphen, H. von, 361, 367
Zwickau, 326, 348
Zwilling, Gabriel, 322
Zwingle, Anna, 298, 662, 670
Zwingle, Ulrich, pleads against Luther's excommunication, 193; defends him against the Papal bull, 203; family of, 258; education, 259; elected pastor of Glaris, 262; receives a pension from the Pope, Julius II., 263; publishes the Labyrinth, 263; in Italy, 263; meets Erasmus, 265; at Marignan, 266; called to Einsidlen, 268; appointed acolyte, 271; his charity, 271; his friends, 272; elected to Zurich Cathedral, 273; his first sermons, 274; cultivates music, 276; his daily life, 276; attacks the sale of indulgences, 278; at Pfeffers, 279; attacked by the plague, 280; visit to Basle, 282; his doctrine, 283; at Baden, 286; attacks human traditions, 290; dispute with Battli before the Great Council, 291; plots against him, 293; publishes his Architeles, 293; sent to the nuns of Œtenbach, 294; dispute with Lambert, 295; marries Anne Reinhardt, 298; convenes a meeting at Einsidlen, 299; consoles Myconius, 303; letters to his brothers, 304; effect of Gospel upon, 394; his theses, 394; overtures from Adrian VI., 396; on the Church, 397; characteristics of his reform, 401; his dream, 406; on original sin, 407; letter from Margaret Watteville, 409; rejection of anabaptism, 418; encourages French refugees, 474; replies to Luther on transubstantiation, 525; conference with Melanchthon, 527; his confession, 575; call to Haller, 602; goes to disputation at Berne, 605; on the mass, 606; charge to the Bernese, 607; pastor, statesman, and general, 632; his call to arms, 634; supports the bailiwicks, 634; his hymns, 637; receives letters from Italian reformers, 640; meeting of ministers, 643; his relation to politics, 644; project against the Emperor, 646; seeks an alliance with Venice, 647; preaches the political reformation of Switzerland, 650; his distress, 655; his presentiments on seeing the comet, 657; departure for the war, 661; his gravity and sorrow, 663; at the battle of Cappel, 667; death, 669

876

THE END.